Historical Guide to New South Wales

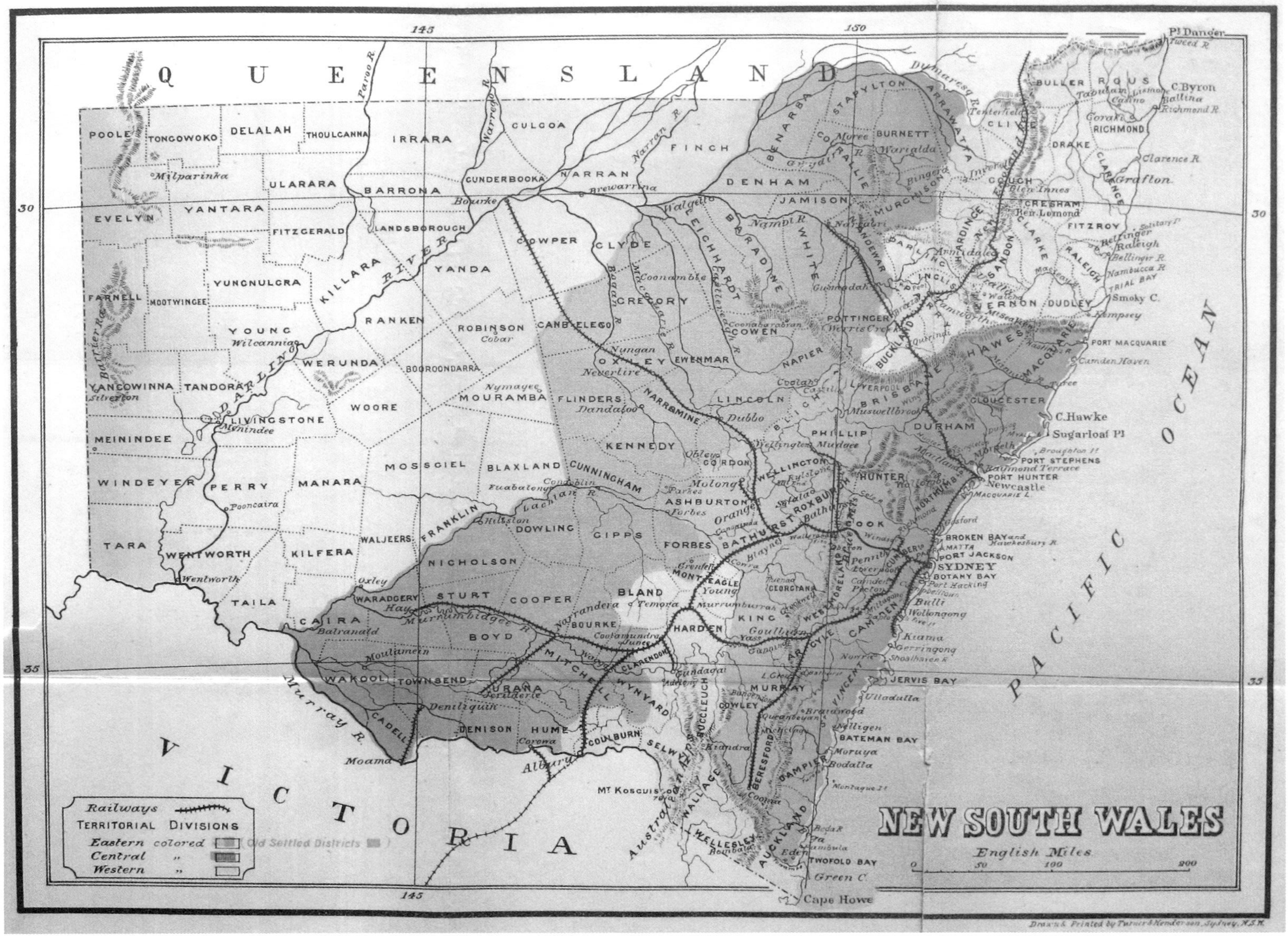

Map of New South Wales, 1891, showing counties. Source: George Ranken, *The Federal Geography of British Australasia*, Turner & Henderson, Sydney, 1891

Historical Guide to New South Wales

PHILLIP SIMPSON

Australian Scholarly

First published 2020 by
Australian Scholarly Publishing Pty Ltd
7 Lt Lothian St Nth, North Melbourne, Vic 3051
Tel: 03 9329 6963 / Fax: 03 9329 5452
enquiry@scholarly.info / www.scholarly.info

ISBN 978-1-922454-00-3

Cover design: Wayne Saunders
Cover photographs taken by Phillip and Margaret Simpson

For Margaret

Foreword

For a century and a half, historians have been heavily indebted to Robert Whitworth, the editor of *Bailliere's New South Wales Gazetteer and Road Guide*. Anyone concerned with the State of New South Wales in the 1860s or before has been readily able to find basic information about every locality, systematically and punctiliously presented. I keep a battered copy of *Bailliere* handy to my desk for frequent reference, while I keep a fine copy, once belonging to Walter Stone, in a bookcase reserved for significant Australiana. *Bailliere* is a book to treasure.

Whitworth had already published a similar, less bulky, gazetteer of Victoria, and was apologetic for the delay in producing the 664 pages of the New South Wales volume. For the delay, he blamed the "longer period of settlement", the "greater area", the "infinitely greater amount of matter to be dealt with", but he triumphed over "many grave, and, in some instances, discouraging difficulties" and published his indispensable work in Sydney in 1866.

Phillip Simpson too has triumphed over such impediments to the task of producing a new "Bailliere". No one else has attempted this monumental venture. No gazetteer has attempted the complex coverage achieved by Whitworth and his colleagues long ago. Phillip has had a long career, specialising in industrial sites and machinery, and produced books of lasting worth, but he has never lost the vision of emulating the sort of universal reference work for New South Wales uniquely produced in the 1860s. The new book goes far beyond Whitworth in content as well as time. I saw and admired drafts of the new book years ago and have nothing but admiration for the pertinacity with which Phillip has finally seen the work to completion.

I look forward to putting "Simpson" among my reference works alongside "Bailliere" and I anticipate that it will appear in every major library and Local Studies collection throughout the State, as well as on the shelves of every researcher.

R. Ian Jack, MA, PhD, FRHistS, FRAHS,
Hon. Fellow University of Sydney
Senior Fellow, St Andrew's College,
University of Sydney

Formerly:
Dean of Faculty of Arts &
Head of Department of History,
University of Sydney

President of Royal Australian Historical Society

Member of Heritage Council of New South Wales

Preface

A comprehensive gazetteer is an essential work of reference for the historian, geographer, genealogist, historical archaeologist, architectural historian, heritage consultant, librarian and archivist, yet the only such compendium on New South Wales was published in 1866: *Bailliere's New South Wales Gazetteer and Road Guide* by Robert P. Whitworth. As such, Whitworth's book continues to be quoted in the bibliographies of many historical publications today.

While Whitworth's approach was to give only a contemporary description or snapshot of places at the time of his visits, this publication concisely records the history and development of the place from European settlement to 2020.

In addition to showing a place's location, the *Historical Guide to New South Wales* endeavours to record the founding, *raison d'être*, products and industries, public buildings, public works and utilities, churches, factories, mills, mines, foundries, cemeteries, calamities, significant weather events and population, etc. over the life of the place to give a succinct historical overview of its development. The inclusion of a place or a building in the *Guide* does not mean that it is necessarily populated today or that the building still exists.

All 141 counties of New South Wales are covered except Sydney (more specifically the County of Cumberland, which constitutes only 0.7% of the State), as there are many books on Sydney and its suburbs, and now the *Dictionary of Sydney* on the internet. It is this remaining 99.3% of New South Wales beyond Sydney that is most ill served in terms of reference material describing its settled places and localities, especially the smaller places or those that have disappeared altogether. Certainly there are reference books covering many country cities and large towns, old post office guides, local histories of smaller towns and books on place names. But the researcher wishing to locate or ascertain anything about any one of the thousands of villages, hamlets, settlements and localities, including those of which all trace has vanished, has until now been obliged to laboriously search out a range of different source material for each place. Even then they may well still find nothing about the smaller, more obscure or defunct places of the State.

It is not claimed that this publication is definitive, or accurate in all its detail, but it can be said that it is the result of over three decades of intensive work locating, identifying, defining, researching and describing thousands of places. This has involved studying many thousands of books, reports, newspapers and maps, and driving thousands of kilometres.

Every effort has been made to address this major gap in the reference works on New South Wales, though unfortunately there are still a number of identified places recorded for which no or very few historical details have been found. However, this book gives the reader a firm basis for further research, whilst its many thousands of names and dates provide a useful key to unlocking the detailed information in the on-line newspaper database (*Trove*) of the National Library of Australia.

Introduction

Places

All identifiable places are included if they are or have been settlements, i.e. hamlets, villages, towns, cities and their suburbs (outside Sydney), as well as many localities that do not appear to have a central or defined place of settlement. In the Western Division of the State in particular there are localities that are synonymous with the main property or landholding in the area.

Headwords

Nearly all places were first formally named by the postal authorities or the Department of Lands, though sometimes by the railway authorities or the Department of Education. The spelling of place-names herein is usually now determined by the Geographical Names Board, but otherwise has regard to the spelling used by Australia Post, the Australian Bureau of Statistics and cartographers. Former names and changes in their spelling are shown and cross-indexed, together with the former names of post offices, railway stations and public schools, as well as subdivisions and estates. A former place that has been absorbed into an expanded contiguous larger place (such as Newcastle, Wollongong or Albury) is still indexed under its own name and is not considered to be a name change. Similarly, where information about a suburb is included under the relevant city, the suburb will be cross-indexed, whereas other suburbs which are larger or on the outskirts may warrant their own separate entries.

Arrangement

The alphabetical arrangement of entries is by the letter-by-letter system, in conformance with universal geographical reference-work standards. Place-names commencing with the words "Central", "Lower", "Upper" or "The" are indexed as such, whereas those containing cardinal points are indexed as if such qualifiers are suffixes. This is so the reader referring to the entry, for example, on Grafton, Maitland or Wyalong, can in the succeeding entry also see the information on the contiguous town, namely, South Grafton, East Maitland or West Wyalong, even though not all towns of this type are contiguous. Otherwise, the body of the text adheres to the long established descriptive method of the qualifier preceding the name. In the case of a place-name with a directional qualifier for which there is no equivalent place-name without the qualifier, it is usually indexed with the qualifier as the prefix, for example, North Haven.

Counties

The primary locational identifier of a place is the county, which is shown in brackets after the place-name. The State is divided into 141 counties of very similar size. This fundamental division of land commenced in 1788 with the County of Cumberland and, unlike the frequently changing boundaries of local government, electoral districts and census districts, has remained stable and reliable. As such, counties are the basis of all land administration in the State, being used in the alienation, surveying, transfer, subdivision and sale of land, mineral leases, water licences, and all other formal descriptions of land. Until recent years they were also used in the Australian census. Counties are the basis of cadastral mapping and are clearly delineated on all the latest large scale topographic maps of the State. Moreover, the official directories of railway stations and public schools have always used counties as their locational identifier.

Co-ordinates

Following on from the county name, the second, and more precise, identifier is given by the place's geographical co-ordinates. All atlases and topographic maps, and now even most proprietary touring maps, show the location of places by means of co-ordinates. This universal locational system has in recent years become even more widely used with the increasing popularity of global positioning systems amongst bushwalkers and four-wheel-drive vehicle users for navigating and fixing their positions, as well as on-line maps. Position is shown here to the nearest minute of latitude and longitude, the actual position of each place being regarded as the site of its post office or, where this is indeterminate or non-existent, the centre of the settlement. The co-ordinates of every place have necessarily been scaled off the largest scale maps available (or in some cases by using a GPS device) as it was found that published co-ordinates of places could not be relied upon for accuracy, nor lists for their comprehensiveness.

Distances

A further indicator to the location of a place is given by its distance and direction from the nearest larger place outside the Australian Capital Territory and County of Cumberland (except Sydney itself) with a population exceeding 500 people according to the 1986 census. Distance is measured in a straight line between post offices where possible, otherwise between what appears to be the centres of the respective places. Distances are rounded up to the nearest kilometre but any distance less than 0.5 km is not recorded. Using grid north as the reference, the direction of the subject place from the nearest larger place is shown to the nearest semi-cardinal point.

Watercourses

If any part of the place is within 500 metres of a watercourse or body of water, this is shown. If the body of water is the South Pacific Ocean, it is recorded more specifically as the Coral Sea or Tasman Sea depending on whether it is above or below the 30th parallel of latitude. Where a place is at the mouth of a river or the confluence of two creeks, etc., the body of water or watercourse closest to the bulk of the settlement is recorded, or otherwise the major one. However, it should be borne in mind that the names of watercourses have frequently been changed. Furthermore, individual watercourses often tend to be known by various names, so that the name of a watercourse shown on one map will often be different to that shown on a map of another date, scale or type. The name shown here is the most recent official name that can be ascertained.

Description

Any smaller or former places included in or subsumed by the subject place, as well as subdivisions, are shown in brackets, followed by any of their former names. As to the description of places, the first grouping of information relates to the place's discovery (by the British), settlement, establishment, founding, survey, gazettal, laying out, subdivision and first land sales, etc. and is arranged chronologically. The availability of this information is often related to the size or importance of the place, and for many places only a few of these events apply. For many other places no record of any such events occurring has been found. The next item of information describes the known purpose, function, activities or products of the place or its surrounding district and, where this can be established, they are shown generally in order of occurrence.

Infrastructure

The bulk of most entries is taken up with an alphabetical listing of the place's public buildings and utilities, churches and cemeteries, factories and industries, mines and mills, significant events and population statistics. Original descriptions of facilities are maintained for historical accuracy wherever possible (e.g. asylums and gaols), and have not usually been replaced by fashionable euphemisms, unless they opened as such or the dates of those changes are known. The other reason is to preserve consistent descriptions throughout the *Guide* so that the reader will find the same facility described in the same way in all entries, which is especially helpful in the entries for cities or large towns. However, this uniformity of arrangement sometimes necessitates a standard descriptor being adopted for essentially the same activity, for example, carriage-works and coach factories are all shown as the former, aerated water works and cordial factories are shown as the latter, and the various types of railway facilities (except stations) such as barracks, bridges, coal stages and turntables are usually preceded by the descriptor, "railway". Road bridges over watercourses are simply shown under "bridges", whereas "foot-bridges" are show separately. Historically, the surnames of builders and proprietors, etc., with the modern prefix of Mc or Mac were frequently just spelt with M' instead, and wherever this was done such spelling has usually been retained.

All known dates of structures and events are given, together with the designers and builders of many of the structures (including additions, extensions and renovations) and those responsible for the industries of the place. Not surprisingly, dates are problematical in themselves. For instance, most sources merely quote a building date which may actually be the commencement date, completion date or opening date, and a few years may have elapsed between the laying of a foundation stone and the opening ceremony. Wherever possible the date shown here for a building or facility is its opening date rather than the commencement of construction or its completion. If it is known that a structure or facility took more than two years to build, the period is specified. It should not be assumed that buildings were not rebuilt or replaced just because evidence of when this occurred has not been found.

Primary production as well as cemeteries, mines and quarries are usually included if they are within several kilometres of the place. Cemeteries were nearly always for general use in a place, though they may have sections reserved for different religions, whereas graveyards were attached to a church in which burial was usually restricted to the parishioners of that church. It should be noted that various sources denote the number of people interred at a place as burials, graves or inscriptions, and though they are here usually shown as graves, the number indicated is debateable. The dates given for the dedication of general cemeteries, and the establishment of public pounds, do not necessarily reflect when they were actually used as such. Airports and rifle ranges are included even though they are often located out of town and sometimes railway stations are as well, the direction and distance often being indicated. Bridges, sawmills, wool-scours and boiling-down works are usually included if they are within a couple of kilometres.

Whenever a period of time is shown (and not indicated as the time taken to build the structure) rather than a single date, this refers to the span of operation of the facility. It could also indicate the provision of the service (e.g. a railway), or an activity which may not always have been provided in the same building (e.g. a public school or post office). Schools and post offices are shown only under their last known location, though previous names or locations are cross-indexed. Public schooling and postal services, for example, were often originally undertaken in private or non-purpose-built premises, and sometimes police stations were in rented premises till they obtained their own building. These periods of official activity are included as they give a better overall picture than the opening dates of specific purpose-built structures. Breaks in school activity of up to five years within the period of operation are not usually indicated. Although most later post offices and telegraph offices were housed together, they are shown separately because they often began in separate buildings (e.g. telegraph offices were sometimes at railway stations). Private, special, provisional, half-time and house-to-house schools have not been included.

A period of time indicates the known existence or use of a structure or facility, or occurrence of an event, during that time at least, but possibly longer. However, if the date of construction (and name of the builder) of a particular railway station, school or post office, etc. is available then this is also given. Silos are shown if they are of cylindrical concrete, but other types of wheat storage or depots are not recorded.

As the great bulk of the infrastructure recorded, for example, dams, bridges, reservoirs and tunnels, were built according to imperial measurements, these are always recorded first, followed by the metric equivalent.

Events

In illustrating the historical development of a place, adversities and events such as droughts, nearby bushfires and floods, epidemics, strikes, the provision of street lighting, reticulated water, sewerage, gas and electricity, and other noteworthy incidents are often included. Town fires (in commercial premises, not houses) are also indicated, as is snow where it is uncommon. When calamities affected much of the State they are not separately shown. These include the 1918–19 influenza pandemic, the great drought of 1895–1902, the more recent droughts in the first nineteen years of this century, the heat waves of 2017–18 and the bushfires of 2019–20.

Population

Lastly, population figures, almost always from official censuses, but sometimes other sources, are usually included where available, but these can be misleading. The major difficulty arises because of the changing areas over the past two centuries to which sequential statistics purport to relate. This is typical of the large rural towns and cities that have dramatically increased their populations by expanding their areas to include more and more surrounding villages which may then become suburbs. The population figures for the former villages are then no longer available whilst at the same time they are included in the town's population, which may in the process have become a city. In addition, the published population statistics relating to towns and villages sometimes included the surrounding district but this was not always ascertainable. Another reason for a major change in a place's population between censuses is often due to the success or failure of mining in the area, a world war or one of the great depressions of the 1840s, 1890s or 1930s.

Whilst once the collection and publication of the population of a place was straightforward, this is now far from the case. For example, population figures are now published for several different, often overlapping areas, all with the same name. A typical example is the various official populations for Ballina in 2006, being 38,461 for the Local Government Area, 25,660 for the Postal Area, 16,477 for the Urban Centre/Locality, and 7,901 for the State Suburb. Moreover, in the 1954 and 1961 censuses, separate figures are given for the town and the locality immediately surrounding it. It will also be noticed that census collection varies significantly in coverage, with 1933 being the most comprehensive. Unfortunately, population figures are no longer released for many villages or any gazetted localities. It is with these types of significant shortcomings with later censuses in mind that population figures should be used or compared most judiciously.

Conventions

To keep the work within a reasonable size, considerable abbreviation (albeit quite straightforward) has had to be used, particularly in the main body of the entries. However, all information in the entries follows a standard order, is recorded alphabetically and is largely self-explanatory. A list of the abbreviations used is included. Nevertheless, personal names are given in full wherever they are known because not only does this limit potential confusion for family historians but it assists the reader who wishes to undertake further research about a particular person.

Abbreviations

&	and (in firms and company names, but not partnerships)
Angl.	Anglican, Church of England or Episcopalian
Assoc.	Association
b.	built
BHP	The Broken Hill Proprietary Company Limited
C.	church (including cathedral, chapel, citadel, kirk, mosque, synagogue, tabernacle and temple)
CAE	College of Advanced Education
CH	court-house
Christ.	Christian
Ck	Creek (not abbreviated in place-names)
Co.	County
Co.	Company
Cong.	Congregational
Co-op.	Co-operative
Corp.	Corporation
CSR	Colonial Sugar Refining Co.
d.	designed
decl.	declared
disc.	discovered
Dist.	District
estab.	established
FB	fire brigade, bushfire brigade or fire station
gaz.	gazetted
HS	high school
incl.	includes or including
incorp.	incorporated
Indep.	Independent
kl	kilolitres
LDS	Jesus Christ of Latter-Day Saints
munic.	municipal or municipality
nr	near
o.	opened
orig.	originally
PO	post office (not just a receiving office)
POW	prisoner of war
Prim.	Primitive
proc.	proclaimed
PWD	Public Works Department
PS	police station (or barracks)
RS	railway service or railway station
Salv.	Salvation
SD	Seventh-day
telephone	telephone service to the subject place
TC	technical college
TX	telephone exchange
UNE	University of New England
Unit.	Uniting
WC & IC	Water Conservation and Irrigation Commission
Wes.	Wesleyan

A

Abbey Green (*Co. Northumberland*) 32°37'S. 151°08'E., 6 km SW of Singleton, on Hunter R.; Angl. C. (St John's) 1922; bushfire 1875; flood 1867; meat works estab. 1867 by George Loder, closed; storms 1905 and 1936.

Abbotsford (*Co. Durham*) see Wallalong.

Aberbaldie (*Co. Vernon*) 31°06'S. 151°27'E., 20 km SW of Walcha; bridge (low-level timber) 1934, over Macdonald R.; pop. 22 (1933).

Abercrombie (*Co. Bathurst*) see Bathurst.

Abercrombie (*Co. Georgiana*) 33°57'S. 149°19'E., 48 km S. of Blayney, on Abercrombie R.; village gaz. 1891, spelt as Abercromby 1912–16; goldmining and grazing; bridge b. 1876–79 by W. Davoren and John Aherne, destroyed 1916, replaced 1919 by D.J. M'Clelland, new one 1931, over Abercrombie R.; flood 1916; mine (Pine Ridge or Hells Hole or Omrah) <1875, 1879–87, 1937, 1940; PO 1899; punt across Abercrombie R.; school (The Junction till 1906) 1897, new one b. 1898 by W.A. Stephens, closed 1923; telephone 1921; pop. *c.*200 (1879), 59 (1901), 200 (1911), 1,011 (2011).

Abercrombie Caves (*Co. Georgiana*) 33°55'S. 149°21'E., 43 km S. of Blayney, on Grove Ck; caves disc. 1843 by Walker Rannie Davidson; mining (Mount Gray, gold disc. 1854) 1890s–1930s; airfield; flood 1950 (caves closed till 1952); stamper batteries: 20 head, and 30 head erected by C.H. Clarth; telephone 1921; TX 1957.

Abercromby (*Co. Georgiana*) see Abercrombie.

Aberdare (*Co. Northumberland*) see Cessnock.

Aberdeen (*Co. Durham*) 32°10'S. 150°53'E., 11 km N. of Muswellbrook, on Hunter R.; disc. 1824 by Henry Dangar, surveyed 1838 by J.S. Rusden, town laid out and gaz. 1838, estab. 1840, first lots sold 1845, second land sale 1853, more lots sold 1859, munic. proc. 1894; dairying, horses, grazing, wheat, lucerne; Angl. C. b. 1885 by Schroter and Jansen, closed and reused, new one (St Mark's) 1914 d. by Frederick George Castleden; bridges: one b. 1878 by W. Burnett, destroyed, (second) 1887, destroyed, Fitzgerald Bridge (iron lattice) b. 1891–93 by O. M'Master, d. by John Alexander McDonald, re-decked 1937 by A. Goninan and Charles Hardy Contracting Co. Ltd, reused 2014, new one (welded steel Warren truss) 1986 d. by McMillan, Britton & Kell Pty Ltd, demolished and replaced 2014, over Hunter R.; butter and bacon factory (Aust. Chilling & Freezing Co. Ltd) 1899, fire 1934, closed 1962, derelict; cemetery (883 graves) 1867, incl. lawn cemetery and columbarium; CH b. 1908 by Walter Barrett; cordial factory (Thomas Pierce Hopkins), in former flour mill, closed and reused; drought 1894–96; electricity 1929; FB 1945 (station b. 1953, new one 1981); fires 1913 and 1937; floods 1870, 1877, 1955; flour mill (horse powered) b. 1825–27 by John Portus for Thomas Potter Macqueen, sold 1838 to Sparkes, Weight & Co., converted to steam 1840, reused, additions 1875 by James White, ruined; Free Presb. C.; meat works (Aust. Chilling & Freezing Co. Ltd) b. 1892 by Thomas, Perry and Rowledge, d. by Frank

Coxon, closed, reopened 1904, closed 1914, taken over 1923 by F.J. Walker Ltd and modernised, dehydration plant 1943, taken over 1983 by Elders IXL Ltd, traded from 1986 as Aberdeen Beef Co., taken over 1994 by Aust. Meat Holdings, closed 1999; Meth. C. b. 1902 by J. Cambourne, d. by James Hicks; PO 1856, new one b. 1900 by Charles Baker; pound (stock) 1856; Presb. C. 1864; PS (in old watch-house) 1892, new one b. 1908 by Walter Barrett; quarry; railway accident (5 killed) 1926; railway bridge (continuous wrought-iron lattice girders) fabricated by Park Gate Iron Co., Rotherham, England, erected 1868–71 by Amos & Co. and Thomas Smithyman, d. by Sir John Fowler and John Whitton, 477 ft (145.4 m), demolished 1982, replacement (plate web girder, steel deck) 1980, over Hunter R.; 4 reservoirs (incl. concrete one, 150,000 gal. or 681.9 kl); rifle range (man killed 1903); Rom. Cath. C. b. 1894 by Walter Barrett, extended 1937 by B. Idstein, demolished 1987, new one (St Thomas's) 1986 d. by Peter Jerome Gannon; RS 1870 (orig. station demolished); sawmill (Haggarty and Morrison) 1972; school 1864, additions 1908 by Charles Benaud Smith, additions 1975, 1994, 2010; tannery (Walfertan Pty Ltd) 1973–2012; telegraph 1890; TX 1910, automatic 1979; typhoid 1894 and 1901; Unit. C. (St Paul's, orig. Presb.) b. 1890 by Andrew Boyd, d. by John Wiltshire Pender, closed, sold 2017; watch-house b. 1864 by William Cains, reused 1872 as post office, reused 1892 as police station, demolished; water supply 1938, augmentation 1994; pop. 27 (1851), 71 (1856), *c.*100 (1866), 185 (1871), 125 (1881), 105 (1891), *c.*700 (1895), 749 (1901), 849 (1911), 958 (1933), *c.*1,000 (1941), 1,072 (1947), 1,154 (1954), 1,056 (1961), 1,127 (1966), 1,118 (1971), 1,133 (1976), 1,410 (1981), 1,741 (1986), 1,797 (1991), 1,737 (1996), 1,710 (2001), 1,791 (2006), 1,837 (2011).

Aberfoil (*Co. Clarke*) see Aberfoyle.

Aberfoyle (*Co. Clarke*) 30°16'S. 152°01'E., 34 km E. of Guyra, on Aberfoyle R.; formerly Aberfoil; airfield; cemetery (51 graves 1899+) 1894; school 1888–91; telegraph 1906; TX 1910, automatic 1972; pop. 104 (1911), 51 (1961), 121 (2006), 233 (2011).

Aberglasslyn (*Co. Northumberland*) 32°41'S. 151°32'E., 5 km NW of Maitland, on Hunter R.; agric.; brewery (Dusty Miner) 2014; bridge (Melville Ford Bridge) b. 1897 by Taylor and Littleproud, destroyed 1904, replaced 1905 by Walter Frank Oakes, new one b. 1939 by Jackson's Bridge Building Co. Pty Ltd, over Hunter R.; grasshopper infestation 1921; hailstorm 1937; PO 1927; school 1859–1934; storm 1962; telegraph 1924; TX 1927–60; pop. 125 (1901), 64 (1911), 80 (1933), 51 (1954), 2,857 (2011).

Abermain (*Co. Northumberland*) 32°49'S. 151°26'E., 3 km W. of Weston, on Swamp Ck; settled 1902, surveyed and laid out 1903 as a private village by Albert Francis Hall, lots sold 1904, govt village surveyed and gaz. 1907, lots auctioned 1908 and building began; mining (coal disc. 1884 by William Tester); Angl. C. (Holy Trinity) b. 1909 by T. Kirk, d. by James Warren Scobie, closed, sold and reused; Bapt. C. b. 1912 by J. Davies, burnt down 1925, rebuilt 1926; bridges: timber beam one, b. 1905 by John McNulty, 73 ft (22.3 m), damaged 1931, damaged and closed 2015, replaced (concrete) 2017, over Deep Ck and one over Swamp Ck; bushfires 1944, 1951, 2016; clock tower 2001; collieries: Abermain No. 1 (estab. as Silkstone Coalmine, o. and renamed 1903 by Abermain Colliery Co. Ltd, strike 1912, 3 men killed 1913–19, taken over 1922 by Abermain Seaham Collieries Ltd, strikes 1923, 1924, 1925, 1930, taken over 1930 by J. & A. Brown & Abermain Seaham Collieries Ltd, strike 1932, man killed 1934, strikes 1935, 1937, 1942, 1947, man killed 1951, taken over and closed 1960 by Coal & Allied Industries Ltd, razed), Greta Main (estab. 1921 by Charles Jeffries, men killed 1927 and 1928, strike 1930–31, closed 1935, razed), Sore Eye; Community C. (The Vines), closed; earth tremor 1925; FB 1909 (station b. 1913 by Arthur Howarth, new one 1959, demolished 2016, replaced 2017); fires 1918 and 1921; floods 1931, 2007, 2015; 2 footbridges over Swamp Ck; gales 1899 and 1944; Meth. C. b. 1909 by Mullally, E. Hedley and T. Sullivan; mines rescue station (South Maitland) b. 1926 by Leslie Elgin Brander, d. by Pitt and Merewether, closed 1983, sold and reused; PO 1904, new one b. 1914; Presb. C. b. 1906 by Hughes and Nelson, closed, sold and reused; PS 1906, new one b. 1927; railway (colliery); railway bridge over Swamp Ck; reservoir; rifle range 1915; Rom. Cath. C. b. 1904 by T. Woodbury, new one (St Francis Xavier's) b. 1972 by Doran Constructions Pty Ltd, d. by Terence A. Daly; RS (on South Maitland Railway) 1903, station rebuilt 1936 by R.H. Hewitt; school (private town) 1905, new one b. 1906 by Reece Lewis, new one (govt town) b. 1909 by George Taylor, new building b. 1927 by J. Mitchell & Son, fire 1932; telephone 1905; TX (automatic); Unit. C.; pop. *c.*300 (1905), 1,849 (1911), 2,491 (1933), 2,182 (1947), 2,104 (1954), 2,006 (1961), 2,322 (2011).

Abermain Shaft No. 2 (*Co. Northumberland*) see Kearsley.

Abernethy (*Co. Northumberland*) 32°53'S. 151°24'E., 7 km SE of Cessnock, on Swamp Ck; village gaz. 1915; coalmining and poultry; Angl. C. (St James's) b. 1923 by Charles Waugh, d. by Ernest Tingle; brickworks (colliery); bushfires 1951, 2002 (man died and 13 houses destroyed), 2016; cemetery; colliery (Aberdare South) estab. 1911 by Alexander and A.H. Shedden as Abernethy Main, acquired 1913 by Caledonian Collieries Ltd and renamed, o. 1918, strikes 1923 and 1924, closed 1927, largely demolished; dam (colliery) 1917; earth tremor 2014; PO 1915; railway (colliery) b. 1917 by J.M. and H.E. Coane, closed 1927; school 1916, new one b. 1918 by A.P. Wall, closed 1966; storm 1937; telephone 1917; pop. 316 (1933), 186 (1947), 189 (1954), 143 (1961), 221 (2011).

Abington (*Co. Hardinge*) 30°17'S. 151°12'E., 37 km S. of Tingha, on Abington Ck; bridge 1924, over Abington Ck; PO 1898; school 1957–69; telephone 1906; pop. 105 (1911), 57 (1954).

Abrahams Bosom (*Co. Goulburn*) 35°58'S. 147°34'E., 33 km SE of Holbrook, on Murray R.

Abroi (*Co. Clarke*) 30°17'S. 152°08'E., 46 km E. of Guyra; telephone 1921; TX 1925.

Acacia (*Co. Yancowinna*) see Limestone.

Acacia Creek (*Co. Buller*) 28°22'S. 152°20'E., 70 km W. of Kyogle, on Acacia Ck; timber, farming, dairying; Angl. C. (St Paul's) 1910; butter factory (Acacia Co-op. Dairy Co. Ltd) 1908; CH b. 1908 by J. Day; PO 1880–1959; PS b. 1901 by William Laws; sawmills: Federal Timber Co. Ltd (sold 1907 to Peterson), J.W. Lewis, J.O.W. Mangleson (fire 1923), Charles Smith; school 1910–34; telephone 1906; TX 1924; Union C.; pop. 181 (1901), 304 (1911), 92 (1933), 50 (1954).

Acacia Creek (*Co. Buller*) see also Legume.

Acacia Dam (*Co. Yancowinna*) see Limestone.

Acacia Park (*Co. Sandon*) 30°33'S. 151°41'E., 5 km SE of Armidale.

Acacia Plateau (*Co. Buller*) 28°23'S. 152°23'E., 63 km NW of Kyogle; farming and dairying; bushfire 1926; PO 1936; school 1957–67; telephone 1923; TX 1936; pop. 99 (1933), 117 (1947), 114 (1954), 84 (1961).

Adaminaby (*Co. Wallace*) 36°00'S. 148°46'E., 41 km NW of Cooma; (incl. Old Adaminaby, submerged in 1957 under Lake Eucumbene); Chalkers till 1885, then Seymour till 1886; surveyed 1860 by Wilbraham Edwards, town gaz. 1861 as Seymour, first town lot sold 1861, 101 buildings relocated and rebuilt 1956–57 on new site laid out by Denis Winston 8 km from Old Adaminaby; gold (disc. 1860), sheep, lucerne, oats, fruit, potatoes, fishing; Angl. C. 1863, reused, replacement (St John the Evangelist) b. 1907 by Arthur Mawson, d. by George Donald Cochran, dismantled 1956 and rebuilt 1957 on new site, and graveyard; butter factory (NSW Creamery Butter Co. Ltd) 1895 d. by Charles C. Lance; cemetery (458 graves 1863+) 1863, new one, incl. columbaria; CH (incl. lock-up) b. 1899 by H.H. Mawson, relocated and reused, new one 1957 on new site; earth tremor 1910; fires

1880 and 1885; Meth. C. b. 1906 by James Frederick Allan and Robert George Allan, extant in situ, reused; PO 1861, new one b. 1893 by David Montgomery, relocated 1957; Presb. C. (St Andrew's) b. 1888 by Thomas Try, closed 1956; PS 1864, new one b. 1901 by Arthur Mawson, closed 1935, new one 1957 on new site; Rom. Cath. C. 1875, new one b. 1911 by J.G. Taylor, d. by George Donald Cochran, dismantled and rebuilt 1957 on new site, burnt down 2006, replacement (St Mary's) b. 2011 by Dewram Constructions Pty Ltd, and graveyard; sawmills: Alpine (A.S. Kelly), Herbert Betts 1946 (sold 1958 to George Vodicka, closed 1962), Rayner Bros 1962 (sold 1972 to Tableland Sawmills Pty Ltd); school 1877, new one b. 1890 by Mark Duffy, repairs 1892 by Robert George Allen, additions and alterations 1910 by Arthur Mawson, extant in situ; sewerage 1960; telegraph 1875; TX 1907; Unit. C. (orig. Presb.) 1957; water reticulation 1959; Wes. Meth. C. 1874, extended 1879, demolished; pop. *c.*67 (1866), *c.*400 (1877), 156 (1891), 608 (1901), 1,250 (1911), 580 (1933), 552 (1947), 523 (1954), 336 (1957), 460 (1961), 412 (1971), 366 (1976), 378 (1981), 283 (1986), 375 (1991), 366 (1996), 465 (2001), 388 (2006), 226 (2011).

Adaminaby Dam (*Co. Wallace*) see Eucumbene.

Adams Crossing (*Co. Gresham*) 29°49'S. 152°36'E., 35 km SW of Grafton, on Nymboida R.

Adams Scrub (*Co. Burnett*) 29°40'S. 150°36'E., 14 km S. of Warialda.

Adamstown (*Co. Northumberland*) 32°56'S. 151°43'E., 6 km W. of Newcastle; (incl. Adamstown Heights); estab. 1870 as a residential area for miners, surveyed by Philip Francis Adams, subdivided by A.S. Huntley, first land sale 1875, munic. 1885–1938 but became part of City of Greater Newcastle; brickmaking, coalmining, agric.; Angl. C. b. 1893 by Dyson & Co., d. by Frederick Burnhardt Menkens, new one (St Stephen's) b. 1954 by T.E. Taylor, d. by Louis Reginald Williams, additions 1960 and 1973; army training depot; brass and iron foundry (Wilson and Cowan); brickworks: Adamstown Steam Brick Co. Ltd 1900–26, Edward Banks 1905, Charles Freeman 1883 (taken over 1898 by Thomas Cottrell); bushfires 1884 and 1951; Christ. Brethren Assemblies C. (Community), refurbished 2003, now Livefree C.; clock tower 1977; collieries: Ebbw Vale (New Lambton Coal Co. Ltd) 1883–1935, Grafton, New Lambton (John and Alexander Brown), Shortland (estab. 1897 by James Ruttley, strikes 1907, 1911, 1912, 1923, fire and closure 1933, abandoned 1935 and plant and equipment sold); cordial factory (Searle Bros); FB 1890 (station b. 1891 by G. Turner, alterations 1917, new station b. 1922 by William Venon Southon, d. by William Hull McNiven, closed, sold and reused); floods 1893, 1897, 1898; foundries: Hardware Foundry Co. and Wilson & Cowan Ltd 1921; Full Gospel C. (Adamstown Heights); hosiery factory (Lustre Hosiery Pty Ltd) b. 1953 by J.C. Davis & Sons, d. by Rodd and Hay, closed, conversion d. by John Patrick, Peter Jerome and John Kevin Gannon, reused 1961; hurricane 1899; lock-up b. 1887 by William Dart; PO: Adamstown 1877 (new one b. 1895 by Southon Bros, extensions 1965 and 1979, partly reused) and Adamstown Heights 1946; Presb. C. 1905 d. by Thomas James Pepper; Prim. Meth. C. 1875, extended 1879, new one 1884; PS 1885, new one (incl. cells) b. 1911, closed, sold and reused; pudding factory 1971; quarry; railway (New Redhead Estate & Coal Co.) to Belmont; railway tunnel (Fernleigh), 198 yds (181 m), 1892, closed, restored and reused; 4 reservoirs; rifle range b. 1901 by Robert Comley; Rom. Cath. C. b. 1885 by Clancy, destroyed 1899, replacement b. 1900–22, d. by Peter Joseph Gannon, closed and reused 1963, new one (St Columba's) 1963 d. by Peter Jerome Gannon; RS 1887, station b. 1891 by John Rollo Rodgers, demolished, replaced 1977 by Steel Building Systems Pty Ltd; Salv. Army C. 1926; schools: Adamstown 1877 (new one

b. 1879, additions 1884 by J. Shaw, additions 1905, additions 1910 by G. Taylor, additions 1965, closed 1971, reused 1973, new infants school b. 1922 on new site by H.W. Jones, additions 1934, damaged 1989, closed, sold and reused, new primary school 1971 on new site), Adamstown Heights 1950–90, Belair 1968 (additions 2010), Kotara HS 1968, additions by R.T. Parker Pty Ltd, re-roofed 2013; sewerage 1915; squall 1913; storm (boy killed) 1899; streets gas lit 1911; tannery 1900; telegraph 1889, new office b. 1895 by Southon Bros; telephone 1908; tramway (steam) to Newcastle 1900, electrified 1925; TX 1889; typhoid 1886 and 1888; Ukrainian Cath. C. (Protection of the Mother of God) 1969; Unit. C. (Jubilee, orig. Meth.) b. 1924 by William Stronach, d. by Benjamin George Pearce, additions and alterations 2008; United Meth. Free C. 1885; water supply 1892; pop. 561 (1881), 2,030 (1891), *c.*2,200 (1895), 2,112 (1900), 2,420 (1901), 2,548 (1911), *c.*4,000 (1921), 4,888 (1933), *c.*5,300 (1947), *c.*4,800 (1954), *c.*6,600 (1961), *c.*7,600 (1966), *c.*10,100 (1971–76), 10,454 (2006), 10,816 (2011).

Adamstown Heights (*Co. Northumberland*) see Adamstown.

Adavale West (*Co. Kennedy*) 32°55'S. 147°55'E., 19 km E. of Trundle; school 1914–64.

Addicumbene (*Co. Wallace*) 36°02'S. 148°36'E., 52 km NW of Cooma; PO 1927–31; telephone 1915; TX.

Adelargo (*Co. Forbes*) 33°48'S. 148°18'E., 16 km NE of Grenfell, on Native Dog Ck.

Adelong (*Co. Wynyard*) 35°19'S. 148°04'E., 14 km W. of Tumut, on Adelong Ck; settled in 1840s, estab. 1856, thrived 1865–85, town gaz. 1880; goldmining (alluvial gold disc. 1853, reef gold disc. 1857 by William Williams, gold rushes 1855, 1860, 1872) mainly 1853–78 and dredging 1901–39, beef, wool, timber, orchards, hort.; Angl. C. (St Paul's) 1872, damaged and repaired 1888; benevolent asylum; brewery (W.S. Eaton & Co.) 1897, sold 1903 to H.S. Headley; bridge b. 1874 by W. and D. Boston, new one 1902, replaced (4 span concrete) 2011, 203 ft (62 m), over Adelong Ck; buddle (Lewis and Munday's patent) 1876; bushfires 1900 and 1939; carriage-works: Boston & Sons and Charles Passlow; cemetery (572 graves) 1879; CH 1874, additions and repairs 1878 by William M. Hotten, alterations and repairs 1908 by W.J. Ritchie, reused; cordial factories: L. Flakelar 1914, and Patrick Kenny and Harry Tweedie (Alphonse Legorie Bourgoin joined partnership 1868, left 1869, Webster replaced Tweedie as Kenny's partner, then R. Dear replaced Webster, then Kenny traded alone till selling to W.S. Eaton & Co., sold 1903 to H.S. Headley, acquired 1903 by James Considine and named Waranga); cyanide plant 1900; cyclone 1888; diphtheria 1917, 1920, 1921; earth tremors 1871, 1908, 1917, 1918; FB 1929 (station b. 1979); fires 1887, 1892, 1924, 1943; floods 1874, 1879, 1931, 2010; hospital (Outpost), reused; jam factory 1917; measles epidemics 1893 and 1923; miners' strike 1898; mines: W. Annetts, A. Bruce, Camp Reef Gold Mining Co., T. Channon, R. Crandell, Crown of Old Reef Gold Mining Co., Currajong Gold Mining Co., N. Emanuel, Flagstaff Gold Mining Co. (Amos), J. Gale, Great Victoria Gold Mining Co., Hamilton, W. Hendon, M. Hodge, J. Ilott, Kennedy and McCutchen, Leviathan Gold Mining Co., Little Victoria Gold Mining Co., North Williams Gold Mining Co., Old Reef Gold Mining Co., Our Own Gold Mining Co., Research Gold Mining Co., R. Rogers, R.E. Thomas, J. Tonking, R. Trudgen, Union Gold Mining Co., J. Watson, Welcome Home Gold Mining Co., Williams Gold Mining Co. (incl. 8 head stamper battery), D. Wilson; PO 1859, new one 1866, replacement b. 1886 by George Lipscombe, additions 1900 by W.J. Ritchie; police barracks, bought, dismantled and removed 1885 by Boston, replaced 1886 by Woodhouse, Fisher and Holder; pound (stock) 1865; PS 1874, reused; quarry; reservoir; reverberatory furnace 1876; rifle range 1907; Rom. Cath. C. (St James's) b. 1865–68, new chancel 1880; sale-yards 1950; Salv. Army C.; sandfly infestation 1886; school 1860, new one b. 1878 by Kinred Bros, d. by John Gordon, new building and alterations 1885 by D. Boston, repairs 1895 by Phillips and Boston, additions and repairs 1903 by W.J. Ritchie, additions 1959 and 1966, additions 2010 by Burton Constructions Pty Ltd; sewerage 1968; snowstorm 1899; stamper batteries: Perseverance Gold-mining Co., Pioneer erected by David Wilson, Reefer (b. 1858 by David Wilson et al., relocated 1870 by William Ritchie et al., used two waterwheels 1870 and 1882); storms 1913 and 1926; telegraph 1866, new office b. 1886 by George Lipscombe; tornado 1923; TX 1909, automatic 1970; Unit. C.: St Andrew's (orig. Presb.) b. 1878 by D. Boston, d. by David Wilson, closed and reused, and Wesley (orig. Wes. Meth.) 1867, closed and reused; water supply 1944, augmentation 1985; pop. *c.*5,000 (1855), *c.*20,000 (1860), 186 (1861), *c.*400 (1866), 864 (1871), 753 (1881), *c.*800 (1887), 1,173 (1891), 1,410 (1901), 1,866 (1911), 819 (1933), 738 (1947), 789 (1954), 800 (1961), 741 (1966), 759 (1971), 766 (1976), 806 (1981), 855 (1986), 795 (1991), 782 (1996), 809 (2001), 829 (2006), 884 (2011).

Adelong Crossing (*Co. Wynyard*) see Tumblong.

Adelong Crossing Place (*Co. Wynyard*) see Tumblong.

Adelong Grove (*Co. Wynyard*) 35°22'S. 148°05'E., 6 km S. of Adelong, on Adelong Ck; school 1876, new one b. 1879 by William Balman, closed 1917; TX.

Adjungbilly (*Co. Buccleuch*) 35°05'S. 148°25'E., 28 km E. of Gundagai, on Adjungbilly Ck; Tomooroma till 1899; goldmining (alluvial) and grazing; bushfire 1979; cemetery; PO 1896; sawmill (Hallstrom's), sold 1922 to Withers; school (Bongongo) 1902; telephone 1924; TX 1928, automatic 1968; pop. 119 (1901), 126 (1911), 135 (1933), 119 (1947), 111 (1954), 147 (1961), 158 (2006).

Aellalong (*Co. Northumberland*) see Ellalong.

Afterlee (*Co. Rous*) 28°35'S. 152°49'E., 19 km W. of Kyogle, on Cob o' Corn Ck; Cob o' Corn till 1920; timber then dairying; gale 1933; PO 1911; sawmills: Barrett and O'Neill, E.G.A. King, Thomson Bros 1918–24; school 1957; telephone 1922; TX 1923; pop. 110 (1933), 102 (1947), 101 (1954), 90 (1961), 407 (2006).

Ahdaman (*Co. Bourke*) 34°14'S. 147°10'E., 27 km NE of Ardlethan.

Ailsa (*Co. Bligh*) 32°03'S. 150°10'E., 21 km NW of Merriwa, on Krui R.; laid out by J.S. Rusden and town gaz. 1840; agric.; pop. 13 (1846), 14 (1851).

Airdrie (*Co. Durham*) 32°35'S. 151°38'E., 15 km N. of Bolwarra; RS 1948–75.

Airlie Brake (*Co. Arrawatta*) 29°34'S. 151°11'E., 25 km N. of Inverell; hailstorm 1907; mine; Presb. C. 1879, moved 1910 to Nullamanna; school (Dinton Vale 1904–7) 1901–20; pop. 57 (1933).

Airly (*Co. Roxburgh*) 33°07'S. 150°02'E., 27 km N. of Portland, on Gap Ck; estab. by Genowlan Shale Co., village gaz. 1897, lots sold 1898, thrived 1883–1908, failed by 1918; formerly oil-shale mining (oil-shale disc. 1883 by Bulkeley, J. Larkin, Massey, Melliday and S. Nicholson) till 1903, now coalmining; coalmines: Centennial Coal Co. Ltd, estab. 2010, and Torbane Tunnel; gale 1901; landslide 1913; miners' strikes 1900–2, 1904, 1907–8; oil-shale mine (Genowlan Shale Co.) 1883 (adits incl. Davis's Heading, Elliott's Heading, Oxley's Heading, Penrose No. 1 Tunnel, Porter's Bord, Sinclair's Heading), acquired 1895 by Aust. Shale Syndicate Ltd, taken over 1897 by Aust. Kerosene Oil & Mineral Co., closed 1903, reopened 1903 by Aust. Shale Syndicate Ltd, acquired 1906 by Commonwealth Oil Corp. Ltd, taken over 1916 by Commonwealth Oil Federation, closed 1918; PO 1897–1920; school (Genowlan till 1910) 1897–1920; tramway (mineral) b. 1897–1900; whooping cough epidemics 1901 and 1917; pop. 406 (1901), 234 (1911).

Akolele (*Co. Dampier*) 36°21'S. 150°04'E., 7 km N. of Bermagui, on Wallaga Lake; bridge b. 1894 by Ring and Spencer, d. by John Alexander McDonald, over Wallaga Lake; pop. 132 (2011).

Akuna (*Co. Phillip*) 32°44'S. 150°07'E., 15 km

NE of Rylstone, on Coxs Ck; TX 1925.

Alagala (*Co. Kennedy*) 32°25'S. 147°43'E., 53 km W. of Narromine; grazing; PO 1927.

Alambie (*Co. Rous*) 28°47'S. 153°31'E., 10 km NE of Alstonville.

Albermarle (*Co. Livingstone*) 32°18'S. 142°39'E., 117 km E. of Broken Hill, on Darling R.; pop. 30 (1933).

Albert (*Co. Kennedy*) 32°21'S. 147°30'E., 70 km W. of Narromine, on Bullock Ck; The Alberts till 1916; village gaz. 1915; farming, grazing, mining (copper and gold); Angl. C. (All Saints') b. 1931 by W. Page, damaged 1932; cemetery (92 graves) 1916; gale 1932; mine (Iron Duke) 1899–*c.*1920, bought 2008 by Kimberley Metals from CBH Resources; PO 1917, burnt down 1921; Presb. C. (Mailer Memorial) 1928; PS 1933, new one b. 1934 by Bert Palmer and A.J. Hepburn; railway (mineral), abandoned; Rom. Cath. C. (Corpus Christi) 1928; RS 1916–74; sawmills: Breaden and Selmes (man killed 1927) and Andrew Strudwick; school 1929–72; telephone 1919; TX 1919; pop. 215 (1933), 100 (1947), 165 (1954), 108 (1961), 94 (2006).

Albert (*Co. Tongowoko*) 29°31'S. 141°50'E., 268 km NW of Wilcannia; estab. 1882, abandoned before 1900; goldmining 1881+.

Albert Park (*Co. Rous*) see Lismore.

Albion (*Co. Pottinger*) see Gunnedah.

Albion (*Co. Yancowinna*) 31°44'S. 141°34'E., 27 km N. of Broken Hill; mines: Albion, Bendigo, Rise and Shine.

Albion Flat (*Co. Hardinge*) 29°57'S. 151°15'E., 5 km E. of Tingha, on Copes Ck; 2 mines; pop. 44 (1933).

Albion Hill (*Co. Gough*) see Inverell.

Albion Park (*Co. Camden*) 34°34'S. 150°46'E., 8 km S. of Dapto, on Frazers Ck; (incl. Croom, Mount Terry, Wentworth Hills); Terry's Meadows till 1840; estab. 1861, expanded 1892, subdivisions 1974, 1977, 1981, 1982; wheat till 1860, then cattle, maize, oats, barley, rye till 1873, then dairying, especially butter; Angl. C. (All Saints') b. 1875 by John Schadel, d. by Blacket, re-roofed 1963, and graveyard (457 graves) 1869, incl. columbarium; Assemblies of God C. (Shellharbour); Bapt. C.; bushfires 1905 and 1909; butter factory (Albion Park Dairy Co.) b. 1885 by James Dawes, d. by Waugh and Josephson, closed 1908; carriage-works (Mood Bros) 1895 (removed from Shellharbour); caterpillar infestation 1893; cemeteries: pioneer (orig. Presb., 71 graves 1851–1969) 1876 and general (409 graves) 1900; CH 1894, new one b. 1908 by Frederick Lemm, d. by Walter Liberty Vernon; Christ. City C.; dairy factory (Yellow Rock Dairy Co.) 1890–1903; earth tremor 1949; electricity 1928; FB 1952 (station b. 2014); flood 2011; lock-up 1894, new one 1908; Meth. C. 1953, extended 1965; PO: Albion Park 1861, new one b. 1895 by George Humphreys, repairs 1907 by A. Porter, and Croom 1889; pound (stock) 1854; Presb. C. 1866, demolished 1907, replacement (St Andrew's) b. 1908 by Frederick Lemm, d. by George Herbert Godsell, and graveyard; PS 1884, new one b. 1908 by Frederick Lemm; quarries: Cleary Bros, and Farley and Lewers; railway tunnel (Croom), 44 yds (40.2 m), 1887; reservoir; Rom. Cath. C. (St Paul's) 1874, extended 1883, additions 1900, demolished 1973, new one (St Paul the Apostle) 1975 d. by Glendenning and King, additions and alterations 2009, and graveyard (442 graves) 1874, incl. columbarium 1994; RS: Croom 1925–50 and Shell Cove b. 2014 by Haslin Constructions Pty Ltd; sawmills: E.J. Bresnahan, C. Buchanan, Macquarie Timber Co., Thomas Bros 1918, Upton Bros; schools: Albion Park 1872 (new one b. 1893 by Dawes Bros, additions 1908 by F.G. Bidgood, additions 1963), Albion Park HS 1991, Croom (b. 1884 by J. Atkinson, closed 1911, demolished), Mount Terry 1995; streets oil lit 1899, then electric lit 1928; tannery estab. 1892 by James Missingham, burnt down 1897, rebuilt, closed; telegraph 1889; telephone 1886; TX 1911; typhoid 1889; Unit. C.; water supply 1955; Wes. Meth. C. 1866; pop. *c.*1,000 (1866), 458 (1911), 12,156 (2006), 12,872 (2011).

Albion Park (*Co. Camden*) see also Yallah.

Albion Park Rail (*Co. Camden*) 34°34'S. 150°48'E., 7 km S. of Dapto, on Koona Bay; subdivided 1921; airport (Illawarra Regional, renamed Shellharbour) 1941, air force base during World War II, new terminal 1993, new hangar 2005; Assemblies of God C. (Lighthouse); Bapt. C.; butter factory (Illawarra Co-op. Central Dairy Society Ltd) 1899, rebuilt 1926 and 1951, closed 1985, reused; cement works (Specified Concrete Pty Ltd); cemetery (Albion Park, formerly Croome, 407 graves 1901+) 1900; FB (station b. 1971); flood 2011; foot-bridge (Slaters Bridge) to Oak Flats, over Horsley Ck; Meth. C. 1928, extended 1941 and 1952, new one 1964; PO 1927; RS (Oak Flats till 1888, then Albion Park) 1887, new station b. 1889; sawmills: Albion Park Building Supplies Pty Ltd, closed 1954, Brush's 1915, Upton Bros 1945, sold 1947; school 1959, additions 1961, 1964, 1970, 1982; telephone 1927; TX (automatic) 1959, new one b. 1969 by A.F. Little Pty Ltd; Union C.; Unit. C., closed; pop. 7,003 (2011).

Albiontown (*Co. Yancowinna*) 31°44'S. 141°34'E., 28 km N. of Broken Hill.

Albury (*Co. Goulburn*) 36°05'S. 146°55'E., 115 km S. of Wagga Wagga, on Murray R.; (incl. East Albury, East Lavington, Glen Morris, Glenroy, Hamilton Valley, Lavington formerly Black Range till 1909, settled 1881 by Joseph Box, North Albury, South Albury, Springdale Heights, West Albury); The Crossing Place till 1839, then Sleepy Hollow and later sometimes also known as Federal City; founded 1824 by Hamilton Hume and William Hilton Hovell, settled 1836 by Robert Brown, surveyed and laid out 1839 by Thomas Scott Townsend, first lots sold 1839 and 1842, expanded 1855+, munic. proc. 1859, thrived 1860 and 1880, town gaz. 1879, designated as chief town of the county, thrived 1923, city proc. 1946, decl. a growth area 1973; orig. wool, wheat and wine-making 1851–70s, then a river port 1855+ with shipbuilding 1858+, mining (gold disc. 1852 by Richard Heaver and James Dennison) 1860–65, oats till *c.*1876, barley, tobacco 1860s–80s, silk 1873–80s, orchards, brandy, butter, cheese, ham, bacon till 1900, honey 1920s+, tourism 1940+, skins, tallow, now agric., hort., grazing, dairying, secondary industry; abattoir b. 1938 by F.W. Lemcke, closed; airport (4 km NE) 1938, World War II airfield, reconstructed and enlarged 1964, new terminal and control tower 1983, terminal redeveloped 2009; ambulance station b. 1934 by Ezra Griffin, new one b. 2014 by Joss Constructions; Angl. C.: St James's (Lavington, first one b. 1873, new one 1907, additions 1932), St Mark's (North Albury) 1970, St Matthew the Apostle and Evangelist (b. 1857–59 by J.H. Kirkpatrick, A.D. Livie and John Robertson, d. by Edmund Thomas Blacket, new one b. 1873–76 by Frew & Co., d. by William Boles, extensions and renovations 1904, alterations 1914 by R.A. Statton, d. by Thorne and Summers, extensions 1974–76, spire added 1977, fire 1991, rebuilding d. by Ian O'Connor, reopened 1994); Assemblies of God C. (North Gate Christ.); Bapt. C. 1930 d. by Harrison and Glaskin, extensions and alterations 1980; bicycle works (Crown) estab. 1899 by Kalbrunner and Uren; biscuit and jam factory 1893; boiling-down works: Morris Asher, later converted to flour mill by Alexander Moon, and Scrivener's 1892 (became Dundas & Co., burnt down 1896, rebuilt, sold 1904 to Collins and Mason); bond store (Mate's), inundated 1889; boot factories: Carew's, Kidd's, M'Guffin's; bottled water plant (Mountain H_20 Pty Ltd) 2000, sold 2011 to Asahi Group Holdings Ltd; breweries: Albury Brewery (first) 1857–72 (b. by Robert Davison and John Kaleski), Albury Brewery (second one, estab. 1874 by Richard O'Keeffe, acquired 1879 by George H. Billson, greatly expanded 1879–82, acquired 1888 by Albury Brewing & Malting Co., taken over 1911 by Border United Co-op. Breweries Ltd, improvements 1913), W.J. Billson 1895, Hume Brewery (first) 1871–74 (estab. by Frederick Gleich and A. Frew), Hume Brewery (second) 1872–88 (estab. by Robert Manning as

Colonial Porter Brewery, bought 1882 by W.S. Eaton, firm known as Headley and Langhammer), Liddle's Brewery 1871–72 (estab. by James Liddle), Robert Manning 1883–84, Thomson's; brickworks: E. Bunton, Flynn and Miller, S. McKay Logan, Mates Ltd, E.W. Sharp, Walkerden Bros; bridges: Union Bridge 1861, 256 ft (78 m), demolished, replacement b. 1899 by J.B. and W. Farquharson, 325 ft (99.1 m), new one (concrete) b. 1957–61 by Brown's Constructional Enterprises Pty Ltd, widened 1990, over Murray R., Smollett Street Bridge (wrought iron arch) 1887, 45 ft (13.7 m), d. by John Alexander McDonald, over Bungambrawatha Ck, Spirit of Progress Bridge (box girder) b. 2006 by Fitzgerald Constructions Aust., over Murray R.; bushfires 1851, 1868, 1878, 1882, 1905, 1923, 1990, 2013; butter factories: Albury Co-op. Butter Factory & Produce Co. Ltd 1897 (sold 1921 to Holderson & Neilson Fresh Food Pty Ltd, demolished 1926) and Albury Dist. Rural Co-op. Society Ltd; CAE (Riverina) 1972, became Riverina-Murray Institute of Higher Education in 1985, became univ. (Charles Sturt) in 1989; candle factory (M'Govern's); carriage-works: George Dallinger & Co. 1884, Edwin Charles Ellis & Son 1893, fire 1898, Helm Bros, J. Higgins, burnt down 1885, Higgins and Baker, burnt down 1879, G.E. Robinson, burnt down 1879; case factory (E. Arnold); cemeteries: Glenmorus Memorial Gardens crematorium 1969 and lawn cemetery, pioneer 1867, Waugh Road 1925 (and lawn cemetery 1958); CH b. 1860 by Thomas Allen, d. by Alexander Dawson, additions 1877, extensions 1881 d. by James Johnstone Barnet, additions 1883 by J. Hartley, additions 1898 d. by Walter Liberty Vernon, additions and alterations 1911 by Hanna and Spalding, renovations 1933, alterations 1961, 1966, 1975, additions 1982, new one b. 1985–87 d. by John Whyte Ian Thomson; Chinese joss house 1876, burnt down 1915; Christ. Fellowship C.; Christ. Revival Crusade C. (Twin City); Churches of Christ: Lavington and River Community; clothing factory (H.D. Lee & Co.) 1973; Cong. C. 1875, closed, reopened 1902, closed, reused 1928; cordial factories: Albury Aerated Waterworks (William H. Gilbert), fire 1880, Albury Brewing & Malting Co. 1897, George Peirson, Phibbs Bros 1909, C. Reis, A. Krueger and Kolk (closed and burnt down 1896, site sold 1896 to Phibbs), Sharpe Bros (estab. by John and Ewart Sharpe) 1920–41, J.F. Willson; customs-house 1864; cyclone 1886; dairy factory (Riverina Dairy Pty Ltd) 2005; dengue fever 1942; diphtheria 1889, 1919 (boy died), 1931; droughts 1850, 1861–62, 1866, 1868, 1877, 1944–45; earth tremors 1871, 1901, 1917; electricity 1916; engineering works: Albury Hydraulics 1987, Lavenco Engineering Pty Ltd 1985, Milspec Manufacturing 2002, Yeo Engineering Pty Ltd 1980; fabric mills: Geofabrics A'asia Pty Ltd 1985, Kimberly-Clark Aust. Pty Ltd 1987–2015, Macquarie Worsteds Ltd 1925; FB 1863 (stations b. 1889, 1916, 1968, 1982, 2008); fibrous plaster works (J.E. Winzer); fires 1868, 1879, 1880, 1884, 1885, 1893, 1896, 1898, 1910, 1915, 1930; floods 1844, 1847, 1851, 1852, 1866, 1867, 1870, 1871, 1875, 1879, 1889, 1906, 1916–17, 1921, 1936, 1939, 1946; flour mills: Fanny Ceres (b. 1851 by James McLaurin, taken over 1862 by George Day, taken over 1871 by Hayes Bros, closed 1887, replacement b. 1887 by James Hayes, boiler explosion 1899 killed boy, burnt down 1909), Richard Heaver 1850, Hume (bought 1869 by John Burrows Pty Ltd, closed 1908, dismantled 1909, rebuilt 1910, sold 1946 to Bunge Aust. Pty Ltd), Meddler and Brebner (taken over 1858 by Joseph Eager), Alexander Moon; foot-bridge over Bungambrawatha Ck; gaol 1860, replaced 1862, additions 1880 by Alkemade and Dickson, modified 1884, closed 1943; gasworks (Albury Gas Co. Ltd) 1882; gate works (Frauenfelder Gates) 1948; gold crushing mill (Lavington) 1865–67; grain processing mill (Bunge's); Greek Orthodox C. (The Archangels) 1964; hailstorms 1896 and 1950; heatwaves 1878,

1880, 1881, 1882, 1900; hospital b. 1859–61 by Thomas Allen, additions 1879, extended 1883, closed 1918, new one b. 1914–18 by John Cochrane, enlarged 1938, additions 1940, 1956, 1972, new one 1994; ice works: Wade Bros Pty Ltd, and D.S. Watson and D.C. Young 1886; Indep. C. d. and b. 1875 by Alexander Jackson; injection moulding machinery plant (Battenfeld Aust. Pty Ltd); iron foundries: Hume (Charles Henry Lampitt) and John P. Laughton 1901; Islamic C. 2008, relocated 2013; joinery (F.A. Stow); LDS (Mormon) C.; leadlight works (H.B. Styles), fire 1936; lock-up, demolished 1878; Lutheran C.: Trinity (in former Cong. C.) 1928, closed 1966, reused, demolished 1973, St Luke's 1938 (enlarged 1967, renovated 2002), St Peter's (Lavington); meat freezing works 1894; metal fabrication works: Albury Steel Fabricators 1994, Macfab Engineering 1998, Southern Technology Pty Ltd 1980; Meth. C.: Lavington 1924 and one o. 1958; milk factory (Haberfields Milk Pty Ltd); mineral water factory (D.S. Watson and D.C. Young) 1877; mines: Black Range Deep Lead, Border City, China Claim, Ethiopian, W. Jones and party, May Day, Nailcan (reef gold) 1863–80, One Tree Hill Reef, Wealands Deposit; monumental stone works: Barklamb Bros Pty Ltd 1884, G. and J. Bennett, V. Brosolo, Thomas Greenfield 1884, Thomas Molloy, J.J. Wartzelhan; munitions factory 1941, reused; paper mill (Aust. Newsprint Mills Ltd) 1980; plastics factory (Fjord Manufacturing Pty Ltd) 1988; PO: Albury 1843 (new one b. 1878–80 d. by James Johnstone Barnet, additions and alterations 1883 by J. Hartley, extensions 1904 and 1913, additions 1942 by F.W. Lemcke, alterations 1954, closed, renovated and reused), East Albury 1937, East Lavington 1950, Lavington 1889, North Albury 1928, West Albury 1936–79; police barracks 1962; pottery (Gulson Bros) 1868; pound (stock) 1865; powerhouse 1916; Presb. C. b. 1859 by Rogers and Prior, closed and sold 1904 to Rom. Cath. C.; prune factory (John Frauenfelder); PS 1839, (second) 1865, (third) b. 1874 by Bourke and Jennings, (fourth) 1962, additions and alterations 1976, extensions 1994; punts: Robert Brown 1844, Crisp's, govt one, across Murray R.; railway barracks b. 1881 by Charles Hardy, additions 1890; railway bridge (iron lattice trusses) fabricated by Westwood, Baillie & Co., London, England, erected 1884 by A. Frew and J.S. Bennett, d. by Sir John Fowler and John Whitton, 600 ft (182.9 m), over Murray R.; railway coal stage b. 1881 by A. Frew; railway engine shed b. 1881 by A. Frew, fire 1890; railway turntable installed 1881 by A. Frew, replaced 1904 and 1926, mechanised 1979; 7 reservoirs (b. 1886, 1891, 1924, 1925, 1941, 1952, 1976); Rom. Cath. C.: Holy Spirit (Lavington), Sacred Heart (Black Range) b. 1904 by J.S. Adams, new one b. 1959 by Bob, Reg and Ken Garland, d. by Bill Purtell, St Brigid's 1858, demolished 1938, St Patrick's b. 1872 by James Walsh, d. by John Gordon, alterations, renovations and repairs 1903, enlargement 1930–33 d. by Harrison and Glaskin; RS 1881, station b. by J. Kyle, J. Stevens, J. Cummins and C. Harris, d. by John Whitton, platform 1,510 ft (460.2 m); sale-yards: G.L. Griffiths 1882, replaced, and Newmarket 1888, demolished; 2 Salv. Army C. (incl. one b. 1889); sawmill (T.H. Mate & Co. Ltd) 1902; scarlet fever 1861; schools: Albury 1850 (b. by Henry Wyse, new one b. 1861 on new site by Rogers and Poole, new one 1881 d. by William Edmund Kemp, new building b. 1892 by Charles Hardy, also d. by Kemp, alterations and repairs 1898 by Grant and Berry, additions and remodelling 1922 by Robert Daniel Quiggin, additions 1942 by F.W. Lemcke, additions 1965 and 1972), Albury HS 1920 (new one b. 1926–28 by P.W. Richardson, enlarged 1935, additions 1955, 1958, 1960, 1971–73, 1979), East Lavington 1959 (additions 1967, 1980, 2010), Glenroy 1975 (additions 1979), Hume 1969 (additions 1978), James Fallon HS (North Albury HS till 1995) 1961, additions 1962, 1963, 1967, 1972, fire 1973, additions 1976, Lavington (Black Range till 1909) 1865–68, reopened 1874, additions 1897 by Grant and Berry, additions 1956, 1959, 1962, 1966, Murray HS 1977, North Albury infants 1927–53, North Albury primary 1954 (additions 1956, 1960, 1963, 1965, 1968), Springdale Heights 1981, West Albury 1936 (additions 1970 and 1982); SD Adventist C. 1889, new one 1924; sewerage 1919, scheme completed 1930; shooting target factory (Australasian Training Aids) estab. 1959 by Lindsay Charles Knight, became Dart Defence Industries Pty Ltd in 1986, bought 1989 by Aust. Defence Industries, sold 1999; snow 1857, 1863, 1899, 1890, 1901, 1920, 1922; soap-works: IXL (reopened 1904 by Brandt and Andrews), A. Krueger 1893, M'Govern's 1857; stamper battery (Lavington) 1865; storms 1882, 1907, 1923 (child killed), 2005; streets gas lit 1882, electric lit 1916; strike (navvies) 1882; tanneries: August Krueger and Gorte (estab. 1869, Gorte left partnership 1875, burnt down 1898, rebuilt, taken over 1904 by Percival A. Pullan) and Podmore's 1857; TC 1899 d. by Walter Liberty Vernon, new one 1908, moved 1914 into old telegraph office, premises enlarged 1940, additions 1978, 1981, 1991, became a campus of Riverina Institute in 1992, additions 1994, 1996, 2014; telegraph: Albury 1858 (new office b. 1861, new one b. 1867 by Charles Hardy, sen. and Thomas Hodson, new one 1885, reused 1905), East Albury 1937, North Albury 1928, West Albury 1936; telephone: East Lavington 1950 and Lavington 1911; textile mill (Crestknit-Aywon), extended 1985; tile and pipe works (Rocla Pty Ltd); tinware factory (J.B. Hilton); toll-gate; tool and hardware factories: Apex Tool Group and Cooper Tools Pty Ltd 1971; trees (ornamental) planted in streets 1879 and 1993; TX: Albury 1898 and Lavington (automatic) 1949; typhoid (woman died) 1894; Union C. (Lavington) 1865; Unit. C.: St David's (orig. Presb., b. 1906 by A.C. Frew and S.M. Logan, d. by Campbell and Kernot), Trinity (extended 2000), Wesley; United C. (West Albury) o. 1940 (removed from Table Top); univ. (Charles Sturt) 1989; vehicle transmission factory (Borg-Warner Aust. Ltd) b. 1971 by Austin Anderson Pty Ltd, sold 1987 to BTR Nylex Ltd, renamed BTR Automotive, sold 2002 to ION Ltd, sold 2006 by Drivetrain Systems International, acquired 2009 by Geely Automotive Holdings, closed 2014; water reticulation (Lavington) 1952; waterworks b. 1884–86 by Evans, Son and Lipscomb, pumping machinery by Appleby Bros, water supply augmentation 1987 and 1994; Wes. Meth. C. 1865, new one b. 1875 by Charles Rosinsky, d. by Crouch and Wilson; wharf 1871, demolished 1896; wine cellars: J.T. Fallon & Co. 1869 (d. by John Gordon, reused 1965) and Greer & Co. (b. 1874 by John Jennings, d. by Thomas A. Bourke); woollen mill 1925 (orig. Amalgamated Textiles Aust. Ltd, became Macquarie Worsteds Ltd in 1956, taken over 1987 by General Investments Aust. Ltd, major expansion 1993, became Macquarie Textiles Group Ltd in 1994, sold 2013); wool-scour (Federal, Hunter Bros and Langdon); wool stores: Farmers and Graziers' (b. 1929 by Stuart Bros, d. by Louis Harrison, sold 1985 and reused), Riverina Wool, Hide & Skin Co., Younghusband & Co.; pop. 7 (1841), 65 (1846), 442 (1851), 645 (1856), 642 (1858), 981 (1861), 1,906 (1871), 4,040 (1881), 5,447 (1891), *c.*5,900 (1895), 6,257 (1901), 6,448 (1911), 7,810 (1923), 11,540 (1933), 15,764 (1947), 18,458 (1954), 22,028 (1961), 23,379 (1966), 27,383 (1971), 31,954 (1976), 35,072 (1981), 37,164 (1986), 39,975 (1991), 41,491 (1996), 42,148 (2001), 50,235 (2006).

Alcheringa (*Co. Hunter*) 32°27'S. 150°45'E., 9 km SE of Denman, on Hunter R.

Aldavilla (*Co. Dudley*) 31°05'S. 152°46'E., 7 km W. of Kempsey; farming and dairying; airport (Kempsey) b. 1937 by A.J. McKenzie, new runway b. 1950–53 by Logging & Earthmoving Co. Pty Ltd, major airport upgrade 2015; gaol b. 2004 by Lahey Constructions Pty Ltd and John Holland (Constructions) Pty Ltd, d. by Perumal Pedavoli, additions 2018 by Watpac Construction; PO 1919–47; school 1871, new school b. 1911 by George Parkins; telephone

1919; TX 1929; pop. 56 (1933), 88 (1947), 103 (1954), 93 (1961), 1,154 (2011).

Alderley (*Co. Gloucester*) 32°26'S. 151°58'E., 20 km E. of Dungog.

Alec's Flat (*Co. Kennedy*) see Alectown.

Alectown (*Co. Kennedy*) 32°56'S. 148°14'E., 24 km N. of Parkes, on Burrandong Ck; Bachelors Rush till 1889 (also known as Alec's Flat and Alick's Flat), then Alicktown till 1891; village gaz. 1889; mining (gold disc. 1889 by Alec Whitelaw, Alec Patton and Alec Cameron) till *c.*1900, grazing, now wheat; Angl. C. (St Stephen's); bushfire 1926; cemetery (123 graves 1891+) 1891; FB; fires 1900 and 1915; flood 1928; mines: Alick's Paddock 1889–1911, Bachelor's 1898, 1900, *c.*1946, Cobweb (Kennedy) *c.*1900, Dead Bird *c.*1895, Live Bird *c.*1890, Sherlaw and Jones 1891, A.N. Snow 1937, Spider *c.*1895, Stockman's 1891 and 1940–50; PO 1899–1983; Presb. C. (orig. Union) 1902; PS 1889–1930, sold and reused, dismantled 1963; Rom. Cath. C. (St Mary's) b. 1918 by Chris Bevis, closed, sold and reused; school 1890, extended and renovated 1928, closed 1974; storm 1900; telegraph 1891; TX 1916, automatic 1975; pop. 264 (1901), 317 (1911), 211 (1933), 194 (1947), 152 (1954), 301 (1961), 201 (2006).

Alectown West (*Co. Kennedy*) 32°56'S. 148°11'E., 23 km N. of Parkes; RS 1914–74; silo 1930; telephone 1922; pop. 65 (1933).

Alfred Lodge (*Co. Rous*) 28°41'S. 153°34'E., 4 km E. of Bangalow.

Alfredtown (*Co. Wynyard*) 35°10'S. 147°31'E., 14 km E. of Wagga Wagga, on Kyeamba Ck; bridge 1978 over Kyeamba Ck; bushfire 1930; creamery 1901; TX; Wes. Meth. C. 1890; pop. 26 (1933), 51 (1954), 64 (1961).

Alfredtown (*Co. Wynyard*) see also Ladysmith.

Alice (*Co. Drake*) 29°03'S. 152°35'E., 50 km SW of Casino, on Clarence R.; orig. Yates's Flat; surveyed 1860 by William Albert Braylesford Greaves, first lots sold 1860, declined 1886+; agric. and gold; bridge (Yates Crossing) 1931, over Clarence R.; flood 1863; prison farm (Balund-a, for Aborigines) 2009; punt, destroyed 1863, across Clarence R.; pop. 24 (1933).

Aliceton (*Co. Gloucester*) see Karuah.

Alick's Flat (*Co. Kennedy*) see Alectown.

Alicktown (*Co. Kennedy*) see Alectown.

Alison (*Co. Gloucester*) 32°27'S. 151°46'E., 6 km S. of Dungog, on Williams R.; farming and dairying; PO 1890; school 1865, new building 1928, closed 1961, reused; telephone 1919; TX 1928; pop. 117 (1933), 88 (1947), 76 (1954), 59 (1961), 291 (2011).

Alison (*Co. Northumberland*) see Jilliby.

Allan Cunningham (*Co. Durham*) 32°27'S. 150°46'E., 9 km SE of Denman; telephone 1914; TX 1928.

Allandale (*Co. Northumberland*) 32°43'S. 151°25'E., 9 km SE of Branxton, on Anvil Ck; farming and dairying; creamery (W.C. Green) 1900; diphtheria 1898; PO 1884; RS 1869–1974; school 1882, new one b. 1884 by Robert Sneesby, closed 1927; telegraph 1894; TX 1920–61; pop. 83 (1901), 263 (1911), 33 (1933), 60 (1947), 305 (2011).

Allandale South (*Co. Northumberland*) see Keinbah.

Alleena (*Co. Bland*) 34°04'S. 147°08'E., 18 km S. of West Wyalong; farming and wheat; eucalyptus oil distillery; PO 1927; RS (Moonoon till 1924, then Dinewan till 1925) 1923–74, station removed 1978; school 1957–60; silo 1928; telephone 1925; TX 1930, automatic 1977; pop. 104 (1933), 81 (1947), 64 (1954), 62 (1961).

Allendale (*Co. Roxburgh*) 33°10'S. 149°42'E., 30 km NE of Bathurst, on Big Oaky Ck; goldmining; mines: Lawsons Reef, Magenta Reef, Roxburgh, Scott and Clarke, Solitary Reef 1880–94, 1900–2, 1936, Wattle Flat Hill; 2 quarries.

Allen Mount (*Co. Blaxland*) see Double Peak.

Allgomera Creek (*Co. Raleigh*) 30°49'S. 152°50'E., 14 km SW of Macksville, on Allgomera Ck; farming and dairying; bridge, destroyed 1954; cheese factory (P. McCabe) 1916, bought 1920 by Eungai & Allgomera Co-op. Dairy Co. Ltd, closed; floods 1913 and 1954; PO 1927–56; telephone 1929; TX 1951–59; pop. 78 (1911), 21 (1933).

Allison's Siding (*Co. Oxley*) see Miowera.

Alloway (*Co. Ewenmar*) 31°41'S. 148°30'E., 15 km W. of Gilgandra.

Allworth (*Co. Gloucester*) 32°32'S. 151°58'E., 13 km N. of Karuah, on Karuah R.; New Wharf till 1911; logging, then farming, dairying, poultry, fishing; Angl. C. 1912; bushfire 1913; cemetery; FB; PO 1908; 2 quarries; sawmills: Armstrong & Royse Pty Ltd, fire 1914 and Karuah Hardwood Co.; school 1915–43; telephone 1907; tramway (timber); TX 1950–73; Union C.; wharf, defunct; pop. 84 (1911), 110 (1933), 62 (1947), 73 (1954), 62 (1961), 196 (2011).

Allworth Park (*Co. Gloucester*) 32°32'S. 151°57'E., 14 km N. of Karuah, on Karuah R.

Allynbrook (*Co. Durham*) 32°22'S. 151°32'E., 21 km W. of Dungog, on Allyn R.; timber, tobacco, wine till 1940, dairying; Angl. C. (St Mary-on-Allyn) b. 1843–45 by Greer, d. by William Grant Broughton, rebuilding and enlargement 1889 d. by Arthur Coe Lee and James Warren Scobie, alterations and repairs 1909, restored and floor replaced 1991, and graveyard (207 graves 1852+); brickworks; bridge (St Mary's Bridge) 1900, new ones 1940 and 1970, over Allyn R.; creamery (Richard Barker Boydell) b. 1896 by A. Ebbeck and P. Kealey; electricity 1937; eucalyptus oil distillery (Richard Barker Boydell); footbridge b. 1891 by Meredith and Galloway, over Allyn R.; PO, closed 1977, reused; sawmill (Alex A. Hancock); school (Caergurle till 1908) 1879, new one b. 1882 by John Libby, repairs 1895 by W. Collison, additions 1902, closed 1971, building reused; soap-works (Richard Barker Boydell); telephone 1899; TX 1915; pop. 249 (1901), 254 (1911), 167 (1933), 142 (1947), 132 (1954), 113 (1961), 217 (2011).

Alma (*Co. Bligh*) see Wuuluman.

Alma (*Co. Waljeers*) 33°47'S. 144°36'E., 83 km N. of Hay.

Alma (*Co. Yancowinna*) see Broken Hill South.

Alma Park (*Co. Hume*) 35°37'S. 146°48'E., 23 km W. of Culcairn; settled by German Lutherans; cemetery; Lutheran C. (Salem) 1892, closed, moved to Urangeline and reused, new one b. 1925 by Charles Hardy & Co., d. by W.T. Thorne; mouse plague 1925; school 1943–75, demolished; pop. 81 (1933), 109 (1947), 60 (1961).

Almavale (*Co. Rous*) 28°40'S. 153°32'E., 2 km N. of Bangalow.

Alnwick (*Co. Northumberland*) see Millers Forest.

Alphadale (*Co. Rous*) 28°50'S. 153°23'E., 5 km W. of Alstonville; farming; Angl. C. (St Peter's) 1905–89, sold and reused; FB; macadamia nut processing plant (Macadamia Processing Co. Ltd); PO 1927–28; pop. 94 (1911), 36 (1933), 80 (1947).

Alpine (*Co. Camden*) 34°24'S. 150°31'E., 8 km NE of Mittagong; formerly Forest Hill; subdivided 1904 by Rickard & Co.; farming and orchards; bushfires 1929 and 1953; PO 1913–66; railway tunnel (Aylmerton), 1,005 yds (919.2 m), 1919; telephone 1914; TX 1923; pop. 52 (1933), 54 (1954), 52 (1961).

Alson's Siding (*Co. Waradgery*) see Tnononga.

Alston (*Co. King*) 34°00'S. 148°58'E., 29 km SE of Cowra; telephone 1911.

Alstonvale (*Co. Rous*) 28°47'S. 153°26'E., 6 km N. of Alstonville; pop. 428 (2011).

Alstonville (*Co. Rous*) 28°51'S. 153°26'E., 12 km W. of Ballina, on Maguires Ck; Duck Creek till 1873; settled 1865 by Andrew and Ellen Freeborn; orig. timber then dairying, sugar-cane, pineapples, bananas, hort.; agric. research station (tropical fruit), renamed NSW Centre for Tropical Horticulture in 2002; Angl. C. b. 1896 by S. Philpott, relocated 1905, closed and reused 1915, new one (St Bartholomew's) b. 1913–15 by Brown and Jolly, d. by Alexander Stewart Jolly, damaged 1949, extensions and restoration 1952–60 by Charles Herbert Wright; Assemblies of God C. (Community); Bapt. C. 1960, closed, sold and reused, new one 1987 on new site; butter factories: first one b. 1890 by A. Duncan and NSW Creamery Butter Co. Ltd 1900 (went into liquidation 1904 and replaced by Alstonville Co-op. Refrigerating & Carrying Co. Ltd, rebuilt 1923 by Thackeray and Gallagher,

d. by Richard Wildridge & Co., damaged 1928, merged 1930 with Norco Co-op. Ltd, closed 1947); caravan factory, in former butter factory; cemetery (1,986 graves) 1876, incl. lawn cemetery and columbaria; CH b. 1903 by W. Leben, not used till 1910, closed 1965; crematorium (Avondale); diphtheria 1911; drought 1923; electricity 1933; FB 1927 (station burnt down 1929, replaced 1930, new one 1980); fires 1916 and 1977; foot-bridge over Maguires Ck; gale 1928; gravel crushing plant; heatwave 1903; joinery (C.H. Wright), burnt down 1929; PO 1872, new one b. 1888, replaced 1902, new one b. 1908 by S. Percival, d. by Walter Liberty Vernon, closed 1997, reused; Presb. C. b. 1878 by Thomas Robb, sold 1899, (second) b. 1899 by Duncan and Mulvena, closed and demolished 1939, (third) b. 1939 by C.H. Wright, sold and reused 1999; PS b. 1903 by W. Leben, not used till 1910, damaged 1998; pudding factory (Father Mac's Heavenly Puddings) 1985; quarry (Tuckombil); 2 reservoirs; rifle range; Rom. Cath. C. (St Laurence O'Toole's) b. 1888 by M.P. Farrelly, d. by Fanning, additions 1924, dismantled and moved 1954 to Lennox Head, replacement (Our Lady of the Rosary) b. 1954 by Frank Bennett, d. by Francis Leo Cullen, re-roofed and additions; 4 sawmills (incl. William Freeborn, burnt down, site sold 1905, and Morrish Bros, in old sugar mill, man killed 1907); schools: primary (b. 1875 by John Perry and Adams, new buildings and alterations 1882 by C. West, burnt down 1895, replaced 1896 by Henry Watson, additions 1899, 1908, 1958, additions 1976 by Bennett Constructions, additions 1994), and HS 1986, additions 1994; SD Adventist C.; sewerage 1974; storms 1949 and 1998; street lighting 1915; sugar mills: Barlow Bros 1872, Duncan's 1872, King and Meston 1872, Melbourne Star Co. 1882–87, James Mellis, J. Moore and Wade 1871, Henry Morrish, Robb's, closed 1887, Angus Robertson; telegraph 1890, new office b. 1908 by S. Percival, d. by Walter Liberty Vernon; TX 1910; typhoid 1902; Unit. C. (orig. Meth.) b. 1909 by T.E. Jarman, d. by Frederick Johnson Board, new belfry 2000; water supply 1957, augmentation 1959 and 1991; water tank factory (estab. by John Fleming, now Duraplas Industries); Wes. Meth. C. b. 1873 by William Crawford et al., new one b. 1883 by Tom Robb, moved and reused; pop. 485 (1891), 651 (1901), 1,001 (1911), 2,064 (1924), 1,057 (1933), 643 (1947), 949 (1954), 790 (1961), 576 (1966), 778 (1971), 1,457 (1976), 2,936 (1981), 3,266 (1986), 3,678 (1991), 4,725 (1996), 4,773 (2001), 4,990 (2011).

Alumny Creek (*Co. Clarence*)
see Alumy Creek.

Alumy Creek (*Co. Clarence*) 29°39'S. 152°57'E., 6 km N. of Grafton, on Alumy Ck; Angl. C. 1872, new one (Holy Trinity) 1898; dairy factory (Grafton Dairy Co.) 1893; flood 1861; hailstorm 1925; school (Alumny Creek) b. 1872 by William Kinnear, d. by George Allen Mansfield, repairs 1883 by G. Wunderlich, additions 1908 by Strauss Bros, closed 1969, restored and reused 1988; sugar mill (Martin's); telephone 1910; pop. 102 (1911), 156 (2011).

Amarina (*Co. Richmond*) 28°59'S. 152°59'E., 15 km SW of Casino; dairying and grazing; PO 1927–30; RS 1908–75; sawmill (Noble Bros); telephone 1913.

Amaroo (*Co. Ashburnham*) 33°11'S. 148°55'E., 10 km SE of Molong, on Reedy Ck; farming and grazing; cemetery 1898; copper mine (Mount Keenan); PO 1900; RS 1885, station b. by James Stuart Douglas, closed 1974; school (Bobs Creek till 1886) 1881, new buildings b. 1883 by Price Bros and Shield, closed 1969; telephone 1906; pop. 99 (1901), 180 (1911), 135 (1933), 91 (1947), 73 (1954), 64 (1961), 567 (2006).

American Creek (*Co. Camden*)
see Mount Kembla.

American Yards (*Co. Wynyard*)
see Humula.

Amesbury (*Co. Cooper*) 34°33'S. 146°23'E., 2 km W. of Leeton; PO 1947–71; telephone 1947; pop. 310 (1947).

Ammerdown (*Co. Wellington*) 33°14'S.

149°04'E., 4 km NW of Orange.

Amosfield (*Co. Buller*) 28°39'S. 152°04'E., 43 km N. of Tenterfield; Herding Yard Creek till 1877; tin and grazing; fire 1906; mine; PO 1875; telephone 1908; TX 1917; pop. 55 (1901), 133 (1911), 107 (1933).

Amosfield (*Co. Buller*) see also Liston.

Amos Flat (*Co. Clarence*) 29°55'S. 153°12'E., 21 km N. of Woolgoolga.

Ampdale (*Co. Richmond*) 29°12'S. 152°57'E., 39 km S. of Casino, on Battens Bight Ck; formerly also known as Battens Bight; airfield; RS 1933–75; pop. 42 (1933).

Ampdale Crossing (*Co. Richmond*) 29°13'S. 152°57'E., 41 km S. of Casino.

Amungula (*Co. Murray*) 35°15'S. 149°16'E., 13 km N. of Queanbeyan; farming; PO 1912–25; school (Woodfield till 1908) 1901–13; telephone 1917; TX 1943; Wes. Meth. C. (Woodfield) b. 1901 by J. Deacon and Bingley Bros.

Anabranch (*Co. Tara*) 33°33'S. 141°39'E., 66 km N. of Wentworth; school 1966–71; pop. 103 (1911), 27 (1933).

Anambah (*Co. Northumberland*) 32°40'S. 151°30'E., 9 km NW of Maitland, on Hunter R.; boiling-down works (R. Pringle); bushfires 1905, 1919, 1926; military training camp; quarry.

Anarel (*Co. Westmoreland*) 33°34'S. 149°57'E., 18 km NE of Oberon; school 1885–93.

Andersons Flat (*Co. Parry*) 31°23'S. 151°08'E., 37 km SE of Tamworth, on Chaffey Dam; village gaz. 1914, but never developed; gold (disc. 1852); cemetery.

Ando (*Co. Wellesley*) 36°45'S. 149°16'E., 20 km N. of Bombala; estab. *c.*1911; sheep and farming; FB; PO 1917; school 1934–2012, sold 2015; telephone 1916; TX 1925, automatic 1964; Union C. 1925 (removed from Saucy Creek), closed, sold and removed; pop. 107 (1933), 80 (1947), 77 (1954), 134 (1961).

Anembo (*Co. Beresford*) 35°48'S. 149°26'E., 55 km NE of Cooma; Gingerra Station till 1908, Gingerra till 1915; farming and grazing; PO 1891; PS 1885; telephone 1908; TX 1924; pop. 86 (1933).

Angle Bend (*Co. Cowley*) 35°35'S. 149°06'E., 28 km SW of Queanbeyan, on Murrumbidgee R.; quarry.

Angledale (*Co. Auckland*) 36°38'S. 149°53'E., 7 km NE of Bega, on Bega R.; farming, dairying, hort.; cheese factory (Jauncey's); PO 1927–31; school 1881, additions and repairs 1898 by J. Malcolm, closed 1965; pop. 71 (1901), 67 (1933), 108 (1947), 88 (1954), 90 (1961), 275 (2011).

Angledool (*Co. Narran*) 29°06'S. 147°55'E., 35 km N. of Lightning Ridge, on Narran R.; (incl. New Angledool); founded 1884 by Merry, thrived in 1890s; grazing and opals; Angl. C. (All Saints') 1912; bridge (James Harper Bridge) b. 1925 by Josiah Williams, over Narran R.; cemetery (34 graves 1896+) 1893; CH, additions 1908 by Peter Beddie; cyclone 1945; fires 1905 and 1952; floods 1893, 1947, 1974, 1998, 2010; hospital; PO, burnt down 1963, rebuilt, closed 1974; pound (stock) 1882; PS 1882, additions 1908 by Peter Beddie, closed 1961; Rom. Cath. C. (St Agnes's) 1908; sawmill (Robinson's) 1883; telephone 1906; tornado 1893; TX 1913; pop. 59 (1891), 163 (1901), 303 (1911), 92 (1933), 66 (1947), 100 (1954), 100 (1961), 86 (2006).

Anglers Reach (*Co. Wallace*) 36°00'S. 148°40'E., 49 km NW of Cooma, on Lake Eucumbene; also known as Illawong; surveyed and laid out by John Usher; telephone 1969; pop. 71 (2006), 358 (2011).

Angourie (*Co. Clarence*) 29°29'S. 153°22'E., 5 km S. of Yamba, on Coral Sea; formerly tourism; cemetery; quarry 1892–99; school 1895–99; sewerage augmentation 1995; pop. 205 (1996), 206 (2001), 172 (2006), 184 (2011).

Angourie Point (*Co. Clarence*) 29°29'S. 153°22'E., 5 km S. of Yamba, on Coral Sea; village gaz. 1917.

Angus Place (*Co. Cook*) 33°21'S. 150°06'E., 8 km NE of Wallerawang, on Kangaroo Ck; Angl. C. (St Aiden's) 1942; bushfires 1942 (woman died) and 1951; collieries: Centennial Coal Co. Ltd and Vale of Clywdd No. 2, strike 1929, closed 1930; PO 1927; school 1928–44 and 1961–66; telephone 1927; TX 1954; weir on Coxs Ck; pop. 136 (1933), 68 (1954), 53 (1961).

Anna Bay (*Co. Gloucester*) 32°46'S. 152°04'E., 9 km SW of Nelson Bay, on Tasman Sea; (incl. Birubi Point and Fishermans Bay); Hannah Bay till 1896; hort., poultry, rutile mining, now tourism; bushfires 1897 (house destroyed) and 1933; cemeteries: Birubi Point (75 graves) and lawn (558 plots) 1964, incl. columbaria; Assemblies of God C. (Baylife) 2002; Christ. City C. (Spectrum); FB (station b. 2008); Lutheran C. (Peace) 1966; PO 1900; Presb. C. (Gateway) 2004; Salv. Army C. (Port Stephens) 2012; school 1882, new one b. 1884 by Burg and Carmody, new building b. 1910 by R. Halliday, new building 1961, additions by R.T. Parker Pty Ltd; squall 1905; telephone 1905; TX 1924; Union C. 1931, closed, sold 2015; pop. 120 (1901), 174 (1911), 180 (1933), 224 (1947), 349 (1954), 624 (1961), 458 (1976), 796 (1981), 1,109 (1986), 1,456 (1991), 1,945 (1996), 2,441 (2001), 2,638 (2006), 2,878 (2011).

Annalera (*Co. Killara*) 31°14'S. 144°00'E., 69 km NE of Wilcannia; telephone 1927; TX 1930.

Anona (*Co. Dowling*) 33°45'S. 146°38'E., 55 km W. of West Wyalong; school 1958–71.

Anson (*Co. Bathurst*) 33°20'S. 149°13'E., 12 km SE of Orange, on Swamp Ck; school 1883–1913.

Antiene (*Co. Durham*) 32°21'S. 150°59'E., 12 km SE of Muswellbrook; orig. Toowong; grazing and dairying; Angl. C. (St Matthew's) 1901; PO 1907–58; 6 quarries; RS (Apple Tree till 1891, then Toowong till 1906) 1890–1975; telephone 1923; TX 1935; pop. 55 (1911), 57 (1933), 76 (1947), 88 (1954).

Antonio (*Co. Westmoreland*) 33°36'S. 150°02'E., 16 km SW of Lithgow; Meth. C. 1915; school 1893–97.

Anvil Creek (*Co. Northumberland*) see Greta.

Apanie (*Co. Westmoreland*) 33°47'S. 149°42'E., 7 km SW of Oberon, on Hopes Ck; sapphire fossicking; telephone 1925.

Apollo (*Co. Lincoln*) see Dubbo.

Appleby (*Co. Parry*) 30°58'S. 150°51'E., 16 km NW of Tamworth, on Peel R.; farming; bridge over Peel R.; RS 1901–87; silo 1934, demolished; pop. 33 (1933), 60 (1947).

Apple Tree (*Co. Arrawatta*) 29°23'S. 151°18'E., 22 km E. of Ashford, on Severn R.

Apple Tree (*Co. Durham*) see Antiene.

Appletree Clearing (*Co. Hunter*) 32°49'S. 150°41'E., 53 km SW of Singleton, on Appletree Ck.

Apple Tree Flat (*Co. Arrawatta*) 29°08'S. 151°00'E., 22 km N. of Ashford.

Apple Tree Flat (*Co. Camden*) 34°48'S. 150°18'E., 15 km S. of Bundanoon, on Shoalhaven R.

Apple Tree Flat (*Co. Clarence*) see Winegrove.

Apple Tree Flat (*Co. Georgiana*) 34°02'S. 149°27'E., 47 km N. of Crookwell, on Abercrombie R.; formerly Surveyors Flat.

Apple Tree Flat (*Co. Gowen*) 31°50'S. 148°57'E., 31 km SE of Gilgandra; flood 1874; sawmill.

Appletree Flat (*Co. Hunter*) 32°31'S. 150°51'E., 21 km SE of Denman, on Appletree Ck; quarry.

Appletree Flat (*Co. Macquarie*) 31°48'S. 152°14'E., 16 km NW of Wingham, on Caparra Ck; formerly Apple Tree Flat.

Apple Tree Flat (*Co. Macquarie*) see Ashlea Flat.

Apple Tree Flat (*Co. St Vincent*) see Araluen.

Apple Tree Flat (*Co. Sandon*) 30°48'S. 151°44'E., 26 km NE of Walcha, on Blue Mountain Ck.

Apple Tree Flat (*Co. Wellington*) 32°41'S. 149°42'E., 15 km SE of Mudgee, on Cudgegong R.; goldmining (alluvial), farming, dairying, sheep, pigs, wine; PO 1869; Rom. Cath. C. (St James's) 1939–70, later sold, moved and reused; telephone 1914; TX 1951; Wes. Meth. C. 1883; wineries: Broombee Organic Wines, Gilbert Family Wines (estab. 2004 by Simon Gilbert), Logan Wines (estab. 1997 by Mal and Peter Logan), Martins Hill Wines 1985, Skimstone; pop. 83 (1891), 110 (1901), 139 (1911), 110 (1933), 82 (1947), 70 (1954), 60 (1961).

Apple Tree Flat (*Co. Westmoreland*) 34°17'S. 150°07'E., 29 km NW of Berrima, on

Wollondilly R.

Appletree Flat (*Co. Westmoreland*) 33°51'S. 150°18'E., 15 km S. of Katoomba, on Coxs R.; formerly Apple-Tree Flat.

Apsley (*Co. Bathurst*) see Perthville.

Apsley (*Co. Wellington*) 32°36'S. 148°58'E., 5 km S. of Wellington; mine (copper) *c.*1890; RS (station relocated 1895) 1881–1965; school 1893–1954; pop. 84 (1933), 79 (1947), 66 (1954), 55 (2011).

Arable (*Co. Wallace*) 36°22'S. 149°01'E., 17 km SW of Cooma; PO 1897; school 1887–94; pop. 21 (1933), 202 (2006).

Arajoel (*Co. Mitchell*) 35°02'S. 146°53'E., 26 km NE of Lockhart; RS 1928–88; silo 1936.

Arakoon (*Co. Macquarie*) 30°53'S. 153°05'E., 3 km E. of South West Rocks, on Trial Bay; (incl. Trial Bay); surveyed and laid out 1866 by Ernest William Lewis Herborn, town gaz. 1867, thrived 1878; breakwater b. 1889–1903; bridge (German Bridge) to South West Rocks, over Saltwater Ck; bushfire 1905; cemetery (552 graves 1903+), incl. lawn cemetery and columbaria; gaol (Trial Bay) b. 1877–86 by Daniel Macquarie and W.E. Macquarie, new wing b. 1898–1900 by Harrison & Son, closed 1903, reused 1914–18 as internment and POW camp, stripped 1922–24, reused; PO: Arakoon 1878–1905 and Trial Bay 1917–18; PS b. 1881 by Thomas Russell, closed 1904; quarry; sawmill (A.L. Usher); school 1883, new building b. 1898 by F. Graham, closed 1905; sewerage 1985; storm 1903; telephone: Arakoon 1905 and Trial Bay 1918; TX; water reticulation 1971; pop. 49 (1891), 107 (1901), 23 (1933), 46 (1961), 467 (2006), 513 (2011).

Araluen (*Co. Rous*) 28°38'S. 153°32'E., 6 km N. of Bangalow.

Araluen (*Co. St Vincent*) 35°39'S. 149°49'E., 22 km S. of Braidwood, on Dirty Butter Ck; (incl. Apple Tree Flat, Bourketown, Crown Flat, Deep Creek, Mudmelong, Redbank, Upper Araluen, Weedy Flat, West Araluen); also formerly known as Happy Valley; settled by Badgery, thrived in 1860s, village gaz. 1867, development peaked 1868; mining (alluvial gold, disc. 1851 by Alexander Waddell, gold rush 1852, hydraulic sluicing 1870+, dredging 1899–1939) till *c.*1925, eucalyptus oil, dairying 1920s–50s, orchards and hort. 1930s+, agric., grazing, later peaches and tomatoes; Angl. C. (St John's) b. 1869 by Isley, damaged 1895, closed 1913, collapsed; Bapt. C.; boot factory (Campbell's); brewery (operated by Richard Chynoweth, then Thomas Auld) 1868–72; carriage-works (H. Robertson); cemeteries: Angl. (73 graves 1860+), Rom. Cath. (graves 1861+), West Araluen 1900; CH (incl. lock-up) b. 1862 by Arundel Everett and William Stephens, additions 1871 by Foley and Doswell, defunct, new one (incl. lock-up and police station) b. 1886 by John Kealman, d. by James Johnstone Barnet, court-house closed, but police station continued till 1956, sold and reused; cheese factories: Goward's and Naughton's; Chinese joss house (Mudmelong); creamery (Araluen Co-op. Dairy Co. Ltd); diphtheria 1862, 1910 (2 children died), 1911–12 (girl died); earth tremor 1860; FB; fires 1900 and 1927; floods 1859, 1860, 1864, 1870, 1871, 1914; fruit packing houses: Mather's and Wisbey's; gales 1862, 1900, 1895; gold dredge (Perry's); hailstorm 1874; heatwave 1900; PO: Araluen 1858–1977, Crown Flat 1861, Upper Araluen 1863–78; powerhouse; PS b. 1861 by Tucker and Bowler, closed; Rom. Cath. C., destroyed 1862, rebuilt 1862 by Dillon et al., new one (St Patrick's) b. 1941 by David Larcombe, d. by Norman Leslie Lipman; sawmill; schools: Araluen 1858–59, reopened 1870, new buildings b. 1893 by George W. Hill, new building b. 1906 by A. Allen, closed 1971, Mudmelong 1904–16, Upper Araluen 1872–88, West Araluen (Bourketown till 1869) 1867, burnt down 1871, rebuilt, additions 1898 by C.R. Stubbs, closed 1919; snowstorm 1880; telegraph 1865; TX 1912; typhoid 1897 and 1905; Union C. 1911, later shared by Angl. and Unit.; Wes. Meth. C. 1868; pop. 2,900 (1871), 609 (1881), 229 (1891), 467 (1901), 771 (1911), 243 (1933), 122 (1947), 90 (1954), 60 (1961), *c.*120 (1965), *c.*100 (1987), 215 (2006), 293 (2011).

Araluen North (*Co. St Vincent*) 35°38'S. 149°48'E., 20 km S. of Braidwood, on Dirty Butter Ck; formerly Newtown; cemetery (4 graves); fire 1921; foundry (iron); PO 1913–71; telephone 1911; TX 1950; Union C. 1913; pop. 98 (1933), 87 (1947), 82 (1954), 72 (1961).

Arandin (*Co. Clarence*) see Grafton South.

Aratula (*Co. Townsend*) 35°49'S. 145°23'E., 17 km W. of Tocumwal.

Arcadia Vale (*Co. Northumberland*) 33°04'S. 151°35'E., 1 km NW of Wangi Wangi, on Eraring Bay; (incl. Buttaba); Kirkdale till 1948; subdivided and laid out 1922 by Henry Ferdinand Halloran, first lots sold 1922; jetty, destroyed 1949; reservoir; PO 1949; sawmill (George Hawkins); school 1958, additions 1968; telephone 1947; pop. 1,381 (2011).

Archerfield (*Co. Hunter*) 32°30'S. 151°04'E., 12 km NW of Singleton, on Hunter R.; aeroplane crash 1936; pop. 26 (1933).

Archill (*Co. Clarke*) 30°30'S. 152°02'E., 37 km E. of Armidale.

Archville (*Co. Raleigh*) 30°24'S. 153°03'E., 5 km SW of Sawtell, on Pine Ck; RS 1936–75.

Archys Flat (*Co. Wellesley*) 36°52'S. 149°20'E., 11 km NE of Bombala.

Ardglen (*Co. Buckland*) 31°44'S. 150°47'E., 5 km NW of Murrurundi, on Doughboy Hollow; Doughboy Hollow till 1893; village gaz. 1856 as Doughboy Hollow; farming and grazing; PO 1877; quarry; railway tunnel, 533 yds (487.6 m), 1877; Rom. Cath. C. (St Michael's) b. 1915 by J. Holt; RS (Doughboy Hollow till 1893) 1877, new station 1892, demolished; school (Doughboy Hollow till 1893) 1876, closed 1909, new one b. 1914 by Thomas John Bowen, closed 1965; telegraph 1890; TX 1937–83; pop. 110 (1901), 226 (1911), 122 (1933), 106 (1947), 119 (1954), 88 (1961), 368 (2006).

Ardgour (*Co. Pottinger*) 31°40'S. 150°03'E., 35 km NE of Coolah, on Bundella Ck; formerly Bundella Creek.

Arding (*Co. Sandon*) 30°34'S. 151°33'E., 12 km SW of Armidale; farming and fruit; Angl. C. (Holy Trinity) 1902; PO 1890; school (Rose Hill till 1898) 1881–1957; telephone 1923; TX 1928; Wes. Meth. C. 1883; pop. 167 (1901), 152 (1911), 116 (1933), 179 (1947), 162 (1954), 159 (1961), 278 (2011).

Ardlethan (*Co. Bourke*) 34°21'S. 146°54'E., 50 km NE of Leeton, on Mirrool Ck; orig. Rosebank, then Warri till 1908; surveyed 1907 by Robert William Meldrum, first lots sold 1907, village gaz. 1908; grazing, wheat, hort.; airfield 1970; ambulance station; Angl. C. (St Mark the Evangelist) 1913; Bapt. C. 1912, closed, sold, renovated and reused; brickworks: Drysdale & Co. and S. Dacey; carriage-works (J. Prothero); cemetery (*c.*700 burials, 1911+), extended 1979; CH 1900 d. by Walter Liberty Vernon, damaged 1923, new one b. 1926 by Philip James Killey; cordial factory (T.J. Webster & Son) 1912, removed from Ariah Park, closed; drought 1914; dust storm 1923; FB; fires 1914 and 1935; floods 1928, 1931, 1939, 1952, 2012, 2016; footbridge over Bygoo Ck; hospital; ice works; Meth. C. 1922; PO 1905, new one b. 1916; pound (stock) 1929; powerhouse estab. 1928 by Les Walton, taken over and expanded 1930 by Tom Baker; Presb. C. (St Andrew's) b. 1912 by MacLean & Co.; PS 1910, new one b. 1926 by Philip James Killey; railway dam; reservoir, 200,000 gal. (909.2 kl); Rom. Cath. C. (Our Lady Help of Christians) b. 1911–14 by John Ryan, extended and renovated 1957; RS 1908, station b. by Frank Vernon, closed 1983; sawmills: W.M. Brown, Dumbrell Bros, burnt down 1898, Harrison and Kennedy; schools: Ardlethan 1910, extra building 1921 (removed from Warri school), and Warri 1907–17 (building moved 1921 to Ardlethan school); silo 1923; telephone 1910; TX 1910; Unit. C.; water supply 1941; pop. 465 (1911), 828 (1933), 565 (1947), 562 (1954), 504 (1961), 629 (1966), 659 (1971), 675 (1976), 602 (1981), 520 (1986), 410 (1991), 427 (1996), 397 (2001), 379 (2006), 365 (2011).

Ardlethan Tin Mines (*Co. Bourke*) see Yithan.

Ardnaclack (*Co. Harden*) 34°35'S. 148°36'E., 19 km SW of Boorowa; quarry.

Ardrossan (*Co. Wynyard*) 35°31'S. 148°04'E., 7

km W. of Batlow.

Argalong (*Co. Buccleuch*) 35°19'S. 148°26'E., 19 km E. of Tumut, on Sandy Waterfall Ck; goldmining (alluvial and reef) and grazing; eucalyptus oil distillery (William H. Teggart) 1940; PO 1909; school 1957–58; telephone 1911; TX 1923; pop. 72 (1911), 52 (1933), 73 (1947), 75 (1954).

Argenton (*Co. Northumberland*) 32°56'S. 151°38'E., 3 km W. of Cardiff, on Brush Ck; subdivided and first lots auctioned 1841; Angl. C. (St Aidan's) 1931; earthquake 1989; mines rescue station b. 1927 by Leslie Elgin Brander, d. by Pitt and Merewether, rebuilt 1985 by Civil and Civic, d. by K. Snell; PO 1929; school 1897–1903, reopened 1951, new building b. 1954 by A.H. McKenzie & Sons, additions 1961 and 1966; sewerage 1950; tram (steam) to Speers Point 1912; pop. 164 (1901), 114 (1911), 201 (1933), 538 (1947), 1,323 (2006), 1,370 (2011).

Argents Hill (*Co. Raleigh*) 30°37'S. 152°46'E., 10 km W. of Bowraville, on North Ck; farming, dairying, bananas; cemetery 1892; LDS (Mormon) C. 1915; PO 1882, burnt down 1929, reopened, closed 1993; Presb. C. 1907; school 1882–1946; telephone 1913; TX 1925, automatic 1980; pop. 152 (1911), 122 (1933), 126 (1947), 216 (1954), 123 (1961), 387 (2011).

Argoon (*Co. Boyd*) see Coleambally.

Argoon (*Co. Urana*) 34°48'S. 145°34'E., 28 km W. of Coleambally; PO 1881–1910; Presb. C. 1883; TX (automatic); pop. 52 (1901).

Argyle (*Co. Argyle*) see Goulburn.

Argyle East (*Co. Argyle*) see Goulburn.

Ariah Park (*Co. Bourke*) 34°21'S. 147°13'E., 29 km E. of Ardlethan; village gaz. 1907, laid out 1907 by A. Maitland, lots sold 1908, thrived in 1920s; wheat, oilseeds, beef, sheep, pigs; Angl. C. (St Augustine's) 1910, and columbarium; Bapt. C. 1912; bushfire 1892; cemetery (orig. Broken Dam, *c.*700 burials 1892+) 1897; CH (incl. police station) 1902 d. by Walter Liberty Vernon, new one b. 1928 by F.A. Goodwin; chaff mill, burnt down 1927; Community C. 1910, closed and sold; cordial factory (T.J. Webster & Son), moved 1912 to Ardlethan; dust storm 2019; FB; fire 1914; flood 1931; Meth. C. 1910; PO 1907, new one b. 1915; powerhouse (Berry Bros); railway dam 1928, reused; reservoir, 200,000 gal. (909.2 kl); Rom. Cath. C. (St Joseph's) 1912; RS 1906, station b. by John Allibone and Augustus Ringholm, closed 1983; sawmill (Berry Bros); school 1904, additions 1965 and 2013; silo 1922; telephone 1906; TX 1911; Unit. C., closed, sold 2015; water supply 1941; pop. 589 (1911), 747 (1933), 478 (1947), 586 (1954), 456 (1961), 344 (1971), 311 (1976), 301 (1981), 311 (1986), 312 (1991), 288 (1996), 299 (2001), 293 (2006), 269 (2011).

Arkell (*Co. Georgiana*) 33°44'S. 149°23'E., 25 km SE of Blayney, on Grove Ck; Long Swamp till 1927; village gaz. 1866 as Carrawa, never fully developed; goldmining, agric., grazing; bushfire 1939; cemetery (Long Swamp Rom. Cath., 218 graves); PO 1859–1930; school (Carrawa 1868–81) 1863–70 and 1879–81; telephone 1927; TX 1930; pop. *c.*200 (1866), 64 (1901), 56 (1911), 26 (1933).

Arkstone (*Co. Georgiana*) 34°02'S. 149°41'E., 39 km SW of Oberon; farming and grazing; goldmine (Golden Gully); PO 1886–1930; Rom. Cath. C. b. 1899 by Stapleton; school 1885–88; telephone 1925; TX 1928; pop. 51 (1911), 44 (1933), 56 (1961).

Armatree (*Co. Ewenmar*) 31°27'S. 148°29'E., 12 km S. of Gulargambone; Armatree Railway till 1916; village gaz. 1912, lots sold 1917; grazing and wheat; Angl. C. (St Margaret's) b. 1931 by Sadlier Bros, moved 1971 to Tooraweenah; bridge 1982, over Castlereagh R.; FB; flood 1955; mouse plague 1932; PO 1906; Presb. C.; RS 1903–75; sawmills: Neil Bradley 1905, Jack Miller and Turner (burnt down 1923), Paterson and Rankmore; school 1893, additions 1914 by L. Burgate, closed 1970; silo 1935; telephone 1910; TX 1916; pop. 65 (1901), 166 (1911), 119 (1933), 111 (1947), 180 (1954), 103 (1961), 284 (2011).

Armatree Railway (*Co. Ewenmar*) see Armatree.

Armidale (*Co. Sandon*) 30°31'S. 151°40'E., 95 km NE of Tamworth, on Dumaresq Ck; (incl.

Bellevue, Ben Venue, Bona Vista, Booloominbah, Duval, East Armidale, Madgwick, Newling, North Hill, St Patricks, Soudan Heights, South Hill, West Armidale); founded 1839 by George James Macdonald, surveyed 1848 by John James Galloway, first lots sold 1849, munic. proc. 1863, thrived 1860s–70s, designated as chief town of the county, focus of New State movement 1967, bypassed by highway 1994, city abolished 2000; orig. wheat, maize, oats, cattle and goldmining (alluvial), now sheep, timber, dairying, fruit, potatoes, significant educational and ecclesiastical centre; abattoir (J.S.A. Jackson); agric. implement works and foundry (William Butler) 1880; airport (4 km SW) 1940, new terminals 1994 and 2017; ambulance station b. 1933 by Charles Frank Nott, d. by Robert Newburgh Hickson, additions 1953 by P.J. Knudson; Angl. C.: St Mary's (b. 1896 by George Frederick Nott, d. by William Lee, extended 1910) and St Peter Apostle and Martyr 1850 (replacement b. 1873–78 by A. Smith, d. by John Horbury Hunt, extensions 1911 also d. by Hunt, re-roofed 1912, tower b. 1937–39 by George Frederick Nott, d. by Frederick George Castleden, church re-roofed 1970); Apostolic C.; Assemblies of God C. (Community); ball lightning 1929; Bapt. C.: Armidale 1882, new one b. 1918 by Charles Frank Nott and East Armidale d. and b. 1951 by P. Stace, additions 1977; biscuit factory (Anglo-Aust. Biscuit Co.) 1948; bone mill 1865; boot factory (Barnett Aaron Moses) 1866, acquired 1897 by Aaron Crossman and William Dale, fire 1913; box factory (New England Timbers Pty Ltd) 1944; breweries: John W. Tuck 1850–52, 1858–67, 1869–74 (new one estab. 1882 by Peter Simpson, renamed City Brewery in 1887, closed 1917) and Welder's Dog (estab. 2017 by Tom Croft, Daniel Emery and Phil Stevens); brickworks: Armidale Brick & Tile Co. and Richard Childs (business acquired 1875 by William Palmer, bought 1901 by George Frederick Nott); bridges: Belmore Bridge (Marsh Street) b. 1869 by William Mason (replaced 1927 by State Monier Pipe & Reinforced Concrete Works), Cookes Road Bridge, Dangar Street Bridge 1952, Elm Avenue Bridge b. by M.R. and E.M. Firth, Markam Street Bridge b. 1872 by Joseph William Moore (replaced 1907 by W. Sims, re-decked 1952, replacement b. 1982 by Moggill Constructions Pty Ltd, d. by Bruce Macfarlane), Niagara Street Bridge b. 1971 by W.H. Marshall & Son, Trim's Bridge b. 1865 by John Trim (re-decking and repairs 1873 by Kerr, repairs 1874 by H. Schmutter, demolished), Victoria Bridge 1880; broom factory (New England) estab. 1901 by James Edstein; butter factories: Armidale Co-op. Butter Factory Co. Ltd 1910–21 (sold 1921 to J. Robertson Geddes Ltd) and New England Butter Factory Pty Ltd 1933–50; CAE 1974–89; cannery (Interstate Fruit Foods Pty Ltd) 1946; carriage-works: Claude Dewhurst, Alexander C. McArthur, Ezra Purkiss (Armidale Motor Garage, Coach & Buggy Factory) 1893, Richard Weston 1884, A.J. Zehner & Co.; cemetery 1846–59, new one 1863, incl. lawn cemetery and columbarium; CH 1844–59, sold and reused, new one b. 1860 by William Moore and Edward Grover, d. by Alexander Dawson, enlargement 1871 by C.H. Brashier, d. by James Johnstone Barnet, clock tower added 1878, repairs 1884 by W. Mason, extensions 1897–99 by D. McDonald, d. by Walter Liberty Vernon, renovated 1971, damaged 1996, refurbished by New England Constructions Pty Ltd, new one b. 2014 by National Buildplan Group Pty Ltd, d. by D.W.P. Suters; cordial factories: George R. Borland (1875–1912, acquired by Charles Simmons, acquired 1917 by William H. Logan, closed 1958), Borland Bros and Willis 1913 (acquired 1940 by T.O. Ryan, modernised 1963, closed 1977, reused), E.E. Elliot, Richard Smart Jenkins 1865 (sold 1875 to Bernard Herzog, acquired 1890 by Francis Owens, known as the West Armidale Steam Aerated Water & Cordial Works, taken over 1907 by Henry William and Valentine Fittler, sold 1912 to Charles Simmons and closed);

earth tremors 1865, 1910, 1928, 1948, 2018; electricity 1922; FB 1889 (station b. 1922, reused, replaced 1975); fibrous plaster works estab. 1954 by A. and Eric Elliott (in former soap-works); fires 1887, 1889, 1894, 1932, 1944; floods 1921, 1926, 1932, 1933, 1935, 1949, 1975; flour mills: Edward Allingham (b. by Peter Green) 1850–90, Robert Kirkwood 1846, James McLean, John Moore's New England Flour Co. 1866 (bought by John Richardson), Robert Andrew Pearson (West Armidale); foot-bridges: one b. 1896, one b. 1904 by James Browning, one b. 1907 (demolished and replaced 1936); gale 1902; galvanised iron works: M. Mahoney and John F. Schmidt; gaol b. 1860–62 by Arundel Everett and William Stephens, additions 1878 by Edmund Lonsdale, closed 1920, demolished 1929; gasworks b. 1885 by Granger, inundated 1926, upgraded 1928 by James Hurll & Co. Ltd; German measles epidemic 1954; Gospel Hall; hailstorms 1868, 1895, 1996, 2000, 2006; hospital 1853, replaced 1858, new one b. 1882 by William Seabrook and John Brown, d. by John Horbury Hunt, extended 1909, 1910, 1911, 1938, 1962, 1983, damaged 1996, additions 2018 by Richard Crookes Constructions, d. by Building Studio; ice works: A.E. Petersen and Tenterfield Butter Depot & Ice Works; joineries: Frederick Eiskamp, Carl Joseph Hirschberg, T.F. Mills & Sons, Claude Skinner 1951, Trim & Co. (sold 1913 to George Frederick Nott, fire 1944); LDS (Mormon) C.; lock-up 1870, new one b. 1878 by William Seabrook and John Brown, replaced 1885 by R.T. Harrison, closed, new one b. 1900 by Moses Hern; measles epidemic 1931; monumental stone works (A.L. Callcott & Co.); pneumonia epidemic (man died) 1906; PO: Armidale 1843 (new one b. 1863 by Edward Grover, extended 1865 by Grover, repairs 1872 by Edmund Lonsdale, new one b. 1878–80 by William Seabrook and John Brown, d. by James Johnstone Barnet, extensions 1897 d. by Walter Liberty Vernon, extended 1917, modified 1929, 1938, 1979–80), East Armidale 1944, West Armidale 1911; pound (stock) 1848; POW control centre (World War II); powerhouse 1922–51; Presb. C. 1859, new one (St Paul's) b. 1882 by Edmund Lonsdale and Henry Ernest Elliott, d. by John Wiltshire Pender; PS: Armidale (b. 1872 by Edmund Lonsdale and Henry Ernest Elliott, additions, alterations and repairs 1901 by William S. Stead & Co., extended 1947, damaged 1996, new one b. 2007 by Lahey Constructions Pty Ltd) and West Armidale (b. 1884, repairs 1896 by M. Roberts); rabbit freezing works (F. Lewis & Son) 1949; railway dam 1924; railway turntable, 50 ft (15.2 m), replaced 1899, 60 ft (18.3 m), disused; reservoirs: steel tank 40,000 gal. (181.8 kl), concrete one 400,000 gal. (1,818.4 kl), one 500,000 gal. (2,273 kl) 1970, one 1,600,000 gal. (7,273.6 kl); rifle range, extended 1908 by William Sims; Rom. Cath. C. (Our Lady and St Joseph's) 1848, enlargement and repairs 1854, demolished 1872, replacement (St Mary's) b. 1870–72, closed, demolished 2012, new one (St Mary and St Joseph's) b. 1910–12 by George Frederick Nott, d. by John Francis Hennessy and Joseph Ignatius Sheerin; RS 1883, station b. by Edmund Lonsdale; sale-yards 1909, new yards 1954; Salv. Army C. 1900; sawmills: Harper Bros 1881–1903 and George Frederick Nott; scarlet fever 1916; schools: Armidale City 1861 (new one b. 1865 by Harper, alterations and repairs 1876 by William Seabrook and John Brown, new building b. 1884 by C.T. Cook, new building b. 1898 by George Frederick Nott, additions 1927 and 1931), Armidale HS 1920 (additions 1930, 1962, 1969, 1972, 1979, renamed Armidale Secondary College in 2019), Ben Venue (b. 1900 by J.P. Kirkwood, additions 1914 and 1928, dismantled and removed 1931, new one b. 1931 on new site by S.W. and R.C. Potter, additions 1960, 1965, 1967, extended 1971 by R.J. Bennell Pty Ltd, additions 1996), Drummond Memorial (West Armidale till 1966) 1890 (additions 1930 by Ryan and Hoyle, additions 1966), Duval HS 1974 d. by

T. Schweiger (additions 1979), Duval View 1886–1905, Martins Gully 1923, Newling 1974 d. by Olga Kosterin, Sandon 1957–59, new one 1993, additions 2000; SD Adventist C. b. 1951 by Edwin P. Barrington, new one 1968; sewerage 1936, extended 1966–68, augmentation 1989; snowstorm 1917; soap-works (George C. Mallaby & Sons), taken over 1917 by John and Hedley Mallaby; streets gas lit 1885, electric lit 1923; tanneries: Kelvin Grove (Page and Pearson) 1894, Barnett Aaron Moses and George Moses (incl. horse powered wattle-bark mill) 1866, James Tysoe, Charles Zeitler; TC, additions 1987, became a campus of New England Institute in 1992, additions 1994 and 2006; teachers' college 1928, new one b. 1929–31, d. by Evan Smith; telegraph 1861, new office b. 1863 by Edward Grover, extensions 1865 also by Grover, repairs 1872 by Edmund Lonsdale, replacement b. 1885 by C.T. Cook, reused; telephone: East Armidale 1944 and West Armidale 1911; TX 1901, automatic 1958; typhoid 1881; Unit. C. (Wesley, orig. Wes. Meth.) b. 1893 by Sharp, d. by Evan Evans, re-roofed; univ. college (New England) 1938, extended 1941 by Charles Frank Nott, became univ. in 1954, additions 1956 d. by Edward Herbert Farmer, fire 1958, additions 1959, additions 1961 d. by Michael John Dysart, additions 1965, 1968, 1972, 1976, amalgamated 1989 with Armidale CAE, damaged 1996; vulcanising works (New England Vulcanising and Rubber Works) estab. 1920 by Jack McAvoy; water supply 1892, waterworks 1897, filtration plant, augmentation 1955 and 1989; Wes. Meth. C. 1862 (temporary one in converted store), new one b. 1862–64 by Edward Grover, d. by Thomas Rowe, restored 1885, closed 1893, reused, replaced; pop. 93 (1843), 76 (1845–46), 556 (1851), 640 (1854), 857 (1856), 910 (1861), 950 (1863), 950 (1865), *c.*1,000 (1866), 1,369 (1871), 2,187 (1881), 3,826 (1891), *c.*4,700 (1895), 4,299 (1901), 6,530 (1911), 5,407 (1921), 5,100 (1923), 6,971 (1933), *c.*7,800 (1941), 8,133 (1947), 9,679 (1954), 12,875 (1961), *c.*14,500 (1964), 15,360 (1966), 18,137 (1971), 19,711 (1976), 18,922 (1981), 19,525 (1986), 21,605 (1991), 21,330 (1996), *c.*21,034 (1999), 20,271 (2001), 19,485 (2006), 19,817 (2011).

Armidale Crossing (*Co. Hardinge*) see Tingha.

Armoy (*Co. Narromine*) see Ceres.

Armstrong Forest (*Co. St Vincent*) see Yatteyattah.

Arrawarra (*Co. Fitzroy*) 30°04'S. 153°12'E., 6 km N. of Woolgoolga, on Tasman Sea; hailstorm 2013; pop. 23 (1961), 698 (1986), 1,273 (1991), 1,512 (1996), 1,564 (2001), 1,402 (2006), 1,505 (2011).

Arrawatta (*Co. Arrawatta*) 29°39'S. 151°06'E., 14 km N. of Inverell; sheep, and dairying 1904+; cheese factory (on govt training farm), closed 1925; govt training farm for migrants 1923; school 1919–32; pop. 143 (1911), 50 (1933).

Arthursleigh (*Co. Ewenmar*) 31°39'S. 148°38'E., 8 km NW of Gilgandra; fire 1879.

Arthurs Seat (*Co. Arrawatta*) 29°24'S. 151°05'E., 8 km S. of Ashford, on Frazers Ck; pop. 27 (1933).

Arthurville (*Co. Gordon*) 32°34'S. 148°44'E., 19 km W. of Wellington; farming; cyclone 1907; PO 1875; Rom. Cath. C. (Mount Carmel's) 1877, demolished; RS 1925–74, station removed 1979; school 1879–85 and 1936–70; silo 1929, extended 1934; storm 1876; telephone 1927; TX 1927; whooping cough epidemic 1938; pop. 58 (1901), 89 (1911), 131 (1933), 112 (1947), 118 (1954), 82 (1961).

Arumpo (*Co. Wentworth*) 33°48'S. 142°53'E., 75 km NE of Gol Gol.

Arunde Park (*Co. Westmoreland*) 33°48'S. 149°47'E., 13 km SW of Oberon, on The Parlour Ck.

Ashbridge (*Co. Bourke*) 34°40'S. 146°58'E., 15 km N. of Ganmain; school 1902–21 and 1957–69; pop. 84 (1911), 185 (1933), 81 (1947), 67 (1954).

Ashby (*Co. Clarence*) 29°26'S. 153°12'E., 2 km N. of Maclean, on Clarence R.; village gaz. 1864; agric.; bushfire 1929; cyclone 1904; dry dock (Green Point, incl. wharf and pump houses) b. 1899 by John Wishart & Son, explosion 1914, extended 1931 and 1958–60; punt to Maclean till 1985, across Clarence R.; sawmill (Ashby Sawmill Pty Ltd); school 1897–1925; storm 1944; sugar mills: Gilbert's, James M'Donald & Sons, A. Oatt, D. and W. Shearer; pop. 139 (1881), 272 (1901), 100 (1911), 127 (1933), 142 (1947), 115 (1954), 102 (1961), 346 (2011).

Ashford (*Co. Arrawatta*) 29°19'S. 151°06'E., 55 km NE of Warialda, on Frazers Ck; Frazers Creek till 1863; surveyed 1860, laid out by John James Galloway, village gaz. 1861, designated as chief town of the county; tobacco 1904–19, resumed 1930, fruit, farming, grazing, fossicking; agric. research station; ambulance station 1982; Angl. C. (St Mark's) b. 1924 by A. Cannon, d. by John Francis O'Connor, porch added 1979; bridge 1908, damaged 1955, over Frazers Ck; bushfire 1952; cemetery (442 graves) 1877; CH 1865, additions and alterations 1903 by Ibbotson and Lansdowne; drought 1920; dust storm 2002; electricity 1952; FB; floods 1872, 1953, 1955, 2000, 2009; footbridge; hailstorm 1928; hospital (cottage) 1938, additions 1955; lock-up b. 1865 by W. Kinnear; PO 1853, new one b. 1903 by Howard, sold and moved 2007; pound (stock) 1861; powerhouse (Northpower) 1958–97; Presb. C. (Sinclair Hall) 1950; PS 1865, sold and removed 1935, new one 1979; Rom. Cath. C. (St Patrick's) 1913; sale-yards; sawmills: B. Bannister, Colin Grimes, Howard's 1898, Nicholls, E.H. Smith; school 1890, additions and repairs 1894, new one b. 1900 by Joseph Thomas, extended 1906 by A.M. Howell, extended 1927 by A.S. Fairweather, additions 1929, new one b. 1935 by H.C. Ditzell, additions 1957, 1963, 1967, 1972; sewerage 1970; telephone 1904; trees (ornamental) planted in streets 1937; TX 1914; Union C., closed, sold 1904, replaced 1905; watchhouse; water supply 1903, reticulation 1959, augmentation 1986, new filtration plant 2014; pop. *c.*60 (1866), 67 (1891), 104 (1901), 602 (1911), 588 (1933), 542 (1947), 550 (1954), 681 (1961), 697 (1966), 709 (1971), 692 (1976), 594 (1981), 602 (1986), 567 (1991), 542 (1996), 476 (2001), 495 (2011).

Ash Island (*Co. Northumberland*) see Kooragang.

Ashlea (*Co. Macquarie*) 31°51'S. 152°19'E., 7 km NW of Wingham, on Dingo Ck; farming; bridge (Tetsell's Bridge), replacement (concrete) b. 1927 by McLean Construction Co., 280 ft (85.3 m), over Dingo Ck; Presb. C. 1882–1962, defunct.

Ashlea Flat (*Co. Macquarie*) 31°51'S. 152°18'E., 6 km NW of Wingham; school (Apple Tree Flat till 1883) 1881–1906.

Ashley (*Co. Courallie*) 29°19°S. 149°48'E., 17 km N. of Moree, on Marshalls Ponds Ck; Bogree till 1886; village gaz. 1867 as Bogree; grazing; Angl. C. (St Matthew's) 1911; cemetery; cotton gin (Namoi Cotton Co-op. Ltd) 1979; FB; flood 2011; PO 1899; quarry; RS 1913–74; school (Medgun Creek till 1908) 1901–68; tornado 2005; telephone 1895; TX 1911–39; pop. 70 (1901), 173 (1911), 207 (1933), 144 (1947), 143 (1954), 82 (1961), 253 (2001), 272 (2006), 340 (2011).

Ashmont (*Co. Wynyard*) see Wagga Wagga.

Ashton (*Co. Fitzroy*) 30°14'S. 152°54'E., 21 km W. of Coffs Harbour, on Brimbin Ck; sawmill (Arthur W. King and Abraham Jennings) 1907, acquired by Ashton Timber Co. Ltd; pop. 65 (1911).

Ashtonfield (*Co. Northumberland*) see Maitland East.

Ashville (*Co. Auckland*) 36°39'S. 149°37'E., 20 km W. of Bega, on Bemboka R.; school (Avoca) 1889, new one b. 1890 by J. Roddan, closed 1896.

Ashville (*Co. Monteagle*) 34°04'S. 148°03'E., 21 km SW of Grenfell; school 1957–67.

Athol (*Co. Bathurst*) 33°33'S. 149°18'E., 5 km E. of Blayney; RS 1903–61; bushfire 1902.

Athol Glen (*Co. Fitzroy*) 30°02'S. 153°02'E., 17 km W. of Arrawarra, on Sherwood Ck; Upper Sherwood Creek till 1929; telephone 1928.

Atholwood (*Co. Arrawatta*) 29°00'S. 151°03'E.,

36 km N. of Ashford, on Mandoe Ck; grazing; PO 1913–40.

Attunga (*Co. Inglis*) 30°56'S. 150°51'E., 19 km NW of Tamworth, on Attunga Ck; planned 1863 by Benjamin Charles Flide, village gaz. 1864; copper mining, tobacco, lucerne, wheat, farming, grazing; Angl. C. (Christ) 1914 d. by Charles Rosenthal; cemetery (295 graves 1872+) 1880; FB; flood 1910; limekilns: Bettison and Jackson, and Simon J. Carey; mine (BHP, magnesite); PO 1870; PS 1905, new one b. 1908 by Hocking Bros, closed 1974; quarry (Sulphide Corp.); railway bridge, destroyed 1910, replaced, over Peel R., reservoir (steel), 170,000 gal. (772.8 kl), 1963; Rom. Cath. C. (St Patrick's) b. 1877 by M. Burke, new one (St Patrick and St Joseph's) b. 1905 by Richard Allright Stanfield, d. by Philip Ernest Ranclaud, additions 1916 and 1919; RS 1902, station b. by John Allibone, closed 1987; school 1881, additions and alterations 1910 by J.N. Josephson, additions 1922 by J.H. Ford; silo 1934; telegraph 1901; telephone 1899; TX 1914, automatic 1938; Union C. 1885, moved 1927 to Garthowen; water supply filtration and reticulation 1963, augmentation 1994; pop. 165 (1891), 117 (1901), 606 (1911), 308 (1933), 380 (1947), 554 (1954), 187 (1961), 209 (1971), 269 (1976), 269 (1976), 282 (1981), 339 (1986), 375 (1991), 376 (1996), 343 (2001), 313 (2006), 337 (2011).

Attunga Springs (*Co. Inglis*) 30°54'S. 150°48'E., 19 km S. of Manilla, on Browns Springs Ck; PO 1881–1911; school 1882–1909; pop. 153 (1901).

Auburn Vale (*Co. Hardinge*) 29°51'S. 151°01'E., 11 km SW of Inverell, on Cooks Ck; settled 1839 by William Murray Borthwick; whooping cough epidemic 1934; pop. 143 (1911), 95 (1933), 58 (1947), 997 (1881), 64 (1954), 90 (1961).

Auckland (*Co. Durham*) 32°34'S. 151°06'E., 6 km W. of Singleton, on Hunter R.; defunct; formerly agric.; cemetery 1867.

Aurania (*Co. Fitzroy*) 30°19'S. 152°59'E., 13 km W. of Coffs Harbour, on Orara R.; telephone 1914.

Aurville (*Co. Harden*) 34°33'S. 148°22'E., 2 km E. of Murrumburrah, on Cunningham Plains Ck; mining, farming, poultry; brickworks (Henry Spence and Robert Irvine McKinney); Meth. C., moved to Cunningar; PO 1910; sluicing plant (Golden Valley Sluicing Co.) 1932; telephone 1911; pop. 286 (1933), 101 (1947), 89 (1954), 108 (1961).

Austermere (*Co. Camden*) see Bong Bong.

Austin's Crossing (*Co. St Vincent*) see Runnyford.

Austral Eden (*Co. Macquarie*) 31°02'S. 152°55'E., 10 km NE of Kempsey, on Macleay R.; settled 1839 by John Verge, subdivided 1918; farming and dairying; creamery (Smithtown Dairy Co. Ltd) 1897; floods 1921 and 1929; PO 1926–47; school 1920–63; telephone 1922; pop. 268 (1901), 221 (1911), 285 (1933), 188 (1947), 232 (1954), 219 (1961).

Australian Farm (*Co. Hunter*) see Leets Vale.

Avalon (*Co. Gloucester*) see Paff Hill.

Avenel (*Co. Ashburnham*) 33°25'S. 148°45'E., 18 km NE of Canowindra; farming; PO 1927–30; school 1885–1913; pop. 53 (1911).

Avian Estate (*Co. Lincoln*) see Dubbo South.

Avisford (*Co. Wellington*) 32°44'S. 149°29'E., 19 km SW of Mudgee, on Meroo Ck; orig. Meroo Creek; defunct; goldmining and grazing; earth tremor 1862; mines: Hampden Hill 1875, 1890, 1898, 1900, Maitland Bar (incl. Great Western Pioneer, Little Wonder, Queen of Shebah, Sailors Gully) 1920s and 1934–36, Tuckers Hill (incl. Band of Hope, Foleys, Hit or Miss, Hogan's or Ida, Reef Hill, Sucks All, Turn of Tide) <1875, 1888, 1895, 1898–1908, 1914–17, 1928, *c.*1935, 1951, 1955; PO 1853; Presb. C.; PS, closed 1858; school 1860, 1865–68, 1882–1924; stamper battery (Stephen Tucker); telephone 1925; TX 1928; Wes. Meth. C.; pop. 130 (1861), *c.*279 (1866), 74 (1891), 120 (1901), 93 (1933).

Avoca (*Co. Auckland*) see Ashville.

Avoca (*Co. Camden*) 34°37'S. 150°29'E., 12 km SE of Moss Vale, on Bundanoon Ck; timber, potatoes, cabbages, dairying; bacon factory (Charles Wright), fire 1936; FB 1939; PO 1893; sawmill (Bonnyrigg Milling Co.);

school (Yarrunga till 1913) 1878; telephone 1914; TX 1914; pop. 73 (1911), 129 (1933), 157 (1947), 141 (1954), 110 (1961).

Avoca (*Co. Northumberland*) see Avoca Beach.

Avoca (*Co. Wentworth*) 33°56'S. 141°58'E., 20 km N. of Wentworth; pop. 20 (1933).

Avoca Beach (*Co. Northumberland*) 33°28'S. 151°26'E., 10 km E. of Woy Woy, on Tasman Sea; (incl. North Avoca); also known as Avoca; settled 1830 by John Moore, subdivided 1918 by H.F. Halloran & Co., but few lots sold till the late 1940s and 1950s; farming, then tourism; aeroplane crash 1937; Angl. C. 1942, extended 1960–62, closed, sold 1967, relocated and reused, replacement (St David's) 1967, extended 1995, closed 2015; Christ. Brethren Assemblies C. (Village); FB; Meth. C. b. 1967 by C. Metzke, d. by V.M. Turner; PO 1933; 2 reservoirs; school 1952, additions 1960, new building 1975, additions 2010; storm 2016; telephone 1933; TX 1936; pop. 149 (1933), 215 (1947), 376 (1954), 633 (1966), 6,272 (2011).

Avonbrook Station (*Co. Hardinge*) 30°18'S. 151°29'E., 20 km W. of Guyra.

Avondale (*Co. Camden*) see Dapto West and Yallah.

Avondale (*Co. Denham*) 29°40'S. 148°47'E., 23 km SE of Collarenebri, on Thalaba Ck; PO 1910; telephone 1911; TX 1913.

Avondale (*Co. Northumberland*) see Cooranbong.

Avondale (*Co. Wellington*) see Orange.

Avon Dam (*Co. Camden*) 34°21'S. 150°38'E., 9 km SE of Bargo, on Lake Avon; dam (cyclopean masonry) b. 1921–27, 236 ft (72 m) high, on Avon R.; PO 1920; PS, closed 1926; telephone 1921; TX 1924–27.

Avonside (*Co. Lincoln*) 32°07'S. 149°20'E., 13 km SW of Dunedoo.

Awaba (*Co. Northumberland*) 33°01'S. 151°32'E., 5 km W. of Toronto, on Stony Ck; laid out 1891, first lots sold 1894; timber then mining and poultry; bushfires 1909, 1936, 1940; colliery (Awaba State Coal Mine, Elcom Collieries Pty Ltd) 1948, new administrative building b. 1951 by Orrett Bros, strikes 1952 and 1953; FB; PO 1889–1993; 4 quarries; railway (power station) 1954; RS 1887, station b. by John McDonald; sawmills: George Buckton and Thomas Chapple Hector 1895; school 1891, additions 1926 by P.A. Solman; telegraph 1891; TX 1930–37; Union C. 1898, new one 1913, damaged and rebuilt 1934; water supply 1948; pop. 104 (1901), 282 (1911), 193 (1933), 216 (1947), 293 (1954), 338 (1961), 204 (1971–76), 216 (1981), 219 (1986), 257 (1991), 290 (1996), 327 (2001), 350 (2006), 351 (2011).

Aylmerton (*Co. Camden*) 34°25'S. 150°30'E., 6 km NE of Mittagong; subdivided and first lots sold 1920; PO 1927; RS 1919–75; sawmill (McFarlane Bros); telephone 1923; pop. 67 (1901), 77 (1933), 96 (1947), 105 (1954), 97 (1961), 249 (2011).

Aylmerton (*Co. Camden*) see also Colo Vale.

B

Baan Baa (*Co. Pottinger*) 30°36'S. 149°57'E., 15 km NW of Boggabri, on Baan Baa Ck; village gaz. 1891, thrived 1905–30; cotton, cattle, agric.; Angl. C. 1894, demolished, new one (St Clement's) b. 1919 by R.C. Vine, d. by Robert Newburgh Hickson; cemetery; FB; fire 1927; flood 1864; PO 1885, burnt down 1927; PS (in rented premises) 1913; Rom. Cath. C. (St Mary's) 1916; RS 1883–1974; sawmills: Baan Baa Sawmill Co. Ltd, B.K. Eather (moved 1943 to Kerringle), Cyprus Pine Steam Sawmills, Les W. Kelly; school 1886, extended 1889, new school b. 1891 by William Hayes, additions 1913, burnt down 1927, replaced, additions 1961, closed 2005, sold and reused; silo 1934; telegraph 1890; telephone 1909; TX 1916, automatic 1941; Unit. C. (orig. Meth.); pop. 405 (1911), 208 (1933), 212 (1947), 260 (1954), 157 (1961), 70 (1999–2002), 525 (2011).

Babathnil Lagoon (*Co. Kennedy*) 32°30'S. 147°22'E., 81 km W. of Peak Hill, on Bulbodney Ck.

Babinda (*Co. Flinders*) 31°57'S. 146°28'E., 80 km SW of Nyngan; mine (copper).

Bachelors Rush (*Co. Kennedy*) see Alectown.

Back Creek (*Co. Auckland*) 36°58'S. 149°49'E., 7 km SW of Pambula; airfield; mine (pyrophyllite); quarry.

Back Creek (*Co. Bathurst*) see Newbridge.

Back Creek (*Co. Bland*) 33°57'S. 147°23'E., 18 km E. of West Wyalong; school 1957–63; pop. 115 (1911).

Back Creek (*Co. Clive*) 28°58'S. 151°44'E., 30 km W. of Tenterfield.

Back Creek (*Co. Forbes*) 33°36'S. 147°53'E., 25 km SW of Forbes, on Back Ck; RS 1918–74; pop. 197 (1911).

Back Creek (*Co. Georgiana*) 34°02'S. 149°20'E., 49 km N. of Crookwell, on Back Ck.

Back Creek (*Co. Gloucester*) 31°58'S. 152°03'E., 11 km NE of Gloucester, on Back Ck.

Back Creek (*Co. Gloucester*) see also Copeland.

Back Creek (*Co. Monteagle*) 34°22'S. 148°18'E., 6 km S. of Young; pop. 33 (1933).

Back Creek (*Co. Murchison*) 30°08'S. 150°16'E., 40 km SW of Bingara, on Back Ck.

Back Creek (*Co. Rous*) 28°22'S. 153°11'E., 21 km W. of Murwillumbah; Rom. Cath. C. (St Agnes's) 1907, additions 1918, new one 1937, sold 1995; telephone 1916; pop. 214 (1911), 91 (1933), 75 (1947), 87 (1954).

Back Creek (*Co. St Vincent*) 35°21'S. 149°56'E., 16 km NE of Braidwood; diphtheria 1912; school 1894–1910; pop. 97 (1901), 104 (1911), 35 (1933).

Back Creek (*Co. Selwyn*) 35°44'S. 148°03'E., 4 km NE of Tumbarumba; goldmining.

Back Forest (*Co. Camden*) 34°51'S. 150°41'E., 6 km W. of Shoalhaven Heads, on Shoalhaven R.; farming; bridge b. 1936 by Cram, d. by Gowans, 300 ft (91.4 m), over Broughton Ck; creamery 1895–1901; telephone 1921; TX 1921; winery (Two Figs); pop. 130 (1901).

Backmede (*Co. Rous*) 28°45'S. 153°01'E., 13 km N. of Casino; dairying, pigs, maize; airfield; RS (1 km W.) 1934–65; school (Runnymede till 1918) 1887–97, 1907–18, 1930–69; storm

1936; telephone 1927; TX 1946, automatic 1958; pop. 56 (1933), 87 (1947), 111 (1954), 78 (1961), 275 (2011).

Back Paddock (*Co. Urana*) 35°34'S. 146°07'E., 29 km E. of Berrigan.

Back Station Creek (*Co. Clarendon*) 35°05'S. 148°05'E., 4 km SW of Gundagai, on Murrumbidgee R.; school 1904–18 and 1957–68; pop. 85 (1911), 90 (1933).

Back Swamp (*Co. Bathurst*) 33°26'S. 149°27'E., 13 km W. of Bathurst.

Backwater (*Co. Clarke*) 30°04'S. 151°53'E., 27 km NE of Guyra, on Backwater Ck; tin and grazing; Angl. C. (St Augustine's); PO 1904–56; sawmill (John Crampton); school 1957–67; telephone 1924; TX; pop. 128 (1911), 87 (1933), 66 (1947), 83 (1954), 56 (1961).

Backwater (*Co. Narromine*) 32°14'S. 148°05'E., 16 km W. of Narromine, on The Boggy Cowal; Meth. C. 1912 (removed from McPhail); school (Yarran Farm) 1917 b. by J. Ryan, closed 1924; pop. 85 (1911).

Back Yamma (*Co. Ashburnham*) 33°20'S. 148°09'E., 16 km NE of Forbes; silver; mine (J. Twaddell) 1887–88; sawmill (W. Ashwin); school 1900–13 and 1957–58; pop. 134 (1933), 124 (1947), 74 (1954), 58 (1961).

Baden Park (*Co. Woore*) 32°10'S. 144°12'E., 103 km SE of Wilcannia.

Badger Brush (*Co. Westmoreland*) 33°39'S. 149°55'E., 9 km NE of Oberon, on Slippery Ck; Meth. C.

Badger Ground (*Co. Phillip*) 32°39'S. 149°59'E., 17 km N. of Rylstone.

Badgery's Siding (*Co. Camden*) see Exeter.

Badja (*Co. Beresford*) 36°03'S. 149°33'E., 42 km NE of Cooma, on Big Badja R.; sawmill (James Broadhead) 1905–63; pop. 37 (1933).

Baelcoola (*Co. Auckland*) 37°09'S. 149°27'E., 32 km SE of Bombala; telephone 1915; TX 1953.

Baerami (*Co. Hunter*) 32°23'S. 150°28'E., 20 km W. of Denman, on Baerami Ck; oil-shale mining (disc. *c.*1900) 1939–45, farming, dairying; bushfire 1957; mine (Colonial Petroleum Oil Ltd); PO 1886–1973; Rom. Cath. C. (Our Lady of Perpetual Succour) b. 1936 by G. Reilly, d. by Peter Joseph Gannon, closed 1991, sold 2005, renovated 2013, reused; telephone 1901; TX 1915, automatic 1966; pop. 168 (1911), 117 (1933), 129 (1947), 79 (1954), 59 (1961).

Baerami (*Co. Hunter*) see also Mount Dangar.

Baerami Creek (*Co. Hunter*) 32°29'S. 150°29'E., 24 km SW of Denman, on Baerami Ck; St Elmo till 1927; dairying; bushfire 1957; PO 1918–66; TX 1930; pop. 217 (1933), 101 (1947), 111 (1954), 82 (1961), 154 (2006).

Bagawa (*Co. Fitzroy*) see Nana Glen.

Bagdad (*Co. Bland*) 34°31'S. 147°30'E., 8 km S. of Temora, on Trigalong Ck; Angl. C. (St Stephen's) 1888, restored 1906, demolished 1921, replacement b. 1921 by D.W. Smith and Thomas Sinclair, d. by Allan McDonald; school 1885–1912, reused, burnt down 1971; pop. 66 (1947).

Bagnoo (*Co. Macquarie*) 31°28'S. 152°32'E., 18 km W. of Wauchope, on Thone R.; Cowangara till 1919; dairying; bridge (steel truss) over Thone R.; PO 1927–78; school (Llanthony till 1963) 1957–69; telephone 1919; TX 1928; pop. 69 (1933), 85 (1947), 118 (1954), 76 (1961).

Bago (*Co. Wynyard*) 35°34'S. 147°58'E., 16 km W. of Batlow; snowstorm 1901.

Bago Forest (*Co. Selwyn*) 35°40'S. 148°10'E., 18 km NE of Tumbarumba; pop. 21 (1933).

Bagotville (*Co. Rous*) 28°59'S. 153°25'E., 12 km NE of Woodburn, on Tuckean Broadwater; farming and dairying; bushfire 1951; fire 1937; PO 1916; punt across Tuckean Broadwater; 4 quarries; sawmill (Bagot Bros) 1884, burnt down 1890, rebuilt, boiler exploded and burnt down again 1899; school 1916–26 and 1957–65; telephone 1916; TX 1929, automatic 1957; pop. 113 (1933), 78 (1947), 60 (1954).

Bagtown (*Co. Cook*) see Glen Davis.

Bagtown (*Co. Cooper*) see Griffith.

Bagtown (*Co. Murray*) see Captains Flat.

Baileys Estate (*Co. Clarence*) see Junction Hill.

Bairnsdale (*Co. Richmond*) 28°56'S. 153°05'E., 9 km S. of Casino; school 1909–44.

Bakana (*Co. Buckland*) 31°22'S. 150°33'E., 10 km W. of Werris Creek.

Bakers Creek (*Co. Gloucester*) 31°57'S. 152°06'E., 15 km NE of Gloucester, on Bakers Ck; pop. 133 (1911), 25 (1933).

Bakers Creek (*Co. Hardinge*) 30°16'S. 151°01'E., 38 km SW of Tingha, on Bakers Ck; school 1903 b. by James Henry, closed 1910.

Bakers Creek (*Co. Raleigh*) 30°49'S. 152°43'E., 24 km SW of Macksville; pop. 65 (1933).

Bakers Creek (*Co. Sandon*) 30°28'S. 151°46'E., 10 km NE of Armidale; school 1918–59.

Baker's Siding (*Co. Bathurst*) see Garland.

Bakers Swamp (*Co. Gordon*) 32°46'S. 148°56'E., 22 km S. of Wellington; farming and grazing; PO 1881–1982; Rom. Cath. C. (Immaculate Conception) 1910, closed, sold, relocated and reused; school 1877–1949; telephone 1915; TX 1916, automatic 1982; pop. 81 (1911), 98 (1933), 88 (1947), 84 (1954), 55 (1961).

Bala (*Co. King*) 34°21'S. 148°52'E., 16 km NE of Boorowa; telephone 1918; TX 1930–57.

Balabla (*Co. Bland*) 34°08'S. 148°00'E., 30 km SW of Grenfell, on Bribbaree Ck; school 1886–95.

Balaclava (*Co. Camden*) 34°27'S. 150°29'E., 3 km NE of Mittagong; brickworks; pop. 71 (1933), 58 (1947), 72 (1954), 82 (1961), 417 (2011).

Balaclava (*Co. Yancowinna*) 32°10'S. 141°22'E., 25 km S. of Broken Hill.

Balala (*Co. Hardinge*) 30°37'S. 151°20'E., 16 km W. of Uralla; grazing; PO 1881–1940; telephone 1937; TX 1937; pop. 132 (1901), 91 (1911), 31 (1933), 320 (2011).

Balarang (*Co. Camden*) see Oak Flats.

Balcolyn (*Co. Northumberland*) 33°06'S. 151°33'E., 3 km NE of Bonnells Bay, on Lake Macquarie; (incl. Silverwater and Yarrawonga Park); orig. timber; water supply 1963; pop. 71 (1961), 817 (2011).

Bald Blair (*Co. Clarke*) 30°14'S. 151°47'E., 11 km E. of Guyra; school 1955, additions 2010; pop. 53 (1933), 65 (1954).

Balderodgery (*Co. Gordon*) see Baldry.

Baldersleigh (*Co. Hardinge*) 30°16'S. 151°23'E., 27 km W. of Guyra, on Laura Ck; Presb. C.; pop. 47 (1933), 195 (2006).

Bald Hill (*Co. Bourke*) 34°26'S. 146°50'E., 10 km SW of Ardlethan; tin mining; Meth. C. 1921, burnt down 1923, replaced, moved 1959 to Ardlethan; pop. 92 (1933).

Bald Hill (*Co. Oxley*) 31°52'S. 147°17'E., 35 km S. of Nyngan.

Bald Hill (*Co. Rous*) see Bexhill.

Bald Hill (*Co. Wellesley*) 36°42'S. 149°07'E., 27 km N. of Bombala.

Bald Hill (*Co. Wellington*) see Hill End.

Bald Hills (*Co. Auckland*) 36°55'S. 149°50'E., 4 km NW of Pambula, on Bald Hills Ck; school 1900 b. by J. Koerber, closed 1911; pop. 33 (1933), 147 (2001), 292 (2011).

Bald Hills (*Co. Fitzroy*) 30°21'S. 152°28'E., 25 km W. of Dorrigo, on Allans Water; airfield.

Bald Hills (*Co. Forbes*) 33°46'S. 148°09'E., 14 km N. of Grenfell, on Bald Hills Ck; mines: crystal quartz (A. Holland) 1970–73, tin (Arizona) worked 1921–27 by Bradley, tin (Melyra) worked 1927 by J.M. Hewer.

Bald Knob (*Co. Fitzroy*) 30°15'S. 152°59'E., 13 km NW of Coffs Harbour.

Bald Nob (*Co. Gough*) 29°38'S. 151°58'E., 25 km NE of Glen Innes, on Tommys Ck; grazing; airfield; FB (station b. 2012); PO 1885; school 1892–1911; telephone 1914; TX 1929; pop. 128 (1911), 100 (1933), 95 (1947), 56 (1954), 55 (1961).

Baldry (*Co. Gordon*) 32°52'S. 148°30'E., 32 km SE of Peak Hill; Balderodgery till 1912; farming and grazing; Angl. C. (All Saints') b. 1899 by F. Shield, additions 1904, renovations 1924; cemetery (51 graves 1897+) 1892; freezing works 1918–20, reopened 1927; PO 1890–1984, bought by Gary and Heidi Ward; POW control centre (World War II); school 1952–72; telephone 1911; TX 1913, automatic 1984; pop. 152 (1911), 134 (1933), 93 (1947), 191 (1954), 152 (1961).

Bald Siding (*Co. Harden*) 35°00'S. 148°08'E., 8 km N. of Gundagai.

Baldwin (*Co. Darling*) 30°51'S. 150°36'E., 16 km SW of Manilla, on Bells Plain Gully; earth tremor 2012; school 1901–4; telephone 1926; TX 1929.

Baleveolan (*Co. Gipps*) 33°15'S. 146°52'E., 32

km SW of Condobolin.

Balfour (*Co. Westmoreland*) 33°44'S. 149°44'E., 12 km W. of Oberon; school (Brisbane Valley till 1892) 1882–92 and 1958–69.

Balgonnia (*Co. Northumberland*) see Brightwaters.

Balgownie (*Co. Camden*) 34°23'S. 150°53'E., 2 km SW of Corrimal, on Cabbage Tree Ck; Para Meadow till 1892; surveyed and estab. 1839, subdivided 1873; coalmining; Angl. C. b. 1908 by Stanley E. Elphinstone, damaged 1952, closed, sold 1988 and reused, new one (St Aidan's) b. 1953 by L. Duff and A. Dawson; bridge (Donnans Bridge), re-decked 1911, over Cabbage Tree Ck; caterpillar infestation 1898; collieries: Balgownie (or Daylight), Mount Pleasant (estab. 1854 by Patrick Lahiff and Benjamin Fawcett, acquired by E. Vickery & Sons, sold 1860 to James and William Byrnes, taken over by Illawarra Coal Co., strikes 1873 and 1886, man killed 1902, office burnt down 1907, new powerhouse 1920, colliery closed 1933, taken over 1937 by Aust. Iron & Steel Ltd and underground workings linked with Mount Keira, closed 1955, largely demolished), North Mount Pleasant (estab. 1886 by Illawarra Coal Co.), Owen's (estab. 1909 by Owen, taken over 1910 by Balgownie Coal Co., acquired 1922 by Mount Kembla Extended Coal Co. which renamed it Mount Kembla Extended Colliery, closed 1936); FB 1924 (station b. 1929, new one 1972); Meth. C. b. 1953 by William J. Longhurst; PO 1889; Prim. Meth. C. 1884–1953, demolished 1984; PS 1903–54; reservoir (concrete), 100,000 gal. (454.6 kl), 1915; Rom. Cath. C. b. 1908 by J.A. Waters, d. by John Alfred Ford, renovations and repairs 1930, closed 1947, demolished, new one (Mater Dolorosa) b. 1974 by Longhurst and Cummins; school 1889 b. by John M. Walker, d. by William Edmund Kemp, additions 1909, 1921, 1966, 1969, 1971, 2010; telephone 1892; Unit. C. (orig. Presb.) b. 1905 by George Dean and Robert Ballantyne, d. by Alexander Leckie Elphinstone, closed, sold 1988, reused; pop. 957 (1911), 2,974 (1954), 5,447 (2011).

Balgownie (*Co. Camden*) see also Fairy Meadow.

Ballacara (*Co. Gloucester*) 32°40'S. 151°47'E., 20 km NE of Maitland; pop. 21 (1933).

Balladoran (*Co. Ewenmar*) 31°52'S. 148°39'E., 16 km S. of Gilgandra, on Marthaguy Ck; timber and farming; Angl. C. (St Michael's) 1907, closed, sold and removed; PO 1905; RS 1903, station b. by W.H. Hudson, closed 1974; sawmill; school 1907–68; telegraph 1905; TX 1924, automatic 1984; pop. 117 (1901), 313 (1911), 269 (1933), 153 (1947), 139 (1954), 223 (1961), 160 (2006), 225 (2011).

Ballalaba (*Co. St Vincent*) 35°34'S. 149°38'E., 20 km SW of Braidwood, on Shoalhaven R.; farming and grazing; Angl. C. (St Paul's) d. and b. 1913 by Bill Thompson, new one 1927; bridge (truss spans on concrete piers) b. 1894 by J.W. Page, over Shoalhaven R.; diphtheria 1912; flour mill; freezing works (T.W. Draper) b. 1917 by Butt, leased 1924 to G.E. Siddall, bought 1927 by P. Nomchong; sawmills: George Gunn and Henry Thompson; school (Nithsdale) 1892–96; telephone 1906; TX 1921–65; pop. 145 (1911), 89 (1933), 68 (1954), 61 (1961).

Ballamalito (*Co. Argyle*) see Bullamalito.

Ballandry (*Co. Cooper*) 33°59'S. 145°54'E., 35 km N. of Griffith; bushfire 1931; FB; pop. 225 (1933), 70 (1947), 71 (1954).

Ballarah (*Co. Lincoln*) 32°02'S. 149°20'E., 6 km W. of Dunedoo; school 1881, new buildings b. 1883 by P.H. Lawson, new school b. 1899 by C.J. Campton, closed 1922.

Ballbank (*Co. Wakool*) 35°27'S. 143°56'E., 27 km NW of Barham; RS (Victorian railway) 1928, closed.

Balldale (*Co. Hume*) 35°51'S. 146°31'E., 18 km NW of Howlong; wheat; cemetery; FB; flood 1939; gale 1923; PO 1905, new ones b. 1911 and 1924; Presb. C. 1912, closed and reused 1962, new one 1962; PS 1912, closed during World War II, reopened 1947–74; Rom. Cath. C. (St Patrick's) b. 1911 by J. Mills, d. by William John Monks, closed, sold 2013, reused; RS (Carnsdale till 1905) 1892, station b. by Charles Hardy, removed 1982, services ceased 1984; school 1907, additions 1919 by W. Squires, relocated 1938, closed 2010, sold; silo 1920; telephone 1906; TX 1912; water reticulation 1949; pop. 299 (1911), 299 (1933), 212 (1947), 180 (1954), 134 (1961).

Ballengarra (*Co. Macquarie*) 31°19'S. 152°42'E., 16 km N. of Wauchope; farming; PO 1900; sawmill (MacLaughlin & Son); telephone 1914; TX 1916; pop. 107 (1911), 92 (1933), 82 (1947), 72 (1954), 197 (2006).

Ballengarra (*Co. Macquarie*) see also Gum Scrub.

Ballengarra Wharf (*Co. Macquarie*) 31°20'S. 152°46'E., 15 km N. of Wauchope, on Wilson R.; telephone 1914; wharf b. 1898 by J. Croker; pop. 24 (1933).

Ballimore (*Co. Lincoln*) 32°12'S. 148°54'E., 28 km E. of Dubbo, on Talbragar R.; orig. Mount Baltimore; surveyed 1915, village gaz. 1916, lots sold 1917; wheat, wool, timber, mining (coal disc. 1880 by F.H. Burslem and A. Hamilton); brick-kiln (Albert R. Smith); bridge 1960 d. by Montague Smith, over Talbragar R.; bushfires 1957 and 2004; cemetery (burials 1919+); coalmine (Mount Baltimore) 1881, defunct; FB (station b. 1966); fire 1956; flood 1955; PO 1896, burnt down 1956; Rom. Cath. C. (Our Lady of Lourdes); RS 1918–75; sawmills: Arthur James Hutchins and Richard Utley, and F.E. Smith (man killed 1919); school 1916, additions 1920 by T. Grimsby, additions 2010; spa water (Zetz-Spa Pty Ltd) bore sunk 1886 by McGinnity Bros for Horace Woodley, sold to C.F. Doutreband, sold to Tooth & Co. Ltd, closed; telephone 1923; TX 1923, fire 1956, automatic 1975; Union C. 1959; pop. 64 (1901), 70 (1911), 222 (1933), 162 (1947), 136 (1954), 138 (1961), 188 (2011).

Ballina (*Co. Rous*) 28°52'S. 153°34'E., 29 km E. of Lismore, on Richmond R.; (incl. West Ballina); orig. Deptford, then Bulloona, then Richmond River Heads 1856–68; settled *c.*1847, surveyed 1855, town gaz. 1856, laid out 1857 by Frederick Septimus Peppercorne, first town lots sold 1857 (West Ballina), subdivided 1883, munic. proc. 1883, thrived in 1880s, further subdivision 1919, munic. abolished 1977, bypassed by highway 2012; orig. timber port, tallow, hides, gold (disc. 1870), then dairying and maize, now sugar-cane, mixed farming, fruit, fishing, oysters, prawns, tourism, retirement centre; airport (Ballina Byron Gateway, 5 km N.), extended 2008 by T.F. Woollam & Son Pty Ltd; ambulance station 1945; Angl. C. (St Mary the Virgin) 1876, reused, replacement b. 1906 by James Ainsworth, d. by Albert A. Tayt, new one b. 1998 by Bennett Constructions Pty Ltd; Assemblies of God C. (Life); bacon factories: Ballina Co-op. Creamery Co. 1918, and Richardson and Mitchell 1902; Bapt. C. 1870, new one 1971; Bible C. (Westside); 2 boat harbours; breakwater (southern) b. 1889–1912 by Timothy Toohey, d. by Sir John Coode, rebuilt 1994; bridges: Teven Bridge (b. 1909 by W.E. Oxenford, d. by Percy Allan), new one 2010, over Emigrant Ck, Missingham Bridge 1935, replaced 1985, to East Ballina, over North Ck, Prospect Bridge (replaced earlier one in use 1906–70) to East Ballina, over North Ck, bridge 1955 over North Ck Canal, bridge over Fishery Ck; bubonic plague (woman died) 1905; butter factory 1900, new one 1919 d. by J. Wildridge and Sinclair, renamed Ballina Co-op. Refrigerating & Produce Co. Ltd, taken over 1929 by Norco Co-op. Ltd, rebuilt 1930 by Gallagher, closed 1945; caravan factory (Kimberley Campers); cemeteies: Ballina 1886 and West Ballina 1876; CH (incl. lock-up) b. 1859 d. by Alexander Dawson, burnt down 1862, new one b. 1865 by William Kinnear, new one b. 1882–84 also by Kinnear, d. by James Johnstone Barnet; Christ. Brethren Assemblies C. (Gospel); Christ. City C. 2010 (former factory); Christ. Outreach C. (Seacoast); cordial factories: C. Ashwood, Enterprise (estab. by George Alfred Lewis, bought 1911 by Angus McDonald, bought 1914 by A.E. Phipps), Johnson Bros, E. Solomon and H. Watson 1884 (damaged 1884); creamery (NSW Creamery Butter Co. Ltd) 1897; customs-house; dengue fever

1942; diphtheria 1902 and 1911; dockyard (Thomas Fenwick) 1891, taken over 1943 by Fenwick Steamship Tug & Engineering Co., became Ballina Slipway & Engineering Co.; drought 1862; engineering works: E.R. Barlow & Co. Ltd 1912–21, W.H. Mountfield, E.H. Wood; FB: town fire brigade 1903 (station b. 1928 by Ainsworth Bros, closed, reused 2018, replaced 2016 on new site) and bushfire brigade 1942; fibrous plaster works (New State, A. Mogg); fires 1909, 1923, 1929, 1935, 1939; floods 1861, 1863, 1864, 1870, 1889, 1890, 1893, 1948, 1954, 2001; foundry (Metalcast Aust.) estab. 1992 by Stuart White; fruit canning factory (North Coast Industries Pty Ltd) 1954, damaged 1954; gales 1884, 1892, 1929, 1950, 2013; hailstorm 1907; hospital 1894, new buildings, alterations and renovations 1939 by Schmitzer, additions by Bennett Constructions Pty Ltd, additions by T.F. Woollam & Son Pty Ltd; Jehovah's Witnesses C.; metal fabrication works (Weldcro Fabrication) 1987; motor home factory (Horizon) 1995; pilot station b. 1940 by L.W. Gazzard, closed 1982, reused; PO 1856, new one b. 1886–88 by James Moore, clock tower added 1890, post office closed and reused; powerhouse (Electric Construction Co. of Aust. Ltd) 1911, taken over 1947 by county council; Presb. C. (St Stephen's) 1885, reused, new one b. 1915 by H.R. Gibson, d. by Frederick Johnson Board, spire damaged 1937 and removed, church renovated 1939; PS 1865, alterations 1934 by Diyal Singh, new one 1979; punt (steam) estab. 1872 by Thomas Fenwick, to cross Richmond R.; railway bridge (bascule) 1930, line closed 1949, reused, over North Creek Canal; Rom. Cath. C. b. 1881 by J. Lewis, new one b. 1901 by Patrick Farrelly, replacment (St Francis Xavier's War Memorial) b. 1962 by Reginald Joseph Want, d. by Sydney George Hirst and David Kennedy; RS 1930–49, line dismantled 1949, station removed and reused; Salv. Army C. 1893, burnt down 1927, replaced 1929, rebuilt 1994; sawmills: Bagot Bros Pty Ltd (taken over 1955 by Tulloch Ltd, closed 1964, defunct), and Lewis and Walton (inundated 1889); scarlet fever 1913; schools: primary (West Ballina 1862–68) 1861, new one b. 1863 by William Clement, sold, replacement 1882 d. by William Edmund Kemp, new building 1888, additions 1924 by Holland and Thorn, additions 1931 by H. Brown, additions 1966 and 1969, and HS 1956, additions 1966, 1973, 1977; SD Adventist C. 1954, extended and modernised 1976; sewerage augmentation 1996; slipways: Barlow's 1952 and Fenwick Bros 1891 (bought by Davies Bros, sold 1942 to S.G. White & Co., closed 1989); spoke and handle factory (Bagot Bros Ltd); storm 1937; sugar mills: W. Clement 1882, George Martin, closed 1905, D. Navin, J.C. Ryan, James Skinner 1871; TC, became a campus of North Coast Institute in 1992, additions 2010 by T.F. Woollam & Son Pty Ltd, d. by Perumal Pedavoli; telegraph 1875, new office b. 1886–88 by James Moore; TX 1900; typhoid 1909; Unit. C. (orig. Meth.) 1920 d. by Frederick Johnson Board; water supply 1903, pipes replaced 1915 and 1936, augmentation 1957, 1969, 1988; Wes. Meth. C. 1888; 10 wharves (incl. Fenwick's and North Coast Steam Navigation Co. 1917–54, demolished); pop. *c.*300 (1870–71), 359 (1881), 1,084 (1891), *c.*1,300 (1895), 1,819 (1901), 2,441 (1911), 2,768 (1921), *c.*3,000 (1924), 3,042 (1933), 3,202 (1947), 3,558 (1954), 4,129 (1961), 4,933 (1966), 6,133 (1971), *c.*6,500 (1973), 7,323 (1976), 9,738 (1981), 12,398 (1986), 14,554 (1991), 16,056 (1996), 16,599 (2001), 16,477 (2006), 15,965 (2011).

Ballina East (*Co. Rous*) 28°52'S. 153°35'E., 2 km E. of Ballina, on North Ck; (incl. Shaws Bay); mineral sand mining; ambulance station 1941; breakwater (northern) b. 1889–1905 by Timothy Toohey, d. by Sir John Coode, damaged and repaired 1947, extended 1967 to 600 ft (182.9 m), repairs 2013 by Civil Team Engineering Pty Ltd; bridges to Ballina over North Ck: Missingham Bridge 1935, replaced 1985, and Prospect Bridge (replaced earlier one in use 1906–70); bushfire 1938; cemeteries: general 1884, incl.

lawn cemetery and columbaria, and Pioneer (Shaws Bay), burials 1853–1915, headstones relocated 1961; coast guard tower 1984; FB; gale 1947; lighthouse (Ballina Head) b. 1879 by Henry Watson and John Perry, d. by James Johnstone Barnet, 23 ft (7 m), converted to acetylene 1920, later converted to electricity, automated 1926, oil storeroom demolished 1938; pilot station 1855–1940; PO 1927; reservoirs: 300,000 gal. (1,363.8 kl) and 1,000,000 gal. (4,546 kl), 1966; rifle range (man killed 1904); sawmill (Lemuel Griggs Snow and Christian Hesse) 1856, acquired 1865 by Breckenridge and moved to Wyrallah; school (Southern Cross) 1971, new one 1993 on new site, additions 1995; sugar mill (John Sharpe) 1869, upgraded 1882; telephone 1917; pop. 5,320 (2011).

Ballingall (*Co. Sturt*) 34°13'S. 145°57'E., 11 km NW of Griffith; pop. 285 (1947), 261 (1954).

Ballington (*Co. Durham*) see Halton.

Ballinwarra (*Co. Rous*) 28°44'S. 153°31'E., 5 km S. of Bangalow.

Balls Platform (*Co. Harden*) 35°01'S. 148°07'E., 6 km N. of Gundagai; RS (relocated 1928) 1891–1946.

Ballyryan (*Co. King*) 34°27'S. 148°41'E., 4 km W. of Boorowa, on Boorowa R.

Balmoral (*Co. Camden*) 34°18'S. 150°31'E., 6 km S. of Buxton; Bargo Platform till 1888; fruit growing; bushfire 2013; FB; PO 1890; pottery (Sandy Lockwood); railway accident 1905; RS (Big Hill Lower Siding till 1881, then Bargo Platform till 1888) 1878–1974, station sold and removed 1979; school 1889–1916, reopened 1959; telegraph 1890; TX 1915–69; Union C.; pop. 97 (1901), 71 (1911), 86 (1933), 53 (1947), 59 (1954), 53 (1961), 313 (2011).

Balmoral (*Co. Northumberland*) see Rathmines.

Balmoral Corner (*Co. Durham*) see Muswellbrook.

Balpool (*Co. Wakool*) 35°13'S. 144°25'E., 60 km NW of Deniliquin, on Edward R.; telephone 1926; TX 1930.

Balranald (*Co. Caira*) 34°38'S. 143°34'E., 118 km W. of Hay, on Murrumbidgee R.; disc. 1830 by Capt. Charles Sturt, settled 1845 by George Hobler, founded 1848 by George James Macdonald, surveyed 1849 by F.P. McCabe, town laid out and gaz. 1851, first land sales 1852, resurveyed 1858 by John McCulloch, designated as chief town of the county, munic. proc. 1882; former coaching centre and river port (wool), now sheep, cattle, irrigated cropping, timber, hort., viticulture; airport (2 km NE); ambulance station; Angl. C. (St Barnabas's) b. 1873 by Philip Comitti, alterations and repairs 1887 by O'Donnell, and graveyard; brewery (Henry Simmons then Thomas Boynton) 1883–88; bridge (iron and steel, with central lift span) b. 1878–82 by G.H. Royce & Co., replaced 1973, over Murrumbidgee R.; bushfire 1974–75; cemetery 1874, restored 2007–12 by Peter Blake and Noel Camin, and lawn cemetery; CH 1861 d. by Henry Sheills, new one 1885 d. by James Johnstone Barnet, demolished 1981; dust storm 1928; earth tremor 1921; electricity 1926; FB (station unroofed 1925, new one b. 1930 by Alfred N. Duryea, d. by William Hull McNiven, new one 1954); fires 1884, 1897, 1909, 1923; foot-bridge over Murrumbidgee R.; freezing works (Arthur H. Griffiths) 1932; gaol b. 1885–87 by James O'Donnell, additions and alterations 1890 by Samuel Stead, closed 1932, became lock-up, closed 1977, reused; hospital 1880, additions and alterations 1913 by Alfred N. Duryea, unroofed 1925, additions 1928, fire 1930, additions and alterations 1938 by V.F. Treadwell, refurbishment by Richard Crookes Constructions; ice works (J.J. Power) 1932; measles epidemic (4 died) 1893; pet food factory (Balranald Trading Co.); PO 1850, new one b. 1871, d. by James Johnstone Barnet, extended 1887, additions 1899 d. by Walter Liberty Vernon, extended 1922 and 1958, demolished, replaced 1979; pound (stock) 1865; powerhouse; Presb. C. b. 1889 by James O'Donnell, d. by William Lawrence; PS 1852, (second) 1871, (third) b. 1899 by George Huntley Dixon, (fourth)

1980; punt (Denis Hanan) 1859, bought from Capt. Francis Cadell and relaunched; railway engine shed (2 stall); reservoir (tower) 1888; Rom. Cath. C. (St Dympna's) 1875, damaged 1925, extended 1926 and 1973; RS (4 km S., on Victorian railway) 1926, closed; sale-yards 1953; sawmill (H.J. and C.M. Winter, bought 1976 by A.B. Rowe & Son); school 1865, new one b. 1880, damaged 1882, additions 1882 by P. Wissmann, repairs 1916 by J.C. White, unroofed 1925, additions 1925 by A. Palmer, demolished, new one b. 1934 by W. and R.C. Potter, additions 1963, 1967, 1969, 1980; silo; squall 1882; storms 1925 (most buildings damaged) and 1996; telegraph 1870, new office b. 1871 by Philip Comitti; toll-house, demolished; TX 1910; typhoid 1889 (15 died) and 1896; watch-house 1861; waterworks b. 1889 by Parker, damaged 1925, water supply augmentation 1985 and 1988; wharves: Boynton's and Harben's; wool store (Cram's) 1876; pop. *c.*100 (1866), 233 (1871), *c.*350 (1873), 646 (1881), *c.*670 (1889), 637 (1891), *c.*750 (1895), 741 (1901), 745 (1911), 1,261 (1933), 1,249 (1947), 1,273 (1954), 1,331 (1961), 1,490 (1966), 1,425 (1971), 1,396 (1976), 1,442 (1981), 1,398 (1986), 1,327 (1991), 1,419 (1996), *c.*1,500 (1999), 1,282 (2001), 1,216 (2006), 1,161 (2011).

Balranald Junction (*Co. Cadell*) see Barnes.

Balwarra Heights (*Co. Clarence*) see Grafton South.

Bamarang (*Co. St Vincent*) 34°53'S. 150°32'E., 7 km W. of Nowra, on Shoalhaven R.; farming; dam, 79 ft (24 m) high, 1983; FB; flood 1870; PO 1927–30; Presb. C. 1864; school 1899–1906; waterworks 1982.

Bandon (*Co. Forbes*) 33°30'S. 148°18'E., 11 km SW of Eugowra, on Lachlan R.; formerly also known as Paytens Bridge; bridge (Allan timber truss) 1926, 420 ft (128 m), over Lachlan R.; school (Paytens Bridge) 1956–74; TX (automatic); pop. 74 (1911), 26 (1933).

Bandon Grove (*Co. Gloucester*) 32°18'S. 151°43'E., 12 km N. of Dungog, on Chichester R.; tobacco, agric., citrus fruit, dairying; bridges: truss and beam bridge b. 1891 by Matthew Murphy, d. by John Alexander McDonald, 491 ft (149.7 m), and steel plate girder bridge, 421 ft (128.3 m), fabricated by Thomas C. Pollard, erected 1948 by J.H. Mould, H.W. Cover and K. Midtvik, over Williams R.; cemetery (burials 1844+, 93 graves); concrete sleeper plant; electricity 1947; foot-bridges: one over Chichester R. and one b. 1879 over Williams R.; hailstorm 1927; PO 1858–1974; Presb. C. 1891; sawmill and tramway (Robert Lee) 1912, burnt down 1912; school 1862, additions 1882 by J. Tierney, closed 1984, reused; telephone 1906; tobacco factory (William Alexander Smith), closed 1875; TX 1915, automatic 1961; Union C. (third one) b. 1888 by Harry Alcorn and Ted Marsh, renovated 1938; Wes. Meth. C. 1850; pop. *c.*200 (1866), 111 (1901), 117 (1911), 139 (1933), 119 (1947), 113 (1954), 104 (1961), 189 (2006), 278 (2011).

Banfield (*Co. Durham*) 32°31'S. 151°48'E., 12 km S. of Dungog, on Unwarrabin Ck; farming.

Bangadang (*Co. Wynyard*) 35°15'S. 147°57'E., 12 km NW of Adelong; agric.; bushfire 1909; FB 1960.

Bangalee (*Co. Camden*) see Nowra (*Co. St Vincent*).

Bangalore (*Co. Argyle*) see Komungla.

Bangalow (*Co. Rous*) 28°41'S. 153°31'E., 10 km SW of Byron Bay, on Byron Ck; Byron Creek till 1894; settled 1881 by Thomas Robinson, bypassed by highway 1994; timber, cattle, dairying, sugar-cane, hort.; Angl. C. (Epiphany) b. 1903 by W.S. Rays, relocated 1910, reused, demolished 1966, replacement (All Souls' Memorial) b. 1928 by W. Braid, d. by Frederick Johnson Board; bridge (J.G. Snow Bridge) b. 1948 by Beattie and Frost, over Byron Ck; butter factory (Byron Creek Dairy Co.) 1893; carriage-works (A. Barnes) 1906, destroyed 1915; caterpillar infestation 1914; cemetery (1,536 graves); CH b. 1909 by Lowe and Beckinsale, closed 1964, reused; cheese factory (Foley Bros) 1916, casein made 1920+; Church of Christ

1965; cordial factory (R. Thompson & Co.); electricty (from Mullumbimby hydro-electric plant) 1926; engineering works (Reading Bros), damaged 1928; FB (station b. 1981); fires 1907 and 1920; flood 1921; furniture factory (C.L. Snow); gale 1928; hospital (War Memorial) 1953; joinery and furniture factory (W.S. Rays), closed 1926; lock-up b. 1905 by Doyle and Gilbert; Meth. C. b. 1910 by W.S. Rays, destroyed 1915; monumental stone works (A. Beckinsale & Co.); PO 1891, new one b. 1908 by James Batten, burnt down 1930, new one b. 1935 by A.R. Sansom, d. by W. Wonder; pound (stock), relocated 1909; Presb. C. (St John's) 1912, renovations 1939; PS b. 1904 by Doyle and Gilbert, new one 1964, in former court-house; reservoir b. 1950 by Chesterfield & Jenkins (Queensland) Pty Ltd; rifle range 1907; Rom. Cath. C. 1894, relocated and extended 1908, reused 1935, new one (St Kevin of Glendalough) b. 1935 by R.M. Bowcock, d. by Clement Glancey; RS (o. as Granuaile, new station b. 1909) 1894, station b. by William Mitchell, closed 1990; sawmills: J.N. Hollingworth & Co. and Snow Bros; school (Byron Creek till 1907) 1888, additions and repairs 1892 by Richard Watson, new building b. 1900 by J.T.G. Carson, new building b. 1914 by Edward Boyle and John O'Keefe, new building b. 1925 by S.W. and R.C. Potter, additions 1994; sewage works; storm 1915; streets electric lit 1926; telegraph office b. 1908 by J. Batten; telephone 1896; TX 1907; Unit. C. (orig. Meth.) 1916; water reticulation 1955; weir on Bangalow Ck; pop. 186 (1901), 1,057 (1911), 972 (1933), 742 (1947), 704 (1954), 626 (1961), 479 (1966), 534 (1971), 568 (1976), 614 (1981), 677 (1986), 819 (1991), 896 (1996), 1,230 (2001), 1,327 (2006), 1,521 (2011).

Bangaroo (*Co. Bathurst*) 33°38'S. 148°38'E., 7 km S. of Canowindra; PO 1927; 3 quarries; RS (7 km E.) 1910, station b. by D.H. Reid, closed 1975; school 1916–44; pop. 129 (1911), 89 (1933).

Bangaroo North (*Co. Bathurst*) 33°36'S. 148°40'E., 3 km S. of Canowindra; PO 1927–51; school 1937–64; telephone 1925.

Bangate (*Co. Narran*) 29°17'S. 147°42'E., 33 km NW of Lightning Ridge.

Bang Bang (*Co. Monteagle*) see Koorawatha.

Bang-lo (*Co. Clarence*) see Iluka.

Bango (*Co. King*) 34°44'S. 148°59'E., 13 km NE of Yass; measles epidemic 1893; school 1883–1928; pop. 23 (1933), 402 (2006).

Bank Corner (*Co. Northumberland*) see Newcastle.

Banks Crossing (*Co. Ashburnham*) 33°05'S. 148°14'E., 9 km NE of Parkes, on Goobang Ck; bridge over Goobang Ck.

Bank Vale (*Co. Urana*) 35°03'S. 146°41'E., 19 km N. of Lockhart.

Bannaby (*Co. Argyle*) 34°26'S. 150°00'E., 31 km W. of Berrima; farming and grazing; Angl. C. (St Matthew's) 1898, additions 1915, and graveyard (burials 1893+); grasshopper infestation 1926; measles epidemic 1899; mine (Mount Bannaby Copper Mine, A. Potter) <1908; PO 1875; school 1901–38; telephone 1914; TX 1916; pop. 206 (1901), 187 (1911), 143 (1933), 58 (1947), 78 (1954), 67 (1961), 210 (2011).

Bannister (*Co. Argyle*) 34°36'S. 149°29'E., 15 km S. of Crookwell; Gullen Flat till 1907; farming and grazing; bushfires 1939 and 1944; butter factory (Isaac Shepherd), fire 1897; PO 1927; school (Gullen Flat till 1915) 1880–1915 and 1958–68; telephone 1915; TX 1930; pop. 66 (1911), 171 (1933), 129 (1947), 117 (1954), 142 (1961), 175 (2006), 333 (2011).

Bannockburn (*Co. Arrawatta*) 29°37'S. 151°02'E., 20 km NW of Inverell, on Bannockburn Ck; cemetery (burials 1870s+); quarry; school 1916–51; pop. 181 (1911), 34 (1933).

Banoon (*Co. Darling*) 30°31'S. 150°26'E., 22 km SW of Barraba, on Manilla R.; soldiers' settlement; school 1957–66, building moved to Barraba; pop. 27 (1933).

Banora Point (*Co. Rous*) 28°13'S. 153°33'E., 6 km S. of Tweed Heads, on Tweed R.; (incl. Barneys Point and Sexton Hill); bananas till 1923, sugar-cane till 1948, dairying, tropical fruit, vegetables; Bapt. C. (Community, renamed The Hub); bridge (Barneys Point Bridge), 625 ft (190.5 m), to Fingal Head, with Strauss bascule span fabricated by Clyde Engineering Co. Ltd, erected 1936 by State Monier Pipe & Reinforced Concrete Works, replaced 1993–96, over Tweed R.; electricity 1943; 3 foot-bridges; PO 1927; punt to Chinderah till 1936, across Tweed R.; reservoir 1966; sawmill (Tasman Hart); schools: Banora Point (Kurrara till 1937) b. 1894 by Hugh Minnow, additions 1924 by Tate Bros, additions 1967, 1990, 1995, additions 2007 by T.F. Woollam & Son Pty Ltd, Banora Point HS 2004 (new buildings b. 2006 by Richard Crookes Constructions), Centaur 1994; telephone 1921; TX 1946, automatic 1952; Unit. C. 1993; water reticulation 1963; pop. 125 (1933), 151 (1947), 172 (1954), 327 (1961), 970 (1971), 14,683 (2006), 15,047 (2011).

Banshaw (*Co. Arrawatta*) see Bonshaw.

Banyabba (*Co. Clarence*) 29°21'S. 153°01'E., 21 km NW of Maclean; forestry; bushfire 1994; RS 1905, station b. by H.W. Owen, closed 1974; sawmill, damaged 1951; storm 1951; telephone 1925; TX 1942; pop. 67 (1947), 54 (1961).

Bara (*Co. Phillip*) 32°34'S. 149°50'E., 24 km E. of Mudgee, on Bara Ck; school (Bara Creek) 1884–94; pop. 30 (1933).

Bara Creek (*Co. Phillip*) see Bara.

Baradine (*Co. Baradine*) 30°57'S. 149°04'E., 42 km NW of Coonabarabran, on Teridgerie Ck; town gaz. and first lots sold 1865, designated as chief town of the county; timber, sleeper cutting, agric., grazing, emu and ostrich farming; airport 1951; ambulance station; Angl. C. (St Andrew's); caterpillar infestation 1947; cemetery (882 graves) 1878; CH 1880, new buildings 1956; electricity 1938; FB; Meth. C. 1954; PO 1867, new one b. 1914 by W. McWhirter; pound (stock) 1867; Presb. C. 1940; PS b. 1916 by John D. Ryan; railway sleeper depot 1915; railway turntable, 60 ft (18.3 m), ruined; rifle range 1934; Rom. Cath. C. 1903, new one (St John the Baptist) b. 1924 by G. Palmer, d. by William James Gilroy, and graveyard; RS 1923–75, station dilapidated; sawmills: Bradley, Wightman & Co., A. Enright, A. Ernest Head, E.M. Lord, Pincham Bros, W. Proctor (burnt down 1914), Saunders' (burnt down 1914), Underwood Bros, F.J. Wangmann; school 1877, new one b. 1880 by Andrew English, repairs 1896 by G. and F.B. Martin, replaced 1908 by J.J. Treasure, additions 1934 by Treasure and Wadey, additions 1965 and 1970; sewerage augmentation 1999; silo 1935; storm 1996; telegraph 1876; TX 1910; Union C. 1954; water supply augmentation 1970; pop. *c.*30 (1866), 80 (1885), 213 (1901), 414 (1911), 726 (1933), 930 (1947), 785 (1954), 992 (1961), 751 (1966), 729 (1971), 754 (1976), 723 (1981), 656 (1986), 657 (1991), 609 (1996), 699 (2001), 763 (2011).

Baraimal (*Co. Rous*) 28°43'S. 153°00'E., 11 km S. of Kyogle; RS 1910, station b. by George Albert Leggo and John Allibone, closed 1969.

Baramul (*Co. Hunter*) 32°33'S. 150°21'E., 35 km SW of Denman, on Widden Brook.

Bar Beach (*Co. Northumberland*) see Newcastle.

Barbers Creek (*Co. Camden*) see Tallong.

Barbigal (*Co. Lincoln*) 32°14'S. 148°51'E., 21 km E. of Dubbo, on Talbragar R.; agric.; RS 1918–71.

Barbingal (*Co. Bland*) 33°52'S. 147°48'E., 34 km W. of Grenfell.

Barcoongere (*Co. Clarence*) 29°56'S. 153°13'E., 19 km N. of Woolgoolga.

Bardouroka (*Co. Gloucester*) see Fingal Bay.

Bare Camp (*Co. Vernon*) 31°08'S. 152°11'E., 56 km E. of Walcha, on Camp Ck.

Bareena (*Co. Rous*) 28°47'S. 153°34'E., 2 km NW of Lennox Head.

Barellan (*Co. Cooper*) 34°17'S. 146°34'E., 30 km NE of Leeton; surveyed 1908, village gaz. and first lots sold 1909, thrived 1923–26, declined 1955+; antimony mining, wheat, sheep, fruit; Angl. C. (St Clement's) 1925 d. by George William Albert Welch; cemetery 1909; drought 1914; dust storms 2018 and 2019; FB; fire 1929; flood 2012; gale 1933; hospital 1938; Meth. C. 1919; PO 1909, new one b. 1924; PS 1913, new one b. 1923 by Haynes and Dixon; reservoir (elevated), 150,000 gal. (681.9 kl); Rom. Cath. C. (Little Flower, renamed St Therese's) 1927; RS 1908, station b. by Frank Vernon, closed 1983, station removed 1985; sale-yards; sawmill (J.W. Wilson); school 1912, additions 1967; silo 1923; telephone 1911; TX 1913; Unit. C. (orig. Meth.) 1924; water supply 1941; pop. 295 (1911), 523 (1921), 564 (1933), 379 (1947), 338 (1954), 418 (1961), 394 (1971), 400 (1976), 380 (1981), 391 (1986), 422 (1991), 392 (1996), 366 (2001), 366 (2006), 328 (2011).

Barellan North (*Co. Cooper*) 34°12'S. 146°29'E., 38 km N. of Leeton; pop. 154 (1954), 162 (1961).

Bargo (*Co. Camden*) 34°17'S. 150°35'E., 8 km S. of Tahmoor, on Hornes Ck; formerly West Bargo; settled 1820, developed 1919+, thrived 1926–27, declined in 1970s; orig. wheat, then grazing, then farming and poultry; airfield (World War II); Angl. C. (St Paul's), temporary one opened in church hall b. 1954 by L. McGowan, W. Davidge and H. Cox; Bapt. C., burnt down 1914 while being leased to Angl. C., replaced; bushfires 1952, 1968, 1972, 2013; causeway; cemetery 1898; clothing factory (Bargo Textile Manufacturing Co.) 1945; FB 1939 (station b. 1968, relocated 1972, replaced 1984); lock-up, reused; Meth. C. b. 1937 by I. France; PO 1868; PS, closed 1920, reopened 1926, new one b. 1937 on new site by Arthur Miller; quarry (silica); 2 railway bridges; railway viaduct (5 brick arches) 1919 over Bargo R.; reservoir; Rom. Cath. C. (St Therese, the Little Flower) 1936–95, reused; RS (West Bargo till 1921) 1919; sawmill (E.E. Lupton); school (West Bargo till 1918) 1892 b. by J.R. Whitfield, additions 1928 by J. Layfield, additions 1976, 1995, 2010; storm (man killed) 1923; telephone 1919; toll-gate (toll abolished 1874); TX 1920; pop. 334 (1901), 226 (1911), 845 (1933), 669 (1947), 761 (1954), 813 (1961), 433 (1971), 669 (1976), 868 (1981), 1,246 (1986), 2,149 (1991), 2,669 (1996), 3,064 (2001), 3,078 (2011).

Bargo Brush (*Co. Camden*) see Buxton.

Bargo Platform (*Co. Camden*) see Balmoral.

Bargo West (*Co. Camden*) see Bargo.

Barham (*Co. Wakool*) 35°38'S. 144°08'E., 77 km W. of Deniliquin, on Murray R.; settled and founded 1843 by Edward Bernard D. Green; wheat, orchards, rice, dairying, timber, wool; ambulance station; Angl. C. (St John's) 1957; Assemblies of God C. (Christ. Family); Bapt. C.; brickworks (John Jamieson); bridge (de Burgh composite timber-steel trusses, and steel lift span fabricated by Eureka Foundry) erected 1904 by Monash and Anderson, 327 ft (99.7 m), lift span towers raised 1925, span motorised 1997, bridge upgraded 2012–14, over Murray R.; cemetery 1901, incl. lawn cemetery; CH 1902, new one 1958; clock tower (Noel W. Tyers memorial) fabricated 2001 by Hume Colville, d. by Caroline Totterman; diphtheria 1934; electricity 1928; engineering works (Hume Colville); FB (station b. 1960, new one 2013); hospital (Barham-Koondrook Soldiers' Memorial) 1955; Jehovah's Witnesses C.; PO 1895; powerhouse b. 1928 by A.J. Bakker; PS 1901, new ones 1958 and 1983; punt 1884, sunk 1898, across Murray R.; railway bridge 1904, over Murray R.; reservoir; Rom. Cath. C. (Sacred Heart); sale-yards; sandfly infestation 1926; sawmills: Bonum (bought 1975 by Gavin and Annette Rowe, closed 2010, plant and machinery sold 2014) and J.C. Chanter (burnt down 1907); schools: primary 1901, new building b. 1908 by G.W. Casburn, additions 1956, 1962, 1967, 1969, 1971, and HS 1969, additions 1975; sewerage 1967, augmentation 1989; storm 2000; telephone 1900; TX 1909; Unit. C.; water supply augmentation 1994; pop. 140 (1901), 618 (1911), 818 (1933), 718 (1947), 855 (1954), 969 (1961), 1,139 (1966), 1,131 (1971), 1,108 (1976), 1,039 (1981), 1,041 (1986), 1,217 (1991), 1,167 (1996), 1,186 (2001), 1,132 (2006), 1,567 (2011).

Barham Sawmills (*Co. Wakool*) 35°43'S. 144°15'E., 17 km SE of Barham, on Murray R.; sawmill; school 1926–33.

Barigan (*Co. Phillip*) 32°27'S. 149°59'E., 40 km NE of Mudgee, on Barigan Ck; formerly mining (oil-shale disc. 1887 by G. Smith); mine estab. 1898 by W. Thompson et al.

Barigan Hole (*Co. Phillip*) 32°34'S. 149°58'E., 36 km E. of Mudgee, on Deruen Ck.

Barkers Lodge (*Co. Camden*) 34°09'S. 150°33'E., 6 km W. of Picton.

Barkers Vale (*Co. Rous*) 28°32'S. 153°07'E., 12 km NW of Nimbin, on Leycester Ck; 3 bridges (incl. Gradwell Bridge and Jacksons Bridge) over Jerrys Ck; sawmill (Banana Growers' Federation Co-op. Ltd); school 1937; telephone 1925; TX 1925–60; pop. 120 (1933), 60 (1947), 108 (1954), 74 (1961), 356 (2011).

Bark Hut (*Co. Fitzroy*) 30°06'S. 153°08'E., 7 km W. of Woolgoolga, on Corindi Ck; bananas; PO 1927, burnt down 1933; sawmill; telephone 1924.

Barlings Beach (*Co. St Vincent*) see Tomakin.

Barmedman (*Co. Bland*) 34°09'S. 147°23'E., 30 km SE of West Wyalong; Wyalong till 1882; surveyed and town gaz. 1882; formerly gold (disc. 1872 by Treasure), wheat 1897+, wool, agric.; Angl. C. 1889, removed and reused, (second) 1906, moved 1938 to Bellarwi by A.G. Haddrill, new one (St John's) b. 1938 by R.T. Gillies, d. by Louis Reginald Williams, and graveyard 1889; Bapt. C. 1908, burnt down 1942; brick-kilns (Taylor and Cronin); bushfire 1926; cemetery (graves 1884+) 1886; CH 1883, closed, reopened 1950; cordial factory (M. Lazarus) 1893; FB; fires 1912 and 1937; grasshopper infestation 1928; heatwave 1904; hospital 1938; Lutheran C. (Holy Cross) 1933; mines: Ada (estab. by Treasure and Quail Bros, acquired by Barmedman United Gold Mining Co.), Black Angel, Fanny Park (acquired by Barmedman United Gold Mining Co.), Fiery Cross, Hard to Find, Hunted to Death, Italians, Jackson's, Moonlight, Neversweat, Phoenix, Prospecting Claim (Barmedman United Gold Mining Co.), White Cross, Wright's; PO 1876, new one b. 1904 by A.E. Beaumont; pound (stock) 1889; Presb. C. 1890, moved and reused, new one (St Paul's) b. 1926 by C.E. Williams, d. by Allan McDonald; PS 1882, new one (incl. lock-up) 1934; quarry; reservoir; Rom. Cath. C. b. 1891 by W. Hickey, closed, altered, renovated and reused, new one (St Joseph's) 1916; RS 1903, station removed 1985, services ceased 1988; sawmills: J. Jessup and John Rutherford; school 1883, additions 1899 by Falconer Bros, additions 1935 by F. Mitchell; sewage works; silo 1922; stamper battery; storm 1923; telegraph 1883; TX 1910; typhoid 1953; water supply 1929; pop. 365 (1883), 176 (1891), 293 (1901), 884 (1911), 565 (1933), 535 (1947), 541 (1954), 382 (1961), 270 (1971), 247 (1976), 223 (1981), 237 (1986), 248 (1991), 214 (1996), 230 (2001), 227 (2006), 213 (2011).

Barmedman (*Co. Bland*) see also Wyalong West (*Co. Gipps*).

Barnato (*Co. Booroondarra*) 31°35'S. 145°00'E., 81 km W. of Cobar; telephone 1927; TX 1933.

Barnes (*Co. Cadell*) 36°02'S. 144°47'E., 10 km N. of Moama; PO 1928–42; RS (Victorian railway, Balranald Junction till 1925) 1924, defunct; telephone 1929.

Barnes's Crossing Place (*Co. Wallace*) see Dalgety.

Barnetts Lagoon (*Co. Macquarie*) 31°02'S. 152°54'E., 9 km NE of Kempsey.

Barney Downs (*Co. Clive*) 29°04'S. 152°06'E., 7 km E. of Tenterfield; Angl. C. (St Matthew's) 1893; pop. 70 (1911).

Barney's Hill (*Co. Gresham*) see Newton Boyd.

Barneys Point (*Co. Rous*) see Banora Point.

Barnsley (*Co. Northumberland*) 32°56'S. 151°35'E., 3 km S. of West Wallsend, on Slatey Ck; (incl. Caledonian and Northville); subdivisions 1880 and 1882; orig. fruit, vegetables, dairying; bridge (Cherrys Bridge) 1938, over Slatey Ck; bushfires 1940, 1951, 1991; causeway across Cockle Ck; PO 1907; school (Teralba till 1891) 1865, new school b. 1866, new school b. 1872, a building removed from Fassifern and re-erected 1892 by John Reid, new one b. 1911 on new site by J. Johnston, closed and replaced, additions 1971, new one 1995, additions 2010 by RTC Group; sewage works; tank factory (Out of Town 4WD Pty Ltd) 1986; telephone 1913; water supply 1949; pop. 216 (1911), 274 (1933), 234 (1947), 236 (1954), 444 (1961), 1,799 (2006), 1,813 (2011).

Barokee (*Co. Durham*) 32°33'S. 151°37'E., 17 km N. of Bolwarra; RS (Martin's Creek Metal Quarry till 1927) 1924–39.

Barooga (*Co. Denison*) 35°55'S. 145°41'E., 16 km SE of Tocumwal, on Bullanginya Lagoon; village gaz. 1890; orig. wool and wheat, later lucerne, rice, dairying, tomatoes, orchards, grapes; boomerang factory (Binghi Boomerangs Pty Ltd) estab. by Jack Byham; cemetery (261 graves 1901+) 1892; FB; flood 1917; fruit juice factory (Brentwood); Jehovah's Witnesses C.; PO 1899; punt (Cobram Punt Co. Ltd) 1889–1902; PS 1990; Rom. Cath. C. (St Joseph's) 1905, sold and destroyed, new one 2007; sawmills: F. and Sid Russell, and H. Stillard; school 1898, additions 1970; sewerage augmentation 1992; telephone 1905; tornado 2013; TX 1953, automatic 1957; water reticulation 1966; pop. 92 (1901), 216 (1911), 481 (1933), 240 (1947), 231 (1954), 234 (1961), 235 (1971), 441 (1976), 556 (1981), 710 (1986), 843 (1991), 999 (1996), 1,033 (2001), 1,455 (2006), 1,497 (2011).

Baroona (*Co. Auckland*) 36°45'S. 149°43'E., 14 km SW of Bega; butter canning factory (A.J. Cook & Co.); butter factory (Foley Bros.), bacon factory added 1902, closed and sold 1907 to Coman; cheese factory.

Bar Point (*Co. Northumberland*) 33°31'S. 151°10'E., 4 km W. of Mooney Mooney, on Hawkesbury R.; subdivided 1922; FB; floods 1933, 1934, 1938, 1942, 1947, 1949; pop. 22 (1961), 135 (2006), 361 (2011).

Barraba (*Co. Darling*) 30°23'S. 150°37'E., 41 km N. of Manilla, on Manilla R.; settled 1837, estab. *c.*1845 by John McKid, surveyed by John Valentine Gorman and plan approved 1852, town gaz. 1852, munic. proc. 1906, town thrived 1908, munic. abolished 1953; gold, infusorial earth, wheat, lucerne, cattle, goats, horses, sheep; airfield; ambulance station; Angl. C. (St Laurence's) b. 1875 by Joseph Ross, d. by John Horbury Hunt, dismantled 1906, rebuilt and reused, new one b. 1909 by McKechnie, d. by Charles Rosenthal, vestry added 1950–55; brickworks (S. Newton); bridge b. 1892 by Matthew Murphy, new one (welded steel truss span) b. 1935 by A. Goninan & Co. and State Monier Pipe & Reinforced Concrete Works, 180 ft (54.9 m), over Manilla R.; carriage-works (W. Chad); cemetery (2,165 graves *c.*1850+) 1870, incl. columbarium; CH (incl. lock-up) b. 1881 by William Lee, additions 1887, additions 1908 by E.P. Frost & Co., extensions and renovations 1936, closed; clock tower (war memorial) b. 1924 by J. Myers and A. York; cordial factories: James F. Dowse and William Henry Odell 1891; dengue fever 1927; diphtheria (2 died) 1910; drought 1965; electricity 1914; FB 1935 (station b. 1956, closed, new one b. 2013); fires 1898 and 1935; floods 1955 and 1964; foot-bridge 1923, over Manilla R.; hailstorm 1924; hospital b. 1892 by Lachlan and Jack McKechnie, additions and alterations 1912 by Thorsbys Ltd, d. by Bertram Willoughby Ford, additions 1936 by W.W. Campbell, renovated and upgraded 2004; Meth. C. d. by Alfred Gambier Newman; PO 1851, new one b. 1882 by W. Lee, d. by James Johnstone Barnet, additions 1890 by J.F. Myers & Co., additions 1926, demolished 1972, replacement b. 1972 by Thorby Bros; police barracks b. 1895 by Robert Gillies and John Fraser; pound (stock) 1851; powerhouse; Presb. C.; PS b. 1895 by Sidney J. Pyne, second one 1904, new one 1979 on new site; rabbit freezing works (Barraba Freezing Co.) 1916; railway coal stage 1907; railway turntable, 50 ft (15.2 m), defunct; reservoir (concrete), 300,000 gal. (1,363.8 kl), 1956; Rom. Cath. C. 1884, new one (St John the Evangelist) b. 1905–7 by J.J. Myers, d. by Philip Ernest Ranclaud, rebuilt 1950 by Walter A. York, d. by J.P. Gannon; RS 1908, station b. by W. Gawne & Sons, closed 1987, demolished; sale-yards; Salv. Army C. 1922; school 1861–63, reopened 1874 in new building, new buildings b. 1882 by W. Lee, replacement b. 1890 on new site by F.J. Myers & Co., additions 1895 by D.A.

Beynon, extended 1899 by J. McKechnie, additions and alterations 1907 by A.A. Brown, additions and alterations 1909 by William Robert Ibbotson, extended 1925, additions 1964 and 1967, new one 1974; sewerage 1955; silo; snowstorm 1984; streets kerosene lit, then electric lit 1915; telegraph 1878, new office b. 1882 by W. Lee, d. by James Johnstone Barnet, additions 1890 by J.F. Myers & Co.; TX 1908, automatic 1973; Unit. C. (orig. Wes. Meth., Chad's) 1899 d. by E.S. Henderson; water reticulation 1934, augmentation 1995; pop. *c.*80 (1866), 77 (1871), 229 (1881), 413 (1891), 747 (1901), 1,959 (1911), 1,428 (1933), *c.*1,450 (1941), 1,591 (1947), 1,521 (1954), 1,469 (1961), 1,425 (1966), 1,579 (1971), 1,947 (1976), 1,679 (1981), 1,498 (1986), 1,427 (1991), 1,267 (1996), 1,203 (2001), 1,161 (2006), 1,152 (2011).

Barrack Flat (*Co. Murray*) 35°22'S. 149°15'E., 3 km SE of Queanbeyan, on Queanbeyan R.

Barrack Heights (*Co. Camden*) 34°34'S. 150°51'E., 10 km SE of Dapto, on Tasman Sea; (incl. Barrack Point, disc. 1812 by George William Evans, subdivided 1951 and 1967); subdivisions 1965, 1969, 1970, 1971, 1972, 1973; ambulance station; flood 2011; foot-bridge to Warilla, over Little Lake; PO: Barrack Heights 1969 and Barrack Point 1950; Salv. Army C. (Shellharbour) 1988; schools: Barrack Heights 1976 and Warilla HS 1966, additions 1976 and 1985; telephone (Barrack Point) 1951; Unit. C. (orig. Cong.); pop. 6,016 (2011).

Barrack Point (*Co. Camden*) see Barrack Heights.

Barragan (*Co. Ashburnham*) 33°24'S. 148°42'E., 18 km N. of Canowindra; airfield; Angl. C. (All Saints') 1908–63, ruined; Meth. C. 1902; quarry.

Barraganyatti (*Co. Dudley*) 30°51'S. 152°56'E., 12 km W. of South West Rocks; PO 1908–19 (moved to Eungai Rail); telephone 1907; pop. 57 (1911), 75 (1933).

Barrallier (*Co. Westmoreland*) 34°16'S. 150°03'E., 35 km NW of Berrima, on Wollondilly R.; Talloweena till 1915; grazing; bushfire 1929; PO 1927; telephone 1925; TX 1930; pop. 20 (1933).

Barratta (*Co. Townsend*) 35°17'S. 144°32'E., 48 km NW of Deniliquin; also known as Ten Mile Waterholes; laid out *c.*1857, town gaz. 1861; grazing; pop. 44 (1933).

Barrengarry (*Co. Camden*) 34°43'S. 150°32'E., 17 km W. of Berry, on Millers Ck; farming and dairying; Angl. C. (Good Shepherd) b. 1870–72; bushfire 1905; butter factory (Barrengarry Dairy Co.) b. 1889 by A. Wolf and Peter Ettingshausen, closed 1924; FB; PO 1875–2013; pound (stock) 1879; quarry; rifle range; sawmill (Barrengarry Sawmilling Co.); school 1877, new one b. 1881 by John Tanner, d. by John Horbury Hunt, additions and alterations 1907 by E. Kennedy, closed 1935, reused; telephone 1899; TX 1919–26; Union C. b. 1886 by John Chittick and Sweeney; Wes. Meth. C. 1873, new one b. 1884–87 by West and Uphill; pop. 328 (1901), 244 (1911), 231 (1921), 222 (1933), 211 (1947), 156 (1954), 171 (1961), 252 (2011).

Barren Grounds (*Co. Camden*) 34°40'S. 150°42'E., 13 km W. of Kiama.

Barren Jack (*Co. Harden*) see Burrinjuck.

Barretts Creek (*Co. Clarence*) 29°21'S. 152°45'E., 41 km NW of Grafton, on Barretts Ck; sawmill; telephone 1925; TX.

Barringella (*Co. St Vincent*) 34°54'S. 150°28'E., 10 km SW of Nowra, on Shoalhaven R.; reservoir.

Barrington (*Co. Gloucester*) 31°58'S. 151°55'E., 6 km NW of Gloucester, on Barrington R.; surveyed 1895, founded 1897; wheat 1857+, maize, pigs, dairying, grazing, goldmining; Aboriginal mission; bridge (Allan timber truss) b. 1920 by Munro and Young, 273 ft (83.2 m); cemetery (pioneer, 66 graves 1874–1970); CH 1879; FB; Free Presb. C. 1889, new one b. 1935 on new site by Pickles and McIlroy, d. by Arthur William Mackenzie Mowle, closed, sold and reused; PO 1874; PS; reservoir; rifle range; school 1864, repairs 1891 by James Shelton, additions 1914 by L. Mitchell; telephone 1896; TX 1918, automatic 1949; water supply augmentation 1970; pop.

*c.*180 (1894), 99 (1901), 346 (1911), 277 (1933), 266 (1947), 251 (1954), 156 (1961), 177 (2006), 517 (2011).

Barringun (*Co. Culgoa*) 29°01'S. 145°43'E., 119 km N. of Bourke; former customs post on Queensland border, almost defunct; grazing; bond store (H. and P. Green); brewery (estab. by Lee and Hine and later operated by Gustavus Klaeby and Henry T. Hine) 1883–94; cemetery 1886; CH 1884; cordial factory (Jimmy Watkins, then Felix McKeown); fire 1895; lock-up; PO 1875; PS 1883; pound (stock) 1884; school 1884–1918; telegraph 1878; telephone 1908; TX 1911; pop. 113 (1882), 179 (1891), 95 (1901), 87 (1911), *c.*10 (1999).

Barron Flat (*Co. St Vincent*) 34°47'S. 150°19'E., 13 km S. of Bundanoon.

Barry (*Co. Bathurst*) 33°39'S. 149°16'E., 12 km S. of Blayney, on Coombing Ck; orig. Five Islands; town gaz. 1886; farming and grazing; Angl. C. (Trinity), new one (St James's) 1884; cemetery 1886; FB; PO 1891, closed, sold and reused; Rom. Cath. C. (St Therese of the Child Jesus) b. 1934 by Bulloch and Hardiman, d. by B. Millane, closed, sold 2004 and 2016, reused; school (Five Islands till 1895) 1862–66 and 1873–76, reopened 1884, new one b. 1911 by John Baker, closed 1986; telephone 1914; TX 1916, automatic 1949; pop. 301 (1901), 295 (1911), 186 (1921), 174 (1933), 157 (1947), 158 (1954), 153 (1961), 234 (2006), 266 (2011).

Barry (*Co. Hawes*) 31°35'S. 151°19'E., 50 km NE of Murrurundi, on Barnard R.

Barryrenie (*Co. Forbes*) 33°48'S. 148°28'E., 20 km W. of Cowra, on Cherry Ck; farming; PO 1927–31; sawmill (A.C. Mousley); telephone 1926; TX 1929; pop. 71 (1933), 51 (1947).

Bar Swamp (*Co. Northumberland*) see Ettalong Beach.

Bartley's Creek (*Co. Ashburnham*) see Mugincoble.

Barwang (*Co. Harden*) 34°26'S. 148°29'E., 22 km SE of Young; bushfire 1905; FB; heatwave 1905; PO 1877–1912; school 1907–16; pop. 63 (1911).

Barwang (*Co. Harden*) see also Collingrove.

Baryulgil (*Co. Drake*) 29°13'S. 152°36'E., 59 km SW of Casino, on Josephs Ck; Aboriginal settlement, thrived 1940–79; dairying, farming, grazing, mining; airfield; cemetery; dam (mine), 26 ft (8 m) high, 1996; floods 1925, 1928, 1933; PO 1912; quarry (chrysotile asbestos) and mill, developed by Asbestos Mining Co. of Aust. Ltd, closed 1924, redeveloped 1940 by Wunderlich Ltd, operated from 1944 by Asbestos Mines Pty Ltd, taken over 1953 by James Hardie Asbestos Pty Ltd, sold 1975 to Woodsreef Mines Ltd, closed 1979; school 1950, additions 1978 and 2010; telephone 1917; TX 1924; pop. 178 (1933), 115 (1947), 167 (1954), 121 (1961).

Basin Creek (*Co. Buckland*) 31°33'S. 150°56'E., 24 km E. of Quirindi.

Basin Plain (*Co. Pottinger*) 31°07'S. 150°01'E., 27 km SW of Gunnedah; pop. 81 (1947), 57 (1954).

Basin View (*Co. St Vincent*) 35°06'S. 150°34'E., 6 km W. of Sanctuary Point, on St Georges Basin; FB; PO 1950; quarry; sawmill (Watt and Mathie) 1890, burnt down 1908; school (St Georges Basin) 1956; sewerage augmentation 1994; telephone 1950; water supply augmentation 1983; pop. 82 (1961), 147 (1971), 223 (1976), 334 (1981), 458 (1986), 659 (1991), 1,008 (1996), 1,206 (2001), 1,293 (2006), 1,401 (2011).

Bassendean (*Co. Hardinge*) 30°04'S. 151°11'E., 12 km S. of Tingha, on Moredun Ck.

Bass Point (*Co. Camden*) see Shellharbour.

Batar (*Co. Macquarie*) 31°40'S. 152°40'E., 4 km SW of Kendall, on Batar Ck; RS 1941–71; school 1957–65; pop. 62 (1947).

Bateau Bay (*Co. Northumberland*) 33°23'S. 151°28'E., 5 km S. of The Entrance, on Tasman Sea; village gaz. 1937; retirement centre; ambulance station; Bapt. C. (The Entrance Dist.); FB; hailstorm 2015; Jehovah's Witnesses C.; PO 1954; reservoir, 2,000,000 gal. (9,092 kl), 1966; school 1980, additions 1985; sewerage augmentation 1974; telephone 1952; Unit. C. (Nareen Gardens);

water reticulation 1967; pop. 276 (1961), 11,759 (2011).

Bateau Bay (*Co. Northumberland*) see also Terrigal.

Batehaven (*Co. St Vincent*) 35°44'S. 150°12'E., 4 km SE of Batemans Bay, on Batemans Bay; (incl. Catalina); marina (Catalina); PO 1950; Presb. C. (Catalina); 2 reservoirs; Rom. Cath. C. (St Bernard of Clairvaux) 1987, and graveyard (burials 1874+); school (Batemans Bay HS) 1988; telephone 1946; TX (automatic) 1953; Unit. C.; water supply 1955; pop. 95 (1947), 203 (1954), 1,750 (2011).

Bateman (*Co. St Vincent*) see Batemans Bay.

Batemans Bay (*Co. St Vincent*) 35°43'S. 150°11'E., 47 km SW of Ulladulla, on Batemans Bay; settled 1850 by Edward Corrigan, surveyed 1859 by Rowlands, lots sold 1859, village gaz. 1884 as Bateman; seaport, shipbuilding 1847+, oysters 1860+, sawmilling 1869+, wattle-bark, gold, later timber, dairying, fishing, vegetables, tourism; ambulance station 1968; Angl. C. (St Paul's) 1878, demolished 1914, replaced (Ascension of Our Lord) 1915–86, new one 1987 on new site, and graveyard; boat harbour, extended 1980; breakwater b. 1898–1905; bridge (steel truss spans and steel plate girder spans, incl. lift span) fabricated by Clyde Engineering Co. Ltd and State Dockyard (Carrington), 1,008 ft (307.2 m), erected 1947–56 by Balgue Constructions Pty Ltd, over Clyde R.; bushfires 1895, 1903, 1952, 1965, 1994; cemetery; CH 1885, burnt down 1903, replacement (incl. lock-up) b. 1905 by Nicholas Mudge, jun., d. by Walter Liberty Vernon, closed, moved and reused, new one 1985; cheese factory (J.E. Larvis); Christ. Outreach C. (Bay Life) 1987; electricity 1950; FB 1954 (new station b. 1977); flood 1974–75; gale 1948; hospital 1934, new one 1970 on new site; jetty 1994; Meth. C. 1915; PO 1859, new one b. 1895 by W. Kerr, alterations 1935, replaced 1965, new one 1976, renovations 1988; Presb. C. 1889, and graveyard (burials 1889+), new one on new site; PS 1876, new one b. 1885, burnt down 1903, replaced 1905, new one b. 1921 by Rolfe, reused 1986, relocated 1993, new one 1995; punt (manual) 1871, new one (petrol) 1927, replaced (steam) 1929, damaged 1948, ceased 1956, across Clyde R.; reservoir; Rom. Cath. C. 1882, dismantled and relocated 1910, reopened (St Bernard's) 1911, relocated 1968; sale-yards 1917; Salv. Army C. 1986; sawmills: A.J. Fenning & Sons (burnt down 1952), Francis Guy 1876 (burnt down 1931), Johnson's, Mitchell Bros (burnt down 1939, rebuilt, fire 1963, sold 1967 to Davis & Herbert Pty Ltd, fire 1989, rebuilt), George Sydney Rayner, Sebbens's, August Thompson; shipyard estab. by Francis Guy, sold 1901 to John Perry; TC; telegraph 1876; TX 1915; 2 Unit. C.; water apparel factory (Hot 'n' Dry); water reticulation 1955; wattle-bark mill (H.E. Greatrix); wharves 1891 and 1980; wooden handle and spoke factory (J. Perry Pty Ltd) estab. 1902 by John Perry in old sawmill, burnt down 1910, rebuilt, burnt down 1920, rebuilt, sold 1974 to A.H. Jones & Sons, sold 1975 to Allen Taylor & Co. Ltd, closed 1982, reused 1983, sold 1985, demolished 1986; pop. 2 (1828), 70 (1867), 266 (1881), 253 (1891), 281 (1901), 257 (1911), 593 (1933), 875 (1947), 856 (1954), 1,458 (1966), 2,776 (1973), 3,463 (1976), 4,924 (1981), 6,492 (1986), 8,320 (1991), 9,568 (1996), 10,219 (2001), 10,845 (2006), 11,332 (2011).

Batemans Bay (*Co. St Vincent*) see also Batehaven and Batemans Bay North.

Batemans Bay North (*Co. St Vincent*) 35°42'S. 150°11'E., 1 km NE of Batemans Bay, on Batemans Bay; (incl. Surfside); Assemblies of God (Church on the Bay); Greek Orthodox C. (St John the Forerunner and Baptist); punt (manual) 1871, new one (petrol) 1927, replaced (steam) 1929, damaged 1948, ceased 1956, across Clyde R.; school (Batemans Bay) 1872, new one b. 1874 by George Alexander Wright, demolished 1895, replacement b. 1894 by Edwin T. Isley, closed, sold 1960, new one 1954 on new site, additions 1966, 1969, 1979; sewerage augmentation 1991; pop. 1,711 (2006), 1,948 (2011).

Bathgate (*Co. Cook*) see Kerosene Vale.

Bathurst (*Co. Bathurst*) 33°25'S. 149°35'E., 47 km E. of Orange, on Macquarie R.; (incl. Abercrombie, Edgell Heights, Esrom, Gormans Hill, Llanarth, Mitchell, Mount Panorama, Robin Hill, South Bathurst orig. Milltown, Stewarts Mount, West Bathurst, Windradyne); disc. 1813 by George William Evans, founded 1815 by Gov. Lachlan Macquarie, laid out 1815 by James Meehan, martial law 1824, laid out 1833 on new site by James Byrn Richards, first lots sold 1834, thrived in 1850s, munic. proc. 1862, designated as chief town of the county, designated part of growth region 1972 but short-lived; grazing till 1851, then goldmining centre till 1876, then wheat, maize, barley, oats, lucerne, rye, potatoes, hort., honey, tobacco, wine, soap, candles, furniture, glue, milling, tanning, shoes and boots, then educational centre 1951+, cartographic centre 1976+, now also sheep, cattle, poultry, apples, vegetables, clothing, food processing, light engineering, manufacturing; agric. implement and engineering works (George Fish Pty Ltd); agric. research station estab. 1895, b. 1902, additions 1903 by James Inseal, major building work 1906+, used as an ordnance depot 1941–45, reused 1951 as teachers' college; ambulance station (in converted shop) 1925, new one b. 1929 by McNaughton & Son, d. by Norman D. Weekes; Angl. C.: All Saints' (b. 1845–49 by Thomas Mockett, d. by Edmund Thomas Blacket, tower 1849, tower raised 1852, vestry added 1855 by William Kerr and Andrew Rae, church additions 1860, 1866, 1869 also d. by Blacket, became cathedral in 1870, further additions 1872–74 d. by Benjamin Backhouse, major repairs 1914 by Elisha William Gale, d. by John Holderness Bates, rebuilt 1925–27, demolished 1971, replacement b. 1965–71 by Kell & Rigby Pty Ltd, d. by McPherson, Harrison and Hassall, bell tower 2009), St Barnabas's (South Bathurst, b. 1875–81 by Livermore, d. by Joseph Backhouse, additions 1896 and 1901 by Albert Emanuel Ennis, d. by John Job Copeman, gutted 2014), St Paul's (West Bathurst), closed and sold; Assemblies of God C.; baking powder factory (L. and W. Peate); Bapt. C. 1863 d. by W.F. Curtis, new one 1870, re-roofed and renovated 1895, renovated 1926 by Edward Abraham Wright, renovated 1952; boot factories: W.J. Stevens and E. Webb & Co.; box factory (Joseph Smedley), burnt down 1921; breweries: Albion Brewery (John Neal), Crown Brewery (b. by James Stewart for Daniel James Fitzpatrick) 1883, bought by W.E. Strickland, bought 1919 by Co-op. Brewing Society, closed 1920, Federal Brewery (Patrick J. McGrath) o. 1899 in former flour mill, demolished 1907, Great Western Brewery (estab. 1852 by Henry Heathorn as Burton Brewery, acquired by Coyle, Holman & Co., renamed Defiance Brewery in 1875, closed, reopened 1895, closed 1927), Two Heads Brewery (o. 2016 by Campbell and Greg Hedley in former flour mill), Walker & Co. (b. 1908 by W. McLean, d. by John Job Copeman closed 1926, reused till 1949, sold 1950); brickworks: A.M.C., Bathurst Brick, Tile & Pottery Co. 1921, William Bliss, James Dewar (taken over by Tason, dismantled and sold 1922), M.E. Hector 1929, J. Robinson, Thomas Whatley; bridges: Denison Bridge, to Kelso, b. 1854–56 by William Henry Downey, d. by William Weaver, 256 ft (78 m), damaged and reinforced 1857, destroyed 1867, new one (iron Pratt truss spans), b. 1870–73 by P.N. Russell & Co., d. by Gustavus Alphonse Morell and William Christopher Bennett, 474 ft (144.5 m), concrete deck laid 1981, closed 1992 and reused, over Macquarie R., Evans Bridge 1991, to Kelso, over Macquarie R., Gordon Edgell Bridge (George Street Falls Bridge till 2006) 1995, to Kelso, over Macquarie R., Flanagan's Bridge b. 1868 by Joseph Hider Mills, Keppel Street Bridge b. 1850 by William Timothy Atkins, replacement 1896 d. by John Job Copeman, over Jordan Ck, Lloyds Bridge over Queen Charlottes Ck, McGuigan Bridge b. 1856 by William Henry Downey, over Jordan Ck, Palmer Bridge b. 1856 by William Henry Downey, over Jordan Ck, Ranken's Bridge, to Abercrombie, d. and b. 1856 by George

Ranken, 120 ft (36.6 m), destroyed 1867, rebuilt 1873, replaced (Allan timber truss) 1920, new one, over Macquarie R., Torys Bridge (Russell Street), b. 1860 by William Timothy Atkins, over Queen Charlottes Ck; broom factory (Peate & Co.) 1900, taken over 1920 by L.L. Gordon and C.H. Davis; butter factory (Bathurst Co-op. Dairying Co. Ltd, incl. ice works, which froze rabbit carcasses for export 1916–25) b. 1902 by Albert Emanuel Ennis, d. by John Job Copeman, extended 1947; CAE (Mitchell) 1970 d. by John McKinney, additions 1976 d. by R. Dinham, dissolved 1989, became univ. (Charles Sturt); can factories: Containers Ltd 1959 and Southern Can Co. b. 1953 by John Newton; cannery (Gordon Edgell & Sons Ltd) 1926, asparagus 1932, rabbits 1947, baby food 1959, merged with Peters; carillon (Soldiers' Memorial) b. 1928–33 by J. Sproule, d. by John Drummond Moore, 100 ft (30.5 m), 35 bells cast by John Taylor & Co., Loughborough, England; carriage-works: G.T. Bennett, C.V. Clifton, Cobb & Co. (relocated 1877 to another site) 1862–1893, Maddy, Fleming and Mollison, W. Pittendrigh (estab. 1871 by Pittendrigh and Hume), M. Treanor 1870; cemeteries: (first) 1830, (South Bathurst) 1839–1901, (third) 1868, incl. lawn cemetery (Maranatha) 1977, columbarium and crematorium (Norwood Park) 2013; CH 1815, (second) 1837, (third) b. 1847–49 by Paddy White, d. by Mortimer William Lewis, additions 1857 by W. Evans, demolished 1880, new one b. 1878–80 by David Jones, W. Jones & Son and Joseph Hider Mills, d. by James Johnstone Barnet, repairs 1890 by F.F. Archer, alterations 1913 by J. Bartlett; Church of Christ; commissariat store 1817, reused 1833; Cong. C. b. 1874 by Joseph Hider Mills, d. by James McDonald, re-roofed 1895 by Albert Emanuel Ennis, closed, reused 1941; cordial factories: Aust. Lemonade & Soda Water Factory (Rooney and White) 1861, Bathurst Soda-Water Factory (estab. 1856 by J.L. Alexander, bought 1882 by Arthur B. James, bought 1924 by A.J. Lunt, bought 1925 by N. and F. Ashelford), W.A. Gansberg, Great Western (F. and Peter Furness 1861–67, William Butler 1865–81, Butler & Sons 1881–1909, demolished 1911), Daniel Mayne and Henry Windred (sold 1861 to J.L. Alexander), C.T. Mullens & Co. 1885–87, R.S. Reily, Sharpe Bros (estab. by John and Ewart Sharpe) 1920–39, Joseph H. Sharman; distillery (Stone Pine) estab. 2008 by Ian and Bev Glen; droughts 1837–39 and 1919; dust storms 1882, 1928, 1938; earth tremors 1842, 1872, 1930, 1932, 1934, 1947; electricity 1934; FB (station b. 1887 by John Dunkley and Richard Clifford Bartlett, d. by James Hine, alterations 1917 by Arnold Rigby, renovations 1937, demolished, new station b. 1963, replaced 2008 on new site by David Payne Constructions); female factory 1833 (former commissariat store), new wing added 1835, closed 1843, demolished; fibrous plaster works (William Henry Hopper); floods 1857, 1867, 1872, 1916, 1928, 1950, 1986, 1998; flour mills: Britannia (estab. 1867 by James Cock, bought 1877 by Redgate & Son, acquired by W. Kite, later acquired by Tremain Bros, rebuilt and alterations 1899 by Albert Emanuel Ennis, demolished 1912), J. Ford, Hibernian (estab. 1862 by Alexander Crilly, acquired 1863 by Bonnear and Tremain, acquired 1872 by David Gordon, acquired 1881 by Francis Crago, renamed National Mill in 1882, demolished 1908, new one b. 1906 on new site by Simmons and John Dunkley for Francis Crago & Son Pty Ltd, named Dominion Mills, closed 1954, sold and reused), Mockett's (also variously known as Bathurst Steam Mills, Western City Mills and Acme Roller Mills, estab. 1846 by Thomas Mockett, acquired by W.C. Mockett, bought 1882 by George Matthews & Son, acquired by H.C. Matthews, bought 1899 by P.J. McGrath, closed, refurbished and converted to brewery), Union (b. 1847 by Thomas Mockett for Thomas and John Syer, sold 1870 to Boylson & Sons, burnt down 1884), Victoria Roller Flour Mills (b. 1857–59 by Chapman Bros, operated 1862–75 by J.S. Brown, taken over 1875 by Tremain Bros Pty Ltd, burnt down and rebuilt 1901, first silo b. 1932, converted to electricity 1953, chimney demolished 1972, mill sold to George Fielder & Co. and closed 1980, reused, bought 2015 by Stephen and Glenda Birrell), Wallace's; foot-bridges: one over Macquarie R. (formerly Denison Bridge), one over Queen Charlottes Ck, one over Vale Ck b. 1890 by John Wadsworth Ashworth; foundries (Denison) estab. 1867 by Thomas Denny, bought 1893 by Robert Russell Blair, closed, bought 1915 by H. Flanagan and demolished; furniture factory (Smith Bros); gales 1878 and 1924; gaol 1825, (second) b. 1838–40 by Paddy White, d. by Mortimer William Lewis, alterations 1862 by William Hopkins, repairs 1867 by John Kerr, demolished 1889, (third) b. 1884–88 by William Smith and J.T. Low, d. by William Coles, additions 1898 by Rigby Bros, new cell block b. 1957–62, riot and fire 1974, rebuilt 1979–82, additions 1985 and 1989; gasworks: John Newlands Wark 1872 (bought 1914 by local council) and munic. 1888 (office b. 1888 by John Dunkley and Richard Clifford Bartlett, gasholder b. 1893 by Elisha William Gale, retort house b. 1906 by Andrew McIntyre, d. by John Job Copeman, gasworks inundated 1916, gasholder repairs 1938 by James Hurll & Co. Ltd, retort house 1946, new retort house b. 1953 by Woodall, Duckham (A'sia) Pty Ltd, gasworks leased 1979 to AGL, closed 1987, site derelict); glue factory (Pat Parker); govt house 1817, demolished 1878; hailstorms 1848, 1893, 1919, 1921, 1934; heatwaves 1833 and 1939; hospital (convict) 1824, renamed Bathurst Dist. Hospital in 1842, burnt down 1878, second one b. 1880 by John Willett, d. by William Boles, children's ward b. 1930 by L.H. Ralph, additions 1944, additions 1950 d. by Cobden Parkes, additions and alterations 1967, restoration 1981 and 2008, new building b. 2008 by John Holland (Constructions) Pty Ltd; hurricane 1874; ice works (Hudson's); joineries: John Newton 1947, Rice's (fire 1946), E.A. Wright & Son; knitting mills: Cecile Knitting Works and H.R. Murden; LDS (Mormon) C.; lock-up (South Bathurst) b. 1885 by John Henry Hansen, closed, sold 2001 and 2013, restored and reused; Lutheran C. (Redeemer) 1959, closed; military barracks 1825; milk factory (Aust. Co-op. Foods Ltd); monumental stone works: J. Burns, A.M. Greenhill & Son, J. MacDonald; motor racing circuit (Mount Panorama) 1938, facilities upgraded 2003; ordnance depots; paper bag factory (Paper Bag Supply Pty Ltd), taken over 1949 by J. Mason; PO: Bathurst 1828 (new one b. 1848 by William Thompson, new one b. 1875–77 by Joseph Hider Mills, d. by James Johnstone Barnet, repairs 1895 by Rigby Bros, additions and alterations 1900 by John Dunkley, d. by Walter Liberty Vernon, closed 1976, reused, new one 1976), Esrom 1875–1932, South Bathurst 1909, West Bathurst 1942; police barracks, demolished, new barracks b. 1890–92 on new site by A. Rigby, d. by James Johnstone Barnet, reused 1938; pound (stock) 1845; powerhouse b. 1924 by Albert Emanuel Ennis; Presb. C.: St Stephen's (b. 1835 by Peter and Patrick White, d. by Samuel Atchison, tower added 1847, church additions and repairs 1862 d. by Henry Sadlier, closed, sold 1872 to John Newel Gilmour, demolished 1873, new one b. 1872 on new site by James Stuart Douglas, d. by Thomas Rowe, alterations 1902 by Albert Emanuel Ennis, alterations 1923, re-roofed 1940, and graveyard) and St Mark's 1952 (additions 1954, burnt down 1966); PS 1829, demolished 1851, new one (incl. lock-up) b. 1878 by John Willett, d. by James Johnstone Barnet, additions and alterations to lock-up 1909 by A. Stephens, station rebuilt and renovated 1940, additions and alterations 1979, new one 1991 on new site; 6 quarries; railway accident (4 killed) 1890; railway barracks (boy killed 1944); railway bridge to Kelso (lattice girder) fabricated by Andrew Handyside & Co., Derby, England, erected 1876 by J.S. Cummings, William Mason, Ellsington and Thomas Smithyman, d. by Sir John Fowler and John Whitton, over Macquarie R.; railway coal stage 1877, extended 1878, new ones 1891 and 1916; railway gasworks b. 1881 by John Louis Castner, expanded 1885–86; railway turntable 1878, 50 ft (15.2 m), replaced 1897, 60 ft (18.3 m), removed 1979; railway workshops 1880, additions 1891 by W. Wilson; reservoirs (concrete): 50,000 gal. (227.3 kl), 218,000 gal. (991 kl), 250,000 gal. (1,136.5 kl), 500,000 gal. (2,273 kl), 2,000,000 gal. (9,092 kl) b. 1931 by State Monier Pipe Works; rifle range 1868, man killed 1898, new ones 1910 and 1915; Rom. Cath. C.: Assumption (West Bathurst) 1955, burnt down 1964, replaced 1966, St Michael's (b. 1839–46 by Henry Simmons, closed 1861, reused, demolished 1964), St Michael and St John's (b. 1857–61 by William Kerr and Andrew Rae, taken over by Simmons and Nixon, d. by Charles Francis Hansom, architectural detailing d. by Edward Gell, dedicated 1865 as cathedral, re-roofed 1893, new sanctuary b. 1894 by William Jones & Sons, d. by John Job Copeland, chancel and trancept 1897, sacristy b. 1922 by Albert Emanuel Ennis, d. by William James Gilroy, major additions 1956–62 by F.G. Woodgate, d. by E.R. Green & Sons, re-roofed again 1963, restored 2012), St Philomena's (b. 1901, chancel added 1912, closed and reused 1960, new one 1960–88, sold and demolished 1989); RS 1876, station b. by William and Charles Cains, additions 1881, station renovations 1993; rubber works (W.J. O'Shea, bought 1918 by Havenhand, Best and O'Dea); sale-yards b. 1889 by Mugridge Bros; Salv. Army C. b. 1887 by G. Smith, d. by Edwin Griffiths Hodges, repairs 1897 by Frederick Archer, additions and alterations 1934 by John Bartlett; sauce and pickle factory (Lackersteen & Co. Pty Ltd), additions 1933 to treat apples and cauliflowers; sawmill and joinery (Mugridge Bros), damaged 1874, bought 1890 by Alexander Kethel & Co.; scarlet fever 1950; schools: Bathurst 1853 (new building b. 1876–78 by James Stuart Douglas, d. by George Allen Mansfield, repairs 1883 by F.T. Archer, additions and repairs 1892 by W. Boyd, repairs 1894 by H.S. Clifton, additions 1907 by Frederick R. Jones, closed and reused 1940, new building b. 1935 on new site by Wallace and McGee, new school 1940, additions 1963 and 1975), Boys HS 1883–87, Girls HS 1883–98, HS 1913 (additions 1927 by Welch Bros, additions 1959, 1966, 1981), Denison College 2007 (additions 2014 by Hines Constructions Pty Ltd), South Bathurst 1879, additions 1883 by Mugridge Bros, additions 1960, West Bathurst 1954, additions 1958 and 1980; SD Adventist C. 1904, second one 1930; sewerage 1916, system completed 1930, augmentation 1990; shoe factory (J. Robins & Son Pty Ltd) 1952 d. by Fitzgerald; silo; small arms factory (with air raid shelter) 1941–46, taken over 1946 by California Productions Ltd and reused to produce shoes and clothing; snowstorms 1872, 1900, 1909, 1929; soap-works: William Irwin 1849, Macquarie Soaps Pty Ltd (in former brewery, sold 1950 by Harry Edwell to John Fullerton-Smith), Parker's, Robert Rae 1845; squalls 1898 and 2011; steel fabrication works (B.C. Industries); storms 1891 and 1903; streets gas lit 1872, electric lit 1924; tanneries: John Grant 1848, fire 1894, Francis Halliday (Railway) 1870, William Kenyon, Frank McKenna, John Page 1851; TC (in rented premises) 1885, new one b. 1896–98 by George William Brewer, d. by William Edmund Kemp, alterations 1913, reused, new one built on new site, additions 1980, 1982, 1985, became a campus of Western Institute in 1992, extended and refurbished 2009; teachers' college 1951–67, became CAE; telegraph office b. 1859–61 by William Nixon, additions 1871, demolished 1878, new one b. 1875–77 by Joseph Hider Mills, d. by James Johnstone Barnet, additions, alterations and repairs 1898 by John Dunkley, d. by Walter Liberty Vernon, closed and reused; telephone (West Bathurst) 1943; tomato pulping plant (Holbrooks A'asia Ltd) 1927–53; TX 1896, new building b. 1953 by Bristol Constructions; Unit. C. (orig. Wes. Meth.) b. 1857–60 by William Timothy Atkins, d. by Matthew Henry Sadlier, extensions and spire added 1876 by Josiah James Atkins, d. by Thomas Rowe, spire demolished 1911, spire replaced

1912 by William Alfred McLean, d. by William Dryden, spire damaged 1924 and restored 1924 by William Henry Hopper; univ. (Charles Sturt) 1989; vegetable quick-freeze factory (Ready Made Quick Frozen Foods Co. Ltd) 1951; watch-house 1838; water filtration plant, upgraded 2014; water pumping station b. 1917 by William Alfred McLean; water supply 1888, from Winburndale 1933, augmentation 1957, 1988, 1990; weir on Macquarie R.; Wes. Meth. C.: one b. 1837 by Henry Simmons, d. by Thomas Mockett, extended 1847, additions 1848, closed and reused 1860, new one 1860 and Thompson Memorial (South Bathurst) 1885 d. by James Hine; winery (Mount Panorama) 1991; wool-scours: Harold Crapp & Co., Mockler Bros, Waddell Bros, sold 1911 to K.D. Turton; pop. 129 (1820), 267 (1821), 392 (1822), 708 (1823), 1,109 (1825), 2,072 (1828), 1,883 (1846), 2,252 (1851), 3,249 (1856), 4,042 (1861), *c.*5,000 (1866), 5,030 (1871), 7,221 (1881), 9,440 (1891), *c.*9,350 (1895), 9,601 (1901), 9,328 (1911), 9,300 (1923), 10,566 (1933), *c.*11,000 (1941), 12,511 (1947), 16,170 (1954), 17,137 (1961), 17,230 (1966), 17,169 (1971), 18,589 (1976), 19,640 (1981), 24,250 (1983), 22,237 (1986), 24,682 (1991), 26,029 (1996), 30,670 (1997), *c.*30,053 (1999), 27,036 (2001), 28,992 (2006), 31,292 (2011). (See also Kelso.)

Bathurst Camp (*Co. Roxburgh*) see Forest Grove.

Bathurst Holding Centre (*Co. Roxburgh*) see Forest Grove.

Bathurst Point (*Co. Roxburgh*) see Sofala.

Batlow (*Co. Wynyard*) 35°31'S. 148°09'E., 25 km S. of Tumut, on Reedy Flat Ck; Reedy Flat till 1889; founded 1900, town gaz. 1910, thrived 1923; orig. gold (disc. 1853 by Frazer and Drew, gold rush 1854), then fruit (mainly apples), cider, farming, timber; ambulance station; Angl. C. (St John the Evangelist) b. 1933 by Frank Mitchell, d. by George Mammatt, and graveyard; apple handling complex (Batlow Packing House & Cool Stores Rural Co-op. Society Ltd, became Letona Mountain Maid) 1923–2002; brickworks (R. Horaczek); cannery (Mountain Maid, subsumed 1977 by Letona) 1967–94; cemetery 1870; cider plant; cool store 1923, extended 1928, burnt down 1962; electricity 1934; FB 1951 (station b. 1968); fibrous plaster works (G.C. Brown); fires 1879 and 1938; hailstorm 1931; hospital, alterations 1960, additions 1975, redeveloped 2008; jam factory; measles epidemic 1875; mines: Mayday (Con Deasy and Foley) 1853 and Poverty (Patrick Glynn) 1860; PO 1873; powerhouse (C.G. Brown & Co.); Presb. C. (St Andrew's) 1933, closed, sold and reused 1984; PS b. 1899 by R.A. Bastard, renovations 1924, additions and alterations 1937 by G.F. Briggs, repairs 1949 by Ross Bros; railway turntable 1923, 50 ft (15.2 m), ruined; reservoir; Rom. Cath. C. 1875, new one (St Mary's) b. 1928 by D. Larcombe; RS 1923–84, station demolished; sawmills: Aust. Boat Factory, Bagot Timbers Pty Ltd, Batlow Case & Timber Mills Pty Ltd, George Brown, Hides Bros; school 1873, additions 1915, 1964, 1966, 1986; sewerage 1967; snowstorms 1935 and 1936; telephone 1889; TX 1910; typhoid 1884; Union C., closed, sold to Angl. C., dismantled and moved 1933, sold 1935 to G.M. Timmis, reused; Unit. C. (orig. Meth.) 1931, closed, sold and reused; vegetable dehydration plant 1944; water filtration plant 1972; water supply augmentation 1985; pop. 241 (1901), 384 (1911), 566 (1933), 1,112 (1947), 1,114 (1954), 1,403 (1961), 1,448 (1966), 1,372 (1971), 1,374 (1976), 1,354 (1981), 1,227 (1986), 1,143 (1991), 1,069 (1996), 973 (2001), 998 (2006), 1,028 (2011).

Battens Bight (*Co. Richmond*) see Ampdale.

Batten's Point (*Co. Northumberland*) see Speers Point.

Battle Abbey (*Co. Phillip*) 32°25'S. 149°47'E., 25 km E. of Gulgong; school 1900 b. by D.J. Smede, closed 1920; whooping cough epidemic 1907.

Bauloora (*Co. Harden*) 34°34'S. 148°00'E., 9 km N. of Cootamundra; RS 1893, station b. by Baxter and Saddler, closed 1939.

Baw Baw (*Co. Argyle*) 34°44'S. 149°38'E., 8 km NW of Goulburn, on Green Gully Ck;

farming, grazing, dairying; bridge (4 span, low-level) 1917, over Wollondilly R.; PO 1927–31; school 1879–1929; telephone 1917; TX 1952; pop. 185 (1901), 88 (1911), 80 (1933), 422 (2011).

Bawden Bridge (*Co. Fitzroy*) 29°44'S. 152°49'E., 13 km W. of South Grafton, on Orara R.; bridge (continuous lattice trusses) 1874 d. by Gustavus Alphonse Morell and William Christopher Bennett, 252 ft (76.8 m), over Orara R.; telephone 1914; pop. 20 (1933).

Bawley Point (*Co. St Vincent*) 35°30'S. 150°23'E., 19 km SW of Ulladulla, on Tasman Sea; estab. *c.*1892; timber and shipbuilding; FB; PO 1927–62; sawmills: Francis Guy (estab. 1892, burnt down 1894, rebuilt, fire 1897, acquired 1911 by A. & E. Ellis Ltd, man killed 1913, burnt down 1922) and Henry and Carl Mitchell; school 1895, burnt down 1897, replaced, closed 1904; shipyard (A. & E. Ellis Ltd); telephone 1916; tramway (timber) from Termeil; TX 1926; pop. 67 (1911), 111 (1933), 15 (1961), 261 (1986), 433 (1991), 464 (1996), 510 (2001), 565 (2006), 590 (2011).

Baxter Junction (*Co. Hunter*) 32°49'S. 150°37'E., 57 km SW of Singleton.

Bayldon (*Co. Raleigh*) see Toormina.

Bayly (*Co. Phillip*) 32°31'S. 149°42'E., 14 km NE of Mudgee; school 1881–1905.

Baywood Chase (*Co. Rous*) see Suffolk Park.

Beabula (*Co. Waradgery*) 34°26'S. 145°08'E., 29 km E. of Hay; RS 1897–1975.

Beabula (*Co. Waradgery*) see also Nulabor.

Beaches (*Co. Northumberland*) see Catherine Hill Bay.

Beach Park (*Co. Macquarie*) see Flynns Beach.

Beachport (*Co. Dudley*) see Grassy Head.

Beachside (*Co. Camden*) see Kiama.

Beaconsfield (*Co. Bourke*) see Quandary.

Beaconsfield (*Co. Westmoreland*) 33°51'S. 149°45'E., 18 km SW of Oberon; Angl. C. (St Aidan's) 1891, chancel 1912, church closed, renovated and reopened 1933.

Beanbah (*Co. Leichhardt*) 30°42'S. 148°13'E., 32 km NW of Coonamble.

Beanbri (*Co. Denham*) 29°57'S. 148°24'E., 29 km E. of Walgett; RS 1908, station b. by James William Doherty, closed 1975; pop. 34 (1933).

Bean Creek (*Co. Buller*) 28°35'S. 152°36'E., 39 km W. of Kyogle, on Bean Ck; telephone 1923; TX 1928; pop. 152 (1933), 99 (1947), 77 (1954), 90 (1961).

Bean Tree (*Co. Rous*) see Chillingham and Wiangaree.

Bearbong (*Co. Gowen*) 31°38'S. 148°53'E., 22 km E. of Gilgandra, on Wallumburrawang Ck; ball lightning 1947; pop. 80 (1911), 53 (1933), 130 (1947), 73 (1954), 124 (1961).

Beardy (*Co. Gough*) see Lambs Valley.

Beardy Plains (*Co. Gough*) 29°47'S. 151°47'E., 7 km SE of Glen Innes; pop. 48 (1933).

Beargamil (*Co. Ashburnham*) 33°01'S. 148°17'E., 17 km NE of Parkes; gold; mine (Gibbons, Davis and Bradley) 1949–52; school 1957–60.

Bear Hill (*Co. Clarke*) 30°02'S. 152°06'E., 47 km NE of Guyra, in Engine Gully; village gaz. 1892, defunct; mining (gold disc. by C. Vitnall) 1888–96; cemetery 1892; 10 mines; PO 1889–1906; PS 1889; school 1890 b. by Michael O'Brien, closed 1894; pop. 261 (1891).

Beaufort (*Co. Gough*) 29°43'S. 151°41'E., 9 km W. of Glen Innes, on Reddestone Ck; PO 1883; school 1883–1910; telephone 1916; TX 1928–55; pop. 109 (1901), 77 (1911), 47 (1933), 62 (1947).

Beaulieu (*Co. Hardinge*) 29°46'S. 151°02'E., 8 km W. of Inverell; school 1900 b. by F.J. Buxton, closed 1924; winery estab. 1877 by Louis Segol, acquired 1885 by Joel Barnett, planted with olive trees 1996; pop. 59 (1911), 60 (1933), 73 (1947), 55 (1954).

Beaumont (*Co. Camden*) 34°47'S. 150°34'E., 11 km N. of Nowra; farming; bushfire 1939; butter factory (Kangaroo Valley Dairy Co.) 1888–1910; FB; PO 1899–1984; school 1887, new one 1922, closed 1949; telephone 1910; TX 1925; Union C.; pop. 83 (1901), 76 (1911), 85 (1921), 114 (1933), 102 (1947), 80 (1954), 79 (1961), 198 (2011).

Beaury Creek (*Co. Buller*) 28°27'S. 152°31'E., 51 km NW of Kyogle, on Beaury Ck; pop. 25

(1933), 91 (1947), 106 (1954), 105 (1961).

Beauty Point (*Co. Dampier*) 36°23'S. 150°04'E., 6 km N. of Bermagui, on Wallaga Lake; pop. 201 (1996), 462 (2001).

Beauty Point (*Co. Northumberland*) see Morisset.

Bebeah (*Co. Northumberland*) 33°09'S. 151°15'E., 22 km W. of Wyee, on Brush Ck; farming; PO 1927–53; telephone 1921; TX 1923.

Beckom (*Co. Bourke*) 34°20'S. 146°58'E., 7 km NE of Ardlethan; surveyed 1908 by Eugene Ernest William Herborn, village gaz. and first lots sold 1909; oats, wheat 1884+; FB; fire 1917; floods 1920, 2012, 2016; PO 1909–93; powerhouse (T.T. Williams); railway dam 1912; RS 1908, station b. by Frank Vernon, closed 1983, station removed 1985; sawmill (H.J. Smith); school 1911, new building 1970; silo 1923; telephone 1910; TX 1910; Union C. b. 1926 by Berry Bros; water supply 1941; pop. 308 (1911), 208 (1933), 109 (1947), 142 (1954), 332 (1961), 172 (2006), 218 (2011).

Bective (*Co. Parry*) 30°58'S. 150°44'E., 22 km NW of Tamworth, on Peel R.; town gaz. 1861; farming; PO 1892; school 1881, new one b. 1883 by J. Neate, closed 1885, reopened 1895 in new building b. by W. Acheson, closed 1957; telephone 1907; TX 1945; Union C.; pop. 153 (1901), 188 (1911), 198 (1933), 114 (1947), 97 (1954), 83 (1961), 511 (2006).

Bective Soldiers' Settlement (*Co. Parry*) 31°02'S. 150°41'E., 25 km W. of Tamworth, on Sandy Ck; telephone 1923.

Bectric (*Co. Bourke*) 34°30'S. 147°15'E., 27 km W. of Temora; FB 1948 (station b. 2013); school 1897, new building 1908, closed 1965, bought by Dyason, moved to Tara; pop. 93 (1911), 97 (1933), 141 (1947), 119 (1954), 106 (1961).

Bedding Ground (*Co. Wellesley*) 36°51'S. 149°07'E., 14 km NW of Bombala, on Cambalong Ck.

Bedellick (*Co. Murray*) 35°08'S. 149°01'E., 17 km S. of Murrumbateman; school 1888, burnt down 1903.

Bedgerabong (*Co. Cunningham*) 33°22'S. 147°42'E., 28 km W. of Forbes; formerly Bedgerebong; farming and dairying; cemetery (255 graves) 1887, incl. columbarium; fire 1884; hailstorm 1914; PO 1889; school (Budgerabong till 1914, then Bedgerebong) 1880–87, reopened 1904, additions 1968, new school 1984; telephone 1906; TX 1910, automatic 1968; Union C. 1892, reused, new one (War Memorial) 1968; whooping cough epidemics 1916 and 1921; pop. 93 (1901), 270 (1911), 397 (1933), 242 (1947), 221 (1954), 274 (1961), 221 (2011).

Bedgerebong (*Co. Cunningham*) see Bedgerabong.

Beechwood (*Co. Macquarie*) 31°26'S. 152°40'E., 7 km W. of Wauchope, on Hastings R.; Mortons Creek till 1888; thrived 1900; timber and farming; Angl. C. (St Paul's) 1921; cemetery (345 graves) 1892; FB; fire 1924; flood 1950; PO 1878, new one b. 1913; Rom. Cath. C. 1889, demolished 1957, replacement (St Patrick's) b. 1957 by D. Olsen, d. by Fowell, Mansfield and Maclurcan; sawmills: one o. 1923 and Maxwell Timbers (Colin Campbell Maxwell, Francis William Ninness and Raymond Thomas Latimore); school 1882, repairs 1898 by J. Pead & Son, repairs 1902 by James Read & Son, new building b. 1917 by Baxter Bros, additions 1955 by D. Olsen & Son, additions 1966 and 1991; telephone 1888; TX 1915; Unit. C. (orig. Meth.) 1928; pop. 140 (1901), 164 (1911), 277 (1933), 320 (1947), 252 (1954), 286 (1961), 244 (1971), 211 (1976), 258 (1981), 234 (1986), 421 (1991), 432 (1996), 425 (2001), 451 (2006), 570 (2011).

Beefwood (*Co. Stapylton*) 29°02'S. 150°04'E., 50 km N. of Moree; telephone 1919.

Beelbangera (*Co. Cooper*) 34°15'S. 146°06'E., 5 km NE of Griffith; soldiers' settlement, village gaz. 1921; hort. and wine; distillery (Tarac Technologies Pty Ltd); incinerator; PO 1919; RS 1916, station b. by Ernest Frederick Leggo, closed 1975, station removed 1978; school 1935, additions 1958; telephone 1922; wineries: McWilliam's (estab. by Henry Francis Jones, taken over 1928 by Patrick and William Jones, became Beelbangera

Winegrowers' Co-op. Ltd in 1935, taken over 1943 by McWilliam's), Rossetto's, Tarac, Vico's; pop. *c*.350 (1919), 265 (1933), 273 (1947), 367 (1954), 399 (1961), 280 (1976), 291 (1981), 308 (1986), 303 (1991), 304 (1996), 340 (2001), 305 (2006), 310 (2011).

Bee Mountain (*Co. Robinson*) see Illewong.

Beemunnel (*Co. Ewenmar*) 31°43'S. 148°03'E., 19 km E. of Warren.

Beenbah (*Co. Rous*) 28°32'S. 153°09'E., 15 km NE of Kyogle; telephone 1925.

Bega (*Co. Auckland*) 36°41'S. 149°50'E., 81 km SE of Cooma, on Bega R.; (incl. Hayden Estate 1932, North Bega, West Bega); surveyed by Samuel Parkinson and town gaz. 1851, relocated after 1851 flood, new site laid out 1854 by D.C. Drake, first lots sold 1854, munic. proc. 1883, thrived 1902, bypassed by highway 1975; wool till 1870, cattle, wheat till 1887, tanning, sawmilling, dairying, butter, cheese, bacon, poultry, maize, barley, fruit, potatoes; ambulance station 1954, new one 2015; Angl. C. b. 1854 as a school, new one 1858, enlarged 1868, reused 1878–97, dismantled, replacement (St John the Evangelist) b. 1874–78 by Richard Thomas and George Sercombe, d. by Edmund Thomas Blacket, re-roofed 1909, restored 1974; Assemblies of God C. (Resonate); Bapt. C.; boot factory (Lion) estab. 1885 by Edward Hughes; brewery (Auckland) estab. 1872 by Richard Rogers, closed 1875, reopened 1882 by Peter Sharp, joined 1891 by Robert Sharp, sold 1897 to Augustus Arnold, burnt down 1900; brickworks (William White) 1857; bridge b. 1876–78 by F. Smith, 415 ft (126.5 m), replaced 1898 by Jakob Nybeck, 360 ft (109.7 m), replaced 1975 in concrete, 2,047 ft (624 m), on new site, over Bega R.; bushfires 1885, 1894, 1905, 1939, 1952 (many houses destroyed); butter factories: Bega Co-op. Creamery Co. Ltd (b. 1900 by W. Manning, extended 1903, additions 1907 and 1924, rebuilt 1926 by R.W. Thatcher, became Bega Co-op. Society Ltd in 1944 and made cheese 1954+, demolished, replaced 1969 by Mauri Bros and Thomson Ltd, butter finished 1972) and NSW Creamery Butter Co. Ltd 1894–99; carriage-works: William Bewicke 1907, A. Chamberlin, G.W. Commens and J.R. M'Donald 1881, Haigh and Disher, (closed 1915), Stephen Henry Pearce (new factory b. 1909 by Thatcher and Underhill, bought 1911 by A.H. Newlyn, closed 1915), Pearce and Britten, Standard Coach Factory (Whyman and Brooks, relocated 1900, taken over 1915 by R.S. Whyman alone), Albert Joseph Zehner; cemetery (668 burials 1857+) 1863–1910, new one (*c*.3,000 burials) 1902, incl. columbarium; CH (incl. lock-up) b. 1862–65 by John Malcolm, renovations 1873, new one b. 1882 by Moore and Chidgey, d. by James Johnstone Barnet; cheese factories: Bugle (William Spence), Manning's (burnt down 1898), Orion (P. Hergenhan), E.F. Stiles, The Meadows (D.A. Gowing); clock tower (Montague Frederick Evershed memorial) 1930; cordial factory estab. 1879 by Robert W. Emley, sold 1891 to T.H. Notley, sold 1899 to John E. Jackson, additions 1906, sold 1912 to John Otton; diphtheria 1912, 1923, 1924, 1936; droughts 1864, 1868, 1885, 1941–42; earth tremors 1872, 1875, 1945; electricity (State Electric Lighting Co.) 1927; FB 1900 (old station demolished and replaced 1916, new one 1937); fires 1908, 1909, 1916, 1926; floods 1851 (17 died), 1857, 1860, 1873, 1874, 1878, 1879, 1891, 1893, 1897, 1898, 1900, 1908, 1914, 1919, 1934, 1966, 1971, 2016; flour mill (James Kirkwood) 1860; furniture factory (Clark Bros); gaol, additions and alterations 1903 by Hines, reduced to lock-up in 1940; gasworks (Bega Gas Co.) 1885; hospital b. 1889 by John Malcolm, additions and repairs by Brown and Olaf Rye Lassen, extended 1904, new wing b. 1909 by William Manning, extended 1912 and 1928, redeveloped 1934–5, alterations 1937, closed 1957, reused, replaced 1957, additions and alterations 2010 by Camarda & Cantrill Pty Ltd, new one (South East Regional Hospital) 2016 on new site; ice works (Horace Hayes) during World War II; Jehovah's Witnesses C.; jetty b. 1862 by John O'Neill; joinery (Olaf Rye Lassen)

1915; measles epidemic 1907; monumental stone works (J.F. Ziegler & Sons) 1894; pleuro-pneumonia epidemic 1864; PO: Bega 1856 (new one b. 1877 by William Alfred Isley, additions 1883 by Moore and Chidgey, replaced 1972), North Bega 1959–94, West Bega 1960; Presb. C. (St Andrew's) b. 1870 by Thomas Moorhead, closed 1977, reused, new one (Scots); PS b. 1879 by Richard Thomas, additions and alterations 1899 by J. Malcolm, reused, new one b. 1941 by R.J. Mathers, relocated 1975 to rented premises, new one 1989; reservoir, 370,000 gal. (1,682 kl); quarry (granite); Rom. Cath. C. b. 1862 by Spindler, enlarged 1865, new one (St Patrick's) 1881, additions 1911, extensions and renovations 1953 d. by Norman Leslie Lipman; sale-yards: G. Haslingden 1882 and Rixon and McLeod 1879; Salv. Army C. 1927; sawmills: Isaac Innes (removed from Tanja) 1936 and William Kesterton 1869; schools: Bega 1860 (new building b. 1883 by Moore and Chidgey, d. by William Edmund Kemp, additions 1892, additions and alterations 1914 by Olaf Rye Lassen, additions 1971 and 1985), Bega HS 1952 (additions 1959, 1964, 1972, 1981, additions 2007 by Edwards Constructions Pty Ltd), West Bega 1959 (additions 1969, closed 2012, sold 2014); SD Adventist C.; sewerage 1937; smallpox 1876 and 1881; soap-works (Underhill and McNamara) 1883; tanneries: W.A. Smith and John Spence, burnt down 1903; telephone: North Bega 1959 and West Bega 1960; TC, additions 1987, became a campus of Illawarra Institute of Technology in 1992; telegraph 1868, new office b. 1877 by William Alfred Isley, additions 1883 by Moore and Chidgey; TX 1906–84; typhoid 1898 and 1903; Unit. C. (orig. Meth.) b. 1924 by R.E. Midson, d. by Vernon and Mills; water supply 1929, augmentation 1984 and 1987; Wes. Meth. C. b. 1866–69 by Ernest Zingle, d. by J. Malcolm, cement rendered 1872 by J. Orchard, reused; winery (Grevillea Estate) 1980; pop. 625 (1861), 516 (1871), 1,634 (1881), 2,023 (1891), *c.*2,300 (1895–8), 1,960 (1901), 2,632 (1911), 2,344 (1933), *c.*2,700 (1941), 2,967 (1947), 3,644 (1954), 3,858 (1961), 3,925 (1966), 4,146 (1971), 4,253 (1976), 4,388 (1981), 4,294 (1986), 4,202 (1991), 4,190 (1996), 4,389 (2001), 4,537 (2006), 4,155 (2011).

Beggan Beggan (*Co. Harden*) 34°42'S. 148°14'E., 21 km E. of Cootamundra, on Deep Ck; quarry; school 1883–1900; pop. 37 (1933).

Beilpajah (*Co. Manara*) 32°52'S. 143°48'E., 153 km S. of Wilcannia; RS 1927–75.

Beitibombi Brush (*Co. Macquarie*) 31°50'S. 152°17'E., 10 km NW of Wingham, on Caparra Ck.

Belair (*Co. Northumberland*) see Adamstown.

Bel Air (*Co. Wellington*) see Orange.

Belalie (*Co. Culgoa*) 29°10'S. 145°51'E., 101 km N. of Bourke, on Warrego R.; PO 1866–67.

Belanglo (*Co. Camden*) 34°32'S. 150°15'E., 10 km SW of Berrima; school 1887–97; pop. 60 (1901).

Belar (*Co. Gowen*) 31°23'S. 149°15'E., 12 km S. of Coonabarabran, on Belar Ck; pop. 149 (1911).

Belara (*Co. Bligh*) 32°22'S. 149°14'E., 28 km W. of Gulgong; copper, silver, gold, lead, zinc; mines: Belara *c.*1875–1907 and Native Bee, closed 1907.

Belarabon (*Co. Booroondarra*) 32°00'S. 144°57'E., 100 km SW of Cobar.

Belarbigill (*Co. Lincoln*) see Rawsonville.

Belar Creek (*Co. Gowen*) 31°23'S. 149°11'E., 15 km SW of Coonabarabran, on Belar Ck; school 1883–1925; pop. 52 (1933).

Belaringar (*Co. Oxley*) 31°47'S. 147°36'E., 24 km W. of Warren; PO 1927–32; RS 1891–1975; pop. 68 (1933).

Belbora (*Co. Gloucester*) 31°59'S. 152°09'E., 19 km E. of Gloucester, on Whooribee Ck; grazing and dairying; PO 1927–68; 2 quarries; school 1945–68; telephone 1922; TX 1926; pop. 139 (1933), 111 (1947), 113 (1954), 187 (1961), 177 (2011).

Belbourie (*Co. Macquarie*) 31°51'S. 152°20'E., 4 km NW of Wingham, on Gorman Ck.

Belford (*Co. Northumberland*) 32°39'S. 151°16'E., 8 km W. of Branxton, on Jump Up

Ck; (incl. Pothana); orig. Jump-up Creek; first surveyed 1833 by George Boyle White and again in 1854 by John Rogers, lots sold 1854, town gaz. 1878; agric. and grazing, then dairying, poultry, vineyards; Angl. C. (Good Shepherd) 1886 d. by Blacket, and graveyard (42 graves 1893+); bridge b. 1888 by Charles Knight, over Jump Up Ck; cemetery 1893, defunct; flood 1904; PO 1865; RS 1869–1976; school 1880–1935; telephone 1899; TX 1910–68; Wes. Meth. C. 1886; wineries: Dimbulla Estate 2001, David Hook, Macquariedale Estate 1999, Ridgeview Wines 2000, Sweetwater Wines 1998, Vercoe's Vineyard 2002; pop. 243 (1861), 218 (1901), 312 (1911), 97 (1933), 75 (1947), 68 (1954), 73 (1961).

Belfrayden (*Co. Mitchell*) 35°07'S. 147°04'E., 18 km N. of The Rock; village gaz. 1931; RS 1928–88; school 1957–67; silo 1931; pop. 46 (1933), 55 (1947), 52 (1954).

Belgamba (*Co. Buckland*) 31°16'S. 150°46'E., 17 km NE of Werris Ck; RS 1937–71.

Belgrave (*Co. Durham*) 32°17'S. 151°30'E., 28 km NW of Dungog, on Allyn R.; cemetery (119 graves 1897+); pop. 20 (1933).

Belgrave Falls (*Co. Dudley*) 31°05'S. 152°44'E., 9 km W. of Kempsey; never developed, defunct; brick-kiln; CH (incl. lock-up) 1847, moved 1859 to West Kempsey; PS 1851, defunct.

Belgravia (*Co. Gough*) see Inverell.

Belgravia (*Co. Wellington*) 33°07'S. 149°02'E., 16 km E. of Molong, on Belgravia Ck; Whiteleys Flat till 1887; farming and grazing; marble quarry (Calula Creek); PO 1887–1924; school 1882–1908; pop. 51 (1901), 80 (1911), 42 (1933), 165 (2011).

Belimbla Park (*Co. Camden*) 34°05'S. 150°32'E., 15 km W. of Camden, on Back Ck; pop. 427 (2001), 547 (2011).

Bell (*Co. Cook*) 33°31'S. 150°17'E., 9 km N. of Mount Victoria, on Koombanda Brook; bushfires 1942 and 1952; FB; PO 1878, burnt down 1961; RS (Mount Wilson till 1889) 1875, relocated 1910; school 1955–73; telegraph 1890; telephone 1897; TX 1939; pop. 57 (1911), 50 (1947), 64 (1954), *c.*100 (1987).

Bellambi (*Co. Camden*) 34°22'S. 150°55'E., 1 km NE of Corrimal, on Tasman Sea; formerly Palamba; subdivided and laid out 1842; coalmining and seaport; breakwater, 492 ft (150 m), 1979; bushfire 1953; Church of Christ; clothing factory (King Gee) 1966–2009; coalmine estab. 1857 by Thomas Hale; electricity 1913; flood (person died) 1998; gales 1898 and 1924; jetties: Bellambi Coal Co. (b. 1889, 1,000 ft or 304.8 m, damaged 1893, destroyed 1898), Thomas Hale (b. 1858 for Hale by William Mills, lengthened 1859, destroyed 1898), Taylor and Walker's 1863 (reopened 1885 by Thomas Saywell and William Wilson), South Bulli Colliery (estab. 1887 by Thomas Saywell and William Wilson, sold 1890 to E. Vickery & Co., rebuilt 1909, abandoned 1952, closed 1954); Meth. C. 1904, damaged, moved and reopened 1940, new one 1961; mines rescue station 1927; PO 1889–1988; PS 1911–33; rifle range 1953; RS 1889; rubber factory (Hardie Rubber Co. Ltd); school 1956, additions 1958, 1961, 1966, 1975, 1981; sewage works; telegraph 1862; telephone *c.*1900; Unit. C.; Wes. Meth. C. 1895; pop. 204 (1891), 155 (1901), 690 (1911), 587 (1921), 1,819 (1954), 3,411 (1961), 4,011 (2011).

Bellangry (*Co. Macquarie*) 31°20'S. 152°37'E., 19 km NW of Wauchope, on Mortons Ck; farming and dairying; Angl. C. (St Bartholomew's) b. 1912–14; FB; PO 1927–73; sawmills: Haydon & Dunn Pty Ltd and Allen Taylor & Co. Ltd; school 1956–67; telephone 1914; TX 1923; pop. 123 (1933), 231 (1947), 341 (1954), 232 (1961), 208 (2011).

Bellarwi (*Co. Bland*) 34°06'S. 147°12'E., 20 km S. of West Wyalong; farming; Angl. C. (St Andrew's) 1938, removed from Barmedman; PO 1926–77; RS 1923–75; telephone 1923; TX; pop. 99 (1933), 77 (1947), 99 (1954), 78 (1961).

Bellarwi (*Co. Gipps*) see Weja.

Bellata (*Co. Jamison*) 29°55'S. 149°47'E., 50 km S. of Moree; Woolabra till 1909; village gaz. 1898 as Woolabra; wheat, grazing, gemstones; Angl. C. (St Thomas's) 1913;

artesian bore sunk 1896 by Crawford and M'Cray; cemetery (83 graves 1900+); CH 1911; FB; PO 1899, additions and renovations 1925, repairs 1955 by Wright Bros, closed 1988; Presb. C.; PS 1901, new one b. 1907 by A.J. Hulbert, d. by Walter Liberty Vernon, closed during World War II, reopened 1947; railway dams 1908 and 1912; Rom. Cath. C. (Holy Rosary) 1911; RS 1897 (Woolabra till 1909), station b. by William Mitchell, station closed 1986; sawmill (G. Clarke); school (Woolabra till 1909) b. 1900 by Christopher Harris, additions and alterations 1911 by Joseph Head, new one b. 1939 on new site by Robson and Hegarty, additions 1960; silo; telephone 1898; TX 1911; water reticulation 1955; wool-scour (Henry Berry & Son) 1898; pop. 104 (1901), 337 (1911), 391 (1933), 156 (1947), 463 (1954), 370 (1961), 232 (1971), 186 (1999), 186 (2006), 407 (2011).

Bella Vista (*Co. Gloucester*) see Old Bar.

Bella Vista (*Co. Selwyn*) 36°20'S. 148°17'E., 14 km NW of Perisher Valley; temporary construction camp estab. by Thiess Bros Ltd for Snowy Mountains Hydro-Electric Scheme, defunct 1966; PO 1962–66; PS; school 1962–66.

Bellawongarah (*Co. Camden*) 34°46'S. 150°38'E., 7 km W. of Berry; formerly Kangaroo Mountain; settled 1866 by Graham; farming, dairying, butter, bacon; butter factory (Rockfield Dairy Co.) estab. 1890 by Henry Graham; cemetery (18 graves 1889–1954) 1876; FB 1944; PO 1908; sawmill (sold 1911 by Alex Johnston to J. Molloy & Sons); school 1894 b. by Muller and Purdie, closed 1920; snow 1895 and 1901; telephone 1924; TX 1925–62; Wes. Meth. C. 1868, closed, reused; pop. 106 (1901), 68 (1911), 53 (1954), 52 (1961), 190 (2011).

Bellbird (*Co. Northumberland*) 32°51'S. 151°19'E., 4 km SW of Cessnock, on Bellbird Ck; (incl. Bellbird Heights); estab. 1908, village gaz. 1910; coalmining; Angl. C. (St Matthew's) 1915; collieries: Bellbird No. 1 (estab. 1907–8 as Hetton Extended by Hetton Coal Mining Co., acquired 1911 by Hetton Bellbird Co. and renamed Hetton Bellbird, o. 1912, strikes 1912, 1914, 1918, 1919, boy killed 1920, explosion and fire 1923 killed 21, closed 1923–24, strikes 1924, 1936, 1940, 1941, 1942, 1943, 1944, 1947, 1948, 1950, fire 1950, acquired 1958 by Eric Newham Wallerawang Pty Ltd, fire 1963, acquired 1974 by Southland Coal Mining Co., closed 1976, razed) and Bellbird No. 2, razed; FB (station b. 1995); Meth. C. 1913 d. by C. Jackson; PO 1911, closed; Presb. C. 1923, closed, reopened 1933, closed, reopened 1939; PS 1920–35; 4 quarries; railway (colliery); 2 reservoirs (incl. one b. 1929); school 1913, additions 1923, additions 1929 by White Bros, additions 1981 and 1995; smallpox 1917; telephone 1912; TX; Unit. C. (orig. Meth.) d. and b. 1926 by R.H.S. Hewitt; pop. 185 (1911), 1,843 (1933), 1,502 (1947), 1,501 (1954), 1,475 (1961), 2,066 (2011).

Bellbird Heights (*Co. Northumberland*) see Bellbird.

Bellbird Hill (*Co. Cook*) see Kurrajong Heights.

Bellbrook (*Co. Dudley*) 30°49'S. 152°31'E., 41 km W. of Macksville, on Macleay R.; village gaz. 1892, classified by National Trust; farming and grazing, now tourism; Angl. C. (St James's) b. 1906 by Percy Landers; bridges: one repaired 1910, burnt down 1936, replaced 1936 by D. Stewart, over Nulla Nulla Ck and one b. 1936 over Macleay R.; cemetery (125 graves 1894+); CH 1900–75; electricity 1953; FB; floods 1949, 1974, 2011; hailstorm 1919; lock-up; PO 1884, new one b. 1895 by William McCarney; PS 1892, new ones 1900 and 1922; Rom. Cath. C. (St Patrick's) 1899, disused and dilapidated; school 1913, new one b. 1930, new building 1970 (removed from Carcolla); telegraph 1879; TX 1917, automatic 1976; water supply augmentation 1970; pop. 758 (1908), 161 (1911), 233 (1933), 203 (1947), 100 (1954), 73 (1961), 356 (2011).

Bellevue (*Co. Brisbane*) see Gundy.

Belle Vue (*Co. Durham*) see Mindaribba.

Bellevue (*Co. Sandon*) see Armidale.

Bellevue Heights (*Co. Clarence*) see Grafton South.

Bellimbopinni (*Co. Dudley*) 31°01'S. 152°54'E., 10 km NE of Kempsey, on Macleay R.; bypassed by highway 2016; farming; aeroplane crash (man killed) 1938; floods 1921 and 1929; PO 1917; school (Seven Oaks till 1917) 1865, repairs 1882 by T. M'Neill, repairs 1893 by William Henry, additions 2010, closed 2014, sold 2016; telephone 1913; TX 1958; pop. 65 (1911), 194 (1933), 188 (1947), 168 (1954), 164 (1961).

Bellingen (*Co. Raleigh*) 30°27'S. 152°54'E., 12 km W. of Urunga, on Bellinger R.; Boat Harbour till 1890; settled by Don Burge, surveyed 1861 by Harborn, village gaz. 1870; maize, timber, oranges, farming, dairying, pigs, centre for alternative lifestyles; ambulance station 1938; Angl. C. b. 1896 by Frederick Gerhard, d. by Tobias H. Neuhaus, closed and moved 1935, new one (St Margaret of Scotland) b. 1935 by R. McNiven, d. by Power, Adam and Munnings; Assemblies of God C. (Christ. Life); brewery (Richard Jennings) 2005; brickworks (Bellingen Concrete Brick Co. Ltd) 1907; bridges: one to North Bellingen b. 1912 by Peter McHugh, destroyed 1946, replaced (Lavenders Bridge) 1952, over Bellinger R. and Cahills Bridge over Cemetery Ck; butter factory (Upper Bellinger Co-op. Dairy Co. Ltd, which later became Bellinger River Co-op. Butter & Bacon Society Ltd) b. 1906 by George Edward Moore, additions 1909 also by Moore, bacon factory added 1919, replacement b. 1927 by Thackeray and Gallagher, inundated 1946, fire 1951, closed 1964, reused 1975, sold 1985, reused 1991; carriage-works (Edward James Robert W. Raymond); CH (incl. lock-up) b. 1869 by Alfred Doorey, d. by James Johnstone Barnet, additions 1873 by George Edward Moore, new one b. 1910 also by Moore, d. by Walter Liberty Vernon; cordial factories: J.L. Bailey, J. Coleman, Pollock's 1905, Charles Scullen 1924; creamery (Barr Bros) 1898; diphtheria 1897; FB (station b. 1929 by H.J. McCallum); fire 1924; floods 1921, 1933, 1946, 1950, 1962, 2004, 2006, 2009, 2011, 2012, 2013, 2017; foot-bridges: one b. 1899, over Bellinger R. and one over Cemetery Ck; hailstorm 1967; hospital (Raleigh Dist., renamed Bellinger River Dist.) b. 1903 by George Edward Moore, d. by E. Duggin, additions and alterations 1912 by Samuel David Hines, extended 1927 and 1928, additions 1934 by B.C. Johnson, alterations 1938, 1943, 1948, additions 1953 and 1975–77; lamp factory (Planet Products) 1975; leather factory (Awl Leather) 1991, in old butter factory; PO 1871, new one b. 1909 by George Edward Moore; powerhouse 1926; Presb. C. 1871; PS b. 1910 by George Edward Moore; reservoir (concrete), 200,000 gal. (909.2 kl); Rom. Cath. C. 1881, sold and demolished 1911, replacement (St William's) 1911–19, reused, new one (Mary Immaculate, Virgin Mother of God) b. 1920 by Scott Bros, d. by Austin McKay; sale-yards b. 1912 by T.G. Tarrant; sawmills: Bellingen Timber Co. Pty Ltd, Best and Doepel (burnt down and replaced 1905), Clyde Sawmilling & Shipping Co. Pty Ltd, East End (Frederick Doepel, burnt down 1912, rebuilt, damaged 1946), Hubert Raymond Moods (burnt down 1952); schools: Bellingen (Bellinger till 1890) 1870 b. by George Edward Moore, additions 1880–1910 also by Moore, additions 1926 by E.H. Poole, closed, reused 1975, demolished 1981, new school on new site, additions 1995, and HS 1960, additions d. by John Moran; sewerage 1940, augmentation 1966 and 1994; telegraph 1883; TX b. 1909 by George Edward Moore; typhoid 1907; Union C.; Unit. C. (St Andrew's, orig. Presb.) 1956, reused 1994, new one; water supply 1937; Wes. Meth. C. 1870, replaced 1878, new one b. 1901 by Thomas Sawtell, relocated 1910, closed, sold and reused; wharves: one b. 1879 by T. Boulton, repairs 1899, and one b. 1912 by McHugh; pop. 583 (1881), 316 (1891), 323 (1901), 1,615 (1911), 1,615 (1924), 1,109 (1933), *c.*1,200 (1941), 1,248 (1947), 1,324 (1954), 1,418 (1961), 1,390 (1966), 1,371 (1971), 1,398 (1976), 1,593 (1981), 1,834 (1986), 2,298 (1991), 2,690 (1996), 2,731 (2001), 2,876 (2006), 3,038 (2011).

Bellingen North (*Co. Raleigh*) 30°27'S. 152°54'E., opposite Bellingen, on Bellinger R.; bridges: one to Bellingen b. 1912 by Peter McHugh, destroyed 1946, replaced 1952, over Bellinger R., Frenchs Bridge over Frenchmans Ck, Taylors Bridge over Frenchmans Ck; cemetery (2,208 graves 1874+) 1875, incl. lawn cemetery and columbarium; flood 2009; sewerage augmentation 1967 and 1994; pop. 165 (1933), 153 (1947), 72 (1954), 1,279 (2006).

Bellinger (*Co. Raleigh*) see Bellingen.

Bellingerambil (*Co. Nicholson*) 33°33'S. 145°44'E., 20 km E. of Hillston; pop. 79 (1933).

Bellinger Heads (*Co. Raleigh*) see Urunga.

Bellinger South (*Co. Raleigh*) see Urunga.

Bellmount (*Co. King*) see Bellmount Forest.

Bellmount Forest (*Co. King*) 34°55'S. 149°15'E., 31 km E. of Yass; Bellmount till 1879; farming and grazing; FB; Meth. C. 1902; PO 1907; telephone 1913; TX 1934–68; pop. 80 (1933), 67 (1947), 67 (1954), 66 (1961).

Bell River City (*Co. Ashburnham*) see Molong.

Bells Creek (*Co. St Vincent*) 35°36'S. 149°48'E., 18 km S. of Braidwood; gold (alluvial disc. 1851, and reef); mines: Banner or Shekamuno (King Gold Mines Ltd, Banner Gold-mining Co. NL, Newhope Gold-mining Co. NL, Littlechild and Nomchong) 1870–1934, Golden Gully (W.E. Simpson) 1907–11, Lady Belmore (Littrel and W.H. Stalker) 1903–9; PO 1872–1962; school 1876–1909; telephone 1906; TX; pop. 96 (1901), 23 (1933).

Bells Lagoons (*Co. Goulburn*) 35°38'S. 147°18'E., 9 km N. of Holbrook, on Billabong Ck; school 1889–1914.

Bells Mountain (*Co. Darling*) 30°18'S. 150°36'E., 11 km N. of Barraba; mining 1930s–50s; mine (diatomite) o. 1982 by Aust. Diatomite Mining Co.

Bells Swamp (*Co. Inglis*) see Marne.

Belltrees (*Co. Brisbane*) 31°59'S. 151°08'E., 25 km E. of Scone, on Hunter R.; Angl. C. (St James's) b. 1888 by Taylor, and graveyard (16 graves); bridge (Allan timber truss) 1919, 391 ft (119.2 m), over Hunter R.; PO 1927–74; school 1879, new one b. 1882 by Robert Sneesby; telephone 1910; TX 1926; pop. 215 (1911), 108 (1933), 66 (1947), 73 (1954), 68 (1961).

Bellview (*Co. Wellesley*) 36°52'S. 149°14'E., 5 km N. of Bombala; school 1901–32 and 1957–65; pop. 97 (1911), 31 (1933).

Bellwood (*Co. Raleigh*)
see Nambucca Heads.

Belmont (*Co. Cunningham*) 32°57'S. 147°19'E., 23 km NE of Condobolin.

Belmont (*Co. Northumberland*) 33°02'S. 151°40'E., 6 km N. of Swansea, on Belmont Bay; (incl. South Belmont); estab. by Thomas Williamson and John Anderson, lots sold 1868, subdivisions 1909 and 1919 (Lewers Estate); timber 1871+, fishing 1874+, shipbuilding, farming, fruit, dairying, later hunting, boating, sand mining, tourism; Aboriginal mission estab. 1826 by Lancelot Edward Threlkeld, closed 1830, demolished 1833; ambulance station b. 1942 by J.C. Davis & Sons, d. by John William Oldham and Robert Godwin Lees; Angl. C. (All Saints') b. 1891 by James Lunn and Ernest Yates, reused, and graveyard; Bapt. C. 1978; bushfires 1940, 1951, 1991; cement works (P. & O., P.F.C. Putensen); cemetery (3,114 graves 1879+), incl. columbaria; CH b. 1936 by Bailey and Birrell, new one 1962; collieries: Bolton, Green Hills (o. and closed in 1860s), Normaine, Wallamaine Open-Cut (Wallamaine Colliery Pty Ltd); FB (station b. 1962); hospital 1968 d. by John Kinstler, additions 2003, 2006, 2007; ice works (Quintrell's); jetty 1923; marina; Meth. C. b. 1926 by Campbell and Steele, d. by Benjamin George Pearce; mine (Rutile & Zircon Mines Newcastle Ltd) 1959–69; miners' strikes 1926, 1929–30, 1937, 1938, 1940, 1948, 1949, 1950, 1953; PO: Belmont 1877, new one b. 1926, new one b. 1940 by W. Stronach Pty Ltd, d. by George Newton Kenworthy, and South Belmont 1959–69; pottery (Northern Stoneware Pipe Pty Ltd) 1937–79; pound (stock) 1865; Presb. C. b. 1903 by J.A. Williamson; Prim. Meth. C. 1881; PS 1901, o. 1906 in building removed from

Arakoon and re-erected by T. Carpenter and W. Derkenne, o. 1921 in rented premises, new ones 1962 and 2016; Rom. Cath. C. (St Francis Xavier's) 1933, closed and reused, new one 2015, and graveyard; RS: govt 1916–71 and New Redhead Estate & Coal Co. Railway (services to Adamstown 1916–71); sawmills: Cardiff Mill (1872–73, later reopened 1885 by John Henderson) and H.O. Crockett; schools: primary 1880, new building b. 1911 by John Waugh, additions 1929 by Richard Seed, new school 1963 d. by Michael John Dysart, additions 1970 and 1995, and HS b. 1953 by Orrett Bros, alterations by R.T. Parker Pty Ltd; sewerage 1939; shipyard (Cornelius and Patrick Moynahan) 1868; tank traps 1942; TC b. 1967 by W. Stronach Pty Ltd, d. by M. Zatorski, additions 1972 and 1985, became a campus of Hunter Institute of Technology in 1992; telegraph 1884–94; telephone 1894; TX 1915, automatic 1958; Union C. 1874; United Meth. Free C. 1880; water supply 1929; wharf; pop. *c*.120 (1884), 145 (1891), 269 (1901), 237 (1911), 475 (1921), 2,013 (1933, incl. 73 on John Darling Estate), 4,786 (1947), 6,420 (2011).

Belmont North (*Co. Northumberland*) 33°01'S. 151°40'E., 2 km N. of Belmont; (incl. Floraville and Wommara); subdivision 1925; Angl. C. (Holy Family); bushfire 1933; Christ. Brethren Assemblies C. (Tingira Community); collieries: Dunlock and John Darling (estab. 1922–27 by BHP, men killed 1930, 1931, 1932, 1934, strikes 1934 and 1937, men killed 1937 and 1938, strike 1944, man killed 1945, strikes 1947, 1949, 1950, 1953, closed 1988, shafts filled and capped 1988 and 1990, colliery partly reused); gale 1942; PO 1951; 4 quarries; reservoir; schools: Floraville 1967, additions 1970 and 1973, additions 2010 by Lahey Constructions Pty Ltd and North Belmont 1953, additions 1956, 1959, 1961; Unit. C. (St Luke's); pop. 6,481 (2011).

Belmore (*Co. Ashburnham*) see Moorbel.

Belmore (*Co. Kennedy*) 32°25'S. 147°20'E., 66 km NW of Trundle, on Bulbodney Ck.

Belmore Flat (*Co. St Vincent*) 34°57'S. 150°21'E., 24 km W. of Nowra, on Danjera Ck.

Belmore River (*Co. Macquarie*) 31°04'S. 152°58'E., 12 km E. of Kempsey, on Belmore R.; dairying; Angl. C. (Christ) 1906; flood 1893; gale 1947; punt b. 1874 by Edmund Taylor; Rom. Cath. C. (St Brigid's) b. 1919 by George Welch, d. by Albert Edmund Bates, damaged 1947, repaired 1948, demolished; school 1871 b. by Thomas Nance, sen., extended 1873 by James Hetherton, additions 1883 by W. M'Neil, additions 1923 by Weeks and Holden, closed 1972; Wes. Meth. C. 1885; pop. 342 (1911), 166 (1933), 177 (1947), 293 (1954), 257 (1961), 391 (2011).

Belnona (*Co. Camden*) see Woonona.

Beloka (*Co. Wallace*) 36°32'S. 148°44'E., 17 km SE of Jindabyne; formerly Boloco or Boloko; grazing; Angl. C. (St James's) b. 1873 by J.J. Mawson, d. by Alberto Dias Soares, restoration 1932 and 1935; cemetery (316 graves 1878+); hailstorm 1910; PO 1890; telephone 1927; TX 1927; pop. 65 (1901), 53 (1933).

Belowra (*Co. Dampier*) 36°09'S. 149°43'E., 38 km W. of Tuross Head, on Belimbla Ck; bushfires 1957 and 1968; drought 1954.

Belowra (*Co. Monteagle*) 34°18'S. 148°27'E., 14 km E. of Young; bushfire 1929; school 1885–92 and 1909–24; pop. 50 (1911).

Belubula (*Co. Bathurst*) 33°36'S. 148°33'E., 11 km W. of Canowindra; farming; PO 1915; telephone 1916; TX 1917; pop. 38 (1933).

Belubula (*Co. Bathurst*) see also Burnt Yards.

Bemboka (*Co. Auckland*) 36°38'S. 149°34'E., 25 km W. of Bega; Colombo till 1886, Brown Mountain till 1887, Lyttleton till 1894; surveyed 1876, village gaz. 1877 as Colombo, lots sold 1884; dairying, pig farming, timber, maize, oats, sorghum; Angl. C. b. 1872 by Patrick O'Connor, demolished and replaced 1889, demolished 1929, new one (Christ) b. 1930 by R.W. Thatcher, d. by John Burcham Clamp and Clifford Horace Finch; bridge 1967, over Colombo Ck; bushfires 1868, 1907, 1919, 1939, 1952, 1985; butter factories:

Bemboka Co-op. Butter Co. Ltd 1905 (replacement b. 1925–27 by R.E. Midson, closed 1978) and West End Creamery Co-op. Co. Ltd; carriage-works (Michael J. Condon); cemetery, incl. columbarium; FB (station b. 2012); fire 1911; flood 1971; PO 1871, new one b. 1906 by William Manning, repairs 1925 by E. Fletcher; powerhouse (hydro-electric) b. 1942–44; PS b. 1885 by Peter Manning, additions and alterations 1956; 2 reservoirs; Rom. Cath. C. (St Columbkille's) 1872, new one b. 1884 by Blunt, new one (St Columba's) b. 1908 by H.J. Wilton; sale-yards 1883; sawmills: F.A. Alcock, Fulton's, George Sydney Rayner 1921, burnt down; school (Brown Mountain till 1878, Colombo till 1879, Benbooka till 1880, Brown Mountain till 1896) 1877, new one b. 1882 by J. Malcolm, extended 1884, relocated 1896 by William Manning, extended 1900 and 1910, additions 1914 by H.J. Wilton, repairs 1920 also by Wilton, new one b. 1924 by Wilton, burnt down 1932, replacement b. 1933 by A. Whitely, additions 1984 and 2010; telegraph 1886; TX 1912, automatic 1961; water reticulation 1955; Wes. Meth. C. 1900; pop. 277 (1891), 323 (1901), 593 (1911), 458 (1921), 361 (1933), 495 (1947), 356 (1954), 292 (1961), 220 (1986), 222 (1991), 262 (1996), 244 (2001), 249 (2006), 307 (2011). (See also Old Bemboka.)

Bena (*Co. Gipps*) 33°32'S. 147°09'E., 44 km N. of West Wyalong, on Humbug Ck; grazing; bridge over Humbug Ck; cemetery (78 graves 1893+); grasshopper infestation 1900; PO 1897; silo; telephone 1908; pop. 63 (1901), 136 (1911), 68 (1933), 65 (1954).

Benalla (*Co. Durham*) 32°26'S. 151°19'E., 20 km NE of Singleton.

Benana Plains (*Co. Bligh*) see Hannahs Bridge.

Benandarah (*Co. St Vincent*) 35°39'S. 150°14'E., 8 km NE of Batemans Bay, on Kioloa Ck; timber and dairying; PO 1905; sawmills: Mervyn Backhouse, Francis Guy, Riley and Ireland (bought 1907 by R. McMillan), Ryan Bros; school 1890–1902 and 1954–70; telephone 1907; TX 1924, automatic 1974; pop. 59 (1933), 61 (1947), 65 (1954), 65 (1961), 596 (2006).

Benanee (*Co. Taila*) 34°31'S. 142°50'E., 68 km W. of Balranald; RS (Victorian railway), closed; pop. 155 (1933).

Benarba (*Co. Benarba*) see Weemelah.

Benarca (*Co. Cadell*) 35°58'S. 144°43'E., 16 km N. of Moama; RS (Victorian railway).

Benaroon (*Co. Harden*) 34°27'S. 148°22'E., 10 km N. of Murrumburrah; PO 1927–30.

Benbooka (*Co. Auckland*) see Bemboka.

Ben Buckley (*Co. Wellington*) 32°28'S. 149°16'E., 27 km SW of Gulgong, on Cudgegong R.

Ben Buckley (*Co. Wellington*) see also Twelve Mile.

Ben Bullen (*Co. Roxburgh*) 33°13'S. 150°01'E., 16 km N. of Portland, on Crown Ridge Ck; farming and grazing; PO 1889, new one b. 1914; quarries: Ben Bullen Lime Co. Ltd (acquired 1915 by G. & C. Hoskins Ltd), NSW Lime Co. 1889–1922 (taken over 1900 by Joseph Edwards, Robert Vernon Saddington and J.M. Dixon, acquired 1908 by G. & C. Hoskins Ltd), No. 3 (G. & C. Hoskins Ltd) 1916–21; RS 1882, station b. by William Cameron and John Briton, closed 1974, derelict; school 1883–94; telephone 1915; tramways (to quarries); TX 1924–65; pop. 78 (1901), 93 (1911), 108 (1933), 85 (1947), 108 (1954), 53 (1961).

Bendabo (*Co. Urana*) see Urangeline East.

Bendalong (*Co. St Vincent*) 35°15'S. 150°32'E., 12 km SW of Sussex Inlet, on Tasman Sea; (incl. Red Head); mining (silica till 1926, and kaolin) and tourism; bushfires 1994, 2001, 2006; FB 1958; PO: Bendalong 1960–78 and Red Head 1881–85; 2 quarries; sawmills: Goodlet and Smith (moved 1884 to Kioloa), Kirton & Earnshaw Ltd 1920–23, Allen Taylor & Co. Ltd 1905; telephone 1960; TX; wharf (Kirton & Earnshaw Ltd); pop. 15 (1961), 630 (2011).

Bendalong North (*Co. St Vincent*) 35°14'S. 150°32'E., 11 km SW of Sussex Inlet, on Tasman Sea; quarry.

Bendeela (*Co. Camden*) 34°44'S. 150°28'E., 18

km SE of Bundanoon, on Kangaroo R.; FB; pondage 1973, 59 ft (18 m) high; power station (hydro-electric) 1977; school 1878–1908; pop. 51 (1901), 6 (1921), 30 (1933), 19 (1947), 57 (1954).

Bendemeer (*Co. Inglis*) 30°53'S. 151°09'E., 31 km NE of Tamworth, on Macdonald R.; town gaz. 1851, surveyed 1852 by John James Galloway, designated as chief town of the county, bypassed by highway 1985; gold, later fossicking, farming, grazing; Angl. C. (St Stephen's) 1923, closed, sold and reused 2015; brick-kiln (Archie Hamilton); bridges: one (laminated arch) b. 1863–65 by David Baillie, d. by William Christopher Bennett, lattice girder, 360 ft (109.7 m), replacement (Dare composite timber truss) b. 1905 by Walter Frank Oakes, 302 ft (92 m), bypassed and reused 1985, new one (Muluerindie Bridge, concrete) b. 1985 by Guy Dickensen, over Macdonald R., T.A. Perry Bridge over Macdonald R., Perrys Pond Bridge over Perrys Ck; cemetery (344 graves 1873+) 1881; CH (incl. lock-up) b. 1874 by William Cains; droughts 1880–81, 1918–19, 1946–47, 1965–66, 1980–82; FB; fires 1883, 1905, 1915; floods 1864, 1893, 1910, 1962; flour mill (James M'Lean) b. 1859 by August Stahlhut; foot-bridge over Macdonald R.; lock-up b. 1859 by August Stahlhut, d. by T.A. Perry; PO 1852, new one b. 1894 by Robert Dixon, new one b. 1946 by Harry Truman; pound (stock) 1865; PS 1873; reservoir (concrete), 150,000 gal. (681.9 kl), 1963; Rom. Cath. C. 1881, new one (Holy Innocents) b. 1968 by G.G. Cooper & Sons Pty Ltd, d. by Fowell, Mansfield, Jarvis & Maclurcan Pty Ltd; sawmills: John Faint and James Michie, Farrell's 1953, Mulligan's, Darrel O'Toole and Bill Doring 1946–52, Harley Priest 1953 (sold 1958 to Bernie Reid); school 1860 b. by August Stahlhut, new buildings b. 1883 by T. Murray, new one b. 1924 on new site by E.W. Anderson, additions 1963 and 2010; snowstorm 1864; storm 1937; tannery (Patrick Connor) 1856–83; telegraph 1861; TX 1915, automatic 1955; Unit. C. (St Andrew's, orig. Presb.) b. 1865 by August Stahlhut; water supply filtration and reticulation 1963; wool-scour and fellmongery (Edward Ford Hodder), burnt down 1880; pop. *c.*150 (1866), 110 (1871), 173 (1891), 242 (1901), 368 (1911), 294 (1933), 369 (1947), 482 (1954), 476 (1961), 209 (1971), 231 (1981), 224 (1986), 247 (1991), 265 (1996), 225 (2001), 221 (2006), 478 (2011).

Bendenine (*Co. Harden*) 34°39'S. 148°46'E., 24 km S. of Boorowa; pop. 81 (1901).

Bendenine (*Co. Harden*)
see also Limestone Creek (*Co. King*).

Bendethera (*Co. Dampier*) 35°57'S. 149°45'E., 30 km W. of Moruya, on Con Ck; mines: Bendethera Gossan (George's) *c.*1890 and Bendethera Silver Prospect (Bendethera Silver Mining Co.) *c.*1890.

Bendick Morell (*Co. Monteagle*)
see Bendick Murrell.

Bendick Morrell (*Co. Monteagle*)
see Bendick Murrell.

Bendick Murrell (*Co. Monteagle*) 34°10'S. 148°27'E., 22 km NE of Young, on Wambanumba Ck; Bendick Morell till 1887; farming and orchards; Angl. C. (St Andrew's) b. 1906 by Stewart, closed 2012, sold 2014 and 2016; FB; mouse plague 1922; PO 1898, new one b. 1920, burnt down 1952; PS 1925; Rom. Cath. C. (St Catherine's) b. 1923 by Hugh Robert Blackett and W. Simpson, d. by Frederick James Purvis, closed, sold and reused; RS (Marengo till 1889, then Bendick Morrell till 1915) 1888, station closed and demolished; school 1884, relocated 1886, additions 1923 by Henry Ford, closed 2009, sold 2012; silo 1935; telephone 1911; TX 1917, automatic 1974; pop. 110 (1891), 117 (1901), 193 (1911), 272 (1921), 235 (1933), 262 (1947), 258 (1954), 171 (1961), 303 (2011).

Bendolba (*Co. Durham*) 32°20'S. 151°44'E., 9 km N. of Dungog; farming and dairying; Angl. C. 1861, repairs 1874 and 1878, replacement (St Peter's) b. 1885 by Lamplough and Peete, d. by John Wiltshire Pender, renovations 1923 and 1967, and graveyard (209 graves), incl. columbarium; PO 1877; school 1856–68 and 1883–1919; telephone 1906; TX 1939–

61; pop. 95 (1901), 90 (1911), 108 (1933), 84 (1947), 73 (1954), 89 (1961), 228 (2011).

Bendoura (*Co. St Vincent*) 35°31'S. 149°41'E., 13 km SW of Braidwood, on Back Ck; farming; airfield; PO 1927–30; quarry; school 1895–1919; telephone 1914; TX 1933–43; pop. 20 (1933).

Benefield (*Co. Wallace*) 36°03'S. 148°38'E., 48 km NW of Cooma.

Beneree (*Co. Bathurst*) 33°29'S. 149°06'E., 9 km SW of Millthorpe, on Lumpy Swamp Ck; Angl. C. (St David's), repairs 1911; goldmines: Lumpy Lead <1882, The Blacksmiths <1882, Tigeroo Shaft <1882; school 1879 b. by John Wadsworth Ashworth, extended 1880 by Thomas Taylor, additions 1883 by Edward Lawler, additions 1886 by James Prior Hull, renovations 1918 by C. Archer, closed 1941, sold and reused; telephone 1915; TX 1915–60; pop. 106 (1901), 61 (1954), 59 (1961).

Benerembah (*Co. Sturt*) 34°26'S. 145°49'E., 23 km NW of Darlington Point; RS 1887–1975, station removed 1984; TX (automatic); pop. 50 (1901), 65 (1911), 181 (1947), 262 (1954), 316 (1961), 429 (2011).

Bengalla (*Co. Arrawatta*) 28°39'S. 150°40'E., 29 km E. of Boggabilla, on Dumaresq R.; village gaz. 1863, never developed.

Bengalla (*Co. Brisbane*) 32°15'S. 150°53'E., 2 km NW of Muswellbrook; boiling-down works (Capt. David Charles Frederick Scott); coalmine; pop. 85 (1933), 57 (1954), 129 (1961).

Bengarralong (*Co. Wynyard*) 35°03'S. 148°09'E., 4 km E. of Gundagai, on Murrumbidgee R.; grazing; boiling-down works (Tooth's).

Bengelala (*Co. St Vincent*) see Falls Creek.

Bengerang (*Co. Benarba*) 29°03'S. 149°27'E., 46 km E. of Mungindi; cotton; RS 1914, station b. by Roberts, closed 1975; Union C.

Ben Halls Place (*Co. Ashburnham*) 33°13'S. 147°54'E., 20 km NW of Forbes.

Beni (*Co. Lincoln*) 32°12'S. 148°45'E., 15 km NE of Dubbo, on Talbragar R.; village gaz. 1917; farming and grazing; PO 1881; Rom. Cath. C. 1882, restored 1898, new one (St Aidan's) 1927; RS 1918–74; school 1882–1948; telephone 1923; TX 1936; typhoid 1900; pop. 221 (1901), 178 (1911), 107 (1933), 74 (1947), 57 (1954), 81 (1961), 437 (2011).

Benkennie (*Co. Camden*) see Camden.

Ben Lomond (*Co. Hardinge*) 30°01'S. 151°40'E., 22 km N. of Guyra, on Moredun Ck; wool, vegetables, corn, oats; airfield (2 km NE); Angl. C. 1897, closed and moved to Glencoe, replaced (St Paul's) 1926; cemetery (53 graves) 1892; electricity 1956; FB 1958; landslip 1886; PO 1879; pound (stock) 1879; Presb. C. 1908; PS 1881; rifle range 1921; Rom. Cath. C. (St Patrick's) b. 1928 by Vincent Doran, d. by Peter Joseph Gannon, and graveyard (73 graves 1896+); RS 1884, station b. by Nathan Cohen & Co., closed 1988; sawmill (water powered) 1877–79 b. by M'Innes and Pickering (waterwheel d. and b. by Henry Sheldon Goddard) for Christopher Thomas Bagot, demolished 1880; school (Sidebrook till 1900) 1889, additions 1922 and 1962; pop. 299 (1901), 300 (1911), 279 (1933), 190 (1947), 324 (1954), 364 (1961), 389 (2006), 436 (2011).

Benmore (*Co. Harden*) 34°32'S. 148°24'E., 5 km NE of Murrumburrah; quarry; school 1891–1950.

Bennetts Green (*Co. Northumberland*) see Windale.

Bennetts Springs (*Co. King*) 34°01'S. 148°51'E., 25 km SE of Cowra; telephone 1907; pop. 20 (1933).

Bensville (*Co. Northumberland*) 33°30'S. 151°23'E., 4 km W. of MacMasters Beach, on Cockle Ck; (incl. South Kincumber); settled by Thomas Humphreys; farming; cemetery; Community C. (Coast); Jehovah's Witnesses C.; PO: Bensville 1927–76 and South Kincumber 1927; Rom. Cath. C. (Holy Cross) b. 1838–42 by Michael Burns and James Taylor, renovations 1893 by Michael Burns, now seldom used, new one (Holy Spirit) 2009, and graveyard (burials 1841+); shipyard (Benjamin Davis); telephone: Bensville 1926 and South Kincumber 1927; water reticulation 1979; wharf (Hastings); pop. 196 (1933), 219 (1947), 224 (1954), 242 (1961), 3,288 (2011).

Bentley (*Co. Rous*) 28°47'S. 153°07'E., 11 km NE of Casino, on Back Ck; timber, vegetables, dairying, pigs; bushfire 1953; Church of Christ, reused; FB; PO 1912; RS 1906–75; sawmills: Bennett and Badham, and Bentley Sawmilling Co. (estab. 1948 by Herbert Reginald Hartley and Owen George Casson, burnt down 1951, rebuilt); telephone 1915; TX 1925, automatic 1953; pop. 316 (1933), 300 (1947), 246 (1954), 287 (1961).

Benton (*Co. Hunter*) see Central Macdonald.

Ben Venue (*Co. Sandon*) see Armidale.

Berambing (*Co. Cook*) 33°32'S. 150°27'E., 19 km E. of Mount Victoria, on Hungerfords Ck; settled 1830 by George Meares Countess Bowen; electricity 1954; sawmill (Ian Hungerford); telephone 1949; TX 1950–73.

Berambong (*Co.* Wakool) 35°02'S. 143°57'E., 67 km N. of Barham; RS (Victorian railway), closed.

Beranghi (*Co. Macquarie*) 31°13'S. 152°55'E., 7 km SW of Crescent Head, on Connection Ck; telephone 1926; TX 1926–45.

Berawinnia Downs (*Co. Thoulcanna*) 29°10'S. 143°38'E., 122 km NW of Bourke.

Berebangalo (*Co. King*) 34°51'S. 149°11'E., 24 km E. of Yass; formerly spelt as Berrebangalo; sheep farming, fruit; school 1882–94, moved 1906 to Lade Vale.

Bereen (*Co. Murchison*) 30°14'S. 150°25'E., 25 km NW of Barraba, on Horton R.; Angl. C. (St Mark's) 1913.

Bereena (*Co. Wynyard*) 35°06'S. 148°01'E., 9 km SW of Gundagai; bushfire 1979.

Berembed Weir (*Co. Bourke*) 34°53'S. 146°50'E., 20 km W. of Ganmain, on Murrumbidgee R.; earth tremor 1938; PO 1908–11; school 1908–10; weir 1910 d. by Ernest Macartney de Burgh, extensively modified 1977, on Murrumbidgee R.

Berendebba (*Co. Bland*) 33°57'S. 147°45'E., 37 km W. of Grenfell; electricity 1949; RS 1916–75, station removed 1976; silo 1934; telephone 1923; TX 1925–44; pop. 47 (1933).

Beresfield (*Co. Northumberland*) 32°48'S. 151°39'E., 8 km SE of East Maitland, on Viney Ck; limited development till 1945+; Angl. C. b. 1955 by Arthur Sheppard, new one (St Paul's) 1980; Bapt. C. 1985; colliery (Kent Collieries Pty Ltd), subsidence resulted in closure; Cong. C. b. 1928 by H.R. Brooks; crematorium (Newcastle Memorial Park) b. 1936 by Norman R. Smith, d. by Louis S. Robertson & Son, alterations 1977, and columbarium; metal fabrication works (Hunter Stainless Steel), removed from Morpeth; PO 1927; poultry processing plant (Baiada Poultry Pty Ltd); Presb. C. (St David's); PS 1975; quarry; railway collision (damaged station) 1997; Rom. Cath. C. (Our Lady of Lourdes) 1977 d. by John Kevin Gannon; RS 1925; school (Upper Hexham till 1888 then Tarro till 1926) 1883 b. by John Shaw, additions 1937, 1959, 1966, 1973; pop. 213 (1933), 617 (1947), 1,420 (1954), 3,078 (2011).

Beresford (*Co. Wellesley*) 36°49'S. 149°27'E., 23 km NE of Bombala; school 1888–1906.

Bergalia (*Co. Dampier*) 35°59'S. 150°06'E., 9 km S. of Moruya; settled 1834 by Alexander Weatherhead; goldmining (gold disc. 1865) 1865–*c.*1870, wheat, maize, dairying; bushfires 1884, 1952, 1965; cheese factory (Union) b. 1893 by J. Ross and J. Constable for Bergalia Co-op. Dairy Co. Ltd, removed 1914 and reused, replaced 1914 by Charles Stewart, taken over 1941, closed 1942; PO 1869–1974; school 1870, new one b. 1871 by George Wright, repairs 1891 by J. and W.C. Anderson, closed 1931; telephone 1908; TX 1927–74; pop. 67 (1901), 123 (1911), 79 (1933), 66 (1947), 90 (1954), 77 (1961), 189 (2011).

Bergen-Op-Zoom (*Co. Vernon*) 30°58'S. 151°33'E., 5 km NW of Walcha, on Bergen-Op-Zoom Ck; FB.

Beri (*Co. Wellington*) 33°00'S. 149°00'E., 15 km NE of Molong; wheat, barley, oats, grapes; Angl. C. (Holy Trinity), renovations 1899 by W. Carroll; boiling-down works (E.C. Cousins).

Berida (*Co. Ewenmar*) 31°39'S. 148°37'E., 21 km W. of Gilgandra; pop. 60 (1911).

Berida (*Co. Ewenmar*) see also Kamber.

Berinba (*Co. Murray*) see Yass.

Berkeley (*Co. Camden*) 34°29'S. 150°51'E., 5 km W. of Port Kembla, on Lake Illawarra; (incl. South Berkeley and West Berkeley); orig. Fishing Village, then Fishtown; surveyed 1816 by James Meehan, settled 1817 by Robert Jenkins, subdivided in 1880s; orig. agric. and cattle, then fishing and dairying; Angl. C. (St Philip's) 1862–77, new one 1958, removed 1960, replacement b. 1964 by Des Herraman, and graveyard; Apostolic C. (Illawarra Family Life) 1981; Buddhist C. (Fokuangshan Nan Tien) 1995; 54 coke-ovens 1889, demolished; crematorium; Foursquare Gospel C. (International Christ.); Jehovah's Witnesses C.; 2 jetties; Lutheran C. (St Mark's) 1964; Meth. C. 1958; migrant hostel 1951–67; PO 1957; Pentecostal C.; PS 1974; quarry; reservoirs: No. 1 (concrete) 1,013,600 gal. (4,607.8 kl) 1933 and No. 2 (concrete) 6,000,000 gal. (27,276 kl) 1940; Rom. Cath. C. (St Mary's) b. 1965 by Laurie Hughes, d. by Tony Goode; Salv. Army C.; schools: Berkeley 1858–92, reopened 1907, new building (removed from Port Kembla by J. Knight) 1918, additions 1955 by Graham and Hughes, additions 1966 and 2010, Illawarra Sports HS (Berkeley HS till 1998) 1957, additions 1960, 1990, 1993, South Berkley 1962–2010, sold, West Berkeley 1959, additions 1960, 1963, 1966; tank traps (World War II); Unit. C. (orig. Meth.) 1964; pop. 89 (1936), 140 (1937), 103 (1947), 152 (1954), 5,329 (1961, incl. 741 in migrant hostel), 9,170 (1966), 7,413 (2006), 7,427 (2011).

Berkeley Vale (*Co. Northumberland*) 33°21'S. 151°26'E., 12 km NE of Gosford, on Chittaway Bay; (incl. Fountaindale and Glenning Valley); farming and citrus orchards; bridges: one b. 1906 and replaced (Lees Bridge) 1980, over Ourimbah Ck, and one over Chittaway Ck; Assemblies of God C. (Bayside Christ. Life); bushfire 1944; cemetery (Ronkana, 77 graves 1926+); Church of Christ 1983; concrete plants: Boral Ltd, Easymix, Hymix; engineering works: Avoca Engineering Pty Ltd and Steelworks Engineering Pty Ltd; FB; food factories: Masterfoods 1992 and Sanitarium Health Food Co.; foot-bridges: one over Berkeley Ck and one b. 2014 to Killarney Vale, over Tumbi Umbi Ck; greeting card factory (Koala Publishing); house frame and truss factories: AusSteel Frames Central Coast and National Frame & Truss; jetty; PO 1927; sawmill (Phillip Maloney); schools: Berkeley Vale 1930, additions 1933 by G. Dixon, additions 1973 and 1979, Fountaindale 1883–91, Tuggerah Lakes Secondary College (Berkeley Vale Community HS till 2002) 1983, additions 1986; sewerage 1978; telephone 1925; TX, closed 1931; water reticulation 1964; pop. 233 (1933), 257 (1947), 246 (1954), 264 (1961), 11,167 (2011).

Berkley Park (*Co. Durham*) 32°34'S. 151°48'E., 19 km NW of Karuah, on Williams R.

Berlang (*Co. St Vincent*) 35°39'S. 149°39'E., 26 km SW of Braidwood; school Jan.-Sept. 1871.

Bermaguee (*Co. Dampier*) see Bermagui.

Bermagui (*Co. Dampier*) 36°25'S. 150°05'E., 23 km S. of Narooma, on Tasman Sea; (incl. North Bermagui and South Bermagui); settled in 1830s, planned 1867, village gaz. 1868 as Bermaguee; whaling estab. by William Duggan Tarlinton, seaport 1858+, gold (disc. 1880), agric., timber, dairying, oysters, now mainly fishing and tourism, retirement centre; airport 1936; ambulance station; Angl. C. (All Saints') b. 1911 by A.H. Preddy; Bapt. C. 1977; boiling-down works (William Duggan Tarlinton) 1843–51; breakwater 1959; bridge 1981, over Bermagui R.; bushfire 1952; cemetery 1888, incl. columbarium; diphtheria 1923 and 1939; earth tremor 2013; electricity 1949; FB; flood 1919; freezing works (Smithers Bros) 1914–17; harbour 1958; jetty, 210 ft (64 m), 1969; marina; PO: Bermagui 1883 and South Bermagui 1900–98; pottery (Mudworks) estab. 1985 by Mike and Kim Collingham; PS 1880, new one b. 1907 by W. Manning, new one 1977; reservoir; Rom. Cath. C. (Our Lady Help of Christians) 1953; sawmills: Alexander Percival Beare (fire 1927, sold 1940 to Clyde Sawmilling Co., closed 1975, sold 1977), McMillan Bros (moved 1905 to Corunna), Thomas Moorehead, Reed Bros 1908, George E. Thornton (taken over 1907 by C. Innes); school 1883, additions 1928 by W. Tapper, additions 1960, 1966, 1969, 2010; sewerage 1975; shipyard (William Christian); telephone: Bermagui 1888, North Bermagui 1954, South Bermagui 1891; TX: Bermagui 1916 and South Bermagui 1917, automatic 1959; Union C. b. 1889 by James Geiss, re-roofed and repaired, now only used by Bapt. and Unit.; water reticulation 1955, augmentation 1970 and 1985; wattle-bark mill (Craig, Mostyn & Co.); whaling station (William Duggan Tarlinton); wharves: one b. 1879 by T. Moorhead and one b. 1888, extended 1901, demolished 1971; pop. *c.*100 (1887), 174 (1891), 398 (1901), 374 (1911), 316 (1921), 332 (1933), 544 (1947), 561 (1954), 613 (1961), 556 (1976), 827 (1981), 995 (1986), 1,166 (1991), 1,196 (1996), 1,320 (2001), 1,298 (2006), 1,471 (2011).

Bernard (*Co. Georgiana*) 34°17'S. 149°28'E., 20 km N. of Crookwell; grazing; PO 1927–31; telephone 1914; TX; pop. 28 (1933).

Berrambool (*Co. Auckland*) see Merimbula.

Berrara (*Co. St Vincent*) see Cudmirrah.

Berrebangalo (*Co. King*) see Berebangalo.

Berrellan (*Co. St Vincent*) see Brundee.

Berremangra (*Co. Harden*) 34°48'S. 148°29'E., 29 km S. of Murrumburrah; Berrmemgura till 1893; farming and grazing; PO 1895; school 1959–68; telephone 1910; TX 1911, automatic 1956; pop. 58 (1911), 63 (1933), 60 (1954), 117 (1961), 174 (2006).

Berrico (*Co. Gloucester*) 32°04'S. 151°49'E., 15 km SW of Gloucester, on Berrico Ck; farming and grazing; PO 1927–42; RS (11 km E.) 1934–75; sawmill (Carson's Northern Timber Co. Ltd) 1935, removed from Cedar Brush Creek, closed 1943; school 1899–1913; telephone 1913; TX 1946.

Berrico Junction (*Co. Gloucester*) 32°03'S. 151°57'E., 6 km S. of Gloucester, on Avon R.

Berridale (*Co. Wallace*) 36°22'S. 148°50'E., 19 km E. of Jindabyne, on Myack Ck; Gegedzerick till 1886; settled 1827, estab. 1863 by William Oliver; copper (disc. 1872), farming, grazing; Angl. C.: All Saints' b. 1910 by S.E. Carbine, d. by Edmund Cooper Manfred and St Mary the Virgin b. 1849–60 by Gray and J. Roddan, restored and vestry added 1912, church re-roofed; bushfire 1940; cemetery (878 graves 1842+) 1867, incl. columbaria; earth tremor 2019; electricity (from Cooma) 1951; FB (new station b. 2012); Meth. C. d. by George Allen Mansfield; PO 1869; PS 1896, new ones 1957 and 1974; 3 quarries; Rom. Cath. C. (St Joseph's) 1915 d. by George Donald Cochran; school 1883, new one b. 1884 by Montgomery and Reidy, repairs 1898 by Bottom and Avery, additions 1965, 1967, 1995, 2010; sewerage 1971; telegraph 1890; TX 1910, automatic 1958; Unit. C. (orig. Presb.) b. 1890 by Henry Hoskins, renamed St Stephen's in 1977, closed, sold 2009; water supply augmentation 1956 and 1991; winery (Snowy River); pop. 165 (1901), 425 (1911), 201 (1933), 338 (1947), 434 (1954), 576 (1961), 625 (1966), 521 (1971), 554 (1976), 695 (1981), 670 (1986), 912 (2011).

Berrigal (*Co. Courallie*) 29°57'S. 150°08'E., 53 km NE of Narrabri; pop. 66 (1911), 61 (1933), 62 (2006).

Berrigan (*Co. Denison*) 35°40'S. 145°48'E., 21 km E. of Finley; settled *c.*1854, estab. 1888, surveyed 1889 by William Creed, village gaz. 1890, irrigation 1939; wheat, wool, rice, citrus fruit, sorghum; agric. implement works (incl. H. Davies and M'Guigan's); airfield; ambulance station 1953–2008, sold and reused; Angl. C. (St Aidan's) 1902; Bible Christ. C. 1896, damaged 1901; brick-kiln (acquired 1899 by W. Grenell); bushfire 1892; carriage-works: E. Burwood, F. Ben Carter, Andy M'Guigan; cemetery 1892; CH (incl. lock-up) 1892, new one 1895; cordial factory; earth tremor 1921; FB 1900 (station b. 1995); fires 1894, 1895, 1897, 1899, 1914, 1931, 1943; flood 1939; gale 1923; hospital (War Memorial) 1953, additions 1986, redeveloped 2008; hurricane (damaged nearly every building) 1901; PO 1885, new one b. 1901 by R.L. Thompson, additions and alterations

1928 by E.W. Burwood; pound (stock) 1893; POW control centre 1944; powerhouse 1925; Presb. C. (St John's) b. 1897 by Lapthorne Bros, d. by M'Donald, closed, sold and reused; PS 1891, new one b. 1892 by Livings Bros; 2 quarries; reservoir (tower), 65,000 gal. (295.5 kl); Rom. Cath. C. (St Columba's) 1894, renovations 1917 by B. Burwood, new one 1967; RS 1896, station b. by Charles Baker, closed 1985, station removed 1987; sawmill (George Jamieson); school 1894, remodelled 1914 by B. Burwood, additions 1981, additions 2010 by Barker Constructions Pty Ltd; silo 1922; soap-works (Rudolph G. Struck); streets lit 1892, lit by acetylene 1902; telegraph 1891; TX 1909–78; typhoid 1907 (2 died) and 1908; Unit. C. (Wesley, orig. Meth.) 1953 d. by William C. Brown and E.B. Mowbray; water supply 1924, augmentation 1955 and 1976; Wes. Meth. C. 1896; pop. 254 (1891), 523 (1901), 1,090 (1911), 756 (1933), 698 (1947), 787 (1954), 914 (1961), 924 (1966), 950 (1971), 952 (1976), 960 (1981), 993 (1986), 949 (1991), 1,015 (1996), 929 (2001), 899 (2006), 921 (2011).

Berrigan (*Co. Denison*) see also Lalalty.

Berrima (*Co. Camden*) 34°29'S. 150°20'E., 8 km W. of Bowral, on Wingecarribee R.; Bong Bong till 1837; disc. and surveyed 1829 by Major Sir Thomas Livingstone Mitchell, laid out 1831 by Robert Hoddle, designated as chief town of the county, declined 1867+ (bypassed by railway), village trust estab. 1963, bypassed by highway 1989; wheat 1820s+ and grazing, then peas, turnips, potatoes, maize, oats, barley, rye, dairying 1867+, minerals, now tourist craft village; abattoir (Berrima Dist. Meat Works) 1963–94; Angl. C. (Holy Trinity) b. 1847–49 by William Munro, d. by Edmund Thomas Blacket, re-roofed 1897, and graveyard; brewery (Oldbury, James J. Atkinson) 1858; bridge (first) destroyed, second one b. 1836 by David Lennox, damaged 1858, destroyed 1860, replacement b. 1860 by Matthews and Jennings, damaged 1873, destroyed 1897, replacement b. 1897 by Thomas Loveridge and Herbert Charles Hudson, demolished and replaced again (in concrete) 1962, over Wingecarribee R.; bushfires 1884, 1946, 1951, 1952; cemetery (graves 1833+); CH b. 1835–38 by Young & Co., d. by Mortimer William Lewis, closed 1889, renovated 1925 for reuse, alterations and renovations 1936 by John Crocker Burnett, reused 1936, restored 1976; convict stockade; earth tremor 1934; electricity 1928; eucalyptus oil distillery; FB; floods 1858, 1860, 1873, 1897; gaol b. 1835–39, d. by G.T. Bullar, walls and gateway b. 1863–68 by Richard Nicholls Matthews, d. by James Johnstone Barnet, incl. 3 underground cells, gaol alterations 1901, closed 1909, reused 1914–19 as German internment and POW camp, reused again 1942, fire 1942, rebuilt 1945–49, reopened 1949 as a training centre, additions 1991, closed 2011, reopened 2016; oil-shale works estab. during World War II by Arnold Stanley Taylor, derelict; PO 1829, new one b. 1887 by Richard Nicholls Matthews; pound (stock), closed 1910; Presb. C. (Finlayson Memorial) b. 1867 by James Powell, but not used as a church till 1929, additions 1935, closed, sold 1993, reused; PS b. 1877 by Richard Nicholls Matthews, additions and alterations 1931, closed 1936; 2 quarries; reservoir 1939; Rom. Cath. C. (St Scholastica's) b. 1849–51 by William Munro, d. by Augustus Welby Northmore Pugin, renamed St Francis Xavier's, closed 1973, reopened 1984; sawmills: Berrima Sawmills Pty Ltd (estab. by Arnold Stanley Taylor), Hardwoods Ltd 1920, T.P. Owen 1921; school 1855–62, reopened and new one b. 1869 by Richard Nicholls Matthews, d. by George Allen Mansfield, re-roofed 1893 by McDonald and Moss, additions 1953 by Hughes Bros; sewerage augmentation 1990; telegraph 1858, repairs to office 1865 by R.N. Matthews; toll-house b. 1861 by Richard Nicholls Matthews; TX 1929; water supply augmentation 1964 and 1988; weir on Wingecarribee R.; whooping cough epidemic 1870; pop. 249 (1841), 377 (1846), 192 (1851), 188 (1856), 394 (1861), 475 (1871), 444 (1881),

495 (1891), 305 (1901), 161 (1911), *c.*80 (1914), 330 (1933), 450 (1947), 792 (1954), 596 (1971), 654 (1976), 685 (1981), 654 (1986), 723 (1991), 815 (1996), 879 (2001), 868 (2006). (See also New Berrima.)

Berrima Colliery (*Co. Camden*) see Medway.

Berrima Junction (*Co. Camden*) 34°32'S. 150°23'E., 3 km N. of Moss Vale.

Berringer Lake (*Co. St Vincent*) see Cunjurong Point.

Berrioye (*Co. Nandewar*) 30°31'S. 150°16'E., 30 km NE of Boggabri, on Maules Ck; sawmill 1937; school 1957–69; telephone 1937; TX 1937.

Berrmemgura (*Co. Harden*) see Berremangra.

Berry (*Co. Camden*) 34°47'S. 150°42'E., 14 km NE of Nowra, on Broughton Mill Ck; Broughton's Creek till 1888; surveyed 1882, estab. 1883 as private town by David Berry, laid out 1883 by James Wilson, founded 1884, thrived in 1880s, first subdivision 1892, bypassed by highway 2017; wheat, potatoes, maize, timber, dairying, butter, cheese, pigs, root crops; ambulance station 2018; Angl. C. (St Luke's) 1885, and columbarium; artificial breeding station 1951, moved 1958; bacon factory (L. Geoghegan) 1884; bridge (timber) 1871, 176 ft (53.6 m), new one 1912, replacement (concrete girder spans) 1955, over Broughton Mill Ck; bushfires 1895 and 1939; butter factory (Berry Central Factory) b. 1895 by Joseph Kennedy and Coward, d. by John Wright, became Berry Rural Co-op. Society Ltd in 1911, closed and reused; carriage-works (W.H. Cockerill) 1905–49; caterpillar infestation 1893; cemetery 1883, incl. columbarium; CH b. 1891 by Anton and Paul Ettingshausen, d. by James Johnstone Barnet, closed 1988, reused, sold 1995 to Anthony A. Graham, bought 1999 by Shoalhaven City Council, restored 2001, reused; confectionery factory (The Treat Factory) o. 1992 in former butter factory; cordial factory (Robert Bolt) 1894–1928; creamery (Berry Dairy Co.) 1889–1903; earth tremor 1930; electricity 1927; experiment farm 1912, became training farm for boys in 1934, additions 1959, closed 1977; FB: town fire brigade 1902 (new station b. 1990) and bushfire brigade 1957; fires 1920, 1961, 2004; floods 1873 and 1893; gales 1934 and 1951; hailstorm 1882; hospital (cottage) 1895, fire 1896, closed 1909, new one (David Berry Memorial) b. 1909 by G.F. Cole, d. by Howard Joseland and Walter Liberty Vernon, additions 1936 by N.R. Morris; lancer barracks 1896, extended 1898 by John Hay, closed, sold and reused; measles epidemic 1893; milk factory (Berry Rural Co-op. Society Ltd) 2016; PO 1861, new one b. 1879 by James Wilson, replacement b. 1886 by William Alfred Isley, additions 1887, repairs 1890 by A. Wolf, closed 1992 and reused, new one on new site; Presb. C. 1884, new one (Scots) b. 1934 by Henry White & Son, d. by Thomas J. Darling; PS (incl. lock-up) b. 1895 by J.H. Read, d. by Walter Liberty Vernon; reservoir (concrete), 480,000 gal. (2,182 kl); Rom. Cath. C. 1866, new one b. 1884–86 on new site, closed and reused, third one (St Patrick's) b. 1936 by H.A. Taylor, d. by Clement Glancey; RS 1893, station b. by Gerald Dalton Fetherston and Felix Edward Barbat; sale-yards; sawmills: Bill Binns, Jack Blow (sold to Blissett), Charlie Host, Malloy's 1913–17, Vous and Fox (taken over by Bill Hollands and Jimmy Ebner, bought out by Len Little who moved and renamed it Earlwood Sawmills, bought out by Noel Williams who renamed it Berry Sawmill, bought out 1978 by Davis & Herbert Pty Ltd, closed); school 1860, building relocated and reused, new buildings b. 1883 by Moore and Wolf, additions 1910 by Alexander Johnston, renovations 1925, additions 1954, 1963, 1965, 1974, 2010; sewage works 1976; tanneries: H. Bunce, and James Wilson and T.M. Richard 1857; telegraph 1877, new office b. 1879 by James Wilson, new one b. 1886 by William Alfred Isley, additions 1887, repairs 1890 by A. Wolf, closed 1992 and reused; TX 1911; Union C. 1861; Unit. C. (Gateway, orig. Meth.) b. 1932 by Whitwell Bros, d. by J.C.R. Mills; univ. (Wollongong, Graham Park Campus);

waterworks 1901; Wes. Meth. C. b. 1884 by Herbert Pettit, d. by William Boyd, reused; wharves: Double Wharf and Hardwood Wharf; winery (Jasper Valley Wines) 1976; pop. 26 (1841), *c.*600 (1850), *c.*300 (1866–68), 1,154 (1871), 1,288 (1881), 908 (1891), *c.*2,260 (1895), 1,990 (1901), 829 (1911), 2,628 (1933), 2,780 (1944), 2,777 (1947), 1,349 (1954), 869 (1961), 924 (1966), 1,049 (1971), 1,132 (1976), 1,220 (1981), 1,375 (1986), 1,570 (1991), 1,604 (1996), 1,597 (2001), 1,691 (2011).

Berrygill (*Co. Courallie*) 29°55'S. 150°07'E., 55 km NE of Narrabri; school 1952–69.

Berry Jerry (*Co. Bourke*) 34°42'S. 147°15'E., 14 km NE of Coolamon; farming; sawmill (Hardy's) 1874; Union C. 1883; pop. 211 (1911), 173 (1933).

Berry Jerry North (*Co. Bourke*) 34°42'S. 147°15'E., 14 km N. of Coolamon; farming; cemetery; FB; PO 1880; school (Berry Jerry till 1896) 1881–96 and 1913–43; telephone 1906; TX 1924–50; pop. 51 (1933), 101 (1947), 138 (1954), 81 (1961).

Berry Park (*Co. Northumberland*) see Thornton.

Berthong (*Co. Bland*) 34°20'S. 148°02'E., 25 km W. of Young; TX (automatic); pop. 71 (1911), 121 (2006).

Berween (*Co. Murchison*) 29°49'S. 150°35'E., 6 km NE of Bingara.

Beryl (*Co. Phillip*) 32°21'S. 149°27'E., 8 km W. of Gulgong; mining, grazing, hort.; bridge (Allan truss) 1927, 235 ft (71.6 m), over Wyaldra Ck; mines: Aust. Diamond Mines Co. 1867, 1899, 1900, 1902, Digger Prince (Digger Prince Mining Co. and Caledonian Gold Mining Co.) 1890, 1923–24, Fraser Lead 1870s, Louisa Lead <1875, Salvation Hill (Salvation Hill Gold Mining Co.) 1889, 1897, 1902–3, 1907; PO 1898; school 1881–1962; telephone 1917; TX 1920–64; Union C. 1909; pop. 196 (1901), 168 (1911), 128 (1933), 95 (1947), 80 (1954), 70 (1961).

Bessy Flat (*Co. Georgiana*) 33°51'S. 149°15'E., 36 km S. of Blayney, on Willow Glen Ck.

Bethanga Bridge (*Co. Goulburn*) see Lake Hume Village.

Bethel (*Co. Hume*) 33°52'S. 146°53'E., 11 km S. of Walla Walla; settled by German immigrants; cemetery; Lutheran C. (Trinity) 1926.

Betherwetherloo (*Co. Argyle*) 34°38'S. 149°32'E., 22 km NW of Goulburn, on Wollondilly R.

Bethungra (*Co. Clarendon*) 34°46'S. 147°51'E., 20 km SW of Cootamundra, on Ulandra Ck; town gaz. 1861; mining, grazing, agric.; Angl. C. (St Augustine's) 1905, renovations 1911, additions 1938 by F. Mitchell, d. by Frederick James Purvis, restored 1994; bushfires 1944, 1987, 2006; cemetery (90 graves) 1881; dam, 43 ft (13 m) high, 1895; PO 1875; pound (stock) 1862; PS 1878, new ones 1892 and 1900, closed and sold; railway barracks 1878; railway coal stage (removed from Cootamundra) 1878; railway spiral 1941–46; railway tunnel (No. 2), 82 yds (74.6 m), 1946; rifle range 1928; Rom. Cath. C. (St Peter's) 1899, new one b. 1918 by Davy, sold 1994, reused; RS 1878, station b. by A. and R. Amos, closed; scarlet fever 1886; school 1876, new buildings b. 1882 by G. Dobbyns, closed 1995, bought by Garry and Gaylene Crabtree, reused 2012; smelter (Wallace's) 1881; telegraph 1878; TX 1910; water supply augmentation 1985; pop. *c.*20 (1866), 249 (1891), 212 (1901), 361 (1911), 252 (1933), 280 (1947), 228 (1954), 184 (1961), 414 (2011).

Bettowynd (*Co. St Vincent*) 35°43'S. 149°48'E., 29 km S. of Braidwood; school 1881–89; pop. 58 (1901).

Bevendale (*Co. King*) 34°32'S. 149°07'E., 34 km W. of Crookwell, on Lachlan R.; Blakney Creek till 1887; Angl. C. (St Thomas's) 1871, rebuilt, and graveyard; PO 1879; school 1956–71; telephone 1915; TX 1916; pop. 97 (1933), 90 (1947), 105 (1954), 86 (1961), 98 (2006).

Beverley (*Co. Hardinge*) 30°06'S. 151°00'E., 11 km NW of Bundarra, on Gwydir R.

Bewong (*Co. St Vincent*) 35°05'S. 150°32'E., 9 km W. of Sanctuary Point, on Wandandian Ck; bushfire 2001; water supply 1984.

Bexhill (*Co. Rous*) 28°46'S. 153°21'E., 9 km NE

of Lismore, on Wilsons R.; orig. Bald Hill; village gaz. 1864; timber, beef, farming; boiling-down works (Percy Yager), burnt down 1909; brickworks (Lismore Dry Press Brick Co. Ltd) 1906, upgraded 1937; butter factory (Unara) 1891; cemetery (290 graves 1880+) 1886, incl. columbarium; FB (Boat Harbour); fire 1891; PO 1880, burnt down 1922 (in premises rented from Percy C. Yager), new premises rented; 3 quarries; RS 1894, station b. by Alexander Hamilton Scouller, closed 1974; school 1882, additions 1891 by B. Jackson; telephone 1891; TX 1923, automatic 1958; Unit. C. (Good Shepherd, orig. Meth.) b. 1926 by Walter W. Gaggin; Wes. Meth. C. b. 1885 by McDonald, closed and sold; pop. 393 (1891), 301 (1901), 354 (1911), 381 (1933), 260 (1947), 228 (1954), 249 (1961), 471 (2006), 485 (2011).

Biala (*Co. King*) 34°36'S. 149°15'E., 27 km SW of Crookwell, on Lampton Ck; telephone 1923; TX 1924, automatic 1951; pop. 87 (1933), 67 (1947), 68 (1961), 170 (2006).

Biamble (*Co. Gowen*) 31°46'S. 149°13'E., 33 km NW of Dunedoo.

Bibbenluke (*Co. Wellesley*) 36°49'S. 149°17'E., 12 km NE of Bombala, on Bombala R.; surveyed 1869 by Thomas Evans, first land sale and village gaz. 1870, subdivided 1911; wheat and hunting, then cattle, sheep, dairying, agric., fishing; Angl. C. (St Matthew's) o. 1933 in a building rebuilt as a church by Walter Allen and David Wilson; bridge (McDonald timber truss), b. 1889–91 by J.D. Huntress, 355 ft (108.2 m), planking renewed 1924, bridge replaced 1997, over Bombala R.; cemetery; floods 1872, 1919, 1934, 1971; PO 1870, burnt down 1899; Presb. C. (St John's) 1886, relocated 1911; PS, closed 1897; school 1881, new one b. 1929 by M.A. Allen, closed 2015; storms 1888 and 1915; telephone 1891; TX 1922, automatic 1954; pop. 182 (1901), 261 (1911), 220 (1933), 152 (1947), 112 (1954), 118 (1961), 179 (2006), 302 (2011).

Bibilah (*Co. Stapylton*) 28°52'S. 150°24'E., 29 km S. of Boggabilla; RS 1932–75.

Bickan (*Co. Lincoln*) see Mogriguy.

Bickley Vale (*Co. Camden*) 34°05'S. 150°40'E., 4 km SW of Camden.

Biddabah (*Co. Northumberland*) see Warners Bay.

Biddi (*Co. Wellesley*) 36°43'S. 148°32'E., 30 km SE of Thredbo.

Biddon (*Co. Gowen*) 31°34'S. 148°48'E., 21 km NE of Gilgandra; farming; earth tremor 2011; Meth. C. b. 1911 by Smirthwaite, reused; school 1954–72; telephone 1903; TX 1914; pop. 63 (1901), 60 (1911), 128 (1933), 101 (1947), 50 (1954), 52 (1961), 281 (2011).

Bidgeemia (*Co. Urana*) 35°27'S. 146°30'E., 33 km SW of Lockhart; farming; Community C. 1951, removed from Mangoplah; FB; PO 1927; school 1935–72; telephone 1924; TX 1927, automatic 1955; pop. 113 (1933), 74 (1947), 60 (1954), 55 (1961), 95 (2006).

Bidgermuniga (*Co. King*) 34°28'S. 148°48'E., 8 km E. of Boorowa, on Pipeclay Ck; agric.

Bielsdown (*Co. Fitzroy*) see Dorrigo.

Big Badja (*Co. Beresford*) 36°04'S. 149°31'E., 39 km NE of Cooma; gold (reef).

Big Ben (*Co. Wynyard*) 35°07'S. 148°06'E., 7 km S. of Gundagai; gold (alluvial); earth tremor 1871; pop. 57 (1901).

Big Bog (*Co. Wellesley*) 36°35'S. 149°24'E., 45 km SE of Cooma; farming; PO 1927–42; sawmill (Clarence R. Burke); telephone 1907; pop. 20 (1933).

Big Burney (*Co. St Vincent*) 35°16'S. 149°51'E., 21 km N. of Braidwood.

Big Creek (*Co. Durham*) see Hilldale.

Bigga (*Co. Georgiana*) 34°05'S. 149°09'E., 50 km SE of Cowra; founded by Tom McGuinness, village gaz. 1892; wool; Angl. C. b. 1885 by W. Ticker and J. Ralph, new one (All Saints') d. and b. 1906 by James Miller, and graveyard; bushfire 1900; cemetery; electricity 1952; FB 1932; grasshopper infestation 1934; PO 1861, burnt down 1923, new one 1955; PS 1924, new one b. 1934 by John Walton; Rom. Cath. C. (Our Lady of Fatima) b. 1952 by William J. Knight; school 1902, new building 1915; telephone 1906; TX 1910; Union C. 1884; Unit. C. (orig. Meth.)

1906 d. by Adin Parsons; pop. 233 (1911), 197 (1933), 251 (1947), 223 (1954), 259 (1961), 296 (2011).

Big Hill (*Co. Argyle*) 34°33'S. 150°00'E., 33 km NE of Goulburn, on Bridgy Ck; grazing; cemetery; PO 1869; school 1880, new building b. 1882 by P. Flanagan, closed 1906; telephone 1915; TX 1925–45; Unit. C. (orig. Prim. Meth.) 1879 d. by H.O. Bell, re-roofed, and graveyard (burials 1878+, 45 graves 1882+); pop. 122 (1901), 48 (1933).

Big Hill Lower Siding (*Co. Camden*) see Balmoral.

Big Hill Upper Siding (*Co. Camden*) see Hill Top.

Big Jacks Creek (*Co. Buckland*) 31°45'S. 150°36'E., 22 km W. of Murrurundi, on Jacks Ck; telephone 1923; TX 1924, automatic 1955.

Big Meadow Flat (*Co. Georgiana*) 34°08'S. 149°29'E., 38 km N. of Crookwell, on Cooks Vale Ck.

Big Mimosa (*Co. Bourke*) 34°35'S. 147°22'E., 22 km SW of Temora; farming; PO 1919; telephone 1916; TX 1920.

Big Mimosa (*Co. Bourke*) see also Boundary Villa and Mimosa.

Big Plain (*Co. Macquarie*) 31°20'S. 152°19'E., 37 km NW of Wauchope, on Forbes R.

Big Ridge (*Co. Sandon*) 30°38'S. 151°35'E., 8 km E. of Uralla; school 1882, new one b. 1884 by Scott and Williams, closed 1892; pop. 50 (1901), 30 (1933).

Big Springs (*Co. Wynyard*) 35°19'S. 147°25'E., 24 km S. of Wagga Wagga, on O'Briens Ck; bridge, destroyed 1947; TX (automatic); pop. 178 (1911), 53 (1933), 54 (1947), 572 (2011).

Big Swamp (*Co. Macquarie*) see Coralville.

Big Wallabadah (*Co. Northumberland*) 33°02'S. 151°01'E., 29 km SW of Paxton.

Bilambil (*Co. Rous*) 28°14'S. 153°28'E., 9 km SW of Tweed Heads, on Bilambil Ck; fruit and dairying; PO 1909, burnt down 1923; Presb. C. 1919; Rom. Cath. C. (St Camillus's) b. 1934 by Philp and Appleton, renovations 1984 by Gittoes; sawmills: Standard Sawmilling Co., Tully Bros, Thomas Vidler; school 1900, new ones 1923 and 1992, additions 1995; telephone 1911; TX 1930; pop. 77 (1901), 222 (1911), 219 (1933), 161 (1947), 139 (1954), 105 (1961), 559 (2011).

Bilambil Heights (*Co. Rous*) 28°13'S. 153°29'E., 6 km W. of Banora Point, on Terranora Broadwater; reservoir; pop. 379 (1981), 3,278 (2011).

Bilambil Soldiers' Settlement (*Co. Rous*) see Carool.

Bilbul (*Co. Cooper*) 34°16'S. 146°08'E., 9 km E. of Griffith; village gaz. 1921; rice, hort., grapes; brewery (William Bull) 1998–99; FB; PO 1922; school 1921–2012, sold 2013; telephone 1925; TX (automatic) 1940; winery (Vittorio De Bortoli) 1928; pop. 287 (1933), 345 (1947), 429 (1954), 403 (1961), 212 (1986), 235 (1991), 245 (1996), 284 (2001), 246 (2006), 263 (2011).

Billabong (*Co. Clarendon*) see Illabo.

Billabong (*Co. Goulburn*) see Garryowen.

Billabong (*Co. Hume*) see Culcairn.

Billabong (*Co. Rous*) 28°52'S. 153°31'E., 4 km W. of Ballina.

Billapalap (*Co. Wynyard*) 35°28'S. 147°57'E., 19 km W. of Batlow, on Yaven Ck; storm 1867.

Billeroy (*Co. Leichhardt*) 30°41'S. 148°27'E., 30 km N. of Coonamble, on Gunyillah Ck; grazing; PO 1888–1954; telephone 1906; TX 1930; pop. 54 (1911), 20 (1933).

Billilingra (*Co. Beresford*) 36°01'S. 149°11'E., 25 km N. of Cooma; disc. 1823 by Capt. John Mark Currie and Major John Ovens, settled by John Cosgrove; grasshopper infestation 1872; RS 1894–1941.

Billimari (*Co. Bathurst*) 33°41'S. 148°37'E., 13 km S. of Canowindra; (incl. Soldiers Flat); estab. 1910, allotments sold 1912; lucerne, maize, wheat, sheep, cattle, now vegetables, olives, grapes; electricity 1950; FB (station b. 2002); Meth. C. b. 1928 by J.R. McDonald, closed, sold and reused; military depot (Soldiers Flat); olive processing plant (La Barre) 2005; Plymouth Brethren C. 1952–63, sold and reused; PO 1916; Rom. Cath. C. (St John the Baptist), rebuilt and renovated 1940 by Walter Goodacre, closed and reused, and graveyard; RS 1910, station b. by D.H. Reid, closed 1978; schools: Billimari 1915–83 and Soldiers Flat 1885–90; silo 1929; telephone 1915; TX 1923, automatic 1971; water supply 1970; pop. 66 (1911), 256 (1933), 85 (1947), 150 (1954), 160 (1961).

Billinudgel (*Co. Rous*) 28°30'S. 153°32'E., 5 km NW of Brunswick Heads, on Marshalls Ck; farming, dairying, bananas, orchards; Angl. C. (St Clement's) 1907; Assemblies of God C. (Brunswick Valley Christ. Life); floods 2003 and 2010; hailstorm 1936; Meth. C. 1907; PO 1895; 2 quarries; rifle range 1916; Rom. Cath. C. (Holy Cross) b. 1935 by J. Fisher, d. by Ray Pullinger, closed, sold, restored and reused; RS 1894, station b. by Frederick Lemm, burnt down, replaced 1939, closed 1985; sawmill (Mann Bros); telephone 1904; TX 1915; pop. 444 (1911), 203 (1933), 186 (1947), 230 (1954), 205 (1961), 282 (2011).

Billinudgel (*Co. Rous*)
see also South Golden Beach.

Billyrimba (*Co. Clive*) 29°11'S. 152°14'E., 24 km SE of Tenterfield, on Billyrimba Ck; airfield.

Billys Creek (*Co. Fitzroy*) 30°10'S. 152°35'E., 23 km NW of Dorrigo, on Billys Ck; farming; bushfire 1936; PO 1927; sawmills: E.M. Lord 1925, Munro & Lever Veneer Co., Nymboida Timber Co., C. Schultz; school 1946, additions 1959, closed 1963; storm 1936; telephone 1923; TX 1934; pop. 44 (1933), 127 (1947), 126 (1954), 90 (1961).

Billys Lookout (*Co. Gipps*) 33°42'S. 147°21'E., 29 km NE of West Wyalong; mining (alluvial gold disc. 1873, reef gold disc. 1895 by Neil White, sen., gold rush 1895, another reef disc. 1939), farming, sheep; PO 1915–42; school 1905–20, building moved to Wyrra; stamper battery (Robert Brenner); telephone 1934; TX 1936; pop. 67 (1911), 82 (1933).

Billywillinga (*Co. Roxburgh*) 33°16'S. 149°26'E., 22 km NW of Bathurst, on Billywillinga Ck.

Bilpin (*Co. Cook*) 33°30'S. 150°31'E., 11 km W. of Kurrajong Heights, on Wheeny Ck; Norwood till 1914; settled by soldiers 1830–39; farming and orchards; Assemblies of God C.; bushfires 1936, 1982, 1994, 2013; cemetery; electricity 1953; FB 1947; fruit packing house (Peter Powell); knitting mill (Bertram Horsfield), taken over 1955 by Ken Davey, closed 1959; PO 1909; Rom. Cath. C. (St Martin de Porres) 1962; sawmills: Buckett Bros and Ness 1947 and Hobby Bros; school 1952; telephone 1920; TX 1921; pop. 94 (1933), 189 (1947), 185 (1954), 292 (1961), 840 (2006), 932 (2011).

Bimbaya (*Co. Auckland*) 36°45'S. 149°38'E., 19 km W. of Bega, on Tantawangalo Ck; Clarkson's Crossing till 1914; farming; bridge over Tantawangalo Ck; butter factory (Candelo Co-op. Dairy Society Ltd) 1895–1959, reused; cheese factory (Fernlee); PO 1903; telephone 1906; TX 1925; pop. 139 (1933), 140 (1947), 135 (1954), 51 (1961).

Bimberamala (*Co. St Vincent*) 35°31'S. 150°08'E., 22 km N. of Batemans Bay, on Bimberamala Ck; goldmining 1890–1915.

Bimbi (*Co. Bland*) 34°02'S. 147°56'E., 26 km SW of Grenfell, on Burrangong Ck; estab. in 1880s, village gaz. 1888, thrived 1890–1914, then declined (bypassed by railway); farming and grazing; Angl. C. (St Bartholomew's) b. 1911–17, moved 1963 to Quandialla; bridge 1884–1938, replaced 1939 by Sullivan Bros, over Burrangong Ck; cemetery (400+ graves) 1889; CH 1911–30, moved to Quandialla; droughts 1847–52, 1876, 1915, 1946, 1982; FB 1930 (station b. 2004); floods 1915, 1916, 1950, 1990; gale 1898; PO 1883–1987; pound (stock) 1896; Presb. C. (used as a Union C.) b. 1907 by John Gault, closed, sold and moved 1951 to Moombooldool; PS 1896, new one (incl. lock-up) b. 1908 by Hugh Robert Blackett, closed 1930; Rom. Cath. C. (St John's) 1899, closed; sale-yards; sawmills: Flood's, Thomas Lanigan, P. McGarry, William Samuel Millard (estab. by Harry Nelson, bought 1878 by Hugh Gault, burnt down 1880, also rebuilt by Gault, sold 1888 to William Samuel Millard, burnt down 1904), Thomas Stonham; school 1892, replaced 1899, destroyed and replaced 1931, closed

1947, building moved 1949 to Quandialla; telephone 1900; TX 1911–87; pop. 153 (1901), 467 (1911), 223 (1933), 104 (1947), 109 (1954), 125 (1961), 158 (2006).

Bimbimbie (*Co. St Vincent*) 35°49'S. 150°08'E., 10 km W. of Malua Bay, on Kellys Ck; Kelly's Creek till 1898; estab. 1899; goldmining, mainly 1857–1913, and farming; mine (Bimbimbee Gold Mines) 1875–1938; miners' strike 1904; PO 1927 (closed within a month); sawmill; stamper battery 1902; pop. 68 (1901), 20 (1933).

Bimlow (*Co. Westmoreland*) 34°00'S. 150°26'E., 26 km NW of Picton, on Wollondilly R.; settled by John Lacey; school 1882–83, demolished 1934.

Binalong (*Co. Harden*) 34°40'S. 148°38'E., 27 km S. of Boorowa, on Balgalal Ck; town gaz. 1880, designated as chief town of the county; hort. and orchards 1870s–1950s, now wool and wheat; Angl. C. (St Thomas's) b. 1886 by J. Carr, additions and alterations 1925–27; bridge (Beckhams Bridge) 1854, destroyed 1870, replaced 1871, new one 1941, over Balgalal Ck; bushfires 1905 and 1939; butter factory 1895; cemetery 1869; CH 1849, ruined by 1860, new one b. 1883 by Van Henderstein and Gough, d. by James Johnstone Barnet, closed 1974, reused as police station; earth tremor 1929; fire 1912; flood 1870; flour mill (Miles Murphy); mine (Last Chance) worked by Lewis Litton; PO 1849, new one b. 1906, reused, replaced 1915, sold to Ben Spencer; pound (stock) 1865; PS (incl. lock-up) 1847, new one 1862, additions 1867, alterations 1904 (lock-up reused) by George Donald, demolished 1919; quarry; railway accident (passenger killed) 1915; railway barracks (removed from Bowning) 1876; railway dam 1916; Rom. Cath. C. (St Peter and St Paul's) b. 1861 by Rema, demolished, new one (St Patrick's) b. 1911–13 on new site by Larcombe Bros, d. by William John Monks, restored 2003; RS 1876, station burnt down and replaced 1883, reused, new one 1915 on new site, closed, sold 1921 to John Bergin, sold 1922 to James Doran, acquired by Euphemia Sargent, later acquired by Peter Le Grand and Linda Wootten, restored, sold, rail services ceased 1989; school 1861, new one b. 1890, additions 1925 by A.P. Sewell; snow 1929 and 1956; streets electric lit 1931; telegraph 1877; TX 1911; water supply augmentation 1992; pop. 11 (1841), 113 (1851), 199 (1856), 210 (1861), *c.*210 (1866), 189 (1871), 179 (1881), 314 (1891), 369 (1901), 524 (1911), 590 (1933), 528 (1947), 476 (1954), 374 (1961), 208 (1976), 212 (1981), 256 (1986), 219 (1991), 240 (1996), 256 (2000), 286 (2001), 306 (2011).

Binbinette (*Co. Wakool*) 34°59'S. 143°54'E., 49 km SE of Balranald.

Binda (*Co. Georgiana*) 34°19'S. 149°22'E., 18 km NW of Crookwell, on Binda Ck; disc. 1820 by John Joseph William Molesworth Oxley and James Meehan, settled 1825 by Francis Oakes and Thomas Bray, village gaz. 1851, surveyed and subdivided 1852, declined 1864+; farming and grazing; Angl. C. (St James's) b. 1864 by Macdonnell and Pinn Bros, d. by Richard Leigh, damaged 1884, additions and restoration 1934, restored 1992 by Garry Dutaillis, and graveyard (2 graves); cemetery (graves 1850+) 1882; diphtheria 1887; earth tremor 1852; FB 1932 (station b. 1989); flour mill b. 1893–98 by George King, reused 1906; hailstorm 1884; lock-up; PO 1852; pound (stock) 1840; PS; Rom. Cath. C. (St Peter's) 1909, in former temperance hall, extended 1952, new one b. 1970 by D. Oxley, d. by Terence A. Daly; school 1851–54 and 1865–1949, reopened 1959; snowstorm 1854; telephone 1899; TX 1913, automatic 1987; Wes. Meth. C. 1848; pop. *c.*50 (1866), 152 (1901), 326 (1911), 277 (1933), 240 (1947), 221 (1954), 151 (1961), 130 (2006), 211 (2011).

Binda Caves (*Co. Westmoreland*) see Jenolan Caves.

Bindawalla (*Co. Hardinge*) 30°17'S. 151°17'E., 37 km W. of Guyra, on Abington Ck; telephone 1928; TX 1928–75.

Bindogandi Station (*Co. Ashburnham*) see Cookamidgera.

Bindogundra (*Co. Ashburnham*) 33°08'S. 148°18'E., 12 km E. of Parkes, on

Bindogundra Ck; Angl. C. (St Stephen's) b. 1912 by Jimmy Job, renovated; school 1890, new one b. 1899 by John Job, closed 1906, reopened 1915, closed 1921; TX (automatic); Wes. Meth. C. b. 1883 by James Jelbart and Edwin White, relocated, burnt down; pop. 81 (1901), 57 (1911), 108 (1933), 74 (1947), 66 (1954), 112 (1961).

Bindura (*Co. Kilfera*) 34°09'S. 143°21'E., 56 km N. of Balranald.

Bingara (*Co. Murchison*) 29°52'S. 150°34'E., 53 km W. of Inverell, on Gwydir R.; Bingera till 1890; disc. 1827 by Allan Cunningham, founded 1840, surveyed 1852 by John James Galloway, town gaz. 1852, estab. 1853, designated as chief town of the county, munic. 1889–1943; mining (especially gold, disc. 1852, and diamonds mined 1872–1909), wheat 1900+, oats, maize, barley, sorghum, lucerne, sheep, cattle, pigs, honey, sawmilling; ambulance station; Angl. C. (St Mark's) 1875, new one (St John's) b. 1890 by Kirkham, d. by Arthur Blacket; bridges: Campbell Bridge (metal lattice truss) b. 1884–86 by H. Royce, upgraded 2016, over Gwydir R. and bridge, upgraded 2016, over Halls Ck; cemetery (3,032 graves) 1869, incl. columbaria; CH b. 1879 by William Lee, d. by James Johnstone Barnet, additions and alterations 1898 by E.W. Rowland, repairs 1910 by E.W. Anderson, reused; cordial factory (Henry J. Fay, taken over by O'Dell and new one b. 1889); earth tremor 1903; electricity supply (Cliftons Ltd) 1928, upgraded 1936, taken over 1940; FB (station b. 1953); fires 1907, 1929, 1935, 1937; fish hatchery (Murray Cod) 1980; floods 1864 and 1910; flour mills: Gwydir Lily (estab. 1891 by John Byrnes, closed, bought by Ray Whitfield and Hayes Bros for partial relocation and reuse) and IXL (James Teare Wearne) 1881, bought 1897 by William Finkernagel; hailstorm 1890; heatwave 1940; hospital 1889, extended 1905, new one b. 1915 by E.W. Anderson and W.H. Rogers, d. by James Warren Scobie, additions 1939, 1965, 1980, 2008; Meth. C.; mine (All Nations or New Bingara Gold Mine, incl. 10 head stamper battery 1890) 1860–1907 and 1938–48; PO 1853, new one b. 1879 by William Lee, repairs 1890 by M'Kechnie Bros and Meyers, additions 1896 and 1913; pound (stock) 1864; powerhouse (Clifton's Ltd); Presb. C. (Scots) 1904; PS b. 1882 by S. Senior, additions 1897 by W. Anderson, new one b. 1916 by S. Senior, repairs 1953 by N.G. Rixon; reservoir, 300,000 gal. (1,363.8 kl); Rom. Cath. C. (Holy Rosary) 1872, additions 1888, reused, new one (St Mary's) b. 1907 by Joseph Keenan; sale-yards (E. Dufty) 1949; Salv. Army C. 1990; sawmills: E. Bates, John Byrnes, Stocker and Gibson, James Teare Wearne 1881; school 1862–71, reopened 1878 after alterations by William Lee, additions 1883 also by Lee, alterations 1916 by E. Anderson, new school b. 1951 by Ben Wade & Sons, additions 1955, 1965, 1993; sewerage 1970; storm 1889; telegraph 1875, new office b. 1879 by William Lee, repairs 1890 by M'Kechnie Bros and Meyers, additions 1896 and 1913; tornado 1891; TX 1912; Unit. C. (St Andrew's, orig. Presb.) b. 1904 by William Anderson, d. by John Francis O'Connor; watch-house b. 1862 by Lachlan Kennedy, new one b. 1876 by Charles Grace, additions 1877 also by Grace, additions and repairs 1898 by W. Anderson, renovations and repairs 1916 by Joseph Head; waterworks 1939 d. by J.H. Butters & Associates; Wes. Meth. C. b. 1885 by William Seabrook and John Brown, burnt down 1935; wool-scour and fellmongery (Taylor and Hulbert, partnership dissolved 1899, carried on by F.R. Hulbert); pop. <90 (1861), *c.*150 (1866), <90 (1871), *c.*400 (1881), 414 (1886), 738 (1891), *c.*770 (1895), 879 (1901), 1,632 (1911), 1,018 (1921), 1,448 (1933), 1,511 (1947), 1,465 (1954), 1,485 (1961), 1,504 (1966), 1,401 (1971), 1,295 (1976), 1,257 (1981), 1,363 (1986), 1,231 (1991), 1,236 (1996), 1,227 (2001), 1,207 (2006), 1,091 (2011).

Bingara Gorge Estate (*Co. Camden*) see Wilton.

Bingeebeebra (*Co. Rous*) 28°47'S. 152°46'E., 29 km W. of Casino, on Bingeebeebra Ck;

telephone 1925; TX 1950–63; pop. 79 (1933).

Bingera (*Co. Murchison*) see Bingara.

Bingham (*Co. Georgiana*) 34°05'S. 149°36'E., 44 km N. of Crookwell; never developed.

Bingie (*Co. Dampier*) 36°01'S. 150°09'E., 13 km SE of Moruya, on Tasman Sea.

Binglebrah (*Co. Durham*) 32°23'S. 151°38'E., 12 km W. of Dungog, on Old Mans Ck; school 1882–89.

Bingleburra (*Co. Durham*) 32°24'S. 151°36'E., 15 km W. of Dungog; farming; pop. 67 (1911), 47 (1933), 59 (1947), 205 (2006).

Bingle Hill (*Co. Northumberland*) see Tighes Hill.

Biniguy (*Co. Courallie*) 29°33'S. 150°12'E., 35 km W. of Warialda, on Slaughterhouse Ck; Biniguy Railway till 1949; village gaz. 1915; farming and grazing; flood 1946; PO 1916; RS 1900, station b. by E.W. Rowland, closed 1983; sawmills: Alex. J. Lockhart, Elijah Maidens, Bert Taylor, Benjamin Martin Wade; school (Binneguy till 1895) 1881–95 and 1957–68; silo 1934; telephone 1916; TX 1924; pop. 56 (1901), 57 (1911), 126 (1933), 147 (1947), 183 (1954), 230 (1961), 625 (2011).

Biniguy Railway (*Co. Courallie*) see Biniguy.

Binna Burra (*Co. Rous*) 28°42'S. 153°30'E., 4 km SW of Bangalow, on Byron Ck; farming; bridge b. 1937 by Kennedy Bros, over Byron Ck; butter factory and ice works (Binna Burra Dairy Co. Ltd) 1912, taken over 1925 by North Coast Co-op. Ltd, remodelled by Daniel Gallagher and casein factory added 1937, closed 1947, reused; casein factory (Milk Industries Ltd) 1921; PO 1907–74; RS (Garvan's Siding till 1898) 1894, station b. by William Mitchell, closed 1972; telephone 1907; pop. 107 (1911), 185 (1933), 136 (1947), 142 (1954), 157 (1961), 188 (2011).

Binnaway (*Co. Napier*) 31°33'S. 149°23'E., 32 km S. of Coonabarabran, on Castlereagh R.; settled 1869 by Charles Naseby, village gaz. 1908, lots sold 1909; farming and grazing; Angl. C. (St Andrew's) 1938; brickworks (Abe Sargent); bridge (low-level concrete) b. 1926 by J. Jamieson, d. by Allman, over Castlereagh R.; cemetery (669 graves) 1881; diphtheria 1935; electricity 1938; FB; floods 1921 and 1950; hospital 1941; measles epidemic 1928; PO 1876; PS 1913, new one b. 1925 by C.J. Manuel; rabbit freezing works (Country Freezing Co. Ltd) 1915, renovations 1919, acquired 1927 by Amalgamated Rabbit & Skin Export Co. Ltd, fire 1927, closed 1946; railway barracks 1925, closed, restored and reused; railway round-house (4 bays) 1925; railway turntable 1925, 60 ft (18.3 m); reservoir; rifle range 1922; Rom. Cath. C. 1924 d. by William James Gilroy, closed, sold and reused, new one (St Peter and St Paul's) b. 1939 as a school, reused 1970 as a church, closed and sold; RS 1917, station b. by John Allibone, closed 1975; sale-yards 1913; sawmills: Holt and Naseby 1912 and T. Keran (bought 1940 by Wallace Bros); school 1881, repairs 1900 by Book and Sheumack, additions 1917 by T.R. M'Donald, additions 1921, 1963, 1967, 1980; silos 1935 and 1955; telephone 1901; TX 1911; Unit. C. (orig. Presb., then Union), closed and reused; water supply augmentation 1955, 1970, 1993; whooping cough epidemic 1912; pop. 134 (1901), 254 (1911), 861 (1933), 761 (1947), 912 (1954), 734 (1961), 691 (1966), 640 (1971), 612 (1976), 583 (1981), 562 (1986), 528 (1991), 500 (1996), 519 (2001), 495 (2006), 456 (2011).

Binneguy (*Co. Courallie*) see Biniguy.

Binni (*Co. Bathurst*) 33°45'S. 148°44'E., 11 km N. of Cowra, on Binni Ck.

Binnia (*Co. Napier*) 31°41'S. 149°45'E., 16 km N. of Coolah, on Honeysuckle Ck.

Binni Creek (*Co. Bathurst*) 33°44'S. 148°43'E., 12 km N. of Cowra; goldmine 1890–96, 1901, 1931; PO 1896 (closed within a year); school 1896–97; pop. 70 (1933), 79 (1947), 50 (1954).

Binya (*Co. Cooper*) 34°14'S. 146°21'E., 30 km E. of Griffith, on Binya Ck; wheat; mouse plague 1970; PO 1917; Rom. Cath. C. (Sacred Heart), destroyed 1954, replaced 1957; RS 1916, station b. by Ernest Frederick Leggo, closed 1985, station sold and removed 1985; school 1933; silo 1928, extended 1934; storm 1954; telephone 1918; TX 1918, automatic

1982; pop. 70 (1911), 88 (1933), 40 (1947), 69 (1954), 271 (1961), 238 (2006), 191 (2011).

Binya North (*Co. Cooper*) 34°11'S. 146°24'E., 36 km E. of Griffith; school 1929–49.

Biraban (*Co. Northumberland*) see Toronto West.

Biraganbil (*Co. Wellington*) 32°25'S. 149°25'E., 13 km SW of Gulgong; bushfire 1890; flour mill (formerly owned by Richard Rouse, later by L. Fox); storm 1878; pop. 43 (1933).

Bird Island (*Co. Northumberland*) see St Huberts Island.

Birdlip (*Co. Mitchell*) 35°19'S. 147°11'E., 28 km SW of Wagga Wagga; formerly Mangoplah North and Plahgoman; RS 1925–56; school (Plahgoman) 1957–69.

Birdwood (*Co. Macquarie*) 31°21'S. 152°20'E., 39 km NW of Wauchope, on Forbes R.; PO 1938; sawmill (Forbes River Timbers Pty Ltd); telephone 1915; TX 1930, automatic 1981; pop. 125 (1954), 101 (1961).

Birganbigal (*Co. Townsend*) 35°31'S. 145°08'E., 14 km E. of Deniliquin; Presb. C.; TX (automatic).

Birkalla (*Co. Flinders*) 31°33'S. 146°36'E., 55 km W. of Nyngan; RS 1931–57.

Birmingham Gardens (*Co. Northumberland*) 32°54'S. 151°41'E., 2 km NE of Wallsend; (incl. Callaghan); formerly part of Wallsend, laid out 1922 as garden suburb by Leslie James Kelly, developed by T.M. Burke, but most building activity 1947+; Angl. C. (St Paul's) 1940, closed and sold 2018; bushfire 1936; CAE (Newcastle) 1974 d. by John McKinney, became a campus of Hunter Institute of Higher Education in 1988; cemetery; hailstorm (Callaghan) 2004; Meth. C. 1948; monumental stone works (J. Lewis); PO: Birmingham Gardens 1947 and Newcastle University 1966; school 1951, additions 1956, closed 1993; telephone: Birmingham Gardens 1947 and Newcastle University 1966; univ. (Newcastle, removed 1966–71 from Tighes Hill), incl. Basden Theatre 1966, Griffith Duncan Theatre 1966, McMullin Building 1966, Edwards Hall 1972, Great Hall b. 1971–73, The Forum 1997, Birabahn Building 2002, fire (Union Building) 2004; pop. 2,231 (1954), 1,848 (2006), 2,122 (2011).

Birrego (*Co. Mitchell*) 35°01'S. 146°35'E., 29 km S. of Narrandera; farming; Meth. C. 1913, removed from Boree Creek; PO 1921; sawmill (Nolan & Son); school 1909–38 and 1957–66; telephone 1921; TX 1922; pop. 112 (1911), 83 (1933), 62 (1947), 61 (1954), 104 (1961).

Birriwa (*Co. Bligh*) 32°07'S. 149°28'E., 13 km SE of Dunedoo; farming; Angl. C. (St John the Baptist) 1934 d. by Harold Robert Hardwick; cemetery; hailstorm 1929; PO 1897; RS (Wyaldra till 1912) 1910, station b. by George Albert Leggo and John Allibone, closed 1974; school 1912–73; silo 1941; telephone 1915; TX 1924, automatic 1986; Union C. 1913; pop. 57 (1901), 52 (1911), 215 (1933), 165 (1947), 198 (1954), 166 (1961).

Birubi Point (*Co. Gloucester*) see Anna Bay.

Birumba (*Co. Westmoreland*) 33°31'S. 149°56'E., 23 km N. of Oberon, on Solitary Ck; RS 1910–16.

Bishops Bridge (*Co. Northumberland*) 32°45'S. 151°28'E., 8 km W. of Maitland, on Bishops Ck; farming, dairying, poultry; Angl. C. 1859, burnt down 1904, new one (St Andrew's) 1905, burnt down 1905, and graveyard (129 graves 1862+) 1860; bushfires 1905 and 1951; FB; hailstorm 1873; PO 1861–1973; quarry (Albert Thomas); school 1858 b. by James Sherwood, new building b. 1929 by W.H. Mitchell, closed 1965; storm 1899; tannery (John Sawyer), damaged 1899; telephone 1899; TX 1956; winery (Bishop Grove) estab. 1990 by Harry Wells, acquired 2004 by Chris Hirst; pop. *c.*100 (1866), 116 (1871), 123 (1891), 206 (1901), 161 (1911), 87 (1933), 66 (1947), 70 (1954), 56 (1961), 225 (2011).

Bismuth (*Co. Gough*) 29°16'S. 151°38'E., 44 km SW of Tenterfield; defunct; mine (Fielders Hill) worked by the Torrington Ore Co. for bismuth and wolframite (incl. 10 head stamper battery); PO 1912; 2 quarries; school 1910, new building b. 1912 by J. Adams, closed 1923; telephone 1913; TX 1915; pop. 145 (1911), 30 (1933).

Bithramere (*Co. Parry*) 31°08'S. 150°46'E., 16 km W. of Tamworth; school (Murroon till 1917) 1912–68; telephone 1916; TX 1917, automatic 1955; pop. 106 (1933), 80 (1947), 120 (1954), 150 (1961), 177 (2011).

Blackalls (*Co. Northumberland*) see Blackalls Park.

Blackalls Park (*Co. Northumberland*) 33°00'S. 151°35'E., 2 km NW of Toronto, on Stony Ck; Blackall's Platform till 1954; subdivisions 1883 and 1915; bridge (Homer Bridge) 1906, to Toronto, over Stony Ck; bushfires 1926, 1948, 1951; colliery (South Pacific); Meth. C. 1955; PO 1923; RS (Blackall's till 1956, relocated 1911) 1891, private railway till 1911, closed 1990; school (Blackalls till 1993) 1953, additions 1969, 1980, 2010; sewage works; telephone 1921; wharf 1925; pop. 203 (1933), 496 (1947), 1,101 (1954), 2,763 (2011).

Blackall's Platform (*Co. Northumberland*) see Blackalls Park.

Blackbird Flat (*Co. Dudley*) 30°45'S. 152°21'E., 50 km W. of Bowraville, on Macleay R.

Blackbutt (*Co. Camden*) see Shellharbour.

Black Camp (*Co. Gloucester*) 32°28'S. 151°52'E., 12 km SE of Dungog; pop. 58 (1933).

Black Camp Creek (*Co. Drake*) 28°52'S. 152°42'E., 35 km W. of Casino, on Blacks Camp Ck; sawmills: J.T. Mealing and Yabbra Timber Co. Ltd.

Black Creek (*Co. Macquarie*) 31°35'S. 152°38'E., 9 km NW of Kendall; pop. 38 (1933), 50 (1947).

Black Creek (*Co. Northumberland*) 32°40'S. 151°19'E., 4 km W. of Branxton; flour mill (horse powered) b. 1831 by John Portus and Robert Pringle, sold to Lieut. Col. Henry Dumaresq and moved to St Heliers; Rom. Cath. C. (St Patrick's) 1841; school 1852–60.

Black Creek (*Co. Northumberland*) see also Branxton.

Black Creek (*Co. Wynyard*) 35°20'S. 148°04'E., 2 km S. of Adelong; cemetery 1863; pop. 33 (1933).

Black Flat (*Co. Drake*) 29°07'S. 152°32'E., 50 km E. of Tenterfield.

Black Flat (*Co. St Vincent*) 35°36'S. 150°05'E., 15 km NW of Batemans Bay.

Blackgolar (*Co. Westmoreland*) see Coxs River.

Black Head (*Co. Gloucester*) 32°04'S. 152°33'E., 12 km N. of Tuncurry, on Tasman Sea; FB; foot-bridge; PO; pop. 749 (2011).

Blackheath (*Co. Cook*) 33°38'S. 150°17'E., 9 km N. of Katoomba, on Popes Glen Ck; (incl. Gordy Town 1880s–1920s, Kanimbla, Shipley disc. 1891, settled by R.S. Longton et al.); Hounslow till 1815; settled 1830 by Andrew Gardner, surveyed and village gaz. 1878, first lots sold 1879, laid out 1881 by William Albert Braylesford Greaves, munic. 1919–47 but became part of City of Blue Mountains; orchards at Kanimbla and Shipley, mountain tourism (Blackheath) for over a century, with lookouts, waterfalls, caves, walks (e.g. Govetts Leap track, b. 1898 by T. Williams); airfield 1939–55; Angl. C. (St Aidan's) 1884, extended 1902 by A.G. Ives and A.G. Woodhead; ball lightning 1904; Bapt. C. 1888, reused, new one b. 1929 by G.B. Holt, d. by Francis William Peplow; brewery (Mountain) estab. 1885 by William Allen, sold 1888 to James Daley, closed 1892, reused, demolished; brickworks (House Bros); bushfires 1894, 1895, 1900, 1919, 1928, 1951, 1952 (5 houses destroyed), 2002; cemeteries: military (25+ burials, *c.*12 graves 1845–84) and general (burials 1884+, *c.*1,700 graves) 1887; concrete pipe works 1910; cordial factory estab. 1892 by William Young, in old brewery; dam (Lake Greaves) 1942; earth tremor 1916; electricity 1917; FB (stations b. 1925 and 1933, new one b. 1959 by Robert Hughan & Sons, new one b. 2017 at Shipley); jam factory (Blue Mountains Jam & Preserving Co.) at Shipley, b. by George William Commens and Sherwood, burnt down 1921; lock-up 1849; Meth. C. 1909, in unused church removed from Mount Victoria, sold 1923; PO 1883, new one b. 1885, replaced 1911 by James Nutt, reused and replaced; Presb. C. b. 1901 by A. Woodhead, d. by Harry Rupert Goyder, closed 1925, relocated 1925 by Gibbon and Crouch, reused, new one (Leslie Memorial) b. 1925 by Gibbon and Crouch, d. by Ross and Rowe; PS 1849, new one (in rented premises) 1938, new one b. 1952 by Ashman and Hart, closed 1962; 2 quarries; rabbit freezing works (E. Vickery & Sons) 1905, closed, burnt down 1913; railway dam 1878, deepened and wall raised 1884, second dam 1886; railway weir 1906, on Govetts Leap Brook; reservoir, 500,000 gal. (2,273 kl), b. 1925 by Monier Pipe Works; rifle range, fire 1902, upgraded 1909; Rom. Cath. C. (Sacred Heart) b. 1902 by John Hines, d. by Harry Rupert Goyder, additions 1915 by F.J. King & Co., d. by A. M'Kay; RS 1869, new station b. 1898 by Charles Palmer; sawmills: A. Couston and Henry Gee; school 1885, new building b. 1896 d. by William Edmund Kemp, additions 1912, 1922, 1964, 1976, 1993; sewerage 1937; snowstorms 1910 and 1934; stockade (convict) 1840–49; telegraph 1880; TX 1909; Unit. C. (orig. Meth.) b. 1924 by George Phillips and E. Simon, d. by Alfred Gambier Newman; water supply 1927; wire works; pop. 771 (1891), 734 (1901), 1,318 (1911), 1,451 (1933), *c.*2,000 (1941), 2,349 (1947), 2,090 (1954), 2,177 (1961), 2,077 (1966), 2,226 (1971), 2,371 (1976), 3,027 (1981), 3,599 (1986), 3,749 (1991), 4,119 (1996), 4,104 (2001), 4,177 (2006), 4,350 (2011).

Blackheath (*Co. Murray*) see Hoskinstown.

Black Hill (*Co. Northumberland*) 32°50'S. 151°37'E., 10 km S. of East Maitland, on Four Mile Ck; (incl. Lenaghan); poultry, honey, dairying; asphalt plant (Boral); collieries: Abel and Donaldson Open-Cut; quarry; school 1882, new one b. 1924 by Holmes and Keppie; Unit. C. (orig. Wes. Meth.) 1886, and graveyard (56 graves 1903+), incl. columbarium; Wes. Meth. C. 1862; pop. 63 (1911), 82 (1933), 82 (1947), 95 (1954), 53 (1961), 656 (2011).

Black Jack (*Co. Pottinger*) 31°00'S. 150°12'E., 5 km SW of Gunnedah; colliery, fire 1900, strikes 1908, 1909, 1944, man killed 1986; Meth. C. 1903; pop. 115 (1911), 92 (1933).

Black Lead (*Co. Phillip*) 32°20'S. 149°23'E., 2 km N. of Gulgong; pop. 97 (1954), 77 (1961).

Blackmans Flat (*Co. Cook*) 33°22'S. 150°04'E., 5 km N. of Wallerawang, on Coxs R.; cemetery (39 graves 1877–2003); collieries: Black Diamond (Wallace's) 1896–1902, acquired by G. & C. Hoskins Ltd, Bulkeley's 1874–*c.*1876, Commonwealth No. 1 (W.C. Wallace) *c.*1894, fire 1904, boy killed 1940, Eastern Main No. 1 (Clutha Development Pty Ltd), Ivanhoe No. 2 (Associated Portland Cement Manufacturers Ltd) 1893, Pine Dale (Enhance Place Pty Ltd), Wallerawang (Coalex Pty Ltd, formerly Brawn's) 1910–87, Western Main (formerly Black Diamond, acquired by Clutha Development Pty Ltd) 1905; diphtheria 1912; miners' strikes 1930, 1931, 1932, 1934, 1935–36, 1938, 1940, 1941, 1942, 1943; quarries; school (Lidsdale 1900–36) 1898 b. by Thomas Harding, closed 1936, building dismantled and moved 1938 to Locksley, reopened 1963–75; pop. 64 (1901), 53 (1911), 97 (1933), 91 (1947), 125 (1954), 83 (1961), 178 (2006).

Blackmans Point (*Co. Macquarie*) 31°25'S. 152°52'E., 5 km NW of Port Macquarie, on Hastings R.; farming and dairying; bridge (Dennis Bridge) 1916, new one (steel-truss and plate-girder spans) fabricated by Transfield Pty Ltd, erected 1961 by Electric Power Transmission Pty Ltd, 1,535 ft (467.9 m), over Hastings R.; PO 1886; punt b. 1910 by L.A. Davis, ceased 1961, across Hastings R.; school 1881, additions 1886 by John Bourke, new building b. 1926 by P. Burns, closed 1962; telephone 1915; Wes. Meth. C. 1869, new one 1890; pop. 83 (1933), 130 (1947), 115 (1954), 123 (1961), 264 (2011).

Blackman's Swamp (*Co. Wellington*) see Orange.

Black Margaret Swamp (*Co. Northumberland*) see Swansea.

Black Mountain (*Co. Sandon*) 30°19'S. 151°39'E., 10 km S. of Guyra; potatoes, oats, cherries, apples, wool, cattle; Angl. C. (All Saints') 1900, destroyed 1948; Bapt. C. 1902, renovated 1951, restored 1992; bushfire 1927; butter factory (Black Mountain Co-op. Dairy

Co. Ltd) 1892–1920, demolished; cemetery 1900; cyclone (damaged or destroyed most buildings) 1948; FB (station moved to Wandsworth, replaced 2014); PO 1884, damaged 1948; RS (Boorolong till 1886) 1884, station b. by John White and Charles Coghill, damaged 1948, closed 1989; sawmill; school 1882, new buildings b. 1883 by C.A. Ramsay, additions 1904 by D. Menzies, new building b. 1942 by P.J. Knudson, additions 2010; telegraph 1890; telephone 1913; TX 1920; pop. 218 (1901), 426 (1911), 201 (1933), 215 (1947), 204 (1954), 234 (1961), 332 (2011).

Black Range (*Co. Goulburn*) see Albury.

Black Ridge (*Co. Ashburnham*) see Forbes.

Black Rock (*Co. Beresford*) see Chakola.

Black Rock (*Co. Gordon*) 32°40'S. 148°56'E., 12 km S. of Wellington, on Bell R.; agric. and grazing; mines: Camelford Park Estate and Reid Plateau (A.A. Smith and A.R. Anderson) 1931–37; PO 1859; pop. *c.*50 (1866).

Black Rock (*Co. White*) 30°22'S. 149°13'E., 25 km SW of Wee Waa.

Blacks Camp (*Co. Northumberland*) 33°06'S. 151°21'E., 13 km W. of Morisset.

Blacksmiths (*Co. Northumberland*) 33°05'S. 151°39'E., 2 km NE of Swansea, on Tasman Sea; subdivisions 1948 and 1961; breakwater; bushfire 1946; diphtheria 1950; earth tremor 1939; Meth. C. 1956; PO 1937; school 1962; sewerage 1961; water supply 1937; telephone 1937; pop. 201 (1933), 670 (1947), 1,188 (2006), 1,844 (2011).

Blacksmiths Shop (*Co. Gresham*) 29°49'S. 152°25'E., 51 km W. of Grafton.

Black Spring (*Co. Wellesley*) 36°59'S. 149°14'E., 8 km S. of Bombala.

Black Springs (*Co. Brisbane*) 32°10'S. 150°39'E., 22 km W. of Aberdeen, on Wybong Ck.

Black Springs (*Co. Darling*) 30°27'S. 150°38'E., 7 km S. of Barraba; RS 1908, station b. by W. Gawne & Sons, closed 1963.

Black Springs (*Co. Hawes*) 31°37'S. 151°37'E., 54 km NW of Gloucester, on Tuggolo Ck.

Black Springs (*Co. Murchison*) 29°42'S. 150°31'E., 31 km NE of Bingara.

Black Springs (*Co. Phillip*) see Budgee Budgee.

Black Springs (*Co. Roxburgh*) 33°02'S. 149°52'E., 27 km SW of Rylstone; airfield.

Black Springs (*Co. Vernon*) 31°07'S. 152°04'E., 45 km E. of Walcha.

Black Springs (*Co. Westmoreland*) 33°51'S. 149°44'E., 18 km SW of Oberon; farming and grazing; airfield; cemetery (128 graves 1906+); PO 1870; quarry; Rom. Cath. C. (St Vincent de Paul's, also known as Avoca) 1889, restored, and graveyard (burials 1858–1911); sawmill (I.H. Bircher); school (Mimosa Dell till 1893) 1881–93, reopened 1959, additions 1968; telephone 1914; TX 1917, automatic 1978; pop. 133 (1901), 131 (1911), 166 (1933), 157 (1947), 107 (1954), 283 (1961), 171 (2006), 355 (2011).

Black Swamp (*Co. Clive*) 29°01'S. 152°09'E., 13 km E. of Tenterfield; farming and grazing; airfield; cemetery; PO 1927–71; school 1884–1954; telephone 1914; TX 1928; pop. 143 (1933), 159 (1947), 63 (1954), 51 (1961).

Blacktown (*Co. Northumberland*) see Killingworth.

Blackville (*Co. Pottinger*) 31°38'S. 150°14'E., 44 km W. of Quirindi; village gaz. 1888; grazing and wheat; Angl. C. (St Aidan's) 1966, removed from Yarraman; cemetery; CH 1881, new one b. 1909 by T. Jones, reused; electricity 1957; mouse plague 1922; PO 1875–1994; PS 1875, new one b. 1909 by T. Jones, closed 1934; Rom. Cath. C. (St Philip and St James's), and graveyard (4 graves 1876–84), church closed and moved to Quirindi; school 1878–81, reopened 1911, additions 1923 by E.W. Anderson, additions 1963 and 2010; telegraph 1892; TX 1911; Union C. 1892 d. by Francis Wilson Darby, closed, reused 1966; water supply 1968; pop. 70 (1911), 102 (1933), 91 (1947), 93 (1954), 187 (1961), 181 (2006).

Blackwall (*Co. Northumberland*) 33°30'S. 151°20'E., 2 km SE of Woy Woy, on Brisbane Water; (incl. Orange Grove, formerly Blackwall Point); estab. by Rock Davis; shipbuilding 1829–1953 and tourism; Angl. C. (St Luke's) 1903; bridge (The Rip Bridge),

1,082 ft (330 m) cantilevered arch, to Daleys Point, b. 1974 by John Holland (Constructions) Pty Ltd, d. by Albert Fried, over Brisbane Water; bushfire (Orange Grove) 1944; electricity (from Newcastle) 1929; PO 1875–1993; reservoir; sawmill; shipyard (Rock Davis) 1862, covered 1864, closed 1913; telegraph 1881; telephone 1893; wharves: one b. 1898 by Rock Davis, demolished, and one b. 1901 by George Lawson; pop. 120 (1901), 160 (1911), 343 (1933), 349 (1947), 1,738 (2011).

Blackwall (*Co. Northumberland*) see also Woy Woy.

Blackwall (*Co. Rous*) see Wardell.

Blackwall Point (*Co. Northumberland*) see Blackwall.

Blady Grass Hill (*Co. Cook*) 33°34'S. 150°39'E., 1 km SW of Kurrajong.

Blair Athol (*Co. Nandewar*) 30°39'S. 150°12'E., 17 km NE of Boggabri, on Bollol Ck; school 1931–44 and 1957–58.

Blair Hill (*Co. Gough*) 29°54'S. 151°48'E., 20 km S. of Glen Innes, on Ben Lomond Ck; Union C.; pop. 51 (1901), 20 (1933).

Blairmore (*Co. Brisbane*) 32°10'S. 150°53'E., 1 km W. of Aberdeen; pop. 101 (1933), 91 (1947), 114 (1954), 108 (1961).

Blairsdale (*Co. Parry*) 31°08'S. 150°51'E., 9 km SW of Tamworth; telephone 1915.

Blake (*Co. Nandewar*) 30°25'S. 150°08'E., 32 km N. of Boggabri, on Black Mountain Ck; school 1907–26; pop. 32 (1933).

Blakebrook (*Co. Rous*) 28°46'S. 153°14'E., 6 km NW of Lismore, on Terania Ck; timber, farming, dairying; brickworks (Tirrania) estab. by T. Atkin; PO 1888–1931; quarry; school (Tirrannia Creek till 1907) 1873, additions and repairs 1888 by Frank Pospichal, burnt down 1907, new one b. 1907 on new site by Charles Kinred; telephone 1907; Wes. Meth. C. 1890, dismantled 1905, moved and re-erected at Keerrong; pop. 154 (1901), 130 (1911), 178 (1933), 80 (1954), 69 (1961), 349 (2006).

Blakney Creek (*Co. King*) 34°39'S. 149°02'E., 24 km NE of Yass, on Blakney Ck; goldmining 1858+; airfield (2 km S.); Angl. C. (Holy Trinity) 1911; quarry; school 1884–94 and 1902–20; telephone 1924; pop. 152 (1911), 78 (1933), 106 (1947), 80 (1954), 41 (1961).

Blakney Creek (*Co. King*) see also Bevendale.

Bland (*Co. Bland*) 34°00'S. 147°40'E., 34 km E. of West Wyalong, on Wah Way Ck; farming; PO 1913–48; TX 1930, automatic 1952; pop. 72 (1911), 122 (1933), 110 (2006).

Bland Billabong (*Co. Bland*) see Marsden.

Blandford (*Co. Brisbane*) 31°47'S. 150°54'E., 6 km E. of Murrurundi, on Pages R.; Murulla till 1896; village gaz. 1855 as Murulla, developed in 1860s, village gaz. 1896 as Blandford; vineyards 1858+, grazing, agric., horses; Angl. C. (St Luke's) b. 1880 by Shaw, Dunbar, M'Nair and Holt, d. by John Horbury Hunt, closed, deconsecrated 2015, sold 2016; bridges over Pages R.: Blandford Bridge (b. 1896 by Taylor, Murphy & Co., damaged 1910, destroyed 1949, replaced with steel girder spans, b. 1951–53, new concrete one 2004) and Haydons Lane Bridge; FB; flood 1949; flour mill 1858; foot-bridge b. 1878 by T. Smith, over Pages R.; PO 1861; Rom. Cath. C., extensive improvements 1916; RS (1 km SE) 1872–1990; school 1871–74, reopened 1883, repairs 1894 by J.J. M'Givney; telegraph 1883; toll-gate; pop. 126 (1861), 203 (1891), 177 (1901), 386 (1911), 295 (1933), 305 (1947), 210 (1954), 211 (1961), 323 (2011).

Bland Road Siding (*Co. Bland*) see Quandialla.

Blanket Flat (*Co. Georgiana*) 34°08'S. 149°13'E., 44 km NW of Crookwell, on Blanket Flat Ck; grazing; PO 1898–1971; quarry; school (Memundie) 1886–92; telephone 1909; TX 1921; pop. 97 (1911), 51 (1933).

Blaxland (*Co. Cook*) 33°45'S. 150°37'E., 3 km N. of Glenbrook; (incl. East Blaxland and South Blaxland); orig. The Pilgrim then Wascoe till 1914; mountain tourism in 1920s; Angl. C. (St David's) b. 1913 by Joshua Hargrave, relocated and renovated 1928, burnt down 1968, replaced 1971; bushfires 1936, 1944, 1951, 1968; Christ. Brethren Assemblies C.

(Gospel); Christ. Reformed C.; Church of Christ 1990 d. by Cornelius Jan Van Breda; FB 1958 (station b. 1961, new one 1979); PO: Blaxland 1911, East Blaxland 1968, South Blaxland 1967; Presb. C. (St Margaret's) 1968; 2 reservoirs; RS (Wascoes till 1879) 1868, new station 1902; schools: Blaxland 1926 b. by E. Andrews, additions 1959, 1961, 1981, Blaxland HS 1977, additions 1981, East Blaxland 1962, additions 1980; sewage works 1976; telephone 1914; TX 1926; Unit. C. (orig. Meth.) b. 1966 by F.C. Parrish and Elkington Pty Ltd, d. by Kenwood, Hoile and Allen; water reticulation 1945; wire works; pop. 88 (1911), 143 (1933), 143 (1938), 334 (1947), 543 (1954), 1,725 (1961), 1,281 (1964), 6,893 (1991), 7,330 (2011).

Blaxland (*Co. Fitzroy*) see Blaxlands Flat.

Blaxlands Arm (*Co. Northumberland*) 33°02'S. 151°07'E., 22 km SW of Paxton, on Blaxlands Arm.

Blaxlands Creek (*Co. Fitzroy*) 29°51'S. 152°51'E., 18 km SW of Grafton, on Blaxlands Ck; pop. 102 (1911), 73 (1933).

Blaxlands Flat (*Co. Fitzroy*) 29°55'S. 152°47'E., 29 km SW of Grafton, on Blaxlands Ck; farming and dairying; Angl. C. (removed 1918 from Ti-Tree Creek, enlarged and renovated); PO 1927–31; Presb. C.; school (Blaxland till 1925) 1900 b. by J. Cartmill, closed 1926; telephone 1909; TX 1953; pop. 74 (1901), 25 (1933).

Blaxlands Ridge (*Co. Cook*) 33°30'S. 150°44'E., 9 km NE of Kurrajong, on Turnbulls Arm; farming and fruit; bushfire 1951; FB; PO 1900; school 1905–77; telephone 1923; TX 1925; pop. 64 (1901), 61 (1933), 60 (1947), 71 (1954), 54 (1961), 464 (2011).

Blayney (*Co. Bathurst*) 33°32'S. 149°15'E., 31 km SE of Orange, on Belubula R.; settled 1826, laid out 1843 by R.G. Haddon, village gaz. 1843, first lots sold 1845, munic. proc. 1882, thrived 1870s–80s, more lots sold 1900, munic. abolished 1935; mining (copper, disc. 1881, and gold), chicory, maize, oats, barley, wheat, hay, flour milling, sheep, dairying, potatoes, peas, fruit; abattoir (Blayney Meat Packers) o. 1958 in old meat freezing works, taken over by Huttons, fire 1961, taken over by McPhee Meats, bought 1996 by ANZCO, closed 1998; airfield (1 km SW); ambulance station 1986; Angl. C. (Christ) b. 1870–72 by Josiah Shakespear, d. by Edward Gell, chancel and transepts b. 1891 by J. Bromfield, d. by James Hine, re-roofed 1929 by Peter Beddie, roof restored 1988; Angl. Catholic C. (St Luke the Healer); Assemblies of God C. (Abundant Life); Bapt. C. (Community) 2014; breweries: one estab. 1882 by C. and C.H. Inch, sold 1891 to David J. Inch and renamed Carlisle Brewery, closed 1895 and Wright's; brickworks: Barnes's, Blayney Brickyards Ltd, Hemsley's; bridge (Glasson Bridge) 1979, over Belubula R.; bronchitis epidemic (2 children died) 1900; butter factories: Blayney Butter Factory 1897 (leased by McArthur & Co., closed 1908), Country Freezing Co. Ltd, Farmers & Settlers' Co-op. Society Ltd, Swift's, closed 1950; cannery (peas); carriage-works (James Henry Marsh) 1880; cemetery (burials 1865+) 1867; CH (incl. lock-up) b. 1878–80 by William Ralston, d. by James Johnstone Barnet, additions 1883, additions 1900 d. by Walter Liberty Vernon, additions 1970; chicory mill (Parsons Bros) 1890, fire 1890, closed 1896, reopened 1900, fire 1900 (2 kilns destroyed); container terminal (FCL Interstate Transport Services); cordial factory (estab. by Hugh Heavener, jun. and Alfred John Wellesley Drayton, partnership dissolved 1917, business taken over 1917 by Drayton and Cooper, taken over by N. and F. Ashelford, burnt down 1928); diphtheria 1882 (person died), 1912, 1916; engineering and bicycle works (David Beddie); 2 FB (one station b. 1928); flood 1950; flour mills: Albion (Bernard Stimpson, acquired by John Plumb), Charles Cooper, Perseverance (Clark's, burnt down 1898, replaced 1899); hailstorm (damaged most of town) 1887; heatwave 1896; hospital 1910 d. by John Job Copeman, additions 1929, 1937, 1976, 1983, demolished, new one 2010; lime-kilns (J. Plumb) 1880–1935, derelict;

meat cannery (Hormel Cerebos) 1975; meat freezing works 1942; mines: BY Mine (gold, open-cut) 1990–91, Great Blayney Copper Mining Co. (o. 1882, incl. smelters, closed, reopened 1889 with new shafts and smelter and renamed Annandale, closed, reopened 1897 by Blayney Mining & Smelting Co., closed 1900), Sugarloaf Copper Mine; pea vining plant (R. Gordon Edgell & Sons Ltd) 1943; pet food factory (Nestle Purina) 1989, major upgrade 2014; PO 1857, new one b. 1880–82 by T. Little, additions 1885 by John Dunkley and Richard Clifford Bartlett; pound (stock) 1858; powerhouse; Presb. C. (St Paul's) b. 1862 by Henry Oliver, tower added 1870, church alterations 1902, renovations 1938, restoration 1970; PS, repairs 1892 by John Dunkley, new one 1970 d. by Margaret Watson; 5 quarries; rabbit freezing works (Country Freezing Co. Ltd) 1906, man killed 1923; railway turntable, 50 ft (15.2 m), new one, 60 ft (18.3 m), derelict; 4 reservoirs; Rom. Cath. C. b. 1877 by John Cody, d. by Edward Gell, o. 1881, additions 1932, enlargement 1954 d. by Norman Leslie Lipman, reused 1981, new one (St James the Great) o. 1981 in former cinema; RS 1876, station b. by James Stuart Douglas, man killed 1904, refreshment rooms 1917–57; sale-yards; scarlet fever 1889; schools: Blayney 1858, new one b. 1861 by Robert McEwen, d. by Robertson, demolished 1918, replacement b. 1880 by John Wadsworth Ashworth, d. by John Hale, repairs 1883 by Josiah Shakespear, additions 1886 by J.H. Oates, d. by William Edmund Kemp, additions 1893 by John Henry Gain, alterations 1917 by John Bridgman, new building 1930, new building b. 1934 by Palmer and Powell, additions 1959, 1961, 1964, 1967, and HS 1970, additions 1972 and 1974; sewerage 1966, augmentation 1990; snowstorms 1915 and 1928; soap-works 1880; storm 1913; tanneries; TC 1934, closed, sold; telegraph 1876, new office b. 1880–82 by T. Little, additions 1885 by John Dunkley and Richard Clifford Bartlett; TX 1909, automatic 1973; typhoid 1897 and 1903; Unit. C. (orig. Wes. Meth.) b. 1886 by Josiah James Atkins, d. by James Hine, re-roofed 1939, vestry added 1965; waterworks 1902; Wes. Meth. C. 1843, replaced 1862, reused, extended 1912 and 1928; pop. 91 (1866), 122 (1871), 720 (1881), *c.*750 (1884), *c.*1,000 (1887), 1,254 (1891), *c.*1,300 (1895), 1,529 (1901), 1,729 (1911), 1,345 (1921), 1,588 (1933), 1,592 (1947), 1,688 (1954), 1,852 (1961), 1,909 (1966), 2,164 (1971), 2,535 (1976), 2,694 (1981), 2,593 (1986), 2,652 (1991), 2,672 (1996), 2,613 (2001), 2,745 (2006), 2,810 (2011).

Bletchington (*Co. Wellington*) see Orange.

Blighty (*Co. Townsend*) 35°35'S. 145°19'E., 34 km E. of Deniliquin; soldiers' settlement; bushfire 1922; drought 1927; FB; horse dip 1937; PO 1927; school 1957; telephone 1923; TX 1924, automatic 1949; pop. 71 (1933), 155 (1947), 221 (1954), 163 (1961), 337 (2006), 396 (2011).

Bloomfield (*Co. Bathurst*) see Orange (*Co. Wellington*).

Bloomhill (*Co. Westmoreland*) 33°34'S. 149°41'E., 18 km SE of Bathurst; farming; PO 1927, closed in two months; school 1876 b. by S. Smith, closed 1930; Wes. Meth. C. 1863, replaced 1880; pop. 89 (1901), 30 (1933).

Bloomsdale (*Co. Gordon*) see Suntop.

Blossom Lodge Flat (*Camden*) 34°07'S. 150°26'E., 18 km NW of Picton, on Nattai R.; colliery (Valley Colliery No. 2), abandoned.

Blowclear (*Co. Cunningham*) 33°00'S. 147°52'E., 17 km SE of Trundle; airfield (World War II).

Blow Clear (*Co. Gipps*) 33°43'S. 147°14'E., 23 km N. of West Wyalong; agric.; earth tremor 2005; mine; school 1916–52; telephone 1915; pop. 151 (1933), 109 (1947), 91 (1954), 79 (1961).

Blowering (*Co. Buccleuch*) 35°27'S. 148°16'E., 17 km S. of Tumut, on Blowering Reservoir; disc. 1824 by Hamilton Hume and William Hilton Hovell, settled in 1830s by Benjamin Clayton; orig. tobacco then dairying and mixed farming till 1960s; Angl. C. (St Simon's) b. 1880 by Kinred Bros, d. by Alberto Dias Soares, additions 1925; dam proposed 1876 by Frederick Kinred, b. 1968 by Morrison-Knudsen-Utah-McDonald, 368 ft (112.2 m) high; FB 1942; flood 1952; PO 1878–1912; school 1874–1939; telephone 1910; trout farm 1972; TX 1914; pop. 207 (1911), 96 (1933).

Blowering West (*Co. Selwyn*) 35°29'S. 148°16'E., 11 km NE of Batlow, on Blowering Reservoir; farming and dairying; PO 1927–32; school 1904–25; telephone 1926; TX 1928; pop. 62 (1901), 124 (1933), 110 (1947), 163 (1954), 140 (1961).

Blue Bay (*Co. Northumberland*) 33°21'S. 151°30'E., 2 km S. of The Entrance, on Blue Bay; (incl. Toowoon Bay, also known as Chinamans Bay); Christ. Brethren Assemblies C. (Gospel); PO (Toowoon Bay) 1950; pop. 1,025 (2011).

Blue Gum Flat (*Co. Northumberland*) see Ourimbah.

Blue Haven (*Co. Northumberland*) 33°13'S. 151°30'E., 2 km NW of Charmhaven, on Wallarah Ck; bridge 1916, replaced 1933, to Charmhaven, over Wallarah Ck; school 1999; sewerage 1990; pop. 5,879 (2006), 6,167 (2011).

Blue Hill (*Co. Argyle*) 35°17'S. 149°47'E., 18 km N. of Braidwood, on Sandy Ck.

Blue Knob (*Co. Rous*) 28°33'S. 153°11'E., 7 km NW of Nimbin, on Calico Ck; bridge (Suffolk Bridge) over Calico Ck; FB; rifle range 1915; school 1920–65; telephone 1915; TX 1927; pop. 83 (1911), 172 (1933), 129 (1947), 119 (1954), 130 (1961), 168 (2011).

Blue Mountain (*Co. Cook*) see Lawson.

Bluey (*Co. Durham*) 32°02'S. 151°19'E., 42 km E. of Scone, on Carters Brook; grazing; PO 1893–1921; pop. 50 (1901).

Blueys Beach (*Co. Gloucester*) 32°21'S. 152°32'E., 19 km S. of Forster, on Tasman Sea; orig. Twenty by Twelve; subdivided 1949; sand mining; pop. 135 (2006).

Bluff Bridge (*Co. Cook*) see Linden.

Bluff River (*Co. Clive*) see Sandy Flat.

Bluff Rock (*Co. Clive*) 29°10'S. 152°00'E., 13 km S. of Tenterfield, on Bluff Ck; farming; PO 1927; railway accident (man killed) 1892; RS 1889, station closed and removed 1975; school 1884–85; telephone 1916; TX 1928; pop. 29 (1933), 53 (1954).

Boambee (*Co. Raleigh*) 30°20'S. 153°04'E., 5 km NW of Sawtell, on Boambee Ck; (incl. North Boambee Valley); bypassed by highway 1950; farming and fruit; Assemblies of God C.; bushfire 1936; PO 1927; pottery (Southern Cross) estab. 1987 by Jeff Sosower; quarry (Readymix Holdings Pty Ltd); RS 1915–46; sawmills: Coffs Harbour Timber Co., Moran's, Guy Degory Thorne Seccombe, burnt down 1936; school 1907, new one b. 1918 by C.J. Frank, additions 1994; sugar mills: James Newport 1882, Hermann Pade, August Schneider 1883; telephone 1915; TX 1944, automatic 1955; pop. 79 (1911), 259 (1933), 504 (1947), 511 (1954), 518 (1961), 988 (1996), 1,152 (2001), 1,188 (2006), 1,545 (2011).

Boambee East (*Co. Raleigh*) see Toormina.

Boambee Valley North (*Co. Raleigh*) see Boambee.

Boambolo (*Co. Murray*) 34°58'S. 148°54'E., 13 km S. of Yass; PO 1884.

Boara (*Co. Monteagle*) 34°22'S. 148°16'E., 6 km SW of Young, on Spring Ck; farming and orchards; goldmine; school (Burrangong Heights till 1919) 1880–1975; TX 1928; pop. 24 (1933), 128 (1947).

Boat Alley (*Co. Dampier*) see Bodalla.

Boat Harbour (*Co. Gloucester*) 32°47'S. 152°07'E., 5 km SE of Anna Bay, on Tasman Sea; (incl. One Mile); quarry; reservoir; pop. 11 (1961), 313 (1986), 327 (1991), 500 (1996), 509 (2001), 813 (2006), 1,478 (2011).

Boat Harbour (*Co. Macquarie*) see Mariaville.

Boat Harbour (*Co. Raleigh*) see Bellingen and Utungun.

Boat Harbour (*Co. Rous*) 28°46'S. 153°22'E., 6 km NW of Wollongbar; farming; PO 1927–30; telephone 1925; TX 1927; pop. 219 (1911), 147 (1933), 153 (1947), 120 (1954), 150 (1961).

Boat Harbour (*Co. St Vincent*) see Ulladulla.

Bobadah (*Co. Flinders*) 32°18'S. 146°42'E., 94 km SW of Nyngan; silver and goldmining 1896+, copper till *c.*1914; cemetery 1899;

hailstorm 1906; rabbit freezing works; mines: Long Panel, Overflow, Recovery, Star of the Range, West Bogan; PO 1897, burnt down 1938; pound (stock) 1899; PS 1897, new one b. 1899 by A.G. Litchfield, closed 1934; school 1897–1919 and 1957–72; telephone 1916; TX 1945, automatic 1979; pop. 96 (1901), 102 (1911), 99 (1933), 69 (1947), 71 (1954), 72 (1961), 204 (2006).

Bobby Whitlow (*Co. Murchison*) see Whitlow.

Bobin (*Co. Macquarie*) 31°43'S. 152°17'E., 19 km NW of Wingham, on Dingo Ck; thrived 1918+; orig. timber, farming, dairying *c.*1918–75; Angl. C. (St Stephen's) b. 1903 by O'Brien and Joyce, closed 1965, demolished; butter factory (Wingham & Upper Manning Dist. Co-op. Butter & Bacon Co., which became Wingham Rural Co-op. Society Ltd) b. 1918 by Harry Brewer and R. Clinch, d. by Grant, closed 1926; PO 1909; Presb. C. b. 1906 by Arthur Rye; sawmill (Stuart J. Donaldson & Sons), burnt down 1926; school (Bobin Flat till 1974) 1902 b. by John M'Pherson, extended 1912 by John Wallace, additions 1982 and 2010, fire 2019; storm 1907; telephone 1914; TX 1919; pop. 197 (1911), 229 (1933), 234 (1947), 167 (1954), 148 (1961).

Bobin Flat (*Co. Macquarie*) see Bobin.

Bobingah (*Co. Wellesley*) 36°28'S. 149°15'E., 28 km S. of Cooma; bushfire 1952; RS (Dalkeith and Baker's Siding till 1921) 1920, public platform 1941, closed 1975.

Bo Bo Creek (*Co. Gloucester*) 31°57'S. 152°18'E., 11 km SW of Wingham, on Bo Bo Ck; bridge b. 1898 by H. Gore, over Bo Bo Ck; cemetery (268 graves 1888+) 1863; PO 1906–10; Presb. C. 1858; sawmill (Mulhearn Bros Ltd); school (Bow Bow Creek till *c.*1900) 1859–68, reopened 1882, new building b. 1884 by G.E. Levick, new building b. 1925 by F.C. Schmitzer, closed 1967; Union C. 1899; pop. 50 (1901), 85 (1911), 23 (1933).

Bobs Creek (*Co. Ashburnham*) see Amaroo.

Bobs Farm (*Co. Gloucester*) 32°46'S. 152°01'E., 5 km W. of Anna Bay; oysters, hort., rutile mining 1967–71; brewery (Murray's Craft Brewing Co.); Jehovah's Witnesses C.; PO 1925; school 1932; telephone 1920; TX 1921; wineries: Diver's Luck (Ray Family Holdings, sold 2017 to Hometown Australia), Port Stephens (estab. 1984, o. 1993), Wonganella Estate (estab. by Kim and Natalie Stevens); pop. 111 (1933), 146 (1947), 116 (1954), 134 (1961), 236 (2006), 504 (2011).

Bob's Range (*Co. Camden*) see Orangeville.

Bobundara (*Co. Wallace*) 36°29'S. 148°59'E., 20 km SE of Berridale, on Woolpack Ck; grazing; bridge over Bobundara Ck; cemetery 1885; FB; PO 1863–93; TX (automatic); pop. *c.*40 (1866), 23 (1933).

Bocoble (*Co. Wellington*) 32°48'S. 149°43'E., 23 km W. of Rylstone, on Triangle Ck; grazing; PO 1927–30; pop. 63 (1901), 243 (2006).

Bocobra (*Co. Ashburnham*) 33°06'S. 148°32'E., 33 km E. of Parkes; FB; pop. 34 (1933).

Boconnoc (*Co. Wallace*) see Buckenderra.

Bodalla (*Co. Dampier*) 36°05'S. 150°03'E., 7 km W. of Tuross Head; formerly known as Boat Alley; surveyed and laid out 1851 by Samuel Parkinson, subdivided 1856 by John Hawdon, founded and relocated 1870, rebuilt by Thomas Sutcliffe Mort, thrived 1878, subdivided 1893, private village commenced to be sold off 1923–26, final sales 1989; agric., grazing, vegetables, dairying, cheese, bacon; airfield; Angl. C. (All Saints') first stage b. 1880–83 by Joseph Ziegler, d. by Edmund Thomas Blacket and Cyril Blacket, second stage b. 1899–1902; bushfires 1895, 1929, 1965, 1968; cemetery (graves 1874+); CH o. 1928 (removed from Nerrigundah), closed 1971; cheese factories: Bodalla Co-op. Cheese Society Ltd (b. 1954 by A. Christensen & Co., d. by Cropper and Andrew, closed 1987, disused) and Bodalla Dairy Cheese Factory (Sandra McCuaig) 2011; creamery (Bodalla Co. Ltd), incl. bacon factory; electricity 1951; FB; floods 1860, 1867, 1870, 1891, 1914, 1925, 1934 (man died); flour mill 1855; lock-up, closed; milk factory (Bodalla Marketing Ltd); PO 1857, new one b. 1877, replacement 1899, closed, bought 1989 by John Gosbell, restored 2000 by John Hackwell; PS o. 1926 (removed from Nerrigundah), closed during

World War II, reopened 1948; punt 1863, across Tuross R.; Rom. Cath. C. (orig. St Edmund and Our Lady of the Assumption, now Star of the Sea) b. 1886 by Laidley Mort, d. by John Horbury Hunt; sawmills: Clyde Sawmilling Co., Tuross Steam-sawmills (estab. 1866 by J.H. Longworth, alias James Brooks, acquired by E. Brown, Goodwin and Hicks Bros), Ironbark Timber Co. (removed 1914 from Conjola); school 1867–68, reopened 1876, new one b. 1878, additions 1880 and 1900, new building b. 1921, reused, replaced; tannery; telegraph 1876, new office b. 1877; tramway (to Narooma) b. by Thomas Sutcliffe Mort; TX 1918, automatic 1959; Unit. C. (orig. Meth.) 1966; pop. 136 (1871), 375 (1881), 388 (1891), 323 (1901), 319 (1911), 255 (1933), 239 (1947), 272 (1954), 242 (1961), 230 (1976), 224 (1981), 291 (1986), 319 (1991), 309 (1996), 316 (2001), 308 (2006), 294 (2011).

Bodangora (*Co. Bligh*) 32°27'S. 149°00'E., 14 km NE of Wellington; Mitchell's Creek till 1892, then Daviesville till 1897; village gaz. 1897, thrived in 1890s, now largely abandoned; mining (gold disc. 1849) till 1917 and farming; airfield; Angl. C. (St John's) removed 1901 from Maryvale and re-erected by Ford, destroyed 1907; Bapt. C. 1902, damaged 1907; boot factory (Foley's), burnt down 1903; cemetery (150 graves 1870s–1974) 1899; cyclone 1907; fires 1899, 1903, 1911; mine (Bodangora Gold Mining Co. and Mitchell's Creek Gold Mining Co.) 1875, man killed 1905, closed 1918, plant dismantled and sold 1919, reopened 1941 for sulphur treatment; PO 1893, new one b. 1905 by Peter Beddie; PS b. 1896 by Lowe and Deans, repairs 1905 by William Carter, closed 1932, moved 1934 to Gulargambone by Charles Alexander Stewart Boag, re-erected and reused; Rom. Cath. C. (St Joseph's), removed 1899 from Kaiser, destroyed 1907, replacement (St Paul's) b. 1907–9 by William Jones & Sons, d. by A. Kennard, seldom used after 1964; school (Mitchells Creek till 1893 then Daviesville till 1906) 1892, additions 1894 by F.H. Kennard, new one b. 1900 by A.W. Lowe, damaged 1907, closed 1970, reused; stamper battery (McGregor's Reef) 1869; storm 1900; telephone 1896; TX; Wes. Meth. C. 1895, damaged 1907; pop. 871 (1901), 684 (1911), 191 (1933), 102 (1947), 158 (1954), 154 (1961), 271 (2006).

Boeill Creek (*Co. Wentworth*) 34°09'S. 142°06'E., 8 km SE of Dareton.

Bogabri (*Co. Pottinger*) see Boggabri.

Bogaduck (*Co. Argyle*) see Hanworth.

Bogaldie (*Co. Baradine*) see Bugaldie.

Bogamildie (*Co. Courallie*) see Marambir.

Bogan (*Co. Oxley*) 32°03'S. 147°28'E., 51 km SW of Warren; pop. 126 (2006).

Bogangar (*Co. Rous*) 28°20'S. 153°34'E., 8 km S. of Kingscliff, on Coral Sea; (incl. Cabarita Beach); mineral sand processing; Bapt. C. (Tweed Coast Community); dredge (Zircon-Rutile Ltd) 1952; PO 1966; reservoir; school 2004; sewerage augmentation 1985; pop. 400 (1976), 956 (1981), 1,207 (1986), 1,535 (1991), 2,681 (1996), 3,043 (2001), 3,050 (2006), 3,099 (2011).

Bogan Gate (*Co. Cunningham*) 33°06'S. 147°48'E., 22 km S. of Trundle; settled by William Tom, estab. 1877, surveyed 1897 by Edwin J. Witts, thrived in 1920s; wheat and wool; ammunition depot (World War II), reactivated 1993 by air force, fire 2011, explosion 2014 destroyed a building; Angl. C. (St Luke's) b. 1902 by J.M. Job, d. by H.B. Pulver, renovated 1990; brick-kiln; bushfires 1926, 1957, 2014; cemetery (252 graves 1900+); CH b. 1902 by Henry Hollibone, new one 1913; clock tower 1922; droughts 1912 and 1919; dust storm 1930; FB; flood 1956; grasshopper infestation 1931; hailstorm 1991; heatwave 1912; PO 1896, new one b. 1914; Presb. C.; PS 1899, reused, burnt down, replaced; quarry 1929; railway turntable 1909, 50 ft (15.2 m), removed 1956; Rom. Cath. C. (All Saints') 1910; RS 1896, station b. by John Allibone, closed 1989, station reused; sawmills: Buchanan Bros, Cypress Pine Co., S.L. West; school 1898 b. by F.J. Goodwin, additions 1902 and 1904, extended 1905 by J.J. Joab, additions 1907 and 1910, new one

b. 1923 by W. Fuller; silo 1919; telegraph 1901; telephone 1899; TX 1910, automatic 1967; Union C. 1901; Unit. C., restored; water supply 1962; pop. 256 (1901), 668 (1911), 384 (1933), 416 (1947), 404 (1954), 218 (1961), *c.*200 (2000), 254 (2006), 307 (2011).

Bogee (*Co. Roxburgh*) 32°58'S. 150°06'E., 17 km SE of Kandos, on Warrangee Ck; telephone 1915; TX 1925; pop. 75 (1933), 107 (2006).

Boggabilla (*Co. Stapylton*) 28°37'S. 150°22'E., 106 km N. of Warialda, on Macintyre R.; village gaz. 1863, land sale 1894; tobacco, cotton, wheat, sheep, cattle; Angl. C. (St Alban's); Apostolic C. (Oasis Family and Community) 2017; cemeteries: old one (8 graves) and new one (293 graves); CH b. 1896 by A. Thorley; cyclone (damaged every building) 1964; FB; flood 2011; paper mill (Euraba); PO 1886, new one b. 1942 by C. Sutton; pound (stock) 1899; PS 1879, additions and alterations 1899, new one b. 1909 by F. Baker, additions and alterations 1931 by W.M. Sinton, new one b. 1973–75; railway turntable, 50 ft (15.2 m), ruined; reservoir; Rom. Cath. C. (St Francis's) 1900; RS 1932, station closed 1979, services ceased 1987, station derelict; sawmill; school 1884, additions 1892 by Thorley and Regazzi, new one 1991; TC 1990, additions 1992, became a campus of New England Institute in 1992; telegraph 1892; TX 1911; water supply augmentation 1986; wool-scour; pop. 298 (1901), 490 (1911), 469 (1933), 376 (1947), 409 (1954), 472 (1961), 393 (1971), 415 (1976), 528 (1981), 653 (1986), 751 (1991), 639 (1996), 667 (2001), 647 (2006), 628 (2011).

Boggabri (*Co. Pottinger*) 30°42'S. 150°03'E., 36 km NW of Gunnedah, on Coxs Ck; settled 1835 by Edward Cox, surveyed 1859 by John Valentine Gorman, laid out 1859 by Benjamin Charles Flide, town gaz. 1860 as Bogabri, first lots sold 1862, old village destroyed and relocated 1864 to present site; wheat, tobacco, sheep, barley, maize, lucerne hay, oats, sorghum, oilseeds, honey, cotton, fossicking; ambulance station, at hospital; Angl. C. 1891–1960, new one (St Barnabas's) 1963 (also used by Unit. C.); brickworks (W. and G. Hall); bridges: one b. 1868, replaced 1930 and 1987, over Coxs Ck, and one (lattice truss span, fabricated in England), erected 1883 by G.H. Royce & Co., re-decked 1940 by Chesterfield & Jenkins Pty Ltd, over Namoi R.; carriage-works (W. Horne); cemeteries: general (1,312 graves 1876+) and lawn (67 graves), incl. columbarium; CH b. 1878 by Alexander Hamilton Scouller, additions and alterations 1905 by Alfred Stephens, new one b. 1935 by G. Ryan, closed 1974, reused; clock tower b. 1986 by D.B. McDonald; cordial factory (Albert S. Baker), closed 1986, reused; cotton gin (Namoi Cotton Co-op.) 1994; drainage system (Caxton Street) 1882; dust storm 1920; 2 FB (station b. 1952, replaced 1997); floods 1864, 1890, 1904, 1910, 1920, 1955; flour mill (Britannia) estab. 1910 by Tremain Bros, acquired by N.B. Love & Co., fire 1948, burnt down 1951; freezing works (Boggabri Freezing Co. Ltd), taken over 1921 by Garratt Scandrett Freezing Companies Ltd, burnt down 1930; hailstorm 1921; honey factory (Michael Nelson); hospital 1913, additions 1919 by R. Wilson & Son, additions 1930, 1934, 1959, 1966; Meth. C. 1910 d. by Mitchell; mouse plague 1922; PO 1870, new one b. 1881 by Joseph Conlon, d. by James Johnstone Barnet, additions 1904 by Moses Hern; pound (stock) 1899; powerhouse (Boggabri Electric Light Co.) 1930, burnt down 1946; PS b. 1878 by Alexander Hamilton Scouller, additions and alterations 1905 by Alfred Stephens, additions and alterations 1931 by W.E. Lightfoot, additions and alterations 1934, new one 1979; railway bridge over Coxs Ck; Rom. Cath. C. b. 1887 by Curry and Elliott, relocated and reused, new one (Sacred Heart) b. 1939 by Peter J. Knudson, d. by E.A. Tolhurst; RS 1882, station b. by Joseph Conlon; sale-yards; sawmills: Eather Bros, Elliott and Humphries, sold 1917, James W.R. Horne, damaged 1920, John Humphries (became Hodson's), Humphries and Hawke, burnt down 1893, rebuilt, burnt down 1900, P. Josephson, McKechnie Bros, H. Pike,

Willowdale Saw Mill Co.; school 1873 b. by Joseph Conlon, new one b. 1882 by C. Taylor, additions 1883 by Burke and Wilson, additions 1895 by E.J. Britton, additions 1904 by A.J. Hulbert, new one 1953; sewerage 1956; silos 1934 and 1955; storm 2000; telegraph office b. 1881 by Joseph Conlon, additions 1904 by Moses Hern; TX 1908; typhoid 1878, 1899, 1903; Union C. b. 1877 by Alexander Hamilton Scouller, bought 1910 by Presb. C., closed 1915, demolished 1930, new one 1957; water supply 1940; pop. *c.*50 (1866), 94 (1871), 453 (1881), 506 (1891), *c.*500 (1895), 560 (1901), 1,953 (1911), 1,218 (1933), 1,197 (1947), 1,378 (1954), 1,256 (1961), 1,199 (1966), 1,065 (1971), 973 (1976), 1,023 (1981), 967 (1986), 958 (1991), 875 (1996), 803 (2001), 865 (2011).

Boggibri (*Co. Brisbane*) see Bow.

Boggumbil (*Co. Rous*) 28°45'S. 153°12'E., 11 km NW of Lismore, school 1888–1945.

Boggy Camp (*Co. Hardinge*) see Copeton.

Boggy Camp Flat (*Co. Clive*) 29°03'S. 151°42'E., 33 km W. of Tenterfield, on Mole R.

Boggy Creek (*Co. Bourke*) see Ganmain.

Boggy Creek (*Co. Raleigh*) 30°27'S. 152°51'E., 5 km W. of Bellingen; creamery (Foley Bros) 1897; sawmill (Hinds') 1914; pop. 55 (1933), 615 (2006).

Boggy Creek (*Co. Rous*) see Tregeagle.

Boggy Creek (*Co. Vernon*) 31°12'S. 151°51'E., 32 km SE of Walcha.

Boggy Plain (*Co. Beresford*) 36°08'S. 149°29'E., 34 km E. of Cooma, on Boggy Plain Ck; grazing; PO 1927–31; sawmill (Albert A. Broadhead); telephone 1922; TX 1934.

Boggy Swamp Creek (*Co. Hunter*) 32°57'S. 150°42'E., 60 km SW of Singleton, on Boggy Swamp Ck; cemetery (3 graves), disused.

Boginderra (*Co. Bland*) 34°13'S. 147°38'E., 27 km NE of Temora; telephone 1928; TX 1928.

Bogleburn (*Co. Durham*) see Dellhurst.

Bogolong (*Co. Forbes*) 33°51'S. 148°05'E., 9 km NW of Grenfell; mining; cemetery (4 infant burials); dam (2 km E.); mines: Bell Bird (manganese) 1915–41, Bogalong (tin) 1870–1927, Simpson's (manganese) *c.*1915–1941; school 1886–1904 and 1957–71; pop. 106 (1933), 124 (1947), 112 (1954).

Bogolong (*Co. Harden*) see Bookham.

Bogree (*Co. Courallie*) see Ashley.

Bogtown (*Co. Murray*) see Captains Flat.

Bohena (*Co. White*) 30°30'S. 149°39'E., 24 km SW of Narrabri, on Bohena Ck; pop. 72 (1933), 209 (1947).

Bohena Creek (*Co. White*) 30°25'S. 149°43'E., 13 km SW of Narrabri; pop. 25 (1933), 209 (1947), 95 (1954), 403 (2006).

Bohnock (*Co. Gloucester*) 31°57'S. 152°34'E., 3 km NW of Old Bar, on Manning R. (South Channel); farming; bridge (Neville Weiley Bridge) b. 1958 by E.S. Clementson Pty Ltd, 571 ft (174 m), to Oxley Island, over Manning R. (South Channel); PO 1916; sawmill (Street's); school 1900–68; telephone 1913; TX 1927; pop. 99 (1911), 111 (1933), 65 (1954), 63 (1961).

Bokhara (*Co. Narran*) 29°38'S. 147°02'E., 95 km W. of Lightning Ridge; village gaz. 1878; telephone 1933.

Bokhara (*Co. Narran*) see also Goodooga.

Bolagamy (*Co. Gipps*) 33°47'S. 146°56'E., 28 km NW of West Wyalong; village gaz. 1916; PO 1918; school 1957–66; telephone 1918; pop. 59 (1954).

Bolagamy (*Co. Gipps*) see also Girral.

Bolah Gap (*Co. Buckland*) see Borambil.

Bolaro (*Co. Beresford*) 35°59'S. 148°50'E., 38 km NW of Cooma, on Murrumbidgee R.; grazing; butter factory (Scottish Aust. Invesment Co.) 1899; creamery (NSW Creamery Butter Co. Ltd) 1895; PO 1927–30; school 1898–1908; Union C. b. 1901 by Witts and Bell; pop. 30 (1933), 60 (1954).

Bolaro (*Co. Lincoln*) see Dunedoo.

Bolaro (*Co. St Vincent*) 35°40'S. 150°00'E., 16 km W. of Batemans Bay, on Buckenbowra R.; cheese factory (P. Egan).

Bolderogery (*Co. Gordon*) 32°52'S. 148°30'E., 33 km SE of Peak Hill.

Bolivia (*Co. Clive*) 29°18'S. 151°58'E., 28 km S. of Tenterfield, on Splitters Swamp Ck; farming and grazing; estab. *c.*1882; cemetery 1884–1986; flour mill (Champion, water powered) b. by Edward Irby, closed; hailstorm 1925; PO 1883–1979; Presb. C.; PS 1883; RS 1886, station b. by Henry Hendrick, closed 1974; sawmills: W.W. Edwards, Henry W. Perrin, Benjamin Martin Wade; school 1883 b. by Cobb & Co., new one b. 1900 by H. Cooper, burnt down 1905, replacement b. 1905 by James Dwyer, closed 1966, sold and removed 1970; telegraph 1883; TX 1918; pop. *c.*650 (1883), 90 (1901), 157 (1911), 149 (1933), 165 (1947), 131 (1954), 85 (1961).

Boloco (*Co. Wallace*) see Beloka.

Boloko (*Co. Wallace*) see Beloka.

Bolong (*Co. Camden*) 34°51'S. 150°40'E., 6 km NE of Nowra, on Shoalhaven R.; farming and dairying; caterpillar infestation 1911; floods 1860 and 1867; paper mill (Shoalhaven Paper Mills Pty Ltd) b. 1954–56, o. 1957, merged 1970 with Associated Pulp & Paper Mills, inundated 1974, sold 1993 to Amcor, bought 2009 by Nippon Paper Group, closed 2015; PO 1886; railway to paper mill; school (Boolong till *c.*1900) 1861, new building b. 1894 by Muller Bros, closed 1963; telephone 1915; TX 1915, automatic 1947; Union C.; water supply 1913; pop. 119 (1911), 119 (1954), 97 (1961).

Bolong (*Co. Camden*) see also Bomaderry.

Bolong (*Co. Georgiana*) 34°14'S. 149°33'E., 26 km N. of Crookwell, on Phils R.; Angl. C. (St John's) 1864 d. by Richard Leigh, re-roofed 1902, renovated 1911, damaged and closed 1947, new one b. 1951 by David Larcombe, Lyle Croker and Selby Croker, d. by K. Oliphant, and graveyard; storm 1947.

Bolton Point (*Co. Northumberland*) 33°00'S. 151°37'E., 2 km NE of Toronto, on Kooroora Bay; orig. Broughton Point; settled 1847 by Richard Fennell; PO 1933–71; school 1944–66; telephone 1927; pop. 82 (1933), 186 (1947), 275 (1954), 2,156 (2006), 2,298 (2011).

Bolton Vale (*Co. Westmoreland*) 33°37'S. 149°47'E., 13 km NW of Oberon; pop. 22 (1933).

Bolwarra (*Co. Durham*) 32°43'S. 151°34'E., 3 km N. of Maitland, on Hunter R.; (incl. Bolwarra Heights and Glenarvon); maize, millet, vegetables; diphtheria 1930; FB; floods 1857, 1867, 1870, 1874, 1893; grasshopper infestation 1907; levee b. 1865 by David Dickson; PO (Bolwarra Heights) 1953; quarry; railway bridge (steel truss) to Oakhampton, fabricated by Clyde Engineering Co. Ltd, erected 1911 by Carson, Carey and Simpson, d. by James Waller Roberts, over Hunter R.; reservoir; school 1852–70, reopened 1891 in new building b. by William King, additions 1898 by J. Irwin, additions 1954 by B. Greedy, additions 1965 and 1970, new school 1987 on new site, additions by R.T. Parker Pty Ltd; telephone (Bolwarra Heights) 1953; typhoid 1898 and 1930; Unit. C. 1958; Wes. Meth. C. b. 1878 by Henry Sherwood, d. by John Wiltshire Pender, re-roofed and renovated 1923; wharf 1894; pop. 447 (1891), 515 (1901), 409 (1911), 527 (1933), 509 (1947), 523 (1954), 589 (1961), 791 (1971), 1,095 (1976), 1,362 (1981), 1,636 (1986), *c.*1,850 (2000), 3,678 (2011).

Bolwarra Heights (*Co. Durham*) see Bolwarra.

Bomadary (*Co. Camden*) see Bomaderry.

Bomaderry (*Co. Camden*) 34°51'S. 150°37'E., 3 km N. of Nowra, on Bomaderry Ck; Bolong till 1874 then Bomadary till 1893; estab. 1859 by Berry, munic. proc. 1868, laid out 1891 by John Hay, subdivided and first lots sold 1892; dairying, farming, manufacturing; ambulance station 1973; Angl. C. 1957, fire 1977, restoration 1978, new one (St Stephen's) 1993; bacon factory estab. 1895 by L. Geoghegan, acquired 1896 by Denham Bros, additions 1897 by Munro, taken over 1905 by Shoalhaven Co-op. Bacon Curing Co. Ltd, acquired 1910 by York Castle Bacon Co. Ltd; Bapt. C.; bridges: one (wrought iron spans fabricated by Edgemoor Iron Co., Delaware, USA), erected 1881 by Onward Bates, d. by C. Shaler Smith, 1,115 ft (340 m), re-decked 1981, new one adjacent (pre-stressed concrete box girders) b. 1980 by Codelfa Constructions Pty Ltd, 1,181 ft (360 m), over Shoalhaven R., and one b. 1903 by Lawson over Bomaderry Ck; bushfire 2018; butter factories: Nowra Co-op. Dairy Co. Ltd

1902 and Shoalhaven Central Butter Factory, acquired by Denham Bros; casein factory 1943; cheese factories: S. Andronico 1933 (in old milk factory) and Nowra Co-op. Dairy Co. Ltd 1939 d. by Bryant and Stanley; clothing factory (Pelaco Ltd) 1969–70; dairy factory (Bolong Dairy Co.) 1896–1902; electricity 1927; FB (station b. 1961, closed); flood 1990; flour mill (F. Poncet) 1896; joinery (Rybrook) estab. by Michael Ryan and Scott Brookes; milk factories: Bacchus Marsh Concentrated Milk Co. 1895–1921, British Aust. Milk Condensing Co. 1923, Horlicks Pty Ltd 1937 (new one b. 1949–52 by Elweld Pty Ltd, d. by Percy James Gordon), Nowra Co-op. Dairy Co. Ltd 1912; PO 1861; Presb. C.; punt 1866, across Shoalhaven R.; railway barracks 1924, closed, sold 1990 and 2014; railway coal stage 1893; railway engine shed 1893; railway turntable (Butler's) 1893, 50 ft (15.2 m), new one (William Sellers & Co.) 1914, 60 ft (18.3 m); reservoir (concrete), 100,000 gal. (454.6 kl); Rom. Cath. C. (Sacred Heart) 1963; RS (1 km E.) 1893, station b. by Gerald Dalton Fetherston and Felix Edward Barbat, burnt down 1944, new one 1945; rubber works (John Bull Pty Ltd) 1951; sale-yards 1966; Salt C. (in old school); sawmills: Richard Shepherd (estab. by Reuben Mison, burnt down 1915) and Molloy & Sons (estab. 1917, bought 1922 by Charles Robert Winley and Aubrey George Franklin Winley and traded as Nowra Timber Co., fire 1927); schools: primary 1880, new building b. 1893 by Anton C. Wolf, d. by William Edmund Kemp, extensions and repairs 1912 by George Muller, additions 1919 by H.A. Eagles, renovations and repairs 1928, repairs 1937, additions 1955, new school 1959 on new site, additions 1961, 1963, 1967, 1978, and HS 1968, new school 1970, additions 1986; sewerage augmentation 1992; starch factory (Manildra Group) 1970, glucose plant added 1973, ethanol plant added 1991; tannery (Tom Shepherd); TC 1955, new buildings 1963, became Illawarra Institute of Technology, Nowra Campus, in 1992; telephone 1895; Unit. C. (orig. Meth.) 1951; water supply 1898, new supply 1938 from dam on Bomaderry Ck; wharf 1871; pop. *c.*50 (1866), 140 (1879), 237 (1901), 353 (1911), *c.*600 (1941), 1,465 (1954), 2,210 (1961), 2,914 (1971), 3,909 (1976), 6,600 (2006), 6,566 (2011).

Bombah Flat (*Co. Georgiana*) 33°58'S. 149°21'E., 49 km S. of Blayney, on Abercrombie R.

Bombah Point (*Co. Gloucester*) 32°30'S. 152°18'E., 14 km SE of Bulahdelah, on The Broadwater; telephone 1925; TX 1955–73.

Bombala (*Co. Wellesley*) 36°55'S. 149°14'E., 60 km W. of Merimbula, on Bombala R.; laid out by Thomas Scott Townsend and town gaz. 1849, lots sold 1854, designated as chief town of the county, munic. proc. 1890, thrived in 1890s and 1920s, munic. abolished 1977; mining, wheat till 1920, wattle-bark, forestry, vegetables, beef, wool; ambulance station; Angl. C. (St Matthias's) 1857, alterations and repairs 1861; brick-kiln (W. Reed), damaged 1873; bridges over Bombala R.: one b. 1891–93 by A.D. Taylor (McDonald timber truss, 290 ft or 88.4 m) and Cunninghams Point Bridge 1893 (McDonald timber truss, 366 ft or 111.6 m); bushfires 1884, 1895, 1896, 1929; butter factory (Bombala Co-op. Dairying Co. Ltd) 1894–1906; cemetery 1868, incl. columbarium; CH 1848, repairs 1870 by J. Roddan, new one b. 1880–82 by T. Moore, d. by James Johnstone Barnet, renovated 1926 by Mawson; cordial factories: Bell's (bought 1905 by W.J. Rogers) and James Parkinson 1872; droughts 1837–43, 1848, 1885–87; dust storm 1898; earth tremors 1872, 1877, 1885; electricity 1926; FB (station b. 1981); fires 1885, 1912, 1916; floods 1867, 1870, 1873, 1892, 1919, 1934, 2016; flour mills: Garnock Bros (leased to Bombala Milling Co. Ltd), closed 1911, Joint Stock Milling Co. (leased from M.M. Cohen), burnt down 1885, Henry Kesterton 1856, McClung Bros (water powered), Trevanion Bros; gale 1885; hailstorms 1906, 1908, 1922; hospital 1884, new one b. 1924–28, additions 1963, redeveloped 2008; lock-up b. 1891 by T. Moore, additions 1893 by John Harris; PO 1849, new one b. 1878 by F.H. Teague, additions 1880 by T. Moore, additions and alterations 1897 by Oliver & Co., additions 1908 by Moore Bros, replaced 1915; police barracks b. 1877 by J.H. Plant and G. Chidgley, additions 1879 by T. Moore, new barracks b. 1903 by D. Livingstone; pound (stock) 1849; powerhouse (Town Lighting Ltd); Presb. C. (St Andrew's) 1872, rebuilt 1912 on new site by Moore Bros; rabbit freezing works (Bombala Freezing Co. Ltd) 1916, taken over by Garratt Scandrett Freezing Companies Ltd; railway turntable, 60 ft (18.3 m), closed; reservoir; Rom. Cath. C. (St Mary's) d. and b. 1867 by Peter Ressler, replacement (Shrine of Our Lady of the Blessed Sacrement) 1941, restored 2008; RS 1921–74; sale-yards b. 1905 by P.H. Williams; sawmills: Dongwha Timbers 2013, T. Hite, George Sydney Rayner, Tableland Sawmills Pty Ltd (estab. 1963 by Jack Cuthbertson and Ray Richards); scarlet fever 1911; schools: primary 1863, additions and alterations 1925 by H.G. Allen, additions 1935, 1960, 1965, 1972, 2010, and HS 1973, additions 1982; sewage works; snowstorms 1853 and 1870; storms 1882, 1888, 1936; streets electric lit 1926; tanneries: D. Beileiter, Edward Hyde 1871 (burnt down 1872), George Lemon 1872; TC; telegraph 1867, new office b. 1878 by F.H. Teague, additions and alterations 1897 by Oliver & Co.; telephone (South Bombala) 1950; TX 1910; Unit. C. (orig. Wes. Meth.) 1873 d. by Thomas Rowe, extended 1944, closed and sold 2018; water supply 1940; wattle-bark mill (Craig, Mostyn & Co.); weir on Coolumbooka R.; woollen mill (Toorallie); pop. 123 (1851), 319 (1856), 405 (1861), *c.*500 (1866), 565 (1871), *c.*800 (1876), *c.*1,000 (1881), 1,101 (1891), *c.*1,020 (1895), *c.*1,100 (1896), 986 (1901), 1,039 (1911), 931 (1933), *c.*950 (1941), 1,111 (1947), 1,258 (1954), 1,389 (1961), 1,495 (1966), 1,490 (1971), 1,474 (1976), 1,504 (1981), 1,458 (1986), 1,404 (1991), 1,380 (1996), 1,226 (2001), 1,206 (2006), 1,210 (2011).

Bombay (*Co. Murray*) 35°26'S. 149°39'E., 13 km W. of Braidwood, on Bombay Ck; barytes mining; airfield; bushfire 1918; FB; mine (General Mining & Investment Co. Ltd et al.) 1917–19, 1941–44, 1946–47; sawmill, closed 1928; telephone 1934; TX 1934; typhoid (man died) 1897; pop. 54 (1901), 49 (1933), 55 (1954), 243 (2006).

Bombira Hill (*Co. Phillip*) 32°35'S. 149°36'E., 2 km NE of Mudgee, on Lawsons Ck; aeroplane crash (2 killed) 2014; airport (Mudgee) 1937–49, new one 1955 on new site, terminal upgraded 2018; brickworks (Mudgee); cemetery (Mudgee) 1886; distillery (Baker Williams) estab. 2011 by Helen Baker and Nathan Williams; wineries: Gooree Park (Eduardo Cojuangco, jun.) 1979, High Valley Wine & Cheese Co., Mudgee Wines 1977, Platt's Wines Mudgee Pty Ltd 1895 (acquired 2004 by Mudgee Growers), Queens Pinch Vineyard (estab. 1995 by Braddock as Cedars Vineyard, bought 2004 by Andrew Buchanan), Red Clay Estate 1997, Frederick Roth 1902, Shawwood Estate (Craig Bishop) 1998, Vinifera Wines (Tony and Debbie McKendry); pop. 101 (1911), 53 (1933).

Bombo (*Co. Camden*) 34°40'S. 150°51'E., 2 km N. of Kiama, on Tasman Sea; farming and basalt quarrying; Angl. C. (St Oswald's) 1913, removed from Crawley Forest, closed, sold 1949; cemetery (Kiama, 2,881 graves 1855+), incl. lawn cemetery and columbaria; gale 2013; jetty 1882, collapsed; PO 1892; quarries (incl. William Carson 1890, George Hill 1883–90, William Meader & Co., one operated 1921–47); quarry accident (man killed) 1891; railway turntable 1887, removed 1893; railway viaduct (timber) 1893, replacement (concrete) 1993; RS (North Kiama till 1889, Kiama till 1893, North Kiama till 1907) 1887, station b. by A. Brown; sawmill (Madden and Madden), fire 1947; school 1890–1948; sewage works; telephone 1922; tramway (for basalt transport) to Kiama 1880, replaced 1914, closed 1961; pop. 150 (1911), 191 (1961), 30 (2011).

Bom Bom (*Co. Clarence*) 29°46'S. 152°56'E., 6 km S. of South Grafton; lawn cemetery

(Clarence, 8,741 plots *c.*1965+), incl. columbaria.

Bombowlee (*Co. Buccleuch*) 35°16'S. 148°15'E., 6 km N. of Tumut; FB 1951; school 1882, new one b. 1884 by Frederick Eberlin and Thomas Brashier, closed 1914; telephone 1926; pop. 377 (1911), 278 (1933), 255 (1947), 192 (1954), 221 (1961), 268 (2011).

Bomen (*Co. Clarendon*) 35°04'S. 147°25'E., 6 km NE of Wagga Wagga, on Dukes Ck; farming; abattoir (Wagga Country Killing Works) b. 1951 by John Grant & Sons Pty Ltd, closed 1981, reopened 1985 by Charles David Pty Ltd, bought 1991 by Cargill; PO 1878; railway barracks 1879; railway turntable, removed; RS (North Wagga Wagga till 1882) 1878, station b. by Charles Hardy, closed; school (North Wagga Wagga) 1880; telephone 1915; winery (Bidgeebong Wines Ltd) 2000; pop. 84 (1911), 146 (1933), 157 (1991), 157 (1996).

Bomera (*Co. Pottinger*) 31°33'S. 149°48'E., 32 km N. of Coolah; RS 1923–75; pop. 51 (1933), 143 (2006), 269 (2011).

Bon Accord (*Co. Mitchell*) 35°14'S. 147°12'E., 8 km NE of The Rock; RS 1891–1962.

Bonalbo (*Co. Buller*) 28°44'S. 152°37'E., 40 km W. of Kyogle, on Peacock Ck; estab. 1911 by McNamee, village gaz. 1935; cattle, dairying, pigs, maize, pumpkins, logging, mining; ambulance station 1949; Angl. C. built 1921 as hall, converted 1929 to church, closed, new one (Our Lady) 1962; brick-kiln; bridge, destroyed 1953, temporary bridge 1953, new one (Jane Robertson Bridge) 1960, over Peacock Ck; butter factory and ice works (Bonalbo Co-op. Dairy Co.) d. and b. 1911 by M'Donald-Hercules Refrigerating Co., new one 1928, taken over 1929 by Norco Co-op. Ltd, closed, reused; cemetery (261 graves); coalmine (Peacock Creek) estab. 1945 by S. Rundle, George Allen and Harry Greenwood, acquired by Bonalbo Collieries Pty Ltd, closed 1972; cordial factory (Jack McQueen) 1929–46; dam, 43 ft (13 m) high, 1968; electricity 1950; FB (station b. 1959); fire 1957, largely destroyed town; floods 1930, 1947, 1953, 2011; Jehovah's Witnesses C.; Meth. C. (Union C. till 1929); PO 1912, burnt down 1957, replaced 1958; Presb. C. (St Andrew's) 1913–2018; PS 1928–69, new one 1969; reservoir, 200,000 gal. (909.2 kl), 1968; Rom. Cath. C. (St Patrick's) 1929; saleyards (Ted Johnston) 1934; sawmills: F.J. Canon 1900, Duncan's Holdings Ltd, Stan Priest (taken over 1921 by Bonalbo Timber Co. Ltd, rebuilt); school 1919, additions 1938 by Ryan and Hoyle, additions 1964 and 1969; SD Adventist C.; storm 2007; telephone 1913; TX 1914; Union C., reused; Unit. C. (West of the Range Community, orig. Meth.) 1959; water reticulation 1968; pop. 129 (1911), 480 (1933), 485 (1947), 632 (1954), 539 (1961), 533 (1966), 494 (1971), 478 (1976), 466 (1981), 440 (1986), 448 (1991), 363 (1996), 337 (2001), 313 (2006), 287 (2011). (See also Old Bonalbo.)

Bonalbo Creek (*Co. Buller*) 28°35'S. 152°40'E., 33 km W. of Kyogle, on Bonalbo Ck; sawmill.

Bona Vista (*Co. Durham*) 32°41'S. 151°38'E., 9 km S. of Paterson; tobacco factory (James Phillips).

Bona Vista (*Co. Inglis*) 30°55'S. 150°41'E., 19 km S. of Manilla; earth tremor 2012.

Bona Vista (*Co. Sandon*) see Armidale.

Bondo (*Co. Buccleuch*) 35°15'S. 148°28'E., 24 km E. of Tumut; pop. 20 (1933).

Boneshaw (*Co. Arrawatta*) see Bonshaw.

Boneys Rocks (*Co. Ashburnham*) see Burdett.

Bongalong (*Co. Harden*) 34°49'S. 148°07'E., 21 km S. of Cootamundra, on Muttama Ck; cemetery; RS 1887–1969.

Bong Bong (*Co. Camden*) 34°32'S. 150°23'E., 2 km NE of Moss Vale, on Wingecarribee R.; estab. 1820, surveyed 1821 by William Harper, abandoned 1837, defunct (except for church); agric., grazing, potatoes; Angl. C. (Christ or Throsby Church) 1845 d. by John Verge, re-roofed and renovated 1884 by Rigby, Hopkins and Rigby, d. by Blacket Bros, and graveyard (16 graves 1847+); bridge (concrete) 1917, demolished 1976, replaced, over Wingecarribee R.; bushfire 1904; commissariat store 1831; lock-up; military barracks 1829; PO 1829–37; pound (stock)

1843, relocated 1858; PS; reservoir; RS (Austermere till 1889) 1879–1913; snowstorm 1935; weir 1894, on Wingecarribee R.

Bong Bong (*Co. Camden*) see also Berrima.

Bongongalong (*Co. Harden*) 34°56'S. 148°03'E., 15 km N. of Gundagai, on Bongongalong Ck; farming and grazing; PO 1892–1930; school 1884–89 and 1952–61; pop. 77 (1901), 52 (1911), 61 (1933).

Bongongo (*Co. Buccleuch*) 35°05'S. 148°24'E., 27 km E. of Gundagai; bushfire 1908; Rom. Cath. C. (St Patrick's) b. 1912 by Thomas Owen, d. by Butler; school 1902; pop. 67 (1901), 61 (1911).

Bongongo (*Co. Buccleuch*) see also Adjungbilly.

Bonnells Bay (*Co. Northumberland*) 33°06'S. 151°31'E., 5 km N. of Mannering Park, on Lake Macquarie; (incl. East Morisset, Morisset Park subdivided 1878, Scarborough, Windermere Park); Assemblies of God C. (Lake Macquarie); jetty; PO: Bonnells Bay 1957 and Morisset Park 1956; Salv. Army C.; school 1912–38, reopened 1955, additions 1966, new one b. 1993; SD Adventist C. (Lakeside); telephone: Bonnells Bay 1948 and Morisset Park 1956; water supply 1951; pop. 82 (1933), 53 (1947), 231 (1954), 400 (1961), 349 (1971), 552 (1976), 849 (1981), 1,087 (1986), 2,566 (1991), 3,186 (1996), 4,042 (2001), 4,423 (2011).

Bonnie Dell (*Co. Ashburnham*) 33°25'S. 148°15'E., 22 km E. of Forbes; school (sometimes spelt Bonny Dell) 1913–25; pop. 141 (1947).

Bonnie Doon (*Co. White*) 30°23'S. 149°22'E., 19 km S. of Wee Waa.

Bonnington Park (*Co. Durham*) 32°17'S. 151°33'E., 24 km NW of Dungog, on Chads Ck; grazing and dairying; telephone 1911.

Bonny Dell (*Co. Ashburnham*) see Bonnie Dell.

Bonny Hills (*Co. Macquarie*) 31°36'S. 152°51'E., 7 km NE of Laurieton, on Tasman Sea; Suterville till 1948; Assemblies of God C. (Christ. Life); bridge over Saltwater Ck; FB; PO 1966; 3 reservoirs; school (Lake Cathie) 2015; sewage works; telephone 1948; TX 1958, automatic 1971; Unit. C., closed 2015; pop. 43 (1961), 261 (1976), 538 (1981), 873 (1986), 1,204 (1991), 1,469 (1996), 2,195 (2001), 2,540 (2006), 2,661 (2011).

Bonshaw (*Co. Arrawatta*) 29°03'S. 151°16'E., 35 km NE of Ashford; orig. Boneshaw; village gaz. 1866 as Banshaw; grazing, tobacco, fishing; Angl. C. (St Luke's) 1938, closed, sold 2004; cemetery (29 graves); PO 1866, burnt down 1963; Rom. Cath. C. (Sacred Heart) 1950, closed, sold and reused; school 1939, additions 1962; telephone 1913; TX 1913; pop. 36 (1891), 133 (1911), 785 (1933), 69 (1947), 256 (1954), 287 (1961), 172 (2006).

Bonville (*Co. Raleigh*) 30°22'S. 153°02'E., 4 km W. of Sawtell, on Bonville Ck; bypassed by highway 2008; forestry, hort., bananas; Angl. C. (Holy Faith) b. 1914–23 by W. Jacobs, Patterson and Mathis, d. by A.E. Fowler, burnt down 2015; cheese factory (Cecil D. Herdegen) 1906–14; Christadelphian C.; FB; Jehovah's Witnesses C. 1985; PO 1905; RS (Bonville Creek till 1923) 1915, station b. by Ernest Frederick Leggo, closed 1974; sawmills: Coffs Harbour Timber Co. 1912–31, Dud and Vic Lindsay (estab. 1937, relocated 1938 by Jack Kelsall, acquired by T. Seccombe & Sons Transport Pty Ltd), W. Paulger and A. Oxenbridge (estab. 1948, acquired by Adam's Sawmill Pty Ltd); school 1895 b. by Thomas Craig, additions 1910 and 1916 by N. McPherson, additions 1967, 1978, 2010; telephone 1915; TX 1923, automatic 1971; pop. 76 (1901), 316 (1911), 322 (1933), 326 (1947), 424 (1954), 479 (1961), 401 (2006), 373 (2011).

Bonville North (*Co. Raleigh*) 30°22'S. 153°02'E., 8 km W. of Sawtell; dam; pop. 269 (2006).

Bonville Reserve (*Co. Raleigh*) see Sawtell.

Booberoi (*Co. Blaxland*) 33°02'S. 146°31'E., 33 km N. of Lake Cargelligo; RS 1919–74; pop. 39 (1933).

Booerie (*Co. Rous*) 28°47'S. 153°15'E., 5 km NW of Lismore, on Booerie Ck; bridge over Booerie Ck; school (Lower Booerie till 1922) 1893, new building b. 1923 by W. Duggan, closed 1955; pop. 77 (1911).

Booerie (*Co. Rous*) see also Tullera.

Boogaldie (*Co. Baradine*) see Bugaldie.

Boogumgoridge (*Co. Dampier*) 36°04'S. 150°09'E., 1 km S. of Tuross Head, on Tasman Sea.

Book Book (*Co. Wynyard*) 35°22'S. 147°34'E., 33 km SE of Wagga Wagga; school 1957, additions 1960, closed 1987; TX (automatic); pop. 156 (1911), 97 (1933), 92 (1947), 98 (1954), 95 (1961).

Booker Bay (*Co. Northumberland*) 33°31'S. 151°21'E., 3 km SE of Woy Woy, on Brisbane Water; tourism; Assemblies of God C.; bridge (The Rip Bridge) 1974, 1,082 ft (330 m), to Daleys Point, d. by Albert Fried, over Brisbane Water; bushfire 1928; cemetery 1850; electricity (from Newcastle) 1929; 2 marinas; PO 1923; telephone 1920; wharf (Guyra Street); pop. 167 (1933), 751 (1947), 1,136 (2011).

Bookham (*Co. Harden*) 34°49'S. 148°38'E., 25 km W. of Yass, on Bogolong Ck; formerly also known as Bogolong; village gaz. 1839, bypassed by highway 2001; farming, wool, beef; airfield; bridge b. 1860 by Hammond and Bocking, over Bogolong Ck; bushfires 1952, 1965, 2003; cemetery; electricity 1955; FB; iron blast furnace (Bogolong Iron Mining Co.) 1874; PO 1864; quarries (abandoned): ironstone and limestone; Rom. Cath. C. (St Columba's) b. 1911 by Larcombe Bros, d. by William John Monks, closed; school 1883–96, reopened 1920 in school b. by William Scurr, burnt down 1935, replaced 1935 by J. Johnson, relocated 1952, additions 1967, closed 1983; telephone 1899; TX 1910, automatic 1957; typhoid 1933; Unit. C. (Pioneer Memorial, orig. Presb.) b. 1927 by D.L. Lawrence; pop. *c.*80 (1891), 135 (1901), 187 (1911), 157 (1933), 88 (1947), 82 (1954), 90 (1961), 120 (2006), 156 (2011).

Bookookoorara (*Co. Buller*) 28°46'S. 152°08'E., 33 km N. of Tenterfield; PO 1872–75.

Bookoola (*Co. Gough*) 29°45'S. 151°04'E., 7 km NW of Inverell; RS (McKenzies Siding till 1926) 1909, station b. by John Allibone, closed 1961.

Boolaboolka (*Co. Livingstone*) 32°35'S. 143°08'E., 114 km S. of Wilcannia, on Boola Boolka Lake.

Boolambayte (*Co. Gloucester*) 32°24'S. 152°16'E., 6 km E. of Bulahdelah, on Boolambayte Ck; thrived in 1860s; timber, shipbuilding, farming; Angl. C. (St Aidan's) 1934, closed, sold 1968 to L.R. Bonney; brickworks; bridge 1968, over Boolambayte Ck; bushfire 1951; cemetery; PO 1879; sawmills: Dee Bros (estab. 1914, fire 1935, bought 1944 by Northern Timbers and moved to Bulahdelah), Newman Bros 1939–44, Duncan McRae; school 1865–82 and 1914–57; telephone 1912; TX 1929; pop. 81 (1901), 117 (1911), 116 (1933), 99 (1947), 60 (1954), 207 (2011).

Boolaroo (*Co. Northumberland*) 32°57'S. 151°38'E., 4 km SW of Cardiff, on Cockle Ck; (incl. Cockle Creek); subdivisions 1896, 1899, 1902; coalmining and fruit growing; ambulance station b. 1922 by W.B. Timmins, d. by Ernest Tingle, new one b. 1954 by V.S. Doran & Son Pty Ltd, d. by Rodd and Hay; Bapt. C.; bridge (Watkins Bridge) 1899, to Teralba, demolished, over Cockle Ck; bushfire 1991; Christadelphian C.; cyclone 1931; electricity 1920; FB 1910 (station b. 1921, new one 1976, renovated 2007); fire 1906; Meth. C. 1922, new one 1930; PO: Boolaroo 1901, new one b. 1924 by W.B. Timmins, and Cockle Creek 1929; power station (Caledonian Collieries Ltd) 1927, damaged 1931, closed 1976, demolished; Presb. C. 1905; PS: Boolaroo 1905–2017 and Cockle Creek 1899–1905; railway bridge (Pratt truss) 1957, to Terabla, 147 ft (44.8 m), over Cockle Ck; reservoirs: Boolaroo 1,398,500 gal. (6,357.6 kl) and Cockle Creek 101,800 gal. (462.8 kl); Rom. Cath. C. (Our Lady Help of Christians) b. 1918 by W.G. Sparke, d. by A. Mackay, damaged 1928, closed 1952, reused, demolished 1998; RS: Boolaroo 1942 and Cockle Creek 1887, station b. by Thomas, Perry and Rowledge; sawmill (Finlay's); school 1900 b. by George Froome, additions 1903 by J.P. Tyler, additions and repairs 1911 by James Frizelle, additions 1923, additions 1934 by Pickles and McIlroy; sewerage 1945; smelter (silver, lead, zinc) and works (cement, sulphuric acid, superphosphate, fertilizers) operated 1896–1922 by Sulphide Corp. Ltd, then Pasminco Metals-Sulphide Pty Ltd, closed 2003; streets electric lit 1920; telegraph 1901; tornado 1992; TX 1912; Unit. C.; water supply 1905; Wes. Meth. C. 1900 (removed from Jesmond); wool-scour (Arthur Thompson); pop. 405 (1901), 720 (1911), 1,602 (1933), 1,576 (1947), 953 (2006), 933 (2011).

Boolboolma Crossing (*Co. Beresford*) 35°45'S. 149°23'E., 47 km S. of Queanbeyan, on Queanbeyan R.

Boolcarroll (*Co. Jamison*) 30°00'S. 149°26'E., 25 km N. of Wee Waa; pop. 58 (1911).

Booligal (*Co. Nicholson*) 33°52'S. 144°53'E., 73 km SW of Hillston, on Lachlan R.; disc. 1817 by John Joseph William Molesworth Oxley et al., estab. *c.*1859 by Edward Roset, laid out by Edward Twynam, town gaz. and lots sold 1860, designated as chief town of the county; sheep and cattle; Angl. C. (St Alban's) b. 1899 by Massie; bridges (1872 and 1912), over Lachlan R.; cemetery 1889; CH 1865; cordial factories: J.B. Elworthy (Ajax Cordial & Soda Water Manufactory) and John Sloan 1893; fire 1891; dust storm 1945; flood 1870; PO 1861, new one b. 1881 by J. Witcombe; pound (stock) 1861; PS (incl. court-room) b. 1899 by George Huntley Dixon; punt (Edward Roset) 1866, across Lachlan R.; Rom. Cath. C. (St Michael's) b. 1890 by Andrew Walsh, destroyed 1945, new one; school 1880–1947, reopened 1957; telegraph 1878, new office b. 1881 by J. Witcombe; TX 1913; weir b. 1907 by F.J. Cornwell and W. Castles, on Lachlan R.; wool-scour (Howson & Co.), bought 1888 by Thomas Honeyman; pop. 120 (1871), 146 (1891), 177 (1901), 335 (1911), 75 (1933), 26 (1947), 43 (1954), 238 (1961), 224 (2006), 162 (2011).

Boolong (*Co. Camden*) see Bolong.

Booloominbah (*Co. Sandon*) see Armidale.

Boomanoomana (*Co. Denison*) 35°53'S. 145°48'E., 10 km E. of Barooga; Presb. C. 1929; TX (automatic); pop. 86 (1911), 27 (1933), 164 (1947), 145 (1954), 187 (1961), 203 (2006), 318 (2011).

Boomerang Beach (*Co. Gloucester*) 32°21'S. 152°32'E., 18 km S. of Forster, on Tasman Sea; school (Charlotte Bay till 1966, then Pacific Palms) 1957; pop. 286 (2006), 434 (2011).

Boomey (*Co. Wellington*) 33°00'S. 148°59'E., 15 km NE of Molong; cemetery 1893; FB; phosphate mine (Nandillyan) *c.*1913 and 1944; PO 1881; school 1883–86 and 1899–1909; pop. 81 (1901), 108 (1911), 148 (1933), 84 (1947).

Boomi (*Co. Benarba*) 28°44'S. 149°34'E., 63 km NE of Mungindi; sheep and cattle; Angl. C. (All Saints') b. 1905 by Philip Smith; artesian bore 1906; cemetery 1897; CH b. 1913 by R. Wilson & Son; cheese factory (R.O. Pethers); grasshopper infestation 1937; PO 1900; pound (stock) 1906; Presb. C. (St Stephen's) b. 1929 by A.M. Duncan, d. by Hugh Henry McCourt, closed, sold 2019; PS 1901; Rom. Cath. C. (St Patrick's) 1911; sandfly infestation 1935; school 1901 b. by Philip Smith, extended 1907 by Joseph Easterbrook, additions 1915 by G. Smith, new building 1964, additions 2010; telephone 1900; TX; water supply 1963; pop. 562 (1911), 252 (1933), 268 (1947), 113 (1954), 138 (1961), 241 (2006).

Boomiaricool (*Co. Taila*) 34°14'S. 143°00'E., 100 km E. of Wentworth.

Boomi Creek (*Co. Buller*) 28°26'S. 152°37'E., 43 km NW of Kyogle, on Boomi Ck; sawmill; cheese factory (Prescott Ltd) 1919; pop. 150 (1933), 139 (1947), 105 (1954), 82 (1961), 315 (2006).

Boomley (*Co. Lincoln*) 32°02'S. 149°06'E., 28 km W. of Dunedoo, on Boomley Ck; farming and grazing; cemetery; PO 1927; RS (Boomley Sleeper Siding till 1921) 1918–74; telephone 1923; pop. 73 (1933), 53 (1947).

Boomoodeerie (*Co. Richmond*) 28°55'S. 153°01'E., 6 km SW of Casino; RS (relocated 1909) 1905–27; telephone 1926.

Boonal (*Co. Benarba*) 28°52'S. 149°40'E., 67 km E. of Mungindi.

Boona Mount (*Co. Kennedy*) 32°37'S. 147°11'E., 60 km NW of Trundle; telephone 1927; TX 1927–78; pop. 96 (2006).

Boonanga (*Co. Stapylton*) 28°50'S. 150°27'E., 26 km S. of Boggabilla; school 1956–64.

Boonangar Crossing (*Co. Benarba*) 28°35'S. 149°33'E., 71 km NE of Mungindi, on Barwon R.; bridge (Allan timber truss) 1928, 147 ft (44.8 m), replacement (concrete) b. 2010 by Queensland Bridge & Civil, over Barwon R.

Boonanghi (*Co. Dudley*) 31°05'S. 152°37'E., 20 km W. of Kempsey, on Dungay Ck.

Boona Tank (*Co. Cunningham*) 32°44'S. 146°59'E., 41 km N. of Condobolin; PO 1897; telephone 1916.

Boona West (*Co. Cunningham*) 32°47'S. 147°09'E., 55 km W. of Trundle; gold (disc. 1886); mines: Anaconda and Big Ben.

Boonda (*Co. Murchison*) 29°48'S. 150°49'E., 23 km E. of Bingara, on Staggy Ck; school 1957–60, building moved to Bingara and reused.

Boonjaub (*Co. Fitzroy*) 29°57'S. 152°59'E., 25 km NW of Arrawarra.

Boonoke (*Co. Townsend*) 35°17'S. 145°06'E., 30 km N. of Deniliquin, on Billabong Ck; 2 airfields; pop. 51 (1933), 60 (1947), 56 (1961).

Boonoo Boonoo (*Co. Buller*) 28°53'S. 152°06'E., 19 km NE of Tenterfield, on Boonoo Boonoo R.; thrived 1861; mining (gold disc. and gold rush 1874), timber, grazing; cemetery; mine (Lady Mary); sawmills: Armstrong Bros & Rand, closed 1922, and Hugh Clark & Sons; PO 1899–1971; school 1888–1910; telephone 1922; TX; pop. 28 (1933).

Boorabee Park (*Co. Rous*) 28°43'S. 153°03'E., 11 km SE of Kyogle, on Boorabee Ck; cyclone 1937; school 1908–91; pop. 300 (2006).

Boorabil (*Co. Dowling*) see Tullibigeal.

Booragul (*Co. Northumberland*) 32°58'S. 151°36'E., 3 km SW of Boolaroo, on Cockle Bay; (incl. Marmong Point, subdivided *c.*1888 by James Brady and W.D. Walker then settled by Richard Hepplewhite, and Woodrising); orig. Marmong; subdivisions 1908 and 1909, first lots sold 1911, further subdivided 1921; bushfire 1946; cemetery (13 graves); earthquake 1989; foot-bridge over Marmong Ck; jetty; marina; Mennonite C. (Hope); Meth. C. 1958; PO: Booragul 1953 and Marmong Point 1933; Rom. Cath. C. o. 1963 in renovated hut removed for Greta, reused, new one on new site (St Michael the Archangel) 1985; RS 1926, station damaged 1989; sawmill (William Quigley); schools: primary 1955, additions 2010, and Lake Macquarie HS (Booragul till 1992) 1958, additions 1962, 1967, 1988; sewage works (Marmong Point), closed 1995; telephone: Booragul 1953 and Marmong Point 1930; Unit. C.; water supply 1929; pop. 339 (1933), 519 (1947), 1,415 (2011).

Booral (*Co. Gloucester*) 32°28'S. 151°58'E., 20 km N. of Karuah, on Karuah R.; founded by the Aust. Agric. Co.; wheat, tobacco, silk till 1900, then timber and dairying; aeroplane crash (pilot killed) 1952; Angl. C. b. 1835 by Aust. Agric. Co., d. by Sir William Edward Parry, demolished, new one (St Barnabas's) b. 1874 by Robert Carnell, relocated 1876, and graveyard (264 graves); brickworks; bridge b. 1876 by E. Taylor and D. M'Lachlan, 327 ft (99.7 m), new one (continuous concrete girder) 1946, over Karuah R.; bushfire 1938; cemetery, disused; CH 1876–1974, reused; engineering works (R.C. Grey) 1975; FB; floods 1857 and 1927; gale 1925; PO 1874; sawmill (Yates Bros); school 1865, additions 1883 by W. Humphreys, repairs 1898 by George Cornell, repairs 1913 by W.J. Hallett, additions 1920 by T. Southon; TX; Union C. 1908, damaged 1925; watch-house (Aust. Agric. Co.) 1832; wharf (Aust. Agric. Co.) 1834; pop. 247 (1901), 228 (1911), 181 (1933), 223 (1947), 214 (1954), 196 (1961), 398 (2011).

Boorara (*Co. Finch*) 29°06'S. 148°28'E., 50 km N. of Collarenebri.

Boorawhanga Brush (*Co. Macquarie*) 31°51'S. 152°18'E., 7 km W. of Wingham, on Dingo Ck.

Boorga (*Co. Sturt*) 34°01'S. 145°57'E., 30 km N. of Griffith; telephone 1929; TX 1930; pop. 128 (1933).

Boorganna (*Co. Macquarie*) 31°38'S. 152°24'E.,

27 km N. of Wingham; dairying; PO 1927; TX 1925; pop. 79 (1933).

Boorindal (*Co. Cowper*) 30°22'S. 146°10'E., 37 km SE of Bourke; Mooculta Siding till 1919; grazing; PO 1909–60; RS (Mooculta till 1919) 1885–1974; telephone 1936; TX 1939; pop. 72 (1911), 23 (1933).

Boorolong (*Co. Sandon*) 30°19'S. 151°32'E., 17 km SW of Guyra, on Boorolong Ck; grazing; cemetery (22 graves); PO 1927–28; sawmill (Richard Pearson, jun.); school 1885–1914; TX (automatic); pop. 104 (1911), 20 (1933), 83 (1954), 94 (1961), 116 (2006), 183 (2011).

Boorolong (*Co. Sandon*)
see also Black Mountain.

Booroobanilly (*Co. Urana*) 35°29'S. 145°37'E., 17 km SW of Jerilderie; FB 1938 (new station b. 2014); Presb. C. (removed 1919 from North Finley); school 1946–52.

Boorook (*Co. Buller*) 28°50'S. 152°16'E., 31 km NE of Tenterfield; village gaz. 1880; mining (gold and silver disc. 1878 by Thomas Horton, rush 1878) till 1886; airfield; cemetery 1881; mines: Addison, Alderman Reef, Golden Age (incl. furnaces, estab. by Thomas Horton), Golden Crown, Grand Junction, Honeyman's Reef, New Reef, Silver King; PO 1879; school 1881–86; stamper battery (3 head); pop. *c.*250 (1879), *c.*200 (1886).

Boorooma (*Co. Clarendon*) 35°04'S. 147°22'E., 6 km N. of Wagga Wagga; agric. experiment farm (incl. butter factory) estab. 1892–96, additions 1898 by J. M'Intosh, additions 1911 by C. Hardy & Co., became agric. college in 1949, additions 1955, 1959, 1963, 1968, 1971, and agric. research institute 1953, merged 1976 with Riverina CAE, became Riverina-Murray Institute of Higher Education in 1985, became univ. (Charles Sturt) in 1989; cheese factory (at Charles Sturt Univ.) 1998; PS 1905; winery (at Charles Sturt Univ.) 1977.

Boorooma (*Co. Finch*) 30°04'S. 147°32'E., 56 km W. of Walgett, on Barwon R.; grazing; PO 1898–1963; telephone 1894; TX 1928; pop. 65 (1933), 112 (2011).

Booroomin (*Co. Pottinger*) 30°44'S. 149°58'E., 7 km W. of Boggabri; school 1915–25.

Booroorban (*Co. Townsend*) 34°55'S. 144°45'E., 47 km S. of Hay, on Coleambally Outfall Drain; surveyed and village gaz. 1867; grazing; airfield; cemetery 1901; PO 1881; school 1913–37 and 1961–81; telephone 1900; TX 1924; pop. 200+ (1885), 59 (1901), 106 (1911), 146 (1933), 34 (1947), 37 (1954), 117 (1961).

Boorowa (*Co. King*) 34°27'S. 148°43'E., 41 km E. of Young, on Boorowa R.; (incl. East Boorowa); Burrowa till 1914; surveyed 1850 by John Frederick Mann, village gaz. 1850, first lots auctioned 1851, town gaz. 1880, munic. proc. 1888 as Burrowa, munic. abolished 1944; formerly mining (gold, copper, tin), maize, barley, lucerne, oats, rye, potatoes, wine, butter, cheese, ham, bacon, now wheat, sheep, cattle; agric. research station (CSIRO) 2019; ambulance station; Angl. C. (St John the Baptist) b. 1861–63 by George Cook and William Bundock, d. by H.H. Voss, extended 1868 and 1882, additions and renovations 1922 by Oliver John Stuart; breweries: G.D. Milne 1881–82 and Patrick Murphy (Old Mill House Brewery) 1891–94; brickworks: J.J. Cummins and Preston's (taken over 1912 by Oliver John Stuart, modernised and renamed Enterprise Steam Brickworks in 1914, later taken over by William Henry Wilson); bridges over Boorowa R.: Acramans Bridge 1892, (McDonald timber truss, 225 ft or 68.6 m, demolished and replaced 1987), Boorowa Bridge 1863 (damaged 1870, repairs by Gilbert, closed 1876, replaced), Jubilee Bridge 1949; bushfires 1869, 1905, 1975; carriage-works: A.C. Kitchener and Marrion's, demolished; causeway; cemetery (graves 1856+) 1864; CH b. 1860 by John Allen, demolished 1883, new one b. 1883–86 by Thomas Colls, d. by James Johnstone Barnet, renovated 1984, closed 1988, reused; clock tower (war memorial) b. 1933 by T. Barlow, d. by R. Richardson; clothing factory (Aust. Silknit Ltd) 1946; cordial factory (Ryan Bros); dam, 30 ft (9.1 m); droughts 1860–62, 1865–67, 1888, 1914, 1939; dust storms 1865, 1899, 1902, 1933; earth tremors 1852, 1886,

1911, 1930, 1938, 1948, 1952, 1961; electricity 1925; FB 1910 (station b. 1925 by W.H. Wills, d. by Jack Oxley, replaced, new one 2000); fires 1875, 1931, 1951; floods 1863, 1867, 1870, 1911, 1931, 1950, 1952, 1974, 1984; flour mills: one b. 1852 by John Phillip Sheahan and Patrick Hurley (leased 1857 to Joseph Hayes, extended 1860, modernised 1862, sold 1880 to Charles Weifert, extended and modernised 1881, sold to A.E. Middleton, bought 1898 by John Boyd Dunlop and Isaac Stevenson, altered and renamed Laurels Patented Roller Mill, closed 1908, demolished 1930) and Union Steam Mill b. 1860 by David Harpur and John Colls for John Mallaly (taken over and altered 1867 by Patrick Henry Scott, sold 1884 to Morgan Bros and renamed The Roller Mills, closed 1897, reused 1915 by Country Freezing Co. Ltd, chimney demolished 1917, closed, sold 1935 to O.W. Burnes, demolished 1936); foot-bridge over Ryans Ck; hailstorms 1914, 1931, 1932, 1951; hospital b. 1903 by Oliver John Stuart, additions 1910, 1940, 1944, 1955, 1977; hunting gear factory (Hunt and Hook, Karren Lefevre); lock-up b. 1858 by John Allen; PO: Boorowa 1854 (new one b. 1876, renovated 1885, re-roofed 1890, additions 1893 by Thomas Leslie) and East Boorowa 1950; pound (stock) 1846; powerhouse (Burrowa Electric Lighting Franchise Ltd) 1924; Presb. C. (St James's) 1885, renovated 1962, closed 1982, sold and reused 1983; PS b. 1863 by George Cook, new one (incl. lock-up) b. 1884 by Henry and Charles Ford, closed, sold and reused; rabbit freezing works 1925; railway bridge over Ryans Ck; railway turntable, 60 ft (18.3 m), closed; reservoir, 200,000 gal. (909.2 kl); rifle range (3 km NE); Rom. Cath. C. b. 1855–58, reused, later largely demolished, new one (St Patrick's) b. 1874–77 on new site by William Duncan and William Keating, d. by Andrea Giovanni Stombuco, porch added 1928, church re-roofed 1929, restored 1980; RS 1915, station b. by Robert Daniel Quiggin, closed 1974, removed 1984; sale-yards (Dwyer and Butler) 1914; school 1870 b. by W. Bundock and William Keating, additions 1878 and 1882, additions 1885 by Bundock & Son, d. by William Edmund Kemp, reused, new one b. 1890 by David Stuart, additions 1903, extended 1930 by S.G. McFarland, extended 1934 by Oliver John Stuart, additions 1960, extended 1965–67 by A.G. Harris Pty Ltd, additions 1985, 1990, 1992; sewage works 1963; silo 1929; snow 1865, 1869, 1890, 1896, 1901, 1956; storms 1873 and 1900; streets candle lit 1890, kerosene lit 1892, gas lit 1905, electric lit 1925; tannery (F. Russell), destroyed 1870, rebuilt, bought 1879 by William Davoren, burnt down 1881; telegraph 1866, office renovated 1885, re-roofed 1890, additions 1893 by Tom Leslie; telephone: Boorowa 1906 and East Boorowa 1950; tornado 1926; TX 1908, upgraded 1915 and 1923, automatic 1975; typhoid 1927; Unit. C. (orig. Wes. Meth.) b. 1869 by John Preston; water supply 1902, new scheme (incl. filtration plant) 1940, augmentation 1994; waterworks 1897 d. by N.E. Dowden; weir b. 1902, 201 ft (61.3 m), on Boorowa R.; pop. 544 (1836), 320 (1861), 446 (1871), 653 (1881), 767 (1891), *c.*750 (1895), 839 (1901), 1,072 (1911), 1,504 (1933), 1,536 (1947), 1,291 (1954), 1,515 (1961), 1,181 (1966), 1,147 (1971), 1,192 (1976), 1,183 (1981), 1,069 (1986), 1,090 (1991), 1,112 (1996), 1,070 (2001), 1,070 (2006), 1,211 (2011).

Booshang (*Co. Burnett*) 29°37'S. 150°39'E., 10 km SE of Warialda; RS (Ballast Siding till 1924, relocated 1935) 1909, station b. by John Allibone, closed 1975.

Bootawa (*Co. Gloucester*) 31°55'S. 152°22'E., 6 km S. of Wingham, on Fatorini Ck; dam, 82 ft (25 m) high, 1967; school 1912–35; pop. 88 (1911), 107 (1933), 99 (1947), 69 (1954), 50 (1961).

Boothenba (*Co. Lincoln*) 32°12'S. 148°42'E., 10 km NE of Dubbo; RS 1918–59; pop. 42 (1933).

Booth Town (*Co. Macquarie*)
see Mitchells Island.

Booti Booti (*Co. Gloucester*) 32°19'S. 152°31'E., 15 km S. of Forster, on Tasman Sea; telephone 1912; TX 1930.

Bootoowa (*Co. Dowling*) 33°30'S. 146°10'E., 34

km SW of Lake Cargelligo; pop. 97 (1933), 66 (1947), 71 (1954).

Bootra (*Co. Yantara*) 30°01'S. 142°57'E., 175 km N. of Wilcannia.

Booyong (*Co. Rous*) 28°45'S. 153°27'E., 10 km SW of Bangalow, on Skinners Ck; village gaz. 1892; farming; abattoir (Northern Co-op. Meat Co. Ltd); bridge 1917 over Wilsons R.; fire 1916; flood 2010; PO 1903; PS 1925–26; railway to Ballina, dismantled 1949; railway bridge b. 1892 by Patent Shaft & Axletree Co. Ltd, over Pearces Ck; railway tunnel, 142 yds (130.1 m), 1894–2004; RS 1894, station b. by Alexander Hamilton Scouller, closed 1974, station defunct; telephone 1906; pop. 156 (1911), 125 (1933), 65 (1947), 75 (1954), 107 (1961).

Boppy Mountain (*Co. Robinson*) 31°32'S. 146°17'E., 43 km E. of Cobar; PO 1896; RS 1892, station b. by R. Funnell, services ceased 1975, station closed 1982; telephone 1899.

Bora Creek (*Co. Hardinge*) see Howell.

Borah (*Co. White*) 31°00'S. 149°32'E., 44 km NE of Coonabarabran, on Borah Ck.

Borah Crossing (*Co. Darling*) 30°47'S. 150°33'E., 18 km W. of Manilla; earth tremor 2012; Meth. C. 1904, defunct; pop. 40 (1933).

Borambil (*Co. Bligh*) 32°02'S. 150°00'E., 35 km SE of Coolah, on Two Mile Hollow Ck; village gaz. 1871; farming and grazing; bridge (Fitzpatrick Bridge) 1897; PO 1900, burnt down 1915; school 1879–1962; telephone 1907; pop. 190 (1901), 128 (1911), 217 (1933), 121 (1947), 116 (1954), 64 (1961).

Borambil (*Co. Buckland*) 31°30'S. 150°38'E., 5 km W. of Quirindi; (incl. Bolah Gap); Angl. C. (St Mark's) 1908; Meth. C.; PO (Bolah Gap) 1928; school (Bolah Gap) 1898, additions 1930 by C. Davies, closed 1953; telephone 1928; pop. 91 (1901), 91 (1947).

Borambil (*Co. Gipps*) 33°10'S. 147°17'E., 15 km SE of Condobolin; weir b. 1902 by R. Whitehead, on Lachlan R.

Borambil North (*Co. Cunningham*) 33°05'S. 147°16'E., 10 km E. of Condobolin; silver; mines: Blue Bell (J. Sinclair 1898 and R. Leese 1906) and Eureka 1888–92; RS 1902–41.

Borambola (*Co. Wynyard*) 35°10'S. 147°39'E., 29 km E. of Wagga Wagga; RS 1917–75; school 1921–70; telephone 1924; TX (automatic); pop. 54 (1911), 172 (1933), 140 (1947), 154 (1954), 122 (1961), 129 (2006), 355 (2011).

Borapine (*Co. Dowling*) 33°20'S. 146°39'E., 26 km E. of Lake Cargelligo; telephone 1927; TX 1927.

Bora Ridge (*Co. Richmond*) 29°03'S. 153°15'E., 8 km SW of Coraki, on Bora Ck; farming and tobacco; PO 1927–31; school 1900 b. by T.W. Keith, closed 1974; telephone 1924; TX 1932, automatic 1953; pop. 111 (1933), 107 (1947), 60 (1954), 81 (1961), 210 (2011).

Border Loop (*Co. Rous*) 28°21'S. 152°58'E., 31 km N. of Kyogle, on Logan Ck; railway tunnel, 1,269 yds (1,160.6 m), 1930; RS 1930.

Boree (*Co. Ashburnham*) 33°15'S. 148°49'E., 13 km SE of Manildra, on Boree Ck.

Boree (*Co. Clarendon*) 34°51'S. 147°36'E., 3 km NE of Junee; school 1882–98.

Boree (*Co. Northumberland*) 33°04'S. 151°00'E., 32 km SW of Paxton, on Big Boree Ck; bushfire 1994.

Boree Cabonne (*Co. Ashburnham*) 33°14'S. 148°50'E., 13 km SE of Manildra, on Boree Ck; school 1881–88.

Boree Creek (*Co. Urana*) 35°07'S. 146°36'E., 16 km NW of Lockhart, on Boree Ck; estab. by Fred Orme, thrived 1912; wool and wheat; Angl. C. (St Oswald's) 1912–75, sold for demolition; bushfires 1892 and 1952; cemetery; Community C. 1975; electricity 1939; floods 1931, 1936, 1939; measles epidemic 1953; mouse plague 1922; PO 1911; Presb. C. (St David's) 1913, destroyed 1922, new one 1922–75; PS 1923; reservoir, 50,000 gal. (227.3 kl); rifle range; Rom. Cath. C. b. 1934 by Cashburn, d. by G.W.A. Welsh, burnt down 1980; RS 1910, station closed 1980, removed 1983, services ceased 1992; sale-yards; sawmills: Ashton and Plant, boy killed 1918, and Richard Marsh; school 1902, new building 1969; silo 1919; telephone 1912; tornado 1922; TX 1917, automatic 1983; Union C., bought 1912 by Meth. C. and moved 1913 to Greenvale; water supply 1946; pop. 476 (1911), 292 (1933), 194 (1947), 235 (1954), 192 (1961), 212 (2011).

Boree Siding (*Co. Clarendon*) see Marinna.

Bore Hole (*Co. Northumberland*) see Hamilton.

Borenore (*Co. Ashburnham*) 33°15'S. 148°59'E., 13 km W. of Orange, on Borenore Ck; berries, apples, pears, peaches, plums, grapes, marble; Angl. C. (Christ) 1878; brewery (Marty Oliver); creamery (Molong Dist. Dairying Co.) b. 1901 by William J. Harding; FB (station b. 1998 by Peter Woodhouse Constructions); dam, 56 ft (17 m) high, 1928; mine (phosphate); PO 1877–1991; quarries (marble): E. Murphy & Sons and one estab. 1901 by Francis Philip Rusconi, taken over by Commonwealth Marble Quarries, closed; Rom. Cath. C. (Sacred Heart) b. 1887–89 by Mitchell and Perry, d. by William Lamrock, jun., closed, sold and reused; RS 1885, station b. by James Stuart Douglas, closed 1989; school 1878–1938, reopened 1957; telegraph 1888; TX 1917, automatic 1941; pop. 265 (1901), 286 (1911), 257 (1933), 221 (1947), 299 (1954), 297 (1961), 432 (2011).

Boridgery (*Co. Bathurst*) 33°36'S. 148°34'E., 9 km SW of Canowindra, on Belubula R.

Boro (*Co. Murray*) 35°09'S. 149°40'E., 24 km NE of Bungendore, on Boro Ck; mining (silver, lead, zinc, copper), farming, grazing; bushfire 1895; mine (The Great Boro Mine) 1888–1928; PO 1859–1968; pound (stock) 1864; telephone 1907; TX 1928; typhoid 1905; pop. 63 (1901), 96 (1911), 59 (1933).

Boronga (*Co. Stapylton*) 28°38'S. 149°40'E., 75 km NE of Mungindi.

Boss Flat (*Co. Buller*) 28°40'S. 152°06'E., 43 km N. of Tenterfield, on Wylie Ck; mine.

Bostobrick (*Co. Fitzroy*) 30°17'S. 152°38'E., 11 km NW of Dorrigo, on Cutbank Ck; logging; PO 1938; 2 quarries; sawmill (hardwood) estab. by Earp, Woodcock, Beveridge & Co. Pty Ltd, burnt down 1929, rebuilt, taken over by Allen Taylor & Co. Ltd; school 1937 b. by N. McPherson, closed 1970; telephone 1924; TX 1928; pop. 162 (1933), 188 (1947), 169 (1954), 141 (1961).

Boston (*Co. St Vincent*) see Nowra.

Botfield (*Co. Cunningham*) see Botfields.

Botfields (*Co. Cunningham*) 33°00'S. 147°46'E., 10 km SE of Trundle; formerly Botfield; iron; pound (stock) 1899; RS (Botfield) 1907, station b. by Peter Herbert, closed 1974; pop. 50 (1933).

Botobolar (*Co. Phillip*) 32°31'S. 149°48'E., 22 km NE of Mudgee, on Stony Ck; Rom. Cath. C. (St Matthew's) 1901; school 1882, new one b. 1884 by S. Thurgood, additions and repairs 1892 by J. Miller, closed 1905; pop. 107 (1911).

Bottle Bend (*Co. Wentworth*) 34°18'S. 142°18'E., 15 km S. of Gol Gol, on Murray R.

Bottle Corner (*Co. Gloucester*) 32°26'S. 151°53'E., 12 km E. of Dungog.

Bottle Creek (*Co. Buller*) 28°48'S. 152°39'E., 40 km W. of Casino, on Bottle Ck; bushfire 1926; school 1931, new school 1935, closed 1958; storm 1937; telephone 1925; TX 1925; pop. 80 (1933), 119 (1947), 112 (1954), 80 (1961), 158 (2006).

Boulder Flat (*Co. Clarke*) 30°36'S. 152°15'E., 57 km E. of Armidale, on Georges R.

Boundary Creek (*Co. Richmond*) 29°00'S. 153°28'E., 13 km NE of Woodburn; sugar mill (Blanch's) 1882; pop. 42 (1933), 67 (1961).

Boundary Flat (*Co. Clarence*) 29°36'S. 153°14'E., 15 km S. of Maclean.

Boundary Villa (*Co. Bourke*) 34°36'S. 147°26'E., 31 km N. of Junee; school (Big Mimosa till 1913, Mimosa till 1914) 1895–1920.

Bourah (*Co. Culgoa*) see Dennawan.

Bourbah (*Co. Gregory*) 31°17'S. 148°16'E., 20 km W. of Gulargambone, on Merri Merri Ck; grazing; artesian water struck 1897; PO 1885–1923; sawmill (Nelson's) 1934–38, moved to Gulargambone; pop. 86 (1901), 151 (1911), 137 (2006).

Bourke (*Co. Cowper*) 30°05'S. 145°56'E., 157 km N. of Cobar, on Darling R.; orig. Eighteen Mile Point; settled 1859, estab. by Thomas Dangar and Joseph Becker, surveyed 1861 by Charles Arthur, laid out 1862 by James Glen Wilson, town gaz. and first lots sold 1863, designated as chief town of the county, munic. proc. 1878 (bankrupt 1906), town thrived 1887–92 and 1934–37, munic. abolished 1955; former river port (declined 1885+), sheep and cattle, then oranges, sorghum, vegetables, cotton 1966+, light engineering; ambulance station b. 1953 by H. Collins, additions (A.J. Davey Wing) 1961; Angl. C. (St Stephen's) b. 1875 by Edward Heseler, d. by John Horbury Hunt, burnt down 1895, replaced 1897, closed, sold 1940 to Rushton, demolished 1941, new one (Holy Innocents) b. 1940 by R.T. Gillies, d. by Louis Reginald Williams; Apostolic C. (Full Gospel Family); boiling-down works (Bourke Meat Preserving Co.) 1893 d. by Coxon, additions 1896; 6 bond stores (incl. Becker's b. 1871 by Ramsay and Peck, and Kirkpatrick & Co., burnt down 1884); brewery (Red Lion Steam Brewery, Aerated Water & Cordial Manufactory) estab. 1879 by Henry Lill Lindsay, closed 1901; brickworks (Thomas Topham) 1884; bushfire 1885; carriage-works: Richardson and Bennet, closed 1883, Cobb & Co.'s Steam Coach and Wagon Factory 1883–99, burnt down 1908, John Myles's City Coach and Buggy Works 1899; cemetery 1879; CH (incl. lock-up) b. 1865 by Andrew McCauley, restored, (second) 1876 d. by James Johnstone Barnet, reused, (third) b. 1897–1900 by James Stuart Douglas, d. by George John Oakeshott, alterations and renovations 1968 by H. Lukas, refurbished by New England Constructions Pty Ltd; Christ C.; cordial factories: T. Clancy, Eli Glover 1885 (sold 1907 to J. Hives & Son), Orbell's (in former powerhouse) 1969, L. Peters (damaged 1872), John Rice (bought 1907 from D. Shaw, new factory 1951); cyclones 1903 and 1932; dengue fever 1926; diphtheria 1891; droughts 1862, 1865–66, 1919, 1927–29, 1964–67; dust storms 1908, 1914, 1941; electricity 1932; engineering works (Gibson's); FB (station b. 1895, renovations and repairs 1918 by C.J. Pacey, new one b. 1938 by E.L. Francis, new one 1978, renovated 2007); fibrous plaster works 1954; fires 1880, 1883, 1884, 1890, 1894, 1899, 1901, 1903, 1905, 1929; floods 1861, 1863, 1864, 1867, 1870, 1873, 1878, 1886, 1890, 1921, 1950, 1951, 1955, 1956, 1971, 1974, 1976, 2009; Full Gospel Family Fellowship C.; gale 1910; gaol (incl. 36 cells) b. 1870–72 by W. Robinson, d. by James Johnstone Barnet, high wall added 1885, additions and alterations 1897 by J. Crimson, closed 1909, reused 1914–18 as German internment camp, demolished; German measles epidemic 1956; hailstorm 1967; heatwaves 1896 (47 died), 1901, 1909, 1938–39, 1940, 1969; hospital b. 1863–65, new one 1878, additions and alterations 1940 by E.L. Francis, additions 1961, additions 1964 by Walmac Construction Pty Ltd, additions 1965 by P. Ross Smith, d. by R. Armstrong; ice works (Wormall Bros and Green) 1884; Islamic C.; Jehovah's Witnesses C.; meat works (Tancred Bros Pty Ltd) b. 1938 by Gaskin Bros; mouse plague 1873; PO 1862, new one b. 1878–80 by Edward Heseler, d. by James Johnstone Barnet, additions 1889 by Henry Ford, alterations 1898 by Bailey, additions 1900 by James Stuart Douglas, repairs 1908 by C. Jones; pound (stock) 1865; powerhouse (Bourke Lighting Co.) 1932–58, new one b. 1958 by Atlas Construction Pty Ltd, closed 1967, reused 1969; Presb. C. (St Andrew's) b. 1890 by R.C. Park, renovated 1962; PS b. 1863–65, replaced 1877, reused, new one (incl. lock-up) b. 1887–89 by Henry Ford, d. by James Johnstone Barnet, fire 1954, renovations and repairs 1955, new cell block b. 1963 and old one renovated, additions and alterations to station 1964 and 1980; punt 1868, new one b. 1893 by J. Lynch and D. Sullivan, new one b. 1934 by Mort's Dock & Engineering Co. Ltd; railway barracks 1891, demolished 1980; railway engine shed; railway turntable, 50 ft (15.2 m), replaced 1927, 60 ft (18.3 m); reservoir, 1,000,000 gal. (4,546 kl), 1972; Rom. Cath. C.: Holy Spirit War Memorial b. 1969 by Cobar Home Industries, d. by Terence A. Daly and St Ignatius of Antioch b. 1871–74, d. by Edward Gell, additions 1895 d. by W.T. Knox; RS 1885, station b. by James Stuart Douglas, burnt down 1965, replaced 1968, closed

1975; sale-yards 1949, new yards 1969; Salv. Army C., damaged 1907 and 1908; sawmills: C. Flower, W.C. Gale, F. Maitland, Roy Wangmann 1969; schools: Bourke 1866 (new one b. 1876–78 by Edward Heseler, additions 1890 by K.C. McKenzie, additions and repairs 1891 by G.G. Payne, additions and repairs 1895 by James Prior Hull, additions 1900 by W.A. M'Lean, remodelled 1921, extended 1928 by Philip James Killey, renovations and repairs 1935 by H. Willett, new buildings b. 1958 by Walmac Construction Pty Ltd, new school b. 1964 also by Walmac, additions 1968 and 1975), HS 1969, additions 1990, Meat Works 1895–1901; SD Adventist C.; sewage works b. 1948–53, augmentation 1985; soap and candle factory (R. Barton) 1873; soap-works: Bankside (Tidmarsh and Baker), Great Western (J. Carr), Topham's; storms 1872 and 1936; streets were candle lit, then kerosene lit, then electric lit 1932; TC (a campus of Western Institute); telegraph 1873, new office b. 1878–80 by Edward Heseler, d. by James Johnstone Barnet, additions 1890 by Henry Ford; telephone 1908; TX 1912; typhoid 1898 (9 died), 1899 (2 died), 1900, 1904; Unit. C.; United Fellowship C. 1967; vulcanising works (R.F. King), taken over 1932 by A. Dorrington; water supply 1892, filtration plant b. 1957–59 by G.E. Todd & Co. Pty Ltd, augmentation 1972 and 1988; weir 1897, new one 1941, on Darling R.; Wes. Meth. C. 1887; wharves (incl. one b. 1885 by Charles Dundass and one b. 1897 by J.S. Gamm), with steam cranes, used till 1931; wool-scours: Hayes Bros (burnt down 1928), P.W. Higgins (bought 1920 by Joah H. Sugden & Co. Ltd), H.G. Morgan 1939, Robinson and Hughes, Arthur Senior 1893, Union Steam Woolscouring & Soapmaking Works (J.T. Gibson & Co., acquired 1893 by Thomas Topham) 1881, M.E. Wring; 2 wool stores; pop. 318 (1871), 450 (1873), *c.*800 (1878), 1,378 (1881), 3,149 (1891), 3,145 (1892), *c.*3,500 (1895), 2,609 (1901), 1,571 (1911), 1,430 (1921), 1,778 (1933), 2,025 (1947), 2,642 (1954), 3,001 (1961), 3,300 (1966), 3,620 (1971), 3,534 (1976), 3,326 (1981), 3,018 (1986), 2,976 (1991), 2,775 (1996), 2,562 (2001), 2,145 (2006), 2,047 (2011), *c.*2,465 (2018).

Bourkelands (*Co. Wynyard*) see Wagga Wagga.

Bourke North (*Co. Gunderbooka*) 30°03'S. 145°57'E., 4 km N. of Bourke, on Darling R.; formerly West Bourke; village gaz. 1867 as West Bourke; farming and grazing; airfield, taken over 1942 by RAAF, now Bourke airport, rebuilt 1959 by R.G. Furney; bridge (lift span) b. 1880–83 by David Baillie and William McCulloch & Co. Ltd, d. by J.H. Daniels, 650 ft (198 m), alterations 1895, modified 1902, reused as foot-bridge, new one (Gateway Bridge) 1997, over Darling R.; cotton gin (Bengerang Ltd, bought 2015 by Namoi Cotton); floods 1893 and 1921; gale 1946; lock-up; PO 1884–1949; PS, closed 1914; sawmill 1969; school 1887–1906; TX 1922–48; pop. 39 (1933), 74 (1954), 116 (1961), *c.*20 (1999).

Bourketown (*Co. St Vincent*) see Araluen.

Bourke West (*Co. Gunderbooka*) see Bourke North.

Bournda (*Co. Auckland*) 36°48'S. 149°54'E., 10 km N. of Merimbula, on Moncks Ck; pop. 124 (2011).

Bournda North (*Co. Auckland*) 36°46'S. 149°54'E., 9 km SW of Tathra; school 1897, new one b. 1906 by W. Manning, closed 1918.

Bournewood (*Co. Gordon*) 32°45'S. 148°45'E., 28 km SW of Wellington; farming; Bapt. C. b. 1897 by Robert Sherringham, d. by J. Mayo, reused, new one b. 1926 by B. Dunkley; FB (station b. 2016); PO 1901; school 1909–61; pop. 89 (1901), 110 (1911), 164 (1933), 174 (1947), 137 (1954), 145 (1961).

Boveedy (*Co. Rous*) see Wongavale.

Bow (*Co. Brisbane*) 32°07'S. 150°15'E., 9 km W. of Merriwa, on Bow R.; formerly Boggibri; village gaz. 1869; farming and grazing; bridge 1964, over Bow R.; cemetery, defunct; flour mill (C.B. Scott, horse powered) 1881; PO 1906; telephone 1907; TX 1917; pop. 134 (1911), 91 (1933), 58 (1947).

Bowan (*Co. Ashburnham*) see Bowan Park.

Bowan Park (*Co. Ashburnham*) 33°19'S. 148°49'E., 18 km SE of Manildra, on Bourimbla

Ck; The Big Flat till 1876; settled *c.*1870; mining (gold disc. 1886), farming, dairying; Angl. C. (St Paul's) b. 1906 by Tillet, closed and dismantled 1937; butter factory b. 1895 by Blunt Bros, sold 1901 by R. Reed to Green Bros, sold 1901 to Molong Dist. Dairying Co.; FB; mines: Paling Yards (copper and gold) 1886–1891 and Cudal Gold Mining Syndicate (Reuben Fairall and Hec Zeidler) 1924–33; PO 1884–1927; quarry (marble); school (Bowan) 1879–1935; telephone 1907; TX 1924; pop. 134 (1901), 249 (1911), 82 (1933), 57 (1947), 63 (1954), 89 (1961), 499 (2011).

Bowan Park South (*Co. Ashburnham*) 33°22'S. 148°49'E., 23 km SE of Manildra; school 1905–23.

Bow Bow Creek (*Co. Gloucester*) see Bo Bo Creek.

Bowen (*Co. Bathurst*) see Orange (*Co. Wellington*).

Bowenfels (*Co. Cook*) see Bowenfels South and Lithgow.

Bowenfels South (*Co. Cook*) 33°31'S. 150°07'E., 5 km SW of Lithgow, on Good Luck Hollow; (incl. Old Bowenfels and Strathlone); Bowenfells till 1879; airfield; bushfire 1940; cemetery (Rom. Cath., 91 graves); colliery 1897; convict stockade (Bowens Hollow), demolished 1936; earth tremor 1903; gale 1928; PO 1852; Presb. C. (Knox) b. 1842 by Andrew Brown, extended 1885, restored and re-roofed 1966, and graveyard (409 graves) 1844; school (Bowenfels till *c.*1900) 1851, new building 1866, closed 1969, reused; telegraph 1869; telephone 1905; toll-gate 1861–72; Wes. Meth. C. 1851, closed, abandoned and dilapidated, bought by T. Sutton, demolished 1921; pop. 219 (1933), 161 (1947), 234 (1954), 299 (1961), 765 (2006), 1,004 (2011).

Bowen Mountain (*Co. Cook*) 33°35'S. 150°38'E., 4 km SW of Kurrajong, on Hooemroy Ck; bottled water plant (Blue Mountains Natural Spring Water) 1989; bushfires 1994 and 2001; FB; pop. 957 (1991), 1,211 (1996), 1,344 (2001), 1,438 (2006), 1,339 (2011).

Bowling Alley Point (*Co. Parry*) 31°24'S. 151°08'E., 39 km SE of Tamworth, on Peel R.; orig. Peel River, then Golden Point till 1858; gold (disc. by Thomas Laurie) 1849–1960 and pigs 1877+; cemetery (151 graves 1884+), surveyed 1874, dedicated 1877; foot-bridge (fabricated of wrought iron in England) 1863, destroyed 1984, over Peel R.; PO 1858–1976, demolished 1979; Prim. Meth. C. 1873; school 1869, repairs 1881 by S. Pyrke, repairs 1895 by William Frederick Gazzard, replaced 1912 by Robert Hamilton Gillies, closed 1970; stamper battery 1863; telephone 1898; TX 1921; Union C. 1906; pop. *c.*400 (1866), 276 (1891), 317 (1901), 222 (1911), 238 (1933), 131 (1947), 163 (1954), 129 (1961).

Bowman (*Co. Gloucester*) 31°56'S. 151°50'E., 14 km NW of Gloucester, on Bowman R.; village gaz. 1880; tobacco; TX 1973.

Bowman Farm (*Co. Gloucester*) 31°56'S. 151°56'E., 8 km N. of Gloucester; FB; pop. 56 (1933), 69 (1947), 62 (1954), 65 (1961).

Bowmans Creek (*Co. Durham*) 32°16'S. 151°09'E., 24 km E. of Muswellbrook, on Bowmans Ck; grazing; PO 1907; Rom. Cath. C. (Our Lady of Perpetual Succour) b. 1902 by W. Schmierer; RS 1893, closed; telephone 1914; TX 1926; pop. 56 (1901), 25 (1933).

Bowna (*Co. Goulburn*) 35°57'S. 147°07'E., 24 km NE of Albury, on Mullanjandra Ck; village gaz. 1866, later bypassed by highway; grapes, tobacco, grazing, wheat; boomerang factory (Yarakila's) estab. 1969 by Jeff Lewry, closed; cemetery (28 graves) 1882; FB 1917; flour mill (W.T. Pyke) d. by Kirkpatrick; foundry (T. Hicks & Co.); PO 1869; Presb. C. (St Andrew's) 1866, closed and demolished 1933 (for Hume Reservoir); PS b. 1893 by A. and J. Kyle, closed 1933; Rom. Cath. C. 1865 (submerged 1934 under Hume Reservoir), new one (St Francis de Sales, Church of the Pioneers) 1934; school 1862, additions 1883 by W.H. Byrne, closed 1934; telegraph 1881; TX 1912; pop. 122 (1891), 268 (1901), 270 (1906), 295 (1911), 85 (1933), 88 (1947), 78 (1954), 84 (1961).

Bowna (*Co. Goulburn*) see also Table Top.

Bowna Railway Station (*Co. Goulburn*) see Table Top.

Bowning (*Co. Harden*) 34°46'S. 148°49'E., 12 km NW of Yass, on Bowning Ck; village gaz. 1846, bypassed by highway 1973; grazing then wheat; Angl. C. (St James's) 1879; cemetery (1 km SW) 1891; earth tremor 1929; electricity 1929; fire 1862; Meth. C. 1902; PO 1874; pound (stock) 1840; PS 1881, new one b. 1903 by Gerald McGee; railway barracks 1876; railway coal stage 1876, new one 1880; Rom. Cath. C. (St Columba's) 1910–2003; RS 1876, station b. by Frederick Horn, closed 1992, sold and reused; school 1849 b. by Nicholson, closed 1859, repaired and reopened 1871, reused, replaced 1876, additions 1882, additions and alterations 1905 by D.J. Grogan, new building b. 1913 by J. Burnett; snow 1929 and 1930; streets electric lit 1931; telegraph 1876; telephone 1909; TX 1911; water supply augmentation 1988; pop. 50 (1851), 193 (1891), 126 (1901), 197 (1911), 273 (1933), 273 (1947), 352 (1954), 241 (1961), 295 (2011).

Bowra (*Co. Raleigh*) see Bowraville.

Bowral (*Co. Camden*) 34°29'S. 150°25'E., 45 km W. of Wollongong, on Mittagong Ck; (incl. East Bowral); orig. Wingecarribbee, then Burradoo, then Bowrall till 1888; settled by Adam Windsor, surveyed 1859, subdivided 1862 by John Norton Oxley and Henry Molesworth Oxley, estab. 1862 by Foulkes, first lots sold 1863, munic. proc. 1886, thrived 1881–93 and in 1920s; favourite highland resort for metrop. gentry and much favoured sanatorium 1884+, then mushrooms, dairying, farming, grazing, quarrying till 1986, tourism; ambulance station (Berrima Dist.) b. 1933 by Alfred Stephens & Sons, d. by Collin and H. Sheaffe; analytical laboratory (Robertson Research Aust. Pty Ltd) 1971; Angl. C. 1863, new one 1874 d. by Edmund Thomas Blacket, demolished 1886, replacement (St Simon and St Jude's) b. 1887 by C. Grove, d. by Thomas Wilson Parrott, alterations 1900 by F.J. Potter, additions 2015, and graveyard; Assemblies of God C. (Lighthouse); Bapt. C. 1939 d. by Pendrill Cyril Blacket, rebuilt 2010; boiling-down works (Charker's), burnt down 1886; brewery (Bowral Brewing Co. Pty Ltd) 2005; brickworks: F. Baker & Sons, Bowral Brick & Tile Works (estab. 1915 by M. Hodkinson, taken over 1922 by F. Baker & Sons, kiln collapsed (2 killed) 1924, new kiln 1924, and new chimney 1924, 150 ft or 45.7 m high), Bowral Brickworks Pty Ltd (expanded 1970, bought 1973 by A.V. Jennings Industries Aust. Ltd, taken over 1984 by Nefco Nominees), C. and J. Willis 1886; bushfires 1883 and 1904; butter factory (Berrima Dist. Farm & Dairy Co. Ltd) 1924 d. by May, modernised 1933; carriage-works: G. Harvey (taken over 1903 by Hector McCallum and Archibald Duncan McCallum, sold 1908), W. Southall 1900, F. Wylie; cemetery (burials 1892+) 1891; CH b. 1896 by Alfred Stephens, d. by Walter Liberty Vernon, additions 1953 d. by Cobden Parkes, closed 2005 and sold; cheese factory (Wingecarribee Butter Factory Co. Ltd) 1902; Christ. Revival Crusade C. (Lighthouse); Christ. Science C.; Church of Christ 1956; concrete pipe works (Rocla Pipe Co.) 1933; Cong. C.; cordial factories: M. Anderson and Springett's Pty Ltd; dust storm 1902; earth tremors 1886, 1934, 1961, 1999; electricity 1925; engineering works (MG Industries Pty Ltd) 1999; eucalyptus oil distillery (W. Marsden); FB (station b. 1894 by Alfred Stephens, d. by E.N. Vennard, sold 1934, new one 1925 by Lowther and Horrocks); floods 1893 and 1943; gale 1900; gasworks (Munic. Gas Co.) 1889, bought 1892 by local council, inundated 1943, improvements 1945 by Alfred Stephens & Sons, explosion 1953, new gasholder b. 1954 by Favelle and Cole, sold 1970 to Aust. Gaslight Co.; grasshopper infestation 1898; hailstorms 1907 and 1933; Highlands Christ. Fellowship C. (in former Roman Catholic C.); hospital (orig. Berrima Dist., now Bowral & Dist.) b. 1889 by John J. Campbell, d. by Harry Chambers Kent, additions 1890 by John Bevan, d. by Harry Chambers Kent, extended 1898 also by Bevan, new building b. 1902 by Alfred Stephens, d. by Charles Herbert Halstead, additions and alterations 1911 d. by James Campbell, additions 1926, isolation block 1928, morgue b. 1932 by S.G. Macfarlane, new hospital b. 1935 by Alfred Stephens & Sons, additions 1954 and 1959, extended 1961 and 1965, additions 1970, 1978, 1985; ice works (Springett's Pty Ltd); joineries: James Ford Walker Alldis 1886 and Alfred Stephens & Sons; milk factory (NSW Fresh Food & Ice Co. Ltd) 1921, closed and reused; monumental stone works (H. Taylor); PO 1864, new one b. 1887 by Henry Ford, d. by James Johnstone Barnet, alterations 1891 by R.A. Bastard, additions and alterations 1908 by Steel Bros, d. by Walter Liberty Vernon, demolished 1989 and replaced; pound (stock) 1882; Presb. C. (St Stephen's) 1892 d. by Hardwick, relocated 1910 by Alfred Stephens, relocated again 1930, relocated again and reused, new one (St Andrew's) b. 1954 by Alfred Stephens & Sons, d. by J. Spencer Stansfield; Prim. Meth. C. 1868, new one b. 1885 by James Ford Walker Alldis, closed 1903, reused 1905, dismantled; PS 1882, new one (incl. lock-up) b. 1887 by Charles Goode & Son, additions and alterations 1931; quarries (syenite): Leggatt's, NSW Trachyte Stone Quarrying Co. (estab. 1885 by William Charker, taken over 1888 by Thomas Loveridge and Herbert Charles Hudson), F.J. Pope & Son; railway accident 1886; railway tunnel (Mt Gibraltar) 1867–1919 b. by Wolf and Humphries, 574 yds (524.8 m), reused, new one o. 1919, 564 yds (516 m); 3 reservoirs (1908, 1931, 1951); rifle range; Rom. Cath. C. (St Thomas Aquinas's) b. 1891 by A. and D. Elphingstone, extended 1916, closed, sold and reused, new one 1986; RS 1867, station. b. by G.A. Tillett, new station b. 1890 by James Searle, upgraded 2008 by Degnan Constructions Pty Ltd; sale-yards (J. Goodfellow) 1917; Salv. Army C. 1925, demolished, new one 1980, closed, sold 2016; 3 sawmills (incl. W.A. Selems and S. Willis); schools: primary 1867, additions 1882 by J.J. Campbell, additions 1885, additions 1889 by Gee and Lusted, new building b. 1894 by R.L. Thompson, additions 1898 by E.A. Allerdice, additions 1917, 1960, 1970, 1975, 1988, 2010, and HS 1930 d. by Edwin Evan Smith, additions 1971, 1985, 1990, 1993; SD Adventist C. 1923, new one 1996; sewerage 1935, augmentation 1994; snowstorm 1899; streets lit by kerosene 1888, gas lit 1889, electric lit 1925; tannery (Henry Pain); telegraph 1877; trees (ornamental) planted in streets 1886 and 1897; TX 1909, automatic 1971; Unit. C. (orig. Meth.) b. 1926 by S.G. Lipscombe, d. by McCredie and Anderson; water supply 1908, reticulation 1922, filtration plant 1929, augmentation 1964; Wes. Meth. C. b. 1865 by Jacob Ward, moved 1881, renovated 1903; wineries: Centennial Vineyards and Greenbrier Park estab. by Robert Constable; Zion Full Salv. Ministry C.; pop. 133 (1871), 363 (1881), *c.*1,200 (1886), 2,258 (1891), 1,752 (1901), 1,911 (1911), 2,620 (1921), 3,005 (1933), *c.*3,300 (1941), 3,660 (1947), 3,840 (1951), 3,926 (1954), 4,922 (1961), 5,210 (1966), 5,913 (1971), 6,283 (1976), 6,862 (1981), 7,390 (1986), 7,929 (1991), 8,705 (1996), 10,402 (2001), 11,493 (2006), 9,603 (2011).

Bowraville (*Co. Raleigh*) 30°39'S. 152°51'E., 9 km NW of Macksville, on South Ck; site reserved 1868, surveyed and village gaz. 1871 as Bowra, estab. *c.*1875; orig. timber, later antimony, maize, pigs, poultry, dairying, bananas, now centre for alternative lifestyles; Angl. C. (St James's) b. 1898 by Campbell; bacon factory b. 1918 by Standard Waygood Hercules Ltd for Bowraville Co-op. Butter Factory Ltd; bridges: Brouggys Bridge 1912 over South Ck and Lanes Bridge, b. 1926 by W.G. Boulton, over Nambucca R.; butter factory (Bowraville Co-op. Butter Factory Ltd) 1907, rebuilt 1914 by George Parkins, new one 1926; carriage-works (Ewin Kennedy); cemetery (1,205 graves 1873+) 1870, incl. columbarium; CH 1872, new one (incl. lock-up) b. 1899 by William Robert Ibbotson, d. by Walter Liberty Vernon, closed 1968; clock tower; cordial factory (Pioneer, Harold Humphris) 1912; FB (station b. 1973); flood 1870; hide works; LDS (Mormon) C.;

PO 1870, new one b. 1893 by James Moloney, another new one b. 1900 by Manning and Morrison; pound (stock) 1900; Presb. C. 1885, reused; PS 1885, new one b. 1899 by William Robert Ibbotson, d. by Walter Liberty Vernon; reservoir (tower); Rom. Cath. C. b. 1873 by John Howle and Edwin Crispin, moved 1912, reused 1913, demolished 1963, replacement (All Saints') 1913, reused 1928, new one (Corpus Christi) b. 1928 by Scott Bros, d. by Austin McKay; sawmills: J. Callinan, Fuller Bros, Gibson and Daly, Guidoux's 1906 (burnt down 1910), George Parkins, Allen Taylor & Co. Ltd, E.M. Walker (bought 1940 by Pidcock Bros Ltd, rebuilt 1948, sold 1949 to Allen Taylor & Co. Ltd); school (Bowra till 1890) 1875, additions and repairs 1894 by George Parkins, removed and disposed of 1900 by P. Maloney, new building b. 1900 by C.B. Smith, additions 1922 by B.W. Skinner, additions 1956, 1959, 1966, 2009; sewerage 1968; streets electric lit 1934; telegraph 1892; telephone 1884; TX 1910; Unit. C. (orig. Meth.) b. 1918, begun by George Edward Moore but completed by Allan Bros; water reticulation 1957, augmentation 1969; Wes. Meth. C. 1872; wharves: one b. 1896 by George Edward Moore, and Sullivan's 1912; pop. 119 (1891), 277 (1901), 576 (1911), *c.*700 (1924), 1,008 (1933), 972 (1947), 1,047 (1954), 1,003 (1961), 883 (1966), 843 (1971), 801 (1976), 848 (1981), 1,024 (1986), 963 (1991), 933 (1996), 956 (2001), 976 (2006), 1,092 (2011).

Bowthorne (*Co. Durham*) see Wallalong.

Box Bump (*Co. Hunter*) 32°55'S. 150°38'E., 61 km W. of Paxton, on Putty Ck.

Box Corner (*Co. Wellington*) 33°03'S. 149°23'E., 35 km NE of Orange, on Stringybark Ck.

Boxers Creek (*Co. Argyle*) 34°44'S. 149°49'E., 9 km E. of Goulburn; Wes. Meth. C. 1860, extended 1872, closed 1881, reused 1886; pop. 203 (1901), 52 (1911), 46 (1933), 456 (2006).

Box Gap (*Co. Hunter*) 33°00'S. 150°37'E., 63 km W. of Paxton, on Reedy Ck.

Box Head (*Co. Northumberland*) see Killcare.

Box Hill (*Co. Cook*) 33°34'S. 150°39'E., 3 km SW of Kurrajong, on Cabbage Tree Ck.

Boxlands (*Co. Bathurst*) 33°31'S. 148°59'E., 18 km NW of Carcoar, on Rodds Ck.

Boxley (*Co. Vernon*) 31°02'S. 151°26'E., 16 km W. of Walcha, on Macdonald R.

Box Ridge (*Co. Leichhardt*) 31°15'S. 148°49'E., 34 km E. of Gulargambone; pop. 73 (1911).

Box Ridge (*Co. Roxburgh*) see Turondale.

Box Tank (*Co. Tandora*) 32°12'S. 142°14'E., 77 km E. of Broken Hill; RS 1919–74.

Box Tree Clearing (*Co. Northumberland*) 32°58'S. 150°35'E., 66 km W. of Paxton.

Box Vale (*Co. Camden*) 34°25'S. 150°26'E., 4 km NW of Mittagong, on Nattai R.; coalmine o. 1883 by Mittagong Coal Mining Co. Ltd, acquired 1890 by Owen Snowden & Co. and named Box Vale Colliery, bought 1896 by Lambert Bros, closed; dam; railway (colliery) 1888, dismantled and reused; school 1901 b. by A. Stephens, closed 1914; wineries: Bousaada Vineyard, estab. 1997 by Alastair and Michele Graham, closed 2015 and Tertini Wines, estab. 2000, o. 2005.

Boyben (*Co. Gowen*) 31°50'S. 149°01'E., 35 km E. of Gilgandra, on Castlereagh R.; farming and grazing; PO 1927–42; telephone 1925; TX 1925; pop. 56 (1933), 58 (1961).

Boyd (*Co. Forbes*) 33°35'S. 147°54'E., 26 km S. of Forbes; defunct; gold (disc. 1883) mining 1883–1937; cemetery 1898; PO 1897; school (Pinnacle Reefs till 1898) 1897–1903; stamper battery (5 head); pop. 79 (1911).

Boyd (*Co. Wynyard*) see Tumut.

Boyd's Plains (*Co. Gough*) see Stonehenge.

Boydsville (*Co. Rous*) see Nunderi.

Boydtown (*Co. Auckland*) 37°06'S. 149°53'E., 5 km SW of Eden, on Nullica Bay; surveyed 1842, estab. 1843 by Benjamin Boyd, thrived 1843–47, collapsed 1849; Angl. C. b. 1844–47 (but never completed), ruined, and graveyard (3 graves); boiling-down works 1844; brickkiln 1843; dam 1844; jetty, 300 ft (91.4 m), b. for Benjamin Boyd; lock-up (private); quarry; salting house 1847; whale look-out tower, 76 ft (23.2 m), 1843 d. by Sir Oswald Walters Brierly as a lighthouse, but never used as such; wharf 1844; wool stores 1843 and 1844; pop. 162 (2011).

Boylston (*Co. Clarence*) 29°24'S. 153°00'E., 20 km W. of Maclean; PO 1927–31; telephone 1919; TX 1930–32; pop. 24 (1933).

Braal (*Co. Kennedy*) 32°36'S. 147°20'E., 49 km NW of Trundle, on Bulbodney Ck; telephone 1927; TX 1930.

Brabri (*Co. Darling*) 30°42'S. 150°41'E., 6 km NW of Manilla; RS 1908, station b. by W. Gawne & Sons, closed 1964.

Brackendale (*Co. Vernon*) 31°13'S. 151°42'E., 28 km S. of Walcha; Orundumbi till 1924; farming and grazing; airfield; Angl. C. (Good Shepherd); PO 1892; school (Tia till 1928) 1894–1934 and 1957–68; telephone 1923; TX 1924; pop. 75 (1911), 94 (1947), 99 (1954), 81 (1961).

Bradfordville (*Co. Argyle*) 34°44'S. 149°44'E., 4 km NE of Goulburn, on Wollondilly R.; (incl. Crestwood and Kenmore); orchards and dairying; abattoir (R.H. Tuttlebee) 1928; Angl. C. (St John's) 1907, chancel added 1926; bridges (to Goulburn) over Wollondilly R.: Kenmore Bridge and Victoria Street Bridge; CAE 1975, then Riverina Institute of Technology 1982–83, reused; cemetery (orig. Rom. Cath., taken over by local council and renamed Kenmore in 1998), burials 1889+, incl. lawn cemetery 2003 and columbaria 2010; dam 1917; electricity 1917; fibrous plaster works (Thomas D. Godfrey); 2 foot-bridges, to Goulburn, over Wollondilly R.; hospital for the insane (Kenmore) b. 1894–97 by John Baldwin and J.C. O'Brien, d. by Walter Liberty Vernon, first patients admitted 1895, additions 1899 by N. Kingston & Co., additions 1908 by W. Gawne & Sons, additions 1910 by E.C. Luster, fires 1912 and 1915, additions 1934 by Robert Daniel Quiggin, used as military hospital 1942–46, ha-ha walls 1955, hospital additions 1958, renovations 1964, additions 1971, 1974, 1978, sold 2003 to Longreach Capital Pty Ltd, additions 2007 by Edwards Constructions (NSW) Pty Ltd, disused, acquired 2015 by Aust. China International Pty Ltd; Meth. C. b. 1930 by J. Wright; PO: Bradfordville 1927–94 and Kenmore 1899; police academy o. 1984 in former CAE, additions 1985, 1989, 1990, became part of Charles Sturt University (Goulburn Campus) in 1998; railway siding for woollen mills 1923–64; 2 reservoirs (incl. Craigs Hill); rifle range (Kenmore); RS: Bradfordville 1934–64 and Kenmore 1902–76; schools: Bradfordville 1970, Kenmore 1904, new one b. 1906 by E.P. Frost & Co., closed 1921, Mulwaree HS 1971; SD Adventist C. (Crestwood); teachers' college (Goulburn) 1970 d. by John Kinstler, closed 1974, became CAE; telephone: Bradfordville 1924 and Kenmore 1913; Wes. Meth. C. 1897; woollen mills (Goulburn Woollen Mills Ltd) 1923 d. by Manfred & Son, taken over 1929 by Amalgamated Textiles (Aust.) Ltd; pop. 884 (1901), 1,399 (1911), 1,632 (1933, incl. 1,243 in Kenmore hospital), 1,179 (1947, incl. 738 in Kenmore hospital).

Bradshaws Flat (*Co. Roxburgh*)
see Wallaby Rocks.

Bradys Gully (*Co. Northumberland*)
see Gosford.

Braeburn (*Co. Oxley*) 32°04'S. 147°36'E., 36 km W. of Trangie.

Braefield (*Co. Buckland*) 31°34'S. 150°42'E., 7 km S. of Quirindi; farming and grazing; airport (Quirindi) 1939, defunct; PO 1926; RS (Mackay's till 1879) 1878–1989; school 1903–53; telephone 1926; TX; pop. 58 (1911), 72 (1933), 96 (1947), 79 (1954), 70 (1961).

Braemar (*Co. Camden*) 34°26'S. 150°29'E., 4 km NE of Mittagong, on Sheep Wash Ck; subdivided 1892 by Bartholomew Rush; orchards and farming; bushfire 1928; engineering works (Mittagong Engineering NSW Pty Ltd); PO 1927; railway viaduct (timber); RS (Rush's Platform till 1892) 1867–1978; telephone 1939; pop. 95 (1911), 70 (1933), 85 (1947), 121 (1954), 154 (1961), 308 (2011).

Braemar (*Co. Wallace*) 36°07'S. 148°39'E., 34 km N. of Jindabyne, on Lake Eucumbene.

Bragg's Siding (*Co. Narromine*)
see Mungeribar.

Braidwood (*Co. St Vincent*) 35°27'S. 149°48'E., 45 km NW of Batemans Bay, on Gillamatong

Ck; Strathallan till 1837; town site selected 1833, surveyed by James Larmer, first lots sold 1840, thrived 1859, designated as chief town of the county, depression 1920–21, thrived in 1950s, classified by National Trust, added to National Estate 1980; formerly, gold, wattle-bark, wheat, maize, barley, lucerne, oats, rye, potatoes, wine, butter, cheese, ham, bacon, rabbit meat, eucalyptus oil (mainly 1946–48), dairying till 1966, now cattle, sheep, horses, timber, fruit; ambulance station 1943, new one 1964; Angl. C. b. 1854–56 by Andrew Badgery, gallery added 1858, church defunct, replacement (St Andrew's) b. 1881–92 by William Alfred Isley, d. by Blacket & Son, tower added 1899; 4 boot factories; breweries: one estab. 1851 and Britannia Brewery (Edward Smith) 1859–60; brickworks (Robinson's); bridges: Archer Bridge over Flood Ck and Jews Bridge b. 1930 by W. Sims & Son, new one 1964, over Gillamatong Ck; bushfires 1888 and 1939; butter factory (Braidwood Butter Factory Co. Ltd) 1894; carriage-works: Arthur Campbell & Co., Bridgement & Co., Grant and O'Heir; cemeteries: general 1847–2007 and lawn, 417 plots; CH (incl. lock-up) b. 1838 by Thomas Braidwood Wilson, d. by Mortimer William Lewis, alterations 1864, repairs 1870 by Thomas Davis, repairs 1878 by William Augustus Kershaw, demolished, replacement b. 1900–2 by Underhill and Thatcher, d. by Walter Liberty Vernon, closed and reused; Chinese joss house; coffin factory (Edward Grizzlestone Morris); cordial factories: Arthur Marrin (burnt down 1895), William John McKay 1896–1931 (acquired 1934 by H. Young), Charles Sacagio (burnt down 1901); diphtheria 1860, 1911, 1912, 1914 (3 died); droughts 1833, 1838–39, 1931; earth tremors 1852, 1871, 1872, 1883, 1900, 1925, 1935; electricity 1936; FB: town fire brigade 1896, bushfire brigade 1936, stations b. 1967 and 1999; fire 1917; floods 1853, 1860, 1867, 1874, 1879, 1925, 1931; flour mills: W.T. Bennison (closed), D.F. Cogill (Mona), demolished, Hendrick and Jacobs 1859, reused, George Macleod, Rodd Bros (b. 1869 by P.N. Russell & Co., became a freezing works, sold 1947 to E.N. Bell & Co.), Thomas Braidwood Wilson (demolished 1901); gales 1897, 1900, 1952; gaol 1862–1936, demolished; grasshopper infestations 1926, 1928, 1931; hailstorm 1877; hospital 1860, remodelled 1893, demolished 1941, new one b. 1942 by Charles Alexander Stewart Boag; hurricane 1881; measles epidemic 1893; Meth. C. 1966–77; PO 1835, new one b. 1865, repairs 1882 by William Alfred Isley, repairs 1886 by Edwin T. Isley, new one 1892, repairs 1925 by R. Russell, renovated; police barracks 1836, new barracks 1865; pound (stock) 1839; powerhouse (Braidwood Electric Supply Co.); PS b. 1880 by William Augustus Kershaw; rabbit freezing works (Braidwood Refrigerating Co. Ltd) b. 1909 by Paterson, closed, taken over 1930 by Davis & Co., taken over 1934 by Country Freezing Co.; reservoir; rifle range b. 1908 by W. Fielding; Rom. Cath. C. 1854, replacement (St Bede's) b. 1858–66 by Thomas Purcell, d. by William Weaver, William Edmund Kemp and William Munro, re-roofed 1890 by R.W. Hunt; sale-yards; Salv. Army C.; sawmills: J.C. and H. Collett, Firewood King 2006, Robert William Jackson, demolished, Sawmillers Pty Ltd, Peter Sebbens 1952, J. Wilder; scarlet fever (many children died) 1860; school 1849, additions 1883 by William Alfred Isley, new building b. 1950 by R. Lamont, additions 1966, 1975, 1992; sewage works 1965; snowstorm 1861; storm 1859; streets electric lit 1936; 3 tanneries (incl. E. Grenenger and Thomas Wiley); telegraph 1861, new office b. 1865, repairs 1886 by Edwin T. Isley, additions 1892, renovated, closed, sold 1993 and reused; TX 1907; typhoid 1897, 1898 (woman died), 1900 (2 died), 1904 (man died), 1905; Unit. C. (St Andrew's, orig. Presb.) 1861; water reticulation 1957, augmentation 1990; wattle-bark mill (Craig, Mostyn & Co.); Wes. Meth. C. b. 1855 by Holder and Clowry, enlarged 1867, re-roofed 1888, closed; pop. 127 (1841), 206 (1846), 212 (1851), 507 (1856), 959 (1861), *c.*1,000 (1866), 1,197 (1871), 1,066 (1881), 1,496 (1891), *c.*1,780 (1895), 1,551 (1901), 1,366 (1911), 1,073 (1933), 1,065 (1947), 1,088 (1954), 1,052 (1961), 929 (1966), 959 (1971), 989 (1976), 944 (1981), 958 (1986), 976 (1991), 940 (1996), 1,006 (2001), 1,108 (2006), 1,159 (2011).

Brambles Green (*Co. Gloucester*) 32°35'S. 152°17'E., 15 km NE of Hawks Nest, on Tasman Sea.

Branch Creek (*Co. Rous*) 28°38'S. 153°17'E., 8 km SE of Nimbin; Meth. C. b. 1908 by Charles Johnson, closed 1968, demolished; telephone 1925.

Branch River (*Co. Gloucester*) see The Branch.

Brandon (*Co. Durham*) 32°40'S. 151°43'E., 15 km NE of Maitland; bushfire 1928; pop. 72 (1901), 55 (1911), 51 (1933).

Brandon Hill (*Co. Camden*) see Mount Brandon.

Brandy Hill (*Co. Durham*) see Seaham.

Branga (*Co. Vernon*) 31°10'S. 151°33'E., 20 km S. of Walcha; school 1888–1902.

Branga Plains (*Co. Vernon*) 31°16'S. 151°33'E., 30 km S. of Walcha, on Ingleba Ck.

Branxton (*Co. Northumberland*) 32°40'S. 151°21'E., 20 km SE of Singleton, on Anvil Ck; (incl. East Branxton); Black Creek till 1862; surveyed by Henry Dangar, planned 1841 by George Boyle White, estab. 1848, village gaz. 1881, subdivided 1913; formerly hunting and grazing, later farming, dairying, wine, fruit, coal; Angl. C. (St John the Baptist) 1849, (St John the Evangelist) b. 1875–81 by Miles, Alcorn and Stewart, d. by John Horbury Hunt, and columbaria; brewery (Hunter Valley Brewing Co. Pty Ltd) 1951–53; bridges: one b. 1911 by Ferry over Anvil Ck, Becan Bridge over Anvil Ck, one over Red House Ck; bushfires 1895, 1909, 1939, 1952; butter factory (George Forrester & Son) b. 1901 by Russell Bros, d. by George Forrester & Son, remodelling 1925 by Grainger, d. by Wildridge and Sinclair, reused 1951 as brewery; bushfire 1939; carriage-works (J. Brown); cemetery (666 graves 1850s+) 1883; CH b. 1879–81 by E. James, d. by James Johnstone Barnet, closed 1969, reused; dairy factories: Branxton Co-op. Dairy Co. Ltd 1918 and Hunter Valley Co-op. Dairy Co. Ltd; diphtheria 1921; drought 1919; FB (station b. 1962); floods 1893 (3 died), 1955, 2007; flour mills: Crago's (sawmill added 1876), Thomas Lindsay, Thomas Brereton Watson 1872; hailstorm 1875; ice works (Branxton Dairy Co. Ltd); lock-up b. 1884 by S. Dumbrill, d. by James Johnstone Barnet; PO 1860, new one b. 1927; PS 1880 d. by James Johnstone Barnet, additions and repairs 1897 by J. Cox; rifle range; Rom. Cath. C. (St Patrick's) 1840, re-roofed, demolished and replaced 1866, reused 1886, demolished 1960, new one (St Brigid's) b. 1887 by William Taylor & Son, d. by Arthur Coe Lee, enlarged and renovated 1961 by Peter Jerome Gannon, and graveyard (997 graves 1840s+); RS 1862; sawmill: H. Russell and Whysall's; school 1863, new one b. 1899 by William Henry Noad, additions 1960, closed, sold and reused 1986, new school 1986 on new site, in reused buildings; sewage works; storms 1899 and 1905; telegraph 1875; telephone 1908; tornado 2003; TX 1910; Unit. C. (orig. Meth.) b. 1919 by Taylor and Bouffier, d. by James Hicks, and columbarium; Wes. Meth. C. 1866 d. by G. Mansfield; winery (Pierre's Wines, Peter and Anne Went); pop. *c.*500 (1860–66), 254 (1871), 87 (1881), 490 (1891), 586 (1901), 713 (1911), 1,289 (1933), 1,107 (1947), 1,181 (1954), 1,144 (1961), 2,544 (1966, incl. Greta), 2,466 (1971, incl. Greta), 2,485 (1976, incl. Greta), 2,849 (1981, incl. Greta), 3,208 (1986, incl. Greta), 3,414 (1991, incl. Greta), 3,734 (1996, incl. Greta), 3,805 (2001, incl. Greta), 4,678 (2006, incl. Greta), 5,190 (2011, incl. Greta).

Brasfort (*Co. Cook*) see Wentworth Falls.

Brassi (*Co. Townsend*) 35°30'S. 144°44'E., 22 km W. of Deniliquin, on Wakool R.; village gaz. 1886; bridge b. 1881 by James Lawrence, over Wakool R.; school 1882–86; TX (automatic).

Braunstone (*Co. Clarence*) 29°48'S. 152°58'E., 12 km S. of Grafton; RS 1915, closed; school (Bundarigo till 1936) 1893–1905 and 1919–

48; telephone 1923; TX 1929–61; pop. 145 (1933), 96 (1947), 74 (1954), 68 (1961), 291 (2011).

Brawboy (*Co. Brisbane*) 31°57'S. 150°38'E., 24 km NW of Scone, on Guan Gua Ck; school 1960–68; TX (automatic).

Brawlin (*Co. Harden*) 34°44'S. 148°03'E., 11 km S. of Cootamundra, on Muttama Ck; farming and grazing; bushfire 1987; eucalyptus oil distillery (Colemane & Sons); PO 1886; RS 1886, station b. by Thomas M'Beath, closed 1975, station demolished 1979; school 1879–95, 1898–1920, 1957–60; telephone 1914; TX 1920; pop. 97 (1901), 157 (1911), 125 (1933), 90 (1947), 75 (1954), 53 (1961).

Bray Park (*Co. Rous*) see Murwillumbah.

Brays Creek (*Co. Rous*) 28°24'S. 153°11'E., 22 km W. of Murwillumbah, on Brays Ck; farming and dairying; bushfire 1936; PO 1927; school 1929–77; telephone 1914; TX 1926; pop. 153 (1933), 108 (1947), 159 (1954), 112 (1961).

Brayton (*Co. Argyle*) 34°39'S. 149°58'E., 26 km NE of Goulburn; Long Reach till 1913; farming and grazing; airfield; Angl. C. (St Mary's) 1896, burnt down 1965, and graveyard; bushfire 1965; lime-works: Brayton Lime Burning Co. (Albert Verner Lacey, David Sharp and Leslie Berry), closed 1923, John E. Leahy, fire 1932 damaged kiln, Sieler and Hogg; PO 1862; quarry (Edward Richards); school (Long Reach) 1859–63 and 1884–1913; telephone 1914; TX 1928; pop. *c.*300 (1866), 133 (1901), 77 (1911), 80 (1933), 53 (1947), 58 (1954), 436 (2006).

Breadalbane (*Co. Argyle*) 34°47'S. 149°30'E., 21 km W. of Goulburn; Mutt Billy till 1875; village gaz. 1871; mining (iron ore) 1895+, farming, grazing; Angl. C. (St Silas's) 1866–1937, demolished, new one (St Silas's, Gerald Chisholm Memorial) b. 1938 by Cox Bros, d. by Bertram Chisholm; bushfire 1905; copper mine (estab. by S. Murray) 1895 and 1906–17; iron ore quarry (G. & C. Hoskins Ltd 1918–29 and BHP 1941–45); PO 1860; Rom. Cath. C. (St Brigid's) b. 1866–79, and graveyard; RS 1875–1976; school 1876, repairs 1882 by T. Apps, additions and alterations 1886 by Joseph Newman, closed 1906, reopened 1918; smelter and railway siding (Breadalbane Mining & Smelting Co.) 1910; telegraph 1890; TX 1911, automatic 1955; pop. *c.*400 (1866), 239 (1891), 218 (1901), 195 (1911), 117 (1933), 79 (1947), 157 (1954), 167 (1961), 275 (2011).

Bread and Butter Flat (*Co. Roxburgh*) 33°19'S. 149°41'E., 15 km NE of Bathurst, on Bread and Butter Ck; mine.

Breakfast Creek (*Co. Monteagle*) 34°07'S. 148°44'E., 31 km S. of Cowra, on Breakfast Ck; gold (disc. 1929); bushfire 1929; earth tremor 2012; electricity 1958; pop. 68 (1911), 34 (1947).

Breakfast Creek (*Co. Phillip*) 32°41'S. 150°01'E., 14 km N. of Rylstone, on Breakfast Ck; quarry; school 1895–1925; telephone 1918; pop. 52 (1933), 229 (2006), 273 (2011).

Breakfast Point (*Co. Cook*) 33°46'S. 150°38'E., 2 km NE of Glenbrook; subdivided 1881; RS 1877–89.

Breakneck Hill (*Co. Gloucester*) 32°00'S. 152°25'E., 11 km S. of Taree.

Bream Beach (*Co. St Vincent*) 35°07'S. 150°40'E., 2 km SE of Erowal Bay, on St Georges Basin.

Brecon (*Co. Durham*) 32°31'S. 151°34'E., 25 km N. of Maitland, on Allyn R.; school 1850–52.

Bredbo (*Co. Beresford*) 35°57'S. 149°09'E., 29 km N. of Cooma, on Bredbo R.; village gaz. 1888; mining (copper, lead, silver, iron), farming, wool, grapes; Angl. C. 1900, dismantled and moved to Chakola, new one (St Bartholomew's) 1929; bridge b. 1869–72, new one b. 1893 by W. Pickering, 285 ft (87 m), replacement (421 ft or 128.4 m) b. 1979 by Nelmac Pty Ltd, over Bredbo R.; cemetery (159 graves 1894+) 1890; electricity 1955; FB; mine fatality (man killed) 1889; mines: Baalgammon, *c.*1880 and 1907, Reed's, Woolshed; PO 1875, new one b. 1901; Rom. Cath. C. (All Saints') 1899; RS 1891, station b. by William Wilson, closed 1989; school 1887, new building b. 1910 by W.H.D. Avery; telephone 1898; TX 1913; water reticulation

1969, augmentation 1989; pop. 82 (1901), 137 (1911), 125 (1933), 144 (1947), 184 (1954), 183 (1961), 172 (2006).

Bredbo North (*Co. Beresford*) 35°53'S. 149°09'E., 39 km N. of Cooma.

Breelong (*Co. Gowen*) 31°48'S. 148°48'E., 17 km SE of Gilgandra, on Breelong Ck; laid out by Edward Fisher and village gaz. 1866, but never fully developed (bypassed 1899 by railway); timber and charcoal burning (World War II); bridge b. 1980 by Greg Brennan, over Wallumburrawang Ck; cemetery; dust storm 1983; FB 1946; hailstorm 1925; sawmill (F. Walker); telephone 1927; TX (automatic) 1976; pop. 108 (1901), 106 (1911), 32 (1933), 110 (1947), 50 (1954).

Breewarrina (*Co. Clyde*) see Brewarrina.

Breeza (*Co. Pottinger*) 31°15'S. 150°28'E., 21 km NW of Werris Creek, on Mooki R.; farming and grazing; Angl. C. (St Stephen's) 1901, burnt down, new one 1966, and graveyard; bridge b. 1867 by Amos Davies; bushfires 1909 and 2012; cemetery (73 graves) 1900; creamery and cheese factory (Cliff Bros); drought 1918; 2 FB; fire 1866; flood 2000; PO 1856, burnt down 1932; pound (stock) 1865; PS 1878–1933; Rom. Cath. C. (St Mary's) b. 1899 by Lees, d. by Scobie; RS 1879, station b. by Joseph Conlon, W. Dowell and J. O'Keeffe, closed 1986; school 1879–1988; silo 1934; telegraph 1879; TX 1914; pop. *c.*65 (1866), 158 (1891), 244 (1901), 275 (1911), 175 (1933), 141 (1947), 247 (1954), 177 (1961), 134 (2006).

Brelsford (*Co. Fitzroy*) see Coffs Harbour.

Brenda (*Co. Narran*) 29°02'S. 147°19'E., 77 km NW of Lightning Ridge, on Culgoa R.; grazing; bridge (Allan timber truss) 1922, 208 ft (63.4 m), over Culgoa R.; PO 1862.

Brenda Gate (*Co. Culgoa*) 29°00'S. 147°17'E., 82 km NW of Lightning Ridge.

Brenta (*Co. King*) 34°24'S. 148°51'E., 12 km E. of Boorowa; telephone 1921; TX 1928.

Brereton Bend (*Co. Cook*) 33°54'S. 150°28'E., 18 km S. of Hazellbrook, on Pelham Ck.

Bretti (*Co. Hawes*) 31°47'S. 151°55'E., 24 km N. of Gloucester, on Manning R.; farming and grazing; PO 1927–72; telephone 1921; TX 1926.

Brewarrina (*Co. Clyde*) 29°58'S. 146°52'E., 89 km E. of Bourke, on Barwon R.; orig. Walcha Hut, then known as Fishery and The Fishing Village; settled *c.*1842, surveyed and laid out 1862 by James Glen Wilson, first lots sold 1862, town gaz. 1863 as Breewarrina, designated as chief town of the county, thrived in 1870s, munic. 1901–54; river port 1859–*c.*1901, fishing, now sheep, cattle, citrus fruit, cotton; airport (4 km W.) 1967; ambulance station; Angl. C. (Christ) b. 1877–79, d. by Edmund Thomas Blacket, damaged 1910, repaired and enlarged 1910; brick-kiln (Charlie Crane); bridges: one (pontoon) b. 1872 by James Govan, replacement (lift span fabricated by F.J. Appleby), b. 1888 by Childs and McClements, d. by Percy Allan, modified 1896, closed and reused, replaced, over Barwon R. and Billabong Bridge; cemetery (1 km SW) 1874; CH (incl. lock-up) b. 1872 by James Batten, alterations 1885, additions 1888 by George Burrows, additions 1899, additions 1909 by W.J. Brown, damaged 1910, restored 1987; cordial factories: John Joseph McDougall and Simmons' (bought 1963 by John Edwards); cyclone (damaged most of town) 1910; dust storms 1875 and 1912; earth tremors 1910 and 1954; electricity 1929; FB 1953 (station b. 1970); fires 1900, 1901, 1930; floods 1864, 1890, 1893, 1974; heatwaves 1892 and 1909; hospital b. 1880–83, d. by Herbert S. Thompson, additions 1893, damaged 1910, alterations 1958, new one 2004; hurricane 1874; PO 1866, new one b. 1880 by M. Robinson, alterations 1896 by A.A. Woolfrey, damaged 1910, demolished 1957, replaced 1958; powerhouse estab. 1929 by Harry Parrott, acquired 1933 by local council; Presb. C. 1912; PS 1866, new one 1873, additions and repairs 1908 by A. Porter, damaged 1910, new one 1960; punt b. 1874 by James Batten; railway barracks, damaged 1910; railway coal stage 1900; railway engine shed, damaged 1910; railway turntable, 50 ft (15.2 m); reservoir, 30,000 gal. (136.4 kl);

Rom. Cath. C. b. 1893 by A. Wolfrey, d. by Fred Harrison, new one (St Patrick's) b. 1940 by John D. Ryan, d. by William Lamrock, jun.; RS 1901, station b. by Charles Baker, damaged 1910, burnt down 1981; sale-yards 1962; sandfly infestation 1930; sawmill (A.B. Maidens); school 1875 b. by James Batten, additions 1877 also by Batten, new building 1893, repairs 1898 by P. Duffy, renovated 1902, damaged 1910, new buildings 1912 and 1960, additions 1967 and 1970; sewerage 1971; soap-works (Ted Marsh); TC (a campus of Western Institute); telegraph 1873, new office b. 1875 by James Batten, replacement b. 1880 by M. Robinson, alterations 1896 by A.A. Woolfrey; TX 1913; water supply 1917, filtration plant 1970, augmentation 1992; weir 1968, on Barwon R.; Wes. Meth. C.; wharf; wool-scours: Joe Hayes and T. Robinson 1875; pop. 95 (1871), 344 (1881), 489 (1891), 683 (1901), 1,137 (1911), 804 (1933), 841 (1947), 905 (1954), 1,225 (1961), 1,282 (1966), 1,444 (1971), 1,386 (1976), 1,236 (1981), 1,166 (1986), 1,168 (1991), 1,113 (1996), 1,201 (2001), 1,121 (2006), 923 (2011).

Brewer (*Co. Dowling*) 33°29'S. 146°07'E., 30 km SW of Lake Cargelligo; telephone 1929; TX 1929; pop. 31 (1933).

Brewers Hill (*Co. Rous*) see Wollongbar.

Brewon (*Co. Clyde*) 30°15'S. 147°31'E., 62 km SW of Walgett; PO 1927–31; wool-scour (W.J. Williams).

Brewongle (*Co. Roxburgh*) 33°29'S. 149°43'E., 14 km SE of Bathurst; Macquarie Plains till 1880; feldspar, wheat, maize; Angl. C. (St George's) 1880; fire 1899; grasshopper infestation 1925; PO 1872–1970; Rom. Cath. C. (St Columbkille's), renovated 1928, closed and reused, burnt down 2013; RS (Macquarie Plains till 1879) 1872, station b. by James Stuart Douglas, closed 1974; school (Macquarie Plains till 1880) 1865, new building b. 1877 by John Wadsworth Ashworth and Rowe, closed 1966; TX 1912; Wes. Meth. C. 1844, new one b. 1858 by William Timothy Atkins, William Kerr and Andrew Rae, and graveyard (22 graves 1830s–1900); pop. 185 (1891), 198 (1901), 90 (1911), 146 (1933), 126 (1947), 154 (1954), 88 (1961), 189 (2011).

Brianderry (*Co. Auckland*) 36°43'S. 149°47'E., 7 km SW of Bega; cheese factory (George Guthrey) in rented premises, burnt down 1908; telephone 1916.

Briar Flat (*Co. Roxburgh*) 33°19'S. 150°01'E., 5 km N. of Portland, on Hunts Ck; cemetery (Back Cullen, 19 burials 1849–1915).

Bribaree Creek (*Co. Bland*) see Bribbaree.

Bribbaree (*Co. Bland*) 34°07'S. 147°53'E., 36 km SW of Grenfell, on Bribbaree Ck; orig. Bribera, then Bribaree Creek till 1917; settled and founded 1915 by John William Byrne, surveyed 1916, village gaz. and lots sold 1917; gold (disc. 1922) mines (7 km SW), farming, grazing; Angl. C. (St Matthew's) 1935, closed, sold 2007 and 2017, reused; brickworks (F.R. Sweeny); cemetery (7 km NE); electricity 1951; FB 1928; German measles epidemic 1940; Lutheran C. (Bethlehem); mines: Bonanza (W. Spring) 1922–36, Brilliant (J.P. Rhall) 1931–37, Golden Lamb (P. Light) 1922–38; PO 1917, new one b. 1933 by Rogers and Chambers, d. by Purvis and Lipman, closed 1993; Presb. C. b. 1928 by H.R. Blackett & Son, sold 1977 to Lutheran C.; PS 1929; 7 quarries; Rom. Cath. C. 1927 (removed from Wyalong and renovated), new one (St Columba's) 1962; RS 1916, station b. by W.S. Millard & Sons Ltd, closed 1985, station sold to Baker; sale-yards (Bribbaree Co-op. Saleyards Ltd) 1933; sawmills: A. Aston, J.C. Flood, Stonham & Son; school 1922, extended 1929 by S. Davis, new building 1950, additions and alterations 1962, new building 1963; silo 1922; stamper battery (10 head) 1923; telephone 1916; TX 1919, new building 1926, automatic 1987; Unit. C. (orig. Meth.) 1926; pop. 30 (1919), 88 (1921), 127 (1926), 199 (1933), 329 (1947), 125 (1954), 365 (1954), 159 (1961), 221 (2006), 267 (2011).

Bribera (*Co. Bland*) see Bribbaree.

Brickella (*Co. Richmond*) 29°07'S. 153°20'E., 5 km S. of Woodburn; school (Riley till 1899) 1892–99 and 1923–47.

Brickfields (*Co. Sandon*) 30°31'S. 151°39'E., 2 km W. of Armidale, on Martins Gully; brickworks; sawmill.

Bridgelo (*Co. Phillip*) 32°22'S. 150°08'E., 33 km SW of Merriwa.

Bridgewater (*Co. Ashburnham*) 33°01'S. 148°52'E., 9 km N. of Molong, on Molong Ck; PO 1880.

Bridgewater (*Co. Ashburnham*) see also Larras Lee.

Bridgman (*Co. Durham*) 32°30'S. 151°10'E., 9 km N. of Singleton; Angl. C. (St Andrew's) 1886, enlarged 1899, rebuilt 1958, and graveyard (56 graves 1892+); coalmine (Integra); PO 1912–15; school (Clairwood) 1888–97; telephone 1912; TX 1928; pop. 96 (1901), 135 (1911), 130 (1933), 396 (2011).

Brierfield (*Co. Raleigh*) 30°31'S. 152°53'E., 6 km W. of Urunga, on Kalang R.; Upper South Arm till 1891; timber, maize, dairying 1890s+; PO 1916–39; quarry (Barry and Cowdery); school 1884–94, reopened 1906, new one erected 1908 (removed from Fernmount), closed 1968; telephone 1919; TX (automatic); wharf 1913; pop. 112 (1933), 67 (1947), 97 (1954), 86 (1961), 268 (2006), 339 (2011).

Brigalow (*Co. Leichhardt*) 31°09'S. 148°48'E., 36 km NE of Gulargambone; formerly Briglo Station.

Brigalows (*Co. Murchison*) 30°13'S. 150°23'E., 29 km NW of Barraba, on Duckholes Ck; school 1957–72.

Briggsvale (*Co. Fitzroy*) 30°15'S. 152°47'E., 11 km NE of Dorrigo; logging; PO 1928–71; quarry; RS (5 km NW) 1924, b. by Charles Briggs & Sons Ltd, closed 1975; sawmills: Bellingen Timber Co. Pty Ltd and G.L. Briggs & Sons Pty Ltd 1923, burnt down 1946; telephone 1926; tramway (steam) for log haulage; TX 1927–62; pop. 74 (1933), 73 (1947), 84 (1954), 51 (1961).

Bright Hill (*Co. Argyle*) 34°26'S. 149°45'E., 25 km E. of Crookwell; telephone 1926; TX 1930.

Brightling (*Co. Leichhardt*) 31°13'S. 148°24'E., 15 km NW of Gulargambone; grazing; PO 1927–31; RS 1903–64; telephone 1910; TX 1913–26.

Brighton (*Co. Macquarie*) see Manning Point.

Brightside (*Co. Wynyard*) 35°31'S. 148°09'E., 2 km N. of Batlow; RS 1925–68.

Brightwaters (*Co. Northumberland*) 33°07'S. 151°33'E., 2 km E. of Bonnells Bay, on Lake Macquarie; (incl. Mirrabooka, subdivided 1926, and Sunshine, subdivided 1925, formerly Gorrick's Point); orig. Sugar Bay, then Bulgonia, then Balgonnia; surveyed and subdivided 1913 by Henry Ferdinand Halloran; timber and fishing; bushfire 1875; FB (Mirrabooka); jetty; PO 1963–79; quarry (gravel, at Mirrabooka); reservoir (Sunshine); sugar mill estab. 1870 by Joseph Marshall, burnt down 1875; telephone: Brightwaters 1963 and Mirrabooka 1921; water supply 1963; wharf; pop. 87 (1933), 59 (1954), 245 (1961), 642 (1971), 923 (1976), 1,539 (1981), 1,918 (1986), 1,258 (1991), 1,420 (1996), 1,583 (2001), 1,637 (2006), 2,062 (2011).

Briglo Station (*Co. Leichhardt*) see Brigalow.

Bril Bril (*Co. Macquarie*) 31°16'S. 152°32'E., 28 km NW of Wauchope; pop. 70 (1933), 59 (1954).

Brimbin (*Co. Macquarie*) 31°51'S. 152°27'E., 7 km N. of Taree; orig. Brymbyn; pop. 11 (1841).

Brinawa (*Co. Macquarie*) 31°37'S. 152°16'E., 30 km N. of Wingham; school 1957–62; telephone 1921; TX 1928.

Brindabella (*Co. Cowley*) 35°23'S. 148°45'E., 44 km W. of Queanbeyan, on Goodradigbee R., mining (gold disc. 1864 by Michael Sheedy and John McDonald) 1860s–90s and grazing; PO 1886; telephone 1929; TX 1929, automatic 1973; pop. 44 (1933), 23 (2006).

Brindingabba Station (*Co. Irrara*) 29°06'S. 144°54'E., 149 km NW of Bourke; pop. 26 (1933), 71 (1947).

Brindley Park (*Co. Brisbane*) 32°07'S. 150°22'E., 2 km N. of Merriwa, on Merriwa R.; pop. 136 (1901), 22 (1933).

Brinerville (*Co. Raleigh*) 30°29'S. 152°33'E., 21 km SW of Dorrigo, on Bellinger R.; telephone 1926; TX 1929; pop. 33 (1933).

Bringagee (*Co. Sturt*) 34°26'S. 145°42'E., 30 km NW of Darlington Point; PO 1888; railway turntable 1909, 51.5 ft (15.7 m), removed 1984; RS 1882–1975, station removed 1984; telegraph 1890; TX 1911; pop. 72 (1911), 42 (1933).

Bringan (*Co. Wakool*) 35°36'S. 144°09'E., 74 km W. of Deniliquin; school 1918–40.

Bringenbrong (*Co. Selwyn*) 36°10'S. 148°03'E., 42 km NW of Perisher Valley, on Swampy Plain R.; telephone 1948; pop. 27 (1933).

Bringle (*Co. Gowen*) 31°26'S. 148°48'E., 31 km E. of Gulargambone; grasshopper infestation 1931.

Brisbanefields (*Co. Northumberland*) see Thornton.

Brisbane Grove (*Co. Argyle*) 34°48'S. 149°42'E., 5 km S. of Goulburn, on Mulwaree R.; quarry; wool-scour and fellmomgery (Thorn & Co.) 1882; pop. 73 (1933), 64 (1947), 61 (1954), 50 (1961), 218 (2011).

Brisbane Valley (*Co. Westmoreland*) 33°44'S. 149°44'E., 12 km W. of Oberon, on Brisbane Valley Ck; goldmining then agric.; bushfire 1897; Rom. Cath. C. (St Francis Xavier's), rebuilt 1915, closed, and graveyard (19 burials 1857–1950); pop. 51 (1901), 51 (1911), 41 (1933).

Brisbane Valley (*Co. Westmoreland*) see also Balfour.

Brisbane Water (*Co. Northumberland*) see Gosford, Umina Beach and Woy Woy.

Brisbania (*Co. Northumberland*) see Saratoga.

Broad Crossing (*Co. Brisbane*) 32°08'S. 150°58'E., 7 km NE of Aberdeen, on Hunter R.; bridge 2013, over Hunter R.

Broadfield (*Co. Phillip*) 32°20'S. 149°35'E., 5 km NE of Gulgong.

Broadfield (*Co. Phillip*) see also Wyaldra.

Broadmeadow (*Co. Northumberland*) 32°55'S. 151°44'E., 5 km W. of Newcastle, on Styx Ck; (incl. South Hamilton); former industrial suburb; airport (District Park) 1934–63; Angl. C. (St George's) 1924, at South Hamilton; CH (Hunter Children's Court) b. 2006 by Richard Crookes Constructions; earthquake 1989; earth tremor 1925; colliery (Hamilton, estab. by Aust. Agric. Co., also known as H Pit, Glebe Pit or New Pit) 1872, roof-fall 1889 killed 11 men, closed 1901; crumpet factory (Golden Crumpet Co.) 1953; engineering works and foundry (A. Goninan & Co. Ltd) b. 1921 by J.T. Mullen, pattern store burnt down 1941, works taken over 1964 by Howard Smith & Co., sold 1999 to United Group Ltd and became United Goninan, renamed United Group Rail in 2005; FB (No. 1 station 1905–25, reused); fibrous plaster works (Reginald P. Rich); floods 1897, 1898, 1932, 2007; 3 footbridges over Styx Ck; Free Serbian Orthodox C. (Naum Ohridski) 1964; furniture factory (Charles Dickinson & Son), burnt down 1949; ice works (Central Ice & Cold Storage Works Pty Ltd); LDS (Mormon) C. b. 1896 by H. Broadway; Lutheran C. (St Philip's, renamed Lifeway) 1978; Macedonian Orthodox C. (St Mary's) b. 1969 by Leo Todisco; Meth. C. 1928, closed and reused; PO: Broadmeadow 1900 (new one b. 1924 by Leslie Elgin Brander) and South Hamilton 1927–86; Prim. Meth. C. 1887; PS (incl. lock-up) b. 1926 by Herbert Taylor, closed 1936; railway barracks 1924–2010, new barracks; railway depot 1924–94; railway round-houses: No. 1 b. 1924, 21 bays, damaged 1989, demolished 1990 and No. 2 b. 1948, 21 bays, restored 2010 by Degnan Constructions Pty Ltd; railway turntables: No. 1, 79 ft (24 m), 1924 and No. 2, 105 ft (32 m), restored 2010; Rom. Cath. C.: first one 1904, reused 1933, demolished 1956, replacement (St Laurence O'Toole's) b. 1933 by Ryan and Hoyle, d. by Peter Joseph Gannon, damaged 1989, restored and remodelled 1992, and St Martin de Tours 1966–93; RS 1887; sawmill (Heron's Creek Timber Mills Ltd); schools: Hunter School of Performing Arts (which previously had many other names) 1923, additions 1966, 1971, 1979, fire 1994, repairs 1995, additions 2006 and 2012, and Merewether HS (Newcastle Technical HS 1939–76) 1977, additions 1978 and 1981, damaged 1989, additions by R.T. Parker Pty Ltd; sheet metal works (Insulation Industries Pty Ltd) 1967; shoe (infants') factory; smelter (copper) estab. 1871 by English & Aust. Co., closed 1894; teachers' college (Newcastle) 1949, moved 1951 to Newcastle; telephone (South Hamilton) 1923; tramway to Newcastle, electrified 1924; Unit. C. (orig. Meth.) 1958; pop. 434 (1911), 1,552 (2011).

Broadmeadows (*Co. Gresham*) 29°51'S. 152°18'E., 64 km W. of Grafton, on Boyd R.

Broadmouth Creek (*Co. Clarence*) see Coldstream.

Broadwater (*Co. Richmond*) 29°01'S. 153°26'E., 11 km NE of Woodburn, on Richmond R.; orig. known as Cooktown and also McDonaldtown; settled 1863 by Henry Cook and Alexander Duncan McDonald and village founded 1881; farming and sugar-cane; brickworks: Olaf Larsen, Lyne and Amos, H. Cook & Co.; bridge 2005, 545 ft (166 m), over Richmond R.; CH (incl. lock-up) b. 1895 by C. Baker, new one 1905; cordial factory (Champion Steam Aerated Water & Cordial Works) estab. by John G. Balzer, bought 1902 by Charles Lauritzen; FB 1957; floods 1893, 1945, 1988; hailstorms 1907 and 1940 (many houses damaged); meat preserving works (Atchison's) 1859; PO 1880, inundated 1893, new one b. 1901 by Alfred Peterson, repairs 1925 by C.A. Larsen; PS 1882–1965; punt across Richmond R.; 3 quarries; reservoir; Rom. Cath. C. b. 1889 by Patrick Farrelly, burnt down 1922, replacement (St Columbkille's) 1925, burnt down 1937, new one b. 1938 by Dayal Singh, d. by F.J. Board & Son, closed, sold and renovated, reused 2012; school 1881, new one b. 1885, repairs 1891 by Rotts and Selkirk, additions 2010; sugar mills: Blanch and Patterson, CSR 1881 (man killed 1936, flooded 1948, sold 1978 to NSW Sugar Milling Co-op. Ltd, co-generation power plant b. 2005–8 by Downer Engineering and Clyde Babcock Hitachi), Richmond River Cane Growers' Assoc., Thompson's (removed 1879 from Wyrallah); telegraph 1885, new office b. 1901 by Alfred Peterson; TX 1917, automatic 1954; Union C. 1881, fire 1932, rebuilt 1933 by Baker, closed, sold; wharf b. 1895 by J. Walsh; pop. 492 (1891), 637 (1901), 550 (1911), *c.*500 (1924), 507 (1933), 614 (1947), 486 (1954), 426 (1961), 387 (1971), 363 (1976), 397 (1981), 424 (1986), 488 (1991), 504 (1996), 408 (2001), 463 (2006), 434 (2011).

Brobenah (*Co. Cooper*) 34°23'S. 146°30'E., 19 km NE of Leeton; PO 1898–1911; telephone 1923; pop. 125 (1911), 145 (1933), 77 (1947), 63 (1954), 56 (1961).

Brobenah (*Co. Cooper*) see also Stony Point.

Brocklehurst (*Co. Lincoln*) 32°11'S. 148°38'E., 9 km N. of Dubbo; village gaz. 1874; farming; Angl. C. (Holy Ascension) b. 1902–6 by Ferguson, d. by Thomas William Heaydon, moved 1924 to Mogriguy; FB; PO 1879; school 1878, additions 1900 by H.T. Seymour, closed 1974; telephone 1913; TX (automatic) 1969; Union C. 1899; pop. 86 (1901), 163 (1911), 59 (1933), 80 (1947), 98 (1954), 153 (1961), 190 (2006), 474 (2011).

Brocklesby (*Co. Hume*) 35°49'S. 146°41'E., 19 km N. of Howlong; founded 1870 by Maxwell Bros, orig. a private village; farming; bushfire 1905; cemetery; chaff mill (J. Hunter); drought 1982; earth tremor 1914; electricity 1948; FB 1922; floods 1939 and 1941; lock-up 1927; measles epidemic 1898; PO 1893; PS 1908; Rom. Cath. C. (St Joseph's) b. 1911 by Woodland; RS 1892, station b. by Charles Hardy, closed 1987; school 1898 b. by John W. Johnson, additions 1904 by James Wybro, remodelled 1914 by William Murdoch, new building b. 1929 by W.G. Thompson, school re-roofed 1993; silo 1922; telegraph 1893; telephone 1895; TX 1910, automatic 1961; Union C. b. 1901 by A.C. Frew and S.M. Logan; Unit. C., closed 2014; water reticulation 1983; pop. 158 (1901), 293 (1911), 293 (1933), 138 (1947), 125 (1954), 148 (1961), 90 (1981), 240 (2006), 225 (2011).

Brocklesby West (*Co. Hume*) 35°49'S. 146°38'E., 18 km N. of Howlong; school 1878 b. by Adolph Reiff and J. Adams, closed 1894.

Brockley (*Co. Clarke*) 30°15'S. 151°52'E., 20 km E. of Guyra, on Boundary Ck; farming and grazing; Meth. C. 1951–73; PO 1910–52;

telephone 1924; TX 1928; Wes. Meth. C. 1890, demolished 1951; pop. 38 (1933), 89 (1947).

Brockoble (*Co. Ashburnham*) see Pinecliffe.

Brocks Flat (*Co. Dudley*) 30°41'S. 152°24'E., 45 km W. of Bowraville, on Five Day Ck.

Brodies Plains (*Co. Gough*) 29°47'S. 151°12'E., 8 km E. of Inverell, on Macintyre R.; farming and grazing; PO 1891; school 1874–1953; telephone 1911; TX; pop. 150 (1901), 126 (1911), 111 (1933), 126 (1947), 80 (1954), 63 (1961).

Brogans Creek (*Co. Roxburgh*) 33°00'S. 149°58'E., 15 km S. of Kandos, on Brogans Ck; limestone; aerial cableway; colliery (Vulcan Portland Cement Co. Ltd) 1916; 3 lime-kilns (Vulcan Portland Cement Co. Ltd) 1916; quarry (Vulcan Portland Cement Co. Ltd) 1916, taken over by Blue Circle group, closed 1977; RS (opened as Tank) 1884–1974; telegraph 1894; pop. 42 (1933), 126 (1947), 56 (1954), 54 (1961).

Brogers Creek (*Co. Camden*) 34°45'S. 150°37'E., 8 km NW of Berry, on Brogers Ck; Angl. C.; FB; Meth. C.; pop. 27 (1921), 45 (1947).

Brogheda (*Co. Brisbane*) 32°14'S. 150°40'E., 18 km N. of Denman, on Wybong Ck; cemetery.

Brogo (*Co. Auckland*) 36°34'S. 149°49'E., 12 km N. of Bega; farming and dairying; bridge 1885, destroyed 1934, over Brogo R.; bushfire (2 girls died) 1952; cheese factories: Broadview (O. Schomberg), Walter Curtis, Willow Creek (William Cochrane); floods 1898 and 1934; PO 1874; sawmill (Thomas C. White); school; telephone 1906; TX 1926; Union C. 1878; pop. 204 (1901), 294 (1911), 220 (1933), 152 (1947), 135 (1954), 365 (2001), 435 (2006), 507 (2011).

Brogo North (*Co. Auckland*) 36°32'S. 149°50'E., 17 km N. of Bega; milking machine (Rotolactor); telephone 1926; TX 1930; pop. 43 (1933), 56 (1947), 84 (1954).

Broke (*Co. Northumberland*) 32°45'S. 151°06'E., 21 km S. of Singleton, on Yellow Rock Ck; settled 1824, founded 1860 by Joseph Clarke, village gaz. and lots sold 1860; grazing, dairying, agric., vineyards; agric. implement works; Angl. C. 1865, replacement (St Andrew's) b. 1889 by Partridge, d. by John Charles Luscombe, enlarged and renovated 1907, and graveyard; brick-kiln; bridge (Herbert Street Bridge) 1965, new one 2012, over Wollombi Brook; bushfire 1994; cemetery (350 graves 1844+) 1876, incl. columbarium; CH (incl. lock-up and police barracks) b. 1878 by Joseph Clark; colliery (South Bulga); creamery (James Moore & Co.) 1897; FB 1944; flour mills: Arthur Blaxland and Paton's; PO 1882, disused; PS (incl. lock-up) b. 1899 by I. Banks & Son, closed 1934, reused; 2 quarries; Rom. Cath. C. 1869, demolished, new one (Immaculate Conception) 1904, and graveyard (11 graves 1911–93); school 1878 b. by Joseph Clark, repairs 1881 also by Clark; telegraph 1882; telephone 1898; TX 1913, automatic 1982; wineries: Broke Estate 1988 (bought 2012 by Max and Bernadette Tolson), Brushbox Vineyard (estab. 1997 by Paul and Suzanne Mackay), Echo Hill Wines (Steve Day, David Epper and Glen Butler) 1998, Glenguin Estate (Robin Tedder) 1993, Hollyclare Wines (John Holdsworth), Margan Family (estab. 1997 by Andrew and Lisa Margan), Mount Broke (estab. 1997 by Phil McNamara, o. 2001), Mount Eyre (estab. 1970 by Neil Grosser), Nightingale Wines (estab. 1997 by Paul and Gail Nightingale), Stomp Wines, Tinonee Vineyard (Tony and Robyn Mears), Whispering Brook (estab. 2000 by Adam Bell and Susan Frazier), Yellow Rock Estate; pop. 117 (1871), 119 (1891), 302 (1901), 381 (1911), 115 (1933), 135 (1947), 191 (1954), 212 (1961), 238 (1991), 292 (1996), 226 (2001), 222 (2006), 260 (2011).

Brokenback (*Co. Northumberland*) see Brunkerville.

Broken Dam (*Co. Bourke*) 34°19'S. 147°14'E., 30 km E. of Ardlethan, on Mirrool Ck; estab. 1863 by William Sanderson; bridge b. by Thomas Sanderson, destroyed and replaced, destroyed again 1917, new one (3 spans) b. 1933 by W. Argaet, 90 ft (27.4 m), over Mirrool Ck; bushfire 1892; cemetery (renamed Ariah Park); PO 1909–17; sawmill; pop. 101 (1911).

Broken Head (*Co. Rous*) 28°43'S. 153°37'E., 7 km S. of Byron Bay, on Coral Sea; farming and dairying; Angl. C. (St Oswald's) b. 1922 by William Henry Unicomb et al., damaged 1940; cheese factory (Rockleigh) estab. 1935 by James Ainsworth; 2 quarries (gravel); sawmill (Charlton and Richardson); school 1918–75; storm 1940; telephone 1924; TX 1929; pop. 188 (1911), 190 (1933), 177 (1947), 194 (1954), 175 (1961), 225 (2011).

Broken Hill (*Co. Yancowinna*) 31°58'S. 141°28'E., 651 km NW of Wagga Wagga; (incl. North Broken Hill, Railway Town, West Broken Hill, Willyama); orig. Willa-Willyama, then Willyama, also formerly known as The Silver City; disc. 1883 by Charles Rasp, surveyed 1886 by T.H. Goodwin, munic. proc. 1888, thrived 1887, 1904–14, 1950–56; silver-lead (disc. 1883 by Charles Rasp), zinc, copper, gold and tin mining, smelting till 1898, grazing, now tourism; abattoir 1908–80; ambulance station b. 1952 by M. Gava, d. by C. Knott, new one 1982; Angl. C.: St Peter's 1888, moved and enlarged, second one b. 1903 by E.V. Woodman, d. by Vincent Hanson, demolished 1928, third one b. 1928 by S. Haunstrup & Co., d. by Louis Reginald Williams) and St Philip's (Railway Town) 1904 d. by Vincent Hanson; army barracks d. by A. Kerr; Assemblies of God C. (Liberty Christ.); Bapt. C.: Beryl Street 1888–1918, Chapple Street (b. 1917–20 by F. Deckert, fire 1927, rebuilt 1928 by L.J. Lawson), Railway Town 1913; Bible Christ. C. (Oxide Street, relocated from Blende Street), became Meth.; biscuit factory (George Adams) 1946; breweries: Barrier Brewery (Clayton's or Lee's), Broken Hill Brewing Co. (b. by Theodore Bruce, o. 1888, in liquidation but acquired 1889 by South Aust. Brewing Co. Ltd), Burton Brewery Co. Ltd (estab. 1891 by Peter McIndoe and James Sloan, the latter being replaced in 1895 by W.H. Alton, bought out and closed 1900 by Waverley Brewery, bought 1902 by J. Sloan, bought 1926 by British Imperial Oil Co. Ltd, tower demolished 1932, brewery demolished 1950), D'Arcy Barker & Co., E. Resch & Co., South Aust. Brewing Co. Ltd 1888–1926, Waverley Brewery (estab. 1887 by George Simpson and Thomas Burke, bought out and closed 1906 by South Aust. Brewing Co. Ltd, demolished 1907), West End Brewery (estab. 1888 as Shamrock Brewery by J.F. Molony, James Sloan and Hince, bought out and closed 1918 by South Aust. Brewing Co. Ltd, demolished 1930); brickworks: Globe Co. Pty Ltd, Pincombe's, Sperber's, Sumison's; carriage-works (Barrier Carriage Factory, J. Perry); caterpillar infestation 1915; cemetery (27,950 graves) 1888; CH (incl. lock-up) b. 1890 by Richard Honey, d. by James Johnstone Barnet, additions 1892 by Reid and Emes, d. by Walter Liberty Vernon, additions and alterations 1898 by A. Brown, additions and alterations 1950 by Hutcherson Bros, additions and alterations 1961, restored 1979, additions and alterations 1985; chocolate factory; Christadelphian C.; Christ. Revival Crusade C.; Church of Christ: Lane Street 1982 (in former convent), Wills Street (Railway Town), Wolfram Street b. 1909 by Orton, d. by E.J Tuck; confectionery factory (William Hepburn); Cong. C. 1888, closed, sold 1946 to W.J. Anderson and J. Brady; cordial factories: F.W. Adams (estab. 1888 by Emil Karl Resch and J. Penrose, new one b. 1938 by Fricker Bros, closed 1971), Barrier Cordial Co. Ltd (sold 1894), Broken Hill Co-op. Aerated Water Co. Ltd, John Eastman (bought by Albert Sumsion), W. Fairchild, R.N.J. Fletcher, W. Hepburn, W.W. Lindstrom, E. O'Malley, OK (Charles Berkholz, burnt down 1912), Ryan & Co., Shelley's (estab. 1893 by John Augustine M. Sheehy, upgraded and modernised 1949), Silver City Mineral Water Co. (Walter E.N. Hince), Stephen's, Young's; crematorium (Fred J. Potter & Son); customs-house 1888, closed; 2 dams 1888; depression 1908; diphtheria 1910, 1913, 1954; droughts 1888, 1903, 1907, 1909, 1926, 1940–45, 1969–70;

dust storms 1892, 1896, 1899, 1901, 1906, 1907, 1922, 1923, 1924, 1930, 1935, 1941, 1944, 1945, 1951, 1953, 1967, 2018, 2020; earth tremors 1903 and 1952; electrical apparatus factory (Aust. General Electric Pty Ltd); electricity 1890; FB: Broken Hill brigade 1887, Central station (b. 1892 by Hewitt and Smethurst, d. by Withall and Wells, additions and alterations 1915 by F.R. Gray & Son, closed, partly demolished and reused, new one b. 1962), Railway Town station (b. 1910 by H. Hutchins, closed 1921); fibrous plaster works: George Thomas Ellis, G. Harris, Lehman Bros, damaged 1946; fires 1888, 1891, 1892, 1893, 1896, 1899, 1900, 1901, 1907, 1952; floods 1898, 1931, 1962, 1971, 1992, 1998, 2000, 2012; flour mills: Adelaide Milling Co. Ltd, Brunton & Co., Roach Bros Ltd; foundries: Barrier Crystal Foundry Co. 1900–42, Block 10, Brownell's Central, Durnell & Co., R.J. Hooper & Co., Federal, P.J. Fogarty, R.J. Hooper & Co. (strike 1917, taken over by W.A. Parnham & Sons), Lehman and Phillips, Proprietary, Sanderson Bros (fire 1914), Silverton Tramway Co., Zinc Corp. Ltd; gale (many buildings damaged) 1895; gaol 1888, new one b. 1892 by John Dobbie, reused 1942–46, then reverted to gaol; gasworks (Broken Hill & Suburban Gas Co. Ltd) 1888; German measles epidemic 1939; grasshopper infestations 1910 and 1950; hailstorms 1978 and 2016; heatwaves 1895–96 (25 died), 1905, 1906, 1939; hospital 1887, (second) b. 1889 by Richard Honey, d. by Frederick William Dancker, new wing b. 1890 by M.J. Kelly, also d. by Dancker, hospital damaged 1895, extended 1930, (third) b. 1939–41 by J.R. & E. Seccull Ltd, d. by Leighton Irwin, extended 1949 by Hansen and Yuncken, extended 1977, demolished 1999, replacement b. 2000 by Maclay Mowlem, d. by D.W.P. Suters; ice-cream factories: Broken Hill Ice & Produce Co. and A.B. Glenn; ice works: Barrier 1889, Crystal (burnt down 1951), Grant's, Ice & Produce Co. (additional plant 1946), New Ice Works, Railway Town, Roberts' (fire 1954); incinerator 1916; Islamic C. 1891, abandoned, renovated 1968; Jehovah's Witnesses C.; Jewish C. 1911–62, reused, restored; joinery (George J. Adkins), fire 1951; LDS (Mormon) C. 1964; Lutheran C. (St Paul's) 1933; magnetic separation plant (Aust. Metal Co.) 1899; measles epidemics 1893 (many died) and 1902; Meth. C.: Blende Street North 1887 (fire 1933, relocated 1936 to Oxide Street, enlarged and renovated), Central Street (renovated 1939), Hebbard Street (enlarged and renovated 1910, closed 1916), Lane Street 1890, McCulloch Street, Mica Street (extended 1904), Nicholls Street (Railway Town) alterations 1905, Oxide Street (b. 1936 by Miller, Garrard and Sugars, d. by H.G. Alexander), Picton Street (moved and reopened 1912), Pirie Street, Railway Town (b. 1959 by Gordon Brown), Sulphide Street 1911–65, Thomas Street 1912; mine creep 1895, 1901, 1902, 1905, 1906, 1908, 1912; mine fatalities 1892, 1893, 1895 (9 killed), 1897 (3 killed), 1898 (2 killed), 1900, 1901 (7 killed), 1902 (2 killed), 1903, 1904, 1905, 1906 (2 killed), 1912, 1939 (4 killed), 1985 (2 killed); miners' strikes 1889, 1890, 1892, 1897, 1909, 1913, 1916, 1917, 1919–20, 1923, 1925, 1926, 1928, 1930, 1933, 1935, 1936, 1939, 1950, 1951; mines: Big (or Proprietary) Mine (2 smelters 1886, mill 1889, fires 1895 and 1906, absorbed 1930 by South Mine, mill demolished 1937) 1885–1930, Blackwood's Shaft, Block 5 Mine, Block 10 (BHP) Mine (incl. Campbell's Shaft, Kelly's Shaft, mill b. 1894 by Jack Warren, new mill 1903–23), Block 11 (BHP) Mine (fire 1895, chimney demolished 1937), Block 12 (BHP) Mine (Brodribb's Shaft, Jamieson's Shaft, Patterson's Shaft), Block 13 (BHP) Mine (McCulloch's Shaft), Block 14 (BHP) Mine (smelter 1889–94, fire 1908), British Mine (smelters 1889, No. 3 shaft destroyed 1890, mill demolished 1936), Central Mine (Sulphide Corp., smelter 1890, mine and mill ruined by creep, explosion 1904, underground fire 1923, foundry closed 1924, mine closed 1940, treatment plant mill demolished 1940, absorbed by South Mine, poppet heads of Kintore Shaft dismantled 1944), Consols Mine, Cosgrove Mine, Delprat's Shaft, Dickenson's Shaft, Globe Mine, Imperial Mine, Junction Mine (fire 1906, bought 1923 by Sulphide Corp., closed 1928, sold 1929), Junction North Mine, Knox's Shaft, Marsh's Shaft, Naabuck Mine, North Mine (Block 17, estab. 1883 by Julius Nickel and James Anderson as the Cosmopolitan Mine, sold 1885 to North Broken Hill Silver Mining Co. Ltd, became North Broken Hill Ltd in 1912, new mill 1939, mine acquired 1988 by Pasminco, closed 1993), Pinnacles Mine (closed 1972), Rasp's Mine (Consolidated Broken Hill Resources) 2007, Rasp's Shaft 1887, Rising Sun Mine, Rising Sun South Mine, Round Hill Mine, South Mine (o. 1885 as Great Bonanza, mill 1894, mill replaced 1908, burnt down 1919, No. 7 shaft o. 1932, mine closed 1972), South Blocks Mine, South Extended Mine, Stewart's Shaft, Thompson's Shaft, Victoria Cross Mine, White Leads Mine, Zinc Corp. Mine (mill demolished 1941); munitions factory 1942–45, reused; ore dressing mill (BHP) 1889; pneumonia epidemic 1895; PO: Broken Hill 1886 (new one b. 1890–92 by John Dobbie, d. by James Johnstone Barnet, clock tower added 1902, office additions 1909 by Michael Kenna Power, additions 1912, renovated and refurbished 1979), North Broken Hill 1897, Railway Town 1888 (new building b. 1900, additions 1905 by Michael Kenna Power, new one b. 1925 by J.H. Wicks, alterations and repairs 19550, West Broken Hill 1901, Wyman Street 1927; police barracks b. 1898 by T. O'Mara; pound (stock) 1889; powerhouse (City) 1935, chimney demolished 1945, alterations 1947, additions and alterations 1951 by Hansen and Yunchen; Presb. C. (St Andrew's) b. 1892 by Mell and Todd, d. by W.T. Knox, relocated and reused; Prim. Meth. C. 1887, extended 1888, closed 1926; PS: Broken Hill (Central) 1890, additions 1911 by C. Sayers, renovated 1931, alterations 1948, additions 1962, North Broken Hill 1893, new one b. 1910 by Michael Kenna Power, Railway Town, closed 1951, West Broken Hill 1902–45; railway barracks, fire 1953; railway coal stage 1928; railway round-house 1928; railway turntable, 75 ft (22.9 m); railway workshops (Silverton Tramway Co.) b. 1891 by Malcolm Reid; reservoirs: 500,000 gal. (2,273 kl), 1,000,000 gal. (4,546 kl), 1,300,000 gal. (5,909.8 kl), steel one, 2,000,000 gal. (9,092 kl), b. 1955 by Perry Engineering Co.; rifle range (West Broken Hill) 1900; riot 1892; Rom. Cath. C.: first one 1887, damaged 1895, replacement (Sacred Heart) b. 1903–5 by J.N. Power, d. by W.T. Knox, renovations 1940 d. by Russell and Yelland, renovations 1960, re-roofed, St Mary's (Railway Town) 1924, St Peter and St Paul's (North Broken Hill) b. 1929 by W.J. Brady; RS 1919, station relocated and rebuilt 1957 by Constructions Ltd, new one 1969; Salv. Army C. (North Broken Hill) 1897, new one (Wolfram Street) 1905, destroyed 1922, replaced 1923, closed, sold and reused; sauce and pickle factory (Rosella Preserving & Manufacturing Co. Ltd); sawmills: Globe Timber Co. Ltd and Heron's Creek Timber Mills Ltd; scarlet fever 1937; schools: Broken Hill 1886 (new buildings b. by Albert Sumsion, additions 1909 by Michael Kenna Power, additions 1956, new one 1965 d. by Don Coleman), Broken Hill HS 1920 b. by Michael Kenna Power (additions d. by A. Van der Steen), Burke Ward 1895 (new one b. 1898 by Albert Sumsion, additions 1907 by Michael Kenna Power, additions 1987), East Broken Hill 1903–62, Morgan Street 1917 (additions 1960, 1965, 1970), North Broken Hill 1890 (additions 1907 by T.H. Brockway, new buildings b. 1909 by Michael Kenna Power, additions and alterations 1916 by Michael Kenna Power, additions 1958, new school 1974), Railway Town 1914 (additions 1960), Willyama HS 1974; SD Adventist C.; septic pneumonia epidemic (6 died) 1912; sewerage 1941; smallgoods factory, burnt down 1926; 2 smelters 1886; snow 1951; soap-works: W.H. Burford & Sons Ltd, burnt down 1919 and J. Kitchen & Sons Pty Ltd; storms 1887, 1912, 1946, 2007, 2011; streets electric lit 1890; TC b. 1898 by Albert Sumsion, new one 1901, additions 1923 by Michael Kenna Power, additions 1980 and 1983, became a campus of Western Institute in 1992; telegraph: Broken Hill 1886 (new office b. 1890–92 by John Dobbie, d. by James Johnstone Barnet, alterations 1912), North Broken Hill 1897, Railway Town 1892, additions 1905 by Michael Kenna Power; telephone: North Broken Hill 1909 and West Broken Hill 1944; terrazzo works (De Nicholo Bros); tile factory (Community Advancement Co-op. Building Society, in old soap-works), closed 1948; tramways: Broken Hill (steam) 1902–26, Silverton 1887, first station 1888, second one b. 1905 by Axtell and Waldie, closed 1970, reused, Torrowangee b. 1892 by Baxter and Saddler for Tarrawingie Flux & Tramway Co. Ltd, closed 1932; TX 1891, automatic 1957; typhoid 1888 (123 died), 1896, 1898, 1901 (man died), 1903, 1904 (man died), 1906, 1914 (2 died), 1925, 1931–32; Unit. C.: St Andrew's (orig. Presb.) b. 1905 by E.V. Woodman, d. by Vincent Hanson and Wesley (orig. Wes. Meth.) b. 1888 by Walter and Morris, d. by Frederick William Dancker, renovated 1987; univ. college 1959; vegetation regeneration scheme 1936+; vulcanising works (Sheppard's); water reticulation from Menindee 1952; whooping cough epidemic 1924; pop. 20 (1883), *c.*3,000 (1886), *c.*5,000 (1887), 11,288 (1888), 19,905 (1890), 19,789 (1891), 22,135 (1892), *c.*19,100 (1895), 26,711 (1899), 27,500 (1901), 27,890 (1906), 30,953 (1911), 26,337 (1921), 26,250 (1922), 24,010 (1926), 22,990 (1930), 26,925 (1933), 26,750 (1934), 26,358 (1936), *c.*27,000 (1941), 27,054 (1947), 30,500 (1950), 32,805 (1952), 31,351 (1954), 32,170 (1956), 31,267 (1961), 30,043 (1966), 29,743 (1971), 27,647 (1976), 26,913 (1981), 24,460 (1986), 23,263 (1991), 20,963 (1996), 19,834 (2001), 18,854 (2006), 18,431 (2011).

Broken Hill South (*Co. Yancowinna*) 31°59'S. 141°28'E., 2 km S. of Broken Hill; (incl. Alma, gaz. 1888); airfield (World War II); airport 1925, new one 1939 on new site, terminal reused 1988, new one 1986; Angl. C. 1890, new one (St James's) 1909; Bapt. C.: Eyre Street 1907, additions 1916 and Patton Street 1912–40, renovated and reopened 1947, closed 1966, sold 1974, reused; Bible Christ. C. 1888; brewery (Berliners') 1891–1902; cyclone 1922; dust storm 1911; earth tremors 1933 and 1952; FB (station b. 1926 by S.W. Potter, d. by William Hull McNiven); fires 1898 and 1900; flood 1931; Meth. C., relocated 1915 by Polkinghorne & Co., reused; PO 1888, new one b. 1898 by Albert Sumsion, d. by Walter Liberty Vernon; powerhouse (Western NSW Electric Power Pty Ltd) b. 1929–31 by Concrete Constructions Ltd; PS b. 1890 by William Sara and Dunstan; quarry (blue metal); reservoir; rifle range; Rom. Cath. C. (All Saints') b. 1891 by Reid and Eames, d. by Porter and Thomas, enlargement and renovations 1941 d. by C.A. Russell; Salv. Army C. 1900; school (Alma) 1889, alterations and repairs 1911 by C.C. Sayers, additions 1956, 1958, 1963, 1966, 1971; silo (Tandou); storm 2005; telegraph 1891, new office b. 1898, d. by Walter Liberty Vernon; univ. (Charles Sturt) 1993; Wes. Meth. C. 1890.

Brolgan (*Co. Ashburnham*) 33°08'S. 148°03'E., 11 km W. of Parkes; farming; bushfire 1926; PO 1927; RS 1896, station b. by John Allibone, closed 1972; school 1901–20; telephone 1911; TX 1917; pop. 113 (1911), 58 (1933), 55 (1954).

Brolgan (*Co. Ashburnham*) see also Tichborne.

Brolgar (*Co. Ashburnham*) see Tichborne.

Brombin (*Co. Macquarie*) 31°27'S. 152°39'E., 9 km W. of Wauchope, on Pappinbarra R.; farming and dairying; bridge 1971, over Pappinbarra R.; school (Pabbinbarra till 1931) 1881–93, 1906–41, 1957–65; telephone 1913; whooping cough epidemic 1913; pop. 72 (1933), 50 (1947), 59 (1954), 71 (1961).

Bronti (*Co. Argyle*) 34°59'S. 149°48'E., 26 km S. of Goulburn; Angl. C. (St Mark's) 1871, additions and repairs 1922, and graveyard (graves 1877–1993); school (Mullengullenga till 1890) 1878, new one b. 1881 by Gideon Cranston and Phillipson, d. by George Allen

Mansfield, closed 1905; pop. 76 (1901), 62 (1911).

Brookdale (*Co. Cook*) see Glenbrook.

Brookdale (*Co. Mitchell*) 35°06'S. 146°53'E., 20 km NE of Lockhart; pop. 76 (1933), 181 (1947), 186 (1954), 151 (1961), 275 (2011).

Brooke Avenue (*Co. Northumberland*) see Killarney Vale.

Brookfield (*Co. Durham*) 32°30'S. 151°46'E., 11 km S. of Dungog, on Unwarrabin Ck; farming and dairying; diphtheria (child died) 1897; PO 1856; Rom. Cath. C. (St Kilian's) 1880, new sacristy b. 1902 by J. Griffiths, closed 1982, sold 2000 and 2015, reused; school 1851–70, 1876–1925, 1958–69; tannery (Carlton's); telephone 1905; TX 1926; pop. 161 (1901), 221 (1911), 120 (1933), 106 (1947), 91 (1954), 75 (1961), 235 (2011).

Brookglen (*Co. Wallace*) 36°22'S. 148°54'E., 6 km E. of Berridale.

Brooklana (*Co. Fitzroy*) 30°16'S. 152°51'E., 16 km NE of Dorrigo, on Bobo R.; timber; cemetery; Meth. C. 1913; PO 1911; RS (3 km NW) 1924–1975; sawmills: Mulhearn Bros, Guy Seccomb, Thomas Timms; school 1920–32; telephone 1916; TX 1919; pop. 97 (1933), 112 (1947), 101 (1954), 65 (1961).

Brooklands (*Co. King*) see Crookwell.

Brooklands (*Co. Murray*) 35°10'S. 148°59'E., 23 km S. of Murrumbateman; school 1898–1906.

Brooklet (*Co. Rous*) 28°44'S. 153°31'E., 5 km S. of Bangalow; farming; bridge 1928 d. by Montague Smith, 35 ft (10.7 m), over Skinners Ck; butter factory (Brooklet Co-op. Dairy Co. Ltd) b. 1893 by Carson; macadamia nut processing plant (Pacific Farms); PO 1904–31; school 1888–1964; telephone 1905; pop. 165 (1911), 130 (1933), 108 (1947), 93 (1954), 81 (1961), 262 (2011).

Brooklyn (*Co. Cunningham*) 32°42'S. 147°04'E., 43 km N. of Condobolin.

Brooklyn (*Co. Sandon*) 30°26'S. 151°50'E., 19 km NE of Armidale; goldmining; pop. 23 (1933).

Brookong (*Co. Urana*) 35°12'S. 146°38'E., 8 km NW of Lockhart; PO 1899–1915; sawmill (T. Glasgow) 1916; school 1934–50; pop. 91 (1911), 59 (1933).

Brookongia (*Co. Urana*) 35°13'S. 146°47'E., 6 km E. of Lockhart; school 1902–15.

Brooks Creek (*Co. Murray*) 35°05'S. 149°18'E., 22 km NW of Bungendore; gold (alluvial disc. 1861 and reef disc. 1878); Chinese joss house; school 1884–96; pop. 35 (1933).

Brooks Flat (*Co. Northumberland*) see Buchanan.

Brookside (*Co. Gough*) 29°35'S. 151°57'E., 28 km NE of Glen Innes, on Severn R.; school 1882–90.

Brooks's Paddock (*Co. Argyle*) see Goulburn.

Brookstead (*Co. Sandon*) 30°32'S. 151°44'E., 7 km E. of Armidale, on Commissioners Waters; bridge over Commissioners Waters; school 1882–1906; wool-scour and fellmongery estab. by Matthew Garthwaite.

Brooks Terrace (*Co. Camden*) see Kanahooka.

Brookstown (*Co. Northumberland*) see Wallsend.

Brookwood (*Co. Argyle*) 34°57'S. 149°31'E., 28 km SW of Goulburn; telephone 1914.

Brooman (*Co. St Vincent*) 35°28'S. 150°14'E., 24 km SW of Ulladulla, on Clyde R.; timber and farming; bushfire 1957; cheese factory (Gill Bros); FB; PO 1881; sawmills: Ellis & Co., T. Shoebridge & Son 1908, Albert Veitch; school 1957–66; telephone 1907; TX 1937; pop. 61 (1901), 85 (1911), 37 (1933), 77 (1947), 62 (1954), 55 (1961).

Brooms Head (*Co. Clarence*) 29°36'S. 153°20'E., 19 km S. of Yamba, on Coral Sea; estab. in 1920s, village gaz. 1964; mineral sand mining 1979+ and tourism; bridge over Cakora Lake; FB; PO 1947; reservoir (Clarence Peak); telephone 1950; TX 1950; water reticulation 1978; pop. 16 (1961), 266 (1991), 307 (1996), 279 (2001), 245 (2006), 193 (2011).

Broughton (*Co. Camden*) 34°45'S. 150°45'E., 6 km NE of Berry, on Broughton Ck; formerly Broughton Village; first land sales 1857; farming; Angl. C. 1873, impovements 1874 by Elliott Bros, burnt down 1954; butter factory (Broughton Village Dairy Co.) 1889–1903; Cong. C. 1873; floods 1870 and 1873; PO 1889–1963; school (Broughton Village) 1871, new one b. 1872, closed 1901, reused, defunct; pop. 322 (1901), 236 (1911), 286 (2006).

Broughton Point (*Co. Northumberland*) see Bolton Point.

Broughton's Creek (*Co. Camden*) see Berry.

Broughtonsworth (*Co. Harden*) see Hughstonia.

Broughton Vale (*Co. Camden*) 34°45'S. 150°43'E., 4 km N. of Berry, on Broughton Mill Ck; estab. 1856, first land sales 1857, munic. proc. 1871 as Broughton's Vale, munic. abolished 1948; dairying; bushfires 1867, 1874, 1895; butter factory (Broughton Vale Dairy Co.) 1892–97; PO 1892–1909; school 1877–1917 and 1921–43; telephone 1923; Wes. Meth. C. 1865; winery (Woodhill Mountain) 1998; pop. 457 (1881), 424 (1891), *c.*450 (1895), 322 (1901), 123 (1911), 333 (1933), 310 (1944), 184 (1947), 184 (1949), 56 (1954), 64 (1961), 268 (2006), 443 (2011).

Broughton Village (*Co. Camden*) see Broughton.

Broula (*Co. Forbes*) 33°53'S. 148°33'E., 15 km W. of Cowra, on Red Ck; ironstone and copper mining; iron mine (Colorcoat Process Co.) 1941–45; school 1890–1951; pop. 138 (1911), 118 (1933), 76 (1947), 62 (1954).

Broulee (*Co. St Vincent*) 35°51'S. 150°11'E., 11 km NE of Moruya, on Broulee Bay; surveyed by James Larmer and town gaz. 1837 as Browley, first lots sold 1840, thrived 1848, abandoned, new village gaz. 1891, resettled 1926, new subdivision 1969; shipping port till 1873, wheat, potatoes; bridge 1966 to Mossy Point, closed and demolished 2015, replaced 2015 by Nelmac Pty Ltd, over Candlagan Ck; bushfire 1952; cemetery (lawn) and crematorium (Broulee Memorial Gardens & Crematorium Pty Ltd) 2003; CH 1841; earth tremor 1989; flood 1841; flour mill (F.W. Ellison); foot-bridge to Mossy Point, over Candlagan Ck; lock-up 1841; PO 1840–57; pound (stock), removed 1850; PS 1841; school 1852, new one 1995; sewerage 1984; telephone 1949; pop. 46 (1841), 22 (1846), 57 (1961), 709 (1981, incl. Mossy Point), 950 (1986, incl. Mossy Point), 1,152 (1991, incl. Mossy Point), 1,389 (1996, incl. Mossy Point), 1,627 (2001, incl. Mossy Point), 1,724 (2006, incl. Mossy Point), 1,939 (2011, incl. Mossy Point).

Browley (*Co. St Vincent*) see Broulee.

Brownlea (*Co. Bathurst*) 33°40'S. 149°30'E., 26 km SE of Blayney; grazing; flour mill (J. Backes); quarry (Bringellet Marble Quarry); school 1883–1921; pop. 30 (1933).

Brownlow Hill (*Co. Camden*) 34°02'S. 150°40'E., 4 km NW of Camden, on Nepean R.; farming and dairying; bridges: Cobbitty Bridge over Nepean R. and Lower Mount Hunter Bridge over Mount Hunter Rivulet; gale 1913; Meth. C. b. 1902 by A. Liggins, damaged 1913; PO 1861; telephone 1911; univ. (Sydney) farms: Camden Farms, Mayfarm, Mt Hunter; pop. 77 (1901), 148 (1911), 95 (1933), 52 (1954), 372 (2001), 379 (2006), 364 (2011).

Brownmore (*Co. Durham*) 32°17'S. 151°39'E., 17 km NW of Dungog, on Williams R.; bridge over Quartpot Ck; cemetery (Quart Pot, 84 graves); telephone 1919; TX 1922–61.

Brown Mountain (*Co. Auckland*) see Bemboka.

Brown's (*Co. Camden*) see Dapto.

Browns Camp (*Co. Wellesley*) 36°58'S. 148°47'E., 41 km W. of Bombala, on Currowang Ck; gold; school 1909–21; pop. 65 (1901).

Browns Corner (*Co. Harden*) 34°37'S. 148°10'E., 13 km E. of Cootamundra.

Browns Creek (*Co. Bathurst*) 33°32'S. 149°10'E., 9 km W. of Blayney, on Cowriga Ck; settled in 1860s; gold (disc. 1867 by Norvis Goggerty), iron ore (disc. 1874 by Rees Davies), farming, grazing; Angl. C. (St Luke's, orig. Union till 1970), closed 1985, reused; dams: BHP Gold Mines Ltd 1991, 82 ft (25 m) high and Browns Creek Gold Mining Co., destroyed 1887; floods 1900 and 1934; mines: Browns Creek Gold Mining Co.

(estab. by Jack Finnall, Jack Flynn and Tom Maloney, sold 1876, closed 1888, bought 1895 by Compagnie Des Mines d'Or Ltd, closed 1901, reopened 1904 as open-cut, acquired 1979 by M. Hickey, sold 1986 to BHP Minerals Ltd, transferred to BHP Gold Mines Ltd, transferred 1990 to Newcrest Mining Ltd, sold 1993 to Hargraves Resources Ltd) and Golden Springs (estab. 1866 by James Rutherford, Walter Hall and Jack Fagan); PO 1873; quarry; Rom. Cath. C. (St John the Baptist) b. by Pat Flood, damaged 1952, closed, moved to Blayney and reused, later demolished; school 1877, new one b. 1879 by John Wadsworth Ashworth, d. by George Allen Mansfield, repairs 1900 by J.E. Brailey, alterations 1911 by W.J. Brown, closed 1935; stamper battery (60 head); storm 1887; telephone 1923; TX 1924; Union C. b. 1911 by J. Bridgman; pop. 246 (1901), 219 (1911), 169 (1933), 59 (1947), 93 (1954), 89 (1961).

Browns Creek (*Co. Macquarie*) see Taree.

Browns Crossing (*Co. Raleigh*) 30°48'S. 152°54'E., 10 km S. of Macksville; pop. 46 (1933).

Browns Mountain (*Co. Camden*) 34°48'S. 150°31'E., 11 km NW of Nowra; pop. 57 (1901).

Brown's Paddock (*Co. Cook*) see Lithgow.

Brown Springs (*Co. Inglis*) see Sulcor.

Browns Road (*Co. Camden*) 34°24'S. 150°43'E., 13 km NW of Unanderra.

Browns Rocks (*Co. Clarence*) see Goodwood Island.

Brown's Sawmill Siding (*Co. Cook*) see Medlow Bath.

Brown's Siding (*Co. Urana*) see New Park.

Brownstown (*Co. Gregory*) see Canonba.

Brownsville (*Co. Camden*) see Dapto.

Brown Town (*Co. Cook*) see Mount Victoria.

Brucedale (*Co. Clarendon*) 35°02'S. 147°25'E., 10 km NE of Wagga Wagga; farming; earth tremor 1876; FB; hailstorm 1875; PO 1899; Rom. Cath. C. (Holy Family), closed, restored, reused; school 1872, new one b. 1879 d. by George Allen Mansfield, additions 1915, closed 1915, reopened 1920, additions 1929, closed 1967; Wes. Meth. C. 1872, burnt down 1875, replacement b. 1876 by Thomas Hodson, d. by G. Sheppard, renovations 1889 also d. by Sheppard; pop. 73 (1911), 97 (1933), 72 (1947), 65 (1954), 73 (1961), 472 (2006).

Bruces Bend (*Co. Wentworth*) 34°12'S. 142°14'E., 3 km S. of Gol Gol, on Murray R.

Bruie Plains (*Co. Kennedy*) 32°47'S. 147°51'E., 20 km NE of Trundle; bauxite; school 1959–70; Union C. 1914; pop. 64 (1947).

Bruinbun (*Co. Roxburgh*) 33°08'S. 149°27'E., 33 km N. of Bathurst; PO 1878; quarry; pop. 23 (1933).

Brumby Plains (*Co. Buller*) 28°27'S. 152°40'E., 38 km NW of Kyogle.

Brundah (*Co. Monteagle*) 34°00'S. 148°20'E., 19 km SE of Grenfell; disc. and settled by John Wood; wheat; cemetery; RS 1901, station b. by F.W. Kinch, closed 1972; silo 1932, disused; pop. 198 (1911), 78 (1933), 64 (1947), 63 (1954).

Brundah North (*Co. Monteagle*) 33°54'S. 148°18'E., 13 km E. of Grenfell, on Brundah Ck; school 1957–69.

Brundee (*Co. St Vincent*) 34°54'S. 150°40'E., 7 km SE of Nowra, on Crookhaven Ck; Berrellan till 1910; potatoes, maize, dairying; FB; PO 1894–1961; telephone 1903; windmill factory (Arnold Aldous); pop. 115 (1911), 112 (1954), 81 (1961).

Brungle (*Co. Buccleuch*) 35°09'S. 148°14'E., 15 km SE of Gundagai, on Brungle Ck; estab. 1888 as Aboriginal mission (closed 1955), village gaz. 1888; mining (arsenic and barytes), wheat, maize, dairying; Angl. C., renovations and repairs 1905 by J.J. O'Dwyer; bridge b. 1876 by Kingdom; cemetery; creamery (George Murray) 1905; electricity 1927; FB 1933, station replaced; PO 1868–1975; Presb. C. (St John's) b. 1886 by Frederick Eberlin and Thomas Brashier, d. by David Wilson, closed, sold 2019; school 1901, additions 1960; snowstorm 1899; telephone 1913; TX 1918, automatic 1952; water supply 1963; pop. 284 (1901), 217 (1911), 219 (1933), 193 (1947), 159 (1954), 218 (1961), 307 (2011).

Brunkerville (*Co. Northumberland*) 32°57'S.

151°29'E., 11 km SW of West Wallsend, on Brunkerville Ck; farming; cyclone 1899; PO 1900; sawmills: Clifton, Blissett & Co., destroyed 1899 and Thomas Lester; school (Brokenback till 1893) 1870, additions 1889 by Burg Bros, closed 1962; telephone 1914; TX 1923; Unit. C. (orig. Wes. Meth.), and graveyard (217 graves 1872+), incl. columbarium; pop. 165 (1901), 158 (1911), 140 (1933), 92 (1947), 65 (1954), 55 (1961).

Brunswick (*Co. Rous*) see Brunswick Heads.

Brunswick Heads (*Co. Rous*) 28°33'S. 153°33'E., 5 km E. of Mullumbimby, on Simpsons Ck; village gaz. 1882 as Brunswick, substantially declined 1894+ after being bypassed by railway, revived 1902+, bypassed by highway 1998; timber, fishing, prawns, oysters 1902+, bananas, tourism 1920s+; ambulance station b. 1936 by John P. Slapp; Angl. C. (St Thomas the Apostle) 1923, closed, sold and reused; boat harbour; breakwaters 1961; bridges: Durungbil Bridge over Brunswick R., Matthew Devine Bridge 2007 over Brunswick R., Torakina Bridge over Simpsons Ck; cemetery 1884; CH 1886; electricity 1933; FB 1951 (station b. 1952, new one 1980, additions and alterations 2008 by T.F. Woollam & Son Pty Ltd); foot-bridge 1937, replaced 1994, over Simpsons Ck; gale 1950; jetty 1990; Meth. C. 1912; PO: Brunswick 1882 and Brunswick Heads 1909, new one 1950; PS 1886–97, new ones 1949 and 1976; punt b. by Matthew Devine; quarry; Rom. Cath. C. 1914 (in converted house), relocated and reused 1936, new one (Our Lady of Lourdes) b. 1936 by John P. Slapp, d. by Ray Pullinger; school (Brunswick River till 1896) b. 1892 by Hughes and Yates, closed 1896, reopened 1908, additions 1924 and 1968; sewerage 1972; storm 1927; telegraph 1884; telephone 1906; TX 1913, automatic 1942; Unit. C.; pop. *c.*20 (1903), 179 (1911), 342 (1933), 767 (1947), 992 (1954), 975 (1961), 1,069 (1966), 1,197 (1971), 1,402 (1976), 1,877 (1981), 1,585 (1986), 1,662 (1991), 1,835 (1996), 1,862 (2001), 1,614 (2006), 1,451 (2011).

Brunswick River (*Co. Rous*) see Brunswick Heads.

Brush (*Co. Northumberland*) see Martinsville.

Brush Creek (*Co. Northumberland*) see Cedar Brush Creek.

Brushgrove (*Co. Clarence*) 29°34'S. 153°05'E., 16 km SW of Maclean, on Woodford Island, in Clarence R.; village gaz. 1877; former river port, maize, poultry, pigs, sugar-cane, dairying till 1950s; Angl. C. (St John's) b. 1910 by F.J. Robertson, d. by Frederick William Conrad Schaeffer, destroyed 1913, replaced, closed 1956, sold and reused; bridge (Wingfield Bridge) to Cowper 1958, over Clarence R.; creamery (Clarence River Pioneer Dairy Co. Ltd) 1893–1912; FB; fire 1909; floods 1890, 1963, 2001, 2013; gale 1878; hospital (moved to Ulmarra); hurricane 1952; PO 1866, inundated 1890, new one b. 1895, additions 1904; Presb. C. 1873, new one b. 1899 by John M'Kay, reused; PS 1883, new one (incl. lock-up) 1891, additions 1919 and 1923, closed 1983; punt (to Cowper) 1871, across Clarence R. (South Arm); Rom. Cath. C. b. 1871 by Thomas Foggo, destroyed 1878, new one (Holy Trinity) 1880; sale-yards; storm 1913; telegraph 1878; TX 1909, automatic 1958; Unit. C. (orig. Wes. Meth.) b. 1901 by John M'Kay, damaged 1913; Wes. Meth. C. 1873, damaged 1878, demolished; wharves: one b. 1877 by J. Walsh, govt one 1900, one b. 1914; pop. 162 (1901), 332 (1911), 116 (1881), 332 (1924), 193 (1933), 196 (1947), 135 (1954), 199 (1961), 190 (2001), 334 (2011).

Brushgrove (*Co. Hardinge*) 30°36'S. 151°15'E., 24 km W. of Uralla; Angl. C. (St Matthew's); school 1957–64.

Brushwood (*Co. Bourke*) 34°48'S. 147°06'E., 6 km E. of Ganmain, on Boggy Ck; sheep; RS 1910–75; school 1897 b. by J. Harrison, closed 1908; silo 1922; pop. 50 (1911).

Brushy Creek (*Co. Hardinge*) 30°10'S. 151°28'E., 19 km W. of Guyra.

Brushy Hill (*Co. Brisbane*) 32°06'S. 150°59'E., 11 km NE of Aberdeen; farming and dairying; Angl. C. (St Paul's) 1898, moved 1952 to Segenhoe; cemetery; PO 1885–1952; school (Upper Hunter till 1889) 1882–1940;

telephone 1911; TX 1916; pop. 75 (1901), 136 (1911), 104 (1933), 123 (1947), 57 (1954), 65 (1961).

Bruton (*Co. Rous*) 28°48'S. 153°00'E., 9 km NW of Casino; pop. 60 (1911), 55 (1933), 53 (1947), 83 (1954), 97 (1961).

Bruxner Park (*Co. Fitzroy*) 30°15'S. 153°07'E., 6 km N. of Coffs Harbour.

Bryans Gap (*Co. Clive*) 29°02'S. 152°05'E., 7 km NE of Tenterfield, on Bryans Gap Ck; farming; flour mill (C. Geldart), moved to Tenterfield; PO 1886; scarlet fever 1903; school 1876, new building b. 1910 by J.R. Day, closed 1946; telephone 1912; TX 1949; pop. 136 (1911), 117 (1933), 100 (1947), 69 (1954), 69 (1961), 187 (2006).

Brymbyn (*Co. Macquarie*) see Brimbin.

Brymedura (*Co. Ashburnham*) 33°09'S. 148°43'E., 5 km NE of Manildra, on Mandagery Ck.

Bucca (*Co. Fitzroy*) 30°09'S. 153°06'E., 9 km W. of Emerald Beach; cemetery (32 graves 1910+); pop. 233 (1911), 523 (2011).

Bucca Creek (*Co. Fitzroy*) see Lower Bucca.

Buccarumbi (*Co. Gresham*) 29°50'S. 152°35'E., 38 km SW of Grafton, on Nymboida R.; town gaz. 1871; bridge b. 1869–75, ironwork fabricated by Rogers Bros foundry (Newcastle), repairs 1898, repairs 1918 by F. Englert, destroyed 1946, replaced, over Nymboida R.; flood 1946; punt 1870; school 1880–84; telephone 1943; TX 1950; pop. *c.*40 (1871), 50 (1933).

Bucca Wauka (*Co. Gloucester*) 32°06'S. 152°09'E., 22 km SE of Gloucester, on Wallamba R.; school 1957–62; telephone 1964; TX; pop. 76 (1933), 70 (1947), 73 (1961).

Buccrabendinni (*Co. Raleigh*) see Buckra Bendinni.

Buchanan (*Co. Northumberland*) 32°49'S. 151°32'E., 5 km E. of Kurri Kurri, on Wallis Ck; formerly Brooks Flat; farming; Angl. C. (St Luke's) 1885; bridge 1896; collieries: Bloomfield Main (Bloomfield Collieries Pty Ltd) and Bloomfield Open-Cut (Bloomfield Collieries Pty Ltd); earth tremor 1868; flood 1904; miners' strikes 1943, 1950, 1952; PO 1873; Rom. Cath. C. (St Patrick's) 1871, demolished; school 1850–51, reopened 1880, new one b. 1883 by W. Humphreys, additions 1898 by J. Cook, closed 1961, sold and reused; telephone 1898; TX; pop. 118 (1891), 161 (1911), 97 (1933), 88 (1947), 73 (1954), 59 (1961).

Buchanans Valley (*Co. Brisbane*) 32°03'S. 150°41'E., 18 km W. of Scone, on Cuan Ck; 3 quarries.

Buckajo (*Co. Auckland*) 36°42'S. 149°43'E., 11 km W. of Bega; farming; cheese factory (T.J. Bateman); FB (station b. 2017); flour mill 1850; PO 1933; school 1904–7 and 1922–51; telephone 1914; TX 1926; pop. 64 (1901), 76 (1911), 104 (1933), 97 (1947), 70 (1954), 63 (1961), 404 (2011).

Buckalow (*Co. Windeyer*) 32°40'S. 141°14'E., 81 km S. of Broken Hill; pop. 36 (1933).

Buckaroo (*Co. Phillip*) 32°33'S. 149°39'E., 8 km NE of Mudgee; farming and pottery clay; PO 1927, burnt down 1954; 2 quarries; school (Pipeclay Creek till 1912) 1867–1955; telephone 1924; TX 1929; wineries: Abercorn (acquired 1996 by Tim and Connie Stevens), Blue Wren Wines, Farmer's Daughter Wines (estab. 1995 by Lance and Gwen Smith), Huntington Estate (estab. 1969 by Robert and Wendy Roberts, sold 2005 to Tim and Nicky Stevens), Adam Roth, Pieter van Gent; pop. 186 (1933), 80 (1947), 133 (1954), 90 (1961).

Buckenbowra (*Co. St Vincent*) 35°44'S. 150°03'E., 12 km W. of Batemans Bay, on Buckenbowra R.; settled 1828; bushfires 1896, 1905, 1953; flood 1914; sawmills: Henry Bland (sold 1863 to William Kearley and W. de Jersey) and Darra (b. 1884 by Thompson); tannin works (Buckenbowra Wattle Bark Co. Ltd) 1913, burnt down 1914.

Buckenderra (*Co. Wallace*) 36°10'S. 148°45'E., 22 km N. of Berridale, on Lake Eucumbene; Boconnoc till 1913; farming and grazing; PO 1927–30.

Buckendoon (*Co. Rous*) 29°03'S. 153°20'E., 3 km N. of Woodburn, on Richmond R.; farming and dairying; brickworks (Horten and Farley); creamery (NSW Creamery

Butter Co. Ltd) 1897; PO 1891–1956; school 1882–1954; sugar mill (Buchanan's) 1873; wharf b. 1891 by David Rankin; pop. 57 (1901), 85 (1911), 112 (1933), 125 (1947), 78 (1954), 91 (1961).

Bucketty (*Co. Northumberland*) 33°07'S. 151°08'E., 33 km W. of Wyee; bushfires 1972–73 and 1994; cyclone 1984; FB (station b. 1993); observatory (Koolang); pop. 180 (2002).

Buckhobble (*Co. Ashburnham*) see Pinecliffe.

Buckinbah (*Co. Gordon*) see Yeoval.

Buckinguy (*Co. Gregory*) 31°01'S. 147°22'E., 59 km N. of Nyngan, on Marra Ck; pop. 25 (1933), 51 (1961).

Buckley's Crossing Place (*Co. Wallace*) see Dalgety.

Buckra Bendinni (*Co. Raleigh*) 30°38'S. 152°43'E., 12 km W. of Bowraville, on Bendinni Ck; antimony; bubonic plague 1902; school (Buccrabendinni) 1885–93; telephone 1924; pop. 168 (1911), 118 (1933), 114 (1947), 99 (1954), 57 (1961).

Buck Swamp (*Co. Wellington*) 32°52'S. 149°03'E., 31 km NE of Molong.

Budawang (*Co. St Vincent*) 35°27'S. 149°58'E., 16 km E. of Braidwood, on Feagans Ck; bushfires 1919 and 1926; eucalyptus oil distillery (Spencer Green); sawmill (McRae and Burke) 1916; pop. 57 (1901).

Budawong (*Co. Nicholson*) 33°54'S. 145°39'E., 48 km S. of Hillston; RS 1927–62.

Budda (*Co. Rankin*) 31°09'S. 144°10'E., 92 km NE of Wilcannia.

Buddabaddah (*Co. Oxley*) 31°56'S. 147°13'E., 42 km S. of Nyngan, on Bogan R.; bridge b. 1895 by J.B. Fitzgerald, over Bogan R.; PO 1876–77.

Buddah (*Co. Narromine*) 32°04'S. 148°13'E., 20 km N. of Narromine; Presb. C. (removed from Timbrebongie) 1910–77, removed; pop. 26 (1933).

Budden (*Co. Phillip*) 32°30'S. 150°05'E., 47 km E. of Mudgee; pop. 29 (1933).

Budderoo (*Co. Camden*) 34°42'S. 150°37'E., 10 km NW of Berry.

Buddigower (*Co. Bourke*) 34°03'S. 147°01'E., 22 km SW of West Wyalong; surveyed 1901; tin (disc. 1901), eucalyptus oil, farming; FB 1939; PO 1926–66; rifle range 1909; RS 1923–75, station removed 1984; school 1957–72; silo 1928; telephone 1925; TX 1925; pop. 117 (1911), 222 (1933), 90 (1947), 114 (1954), 76 (1961).

Buddong (*Co. Selwyn*) 35°42'S. 148°13'E., 20 km NE of Tumbarumba; sawmill (National Timber Co. Ltd).

Budgambi (*Co. Clarence*) see Copmanhurst.

Budgee Budgee (*Co. Phillip*) 32°32'S. 149°40'E., 10 km NE of Mudgee; goldmining and farming; Angl. C., renovated 1952, closed 1964, defunct; goldmine 1876, 1911, 1925; hailstorm 1912; PO 1873; school (Black Springs till 1905) 1891, additions 1917 by W. Carmichael, closed 1954, defunct; telephone 1913; TX 1924; whooping cough epidemic 1907; winery (Robert Stein Vineyard) 1976; pop. 163 (1911), 144 (1933), 107 (1947), 73 (1954), 61 (1961), 261 (2006), 325 (2011).

Budgerabong (*Co. Cunningham*) see Bedgerebong.

Budgery (*Co. Canbelego*) 31°32'S. 146°37'E., 48 km W. of Nyngan; copper mining; PO 1907–9.

Budgewoi (*Co. Northumberland*) 33°14'S. 151°34'E., 4 km N. of Toukley, on Budgewoi Lake; (incl. Budgewoi Peninsula); village gaz. 1941; Angl. C. (St John's) 1971; bridge b. 1903 by Freeman, (second) b. 1936 by Jack Devine, (third) b. 1947 by Beattie and Frost, (fourth) b. 1967, over Budgewoi Ck; electricity 1952; FB 1946 (station b. 1971, renovated 2007); flood 1889; foot-bridge over Budgewoi Ck; jetty; PO 1947, new one b. 1982; quarry; sawmill (Joe Wooffindin); telephone 1947; water supply began 1956, connections completed 1967; pop. 146 (1954), 531 (1961), 2,954 (2006), 3,254 (2011).

Budgewoi (*Co. Northumberland*) see also Halekulani.

Budgewoi Peninsular (*Co. Northumberland*) see Budgewoi.

Budgong (*Co. Camden*) 34°47'S. 150°28'E., 16 km NW of Nowra; farming; bushfires 1926,

1929, 1951; cheese factory estab. by Bert and Charlie Brooks; FB 1944; flood 1867; PO 1927–31; sawmill (Illaroo Timber Co.) 1950, burnt down 1951; telephone 1926; pop. 149 (1901), 54 (1911), 50 (1921), 61 (1933), 27 (1947), 34 (1961).

Budgong Gap (*Co. Camden*) 34°46'S. 150°28'E., 17 km NW of Nowra; school 1889–1909.

Budjong Vale (*Co. Camden*) 34°50'S. 150°28'E., 13 km NW of Nowra, on Kellets Ck; school 1886–98; winery (Lyrebird Ridge) 1994.

Buena Vista Estate (*Co. Cook*) see Bullaburra.

Buffalo City (*Co. Argyle*) see Goulburn.

Buffer Creek (*Co. Raleigh*) 30°23'S. 152°51'E., 8 km N. of Bellingen, on Buffer Ck.

Buff Point (*Co. Northumberland*) 33°14'S. 151°32'E., 2 km W. of Budgewoi, on Budgewoi Lake; bushfire 1951; foot-bridge over Hammond Canal; jetty; PO 1945; telephone 1938; TX (automatic); pop. 27 (1933), 123 (1947), 120 (1954), 266 (1961), 3,285 (2011).

Bugaboo Point (*Co. Narromine*) 32°04'S. 148°14'E., 20 km N. of Narromine, on Macquarie R.

Bugaldi (*Co. Baradine*) see Bugaldie.

Bugaldie (*Co. Baradine*) 31°07'S. 149°07'E., 21 km S. of Baradine; Bugaldi till 1924; village gaz. 1921; diatomite mining, farming, grazing; bushfire 2013; cemetery (15 graves 1896–1933) 1895; fire 1926; mine (Minerals Ltd); PO 1896; Presb. C.; railway accident (7 killed) 1935; Rom. Cath. C. (St Joseph's) 1924, closed and derelict; RS 1923–76, platform removed 1985; sawmills: G. Douglas, J. Parsons, Pincham Bros; school (Bogaldie till 1890 then Boogaldie till 1907) 1884–90 and 1896–1967; silo; telephone 1913; TX 1915; water supply 1963; pop. 199 (1911), 209 (1933), 257 (1947), 215 (1954), 201 (1961), 236 (2011).

Buggil (*Co. Leichhardt*) 30°42'S. 148°16'E., 30 km N. of Coonamble; PO 1878–88.

Bugilbone (*Co. Denham*) 30°15'S. 148°50'E., 58 km W. of Wee Waa; Pian Creek till 1886; grazing; cemetery; PO 1883–1917; telephone 1893; TX 1915; pop. 174 (1911), 57 (1933).

Bugilbone Railway (*Co. Denham*) 30°02'S. 148°43'E., 56 km S. of Collarenebri; PO 1927–47; RS 1905, station b. by John Allibone, closed 1975.

Bugong (*Co. Camden*) 34°47'S. 150°28'E., 7 km SW of Kangaroo Valley, on School Ck.

Bugtown (*Co. Wallace*) 35°56'S. 148°45'E., 48 km NW of Cooma.

Bukalong (*Co. Wellesley*) 36°48'S. 149°12'E., 14 km N. of Bombala, on Buckalong Ck; Angl. C. (St John's) b. 1880 by John Boucher, and graveyard; RS 1921–74, station derelict; TX (automatic).

Bukkulla (*Co. Arrawatta*) 29°30'S. 151°08'E., 20 km S. of Ashford; vineyards, farming, grazing; brewery (Wadham Wyndham) 1882; cemetery; cheese factory (George E. Cardale) 1904, closed; FB (station b. 2013); mine (diamond), closed and reused; PO 1876; school 1898–1939 and 1957–58, building moved to Ashford; telephone 1913; TX 1913, automatic 1980; Union C. 1906, moved to Ashford; winery (Emminthal) estab. by Christian and Jacob Seitz; pop. 60 (1901), 235 (1911), 187 (1933), 108 (1947), 134 (1954), 174 (1961), 396 (2011).

Bulahdelah (*Co. Gloucester*) 32°25'S. 152°12'E., 35 km N. of Nelson Bay, on Myall R.; also known as Myall River till 1877; village gaz. 1864 as Bullah Delah, bypassed by highway 2013; alunite 1878–1927 and 1934–52, timber, dairying, farming; ambulance station; Angl. C. (St John's) b. 1873 by A. and John Donaldson and Kinnaird, enlarged 1903, new one b. 1912 by G.F. Heath, jun. and G. Maybury, re-roofed 1989; brickworks; bridge 1892, 215 ft (65.5 m), new one 1933, replaced (concrete) 1969, new bridge on new site, over Myall R.; bushfire 1951; butter factories: Joseph Blanch 1900, later relocated, and Bulahdelah Co-op. 1917; calcining plant 1890; cemetery (1,220 graves) 1867; CH 1869, destroyed, new one (incl. cells) b. 1888 by White, d. by James Johnstone Barnet, additions and repairs 1909 and 1919 by Joseph Head, closed, restored and reused; earth tremor 1949; engineering works

(R. Goldstein); FB; floods 1903, 1927, 1946, 1952, 2016; German measles epidemic 1940; hailstorms 1932 and 2005; hospital 1930, additions and alterations 1976; LDS (Mormon) C. b. 1904 by Wesley Tunks, closed, sold and reused, new one (Community of Christ) 1965 on new site; 2 marinas; mine fatalities (2 killed) 1909; mines: Alunite (Aust.) Pty Ltd and Aust. Alum Co. Ltd; pneumonia epidemic (2 died) 1937; PO 1863, new one b. 1904 by R. Mitchell; PS b. 1869 by Alfred Doorey, repairs 1919 by Joseph Head, new one 1956; punt; quarries (alunite): Big Quarry 1888–1910, Kimberley Quarry, Ladysmith Quarry, Myall Quarry, Tunnel Quarry; reservoir; Rom. Cath. C. 1882, new one (St Brigid's) b. 1927 by Piper and Solari, d. by Peter Joseph Gannon; sale-yards 1917; sawmills: C. Dee, G.F. Heath, sen. and G.F. Heath, jun. 1884, Hitchcock and Robertson, Henry Grove Howard, Duncan McRae, W. Masters, W. Maybury, Northern Timbers (taken over 1946 by Newman Bros, closed 1973), S. Relf, Smith Gooch & Co., Allen Taylor & Co. Ltd (bought 1914 from McSweeney), F. Viggers (closed 1968); school (Bulladelah till 1935) 1878, new buildings b. 1881 by W. Humphreys, alterations 1912 by J. Head, additions 1955 by C.H. Hawkins, additions 1959, 1965, 1967, 1979, 1980, 2006, 2008; sewerage augmentation 1996; slipway (S. Relf, sen.); telegraph 1877, new office b. 1904 by R. Mitchell; tornado 1970; TX 1915, automatic 1975; typhoid (2 died) 1898; Unit. C. (orig. Meth.) 1908, restored 1997; water reticulation 1964, augmentation 1987; wharf b. 1882 by R.H. Worthing; pop. 92 (1871), 299 (1891), 559 (1901), 631 (1911), 627 (1933), 766 (1947), 1,000 (1954), 978 (1961), 966 (1966), 923 (1971), 986 (1976), 972 (1981), 1,098 (1986), 1,097 (1991), 1,113 (1996), 1,161 (2001), 1,093 (2006), 1,117 (2011).

Bulahdelah Plain (*Co. Gloucester*) 32°26'S. 152°12'E., 4 km SW of Bulahdelah.

Bulbudgeree (*Co. Bligh*) 32°31'S. 149°06'E., 15 km E. of Wellington; school (Wolloman till 1889) 1880–1927.

Bulby (*Co. Gloucester*) 32°08'S. 152°16'E., 21 km W. of Tuncurry; pop. 82 (1933), 86 (1954), 82 (1961).

Bulby Brush (*Co. Gloucester*) 32°08'S. 152°13'E., 27 km W. of Tuncurry, on Bunyah Ck; school 1920–46 and 1957–71, building sold to Deer; telephone 1916; TX 1926.

Bulcolcol (*Co. Rankin*) 31°18'S. 144°04'E., 74 km NE of Wilcannia.

Bulga (*Co. Gowen*) 31°36'S. 148°47'E., 17 km NE of Gilgandra; pop. 21 (1933).

Bulga (*Co. Hunter*) 32°39'S. 151°01'E., 17 km SW of Singleton, on Wollombi Brook; The Bulga till 1894; farming; airfield (World War II); Angl. C. b. 1856 by William McAlpin, sen. and Woodberry, new one (St Mark's) b. 1888 by William Partridge, and graveyard (204 graves 1868+), incl. columbarium; bridge 1879, new one (Dare timber truss) b. 1912 by William Murphy and James Taylor, 424 ft (129.2 m), repairs 2004, over Wollombi Brook; bushfires 1951 and 2001; cemetery; colliery; FB (station b. 2005); hailstorm 1914; PO 1878–1993; PS 1903, new buildings b. 1910 by Thomas Simpson; school 1880–1970; telephone 1893; TX 1912, automatic 1980; Wes. Meth. C. 1885; winery (Peschar's Family Vineyard) bought 1995 by John and Mary Peschar; pop. 179 (1901), 223 (1911), 191 (1933), 213 (1947), 252 (1954), 202 (1961), 322 (2006), 358 (2011).

Bulga (*Co. Macquarie*) 31°36'S. 152°17'E., 30 km N. of Wingham, on Ellenborough R.; sawmill (Elands Timber Ltd), axe handle production began 1920; pop. 51 (1933).

Bulgandra (*Co. Hume*) see Bulgandry.

Bulgandramine (*Co. Narromine*) 32°36'S. 148°06'E., 15 km NW of Peak Hill, on Bogan R.; bridge b. 1883 by J.B. Fitzgerald, over Bogan R.; mine; PO 1875–96; pop. 128 (1901), 90 (1933), 64 (1961).

Bulgandramine Estate (*Co. Narromine*) see Narromine.

Bulgandry (*Co. Hume*) 35°37'S. 146°37'E., 38 km W. of Culcairn, on Billabong Ck; Walbundrie Reefs till 1900; thrived 1898; mining (gold disc. 1855, and more in 1898) 1855+ and farming; FB; mines: Coonerty and Murphy's Reef, Goodwood Reef, Lone Hand Reef, Show Day Reef, Welcome Find Reef; PO 1895; Presb. C. 1909, removed 1950; school (Bulgandra) 1896–1944; snow 1927; stamper batteries (5 head and 10 head); telephone 1900; TX 1913; pop. 113 (1901), 183 (1911), 179 (1933), 65 (1947), 52 (1954).

Bulgary (*Co. Mitchell*) 35°04'S. 146°57'E., 28 km NE of Lockhart; RS 1928–75; school 1957–69.

Bulgong (*Co. Macquarie*) 31°37'S. 152°17'E., 28 km N. of Wingham, on Little Ck; surveyed 1914, village gaz. 1915, never developed; orig. timber then dairying *c.*1918–75; TX 1916.

Bulgonia (*Co. Northumberland*) see Brightwaters.

Bulingarry (*Co. Raleigh*) 30°47'S. 152°45'E., 18 km W. of Macksville, on Taylors Arm; dairying; PO 1927–67; school 1957–68; telephone 1916; TX 1926; pop. 30 (1933), 69 (1947), 74 (1954), 74 (1961).

Bulla (*Co. Monteagle*) see Monteagle.

Bullaburra (*Co. Cook*) 33°44'S. 150°25'E., 1 km W. of Lawson; orig. Coleridge, then developed by Sir Arthur Rickard & Co. as Buena Vista Estate; bushfires 1936, 1956, 1977; FB 1955; PO 1927; Presb. C. (St James's) 1949; railway dam 1906; reservoir, 500,000 gal. (2,273 kl); RS 1925 (private station, bought 1945 by govt); sewerage 1965; telephone 1927; water supply 1940; pop. 73 (1933), 184 (1947), 242 (1954), 275 (1961), 374 (1964), 1,215 (2011).

Bulla Creek (*Co. Monteagle*) 34°07'S. 148°16'E., 22 km N. of Young, on Bulla Ck; school (Bullokreek) 1889–1912; pop. 23 (1933).

Bulla Creek (*Co. Monteagle*) see also Monteagle.

Bulladelah (*Co. Gloucester*) see Bulahdelah.

Bullagreen (*Co. Ewenmar*) 31°25'S. 148°05'E., 39 km NE of Warren; cemetery 1893; PO 1895–1915; Presb. C. b. 1900 by Shaw and Parker, closed, abandoned, sold.

Bullah Delah (*Co. Gloucester*) see Bulahdelah.

Bullamalito (*Co. Argyle*) 34°54'S. 149°47'E., 17 km S. of Goulburn, on Bullamalito Ck; Ballamalito till 1925; cemetery; telephone 1918; TX.

Bullamiah (*Co. Camden*) see Cambewarra.

Bullan (*Co. Camden*) 34°48'S. 150°14'E., 16 km S. of Bundanoon, on Shoalhaven R.

Bullarah (*Co. Benarba*) 29°28'S. 149°13'E., 58 km S. of Mungindi, on Goonal Branch; Meroe till 1895; grazing; PO 1872–1921; pound (stock) 1869; PS 1876–1934, sold 1935 to Country Women's Assoc., remodelled, reused 1937; school 1959, additions 2010; pop. 145 (1911), 270 (2006).

Bullatale (*Co. Townsend*) 35°45'S. 145°10'E., 25 km E. of Mathoura; agric., forestry, fishing; telephone 1933.

Bullawa Creek (*Co. Nandewar*) 30°19'S. 150°00'E., 21 km E. of Narrabri, on Bullawa Ck; diamonds; Angl. C. (St Barnabas's) 1913; bridge (steel tubular truss) b. 1954 by S.J. Donaldson, over Bullawa Ck; creamery (A.R. Stafford) 1903; mine (Alpha); school 1912–43; pop. 221 (1933), 92 (1947), 69 (1954), 65 (1961).

Bullenbalong (*Co. Wallace*) 36°16'S. 148°43'E., 15 km NW of Berridale, on Stony Ck; earth tremor 2012; quarry; trout farm (Eucumbene).

Bullenbong (*Co. Mitchell*) 35°10'S. 146°56'E., 21 km E. of Lockhart, on Bullenbong Ck; PO 1894–1903; Rom. Cath. C. (St Francis's); pop. 61 (1911), 61 (1933).

Buller (*Co. Buller*) see Legume.

Bullerawa (*Co. Baradine*) 30°18'S. 149°08'E., 30 km W. of Wee Waa, on Namoi R.

Bulli (*Co. Camden*) 34°20'S. 150°55'E., 2 km N. of Woonona, on Tasman Sea; settled *c.*1823 by Cornelius O'Brien, estab. *c.*1857, thrived in 1870s; mining (coal disc. by Mackenzie) 1863+, timber, dairying, blackberries, rutile mining 1953+; ambulance station b. 1939 by Williams, d. by H. Longhurst, additions 1946 also d. by Longhurst, closed, converted 1990 and reused, new one d. by Denis Magoffin; Angl. C. 1856, new one (St Augustine's) b. 1882 by Orphin and Newson, d. by Blacket & Son, re-roofed 1912, additions 1925 by W.G. Willis, d. by John Burcham Clamp and Clifford Horace Finch, tower rebuilt 1965, and graveyard (484 graves 1853+), incl.

columbaria; brickworks: Bulli Brick & Tile Co., mechanised 1959, closed 2004, Illawarra Fire Clay & Brick Co., Pendlebury & Son; bushfires 1940 and 1968; cemetery (5,790 graves 1869+) 1868, incl. columbaria; CH b. 1884 by Wilson and Walker, d. by James Johnstone Barnet, repairs 1908 by John M'Donald, extended 1961, closed and reused, sold 2012; coke-works: George Adams (20 ovens b. 1889, 20 ovens added 1908, closed 1930, demolished) and Bulli Coke Co. Ltd (54 Welsh-type ovens estab. 1889); collieries: A Pit (estab. 1861, o. 1863 by Bellambi & Bulli Coal Co., acquired 1936 by Aust. Iron & Steel Ltd, closed 1987), B Pit (o. 1878 by Bulli Coal Co., abandoned, reopened 1891 by Williams and Garlick, closed 1894, reopened 1895 by Bulli Steam Coal Co., taken over 1896 by George Adams, closed 1902, taken over 1937 by Aust. Iron & Steel Ltd, No. 2 ventilation shaft sunk 1940, drift driven 1944–53, modernisation 1950–53, fire 1967, closed 1987, razed), Bulli No. 3 (Corn Beef) 1902–8, reopened in 1940s, Bulli No. 4 worked 1909–14; cordial factories: Sydney and Thomas Ball (acquired by Lockett Bros, and later by Parkinsons), H.E. Hedley, E.L. Holmes Ltd; earth tremor 1902; electricity 1913; engineering works (David Brown Gear Industries Ltd) 1988; FB (station b. 1919, new one 1924); gales 1907 and 1952; heatwave 1905; hospital (cottage) b. 1892–94 by John Myles, d. by Kenwood and Kerle, additions and alterations 1906 d. by Alexander Leckie Elphinstone, additions 1913, 1924, 1925, 1934, 1938, additions and alterations 1945–47 by L.G. Price, additions 1948, 1956, 1957, 1969; Jehovah's Witnesses C. 2005; jetty (Bulli Bight) b. 1863 by William Weaver, damaged 1864, rebuilt 1867, extended 1877 and 1895, collapsed 1907, rebuilt 1908, collapsed 1912, rebuilt, closed 1938, collapsed 1943; measles epidemic (person died) 1893; mine fatalities 1887 (81 killed), 1965 (4 killed), 1967 (6 killed); miners' strikes 1880, 1885, 1886–87, 1911, 1938, 1942, 1943; PO 1869, new one b. 1903, new one b. 1926 by Lowther and Horrocks; Prim. Meth. C. 1867, demolished and replaced 1885 by Craddock and Icely, alterations and renovations 1895, closed, sold, reused 1908; PS 1850, new one b. 1880 (incl. lock-up), repairs 1908 by H. Pollock, demolished 1918, replacement b. 1919 by Alfred Ede, d. by George McCrae, additions 1934 by Dyal Singh, closed, sold 2012; railway bridge; rayon factory (John Vicars & Co.) b. 1945 by E.H. Donnelly & Son, d. by William Laurie, became Bulli Spinners Pty Ltd in 1955; 2 reservoirs (incl. concrete one, 355,000 gal. or 1,613.8 kl, 1915); rifle range 1912; Rom. Cath. C. 1863, new one b. 1881 by Cavanagh, new one (St Joseph's) b. 1900 by Shaw & Son, d. by P. Hayes, renovated and remodelled 1986; RS 1887, station b. by Alexander Hamilton Scouller, additions 1923, reused 1990; Salv. Army C. 1886; sawmills: J. Molloy Ltd, John Somerville 1864, Robert Somerville 1858, William Somerville; schools: Bulli primary 1869, repairs 1910 by D. Cullingham, additions 1923 by A.F. Webb, additions 1954 by S. Robinson, additions 1958, 1969, 2010, Bulli HS 1956, additions 1964, fire 1975, additions 1976 and 1980, Waniora 1954, additions 1956; sewage works; storm 1912; telegraph 1877; toll-gate; tramway (mine) 1863; TX 1906; Unit. C. (Northern Illawarra, orig. Wes. Meth.) b. 1865 by Benjamin Thackeray, d. by Thomas Rowe, renovations 1922 by A.F. Webb, d. by McCredie and Anderson, spire collapsed 1939 and replaced 1962, extensive church repairs 1955–60; water supply 1910, reticulation 1915; Wes. Meth. C. o. 1862, in converted barn; pop. 1,187 (1881), 1,352 (1891), 962 (1901), 1,397 (1911), 1,765 (1921), 2,251 (1933), 2,478 (1947), 3,997 (1954), 4,829 (1961), 5,376 (2001), 5,455 (2006), 5,671 (2011).

Bulliac (*Co. Gloucester*) 31°55'S. 152°02'E., 12 km NE of Gloucester, on Gloucester R.; Cong. C. b. 1925 by Dun, d. by Shepherd, closed, sold and reused; FB; railway tunnel, 243 yds (222.2 m), 1913; RS 1913, station b. by John Allibone, closed and removed 1984; telephone 1953; TX 1956; pop. 93 (1933), 54 (1947), 52 (1954).

Bulliac (*Co. Gloucester*) see also Pitlochry.

Bullio (*Co. Camden*) 34°21'S. 150°11'E., 22 km NW of Berrima, on Bullio Ck; pop. 22 (1933), 297 (2006).

Bulloak (*Co. Bourke*) 34°37'S. 146°48'E., 26 km NE of Narrandera; telephone 1925; TX 1926; pop. 33 (1933).

Bullock Creek (*Co. Kennedy*) see Tullamore.

Bullock Flat (*Co. Gloucester*) 32°13'S. 152°23'E., 12 km W. of Tuncurry, on Wallingat R.

Bullock Flat (*Co. Roxburgh*) 33°11'S. 149°44'E., 30 km NE of Bathurst; quarry.

Bullock Flats (*Co. Westmoreland*) see Oberon.

Bullock Island (*Co. Northumberland*) see Carrington.

Bullocks Bow (*Co. Macquarie*) 31°43'S. 152°03'E., 33 km N. of Gloucester, on Rowleys R.

Bullocks Flat (*Co. Wallace*) 36°27'S. 148°27'E., 5 km SE of Perisher Valley, on Little Thredbo R.; bridge over Snowy R.; hurricane 2011; 3 reservoirs; RS (ski tube from Perisher Valley) 1987.

Bullocks Wharf (*Co. Gloucester*) see Nabiac.

Bullocks Wharf (*Co. Hunter*) 33°25'S. 150°48'E., 20 km N. of North Richmond, on Colo R.

Bullock Wharf (*Co. Northumberland*) see St Albans.

Bullokreek (*Co. Monteagle*) see Bulla Creek.

Bulloona (*Co. Rous*) see Ballina.

Bull Plain (*Co. Denison*) 35°46'S. 146°08'E., 28 km NE of Mulwala; PO 1882–97; pop. 90 (1911), 79 (1933).

Bull Ridge (*Co. Cook*) 33°30'S. 150°48'E., 4 km N. of Glossodia; orchards; Bapt. C. 1900; PO 1895–96; pop. 85 (1901), 83 (1911).

Bull Ridge (*Co. Cook*) see also Kurrajong East.

Bulls Camp (*Co. Cook*) 33°43'S. 150°29'E., 2 km NE of Woodford, on Bulls Ck; orig. Eighteen Mile Hollow; military stockade 1835–44; PO 1863–66; PS 1863.

Bulls Flat (*Co. St Vincent*) 34°48'S. 150°20'E., 17 km S. of Bundanoon, on Shoalhaven R.

Bulls Nest (*Co. Drake*) 29°12'S. 152°43'E., 51 km SW of Casino, on Bulls Nest Ck; formerly The Bulls Nest.

Bulpunga (*Co. Wentworth*) 33°46'S. 141°44'E., 84 km NW of Wentworth.

Bulyeroi (*Co. Benarba*) 29°47'S. 149°05'E., 57 km SE of Collarenebri; grazing; PO 1898; PS b. 1901 by George Grace, closed 1920; Rom. Cath. C. b. 1904 by James William Doherty, dismantled and moved 1927 to Rowena; telegraph 1898; TX 1910; pop. 147 (1911).

Bumbaldry (*Co. Monteagle*) 33°55'S. 148°27'E., 26 km E. of Grenfell, on Bumbaldry Ck; largely defunct; mining (gold disc. 1901), wheat, fruit; cemetery; diphtheria 1908; Meth. C. 1929; mines: H. Balston (gold) 1906, Boori (copper) 1903, Broula King (gold) 1901–39, Bumbaldry Creek (iron), J.B. Cannon (gold) 1939, Cowfell (copper) 1903–32, Kellys Creek (gold) 1939, P. Wood (silver) 1889, Tyagong Creek (rutile) 1940–41; PO 1903; 2 quarries; Rom. Cath. C. (St Andrew's) b. 1905 by Pease; school 1904 b. by H. Francis, closed 1960; stamper battery (20 head) 1903; telephone 1903; TX 1918; pop. 196 (1911), 169 (1933), 102 (1947), 98 (1961), 226 (2006).

Bumberra (*Co. Phillip*) see Mount Frome.

Bumberry (*Co. Ashburnham*) 33°10'S. 148°27'E., 25 km E. of Parkes, on Billabong Ck; farming; cemetery (72 graves) 1880; PO 1883–1945; PS, closed 1894; rifle range 1909; RS (6 km SE) 1893, station b. by Frederick Lemm, jun. and Thomas Edward Spencer, closed 1989; school (Bumbury) 1880–1914; telephone 1923; TX 1923–26; pop. 144 (1901), 81 (1911), 109 (1933), 75 (1947), 86 (1954), 78 (1961).

Bumbury (*Co. Ashburnham*) see Bumberry.

Bunaloo (*Co. Cadell*) see Bunnaloo and Thyra.

Bunaloo East (*Co. Cadell*) see Thyra.

Bunarba (*Co. Benarba*) 29°02'S. 149°15'E., 26 km E. of Mungindi; PO 1917; telephone 1915; TX 1915.

Bundabah (*Co. Gloucester*) 32°40'S. 152°04'E., 9 km W. of Tea Gardens, on North Arm Cove; fishing and oysters; pop. 9 (1961), 291 (2011).

Bundaburrah (*Co. Gipps*) 33°33'S. 147°43'E.,

31 km SW of Forbes; PO 1857–61; 2 quarries; school (Bundaburrah Gap) 1890, closed same year; TX (automatic); pop. 245 (2006), 289 (2011).

Bundaburrah Gap (*Co. Gipps*) see Bundaburrah.

Bundagen (*Co. Raleigh*) 30°25'S. 153°04'E., 10 km NE of Urunga; pop. 43 (1933), 128 (2011).

Bundah (*Co. Ewenmar*) 31°40'S. 148°31'E., 14 km W. of Gilgandra, on Marthaguy Ck

Bunda Hall (*Co. Nicholson*) 33°41'S. 145°46'E., 31 km SE of Hillston; telephone 1929; TX 1929–36.

Bundanoon (*Co. Camden*) 34°39'S. 150°18'E., 14 km SW of Moss Vale, on Coal Ck; Jordan's Crossing till 1881; disc. 1818 by Charles Throsby, surveyed 1821 by William Harper, lots sold 1883 and 1884, thrived 1891–1907 and 1920s–30s; orig. potatoes, coalmining 1867+, timber 1870s+, hay till *c.*1892, farming, dairying, tourism 1888+, highland holiday resort 1891–*c.*1945; abattoir; Angl. C. 1879, burnt down 1904, replacement (Holy Trinity) b. 1905 by J.R.W. Walker, and graveyard (graves 1880+); bushfires 1904 (11 houses destroyed), 1939, 1965; cemetery (234 graves 1910+) 1903; coalmine estab. 1867 by Martin Larkin, closed 1871, sold 1881 to Ezekial Alexander Baker who reopened and named it Erith, strike 1884, closed 1886, sold to James Fletcher and Samuel Palmer and reopened 1896, soon closed; earth tremor 1897; electricity 1929; FB (station b. 1945 by Charles Alexander Stewart Boag, demolished, new one 1996); hailstorm 1907; pill factory (Nicholas' Golden Cross Ointment & Pill Factory) estab. 1898 by W.A. Nicholas, bought 1930 by Elsie Morris, renovated and reused, sold 1976 to Heinz and Gerda Loock; PO 1872, new one b. 1958; Presb. C. 1959, closed; PS 1897, new one (in rented premises) 1905, new one (incl. lock-up) b. 1936 by Charles Alexander Stewart Boag; quarry (Edward Hayman); rifle range 1926; Rom. Cath. C. (St Brigid's) b. 1891–95, additions 1935 by A. Stephens & Sons, d. by Ernest A. Scott, Green and Scott; RS 1869; sawmills: Amos Bros, H. Larkins, Edward Selems (moved to Mittagong 1911), Arthur Tooth 1892, fire 1952; school 1876, new one b. 1882, new building b. 1909 by A. Allen, additions 1995; sewage works; telegraph 1899; TX 1883; Unit. C. (orig. Prim. Meth.) b. 1885 by Sam Tooth, and graveyard (graves 1872+); water reticulation 1956; pop. 465 (1891), 474 (1901), 455 (1911), 525 (1933), 871 (1947), 741 (1954), 727 (1961), 696 (1966), 748 (1971), 843 (1976), 1,018 (1981), 1,291 (1986), 1,513 (1991), 1,763 (1996), 1,852 (2001), 1,950 (2001), 2,035 (2006), 2,417 (2011).

Bunda North (*Co. Nicholson*) 33°39'S. 145°42'E., 25 km SE of Hillston; telephone 1929; TX 1929–52.

Bundarbo (*Co. Buccleuch*) 34°55'S. 148°25'E., 34 km NE of Gundagai; pop. 23 (1933).

Bundarigo (*Co. Clarence*) see Braunstone.

Bundarra (*Co. Hardinge*) 30°10'S. 151°04'E., 27 km SW of Tingha, on Gwydir R.; also known as Clerkness; settled 1836 by Edward G. Clerk and John Rankin, estab. 1846 by Edward G. Clerk, planned 1849 by John James Galloway, surveyed 1855 by Patrick Heron Henderson, laid out 1861 by Thomas J. Oliver, town gaz. 1863, designated as chief town of the county, thrived 1870s–80s; cattle, sheep, oats, barley, sorghum, millet; Angl. C. (St Mary the Virgin) 1857, demolished, new one b. 1874–78, begun by Joseph Ross but completed by others, d. by John Horbury Hunt; Bapt. C. 1959, closed, sold 2001, reused; bridges: iron lattice truss bridge b. 1881 by F.A. Franklin, d. by Sir John Fowler, 635 ft (193.5 m), re-decked by Chesterfield and Jenkins, over Gwydir R., and Maclean Bridge (concrete and steel) 1939 d. by L.G. Day, over Clerks Ck; cemetery (600 graves) 1863; CH 1862, demolished 1873, new one (incl. lock-up) b. 1869 by Siseri Eastment, additions 1870 also by Eastment, additions 1883 by J. Ross, repairs 1911 by J.A. Keenan, closed 1967, reused; cordial factories: Federal (estab. 1901 by James Edward Henry) and John and E. Parker 1901 (taken over 1918 by F. and E. Thomas); electricity 1951; FB; floods

1861, 1890, 1893, 1956; flour mills: Edward G. Clerk 1857 and Theodore Cooper; hailstorm 1905; hospital (cottage) b. 1911 by S.H. Curry, d. by John Francis O'Connor, additions and alterations 1939 by A.R. Smith; lock-up b. 1861 by Edward G. Clerk; mine (copper); PO 1852, new one 1886; pound (stock) 1858; PS, additions and alterations 1939 by A. McDonald, new one 1981 d. by John Whyte Ian Thomson; 2 quarries; reservoir; Rom. Cath. C. b. 1862 by John Heffernan, new one (St Mary of the Angels) b. 1913 by S.H. Curry, d. by John Francis O'Connor; sawmills: James Edward Henry 1906 and A. McDonald; school 1869 b. by Siseri Eastment, repairs 1898 by James Edward Henry, additions 1900 by James Lonsdale, additions 1959 and 1967, closed 1980, reused, new one on new site; telegraph 1874, new office b. 1886; TX 1910; water supply augmentation 1992; pop. 184 (1871), 301 (1881), 330 (1891), 453 (1901), 814 (1911), 669 (1933), 292 (1947), 782 (1954), 478 (1961), 358 (1971), 388 (1976), 377 (1981), 329 (1986), 324 (1991), 319 (1996), 299 (2001), 331 (2006), 402 (2011).

Bundawarrah (*Co. Bland*) 34°23'S. 147°33'E., 7 km N. of Temora; school 1900–13; pop. 110 (1911), 144 (1933).

Bundella (*Co. Pottinger*) 31°34'S. 149°59'E., 39 km NE of Coolah, on Bundella Ck; village gaz. 1876; grazing; cemetery 1881; drought 1878; mouse plague 1922; PO 1875, burnt down 1932; Presb. C. (St Andrew's) 1900; Rom. Cath. C. (St John's) 1910, demolished 1979; school 1957–83; telephone 1892; TX 1910, automatic 1968; tornado 1996; pop. 69 (1901), 188 (1911), 97 (1933), 96 (1947), 182 (1954), 128 (1961).

Bundella Creek (*Co. Pottinger*) see Ardgour.

Bundemar (*Co. Ewenmar*) 31°50'S. 148°11'E., 36 km SE of Warren, on Ewenmar Ck; Drillwarrina till 1897; Angl. C. (All Saints') 1893; FB; pop. 29 (1933), 55 (1954), 68 (1961).

Bundewallah (*Co. Camden*) 34°46'S. 150°40'E., 3 km NW of Berry, on Bundewallah Ck; school (Bundywalla) 1872–87; pop. 54 (1911).

Bundgeam (*Co. Rous*) 28°26'S. 152°53'E., 25 km N. of Kyogle, on Terrace Ck; sawmill; school (Terrace Creek till 1923) 1919–78; telephone 1916; TX 1923–68; pop. 65 (1933), 72 (1947), 73 (1954), 85 (1961).

Bundi (*Co. Wellington*) 32°58'S. 149°19'E., 39 km NE of Orange.

Bundjalung (*Co. Richmond*) see Evans Head.

Bundocks Crossing (*Co. Richmond*) 29°11'S. 153°03'E., 31 km W. of Woodburn, on Myrtle Ck; Presb. C. b. 1909 by Mackney, closed, moved to Coraki and reused; Rom. Cath. C. (St Anne's); sawmill.

Bundook (*Co. Gloucester*) 31°54'S. 152°07'E., 20 km NE of Gloucester, on Bakers Ck; grazing; FB; fire 1927; PO 1917; RS 1913, station b. by John Allibone, closed 1978; sale-yards (J.J. Gallagher) 1917; sawmills: Clyde Sawmilling Co., burnt down 1947 and H. Walters Pty Ltd, moved to Lansdowne; school 1929–84; telephone 1916; TX 1922; pop. 160 (1933), 146 (1947), 113 (1954), 77 (1961), 173 (2006), 192 (2011).

Bundure (*Co. Urana*) 35°10'S. 146°01'E., 33 km NE of Jerilderie; bushfire 1884; earth tremor 1871; PO 1926; RS (5 km SE) 1884–1975; telephone 1926; TX (automatic) 1954; pop. 81 (1947), 74 (1954), 77 (1961), 273 (2006).

Bundyulumblah (*Co. Wakool*) 35°02'S. 144°27'E., 72 km NE of Barham, on Coleambally Outfall Drain; earth tremor 2015; Presb. C.

Bundywalla (*Co. Camden*) see Bundewallah.

Bunga (*Co. Dampier*) 36°34'S. 150°02'E., 16 km S. of Bermagui; telephone 1908; TX 1954–60.

Bungaba (*Co. Bligh*) 32°10'S. 149°39'E., 24 km NE of Gulgong.

Bungabbee (*Co. Rous*) 28°47'S. 153°09'E., 13 km W. of Lismore, on Back Ck; Angl. C. (St Thomas's) 1907; PO 1936–42; RS 1903–73; pop. 140 (1911), 84 (1933), 75 (1947), 88 (1954).

Bungadore (*Co. Parry*) see Niangala.

Bungalong Creek (*Co. Monteagle*) see Cowra Road.

Bungalora (*Co. Rous*) 28°15'S. 153°28'E., 11 km SW of Tweed Heads, on Duroby Ck; cheese factory b. 1909 by Cork Bros; pop. 94

(1911), 75 (1933).

Bungalora (*Co. Rous*) see also Terranora.

Bungalow Flat (*Co. Northumberland*) 33°15'S. 151°20'E., 10 km W. of Wyong.

Bungalow Park (*Co. St Vincent*) 35°23'S. 150°26'E., 5 km SW of Ulladulla, on Burrill Lake.

Bunganbil (*Co. Cooper*) see Colinroobie.

Bunga Pinch Road (*Co. Dampier*) 36°34'S. 150°02'E., 17 km S. of Bermagui.

Bungarby (*Co. Wellesley*) 36°40'S. 149°01'E., 32 km NW of Bombala; grazing; Angl. C. (St Peter's) 1895, demolished, replaced 1927, closed and sold; PO 1908; school 1884–85 and 1944–72; telephone 1924; TX 1925; pop. 53 (1901), 85 (1911), 65 (1933), 81 (1947), 105 (1954), 52 (1961), 214 (2011).

Bungaree Norah (*Co. Northumberland*) see Norah Head.

Bungawalbin (*Co. Richmond*) 29°02'S. 153°17'E., 7 km S. of Coraki, on Richmond R.; timber, tea-tree oil, sugar-cane, farming, dairying; bridge b. 1910 by Oakes Bros, replacement (5 spans), 350 ft (106.7 m), b. 1967 by Central Constructions Pty Ltd, over Bungawalbin Ck; bushfire 1952; caterpillar infestations 1919, 1929, 1931; Church of Christ; floods 1893, 1895, 1928, 2008; PO 1890; punt b. 1889 by Conroy Bros to cross Richmond R.; school (Bungawalbyn) 1883–1965; sugar mill (Robert Henry Leeson) 1873; telephone 1905; TX 1915; Union C.; wharf b. 1891 by William M'Donald; pop. 228 (1901), 245 (1911), 173 (1933), 118 (1947), 115 (1954), 94 (1961).

Bungawalbyn (*Co. Richmond*) see Bungawalbin.

Bungay (*Co. Macquarie*) 31°55'S. 152°20'E., 5 km SW of Wingham, on Manning R.; orig. Bungy Bungy; bushfire 1937; gale 1925; school 1880, additions 1895 by F. Craven, closed 1908; pop. 38 (1841), 62 (1901), 70 (1911), 42 (1933).

Bungendore (*Co. Murray*) 35°15'S. 149°27'E., 23 km NE of Queanbeyan, on Turallo Ck; (incl. Elmslea and Smiths Gap); disc. 1820 by Joseph Wild, settled 1835 by Richard Brooks, surveyed 1837 by James Larmer, town gaz. 1837, thrived in 1880s; formerly sheep and fruit, now hobby farming and tourism; ambulance station 2019; Angl. C. (St Philip's) 1865 d. by Alberto Dias Soares, vestry added and church re-roofed, and graveyard; bridge b. 1876 by Bradbury, over Turallo Ck; caterpillar infestations 1903 and 1904; cemetery; CH 1864, new one b. 1875 by G. Smith, renovated 1923 by McKie & Sons, reused as police station, alterations and repairs 1953 by A. Butterfield; clay mine (Lundie and Griffith) <1928; cordial factories: H.H. Daniel & Son 1906 and D.J. Sparrow; creamery (A. Robinson & Co.) 1894; earth tremors 1871, 1883, 1925; electricity 1949; FB 1939; floods 1870, 1887, 1898 (whole town inundated); flour mill (Alexander McClung) 1861, repaired and modernised 1904, reused; gale 1924; grasshopper infestation 1898; lock-up 1838; measles epidemic 1893; PO 1840, new one b. 1882, renovated 1936 by Gardiner and Moulds; police barracks, closed and reused, fire 1862; pound (stock), relocated 1852; Presb. C. (St John's) b. 1875 by John Kealman, dismantled 1883, re-erected on new site; PS b. 1900 by J. Burnett, additions 1903 by John McKie; quarry; rabbit freezing works (in old flour mill), estab. 1908 by Oscar Curtis and W. White, leased to Garratt Scandrett Freezing Companies Ltd; reservoirs; rifle range; Rom. Cath. C. (St Mary's) b. 1851–62 by McLean and Ross, additions 1875 by T. Priest and E. Evans, re-roofed 1907 by John McKie, and graveyard; RS 1885, station b. by Joseph Jordan and G. Williams; sawmills: George Daniel and W.L. Hopkins; school 1877, new one b. 1879 by John Kealman, re-roofed 1902 by Peter Poidevin, additions 1916 by Portus and Ibbotson, additions 1964; sewerage 1976, augmentation 1994; telegraph 1878; TX 1910; Unit. C. (St John's, orig. Presb.) b. 1886 by Charles Ross, closed, sold 1997 and reused; water reticulation 1967, augmentation 1985; winery (Lark Hill) 1978; pop. 30 (1846), 63 (1851), 154 (1856), 195 (1861), *c.*200 (1866), 188 (1871), 270 (1881), *c.*700 (1885), 629

(1891), 731 (1901), 584 (1911), 655 (1933), 545 (1947), 562 (1954), 508 (1961), 493 (1966), 514 (1971), 601 (1976), 683 (1981), 1,028 (1986), 1,153 (1991), 1,348 (1996), 1,690 (2001), 2,183 (2006), 2,755 (2011).

Bungendore Junction (*Co. Murray*) 35°18'S. 149°26'E., 5 km S. of Bungendore; quarry.

Bunghery (*Co. Gloucester*) see Violet Hill.

Bungiebomar (*Co. Lincoln*) 32°19'S. 149°08'E., 32 km NE of Wellington; farming and grazing; PO 1927–30.

Bungleboori (*Co. Cook*) 33°24'S. 150°12'E., 9 km NE of Lithgow, on Marrangaroo Ck.

Bunglegumbie (*Co. Gordon*) 37°08'S. 148°35'E., 7 km NW of Dubbo; diphtheria 1898; mouse plague 1922; school 1885–1916; storm 1918; telephone 1924; pop. 54 (1911), 49 (1933), 164 (2011).

Bungonia (*Co. Argyle*) 34°51'S. 149°57'E., 24 km SE of Goulburn, on Bungonia Ck; Inverary till 1836; settled 1821, surveyed 1831 by Robert Hoddle, laid out 1832 by Hoddle, town gaz. 1833, founded by Robert Futter; tourism from 1889 to caves (disc. 1824 by Allan Cunningham) and gorge, peaked in 1900, cobalt 1910, farming, grazing; Angl. C. b. 1834–36 but not finished, d. by John Verge, temporary one (St Luke's) 1841, new one (Christ) b. 1878 by Robert B. Turner, d. by William Edmund Kemp, re-roofed 1935; bridge 1862, new one b. 1893 by Thomas Bell, over Bungonia Ck; bushfire 1965; cemetery (burials 1836+), restored 1988; CH 1835; FB 1942; gale 1923; lock-up 1832, closed, reused; PO 1832; pound (stock) 1866; Presb. C.; PS b. 1907 by G.E. Fraser, closed 1933, sold and reused; quarry; rifle range 1908; Rom. Cath. C. (St Michael the Archangel) b. 1847 by Patrick Kelly, repairs 1997 d. by Garry Dutaillis & Associates; school 1880, new one b. 1882 by Gideon Cranston and Phillipson, closed 1973; telephone 1906; TX 1925; pop. 82 (1841), 98 (1846), 67 (1851), 108 (1856), *c.*100 (1866), 285 (1891), 109 (1901), 223 (1911), 154 (1933), 135 (1947), 142 (1954), 132 (1961), 259 (2006), 355 (2011).

Bungowannah (*Co. Hume*) 36°00'S. 146°46'E., 17 km NW of Albury; goldmining, vineyards, wheat, grazing; Angl. C. 1870, new one (St Mark's) b. 1905 by Cochrane Bros, closed 1976; boiling-down works 1893; bushfires 1900 and 1905; cemetery (burials 1870+); FB; fire 1894; flood 1917; flour mill (John Dight, water powered); gale 1914; PO 1867; pound (stock) 1869; Presb. C. b. 1896 by James Whybro; school 1867–69, new one b. 1876, reopened 1877, closed 1930, sold 1977, reused; storm 1923; telephone 1919; TX 1921, automatic 1950; Wes. Meth. C. 1883 (removed from Howlong), re-roofed, destroyed 1914; Unit. C. (orig. Meth.) d. and b. 1919 by James Whybro; pop. 112 (1901), 187 (1911), 142 (1933), 102 (1947), 132 (1954), 141 (1961), 208 (2011).

Bungulla (*Co. Clive*) 29°07'S. 152°00'E., 9 km S. of Tenterfield; Jump Up till 1892; farming and grazing; PO 1909, burnt down 1941, reopened, closed 1973; quarry; RS (Jump Up till 1892) 1891–1975; school (Groombridge Swamp till 1893) 1881, new building b. 1928 by M. Johnston, closed 1940; telephone 1914; TX 1956; Wes. Meth. C. 1891, closed, sold 1940; pop. 111 (1901), 101 (1911), 93 (1933), 68 (1947), 60 (1954), 50 (1961).

Bungunyah Valley (*Co. Wakool*) 35°10'S. 143°25'E., 60 km S. of Balranald.

Bungunyah Valley (*Co. Wakool*) see also Koraleigh.

Bungwahl (*Co. Gloucester*) 32°24'S. 152°26'E., 21 km E. of Bulahdelah, on Myall Lake; (incl. Neranie formerly Narani); Bungwall Flat till 1896; timber, farming, fishing; Angl. C. (St James's) b. 1884 by Alexander Croll, closed, sold 2018, and graveyard (graves 1877+); cemeteries: old (10 graves), new (231 graves 1890s+), incl. columbarium, Neranie Point (8 graves 1886+) 1890, disused; CH; FB; fire 1912; limestone quarry (Patent Asphaltum Co. of NSW); PO 1875; PS 1881, repairs 1919 by Joseph Head, closed 1932, sold 1940; sawmills: Bungwahl (estab. 1873 by Alexander Croll, sen., John Wright and J.S. Rodger, fire 1911, burnt down 1924, rebuilt by Thomas Bros, burnt down 1948, rebuilt, burnt down 1962, rebuilt by Thomas Palmer for Thomas Bros and sold by them in 1978 to Paul Herbert Pty Ltd, closed 1997), George Ireland, Neranie (estab. 1873 by Hudson Bros, closed 1894, reopened 1895 by George Wilton Mitchell, closed 1907, plant bought 1907 by Frederick Phillips and removed), Norco Timber Co. 1924, burnt down 1926, Elwyn Pascoe; schools: Bungwahl (Bungwall till 1884, then Bungwall Flat till 1896) 1876, additions 1970 and Narani 1880–93 and 1899–1908; telegraph 1879; tramway (timber) to Smiths Lake, b. 1884 by Hudson Bros; TX 1927; wharf b. 1897 by A. Croll; pop. *c.*400 (1891), 142 (1901), 181 (1911), 134 (1933), 161 (1947), 182 (1954), 161 (1961), 210 (2006), 254 (2011).

Bungwall (*Co. Gloucester*) see Bungwahl.

Bungwall Flat (*Co. Gloucester*) see Bungwahl.

Bungy Bungy (*Co. Macquarie*) see Bungay.

Bungymulla (*Co. Darling*) 30°47'S. 150°57'E., 22 km E. of Manilla, on Halls Ck; telephone 1926; TX 1926, automatic 1956.

Buninyong (*Co. Lincoln*) see Dubbo.

Bunna Bunna (*Co. Benarba*) 29°48'S. 149°17'E., 46 km N. of Wee Waa, on Thalaba Ck.

Bunnabunoo (*Co. Durham*) see Fishers Hill and Summer Hill.

Bunnaloo (*Co. Cadell*) 35°47'S. 144°36'E., 27 km W. of Mathoura, on Deniboota Canal; farming and grazing; PO 1926; RS (11 km W., on Victorian railway); sawmill (Jacka Bros); school (Bunaloo till 1935) 1931–46, reopened 1955, additions 1958; telephone 1927; TX 1928; pop. 92 (1911), 152 (1933), 88 (1947), 143 (1954), 190 (1961), 127 (2006).

Bunnaloo East (*Co. Cadell*) 35°48'S. 144°44'E., 15 km W. of Mathoura.

Bunnaloo East (*Co. Cadell*) see also Thyra.

Bunnan (*Co. Brisbane*) 32°02'S. 150°35'E., 27 km W. of Scone, on Wybong Ck; village gaz. 1886; grazing; Angl. C. 1883, demolished and replaced (St Jude's) 1928, and graveyard (42 graves 1887–1974); bridge (reinforced concrete continuous girder) b. 1936 by Charles Hardy Contracting Co. Ltd, over Wybong Ck; FB; mouse plague 1904; PO 1876; Presb. C. 1907; school 1882, closed later that year, reopened 1901, additions 1914 by G. Cavanough, closed 1973; telephone 1900; TX 1912; Unit. C. (St Andrew's, orig. Presb.) 1907; pop. 78 (1901), 277 (1911), 139 (1933), 124 (1947), 109 (1954), 61 (1961), 213 (2011).

Bunneringee (*Co. Tara*) 33°36'S. 141°46'E., 58 km N. of Wentworth; cemetery (2 graves) 1864.

Bunyah (*Co. Gloucester*) 32°10'S. 152°13'E., 27 km W. of Tuncurry, on Wang Wauk R.; farming and dairying; Free Presb. C.; PO 1923; school 1959–84; telephone 1916; TX 1930; pop. 132 (1933), 169 (1947), 96 (1954), 104 (1961).

Bunyan (*Co. Beresford*) 36°10'S. 149°09'E., 8 km N. of Cooma, on Cooma Ck; orig. Reid's Flat, then Jews Flat, then Pindjera till 1858; estab. *c.*1828, village gaz. 1880; lucerne and grazing; airfield; boiling-down works (Loutit, Hobson and Ryder) 1893; bridge b. 1881 by David Montgomery, new one b. 1899 by J.M. Fitzgerald, over Cooma Ck; electricity 1955; PO 1860–91; quarry (diatomite); RS 1889, station b. by Alexander Hamilton Scouller, closed 1989, demolished; school 1911–36; TX; pop. *c.*60 (1866), 69 (1901), 103 (1911), 90 (1933), 94 (1947), 73 (1954), 68 (1961), 374 (2011).

Buraja (*Co. Hume*) 35°52'S. 146°22'E., 16 km N. of Corowa; Angl. C. (All Saints') 1891, renovated 1925; cemetery 1878; electricity 1948; FB; Wes. Meth. C. 1881; pop. 68 (1933).

Buralyang (*Co. Cooper*) 33°58'S. 146°46'E., 41 km W. of West Wyalong; formerly Buralyang Siding; goldmining (reef); FB 1939; PO 1927–64; RS 1923–75, station removed 1984; school 1930–54; silo 1936; telephone 1925; TX 1926; pop. 38 (1933).

Buralyang Siding (*Co. Cooper*) see Buralyang.

Buramilong (*Co. Ewenmar*) 31°40'S. 148°30'E., 16 km W. of Gilgandra, on Marthaguy Ck.

Burbong (*Co. Murray*) 35°20'S. 149°19'E., 8 km E. of Queanbeyan, on Molonglo R.; laid out by William Henry O'Malley Wood, village gaz. 1888; bridge (De Salis Bridge) 1875, new one (timber truss) b. 1897 by Edward William Fitzgerald, replaced by steel one 1926, over

Molonglo R.; cemetery 1889; quarry; RS (Molonglo till 1890) 1887–1975.

Burburgate (*Co. Pottinger*) 30°54'S. 150°11'E., 12 km NW of Gunnedah; boiling-down works; FB; pop. 161 (2006).

Burburgate (*Co. Pottinger*) see also Rosewarne.

Burcher (*Co. Gipps*) 33°31'S. 147°15'E., 46 km N. of West Wyalong; Euglo till 1936; village gaz. 1930 as Euglo; gold and wheat; mine (Kayser) worked by H.W. Kayser 1907 and H.F. Fitzgerald 1941; PO 1933; railway coal stage; railway turntable, 60 ft (18.3 m), ruined; Rom. Cath. C. (Immaculate Heart of Mary) 1950; RS (Euglo till 1936) 1929–72; school 1955, additions 1967, closed 2010, sold; silo 1936; telephone 1934; TX 1934, automatic 1973; Union C. (Good Shepherd) 1955; water supply augmentation 1955; pop. 232 (1933), 139 (1947), 128 (1954), 157 (1961), 187 (2006).

Burdekins Gap (*Co. Gloucester*) 32°29'S. 152°12'E., 9 km S. of Bulahdelah.

Burdenda (*Co. Kennedy*) 32°07'S. 147°25'E., 54 km W. of Trangie.

Burdett (*Co. Ashburnham*) 33°25'S. 148°38'E., 17 km N. of Canowindra; Boneys Rocks till 1899; defunct; goldmining and farming; mine o. 1866, bought 1894 by Lady Burdett Coutts Gold Mining Co., became Burdett Ltd in 1899, abandoned 1907 and machinery sold; PO 1907–62; quarry; school 1897–1903 and 1927–48; pop. 67 (1911), 125 (1933), 104 (1947), 91 (1954).

Bureen (*Co. Hunter*) 32°28'S. 150°43'E., 9 km S. of Denman; dairying; FB; school 1957–70; telephone 1946; TX 1946, automatic 1952; pop. 66 (1954), 69 (1961).

Burgaria (*Co. Burnett*) see Warialda Rail.

Burgoon (*Co. Gordon*) 32°59'S. 148°43'E., 19 km NW of Molong, on Buckinbah Ck.

Burgooney (*Co. Dowling*) 33°23'S. 146°35'E., 21 km SE of Lake Cargelligo; settled 1914 by F. Davis; farming; bushfires 1956 and 1957; PO 1921, new one b. 1926 by E.A. Turner; RS 1917–75, station removed 1982; school 1931–42; silo 1934; telephone 1923; TX 1925; pop. 319 (1933), 102 (1947), 134 (1954), 140 (1961).

Buri (*Co. Inglis*) see Limbri.

Burindi (*Co. Darling*) 30°27'S. 150°27'E., 17 km SW of Barraba; squall (buildings unroofed) 1938; pop. 26 (1933).

Burinegeel (*Co. Narromine*) 31°55'S. 148°05'E., 16 km NE of Trangie, on Macquarie R.; farming; PO 1927; telephone 1925; TX 1957; pop. 78 (1933).

Burkeville (*Co. Bathurst*) see Garland.

Burke Ward (*Co. Yancowinna*) see Broken Hill.

Burley Jacky's (*Co. Bathurst*) see Waugoola.

Burmpabank (*Co. Rous*) see Wyneden.

Burnima (*Co. Wellesley*) 36°52'S. 149°16'E., 5 km N. of Bombala; soldiers' settlement; sheep; PO 1927–45; telephone 1925; pop. 20 (1933).

Burnt Bridge (*Co. Dudley*) 31°06'S. 152°49'E., 4 km SW of Kempsey, on Sandy Ck; Aboriginal mission; pop. 81 (1933), 213 (1947), 281 (1954), 86 (2011).

Burnt Flat (*Co. Westmoreland*) 34°16'S. 150°14'E., 29 km NW of Mittagong, on Wollondilly R.

Burnt Hut Crossing (*Co. Wellesley*) see Rodney.

Burnt Yards (*Co. Bathurst*) 33°35'S. 149°01'E., 21 km SW of Millthorpe, on Burnt Yards Ck; gold (disc. 1870) mining 1870–77, farming, grazing; mine (Prince of Wales, o. 1870, closed 1877, reopened 1882, closed 1884, sold 1887 to Golden Hill Gold Mining Co., reopened 1888, closed 1890, reopened 1899 by Henry Newman as the New Prince of Wales, closed 1910, reopened 1933 by Arthur Moad, closed 1940); PO 1897; quarry; school (Belubula 1904–25) 1884, repairs by Christopher Shandley, new one b. 1889 by W.R. Gorringe, closed 1893, re-erected on new site by W.R. Jarvis and reopened 1897, closed 1946; telephone 1922; TX 1924; Wes. Meth. C. 1871; pop. 93 (1901), 66 (1911), 96 (1933), 57 (1947).

Buronga (*Co. Wentworth*) 34°10'S. 142°11'E., 4 km W. of Gol Gol, on Murray R.; Hendy Town till 1935, then Mildura Bridge till 1937;

village gaz. 1939; grapes, olives, tomatoes; bridge b. 1925–27 by Armstrong Whitworth Pty Ltd and Gilbert Lodge & Co., 820 ft (250 m), demolished, replacement (George Chaffey Bridge) b. 1983–85 by Transfield Pty Ltd, pre-stressed concrete box girder, 1,086 ft (331 m), over Murray R.; electricity 1951; FB 1959; flood 1956; metal fabrication works; PO 1941; PS 1954, new ones 1962 and 1977; punt, ceased 1927, over Murray R.; reservoir 1964; Rom. Cath. C. (St Michael the Archangel) 1967; school 1942, additions 1968; sewerage augmentation 1996; slipway estab. 1927 by Murray Anderson; storm 1949; telephone 1941; TX (automatic) 1959; water reticulation 1955, augmentation 1994; pop. 306 (1947), 505 (1961), 378 (1971), 561 (1976), 550 (1981), 551 (1986), 558 (1991), 896 (1996), 929 (2001), 807 (2006), 1,132 (2011).

Burra (*Co. Harden*) 34°55'S. 148°04'E., 18 km N. of Gundagai; bushfire 1979.

Burra (*Co. Murray*) 35°33'S. 149°13'E., 22 km S. of Queanbeyan, on Burra Ck; mining (silver, lead, iron), farming, grazing; Angl. C. (St Paul's) 1867 d. by Alberto Dias Soares, vestry added 1887; FB; PO 1906–30; pop. 44 (1933), 73 (1947), 70 (1954), 76 (1961), 477 (2006), 715 (2011).

Burra (*Co. Selwyn*) 34°49'S. 148°03'E., 5 km SE of Tumbarumba; sawmill (Burra Creek Mill, water powered) estab. 1883 by F. Hussell and Gaylard, closed 1916; pop. 60 (1901), 26 (1933).

Burra Bee Dee (*Co. Gowen*) 31°13'S. 149°22'E., 10 km NE of Coonabarabran; Aboriginal mission founded 1911 by Mary Jane Cain; United Aborigines Missionaries C., removed, reused, demolished; pop. 114 (1933), 71 (1947), 56 (1954).

Burrabeena (*Co. Bland*) 33°52'S. 147°52'E., 28 km W. of Grenfell, on Clearys Ck; telephone 1926; TX 1926.

Burrabogie (*Co. Waradgery*) 34°30'S. 145°12'E., 32 km E. of Hay, on Murrumbidgee R.; cemetery; pumping station (irrigation); pop. 81 (1911).

Burraboi (*Co. Wakool*) 35°24'S. 144°19'E., 32 km NE of Barham; PO 1929; RS (1 km E., on Victorian railway); school 1954, additions 1956, closed 2007, sold; telephone 1930; TX 1930–37; pop. 47 (1933), 61 (1947), 89 (1954), 107 (1961), 418 (2006).

Burra Burra (*Co. Kennedy*) 32°41'S. 147°21'E., 43 km NW of Trundle; pop. 112 (1911).

Burra Creek (*Co. Harden*) 34°54'S. 148°04'E., 19 km N. of Gundagai, on Burra Ck; Rom. Cath. C. (St Joseph's) b. 1901 by James Toner; school (Yammatree 1897–1906) 1886–90 and 1897–1912; pop. 64 (1933).

Burradoo (*Co. Camden*) 34°30'S. 150°24'E., 3 km S. of Bowral, on Wingecarribee R.; airport; brickworks 1884; bushfire 1905; cemetery; electricity 1925; PO 1887; railway viaduct (timber), 1,320 ft (402.3 m), replacement (23 steel spans) 1914, over Wingecarribee R.; RS 1870, station relocated 1891, closed 1975, reopened 1976; sewage works; telephone 1891; Unit. C. (Wesley) and graveyard; pop. 165 (1901), 215 (1911), 231 (1933), 318 (1947), 807 (1954), 2,071 (2006), 2,555 (2011).

Burradoo (*Co. Camden*) see also Bowral.

Burraduc (*Co. Gloucester*) 32°23'S. 152°23'E., 17 km E. of Bulahdelah; school 1886–94.

Burraga (*Co. Georgiana*) 33°57'S. 149°32'E., 40 km SW of Oberon; surveyed 1884 by Thomas Lindon Biddulph and village gaz. 1887; formerly mining then farming and grazing; Angl. C. (St Paul's), dismantled, removed, and rebuilt 1924 on new site; brick-kilns (Green's); bushfire 1939; cemetery (126 graves 1910+) 1888; CH 1886; cordial factory (Heavener's), bought 1913 by Albert Riley; dam (Lloyd Copper Co.) 1901, opened to fishing 1907; dust storms 1902 and 1907; electricity 1956; eucalyptus oil distillery; fire 1901; hailstorm 1901; hospital 1905, new one b. 1907 on new site by J. Clarke and J. Moore; measles epidemic 1894; miners' strike 1895; mines: Lloyd Copper Mine (o. 1878 as Thompson's Creek Mine, remodelled 1900, closed 1914, reopened 1918 as Excelsior Mine, closed 1919, works demolished 1925), Lucky Draw, Sprague's or Mount Burraga (incl. 10 head stamper battery); PO 1876, new one 1903; PS (incl. lock-up) 1883, new one 1886, repairs 1897 by R. Harper, closed and sold 1903 to T. Martin, replaced 1904; Rom. Cath. C. 1883, relocated 1897, demolished 1940, replacement (St Dympna's) b. 1941 by A.E. Rauch, d. by Edward Rodwell Green; school 1882, additions 1888 by James Prior Hull, new building b. 1954 by Hughes Bros, closed 2016; storm 1903; telegraph 1892; TX 1917, automatic 1986; typhoid 1905; Union C., damaged 1903 and 1907; Wes. Meth. C. 1884; pop. *c.*250 (1882), *c.*500 (1883), 528 (1891), 954 (1901), *c.*1,500 (1905), *c.*1,800 (1907), 472 (1911), 475 (1913), 1,570 (July 1914), 450 (Aug. 1914), *c.*250 (1915), *c.*1,300 (1918), 248 (1933), 211 (1947), 217 (1954), 150 (1961), 71 (1984), 116 (2006), 251 (2011).

Burragan (*Co. Fitzroy*) 29°51'S. 152°54'E., 19 km S. of Grafton; school 1880, additions 1891 by James Trent, closed 1909.

Burragate (*Co. Auckland*) 37°01'S. 149°37'E., 24 km W. of Pambula, on Towamba R., village gaz. 1867; goldmining and farming; bridge b. 1937 by Armstrong, over Towamba R.; bushfire 1900; butter factory (Burragate Co-op. Co.) 1895, burnt down 1900; cemetery 1897; cheese factory (Burragate Dairy Co. Ltd) b. by Waterson and Moore; FB; mine (Williams's); PO 1896–1971; school 1894–1924 and 1957–59; telephone 1900; TX 1920; pop. 155 (1901), 114 (1911), 97 (1933), 61 (1947), 78 (1954), 23 (1961).

Burragorang (*Co. Camden*) 34°00'S. 150°26'E., 25 km NW of Picton, on Lake Burragorang; orig. Burragurrang, formerly also known as Woodville; disc. 1823 by William Hilton Hovell; maize and dairying; caterpillar infestation 1923; cheese factory 1937; colliery (Brimstone, owned by Clutha Development Pty Ltd); earth tremor 1910; floods 1952 and 1956; flour mill; PO 1858, new one b. 1934; Rom. Cath. C. 1840, new one (St Paulinus and the Guardian Angels) b. 1867–74 by Charles Minell, d. by William Munro, damaged 1937, demolished 1957, and graveyard; sawmill; telephone 1918; TX 1926; pop. *c.*550 (1866), 531 (1891), 184 (1901), 411 (1911), 220 (1933), 206 (1947), 112 (1954), 525 (2006).

Burragorang (*Co. Camden*)
see also Central Burragorang.

Burragurrang (*Co. Camden*) see Burragorang.

Burrajaa (*Co. Hume*) see Lowesdale.

Burra Lake (*Co. Georgiana*) 34°21'S. 149°47'E., 32 km NE of Crookwell; school 1882–97 and 1912–55, disused and dilapidated.

Burrandana (*Co. Mitchell*) 35°25'S. 147°21'E., 27 km SE of The Rock, on Burkes Ck; goldmine; RS 1925–52; school 1957–75; telephone 1923; TX 1925, automatic 1953; pop. 82 (1961).

Burrandong (*Co. Wellington*) 32°41'S. 149°07'E., 22 km SE of Wellington, on Macquarie R., village now submerged under Lake Burrendong; Burrendong till 1911; goldmining and grazing; Angl. C. 1928, moved to Mumbil; cemetery 1856–73; dam b. 1958–67, wall 249 ft (75.9 m) high and 3,661 ft (1,115.9 m) long, wall raised and other upgrading works 2010–14, on Macquarie R.; dust storm 1946; earth tremor 1862; PO 1862–1938; power station (hydro-electric) 1996, orig. managed by Power Facilities Pty Ltd, now AGL Energy Ltd; Presb. C. b. 1906 by Thomas Campbell; rifle range; school 1911–22; telephone 1913; TX 1915–22; pop. 157 (1911), 108 (1933), 241 (1961).

Burrangong (*Co. Monteagle*) 34°17'S. 148°16'E., 4 km NW of Young, on Burrangong Ck; settled 1826 by James White; goldmining; Cong. C. 1863; hospital 1862, replaced 1900; Indep. C.; pound (stock) 1899; Rom. Cath. C. (Guardian Angels) 1874, new one (St Philomena's) 1929; RS 1889–1975; school 1889–1958; pop. 138 (1911), 78 (1921), 140 (1933), 207 (1947), 121 (1954), 73 (1961), 240 (2011).

Burrangong Heights (*Co. Monteagle*)
see Boara.

Burrapine (*Co. Raleigh*) 30°43'S. 152°38'E., 21 km W. of Bowraville, on Taylors Arm; farming; mine (antimony); PO 1900; sawmill (George Fortescue); school 1909, new one b. 1930 by Charles Alexander Stewart Boag, closed 1967; telephone 1916; TX 1927–64;

pop. 74 (1901), 61 (1911), 149 (1933), 82 (1947), 51 (1954), 50 (1961).

Burrawang (*Co. Camden*) 34°36'S. 150°31'E., 14 km E. of Moss Vale; Mount Pleasant till 1865; estab. 1865, thrived 1877, town lots sold 1885, 1887, 1889; cabbages 1887+, potatoes, fodder crops, cereals, hort., dairying; Angl. C. 1867, new one (St David's) 1886 on new site; bacon factory (John R. Battye); bushfire 1905; butter factories: Beehive estab. by Walmsley, and Emu b. by E. Hawkens; cemetery (366 graves) 1881; drought 1893–1902; earth tremor 1875; FB (station b. 2009); flour and timber mill (Barrett, Hayter & Co.) 1879; grasshopper infestation 1945; PO 1865; Presb. C. (St John's) 1888, closed, sold 2009, reused; PS 1894, new one b. 1911, closed 1920, dismantled and removed 1927; 3 quarries; Rom. Cath. C. (St Peter's) 1875, and graveyard (182 graves); RS 1932–75; school 1878 b. by John Staggs, d. by George Allen Mansfield, repairs 1895 by J.S. Parker, jun., remodelled 1925 by E. Symons, building sold 1993 to G. Sutton; snow 1887 and 1934; telegraph 1879; TX 1922, automatic 1953; water pumping station; water supply augmentation 1995; Wes. Meth. C. 1875; pop. *c.*300 (1866), 276 (1901), 261 (1911), 233 (1933), 211 (1947), 241 (1954), 243 (1961), 176 (2006), 238 (2011).

Burrawang East (*Co. Camden*) see Myra Vale.

Burrawong Bay (*Co. Northumberland*) see Woy Woy Bay.

Burrell Creek (*Co. Gloucester*) 31°57'S. 152°18'E., 12 km SW of Wingham, on Red Gully; farming and dairying; FB; foot-bridge over Burrell Ck; Meth. C. 1924, renovated 1940, closed, sold and reused; PO 1906; telephone 1905; TX 1917; pop. 92 (1933), 129 (1947), 155 (1954), 148 (1961), 247 (2011).

Burrembooka (*Co. Wellesley*) 36°58'S. 149°17'E., 8 km SE of Bombala, on Warburton Ck; school 1882–96 and 1903–10.

Burren (*Co. Jamison*) 30°03'S. 148°58'E., 49 km NW of Wee Waa, on Pian Ck; PO 1898; PS 1893–1901; telephone 1898; TX 1915. (See also Old Burren.)

Burren (*Co. Jamison*) see also Burren Junction.

Burren Burren (*Co. Finch*) 29°17'S. 148°47'E., 40 km SW of Mungindi.

Burrendong (*Co. Wellington*) see Burrandong and Mumbil.

Burrendoon (*Co. Benarba*) 29°27'S. 149°06'E., 53 km S. of Mungindi.

Burren Junction (*Co. Jamison*) 30°06'S. 148°57'E., 47 km W. of Wee Waa; village gaz. 1903; sheep, wheat, cotton; Angl. C. (All Saints') 1905, destroyed 1929, replaced 1936; cemetery (68 graves 1919+) 1903; CH b. by William Houlahan; fires 1921 and 1926; hospital 1932; hurricane (many buildings unroofed) 1929; lock-up b. 1904 by C.A. Freeman; mouse plague 1940; PO 1904, new one b. 1915 by Donald Campbell; Presb. C.; railway barracks, removed 1984; Rom. Cath. C. (St Joseph's) 1909; PS 1903; RS (renamed Burren in 1940) 1903, station b. by John Allibone and McCarthy, closed 1973; school 1904 b. by B.B. Kinnear, burnt down, new one b. 1911 by W.J. Wallace, additions 1927 and 2010; silo; telegraph 1905; TX 1910; pop. 460 (1911), 250 (1933), 275 (1947), 327 (1954), 235 (1961), 223 (1971), 300 (2011).

Burrier (*Co. St Vincent*) 34°52'S. 150°27'E., 14 km W. of Nowra, on Meadow Ck; orig. Purreah; farming; bushfire 1965; cemetery; FB; floods 1867 and 1870; PO 1863; school 1870–1911 and 1916–52; telephone 1919; TX 1926; Union C.; water pumping station 1955; pop. *c.*200 (1866), 70 (1911), 66 (1933), 83 (1954).

Burrill (*Co. St Vincent*) 35°21'S. 150°24'E., 5 km SW of Milton; school 1876–1934, demolished 1947; pop. 54 (1911).

Burrill Lake (*Co. St Vincent*) 35°23'S. 150°27'E., 4 km SW of Ulladulla, on Burrill Lake; (incl. Kings Point); timber and lime burning, later tourism; Angl. C. (St Michael and All Angels') 1952, closed and sold; bridge 1881, replaced 1958, 180 ft (54.9 m), demolished 2017, replacement (16 span pre-cast concrete girder) b. 2017 by BGC Contracting Pty Ltd, over Burrill Lake; bushfires 1952, 2006, 2018; FB; PO 1934; reservoir; sawmill (Hibberd's); telephone 1935; pop. 1,610 (1991), 1,785

(1996), 1,883 (2001), 2,059 (2006), 1,890 (2011).

Burringbar (*Co. Rous*) 28°26'S. 153°28'E., 14 km SE of Murwillumbah, on Burringbar Ck; bananas and dairying; Angl. C. (St Michael and All Angels') 1910, closed, sold 2013; cemetery; cordial factory (Skinner's); electricity 1950; FB (station b. 1976); fires 1915, 1923, 1926, 1932, 1957; Meth. C. 1920; PO b. 1902 by J. Devereaux, burnt down 1915, replacement burnt down 1926, replacement burnt down 1957, replaced 1958; PS 1910–38; quarry; rifle range 1909; Rom. Cath. C. (St Brigid's) 1904, enlarged 1923 and 1954, renovated 1989; RS 1894, station b. by Frederick Lemm, damaged 1914, closed 1967, demolished 1993; school 1894, new one 1901 on new site, additions 1907 and 1994; SD Adventist C., demolished; storm 1914; streets electric lit 1959; telephone 1892; TX 1911, automatic 1955; Unit. C. (orig. Meth.) 1925, removed from North Arm; pop. 88 (1901), 422 (1911), 248 (1933), 305 (1947), 331 (1954), 300 (1961), 243 (1971), 294 (1981), 349 (1986), 380 (1991), 424 (1996), 332 (2001), 557 (2006), 544 (2011).

Burrinjuck (*Co. Harden*) 35°00'S. 148°35'E., 35 km SW of Yass, on Murrumbidgee R.; Barren Jack till 1911; Angl. C. (St Saviour's) 1907; cemetery (children's); dam (works and village supply) 1908, 42 ft (12.8 m) high, on Barren Jack Ck; dam (Burrinjuck) b. 1907–28 by Lane and Peters, d. by Leslie Augustus Burton Wade, 247 ft (75.3 m) high, wall strengthened and raised 1938–57 by 13 ft (4 m), modified 1988, wall raised again 1994; floods 1916, 1922, 1925; PO 1907; power station (hydro-electric) 1928; PS 1907–56; quarry; Rom. Cath. C. (St Stanislaus') 1908, new one 1941; school 1907–70; telephone 1909; TX; pop. 768 (1911), 123 (1933), 509 (1947), 170 (1954), 108 (1961).

Burrowa (*Co. King*) see Boorowa.

Burroway (*Co. Ewenmar*) 32°04'S. 148°16'E., 20 km N. of Narromine; FB; TX 1966; pop. 77 (1911), 32 (1933), 364 (2011).

Burrumbelong Flat (*Co. Phillip*) 32°27'S. 150°04'E., 43 km SW of Merriwa, on Growee R.

Burrumbuttock (*Co. Hume*) 35°50'S. 146°48'E., 12 km SW of Walla Walla; settled by German immigrants, surveyed 1901; grazing till 1860s then grain farming; Bethel C. 1871, replaced 1926; bushfire 1905; cemetery 1886; electricity 1947; FB 1930; fire 1882; gale 1923; hailstorm 1941; Lutheran C. 1878, new one (Holy Cross) b. 1888 by Henry Menz, d. by E. Teppe, alterations and renovations 1913 by W.T. Thorne, and graveyard, incl. columbarium; measles epidemic 1923; PO 1886, new one 1914; RS 1892, station b. by Charles Hardy, closed 1975; schools: Burrumbuttock (East Burrumbuttock till 1929) 1917 and West Burrumbuttock (Burrumbuttock till 1900) 1883–1904; silo 1920; snow 1927; telegraph 1899; telephone 1908; TX 1914, automatic 1941; Unit. C. (orig. Union) b. 1923 by Gamble; whooping cough epidemic 1941; pop. 163 (1901), 205 (1911), 80 (1933), 69 (1947), 87 (1954), 81 (1961), *c.*100 (1981), *c.*150 (2002), 337 (2011).

Burrundulla (*Co. Wellington*) 32°38'S. 149°38'E., 5 km SE of Mudgee, on Oaky Ck; agric.; brewery estab. 1861 by Andrew Caxton, bought 1876 by George John Southward, later known as Sydney Brewery, acquired by E.W. Daley, bought 1891 by George Douglas Young and Robert Heather Ferrier, closed 1898; brick-kiln; butter factory (Burrundulla Dairy Co. Ltd) 1892; flour mills: George Cox (horse powered) 1840 (taken over by J. and W. Mears, converted to steam 1852, taken over 1858 by William Ellison and Edwin Mears, converted 1861 to brewery) and J.H. McCarthy & Sons; gale 1952; hailstorm 1873; school 1859–1954; storms 1916 and 1952; telephone 1915; Wes. Meth. C. b. 1857 by Stoddart and Cassimer, new one 1897, damaged and repaired 1952, demolished 1958; wineries: Burrundulla 1995 and Clearview Estate; pop. 208 (1911), 162 (1933), 79 (1947), 59 (1954), 85 (1961), 159 (2011).

Burta (*Co. Menindee*) 32°27'S. 141°04'E., 64 km SW of Broken Hill, on Burta Ck.

Burtenshaw (*Co. Rous*) 28°42'S. 153°05'E., 12 km SE of Kyogle, on Back Ck; telephone 1916.

Burtundy (*Co. Wentworth*) 33°44'S. 142°17'E., 45 km NE of Dareton, on Darling R.; sheep; PO 1918–59; telephone 1918; pop. 32 (1933).

Burwood (*Co. Northumberland*) see Merewether.

Busbys Flat (*Co. Richmond*) 29°02'S. 152°48'E., 31 km SW of Casino, on Sandy Ck; Angl. C. (St Alban the Martyr); sawmills: Busby's Sawmilling Co., Slade Bros 1912, Wood & Wood Ltd, in liquidation 1914; school 1955–65; telephone 1923; TX 1929–75; pop. 66 (1911), 106 (1933), 96 (1947), 135 (1954), 65 (1961).

Bushells Ridge (*Co. Northumberland*) see Doyalson.

Bushmans Lead (*Co. Ashburnham*) see Parkes.

Bushrangers Creek (*Co. Gordon*) 32°33'S. 148°54'E., 4 km W. of Wellington; pop. 58 (1947), 66 (1954), 55 (1961).

Bushy Hill (*Co. Beresford*) 36°13'S. 149°09'E., 3 km NE of Cooma; goldmining 1897–1929; mines: Birthday, Bushy Hill Pty Gold Mining Co., Coronation (orig. Blake's Claim); stamper battery (10 head) 1928.

Bushy Park (*Co. Clarence*) 29°47'S. 152°53'E., 12 km SW of Grafton, on Sandstone Ck.

Buss's (*Co. Cook*) see Woodford.

Buss's Platform (*Co. Cook*) see Woodford.

Bustle Hill (*Co. Camden*) see Minnamurra.

Butcher Boy Reef (*Co. Roxburgh*) 33°11'S. 149°44'E., 31 km NE of Bathurst; goldmining.

Butlers Crossing (*Co. Hunter*) 33°22'S. 150°57'E., 37 km W. of Ourimbah, on Macdonald R.; quarry.

Butlers Falls (*Co. Lincoln*) 32°18'S. 148°38'E., 7 km SE of Dubbo, on Macquarie R.; cemetery (Dubbo pioneer, 108 burials *c.*1840–1882 incl. 21 graves), damaged 1955 and 1956; floods 1955 and 1956; winery (Lazy River Estate) 1997.

Butmaroo (*Co. Murray*) 35°13'S. 149°31'E., 8 km NE of Bungendore; bridge 1879; RS 1901–71.

Buttaba (*Co. Northumberland*) see Arcadia Vale.

Buttabone (*Co. Gregory*) 31°20'S. 147°40'E., 76 km W. of Gulargambone, on Macquarie R.; pop. 69 (1911), 39 (1933), 51 (1954).

Buttai (*Co. Northumberland*) 32°50'S. 151°34'E., 8 km E. of Kurri Kurri, on Buttai Ck; boiling-down works (James Price) 1860; cemetery; FB; PO 1949–63; reservoir, 1,051,000 gal. (4,777.8 kl), b. 1880–82 by Thomas A. Bourke, d. by C.W. Darley; school (Stockrington till 1920) 1904–20 and 1939–48; telephone 1955; pop. 59 (1933), 92 (1947), 63 (1954).

Butterwick (*Co. Durham*) 32°39'S. 151°38'E., 12 km NE of Maitland; town gaz. 1881; cemetery, defunct; CH 1838 d. by Mortimer William Lewis; pop. 623 (1881).

Buxton (*Co. Camden*) 34°15'S. 150°32'E., 6 km NW of Bargo; formerly Bargo Brush; estab. 1883; orchards and poultry; Angl. C. (St John's) 1955; bushfire 1953; Community C. b. 1953–55 by Arthur Lewis Hick; FB; fire 1977; PO 1895–1993; RS 1893–1978; quarry; sawmill (Henry J. Cock); school 1897, additions 1917 by A. Hitchcoe, closed 1922, reopened 1949; streets electric lit 1948; telephone 1915; TX 1929; pop. 98 (1901), 71 (1911), 104 (1933), 144 (1947), 211 (1954), 247 (1961), 788 (1986), 1,013 (1991), 1,304 (1996), 1,475 (2001), 1,699 (2006), 1,627 (2011).

Byabarra (*Co. Macquarie*) 31°32'S. 152°32'E., 19 km NW of Kendall, on Thone R.; Greenburn till 1913; farming; Angl. C. (St James's) 1930; bushfire 1926; PO 1913, burnt down 1926; Presb. C. 1899; Rom. Cath. C. (Christ the King) 1960–70, later moved to Lake Cathie and reused; school 1920, additions 1933 by W. Condon, additions 2010, closed 2011, sold; telephone 1914; TX 1926; pop. 210 (1933), 237 (1947), 237 (1954), 188 (1961), 328 (2011).

Byamee (*Co. Parry*) 31°03'S. 150°49'E., 11 km NW of Tamworth, on Taugaratta Ck; PO 1927–58; school 1927–60; telephone 1927; TX 1929; pop. 70 (1947), 82 (1954), 66 (1961).

Byangum (*Co. Rous*) 28°22'S. 153°21'E., 5 km SW of Murwillumbah, on Tweed R.; estab.

1876; dairying and fruit; bridge (low-level timber beam) b. 1926 by C.V. Lawson, d. by Percy Allan, replaced 2005, over Tweed R.; cemetery 1892; flood 2017; PO 1891; punt across Tweed R.; quarry; sawmills: Garvey and Hines, and James White, later moved to Condong; school 1885–93 and 1904–18; telephone 1890; TX 1913; wharf b. 1890 by Thomas Clark; pop. 46 (1891), 158 (1911), 185 (1933), 126 (1947), 152 (1954), 92 (1961), 335 (2011).

Bye-Rock (*Co. Cowper*) see Byrock.

Bygalorie (*Co. Gipps*) 33°28'S. 146°47'E., 41 km E. of Lake Cargelligo; farming; PO 1925, burnt down 1943; RS 1917–75; telephone 1923; TX 1927; pop. 52 (1933).

Bygee (*Co. Cooper*) see Kamarah.

Bygoo (*Co. Bourke*) 34°14'S. 146°49'E., 16 km NW of Ardlethan; mining (tin); cemetery; mines: Big Bygoo Mining Co. Ltd and Dumbells Bygoo Mining Co. Ltd; pop. 90 (1911), 85 (1933).

Bylong (*Co. Phillip*) 32°25'S. 150°07'E., 38 km SW of Merriwa, on Bylong R.; farming and grazing; Angl. C. (St Stephen's) 1876, closed, and graveyard (44 graves 1881+); cheese factory estab. 1911 by W.H. McIllree, closed 1926, defunct; gale 1923; hailstorm 1915; PO 1880, new one (in rented premises) 1915; Rom. Cath. C. (Our Lady of the Sacred Heart) b. 1915 by Archer Bros, closed 2000, sold 2008, and graveyard (4 graves); telephone 1915; TX 1916, automatic 1984; pop. 269 (1911), 172 (1933), 198 (1947), 214 (1954), 191 (1961).

Bylong Flat (*Co. Phillip*) 32°31'S. 150°05'E., 33 km N. of Rylstone, on Growee R.

Bylong South (*Co. Phillip*) 32°30'S. 150°02'E., 33 km N. of Rylstone, on Burrumbolong Ck.

Byng (*Co. Bathurst*) 33°21'S. 149°15'E., 12 km NE of Millthorpe, on Sheep Station Ck; orig. Springfield, also known as Cornish Settlement, then Carangara; settled 1830 by William Thom and Cornish Methodists, village gaz. 1881; farming, grazing, mining (copper disc. 1849); cemetery (110 graves 1843–1962); mines: Carangara (estab. 1850 by John Glasson, closed *c.*1875) and Crows Nest; PO 1873; school (Cornish Settlement till 1868, then Carangara 1874–82) 1864–68, 1874–1926, 1957–58; smelter (copper) 1850; Unit. C. (orig. Bible Christ., then Wes. Meth., then Meth.) 1873 d. by Thomas Rowe, restoration 1934 and 1986–88; Wes. Meth. C. 1842, demolished, and graveyard (4 graves); pop. 181 (1901), 107 (1911), 80 (1933), 54 (1954), *c.*50 (1987).

Byrnedale (*Co. Hume*) 35°35'S. 146°25'E., 46 km N. of Corowa.

Byrnes Point (*Co. Richmond*) 28°53'S. 153°32'E., 2 km SW of Ballina, on Richmond R.; sugar-cane.

Byrock (*Co. Cowper*) 30°40'S. 146°24'E., 77 km SE of Bourke; laid out 1882, first land sale and village gaz. 1884 as Bye-Rock; grazing; Angl. C. (St John the Baptist) 1929; airfield; cemetery 1886; CH; drought 1929; gale (houses unroofed) 1918; PO 1884; pound (stock), closed 1910; Presb. C., renovated 1921; PS 1884, additions 1898 by A.J. O'Grady; railway coal stage 1900; railway engine shed, destroyed 1918; railway turntable, 50 ft (15.2 m), removed 1983; Rom. Cath. C. (St Brigid's) 1890, destroyed 1938; RS 1884, station b. by Alexander Hamilton Scouller, damaged 1938, closed 1989; school 1885 b. by Thomas Hull, extended 1889, new one b. 1915 by T.E. Quiggin, closed 2009; storm 1938; telegraph 1884; TX 1912–89; typhoid 1900; water supply augmentation 1986; pop. *c.*500 (1884), 249 (1891), 234 (1901), 211 (1911), 164 (1933), 139 (1947), 89 (1954), 96 (1961), 89 (2006).

Byron (*Co. Arrawatta*) 29°41'S. 151°06'E., 10 km N. of Inverell, on Macintyre R.; disc. *c.*1837 by Alexander Campbell, surveyed by Patrick Heron Henderson, town gaz. 1858, first lots sold 1859, never developed; flour mill and sawmill (Stephen Neate Dark) 1868; PO 1855–59; RS (6 km S.) 1902, station b. by J. Bromley and J.N. Holloway, closed 1971; pop. 85 (1911), 36 (1933).

Byron Bay (*Co. Rous*) 28°39'S. 153°37'E., 26 km N. of Ballina, on Byron Bay; (incl. Palm Valley and Watego's Beach subdivision 1961); orig. Cavanbah; surveyed 1884 by Fred

Poate, village gaz. 1885 as Cavvanba, first lots sold 1886, gaz. 1894 as Byron Bay, more lots auctioned 1910; orig. seaport (till 1954), timber, tropical fruit, mineral sand processing (rutile and zircon) 1935–74, fishing till 1954, whaling 1954–62, sugar-cane, dairying, pigs, surfboard manufacturing, tourism, alternative lifestyle centre; ambulance station 1955, sold 2012; Angl. C. 1898, inundated and damaged 1940, reused 1961, new one (St Paul's) b. 1961 by Alex. Roberts Constructions Pty Ltd, d. by Frederick Johnson Board; Assemblies of God C. (Eastgate); beach erosion (Clarkes Beach) 2019; biscuit factory (Byron Bay Cookies); breakwater 1889; breweries: Fixation Brewing Pty Ltd 2015 and Stone & Wood Brewing Co., founded 2008 by Brad Rogers, Jamie Cook and Ross Jurisich; brickworks (Glasgow & Co.) 1907; butter factory (North Coast Fresh Food & Cold Storage Co-op. Co. Ltd) 1895, bacon curing 1896, factory extended 1897, company became North Coast Co-op. Ltd in 1904, factory demolished 1925, became Norco Co-op. Ltd, new one b. 1926 by John Dunton, butter manufacturing ceased 1972, factory closed 1975, reused; carriage-works (J.W. Banner); casein factory estab. 1914 by S.M. Cottee; cemetery (1,060 graves) 1890, incl. lawn cemetery and columbarium; CH (incl. police station) b. 1892 by P. Flaherty, closed and sold to G.D. Wylie, then sold to F. Baker, moved 1928 to Murwillumbah and reused, new one b. 1921 by Arthur Beckinsale, new court-house 1991; Church of Christ; cordial factories: W.E. Balzer (b. 1904 by Jim Wilson, sold 1911 to George Bryant) and F.L. Playford; Christ. City C.; creamery (P. Buckley); cyclone 1904; diphtheria 1952; electricity (from Mullumbimby hydro-electric plant) 1926; FB (station b. 1952, new one 1978); fires 1928, 1936, 1949; floods 1921 and 2020; gale 1928; hospital b. 1952 by J. Henderson, d. by Val Miller, major redevelopment 1994–96, closed 2016; jetty b. 1886–89, 1,320 ft (402.3 m), alterations and repairs 1897 by G. Lawson, extended 1912 by F.J. Oakes, demolished 1948, new one b. 1925–29, damaged 1954 but not repaired and then used only for whaling, damaged 1963, demolished 1972, remains removed 1989; lighthouse (Cape Byron) b. 1901 of concrete by Mitchell and King, d. by Charles A. Harding, 74 ft (22.6 m), light upgraded 1914 and 1922, converted from kerosene to electricity 1959, automated 1986, demanned 1989; meat works (Byron Bay Co-op. Canning & Freezing Co. Ltd) 1913, leased 1916 to W. Reynolds & Son Pty Ltd, closed 1919, reopened 1920 by Kensington Preserving Co. Pty Ltd, closed 1921, reopened 1922, sold to Norco, leased to A.W. Anderson, reopened 1930, taken over 1968 by F.J. Walker, closed 1983; Meth. C. 1911; mineral sand processing plant (Zircon-Rutile Ltd) 1935, fire 1957, rebuilt and improved, closed and removed 1977; PO 1888, new one b. 1897, repairs 1905 by Gostelow, additions and alterations 1907 by G. Brooke; poultry processing plant (Sunnybrand Chickens Pty Ltd 1972, bought 2011 by Inghams Enterprises, closed 2014); Presb. C. b. 1904 by M'Intosh, new one (John Knox's) 1969; quarry; railway coal stage b. 1893 by W. Mitchell; railway turntable 1904, 50 ft (15.2 m); 2 reservoirs (incl. one b. 1950 by Chesterfield & Jenkins Queensland Pty Ltd); rifle range; Rom. Cath. C. (St Finbar's) b. 1901 by Wilson, d. by W.J. Grainger, extended 1922, new one; RS 1894, station b. by William Mitchell, closed 2004, railway partly reused 2017; sawmills: Byron Bay Saw Milling Co., Carlton and Richardson, Duncan and Campbell 1905 (man killed 1905), John E. Glasgow (moved 1897 to Mullumbimby), William Thomas 1904 (sold 1905 to Frank Russell and T.H. Booker); schools: primary 1892 b. by John W. Sheppard, additions 1914 by Alfred Ede, additions 1923 by F. Bolton, additions 1961, and HS 1987; SD Adventist C.; storms 1889, 1911, 1932, 1936, 1940, 1952, 1954, 1963; streets electric lit 1926; sugar mill, failed; telegraph 1888, new office b. 1897; TX 1910, automatic 1969; Unit. C.; water supply 1938, augmentation 1955 and 1985; whaling station (Byron Whaling Co., founded by A.W. Anderson) 1954–62; pop. 380 (1901), 1,222 (1911), 2,659 (1924), 1,717 (1933), 1,750 (1938), 2,036 (1947), 2,001 (1954), 2,172 (1961), 2,315 (1966), 2,320 (1971), 2,525 (1976), 3,187 (1981), 3,730 (1986), 5,001 (1991), 6,130 (1996), 7,032 (2001), 4,981 (2006), 4,957 (2011).

Byron Creek (*Co. Rous*) see Bangalow.

Byron Hills (*Co. Rous*) see Suffolk Park.

Byron View (*Co. Rous*) 28°40'S. 153°34'E., 5 km E. of Bangalow.

Byrrill (*Co. Rous*) 28°27'S. 153°17'E., 17 km SW of Murwillumbah, on Tweed R.

Byrrill Creek (*Co. Rous*) 28°27'S. 153°12'E., 23 km SW of Murwillumbah, on Byrrill Ck; bridge 1928, new one 1944, destroyed 1956, over Byrrill Ck; bushfires 1926 and 1936; floods 1933 and 1956; sawmill b. 1956 by Ken and John McNamara, sold 1961 to Bill Choat, dismantled and removed; school 1957–62; pop. 64 (1933), 71 (1947), 73 (1954), 219 (2011).

Bywannah (*Co. Narromine*) 32°16'S. 147°53'E., 27 km S. of Trangie.

Bywong (*Co. Murray*) 35°10'S. 149°20'E., 15 km NW of Bungendore, on Brooks Ck; surveyed 1895 by John Fowell Camden Goodridge; mining (gold disc. 1894 by Thomas Alchin) 1894–1964, grazing, honey; mines: Alchin and Lowe *c.*1895 (dynamite magazine exploded 1897), Cartwright's, Clancy and East, Coolgardie (Giles) *c.*1895, Erenshaw and Whalan *c.*1895, Government Aid, Johnston's *c.*1895, Little Wonder 1894, Lone Hand (McCabe) *c.*1897, Long Corner, Mac's 1866, Millyn's *c.*1895, Mystery, New Year's Gift, Prospector's Shaft, Robbins and Cartwright *c.*1895, Tunnel, Victory, Walsh's *c.*1890, Williams's; PO 1895, burnt down 1936; school 1895–1906; snow 1898; stamper batteries: Seymour's 1904 and Shepherd's 1942; wineries: Affleck 1976, Brooks Creek 1973, Koonaburra, Milimani Estate; pop. 51 (1933), 64 (1954), 74 (1961), 784 (2006), 1,195 (2011).

C

Cabarita Beach (*Co. Rous*) see Bogangar.

Cabbage Tree (*Co. Camden*) see Fairy Meadow.

Cabbage Tree Island (*Co. Gloucester*) 31°57'S. 152°35'E., 1 km N. of Old Bar, in Manning R.

Cabbage Tree Island (*Co. Rous*) 28°59'S. 153°27'E., 13 km NE of Woodburn, in Richmond R.; Aboriginal mission; flood 1945; PO 1960–71; school (Aboriginal till 1968) 1952; telephone 1960; Union C. 1960; pop. 95 (1933), 99 (1947), 137 (1954), 98 (2011).

Cable's Siding (*Co. Camden*) see Penrose.

Cabramurra (*Co. Selwyn*) 35°56'S. 148°22'E., 38 km SE of Tumbarumba; orig. Ghent's Camp and Saddle Camp, then Cubmurra; surveyed by Ghent; estab. 1954 as temporary construction camp for Snowy Mountains Hydro-Electric Scheme; airfield; PO 1953; PS 1959–66; school 1955; telephone 1953; TX 1957; pop. 424 (1954), 934 (1961), 234 (1991), 203 (1996), 364 (2011).

Caddigat (*Co. Wallace*) 36°02'S. 148°54'E., 30 km NW of Cooma; grazing; bushfire 1951; creamery 1898; PO 1927; school 1882–1904.

Cadgee (*Co. Dampier*) 36°09'S. 149°55'E., 19 km W. of Dalmeny, on Gulph Ck; farming; Angl. C. (Christ) 1913–46, sold and reused; bridge (Stony Crossing Bridge) 1936, over Tuross R.; butter factory (Cadgee Co-op. Butter Co.) 1908–16; flood 2016; PO 1927–46; telephone 1915; pop. 33 (1933).

Cadia (*Co. Bathurst*) 33°27'S. 149°00'E., 16 km W. of Millthorpe, on Cadiangullong Ck; estab. 1865 by the Cadiangullong Mining Co., abandoned 1945; mining (gold disc. 1851, copper disc. 1851 by Samuel Stutchbury, iron 1918+), forestry, grazing; cemetery (111 burials 1864–1927), relocated 1998; earth tremors 2011, 2012, 2017; fire 1927; Meth. C. 1914; mines: Cadia (Oakey Creek till 1861, then Cadiangullong or Old Cadia or White Engine, incl. Cornish engine house with beam engine 1865, re-roofed 1993, boiler house demolished) 1861–67, Chilcott 1914–18 and 1942–43, East Cadia 1914–18 and 1942–43, Iron Duke (Hoskins Iron & Steel Co. Ltd then Aust. Iron & Steel Ltd) 1918–28 and 1941–45, Little Cadia or Cadia Extended or Canobolas Copper Gully 1851–*c.*1908, New Cadia or Big Cadia or Iron Duke Copper (Cadia Copper Mining Co.) 1882–98, Newcrest Mining Ltd 1998, Ridgeway, West Cadia 1861; PO 1864–1935; pound (stock) 1867; PS 1923–29; quarry, accident (9 killed) 1921, closed 1945; railway (iron ore) from Spring Hill 1919–29 (G. & C. Hoskins Ltd) and 1941–45 (Aust. Iron & Steel Ltd); school 1865–1930 and 1943–45; smelters (copper) 1862 and 1912; Rom. Cath. C. (St Brigid's), closed, dismantled and moved to Spring Hill; telephone 1907; TX 1915; Union C.; Wes. Meth. C. 1868, demolished 1914; pop. *c.*250 (1863), *c.*500 (1865), *c.*600 (1866), *c.*150 (1870), 72 (1901), 153 (1911), *c.*300 (1925), 137 (1933).

Cadow (*Co. Gipps*) 33°16'S. 147°29'E., 37 km SE of Condobolin, on Lachlan R.

Caergurle (*Co. Durham*) see Allynbrook.

Caerleon (*Co. Wellington*) 32°34'S. 149°33'E., 4 km NW of Mudgee.

Caffreys Flat (*Co. Macquarie*) 31°48'S. 152°04'E., 30 km W. of Wingham, on Nowendoc R.; school 1960–63; telephone 1957; TX 1958.

Caidmurra (*Co. Benarba*) 29°13'S. 148°46'E., 35 km SW of Mungindi; PO 1861–62.

Cainbil (*Co. Bligh*) 32°05'S. 149°39'E., 25 km E. of Dunedoo, on Cainbil Ck; bridge (Dennis McGrath Bridge) over Cainbil Ck; quarry (abandoned); Rom. Cath. C., dilapidated by 1903, demolished; telephone 1930; TX 1930; pop. 22 (1933).

Cajildry (*Co. Oxley*) 32°00'S. 147°20'E., 48 km S. of Nyngan, on Bogan R.

Calabash (*Co. Monteagle*) 34°19'S. 148°31'E., 19 km E. of Young; bushfires 1900 and 1905; creamery (Young Butter & Dairy Products Co-op. Factory Co. Ltd) 1894; heatwave 1905.

Calala (*Co. Parry*)
see Tamworth (*Co. Inglis*).

Calamia (*Co. Clarence*) 29°51'S. 153°07'E., 23 km SE of South Grafton; pop. 256 (2006).

Calare (*Co. Forbes*) see Conimbla.

Calare (*Co. Wellington*) see Orange.

Calarie (*Co. Ashburnham*) 33°20'S. 148°01'E., 5 km N. of Forbes; Lachlan Gold Mine till 1905; village gaz. 1904; goldmining 1896–1909, 1916, 1958–59; mines: Bald Hill (W.B. Hodgetts) 1927, Britannia (incl. Trojan shaft) 1861–1909, Dead Dog, Iakwa (Iakwa Pty Ltd) *c.*1900, Lachlan (Sinclair's) 1896–1909 and 1958–59, Nil Desperandum (Morris) <1898–1905, North Lachlan (North Lachlan Gold Mining Co. 1901–7 and Hauraki Gold Mining Co. 1930–33); PO 1904; quarry; Rom. Cath. C., damaged, dismantled, moved 1908 to Gunning Gap and reused; school (North Forbes till 1943) 1901–69, reused; telephone 1925; pop. 160 (1911), 167 (1933), 109 (1947), 100 (1954), 87 (1961), 278 (2011).

Calderwood (*Co. Camden*) 34°33'S. 150°42'E., 9 km SW of Dapto, on Mount Marshall Ck; bridge (Manson's Bridge) b. 1882 by Joseph Atkinson, dismantled and replaced 1950, over Macquarie Rivulet; FB; pop. 175 (2011).

Caldwell (*Co. Cadell*) 35°38'S. 144°30'E., 34 km E. of Barham; village gaz. 1928; PO 1926–67; RS (Victorian railway); school 1957–87; telephone 1927; TX 1928; pop. 54 (1933), 85 (1961).

Caledonia (*Co. Lincoln*) 32°01'S. 148°37'E., 25 km N. of Dubbo.

Caledonia (*Co. Northumberland*)
see Cessnock.

Caledonian (*Co. Northumberland*)
see Barnsley.

Calga (*Co. Northumberland*) 33°26'S. 151°13'E., 12 km W. of Gosford, on Christy Gully; bottled water plant (Mangrove Mountain Springs Pty Ltd); bushfire 1951; quarry; telephone 1940; TX 1951; pop. 24 (1933), 78 (1947), 93 (1954), 71 (1961), 300 (2006).

Califat (*Co. Wynyard*) 35°14'S. 148°05'E., 8 km N. of Adelong, on Bunnabuckbuck Ck; quarry; RS 1903, station b. by F.G. Filmer, closed 1975, removed 1984.

California Flats (*Co. Cowley*) 35°14'S. 148°46'E., 37 km SW of Murrumbateman.

Calimo (*Co. Townsend*) 35°25'S. 144°34'E., 38 km W. of Deniliquin, on Colligen Ck; TX (automatic); pop. 134 (1911), 144 (2006), 232 (2011).

Calimpa (*Co. Courallie*) 29°22'S. 150°09'E., 31 km E. of Moree; RS 1932–74; pop. 23 (1933).

Callaba (*Co. Georgiana*) see Glengarry.

Callaghan (*Co. Northumberland*)
see Birmingham Gardens,
Jesmond, Wallsend, Waratah.

Callaghans Creek (*Co. Macquarie*) 31°51'S. 152°04'E., 20 km NE of Gloucester, on Manning R.

Callaghans Creek (*Co. Macquarie*)
see also Cundle Flat.

Cal Lal (*Co. Tara*) 34°03'S. 141°06'E., 75 km W. of Wentworth, on Murray R.; grazing; cemetery (24 graves); CH 1900–38, reused, abandoned; PO 1895, new one b. 1920, derelict; PS 1900, new one b. 1909 by James W. Duncan, closed 1938, reused, abandoned; telegraph 1895; telephone 1899; TX 1921; pop. 63 (1901), 96 (1911), 76 (1933).

Callala (*Co. St Vincent*) see Callala Bay.

Callala Bay (*Co. St Vincent*) 35°00'S. 150°43'E., 3 km E. of Callala Beach, on Hare Bay; Angl.

C. (St Mark's); FB; PO 1956; school (Callala) 2000; sewerage 1981, augmentation 1999; telephone 1955; TX 1955, automatic 1977; pop. 10 (1961), 95 (1971), 201 (1976), 623 (1981), 947 (1986), 1,379 (1991), 1,741 (1996), 2,340 (2001), 2,717 (2006), 3,001 (2011).

Callala Beach (*Co. St Vincent*) 35°01'S. 150°42'E., 4 km NE of Huskisson, on Jervis Bay; orig. Honeysuckle Beach; FB; PO 1981; pop. 19 (1961), 767 (2006), 774 (2011).

Calleen (*Co. Gipps*) 33°47'S. 147°06'E., 18 km NW of West Wyalong; village gaz. 1918; farming; PO 1927; RS 1917–75; school 1957–60; silo 1922; telephone 1926; TX 1930; pop. 200 (1933), 55 (1947), 50 (1961).

Callemondah (*Co. Beresford*) 35°55'S. 148°57'E., 39 km N. of Cooma; telephone 1927; TX 1930.

Calliope (*Co. Clarence*) 29°37'S. 153°04'E., 16 km NE of Grafton, on Calligans Ck; Bapt. C. 1903, closed, sold 1999, 2013, 2019, reused; creamery (Pioneer Dairy Co.), closed 1909; hailstorms 1925 and 1953; school 1890, new one b. 1892 by William Jones, closed 1983; pop. 131 (1911), 119 (1961).

Callo (*Co. Dampier*) 36°37'S. 150°02'E., 18 km E. of Bega, on Wapengo Lake.

Caloma (*Co. Narromine*) 32°33'S. 148°22'E., 25 km NE of Peak Hill.

Caloola (*Co. Bathurst*) 33°37'S. 149°26'E., 19 km SE of Blayney, on McGeorges Ck; village gaz. 1871 as Egan, largely defunct; mining (gold disc. 1895), farming, grazing; copper mine (Rise and Shine) 1906; flour and woollen mill (Caleula) o. 1845 by Henry Herman Kater, woollen mill ceased 1852, flour mill ceased 1871; goldmine (Caloola Creek) 1895–1909, 1912–14, 1917; PO 1858–1931; quarries (marble): Caloola and Commonwealth; school 1877 b. by James Wiburd, closed 1891, rebuilt; tannery (L. Byrnes), closed 1860; Union C. 1865, and graveyard (4 graves); pop. 64 (1901), 117 (1911), 60 (1933), 103 (1947), 59 (1954), 327 (2006).

Caloola (*Co. Pottinger*) 30°39'S. 149°54'E., 14 km NW of Boggabri.

Caloona (*Co. Benarba*) 28°53'S. 149°15'E., 28 km NE of Mungindi.

Calorafield (*Co. Cooper*) 34°27'S. 146°13'E., 24 km SE of Griffith; school 1957–87.

Calwalla (*Co. Camden*) 34°34'S. 150°29'E., 10 km E. of Moss Vale; village gaz. 1932; airfield (World War II); dam (Wingecarribee) 1974, 66 ft (20 m) high; RS 1932–76.

Cambalong (*Co. Wellesley*) 36°53'S. 149°07'E., 12 km W. of Bombala, on Bombala R.; pop. 55 (1901), 25 (1933).

Cambawongla (*Co. Rous*) see Cawongla.

Camberwell (*Co. Durham*) 32°29'S. 151°05'E., 12 km NW of Singleton, on Glennies Ck; grazing, agric., dairying, coalmining; planned 1840, village gaz. 1880; Angl. C. (St Clement's) b. 1842–51, porch added 1908 by R.E. Moore and O.G. Morton, vestry replaced 1918, church re-roofed and restored 1964–68, fire 2008, closed 2013, and graveyard (225 graves 1860+), incl. columbarium; bridge 1841, destroyed, replacement b. 1884 by W. Burnett, new one 1957, over Glennies Ck; mine (open-cut) o. 1991 by Camberwell Coal Pty Ltd, bought 2015 by Bloomfield Group; PO 1860; Presb. C., damaged 1928, defunct, and graveyard; Rom. Cath. C. 1869; school (Falbrook till 1892) 1853, new building b. 1883 by D. Gardiner, closed 1958, demolished; storms 1898 and 1928; telephone 1914; toll-gate; TX; pop. *c.*100 (1866), 81 (1891), 151 (1901), 115 (1911), 102 (1933), 125 (1947), 104 (1954), 106 (1961), 36 (1977), 376 (2006), 181 (2011).

Camberwell (*Co. Durham*) see also Ravensworth.

Camberwell Railway Station (*Co. Durham*) see Ravensworth.

Cambewarra (*Co. Camden*) 34°49'S. 150°34'E., 7 km NW of Nowra, on Good Dog Ck; (incl. Cambewarra Village); formerly known as Good Dog and Bullamiah; founded 1859; oranges, maize, tanning, dairying; bushfires 1939 and 1968; cheese factory (Cambewarra & Meroo Dairy Co.) estab. 1889 by Thomas Binks, sen., acquired 1899 by Foley Bros Ltd, made butter instead from 1902, closed 1906; cemetery (409 graves 1874+) 1874;

3 dams 1893; FB; flood 1959; milk factory (Cambewarra Dairy Co. Ltd) 1889–1905; PO 1866; reservoir 1983; school 1859, new building b. 1884 by A. Mathie, new school 1989, additions 2010; storm 1959; tanneries: Johann Schultz, Robert Shepherd 1884, Thomas Shepherd 1870; telegraph 1884; TX 1928; Union C. 1866, new one b. 1900 by Kenneth M'Kenzie, renovated 1964; pop. 517 (1891), 342 (1901), 402 (1911), 154 (1933), 158 (1947), 167 (1954), 186 (1961), 349 (1981), 501 (1986), 696 (1991), 984 (1996), 1,057 (2001), 1,229 (2011).

Cambewarra Village (*Co. Camden*) see Cambewarra.

Cambewarra West (*Co. Camden*) 34°49'S. 150°31'E., 9 km NW of Nowra, on Tapitallee Ck; bushfire 1928; butter factory (West Cambewarra Dairy Co.) 1889; cemetery (burials 1874+); PO 1880–1909; school 1880, new one b. 1889, closed 1927; Union C. b. 1888 by Charles Sinclair, d. by W.H. Wood.

Camboon (*Co. Phillip*) 32°43'S. 149°58'E., 11 km N. of Rylstone; school 1881, repairs 1891 by J. Miller, closed 1908; pop. 61 (1933).

Cambra (*Co. Gloucester*) 32°27'S. 151°50'E., 9 km SE of Dungog, on Nolans Ck; Meth. C. 1958; school 1957–64.

Cambridge Hills Estate (*Co. Northumberland*) see Elermore Vale.

Camden (*Co. Camden*) 34°03'S. 150°42'E., 41 km NW of Wollongong, on Nepean R.; (incl. Camden Park, East Camden, Grasmere formerly Grassmere, South Camden formerly Benkennie); orig. The Cowpastures; settled by James Macarthur, surveyed 1836, laid out 1840 by Murray, founded and first lots sold 1840, munic. proc. 1889; dairying 1826+, wool till 1860s, wheat till 1863, maize, oats, barley, rye, potatoes, brandy, wine, butter, cheese, bacon, now farming, orchards, vineyards, cattle, pigs, poultry; abattoir (Lakeman's); agric. institute (Elizabeth Macarthur); ambulance station 1943, new one 1957; Angl. C. (St John the Evangelist) b. 1840–49 by Richard Basden, John Le Fevre and Johnathan Wheeler, d. by John Cunningham and Mortimer William Lewis, extensions 1872 d. by Edmund Thomas Blacket and Sir George Gilbert Scott, re-roofed 1872, 1901, 1929, restoration d. by Fisher and Jackson, and graveyard (901 graves); Assemblies of God C. (Christ.); bacon and butter factory (Camden Park Estate) 1895, reused 1913 as rabbit freezing works; Bapt. C. 1969; brickworks: Ephraim Cross, Richard Cross (taken over by Walter F. Peters), John Lacey; bridges over Nepean R.: Cowpasture Bridge (d. and b. 1827 by Wainwright, strengthened 1835, rebuilt 1861 and named Cowper Bridge), new one (also with railway tracks) 1901, consisting of steel girder spans (supplied by Pope, Maher & Co.) on concrete piers and timber beam spans totalling 403 ft (122.8 m), destroyed 1975, replaced 1976 and Macarthur Bridge (concrete) 1973; bushfire 1895; caterpillar infestations 1894 and 1903; carriage-works (Poole & Sons); cemetery 1898; CH (incl. cells) b. 1855–57 by Edward Mumford, d. by William Weaver, additions 1885 by Joseph Packenham, extended; cordial factories: Druitt's, F.E. and P. Fox, P. Fuchs & Son; droughts 1839, 1849, 1907, 1936; electricity 1927; FB: Camden 1900 (station b. 1902, new one b. 1917 by S. Box, d. by William Hull McNiven) and Grasmere (station b. 2014); fires 1888, 1892, 1893, 1905, 1906, 1907, 1933; floods 1806, 1816–17, 1835, 1857, 1859, 1860, 1861, 1867, 1873, 1890, 1891, 1892, 1893, 1898, 1899, 1900, 1913, 1919, 1929, 1934, 1949, 1950, 1961, 1964, 1975, 1978; fires 1878, 1893, 1905, 1906, 1907, 1931, 1933; flour mills: Thomas's and Joseph Thompson & Sons 1843, converted 1847 from water power to steam, additions 1848, inundated 1860, reused, new one b. 1860 on higher ground for Henry Thompson by Minnells and Furners, closed 1863, reused 1885; gasworks (Camden Gas Co. Ltd) 1912; heatwave 1904; hospital (cottage) 1899, new one b. 1902 by James Downie Rankin, additions 1916, 1917, 1919, 1934, additions and alterations 1939 by Robert Daniel Quiggin, maternity unit 1951, enlarged 1971, additions 1990 and 2010; lock-up b. 1850 by John Le Fevre, replacement b. 1859–61, additions and alterations 1900 by John Bruce; measles epidemic 1912; milk factory (Camden Vale Milk Co. Ltd) 1926, burnt down 1926, rebuilt 1927; PO: Camden 1841 (new one b. 1882 by J. and W. Packenham, additions and alterations 1898 by G.W. Cleveland, alterations 1906 by O.E. Priest) and East Camden 1960; pound (stock) 1844; Presb. C. (St Andrew's) b. 1850–53, closed 1882, new one 1938; Prim. Meth. C. 1859, reused, demolished 1981; PS b. 1878 by Walter Charles Furner, additions and alterations 1900 by John Bruce, additions, alterations and repairs 1910 by W. Peters, restored and modernised 1981, closed 2011; reservoir; Rom. Cath. C. (St Paul's), reused, demolished 1901, second one b. 1859 by J.B. Elphinstone, d. by William Munro, third one b. 1987, and graveyard; RS 1882, trains replaced trams in 1901, closed 1963; sale-yards estab. 1940 by William Inglis & Son Pty Ltd; sawmills: P. Peters and Arthur Rideout (man killed 1894); schools: Camden 1849 (new one b. 1851, additions 1876 and 1878, closed 1902, building reused 1909, new one b. 1909 by Richard Hindes and Henry Farindon, new one b. 1956 by A.F. Little Pty Ltd, d. by Cobden Parkes), Camden HS (old site, new one at Cawdor) 1956 d. by Cobden Parkes, additions 1966 and 1972, Camden Park 1879–87, South Camden 1961; sewerage 1939; shoe factory (Fostars Shoes Pty Ltd) 1948; streets gas lit 1912, electric lit 1932; telegraph 1877, new office b. 1882 by J. and W. Packenham, alterations 1906 by O.E. Priest; telephone 1905; TX 1910, replaced; Unit. C. (orig. Wes. Meth.) b. 1889 by George Furner; waterworks 1899; weirs on Nepean R.: Camden and Thurns; Wes. Meth. C. 1844, new one 1858; winery (Kirkham Estate) estab. by Stan Aliprandi; woollen mill estab. 1883 (in old flour mill) by F.H. Burne and James McKenzie, later joined by C.A. Thompson, bought by C.T. Whiteman and Frank Barter, became J.H. Gale & Co. in 1895, burnt down 1899; pop. 242 (1847), 342 (1851), 458 (1856), 685 (1861), *c.*700 (1866), 604 (1871), 505 (1881), 342 (1889), 1,303 (1891), *c.*1,550 (1895), 1,907 (1901), 1,314 (1911), 2,394 (1933), 2,935 (1947), 4,934 (1954), 4,080 (1961), 3,427 (1966), 5,357 (1971), 7,644 (1976), 9,000 (1981).

Camden (*Co. Camden*) see also Cawdor.

Camden Forest (*Co. Goulburn*) see Holbrook.

Camden Haven (*Co. Macquarie*) see Kendall, Kew and Rossglen.

Camden Haven Punt (*Co. Macquarie*) see Rossglen.

Camden Haven River (*Co. Macquarie*) see Rossglen.

Camden Head (*Co. Macquarie*) 31°39'S. 152°50'E., 1 km E. of North Haven, on Gogleys Lagoon; breakwater, rebuilt 1968; pilot station, reused; reservoir.

Camden Park (*Co. Camden*) see Camden.

Camel Yard Corner (*Co. Irrara*) 29°46'S. 144°43'E., 123 km W. of Bourke.

Cameron Corner (*Co. Poole*) 29°00'S. 141°00'E., 332 km N. of Broken Hill.

Cameron Park (*Co. Northumberland*) 32°55'S. 151°36'E., 3 km E. of West Wallsend, on Cocked Hat Ck; Estelville till 2001; surveyed and subdivided 1905; brewery (Bluetongue Brewery Pty Ltd) estab. 2003 by Philip Hele, Bruce Tyrrell, Ian Burford and Paul Hannan, sold 2007 to Pacific Beverages Ltd; colliery; Foursquare Gospel C. (Indonesian); tramway (steam) to Newcastle 1887; pop. 157 (1911), 189 (1933), 161 (1947), 3,720 (2006), 5,166 (2011).

Camerons Camp (*Co. Boyd*) 34°51'S. 145°28'E., 68 km SE of Hay.

Camerons Camp (*Co. Macquarie*) 31°12'S. 152°24'E., 42 km NW of Wauchope.

Camira Creek (*Co. Richmond*) 29°15'S. 152°58'E., 32 km NW of Maclean; farming; Angl. C. (St Andrew's) 1914; PO 1909; RS 1905, station b. by H.W. Owen, closed 1974; sawmill (Ventura) estab. 1921 by A.C. Cordner; school 1957–69; telephone 1919; TX 1933; pop. 74 (1911), 88 (1933), 54 (1947), 88 (1954), 60 (1961).

Campbells Corner (*Co. Bathurst*) 33°20'S. 149°03'E., 6 km SW of Orange, on Brandy Ck; wineries: Brangayne of Orange (estab. 1994 by Hoskins), Ross Hill Wines (estab.

1994 by Peter and Terri Robson), Word of Mouth Wines (Peter Gibson).

Campbells Creek (*Co. Wellington*) 32°52'S. 149°42'E., 26 km W. of Kandos, on Hundys Ck; goldmining (alluvial); PO 1859–61; pop. 82 (1911), 99 (1933), 79 (1947), 60 (1954).

Campbellsfields (*Co. Monteagle*) 34°27'S. 148°37'E., 10 km W. of Boorowa, on Yellow Waterhole Ck.

Campbells Hill (*Co. Northumberland*) see Rutherford.

Campbells River (*Co. Bathurst*) 33°35'S. 149°39'E., 20 km S. of Bathurst, on Campbells R.; Wes. Meth. C. 1850.

Campbells River (*Co. Bathurst*) see also The Lagoon.

Campbells River (*Co. Georgiana*) 33°53'S. 149°38'E., 30 km SW of Oberon, on Walbrook Ck; pop. 21 (1933).

Campbells River (*Co. Georgiana*) see also Walbrook.

Campfield (*Co. Georgiana*) 33°47'S. 149°17'E., 28 km S. of Blayney, on Rocky Bridge Ck; school 1903–4.

Campfire (*Co. Vernon*) 31°09'S. 151°23'E., 28 km SW of Walcha, on Campfire Ck; gold (disc. 1895 by John Mullins); mine (incl. 5 head stamper battery); pop. 24 (1933), 121 (2006).

Campo Santo (*Co. Darling*) 30°22'S. 150°28'E., 14 km W. of Barraba; pop. 51 (1933).

Campsie (*Co. Durham*) see Trevallyn.

Campvale (*Co. Gloucester*) 32°46'S. 151°51'E., 4 km SW of Medowie, on Grahamstown Lake; sand mining; bushfire 2018; swamp drainage works completed 1911 by Pepper and Moy.

Cams Wharf (*Co. Northumberland*) see Nords Wharf.

Camurra (*Co. Courallie*) 29°24'S. 149°55'E., 10 km NE of Moree; bridge (Boolooroo Bridge) b. 1886 by John Gray, replaced 1920, over Gwydir R.; railway bridge (steel truss) 1913, over Gwydir R.; RS 1913–74.

Camyr Allyn (*Co. Durham*) 32°25'S. 151°33'E., 19 km W. of Dungog, on Allyn R.; grazing, dairying, agric., wine; bridge, destroyed 1931, replacement b. 1933 by R.P. Sylvester, 135 ft (41.1 m), over Allyn R.; quarry; tobacco factory (James Boydell); winery (John and Judy Evers) 1999; pop. 29 (1933).

Canadian Lead (*Co. Phillip*) 32°25'S. 149°35'E., 8 km SE of Gulgong; defunct; mining (gold disc. 1871) and farming; Cong. C.; mines: Gulgong Reef (Dietz and Trinity Reef Co.) 1866–76, 1883–84, 1889, Louisiana Reef 1875 and 1883; Magpie (incl. Springfield and Rapps Gully Leads) 1871–76, Three Mile Lead (Gulgong Alluvial Goldfields Co.) 1871 and 1891; PO 1872–1960, ruined; school 1879, additions and repairs 1883 by S. Thurgood, new one b. 1915, closed 1923, building moved 1930 to Eurunderee; telephone 1914; tornado 1901; TX 1936; pop. 175 (1911).

Canarca (*Co. Denison*) 35°50'S. 146°01'E., 13 km N. of Mulwala; telephone 1917.

Canbelego (*Co. Robinson*) 31°33'S. 146°19'E., 47 km E. of Cobar; Mount Boppy Mine till 1901; surveyed 1900, village gaz. 1902, thrived 1901–9; formerly mining (gold disc. 1896 by Thomas Reid) 1901+; Angl. C. (Good Shepherd) 1909; cemetery (135 graves); CH b. 1904 by Gudgeon and Clifton; cyanide plant; gale (damaged most of town) 1925; Meth. C. b. 1910 by C. Buttenshaw; mines: Baker's Claim or The Snakes, Birthday, Boppy Boulder, East Mount Boppy or Hogan's, Hardwick's, Hoffnung's Shaft, Jack Lock, Mount Boppy 1898–1923, Newhaven, North Mount Boppy, Reid and Ranken's, South Mount Boppy, Wealth of Nations, West Boppy; morgue, destroyed 1925; PO 1901, new one b. 1910 by J.T.J. Viant, repairs 1935 by H. Janes, reused; Presb. C. 1901; PS 1901–57; rifle range 1911; Rom. Cath. C. (St Philip's) 1907, destroyed 1925; sawmill; school 1901–69; stamper batteries: 40 head 1901 and 20 head erected 1904 by Robert Gregory; telephone 1905; TX 1912, automatic 1987; pop. 179 (1901), *c.*900 (1904), *c.*2,000 (1907), *c.*3,000 (1908), 1,671 (1911), 189 (1933), 115 (1947), 114 (1954), 143 (1961), *c.*20 (1999).

Candelo (*Co. Auckland*) 36°46'S. 149°42'E., 17 km SW of Bega, on Candelo Ck; surveyed

1860, town gaz. and first lots sold 1865, further sale 1874; dairying, butter, cheese; airfield; Angl. C. (Holy Trinity) 1888, damaged 1898, new one (St Peter's) b. 1909 by J. Hines; bridge b. 1879 by M.F. Smith, new one b. 1921 by J.A. Jackson, new one 1975, over Candelo Ck; bushfires 1905 and 1926; butter factory (Candelo Co-op. Dairy Co. Ltd) 1895, additions 1903 by Glenn and Tapper; carriage-works (White and Hammond); cemeteries: old one (burials 1840s+) and new one 1877; CH b. 1885 by John Malcolm; cheese factories: Bright Hills and Rose Brook (Lucas Bros); cordial factory (John Pike) 1886; diphtheria 1910; drought 1885; electricity 1944; FB (old station sold 1925 to D.D. Sheehan); fires 1889, 1903, 1907; flood 1971; foot-bridge (rebuilt 1893 by E. Taylor) over Candelo Ck; gale 1898; Meth. C. 1903; PO 1870, additions 1896 by Underhill and Thatcher; PS 1877, new one b. 1885 by John Malcolm; Rom. Cath. C. (St Joseph's) b. 1873–75 by Thomas Ryan, d. by P. Slattery; school 1869, additions 1887 by H. Puxley, new buildings 1952; storm 1948; telegraph 1875; TX 1907, automatic 1962; Union C.; water supply 1950; pop. 118 (1871), 146 (1881), 473 (1891), 542 (1901), 643 (1911), 424 (1921), 350 (1933), 309 (1947), 388 (1954), 341 (1961), 248 (1971), 227 (1976), 255 (1981), 298 (1986), 347 (1991), 367 (1996), 350 (2001), 393 (2006), 417 (2011).

Candos (*Co. Roxburgh*) see Kandos.

Cangai (*Co. Gresham*) 29°30'S. 152°29'E., 49 km NW of Grafton, on Yantalla Ck; copper (disc. 1901 by John Sellars); mine (Grafton Copper Mining Co. Ltd) 1904, shafts incl. Greenberg's, McDonough's, Marks', Sellar's, Volkhardt's; PO 1908; PS (in rented premises) 1909, closed 1921; school; smelters (copper) 1906–14, incl. sawmill; telephone 1910; TX 1911–20; pop. 77 (1933), 74 (1947), 57 (1961), 182 (2011).

Caniaba (*Co. Rous*) 28°50'S. 153°14'E., 7 km W. of Lismore; bushfire 1953; FB; Meth. C. 1910; school 1916, additions 1967; telephone 1947; pop. 64 (1933), 117 (1947), 118 (1954), 99 (1961), 517 (2006), 578 (2011).

Canimbla (*Co. Forbes*) see Conimbla.

Cannonbar (*Co. Gregory*) see Canonba.

Cannon Point (*Co. Rous*) 29°00'S. 153°18'E., 2 km E. of Coraki, on Wilsons R.

Canns Plain (*Co. Parry*) 31°25'S. 151°06'E., 39 km SE of Tamworth, on Canns Ck.

Canoblas (*Co. Wellington*) see Canobolas.

Canobolas (*Co. Wellington*) 33°18'S. 149°03'E., 6 km SW of Orange; Canoblas till 1913; farming and orchards; apple processing plant (Avondale Foods) 1995; Angl. C. (St Luke's), damaged 1919; bushfire 1882; dam, 39 ft (12 m) high, 1918; earth tremor 1936; hailstorm 1907; PO 1881–1949; RS (3 km NE, Orange Racecourse till 1913) 1885–1955; school (Canoblas till *c.*1920) 1864, new school 1878, repairs 1881 by John Henry Gain, repairs 1908 also by Gain, remodelled 1926; storm 1919; telephone 1915; TX 1915, automatic 1941; Wes. Meth. C. 1872; pop. 201 (1901), 196 (1911), 193 (1933), 253 (1947), 228 (1954), 514 (2011).

Canobolas (*Co. Wellington*) see also Orange.

Canomodine (*Co. Ashburnham*) 33°30'S. 148°48'E., 15 km NE of Canowindra, on Canomodine Ck; phosphate mine (Limestone Valley) 1918–20.

Canonba (*Co. Gregory*) 31°21'S. 147°21'E., 28 km NE of Nyngan, on Duck Ck; orig. Brownstown, then Cannonbar; disc. 1846 by Major Sir Thomas Livingstone Mitchell, founded *c.*1862 by John Brown, laid out by R.J. Campbell and village gaz. 1866, declined 1883+ (bypassed by railway); sheep; Angl. C. b. 1877 by James M'Cauley, destroyed 1883; bridge b. 1874 by John Herrick, over Duck Ck; cemetery 1888; CH (incl. lock-up) b. 1877 by D. McFarlane and G. Henry; drought 1877; earth tremor 1887; flood 1870; grasshopper infestation 1896; PO 1858, new one b. 1882, begun by J. Hendery but completed by William Moffatt; pound (stock), closed 1901; PS 1877–1917, reopened, closed 1925; school 1871–72 and 1878–82; storm 1883; telegraph 1878, new office b. 1882, begun by J. Hendery but completed by William Moffatt; telephone

1896; pop. *c*.20 (1866), 129 (1871), *c*.500 (1872), 472 (1881), *c*.140 (1886), 58 (1891), 101 (1901), 51 (1911), 34 (1933), 158 (2006).

Canowindra (*Co. Ashburnham*) 33°34'S. 148°40'E., 30 km N. of Cowra, on Belubula R.; (incl. South Canowindra, gaz. as a village 1934); estab. 1849, thrived in 1850s, surveyed and town gaz. 1860; lucerne 1863+, mining, canola, wheat, horses, sheep, pigs, clothing; airfield; ambulance station; Angl. C. 1878, burnt down 1891 during enlargement, replacement b. 1892 by Henry Hart, d. by James Hine, closed, reused 1929, replacement (All Saints') b. 1927–29, d. by Louis Reginald Williams, additions 1956; bridges over Belubula R.: one b. 1873–75 by Joseph Child, Waddell Bridge b. 1901 by J. Jackson (de Burgh timber truss, 171 ft or 52.1 m), John Grant Bridge 1996; bushfire 1900; butter factory (Canowindra Butter & Refrigeration Co.) 1911 d. by Richard Wildridge & Co.; carriage-works: Richard Ayrton 1885 and Federal (J.C. Marka, taken over 1907 by Thomas Curry); cemetery 1886; CH (incl. lock-up) b. 1880–82 by C.M. Murray, d. by James Johnstone Barnet, reused 1937, additions and repairs 1899 by Henry Hart, new one b. 1937 by Charles Alexander Stewart Boag; chaff mill (Goulburn Produce Co. Pty Ltd); cordial factories: Derwin Bros and William Abraham Newling; diphtheria 1935; earth tremor 1930; electricity initially supplied 1912 by William Cobley, new powerhouse estab. 1917 by Cobley, became Canowindra Electric Light & Power Supply Co. Ltd, reused; floods 1934, 1955, 2010; flour mills: Great Western Milling Co. Ltd (b. 1911 by Albert Emanuel Ennis, silo added 1926) and Tee Bros (estab. 1910 by John H. Tee & Sons, closed); foot-bridge 1928, destroyed 1934, new one 1938, replaced 1998, over Belubula R.; heatwave 1896; hospital (Soldiers' Memorial) 1922, additions 1930, 1935, 2017; lucerne mill (Canowindra Produce Co. Pty Ltd); Meth. C. b. 1914 by E.V. Campbell, d. by J. Boyd McDonald, demolished 1969; mouse plague 1888; PO 1847, damaged 1902, dismantled and moved 1904, new one b. 1905 by Henry Hugh Suttor Francis, additions 1915 by G.A. Marlin; pound (stock) 1844; Presb. C. (St Paul's) b. 1902 by W.H. Atkinson, damaged 1902, rebuilt 1903 by Grimshaw, closed 1970; PS 1878, new one o. 1937 in former court-house, new one 1962; 5 quarries; rabbit freezing works (Country Freezing Co. Ltd) 1910; railway bridge (timber truss) 1910, over Belubula R.; railway coal stage 1924; railway engine shed, moved 1921 to Humula; railway turntable, 50 ft (15.2 m), derelict; reservoir; rifle range (7 km NE); Rom. Cath. C. d. and b. 1875 by John Cody, relocated, re-erected and enlarged 1892, destroyed 1902, replacement (St Edward the Confessor) b. 1903 by Henry Hart, d. by John Job Copeman, additions 1914 by G.A. Marlin, d. by John Holderness Bates, additions 1969; RS 1910, station b. by D.H. Reid, closed 1974; Salv. Army C. b. 1930 by Egan; sawmills: W. Goodacre and D. Sames; schools: primary 1877, new one b. 1879 by W.M. Murray, additions 1887 and 1891, additions and alterations 1898 by Henry Hart, additions and alterations 1922 by D.E. Sames, additions 1929 by De Baskerville Edward Edwin Carden, additions 1934 by Peter Beddie and J.W. Brown, renovations 1937, additions 1955 by Sawyer Bros, additions 1959, 1968, 1969, 2010, and HS 1976; sewerage 1967; silo 1926; stamper battery; storms 1890 and 1932; telegraph 1881; tornado (destroyed much of town) 1902; TX 1910, automatic 1980; typhoid 1896; Unit. C. (Peace Memorial, orig. Presb.) b. 1969 by Reg Sawyer; water supply 1928, reticulation 1956; pop. *c*.120 (1866), 179 (1871), 399 (1891), 416 (1901), 1,535 (1911), 1,716 (1933), *c*.2,000 (1941), 2,271 (1947), 1,913 (1954), 1,747 (1961), 1,717 (1966), 1,679 (1971), 1,743 (1976), 1,720 (1981), 1,742 (1984), 1,717 (1986), 1,721 (1991), 1,656 (1996), 1,512 (2001), 1,499 (2006), 1,424 (2011).

Canton Beach (*Co. Northumberland*) see Toukley.

Canyan Leigh (*Co. Camden*) see Canyonleigh.

Canyonleigh (*Co. Camden*) 34°35'S. 150°07'E.,

19 km NW of Bundanoon, on Pivets Ck; formerly Canyan Leigh; timber replaced by pasture in 1950s–60s; coalmines: Araluen (or Southern or Black Bob's) 1878–90 and open-cut 1948; hailstorm 1907; PO 1893–1915; sawmill (Tooth and Murray); school (Canyan Leigh) 1896–1920; pop. 50 (1911), 96 (1933), 51 (1954), 45 (1961), 291 (2006), 193 (2011).

Caoura (*Co. Camden*) 34°47'S. 150°10'E., 40 km E. of Goulburn, on Caoura Ck; school 1882–92; pop. 32 (1933).

Caparra (*Co. Macquarie*) 31°44'S. 152°15'E., 19 km NW of Wingham, on Caparra Ck; farming; PO 1927, burnt down 1952; sawmill (William and James Eriksson), burnt down 1945; telephone 1925; TX 1926; Union C.; pop. 59 (1933), 84 (1947), 60 (1954), 68 (1961).

Capeen (*Co. Buller*) 28°35'S. 152°40'E., 33 km W. of Kyogle, on Duck Ck; Oorin till 1953; farming and dairying; bushfire 1970; cemetery; flood 1954; sawmill estab. 1938 by Hugh, John and Robert McKee, bought 1947 by Harold, Charles, William and Noel Keys, acquired 1954 by Brandon Timbers, closed 1971; school 1954–72; telephone 1924; TX 1925, automatic 1972; pop. 74 (1954), 57 (1961).

Cape Hawke (*Co. Gloucester*) see Nabiac.

Capertee (*Co. Roxburgh*) 33°09'S. 149°59'E., 23 km N. of Portland, on Turon Ck; Capertee Camp 1877–82; disc. 1821 by James Blackman, jun., settled by William Lee, estab. *c.*1870, laid out 1883 by Henry Augustus Crouch, village gaz. 1885, declined 1960s+; mining, farming, bees, grazing; airfield; Angl. C. (St Augustine's) 1923, closed, sold; cemetery (205 graves 1900+) 1874, incl. columbarium; CH 1899, new one b. 1936 by Peter Beddie and J.W. Brown, closed and reused; dam; FB 1939; fire 1931; freezing works (estab. by O'Brien Bros, became Thomas Borthwick & Sons A'asia Ltd) 1916; hailstorm 1883; PO 1875, new one 1913; PS 1882, new one (incl. lock-up) 1897, new one 1903, new one b. 1936 by Peter Beddie and J.W. Brown; railway dam 1913; railway tunnel, 191 yds (174.3 m), 1882; rifle range (2 km S.) 1906, repairs 1933; Rom. Cath. C. (St Jude's) b. 1930 by Ernest Bartlett; RS 1882, station b. by William Cameron and John Briton, closed, restored; school 1882–89, reopened 1896, new one b. 1923 by N.R. Morris; telegraph 1882; TX 1917, automatic 1987; whooping cough epidemics 1901, 1919, 1931; pop. 160 (1901), 336 (1911), 230 (1933), 267 (1947), 240 (1954), 234 (1961), 372 (2011).

Capertee Camp (*Co. Roxburgh*) see Capertee.

Captains Creek (*Co. Buckland*) 31°49'S. 150°42'E., 14 km W. of Murrurundi.

Captains Flat (*Co. Murray*) 35°36'S. 149°27'E., 33 km SE of Queanbeyan, on Molonglo R.; (incl. Bagtown, Bogtown, Coppertown, Newtown, Oakvale); founded 1883, village gaz. 1886, laid out by William Henry O'Malley Wood, town gaz. 1888, thrived till 1899 then 1937–62, declined 1962+, more recently a dormitory town; grazing and mining (reef gold disc. 1881, copper disc. 1882, silver-lead, zinc) mainly 1882–99 and 1926, finished 1962; Angl. C. (St Luke's) 1895, additions 1925, interior restored 2000, now also used by Rom. Cath. C.; brewery (Henry W. Leon) 1892–97; brickworks (Mason Bros) 1926; bridge 1863 over Molonglo R.; bushfires 1891, 1948, 1982; cemetery (burials 1890s–1960s) 1889; CH (incl. lock-up) b. 1899 by G. Kidney; cordial factories: Commonwealth Cordial Co. Ltd (incl. ice works) and William Pike & Son (acquired 1899 by P. Coffey and W. Hammond); cyanide plant d. and b. 1900 by William Alfred Isley; dam b. 1938 by Lake George Mines Pty Ltd, 41 ft (12.5 m) high, wall raised 1942 by 10 ft (3 m), on Molonglo R.; electricity 1937; FB (station b. 1979); fire 1898; floods 1939, 1942, 1945, 1959; grasshopper infestation 1899; hospital b. 1945–50, closed 1962, sold 1985, reused; lock-up 1886; measles epidemic 1909; miners' strikes 1898, 1899, 1928, 1941, 1945, 1947, 1948–49, 1951, 1952, 1953, 1954, 1959; mines: Dam Shaft, El Capitan (estab. 1886 by Blatchford, taken over 1888 by BHP and renamed Commodore), Federal (Old Copper Shaft), Kohinoor (estab. 1886 by Ralf Montgomery and in 1894 combined with Commodore and Vanderbilt mines and became Lake George United Mining & Smelting Co., closed 1900, reopened 1926 by National Mining Corp., reworked 1937–62, surface works sold and removed 1963), North Vanderbilt Amalgamated Silver Mining Co. 1888–90, Vanderbilt (o. 1887 by William Garland); PO 1884, new one b. 1898 by Charles Bruce, closed, sold and reused; powerhouse (Lake George Mines Ltd); Presb. C. 1938; PS (in rented premises) 1886, new one 1896, repairs 1954 by A. Butterfield; quarry; railway turntable (William Sellers & Co.), 60 ft (18.3 m), closed; reservoir; Rom. Cath. C. (St Joseph's) 1891, demolished 1952, new one (St Brigid's) 1948; RS 1940–68, station reused; sawmills: Frederick Gibson, Samuel Martin, Tablelands, Henry Thompson; school 1886, new building b. 1889 by William Nicholls, extended 1897; smelters 1885, 1889, 1896, 1897; stamper batteries; telegraph 1887; TX 1921; typhoid 1897, 1900 (woman died), 1954; water supply augmentation 1990; Wes. Meth. C. b. 1898 by John Jordan; pop. 488 (1891), 558 (1901), 206 (1911), *c.*300 (1928), 276 (1933), *c.*1,200 (1938), 1,475 (1947), 1,778 (1954), 1,548 (1961), 598 (1966), 505 (1971), 412 (1976), 309 (1981), 393 (1986), 446 (1991), 418 (1996), 421 (2001), 447 (2006), 437 (2011).

Cara (*Co. Sandon*) see Hillgrove.

Carabost (*Co. Wynyard*) 35°36'S. 147°43'E., 33 km NW of Tumbarumba; soldiers' settlement; farming and forestry; Angl. C. (St Alphege's) 1961, closed; bushfires 1904, 1952, 2014; PO 1916; school 1957, additions 1960, closed 1971; telephone 1924; TX 1930, automatic 1963; typhoid 1912; pop. 80 (1911), 137 (1933), 124 (1947), 119 (1954), 142 (1961).

Caragabal (*Co. Gipps*) 33°51'S. 147°44'E., 39 km W. of Grenfell, on Caragabal Ck; village gaz. 1917; sheep and cattle, then wheat; Angl. C. (St Peter's) 1928, demolished, rebuilt 1987 by David Buttenshaw, deconsecrated 2017; bushfire 1906; cemetery (60 graves); electricity 1948; floods 1931, 1962, 1963, 1977, 1990, 1993; gale 1925; grasshopper infestation 1934; mouse plague 1951; PO 1917, new one b. 1933, closed 1994; Presb. C. 1955 d. by Peck; PS 1931, new one 1957, additions and alterations 1976; railway coal stage, removed 1941; reservoir (elevated, steel), 100,000 gal. (454.6 kl), b. 1953 by V.G. Saunders; Rom. Cath. C. (St Patrick's) b. 1935 by Harveyson Bros, d. by Norman Leslie Lipman, closed; RS 1916, station b. by Ernest Frederick Leggo, closed 1979, removed 1984; sale-yards b. 1951 by Tom Austin; 2 sawmills (1923 and 1924); school (Little Caragabal till 1914) 1907–14, reopened 1941, new one b. 1988; silo 1922; storms 1958 and 1959; telephone 1920; TX 1923, automatic 1987; pop. 201 (1933), 324 (1947), 281 (1954), 381 (1961), 199 (2006), 214 (2011).

Carangara (*Co. Bathurst*) see Byng.

Carat Flat (*Co. Argyle*) 34°55'S. 150°01'E., 32 km SE of Goulburn, on Washedaway Ck.

Carbeen (*Co. Jamison*) 30°11'S. 149°13'E., 22 km W. of Wee Waa; RS 1903–75.

Carberry (*Co. Urana*) 35°31'S. 146°12'E., 39 km NE of Berrigan; estab. 1924 but never developed; coal and kaolin; mines: coalmine (Riverina Collieries Ltd) 1924 and kaolin mine (McDonalds Ltd) 1949, sold to Minerals Pty Ltd, taken over by James Hardie Pty Ltd.

Carbine (*Co. Bathurst*) 33°28'S. 149°03'E., 12 km W. of Millthorpe, on Pennyweight Gully; goldmine (Little Emma or Beneree) <1935.

Carboona (*Co. Goulburn*) 35°50'S. 147°44'E., 27 km W. of Tumbarumba; Copabella Mines till 1905; silver-lead and fluorspar mining; PO 1906; telephone 1906; TX 1911.

Carcalgong (*Co. Wellington*) 32°51'S. 149°43'E., 24 km W. of Kandos, on Campbells Ck; telephone 1951; TX 1951; pop. 50 (1933).

Carcoar (*Co. Bathurst*) 33°37'S. 149°08'E., 14 km SW of Blayney, on Belubula R.; orig. Carcuan, also known as Corcoran; settled 1829 by Thomas Icely, surveyed 1829 by James Byrn Richards, founded 1838 by Icely, laid out 1839 by Walker Rannie Davidson, village gaz. 1839 as Carcor, first lots sold 1840, further sales 1841, declined 1876+, munic. 1878–1935, decl. historic site 1974, bypassed by highway 1975; copper 1850+, gold (disc. 1851, gold rush 1871) 1876–81, cobalt 1888, iron, wheat, maize, lucerne, hay, barley, oats, rye, potatoes, peas, tobacco, wine, butter, ham, bacon, beef, sheep, goats, horses; Angl. C. (St Paul's) b. 1845–48 by Thomas Kirkpatrick, d. by Edmund Thomas Blacket, tower and spire b. 1875 by Josiah Shakespear, church restored 1988, spire reclad 2010, and graveyard (23 graves 1850+); brewery (Aust. Brewery) estab. 1889 by William John Derwin, taken over by Charles James Derwin and J.G. Derwin, sold 1910 to Robert S. Raymond, leased 1912 by H. Sleigh; bridge (timber truss) 1856, d. by William Weaver, 172 ft (52.4 m), rebuilt 1896, over Belubula R.; cemetery (1 km NE) 1852; CH (incl. lock-up) 1850 d. by Edmund Thomas Blacket, dilapidated by 1872, repairs 1874 by Patrick Brady, demolished 1880, new one b. 1880–82 by John Willett & Son, d. by James Johnstone Barnet, closed 1936, reused, partly restored 1969; cordial factories: William John Derwin 1864 (taken over by Charles James Derwin) and Yoxall's; dam 1970, 174 ft (53 m) high, on Belubula R.; diphtheria 1886 (several deaths), 1893 (3 children died), 1912, 1914; earth tremors 1886, 1906, 1917; FB; fires 1888, 1889, 1909, 1943; flood 1906; flour mills: Aust. Steam Flour Mills (estab. 1856 by S. Meyer, acquired by T. Hilliar), Caledonian (Bayliss and Isaacs), James Dalton, sen., Great Western Mill (estab. 1877 by John Kenworthy, bought by T. Morgans, demolished), Union; hailstorms 1858 and 1916 (every house damaged); hospital 1852, proc. a public hospital 1859, replacement 1861 d. by Edward Gell, renovations 1903 by Edward Abraham Wright, d. by John Job Copeman, additions 1908 also by Wright, also d. by Copeman, re-roofed 1909, additions and alterations 1914 by Patrick Flood, d. by William Lamrock, jun., additions 1934, 1935, 1947, 1949, closed and reused; lock-up, additions 1885 by Henry Ford; measles epidemic 1888; mine (Geraldine Copper Mine) worked 1848–51 by Thomas Icely, reopened 1875 by Sir Saul Samuel and Lewis Lloyd, whim erected 1877, smelter 1876–78; miners' strike 1911; PO 1843, new one b. 1879 by Findlay and Cody, d. by James Johnstone Barnet, additions d. by Walter Liberty Veron; pound (stock) 1865; Presb. C. (St James's) b. 1860–62, closed, sold 2019; PS 1864, new one b. 1884 by John Henry Hansen, d. by James Johnstone Barnet, closed 1943–46, reopened; 5 quarries (incl. Carcoar Iron Quarry 1898–1905 and worked 1907–23 by G. & C. Hoskins Ltd); railway tunnel, 307 yds (281 m), 1887; reservoir 1955; rifle range 1912; Rom. Cath. C. (St Mary's) 1857, reused, replacement (Immaculate Conception) b. 1867–71 by John Cody, d. by Edward Gell; RS 1888, station b. by Alexander Hamilton Scouller, closed 1987; scarlet fever 1898; school 1857 b. by Englebert Hahn, demolished 1885, new one b. 1885 by W. O'Brien, d. by William Edmund Kemp, additions 1915 by P. Flood, additions 1978; sewage works; Shalom House of Prayer; storms 1906 and 1932; telegraph 1871, new office b. 1879 by Findlay and Cody; TX 1911; typhoid 1886, 1887 (boy died), 1899, 1904, 1914; watch-house b. 1875 by W. Budcock; water reticulation 1956; Wes. Meth. C.; pop. 73 (1846), 303 (1851), 364 (1856), 374 (1861), 395 (1871), *c.*500 (1876), 540 (1881), *c.*600 (1886), 562 (1891), *c.*650 (1895), 578 (1901), 737 (1911), 478 (1933), 452 (1947), 524 (1954), 364 (1961), 377 (1971), 335 (1976), 277 (1981), 244 (1986), 242 (1991), 223 (1996), 218 (2006), 214 (2011).

Carcolla (*Co. Dudley*) 30°42'S. 152°30'E., 34 km W. of Bowraville, on Nulla Nulla Ck; formerly Upper Nulla Nulla; farming; PO 1927–39; school 1957, additions 1961, closed 1967, moved 1970 to Bellbrook; telephone 1924; TX 1928.

Carcor (*Co. Bathurst*) see Carcoar.

Carcuan (*Co. Bathurst*) see Carcoar.

Cardiff (*Co. Northumberland*) 32°56'S. 151°40'E., 4 km S. of Wallsend, on Winding Ck; (incl. Cardiff Heights, Evelien, Macquarie Hills, Macsville, North Cardiff, South Cardiff, was Ulinga till 1930); orig. Winding Creek, later known as Lymington; estab.

1862, subdivided 1875; formerly orchards and poultry, then coalmining; Angl. C. b. 1904 by R.L. Cherry, new one (built as a hall) 1926, new one (St Thomas Apostle and Martyr) 1994; Assemblies of God C. (Macquarie Life); Bapt. C.: Cardiff 1933, Cardiff Heights, Evelien 1924, Liberty; beekeeping equipment factory (Pender Beekeeping Supplies) 2002; brewery (Hunter Brewery, estab. by Toohey's Ltd) 1970–87; bushfires 1936, 1938 (2 houses destroyed), 1940, 1941, 1952, 1991; Church of Christ (South Cardiff) 1951; collieries: Ajax, Austral, Cardiff (dewatered 1920 and renamed Cardiff Borehole, strikes 1894, 1896, 1900, 1901, 1928), Evelien (O'Halloran and Ellis), Jubilee, Lymington (Lymington Collieries Ltd, o. 1882, strikes 1908, 1909, 1911, 1914, men killed 1916 and 1917, strikes 1917 and 1918, man killed 1920), Myall, Myall Extended, Rising Sun, Rosebank, South Wallsend (strikes 1925, 1928, 1929), Tickhole; electroplating works (Cardiff Industrial Platers Pty Ltd); Evangelical Christ. C.; FB (station b. 1928, new one 1971, alterations 2013); fibrous plaster works (Crockett and Hoffman); fire (man died) 1894; flood 2015; foot-bridge over Winding Ck; gale (South Cardiff) 1951; joinery 1950; metal fabrication works (Cameron Drew Industries); Meth. C. (Cardiff Heights) 1959; monumental stone works (Delic & Co. Pty Ltd); PO: Cardiff 1891, new one b. 1910, Cardiff Heights 1927, South Cardiff 1927–93; poultry processing plant (Inghams Enterprises); Presb. C. 1925, new one 1940; PS 1901, new one 1943; 2 quarries; 3 reservoirs; Rom. Cath. C. b. 1906 by T. Bevan, damaged 1913, extended 1917, reused, burnt down 1942, new one (St Kevin's) b. 1928 by Ratcliffe and Kirsopp, d. by Peter Joseph Gannon, and columbarium; RS: Cardiff 1889, station relocated 1900 and Sulphide Junction 1926; Salv. Army C.; sawmills: Leslie Delatorre and Fatal Mill (formerly owned by Cummings and Lane, acquired by Henderson); schools: Cardiff 1891 (additions and repairs 1909 by W.J. Wooden, additions 1924 by T.C. Southon, additions and alterations 1927 by Arthur Partridge-Wall, additions 2010 by R.T. Parker Pty Ltd), Cardiff HS 1962, new school 1964, additions 1968 and 1983, North Cardiff 1956, additions 1960, South Cardiff 1952, additions 1956, 1960, 1962, 1969, 1981; sewerage 1945; squall 1913; telephone: Cardiff 1900, Cardiff Heights 1926, South Cardiff 1925; TX (automatic) 1935; Unit. C. (orig. Prim. Meth.) 1891, additions 1925; water supply 1922, extended 1927; pop. 114 (1891), 598 (1901), 667 (1911), 1,522 (1921), 3,843 (1933), 4,755 (1947), 10,002 (2011).

Cardiff Heights (*Co. Northumberland*) see Cardiff.

Cardiff West (*Co. Northumberland*) see Glendale.

Cardington (*Co. Gordon*) 32°53'S. 148°54'E., 23 km N. of Molong; bushfire 1901.

Carey Bay (*Co. Northumberland*) see Coal Point.

Cargelligo (*Co. Dowling*) see Lake Cargelligo.

Cargo (*Co. Ashburnham*) 33°25'S. 148°49'E., 21 km NE of Canowindra; village gaz. 1869, thrived till 1899; orig. grazing, then mining (gold disc. 1868, gold booms 1869–79 and 1885–99) till 1904, then agric. (mainly wheat); airfield; Angl. C. 1870, demolished, new one (St John's) 1905; cemetery (457 graves 1870s+); earth tremor 1924; fires 1912 and 1920 (2 died); flour mill (Gem of the West) estab. 1883 by Blay Bros, acquired by W.H. Couch, sold to James Rhodes Worrall and Sid Worrall, moved 1907 to Manildra; heatwave 1905; Meth. C. 1902, sold and demolished 1915; mines: Cargo Consols, Commonwealth 1899–1900, Dalcoath or Mt Derwood <1875, Essex, Golden Clad or Rise and Shine 1875–80 and 1890, Gum Flat 1872–1911, Ironclad 1875–90; PO 1868; PS 1887; quarry; reservoir 1959; Rom. Cath. C. 1875 d. by Edward Gell, additions 1886, reused 1907, demolished 1939, new one (St Patrick's) 1908 d. by William Lamrock, jun., additions 1940 d. by Norman Leslie Lipman; scarlet fever 1904; school 1871, new one b. 1878 by T. Taylor, repairs 1903 by H. Palmer; stamper batteries: Ironclad, Wall Church & Co., Wickens & Co.; telegraph 1882; TX 1910; waterworks b. 1882 by Wright and Sharp, reticulation 1959; pop. 396 (1871), 286 (1881), 610 (1891), 462 (1901), 608 (1911), 274 (1933), 324 (1947), 388 (1954), 397 (1961), *c.*100 (1975), *c.*100 (1987), 242 (1996), 259 (2001), 278 (2006), 238 (2011).

Cargo Road (*Co. Wellington*) see Nashdale.

Carinda (*Co. Clyde*) 30°28'S. 147°42'E., 63 km SW of Walgett, on Marthaguy Ck; village gaz. 1890; orig. cattle, then sheep, cotton 1982+; airfield 1953; Angl. C. (St John the Evangelist) 1934; artesian bore, 1,660 ft (506 m), 1897; bridge 1941, over Marthaguy Ck; cemetery (2 km SE); CH (incl. police station and lock-up) 1912, burnt down 1963, new one 1968 d. by Leif Kristensen; cotton gin (Namoi Cotton Co-op. Ltd); drought 1982; electricity 1936; FB; floods 1950, 1974, 1976, 2010; ice works (Theo Conomos); PO 1874; powerhouse (Theo Conomos) 1942; Presb. C. (St Andrew's) 1961; PS 1883; Rom. Cath. C. (Our Lady of the Sacred Heart) b. 1908 by Mooy Bros, d. by William Lamrock, jun., burnt down 1983; school 1904 b. by Cormack and Stanley, new one b. 1929, replacement b. 1969 by A.H. Cooper Pty Ltd; telegraph 1899; telephone 1895; TX 1911; whooping cough epidemic 1932; wool-scour (Gill and Pearce); pop. 113 (1901), 211 (1911), 230 (1933), *c.*150 (1941), 131 (1947), 286 (1954), 122 (1961), 185 (2011).

Carlachy (*Co. Cunningham*) 33°07'S. 147°44'E., 22 km S. of Trundle, on Gunningbland Ck; Carlachy Tank till 1900; PO 1910; RS 1898–1971; school 1900 b. by J.M. Job, closed 1910, building moved 1915 to Cookeys Plains; telephone 1914.

Carlachy Tank (*Co. Cunningham*) see Carlachy.

Carlaminda (*Co. Beresford*) 36°16'S. 149°18'E., 16 km E. of Cooma.

Carlisle (*Co. Cunningham*) 32°52'S. 147°25'E., 28 km W. of Trundle.

Carlisle Gully (*Co. Inglis*) 30°52'S. 151°20'E., 27 km NW of Walcha, on Tara Springs Ck; grazing; PO 1874; pop. 51 (1911).

Carlisle Park (*Co. Cunningham*) 32°52'S. 147°23'E., 31 km W. of Trundle; mine (Golden Gulch).

Carlos Gap (*Co. Roxburgh*) 33°02'S. 149°59'E., 20 km S. of Kandos; alum; coalmine (Carlos Gap Coal & Iron Co.) 1884–1903; railway tunnel, 418 yds (381.9 m), 1884; RS 1887–1931.

Carlwood (*Co. Westmoreland*) 33°35'S. 149°53'E., 13 km N. of Oberon, on Snakes Valley Ck; bushfire 1936; 3 quarries; RS 1923–73; school (Keirson till 1903, then Kierstone) 1887–1915.

Carlyle (*Co. Denison*) 35°51'S. 145°59'E., 15 km N. of Mulwala; school 1919–27.

Carmarthen Hills (*Co. Cook*) see Kurrajong Heights.

Carnham (*Co. Drake*) 29°20'S. 152°32'E., 54 km NW of Grafton, on Clarence R.; village reserve surveyed 1883; bridge (concrete) 1934, 910 ft (277.4 m), over Clarence R.; flood 1948.

Carnsdale (*Co. Hume*) 35°52'S. 146°31'E., 17 km NW of Howlong; Richmond till 1876; PO 1876–1915.

Carnsdale (*Co. Hume*) see also Balldale.

Caroda (*Co. Murchison*) 30°01'S. 150°22'E., 23 km SW of Bingara, on Horton R.; grazing; telephone 1909; TX 1912, automatic 1988; pop. 160 (1933), 88 (1947), 131 (1954), 158 (1961).

Carolgi (*Co. Sturt*) 34°03'S. 145°48'E., 34 km NW of Griffith; RS 1932–71.

Carool (*Co. Rous*) 28°14'S. 153°25'E., 11 km N. of Murwillumbah, on Cobaki Ck; (incl. Bilambil soldiers' settlement, 3 km SW, 1919+); bushfire 1936; PO 1927; school (Bilambil Soldiers' Settlement till 1927) 1922; telephone 1923; TX 1930; winery (Ilnam Estate); pop. 203 (1933), 211 (1947), 119 (1954), 104 (1961).

Caroona (*Co. Pottinger*) 31°24'S. 150°25'E., 22 km W. of Werris Creek, on Mooki R.; village gaz. 1922; farming and grazing; bridge over Mooki R.; FB; PO 1900; Rom. Cath. C. (Queen of the Angels) 1936; RS (1 km NE)

1923–75, station demolished 1979; school (Walhallow till 1907) 1892–1941 and 1955–83; telephone 1914; TX 1923, automatic 1985; Union C. (Croaker Memorial) 1924; water supply 1980; pop. 131 (1933), 124 (1947), 136 (1954), 262 (1961), 90 (2011).

Carrabean (*Co. Gloucester*) see Carrington.

Carrabolla (*Co. Durham*) 32°15'S. 151°23'E., 40 km NW of Dungog, on Paterson R.; orchards, farming, grazing, dairying; PO 1917–62; telephone 1929; TX 1930; pop. 87 (1901), 66 (1911), 23 (1933).

Carrabungla (*Co. Georgiana*) 34°24'S. 149°39'E., 18 km E. of Crookwell; pop. 53 (1901), 29 (1933).

Carrai (*Co. Dudley*) 30°49'S. 152°15'E., 64 km NW of Kempsey; gold and tin; PO 1947–60; sawmill estab. by William Haydon (moved to Kookaburra).

Carranya (*Co. Cooper*) 33°59'S. 146°21'E., 44 km NE of Griffith.

Carrathool (*Co. Sturt*) 34°24'S. 145°25'E., 55 km E. of Hay; (incl. West Carrathool); first lots sold 1865, village gaz. 1880 as Currathool, relocated 1882 when railway opened, more lots sold 1883; orig. a river port, then wheat *c.*1928+, sheep, cattle, rice, vineyards, cotton, vegetables, orchards; Angl. C. (St George's) 1925, restoration 1996–97 d. by Ruth Daniell; boiling-down and freezing works (Graziers' Meat Export Co.) 1896 d. by Coxon and Greenstreet; bridge (Alan timber truss, with steel bascule span) b. 1924 by Poole and Steele Ltd, new one over Murrumbidgee R.; bushfires 1919 and 1975; cemetery 1886; CH 1890; drought 1967–68; dust storm 1944; electricity 1963; FB; fires 1929 and 2010; floods 1956 and 1974; grasshopper infestation 1955; PO 1882, new one b. 1893 by W.G. Butterworth; police barracks; Presb. C. (St David's) 1885, renovated; PS 1882, additions and alterations 1976; punt, ceased 1924; railway coal stage, removed 1941; Rom. Cath. C. (Sacred Heart) b. 1929 by O'Meara and Drummond, d. by Lorna Smith; RS 1882, station b. by A. Johnson, removed 1984, services ceased 1985; school 1883, new one b. 1887 by Lewis Cawsey, repairs 1898 by William Eyles, replacement b. 1918 by C. Styman, extended 1939, additions 1972, closed 1995; streets electric lit 1963; telegraph 1882; TX 1910; water supply augmentation 1990; wool-scour (James Looby); pop. 163 (1891), 210 (1901), 271 (1911), 222 (1933), 142 (1947), 147 (1954), 132 (1961), 72 (1982), *c.*100 (1987), 328 (2006), 296 (2011).

Carravale (*Co. Georgiana*) 34°25'S. 149°36'E., 13 km NE of Crookwell; telephone 1914; TX 1917.

Carrawa (*Co. Georgiana*) see Arkell.

Carrawabbity (*Co. Ashburnham*) 33°22'S. 147°51'E., 15 km W. of Forbes; formerly Carrawobity; school 1880–90; TX (automatic); pop. 20 (1933).

Carrawobity (*Co. Ashburnham*) see Carrawabbity.

Carrick (*Co. Argyle*) 34°42'S. 149°53'E., 16 km NE of Goulburn, on Wollondilly R.; PO 1872; railway viaduct (Wollondilly No. 1), replacement (9 brick arches) 1915, over Wollondilly R.; RS (Towrang till 1879) 1869–1975; school 1876–87; telephone 1905; pop. 46 (1933).

Carrington (*Co. Gloucester*) 32°40'S. 152°01'E., 5 km E. of Karuah, on Port Stephens; orig. Carrabean; founded and laid out 1826 by Robert Dawson as first headquarters of Aust. Agric. Co. but largely abandoned by the 1870s and now almost defunct; wheat, tobacco, grapes, cattle, oysters; abattoir; Angl. C. (Holy Trinity) b. 1847 by Thomas Laman for Aust. Agric. Co., closed 1862, restored 1888, reopened 1892 as St Andrew's, closed 1949, reused 1965–93, returned to parish 1993, sold 1997 and 2017, and graveyard (13 burials) 1837–1906; brick-kiln; cemetery (25 graves) 1834; convict barracks; FB; flour mill (horse powered); foot-bridge; hospital; lime-kiln 1834, ruined; lock-up; military barracks; PO 1831–51; slipways; tannery; watch-house; wharf 1834; winery 1831; pop. *c.*500 (1830), 1 (1866).

Carrington (*Co. Northumberland*) 32°55'S. 151°46'E., 2 km NW of Newcastle, on

Hunter R.; orig. Chapman Island, then Onebygamba 1885–88, also known as Bullock Island; subdivided by Thomas Adam and John Howden, first lots sold 1854, futher subdivided 1865, munic. 1887–1938 but became part of City of Greater Newcastle; Angl. C. b. 1877 by Smith, demolished 1924, replacement (St Thomas's) 1924–2014, sold 2014 and reused; boiler works (T.C. Pollard); bridges: one b. 1875 by J. and M. Burley, one b. 1885 by Flynn, Denison Street Bridge 1900, Cowper Street Bridge, widened 1933, new one (floating span) 1934, over Throsby Ck; cistern factory (T.V. Richards & Son Pty Ltd), in liquidation 1983; coal loader, closed 1980; collieries: Wickham & Bullock Island Coal Mining Co. estab. 1882, o. 1884, fire 1903, closed 1905, and Hetton Coal Mining Co. 1885, man killed 1896, new powerhouse 1905, colliery closed 1915, dismantled 1916; diphtheria 1936; dockyard (State) 1942–87; earthquake 1989; engineering works (Thomas C. Pollard Pty Ltd); engineering works and iron foundry (Vulcan) estab. by John Howden & Son, acquired 1874 by Robert and James Morison and Edwin Bearby, became Morison & Bearby Pty Ltd, new building 1877, fire 1903, new rolling mill 1917, taken over 1963 by Brambles Ltd; FB 1885 (station b. 1890 by John Lacy, damaged 1913, new one b. 1918 by S. Box); floating dock (Forgacs Engineering Pty Ltd); hailstorm 1895; hydraulic power station b. 1877 by W.H. Jennings, d. by James Johnstone Barnet, extended 1891 by F.A. King, extended 1914, closed 1967, reused; jetties (incl. ballast jetties b. 1867 by Ross and one b. 1959); mine subsidence 1901 and 1902; miners' strikes 1888 and 1896; oil terminal (BP); PO 1875, new one b. 1898 by R.L. Thompson, d. by Walter Liberty Vernon; Prim. Meth. C. 1888, destroyed 1895, rebuilt 1896 by George Cave; PS 1878, additions and repairs 1905 by Myers, demolished 1935; Rom. Cath. C. (St Francis Xavier's) b. 1887 by McDonald and Nicholl, d. by Frederick Bernhardt Menkens, additions 1897 also d. by Menkens, renovated 1912; sawmills: Thomas Adam and William Bowden 1857, Armstrong & Royse Ltd (incl. joinery) 1919, largely burnt down 1923, additions 1937, Earp, Woodcock, Beveridge & Co. Pty Ltd (largely burnt down 1922), J.C. Ellis; school (Onybigambah till 1889) 1873 b. by Cropley & Sons, additions 1879 by W. Humphreys, additions 1888 by Myers and Thompson, additions 1902 by Charles Baker, alterations 1907 by William Frederick Gazzard, additions 1910, new buildings and remodelling 1926 by G.E. Hogden, damaged 1989, new building 2010; sewerage 1936; shipyard (John W. Scott) 1869–86; silo 1937; slipway estab. 1957 by John Laverick, snr, became Carrington Slipways, closed 1990; squall 1913; storm 1898; streets gas lit 1903, electric lit 1913; telegraph 1888; tramway (steam) to Newcastle 1912, electrified 1926, closed 1938; typhoid 1896; watch-house b. 1878 by William Dart; Wes. Meth. C. 1888; wharves: Armstrong & Royse Pty Ltd 1917, Callen Bros 1886, cattle wharf (built 1899 by Peter Callen), Dyke 1874, Western Basin wharf 1915; works: ADI, Boral Building Services, Commercial Minerals Ltd, Glazed Waterproof Tile Co. 1918, State Monier Pipe Works; pop. 120 (1872), *c.*500 (1878), 805 (1881), 1,256 (1885), 2,112 (1891), *c.*2,275 (1895), 2,505 (1900), 2,547 (1901), 2,685 (1911), *c.*3,100 (1921), 3,236 (1933), *c.*3,200 (1947), *c.*3,100 (1954), *c.*2,800 (1961), *c.*1,700 (1966), *c.*2,100 (1971), 1,907 (1976), 1,794 (2006), 1,874 (2011).

Carrington Falls (*Co. Camden*) 34°38'S. 150°40'E., 12 km SW of Albion Park, on Kangaroo R.; sawmill.

Carroll (*Co. Buckland*) 30°59'S. 150°27'E., 18 km E. of Gunnedah, on Namoi R.; town gaz. 1860; farming and grazing; Angl. C. (St Luke's) 1860; Bible Christ. C.; cemetery (136 graves 1879+) 1887; earth tremor 2012; FB; floods 1908, 1950, 1955; PO 1851–1990; pound (stock) 1850; PS 1881, additions 1901 by Thomas John Bowen, additions 1905 also by Bowen, closed 1934; Rom. Cath. C. (St John's) 1907; sawmill (Jensen Bros); school

1880, new buildings b. 1902 by Montague Audet, alterations 1911 by Throsby's Ltd, additions 2010; telephone 1890; TX 1915; typhoid 1912; Wes. Meth. C. 1892; pop. *c.*50 (1866), 231 (1881), 178 (1891), 454 (1901), 421 (1911), 205 (1933), 242 (1947), 308 (1954), 180 (1961), 176 (2011).

Carroll Gap (*Co. Parry*) 30°57'S. 150°32'E., 26 km E. of Gunnedah, on Peel R.; farming and grazing; bridge 1938; PO 1904; school 1882, additions and repairs 1908 by Thomas John Bowen, closed 1914; telephone 1911; TX 1927; pop. 47 (1933), 70 (1954), 58 (1961).

Carrolls Creek (*Co. Buller*) 28°51'S. 152°06'E., 24 km N. of Tenterfield, on Carrolls Ck; school 1914–16.

Carrowbrook (*Co. Durham*) 32°17'S. 151°18'E., 34 km N. of Singleton, on Carrow Brook; dairying and grazing; Cong. C. 1905; hailstorm 1908; PO 1894–1982; sawmills: Gould Bros, burnt down 1948, and Wilkinson Bros and McNielley; telephone 1914; TX 1914; pop. 83 (1901), 79 (1911), 78 (1933), 85 (1947), 55 (1954), 56 (1961).

Carrs Creek (*Co. Clarence*) 29°38'S. 152°56'E., 6 km N. of Grafton; Angl. C. (St George's) b. 1899 by Hermann Schaeffer, d. by Frederick William Conrad Schaeffer, closed; butter factory (Grafton Dairy Co.); punt; school 1877, new buildings b. 1882 by J. Moyes, closed 1964, reused; sugar mill (Carrs Creek Co-op.) 1869, burnt down; TX (automatic); water reticulation 1966; Wes. Meth. C. b. 1863 by Kinnear and Ring; pop. 160 (1911), 130 (1933), 105 (1947), 85 (1954), 101 (1961).

Carr's Creek (*Co. Wellington*) see Kerrs Creek.

Carr's Creek Junction (*Co. Clarence*) see Junction Hill.

Carrs Island (*Co. Clarence*) 29°40'S. 152°55'E., 3 km NW of Grafton, on Clarence R.; maize; flood 1893; pop. 24 (1933).

Carrs Peninsula (*Co. Clarence*) 29°39'S. 152°54'E., 6 km NW of Grafton; pop. 32 (1933).

Carson's Siding (*Co. Roxburgh*) see Cullen Bullen.

Carsonville (*Co. Gloucester*) 32°06'S. 151°48'E., 18 km SW of Gloucester, on Berrico Ck; PO 1936–44; sawmill (Carsons Northern Timber Co. Ltd) estab. 1933 by Frederick James Carson, burnt down 1955; telephone 1935; TX 1935.

Carters Bridge (*Co. Richmond*) 29°10'S. 152°53'E., 36 km S. of Casino.

Cartmills (*Co. Fitzroy*) 29°54'S. 152°51'E., 22 km SW of Grafton; telephone 1915.

Cartwrights Hill (*Co. Clarendon*) 35°05'S. 147°23'E., 5 km N. of Wagga Wagga.

Carumbi (*Co. Bland*) 34°18'S. 147°49'E., 30 km NE of Temora, on Yeo Yeo Ck; pop. 110 (1911).

Carwell (*Co. Roxburgh*) 32°50'S. 149°54'E., 7 km SW of Rylstone, on Carwell Ck; bushfire 1909; cemetery (14 graves 1849–69); mine (Rockwell Antimony & Gold Mining Co.) 1881; school 1881–85 and 1899–1916; telephone 1929; TX 1929.

Carwell (*Co. Roxburgh*) see also Clandulla.

Carwoola (*Co. Murray*) 35°26'S. 149°23'E., 16 km SE of Queanbeyan; Angl. C. (St Thomas the Apostle) b. 1872–74 by Thomas Rutledge, d. by Alberto Dias Soares, and graveyard (graves 1840+); bushfire 2017; school 1877–87; pop. 56 (1911), 785 (2006), 1,431 (2011).

Cary Bay (*Co. Northumberland*) see Coal Point.

Cascade (*Co. Fitzroy*) 30°14'S. 152°47'E., 14 km NE of Dorrigo, on Cascade Ck; logging; PO 1927; RS (6 km NW) 1925, station b. by Earp, Woodcock, Beveridge & Co. Pty Ltd, closed 1975; sawmills: Eades & Co. (acquired by Earp, Woodcock, Beveridge & Co. Pty Ltd), burnt down 1942 and Earp, Woodcock, Beveridge & Co. Pty Ltd, burnt down 1931; school 1941–75; telephone 1926; TX 1929–71; pop. 96 (1933), 175 (1947), 182 (1954), 154 (1961).

Casino (*Co. Rous*) 28°52'S. 153°03'E., 23 km W. of Lismore, on Richmond R.; (incl. Gays Hill, South Casino, West Casino); formerly The Crossing and The Falls, then Richmond River till *c.*1853; settled 1840 by Henry Clay and George Stapleton, surveyed 1853 by William Wedge Darke, laid out 1855 by Frederick Septimus Peppercorne, town gaz. 1855, first lots sold 1856, second land sale 1857, third land sale 1873, munic. proc. 1880, fourth land sale 1884, thrived 1905–6; timber, cattle, dairying, sugar-cane, horses, pigs, tropical fruit, tobacco, cotton, maize; abattoir (Northern Co-op. Meat Co. Ltd) 1939, fire 1954; airport 1934, new runway 1947, acquired 1950 by Commonwealth govt, rebuilt 1955; ambulance station b. 1939 by McIntosh and Scott, d. by Valentine Lee Miller, extensions 1948; Angl. C. b. 1871 by George Walters, closed 1904, relocated and reused, new one (St Mark's) b. 1905 by J.G. Taylor, d. by Frederick Johnson Board; Apostolic C.; Assemblies of God C. (Christ. Family); Bapt. C. b. 1907 by W. Anthony, d. by William Gill; boiling-down works (Clark Irving) 1847; bridges: Black Gully Bridge b. by E.L. Lawson over Black Gully, Irving Bridge b. 1873–76 by Robert Donaldson, 140 ft (42.7 m) McCallum truss, new one (steel truss) b. 1909 by Walter Frank Oakes, damaged 1954, temporary repairs 1954, replacement (concrete) 1959, over Richmond R., Short Street Bridge b. by K.F. Ariel over Richmond R.; broom and coffin factory (Trevor D. Bevan), burnt down 1930; butter factory (Casino Co-op. Dairy Co. Ltd) 1894, incl. ice works, sold 1897 to NSW Creamery Butter Co. Ltd, new one b. 1907 by M'Donald, damaged 1919, rebuilt 1926, damaged 1952, merged 1974 with Norco Co-op. Ltd, new factory 2016; carriage-works: Andrews Bros 1904 (became G.A. Andrews), Bowers and Duffy (fire 1913), T. Morrissey, C.H. Riley (became Riley & Co.); cemeteries: general (3,739 graves 1859+) 1876 and lawn (5,785 plots) 1961, incl. columbaria; CH 1861, new one b. 1881 by George Hughes, d. by James Johnstone Barnet, additions 1914; clock tower; cordial factories: Chris Balzer 1869 (became P. Balzer & Co. 1879–1938, then Casino Cordial Co. 1938, merged 1956 with O'Connor's Cordials), R.J. Jordan, N.G. Maguire 1933, Joseph O'Connor, sold 1916 to Denis Kelly, A.E. Olive, Pollock's; cyclone 1907; dairy factory (Foley Bros); dengue fever 1926; diphtheria 1913 and 1927; dust storms 1900 and 1926; electricity 1926; FB 1908 (station b. 1911 by Bannerman and Crawford, d. by J.G. Popplewell and J. Sykes, closed, sold 1919 to Casino Co-op. Dairy Co. Ltd and reused 1920, second one b. 1919 by S. Box, d. by William Hull McNiven); fibrous plaster works: Thomas Pidcock & Sons Pty Ltd, fire 1942 (4 boys died), and Jack Shannon, fire 1954; fires 1932, 1934, 1936; floods 1862, 1863, 1864, 1887, 1889, 1893, 1921, 1954, 2008; foot-bridge over Richmond R.; Foursquare Gospel C.; gale 1864; gaol, additions 1892 by W.R. Mackney & Son; gasworks b. 1911 by R. Hughes; hailstorms 1877 and 1919 (man killed and nearly every building damaged); hospital b. 1886 by George Hughes, d. by Stuart and Moyes, additions 1911, new one (Casino and Dist. Memorial) 1933, extended 1938 by Ryan and Hoyle, extended 1946, 1949, 1962, 1968, additions by Bennett Constructions Pty Ltd; joineries: T.A. Frater (fires 1928 and 1942), Elsmer Jones and John Brewster 1909 (incl. furniture factory, fire 1941), W.G. Mackney (burnt down 1905), W.S. Mackney; LDS (Mormon) C.; lock-up, alterations 1889 by Samuel Stead; measles epidemic 1916; meat canning works 1953; military detention camp for Indonesians during World War II; milk factory (Norco Co-op. Ltd) 1949; monumental stone works: C.J. Langker, P. McGeary, Monumental Masonry Pty Ltd; PO: Casino 1849, inundated 1877 (new one b. 1880 by Henry John Van der Waerden, additions 1884 by George Hughes, additions 1891 by Wheeler and Brown, additions 1892 by Mackney & Son, additions 1909 by J. Barnsley, additions 1915 and 1976), South Casino 1872–74, West Casino 1961; police barracks b. 1879 by Henry John Van der Waerden; powerhouse b. 1925–27 by P.F. Small, damaged 1927, closed 1934; Presb. C. 1881, relocated 1907 by W.G. Mackney, replacement (St Paul's) b. 1908 by W. Richard Hughes, d. by Popplewell and Sykes; PS 1853, new one 1961, additions 1984; punt 1865–67, across Richmond R.; railway barracks; railway bridge (steel Pratt truss) 1905, 180 ft (54.9 m), fabricated by Pope, Maher & Co., replaced, over Richmond R.; railway coal loader (Harman) 1947; railway engine shed; railway round-house (8 bays) 1928–86; railway turntable 1933, 75 ft (22.9 m); railway workshops 1932; reservoirs: one of 406,000 gal. (1,845.7 kl) 1905 and tower 1940; rifle range (South Casino) 1911; Rom. Cath. C. b. 1876 by Henry John Van der Waerden, d. by J.A. Despoints, additions 1902, demolished 1939, replacement (St Mary's) 1940 d. by Austin McKay; RS: Casino (2 km W.) 1905, station b. by Patrick Farrelly, refreshment rooms 1909, new station 1930 and South Casino 1905–74; sale-yards 1916 d. by Popplewell and Sykes, new yards 1930; Salv. Army C. b. 1907 by Tripp; sawmills: J.T. Bennett & Son (fire 1946), McCarthy's 1886, Pioneer (Alfred C. Simpson) 1907, bought 1918 by NSW Box Co. Ltd, Railway (Pidcock Bros Ltd, damaged 1919, burnt down 1934, rebuilt, fire 1942); schools: Casino 1861 (new building b. 1882 by J. Fanning, additions 1909 by William Anthony, additions 1920 by P.F. Small, additions 1925 by Fred Dinham, additions 1958, additions 2012 by T.F. Woollam & Son Pty Ltd), Casino HS 1945 (additions 1954 by B.L. Unicomb, additions 1959, new one 1965, additions 1971 and 1976, fire 2018), Casino Intermediate HS 1926 (additions 1933 by S.W. and R.C. Potter, additions 1941 by J. Schmitzer, closed 1944), West Casino 1952 (additions 1978 and 1990, additions 2010 by T.F. Woollam & Son Pty Ltd); SD Adventist C. 1951; sewerage 1934, augmentation 1991; storms 1879, 1888, 1927, 1952, 2001; streets lit by acetylene gas 1910, then coal gas 1911; tannery (Casino Hide Processors Pty Ltd) 1975; TC, additions 1959, became a campus of North Coast Institute in 1992, additions 2009 by T.F. Woollam & Son Pty Ltd; telegraph: Casino 1871 and Casino Railway 1930; telephone: Casino 1894, South Casino 1958, West Casino 1961; TX 1900, automatic 1975; typhoid 1903; Unit. C. (orig. Meth.) 1962 d. by Milo Kanangra Dunphy and Bruce Donald Loder; vulcanising works (Advanx); waterworks b. 1905 by G. Maddison, d. by W. Gill, filtration plant 1938, water supply augmentation 1985; weirs: Gulley Weir, Jabour Weir, Manyweathers Weir 1966–2009; Wes. Meth. C. 1888 d. by J. Robinson; wharves 1864 and 1881; whooping cough epidemic 1921; pop. *c.*150 (1866), *c.*300 (1870), 284 (1871), 718 (1881), 1,486 (1891), *c.*1,950 (1895), 1,926 (1901), 3,635 (1911), *c.*4,500 (1924), 5,287 (1933), 6,698 (1947), 7,844 (1954), 8,091 (1961), 8,507 (1966), 9,048 (1971), 9,456 (1976), 9,743 (1981), 10,067 (1986), 10,164 (1991), 9,990 (1996), 9,167 (2001), 9,400 (2006), 9,629 (2011).

Casino (*Co. Rous*) see also Old Casino.

Casino North (*Co. Rous*) 28°50'S. 153°04'E., 4 km NE of Casino; reservoir (steel), 450,000 gal. (2,045.7 kl); rifle range 1916; RS (formerly Tenby) 1903–66; school (One Tree Farm till 1936) 1918–36 and 1955–65; telephone 1921; TX 1925; pop. 156 (1947), 127 (1954), 120 (1961), 714 (2006), 975 (2011).

Casino South (*Co. Richmond*) see Greenridge.

Cassilis (*Co. Bligh*) 32°00'S. 149°59'E., 32 km SE of Coolah, on Munmurra R.; estab. as a private village by Robert Scott, laid out 1835, village gaz. 1869 as Dalkeith but known as Cassilis, designated as chief town of the county; sheep, wheat, goldmining; airfield; Angl. C. (St Columba of Iona) b. 1900 by Robert Thompson Highfield, d. by George Sanders & Son, and graveyard (208 graves 1882+); bridge 1878, new one (concrete) b. 1936 by Charles Hardy Contracting Co., over Munmurra R.; bushfire 2017; cemetery; CH (incl. lock-up) 1835, replacement 1860 d. by Alexander Dawson, additions 1870 by Patrick Ryan, additions 1882 by Oliver Saunders, repairs 1891 by Stoddart Bros, repairs 1907 by Albert Murphy; FB; fire 1899; floods 1862 and 1874; grasshopper infestation 1921; mouse plague 1943; PO 1836, new one b. 1880–82 by Oliver Saunders, repairs 1935 by J.H. Kertz; pound (stock) 1842; powerhouse

(Keith Vincent Lennox), plant repaired by John Henry Agnew after fire in 1949; PS 1860 d. by Alexander Dawson, new one b. 1891 by Patrick Berecry, d. by Walter Liberty Vernon; rifle range 1925, new one 1937; Rom. Cath. C. 1876, new one (St Joseph's) b. 1894 by John Miller, d. by Frederick Burnhardt Menkens, closed, and graveyard (143 graves 1876+); school 1875, new one b. 1876 by James Pritchard, renovated 1929 by Kurtz, new building b. 1938 by J.C. Pickles, moved to new site, additions 1962; snowstorm 1939; storms 1876, 1903, 1921; telegraph 1865, new office b. 1880–82 by Oliver Saunders; TX 1910; water reticulation 1969; pop. 49 (1846), 79 (1851), 82 (1856), 109 (1861), *c.*200 (1866), 141 (1871), 99 (1881), 164 (1891), 321 (1901), 383 (1911), 232 (1933), 235 (1947), 213 (1954), 168 (1961), 342 (2006), 350 (2011).

Cassons Camp (*Co. Clarence*) 29°54'S. 153°13'E., 23 km N. of Woolgoolga.

Castille (*Co. Buller*) 28°28'S. 152°37'E., 41 km W. of Kyogle, on Boomi Ck; telephone 1926; TX 1926.

Castle Doyle (*Co. Sandon*) 30°36'S. 151°46'E., 13 km SE of Armidale, on Powers Ck; farming and grazing; PO 1884–1941; school 1882–1921; telephone 1914; TX 1927; pop. 67 (1911), 62 (1954), 59 (1961), 457 (2011).

Castle Flat (*Co. St Vincent*) 35°20'S. 150°13'E., 22 km W. of Milton, on Clyde R.

Castle Forbes (*Co. Northumberland*) 32°38'S. 151°14'E., 9 km SE of Singleton, on Hunter R.

Castle Mountain (*Co. Buckland*) 31°32'S. 150°45'E., 7 km E. of Quirindi, on Quirindi Ck; farming; butter factory (Castle Mountain Co-op. Butter Factory Ltd) 1894, burnt down 1913; hailstorm 1900; Meth. C. 1902; PO 1883–1952; school 1882 b. by E. Douglas, closed 1947, reopened 1957–64; telephone 1908; TX 1928; Unit. C. (orig. Presb.) 1915, vestry added 1958; pop. 137 (1911), 130 (1933), 61 (1947), 72 (1954), 80 (1961).

Castle Rock (*Co. Brisbane*) 32°16'S. 150°44'E., 15 km W. of Muswellbrook; Angl. C.; 3 quarries; school 1919–20 and 1938–50; pop. 329 (2011).

Castlestead (*Co. King*) 34°30'S. 148°42'E., 7 km S. of Boorowa.

Casuarina (*Co. Rous*) 28°17'S. 153°34'E., 5 km S. of Kingscliff, on Coral Sea; (incl. Kings Forest and Salt Village developed by Don O'Rorke); former rutile mining area, now redeveloped.

Caswell (*Co. Durham*) 32°29'S. 151°08'E., 10 km N. of Singleton; farming and coalmining; PO 1907; telephone 1914; pop. 58 (1933).

Catalina (*Co. St Vincent*) see Batehaven.

Cataract (*Co. Camden*) see Cataract Dam

Cataract City (*Co. Camden*) see Cataract Dam.

Cataract Dam (*Co. Camden*) 34°16'S. 150°48'E., 13 km NW of Bulli, on Lake Cataract; orig. known as Cataract and Cataract City; site surveyed 1902, town dismantled 1907; Angl. C. (St Paul's) 1903; bushfire 1952; dam (cyclopean masonry) b. 1903–7 by Lane and Peters, d. by Leslie Augustus Burton Wade, 184 ft (56 m) high, spillway widened 1911–15, spillway modified 1983, dam strengthened 1988, on Cataract R.; PO (Cataract) 1902–7; powerhouse; Rom. Cath. C. 1903; sawmill; school 1903–7; tramway (quarry) 1903; pop. *c.*700 (1905).

Cateye (*Co. Macquarie*) 31°53'S. 152°38'E., 5 km W. of Harrington; pop. 6 (1841).

Cathcart (*Co. Wellesley*) 36°51'S. 149°24'E., 15 km NE of Bombala, on Dragon Swamp; orig. Taylors Flat; village gaz. 1854, surveyed 1857 by E.H. Arnheim; timber, mining, grazing, agric., dairying 1870s+, potatoes; Angl. C. (St Paul's) b. 1907 by William Gaunson; bridge 1884, new one b. 1914 by J. Love, repairs 1937 by A. Cowell; butter factory (Cathcart Co-op. Dairy Co. Ltd) 1895–1927; cemetery 1885; diphtheria (person died) 1909; droughts 1877, 1884, 1885, 1888, 1903–4, 1915, 1940–41; floods 1867, 1870, 1871, 1873, 1898, 1913, 1925, 1934, 1971; hailstorms 1907 and 1917; military barracks b. for Major Cathcart; PO 1860, new one b. 1900; PS 1897, new one b. 1907 by Thomas Moore & Son, new one (incl. lock-up) 1914–48; rifle range 1914; Rom. Cath. C. (St John's) 1880, and graveyard, church closed 1970 and sold; sale-yards 1914–55; sawmills: Burke and Fitch, Day and O'Brien, A.M. Fulton, Maurice McKinnery; school 1877, additions 1909 by Devitt Bros, closed 1975, building reused; snowstorm 1904; telegraph 1900; telephone 1891; TX 1912; Union C., closed 1931; pop. *c.*100 (1866), 345 (1901), 348 (1911), 190 (1929), 151 (1933), 107 (1947), 88 (1954), 90 (1961), 267 (2006).

Catherine Creek (*Co. King*) see Jerrawa.

Catherine Hill Bay (*Co. Northumberland*) 33°10'S. 151°38'E., 3 km SE of Nords Wharf, on Tasman Sea; (incl. Beaches subdivision, Cowper, gaz. 1870, Middle Camp, South Catherine Hill Bay); also known as New Wallsend; estab. 1873, largely abandoned 1877, deserted by 1879, re-estab. 1889 by Wallarah Coal Co., thrived 1894, classified 1983 by National Trust; mining (coal disc. by Pembledon) 1873–2002, sand mining in 1960s, seaport; Angl. C. (Holy Trinity), extended and renovated 1910, relocated and reopened 1923, closed, sold 2013 and reused, and graveyard; bushfires 1940, 1944, 1951, 2013; cemetery (956 graves 1896+) 1894; CH 1906; coal loader; coal preparation plant 1964–2002, demolished 2003; collieries: A Pit 1873–75, B Pit 1893, C Pit, D Pit, E Pit (Wallarah, closed 1963), F Pit (Moonee, modernised 1982, owned by Coal Operations Aust. Ltd, closed 2002), New Wallsend Mining Co. (estab. 1873 by Thomas Hale, closed 1875, abandoned 1877, reopened 1889 by Wallarah Coal Co. Ltd, taken over by J. & A. Brown & Abermain Seaham Collieries Ltd); dam; FB; jetty b. 1873 for Thomas Hale, 500 ft (152.4 m), burnt down, replaced 1888 by Kerl and Kerl, damaged 1974, rebuilt 1975, disused 2002, damaged 2013; lock-up 1890; measles epidemic 1898; Meth. C. 1965; miners' strikes 1874, 1896, 1899, 1906, 1911, 1913, 1917, 1920, 1921, 1924, 1927, 1928, 1929, 1930, 1932, 1935, 1936, 1938, 1939, 1954; PO 1874–1993, reused; powder magazines; PS 1875, moved 1924 into reused building, closed and reused; 3 quarries; radar station (No. 208) 1943–47; railway (Wallarah Coal Co. Ltd) to Mine Camp 1890; sawmill; scarlet fever 1898; school 1890–1985, building reused; storm 1974; telegraph 1894; telephone 1890; TX 1912, automatic 1952; United Meth. Free C. 1890; water supply 1934; pop. 354 (1891), 440 (1893), 651 (1901), 476 (1911), 896 (1933), 589 (1947), 375 (1973), *c.*350 (1987), 202 (1991), 230 (1996), 432 (2011).

Cathona (*Co. Rous*) 28°34'S. 153°32'E., 3 km SE of Mullumbimby.

Cathundral (*Co. Oxley*) 31°55'S. 147°50'E., 19 km NW of Trangie; grazing; PO 1910; RS 1901–74; pop. 64 (1911), 40 (1933), 58 (1947).

Catombal (*Co. Gordon*) 32°49'S. 148°48'E., 31 km N. of Molong; copper mine (Blatherys Gap); pop. 54 (1961).

Cattai Creek (*Co. Macquarie*) see Rawson.

Cattle Creek (*Co. Buckland*) 31°48'S. 150°17'E., 38 km N. of Merriwa.

Caulderwood (*Co. Harden*) 34°50'S. 148°14'E., 28 km N. of Gundagai.

Cavan (*Co. Cowley*) 35°01'S. 148°45'E., 26 km SW of Yass; PO 1877–1901; school 1883–93; telephone 1915; TX 1921, automatic 1951; pop. 103 (1911), 104 (1933), 112 (1947), 144 (1954), 134 (1961).

Cavan (*Co. Raleigh*) see Orama.

Cavan (*Co. Wentworth*) 33°42'S. 142°22'E., 54 km NE of Dareton, on Darling R.; school 1969–79.

Cavanbah (*Co. Rous*) see Byron Bay.

Cavan Park (*Co. Georgiana*) 34°07'S. 149°29'E., 40 km N. of Crookwell, on Cooks Vale Ck.

Cave Creek (*Co. Ashburnham*) 33°19'S. 148°55'E., 16 km W. of Orange; butter factory b. 1901 by Martin Clancey; school (Germans Hill till 1880) 1875–88 and 1915–18; pop. 163 (1901), 102 (1911), 22 (1933).

Cavell Hill (*Co. Burnett*) 29°40'S. 150°24'E., 22 km SW of Warialda.

Cave Point (*Co. Rous*) see Fingal Head.

Caves Beach (*Co. Northumberland*) 33°06'S. 151°39'E., 1 km SE of Swansea, on Tasman Sea; (incl. Pinny Beach); orig. The Plains, then The Plains Beach, then Caves Beach till 1960, then Mawson till 1965; subdivided

1935; Bapt. C. (Swansea Dist.); 4 quarries; reservoir (Pinney Beach); schools: Caves Beach 1968 and Swansea HS b. 1963 by A.E. Davis Pty Ltd, additions 1966 and 1979; Unit. C.; water supply 1955; pop. 3,936 (2011).

Cavvanba (*Co. Rous*) see Byron Bay.

Cawdor (*Co. Camden*) 34°05'S. 150°40'E., 5 km S. of Camden, on Matabil Ck; settled 1804, abandoned 1841, but later resettled; sheep, farming, dairying, poultry, horse studs; Angl. C. (St Jerome's) b. 1905 by Richard Hindes and Henry Farindon, d. by John Sulman, restored 2010; cemeteries: Camden general (1,795 graves 1901+), incl. columbarium, and Camden Rom. Cath. (920 graves 1845+); CH (Fletcher's Gaol) 1824; creamery (Camden Park Estate) 1895; drought 1839; FB; PO 1836–41 then 1927–31; schools: Cawdor 1858, new one b. 1888, fire 1923, additions 2010, and Camden HS (new site, old one at Camden) b. 2001 by Lahey Constructions Pty Ltd; telephone 1925; Unit. C. (orig. Meth.) b. 1902 by J. Peat; Wes. Meth. C. 1851, enlarged 1861, demolished, and graveyard (802 graves 1845+), incl. columbaria; pop. 428 (1825), 178 (1901), 173 (1911), 56 (1933), 73 (1954), 85 (1961), 195 (2001).

Cawdor (*Co. Camden*) see also Camden.

Cawongla (*Co. Rous*) 28°36'S. 153°06'E., 10 km E. of Kyogle, on Leycester Ck; Cambawongla till 1911; settled 1898 by Atkin; farming; Angl. C. (All Saints' Roach Memorial) b. 1927–29 by George James Grove, d. by C. Burrowes; butter factory (Norco Co-op. Ltd) b. 1919 by George James Grove, closed 1940; PO 1924; quarry (blue metal); sawmill (Edwin Roach & Co.) 1911; school 1928, additions 1933 by Diyal Sing & Son, closed 1975, building reused; telephone 1914; tornado 1935; TX 1920, automatic 1953; pop. 207 (1933), 187 (1947), 175 (1954), 156 (1961), 221 (2011).

Cedar Brush Creek (*Co. Northumberland*) 33°10'S. 151°17'E., 19 km W. of Wyee, on Cedar Brush Ck; orig. Brush Creek; timber, farming, dairying; cheese factory; PO 1907, burnt down 1930; sawmills: Thomas Cantrell Bradley (taken over 1946 by Reginald Thomas Bradley and Horace Edgar Bradley) and Frederick J. Carson (moved 1935 to Berricoe); school 1905–27 and 1957–80; telephone 1914; TX 1926, automatic 1954; pop. 78 (1911), 60 (1933), 106 (1947), 78 (1954), 64 (1961), 278 (2006).

Cedar Butt (*Co. Raleigh*) see Girralong.

Cedar Creek (*Co. Northumberland*) 32°51'S. 151°11'E., 13 km NW of Paxton, on Cedar Ck; sawmill (Jack Graham), moved to Quorrobolong; pop. 26 (1933).

Cedar Creek (*Co. Rous*) 28°25'S. 153°16'E., 17 km SW of Murwillumbah, on Cedar Ck.

Cedar Dump (*Co. Durham*) 32°07'S. 151°28'E., 47 km W. of Gloucester.

Cedar Grove (*Co. Rous*) see Tregeagle.

Cedar Party (*Co. Macquarie*) 31°48'S. 152°23'E., 8 km N. of Wingham, on Cedar Party Ck; farming; Angl. C. b. 1887 by Jim Evans, enlarged 1904 by E. Potts, closed, sold 1940, new one (St Alban's) b. 1941 by George Douglas, closed 1992, sold; bridge over Reynolds Ck; cemetery; creamery (Aust. Dairying Co.), relocated 1900; Meth. C. b. 1906 by Nesbitt; PO 1881; sawmill (Richard H. Worthing) 1902; school 1883 b. by Francis John Dennes, new one b. 1925, closed 1968; telephone 1915; TX 1916; Wes. Meth. C. 1881; pop. 12 (1841), 142 (1901), 217 (1911), 116 (1933), 238 (1947), 178 (1954), 178 (1961), 327 (2011).

Cedar Point (*Co. Rous*) 28°41'S. 153°00'E., 6 km S. of Kyogle, on Richmond R.; farming and dairying; bridge (concrete and steel) 1941, over Richmond R.; cheese factory (Urch and Clapp) 1912; hailstorm 2016; PO 1926; RS 1910, station b. by George Albert Leggo and John Allibone, closed 1969; sawmill (William Seccombe); telephone 1917; TX 1930; pop. 55 (1911), 149 (1933), 78 (1954), 108 (1961).

Cedar Tree Flat (*Co. Vernon*) 30°46'S. 152°11'E., 59 km SE of Armidale, on Macleay R.

Centaur (*Co. Rous*) see Banora Point.

Central Bucca (*Co. Fitzroy*) 30°13'S. 153°06'E., 9 km N. of Coffs Harbour, on Bucca Bucca Ck; bushfire 1946; Meth. C. 1916, relocated and extended 1940; sawmills: William Seccombe 1912, taken over 1934 by T.C. Seccombe, burnt down 1951 and Lyle Brisbane Swan; school 1910–63; telephone 1916; TX 1928; pop. 115 (1933), 93 (1947), 125 (1954), 100 (1961).

Central Burragorang (*Co. Camden*) 34°06'S. 150°26'E., 20 km NW of Picton, on Nattai R.; bridge over Nattai R., closed 1959; bushfire 1936; colliery (Valley Colliery No. 1); PS 1940–56; Rom. Cath. C. (St Paulinus's) 1840–1957, and graveyard (73 graves); school (Burragorang till *c.*1917) 1896–1904 and 1910–57.

Central Colo (*Co. Cook*) 33°25'S. 150°48'E., 18 km N. of North Richmond, on Colo R.; farming and orchards; bridge 1941, over Colo R.; PO 1881–1927; school 1916–34; telephone 1921; wharf (variously known as Blundell's, Bullock and Gee's) 1894, derelict after 1940; pop. 94 (1901), 105 (1933).

Central Doon Doon (*Co. Rous*) 28°30'S. 153°18'E., 13 km NE of Nimbin, on Griers Ck; telephone 1924; TX 1945.

Central Dyraaba (*Co. Rous*) 28°43'S. 152°52'E., 17 km SW of Kyogle, on Doubtful Ck; farming; PO 1926–73; quarry; telephone 1924; TX 1925–68; pop. 61 (1954), 55 (1961).

Central Kempsey (*Co. Dudley*) see Kempsey.

Central Lansdowne (*Co. Macquarie*) 31°45'S. 152°29'E., 18 km NE of Wingham, on Koppin Yarratt Ck; (incl. Koppin Yarratt); farming and dairying; airfield; PO 1905; Meth. C. 1948 d. by C.J. Mathers; Salv. Army C. 1904; school (Koppin Yarratt till 1939) 1885–1971; telephone 1908; TX 1947; typhoid 1900; Wes. Meth. C. b. 1901 by William Henry Unicomb, closed, bought 1949 by G.A. Minett, demolished; pop. 53 (1933), 120 (1947), 96 (1954), 93 (1961).

Central Macdonald (*Co. Hunter*) 33°20'S. 150°59'E., 35 km W. of Ourimbah, on Macdonald R.; orig. Benton; farming and orchards; Angl. C. (St Jude's) 1918, closed, sold and reused, and graveyard (graves 1883–1904); bushfire 1898; cemetery; flood 1949; PO 1870; sawmill (C.E. Butler, E. Butler and S.J. Butler); school (McDonald River till 1870, Central McDonald River till 1875, Central McDonald till 1981, then Macdonald Valley) 1850, new one 1880, additions 1902 by J.H. Fleming, new building b. 1929 by C. Sheaves, destroyed 1949, rebuilt; telephone 1916; TX 1924; wharf b. 1903 by Francis Hearne; pop. 201 (1891), 132 (1901), 89 (1933), 92 (1947), 77 (1954), 55 (1961), 27 (1966).

Central McDonald (*Co. Hunter*) see Central Macdonald.

Central McDonald River (*Co. Hunter*) see Central Macdonald.

Central Mangrove (*Co. Northumberland*) 33°18'S. 151°14'E., 15 km NW of Ourimbah, on Popran Ck; orchards; food factory (Agrana Fruit Aust. Pty Ltd); fruit packing house (Producers' Co-op. Distributing Society); Greek Orthodox C. (St Dionysios's); Rom. Cath. C. (St Francis of Assisi); sawmill; school 1957, new school 1958; pop. 286 (2011).

Central Pappinbarra (*Co. Macquarie*) see Hollisdale.

Central Raleigh (*Co. Raleigh*) see Raleigh.

Central Sherwood (*Co. Fitzroy*) 30°01'S. 153°02'E., 20 km NW of Woolgoolga, on Sherwood Ck.

Central Tilba (*Co. Dampier*) 36°19'S. 150°05'E., 11 km SW of Narooma, on Bobundara Ck; subdivided by Samuel William Bate and lots sold 1895, classified 1974 by National Trust, bypassed by highway 1990; goldmining, farming, dairying (declined in 1960s), now tourist craft village; cemetery (Tilba District, 102 graves) 1901, restored 2013 by Jacob Castagna; CH, damaged 1904; cheese factory (ABC Dairy Factory Co. Ltd) 1891, new one b. 1925 by A.G. Brown, d. by H.W. May & Co., amalgamated 1972 with Bega Co-op. Society Ltd, sold 1982, reopened 1983 by ABC Cheese Factory Pty Ltd, bought 1999 by King Island Co., bought 2001 by National Foods, taken over 2005 by San Miguel Corp., sold 2006, bought 2012 by Nick and Erica Dibden, who also produce milk; electricity 1952; FB (old station sold 2017, new station

b. 2012); mine (Lake View Gold Mining) 1911, incl. cyanide plant and 5 head stamper battery, closed 1916; PO 1897, new one b. 1905, closed and reused, new one in rented premises; PS 1897–1942; rifle range b. 1914 by Newman; school (Noorooma till 1889, then Tilba Tilba till 1962) 1884, new school b. 1885 by C.R. Stubbs, new one b. 1900 on new site by Jacob John Shottin; telephone 1897; TX 1921; Unit. C. (orig. Meth.) b. 1907 by Jacob John Shottin, closed and sold 2007 to Esther Faerber, restored and reused; water supply 1970; pop. 277 (1901), 301 (1911), 143 (1921), 252 (1933), 185 (1947), 198 (1954), 180 (1961), 222 (2006), 391 (2011).

Central Tyndale (*Co. Clarence*) 29°33'S. 153°12'E., 5 km S. of Maclean, on Shark Ck; Shark Creek till 1925; maize then sugar-cane; bridge 1882, (second) b. 1916 by Country Concrete Constructions Ltd, (third) b. 1934–36 by State Monier Pipe & Reinforced Concrete Works (reinforced concrete bowstring arch), 151 ft (46 m), d. by Alexander Theodore Britton, disused, new one, over Shark Ck; caterpillar infestation 1919; flood (whole village inundated) 1890; PO 1917–86; punt (James O'Mara) 1872, across Shark Ck; school 1877–1927; telephone 1901; TX 1942–69; pop. 104 (1911), 38 (1933).

Central Wyalong (*Co. Gipps*) see Wyalong West.

Ceres (*Co. Narromine*) 32°11'S. 148°10'E., 9 km NW of Narromine; RS 1880–1964; school (Armoy) 1911–36.

Cessnock (*Co. Northumberland*) 32°50'S. 151°21'E., 22 km SW of Maitland, on Black Ck; (incl. Aberdare, surveyed by T.H. Smith, laid out 1905, Caledonia, East Cessnock, North Cessnock, South Cessnock, West Cessnock); settled by John and David Campbell, surveyed by Blakers, founded and first lots sold 1853, land boom 1903–23, housing boom 1918–26, munic. proc. 1926, munic. proc. (Greater Cessnock) 1957, city proc. (Greater Cessnock) 1958; orig. wheat, declined 1870+, grapes 1866+, tobacco, then maize, grazing, dairying, farming, timber, mining (coal disc. 1891 by Hammond, confirmed 1892 by George Brown), textiles; ambulance station (in converted premises) 1937, new one b. 1953 by C. Turnbull, d. by J. Bartlett, new one 2012; Angl. C.: St Luke's 1867, demolished 1906, new one b. 1890 by James Richardson and St John's 1910 d. by Cyril Blacket, spire added later, church extended 1975, and columbaria; Apostolic C.; Assemblies of God C. (Hope Valley Christ.); baby carrier factory (Cuddleseat Manufacturing Co.) estab. 1944 by George Ryder; Bapt. C. b. 1913 by McNaughton and Hafey, fire 2017, closed, and columbarium; boot factory (Thomas Sanders); brickworks (C. Bush); bridge over Black Ck; bushfires 1928, 1936, 1944, 1952, 1965, 2010, 2013; butter factory estab. 1899 by Vincent Doyle, taken over 1904 by Walker Lane and Thomas Peters, bought by them in 1906, partnership dissolved 1907, incorp. 1907 as Cessnock Co-op. Dairy Co. Ltd, merged with Raymond Terrace Dairy Co. Ltd, closed, reused 1926 as ice works, demolished 1937, new factory 1926; carriage-works (G. McCullock); cemeteries: Cessnock (5,000+ burials, incl. 3,500+ graves) 1877 and Gordon Williams Memorial, formerly Aberdare, (2,025 graves) 1906, incl. lawn cemetery and columbaria; CH 1871 (incl. lock-up), demolished 1899, replacement b. 1883 by George Brown, demolished 1915, new one b. 1913–15 d. by George McRae, renovations and repairs 1925, additions and alterations 1990; Christ. Brethren Assemblies C. (Gospel); Church of Christ 1923, renovated 1946; clothing factory 1944; collieries: Aberdare (Caledonian Collieries Ltd, fire 1910, men killed 1912, 1914, 1930, 1945), Aberdare East (estab. 1966 by Coal & Allied Industries Ltd, o. 1968, closed 1982, largely demolished 1982, remainder reused 1983–88), Aberdare Extended (estab. 1904, o. 1907 by Caledonian Coal Co., became Caledonian Collieries Ltd in 1912, strikes 1916, 1926, 1927, 1928, 1929, 1934, 1936, 1937, 1938, 1940, 1941, 1943, 1944, 1947, flood 1949 killed 22 pit ponies, closed 1963, demolished 1973–83), Aberdare North (estab. 1914 by Caledonian Collieries Ltd as Aberdare Tunnel, o. 1915, upcast air shaft 1951, renamed 1952, bath-house and extra drift 1954, closed 1959, acquired 1960 by Coal & Allied Industries Ltd, reopened 1964, fires 1965, 1966, 1975, closed and largely demolished 1988), Aberdare No. 7 (o. 1957 by Caledonian Collieries Ltd, acquired 1960 by Coal & Allied Industries Ltd, fires 1961 and 1963, closed 1968, worked as open-cut 1969–72, razed), Aberdare Shaft (estab. 1904 by Caledonian Coal Co., o. 1905, taken over 1913 by Caledonian Collieries Ltd, drift tunnel 1915, flooded 1926, closed 1931, reopened 1934, flooded 1937, acquired 1960 by Coal & Allied Industries Ltd, closed except for washery 1960, washery dismantled 1982, colliery razed 1985), Aberdare West (estab. 1954 by Caledonian Collieries Ltd, o. 1955, acquired 1960 by Coal & Allied Industries Ltd, closed 1965, reopened 1966, closed 1968, razed), Abernock (estab. 1931 by James Brown, transferred 1942 to Joshua Brown, closed 1944, razed), Caldare No. 1 Open-Cut (o. 1944 by Caledonian Collieries Ltd, flooded 1949, closed 1952), Caldare No. 2 Open-Cut (o. 1949 by Caledonian Collieries Ltd, flooded and filled in 1949, never produced coal), Caledon Open-Cut (o. 1946 by Caledonian Collieries Ltd, closed 1952, reopened, closed 1968, site rehabilitated), Cessnock No. 2 also known as Little Cessnock (estab. 1917 by Wickham & Bullock Island Co., d. by Clem Jones, o. 1918, taken over 1927 by Cessnock Collieries Ltd, man killed 1940, fire 1946, closed and demolished 1948, worked as open-cut 1948–55, open-cut reopened, closed 1972), Hill End (estab. 1924 by Peter Noble, Thomas Russell and Thomas Bartlett, o. 1925, taken over 1928 by Hill End Coal Mining Co., closed by fire 1930, reopened 1931, closed 1932, fire and subsidence 1933), Neath Open-Cut (Caledonian Collieries Ltd, operated 1951–59 by N.H. Bowers Pty Ltd); confectionery factory (White Rose Cessnock Ltd); Cong. C.: Bridge Street one b. 1909 by J. Hughes-Jones, d. by F.A. Jackson and West Cessnock 1922; cordial factories: Elliott and Brown, John Ellis (taken over 1951 by Reg Astley, taken over 1968 by Brian Scott), Healey Bros, Arthur Needham & Son, Ryan and Rolfe (b. 1915 by J.J. Ryan, taken over 1919 by W.D. Glynn & Co., later sold to Scott's Cordials), Sharpe Bros (estab. by John Sharpe and A.C. Bellini) 1913–15, Les Slack and Edwin Alfred Slack 1941 (became Slack's Cordials Pty Ltd in 1963, closed 1977), James Wolstenholme (sold 1923 to Martin and George Knipe, new factory 1971, closed 1988; dam; earth tremors 1925 and 2014; electricity 1912; FB (station b. 1916 by Thorne); fibrous plaster works (John Crockett); fires 1906 and 1924; floods 1913, 1926, 1927, 2007; foot-bridge over Black Ck; Foursquare Gospel C. (City); gales 1928 and 1944; gaol 1972 d. by D. Moline, additions 1976, 1979, 1985, new one (Shortland) b. 2011 by John Holland (Constructions) Pty Ltd, d. by Perumal Pedavoli, new one (Hunter) 2018, extensions (Shortland) 2019 by Richard Crookes Constructions, d. by Guymer Bailey Architects; gasworks (Aberdare) 1958; German measles epidemic 1937; hailstorm 1948; heatwave (man died) 1939; hospital b. 1912–14, additions 1923 and 1927, damaged 1936, additions 1937 and 1961; ice-cream factory (A. Williams & Co. Ltd); ice works; LDS (Mormon) C.; Meth. C.: Aberdare 1907, closed, reopened 1939 and Cessnock 1908, replaced 1911; miners' strikes 1915, 1916, 1920, 1921, 1924, 1925, 1927, 1929–30, 1932, 1934, 1936, 1939, 1940, 1941, 1942, 1943, 1944, 1948, 1949, 1950, 1954, 1957; monumental stone works: Thomas Browne Pty Ltd, E.B. Roberts, William Wallace, jun. (Aberdare); pneumonia epidemic (woman died) 1908; PO: Aberdare 1907, Cessnock 1864 (new one b. 1910 by W.J. Wooden, extensions and alterations 1955 by N.F. Mitchell), East Cessnock 1955–78, North Cessnock 1961, South Cessnock 1927, West Cessnock 1925; pottery (Northern Potteries Pty Ltd); Presb. C.: Aberdare 1909 and

Cessnock (St Andrew's) 1906, and graveyard; PS 1871, demolished 1899, (second) b. 1899 by William Henry Noad, (third, incl. lock-up) b. 1934 by Pickles and McIlroy, additions 1964 and 1975; psychiatric hospital for the elderly (Allandale) 1962, additions 1967; quarry; 2 reservoirs (one b. 1923 by Paterson Bros and Teasdale Smith); rifle range 1917; Rom. Cath. C. (St Joseph's) 1954 d. by John Patrick Gannon; RS (on South Maitland Railway 1904–72): Aberdare 1904, Cessnock (old station demolished 1924, new one b. 1924 by James Lawson, razed), Caledonia; Salv. Army C. 1912, new one 1963; sawmills: Excelsior Steam Sawmills (Gould Bros & Co. Pty Ltd, burnt down 1921), J. Graham, William Harman 1883, O'Hara's, A. Shedden, A.J. Turner (removed 1883 by George Brown from Deadmans Ck, 4 km NE of Cessnock); schools: Cessnock 1859 (repairs 1895 by A.J. Ingles, new one b. 1908, additions 1910 by G. Taylor, d. by Walter Liberty Vernon, additions 1918 d. by Colonel Wells, additions 1924 by Montague Audet, additions 1925 by E.R.S. Potter, additions 1995, additions 2010 by Kingston Building Aust. Pty Ltd), Cessnock HS 1934 (new one b. 1937 d. by Cobden Parkes, additions 1952, 1958, 1967, 1979, 1985, additions 2013 by O'Donnell & Hanlon Pty Ltd), East Cessnock 1928 (b. by Kent and Kent, d. by Richard McDonald Seymour Wells, additions 1959 and 1968, major upgrade 1995), Mount View HS 1985, additions 1991, South Cessnock 1926–36 and 1959–87, West Cessnock 1920, additions 1925 by Montague Audet, additions 1956 and 1985; SD Adventist C.; sewerage 1933; smallpox 1915; storm 1936; streets electric lit 1912; TC 1916, new building b. 1924 by C. Davis & Sons, new building b. 1956 on new site by F.H. Compton & Sons, additions 1985, became a campus of Hunter Institute of Technology in 1992, additions 2001; telegraph 1888, new office b. 1910 by W.J. Wooden; telephone: Aberdare 1909, Cessnock 1892, East Cessnock 1955, North Cessnock 1961, South Cessnock 1924; toll-gate 1861; towel factory (Bonds Industries Ltd) 1949–2009; TX 1909; typhoid 1908 and 1921; underwear factory (Bonds Industries Ltd) 1947; Unit. C. (orig. Meth.) 1974, and columbarium; vulcanising works (Tom R. Saunders); water supply 1905; winery (Kelman Vineyard) 1999; pop. 11 (1861), 11 (1866), 62 (1871), 130 (1881), 203 (1891), 165 (1901), 5,102 (1911), *c.*8,000 (1912), 9,340 (1921), *c.*12,000 (1926), 14,385 (1933), 13,029 (1947), 14,417 (1954), 13,833 (1961), 15,332 (1966), 16,141 (1971, incl. Bellbird), 16,256 (1976, incl. Bellbird), 16,916 (1981, incl. Bellbird), 17,506 (1986, incl. Bellbird), 17,932 (1991, incl. Bellbird), 17,540 (1996, incl. Bellbird), 17,825 (2001, incl. Bellbird), 18,316 (2006, incl. Bellbird), 20,015 (2011, incl. Bellbird).

Chain of Ponds (*Co. King*) 34°48'S. 149°09'E., 21 km E. of Yass, on Jerrawa Ck; school 1878–1904.

Chain Valley Bay (*Co. Northumberland*) 33°10'S. 151°34'E., 3 km N. of Lake Munmorah, on Chain Valley Bay; (incl. Kingfisher Shores and Valhalla Village); footbridge over Karignan Ck; 2 jetties; sewerage 1990; pop. 78 (1933), 89 (1961), 840 (1986), 1,658 (1991), 2,266 (1996), 2,632 (2001), 2,452 (2011).

Chakola (*Co. Beresford*) 36°06'S. 149°11'E., 15 km N. of Cooma, on Numeralla R.; farming and grazing; PO 1894; quarry; railway bridge (timber truss) 1889, damaged and repaired 1900, replaced (steel Warren truss) 1926, over Numeralla R.; RS (Umaralla till 1921) 1889, station b. by Walker and Swan, closed 1976; school (Black Rock till 1889, then Umaralla Siding till 1921) 1883–1959; telephone 1907; TX 1922; pop. 136 (1901), 124 (1933), 73 (1947), 54 (1954), 85 (1961).

Chalkers (*Co. Wallace*) see Adaminaby.

Chalker's Flat (*Co. Camden*) see Lower Mittagong.

Chalkerville (*Co. Camden*) see Colo Vale.

Chambers Creek (*Co. Bathurst*) 33°08'S. 149°24'E., 37 km NW of Bathurst, on Chambers Ck; settlement defunct; goldmining 1872+ and 1959+; 10 mines; PO

1872; school 1874–75; 4 stamper batteries (incl. Sir John Moore's 25 head).

Chambigne (*Co. Fitzroy*) 29°44'S. 152°47'E., 14 km W. of South Grafton; dairying and grazing; Community C., PO 1927–31; school 1896–1902 and 1907–16; telephone 1920; TX 1945; pop. 84 (1911), 51 (1933).

Chandler (*Co. Clarke*) 30°31'S. 152°03'E., 37 km E. of Armidale; cemetery 1881; school 1882–85, reopened 1913, new building b. 1914 by Alfred Ede, additions 2010; pop. 52 (1911).

Channon Grass (*Co. Rous*) see The Channon.

Chapman Island (*Co. Northumberland*) see Carrington.

Chapmans Farm (*Co. Parry*) 31°27'S. 151°11'E., 6 km E. of Nundle.

Charawarra (*Co. Richmond*) 29°11'S. 152°49'E., 42 km SW of Casino, on Four Mile Ck.

Charbon (*Co. Roxburgh*) 32°53'S. 149°58'E., 3 km S. of Kandos; estab. 1928; aerial cableway; bushfire 1990; cement works (Standard Cement Co.) 1926, strike 1929; coalmines: Centennial Coal Co. Ltd and Kandos-Coomber Mining Co. Pty Ltd; PO 1927, burnt down and replaced 1929; quarry; RS 1927–74; sawmill (Jack Grady); school 1928 b. by M. Johnston, closed 1972; telephone 1926; water augmentation 1955; pop. 336 (1933), 190 (1947), 293 (1954), 341 (1961), 226 (1971), 145 (2006), 231 (2011).

Charcoal Creek (*Co. Camden*) see Unanderra.

Charity Creek (*Co. Macquarie*) 31°54'S. 152°13'E., 14 km W. of Wingham, on Manning R.; bridge (concrete) b. 1926 by Bradshaw and MacIntyre, d. by R.S. Morris & Co.; railway bridge (steel truss), 120 ft (36.6 m), fabricated by R.L. Scrutton & Co., erected 1913 by Smith, Timms & Co., over Charity Ck; RS 1913, station b. by John Allibone, closed 1975; pop. 48 (1933).

Charles Pit (*Co. Northumberland*) see Charlestown.

Charles Town (*Co. Northumberland*) see Charlestown.

Charlestown (*Co. Northumberland*) 32°58'S. 151°42'E., 9 km SW of Newcastle, on Winding Ck; orig. Charles Pit, then Raspberry Gully, then South Waratah, then Charles Town; surveyed and subdivided 1876, first lots sold 1876; orig. mining, then also fruit and poultry; Angl. C. (St Alban's) 1922, closed; Assemblies of God C. (Abundant Life); Bapt. C. 1944, new one 1947; bushfires 1884 (7 houses destroyed), 1933, 1951, 1994; Celebration City Church International; cemetery (Whitebridge) 1891; CH 1901–36, reused; Christadelphian C.; Church of Christ; collieries: South Waratah or Raspberry Gully Pit (estab. 1873–75, o. 1876 as Charles's Pit by Waratah Coal Co., strikes 1888 and 1894, acquired 1895 by Caledonian Coal Co., strike 1903, fire 1947, closed 1961, fire 1964, largely demolished 1969) and Newcastle Myall (Scottish-Australian Coal Mining Co.); FB (station o. 1936 in old court-house); flood 2007; Lay Meth. C. b. 1902 by Edward Pickering, closed, dismantled, moved 1950 to Garden Suburb and reused; LDS (Mormon) C.; lock-up b. 1887 by William Dart; New Apostolic C.; PO: Charlestown 1877 and South Waratah 1951–84; Presb. C. 1923, new one (St David's) 1962; Prim. Meth. C. 1880; PS 1879, new one 1978; railway (Caledonian Collieries Ltd) to Port Waratah; Rom. Cath. C. (Immaculate Conception) b. 1904 by G. Taylor, d. by Thomas A. Bourke, new one (St Mary Immaculate); schools: Charlestown b. 1879 by James Cropley, additions 1890, 1900, 1923, 1927, fire 1933, additions 1958 and 1976, East Charlestown 1959, additions 1964, South Charlestown 1963, additions 1976; SD Adventist C.; sewerage 1959; storm 2007; TC 1979, became a campus of Hunter Institute of Technology in 1992, closed 2003; telegraph 1890; telephone 1899; TX 1925, automatic 1947; Unit. C.: Charlestown and Whitebridge (orig. Meth.) 1959 d. by Milo Kanangra Dunphy and Bruce Donald Loder; water supply 1927; Wes. Meth. C. 1880, dilapidated, repaired and reopened 1937; pop. *c.*200 (1877), 268 (1881), 448 (1891), 662 (1901), 515 (1911), 736 (1921), 1,357 (1933), 2,400 (1947),

11,725 (2006), 12,411 (2011).

Charlesworth Bay (*Co. Fitzroy*) see Coffs Harbour.

Charleville (*Co. Bathurst*) see Four Mile Creek.

Charleyong (*Co. St Vincent*) 35°15'S. 149°55'E., 24 km NE of Braidwood, on Mongarlowe R.; Hush's 1901–17; grazing; bridge (Allan timber truss) b. 1901 by Jakob Nybeck, 293 ft (89.3 m), over Mongarlowe R.; FB; flood 1860; PO 1927–71; telephone 1912; TX 1923; pop. 60 (1901), 26 (1933).

Charleyong (*St Vincent*) see also Marlowe.

Charleys Forest (*Co. St Vincent*) 35°24'S. 149°59'E., 17 km E. of Braidwood; farming and grazing; bushfire 1905; PO 1927–31; sawmill (Reuben Burke); telephone 1925; TX 1949; pop. 57 (1901), 46 (1933), 74 (1947), 373 (2006).

Charlmont (*Co. Raleigh*) 30°28'S. 152°58'E., 7 km E. of Bellingen, on Bellinger R.; telephone 1925; TX 1954.

Charlotte Bay (*Co. Gloucester*) see Boomerang Beach and Pacific Palms.

Charlotte Pass (*Co. Wallace*) 36°26'S. 148°20'E., 8 km W. of Perisher Valley, on Spencers Ck; telephone 1961; TX 1961.

Charlottes Vale (*Co. Bathurst*) see Perthville.

Charlton (*Co. Clyde*) 30°14'S. 146°44'E., 32 km S. of Brewarrina, on Boomi Ck; RS 1925–74.

Charlton (*Co. Westmoreland*) 33°41'S. 149°37'E., 22 km W. of Oberon, on Campbells R.

Charmhaven (*Co. Northumberland*) 33°14'S. 151°30'E., 4 km NW of Gorokan, on Budgewoi Lake; (incl. Woongarrah); Assemblies of God C.: Northlakes Christ. Life and Sparks Road Christ.; bridge 1916, replaced 1933, to Blue Haven and San Remo, over Wallarah Ck; FB 1956; fibreboard plant (Borg Manufacturing); food factory (Kellogg's) 2000; PO 1956; school (Woongarrah) 2005; sewage works 1991; telephone 1956; pop. 202 (1961), 5,532 (2006), 6,832 (2011).

Chatham (*Co. Macquarie*) see Taree.

Chatham Valley (*Co. Westmoreland*) 33°52'S. 149°54'E., 18 km S. of Oberon, on Duckmaloi R.; mine (gold) 1936; pop. 27 (1933).

Chatmans Flat (*Co. Gordon*) 32°48'S. 148°38'E., 39 km SW of Wellington.

Chatsbury (*Co. Argyle*) 34°33'S. 149°48'E., 24 km N. of Goulburn, on Chatsbury Ck; farming and grazing; Angl. C. (Christ) 1895, demolished 1972, and graveyard (burials 1903–29) 1904; PO 1884; Presb. C. (Redhill) b. 1871 by Armstrong, new one (St Andrew's) 1906; school 1871–1909 and 1928–39; slate quarries (5 km SW) 1874; telephone 1905; TX 1912; pop. 109 (1901), 71 (1911), 91 (1933), 71 (1954), 254 (2006).

Chatsworth (*Co. Clarence*) see Chatsworth Island.

Chatsworth Island (*Co. Clarence*) 29°24'S. 153°15'E., 8 km NE of Maclean, in Clarence R.; (incl. Chatsworth, bypassed by highway 1986); sugar-cane, maize, dairying, mixed farming; Angl. C. (St Luke's) 1883; bridge (Warregah Bridge), 489 ft (149 m), 1976, over Clarence R.; cordial factory (Clare & Co.), burnt down 1885; creamery (Fresh Food & Ice Co.) 1896; fires 1876 and 1885; floods 1890 and 1893; Free Presb. C. b. 1939 by Allan Cameron, d. by F.J. Robertson, closed 1975; measles epidemic 1920; Meth. C. 1964; PO 1870; PS: Chatsworth, closed 1888 and Chatsworth Island 1875–1928; punt, ceased 1976, across Clarence R.; Rom. Cath. C. (St Patrick's) 1880; sawmill (R.H. Addison); school 1868, new buildings 1883 by G. Wunderlich, repairs 1898 by T.H. Fago, additions 2010; sugar mills: CSR 1870–87, David Kirk (b. 1872 by Lane and Lacey, horse powered, upgraded 1878 to steam, sold to Martin, Law and Perrego), Jones & Sons, McAulay's (mill moved 1888 to Ewingsdale by Edward Stephen Atkins), G. Morrison, R. Rankin; telegraph 1884; telephone 1914; TX 1919; Union C.; water reticulation 1966; wharf b. 1885 by J. Walsh; pop. 393 (1881), 369 (1891), 294 (1901), 329 (1911), 855 (1924), 255 (1933), 287 (1954), 281 (1961), 282 (1947).

Chaucer (*Co. Bathurst*) 33°36'S. 148°46'E., 11 km SE of Canowindra, on Emu Ck; FB; school 1907 b. by W.A. Hickey, closed 1922; telephone 1955; pop. 40 (1933).

Cheero Point (*Co. Northumberland*) see Mooney Mooney.

Cheesemans Creek (*Co. Ashburnham*) 33°14'S. 148°53'E., 15 km S. of Molong, on Boree Ck; farming and grazing; PO 1875; telephone 1917; TX 1924; pop. 130 (1911), 39 (1933), 50 (1947).

Cheetham Flats (*Co. Westmoreland*) 33°33'S. 150°03'E., 12 km SW of Lithgow, on Cheethams Ck; also known as Cheetham's Flats; Meth. C. 1915; pop. 70 (1911).

Cheetham's Flats (*Co. Westmoreland*) see Cheetham Flats.

Chellas (*Co. Hardinge*) 29°55'S. 151°17'E., 7 km NE of Tingha; school 1906 b. by H.C. Stortenbecker, closed 1957.

Chellington (*Co. Bland*) 34°15'S. 147°36'E., 22 km N. of Temora; PO 1910–16.

Chelmsford (*Co. Rous*) 28°42'S. 153°08'E., 14 km SW of Nimbin, on Leycester Ck; farming and dairying; PO 1927–31; telephone 1913; pop. 61 (1933), 85 (1947).

Chelmsford (*Co. Rous*) see also Wongavale.

Cherry Tree (*Co. Gloucester*) 32°35'S. 152°14'E., 11 km NE of Hawks Nest, on Myall R.

Cherry Tree (*Co. Roxburgh*) 33°17'S. 149°32'E., 16 km N. of Bathurst, on Dicks Ck; airfield.

Cherry Tree Hill (*Co. Arrawatta*) 29°32'S. 151°00'E., 26 km S. of Ashford; farming and grazing; cemetery 1895; PO 1905; Rom. Cath. C. (St David's) 1892, new one (removed from Delungra) 1939, moved 1941 to Coolatai; storm 1961; telephone 1904; TX 1911; pop. 60 (1901), 75 (1933), 52 (1961).

Cherry Tree Hill (*Co. Roxburgh*) 33°01'S. 149°53'E., 20 km SW of Kandos, on Warrangunia Ck; goldmining; mines: Bowcocks Tunnel, Cherry Tree Hill Deep Lead 1936–38, Evans Shaft, Franki Tunnel, Galloways Tunnel, Hagans Shaft, Ilford Shaft, Kaolin Tunnel, Leaders 1937, Withers Tunnel; 2 quarries; toll-gate.

Chertsey (*Co. Northumberland*) see Springfield.

Cheshunt (*Co. Hunter*) 32°31'S. 151°01'E., 14 km W. of Singleton.

Cheviot (*Co. Clarence*) 29°26'S. 153°05'E., 11 km W. of Maclean; school 1894, additions 1897 by F.J. Robertson, closed 1910.

Chichester (*Co. Gloucester*) 32°12'S. 151°37'E., 26 km NW of Dungog, on Chichester R.; Angl. C. (St James's) 1903–36, renovated by Saxby, reopened 1940; bridge 1944; bushfire 1905; foot-bridge; sawmill (estab. 1931 by G.F. Heath, acquired and relocated by J. Croll & Sons); school 1880, new one b. 1882 by W. Smith, closed 1969; telephone 1914; TX 1930; Unit. C. (orig. Meth.) 1906; waterworks (to supply water to Maitland and Newcastle) 1925; Wes. Meth. C. 1883; pop. 153 (1911), 86 (1933), 95 (1947), 80 (1954), 65 (1961).

Chidowla (*Co. Buccleuch*) see Nanangroe.

Chifley (*Co. Cook*) see Lithgow.

Chifley Vale (*Co. Bathurst*) 33°27'S. 149°34'E., 3 km S. of Bathurst.

Chilcotts Creek (*Co. Buckland*) 31°40'S. 150°51'E., 12 km N. of Murrurundi.

Chilcotts Grass (*Co. Rous*) 28°50'S. 153°20'E., 5 km SE of Lismore, on Tucki Tucki Ck; farming; bridge (Mathiesons Bridge), over Tucki Tucki Ck; creamery 1895; Meth. C. 1930; PO 1903–31; Wes. Meth. C. 1893; pop. 99 (1901), 95 (1911), 56 (1933), 182 (2011).

Childowla (*Co. Harden*) 34°55'S. 148°33'E., 34 km W. of Yass, on Murrumbidgee R.; earth tremor 2007.

Chillingham (*Co. Rous*) 28°19'S. 153°17'E., 12 km W. of Murwillumbah, on Rous R.; Bean Tree till 1913; dairying and bananas; bridge (Zara Bridge), destroyed 1921, second one b. 1928 by W.R. Isaacs, third one (concrete) b. 1977 by Chris Adams; bushfire 1936; floods 1921, 1928, 1945; hailstorm 1917; landslip 1928; Meth. C. (Numinbah), closed, sold and reused; PO 1926; Presb. C. 1914; sawmill (Chillingham Timber Co.); school (Zara 1908–23) 1905, additions 2010; telephone 1913; TX 1924; pop. 175 (1911), 192 (1933), 128 (1947), 142 (1954), 155 (1961), 286 (2011, incl. Zara).

Chinamans Bay (*Co. Northumberland*) see Blue Bay.

Chinamans Camp (*Co. Buller*) 28°34'S.

152°14'E., 59 km N. of Tenterfield, on Maryland R.

Chinamans Flat (*Co. Gordon*) 32°47'S. 148°38'E., 38 km SW of Wellington.

Chinamans Hill (*Co. Darling*) 30°47'S. 150°57'E., 21 km E. of Manilla, on Halls Ck; mine.

Chinamans Hollow (*Co. Northumberland*) see Weston.

China Town (*Co. Wellesley*) see Craigie.

Chinderah (*Co. Rous*) 28°15'S. 153°33'E., 2 km W. of Kingscliff, on Tweed R.; Cudgen till 1894; village gaz. 1884; orig. timber, then farming and sugar-cane; cemetery (27 graves 1872–1960); fire 1923; floods 1933, 2012, 2013, 2017; PO 1903, burnt down 1923; punt to Banora Point, replaced 1936 by Barneys Point Bridge, across Tweed R.; Rom. Cath. C. (St Mark's) 1899; SD Adventist C. (Kingscliff); sewage works; telephone 1891; TX 1913, automatic 1951; wharf; pop. 176 (1911), 265 (1933), 368 (1947), 370 (1954), 191 (1961), 1,340 (2006), 1,480 (2011).

Chinnock (*Co. Auckland*) 36°42'S. 149°57'E., 10 km E. of Bega.

Chisholm (*Co. Northumberland*) see Thornton.

Chittaway Bay (*Co. Northumberland*) 33°20'S. 151°27'E., 5 km SE of Wyong, on Ourimbah Ck; bridge 1906, new one (Lees Bridge) 1980, duplicated 1997, over Ourimbah Ck; foot-bridge; school 1982, new building 1987; pop. 1,901 (2011).

Chittaway Point (*Co. Northumberland*) see Tuggerah.

Chittaway South (*Co. Northumberland*) 33°20'S. 151°26'E., 5 km SE of Wyong, on Tuggerah Lake.

Chowan Creek (*Co. Rous*) 28°26'S. 153°21'E., 13 km SW of Murwillumbah.

Chowar (*Co. Wakool*) 35°16'S. 144°16'E., 41 km N. of Barham, on Niemur R.

Christmas Swamp (*Co. Cook*) see Lawson.

Christo Road (*Co. Northumberland*) see Waratah.

Church Creek (*Co. Wellesley*) 37°01'S. 149°00'E., 24 km SW of Bombala, on Delegate R.; Angl. C., destroyed 1849, rebuilt; school 1883–85.

Churchill Gardens (*Co. Gordon*) see Dubbo West.

Church Plain Camp (*Co. Burnett*) 29°15'S. 150°29'E., 33 km N. of Warialda.

Circular Reach (*Co. Rous*) see Kilgin.

Cirrigan (*Co. Gloucester*) 32°04'S. 152°28'E., 12 km N. of Tuncurry.

Civic (*Co. Northumberland*) see Newcastle.

Clairvaulx (*Co. Gough*) see Reddestone.

Clairville (*Co. Gough*) 29°42'S. 151°42'E., 6 km NW of Glen Innes; farming; airport (Glen Innes), rebuilt 1966; PO 1927–53; school 1896, new building b. 1910 by E.R.S. Potter, closed 1927; telephone 1924; pop. 59 (1901), 100 (1911), 40 (1933).

Clairwood (*Co. Durham*) see Bridgman.

Clandulla (*Co. Roxburgh*) 32°55'S. 149°57'E., 6 km SW of Kandos; Ilford Railway Station till 1900, Mornington till 1903, Carwell till 1905; mining (oil-shale disc. 1865 by Moore and Stuart); grazing; bridge over Carwell Ck; bushfires 1990 and 2009; cemetery; FB; mine (Mornington Pty Oil Co.) 1900, incl. retort (Clyde Engineering Co. Ltd) 1901; PO 1902; quarry; RS (Ilford till 1900, Mornington till 1903, Carwell till 1905) 1884, station b. by Alexander Hamilton Scouller, closed 1985; school 1882–85 and 1929–78; telephone 1905; TX 1920, automatic 1978; water supply augmentation 1987; pop. 58 (1911), 158 (1933), 174 (1947), 188 (1954), 205 (1961), 367 (2006), 211 (2011).

Clare (*Co. Manara*) 33°25'S. 143°57'E., 145 km NW of Hay; grazing; PO 1880; PS, reopened 1915; school 1985; pop. 51 (1911), 64 (1933).

Clare (*Co. Perry*) see Wilkurra.

Clare Corner (*Co. Manara*) 33°29'S. 143°52'E., 143 km NW of Hay; telephone 1949; TX 1950.

Clarence (*Co. Cook*) 33°29'S. 150°14'E., 6 km E. of Lithgow, on Browns Swamp; coalmine and washery (Centennial Coal Co. Ltd); FB; iron mine 1882; PO 1878; PS 1908; railway tunnel, 540 yds (494 m), 1869–1910; reservoir, 250,000 gal. (1,136.5 kl), 1932; RS (on old Zig Zag) 1874–1910 and (on new deviation) 1910–

74; sawmill; school 1909–11; snowstorm 1910; telegraph 1890; telephone 1950; TX 1951; pop. 109 (1911), 24 (1933), 209 (2006), 224 (2011).

Clarence River (*Co. Clarence*) see Grafton.

Clarence River Heads (*Co. Clarence*) see Yamba.

Clarence Town (*Co. Durham*) 32°35'S. 151°47'E., 19 km NW of Karuah, on Williams R.; Erringhi till 1826; disc. 1801, estab. 1826, surveyed by Major Sir Thomas Livingstone Mitchell, lots offered for sale 1832, thrived in 1860s, declined 1911+; former river port, timber 1801+, shipbuilding, wheat, tobacco, then dairying, maize and other cereals; Angl. C. 1857, destroyed 1868, replaced, new one (St John the Evangelist) b. 1906 by P.T. Street, d. by Robert Wilkins, and graveyard (61 graves), incl. columbarium; bacon factory estab. 1892 by Stephen Thwaites Robards and A. Wansey, additions 1899, fire 1935; Bapt. C. 1862; bridge (Brig o' Johnston) b. 1880 by J.K. Mackenzie, McDonald timber truss, 425 ft (129.5 m), rebuilt 1927, reinforced 1966, modified 1974, 380 ft (115.8 m), over Williams R.; bushfire 1979; cemetery (731 graves 1840s+) 1863, damaged 2007; CH 1869 d. by James Johnstone Barnet, repairs 1878 by A. M'Laren, closed 1970, reused 1971; earth tremors 1868 and 2012; electricity 1945; FB; fire 1920; floods 1851, 1857 (many died), 1875, 1892–95, 1946, 2007; flour mills: Allen's (damaged 1857), Campbell's, Daley's, Stephen Neate Dark (damaged 1857), Singleton Bros (destroyed 1857), Victoria (George Achurch, damaged 1857); Free Church of Scotland (Chalmers') 1856, burnt down, replacement (St David's) b. 1905 by Gaggin; gale 1928; kayak factory (Elliott's); Meth. C. b. 1907 by Amos Moore; PO 1839, new one b. 1880 by Alexander McLaren, closed and dilapidated; pound (stock) 1844; PS (incl. lock-up) b. 1879 by W.H. Galbraith, rebuilt 1912, additions 1987; punt (Stephen Neate Dark) 1858; quarry; 2 reservoirs; Rom. Cath. C. 1856, new one 1863, replacement (St Patrick's) b. 1892 by Andrew Burg; sawmills: Armstrong & Royse Pty Ltd, Enterprise (J.C. Ellis) 1883, Hardy & Son, Healy Bros (fire 1943), Jones Bros; school 1849, additions and repairs 1882 by J. Libby, additions 1927, additions 2010 by RTC Group; shipyard (Deptford) estab. 1830 by James Marshall and William Lowe, partnership dissolved 1836, carried on by Lowe till 1855, closed; spoke factory (Shaft, Spoke & Wood Turning Ltd); tanneries: A. Lloyd and James Lyall; telegraph 1874, new office b. 1880 by Alexander McLaren; 2 tobacco factories (incl. James Lyall); tool handle factory (J. Wellings and Lyons), fire 1937; TX 1915, automatic 1967; watch-house b. 1854 by Samuel Walters; water reticulation 1960; Wes. Meth. C.; wharves: David Farquahar and Williams River Steam Navigation Co. (destroyed 1906); pop. 93 (1840), 93 (1846), 193 (1851), 295 (1856), 301 (1861), 350 (1871), 370 (1881), 491 (1891), 371 (1901), 730 (1911), 440 (1933), 338 (1947), 401 (1954), 349 (1961), 252 (1971), 281 (1976), 394 (1981), 489 (1986), 649 (1991), 758 (1996), 807 (2001), 794 (2006), 861 (2011).

Clarendon (*Co. Clarendon*) see Eurongilly.

Clarenza (*Co. Clarence*) 29°41'S. 152°59'E., 4 km NE of Grafton, on Swan Ck; flood 1863; sale-yards b. 1916 by C.K. Maxwell; sewage works; wharf b. 1892 by D. Johnstone, on Clarence R.; pop. 164 (1911), 27 (1933), 246 (1947), 199 (1954), 563 (2011).

Clareval (*Co. Gloucester*) 32°19'S. 151°55'E., 18 km NE of Dungog, on Karuah R.; dairying; butter factory (Gloucester Dist. Co-op.) 1902; PO 1927–30; school 1885–1901; pop. 69 (1911).

Clarevaulx (*Co. Gough*) 29°39'S. 151°41'E., 11 km NW of Glen Innes, on Reddestone Ck; PO 1883.

Clarkes Creek (*Co. Wellington*) 32°48'S. 149°34'E., 23 km S. of Mudgee, on Clarkes Ck; orig. Devil's Hole; gold; Angl. C. d. by Harold Robert Hardwick; Union C. 1862.

Clarkson's Crossing (*Co. Auckland*) see Bimbaya.

Clarkson's Crossing (*Co. Gloucester*)

see Nabiac.

Claydon (*Co. Ewenmar*) 32°02'S. 148°25'E., 28 km NE of Narromine.

Clear Creek (*Co. Roxburgh*) 33°19'S. 149°42'E., 16 km NE of Bathurst; farming and grazing; brick-kiln (Edward Tebbell); PO 1879–1929.

Clearfield (*Co. Richmond*) 29°09'S. 152°56'E., 33 km S. of Casino; farming and grazing; PO 1913; RS (Watertank till 1913) 1905–74; school 1938–40; telephone 1919; pop. 99 (1933).

Clear Hills (*Co. Forbes*) 33°33'S. 148°11'E., 24 km SE of Forbes; building stone; quarry (Grandee Dark) operated by Central West Granite Pty Ltd 1969–73.

Clear Hills (*Co. Urana*) see Oaklands.

Clearmont (*Co. Wynyard*) 35°16'S. 147°56'E., 27 km SW of Gundagai; school 1915–26.

Clear Ridge (*Co. Gipps*) 33°46'S. 147°18'E., 20 km NE of West Wyalong; RS (1 km S., Girdlers till 1934) 1929–75, station removed 1984; school (building removed from Wamboyne) 1929–57; telephone 1934; TX 1934; pop. 92 (1933), 63 (1954), 69 (1961).

Clergate (*Co. Wellington*) 33°11'S. 149°07'E., 10 km N. of Orange; mining (zinc and lead), orchards, farming; PO 1906, burnt down 1925; RS (March till 1904) 1902–74; school (Mulyan till 1942) 1882; telephone 1913; TX 1924; woollen mill (H.J. Griffith) 1910, moved 1915 to Orange; pop. 100 (1911), 122 (1933), 109 (1947), 102 (1954), 83 (1961).

Clerkness (*Co. Hardinge*) see Bundarra.

Cleveland (*Co. Camden*) see Dapto.

Cleveland Crossing (*Co. Drake*) 29°02'S. 152°36'E., 48 km SW of Casino, on Clarence R.; telephone 1925; TX 1928.

Clifden (*Co. Clarence*) 29°34'S. 152°55'E., 14 km N. of Grafton; gale 1926; quarry; school 1879–86.

Cliftlands (*Co. Brisbane*) 32°03'S. 150°51'E., 2 km SW of Scone; storm 1928; pop. 66 (1911), 24 (1933).

Cliftleigh (*Co. Northumberland*) 32°47'S. 151°31'E., 5 km NE of Kurri Kurri, on Wallis Ck; (incl. Testers Hollow); bushfires 1928 and 2002; collieries: Ayrfield No. 1 (estab. 1920 by Thomas Evans and Robert William Miller, acquired 1923 by R.W. Miller & Co. and Ayrfield Colliery Co. Ltd, flooded 1927 and 1928, man killed 1928, strikes 1928 and 1929, flooded 1930, strike 1931, subsidence 1934, fire 1935, man killed 1937, closed by fire 1938, razed 1947) and Glen Ayr (o. 1914, fire 1927, flooded 1928, acquired 1929 from E.M. Robbins by James Fallins, destroyed and closed by flood 1930, razed); railway (colliery); pop. 180 (2011).

Clifton (*Co. Buckland*) 31°04'S. 150°32'E., 28 km E. of Gunnedah.

Clifton (*Co. Clive*) see Waropurra.

Clifton Gates (*Co. Clive*) see Leefield.

Clifton Grove (*Co. Bathurst*) 33°15'S. 149°09'E., 5 km NE of Orange, on Summerhill Ck; FB; pop. 598 (1986), 625 (1991), 578 (1996), 597 (2001), 620 (2006), 653 (2011).

Climsland (*Co. Cooper*) see Myall Park.

Clinton (*Co. Wellington*) see Orange.

Clive (*Co. Clive*) 29°14'S. 151°50'E., 27 km SW of Tenterfield, on Pyes Ck; village gaz. 1887; PO 1888.

Clogham (*Co. Kennedy*) 32°46'S. 147°42'E., 17 km N. of Trundle.

Clonegonnell (*Co. Clarendon*) 34°59'S. 147°17'E., 16 km NW of Wagga Wagga; farming; PO 1927–31; TX 1928.

Clothiers Creek (*Co. Rous*) 28°20'S. 153°30'E., 10 km E. of Murwillumbah, on Clothiers Ck; bananas; bushfire 2016; school 1949–68; telephone 1940; TX 1940; pop. 93 (1947), 117 (1954), 115 (1961), 363 (2011).

Clouds Creek (*Co. Fitzroy*) 30°05'S. 152°38'E., 29 km N. of Dorrigo, on Clouds Ck; gold disc. 1852; bushfire 1951; PO 1935; sawmills: Northern Sawmills Pty Ltd 1935, E.D. Pike & Co. Ltd, S. Smyth, burnt down 1937; school 1950–64; telephone 1934; TX 1936; pop. 35 (1933), 148 (1947), 170 (1954), 147 (1961).

Clovass (*Co. Rous*) 28°52'S. 153°09'E., 10 km E. of Casino; farming and dairying; Angl. C. (All Saints') 1900; Meth. C. 1904 (removed from Irvington); PO 1927–63; school 1901, additions 1924 by W.S. Mackney, closed 1982; telephone 1923; TX 1923; pop. 91

(1911), 107 (1933), 84 (1947), 72 (1954).

Clover Hill (*Co. Wellington*) see Orange.

Clover Lee (*Co. Rous*) 28°38'S. 153°33'E., 7 km W. of Byron Bay.

Clover Park (*Co. Buller*) 28°33'S. 152°35'E., 41 km W. of Kyogle, on Bean Ck; quarry; telephone 1925; TX 1943.

Clowery (*Co. Dowling*) 33°46'S. 146°39'E., 53 km W. of West Wyalong; telephone 1927; TX 1930.

Cluckens Bend (*Co. Raleigh*) 30°29'S. 152°32'E., 22 km SW of Dorrigo.

Clunes (*Co. Rous*) 28°44'S. 153°24'E., 13 km SW of Bangalow; farming and dairying; Angl. C. (St Peter's) b. 1906 by W.S. Rays and E.M. Lowe, closed 2015, sold 2016, reused; bushfire 1890; butter factory (Perseverance, Clunes Dairy Co. Ltd) 1893, burnt down 1901; cemetery (719 graves 1893+) 1888, incl. columbarium; cyclone 1916; dengue fever 1926; FB 1968; fire 1892; PO 1883; Presb. C. (St John's) b. 1910 by R. Hughes, d. by Frederick Johnson Board, closed, sold and reused; reservoir; sawmill; school 1883, additions 1915 by A. Sansom, new one 1995; storm 1890; telegraph 1890; TX 1915, automatic 1940; Unit. C. (orig. Meth.) 1905 d. by H. Lumley, destroyed 1916, rebuilt 1916 by Gaggin; pop. 346 (1901), 488 (1911), 289 (1933), 227 (1947), 266 (1954), 333 (1961), 443 (1996), 417 (2001), 520 (2006), 560 (2011).

Clybucca (*Co. Dudley*) 30°56'S. 152°57'E., 11 km SW of South West Rocks; bypassed by highway 2016; dairying; bushfire 1895; cheese factory b. 1918 by James Drummond & Co., destroyed 1918; creamery (Record Reign, E.I.C. Scott) 1897; cyclone 1918; FB; PO 1884, demolished 1985; reservoir (steel), 250,000 gal. (1,136.5 kl), 1968; sawmills: McDougall's, burnt down 1928 and Swan Bros, burnt down 1942; school 1891, additions 1895 by A.H.G. Taylor, closed 1970, building sold 1973; telephone 1907; TX 1924, automatic 1968; Wes. Meth. C. 1879; whooping cough epidemic 1927; pop. 292 (1911), 266 (1933), 220 (1947), 167 (1954), 188 (1961), 466 (2011).

Clyde (*Co. St Vincent*) 35°42'S. 150°12'E., 2 km NE of Batemans Bay.

Clydesdale (*Co. Durham*) 32°35'S. 151°13'E., 4 km SE of Singleton; sale-yards 1908; pop. 59 (1933), 59 (1947), 103 (1954), 58 (1961).

Coads Tank (*Co. Hume*) 35°44'S. 146°18'E., 31 km N. of Corowa; school 1957–69.

Coalbaggie (*Co. Ewenmar*) see Eumungerie.

Coalcroft (*Co. Clarence*) see Coaldale.

Coaldale (*Co. Clarence*) 29°24'S. 152°49'E., 31 km N. of Grafton; Lower Coaldale till 1978; agric. and beef; bushfire (house destroyed) 1936; school (Coalcroft) 1915–20, reopened 1957, closed 1971, reused; tea-tree oil still (L. Chevalley); telephone 1923; TX 1928; pop. 83 (1911), 121 (1933), 76 (1947), 84 (1954), 55 (1961).

Coal Hole Flat (*Co. Georgiana*) 33°45'S. 149°18'E., 24 km S. of Blayney.

Coal Point (*Co. Northumberland*) 33°02'S. 151°37'E., 4 km SE of Toronto, on Lake Macquarie; (incl. Carey Bay, formerly Cary Bay, settled 1890, and Kilaben Bay); subdivided 1891+ by Excelsior Land, Investment, & Building Co. & Bank Ltd; mining (coal disc. 1834 by Lancelot Edward Threlkeld); Angl. C. (St Saviour's) b. 1921 by J.W.T. Chapman, d. by Ernest Tingle, closed, sold and reused; Bapt. C. (Westlakes); bushfires 1933 (2 houses destroyed), 1936, 1940, 1946; coalmine (Ebenezer Coal Works) estab. 1840 by Lancelot Edward Threlkeld, sold 1844 to Ralph Mayer Robey, man killed 1848, sold 1853 to NSW Coal & Intercolonial Steam Navigation Co., worked 1890s–1906 as South Hetton Colliery, abandoned; 4 jetties; PO: Cary Bay 1927 (closed, sold and reused), Coal Point 1946, Kilaben Bay 1933; quarry; Rom. Cath. C. (St Joseph's) 1984; school 1955, additions by R.T. Parker Pty Ltd; sewerage 1959; telephone: Carey Bay 1924, Coal Point 1947, Kilaben Bay 1933; water supply 1928; pop. 251 (1933), 781 (1947), 917 (1954), 1,730 (2011).

Coal River (*Co. Northumberland*) see Newcastle.

Cobaki (*Co. Rous*) 28°13'S. 153°29'E., 10 km SW of Tweed Heads, on Cobaki Ck; bridge over Cobaki Ck; causeway across Cobaki Ck; cemetery; reservoir; pop. 48 (1933), 114 (1947), 85 (1954), 225 (2011).

Cobaki Lakes (*Co. Rous*) 28°11'S. 153°29'E., 7 km W. of Tweed Heads, on Cobaki Ck.

Cobar (*Co. Robinson*) 31°30'S. 145°50'E., 275 km W. of Dubbo; (incl. Cornishtown and Dapville); surveyed by Evans, town gaz. 1873, lots sold 1883, munic. proc. 1884, declined 1920s+; mining (copper disc. 1869 by Charles Campbell, George Gibb and Thomas Hartman, and gold disc. 1871) mainly 1870–1929, sheep, cattle; airfield (World War II); airport (6 km SW) 1958, upgraded 2015; ambulance station 1955; Angl. C., burnt down 1902, new one (St Paul's) 1904 d. by John Holderness Bates; Assemblies of God C.; Bapt. C. 1962; bicycle works: M.J. Corbett, burnt down 1902 and Cosmos Cycle Co. (Kinch and Todd); breweries: Australian (formerly Fair Hill), Red Lion Steam Brewery, Aerated Water & Cordial Manufactory (estab. by Henry Lill Lindsay) 1882–90, Thomas O'Brien et al. 1879–95, G. Williams et al. 1880–85, Samuel R. Wood 1888; bushfires 1957, 1974–75, 1985; carriage-works (Western Coach & Buggy Factory, Tomlins and Simon); cemetery (2 km W.) 1881; CH b. 1887 by Hugh Sutherland, d. by James Johnstone Barnet, additions 1899 by William Robert Ibbotson, d. by Frederick George Castleden; cordial factories: H. Harris (bought 1880 by Henry Lill Lindsay), Hives & Sons, William Hopkins, Samuel R. Wood; cyclones 1944 (most houses damaged) and 1945; diphtheria 1910 (2 died) and 1945; drought 1877; dust storms 1881, 1895, 1900, 1903, 1913, 1914; earth tremors 1875 and 1886; electricity 1910; FB (station b. 1913); fires 1881, 1895, 1897, 2014 (man killed); floods 1908, 1910, 1914; foot-bridge; gales 1902 and 1933; heatwaves 1897, 1899, 1914; hospital 1881, additions 1882, 1900, 1904, 1908, new one b. 1968; Jehovah's Witnesses C.; mine fatalities 1885, 1886, 1895, 1896 (2 killed), 1898, 1900 (5 killed), 1901 (2 killed), 1902, 1904 (2 killed), 1906, 1908 (3 killed), 1910, 1912, 1913, 1916 (2 killed), 1980 (2 killed); miners' strikes 1896, 1901, 1907, 1908, 1910, 1915, 1916, 1936, 1937, 1941; mines: Chesney (New Occidental Gold Mines NL 1932–52, company bought out 1957 by Cobar Mines Pty Ltd and Cobar South Pty Ltd) 1887, Cobar Copper (closed *c.*1874), Cobar East, Cobar Gold (formerly Fort Bourke, incl. 100 stamp mill, cyanide and slimes plant) 1890, Cobar Occidental (incl. 100 stamp mill and cyanide plant, mine closed 1952), Coronation, CSA (copper, lead, silver, gold disc. 1871, mine o. 1872, closed, reopened 1905, closed 1920, acquired 1960 by Cobar Mines Ltd from Consolidated Zinc Pty Ltd, reopened 1965, closed 1998, reopened 1999 by Cobar Management Pty Ltd), Dapville, Diane, East Cobar, Gladstone 1908, Great Cobar (copper, gold, silver, incl. Barton's Shaft, Becker's Shaft, Bradley's Shaft, Hardie's Shaft, Main Shaft, Renwick's Shaft, and 4 blast furnaces) 1871–1919, Great Cobar Extended, Great Cobar North (copper), Great Peak, Great Western, King Edward, Ivanhoe, Lady Greaves (gold), McKinnons 1995, Mount Pleasant, New Burra Burra, New Cobar (New Occidental Gold Mines NL 1932–52, company bought out 1957 by Cobar Mines Pty Ltd and Cobar South Pty Ltd), North Gladstone (gold), Occidental (New Occidental Gold Mines NL 1932–52, company bought out 1957 by Cobar Mines Pty Ltd and Cobar South Pty Ltd) 1889, Phoenix, Royal George (iron), South Occidental (copper), Tharsis (copper), Wood Duck (gold), Young Australian (gold) 1896; monumental stone works (C. Bray); PO 1873, new one b. 1885, additions 1890 by D. Soame, additions 1908 by Gudgeon & Co.; police barracks; pound (stock) 1877; powerhouse (Provincial Electric Supply Co. Ltd) b. 1910 by Gudgeon & Co., closed 1960; Presb. C. (St Margaret's) 1901, closed, sold 1980 and reused; PS 1876, repairs 1897 by G.F. Grill, additions and alterations 1907 by T. Jones; radar station (weather); railway to copper mine 1897, new one (to CSA mine) 1918–37; railway turntable, 50 ft (15.2 m);

reservoirs: one b. 1884 by T. Salmond, one b. 1901 by Clyde Engineering Co. Ltd, one b. 1958, one b. 1965 (1,000,000 gal. or 4,546 kl); rifle range (2 km NE); Rom. Cath. C. (Sacred Heart) b. 1883 by James Burns, new one (St Laurence O'Toole's) b. 1905–7 by William Alfred McLean, d. by W.T. Knox, damaged during construction; RS 1892, station b. by R. Funnell, closed 1975, restored 1996, reused; Salv. Army C.; sawmill (Cobar Sawmills Ltd), burnt down 1957; scarlet fever 1898 and 1910; schools: primary 1878 (in billiard room b. for Barton and Goold), new one b. 1881–83 by Hugh Sutherland, new building b. 1902 by Gudgeon and Clifton, additions 1913 and 1980, and HS 1969 d. by Owen Main Podger, additions 1974; sewerage 1971; smelters; storm 1883; streets electric lit 1910; TC (a campus of Western Institute); telegraph 1881, new office b. 1885, additions 1908 by Gudgeon & Co.; TX 1896, automatic 1979; typhoid 1896, 1897, 1898, 1900 (4 died), 1903, 1906, 1907, 1908, 1910 (3 died); Unit. C. (orig. Meth.) b. 1914 by Gudgeon & Co., d. by T. Owen; waterworks 1901, water supply (from Nyngan) 1965, augmentation 1985, new water treatment plant b. 2017–19 on new site by Laurie Curran Water Pty Ltd; Wes. Meth. C., burnt down 1881, replaced 1882, closed 1914, reused; whooping cough epidemic 1904; pop. *c.*190 (1873), *c.*500 (1875), 1,859 (1881), 1,189 (1891), *c.*3,000 (1896), 3,371 (1901), 4,745 (1911), 1,163 (1933), *c.*1,800 (1941), 2,277 (1947), 2,224 (1954), 2,178 (1961), 2,350 (1966), 3,744 (1971), 3,339 (1976), 3,583 (1981), 4,287 (1986), 4,138 (1991), 4,524 (1996), 4,117 (2001), 4,128 (2006), 3,817 (2011).

Cobargo (*Co. Dampier*) 36°23'S. 149°53'E., 16 km W. of Bermagui, on Narira Ck; orig. The Junction, then Wattle Town till 1870; disc. 1829 by William Duggan Tarlinton, estab. in 1830s, thrived in 1880s; sawmilling, dairying 1870s+, mimosa bark till 1964, maize, pigs, now tourist craft village; Angl. C. 1881, demolished 1928, new one (Christ) b. 1924 by R.W. Thatcher; bridges: one b. 1882 by R.H. Worthing, repairs 1898 by Alick Blomquist, replaced 1920 by Alick Blomquist, replaced 1943 by H. Worthing, replaced (T.F. Kennelly Bridge) 1960, over Narira Ck and one b. 1959 over Murrabine Ck; bushfire (5 houses destroyed) 1952; butter factories: Cobargo Dist. Co-op. Creamery Butter Co. Ltd 1901 (remodelled 1922 by Grainger, burnt down 1926, rebuilt 1927 by R.W. Thatcher, closed 1980) and NSW Creamery Butter Co. Ltd 1896–1903; carriage-works (Morrison and Harlow, taken over 1903 by A. Boyd); cemetery 1876; CH 1883, new one b. 1904 by John Hines; cheese factories: William Blaka, Wangruka (J.G. Boxsell), John Whiffen; clothing factory (Kinetix); cordial factory (C. Bown) 1921; creamery (Cobargo Co-op. Creamery Society) 1902; diphtheria 1939; earth tremors 1885 and 1912; FB; grasshopper infestation 1901; PO 1870, new one b. 1888–90 by Robert Underhill, additions and alterations 1903 by John Hines, repairs 1919 by Jack Martin; pound (stock) 1871; PS b. 1882 by R.H. Worthing, d. by Walter Liberty Vernon; reservoir (concrete) 1955; Rom. Cath. C. b. 1875 by Lawler, new one (Our Lady of Good Counsel) b. 1896–98 by Underhill and Thatcher, d. by John Francis Hennessy and Joseph Ignatius Sheerin; school 1871, renovations and repairs 1934; sewerage augmentation 1985; telegraph 1876, additions and alterations to office 1903 by John Hines; TX (automatic) 1981; Union C. 1874, re-roofed and renovated 1908; Unit. C. (orig. Meth.) 1962; waterworks 1900, reticulation 1959; pop. 346 (1891), 519 (1901), 610 (1911), 520 (1921), 390 (1933), 527 (1947), 413 (1954), 373 (1961), 251 (1971), 285 (1976), 285 (1981), 345 (1986), 376 (1991), 397 (1996), 403 (2001), 426 (2006), 441 (2011).

Cobark (*Co. Gloucester*) 31°57'S. 151°42'E., 25 km W. of Gloucester, on Cobark R.; 3 quarries.

Cobar Paddock (*Co. Cook*) see Lithgow.

Cobar Park (*Co. Cook*) see Lithgow.

Cobbadah (*Co. Murchison*) 30°14'S. 150°35'E., 17 km N. of Barraba, on Sheep Station Ck;

surveyed by Thomas J. Oliver and first lots sold 1863, town gaz. 1865; grazing; Angl. C. (Annunciation) 1909; bridge over Sheep Station Ck; bushfire 1871; cemetery; FB; mine (antimony); PO 1868; school 1957–65; telephone 1899; TX 1910; pop. 135 (1911), 96 (1921), 78 (1933), 35 (1947), 69 (1954), 104 (1961).

Cobbitty Paddocks (*Co.* Camden) see Ellis Lane.

Cobblers Hill (*Co. Camden*) 34°27'S. 150°51'E., 2 km NE of Unanderra, on American Ck.

Cobbobra (*Co. Dampier*) see Verona.

Cobbora (*Co. Lincoln*) 32°03'S. 149°15'E., 14 km W. of Dunedoo; also known as Martin Town; surveyed 1862 by William Jacomb Conder, village gaz. 1863 as Cobborah, laid out 1883 by Liddell; grazing, mining, agric.; Angl. C. (St Paul's) 1897; cemetery (109 graves 1868+) 1870; flood 1955; PO 1859–1985; pound (stock) 1877; PS (incl. court room) b. 1883–85 by W. Summerhayes, closed 1933, reused; rifle range 1908; Rom. Cath. C. (Immaculate Conception) 1904; sawmills: Craft Bros, and Kelly and Sweeney; school (Cobborah till 1902) 1880, extended and re-roofed 1907 by G. Collyer and W. Carmichael, additions 1966, closed 1968, reused; telegraph 1881–1914; TX 1910; pop. *c.*80 (1866), 120 (1871), 196 (1901), 210 (1911), 188 (1933), 146 (1947), 133 (1954), 110 (1961).

Cobborah (*Co. Lincoln*) see Cobbora.

Cobbora West (*Co. Lincoln*) 32°03'S. 149°14'E., 16 km W. of Dunedoo, on Talbragar R.; surveyed 1865 by William Jacomb Conder, lots sold 1868 and 1873, abandoned.

Cob o' Corn (*Co. Rous*) see Afterlee.

Cobodong (*Co. Georgiana*) 34°13'S. 149°50'E., 41 km NE of Crookwell, on Wiarborough Ck.

Cobramunga (*Co. Wakool*) 35°27'S. 143°52'E., 31 km NW of Barham.

Cochrane Creek (*Co. Wakool*) 35°18'S. 144°18'E., 39 km N. of Barham; pop. 65 (1911), 44 (1933).

Cockatoo Flat (*Co. Gough*) 29°50'S. 151°58'E., 26 km SE of Glen Innes, on Gold Diggers Ck; mine (sapphires).

Cockatoo Flat (*Co. Vernon*) 31°03'S. 151°33'E., 7 km SW of Walcha; school 1885–96.

Cockburn River (*Co. Inglis*) see Kootingal.

Cocked Hat Creek (*Co. Northumberland*) see Edgeworth.

Cockle Creek (*Co. Northumberland*) see Boolaroo, Davistown and Empire Bay.

Cockwhy (*Co. St Vincent*) 35°33'S. 150°19'E., 21 km NE of Batemans Bay; bushfire 1952; pop. 71 (1911).

Cocomingla (*Co. Monteagle*) 34°01'S. 148°48'E., 22 km S. of Cowra; school 1886–90.

Cocumbark (*Co. Gloucester*) 32°06'S. 152°16'E., 23 km W. of Tuncurry, on Fire Fly Ck; school 1880, new one b. 1884 by Henry Miles, moved 1936 to Dyers Crossing and reused, new one b. 1937 by Alf E. Woodward, closed 1947, moved 1948 to Forster; Union C.; pop. 128 (1901), 87 (1911).

Codners Flat (*Co. Wellington*) 32°46'S. 149°12'E., 33 km SE of Wellington, on Macquarie R.; goldmine (Junction Point Co.) 1883–85; pop. 22 (1933).

Codrington (*Co. Richmond*) 28°57'S. 153°15'E., 6 km NW of Coraki, on Seleems Ck; laid out *c.*1856 by Frederick Septimus Peppercorne, but never fully developed; timber, farming, dairying; boiling-down works (Clark Irving); measles epidemic 1890; PO 1866; sawmill (William Baillie); school 1881–1933 and 1954–78; storm 1886; sugar mill (horse powered) estab. 1869 by William Baillie; telephone 1924; TX 1929, automatic 1953; pop. 136 (1891), *c.*140 (1903), 292 (1911), 62 (1933), 96 (1947), 78 (1954), 58 (1961).

Codrington North (*Co. Rous*) see Ruthven.

Coffee Camp (*Co. Rous*) 28°40'S. 153°14'E., 7 km S. of Nimbin, on Goolmangar Ck; 3 bridges; FB; school 1911; telephone 1908; pop. 61 (1911), 98 (1933), 101 (1947), 99 (1954), 88 (1961), 233 (2011).

Coffe Hill (*Co. Ashburnham*) 33°21'S. 148°54'E., 19 km W. of Orange; school (Coffey Hill) 1878, additions 1898 by J.H. Gain, closed 1911; pop. 50 (1901), 60 (1911).

Coffey Hill (*Co. Ashburnham*) see Coffe Hill.

Coffs Harbour (*Co. Fitzroy*) 30°18'S.

153°07'E., 140 km E. of Armidale, on Coffs Ck; (incl. Charlesworth Bay, Coffs Harbour Jetty, Park Beach); Korff's Harbour till 1861, Coffs Harbour 1861–86, Brelsford 1886–97, reverted to Coffs Harbour 1897; disc. 1847 by John Korff, settled 1880, village gaz. 1886 as Brelsford, first lots sold 1888, subdivision 1909, further town lots surveyed and laid out 1912 by Drummond, city proc. 1987; sugar-cane 1881+, bananas (industry now declining), tomatoes, peas, beans, fish, timber, cattle, pigs, paspalum, coastal shipping till 1915 which lingered on till 1975, mineral sand mining, engineering, manufacturing, tourism 1960s+, retirement centre; aeroplane beacon 1936; airfield (2 km S.) 1930, requisitioned by air force during World War II, redesignated an airport 1947, new terminal 1954, upgraded 2000 and 2013; ambulance station; Angl. C. (St John the Evangelist) 1899, relocated 1909, relocated 1911 to Coffs Harbour Jetty and renamed St Aidan's, new one at Coffs Harbour Jetty b. 1932 by T. Crombie, new St John's b. 1911, another new St John's b. 1973 by Col Shelton, d. by Trevor James Reddacliff; Assemblies of God C. (Life House); Bapt. C.; boat harbour 1976; box factory (J. Gregor and Bob McKay); brass and iron foundry (E.W. Smith Pty Ltd); breakwaters: eastern one 1,530 ft (466.3 m) b. 1918–39 and northern one 3,200 ft (975.4 m) b. 1915–24, reinforced 1960; brickworks: Coffs Harbour Brick & Tile Co. 1948–53 and J. Laverty; bridges: one b. 1882 by McPherson over Coffs Ck, one b. 1947 (3 concrete spans) over Coffs Ck, Bamgalor Bridge over Coffs Ck, Harry Jensen Bridge over Newports Ck, McCanns Bridge over Coffs Ck, Park Beach Bridge 1936 over Coffs Ck; bunker (RAAF, World War II), closed and derelict, restored and, reused; bushfire (house destroyed) 1952; butter factories: Coffs Harbour-Orara Co-op. Dairy Society (sold 1949 to Cow & Gate Pty Ltd, sold 1952 to Co-op. Dairy Assoc.) and Coffs Harbour Co-op. Dairy & Refrigerating Co. Ltd (b. 1909 by Lonsdale); cemetery (4,753 graves 1888+) 1887; CH (incl. police station) 1907 d. by Walter Liberty Vernon, additions 1919, new one b. 1930 by F. Hampson, replaced 1963, additions and alterations 1983, closed, sold 2015, new one b. 2015 on new site by Richard Crookes Constructions, d. by P.T.W. Architects; Church of Christ; cordial factories: Glynn Bros and Griffin's (sold 1911 to F. Robinson); cyclones 1908 (most houses damaged), 1952, 1962; drought 1960–61; engineering works: Isles Forge & Engineering Works 1951 and A.W. Renshaw (b. 1954 by Alf Bird); FB 1911 (station b. 1919 by S. Box, d. by William Hull McNiven, demolished, new one on new site b. 1977); fibrous plaster works (Condon's), fire 1936; fires 1914 and 1938; fish packing shed b. 1950 by H. Fanning and W. Mackay; floods 1938, 1950, 1963, 1996, 2001, 2009, 2016, 2017; 2 foot-bridges over Coffs Ck; foundry (E.W. Smith); Foursquare Gospel C. (Heartbeat); gales 1894 and 1949; German measles epidemic 1934; harbour b. 1915–39; hospital b. 1917 by T. Jones, additions 1930, additions 1938 by W.P. Mellefont, additions 1940, additions 1960 by D.E. Lahey, additions 1963 by King and Lightfoot, new one 1970 d. by I. Roberts, additions 2012; ice works (R. Dowling); jetty b. 1890–92 by G. and T. Lawson, 1,641 ft (500.2 m), crane erected 1892 by J.S. Rodgers & Sons, jetty repairs 1907 by M'Phillips, crane erected 1907 by McWilliams, jetty repairs 1908 by G. Mooney, widened 1910 and 1912–14, lengthened 320 ft (97.5 m) in 1914, strengthened 1915–20, lengthened 300 ft (91.4 m) 1943–46, lengthened and widened 1946–55, railway lines and cranes removed 1984, closed 1990, restored 1996; LDS (Mormon) C.; lock-up (at Coffs Harbour Jetty) 1920; Lutheran C. (Peace); marina 1979; metal fabrication works (Advance Metal Industries Aust.) 1984; mineral sand mining plants: Aust. Rutile Pty Ltd 1956 and Coffs Harbour Rutile NL 1957 (dismantled and moved 1958 to Redhead); monumental stone works (A. Beckinsale & Co.) 1938; plywood factory (Pacific Plywood & Timber Pty Ltd), removed from Ulong, re-erected 1940 by

J.S. Maloney, d. by Cumming, Henderson & Co. Pty Ltd; PO: Coffs Harbour 1890, new one b. 1895, replaced 1910 by E.B. Bernie, alterations 1932, demolished 1938, new one 1938, closed 1969, Coffs Harbour Beach 1958, Coffs Harbour Jetty 1906, new one b. 1926 by E.R. Greenfield, Coffs Harbour Plaza 1982; pound (stock) 1912; Presb. C.: St Andrew's (b. 1907, relocated 1961, reused, demolished 1983, new one b. 1962 by R.J. Want Pty Ltd, later renamed Harbourside) and Jetty (b. 1917 by Benjamin Donn-Patterson); PS: Coffs Harbour 1906, new one b. 1913 by Alfred Fowler, new one 1963, additions and alterations 1978 and Coffs Harbour Jetty 1920–36; railway barracks (Coffs Harbour Jetty), burnt down 1935; railway turntable, 60 ft (18.3 m); reservoir, 300,000 gal. (1,363.8 kl); rifle range (2 km SE); Rom. Cath. C.: Mary Immaculate Star of the Sea (b. 1936, closed and reused) and St Anthony's (b. and destroyed 1908, rebuilt 1909 and renamed St Augustine's, additions 1915 and 1938, reused 1962, demolished 1975, new one 1962 d. by Fowell, Mansfield and Maclurcan); RS: Coffs Harbour 1915, station b. by Ernest Frederick Leggo, refreshment rooms 1923, new one 1970, North Coffs Harbour 1924–58, Park Beach 1925–74; Salv. Army C. 1956; sawmills: William Best (at Jetty), Langley Bros (incl. timber tramway) 1907, George William Nicoll (o. 1903 as Harbour Saw Mills, acquired 1905 by North Coast Steam Navigation Co. Ltd, bought 1906 by Dalgety & Co., burnt down 1915), Pike and Burrows (b. by G.F. Heath, jun., burnt down 1906), Allen Taylor & Co. Ltd (burnt down 1960, rebuilt 1961); schools: Coffs Harbour primary 1896 (new one b. 1897 by Sydney Edward Moore, additions 1907 by W.J. Brown, additions 1909 by William Herd, moved and rebuilt 1914 on new site by Ernest Frederick Leggo, additions 1920 by R.H. Rennie, new building b. 1950 by W.P. Mellefont, additions 1952 also by Mellefont additions 1955, 1960, 1967, 1970), Coffs Harbour HS 1939 (b. by F.C.W. Powell, additions 1959 by Reginald Joseph Want, additions 1968 and 1974, new wing b. 1978 by R. & B. Constructions Pty Ltd, additions 2010 by T.F. Woollam & Son Pty Ltd), Coffs Harbour senior college 1995, Narranga 1968, Orara HS 1971, additions 1973 by R.J. Want Pty Ltd, fire 2015, Tyalla 1978, additions 1981; SD Adventist C. 1952, extended, new one 1972; seed cleaning plant (Anderson's Seeds Ltd) 1953; sewerage 1959, augmentation 1969, 1973, 1992, 1997; storm 1914; TC 1952, additions 1956 by King and Lightfoot, additions 1973, became a campus of North Coast Institute in 1992, relocated 1995; technology park 1995; telegraph: Coffs Harbour 1891 and Coffs Harbour Jetty 1908; telephone: Coffs Harbour Beach 1958 and Coffs Harbour Jetty 1893; tornado 1908; TX 1908, new one 1955, automatic 1973; Unit. C. (orig. Meth.) 1915; United Pentecostal C. of Aust.; univ. (Southern Cross) 1995; water supply 1937, augmentation 1949 d. by J.W. Campbell, further augmented 1958, 1980, 1988; Wes. Meth. C.; whooping cough epidemic 1907; pop. 299 (1891), 123 (1901), 770 (1908), 1,422 (1909), 1,730 (1910), 1,114 (1911), 2,244 (1912), *c.*2,750 (1924), 2,884 (1933), 4,816 (1947), 6,215 (1954), 7,188 (1961), 7,683 (1966), 10,107 (1971), 12,197 (1976), 16,020 (1981), 18,074 (1986), 20,326 (1991), 22,177 (1996), 26,083 (2001), 26,353 (2006).

Coffs Harbour Beach (*Co. Fitzroy*) see Coffs Harbour.

Coffs Harbour Jetty (*Co. Fitzroy*) see Coffs Harbour.

Coffs Harbour Plaza (*Co. Fitzroy*) see Coffs Harbour.

Coggan (*Co. Phillip*) 32°21'S. 150°05'E., 35 km SW of Merriwa, on Goulburn R.

Cogo (*Co. Macquarie*) 31°15'S. 152°40'E., 24 km N. of Wauchope, on Wilson R.; school 1889–1935.

Cogra Bay (*Co. Northumberland*) see Wondabyne.

Coila (*Co. Dampier*) 36°01'S. 150°06'E., 6 km N. of Tuross Head, on Coila Lake; town gaz. 1863; agric. and fishing; Angl. C. (St Peter's)

1871, ruined; bridge, damaged and rebuilt 1867, new one 1898, over Coila Ck; cheese factory (Thomas Davis); Presb. C. 1872, new one 1904.

Colane (*Co. Gregory*) 31°15'S. 147°15'E., 35 km N. of Nyngan, on Duck Ck; PO 1884–1901.

Colchester (*Co. Cooper*) 34°21'S. 146°11'E., 14 km SE of Griffith; RS 1946–75.

Coldstream (*Co. Clarence*) 29°35'S. 153°07'E., 15 km SW of Maclean; Broadmouth Creek till 1881; village gaz. 1873; farming; creamery (Fresh Food & Ice Co.) 1897; flood 1892; PO 1877; telephone 1909; TX 1928; Wes. Meth. C. 1876; pop. 40 (1881), 156 (1901), 313 (1911).

Coleambally (*Co. Boyd*) 34°48'S. 145°53'E., 29 km SW of Darlington Point, on Boona Channel; planned 1952 as centre of irrigation area, town d. 1954 by Clarke Gazzard, founded 1968; cotton 1963–73, hort. 1965+, sorghum and rice 1968+, vegetables till 1970, cattle in 1970s, potatoes 1970+, maize, lucerne, sunflowers, wheat; ambulance station 1975; Angl. C. (St Mark's) b. 1969 by Stewart McDonald; Christ. Revival Crusade C.; FB; PO 1970; PS b. 1982 by Forlico; reservoir (tower) b. 1968 by F.J. Thomson & Co.; rice mill (Ricegrowers' Co-op. Mills Ltd) 1968, additions 1980; Rom. Cath. C. (St Peter's) 1982; sale-yards 1970; school (Argoon till 1965, then North Coleambally till 1968) 1963, new school 1967, additions 1985; sewerage 1974; TX (automatic); Unit. C. 1968, renovated 1980 by Reg Cowie; water reticulation 1969; pop. 120 (1961), 245 (1971), 367 (1976), 565 (1981), 562 (1986), 580 (1991), 647 (1996), 656 (1997), 686 (2001), 658 (2006), 630 (2011).

Coleambally (*Co. Boyd*) see also Egansford.

Coledale (*Co. Inglis*) see Tamworth.

Colemans Bend (*Co. Selwyn*) 36°20'S. 148°03'E., 33 km W. of Perisher Valley, on Murray R.

Coleman's Siding (*Co. Camden*) see Colo Vale.

Coleridge (*Co. Cook*) see Bullaburra.

Colima (*Co. Townsend*) 35°25'S. 144°34'E., 40 km W. of Deniliquin, on Colligen Ck.

Colinroobie (*Co. Cooper*) 34°27'S. 146°35'E., 20 km NE of Leeton; village gaz. 1899 as Collinroobie; farming; cemetery (burials 1907+) 1900; PO 1899–1951; school (Bunganbil till 1906) 1897–1921 and 1928–46; telephone 1914; TX 1917, automatic 1952; Union C. b. by Walter Samuel Yandell; pop. 205 (1901), 121 (1911), 117 (1933), 79 (1947), 63 (1954), 87 (1961).

Colinton (*Co. Beresford*) 35°52'S. 149°09'E., 41 km N. of Cooma, on Colyers Ck; Collington till 1885; village gaz. 1862; goldmining 1888–98, silver, farming; mines: Colinton Gold Mining Co. and Cooma Pty Mine; PO 1866; RS 1889–1975; school 1886–1904; stamper battery (10 head); telephone 1905; TX 1927; pop. 75 (1911), 68 (1933), 57 (1947).

Collarendabri (*Co. Benarba*) see Pokataroo.

Collarenebri (*Co. Finch*) 29°32'S. 148°34'E., 60 km E. of Lightning Ridge, on Barwon R.; first land sales 1865, laid out 1867 by Christie and Greaves, town gaz. 1867 as Collarindabri; sheep; airport (2 km N.); Angl. C. (St John the Evangelist), destroyed 1953; bridge (Gladstone Bridge) b. 1882–86 by Frederick C. Staveley, new one b. 1920 by C. McClure & Co., over Barwon R.; cemetery (383 graves) 1888; CH (incl. lock-up) b. 1902 by William Refshaw, d. by Walter Liberty Vernon, closed and reused; cordial factory (Stephen A. Gray, jun.); electricity 1930; FB; fires 1905, 1936, 1938 (main business block destroyed), 1940; floods 1864 and 1890; hailstorm 1953; hospital 1898, additions 1974; ice works (E.E. Vitnell); Meth. C. 1902; PO 1867, new one b. 1898, additions and alterations 1909 by B.B. Kinnear, burnt down 1994; powerhouse (R.C. Vincent Pty Ltd); Presb. C. 1925; PS 1882, now in former court-house, new cells 1961; punt; reservoir; Rom. Cath. C. (St Vincent de Paul's) b. 1905–7 by James William Doherty, new one 1959; school 1885, new buildings b. 1893 by J.E.A. Clarke, extended 1900, sold 1912, replacement b. 1909 by A.J. Hulbert, new building b. 1954 by Peter and D. Gooding, additions 1964 and 1968, extended 1971 by Harris-James Pty Ltd, additions 1981 and 2010; telegraph 1888; telephone 1910; TX

1912, automatic 1988; typhoid (man died) 1903; water supply augmentation 1990 and 1996; 2 wool-scours; pop. 127 (1891), 257 (1901), 551 (1911), 394 (1933), *c.*450 (1941), 519 (1947), 605 (1954), 599 (1961), 581 (1966), 608 (1971), 599 (1976), 602 (1981), 623 (1986), 617 (1991), 544 (1996), 505 (2001), 478 (2006), 386 (2011).

Collarenebri East (*Co. Benarba*) see Pokataroo.

Collarindabri (*Co. Finch*) see Collarenebri.

Collaroy (*Co. Brisbane*) 32°06'S. 150°07'E., 24 km W. of Merriwa, on Krui R.; soldiers' settlement; agric.; Angl. C. (St Mark's) 1872, renovated 1938; bridge, orig. timber, replacement (concrete) b. 1933–35 by State Monier Pipe & Reinforced Concrete Works; drought 1978; FB (station b. 2014); flood 1933; pop. 66 (1911), 25 (1933).

Collector (*Co. Argyle*) 34°55'S. 149°26'E., 31 km SW of Goulburn, on Collector Ck; founded by Terrence Murray, laid out 1841, resurveyed 1859 on higher ground, town gaz. 1859; agric., grazing, dairying; Angl. C. 1838, demolished, new one (All Saints') 1860 d. by Alberto Dias Soares, and graveyard (108 graves 1849+); CH b. 1875 by William Duncan, demolished 1952; earth tremor 1953; FB; flour mill (wind) estab. 1849 by John Hincksman, leased 1855 to John Higman; hailstorm 1932; mine (Mountain Ash); PO 1849, new one b. 1931 by Fielding & Son; pound (stock) 1865; PS, repairs 1896 by Brown and Anderson, closed during World War II, reopened 1947; Rom. Cath. C. (St Bartholomew's) 1850, enlarged 1871, and graveyard (138 graves 1852+); school 1866, repairs 1892 by Peter Poidevin, additions 1902 also by Poidevin, further repairs 1912 by Poidevin, burnt down 1914, replaced 1916 by Portus and Ibbotson; snowstorm 1854; streets oil lit 1850; telephone 1898; TX 1912; Unit. C. (orig. Wes. Meth.) b. 1863–65 by Sampson Ranger and John Lane, and graveyard (77 graves 1875+); pop. 169 (1871), 230 (1891), 263 (1901), 208 (1911), 183 (1933), 105 (1947), 135 (1954), 80 (1961), 326 (2006), 403 (2011).

Collector (*Co. Argyle*) see also Yarra.

Collendina (*Co. Denison*) 36°00'S. 146°08'E., 12 km E. of Mulwala, on Lake Mulwala; school 1915–20; TX (automatic); pop. 71 (1911), 195 (2006), 231 (2011).

Collerina (*Co. Narran*) 29°42'S. 146°38'E., 36 km NW of Brewarrina, on Culgoa R.; PO 1897–1972; telephone 1897; TX 1930; pop. 20 (1933), 113 (2006).

Collerina Hall (*Co. Flinders*) 32°03'S. 147°04'E., 55 km S. of Nyngan; mining; mines: Chrome (gold) 1905–9, Collerina (copper) 1914–21, Tindall's (copper) 1909.

Collie (*Co. Ewenmar*) 31°40'S. 148°18'E., 34 km W. of Gilgandra, on Marthaguy Ck; surveyed 1892, village gaz. and lots sold 1893, designated as chief town of the county; grazing and wheat; Angl. C. (St Oswald's) 1917; bridge 1911, over Marthaguy Ck; bushfires 1951 and 1952 (man killed); cemetery (31 graves 1901–2001) 1890; FB; floods 1955 and 1969; PO 1862; PS b. 1899; Rom. Cath. C. 1911, closed, sold 1954 to Neville Hannan, new one (Holy Cross) b. 1953 by Allan Weaver, d. by Fowell, Mansfield and Maclurcan; school 1881, new one b. 1884 by W.J. White, closed 1890, reopened 1896, extended 1898, replaced 1918, closed 2001, sold; sewage works; telephone 1913; TX 1915, automatic 1975; Union C. 1903; pop. 24 (1866), 167 (1901), 269 (1911), 203 (1933), 135 (1947), 171 (1954), 76 (1961), 109 (2006), 158 (2011).

Collina (*Co. Cooper*) see Griffith.

Collingrove (*Co. Harden*) 34°25'S. 148°28'E., 20 km SE of Young; school (Barwang till 1883, then Douglas till 1893) 1880–95.

Collington (*Co. Beresford*) see Colinton.

Collingullie (*Co. Mitchell*) 35°05'S. 147°08'E., 20 km N. of The Rock, on Beavers Island Ck; formerly Cross Roads; farming and grazing; FB; fire 1931; PO 1907; 2 quarries; Rom. Cath. C. (St Michael's) b. 1908 by C. Hardy & Co.; RS (9 km S.) 1928–75; school 1881, new one b. 1883 by C. Hardy & Co., closed 1895, reopened 1908; telephone 1906; TX 1919; Unit. C. (St Margaret's, orig. Presb.)

b. 1927 by Rowlands, d. by Eric Clarke Pitt and John Donald Morrow, closed, sold 2019; water supply augmentation 1985; pop. 191 (1911), 54 (1933), 82 (1947), 230 (1954), 218 (1961), 134 (2011).

Collingwood (*Co. Wellington*) 32°35'S. 149°27'E., 13 km W. of Mudgee; Meth. C. b. 1929 by C. Wright, d. by Harold Robert Hardwick; Wes. Meth. C. 1875, demolished; pop. 22 (1933).

Collinroobie (*Co. Cooper*) see Colinroobie.

Collins Creek (*Co. Rous*) 28°29'S. 153°01'E., 15 km N. of Kyogle, on Collins Ck; school 1924, new one b. 1925 by W. Tyrrell; telephone 1915; pop. 227 (1933), 125 (1947), 188 (1954), 205 (1961).

Collits Inn (*Co. Cook*) 33°32'S. 150°13'E., 6 km N. of Mount Victoria; estab. 1823 by Pierce Collits; PO 1831–33.

Collombatti (*Co. Dudley*) 30°57'S. 152°45'E., 19 km NW of Kempsey, on Trial Bay Ck; farming; PO 1927–43; school 1904–15 and 1928–51; telephone 1923; pop. 102 (1911), 87 (1933), 99 (1947), 55 (1954), 361 (2006), 601 (2011).

Collombatti Rail (*Co. Dudley*) 30°58'S. 152°50'E., 11 km N. of Kempsey; farming and dairying; PO 1927; RS (4 km NW of Collombatti) 1919–75; school 1928–38 and 1953–2001, sold; telephone 1922; TX 1936; pop. 168 (1933), 50 (1947), 77 (1954).

Colly Blue (*Co. Pottinger*) 31°28'S. 150°09'E., 50 km W. of Quirindi; village gaz. 1904; farming and grazing; bushfire 1946; cemetery (14 graves) 1903; PO 1875–1972; RS 1948–75; school 1885–87 and 1957–73; telephone 1937; TX 1937; pop. 66 (1911), 32 (1933), 58 (1961), 25 (1968).

Collymongle (*Co. Benarba*) 29°27'S. 148°43'E., 18 km NE of Collarenebri; bushfire 1901; pop. 64 (1933).

Colmount (*Co. Forbes*) 34°00'S. 148°46'E., 20 km S. of Cowra; telephone 1932.

Colo (*Co. Camden*) see Hill Top.

Colo (*Co. Cook*)
see North Richmond and Upper Colo.

Colo (*Co. Hunter*) 33°26'S. 150°49'E., 20 km NE of North Richmond, on Colo R.; agric.; Angl. C., destroyed 1867, new one (St John's) b. 1878–80; PO 1964.

Colo Creek (*Co. Georgiana*) see Scabben Flat.

Colo Heights (*Co. Hunter*) 33°22'S. 150°44'E., 21 km N. of Kurrajong; (incl. Mile Ridge); bushfire 2001; FB 1949; quarry; sawmills: Jim Buckett & Co. and MacIntosh's; school 1957; telephone 1949; TX 1951, automatic 1975; pop. 64 (1954), 80 (1961), 339 (2006), 332 (2011).

Colombo (*Co. Auckland*) see Bemboka.

Colombo (*Co. Urana*) see Morundah.

Colombo Creek (*Co. Urana*) see Morundah.

Colongra (*Co. Northumberland*) 33°13'S. 151°33'E., 2 km N. of Halekulani, on Colongra Lake; (incl. North Doyalson); collieries (Powercoal): Endeavour (o. 1967 as Newvale No. 2, renamed in 1995, operated by Elcom Collieries Pty Ltd) and Munmorah State Mine (formerly Elcom Collieries Pty Ltd) 1967; foot-bridge over Hammond Canal; PO (North Doyalson) 1966–81; power station (Munmorah) b. 1961–67, operated by Delta Electricity, closed 2012.

Colonna (*Co. Darling*) 30°27'S. 150°39'E., 8 km S. of Barraba; school 1890–1926.

Colo Vale (*Co. Camden*) 34°24'S. 150°29'E., 7 km NE of Mittagong, on Bargo R.; estab. by Lindesay Crawford Shepherd, subdivided and first lots sold 1889; poultry, orchards, farming; Angl. C. (St Paul's) 1884; bushfire 1952; cemetery; FB; PO 1883; quarry; reservoir, 150,000 gal. (681.9 kl), 1972; RS (Coleman's Siding till 1885) 1883–1975, station restored; sawmills: Colo Vale Wood Co. and E. Starslinoff; school (Chalkerville till 1895, Colo Vale till 1930, then Aylmerton till 1985) 1882, building re-erected 1895 by George Fleming, new one 1985 on new site; telegraph 1890; TX 1917; typhoid (woman died) 1897; water reticulation 1972; pop. 59 (1901), 147 (1933), 142 (1947), 149 (1954), 159 (1961), 332 (1986), 691 (1991), 1,035 (1996), 1,180 (2001), 1,212 (2006), 1,382 (2011).

Colrose (*Co. Leichhardt*) 30°37'S. 148°31'E., 39 km N. of Coonamble; grazing; PO 1927–35;

sawmill; telephone 1915; TX 1916; pop. 81 (1933).

Colstoun (*Co. Durham*) see Coulston.

Columbo Flat (*Co. Brisbane*) see Coolumbo Flat.

Comara (*Co. Dudley*) 30°46'S. 152°23'E., 52 km W. of Macksville, on Macleay R.; farming; Angl. C. (St Paul's) 1918, removed from Moparrabah; bridge (timber truss and girder span) 1892 d. by John Alexander McDonald, over Five Day Ck; cemetery; fire 1952; PO 1896, demolished 1960; school 1957–83; telephone 1898; TX 1917, automatic 1984; pop. 98 (1911), 69 (1933).

Comarong (*Co. St Vincent*) see Comerong.

Combadello (*Co. Courallie*) 29°34'S. 149°37'E., 25 km SW of Moree, on Gwydir R.; cotton gin (Namoi Cotton Co-op. Ltd); pop. 59 (1911).

Combamolang (*Co. Roxburgh*) see Kandos.

Combaning (*Co. Bland*) 34°28'S. 147°41'E., 15 km E. of Temora; goldmining (reef) and farming; mine (Hill 304); PO 1927; RS (8 km N., relocated 1911) 1893, station b. by Franklin and Finlay, closed 1975; school (Combaning Siding) 1912–67, later removed and reused; silo 1922; telephone 1913; TX 1936, automatic 1953; pop. 217 (1911), 70 (1933), 81 (1947), 95 (1954), 86 (1961), 211 (2006).

Combaning Siding (*Co. Bland*) see Combaning.

Combaning South (*Co. Bland*) 34°32'S. 147°40'E., 16 km SE of Temora; school (Combaning till 1917) 1906–17 and 1952–84, later demolished; pop. 205 (1933).

Combara (*Co. Leichhardt*) 31°07'S. 148°22'E., 19 km S. of Coonamble; sheep; bridge 1935, 283 ft (86.3 m), over Castlereagh R.; PO 1904; Rom. Cath. C. (Blessed Oliver Plunket) b. 1939 by J.F. Brown, d. by J. Cozens; RS 1903, station b. by John Allibone and McCarthy, closed 1975; sawmills: Combara Sawmilling Co. 1911 and Whitton & Sons; school 1916–20 and 1930–47; telephone 1910; TX; pop. 83 (1911), 189 (1933), 78 (1947), 96 (1954), 126 (1961).

Combimelong (*Co. Roxburgh*) see Kandos.

Combo (*Co. Lincoln*) 32°26'S. 148°54'E., 14 km N. of Wellington; copper mine (Rose Hill) 1888–89; RS 1897–1950; school 1911–41.

Combo (*Co. Northumberland*) see Singleton.

Combo (*Co. Phillip*) 32°22'S. 149°53'E., 33 km E. of Gulgong, on Cumbo Ck; pop. 86 (1911), 54 (1933).

Comborah (*Co. Finch*) see Cumborah.

Comborah Springs (*Co. Finch*) see Cumborah.

Comboyne (*Co. Macquarie*) 31°36'S. 152°28'E., 22 km W. of Kendall, on Thone R.; disc. 1882 by William Albert Braylesford Greaves, settled *c.*1899 by G. Brown, W. Graham and T. Jones, village gaz. 1902, thrived in early 1920s; orig. timber, then farming and dairying; Angl. C. (St Mark's) b. 1922 by Dun and Amos, deconsecrated and sold 2019; bushfire 1944; butter factory (Comboyne Co-op. Dairy & Produce Co. Ltd) b. 1914 by H. Amos and A.E. Robinson, alterations 1925; cemetery (316 graves 1906+), incl. columbarium; cheese factories: Lancelot Bosanquet and William Debreceny 1914; electricity 1950; milk factory (Comboyne Rural Co-op. Society Ltd) 1910; PO 1905; Presb. C.; PS 1912; Rom. Cath. C. (Our Lady of Mount Carmel) b. 1918 by R.T. Dun and Alec Busteed, renovated, closed, sold 2012; sawmills: Bell's, Prando Borga (burnt down 1915), W.G. Carter & Son, V.C. Duck 1948 (burnt down 1953), Paddy Keough, A.E. Robinson 1910, J.W. Schmidt 1914, Geoffrey Schubert 1920–63; school 1922, new one b. 1924 by N. McPherson, additions 1962; telephone 1911; TX 1916; Unit. C. (Community, orig. Meth.) 1914; water supply 1973; pop. 70 (1907), 249 (1911), 777 (1921), 532 (1933), 636 (1947), 429 (1954), 321 (1961), 546 (2006), 453 (2011).

Comboyne (*Co. Macquarie*) see also Comboyne West.

Comboyne East (*Co. Macquarie*) 31°37'S. 152°29'E., 20 km W. of Kendall, on Upsalls Ck; school 1915–42 and 1957–68; pop. 99 (1933), 58 (1954).

Comboyne Road (*Co. Macquarie*)

see Melinga.

Comboyne West (*Co. Macquarie*) 31°36'S. 152°27'E., 25 km W. of Kendall, on Branch Gully; school (Comboyne till 1922) 1906–75; telephone 1916; pop. 163 (1933).

Come By Chance (*Co. Baradine*) 30°21'S. 148°29'E., 50 km SE of Walgett, on Baradine Ck; settled *c.*1862 by George and William Colless; grazing; bushfire 1951; cemetery (52 graves); PO 1890; PS 1898–1933; sawmill (Perseverance, G. Wilkins); telegraph 1891; TX 1911, automatic 1987; pop. 175 (1901), 170 (1911), 211 (1933), 45 (1947), 55 (1954), 158 (1961), 186 (2006), 115 (2011).

Comerang (*Co. Dampier*) 36°05'S. 150°01'E., 11 km W. of Tuross Head, on Tuross R.; bacon factory (Thomas Sutcliffe Mort) 1873; bushfire 1968; cheese factory (Bodalla Co-op. Cheese Society Ltd) 1862, demolished 1926.

Comerong (*St Vincent*) 34°52'S. 150°45'E., 2 km S. of Shoalhaven Heads, on Tasman Sea; surveyed 1862 by John Mann, further surveyed 1871 by Binstead; farming; butter factory (Comerong Dairy Co.) 1891–1903, demolished 1940; canal, 627 ft (191.1 m), b. 1822 for Alexander Berry; caterpillar infestation 1911; PO 1885; punt (second) 1903, (third) 1907, (fourth) 1908, (fifth) 1957, (sixth) 1993; school (Comarong) 1882–93; telephone 1914; TX 1927.

Comleroy Road (*Co. Cook*) 33°32'S. 150°42'E., 4 km NE of Kurrajong; orchards; Angl. C. 1907, dedicated 1926 as St John the Evangelist, burnt down 1944, new one 1946, removed; bushfires 1928, 1936, 1944; hailstorm 1897; PO 1890; PS; telephone 1905; Wes. Meth. C. 1854, burnt down 1944, and graveyard; pop. 138 (1911), 99 (1933).

Comleroy Road (*Co. Cook*) see also Blaxlands Ridge.

Commandant Hill (*Co. Macquarie*) see Kempsey South.

Commissioners Creek (*Co. Rous*) 28°30'S. 153°19'E., 20 km SW of Murwillumbah, on Commissioners Ck; sawmill (Bill and Frank Hambley), sold to Creegan Bros; telephone 1925; TX 1927; pop. 38 (1933), 86 (1947), 80 (1954).

Commissioners Waters (*Co. Sandon*) 30°31'S. 151°41'E., 3 km E. of Armidale; pop. 24 (1933).

Comobella (*Co. Lincoln*) 32°21'S. 148°58'E., 23 km N. of Wellington, on Mitchell Ck; orig. Tenundra; settled by Grey; bushfire 1902; cyclone 1907; FB 1931 (station b. 2014); PO 1879–1909; school 1881–87; pop. 96 (1901), 130 (1911), 57 (1933), 65 (1947), 84 (1954), 79 (1961), 57 (2011).

Compton Downs (*Co. Cowper*) 30°25'S. 146°34'E., 71 km SE of Bourke; grazing; PO 1927–63; RS 1901, station b. by Charles Baker, closed 1974; telephone 1926; TX 1939; pop. 27 (1933).

Conapaira (*Co. Cooper*) see Taleeban.

Conargo (*Co. Townsend*) 35°18'S. 145°11'E., 32 km NE of Deniliquin, on Billabong Ck; surveyed 1859, town gaz. 1860, laid out 1860 by John McCulloch; grazing; drought 1914; FB; fire 2014; flood 1931; PO 1864; Presb. C. 1914, abandoned; PS 1908; school 1880–97, reopened 1960, additions 2010; telegraph 1886; TX 1910, automatic 1985; pop. *c.*40 (1866), 50 (1891), 62 (1901), 199 (1911), 126 (1933), 62 (1947), 66 (1954), 235 (1961), 189 (2006), 244 (2011).

Condell Park (*Co. Dowling*) 33°33'S. 146°20'E., 28 km S. of Lake Cargelligo; PO 1927–38; telephone 1925; TX 1932.

Condobolin (*Co. Cunningham*) 33°05'S. 147°09'E., 86 km W. of Forbes, on Lachlan R.; disc. 1836 by Major Sir Thomas Livingstone Mitchell, village site reserved by Walker Rannie Davidson, surveyed 1859 by Lewis Gordon, town gaz. 1859 as Condoublin, first lots sold 1860, designated as chief town of the county, munic. 1890–1977; mining (gold, silver, copper) 1898–*c.*1910, timber, wheat, lucerne, barley, cotton, cattle, sheep, fruit, nuts; abattoir (Condobolin Industries) b. 1973–75, closed 1979; Aboriginal mission (Willow Bend); agric. research station 1913; airport (6 km E.) 1939; aluminium outdoor furniture factory (Felton Industries); ambulance station

1952 d. by J.W. Sproule; Angl. C. (All Saints') b. 1878–80 by Brinsmead, d. by Edmund Thomas Blacket, renovated 1926, re-roofed 1940, restored 1978; brewery estab. 1892 by Graf and Williams, acquired by Dowling, burnt down 1903; brickworks, demolished; bridges: first bridge b. by Morton, second one b. 1879 by Staveley and Smith, replaced 1900, destroyed 1976, replaced 1979, J. Brady Bridge over Lachlan R., Chinaman's Bridge over Goobang Ck, Stock Bridge 1966, over Lachlan R.; bushfires 1891, 1898, 1899, 1900, 1905, 1906; carriage-works (Scourfield and Murray) 1899; cemeteries: old one (55 graves 1861–78, razed) and new one (4,211 graves 1878+) 1877, extended 1937, incl. lawn cemetery and columbarium; CH b. 1869 by H. Rogers, relocated, reused, burnt down 1903, new one b. 1880–82, d. by James Johnstone Barnet, additions 1900 by H.P. Hamilton, d. by Walter Liberty Vernon, renovated 1918 by W.A. Miller; Chinese joss house, burnt down 1902; Christ. Revival Crusade C. (Lachlan Valley) 1977; cordial factory estab. by W. Graf, sold to W. Green, sold to John Oppy who opened new one in 1905 and later sold it to William and Albert Oppy, taken over 1954 by Atkinson;_diphtheria 1891;_droughts 1880, 1912, 1914; dust storms 1897, 1917, 1930, 1933, 1965, 2019; FB 1898 (station b. 1901, demolished and replaced 1940, closed, bought 2015 by Terrence O'Bryan, new one 1999 on new site); fires 1889, 1893, 1895, 1896, 1899, 1903, 1906, 1911, 1913, 1927, 1934; floods 1870, 1891, 1894, 1900, 1916, 1926, 1950, 1951, 1952, 1956, 1974; flour mill o. 1881 by R. Blackwood, sold 1882 to Auguste Nicolas and Joseph Bernard Reymond, rebuilt 1890, acquired by A. Nichols, modernised 1899, remodelled 1920, fire 1921, burnt down 1924; freezing works (John David & Son) upgraded 1926, burnt down 1936; heatwaves 1896, 1898, 1946; hospital b. 1884 by Nolty, extended 1910, additions 1927 and 1958, new one 1975; ice works (Francis Hubert Cowlishaw), burnt down 1940; joinery; lock-up 1862; mines: Gold Paint, Great Condobolin Gold & Copper Mine (o. 1898 by Benjamin Roberts, battery erected 1899), Julia Reubens or Lady Julia or Red Paint and Red Paint Extended (Officer, Shepherd & Co.) 1891–1900, Mascotte or Per Ardua, Phoenix or Shepherd's (Condobolin Gold Mining Co.) 1893–1907, Piebald *c.*1890, T.A.R. Potter 1905–25, Rifle Butt, Sultan and Ramping Lion (Smith 1899–1900 and C. Miller 1916), Surprise or Magnolia (Lough, Pennycuick and Smyth) 1892–1902; moth infestation 1906; PO 1858, new one b. 1886 by M. Kelly, additions and alterations 1914 by H.R. Davidge, renovated 1929; pound (stock) 1859; powerhouse 1925, extended 1927, removed 1968; Presb. C. 1877, new one (St Paul's) 1879, re-roofed 1923, reused, demolished 1963, replacement (Keith Memorial) b. 1954 by Brannan and Inman, d. by Finlay Munro, jun.; PS b. 1881 by R.M. Vaughan, additions 1961, additions and alterations 1974; railway barracks, reused; railway engine shed, damaged 1928; railway turntable, 60 ft (18.3 m); 4 reservoirs (one b. 1929, one b. 1954, one b. 1956, one b. 1967); rifle range 1939; Rom. Cath. C. b. 1882 by Joseph Nulty, d. by Rudden and Budd, extended 1908 by S. Davidge, renovated and reused 1963, new one (St Joseph's) b. 1936–38 by E. Walker, d. by Peter Jerome Gannon; RS 1898, station b. by John Allibone, upgraded 1901, extended 1935, closed 1989; sale-yards (munic.) b. 1947 by Smith and Lulham; Salv. Army C. 1919–42, reopened 1947, reused 1977; sawmills: William Baxter, W. Birch, R. Blackwood 1881, Grant's, H. Holm, Auguste Nicolas and Joseph Bernard Reymond, H.F. Selmes; schools: Condoblin 1872, new one b. 1876 by H. Rogers, additions 1879 by Keilly, burnt down 1883, replaced 1884, extended 1890, additions and alterations 1909 by Charles Benaud Smith, additions 1921 and 1924, new one 1934, additions 1956, 1958, 1964, 1983, and HS b. 1967 by K.D. Morris & Sons Pty Ltd, d. by F.D. Underwood, additions 1975 and 2010; SD Adventist C.; sewerage 1952; silos 1933 and 1961; stamper batteries (incl. one erected 1899); storm 1928;

street tree plantings 1892; streets lit by oil 1891, then acetylene gas, then kerosene, then methylated spirits, then electricity 1925; TC (a campus of Western Institute); telegraph 1878, new office b. 1886 by M. Kelly; TX 1907, automatic 1971; typhoid 1903; Unit. C. (Freedom in Christ Ministries, orig. Meth.) b. 1930 by W.J. Hassen; vulcanising works (C.H. Leifermann); water supply 1898; waterworks (new boiler installed 1915 and filtration plant 1941); weirs: one on Goobang Ck 1899 and one on Lachlan R. 1922; wool-scour (bought 1905 by John Dill from Robert Bentley Nightingale), demolished; pop. 71 (1861), *c.*100 (1866), 95 (1871), 467 (1881), *c.*600 (1885), *c.*700 (1889), 742 (1891), 850 (1896), 1,078 (1901), 1,230 (1910), 1,918 (1911), 1,250 (1915), 1,469 (1921), *c.*1,600 (1922), 1,360 (1924), 2,642 (1927), 2,572 (1933), 2,616 (1947), 2,840 (1954), 3,150 (1961), 3,250 (1963), 3,593 (1966), 3,214 (1971), 3,273 (1976), 3,355 (1981), 3,229 (1986), 3,163 (1991), 3,100 (1996), 3,054 (2001), 2,847 (2006), 2,754 (2011).

Condobolin North (*Co. Cunningham*) 32°57'S. 147°10'E., 15 km N. of Condobolin.

Condong (*Co. Rous*) 28°19'S. 153°26'E., 4 km E. of Murwillumbah, on Tweed R.; settled 1866 by John McLeod, bypassed by highway 1980; cattle, farming, sugar-cane; bridge over Tweed R.; caterpillar infestation 1921; diphtheria 1914; floods 1945, 1954, 2017; PO 1898; quarry; railway siding 1894; sawmill (Standard Sawmilling Co.) 1897; school 1896, additions 1923 by T.J. Baker, additions 1929; storm 1892; streets electric lit 1959; sugar mill 1880, damaged 1892, sold 1978 by CSR to NSW Sugar Milling Co-op. Ltd, became Manildra Harwood Sugars in 1989, co-generation power plant b. 2005–8 by Downer Engineering and Clyde Babcock Hitachi, mill inundated 2017; telephone 1908; wharf b. 1901 by E.J. Fackerell; pop. 98 (1901), 531 (1911), 577 (1933), 538 (1947), 431 (1954), 393 (1961), 256 (2006), 298 (2011).

Condoublin (*Co. Cunningham*) see Condobolin.

Condoulpe (*Co. Caira*) 34°46'S. 143°23'E., 15 km S. of Balranald; Hillerman's till 1909; farming; PO 1908; rifle range 1913; telephone 1908; TX *c.*1910.

Coneac (*Co. Gloucester*) 31°51'S. 151°49'E., 22 km NW of Gloucester, on Manning R.; pop. 24 (1933).

Congarinni (*Co. Raleigh*) 30°44'S. 152°53'E., 4 km SW of Macksville, on Taylors Arm; bridge 1940, over Taylors Arm; punt b. by W. Robertson; pop. 130 (1911), 38 (1933), 64 (1947), 87 (1961), 450 (2006), 522 (2011).

Congera (*Co. Monteagle*) 34°21'S. 148°46'E., 11 km N. of Boorowa.

Congewai (*Co. Northumberland*) 33°00'S. 151°20'E., 11 km SE of Paxton, on Congewai Ck; (incl. Mootai); wheat, corn, timber, dairying 1905–1960s, orchards; Angl. C. (St Barnabas's) b. 1928 by William Beckett, closed 1969, demolished; bridge over Congewai Ck; droughts 1939, 1940, 1941, 1944, 1979, 1980; earth tremor 1888; floods 1938, 1949, 1955, 1977; hailstorm 1932; PO 1896; quarry (Mootai); sawmills: Burgess and Harrison 1919 and Charlie Thursby; school (Eglinford till 1973) 1889, burnt down 1944, rebuilt; telephone 1923; TX 1923; pop. 260 (1933), 184 (1947), 173 (1954), 103 (1961), 254 (2011).

Congo (*Co. Dampier*) 35°57'S. 150°09'E., 8 km SE of Moruya, on Congo Ck; settled 1840 by Patrick Staunton; pop. 139 (2006), 225 (2011).

Congudang (*Co. Wellington*) 32°28'S. 149°18'E., 25 km SW of Gulgong.

Conifer (*Co. Hardinge*) 29°59'S. 151°16'E., 27 km SE of Inverell, on Darbys Ck; school (Darbys Branch till 1899) 1896, relocated 1904 by H. Stortenbeker, closed 1936.

Conimbia (*Co. Leichhardt*) 30°41'S. 148°00'E., 48 km NW of Coonamble, on Nedgera Ck; TX (automatic).

Conimbla (*Co. Forbes*) 33°47'S. 148°33'E., 13 km NW of Cowra, on Conimbla Ck; formerly Canimbla; PO 1898; school (Calare 1891–1914) 1881–1928; pop. 92 (1901), 125 (1911).

Coniston (*Co. Camden*) 34°26'S. 150°53'E., 2 km S. of Wollongong, on Tasman Sea; (incl. Mangerton and Mount St Thomas); formerly farming; ambulance station 1987; Assemblies of God C. (Slavic); brickworks: Newbold General Refractories Ltd (demolished 1965) and Wollongong Brick Works Ltd; bridge (Jack Kimble Bridge); bushfire 1939; electricity 1927; fort (Fort Drummond) 1943, closed, guns removed 1962, reused; Foursquare Gospel C.; PO: Coniston 1921, Mangerton 1951, Mount St Thomas 1950; Presb. C. 1951; 3 reservoirs (incl. Mangerton, 1,273,000 gal. or 5,787.1 kl, 1938); Rom. Cath. C. (St Therese of Lisieux) b. 1939 by H.A. Taylor, d. by Clement Glancey, extended 1980; RS o. 1916 as Mount Drummond, closed 1923, reopened 1925 as Coniston, relocated 1941; schools: Coniston (South Wollongong till 1925) 1921, new one b. 1923 by A. Ede, extended 1935, additions 1980, additions 2010 by Patterson Building Group Pty Ltd and Mount St Thomas 1952, additions 1960 and 1963; sewage works; TC 1928; telephone 1917; Union C. b. 1917 by Fred Wishaw, renovated 1966, renamed United C.; water supply (Mangerton) 1922; pop. 1,584 (1947), 2,181 (1954), 5,001 (2011).

Conjola (*Co. St Vincent*) 35°13'S. 150°26'E., 11 km N. of Milton, on Conjola Ck; farming; bridge (concrete) 1938, new one 2008, over Conjola Ck; bushfire 1905; cemetery (96 graves 1890+) 1883; creamery (Conjola Co-op. Dairy Co. Ltd) 1895–1910; FB 1943; PO 1879; Rom. Cath. C. (St Patrick's) 1914–69, moved 1972 to Sussex Inlet; sawmill (Ironbark Timber Co.), dismantled and moved 1914 to Bodalla; school 1880–93; telephone 1909; TX 1925; pop. 116 (1901), 136 (1911), 79 (1933), 82 (1947), 94 (1954), 52 (1961), 210 (2006), 395 (2011).

Connell's Point (*Co. St Vincent*) see Mossy Point.

Connemarra (*Co. Pottinger*) 31°35'S. 149°46'E., 26 km N. of Coolah; RS 1939–75.

Connorton (*Co. Mitchell*) 35°10'S. 147°18'E., 9 km SW of Wagga Wagga; school 1896–1913.

Conoble (*Co. Mossgiel*) 32°57'S. 144°42'E., 96 km NW of Hillston; PO 1948; RS (5 km S.) 1925–89; telephone 1950; TX 1950; pop. 50 (1961).

Conrad (*Co. Hardinge*) see Howell.

Cooba (*Co. Clarendon*) 34°58'S. 147°52'E., 24 km NW of Gundagai, on Cooba Ck; farming; bushfire 1979; cemetery 1886; gale 1904; Rom. Cath. C. (St Mary's) 1886, damaged 1904; school 1883–94 and 1914–22.

Coobool (*Co. Wakool*) 35°14'S. 143°44'E., 55 km NW of Barham; RS (Victorian railway) 1928, closed.

Coocooboonah (*Co. Pottinger*) 30°59'S. 150°09'E., 10 km W. of Gunnedah; farming; FB; PO 1927–31; school 1900–6; pop. 74 (1901), 21 (1933), 338 (2006).

Coocumbit (*Co. Macquarie*) 31°51'S. 152°18'E., 7 km W. of Wingham.

Coodah (*Co. Georgiana*) 33°59'S. 149°23'E., 52 km S. of Blayney, on Abercrombie R.; goldmines: Mount Grey 1875, 1888, 1891, 1893–98 and Scrubby Rush 1883–84, 1887, 1889, 1894–95.

Cooerwull (*Co. Cook*) see Lithgow.

Cookamidgera (*Co. Ashburnham*) 33°12'S. 148°18'E., 14 km SE of Parkes, on Bartleys Ck; Bindogandi Station or Flagstone till 1895; surveyed 1895; farming; cemetery (15 graves); electricity 1950; fires 1922 and 1926; PO 1896, burnt down 1909; RS 1893, station b. by Frederick Lemm, jun. and Thomas Edward Spencer, closed 1974; sawmills: David Bell and Herbert E. Mullins; school 1914–70, reused; telephone 1902; TX 1924; Unit. C. (orig. Meth.) b. 1930 by A.R. Davis; Wes. Meth. C. 1900; pop. 134 (1911), 215 (1933), 184 (1947), 167 (1954), 183 (1961), 214 (2011).

Cookannalla (*Co. St Vincent*) see Cookanulla.

Cookanulla (*Co. St Vincent*) 35°20'S. 149°55'E., 17 km NE of Braidwood; formerly Cookannalla; grazing; flood 1860; PO 1927–31; sawmill (Archibald's), destroyed 1860; telephone 1921; TX 1953.

Cookardinia (*Co. Goulburn*) 35°33'S. 147°14'E., 20 km NW of Holbrook; farming and grazing; bridge over Jerra Jerra Ck; cemetery (2 km E.); FB; PO 1873; Presb. C. (Chalmers) 1883, and graveyard; sawmill; school 1883 b. by Adolph Reiff, additions and repairs 1892 by

R.G. Allen, closed 1906, reopened 1943–54; telephone 1897; TX 1915; Union C.; pop. 159 (1901), 289 (1911), 192 (1933), 177 (1947), 123 (1954), 225 (1961), 240 (2011).

Cookeys Flat (*Co. Wellington*) 32°45'S. 149°10'E., 29 km SE of Wellington, on Macquarie R.

Cooks Crossing (*Co. Napier*) 31°47'S. 149°46'E., 6 km NE of Coolah, on Coolaburragundy R.

Cooks Gap (*Co. Phillip*) 32°22'S. 149°43'E., 18 km E. of Gulgong; grazing; FB; PO 1927; quarry; telephone 1913; TX 1928, automatic 1982; pop. 61 (1933), 62 (1961), 298 (2006), 490 (2011).

Cooks Hill (*Co. Northumberland*) see Newcastle.

Cooks Myalls (*Co. Ashburnham*) 33°02'S. 148°02'E., 19 km NW of Parkes, on Myall Ck; mines: Copper Ridge East *c.*1890 and Copper Ridge West *c.*1890; TX (automatic); Union C.; pop. 26 (1933), 63 (1954), 58 (1961), 385 (2011).

Cooks Ridge (*Co. Townsend*) 35°04'S. 144°42'E., 57 km NW of Deniliquin.

Cooktown (*Co. Richmond*) see Broadwater.

Coolabah (*Co. Canbelego*) 31°02'S. 146°43'E., 74 km NW of Nyngan; founded by George Werner, village gaz. 1886; grazing; cemetery (18 graves 1889+) 1887; CH 1899; experiment farm 1898; FB (station b. 2017); fire 2014; PO 1885, burnt down 1931; PS 1890, new one b. 1928 by Albert Rosette, burnt down 1988; reservoir 1959; RS 1884–1989; sawmills: D. Gregson and William Mackinnon; school 1892–1933 and 1955–2008; telegraph 1890; TX 1915; water reticulation 1959, augmentation 1986; pop. 137 (1901), 98 (1911), 50 (1933), 167 (1947), 137 (1954), 111 (1961), 136 (2006).

Coolac (*Co. Harden*) 34°56'S. 148°10'E., 16 km N. of Gundagai, on Muttama Ck; town gaz. 1862, bypassed by highway 2009; mining (gold, chromite, talcum), dairying, grazing; Angl. C. (St Jude's) b. 1879 by Arnott and Biggs, rebuilt 1910 by G. Armstrong, restored 1925, renovated 1953, reused; bushfires 1952 and 1990; cemetery 1881; FB; mine (Sandy Falls Mining Co. Ltd); PO 1870, reused; PS 1884–1933, reused; rabbit freezing works (Regan and Davis, bought 1922 by Adjungbilly Freezing Co.); rifle range 1908; Rom. Cath. C. (St Peter's) b. 1927 by E.C. Williams, d. by A.F.I. Somerville, closed, sold 2008, reused; RS (2 km N.) 1886, station b. by John Miller, closed 1983, sold and demolished 1987; school 1874, additions and repairs 1910 by J.W. Richardson, closed 1981, sold and reused; talcum mine (Somerset); telegraph 1887; TX 1910, automatic 1938; pop. *c.*12 (1866), 232 (1891), 247 (1901), 363 (1911), 249 (1933), 163 (1947), 184 (1954), 140 (1961), 387 (2006), 365 (2011), 216 (2016).

Coolagolite (*Co. Dampier*) 36°24'S. 149°55'E., 13 km W. of Bermagui; TX 1928; pop. 63 (1911), 57 (1933), 70 (1947), 71 (1954), 70 (1961), 285 (2006), 360 (2011).

Coolah (*Co. Napier*) 31°50'S. 149°43'E., 36 km NE of Dunedoo, on Coolaburragundy R.; (incl. Oban Soldiers' Settlement estab. 1917); estab. *c.*1848, surveyed and laid out by Edward Fisher, village gaz. 1885; sheep, lucerne, farming; airport (12 km NW) 1954; ambulance station; Angl. C. (St Andrew's) b. 1874–82, extended 2014, and graveyard; brewery (Richard Mead) 1886–93; bridge b. by John Ahearn, over Coolaburragundy R.; bushfire 1912; butter factory (Oban) b. 1919 by E. Boyne, new one (Coolah Co-op.) 1922, closed 1925, alterations and renovations 1933, reopened 1934 by Coolah Valley Dairy Society Ltd, closed 1936, sold 1941 to W.H. Brown; carriage-works: Perseverance (bought 1917 by J. Pearce from F. Patterson) and E. Whitfield; cemetery (1,020 graves 1871+) 1880; CH (incl. lock-up) b. 1878–80 by Henry S. Winter, d. by James Johnstone Barnet, alterations and repairs 1898 by J.T. Saunders; cordial factory (A. Morrow), sold 1914 to Devoy Bros; FB 1946 (station b. 1947 by D.G. Murphy, reused, new one 1968); fire 1928; hospital b. 1909 by M.H. Bennett, additions 1913 and 1960; PO 1849, new one b. 1882 by W. Summerhayes, additions 1915 by John Hutson; pound (stock) 1864; powerhouse

(Tucker Bros); Presb. C. (St James's) b. 1870 by John Campbell, rebuilt and reopened 1904, and graveyard; PS 1874–80, second one b. 1878–80 by Henry S. Winter, d. by James Johnstone Barnet, extended 1898 by J.T. Saunders, d. by Walter Liberty Vernon, renovations and repairs 1917 by C. Archer, additions and repairs 1931 by G. Palmer & Sons, third one 1979; rabbit freezing works 1921, burnt down 1922; railway turntable (William Sellers & Co.), 60 ft (18.3 m), closed; reservoirs; Rom. Cath. C. b. 1882 by Michael Murphy, replacement b. 1906 by John S. Nutt, d. by Harold Robert Hardwick, reused, new one (Sacred Heart) 1982; RS 1920–75; sale-yards 1947; sawmills: Coolah Sawmills Pty Ltd (estab. 1943 by Michael and William Malouf), Probert's 1909, G. Rodgers 1919, Young and Bray; school 1875, new buildings b. 1882 by W. Summerhayes, additions and alterations 1914 by J. Hutson, additions 1956, 1966, 1981; sewerage 1970; storm 1885; telegraph 1872; TX 1910, automatic 1978; Wes. Meth. C. 1871; wool store (Wilcox and Mofflin) 1920; pop. *c.*60 (1866), 263 (1891), 254 (1901), 765 (1911), 768 (1933), 851 (1947), 1,007 (1954), 911 (1961), 904 (1966), 827 (1971), 851 (1976), 878 (1981), 863 (1986), 889 (1991), 828 (1996), 785 (2001), 798 (2006), 794 (2011).

Coolah Bridge (*Co. Bligh*) 31°57'S. 149°39'E., 15 km S. of Coolah; school 1896–99; telephone 1911.

Coolah Bridge (*Co. Bligh*) see also Hannahs Bridge.

Coolalie (*Co. King*) 34°47'S. 148°59'E., 9 km NE of Yass; airfield; lime-works (Henry James); PO 1910–64; quarries (limestone and marble); RS (station relocated 1914) 1891–1975; school (Farrington till 1886, then Drofwal till 1920) 1882, new building b. 1883 by J. Caldwell, closed 1922; telephone 1910; TX 1928; typhoid 1914; pop. 54 (1901), 75 (1911), 92 (1933), 64 (1954), 57 (1961).

Coolaman (*Co. Bourke*) see Coolamon.

Coolamatong (*Co. Wallace*) 36°24'S. 148°47'E., 6 km SE of Berridale, on Kara Ck.

Coolamigal (*Co. Roxburgh*) 33°17'S. 149°53'E., 13 km NW of Portland, on Coolamigal Ck; gold disc. 1917 by J. M'Quillen and H.T. Ashby.

Coolamon (*Co. Bourke*) 34°49'S. 147°12'E., 35 km W. of Junee; Cowabbie till July 1881, then Ganmain till Aug. 1881; surveyed 1881 by C.F. Bolton, laid out by B.C. Garland and village gaz. 1881, first lots sold 1882, second auction 1883; wheat, hay, chaff, sheep, turkeys; airfield 1970; ambulance station 2018; Angl. C. (St Andrew's) 1885, new one 1905 d. by William John Monks, extensions 1928 d. by E.R. Laver and George Mammatt; brick-kilns (Ashwood Bros); bushfire 1897; carriage-works (Vandewater and McGrath); caterpillar infestation 1936; cemetery 1889, restored 1931; CH 1892, burnt down 1896, new one (incl. lock-up) 1900; chaff mill (N. Mutton & Co.), burnt down 1978; cheese factory (Barry Lillywhite) 2016; clock tower (Pioneer) 1988; cordial factory (William Steele), bought 1907 by Dave J. Iverach, burnt down 1916; dust storms 1896, 1898, 1902; earth tremors 1938 and 1952; electricity 1925; FB 1927 (station b. 1933, new one 2013); fires 1897, 1917, 1918, 1990; floods 1902 and 1928; flour mill (Devon Roller Flour Mills) b. 1897 by William Steele and B. Costin for William Tucker Pyke, taken over by Randall King and W.E. Pyke, taken over 1945 by Lance Pyke, demolished 1962, chimney demolished 1970; gale 1923; grasshopper infestation 1907; hailstorms 1902, 1914, 1969; heatwave 1900; hospital 1952; iron foundry (M.E. Baird); flood 1931; Meth. C. b. 1928 by R.A. Tiltman, d. by Eric Clarke Pitt and John Donald Morrow; mouse plague 1917; PO 1881, alterations 1903 by George Huntley Dixon and William Godfrey Butterworth, extended 1909 by William Edwards; Presb. C. b. 1904 by J.I. Massey, d. by William Steele; PS 1885; reservoir, 200,000 gal. (909.2 kl); Rom. Cath. C. 1888, new one (St Michael's) b. 1912 by M. Mellor, extended 1928; RS o. 1881 as Cowabbie Road, renamed Cooleman 1881 till 1895, closed 1989; sale-yards 1929; sawmills:

T.W. Milne & Co. and William Tucker Pike, burnt down 1896; scarlet fever 1952; school (Coolaman till 1894) b. 1884 by Charles, new buildings b. 1892 by Turner and Hindes, additions and alterations 1912 by William Breakell, additions 1915, 1918, 1966, 1972, additions 1999 by Burton Constructions Pty Ltd; sewerage 1966; silos 1922 and 1937; snow 1899 and 1903; steel fabrication works (Coolamon Steelworks Pty Ltd) estab. 1973 by H.K. Menzies and B. Holden; storm 1946; telegraph 1885; TX 1908, automatic 1980; typhoid 1898 (man died) and 1903; Unit. C. (St Peter's, orig. Presb.) b. 1958 by Jackson and Jones; water supply 1941; Wes. Meth. C. 1899, renovated 1907, closed, moved and reused; pop. 319 (1891), 418 (1901), 1,694 (1911), 1,286 (1933), 1,064 (1947), 1,048 (1954), 988 (1961), 1,036 (1966), 1,056 (1971), 1,084 (1976), 1,088 (1981), 1,088 (1986), 1,184 (1991), 1,261 (1996), 1,267 (2001), 1,339 (2006), 1,590 (2011).

Coolan (*Co. Forbes*) see Wirrinya.

Coolaness (*Co. Rous*) 28°50'S. 153°07'E., 7 km NE of Casino, on Tomki Ck; Lower Spring Grove till 1932; 2 quarries; school 1957–59; telephone 1926; pop. 47 (1933), 86 (1954).

Coolangatta (*Co. Camden*) 34°52'S. 150°43'E., 2 km W. of Shoalhaven Heads, on Shoalhaven R.; orig. Cooloomgatta; settled 1822 by Alexander Berry and Edward Wollstonecraft, subdivided and lots sold 1946; logging 1822+, shipbuilding 1824+, then wheat, maize, barley, potatoes, dairying, now tourism; bushfire 1895; cemetery 1899; condensed milk factory (estab. by John Hay, taken over by Jersey Milk Co. Ltd) 1896–1901; FB 1944; flour mill (Alexander Berry); PO 1886; telephone 1915; TX 1927, automatic 1954; Union C., reused; wineries: Coolangatta Estate (Colin Bishop) 1990 and Mountain Ridge 2007; pop. 100 (1841), 237 (1901), 154 (1911), 59 (1954), 61 (1961), 291 (2011).

Coolangatta (*Co. Camden*) see also Shoalhaven Heads.

Coolatai (*Co. Burnett*) 29°15'S. 150°45'E., 34 km W. of Ashford, on Ottleys Ck; grazing; surveyed 1902; Angl. C. (St Peter's) b. 1912 by Jack Robertson and Teddy Slack; cemetery 1910; PO 1904–79; quarry (gravel); Rom. Cath. C. (St Therese of Lisieux) 1941, removed from Cherry Tree Hill, closed, sold; school 1954, additions 1963, closed 1969; telephone 1898; TX 1911; pop. 141 (1901), 276 (1911), 138 (1933), 123 (1947), 259 (1954), 82 (1961), 183 (2006).

Coolbaggie (*Co. Lincoln*) 32°01'S. 148°31'E., 27 km N. of Dubbo, on Coolbaggie Ck; TX (automatic); pop. 69 (1947), 57 (1961).

Coolbaggie Creek (*Co. Ewenmar*) see Eumungerie.

Coolbool (*Co. Wakool*) 35°17'S. 143°42'E., 56 km NW of Barham; RS (Victorian railway) 1927, defunct.

Cooleman (*Co. Bourke*) see Coolamon.

Coolendel (*Co. St Vincent*) 34°50'S. 150°25'E., 17 km W. of Nowra, on Shoalhaven R.

Coolgardie (*Co. Rous*) 28°55'S. 153°27'E., 8 km S. of Alstonville; sawmill (Robert J. Randle), closed; pop. 39 (1933).

Coolongolook (*Co. Gloucester*) 32°13'S. 152°19'E., 17 km W. of Tuncurry, on Coolongolook R.; settled by George Worth, surveyed 1890 by Henry Fraser Hall; mining (gold disc. *c.*1878 by George, John and William Worth), sawmilling, farming, dairying *c.*1910+; airfield; Angl. C. (St Luke's) b. 1904 by William T. Batchelor and Philip Munro, closed, sold 1996 and reused; bushfire 1968; cemetery (268 graves 1900+) 1891, incl. columbarium; FB; mines: Big Wonder, Curreeki, Gold Bar (Lulham's), Golden Butterfly, Golden Star, Great Wonder, Farnell (J. Donaldson), Lady Mary, Little Wonder (V. Murray), Mount Springfield, Mountain Maid, Mountain Widow (S. M'Kay), Nil Desperandum (Clayton's), Perseverance (Cannell's), Rose and Thistle (Worth's), Queen Mary (Hoare's), The Suttor, Who'd-have-thought-it; PO 1878; punt; 2 quarries; sale-yards; sawmills: John Donaldson (sold to Goodlet and Smith, closed) and Victor Nosworthy (estab. 1939, burnt down 1944, rebuilt on new site, closed 1961); school

1884 b. by John Donaldson, extended 1897, demolished and replaced 1941 by J.A. Butler, additions 2010; stamper batteries (10 head and 15 head); telephone 1906; TX 1924–75; wharf; pop. 68 (1901), 248 (1911), 315 (1933), 267 (1947), 257 (1954), 181 (1961), 404 (2006), 417 (2011).

Cooloomgatta (*Co. Camden*) see Coolangatta.

Cooloon (*Co. Rous*) see Tweed Heads.

Coolringdon (*Co. Beresford*) 36°17'S. 148°58'E., 16 km SW of Cooma, on Slack Ck; sheep; airport (Cooma-Snowy Mountains); school 1907–16; pop. 39 (1933).

Coolumbo Flat (*Co. Brisbane*) 32°20'S. 150°04'E., 35 km SW of Merriwa, on Goulburn R.; formerly Columbo Flat.

Coolumbooka (*Co. Wellesley*) 36°55'S. 149°20'E., 8 km E. of Bombala; bushfire 1884.

Cooma (*Co. Beresford*) 36°14'S. 149°08'E., 99 km S. of Queanbeyan, on Cooma Ck; (incl. East Cooma and North Cooma); orig. Kuma, then Coombah; surveyed 1849 by Thomas Scott Townsend, village gaz. 1849, first lots sold 1850, more lots sold 1854, designated as chief town of the county, munic. proc. 1879, thrived 1949–72; mining (gold rush 1861), animal skin industry (wallaby, possum, hare), wheat till 1920, barley, oats, rye, maize, potatoes, butter, cheese, ham, bacon, now mainly sheep and cattle, tourism *c.*1900+, trout fishing, headquarters for Snowy Mountains Hydro-Electric Scheme 1949+; abattoir (Monbeef Pty Ltd) 1998; ambulance station 1952; Angl. C.: Christ (b. 1845–50 by A. and D. McDonald, d. by William Grant Broughton, closed 1872, derelict, re-roofed and renovated 1936, restored 1960, reused) and graveyard (graves 1846+) and St Paul's (b. 1865–69 by James Jackson Mawson, Charles Potter and David Scarlett, d. by Alberto Dias Soares, re-roofed and spire b. 1892 by D. Montgomery, d. by Harry Chambers Kent, renovated 1959, vestry added 1966, church re-roofed again 1983, restored); Assemblies of God C. (Snowy Monaro); asylum (lunatic) 1877 (in former gaol), closed 1884; Bapt. C. (Redemption) 1972; brewery estab. 1886 by Sir James Ashton and Hugh Stewart, closed 1892; bushfires 1952 and 2003; carriage-works: Cooma Coach Works (Samuel Scanes, then John A. Butler, then J.H. Rogan 1906), Cooma Steam Coach Factory (A.W.G. Ryall, acquired 1908 by Thomas Kilborn & Co.), A.J. Zehner and W.R. Smith 1876; 2 cemeteries; CH (incl. lock-up) 1849, second one b. 1862–64 by John Malcolm, d. by James Johnstone Barnet, additions 1878 by J. Harris, reused as police station, third one b. 1886–88 by J.G. Gough & Co., also d. by Barnet, renovated 1892 by Mawson Bros, additions 1990; Christ. Brethren Assemblies C. (Community); cordial factories: Edward Agnew, Bookallil & Co., D. Myles, Parkinson Bros 1873, Woodcroft's; diphtheria 1906 and 1909; droughts 1884, 1885–87, 1923; dust storm 1896; earth tremors 1872, 1878, 1885, 1892, 1898, 1901, 1902, 1905, 1910, 1917, 1931, 1933; electricity 1922; FB 1917 (station b. 1924, replaced 1974); fires 1911, 1930, 1935; floods 1862, 1870, 1873, 1879, 1922, 1956, 2012; flour mills: one b. 1861 by Alexander Montague, taken over 1872 by John Elihu Body, inundated 1879, and Monaro Co-op. Mill & Flour Co. b. 1884 by John Harris; gaol b. 1862–64 by John Malcolm, d. by James Johnstone Barnet, new one b. 1870–73 by James Hinton, also d. by Barnet, converted 1877 to lunatic asylum by H. Thornton, then used as offices 1885, re-roofed 1896, reopened as gaol, closed 1909, reused, additions and alterations 1953–56, reopened 1957 as (homosexual) gaol, closed and reused 1998, reopened 2001 as gaol; hailstorms 1871, 1883, 1935, 1959; hospital 1861, extended 1867 by James Jackson Mawson, extended 1872, 1879, 1905, 1939, 1952, 1953, additions 1954 by F.R. Coyle, additions 1956 and 1961, new one 1986; Jehovah's Witnesses C. 1968; Lutheran C. (Trinity) 1967 d. by A. Rimka; measles epidemics 1875 (infant died), 1893 (3 died), 1898, 1909; PO: Cooma 1847 (new one b. 1877–79 by John Harris, d. by James Johnstone Barnet, additions 1897 by Avery, extended 1909 by Arthur Mawson, sold), East Cooma 1956, North Cooma 1952–2014; police barracks b. 1878–80 by Peter Poidevin and David O'Rourke, additions 1892 by Mawson Bros, repairs 1909 by A. Stephens; pound (stock) 1848; powerhouse 1922, alterations 1924, demolished 1954; rabbit canning works (G.E. Curtis) 1920; rabbit freezing works; railway barracks, additions 1891 by D. Montgomery, closed and reused; railway engine shed 1889, burnt down 1923; railway turntable, 50 ft (15.2 m), replaced 1902 (William Sellers & Co.), 60 ft (18.3 m); reservoirs (one failed 2020 and flooded North Cooma); rifle range (2 km SE) 1908; Rom. Cath. C.: Our Lady Help of Christians 1960 and St Patrick's 1860, new one b. 1874–77 by Richard Hannaford, d. by D.W. Ryan, remodelled 1957, additions and alterations 1981 by Hughes Bros, d. by Terence A. Daly; RS 1889, station b. by Alexander Hamilton Scouller, refreshment rooms 1922–74, station closed 1990, restored and reused; sale-yards; Salv. Army C. 1890–1903; sawmill (Sarnia, H.E. Joy); scarlet fever 1909; schools: Cooma 1863 (new building b. 1886 by John Harris, additions 1908 by A. Manson, additions 1926 by W. Mawson, additions 1962, 1966, 1970, 1975), East Cooma 1955 b. by Architon Construction Co., closed 1972, Monaro HS 1954 b. by Hughes Bros (additions 1956, 1958, 1962, 1965, 1968, 1980), North Cooma 1953, additions 1956 and 1985; SD Adventist C.; sewerage 1938, augmentation 1959 and 1997; storms 1861, 1897, 1900 (many houses damaged); TC o. 1908 (in old gaol), relocated, became a campus of Illawarra Institute of Technology in 1992, additions 2007, additions 2014 by Edwards Constructions (NSW) Pty Ltd; telegraph 1865, additions to office 1897 by Avery, office extended 1909 by Arthur Mawson, closed 1969; telephone: East Cooma 1956 and North Cooma 1952; TX 1904, automatic 1964; typhoid 1906; Unit. C. (St Andrew's, orig. Presb.) b. 1880–82 by Charles Freeby and J.L. Fisher, d. by Alexander Leckie Elphinstone; water supply 1912, augmentation 1985; Wes. Meth. C. 1881, demolished 1928, new one 1890, reused 1977; wool-scours: Anderson's 1860–80 and A.M. Lloyd (incl. fellmongery) 1900; pop. 47 (1851), 166 (1856), 369 (1861), 370 (1866), 492 (1871), 1,042 (1881), 1,729 (1891), *c.*2,000 (1895), 1,938 (1901), 2,330 (1911), 1,969 (1933), 2,249 (1947), 6,506 (1954), 8,716 (1961), 9,350 (1965), 9,106 (1966), 7,784 (1971), 7,353 (1976), 7,978 (1981), 7,406 (1986), 7,385 (1991), 7,150 (1996), 6,949 (2001), 6,587 (2006), 6,301 (2011).

Coomba (*Co. Gloucester*) 32°15'S. 152°28'E., 8 km SW of Forster; pop. 72 (1911), 35 (1933).

Coombadjha (*Co. Drake*) 29°20'S. 152°32'E., 53 km NW of Grafton, on Clarence R.; sawmills: J.T. M'Kittrick and Priest's; telephone 1926; pop. 273 (2006).

Coombah (*Co. Benarba*) 29°39'S. 149°18'E., 58 km SW of Moree.

Coombah (*Co. Beresford*) see Cooma.

Coombah (*Co. Windeyer*) 32°59'S. 141°38'E., 114 km S. of Broken Hill, on Coombah Lake; pop. 37 (1933), *c.*5 (1999).

Coomba Park (*Co. Gloucester*) 32°15'S. 152°28'E., 8 km SW of Tuncurry, on Wallis Lake; FB (station b. 1988); pop. 269 (1996), 329 (2001), 396 (2006), 449 (2011).

Coombell (*Co. Richmond*) 29°01'S. 152°58'E., 18 km S. of Casino; farming and dairying; Angl. C. (St Michael and All Angels'); brickworks (The Coombell Brickmaking Co. Ltd) o. 1912 by F.W. Knapman, acquired 1915 by Robert Ernest Gunthorpe, closed, derelict; PO 1911; RS (3 km W.) 1905, station closed and removed 1975; school 1957–85; telephone 1913; TX 1930; pop. 73 (1933), 99 (1947), 100 (1954), 88 (1961).

Coomber (*Co. Roxburgh*) see Kandos.

Coombermelon (*Co. Roxburgh*) see Kandos.

Coombing Park (*Co. Bathurst*) 33°38'S. 149°07'E., 4 km SW of Carcoar, on Coombing Ck; surveyed 1831 by James Byrn Richards, estab. by Thomas Icely, acquired 1881 by Cobb & Co.; iron ore mining; railway (mineral); police barracks 1838; quarry (ironstone); pop. 34 (1933).

Coomealla (*Co. Wentworth*) see Dareton.

Coonabarabran (*Co. Gowen*) 31°16'S. 149°16'E., 92 km E. of Coonamble, on Castlereagh R.; settled in 1840s, surveyed 1859 by Walker Rannie Davidson, founded by James Weston, laid out 1859 by Lewis Gordon, first lots sold 1860, town gaz. 1869, thrived 1870s–80s and 1928–30; wheat, maize, sheep, cattle, sawmilling, fruit, tourism (Warrumbungle National Park and Siding Spring Observatory); abattoir (Chillana Pty Ltd), closed 2012; airport (7 km S.) 1963; ambulance station 1953; Angl. C. (Christ) b. 1873 by John Isaac Neate, relocated and re-roofed 1911, closed and reused, bought 1947 by Yelland, new one 1939; brick-kilns: Fred W. Liebentritt and J. Taylor 1912; bridges: one b. 1885 by Mitchell and Jones, replaced 1926, new one (Mary Jane Cain Bridge) 1996, over Castlereagh R. and Max Mapleson Bridge over Nandi Ck; carriage-works (William Gardiner); cemeteries: Anglican (1,082 graves 1870s+), general (987 graves 1870+) 1864, lawn (338 plots 1987+); CH (incl. lock-up) b. 1861 by James Smith and William Grose, d. by Alexander Dawson, demolished, new one b. 1878 by D. McFarlane and G. Henry, d. by James Johnstone Barnet, additions 1896 by J.J. Treasure & Co., renovations and repairs 1937 by H. Willett, additions and restoration 1967 d. by John Rabong; clock tower (war memorial) b. 1928 by Pye; cordial factories: J. Clare, H. Fisk, P.J. Garland (sold 1899), E.J. Jones (taken over 1912 by J.T. Young and Les Bibb), Michael Putney, G.H. Weily 1930; diphtheria 1910; drought 1877–78; electricity 1930; FB (station b. 1936); fibrous plaster works (Harold Gordon); floods 1840, 1864, 1874, 1890, 2007; 2 floodways across Castlereagh R.; flour mills: Co-op. Roller Milling Co. (b. 1892 by Rhodes & Co., burnt down 1898, replaced 1900 by Robinson & Son, sold 1908 to D. Hagan), McIntyre Bros (estab. 1924 by Charles and Colin McIntyre, closed 1928, burnt down 1929), Neilson & Co. (Robert Neilson and Thomas Cadell) b. 1874 by English and Dean, new one b. 1892 by Robinson & Son, James Weston (water powered); foot-bridge; freezing works: Bill Hadfield (turkeys) and Lachlan Freezing Co. (rabbits) 1916; granary; grasshopper infestation 1937; hailstorm 1946; heatwaves 1878 and 1940; honey processing plant; hospital b. 1893 by John Isaac Neate, additions and alterations 1935 by Robinson and Ward, additions 1948, new one 1985; Jehovah's Witnesses C.; Lutheran C.; observatory (Skywatch); PO 1850, new one b. 1879 by Allen McLean, repairs 1925 by G. Woolley; pound (stock) 1860; POW control centre 1943 (in old police station); powerhouse, burnt down 1942, new one 1943, closed; Presb. C. (St Andrew's) 1914, new one 1967; PS b. 1882 by J. Neale, renovations and repairs 1937 by H. Willett, demolished, replacement 1967 d. by John Rabong, additions 1985; quarry (blue metal); railway bridge over Castlereagh R.; railway turntable, 60 ft (18.3 m); reservoir (concrete), 150,000 gal. (681.9 kl); rifle range; Rom. Cath. C. b. 1873–75 by Andrew English, reused 1901, second one 1901, reused 1929, third one 1929, reused 1966, fourth one (St Laurence O'Toole's) b. 1966 by Throsby Bros; RS 1917, station b. by John Allibone, closed 1989; sale-yards; sawmills: Bradley and Wightman, and William and James Pincham (later moved to Baradine); scarlet fever 1876; schools: primary b. 1870 by John Isaac Neate, extended 1874, reused, new one b. 1889 by Kennard Bros, d. by William Edmund Kemp, additions 1910 by J.L. Smith, new school b. 1939 on new site by Kent and Kent, new building 1955, and HS 1962, additions 1973; SD Adventist C.; sewerage 1963; smallpox 1917; storm 1996; streets electric lit 1930; TC, additions 1965 and 1989, became a campus of New England Institute in 1992, additions 2017 d. by Brewster Hjorth Architects; telegraph 1875, new office b. 1879 by Allen McLean; TX 1910; Unit. C. (orig. Meth.) 1933, new one 1987; water supply 1933, augmentation 1993; weirs (Pound Yard Weir and Warrana Weir); Wes. Meth. C. 1875, vestry added 1876; pop. *c.*200 (1866), 163 (1871), 405 (1881), 580 (1891), 662 (1901), 1,172 (1911), 1,923 (1933), 2,240 (1947),

2,210 (1954), 2,547 (1961), 2,793 (1966), 3,045 (1971), 3,068 (1976), 3,001 (1981), 3,033 (1986), 2,959 (1991), 3,012 (1996), 2,748 (2001), 2,609 (2006), 2,578 (2011), *c*.3,174 (2017).

Coonamble (*Co. Leichhardt*) 30°57'S. 148°22'E., 146 km N. of Dubbo, on Castlereagh R.; disc. 1829 by Capt. Charles Sturt, settled 1848 by John Walker, town reserve decl. 1855, surveyed 1859 by Lewis Gordon, laid out 1861 also by Gordon, founded by James Walker, town gaz. and first lots sold 1861, munic. 1880–1952; cattle, then sheep, wheat, barley, citrus orchards; abattoir, taken over 1974 by Scott Bros, closed 2000, sold and refurbished 2012; airport (2 km S.) 1935, terminal 1959; ambulance station (War Memorial) 1958, new one 2012; Angl. C. b. 1876 by Pascoe, replacement (St Barnabas's) b. 1909 by Mooy Bros, d. by Charles Herbert Davy Button; artesian bore, 1,365 ft (416 m), sunk 1894 by William Watkins, second one 1907, third one 1909 (2,180 ft or 664.5 m), fourth one 1924; baking powder factory (N. Fetherstone) 1902; breweries: Aerated Water & Milling Co., Ernst Ernstein, Red Lion Brewery (estab. 1887 by R.E. Rule and E.R. Shone, bought 1889 by Samuel Carmichael and R.J. Boyle, became Coonamble Brewing & Cordial Manufacturing Co. Ltd in 1891, sold 1893 to Henry Parsons, closed 1900, reopened 1904 by John and Ernest Fletcher, closed 1904), Riverine Brewery; bridges: one b. 1883, new one 1919, renovated 1923, demolished, replaced (Sir Edward Hallstrom Bridge) 1983, over Castlereagh R. and one b. 1888 over Warrana Ck; bushfire 1951; carriage-works: Coonamble Coach & Harness Factory (estab. 1883 by Thomas Wilkins, Robert Kennedy and Spence, taken over 1892 by Edwin Perram and Henry Clarkson Firth, sold 1925) and P.B. Sheridan and Meagher; cemeteries: old one (643 graves 1869–1912, razed) 1870 and new one (3,190 graves 1892+), incl. lawn cemetery and columbarium; CH (incl. lock-up) b. 1863 by Benjamin Walker, (second) b. 1877 by Henry and M'Farlane, (third) b. 1883 by W.J. White, additions and repairs 1899 by John Dunkley, (fourth) b. 1972 by Hughes Bros, d. by Margaret Watson; cordial factories: Bob Hickson and Christian, E.J. Graff, W. Pedley, William Smith, Young and Bibb; droughts 1829 and 1877; electricity 1916; experiment farm 1911–30; FB 1887, new station b. 1959; fires 1884, 1902, 1909, 1913, 1929 (destroyed much of town), 2018; floods 1817, 1862, 1870 (nearly destroyed town), 1873, 1887, 1890, 1910, 1920, 1926, 1950, 1955, 2000, 2007, 2009–10; grasshopper infestation 1934; gaol, alterations and additions 1885 by W.J. White; hospital 1878, new one b. 1884 by Mooy Bros, d. by Edmund Thomas Blacket, extended 1897 by T.W. Richards, additions 1903 by Mooy Bros, d. by Charles Herbert Davy Button, additions 1917 by John D. Ryan, additions 1928, alterations and renovations 1936 by William Lishman Jemison, additions 1955, new one b. 2010 by Lahey Constructions Pty Ltd; ice works; Jehovah's Witnesses C.; PO 1859, new one b. 1881, additions 1893 by Mooy Bros; police barracks 1870, new barracks b. 1885 by T. Atkinson; pound (stock) 1862; powerhouse (Aust. Electric Supply Ltd), acquired 1926 by local council; PS 1879, alterations and repairs 1916 by Steel Bros, closed, sold 1970, reused, new one 1961, since 1972 incorporated in the new court-house complex; railway turntable (William Sellers & Co.), 50 ft (15.2 m), closed; 3 reservoirs (incl. one 60 ft or 18.3 m high tower of 26,000 gal. or 118.2 kl); Rom. Cath. C. 1870, replacement b. 1892 by Mooy Bros, d. by T.J. Kelly, dismantled 1938 and moved to Gulargambone, new one (Our Lady of Perpetual Help) b. 1939 by Wallace & McGee Pty Ltd, d. by Hennessy, Hennessy & Co.; RS 1903, station b. by John Allibone and McCarthy, burnt down 1910, replaced, closed 1975, disused; sale-yards (F.S. Caswell), new yards 1935; sawmills: R.A. Colwell, Kennedy Bros, Mooy Bros (estab. 1881, relocated twice, converted 1916 from steam to electricity), R.J. Nelson & Sons Pty Ltd (burnt down 1944, rebuilt, burnt down 1953), G. Sayers; schools: primary b. 1868 by Adam Gordon, new one b. 1880, additions 1891 by Mooy Bros, additions 1908 by Mooy Bros, additions 1931, 1959, 1961, 1973, 1980, and HS 1968, new school 1970, additions 1986; SD Adventist C.; sewerage 1963; silo; soap-works; streets were kerosene lit, then acetylene lit, then electric lit 1916; TC, additions 1984, became a campus of Western Institute in 1992; telegraph 1875, new office 1881, additions 1893 by Mooy Bros; TX 1906, automatic 1976; typhoid 1903 (15 died); Unit. C. (orig. Presb.) 1917–2010, sold and reused; vinegar works; watch-house 1877, decl. a gaol 1878; water supply (from artesian bore) 1892, reticulation 1897, new treatment plant d. and b. 2013 by Aquatec Maxcon Pty Ltd; weir on Warrana Ck; Wes. Meth. C. 1890; wool-scour (William Murray Pty Ltd); pop. 209 (1871), 1,226 (1881), *c.*1,220 (1885), *c.*1,000 (1887), *c.*1,300 (1889), 1,141 (1891), *c.*1,500 (1894), *c.*1,100 (1895), 1,680 (1901), 3,280 (1911), 2,717 (1933), 2,567 (1947), 2,910 (1954), 3,235 (1961), 3,410 (1966), 3,152 (1971), 3,054 (1976), 3,090 (1981), 3,058 (1986), 2,886 (1991), 2,754 (1996), 2,661 (2001), 2,549 (2006), 2,445 (2011).

Coonawaragan (*Co. Gowen*) 31°22'S. 148°31'E., 5 km SE of Gulargambone.

Coonerang (*Co. Beresford*) 36°26'S. 149°11'E., 22 km S. of Cooma, on Brick Kiln Ck; RS 1912, station b. by D.L. Reid, closed 1975.

Cooners Flat (*Co. Wellington*) 32°46'S. 149°12'E., 34 km SE of Wellington, on Macquarie R.

Coongbar (*Co. Drake*) 29°06'S. 152°41'E., 43 km SW of Casino.

Coonong (*Co. Urana*) 35°14'S. 146°10'E., 49 km W. of Lockhart; Presb. C. 1899; RS (12 km NW) 1884–1975; school 1899–1907; pop. 65 (1911), 21 (1933).

Cooper (*Co. Argyle*) 35°01'S. 149°42'E., 27 km S. of Goulburn, on Lake Bathurst; village gaz. 1886.

Cooperabung (*Co. Macquarie*) 31°17'S. 152°48'E., 18 km NW of Port Macquarie; telephone 1924; pop. 35 (1933), 375 (2011).

Coopernook (*Co. Macquarie*) 31°49'S. 152°37'E., 9 km NW of Harrington, on Coopernook Ck; surveyed 1885, village gaz. 1886, bypassed by highway 2006; sawmilling, shipbuilding, dairying, farming, grazing, fruit, fishing, oysters; Angl. C. (St Luke's) 1886, damaged 1903; bridges: one b. 1885 by J. Johnstone, 10 iron spans, incl. retractile draw span, demolished, replaced in steel, with Strauss 50 ft (15.2 m) bascule span, fabricated by Steel Constructions Ltd, b. 1932–34 by Hancock & Webb Pty Ltd, demolished 2006, new one (Francis Longworth Bridge) 2006, over Lansdowne R. and Isaac Rose Bridge 2006, over Coopernook Ck; cemetery (336 graves 1889+) 1884; CH (incl. lock-up) b. 1900 by Rudolph George Ochs, d. by Walter Liberty Vernon; creamery (Lower Manning Co-op. Dairy Co.) 1897; FB; floods 1929 and 1950; Meth. C. b. 1907 by William Henry Unicomb, new one 1915; PO 1876, new one b. 1934 by F. Unicomb; PS 1883; punt 1874–84; quarry; reservoir; Rom. Cath. C. (Holy Angels) b. 1899 by G. Craig, sen., demolished 1953; RS (2 km NW) 1915, closed; sawmills: Aust. Timber Mill Co. Ltd 1898, C.S. Ellis, Allen Taylor & Co. 1903; school 1877, additions 1906; shipyard (Denis Sullivan); storm 1903; telegraph 1914; telephone 1889; TX 1915; Unit. C.; pop. 270 (1891), 284 (1901), 450 (1911), 410 (1933), 545 (1947), 480 (1954), 414 (1961), 287 (1971), 262 (1976), 285 (1981), 333 (1986), 328 (1991), 352 (1996), 380 (2001), 365 (2006), 301 (2011).

Coopers Creek (*Co. Auckland*) 36°40'S. 149°56'E., 8 km E. of Bega.

Cooper's Creek (*Co. Rous*) see Corndale.

Coopers Flat (*Co. Dudley*) 30°49'S. 152°23'E., 53 km W. of Macksville, on Macleay R.

Coopers Flat (*Co. Wellington*) 32°56'S. 149°06'E., 28 km NE of Molong; airfield.

Coopers Glen (*Co. Auckland*) 36°39'S. 149°49'E., 5 km NW of Bega; school 1897–1922.

Coopers Shoot (*Co. Rous*) 28°41'S. 153°36'E., 4 km S. of Byron Bay; flood 2011; school 1905–49; pop. 88 (1911), 143 (1933), 82 (1947), 97 (1954), 75 (1961), 321 (2011).

Cooplacurripa (*Co. Hawes*) 31°37'S. 151°55'E., 44 km N. of Gloucester, on Cooplacurripa R.; airfield; school 1959 b. by Geoff Rowe, additions 1976, closed 1986; snowstorm 1921; telephone 1927; TX 1957; pop. 26 (1933), 141 (2006).

Cooplacurripa (*Co. Macquarie*) see Number One.

Coorabell (*Co. Rous*) 28°37'S. 153°28'E., 7 km N. of Bangalow, on Coorabell Ck; orig. timber, then farming, dairying, bananas; Angl. C. (Epiphany) 1908, Meth. till 1969, closed, sold and reused; hailstorm 1936; landslip 1955; school 1897, additions and alterations 1928 by Edwin Charles Cupitt; pop. 229 (1911), 126 (1933), 160 (1947), 145 (1961), 451 (2006), 421 (2011).

Coorabell Creek (*Co. Rous*) 28°38'S. 153°29'E., 8 km N. of Bangalow; PO 1890; telephone 1891; pop. 21 (1933).

Coorabin (*Co. Urana*) 35°30'S. 146°13'E., 41 km NE of Berrigan; village gaz. 1917; coal (disc. 1915 by J.T. Lane) and kaolin (disc. 1918); butter factory, closed 1895; coalmine (Coorabin Coal Ltd), explosives magazine 1923; hailstorm 1951; Meth. C. b. 1908 by W.S. Ray, damaged and renovated 1951, closed 1987, reused; RS 1912, station b. by Ernest Frederick Leggo, closed 1975; telephone 1950; TX 1950.

Cooradulla (*Co. Buller*) 28°32'S. 152°26'E., 57 km W. of Kyogle; school (Upper Tooloom till 1941) 1938–43; telephone 1925.

Cooranbong (*Co. Northumberland*) 33°05'S. 151°27'E., 6 km W. of Dora Creek, on Dora Ck; (incl. Avondale); Coorumbung till 1866; estab. 1861 (founded by Americans), land sales 1861, thrived in 1880s, declined 1887+; formerly timber and shipbuilding, then orchards; airfield; ambulance station 1953; Angl. C. (St John's) 1869, chancel 1873, and graveyard (burials 1871+); badge and insignia factory (Crusader Industries); bridges: one (3 spans) b. 1876 by Thomas Blissett, over Dora Ck and Avondale Bridge (steel) 1916; bushfires 1951 and 1994; cemetery 1878; CH (incl. lock-up) b. 1877 by E. Davis, repairs 1897 by N.A. O'Leary, renovations and repairs 1910 by H.E. Thompson & Sons; FB; floods 1868 and 1927; flour mills; food factory (Sanitarium Health Food Co.) estab. 1898 by Edward Halsey, new one b. 1934 by H.W. Thompson Ltd, d. by Peddle, Thorp and Walker; foot-bridge over Dora Ck; hospital 1899; PO 1866, new one b. 1881 by William Humphreys, repairs 1911 by Thomas Curran, reused; PS 1873–1920; quarry (sand); Rom. Cath. C. 1861, second one 1869, third one (St Patrick and St Brigid's) b. 1906 by J.R. Berg & Son, d. by Joseph Ignatius Sheerin and John Francis Hennessy, renovated 1971 by Charles A. Lonergan, and graveyard (468 burials 1862+), incl. columbaria 2006; sawmills: Victoria Steam Sawmills (o. 1874, sold 1883 by King), Thomas Russell, George A. Wright; school 1861, new one b. 1879 by Robert Creighton, new building b. 1941 by F. Chambers; SD Adventist C. (Avondale Memorial) 1897, demolished, replaced, and graveyard; telegraph 1878, new office b. 1881 by William Humphreys, repairs 1911 by Thomas Curran; TX 1921; typhoid 1894; water supply 1942; pop. *c.*150 (1865), *c.*700 (1884), 206 (1891), 412 (1901), 492 (1911), 922 (1933), 767 (1947), 1,411 (1954), 1,744 (1961), 1,332 (1966), 2,050 (1971), 1,929 (1976), 2,265 (1981), 2,998 (1991), 3,398 (1996), 3,290 (2001), 3,771 (2006), 5,030 (2011).

Coorumbung (*Co. Northumberland*) see Cooranbong.

Coota (*Co. Bathurst*) see Holmwood.

Cootamundra (*Co. Harden*) 34°38'S. 148°02'E., 44 km SW of Young, on Muttama Ck; (incl. West Cootamundra); Coramundra till 1877; settled in 1830s, surveyed 1859 by Philip Francis Adams, planned 1860, town gaz. 1861 as Cootamundry, first lots sold 1862, thrived 1877+, munic. proc. 1884, 87 lots sold 1887, land boom *c.*1891, munic. abolished 1975; mining, sheep, wheat, dairying, hort., furniture, concrete, smallgoods; abattoirs: Conkey & Sons Ltd 1947 (sold 1979 to Metro Meats Ltd, closed 1984) and G.M. Scott Pty Ltd (sold 2014 by Manildra Meat Co., closed

2017); air force base (World War II); airport 1934, hangar burnt down 1970; ambulance station b. 1953 by S. Mitchell; Angl. C. b. 1878 by Thomas Jobson, fire 1896, demolished 1972, new one (Christ) 1973; Assemblies of God C.; Bapt. C. (orig. Wes. Meth.) b. 1899 by Herbert Butler, d. by David Thomas Morrow, new one re-erected 1954 (removed from Gidginbung), burnt down 1983; bicycle works (W.D. Hutchinson); boiling-down works (Connell and Graham) 1892; boot factory (J. Mullins) 1899; breweries: Burton Brewery (b. 1881 by Rochester, Morton and Jackson, acquired 1883 by Edmund Resch and Richard Frederick Edward Nicolas Resch who renamed it the Lion Brewery, Edmund left partnership in 1885, reopened 1902 by Richard N.J. Resch), Cootamundra Brewery (estab. 1879 by J. and E. Barnes and later became Thomas Rankin's Excelsior Brewery till 1913), Excelsior (Bartley & Co., closed, sold to Frank Mitchell), McIntyre, Lincoln & Co.; brickworks: John F. Brady, Thomas McBeath, Falconer Bros 1890, Giles & Co.; bridge (John Rees Bridge), over Muttama Ck; bushfires 1933, 1987, 1990; butter factories: Albury Co-op. Butter Factory & Produce Co. Ltd (and rabbit freezing works) 1902, Cootamundra Co-op. Butter Factory 1902, Conkey & Sons Ltd 1932, burnt down 1966, Foley Bros (and rabbit freezing works, b. 1901 by P. McBeath & Co., sold 1919 to William White Ltd, later sold to Cowley); carriage-works: Cootamundra Steam Carriage & Engineering Works (estab. by William Brown) and William Henry Richardson (unroofed 1903); cemetery 1868; CH b. 1879 by William Duncan, d. by James Johnstone Barnet, additions 1895 by R.L. Thompson, reused, new one b. 1901 by Sanbrook Bros, d. by Walter Liberty Vernon, portico added 1924, new court-house 1940; clothing factory (F.F. Robinson) 1943–52, reused; cordial factories: Bartley & Co. (acquired 1938 by Arthur Pile), Duhigg and Griffen 1879, Excelsior (Pund and Rankin, bought from Thomas John Webster), Kent (Wyman and Baker), McIntyre, Lincoln & Co., Resch's 1946–74, J. Whitfield; drought 1888; dust storm 1915; earth tremors 1916, 1925, 1935, 1998; electricity 1924; FB 1892 (station b. 1896, steel bell tower 70 ft or 21.3 m high b. 1904 by William Brown, new station b. 1914 by Mitchell Bros, d. by Frederick James Purvis); fibrous plaster works: Cootamundra Art Ceiling Co. (Wal Schoer) 1927 and Southern (Alan Manwaring) 1937; fires 1898, 1926, 1946; floods 1919 and 2016; flour mills: Commercial (estab. 1874 by Patrick Henry Scott and Michael John Mullaly, additions and improvements 1882, acquired by James Gibb, acquired 1891 by Cootamundra Farmers' Co-op. Roller-milling Co.), Excelsior (J. Wearne & Sons), Jansen's (burnt down 1899), Stratton & Sons Ltd (o. 1894, damaged 1947, taken over 1955 by Clifford Love & Co.); foot-bridge, destroyed 1919, over Muttama Ck; foundry (William Brown); Foursquare Gospel C.; freezing works (Robertson & Geddes Ltd); gales 1909, 1947, 2016; gaol b. 1886 by Thomas McBeath, extensions 1886 also by McBeath, closed 1909, reused as lock-up, closed 1935; gasworks (Cootamundra Munic. Gas Co.) b. 1892 by W.W. Monk, inundated 1903, gasholder repairs 1934, gasworks alterations 1944, reticulation improved 1952, fire 1954, natural gas connected 1981; hailstorms 1913 and 1948; hospital b. 1887–89 by Falconer Bros, reused, new one b. 1910 by G.I. Armstrong, d. by Ernest Rees Laver, additions and alterations 1935 by F. Mitchell, additions 1942 and 1973, closed 1987; ice-cream factory (J. Whitfield); Jehovah's Witnesses C.; joineries: Cootamundra Components Pty Ltd 1984 and Frank Mitchell, burnt down 1922; lock-up 1865, repairs 1879 by W. Falconer; monumental stone works (S. Dickson) 1883; oilseed refinery (Cootamundra Oilseeds Pty Ltd) 1992; PO: Cootamundra 1864 (new one b. 1881 by Thomas McBeath, d. by James Johnstone Barnet, tower raised 1894 by G.M. Bundock, office additions 1897 by Falconer Bros) and West Cootamundra 1924; police barracks b. 1878 by Thomas McBeath, new barracks 1901; pound (stock) 1863; Presb. C. b. 1870 by Thomas McBeath, new one b. 1884 also by McBeath, demolished 1970, new one (Scots) 1983; Prim. Meth. C. 1876–1988; PS b. 1900 by G.H. Bundock, additions and alterations 1973; quarry; railway barracks 1877, moved 1878 to Bethungra, new barracks 1927, closed, reused; railway coal stage 1877, moved 1878 to Bethungra, new one b. 1893 by Eaton Bros; railway engine shed 1889, extended 1898; railway turntable 1891, 50 ft (15.2 m), new one 1910, 60 ft (18.3 m); 2 reservoirs (one b. 1892 by James Donohue and one b. 1930 by Frank Mitchell); rice mill (Conqueror, Stratton & Sons) 1943; rifle range 1907; Rom. Cath. C.: St Columba's b. 1879 by Thomas Jobson, d. by Andrea Giovanni Stombuco, additions and alterations 1909 by P. McBeath & Co. and Fisher and Green, closed and reused, and Sacred Heart 1916 d. by Ernest Rees Laver; RS: Cootamundra 1877, station b. by William Sharp, new one b. 1888 by Evans, refreshment rooms 1893, extended 1904, and West Cootamundra 1911, new station 1918 (incl. refreshment rooms), closed and reused; rubber works (G. Adams); sale-yards (G. Thompson & Co.) 1908, (second) 1920, (third) 1930; Salv. Army C. 1960; sawmills: Frank Mitchell and Henry Turner, burnt down 1891; scarlet fever 1886; schools: primary 1875, additions 1885 by Woodhouse, Fisher and Holder, additions 1909 by G.I. Armstrong, additions 1914 by Mitchell Bros, additions 1926 by Philip James Killey, additions 1948 by Blackett and Dreyer, additions 1956, 1987, 2011, HS 1955, additions 1959, 1965, 1971, re-roofed 2013, damaged 2016; SD Adventist C.; sewerage 1939; silo 1920; snow 1899 and 1938; soap and candle factory estab. by McGovern, leased to Charles Pigram, sold 1907 to Polatsek & Co., taken over by Bert Wood, taken over by J. Kitchen & Sons Pty Ltd, closed and sold 1949; storms 1886, 1903, 1914, 1923; streets gas lit 1892, electric lit 1924; TC 1928, additions and alterations 1961, new campus 1983, became a campus of Riverina Institute in 1992; telegraph 1875, new office b. 1881 by Thomas McBeath, d. by James Johnstone Barnet, tower raised 1894 by G.M. Bundock, additions 1897 by Falconer Bros; telephone (West Cootamundra) 1924; TX 1906, new exchange 1955 in former clothing factory converted by Alan Strangman, automatic 1975; typhoid 1903; Unit. C. (orig. Presb.) b. 1936 by Frank Mitchell, William Simpson and Dave Larcombe, d. by Frederick James Purvis; water supply 1869, reticulation (Hardy's Folly Gravitation Scheme) 1892, second supply 1898, third supply 1933, augmentation 1955, 1958, 1969; Wes. Meth. C. 1872, second one b. 1876 by B. Ford, demolished 1939, third one b. 1899 by H. Butler, d. by David Thomas Morrow; woolskins factory (Shepherd Woolskins) 1972; pop. *c.*100 (1866), 612 (1870), 237 (1871), 938 (1881), 1,604 (1885), *c.*1,000+ (1887), 2,016 (1891), *c.*2,500 (1895), 2,424 (1901), 3,352 (1911), 4,683 (1933), *c.*5,000 (1941), 5,250 (1947), 5,760 (1954), 5,939 (1961), 6,219 (1966), 6,530 (1971), 6,384 (1976), 6,540 (1981), 6,314 (1986), 6,386 (1991), 5,879 (1996), 5,486 (2001), 5,566 (2006), 5,576 (2011).

Cootamundry (*Co. Harden*) see Cootamundra.

Cootinget (*Co. Inglis*) see Danglemah.

Cootralantra (*Co. Wallace*) 36°16'S. 148°52'E., 11 km N. of Berridale; grazing and copper (disc. 1872); mine (Solomon's); PO 1927–31; school 1881–90 and 1903–18.

Cooyal (*Co. Phillip*) 32°27'S. 149°46'E., 23 km NE of Mudgee, on Cooyal Ck; farming and grazing; Angl. C. (St Andrew's, Meth. till 1930) b. 1914 by Horswell and Hicken, and graveyard (28 graves 1884–1922) 1881, restored 2007; bushfires 1888 and 1902; butter factory 1891, sold 1904 to Curran, sold 1905 to E. Woolley and W. Brown, closed, burnt down 1913; causeway across Cooyal Ck; PO 1882; rifle range 1915; Rom. Cath. C. (St John the Baptist) 1888–1957, sold and reused; sawmill (John H. McGrath); school 1877, new one b. 1920 by Wurth and Wright, closed 1962; telephone 1914; TX 1927; pop.

113 (1901), 222 (1911), 214 (1933), 107 (1947), 126 (1954), 102 (1961), 436 (2011).

Cooyal (*Co. Phillip*) see also Stony Creek.

Cooyal Diggings (*Co. Phillip*) see Linburn.

Copabella Mines (*Co. Goulburn*) see Carboona.

Copacabana (*Co. Northumberland*) 33°30'S. 151°26'E., 10 km E. of Woy Woy, on Tasman Sea; failed subdivision 1954 by Willmore and Randell which remained vacant for many years; FB (station b. 2009); PO 1966; school 1983, new building 1987; water reticulation 1979; pop. 25 (1961), 2,690 (2011).

Copeland (*Co. Gloucester*) 32°00'S. 151°50'E., 11 km W. of Gloucester, on Copeland Ck; Back Creek till 1879 then North Copeland till 1936; surveyed 1878 and village gaz. 1879; mining (gold disc. 1876 by Ned Saxby and Ted Bartlett, gold rush 1876) peaked 1879, largely finished by 1908, timber, grazing, agric., orchards; Angl. C. (St James's) 1954; cemetery 1882; CH 1880, burnt down 1886; Cong. C. 1926; FB 1954; gale 1886; hospital 1880; mines: Bank, Caledonian, Centennial 1876, Christmas Box, Golden Spur, Hidden Treasure 1877, Homeward Bound, Lady Belmore or Anderson 1877, Lady Lizzie, Lord of the North, Mechanics, Mint, Morning Star, Mountain Maid (1876–1979, reused), Queen of Beauty, Rainbow, Rose and Thistle or Sydney Flag, Star of the South (George Dasey and Fred Aitken); PO 1876, repairs 1901 by T. and W. Cowan; Presb. C. 1926; PS, closed 1919, reopened 1921, closed 1934; school 1880–1912 and 1938–65, reused; stamper batteries: Driscoll and White (10 head) 1877, Ernie Harris (8 head), 5 head 1934; telegraph 1879; telephone 1906; TX 1928; Wes. Meth. C. 1880; pop. 472 (1881), 226 (1891), 135 (1901), *c.*230 (1903), 189 (1911), 152 (1933), 96 (1947), 77 (1954), 66 (1961), 310 (2006).

Copeland Common (*Co. Gloucester*) 31°58'S. 151°52'E., 11 km W. of Gloucester, on Copeland Ck; cemetery (Copeland, 63 graves 1886–1956); quarry.

Copeland North (*Co. Gloucester*) see Copeland.

Copelands (*Co. Phillip*) 32°13'S. 149°55'E., 39 km NE of Gulgong, on Goulburn R.

Copes Creek (*Co. Hardinge*) 29°54'S. 151°04'E., 15 km NW of Tingha, on Copes Ck; tin mining; dredge (Copes Creek Dredging NL Co.) 1901; drought 1919–20; mine (Britannia); pop. 134 (1901), 260 (1911), 46 (1933).

Copeton (*Co. Hardinge*) 29°55'S. 151°01'E., 21 km W. of Tingha, on Copes Ck; Boggy Camp till 1899; village gaz. 1900, submerged 1973 under Copeton Dam; diamonds 1883–1922 and grazing; Angl. C. (St Andrew's) 1903; brickworks; bushfire 1951; cemetery (burials 1901–63, 41 graves) 1902; cordial factory; fire 1898; foot-bridge; PO 1898; PS 1899–1901; school (Round Mount till 1900) 1890–1940 and 1957–65; telephone 1900; TX 1929; Wes. Meth. C. 1899; pop. 158 (1901), 225 (1911), 90 (1933), 83 (1947), 52 (1954), 125 (2006).

Copeton Dam (*Co. Murchison*) 29°54'S. 150°55'E., 30 km W. of Tingha, on Gwydir R.; dam b. 1968–76, 371 ft (113 m) high, upgraded 2011–13, on Gwydir R.; PO 1968–74; PS 1969; school 1969–73; telephone 1968.

Copmanhurst (*Co. Clarence*) 29°35'S. 152°46'E., 19 km NW of Grafton, on Clarence R.; Budgambi for 3 months in 1892, also formerly known as Grose's; planned 1859 by William Albert Braylesford Greaves, town gaz. 1860; former river port, timber, maize, potatoes, mining, dairying 1890s–1960s, pigs, cattle; Angl. C. 1872, new one (Holy Apostles) b. 1915 by Strauss Bros; bridge (Rogan Bridge) 1960; butter factory (Copmanhurst Co-op. Dairy Co. Ltd) b. 1906 by Strauss Bros, closed 1920; CH b. 1904 by W.J. Brown; creamery (Fresh Food & Ice Co.); electricity 1931; FB; floods 1890, 1893, 2013; hurricane (unroofed most houses) 1946; PO 1892; powder magazine, disused; Presb. C. 1874, damaged 1903, dismantled and relocated, rebuilt b. 1922 by A.W. Phemister, damaged 1946; PS b. 1881 by Hermann Schaeffer, new one b. 1903 by W.J. Brown; Rom. Cath. C. (St John of the Cross) b. 1882 by J. Moyes; sawmill (W. Shaw and A. Schwinghammer) 1909; school 1891, new building b. 1918 by Strauss Bros; storm 1903; telephone 1892; TX 1912, automatic 1938; wharves: govt one b. 1878 by J. Walsh and one estab. by Joseph Hickey Grose; pop. *c.*150 (1866), 241 (1891), 300 (1901), 323 (1911), 184 (1933), 154 (1947), 124 (1954), 150 (1961), 212 (1996), 212 (2001), 231 (2006).

Copmanhurst (*Co. Clarence*)
see also Upper Copmanhurst.

Coppabella (*Co. Goulburn*) 34°46'S. 148°30'E., 28 km SE of Murrumburrah, on Coppabella Ck; grazing; school 1886–87; TX (automatic); pop. 75 (1901), 75 (1911), 49 (1933).

Copper Hill (*Co. Wellington*) 33°03'S. 148°52'E., 4 km N. of Molong, on Molong Ck; mining (copper disc. 1845, and gold), farming, grazing; bridge, destroyed 1900, replaced 1901 by G.A. Jones, over Molong Ck; flood 1900; mines: Copper Hill 1845–51, 1871, 1888, 1907–8, 1919–31 and Little Copper Hill 1848 and 1906–7; PO 1915–30; 3 quarries; school 1918–33; telephone 1911; pop. 80 (1933), 67 (1947).

Coppertown (*Co. Murray*) see Captains Flat.

Coppy Murrumbilla (*Co. Stapylton*) 28°44'S. 150°15'E., 17 km SW of Boggabilla, on Whalan Ck; pop. 56 (1911).

Coradgerie (*Co. Ewenmar*) 31°35'S. 148°12'E., 47 km W. of Gilgandra, on Merrigal Ck; school 1886–90 and 1898–1906.

Coradgery (*Co. Kennedy*) 32°55'S. 148°03'E., 23 km SW of Peak Hill; gold (disc. 1905); Angl. C. (St Michael's) b. 1930 by Page; bushfire 1926; mine (G. Humphreys 1905–9 and Bogan Gold Mining Syndicate 1935); PO 1907–19; school 1957–67; pop. 173 (1911), 120 (1947).

Coraki (*Co. Richmond*) 28°59'S. 153°17'E., 20 km S. of Lismore, on Richmond R.; formerly The Junction; settled and founded 1849 by William Yabsley, village gaz. 1866 and laid out by Patrick R. Donaldson, first lots sold 1867, subdivided 1886, munic. proc. 1891, thrived 1915, munic. abolished 1934; former river port, shipbuilding 1848+, sugar-cane 1866+, timber, coalmining, dairying, tea-tree oil, maize, potatoes, beef, pigs, soya beans; agric. implement works (Patrick Claffey); Angl. C. b. 1878 by Chalmers, closed and reused, destroyed 1931, new one (St Mary Magdalene) b. 1913 by Robertson and Hawkins, d. by Popplewell and Sykes; Bapt. C. b. 1925 by G. Smith, relocated 1948, closed, sold 2014 and 2018, reused; boot factory (Reynold's); brick-kiln (Wheeler and Brown) 1886; brickworks (Turner Bros) 1911; bridges over Richmond R.: The Glebe Bridge (with steel bascule span) b. 1905 by Mountney & Co. Ltd, repairs 1938, 1945, 2015, and East Coraki Bridge (concrete) 1990; bushfire 1946; butter factory (Aust. Dairying Co.) 1898, taken over 1901 by Coraki Co-op. Butter Co. Ltd, extended 1905, enlarged 1908 by Hodge and Everingham, d. by Popplewell and Sykes, new one b. 1921 by English Electric Co., fire 1932, repairs by Turner Bros, closed 1957; carriage-works (McMullen's); caterpillar infestations 1928 and 1937; cemetery 1880; CH 1883, new one b. 1888 by James McMorrine, d. by James Johnstone Barnet, renovated 1901 by D. Quain, closed 1966, reused, new one 1966; cholera 1900; condensed milk factory b. 1922 by Turner Bros for Richmond River Condensed Milk Co., acquired 1925 by Nestle & Anglo-Swiss Condensed Milk Co. (A'asia) Ltd; cordial factories: M. Balzer and C. Stamford; creamery (NSW Creamery Butter Co. Ltd) 1896–99, moved to Greenridge; dengue fever 1926 and 1927; diphtheria 1898; FB 1921 (station b. 1924 by Lowther and Horricks, d. by William Hull McNiven); fires 1886, 1897, 1904, 1905, 1911, 1913, 1923; floods 1864, 1870, 1892, 1893, 1921, 1948, 1967, 2001, 2008; gales 1891, 1928, 1931; hailstorm 1951; hospital (John Campbell) b. 1904 by R.S. Messent, d. by Frederick Johnson Board, extensions 1905 d. by W. Burgess, additions 1952, 1954, 1956, 1966, 1985; ice works (Coraki Co-op. Butter & Refrigeration Co. Ltd); knitting mill (Forrest Knitting Co.); measles epidemic 1936; Meth. C. 1904; PO 1870, new one b. 1890 by Brown and Jolly; powerhouse 1923; Presb. C. 1867 d. and b. by William Chambers, new one 1886, sold 1900 to O. McPherson and demolished, replacement b. 1900 by D. Quain; PS 1881, additions 1901; punt 1879, new one 1898–1990, across Richmond R.; quarry; Rom. Cath. C. b. 1877 by John Curtain, burnt down 1904, replaced 1905, new one (St Joseph's) b. 1923 by P.F. Small, d. by Frederick Johnson Board; sale-yards b. 1933 by D. Twomey; sawmills: Thomas Gainford, Meagher's, William Yabsley, jun. 1866, fire 1909, burnt down 1913, chimney demolished 1930; scarlet fever 1913; school 1872 b. by William Yabsley, jun. and Thomas King, rebuilt 1873, demolished, new one b. 1898 by Patrick Farrelly, additions 1910, 1923, 1924, 1953, 1962; sewerage 1968; shipping depot (Yeager's); shipyard (William Yabsley) 1850, ship shed added 1866, reused 1881 as sawmill; slipway (Turner and Conroy) 1902; soap-works (bought by Richmond River Soap Co. from John White) 1882; storms 1902, 1908, 1942; sugar mills: Ewen Kennedy (Spring Hill) 1880–91, and Donald and John MacKinnon 1869–91; telegraph 1879, new office b. 1890 by Brown and Jolly; tinsmithing works (Turner's); TX 1900; typhoid 1889; Unit. C. (St John's, orig. Presb.); wharves: govt one 1891, Keiran Nolan, William Yabsley, William Tudor Yeager (new one b. 1897 by G. Rankin); whooping cough epidemic (infant died) 1891; wire works (Jasen) estab. by A.E. Jacobsen; pop. 538 (1891), *c.*620 (1895), 926 (1901), 1,419 (1911), 1,231 (1933), 1,097 (1947), 970 (1954), 905 (1961), 650 (1966), 857 (1971), 912 (1976), 895 (1981), 1,047 (1986), 1,103 (1991), 1,223 (1996), 1,159 (2001), 1,180 (2006), 1,214 (2011).

Coralville (*Co. Macquarie*) 31°47'S. 152°41'E., 10 km N. of Harrington; Big Swamp till 1926; farming, dairying, orchards, white clay; PO 1908; school 1905–65; telephone 1924; TX 1938; Union C. 1939; pop. 114 (1911), 82 (1933), 126 (1947), 105 (1954), 74 (1961), 95 (2011).

Coramba (*Co. Fitzroy*) 30°13'S. 153°01'E., 13 km NW of Coffs Harbour, on Orara R.; site selected 1886 by William Gale, thrived 1897; mining (gold disc. 1895) then sawmilling and dairying; Angl. C. (St Paul's) b. 1898 by A. Townshend and C. Shephard; bridge 1909, new one (Old White Bridge) 1922, Allan timber truss, 356 ft (108.5 m), closed, new one (concrete) 2003, over Orara R.; bushfire 1936; butter factory (Orara Co-op. Dairy Co. Ltd) 1902–26, new one d. by J. Wildridge & Sinclair Ltd, closed 1950 and sold to Fawcett Bros, sold to Peters American Delicacy Co. Ltd; cemetery (182 graves 1895+) 1895; CH (incl. lock-up) b. 1899 by T. Smart; cheese factory (Apollo) estab. by W.G. Mussared, taken over 1917 by W.A. Mussared; cordial factory (Pollock's) 1897; earth tremor 1929; FB (station b. 1982, additions 1994); floods 1938, 1945, 1950, 2020; hailstorm 1916; Meth. C. 1908; mines: Coramba King, Coramba Queen, Lady Elsie, Star Creek; PO 1889; Presb. C.; PS 1896, repairs 1937 by J.T. Henry; reservoir 1949; Rom. Cath. C. (St Therese's) b. 1927 by D.J. Ross, d. by Frederick Johnson Board; RS 1922, station sold and demolished 1987; sawmills: Coramba Milling Co. Ltd and Mulhearn Bros (sold 1912); school 1896, new one b. 1910 by W. Morris; storm 1911; telephone 1897; TX 1913; water pumping station 1949, destroyed 1950; pop. 148 (1901), 385 (1911), *c.*550 (1924), 325 (1933), 353 (1947), 395 (1954), 320 (1961), 201 (1971), 280 (1986), 347 (1991), 329 (1996), 297 (2001), 297 (2006), 372 (2011).

Coramundra (*Co. Harden*) see Cootamundra.

Corang (*St Vincent*) 35°11'S. 150°01'E., 35 km NE of Braidwood, on Corang R.; Nerriga till 1865; defunct; grazing; airfield; bushfire 1986; PO 1859–76 and 1927–31; Rom. Cath. C. (St Patrick's), closed, sold and removed, and graveyard (graves 1854+); school 1897–1909; telephone 1924; TX 1950; pop. *c.*50 (1866), 26 (1933).

Corangula (*Co. Dudley*) 31°00'S. 152°40'E., 16 km NW of Kempsey; largely abandoned 1908; mining (antimony, deposit opened up 1879) mainly 1880–84; Meth. C. 1903, renovated 1922; mines: Corangula Antimony Co. 1880–1908 and Munga Creek Minerals

NL Co. 1970–74; ore treatment plant; PO 1881–86; PS; schools: Corangula 1902 b. by G. Lowe, closed 1942 and Corangula Mines 1882 and 1885; pop. *c.*200 (1880), 40 (1933).

Corbie Hill (*Co. Cooper*) 34°34'S. 146°27'E., 5 km E. of Leeton; village gaz. 1924; PO 1923; rifle range; school 1930–70; telephone 1925; TX 1934; pop. 184 (1933), 323 (1947), 260 (1954), 300 (1961), 296 (2011).

Corcalgong (*Co. Wellington*) 32°50'S. 149°43'E., 24 km W. of Kandos, on Campbells Ck; grazing; PO 1927–30; telephone 1926.

Corcoran (*Co. Bathurst*) see Carcoar.

Cordeaux (*Co. Camden*) see Tahmoor.

Cordeaux Dam (*Co. Camden*) 34°20'S. 150°45'E., 16 km W. of Corrimal, on Lake Cordeaux; dam (cyclopean masonry) b. 1918–26, 174 ft (53 m) high, on Cordeaux R.; PO 1917; PS, closed 1926; school 1918–26; telephone 1923; TX 1925; pop. 20 (1933).

Cordeaux Heights (*Co. Camden*) see Unanderra.

Cordillera (*Co. Georgiana*) 34°05'S. 149°25'E., 43 km N. of Crookwell, on Peelwood Ck; thrived 1888; mining (silver disc. by Phillip Hyde, lead-zinc-copper); cordial factory (Chrystal Fountain) estab. 1888 by A.E. Cameron; earth tremor 1890; mine o. 1888 by Cordillera Lead & Silver Mining Co., closed 1889, dismantled 1891, reopened 1907 by Mount Costigan & Cordillera Co., closed 1908, chimney demolished 1934; PO 1888; quarry; school 1888–91; pop. 64 (1891), 23 (1933).

Coree (*Co. Townsend*) 35°21'S. 145°28'E., 24 km W. of Jerilderie, on Billabong Ck; village gaz. 1868; PO 1875–92; pop. 23 (1891), 27 (1933), 89 (2006).

Coreen (*Co. Flinders*) see Tikkara.

Coreen (*Co. Hume*) 35°45'S. 146°21'E., 28 km N. of Corowa; village gaz. 1879; farming; cemetery 1893; electricity 1950; FB; hailstorm 1916; PO 1906; Presb. C. b. 1936 by Kevin Wilson; school 1908–46; telephone 1905; TX 1915; pop. 90 (1901), 347 (1911), 347 (1933), 210 (1947), 174 (1954), 199 (1961), 396 (2011).

Coreen (*Co. Hume*) see also Daysdale.

Coree South (*Co. Urana*) 35°31'S. 145°33'E., 24 km SW of Jerilderie; telephone 1925; TX 1925, automatic 1959; pop. 65 (1933), 107 (1947), 126 (1954), 68 (1961).

Coreinbob (*Co. Wynyard*) 35°14'S. 147°36'E., 26 km SE of Wagga Wagga, on Coreinbob Ck; bushfire 1952; Meth. C. b. 1912 by Gideon P. Watson, burnt down 1952, replaced 1956; RS 1917–75; school 1952–65; pop. 78 (1911), 106 (1933), 91 (1947), 92 (1954), 102 (1961).

Corella (*Co. Culgoa*) 29°38'S. 146°27'E., 56 km NW of Brewarrina; pop. 62 (1911), 56 (1933).

Corella (*Co. Darling*) 30°45'S. 150°30'E., 22 km W. of Manilla; earth tremor 2012.

Corella (*Co. Darling*) see also Head Vale.

Corinda (*Co. Northumberland*) 32°37'S. 151°16'E., 9 km NW of Branxton; boiling-down works (A. Bell); creamery (Kurrindar) estab. 1892 by R.C. M'Douall, who later converted it to a condensed milk factory, taken over by NSW Concentrated Milk Co., closed 1907; Wes. Meth. C. 1866, damaged, repaired 1911; pop. 157 (1901), 22 (1933).

Corindi (*Co. Fitzroy*) 30°01'S. 153°11'E., 7 km N. of Arrawarra; farming; 2 bridges b. 1888 by Charles Avery; cemetery (8 graves 1911–94); cheese factory 1909; pop. 65 (1901), 150 (1911), 87 (1933), 106 (1947), 166 (1954), 150 (1961).

Corindi (*Co. Fitzroy*) see also Corindi Beach.

Corindi Beach (*Co. Fitzroy*) 30°02'S. 153°12'E., 4 km N. of Arrawarra, on Tasman Sea; Corindi Clarence till 1972; bypassed by highway 1980; bridge 1980, over Corindi R.; FB; hailstorm 2015; PO 1892; school (Corindi) 1890–1910, reopened 1951; telephone 1907; TX 1915; pop. 274 (1986), 548 (1991), 696 (1996), 726 (2001), 834 (2006), 1,200 (2011).

Corindi Clarence (*Co. Fitzroy*) see Corindi Beach.

Corinella (*Co. Gipps*) 33°26'S. 147°31'E., 45 km W. of Forbes; FB (station b. 2017); school 1961–2014; pop. 57 (1961).

Corlette (*Co. Gloucester*) see Nelson Bay.

Cormal Park (*Co. Wellington*) 33°16'S. 149°02'E., 6 km W. of Orange; quarry.

Cormick's Creek (*Co. Clarence*) see Tullymorgan.

Cornalla (*Co. Townsend*) 35°43'S. 145°07'E., 24 km SE of Deniliquin; pop. 59 (1911).

Cornbury Park (*Co. Macquarie*) see Telegraph Point.

Corndale (*Co. Rous*) 28°42'S. 153°22'E., 15 km NE of Lismore, on Boomerang Ck; Cooper's Creek till 1895; settled 1880; farming and dairying; bridge (Ewing Bridge) 1888, new one 1948, over Coopers Ck; butter factory (Lismore Dairy Co.) 1912, taken over 1921 by North Coast Co-op. Ltd, fire damaged 1937, rebuilt by Daniel Gallagher, closed 1946; creamery 1897; Meth. C.; PO 1896; quarry; rifle range; school (Coopers Creek till 1912) 1889, new one b. 1924 by John P. Slapp; SD Adventist C. 1901, demolished 1937, moved to Burringbar; telephone 1913; TX 1928; pop. 138 (1901), 272 (1911), 292 (1933), 222 (1947), 199 (1954), 194 (1961), 393 (2006), 350 (2011).

Corner Camp (*Co. Murchison*) 30°10'S. 150°48'E., 29 km NE of Barraba.

Corner Cattle Camp (*Co. Bland*) 33°52'S. 148°00'E., 14 km W. of Grenfell, on Barbingal Ck.

Corney Town (*Co. Cook*) see Lithgow.

Cornish Point (*Co. Wellington*) 32°46'S. 149°13'E., 36 km SE of Wellington, on Macquarie R.

Cornish Settlement (*Co. Bathurst*) see Byng.

Cornishtown (*Co. Robinson*) see Cobar.

Cornucopia Estate (*Co. Narromine*) see Narromine.

Corobimilla (*Co. Mitchell*) 34°52'S. 146°24'E., 18 km SW of Narrandera; Cuddell Siding till 1904; farming; mouse plague 1918; PO 1895; reservoir; RS (Cuddell till 1904) 1890–1975, station removed 1985; sawmill (H.C. Sweeting); school 1887–1905 and 1938–49; silo 1936; storm 1923; telephone 1906; TX 1926; Union C. 1935; pop. 51 (1901), 77 (1911), 198 (1933), 155 (1947), 130 (1954), 92 (1961).

Corona (*Co. Farnell*) 31°16'S. 141°25'E., 77 km N. of Broken Hill; pop. 83 (1911), 21 (1933).

Corowa (*Co. Hume*) 36°00'S. 146°23'E., 47 km W. of Albury, on Murray R.; orig. North Wahgunyah; disc. 1838 by Capt. Charles Sturt, settled by Brocklesbury, surveyed 1857 by Samuel Parkinson, laid out 1858 by Philip Francis Adams, plan approved and first lots sold 1859, founded 1859 by John Foord, thrived 1861, town gaz. 1879, designated as chief town of the county, munic. proc. 1903, thrived 1911, munic. abolished 1955; former river port, orig. wheat, then gold (gold rush 1861), silk, wool, wine 1872+, oilseed rape, barley, oats, sawmilling, stock feed, pigs; abattoir (QAF Meat Industries); agric. implement works: Neil Jamieson, Riverina Harvester Co. Ltd 1893–1924, Upton Engineering 1944; airport (3 km W.) 1941, new terminal 1952; ambulance station b. 1940 by A.A. M'Bride; Angl. C. b. 1861–63, replacement (St John's) b. 1882–84 by William Squires, sen., additions 1911, and graveyard; Assemblies of God C. (River Life Country); Bapt. C. 1998; boiling-down works (Chilling Meat & Boiling Down Co.) 1893; bond store; boot factory (A.G.T. Phillips); brewery b. 1871 by Thomas William Brady, taken over 1874 by Denis Hallahan, later taken over by Larkin and Clifton, closed 1889, bought, rebuilt and renamed 1889 by Thomas Ogilvie as Corowa & Wahgunyah Brewing & Malting Co. Ltd, closed and reopened 1891, closed 1892, reopened 1893, damaged 1897, closed 1917; brickworks (taken over 1928 by Thomas H. Armour, closed, reopened 1946); bridge (laminated timber arch) 1862, purchased 1881 by govt and tolls removed, dismantled and sold 1894, replaced by John Foord Bridge (iron lattice trusses) 1892 d. by John Alexander McDonald, 366 ft (111.6 m), new one (Federation Bridge) b. 2003–5, over Murray R.; bushfires 1882 and 1904–5; butter factory and ice works (Corowa & Wahgunyah Dairy Co. Ltd); cemeteries: pioneer (graves 1859+) 1870 and lawn; CH (incl. lock-up) b. 1868 by Charles Hardy and Thomas Hodson, demolished 1886, replaced 1887 by William Squires, jun., d. by James Johnstone Barnet, wings added 1888–90 by Neill and Jackson, additions and alterations 1961, restored 1991; chocolate factory, in former flour mill; Church of Christ (Christ. Tabernacle) 1893, closed, sold and reused; clock tower (war memorial) b. 1922 by A.J. Goode; clothing factory (Alamac Clothing Co.) 1946, fire 1948; concrete products plant (A. Bernard) 1953; cordial factories: Jackson Bros (burnt down 1917), J.H. Oswald (ice works added 1908), Joseph Webster 1876; customs-house 1864, reused, new one b. 1895 on new site by George William Brewer, demolished 1901; distillery (whisky) estab. 2013 by Dean Druce in former flour mill; drought 1878; dust storm 1910; electricity 1914; engineering works (Dickins) 1947; FB 1878 (old station closed, reused 1927, sold 1928, new one b. 1927 by J. Mills); fellmongery; fires 1872 and 1878; flood 1879; flour mills: Corowa Milling Co. Ltd (b. 1858 by F. Foord, acquired by Wangaratta Milling Co.), Elliott's, Graham Bros, Leyser Levin 1872 (reused as wool store then butter factory, demolished 1934), Netherby (Joseph Chicken, improvements and repairs 1896, damaged 1898, new one 1906, sold 1910 to Teague Bros, sold 1919 to Bayliss & Co., burnt down 1920, replaced 1922 on new site by T.H. Armour, closed 1970, sold 2009, renovated and reused 2010); freezing works; gales 1897 and 1923; grasshopper infestation 1907; heatwaves 1901 and 1904–5; hospital b. 1893 by Wilson, extended 1908, 1937, 1938, 1940, 1954; hurricane 1914; ice works (D. McPherson); lock-up b. 1893 by A. and J. Kyle; Lutheran C. (St Andrew's) 1967, removed from Victoria; mineral water plant (D.S. Watson and D.C. Young) 1883; mines: Corowa Deep Lead Gold Mining Co. 1900–4 and Corowa Perseverance Mine 1916–19; mouse plague 1917; PO 1861, new one b. 1881 by William Squires, jun., repairs 1890 by Thomas Machin; pound (stock) 1865; powerhouse 1913; Presb. C. b. 1895 by John Swan, closed 1934, reused, replacement (St Andrew's) 1934; Prim. Meth. C.; PS, additions 1871, additions 1879 by C. Johnson, new building b. 1890 by William Refshange, additions and repairs 1919 by R.W. Alston; punt estab. 1857 by John Foord, across Murray R.; quarry 1923; railway coal stage, 90 ft (27.4 m), removed 1938; railway turntable, 50 ft (15.2 m), replaced 1915, 60 ft (18.3 m), closed; 4 reservoirs (incl. concrete one b. 1906 by Gummow, Forrest & Co., one b. 1926, one b. 1939); Rom. Cath. C. 1875 b. by William Squires, sen., additions 1882, replacement (St Mary, Star of the Sea) b. 1921 by Armour, d. by Augustus Andrew Fritsch, and graveyard (graves 1883+); RS 1892, station b. by William Haslem, closed 1989, reused 1998; sale-yards (Higgin & Co.) 1889, new yards b. 1911 by Webster and O'Brien; sawmills: Carroll & Sons and Elliott's; schools: primary b. 1878 by Charles Johnson, new buildings 1917, new building b. 1929 by Kent and Kent, additions 1960 and 1972, and HS 1965, new building 1968; sewerage 1937, augmentation 1989 and 1995; silo; stamper battery (8 head); storms 1898 and 1928; streets electric lit 1913; TC (in old school) 1973, became a campus of Riverina Institute in 1992; telegraph 1873, new office b. 1881 by William Squires, repairs 1890 by Thomas Machin; tobacco factory; TX 1907, building enlarged 1948 by Jim Camplin; typhoid 1899; Unit. C. (Calvary Memorial, orig. Meth.) 1967; waterworks b. 1907 by McDonald and Younger, d. by Leslie Augustus Burton Wade, upgraded 1912, extended 1920, new (electric) pumping station b. 1924–26, extended 1950, new treatment plant 2001; Wes. Meth. C. b. 1884 by William Squires, d. by T. Parkin, demolished and replaced; woodware factory (Darby Woodware); wool-scour (George Frederick Sugden) 1879, sold 1905 to William Sherwin; wool store (Synnot & Co.), in old flour mill; pop. *c.*200 (1866), 189 (1871), *c.*300 (1872), *c.*700 (1875), 495 (1881), 1,171 (1891), 2,046 (1901), 2,272 (1911), 2,757 (1933), 2,751 (1947), 3,045 (1954), 2,593 (1961), 2,709 (1966), 3,013 (1976), 3,390 (1981), 4,315 (1986), 5,064 (1991), 5,161 (1996), 5,220 (2001), 5,450 (2011).

Corowa South (*Co. Hume*) 36°02'S. 146°22'E.,

3 km SW of Corowa, on Murray R.; Lower Corowa till 1897; surveyed 1856 by Samuel Parkinson, laid out 1858 by Philip Francis Adams, first lots sold 1859; flood 1906; PO 1900–71; school 1898, additions 1938, additions 2010 by Barker Constructions Pty Ltd; telephone 1908; Union C.; pop. 237 (1961).

Corridgeree (*Co. Auckland*) 36°39'S. 149°51'E., 3 km N. of Bega; flour mill (Robert Spence); cemetery (burials 1844+).

Corridgery (*Co. Cunningham*) 33°18'S. 147°47'E., 24 km NW of Forbes.

Corrimal (*Co. Camden*) 34°22'S. 150°54'E., 6 km N. of Wollongong, on Tasman Sea; (incl. East Corrimal and Tarrawanna); laid out and first land sales 1884; Angl. C.: Corrimal 1896 d. by Cyril Blacket, relocated 1914, new one (St Alban's) b. 1914 by R. Ballantyne, d. by Blacket & Son and Tarrawanna 1886; baking powder factory; Bapt. C. (Living Hope) 1959; bushfires 1946 and 1953; carriage-works (A.C. Kitchener); cemetery (Rom. Cath., 794 graves); Christ. Brethren Assemblies C. (Gospel); Christadelphian C.; clothing factory (King Gee Clothing Co. Pty Ltd) 1952; coke-works: Thomas Bertram (7 beehive ovens) 1886–90, Corrimal-Balgownie Collieries Ltd (40 rectangular beehive ovens b. 1912 by G.S. Yuill & Co. Ltd, 8 ovens added 1930, new battery of 32 ovens b. 1959–62, bought 1964 by Aust. Iron & Steel Ltd, sold 1969 to Bellambi Coal Co., acquired 1980 by Aust. Coal & Coke Co., sold 1983 to Kembla Coal & Coke, sold 1996 to Illawarra Coke Co. Pty Ltd, closed 2014), Tarrawanna (experimental) 1886–90; collieries: Bellambi (orig. Woonona Colliery, estab. 1857 by Thomas Hale, closed 1863, reopened by Bellambi Coal Co. and reworked as Model Colliery 1887, closed 1921, absorbed 1926 into South Bulli Colliery), Broker's Nose (estab. 1885 by Thomas Bertram for Broker's Nose Coal Co., closed 1885, reopened 1888, acquired by Southern Coal Co. of NSW and became Corrimal Colliery in 1889, taken over 1902 by Corrimal-Balgownie Collieries Ltd, which became Corrimal Coal & Coke Co. Pty Ltd in 1937, strikes 1942 and 1943, bought 1964 by Aust. Iron & Steel Ltd, closed 1986), South Bulli (estab. 1861 by Taylor, Walker and Longmore, closed 1864, acquired 1885 by South Bulli Coal Mining Co. and reopened 1887 as South Bulli Colliery, bought 1890 by Ebenezer Vickery, strike 1900, acquired 1901 by Bellambi Coal Co., strikes 1913 and 1917, powerhouse 1928, strikes 1938, 1942, 1943, upgraded 1960–62, 3 men killed 1991, colliery acquired 2004 by Gujarat Nre); FB 1924 (station b. 1929 by W.J. Williams, renovated 2007); floods 1904 and 1914; foot-bridge over Towradji Ck; gale (Tarrawanna) 1895; house frame and truss factory (Wonson Frames & Trusses Pty Ltd); ice-cream factory (Streets Ice Cream Pty Ltd) estab. 1934 by Edwin Street (in old ice works), bought 1961 by Unilever Aust. Pty Ltd, closed 2001; Meth. C. b. 1905–8, demolished, replaced 1968; pneumonia epidemic 1908; PO: Corrimal 1890, new one 1900, new one built 1911 by Hubert C. Elphinstone, East Corrimal 1941, Tarrawanna 1899; powerhouse (Corrimal Coal & Coke Pty Ltd); Presb. C. 1890, burnt down 1910; Prim. Meth. C. 1899; PS 1939, new one 1962, refurbished 2007; reservoirs: first one (concrete), 254,000 gal. (1,154.7 kl), 1915 and second one 1949; rifle range 1915; Rom. Cath. C. (St Columbkille's) b. 1902 by J. M'Intosh, d. by Shaw, reused 1913, new one b. 1913 by J.A. Waters, d. by J.T. M'Carthy; RS 1887, station b. by John D. Mackie; Russian Orthodox C. (Holy Dormition of Our Lady); Salv. Army C. 1964–81; sawmill (Sassafras) b. 1917 by Robert Cram, sen., Jack Cram and Arthur Cram for South Bulli Coal Co., burnt down 1923, rebuilt, burnt down again; schools: Corrimal 1890, additions 1906 by J. Devitt, additions 1929 by W.J. Anderson, additions 1964, Corrimal HS 1951, additions 1956, 1966, 1975, 1983, fire 2018, East Corrimal 1952, new building b. 1954 by G.C. Kirkman, additions 1976, Tarrawanna 1952, additions 1968; SD Adventist C. 1972; streets electric lit 1918; telephone: Corrimal 1897 and East Corrimal 1942; tramway (colliery); TX 1925, automatic 1956; Unit. C. (orig. Presb.) b. 1913 by W. Bryce, extended 2002; water supply (Tarrawanna) 1922; Wes. Meth. C. 1899, relocated and reused 1908; pop. 300 (1892), 2,133 (1911), 7,451 (1954), 10,690 (1961), 9,521 (2001), 7,446 (2011).

Corringle (*Co. Gipps*) 33°38'S. 147°21'E., 35 km N. of West Wyalong; goldmine (Wamboyne) *c.*1907, 1935, 1939; RS 1929–71.

Corroba (*Co. Gloucester*) see Stockton.

Corroboree Flat (*Co. Hawes*) 31°40'S. 151°45'E., 43 km NW of Gloucester, on Barnard R.; telephone 1917; TX 1932.

Corrong (*Co. Waljeers*) 34°13'S. 144°28'E., 47 km NW of Hay, on Lachlan R.; bridge (timber beam) 1948, over Lachlan R.; pop. 24 (1933).

Corrowidgin (*Co. Wellesley*) 36°57'S. 148°51'E., 35 km W. of Bombala, on Rossys Ck; grazing; pop. 24 (1933).

Corrowong (*Co. Wellesley*) 36°56'S. 148°50'E., 37 km W. of Bombala, on Rossys Ck; flour mill; hailstorm 2000; PO 1872; quarry; Rom. Cath. C. (St Peter's) b. 1877 by O'Hare, and graveyard; school 1880–85; telephone 1908; TX 1913; pop. 78 (1911), 45 (1933), 58 (1954).

Corruga (*Co. Yancowinna*) 31°57'S. 141°25'E., 5 km W. of Broken Hill, on Nine Mile Ck.

Corrys Wood (*Co. Goulburn*) 36°03'S. 146°59'E., 7 km NE of Albury.

Corunna (*Co. Dampier*) 36°17'S. 150°06'E., 7 km S. of Narooma, on Corunna Lake; Noorooma till 1880; goldmining, farming, dairying; Angl. C. (St Philip's) 1886, burnt down 1928; bushfire 1928; cemetery; cheese factory (Corunna Dairy Co. Ltd) 1895–1926; PO 1880; sawmills: McMillan Bros (removed 1905 from Bermagui, burnt down 1914) and William Innes; school 1895–1920; telephone 1909; Wes. Meth. C. 1883, renovated 1914, and graveyard (burials 1883–1967); pop. 91 (1901), 69 (1911), 82 (1933).

Cottawalla (*Co. Argyle*) 34°29'S. 149°31'E., 5 km SE of Crookwell; butter factory (Crookwell) 1890; Prim. Meth. C.; school 1876–1945; snow 1865; telephone 1917; pop. 135 (1901), 144 (1933), 101 (1947), 56 (1954), 76 (1961).

Cottee (*Co. Bourke*) 34°57'S. 147°06'E., 17 km S. of Ganmain; school (Currawarna till 1899) 1884–1911; pop. 174 (1911), 80 (1933), 62 (1947), 62 (1961).

Cottesbrook (*Co. Clive*) see Sandy Flat.

Cougal (*Co. Rous*) 28°22'S. 152°58'E., 29 km N. of Kyogle, on The Logan Ck; Upper Grady's Creek till 1932; farming; plywood and veneer factory (William Seccombe and Hardy) 1927, burnt down 1928; PO 1927, burnt down 1933; PS; RS 1930–71; sawmill (Cougal Timber Co.); school (Tunnel Camp till 1932) 1929–62; telephone 1927; TX 1927; pop. 127 (1933), 96 (1947), 63 (1954).

Coulsons Creek (*Co. Brisbane*) 31°55'S. 150°24'E., 25 km N. of Merriwa; TX (automatic); pop. 75 (1947), 83 (1954).

Coulston (*Co. Durham*) 32°23'S. 151°29'E., 23 km W. of Dungog, on Paterson R.; also known as Colstoun; school (Colstoun) 1883–1932; pop. 53 (1901).

Countegany (*Co. Dampier*) 36°11'S. 149°27'E., 30 km E. of Cooma, on Guinea Ck; grazing; PO 1908–45; sawmill (Albert A. Broadhead); telephone 1911; TX 1934; pop. 38 (1933), 128 (2006).

Countryside Estate (*Co. Rous*) 28°20'S. 153°22'E., 2 km W. of Murwillumbah, on Rous R.; cemetery.

Courabyra (*Co. Wynyard*) 35°40'S. 148°03'E., 12 km N. of Tumbarumba; Upper Tumberumba till 1895; goldmining and farming; earth tremor 1905; FB; PO 1895; school 1882–1923; telephone 1900; TX 1927, automatic 1954; pop. 72 (1901), 71 (1911), 74 (1933), 89 (1947), 77 (1954), 84 (1961), 244 (2011).

Couragago (*Co. Buccleuch*) 35°10'S. 148°33'E., 33 km NE of Tumut, on Swamp Gully; telephone 1926; TX 1929; pop. 25 (1933).

Courallie (*Co. Courallie*) see Moree.

Couria Creek (*Co. Dampier*) 36°20'S. 150°02'E., 9 km N. of Bermagui, on Couria Ck; farming; PO 1927–35; telephone 1919; pop. 28 (1933).

Couridjah (*Co. Camden*) 34°14'S. 150°33'E.,

4 km W. of Tahmoor, on Thirlmere Lakes; surveyed and village gaz. 1881; cemetery 1881; PO 1936–71; RS (o. as Picton Lagoons Tank, then Lagoons till 1929) 1867; pop. 60 (1933), 80 (1947), 55 (1954), 90 (1961), 280 (1991), 455 (1996), 481 (2001), 456 (2006).

Coursing Park (*Co. Clarendon*) 34°57'S. 147°22'E., 18 km N. of Wagga Wagga; school 1957–71.

Coutts Crossing (*Co. Fitzroy*) 29°50'S. 152°53'E., 17 km S. of Grafton, on Orara R.; settled by William Forster; farming and dairying; bridge (welded steel truss span) b. 1939–41 by Oxenfords Pty Ltd, over Orara R.; cemetery (186 graves 1895+) 1890; creamery (Fresh Food & Ice Co.) b. 1896 by Smart and Jordan, d. by J.H. Garratt; 2 FB; PO 1890; Presb. C.; school 1914, additions 1986, 1990, 1995; sewerage augmentation 1993; telephone 1909; TX 1926, automatic 1959; Union C. b. 1886 by Charles Avery, additions 1899, additions 1907 by Faulks, dismantled 1945, replaced 1951; water reticulation 1967; pop. 59 (1901), 102 (1911), 234 (1933), 80 (1947), 64 (1954), 70 (1961), 336 (1986), 446 (1991), 510 (1996), 523 (2001), 571 (2006), 556 (2011).

Coutts Water (*Co. Fitzroy*) see Deer Park.

Covan Creek (*Co. Argyle*) 35°00'S. 149°35'E., 29 km SW of Goulburn, on Covan Ck.

Cowabbie (*Co. Bourke*) 34°36'S. 146°58'E., 23 km N. of Ganmain; mining (gold rushes 1872 and in 1890s); mine; Presb. C.; stamper battery 1904; pop. 66 (1933), 64 (1947).

Cowabbie (*Co. Bourke*) see also Coolamon.

Cowabbie Road (*Co. Bourke*) see Coolamon.

Cowabbie West (*Co. Bourke*) 34°38'S. 146°54'E., 24 km NW of Ganmain, on Cowabbie Ck; school 1957–72; pop. 120 (1933), 58 (1954).

Cowangara (*Co. Macquarie*) see Bagnoo.

Cowanna Bend (*Co. Wentworth*) 34°06'S. 142°03'E., 2 km S. of Dareton, on Murray R.

Cowans (*Co. Gloucester*) see Firefly.

Cowarra (*Co. Beresford*) 36°00'S. 149°18'E., 31 km NE of Cooma; estab. 1935; mining; goldmine (BHP), closed 1942; gold treatment mill (BHP) 1940; PO 1940; powerhouse (BHP) 1940; telephone 1941; pop. *c.*300 (1941), 63 (1947).

Coweambah (*Co. Gloucester*) see Tea Gardens.

Cow Flat (*Co. Bathurst*) 33°34'S. 149°32'E., 18 km S. of Bathurst; defunct; copper, silica, talc, grazing, agric.; copper mines: Apsley 1875–81 and 1898–1920, Balmoral 1870s and 1906, Belmore (Morgan's Mining Co.) 1875, 1877–81, 1899, 1901–2, 1905–7, Cow Flat Copper Mining Co. 1875–81 and 1900, Cow Flat North, Esmeralda (J. Thomas) 1877 and 1906–7, Red Hill 1901, 1903, 1906–7, 1959, Rockley Mount or The Mount 1918 and 1959, Shepherds (Amos and Shannon) 1870s, 1895, 1907, Sugarloaf or Mountain Run (Mining & Exploration Co.) 1899–1900, 1905–7, 1909, 1914, 1919, 1921; hailstorm 1895; Meth. C. b. 1939 by Roy and Herbert Eldridge, d. by William Henry Hopper; PO 1872–1931; quarry (Bellville) operated by Joe Bell; school 1875, new one b. 1879 by Alfred George Stanger, d. by George Allen Mansfield, closed 1915, reused, fire 1985, derelict, sold 2016; smelters (copper); telephone 1914; Wes. Meth. C. 1871, sold and dismantled 1918; pop. 99 (1901), 57 (1911), 36 (1933).

Cow Flat (*Co. Clive*) 29°15'S. 151°39'E., 42 km SW of Tenterfield.

Cowlong (*Co. Rous*) 28°47'S. 153°25'E., 8 km NW of Alstonville; Meth. C. 1910; PO 1890; storm 1942; Wes. Meth. C. 1884; pop. 108 (1901), 134 (1911).

Cowlong (*Co. Rous*) see also Eltham.

Cowper (*Co. Clarence*) 29°34'S. 153°05'E., 17 km SW of Maclean, on Clarence R. (South Arm); village gaz. 1870, laid out 1879, never fully developed, declined 1945+, bypassed by highway 1993; shipbuilding, sugar-cane, farming, dairying; bridge (Wingfield Bridge) 1958, over Clarence R. (South Arm), to Brushgrove, on Woodford Island; creamery (Clarence River Pioneer Dairy Co.) b. 1899 by John M'Kay, closed 1909; hailstorm 1953; PO 1901, damaged 1913; Presb. C., demolished 1898, replacement (St David's) b. 1900 by L.C. Finlay, d. by J. Strauss, new vestry 1948, church relocated 1991, closed, sold and reused; punt, ceased 1956; Rom. Cath. C. 1880 d. by

James Moyes, re-roofed 1905, closed 1970, sold and reused, new one (Mary Immaculate) 1965 on new site; sawmill; school 1874, new one b. 1876, repairs 1887 by J.D. Avery, burnt down 1910, rebuilt 1910 by F. Robertson, additions 1915 by E. Comerford, additions 2010; slipway (William Toft Pullen) 1882; storm 1913; telephone 1903; wharves (incl. one b. 1885 by J. Walsh); pop. 249 (1911), 27 (1933), 234 (1961), 432 (2006).

Cowper (*Co. Northumberland*)
see Catherine Hill Bay.

Cowra (*Co. Bathurst*) 33°50'S. 148°41'E., 72 km SW of Orange, on Lachlan R.; (incl. North Cowra and South Cowra); settled 1833 by John Grant, founded 1846, surveyed and village gaz. 1849, first lots sold 1854, thrived in 1860s and 1880s, town gaz. 1880, southern subdivision 1882, munic. proc. 1888; orig. grazing, then wheat (estab. *c.*1849 by Tindal Bros), fruit, pigs, dairying, oats, barley, canola, lucerne, vegetables, vineyards 1970s+, food processing, manufacturing, light engineering; agric. research station 1903; ambulance station 1990; Angl. C. (St John the Evangelist) b. 1879 by Foley, d. by Alexander Leckie Elphinstone, jun., major repairs 1881, demolished 2001, new one (St John's War Memorial) b. 1956 by Walsh, Tillet and Tilston, d. by N.W. McPherson, fire 2015; army training camp 1940–45, reused; Assemblies of God C. (Abundant Life); Bapt. C. 1955; breweries: Clifton's (estab. by William Larkin and David Clifton) 1882–98 and Connolly's (estab. by John Connolly, closed 1895, reopened 1902 by Tom Comerford and renamed Phoenix Brewery, closed 1904); brickworks: Cowra Machine Brickworks Products (P.H. Francis), C.E. Newcombe & Sons, Sergeant's; bridges: one (McCallum truss) b. 1867–70 by Baillie and Chalder, d. by William Christopher Bennett, replacement (composite steel and timber bowstring truss) b. 1891–93 by John Wishart & Sons, d. by John Alexander McDonald, demolished 1988, new one (concrete) b. 1986 by McDougall-Ireland Pty Ltd, d. by Rankine & Hill Pty Ltd, over Lachlan R. and Cyril Treasure Bridge over Waugoola Ck; bushfire 1952; butter factory (A. Rothwell's Cowra Dairy Co.); cannery (Gordon Edgell & Sons Ltd) 1943; carriage-works (Poignand Bros); caterpillar infestation 1899; cemeteries: general 1863 and Japanese (522 graves); CH 1873, new one b. 1880 by Henry Ford, d. by James Johnstone Barnet, additions 1883 also by Ford, additions 1899 d. by Walter Liberty Vernon, remodelling and additions 1909 by Peter Beddie, also d. by Vernon, restored 1990; clothing factory (Rajer Manufacturing Co.) 1946–60, in former small arms factory; cordial factories: John Arnold and W. Guild, Boxhall's, fire 1887, Connelly's, W.P. Costello, Charles James Derwin 1905, relocated 1910, D. Duncan, burnt down 1929, E. Fitzgerald, Great Western Aerated & Medicinal Waters & Cordials Manufactory (James Mulally) 1884–87, J. Lamplough, Newling Cordials (Newling and Ginns, sold 1971 to Malcolm and Effie Langfield, relocated 1976), Phoneix Cordial Factory (Austin and George Taylor, bought by Derwin Bros, closed 1924), Prior & Co. 1911, Sharpe Bros, Sparkling Cordial Factory, White Star Steam Aerated Water & Cordial Works (William Howey); diphtheria 1893 (many died) and 1895; droughts 1839, 1840, 1841, 1888; dust storm 1902; earth tremors 1916 and 1926; electricity 1924; engineering works (H.H. Yuill) 1911; engineering and metal fabrication works (Active Group Pty Ltd); FB 1910 (new station b. 1929); fibrous plaster works (R. Jones); fires 1897 and 1949; floods 1844, 1863, 1870, 1891, 1916, 1952, 2010; flour mills: Adams & Sons, Phoenix 1884 (Dennis C.J. Donnelly, boiler explosion 1887, taken over 1889 by Adkins), Patrick and Thomas Walsh (b. 1859–61 by McEwan, d. by Edward Gell, bought 1898 by Henry Hugh Suttor Francis, boiler explosion 1898, inundated 1900, closed 1905, reused), W.H. Corp Pty Ltd 1953; freezing works: Lachlan Pty Ltd, burnt down 1945, replaced 1948, and John Paterson Ltd 1910; gale 1923; gaol b. 1886 by Henry Hugh

Suttor Francis, additions and alterations 1918 also by Francis, new one 1939; gasworks 1912; heatwave 1904–5; hospital 1885, additions 1928 by S.S. Barr, additions 1936, 1941, 1955, 1959; hurricane 1877; ice works (C. Pryce); Ignite C. (formerly Christ. Outreach C.); LDS (Mormon) C.; Lutheran C.; metal fabrication works (Lachlan Steel Power Tools Plus); migrant camp 1949–55, at former army training camp; milk factory (Cowra Milk Supply Co.); mineral water factory; monumental stone works: W. Jones, W. McCarthy, T.M. Murphy; mouse plague 1987; Plymouth Brethren C.; PO: Cowra 1850, new one b. 1881–83 by Henry Ford, additions 1894 by Henry Hart, additions and alterations 1909 by Rigby Bros, North Cowra 1947–71, South Cowra 1955–71; pound (stock) 1865; powerhouse 1925–29, then electricity obtained from Burrinjuck; POW camp 1941–47 (suicidal breakout 1944 resulted in 234 Japanese deaths), reused as migrant camp, razed; Presb. C. (St Peter's) 1861, new one b. 1911–13 by Robert Walsh and Henry Hugh Suttor Francis, d. by Power and Adam; PS 1864, new one b. 1885 by Henry Ford, new one b. 1913 by Henry Hugh Suttor Francis, additions and alterations 1919 by Henry Ford, new one 1939; railway bridge (lattice girder), 159 ft (48.5 m) span, fabricated by A. Lecoq, Belgium, erected 1887 by Fishburn & Co. and D. and W. Robertson, d. by Sir John Fowler and John Whitton, over Lachlan R.; railway coal stage 1902; railway engine shed 1889, burnt down 1897, rebuilt 1898 by G. Boothley; railway round-house 1923; railway turntable, 60 ft (18.3 m), moved 1928 to Culcairn, new one 1923, 75 ft (22.9 m); 4 reservoirs (incl. two b. 1929); rifle range 1915, new one 1923; Rom. Cath. C. b. 1859–61 by O'Mara, reused 1878, second one b. 1877–81 by O'Mara and Ralston, d. by Edward Gell, additions 1902 by Albert Emanuel Ennis, d. by John Job Copeman, demolished 1938, third one (St Raphael's) b. 1939 by Wallace and McGee, d. by E.A. Scott, Green and Scott; RS 1886, station b. by John George Gough, refreshment rooms 1917, closed and reused; sale-yards 1927; Salv. Army C. 1927, renovated 1980 by Ian Hartwig, extended 1999; sawmills: Henry Hugh Suttor Francis (fire 1914, inundated 1916), J.R. McDonald, Nicholas Markham; schools: Cowra 1858, additions and alterations 1882 by Henry Ford, additions 1887 by G.J.B. Wood, additions and alterations 1909 by Arnold Rigby, additions 1920 by L.H. Ralph, additions 1931 and 1979, HS 1942, additions 1956, 1965, 1969, 1980, Migrant Camp 1949–55, Mulyan 1953, additions 1962, 1967, 1969, 1975; SD Adventist C. 1934; sewerage 1936; small arms factory (World War II), reused; soap-works: Great Central Soap Co. and Lachlan Soap Works (Aubrey Lane and H.C. Lane), man killed 1900; stock food plant (NSW Produce Co. Pty Ltd) 1948; storms 1897 (boy killed) and 1900; TC 1969 d. by R. Tanner, became a campus of Western Institute in 1992; telegraph 1874, new office b. 1881–83 by Henry Ford, burnt down 1892, replaced; tile works 1950; TX 1903; Unit. C. (orig. Wes. Meth.) 1890, sanctuary remodelled 1950, porch added 1989; water tank factory (Amos's) 1993; waterworks b. 1908 by F.J. Cornwell and Wesley Castles, augmentation 1994; winery (River Park, Bill and Chris Murphy) 1994; wool-scour (Lachlan Industries); pop. 193 (1861), *c.*200 (1866), 265 (1871), 628 (1881), *c.*700 (1887), 1,546 (1891), 1,811 (1901), 3,981 (1911), 3,733 (1921), 5,056 (1933), 5,473 (1947), 6,789 (1954, incl. 692 at migrant centre), 6,288 (1961), 7,092 (1966), 7,282 (1971), 7,734 (1976), 7,900 (1981), 8,207 (1986), 8,422 (1991), 8,544 (1996), 8,722 (2001), 8,430 (2006), 8,107 (2011).

Cowra Creek (*Co. Beresford*) 36°00'S. 149°19'E., 31 km NE of Cooma, on Cowra Ck; estab. 1888; gold (disc. 1888); cemetery 1899; mines: Cowra King, Democrat, Ironclad, Just in Time, Kitchingmans, Nellie Darling, Polar Star, Princess, Southern Star, Star of Cooma, Vanderbilt, Victoria, Waratah; PO 1895–1910; school 1897–1910; stamper batteries: Back Creek, Democrat (8 head, removed 1893 by

John Murray from Michelago), Lewis's 1891; pop. 148 (1901).

Cowra Road (*Co. Monteagle*) 33°56'S. 148°20'E., 17 km E. of Grenfell, on Bungalong Ck; settled 1906+; bridge over Bungalong Ck; Meth. C., removed from Brundah Creek and re-erected 1916 by J.T. Darrington, d. by Drury; school (Bungalong Creek) 1912–15.

Cowra West (*Co. Forbes*) 33°50'S. 148°41'E., 1 km W. of Cowra, on Lachlan R.; town gaz. 1879; abattoir (Cowra Abattoir Pty Ltd) 1970; aircraft factory (Brumby Aircraft Aust. Pty Ltd) 2004; airport (Cowra) 1951; quarry; RS 1910, station b. by D.H. Reid, closed 1971; silo.

Cox Estate (*Co. Northumberland*) see Woy Woy.

Coxs Creek (*Co. Phillip*) 32°45'S. 150°07'E., 14 km E. of Rylstone; pop. 52 (1911), 47 (1933), 182 (2006), 160 (2011).

Cox's Flat (*Co. Northumberland*) see Woy Woy.

Coxs Gap (*Co. Brisbane*) 32°15'S. 150°39'E., 17 km N. of Denman; PS 1941–42; school 1885–86 and 1896–1901.

Coxs River (*Co. Westmoreland*) 33°56'S. 150°21'E., 24 km S. of Wentworth Falls; farming; Angl. C. (St John's); bushfire 1905; PO 1874, burnt down 1926; Rom. Cath. C. 1872, new one (St Joseph's) b. 1918 by Frank Wedesweiler, closed 1955, demolished, and graveyard; school (Blackgolar till 1909) 1888–1913 and 1931–54; telephone 1923; TX 1936; pop. 80 (1911), 116 (1933), 107 (1947).

Crabbes Creek (*Co. Rous*) 28°28'S. 153°30'E., 10 km SW of Pottsville, on Crabbes Ck; farming, dairying, bananas, sugar-cane; electricity 1956; Macedonian C. 1949, closed, sold and reused; PO 1896; RS (Mooball till 1895) 1894–1975; sawmill; school 1906, new building b. 1916 by Alfred John Modini, additions 2010; telephone 1905; TX 1925, automatic 1954; pop. 126 (1911), 203 (1933), 270 (1947), 371 (1954), 332 (1961), 294 (2011).

Craboon (*Co. Bligh*) 32°02'S. 149°28'E., 6 km E. of Dunedoo; lots sold 1910, declined 1920+; wheat and lucerne; PO 1910; RS 1910, station b. by George Albert Leggo and John Allibone, closed 1975; school 1912–40; telephone 1911; TX 1917; pop. 81 (1933), 50 (1954), 52 (1961).

Crackenback (*Co. Wallace*) 36°26'S. 148°28'E., 13 km W. of Jindabyne; PO 1958; telephone 1959; TX (automatic); pop. 53 (1911), 322 (2006).

Craeton (*Co. Bligh*) see Idaville.

Craigie (*Co. Wellesley*) 37°05'S. 149°03'E., 24 km SW of Bombala, on Little Plains R.; orig. China Town; goldmining and grazing; Angl. C. (St Stephen's) b. 1885 by John Groves, relocated 1905 by Thomas Moore & Sons, renovated 1933; bridge 1903, over Little Plains R.; cemetery; Chinese joss house, inundated 1900, burnt down 1902; fires 1868 (destroyed most of town) and 1922; flood 1900; hailstorm 1872; PO 1872; school 1882–1931; telephone 1893; TX 1925–71; pop. 118 (1901), 108 (1911), 115 (1933), 83 (1947), 75 (1954), 68 (1961), 170 (2006).

Craigie Lea (*Co. Narromine*) 32°19'S. 148°11'E., 10 km SW of Narromine.

Craigilea (*Co. Buckland*) 31°43'S. 150°37'E., 25 km S. of Quirindi, school 1914–16.

Craig Lea (*Co. Vernon*) see Ingalba.

Cramsville (*Co. Camden*) see Fairy Meadow.

Cranbury (*Co. Ashburnham*) 33°25'S. 148°39'E., 18 km N. of Canowindra; Angl. C. (All Saints') b. 1909 by Parker and Gadd; Meth. C. 1903, closed, dismantled 1954; PO 1880–1914; school (Nyrang till 1885) 1878–89 and 1900–20; Unit. C. (orig. Meth.) 1955; pop. 68 (1901), 143 (1911), 62 (1933).

Crangan Bay (*Co. Northumberland*) see Nords Wharf.

Cranky Corner (*Co. Durham*) 32°34'S. 151°24'E., 11 km N. of Branxton; snow 1964.

Craven (*Co. Gloucester*) 32°10'S. 151°57'E., 17 km S. of Gloucester, on The Swamp; bushfire 1953; FB 1953 and 1965 (station b. 1993); PO 1916; quarry; RS 1913, station b. by Robert Daniel Quiggin, closed, removed 1984; sawmills: Taylor and Sheddon (estab. 1914, sold 1917, burnt down 1920), F. Viggers & Co. Pty Ltd (acquired 1969 by Allen Taylor

& Co., closed 1978), W.D. Wood Ltd (closed 1925 and moved to Stroud Road); school 1916 b. by J.T. Henry, closed 1978, building moved 1981 to Stratford; telephone 1914; TX 1920–78; Union C. b. 1916 by W. Wright; pop. 158 (1933), 141 (1947), 139 (1954), 109 (1961), 267 (2011).

Craven Creek (*Co. Gloucester*) see Rookhurst.

Craven Plateau (*Co. Gloucester*) 31°52'S. 151°46'E., 25 km NW of Gloucester, on Cravens Ck; goldmining and dairying; sawmill estab. by Ernie and Beau Price, taken over by Carson's Timber Co., acquired by Ted Bromley, taken over by Harold Stuart; pop. 65 (1933), 66 (1947), 55 (1954).

Crawford River (*Co. Gloucester*) 32°27'S. 152°09'E., 7 km SW of Bulahdelah, on Crawford R.; sawmill (F. Stacey) 1933; school 1882–95; pop. 78 (1933), 68 (1947).

Crawfordville (*Co. Northumberland*) see Millfield.

Crawler's Forest (*Co. Camden*) see Crawley Forest.

Crawley Forest (*Co. Camden*) 34°42'S. 150°50'E., 4 km SW of Kiama; also known as Crawler's Forest; Angl. C. 1885, rebuilt (St John's) 1894 by Faux, closed, moved 1912 to Bombo by O. Alexander, T. Brown and W. Grey, jun. and reused.

Crawney (*Co. Brisbane*) 31°34'S. 151°01'E., 28 km NE of Murrurundi; pop. 35 (1933).

Creeper Gate (*Co. Flinders*) 31°53'S. 146°50'E., 49 km SW of Nyngan.

Creewah (*Co. Wellesley*) 36°45'S. 149°23'E., 23 km NE of Bombala, on Bombala R.

Crescent Head (*Co. Macquarie*) 31°12'S. 152°59'E., 18 km SE of Kempsey, on Tasman Sea; village gaz. 1894; fishing, surfing, tourism; airfield; Angl. and Unit. C. (orig. Meth.) 1925; bushfires 1968 and 1970; cemetery (2 graves) 1926; columbarium (unused); FB; foot-bridge over Killick Ck; gun battery (World War II); PO 1927; PS; 5 reservoirs; Rom. Cath. C. (Our Lady Star of the Sea) 1968–2003; school 1922 b. by Tom Lions and Bill Hyde, new one b. 1979 by E.E. Lahey Constructions, additions 1994; sewerage 1976; telephone 1916; TX 1926, automatic 1954; water reticulation 1967, augmentation 1988; pop. 73 (1933), 186 (1947), 253 (1954), 338 (1961), 623 (1971), 798 (1976), 944 (1981), 1,098 (1986), 1,208 (1991), 1,175 (1996), 1,186 (2001), 1,076 (2006), 978 (2011).

Crestwood (*Co. Argyle*) see Bradfordville.

Crestwood (*Co. Murray*) see Queanbeyan.

Criefton (*Co. Lincoln*) 32°25'S. 148°57'E., 15 km N. of Wellington; school 1906–15.

Cringila (*Co. Camden*) see Port Kembla.

Crockwell (*Co. Georgiana*) 33°51'S. 149°30'E., 37 km SW of Oberon.

Croki (*Co. Macquarie*) 31°53'S. 152°36'E., 9 km W. of Harrington, on Manning R.; surveyed 1898 as a private village, thrived till 1908; former river port, oysters, fish, maize, dairying; butter factory and creamery (Lower Manning Co-op. Dairy Co.) 1893; cheese factories: Drummond & Co. 1919 and C.A. Lane; floods 1893, 1929, 1950, 1978; jetty; punt (4 car capacity) to Mitchells Island, across Manning R.; Wes. Meth. C. 1858; wharf b. 1879 by H. Moscatt, destroyed 1895; pop. 20 (1841), *c.*300 (1891), 141 (1911), 141 (1924), 97 (1947).

Croki (*Co. Macquarie*) see also Jones Island.

Cromartys Bay (*Co. Gloucester*) see Taylors Beach.

Crooble (*Co. Burnett*) 29°16'S. 150°15'E., 43 km NW of Warialda; village gaz. 1940; PO 1938; RS 1932–76; school 1956–69; telephone 1953; TX 1954, automatic 1969; pop. 88 (1933), 127 (1954), 110 (1961).

Croobyar (*Co. St Vincent*) 35°21'S. 150°18'E., 13 km W. of Milton; FB; school 1862 b. by David Warden, new one b. 1878, closed 1934; pop. 81 (1954), 64 (1961).

Crooked Corner (*Co. Georgiana*) 34°14'S. 149°18'E., 30 km NW of Crookwell, on Mulgowrie Ck; PO 1937; quarry; school (Five Mile Tree) 1956–2010, sold and reused; telephone 1937; TX 1938; pop. 58 (1933), 226 (2006).

Crookes Valley (*Co. Rous*) 28°20'S. 153°19'E., 8 km W. of Murwillumbah; bananas; bushfire

1936.

Crookhaven (*Co. St Vincent*) 34°55'S. 150°46'E., 2 km NW of Culburra, on Tasman Sea; FB; jetty 1959; lighthouse (Crookhaven Heads) b. 1882 of timber, demolished 1904, replacement b. of concrete in 1904 by Fetherston and Paulson, 23 ft (7 m); telegraph 1881; wharf 1921; pop. 50 (1911).

Crookwell (*Co. King*) 34°28'S. 149°28'E., 40 km NW of Goulburn, on Crookwell R.; (incl. Brooklands and North Crookwell); orig. Kiama; disc. 1820 by James Meehan, settled 1828+, site reserved 1848, laid out by John Barry Armstrong and town gaz. 1860, first lots sold 1869, thrived in 1870s; formerly gold, then sheep, wheat, potatoes, cattle, dairying, oaten hay, apples, pears, cherries, meat processing, veterinary products; airfield; ambulance station 1940; Angl. C. (St Paul's) b. 1864–66 by McDonald, Murray and Kennedy, d. by Leigh, reused, second one (St Bartholomew's) b. 1904 by King and Armstrong, d. by Edmund Cooper Manfred, new one (St Bartholomew's War Memorial) 1969, and graveyard; brickworks: Crookwell Bricks (D. Grimson, J. Parker and C. Bunker) 1884–91, John Willis & Son 1885–90, Willis Bros 1917–40; bridge 1870, destroyed, rebuilt 1879 by Brooks and Wardle, demolished 1934, new one (concrete beam) b. 1935 by F. Hampson, over Crookwell R.; bushfires 1952 and 1975; butter factory (Crookwell Dairy Society Ltd) d. and b. 1890 by William Steele, new one 1926 d. by Richard Wildridge & Co.; carriage-works: N.E. Bassingthwaite, J.H. Rogan 1904, A.J. Rowe; cemetery (2,000+ burials 1871+) 1870; CH b. 1875 by Thomas Davies, additions 1881 by A. Ferguson, repairs 1892 by William Steele, reused, new one b. 1892 by William Pearman, d. by Walter Liberty Vernon, additions 1899 by Arthur Allen; clock tower 2004; cordial factories: W. Rolfe 1890–1906 (bought 1907 by A.E. Cameron) and W.H. Searle; earth tremors 1870 and 1954; electricity 1920; FB (station b. 1939, new one 1976); fellmongery (John Mortimer & Co.) 1888; fires 1889, 1902, 1913, 1916, 1938; flood 1893; flour mills: Samuel Cox 1882–1908, reused 1914, Anthony Stephenson 1871 (taken over 1881 by James Warne, closed 1901, reused, sold 1989 and restored, bought 2017 by Susan Hutton), United Steam Mill (Mathlin and Bonfield); foot-bridge over Crookwell R.; gastroenteritis epidemic 1952; hailstorm 1951; hospital (cottage) b. 1907 by King and Armstrong, d. by Walter Spiers, new wing b. 1934 by D.E. Foster, additions 1943 and 1956; measles epidemic 1933; PO 1867, new one b. 1888–90 by Henry Ford, alterations 1938 by H. Gould; pound (stock) 1878; powerhouse 1920; Presb. C. (St Andrew's) b. 1882 by Williams and Balgowan; Prim. Meth. C. 1871–1901, reused, demolished; PS (incl. lock-up) 1878, additions and alterations 1895 by G.F Cole and W. Frost, new one 1994; quarries: iron ore, incl. powder magazine, o. by A.I. & S. Co. Ltd and stone (John Howard); rabbit freezing works: Davis Packing Co. 1914 (in former flour mill), Highland Refrigerating Co. 1909 (burnt down 1930), R.S. Phillips 1925–37; railway coal stage; railway turntable (William Sellers & Co.), 60 ft (18.3 m), closed; reservoirs (incl. one b. 1937 by A.F. Hood); rifle range 1909, new one 1913; Rom. Cath. C. (St Mary's) b. 1889–91 by John Howard, d. by Charles Spadaccini, additions 1929, extended 1951, fire 1958, rebuilt 1959 by S.G. McFarlane & Sons, d. by Fowell, Mansfield and Maclurcan; RS 1902–85; sale-yards (Cox Bros) 1875, new yards b. 1885 by Charles Harvey, new yards 1967; Salv. Army C. 1884, damaged 1896; schools: primary 1865, closed later that year, reopened 1874, additions 1882 by A. Ferguson, demolished 1897, replaced 1897 by Stubbins and Edwards, alterations 1918 by A. Allen, new building 1938, additions 1960, 1968, 1971, and HS 1968, additions 1974 and 1979; sewage works 1960, augmentation 1995; snowstorms 1869, 1896, 1900, 1921; sock factory (Lindner Quality Socks Pty Ltd) estab. 1997 by Wilfred and Gisela Lindner; storm 1896; tank works (Grove's); tannery (E. Denning) 1899–1904; telegraph 1880, new office b. 1888–90 by Henry Ford; telephone 1906; TX 1909, automatic 1966; typhoid 1896 (woman died), 1906, 1907; Unit. C. (orig. Wes. Meth.) b. 1866 by Willmot and O. Robinson, renovated and transept added 1903, alterations 1959; watch-house b. 1875 by Thomas Davies; water supply 1938, augmentation 1990; weaving mill; whooping cough epidemics 1890 and 1934; pop. 130 (1864), 1,000+ (1872), 240 (1881), 925 (1891), 1,395 (1901), 1,696 (1911), 1,908 (1933), 2,117 (1941), 2,214 (1947), 2,112 (1954), 2,340 (1961), 2,267 (1966), 2,120 (1971), 2,147 (1976), 2,063 (1981), 1,966 (1986), 1,966 (1991), 2,016 (1996), 1,926 (2001), 1,993 (2006), 2,016 (2011).

Crookwell River (*Co. King*) 34°23'S. 149°19'E., 16 km NW of Crookwell; school 1882, new building b. 1884 by G. Parker, closed 1898, reopened 1957, closed 1968.

Croom (*Co. Camden*) see Albion Park.

Croom Park (*Co. Gloucester*) see Fosterton.

Croppa Creek (*Co. Burnett*) 29°08'S. 150°17'E., 53 km NW of Warialda; Angl. C. (removed from Moree and rebuilt 1936) dedicated 1939 as St David's; PO 1937; Rom. Cath. C. (St Anne's) 1976, shared with Anglicans; RS (10 km NW) 1932–76; school 1951, additions 2010; silo; telephone 1928; TX 1928, automatic 1974; pop. 105 (1933), 70 (1947), 159 (1954), 214 (1961), 186 (2006).

Crosslands (*Co. Macquarie*) 31°27'S. 152°43'E., 3 km NW of Wauchope, on Hastings R.; bridge (Bains Bridge) 1907, over Hastings R.; pop. 425 (2011).

Crossmaglen (*Co. Raleigh*) 30°22'S. 152°59'E., 11 km W. of Sawtell, on Bonville Ck; PO 1927; sawmill 1912–32; school 1957; telephone 1923; TX 1930; pop. 59 (1933), 73 (1947), 85 (1954), 72 (1961).

Cross Roads (*Co. Bathurst*) see Millthorpe.

Cross Roads (*Co. Camden*) 34°36'S. 150°15'E., 9 km NW of Bundanoon; PO 1869; telephone 1925; TX 1952; pop. 59 (1911).

Crossroads (*Co. Gordon*) see Cumnock.

Cross Roads (*Co. Macquarie*) see Lansdowne.

Crossroads (*Co. Macquarie*) 31°28'S. 152°41'E., 5 km W. of Wauchope; cemetery (238 graves 1868+).

Cross Roads (*Co. Mitchell*) see Collingullie.

Cross Roads (*Co. Northumberland*) 32°56'S. 151°39'E., 2 km NW of Cardiff, on Winding Ck; sawmill (Richard Colin Carroll) 1941.

Cross Roads (*Co. Phillip*) 32°31'S. 149°42'E., 15 km NE of Mudgee; pop. 41 (1933).

Croudace Bay (*Co. Northumberland*) see Valentine.

Crowdy Head (*Co. Macquarie*) 31°51'S. 152°45'E., 7 km NE of Harrington, on Tasman Sea; village gaz. 1973; fishing and tourism; breakwater 1964; harbour 1972; 2 jetties, 295 ft (90 m) each, 1976; lighthouse (stone) b. 1879 by William John Smith, d. by James Johnstone Barnet, 24 ft (7.3 m), converted 1920 from oil to acetylene and to electricity in 1972; PO 1962–89; quarry 1894–1904, reopened 1964, closed, reopened 1972; railway from quarry to Harrington breakwater, 4.5 miles (11.7 km); reservoir; school 1958, additions 2010, closed 2014; telephone 1912; TX 1957; wharf 1986; pop. 60 (1901), 59 (1933), 50 (1954), 61 (1961), 221 (2011).

Crow Mountain (*Co. Darling*) 30°29'S. 150°46'E., 18 km SE of Barraba; goldmining and grazing; PO 1896–1961; sawmill (John Coote); school 1896–98; telephone 1924; TX 1928; pop. 196 (1901), 60 (1911), 57 (1933), 59 (1947), 56 (1961).

Crown Flat (*Co. St Vincent*) see Araluen.

Crown View (*Co. Westmoreland*) 33°34'S. 149°57'E., 18 km NE of Oberon.

Crowther (*Co. Monteagle*) 34°06'S. 148°30'E., 31 km NE of Young, on Opening Ck; farming and orchards; bushfire 1932; PO 1912; RS 1888–1975, demolished 1985; school 1917–39; telephone 1913; TX 1918, automatic 1974; pop. 71 (1901), 106 (1911), 108 (1954), 101 (1921), 131 (1933), 82 (1947), 108 (1954), 107 (1961), 196 (2006).

Crowther's Camp (*Co. Cooper*) see Griffith.

Crudine (*Co. Roxburgh*) 32°57'S. 149°42'E., 27 km W. of Kandos, on Crudine R.; goldmining (alluvial), farming, grazing; Angl. C. b. by

Foster; cemetery (46 graves 1893–1950) 1884; drought 1875–79; PO 1875–1931; pound (stock) 1886; school 1867, additions 1876 by Foster, closed 1916; 2 stamper batteries (incl. Elkin's 10 head); telephone 1953; TX 1953; Union C., repairs 1904 by Southcott; pop. 193 (1911), 107 (1933), 56 (1947).

Crumps Retreat (*Co. Northumberland*) 33°02'S. 151°21'E., 11 km NW of Cooranbong, on Reedy Ck.

Crusher (*Co. Leichhardt*) 31°02'S. 148°35'E., 23 km W. of Coonamble, on Magometon Ck.

Crusher Camp (*Co. Cooper*) see Leeton.

Crushers (*Co. Cook*) see Katoomba.

Cryon (*Co. Denham*) 30°00'S. 148°36'E., 56 km E. of Walgett; grazing; PO 1921; PS, damaged 1911, closed 1920; RS (12 km SW) 1905, station b. by John Allibone, closed 1980; school 1957–68; telegraph (office at railway station) 1908–25; telephone 1924; tornado 1911; TX 1928; pop. 133 (1911), 52 (1933), 47 (1947), 182 (1954), 154 (1961).

Crystal Creek (*Co. Rous*) 28°19'S. 153°19'E., 7 km W. of Murwillumbah, on Rous R.; farming and bananas; bridge (Korns Crossing) 1916, timber truss, 144 ft (43.9 m), over Rous R.; PO 1925; Rom. Cath. C. (St Michael's) 1907, closed, sold and reused; sawmill (Stan Boxill); school 1900, new one b. 1911 by Alfred John Modini; telephone 1913; TX 1930; pop. 142 (1911), 228 (1933), 118 (1947), 62 (1954), 55 (1961), 395 (2011).

Crystal Waters (*Co. Clarence*) 29°25'S. 153°19'E., 4 km W. of Yamba, on Clarence R.; (incl. Kolora Estate); ambulance station; bridge (Oyster Channel Bridge) 1908, to Micalo Island, over Oyster Channel; Christ. Life C.; river training wall (Middle Wall); wharf.

Cuan (*Co. Brisbane*) 32°00'S. 150°39'E., 22 km W. of Scone; school 1882–88; pop. 58 (1911).

Cubawee (*Co. Rous*) 28°48'S. 153°12'E., 6 km W. of Lismore; RS 1909–66; school 1957–63; pop. 105 (1961).

Cubbal (*Co. Buller*) 28°24'S. 152°41'E., 40 km NW of Kyogle; telephone 1922.

Cubbaroo (*Co. Jamison*) 30°10'S. 149°08'E., 31 km W. of Wee Waa, on Pian Ck; RS 1903, station b. by John Allibone and McCarthy, closed 1975; school 1957–59; pop. 63 (1933), 56 (1947), 59 (1954), 58 (1961).

Cubmurra (*Co. Selwyn*) see Cabramurra.

Cucumgilliga (*Co. Forbes*) 34°01'S. 148°42'E., 19 km S. of Cowra; school 1901–76; TX (automatic); pop. 35 (1933).

Cudal (*Co. Ashburnham*) 33°17'S. 148°44'E., 12 km S. of Manilla, on Boree Ck; surveyed by Edward Fisher and village gaz. 1867, munic. proc. 1890; goldmining, grazing, wheat, oats, maize, barley, canola; airport (2 km NE), closed, reused 2020; Angl. C. 1876, new one (St James's) b. 1904 by Joseph Wells, d. by John Holderness Bates; brick-kiln; bridge (R.H. Herbert Bridge) 1960, over Boree Ck; butter factory (L. Carman), leased 1901 to Molong Dist. Dairying Co. as a creamery; carriage-works (E. Atherton) 1906, sold 1907; cemetery (731 graves 1870s+) 1870, incl. columbarium; CH (incl. lock-up) b. 1885 by Thomas Atkinson, additions 1900 by C.W. Muller and J.F. Byrne; cordial factories: W. Barrett 1881 and J. Travers; dust storm 1901; electricity 1938; FB (station b. 2017); fires 1898, 1905, 1909, 2015; flour mill (Sam Landauer) 1878–1913, destroyed; hospital 1928, new one (War Memorial) 1951, closed, demolished, replaced; ice works (K.G. Group Pty Ltd) estab. 1997 by Ken Brooke; PO 1872, new one b. 1889 by R.B. Spicer; pound (stock) 1874; PS 1881–1943, reopened 1947, new building 1960; 2 quarries; rifle range 1908; Rom. Cath. C. (St Columbanus's) b. 1880 by Francis Rule and John Henry Gain, d. by Edward Gell, renovations 1896, additions 1937 by J.H. Clarke; sawmill (Arthur Davis); school 1876, new one b. 1879, additions 1881, 1956, 1966; telegraph 1880; TX 1910, automatic 1980; Unit. C. (orig. Meth.) b. 1923 by W. Gifford and E. Goodacre, d. by L.B. Watson, closed, sold 2014; water supply augmentation 1995; pop. 235 (1881), 447 (1891), *c.*550 (1895), 599 (1901), 577 (1911), 362 (1933), 352 (1947), 491 (1954), 405 (1961), 324 (1971), 373 (1976), 400 (1981), 352 (1986),

380 (1991), 420 (1996), 417 (2001), 389 (2006), 338 (2011).

Cuddell (*Co. Mitchell*) 34°48'S. 146°21'E., 19 km W. of Narrandera, on Cuddell Ck; surveyed and village gaz. 1867; sawmill (George Henri Risby) 1878; school 1882–83.

Cuddell (*Co. Mitchell*) see also Corobimilla.

Cuddell Siding (*Co. Mitchell*) see Corobimilla.

Cudgebegong Creek (*Co. Bligh*) see Mebul.

Cudgegong (*Co. Wellington*) 32°48'S. 149°49'E., 14 km W. of Rylstone, orig. on Cudgegong R., but now old town submerged under Lake Windamere; surveyed by John A.H. Price, village gaz. 1858, munic. proc. 1860, resumed 1971; vegetables, dairying, sheep, mining; Angl. C. (St James the Less) b. 1863 by Robert Charlesworth, demolished; bridge (Lambert Bridge) b. 1875 by T. and F. Atkinson; cemetery (100 graves 1868–1973) 1875; flood 1862; marble quarry (Holdsworth Macpherson & Co.); milk factory, became butter factory, then rabbit-boning works; mines: Cheshire (copper) 1882–85 and 1897 and Rhobadah (gold) 1881–89 and 1895; PO 1865; school 1868, new one b. 1877 by William Readford and William Babbage, repairs 1896 by William Readford, closed 1925, reopened 1957, closed 1970; telephone 1914; TX 1925; pop. 1,595 (1861), 2,342 (1871), 2,533 (1881), 2,519 (1891), *c.*2,500 (1895), 182 (1911), 75 (1933), 117 (1947), 85 (1954), 120 (1961).

Cudgegong Valley (*Co. Wellington*) see Mudgee.

Cudgell Creek (*Co. Monteagle*) 34°11'S. 148°13'E., 17 km NW of Young, on Cudgell Ck; Presb. C.; school 1881, new buildings b. 1883 by Van Iderstine and John George Gough, closed 1893.

Cudgen (*Co. Rous*) 28°16'S. 153°33'E., 2 km W. of Kingscliff, on Cudgen Ck; Cudgen Scrub till 1894; town gaz. 1865; sugar-cane 1869+, mineral sand mining, beans, farming; Angl. C. (St Mark's) 1882, new one 1916 on new site, damaged and repaired 1929, sold 1960; CH; FB; gales 1929 and 1950; Kanaka C. (St John's) 1895; Meth. C. 1902, new one 1925; PO 1884; police barracks 1891; PS 1883–1937; school 1882, additions 1915 by Walter Bray, extra accommodation 1946 (in building removed from Middle Pocket), school closed, sold, relocated and reused 1983, new one 1982; sugar mills: Henry Robert Cazala and CSR (estab. 1882 as Eddyvale by William W. Julius, demolished and rebuilt 1884, sold 1892 to Robb & Co., bought 1912 by CSR, closed, demolished 1962); telegraph 1890; telephone 1907; trees (memorial) planted in streets 1918 and 1945; TX 1913, automatic 1938; water supply augmentation 1963; wharf b. 1885 by David Rankin; pop. 338 (1891), 380 (1901), 185 (1911), 198 (1933), 296 (1947), 336 (1954), 321 (1961), 526 (2011).

Cudgen (*Co. Rous*) see also Chinderah.

Cudgen Headland (*Co. Rous*) see Kingscliff.

Cudgen Scrub (*Co. Rous*) see Cudgen.

Cudgera Creek (*Co. Rous*) 28°24'S. 153°31'E., 5 km W. of Pottsville, on Cudgera Ck; bananas and dairying; PO 1916, burnt down 1933; school 1908–75; telephone 1914; TX 1915; pop. 228 (1933), 183 (1947), 157 (1954), 138 (1961), 386 (2011).

Cudgera Headland (*Co. Rous*) see Hastings Point.

Cudmirrah (*Co. St Vincent*) 35°12'S. 150°34'E., 5 km SW of Sussex Inlet, on Tasman Sea; (incl. Berrara, settled 1866 by Daniel and Eliza Glanville); settled 1948 by Nicholas Collier; FB 1958 (new station b. 2000, extended 2009); PO 1957; telephone 1958; TX 1958; pop. 16 (1961), 316 (1981), 346 (1986), 498 (1991), 551 (1996), 579 (2001), 600 (2006), 559 (2011).

Cugong (*Co. Cunningham*) 32°58'S. 146°43'E., 42 km W. of Condobolin; gold (disc. 1895 by McClure and Linden); mines: Dry Blower 1902 and 1936–38, and Yellow Streak (or No. 1 South) 1895–96, 1902, 1903, 1926, 1936–37; PO 1880–97; school 1966–70.

Culburra (*Co. St Vincent*) 34°56'S. 150°47'E., 17 km E. of Nowra, on Tasman Sea; Union C.; pop. 136 (1961).

Culburra Beach (*Co. St Vincent*) 34°56'S. 150°45'E., 15 km SE of Nowra, on Tasman Sea; Warrain Beach till 1970; d. by Walter

Burley Griffin; tourism; ambulance station; Angl. C. (St John's); Bapt. C.; FB; PO 1970; PS; Rom. Cath. C. (Our Lady Help of Christians) 1978; school 1976; sewerage augmentation 1985; pop. 1,416 (1976, incl. Orient Point), 2,068 (1981, incl. Orient Point), 2,525 (1986, incl. Orient Point), 3,145 (1991, incl. Orient Point), 3,533 (1996, incl. Orient Point), 3,622 (2001, incl. Orient Point), 3,416 (2006, incl. Orient Point), 3,289 (2011, incl. Orient Point).

Culcairn (*Co. Hume*) 35°40'S. 147°02'E., 26 km W. of Holbrook, on Billabong Ck; estab. by German Lutherans, laid out 1880 by James Balfour as private town, till 1890; wheat, chaff, clover seed, wool; abattoir (Alec Beer); Angl. C. (St Paul's) b. 1912–15 by Barrie and Binding, d. by Thompson; Assemblies of God C. (Living Word); brickworks (Manning's) 1907; bridge 1907 by W. Farquharson, new one 1967, over Billabong Ck; bushfire 1969; cemetery (918 graves 1902+) 1898, incl. columbarium; CH b. 1926 by D.M. Mitchell, repairs 1938 by J.S. and H. Gamble; chaff mill estab. 1916 by Gus. R. Kleinig, J.E. Kleinig and Arthur Stockman, became A.H. Stockman & Co. Pty Ltd in 1921, taken over 1926 by John Crennan & Co. Ltd, bought by Alfred Haberecht; concrete (Pre-Mix) plant 1976, new plant 1977; diphtheria 1905; engineering works (Wilson's) b. 1913 by F.W. Scholz; FB (station b. 1973); flood 1931; flour mill (J. Burrows Pty Ltd); gale 1905; hospital (cottage) 1939, became district hospital in 1947, additions 2018; ice works (Walter Craig); Lutheran C. (St Stephen's) 1967 d. by M.L. Schoff; Meth. C. b. 1918 by J.S. Gamble, demolished 1981; mouse plague 1917; PO 1880, new one b. 1909 by Hardy & Co., additions 1914 by Barrie and Binding; powerhouse estab. by F.W. Scholz, taken over by Stockman & Co., taken over by A.L. Haberecht, taken over 1934 by Murrell Bros, trading as Culcairn Electricity Co., closed 1952; Presb. C. 1888, additions 1913 by Gamble Bros, reused; PS b. 1914 by Barrie and Binding, new one b. 1926 by D.M. Mitchell, repairs 1938 by J.S. and H. Gamble; quarry; railway coal stage 1899; railway turntable 1899, 50 ft (15.2 m), new one 1928, 60 ft (18.3 m); reservoirs: concrete tower 76 ft (23.2 m), 200,000 gal. (909.2 kl) and steel tower 1981; Rom. Cath. C. 1902, additions and alterations 1928 by C. Hardy & Co., new one (St Patrick's) 1967, fire 1969; RS 1880, station b. by Charles Hardy; sale-yards estab. 1928 by New Zealand Loan & Co., bought by Jack Hynes, bought 1950 by W. Hayes, bought by Goldsbrough Mort & Co., later bought back by Hynes; schools: Billabong HS b. 1978 by Seibel Bros, additions 1980, and Culcairn primary b. 1889 by E. Scanlon, additions 1890 by C. Hardy, additions 1903 by J. Wyatt, additions 1913 by Gamble Bros, additions 1924, 1953, 1959, 1966, additions 2010 by Barker Constructions Pty Ltd; sewerage 1972; silo 1920, extended 1923 and 1929; snow 1899; steel fabrication works (Culcairn Steel Fabrication) 1997, formerly W.O.K. Engineering; storm 1923; straw envelope factory (Jack G. Dallwitz) 1949–53; telegraph 1880, new office b. 1909 by Hardy & Co., additions 1914 by Barrie and Binding; TX 1910, automatic 1966; Unit. C. (St Andrew's, orig. Presb.) 1966; water supply (artesian) 1926, reticulation 1934, aeration plant and pumping station 1981; pop. 197 (1891), 253 (1901), 667 (1911), 1,169 (1933), *c.*1,100 (1941), 1,054 (1947), 1,093 (1954), 932 (1961), 1,019 (1966), 965 (1971), 933 (1976), 1,027 (1981), 1,138 (1986), 1,175 (1991), 1,164 (1996), 1,019 (2001), 1,120 (2006), 1,120 (2011).

Culgoora (*Co. White*) 30°17'S. 149°35'E., 15 km E. of Wee Waa; observatory (CSIRO) 1967; PO 1927; RS (Round Swamp till 1913) 1903, station b. by J. Bromley, closed 1975; sawmill (Budd Ireland), burnt down 1924; telephone 1916; pop. 63 (1911), 20 (1933).

Cullarin (*Co. Argyle*) see Cullerin.

Cullen (*Co. Roxburgh*) see Portland.

Cullenbone (*Co. Wellington*) 32°29'S. 149°30'E., 14 km S. of Gulgong, on Cudgegong R.; (incl. Slashers Flat, formerly Splashers Flat); goldmining, farming, grazing; bridge

(Belinfante Bridge) b. 1875 by J.G. Cummins, replaced 1919 by Herbert Ernest Ibbotson, over Cudgegong R.; bushfire 1875; fires 1905 and 1912; mine (Royal George Gold Mining Co.) 1870–71 and 1897–99; PO 1873; school (Green Swamp till 1863) 1862–1963; telephone 1911; Union C.; wool-scour (Atkinson and Dean) 1869; pop. 53 (1901), *c.*100 (1903), 227 (1911), 24 (1933), 65 (1947), 105 (1954), 82 (1961).

Cullen Bullen (*Co. Roxburgh*) 33°18'S. 150°02'E., 7 km N. of Portland, on Cullen Ck; grazing then mining; Angl. C. (St Aidan's), demolished; bushfires 1933 and 1951; cemetery (244 graves 1917+), incl. columbarium (unused); collieries: Baal Bone (Xtrata), Cullen Bullen Coal & Coke Co. (sold and closed 1900), Cullen Valley Open-Cut (Lithgow Coal Co.), Invincible (estab. 1905 by William Crawford, jun. and William Hart, later bought by Joe Cornock from Austen & Bullen Pty Ltd, acquired by Invincible Colliery Ltd), Renown (closed 1930, reopened 1934, 2 killed 1941); electricity 1929; FB; Meth. C. 1915, demolished; miners' strikes 1890, 1909, 1916, 1925, 1929, 1942, 1943, 1945, 1953; PO 1861, burnt down 1915, reopened, closed 1993; PS 1915–62; railway turntable, 60 ft (18.3 m), ruined; Rom. Cath. C. (St Canice's) 1925, new one (St Brendan's) 1943, removed from Sunny Corner and re-erected by James Hoctor; RS (Carson's Siding till 1896) 1889, new station 1927 on new site, closed 1976; school 1890, repairs 1898 by J.W. Frazer, additions 1918 by W.J. Bailey; telephone 1896; TX 1921; pop. 87 (1901), 283 (1911), 622 (1933), 464 (1947), 480 (1954), 439 (1961), 240 (1971), 232 (1976), 231 (1981), 263 (1986), 198 (1996), 207 (2001), 197 (2006), 183 (2011).

Cullendore (*Co. Buller*) 28°27'S. 152°09'E., 68 km N. of Tenterfield, on Cullendore Ck; grazing; cemetery; PO 1927; pop. 54 (1911), 44 (1933).

Cullendulla (*Co. St Vincent*) 35°40'S. 150°13'E., 5 km NE of Batemans Bay, on Cullendulla Ck; sawmill (Francis Guy); tramway; wharf.

Cullen Siding (*Co. Roxburgh*) see Portland.

Cullerin (*Co. Argyle*) 34°47'S. 149°25'E., 29 km W. of Goulburn; largely defunct; farming and grazing; PO 1909; RS 1880–1973; school (Cullarin till *c.*1920) 1880, new one b. 1884 by G. Dalton, repairs 1903 by Peter Poidevin, new building b. 1918 by A. Allen, closed 1964; telephone 1914; TX 1928; pop. 70 (1911), 103 (1933), 79 (1947), 70 (1954), 72 (1961).

Cullinga (*Co. Harden*) 34°36'S. 148°10'E., 14 km E. of Cootamundra; mining (gold disc. by Johnson) till 1940 and farming; Angl. C. (St John's, renamed St Augustine's) 1884, closed, ruined; creamery (Co-op. Creamery Co.) 1895; gale 1893; mines: Christmas Gift 1908 (incl. stamper battery), Cullinga Extended 1910 (incl. 10 head stamper battery), Federal (gold disc. by Tilden and McLeod, incl. 15 head stamper battery and dam); PO 1878; Presb. C., in former Angl. C. removed from Currawang by McLeod and Affleck Bros, burnt down 1926, replaced 1928; scarlet fever 1882; schools: Cullinga (Wallendbeen till 1881) 1876–1914 and Cullinga Mines 1904–43; Wes. Meth. C. b. 1884 by B. Ford, renovated and rededicated 1952; pop. 117 (1901), 195 (1911), 58 (1947), 59 (1961).

Cullinga Mines (*Co. Harden*) see Cullinga.

Cullivel (*Co. Urana*) 35°16'S. 146°23'E., 31 km W. of Lockhart; horse dip 1937; RS 1911, station b. by John Allibone, closed 1975; school 1915, additions 1920 by J. Henderson, closed 1962; silo 1920; pop. 55 (1911), 79 (1933), 110 (1947), 87 (1961).

Cullulla (*Co. Argyle*) 35°06'S. 149°49'E., 38 km N. of Braidwood, on Nadgigomar Ck; silver-lead (disc. 1889 by O'Neill, Blake et al.); mines: Cullulla silver-lead mine 1893 and Curra Creek copper mine 1890.

Cullya (*Co. Wellington*) 33°12'S. 149°07'E., 9 km N. of Orange; quarry; RS 1910–72; winery (Mortimers of Orange); pop. 59 (1947).

Culmaran Creek (*Co. Drake*) 28°52'S. 152°42'E., 35 km W. of Casino, on Culmaran Ck; telephone 1926; TX 1952; pop. 57 (1933), 75 (1947), 53 (1961).

Culpaulin (*Co. Young*) 31°44'S. 143°13'E., 24

km SW of Wilcannia, on Darling R.; pop. 39 (1933).

Cultowa (*Co. Werunda*) 31°29'S. 144°01'E., 65 km E. of Wilcannia.

Cumavon (*Co. Sturt*) 34°07'S. 145°58'E., 19 km N. of Griffith; telephone 1929; TX 1930.

Cumbalum (*Co. Rous*) 28°50'S. 153°32'E., 6 km NW of Ballina, on Emigrant Ck; Emigrant Creek till 1893; farming and dairying; bridge (Garney Koellner Bridge) over Emigrant Ck; PO 1907–42; school 1889–1934; telephone 1913; pop. 81 (1901), 127 (1911), 89 (1933), 63 (1947), 74 (1954), 76 (1961), 871 (2011).

Cumbamurra (*Co. Harden*) 34°36'S. 148°28'E., 13 km SE of Murrumburrah, on Rocky Ponds Ck; laid out 1864, village gaz. 1865, never developed; pop. 20 (1933).

Cumbijowa (*Co. Forbes*) 33°27'S. 148°11'E., 18 km SE of Forbes; TX (automatic); pop. 55 (1911).

Cumbil (*Co. Baradine*) 30°47'S. 149°07'E., 18 km N. of Baradine; PO 1927; pop. 56 (1933).

Cumboogle (*Co. Gordon*) 32°19'S. 148°36'E., 9 km S. of Dubbo; RS 1925–74, station removed 1983.

Cumborah (*Co. Finch*) 29°45'S. 147°46'E., 40 km SW of Lightning Ridge; Comborah till 1910; gemstones, gravel pits, grazing; Angl. C. (St Peter's in the Pines) 1912; cemetery (78 graves) 1897; PO 1898, burnt down 1938; PS 1897–1934; sawmill (Robert Potts); school (Comborah Springs till 1912) 1904–42; telephone 1901; TX 1912; pop. 79 (1911), 81 (1933), 82 (1947), 65 (1961), 360 (2011).

Cumeroogunja (*Co. Cadell*) 36°02'S. 144°57'E., 19 km NE of Moama; Aboriginal mission; school (Cummeragunja) 1881–1951 and 1957–71; pop. 236 (1901), 240 (1911), 226 (1933), 79 (1947).

Cummeragunja (*Co. Cadell*) see Cumeroogunja.

Cumnock (*Co. Gordon*) 32°56'S. 148°45'E., 21 km NW of Molong, on Doughboy Ck; orig. Doughboy Creek then Crossroads *c.*1860–78; farming and grazing; Angl. C. 1882, re-roofed 1899 by J. Marston, extensions 1904 by William Gadd, d. by William Lamrock, jun., transepts 1907, closed 1928 and acquired by Rom. Cath. C., new one (St Matthew's) b. 1929 on new site, begun by Hoepper and Shaw but completed by C.W. Evans, d. by Louis Reginald Williams, additions 1986; brick-kiln (D. Starr) 1899; butter factory (Christian Miller) 1891; cemetery (409 graves 1884+); CH (incl. police station and lock-up) b. 1902 by Rigby Bros, d. by Walter Liberty Vernon, reused; copper mine (Boomalli Ltd); creamery (Molong Dist. Dairying Co.) 1901; dust storm 1929; earth tremor 1934; FB; flood (man died) 1914; fruit canning and jam factory (Burrawong Fruit Co.) 1895, burnt down 1910; grasshopper infestations 1904 and 1907; Meth. C. 1904 (removed from Dilga); PO 1879, new one o. 1899 in rented premises, new one b. 1901 by Rigby Bros, renovated 1907 by William Gadd; pound (stock) 1891; Presb. C. (John Bruce Memorial) b. 1909 by Joseph Fleming Walker, d. by William Lamrock, jun., closed, sold 2005 and 2017; PS b. 1889 by Black; 3 quarries; Rom. Cath. C. (St Dympna's) 1882; RS 1925–89; school 1880, new buildings b. 1881 by James Prior Hull, additions 1888 by James Mitchell, new building b. 1910 by J. Bartlett, new building 1921, additions 1961; silo 1928; telegraph 1899; telephone 1891; TX 1911; Union C.; pop. 305 (1901), 629 (1911), 759 (1933), 418 (1947), 474 (1954), 355 (1961), 230 (1971), 259 (1976), 252 (1981), 236 (1986), 263 (1991), 297 (1996), 266 (1999), 260 (2001), 288 (2006), 276 (2011).

Cundle Cundle (*Co. Macquarie*) see Kundle Kundle.

Cundle Flat (*Co. Macquarie*) 31°50'S. 152°01'E., 20 km N. of Gloucester, on Khatambuhl Ck; farming and dairying; earth tremor 1948; PO 1927; school (Callaghans Creek till 1893) 1888–93 and 1957–61; telephone 1915; TX 1927, automatic 1980; pop. 40 (1933), 57 (1954).

Cundletown (*Co. Macquarie*) 31°54'S. 152°31'E., 6 km E. of Taree, on Manning R.; first lots sold 1855 by Manning River Co., estab. 1856 as a private town, second land sales 1873, further lots sold 1907; former river port, dairying and agric.; airport (Taree) 1930, new one b. 1953 by L.G. Gleeson, navigational beacon installed 1962, night landing facilities installed 1963; Angl. C. 1870, new one (St Thomas's) b. 1916 by Stewart Adolphus Levick, d. by H. Wilfred Webster, extended, closed 2014; brick-kilns; bridges: Burdett-Smith Bridge 1879, to Taree, replacement (steel truss) 1933, over Dawson R., L.C. Jordan Bridge 1968 over North Passage of Manning R., Henry Hawkeye Edwards Bridge to Dumaresq Island over North Passage of Manning R.; cemetery (Dawson River, 3,757 graves 1848+), incl. lawn cemetery (2,998 plots) and columbaria; CH (incl. lock-up) b. 1869–71 by William John Smith, court-house section closed 1905, police station section closed 1936, sold 2002 and reused; Christ. Coptic Orthodox C. (St Mary and St Pope Kirolos) 2017 d. by Austin McFarland; dock (govt) 1888, 100 ft (30.5 m), dock crane supplied 1891 by Davy and Sands, dock extended 1908 by C. Henderson; engineering works (United Goninan & Co. Ltd); fires 1893, 1915, 1927, 1952; floods 1866, 1867, 1929, 1930, 1950, 1955, 1959, 1967, 1978; PO 1856, new one b. 1890–93 by J. Healy; Presb. C. 1886 (removed from Ghinni Ghinni), repairs 1899 by J.C. Dorward, renovated 1900, demolished 1958, new one (St Andrew's) 1960–99, sold and reused; PS, closed 1936; punts: one to Dumaresq Island (2 car capacity) across North Passage of Manning R. and one to Oxley Island (4 car capacity) across Manning R.; reservoir 1974; Rom. Cath. C. 1856, relocated 1908 by Stewart Adolphus Levick, new one (St Patrick's) 1909; sawmills; school 1857, additions 1876 by Albury, new one b. 1892 by James Levick, d. by William Edmund Kemp, repairs 1910 by Holden and Carle, additions 1970; sewerage 1973, augmentation 1986; slipway; smallpox 1916; streets electric lit 1930; telegraph 1878, new office b. 1890–93 by J. Healy, telegraph ceased 1907; telephone 1907; TX 1911, automatic 1955; Unit. C. (orig. Meth.) b. 1967 by R.J. Burg Pty Ltd; water reticulation 1961; Wes. Meth. C. b. 1870 by James Levick, renovated 1930, closed 1966; wharves: Carle's, demolished 1995, govt one b. 1878 by W. Smith, N.C.S.N. Co.; pop. 150 (1861), 121 (1871), 217 (1881), 279 (1891), 266 (1901), 446 (1911), *c.*500 (1924), 497 (1933), 555 (1947), 670 (1954), 2,064 (2011).

Cundumbul (*Co. Gordon*) 32°50'S. 148°54'E., 29 km N. of Molong, on Two Mile Ck; farming and grazing; bushfire 1909; PO 1916; school 1880–94; TX 1927; pop. 25 (1933), 57 (1954), 56 (1961).

Cungegong (*Co. Harden*) see Frampton.

Cunjaree Basin (*Co. Fitzroy*) 29°59'S. 153°04'E., 20 km NW of Woolgoolga.

Cunjegong (*Co. Harden*) see Frampton.

Cunjurong Point (*Co. St Vincent*) 35°16'S. 150°31'E., 9 km NE of Milton, on Tasman Sea; (incl. Berringer Lake and Manyana); tourism; bushfire 1994; FB 1972; PO 1964–80; reservoir; pop. 6 (1961), 364 (1986), 429 (1991), 468 (1996), 488 (2001), 571 (2006), 577 (2011).

Cunningar (*Co. Harden*) 34°34'S. 148°25'E., 7 km E. of Murrumburrah, on Cunningham Plains Ck; Cunningham till 1919; laid out 1857, first lots sold 1858, town gaz. 1881; farming and grazing; FB; Meth. C. 1917 (removed from Aurville); olive oil factory (Michael and Lorraine Brown); PO 1871; RS 1877–1975, station removed 1976; school 1870, burnt down 1889, rebuilt, closed 1960; silo 1931; telephone 1915; pop. 179 (1933), 143 (1947), 118 (1954), 95 (1961).

Cunningham (*Co. Harden*) see Cunningar.

Cunningham Creek (*Co. Harden*) 34°35'S. 148°20'E., 4 km S. of Murrumburrah; school 1894 b. by Farrow and Farrow, additions 1895 by John A. Vogt, closed 1911.

Cunninyeuk (*Co. Wakool*) 35°12'S. 143°51'E., 52 km NW of Barham, on Cunninyeuk Ck; bridge over Cunninyeuk Ck; TX (automatic); pop. 56 (1954), 78 (1961).

Curagudde (*Co. Auckland*) 37°00'S. 149°55'E., 6 km S. of Pambula Beach, on Tasman Sea.

Curban (*Co. Ewenmar*) 31°33'S. 148°35'E., 20 km N. of Gilgandra, on Castlereagh R.;

farming; bridges: one b. 1929 by J.A. Jackson & Son, new one 2004, over Castlereagh R. and one b. 1933, new one (concrete) 2014 d. by Barnson, over Terrabile Ck; cemetery (19 graves 1886–1997); floods 1950 and 1955; PO 1878; pound (stock) 1869; RS (4 km SW) 1903, station b. by John Allibone and McCarthy, closed 1974; silo (4 km SW) 1930; telephone 1898; TX 1915, automatic 1985; Union C. 1895, (second) 1915, (third) 1955; pop. 106 (1901), 214 (1911), 231 (1933), 97 (1947), 135 (1954), 251 (1961).

Curenbenya (*Co. Gordon*) 32°59'S. 148°37'E., 27 km NW of Molong, on Paling Yards Ck.

Curia Creek (*Co. Dampier*) 36°20'S. 150°02'E., 9 km N. of Bermagui; school 1892–1914.

Curlew (*Co. Dowling*) 33°15'S. 146°26'E., 9 km NE of Lake Cargelligo; irrigated orchards; FB; pop. 38 (1933).

Curlewis (*Co. Pottinger*) 31°07'S. 150°16'E., 15 km S. of Gunnedah; disc. 1818 by John Joseph William Molesworth Oxley, founded by Henry Thomas Pike, surveyed 1885 by Edwin W. Turner, laid out and village gaz. 1886; wheat, timber, coal (disc. 1887 by Alfred Lithgow Poole), fruit, vegetables; Angl. C. (St Peter's) 1907, closed; bushfire 1905; cemetery (206 graves 1903+) 1888; coalmine (Centenary Coal & Coke Co.) 1888, acquired by Preston Iron, Coke & Coal Mining Co. Ltd, renamed Preston Colliery, closed 1936, reopened 1941 as Nevil Mine, renamed Preston Extended Mine, bought 1989 by Bob Cameron, closed 1999; Community C. (formerly Unit.); dam b. 1902 by H. Ryman; electricity 1951; FB (station b. 1968); Meth. C. b. 1905 by Jonathon Cook, (second) b. 1924 by Walter Richmond, d. by Vernon and Mills, (third) b. 1982; miners' strike 1947; PO 1883, new one b. 1908 by Thomas John Bowen, repairs 1955 by E.T. Thompson; plant breeding station (Waterhouse) 1945–62; PS 1900, new one (incl. lock-up) b. 1908 by Alfred Stephens; 2 reservoirs, 40,000 gal. (1,81.8 kl) each; Rom. Cath. C. (St Alphonsus's) b. 1905 by Thomas John Bowen; RS 1880, new station 1891, burnt down 1898, replaced, closed 1975, demolished 1979; sawmills: John H. Kettlewell and Henry Pike 1879; school 1886, new one b. 1892 by Robert Williams, additions 1907 and 1913; sewerage augmentation 1991; silo 1934; telegraph 1890; telephone 1909; TX 1910; water reticulation 1972, augmentation 1981 and 1984; pop. 112 (1901), 992 (1911), 501 (1933), 476 (1947), 579 (1954), 438 (1961), 330 (1971), 291 (1976), 487 (1981), 583 (1986), 651 (1991), 613 (1996), 575 (2001), 603 (2006), 590 (2011).

Curlwa (*Co. Wentworth*) see Curlwaa.

Curlwaa (*Co. Wentworth*) 34°06'S. 141°59'E., 7 km E. of Wentworth, on Murray R.; Curlwa till 1941; orchards and vineyards; bridge (Abbotsford Bridge) b. 1925–28 by Christiani & Nielson (Aust.) Pty Ltd as a railway bridge but never used as such, steel Pratt trusses and lift-span, 790 ft (240.8 m), over Murray R.; FB 1979 (station b. 1987); flood 1956; fruit packing houses: Curlwaa Co-op. Fruit Packing Co. Ltd 1929 and Mildura Co-op. Fruit Co. Ltd 1911, extended 1939; hailstorm 1998; Jehovah's Witnesses C. 1974; levee 1958; PO 1916; punt (Abbotsford), ceased 1928, across Murray R.; school 1917 b. by W. Wood, additions 1926 by J.A. McGeorge, additions 1934, closed 1974; telephone 1916; TX 1941, automatic; Unit. C. (orig. Meth.) b. 1936 by McWaters; water pumping station (pumping capacity doubled 1921); pop. 658 (1933), 587 (1961), 403 (2006), 413 (2011).

Currabubula (*Co. Buckland*) 31°16'S. 150°44'E., 12 km NE of Werris Creek, on Currabubula Ck; surveyed 1851 by John Valentine Gorman, founded by John Martin Davis, first land sale 1854, town gaz. 1860; wheat and wool; Angl. C. (St Matthew's) 1901, damaged 1995 and removed; brickworks (C. and J. White); bridge (Bennetts Bridge) over Currabubula Ck; cemetery (129 graves 1876+) 1886; electricity 1931; FB; PO 1861; PS 1879, demolished 1898, replaced 1898 by Moran Bros; rabbit freezing works b. 1922 by W. Tighe and A.J. Rollo, burnt down 1932; railway collision 1898; Rom. Cath. C. b. 1897 by Alexander Lees, demolished, new one (St

Michael's) b. 1908 by J. Holt, d. by Philip Ernest Ranclaud, renovated 1979, closed, sold 1998 and 2008, reused; RS 1878–1985; school 1882 b. by Lambert & Co., alterations 1888 by Byron and Schwartz, additions 2010; storm 1995; telegraph 1890; TX 1916; Unit. C. (orig. Union) b. 1883 by Elsley; pop. *c.*100 (1866), 360 (1901), 557 (1911), 235 (1933), 223 (1947), 411 (1954), 156 (1961), 388 (2006), 321 (2011).

Curra Creek (*Co. Gordon*) 32°42'S. 148°49'E., 20 km SW of Wellington, on Curra Ck; mining (gold disc. 1890 by Gates) and farming; cemetery (Rozelayne, 36 graves 1883–1959); mine (Gunner's Dam or Southern Cross or Corkers, o. 1890, worked by Southern Cross Gold Mining Co., H. Mearns and Boomalli Ltd) 1908–9 and 1914–18; PO 1902–36; school 1884–1902 and 1957–65; Union C. 1899; pop. 232 (1901), 174 (1911), 221 (1933), 129 (1947), 139 (1954), 210 (1961).

Curragh (*Co. Georgiana*) 33°58'S. 149°12'E., 47 km S. of Blayney; goldmine (Boltrells Tunnel).

Curraghmohr (*Co. Denison*) 35°40'S. 145°37'E., 4 km SE of Finley; RS 1898–1958.

Currajong (*Co. Ashburnham*) see Parkes.

Curramanga (*Co. Jamison*) 30°01'S. 149°57'E., 37 km NE of Narrabri; school 1964–82.

Curramore (*Co. Camden*) 34°37'S. 150°47'E., 9 km NW of Kiama; pop. 228 (2011).

Currandooley (*Co. Murray*) 35°10'S. 149°30'E., 11 km NE of Bungendore, on Wrights Ck; pop. 29 (1933), 54 (1954).

Currans Creek (*Co. King*) 34°26'S. 149°23'E., 8 km W. of Crookwell; school 1895, new building b. 1903 by A. Allen, closed 1925.

Curranyale (*Co. Livingstone*) 32°07'S. 142°49'E., 79 km SW of Wilcannia, on Darling R.

Curranyalpa (*Co. Rankin*) 30°54'S. 144°41'E., 141 km NE of Wilcannia, on Darling R.; PS 1883–91.

Currarong (*Co. St Vincent*) 35°01'S. 150°49'E., 14 km E. of Huskisson, on Crookhaven Bight; village gaz. 1947; crayfish 1926+, coastal fishing and tourism; Angl. C. (St Luke's); bushfire 1965; Church of God; electricity 1956; FB; PO 1945; sewage works; telephone 1938; TX 1943–46; pop. 79 (1947), 100 (1954), 126 (1961), 176 (1966), 408 (1971), 466 (1976), 518 (1981), 566 (1986), 572 (1991), 554 (1996), 549 (2001), 513 (2006), 457 (2011).

Currathool (*Co. Sturt*) see Carrathool.

Currawananna (*Co. Bourke*) see Currawarna.

Currawang (*Co. Argyle*) 34°59'S. 149°31'E., 32 km N. of Bungendore; formerly Currawong and Currowang; estab. *c.*1865, thrived 1873, declined 1878+, now largely defunct; mining (copper disc. 1853) 1865–82 and 1897–1907, agric., sheep and dairying 1882+; Angl. C. (St Matthias's) 1875 d. by Andrea Giovanni Stombuco, re-roofed, damaged 1923, re-roofed again, renovated, and graveyard; brewery (Samuel Williams) 1876–78; dairy factory (Frederick McKinley); gale 1923; mine estab. 1866 by Currawang Copper Mining Co., reformed 1872 as Phoenix Copper Mining Co., bought by Esk Co., closed 1879, reopened 1880 by Currawang Copper Mining Co. (wound up 1882), taken over 1987 by Woodlawn for the mining of lead-silver-zinc suphides; PO 1866; school 1870, new one b. 1872 by John Armstrong, closed 1944; 5 smelters; telephone 1914; TX 1930, automatic 1962; Wes. Meth. C.; pop. *c.*300–400 (1866–75), *c.*150–250 (1876–85), 140 (1901), 135 (1911), 126 (1933), 53 (1947), 180 (2006).

Currawang South (*Co. Argyle*) 35°00'S. 149°31'E., 29 km N. of Bungendore; Willaroo till 1917; PO 1899; telephone 1914; TX 1926–32.

Currawarna (*Co. Bourke*) 35°01'S. 147°04'E., 25 km SW of Coolamon, on Murrumbidgee R.; village gaz. 1880 as Currawananna; farming and dairying; cemetery (graves 1904+); cheese factory (Crubben Pty Ltd); FB; grasshopper infestation 1928; PO 1900; Rom. Cath. C. b. 1890 by Morgan, new one 1909; sawmills: William and Edmund N. Gibbs, and T. Milne 1908; school 1900 b. by Hardy & Co., closed 2004; telephone 1905; TX 1923, automatic 1972; Union C. b. 1907 by J. Gowland; pop. 65 (1901), 219 (1911), 232

(1933), 83 (1947), 113 (1954), 109 (1961), 245 (2006), 226 (2011).

Currawarna (*Co. Bourke*) see also Cottee.

Curraweela (*Co. Georgiana*) 34°16'S. 149°47'E., 36 km NE of Crookwell; grazing; Angl. C. (St John's) b. 1900 by J. and G. Pollock; PO 1872–1936; telephone 1913; TX 1924; pop. 65 (1901), 44 (1933).

Currawinga (*Co. Irrara*) see Hungerford.

Currawong (*Co. Argyle*) see Currawang.

Currawong (*Co. Harden*) 34°28'S. 148°22'E., 10 km N. of Murrumburrah, on Currawong Ck; laid out 1864 by W. Edwards, village gaz. 1865; agric.; Angl. C. (variously known as St Mark's, St Matthew's and St Matthias's) 1888, replacement (Roberts Memorial) b. 1919 by W.S. Millard & Sons Ltd, d. by Henry Hamilton Crigan, closed 1956, reopened 1962, and graveyard (34 graves 1919+); cemetery; school (Harden till 1885, then Tiverton) 1875, additions 1914 by M. Lawless, closed 1919; pop. 94 (1911), 39 (1933).

Currawong (*Co. Wellesley*) 36°57'S. 148°51'E., 35 km W. of Bombala, on Currowang Ck.

Currency Creek (*Co. Cook*) see Glossodia.

Curriba (*Co. Dowling*) 33°30'S. 146°37'E., 32 km SE of Lake Cargelligo; school 1957–66.

Curricabark (*Co. Hawes*) 31°43'S. 151°41'E., 40 km NW of Gloucester, on Curricabark Ck; grazing; pop. 54 (1947).

Currockbilly (*Co. St Vincent*) 35°23'S. 149°59'E., 17 km E. of Braidwood; bushfire 1929; school 1882–85, sold 1899, new one b. 1898 by Hugh McCrae, reopened 1902, burnt down 1917, replaced 1919, closed 1927, burnt down 1929.

Currowan (*Co. St Vincent*) 35°34'S. 150°10'E., 15 km N. of Batemans Bay, on Currowan Ck; village gaz. 1844; mining (gold disc. 1859); causeway across Currowan Ck; school 1884–88; starch factory (Austral Starch Co. Ltd) 1920–22; pop. 79 (1891), 90 (1911), 30 (1933).

Currowan Creek (*Co. St Vincent*) 35°34'S. 150°03'E., 19 km NW of Batemans Bay, on Currowan Ck; causeway across Currowan Ck.

Currowang (*Co. Argyle*) see Currawang.

Curryall (*Co. Bligh*) 32°02'S. 149°52'E., 28 km SE of Coolah, on Sawpit Ck; school 1907–46 and 1957–64; pop. 53 (1911).

Curryjong (*Co. Cook*) see Kurrajong.

Cuthero (*Co. Windeyer*) 33°02'S. 142°21'E., 125 km N. of Wentworth, on Darling R.; school 1889–1914; telephone 1953; TX 1953; pop. 84 (1911), 43 (1933).

Cuttabri (*Co. White*) 30°20'S. 149°13'E., 25 km SW of Wee Waa, on Coghill Ck; farming and grazing; PO 1892–1971; sawmill (Burke and Schwager); telephone 1915; TX 1917; pop. 148 (1933), 82 (1947), 82 (1954), 83 (1961).

Cuttagee (*Co. Dampier*) 36°29'S. 150°03'E., 6 km S. of Bermagui; bridge over Cuttagee Lake; sawmill (Thornton's), burnt down 1913; pop. 50 (1911), 54 (1933).

D

Dabee (*Co. Phillip*) 32°49'S. 150°01'E., 5 km E. of Rylstone, on Cudgegong R.; never developed; wool; airfield; school 1882–89; pop. 149 (2006).

Dagworth (*Co. Northumberland*) see Louth Park.

Dahwilly (*Co. Townsend*) 35°25'S. 144°53'E., 15 km NW of Deniliquin, on Dahwilly Main Channel; village gaz. 1879.

Dairy Arm (*Co. Northumberland*) 33°02'S. 151°09'E., 19 km SW of Paxton, on Dairy Arm; pop. 33 (1933).

Dairy Flat (*Co. Rous*) 28°23'S. 152°43'E., 38 km NW of Kyogle, on Richmond R.; creamery (Foley Bros); telephone 1933; TX 1933; pop. 63 (1933), 71 (1947), 124 (1954), 68 (1961).

Dairymans Plains (*Co. Beresford*) 36°13'S. 149°03'E., 8 km W. of Cooma; school 1884–90 and 1899–1913; pop. 86 (1954).

Dairyville (*Co. Fitzroy*) 30°16'S. 152°58'E., 14 km W. of Coffs Harbour, on Urumbilum Ck; dairying; foot-bridge, damaged 1914; gale 1914; PO 1908, burnt down 1939; school 1915–50; telephone 1912; TX 1916; pop. 81 (1911), 70 (1933), 80 (1947).

Daisy Bank (*Co. Westmoreland*) 33°52'S. 149°42'E., 23 km SW of Oberon; school 1899–1927 and 1957–68.

Daisydale (*Co. Goulburn*) see Dighton.

Daisy Hill (*Co. Auckland*) 36°41'S. 149°46'E., 6 km W. of Bega; pop. 36 (1933).

Daisy Park (*Co. Cunningham*) 33°15'S. 147°48'E., 25 km NW of Forbes.

Daisy Patch (*Co. Hawes*) 31°22'S. 151°56'E., 52 km SE of Walcha.

Daisy Plains (*Co. Dudley*) 30°56'S. 152°18'E., 53 km W. of Kempsey; sawmill; school 1957–60.

Daisy Plains (*Co. Nicholson*) see Hillston.

Daleys Point (*Co. Northumberland*) see Empire Bay.

Dalgety (*Co. Wallace*) 36°30'S. 148°50'E., 15 km S. of Berridale, on Snowy R.; Buckley's Crossing Place till 1900, and formerly also known as Barnes's Crossing Place; surveyed 1874 by J.R. Campbell, plan approved 1875, village gaz. 1880, first lots sold 1881, thrived 1890; wheat, grazing, fishing; Angl. C. (St Peter's) 1924; bridge (iron lattice truss) b. 1889 by J. Gay, d. by John Alexander McDonald, over Snowy R.; CH (incl. lock-up) b. 1875 by David Scarlett; earth tremor 1878; FB (station b. 2012); flood 1922; PO 1860; PS b. 1876 by David Scarlett, closed 1957, reused; punt (Buckley Bros) 1860, destroyed 1870, replaced, across Snowy R.; reservoir 1956; rifle range 1910; Rom. Cath. C. (Our Lady Star of the Sea) b. by Peter Poidevin, additions 1910 by Arthur Mawson, d. by George Donald Cochran, restored 1978 by Kevin Schaefer; sale-yards 1937; school 1889, new building b. 1909 by M. Avery; telephone 1891; TX 1917, automatic 1988; water supply augmentation 1956, 1986, 1991; wattle-bark mill (Craig, Mostyn & Co.); winery (Snowy Valley); pop. *c.*59 (1859), 23 (1864–66), 76 (1901), 113 (1911), 132 (1933), 179 (1947), 78 (1954), 121 (1961), 214 (2011).

Dalhousie Creek (*Co. Raleigh*) 30°33'S. 153°01'E., 5 km S. of Urunga; RS 1950–63.

Dalkeith (*Co. Bligh*) see Cassilis.

Dallas (*Co. Cooper*) 34°34'S. 146°13'E., 18 km W. of Leeton; TX (automatic).

Dalman (*Co. Buller*) 28°22'S. 152°31'E., 54 km NW of Kyogle, on Woodenbong Ck; cheese factory (J. Watson); sawmill; telephone 1918; TX 1922; pop. 51 (1947), 83 (1954), 70 (1961).

Dalmeny (*Co. Dampier*) 36°10'S. 150°08'E., 6 km N. of Narooma, on Tasman Sea; subdivided 1930, 1933, 1937; orig. dairying, formerly tourism, retirement centre 1984+; bushfires 1963 and 1965; electricity 1953; FB 1960; foot-bridge 1980, over Mummuga Lake; Jehovah's Witnesses C.; PO 1952, closed, dismantled and removed 2012 by Graham Cannon; Rom. Cath. C. o. 1956 (removed from Eurobodalla), now seldom used; sawmill (Dalmeny Sawmills Pty Ltd) 1955, new adjacent one 1965–82; sewerage 1985; street tree plantings 1951; telegraph 1952; TX 1953, automatic 1979; pop. 72 (1961), 378 (1976), 670 (1981), 1,104 (1986), 1,476 (1991), 1,631 (1996), 1,785 (2001), 1,928 (2006), 1,931 (2011).

Dalmorton (*Co. Gresham*) 29°52'S. 152°27'E., 50 km W. of Grafton, on Boyd R.; village gaz. 1874, defunct; goldmining (reef), timber, grazing; brick-kiln 1898; bushfire 1936; cemetery 1899–1931; CH (incl. lock-up) b. 1899 by J.P. Josephson; PO 1872, burnt down 1950; PS, closed 1961; sawmill (Wade's), burnt down 1936; school 1891–1906; storm 1893; telegraph 1892; TX 1928; pop. 137 (1891), 86 (1901), 67 (1911), 44 (1933), 54 (1947).

Dalswinton (*Co. Durham*) 32°25'S. 150°42'E., 4 km S. of Denman; FB; TX (automatic); pop. 57 (1954), 71 (1961).

Dalton (*Co. King*) 34°44'S. 149°11'E., 28 km NE of Yass, on Oolong Ck; formerly Wesley Vale; settled 1847, surveyed 1861 by John Armstrong, jun., first lots sold 1862, town gaz. 1862; mining (gold disc. 1859) 1874–89 and 1930–41, wheat, dairying, wool, vineyards, apple orchards; Angl. C. (St Matthew's) 1878, chancel 1903, and graveyard; boot factory; bridge (timber beam) b. 1896 by Richard Hughes, 120 ft (36.6 m), over Oolong Ck; bushfire 1979; carriage-works; cemetery 1884; creamery (Dalton Creamery Co.) b. 1901 by Fred Dawe, d. by T.H. Gibson; diphtheria 1861; earth tremors 1886, 1934, 1949, 2000, 2008, 2015; electricity 1954; flour mill (John Wheatley) b. 1879 by R. Humphries, d. by W. Crispin, damaged 1883, reopened 1885, damaged 1897, reopened 1898, acquired 1900 by Robert Dowling, burnt down 1913; mines: T. Alchin 1937, Big or Budget or Collins Big or Dalton (J.P. Collins 1932–33, Murray Bros 1933, Dalton Gold Development NL 1934), Golden Dyke 1938, Honeyfields Lookout 1960, Jerrawa Creek 1888, King Solomon, Queen May, Star of Dalton (T. Starr), Wiseman and Holzigal; PO 1863, additions and repairs 1895 by Richard Hughes; pound (stock) 1878; PS (incl. lock-up) 1880, new one b. 1889 by Wheatley and Brander, additions 1919 by P.R. Thorn, closed 1943, sold and reused; reservoir b. 1889 by T.B. Brown; school (Wesley Vale 1860–63 and 1865–67) 1860, new one b. 1878 by Wheatley and Brander, additions 1959; stamper batteries (5 head, 15 head, 16 head); tannery; telegraph 1892; telephone 1908; TX 1915, automatic 1973; Unit. C. (orig. Wes. Meth.) b. 1858–60, and graveyard; water reticulation 1980; Wes. Meth. C. 1854, reused; winery; pop. 61 (1866), 342 (1891), 160 (1901), 382 (1911), 277 (1933), 228 (1947), 244 (1954), 204 (1961), *c.*100 (1991), 108 (2011).

Dalwood (*Co. Northumberland*) 32°38'S. 151°25'E., 7 km NE of Branxton, on Hunter R.; farming and dairying; creamery (W.H. Wyndham) 1892, bought 1904 by Frank Joseph Lappen Measures who estab. a butter factory instead, closed 1913; earth tremor 1868; flour mill b. 1831 by John Portus for George Wyndham; gravel pit; mine; PO 1889–1961; school (Marshwood till 1934) 1899–1970; storm 1962; telephone 1919; TX 1923, automatic 1954; winery (Dalwood Wines, renamed Wyndham Estate in 1970) estab. 1828 by George Wyndham; pop. 95 (1901), 145 (1933), 56 (1947), 87 (1954), 120 (1961).

Dalwood (*Co. Rous*) 28°52'S. 153°26'E., 3 km S. of Alstonville, on Gum Ck; Angl. C. (St Thomas's) 1897, moved 1945 by G. Wright to Meerschaum Vale; school 1891 b. by Arthur J. West, closed 1926; pop. 137 (1901), 50 (1933), 51 (1947), 53 (1954), 255 (2011).

Dalwood (*Co. Rous*) see also Rous.

Dalwood Richmond River (*Co. Rous*) see Rous.

Dandaloo (*Co. Narromine*) 32°16'S. 147°38'E., 57 km W. of Narromine, on Bogan R.; settled *c.*1857 by Florant John Martel, village gaz. 1873, laid out 1877, declined 1916+, now largely defunct; mining, agric., grazing; bridge b. 1886 by Alexander Biggs, new one (9 span) 1935, over Bogan R.; bushfire 1890; cemetery 1892; CH (incl. lock-up) 1872, new one 1895; fire 1928; floods 1905 and 1950; PO 1867; pound (stock) 1871; PS 1871–1933, moved 1938 to Trangie by Percy Young; school 1902–5 and 1910–32; telegraph 1889–1913; telephone 1886; TX 1929; Union C.; Unit. C. (Mausoleum, orig. private, then Presb. 1906–77) 1888, extended and restored 1965, and graveyard (11 burials 1869+); pop. 194 (1901), 396 (1911), 170 (1933), 88 (1947), 362 (2006).

Dandarbang (*Co. Wellington*) 33°01'S. 148°58'E., 13 km NE of Molong.

Dandinya (*Co. Cooper*) 34°33'S. 146°16'E., 14 km W. of Leeton; RS (Gogeldrie till 1915) 1905–25.

Dangar Bridge (*Co. Baradine*) 30°01'S. 148°04'E., 5 km W. of Walgett, on Barwon R.; bridge b. 1874–77, new one (Dare timber truss) b. 1930 by J.A. Jackson & Sons, 392 ft (119.5 m), over Barwon R.; telephone 1909.

Dangarfield (*Co. Durham*) 32°09'S. 151°00'E., 10 km E. of Aberdeen; subdivided 1895; dairying; cemetery; PO 1924; school (Segenhoe till 1923) 1905, new building b. 1930 by R.L. Hutchings, closed 1965; telephone 1900; TX 1925; pop. 63 (1933), 57 (1947), 53 (1954), 63 (1961).

Dangars Lagoon (*Co. Sandon*) 30°41'S. 151°30'E., 5 km S. of Uralla, on Dangars Lagoon; school 1886–1906.

Dangarsleigh (*Co. Sandon*) 30°36'S. 151°41'E., 10 km S. of Armidale; airfield; Angl. C. b. 1913 by S. Swanson, d. by Robert Newburgh Hickson; FB; school 1911–57; TX (automatic); pop. 111 (1933), 150 (1947), 143 (1954), 113 (1961), 99 (2006).

Dangar Village (*Co. Nandewar*) see Narrabri.

Dangelong (*Co. Beresford*) 36°21'S. 149°18'E., 20 km SE of Cooma, on Dangelong Ck; school 1880–86; pop. 24 (1933).

Danglemah (*Co. Inglis*) 31°00'S. 151°13'E., 30 km E. of Tamworth, on Jamiesons Ck; grazing; PO 1905; RS (Jamieson's Siding till 1912, then Cootinget till 1918) 1897–1985; telephone 1941; TX 1941; pop. 61 (1933).

Dapper (*Co. Lincoln*) 32°13'S. 149°13'E., 28 km SW of Dunedoo; farming; school (building removed from Ballarah, later moved to Mendooran) 1884–1901; Union C. 1910; pop. 103 (1911).

Dapto (*Co. Camden*) 34°30'S. 150°48'E., 10 km W. of Port Kembla, on Mullet Ck; (incl. Brownsville, bypassed by highway 1975 and Cleveland); orig. Brown's; settled 1829 by Osborne, founded 1834 by George Brown, thrived in 1870s and 1902; orig. cattle and wheat, then potatoes, sheep, dairying 1848+; ambulance station 1970; Angl. C.: St Luke's (b. 1842–45, reused), Osborne Memorial Church of St Luke (b. 1880–82 by Reynolds, d. by John Horbury Hunt, damaged 1883 and 1887) and graveyard (1,071 graves 1855+) 1848, St Aidan's 1972; Bapt. C. 1966; bridges over Mullet Ck: one b. 1861 by Moore and Vaughan, d. by Weaver, one b. 1890, one b. 1916 (4 spans), new one 1975; bushfire 1939; butter factories: Dapto Co-op. Dairy Co. Ltd (sold 1923 to Dairy Farmers' Co-op. Milk Co. Ltd) and Country Milk Co. o. 1886 in old flour mill, inundated 1893; cemetery (graves 1900–30); cheese factories: George Lindsay 1880–82, and James and Thomas Wilson 1879 (in old flour mill); clothing factory (Crystal Shirt Manufacturing Co.) 1953; colliery (South Kembla); creamery (Fresh Food & Ice Co.) 1890–1902; diphtheria 1897 (2 died) and 1905; FB (station b. 1938, new one 1984); floods 1893, 1984, 2011; flour mill (wind) b. 1839 by Bourne for George Brown, replaced (steam) 1841, acquired 1850 by John Brown, closed, reused; gale 1891; Jehovah's Witnesses C.; Lutheran C. (St Peter's) 1976; Meth. C. 1904; PO 1840, new one b. 1904 by Ford and Mansfield, replaced 1978; Presb. C. 1841, (second) 1851, (third) 1894; PS, closed 1934, reopened 1940, new one 1985; reservoir (cast iron), 53,000 gal. (240.9 kl), 1920; rifle range 1871, new one 1895; Rom. Cath. C. 1838, new one (St John the Evangelist) b. 1900 by Denning and Darley, d. by John Francis Hennessy and Joseph Ignatius Sheerin, new one 1958, demolished 1986, replacement 1987 d. by Don Kennedy, and graveyard (graves 1850s+); RS 1887, station b. by Robert B. Spiers; Salv. Army C. 1974; sawmill (Clarke's), demolished; schools: Dapto HS 1958 (additions 1960, 1962, 1964, 1972, 1976), Lakelands 1896–1904 (new one 1961, additions 1963 and 1967), Mount Brown 1971 (additions 2010); squall 1887; storm 2002; TC 1975 d. by J. Lowing, became a campus of Illawarra Institute of Technology in 1992; telegraph 1894, new office 1904; TX 1913, automatic 1967; Unit. C. (St Andrew's, orig. Presb.) 1958; univ. (NSW Univ. of Technology) 1951; water supply 1920; Wes. Meth. C. 1848, moved 1861, later replaced; pop. 1,060 (1911), 1,428 (1947), 3,208 (1954), 5,706 (1961), 10,991 (2006), 11,258 (2011).

Dapto (*Co. Camden*) see also Wongawilli.

Dapto Estate (*Co. Narromine*) see Narromine.

Dapto West (*Co. Camden*) 34°29'S. 150°47'E., 2 km NW of Dapto, on Robins Ck; (incl. Penrose); Bapt. C. 1995; bushfire (2 houses destroyed) 1939; cemetery; LDS (Mormon) C. at Penrose; diphtheria (child died) 1876; flood 1984; school (Avondale) 1860–1918 and 1943–55; Serbian Orthodox C. (St John the Baptist) at Penrose; pop. 132 (1947), 156 (1954), 154 (1961).

Dapto West (*Co. Camden*) see also Kembla Grange.

Dapville (*Co. Robinson*) see Cobar.

Darawank (*Co. Gloucester*) 32°08'S. 152°29'E., 6 km N. of Tuncurry, on Wallamba R.; farming; creamery (Aust. Dairy Co.) b. 1898 by Brewer and Bradley; school 1889–1923 and 1928–58; telephone 1938; pop. 51 (1901), 68 (1911), 56 (1933), 87 (1947), 63 (1954), 294 (2006), 325 (2011).

Darbalara (*Co. Buccleuch*) 35°02'S. 148°13'E., 10 km NE of Gundagai, on Adjungbilly Ck; settled 1830; farming, dairying, grazing; butter factory (Scottish Aust. Investment Co. Ltd) 1908, bought 1926 by J.M. Hyndes and reused as cheese factory; goldmine (Shady Brook); grasshopper infestation 1931; PO 1927, closed; school 1911–49; telephone 1927; TX 1927, automatic 1953; pop. 117 (1911), 122 (1933), 62 (1947), 66 (1954), 53 (1961).

Darbys Branch (*Co. Hardinge*) see Conifer.

Darbys Falls (*Co. Bathurst*) 33°56'S. 148°52'E., 19 km SE of Cowra; grazing; Angl. C. (Holy Trinity) 1925; cemetery (134 graves); FB (station b. 2012); freezing works (Darby Freezing Co. Ltd) 1920, taken over 1921 by Garratt Scandrett Freezing Companies Ltd, burnt down 1924; goldmine (Battery Range); PO 1877–1984; Rom. Cath. C. (St Joseph's) 1925 d. by William James Gilroy, closed, sold 2006, reused; sawmill (Nick Markham), closed 1939; school 1884–1903 and 1910–71; streets electric lit 1931; telephone 1909; TX 1915, automatic 1983; pop. 123 (1911), 160 (1933), 119 (1947), 116 (1954), 125 (1961), 316 (2011).

Darby Street (*Co. Northumberland*) see Newcastle.

Dareton (*Co. Wentworth*) 34°06'S. 142°02'E., 12 km E. of Wentworth, on Murray R.; formerly Nine Mile; estab. 1923, town gaz. 1924; irrigation farming 1922+, orchards, vineyards; Angl. C. (St Martin's) 1959; cemetery, incl. crematorium (Coomealla Memorial Gardens) 1962; earth tremor 1954; electricity 1944; FB 1955 (stations b. 1981 and 2006); fruit packing houses: one estab. by Freeman, taken over 1932 by Crowe and Newcombe, taken over 1936 by Coomealla Packers Pty Ltd, closed 2002, reused, and one b. 1950 for Mildura Co-op. Fruit Co. Ltd, demolished and replaced 1954, reused; ice works, closed 1954; Meth. C. 1937; PO 1928; PS 1954, new one 1963; reservoirs b. 1945, 1964, 1982; Rom. Cath. C. (St Maria Goretti) b. 1953 by Sandor Bros; schools: Dareton 1931, additions 1960 and 1972 and Coomealla HS 1976 d. by P. Rochaix, fire 1976, repairs 1977, additions 1979; SD Adventist C. 1937; sewerage 1970; TC; telephone 1929; TX 1930, automatic 1935; Unit. C. (orig. Church of Christ) b. 1934 by R. Tatchell; water supply augmentation 1994; pop. 557 (1933), 1,449 (1961), 414 (1966), 553 (1971), 601 (1976), 612 (1981), 630 (1986), 650 (1991), 652 (1996), 620 (2001), 567 (2006), 516 (2011).

Dark Corner (*Co. Roxburgh*) 33°18'S. 149°53'E., 10 km NW of Portland, on Needles Ck; defunct; mining (gold disc. by Patrick Lahy), farming, grazing; bushfires 1909 and 1939; cemetery (80 graves 1872+); mines: Blackbutt Mountain, Dunn's Reef (became The Great Victoria) 1896 and 1933, Homeward Bound 1878 (became St George Gold Mine and then Ashton Gold Mine, incl. a stamper battery), Paddy Lackey (estab. *c.*1868 by Patrick Lahy, taken over 1870 by Donald Campbell, taken over 1882 by John Cook, who estab. a 5 head stamper battery and, in 1899, a cyanide plant, closed 1906, reopened 1914, razed), Reedy, Verdun; PO 1872; Rom. Cath. C. 1920; school 1882, new one b. 1884 by Thomas Kirk, replacement b. 1900 by Cook and Simpkins, closed 1941, reopened 1947, closed 1951, building removed; telephone 1924; TX 1928–73; pop. *c.*150 (1872), 133 (1911), 45 (1933), 61 (1947).

Dark Creek (*Co. Northumberland*) see Jesmond.

Darkwater (*Co. Macquarie*) see Gladstone.

Darkwood (*Co. Raleigh*) 30°27'S. 152°39'E., 13 km SW of Dorrigo, on Bellinger R.; farming; bridge b. 1937 by M.A. Anderson and Matherson, over Bellinger R.; floods 2001, 2009, 2011; PO 1912–68; telephone 1924; TX 1944; pop. 27 (1933), 243 (2011).

Darlington (*Co. Cooper*) see Willbriggie.

Darlington (*Co. Durham*) see Singleton (*Co. Northumberland*).

Darlington Point (*Co. Cooper*) 34°34'S. 146°00'E., 31 km S. of Griffith, on Murrumbidgee R.; disc. 1829 by Capt. Charles Sturt, site reserved *c.*1853 by Thomas Scott Townsend, estab. 1864 by George Rogers, village gaz. 1901; former river port, then timber, cattle, sheep, vegetables, poultry, cotton; Angl. C. (St Paul's) b. 1923–26 by T.G. Taylor, d. by John Hill Robertson; bridge (pontoon) 1880, replaced 1905 in steel (with bascule span), 670 ft (204.2 m), d. by Henry Harvey Dare, new one (concrete) b. 1977–79 by Siebels Concrete Constructions Pty Ltd, 675 ft (205.7 m), d. by Taylor and Herbert, over Murrumbidgee R.; cemetery; CH 1883 d. by James Johnstone Barnet, reused; dust storm 1944; FB; floods 1922, 1925, 1931, 1950, 1956; gale (child killed) 1998; grasshopper infestations 1899 and 1948; mouse plague 1970; PO 1877, new ones b. 1937 and 2010; Presb. C. 1893; PS 1878, new one b. 1954–57, closed, reused; punt 1866, new one 1881; Rom. Cath. C. (St Oliver Plunket's) b. 1925 by Haynes and Dixon, d. by George William Albert Welch; sawmill (George Henri Risby); school 1882, new one 1902 on new site, additions 1960; telegraph 1884; TX 1910, automatic 1966; Unit. C. (orig. Presb.); wharves 1876, 1881, 1883; whooping cough epidemic 1899; wool store (McCulloch & Co.) 1876; pop. 120 (1881), 57 (1891), 64 (1901), 250 (1911), 539 (1933), 427 (1947), 472 (1954), 662 (1961), 706 (1966), 640 (1971), 658 (1976), 599 (1981), 735 (1986), 750 (1991), 881 (1996), 991 (2001), 1,026 (2006), 1,018 (2011).

Darlington Point Railway Station (*Co. Cooper*) see Willbriggie.

Darlington Railway Station (*Co. Cooper*) see Willbriggie.

Darlow (*Co. Wynyard*) 35°23'S. 147°55'E., 15 km SW of Adelong, on Yaven Yaven Ck; FB 1954; TX (automatic).

Darnick (*Co. Manara*) 32°51'S. 143°37'E., 146 km S. of Wilcannia; PO 1947, burnt down 1957; RS 1927–89; school 1957–68; telephone 1949; TX 1957; pop. 109 (1954), 165 (1961).

Daroobalgie (*Co. Ashburnham*) 33°20'S.

148°03'E., 8 km NE of Forbes; goldmining and farming; bushfire 1926; gale 1948; meat works o. 1911 by Forbes Freezing Co. Ltd, in liquidation 1914, sold 1915 to W. Angliss & Co. (Aust.) Pty Ltd, extended and modernised 1916, closed 1920, reopened 1922, fire 1924, closed and rebuilt 1925, reopened 1931, closed, reopened 1943, closed 1948, fire 1963, derelict; Meth. C. 1911; mines: Cook's 1890, Cripple's (Merris) 1903, King *c.*1860, Magpie (Remington) 1884–89, Mary's Dream or Strickland 1862–86, 1902, 1915, Queen's 1860s and 1879–81, Toss of a Penny (Franks, Williams et al.) 1905–8; PO 1912; RS 1893, station b. by Gerald Dalton Fetherston and Felix Edward Barbat, closed 1975; school 1896–1971, sold and reused; telephone 1913; TX 1928–64; pop. 97 (1911), 140 (1933), 68 (1947), 56 (1954), 88 (1961).

Darouble (*Co. Oxley*) 31°40'S. 147°11'E., 13 km S. of Nyngan, on Bogan R.

Darralume (*Co. Lincoln*) 32°07'S. 148°39'E., 16 km N. of Dubbo; pop. 20 (1933).

Darrung (*Co. Wynward*) see Wagga Wagga.

Dartbrook (*Co. Brisbane*) 32°09'S. 150°51'E., 4 km W. of Aberdeen; subdivided for soldiers' settlement *c.*1919; bridge over Dart Brook; FB 1926; school 1929–51 and 1957–72; TX (automatic); pop. 72 (1911), 171 (1933), 147 (1947), 167 (1954), 147 (1961).

Dartmoor (*Co. Beresford*) 36°17'S. 149°15'E., 12 km SE of Cooma, on Thubergal Lake; copper and silver mining 1897–98; school (Thubergal Lake) 1889–91.

Dartmouth (*Co. Durham*) 32°12'S. 150°53'E., 4 km S. of Aberdeen, on Hunter R.; pop. 31 (1933).

Davidges Crossing (*Co. Dampier*) 36°15'S. 149°58'E., 15 km W. of Narooma, on Red Bank Ck; telephone 1925.

Davidson's Siding (*Co. Oxley*) see Warrigal.

Davies Creek (*Co. Durham*) see Davis Creek.

Daviesville (*Co. Bligh*) see Bodangora.

Davis Creek (*Co. Durham*) 32°10'S. 151°09'E., 24 km E. of Aberdeen, on Davis Ck; Davies Creek till 1923; grazing; PO 1880; school 1884–1903 and 1957–66; telephone 1913; TX 1915; Union C. 1901; Unit. C.; pop. 116 (1901), 61 (1911), 74 (1933), 54 (1947), 65 (1954), 56 (1961).

Davistown (*Co. Northumberland*) 33°29'S. 151°22'E., 3 km E. of Woy Woy, on Kincumber Broadwater; (incl. Yow Yow Estate subdivided 1908 by H.F. Halloran & Co.); Cockle Creek till 1888; estab. *c.*1851 by Benjamin, Edward, Rock and Thomas Davis; orig. shipbuilding, then fern gathering, citrus fruit, oysters; electricity 1937; FB (station b. 1954); gale 1920; Meth. C. b. 1953 by Host; PO 1888; sandfly infestation 1949; shipyards: Benjamin Davis 1869–79, Rock Davis 1854–62, Thomas Davis 1854 (bought 1869 by Adam Houlsby who later sold it to Giles Jenkins), Giles Jenkins 1876–89, Alfred William Settree 1869–79; telephone 1914; TX 1918–65; wharves: Central, Davidson's, Eulalia, Lintern Street, Pine Avenue, Yow Yow; pop. 79 (1901), 96 (1911), 237 (1933), 484 (1947), 563 (1954), 626 (1961), 1,942 (2001), 2,298 (2006), 2,394 (2011).

Davistown (*Co. Northumberland*) see also Empire Bay.

Dawsons Gates (*Co. Wellington*) 33°13'S. 149°06'E., 7 km N. of Orange.

Dawsons Hill (*Co. Durham*) 32°19'S. 151°12'E., 30 km E. of Muswellbrook, on Goorangoola Ck; farming and grazing; PO 1927–83; telephone 1913; TX 1927; pop. 52 (1933).

Dawsons Spring (*Co. Nandewar*) 30°17'S. 150°10'E., 37 km E. of Narrabri, on Horsearm Ck.

Day Dream (*Co. Yancowinna*) 31°49'S. 141°21'E., 19 km NW of Broken Hill; formerly also known as Wilson; largely defunct by 1888, razed in 1890s; mining (silver-lead disc. 1881 by Joe Meech); mines (within 5 km): Apollyon (Barrier Ranges Silver Mining Assoc.) 1884–89, Apollyon South, Barrier Chief, Bendigo, Bonnie Dundee, Day Dream or Meech's Blow (o. 1882 by Day Dream Silver Mining Co. bought 1907 by John Spargo Grose & Sons, taken over 1964 by Robert Pittaway, reused 1983 by Pittaway), Gem (formerly Bobby Burns) 1883–91, Gemini (Gemini

Silver Mining Co.) 1889–90, Germania, Hen and Chickens, Lady Dorothy 1885 and 1910–13, Leo, New Year (Barrier Ranges Silver Mining Assoc., acquired 1888 by New Year Silver Mining Co.) 1885–90, Richard Ruby 1888–89, Tom Thumb; PO 1885–98; refinery 1885; smelter (Barrier Ranges Silver Mining Assoc. 1885–88, slag heaps picked over 1889 by Day Dream Slag Dump Co.); pop. 400–500 (1884).

Daysdale (*Co. Hume*) 35°39'S. 146°18'E., 40 km N. of Corowa; grazing and agric.; bushfire 1926; cemetery; CH 1899; electricity 1950; fires 1879 and 1899; flood 1931; horse dip 1937; lock-up (moved to Pooncarie); Meth. C. (bought from Anglicans) 1971; PO 1876, burnt down 1878; PS (incl. lock-up) b. 1896 by A. M'Guffin, closed during World War II, reopened 1948–52, sold and reused; Rom. Cath. C. (St Paul's) b. 1929 by A.G. Purchase, d. by A.C. Macknight, closed, sold 2016; school (Coreen till 1898) 1890–1997; telegraph 1897–1904; telephone 1895; TX 1910, automatic 1977; pop. 85 (1901), 432 (1911), 191 (1933), 209 (1947), 159 (1954), 96 (1961), 193 (2006).

Dead Horse Gap (*Co. Wallace*) 36°32'S. 148°15'E., 19 km SW of Perisher Valley, on Thredbo R.; formerly Groggins Gap; bridge over Thredbo R.

Dead Man's Waterhole (*Co. Baradine*) see Wooleybah.

Deanes Siding (*Co. Cook*) 33°17'S. 150°14'E., 21 km NE of Wallerawang; explosion (3 killed) 1907; RS (Wolgan Valley).

Deans Flat (*Co. St Vincent*) 34°56'S. 150°25'E., 18 km SW of Nowra, on Yarramunmun Ck.

Deauville (*Co. Macquarie*) 31°40'S. 152°48'E., 1 km S. of Laurieton, on Camden Haven Inlet.

Decca (*Co. Georgiana*) 33°57'S. 149°04'E., 36 km E. of Cowra.

Deep Creek (*Co. Drake*) 29°09'S. 152°38'E., 54 km SW of Casino; pop. 76 (1911).

Deep Creek (*Co. Dudley*) 30°58'S.152°42'E., 19 km NW of Kempsey, on Deep Ck; pop. 29 (1933).

Deep Creek (*Co. King*) 34°09'S. 148°53'E., 36 km NE of Boorowa, on Hovells Ck; Rom. Cath. C. 1913.

Deep Creek (*Co. Nandewar*) 30°22'S. 149°51'E., 6 km SE of Narrabri; FB (station b. 2017); pop. 40 (1933).

Deep Creek (*Co. Northumberland*) see Martinsville.

Deep Creek (*Co. Raleigh*) see Valla.

Deep Creek (*Co. Richmond*) 28°54'S. 153°01'E., 5 km S. of Casino, on Deep Ck; railway bridge (timber truss) 1905, replaced 1926, over Deep Ck.

Deep Creek (*Co. Richmond*) see also Leeville.

Deep Creek (*Co. St Vincent*) see Araluen.

Deep Lead (*Co. Ashburnham*) 33°06'S. 148°07'E., 7 km NW of Parkes; goldmine (No Mistake and Reids Gully leads) 1871–80; school 1888–1947; pop. 76 (1947), 58 (1954).

Deepwater (*Co. Gough*) 29°27'S. 151°51'E., 35 km N. of Glen Innes, on Deepwater R.; village gaz. 1863; formerly tin mining, timber, dairying, then sheep, beef, honey, fossicking; airfield; Angl. C. (St John's) 1898, and graveyard; bridge (concrete) 1950, over Deepwater R.; butter factory (Deepwater Butter Factory Ltd) b. 1909 by J.H. Jones, d. by J.H. Madden; cemetery (292 graves 1887+) 1873, incl. columbaria; CH 1890; cordial factory and ice works (Carl Baer); FB; hospital (cottage) 1930; PO 1870, new one b. 1914; Presb. C. and graveyard; PS b. 1890 by Nathan Cohen, renovated 1924 by Hinchliffe and Watson; quarry (abandoned); rabbit freezing works 1918; reservoir; Rom. Cath. C. b. 1895 by James Mangleson, new one (St Michael the Archangel) 1954, and graveyard; RS 1886, station b. by Nathan Cohen, closed, restored and reused; sawmills; school 1884, new one b. 1889 by William Morris, sold and demolished, replaced 1927, additions 1976; sewerage augmentation 1986; telegraph 1876; telephone 1910; TX 1914, automatic 1981; water reticulation 1969; pop. *c.*40 (1866), 362 (1891), 423 (1901), 710 (1911), 454 (1933), 499 (1947), 452 (1954), 334 (1961), 305 (1971), 277 (1976), 260 (1981), 283 (1986), 297 (1991), 268 (1996), 269 (2001), 319 (2011).

Deer Park (*Co. Fitzroy*) 30°21'S. 152°29'E., 22 km W. of Dorrigo; school (Coutts Water) 1940–41.

Deer Vale (*Co. Fitzroy*) 30°22'S. 152°32'E., 16 km W. of Dorrigo; farming; cemetery; PO 1927, burnt down 1928; 4 quarries; school 1957–65; telephone 1913; TX 1925; Union C. 1929; pop. 105 (1911), 131 (1933), 99 (1947), 114 (1954), 90 (1961), 257 (2011).

Deer Vale (*Co. Fitzroy*) see also Meldrum.

Delegate (*Co. Wellesley*) 37°03'S. 148°56'E., 31 km SW of Bombala, on Delegate R.; settled 1823, surveyed 1875 by Charles Harper; goldmining, timber, grazing, fishing; Angl. C. 1855, new one (St Philip's) 1880, re-roofed 1916; bridge b. 1883 by J.A. Dorron, over Delegate R.; bushfire 1905; butter factory b. 1897 by Oliver & Co.; cemetery 1872, incl. columbarium; CH and police station b. 1879 by M.C. Hayes, d. by James Johnstone Barnet, additions 1899 by Oliver & Co., extended 1920, closed 1981, reused as police station only; drought 1869; earth tremor 1877; flood 1916; flour mill (water powered, Hayes and Body), burnt down 1876; hailstorm 1909; hospital 1926, additions and alterations 1937; PO 1858, new one b. 1897 by H.T. Allen; Presb. C. (St Andrew's) b. 1878 by William Moore, re-roofed 1912, closed 2001; PS 1876, additions 1897 by Arthur Mawson; Rom. Cath. C. (St Joseph's) 1877, new one b. 1916 by Arthur Mawson, d. by George Donald Cochran; sawmills: Jamieson Bros and W.J.J. Reed; school 1877, new one b. 1881 by George Kellond, additions 1909 by A. Mawson, additions 1995; sewerage augmentation 1990; streets electric lit 1928; telegraph 1882, new office b. 1897; TX 1910, automatic 1976; water reticulation 1956; pop. 144 (1881), 365 (1891), 508 (1901), 569 (1911), 503 (1933), 496 (1947), 491 (1954), 477 (1961), 456 (1971), 427 (1976), 347 (1981), 304 (1986), 324 (1991), 336 (1996), 255 (2001), 269 (2011).

Delelvin (*Co. Rous*) 28°58'S. 153°20'E., 6 km NE of Coraki; farming and dairying; PO 1927–31; telephone *c.*1925; pop. 60 (1947), 53 (1954).

Dellhurst (*Co. Durham*) 32°17'S. 151°13'E., 30 km E. of Muswellbrook, on Goorangoola Ck; Bogleburn till 1929; telephone 1929; TX 1929–80.

Dellward (*Co. Macquarie*) 31°39'S. 152°35'E., 11 km W. of Kendall, on Camden Haven R.; school 1927–75.

Delroy (*Co. Gordon*) 32°16'S. 148°34'E., 5 km W. of Dubbo; farming and pipeclay; PO 1927–31; school 1898–1930; pop. 90 (1911), 81 (1933), 93 (1947).

Delroy (*Co. Gordon*) see also Dubbo West.

Delroy Gardens (*Co. Gordon*) see Dubbo West.

Delroy Heights (*Co. Gordon*) see Dubbo West.

Delroy Park (*Co. Gordon*) see Dubbo West.

Delungra (*Co. Burnett*) 29°39'S. 150°50'E., 27 km SE of Warialda; Reedy Creek till 1906; surveyed, town gaz. and first lots sold 1906; sheep, wheat, cattle, pigs; aeroplane crash 1931; Angl. C. 1908, relocated 1924, closed and reused 1958, new one (St Columba's War Memorial) b. 1958; cemetery (369 graves 1908+); FB 1952; fires 1914 and 1988; flood 1910; hospital (cottage) 1916; PO 1906, new one b. 1917, repairs 1925 by A.J. Preston; Presb. C. b. 1907 by John Fraser, relocated 1913, new one (St Stephen's) 1963 d. by Robert Lockwood; PS 1908–34, new one (incl. lock-up) b. 1934 by S. Featherstone, closed during World War II, reopened 1948; Rom. Cath. C. 1912 d. by John Francis O'Connor, moved to Cherry Tree Hill, new one (St Patrick's) b. 1939 by B.M. Wade Ltd, d. by Frederick John Madigan; RS (Reedy Creek till 1906) 1901, station b. 1911 by John Allibone, closed 1979; sale-yards (H.C. Lamrock & Son) 1951; sawmills: A. Arnold, Cecil J. Dufty and Sid McDonald, fire 1952, Mick Hobday, Jack Magann; schools: Delungra 1907 b. by Benjamin Martin Wade, additions 1911 by James Devitt, additions 1917 by Cameron, additions 1918 by John Lenord, additions 1922 by Philip James Killey, renovated 1935, additions 2010, and Reedy Creek 1884–91; silo 1934; snow 1984; telegraph 1904; telephone 1906; TX 1910, automatic 1987; Unit. C. (orig. Meth.) b. 1957 by Eddy & Sons, closed, sold and reused; water supply 1958, augmentation 1995; Wes. Meth. C. 1857; pop. 819 (1911), *c.*1,000 (1917), 479 (1933), 585 (1947), 769 (1954), 508 (1961), 387 (1971), 331 (1976), 332 (1981), 334 (1986), 327 (1991), 318 (1996), 269 (2001), 289 (2006), 290 (2011).

Demondrille (*Co. Harden*) 34°32'S. 148°20'E., 3 km NW of Murrumburrah; Demondrille Junction till 1900; farming and grazing; butter factory (C. Craddock) 1891; 2 cemeteries; PO 1927, closed and reused; quarry; railway coal stage 1922–64, 167 ft (50.9 m) long, demolished 1980; RS 1885, station burnt down 1892, replaced, closed 1974; school 1885–1911 and 1919–29; telephone 1923; pop. 285 (1901), 161 (1911), 27 (1933).

Demondrille (*Co. Harden*) see also Redbridge.

Demondrille Junction (*Co. Harden*) see Demondrille.

Dempsey Island (*Co. Northumberland*) see Kooragang.

Denebry (*Co. Stapylton*) 29°13'S. 150°08'E., 37 km NE of Moree; telephone 1924–25; TX 1924–25.

Denhams Beach (*Co. St Vincent*) 35°45'S. 150°13'E., 5 km NW of Malua Bay, on Batemans Bay; (incl. Sunshine Bay and Surf Beach); ambulance station 2012; Bapt. C. (Surf Beach) 1981; bridge over Short Beach Ck; FB (Sunshine Bay); pottery (Rosebud Farm); reservoir; school (Sunshine Bay) 1985; sewage works (Surf Beach); pop. 3,829 (2011).

Deniliquin (*Co. Townsend*) 35°32'S. 144°57'E., 57 km W. of Albury, on Edward R.; The Sandhills till 1848; (incl. North Deniliquin gaz. 1881 and South Deniliquin gaz. 1881); founded 1847, surveyed 1848 by Thomas Scott Townsend, laid out 1849 by Samuel Parkinson, town gaz. 1850, first lots sold 1851, settled 1858, munic. proc. 1865, designated as chief town of the county, thrived 1874–75 and 1882; orig. stock crossing-place, then oats and stock-selling centre in 1860s, wheat *c.*1890+, timber, vineyards, barley, pigs, cattle, sheep, vegetables, fruit, rice, oilseeds, dairying till 2019; abattoir (Famicorp Pty Ltd), acquired 2013 by Global Crown Pty Ltd; agric. implement and engineering works (Turner Harrows Pty Ltd) 1989; air force training school 1941; airport, upgraded 1965; ambulance station 1950; Angl. C. (Christ) b. 1859 by John Taylor, destroyed 1861, replacement (St Paul's) b. 1866 also by Taylor, d. by Smith and Watts, enlarged 1882, closed 1977, sold to local council, reused, new one 1977; Assemblies of God C. (Sanctuary); Bapt. C. o. 1978 in former theatre; benevolent asylum; boiling-down works; breweries: Elliott's (b. 1866 by George Elliott, malt-house added 1873, acquired 1884 by Riverine Brewery Co., damaged 1890, modernised, sold 1926, closed 1952, demolished 1979) and Ernsten's (estab. 1878 by Ernst Ernsten, closed 1902); brickworks (L.L. Bode); bridge 1861, (second) 1864, 800 ft (243.8 m), demolished 1895, (third) 1896, (fourth) b. 1969 by Central Constructions Pty Ltd, d. by Gordon Bull & Associates, 570 ft (173.7 m), over Edward R.; bushfires 1939 and 1987 (man killed); butter factory (Deniliquin Co-op. Butter & Farm Produce Co.) 1906; carriage-works (Burchfield Bros) 1858, remodelled 1938; cemetery; CH 1859, (second) 1863, additions 1869 by Thomas Robertson, repairs 1872 by A.W. Lane, reused, sold 1934, (third) b. 1883–87 by H.W. Hunter, d. by James Johnstone Barnet, occupied 1892, additions 1892–95 by Johnson and Fox, d. by Walter Liberty Vernon; Chinese joss house; Christ. Revival Crusade C.; clock tower 1996; cordial factories: Collins & Sons, and Giulieri and Halliday (taken over 1900 by Elliott's Riverine Brewery, Aerated Waters & Milling Co. Ltd); cyclone 1861; diphtheria 1894, 1911, 1934; droughts 1838–39, 1865, 1915; dust storms 1878, 1882, 1900, 1902, 1915; FB 1878 (station b. 1889 by Thomas Campbell, new one 1938, extended 1992, new one 2012); fibrous plaster works; fires 1861 (man died), 1872, 1876, 1880, 1882, 1883, 1884, 1893, 1895, 1896, 1911, 1914, 1946, 1948; floods 1859, 1863, 1867, 1870, 1917, 1931, 1955, 1956; flour mills: Charles Elliott 1872 (taken over 1884 by Riverine Brewing Co.) and Finley Flour Milling & Agency Co. Pty Ltd; gaol b.

1863 by Charles Hardy and Thomas Hodson, extended 1878, additional cells b. 1896 by R.T. Hill, gaol closed 1935 and converted to lock-up, demolished and replaced 1966; gasworks 1865, new works b. 1887 by S. Hutchinson & Co.; grasshopper infestations 1874 and 1898; hospital b. 1856 by John Taylor, (second) 1858, additions 1859, (third) 1860, additions 1866, (fourth) 1872, additions 1880 and 1888, (fifth) b. 1904 by Samuel Fox, additions 1911, 1933, 1942; ice works 1905; Jehovah's Witnesses C.; joinery; levee 1956, upgraded 2014; lock-up 1858, moved 1909 to Wanganella; meat freezing works (Riverine Frozen Meat Co.) 1895 d. by Coxon and Greenstreet, sold 1910 to J.A.M. Elder, renovations and repairs 1910, closed and dismantled 1918; Meth. C. b. 1938 by Glen Bye, d. by Raymund G. Wilson, closed and reused 1977; milk factory (Kraft Foods Ltd); mouse plague 1932; PO: Deniliquin 1850 (new ones 1863 and 1869, additions 1889 by Samuel Stead, demolished and replaced 1974) and North Deniliquin 1957; police barracks b. 1885 by Heales and Weatherstone, new barracks 1964; pound (stock) 1851; powerhouse 1909, acquired 1913 by Deniliquin Electric Co., acquired and relocated 1914 by Aust. Electric Supply Co., relocated again 1929, taken over 1930 by local council, closed 1961; PS (North Deniliquin) b. 1879 by J. Dobbie, new one (Deniliquin) 1964, new one 2018; punts (across Edward R.): one estab. 1847 by James Maiden, taken over by govt 1848, acquired 1856 by Will and Vaughan, ceased 1861, derelict 1862, sunk 1869, and one estab. 1864 by John Taylor; railway (private) from Echuca o. 1876 by Deniliquin and Moama Railway Co.; railway turntable, 70 ft (21.3 m); reservoirs: Ping Pong 1938 and 2 towers (incl. one b. 1883); rice mill (Ricegrowers' Co-op. Mills Ltd) 1970–2008; Rom. Cath. C. b. 1859 by John Taylor, new one (St Michael's) 1876 d. by T.M. Brady, damaged 1890, additions 1909 d. by Montgomery, enlarged 1961; RS (Victorian railway) 1876, station burnt down 1924, replaced, demolished; sale-yards 1931; Salv. Army C. 1930, new one o. 1977 in former Meth. C.; sawmills: T.O. Atkinson, J.M. Fitzpatrick, Gulpa Sawmill Pty Ltd, Johnston and Fox 1898; schools: Deniliquin primary 1862 (b. by Donald Mackenzie, additions and repairs 1883 by Hunter & Son, additions 1910 by G.H. Perrin, remodelled 1924 by Haynes and Dixon, new building b. 1928 by Ryan and Moore, closed and reused 1972), Deniliquin HS 1954 (additions 1956, 1960, 1966, 1977, 1990), Edward 1972 (additions 1977 and 2010), North Deniliquin 1897–1935 (reopened 1963, additions 1974 and 2010), South Deniliquin 1956 (additions 1965, 1968, 1995, 2010); sewerage 1938, augmentation 1972 and 1995; silo; storms 1861 and 1890 (both damaged almost every building); streets gas lit 1887–1913; TC, additions 1971 d. by P. Stephens, additions 1983 and 1990, became a campus of Riverina Institute in 1992, additions 2010; telegraph 1863, new office b. 1869, additions 1877 by Hunter & Son, additions 1889 by Samuel Stead; telephone (North Deniliquin) 1957; TX 1903, automatic 1970; typhoid 1878, 1882, 1886, 1889 (girl died), 1892 (boy died), 1901, 1902, 1903 (person died), 1906 (man died); Unit. C. (St Andrew's, orig. Presb.) b. 1877 by Dobbie, alterations 1915 by W.W. Moore & Sons, d. by Louis Harrison, alterations 1930; watch-house, additions 1861 by John Gibson; waterworks b. 1882–84 by Hunter & Sons, fire 1912, reticulation 1966, water supply augmentation 1972 and 1986; Wes. Meth. C. b. 1871 by Henry William Hunter, d. by Crouch and Wilson, closed and sold 1938; wool-scour and soap-works (John Oddy & Son) 1885, destroyed 1890, rebuilt, fire 1936; pop. 155 (1856–58), 632 (1861), *c.*600–700 (1866), 1,118 (1871), *c.*1,500 (1876), 2,506 (1881), 2,273 (1891), 2,486 (1895), 2,644 (1901), 2,858 (1911), 3,192 (1933), 3,668 (1947), 4,704 (1954), 5,575 (1961), 6,277 (1966), 6,604 (1971), 6,865 (1976), 7,354 (1981), 7,566 (1986), 7,895 (1991), 7,816 (1996), 7,786 (2001), 7,431 (2006), 7,494 (2011).

Denison (*Co. Bathurst*) see Bathurst.

Denison (*Co. Wallace*) 35°58'S. 148°38'E., 50 km N. of Jindabyne; PS.

Denison Town (*Co. Bligh*) 32°02'S. 149°30'E., 10 km E. of Dunedoo; surveyed 1856 by William Armstrong; agric., grazing, gold and silver mining; Angl. C. (Holy Spirit), additions and renovations 1905, abandoned, repairs 1935 by Gardner; cemetery (pioneer) 1850–1915; lock-up; PO 1860–93; storm 1893; telegraph 1890; telephone 1893; pop. *c.*150 (1866), 79 (1891), *c.*30 (1903).

Denison West (*Co. Wallace*) 35°57'S. 148°36'E., 51 km N. of Jindabyne, on Lake Eucumbene; bridge over Lake Eucumbene.

Denman (*Co. Brisbane*) 32°24'S. 150°41'E., 24 km SW of Muswellbrook, on Sandy Ck; (incl. Merton, nearby, settled 1825 by Lieut. William Ogilvie, declined 1853+, flood 1857, deserted by 1870, defunct); estab. and village gaz. 1853, town gaz. 1880; dairying, horses, cattle, viticulture, lucerne hay, lucerne seed, wheat, maize, sorghum, pumpkins; Angl. C. 1851, enlarged 1861, new one (St Matthias's) b. 1871–74 by Owen Hudson et al., d. by John Horbury Hunt, and columbarium; brickworks 1922; bridge b. 1877 by D. and F. Rankin, new one (General Gordon Bridge), 690 ft (210.3 m), b. 1885 by Matthew Murphy, replacement (steel trusses) fabricated by Sir William Arrol & Sons, erected 1956 by Electric Power Transmission Pty Ltd, 665 ft (202.7 m), over Hunter R.; bushfire 1905; butter factory and ice works (Denman Co-op. Dairy Co. Ltd) o. 1907 in old flour mill, new one b. 1925 by R.H. Taylor, d. by Richard Wildridge & Co., amalgamated 1933 with Raymond Terrace Co., became Hunter Valley Co-op. Dairy Co. Ltd, closed; carriage-works: E. Gardner 1914 and Jamison's, taken over 1908 by Denman Co-op. Coach-building & Blacksmithing Co.; cemetery (914 graves) 1902, incl. lawn cemetery and columbarium; CH 1826, replaced 1838, new one b. 1880–82 by Hudson and Oxford, d. by James Johnstone Barnet, additions 1883 by O. Hudson, repairs 1890 by M. Anderson, closed 1973, sold and reused; concrete sleeper plant (Rocla, later Amatek), closed 1992; cordial factory (Thomas James Purvis) 1909; earth tremor 2019; electricity 1932; FB: Denman 1950 (new station b. 1982) and Mangoola; fires 1928 (destroyed much of town) and 1939; floods 1870 (7 died), 1890, 1921, 1928, 1913, 1930, 1935, 1955; flour mill (John H. Saunders), converted 1907 to butter factory, reused again 1930; gale 1925; German measles epidemic 1927; grasshopper infestation 1921; hospital, closed 1925, relocated, closed 1930, third one on new site taken over 1951 by Hospitals Commission; levee 1988; lock-up b. 1868 by Alexander Watt, additions 1880 by Hudson and Oxford, demolished; PO: Denman 1862 and Merton 1835–62; pound (stock) 1861; Presb. C. b. 1874 by Imrie, closed 1933, demolished 1937; PS 1881 d. by James Johnstone Barnet, reused, new one 1973; quarry; rabbit freezing works 1930 (in old flour mill), closed and reused 1974 as lucerne pellet factory, closed, demolished 1982; reservoir; rifle range 1906; Rom. Cath. C. 1872, enlarged and renovated 1886, replacement b. 1915 by David Jordan, d. by James Hicks, new one (St Bernard of Clairvaux) 1980 d. by Peter Jerome Gannon; RS 1915–74; school 1883 b. by O. Hudson, additions 1908 by A.H. Thorsby, new building b. 1918 by T.R. Simpson, additions 1958, 1962, 1976, 2010; sewerage 1974; telegraph 1868; telephone 1911; TX 1913, automatic 1972; typhoid 1887; water reticulation 1966; wineries: Chocolate Hills (Craig and Margaret Benjamin), Rosemount Estate (estab. by Carl J.P. Brecht, acquired by William Louis Carl Brecht and E.C. Brecht, reused 1916, revived 1969 by Bob Oatley, merged 2001 with Southcorp), Two Rivers Wines 1988; pop. *c.*50 (1828), 137 (1841), *c.*200 (1866), 557 (1881), 268 (1891), 260 (1901), 527 (1911), 725 (1933), 705 (1947), 737 (1954), 743 (1961), 775 (1966), 782 (1971), 808 (1976), 1,122 (1981), 1,321 (1986), 1,440 (1991), 1,509 (1996), 1,406 (2001), 1,385 (2006), 1,405 (2011).

Dennawan (*Co. Culgoa*) 29°06'S. 147°03'E., 96 km N. of Brewarrina; Bourah till 1907; grazing; PO 1911; PS, reopened 1918–20; TX 1913; pop. 46 (1933).

Dennis Island (*Co. Bathurst*) 33°34'S.

149°30'E., 23 km E. of Blayney, on Vale Ck; agric.; airfield; school 1858 d. by Edward Gell, repairs 1876 by E. Sargant, closed 1878; Wes. Meth. C. 1857, new one 1874, closed, and graveyard.

Depot Beach (*Co. St Vincent*) 35°38'S. 150°19'E., 16 km NE of Batemans Bay, on Tasman Sea; FB.

Depot Glen (*Co. Evelyn*) 29°40'S. 141°48'E., 259 km NW of Wilcannia, on Preservation Ck; cemetery (4 graves).

Deptford (*Co. Rous*) see Ballina.

Derain (*Co. Bourke*) 34°47'S. 146°58'E., 6 km W. of Ganmain; RS 1904–75; school 1896–1942; pop. 35 (1933).

Deringulla (*Co. Napier*) 31°23'S. 149°20'E., 14 km S. of Coonabarabran, on Castlereagh R.; abattoir; bridge 1937, replacement (David Knight Bridge) 2006, over Castlereagh R.; RS 1917, station b. by John Allibone, closed 1974.

Dermal Lake (*Co. St Vincent*) 35°27'S. 150°24'E., 13 km SW of Ulladulla; PO 1927; telephone 1927; TX 1928.

Derra Derra (*Co. Murchison*) 29°56'S. 150°23'E., 18 km W. of Bingara, on Pallal Ck; school (Ermelo 1958–59) 1897–1913 and 1958–67; pop. 54 (1947).

Derringullen (*Co. King*) 34°44'S. 148°51'E., 13 km NW of Yass; school 1884–1907; pop. 64 (1911), 28 (1933).

Derriwong (*Co. Cunningham*) 33°06'S. 147°20'E., 18 km E. of Condobolin; wheat; FB; hailstorm 1930; PO 1916; RS 1898, station b. by John Allibone, closed 1976; school 1907, additions 1908 by J. Whiley, additions 1930 by Cunningham, closed 1949, reused, removed 1957; silo 1933; telephone 1914; tornado 1994; TX 1921–79; pop. 62 (1911), 207 (1933), 101 (1947), 81 (1954), 73 (1961).

Derry (*Co. Bourke*) see Ganmain.

Derrymore (*Co. Kennedy*) 32°58'S. 148°16'E., 21 km N. of Parkes.

De Salis (*Co. Murray*) see Queanbeyan.

Deua River (*Co. Dampier*) 35°44'S. 149°53'E., 32 km S. of Braidwood, on Deua R.; bushfires 1905 and 1953; cheese factory 1908; creamery (Deua River Co-op. Dairy Co. Ltd); Rom. Cath. C., removed 1949 from Jembaicumbene; telephone 1905; pop. 91 (1933).

Devils Delight (*Co. Vernon*) 31°17'S. 151°54'E., 45 km SE of Walcha, on Jackeys Ck.

Devil's Elbow (*Co. Clarence*) see Lawrence.

Devil's Elbow (*Co. King*) 34°42'S. 149°04'E., 20 km NE of Yass.

Devils Hole (*Co. Auckland*) 36°53'S. 149°39'E., 23 km W. of Pambula, on Mataganah R.; sawmill (removed from Montgomery Park by William Charles Rayner).

Devils Hole (*Co. Northumberland*) 32°50'S. 150°53'E., 38 km W. of Paxton, on Devils Hole Ck.

Devil's Hole (*Co. Wellington*) see Clarkes Creek.

Devlins Siding (*Co. Bourke*) see Matong.

Dewrang (*Co. Gloucester*) 32°19'S. 151°57'E., 22 km NE of Dungog, on Johnsons Ck; RS 1926–63; pop. 27 (1933).

Dhulura (*Co. Clarendon*) 35°01'S. 147°18'E., 13 km NW of Wagga Wagga; telephone 1910; pop. 64 (1933).

Dhuragoon (*Co. Wakool*) 35°12'S. 144°09'E., 47 km N. of Barham; RS (Victorian railway); school 1955–66; TX (automatic).

Diamond (*Co. Georgiana*) 34°16'S. 149°26'E., 21 km N. of Crookwell; school 1882, new one b. 1884 by John Howard, closed 1887.

Diamond Beach (*Co. Gloucester*) 32°03'S. 152°32'E., 9 km SW of Old Bar, on Tasman Sea; (incl. Diamond Beach North); FB; school (Hallidays Point) 1994, additions 2010; pop. 365 (1991), 436 (1996), 569 (2001), 847 (2011).

Diamond Beach North (*Co. Gloucester*) see Diamond Beach.

Diamond Creek (*Co. Georgiana*) 34°20'S. 149°27'E., 15 km N. of Crookwell, on Diamond Ck.

Diamond Flat (*Co. Clarke*) 30°34'S. 152°20'E., 43 km SW of Dorrigo, on Cunnawarra Ck.

Diamond Head (*Co. Fitzroy*) see Sandy Beach.

Diamond Head (*Co. Macquarie*) 31°43'S. 152°48'E., 8 km S. of Kendall, on Tasman Sea; rutile mine.

Diamonds Crossing (*Co. Macquarie*) 31°48'S. 152°22'E., 8 km N. of Wingham, on Cedar Party Ck.

Diamond Swamp (*Co. Roxburgh*) 33°26'S. 149°53'E., 17 km W. of Wallerawang; pop. 34 (1933).

Diamond Valley (*Co. Georgiana*) 33°49'S. 149°23'E., 34 km S. of Blayney; Angl. C. 1873.

Dicks Camp (*Co. Ewenmar*) 31°41'S. 148°13'E., 43 km W. of Gilgandra, on Boothaguy Ck; cemetery (69 graves 1839+).

Dicks Crossing (*Co. Rous*) 28°42'S. 153°14'E., 13 km N. of Lismore, on Goolmangar Ck; telephone 1925.

Dicks Flat (*Co. Clarke*) 30°41'S. 152°13'E., 57 km E. of Armidale, on Georges Ck.

Dicks Hill (*Co. Macquarie*) 31°39'S. 152°50'E., 3 km E. of Laurieton, on Gogleys Bay; pop. 604 (2006).

Dicks Mount (*Co. Macquarie*) 31°19'S. 152°52'E., 14 km N. of Port Macquarie.

Dicks Point (*Co. Dudley*) 30°50'S. 152°32'E., 40 km W. of Macksville, on Macleay R.

Dickygundi (*Co. Narromine*) 32°12'S. 148°27'E., 21 km E. of Narromine; Minore till 1902; farming and grazing; pop. 57 (1911).

Diega Flat (*Co. Northumberland*) see Wakefield.

Diggers Camp (*Co. Clarence*) 29°49'S. 153°17'E., 28 km N. of Arrawarra, on Coral Sea.

Diggers Creek (*Co. Wallace*) 36°22'S. 148°29'E., 9 km NE of Perisher Valley.

Dighton (*Co. Goulburn*) 36°03'S. 146°50'E., 8 km W. of Albury; school (Daisydale) 1883–89.

Dight's Forest (*Co. Goulburn*) see Jindera.

Dignams Creek (*Co. Dampier*) 36°21'S. 149°59'E., 10 km NW of Bermagui, on Dignams Ck; gold (disc. 1852), farming, dairying; Angl. C. (Union till 1926) restored 1927–29 and dedicated (Transfiguration) 1929, closed, sold 1969; flood 1956; PO 1896–1935; sawmill (A.P. Beare), closed 1965; school 1881–89; telephone 1905; TX 1926; pop. 91 (1911), 43 (1933), 281 (2001), 160 (2011).

Dilga (*Co. Gordon*) 32°57'S. 148°37'E., 28 km NW of Molong, on Little R.; farming and grazing; bushfire 1901; Meth. C. b. 1902 by F. Shield, moved 1904 to Cumnock; PO 1927–31; sawmill (Mazoudier & Co.) 1900, taken over 1901 by James A. Pender, taken over 1902 by A.G. Brown; telephone 1912; TX 1914; Wes. Meth. C.; pop. 98 (1901), 56 (1911), 50 (1933).

Dilgry (*Co. Gloucester*) 31°56'S. 151°43'E., 24 km W. of Gloucester; grazing; PO 1927–42; pop. 24 (1933).

Dilkoon (*Co. Clarence*) 29°30'S. 152°59'E., 21 km W. of Maclean; farming and grazing; gales 1926 and 1935; RS 1907–73; PO 1926–67; TX 1932; pop. 34 (1933).

Dillans Scrub (*Co. Northumberland*) 32°42'S. 151°22'E., 4 km S. of Branxton, on Sawyers Ck; rifle range.

Dilpurra (*Co. Wakool*) 35°09'S. 143°40'E., 58 km S. of Balranald; RS (Victorian railway) 1928, closed; TX (automatic).

Dinewan (*Co. Bland*) see Alleena.

Dingadee (*Co. Gloucester*) 32°22'S. 151°47'E., 5 km NE of Dungog, on Carowiry Ck; (incl. Stroud Hill); bridges: one b. 1956 over Phillips Ck and Rocky Hill Bridge over Carowiry Ck; creamery estab. 1893 by F.A. Hooke; PO: Dingadee 1927–31 and Stroud Hill 1911–13; quarry; RS 1913, station b. by Robert Daniel Quiggin, closed 1975; sawmills: Mitchell's, taken over 1919 by Millar & Sons and James Wolstenholme 1910; tannery (William Young); telephone 1916; pop. 52 (1933).

Dinga Dingi (*Co. Bland*) 34°26'S. 147°51'E., 28 km E. of Temora; wheat; flood 1920; school 1886, burnt down 1894, new one 1916 on new site, closed 1929, sold to H.J. Loiterton and removed; pop. 107 (1933).

Dingle (*Co. Raleigh*) 30°28'S. 152°49'E., 8 km W. of Bellingen; dairying and timber; 3 sawmills.

Dingo Creek (*Co. Macquarie*) 31°50'S. 152°19'E., 6 km NW of Wingham; farming and dairying; flour mill; PO 1862; telephone 1913; TX 1926; pop. 400 (1911), 169 (1933), 143 (1947), 103 (1954), 127 (1961).

Dingo Creek (*Co. Macquarie*) see also Wherrol Flat.

Dingo Dell Flats (*Co. Cowley*) 35°14'S. 148°51'E., 33 km S. of Murrumbateman.

Dinnykymine (*Co. Napier*) 31°47'S. 149°20'E., 25 km N. of Dunedoo; pop. 32 (1933).

Dinoga (*Co. Murchison*) 30°00'S. 150°36'E., 15 km S. of Bingara, on Halls Ck; farming and grazing; PO 1927; telephone 1915; TX 1929–61; pop. 91 (1911), 54 (1933), 55 (1947), 51 (1954), 179 (2006).

Dinton Vale (*Co. Arrawatta*) 29°34'S. 151°08'E., 25 km N. of Inverell; farming and grazing; Angl. C. (St John's) 1892–1978; cemetery (25 graves 1899–1979); cheese factory (G.E. Cardale); hailstorm 1907; PO 1908; telephone 1913; pop. 53 (1911), 83 (1933), 56 (1961).

Dinton Vale (*Co. Arrawatta*) see also Airlie Brake.

Dirnaseer (*Co. Clarendon*) 34°38'S. 147°42'E., 25 km SE of Temora; soldiers' settlement; Presb. C. (though used as a Union C.) b. 1933 by Frank Mitchell; TX (automatic); pop. 74 (1911), 93 (1933), 108 (1947), 109 (1954), 140 (1961), 173 (2006).

Dirrung (*Co. Nicholson*) 33°35'S. 145°32'E., 13 km S. of Hillston; RS 1925–72; school 1957–59; pop. 22 (1933).

Dirty Creek (*Co. Fitzroy*) 29°59'S. 153°09'E., 15 km N. of Woolgoolga; sawmills: Pike & Co., fire 1929, and Rosenthal's; pop. 555 (2006).

Dirty Swamp (*Co. Roxburgh*) see Locksley.

Dixson's Swamp (*Co. Goulburn*) see Mullengandra.

Dobies Bight (*Co. Richmond*) 28°49'S. 152°57'E., 12 km NW of Casino, on Dyraaba Ck; gale 1916; school 1909–64; pop. 86 (1911), 125 (1933), 118 (1947), 125 (1954), 121 (1961).

Dobikin (*Co. Jamison*) 29°52'S. 149°42'E., 48 km S. of Moree, on Gehan Ck.

Dockyard (*Co. Northumberland*) see Millers Forest.

Doctor George Mountain (*Co. Auckland*) 36°40'S. 149°54'E., 5 km E. of Bega; pop. 23 (1933).

Doctors Creek (*Co. Murchison*) 29°51'S. 150°31'E., 4 km W. of Bingara, on Doctors Ck; school 1896–1909.

Doctors Gap (*Co. Cook*) 33°30'S. 150°10'E., 2 km SE of Lithgow; telephone 1943; pop. 56 (1954).

Dodsworth (*Co. Murray*) see Queanbeyan.

Dogherty's Beach (*Co. Northumberland*) see Ettalong Beach.

Dog Rocks (*Co. Westmoreland*) 33°44'S. 149°35'E., 25 km W. of Oberon; mines: Carter's Hill Consolidated Gold Mines NL 1923–32, Hansard's Rockley Gold Developments NL 1937, Jackass (copper) <1878.

Dog Trap Crossing (*Co. Murray*) 35°06'S. 148°56'E., 16 km SW of Murrumbateman, on Murrumbidgee R.; orig. Dog Trap Ford; farming and grazing; PO 1927–30.

Dog Trap Ford (*Co. Murray*) see Dog Trap Crossing.

Dog Trap Junction (*Co. Rous*) 28°24'S. 153°02'E., 36 km W. of Murwillumbah.

Dolgelly (*Co. Stapylton*) 28°48'S. 149°53'E., 72 km N. of Moree; grazing; PO 1907; telephone 1906; TX 1911–26.

Dollys Flat (*Co. Macquarie*) 31°53'S. 152°19'E., 5 km W. of Wingham.

Dolphin Point (*Co. St Vincent*) 35°24'S. 150°27'E., 5 km SW of Ulladulla, on Tasman Sea; pop. 214 (2011).

Dombarton (*Co. Camden*) 34°27'S. 150°46'E., 6 km NW of Dapto, on Forest Ck; collieries: Dombarton, Dombarton Open-Cut, South Kembla (estab. by A.J. Fleming, acquired by H.W. Buck, acquired 1932 by Cam Bros, sold 1932 to Aust. Iron & Steel Ltd); railway bridge, 15 ft (4.6 m), 1962; RS 1943–60.

Donald Creek (*Co. Sandon*) 30°25'S. 151°45'E., 12 km NE of Armidale; school 1883–1913.

Dondingalong (*Co. Dudley*) 31°07'S. 152°44'E., 10 km W. of Kempsey, on Dungay Ck; farming; bushfires 1895 and 2017; FB 1942; flood 1893; gale 1870; PO 1927–31; school 1865–69, 1882–1916, 1933–65; storm 1927; Unit. C. (orig. Wes. Meth.) 1892, damaged 1927, closed, sold 2015; Wes. Meth. C. 1869; pop. 100 (1901), 119 (1911), 92 (1933), 88 (1947), 78 (1954), 688 (2011).

Dondymun (*Co. Clarence*) 29°47'S. 152°55'E.,

9 km S. of South Grafton; school 1888–1912.

Donnellyville (*Co. Raleigh*) 30°45'S. 152°55'E., 5 km S. of Macksville, on Warrell Ck.

Doodle Cooma (*Co. Hume*) see Henty.

Dooga (*Co. St Vincent*) 35°53'S. 150°05'E., 3 km N. of Moruya.

Doon Ayre (*Co. Gloucester*) 31°54'S. 152°05'E., 17 km NE of Gloucester, on Gloucester R.; RS 1941–75.

Doonbah (*Co. Richmond*) 29°05'S. 153°23'E., 6 km NW of Evans Head, on Evans R.; rutile mining; quarry; pop. 244 (2011).

Doondongorra Plain (*Co. Monteagle*) 34°25'S. 148°43'E., 3 km N. of Boorowa.

Doon Doon (*Co. Rous*) 28°31'S. 153°19'E., 12 km NE of Nimbin, on Griers Ck; flood 1956; Meth. C. 1958; sawmill estab. 1921 by Bob and James Cram, burnt down 1927, rebuilt by Bill Charlton and George Richardson, operated by Charlie and James Cram, sold 1940 to Slys Bros; school 1920–69; storm 1914; telephone 1923; TX 1928, automatic 1971; whooping cough epidemic 1938; pop. 75 (1911), 205 (1933), 205 (1947), 218 (1954), 157 (1961), 429 (2006).

Dooralong (*Co. Northumberland*) 33°11'S. 151°21'E., 12 km W. of Wyee, on Jilliby Jilliby Ck; orig. timber then agric., dairying, citrus orchards, horses; Angl. C. (St Anne's) b. 1922 by Hugh D'Arcy, closed, reused; bridge (Birk's Bridge); bushfire (2 houses destroyed) 1939; FB; PO 1913; sawmills: William Bridge, George Goldsmith (closed 1914, burnt down 1915), J. Holzhouser, John H. Mumford, Walters and Middleton 1916; school 1909, extended 1914 and 1969, closed 2011; telephone 1913; TX 1928, automatic 1969; pop. 154 (1911), 157 (1933), 168 (1947), 156 (1954), 180 (1961).

Dora Creek (*Co. Northumberland*) 33°05'S. 151°30'E., 3 km N. of Morisset, on Dora Ck; (incl. Stingaree); Newport 1840–85, then Doree till 1894; estab. and first lots sold 1840, orig. settlement declined 1843+; orig. timber, then hort., orchards, fishing; Angl. C. (St Paul's) 1903, closed; colliery (Cooranbong, Newcom Collieries Pty Ltd) 1981; FB; floods 1927, 1954, 1978, 1981; jetty; Meth. C. 1912; PO 1887, burnt down 1923; Presb. C.; railway bridge 1889, replaced with 6 steel spans carried on concrete piers; reservoir; RS 1889; sawmill estab. 1884 by E.W. Hely, taken over 1894 by F.C. and E.W.J. Hely, became Hely Bros Ltd in 1912, made tool handles from 1914, burnt down and rebuilt 1919, moved 1921 to Hamilton; school (Newport till 1901) 1884, additions 1913, burnt down 1916, new one b. 1917; SD Adventist C. 1951; sewerage augmentation 1995; telephone 1902; training farm 1900–13; TX 1921, automatic 1958; wharf, 50 ft (15.2 m), 1841; pop. 15 (1841), *c.*100 (1875), 237 (1901), 364 (1911), 516 (1933), 551 (1947), 541 (1954), 617 (1961), 492 (1971), 583 (1976), 615 (1981), 696 (1986), 1,139 (1991), 1,199 (1996), 1,322 (2001), 1,312 (2006), 1,671 (2011).

Dora Creek (*Co. Northumberland*) see also Martinsville.

Doradilla (*Co. Cowper*) 30°20'S. 146°19'E., 47 km SE of Bourke; village gaz. 1920; copper (disc. 1906 by Alf Olssen and W. Tully); mine (Doradilla Copper Mining & Smelting Co. Ltd).

Dora Dora (*Co. Goulburn*) 35°56'S. 147°24'E., 24 km S. of Holbrook, on Home Flat Ck; settled 1835–45; sheep, oats, barley, corn; bushfire 1914; cheese factory (Lamb Bros); gale 1923; mine (Home Flat Creek); pop. 120 (1901), 94 (1911), 81 (1933).

Doree (*Co. Northumberland*) see Dora Creek.

Doreen (*Co. Jamison*) 30°00'S. 149°19'E., 27 km NW of Wee Waa.

Dorrigo (*Co. Fitzroy*) 30°21'S. 152°43'E., 21 km NW of Bellingen, on Bielsdown R.; (incl. South Dorrigo and West Dorrigo); Bielsdown till 1905; settled 1848, village gaz. 1900, estab. *c.*1906; logging, dairying, farming, fruit, butter, cheese, bacon, beef, root crops, potatoes 1932+; abattoir (Pan's Aust. Pty Ltd); ambulance station 1950; Angl. C. b. 1909 by W. Morris, new one (St Stephen the Martyr) 1970; bacon factory 1915, burnt down 1918, replaced 1919; brickworks (L.R. Blamey and H.T. Shaw); bushfire 1919; butter factory

(Dorrigo Co-op. Dairy Co.) 1906, new one 1922, closed; cemetery (1,583 graves 1897+) 1899, incl. columbarium; CH b. 1910 by George Edward Moore; cheese factory (W.H. Jarrett); distillery (Red Dirt) 2007; earth tremor 2018; electricity 1922; FB (station b. 1937); flood 1950; hailstorm 1909; hospital b. 1936 by B.C. Johnson, additions 1971, alterations 1999; joineries: G.H. Gostelow 1908 and Millikin and Hollingworth; Meth. C. 1907, new one 1928, closed and reused; PO 1900, new one b. 1913 by C.A. Morris; pound (stock) 1926; powerhouse (hydro-electric) 1922; Presb. C. 1918; PS b. 1904 by George Edward Moore, additions and alterations 1931 by Condon Bros, repairs 1954 by H.R. Shaw; 2 quarries; rabbit freezing works (Dorrigo Co-op. Dairy Co., but leased to Country Freezing Co. Ltd) b. 1929 by Thomson and Yates; railway turntable, 60 ft (18.3 m), closed; reservoir; rifle range 1901, upgraded 1915; Rom. Cath. C. 1910, demolished, replacement (Sacred Heart) 1960; RS 1924–72, railway partly reused; sale-yards; Salv. Army C. o. 1920 (in former shop); sawmills: Backhouse Roebuck Pty Ltd 1949, T. Battle, Briggs & Co. (burnt down 1913), Dorrigo Softwood Co., David Jones Ltd, A.M.R. McKay, Allen Taylor & Co. Ltd; schools: Dorrigo (Bielsdown till 1906) 1903, additions 1909 by W. Morris, additions 1938 by G. Shelmerdine, additions 1956, 1959, 1962, 1966, 1981, HS 1968, additions 1973, South Dorrigo 1914–45, West Dorrigo 1918–51; SD Adventist C.; sewage works; storm (East Dorrigo) 1914; telephone 1909; TX 1914, automatic 1980; Unit. C.; water reticulation 1956, augmentation 1994; pop. 1,395 (1911), 890 (1933), 1,080 (1954), 1,027 (1961), 1,111 (1966), 1,078 (1971), 1,152 (1976), 1,192 (1981), 1,167 (1986), 1,135 (1991), 1,013 (1996), 969 (2001), 967 (2006), 1,074 (2011).

Dorrigo (*Co. Fitzroy*)
see also Dorrigo North.

Dorrigo North (*Co. Fitzroy*) 30°18'S. 152°41'E., 6 km NW of Dorrigo, on Little Plain Ck; Dorrigo till 1905; Meth. C. 1909; PO 1895; quarry; sawmills: Earp, Woodcock, Beveridge & Co. Pty Ltd (softwood) and A.U. Trim 1903; school (Dorrigo till 1906) 1899, new building b. 1918 by N. M'Pherson, closed 1970; telephone 1909; TX 1920; pop. 322 (1933), 279 (1954), 209 (1961), 305 (2011).

Dorroughby (*Co. Rous*) 28°39'S. 153°21'E., 14 km SE of Nimbin; Dorroughby Grass till 1896; farming and dairying; Meth. C.; PO 1906; sawmill (West and Sharpe); school 1898, additions 1899 by T. M'Morrin, new one b. 1908 by E.D. Seamark, closed 1973; telephone 1910; TX 1924–68; pop. 98 (1901), 241 (1911), 208 (1933), 234 (1947), 178 (1954), 154 (1961).

Dorroughby Grass (*Co. Rous*) see Dorroughby.

Double Creek (*Co. Auckland*) 36°36'S. 149°49'E., 8 km N. of Bega, on Double Ck; pop. 24 (1933).

Double Gates (*Co. Booroondarra*) 31°42'S. 145°29'E., 40 km SW of Cobar.

Double Peak (*Co. Blaxland*) 32°42'S. 145°52'E., 41 km NW of Lake Cargelligo; Allen Mount till 1894; PO 1896; school 1896–97.

Doubtful Creek (*Co. Rous*) 28°45'S. 152°55'E., 18 km NW of Casino, on Eden Ck; dairying; Angl. C. (St Faith's) 1958; butter factory (Casino Co-op. Dairy Co. Ltd) 1924 d. by Richard Wildridge & Co.; hailstorm 1936; PO 1924; school 1936; telephone 1923; TX 1924–68; pop. 116 (1911), 238 (1933), 207 (1947), 137 (1954), 182 (1961), 263 (2011).

Doughboy (*Co. Murray*) 35°15'S. 149°40'E., 20 km E. of Bungendore.

Doughboy Creek (*Co. Gordon*) see Cumnock.

Doughboy Hollow (*Co. Buckland*)
see Ardglen.

Douglas (*Co. Camden*) see Douglas Park.

Douglas (*Co. Harden*) see Collingrove.

Douglas Park (*Co. Camden*) 34°11'S. 150°43'E., 9 km E. of Picton, on Nepean R.; orig. Hoaretown, then Douglass Park till 1882 and Douglas till 1904; farming; Angl. C. (St Alban's), closed; bridges: Blades Bridge (strengthened 1930) over Harris Ck and one b. 1980 over Nepean R.; FB; PO 1860; Rom. Cath. C. (Sacred Heart) o. 1939 (built 1937 as a hall); RS 1864, station b. by Matthew Jamieson, relocated 1892, burnt down 1900, rebuilt 1901; school (Spaniards Hill till 1908) 1883, new buildings b. 1893 by William Frederick Gazzard; telegraph 1879; telephone 1912; TX 1917, automatic 1961; pop. 203 (1901), 186 (1911), 302 (1933), 318 (1947), 228 (1954), 432 (1961), 261 (1981), 492 (1986), 628 (1991), 743 (1996), 834 (2001), 827 (2006), 1,053 (2011).

Douglass Park (*Co. Camden*) see Douglas Park.

Douglass's Hill (*Co. Cook*) see Kurrajong Heights.

Douribang (*Co. Durham*) 32°37'S. 151°37'E., 14 km N. of Maitland, on Paterson R.; village gaz. 1881; bridge over Paterson R.; flood 1864.

Dovedale (*Co. Clarence*) see Grafton.

Dovedale (*Co. Raleigh*) see Fernmount.

Downfalls (*Co. Wynyard*) 35°35'S. 147°50'E., 27 km NW of Tumbarumba, on Umbango Ck; pop. 38 (1933).

Downside (*Co. Clarendon*) 35°00'S. 147°21'E., 13 km N. of Wagga Wagga; sheep, wheat, canola, peas, lupins, barley, pigs, cattle; bridge b. 1879, re-decked 1907, second one b. 1934 by L.J.C. Mansfield, third one b. 1974 by Siebels Concrete Constructions, over Houlaghans Ck; FB 1949; flood 1974; PO 1891–1905; Presb. C. (St Stephen's) b. 1907 by Richard Morris, closed and demolished 1937, replacement b. 1938 by F.D. Gordon, d. by John Donald Morrow; school 1878–1936 and 1957–70; telephone 1910; TX 1924, automatic 1960; Unit. C.; pop. 88 (1901), 170 (1911), 153 (1933), 85 (1947), 76 (1954), 83 (1961), 419 (2011).

Doyalson (*Co. Northumberland*) 33°12'S. 151°31'E., 1 km N. of San Remo; (incl. Bushells Ridge); East Wyee till 1945; ambulance station; Bapt. C.; brick and tile works (Boral Montoro Pty Ltd); FB; PO 1946–86; quarry (Boral Montoro Pty Ltd); reservoir 1976; telephone 1938; TX (automatic); water reticulation 1975; pop. 53 (1947), 134 (1954), 193 (1961), 275 (2006), 306 (2011).

Doyalson North (*Co. Northumberland*) see Colongra.

Doyle Clearing (*Co. Hunter*) 32°40'S. 150°49'E., 34 km W. of Singleton, on Doyles Ck.

Doyles Creek (*Co. Hunter*) 32°33'S. 150°48'E., 20 km SE of Denman, on Doyles Ck; farming; Angl. C. (St Paul's), and graveyard (58 graves); PO 1927–42; school 1882–86 and 1901–13; telephone 1923; TX 1928; pop. 96 (1911), 58 (1933), 62 (1961).

Doylton (*Co. Cooper*) 34°28'S. 146°23'E., 8 km N. of Leeton; farming; PO 1915–29; telephone 1922.

Drake (*Co. Drake*) 28°56'S. 152°23'E., 37 km E. of Tenterfield, on Plumbago Ck; Fairfield till 1858, then Timbarra till 1867; disc. 1840 by Ogilvie, settled 1842 by Walter Hindmarsh, first lots sold 1860, town gaz. 1861, designated as chief town of the county, thrived 1886–1906, declined 1939+; mining (gold disc. by Samuel Costa, and copper disc. 1886) 1886–1939 and cattle; Angl. C. (St Peter the Apostle) b. 1895 by Bailey and Satter, and graveyard; brewery (James Thomas and George Beet) 1888–89; 3 brickworks; bridge 2001, over Plumbago Ck; cemetery (120 graves) 1892; CH (incl. lock-up) b. 1863 by Anthony Linedale, new one b. 1895–97 by Robert James Leamon, closed 1963; cordial factory; Meth. C. b. 1902 by Frederick Morton, C.J. McAulay and Alfred Hicks, closed 1972; mines: Adeline (Samuel Costa) 1886, All Nations (sold 1897 to F.J. Thomas), Barker's, Beagley's, Bill Butlaw, Curringlow, Great Northern, Guy Bill, Hot Scone, Kybie, Kyogle, Lady Hampden, Lady Jersey 1888, Lady Mary, Lead Block, Lone Hand, Mascotte, Mount Carrington (formerly Mount Pleasant), Nil Desperandum, No. 9, Perseverance, Pig and Whistle, Pioneer, Rainbow, Red Rock, Sawpit Gully, Silver King (Kelly's), Spirit of Iron, Strauss, White Rock; PO 1858, new one b. 1899 by W.L. Bailey, burnt down 1983; PS, closed 1963, sold and reused; Rom. Cath. C. (St Joseph's) 1905, moved 1960 to Tabulam, and graveyard; 3 sawmills (incl. one estab. 1929 by Armstrong and Clark, bought by Ernie M. Ford, burnt down 1944, rebuilt, burnt down again 1957, rebuilt again, fire damaged 1965, acquired 1968 by Ford Timbers Pty Ltd, closed 1995); school 1887, new building b. 1912 by J.R. Day, additions 2010; stamper batteries: Adeline Gold Mining Co. (25 head) 1886, All Nations (10 head) 1894, Carmichael's (10 head) 1886, Great Red Rock Gold Mining Co. (25 head) 1887, Kelly Gold Mining Co. (5 head) 1887, Mount Carrington Gold Mining Co. (15 head) 1887, Red Rock Gold Mining Co. (20 head) 1887, Strauss Gold Mining Co. (15 head) 1887, White Rock Silver Mining Co. (20 head) 1887; telegraph 1886; telephone 1917; TX 1918, automatic 1985; Union C. 1894; Wes. Meth. C. 1890; pop. *c.*50 (1866), *c.*500 (1885), *c.*1,700 (1887), *c.*500 (1889), 71 (1891), 814 (1901), 347 (1911), 159 (1933), 112 (1947), 135 (1954), 127 (1961), 395 (2011).

Driftway (*Co. Forbes*) 33°47'S. 148°05'E., 15 km NW of Grenfell, on Ooma Ck; school 1955–71; TX (automatic).

Drill Creek (*Co. Lincoln*) 32°22'S. 149°04'E., 24 km NE of Wellington; farming and grazing; PO 1927–33; school 1901–10 and 1925–34; pop. 66 (1911), 50 (1933).

Drillwarrina (*Co. Ewenmar*) see Bundemar.

Drinane (*Co. Ewenmar*) 31°59'S. 148°23'E., 31 km NE of Narromine, on Ewenmar Ck; school 1957–2007.

Dripstone (*Co. Wellington*) 32°39'S. 148°59'E., 11 km SE of Wellington; Springs till 1890, then Morungulan till 1907; orig. part of The Springs Pastoral Co. estate; lime burning 1870s–1900 and hort.; Angl. C. (St Peter's) b. 1926 by Bert Male; brickworks, demolished; mill (oxide and pyrites); FB; PO 1880; quarries (stone); Rom. Cath. C. (St Agnes of the Springs) b. 1877–79, enlarged and renovated 1909, cement rendered 1930, closed and sold; RS (Springs till 1890) 1880–1975; school (Red Hill till 1881, then Morungulan till 1907) 1880, new building b. 1882 by G. Kennard, closed 1966; telegraph 1890; telephone 1916; TX 1927–76; 3 wineries; pop. 212 (1901), 172 (1911), 211 (1933), 172 (1947), 168 (1954), 162 (1961).

Driscolls Flat (*Co. Westmoreland*) 33°45'S. 149°46'E., 9 km SW of Oberon, on Ben Bingle Ck.

Driver (*Co. Cooper*) see Griffith.

Drofwal (*Co. King*) see Coolalie.

Dromoland (*Co. Georgiana*) 33°58'S. 149°37'E., 36 km SW of Oberon; school 1957–69.

Dromore (*Co. Livingstone*) 32°02'S. 143°39'E., 60 km SE of Wilcannia; telephone 1920; TX 1941–55.

Dromore North (*Co. Livingstone*) 32°14'S. 143°46'E., 83 km SE of Wilcannia; telephone 1955; TX 1955–84.

Drungalee (*Co. Gregory*) 31°25'S. 147°44'E., 33 km N. of Warren, on Cowal Ck; PO 1859–64.

Dry Creek (*Co. Brisbane*) 31°53'S. 150°50'E., 13 km S. of Murrurundi.

Dry Dock (*Co. Rous*) see Tweed Heads South.

Dry Lake (*Co. Gunderbooka*) 29°48'S. 146°00'E., 30 km N. of Bourke; grazing; fire 1892; PO 1907, burnt down 1959; telephone 1905; TX 1923.

Dry Plain (*Co. Wallace*) 36°06'S. 148°54'E., 25 km NW of Cooma, on Back Ck; farming and grazing; FB; PO 1877–1957; telephone 1924; TX 1926, automatic 1958; pop. 50 (1901), 122 (1911), 59 (1933), 68 (1947), 76 (1954), 66 (1961), 122 (2006).

Dry River (*Co. Dampier*) see Quaama.

Dubbo (*Co. Lincoln*) 32°15'S. 148°36'E., 124 km N. of Orange, on Macquarie R.; (incl. Apollo, Dulhunty, Eastridge, Equus, Manera Heights, North Dubbo, Orana Heights, Sheraton Meadows, Yarrawonga Estate); disc. 1818 by John Joseph William Molesworth Oxley, settled *c.*1832 by Robert Venour Dulhunty and Lawrence Vance Dulhunty, founded 1841 by Jean Emile Serisier, established 1847, surveyed 1848 by Walker Rannie Davidson, laid out by George Boyle White and village gaz. 1849, first lots sold 1850, second land sale 1851, third land sale 1856, expanded 1868+, designated as chief town of the county, munic. proc. 1872, thrived in 1880s and 1960s+, city proc. 1966; orig. grazing, then wheat 1861+, oats, maize, fruit, barley, potatoes, onions, wine, now sheep, cattle, poultry, pigs, lucerne, vegetables, dairying, food processing, light engineering, manufacturing; ambulance station b. 1942 by Foxall, d. by E.L. James; Angl. C.: Holy Trinity b. 1859 by Adam Gordon, tower added 1865, new church b. 1874–76 by William Moffatt, d. by Edmund Thomas Blacket, re-roofed 1908, tower added 1923 by A.G. Brown, d. by J.B. Macdonald, church restoration 1956 and 1974, and St Luke's (North Dubbo), additions 1963; Apostolic C. (City); baking powder factory (James and John Leslie) 1883; Bapt. C. 1928; bicycle works: Lynch and Phipps, and J.H. Warr; boiling-down and refrigerating works estab. 1893 by W.L. Brown; breweries: Devil's Elbow Brewery (Brendon O'Sullivan, David Rich, Paul Knaggs and Melissa Knaggs) 2019, Macquarie Brewery (estab. 1875 by Archibald and John McCallum, bought 1896 by Narcisse Muller, closed 1900, reused 1906 as butter factory), Well Park Brewery (estab. by James Osborne and Narcisse Muller) 1875–78; brickworks (Charles Bates) 1877, taken over by John Bates, then taken over by H. Hector; bridges over Macquarie R.: Oxley Bridge (renamed Albert Bridge, b. 1864–66 by A. McAuley, 334 ft or 102.1 m, demolished 1905), bridge 1884–86, 300 ft (91.4 m), White Bridge (composite truss, b. 1905 by Murphy and Taylor, closed 1969, demolished), L.H. Ford Bridge (concrete, b. 1969 by M.R. Hornibrook NSW Pty Ltd, 2,013 ft or 613.6 m, major structural repairs 1972), Emile Serisier Bridge 1987; butter factories: Central Western Co-op. Dairy Society Ltd 1932 and Thomas A. Wright (incl. cheese, in former brewery converted 1906 by Albert Murphy, later acquired by Dubbo Freezing Co.); carriage-works: J. Anderson 1895, S.J. Greer 1895, Thomas Wilkins and Robert Kennedy (R. Spence was also an original partner, but later died) 1874, E.H. Williams (acquired 1911 by Wilson and Carveth); cemeteries: old one (graves 1843+) 1863 and new one 1966; CH (incl. lock-up) 1848, demolished, (second) b. 1863 by James Atkinson, jun., d. by Alexander Dawson, additions 1869 by Silas Winter, additions 1876 by Moffatt & Co., extensions 1878, reused 1890, demolished 1909, (third) b. 1885–89 by James Stuart Douglas, d. by James Johnstone Barnet, renovated 1905 by Archer, restored and reused, enlargement b. 1978–81 by Hughes Bros, d. by John Whyte Ian Thomson, refurbishment 2008 d. by Perumal Pedavoli; Christ. Brethren Assemblies C. (Gospel); Christ. Outreach C. (Riverside); Church of Christ (North Dubbo) 1953; clothing factory (Bonds Industries Ltd) 1944–56, in former small arms factory; concrete pipe works (Monier) 1938; convict stockade 1824–31; cordial factories: Butler and Buckley (F.C. Butler bought out J.T. Buckley's interest in 1917), Excelsior Cordial Works (G.A. Ferguson), A.S. George, W. Hangan (taken over 1927 by Laughton & Sons), George G. Mitchell, Narcisse Muller and J.A. Hives (fire 1900, Neil Hives bought out J.A. Hives's interest in 1909, burnt down 1914), Albert Ellis Orbell 1914 (alterations 1918 by W. Fuller, d. by J.B. Macdonald, fire 1957), James Osborne (in former Well Park Brewery, taken over by R. Greaves & Son) 1878, Stanwells Cordials Pty Ltd; crematorium 2013; diphtheria 1913, 1921, 1931, 1943; droughts 1838–43, 1876–77, 1880–84; dust storms 1902, 1923, 1924, 1941, 1944, 1945, 2018, 2020; earth tremor 1933; electricity 1925; engineering works (R. Bates); FB 1880 (new station b. 1920 by S. Box and Thomas Bain, reused 2013, new one 2000); fellmongery (Fletcher International Exports Pty Ltd) 1990; fibrous plaster works: E.J. Collins 1926, Garfield Fibrous Plaster Co., A.J. Hutchins, Wonderbord Co. (L.H. and F. Kingsley, leased 1939 to G. Davey); fires 1882, 1891, 1898, 1900, 1908, 1914, 1923, 1924, 1946, 1966; floods 1867, 1870, 1874, 1884, 1885, 1887, 1890, 1896, 1924, 1926, 1950, 1954–55, 1971, 1990, 2010; flour mills: Burrows and Dickson 1865 (acquired by William Moffatt, became Burrows and Moffatt in 1868, then Davies and Moffatt by 1870, then Moffatt & Co. in 1873, mill upgraded 1890, firm became Dubbo Milling Co. Ltd in 1894, eventually became known as the Old Berrima, closed 1902), Dubbo Co-op. Milling Co. Ltd (b. 1902 by John Dunkley, silo b. 1908 also by Dunkley, mill bought 1921 by McLeod & Co., extensive improvements 1923, fire 1941, taken over by Gillespie Bros Pty Ltd, fire 1974, rebuilt, closed 1981, bought by Ben Furney Bettaview Pty Ltd), H. McLeod & Co. (formerly Great Western), Victoria (Tremain Bros), burnt down 1901; foot-bridge, damaged 2010, repaired 2012; gale 1994; gaol 1871, additions 1874 by William Moffatt, extensions 1877–80, additions 1888 by James Douglas, extensions 1895–98, additions and alterations 1930, closed 1966, restored and reused 1975; gastroenteritis epidemic (children died) 1939; gasworks (Dubbo Gas Co. Ltd) 1884, inundated 1884 and 1924, acquired 1944 by local council; Generocity C.; Greek Orthodox C. (The Lady of Myrtles); hailstorms 1900 and 2017; heatwave 1940; hospital b. 1868–70 by J. Edwards, d. by G.A. Hartley, additions 1888 and 1894, extended 1908 by H. Whittle, additions 1913, 1919, 1930, 1936, 1947, 1952, 1956, 1962, 1968, 1972, 1973, 1976, 1979, 1998, 2016; ice works (Dubbo Ice & Freezing Co. Ltd); Jehovah's Witnesses C.; joineries: W.T. Lewis 1873, destroyed 1883 and rebuilt, C.H. Price 1916, fire 1953, Wallace & McGee Ltd; juvenile justice centre (Orana) 1999; lock-up b. 1900 by J. Kermode, closed 1916; Lutheran C. (St Mark's) 1978; measles epidemic 1954; milk factory (Aust. Co-op. Foods Ltd); monumental stone works: William Larcombe & Son, Christopher J. Shakespeare & Sons 1926, Thomas K. Shakespeare & Co.; mouse plague 1984; PO: Dubbo 1848 (new one b. 1867 by William Moffatt, replacement b. 1885–87 also by Moffatt, d. by James Johnstone Barnet, reused, new one b. 1983) and North Dubbo 1927; police barracks 1877; pound (stock) 1865; powerhouse (Dubbo Lighting Co. Ltd) 1924, acquired 1944 by local council; Presb. C. (St Andrew's) b. 1874–76 by William Moffatt, demolished 1926; PS 1847, replaced 1889, new cells 1931 by Condon Bros, new police station 1965 d. by Peter Proudfoot, demolished 2007, new one b. 2009 by Richard Crookes Constructions, d. by Collard Maxwell; punt (C.L. Purvis); railway bridge (3 span continuous iron lattice girder) fabricated by Cochrane & Co., Middlesborough, England, erected 1884 by A. and R. Amos and Benjamin Barnes, d. by Sir John Fowler and John Whitton, over Macquarie R.; railway coal stage 1891; railway engine shed b. 1879 by H.A. Brigg; railway turntable 1902, 60 ft (18.3 m); railway viaduct 1884, replacement (concrete) 1993 d. by Rankine Hill Pty Ltd; 2 reservoirs; rifle range 1935; Rom. Cath. C.: St Brigid's (b. 1855, destroyed 1869, replacement b. 1869–74 by Wilcox and Babbage, d. by Edward Gell, enlarged and re-roofed 1882, transepts added 1906 by W.W. Sutton, d. by Arthur John Paul Watson, baptistry added 1956, church closed, reused 1990, new one 1990 d. by Bill and Dan Gibbons) and St Mary of the Angels 1910–89 (sold, later demolished); RS 1881, station b. by H.A. Brigg, refreshment rooms 1925; rubber works (Robertson's); sale-yards 1925–50; Salv. Army C. b. 1903 by E.S. Ferguson, renovated 1909, remodelled 1935; sawmills: Artz and Russell 1901, Centennial Steam Sawmills & Joinery Works (Edwin Davies and Edwin Henry Utley) 1867, burnt down 1887, rebuilt, fire 1923, William Moffatt and Edwin Davies (b. by Martin Kerz), Starr's, fire 1950, M.F. Turner, Wallace & McGee Ltd, W.E. Waser, fire 1946; scarlet fever 1931; schools: Buninyong 1882 (new buildings b. 1883 by Moulton and Shadbolt, burnt down 1903, replaced, closed 1922, reopened in new building 1996, fire 2016), Dubbo 1858 (new one b. 1874 by Adam Gordon, d. by William Edmund Kemp, additions 1881, 1882, 1883, additions 1909 by W.H. Bryant, new building b. 1910 by Charles Benaud Smith, additions 1927 by W. Fuller, additions 1955, new school 1996), Dubbo HS 1917 (b. by E. Denham, d. by George McRae, additions 1919 by Wallace and McGee Ltd, additions 1935, fire 1941, additions 1951 by Walmac Construction Co., additions 1953, 1960, 1974, became Dubbo

College in 2001), North Dubbo 1931 (additions 1962 and 2010), Orana Heights 1983; SD Adventist C. 1954 d. by E.S. House; sewerage 1928; silo 1920; small arms factory 1941–44, reused; smallgoods factory (Ganarrin Meat Service Pty Ltd) 1937–43; snow 1900; soap-works: Jabez Carr 1883 (taken over by J. Kitchen & Sons Pty Ltd), W.A. Harris & Co., N.O. Lane (bought 1872 by Jabez Carr); squall 1912; storms 1869, 1895, 2001; streets gas lit 1882, electric lit 1925; tanneries: Byrne's 1870, Jabez Carr, Great Western (Henry Nancarrow) 1873; TC b. 1947–50 by Walmac Construction Co., additions 1977, 1980, 1984, 1990, became a campus of Western Institute in 1992, additions 1994; telegraph 1864, new office b. 1885–87 by William Moffatt, d. by James Johnstone Barnet; telephone (North Dubbo) 1927; tornado 2015; TX 1897, new one b. 1953 by Walmac Construction Co., automatic 1971; typhoid 1884, 1892 (woman died), 1896, 1900, 1902, 1906 (3 died), 1908; Unit. C.: St Andrew's (orig. Presb.) b. 1927 by Wallace and McGee, d. by John Boyd MacDonald, closed, sold 2012 to W. Larcombe & Son, reused, and Wesley Centre (orig. Wes. Meth.) b. 1888 by C. Grace, d. by Thomas William Heaydon, renovated 1940; univ. (Charles Sturt) 1999; watch-house b. 1871 by Moffatt and Davis; water pumping station b. 1894 by W. Refshange, machinery installed by R.T. Ball & Co., new filtration plant 1981, water supply augmentation 1986; weir 1933, on Macquarie R.; Wes. Meth. C. b. 1875 by Benham and Payne, enlarged 1882, reused 1888; wool-scours: Aust. Carbonising Wool & Textile Co. Ltd, P. Butterworth & Co., Fletcher International Exports Pty Ltd 1995, Moffatt's 1873 (bought 1878 by Joseph Thoms, closed 1884, reopened), Riverbank (George Gordon) 1900, taken over 1912 by Ralph Gordon; wool store (North Dubbo) 1946, reused, demolished 2001; pop. 47 (1851), 381 (1861), *c.*400 (1866), 836 (1871), 3,334 (1881), 3,551 (1891), 5,113 (1901), 5,368 (1911), 8,344 (1933), 9,545 (1947), 12,009 (1954), 14,118 (1961), 15,623 (1966), 17,767 (1971), 20,149 (1976), 23,986 (1981), 25,796 (1986), 28,064 (1991), 30,102 (1996), 30,937 (2001), 30,574 (2006), 32,326 (2011).

Dubbo Grove (*Co. Lincoln*) see Dubbo South.

Dubbo South (*Co. Lincoln*) 32°15'S. 148°37'E., 3 km S. of Dubbo, on Macquarie R.; (incl. Avian Estate, Dubbo Grove, Holmwood, Keswick, Newtown); air force stores depot (30 buildings, incl. 4 hangars and bunker) 1943–95; Angl. C. (St Michael's); Assemblies of God C. (Christ. Community) 1954, additions and alterations 2009; Bapt. C.; boot factory and tannery (McDermott & Co.) 1863; brewery estab. 1880 by James Stevens, bought 1911 by Treacey and Seage, closed 1914, brickworks (Western Brickworks, Robinson and Logue); flood 1874; Islamic C.; Lutheran C. (Open Brethren Assembly); Meth. C. b. 1948 by Walmac Construction Co., d. by William C. Brown; PO (Dubbo Grove) 1966; railway bridge (Dundullimal Bridge) 1925, 2 steel Pratt truss spans, d. by James Waller Roberts, over Macquarie R., closed; reservoir; Revival C.; Rom. Cath. C. 1953, new one (St Laurence O'Toole's) 1972; schools: Dubbo College (South Dubbo HS till 2001) 1942, additions 1965, 1970, 1974, 2007, and South Dubbo 1942, additions 1946, 1956, 1960, 1962, 1966, 1976; SD Adventist C. b. 1951 by E. Ferguson, d. by E.S. House; telephone (Dubbo Grove) 1966; Unit. C.; waterworks 1981; weir 1941, on Macquarie R.

Dubbo West (*Co. Gordon*) 32°15'S. 148°36'E., 1 km W. of Dubbo, on Macquarie R.; (incl. Churchill Gardens, Delroy Gardens, Delroy Heights, Delroy Park, Grangewood, Kintyre Estate, Yuulong); farming and dairying; aeroplane crash 1949; aircraft engineering workshops (Ansett) 1969; airport, upgraded 1950, 1972, 2014; Angl. C. (Good Shepherd) 1977; army camp (World War II), site reused 1978; FB (station b. 1983, upgraded 2013); floods 1874 and 1950; observatory (Peter Starr); PO 1942; Presb. C.; reservoir; rifle range (4 km SW) 1935; Rom. Cath. C. (St Pius X) 1989; sale-yards (Commonwealth Wool & Produce Co.) 1925, fire 1944, new yards 1950; schools: Dubbo College (Delroy HS till 2001)

1980, damaged 1991, and Dubbo West 1944, additions 1975; sewage works 1919; tannery (A. Liddell); wineries: Mount Olive estab. by Friedrich Kurtz and Red Earth Estate 2001; pop. 208 (1933), 418 (1947), 78 (1961).

Duck Creek (*Co. Bland*) see Trungley Hall.

Duck Creek (*Co. Buller*) 28°43'S. 152°33'E., 45 km W. of Kyogle, on Tooloom Rivulet; farming; cemetery; pop. 159 (1933), 141 (1947), 94 (1954), 96 (1961).

Duck Creek (*Co. Rous*) see Alstonville and Uralba.

Duckenfield (*Co. Northumberland*) 32°44'S. 151°41'E., 7 km W. of Raymond Terrace, on Hunter R.; horses; butter factory (Duckenfield Park Central Creamery & Butter Factory) estab. 1895 by John Eales, jun. in a converted grain store, leased 1899 to McArthur & Co., leased 1900 to William McMillan, became a co-op. in 1902, moved 1906 to Morpeth, old factory demolished 1931; flood 2007; gale 1905; pop. 62 (1911), 95 (1933), 54 (1947), 74 (1954), 78 (1961), 357 (2011).

Duckmaloi (*Co. Westmoreland*) 33°42'S. 149°57'E., 10 km E. of Oberon; orig. Irish Corner; mining (bismuth, disc. 1906) 1906–20, farming, grazing; mine (Mount Bindo Bismuth Ltd and Duckmaloi Bismuth Mines Ltd) 1918–21 and 1932–34; PO 1884; school 1882–94; telephone 1919; TX 1932–81; pop. 105 (1901), 71 (1911), 56 (1933), 73 (1947), 58 (1954), 99 (1961), 196 (2011).

Duckmaloi Junction (*Co. Westmoreland*) 33°40'S. 149°58'E., 12 km E. of Oberon, on Fish R.

Dudauman (*Co. Bland*) 34°35'S. 147°53'E., 14 km W. of Cootamundra; farming; bushfire 1926; PO 1890–1926; school 1884–93; TX (automatic) 1970; Union C. 1892; Wes. Meth. C. b. 1892 by Falconer Bros, d. by Thomas McBeath; pop. 90 (1911), 75 (1933), 60 (1947), 90 (1954), 53 (1961).

Dudley (*Co. Northumberland*) 32°59'S. 151°43'E., 4 km SW of Charlestown, on Tasman Sea; subdivisions 1889 and 1891; orchards and coalmining; Angl. C. (St Mary the Virgin) b. 1927 by J. Hafey; bushfires 1933, 1951, 2013; Church of Christ (Whitebridge); collieries: Dudley (o. 1888 as South Burwood, also known as Burwood No. 3, 4 killed 1889, renamed 1891, closed by explosion 1898 which killed 15, flooded and sealed, reopened 1899, strikes 1899, 1905, 1909, 1910, 1914, 1917, man killed 1919, strikes 1919, 1920, 1924, 1925, 1934, closed 1939, demolished 1940) and Fern (John Roger Stevenson); electricity 1927; PO 1891; Presb. C. b. 1908 by W. Beath, d. by J.E. Moffatt and W. Harper, burnt down 1933; Prim. Meth. C. 1892; PS 1893, new one 1961; reservoir, 283,000 gal. (1,286.5 kl); Rom. Cath. C. b. 1907 by G.J. Burg; RS 1908–31; school 1892 b. by William Venor Southon, additions 1967 and 1976; sewerage 1964; telephone 1901; TX 1914, automatic 1954; water supply 1928; pop. *c.*350 (1892), 630 (1901), 659 (1911), 786 (1933), 764 (1947), 2,239 (2006), 2,267 (2011).

Duffys (*Co. Cook*) 33°34'S. 150°40'E., 1 km S. of Kurrajong; RS 1928–52.

Dukes Crossing (*Co. Forbes*) 33°26'S. 148°04'E., 7 km SE of Forbes, on Bundaburrah Ck.

Dukes Flat (*Co. Wellington*) 32°46'S. 149°05'E., 27 km SE of Wellington.

Dukes Springs (*Co. Wellesley*) 36°37'S. 149°05'E., 21 km SW of Nimmitabel.

Dulah (*Co. Bourke*) 34°39'S. 147°05'E., 17 km N. of Ganmain; tin; mine (Red Cross); school (Dullah) 1916–46; storm 1935; pop. 173 (1911), 102 (1933), 100 (1947), 61 (1954), 87 (1961).

Dulguigan (*Co. Rous*) 28°17'S. 153°24'E., 6 km N. of Murwillumbah, on Dulguigan Ck; sugar-cane; airfield; bushfire 1936; pop. 110 (1933), 86 (1947), 77 (1954), 67 (1961), 320 (2011).

Dulhunty (*Co. Lincoln*) see Dubbo.

Dulla Dulla (*Co. Ewenmar*) 32°07'S. 148°22'E., 16 km NE of Narromine, on Cookaburra Ck; school 1901–10.

Dullah (*Co. Bourke*) see Dulah.

Dumaresq (*Co. Sandon*) 30°28'S. 151°35'E., 10 km NW of Armidale; farming; dam 1897, 39 ft (12 m) high; PO 1884–1963; RS 1884, station b. by George Michael and J. Walsh, closed 1974; school 1882–1969; telegraph 1890; telephone 1963; TX (automatic) 1966; pop. 121 (1901), 284 (1911), 111 (1933), 88 (1947), 156 (1954), 225 (1961).

Dumaresq Island (*Co. Macquarie*) 31°55'S. 152°30'E., 5 km E. of Taree, in Manning R.; orig. maize and wheat, then dairying; bridges: Henry Hawkeye Edwards Bridge and L.C. Jordan Bridge (concrete) 1968 to Cundletown, over North Passage of Manning R. and Ella Simon Bridge to Pampoolah, over South Passage of Manning R.; creamery (Mathers') b. 1897 by P. Clark, closed 1905; floods 1929 and 1978; punts: one to Cundletown (2 car capacity), across North Passage of Manning R. and one to Pampoolah (4 car capacity), across South Passage of Manning R.; school 1863–1947 and 1957–73; sugar mills: Darwood's, Malcolm's, Norton's, Salter's; pop. 213 (1901), 166 (1911), 157 (1933), 131 (1947), 110 (1954), 105 (1961), 72 (2011).

Dumbudgery (*Co. Drake*) 29°18'S. 152°31'E., 58 km NW of Grafton; pop. 20 (1933).

Dum Dum (*Co. Rous*) 28°23'S. 153°20'E., 8 km SW of Murwillumbah, on Tweed R.; school 1920 b. by Alfred John Modini, closed 1936; pop. 60 (1961).

Dumpe (*Co. Gresham*) 29°28'S. 152°27'E., 53 km NW of Grafton; telephone 1924; TX 1957.

Dunbars Creek (*Co. Durham*) 32°13'S. 151°02'E., 14 km E. of Aberdeen, on Limestone Ck; farming and dairying; PO 1880–1942; school 1880, additions and repairs 1882 by J. Skinner, closed 1893; telephone 1926; TX 1927–77; pop. 36 (1933).

Dunbars Flat (*Co. Cook*) 33°43'S. 150°17'E., 2 km W. of Katoomba, on Megalong Ck; defunct hamlet in Nellie's Glen that served Megalong mines.

Dunbible (*Co. Rous*) 28°23'S. 153°24'E., 6 km S. of Murwillumbah, on Dunbible Ck; dairying; fire 1893; PO 1892; railway bridge (Pratt steel truss) 1894, d. by Henry Deane, 120 ft (36.6 m), over Dunbible Ck; RS 1894, station b. by Frederick Lemm, closed 1974; school (Main Camp till 1895) 1893–1943, dismantled, moved to Murwillumbah, re-erected and reused; telephone 1893; pop. 190 (1911), 103 (1933), 136 (1947), 146 (1954), 119 (1961), 329 (2011).

Dunbible Siding (*Co. Rous*) see Stokers Siding.

Dunbogan (*Co. Macquarie*) 31°39'S. 152°49'E., 2 km E. of Laurieton, on Camden Haven Inlet; fishing and tourism; bridge to Laurieton over Camden Haven Inlet; flood 1963; PO 1955; sawmill; telephone 1955; pop. 50 (1947), 183 (1954), 144 (1961), 417 (2006), 962 (2011).

Duncans Creek (*Co. Parry*) 31°22'S. 151°11'E., 38 km SE of Tamworth, on Duncans Ck; school 1895–1905; telephone 1911; TX 1925, automatic 1956; Union C. 1907; pop. 142 (1901), 131 (1911), 156 (1933), 131 (1947), 102 (1954), 70 (1961), 103 (2006).

Dundarbang (*Co. Wellington*) 33°00'S. 148°59'E., 15 km NE of Molong.

Dundee (*Co. Gough*) 29°34'S. 151°52'E., 23 km NE of Glen Innes, on Severn R.; village gaz. 1859 as Severn, declined in 1880s; tin, farming, sheep, cattle, honey; Angl. C. (Christ, Union till 1894) 1879, extended 1901, demolished 1951, new one b. 1952 by Freak & Son; bridge b. 1881 by E. Taylor, replaced 1928, widened 1979, over Severn R.; cemetery (215 graves 1862+) 1863; FB; floods 1863 and 1870; flour mill (Bowers's, water powered) b. 1845 by John Baker, acquired by C.W. Gardiner, converted to steam, acquired 1861 by Oswald Bloxsome, closed, bought 1872 for machinery removal by Edward Irby; PO 1851, new one b. 1967; sawmill (Northern Sawmills Pty Ltd), burnt down 1929; school 1853–55, 1875–1931, 1953–74; telephone 1913; TX 1920, automatic 1966; wool-scour and fellmongery estab. 1868 by John R. Chappell, damaged 1870, modernised 1904, expanded 1908, closed 1914, reopened 1920, closed 1925, reopened 1930, closed 1941; pop. *c.*60 (1866), 317 (1901), 315 (1911), 70 (1933), 72 (1947), 190 (1954), 191 (1961), 206 (2011).

Dundee Rail (*Co. Gough*) 29°33'S. 151°49'E., 22 km N. of Glen Innes; farming and grazing; PO 1888; RS (5 km W. of Dundee) 1886, station b. by Nathan Cohen, closed 1976; telegraph 1887; telephone 1921.

Dundoo (*Co. Clarence*) 29°54'S. 153°07'E., 20 km NW of Arrawarra; sawmill (Northern Sawmills Pty Ltd), burnt down 1929.

Dundullimal (*Co. Narromine*) 32°18'S. 148°28'E., 15 km W. of Dubbo; Presb. C., closed, moved 1921 to Globelands and reused; school 1908–14.

Dun Dun (*Co. Wellington*) 32°54'S. 149°27'E., 48 km W. of Kandos; goldmining; mine.

Dundurrabin (*Co. Fitzroy*) 30°12'S. 152°32'E., 23 km NW of Dorrigo, on Blicks R.; bridge b. 1865 by John Strauss, jun., repairs 1928 by C.W. Wilson, new one b. 1975 by M. & E. Firth Civil Constructions (Tamworth) Pty Ltd; cemetery; PO 1936, burnt down; sawmill (Joseph Reid Pty Ltd) 1937; school (Tyringham till 1937) 1931, additions 1958, 1961, 2010; telephone 1949; TX 1953; pop. 99 (1933), 109 (1947), 118 (1954), 139 (1961), 140 (2006), 185 (2011).

Duneba (*Co. Mitchell*) see Pulletop.

Dunedoo (*Co. Lincoln*) 32°01'S. 149°24'E., 40 km N. of Gulgong, on Talbragar R.; Bolaro till 1909; surveyed 1868 by William Jacomb Conder, town gaz. 1869, first lots sold 1875, town relocated 1908, new lots sold 1910, town extension surveyed 1918 by E.E. Sampson; timber, sheep, cattle, wheat, lucerne; ambulance station; Angl. C. (All Saints') 1925, and columbarium; bridge b. 1939 by Sullivan Bros, 240 ft (73.2 m), over Talbragar R.; carriage-works (BRB Coach Factory) estab. 1914 by Eyles, Carter and Brayley, factory re-erected 1931 on new site; cemetery (729 graves); CH 1912, new one b. 1928 by William Bailey; clock tower 1960; cordial factory (William Heslin) 1913; diphtheria 1915 and 1941; earth tremors 1937 and 1997; electricity 1937; FB 1946 (station removed from Sydney, re-erected 1951, replacement b. 1971 by Mudgee Woodworking Pty Ltd, new one b. 2016); fire 1935; floods 1920 and 1955; freezing works b. 1911 by G. Hardy; hospital (War Memorial) b. 1945 by Wallace & McGee Pty Ltd, additions 1964 and 1965, closed 2007, demolished 2016; moth plague 1936; PO 1901, new one b. 1912 by C. Craft, new one b. 1925 by E. Campbell; POW control centre 1944; powerhouse (taken over by E.G. Hooper from Alex Massie); Presb. C. (St David's) d. and b. 1924 by M.H. Bennett; PS 1910, new one b. 1925 by E.V. Campbell; railway bridge (timber truss spans) 1917, over Talbragar R.; railway coal stage b. 1909 by John Allibone; railway turntable 1909, 50 ft (15.2 m), replaced 1914, 60 ft (18.3 m); Rom. Cath. C. (Holy Angels) d. and b. 1913 by S. Maudsley, reused 1973, re-roofed and repaired 1995, new one (St Michael's War Memorial) 1971; RS 1910, station b. by George Albert Leggo and John Allibone, closed 1975; sale-yards (O.L. Milling & Co. Ltd) 1917; sawmill; school 1911 b. by Maudsley and Hainwright, additions 1956, 1963, 1966, 1968, 1970, 1976; sewerage 1970; silo 1936; TC (a campus of Western Institute); telephone 1910; TX 1910, automatic 1987; Union C. b. 1906 by Charles Campton, closed 1937, sold 1939 to Arnold Fitzgerald, demolished 1939; Unit. C. (orig. Meth.) 1937, closed, sold and reused; water supply 1940; pop. 71 (1901), 405 (1911), 845 (1933), 752 (1947), 943 (1954), 766 (1961), 811 (1966), 805 (1971), 797 (1976), 836 (1981), 875 (1986), 829 (1991), 781 (1996), 837 (2001), 836 (2006), 804 (2011).

Dunee (*Co. Murchison*) 30°12'S. 150°26'E., 26 km NW of Barraba, on Horton R.; school 1915–22.

Dungalear (*Co. Finch*) 29°42'S. 148°12'E., 35 km SE of Lightning Ridge; pop. 58 (1911), 60 (1933), 73 (1954).

Dungarubba (*Co. Rous*) 29°00'S. 153°22'E., 9 km N. of Woodburn, on Stibbards Ck; dairying, pigs, sugar-cane; Angl. C. (St Columba's) 1921; electricity 1959; floods 1870 and 1954; PO 1908; Rom. Cath. C. (St John the Evangelist and Our Lady of the Rosary), removed from Rileys Hill and rebuilt 1934 by E. Grainger et al., closed, sold 1974; school (Dungarubba Creek till 1911) 1899, additions 1920 by O.L. Larsen, closed 1988; sugar mill (Harrison and Leigh) 1872; telephone 1907; pop. 100 (1901), 156 (1911), 211 (1933), 85 (1947), 89 (1954), 86 (1961).

Dungarubba (*Co. Rous*) see also Kilgin.

Dungarubba Creek (*Co. Rous*) see Dungarubba.

Dungate (*Co. Vernon*) 31°01'S. 151°38'E., 8 km SE of Walcha; school (Morgans Gully till 1931) 1915–34.

Dungay (*Co. Rous*) 28°17'S. 153°22'E., 6 km NW of Murwillumbah, on Dungay Ck; sawmill; school (Dungay Creek till 1954) 1894, enlarged 1897 by C. McCarthy, extended 1904 by Edward Fackerell, repairs 1913 by Alfred John Modini, new building 1921, additions 1958 by Peter Furness; pop. 186 (1911), 122 (1933), 233 (1947), 183 (1954), 195 (1961), 316 (2011).

Dungay Creek (*Co. Rous*) see Dungay.

Dungeree (*Co. Phillip*) 32°39'S. 149°52'E., 18 km NW of Rylstone, on Lawsons Ck; Angl. C. 1907; mine (iron) 1950s–1970; PO 1874; Rom. Cath. C. (St Martin's) b. 1906 by Patrick Callaghan, closed, dismantled and moved 1936 to Mudgee; sawmill (Hinton and Jerome) 1875; typhoid 1884; pop. 76 (1901), 61 (1911).

Dungeree (*Co. Phillip*) see also Lue.

Dungog (*Co. Durham*) 32°24'S. 151°45'E., 40 km N. of Raymond Terrace, on Williams R.; Upper Williams till 1834; site reserved 1830, surveyed and village gaz. 1838, estab. 1840, munic. proc. 1893, thrived in 1880s and 1911+, munic. abolished 1958; orig. timber and wheat, then cattle, maize, tobacco, barley, hay, oats, rye, potatoes, maizena, arrowroot, oranges, wine, butter, cheese, ham, bacon, poultry, olives, dairying; abattoir (Finch's); ambulance station (in reused house) 1939, new one 1962; Angl. C. (temporary one) 1842, demolished 1894, (Christ) b. 1849–58 by R. Lamplough and W. Peet, d. by Edmund Thomas Blacket, bell tower 1861, church re-roofed 1873, re-roofed, refloored and renovated 1906, and columbarium 1956; Bapt. C. 1917; barracks (mounted troopers) 1838; boiling-down works: Aust. Agric. Co. and Hooke's; brewery (Tinshed) estab. by David Cox and Haley Collis; brick-kiln (Paddy Gleeson); bridges: Cooreei Bridge 1851, one b. 1874 by Thomas Smith, one b. 1900, one b. 1904–6 (Dare composite timber truss) by Walter Frank Oakes, 376 ft (114.6 m), Bennett Bridge 1970; bushfires 1903, 1939, 1985; butter factories: Dairy Farmers' Co-op. Milk Co. Ltd (bought 1932 by Dungog Co-op. Butter Factory Co. Ltd), Dungog Co-op. Butter Factory Co. Ltd (b. 1905 by William Mitchell, relocated 1914, extensions and alterations 1930 d. by Richard Wildridge & Co., additions 1939 by J.C. Pickles, d. by J. Wildridge and Sinclair), Heather Bell (estab. 1898 by W.O. Skillen and George Walker), Williams River Co-op. Manufacturing & Butter Co. Ltd; caterpillar infestation 1869; cemetery (burials 1838+, *c.*1,750 graves) 1828; CH 1834 (incl. lock-up), new one o. 1849 (in former police station), conversion by W. Irwin, d. by Mortimer William Lewis, alterations 1864 by Richard Davey, repairs 1871 by Philip Houguet, repairs 1876 by W.H. Galbraith, additions and alterations 1907 by A.A. Moore, new one b. 1933 by G.A. Zeininger & Sons, repairs 1935 by Bailey and Birrell; clothing factory (Fit-Rite Pty Ltd) 1944; cordial factories: Roy C. Bacon, E. Bradbery 1920, H. Pitt 1916, Rolfe Bros 1918, George Taylor; cornflour mill (Cooreei) estab. 1878 by John Wade and R.L. Alison, closed 1902, razed; diphtheria 1898 (child died) and 1934; drought 1965; earth tremor 1868; FB (station b. 1928 by James Musgrove); fires 1897, 1902, 1920, 1923; floods 1851, 1857, 1894, 1913, 1915, 1929, 1946, 1955, 1963, 1967, 1978, 1985, 2015 (3 died), 2016, 2018; flour mills: J.K. Allen (Wiry Gully), destroyed 1857, Allendale (estab. by John Walker, inundated 1870 and 1873, modernised 1898, bought 1916 by J. Croll & Sons and reused as sawmill, closed 1987), Thomas Benjamin Kermode (burnt down 1861), James Stephenson 1848; Free Presb. C. (John Knox's) b. 1855–58; heatwave 1939; hospital (cottage) b. 1892 by Boots Bros, d. by Louat, additions 1910 by B. Bosworth, d. by W. Atkins, additions 1915 and 1929, taken over 1929 by Hospitals Commission, additions 1934, fire 1944, additions 1946 by J.C. Pickles, additions 1958; ice works: Dungog Electric Lighting Co. Ltd, and Skillen and Walker; knitting mill (Stevens Knitting Mills Pty Ltd) 1965–80; lock-up 1858 d. by Alexander Dawson, repairs 1876 by W.H. Galbraith, new one b. 1883 by James and Fleming, exercise yard b. 1935 by Bailey and Birrell, reused; measles epidemic 1902; milk factories: Dairy Farmers' Co-op. Milk Co. Ltd, closed 1989 and Dungog Dairymen's & Farmers' Milk & Ice Co., taken over 1929 by Dairy Farmers' Co-op. Milk Co. Ltd, sold 1931 to Dungog Co-op.; PO 1835, new one b. 1880 by A. M'Laren, repairs 1896 by J.A. Hall, repairs 1909 by Pollock & Co., additions and alterations 1910 by C.A. Hutcherson, d. by Walter Liberty Vernon; pound (stock) 1865; powerhouse (Dungog Electric Supply Co. Ltd) 1912, fire 1929; Presb. C. 1856–1905, reused, demolished 1913, new one (St Andrew's) b. 1905 by William Henry Noad, d. by James Warren Scobie, and graveyard, incl. columbarium; PS 1839, reused 1849 as court-house, replaced, additions 1882 by James and Fleming; 3 quarries; railway barracks 1913, new barracks b. 1929 on new site by James Dean; railway bridge (steel truss), 120 ft (36.6 m), fabricated by H. Vale & Sons, erected 1913 by G. Wilcocks, over Williams R.; railway engine shed b. 1911 by R.D. Quiggan; railway turntable, 60 ft (18.3 m); reservoir, 200,000 gal. (909.2 kl), 1910; rifle range (2 km W.) 1909; Rom. Cath. C. (Maternity of the Ever Blessed Virgin) b. 1870 by Moylan and Tierney, demolished 1933, new one (St Mary's) b. 1933 by McGrorey and Keernan, d. by Peter Joseph Gannon; RS 1911, station alterations 1924, demolished 1981; sale-yards 1901; Salv. Army C. 1984; sawmills: J. Croll & Sons Pty Ltd (estab. 1916 by James Croll in old flour mill, fruit boxes made from 1917, man killed 1929, burnt down 1947, rebuilt, veneer mill added 1955, bought 1969 by Allen Taylor & Co. Ltd, closed 1987), K.A. Gam, G.F. Heath & Son, Thomas Benjamin Kermode (burnt down 1861), W. O'Neill, Skillen and Walker; schools: primary 1851 (new one b. 1865, additions 1881, additions 1887 by Boots and Redman, new one 1910, alterations 1923, extensions 1935 by Pickles and McIlroy, additions 1959, renovations 1999) and HS 1971, additions 1973–75 by R.A. Wenham Builders Pty Ltd, additions 1989; SD Adventist C. 1979; self-raising flour factory (T.D. Hutchinson); sewerage 1941; silo; storms 1899, 1907, 1925, 1932; streets lit by acetylene gas 1904, electric lit 1925; tannery (Edward James Hayman), burnt down 1880; telegraph 1874, new office b. 1880 by A. M'Laren; telephone 1905; tobacco factories: G.W. Lloyd, and Peter and Thomas McWilliam; TX 1909, automatic 1961; typhoid 1898, 1900 (boy died), 1902, 1903; Unit. C. (orig. Meth.) 1911, damaged 1925, repairs 1996, and columbarium; water supply 1910; Wes. Meth. C. b. 1852–54, reused, demolished 1921, new one 1865; wharf, rebuilt 1930 by G.A. Engel & Sons Ltd; pop. 124 (1846), 286 (1851), 356 (1856), 458 (1861), *c.*500 (1866), 396 (1871), 436 (1881), 878 (1891), *c.*900 (1895), 1,169 (1898), 1,082 (1901), 1,712 (1911), 2,128 (1933), 2,041 (1947), 2,154 (1954), 2,211 (1961), 2,101 (1966), 2,119 (1971), 2,175 (1976), 2,126 (1981), 2,106 (1986), 2,187 (1991), 2,181 (1996), 2,115 (2001), 2,102 (2006), 2,132 (2011).

Dungowan (*Co. Parry*) 31°13'S. 151°07'E., 23 km SE of Tamworth, on Dungowan Ck; planned 1860 by Benjamin Charles Flide; agric., grazing, dairying; Angl. C. (St Thomas's) 1913, new one 1931; butter factory, bought 1895 by Robert Johnston, closed 1904; cemetery 1877, incl. columbarium; copper mines: Fisher's 1899–1900, reworked 1968–74 by Janko Krco, and Trough Gulley; FB 1965; gale 1914; PO 1868; Rom. Cath. C. 1883, dismantled and sold 1916 to Arthur Wilson, new one (St Michael's) b. 1916 by W. Moran, d. by Frederick James Bishop; school 1880, new one b. 1884 by E. Henry, additions 2010; telephone 1898; TX 1914, automatic 1951; Union C. 1873; water reticulation 1966; pop. 251 (1901), 525 (1911), 503 (1933), 454 (1947), 380 (1954), 357 (1961), 524 (2011).

Dunkeld (*Co. Bathurst*) 33°25'S. 149°29'E., 9 km W. of Bathurst, on Evans Plains Ck; farming and grazing; bridge b. 1890 by William Hall, over Evans Plains Ck; PO 1867; school (Malmsbury till 1884) 1882–1922; telephone 1924; TX 1924, automatic 1970; Wes. Meth. C. 1871; pop. 68 (1901), 84 (1911), 39 (1933), 82 (1947), 82 (1954), 81 (1961).

Dunlop (*Co. Yanda*) 30°38'S. 145°01'E., 107 km SW of Bourke; pop. 24 (1933).

Dunlop Vale (*Co. Camden*) see Kembla Grange.

Dunmore (*Co. Camden*) 34°36'S. 150°50'E., 7 km N. of Kiama, on Minnamurra R.; Shellharbour Railway Station till 1890; basalt and sand mining, and farming; butter factory b. 1888 by C. Bursill, closed 1902; earth tremor 1842; FB; PO 1890–1993; quarries: Blue Metal & Gravel, Federal 1921, Locking Hill (blue metal, J.W. Manning) 1921; RS (Shellharbour till 1981, then Dunmore Shellharbour till 2014, then Shellharbour Junction on new site) 1887, station b. by Robert B. Spiers, new station 2014 on new site; school (Peterborough till 1886, then Minnamurra) 1862, new one b. 1881 by Anton Ettingshausen, John Dwyer and Frederick Watson, d. by William Edmund Kemp, closed 1907, sold, restored and reused; telephone 1902; TX 1928–63; pop. 151 (1911), 264 (2011).

Dunmore (*Co. Durham*) see Largs and Mindaribba.

Dunmore (*Co. Kennedy*) 32°44'S. 148°02'E., 15 km W. of Peak Hill; school 1937–46; pop. 90 (1947).

Dunmore Shellharbour (*Co. Camden*) see Dunmore.

Dunnadie Creek (*Co. Pottinger*) 30°58'S. 149°49'E., 41 km W. of Gunnedah, on Dunnadie Ck; school 1957–71.

Dunns Creek (*Co. Durham*) see Duns Creek.

Dunns Plains (*Co. Bathurst*) 33°41'S. 149°32'E., 30 km S. of Bathurst, on Peppers Ck.

Dunnwell (*Co. Bourke*) 34°29'S. 147°22'E., 15 km W. of Temora, on Mirrool Ck.

Dunolly (*Co. Durham*) see Singleton (*Co. Northumberland*).

Dunoon (*Co. Rous*) 28°41'S. 153°19'E., 13 km SE of Nimbin, on Numulgi Ck; timber, sugar-cane, dairying 1891+, cattle, bananas, orchards, macadamia nuts 1962+; abattoir (Elliott's) 1905–21; Angl. C. 1911, damaged then demolished 1954, replacement (St Matthew's) b. 1955 by G. Jones, d. by K. Crandon, damaged 2007; butter factory 1891, sold to NSW Creamery Butter Co., taken over by North Coast Fresh Food & Cold Storage Co-op. Co. Ltd, closed 1898, new ones 1898 and 1914, closed 1939; cemetery (436 graves 1886+) 1892, incl. columbarium; cheese factory (Norco Co-op. Ltd) b. 1940 by Daniel Gallagher (in converted butter factory), closed 1958; cyclone 1954; electricity 1933; FB (station b. 1982); fires 1925, 1926, 1927; nut processing plant (Macadamia Plantations of Aust. Pty Ltd) 1978; PO 1886, burnt down 1925, new one b. 1926; Presb. C. (St Andrew's) b. 1912 by Gaggin, d. by Alexander Stewart Jolly, renovations 1936; rifle range 1906; Rom. Cath. C. (St Dympna's) 1907, relocated and re-erected 1922 by Jack Williams and E. Lattimore; sawmills: H. Gulliver 1948 (burnt down 1960, rebuilt, burnt down again 1970), Duck & Son, L. Parmenter, Edwin Roach & Co., West and Sharpe; school 1884 b. by John Dorrough, relocated 1891, moved 1921 to The Channon, new one b. 1922, additions 1986 and 1994, damaged 2007; street lighting 1954; telephone 1905; tornado 2007; TX 1916, automatic 1968; Unit. C. (orig. Meth.) 1903; water supply 1971; Wes. Meth. C. 1890, fire 1901; pop. 168 (1901), 771 (1911), 235 (1933), 356 (1947), 480 (1954), 380 (1961), 461 (1996), 398 (2001), 372 (2006), 379 (2011).

Duns Creek (*Co. Durham*) 32°38'S. 151°38'E., 14 km NE of Maitland, on Dunns Ck; formerly Dunns Creek; sawmill (T. Gordon); pop. 33 (1933), 491 (2011).

Dunvegan (*Co. Fitzroy*) 30°18'S. 153°01'E., 9 km W. of Coffs Harbour, on Orara R.; Presb. C. 1932; Union C.

Dunvegan (*Co. Fitzroy*) see also Upper Orara.

Duramana (*Co. Bathurst*) see Newbridge.

Duramana (*Co. Roxburgh*) 33°18'S. 149°33'E., 13 km N. of Bathurst; farming and grazing; Angl. C. 1885, new one (St Paul's) 1919, closed, sold; bushfire 2009; gale 2015; PO 1883; school 1869–72, 1880–1912, 1938–50; telephone 1923; TX 1955–82; Wes. Meth. C. b. 1869 by William Jones and John Burns; pop. 156 (1901), 127 (1911), 153 (1933), 78 (1947), 99 (1954), 124 (1961), 280 (2006).

Duramba (*Co. Macquarie*) 31°48'S. 152°29'E., 12 km N. of Taree; pop. 11 (1841).

Duranbah (*Co. Rous*) 28°19'S. 153°31'E., 5 km NW of Bogangar; dairying, cattle, sugar-cane, bananas, avocados; cemetery (Tweed Valley); PO 1927; quarry; Rom. Cath. C., removed 1926 from Stotts Creek, closed 1961, demolished; school 1896, additions 1924 by Lanham, Deacon and Watkins, additions 2010; telephone 1923; TX 1929, automatic 1969; pop. 51 (1901), 125 (1911), 217 (1933), 191 (1947), 205 (1954), 205 (1961), 262 (2011).

Duri (*Co. Parry*) 31°13'S. 150°49'E., 17 km SW of Tamworth; agric.; Angl. C. (All Saints') 1913 d. by William Powell, severely damaged 1914, rebuilding and restoration 1914 by Gillies, d. by Frederick James Bishop; cyclone 1914; FB; Meth. C. d. and b. 1911 by Charles Kinred, closed 1992, sold and reused; PO 1891; Rom. Cath. C. (St James's) 1913–62, reused; RS 1879–1985; school 1894, new one b. 1895 by Moran Bros, additions 1906 by Richard Allright Stanfield, additions 1995 and 2010; silo 1934; telephone 1905; TX 1923, automatic 1981; Union C., sold 1913; Wes. Meth. C. 1886; pop. 221 (1901), 445 (1911), 409 (1933), 392 (1947), 374 (1954), 405 (1961), 534 (2011).

Duroby (*Co. Rous*) 28°14'S. 153°28'E., 11 km SW of Tweed Heads, on Duroby Ck; pop. 51 (1911), 70 (1933), 54 (1947).

Durran Durra (*Co. St Vincent*) 35°19'S. 149°53'E., 16 km NE of Braidwood, on Eastlea Ck; mine (manganese) 1929; PO 1942–56; telephone 1912; TX 1928; pop. 76 (1911), 42 (1933), 61 (1954), 53 (1961).

Durras (*Co. St Vincent*) 35°40'S. 150°18'E., 12 km NE of Batemans Bay, on Beagle Bay; village gaz. 1932; electricity 1960; FB (South Durass); PO 1954–73; telephone 1951; TX 1951, automatic 1974; pop. 291 (1991), 328 (1996), 326 (2001), 326 (2006).

Durras Lake (*Co. St Vincent*) 35°39'S. 150°18'E., 13 km NE of Batemans Bay, on Durras Lake; estab. 1945; electricity 1960.

Durras North (*Co. St Vincent*) 35°38'S. 150°18'E., 14 km NE of Batemans Bay, on Durras Lake; PO 1960; telephone 1960; pop. 13 (1961), 250 (2006), 288 (2011).

Durren Durren (*Co. Northumberland*) 33°12'S. 151°24'E., 9 km W. of Wyee, on Buttonderry Ck; pop. 69 (1911).

Durridgere (*Co. Bligh*) 32°10'S. 149°55'E., 43 km NE of Gulgong, on Durridgere Ck; pop. 43 (1933).

Durrumbul (*Co. Rous*) 28°31'S. 153°26'E., 6 km NW of Mullumbimby, on Brunswick R.; sawmill; school 1901.

Dusodie (*Co. Gloucester*) 32°16'S. 151°42'E., 17 km N. of Dungog, on Chichester R.; farming; bushfire 1915; PO 1916; sawmill, fire 1915; TX 1928–61; pop. 33 (1933).

Dusodie (*Co. Gloucester*) see also Wangat.

Dutchmans Bay (*Co. Gloucester*) see Nelson Bay.

Duval (*Co. Sandon*) see Armidale and Exmouth.

Duval View (*Co. Sandon*) see Armidale.

Dwyers (*Co. Cooper*) 30°25'S. 146°13'E., 45 km SE of Bourke; RS (relocated 1946) 1892–1974.

Dwyers Creek (*Co. Dampier*) 35°58'S. 150°01'E., 9 km SW of Moruya; gold, arsenic, silver (disc. 1849) mining 1861+, timber; mine (Donkey Hill, Francis Guy) 1870–1914, reopened 1923 by Moruya Gold & Arsenic Syndicate, failed and demolished; stamper batteries: one erected 1859 and a 10 head one erected 1890 by Francis Guy.

Dyers Crossing (*Co. Gloucester*) 32°06'S. 152°18'E., 21 km NW of Tuncurry, on Firefly Ck; farming and dairying; Angl. C., first one removed 1923 from Koribar and re-erected by W. Batchelor et al., reused, new one (St John's) b. 1940 by Alf E. Woodward; bridge

b. 1938 by S.J. Donaldson, replaced 2015 by Delaney Civil; butter factory (Upper Wallamba River Co-op. Dairy Co. Ltd) b. 1905 by H.E. Milligan, taken over by Peters American Delicacy Co. Ltd, closed 1959, sold and reused, fire 2016; cemetery; fire 1945; PO 1910; quarry; school 1938–69; telephone 1910; TX 1919; water reticulation 1969; winery (Villa d'Esta) 1997; pop. 76 (1911), 273 (1933), 164 (1947), 180 (1954), 203 (1961), 340 (2011).

Dyraaba (*Co. Rous*) 28°47'S. 152°51'E., 21 km NW of Casino; formerly Upper Pigman Creek; soldiers' settlement 1922–23, subdivided *c.*1939; dairying; butter factory (Casino Co-op. Dairy Co. Ltd) b. 1924 by Farrow, additions and alterations 1929; cemetery 1926; Rom. Cath. C. (St Patrick's) b. 1934 by J. Watt, d. by Nicol, closed, sold 1984; school 1957–71; pop. 71 (1911), 128 (1933), 66 (1947).

Dyraaba Arm (*Co. Rous*) 28°50'S. 152°52'E., 18 km W. of Casino, on Rileys Ck; farming; PO 1927; telephone 1923; TX 1928–56; pop. 44 (1933), 58 (1954).

Dyraaba Creek (*Co. Rous*) 28°46'S. 152°49'E., 25 km NW of Casino, on Dyraaba Ck; Pigman Creek till 1933; telephone 1929; TX 1930; pop. 124 (1933), 168 (1947), 174 (1954), 113 (1961).

E

Eager's Platform (*Co. Cook*) see Valley Heights.

Eaglehawk (*Co. Wallace*) see Eucumbene.

Eaglehawk (*Co. Yancowinna*) 31°52'S. 141°34'E., 16 km NE of Broken Hill; reservoir (Stephens Creek) b. 1890–92, modified 1909, 49 ft (15 m) high; pop. 67 (1891).

Eaglehawk (*Co. Yancowinna*) see also Mount Gipps.

Eagleton (*Co. Gloucester*) 32°42'S. 151°45'E., 7 km N. of Raymond Terrace, on Williams R.; Eagleton 1885, Eskdale 1886–1914, Eagleton 1914–23, Portree 1923, Eagleton 1923+; shipbuilding and farming; broom factory (Williams River), sold 1888 to James Crane; creamery (Eagleton Co-op. Creamery Co.) 1892–97; PO 1886–1932; punt across Williams R.; quarry; school 1865–1948; shipyard (William McPherson) 1860–86; telephone 1910; TX 1928; pop. 58 (1901), 80 (1933), 234 (2011).

East Arramagong (*Co. Monteagle*) 34°05'S. 148°10'E., 21 km S. of Grenfell, on Burrangong Ck; pop. 32 (1933), 53 (1947).

Eastbourne (*Co. Wallace*) 36°11'S. 148°40'E., 24 km NW of Berridale; grazing; PO 1898; telephone 1914; TX 1917–56; pop. 25 (1933).

East Boyd (*Co. Auckland*) 37°07'S. 149°56'E., 5 km S. of Eden, on East Boyd Bay; founded 1843 by Benjamin Boyd; whaling; PO 1927; telephone 1915; TX 1928; 2 whale look-out towers, incl. one b. 1846–48 of sandstone, 76 ft (23.2 m); whaling stations: Barclay, Faulkner and Rixon's, Benjamin Boyd 1843, Davidsons' 1861–1927, Imlays' No. 2 station; woodchip mill (Harris-Daishowa Aust. Pty Ltd) estab. 1968, became South East Fibre Exports in 2003, sold 2015 to Allied Natural Wood Exports Pty Ltd, fire 2020; pop. 25 (1933).

East End (*Co. Raleigh*) 30°28'S. 152°54'E., 1 km E. of Bellingen, on Bellinger R.; pop. 26 (1933).

Eastgrove (*Co. Argyle*) see Goulburn.

Eastholme (*Co. Cooper*) 34°02'S. 146°09'E., 30 km N. of Griffith; wheat; PO 1928–34; telephone 1927; TX 1928.

East Lynne (*Co. St Vincent*) 35°37'S. 150°16'E., 14 km NE of Batemans Bay, on Ryans Ck; airfield; PO 1958; sawmills: Davis & Herbert Pty Ltd 1968 and Ryan Bros; telephone 1924; TX 1953–74; pop. 26 (1933), 52 (1954).

East Marowie (*Co. Nicholson*) 33°27'S. 145°51'E., 28 km E. of Hillston; telephone 1929; TX 1930.

Eastridge (*Co. Lincoln*) see Dubbo.

Eastville (*Co. Northumberland*) see Maitland East.

East Wyee (*Co. Northumberland*) see Doyalson.

Eaton (*Co. Jamison*) see Rowena.

Eatonsville (*Co. Clarence*) 29°38'S. 152°50'E., 12 km NW of Grafton, on Clarence R.; village gaz. 1880 as First Falls; farming and dairying; Angl. C. (Holy Name of Jesus) b. 1931 by Stephenson and Spencer, d. by Cyril Blacket, badly damaged 1935, closed, sold and reused; cemetery 1893; floods 1876 and 1945; gale 1935; PO 1892–1962; PS; punt (6 car capacity) 1905, across Clarence R.; school

1881, new one b. 1882 by Hermann Schaeffer, repairs 1900 by Timothy Mullane and James McKay, closed 1961; telephone 1911; TX 1928–1962; water supply augmentation 1986; wharf b. 1891 by J. Walsh; pop. 166 (1901), 164 (1911), 85 (1933), 68 (1947), 51 (1954), 397 (2011).

Eauabalong (*Co. Blaxland*) see Euabalong.

Ebenezer (*Co. Cook*) 33°32'S. 150°53'E., 5 km NE of Wilberforce, on Hawkesbury R.; (incl. Portland Head); founded by Owen Cavanough; farming, then poultry and orchards; FB; floods 1806 and 1867; flour mill (Victoria, water powered) estab. by Denis Benjamin Kirwan; PO 1863; 2 quarries (sand); sawmill (I.N. Woods) 1907; school 1887, new one b. 1902 by Lawrence Pickup, additions 2010; telephone 1905; TX 1924, automatic 1954; Unit. C. (orig. Presb., and also used by Meth. till 1824) b. 1809 by William Harvey, William Barren and Jacintho Barrero, finished by James Smith and David Dunstan, d. by Andrew Johnston, additions 1829, inundated 1867, additions 1926, vestry 1959 d. by Morton Earle Herman, church additions 1966, and graveyard (717 graves 1819+); winery (Tizzana) estab. 1887 by Thomas Henry Fiaschi, fire 1955, restoration 1969 by Peter and Carolyn Auld, restored again 1999, reused 2000; wharf; pop. 7 (1866), 138 (1901), 153 (1911), 251 (1933), 182 (1947), 319 (1954), 360 (1961), *c.*250 (1987), 563 (2006), 968 (2011).

Ebenezer (*Co. Hume*) see Walla Walla.

Ebenezer (*Co. Northumberland*) see Toronto.

Ebor (*Co. Clarke*) 30°24'S. 152°21'E., 35 km W. of Dorrigo, on Guy Fawkes R.; village gaz. 1905; agric. and grazing; butter factory (Guy Fawkes Co-op. Dairy Co. Ltd) b. 1908 by J. Walsh, burnt down and replaced 1912; cemetery (123 graves *c.*1890+); PO 1868; Presb. C.; PS, burnt down 1944; Rom. Cath. C. (St Patrick's), removed 1914 from Metz, burnt down 1946; school 1910–33, reopened 1955, additions 1960 and 2009; snowstorm 1949; telephone 1911; TX 1913, automatic 1982; Union C.; pop. 163 (1911), 91 (1933), 143 (1947), 151 (1954), 202 (1961), *c.*100 (1987), 160 (2006), 304 (2011).

Eccleston (*Co. Durham*) 32°16'S. 151°30'E., 29 km NW of Dungog, on Allyn R.; timber, agric., tobacco, dairying, citrus fruit; Angl. C. (St Paul's), rebuilt 1924, closed and sold 2017, and graveyard; cemetery (Belgrave, 119 graves) 1895; Cong. C. 1895, closed; electricity 1948; flood 1886; foot-bridge (Como Bridge) 1904 d. by R. Figgis, over Allyn R.; PO 1859; Presb. C. 1871; school 1867–68, reopened 1880, additions 1885 by W. Smith, replaced 1944, closed 1986, sold and reused; telephone 1911; tobacco factory (J. Sivyer); TX 1915, automatic 1961; Wes. Meth. C., used 1884–95 by Cong. C.; pop. *c.*180 (1866), 114 (1901), 158 (1911), 126 (1933), 111 (1947), 114 (1954), 85 (1961).

Eddenville (*Co. Northumberland*) see Kearsley.

Eden (*Co. Auckland*) 37°04'S. 149°55'E., 19 km S. of Merimbula, on Twofold Bay; (incl. South Eden); orig. Twofold Bay; settled 1828 by Thomas Raine, estab. 1836, surveyed 1842 by Thomas Scott Townsend, town gaz. and first lots sold 1843, designated as chief town of the county; shore whaling 1828–1929, wattle-bark 1830–1950s, brickmaking 1850–1900, cattle till 1896, timber 1903–55, shipbuilding, wheat, maize, barley, oats, potatoes, rye, butter, cheese, bacon, horses, woodchips 1970s+, now dairying, grazing, fishing, tourism; ambulance station b. 1964 by Whiter Bros; Angl. C. (St John's) 1885; benevolent asylum; breakwater 1965, 530 ft (161.5 m), extended 1985–88; brewery (Thomas Auld) 1861; brick-kiln (John Hines); brickworks (Adelaide); bushfires 1926, 1939, 1952 (11 houses destroyed); cemetery (burials 1834+) 1863, incl. columbaria 1994 and 2003; CH (incl. lock-up) 1858 d. by Alexander Dawson, additions 1860 by Arundel Everett and William Stephens, damaged 1863, additions 1893 d. by Walter Liberty Vernon, alterations and renovations 1910, new one 1914; Church of Christ; customs-house 1849 d. by Mortimer William Lewis, demolished; FB (station b. 1971); fish canneries: Aust.

Fishing Industries Ltd, Green's Products 1948 (bought 1961 by Kraft Foods, bought 1974 by H.J. Heinz Co. Aust. Ltd, closed 1999 by Heinz Wattie's), Twofold Bay Canneries Pty Ltd; flood 1919; flour mills; jetties: one one b. 1857, 115 ft (35.1 m), one b. 1861, 470 ft (143.3 m), one b. 1984, 492 ft (150 m); lighthouse (Lookout Point) 1862, demolished, replacement b. 1970, 46 ft (14 m); lock-up b. 1901 by John Hines; pilot station 1862; PO (in rented premises) 1847, new one b. 1888–91 by George Hodgson, extended 1907, reused, demolished 1967, replaced 1971; powerhouse (Eden Power Station Pty Ltd, in liquidation 1948); 3 reservoirs; Rom. Cath. C. 1864–1992, restored, reused, new one (Our Lady Star of the Sea) 1992; sawmills: Duncan's Holdings Ltd, Federal (Edward Legge), T. Goward, O.L. Harrison (moved 1924 to Mt Darragh), John Hines; schools: primary 1857, additions and alterations 1907 by Peterson and Wellings, additions 1960, 1963, 1979, 1994, and HS 1974, additions 1978, 1991, 1995; sewerage augmentation 1972 and 1988; storms 1863 and 1948; TC (Illawarra); telegraph 1868, new office b. 1888–91; TX 1909, automatic 1972; strike (sleeper cutters) 1915; Unit. C. (St George's, orig. Presb.) b. 1866 by William Ogle, cement rendered 1931, re-roofed 1961, bell tower restored 2007 by Geoff Uebergang; wattle-bark mill (Craig, Mostyn & Co.); whale look-out tower; whaling stations: Greig's, Imlay Bros No. 1 station 1834 (taken over by W. Walker & Co., demolished), Thomas Raine 1828–32; wool store b. 1910 by R.W. Henry; pop. 63 (1846), 120 (1851), 235 (1856), 482 (1861), *c.*200 (1866), 214 (1871), 231 (1881), 280 (1886), 351 (1891), 347 (1901), 626 (1911), 661 (1933), 993 (1947), 1,095 (1954), 1,245 (1961), 1,416 (1966), 2,210 (1971), 2,978 (1976), 3,107 (1981), 3,248 (1986), 3,277 (1991), 3,106 (1996), 3,157 (2001), 3,006 (2006), 3,044 (2011).

Eden Creek (*Co. Rous*) 28°35'S. 152°54'E., 11 km W. of Kyogle, on Eden Ck; Meth. C. 1912, reused; school (Geneva till 1926) 1918–26 and 1939–69; TX 1926, automatic 1953; pop. 90 (1911), 74 (1933), 122 (1947), 80 (1954), 98 (1961), 561 (2011).

Edenhurst (*Co. Rous*) see Upper Eden Creek.

Edenville (*Co. Rous*) 28°42'S. 152°58'E., 9 km SW of Kyogle; Glentimon till 1927; quarry; school 1919 b. by W. Tyrrell, closed 1966; telephone 1918; TX 1928, automatic 1953; pop. 128 (1933), 125 (1947), 107 (1954), 98 (1961).

Edgehill (*Co. Mitchell*) 35°29'S. 146°56'E., 11 km NW of Henty; settled by German immigrants; school 1892–1924; pop. 27 (1933).

Edge Hill (*Co. Wellington*) 32°54'S. 149°23'E., 39 km SW of Mudgee.

Edgell Heights (*Co. Bathurst*) see Bathurst.

Edgeroi (*Co. Jamison*) 30°07'S. 149°48'E., 23 km N. of Narrabri; soldiers' settlement (World War II) 1948; grazing, wheat, sorghum, cotton; PO 1912; RS 1897, station b. by William Mitchell, closed 1972, reopened 1993; silo 1962; telephone 1910; TX 1934, automatic 1983; pop. 104 (1933), 103 (1947), 226 (1954), 272 (1961).

Edgeroi Wool Siding (*Co. Jamison*) see Woolenget.

Edgewood (*Co. St Vincent*) 35°45'S. 150°12'E., 2 km SE of Batehaven, on Batemans Bay.

Edgeworth (*Co. Northumberland*) 32°55'S. 151°37'E., 4 km SE of West Wallsend, on Cocked Hat Ck; Cocked Hat Creek till 1885, Young Wallsend till 1960; surveyed 1885 by Percy Hodgkinson, subdivided 1885, land sales 1885, 1887, 1889, further subdivided 1890; farming and mining; Angl. C. (St Ann's) 1910; Bapt. C. (Northville Community); brickworks (A. Grant & Son); bushfires 1909, 1928, 1991, 1994; colliery (Young Wallsend) estab. 1887–89 by Young Wallsend Coal Co., o. 1890, closed 1893, reopened 1908, closed; Cong. C. (removed from Wallsend) re-erected 1906 by Tyler Bros; earthquake 1989; earth tremor 1925; electricity 1929; miners' strike 1909; New Heights Christ. C.; PO 1891; railway (colliery); sawmill (Richard Colin Carroll); schools: Edgeworth

(Young Wallsend till 1960) 1891 b. by John Rollo Rodgers, repairs 1897 by A. Laverick, additions 1924 by T.C. Southon, additions 1954, 1959, 1970, 1973, additions by R.T. Parker Pty Ltd) and Edgeworth Heights (Salty Creek till 1968) 1958, additions 2010; sewerage 1959; telephone 1913; tramway (steam) to Newcastle 1887; water reticulation 1926; pop. 233 (1901), 268 (1911), 384 (1921), 461 (1933), 557 (1947), 1,555 (1961), 5,904 (2006), 6,252 (2011).

Edinglassie (*Co. Durham*) see Muswellbrook.

Edith (*Co. Westmoreland*) 33°47'S. 149°55'E., 11 km SE of Oberon, on Duckmaloi R.; estab. by John McLean Whalan; farming; butter factory (Oberon Co-op. Dairy Co.) 1892, moved to Gingkin; PO 1900–73; Rom. Cath. C. o. 1908 in former shed; school 1884–1973, reused; telephone 1906; TX 1944–72; Wes. Meth. C., demolished 2002; pop. 151 (1901), 146 (1911), 148 (1933), 94 (1947), 108 (1954), 121 (1961), 221 (2011).

Edron (*Co. Auckland*) 37°06'S. 149°56'E., 5 km SE of Eden, on East Boyd Bay.

Edward (*Co. Townsend*) see Deniliquin.

Edward (*Co. Wakool*) 35°08'S. 144°04'E., 54 km N. of Barham; village gaz. 1931; pop. 43 (1933).

Edwardstown (*Co. Wynyard*) 35°07'S. 148°04'E., 7 km SW of Gundagai, on Big Ben Ck; quarry; school 1873, additions 1885 by W.H. Hilton, closed 1962; pop. 28 (1933), 85 (1954).

Edwells Flat (*Co. Clarence*) 29°56'S. 153°09'E., 20 km N. of Woolgoolga, on Wolli Wolli R.

Edzell (*Co. Dudley*) 30°55'S. 152°35'E., 29 km NW of Kempsey, on Macleay R.; telephone 1928.

Eenaweena (*Co. Oxley*) 31°31'S. 147°33'E., 34 km E. of Nyngan, on Duck Ck; pop. 24 (1933).

Egan (*Co. Bathurst*) see Caloola.

Egansford (*Co. Boyd*) 34°45'S. 146°04'E., 38 km SW of Leeton; school (Coleambally till 1965) 1961–71; telephone 1961; TX (automatic) 1962.

Eganton (*Co. Bathurst*) see Hazelwood.

Egelabra (*Co. Oxley*) 31°45'S. 147°47'E., 7 km SW of Warren, on Beleringar Ck; RS (Sandy Creek till 1924) 1898–1973; storm 1900; pop. 40 (1933), 56 (1954).

Eglinford (*Co. Northumberland*) see Congewai.

Eglinton (*Co. Roxburgh*) 33°23'S. 149°33'E., 6 km NW of Bathurst, on Macquarie R.; estab. 1822 by George Ranken, subdivided, laid out and lots sold 1855 by George Ranken; farming and grazing; Bapt. C. 1896, defunct; boiling-down works and tannery (George Ranken); brewery (Kelloshiel) estab. by George Ranken, taken over by Heathorn and Price, converted 1841 from water power to steam, burnt down 1858; bridge (Ranken's Bridge), to Abercrombie, d. and b. 1856 by George Ranken, 120 ft (36.6 m), destroyed 1867, rebuilt 1869–73 by William Timothy Atkins, replaced (Allan timber truss) 1920 by Ford, new one b. 1998 by N.J. McIntosh Pty Ltd, over Macquarie R.; bushfire 2009; cheese factory (George Ranken); drought 1838–40; electricity 1947; FB (station b. 1999); floods 1867 and 1950; flour mills: Blackdown (brick tower mill b. 1824 by Thomas Fitzherbert Hawkins, refitted 1834, taken over 1837 by Solomon Mocatta, taken over 1848 by James Coombes, burnt down 1852), Kelloshiel (estab. 1831 by George Ranken, converted 1841 from water power to steam, burnt down 1858, rebuilt 1860, burnt down again 1867), Stain's; PO 1869; Rom. Cath. C. (Our Lady of Fatima) 1954, demolished; school 1868, repairs 1891 by Albert Emanuel Ennis, demolished and replaced 1956, additions 1990 and 2010; sewerage augmentation 1985; telephone 1911; TX (automatic) 1957; Union C. (Muller Memorial) b. 1900 by W. Boyd, became Angl. C. (St Luke's), closed 1986, reused; water supply augmentation 1985; winery (George Ranken); pop. 170 (1901), 181 (1911), 197 (1933), 186 (1947), 220 (1954), 227 (1961), 2,109 (2011).

Eighteen Mile Hollow (*Co. Cook*) see Bulls Camp.

Eighteen Mile Point (*Co. Cowper*) see Bourke.

Elands (*Co. Macquarie*) 31°38'S. 152°18'E., 27 km N. of Wingham, on Little Ck; timber, farming, dairying *c.*1918–75; PO 1916; sawmills: Duncan's Holdings Ltd, Eriksson Bros, Goldsmith and Rose, Henry Machin & Sons Pty Ltd, Edmund Wallace; school 1935, additions 2010; telephone 1916; TX 1922, automatic 1977; pop. 207 (1933), 173 (1947), 200 (1954), 152 (1961), 277 (2006), 400 (2011).

Elcombe (*Co. Murchison*) 29°45'S. 150°23'E., 20 km NW of Bingara; farming; PO 1913; telephone 1916; TX 1916, automatic 1966; pop. 67 (1933).

Elderbury (*Co. Hardinge*) 30°16'S. 151°34'E., 11 km SW of Guyra, on Abington Ck; pop. 26 (1933).

Elderslie (*Co. Durham*) 32°36'S. 151°20'E., 6 km N. of Branxton, on Hunter R.; farming and orchards; airfield; bridge (Burns Bridge), 236 ft (71.9 m), b. 1876 by E. Taylor and D. M'Lachlan, new one (iron lattice) b. 1889–91 by J.F. Carson, d. by John Alexander McDonald, 533 ft (162.5 m), over Hunter R.; creamery (Joseph Bercini) b. 1892 by W. Taylor & Son; PO 1876–1969; 3 quarries; school 1878 b. by James Pritchard, closed 1982; telephone 1919; TX 1920, automatic 1969; pop. 75 (1901), 95 (1911), 106 (1933), 68 (1954), 97 (1961).

Eleebana (*Co. Northumberland*) 33°00'S. 151°38'E., 4 km NE of Toronto, on Lake Macquarie; (incl. Tingira Heights, formerly Violet Town); subdivisions 1918, 1938, 1951, 1953; bushfires 1952, 1982, 1991; Christ. Brethren C.; FB (Tingira Heights), station b. 2006 by R.T. Parker Pty Ltd; PO 1948; quarry; school 1955, additions 1957 and 1970, new one b. 1991 by R.T. Parker Pty Ltd; sewerage 1977; telephone 1946; water supply 1955; pop. 78 (1947), 5,498 (2011).

Elermore Vale (*Co. Northumberland*) 32°55'S. 151°40'E., 2 km S. of Wallsend, on Ironbark Ck; (incl. Rankin Park, orig. Cambridge Hills Estate); formerly South Wallsend; bushfire 1935; colliery (Kirkdale); PO 1958; 2 reservoirs; schools: Elermore Vale (Jubilee Road till 1979) 1957, additions by R.T. Parker Pty Ltd, and South Wallsend 1952, additions 1958 and 1991; SD Adventist C. (Wallsend); pop. 5,186 (2011).

Eleven Mile Turn Off (*Co. Murray*) 35°24'S. 149°23'E., 15 km E. of Queanbeyan, on Molonglo R.; mine (The Briars Mine operated by Mount Malcombe Syndicate and Scottsdale Copper-mining & Smelting Co.) *c.*1921.

Eli Elwah (*Co. Waradgery*) 34°39'S. 144°52'E., 17 km S. of Hay; pop. 97 (1911).

Elizabeth Bay (*Co. Northumberland*) 33°12'S. 151°35'E., 2 km SE of Lake Munmorah, on Lake Munmorah; rutile mining; 2 quarries.

Elizabeth Beach (*Co. Gloucester*) 32°20'S. 152°32'E., 18 km S. of Forster, on Elizabeth Bay; reservoir; pop. 33 (1961), 230 (2011).

Elizabeth Fields (*Co. King*) 34°53'S. 149°05'E., 15 km E. of Yass, on Yass R.; school 1876, new buildings b. 1882 by G. Thomson, closed 1889, demolished.

Elizabeth Vale (*Co. Cook*) 33°26'S. 150°02'E., 3 km SW of Wallerawang.

Ellalong (*Co. Northumberland*) 32°55'S. 151°19'E., 3 km SE of Paxton, on Quorrobolong Ck; (incl. Wallaby Gully); settled 1848 by Samuel Cadman, Benjamin Bridge and James Hamilton, surveyed 1856, village gaz. 1880 as Aellalong; timber, wheat till 1870s, salt (disc. 1889), coalmining, grazing, farming, dairying; Angl. C. (St Thomas's) b. 1873 by Libbey, d. by B.E. Shaw, extended 1879, closed 2014, sold 2015; brickworks 1909–12; bushfire 1951; cemetery (752 graves 1863+) 1863; CH 1872; collieries: Cessnock No. 1 (o. 1921 by Great Northern Coal Co. as Kalingo Colliery, bought 1922 by Wickham & Bullock Island Co., strikes 1922, 1923, 1924, taken over 1937 by Cessnock Collieries Ltd, name changed 1937, strikes 1939, 1940, 1943, 1944, men killed 1944 and 1952, strikes 1948 and 1952, closed 1959, acquired 1959 by Caledonian Collieries Ltd, acquired and reopened 1960 by Coal & Allied Industries Ltd, closed 1961, derelict) and Ellalong (estab. 1976 by Peko-Wallsend Ltd, merged 1988 with North Broken Hill

Ltd, taken over 1988 by Elders Resources, taken over 1990 by a consortium); creamery (Thursby and Rae) 1898; dam (colliery) 1920; diphtheria 1921; FB; flour mill (Alex Kennedy) 1860; PO 1862; Presb. C.; PS 1884–1905; railway (colliery); Rom. Cath. C. (St Isidore's); sawmill estab. 1880 by William Snape, sen., sold to Harry Bridge and Charles Chapman, sold to G. Chapman, burnt down and rebuilt, sold to Gould Bros who moved it to Cessnock; school 1858, new one b. 1879, burnt down 1908, replaced 1911, extended 1928 by H.B. Sudlow; telephone 1901; TX 1927; pop. *c.*50 (1866), 294 (1901), 333 (1911), 334 (1933), 342 (1947), 327 (1954), 278 (1961), 264 (1986), 367 (1991), 504 (1996), 561 (2001), 620 (2006), 788 (2011).

Elland (*Co. Clarence*) 29°46'S. 152°55'E., 6 km S. of South Grafton.

Ellangowan (*Co. Richmond*) 29°02'S. 153°04'E., 19 km S. of Casino; farming; Angl. C. (St George the Martyr) 1918, damaged, repaired and reopened 1938; bushfires 1918, 1926, 1946; gale 1938; PO 1927–31; school 1913, burnt down 1918, new one b. 1920 by Percival F. Small, additions 2010, closed 2014, sold 2015; telephone 1915; TX 1928; pop. 72 (1911), 206 (1933), 168 (1947), 143 (1954), 115 (1961), 255 (2011).

Ellenborough (*Co. Macquarie*) 31°27'S. 152°27'E., 28 km W. of Wauchope, on Ellenborough R.; village gaz. 1905; timber, farming, grazing, dairying *c.*1918–75; Angl. C. (St Cuthbert's) 1908; bridges: one b. 1869–71 and suspension bridge b. 1936 over Hastings R.; cemetery (75 graves 1905+) 1875; PO 1865; PS b. 1899 by G.A. Stokes; sawmills: Beale's (estab. by Donaldson) and Myall Timber Co. (Glenwarrin Mill, estab. 1947 by Ron Harris, George Dunford, George Ducat and Bert Cooper, closed 1975); school 1919–71; telephone 1915; TX 1916, automatic 1971; pop. 58 (1901), 120 (1911), 169 (1933), 208 (1947), 147 (1954), 130 (1961), 294 (2011).

Ellerslie (*Co. Wentworth*) 33°49'S. 142°02'E., 33 km N. of Wentworth, on Darling R.

Ellerslie (*Co. Wynyard*) 35°19'S. 147°56'E., 12 km W. of Adelong; pop. 61 (1911), 64 (1954), 55 (1961).

Ellerston (*Co. Durham*) 31°49'S. 151°18'E., 44 km E. of Murrurundi, on Hunter R.; grazing; airfield; bridge b. 1970 by M.R. and E.M. Firth, 166 ft (50.6 m); FB (station b. 2014); PO 1925; school 1957; telephone 1910; TX 1916, automatic 1972; pop. 92 (1911), 148 (1933), 175 (1947), 132 (1954).

Ellimo (*Co. Cooper*) 34°10'S. 146°08'E., 16 km NE of Griffith; village gaz. 1924, razed.

Ellis Lane (*Co.* Camden) 34°02'S. 150°41'E., 4 km NW of Camden, on Nepean R.; orig. Cobbitty Paddocks; dairying, then hort. and turf; FB; pop. 808 (2011).

Ellison (*Co. Cook*) see Springwood.

Ellon (*Co. Bourke*) 34°07'S. 147°02'E., 28 km N. of Ardlethan; school 1957–70.

Elmgrove (*Co. Auckland*) 36°38'S. 149°51'E., 5 km N. of Bega; cheese factory (William Allen) 1877, bought 1909 by George Guthrey; pop. 31 (1933).

Elmslea (*Co. Murray*) see Bungendore.

Elmwood (*Co. Camden*) see Yarrunga.

Elong Elong (*Co. Lincoln*) 32°07'S. 149°02'E., 35 km W. of Dunedoo; village gaz. 1917; wheat and grazing; cemetery (33 graves 1913+) 1911; FB; PO 1919, burnt down 1931; Presb. C. 1899; Rom. Cath. C. (St Therese of the Child Jesus) 1930; RS 1918–74; sawmill (James J. Sweeney); school 1929–69, reused; telegraph 1922; telephone 1923; tornado 1996; TX 1923, automatic 1973; Union C., closed, and graveyard; pop. 187 (1933), 136 (1947), 131 (1954), 126 (1961), 225 (2006).

Elouera (*Co. Robinson*) 31°10'S. 145°47'E., 10 km NW of Cobar; copper mine; PO 1907; school 1908–15; telephone 1917.

Elrington (*Co. Northumberland*) 32°53'S. 151°25'E., 9 km SW of Kurri Kurri; settled by Clement Cains Elrington; bushfire 1994; cemetery 1863; collieries: Elrington (estab. 1924–28 as Hebburn No. 3 by BHP Collieries Pty Ltd, strike 1928, o. and renamed 1930, man killed 1937, strikes 1938, 1939, 1941, 1942, 1943, 1944, 1950, 1954, closed 1962, reused 1964) and Hebburn No. 2 (estab. 1918–

21 by Hebburn Ltd, o. 1921, men killed 1922 and 1942, strikes 1942, 1943, 1944, 1946–47, 1950, 1954, man killed 1954, washery 1956, company reconstituted 1958 as Hebburn Collieries Ltd, acquired 1961 by Bitumen & Oil Refineries Aust. Ltd, reconstituted 1964 as Boral Ltd, colliery taken over 1967 by Coal & Allied Industries Ltd, closed 1972, partly reused, powerhouse closed and demolished 1976); railway (colliery); rifle range (Hebburn) 1915; school (Hebburn) 1927–35, building removed; pop. 37 (1933), 275 (2011).

Elrington (*Co. St Vincent*) see Majors Creek.

Elsinora (*Co. Delalah*) 29°27'S. 143°37'E., 233 km N. of Wilcannia.

Elsmore (*Co. Gough*) 29°48'S. 151°18'E., 16 km E. of Inverell; Glenmore till 1846; settled largely by Cornishmen; mining (tin disc. 1871 by Joseph Wills), declined 1918+, hay, chaff, corn, apiculture, grazing; bridges over Macintyre R.: one b. 1910 (low-level timber) by W.A. Sims and one b. 1954 by W.F. Stephenson; cemetery (170 graves 1895+) 1879; earth tremor 1915; FB; 3 mines (incl. C.S. McGlew 1871); PO 1873, new one b. 1906, closed 1991; scarlet fever 1911; school 1881, new buildings b. 1883 by A. Thorley, closed 1966; tornado 1989; telephone 1900; TX 1910, automatic 1989; Wes. Meth. C. 1901, burnt down; pop. 383 (1911), 155 (1933), 218 (1947), 248 (1954), 242 (1961), 326 (2006), 567 (2011).

Elswick (*Co. Cunningham*) 33°00'S. 147°19'E., 18 km NE of Condobolin.

Eltham (*Co. Rous*) 28°45'S. 153°24'E., 10 km NW of Alstonville, on Wilsons R.; farming; Angl. C. (St Mark's) b. 1897 by Alexander Robertson, closed, sold, moved, reused; bridge (timber truss) 1934, over Wilsons R.; floods 2001 and 2010; PO 1896; railway bridge (steel truss) 1894, 120 ft (36.6 m), over Wilsons R.; RS (orig. Mayfield) 1894, station b. by Alexander Hamilton Scouller, closed 1974; sawmill, man killed 1899; school (Cowlong till 1907) 1888, new one b. 1907 by T.E. Jarman; telephone 1899; TX 1925–64; pop. 134 (1901), 266 (1911), 173 (1933), 144 (1947), 97 (1954), 106 (1961), 351 (2011).

Embie (*Co. Gregory*) 31°07'S. 148°02'E., 39 km SW of Coonamble.

Emden Vale (*Co. Georgiana*) 34°05'S. 149°37'E., 43 km N. of Crookwell; PO 1927–30.

Emerald Beach (*Co. Fitzroy*) 30°10'S. 153°11'E., 6 km S. of Woolgoolga, on Tasman Sea; airfield (2 km SW); flood 2001; 2 quarries; water reticulation 1980; pop. 917 (1986), 1,208 (1991), 1,688 (1996), 1,847 (2001), 1,912 (2006). 2,135 (2011).

Emerald Hill (*Co. Pottinger*) 30°53'S. 150°07'E., 17 km NW of Gunnedah; farming and grazing; Angl. C. (St Thomas's); electricity 1954; FB; PO 1891; Rom. Cath. C. (St Peter and St Paul's) 1872; RS 1883, station relocated 1913; school 1957–67; silo 1934; TX 1910, automatic 1949; pop. 61 (1901), 154 (1911), 182 (1933), 112 (1947), 82 (1954), 101 (1961), 256 (2011).

Emigrant Creek (*Co. Rous*) see Cumbalum.

Emmagool (*Co. Gordon*) 32°32'S. 148°33'E., 36 km W. of Wellington, on Meadows Ck; Angl. C. (St John the Baptist) 1928.

Emmaville (*Co. Gough*) 29°27'S. 151°36'E., 35 km N. of Glen Innes; Vegetable Creek till 1882; estab. 1872; tin (disc. 1872 by Thomas Carlean), production peaked 1881, silver (disc. *c.*1895 by Webb), sheep, fossicking; Angl. C. (St Paul's) b. 1875 by Clarke and Schedel, relocated and enlarged 1879, closed 1953, demolished, replaced 1953; bushfire 1952; cemetery (1,037 graves 1876+), incl. columbarium; CH (incl. lock-up) b. 1882–84 by J. Strauss, new one b. 1920 by Benjamin Martin Wade; Chinese joss house 1887, burnt down 1932; Chinese Mission C. 1893; cordial factory (E.A. Fisher); diphtheria 1909; electricity 1951; FB; flood 1912; hailstorm 1887; hospital (Vegetable Creek) b. 1882 by Clarke and Schedel, rebuilt 1947; measles epidemic 1912; mines: Associated Extended, Britain Tin Mining Co., Buffalo Tin Mining Co., Burkes Tin Mining Co., East Britain Tin Mining Co., Great Britain Tin Mining

Co. (estab. by Thomas Carleen, closed 1921), Mining Recovery of Aust. (open-cut tin mine), Vegetable Creek Tin Mining Co., Y-Water Tin Mining Co.; PO 1873, new one b. 1883 by J. Strauss; police barracks b. 1891 by Clarke and Schedel; PS, new one 1954; 10 quarries; Rom. Cath. C. 1874, new one (St Mary's) 1910, and graveyard; school (Vegetable Creek till 1882) 1878, new one b. 1880 by William Seabrook and John Brown, additions 1882 by J. Strauss, additions 1893 by Nicholas Josephson, additions and repairs 1908 by H. Clarke, replacement b. 1928 on new site by Benjamin Martin Wade, extended 1970 by Fred Huntley Constructions; streets electric lit 1939; tin treatment plants: Base Minerals Ltd 1970 and one of 1971; telegraph 1876; TX 1911, automatic 1970; typhoid 1899 (3 died), 1912, 1953; Wes. Meth. C. b. 1874 by Clarke and Schedel, enlarged 1877, new one 1881 d. by Reid, reused 1975; whooping cough epidemics 1908 and 1912; pop. *c.*800 (1873), 2,670 (1881), 978 (1891), 978 (1901), 1,585 (1911), 908 (1933), 764 (1947), 897 (1954), 604 (1961), 506 (1971), 446 (1976), 503 (1981), 405 (1986), 379 (1991), 347 (1996), 308 (2001), 247 (2006), 300 (2011).

Emmdale (*Co. Werunda*) 31°39'S. 144°15'E., 84 km E. of Wilcannia; pop. *c.*5 (1999).

Empire Bay (*Co. Northumberland*) 33°30'S. 151°22'E., 4 km E. of Woy Woy, on Brisbane Water; (incl. Daleys Point and Merritts Wharf); Sorrento till 1908; subdivided 1905 by Arthur Rickard & Co., estab. 1906; orig. hunting, boating, fishing, then farming and oysters; Angl. C. (All Saints'); bridge (The Rip Bridge), 1,082 ft (330 m), from Daleys Point to Blackwall and Booker Bay, b. 1974, d. by Albert Fried, over Brisbane Water; bushfire 1928; electricity 1938; FB; PO 1909; sawmill (John Settree); school (Cockle Creek till 1902, then Davis Town till 1910) 1881 b. by A. Davis, additions 1981 and 1993; telephone: Daleys Point 1953 and Empire Bay 1914; TX 1917–65; Union C.; Unit. C. 1913; wharves: Kendall Road, Merritts, Shelly Beach Road; pop. 72 (1911), 150 (1933), 196 (1947), 174 (1954), 355 (1961), 205 (1971), 2,862 (2011).

Empire Vale (*Co. Richmond*) 28°55'S. 153°31'E., 7 km SW of Ballina, on Richmond R.; German Creek till 1915; farming and sugar-cane; Meth. C. (moved to Woodburn); PO 1884; school (Pimlico till 1895, then German Creek till 1915) 1880, new one b. 1891 on new site, additions 1895 by Brown and Jolly, additions 1903 by J. Henderson, alterations 1920 by F. Bolton, additions 1964; telephone 1907; Union C. 1890; Wes. Meth. C.; wharf b. 1893 by Charles Hodgson; pop. 147 (1901), 201 (1911), 221 (1933), 204 (1947), 145 (1954), 194 (1961), 395 (2011).

Emu (*Co. Cook*) see Emu Plains.

Emu Creek (*Co. Monteagle*) 33°59'S. 148°08'E., 10 km S. of Grenfell, on Emu Ck.

Emu Creek (*Co. Monteagle*) see also Grenfell.

Emu Creek (*Co. Vernon*) 30°57'S. 151°43'E., 11 km E. of Walcha; electricity 1953; pop. 22 (1933).

Emu Ferry (*Co. Cook*) see Emu Plains.

Emu Flat (*Co. Murray*) 35°44'S. 149°39'E., 34 km S. of Braidwood, on Shoalhaven R.; cemetery (Gundillion); PS.

Emu Heights (*Co. Cook*) see Emu Plains.

Emu Island (*Co. Cook*) see Emu Plains.

Emu Park (*Co. Denison*) 35°42'S. 146°13'E., 37 km NW of Corowa; school 1912–18 and 1936–47.

Emu Park (*Co. Richmond*) 29°00'S. 153°08'E., 16 km W. of Coraki.

Emu Plains (*Co. Cook*) 33°45'S. 150°40'E., 5 km NE of Glenbrook, on Nepean R.; (incl. Emu Heights, estab. 1976); Emu Island 1808–14, then Emu, then Emu Ferry 1863–82; surveyed by Major Sir Thomas Livingstone Mitchell, laid out 1832 by White, town gaz. 1881; orig. maize then grazing, agric., dairying, fruit; Angl. C. b. 1848 by Crotts and Mealy, d. by Edmund Thomas Blacket, alterations 1872, chancel b. 1887 by Donald, d. by Sykes, new one (St Paul's) 1991, and graveyard (now the general cemetery); bridges: one b. 1854–56 by Penrith Nepean Bridge Co., d. by David McBeath, (689 ft or 210 m), destroyed 1857, rebuilt, destroyed 1860, Victoria Bridge (wrought iron box girders) b. 1867 by William Watkins and Peto, Brassey and Betts, d. by Sir John Fowler and John Whitton, 198 ft (60.4 m), damaged 1867, iron span (135 ft or 41.1 m) added, shared by motor vehicles and trains till 1907 when a separate railway one was built, Penrith Valley Bridge 1971, over Nepean R.; bushfires 1923 and 1929; cemetery (966 graves 1860+) 1863, orig. St Paul's graveyard; chocolate factory (Zokoko) 2009; Church of Christ; crate, case and pallet factory (Douglas Box); floods 1799, 1806, 1809, 1817, 1819, 1857, 1864, 1867, 1900, 1904, 1925, 1943, 1949, 1961, 1978, 1986, 1988, 1990; foot-bridge b. 2018 by Seymour Whyte Constructions Pty Ltd, over Nepean R.; govt agric. station 1819–32; house frame and truss factory (Western Sydney Frame & Truss); LDS (Mormon) C.; metal fabrication works (J.H. Bonwick & Co.) 1970; motor home factory (Winnebago Industries) 2001, became Avida in 2013; PO 1852; pound (stock) 1865; prison farm 1914, enlarged 1940, remodelled 1957, additions 1990, female prisoners only from 1994, additions 1995 and 2000; PS, sold 1891, new one b. 1908 on new site by J.J. Giles, closed 1921; punt 1823, destroyed 1867, across Nepean R.; quarries (Boral); railway accident (3 killed) 1878; railway bridge (Victoria Bridge) b. 1867 (wrought iron box girders) by William Watkins and Peto, Brassey and Betts, d. by Sir John Fowler and John Whitton, 198 ft (60.4 m), damaged 1867, iron span (135 ft or 41.1 m) added, reused solely for road traffic from 1907, new railway one one (steel truss) 1907, 120 ft (36.6 m), fabricated by R. Tulloch & Co., Phoenix Iron Works, d. by James Fraser, over Nepean R.; Rom. Cath. C. b. 1976 by J.W. Broomhead & Sons Pty Ltd, d. by Matthew Gooden, new one (Our Lady of the Way) 1993; RS 1868, old station removed, new station b. 1884 on new site by M. Read; schools: Emu Plains 1877, reused (new one, additions 1907 by J.J. Giles, additions 1967, 1970, 1980), Emu Heights 1972, Nepean HS 1963 d. by R.A. Johnson, additions 1971; shade structures factory (Abacus); stockade, sold 1840 to Hogan; storm 1857; telegraph 1885; telephone: Emu Heights 1951 and Emu Plains 1910; toll-gate; tweed mill and flour mill in former stockade (Abraham and John Rayner) 1851, burnt down 1861, rebuilt, demolished; typhoid 1904; Unit. C. (orig. Wes. Meth.) 1863, re-roofed and renovated 1903; wool-scour (William George McGrath and Robert W. Smith-Gow) 1894, damaged 1900, fire 1941; pop. 61 (1851), 125 (1856), 107 (1861), *c.*550 (1866), 136 (1871), 530 (1881), 642 (1891), 610 (1901), 622 (1911), 680 (1933), 867 (1947), 914 (1954), 1,080 (1961), 11,459 (2011).

Emu Swamp (*Co. Bathurst*) 33°19'S. 149°12'E., 9 km E. of Orange; gold (alluvial); Wes. Meth. C. 1872, closed, sold and reused; pop. 134 (1901), 124 (1911), 62 (1933), 70 (1947), 62 (1954), 50 (1961).

Endsleigh (*Co. Wellington*) see Orange.

Enfield (*Co. Cook*) see North Richmond.

Enfield (*Co. Northumberland*) see Maitland East.

Enmore (*Co. Narromine*) 32°05'S. 147°46'E., 21 km W. of Trangie.

Enmore (*Co. Sandon*) 30°43'S. 151°46'E., 24 km S. of Armidale; formerly Melrose; estab. 1889; gold rush; mine (Bora, disc. by Jack Ward) 1914; PO 1889–91; PS 1889; Rom. Cath. C. (St Mary's); school 1890–91 and 1957–80; Union C. 1954; Wes. Meth. C. 1890; pop. 83 (1911), 90 (1933), 100 (1947), 123 (1954), 94 (1961), 352 (2006).

Enngonia (*Co. Culgoa*) 29°19'S. 145°51'E., 85 km N. of Bourke, on Warrego R.; Enngonia since 1884; settled by Con Bride, surveyed 1869 by Henry V. Evans, town gaz. 1869 as Eringonia, first lots sold 1870; grazing; bridge b. 1889 Richard Biggs, over Warrego R.; cemetery 1893; CH 1898; cordial factories: D. Caine and G.E. Klaeby; PO 1871, burnt down 1941; PS 1878, new one b. 1899 by John Dunkley; Rom. Cath. C. (St Francis Xavier's) 1892; school 1884–1904, reopened 1955, additions 1966, new one 1979; telegraph 1884; water reticulation 1967; TX 1912–89;

pop. 78 (1891), 70 (1901), 91 (1911), 40 (1933), 78 (1947), 116 (1954), 90 (1961), *c.*100 (1999), 125 (2006), 210 (2011).

Ennis (*Co. Macquarie*) 31°27'S. 152°45'E., 3 km NE of Wauchope, on Hastings R.; farming; Angl. C. (St Peter's), defunct; PO 1868–1915; punt across Hastings R.; school 1876–81; telephone 1914; Wes. Meth. C. 1864, new one 1883, demolished 1896, rebuilt 1896 by G. Freeman; wharf 1898; pop. 65 (1911), 43 (1933).

Ennisdale (*Co. Darling*) 30°33'S. 150°37'E., 19 km S. of Barraba; RS 1946–65.

Environ (*Co. Rous*) 28°19'S. 153°29'E., 9 km E. of Murwillumbah; sugar-cane.

Environa (*Co. Murray*) 35°24'S. 149°11'E., 7 km SW of Queanbeyan; bought 1924 by Henry Ferdinand Halloran for subdivision, but never developed; pop. 894 (2006).

Enwylong (*Co. Gloucester*) 32°40'S. 151°50'E., 12 km W. of Karuah; Euwylong till 1896; farming; bushfire 1914; PO 1927–30; quarry; school 1891–1910; telephone 1925; pop. 121 (1901), 64 (1911).

Equus (*Co. Lincoln*) see Dubbo.

Eraring (*Co. Northumberland*) 33°04'S. 151°31'E., 3 km NE of Dora Creek, on Lake Eraring; subdivided 1910 by Excelsior Land, Investment, & Building Co. & Bank Ltd; hort. and orchards 1910+; dam (ash) 1982, 82 ft (25 m) high; electricity 1936; PO 1927–73; power station b. 1975–84, sold 1983 by Pacific Power to Eraring Power Co., explosion 2011; school 1924 b. by Richard Partridge-Wall, closed 2014, sold 2016; telephone 1925; water supply 1941; winery; pop. 143 (1933), 133 (1947), 294 (1954), 308 (1961), 212 (2006), 274 (2011).

Eremeran Station (*Co. Blaxland*) 32°30'S. 146°26'E., 95 km NW of Condobolin; pop. 69 (1933), 70 (1947), 55 (1954).

Eribung (*Co. Kennedy*) 32°40'S. 147°46'E., 29 km N. of Trundle; school 1957–72.

Erigolia (*Co. Cooper*) 33°51'S. 146°22'E., 56 km NE of Griffith; Naradhun till 1924; soldiers' settlement 1920, village gaz. 1925, declined by 1929; farming; bushfire 1969; cemetery; FB; PO 1924, burnt down 1926; RS (Naradhun till 1924) 1923–75, station removed 1984; school 1931–43; silo 1930; storm 1939; telephone 1925; TX 1925; pop. 126 (1933), 24 (1947), 25 (1954), 106 (1961), 214 (2006).

Erin (*Co. Cooper*) see Moombooldool.

Erina (*Co. Northumberland*) 33°26'S. 151°23'E., 4 km E. of Gosford, on Erina Ck; (incl. Erina Heights and West Erina); formerly also known as Woodport; founded 1885, surveyed, subdivided (Runnimede Estate) and laid out 1888; orig. timber then citrus orchards; Angl. C. (St Philip the Deacon) 1916, chancel and porch added, church closed, moved 1986 to Somersby and reused; army training depot 1970, additions by R.T. Parker Pty Ltd; Assemblies of God C. (Coastlife), burnt down 2010; Bapt. C. (Central Coast); brewery (Six String Brewing Co.) estab. 2010 by Chris Benson and Adam Klasterka; bridges over Erina Ck: The Punt Bridge to East Gosford (b. 1884–86 by John Johnstone, 2 plate web girder fixed spans, opening span locked 1930, demolished 1963, replacement b. 1962 by Beattie & Frost Pty Ltd, 135 ft 9 in. or 41.4 m) and Yerin Bridge (to Springfield) 1998; bushfires 1909, 1952, 1994; chocolate factory (Faith Chocolate Co.) estab. 2014 by Brett Mayhew; cordial factory (George Margin), relocated 1969 from Gosford; distillery (St Fiacre) estab. 2006 by Philip Moore, renamed Botanica in 2010; Evangelical C. (Central Coast) 2009; flood 1956; PO 1880; Salv. Army C. 1982; sawmills: Alfred George Aldrick (burnt down), George Clark (destroyed 1956), I.B. Day & Sons (fire 1953), W.E. Kirkness 1925, Pioneer (estab. 1879 by George Henry Howard, replaced by Hylton J. Moore's sawmill, fire 1944, sold 1953 to E.K. Clarke); schools: Erina Heights (Erina till 1950) 1880, new school b. 1892 by Wright Bros, alterations 1914, additions 1919, 1963, 1967, 1974, Erina HS 1964, additions 1975 and 1985, Woodport (West Erina 1927–50 and 1954–92) 1893 b. by Spurway, additions 1982 and 1993; SD Adventist C.; telephone 1905; TX (automatic) 1962; wharf; pop. 288

(1901), 375 (1911), 311 (1933), 503 (1947), 748 (1954), 883 (1961), 835 (1971), 5,055 (2011).

Erina Heights (*Co. Northumberland*) see Erina.

Eringanerin (*Co. Gowen*) 31°46'S. 148°44'E., 9 km E. of Gilgandra, on Castlereagh R.; town gaz. 1863; floods 1874 and 1955.

Eringonia (*Co. Culgoa*) see Enngonia.

Eringowarra (*Co. Clarendon*) 35°05'S. 147°40'E., 25 km E. of Wagga Wagga.

Erin Vale (*Co. Clarendon*) 34°40'S. 147°32'E., 23 km N. of Junee; school (Gwynne) 1892–1914; pop. 31 (1933), 55 (1947), 169 (2006).

Ermelo (*Co. Murchison*) see Derra Derra.

Ermelo (*Co. Richmond*) 29°03'S. 153°04'E., 21 km W. of Coraki; telephone 1916; TX 1922.

Erowal Bay (*Co. St Vincent*) 35°06'S. 150°39'E., 2 km NE of Sanctury Point, on Erowal Bay; (incl. Old Erowal Bay); fishing; brick-kilns; FB; flood 2015; Greek Orthodox C. (St John the Forerunner and Baptist); PO 1947; telephone 1947; TX 1947–69; pop. 139 (1954), 80 (1961), 162 (1971), 209 (1976), 481 (1981), 705 (1986), 1,000 (1991), 1,214 (1996), 1,506 (2001), 1,755 (2006), 1,963 (2011).

Erringhi (*Co. Durham*) see Clarence Town.

Errol (*Co. Bathurst*) 33°36'S. 149°10'E., 3 km NE of Carcoar.

Errowanbang (*Co. Bathurst*) 33°33'S. 149°03'E., 18 km SW of Millthorpe, on Flyers Ck; earth tremor 1920; school 1957–2014, sold 2016; TX; pop. 42 (1933), 75 (1961).

Erskine Flat (*Co. Roxburgh*) see Sofala.

Erskine Island (*Co. Roxburgh*) see Sofala.

Erudgere (*Co. Wellington*) 32°35'S. 149°29'E., 9 km W. of Mudgee; farming; PO 1912–62; telephone 1913; TX 1915; wineries: Burnbrae Vineyard 1968 and Thistle Hill Vineyard estab. 1975 by Dave and Leslie Robertson; pop. 100 (1933), 52 (1947), 58 (1961).

Eschol (*Co. Lincoln*) 32°20'S. 148°39'E., 9 km SE of Dubbo; goldmine (D.B. Thompson and A.D. Huckel) 1934–37; school 1883 b. by Moulton and Shadbolt, closed 1921, reopened 1957–58; pop. 79 (1933), 74 (1947), 60 (1954), 338 (2011).

Esdai (*Co. Hunter*) 32°28'S. 150°39'E., 9 km S. of Denman, on Horseshoe Ck; telephone 1928; TX 1942.

Eskbank (*Co. Cook*) see Lithgow.

Eskdale (*Co. Gloucester*) see Eagleton.

Esrom (*Co. Bathurst*) see Bathurst.

Essington (*Co. Westmoreland*) 33°43'S. 149°41'E., 16 km W. of Oberon, on Native Dog Ck; estab. 1892 as mining village, defunct; mining (gold and copper), farming, grazing, timber; airfield; bushfire 2006; mines: Cash-Essington or Essington (Lloyd Copper Mining Co.) <1877, 1905, 1907–8, 1920, 1958, Chain of Ponds, Fullback or Dingo (Dingo Copper Mining Co.) 1901 and 1907, Mount Stromlo (tungsten) 1906, North Essington 1904 and 1908, Prosper Copper Mining Co. 1907–8; PO 1876; school 1881–90 and 1903–15; telephone 1915; TX 1941, automatic 1964; pop. 83 (1901), 108 (1911), 74 (1947), 51 (1954), 272 (2006).

Essington Park (*Co. Westmoreland*) 33°43'S. 149°46'E., 8 km W. of Oberon, on Prospecting Ck.

Estella (*Co. Clarendon*) 35°04'S. 147°21'E., 5 km N. of Wagga Wagga; Unit. C.; pop. 508 (1991), 1,080 (1996), *c.*1,156 (1999), 1,537 (2006), 1,876 (2011).

Estelville (*Co. Northumberland*) see Cameron Park.

Eton (*Co. Jamison*) see Rowena.

Ettalong Beach (*Co. Northumberland*) 33°31'S. 151°20'E., 2 km SE of Woy Woy, on Brisbane Water; orig. Bar Swamp, then also known as Gittins' Lagoon and Dogherty's Beach; disc. 1788 by Capt. Arthur Phillip, estab. 1906; ambulance station 1952; Angl. C. (St Paul's); Bapt. C.; bushfires 1926, 1928, 1936; electricity (from Newcastle) 1929; FB (station b. 1954); foreshore upgraded 2014; gale 1910; jetty (Restwell), destroyed 1910; Meth. C. b. 1932 by S.W. and R.C. Potter; PO 1919; Presb. C. 1930, renovations 1963; PS 1957; school 1928 b. by Ryan and Moore, additions 1935 by C.L. Meakin & Son, additions 1956 and 1961, new one 1977; telephone 1916; Unit. C.; 2 wharves; pop. 385 (1933), 1,260 (1947), 4,205 (2006), 4,628 (2011).

Ettalong Beach Estate (*Co. Northumberland*) see Umina Beach.

Ettamogah (*Co. Goulburn*) 36°01'S. 146°59'E., 9 km NE of Albury; vineyards; ammunition depot (World War II); container terminal 2009; paper mill (Norske Skog Paper Mills Aust. Pty Ltd) 1981, re-cycling facility 1993, gas leak (2 died) 2018; RS 1881–1975; telephone 1915; TX 1928; winery (Harbottle, Alsop & Co.) estab. 1863 by Philip Francis Adams, sold; pop. 25 (1933), 52 (1947).

Ettrick (*Co. Rous*) 28°40'S. 152°55'E., 10 km SW of Kyogle, on Eden Ck; dairying; bridges: one over Eden Ck 1924 and Whites Bridge over Iron Pot Ck; butter factory (Kyogle Co-op. Dairy Co.) b. 1911 by George James Grove, bought 1925 by Norco Co-op. Ltd, closed 1940; PO 1910; school 1919, additions 1924 by E. Comerford, closed 1968; telephone 1914; TX 1924, automatic 1970; pop. 165 (1911), 293 (1933), 186 (1947), 204 (1954), 203 (1961), 230 (2011).

Euabalong (*Co. Blaxland*) 33°07'S. 146°28'E., 22 km NE of Lake Cargelligo, on Lachlan R.; Eauabalong till 1921; village gaz. and first lots sold 1873, second sale of lots 1876; goldmining, then cropping, cattle, sheep; bridge (swing); cemetery (graves 1899+); CH 1880; flood 1952; lock-up; PO 1868; pound (stock) 1876; PS 1876; school 1889–1991; storm 1873; telegraph 1880; TX 1913, automatic 1989; Union C. b. by William McFadzean; pop. 83 (1891), 108 (1901), 101 (1911), 209 (1933), 174 (1947), 178 (1954), 196 (1961), *c.*150 (2000), 212 (2006), 378 (2011).

Euabalong West (*Co. Blaxland*) 33°03'S. 146°24'E., 27 km N. of Lake Cargelligo; village gaz. 1919; cropping and grazing; electricity 1957; freezing works (Carabubula) b. by Tighe Bros; Meth. C. 1958 (removed from Girral); PO 1929; RS 1919–89; sawmill (Western Sawmilling Co.), fire 1954; school 1953; telephone 1921; TX 1928; pop. 57 (1933), 123 (1947), 166 (1954), 140 (1961), *c.*70 (2000).

Eualdrie (*Co. Forbes*) 33°56'S. 148°04'E., 10 km SW of Grenfell; pop. 134 (1933), 56 (1947), 83 (1954).

Euambeline (*Co. Flinders*) 32°02'S. 147°11'E., 52 km S. of Nyngan, on Bulbodney Ck.

Euberta (*Co. Bourke*) 35°04'S. 147°12'E., 17 km W. of Wagga Wagga; FB; school 1912–72; telephone 1917; TX 1950, automatic 1963; pop. 130 (1933), 115 (1947), 87 (1954), 129 (1961), 375 (2006).

Eubindal (*Co. Harden*) 34°37'S. 148°40'E., 21 km S. of Boorowa; pop. 21 (1933).

Euchareena (*Co. Wellington*) 32°57'S. 149°06'E., 27 km NE of Molong, on Gibbers Ck; Warne till 1899; farming and grazing; Angl. C., renovations 1937, new one (St Thomas's) 1959; bushfire 1975; cemetery (117 graves) 1893; FB; fires 1928 and 1959; goldmine (F.J. Hubbard) 1900 and 1935; PO 1880; Rom. Cath. C. (St Brigid's) 1902–70; RS (Warne till 1899) 1880–1976; Salv. Army C.; school (Warne till 1900) 1882, renovated 1944; telegraph 1890; TX 1920, automatic 1985; typhoid 1905; pop. 274 (1901), 257 (1911), 199 (1933), 205 (1947), 198 (1954), 201 (1961), 313 (2006).

Eucumbene (*Co. Wallace*) 36°08'S. 148°38'E., 35 km NE of Perisher Valley; Adaminaby Dam till 1959; PO 1952; PS 1955–58; school (Eaglehawk till 1960) 1954–67; telephone 1952; pop. 1,357 (1954), 238 (1961).

Eucumbene Cove (*Co. Wallace*) 36°08'S. 148°37'E., 35 km NE of Perisher Valley, on Lake Eucumbene; dam b. 1956–58 by Kaiser-Walsh-Perini-Raymond, 381 ft (116 m) high and 1,900 ft (579.1 m) long, on Eucumbene R., which inundated Old Adaminaby.

Eucumbene Portal (*Co. Wallace*) 36°05'S. 148°36'E., 40 km NE of Perisher, on Lake Eucumbene; PO 1955–59; telephone 1955.

Euglo (*Co. Gipps*) see Burcher.

Eugowra (*Co. Ashburnham*) 33°26'S. 148°22'E., 31 km NW of Canowindra, on Mandagery Ck; estab. 1834, surveyed by Thomas Lindon Biddulph, laid out 1881, town gaz. 1883; copper (disc. 1881 by Sloan and Pateman), wheat, lucerne, sheep; Angl. C. b. 1892 by Edwin Rymer, new one (St Matthew's) b. 1964 by R.J. Hubbard, d. by N.W. McPherson and D.A. Harrison; bridge 1869, new one b. 1888 by G.D. Williams, new one 1941, over Mandagery Ck; bushfire 2001; cemetery (931 graves) 1881, incl. columbarium; CH b. 1914 by Duggan, new one 1933, reused; creamery (Eugowra Creamery Co. Ltd) 1901, became butter factory (Eugowra Co-op. Dairy Co. Ltd); dust storm 1902; FB; fire 1930; floods 1950, 2005, 2010; foot-bridge; hospital 1930, replacement (Memorial) 1947; lucerne mill (Eugowra Produce Milling Co.) 1952; mines: Eurow 1881–1956 and Vychan 1881–1957; monumental stone works; PO 1873, new one b. 1884 by W.H. Murray, repairs 1902 by Arnold Rigby, closed, sold, restored and reused; pound (stock) 1877; PS b. 1862 by Arundel Everett and William Stephens, new one b. 1881 by J.B. Fitzgerald, additions and repairs 1910 by John Baker; railway turntable, 50 ft (15.2 m); reservoir 1955; Rom. Cath. C. 1908, new one (St John the Baptist) b. 1921 by E.A. Wright & Son, d. by William Lamrock, jun. and John Holderness Bates; RS 1922, railway closed and reused, station demolished 1986; sawmills: Federal (William Moss) and E. & R.J. Hay & Co. Pty Ltd 1897; school 1879, new one b. 1881 by Hugh Sutherland, additions 1934 by Moore and Richardson Bros, additions 1965 and 1973; SD Adventist C., closed; silo 1927; storm 1863; telegraph 1880, office repairs 1902 by Arnold Rigby; TX 1910, automatic 1976; typhoid 1906 and 1910; Unit. C. (Welsh Memorial, orig. Presb.) b. 1912 by Robert Joyce, d. by John Holderness Bates; water reticulation 1956; pop. *c.*24 (1866), 137 (1891), 668 (1901), 911 (1911), 704 (1933), 714 (1947), 665 (1954), 669 (1961), 609 (1966), 651 (1971), 651 (1976), 577 (1981), 579 (1986), 572 (1991), 612 (1996), 589 (2001), 535 (2006), 530 (2011).

Eulah Creek (*Co. Nandewar*) 30°21'S. 149°56'E., 14 km E. of Narrabri, on Eulah Ck; cemetery 1895; school 1882–1946 and 1957–67; telephone 1926; TX 1926, automatic 1971; pop. 146 (1933), 90 (1947), 80 (1954), 74 (1961), 190 (2011).

Eulenstein (*Co. Urana*) see Munyabla.

Eulimore (*Co. Ashburnham*) 33°22'S. 148°26'E., 10 km NE of Eugowra, on Eulimore Ck; FB (station b. 2012); sawmill; school 1928–44; pop. 54 (1947).

Eulomogo (*Co. Lincoln*) 32°17'S. 148°41'E., 8 km SE of Dubbo; yellow ochre and wheat; electricity 1951; FB; PO 1927–42; RS 1896, station b. by W.H. Hudson, closed 1964; school 1880–1913; telegraph 1912; telephone 1914; winery (Tombstone Estate) estab. by Rod and Patty Tilling; pop. 242 (1901), 147 (1911), 132 (1933), 61 (1954), 760 (2011).

Eulourie (*Co. Murchison*) 30°03'S. 150°24'E., 26 km SW of Bingara; also spelt as Eulowrie; PO 1878; pound (stock) 1876; PS 1882, closed, moved 1898 to Upper Horton by T. Potts.

Eulowrie (*Co. Murchison*) see Eulourie.

Eumungerie (*Co. Ewenmar*) 31°57'S. 148°37'E., 27 km S. of Gilgandra, on Drillwarrina Ck; Coalbaggie till 1903; estab. 1903 by Ewen McMillan, village gaz. 1904; yellow ochre and farming; Angl. C., first one burnt down 1932, new one (St Andrew's) b. 1932 by H. Smith; bridges: one over Dohnts Ck and one b. 1974 over Drillwarrina Ck; cemetery 1905; cyclone 1949; FB; fires 1919 and 1931; hailstorm 1954; PO 1907, new one b. 1943 by N. Foxall; PS 1924–40; Rom. Cath. C. (St Therese's) 1925, sold and reused, burnt down 2003; RS (orig. Coolbaggie Creek) 1903–75; sawmills: Brown and E.C. McMillan, Edwin Davies, W. Moffatt, Edwin Henry Utley; school 1908, additions 1913 by Lyons and McEwen, new building 1948; silo 1920; telephone 1908; TX 1914–84; pop. 85 (1901), 231 (1911), 321 (1933), 202 (1947), 210 (1954), 367 (1961), 264 (2006), 426 (2011).

Eungai Creek (*Co. Raleigh*) 30°50'S. 152°53'E., 14 km S. of Macksville, on Eungai Ck; Unkya Creek till 1911; surveyed by Ernest William Lewis Herborn, settled by John William Miles; orig. timber, then maize till 1893, dairying till 1989, later peas and beans; Angl. C. (St Paul's) 1903, relocated 1925; cemetery (339 graves) 1901; cheese factory (P. McCabe) 1916; electricity 1939; FB; fire 1905; Meth. C. b. 1916 by Allen Bros, dismantled; PO 1899;

school (Unkya Creek till 1912) 1895, new one b. 1898, additions 1918; telephone 1907; TX 1922, automatic 1971, upgraded 1977; Wes. Meth. C. 1897, closed, sold; pop. 179 (1901), 179 (1933), 173 (1947), 146 (1954), 124 (1961), 377 (2011).

Eungai Rail (*Co. Raleigh*) 30°51'S. 152°54'E., 14 km W. of South West Rocks; butter factory (Nambucca Dairy Co. Ltd) b. 1920 by Bert Skinner; FB; PO 1919 (removed from Barraganyatti); quarry; Rom. Cath. C. (Our Lady of Dolores) 1953–89 (removed from Jerseyville), sold and reused; RS 1919; sawmills: Ron and Lloyd Johnson (bought by Albert Thurgood and later destroyed), Frederick William Lane 1919 (destroyed and rebuilt 1928, sold to George Smith and Warren Jeffery, destroyed and rebuilt 1941, later taken over by Allen Taylor & Co. Ltd, destroyed 1970), Wally Thurgood; school 1924–74; telephone 1920; TX 1924–71; pop. 189 (1933), 183 (1947), 262 (1954), 216 (1961), 137 (2006), 281 (2011).

Eungella (*Co. Rous*) 28°21'S. 153°19'E., 8 km W. of Murwillumbah, on Oxley R.; farming, dairying, fruit; airfield; bridge, destroyed 1989; bushfire 1936; flood 1989; gale 1930; hailstorm 1925; PO 1903; rifle range 1914; sawmill and case factory (Russell Gresinger); school (Wollumbin till 1909) 1906, new buildings b. 1912 by A.A. Gaggin, damaged 1930, closed 1969; telephone 1908; TX 1915–64; pop. 152 (1911), 309 (1933), 284 (1947), 235 (1954), 227 (1961), 285 (2011).

Eunonyhareenyha (*Co. Clarendon*) 35°04'S. 147°28'E., 11 km NE of Wagga Wagga; school 1873–75 and 1957–69.

Euraba (*Co. Benarba*) 28°47'S. 149°38'E., 65 km E. of Mungindi, on Whalan Ck; bridge (low-level timber beam) b. 1907 by Murphy and Taylor.

Euraba (*Co. Buckland*) 31°30'S. 150°40'E., 1 km NW of Quirindi.

Eurabba (*Co. Bland*) 34°04'S. 147°50'E., 36 km SW of Grenfell; RS 1916–75.

Euradux (*Co. St Vincent*) 35°20'S. 149°49'E., 12 km N. of Braidwood; also known as Uradux; farming and grazing; PO 1927–30.

Euralie (*Co. Murray*) 34°53'S. 148°50'E., 10 km SW of Yass; school (Spring Creek till 1883) 1877–95 and 1913–29.

Euratha (*Co. Cooper*) 33°52'S. 146°33'E., 59 km W. of West Wyalong; village gaz. 1925; mining (gold disc. 1900 by Stanley) 1900–30 and farming; cemetery 1928; mine; PO 1926; RS 1923–75; telephone 1925; TX 1937–77; pop. 82 (1933), 53 (1947).

Eureka (*Co. Rous*) 28°41'S. 153°26'E., 9 km W. of Bangalow, on Little Bennys Ck; orig. timber, then farming and dairying, now macadamia nuts; Angl. C. (St Aidan's) 1895, new sanctuary 1930; butter factory (Rosevale Dairy Co.) b. 1890 by Noonan Bros, closed 1904; PO 1885–1994; school (Whian Whian till 1908) 1894, additions 1935 by R. Condon; storm 1929; telephone 1910; TX 1917–58; Unit. C. (orig. Wes. Meth.) b. 1887 by J. and E. Noonan, known as North Clunes church till 1894, closed and reused 1905, new one 1905, damaged and rebuilt 1929, closed 2017; pop. 211 (1901), 246 (1911), 254 (1933), 237 (1947), 191 (1954), 165 (1961), 306 (2011).

Eurie Eurie (*Co. Denham*) 29°58'S. 148°15'E., 15 km NE of Walgett; RS 1908, station b. by James William Doherty, closed 1975; pop. 52 (1911).

Eurimbula (*Co. Gordon*) 32°53'S. 148°50'E., 24 km N. of Molong; farming; Angl. C. (St Paul's) b. 1912 by J.M. Job, rebuilt 1920; PO 1927; school 1881–83 and 1890–96; telephone 1928; TX 1929–38; pop. 72 (1911), 93 (1933), 56 (1954).

Euriowie (*Co. Farnell*) 31°23'S. 141°37'E., 66 km N. of Broken Hill; defunct; silver and tin (disc. 1884 by Ralph Hodgson, John Marsh and Henry Hines); cemetery; earth tremor 1915; mine (Huel Byjerkerno) *c.*1884–1920; PO 1887; PS 1887–95; telegraph 1888–1904; telephone 1904; TX 1918–36; pop. 551 (1888), 62 (1891).

Eurobodalla (*Co. Dampier*) 36°08'S. 149°58'E., 14 km W. of Dalmeny, on Tuross R.; Urabodalla till 1870; agric., beans *c.*1947+; bridge (Tyrone Bridge), 272 ft (83 m), b.

1893 by Kyngdon and Blumgvist, replaced 2018 in concrete, 282 ft (86 m), over Tuross R.; bushfires 1895 and 1968; cemetery 1867; CH 1890; cheese factories: Eurobodalla Co-op. Dairy Co. and Tyrone; earth tremor 1870; floods 1914, 1934, 1944, 1971; PO 1870, inundated 1914; pound (stock) 1872; PS 1883–95; Rom. Cath. C. 1871, new one 1913, closed, moved 1956 to Dalmeny; sawmill (Reed Bros) 1912; school 1864–69 and 1878–1944; telegraph 1888–92; telephone 1892; TX 1927–68; water supply augmentation 1988; pop. 79 (1901), 146 (1911), 61 (1933), 74 (1947), 55 (1954), 64 (1961), 218 (2011).

Euroka (*Co. Cook*) 33°46'S. 150°14'E., 9 km SW of Katoomba; mine, closed.

Euroka (*Co. Dudley*) 31°05'S. 152°48'E., 4 km W. of Kempsey, on Euroka Ck; farming; bridge over Euroka Ck; bushfire 1895; cemetery (57 graves 1880+); gale 1870; Meth. C. b. 1922 by Blight Bros, d. by George Blight, burnt down 1938; Prim. Meth. C. 1870; school 1863, new one b. 1867, additions 1877 and 1885, closed 1968; Unit. C. (orig. Meth.) 1940 d. by William C. Brown; Wes. Meth. C. 1872; pop. 166 (1901), 247 (1911), 156 (1933), 150 (1947), 125 (1954), 135 (1961), 323 (2011).

Euroka Clearing (*Co. Cook*) 33°48'S. 150°37'E., 4 km S. of Glenbrook, on Euroka Ck.

Euroka Siding (*Co. Bland*) see Quandialla.

Euroley (*Co. Boyd*) 34°39'S. 146°22'E., 11 km S. of Leeton, on Murrumbidgee R.; formerly Uroly; farming and grazing; bridge (Dare timber truss) 1929, 314 ft (95.7 m), over Murrumbidgee R.; flood 1952; PO 1917–65; schools: Uroly 1903–11 and Yanco Agric. HS (McCaughey Memorial Agric. HS 1939–42) 1922, additions 1927, 1935, 1938, 1964, 1971, 1976, 1988, 1993; telephone 1914; TX 1917, automatic 1972; pop. 63 (1911), 164 (1933), 84 (1947), 90 (1954), 65 (1961).

Eurolie (*Co. Waradgery*) 34°45'S. 145°08'E., 39 km SE of Hay, on Eurolie Ck; pop. 32 (1933).

Euromedah (*Co. Narromine*) 32°12'S. 148°23'E., 13 km E. of Narromine, on Macquarie R.; FB; school 1900, new building b. 1903 by W. Louden, closed 1909.

Eurongilly (*Co. Clarendon*) 34°57'S. 147°46'E., 19 km SE of Junee, on Eurongilly Ck; Clarendon till 1886; goldmining (alluvial and reef), grazing, agric.; cemetery 1886; FB; lock-up, defunct; PO 1866–1926; pound (stock) 1878; PS; school 1918–33, reopened 1955; TX (automatic) 1961; pop. *c.*250 (1903), 75 (1911), 115 (1933), 83 (1947), 84 (1954), 81 (1961).

Europambela (*Co. Vernon*) 30°59'S. 151°41'E., 8 km E. of Walcha, on Apsley R.; earth tremor 1880; pop. 26 (1933).

Eurugabah (*Co. Nicholson*) 33°49'S. 144°59'E., 64 km SW of Hillston; bushfire 1979.

Eurunderee (*Co. Phillip*) 32°32'S. 149°37'E., 8 km N. of Mudgee; New Pipe Clay till 1877; iron and goldmining (gold disc. 1857 by Frederick Wurth and Henry Hill, more disc. 1863 by Hill, and more in 1874), orchards, farming; mines: Eurunderie (Wall and Bucholtz) 1908, Log Paddock Lead 1857, 1876–84, 1898, Wilbertree (W.C. Wall) 1908; PO 1875; school 1877, new one b. 1879 by Peter Lawson, closed 1925, demolished 1930, replacement (removed from Canadian Lead) o. 1957, closed 1970, restored and reused 1989; telephone 1914, automatic 1968; wineries: Amberton Wines 1975–90, Caloola, Elliot Rocke Estate, Knights Vines, Lawson's Hill Vineyard, Mansfield Wines 1975, Montrose Wines, Poet's Corner Wines (formerly Craigmoor), Willow Lane Vineyard; pop. 235 (1911), 138 (1933), 86 (1947), 101 (1954), 90 (1961).

Euston (*Co. Taila*) 34°35'S. 142°45'E., 76 km W. of Balranald, on Murray R.; settled 1846 by E. Morey, town gaz. 1851, designated as chief town of the county; orig. stock crossing place, former river port, then fishing and grazing, now irrigation farming, wine; almond packing plant (Select Harvests Ltd); boiling-down works; bond store; bridge (road and rail) 1923–28 (steel plate girders with central lift span), 570 ft (173.7 m), replacement d. and b. 2004–6 by Baulderstone Hornibrook Pty Ltd, over Murray R.; cemetery 1870; CH (incl. lock-up) b. 1879 by F.M.H. Parker, additions

1899 by Hocking Bros, closed, reused 1981, restored 1996; customs-house 1864; FB; floods 1931 and 1956; fruit packing house (Scalora); PO 1852, new one b. by Charles Hardy, sen., additions 1900 by George Huntley Dixon; pound (stock) 1865; PS, additions and alterations 1901 by George Huntley Dixon, renovations and repairs 1936 by T. Burrage, new one 1981; punt across Murray R.; 2 reservoirs; Rom. Cath. C. (St Fintan's) 1911; RS (Victorian railway), closed; school 1865, new buildings b. 1882 by F.M.H. Parker, alterations 1899 by George Huntley Dixon, additions 1972; sewerage augmentation 1995; telegraph 1867, new office b. by Charles Hardy, sen. and Thomas Hodson, additions 1900 by George Huntley Dixon; TX 1910–81; typhoid 1880; Unit. C. (orig. Presb.) 1887, inundated 1931; water supply augmentation 1985; wharf; winery (Eustonia Vineyards Pty Ltd) estab. by Frank Garreffa; wool-scour (George Graham) 1869; pop. *c.*50 (1866), 100 (1871), 170 (1891), 175 (1901), 265 (1911), 146 (1933), 158 (1947), 167 (1954), 323 (1961), 216 (1971), 244 (1976), 409 (1986), 375 (1991), 459 (1996), 511 (2001), 462 (2006), 441 (2011).

Euwylong (*Co. Gloucester*) see Enwylong.

Evans Head (*Co. Richmond*) 29°07'S. 153°26'E., 30 km SW of Ballina, on Evans R.; (incl. Bundjalung, Iron Gates, South Evans Head); founded 1884 by Thomas Paddon, subdivided 1906; farming, oysters, prawns, lobsters, fishing, tourism, sand mining 1960s–80s; aeroplane crash (2 killed) 1934; airfield 1936, aerodrome b. 1935–37, taken over 1937 by Commonwealth govt, air force base b. 1936–40, upgraded to airport for World War II, incl. 17 Bellman hangars, bombing and gunnery school 1941–43, closed 1946 and commercial flights began; ambulance station b. 1951 by E. Raphael; Angl. C. 1924, sanctuary 1930, new church (St John's) 1985; Assemblies of God C. (Wellspring); Bapt. C. 1965; boat harbour b. 1966–69; breakwaters b. 1959–63, new one 1968; bridge 1962, over Evans R.; cemetery (1,420 graves) 1938, incl. lawn cemetery and columbaria; FB (station b. 1957); hailstorm 1998; lighthouse 1976; marina (South Evans Head); Meth. C.; PO 1909; Presb. C. (St David's) 1956; PS 1948, new one 1973; 3 reservoirs; Rom. Cath. C. (St John the Evangelist) 1941; school (Evans River since 2000) 1921 in building re-rected by F. Bolton, new building b. 1935 by Les Baker, new building 2000; sewerage 1971, augmentation 1991; storm 1945; telephone 1907; TX 1917, automatic 1937; Unit. C. (Caroona); wharf 1994; pop. 76 (1911), 249 (1933), 764 (1947), 1,057 (1954), 969 (1961), 1,098 (1966), 1,313 (1971), 1,591 (1976), 1,802 (1981), 1,903 (1986), 2,375 (1991), 2,613 (1996), 2,614 (2001), 2,631 (2006), 2,720 (2011).

Evans Plains (*Co. Bathurst*) 33°26'S. 149°30'E., 8 km W. of Bathurst, on Evans Plains Ck; village gaz. 1847 as Mount Pleasant; agric.; butter factory estab. 1892 by E. Webb & Co., in old flour mill, sold 1901 to Bathurst Co-op. Dairying Co. Ltd, bought by David Pratley; flood 1862; flour mill (Job Boardman) b. 1861 by William Timothy Atkins, d. by Matthew Henry Sadlier, closed 1878, fire 1881, closed and reused; PO 1862; Presb. C. 1865, closed, reopened 1924, closed, sold to Burrow, reused; quarry; school 1859 d. by Matthew Henry Sadlier, additions 1898 by Edward Abraham Wright, closed 1926; telephone 1923; TX 1925; Wes. Meth. C. 1859, new one 1865; pop. 124 (1901), 104 (1911), 114 (1933), 103 (1947), 73 (1954), 80 (1961), 232 (2011).

Evans River (*Co. Richmond*) see Evans Head.

Evans Swamp (*Co. Bathurst*) see also Osborneville.

Evelien (*Co. Northumberland*) see Cardiff.

Evelyn Creek (*Co. Evelyn*) see Milparinka.

Everett (*Co. Hardinge*) 30°10'S. 151°37'E., 8 km NW of Guyra, on Laura Ck; school 1893–1911 and 1919–64; pop. 62 (1901).

Everetts Flat (*Co. Hardinge*) 30°09'S. 151°40'E., 7 km N. of Guyra.

Eversleigh (*Co. Sandon*) 30°25'S. 151°32'E., 17 km NW of Armidale, on Saumarez Ck; Inverella till 1885; PO 1884; school 1900–27; pop. 55 (1901), 22 (1933).

Eversleigh (*Co. Sandon*) see also Wyndella.

Everton (*Co. Ewenmar*) 31°45'S. 148°36'E., 7 km SW of Gilgandra; school 1915–21 and 1929–30; pop. 44 (1933).

Everton Vale (*Co. Sandon*) 30°34'S. 151°29'E., 8 km N. of Uralla; school 1887–1905.

Eviron (*Co. Rous*) 28°19'S. 153°29'E., 9 km E. of Murwillumbah; sugar-cane; pop. 22 (1933), 165 (1947), 125 (1954), 107 (1961), 281 (2011).

Ewingar (*Co. Drake*) 29°05'S. 152°33'E., 54 km SW of Casino, on Ewingar Ck; grazing; FB 1953; flood 2011; PO 1915–52; telephone 1923; TX 1926; pop. 25 (1933), 161 (2006), 252 (2011).

Ewingsdale (*Co. Rous*) 28°38'S. 153°33'E., 6 km W. of Byron Bay, on Simpsons Ck; ambulance station 2012; Angl. C. (St Columba's) b. 1915 by Hobbs and Edmund Shrubb, d. by W.B. King, damaged 1936, repairs by A.R. Sansom; cyclone 1936; hospital (Byron Central) 2016; school (Tyagarah till 1909) 1900, new school b. 1911 by Walter Bray, unroofed 1936, closed 1976; sugar mill (Edward Stephen Atkins) 1888, removed from Chatsworth Island; telephone 1936; TX 1936, automatic 1953; pop. 53 (1911), 194 (1933), 152 (1947), 163 (1954), 124 (1961), 462 (2011).

Excelsior (*Co. Roxburgh*) 33°04'S. 149°59'E., 24 km S. of Kandos; limestone and honey; drought 1927; lime-kiln, demolished; 4 mines; PO 1912; quarry estab. by Excelsior Lime Co., acquired 1892 by Goodlet & Smith Ltd, man killed 1901, acquired 1919 by G. & C. Hoskins Ltd, man killed 1923, closed 1929; RS 1886–1974; school 1913–41; telephone 1915; TX 1921–32; pop. 61 (1911), 47 (1933).

Exeter (*Co. Camden*) 34°37'S. 150°19'E., 5 km N. of Bundanoon, on Indigo Ck; Badgery's Siding till 1890; settled by James Badgery, estab. 1889, subdivided 1891, first lots sold 1892; dairying, farming, grazing, nurseries, highland holiday location 1920–45; Angl. C. (St Aidan's) b. 1896 by William Jones, extended 1904 and 1995; causeway across Reedy Ck; creamery (NSW Fresh Food & Ice Co. Ltd) 1900; earth tremor 1897; electricity 1929; FB; hailstorm 1907; PO 1890; quarry; railway accident (14 killed) 1914; RS (Badgery's Siding till 1890) 1878; school 1891, additions 1893 by Charles Palmer, new school 1907, additions 1924 by A. Clough, additions 1995; seed nursery (Arthur Yates & Co. Ltd) 1891; telegraph 1890; TX 1913, automatic 1960; pop. 251 (1901), 351 (1911), 365 (1933), 357 (1947), 296 (1954), 247 (1961), 296 (1991), 317 (1996), 359 (2001), 397 (2006), 531 (2011).

Exmouth (*Co. Sandon*) 30°23'S. 151°35'E., 16 km NW of Armidale; RS (Duval till 1904) 1886–1976.

Extension Estate (*Co. Cook*) see Lithgow.

F

Failford (*Co. Gloucester*) 32°06'S. 152°27'E., 10 km NW of Tuncurry, on Wallamba R.; estab. 1883, declined in 1950s; timber, farming, dairying; cemetery (700 graves 1882+); creamery (Aust. Dairying Co.); flood 1927; Meth. C. b. 1924 by Robert Croker, jun. (moved 1971 to Nabiac); PO 1886; punt across Wallamba R.; quarry (Allard's); sawmill and shipyard (John Breckenridge & Sons Ltd); scarlet fever 1910; school 1886, additions 1898 by Silas Brewer, additions 1912 by Dunn, closed 1963; telephone 1900; TX 1928, automatic 1965; pop. 144 (1901), 286 (1911), 282 (1933), 177 (1947), 179 (1954), 69 (1961), 495 (2011).

Fairbridge (*Co. Ashburnham*) 33°07'S. 148°54'E., 3 km SE of Molong; child migrant farm 1938–74, sold to T.A. Barrett Pty Ltd and reused, sold again 1988; school (Fairbridge Farm till 1970) 1938–73; pop. 214 (1954).

Fairfax (*Co. Nandewar*) 30°30'S. 150°08'E., 26 km N. of Boggabri; school 1932, additions 1965 and 2010.

Fairfield (*Co. Drake*) see Drake.

Fairfield (*Co. Murray*) 35°00'S. 149°16'E., 36 km SE of Yass, on Gundaroo Ck; grazing; bridge over Gundaroo Ck; PO 1867.

Fairfield South (*Co. Drake*) 29°03'S. 152°25'E., 37 km E. of Tenterfield.

Fairhaven (*Co. Dampier*) 36°23'S. 150°03'E., 5 km N. of Bermagui, on Wallaga Lake; pop. 133 (2001).

Fair Hill (*Co. Ashburnham*) 33°15'S. 148°42'E., 10 km S. of Manildra; school 1887–94 and 1904–15.

Fairholme (*Co. Gipps*) 33°17'S. 147°23'E., 31 km SE of Condobolin, on Island Ck; grazing; TX 1926–71; pop. 27 (1933), 102 (1954), 91 (1961), 195 (2006).

Fairley (*Co. Northumberland*) 32°55'S. 151°33'E., 3 km W. of West Wallsend, on Slatey Ck; estab. 1905, surveyed 1906; bushfire 1936; colliery (Seaham No. 2) estab. 1904, o. 1905, strike 1943, closed 1945, fire 1946, demolished; railway (colliery); pop. 48 (1933).

Fairview (*Co. Buckland*) 31°36'S. 150°48'E., 15 km SE of Quirindi; PO 1886–1900; school 1879–1917.

Fair View (*Co. Dowling*) 33°11'S. 146°39'E., 29 km NE of Lake Cargelligo.

Fairview (*Co. Gloucester*) see Paff Hill.

Fairview (*Co. Mouramba*) 31°44'S. 146°21'E., 82 km W. of Nyngan.

Fairview (*Co. Narromine*) 32°23'S. 148°10'E., 18 km SW of Narromine; RS 1910, station b. by T.E. Quiggin, closed 1974.

Fairview Estate (*Co. Narromine*) see Narromine.

Fairweather Vale (*Co. Clive*) 29°06'S. 152°08'E., 13 km SE of Tenterfield.

Fairy Hill (*Co. Rous*) 28°47'S. 152°59'E., 11 km NW of Casino, on Richmond Lagoon; dairying and pigs; FB; hailstorm 1936; PO 1914; RS (2 km E.) 1910, station b. by George Albert Leggo and John Allibone, closed 1974, demolished 1978; school 1933–79; TX 1947, automatic 1958; pop. 77 (1911), 180 (1933), 161 (1947), 121 (1954), 90 (1961), 298 (2011).

Fairy Meadow (*Co. Camden*) 34°24'S.

150°54'E., 1 km SE of Balgownie, on Tasman Sea; (incl. Fernhill and Reidtown); Cabbage Tree till 1883; subdivided 1839, first lots offered 1841; Angl. C. 1859, extended and re-roofed 1901 by J.S. Reid and William Harrigan, renovated 1913, new one b. 1928 on new site by W.R. Dawson, d. by David R. Masters, new one (St Paul's) 1999; army camp (World War II) at Reidtown; Assemblies of God C. (Citylife); brewery (Five Islands, renamed Illawarra Brewing Co. in 2011); bridge over Para Ck; Christ. Brethren Assemblies C. (Evangelical); Christ. Reformed C. 1959, new one 1971; Cong. C. 1955; cordial factories: Illawarra Mineral Water Manufacturers (W. and T. Riley) and Ryan and Moore 1939; fibrous plaster works; flour mill (Palmer's, dismantled 1875); food factory (Lockett Bros Pty Ltd) 1947; foot-bridge; gale 1891; Jehovah's Witnesses C.; joinery (Highway) 1949; Meth. C. 1919, new one 1958; migrant hostel 1950–82; PO: Fairy Meadow 1881 and West Fairy Meadow 1957–78; PS 1954; Rom. Cath. C. 1861, new one (St John Vianney) 1952; RS (Cramsville till 1888, Para Meadow till 1909, Balgownie till 1956) 1887; Salv. Army C. 1981; schools: Fairy Meadow 1858, additions 1892, new buildings 1956 and 1966, Mount Ousley 1959, additions 1960 and 1963, Towradgi 1953; streets electric lit 1925; 2 TC; telephone: Fairy Meadow 1920 and West Fairy Meadow 1957; Unit. C.; univ. (Wollongong, East Campus) b. by Baulderstone, d. by Bates Smart, Graham Bell Bowman and Perumal Pedavoli; water supply: Fairy Meadow 1918 and Fernhill 1922; pop. 418 (1911), 5,603 (1954), 7,609 (2011).

Fairy Mount (*Co. Murray*) see Mount Fairy.

Fairy Mount (*Co. Rous*) see Kyogle.

Faithfull (*Co. Mitchell*) 35°01'S. 146°39'E., 24 km N. of Lockhart; school 1918–47; pop. 145 (1933), 78 (1954).

Falbrook (*Co. Durham*) 32°25'S. 151°09'E., 16 km N. of Singleton; Angl. C. (St Clement's) 1863; PO 1875; Rom. Cath. C. 1869; telephone 1926; TX 1927–77.

Falbrook (*Co. Durham*) see also Camberwell.

Falconer (*Co. Sandon*) 30°11'S. 151°42'E., 5 km NE of Guyra, on Washpool Ck; village gaz. 1852 and lots sold 1854; cattle, wheat, oats, potatoes; PO 1857–79; school 1890–1906; pop. *c.*100 (1866), 60 (1911), 27 (1933).

Falkner's Platform (*Co. Northumberland*) see Whittingham.

Falls Creek (*Co. St Vincent*) 34°58'S. 150°36'E., 10 km S. of Nowra, on Currambene Ck; Bengelala till 1904; timber, farming, dairying, grazing; Angl. C. (St Andrew's) b. 1874 by Charles Harvey, replacement 1888 also b. by Harvey, additions 1933, moved 1965 by Ack Wilton to Wandandian and reused; bridge, destroyed 1911; bushfires 1909 (house destroyed), 1919, 1939; butter factory (Bengelala Dairying Co. Ltd) estab. 1894 by John Monaghan, closed 1902, burnt down 1904; Church of God (Shoalhaven); FB 1947; floods 1891 and 1894; Meth. C. 1910, closed, reopened 1932, demolished; PO 1904, new one b. 1910; sawmill (I. Kimpton & Sons) 1915; school (The Falls till 1896) 1887, replaced 1924; telephone 1912; TX 1922, automatic 1956; Union C. 1874; Wes. Meth. C., removed from Forest Lodge and re-erected 1892, burnt down 1909; pop. 61 (1901), 71 (1911), 97 (1933), 130 (1954), 238 (1961), 951 (2011).

Fargunyah (*Co. Urana*) 35°08'S. 146°43'E., 9 km N. of Lockhart; school 1957–71.

Farley (*Co. Northumberland*) 32°44'S. 151°31'E., 3 km W. of Maitland, on Stony Ck; farming; boiling-down works (Emanuel Hungerford, jun.) 1850; bushfires 1905, 1939, 1944; floods 1867 and 1875; hailstorm 1938; PO 1877; railway accident (man killed) 1890; RS (Wollombi Road till 1882) 1860, station additions 1891 by Charles Baker, closed 1975; telegraph 1890; telephone 1915; pop. 176 (1901), 150 (1911), 39 (1933), 112 (1961), 236 (2011).

Farmborough Heights (*Co. Camden*) see Unanderra.

Farmborough Road (*Co. Camden*) see Unanderra.

Far Meadow (*Co. Camden*) 34°49'S. 150°43'E.,

4 km SE of Berry; dairying; FB; milk factory b. 1896 by G. Wynyard, later converted to creamery, closed 1904; school 1897–1970; pop. 83 (1954), 85 (1961), 286 (2011).

Farnham (*Co. St Vincent*) see Jerrawangala.

Farnham (*Co. Wellington*) 32°50'S. 149°05'E., 34 km SE of Wellington, on Boduldura Ck; estab. *c.*1860, defunct; mining (gold rush 1855), farming, grazing; Angl. C. 1920, demolished; cemetery, closed 1890; mines: Beehive 1859–1912, Chump 1870s and 1890, Daisy, Elslie, Fitzsimmons, Great Britain <1877–1884, Great Northern, J. Hughes 1925–27, Iron Duke (Marshall & Co.), Kaiser Wilhelme or Billy or Golden Gully or King Billy or Prince Billy or Prince William (Golden Gully Co. and J. Pearse) <1878 and 1887–1916, Lady Carrington, Mascotte (Wentworth Gold Fields Pty Ltd), Monks (Ironbarks Goldmining Co. and Marshall & Co.), Redfern, Sailors Gully, Splitters Gully (Curnow) 1877, 1884, 1894, 1904, 1932, Stringy Bark <1885 and 1916, Swallows Nest <1878; PO 1873; RS 1897–1975, defunct; Salv. Army C., demolished; school 1880, new building b. 1898 by J.T. Deans, closed 1965 (building moved 1968 to Mullion Creek); telephone 1901; TX 1928–70; Wes. Meth. C. 1898, demolished; pop. 171 (1901), 207 (1911), 165 (1933), 76 (1947), 107 (1954), 86 (1961).

Farquhar Park (*Co. Gloucester*) 31°57'S. 152°37'E., 15 km E. of Taree, on Tasman Sea; telephone 1920.

Farquharson (*Co. Inglis*) see Limbri.

Farrendale (*Co. Narromine*) 32°21'S. 147°53'E., 36 km W. of Narromine; TX (automatic) 1968.

Farrer (*Co. Parry*) see Tamworth.

Farringdon (*Co. Murray*) 35°31'S. 149°40'E., 13 km SW of Braidwood, on Shoalhaven R.; FB.

Farrington (*Co. King*) see Coolalie.

Farthings (*Co. Northumberland*) see Greta.

Fashions Mount (*Co. Wellington*) 32°41'S. 149°07'E., 22 km SE of Wellington, under Lake Burrendong; farming and goldmining; dam (Burrendong) b. 1946–68 by WC & IC, 250 ft (76.2 m) high, on Macquarie R.; PO 1925; rifle range; Rom. Cath. C. (St Therese of the Infant Jesus) b. 1937 by Ted Weeks, closed, moved to Mumbil and reused; school 1900–38; telephone 1915; TX 1935; pop. 82 (1933).

Fassifern (*Co. Northumberland*) 32°59'S. 151°35'E., 3 km NW of Toronto, on LT Ck; bushfires 1933, 1936, 1951; collieries: Newstan (formerly Elcom Collieries Pty Ltd, acquired by Centennial Coal) 1949, Northumberland No. 1 (estab. 1888 by Northumberland Land & Coal Co., taken over 1894 by Ocean Steam Coal Co., sold 1916 to Fassifern Coal Co., strike 1944, sold 1949 to Electricity Commission), Northumberland No. 2 (o. 1914, sold 1916 to Fassifern Coal Co., strike 1944, sold 1949 to Electricity Commission), Oldstan (o. 1919 by Fassifern Coal Co., sold 1949 to Electricity Commission); PO 1888; quarry; railway (private) to Toronto o. 1891 by Excelsior Land, Investment, & Building Co. & Bank Ltd, taken over 1910 by govt, reused; RS 1888, station b. by John M'Donald, burnt down and replaced 1933; schools: Fassifern 1922, additions 1929 by Richard Seed, and Northumberland Colliery 1889–91; telegraph 1894; water supply 1928; pop. 55 (1901), 91 (1911), 179 (1933), 260 (1947), 364 (1954), 598 (2006), 621 (2011).

Faulconbridge (*Co. Cook*) 33°42'S. 150°32'E., 3 km W. of Springwood, on Sassafras Gully; part of Springwood till 1877; bushfires 1895, 1936, 1944, 1951, 1956, 1968, 2013; cemetery (28 burials 1880–1941), incl. columbaria 1967 and 1975; Community C.; electricity 1924; FB; ice works (Wheatley Bros); PO 1891; reservoir; RS 1877, new station 1894, replaced 1902 on new site by Charles Palmer; Salv. Army C. 1990; sawmills: Graham Bros (burnt down 1944), Henry Joyce 1913 (acquired by Augustus Wilson, sold 1920 to Charles Frederick Snell, closed), Francis James Searle and Lawrence George Moncrieff; schools: Faulconbridge 1965, additions 1967 and 1976, and Springwood HS 1967, additions 1971 and 1975; telephone 1916; Unit. C. (orig. Meth.) 1926, chancel b. 1964 by Charles Crowson, closed; water supply 1936; pop. 66 (1911), 156

(1933), 405 (1947), 537 (1954), 838 (1961), 1,029 (1964), *c.*2,400 (1987), 3,990 (2011).

Faulkland (*Co. Gloucester*) 32°04'S. 151°53'E., 10 km SW of Gloucester, on Gloucester R.; Presb. C.; telephone 1915; TX 1920.

Fawcetts Plain (*Co. Rous*) 28°35'S. 153°02'E., 5 km NE of Kyogle; pop. 57 (1933), 61 (1947), 84 (1954), 107 (1961), 374 (2011).

Federal (*Co. Rous*) 28°39'S. 153°27'E., 8 km NW of Bangalow, on Stony Ck; orig. timber then farming and dairying; Angl. C. (Holy Trinity) b. 1909 by Lowe and Beckinsale; butter factory; cheese factories: E.H. Codrington and S.T. Kirkland; FB; Meth. C. b. 1909 by Lowe and Beckinsale, new one 1961; PO 1899, burnt down 1920, replaced; school (Jasper till 1906) 1898, new building b. 1907 by Charles Benaud Smith, closed 1978; storm (man killed) 2018; telephone 1900; TX 1924, automatic 1958; pop. 251 (1901), 446 (1911), 194 (1933), 218 (1947), 254 (1954), 211 (1961), 712 (2011).

Federal City (*Co. Goulburn*) see Albury.

Federal Park (*Co. Bourke*) 34°42'S. 146°49'E., 25 km E. of Narrandera, on Yarran Ck; school 1903–38.

Federation (*Co. St Vincent*) see Wrights Beach.

Felled Timber Creek (*Co. King*) see Greendale.

Fellow Hills (*Co. Hume*) 35°42'S. 147°10'E., 12 km E. of Culcairn; RS 1902, station b. by John Allibone, closed 1975.

Fennell Bay (*Co. Northumberland*) 32°59'S. 151°36'E., 2 km N. of Toronto, on Fennell Bay; subdivided 1882; bridge 1902, new one, 664 ft (202.4 m), 1967, over Fennell Bay; bushfire 1936; colliery (South Stockton); PO 1947; quarry; RS (Fennell's Platform) 1891–1910; sawmill; school 1959, additions 1985; telephone 1947; wharf 1921; pop. 57 (1901), 59 (1933), 289 (1947), 655 (1954), 1,474 (2011).

Fennell's Platform (*Co. Northumberland*) see Fennell Bay.

Fernances (*Co. Northumberland*) 33°12'S. 151°00'E., 38 km NW of Ourimbah, on Wallambine Ck; Wallambine till 1900; farming; Angl. C. (St John the Baptist) 1906, closed, moved 1983 by Don McKillop to St Albans and reused; PO 1927; school (Wallambyne Creek) 1896–1909; telephone 1924.

Fernbank (*Co. Argyle*) 35°06'S. 150°01'E., 42 km NW of Braidwood, on Shoalhaven R.; goldmining; mines; stamper battery; pop. *c.*150 (1873).

Fernbank Creek (*Co. Macquarie*) 31°25'S. 152°50'E., 7 km W. of Port Macquarie; cemetery (Riverside, 4 graves 1850s+); winery (John Cassegrain) 1985; pop. 80 (1911), 60 (1933).

Fern Bay (*Co. Gloucester*) 32°52'S. 151°48'E., 5 km N. of Stockton, on Hunter R.; (incl. North Stockton, a garden suburb); anti-aircraft battery and command post (World War II); PO: Fern Bay 1953 and North Stockton 1912–42; PS (North Stockton) 1905–36; rifle range 1940, closed, acquired 2015 by Defence Housing Aust. for future redevelopment; school 1955; smallpox 1914; telephone: Fern Bay 1948 and North Stockton 1912; pop. 131 (1947), 289 (1954), 411 (1961), 1,137 (2006), 1,625 (2011).

Fernbrook (*Co. Fitzroy*) 30°22'S. 152°34'E., 13 km W. of Dorrigo, on Little Murray R.; Tangulla till 1938; telephone 1924; TX 1925, automatic 1959; pop. 184 (1933), 212 (1947).

Ferndale (*Co. Camden*) 34°38'S. 150°15'E., 5 km NW of Bundanoon.

Ferndale (*Co. Clarendon*) 34°40'S. 147°49'E., 20 km W. of Cootamundra; Ironbong till 1898; church (St Paul's) b. 1881 by Elliott Bros; school 1882, new building b. 1883 by J. M'Beath, closed 1905; pop. 52 (1911), 23 (1933).

Ferndale (*Co. Gough*) 29°50'S. 151°11'E., 8 km SE of Inverell; abandoned in 1920s; boiling-down works and wool-scour estab. by John, Richard and William Ellicott, acquired by Thomas and Ann Rowland, acquired 1897 by Frederick Chappell, filtration dam b. 1899, establishment closed 1921; drought 1919–21.

Ferndale (*Co. Hume*) 35°32'S. 146°37'E., 38 km W. of Henty; RS 1920–75; silo 1932; pop. 34 (1933).

Ferndale (*Co. Hunter*) 32°26'S. 150°36'E., 14 km SW of Denman, on Kings Ck.

Ferndale (*Co. Roxburgh*) 32°51'S. 149°57'E., 7 km SW of Rylstone; quarry.

Ferndale (*Co. Wynyard*) 35°27'S. 148°12'E., 10 km N. of Batlow, on Gilmore Ck.

Ferndale (*Co. Wynyard*) see also Upper Gilmore.

Fern Glen (*Co. Clarence*) see Stockyard Creek.

Fernhill (*Co. Camden*) see Fairy Meadow.

Fern Hill (*Co. Rous*) see Fernside.

Fernleigh (*Co. Northumberland*) see Spencer.

Fernleigh (*Co. Rous*) 28°46'S. 153°30'E., 10 km NE of Alstonville; dairying, tropical fruit, macadamia nuts, sweet potatoes; Meth. C. 1910 (in former school); PO 1927–31; school 1896, new buildings b. 1909 and 1920 by T.E. Jarman, closed 1940, reopened 1956, additions 2010; telephone 1924; pop. 57 (1911), 67 (1933), 82 (1947), 83 (1954), 75 (1961), 277 (2011).

Fernmount (*Co. Raleigh*) 30°28'S. 152°56'E., 5 km SE of Bellingen, on Bellinger R.; Dovedale (designated as chief town of the county) till 1871; village gaz. as Weekes 1871; former river port, shipbuilding, dairying, maize; Angl. C. (St Vincent's) b. 1897 by E. Brandrick; cemetery (355 graves 1872+) 1896; cheese factory (T. Rowe) 1917; cordial factories: P. Logan (bought 1903 by Tom Hogan) and Pollock's (closed 1905); creamery estab. 1892 by George Tyson and became the Bellinger Central Butter & Ice Factory; FB; PO 1865, burnt down 1923; Presb. C. 1872, moved 1979; PS 1883, new one (incl. lock-up) b. 1895 by P. Keogh; punt; Salv. Army C.; school 1872, new one b. 1880, repairs 1898 and 1903 by George Edward Moore, building dismantled 1908 and moved to Brierfield, school closed 1963; storm 1877; telegraph 1877; Wes. Meth. C. 1869, demolished and replaced 1877, demolished; wharves: one b. 1879 by Taylor and Johnstone and one b. 1895 by W.G. Boulton; pop. 204 (1891), 288 (1901), 363 (1911), 363 (1924), 165 (1933), 181 (1947), 173 (1954), 132 (1961), 376 (2011).

Fern Ridge (*Co. Macquarie*) see Langley Vale.

Fernside (*Co. Rous*) 28°47'S. 153°10'E., 11 km W. of Lismore, on Back Ck; formerly Fern Hill; Angl. C. (St Thomas's) 1909 d. by Charles Rosenthal, later moved to Wyrallah; bushfire 1936; PO 1934–43; RS 1904–72; telephone 1934; TX 1934–43; pop. 90 (1933), 58 (1947), 75 (1954).

Fernthorpe (*Co. Hume*) 35°31'S. 146°36'E., 40 km W. of Henty; school 1915–69.

Fern Top (*Co. Parry*) 31°08'S. 150°51'E., 16 km S. of Tamworth; Union C. 1918.

Fernvale (*Co. Rous*) 28°22'S. 153°26'E., 6 km SE of Murwillumbah; school 1954–76, reused; pop. 52 (1933), 84 (1947), 72 (1954), 75 (1961), 238 (2011).

Ferodale (*Co. Gloucester*) see Raymond Terrace.

Ferriers (*Co. Urana*) see Lockhart.

Fiefield (*Co. Kennedy*) see Fifield.

Fiery Creek (*Co. Beresford*) 36°08'S. 149°20'E., 21 km NE of Cooma; mining (gold rush 1888); dam; mines; stamper battery.

Fifield (*Co. Kennedy*) 32°48'S. 147°27'E., 27 km NW of Trundle; Fiefield till 1894; estab. 1893, village gaz. 1896 as Fiefield; gold (disc. 1893 by Fifield and Rand), platinum (disc. 1887 by F.J. Connelly) mining 1893+, magnesite (disc. 1907), farming, grazing; cemetery (60 graves); FB (station b. 2016); mines (within 5 km): Fifield Lead 1893–1964, Gillenbine Tank Lead (disc. 1918), Jack's Lookout (incl. 3 puddling machines) 1907–*c.*1914, magnesite (BHP *c.*1915–1965 and Fifield Magnesite & Refractories Pty Ltd *c.*1922), Platina Lead (disc. 1893), Reynold's Tank; mouse plague 1956; PO 1894; PS 1895–1930; rifle range 1915; Rom. Cath. C. (St Dympna's) 1924; sawmill (James H. Smith); school 1894–1973; telephone 1898; TX 1911, automatic 1980; pop. 93 (1901), 205 (1911), 216 (1933), 184 (1947), 231 (1954), 122 (1961), 244 (2006), 287 (2011).

Figtree (*Co. Camden*) 34°26'S. 150°52'E., 4 km SW of Wollongong, on American Ck; (incl. Nareena Hills); farming; Angl. C. b. 1911 by George Waters, d. by H.A. Blomfield, sold, new one (All Saints') 1983; bridge b. 1861 by Moore and Vaughan, new one (concrete) 1914, replaced 1982, over American Ck; Christ. Science C.; Croatian Catholic C. (Mary Queen of Croats) 1983; Church of Christ (Newday); floods 1914 and 2007; foot-bridge over American Ck; Jehovah's Witnesses C. 1959; PO 1867; PS 1886, new one 1907, closed 1933; quarry (Central Kembla Quarries Co.); 2 reservoirs (incl. Mount Nebo, 50,000 gal. or 227.3 kl, 1915); schools: Figtree 1956 (additions 1977), Figtree HS 1969 (additions 1973 and 1975, additions 2007 by Edwards Constructions NSW Pty Ltd), Figtree Heights 1972 (additions 2010), Nareena Hills 1977; Slovenian Catholic C. (All Saints') 1983; telephone 1904; Unit. C. (orig. Presb.) 1969; water supply 1915; pop. 258 (1911), 458 (1947), 640 (1954), 1,889 (1961), 10,387 (2006), 10,629 (2011).

Fig Tree Flat (*Co. Clarke*) 30°51'S. 152°06'E., 50 km E. of Walcha, on Macleay R.

Figtree Heights (*Co. Camden*) see Figtree.

Finchs Caves (*Co. Wellington*) 32°55'S. 149°03'E., 27 km NE of Molong, on Coopers Ck.

Findlays Siding (*Co. Argyle*) 34°36'S. 149°42'E., 18 km N. of Goulburn.

Findon Creek (*Co. Rous*) 28°22'S. 152°53'E., 30 km NW of Kyogle; sawmill (Fraser Bros & Co.), moved to Wiangaree; school 1957–69; pop. 45 (1933), 56 (1947).

Fine Flower (*Co. Drake*) 29°23'S. 152°40'E., 43 km NW of Grafton, on Gordon Brook; orig. Koorway then Fine Flower Creek; mining (copper disc. 1905 by J. Torrance and T. Smith) and farming; mine (copper) estab. by Smith and Wiley, sold to Fine Flower Syndicate; PO 1927; smelter (Gordon Brook Co.), closed 1913; telephone 1917; tramway (between mine and smelter); TX 1939–82; pop. 99 (1933), 77 (1947), 59 (1961).

Fine Flower Creek (*Co. Drake*) see Fine Flower.

Fingal (*Co. Rous*) see Fingal Head.

Fingal Bay (*Co. Gloucester*) 32°45'S. 152°10'E., 4 km SE of Nelson Bay, on Fingal Bay; Bardouroka till 1982; tourism; bushfire 2013; FB (station b. 2018); gale 1891; hurricane 1898; lighthouse (Point Stephens) b. 1862 of sandstone by James Elphinstone, d. by Alexander Dawson, 69 ft (21 m), converted from kerosene to automatic acetylene 1922, converted to electricity 1960, converted to solar power 1990, restored 1998; PO 1961; telephone 1961; sewage works (Boulder Bay); pop. 37 (1961), 954 (1991), 1,392 (1996), 1,581 (2001), 1,473 (2006), 1,501 (2011).

Fingal Head (*Co. Rous*) 28°12'S. 153°34'E., 4 km SE of Tweed Heads, on Coral Sea; formerly Fingal; tourism; Aboriginal & Islander Christ. Fellowship C. (Cross Flow Ministries); army camp (USA) 1943, defunct; Assemblies of God C. 1920; breakwater 1902; bridge (Barneys Point Bridge), 625 ft (190.5 m), to Banora Point, with Strauss bascule span fabricated by Clyde Engineering Co. Ltd, erected 1936 by State Monier Pipe & Reinforced Concrete Works, replaced 1993–96, over Tweed R.; cemetery; lighthouse (timber) b. 1872 by McGregor et al., demolished 1879, new one b. 1879 by Shepherd and Mortley, d. by James Johnstone Barnet, 23 ft (7 m), converted 1920 from kerosene to automatic acetylene, converted 1980 to electricity, closed 2003 and reused; PO 1927; quarry; school (Cave Point) 1897–99, reopened (Fingal Point till 1962) 1914; sewage pumping station; telegraph 1890; telephone 1911; TX 1929–63; wharf; pop. 118 (1933), 276 (1947), 531 (1971), 544 (2011).

Fingal Point (*Co. Rous*) see Fingal Head.

Fingerboard (*Co. Gloucester*) 32°03'S. 151°53'E., 9 km SW of Gloucester, on Barrington R.

Finger Post (*Co. Gordon*) 32°37'S. 148°53'E., 8 km SW of Wellington, on Curra Ck; farming; PO 1927; telephone 1909; Union C. 1906, renovations 1928, abandoned; pop. 51 (1911), 48 (1933).

Finlay Rise (*Co. Rous*) 28°23'S. 153°04'E., 33 km W. of Murwillumbah.

Finley (*Co. Denison*) 35°39'S. 145°34'E., 57 km E. of Deniliquin, on Mulwala Canal;

Ulupna till 1881, then Murray Hut till 1893; surveyed 1884 by Andrew Robb, village gaz. 1884 as Ulupna, land sales 1884, 1892, 1894, irrigation 1939; sheep, wheat, cattle, pigs, dairying, vegetables, rice; airport; ambulance station; Angl. C. (Holy Trinity) b. 1925 by M. Sheppard; butter factory (Berriquin Dairy Co. Ltd) 1946, taken over 1963 by Murray Goulburn Co-op. Co. Ltd; carriage-works: Finley Steam Implement Works, incl. foundry, estab. 1893 by John Thomas Close, became J.T. and E.N. Close, and Smith's; cemetery (burials 1898+) 1896, incl. lawn cemetery; CH b. 1919 by John Waugh, new one 1982; Christ. Revival Crusade C. (River of Life), in former hall; cordial factories: Frederick Beasley 1904 and Summers Bros 1946; electricity (from Berrigan) 1929; FB 1901 (station b. 1952, new one 2006); fires 1908, 1927 (8 shops destroyed), 1928; foundry (Pioneer) estab. 1894 by William Downie; hospital b. 1962 by A.R.P. Crowe & Sons; LDS (Mormon) C.; PO 1881, burnt down 1914, rebuilt 1915 by McDevitt, demolished 1961, new one b. 1962 by Cowie Bros; Presb. C. (Thomas Fulton Memorial) 1887, relocated 1902, closed, moved 1919 to Booroobanilly, new one (Scots) 1920 d. by Laird and Buchan; PS 1897, new one b. 1919 by John Waugh; railway dam 1898; railway engine shed 1898, restored; railway turntable, 50 ft (15.2 m); reservoir (elevated, concrete), 250,000 gal. (1,136.5 kl); Rom. Cath. C. (St Mary's) 1919, additions 1920; RS 1898, station b. by Charles Baker, d. by Henry Deane, closed 1987, reused; sale-yards; schools: primary 1896 b. by William Haslem, extended 1897, additions 1900, additions 1925 by A.G. Leech, new building b. 1953 by D. Noordewier & Son, additions 1961, additions 1966 by A.G. and R.G. Cowie, additions 2010 and HS 1961, additions 1967, 1973, 1976, 1985, 2008; sewerage 1970; silo 1922; storm 1901; TC, additions 1984, became a campus of Riverina Institute in 1992; telegraph 1897, office burnt down 1914; TX 1910, automatic 1971; Unit. C. (orig. Meth.) 1953 d. by William C. Brown and Mowbray; water supply 1939, augmentation 1976; pop. 294 (1901), 678 (1911), 613 (1933), 828 (1947), 1,294 (1954), 1,505 (1961), 1,783 (1966), 2,004 (1971), 2,072 (1976), 2,193 (1981), 2,216 (1986), 2,220 (1991), 2,137 (1996), 1,912 (2001), 2,054 (2006), 1,921 (2011).

Finns Crossing (*Co. Lincoln*) 32°21'S. 148°56'E., 32 km E. of Dubbo, on Mitchell Ck.

Firefly (*Co. Gloucester*) 32°05'S. 152°15'E., 26 km W. of Tuncurry, on Firefly Ck; Cowans till 1912; farming and grazing; PO 1912; telephone 1914; TX 1921, automatic 1973; pop. 41 (1933), 100 (1954), 96 (1961), 390 (2006), 489 (2011).

Firefly Creek (*Co. Gloucester*) 32°05'S. 152°13'E., 28 km W. of Tuncurry, on Firefly Ck; farming and grazing; FB; PO 1877.

Firgrove (*Co. Lincoln*) 32°21'S. 148°46'E., 19 km SE of Dubbo; pop. 565 (2006), 595 (2011).

First Falls (*Co. Clarence*) see Eatonsville.

First Moonbi (*Co. Inglis*) 30°59'S. 151°06'E., 20 km NE of Tamworth.

Fishermans Bay (*Co. Gloucester*) see Anna Bay.

Fishermans Paradise (*Co. St Vincent*) 35°14'S. 150°27'E., 10 km N. of Milton, on Conjola Ck; cemetery; FB; quarry; pop. 278 (1991), 295 (1996), 333 (2001), 378 (2006), 420 (2011).

Fishermans Reach (*Co. Dudley*) 30°52'S. 153°00'E., 6 km NW of South West Rocks, on Macleay Arm; pop. 281 (2011).

Fishers Hill (*Co. Durham*) 32°30'S. 151°32'E., 25 km SW of Dungog, on Paterson R.; dairying; PO 1909–59; school (Summer Hill till 1884, then Bunnabunoo till 1934) 1880, new one b. 1883 by James Richardson and Reuben Taylor, closed 1943, reopened 1957, closed 1975, sold and reused; telephone 1914; TX 1928; pop. 78 (1933), 67 (1947), 67 (1954), 84 (1961).

Fishery (*Co. Clyde*) see Brewarrina.

Fishery Creek (*Co. Northumberland*) see Gillieston Heights.

Fishing Point (*Co. Northumberland*) see Rathmines.

Fishing Village (*Co. Camden*) see Berkeley.

Fish River (*Co. King*) 34°46'S. 149°19'E., 37 km W. of Goulburn, on Lerida Ck; railway accident (man killed) 1888; RS (Tank till 1877) 1875, platform b. 1877 by D. Williams, relocated 1915, closed 1975; Wes. Meth. C. 1872; pop. 30 (1933), 56 (1954), 51 (1961).

Fish River Caves (*Co. Westmoreland*) see Jenolan Caves.

Fish River Creek (*Co. Westmoreland*) see Oberon and Titania.

Fishtown (*Co. Camden*) see Berkeley.

Fitzgerald's Platform (*Co. Bathurst*) see Wimbledon.

Fitzgeralds Valley (*Co. Bathurst*) 33°32'S. 149°24'E., 13 km E. of Blayney, on Evans Plains Ck; gold (disc. 1851), wheat, maize, lucerne, dairying, vegetables 1930s+; Angl. C. (St Stephen's) b. 1869–71, re-roofed, re-roofed again 1960, and graveyard; mines: Hodson's 1932–39, Mount Willis or Star of the West (estab. by James and Joseph Collins) 1897–1900, Sugarloaf Hill 1933; PO 1878–98; TX (automatic) 1970; pop. 75 (1933).

Fitzgeralds Valley (*Co. Bathurst*) see also Wimbledon.

Fitzgerald's Valley (*Co. Cook*) see Valley Heights.

Fitz Roy (*Co. Camden*) see Welby.

Fitzroy Falls (*Co. Camden*) 34°39'S. 150°29'E., 15 km SE of Moss Vale, on Fitzroy Falls Reservoir; laid out *c.*1882; farming; Angl. C. (Emmanuel) 1937, closed, sold 2018, reused; bridge b. 1892 by Parker and Leonard, over Yarrunga Ck; dam 1974, 46 ft (14 m) high; earth tremor 1925; eucalyptus oil distillery (Finneran & Co.); PO; sawmill (J.E. McCleery); TX (automatic) 1956; pop. 53 (1901), 82 (1933), 80 (1947), 87 (1954), 105 (1961), 208 (2011).

Fivebough (*Co. Cooper*) 34°32'S. 146°27'E., 5 km NE of Leeton, on Fivebough Swamp; Salv. Army C. 1928; school 1913–69, sold and reused; telephone 1923; pop. 182 (1933), 162 (1947), 445 (1954).

Five Corners (*Co. Culgoa*) 29°16'S. 146°34'E., 81 km N. of Brewarrina.

Five Corners (*Co. Dowling*) 33°36'S. 146°42'E., 45 km SE of Lake Cargelligo.

Five Corners (*Co. Flinders*) see Five Ways.

Five Corners (*Co. Townsend*) 35°11'S. 144°39'E., 48 km NW of Deniliquin; formerly The Five Corners.

Five Day Creek (*Co. Dudley*) 30°43'S. 152°24'E., 44 km W. of Bowraville, on Five Day Ck; sawmill (J.R. Coverdale & Son); pop. 72 (1933), 94 (1947), 89 (1954), 63 (1961).

Five Islands (*Co. Bathurst*) see Barry.

Five Islands (*Co. Camden*) see Port Kembla.

Five Islands Estate (*Co. Camden*) see Port Kembla.

Five Mile Creek (*Co. Clarendon*) 35°00'S. 148°07'E., 7 km N. of Gundagai; school 1899–1905.

Five Mile Creek (*Co. King*) see Rugby.

Five Mile Flat (*Co. Georgiana*) see Peelwood.

Five Mile Tree (*Co. Georgiana*) see Crooked Corner.

Five Ways (*Co. Flinders*) 32°07'S. 147°02'E., 62 km S. of Nyngan; formerly Five Corners.

Five Ways (*Co. Rous*) 28°24'S. 153°25'E., 8 km SE of Murwillumbah, on Dunbible Ck.

Fladbury (*Co. Gough*) 29°30'S. 151°41'E., 26 km N. of Glen Innes, on Severn R.; bridge b. 1910 by Arthur J. Butt, over Severn R.; PO 1911; sawmill; school 1885–1920; telephone 1914; TX 1928; pop. 102 (1901), 94 (1911), 31 (1933).

Flaggy Creek Camp (*Co. Burnett*) 29°18'S. 150°33'E., 26 km N. of Warialda.

Flagstaff Corner (*Co. Landsborough*) 30°19'S. 144°51'E., 108 km W. of Bourke.

Flagstone (*Co. Ashburnham*) see Cookamidgera.

Flash Jack Creek (*Co. Ashburnham*) see Manildra.

Flash Jack's Flat (*Co. Ashburnham*) see Manildra.

Flat Rock (*Co. Cook*) 33°28'S. 150°35'E., 8 km NW of Kurrajong Heights.

Flat Rock (*Co. St Vincent*) 35°26'S. 150°20'E., 16 km SW of Ulladulla, on Flat Rock Ck; bushfires 1948 and 1965; sawmills: R. Mison & Sons 1916, Mitchell Bros (burnt down 1948), Pearman and Allan; wharf.

Flat Tops (*Co. Gloucester*) 32°28'S. 151°49'E., 8 km SE of Dungog; FB; British Israel Mission C. 1921; pop. 44 (1933).

Fletcher (*Co. Northumberland*) see Maryland.

Flinders (*Co. Camden*) see Shellharbour.

Floraville (*Co. Northumberland*) see Belmont North.

Florida (*Co. Canbelego*) 31°32'S. 146°21'E., 48 km E. of Cobar; RS 1892–1974.

Flowerburn (*Co. Georgiana*) 34°10'S. 149°27'E., 32 km N. of Bathurst, on Middle Ck; school 1882, new building b. 1884 by John Howard, closed 1894.

Flowerdale (*Co. Bourke*) 34°57'S. 147°16'E., 19 km NW of Wagga Wagga; pop. 31 (1933).

Flowerdale (*Co. Wynyard*) see Wagga Wagga.

Flyers Creek (*Co. Bathurst*) 33°31'S. 149°02'E., 16 km SW of Millthorpe, on Flyers Ck; copper, gold (alluvial and reef), grazing; copper mine (Infirtaris) 1880+; earth tremor 1919; PO 1927–30; stamper battery (Bright and MacKenzie) 1892; pop. *c.*50 (1866), 108 (1901), 79 (1911), 29 (1933).

Flynns Beach (*Co. Macquarie*) 31°27'S. 152°55'E., 2 km SE of Port Macquarie, on Tasman Sea; Beach Park till 1961; PO 1960; telephone 1951.

Foleys Creek (*Co. Westmoreland*) 33°44'S. 149°45'E., 11 km W. of Oberon, on Brisbane Valley Ck; farming and grazing; cemetery (Brisbane Valley, Rom. Cath., 17 graves 1857+); goldmines: Dad's Millions or Mount Baring or Baring Hill or Leviathan (Dad's Millions Gold Mining Co. and Baring Hill Gold Mining Co.) 1911 and 1915 and Jocelyn's Reef <1878; PO 1927; telegraph 1925; telephone 1925; pop. 75 (1933), 77 (1947), 73 (1954), 58 (1961).

Forbes (*Co. Ashburnham*) 33°23'S. 148°00'E., 31 km SW of Parkes, on Lake Forbes; (incl. North Forbes and South Forbes); Black Ridge till 1861; disc. 1817 by John Joseph William Molesworth Oxley, settled by George Ranken, thrived 1861–63, town gaz. 1863, designated as chief town of the county, munic. proc. 1870; orig. sheep and mining (gold disc. 1861 by Pierce Strickland, gold rush 1861–66, production peaked 1862), then wheat, cattle, dairying, apples, grapes, vegetables, maize, barley, oats, honey, wine, butter, cheese, ham, bacon, potatoes, chickens, now wool, hay, grain seeds, oilseeds, lucerne, poultry, hort., canning, timber, cement, light engineering; abattoir 1963–2003, sold by Lachley Meats to Tasman Group Services Pty Ltd; aeroplane crash (5 killed) 1955; airport (9 km W.) 1939, hangar damaged 1939; ambulance station 1937 (in former clubhouse), new one (in former bank) 1944, fire 2001, closed, bought by Raymond John Sharpe, derelict, new one on new site, fire 2015; Angl. C. 1861, new one (St John's) b. 1874–77 by Rogerson & Co. and Peter Mantora, d. by Benjamin Backhouse, extensions b. 1909 by Davidson and Worrall, d. by John Holderness Bates, re-roofed 1933, extended 1969; Assemblies of God C. (Generocity) 2005; bacon factory (F.A. Heinke), burnt down 1919, rebuilt, burnt down 1928; Bapt. C. 1952–94, removed 1998 and reused, new one 2003 on new site; breweries: Kent Brewery (estab. by William Bray, major fire 1892) 1885, burnt down 1898, Park Brewery (estab. by James Howison, acquired 1896 by Arthur Marrin, joined 1898 by Thomas Vincent, new one at South Forbes built for them in 1898 by Harrison and Corscaden, fire 1899, sold 1905 to Newell and Broughton, closed 1906, reopened 1907) 1879–1928, Red Lion (acquired 1898 by P.J. M'Grath), burnt down 1898; brickworks: G.A. Adams and A. Sam; bridges: one b. 1863 by Richard Bishop, W.R. Spencer and John Moulton, over Lachlan R., Bates Bridge 1919, over Lake Forbes, renovated 2012, Camp Street Bridge 1927, over Lake Forbes, Fitzgerald Bridge b. 1891 by J.B. Fitzgerald, new one 1995, over Lachlan R., Iron Bridge 1893, over Lachlan R., Oxley Bridge 1970, over Lake Forbes; bushfire 1926; butter factories: Henry James Brooke (bought 1909) and Forbes Co-op. Dairy Co. Ltd 1899 (d. by John Holderness Bates, new one b. 1933 by Ferguson); canneries: rabbits 1905 and vegetables (Forbes & Dist. Canning Co. Pty

Ltd) 1949, in old powerhouse; carriage-works: Farnsworth and Combe, F.W. Gaggin 1895, F. Rath & Co. 1879 (additions 1915 by W.J. Thomson, d. by John Holderness Bates), E.T Pettett (taken over 1914 by Fred Peters); caterpillar infestation 1899; causeway across Lake Forbes; cemeteries: pioneer (166 graves 1861–63) 1860 and general (6,608 graves 1860s+) 1864; CH b. 1863 by Peterson and James Rixon, additions and repairs 1864, reused, new one b. 1880 by William Adolphus Steinan, d. by James Johnstone Barnet, alterations 1884 by William Hewson; Christ. Brethren C.; concrete pipe works (Debenham Pipe Co. Ltd); cordial factories: Adams' (fire 1923), Reginald Charles Astley and Henry Edward Tribolet 1939 (incl. sauce factory, partnership dissolved 1943 but Astley remained, taken over 1951 by J. and R. Genge), M., L. and T. Doyle (sold 1923 to H.J. Lewis), George G. Eddy, A.J. Gunn, J. Hugo, Lachlan (burnt down 1933), D. and W. Peter 1861, Sharpe Bros (estab. by Ewart Sharpe), closed 1931, Roy H. Strickland (sold 1921 to G.E. Cross); cyanide plant (Hough's); diphtheria 1890, 1913, 1918, 1922, 1928, 1934 (boy died); dust storms 1891, 1902, 1904–5, 1914, 1918, 1924; electricity 1928; engineering works: C.H. Cocksedge, Forbes Engineering Pty Ltd, Johnson and Combe, W.J. Leaney & Son, R.L. Peitsch, E.W. Venables & Co.; FB 1872 (station b. 1905, closed, reused 1929, new one 1929); fibrous plaster works and joinery (estab. by N.D. Baldock, taken over by R.W. Baldock); fires 1863, 1884, 1893, 1898, 1902, 1922, 1936; floods 1870, 1900, 1916, 1931, 1950, 1951, 1952, 1974, 1990, 1994, 2012, 2016; flour mills: Clark's (bought 1916 by P.T. Stinson), Forbes Co-op. Milling Co. (b. 1899 by H. Luthje, d. by John Holderness Bates), Harris & Co. (Forbes) Pty Ltd (estab. by F.H. Harris), J.B. Reymond & Sons Ltd (estab. 1873 by Auguste Nicolas and Joseph Bernard Reymond, d. by Edward Gell, sold 1925 to Harris & Co.), Alfred Stokes (bought 1918 by W. Bassett); foot-bridge, destroyed 1950, replaced, over Lake Forbes; gale 1948; gaol (lock-up proc. gaol 1870) b. 1897 by J. Crimson, additions and alterations 1898 by C.W. Muller and J.F. Byrne, closed 1916, reused 1916–19 by military, demolished 1920; gasworks (Forbes Munic. Gas Co.) 1904, new retorts 1930 and 1947, closed 1956; hailstorm 1897; heatwaves 1904–5, 1932, 1952; hospital 1866, additions 1875, extended 1893, new one b. 1902 by Rigby Bros, d. by John Holderness Bates, alterations 1914 by J. Peterson and William Hewson, also d. by Bates, children's ward b. 1927 by William Raper Acret, hospital additions 1937, 1960, 1971, 1982, 2016; ice works (H.J. Lewis); incinerator 1964–90; Jehovah's Witnesses C. 1975, extended 1994; Jewish C. 1862–70; linseed crushing plant; lucerne meal mill (Bob and Jack Maher) 1947; Lutheran C. (St John's) 1934; measles epidemic 1893; meat works (W. Angliss & Co. Aust. Pty Ltd); mines: Boyle's (incl. Trafalgar and Apex) <1905–1908 and 1930, Brilliant, Caledonia 1862–90, 1913–15, 1922–24, 1930, Consols, Consols No. 2, Crocker's, Golden Horseshoe, Grassett's Lead, Hayes's, Judd's 1886, Lachlan Consols, Matheson's, Pinnacles, Rise and Shine (Pennington's) 1861, 1889–90, 1895, Sinclair's, Strickland's, Sullivan's, The South Lead 1862–93, Thompson's Lead; monumental stone works (C.J. Shakespeare & Sons); pet food factory (Petchef International Pty Ltd); pickle factory (Bray Bros) 1901; PO: Forbes 1861 (new one b. 1863, new one b. 1879–81 by R.M. Vaughan, d. by James Johnstone Barnet, additions and alterations 1914–16 by J.J. Patterson, alterations and restoration 1984), North Forbes 1957–78, South Forbes 1945; police barracks 1861, new barracks b. 1898 by T.F. Rowe, d. by Walter Liberty Vernon; pound (stock) 1864; powerhouse b. 1928 by William Raper Acret, damaged 1945; Presb. C. 1862, burnt down, new one (St Andrew's) 1874–77 d. by Thomas Rowe, re-roofed 1927, spire replaced 1991; PS 1862, new one 1898, additions and alterations 1976; quarry (blue metal); railway bridge (steel truss) 1914, fabricated by Haes & Eggers Ltd, erected by W.J. Bradham, 157 ft (48 m), over Lachlan R.; railway coal stage b. 1893 by Gerald Dalton Fetherston and Felix Edward Barbat; railway engine shed; railway turntable, 50 ft (15.2 m), replaced 1902, 60 ft (18.3 m); 4 reservoirs (one on Camp Hill 1884 and 3 on Turners Hill, one failed 1900); rifle range 1902; Rom. Cath. C.: first one destroyed 1862, new one (St Laurence O'Toole's) b. 1878–80 by T.A. Crowe on new site, d. by Edward Gell, sanctuary and sacristy added 1905 by Mitchell and Dodd, d. by John Holderness Bates, church extended 1923, re-roofed 1936, extended 1958 and St Mary's (South Forbes) 1928–74; RS 1893, station b. by Gerald Dalton Fetherston and Felix Edward Barbat, closed 1990, reused; sale-yards (E. Weaver & Co. 1906, new yards 1928 d. by Kemmis and Seymour); Salv. Army C. 1890, renovated 1972, extended 1977; sawmills: Cockram & Sons, Herbert and Fieldland, Charles Mathieson, J.B. Reymond & Sons Ltd (estab. 1861 by Auguste Nicolas, Joseph Bernard Reymond, Phillip John Beckett and Arthur Mott); schools: Forbes 1862 (new building b. 1883 by J.G. Martin, new building 1891, repairs 1909 by D.J. Fraser, additions 1917, 1942, 1956, 1962, 1969), Forbes HS 1955, additions 1966, 1974, 1979, North Forbes (see also Calarie) 1957, additions 1960 and 1966; SD Adventist C., closed 1966; sewerage 1931, augmentation 1994; silo 1920; silo fabrication works (H.E. Silos) 1984, expanded 2005 and 2011; small arms factory, closed 1945; snow 1900; steel fabrication works: Duncans 1987 and MD Steel Fabrication Pty Ltd 2004; storms 1862, 1863, 1888; streets were gas lit 1904; TC 1958, additions 1971, 1982, 1991, became a campus of Western Institute in 1992; telegraph 1862, new office b. 1863, replacement b. 1879–81 by R.M. Vaughan, d. by James Johnstone Barnet; telephone: North Forbes 1957 and South Forbes 1945; tobacco factory (W.D. & H.O. Wills Aust. Ltd) o. 1946 in former munitions factory; tomato pulping factory 1948; TX 1900, automatic 1965; typhoid 1899, 1903, 1909, 1953; Union C. (South Forbes), burnt down 1920; Unit. C. (orig. Meth.) b. 1906 by William Raper Acret, d. by John Holderness Bates, vestry b. 1921 also by Acret, church re-roofed 1965; waterworks b. 1884 by H. Hand, filtration plant 1946 d. by PWD, augmentation 1956, 1987, 1995; 3 weirs (incl. Cotton's, and Auguste Nicolas and Joseph Bernard Reymond's) on Lachlan R.; Wes. Meth. C., destroyed 1862, new one 1877, enlarged 1892; whooping cough epidemic 1921; wineries: Chateau Champsaur estab. 1886 by Auguste Nicolas and Joseph Bernard Reymond, and Sandhill's Vineyard estab. 1920 by Lucien Bourcier; wool-scours: Harrison Corscaden & Co. 1888, fire 1902, burnt down 1919, and Springbank (Cunningham and Cabot) 1888, extended 1890; pop. 124 (1861), 710 (1871), 2,191 (1881), 3,011 (1891), *c.*3,700 (1895), 4,294 (1901), 4,654 (1911), *c.*5,000 (1915), 5,355 (1933), 5,949 (1947), 6,514 (1954), 6,826 (1961), 7,370 (1966), 7,467 (1971), 7,754 (1976), 8,029 (1981), 7,915 (1986), 7,552 (1991), 7,467 (1996), 7,102 (2001), 6,954 (2006), 6,804 (2011).

Forbes Creek (*Co. Murray*) 35°26'S. 149°29'E., 19 km S. of Bungendore; storm 2016.

Forbesdale (*Co. Gloucester*) 32°04'S. 151°53'E., 10 km SW of Gloucester, on Gloucester R.; dairying; school 1909–69; telephone 1926; TX (automatic) 1955; pop. 84 (1933), 117 (1947), 70 (1954), 125 (1961).

Forbes River (*Co. Macquarie*) 31°22'S. 152°20'E., 39 km W. of Wauchope, on Forbes R.; school 1957–78; pop. 95 (1933), 79 (1947).

Forbestown (*Co. Durham*) see Muswellbrook.

Fords Bridge (*Co. Barrona*) 29°45'S. 145°26'E., 64 km NW of Bourke, on Warrego R.; grazing; artesian bore; bridge b. 1888 by T. Bell, over Warrego R.; cemetery 1900; PO 1892, new one 1900; PS b. 1898 by A.G. Litchfield, closed 1940; telegraph 1891; telephone 1903; TX 1922; pop. 96 (1901), 62 (1911), 27 (1933), 114 (1947), 122 (1954), 139 (1961), 29 (2006).

Fordwich (*Co. Northumberland*) 32°43'S. 151°03'E., 20 km SW of Singleton, on

Wollombi Brook; vineyards and soldiers' settlement; boiling-down works (A. Blaxland) 1853; flood 1867; flour mill (A. Blaxland) 1860; PO 1859, building destroyed 1867, replaced; pound (stock) 1865; telegraph 1877; wineries: Bacchus Fine Wines, Beyond Broke (Lindemans till 1997), Broke's Promise Estate 1996, Caprea Grove (estab. 1995 by Chris and Bindy Elsmore), Castle Rock, Catherine Vale (estab. 1993–97 by Bill and Wendy Lawson), Elysium (bought 1985 by Victoria Foster and Pam Waugh, estab. 1990–93, bought 2018 by Aaron Ching), Esselmont Estate (McGowan's), Foate's Ridge, Fordwich Estate (estab. 1990 by Warren and Julia Moore), Fordwich Hill, Fordwich Wines (estab. by Elliot, taken over by Tulloch, then Wyndham Estate), Harry's Run, Hill of Hope 1997, Lavender Ridge 1996, Louis-Laval Wines, Redstone, Saxonvale 1974, Smithleigh, Timbervines, Wattlebrook (Peter McClellan) 1994, Watts Creek; pop. 56 (1947).

Forest Creek (*Co. King*) 34°11'S. 148°52'E., 31 km NE of Boorowa; school 1897–1925; telephone 1923.

Forest Grove (*Co. Roxburgh*) 33°23'S. 149°40'E., 9 km NE of Bathurst; army camp (incl. hospital) 1940, 5 men killed 1946, closed 1947, became migrant camp (incl. hospital) 1948–52; PO (Bathurst Camp) 1948–52; school (Bathurst Holding Centre) 1949–52.

Forest Hill (*Co. Camden*) see Alpine.

Forest Hill (*Co. Wynyard*) 35°09'S. 147°28'E., 10 km SE of Wagga Wagga; subdivided 1892 and 1900; farming; aeroplane crash (pilot killed) 1953; air force training school (World War II) b. 1940 by McConnell & Co. Pty Ltd, became RAAF base in 1952; air force hospital (No. 1) b. 1944 by M'Gilvray and Wise; airport (Wagga Wagga) 1938, upgraded 2009; PO 1900; radar station (weather); 4 reservoirs; RS 1917–75; sawmill (George Clayton); school 1878, repairs 1896 by C. Hardy & Co., repairs 1913 by J. Hogan, additions 1959 and 2010; silo; TC (a campus of Riverina Institute); telephone 1915; Wes. Meth. C. 1897, moved 1959 to Ladysmith; pop. 72 (1901), 93 (1911), 119 (1933), 714 (1947), 164 (1954), 323 (1961), 1,807 (1971), 1,591 (1976), 1,977 (1981), 2,068 (1986), 2,454 (1991), 2,276 (1996), 2,142 (2001), 1,939 (2006), 2,186 (2011).

Forest Lodge (*Co. Camden*) 34°49'S. 150°36'E., 7 km N. of Nowra; Wes. Meth. C. 1879, dismantled and moved 1891 to Falls Creek.

Forest Reefs (*Co. Bathurst*) 33°27'S. 149°05'E., 9 km W. of Millthorpe; largely defunct; goldmining 1876–1909, agric., grazing; Angl. C. (St James the Apostle) b. 1883–85, new one 1929; Bapt. C. 1931; cemetery 1884; mines: Austral, Ballarat (Henry Newman), Band of Hope, Benora Extended, Duke, Finnerans Hill (incl. Ironclad, Stewarts, Williams, operated by Forest Reefs Gold Mining NL) 1901–16, Grand Junction, Great Extended 1877–84, Newton's; PO 1870–1974; Rom. Cath. C. (St Patrick's) b. 1893 by John Henry Gain, d. by William Lamrock, jun., closed, sold and reused; school (Waldegrave till 1920) 1882, new one b. 1885 by R. Brownrigg, repairs 1908 by Peter Beddie, replaced 1920 by F.A. Collins, renovated 1936 and 1937, closed 1990; snowstorm 1918; telephone 1900; TX 1928, automatic 1969; Unit. C. (orig. Meth.) 1911; pop. 358 (1901), 408 (1911), 383 (1921), 104 (1933), 320 (1947), 291 (1954), 231 (1961), 465 (2011).

Forked Mountain (*Co. Gowen*) 31°14'S. 149°21'E., 9 km NE of Coonabarabran.

Forresters Beach (*Co. Northumberland*) 33°25'S. 151°28'E., 8 km S. of The Entrance, on Tasman Sea; settled 1861 by Robert Forrester; water reticulation 1979; pop. 58 (1954), 127 (1961), 2,289 (2006), 2,496 (2011).

Forresters Beach (*Co. Northumberland*) see also Wamberal.

Forster (*Co. Gloucester*) 32°11'S. 152°31'E., 30 km S. of Taree, on Tasman Sea; settled 1856 by William Godwin, surveyed 1869 by John Hall, village gaz. 1870, laid out 1871; sawmilling, shipbuilding, fishing, oysters 1884+, dairying, tourism 1945+, retirement centre; Angl. C. (St Albyn the Martyr) b. 1911 by G. Perkins, d. by Cyril Blacket, closed 1980, sold to Presb. C., replaced; Assemblies of God C. (Christ. Life); Bapt. C. 1973; boat harbour; breakwater b. 1899–1901 by Hungerford & Co., extended 1966; brewery (Coastal Brewing Co.); bridge (47 concrete spans) to Tuncurry, b. 1957–59 by John Holland (Constructions) Pty Ltd, 2,070 ft (631 m), over Wallis Lake; cement tile works (Arnold Robinson); cemeteries: historic (8 graves 1880–92) and general (1,854 graves 1870+), incl. columbarium; CH 1884, new one (incl. lock-up) b. 1906 by H.E. Milligan, demolished, replacement 1970 d. by T. McGregor, additions and alterations 1990; earth tremor 1925; FB (station b. 1961); fire 1897; flour mill (John Wright); foundry (Cape Hawke Foundry & Engineering Co., Haden Bros); gale 1897; hailstorm 2014; Jehovah's Witnesses C.; marina; measles epidemic 1898; Meth. C. b. 1909 by G.L. Perkins, damaged 1910; pilot station (Cape Hawke) 1872; PO 1872, new ones b. 1877 and 1902; Presb. C. (St Andrew's), in former Angl. C.; PS, repairs 1896 by A. Rye, new one b. 1906 by H.E. Milligan, d. by Walter Liberty Vernon, new one 1970 d. by T. McGregor, replaced 1995, additions and alterations 2018; punts across Wallis Lake: pedestrian one (Charles A. Blows) 1921–59 and vehicular one (Charles A. Blows) 1924–59; quarry; reservoirs; Rom. Cath. C. b. 1957 by P.J. Smyth, new one (Holy Name of Jesus) 1980; sawmills: John Barling (acquired 1871 by John Wiley Breckenridge, sen., taken over by John Breckenridge, jun., sold to Josiah and Thomas Miles, burnt down, site sold 1930), Milton Hadley, James McCann, Henry Miles, Oscar Thompson, J. Wright; schools: primary (Minimbah till 1880) 1873, new building 1876 and one b. 1896 by Rye, additions 1918, 1938, 1966, 1974, new one 1991, and Great Lakes College (Forster HS 1978–2002) 2003; sewerage 1969, augmentation 1981, 1988, 1994; shipyard (estab. 1872 by Henry Miles, sen., joined 1896 by Thomas Miles and Henry Miles, jun., became T. and H. Miles, and later Henry Miles & Sons); slipway (Richard Phegan) 1871; steel fabrication works (BM Steel Fabrication) 2009; storm 1910; telegraph 1882; TX 1910, automatic 1977; typhoid 1884; Unit. C.; water reticulation 1969; Wes. Meth. C. 1876; wharves: one b. 1880 by M'Ardle and Thompson and one b. 1899 by S.J. Donaldson, in Cape Hawke Harbour; pop. 328 (1891), 298 (1901), 523 (1911), 560 (1933), 1,235 (1947), 1,436 (1954), 1,426 (1961), 2,869 (1966, incl. Tuncurry), 3,682 (1971, incl. Tuncurry), 6,195 (1976, incl. Tuncurry), 9,261 (1981, incl. Tuncurry), 11,239 (1986, incl. Tuncurry), 14,578 (1991, incl. Tuncurry), 15,943 (1996, incl. Tuncurry), 17,996 (2001, incl. Tuncurry), 18,372 (2006, incl. Tuncurry), 18,904 (2011, incl. Tuncurry).

Forster (*Co. Gloucester*)
see also Forster Keys.

Forster (*Co. Sandon*) 30°30'S. 151°39'E., 2 km NW of Armidale, on Dumaresq Ck.

Forster Keys (*Co. Gloucester*) 32°13'S. 152°31'E., 4 km S. of Forster, on Pipers Ck; (incl. Pipers Bay); school (Forster HS till 2002, then Forster Campus of Great Lakes College) 1978; sewerage augmentation (Pipers Bay) 1981.

Forster North (*Co. Gloucester*) see Tuncurry.

Fort Bourke (*Co. Gunderbooka*) 30°02'S. 145°47'E., 16 km W. of Bourke; artesian bore, 1,280 ft (390.1 m), sunk by Petrolia Boring Co.; PO 1860–65.

Forty Acres (*Co. Richmond*) 29°03'S. 152°44'E., 37 km SW of Casino, on Busbys Ck.

Fosters Valley (*Co. Bathurst*) 33°39'S. 149°33'E., 25 km S. of Bathurst, on Fosters Valley Ck; airfield; mines: Back Creek manganese deposit (G. & C. Hoskins Ltd and Newbridge Quarries Ltd) 1884–87, 1892, 1906, 1918, 1929–41 and Back Creek Silver Mining Co. (incl. Boss, Lord Roberts, No Objection, Mount Clarkson, Rolph's Lode, The First and Last) 1886–87 and 1893; pop. 188 (2011).

Fosterton (*Co. Gloucester*) 32°20'S. 151°45'E., 8 km N. of Dungog, on Williams R.; bridge (low-level, at Newell's Crossing) 1920, destroyed, replaced 1922 by W.G. Marsh, over Williams R.; bushfire 1915; Presb. C.; sawmill (estab. 1919 by G.F. Heath & Son, closed 1932, bought 1934 by J. Croll & Sons Ltd); school (Croom Park till 1890) 1865; telephone 1924; TX 1930, automatic 1955; Union C. 1906, new one 1913, closed; pop. 143 (1911), 151 (1933), 128 (1947), 139 (1954), 129 (1961), 244 (2011).

Fountaindale (*Co. Northumberland*) see Berkeley Vale.

Four Corners (*Co. Mouramba*) 32°08'S. 146°17'E., 105 km SW of Nyngan.

Four Corners (*Co. Urana*) 35°24'S. 145°50'E., 11 km SE of Jerilderie.

Four Corners (*Co. Thoulcanna*) 29°18'S. 144°06'E., 51 km NW of Bourke.

Four Corners (*Co. Townsend*) 34°51'S. 145°25'E., 62 km SW of Darlington Point.

Four Corners (*Co. Wakool*) 34°55'S. 143°24'E., 35 km SW of Balranald.

Four Mile (*Co. Clive*) 29°24'S. 151°54'E., 40 km S. of Tenterfield; pop. 31 (1933).

Four Mile Clump (*Co. Benarba*) 29°01'S. 149°39'E., 52 km N. of Moree.

Four Mile Creek (*Co. Bathurst*) 33°27'S. 148°57'E., 23 km SW of Orange, on Swallow Ck; mining (alluvial gold disc. *c.*1869 by Jolly) till 1911, then farming, grazing, dairying; airfield; earth tremor 2013; mines; PO 1911; quarry; school (Charleville) 1889–1911; stamper battery (10 head); telephone 1915; TX 1917, automatic 1958; Wes. Meth. C. 1882; pop. 65 (1933), 55 (1954), 67 (1961), 233 (2006).

Four Mile Creek (*Co. Northumberland*) 32°48'S. 151°35'E., 5 km S. of East Maitland, on Four Mile Ck; boiling-down works (C. Gale) 1853; coalmine (James Brown) 1844; Prim. Meth. C. 1856; school 1856, additions 1881 by T. Cooper, closed 1910, moved 1919 by Arthur Partridge-Wall to Thornton and reused; pop. 29 (1933), 242 (2006).

Four Mile Creek (*Co. Sandon*) 30°31'S. 151°59'E., 30 km E. of Armidale.

Four Ways (*Co. Ashburnham*) 33°22'S. 148°22'E., 8 km N. of Eugowra.

Fowlers Gap (*Co. Farnell*) 31°06'S. 141°42'E., 102 km N. of Broken Hill, on Fowlers Ck.

Foxground (*Co. Camden*) 34°44'S. 150°46'E., 6 km W. of Gerringong, on Foxground Ck; settled 1850 by John Blow, bypassed by highway 2017; agric. and dairying; Angl. C. 1850, replacement (St James's) 1880, burnt down 1954; butter factory (Foxground Co-op. Dairy Co. Ltd) b. 1889 by J.B. Taylor, burnt down 1892, replacement b. 1893 also by Taylor, burnt down 1914; cemetery; milk factory (Fresh Food & Ice Co.) 1917; PO 1889, relocated and renovated 1945; Prim. Meth. C. 1859; school 1883, relocated 1914, closed 1950, reused; TX (automatic) 1953; Wes. Meth. C. b. 1861 by W. Burless, and graveyard (2 burials), church and graveyard defunct, site sold and reused; pop. 74 (1911), 61 (1961).

Fox Hill (*Co. Dampier*) 36°24'S. 149°57'E., 10 km W. of Bermagui, school 1896–1935.

Foxlow (*Co. Murray*) 35°29'S. 149°27'E., 25 km SE of Queanbeyan, on Molonglo R.; gold prospecting; bridge b. 1896 by J.S. Gam, over Molonglo R.; PO 1875–88; RS 1940–68.

Frampton (*Co. Harden*) 34°42'S. 147°55'E., 12 km SW of Cootamundra; orig. Cunjegong, then Cungegong till 1889, then Moatefield till 1905; village gaz. 1866 as Cunjegong; farming; bushfire 1987; PO 1875; RS (Cungegong till 1889) 1878, new station 1905, closed 1975, demolished; school (Cungegong till 1894) 1884–1906; pop. 135 (1891), 54 (1901), 87 (1911), 130 (1933), 89 (1947), 93 (1954), 85 (1961).

Frankfield (*Co. King*) 34°48'S. 149°21'E., 35 km W. of Goulburn.

Franklin (*Co. Wynyard*) see Tumut.

Frank Lynne (*Co. Pottinger*) 31°01'S. 150°06'E., 14 km W. of Gunnedah.

Franks Wharf (*Co. Raleigh*) 30°44'S. 152°52'E., 7 km W. of Macksville, on Taylors Arm; bushfire 1915; telephone 1916; Union C., burnt down 1915; wharf, additions 1912 by G.T. Boyes.

Frazer Park (*Co. Northumberland*) 33°11'S. 151°36'E., 2 km NE of Lake Munmorah, on Tasman Sea; (incl. Freemans, Moonee, Wybung); mine (red oxide); 2 quarries (D. & J. Quarries).

Frazers Creek (*Co. Arrawatta*) see Ashford.

Frazers Creek (*Co. Macquarie*) 31°25'S. 152°38'E., 11 km NW of Wauchope; pop. 48 (1933).

Frazers Creek Station (*Co. Arrawatta*) 29°13'S. 151°07'E., 14 km N. of Ashford; coalmine and power station (Ashford, owned by North West County Council), power station 1958–97, demolished.

Frecklingtons Crossing (*Co. Narromine*) 32°34'S. 148°01'E., 24 km NW of Peak Hill, on Bogan R.

Frederick (*Co. Bathurst*) see Shadforth.

Frederick's Valley (*Co. Bathurst*) see Shadforth.

Frederickton (*Co. Dudley*) 31°02'S. 152°53'E., 6 km NE of Kempsey, on Macleay R.; settled 1841 by Gillies, estab. 1857 by William Henry Chapman, village gaz. 1879 as Fredericton, bypassed by highway 2013; agric., grazing, timber, shipbuilding, dairying; abattoir (Tolsat Pty Ltd); Angl. C. 1874, closed and reused, new one (St Peter's) 1960; Assemblies of God C. (Christ. New Life); bushfires 1895 and 1970; butter factory estab. 1892 by Edmund Debenham, taken over 1920 by Frederick Debenham, bought 1920 by Macleay River Co-op. Dairying Co. Ltd and converted 1922 to cheese factory, company changed name 1925 to Macleay River Dairying Co. Ltd, factory extended 1948 by A. Christensen for cheese making, butter making recommenced 1956, factory damaged 1964, taken over 1975 by United Dairies (By-Products) Pty Ltd, closed 1993, reused; cemetery (3,279 graves) 1869; creamery (Jacob Allen and Cowin, East Frederickton) 1897, burnt down 1904; FB; flood 1870; measles epidemic 1910; monumental stone works (Eric Dunn); PO 1860, new one b. 1886 by E. Debenham; Presb. C. 1886, damaged 1910, closed, sold and reused; PS 1881–1962; punt b. 1881 by Callen Bros, new one 1934–73; quarry; reservoir (steel), 250,000 gal. (1,136.5 kl), 1968; Rom. Cath. C. (St John's) 1905, porch and sacristy added later, church closed 1990, sold and reused; sawmill (R.J. Jamieson & Sons) 1911, burnt down 1945; school 1861–62, reopened 1877, new one b. 1879–81 by G.J.T. Lawson and Reynolds & Son, d. by John Horbury Hunt, additions 1903, additions and alterations 1951 by Gill Bros; shipyard estab. 1841 by J. Gillies, acquired 1843 by Christopher Lawson; storms 1910 and 1968; sugar mill (Macleay River Sugar Co.), additions and alterations 1869, acquired 1871 by M'Donald; telegraph 1878, new office b. 1886 by E. Debenham; telephone 1907; tornadoes 1897 and 1964; TX 1922, automatic 1957; Unit. C. (orig. Wes. Meth.) 1882, damaged 1968, replaced 1977; Wes. Meth. C. 1862; wharves: one b. 1871 by Ruskin and Batty, alterations and repairs 1882 by G. and T. Lawson and one b. 1894 by John Lawson; pop. *c.*100 (1866), 188 (1871), 221 (1881), 343 (1891), 443 (1901), 539 (1911), 492 (1933), 718 (1947), 644 (1954), 616 (1961), 526 (1966), 549 (1971), 611 (1976), 616 (1981), 762 (1986), 826 (1991), 881 (1996), 903 (2001), 986 (2006), 1,075 (2011).

Fredericton (*Co. Dudley*) see Frederickton.

Freemans (*Co. Northumberland*) see Frazer Park.

Freemans Reach (*Co. Cook*) 33°34'S. 150°48'E., 2 km SE of Glossodia, on Hawkesbury R.; orchards, farming, dairying, poultry, turf; Angl. C. (St Mark's) 1936; Cong. C. 1871, closed, sold 1917 to R.C. Greentree; FB; floods 1867, 1892, 1925, 1949; PO 1884; quarry; schools: Freemans Reach 1867, new school 1877, repairs 1888 by Charles Sheen, additions 1906 by R.W. Dunstan, additions 1908 by George Bennett, demolished 1935, new schools 1934 and 1990, and Hawkesbury HS 1983, additions 1989; telephone 1910; TX 1922, automatic 1965; pop. 331 (1911), 374 (1933), 313 (1947), 287 (1954), 343 (1961), 1,279 (1986), 1,378 (1991), 860 (1996), 874 (2001), 842 (2006), 1,239 (2011).

Freemans Waterhole (*Co. Northumberland*) 32°59'S. 151°29'E., 11 km W. of Toronto, on

Lords Ck; bridge (Nobles Bridge) over Lords Ck; PO 1966–79; 2 sawmills; telephone 1966; TX (automatic) 1966.

Freemantle (*Co. Bathurst*) 33°16'S. 149°23'E., 24 km NW of Bathurst; short-lived soldiers' settlement; airfield; bridge (timber beam spans) b. 1931 by H.H. Woodward, over Macquarie R.; bushfires 1907 and 1939; earth tremor 1934; FB; PO 1880; TX; Union C. 1897; pop. 64 (1933), 78 (1947), 70 (1954), 72 (1961).

French Park (*Co. Mitchell*) 35°16'S. 146°55'E., 17 km W. of The Rock; farming; PO 1914; RS 1901, station b. by C. Hardy & Co., closed 1975; school 1957–73; telephone 1913; TX 1923–66; pop. 125 (1933), 101 (1947), 94 (1954), 91 (1961).

Freshwater (*Co. Clarence*) 29°56'S. 153°16'E., 14 km N. of Arrawarra; pop. 50 (1901).

Freshwater Creek (*Co. Northumberland*) see Teralba.

Friday Flat Camp (*Co. Wallace*) see Thredbo.

Friday Mount (*Co. Goulburn*) see Holbrook.

Fridays Creek (*Co. Fitzroy*) 30°19'S. 153°01'E., 9 km W. of Coffs Harbour, on Fridays Ck; telephone 1924; TX 1955–58; pop. 61 (1947), 55 (1954), 60 (1961).

Friendship Point (*Co. Gloucester*) see Soldiers Point.

Frizells (*Co. Clarence*) 29°47'S. 152°56'E., 9 km S. of Grafton; telephone 1927; TX 1953–63.

Frog Hollow (*Co. Northumberland*) 33°18'S. 151°05'E., 27 km W. of Ourimbah.

Frogmoor (*Co. King*) see Frogmore.

Frogmore (*Co. King*) 34°16'S. 148°51'E., 22 km NE of Boorowa; Frogmoor till 1909; surveyed and laid out 1889 by Lester; copper (disc. 1860, rush 1872) 1870+, wolfram, farming, grazing; bushfires 1944 and 1964; cemetery (80 graves 1877–1996) 1878; CH 1887, reused, new one b. 1911 by Oliver John Stuart; electricity 1954; FB; hurricane 1877; Meth. C. 1906; mines: Aust. Copper Mines (failed 1874), Burrowa Copper, Silver & Slate Mining Co. 1872, Federal, Frogmore Copper Mine 1873–75, 1880–85, 1888–91, Frogmore Scheelite Ltd (closed, reopened 1951, closed again and sold 1957), Glenavon, A. McInnes and Cook 1898–1900, Phoenix or Mt Charlestead or Frogmore Wolfram Mine 1914–20, 1937–44, 1952–55, Pride of Frogmore (or Bensusans) 1870–1907, John Sheedy 1870, Southern Copper Mines 1872, Southern Mining Co., Yando Copper Mines; PO 1875; pound (stock) 1879; PS 1878, reused, new one (incl. lock-up) b. 1911 by Oliver John Stuart, closed 1966; Rom. Cath. C. 1880, new one (St John the Baptist) b. 1926 by N.J. Markham, and graveyard (121 graves 1865+); sawmill; school (Frogmoor till 1903) 1875, new one b. 1878, replaced 1961, closed 1982; smelter (copper) 1875–85 and 1888–91; stamper battery; telephone 1908; tornado 1912; TX 1919, automatic 1955; Unit. C. (orig. Meth.) 1961; pop. *c.*120 (1875), *c.*300 (1877), 178 (1901), 345 (1911), 111 (1933), 64 (1947), 59 (1954), 272 (1961), 382 (2011).

Frogmore (*Co. Macquarie*) 31°04'S. 152°55'E., 8 km E. of Kempsey; cemetery; storm 1890.

Frogmore Park (*Co. Buckland*) 31°00'S. 150°20'E., 11 km E. of Gunnedah; pop. 20 (1933).

Frog Rock (*Co. Phillip*) 32°28'S. 149°41'E., 17 km NE of Mudgee; quarry.

Frogs Hollow (*Co. Auckland*) 36°46'S. 149°49'E., 10 km S. of Bega; airport (Bega) 1937; flood 1956.

Fromes Creek (*Co. Wellington*) 32°31'S. 149°29'E., 14 km NW of Mudgee; school 1884–1921.

Frying Pan (*Co. Roxburgh*) see Yetholme.

Frying Pan (*Co. Wallace*) 36°09'S. 148°49'E., 31 km W. of Cooma, on Lake Eucumbene; pop. 24 (1933).

Fulham (*Co. Woore*) 31°55'S. 144°25'E., 105 km E. of Wilcannia.

Fullerton (*Co. Georgiana*) 34°13'S. 149°32'E., 27 km N. of Crookwell; farming and grazing; Angl. C. (St John's) 1863–1947, demolished, new one 1958, and graveyard (burials 1863+) also known as Bolong cemetery; PO 1871–1974; school 1893, burnt down 1897, replaced, closed 1924; telephone 1915; TX 1924, automatic 1982; pop. 67 (1901), 94 (1911), 123 (1933), 37 (1947), 95 (1961), 103 (2006).

Fullerton Cove (*Co. Gloucester*) 32°50'S. 151°50'E., 11 km NE of Newcastle, on Fullerton Cove; sand mining; Angl. C. (St John's) 1899 d. by George Sanders & Son; quarry; telephone 1912; pop. 199 (1901), 199 (1933), 131 (1947), 132 (1954), 156 (1961), 300 (2011).

Furracabad (*Co. Gough*) 29°47'S. 151°40'E., 8 km SW of Glen Innes, on Furracabad Ck; oats, chaff, grazing; bridge (United Bridge) 1911 d. by Wickner, 104 ft (31.7 m), over Furracabad Ck; hailstorm 1915; PO 1904; school 1894–1958; storm 1906; telephone 1907; TX 1934, automatic 1952; pop. 265 (1901), 149 (1911), 230 (1933), 173 (1947), 94 (1954), 104 (1961).

G

Gadara (*Co. Wynyard*) 35°18'S. 148°08'E., 6 km E. of Adelong; PO 1956; RS 1903, station b. by F.G. Filmer, closed 1975; school 1881–1916; telephone 1956; pop. 138 (1911).

Gainsborough (*Co. Camden*) see Mittagong.

Gainsborough (*Co. Sandon*) 30°34'S. 151°41'E., 6 km S. of Armidale; school 1883–89.

Galambine (*Co. Phillip*) 32°25'S. 149°31'E., 7 km S. of Gulgong; school (Springfield) 1878–91.

Galargambone (*Co. Gowen*) see Gulargambone.

Gala Vale (*Co. Urana*) 34°59'S. 145°46'E., 22 km SW of Coleambally; telephone 1926; TX 1927, automatic 1954.

Galba (*Co. Dampier*) 36°21'S. 149°50'E., 20 km W. of Bermagui; telephone 1927; TX 1927, automatic 1959; pop. 29 (1933).

Gale (*Co. Murray*) see Queanbeyan.

Galgabba (*Co. Northumberland*) see Swansea.

Galley Swamp (*Co. Bathurst*) see Gallymont.

Gallymont (*Co. Bathurst*) 33°44'S. 149°06'E., 26 km SW of Blayney, on Gallymont Ck; Galley Swamp till 1898; village gaz. 1899; mining (gold disc. 1886 by Tom Lane) 1886–96 and 1908, farming, grazing; airfield (1 km NE); bushfire 1944; 2 dams (mine); dust storm 1944; earth tremor 1919; hailstorm 1899; mines: Black Hill Reef, Gallymont (E. Gregory and Anglo-Exploration Co.), Homeward Bound (estab. by Tucker and Osborne, sold 1887 to Henry Newman); PO 1889; powder magazines; PS 1898; quarry; school (Mandurama Ponds till 1888, Milpost till 1889, then Galley Swamp till 1900) 1880, new one b. 1882 by John Cody, burnt down 1909, replaced 1910 by W.J. Leabeater, additions 1911 by W.W. Nixon, closed 1959; stamper battery (40 head) 1898; telephone 1903; tramway (mine); TX 1923–62; pop. 360 (1901), 213 (1911), 186 (1921), 153 (1933), 106 (1947), 70 (1954).

Galoand (*Co. Gowen*) 31°42'S. 148°41'E., 2 km NE of Gilgandra, on Castlereagh R.

Galong (*Co. Harden*) 34°36'S. 148°33'E., 19 km E. of Murrumburrah; orig. a private town, subdivided 1907 and 1915; farming, dairying, grazing; butter factory 1906; cemetery (burials 1830s+, 365 graves) 1884, restored 1999; freezing works (Wilson, Flood & Co.) 1915; gale 1947; lime-kilns (McShane's); PO 1888; PS 1927–39; quarry; Rom. Cath. C. b. 1902 by Thomson and Bates, d. by Sheerin and Hennessy, additions 1917, new one (St Michael's) 1935; RS (relocated 1915) 1877–1980, reused; school 1896 b. by John Carter, closed 2007, sold; storm 1932; streets electric lit 1931; telegraph 1890; TX 1914, automatic 1973; Unit. C. (orig. Meth.) b. 1922 by Mitchell; pop. 147 (1901), 302 (1911), 325 (1933), 419 (1947), 312 (1954), 314 (1961), 123 (2006), 338 (2011).

Galore (*Co. Mitchell*) 35°00'S. 146°49'E., 26 km N. of Lockhart; farming; Angl. C. (St Michael and All Angels') 1953; FB 1939; PO 1933; Rom. Cath. C. (St Kevin's) 1956; RS 1928–75; telephone 1934; TX 1935, automatic 1971; pop. 78 (1911), 147 (1933), 81 (1947), 158 (1954), 161 (1961), 223 (2006).

Galwadgere (*Co. Wellington*) 32°37'S.

149°04'E., 12 km SE of Wellington, on Macquarie R.; mining (gold, copper, silver); mines: Christies' 1967–71, Galwadgere or Dawn of Galwadgere 1935–48, McDowall's or Old Paint 1936–37; school 1883–1907; pop. 85 (1911).

Gamble Creek (*Co. Napier*) 31°41'S. 149°27'E., 16 km S. of Binnaway; pop. 52 (1933).

Ganbenang (*Co. Westmoreland*) 33°39'S. 150°08'E., 27 km E. of Oberon; formerly Marsdens Swamp; school 1882–92; pop. 41 (1933), 87 (1947), 355 (2011).

Gan Gan (*Co. Gloucester*) see Nelson Bay.

Gangara (*Co. Fitzroy*) 30°19'S. 152°37'E., 9 km W. of Dorrigo, on Borra Ck; 2 quarries; sawmill; telephone 1913; TX 1923–29; pop. 59 (1933).

Gangat (*Co. Gloucester*) 32°01'S. 152°04'E., 10 km E. of Gloucester, on Bakers Ck; FB; school 1938–67; telephone 1936; TX 1937; pop. 64 (1933), 72 (1947), 64 (1954), 67 (1961).

Ganmain (*Co. Bourke*) 34°48'S. 147°02'E., 15 km W. of Coolamon, on Boggy Ck; Boggy Creek till Jan. 1894 then Derry till Mar. 1894; village gaz. 1892, settled mainly by Victorians, thrived 1907–12; grazing, hay, chaff, wheat, canola, barley, oats; Angl. C. (St Peter's) b. 1912 by A.C. Witts, d. by Ernest Rees Laver; brick-kiln; bridge 1914, over Boggy Ck; cemetery 1899; CH 1911, new one 1927; chaff mills: Mellor and Murphy, and Stockman & Co. Ltd, damaged 1923, sold 1925; diphtheria 1910, 1913, 1934; electricity 1937; FB; fires 1908, 1912, 1914, 1927, 1930; floods 1925, 1928, 1931, 2012; grasshopper infestation 1946; measles epidemic 1901; PO 1891, new one b. 1911 by A.C. Witts; PS (in rented premises) 1902, new building 1926; railway dam; reservoir (elevated), 150,000 gal. (681.9 kl); Rom. Cath. C. 1898, damaged 1902, reused, new one (St Brendan's) b. 1912 by A.G. Plowman, d. by Kempson and Conolly; RS (Boggy Creek till 1894) 1883, damaged 1902, new station 1910, closed 1988; sale-yards (Mellor and Murphy) 1937; sawmill (J.F. Dunn), man killed 1936, taken over 1943 by Ganmain Sawmill Co. Pty Ltd, burnt down 1944; scarlet fever 1934, 1943, 1952; school (Derry till 1895) 1893 b. by James M'Intosh, additions 1913 by George Huntley Dixon and William Godfrey Butterworth; sewerage augmentation 1999; silo 1922; storms 1902 and 1923; telegraph 1906; telephone 1896; TX 1910, automatic 1984; typhoid 1895, 1896, 1899, 1904, 1909 (woman died), 1912 (2 died); Unit C. (orig. Meth.) 1912, restored 1997; water supply 1941; Wes. Meth. C. 1894, closed and reused; pop. 533 (1901), 1,033 (1911), 944 (1933), 784 (1947), 792 (1954), 769 (1961), 731 (1966), 691 (1971), 656 (1976), 650 (1981), 614 (1986), 597 (1991), 578 (1996), 632 (2001), 614 (2011).

Ganmain (*Co. Bourke*) see also Coolamon.

Ganmurra (*Co. Bourke*) 34°59'S. 146°59'E., 19 km S. of Ganmain, on Murrumbidgee R.; cheese factory (Ganmain); school 1957–63; pop. 62 (1933).

Gannons Creek (*Co. Macquarie*) 31°29'S. 152°37'E., 12 km W. of Wauchope, on Hastings R.; dairying; PO 1893–1967; quarry; school 1895 b. by Tom Maher, closed 1909, burnt down 1926; telephone 1913; TX 1928–67; pop. 51 (1947), 58 (1954).

Gap (*Co. Buckland*) 31°21'S. 150°36'E., 5 km W. of Werris Creek, on Werris Ck; abattoir estab. 1895 by Graziers Meat Export Co. of NSW Ltd, renamed Stock Owners' Meat Co., sold 1901 to Austral Freezing Works Ltd, closed and dismantled 1902; railway bridge replaced 1915; railway dam 1902, rebuilt 1912, wall raised 1920, silted up by 1924; RS 1879–1971.

Gara (*Co. Sandon*) 30°35'S. 151°48'E., 16 km SE of Armidale; antimony (disc. 1853); dam 1954; pop. 82 (1911).

Garah (*Co. Stapylton*) 29°04'S. 149°38'E., 47 km NW of Moree, on Gil Gil Ck; village gaz. 1894, first lots sold 1902; wool and cotton; cemetery 1894; PO 1881; Presb. C. b. 1929 by Trueline Brick Construction Co. Ltd, d. by Hugh Henry McCourt; PS 1892, new one b. 1908 by R.E. Humphries, new one b. 1923; railway turntable, 50 ft (15.2 m); Rom. Cath. C. (Our Lady Help of Christians) d. and b.

1938 by Bob Morgan; RS 1913, station b. by C. Harris, closed 1974; school 1913, new one b. 1914 by Thomas John Bowen, additions 1960 and 1983; telephone 1905; tornado 1937; TX 1910, automatic 1987; pop. 136 (1911), 241 (1933), 257 (1947), 204 (1954), 210 (1961), 305 (2001), 338 (2006), 551 (2011).

Garangula (*Co. Harden*) 34°41'S. 148°17'E., 15 km S. of Murrumburrah; gold (alluvial, gold rush 1894); bushfire 1905; PO 1894–1927; PS 1894–96; school 1895–99; stamper battery (Martin's, 5 head); TX (automatic) 1955; pop. 57 (1901), 57 (1911).

Garden Suburb (*Co. Northumberland*) 32°57'S. 151°41'E., 2 km E. of Cardiff, on Tickhole Ck; Kotara Heights till 1964; subdivided 1918; formerly orchards; bushfire 1994; colliery (Cardiff Tickhole) 1925; Meth. C. (removed 1950 from Charlestown) re-erected, renovated and reopened 1951; PO 1956; Rom. Cath. C. (St James's) 1961, demolished; school 1958, additions 1960 and 1966; telephone 1956; Unit. C.; pop. 1,716 (2006), 1,927 (2011).

Garema (*Co. Forbes*) 33°33'S. 147°56'E., 20 km S. of Forbes, on Ooma Ck; village gaz. 1918; farming; FB (station b. 2011); floods 1950 and 1955; school (Garema Siding) 1956–71; PO 1924; RS 1918–76; silo 1928; telephone 1923; TX 1927, automatic 1965; pop. 147 (1933), 121 (1947), 100 (1954), 145 (1961), 131 (2006).

Garema Siding (*Co. Forbes*) see Garema.

Garfield (*Co. Argyle*) see Goulburn.

Garfield (*Co. Auckland*) 36°37'S. 149°46'E., 9 km NW of Bega; school 1880–96 and 1933–70.

Garibaldi (*Co. Monteagle*) 34°23'S. 148°15'E., 8 km S. of Young; gold; mines: Davison's, Garibaldi Reef, Mary's Dream, Stoney Creek; school (Tumbleton till 1934) 1893, new building b. 1914 by W.S. Millard & Sons, closed 1942.

Garland (*Co. Bathurst*) 33°43'S. 149°02'E., 29 km SW of Blayney, on Grubbenbun Ck; farming and grazing; PO 1901; 2 quarries; RS (Baker's Siding till 1890) 1888, station b. by Charles Palmer, closed 1975; school (Burkeville till 1900) 1870, repairs 1882 by H. Snowdon, new building b. 1891 by W.R. Gorringe, repairs 1896 by C. Bloomfield, new building b. 1900 by Henry Hart, closed 1912, reopened 1919, closed 1979; telephone 1911; TX 1918–86; pop. 117 (1901), 111 (1911), 105 (1921), 168 (1933), 141 (1947), 123 (1954), 134 (1961).

Garlandtown (*Co. St Vincent*) 35°54'S. 150°08'E., 5 km E. of Moruya, on Moruya R.; (incl. Granite Town estab. 1924 by Dorman Long & Co. for Scottish and Italian workers cutting stone for Sydney Harbour Bridge pylons, abandoned 1931); founded by James Garland; airport (Moruya) 1939, used by air force during World War II (incl. bomb shelters and bunker), new one 1950, upgraded 2019; breakwater b. 1876+ by John White et al.; bushfires 1896 and 1968; dam; flood 1913; granite quarries: govt one 1876 (acquired 1925 by Dorman Long & Co., closed 1931, later reopened by PWD, closed 1954, later reopened), McCredie Bros 1884, Henry Christian Ziegler and Joseph Ard 1867 (acquired 1894 by Henry Thompson, acquired 1900 by Henry Eshalby Boot, acquired 1925 by Dorman Long & Co., closed 1931); school (Granite Town) 1926–31; tannery (D. Beileiter), burnt down 1894, rebuilt, burnt down 1900; training wall b. 1897–1901, later extended, completed 1954; tramway (govt quarry to breakwater); wharf; pop. 30 (1933), 83 (1947), 57 (1954).

Garland Valley (*Co. Hunter*) 32°56'S. 150°45'E., 50 km W. of Paxton; telephone 1958; TX 1960–81.

Garoo (*Co. Parry*) 31°24'S. 150°59'E., 34 km S. of Tamworth; FB (station b. 2012); school 1957–66; TX (automatic); pop. 236 (2006).

Garoolgan (*Co. Cooper*) 34°15'S. 146°26'E., 43 km W. of Ardlethan; wheat; RS 1916, station b. by Ernest Frederick Leggo, closed 1975; silo 1936; telephone 1919; TX 1923–24; pop. 111 (1933), 56 (1947).

Garra (*Co. Ashburnham*) 33°07'S. 148°45'E., 10 km NE of Manildra, on Mandagery Ck; farming; Angl. C. 1881, new one (St Andrew's) 1891, renovated 1899, and graveyard; Bapt. C. 1890; cemetery (138 graves 1896+) 1886; FB; flour mill (W. Spurr); PO 1883; school 1879, new one b. 1882 by William Gadd, additions 1912, closed 1970; storm 1902; telephone 1914; TX 1915–80; Wes. Meth. C. 1877, new one b. 1880–83 by William Gadd; pop. 235 (1901), 211 (1911), 139 (1933), 81 (1947), 81 (1954), 97 (1961), 186 (2011).

Garrawilla (*Co. Pottinger*) 31°10'S. 149°39'E., 36 km E. of Coonabarabran, on Girrawillie Ck; pop. 84 (1933), 68 (1954).

Garryowen (*Co. Goulburn*) 35°40'S. 147°26'E., 12 km NE of Holbrook, on Little Billabong Ck; orig. Billabong; site reserved 1852, village gaz. 1875, never developed, defunct; wheat, oats, maize, barley, tobacco, sheep; brewery (Gregson Bros) 1878–79; flood 1870; mine (Dalriada); PO 1869–77; PS (moved 1862 to Holbrook); pop. *c.*50 (1866), 143 (1901), 232 (1911).

Garryowen Estate (*Co. Murray*) see Queanbeyan.

Garthowen (*Co. Inglis*) 30°53'S. 150°53'E., 21 km SE of Manilla, on Attunga Ck; Angl. C. (St Mark's), removed 1927 from Attunga, closed, moved 1960 to Moonbi; school 1948–69; telephone 1925; TX 1926, automatic 1954; pop. 157 (1933), 52 (1947), 100 (1961).

Garvan's Siding (*Co. Rous*) see Binna Burra.

Gaspard (*Co. Buckland*) 31°29'S. 150°49'E., 13 km E. of Quirindi, on Jacob and Joseph Ck; school 1885–1913; telephone 1918; TX 1920–29; pop. 88 (1911), 50 (1933), 52 (1947), 70 (1954).

Gateshead (*Co. Northumberland*) 32°59'S. 151°41'E., 2 km S. of Charlestown, on Johnsons Ck; (incl. Oak Dale and West Gateshead); planned 1877 by William Thomas Verge; formerly timber, farming, fruit; Assemblies of God C. (Eastlakes Christ. Life); colliery (Wattle Glen, Date Bros) 1917; PO: Gateshead 1946, additions 1959, and West Gateshead 1965–93; Rom. Cath. C. (St Paul's) d. by John Kevin Gannon; schools: Hunter Sports HS (Gateshead HS till 1997) 1959, additions 1966, 1978, 1981, additions 2011 by Artel Constructions Pty Ltd, West Gateshead 1967–2013, Wiripaang (Gateshead till 2012) 1950, additions 1965; sewerage 1961; telephone: Gateshead 1946 and West Gateshead 1965; pop. 61 (1901), 66 (1911), 71 (1933), 419 (1947), 3,574 (2011).

Gays Hill (*Co. Rous*) see Casino and Nashua.

Gearys Flat (*Co. Macquarie*) 31°11'S. 152°35'E., 27 km SW of Kempsey, on Glencoe Ck.

Gearys Gap (*Co. Murray*) 35°06'S. 149°22'E., 19 km N. of Bungendore, on Lake George; orig. Lake George; estab. by Daniel Geary; goldmining; earth tremor 1852; grasshopper infestation 1898; PO 1837–39; TX.

Geebung Ground (*Co. Hunter*) 33°03'S. 150°21'E., 48 km NE of Wallerawang; The Geebung Ground till 1975; airfield.

Geegullalong (*Co. Monteagle*) 34°21'S. 148°42'E., 10 km N. of Boorowa, on Geegullalong Ck; earth tremor 1946; school (orig. Gegullalong) 1888–93.

Geehi (*Co. Selwyn*) 36°24'S. 148°11'E., 16 km NW of Thredbo, on Swampy Plain R.; estab. 1958, relocated 1960; PO 1959–61; telephone 1959; pop. 61 (1961).

Geera (*Co. Clyde*) 30°08'S. 147°23'E., 53 km E. of Brewarrina, on Barwon R.

Gees Wharf (*Co. Cook*) 33°25'S. 150°48'E., 19 km N. of North Richmond, on Colo R.; farming and orchards; PO 1927; telephone 1921; TX 1922–44.

Gegedzerick (*Co. Wallace*) see Berridale.

Gegullalong (*Co. Monteagle*) see Geegullalong.

Gemalla (*Co. Roxburgh*) 33°32'S. 149°50'E., 20 km N. of Oberon, on Fish R.; farming and molybdenite; Meth. C.; PO 1927; quarry; RS (Stoney Creek Loop till 1909) 1907–74; telephone 1924; TX 1925–70; pop. 61 (1911), 61 (1933), 53 (1947).

Gemville (*Co. Yungnulgra*) 30°55'S. 142°56'E., 91 km NW of Wilcannia; surveyed and established 1907, declined 1909+; mining (opals disc. 1893) 1893–98, then 1906+; PO 1906–18; PS 1907–10; school (removed from White Cliffs) 1908–9; pop. *c.*20 (1909).

Geneva (*Co. Rous*) see Eden Creek and Kyogle.

Genista (*Co. Cooper*) 34°09'S. 146°38'E., 34 km NW of Ardlethan; school (Roachs Saw Mills till 1919) 1913–21.

Genowlan (*Co. Roxburgh*) see Airly.

Georges Creek (*Co. Clarke*) 30°45'S. 152°12'E., 56 km SE of Armidale, on Georges R.; grazing; PO 1906; PS b. 1906 by Culverwell and Scott; telephone 1907; TX 1915–61; pop. 47 (1933).

Georges Creek (*Co. Hardinge*) 30°11'S. 151°11'E., 25 km S. of Tingha, on Georges Ck; school 1880–97; pop. 39 (1933).

Georges Plains (*Co. Bathurst*) 33°31'S. 149°31'E., 12 km SW of Bathurst, on Georges Plains Ck; farming; Angl. C. (St John's) 1868 d. by Edward Gell, closed 1986, and graveyard (118 graves 1868+); bridge 1965; FB; flood 1955; PO 1876–1982; RS 1876, station b. by James Stuart Douglas, closed 1989; school 1889–94, reopened 1900, new building b. 1909 by H.C. Bruce, new building b. 1912 by Albert Emanuel Ennis, burnt down 1973; telegraph 1877; telephone 1903; TX 1925–81; Wes. Meth. C. 1844, new one 1856; pop. 221 (1901), 203 (1911), 178 (1933), 158 (1947), 145 (1954), 197 (1961), 361 (2011).

George Town (*Co. Macquarie*) 31°54'S. 152°12'E., 17 km W. of Wingham, on Manning R.; surveyed 1841, first lots offered 1842 but first ones sold 1855, never developed.

Georgetown (*Co. Northumberland*) see Waratah.

Georgeville (*Co. Pottinger*) 31°21'S. 149°54'E., 52 km SW of Gunnedah, on Bundella Ck.

Georgica (*Co. Rous*) 28°40'S. 153°10'E., 8 km SW of Nimbin, on Georgica Ck; dairying; bridges: Murphy Bridge over Georgica Ck and 2 bridges over Oakey Ck; FB; flood 1935; Meth. C. (The Tower) b. 1909 by James; PO 1913, burnt down 1928; school 1957–61; telephone 1914; TX 1927–60; pop. 194 (1933), 199 (1947), 201 (1954), 123 (1961), 246 (2011).

Geradan (*Co. Ashburnham*) see Geradon.

Geradon (*Co. Ashburnham*) 33°34'S. 148°30'E., 16 km W. of Canowindra; RS (Geradan) 1927–68.

Geraldene (*Co. Parry*) 31°12'S. 151°21'E., 33 km SW of Walcha, on Gunyah Ck.

Geran (*Co. Gipps*) see Warroo.

German Creek (*Co. Richmond*) see Empire Vale.

Germans Hill (*Co. Ashburnham*) see Cave Creek.

German's Hill (*Co. Wellington*) see Lidster and Nashdale.

Germanton (*Co. Goulburn*) see Holbrook.

Germantown (*Co. Wellington*) see Hill End.

Gerogery (*Co. Goulburn*) 35°50'S. 147°00'E., 12 km SE of Walla Walla; disc. 1824 by Hamilton Hume and William Hilton Hovell, settled by German immigrants, village gaz. 1869; farming, grazing, wheat, now mainly hobby farms; Angl. C. (St Alban's) d. and b. 1909 by J.H. Berry, restored 1922, closed, sold 2015, reused; bushfires 1905, 1926, 2009 (5 houses destroyed); cemetery; electricity 1948; FB 1927; PO 1875; PS 1880–97; RS (2 km SE) 1880, station b. by Charles Hardy, closed 1984; school (Gerogery Railway Station till 1928) 1884 b. by J. Matthews, additions 1923; telegraph 1880; TX 1913, automatic 1959; pop. 227 (1881), 224 (1891), 206 (1901), 302 (1911), 127 (1933), 226 (1947), 225 (1954), 284 (1961), 120 (1981), 510 (2011).

Gerogery (*Co. Goulburn*) see also Gerogery West.

Gerogery Railway Station (*Co. Goulburn*) see Gerogery.

Gerogery West (*Co. Goulburn*) 35°52'S. 146°58'E., 11 km SE of Walla Walla; bushfire 2009; cemetery; Lutheran C. 1880, new one (St Peter's) b. 1920 by W.T. Thorne, and graveyard; PO 1927–59; school (Gerogery till 1903) 1882–99, 1904–53, 1961–68; telephone 1923; TX 1926–59; pop. 115 (1933), 79 (1947).

Gerringong (*Co. Camden*) 34°45'S. 150°50'E., 9 km S. of Kiama, on Tasman Sea; (incl. Werri Beach, subdivided by J.M. Miller); site reserved 1824, surveyed 1826 by James McBrien, settled 1827 by Michael Hindmarsh, first lots sold 1855, munic. proc. 1871 (amalgamated with Kiama 1954), declined 1893+; timber 1814+, shipping port 1884–93, farming, grazing, dairying, tourism 1945+; Angl. C. b. 1856 by George and Henry Gray, burnt down 1872, replacement (St George's) b. 1874 by Peter Walker & Sons, d. by Edmund Thomas Blacket, additions 1884 by Frederick

Watkins, and graveyard; bacon factory (W. Cooke); butter factory (Gerringong Co-op. Dairy Society Ltd) b. 1888 by J.B. Taylor, burnt down 1914, rebuilt, additions 1927; carriage-works: J.W. Cockerill and John Kelly; cemetery (1,155 graves 1860s+), incl. columbarium; Cong. C. 1856, new one b. 1884 by Thomas Kirby and James Galloway, d. by Herbert S. Thompson, new one (Jubilee) 1906; electricity 1928; FB 1953; fires 1866, 1872 (town nearly destroyed), 1928; foot-bridge over Werri Lagoon; gales 1899 and 1947; jetty, 300 ft (91.4 m), extensions 1884 by John Britain Taylor, destroyed 1891; lock-up b. 1883 by G. Osborne; PO: Gerringong 1857, new one b. 1966, closed 1997, and Werri Beach, closed 1979; pound (stock) 1842; Presb. C. 1855; PS 1877, new one 1884, reused, new one 1990; rifle range 1912; Rom. Cath. C. 1864, new one (St Mary's Star of the Sea) b. 1882 by Frederick Watkins, d. by George Osborne, extended 1995; RS 1893, station b. by Gerald Dalton Fetherston and Felix Edward Barbat, burnt down 1941, rebuilt 1942; sawmill 1942; school 1876, additions 1885 by J. Stokes, repairs 1913 by H.A. Baglee, additions 1924 by F. Jones, new building (removed from Toolijooa) 1954, new school b. 1994 on new site, additions 2010; sewerage 2002; storms 1891 and 1903; streets were formerly kerosene lit; telegraph 1879; telephone: Gerringong 1913 and Werri Beach 1947; TX 1915, automatic 1965; Unit. C.: Chittick Lodge Chapel (orig. Wes. Meth., b. 1870 by James Dinning, d. by Thomas Rowe, renovated and vestry added 1923, church re-roofed, renovated 1995) and former Cong. C. (b. 1884, re-roofed 1900, vestry added 1969); water reticulation 1971; Wes. Meth. C. 1850; wineries: Crooked River Wines estab. 1998, winery o. 2001 and Roselea Vineyard 1998; pop. 7 (1841), 68 (1856), *c.*100 (1866), 1,047 (1881), 1,534 (1891), *c.*1,100 (1895), 1,051 (1901), 489 (1911), 855 (1933), 881 (1947), 1,058 (1954), 995 (1961), 805 (1966), 1,240 (1976), 1,775 (1981), 2,326 (1986), 2,478 (1991), 2,891 (1996), 3,492 (2001), 3,588 (2006), 3,998 (2011).

Gerroa (*Co. Camden*) 34°46'S. 150°49'E., 3 km S. of Gerringong, on Shoalhaven Bight; surveyed 1824 by James McBrien; bridge over Crooked R.; electricity 1929; foot-bridge, rebuilt 1951, over Crooked R.; PO 1933; sewage works d. and b. 2002 by Veolia Water; telephone 1933; pop. 97 (1961), 422 (1991), 541 (1996), 497 (2001), 477 (2006), 496 (2011).

Gerrymberryn (*Co. Clarence*) 29°41'S. 152°54'E., 5 km W. of Grafton; cemetery 1884; PO 1882–1912; school 1881, additions 1883 by J. Rooke, closed 1911; pop. 68 (1911).

Geurie (*Co. Lincoln*) 32°24'S. 148°50'E., 21 km NW of Wellington, on Boori Ck; Ponto Railway Station till 1888; declined 1920+; wheat; Angl. C. (St Matthew's) b. 1906–9 by Benjamin Aldridge Tillett, closed; brickworks: Joseph Payne and Reynolds; cemetery (360 graves 1891+), incl. columbarium; cyclone 1907; dust storm 1920; FB; floods 1926 and 1929; lime-kilns: Alf Baker, Joseph Payne, Reynolds; PO 1888, new one b. 1916; PS 1896, new one b. 1909 by Benjamin Aldridge Tillett; quarry (BHP, blue metal); railway collision 1963; rifle range 1907; Rom. Cath. C. (Holy Name of Jesus) b. 1906 by James Connors, d. by A. Kennard, renovations and repairs 1927; RS (Ponto till 1889) 1885, closed; sawmill (acquired from William Heath by Frederick Bell, later acquired by J.T. Atkins, then by Tom Smith and Arthur Davis); school 1886, new one b. 1895 by John Lane, additions and alterations 1910 by Charles Benaud Smith, additions 1920; sewage works; silo 1920; storm (man killed) 2018; telegraph 1890; telephone 1908; TX 1910, automatic 1983; Union C. 1897, renovated 1953; water supply 1958, filtration plant, augmentation 1995; pop. 396 (1911), 418 (1933), 590 (1947), 410 (1954), 381 (1961), 291 (1971), 264 (1976), 290 (1981), 317 (1986), 412 (1991), 488 (1996), 509 (2001), 466 (2006), 453 (2011).

Ghent's Camp (*Co. Selwyn*) see Cabramurra.

Ghinni Ghi (*Co. Rous*) 28°37'S. 152°50'E., 17 km W. of Kyogle, on Iron Pot Ck; formerly

Iron Pot Creek; Rom. Cath. C. (Holy Family) b. 1935 by J. Watt, closed, sold 1984; school (Oakburn till 1952) 1930–72; telephone 1924; TX 1928–70; pop. 55 (1911), 86 (1933), 59 (1947), 66 (1954), 53 (1961).

Ghinni Ghinni (*Co. Macquarie*) 31°53'S. 152°33'E., 10 km NE of Taree, on Ghinni Ghinni Ck; farming and dairying; bridge 1963, demolished, new one (Harold Eggins Bridge) 2005, over Ghinni Ghinni Ck; creamery (Aust. Dairying Co.) 1897; PO 1868–1960; punt; school 1861, new one b. 1870 by A. Whitton, replaced 1913 by R. Cairns and E. Schmitzer, closed 2009, sold; telephone 1908; TX 1952; Wes. Meth. C. 1865, new one 1896; wharf b. 1888 by R.H. Worthing; pop. 77 (1901), 62 (1911), 141 (1933), 65 (1947), 100 (1954), 77 (1961).

Ghoolendaadi (*Co. Pottinger*) 30°50'S. 149°55'E., 18 km SW of Boggabri, on Bara Ck; FB; Presb. C.; TX (automatic); pop. 69 (1911), 32 (1933).

Giants Creek (*Co. Brisbane*) 32°19'S. 150°33'E., 15 km NW of Denman, on Halls Ck; dairying; Angl. C. (St John's) 1877, re-roofed; cemetery (121 graves 1888+) 1886; PO 1901; sawmill (W. Hogan); telephone 1898; TX 1914–37; pop. 142 (1911), 136 (1933), 117 (1947), 192 (2006), 196 (2011).

Giants Creek (*Co. Brisbane*) see also Sandy Hollow.

Gibbagunyah (*Co. Wallace*) 36°23'S. 148°41'E., 7 km NE of Jindabyne.

Gibberagee (*Co. Richmond*) 29°14'S. 153°06'E., 29 km SW of Woodburn, on Myall Ck; pop. 34 (1933), 282 (2006).

Gibsonvale (*Co. Dowling*) 33°41'S. 146°43'E., 51 km NW of West Wyalong; estab. 1939; mining (tin disc. 1939 by J. Gibson); PO 1940; telephone 1941; TX 1941–72; pop. 128 (1947), 71 (1954).

Gidgell (*Co. Boyd*) 34°50'S. 146°06'E., 39 km SW of Leeton; school 1964–73; TX (automatic); pop. 26 (1933).

Gidginbung (*Co. Bland*) 34°20'S. 147°28'E., 15 km N. of Temora; goldmining and farming; Lutheran C. 1911, closed, dismantled and moved 1953 to Cootamundra; mine (Paragon Gold Pty Ltd) 1986–96; PO 1902; RS 1902–75; school 1904, additions 1923 by John Garlick, closed 1969; silo 1930; telephone 1912; TX 1916–78; pop. 213 (1911), 164 (1933), 134 (1947), 101 (1954), 123 (1961).

Gidleigh (*Co. Murray*) 35°19'S. 149°28'E., 6 km SE of Bungendore, on Turallo Ck; private town surveyed by Thomas Rutledge, failed in 1890s; pop. 86 (1911), 44 (1933), 50 (1947), 53 (1954), 59 (1961).

Gidley (*Co. Parry*) 31°01'S. 150°50'E., 12 km NW of Tamworth, on Peel R.; farming; airfield (World War II); Meth. C. 1902; PO 1904; RS (5 km S.) 1902–75; school 1902 b. by J. Russell, closed 1929; silo 1934; telephone 1907; TX 1925–34; pop. 107 (1933), 56 (1947).

Gilgai (*Co. Gough*) 29°51'S. 151°07'E., 8 km S. of Inverell; estab. 1864; mining (tin and precious stones), cattle, fruit; airport (4 km SE) 1954; Angl. C. (All Saints') 1915, closed and sold 2018; cemetery 1904; FB; flood 1955; mine (Wattle Glen Tin Mining Co.); PO 1879, burnt down 1945, rebuilt; Salv. Army C. 1914; sawmill (W. Thorne); school 1880, new buildings b. 1883 by Moore Bros, additions 1908 by Benjamin Martin Wade, additions 1962 and 2010; sewerage augmentation 1994; telephone 1911; TX 1928, automatic 1980; water supply augmentation 1994; winery estab. 1968 by Keith Whish, taken over 2005 by Alan Turvey; pop. 148 (1891), 154 (1901), 271 (1911), 297 (1933), 192 (1947), 355 (1954), 423 (1961), 243 (1971), 284 (1976), 257 (1981), 247 (1986), 315 (1991), 250 (1996), 271 (2001), 289 (2006), 394 (2011).

Gilgandra (*Co. Ewenmar*) 31°43'S. 148°40'E., 60 km N. of Dubbo, on Castlereagh R.; estab. 1866, first lots sold 1889, more lots sold 1900, thrived 1910; sheep 1830+, mining, wheat, barley, oats, rye, sorghum, oilseeds, legumes, pigs, cattle, fruit, timber; airport; ambulance station 1944 (in former bank), damaged 1955, new one d. by F.C. Graf; Angl. C. (Resurrection) b. 1903 by M. Brown and Neate, d. by Harold Robert Hardwick, demolished 1921, new one (St Ambrose's

Memorial) b. 1920–22 by John D. Ryan, d. by Louis Reginald Williams, porch replaced 1975; Assemblies of God C. (New Life); bridges: first one 1884, replaced 1929 by Jackson & Sons, and Jack Renshaw Bridge 1987, over Castlereagh R.; bushfire 1951; cemetery (2,663 graves 1895+) 1884, incl. lawn cemetery and columbarium; CH 1885, new one 1929; Church of Christ 1927; clock tower 1991; concrete-brick works (Jack Ryan); cordial factory (S.G. Turley) 1929, bought 1936 by R.N.J. Fletcher; diphtheria 1935 and 1937; dust storm 1925; earth tremor 1937; electricity 1917; FB 1911 (station b. 1915, new one 1989); fires 1903, 1904, 1909, 1926, 2009; floods 1874, 1950, 1955 (3 died); flour mill (Castlereagh) b. 1909 by John Dunkley, d. by Henry Simon Ltd, for Murdoch McLeod & Co., extended, taken over by Gillespie Bros Ltd and renamed Anchor Mills, closed 1974, acquired 1976 by Terry Nagle, burnt down 1997; freezing works (Country Freezing Co. Ltd); grasshopper infestation 1942; hailstorms 1891, 1900, 1913, 1920; heatwave 1901–2; hospital b. 1916 by R.J. Nelson, damaged 1925, morgue b. 1932 by Weaver and Greenaway, hospital repairs 1935 by H.E. Fielding, additions and alterations 1941 by A.H. Baglee, additions 1956; Jehovah's Witnesses C.; joineries: Gilgandra Cabinet Works and R.J. Nelson & Sons Pty Ltd; lock-up 1929; Lutheran C., burnt down 1922, replaced 1925, new one (St John's) 2009; Meth. C. 1910; observatory (Jack and Margaret Estens) 1975; PO 1867, new one b. 1904 by W. Refshaw; pound (stock) 1865; powerhouse (Gilgandra Electrical Supply Co.) b. by A.H. Smith, burnt down 1923, new one 1926, additions and alterations 1934 by A.H. Smith; Presb. C. (St Stephen's) b. 1912 by R.J. Carson; PS 1883, new one b. 1934 by Dan E. Foster; reservoir (elevated, steel), 500,000 gal. (2,273 kl), 1964; rifle range (9 km E.) 1909; Rom. Cath. C. 1909, new one b. 1914 by Hill, d. by John Francis Kenny, demolished, new one (St Joseph's) 1974; RS 1903, station b. by W.H. Hudson, burnt down 1930, new one b. 1932 by Joe Worrall, closed and disused; sale-yards 1954; sawmills: A.C. Bailey 1924 (bought by Cliff L. Anderson, and later by Robert John Nelson), John Elsom, T. Jones (burnt down 1902), Scholz's (fire 1912), George Wilkins; schools: primary 1881, new one b. 1884 by George Shaw, replaced 1887, additions 1898, 1914, 1918, 1929, 1956, 1969, 1975, and HS 1965, additions 1971, 1980, 1982; SD Adventist C.; sewerage 1966; silo 1955; storm 1949; streets gas lit 1912, electric lit 1917; TC (a campus of Western Institute); telegraph 1882; tornadoes 1944 (woman killed) and 1996; TX 1908, automatic 1977; Union C. 1887, closed, sold 1911; Unit. C. 1982; water reticulation 1966, filtration plant 1973, augmentation 1985; whooping cough epidemic 1932; pop. 95 (1891), 683 (1901), 2,207 (1911), 2,577 (1933), 2,231 (1947), 2,032 (1954), 2,245 (1961), 2,414 (1966), 2,554 (1971), 2,494 (1976), 2,700 (1981), 2,713 (1986), 2,890 (1991), 2,822 (1996), 2,718 (2001), 2,679 (2006), 2,666 (2011), *c.*3,143 (2018).

Gilgoin (*Co. Clyde*) 30°17'S. 147°13'E., 49 km SE of Brewarrina, on Marra Ck; school 1967–76.

Gilgooma (*Co. Leichhardt*) 30°45'S. 148°31'E., 26 km NE of Coonamble, on Weetaliba Ck; Weetalibah till 1917; surveyed 1902; grazing; PO 1920–58; sawmill (Colin and Mervyn Head) 1969–92; telephone 1906; TX 1914, automatic 1958; Unit. C. (orig. Meth.) re-erected 1958 (removed from Terembone); pop. 70 (1933), 98 (1947), 116 (2006), 176 (2011).

Gilgunnia (*Co. Blaxland*) 32°25'S. 146°02'E., 103 km S. of Cobar; founded *c.*1869 by Henry Kruge, declined 1896+, village gaz. 1897, defunct; mining (gold disc. 1895 by Jacky Owens and copper) mainly 1895–1909 then grazing; cemetery 1897; droughts 1937 and 1957; mines: Cripple's Reward, Daisy Bell, Hand in Hand, Her Dream (Finn's Mary's Dream, closed 1940), Hidden Treasure, Keep it Dark, Last Chance (Martin Siegel), Last Rose of Summer, Mehwar (South

Slanter), Narragadore (formerly The May Day), Pommer and Condon, Silver Ray, The Moonlight, The Rising Sun (Mullen's), The Trilby; PO 1878–1934; PS 1878–1915; sawmills: Henry Kruge and John F. Sweeting 1896 (bought by Billy Kitson); school 1896–1907; stamper battery (15 head); telephone 1924; TX 1928; pop. 20 (1933), 62 (1954).

Gillenbah (*Co. Mitchell*) 34°46'S. 146°31'E., 4 km SW of Narrandera, on Gillenbah Ck; settled 1856; farming; bushfire 1872; fire 1907; Meth. C. 1913; PO 1927–41; RS 1884, closed; sawmill (Beecher Bros); school 1900 b. by G.W. Casburn, closed 1945, reopened 1952, closed 1953; telephone 1928; TX 1928–40; pop. 316 (1911), 333 (1933), 113 (1947), 165 (1954), 118 (1961), 140 (2006).

Gillenbine (*Co. Cunningham*) 32°51'S. 147°29'E.; 24 km NW of Trundle; mining (platinum and gold) and farming; mines: Gillenbine Tank 1918–66 and McConnell's Prospect; PO 1927–30.

Gillens Crossing (*Co. Beresford*) 36°05'S. 149°08'E., 17 km N. of Cooma, on Murrumbidgee R.

Gilletts Ridge (*Co. Clarence*) 29°39'S. 153°06'E., 16 km E. of Grafton, school 1901–71.

Gillian Park (*Co. St Vincent*) see Gilligan Park.

Gilliby Gilliby (*Co. Northumberland*) see Jilliby.

Gillieston (*Co. Northumberland*) see Gillieston Heights.

Gillieston Heights (*Co. Northumberland*) 32°46'S. 151°32'E., 4 km SW of Maitland, on Wallis Ck; East Greta till 1968; estab. by East Greta Coal Mining Co.; Angl. C. (St Thomas's) b. 1899 by James Hinman, d. by C.W. Holmes, relocated, re-erected, enlarged, reopened 1906, enlarged 1912; briquette plant (East Greta Coal Mining Co.) 1907; bushfire 2002; collieries: East Greta No. 1 Tunnel (estab. 1888 by Henry Cartwright, taken over 1891 by East Greta Coal Mining Co., o. 1893, 3 men killed 1898, fire 1914, closed 1926, flooded 1930, razed), East Greta No. 2 Tunnel (estab. 1894 by East Greta Coal Mining Co., o. 1896, strike 1904, closed by strike 1929, flooded 1930, razed 1939), Glenmore Extension; FB (station 1909 d. by Pender); floods 1949 and 1955; gales 1899 and 1925; Meth. C. b. 1903 by A.H. Walker, damaged 1925; PO 1895–1993; PS 1911–22; railway (colliery) to Maitland b. 1893 by Wright and Woodward, d. by W.G. Kerle for East Greta Coal Mining Co., closed 1929; railway (South Maitland Railway) workshops, closed 1984, sold 1986, reused, restored 1988; Rom. Cath. C. (Our Lady Help of Christians) b. 1911 by Andrew Burg; school (Fishery Creek till 1893, then Gillieston) 1858, additions and repairs 1892 by Thomas E. Nott, additions 1904 by James Cook; telephone 1903; typhoid 1896; pop. 404 (1901), 690 (1911), 342 (1954), 305 (1961), 274 (1971), 308 (1976), 398 (1981), 464 (1986), 587 (1991), 636 (1996), 621 (2001), 609 (2006).

Gilligan Park (*Co. St Vincent*) 35°33'S. 149°49'E., 12 km S. of Braidwood, on Reidsdale Ck; also known as Gillian Park.

Gillinbah (*Co. Cooper*) see Narrandera.

Gillinghall (*Co. Lincoln*) 32°20'S. 149°05'E., 29 km NE of Wellington.

Gillwinga (*Co. Clarence*) see Grafton South.

Gilmandyke (*Co. Georgiana*) 33°47'S. 149°33'E., 29 km W. of Oberon, on Gilmandyke Ck; goldmining (reef) 1851–1900; mines: Gilmandyke (gold) 1895–98 and 1900, Nardin Deep Lead (gold), Summerhill (Bathurst Copper-Mining Co.) 1847–58, 1897, 1901; school 1898 b. by W.J. Bailey, closed 1922; pop. 83 (1901), 84 (1911), 53 (1933), 144 (2006).

Gilmore (*Co. Wynyard*) 35°20'S. 148°11'E., 5 km SW of Tumut, on Gilmore Ck; farming; Angl. C. (St Jude's) b. 1921 by Masters Bros, d. by A.E. Robson; bridge b. 1898, 50 ft (15.2 m), new one 1918, over Gilmore Ck; bushfire 1905; butter factory (Rosebank Dairy & Refrigerating Works) estab. 1900 by William Daniel Patrick O'Brien, became Tumut Co-op. Butter Factory Ltd in 1902, freezing works moved 1906 to Tumut; cheese factory (Rosebank) estab. 1904 by Isaacs Bros; FB 1939; flour mill b. by Henry Moon for Frank Taylor, acquired, refurbished and reopened 1905 by P.L. Ramsay; PO 1871, burnt down 1923; 4 quarries (incl. one for marble o. 1891); RS (Killarney till 1904) 1903–84, station removed 1984; sawmill (ACI Timber Products); telephone 1914; TX 1915, automatic 1956; pop. 102 (1901), 252 (1911), 254 (1933), 230 (1947), 210 (1954), 251 (1961), 249 (2011).

Gineroi Crossing (*Co. Burnett*) 29°41'S. 150°26'E., 20 km SW of Warialda, on Gwydir R.; butter factory (Gineroi Co-op. Dairy Products Ltd) 1912, sold 1922, closed 1925; flood 1910.

Gingerra (*Co. Beresford*) see Anembo.

Gingerra Station (*Co. Beresford*) see Anembo.

Gingers Creek (*Co. Hawes*) 31°24'S. 152°07'E., 58 km W. of Wauchope.

Ginghi (*Co. Phillip*) 32°35'S. 150°04'E., 25 km NE of Rylstone, on Ginghi Ck; butter factory; pop. 52 (1947).

Gingie (*Co. Finch*) 30°00'S. 148°01'E., 10 km W. of Walgett; Aboriginal mission; pop. 57 (1933), 118 (1954), 247 (1986).

Gin Gin (*Co. Ewenmar*) 31°55'S. 148°05'E., 16 km NE of Trangie, on Macquarie R.; bridge b. 1893 by Charles John Foord, replaced 1955, over Macquarie R.; school (Gin Gin Bridge) 1907–12; pop. 87 (1911), 24 (1933), 115 (2006), 157 (2011).

Gin Gin Bridge (*Co. Ewenmar*) see Gin Gin.

Gingkin (*Co. Westmoreland*) 33°54'S. 149°56'E., 21 km S. of Oberon; farming and grazing; butter factory (removed from Edith); PO 1876; telephone 1906; TX 1928–78; pop. 60 (1911), 74 (1933), 65 (1947), 69 (1954), 54 (1961), 136 (2006).

Gipps (*Co. Gipps*) 33°47'S. 146°47'E., 41 km W. of West Wyalong; telephone 1929; TX, closed 1936.

Giralambone (*Co. Canbelego*) see Girilambone.

Girards Hill (*Co. Rous*) see Lismore.

Girdlers (*Co. Gipps*) 33°47'S. 147°19'E., 18 km NE of Wyalong; village gaz. 1931; silo; pop. 36 (1933).

Girdlers (*Co. Gipps*) see also Clear Ridge.

Girilambone (*Co. Canbelego*) 31°15'S. 146°54'E., 44 km NW of Nyngan; village gaz. 1884; agric. and grazing; Angl. C. (St Paul's) 1925; brewery (Isaac Mullard) 1882; cemetery (119 graves 1900+) 1888; CH 1885; FB; fire 1885; Meth. C. 1959; PO 1881; PS 1882, new one b. 1899 by Grace and Carr; reservoir (elevated); Rom. Cath. C. 1898; RS (Giralambone till 1889) 1884, station b. by James Stuart Douglas, closed 1986, station dilapidated; school 1897 b. by F. O'Grady; telegraph 1883; TX 1917, automatic 1988; Union C. 1882, new one 1913; water supply augmentation 1956 and 1986; pop. 162 (1891), 369 (1901), 333 (1911), 156 (1933), 281 (1947), 96 (1954), 134 (1961), *c.*100 (1999), 220 (2011).

Girilambone (*Co. Canbelego*) see also Girilambone Mine.

Girilambone Mine (*Co. Canbelego*) 31°15'S. 146°52'E., 45 km NW of Nyngan; mining (copper disc. 1875 by Thomas Hartman, and gold); mine o. 1880 by Hartman, Campbell et al., headframes and furnaces replaced 1896, closed; PO 1894; sawmill (Martin Kerz and T.L. Richardson); school (Girilambone till 1897) 1882–1904; smelting works (copper); pop. *c.*300 (1903), 26 (1933).

Giro (*Co. Hawes*) 31°43'S. 151°48'E., 35 km NW of Gloucester, on Barnard R.; laid out 1861 by John Hall, village gaz. 1862; airfield; telephone 1917; TX 1927; pop. 25 (1933).

Girragulang (*Co. Bligh*) 31°55'S. 149°41'E., 11 km S. of Coolah; RS 1920–75.

Girrakool (*Co. Northumberland*) 33°26'S. 151°17'E., 6 km W. of Gosford, on Piles Ck; 5 quarries.

Girral (*Co. Gipps*) 33°42'S. 147°04'E., 26 km NW of West Wyalong; tin, farming, wheat; airfield; Meth. C. 1926 (moved 1958 to Euabalong West); mine (R.A. Bamford) 1939–41; PO 1919, burnt down 1925, rebuilt, burnt down 1945; RS (Bolagamy till 1919) 1917–75; sawmills: Richard Breardon, L.C. Lewington, Harry J. Smith; school 1931–44; silo 1922; TX 1923–84; pop. 49 (1933), 105 (1954), 88 (1961), 187 (2011).

Girralong (*Co. Raleigh*) 30°34'S. 152°39'E., 21 km NW of Bowraville, on Nambucca R.; formerly Upper North Arm; farming; PO 1927–61; school (Cedar Butt) 1931–58; telephone 1924; TX 1938; pop. 94 (1933).

Girvan (*Co. Gloucester*) 32°28'S. 152°04'E., 14 km SW of Bulahdelah, on Rooty Ck; timber and dairying; Angl. C. (St Luke's) 1912, extended 1915; bushfire 1951; PO 1900; quarry; sawmills: Armstrong & Royse Pty Ltd 1935, C.W. Grey & Bros (Sawmillers) Pty Ltd, man killed 1945, Niagra Saw Milling Co.; school 1904 b. by G. Carnell, closed 1920, reused 1961; telephone 1911; TX 1940, automatic 1975; pop. 65 (1901), 110 (1933), 131 (1947), 110 (1954), 101 (1961).

Gittins' Lagoon (*Co. Northumberland*) see Ettalong Beach.

Gladstone (*Co. Macquarie*) 31°02'S. 152°57'E., 12 km NE of Kempsey, on Macleay R.; Darkwater till 1870; first lots sold 1860, surveyed 1864 by Ernest William Lewis Herborn, town gaz. 1879, munic. proc. 1899; butter and maize; Angl. C. (St Barnabas's) b. 1927 by F.C. Sweeney, d. by L. Dennis, closed 2016; bridges: one b. 1929 by Lawson Bros over Belmore R. and Major Oakes Bridge, 1,125 ft (342.9 m), b. 1971–73 by John Holland (Constructions) Pty Ltd, over Macleay R.; bushfire 1895; CH b. 1885 by M'Morrance and Gabriel, d. by James Johnstone Barnet, reused, renovated and restored 1983; creamery (Smithtown Dairy Co. Ltd); FB; floods 1921, 1929, 1950, 1963, 1967, 2001, 2009; footbridge over Belmore R.; Meth. C. 1921 by George Welch; PO 1864, new one b. 1926; pound (stock) 1884; Presb. C., burnt down and replaced 1885; PS 1877, new one (incl. lock-up) b. 1898 by Manning and Morrison, d. by Walter Liberty Vernon, renovated and restored 1983; punt; school 1877, additions and repairs 1882 by W. M'Neil, repairs 1900 by Manning and Morrison, additions 2010; sewerage augmentation 1985; sugar mill (CSR) 1869, moved 1873 to Harwood Island; telegraph 1879; TX 1914–77; Unit. C. 1921; water reticulation 1969; Wes. Meth. C. 1865, new one 1883, closed, sold and removed 1921; wharf b. 1873 by John Lawson; pop. 176 (1891), 275 (1901), 940 (1908), 276 (1911), 479 (1933), 590 (1947), 462 (1954), 977 (1976, incl. Smithtown), 953 (1981, incl. Smithtown), 979 (1986, incl. Smithtown), 965 (1991, incl. Smithtown), 960 (1996, incl. Smithtown), 973 (2001, incl. Smithtown), 958 (2006, incl. Smithtown), 995 (2011, incl. Smithtown).

Gladstone West (*Co. Dudley*) see Smithtown.

Glamis (*Co. Hawes*) 31°39'S. 151°58'E., 40 km N. of Gloucester, on Cooplacurripa R.; telephone 1927; TX 1941–80.

Glanmire (*Co. Roxburgh*) 33°26'S. 149°42'E., 12 km E. of Bathurst; mining (gold disc. 1864 by Carlo Giuseppe Fontana, rush 1865), agric., grazing; brewery (Edward Combes) 1870–75; diphtheria 1882; mines: Fontana Reef 1886 and Little Wonder <1875; PO 1865–1938; school 1880, new buildings b. 1883 by James Wiburd, closed 1895, building sold 1920, restored, reused; telephone 1925; TX 1928; pop. *c.*500 (1866), *c.*650 (1886), 56 (1901), 77 (1911), 57 (1933), 256 (2006).

Glasston (*Co. Buckland*) 31°48'S. 150°25'E., 39 km W. of Murrurundi, on Pump Station Ck; grazing; PO 1877; telephone 1925; TX 1926.

Glassville (*Co. Northumberland*) see Gouldsville.

Glebe (*Co. Auckland*) 36°41'S. 149°51'E., 1 km S. of Bega.

Glen Alice (*Co. Roxburgh*) 33°03'S. 150°13'E., 29 km SE of Kandos, on Umbiella Ck; village gaz. 1901; mining (oil-shale disc. 1865 by G.R. and J. McLean) 1886+, farming, grazing; cemetery (114 graves 1845+) 1875; Meth. C.; mines: R. Amos & Co. 1897, Capertee Shale & Oil Mining Co. Ltd, Portal No. 1 (C.G. Cameron) 1881, The Glen Alice Coal & Shale Mining Co.; PO 1869; Presb. C., burnt down 1878, replaced 1908, and graveyard; school 1957 (building removed from Glen Davis), burnt down and replaced 1968; telephone 1915; TX 1916–85; pop. 78 (1911), 208 (1933), 34 (1947), 65 (1954), 156 (1961).

Glen Allen (*Co. Wellesley*) 36°42'S. 149°22'E., 27 km NE of Bombala, on Grassy Flat Ck.

Glenara (*Co. Lincoln*) 32°19'S. 148°51'E., 25 km E. of Dubbo, on Long Gully; school 1957–69; pop. 20 (1933).

Glenariff (*Co. Cowper*) 30°49'S. 146°33'E., 99 km SE of Bourke; RS 1884–1974.

Glenarvon (*Co. Durham*) see Bolwarra.

Glenbawn Dam (*Co. Brisbane*) 32°06'S. 151°00'E., 13 km E. of Scone, on Lake Glenbawn; boat harbour; cemetery; dam (earth and rockfill) b. 1946–58, orig. 256 ft (78 m) high, wall raised 72 ft (22 m) 1983–87 by Citra Constructions Ltd; jetty; PO 1955; power station; quarry; school 1955–66; pop. 163 (1954).

Glenbog (*Co. Wellesley*) 36°35'S. 149°21'E., 43 km SE of Cooma; school 1884–93.

Glenbrook (*Co. Cook*) 33°46'S. 150°37'E., 7 km E. of Springwood, on Knapsack Ck; village gaz. 1884; air force base 1953, powerhouse added 1955 by M. & G. Constructions Co.; Angl. C. 1896, new one 1966 d. by E.N. Skarratt, new one (St Peter's) 2013; Bapt. C. 1964; bridge (Lennox Bridge), d. and b. 1833 by David Lennox, 47 ft (14.3 m), closed 1962, restored and reopened 1983, over Lapstone Ck; bushfires 1936 (8 houses destroyed), 1938, 1951 (6 houses destroyed), 2001; FB (station b. 1951, new one 1975); military depot 1815–16; PO 1882, new one b. 1910; PS 1929–33; quarry; railway (Little Zig Zag) d. by John Whitton and George Cowdery, closed 1892 and bypassed by deviation; railway accidents: passenger killed 1976 and 7 passengers killed 1999; railway tunnel b. 1892 by Proudfoot & Co., 722 yds (659.8 m), abandoned 1913, reused, new one b. 1913, 309 yds (282.8 m); railway viaduct (Knapsack Gully) b. 1865–68 by William Watkins, 126 ft (38.4 m) high, 388 ft (118.3 m) long, d. by John Whitton, closed 1913, reused for road traffic 1926, widened 1939 by Hardy Davis Pty Ltd, closed and reused, new one (brick) 1913; Rom. Cath. C. 1912 d. by Charles Fowler, new one 1966, new one (St Finbar's) 1995; RS (Watertank till 1874, Wascoe's Siding till 1878, Brookdale till 1879) 1867, new station 1913 on new site; school 1892, relocated 1903, additions 1911, 1937, 1962, 1964, 1967; telegraph 1890; telephone 1909; TX 1927, automatic 1950; Unit. C. (St Andrew's, orig. Presb.) b. 1954 by A.H. Clague and Gordon Williams, d. by George B. Gray; water reticulation 1946; pop. 123 (1901), 274 (1911), 409 (1933), 754 (1947), 1,368 (1954), 2,499 (1961), 1,929 (1964), 4,945 (2011).

Glenburn (*Co. Westmoreland*) 33°37'S. 149°43'E., 16 km NW of Oberon, on Wisemans Ck; estab. to cater for silver mining at Wisemans Creek; school 1880, new buildings b. 1883 by T.G. Morgan, closed 1928 and 1957–63; pop. 80 (1933).

Glenbye (*Co. Dowling*) 33°15'S. 146°38'E., 25 km E. of Lake Cargelligo; telephone 1927; TX 1928–42.

Glencairn (*Co. Dowling*) 33°28'S. 146°35'E., 26 km SE of Lake Cargelligo.

Glencairn (*Co. King*) 34°30'S. 149°23'E., 11 km SW of Crookwell; school 1914–55.

Glencardie (*Co. Gordon*) 32°33'S. 148°47'E., 15 km W. of Wellington, on Barneys Ck; school 1901–13.

Glencoe (*Co. Benarba*) 29°20'S. 149°10'E., 42 km SE of Mungindi.

Glencoe (*Co. Georgiana*) see Porters Retreat.

Glencoe (*Co. Gough*) 29°56'S. 151°44'E., 21 km S. of Glen Innes, on Marowan Ck; village gaz. 1886; sapphire fossicking; Angl. C., re-erected 1927 (removed from Ben Lomond), closed 1976, sold 1979; butter factory 1893; cemetery (118 graves) 1891; 3 mines (sapphires); PO 1881; PS 1903; RS 1884, station b. by Nathan Cohen & Co., relocated 1910, closed 1975; school 1884–1966; telegraph 1890; telephone 1913; TX 1923, automatic 1989; Unit. C. (orig. Union) b. 1886 by Joseph Thomas Brigdale, d. by George Frederick Nott, closed, sold 2015 and 2017; pop. 268 (1911), 220 (1933), 212 (1947), 165 (1954), 186 (1961), 211 (2006), 353 (2011).

Glencoe (*Co. Kennedy*) 32°32'S. 147°52'E., 36 km NW of Peak Hill.

Glendale (*Co. Northumberland*) 32°55'S. 151°39'E., 2 km NW of Cardiff, on Winding Ck; West Cardiff till 1952; subdivided 1915;

Assemblies of God C. (Christ. Life); bushfire 1974–75; Christ. Reformed C.; Grace Evangelical C. (formerly Baptist Reformed C.); PO 1948; railway turntable, 75 ft (22.9 m); railway workshops (Cardiff) b. 1925–28; Reflections C. (formerly Light C.); Rom. Cath. C. (Holy Cross) 1980, and columbaria; schools: East Glendale 1959, additions 2010, Glendale (West Cardiff till 1951) 1949, additions 1956, 1958, 1960, closed 1990, Glendale HS 1970, additions by O'Donnell & Hanlon Pty Ltd; storm 2007; TC 1981, became a campus of Hunter Institute of Technology in 1992, additions by R.T. Parker Pty Ltd; telephone 1948; tramway (steam) to Newcastle 1887; pop. 2,998 (2006), 3,284 (2011).

Glen Davis (*Co. Cook*) 33°07'S. 150°17'E., 38 km NE of Wallerawang, on Capertee R.; (incl. Bagtown); laid out 1939 by A.A. Cooke, subdivided and first lots sold 1940, thrived 1940–47, town largely defunct by 1952; mining (oil-shale disc. 1873 by Campbell Mitchell and initial mining began 1881 by C.G. Cameron, resumed 1938), retorting and refining 1939–42 by National Oil Pty Ltd, first crude oil produced 1940, taken over by govt and operated till 1952, plant auctioned 1953; ambulance station, closed 1953; Angl. C. (St Mark's) 1940; bushfires 1951 and 2009; cordial factory (C.J. Talbot) 1943; drought 1943; electricity 1939; floods 1949, 1950 (man died), 1952; lock-up; Meth. C. 1941; mine accident (man killed) 1948; miners' strikes 1940, 1942, 1943, 1945, 1946, 1952; pipeline to Newnes 1941; PO 1939, new one b. 1943 by Wallace and McGee, reused; powerhouse (National Oil Co. Ltd); PS (temporary one) 1940, burnt down 1942, new one b. 1944 by Wallace and McGee Pty Ltd, closed 1954, reused; quarry; reservoir, 1,000,000 gal. (4,546 kl), 1943; 64 retorts (Fell-modified Pumpherston, for oil-shale), later increased to 104, abandoned and derelict; Rom. Cath. C. (Most Holy Rosary) b. 1946 by James Hoctor; school 1940–62; telephone 1939; TX 1939, automatic 1986; water reticulation 1943; pop. *c.*2,500 (1946), 1,619 (1947), 316 (1954), 47 (1961), 34 (1974), 288 (2011).

Glen Dhu (*Co. Inglis*) 31°40'S. 151°04'E., 26 km E. of Murrurundi, on Isis R.; Angl. C. (St Mark's) 1913; pop. 46 (1933).

Glendon (*Co. Burnett*) 29°35'S. 150°25'E., 15 km W. of Warialda; RS 1902, station b. by John Allibone, closed 1975.

Glendon (*Co. Durham*) 32°35'S. 151°16'E., 11 km E. of Singleton, on Hunter R.; airfield (World War II); Angl. C. (St Mary the Virgin) b. 1899 by Richard Southon, d. by Anderson and White, closed and reused, and graveyard; boiling-down works (H. Scott); bridge b. 1899 by Sheddon Bros, over Hunter R.; cemetery (23 graves 1907+); creamery; earth tremor 2004; milk factory (Bacchus Marsh Concentrated Milk Co. Ltd), acquired 1920 by Nestle Ltd; pop. 90 (1901), 77 (1911), 79 (1947), 561 (2006).

Glendon Brook (*Co. Durham*) 32°31'S. 151°20'E., 17 km E. of Singleton, on Webbers Ck; tobacco, farming, dairying; bridges over Webbers Ck: Beckers Bridge b. 1902 by Walter Frank Oakes, (de Burgh timber truss), 149 ft (45.4 m) and Boyces Bridge; coalmine 1946; creamery (Brookside) o. 1893 by J.W. Tulloch; FB (station b. 2014); PO 1874; Rom. Cath. C. 1870, new one (St Paul's) b. 1889 by G.D. Campbell, A. Moore and F. Baker, d. by Frederick Burnhardt Menkens, and graveyard; school 1878–1950; telephone 1914; TX 1914, automatic 1971; pop. 260 (1901), 281 (1911), 202 (1933), 179 (1947), 182 (1954), 179 (1961), 267 (2006), 285 (2011).

Glendon East (*Co. Durham*) 32°30'S. 151°25'E., 24 km E. of Singleton, on Webbers Ck; school 1957–60 (building moved 1963 to Lemington); pop. 36 (1933).

Glendore (*Co. Northumberland*) see Maryland.

Glendowda (*Co. Pottinger*) 31°19'S. 149°43'E., 40 km E. of Coonabarabran, on Mitchells Ck; telephone 1926.

Glen Eden (*Co. Forbes*) 33°38'S. 147°58'E., 28 km S. of Forbes; farming; PO 1927; telephone 1924; TX 1926; pop. 26 (1933).

Glenelg (*Co. Forbes*) 33°46'S. 148°05'E., 17

km NW of Grenfell; Angl. C. (St Margaret's) 1935.

Glen Elgin (*Co. Clive*) 29°34'S. 152°08'E., 44 km NE of Glen Innes, on Timbarra R.; goldmining, dairying, grazing; bushfire 1912; mine (defunct, plant and machinery sold 1900); PO 1894–1961; sawmills: Hewetson and Hickey, burnt down 1912 and William Scott; school 1957–63; telephone 1924; TX 1925, automatic 1973; pop. 103 (1911), 103 (1933), 78 (1947), 52 (1954), 54 (1961).

Glenellen (*Co. Goulburn*) 35°55'S. 146°55'E., 16 km S. of Walla Walla, on Dead Horse Ck; FB; school 1957–73.

Glenerin (*Co. King*) 34°30'S. 149°23'E., 8 km W. of Crookwell; farming; electricity 1955; PO 1927–31; telephone 1915; TX; pop. 60 (1933), 72 (1947), 52 (1954), 51 (1961).

Glen Fernaigh (*Co. Fitzroy*) 30°15'S. 152°29'E., 25 km NW of Dorrigo; school 1940–67; telephone 1922; TX 1928–68; pop. 59 (1933), 53 (1954).

Glenfield Park (*Co. Wynyard*) see Wagga Wagga.

Glen Gallic (*Co. Hunter*) 32°32'S. 150°43'E., 15 km S. of Denman, on Martindale Ck; school 1957–67; telephone 1928; TX 1929–57; pop. 75 (1954), 85 (1961).

Glengarrie (*Co. Rous*) 28°14'S. 153°24'E., 11 km N. of Murwillumbah, on Bradys Ck; school 1957–68; pop. 89 (1954), 329 (1961).

Glengarry (*Co. Finch*) 29°41'S. 147°37'E., 45 km SW of Lightning Ridge; opals (disc. 1905 by Charles Phipps).

Glengarry (*Co. Georgiana*) 34°12'S. 149°03'E., 49 km NW of Crookwell, on Lachlan R.; orig. Callaba; surveyed 1855, first lots sold 1856, village gaz. 1889, never developed; agric.

Glengeera (*Co. Gordon*) 32°24'S. 148°35'E., 16 km S. of Dubbo, on Hyandra Ck; RS 1925–74.

Gleniffer (*Co. Raleigh*) 30°24'S. 152°53'E., 7 km N. of Bellingen, on Never Never R.; farming, dairying 1905+; bridges over Never Never R.: McFaydens Bridge and Promised Land Bridge; butter factory (Gleniffer Co-op. Dairy Co. Ltd) 1906–24; Community C. (formerly Angl.); FB; gale 1899; hailstorm 1932; PO 1907; Presb. C. 1907; rifle range 1914; sawmill (Bellingen Timber Co. Ltd); school 1900–69; telephone 1907; TX 1918; Union C. 1908; pop. 276 (1911), 272 (1933), 161 (1947), 166 (1954), 143 (1961), 388 (2006), 416 (2011).

Glen Innes (*Co. Gough*) 29°44'S. 151°44'E., 60 km E. of Inverell, on Rocky Ponds Ck; surveyed 1849, laid out 1851 by John James Galloway, town gaz. 1852, first lots sold 1855, designated as chief town of the county, munic. proc. 1872, thrived 1872–91 and 1926; mining (tin, gold, silver, bismuth, sapphires 1959+), fossicking, fruit, onions, potatoes, linseed, oats, maize, barley, lucerne, millet, rye, sorghum, wheat, cattle, sheep, dairying; aeroplane crash (5 killed) 1944; agric. research station (6 km NW) 1902; ambulance station b. 1946–48 by E. Sully, d. by Frederick John Madigan; Angl. C. (Holy Trinity) b. 1868 by Cortin, Jackson and James Benjamin Winstanley, bell tower 1913 d. by Frederick John Madigan, church additions 1915 by James Lonsdale, also d. by Madigan, bell tower repairs 1970 by W.R. Ford, church re-roofed 1972 by Hardy Marr Constructions Pty Ltd; Assemblies of God C. (Oasis); bacon factories: Glen Innes Co-op. Butchering & Bacon Factory Ltd 1908 and Glen Innes Co-op. Dairy Society b. 1926 by W.E. Lightfoot, d. by John Francis O'Connor, closed 1952; Bapt. C. b. 1932 by Thomas Bacon, new one (Crossroads) b. 2016 on new site; blue metal crushing plant of E.S. Clemenston sold 1954 to A. Shelton; boot factories: J.J. Cotton, Neil M'Leod, New State (estab. 1900 by John James Whyte, burnt down 1941, replacement 1942 d. by Frederick John Madigan, closed 1967); box factory 1944; breweries: Kite & Co. and J.A. Spier and Thomas Craig Gillies (estab. 1883, closed 1886, reopened 1887 as Gillies & Co., closed and reopened 1893, closed 1894, later demolished); brickworks estab. by Arthur Bickam Willis, became Willis Bros, acquired 1922 by Glen Innes Brick & Tile Co. Ltd; bridges: first one b. by William Heydon and Meade Street Bridge b.

by Arthur J. Butt; butter factory (Glen Innes Co-op. Butter Factory Co. Ltd) 1894, new one b. 1901, burnt down 1917, rebuilt 1918, fire 1931, closed 1974; carriage-works: Central New England Coach Factory (R. Johnson), J.F. Chaffey & Co. 1882, Draffin and Potter, Gottfried Manthey & Sons, Henry Green 1865–74, H.S. Sully, Carl Tronier; caterpillar infestation 1933; cemetery (7,530 graves *c.*1860+) 1863, incl. lawn cemetery and columbarium; CH (incl. lock-up) 1859, additions 1872 by W. Kinnear, replacement b. 1874 by William Cains, d. by James Johnstone Barnet, additions 1878 by Edward Grover, additions 1898 by J.N. Josephson, d. by Walter Liberty Vernon, damaged by fire and repaired 1902 by Moffit, extended 1922 and 1964, restoration d. by C. Still, reused 1978; chaff mill (G. Roberts), bought 1883 by Charles Wills; cheese factory (James Osborne) 1888; Christ. Life C.; clock tower 1999; clothing factory (Ross Industries) 1947 (in old flour mill); concrete pipe works (Monier) 1939; concrete plant 1966, sold 1968 to Hardy Marr Constructions Pty Ltd; confectionery factory (Charles Copp) 1900; cordial factories: William Marshall 1888, P. M'Gauran, sold 1884, F. Edward Sayers 1901 (sold to Fred and Ernest Thomas); cyclones 1964 and 2002; diphtheria 1910, 1914, 1917; droughts 1965 and 1994; dust storm 1901; earth tremor 1900; electricity 1922; FB: town fire brigade 1888 (station b. 1916 by E.N. Thorne) and bushfire brigade (station b. 2018); fires 1897, 1910, 1915; floods 1869, 1872 (man died), 1933; flour mills: Edward Grover 1871 (closed), Patrick Heron Henderson 1858 (leased to James Ormandy, ruined), Millennium (burnt down 1949), O'Keeffe & Co., Sunlight (b. 1882 by William Edward Wright for John Frederick Utz, roller plant installed 1891, remodelled and enlarged 1912, bought 1912 by Mackenzie & Sons Ltd, became Sunlight Flour Milling Co. Ltd in 1913, modernised 1921, in liquidation 1924, new company estab. 1925, acquired by Fielders Flour Co., closed, reused 1998), Victor 1855; foundries: William Garibaldi Cleghorn 1910 and Vulcan, estab. 1884 by John Sully, sen., taken over 1904 by H.S. and J.W. Sully; furniture factory (Kwong Sing & Co.); gaol b. 1878 by Edward Grover, new one b. 1886 by J. Baldwin, reused 1928; gasworks b. 1893 by Edward Grover, explosion 1894; hailstorms 1872, 1885, 1892, 1946; hospital b. 1875–77 by William Edward Wright, d. by Mansfield Bros, additions 1904, additions 1920 by S.S. Barr, additions 1936, closed 1956, reused 1970, new one b. 1952–56 by E.S. Clemenston Pty Ltd; iron foundry estab. 1883 by John Sully, became Sully Bros; joineries: Robert Norman, Jacob James Petrie and Keith Percival Hockley (burnt down 1947), Eric Potter and Charles Greenaway (burnt down 1947), Francis Schedel, Matthew Simpkin, Weller and Porter 1875; measles epidemics 1921 and 1954; monumental stone works (J.R. Throwden); paint factory (Rudd Bros); pipe works (Ralph Williams Ltd) 1932; pneumonia epidemic 1936; PO 1854, new one b. 1876 by Francis Schedel, d. by James Johnstone Barnet, additions 1883 by Edward Grover, demolished, replacement b. 1896 by Sanbrook Bros, d. by Walter Liberty Vernon, additions 1913–14 and 1978; pound (stock) 1865; POW control centre 1944; powerhouse 1922–56, reused, demolished 1989; Presb. C. b. 1866–70 by Samuel Jackson, d. by Thomas Rowe, renovations 1887 by Daniel Lannstrom, closed and reused 1921, new one (St Andrew's) 1981 on new site; PS b. 1876–78 by Edward Grover; rabbit freezing works 1918; railway bridge; railway coal stage b. by J. Conlon; railway turntable, 50 ft (15.2 m), replaced 1900, 60 ft (18.3 m), closed; reservoirs; Rom. Cath. C. b. 1865–67 by John and Pat McGauran, new one (St Patrick's) b. 1909 by James Lonsdale, d. by John Francis Hennessy and Joseph Ignatius Sheerin, additions 1938; RS 1884, station b. by Joseph Conlon, refreshment rooms 1896, station closed 1989, reused; sale-yards b. 1910 by S.J. Mahoney, d. by John Francis O'Connor, replaced, extended 1977; Salv. Army C. b. 1926 by Freak Bros; sawmills: Cattell Bros, Duncan's Holdings

Ltd (modernised 1986), Hewetson Hickey & Co. (incl. joinery), J.O.W. Mangleson; schools: Glen Innes 1863 (new one b. 1874 by Matthew Simpkin, additions and repairs 1884 by W. Cottey, additions 1886 by George Arnall, additions 1892 by Edward Grover, repairs 1910 by John Axtell, additions 1921, 1929, 1958, 1961, 1982), Glen Innes HS 1928 (b. by S.W. and R.C. Potter, d. by Gorrie McLeish Blair, additions 1960, 1967, 1972), West Glen Innes 1926; SD Adventist C. 1961; seed cleaning plant; sewerage 1935, augmentation 1986; snowstorm 1875; soap-works (Janitzky & Co.) 1891; storm 1928; streets kerosene lit 1884, gas lit 1893, electric lit 1922; tank works (James Newell), sold 1876 to Charles Stumpf; tanneries: J.S. Dick 1881, Westdale (John Priest) 1891, taken over by M'Lean Bros, J.J. Whyte Pty Ltd 1887; TC 1968, additions 1975, became a campus of New England Institute in 1992, additions 2017 d. by Brewster Hjorth Architects; telegraph 1861, new office b. 1876 by Francis Schedel, d. by James Johnstone Barnet, demolished, replacement b. 1896 by Sanbrook Bros, d. by Walter Liberty Vernon; TX 1906, new building b. 1954, extended 1971, automatic 1981; typhoid 1899 and 1903; Unit. C. (Cameron Memorial, orig. Presb.) b. 1920 by F.W. Hickey, d. by H.E. Ross and Rowe; vegetable freezing factory (Cahill's Quick-Freezers Ltd) 1951, sold 1960 to Pict Pty Ltd, expanded 1966, taken over 1972 by British Tobacco which merged with Watties to become Wattie Pict Pty Ltd, closed 1974, sold 1976, reused; water supply 1918, filtration plant 1930, augmentation 1932, treatment plant 1982, further augmentation 1987 and 1990; weir 1932, on Beardy R.; Wes. Meth. C. 1881, new one b. 1886 by Edward Grover, d. by Evan Evans, extended, closed, sold 1983 to Glen Innes Arts Council Inc., reused 1984; pop. 288 (1861), *c.*350 (1866), 343 (1871), *c.*1,500 (1875), 1,327 (1881), *c.*1,500 (1887), 2,532 (1891), *c.*3,000 (1895), 2,918 (1901), 4,030 (1911), 4,830 (1921), 5,352 (1933), *c.*5,300 (1938), *c.*5,400 (1941), 5,453 (1947), 5,842 (1954), 5,771 (1961), 5,756 (1966), 5,762 (1971), 5,953 (1976), 6,052 (1981), 5,971 (1986), 6,140 (1991), 6,101 (1996), 5,722 (2001), 5,944 (2006), 5,173 (2011).

Glenlegh (*Co. Gough*) see Glen Leigh.

Glen Leigh (*Co. Gough*) 29°45'S. 151°47'E., 11 km SE of Glen Innes; formerly Glenlegh; school (Glenlegh) 1919–42; pop. 40 (1933).

Glen Levet Estate (*Co. Northumberland*) see Hexham.

Glenlogan (*Co. Bathurst*) 33°46'S. 148°39'E., 8 km NW of Cowra; agric.; RS 1910, station b. by D.H. Reid, closed 1970; silo 1935; pop. 63 (1911), 78 (1933).

Glenlogan (*Co. Bathurst*) see also Wynnefield.

Glen Martin (*Co. Gloucester*) 32°34'S. 151°49'E., 17 km NW of Karuah, on Williams R.; bushfire 1951; PO 1924–49; school 1915, new building b. 1923 by W.J. Hallett, closed 1935; telephone 1926; TX 1949; pop. 98 (1933), 233 (2006).

Glen Mitchell (*Co. Northumberland*) see Teralba.

Glen Moan (*Co. Buckland*) 31°46'S. 150°18'E., 46 km SW of Murrurundi.

Glenmore (*Co. Camden*) 34°04'S. 150°36'E., 9 km W. of Camden, on Splitters Gully; settled 1854 by Edward Moore; farming and dairying; PO 1894–1958; quarry; school 1864, new one b. 1869, closed 1911; Unit. C. (orig. Wes. Meth.) b. 1860 by Stokes, additions 1900, and graveyard (60 graves 1864–1996); pop. 74 (1911), 70 (1933), 58 (1947), 71 (1961), 90 (2001).

Glenmore (*Co. Gough*) see Elsmore.

Glen Morris (*Co. Goulburn*) see Albury.

Glen Morrison (*Co. Vernon*) 31°11'S. 151°31'E., 24 km S. of Walcha, on Bald Ck; goldmining (reef) and grazing; cemetery 1894; PO 1873–1957; Rom. Cath. C. (Sacred Heart) b. 1912 by W. Miller; school 1884–1922 and 1955–62; telephone 1916; TX 1916, automatic 1967; pop. 85 (1901), 138 (1911), 129 (1933), 115 (1947), 101 (1954), 98 (1961).

Glen Murray (*Co. Camden*) 34°44'S. 150°33'E., 14 km W. of Berry; butter factory (People's Dairy & Manufacturing Assoc. Ltd, factory removed from Upper Kangaroo River) 1913–25.

Glennies Creek (*Co. Durham*) 32°28'S. 151°06'E., 13 km NW of Singleton, on Glennies Ck; farming and dairying; bridge 1895, over Glennies Ck; coalmine estab. 1860 by B. McCosker; electricity 1957; FB (station b. 2014); floods 1870 and 1893; hailstorm 1963; PO 1883; railway bridge b. 1908 by Clyde Engineering Co. Ltd; floods 1860, 1861, 1870, 1893; gale 1925; Rom. Cath. C. (St Mary and St John Lateran) 1869, unroofed 1925, moved 1925 to Ravensworth, new one b. 1925 by Thomas Burg, d. by Thomas Wilfred Silk, damaged 1925 during construction, closed 1980; RS 1869–1975; school (Middle Falbrook till 1927) 1888–1937; snow 1965; storms 1882 and 1898; telephone 1914; TX 1928–65; Wes. Meth. C. b. 1899 by Thomas Noble, closed 1930; pop. 88 (1901), 220 (1911), 168 (1933), 165 (1947), 154 (1954), 162 (1961).

Glenning Valley (*Co. Northumberland*) see Berkeley Vale.

Glen Oak (*Co. Durham*) 32°37'S. 151°43'E., 20 km NE of Maitland, on Storks Ck; formerly Glenoak; dairying; bridge (Wattle Creek Bridge); PO 1882, burnt down 1925; quarry; school (Oakendale till 1899) 1881–1944; telephone 1893; TX 1922; pop. 95 (1901), 110 (1911), 91 (1933), 54 (1947), 53 (1954), 65 (1961), 328 (2011).

Glenoak (*Co. Gloucester*) see Wangat.

Glenora (*Co. Gloucester*) 32°06'S. 152°24'E., 11 km NW of Tuncurry, on Wallamba R.; school 1905–9.

Glenore (*Co. Hardinge*) 30°13'S. 151°31'E., 15 km W. of Guyra; pop. 52 (1933).

Glenovel (*Co. Argyle*) 35°00'S. 149°46'E., 28 km S. of Goulburn; farming and grazing; PO 1913–52; telephone 1915; TX 1928; pop. 86 (1933), 73 (1947), 64 (1954), 64 (1961).

Glenowra (*Co. Cunningham*) 32°57'S. 147°26'E., 26 km W. of Trundle; school 1930–43.

Glen Oxley (*Co. Hawes*) 31°25'S. 152°10'E., 55 km W. of Wauchope; sawmill; tramway (timber).

Glenpatrick (*Co. Nandewar*) 30°29'S. 150°00'E., 24 km N. of Boggabri.

Glenquarry (*Co. Camden*) 34°31'S. 150°29'E., 8 km SE of Bowral; Upper Mittagong till 1889; farming and dairying; Angl. C. 1862, replaced 1872, closed and sold, new one (St Luke's) b. 1911 by F.J. Potter, damaged 1948 and 1961, and graveyard; cemetery (44 graves 1875–1944); earth tremor 1961; eucalyptus oil distillery (Daniel Chalker) 1906, removed from Mittagong; hailstorm 1927; PO 1889; 4 quarries; Rom. Cath. C. 1888; school (Upper Mittagong till 1890, Glenquarry till 1892, Roberton Park till 1908) 1869, new buildings b. 1892 on new site by Frank A. Raward; storm 1948; telephone 1910; TX 1922, automatic 1956; pop. 59 (1901), 196 (1911), 165 (1933), 110 (1947), 87 (1954), 174 (1961), 249 (2011).

Glenreagh (*Co. Fitzroy*) 30°03'S. 152°59'E., 22 km W. of Woolgoolga, on Orara R.; settled 1860 by J. Shannon, village gaz. 1915; farming and dairying; Angl. C. (Christ) 1914; bridge (steel Warren truss) b. 1918, 266 ft (81 m), over Orara R.; bushfire 1936; cemetery (161 graves 1916+) 1904, incl. columbarium; earth tremor 1929; FB; floods 1948 and 1950; PO 1899; PS (in rented premises) 1925; quarry; railway bridge (steel Pratt truss) 1916, 157 ft (47.9 m), d. by James Waller Roberts, over Orara R.; railway locomotive depot, closed 1960; railway turntable 1916, 60 ft (18.3 m); Rom. Cath. C. (St Paul's) b. 1931 by C. Irving and G. Shepherd, burnt down 2018; RS 1915, station b. by Ebeling, closed 1972; sawmills: Johnson Bros (b. 1917 by Harris Raven, burnt down 1921), John Sullivan and John Blackley 1914, Gillard Wright & Co.; school 1888 b. by McBeath, building sold to Nicholson and removed 1898, replacement b. 1898 by Timothy Mullane and James McKay, additions 1916 by Strauss Bros, new one b. 1930 by A.C. Irving, additions 1962, 1975, 1995; telephone 1908; TX 1916, automatic 1972; water reticulation 1969; pop. 134 (1901), 202 (1911), 556 (1933), 453 (1947), 442 (1954), 390 (1961), 222 (1971), 210 (1976), 233 (1981), 252 (1986), 285 (1991), 276 (1996), 273

(2001), 422 (2006), 479 (2011).

Glenridding (*Co. Northumberland*) see Singleton.

Glen Rock (*Co. Dudley*) 31°04'S. 152°51'E., 4 km N. of Kempsey; flood 1893; pop. 146 (1933), 124 (1947), 66 (1954), 73 (1961).

Glen Rock (*Co. Dudley*) see also Moparrabah.

Glenrock (*Co. Hawes*) 31°40'S. 151°25'E., 56 km E. of Murrurundi, on Orham Ck; PS b. 1910 by Charles Benaud Smith; school 1962–77; telephone 1909; TX 1926–56; pop. 99 (1911), 124 (1947), 370 (2011).

Glen Rock (*Co. Murray*) 35°05'S. 149°08'E., 35 km SE of Yass.

Glenrock (*Co. Wynyard*) 35°30'S. 148°09'E., 3 km N. of Batlow.

Glenrock Estate (*Co. Northumberland*) see Koolewong.

Glenroi (*Co. Bathurst*) see Orange (*Co. Wellington*).

Glen Ross (*Co. Clarke*) 30°13'S. 151°58'E., 29 km E. of Guyra, on Johns Ck; school 1910–19.

Glenrouth (*Co. Mitchell*) see Uranquinty.

Glenroy (*Co. Cook*) 33°33'S. 150°09'E., 7 km S. of Lithgow, on Coxs R.; agric.; disc. 1814, settled 1815, never developed; bridge 1814, (second) 1861, (third) b. 1867 by William Timothy Atkins, replacement (timber beam spans) 1901, 253 ft (77.1 m), new one (steel girders) 1957, over Coxs R.; convict stockade 1816.

Glenroy (*Co. Goulburn*) see Albury.

Glenroy (*Co. Kennedy*) 32°31'S. 147°33'E., 47 km N. of Trundle.

Glenroy (*Co. Selwyn*) 35°45'S. 147°56'E., 8 km W. of Tumbarumba; bridge 1941; RS 1921–75; school (West Glenroy till 1907) 1880, additions 1900 by J. Thomson, burnt down 1905, replaced, closed 1954; Union C.; pop. 90 (1901), 86 (1911), 43 (1933), 74 (1961), 330 (2011).

Glenthorne (*Co. Gloucester*) 31°55'S. 152°29'E., 2 km E. of Taree, on Manning R.; farming; bridge (Martin Bridge) to Taree, 1,518 ft (462.7 m), incl. lift span fabricated by Clyde Engineering Co. Ltd, erected 1938–40 by Monier Industries Ltd, over Manning R.; cemetery (Gilwarra, 60 graves 1870+); droughts 1923, 1927, 1928, 1929; flood 1929; hailstorm 1950; Meth. C. 1913; PO 1887; school 1880–1916 and 1923–40; telephone 1913; Wes. Meth. C. 1856, closed, demolished, replaced 1866, new one 1878; wharf b. 1896 by R.H. Worthing; pop. 95 (1901), 56 (1911), 116 (1933), 130 (1947), 133 (1954), 144 (1961), 263 (2011).

Glentimon (*Co. Rous*) see Edenville.

Glenugie (*Co. Clarence*) 29°47'S. 153°01'E., 11 km SE of South Grafton, on Glenugie Ck.

Glen Warning (*Co. Rous*) 28°26'S. 153°16'E., 17 km SW of Murwillumbah, on Byrrill Ck; telephone 1926; TX 1928–48.

Glenwarrin (*Co. Macquarie*) 31°35'S. 152°16'E., 33 km N. of Wingham; farming; PO 1927; sawmills: Bulga Sawmills Co., and Francis William Drinkwater and Charles Drinkwater, burnt down 1953; school 1955–69; telephone 1923; TX 1924; pop. 75 (1933), 82 (1947), 133 (1954), 83 (1961).

Glen William (*Co. Durham*) 32°32'S. 151°48'E., 14 km S. of Dungog, on Williams R.; farming and grazing; Angl. C. 1855, new one (St Thomas's) b. 1897 by Robert Ford, jun., and graveyard (102 graves 1855+); bridge (Banfield Bridge) b. 1895 by Samuel McGill, destroyed 1946, rebuilt 1947, over Williams R.; creamery (Erringhi) estab. 1892 by E.F. and A.W. Lowe; flood 1946; PO 1878; quarry; telephone 1905; tobacco factory (Robert Muirhead); TX 1928, automatic 1969; pop. 143 (1911), 142 (1933), 126 (1947), 109 (1954), 81 (1961), 233 (2011).

Glenwood (*Co. Murray*) 35°08'S. 149°01'E., 19 km S. of Murrumbateman: school 1883–1934.

Glenworth Valley (*Co. Northumberland*) 33°26'S. 151°10'E., 17 km W. of Gosford, on Popran Ck; cemetery; telephone 1922; TX 1928.

Globelands (*Co. Ewenmar*) 32°02'S. 148°30'E., 26 km NW of Dubbo; Presb. C. (removed 1921 from Dundullimal).

Gloryvale (*Co. Vernon*) 31°51'S. 151°54'E., 18 km N. of Gloucester, on Manning R.

Glossodia (*Co. Cook*) 33°33'S. 150°48'E., 8 km NE of North Richmond, on Currency Ck; Currency Creek till 1922; poultry; Bapt. C. 1992; FB; PO 1927–90; Salv. Army C.; school (Currency Creek till 1923) 1898, new building 1926, burnt down 1961, new building 1990; telephone 1923; winery (Tijuana), burnt down 1980; pop. 155 (1901), 98 (1911), 156 (1933), 142 (1947), 169 (1954), 194 (1961), 524 (1976), 1,634 (1981), 2,113 (1986), 2,509 (1991), 2,576 (1996), 2,574 (2001), 2,426 (2006), 2,543 (2011).

Glossop (*Co. Hume*) 35°44'S. 146°49'E., 21 km W. of Culcairn, on Billabong Ck; bridge (Brooklyn Bridge) over Billabong Ck; school 1957–69.

Gloucester (*Co. Gloucester*) 32°01'S. 151°58'E., 48 km W. of Taree, on Gloucester R.; (incl. Leman's Flat subdivision); surveyed 1855 for Aust. Agric. Co., sold 1902 to Gloucester Estates Ltd, first land sales 1903; orig. sheep, then wheat, barley, maize, oats, potatoes, dairying, now beef, timber, engineering, lime; airfield; ambulance station 1943; Angl. C. (St Clement's) b. 1860 by Aust. Agric. Co., closed, roof collapsed, sold and demolished 1945, new one (St Paul's) 1910; Bapt. C. b. 1952 by W.T. Howard, extended 1984; bridges: one b. 1964 over Avon R. and one b. 1911, new one 2008, over Gloucester R.; broom handle factory (Frank Kelly) 1953; butter factories: Avon & Barrington Co-op. Dairy Co. 1906, acquired by Aust. Co-op. Foods Ltd, and Gloucester Dairy Co. b. 1937 by J.C. Pickles and A. McIlroy, d. by Arthur William Mackenzie Mowle, extensions 1963; candle factory (Mike Anthony); carriage-works (Wilson and Flanagan); cemetery (2,753 graves 1902+), incl. lawn cemetery and columbaria; CH b. 1908 by Charles Joseph Skinner, extensions and alterations 1948; Christ. Outreach C. 1991; clock tower (war memorial) b. 1931 by F.A. Isaac, d. by Frederick George and Archer Cox Castleden; clothing factory (Metas Manufacturing Co.) estab. 1945 by G.R. and Meta Mysels, in former theatre; colliery (Gloucester Main); Cong. C.; cordial factories: Buchan's and Gloucester River (estab. by Charles Heinrich Wilhelm Lostroh, upgraded 1916, bought 1917 by Albert and Leslie Parish); cyclone 1924; electricity 1923; engineering works (A.B. Campbell); FB (station b. 1962); fibrous plaster works (Charles Falconer) 1929; floods 1913, 1929, 1956, 1978; hailstorms 1877 and 1913; hospital (cottage), new one (Soldiers' Memorial) b. 1952 by A.E. Davis; lock-up b. 1896 by A.E. Gould; Meth. C. b. 1913 by W.R. Mitchell, d. by Adin Parsons, moved 1946; PO 1859, new one b. 1900 by Reginald Mitchell; powerhouse b. 1923 by Manning Motor Co., which became Gloucester Light & Power Co. in 1927, supply taken over 1946 by local council, powerhouse reused; Presb. C. (St Andrew's) 1906, belfry added 1916, church damaged and repaired 1924; PS 1878, new one b. 1896 by A.E. Gould, additions 1964; quarry, disused; rabbit freezing works (Midland Freezing Co.) b. 1917 by Standard Waygood Hercules Ltd; railway barracks; railway bridge (steel truss) 1913, 120 ft (36.6 m), over Avon R.; 2 reservoirs (incl. tower 1927); Rom. Cath. C. 1907, new one (St Joseph's) b. 1953 by A.E. Davis, d. by Gannon; RS 1913, station b. by John Allibone, refreshment rooms 1917–56; sale-yards 1975; sawmills: Andrews and Johnston, Carson Northern Timber Co. 1944, Edward W. Geale, Harvey Robinson (bought by Frederick Carson, sold 1976 to Allen Taylor & Co. Ltd, closed 1998), State Sawmills (fire 1920), F. Viggers Pty Ltd; schools: primary 1905, new buildings b. 1908 by T. Carpenter and W. Derkenne, additions 1917 by H.T. Shepherd, additions 1956 and 1967, and HS 1961, additions 1966 and 1972; SD Adventist C. 1978; sewerage 1940, augmentation 1985; telegraph 1877, new office b. 1900 by Reginald Mitchell; TX 1913, automatic 1980; Union C. 1917; Unit. C. (orig. Meth.) 1968, replaced 1993; water supply 1930; water treatment plant 1982; pop. *c.*30 (1866), 79 (1901), 1,472 (1911), *c.*900 (1913), 1,512 (1933), 1,702 (1947), 1,894 (1954), 2,012 (1961), 2,032 (1966), 2,176

(1971), 2,313 (1976), 2,488 (1981), 2,397 (1986), 2,465 (1991), 2,634 (1996), 2,468 (2001), 2,445 (2006), 2,336 (2011).

Glow Worm Glen (*Co. Camden*) 34°40'S. 150°20'E., 3 km E. of Bundanoon.

Glynburn (*Co. Bland*) 34°26'S. 147°28'E., 5 km W. of Temora; school 1902–47.

Gnahpeang (*Co. Gloucester*) 32°24'S. 152°22'E., on Myall Lake, 14 km E. of Bulahdelah.

Gnalta (*Co. Yungnulgra*) 31°04'S. 142°23'E., 110 km NW of Wilcannia, on Amphitheatre Ck; cyclone 1913; PO 1875–84.

Gnomery (*Co. Narran*) 29°10'S. 147°16'E., 75 km W. of Lightning Ridge.

Goambeen (*Co. Ashburnham*) see Mandagery.

Goangra (*Co. Baradine*) 30°09'S. 148°23'E., 29 km SE of Walgett, on Namoi R.; town gaz. 1876; cemetery 1893; telephone 1904; pop. 60 (1911), 58 (1947).

Goba Creek (*Co. Monteagle*) 34°18'S. 148°45'E., 15 km N. of Boorowa, on Goba Ck; mine (bismuth) estab. 1935 by Rolf.

Gobarralong (*Co. Harden*) 34°59'S. 148°16'E., 18 km NE of Gundagai, on Murrumbidgee R.; North Gobarralong till 1909; mining (chromite) and grazing; bridge (low-level), b. 1896 by C. M'Clure, 300 ft (91.4 m), new one (steel decking) b. 1936 by L.J.C. Mannsfield, d. by S.J. Hunnings, 315 ft (96 m), over Murrumbidgee R.; bushfire 1979; mines: Mount Mary, Quilter's, Vulcan; PO 1876; Rom. Cath. C. (Our Lady of the Rosary) b. 1897–99 by C. Harrington, d. by John Goode; school 1886–1903; telephone 1907; TX 1910, automatic 1967; pop. 55 (1901), 76 (1911), 80 (1933), 146 (1947), 213 (1954), 192 (1961), 199 (2011).

Gobarralong North (*Co. Harden*) see Gobarralong.

Gobbagaula Plain (*Co. Mitchell*) 34°48'S. 146°35'E., 6 km SE of Narranderra; school 1899–1906 and 1913–16.

Gobbagombalin (*Co. Bourke*) 35°02'S. 147°17'E., 11 km NW of Wagga Wagga; school (Gobbagumblin) b. 1897 by J. Harrison, closed 1917, reopened 1923, closed 1924; telephone 1910; pop. 128 (1911), 79 (1961), 360 (2011).

Gobbagumblin (*Co. Bourke*) see Gobbagombalin.

Gobondery (*Co. Kennedy*) 32°41'S. 147°36'E., 28 km NW of Trundle, on Bullock Ck; farming and mining (chromite and haematite); chromite mine (Quilter's) 1894–95; PO 1927–31; Rom. Cath. C. 1911 d. by Bates; RS 1908, station b. by Reid and Castles, closed 1974; silo 1933; pop. 54 (1933).

Gobondry (*Co. Kennedy*) see Tullamore.

Gocup (*Co. Wynyard*) 35°14'S. 148°11'E., 8 km N. of Tumut, on Meadow Ck; farming and grazing; FB 1942; PO 1885; quarry; school 1873–1939 and 1949–70; telephone 1907; TX 1929, automatic 1959; typhoid (2 died) 1896; pop. 198 (1901), 156 (1911), 135 (1933), 132 (1947), 127 (1954), 124 (1961), 166 (2011).

Godfreys Creek (*Co. Monteagle*) 34°08'S. 148°43'E., 33 km S. of Cowra; sheep and farming; FB (station b. 2019); Meth. C. 1922; PO 1908; school 1957–68; telephone 1915; TX 1920, automatic 1962; pop. 76 (1961), 151 (2006), 164 (2011).

Gogeldrie (*Co. Cooper*) 34°33'S. 146°17'E., 11 km W. of Leeton; village gaz. 1932; PO 1933–44; RS 1915–75; silo; telephone 1934; TX 1935, automatic 1956; weir 1959, on Murrumbidgee R.; pop. 217 (1933), 131 (1961), 143 (2006).

Gogeldrie (*Co. Cooper*) see also Dandinya.

Gogeldrie South (*Co. Cooper*) 34°35'S. 146°16'E., 14 km W. of Leeton; school 1957–72; pop. 206 (1933), 122 (1947), 99 (1954).

Golden Gully (*Co. Bathurst*) 33°38'S. 149°06'E., 18 km SW of Blayney, on Belubula R.; copper mine (Coombing) 1850–80; goldmine (Three Mile); pop. 20 (1933).

Golden Links Estate (*Co. Rous*) 28°20'S. 153°22'E., 3 km W. of Murwillumbah, on Rous R.; quarry.

Golden Point (*Co. Parry*) see Bowling Alley Point.

Golden Point (*Co. Roxburgh*) see Sofala.

Gol Gol (*Co. Wentworth*) 34°11'S. 142°13'E., 30 km E. of Wentworth, on Murray R.; surveyed and town gaz. 1866, first lots sold 1871; former river port, then fruit and vegetables; abattoir (John W. Strong); bridge (timber beam) b. 1909 by J.H. Hill, over Gol Gol Ck; cemetery 1879; electricity 1944; FB; gunnery range (World War II), plane crashed and pilot killed 1943; PO 1927; punt 1910; reservoir 1976; school 1919, additions 1936 by V.F. Treadwell, additions 1955 by E.A. Graff, additions 1960 and 1972; sewerage augmentation 1996; telephone 1924; TX 1945, automatic 1954; water reticulation 1965, augmentation 1994; wharf; pop. 52 (1891), 66 (1911), 145 (1933), 337 (1947), 390 (1954), 446 (1961), 265 (1976), 383 (1981), 642 (1986), 625 (1991), 619 (1996), 591 (2001), 663 (2006).

Gollan (*Co. Lincoln*) 32°16'S. 149°05'E., 35 km N. of Wellington; farming; Bapt. C. b. 1908 by W. Carter; PO 1894; Rom. Cath. C. (Holy Cross) 1911, closed 1980; school 1895–1936 and 1957–69; telephone 1923; TX 1925, automatic 1982; pop. 155 (1911), 203 (1933), 168 (1947), 244 (1954), 166 (1961), 226 (2011).

Golspie (*Co. Georgiana*) 34°18'S. 149°41'E., 26 km NE of Crookwell; farming and grazing; Angl. C. (St Mark's) 1900; German measles epidemic 1940; PO 1873; Rom. Cath. C. (St Joseph's) b. 1897 by H.M. Maynard; school 1881, new buildings b. 1883 by Cranston & Co., closed 1912; telephone 1913; TX 1921, automatic 1989; typhoid 1899; pop. 102 (1901), 148 (1911), 114 (1933), 103 (1947), 115 (1954), 135 (1961), 183 (2006).

Gonella (*Co. Yanda*) 30°42'S. 145°37'E., 150 km SW of Bourke; goldmining; mines: Christmas Gift, Dodger, The Baalgammon or Black, The German or Who'd A Thought It.

Gongolgon (*Co. Cowper*) 30°21'S. 146°54'E., 43 km S. of Brewarrina, on Bogan R.; settled by Joseph Wye, surveyed by R.J. Campbell and town gaz. 1867, declined 1880+; grazing; cemetery 1880–1997; fire 1930; PO 1862, burnt down 1922, replaced; PS (incl. lock-up) 1866, closed, sold and reused, new one b. 1908 by Peter Beddie; school 1876–91 and 1899–1918, new school 1966; telegraph 1879; telephone 1895; TX 1926; weir; pop. *c.*50 (1872), *c.*30 (1903), 69 (1911), 63 (1933), 95 (1954), 82 (1961).

Gonn (*Co. Wakool*) 35°29'S. 143°58'E., 22 km NW of Barham; pop. 72 (1933).

Gonn Crossing (*Co. Wakool*) 35°30'S. 143°57'E., 20 km NW of Barham, on Murray R.; bridge (steel, with lift span) b. 1924–26, carried road and rail till 1961 when railway closed, over Murray R.; pop. 95 (1933).

Goobang (*Co. Ashburnham*) 33°02'S. 148°14'E., 13 km NE of Parkes, on Goobang Ck; surveyed 1864 and town gaz. 1865; gold; cemetery (37 graves 1875–1946); Meth. C. b. 1902 by E. Bullock, d. by Herbert B. Pulver, reused as Presb. C., reused as Angl. C., closed 1981, moved to Parkes and reused; mines: Homeward Bound 1901–2 and Pukka 1930–37 and *c.*1965; school 1879–1955; pop. 169 (1933), 200 (1947), 172 (1954), 156 (1961).

Goobarabah Point (*Co. Northumberland*) see Lake Haven.

Goobarragandra (*Co. Buccleuch*) 35°24'S. 148°26'E., 21 km SE of Tumut, on Goobarragandra Ck; goldmining (alluvial and reef); FB (station b. 2017); pop. 57 (1911), 123 (2006).

Good Dog (*Co. Camden*) see Cambewarra.

Good Forest (*Co. Westmoreland*) 33°34'S. 150°08'E., 11 km S. of Lithgow; Presb. C. 1935; school 1882–91; telephone 1924.

Good Good (*Co. Beresford*) see Peak View.

Good Hope (*Co. Murray*) 34°55'S. 148°48'E., 13 km SW of Yass, on Lake Burrinjuck; mining (copper 1848–49 and lead 1859); earth tremor 1850; PO 1878; school 1880, new building b. 1883 by J. Caldwell, closed 1912; telephone 1926; TX 1926, automatic 1967; pop. 64 (1901), 102 (1911), 25 (1933), 52 (1961).

Goodiman (*Co. Bligh*) 32°18'S. 149°24'E., 14 km NW of Gulgong, on Goodiman Ck.

Goodmans Ford (*Co. Camden*) 34°18'S. 150°04'E., 32 km NW of Berrima, on Wollondilly R.; bridge over Wollondilly R.

Goodnight (*Co. Wakool*) 34°57'S. 143°20'E., 41 km SW of Balranald, on Bingera Ck; orchards; grasshopper infestation 1934; PO 1927; school 1927–49; telephone 1924; TX

1925–81; pop. 123 (1933), 186 (1947), 170 (1954), 197 (1961), 227 (2011).

Goodooga (*Co. Narran*) 29°07'S. 147°27'E., 61 km NW of Lightning Ridge, on Bokhara R.; Bokhara till 1938; thrived 1900; grazing; airport (9 km NW) 1949; ambulance station, closed 1984; Angl. C. (Good Shepherd) 1910; artesian bore, 2,813 ft (857.3 m), sunk 1897; brick-kiln; bridges: one b. 1884 by W.R. Moore, replaced (Dare truss) 1929, over Birrie R. and one b. 1898 over Bokhara R.; cemetery (129 graves) 1884; CH 1877, new one 1961; cordial factories: Joseph Clark, burnt down 1895, William McDougall, A. Sinclair (taken over by J. Hammond & Sons); cyclone 1945; diphtheria 1898; FB (station b. 2016); floods 1890, 1950, 1956, 1974, 1976, 1983; hospital 1896, new one 1901 on new site, burnt down 1979; PO 1870, new one b. 1882, repairs 1892 by John Black, additions 1913 by C.E. Farley, restored; Presb. C. (St Michael's) 1959; PS b. 1884 by W.R. Moore, new one 1961; Rom. Cath. C. (St Denis's) 1938; school (Bokhara till 1884) 1882, additions 1966 and 1970; telegraph 1877, office repairs 1892 by John Black; TX 1910, automatic 1991; water supply augmentation 1996; wool-scours: Hayes Bros, fire 1907, closed 1942, and C. McWilliams; pop. 198 (1891), 247 (1901), 201 (1911), 160 (1933), 182 (1947), 354 (1954), 214 (1961), 228 (1971), 264 (1976), 248 (1981), *c.*350 (1983), 376 (1986), 396 (1991), 375 (1996), 300 (2001), 265 (2006), 215 (2011).

Goodooga Gate (*Co. Narran*) 29°00'S. 147°45'E., 52 km NW of Lightning Ridge.

Goodradigbee (*Co. Cowley*) 35°00'S. 148°39'E., 29 km SW of Yass, on Lake Burrinjuck; village gaz. 1866.

Goodrich (*Co. Gordon*) 32°46'S. 148°34'E., 35 km E. of Peak Hill, on Little R., mining (copper, disc. *c.*1868, gold and silver); mines: Buckenba, Goodrich Pty Co. (estab. by Wynne and Gibson, taken over by Lewis Lloyd, sold to J. Veitch, taken over 1903 by Goodrich Pty Co.) 1868–1912, Jake's (K. Barker), Mount Rose (Frogs Hollow) 1872, Vaughans Ridge; PO 1873; Rom. Cath. C. 1874; school 1875–86; stamper battery; storm (damaged every house) 1876; pop. *c.*250 (1875), 27 (1933).

Goodwood Island (*Co. Clarence*) 29°23'S, 153°19'E., 5 km NW of Iluka, in Clarence R.; (incl. Browns Rocks); sugar-cane; cyclone 1913; sugar mills: Brown's (chimney demolished 1932) and George Morrison (closed 1906, plant and machinery removed 1912, chimney demolished 1932); telephone 1924; TX 1928–55; wharves: Brown's, destroyed 1928 and one b. 1969 by Dowsett Engineering (Aust.) Pty Ltd; pop. 65 (1881), 60 (1901), 63 (1911), 54 (1933), 63 (1947), 52 (1961).

Googong (*Co. Murray*) 35°26'S. 149°16'E., 9 km S. of Queanbeyan, on Queanbeyan R.; lime-kiln (Morley's); quarry (CSR Readymix); reservoir 1977, 244 ft (74.5 m) high, wall raised 1991, on Queanbeyan R.; school 1887–96; water pumping station; water treatment plant; pop. 24 (1933), 302 (2006), 1,122 (2011).

Goolagong (*Co. Forbes*) see Gooloogong.

Goolaway Plain (*Co. Macquarie*) 31°12'S. 152°55'E., 6 km W. of Crescent Head.

Goolgowi (*Co. Nicholson*) 33°59'S. 145°43'E., 45 km NW of Griffith; second site surveyed and laid out 1884, relocated again, first lots sold 1924; grazing, wheat, hort.; airfield; Angl. C. (St Giles's); cemetery 1928; cyclone 1983; drought 1967–68; electricity 1957; FB 1965 (station b. 1968); hailstorm 1985; mouse plague 1939–40; PO 1925; PS 1960, replaced 1982; quarry (clay); reservoir 1956; Rom. Cath. C. (St John Vianney) 1930, refurbished 2002; RS 1923, closed, station moved 1984 to Griffith and reused; sale-yards b. by Frank Rawlinson; school 1934; silo; storm 1959; TX 1927; Unit. C. (orig. Presb.) 1954, refurbished 2002; water reticulation 1956, augmentation 1995; pop. 189 (1933), 118 (1947), 205 (1961), 224 (1954), 204 (1971), 211 (1976), 245 (1981), 256 (1986), 286 (1991), 289 (1996), 298 (2001), 287 (2006), 287 (2011).

Goolhi (*Co. Pottinger*) 31°00'S. 149°45'E., 42 km SW of Boggabri; Presb. C.; school 1956, additions 1960, closed 1986; pop. 58 (1933), 209 (2006), 250 (2011).

Goolma (*Co. Bligh*) 32°22'S. 149°16'E., 25 km W.

of Gulgong, on Goolma Ck; copper mining, farming, grazing; Angl. C. (St Mark's) 1908; bridges: one b. 1969, over Goolma Ck and one over Sheep Station Gully; diphtheria 1927; earth tremor 1919; FB; mine (Belara); rifle range 1908; Rom. Cath. C. 1877, replacement b. 1893 by George Rush and Parkins, new one (St Francis Xavier's) 1969 d. by Terence A. Daly; school 1888, new building b. 1908 by F. Quinn; TX; pop. 75 (1901), 179 (1911), 59 (1933), 105 (1947), 171 (1954), 188 (1961), 200 (2006).

Goolmangar (*Co. Rous*) 28°45'S. 153°13'E., 9 km NW of Lismore, on Goolmangar Ck; farming and dairying; Angl. C. (St Matthew's Peace Memorial) b. 1920 by John Noonan; cheese factory (Ernest Carter); creamery (NSW Creamery Butter Co. Ltd) b. 1895 by Brown and Jolly; FB; jam and pickle factory (Waratah) 1915; PO 1886; Presb. C. 1908, closed, reopened 1940; quarry; Rom. Cath. C. (St Patrick's) 1893, additions 1912; school 1882, new one b. 1898 by H. Dunsmore, closed 1893, reopened 1905, new building b. 1928 by Diyal Singh, additions 2010; telephone 1907; TX 1916, automatic 1958; pop. 177 (1901), 281 (1911), 159 (1933), 245 (1947), 344 (1954), 317 (1961).

Goolmangar North (*Co. Rous*) 28°43'S. 153°14'E., 11 km NW of Lismore, on Goolmangar Ck; telephone 1924.

Gooloogong (*Co. Forbes*) 33°37'S. 148°26'E., 22 km W. of Canowindra, on Lachlan R.; Goolagong till 1924; village gaz. 1878; maize, lucerne, potatoes, dairying, grazing; Angl. C. (St Paul's) b. 1935 by Joe Lashford, d. by E. Schneider, closed, and graveyard (95 graves); bridge (Holman Bridge), de Burgh timber truss, 808 ft (246.3 m), b. 1904 by Charles Henry Curtis and Charles John Foord, replaced 2014 in concrete, over Lachlan R.; cemetery (400 graves) 1879; PO 1868, new one b. 1938 by Heavener; Presb. C. (St Andrew's) 1902, closed; PS 1883, new one (incl. lock-up) b. 1899 by Henry Hart; quarry; reservoir 1955; Rom. Cath. C. 1881, closed, sold 2016, reused, new one (St Malachy's) b. 1953 by Noel Reid, d. by Louis Philip Burns; RS (5 km N.) 1924–78; school (Goolagong till 1924) 1880, new building b. 1882 by H. Ford, additions 1884 by W.M. Murray, new one b. 1911 by John Waugh; silo 1931; telegraph 1890; telephone 1889; TX 1911, automatic 1987; water reticulation 1956; pop. 153 (1901), 534 (1911), 282 (1933), 407 (1947), 415 (1954), 341 (1961), 228 (1971), 246 (1976), 221 (1981), 207 (1986), 295 (2011).

Goombalie (*Co. Barrona*) see Gumbalie.

Goombargana (*Co. Hume*) 35°48'S. 146°35'E., 21 km N. of Howlong; Bapt. C. 1878, burnt down 1905, new one b. 1906 by A.C. Frew and S.M. Logan, d. by J.T. and G.M. McCredie; bushfires 1905 and 1951; cemetery 1880; FB; hailstorm 1889; PO 1875–1914; pop. 68 (1901), 77 (1911).

Goombargana West (*Co. Hume*) 35°42'S. 146°35'E., 31 km N. of Howlong.

Goomoorah (*Co. Arrawatta*) 29°36'S. 151°10'E., 20 km N. of Inverell; PO 1884–1908; pop. 105 (1901), 152 (1911).

Goonambil (*Co. Urana*) 35°29'S. 146°15'E., 50 km SW of Lockhart; PO 1887.

Goonanyah (*Co. Baradine*) see Gwabegar.

Goondabluie (*Co. Finch*) 29°10'S. 148°38'E., 41 km N. of Collarenebri, on Mooni R.; telephone 1898; pop. 82 (1911), 130 (1933), 54 (1947).

Goondabooka (*Co. Cowper*) see Maroona.

Goondah (*Co. Harden*) 34°44'S. 148°44'E., 20 km NW of Yass, on Dunderalligo Ck; PO 1907; RS (relocated 1916) 1891–1975; school 1910–59; telephone 1923; TX 1935; pop. 113 (1911), 77 (1933), 68 (1947), 58 (1954).

Goonellabah (*Co. Rous*) 28°49'S. 153°19'E., 4 km E. of Lismore, on Tucki Tucki Ck; farming; Angl. C. 1961, new one (St Peter's) 1979, closed; Arise C.; candied peel factory (F. Withers) 1895; cemetery (Lismore crematorium and lawn cemetery, 7,081 plots) 1966; Church of Christ (Northern Rivers); cyclone 1888; FB (station b. 1971); fire 1891; Jehovah's Witnesses C.; LDS (Mormon) C.; PO 1900; 3 reservoirs; Salv. Army C. (Lismore) b. 1997 by Bennett Constructions

Pty Ltd; schools: Goonellabah (Wilsons Ridges till 1880) 1879, new one b. 1881 by Patrick Ryan, damaged 1888, additions and repairs 1895 by John Read, additions and repairs 1910 by T.E. Jarman, new building b. 1935 by Diyal Singh & Son, additions 1959, 1966, 1972, 1982 and Kadina HS 1977 b. by Alex Roberts Constructions Pty Ltd, renamed Rivers Secondary College in 2015; telephone 1916, automatic 1973; United Pentecostal C. of Aust. (Truth and Light); pop. 207 (1901), 262 (1911), 349 (1933), 439 (1947), 781 (1954), 12,137 (2006), 12,537 (2011).

Goonengerry (*Co. Rous*) 28°37'S. 153°26'E., 9 km SW of Mullumbimby; orig. timber, then dairying 1905+, bananas; Angl. C. (St Philip and St James's) 1908; cyclone 1936; PO 1927; sawmills: Egan Bros and J.N. Hollingworth & Co. 1921; school 1901; telephone 1924; TX 1925, automatic 1952; pop. 95 (1911), 221 (1933), 205 (1947), 208 (1954), 167 (1961).

Goonigal (*Co. Ashburnham*) 33°07'S. 148°39'E., 8 km NW of Manildra; copper mine (Gumble) *c.*1886–88.

Goonoo (*Co. Gordon*) 32°40'S. 148°43'E., 28 km SW of Wellington; goldmine (Higgins) 1935–36.

Goonoo (*Co. Lincoln*) see Mogriguy.

Goonoo Goonoo (*Co. Parry*) 31°18'S. 150°54'E., 23 km S. of Tamworth, on Goonoo Goonoo Ck; estab. 1841 by Aust. Agric. Co. as its regional headquarters, acquired 1853 by Peel River Land & Mineral Co., re-acquired 1959 by Aust. Agric. Co., private village sold 1985, sold 2011 to Tony Haggarty, restored 2012–18 and reused; primarily sheep (wool production peaked in 1899); Meth. C. 1911; PO 1853–1952; school 1881–1915 and 1957–66; pop. *c.*40 (1866), 88 (1901), 424 (1911), 178 (1933), 59 (1947), 325 (1954), 316 (1961).

Goonoo Railway Station (*Co. Lincoln*) see Mogriguy.

Goonoowigal (*Co. Gough*) 29°49'S. 151°07'E., 4 km S. of Inverell, on Sheep Station Ck; fellmongering and wool-scouring; brickworks: George Frederick Nott and Willis's (Nott bought out Willis and in 1909 the brickworks was acquired by Benjamin Martin Wade who moved it to Inverell in 1929); 4 quarries; school 1887–1966 (building moved 1973 to Inverell, restored and reused); tanneries: Colin Ross and George Dean (incl. bark mill) and Samuel Rowland; wool-scours: Alderson & Sons (improvements 1874), Colin Ross and Thomson 1877, S. Rowland & Sons (became Rowland Bros); pop. 46 (1891).

Goonumbla (*Co. Ashburnham*) 33°00'S. 148°08'E., 15 km N. of Parkes, on Limestone Plains Ck; village gaz. 1916; farming and mining (copper and gold); cemetery; Meth. C. 1908; mines: Northparkes (o. 1994 by GeoPeko, taken over 1995 by North Ltd, taken over 2000 by Rio Tinto and Sumitomo) and J. Wright 1896–98; PO 1916; RS (Limestone Plains till 1915) 1914–76; sawmill (Vanderfield and Reid) 1925; school 1910–49; silo 1930; telephone 1959; TX (automatic) 1959; pop. 225 (1933), 141 (1947), 224 (1954), 221 (1961), 350 (2011).

Goonyan (*Co. Beresford*) 34°56'S. 149°01'E., 36 km N. of Cooma; cemetery (62 graves).

Gooramma (*Co. Harden*) 34°30'S. 148°37'E., 11 km SW of Boorowa; RS 1915–74; earth tremor 2005.

Goorangoola (*Co. Durham*) 32°18'S. 151°11'E., 28 km E. of Muswellbrook, on Campbells Ck; settled 1838; tobacco, farming, grazing; Angl. C. 1875, demolished 1928, replaced (St Columba's) 1929, and graveyard (95 graves 1880s+); bushfires 1881 and 1898–99; creamery (Glennies Creek & Goorangoola Co-op. Creamery Co. Ltd) 1894; flood 1893; Meth. C.; PO 1872–1943; PS (incl. lock-up) b. 1885 by William Burnett, closed 1894; school 1877, new one b. 1880 by William Burnett, closed 1901, reopened 1905–22; telephone 1909; TX 1952–59; Wes. Meth. C. 1882; pop. 87 (1891), 162 (1911), 49 (1933), *c.*70 (1980).

Gooraway (*Co. Finch*) 29°37'S. 148°02'E., 21 km S. of Lightning Ridge.

Goorawin (*Co. Nicholson*) 33°44'S. 145°36'E., 30 km S. of Hillston; RS 1926–75.

Goorianawa (*Co. Baradine*) 31°05'S. 148°57'E., 19 km SW of Baradine, on Bucklanbar Ck;

TX (automatic).

Gooringoora (*Co. Murchison*) 29°56'S. 150°42'E., 16 km SW of Bingara, on Gwydir R.

Gordon (*Co. Drake*) 29°18'S. 152°43'E., 48 km NW of Grafton, on Gordon Brook.

Gordon Brook (*Co. Drake*) 29°26'S. 152°38'E., 41 km NW of Grafton, on Clarence R.; mining (chromite) 1895; boiling-down works estab. by Ogilvie; butter factory (Field's) 1910; mine (copper) and smelter; pop. 38 (1933).

Gordons Point (*Co. Waradgery*) 34°30'S. 144°47'E., 6 km W. of Hay, on Murrumbidgee R.; school 1898–1905.

Gordonville (*Co. Raleigh*) 30°24'S. 152°51'E., 7 km NW of Bellingen, on Never Never Ck; dairying 1905+; Meth. C. 1916; school 1891–1939; pop. 65 (1933), 59 (1947).

Gordonville Cutting (*Co. Raleigh*) 30°25'S. 152°50'E., 6 km NW of Bellingen, on Bellinger R.

Gordy Town (*Co. Cook*) see Blackheath.

Gorge Creek (*Co. Buller*) 28°44'S. 152°43'E., 30 km SW of Kyogle, on Gorge Ck; pop. 25 (1933).

Gorham (*Co. King*) see Gunnary.

Gormans Hill (*Co. Bathurst*) see Bathurst.

Gorokan (*Co. Northumberland*) 33°16'S. 151°31'E., 25 km NE of Gosford, on Tuggerah Lake; fishing; Assemblies of God C.; Bapt. C. (Lakes), fire 2008, repairs 2010; bridge (Wallarah Point Bridge) 1939, 570 ft (173.7 m), demolished, new one b. 1983–85, to Toukley, over Budgewoi and Tuggerah Lakes; Christ. Brethren Assemblies C.; PO 1927; school 1980; sewerage 1976; telephone 1924; TX (automatic) 1960; Unit. C.; water reticulation 1969; pop. 45 (1933), 71 (1947), 276 (1954), 598 (1961), 7,066 (2006), 7,682 (2011).

Gorokan (*Co. Northumberland*) see also Lake Haven.

Gorrick's Point (*Co. Northumberland*) see Brightwaters.

Gosford (*Co. Northumberland*) 33°26'S. 151°20'E., 50 km N. of Sydney, on The Broad Water; (incl. Bradys Gully, North Gosford, Point Frederick, West Gosford); Brisbane Water till 1841; settled by Thomas Alison Scott, surveyed 1838 by Samuel Dalgety, laid out 1839 also by Dalgety, first lots sold 1841, town gaz. 1879, munic. proc. 1886, subdivisions 1886 and 1887, commercial centre moved northwards 1888+; timber 1820s–70s, citrus orchards 1880+, tourism 1887+, passionfruit, vegetables, farming, poultry, food processing, clothing, building materials; abattoir (Gosford Meats Pty Ltd, sold 1966 to Charles David Pty Ltd) 1960–89; ambulance station (Brisbane Water Dist.) b. 1940 by Ernest Theodore Ohlsson, d. by R.S. Hamilton; Angl. C. (St Mary the Virgin), closed and reused, demolished 1959, new one (St Mary's) 1906, removed from East Gosford (Peeks Point), closed and reused 1960, new one (Christ) 1960; Assemblies of God C. (House of Praise); Bapt. C. b. 1940 by Reginald Joseph Want; blind factory (Lifelong Products Pty Ltd) 1951; bottled water plant (Somersby Springs Natural Water Pty Ltd) 1992; brickworks: Gosford Brick, Tile & Pipe Pty Ltd (West Gosford) 1938, pipes produced 1940, closed 1984, John and Henry Millard (North Gosford), Alex Olsen; bridge (Fagan's Bridge) b. 1892 by Arthur Davis, replacement (Henry Kendall Bridge) b. 1956 by Beattie and Frost, over Narara Ck; bushfires 1909, 1916, 1928, 1940, 1944, 1948, 1953, 1994; cemeteries: Bradys Gully (65 graves) 1882, and Point Frederick (498 burials 1840–1953) 1847, headstones razed or relocated 1974; CH (incl. lock-up) b. 1847–49, d. by Mortimer William Lewis, repairs 1879 by R. Coulter, new one 1887, extended 1892, additions 1911 by D. M'Colgan, additions 1928, alterations 1961, reused, new one 1987; chocolate factory (Bon Bon Fine Chocolate); Christ. City C.; Christ. Science C.; Church of Christ; clock tower (Chapman memorial) 2010; clothing factory (Bonds Industries Ltd) 1964; cordial factories: G. Margin & Sons Pty Ltd (estab. 1906 by George Margin, additions 1921, moved 1969 to Erina), and James Millard; electricity substation (West Gosford); FB (station b. 1939, new one

1986); fibrous plaster works; fires 1893, 1914, 1920, 1923, 1924, 1929, 1934, 1944, 2013; flood 1989; fruit case factories: Capitol and Ray Griffiths; fruit juice factory estab. 1921 as Fruit & Vegetable By-Products Ltd by Col. Garnet I. Adcock to produce oils for perfumes and essences for fruit drinks, became Jusfrute Ltd in 1924, taken over 1960 by Keith Harris & Co. Ltd, closed 1982; fruit packing houses: Gosford Bulk Loading Rural Co-op. Society Ltd (renamed Sungold in 1950) and Gosford Citrus Packing House Co-op. Co. Ltd 1922 (burnt down 1934, replaced 1934 by A.A. Best, d. by B.G. Miller); gale 1910; hospital 1945, additions 1958, extended 1967, upgraded 1980, redeveloped 2001–5; Jehovah's Witnesses C.; joinery (Gosford Machine Joinery Works); Liberty Family C.; Lutheran C. (St Matthew's); measles epidemic 1940; Meth. C. 1926, new one b. 1955 by W.E. Stratford, d. by William C. Brown; PO: Gosford 1835 (new one b. 1880–82 by R. Minell, d. by James Johnstone Barnet, additions 1891 by Frederick Lemm, additions 1908, additions 1912 by W.W. Dunk, additions 1953) and West Gosford 1966; pound (stock) 1865; Presb. C. 1913, (second) 1926, new one (St Andrew's) 1960 d. by Milo Kanangra Dunphy and Bruce Donald Loder, demolished 2002, new one (West Gosford); PS b. 1847–49, d. by Mortimer William Lewis, new one b. 1881 by H. Wilson, extended 1892, additions 1899 by W.J. Green, additions 1928, alterations 1961, reused, new one 1983, additions and alterations 1993; punt (Fagan's), ceased 1891, across Narara Ck; quarries: Freestone Quarries Gosford Ltd and Gosford Quarries Pty Ltd (estab. 1922 by Henry Parry); radar station (World War II); railway bridge (6 steel spans) over Fagans Bay; railway turntable 1926, 75 ft (22.9 m); 3 reservoirs (Gosford, North Gosford, West Gosford); rifle range (Bradys Gully); Rom. Cath. C. (Our Lady of the Rosary) b. 1892 by Hayes, enlarged 1930; RS 1887, station b. by John R. Rogers, refreshment room 1890, new refreshment room 1912, refreshment room additions 1916; Salv. Army C. b. 1925 by Lyell and Gilfillan, closed, sold 1965; sawmills: Gosford Sawmills & Joinery Works (estab. 1917 by William Hastings Kirkness), Marshall Sawmilling Co., Arthur Parsons (destroyed in explosion 1913, man killed), Samuel Ranyard; schools: Gosford primary 1876, new one b. 1877 by Robert Creighton and Thomas Donlon, d. by George Allen Mansfield, additions 1883 by Creighton and White, additions 1886 by H. Coates, additions 1892, renovations and repairs 1910 by Robert Creighton, repairs 1911 by W.W. Dunk, reused, second one 1954 on new site, demolished 2014, new one b. 2012–14 on new site, Gosford HS 1929 b. by William Lishman Jemison, additions 1939 by Short Bros, additions 1967, 1970, 1976, 1981, Henry Kendall HS 1970, additions 1976 and 1979; SD Adventist C. d. and b. 1922 by Murray; sewerage augmentation 1994; shipyard (Edward Davis); sheet metal works (Central Coast Sheetmetal & Fabrication); smallgoods factory (Central Coast Smallgoods Pty Ltd); spring factory (Gibbens Industries Pty Ltd); storm 1974; streets kerosene lit 1902, electric lit 1923; tank works (John William Sterland) 1888; TC o. 1953 (in former school), additions 1983, became a campus of Hunter Institute of Technology in 1992, additions 1994; telegraph 1878, new office b. 1880–82 by R. Minell, d. by James Johnstone Barnet, additions 1891 by Frederick Lemm, additions 1908, additions 1912 by W.W. Dunk, additions 1953; telephone: Gosford 1884 and West Gosford 1966; tie factory (Ensign Ties Pty Ltd); TX 1910, automatic 1958; Unit. C. (orig. Meth.); watch-house b. 1827 by George Paton; water supply (Mooney Dam) 1938, augmentation 1993; Wes. Meth. C. 1890; wharves: govt one b. 1841, one b. 1863 by W.S. Lockhart, one b. 1940; pop. 199 (1841), 53 (1846), 95 (1851), 117 (1856), 138 (1861), 138 (1866), 67 (1871), 239 (1881), 685 (1891), *c.*680 (1895), 751 (1901), 1,100 (1911), 2,606 (1933), 4,495 (1947), 5,320 (1954), 7,601 (1961), 11,310 (1966), 10,056 (2011).

Gosford East (*Co. Northumberland*) 33°26'S. 151°21'E., 2 km SE of Gosford, on Brisbane Water; estab. 1840 by Samuel Peek, surveyed 1840 by W.H. Wells, incorp. 1886; timber 1824–70s, citrus orchards 1880+; Angl. C. (Christ) b. 1858 by Aaron Booth, d. by Edmund Thomas Blacket, closed 1889, dismantled 1905 by P.H. Streit and moved to Gosford; Bapt. C. 1952 by W.E. Stratford; bridge (The Punt Bridge) to Erina, b. 1884–86 by John Johnstone, 2 plate web girder fixed spans, opening span locked 1930, demolished 1963, replacement (steel and concrete) b. 1962 by Beattie & Frost Pty Ltd, 135 ft 9 in. (41.4 m), over Erina Ck; Dutch Reformed C.; FB; Meth. C. 1958; PO 1953; Rom. Cath. C. (St Patrick's War Memorial) b. 1965 by Archbold & Fogarty Pty Ltd, d. by Peter Gilmour; sawmill (Venteman's); school 1960, additions 1966 and 1981; sewage works (Peeks Point), closed, site reused; shipyard (William Woodward) 1883; telephone 1953; wharves: The Fox under the Hill, Punt, Victoria 1841; pop. 116 (1851), 155 (1856), 145 (1861), 101 (1871), 113 (1933), 3,513 (2006), 3,908 (2011).

Gosforth (*Co. Northumberland*) 32°39'S. 151°29'E., 10 km NW of Maitland; village gaz. 1881; farming; Angl. C. (St Clement's) b. 1895 by Fred Brewer, d. by Arthur Coe Lee and Arthur Josling; bushfire 1926; grasshopper infestation 1921; hailstorms 1906 and 1910; PO 1890; quarry; school 1850–1940; storms 1918 and 1925; telephone 1916; pop. 77 (1891), 98 (1901), 737 (1911), 86 (1933), 60 (1947), 61 (1954), 196 (2006).

Gosling Creek (*Co. Bathurst*) see Orange (*Co. Wellington*).

Gospers Downs (*Co. Ashburnham*) 33°11'S. 148°34'E., 11 km W. of Manildra; school 1897, additions 1901 by William Fleeting, closed 1952.

Gospers Point (*Co. Clarence*) 29°31'S. 153°03'E., 16 km W. of Maclean.

Gossan Hill (*Co. Yancowinna*) see Taltingan.

Gostwyck (*Co. Durham*) 32°34'S. 151°36'E., 15 km N. of Bolwarra, on Paterson R.; settled by Edward Gostwyck Cory 1831, sold 1874 to John Ponsford Luke, subdivided 1902, defunct; vineyards, tobacco, wheat; bridge b. 1878 by Mark Burley, d. by William Christopher Bennett, damaged and repaired 1926, new one (steel Pratt truss) b. 1928, 381 ft (116 m), over Paterson R.; butter factory (Raymond Terrace Co-op. Dairy & Produce Co. Ltd) b. 1908 by C.A. McDonald, bought 1915 by Peters Paterson River Dairies Ltd, closed 1926 and sold back to Raymond Terrace Co-op. Dairy & Produce Co. Ltd, renamed Hunter Valley Co-op. Dairy Co. Ltd in 1944, closed; copper mine (Edward Gostwyck Cory); flour mills (Edward Gostwyck Cory): a water powered one 1831 and a steam powered one 1834; punt 1843, across Paterson R.; quarry; sawmill (John Ponsford Luke) 1875; school 1880–92 and 1910–42; wharf; pop. 104 (1911).

Gostwyck (*Co. Sandon*) 30°42'S. 151°35'E., 10 km SE of Uralla, on Salisbury Waters; settled by Edward Gostwyck Cory 1832, sold 1834 to William Dangar; Angl. C. (All Saints') b. 1921 by C.G. Cooper, d. by Robert Newburgh Hickson; bridge (suspension) fabricated by Clyde Engineering Co. Ltd, over Salisbury Waters; pop. 50 (1841), 69 (1901), 109 (1911), 68 (1933).

Goulburn (*Co. Argyle*) 34°45'S. 149°43'E., 81 km NE of Queanbeyan, on Mulwaree R.; (incl. Argyle, Buffalo City, East Argyle, East Goulburn, Eastgrove formerly Brooks's Paddock, Garfield, Ifield, North Goulburn, River Heights, South Goulburn, West Goulburn formerly Newtown); orig. Goulburn Plains; disc. 1820 by John Joseph William Molesworth Oxley, settled 1825 by Andrew Allan, Goulburn Plains surveyed 1828 by Robert Dixon, laid out 1829 by Elliott, founded 1829, new site (Goulburn) chosen 1832 by Gov. Sir Richard Bourke, surveyed 1832 by William Romaine Govett, laid out 1833 by Robert Hoddle, town gaz. and first lots sold 1833, developed 1850+, munic. proc. 1859, city proc. 1863, designated as chief town of the county, thrived 1869–85, city declined 1927+, bypassed by highway 1992; orig. cattle, then sheep *c.*1827+, tobacco and poppies (opium) 1840s, wheat (mainly 1820s–1860s), maize, barley, rye, oats, lucerne, potatoes, apples, vineyards, butter, cheese, ham and bacon, later dairying, poultry, vegetables, textiles, carriage building, engineering, boots, flour, soap, cordials, condiments; abattoir 1951, extended 1964, closed 1979; aeroplane crash (man killed) 2010; airport (6 km S.) 1928, major upgrade 1966; ambulance station b. 1933 by H.C. Gould, d. by Herbert Charles Manfred, additions 1952; Angl. C.: one b. 1848, All Saints' 1899, Christ 1884 (d. and b. by Alberto Dias Soares, chancel and sanctuary added 1912, demolished, church extended 1978), Good Shepherd, St Nicholas's 1861 (d. by Richard Leigh, reused 1938 as cordial factory, replacement b. 1880 by Banks and Minell, d. by Edmund Thomas Blacket, additions 1940 and 1972, and columbarium), St Saviour's (b. 1838–43, demolished 1884, pro-cathedral b. 1874 by R.B. Turner and Louis Le Breton, d. by Edmund Thomas Blacket, reused, cathedral b. 1874–84 by R. and J. Turner, W. Duncan, John Nelson and Louis Le Breton, d. by Blacket & Son, memorial chapel 1922 d. by John Burcham Clamp, tower b. 1986–88); Assemblies of God C. (Christ. Life); baking powder factory (A.M. Hunt) 1871; Bapt. C.: Bourke Street one o. 1901 in former Presb. C. (Trinity) and Clifford Street one o. 1843, demolished, new one 1893, alterations and renovations 1953 d. by E. Petersen; Bible Bapt. C.; boiling-down works: Argyle Steam Works, sold 1852, Benjamin and Moses 1844, Duncan McKellar and Jacob White 1844; boot factories: Gillespie & Co. Ltd (estab. 1844 by Dennis Gillespie, taken over 1851 by Charles Gillespie, new factory b. 1878 by J. Raward and T. Lee, d. by H.O. Bell, upgraded 1895, sold 1907, burnt down 1915, rebuilt 1916 by E. Gould, d. by Oakden, Ballantyne and Donald Thomas Esplin, closed 1926), R.L. Stalker, William Teece & Co. (estab. 1850, sold 1885 to Henry Baxter, became Baxter & Co.), Wood & Co. 1857; breweries: Argyle Brewery (estab. by Edward and Joseph Kennedy, taken over 1887 by H.G. Chard) 1883–94, Capel's (or Argyle) Brewery (estab. by Thomas Capel) 1849, Foston Brewery (estab. by John Blackshaw) 1853–73, Goulburn (or Bradley's or Raymond's) Brewery (b. 1836–38 by William Bradley and William Shelley for James Bradley, closed 1854, taken over 1866 by Walford, Spark and S. Emanuel, acquired 1870 by Goulburn Meat Preserving Co. Ltd, acquired 1875 by William J. Bartlett and J.S. Oddy, known as Bartlett's Brewery 1878–1920, acquired 1921 by Tooth & Co., closed 1929, reused by Tooth & Co. till 1956, sold 1958 to Hedley and Joyce Carman, sold 1975 to Phoenix Community Services Ltd, reused, closed, reopened and reused 1989), Riversdale Brewery (estab. by Matt Healy), Thorne Bros Brewery (b. by George and Daniel Thorne) 1847–49, Tribe Breweries (estab. 2019 by Anton Szpitalak), Wollondale Brewery (estab. by John Farrell and Tom Gulson) 1883–1900; brickworks: Fitzroy Brickworks (estab. by Frederick Lemm, acquired 1884 by J.W. MacGraw), Goulburn Brick & Tile Co., Gulson Pty Ltd (estab. 1884 by Francis Gulson, upgraded 1914, acquired 1922 by Roy and Lyn Gulson, renovated 1923, joined by Artie Watson and became Gulson's Brick & Pottery Co. Pty Ltd), Edward Johnson, William Keeley 1837, Melbourne Place Brickworks (estab. 1863 by Thomas Stubbings, taken over by Stubbings Bros), John Rawood; bridges: first one 1837, replaced by Fitzroy Bridge (b. 1855 by William Weaver, destroyed), second Fitzroy Bridge (304 ft or 92.7 m) 1884, third Fitzroy Bridge (b. 1976 by Transbridge Pty Ltd) over Mulwaree R., Kenmore Bridge (to Bradfordville) 1982 over Wollondilly R., Lansdowne Bridge (b. 1902 by J.J. Paddington, de Burgh timber truss, 320 ft or 97.5 m, new one 2018) over Mulwaree R, Marsden Bridge 1984 over Wollondilly R., Victoria Street Bridge (to Bradfordville) 1970 over Wollondilly R., Wollondilly Bridge (b. 1883 by G.H. Royce & Co.) over Wollondilly R.; bushfires 1882 and 1939; butter factory and ice works (Argyle Co-op. Central Dairy

Co. Ltd) 1901–28, reconstituted as Goulburn & Dist. Co-op. Society Ltd, reopened 1933 following additions and alterations by W.E. Armstrong, new plant and machinery installed by J. Wildridge and Sinclair, acquired 1937 by Taralga Co-op. Dairy Co. Ltd, taken over 1950 by Dairy Farmers' Co-op. Milk Co. Ltd; carriage-works: R. Broadhurst, Cobb & Co. (closed 1893), Charles Cole, Alf Dean, Neil Doneghue 1884, English & American Carriage-Works (estab. 1881, acquired 1882 by J.E. Toohey who b. new factory 1885), H.J. Hackett 1883, Lake and Stewart (estab. 1848 by William Stewart), Penberthy and Donnelly 1887, William Southall 1870 (new one o. 1889), Christopher Walker, Wright Bros and Slayter 1884 (Slayter left the partnership in 1886, closed 1920); cement works (Divall & Son); cemeteries: general 1864 (incl. lawn cemetery and columbaria), Governor's Hill (graves 1904+), Jewish (36 graves 1845+), restored by Stephen Tazewell, Mortis Street (1,342 graves 1839–1954), St Saviour's (980 graves 1833–1957) 1842, closed; CH 1832, replaced, inundated 1842, (third) b. 1848 by James Sinclair, d. by Mortimer William Lewis, alterations 1857, additions 1866 and 1872, reused, (fourth) b. 1884–87 by David Jones, d. by James Johnstone Barnet, extended 1907; chenille factory (Supertex Industries Ltd) o. 1945 in former munitions factory, extended 1964; clothing factories: Chief 1944 and F.W. Sandell 1918–30; confectionary factory (H.E. Jordon) 1877; container terminal (Chicago Freight Rail Services); cordial factories: Atlas, Barrett's, Charles Colbert, Charles A. McAlister (bought 1907 by W. Steele & Co. Ltd, incl. ice works), James Nowlan, Sharpe Bros (estab. by John and Ewart Sharpe) 1920–33, Cornelius Phillip Sheekey (incl. ice works) 1868, man killed 1945, Sinclair and McCallum, Skinner & Co. 1859, Sotheran Bros, W.J. Sullivan & Son (bought 1947 by E. Hope and renamed Goulburn Cordials), Thomas A. Walker; cotton mill 1949; dams: Sooley 1930, modified 1961, 43 ft (13 m) high, on Sooley Ck and Rossiville 1918, on Wollondilly R.; diphtheria 1908, 1922, 1933–34 (child died), 1939; dust storms 1884, 1898, 1902, 1923, 1928, 1929, 1933; dye works (E. Long); earth tremors 1857, 1872, 1883, 1886, 1897, 1916, 1926, 1928, 1940, 1941, 1944, 1946; electricity 1914; engineering works: E. Denney 1917 and Pearson Engineering Pty Ltd; FB: Goulburn 1854 (station b. 1882, new one b. 1888 by Birkin and Ashley, new one b. 1891, d. by Edmund Cooper Manfred, reused, replaced 1971) and North Goulburn (station b. 1886 by John O'Brien, closed 1917); fires 1864, 1874, 1882, 1884, 1888, 1909, 1911, 1915; floods 1842, 1843, 1852, 1857, 1860, 1864, 1867, 1870, 1885, 1891, 1900, 1952, 1956, 2007; flour mills: Argyle (estab. 1849 by James Sinclair, sold 1851 to Byrnes and Oakes, sold 1854 to William Conolly, incorp. 1903 as William Conolly Pty Ltd, roller mill b. 1908 on new site by John Dunkley, sold to Bunge Aust. Ltd, closed 1969, sold and reused), William Bradley and William Shelley (b. 1836–38, sold 1866 to Walford, Spark and S. Emanuel, closed 1869, but brewing continued on the site), City Roller Flour Mills (b. 1869 by John Richardson and Pinn Bros for James and Joseph Smithers Hayes, taken over 1895 by W.S. Kimpton & Sons), Excelsior (estab. 1882 by W.E. Cox and Worrall, sold 1884 to H.B. Douglas and then operated by Short & Co. from 1888, taken over by Walter Adamson Martin, taken over 1911 by Ashley, Stephens & Co. and renamed Warrego, closed and reused, chimney demolished 1918), Duncan McKellar (horse powered); 2 foot-bridges to Bradfordville, over Wollondilly R.; foundries: Atlas Engineering & Foundry Works (sold 1885 by H.D. Manning to Incher and Crossley), Ayling Bros (became Hodkinson and Ayling, then Simpson and Jones, then George Simpson), Burn & Sons 1866 (bought 1881 by Richard Thomas Ball, became M'Fadyen, Ball and Bryant in 1883, then Ball, Incher & Co. in 1885, then R.T. Ball & Co. later in 1885, then Goulburn Foundry, Engineering Co. Ltd later in 1885, boy killed 1887, closed and demolished 1894), John Byrne, Matt Gibbons, Goulburn Engineering & Foundry Works (bought out by Pneumatic Cell Tyre Co., taken over 1929 by Ben R. Nosworthy), W. Wardle; furniture factory (Charles Rogers & Sons Pty Ltd) 1859; gale 1892; gaol b. 1841–43 by James Sinclair, d. by Mortimer William Lewis, alterations 1871, additions and alterations 1880 by Frederick Horn, closed 1884, demolished 1884, new one at North Goulburn b. 1880–84 by Frederick Lemm and Thomas Edward Spencer, d. by James Johnstone Barnet, William Coles and Brown, new wing (114 cells) added 1893 by Donohue and J. Goode, new female cells b. 1897–99, renamed a reformatory in 1928, renamed a training centre in 1949, external wing b. 1957–61, additions 1963, new education block 1967, extended 1986–89, additions 1990, renamed a correctional centre in 1993, renovated 2000, maximum security unit 2001; gastroenteritis epidemic (10 children died) 1919–20; gasworks (City of Goulburn Gas & Coke Co. Ltd) b. 1879 by Jessop, additions 1883 by T. Donohue, taken over 1941 by Gas Supply Co. Ltd, expanded 1942, fire 1952; German measles epidemic 1940; Greek Orthodox C. (St Panteleimon's) 1973; hailstorms 1879 and 1888; hospital 1834, (second) b. 1849 by Henry Wilson, closed, reused, (third) b. 1887–89 by Charles Goode & Son, d. by Edmund Cooper Manfred, additions 1892 by O'Brien, additions 1906, 1911, 1915, 1919, 1925, 1928, 1933, 1937, 1938, 1939, 1940, 1943, 1945, 1949, 1956, 1959, 1966, 1976, 2013; immigration barracks 1841; jam factories: Argyll (G. Fox) 1873, A.M. Hunt & Co., J.W. Middlebrook, E.G. Woodhall & Co.; Jehovah's Witnesses C. (North Goulburn); joineries: John Cody, burnt down 1927, Lansdown Bros, fire 1887, sold 1888, Charles Rogers 1889; knitting yarn mill (Sirdar Wools Aust. Pty Ltd) 1964; lime-works: John Gray and R.D. Gray & Sons; lock-up 1830, new one b. 1879 by William Duncan; Lutheran C.; marble works estab. 1860 by Robert Turner, taken over 1878 by James Turner, expanded 1879; measles epidemics 1893 (boy died), 1933, 1947; Meth. C.: Goulburn 1924 and South Goulburn 1911; migrant hostel 1951; monumental stone works: William Duncan, Greaves, E.I. Richards, James Turner & Sons Pty Ltd; morgue b. 1881 by W. Duncan; munitions factory 1941, closed, reused; PO: Goulburn 1832 (new one b. 1865 by Bull, second one b. 1872 by William Duncan, third one b. 1881 by Frederick Horn, d. by James Johnstone Barnet, alterations 1910 by E. Gould, alterations 1926 and 1981, renovated 1986), East Goulburn 1951, Ifield 1947, North Goulburn 1905 (new one b. 1940), South Goulburn 1949, West Goulburn 1947; pound (stock) 1833; powder magazine (Eastgrove); powerhouse (Goulburn Electric Supply Pty Ltd) b. 1914 by King and Armstrong; Presb. C.: St Andrew's (b. 1839–42, d. by James Hume, closed and replaced 1925) and Trinity (b. 1887 by Charles Goode & Son, d. by Edmund Cooper Manfred, closed 1899, sold 1901 to Baptists and reused, new one b. 1925 by H.C. Gould, d. by Power, Adam and Munnings); Prim. Meth. C. 1859, altered and enlarged, replacement b. 1879 by Richardson & Son, d. by H.O. Bell, damaged 1898, closed 1913, demolished; PS b. 1874 by Thomas Wilkie, sen., new one b. 1884–88 by David Jones, d. by James Johnstone Barnet, additions 1910 by Frederick Lemm, additions and alterations 1975; 2 quarries (stone): one estab. 1849 and one estab. by Burke; rabbit freezing works: Curtis and Curtis 1915 and Mulwaree (Wilson and Flood) 1917; railway (orig. police) barracks, new barracks b. 1888 by Thomas Wilkie, reused, new barracks (South Goulburn) b. 1935, fire 1954; railway bridges: one b. 1869 by Mark Faviell, 862 ft (262.7 m) and one b. 1902 (steel truss) over Wollondilly R.; railway coal stage b. 1870 by Frederick Horn, second one (from Harden) 1880, third one 1891; railway engine shed b. 1869 by W. Webb, reused, new one 1885; railway round-house (South Goulburn), 42 bays, 1917, man killed 1918, upgraded 1951, partly dismantled 1975, reused; railway turntable 1870, 50 ft (15.2 m), new one 1897, 60 ft (18.3 m), South Goulburn one 75 ft (22.9 m), new one (electric) 1935, 90 ft (27.4 m), damaged 2013, repaired 2015 by Betts Welding; railway viaduct (12 spans) 1869–1914, 858 ft (261.5 m), partly dismantled 1930, demolished 1937, replacement (16 brick arches) 1914, over Mulwarree Ponds; railway workshops 1881, re-erection of workshops (South Goulburn) 1935 removed from Wellington, new facility 1980, taken over 2006 by United Group Ltd, taken over 2010 by Chicago Freight Car Leasing Aust.; 9 reservoirs (incl. one b. 1884 by Shaw and Monie); rifle range (3 km SE) 1910; Rom. Cath. C.: Our Lady of Fatima (North Goulburn) 1953, Our Lady of Sorrows (West Goulburn) b. 1954 by East Coast Constructions Pty Ltd, d. by Louis Philip Burns, Sacred Heart (North Goulburn) b. 1882 by W. Duncan, fire 1922, closed, sold and reused, St Peter and St Paul's (b. 1841–49, demolished 1890, replacement b. 1871–90 by C.J. O'Brien and Wilkie Bros, d. by Andrea Giovanni Stombuco and Charles Spadaccini, renovated 1928, spire 2014); RS: Argyle 1902–69, Goulburn 1869 (station b. by J. Taylor, Holdsworth and Rolfe, d. by John Whitton, additions and alterations 1882, alterations 1901 by Daniel H. Taunton, new refreshment rooms 1915, station extended 1922), North Goulburn 1882–1975; sale-yards, improvements 1882 by Webb, new yards 1926; Salv. Army C. b. 1884 by James Armstrong, leased 1892 to Cong. C., Salv. Army relocated to former hall; sawmill (Victoria Steam Saw and Moulding Mills) estab. 1887 by Thomas Wilkie; scarlet fever 1933 and 1940; schools: Argyle 1881 (new one b. 1884 by J. McArthur, closed 1890), East Argyle 1878–88, East Goulburn (Eastgrove till 1900, b. 1887 by J. O'Brien, additions 1889 by G.H. Daniel, additions and renovations 1931 d. by Leslie Elias Lyons, additions 1966), Goulburn 1858–62 (reopened 1868, repairs 1878 by Thomas Wilke, sen., additions 1883 by Goode and Le Breton, additions and alterations 1918 by R. Miles, additions 1924 by William Lishman Jemison, additions 2010), Goulburn Boys HS 1883–86, Goulburn Girls HS 1883–86, Goulburn HS 1913 (new one b. 1927 by John Crocker Burnett, additions 1954 by P.A. Bissaker, additions 1960, 1967, 1972, 1978), Mulwaree HS 1971 (additions 1979), North Goulburn 1877 (b. by Thomas Lee, additions 1886, additions 1927 by A. Ede), South Goulburn 1881 (b. by William Duncan, d. by William Edmund Kemp, new building b. 1908 by A. Thompson, additions 1908 by Alfred Stephens, additions 1966 and 1977), West Goulburn 1952, Wollondilly 1970; SD Adventist C. 1948, new one; sewage works b. 1915–18, extended 1930, augmentation 1992 and 1996, Ifield sewered 1930; snowstorms 1865, 1867, 1869, 1870, 1876, 1881, 1896, 1898, 1917, 1925; soap-works: Hunt, Mills and Evenis 1886, McGovern's (estab. 1848 by James McGovern, taken over by Anne McGovern), Pioneer Manufacturing Co. Pty Ltd; sock factory (Lindner Quality Socks Pty Ltd) estab. 1987 by Wilfred and Gisela Lindner; squall 1882; storms 1845, 1869, 1879, 1894, 1949; streets kerosene lit 1869, gas lit 1879, electric lit 1914; tanneries: Baxter & Co. Ltd (damaged 1900, fire 1914, burnt down 1938, rebuilt), David Beattie, Beer's, Gillespie & Co. Ltd (incl. bark mill, b. 1918 by Herbert Ernest Ibbotson, d. by Oakden, Ballantyne and Donald Thomas Esplin, closed 1926, sold, renovated and reused 1940, burnt down 1974), Glebe (W.T. Woods & Co.) 1857, Hadfield and Powell, Zachariah Hawkins; TC 1889, closed, sold and reused, new one b. 1902 on new site by R. Wall & Sons, d. by Walter Liberty Vernon, additions 1909 by W. Fielding, reused, new one became a campus of Illawarra Institute of Technology in 1992; telegraph 1858, repairs to office 1864 by Murray and Clegg, additions 1871, new office b. 1881 by Frederick Horn, d. by James Johnstone Barnet; telephone: East Goulburn 1951, Ifield 1947, North Goulburn 1906, South Goulburn 1949, West Goulburn 1947; TX 1891, automatic 1951; typhoid 1889, 1894, 1897,

1905, 1926; Unit. C. (orig. Wes. Meth.) b. 1871 by John Richardson and Pinn Bros, d. by Thomas Rowe, gallery added 1881 by Louis Le Breton, spire damaged 2014 and removed; water pumping station (operated by Appleby Bros beam engine installed by R.T. Ball & Co., restored) b. 1886 by Evans, Son and Lipscomb, additions 1897 and 1918, beam engine replaced 1918 by Kelly and Lewis electric pump assisted by duplex steam pump by G.F. Blake & Co. installed 1897, pumping station rebuilt 1924–32, Galloway boilers decommissioned 1932, Clyde electric pumps installed 1932, well flooded 1947, new electric engines installed 1947 and 1969, closed 1977, reused; weir (Marsden Weir) b. 1889 by G. Gatty and Richard Flook, on Wollondilly R.; Wes. Meth. C.: Goulburn 1843, replaced 1848, enlarged, and North Goulburn b. 1889 by F. Everett and T. Godfrey; wool-scour (Chatfield's); wool stores: Ray Bladwell & Co. 1936 (sold 1942 to Farmers & Graziers', reused), R.D. Gray 1931 (sold to Farmers & Graziers'), P. M'Shane, Winchcombe Carson Ltd (d. and b. 1960 by Stuart Bros Pty Ltd); pop. 655 (1841), 1,171 (1846), 1,518 (1851), 1,779 (1856), 3,241 (1861), 4,453 (1871), 5,881 (1881), *c.*10,000 (1888), 10,916 (1891), *c.*6,000 (1895), 10,612 (1901), 10,187 (1911), 12,715 (1921), 14,849 (1933), 15,380 (1939), 15,991 (1947), 19,122 (1951), 19,183 (1954), 20,544 (1961), 20,871 (1966), 21,568 (1971), 21,735 (1976), 21,755 (1981), 21,552 (1986), *c.*24,000 (1988), *c.*23,500 (1989), 21,451 (1991), 21,293 (1996), 20,884 (2001), 20,127 (2006), 21,092 (2011). (See also Bradfordville.)

Goulburn Plains (*Co. Argyle*) see Goulburn.

Gouldsville (*Co. Northumberland*) 32°35'S. 151°05'E., 8 km W. of Singleton; formerly Wiley's Flat; farming and dairying; FB; PO 1890; school (Glassville till 1891) 1886–1975; telephone 1915; TX 1921–67; pop. 75 (1901), 77 (1911), 104 (1933), 56 (1947), 59 (1954), 58 (1961).

Gourlay (*Co. Auckland*) 36°41'S. 149°40'E., 16 km W. of Bega; school 1886–1913; pop. 60 (1901).

Gowan (*Co. Bathurst*) 33°12'S. 149°22'E., 27 km NE of Orange, on Daddys Hole Ck; airfield.

Gowang (*Co. Gowen*) 31°26'S. 149°06'E., 24 km SW of Coonabarabran; pop. 83 (1933), 60 (1947), 201 (2006).

Gowrie (*Co. Durham*)
see Singleton (*Co. Northumberland*).

Gowrie (*Co. Parry*) 31°19'S. 150°51'E., 21 km E. of Werris Creek; farming; flood 1920; PO 1916–61; Rom. Cath. C. (St Brigid's), destroyed 1928, replacement b. 1929 by Les Wake, d. by Peter Joseph Gannon; school 1884–1902, reopened 1915, additions 1919 by W. Moran, closed 1969, burnt down 1971; storm 1928; telephone 1922; TX 1923, automatic 1976; Union C. 1893, destroyed 1928; Unit. C. (orig. Meth.) b. 1933 by Alan Shelton; pop. 63 (1911), 125 (1933), 81 (1947), 156 (1954), 151 (1961), 251 (2006).

Gowulma (*Co. Gordon*) 32°52'S. 148°35'E., 37 km NW of Molong, on Dilga Ck; goldmine (Dilga Creek) *c.*1900.

Grabben Gullen (*Co. King*) 34°32'S. 149°24'E., 12 km SW of Crookwell; disc. 1820 by James Meehan, village gaz. 1870; farming, dairying, grazing, sapphires; butter factory (Grabben Gullen Butter Factory Ltd) 1897, repairs and renovations 1905 by P. Kennedy; electricity 1955; FB; hailstorm (many houses damaged) 1931; Meth. C. b. 1915 by S. Marks; PO 1891; pound (stock) 1865; quarry; Rom. Cath. C. (St Mary's) 1865 d. by John Gordon, renovated 1886, closed; telephone 1913; TX 1917, automatic 1960; Wes. Meth. C. 1871; pop. 240 (1901), 277 (1911), 154 (1933), 96 (1947), 109 (1954), 150 (1961), 428 (2006), 476 (2011).

Grabine (*Co. Georgiana*) 33°57'S. 149°01'E., 33 km E. of Cowra, on Lake Wyangala; gold (alluvial); pop. 49 (1933).

Graburn (*Co. Urana*) 35°22'S. 146°33'E., 22 km SW of Lockhart; school (Urangeline) 1915–21.

Graces Road (*Co. Raleigh*) 30°36'S. 152°48'E., 6 km NW of Bowraville, on Nambucca R.; telephone 1925.

Gradgery (*Co. Gregory*) 31°14'S. 147°51'E., 58

km SW of Coonamble, on Marthaguy Ck.

Gradys Creek (*Co. Rous*) 28°22'S. 152°58'E., 29 km N. of Kyogle; gale 1933; railway tunnels: Spiral Tunnel No. 1, 210 yds (192 m), 1930 and Spiral Tunnel No. 2, 194 yds (177 m), 1930; sawmill (Seccombe's); pop. 88 (1911), 20 (1933).

Gradys Creek (*Co. Rous*) see also The Risk.

Grafton (*Co. Clarence*) 29°41'S. 152°56'E., 69 km N. of Coffs Harbour, on Clarence R.; (incl. Dovedale, North Grafton, Northmeadow, West Grafton, Westlawn); The Settlement till 1846, then Clarence River till *c.*1849, also known as Woolport; estab. 1841 by Robert Bentley, surveyed 1849 by William Wedge Darke, first lots sold 1851, thrived in 1850s, munic. proc. 1859, town gaz. 1879, designated as chief town of the county, local council replaced 1916 by administrator, city enlarged 1957, city incl. in Clarence Valley 2004; sawmilling, shipbuilding, agric., brewing, maize, potatoes, sugar-cane, oranges, dairying, cattle, horses, pigs, fish, light engineering; agric. implement works: E. Cox & Co., S. Kritsch 1860, Charles Page; ambulance station b. 1936 by Fred and Jack Schmitzer, additions 1953 by Reginald Joseph Want; Angl. C.: first one 1854, demolished 1900, replacement (Christ the King) b. 1880–84 by G.J.T. Lawson and Reynolds & Son, d. by John Horbury Hunt, extended 1934–37 by S.D.C. Kennedy & Bird Pty Ltd, d. by John Horbury Hunt, and Power, Adam and Munnings, restored 1984, and St Luke's (North Grafton) b. 1921 by Richards; Assemblies of God C. (Clarence Valley Community); Bapt. C. 1876–85, new one b. 1885 by Henry Frank Sault, d. by W.H. Waterhouse, remodelled 1943; benevolent asylum, renovated 1910 by Strauss Bros; boiling-down works estab. 1844 by Wilhelm Kirchner and Joseph Sharp, converted to a soap and candle factory, partnership dissolved 1861, sold and converted to a sawmill; breweries: Grafton Brewing Co. Ltd (b. 1950–52 by J. Tye, upgraded 1955, acquired 1961 by Toohey's Ltd, upgraded again 1968, closed 1997) and Robert Muir 1861–63; brickworks: Sam George and John Giese (sold to Richard Palmer, firm became Palmer & Son); bridges: Dobie Street Bridge (orig. Susan Bridge) b. 1862 by John Strauss, jun., over Alumy Ck, Duke Street Bridge b. 1861 by John Cane, Pound Street Bridge b. 1860 by Thomas Cook, new one b. 1891 by J. Crimson, over Alumy Ck, road and rail bridge to South Grafton (with Rall bascule span) fabricated by Clyde Engineering Co. Ltd, erected 1928–32, d. by James Waller Roberts, 1,500 ft (457.2 m), bascule span closed permanently 1970, over Clarence R.; butter factories: Grafton Dairy Co. Ltd (b. 1893 by G. Wunderlich, d. by George Finlay, jun., new one b. 1925 by John Dunton, d. by Waugh and Josephson) and NSW Fresh Food & Ice Co. Ltd (b. 1896 by J.G. Popplewell & Co., d. by W.W. Crawford, taken over 1909 by Grafton Dairy Co. Ltd, bacon factory added 1946, b. by White & Thompson Pty Ltd, d. by A.E. Harrison, taken over 1949 by Dairy Farmers' Co-op. Milk Co. Ltd, amalgamated 1970 with Clarence River Pioneer Dairy Co. Ltd to become Grafton-Ulmarra Co-op. Dairy Co. Ltd, merged 1990 with Norco Co-op. Ltd); carriage-works: Clarence River Coachbuilding Co. (Cox, Greentree and Stevens), Kritsch Bros (estab. 1860 by Sebastian Kritsch), Charles Page 1858 (additions and alterations 1889), Stokes and Englert, Wicks and Reilly, burnt down 1942; caterpillar infestation 1953; cemetery (4,868 graves 1846+) 1869; CH 1847, (second) b. 1861 by John French and Thomas Wray, d. by Alexander Dawson, reused 1880, alterations 1882 by Henry Frank Sault, largely demolished 1974, (third) b. 1878–80 by J.C. Low, d. by James Johnstone Barnet, repairs 1888 by D. McDonald, extended 1935 by Plunkett Bros, restoration 1968 d. by Peter Bridges, restoration 1975 d. by Colin Still; clock tower b. 1909 by Jacob Walter, d. by Sherard M. Becher; clothing factory (Snowball Bros) b. 1944 by White & Thompson Pty Ltd, sold 1953; cordial factories: W. Clare & Co. 1880 (modernised 1884, fire 1897), W.H. Henson 1876, William Southion, Zietsch Bros Pty Ltd 1889; customs-house b. 1862 by John French and Thomas Wray, d. by Alexander Dawson, alterations and repairs 1878 by J. Mayes, demolished 1924; cyclone 1964; drought 1914–15; dye works (in former hotel b. 1856), closed, reused; electricity 1924; engineering works: Hastings Bros, Mackie and Donaldson (partnership dissolved 1887 and J. Donaldson carried on alone while Mackie set up separately), Star Foundry (George and William Mackie) 1887; FB 1879 (station b. 1909 by Strauss Bros, additions 1924 d. by William Hull McNiven); fibrous plaster works (Thomas Pidcock & Sons Pty Ltd) 1938; fires 1860, 1879, 1888, 1903, 1904, 1908, 1909, 1930; flood mitigation project 1967; floods 1839, 1841, 1848, 1857, 1861, 1863, 1864, 1867, 1870, 1876, 1887, 1889, 1890, 1892, 1893, 1921, 1928, 1945, 1946, 1948, 1950, 1952, 1954, 1955, 1956, 1959, 1962, 1963, 1967, 1968, 1972, 1974, 1976, 1980, 1988, 1989, 1996, 2001, 2009, 2011, 2013; flour mill b. 1863 by Daniel Moyes, closed 1873, reused as sawmill; Foursquare Gospel C. (New Life); Free Presb. C. b. 1872 by Mackney and Tombs, new one b. 1941 by White and Thompson; furniture factories: Frank Frederick Charleston 1909, burnt down 1910 and Clarence Furniture Manufacturing Co., burnt down 1916; gales 1900 and 1903; gaol b. 1861 by John French and Thomas Wray, d. by Alexander Dawson, converted for reuse 1896 by C. Baker, demolished, new one b. 1893 by Holloway Bros, d. by Henry Austin Wilshire, alterations 1942, additions 1986, redeveloped 1988, downgraded 1991 to a periodic detention centre, women's wing closed 2011, downgraded 2012 to a remand centre; gasworks (Grafton Lighting Co. Ltd) b. 1884 by W.M. Coward; hailstorms 1945, 1952, 2015; hospital b. 1863–65 by Daniel Moyes, new wings b. 1880 by William Kinnear, d. by J. Moyes, additions 1902, 1905, 1910, additions 1919 by Strauss Bros, additions and alterations 1935 by Condon, additions 1941 by W.P. Mellefont, d. by Cobden Parkes, additions 1941–43 by F.C.W. Powell & Son, additions 1955 by Reginald Joseph Want, additions 1968 and 1979, additions by Bennett Constructions Pty Ltd; ice-cream factories: Clarence Pasteurized Milk Co. and Conrad Kunzle (moved 1882 to new premises); ice works (J.F. Busch); Independent Bapt. C.; jetty 1990; joineries: John Giovanelli, W.K. Mackney & Sons, Stucley and Leighton 1862 (taken over by H.H. Sanders, additions 1915 d. by Strauss Bros), George Wunderlich; levee b. 1969–72; lock-up, additions and alterations 1931 by A. Ayre, repairs 1953 by Reginald Joseph Want; Lutheran C. d. and b. 1876 by H.E. Briggs; match factory (Federal Match Co. Pty Ltd) b. 1942 by H.W. Gibbons, moved 1967 to Great Marlow; mattress factory (E.P. Sampson) 1878; measles epidemics 1920 and 1948; Meth. C. b. 1925 by W. Lambert; milk factory (Peters Creameries Grafton Pty Ltd) b. 1950–54 by White & Thompson Pty Ltd, butter production ceased 1962, powered milk production ceased 1972, closed 1983; monumental stone works (Thomas Matheson) 1893; pneumonia epidemic 1902; PO: Grafton 1849 (new one b. 1874–78 by William Kinnear, d. by James Johnstone Barnet, damaged 1878, alterations 1897 by Strauss Bros, restored 1978), North Grafton 1948, West Grafton 1946; police barracks b. 1873 by William Kinnear; pound (stock) 1858, new one estab. 1953 on new site; powerhouse (Grafton Lighting Co. Ltd); Presb. C. 1858, second one (St Andrew's) b. 1887 by Duncan M'Rae, d. by G. and A.L. M'Credie, re-roofed 1957; PS 1847, reused, new one 1881 d. by James Johnstone Barnet, additions 1890 by Henry Frank Sault, repairs 1897 by Strauss Bros, repairs 1953 by Reginald Joseph Want, new one b. 1975 by R.J. Want Pty Ltd, d. by Colin Still; punt to South Grafton 1859, sunk 1867, new ones 1868 and 1900, later one overhauled 1929, replaced 1932 by bridge, across Clarence R.; railway barracks; railway turntable, 60 ft (18.3 m), closed; reservoir, 7,000,000 gal. (31,822 kl), 1966; Rom. Cath. C. 1867, additions 1877, burnt down 1913, replacement (St Mary's) b. 1914 by C. Fitzgerald, d. by Eaton and Bates; RS 1905, station b. by H.W. Owen, closed 1974; Salv. Army C. 1900, burnt down 1951, replaced 1952; sawmills: F.W. Chapman, G.W. and F.R. Gibbins (fire 1952), Thomas Hewitt 1855 (failed, dismantled 1855), Ingpen and Carter 1871 (acquired 1874 by William Kinnear, taken over by Patrick L. Fraser, bought 1891 by William Fraser and Frank Norrie, became Fraser & Co. Ltd, fires 1907 and 1909, burnt down 1915, rebuilt, burnt down 1930, rebuilt, fire 1937), Owen Hynes (incl. joinery, taken over by T.B. Timms, acquired by J. Notaras & Sons, modernised 1966), Wilhelm Kirchner (acquired by Daniel B. Selman), Pidcock Bros Ltd, E.D. Pike & Co. Ltd; schools: Grafton primary 1852, new one b. 1855, additions 1865, additions 1882 by G. Wunderlich, d. by William Edmund Kemp, additions 1898 by Hermann Schaeffer, additions 1909 by Strauss Bros, additions 1911 by W. Ward, demolished, new buildings 1968 and 1971, Grafton HS 1912 (additions and alterations 1940 by A.C. Palmer & Son, additions 1958, 1963, 1971, 1989, 2014), Westlawn infants 1955 b. by D.J. Donnelly, closed 1963, Westlawn primary 1963; sewerage 1934, augmentation 1989; slipway (Fraser Bros), additions and improvements 1907 by M'Arthur; soap and candle factory (Wilhelm Kirchner and Joseph Sharp), later reused as sawmill; soap-works: Grafton Soap Co. and Frederick Layton; storm 1878; streets gas lit 1884; tannery (Frederick Layton) 1871; TC b. 1954 by D.J. Donnelly, new one 1976, became a campus of North Coast Institute in 1992; tea-tree oil factory (Melacare); telegraph 1862, new office b. 1874–78 by William Kinnear, d. by James Johnstone Barnet, alterations 1897 by Strauss Bros; telephone: North Grafton 1946 and West Grafton 1946; telephone tower 1984; trees (ornamental) planted in streets 1874, 1879, 1907–8 (many by Henry August Volckers); TX 1903, automatic 1969; typhoid 1889, 1890, 1901, 1902, 1907, 1916; Union C.; Unit. C. (orig. Meth.) b. 1922 as church hall, refurbished 1927 as church, modernised 1974; vulcanising works (C.I. Wykes); water supply 1915, augmentation 1990; Wes. Meth. C. b. 1861 by W. Lambert, enlarged 1874 also by Lambert, closed 1927; wharves (incl. one b. 1882 by Denning and Atkinson and one b. by Joseph Sharp); whooping cough epidemics 1928 and 1939 (2 children died); pop. 120 (1846), 193 (1851), 655 (1856), 1,441 (1861, incl. South Grafton), *c.*1,500 (1866), 1,714 (1868), 2,250 (1871), 3,891 (1881), 4,445 (1891), 4,171 (1901), 6,411 (1933), *c.*8,000 (1941), 8,283 (1947), 9,759 (1954), 10,205 (2011).

Grafton City (*Co. Clarence*)
see Grafton South.

Grafton South (*Co. Clarence*) 29°42'S. 152°56'E., 1 km S. of Grafton, on Clarence R.; (incl. Balwarra Heights, Bellevue Heights, Hawthorneville, Musk Valley); settled 1838 by William Phillips, town gaz. 1879, munic. 1896–1957 but became part of City of Grafton; shipbuilding 1839+, dairying, maize, grazing, mining; abattoirs: Fresh Food & Ice Co. (Musk Valley) 1896 d. by J.H. Garratt and OK Meat Co. (bought 1931 by Tancred Bros, taken over 1937 by Grafton Co-op. Dairy Co., taken over 1946 by Clarence River Co-op. Meat Society Ltd, alterations and upgrading 1954 d. by C. Richards, taken over 1980 by R.J. Gilbertson Pty Ltd, closed 1997, sold and reopened 1998, closed again); agric. implement works (D. M'Dermid) 1873; airport, hangar destroyed 1937, airport upgraded 2017; Angl. C. 1879, closed 1908, reused, demolished 1951, new one b. 1908 by F. Salt, d. by Frederick William Conrad Schaeffer, enlarged and renovated 1946 by White & Thompson Pty Ltd, new one (St Matthew's) 2000; Assemblies of God C. (Riverside); Bapt. C. o. 1949 in former Union C. removed from Southgate by Earl G. Shepherd, who re-erected it; brickworks

(Clarence Earthenware & Tile Co.), acquired 1958 by Reginald Joseph Want, later acquired by Noel Mason; bridges: Grafton Bridge, with Rall bascule span fabricated by Clyde Engineering Co. Ltd, erected 1928–32, d. by James Waller Roberts, 1,500 ft (457.2 m), bascule span closed permanently 1970, carries road and rail, new one b. 2016–19 by Fulton Hogan, over Clarence R. and bridge b. 1932 by Bugden and Bugden, rebuilt and enlarged 1953, over Musk Valley Ck; carriage-works: J.F. Foran, D. M'Dermid 1873, Thomas Morrissey, Neale and Layton, T.J. Roberts (relocated 1895), C.A. Schmidt; caterpillar infestation 1953; cemeteries: Clarence lawn (7,055 graves) incl. columbaria, and general (2,084 graves 1852+) 1863; cordial factory (Zuber's); electricity 1924; FB (station b. 1915 by William Robertson); fires 1886, 1887, 1901, 1955; floods 1839, 1841, 1848, 1857, 1861, 1863, 1864, 1867, 1876, 1887, 1889, 1890, 1892, 1893, 1921, 1928, 1945, 1946, 1948, 1950, 1952, 1954, 1955, 1956, 1959, 1962, 1963, 1967, 1968, 1972, 1974, 1976, 1980, 1988, 1989, 1996, 2001, 2013; flour mill (Patrick L. Fraser) 1861, destroyed 1863; hailstorms 1937 and 1952; handle factory (Trojan's); juvenile justice centre (Acmena) 1999; levee 1973; marina 2005; meat canning works (Rivers Preserving Co.); parquetry flooring factory; plywood and veneer factories: Northern Sawmills Pty Ltd 1948 and South Grafton Veneer Co., fire 1953; PO 1866, fire 1884, additions 1892 by William Charles Hanson, new one 1905, additions and alterations 1910 by W.J. Green; poultry processing plant (Clarence River Chicken Co.) b. 1948 by Reginald Joseph Want; pound (stock) 1878; Presb. C. (St Stephen's) b. 1922 by H. Bull, d. by G. Finlay, renovated 1936; PS (incl. lock-up) b. 1894 by Alexander David Henry Scouller, alterations and renovations 1929 by Irving, closed 1962; punt to Grafton 1859, new one 1868, overhauled 1929, replaced by bridge 1932, across Clarence R.; railway accident (person killed) 1915; railway engine shed 1908; railway turntable, 50 ft (15.2 m), replaced 1925, 60 ft (18.3 m); reservoirs: 600,000 gal. (2,727.6 kl), and 7,000,000 gal. (31,822 kl) b. 1948–50 by Thiess Bros (Queensland) Pty Ltd; rifle range (Susan Island) 1887; Rom. Cath. C. 1857, replaced 1882 by James Moyes, new one (St Patrick's) b. 1936 by Fred and Jack Schmitzer, d. by Austin McKay; RS (renamed Grafton City in 1976) 1915, refreshment rooms 1923, station burnt down 1978; sale-yards 1922, new yards 1933; Salv. Army C. 1938; sawmills: Enterprise (Joseph Reid Pty Ltd), General Timber Products, George Mills, Michael M'Enerney, McGee Bros, Northern Sawmills Pty Ltd, Webber's (Clarence River Timber Co., incl. joinery and ice works, burnt down 1915, rebuilt, fire 1929, burnt down 1936, rebuilt, fires 1945 and 1948); schools: Arandin 1916–32, Gillwinga 1971, additions 1978, South Grafton 1867, additions 1903 by F. Sault, new buildings 1917, new building b. 1949 by White & Thompson Pty Ltd, new building b. 1954 by H.H. Thompson, additions 1968 and 1975, South Grafton HS 1964, additions by Bennett Constructions Pty Ltd; SD Adventist C. 1941; sewerage 1940; shipyard (Cole and William Phillips) 1839; sugar mill; telegraph 1877; TX 1905–69; typhoid 1890; Unit. C. (orig. Meth.) b. 1908 by F. Sault, d. by Frederick William Conrad Schaeffer, renovated 1945 by G.W. Shepherd; water supply 1915, augmentation 1967; wharf b. 1882 by Denning and Atkinson; wire works (Jasen) estab. 1953 by Jacobsen Bros; pop. 126 (1851), 638 (1881), 976 (1901), 2,309 (1933), 3,742 (1947), 4,442 (1954), 5,930 (2006), 6,392 (2011).

Gragin (*Co. Burnett*) 29°31'S. 150°45'E., 17 km E. of Warialda; telephone 1953; TX 1954, automatic 1955.

Gragin (*Co. Murchison*) see Koloona.

Graham (*Co. King*) 34°06'S. 148°53'E., 36 km SE of Cowra, on Hovells Ck; FB (station b. 2014); PO 1873–85; school 1884–91 and 1957–66; telephone 1907; TX 1927, automatic 1979; pop. 71 (1911), 76 (1933), 61 (1947), 87 (1954), 67 (1961).

Grahams Flat (*Co. Gough*) 29°52'S. 151°40'E., 16 km S. of Glen Innes.

Grahamstown (*Co. Gloucester*) see Raymond Terrace.

Grahamstown (*Co. Wynyard*) 35°16'S. 148°02'E., 5 km NW of Adelong, on Adelong Ck; goldmining till 1916, dairying, grazing; bridge, replaced 1972; fires 1913 and 1918; flood 1879; gold dredge (Grahamstown Gold Estates, later Davies & Kershaw Gold Estates Pty Ltd) 1901–14; mine (Adelong United Gold Mining Co.); PO 1881; PS, closed 1917; Rom. Cath. C. (St Patrick's) 1900, extended 1911, remodelled and reopened 1926; telephone 1903; TX 1928–68; pop. 298 (1901), 480 (1911), 231 (1933), 146 (1947), 147 (1954), 125 (1961), 222 (2011).

Grahams Valley (*Co. Gough*) 29°53'S. 151°41'E., 17 km S. of Glen Innes, on Beardy Waters; airfield; PO 1886–1912; telephone 1926; TX 1928–55; pop. 102 (1901), 116 (1911), 81 (1933), 60 (1947), 62 (1954), 46 (1961).

Grahweed (*Co. Canbelego*) 31°20'S. 147°00'E., 31 km NW of Nyngan; RS 1909–74.

Gralee (*Co. Cooper*) see Leeton.

Graman (*Co. Arrawatta*) 29°28'S. 150°56'E., 23 km SW of Ashford; farming and grazing; Angl. C. (Community) 1960; cemetery (graves 1875+) 1896; FB; PO 1885; Rom. Cath. C. (St John's) b. 1935 by R. Smith, d. by John Francis O'Connor, sold and reused 1994; school 1888–1906 and 1955–98, sold; telephone 1901; TX 1911, automatic 1988; Wes. Meth. C. 1895; pop. 104 (1911), 113 (1933), 61 (1947), 83 (1954), 88 (1961), 196 (2011).

Grangewood (*Co. Gordon*) see Dubbo West.

Granite Diggings (*Co. Tongowoko*) see Tibooburra.

Granite Rush (*Co. Tongowoko*) see Tibooburra.

Granite Town (*Co. St Vincent*) see Garlandtown.

Grantway (*Co. Nandewar*) 30°46'S. 150°26'E., 28 km W. of Manilla; school 1957–64.

Granuaile (*Co. Rous*) see Bangalow.

Grasmere (*Co. Camden*) see Camden.

Grass Hut (*Co. Gunderbooka*) 29°40'S. 145°53'E., 45 km N. of Bourke; PO 1927; telephone 1898; TX 1928.

Grassmere (*Co. Camden*) see Camden.

Grasstree (*Co. Durham*) 32°17'S. 150°58'E., 9 km E. of Muswellbrook; PO 1874–76; RS 1877–1975.

Grassy Gully (*Co. St Vincent*) 34°51'S. 150°24'E., 18 km W. of Nowra; gold (disc. 1895 by R. Ison and Charles Moffatt); mine 1895; PO 1900–2; stamper battery (10 head) 1900; pop. 66 (1901).

Grassy Head (*Co. Dudley*) 30°48'S. 152°59'E., 11 km NW of South West Rocks; cemetery; earth tremor 1889; flood 1893; pilot station 1862; PO (Beachport); pop. 50 (1954), 57 (1961).

Grassy Hill (*Co. Hunter*) 33°15'S. 150°39'E., 30 km N. of Kurrajong Heights, on Dooli Ck.

Grattai (*Co. Wellington*) 32°39'S. 149°29'E., 12 km SW of Mudgee, on Grattai Ck; goldmining, agric., grazing; Angl. C. (St George's) 1913 d. by Harold Robert Hardwick, closed and reused; Meth. C. 1913; PO 1927–62; quarry (slate) 1899; rifle range 1914; school 1881–1930; telephone 1914; TX 1927, automatic 1980; pop. 165 (1911), 91 (1933), 73 (1947), 78 (1954), 57 (1961), 380 (2011).

Gravel Pits (*Co. Northumberland*) see Teralba.

Gravesend (*Co. Burnett*) 29°35'S. 150°20'E., 23 km W. of Warialda; orig. a teamsters' camp, then farming and grazing; Angl. C. (Holy Trinity) 1909, additions 1925, relocated 1952, closed 2005, sold and reused; bridge b. 1930 by William T. Addison and E. McGregor, 567 ft (172.8 m), over Gwydir R.; cemetery (15 graves 1927–44); electricity 1936; FB (station 2015); floods 1910 and 1946; freezing works (Gwydir Freezing Co. Ltd) 1916, taken over 1921 by Garratt Scandrett Freezing Companies Ltd, acquired 1927 by Amalgamated Rabbit & Skin Export Co. Ltd, burnt down 1936; Meth. C. (removed from Moree) re-erected 1938 by Ephraim Tomkins; PO 1900, new one b. 1912 by Peter Musk; PS 1914, new one b. 1928 by F.D. McKenzie; rabbit freezing works 1940; railway bridge (Pratt steel truss arches) 1901, over Gwydir R.; Rom. Cath. C.

(St Sophie's) 1925, closed, sold and reused; RS 1900, station b. by E.W. Rowland, closed 1979; sawmills: Brooklyn (Henry Fenn), H. Cook & Son, Federal (R. Magee); school 1907 b. by William F. Parsons, new one b. 1914 on new site by Robert and Clarence Wilson, old school relocated 1915, additions to new one 1924 by T.D. McKenzie, additions 1959 and 2010; silo 1934; telegraph 1900; telephone 1913; TX 1914, automatic 1987; water supply augmentation 1970; Wes. Meth. C. 1895; wool-scour; pop. 114 (1901), 394 (1911), 263 (1933), 222 (1947), 267 (1961), 278 (2006), 322 (2011).

Grawin (*Co. Finch*) 29°38'S. 147°39'E., 40 km SW of Lightning Ridge; opals (disc. 1908) and grazing; PO 1927; PS 1883–97; telephone 1927; TX 1928–51; pop. 37 (1933).

Grawlin (*Co. Forbes*) 33°28'S. 148°02'E., 9 km S. of Forbes, on Bundaburrah Ck; pop. 49 (1933), 87 (1947), 285 (2011).

Grawlin Plains (*Co. Forbes*) 33°30'S. 148°05'E., 14 km SE of Forbes; RS 1918–74; silo; telephone 1923.

Grays Crossing (*Co. Raleigh*) 30°44'S. 152°47'E., 14 km W. of Macksville, on Taylors Arm; Meth. C. 1926.

Grays Crossing (*Co. Raleigh*) see also Yarranbella.

Graywood Siding (*Co. Argyle*) 34°35'S. 149°39'E., 20 km N. of Goulburn.

Great Central (*Co. Blaxland*) see Mount Hope South.

Great Lakes (*Co. Gloucester*) see Forster and Tuncurry.

Great Marlow (*Co. Clarence*) 29°40'S. 152°57'E., 3 km N. of Grafton; laid out by William Albert Braylesford Greaves; floods 1890 and 1946; levee 1893, damaged 1946, repaired 1948; match factory (Federal Match Co. Pty Ltd) 1967–84; pop. 116 (1911), 145 (1933), 139 (1947), 100 (1954), 137 (1961), 249 (2006).

Green Arm (*Co. Brisbane*) 32°07'S. 150°12'E., 16 km W. of Merriwa.

Greenbah (*Co. Courallie*) 29°27'S. 149°44'E., 10 km W. of Moree, on Tarran Ck.

Greenbank (*Co. Wynyard*) 35°18'S. 148°00'E., 13 km W. of Adelong, on Nacki Nacki Ck; school 1884–91 and 1898–1913.

Greenbank Island (*Co. Rous*) see Tweed Heads.

Greenburn (*Co. Macquarie*) see Byabarra.

Green Cape (*Co. Auckland*) 37°16'S. 150°03'E., 26 km SE of Eden, on Tasman Sea; cemetery (Ly-ee Moon); lighthouse (kerosene-powered light), 68 ft (20.7 m), b. 1881–83 of concrete by Albert W. Aspinall, d. by James Johnstone Barnet, closed 1962, reused, replaced by lattice tower (solar-powered light); PO 1892–1922; telegraph 1882; telephone 1898.

Green Creek (*Co. Brisbane*) 31°47'S. 151°02'E., 18 km E. of Murrurundi; pop. 57 (1933).

Greendale (*Co. Auckland*) 36°36'S. 149°51'E., 10 km N. of Bega; flood 1956.

Greendale (*Co. King*) 34°42'S. 149°08'E., 25 km NE of Yass, on Felled Timber Ck; school (Felled Timber Creek) 1881–1920, bought by Merv Offley; Unit. C. (orig. Prim. Meth.) b. 1863 by Wilmont, repairs 1911 and 1923 by P.R. Thorn, porch added 1930 by Percy Thorn, re-floored 1946 by C. Veness, closed 1965, restored 1972 by Tom Maguire, reopened for occasionl reuse, and graveyard.

Greenethorpe (*Co. Monteagle*) 34°00'S. 148°24'E., 25 km SE of Grenfell, on Tyagong Ck; Iandra Siding till 1908; estab. and founded 1908 by George Henry Greene and laid out 1909 by Capt. William Pomeroy Crawford Greene; wheat, oats, barley, grazing, rape seed, lupins, sunflowers; Angl. C. (St James's) b. 1910–12, additions 1916, and columbarium; bridge (4 spans) b. 1913 by John R. Hyland, over Tyagong Ck; bushfire 1932; chaff mills: Greenethorpe (NSW) Primary Producers 1924 and Amos Southwell; electricity 1930; FB; fires 1919, 1926, 1935, 1968; Meth. C. 1908; PO 1908; PS 1912; rifle range 1910; Rom. Cath. C. b. 1912 by Joseph Robert Throwden, demolished, new one (St Columba's) b. 1933 by William Simpson, d. by Norman Leslie Lipman; RS (Iandra till 1908) 1901, station built by F.W. Kinch, closed 1975, station removed 1985; school (Iandra till 1909) 1906, new one b.

1923, additions 1928; silo 1926; tornado 1979; TX 1913, automatic 1983; Unit. C. (orig. Meth.) b. 1928 by H.R. Blackett & Son, d. by Arthur Lanyon Clark; water supply 1921; whooping cough epidemic 1943; pop. 277 (1911), 352 (1933), 279 (1947), 248 (1954), 213 (1961), 320 (2011).

Greenfield Farm (*Co. Murray*) 34°55'S. 149°06'E., 19 km SE of Yass, on Yass R.; farming and grazing; PO 1874; telephone 1921; TX 1924, automatic 1967.

Green Forest (*Co. Rous*) 28°59'S. 153°21'E., 7 km E. of Coraki; farming and dairying; PO 1927; pop. 23 (1933), 73 (1947).

Greengrove (*Co. Ashburnham*) 33°16'S. 148°40'E., 10 km S. of Manildra, on Mandagery Ck; airfield; quarry, disused; school 1881–99.

Greengrove (*Co. Northumberland*) 33°23'S. 151°09'E., 21 km W. of Ourimbah, on Mangrove Ck; Angl. C. (St Peter's) b. by James Everingham, replaced 1910, and graveyard (47 graves 1850–1981); telephone 1917; TX 1928–69.

Green Gully (*Co. Bathurst*) see Milburn Creek.

Green Gully (*Co. Wellington*) 32°47'S. 149°40'E., 28 km W. of Rylstone; pop. 25 (1933).

Greenhill (*Co. Dudley*) 31°04'S. 152°48'E., 4 km NW of Kempsey, on Macleay R.; farming; plywood and veneer factory (Daisy Plains Sawmill Pty Ltd) 1951; PO 1877; punt b. 1881 by Callen Bros; quarry; reservoir; sawmill (Mitchell Bros), removed 1913 from Hickeys Creek; school 1890 b. by William Neal; telephone 1897; TX 1915–28; wharf b. 1885 by G. and T. Lawson; pop. 166 (1901), 178 (1911), 322 (1933), 215 (1947), 366 (1954), 254 (1961), 347 (1991), 415 (1996), 685 (2011).

Green Hills (*Co. Bligh*) 32°08'S. 149°48'E., 35 km NE of Gulgong, on Currycurryall Ck; flour mill (Charles Lawn) 1872; quarry; pop. 29 (1933).

Green Hills (*Co. Northumberland*) see Morpeth.

Greenhills (*Co. Northumberland*) see Maitland East.

Greenhills (*Co. Rous*) 28°21'S. 153°24'E., 2 km S. of Murwillumbah, on Tweed R.; dairying; gale 1892; fibrous plaster works (H.A. Diprose); quarry; sawmill (Sly Bros) 1932; pop. 20 (1933), 103 (1947).

Green Hills (*Co. Wynyard*) 35°22'S. 148°02'E., 8 km SW of Adelong, on Nacka Nacka Ck.

Greenhills (*Co. Wynyard*) see Sharps Creek.

Greenland (*Co. Durham*) see Greenlands.

Greenlands (*Co. Durham*) 32°23'S. 151°11'E., 20 km N. of Singleton, on Goorangoola Ck; formerly Greenland; dairying; PO 1927; telephone 1912; TX 1926; pop. 85 (1933), 74 (1954), 68 (1961), 171 (2006).

Greenleigh (*Co. Murray*) see Queanbeyan.

Greenmantle (*Co. Georgiana*) 33°58'S. 149°05'E., 40 km E. of Cowra, on Davis Ck; PO 1875–1918.

Greenmount (*Co. Auckland*) 36°48'S. 149°40'E., 21 km SW of Bega; butter factory (John Farraher).

Green Pidgeon (*Co. Rous*) 28°29'S. 153°05'E., 18 km NE of Kyogle, on Fawcetts Ck; farming; PO 1927; sawmill (Moore Bros) 1943–71; school 1928–75; telephone 1923; TX 1923; pop. 137 (1933), 125 (1947), 164 (1954), 135 (1961).

Green Point (*Co. Dudley*) 30°54'S. 152°36'E., 31 km NW of Kempsey, on Macleay R.

Green Point (*Co. Gloucester*) 32°15'S. 152°31'E., 7 km S. of Forster, on Wallis Lake; FB; pop. 430 (1991), 522 (1996), 526 (2001), 568 (2006), 587 (2011).

Green Point (*Co. Northumberland*) 33°27'S. 151°21'E., 4 km SE of Gosford, on Brisbane Water; (incl. Lindens Flat); farming and orchards; Bapt. C.; PO 1916–41; 2 reservoirs; telephone 1906; TX 1914, automatic 1965; 2 wharves; pop. 55 (1901), 90 (1911), 88 (1933), 97 (1947), 181 (1954), 270 (1961), 6,462 (2006), 6,577 (2011).

Green Point Beach (*Co. Northumberland*) see Pearl Beach.

Greenridge (*Co. Richmond*) 28°54'S. 153°07'E., 8 km SE of Casino; maize, sugar-cane, then dairying, grazing, pigs, fodder crops; Angl. C. (St Columba's) 1899–1952, demolished 1955; broom factory (Tom Johnson); creamery (NSW Creamery Butter Co.) 1889, removed from Coraki; gale 1930; mouse plague 1917; PO 1891; quarry; school (South Casino till 1911) 1880, repairs 1882 by J. Gould, new building b. 1885 by G. Hughes, closed 1974; storm 1927; telephone 1906; TX 1924, automatic 1952; wharf b. 1898 by A. Cameron; pop. 76 (1901), 196 (1911), 166 (1933), 153 (1947), 138 (1954), 132 (1961).

Greens (*Co. Northumberland*) 33°26'S. 151°02'E., 29 km W. of Gosford, on Hawkesbury R.; drought 1826; fire 1826; floods 1806, 1867, 1887, 1893, 1933, 1934, 1938, 1942, 1947, 1949; Wes. Meth. C. (Lower Hawkesbury) b. 1855 by Greentree Bros, closed 1963, reused 1967, restored.

Green's Gunyah (*Co. Urana*) see Lockhart.

Green Swamp (*Co. Gough*) see Inverell.

Green Swamp (*Co. Roxburgh*) see Walang.

Green Swamp (*Co. Wellington*) see Cullenbone.

Green Swamp Road (*Co. Denison*) 35°33'S. 145°45'E., 12 km NW of Berrigan; Meth. C. 1950; quarry; RS 1896–1975; school 1957–65; TX (automatic).

Green Tree (*Co. Parry*) 31°15'S. 151°05'E., 22 km SE of Tamworth; telephone 1929; TX 1929.

Greenvale (*Co. Urana*) 35°02'S. 146°32'E., 27 km NW of Lockhart; Meth. C. o. 1913 (removed from Boree Creek); PO 1909; storm 1925; telephone 1915; Union C. 1913; pop. 53 (1933), 58 (1947), 53 (1954).

Green Valley (*Co. Inglis*) 30°46'S. 151°15'E., 46 km NE of Tamworth, on Carlisles Gully.

Green Valley (*Co. Inglis*) see also Townsend.

Greenwattle (*Co. Georgiana*) see Thalaba.

Green Wattle (*Co. Westmoreland*) 33°58'S. 150°00'E., 31 km SE of Oberon.

Green Wattle Flat (*Co. Roxburgh*) see Wattle Flat.

Greenwell Point (*Co. St Vincent*) 34°55'S. 150°44'E., 6 km S. of Shoalhaven Heads, on Crookhaven R.; former port, oysters (estab. by George Haiser) *c.*1883+, fishing 1945+, tourism; airport 1932; electricity 1941; FB (station b. 1998); flood 1867; PO 1879; reservoir 1955; school 1878, new buildings b. 1893 by H.C. Wolf and S. Elliott, repairs 1908 by George Albert Leggo, closed 1939, reopened 1952, additions 2010; streets electric lit 1941; telegraph 1878; TX 1915, automatic 1960; Union C. (Berry Memorial) d. and b. 1891 by William A. Isley & Sons, renovated 1942, re-roofed 1960; water reticulation 1959; wharves: one b. 1829 by Alexander Berry, govt one b. 1880 by Henry Bryce, fishermen's wharves 1939 and 1980; pop. 19 (1841), *c.*50 (1866), 117 (1911), 21 (1933), 258 (1954), 368 (1961), 373 (1971), 768 (1976), 944 (1981), 1,027 (1986), 1,130 (1991), 1,217 (1996), 1,274 (2001), 1,276 (2006), 1,198 (2011).

Greenwich Park (*Co. Argyle*) 34°35'S. 149°56'E., 27 km NE of Goulburn; farming and grazing; Angl. C., first one demolished, replacement (Christ) 1934; PO 1876; school 1883–92 and 1899; telephone 1916; TX 1928, automatic 1953; pop. 54 (1901), 75 (1911), 51 (1933).

Greenwood (*Co. Arrawatta*) 29°44'S. 151°01'E., 11 km NW of Inverell; RS 1902, station b. by J. Bromley and J.N. Holloway, closed 1972.

Greenwood (*Co. Selwyn*) 35°50'S. 148°05'E., 9 km SE of Tumbarumba; school 1885–1911.

Gregadoo (*Co. Wynyard*) 35°13'S. 147°25'E., 13 km S. of Wagga Wagga, on Coxs Gully; soldiers' settlement; farming and grazing; flour mill (water powered, Robert Nixon); hurricane 1878; PO 1927; school 1889–1969; telephone 1925; TX 1925, automatic 1953; winery (John and Charles Nixon); pop. 109 (1911), 136 (1933), 126 (1947), 132 (1954), 134 (1961), 347 (2006).

Greg Greg (*Co. Selwyn*) 36°03'S. 148°03'E., 31 km S. of Tumbarumba; pound (stock), abolished 1891; PS 1875; school 1881–87 and 1957–68; telephone 1953; TX 1953, automatic 1960; pop. 22 (1933), 80 (1954), 79 (1961).

Greghamstown (*Co. Bathurst*) 33°28'S. 149°15'E., 6 km SE of Millthorpe; farming; Angl. C. (St Matthew's) 1901–81; PO 1927–31; school 1875 b. by John Renny and William Cosgrove, d. by George Allen Mansfield, additions 1882 by Ebenezer Davis, renovated 1912 by W.W. Nixon, closed 1947; snowstorm 1937; telephone 1928; TX 1928; pop. 157 (1901), 103 (1933), 93 (1947), 70 (1954).

Gregra (*Co. Ashburnham*) 33°11'S. 148°46'E., 7 km E. of Manildra; Gregra Railway Station till 1922; farming; PO 1907; RS 1893, station b. by Frederick Lemm, jun. and Thomas Edward Spencer, closed 1974; school 1879–1921 and 1938–60; pop. 59 (1911), 81 (1933), 94 (1947), 53 (1954), 59 (1961), 201 (2006).

Gregra Railway Station (*Co. Ashburnham*) see Gregra.

Greigs Flat (*Co. Auckland*) 36°58'S. 149°52'E., 5 km SW of Pambula Beach, on Yowaka R.; oysters and farming; 2 mines (pyrophyllite); PO 1891; telephone 1916; TX 1928; pop. 101 (1901), 109 (1911), 67 (1933), 65 (1947), 73 (1954), 56 (1961), 323 (2011).

Greigs Flat (*Co. Auckland*) see also Yowaka.

Grenelle (*Co. Bland*) 34°10'S. 147°34'E., 31 km N. of Temora, on Duck Ck; bridge over Duck Ck; school o. 1959 (in building removed from Chellington), closed 1969, later burnt down.

Grenfell (*Co. Monteagle*) 33°54'S. 148°10'E., 49 km W. of Cowra, on Emu Ck; orig. Emu Creek and Weddin Mountains, then Weddin till 1866; settled by John Wood and sons 1833, surveyed 1867 by Edward Twynam, first lots sold 1867, munic. 1883–1975; mining (gold disc. 1866 by Cornelius O'Brien, gold rush 1866–70) 1866–73, wheat, sheep, cattle till 1900, horses, oats and hay 1900+, flour milling, barley, maize, sorghum, lupins, safflower, potatoes, fruit, canola, peas, wine, honey, dairying, sawmilling; aeroplane crash (2 killed) 1929; ambulance station o. 1949 (in converted bank); Angl. C.: first one 1867, bought and demolished 1902 by T. Todd, new one (Holy Trinity) b. 1877–79, d. by John Kirkpatrick, vestry b. 1928 by W. Guthrie & Son, d. by J. Stuart Williams; Assemblies of God C. (Family); brewery (Union Brewery, estab. by Thomas E. Fisher and James Frazer) 1889–1914; bushfires 1884, 1900, 1905; carriage-works (W.S. Thomson), burnt down 1896; cemetery 1867; CH 1867, new one (incl. lock-up) b. 1874–77 by William Sharpe, d. by James Johnstone Barnet, additions 1879 by J.M. Hewen; Chinese joss house; clothing factory (Rajer Manufacturing Co.) 1949; Cong. C. 1867, replaced 1876, destroyed 1877; cordial factories: Reginald Astley (relocated 1951), Grenfell Cold Stores & Cordial Co., M'Callum's (burnt down 1888), Thomas Nelson 1857 (sold 1866 to Thomas E. Fisher and James Frazer, closed), Rich and Pritchard 1876; cyanide plants: Enterprise (b. 1897 by James O'Connor, d. by William Henry Sadlier), Irvine & Co. 1898 (burnt down 1899), Wilson & Co. 1896; diphtheria 1903; dust storm 1901; earth tremors 1871, 1934, 1938, 1949, 2001; electricity 1927; engineering works (Bromar Engineering) estab. 1990 by Mark Liebich; eucalyptus oil distillery; 2 FB (first one 1899, incl. station b. 1902, new one 1929, renovated 2013); fires 1875, 1878, 1879, 1881, 1887, 1888, 1896; flour mills: G. Black & Sons, Challenge (burnt down, replaced 1901, severely damaged 1912, closed), Great Western Milling Co. Ltd, Grenfell Joint Stock Flour Mill Co. (b. 1875 by Henry Hayes, bought 1876 by Charles John Ingrey and C. Mattison, upgraded and reopened 1897 by Henry Allsopp, burnt down 1898), Grenfell Roller Mills (b. 1901 by William Guthrie for Rod and G.H. Black), George Jacobs, D. Pyne and Watts 1884, J.J. Sullivan Pty Ltd 1904, reused by Lachlan Fertilizers; foundry (D. Reece), removed 1868; gale 1923; gasworks 1910; grasshopper infestation 1934; heatwave 1905; hospital b. 1867 by Holmes and Martin, d. by Backhouse, closed 1878, reopened 1880, replacement b. 1890 by R. McKinnon, d. by Walter Liberty Vernon, additions 1900, 1914, 1924, 1926, 1941, 1946, 1948, 1958, 1986; ice works (Rankin's) 1899; measles epidemic 1888; mines: Abbly's, Band of Hope, Britannia, Connelly's, Consols (gold) 1866–80 and 1931–32, Enterprise, Frenchman's Welcome, Golden Point, Homeward Bound (disc. by Engel Gravenmaker), Hoskins' (manganese) 1915–41, Lawson's Gully (gold) *c.*1880 and 1932, Lucknow (Wilson's, reef disc. by Eaton), Main Grenfell (gold) *c.*1875–1876, W. Moran, Oriental, Outward Bound, Payne's (tin), Prussian, Quartz Hill (gold) *c.*1895 and 1935, Quigley's, Result, Star Gully (gold), Victory (O'Brien's), Welcome, White Rose, Who'd a Thought It, Young Farmer (gold) *c.*1900 and 1935–38, Young O'Brien (gold) 1875–95 and 1932–35; monumental stone works: W.T. Jones and J.P. Neagle; mouse plague 1917; PO 1866, additions 1877 by William Sharp, additions 1884, repairs 1890 by Brown and Hill, alterations and repairs 1903 by Rigby Bros, alterations 1912, replaced 1924; powerhouse (Grenfell Electric Light Co.); Presb. C. (St Andrew's) b. 1871 by George Grimm, replaced 1897, re-roofed 1902, renovated 1926; Prim. Meth. C. 1867, closed; PS b. 1877 by William Sharp; railway turntable (William Sellers & Co.), 50 ft (15.2 m); reservoir (concrete), 300,000 gal. (1,363.8 kl); Rom. Cath. C. 1867, burnt down 1875, replaced 1877, new one (St Joseph's) b. 1907 by James Michael Durning, d. by John Job Copeman, additions 1924–27 d. by William John Monks; RS 1901, station closed and reused; sale-yards; Salv. Army C. b. 1904 by James Michael Durning, burnt down, replaced 1924 by J. Liscombe; sawmills: Robert Bolton, W.G. Campbell, Duncan's Holdings Ltd, Charles Flood, McClymont and Callis, fire 1930; school 1867, new one b. 1871 by Sharp, Guidice and Howes, additions 1872 by William Sharp, remodelled 1880, extended 1886 by S. Cookman, additions 1888, additions 1903 by E.P. Frost & Co., additions 1908 by C.B. Smith, additions 1919 by Thomas Norman Grimsley, new building b. 1931 and extended 1939, fire 1940, additions 1955 by Robinson, additions 1958, 1967, 1969, and Henry Lawson HS 1965, new school 1973 on new site; SD Adventist C. 1935; sewage works; silo 1926; snow 1901; stamper batteries: Aubrey's (10 head), Bevan and Allsop (12 head), Donald Campbell (10 head), Closeburn (10 head), Hill and Hall (10 head), Koh-i-noor (Joseph and George Rich, 12 head), McConnell & Co. (10 head), Mattheson and Clyburn (10 head), May and Vaughan (10 head), James Parker (20 head), Victoria (Charles Cunningham's 15 head), Peter Wellington (12 head), J.B. Wood (20 head); storms 1877 and 1912; streets gas lit 1912, electric lit 1927; tannery; TC (a campus of Western Institute); telegraph 1867, additions to office 1877 by William Sharp, additions 1884, repairs 1890 by Brown and Hill, alterations and repairs 1903 by Rigby Bros; TX 1907, automatic 1967; Unit. C. (orig. Meth.) b. 1928 by W. Guthrie & Son, d. by Arthur Lanyon Clark; water supply 1932, reticulation 1957; Wes. Meth. C. 1867, closed, sold 1877 to William Irvine and dismantled, replacement b. 1888 by J.B. Gough, closed, reused, later demolished; pop. 1,657 (1871), 1,575 (1881), *c.*1,700 (1887), 745 (1891), *c.*746 (1895), 212 (1901), 3,007 (1911), 1,192 (1921), 2,488 (1933), 2,425 (1947), 2,584 (1954), *c.*2,640 (1959), 2,360 (1961), 2,377 (1966), 2,192 (1971), 2,156 (1976), 2,070 (1981), 1,986 (1986), 2,037 (1991), 1,956 (1996), 1,928 (2001), 1,994 (2006), 1,996 (2011).

Gresford (*Co. Durham*) 32°26'S. 151°32'E., 21 km W. of Dungog, on Paterson R.; orig. maize, wheat, grapes, turnips, tobacco, then timber and sawmilling, now cattle and dairying; Angl. C. 1849, demolished 1898, replacement (St Anne's) b. 1898 by Walter Barrett, d. by John Charles Luscombe, and graveyard (433 graves 1851+), incl. columbaria; brickworks; bridge b. 1883 by B. Henry, new ones 1911 and 1936, over Paterson R.; bushfire 1958; butter factory (Bowthorne Co-op. Butter Factory Ltd) 1907, new one 1908, burnt down 1912, replacement b. 1913 by Litchfield and Howard, d. by James Warren Scobie, condemned 1928; electricity 1937; FB 1953 (station b. 1967 by Dark and Dean, extended 1999); fire 1930; flood 1875; hospital 1956–84; PO 1841; pound (stock) 1844; reservoir 1954; sawmill (Thomas R. Hancock), closed 1963; school 1879, new one b. 1882 by D. Gardiner, additions 1909 by William Frederick Gazzard, additions 1970 and 2010; telephone 1884; TX 1915; water reticulation 1954; winery (Cawarra Estate, Henry Lindeman) 1843–1918; pop. *c*.400 (1891), 267 (1901), 512 (1911), 186 (1933), 234 (1947), 230 (1954), 135 (1961), 305 (2011).

Gresford East (*Co. Durham*) 32°26'S. 151°33'E., 19 km W. of Dungog, on Allyn R.; farming and dairying; bushfire 1958; butter factory (Gresford Butter Factory Co. Ltd), reused; cemetery (117 graves 1937+), incl. columbarium; CH b. 1885 by A. M'Laren, reused; Cong. C. 1903, extended 1953; flour mill (Charles Boydell), destroyed 1857; ice works (Ralph Stein); PO 1901, new one b. 1938; PS d. by James Johnstone Barnet; quarry; Rom. Cath. C. (St Helen's) b. 1867 by Thomas Hyndes, d. by Edmund Thomas Blacket, renovated 1883, and graveyard (258 graves 1875+); telephone 1900; tobacco factories: J. Beattie and M'Cormick's; TX 1912, automatic 1977; winery (Glendonbrook, Andrew Leembruggen); pop. 326 (1933), 298 (1947), 302 (1954), 271 (1961), 236 (1971), 290 (2006), 315 (2011).

Gresham (*Co. Bathurst*) 33°34'S. 149°24'E., 14 km E. of Blayney; airfield (1 km W.); quarry; RS 1891–1974.

Greswick (*Co. Gloucester*) 32°38'S. 151°45'E., 20 km NE of Maitland; school 1895–1910.

Greta (*Co. Northumberland*) 32°41'S. 151°23'E., 5 km SE of Branxton, on Anvil Ck; (incl. Harpers Hill and Illalong laid out by Anvil Creek Mining Co., lots sold 1874); Anvil Creek till 1886; surveyed 1842 by George Boyle White, village gaz. 1843, munic. 1890–1933; mining (coal and oil-shale disc. 1864 by Thomas Frost) and vineyards; Angl. C. 1876, replaced 1913 by W. Bailey, damaged 1914, new one (St Mary's) b. 1926 on new site by Thorpe and Shehan, d. by J.W. and W.H. Scobie, closed 2011, sold 2013, reused; bridge over Anvil Ck; bushfire 1895; causeway across Sawyers Ck; cemetery (900 graves 1879+) 1876; CH b. 1896 by Benjamin George Pearce, d. by Walter Liberty Vernon, closed 1935, reused; collieries: Anvil Creek (estab. 1861 by William Farthing, fire 1871 and closed, reopened 1872, acquired 1873 by Anvil Creek Coal Mining Co., fire 1877 and closed, reopened and closed 1881, acquired and reopened 1886 by New Anvil Creek Colliery Co. and renamed New Anvil Creek Colliery, sold 1892 to A. Thomas et al., closed 1902, acquired 1908 by William Humphrey and renamed Central Greta Colliery, man killed 1913, boiler explosion 1915, closed 1932, razed), Farthing's Pit (William Farthing) 1862–64, Greta (estab. 1873 by Greta Coal & Shale Mining Co., o. 1874, taken over 1876 by E. Vickery & Son, acquired 1888 by Greta Coal Co. Ltd, fire 1884, acquired 1895 by Greta Coal Co., creep 1898, fire 1900 killed 5 men and mine closed, acquired 1900 by Mahlon Clark Cowlishaw, reopened 1923, demolished), Greta Extended No. 1 (estab. 1937 by Garnett and Henry Hodges, closed 1938, razed), Greta Extended No. 2 also known as Hodges' Pit (estab. 1938 by Garnett and Henry Hodges, sold 1942 to A.F. Lyons, closed 1945, defunct), Little Anvil Creek, Little Greta (estab. 1931 by W.H. Burdon, closed and reopened 1932, closed 1934, reopened and closed 1937, razed), Newfield Open-Cut (estab. 1948 as New Greta Open-Cut by Joint Coal Board, closed 1950), New Greta (o. 1908 by Ebbw Coal Mining Co. Ltd as Ebbw Main Colliery, acquired 1909 by A. Kethel & Co. Ltd, acquired 1911 by Broxburn Coal & Shale Co. and renamed Broxburn-Maitland, acquired 1917 by Excelsior Colliery & Coke Works Ltd and renamed Broxburn-Leconfield, renamed 1918, fire 1924, closed 1932, leased 1934 to syndicate, closed 1935, works sold 1936), Ringwood (estab. 1953 by Alan M. Drayton, closed 1957, razed), Whitburn (estab. 1902 by Mark North and John Rylatt as North Greta Colliery, bought 1907 by Newcastle Coal Mining Co. and renamed, fire 1915, man killed 1915, closed 1928, reopened 1929, closed 1930, reopened 1938, fire 1947, closed 1948, largely demolished), Whitburn No. 2 (o. 1938 by Newcastle Coal Mining Co., closed 1939); cordial factory (Gibson Bros); dam (Anvil Creek Colliery) 1874; earth tremor 1902; FB; fires 1892 and 1901; gale 1914; hailstorm 1875; measles epidemics 1898 and 1949; military camp 1939–45, largely b. by Hewitt and Powe, reused as migrant hostel 1949–60 (incl. St Anthony's Rom. Cath. Chapel, sold 1963); milk factory (Morgan's Dairy); miners' strikes 1878, 1888, 1889, 1891, 1895, 1896, 1919, 1921, 1922, 1923, 1924, 1928, 1952; PO 1874, new one b. 1912, reused; pound (stock) 1843; Presb. C. b. 1890 by Frederick Claffer, closed 1926, reused, destroyed 1959; Prim. Meth. C. b. 1875 by John Hartley, new one 1887 d. by James Warren Scobie; PS (incl. lock-up) b. 1879 by Charles Mack, additions 1882 by J. Libley, repairs 1896 by Benjamin George Pearce, damaged 1905, closed, sold and reused; quarry (Illalong) 1914–55; railway workshops (Pacific National) 2012; rifle range b. 1897 by Dann and Walker; Rom. Cath. C. (St Mary's) 1882, demolished, new one (St Catherine's) b. 1962 by Joseph Redhead, d. by J. Gannon; RS (Farthings till 1878) 1869, new station b. 1890 by W. Wilson; sawmill (F. King); school 1875 b. by Peter Cooke, reused, new building b. 1878 by James Pritchard, d. by John Wiltshire Pender, extended 1890, repairs 1893 by James Russell, repairs 1913 by R.F. Harper, additions and alterations 1922 by F. Paroz, additions 2010 by Kingston Building Aust. Pty Ltd; storms 1899, 1905, 1959; telegraph 1894; TX 1910, automatic 1981; typhoid 1892, 1896 (man died), 1898, 1902; Unit. C. (orig. Wes. Meth.) b. 1888 by B. Hodgson & Son, d. by James Warren Scobie, closed, sold 2017, reused; Wes. Meth. C. 1874, enlarged 1885; whooping cough epidemic 1899; wineries: Molly's Cradle Wines Pty Ltd 2000 and Tellas Wines; pop. 570 (1881), *c.*700 (1886), 1,751 (1891), 861 (1901), 918 (1911), 1,381 (1933), 1,135 (1947), 3,012 (1954, incl. 1,626 in migrant hostel), 1,454 (1961), 2,544 (1966, incl. Branxton), 2,466 (1971, incl. Branxton), 2,485 (1976, incl. Branxton), 2,849 (1981, incl. Branxton), 3,208 (1986, incl. Branxton), 3,414 (1991, incl. Branxton), 3,734 (1996, incl. Branxton), 3,805 (2001, incl. Branxton), 4,678 (2006, incl. Branxton), 5,190 (2011, incl. Branxton).

Greta East (*Co. Northumberland*) see Gillieston Heights.

Greta Main (*Co. Northumberland*) 32°53'S. 151°17'E., 2 km N. of Paxton; bushfires 1968 and 1969; colliery (Maitland Main) estab. 1921 by Wyalla-Maitland Coal Co. Ltd as Wyalla-Maitland Colliery, acquired 1922 by Cessnock-Main Collieries Ltd and renamed Cessnock-Main Colliery, acquired 1923 by Gretamain Collieries Ltd and renamed Gretamain Colliery, acquired 1929 by Maitland Main Collieries Pty Ltd and renamed, strikes 1938, 1942, 1943, 1944, 1947, washery installed 1960, colliery closed 1969, reopened 1970, abandoned 1972, shaft sealed 1973, largely razed 1976 except for washery, derelict bath-house and reused colliery office; PO 1925–64; railway (colliery); sawmill (Arthur Craft), moved to Millfield; telephone 1925; pop. 131 (1933), 95 (1947), 79 (1954), 59 (1961).

Greta North (*Co. Northumberland*) see Leconfield.

Grevillia (*Co. Rous*) 28°27'S. 152°50'E., 26 km NW of Kyogle, on Richmond R.; village gaz. 1914; timber and farming; Angl. C. (St Peter's, Walter and Elizabeth Lever Memorial) 1936; electricity 1960; flood 1947; PO 1913; sawmills: Fraser & Co., and Edward Munro and Walter Lever 1912–29; school 1929, additions 1936 by W. Tyrrell, additions 1960, closed 2010, sold; telephone 1912; TX 1916, automatic 1968; veneer factory (Munro and Lever's), removed from Kyogle, closed 1983; pop. 278 (1933), 172 (1947), 146 (1954), 157 (1961). (See also Old Grevillia.)

Grey West (*Co. Kennedy*) 32°55'S. 148°15'E., 27 km N. of Parkes.

Griffins Crossing (*Co. Phillip*) 32°22'S. 149°35'E., 6 km E. of Gulgong, on Cooyal Ck.

Griffith (*Co. Cooper*) 34°17'S. 146°02'E., 151 km NW of Wagga Wagga, on Main Canal; (incl. Bagtown or Crowther's Camp 1910–22, Collina, Driver, East Griffith, Mayfair,

Mooreville, North Griffith, Pioneer, South Griffith, West Griffith, Wickhams Hill); farms available 1912, d. 1914 by Walter Burley Griffin, settled mostly by Italian immigrants, town gaz. and lots sold 1916, first building 1920, city proc. 1987; dairying 1912+, then wheat, barley, oats, sheep, cattle, vineyards 1913+, onions, orchards (oranges 1917+), rice 1924+, cotton, eggs, fruit processing, light engineering; abattoir (Griffith Abattoirs Pty Ltd) 1958; airport (6 km N.) 1948, terminal upgraded 2013; ambulance station 1959; Angl. C.: St Alban the Martyr b. 1955 by Hutcherson Bros Pty Ltd, d. by Louis Reginald Williams, and St James's 1907, moved 1913 to Hanwood; Apostolic C. (One in Christ); Bapt. C. 1925, closed, relocated and reused 1972, new one 1973; bio-mass conversion facility (Ricegrowers' Co-op. Ltd); brickworks (T. Berry); bridge 1979 over Main Canal; cannery (Griffith Growers' Outlet Pty Ltd, renamed Griffith Cannery Pty Ltd in 1943), reused 1950; carriage-works: A.G. Hams and R.J. Thomson; cemeteries: Bagtown (54 burials 1912–22), closed 1923, restored 1988 and Griffith 1920; CH 1929, additions 1985, upgraded 2013; cheese factory (WC & IC) 1916–20, reused; Christ. Revival Crusade C. (renamed Life Source C. in 2006); clothing factory (Oxenham and Oxenham); concrete plant (Bruno Altin & Co. Pty Ltd) estab. 1954 by Bruno Altin; cordial factories: Brown & Co., Joe Burgess (bought 1928 by Charles and Olive Pritchard), Denham & Co.; cyclone 1925; droughts 1910 and 1911; dust storms 1912, 1913, 2018; electricity (WC & IC) 1913; engineering works (Colla Bros); FB (station b. 1951); fibrous plaster works (F.E. Hodson, taken over 1948 by G. Thomas); floods 1924, 1934, 1939, 1944, 1974, 1989; flour mill (Pardey & Co. Ltd) b. 1925 by Thomas Robinson & Son Ltd; Foursquare Gospel C. (Grace Christ.); foundry (J.T. Smith) 1949; freezing works; fruit juice factory (Jusfrute Juice Processors) 1971; fruit packing houses: Griffith Producers 1927 and Leeton Packing Co.; gales 1923 and 1933; gastroenteritis epidemic (2 infants died) 1952; hospital 1922–31, reused, relocated 1977 and reused again, new one 1931, additions 1936, 1953, 1966, 1973, 1980; Jehovah's Witnesses C.; LDS (Mormon) C.; lock-up (Bagtown) 1914, relocated (Griffith) 1922, closed, relocated and reused 1993, new one 1934; Lutheran C. (St Paul's); Meth. C. 1922; milk factory (J.C. Donnelly), bought 1980 by Murrumbidgee Dairy Co.; mouse plague 1970; PO: East Griffith 1967, Griffith 1912, new one b. 1928, North Griffith 1955, West Griffith 1938; Presb. C. b. 1925 by Hurley, new one 1982; PS (temporary) 1915, new buildings 1922, 1928, 1935, additions and alterations 1976; railway turntable 1916, 60 ft (18.3 m); 3 reservoirs (incl. concrete one, 300,000 gal. or 1,363.8 kl and one of 2,000,000 gal. or 9,092 kl b. 1952 by Bernard Smith Pty Ltd); rice mill (Aust. Rice Pty Ltd) o. 1942 in former flour mill, burnt down 1949, replaced 1950, sold 1959 to Ricegrowers' Co-op. Mills Ltd; Rom. Cath. C. (Sacred Heart) b. 1928 by Jones Bros, d. by George William Albert Welch; RS 1916, station b. by Ernest Frederick Leggo; Salv. Army C. 1928; sawmill (W. Day & Son Pty Ltd), fire 1952; schools: East Griffith 1960 (additions 1967 and 1979), Griffith 1920 (new building b. 1941 by A. Still, additions 1968 and 1971), Griffith HS 1939 (additions 1962, 1967, 1972, 1975, renamed Murrumbidgee Regional HS in 2019), North Griffith 1953 (additions 1955 by A.L. Jack, additions 1960, 1966, 1978), Wade HS 1971 (renamed Murrumbidgee Regional HS in 2019); SD Adventist C.; sewerage 1935, augmentation 1957 and 1993; starch factory o. 1950 in former cannery; steel fabrication works (Bruno Altin Steel-Tech Pty Ltd) estab. 1994 by Bruno Altin; TC (temporary buildings) b. 1952 by Bristol Construction Co., additions 1960 and 1985, became a campus of Riverina Institute in 1992, additions 2012; telephone: East Griffith 1967, Griffith 1915, North Griffith 1955, West Griffith 1938; TX 1921, automatic 1967; Unit. C.: one orig. Meth., b. 1953 by Hutcherson Bros, d. by W.C. Brown and B. Mowbray and one orig. Presb.,

b. 1958; water supply 1936, filtration plant 1941, augmentation 1976, treatment plant 1988; wineries: Calamia 1945, Cinzano 1976, Cranswick Estate 1991, Dal Broi (formerly Miranda, estab. 1939), Melange Wines 2000, Penfolds (estab. 1919–21 by Frank Penfold Hyland, damaged 1923, extended 1929), Riverina, San Bernadino (estab. 1973 by Stan Aliprandi), Savage, Swift's Winery Pty Ltd (in former cannery) 1950, West End (estab. 1945 by Frank Calabria), Wickham Hill 1960; pop. 2,468 (1933), *c.*3,200 (1941), 5,727 (1947), 6,608 (1954), 7,696 (1961), 9,553 (1966), 11,930 (1976), 13,187 (1981), 13,630 (1986), *c.*24,000 (1988), 13,296 (1991), 14,209 (1996), 16,003 (2001), 16,182 (2006), 16,972 (2011). (See also Bilbul and Yoogali.)

Grogan (*Co. Bland*) 34°19'S. 147°49'E., 30 km NE of Temora, on Bland Ck; farming; bridge (concrete) b. 1934 by F. Graham & Sons, 98 ft (29.9 m), over Bland Ck; PO 1891, burnt down 1923, new one 1928 on new site; telephone 1916; TX 1923–79; pop. 157 (1911), 112 (1933), 99 (1947), 113 (1954), 108 (1961), 125 (2006).

Groggins Gap (*Co. Wallace*) see Dead Horse Gap.

Grong Grong (*Co. Bourke*) 34°44'S. 146°47'E., 21 km E. of Narrandera, on Cowabbie Ck; settled 1881 by Kennedy, village gaz. 1884; farming; Angl. C. (St Matthew's) b. 1911 by A. Schuler, d. by H.C. Hind, damaged 1923; cemetery 1886; creamery (Wagga Wagga Co-op. Dairy Co.) 1896; dust storm 1915; fire 1904; PO 1881; PS (in rented premises) 1895, new one b. 1899, new buildings b. 1909 by E.P. Frost & Co.; reservoir (elevated), 50,000 gal. (227.3 kl); Rom. Cath. C. (St Patrick's) 1890, burnt down 1917, new one b. 1918 by William McFadzean and Charles Frederick Bland, d. by John Hill Robertson, damaged 1923; RS 1881, station burnt down 1904, rebuilt 1905, closed 1984, demolished 1985; school 1883, new building b. 1896 by C. Hardy & Co., alterations 1922, closed 2013; silo 1920; storm 1923; telegraph 1890; TX 1910, automatic 1981; Unit. C. (St Paul's, orig. Presb., damaged 1923) 1919–2002, sold and reused; water supply 1941; pop. 58 (1891), 248 (1901), 567 (1911), 677 (1921), 297 (1933), 229 (1947), 252 (1954), 247 (1961), 136 (1971), 130 (1981), 391 (2011).

Gronos Point (*Co. Cook*) see Wilberforce.

Groombridge Swamp (*Co. Clive*) see Bungulla.

Groongal (*Co. Sturt*) 34°25'S. 145°34'E., 46 km W. of Griffith; bushfire 1893; RS (Koorangal till 1885) 1882–1975; pop. 54 (1911), 22 (1933).

Grose's (*Co. Clarence*) see Copmanhurst.

Grose Vale (*Co. Cook*) 33°35'S. 150°40'E., 3 km S. of Kurrajong, on Cabbage Tree Ck; oranges and stone fruit; bushfires 1944, 1951, 1956, 1994; FB 1951; PO 1884, new one b. 1929; school (Kurrajong South till 1929) 1875, new building b. 1900 by R. Marlin, burnt down 1944, replaced, closed 1976; silo 1921; telephone 1912; TX 1915, automatic 1964; pop. 248 (1901), 205 (1911), 677 (1921), 233 (1933), 245 (1947), 301 (1954), 299 (1961), 1,276 (2006), 1,135 (2011).

Grose View (*Co. Cook*) see Grose Wold.

Grose Wold (*Co. Cook*) 33°36'S. 150°41'E., 4 km SW of North Richmond, on Grose R.; orchards and farming; FB; flood 1949; PO 1923; schools: Grose View 1977, additions 1993, and Grose Wold 1964–76; telephone 1921; TX 1925–64; pop. 50 (1911), 112 (1933), 112 (1947), 106 (1954), 114 (1961), 632 (2011).

Grosses Plain (*Co. Wallace*) 36°34'S. 148°30'E., 17 km S. of Jindabyne; pop. 22 (1933).

Grovetown (*Co. Northumberland*) see Lambton.

Growee (*Co. Phillip*) 32°38'S. 152°08'E., 23 km NE of Rylstone, on Growee R.; pop. 23 (1933).

Growee Gulph (*Co. Phillip*) 32°37'S. 150°04'E., 22 km NE of Rylstone, on Growee R.; telephone 1935; TX 1935–84.

Grubben (*Co. Mitchell*) 35°23'S. 147°03'E., 35 km SE of Lockhart; school 1899–1936 and 1957–61; pop. 60 (1933), 62 (1954).

Guagong (*Co. Blaxland*) see Gunebang.

Gubbata (*Co. Dowling*) 33°38'S. 146°33'E., 41 km SE of Lake Cargelligo; village gaz.

1930; wheat; cemetery; FB 1936; PO 1930; RS 1929–75; school 1934–46 and 1961–83; telephone 1934; TX 1948–81; pop. 134 (1933), 67 (1961).

Guerilla Bay (*Co. St Vincent*) 35°50'S. 150°13'E., 4 km S. of Malua Bay, on Tasman Sea; lighthouse (Burrewarra Point); radar station (RAAF, No. 17) and bunker 1943–45.

Guests Swamp (*Co. Denison*) 35°55'S. 145°58'E., 8 km N. of Mulwala; earth tremor 1998.

Guinema (*Co. Baradine*) 31°11'S. 148°58'E., 28 km S. of Baradine; telephone 1926; TX 1928–36; pop. 70 (1933).

Gular (*Co. Ewenmar*) 31°19'S. 148°27'E., 3 km W. of Gulargambone; laid out by William M. Thomas and village gaz. 1903, first lots sold 1904; cemetery 1903; PO 1913, burnt down 1934; RS 1903, station b. by John Allibone and McCarthy, closed 1975, station demolished 1986; sawmill (R.J. Nelson & Sons), fire 1937; silo 1959; telephone 1950; pop. 62 (1911), 85 (1933), 78 (1947), 110 (1954), 102 (1961).

Gulargambone (*Co. Gowen*) 31°20'S. 148°28'E., 43 km S. of Coonamble, on Castlereagh R.; village gaz. 1878 as Galargambone, subdivided 1879, surveyed 1880 by Edward McFarlane, first lots sold 1880; timber, wheat, sheep, cattle; ambulance station; Angl. C. (All Saints') 1912, closed and dilapidated; artesian bore sunk 1901 by Edward M'Cray; bridges: one (low-level) b. 1907 by J.H. Shedden, new one 2004, over Castlereagh R. and one over Gulargambone Ck; cemetery (612 graves 1887+) 1884, incl. columbarium; CH 1910, new one b. 1934 by Charles Alexander Stewart Boag; dust storm 1913; FB; fires 1927 and 1968; floods 1920, 1926, 1955; gale 1925; monumental stone works (C.J. Shakespeare); mouse plague 1932; PO 1871, new one b. 1911 by William Robert Ibbotson; Presb. C. 1886, new one (St Margaret's Pioneers' Memorial) b. 1938 by A.H. Smith, d. by Charles Herbert Davy Button; PS 1892, new one 1914, later one removed from Bodangora and re-erected 1934 by Charles Alexander Stewart Boag; reservoir; Rom. Cath. C. 1898, second one (St Philomena's) re-erected 1938 by Wallace and McGee (removed from Coonamble), closed, sold and reused, third one (Sacred Heart) o. 1985 in former school; sawmills: R.J. Nelson & Sons 1938 and R.E. Wallace; school 1882, new one b. 1883, new building b. 1910 by W. Bills, additions 1954 and 1966; sewerage 1976; telegraph 1883; telephone 1907; TX 1910, automatic 1986; water supply 1956, augmentation 1985; pop. 2 (1841), 297 (1901), 486 (1911), 460 (1933), *c.*750 (1938), 636 (1947), 868 (1954), 559 (1961), 408 (1966), 517 (1971), 461 (1976), 457 (1981), 511 (1986), 461 (1991), 490 (1996), 447 (2001), 582 (2011).

Gulf Creek (*Co. Murchison*) 30°12'S. 150°42'E., 22 km N. of Barraba; village gaz. 1903, declined 1916+, largely defunct; grazing and mining (copper disc. 1889) 1892+; cemetery 1902; flood 1910; mine estab. 1892 by Cornish Copper Mining Co. Ltd, taken over 1899 by Mining & Financial Trust Syndicate which floated Gulf Creek Copper Mining Co., mine thrived 1901, closed 1902, reopened, closed 1904, reopened, sold 1907 to London Metal Banking Co., closed 1911; PO 1897–1965; PS 1901; school 1897, new one b. 1900 by McKechnie Bros, closed 1944; smelter 1897, demolished; telephone 1922; TX 1923, automatic 1970; pop. *c.*320 (1899), 393 (1901), 230 (1911), 95 (1933), 114 (1947), 111 (1954), 100 (2006).

Gulgamree (*Co. Wellington*) 32°46'S. 149°45'E., 20 km W. of Rylstone, on Limestone Ck; farming and grazing; Meth. C. 1906; PO 1895; school 1881–1901 and 1910–15; telephone 1926; TX 1927; pop. 51 (1911), 59 (1933).

Gulginni (*Co. Macquarie*) 31°19'S. 152°51'E., 13 km NW of Port Macquarie, on Maria R.; telephone 1927; TX 1928–40.

Gulgo (*Co. Cunningham*) 33°05'S. 147°01'E., 13 km W. of Condobolin; pop. 20 (1933).

Gulgong (*Co. Phillip*) 32°22'S. 149°32'E., 26 km N. of Mudgee; founded by Tom Saunders, surveyed 1870, village gaz. 1872, thrived in 1870s, munic. 1876–1940, decl. National Trust conservation area 1975; formerly mining (gold disc. 1870 by Tom Saunders, more discoveries

1871 and 1872, production peaked 1872), then wool, beef, wheat, oats, flour, kaolin, poultry, pigs, dairying, fruit, hort.; ambulance station; Angl. C. 1871, demolished 1876, new one (St Luke's) b. 1874–76 by Charles Wain, Henry Bennett and James Beattie, d. by Edmund Thomas Blacket and Harold Robert Hardwick, re-roofed 1909, damaged 1912, repairs 1997 d. by Barbara Hickson; brewery (Eli Allan, James Jackson and Thomas Largey) 1872; bushfires 1964 and 2001; butter factory (H.R. Denison) b. 1891 by G. Turner, d. by William Henry Sadlier, burnt down 1897; carriage-works (H.M. Rudd and C. Blane) 1901; cemetery (2,915 graves 1870s+) 1872, incl. lawn cemetery and columbarium; CH 1872, renovated 1877, closed, reused 1899, demolished 1901, new one b. 1899 by R.T. Hill, additions 1935 by H.M. Bennett; cholera 1891; Cong. C. 1872; cordial factories: Alfred Brigden, taken over and modernised 1929 by A.J. Brigden, J. Curran, closed 1903, Albert E. Turner; diphtheria 1894–95; electricity 1923; FB (station b. 1935, new one 2017); fires 1865, 1872, 1944; flour mills: William Lee 1885 and Christopher Reid Young (b. 1894 by G.H. Rhodes, sold 1902 to James Loneragan Ltd, who opened new Golden Gate mill 1913, taken over 1914 by John Edward Loneragan, later became James Loneragan Milling Co. Pty Ltd, closed 2011); hailstorms 1912 and 1918; hospital b. 1872 by White, replaced 1901 by S.J. Pyne, additions 1906 also by Pyne, d. by Harold Robert Hardwick, additions 1939, repairs 1954 by G.F. Knight, additions 1965, closed 2010; ice works (Leslie Whenlock Norris), sold 1945 to Clarence Roy Fragar; lime-kiln (Mark Smith); mines: Adams Lead 1870–71, 1876, 1891, 1925, Black Lead (South Napoleon Co., Gulgong Gold Options Ltd, Black Lead NL Co.) 1870–90, 1924, 1932, 1935, Perseverance Lead (Caledonian Gold Mining Co., Digger Prince Mining Co., Cullengoral Alluvials) 1871–72, 1896, 1923–25, Old 44 Shaft, Red Hill (Golden Hill Co., Mt Boppy Gold Mining Co. Ltd, Red Hill Gold Mining Co.) 1871–72, 1906–8, 1910, 1915–16; PO 1870, new one b. 1879 by D. McFarlane and G. Henry, additions and alterations 1909 by W. Murphy; powerhouse (Leslie Whenlock Norris), sold 1945 to Clarence Roy Fragar, closed 1950; Presb. C. 1872, new one (St Andrew's) b. 1910 by M.H. Bennett, d. by Joseph Porter Power and John Shedden Adam, jun.; PS (incl. lock-up) b. 1881 by D. McFarlane; quarry (limestone) estab. by Mark Smith; rabbit freezing works (Leslie Whenlock Norris) 1932, sold 1945 to Clarence Roy Fragar; railway dam 1909; railway turntable, 50 ft (15.2 m), replaced 1913, 60 ft (18.3 m); reservoirs (concrete): 150,000 gal. (681.9 kl) and 250,000 gal. (1,136.5 kl); rifle range; Rom. Cath. C. (St John the Baptist) b. 1872 by P.W. Kelleher, destroyed 1885, replacement b. 1890 by George Turner, d. by John Francis Hennessy and Joseph Ignatius Sheerin (known as Sacred Heart till 1903 then reverted to St John the Baptist, damaged 1912); RS 1909, station b. by Reid and Castles, closed 1975; sale-yards (John Tuxford) 1900, new yards (H.A. Chick) 1937; Salv. Army C. 1922, reused; sawmills: S. Buckman (2 children killed 1917, mill taken over 1920 by James Loneragan Co.) and James Edwin Davies; schools: primary 1868, reopened 1874 in new school b. by Charles Sillington, damaged 1885, new one 1892, repairs 1900 by Hohnhorst and Barton, new building b. 1924 by J.A. Carle, additions 1966 and 1978, new school 1993, and HS 1981, fire damage restoration 1983; sewerage augmentation 1971; silo 1955; squalls 1871 and 1901; storms 1878, 1885 (nearly every building damaged), 1893; tannery (W.R. Jackson) 1874, destroyed 1878; telegraph 1871, new office 1872, additions 1874 by W.J. White, new one b. 1879 by D. McFarlane and G. Henry; TX 1906, automatic 1980; typhoid 1879; Union C. (Parochial); Unit. C. (orig. Wes. Meth.) b. 1901 by S.J. Pyne, d. by Harold Robert Hardwick; water supply 1933, augmentation 1987; Wes. Meth. C. 1871, reused; pop. 3,228 (1871), 1,642 (1881), 1,283 (1891), *c.*1,550 (1895), 1,579 (1901), 1,577 (1911), 1,723 (1933), *c.*1,600 (1941),

1,580 (1947), 1,473 (1954), 1,396 (1961), 1,441 (1966), 1,486 (1971), 1,618 (1976), 1,740 (1981), 1,988 (1986), 2,042 (1991), 2,018 (1996), 2,018 (2001), 1,907 (2006), 1,866 (2011).

Gulgullendah (*Co. Gordon*) 32°49'S. 148°37'E., 26 km SE of Peak Hill, on Cookamobil Ck; school 1892–95.

Gullamara (*Co. Phillip*) 32°28'S. 149°36'E., 13 km SE of Gulgong; Wilbertree till 1918; farming; PO 1927–52; telephone 1914; TX 1928; pop. 39 (1933).

Gullen (*Co. King*) 34°34'S. 149°26'E., 13 km S. of Crookwell; farming; cemetery (4 km E.) 1884; PO 1868–1931; school (Gullen West till 1889) 1884–1971; telephone 1920; TX 1933–60; typhoid (girl died) 1884; Wes. Meth. C. 1871; pop. 90 (1901), 20 (1933), 59 (1947), 50 (1961).

Gullen (*Co. King*) see also Kialla (*Co. Argyle*).

Gullen Flat (*Co. Argyle*) see Bannister.

Gullen West (*Co. King*) see Gullen.

Gulligal (*Co. Pottinger*) 30°48'S. 150°08'E., 23 km NW of Gunnedah; founded 1854 by Abraham Johnston, surveyed 1863 by Arthur Dewhurst, village gaz. 1865, defunct; sheep; flood (almost destroyed village) 1864; PO 1852; pound (stock) 1865; school 1919–38; pop. 63 (1866), 80 (1933).

Gulmarrad (*Co. Clarence*) 29°29'S. 153°14'E., 5 km SE of Maclean; school 1906; sugar mill (Davis's); pop. 156 (1881), 152 (1901), 335 (1996), 501 (2001), 806 (2006), 1,328 (2011).

Gulpa (*Co. Townsend*) 35°42'S. 144°53'E., 12 km N. of Mathoura; virtually defunct; PO 1925–71; RS (1 km S., on Victorian railway), closed; sawmill (Barker and Hay), burnt down 1955; telephone 1925; TX 1926, automatic 1970; pop. 107 (1933), 115 (1947), 57 (1954), 42 (1961).

Gumbalie (*Co. Barrona*) 29°59'S. 145°23'E., 55 km W. of Bourke, on Warrego R.; village gaz. 1886 as Goombalie; bridge b. 1890 by Richard Biggs, over Warrego R.; cemetery 1887; pop. 148 (2006).

Gumble (*Co. Ashburnham*) 33°05'S. 148°39'E., 13 km N. of Manildra, on Gumble Ck; largely defunct; gold (disc. 1887 by John Delaney), copper, farming; FB; mine 1887–91; PO 1908–38; school 1957–60; TX (automatic) 1980; pop. 54 (1911), 105 (1933), 86 (1947), 81 (1954), 79 (1961), 444 (2006).

Gumble Scrub (*Co. Ashburnham*) 33°04'S. 148°42'E., 13 km N. of Manildra, on Back Ck; 5 quarries.

Gum Creek (*Co. Boyd*) 34°37'S. 145°27'E., 43 km NW of Coleambally.

Gum Flat (*Co. Ashburnham*) 33°26'S. 148°47'E., 18 km NE of Canowindra; settled mainly by the Irish; mining (gold disc. 1872); butter factory (Primrose) estab. 1900 by James Joseph Carman, closed 1901, sold, reopened 1904 by John Green.

Gum Flat (*Co. Macquarie*) 31°09'S. 152°12'E., 58 km E. of Walcha; pop. 36 (1933).

Gum Flat (*Co. Murchison*) 29°46'S. 150°59'E., 12 km W. of Inverell; farming and grazing; cemetery (188 graves 1900+) 1895; drought 1883; dust storm 1952; electricity 1958; grasshopper infestation 1934; PO 1890; school 1883 b. by Moore Bros, additions 1965 and 2008; telephone 1906; TX 1914–71; Wes. Meth. C. d. and b. 1894 by J.W. Moore, closed; pop. *c.*70 (1880), 269 (1901), 225 (1911), 278 (1933), 199 (1947), 196 (1954), 190 (1961), 316 (2011).

Gum Holes (*Co. Urana*) 35°19'S. 146°39'E., 13 km S. of Lockhart.

Gum Holes (*Co. Urana*) see also Osborne.

Gum Lake (*Co. Livingstone*) 32°41'S. 143°10'E., 125 km S. of Wilcannia, on Boolaboolka Lake; RS (Tolarno till 1939) 1926–89, station demolished.

Gumly Gumly (*Co. Wynyard*) 35°07'S. 147°26'E., 6 km E. of Wagga Wagga, on Murrumbidgee R.; estab. 1934; sheep, cattle, lucerne, dairying, fruit, vegetables, quarrying (gravel) 1980+; electricity 1944; fish hatcheries (Murray Cod); floods 1934, 1950, 1952, 1956, 1959, 1960, 1970, 1974, 1975, 1976, 1983, 2010, 2012; PO 1936; Presb. C. (St Ninian's) 1942, renovated 1982, sold 2015; quarry; school 1936–2005, sold and reused; telephone 1935; TX 1950–58; water pumping station 1976; pop. 26 (1933), 208

(1947), 188 (1954), 373 (1961), 206 (1971), 154 (1991), 252 (1996), 227 (2001), 243 (2006), 290 (2011).

Gumma (*Co. Raleigh*) 30°42'S. 152°58'E., 5 km E. of Macksville, on Nambucca R.; pop. 34 (1933), 52 (1947), 408 (2011).

Gum Scrub (*Co. Macquarie*) 31°18'S. 152°44'E., 17 km N. of Wauchope, on Wilson R.; farming; PO 1936; school (Ballengarra till 1943) 1888–92 and 1919–62; telephone 1935; TX 1950–69; pop. 52 (1933), 62 (1947), 93 (1954), 71 (1961).

Gum Springs (*Co. Ashburnham*) 33°22'S. 148°18'E., 9 km NW of Eugowra; school 1891–96.

Gum Tree Flat (*Co. Northumberland*) see Lisarow.

Gum Tree Hole (*Co. Hunter*) 32°48'S. 150°38'E., 45 km S. of Denman, on Mullen Malong R.

Gunbar (*Co. Nicholson*) 34°03'S. 145°24'E., 65 km NW of Griffith; (incl. North Gunbar); estab. 1871 by William Spry, surveyed 1884, town gaz. 1886; farming (incl. rice) and grazing; cemetery (burials 1886+) 1887; droughts 1888, 1944–45, 1967–68; grasshopper infestation 1955; lock-up b. 1901 by George Huntley Dixon, moved 1930 to Merriwagga; PO 1879, burnt down 1903; pound (stock) 1910; Presb. C. b. 1884 by Rutledge and Ausevil, relocated 1914 by Tom Harris, closed; PS b. 1901 by George Huntley Dixon, closed 1933; school 1883 b. by Rutledge and Ausevil, repairs 1891 by H. Jones, closed 1923; storm 1922; telephone 1900; TX 1917; Unit. C. (Pioneers' Memorial, orig. Presb.) b. 1934 by Shannon Bros, repairs 1959 by J. Myott, repairs 1979 by K. Mark; pop. 64 (1901), 310 (1911), 258 (1933), 32 (1947), 69 (1954), 108 (1961), 97 (2006).

Gundabloui (*Co. Finch*) 29°10'S. 148°37'E., 40 km SW of Mungindi, on Moonie R.; town gaz. 1869.

Gundabooka (*Co. Cowper*) 30°24'S. 145°33'E., 51 km SW of Bourke; goldmining.

Gundabooka (*Co. Cowper*) see also Maroona.

Gundagai (*Co. Clarendon*) 35°04'S. 148°06'E., 28 km N. of Tumut, on Murrumbidgee R.; (incl. South Gundagai); orig. The Crossing Place, also formerly known as North Gundagai; disc. 1829 by Capt. Charles Sturt, settled 1836, founded 1838 by Major Joseph Andrews, surveyed and town gaz. 1838, laid out by Capt. William Augustus Perry, lots measured 1840 by James Larmer, first lots sold 1842, orig. town washed away 1852 and rebuilt on higher ground, first lots in new town sold 1853, thrived 1865, designated as chief town of the county, munic. proc. 1889, bypassed by highway 1977; orig. an important crossing place, then river port 1858+, mining (gold disc. 1861 by Gaspard Billardi, gold rushes 1861 and 1894, and chromite), wheat, barley, maize, oats, potatoes, then cattle, sheep, lucerne, millet, tobacco, wine, butter, cheese, ham, bacon, fruit; abattoir (Gundagai Meat Processors); ambulance station (temporary one) 1937, new one b. 1942 by C.W. Colley & Co., d. by John Donald Morrow; Angl. C.: St James's (b. 1899 by William Warbrick, restored 1935, closed 1965, demolished, replaced) and St John the Evangelist (b. 1861–67 by Abraham Marshall, d. by George Hart, renovated 1925, burnt out 1975, restoration 1976 by John Gates, d. by Bryan Dowling, alterations 1986 by Brian Manwaring); Bapt. C.; brewery (Dennis Kenny) 1879–1910; bridges: Byron Street Bridge b. 1902 by J.M. Dodd, over Morelys Ck, Prince Alfred Bridge (b. 1867–69 by Francis Bell, Hammond, Bocking and David Baillie, d. by William Christopher Bennett, 1,030 ft or 313.9 m, repairs 1882 by M'Evoy and Keefe, repairs 1885 by James M'Evoy and Timothy Dunn, extended and realigned in 1896 to 3,025 ft or 922 m by W. Pickering, reinforced during World War II, closed 1984, dilapidated, over Murrumbidgee R.), Sheahan Bridge (b. 1974–77, 3,750 ft or 1,143 m, new one d. and b. 2007–9 by Fulton Hogan Pty Ltd, over Murrumbidgee R.), Yarri Bridge 1984, over Morleys Ck; bushfire 1905; butter factory (Gundagai Co-op. Butter Factory Co. Ltd) 1908, closed, sold to Adjungbilly Freezing Co. and reused, inundated 1922, closed, partly dismantled 1926, fire 1927; carriage-works (F. Wilson) 1901; caterpillar infestation 1938; cemeteries: Gundagai 1878, South Gundagai, lawn cemetery and columbarium; CH 1847, destroyed 1852, new one b. 1860 by Charles Hardy, d. by Alexander Dawson, repairs 1869 by James Francis, repairs 1871 by Charles Hardy, repairs 1877 by J. M'Kenzie, additions 1879 by Thomas Jobson, repairs 1889 by D. M'Donald, renovated 1901 by William Warbrick, burnt out 1943, rebuilt 1944 by L.G. Price, re-roofed and repaired 1961; cheese factory (T.A. and G.R. Woodbridge) b. 1905 by C. Harrington; cordial factories: Eaton and Lincoln (acquired 1875 by Collins and Belford), Charles Goodsall (bought by William George Brannock, sold 1930 to T.S. Bell), Charles McCabe 1885, R.G. Thomas (burnt down 1922); diphtheria 1918, 1934, 1936; droughts 1839 and 1847–51; earth tremors 1871, 1898, 1909, 1932, 1947, 1952; electricity 1928; FB 1930 (station b. 1951); fires 1866, 1919, 1920; floods 1844, 1852 (89 people died), 1853, 1870, 1874, 1879, 1891, 1900, 1922, 1925, 1931, 1934, 1950, 1952, 1956, 1959, 1974, 1976, 1984, 1989, 1991, 2012; flour mills: Brunton & Co. Pty Ltd, Flood's (b. 1849 by Joseph Dillon Morley for Edward Flood and Thomas Hanley, damaged 1852 and 1900, sold and reused 1918 by Regan and Davis as freezing works, taken over 1931 by D.H. Roberts for rabbit export business, bought 1944 by W.T. Ballard & Son, acquired 1964 by A.J. and H.M. McIntyre, and reused again, now disused), J. Moon, Phoneix (estab. 1879 by George F. Hayes, bought 1880 by Walker and Walton, bought 1884 by Patrick Henry Scott and Michael John Mullaly, acquired 1886 by R. and W. Rumble, burnt down, rebuilt and reused), John Spencer (partly damaged 1863), Victoria (William Williams, sen.) 1873; foot-bridge over Morleys Ck; gale 1923; gaol b. 1881 by Joseph Conlon, d. by James Johnstone Barnet, gaol hospital b. 1883 by Thomas McBeath, gaol extensions 1886 also by McBeath, additions 1899 by William Warbrick, remodelled 1954, closed and reused; grasshopper infestation 1874; hailstorm (damaged most of town) 1874; heatwave 1904; hospital 1858, additions 1889 by William Warbrick, d. by Joseph Ignatius Sheerin and John Francis Hennessy, reused, new one b. 1904 by C. Harrs, d. by William Mark Nixon and John Shedden Adam, jun., new buildings 1935, additions and alterations 1936 by C.C. Marshall, additions 1947, 1955, 1961, renovated 1986, closed, sold 2015, new one 2012; lock-up 1847–52, new one 1855; measles epidemic 1893; Meth. C. b. 1930 by Cecil Marshall, closed, reused 1977, bought 2000 by Peter Smart and Judy Hay, reused 2006; mines: Morning Star, Mount Potter, Turn of the Tide; monumental stone works (Francis Philip Rusconi) 1905; PO: Gundagai 1843 (new one b. 1878–80 by Charles Hardy) and South Gundagai 1859; pounds (stock): Gundagai 1878 and South Gundagai 1857; PS, destroyed 1852, new one b. 1878 by Charles Hardy, additions and alterations 1903 by William Abbey, fire 1915, renovations and repairs 1938 by C.B. Gehrig; punts: Michael Doyle 1849–67 and Johnston's, across Murrumbidgee R.; quarries (slate) 1880; rabbit freezing works o. 1918 in old flour mill; railway bridge b. 1901–3, steel truss span, 200 ft (61 m), fabricated by A. & P. Roberts & Co., Pencoyd Iron Works, Pennsylvania, USA, d. by Union Bridge Co., Buffalo, New York, USA, closed 1983, over Murrumbidgee R.; railway coal stage; railway turntable 1891, 50 ft (15.2 m), defunct; railway viaduct b. 1901–3 (77 timber truss spans), 2,695 ft (821.4 m), closed and dilapidated; 4 reservoirs (incl. one 200,000 gal. or 909.2 kl); Rom. Cath. C. b. 1857–59, repairs 1876 by Flynn and Marshall, new one (St Patrick's) b. 1885–87, begun by James Cahir but completed by Dalton Bros, d. by Edmund Cooper Manfred, extended 1953; RS: Gundagai 1886, station b. by John H. Bell, refreshment rooms 1903, station closed 1984, restored and reused 1992, and South Gundagai, station b. 1903 by F.G. Filmer, closed 1975; sale-yards (Kyle & Co.) b. 1926 by W. Wales; Salv. Army C., moved

1900 to Reno and reused; schools: primary 1851 (destroyed 1852, new one b. 1858 by H.J. Thatcher, demolished 1883, replaced 1883 by Thomas McBeath, additions and alterations 1909 by G.J. Armstrong, additions 1929 by J.F. Burns, additions 1968, 1972, 2010, re-roofed 2013), HS 1967 (additions 1992), South Gundagai 1881 (repairs 1897 by J. Bloomfield, additions 1908 by W.J. Ritchie, alterations 1914 by Bill Armstrong, additions 1967); sewerage 1939, augmentation 1972; snow 1892 and 1899; storms 1851 and 1877; telegraph 1858, new office b. 1878–80 by Charles Hardy; telephone (South Gundagai) 1903; toll-gate; TX 1908, automatic 1972; typhoid 1898; Unit. C. (St David's, orig. Presb.) 1908, closed; vulcanising works (A. Dean); watch-house b. 1860 by Charles Hardy, d. by Alexander Dawson, additions 1861 by Charles Hardy and Thomas Hodson, additions 1863 d. by James Johnstone Barnet, wall 1866, reused 1881 as gaol hospital; water supply works b. 1907–9 by F.J. Cornwell and W. Refshaw, steam pump replaced with electric one, augmentation 1990, closed 1991, new treatment plant 1991; Wes. Meth. C. 1865, (second) 1869, (third) 1889; pop. 87 (1846), 397 (1851), 250 (1852, before flood), 347 (1856), 484 (1861), *c.*800 (1866), 1,008 (1871), 787 (1881), *c.*1,000 (1885–87), 1,424 (1891), 1,898 (1901), 1,921 (1911), 1,737 (1933), 1,945 (1947), 2,127 (1954), 2,167 (1961), 2,116 (1966), 2,061 (1971), 2,074 (1976), 2,308 (1981), 2,124 (1986), 2,069 (1991), 2,064 (1996), 1,997 (2001), 1,926 (2011).

Gundarene (*Co. Fitzroy*) 30°12'S. 152°54'E., 23 km NW of Coffs Harbour; farming and grazing; PO 1913, burnt down 1929; sawmill (Mulhearn Bros); telephone 1915.

Gundaroo (*Co. Murray*) 35°02'S. 149°16'E., 30 km NW of Bungendore, on Yass R.; Gundaroo Township till 1877, then Lower Gundaroo till 1892; founded by William Affleck, surveyed 1849 by John Frederick Mann, first land sale 1849, estab. 1855; wheat, rye, maize, oats, barley, potatoes, sheep, now hobby farms; airfield; Angl. C. (St Mark's) o. 1941 in old court-house after extensive renovations; bridge b. 1879 by J. Kingdom, replacement (Allan timber truss) b. 1900 by Jakob Nybeck, 210 ft (64 m), demolished 2014, new one 2009, over Yass R.; butter and cheese factory 1894; cemetery (200 graves 1869+) 1867; CH 1863, new one b. 1876 by William Duncan, d. by James Johnstone Barnet, additions 1877 by S. Hellman, additions 1882 by John Keilman, repairs 1906 by Peter Poidevin, closed 1935, sold 1940, reused; drought 1894; dust storm 1902; earth tremors 1934, 1940, 1942; electricity 1954; floods 1870, 1894, 1900, 1950; flour mill (horse powered) removed 1852 from Queanbeyan by John Wishart; grasshopper infestations 1897–98 and 1902; hailstorm 1896; lock-up b. 1857 by Thomas Hodson; PO 1872; pound (stock) 1838, relocated 1859; PS 1852–1935; quarry; Rom. Cath. C. (St Joseph's) b. 1879–81 by Falconer, Smith and Priest, and graveyard (burials 1857+); school 1865, new one b. 1869, new building b. 1898 by King and Armstrong, additions and repairs 1908 by W.J. Poulton, additions 1993; snow 1896 and 1929; snowstorm 1899; telegraph 1882; telephone 1916; TX 1923, automatic 1967; Unit. C. (orig. Presb.) b. 1864 by William Affleck et al., closed, derelict, subsequently refurbished; whooping cough epidemic 1917; pop. *c.*300 (1866), 108 (1871), 90 (1881), *c.*150 (1891), 187 (1901), 384 (1911), 119 (1933), 89 (1947), 100 (1954), 161 (1961), *c.*75 (1970), *c.*150 (1987), 238 (2001), 331 (2006), 403 (2011).

Gundaroo (*Co. Murray*)
see also Upper Gundaroo.

Gundaroo Township (*Co. Murray*)
see Gundaroo.

Gundary (*Co. Argyle*) 34°50'S. 149°45'E., 9 km S. of Goulburn; pop. 59 (1901), 77 (1933), 71 (1947), 92 (1954), 314 (2011).

Gundary (*Co. Dampier*) see Moruya.

Gunderman (*Co. Northumberland*) 33°27'S. 151°04'E., 25 km W. of Gosford, on Hawkesbury R.; orchards; bushfires 1994 and 2001; floods 1933, 1934, 1938, 1942, 1947, 1949; PO 1921; school 1957–78; telephone

1921; TX 1928, automatic 1981; Wes. Meth. C. 1855, closed, sold and reused; wharf; pop. 32 (1961), 139 (2006).

Gundibindyal (*Co. Bland*) 34°29'S. 147°47'E., 24 km E. of Temora, on Berri Jerri Ck; RS 1893, station b. by Franklin and Finlay, closed 1974; pop. 42 (1933).

Gundibri (*Co. Brisbane*) 32°08'S. 150°30'E., 13 km E. of Merriwa.

Gundillion (*Co. Murray*) 35°46'S. 149°38'E., 38 km S. of Braidwood; gold, farming, grazing; cemetery (74 graves); mine (G.S. Burrows and M. Gallagher) 1935–37; PO 1927–72; quarry; Rom. Cath. C. (St Brigid's); school 1882–84; telephone 1914; TX 1938, automatic 1972.

Gundurimba (*Co. Rous*) 28°51'S. 153°17'E., 5 km S. of Lismore; settled 1843 by Jimmy Pearce, Tommy Chilcott and George Cooper, town gaz. 1859; timber, farming, dairying; Angl. C. (St Matthew's) 1882; cemetery 1892; flood 1870; monumental stone works (Casino Monuments Aust. Pty Ltd); PO 1871; school 1868, new one b. 1873, additions 1883 by J.W. Burless, repairs 1896 by P. Mahony, demolished and replaced 1954, closed 1963; sewage works; sugar mill (Whitney's) 1871; telephone 1890; pop. 71 (1891), 113 (1901), 122 (1954), 110 (1933), 101 (1947), 84 (1961).

Gundurimba South (*Co. Rous*) 28°53'S. 153°15'E., 9 km S. of Lismore, on Pelican Ck; farming and dairying; cemetery (now Northern Rivers Memorial Park) 1882; creamery (Foley Bros) 1897; PO 1910; Presb. C.; quarry; school (Pelican Creek till 1907) 1892, additions 1900 by T.W. Keith, closed 1967; telephone 1914; TX 1928, automatic 1958; pop. 331 (1933), 311 (1947), 262 (1954), 251 (1961), 661 (2011).

Gundy (*Co. Brisbane*) 32°01'S. 151°00'E., 13 km E. of Scone, on Pages R.; orig. Bellevue; estab. *c.*1863, village gaz. 1871; grazing and dairying; Angl. C. (St Matthew's) b. by Matthew Miller, renovated 1874, damaged 1879, renovated 1880, reused, demolished, new one b. 1903 by T. and W. Cowan, d. by Pender and Silk, and graveyard (27 graves 1878–1934); bridge (Dare timber truss) b. 1909 by Taylor, Murphy & Co., 287 ft (87.5 m), new one 1994, over Pages R.; cemeteries: general (177 graves 1899+) and historic (15 graves 1874+) 1877; diphtheria 1885; FB; flood 1955; PO 1874–1994; Presb. C. b. 1874 by Denis Hayes, porch added 1908, new church b. 1929 by H.R. Welsh, and graveyard; Rom. Cath. C. (St Peter and St Paul's) 1896, closed, new one 1922, closed, sold; school 1878, new one b. 1880 by J. Libby, additions and repairs 1907 by Rae and Welsh, replaced 1916, closed 1991, sold and reused; storm 1879; telephone 1891; TX 1911, automatic 1935; pop. 60 (1881), 110 (1901), 276 (1911), 213 (1933), 138 (1947), 214 (1954), 203 (1961), 188 (2011).

Gundys Flat (*Co. Georgiana*) 33°55'S. 149°06'E., 38 km E. of Cowra, on Abercrombie R.

Gunebang (*Co. Blaxland*) 33°01'S. 146°41'E., 42 km NE of Lake Cargelligo; RS (Guagong till 1932) 1919–74.

Gungal (*Co. Brisbane*) 32°16'S. 150°30'E., 20 km SE of Merriwa, on Halls Ck; formerly Wickham; orig. agric., then grapes, dairying, sheep, now cattle; bridge b. 1929 by C. Leahey, over Halls Ck; cemetery 1886, defunct; FB; flood (woman died) 2017; meat works; PO 1876–1997; Rom. Cath. C. (St Anthony of Padua) b. 1911 by Walter Barrett, now seldom used; RS 1917–80; school 1880–85 and 1892–1965; telephone 1911; TX 1927, automatic 1983; winery (London Lodge); pop. 84 (1901), 80 (1911), 135 (1933), 89 (1947), 68 (1954), 122 (1961).

Gungalman (*Co. Leichhardt*) 30°30'S. 147°58'E., 54 km S. of Walgett.

Gunnary (*Co. King*) 34°21'S. 148°50'E., 14 km NE of Boorowa, on Gunnary Ck; Gunnary Creek till 1899; farming and grazing; bridge b. 1929, 75 ft (22.9 m), replaced 1978, over Gunnary Ck; earth tremor 2012; PO 1927–30; school (Gorham till 1900) 1894 b. by Anderson and Birnie, closed 1902.

Gunnary (*Co. King*)
see also Waterhole Flats.

Gunnary Creek (*Co. King*) see Gunnary.

Gunnedah (*Co. Pottinger*) 30°59'S. 150°15'E., 66 km W. of Tamworth, on Namoi R.; (incl. Albion and South Gunnedah); The Woolshed till 1858; settled 1834 by John Johnston, surveyed and laid out 1856 by Hyde, town gaz. 1856, first lots sold 1857, further lots laid out 1864 by Edward P. Mann, designated as chief town of the county, munic. proc. 1885, thrived 1959, munic. abolished 1980; sheep, cattle, wheat, maize, rape, barley, sorghum, lucerne, tobacco, soybeans, sunflowers, potatoes, fruit, butter, cheese, ham, bacon, poultry, cotton, coalmining, sawmilling, light engineering; abattoir b. 1954–57 by Walmac Construction Pty Ltd; airport 1951 (terminal demolished 1982, new one 1984 d. by Mike Silver); ambulance station b. 1957 by R.B. Bowen & Sons, d. by F.R. Donaldson, new one 2006 (at hospital); Angl. C. b. 1863 by George Brown, d. by C.W. Lloyd, new one (Christ) b. 1903 by Thomas John Bowen, d. by William Henderson Lee, additions and tower 1960; Bapt. C.; boiling-down works: Goodall & Co. (inundated 1893, explosion 1895 unroofed building) and William Woods 1893; brewery (Perseverance) b. 1879 by Butts for C.E. Beauvais, d. by G. Francis, closed 1888, sold 1889 to John G. Cock, reused 1890; brickworks: H.J. Cuell and Namoi Valley Bricks (estab. 1959 by Tony Broekman); bridge (Cohens Bridge) b. 1883–85 by Royce Bros, approaches replaced 1916 in concrete, over Namoi R.; bushfire 2009; butter factory (Gunnedah Co-op. Dairy Co.) 1907; carriage-works (Mirow & Sons Pty Ltd); caterpillar infestation 1899; cemetery (3,797 graves) 1864; CH b. 1879 by J.B. Jones, d. by James Johnstone Barnet, additions 1884 by A. Cross, also d. by Barnet, alterations 1896 by A. M'Michael, additions 1900 by Hocking Bros; cholera 1896; Christ. Outreach C. (Turning Point); cordial factories: John G. Cock (o. 1890 in old brewery, sold 1898, tower demolished 1951), J. and E. Cushan, Frederick Gough, Richard Oscar Albert Mirow 1908, became Mirow & Sons; crematorium (Lightfoot & Co.); dengue fever 1926; diphtheria 1889; drought 1888; dust storms 1895 and 1902; earth tremor 1900; FB 1902 (first station b. 1902, second one b. 1910, third one b. 1915 by E.L. Thoyne, fourth one b. 1962 by John W. Roberts & Associates); fires 1884, 1914, 1916, 1927, 1944, 1947, 1951, 1979; floods 1856, 1864, 1870, 1893, 1908, 1910 (2 died), 1955, 1998, 2000, 2012; flour mills: Brunton & Co. Ltd, burnt down 1916, Excelsior Roller Flour Mills (W.H. Short & Co.) 1904, Namoi Milling Co. Ltd (taken over and closed by Fielder and Regan), North Western Milling Co. Ltd; gale 1902; grasshopper infestations 1937, 1953, 1955; hailstorms 1897 and 1899; heatwaves 1878 and 1882; hospital 1882, damaged 1902, new wing 1902, enlarged 1905, additions 1920, additions 1936 by T. Carlin, additions 1962, re-roofed 2016; Jehovah's Witnesses C.; Lutheran C. (Trinity); monumental stone works (R.J. Lightfoot); PO: Gunnedah 1856 (new one b. 1880 by J. McLean, additions and alterations 1901 by Montague Audet, remodelled 1951, demolished 1980, new one b. 1985) and South Gunnedah 1965; powerhouse (Pike Bros) 1910, modernised 1938 by W.H. Pike, sold 1945 to local council, closed 1947; Presb. C. 1921, new one (St Andrew's) 1955; PS (incl. lock-up) b. 1875–77 by Charles Grace, d. by James Johnstone Barnet, additions and alterations 1881 by J. Conlan, demolished, new one 1963, demolished, new one 2018; rabbit freezing works (Gunnedah Freezing Works Ltd); railway (Gunnedah Colliery Co.) 1899; railway engine shed 1879, unroofed 1902; railway turntable 1902, 50 ft (15.2 m); reservoirs: (first) b. 1908 by William Gulliver & Sons, closed and replaced 1954, reused, (third) 1958, (fourth) 1961, (fifth) 1978; Rom. Cath. C. 1875–1919, reused, new one (St Joseph's) b. 1919 by Montague Audet, d. by Frederick James Bishop; RS: Gunnedah 1879 (station b. by Alexander Hamilton Scouller, J. Harrison and N. Turner, new one 1915) and West Gunnedah 1925–55; sale-yards 1915; Salv. Army C. 1888, new one 1938, sold, new one 2016; sawmills: Henry Thomas Pike and White Bros; schools: Gunnedah 1862–64 (reopened 1875, new building 1878, new school b. 1900 by Montague Audet, additions 1929 by Kent and Kent, sold and reused, new one 1971 on new site), Gunnedah HS 1955 (additions 1961 and 1967, restoration 1972 after fire, additions 1975 and 1990), South Gunnedah 1955 (additions 1959, 1961, 1966, 1971, 1985, additions 2007 by O'Donnell & Hanlon Pty Ltd); SD Adventist C.; semolina plant (Manildra Group) 1991; sewerage (pumping station b. by McLean Constructions Pty Ltd and treatment works b. by Norman Davis) 1944, augmentation 1968; silo 1934; silo fabrication works (H.E. Silos) 1997; soap-works; storm 1937; streets aligned 1887; streets kerosene lit 1891, electric lit 1908; tannery (New Wave Leathers Pty Ltd), bought 2009 by A.I. Topper & Co.; TC o. 1943 in reused building, became a campus of New England Institute in 1992; telegraph 1869, new office b. 1880 by J. McLean, additions and alterations 1901 by Montague Audet; telephone: Gunnedah 1897 and South Gunnedah 1965; TX 1906, automatic 1974; typhoid 1903 and 1909; Unit. C. (orig. Meth.) 1957; watch-house 1871; water supply 1893, reticulation infrastructure 1908, augmentation 1924, modernised 1938, further augmented 1956 and 1985; Wes. Meth. C. b. 1878 by J.B. Jones; wool-scours: L.F. Iredale and Arthur Thompson 1895; pop. 247 (1861), *c.*300 (1866), 459 (1871), *c.*500 (1873), 1,331 (1881), *c.*1,000 (1885), *c.*1,500 (1887), 1,362 (1891), *c.*1,250 (1895), 1,910 (1901), 4,100 (1911), 3,591 (1933), 4,314 (1947), 5,129 (1954), 6,543 (1961), 7,522 (1966), 8,219 (1971), 8,689 (1976), 8,909 (1981), 9,144 (1986), 8,874 (1991), 8,315 (1996), 7,871 (2001), 7,542 (2006), 7,888 (2011).

Gunnembene (*Co. Nandewar*) 30°55'S. 150°28'E., 20 km E. of Gunnedah, on Namoi R.; earth tremor 2012; FB; school 1880–1923; pop. 65 (1911), 44 (1933).

Gunnible (*Co. Nandewar*) 30°53'S. 150°20'E., 14 km NE of Gunnedah; earth tremor 2012.

Gunning (*Co. King*) 34°47'S. 149°16'E., 33 km E. of Yass, on Meadow Ck; disc. 1821 by George Barber, William Broughton, Francis Rawdon Hume and Hamilton Hume, settled 1830, surveyed and laid out 1836 by Thomas Scott Townsend, first lots sold 1838, second land sale 1839, designated as chief town of the county, bypassed by highway 1993; agric., sheep, cattle, wine, hort.; Angl. C. (St Edmund's) b. 1845–59, destroyed 1868, replaced 1869, chancel added 1912, church extended 1926, restored 1934, restored again and re-roofed 1985; bridge b. 1857–59 by Hammond and Bocking, d. by William Henry Downey, demolished; cemetery 1879; CH (incl. lock-up) b. 1874–79 by Samuel Bates, d. by James Johnstone Barnet, additions 1893, additions and repairs 1917 by Arthur Allen, restored; cordial factory; creamery (William Grovenor); earth tremors 1852, 1857, 1885, 1886, 1898, 1933, 1934, 1935, 1945, 1946, 1947, 1949, 1952; electricity 1940; FB; floods 1928, 1931, 1959; flour mill b. 1850 by William Grovenor, sen., taken over by Richard and William Grovenor, jun., leased for years to several operators, reverted to William Grovenor, jun., closed, renovated, reopened 1898 by Alfred E. Grovenor as Commercial Steel Roller Mills, burnt down 1911; gale 1868; measles epidemic 1893; PO 1840, new one b. 1881 by Thomas McBeath; polish factory (OHB) estab. by Langdon; pound (stock) 1841; PS 1873, additions and repairs 1917 by Arthur Allen; rabbit freezing works 1915; railway coal stage and turntable 1920; Rom. Cath. C. (St Francis Xavier and St Joseph's) 1860, extended 1907 by J. Cody, demolished, replaced 1973, and graveyard; RS 1875, station b. by Frederick Horn, refreshment room closed 1880, station closed 1989; sawmills: J.K. Clancy, Fitzgerald's, J. Wheatley; school 1858, new one b. 1871, additions 1884 by Falconer Bros, additions 1915, 1957, 1966; sewerage 1974; telegraph 1875, new office b. 1881 by Thomas McBeath; TX 1914, automatic 1970; Unit. C. (orig. Wes. Meth.) b. 1876 by George Coates & Son, d.

by Thomas Rowe; watch-house 1846; water supply filtration 1963; weir on Meadow Ck; Wes. Meth. C. 1849; pop. 95 (1846), 134 (1851), 125 (1856), 192 (1861), *c.*200 (1866), 272 (1871), 409 (1881), 468 (1891), 602 (1901), 816 (1911), 723 (1933), 661 (1947), 684 (1954), 598 (1961), 462 (1966), 483 (1971), 457 (1976), 438 (1981), 424 (1986), 497 (1991), 486 (1996), 415 (2001), 482 (2011).

Gunningbar (*Co. Oxley*) 31°41'S. 147°39'E., 18 km W. of Warren, on Beleringer Ck; pop. 20 (1933).

Gunningbar West (*Co. Oxley*) 31°38'S. 147°35'E., 25 km W. of Warren, on Beleringer Ck.

Gunningbland (*Co. Ashburnham*) 33°08'S. 147°55'E., 24 km W. of Parkes; Gunningbland Siding till 1918; estab. 1896; crops, pigs, sheep, cattle; PO 1907; RS 1896, station b. by John Allibone, closed 1976; school 1919–95; silo 1930; telephone 1915; TX 1917–73; Union C. 1904, enlarged; pop. 149 (1911), 251 (1933), 176 (1947), 192 (1954), 203 (1961).

Gunningbland Siding (*Co. Ashburnham*) see Gunningbland.

Gunning Gap (*Co. Cunningham*) 33°17'S. 147°49'E., 22 km NW of Forbes, on Goobang Ck; flood 1950; Rom. Cath. C. (St Joseph's) o. 1909, removed from Calarie, new sacristy added 1955, seldom used since 1983; school 1957–61; pop. 91 (1947).

Gunning Grach (*Co. Wellesley*) see Gunningrah.

Gunningrah (*Co. Wellesley*) 36°46'S. 149°09'E., 19 km NW of Bombala, on Walkers Ck; formerly Gunning Grach; soldiers' settlement; airfield; pop. 59 (1901).

Guntawang (*Co. Phillip*) 32°24'S. 149°29'E., 7 km SW of Gulgong; disc. 1822 by George and Henry Cox; wheat 1851+, grazing, goldmining (sluicing 1933–35, shafts and drives 1935–38, dredging 1938–49); Angl. C., closed; butter factory (R. Rouse) 1889–1935; cemetery; flood 1870; mine (Cullengoral Alluvial Gold Sluicing NL) 1933–49; PO 1861–1912; school 1860, new building b. 1908 by Walter Murphy, closed 1914; storm 1878; Wes. Meth. C. b. 1860 by McCauley; pop. *c.*200 (1866), *c.*200 (1903).

Gunyerwarildi (*Co. Burnett*) 29°17'S. 150°31'E., 29 km N. of Warialda, on Postmans Gully; cemetery; school 1955–67; TX (automatic); Union C. 1918; pop. 88 (1901), 33 (1933). (See also Old Gunyerwarildi.)

Gurley (*Co. Courallie*) 29°44'S. 149°48'E., 30 km S. of Moree; Gurley Siding till 1917; village gaz. 1913; grazing; FB; PO 1902, burnt down 1926; RS 1897, station b. by William Mitchell, new one b. 1924, closed; school 1919–65; silo; telephone 1898; TX 1913, automatic 1940; pop. 188 (1911), 92 (1933), 200 (1947), 78 (1954), 307 (1961), 217 (2001).

Gurley Siding (*Co. Courallie*) see Gurley.

Gurranang (*Co. Clarence*) 29°28'S. 153°00'E., 19 km W. of Maclean; RS (Sportsmans Creek till 1910) 1905, station b. by H.W. Owen, closed 1974; pop. 51 (1933), 171 (2006), 259 (2011).

Gurrundah (*Co. King*) 34°39'S. 149°25'E., 21 km S. of Crookwell, on Gurrunda Ck; farming, dairying, sheep; butter factory (Gurrunda Co-op. Butter Factory Ltd) 1894; cemetery (3 km S.); PO 1876–1973; Rom. Cath. C. (Sacred Heart) b. 1923 by Larcombe and Perry, d. by Otto Knopp; school 1883–93 and 1957–86; telephone 1914; TX 1921; pop. 219 (1901), 76 (1911), 127 (1933), 67 (1947), 72 (1961), 124 (2006).

Guthega (*Co. Wallace*) 36°23'S. 148°22'E., 4 km NW of Perisher Valley, on Guthega Pondage; temporary construction camp for Snowy Mountains Hydro-Electric Scheme, became small winter snow resort; bushfire 2003; coffer dam 1953.

Guy Fawkes (*Co. Clarke*) 30°25'S. 152°19'E., 38 km W. of Dorrigo; estab. *c.*1884, largely abandoned by *c.*1909, defunct; cemetery (123 graves) 1898; PO 1895–1911; PS b. 1895 by Thomas Morrissy, closed 1944, removed; sawmill (George Frederick Nott); school 1903–29; telephone 1893; TX 1912–61; Union C. 1905; pop. 297 (1901), 130 (1911), 61 (1933).

Guyong (*Co. Bathurst*) see Guyong West.

Guyong East (*Co. Bathurst*) 33°25'S. 149°16'E., 8 km NE of Millthorpe; farming and grazing; Angl. C. (Holy Trinity) 1872 d. by Edward Gell, closed 1982, sold 1986, and graveyard; PO 1904; telephone 1926; TX 1926, automatic 1954; Wes. Meth. C. b. 1856–58 by William Nixon, new one b. 1875 by Frank Rule, additions 1897 d. by John Hale; pop. 114 (1933), 76 (1947), 91 (1954), 91 (1961).

Guyong West (*Co. Bathurst*) 33°24'S. 149°13'E., 7 km NE of Millthorpe; Guyong till 1907; village gaz. 1880 as Guyong; farming and copper mining; cemetery 1871; 7 mines (incl. Diamond Hill 1903); PO 1853–1922; pound (stock) 1858; school 1870, new buildings 1883 by J. Harvey, closed 1931; telephone 1926; toll-house b. 1870 by James Stuart Douglas; pop. 262 (1871), 249 (1901), 255 (1911), 34 (1933).

Guyong West (*Co. Bathurst*)
see also Shadforth.

Guyra (*Co. Sandon*) 30°13'S. 151°40'E., 33 km N. of Armidale, on Mother of Ducks Lagoon; (incl. North Guyra); formerly Gyra and Mother of Ducks; settled 1836 by Peter McIntyre, founded 1883, village gaz. 1884; mining, dairying, maize, oats, potatoes, peas, fruit, cattle, wool; abattoir (New England) 1965–81, sold and reopened 1985 (Guyra Meat Packing Co.), acquired and closed 1996 by Aust. Meat Holdings; airfield; ambulance station; Angl. C. 1886, (second) 1896, relocated 1911, demolished 1942, (St James the Apostle) b. 1914 by Charles G. Cooper; Assemblies of God C. (Northwest, formerly Bluecross); brickworks (Vickery & Co.); butter factory 1893, closed, sold 1896 to John Moffat; carriage-works (Hunter and Rudd, became E.H. Rudd & Co. in 1917); cemetery (1,615 graves 1885+) 1884, incl. lawn cemetery and columbarium; CH 1893; chaff mill (Richard Pearson) 1886; cordial factories: Alexander Lauder and Edwin Winter Thomas 1901 (Thomas left the business in 1923 and set up on his own account, Lauder later sold to H. Burrows, sold to S. McKay, closed 1940); earth tremor 1938; engineering works (Ramage Engineering Pty Ltd) 1995; FB 1929 (new station b. 1963); fires 1925 and 1928; freezing works 1924–30; Full Gospel C. (Freedom); hailstorm 1919; hospital (Guyra Dist. War Memorial) 1947, replaced 2006, additions 2013 by P.J. Trueman Constructions Pty Ltd; measles epidemic 1952; PO: Guyra 1877 (new one b. 1914 by Charles G. Cooper) and North Guyra 1903; powerhouse (Guyra Electric Supply Co. Ltd) 1929; Presb. C. (St Columba's) b. 1926 by Charles Frank Nott, d. by Joseph Fearis Munnings; PS 1885, repairs 1896 by W. Hern, new one (incl. lock-up) b. 1905 by R.A. Bartlett, third one 1932, repairs 1953 by N.A. Graham, fourth one 1979; 2 reservoirs (towers); rifle range 1905; Rom. Cath. C. b. 1888 by H.E. Elliott, additions, new one (St Mary of the Angels) b. 1909 by Paul Kirkwood, d. by Philip Ernest Ranclaud, additions 1930 by Thomas Burg, d. by Peter Joseph Gannon; RS 1884, station b. by George Michael, closed, station reused; sale-yards (T.E. Sole & Co.); sawmill (Pearson & Sons) estab. by Richard Pearson; scarlet fever 1922; school (Loch End till 1893) 1883, new one b. 1884 by R.T. Harrison, extended 1886 by James Dewar, reused, new buildings b. 1893 by Harper Bros, repairs 1895 by S. Chidgey, repairs 1900 by G. Wilson, extended 1919, additions 1935 by Charles G. Cooper, additions 1960, 1971, 1977, 2009; SD Adventist C.; sewerage 1968; silo; snowstorm 1943; storm 2002; telegraph 1885, new office b. 1914 by Charles G. Cooper; telephone: Guyra 1912 and North Guyra 1902; train derailment 1892; TX 1911, automatic 1974; Union C. (St Bartholomew's) 1876, bought 1927 by Meth. C., sold; Unit. C. (orig. Meth.) b. 1928 by Charles G. Cooper, on the site of the former Union C.; vulcanising works (Claude Heagney); water supply 1958, augmentation 1969, treatment plant 1982; whooping cough epidemic 1934; pop. 547 (1901), 1,309 (1911), 1,319 (1933), 1,407 (1947), 1,557 (1954), 1,628 (1961), 1,700 (1966), 1,788 (1971), 1,933 (1976), 1,840 (1981), 1,999 (1986), 1,942 (1991), 1,801 (1996), 1,725 (2001), 1,758

(2006), 1,919 (2011).

Gwabegar (*Co. Baradine*) 30°37'S. 148°57'E., 39 km N. of Baradine; Goonanyah till 1924; village gaz. 1923; timber, wheat, grazing; Angl. C., reused, burnt down 2012; cemetery (172 graves 1933+); Community C.; FB; PO 1924, new one b. 1935 by A. Masmon; Presb. C. 1930; PS 1925, new one (incl. lock-up) b. 1935; Rom. Cath. C. (St Mary's); RS 1923–75; sawmills: Bradley & Whiteman Ltd, burnt down 1933 and Great Western Investments, burnt down 1950, rebuilt 1951; school 1928, new one b. 1936 by Johnson; telegraph 1924; telephone 1924; TX 1925, automatic 1983; whooping cough epidemic 1937; pop. 249 (1933), 302 (1947), 378 (1954), 381 (1961), 240 (2006), 344 (2011).

Gwandalan (*Co. Northumberland*) 33°09'S. 151°35'E., 7 km SW of Caves Beach, on Crangan Bay; (incl. Point Wolstoncroft); tourism; FB 1957 (station b. 1963); fire 1972; jetty; PO 1961; school 1961 (in rented premises), new school 1966 on new site, major upgrade 1990; sewage works; telephone 1961; water reticulation 1976; pop. 99 (1961), 609 (1971), 1,087 (1976), 1,685 (1981), 2,331 (1986), 3,108 (1991), 3,630 (1996), 4,538 (2001), 2,941 (2006), 3,035 (2011).

Gwandalan West (*Co. Northumberland*) 33°08'S. 151°34'E., 2 km W. of Gwandalan, on Lake Macquarie.

Gwando (*Co. Flinders*) 32°23'S. 146°53'E., 95 km S. of Nyngan; telephone 1925; TX 1926–57.

Gwydir Raft (*Co. Courallie*) 29°25'S. 149°44'E., 11 km NW of Moree, on Gingham Watercourse.

Gwynne (*Co. Clarendon*) 34°47'S. 147°28'E., 14 km NW of Junee; pop. 23 (1933).

Gwynne (*Co. Clarendon*) see also Erin Vale.

Gwynne (*Co. Rous*) 28°41'S. 153°09'E., 11 km SW of Nimbin.

Gwynneville (*Co. Camden*) 34°25'S. 150°53'E., 2 km NW of Wollongong, on Fairy Ck; (incl. Keiraville); formerly farming; Angl. C. (St John's) b. 1941 by Paine, new one b. 1973 by Osron Constructions, d. by Robert M. Wilson; Cong. C. 1890–1951, new one 1960; flour mill (A. Graham); Islamic C. (Omar); Jewish C. 1963; Meth. C. 1912; PO: Gwynneville 1942 and Keiraville 1890; Rom. Cath. C. (St Brigid's) b. 1949–51 by A.W. Edwards Pty Ltd, d. by Sydney George Hirst and David Kennedy, new one 1995; schools: Gwynneville 1951, additions 1958 and 2010, Keira HS (Wollongong Junior Technical HS till 1959) 1944, Keiraville 1891, renovations and repairs 1910 by J.W. Poulter, additions 1956, 1961, 1964, Wollongong HS of Performing Arts (Wollongong HS till 1993) 1917, additions 1963 and 1970; TC (Illawarra Institute of Technology, Wollongong Campus); telephone: Gwynneville 1925 and Keiraville 1908; pop. 463 (1911), 1,164 (1954), 2,837 (2011).

Gypsy Point (*Co. Camden*) 34°51'S. 150°33'E., 5 km NW of Nowra, on Shoalhaven R.

Gyra (*Co. Sandon*) see Guyra.

H

Haberworth (*Co. Narromine*) 32°21'S. 148°12'E., 12 km S. of Narromine; TX 1967.

Hacks Ferry (*Co. Macquarie*) 31°20'S. 152°51'E., 12 km NW of Port Macquarie, on Maria R.; school 1957–63.

Haddon Hall (*Co. Cook*) see Woodford.

Hadleigh (*Co. Burnett*) 29°35'S. 150°28'E., 13 km W. of Warialda; RS 1901, station b. by John Allibone, closed 1975.

Hadley (*Co. Georgiana*) 34°09'S. 149°34'E., 35 km N. of Crookwell; farming and grazing; PO 1927–30; school 1901–17 and 1957–68; pop. 21 (1933).

Hadsonville (*Co. Bathurst*) 33°48'S. 149°11'E., 31 km S. of Blayney, on Jackies Ponds; grazing; bushfire 1896; PO 1904–7.

Halekulani (*Co. Northumberland*) 33°13'S. 151°33'E., 1 km NE of Budgewoi, on Lake Munmorah; PO 1967; reservoir, 1,500,000 gal. (6,819 kl), 1966; school (Budgewoi) 1961, additions 1963, 1969, 1974, 1989; telephone 1967; water reticulation 1969; pop. 2,378 (2006), 2,427 (2011).

Half Moon Brush (*Co. Gloucester*) 32°32'S. 151°52'E., 15 km NW of Karuah.

Half Moon Flat (*Co. Buller*) 28°42'S. 152°12'E., 42 km NE of Tenterfield, on Boonoo Boonoo R.

Half Moon Flat (*Co. St Vincent*) 35°23'S. 149°58'E., 17 km NE of Braidwood, on Mongarlowe R.

Halfway Creek (*Co. Clarence*) 29°55'S. 153°04'E., 20 km NW of Arrawarra, on Halfway Ck; timber, dairying, hort.; bushfire 1936; PO 1899–1969; school 1957–66; telephone 1906; TX 1941–69; pop. 71 (1911), 141 (1933), 72 (1947), 124 (1954), 126 (1961), 256 (2001), 264 (2011).

Hallidays Point (*Co. Gloucester*) 32°04'S. 152°32'E., 12 km N. of Tuncurry, on Tasman Sea; (incl. Red Head); farming and dairying; PO 1927; quarry; sewerage augmentation 1988; telephone 1932; TX 1928, automatic 1969; Unit. C. (Community); water reticulation 1969; pop. 90 (1933), 59 (1947), 79 (1954), 98 (1961), 318 (1986), 503 (1991), 611 (1996), 700 (2001), 1,011 (2006).

Hallidays Point (*Co. Gloucester*) see also Diamond Beach.

Halloran (*Co. Northumberland*) see Warnervale.

Halls Block (*Co. Buccleuch*) 35°15'S. 148°32'E., 29 km E. of Tumut.

Halls Creek (*Co. Darling*) 30°45'S. 150°55'E., 19 km E. of Manilla, on Halls Ck; Angl. C. (Christ) b. 1903 by Reardon; FB (station b. 2012); pop. 95 (1911), 154 (1933), 140 (1947), 166 (1954), 156 (1961).

Halls Creek (*Co. Murchison*) 29°57'S. 150°37'E., 9 km S. of Bingara; school 1883 b. by A. Thorley, closed 1928; pop. 61 (1911), 51 (1954), 54 (1961).

Hall's Estate (*Co. Gloucester*) see Old Bar.

Halls Lead (*Co. Gough*) 29°24'S. 151°30'E., 40 km E. of Ashford; mining (tin).

Halls Peak (*Co. Sandon*) 30°44'S. 152°02'E., 43 km SE of Armidale; mining (copper, silver and lead disc. 1913 by Borham and Hawkins).

Halls Point (*Co. Cook*) 33°33'S. 151°53'E., 3 km E. of Wilberforce, on Hawkesbury R.

Hallsville (*Co. Inglis*) 31°01'S. 150°52'E., 10 km NW of Tamworth; PO 1899–1910; school (Woolomol till 1926) 1883, additions 1930 by E.R.S. Potter, closed 1968; TX (automatic) 1966; Unit. C. (orig. Wes. Meth.) b. 1894 by Sneesby, d. by Dixon, new one 1989, and graveyard (19 graves 1901+); pop. 97 (1933), 138 (1947), 94 (1954), 111 (1961), 529 (2011).

Halton (*Co. Durham*) 32°19'S. 151°31'E., 25 km NW of Dungog, on Allyn R.; dairying; bridge b. 1923 by William Benjamin Marsh, over Allyn R.; PO 1927; school (Ballington till 1884) 1882, new one b. 1884 by R.A. Taylor, additions 1902 by G.H. Morton, closed 1949; telephone 1911; tobacco factory (James Laurie & Sons) 1860–1903; TX 1915; pop. 80 (1911), 40 (1933), 69 (1954), 62 (1961).

Hambledon Hill (*Co. Durham*) 32°36'S. 151°07'E., 6 km SW of Singleton; pop. 31 (1933).

Hambridge (*Co. Camden*) 34°27'S. 150°39'E., 14 km W. of Dapto, on Hambridge Ck.

Hamel (*Co. Cooper*) 34°12'S. 146°36'E., 32 km NW of Ardlethan; school 1923–35.

Hamilton (*Co. Macquarie*) see Port Macquarie.

Hamilton (*Co. Northumberland*) 32°55'S. 151°45'E., 3 km W. of Newcastle, on Styx Ck; (incl. East Hamilton, Newtown, North Hamilton, The Commonage, Woodville); orig. Happy Flat, then Bore Hole till 1872, also known as Pit Town; formerly part of the Aust. Agric. Co. estate, estab. 1849, surveyed and laid out 1855, first land sale 1857, munic. proc. 1871, garden subdivision d. 1912 by Sir John Sulman and John Francis Hennessy, munic. subsumed 1938 under City of Greater Newcastle; coalmining; ambulance station (Newcastle Dist.) b. 1923 by J. Jamieson, d. by Frederick George and Archer Cox Castleden, alterations 1937 by N.J. Ladkin, d. by John William Oldham and Robert Godwin Lees, damaged 1989, repaired; Angl. C.: Hamilton (St Peter's) 1864, repairs 1875, new one b. 1885 by Reynolds Bros and R. Saville, d. by John Horbury Hunt, re-roofed 1911, steeple damaged and repaired 1935 by J. Simpson, church restoration 1996 d. by Mark Lawler and North Hamilton (St Aidan's) 1923; Assemblies of God C. (Newcastle) 1938, new one (Generation City); bakery (Arnott's Great Northern Bread Factory) b. 1902 by A. Cook, d. by G. Wayne; Bapt. C. 1929; box factory (Pacific); brewery (Northern Brewery Wine & Spirit Co.) b. 1884–88 by John and Joseph Wood, d. by Peter Bennett and Ernest George Yeomans, closed, sold and reused; brickworks (Waterloo Fire Brick Co. Ltd); brush factory (Cleansall Products Pty Ltd); bushfire 1884; Christ. Science C. (Newcastle) 1955; Church of Christ 1923; clock tower d. by Wallace Lintott Porter; clothing factory (Styl-Master Tailoring Co.); coke-ovens (Aust. Agric. Co.); collieries: D Pit (Aust. Agric. Co.) 1851, E Pit (Aust. Agric. Co.) 1854, No. 1 Pit (Aust. Agric. Co.), No. 2 Pit (Aust. Agric. Co.) 1862–1901, Borehole Pit 1861–1901; cordial factories: Bishop Bros (incl. pickle factory), moved to Kurri Kurri, Healey Bros (became YY Aerated Water Co. in 1921), William Hutchinson; diphtheria 1917; earthquake (4 died) 1989; earth tremors 1925 and 1951; engineering works: A. Bortkevitch and P.J. Taylor (Newcastle) Pty Ltd, bought 1952 by Repco Ltd; FB 1888: Broadmeadow No. 2 station 1907 and Hamilton station b. 1901 by R.R. Wonders, d. by Ernest George Yeomans, additions 1906 also by Wonders, reused, damaged 1989, repaired and renovated, new one b. 1925 on new site by W.A. Gazzard, d. by William Hull McNiven, closed and sold 2016, reused); fibrous plaster works: Austral Fibrous Plaster Products Pty Ltd and Rich & Co. Pty Ltd 1923; floods 1893 and 2007; flour mill (C.S. McIntyre Ltd) estab. 1900 by Peter McIntosh and Charles Shelley McIntyre, upgraded 1936 and 1952, sold 1982 to Allied Mills, then sold to Fielders Pty Ltd, damaged 1989, silo demolished 1990, mill closed, sold and reused; food factory (Nut Food Pty Ltd) b. 1954 by W. Stronach Pty Ltd, d. by O.E. Phillips; foundries: J.B. Barclay, J.P. Davidson, Dick Bros, Henry Lane Pty Ltd, burnt down 1945; furniture factories: Fred Barrie, Modern Homes (Henry James

Pullin), fire 1924, D. Murray, William F. Nicolson; gale 1899; gasworks (The City of Newcastle Gas & Coke Co. Ltd) 1912–85; glass works (Newcastle Glass Works Pty Ltd) 1925–2002; glue factory; Greek Orthodox C.: Holy Apostles and St Demetrios's; handle factories: Dodds' and Hely Bros Ltd (removed 1921 from Dora Creek), fire 1926; hosiery factory (Lustre Hosiery Pty Ltd); incinerator (Eureka Sanitary Patent Co.) estab. 1889 for night soil disposal at Newtown by J.M. Rooke and Henry Monlean De Montemas; insulation factory (Bradford Insulation Pty Ltd); joinery (Cannell Bros) 1885; lamp factory (Electric Lamp Manufacturers Aust. Ltd) 1931, extensions b. 1941 by Murdoch and Turner, d. by Jeater, Rodd and Hay; leadlight works (Newcastle Leadlight Works); lime-works (Newcastle Lime & Cement Co. Pty Ltd); lock-up b. 1882 by William Dart; measles epidemic 1948; miners' strikes 1861 and 1880; petrol pump factory (Gilbert & Barker Manufacturing Co. Aust. Pty Ltd); PO 1861, additions 1909 by T. Carpenter and W. Derkenne; Presb. C. (Scots Kirk) b. 1887 by John Frogley, d. by James Henderson, sen.; Prim. Meth. C. 1870; PS b. 1882 by William Dart, d. by Mortimer William Lewis, jun., additions and alterations 1906 by Southon Bros, additions 1964; rabbit trap factory (Henry Lane Aust. Ltd, became Henry Lane Pty Ltd in 1937) 1921, extended 1934 by C. Davis & Sons, d. by Pitt and Merewether, fire 1951; railway barracks, engine shed and workshops b. 1892 by Alexander Hamilton Scouller; Reorganised LDS (Mormon) C. b. 1926 by J. Imrie and Joseph Richard Crebert, closed, sold 2013 and 2016, reused; reservoir b. 1886 by J. Fox & Co.; RS 1872; Salv. Army C. 2012; sawmills: Andrew and Robert Beveridge, and Shay and Munton (bought 1891 by William Laing); scarlet fever 1917 and 1933; schools: Hamilton (Pit Town till 1873) 1858, new building b. 1872 by J.H. Blake, d. by George Allen Mansfield, repairs 1888 by T. Southon, new building b. 1900 by Southon Bros, additions 1918 and 1958, Hamilton Girls HS 1962–73, North Hamilton 1943; SD Adventist C. 1899, new one 1974 d. by Neville Clouten; shale-oil refineries: British-Aust. Oil Co. 1910, closed 1915, site later acquired by Shell Oil Co., and Viggers Pty Ltd 1942; slag wool insulation factory (Bradford Insulation Pty Ltd) 1935; storms 1879, 1898, 2007; streets gas lit 1886; structural steel fabrication works (James Mullan Pty Ltd) 1920; telegraph 1879; tobacco factory (Newcastle Tobacco Manufacturing Co.); tram depot and workshops, extensions 1926, reused; tramway (steam) 1887, converted 1925 to electricity; TX 1903, new building b. 1940 by C.M. Drinkwater, automatic 1944; typhoid 1886; umbrella factory (C. and M. Martinsen); Unit. C. (Wesley-on-Beaumont, orig. Meth.) b. 1928 by John E. Parry, d. by John William Oldham, damaged 1989 and tower rebuilt; vulcanising works (Grierson's) 1920; Wes. Meth. C. 1859, new one 1882, renovated 1902; works: General Electric Co. Ltd 1928 and Shell Oil Co.; pop. 854 (1871), 2,215 (1881), 4,836 (1891), *c.*5,200 (1895), 6,124 (1901), 7,099 (1911), *c.*14,200 (1921), 18,973 (1933), *c.*20,800 (1947), *c.*19,200 (1954), *c.*17,900 (1961), *c.*16,900 (1966), *c.*16,500 (1971), *c.*14,800 (1976).

Hamilton Gate (*Co. Delalah*) 29°00'S. 143°22'E., 281 km N. of Wilcannia.

Hamilton South (*Co. Northumberland*) see Broadmeadow and Merewether.

Hamilton Valley (*Co. Goulburn*) see Albury.

Hamlyn Terrace (*Co. Northumberland*) 33°16'S. 151°28'E., 6 km NE of Wyong; FB (station b. by R.T. Parker Pty Ltd); hospital (Wyong) b. 1978–80 by Beattie & Frost Pty Ltd, d. by Thompson, Glendenning and Pauli, additions by R.T. Parker Pty Ltd, redeveloped 2001–5; school (Warnervale), removed 2008 from Warnervale; Unit. C. (orig. Meth.) 1921, closed, reused, reopened 1994 as Unit. C. (North Lakes), restored 2007, closed 2015, sold, new one (Warnervale Regional) 2017; pop. 3,981 (2006), 5,225 (2011).

Hampden Hall (*Co. Macquarie*) 31°04'S. 152°51'E., 3 km N. of Kempsey; pop. 43 (1933).

Hampton (*Co. Bathurst*) 33°38'S. 148°59'E., 28 km SW of Blayney; pop. 69 (1933).

Hampton (*Co. Bathurst*) see also Hazelwood.

Hampton (*Co. Westmoreland*) 33°39'S. 150°03'E., 19 km E. of Oberon; Upper Run till 1891; farming (incl. potatoes) and pine plantations; Angl. C. (St Thomas's) b. 1897–1907 by E. Cook; cemetery 1892; PO 1867; quarry; rifle range 1915; Rom. Cath. C. (St Gabriel the Archangel) 1952, closed, sold and reused; sawmills: Normanlea (Moore and Coates), burnt down 1917 and Henry J. Roberts; school (Off Flat till 1899) 1882, buildings relocated and re-erected 1891 by James Donald, new building b. 1914 by George Coates, burnt down 1921, new building 1923; TX 1922, automatic 1985; pop. 123 (1901), 123 (1911), 72 (1933), 122 (1947), 119 (1954), 184 (1961), 179 (2006).

Hampton Court (*Co. Raleigh*) 30°25'S. 152°46'E., 10 km SE of Dorrigo.

Hanbury (*Co. Northumberland*) see Waratah.

Hanging Rock (*Co. Mitchell*) see The Rock.

Hanging Rock (*Co. Parry*) 31°29'S. 151°11'E., 50 km SE of Tamworth, on Burrows Ck; gold (disc. 1851), timber, grazing, potatoes; cemetery (81 burials), surveyed 1869, dedicated 1873, closed 1964; dams (mine); electricity 1967; FB; mine (Black Snake) estab. *c.*1861 by Joseph Clark, closed 1908; PO 1863–1944; Prim. Meth. C. 1882; school 1878, new one b. 1880, replaced 1952, closed 1970; stamper battery; telephone 1915; TX 1920, automatic 1973; pop. *c.*200 (1886), 130 (1891), 92 (1911), 149 (1933), 88 (1947), 70 (1954), 123 (1961), 194 (2006).

Haning (*Co. Inglis*) 30°48'S. 151°07'E., 41 km SW of Uralla, on Macdonald R.; school 1897–1907.

Hanleys Creek (*Co. Durham*) 32°25'S. 151°41'E., 7 km W. of Dungog; storm 1928; pop. 26 (1933).

Hannah Bay (*Co. Gloucester*) see Anna Bay.

Hannahs Bridge (*Co. Bligh*) 31°58'S. 149°39'E., 15 km S. of Coolah; orig. Benana Plains; subdivision surveyed 1874 by William Jacomb Conder; Angl. C. (St Luke's) removed from Leadville and re-erected 1918, demolished, replaced, moved 1968 to Neilrex and renamed; RS 1929–75; school (Coolah Bridge till 1953) 1908–59; pop. 97 (1933), 37 (1947).

Hannam Vale (*Co. Macquarie*) 31°43'S. 152°36'E., 14 km SW of Kendall, on Stewarts R.; dairying; Angl. C. (St Paul's) b. 1926 by Bert Kenniwell; FB 1964; LDS (Mormon) C.; Meth. C. b. 1913–15 d. by H. Wilfred Webster; PO 1909; quarry; Salv. Army C. 1914; sawmills: Everingham's and Percy G. Steinmetz; school 1908, new school b. 1926 by F.C. Schmitzer; telephone 1914; TX 1922, automatic 1974; pop. 72 (1911), 382 (1933), 380 (1947), 350 (1954), 268 (1961), 346 (2006), 422 (2011).

Hannan (*Co. Dowling*) 33°38'S. 146°25'E., 35 km S. of Lake Cargelligo; village gaz. 1931; RS 1929–75; pop. 101 (1933).

Hanover (*Co. Bathurst*) 33°41'S. 149°16'E., 17 km S. of Blayney; school 1890 b. by W.R. Gorringe, closed 1896, demolished.

Hanwood (*Co. Cooper*) 34°20'S. 146°02'E., 5 km S. of Griffith; estab. 1912 and village gaz. 1915; rice, hort., oranges, wine, eggs; Angl. C. (St James's) 1913–71, moved 1971 to Griffith; cemetery; engineering works; flood 2012; freezing works (Griffith Freezing Co. Ltd); gale 1923; Meth. C. 1926; PO 1921, damaged 1923; poultry processing plant (Baiada Poultry Pty Ltd); Rom. Cath. C. (St Anthony's) 1972; school 1914, additions 1985 and 2010; storm 1954; telephone 1923; TX 1930–59; vegetable packing house (Rinaland); wineries: Beelbangera Co-op. Winery (estab. 1925 by Henry Francis Jones, bought 1943 by McWilliam's), McWilliam's (estab. 1913–17 by John James McWilliam), Piromit, Zappacosta Estate (formerly Franco Wines) 1956; pop. 796 (1933), 1,394 (1947), 421 (1954), 424 (1961), 302 (1971), 262 (1976), 306 (1981), 399 (1986), 422 (1991), 509 (1996), 595 (2001), 583 (2006), 562 (2011).

Hanworth (*Co. Argyle*) 34°24'S. 150°03'E., 28 km W. of Berrima, on Hanworth Ck; Bogaduck till 1926; goldmining and grazing;

PO 1927–31; sawmill (William and Albert Smith), closed and removed 1922; telephone 1925; TX 1928; pop. 42 (1933).

Happy Flat (*Co. Northumberland*) see Hamilton.

Happy Jack (*Co. Selwyn*) 36°02'S. 148°29'E., 52 km SE of Tumbarumba; temporary construction camp (1954–59) estab. by Kaiser-Walsh-Perini-Raymond for Snowy Mountains Hydro-Electric Scheme; PO 1955–59; PS (incl. lock-up) 1955–59; quarry; school 1956–59; telephone 1955.

Happy Valley (*Co. Forbes*) 33°40'S. 148°13'E., 26 km N. of Grenfell; gold; mines: Razor *c.*1900 and *c.*1931, and Tin Pot 1878–1931.

Happy Valley (*Co. Hardinge*) 30°04'S. 151°39'E., 18 km N. of Guyra; sawmill.

Happy Valley (*Co. Hunter*) 32°56'S. 150°39'E., 58 km W. of Paxton.

Happy Valley (*Co. Northumberland*) see Killingworth.

Happy Valley (*Co. Rous*) 28°32'S. 152°56'E., 11 km NW of Kyogle; bananas; bushfire 1936; pop. 43 (1933).

Happy Valley (*Co. St Vincent*) see Araluen.

Happy Valley Springs (*Co. Cook*) 33°26'S. 150°14'E., 8 km NE of Lithgow; quarry (sand).

Harben Vale (*Co. Brisbane*) 31°48'S. 150°57'E., 12 km E. of Murrurundi, on Splitters Ck; school 1886–98.

Harden (*Co. Harden*) 34°33'S. 148°22'E., 2 km E. of Murrumburrah, on Cunningham Plains Ck; North Murrumburrah till 1880; munic. (Murrumburrah) proc. 1890, thrived 1927; mining (gold disc. 1856), cereal crops, sheep, cattle; abattoir (Woodbrae Holdings Pty Ltd); ambulance station; butter factory (Coastal Farmers, taken over 1922 by Cootamundra-Harden Co-op. Dairy Society Ltd, extended 1923, closed 1973); concrete pipe works (Hume Pipe Co. Aust. Ltd) 1933–86; earth tremor 1940; electricity 1920; FB 1934 (station b. 1935 by Henry Spence and Robert Irvine McKinney, extended 2007); fires 1895, 1920, 1923; flood 1893; lock-up 1892; Meth. C. 1910; mines; PO 1882; PS 1883, new one 1929; railway barracks 1877, new barracks 1913; railway coal stage, removed 1880 from Goulburn, second one 1891, third one 1896; railway engine shed b. 1879 by H.A. Brigg, second one 1888 (removed from Goulburn), burnt down 1895, replaced; railway turntable, 75 ft (22.9 m); railway workshops; reservoir 1980; Rom. Cath. C. (St Anthony's) b. 1934 by Stanley Gordon Lipscombe and Len Price, d. by William Patrick Conolly; RS (North Murrumburrah till 1880) 1877, station moved 1881 to Tallong, new one b. 1881 by Langley and Thompson, refreshment room b. 1884 by W.H. Downey and closed 1957, station renovated 1919; sale-yards b. 1917 by Robert Gibson & Son; school (Murrumburrah HS) 1971; SD Adventist C., burnt down 1920; sewerage 1940; snow 1900 and 1956; telegraph 1881; TX 1909, automatic 1969; typhoid 1885; Unit. C. (William Ross Memorial, orig. Presb.) b. 1915 by Brown and Haynes, d. by John Reid & Son; water supply 1929; Wes. Meth. C. 1890, additions 1900 and 1933, closed, sold 2014, reused; pop. 182 (1871, incl. Murrumburrah), 1,620 (1881, incl. Murrumburrah), 133 (1891), *c.*700 (1903), 427 (1911), 2,851 (1933, incl. Murrumburrah), 2,595 (1947, incl. Murrumburrah), 2,727 (1954, incl. Murrumburrah), 2,112 (1976, incl. Murrumburrah), 2,070 (1981, incl. Murrumburrah), 2,045 (1986, incl. Murrumburrah), 2,016 (1991, incl. Murrumburrah), 1,700 (1996, incl. Murrumburrah), 1,911 (2001, incl. Murrumburrah), 1,996 (2006, incl. Murrumburrah), 1,925 (2011, incl. Murrumburrah). (See also Murrumburrah.)

Harden (*Co. Harden*) see also Currawong.

Hardys Bay (*Co. Northumberland*) see Killcare.

Hardys Mill (*Co. Selwyn*) 35°41'S. 148°05'E., 12 km NE of Tumbarumba; PO 1950; school 1951–70; telephone 1949; TX 1950–74; pop. 60 (1947), 53 (1954), 62 (1961).

Harefield (*Co. Clarendon*) 34°58'S. 147°31'E., 12 km SW of Junee, on Reedy Ck; farming and grazing; Angl. C. (St Mark's) 1881; floods

1926 and 1928; PO 1914; RS (Wallace Town till 1882) 1878–1984; school 1890–99 and 1919–78; silo 1922; telegraph 1890; telephone 1914; TX 1915, automatic 1954; pop. 132 (1911), 149 (1933), 97 (1947), 118 (1954), 109 (1961).

Hargraves (*Co. Wellington*) 32°48'S. 149°28'E., 25 km SW of Mudgee, on Louisa Ck; Louisa Creek till 1872; surveyed 1859 by John Alexander Horatio Price, town gaz. 1860; mining (gold disc. 1851) mainly 1894–1903, then farming, grazing, fossicking; Angl. C. (St Stephen's) 1852, new one 1860; cemeteries: pioneer (15 graves 1856–89), general (101 graves), Rom. Cath. (71 graves 1858+); CH, closed; dam (Great Nugget Vein Co.); earth tremor 1934; fire 1907; mines: Alma, Big Nugget (incl. headframe), Blackfellow, Blue Spec (North Mt Boppy Co.) 1908–12 and 1933, Brown Eagle, Eldorado Hill (F. Fletcher) <1875, 1896–1900, 1902–4, Eureka (bought 1874 by Redell), Florence, Florrie, Frenchman's, Happy Dick's, Lizzie Watson, Main Axis, Mudgee; PO 1856; pound (stock) 1865; Presb. C. 1856; PS, closed; 2 quarries; Rom. Cath. C. (St Mary's) 1856; school (Louisa Creek till 1862) 1856, new one b. 1858, additions 1882 by G. Leggett, new one b. 1910 by John Baker, additions 2010; stamper battery; telegraph 1888; TX 1927, automatic 1985; watch-house b. 1869 by J. Atkinson, repairs 1905 by G. Collyer and W. Carmichael; pop. 330 (1861), 231 (1871), 221 (1881), *c.*300 (1886), 178 (1891), 212 (1901), 280 (1911), 219 (1933), 229 (1947), 174 (1954), 261 (1961), *c.*150 (1987), 338 (2011).

Harley Hill (*Co. Camden*) 34°47'S. 150°44'E., 4 km E. of Berry; cemetery (36 graves 1901–*c.*1920) 1899; school 1885, dismantled and re-erected on new site 1903 by David Wilson, closed 1926.

Harolds Cross (*Co. Murray*) 35°34'S. 149°33'E., 26 km SW of Braidwood; mine (gold); sawmills: Gumm Bros and Robinson Williams & Co.; pop. 27 (1933), 416 (2011).

Harparary (*Co. Nandewar*) 30°32'S. 150°00'E., 20 km N. of Boggabri; school 1888–93 and 1957–73; telephone 1927; TX 1927, automatic 1968; pop. 36 (1933).

Harpers Hill (*Co. Northumberland*) see Greta.

Harrington (*Co. Macquarie*) 31°52'S. 152°42'E., 22 km E. of Taree, on Manning R.; (incl. Harrington Waters); Manning River Heads till 1885; orig. shipbuilding and former seaport, now fishing and tourism; Angl. C. (St Peter's) b. 1954 by N. Atkins; breakwater b. 1895–1927 by Granter & Co., damaged 1898; cemetery (Pilot Hill, 8 graves); Community C.; FB; fire 1903; foot-bridge; gale 1898; pilot station 1860, defunct; PO 1876, new one b. 1900 by Stewart Adolphus Levick; Presb. C. (St Andrew's) 1905–70, demolished; railway to breakwater from Crowdy Head quarry, 4.5 miles (11.7 km); reservoir; Rom. Cath. C. (Our Lady Star of the Sea) b. 1953 by Schmitzer and Burg, extended and remodelled 1978; school 1896, repairs 1920 by F. Unicomb, renovated 1942, additions 1963 and 1978; sewage works; telegraph 1876, new office b. 1900 by Stewart Adolphus Levick; telephone 1906; TX 1918, automatic 1972; Unit. C. (orig. Meth.) 1971; water supply augmentation 1970; wharf b. 1898 by R.H. Worthing; pop. 204 (1901), 150 (1911), 153 (1933), 384 (1947), 382 (1954), 488 (1961), 543 (1966), 606 (1971), 896 (1976), 1,183 (1981), 1,234 (1986), 1,414 (1991), 1,397 (1996), 1,409 (2001), 1,753 (2006), 2,258 (2011).

Harrington Waters (*Co. Macquarie*) see Harrington.

Hartford (*Co. Vernon*) 31°05'S. 151°44'E., 17 km SE of Walcha; school 1883–1912.

Hartley (*Co. Cook*) 33°33'S. 150°11'E., 8 km S. of Lithgow, on River Lett; Vale of Clwyd 1815–33 then Hassan's Walls till 1841; estab. 1815, founded 1834, surveyed 1836 by Henry Butler, laid out 1836 by Samuel Augustus Perry, first lots sold 1840, second land sale 1841, thrived in 1860s, designated as chief town of the county, declined 1869+, revived 1887+, declined 1946+, decl. historic site 1972, village restored 1978+; formerly wheat, maize, rye, oats, potatoes, apples, tobacco, now fruit and tourism; airfield; Angl. C. (St

John the Evangelist) b. 1857–59 by William Rose, d. by Edmund Thomas Blacket, closed 1988; bridge b. 1877 by Frederick C. Staveley, new one 1935 by Noyd, over River Lett; bushfire 1944; cemetery (286 graves 1847+); CH b. 1835–38 by Robert Reddie and Ross Coulter, d. by Mortimer William Lewis, 6 cells added 1840 but later demolished, courthouse closed 1887, placed in trust of local council 1927, reused, restored 1978; FB; gale 1898; hailstorm 1901; lock-up 1834, extended 1841, ruined; measles epidemic 1939; PO 1834, new one b. 1846, reused; pound (stock) 1865; PS 1831; quarries (feldspar and Cornish stone); Rom. Cath. C. (St Bernard's) d. and b. 1842–48 by Alexander Binning, re-roofed, closed 1965, sold 1974, restored, reused, and graveyard; school 1870–1943 and 1956–71; telephone 1898; TX 1915, automatic 1967; pop. 39 (1841), 62 (1846), 88 (1851), 128 (1856), 118 (1861), *c.*150 (1866), 59 (1901), 552 (1911), 68 (1933), 114 (1947), 63 (1954), 99 (1961), *c.*50 (1987), 299 (2011).

Hartley Vale (*Co. Cook*) 33°32'S. 150°14'E., 6 km N. of Mount Victoria, on Kerosene Ck; (incl. Petrolea Vale); private village estab. 1866 by Hartley Kerosene & Paraffine Co., thrived *c.*1892; mining (oil-shale disc. 1824 by Rene Primevere Lesson) 1865–1910, farming, orchards; brickworks; candle factory 1896; cemetery (152 graves 1837+); coalmine (Hartley Vale No. 4, estab. 1956 by Ted Miller, bought 1960 by Austen & Butta Pty Ltd and renamed Grose Valley, modernised 1962, flooded 1972, closed 1987, reopened 1990 by Coalpac Pty Ltd as Canyon, closed 1997); coke-oven b. 1888 by Sands & Co.; electricity 1943; fires 1886 and 1904; measles epidemic 1939; miners' strikes 1880, 1897, 1901; mines (oil-shale) and works: Kerosene Oil & Paraffine Co. Ltd (estab. 1865) and Western Kerosene Oil Co. Ltd (estab. 1866), distillation began 1866 with 27 retorts, incline and tramway b. 1869, d. by Norman Selfe, companies merged 1871 to become NSW Shale & Oil Co. Ltd, 20 horizontal retorts added 1880, site closed 1903, acquired 1906 by Commonwealth Oil Corp. Ltd, refinery upgraded 1908–10, mining ceased 1910, works closed 1913, partly dismantled and removed 1916–18, remainder demolished 1929; PO 1872–1967; PS 1884–1913; RS 1876, new station b. 1892 by Charles Palmer, relocated 1901, closed 1973, demolished 1975; school 1872, additions 1881 by John Wadsworth Ashworth, additions 1894 by Robert A. Crowe, remodelled 1925, closed 1946; telephone 1891; TX 1928–67; pop. 70 (1871), 797 (1891), 442 (1901), 131 (1933), 86 (1947), 91 (1954).

Hartwood (*Co. Townsend*) 35°21'S. 145°23'E., 32 km W. of Jerilderie, on Billabong Ck; pop. 74 (1911), 26 (1933).

Hartys Plains (*Co. Macquarie*) 31°28'S. 152°38'E., 10 km W. of Wauchope, on Hastings R.

Harwood (*Co. Clarence*) see Harwood Island.

Harwood Island (*Co. Clarence*) 29°25'S. 153°15'E., 9 km NE of Maclean, in Clarence R.; (incl. Harwood); dairying, agric., sugarcane; bridge (steel and concrete, with lift span fabricated by Arcos Industries Pty Ltd), b. 1966 by Reed & Stuart Pty Ltd, 2,915 ft (888.5 m), over Clarence R.; cyclones 1913 and 1916; floods 1890, 1892, 1948; hailstorm 1964; PO 1875; PS 1888, new one (incl. lock-up) b. 1909 by Grace and Boulton; punt, replaced 1966 by bridge, across Clarence R.; Rom. Cath. C. (St Dominic's) 1908, damaged 1913, new one 1914, damaged 1944; school 1876, new school b. 1880 on new site by William Kinnear, additions 1889 also by Kinnear, additions 2010; sugar mills: CSR (o. 1874, removed from Gladstone, distillery closed 1895, fire 1947, mill regularly extended and modernised, sold 1978 to NSW Sugar Milling Co-op. Ltd, refinery added 1989, joined 1994 by Manildra Group), John McLachlan, A. McMillan, George Martin, J. Nicholson (incl. distillery) 1878; storm 1944; telegraph 1884; telephone 1906; TX 1911, automatic 1969; Union C. 1878; water reticulation 1966; wharf (concrete) b. 1941 by Oxenfords Pty Ltd; pop. 391 (1881), 519 (1891), 523 (1901), 563 (1911),

523 (1924), 484 (1933), 605 (1947), 475 (1954), 488 (1961), 258 (1971), 231 (1986), 221 (1991), 211 (1996).

Hassans Walls (*Co. Cook*) 33°31'S. 150°09'E., 4 km S. of Lithgow; lookouts; bushfire 1909; mine (abandoned).

Hassan's Walls (*Co. Cook*) see Hartley.

Hastings (*Co. Macquarie*) see Port Macquarie.

Hastings Point (*Co. Rous*) 28°22'S. 153°34'E., 4 km S. of Bogangar, on Coral Sea; Cudgera Headland till 1950; sand mining, tourism, retirement centre; PO 1947; sewerage augmentation 1985 and 1995; telephone 1947; TX 1947, automatic 1972; pop. 27 (1933), 74 (1947), 99 (1954), 123 (1961), 482 (1981), 385 (1986), 582 (2011).

Hatfield (*Co. Kilfera*) 33°52'S. 143°44'E., 88 km N. of Balranald; grazing; PO 1886, burnt down 1930; PS 1886–95; school 1885–90 and 1989–2001; telephone 1924; TX 1924; pop. 46 (2006).

Hat Head (*Co. Macquarie*) 31°03'S. 153°03'E., 21 km E. of Kempsey, on Tasman Sea; village gaz. 1918; tourism; Angl. C. (Christ) 1965; bridge over Korogoro Ck; flood 1964; footbridge over Korogoro Ck; PO 1946; reservoir (concrete), 625,000 gal. (2,841.3 kl), 1968; telephone 1949; TX 1951, automatic 1973; water reticulation 1969; pop. 63 (1947), 65 (1954), 100 (1961), 280 (1976), 330 (1981), 355 (1986), 349 (1991), 334 (1996), 322 (2001), 298 (2006), 326 (2011).

Hattons Corner (*Co. Murray*) see Yass.

Haverton Hill (*Co. Bathurst*) 33°36'S. 149°07'E., 15 km SW of Blayney, on Dirty Ck; school 1880–85.

Havilah (*Co. Phillip*) 32°37'S. 149°46'E., 17 km E. of Mudgee, on Lawsons Ck; gold (disc. 1851), limestone, dolomite; airfield; Angl. C. (Memorial) b. 1905 by John S. Nutt, for Henry White, d. by Harold Robert Hardwick, now seldom used, and graveyard (12 graves 1900–99); cemetery (Rom. Cath., 18 graves 1859+); hailstorm 1878; lime-kilns (Metrop. Lime Co.) 1918, defunct; PO 1883–84; quarries: G. & C. Hoskins Ltd 1912, Metrop. Lime & Cement Co., William Wall 1911; RS 1890–1975; school 1882–84 and 1915–45; pop. 85 (1911), 75 (1933), 68 (1947).

Hawarden (*Co. Darling*) 30°47'S. 150°32'E., 19 km W. of Manilla, on Lake Keepit; school 1890–95.

Hawdon's Ford (*Co. Wentworth*) see Wentworth.

Hawkesbury (*Co. Cook*) see Freemans Reach.

Hawkesbury Cabin (*Co. Northumberland*) see Wondabyne.

Hawkesbury Heights (*Co. Cook*) see Winmalee.

Hawkins Creek (*Co. Darling*) 30°22'S. 150°32'E., 7 km W. of Barraba, on Hawkins Ck; Angl. C. (St Vincent's) b. 1902 by Rodger and Lawrance; school 1884–1934.

Hawks Nest (*Co. Gloucester*) 32°40'S. 152°11'E., 6 km NE of Nelson Bay, on Myall R.; settled by George and Josephine Engel, first lots offered 1926; tourism 1930+, sand mining (Mineral Deposits Pty Ltd) 1966+, retirement centre; bridge (Singing Bridge) to Tea Gardens b. 1974 by Central Constructions Ltd, over Myall R.; PO 1961; punt to Tea Gardens 1930–74, across Myall R.; sawmill (William Henderson and Jabez Buckman) 1867, taken over 1870 by Richard Henry Southan, closed, bought by McSweeney, moved to Bulahdelah; sewage works; storm 2015; telephone 1937; TX 1939; water reticulation 1966; wharves 1926 and 1952; pop. 57 (1954), 83 (1961), 301 (1971), 599 (1976), 1,071 (1981), 1,102 (1986), 1,250 (1991), 1,174 (1996), 1,173 (2001), 1,027 (2006), 1,123 (2011).

Hawks Nest (*Co. Gloucester*) see also Tea Gardens.

Hawksview (*Co. Goulburn*) see Wirlinga.

Hawthorneville (*Co. Clarence*) see Grafton South.

Hay (*Co. Durham*) see Lemington.

Hay (*Co. Waradgery*) 34°30'S. 144°51'E., 112 km W. of Griffith, on Murrumbidgee R.; Lang's Crossing Place till 1861, when also known as Police Point; estab. 1858, surveyed 1859 by Edward Twynam, laid out by Philip Francis Adams, town gaz. and first lots sold

1859, designated as chief town of the county, munic. 1872–1964; orig. river port and sheep, then irrigated crops and grain, cattle, pigs, vegetables, grapes, melons, tomatoes, lettuce, garlic; airport 1940, flooded 1952; ambulance station b. 1955 by W.G. Butterworth & Co., new one 1981; Angl. C. b. 1868–72 by James Simpson, demolished 1989, new one (St Paul's) 1885, additions 1900 and 1908, renovations 1991, closed, and graveyard; Bapt. C. (Hope); boiling-down works (Henry B. Maclure and Robert Gibson), joined 1892 by John Lewis Tomlinson Corrigan, sold to George Gregson Claughton; bond store b. 1877 by Witcombe Bros, reused 1906; breweries: Black Horse Brewery (estab. 1879 by John Simpson, closed 1880, reopened 1883, closed 1885, reopened and closed 1891, reopened 1897, closed 1899), Excelsior Brewery (estab. 1868 by Albert Elliott and John G. Mennon, acquired 1870 by Thomas Simpson, acquired 1873 by George Elliott and Henry Lill Lindsay, renamed the Red Lion Steam Brewery, aerated water plant added 1874, burnt down 1891 and rebuilt, closed 1912, reused), McGrath's Brewery (estab. 1885 by Patrick McGrath, bought 1891 by Jones, Lincoln & Co.); bridge (iron, with swing span) b. 1871–74 by P.N. Russell & Co. and Bartholomew, d. by Gustavus Alphonse Morell and William Christopher Bennett, 750 ft (228.6 m), repairs 1886 by J. Simpson, new one 1896, replaced 1973, over Murrumbidgee R.; bushfires 1906 and 1990–91; butter factories: W. Gordon and Hay Co-op. Butter Factory Co. Ltd (incl. ice works) o. 1906 in former bond store, extended 1906, made ice-cream 1927, damaged 1947, sold 1956 to Hardman and reused as ice works, sold 1959 and reused; carriage-works: Arcade (estab. by Thomas Simpson, became Smith, Simpson & Co., bought 1877 by King), Cobb & Co. 1877 (fire 1893), George Haines (fire 1895), Heyhoe and Baker, Robertson Wagner & Co., N.J. Trevena; caterpillar infestation 1922; cemeteries: general 1863, Jewish, lawn; CH (incl. lock-up) b. 1860 by Philip Comitti and Charles Theodore Bregartner, (second) b. 1875–77 by Witcombe Bros, reused, (third) b. 1892 by Brown and Hill, d. by Walter Liberty Vernon, repairs 1900 by S. Stead & Son, alterations 1920, re-roofed 1962; Chinese joss house, fire 1893; cordial factories: William Sabine, closed and reused and E.G. Smallhorn, bought 1928 by R.M. Rutledge and then traded as E.G. Smallhorn & Co.; customs-house; dam (David Dam); dust storms 1900, 1902, 1922, 1941, 1945; earth tremor 1921; FB 1880 (station b. 1900, second one b. 1918 by W.G. Butterworth & Co., d. by William Hull McNiven, sold and reused 1989, third one b. 1989); fires 1872, 1884, 1885, 1897; floods 1870, 1891, 1931, 1956; gaol b. 1878–80 by Witcombe Bros, d. by James Johnstone Barnet, closed 1915, reused as hospital 1919–21, reused as maternity home 1921–28, reverted to gaol 1930–40, reused as POW camp 1940–46, reverted to gaol 1946–47, disused, reused as delinquent and incorrigible girls' institution 1961–74, reused 1976; gasworks (Colonial Gas Assoc. Ltd) b. 1885 by Alfred George Stanger and Arthur Budden; heatwave 1904–5; hospital 1866, new one b. 1872 by Witcombe Bros, d. by Frederick Augustus Franklin, reused, new one b. 1895 by J.P. Markey, d. by Sir John Sulman, additions 1904 d. by William John Monks, additions 1921, 1961, 1963, 1972, 1975, 1981, 1991, new one 2003; ice works (Riverina) 1887, burnt down 1947; internment camp 1940–46; irrigation 1892; milk factory (W.T. Baird & Sons) o. 1959 in former butter factory, new one 1981–93; munitions factory (World War II); PO 1859, additions 1877 by Witcombe Bros, new one b. 1882 by E. Noble & Co., d. by James Johnstone Barnet, clock tower added 1901, post office renovated and restored 1974; pound (stock) 1859; powerhouse (G.M. Richards & Co.) 1927, fire 1947, alterations 1953 by H. Hyde; Presb. C. (St Andrew's) b. 1872 by Witcombe Bros, tower and spire d. by Frederick Augustus Franklin, spire capped with copper 1978; PS 1860, new one b. 1874 by Witcombe Bros, d. by James Johnstone Barnet, new one b. 1909 by George Huntley

Dixon and William Godfrey Butterworth, d. by Walter Liberty Vernon, repairs 1937 by J.W. Blake and R.A. Gordon, new one 1989; punts: Bagot's 1857, Disher's 1861, Frank Johns 1866, Henry Leonard 1858; railway barracks; railway engine shed b. 1882 by Charles Hardy, destroyed 1902, replaced, demolished 1961; railway turntable, 60 ft (18.3 m); reservoir, 100,000 gal. (454.6 kl); Rom. Cath. C. (St Virgilius's) b. 1875 by Begg, Rawnsley & Son, d. by Andrea Giovanni Stombuco, new one (St Fergal's) 1981; RS 1882, station b. by Charles Hardy, closed 1989, restored and reused; sale-yards b. 1901 by Robert Massie; Salv. Army C.; sawmills: Enterprise (estab. 1872 by Thomas Simpson) and Murdoch and Murphy (closed and sold 1953); scarlet fever 1902 and 1927; schools: primary 1869, new one b. 1870 by Witcombe Bros, additions and repairs 1883 by G.H. Harrison, additions 1910 by George Huntley Dixon and William Godfrey Butterworth, additions 1964 and 2010, and War Memorial HS 1918, additions 1974; sewage works b. 1902–4, augmentation 1957; silo; soap-works: W.F. Gordon & Co. and Thomas S. Williams; storms 1899 and 1902; streets first kerosene lit, then gas lit 1885, then electric lit 1927; telegraph 1864, additions to office 1877 by Witcombe Bros; TX 1907, automatic 1982; typhoid 1889, 1899 (woman died), 1903; Unit. C. (orig. Meth.) 1964; water supply (engine house b. by Witcombe Bros) 1878, augmentation 1988; Wes. Meth. C. b. 1872 by Witcombe Bros; wharf b. 1879 by C.G. Miller; winery (Ruberto's Cellars) 1982; wool-scour (Lomax's), taken over by John Lewis Tomlinson Corrigan, joined by Harold James Corrigan, taken over 1941 by Lachlan Trading Co., closed 1945, machinery sold 1951; pop. 172 (1861), *c.*300 (1866), *c.*400 (1868), 664 (1871), 2,073, (1881), 2,000+ (1887), 2,741 (1891), 3,078 (1895), 3,012 (1901), 2,582 (1911), 3,156 (1933), 2,963 (1947), 3,009 (1954), 3,134 (1961), 2,959 (1966), 3,206 (1971), 2,872 (1976), 2,958 (1981), 2,961 (1986), 2,817 (1991), 2,896 (1996), 2,703 (2001), 2,636 (2006), 2,298 (2011).

Hayards Crossing (*Co. Fitzroy*) 29°56'S. 152°59'E., 24 km NW of Arrawarra, on Orara R.

Hayden Estate (*Co. Auckland*) see Bega.

Haydonton (*Co. Brisbane*) see Murrurundi.

Hayes Park (*Co. Camden*) see Kanahooka.

Haystack Creek (*Co. Buller*) 28°38'S. 152°33'E., 43 km W. of Kyogle, on Haystack Ck; pop. 58 (1933).

Haywards Bay (*Co. Camden*) see Yallah.

Hazelbrook (*Co. Cook*) 33°44'S. 150°27'E., 2 km E. of Lawson, on Hazelbrook Ck; subdivided 1891; orchards, poultry, dairying; Angl. C. (St James's) b. 1904 by Adams on site of former Union C., enlarged 1917, closed 1957, sold and moved to Winmalee, replaced 1957; bushfires 1909, 1940, 1946, 1952, 1957, 1974, 1977, 1979; FB; fibrous plaster works (Auburn, W.P. Archibald); gale 1904; joinery (C.W. Boyle); Meth. C. 1916; PO 1898, new one b. 1966; Rom. Cath. C. (Our Lady of Nativity) 1929; RS 1884, new station 1901; school 1946, additions 1968 and 1990; sewerage 1965; sheet metal works (Hazelbrook Sheet Metal & Plumbing Works); telephone 1903; TX (automatic) 1957; Union C. 1902, destroyed 1904; Unit. C. (Elizabeth Tremain Memorial, orig. Meth.) b. 1940 by Ledger and Smith, d. by Kenwood and Hoile; pop. 113 (1901), 168 (1911), 509 (1921), 448 (1933), 673 (1947), 816 (1954), 955 (1961), 1,351 (1964), 1,113 (1966), 1,871 (1976), 3,570 (1986), 4,534 (2011).

Hazelgrove (*Co. Westmoreland*) 33°40'S. 149°54'E., 6 km NE of Oberon, on Hazelgrove Ck; Slippery Creek till 1890; formerly mining (gold and silver) then farming; cemetery (228 graves 1853+); eucalyptus oil distillery 1937; goldmine (Fitzpatrick's or Slippery Creek, incl. 5 head stamper battery) <1878; PO 1890; quarry; Rom. Cath. C. (St Dominic's) 1856, closed, sold to Jack O'Connell, dismantled, removed and reused, new one (in old church hall) 1928; RS (3 km NW) 1923–71; school 1901 b. by W.J. Bailey, closed 1969; telephone 1908; TX 1928–73; pop. 66 (1901), 79 (1911), 179 (1933), 174 (1947), 175 (1954), 168 (1961).

Hazel Park (*Co. Jamison*) 29°51'S. 149°19'E.,

39 km N. of Wee Waa; school 1961–71.

Hazelwood (*Co. Bathurst*) 33°37'S. 148°58'E., 29 km W. of Blayney; school (Hampton till 1899 then Eganton till 1911) 1889 b. by James Donald, closed 1893, reopened 1898, demolished 1918, new one b. 1910 by W.J. Leabeater, closed 1930, reopened 1937, closed 1941, moved 1948 to Emu Swamp.

Head Vale (*Co. Darling*) 30°44'S. 150°29'E., 23 km W. of Manilla; earth tremor 2012; school (Corella till 1925) 1906–26; telephone 1926; TX 1926–37.

Heatherbrae (*Co. Gloucester*) 32°47'S. 151°44'E., 2 km S. of Raymond Terrace, on Hunter R.; (incl. Motto Farm); Assemblies of God C. (New Life); bushfires 1926, 1938, 2013; blind factory (Mick Sullivan Blinds) 1989; caravan factory (Opalite Industries); hailstorm 2005; metal fabrication works: Ezi Metal (Warren Lawrence) 1999 and Terrace Fabrications Pty Ltd 1979; particle board factory (Masonite Corp. A'asia Ltd) b. 1939 by W. Stronach, d. by John William Oldham and Robert Godwin Lees, later became Hardboards Aust. Ltd, closed; PO 1955–75; rifle range; sawmill; school (Hunter River HS, Raymond Terrace HS till 2005) 1956, additions 1959, 1961, 1965, 1967, 1969, 1971, 1979; tarpaulin factory (All Tarps); telephone 1955; trailer works (Altair Steel Fabrications); pop. 214 (1961), 479 (2006), 492 (2011).

Heatherdale (*Co. Gloucester*) 32°03'S. 151°50'E., 13 km SW of Gloucester, on Gloucester R.; school (Lower Gloucester River till 1929) 1904–18 and 1957–69; Union C.

Heatherwood Village (*Co. Cook*) see Winmalee.

Heaton (*Co. Northumberland*) see Jesmond.

Hebburn (*Co. Northumberland*) see Elrington.

Hebden (*Co. Durham*) 32°23'S. 151°04'E., 22 km NW of Singleton; dairying and grazing; Angl. C. (St Peter's) 1926, and graveyard; PO 1912; school 1912 b. by G. Sanderman, closed 1973, derelict; telephone 1914; TX 1918–73; pop. 144 (1933), 89 (1947), 93 (1954), 81 (1961).

Heddon (*Co. Northumberland*) see Sawyers Gully.

Heddon Greta (*Co. Northumberland*) 32°48'S. 151°31'E., 3 km NE of Kurri Kurri; estab. 1902 by Heddon Greta Coal Mining Co., first lots sold 1902; abattoir; Angl. C. (St John the Baptist) b. 1908 by Richard Peet, d. by C.W. Holmes; bushfires 1909, 1928, 1933, 1936, 1944, 2002, 2006, 2017; colliery estab. 1889 by Henry Trenchard, Samuel Clift, Henry John Adams et al., acquired and o. 1902 by Heddon Greta Coal Mining Co., man killed 1904, fire 1905, strike 1908, fire 1911, flooded, closed 1912, acquired 1915 by East Greta Coal Mining Co., razed; Meth. C. b. 1906 by Payne and Roberts, closed, moved 1921 to Kurri Kurri, replaced 1922; PO 1903, burnt down 1927; quarry; railway (colliery); RS (colliery) 1903, relocated and renamed Kurri Road, burnt down 1929; sawmills: Gould and Schultz, and Pike Bros, fires 1908 and 1926; school 1904 b. by C. Waters, closed 1969, burnt down 1975; telephone 1904; water supply pump house b. 1923 by W. Horton & Sons; pop. 401 (1911), 312 (1933), 272 (1947), 313 (1954), 374 (1961), 907 (1991), 1,038 (1996), 1,085 (2001), 1,428 (2006), 1,711 (2011).

Heifer Station (*Co. Gresham*) 29°28'S. 152°35'E., 43 km W. of Kyogle; PO 1868–80; sawmill (Northern Sawmills Pty Ltd), burnt down 1942; pop. 61 (1933).

Hell Hole (*Co. Richmond*) 29°13'S. 153°19'E., 15 km SW of Evans Head.

Hells Hole (*Co. Georgiana*) 33°50'S. 149°13'E., 33 km S. of Blayney, on Hells Hole Ck.

Henderson's Platform (*Co. Cook*) see Linden.

Hendy Town (*Co. Wentworth*) see Buronga.

Henriendi (*Co. Pottinger*) 30°35'S. 150°01'E., 13 km N. of Boggabri.

Henty (*Co. Hume*) 35°31'S. 147°02'E., 17 km N. of Culcairn, on Buckargingah Ck; Doodle Cooma till 1891; settled by Bourke, surveyed 1886, laid out and village gaz. 1888, lots auctioned 1888, founded by John Herman Rosler; wheat, chaff cutting, cattle, sheep, dairying 1910–45, poultry 1930s–70s; agric. implement works: C.F. Haberecht 1886 and Whitlock Bros; airfield; Angl. C. (St Barnabas's) 1917; Assemblies of God C. (Riverlife); bridge b. 1892 by John Archer, over Buckargingah Ck; carriage-works: C.F. Haberecht 1886 and Whitlock Bros; cemetery 1891, new one 1910; CH 1899, new one b. 1909 by Hocking Bros; chaff mills: Goulburn Produce Co. Pty Ltd, Kerridge and McMahon 1937, one estab. 1916 by Gus. R. Kleinig, J.E. Kleinig and Arthur Stockman (taken over 1921 by A.H. Stockman & Co. Pty Ltd, bought 1926 by John Crennan & Co., then in 1928 by Stockman's again, sold 1930 to James Dunn & Sons Pty Ltd, acquired by Wettern & Co.), J. Thiemann 1937, Wettern & Co. 1968–77; concrete plant; cordial factory estab. 1900 by J. Derepas, taken over 1904 by W.R. Yates, operated 1918 by W. Graf, factory replaced by Charles A. Graf, taken over by John Rogers trading as Alpha Cordials, bought 1977 by Kilo Bros; dam 1895; drought 1914; dust storm 1898; FB 1947 (station replaced 1968, new one 2018 on new site); fire 1933; flood 1900; frog plague 1971; hospital 1966; ice works 1914; Lutheran C.: St Paul's 1963, Trinity (b. 1937 by Jack Barrie, jun., reused 1970 as Rom. Cath. C. and renamed St Patrick's), Zion 1913, demolished; measles epidemic (boy died) 1898; PO 1886, new one b. 1890, closed 1902, another one b. 1900 by J. Wyatt, additions 1912 by Bond and McMillan; POW control centre 1944; powerhouse (Henty Electric Supply, C.F. Haberecht) 1910; Presb. C. (St John's) b. 1935 by Jack Barrie, jun., d. by William John Monks and Christopher Ernest Jeffs; PS 1899, new one b. 1909 by Hocking Bros; reservoir, 1,000,000 gal. (4,546 kl); rifle range, flooded 1931; Rom. Cath. C. (St Patrick's) 1910, demolished, new one in former Lutheran C.; RS (Doodle Cooma till 1891) 1885, station b. by Charles Hardy, relocated 1904, closed 1989, partly reused; sale-yards (Dalgety's) 1954; school 1893, additions 1905 by Williams and Bruce, additions 1938 by Ryan, additions 1964; sewerage 1972; silo 1920; snow 1899 and 1970; storm 1972; tannery (Wilhelm Schnelle) 1890–1900; telephone 1892; TX 1910, automatic 1980; Union C. 1897, not used 1916–21, reused, replaced, demolished 1955; Unit. C. (orig. Meth.) b. 1928 by Jack Barrie, jun.; water supply 1948; pop. 123 (1891), 521 (1901), 968 (1911), 1,142 (1933), 1,047 (1947), 1,073 (1954), 894 (1961), 863 (1966), 845 (1971), 832 (1976), 883 (1981), 880 (1986), 840 (1991), 878 (1996), 856 (2001), 863 (2006), 882 (2011).

Herding Yard Creek (*Co. Buller*) see Amosfield.

Hermidale (*Co. Flinders*) 31°33'S. 146°44'E., 44 km W. of Nyngan; Hermitage Plains till 1892; village gaz. 1896; grazing and copper (disc. 1906 by R.A. Sorensen); airfield; Angl. C. (St Faith's) 1923; cemetery (41 graves 1915+); FB; mine (Budgery) 1906; PO 1881–1994; PS 1917; reservoir 1959; RS 1892, station b. by R. Furnell, closed 1975, removed 1986; school 1901, new building 1909; telephone 1898; TX 1915, automatic 1986; water reticulation 1959; pop. 132 (1901), 236 (1911), 164 (1933), 140 (1947), 136 (1954), 105 (1961), 132 (2006), 302 (2011).

Hermitage Flat (*Co. Cook*) see Lithgow.

Hermitage Plains (*Co. Flinders*) see Hermidale.

Hermits Peak (*Co. Rous*) 28°32'S. 152°58'E., 10 km N. of Kyogle, on Richmond R.; RS 1941–57.

Hernani (*Co. Fitzroy*) 30°19'S. 152°26'E., 28 km W. of Dorrigo, on Dead Dog Ck; farming; cheese factory (Maida Vale Co-op. Factory Ltd) 1924; PO 1902, burnt down 1929; school 1897, additions 1967 and 2010; telephone 1912; TX 1915, automatic 1975; Union C. 1909; pop. 162 (1911), 147 (1933), 140 (1947), 126 (1954), 106 (1961), 208 (2006), 243 (2011).

Hernani West (*Co. Fitzroy*) 30°18'S. 152°24'E., 30 km W. of Dorrigo.

Herons Creek (*Co. Macquarie*) 31°36'S. 152°44'E., 5 km N. of Kendall, on Herons Ck; settled 1850 by George William Crane, estab. 1890; timber, farming, dairying;

Angl. C. (St Mary the Virgin) 1927–2005, bought 2009 by Martin and Jeanette Parish, restored, reopened 2011 as Community C.; bushfire 1951; cemetery (143 graves 1914+); PO 1908; quarry; RS 1915–74; sawmills: Jack Boyd 1950 (restored 1996–97), Brown's, Alf Noone 1915 (amalgamated with Brown's to form Heron's Creek Timber Mills Ltd, burnt down 1942, replaced, acquired 1947 by Zinc Corp. Ltd, man killed 1951, new one b. 1960, acquired 1985 by Duncan's Holdings Ltd, sold 1992 to Boral Pty Ltd, expanded 2004–6); school 1894, new one b. 1925, additions 2010; telephone 1912; TX 1944, automatic 1953; pop. 159 (1911), 329 (1933), 294 (1947), 335 (1954), 271 (1961), 311 (2011).

Hewetsons Mill (*Co. Buller*) 28°26'S. 152°23'E., 61 km W. of Kyogle, on Little Oaky Ck; PO 1929; telephone 1925; TX 1937–72; pop. 59 (1947), 54 (1961).

Hexham (*Co. Northumberland*) 32°50'S. 151°41'E., 9 km SW of Raymond Terrace, on Hunter R.; lots sold 1840, village gaz. 1856, subdivision (Glen Levet Estate) 1921; hunting, maize, lucerne, dairying, vegetables; Angl. C. (St Paul's), re-roofed 1874; boiling-down works (Hunter River, Thomas Doust); bridges: Ash Island Bridge to Kooragang, b. 1909 by J.H. Shedden, new one 1955, 560 ft or 170.7 m, over Hunter R., steel truss bridge (with lift span) to Tomago, fabricated by Thomas C. Pollard and State Dockyard (Carrington), b. 1945–52 by J. King & Son, 1,254 ft (382.2 m), new adjacent concrete one 1987, over Hunter R., Iron Bark Creek Bridge to Sandgate 1938, destroyed 1956, replaced 1962 (with Bailey bridge being used in the interim); 2 coal shoots; coal washery 1956; dairy factory (Raymond Terrace Dairy & Produce Co.) b. 1927 by J. Conolly, d. by Richard Wildridge; earth tremor 1868; engineering works (J. & A. Brown & Abermain Seaham Collieries Ltd) 1891; floods 1864, 1867, 1893, 1922, 1930, 1934, 1949, 1950, 1955; gale 1951; PO 1840; pound (stock) 1843, relocated 1863; Prim. Meth. C. 1869; punt (John Hannell) 1847, new one (steam) b. 1884 by J.S. Rodgers, ceased 1952, across Hunter R.; railway (coal) to Minmi b. 1856 for John Eales, later extended; railway bridge (steel truss) 1898 to Sandgate, 110 ft (33.5 m), new one (steel truss) 1912, 126 ft (38.4 m), over Ironbark Ck; Rom. Cath. C. (St Patrick's); RS 1871, new station 1902; school 1850–56 and 1865–1976; slaughtering and salting works (Edward Sparke) 1843; storm 2004; telegraph 1882–1902; telephone 1893; Unit. C. (orig. Meth.) b. 1922 by P. Wall, d. by Alfred Gambier Newman, closed, sold and reused; Wes. Meth. C. b. 1867 by John Coulton; wharves: one b. 1892 by Austin Callen and one b. 1937 by C.R. McKenzie (for Raymond Terrace Co-op. Dairy & Produce Co. Ltd); pop. 122 (1856), *c.*200 (1866), 143 (1871), 76 (1881), 335 (1891), 915 (1901), 334 (1911), 512 (1933), 679 (1947), 604 (1954), 339 (1971), 242 (1976), 208 (1981), 153 (2006), 179 (2011).

Hexham (*Co. Northumberland*) see also Tarro.

Hiawatha (*Co. Gipps*) 33°50'S. 147°10'E., 10 km N. of West Wyalong; goldmining; Meth. C. 1908; mines: Coronation or Blow (Conway and Ryan 1898, P. Bonner 1938, M. Hart 1960), Crampton's *c.*1898, Crawley's *c.*1898, Dawson's *c.*1898, Early Morn *c.*1898, Fletcher's *c.*1898, Molloy's *c.*1898, Nelson's, Prospector's *c.*1898; pop. 84 (1911).

Hibbard (*Co. Macquarie*) see Port Macquarie.

Hickeys Creek (*Co. Dudley*) 30°53'S. 152°37'E., 30 km NW of Kempsey, on Hickeys Ck; farming; butter factory (Upper Macleay Co-op. Dairy Co. Ltd) 1906; cemetery (Toms Gully, 64 graves 1878); Meth. C. b. 1903 by W. Hefren; PO 1886; Rom. Cath. C. (St John's) 1896; sawmills: Mitchell Bros (moved 1913 to Greenhill), and Watkins and Watkins; school 1882, additions 1915 by P. Landers, closed 1928; telephone 1898; TX 1914–70; Unit. C. (orig. Meth.) b. 1913 by W. Hefren, renovated 1922; Wes. Meth. C. b. 1890 by James Murphy; pop. 149 (1911), 71 (1933), 58 (1947), 60 (1954), 50 (1961), 263 (2011).

Hickeys Creek (*Co. Dudley*) see also Millbank.

Hickory Hill (*Co. Hume*) 35°36'S. 146°55'E., 14 km NW of Culcairn; school 1923–51, building moved 1953 to Culcairn.

Higham Road (*Co. Northumberland*) see Mount Hutton.

Higher Macdonald (*Co. Northumberland*) 33°13'S. 150°56'E., 45 km NW of Ourimbah, on McDonald R.; abandoned; farming; Angl. C. (St Phillip's) 1900; bridge over McDonald R.; PO 1927–31; telephone 1930; pop. 46 (1933).

Highfield (*Co. Rous*) 28°38'S. 153°00'E., 1 km S. of Kyogle, on Richmond R.; sewage works; pop. 51 (1933), 55 (1947), 83 (1961).

Highfields (*Co. Northumberland*) see Kahibah.

Highland Home (*Co. Gough*) 29°19'S. 151°35'E., 48 km N. of Glen Innes, on Highland Home Ck; toll-gate.

High Range (*Co. Camden*) 34°23'S. 150°18'E., 13 km N. of Berrima; vineyards; Angl. C. (St Thomas's) b. 1891 by William Bunter, renovated 1907, closed 1947, reopened 1971, closed 1999, reopened, and graveyard (28 graves 1900+) 1893; FB; pop. 25 (1933), 473 (2011).

High Street (*Co. Northumberland*) see Maitland.

High View (*Co. Rous*) 28°25'S. 152°59'E., 23 km N. of Kyogle; telephone 1925; TX 1925–27.

Hilans Corner (*Co. Rous*) 28°31'S. 153°31'E., 4 km N. of Mullumbimby.

Hillas Creek (*Co. Wynyard*) 35°10'S. 147°48'E., 29 km NW of Adelong, on Hillas Ck; bridge 1860, new one (concrete bowstring arch) 1938, disused since 1983; PO 1873–80.

Hillas Creek (*Co. Wynyard*) see also Mundarlo.

Hillcrest (*Co. Camden*) see Upper Kangaroo River.

Hillcroft (*Co. Lincoln*) 32°19'S. 149°01'E., 28 km N. of Wellington; PO 1884; school 1916–31; telegraph 1888; telephone 1906; TX 1910, automatic 1972.

Hilldale (*Co. Durham*) 32°30'S. 151°39'E., 15 km SW of Dungog, on Wattle Gully; Big Creek till 1905; settled 1861+; formerly tobacco, wine, nuts, logging till 1930s, orchards till 1955, poultry 1950s+, now dairying and beef; droughts 1965 and 1980; electricity 1950; floods 1955 and 1971; PO 1916–78; quarry; RS 1923; sawmill; school (Big Creek till 1961) 1907–37 and 1946–68; telephone 1914; TX 1926–78; Union C. b. 1899 by Ralph Oliver Borham and Albert Taylor, new one b. 1957 by G.W. Deards, and columbarium; pop. 179 (1911), 135 (1933), 132 (1947), 116 (1954), 108 (1961).

Hill End (*Co. Wellington*) 33°02'S. 149°25'E., 41 km NE of Orange, on Hill End Ck; (incl. Germantown, Irishtown, Newtown); orig. Bald Hill; settled 1851, founded 1853, surveyed 1859 by John Alexander Horatio Price, village gaz. 1860 (erroneously) as Forbes, gaz. 1862 as Hill End, thrived 1871–73, munic. proc. 1873, declined 1874+, munic. abolished 1908, village revived 1908–*c.*1922, decl. historic site 1967, classified by National Trust, most buildings defunct; mining (gold disc. 1851) mainly 1871–74 and 1908–24, hort., artists' colony 1947+, grazing, now fossicking and tourism; Angl. C. (St Matthew's), new one (St Andrew's) b. 1872–75 by Wilcox and Babbage, d. by Edward Gell, condemned, demolished 1917, replaced 1922 with former Salv. Army C., new one 1924 on new site; brewery (Barley Sheaf Brewery) estab. 1873 by Edward Inch and Albert Jeffree; brickworks (Thomas Newcombe); bushfire 1957; cemetery 1874; CH 1872, fire 1883, new one (incl. lock-up) 1900 d. by Walter Liberty Vernon; Chinese joss house; cordial factories: J. Cahill, Excelsior (estab. by Thomas Girvan Weir), Holman's, Weir and Embleton; diphtheria 1914; droughts 1854–55, 1880, 1888; earth tremors 1872 and 1876; FB (station reused); fires 1874, 1880, 1883; hospital 1873, closed, restored and reused 1972; lock-up b. 1872 by Hudson Bros; miners' strike 1916; mines: Amalgamated, Jimmy Brown, Canton, Carroll and Beard, Cornelian, Deep Levels (closed 1924), Devon Gold Mining Co. 1951–53, Emmett and Hughes, Goldenville, Great Western Undaunted, Just in Time, Kings Reef, Krohmann's, Monte Cristo, Northumberland, Patriarch, Paxton and Holman, Pioneer Reef, Porter and Rawsthorne, Rapp's, Red Hill (closed 1917), Reward, Rose of England, Star of Hope, Star of Peace (man killed 1879) 1872–84; PO 1869–1994; pound (stock) 1880; Prim. Meth. C. 1873, closed, sold and reused; PS 1871; rifle range 1906; Rom. Cath. C. (St Joseph's) 1873, demolished, new one (Sacred Heart) o. 1895 in old Prim. Meth. C., restored and reused 1988; Salv. Army C., sold 1922 to Angl. C.; sawmill b. by Garner and Auld, burnt down 1951, replaced; school 1870, new one b. 1872, additions 1884 by W. Mousedale; stamper batteries: Thomas Chappell (25 head) 1871, Macarthur's, Peterson's, William Toft Pullen and Robert Rawsthorne (8 head 1870, replaced 1871 with 15 head), Reward (20 head, at Emmett and Hughes's mine); street tree plantings 1877, 1885, 1928; telegraph 1871; TX 1923, automatic 1982; Unit. C. (St Paul's, orig. Presb.) b. 1872 by Bully & Co., d. by Thomas Rowe, damaged 1883, re-roofed and repaired 1910, condemned and closed 1961, restored and reopened 1967; water reticulation 1980; Wes. Meth. C. 1868, replaced 1870, gallery added 1872; pop. 124 (1861), 656 (1871), *c.*8,500 (1872), *c.*8,700 (1873), *c.*6,400 (1874), *c.*5,000 (1875), *c.*3,900 (1876), 1,223 (1881), *c.*1,200 (1882), *c.*1,000 (1887), 814 (1891), *c.*850 (1895), 643 (1901), 464 (1911), 378 (1933), 347 (1947), 304 (1954), 220 (1961), 129 (1966), 92 (1980), *c.*200 (1987), 120–150 (*c.*1988), *c.*120 (1989), *c.*100 (2000), *c.*150 (2003), *c.*120 (2004), *c.*130 (2005), 167 (2006).

Hillerman's (*Co. Caira*) see Condouple.

Hillgrove (*Co. Sandon*) 30°34'S. 151°54'E., 24 km E. of Armidale; formerly Cara; village gaz. 1889, munic. proc. 1899, thrived 1880s–90s, declined 1907+, town largely abandoned and buildings removed 1921, munic. abolished 1923; gold (disc. 1882 by George Smith) 1882–1921 and 1937–40, then 1969+, antimony (disc. 1853, but payable amounts not till 1877) 1877+, scheelite, stibnite, grazing; Angl. C. (St George's) b. 1892 by Dean and Martin, d. by J.T. French, moved 1957 to Armidale; cemetery (211 graves) 1890; CH b. 1893 by Moses Hern; cordial factories: T.C. Faint, Simms and Gannon, J.J. Wilkinson 1889 (sold 1899 to James Maddox, sold 1904 to William H. Logan, sold 1917 to A.W. Brindell); FB; fires 1894, 1901, 1902, 1904, 1911; gaol; hydro-electric scheme estab. 1893–95 by Crompton Power Co., d. by Sir Richard Threlfall, taken over 1896 by Sandon County Electrical Light & Power Co., later sold to International Railway Corp. of England, closed, derelict; mines: Bakers Creek Co., Bakers Creek North, Bakers Creek South, Cosmopolitan, Earl of Hopetoun 1891, Eleanora Gold-mining Co. NL, Eleanora North, Garibaldi, Golden Gate, Lady Carrington, New England, New Hillgrove, Scheelite and GM, Starlight, Sunlight, West Sunlight Reef Co.; PO 1884, new one b. 1901, sold 1947; Presb. C. 1896; PS 1888 b. by Harper Bros; rifle range; Rom. Cath. C. (St Patrick's) b. 1889 by W. Morris, moved 1918 to Wards Mistake; Salv. Army C. 1891; school 1888, additions 1889, new buildings b. 1897 by W. Hern, additions 1901 by W. Morris, closed 1974, reused; 6 stamper batteries; storm 1905; streets first lit 1895 by hydro-electricity, scheme failed and streets lit again 1900; TC 1902; telegraph 1888, new office b. 1901, sold 1947; telephone 1906; TX 1910, automatic 1972; typhoid 1903; water supply 1891; Wes. Meth. C. 1889, enlarged 1899 by Edmund Lonsdale; winery (Cremorne Gardens) estab. by Theodore Bauer, thrived 1908, faltered 1910; pop. 2,098 (1891), 2,274 (1901), 1,777 (1911), 241 (1933), 169 (1947), 200 (1954), 140 (1961), *c.*180 (1965), *c.*100 (1987), 256 (2006), 290 (2011).

Hillgrove West (*Co. Sandon*) see Metz.

Hillmont (*Co. Monteagle*) 34°15'S. 148°32'E., 23 km E. of Young, on Top Ck; school 1896–1922.

Hill Plain (*Co. Townsend*) 35°39'S. 144°53'E., 16 km SW of Deniliquin; farming; dust storm 1884; FB; PO 1898; RS (Victorian railway), closed 1961; sawmill (Thomas Atkinson); school 1897, new one b. 1898 by Johnston and Fox, closed 1918; telephone 1924; pop. 48 (1933).

Hillrise (*Co. Raleigh*) 30°36'S. 152°51'E., 6 km N. of Bowraville; telephone 1937; TX 1945–62.

Hillsborough (*Co. Northumberland*) see Mount Hutton and Teralba.

Hillside (*Co. Goulburn*) 35°33'S. 147°32'E., 27 km NE of Holbrook, on Little Billabong Ck; settled 1847 by Thomas Ford; grazing; cemetery.

Hillside (*Co. Gowen*) 31°30'S. 148°43'E., 24 km N. of Gilgandra, on Terrabile Ck; pop. 28 (1933).

Hill Sixty (*Co. Forbes*) 33°40'S. 148°04'E., 28 km N. of Grenfell.

Hillston (*Co. Nicholson*) 33°29'S. 145°32'E., 101 km NW of Griffith, on Lachlan R.; orig. Daisy Plains, then Redbank till 1869; disc. 1817 by John Joseph William Molesworth Oxley, estab. 1863 by William Ward Hill, laid out 1863 by John McGee, thrived in 1880s and 1928–29; wheat 1866+, sheep, citrus orchards, vegetables, vineyards, cotton; airport; ambulance station 1971; Angl. C. 1888, enlarged 1892, additions 1951, reused, demolished, new one (War Memorial Church of Christ the King) 1966 d. by Louis Reginald Williams; breweries: Red Lion Steam Brewery, Aerated Water & Cordial Manufactory (estab. 1878 by Henry Lill Lindsay, closed 1895, reopened 1896 by McIntyre, Lincoln & Co.) and W. M'Brown (taken over 1888 by Jones, Lincoln & Co.); brickworks: Dowsmerrie Brick & Tile Works (estab. by T. Griffiths & Son), Hickmott and Spurr 1882, T. Macfarlane 1925; bridge b. 1882 by T. Brooks, new one (Jackson's Bridge) b. 1920 by J.A. Jackson, Allan timber truss, 128 ft (39 m), over Lachlan R.; carriage-works (Bells and Sorrenson); cemetery; CH b. 1884 by J. O'Donnell, repairs 1887 by Donaldson, demolished 1965, new one 1965 d. by Peter Proudfoot; droughts 1888, 1914, 1927, 1967, 1972, 1973, 1977, 1978, 1983; dust storms 1902, 1939, 1983, 2009; electricity 1929; engineering works (Hillston Engineering) 1969–84; FB (station b. 1938); fires 1884, 1896, 1915, 1924, 1948, 1951; floods 1870, 1901, 1932, 1939, 1950, 1952, 1956, 1990; flour mills: Varcoe, Lynn & Co. 1888 (taken over 1893 by Joint Stock Co., sold 1900, reopened 1901, sold 1921) and McKinley's 1888; footbridge (suspension) 1933, over Lachlan R.; gaol, additions 1890 by L. Cawsey & Sons, closed 1916; grasshopper infestation 1955; hospital b. 1884 by Charles Lynn, d. by Varney Parkes, additions 1890 also by Lynn, additions 1895 by John Nicholson, additions and alterations 1935 by G.H. Dixon & Sons Ltd, additions 1988; juice factory (Outback); levees 1950; mouse plagues 1916, 1932, 1970, 1984; PO 1869, new one b. 1883 by John Witcombe, additions 1900 by Charles Lynn, reused, demolished 1983, replacement b. 1968 by Camarda and Cantrill; pound (stock) 1875; powerhouse b. 1930 by Frank Hardy for Hillston Electric Supply Co. Pty Ltd; Presb. C. 1890, renovated 1902 by Thompson and Ryan, demolished 1963; PS b. 1885 by J. Witcombe; rabbit freezing works (Hillston Freezing Co. Pty Ltd), burnt down and rebuilt 1933, closed 1953; railway turntable, 60 ft (18.3 m), closed; reservoir (concrete), 82 ft (25 m) tower, 250,000 gal. (1,136.5 kl), b. 1936 by Robert Hood; riot (Chinese) 1895; Rom. Cath. C. b. 1887–89 by L. Cawsey & Sons, d. by Tappin, Gilbert and Dennehy, destroyed 1944, replacement (Our Lady of Good Counsel) 1954; RS 1923–74, station removed; sale-yards b. 1923 by P.J. Madden, new yards (Wilson & Mackie Ltd) 1934; sawmills: Brown Bros, James Butler, R. Greenwood, G. Haub, J.H. Pearson, Sweeting and Flood, W.J. Turner, N. White; school 1882 b. by James O'Donnell, additions 1885 by L. Cawsey & Sons, additions 1895, additions 1896 by Charles Lynn, repairs 1899 by H.J.C. Jennings, new one b. 1926 by Edwin Potter, additions 1929, extended 1936 by R.W. Saunders and Edmund Beech, additions 1956, 1966, 1973, 1976, 2011; sewerage 1973; silo; storm 1901; streets electric lit 1929; telegraph 1879, new office b. 1883 by John Witcombe, additions 1900 by Charles Lynn; TX 1910, automatic 1988; typhoid 1903; Unit.

C. (St David's, orig. Presb.) 1964; watch-house, declared a gaol 1884; water supply 1937, augmentation 1987; Wes. Meth. C. b. 1882 by John W. Makepeace; pop. 337 (1881), 734 (1891), 704 (1895), 843 (1901), 867 (1911), 1,137 (1933), 829 (1947), 1,019 (1954), 966 (1961), 1,036 (1966), 1,001 (1971), 889 (1976), 999 (1981), 1,052 (1986), 1,030 (1991), 1,099 (1996), 1,217 (2001), 1,054 (2006), 996 (2011).

Hill Top (*Co. Camden*) 34°21'S. 150°30'E., 12 km N. of Mittagong, on Rocky Waterholes Ck; farming and poultry; bridge (concrete) 1897; bushfire 1928; charcoal works (Edward V. Mulhall); electricity 1950; FB (station b. 1959); PO 1887; reservoir; RS (Big Hill Upper Siding till 1881, then Colo till 1883) 1878–1988; sawmill (Brodribb and Robinson); school 1884–88 and 1897–99, reopened 1938; telegraph 1890; TX 1923, automatic 1968; typhoid (2 died) 1897; Union C. 1916–67, demolished; water reticulation 1972, augmentation 1985; pop. 86 (1901), 74 (1911), 154 (1933), 170 (1947), 151 (1954), 213 (1961), 290 (1976), 462 (1981), 641 (1986), 920 (1991), 1,496 (1996), 1,607 (2001), 1,802 (2006), 2,119 (2011).

Hill Top (*Co. St Vincent*) 35°12'S. 150°27'E., 16 km W. of Sussex Inlet, on Luncheon Ck.

Hill Top (*Co. Wallace*) 36°20'S. 148°51'E., 5 km NE of Berridale.

Hillview (*Co. Baradine*) 30°22'S. 150°50'E., 21 km E. of Barraba, on Nangahrah Ck.

Hillview (*Co. Robinson*) 31°42'S. 145°55'E., 23 km S. of Cobar.

Hillview (*Co. Sandon*) 30°42'S. 151°38'E., 15 km SE of Uralla; school 1883–1909.

Hillville (*Co. Gloucester*) 31°59'S. 152°21'E., 12 km SW of Taree, on Bo Bo Ck; telephone 1923; pop. 279 (2011).

Hillvue (*Co. Parry*) see Tamworth.

Hinkler (*Co. Argyle*) 34°29'S. 149°41'E., 19 km E. of Crookwell; RS 1931–57.

Hinton (*Co. Durham*) 32°43'S. 151°39'E., 9 km E. of Maitland, on Paterson R.; estab. and lots sold 1840; former river port, wheat till 1848, now lucerne, maize, millet, potatoes; agric. implement works: Henry Geering 1849 and Charles Lawn, sold 1871 to Dea and Yates, partnership dissolved 1873 and business carried on alone by William Yates; Angl. C. (St John the Evangelist) b. 1848–56 by James Hesp, reused 1996, and graveyard (199 graves 1863+); Bapt. C. b. 1857 by Phillip Lane, remodelled 1945; bridge (Allan timber truss, with steel lift span fabricated by Pope, Maher & Co., deactivated 1940) b. 1898–1901 by Samuel McGill, d. by Ernest Macartney de Burgh, 512 ft (156 m), over Paterson R.; bushfire 1895; cemetery (183 graves 1851+) 1895; CH, closed, sold and reused; floods 1864, 1874, 1893, 1895, 1930, 1950, 1964, 2007; flour mills: Caledonian, and Charles Lawn 1858, demolished 1917; fruit case factory (S. Foster & Sons); grasshopper infestation 1907; hailstorms 1861, 1875, 1996; lock-up b. 1881 by William Dart; PO 1835–1994; pound (stock) 1844; Presb. C. (St Andrew's) 1842, sold and demolished 1962; PS, reused; punt (to Morpeth) 1858, new one b. 1875 by W. Henderson and A. Smith, punt house 1877; Rom. Cath. C. (St Patrick's) 1848, closed, demolished; school 1849, new one b. 1878 by R.B. Cropley, d. by John Wiltshire Pender, additions by R.T. Parker Pty Ltd; storm 1873; tannery; telegraph 1884; TX (automatic) 1956; typhoid 1894, 1895, 1896, 1907, 1908 (person died); Wes. Meth. C. 1861; wharf 1844, new one b. 1870 by Ross, Moyes and Donald, partly collapsed 1932; pop. 418 (1856), 351 (1861), *c.*200 (1866), 349 (1871), 475 (1881), 524 (1891), 427 (1901), 411 (1911), 295 (1933), 375 (1947), 312 (1954), 304 (1961), 242 (1976), 207 (1981), 222 (1986), 237 (1991), 321 (1996), 320 (2001), 363 (2006), 313 (2011).

Hoaretown (*Co. Camden*) see Douglas Park.

Hobbins' Dam (*Co. Bligh*) see Leadville.

Hobbys Yards (*Co. Bathurst*) 33°42'S. 149°20'E., 19 km S. of Blayney; mining (gold disc. 1896) and farming; cemetery 1897; dust storm 1925; gravel pit; mines: Craiglea (Abercrombie Gold Syndicate) 1903, 1916, 1923–24, 1931–32, 1935–36, Podgers Reef, Yellow Streak 1905–8 and 1913; PO 1887–1980; Presb. C. (St Peter's) 1864, demolished;

2 quarries; school 1880, new one b. 1882 by James Wiburd, d. by William Edmund Kemp, repairs 1889 and 1898 by John Wadsworth Ashworth, closed 1975; snowstorm 1900; telephone 1907; TX 1925; Unit. C. (St Peter's, orig. Presb.) 1939, and graveyard (burials 1864+); pop. 214 (1901), 163 (1911), 132 (1921), 181 (1933), 127 (1947), 110 (1954), 89 (1961), 194 (2006).

Hoddles Cross Roads (*Co. Camden*) 34°35'S. 150°15'E., 9 km NW of Bundanoon; formerly The Cross Roads; bridge (concrete) b. 1971 by Peter Verheul Pty Ltd, 282 ft (86 m), over Black Bobs Ck; winery (Eling Forest) estab. 1987 by Leslie Fritz, leased 2012 to Jeff Aston.

Hodgson Park (*Co. Macquarie*) 31°05'S. 152°51'E., 3 km E. of Kempsey, on Bridge Ck.

Hogan's Brush (*Co. Northumberland*) see Narara.

Hogarth Range (*Co. Richmond*) 28°54'S. 152°49'E., 23 km W. of Casino; airfield; bushfire 1936; Angl. C. (St Faith, Virgin and Martyr) 1954; school 1957–67; telephone 1926; TX 1930; pop. 93 (1933), 80 (1954), 55 (1961), 280 (2011).

Holbert's Town (*Co. Gloucester*) see Limestone.

Holbrook (*Co. Goulburn*) 35°43'S. 147°19'E., 53 km NE of Albury, on Ten Mile Ck; Friday Mount and Camden Forest 1824, The German's 1840–57, Ten Mile Creek 1857–75, Germanton till 1915; disc. 1824 by Hamilton Hume and William Hilton Hovell, settled 1836 by John Purtell, surveyed 1852 by Thomas Scott Townsend, laid out 1858 by Samuel Parkinson with the assistance of Constantine Francis Bolton, first lots sold 1858, town gaz. 1879 as Germanton, bypassed by highway 2013; grapes, tobacco, wheat, lucerne, oats, potatoes, orchards, sheep, cattle, timber; airport (5 km N.) 1939; ambulance station; Angl. C. (St Paul's) b. 1887 by Neill and Jackson, d. by C. Jackson, extensions 1959 and 1963–67 by Charles Craig, d. by James Kell; brick-kiln (N. Woods); bridges over Ten Mile Ck: (first) 1860, (second) b. 1876 by P. Adams, (third) b. 1894 by W. Dumbrell, (fourth) 1942; bushfires 1892 and 1952; carriage-works (W.C. Webb), burnt down 1912; cemetery 1879; CH b. 1875 by Adolph Reiff, d. by James Johnstone Barnet, additions and alterations 1899 by William Frost, additions and alterations 1939 by A.H. Baglee; 2 cordial factories (incl. F.W. Nolan); electricity 1914; FB 1906 (station b. 1977); flood 2010; flour mill (Teague Bros) 1878; hospital (cottage) b. 1913 by Frew and Logan; lock-up, additions 1893; Meth. C. 1954; PO 1857, new one b. 1922 by James Ross Ltd; pound (stock) 1865; powerhouse (Percy Lucien Grimwood), acquired 1923 by local council; Presb. C. 1873, closed and reused; PS 1862 (removed from Garryowen), additions 1871, new one b. 1878 by Adolph Reiff; railway turntable, 50 ft (15.2 m); 2 reservoirs (incl. one 250,000 gal. or 1,136.5 kl); Rom. Cath. C. 1867, new one (Our Lady of Sorrows) b. 1887 by Hurst, d. by Gordon and Gordon, additions 1955; RS (Germanton till 1915) 1902, station b. by John Allibone, closed 1975; sale-yards; sawmill (Austral Softwoods); school (Germanton till 1915) 1875, additions 1883 by Adolph Reiff, additions and remodelling 1918 by F.E. Heather, additions 1956, 1960, 1967, additions 2010 by Barker Constructions Pty Ltd; sewerage 1969; silo 1924, disused; snow 1899 and 1904; storm 1923; streets kerosene lit 1888; telegraph 1873; telephone 1904; TX 1909, automatic 1971; Unit. C. (Knox, orig. Presb.) b. 1901 by P. Rodger, d. by W.M. Campbell; water supply augmentation 1989; pop. *c.*100 (1866), 462 (1881), 393 (1891), 560 (1901), 1,169 (1911), 983 (1933), 973 (1947), 1,210 (1954), 1,158 (1961), 1,135 (1966), 1,068 (1971), 1,157 (1976), 1,276 (1981), 1,354 (1986), 1,369 (1991), 1,331 (1996), 1,276 (2001), 1,336 (2006), 1,263 (2011).

Holdfast (*Co. Arrawatta*) 29°47'S. 150°45'E., 41 km SE of Boggabilla, on Macintyre R.; telephone 1926; TX 1927–42.

Holey Flat (*Co. Macquarie*) see Moorland.

Holgate (*Co. Northumberland*) 33°24'S.

151°25'E., 7 km NE of Gosford, on Fires Ck; (incl. Mount Elliot); hort. and orchards; Bapt. C. (Community); bridges over Erina Ck and Fires Ck; bushfire 1994; FB (station b. 2011); PO: Holgate 1927 and Mount Elliot 1889; school 1929, additions 1952 by F. Butt and Eric Benson; telephone 1925; TX 1949–64; wineries: Central Coast Winery Pty Ltd 1976 and Fires Creek Fruit Wines 2003; pop. 130 (1933), 135 (1947), 167 (1954), 197 (1961), 986 (2011).

Hollisdale (*Co. Macquarie*) 31°24'S. 152°33'E., 20 km W. of Wauchope, on Pappinbarra Ck; Central Pappinbarra till 1923; dairying; bushfire 2017; PO 1914; telephone 1914; TX 1915; pop. 51 (1933), 109 (1954).

Hollydeen (*Co. Brisbane*) 32°20'S. 150°37'E., 9 km NW of Denman, on Wybong Ck; farming, grazing, dairying; bridge b. by Thomas Smith, replacement (timber truss) 1894, 293 ft (89.3 m), new one 1984, over Wybong Ck; PO 1917, burnt down 1939; telephone 1914; TX 1928; pop. 58 (1933).

Holmesville (*Co. Northumberland*) 32°55'S. 151°35'E., 2 km S. of West Wallsend, on Slatey Ck; surveyed 1898 by W. Howard, subdivided 1898 by Joseph Holmes, thrived 1907; formerly farming and coalmining; brick-kiln (Frith's); bridge (Friths Bridge) 1910, over Slatey Ck; colliery (Maitland); earthquake (buildings damaged) 1989; FB; Meth. C. 1915; PO, closed 1993, sold and reused; PS; rifle range (West Wallsend); RS (colliery) 1895–1929, largely defunct; tramway (steam) to Newcastle 1887; Unit. C. (Sugarloaf Community, orig. Cong.) 1903; water supply 1902; pop. 416 (1901), 672 (1911), 620 (1933), 455 (1947), 1,419 (2011).

Holmwood (*Co. Bathurst*) 33°48'S. 148°46'E., 7 km NE of Cowra, on Waugoola Ck; wheat and cattle; Angl. C. (St Luke's) 1907; bushfire 1909; copper mine 1906; droughts 1850, 1919, 1944, 1957, 1965, 1966–67, 1972, 1979–80; floods 1852, 1870, 1885, 1900, 1916, 1973; PO 1894–1971; quarry; RS 1888–1972; school (Coota till 1891) 1880, repairs 1900 by H. Hart, new building 1993; silo 1935; storm 1957; telephone 1906; wool-scour (Alford and Kingswell) 1895; pop. 194 (1901), 190 (1911), 126 (1933), 104 (1947), 78 (1954), 72 (1961).

Holmwood (*Co. Lincoln*) see Dubbo South.

Holts Flat (*Co. Wellesley*) 36°38'S. 149°17'E., 32 km N. of Bombala, on Pipe Clay Ck; grazing; airfield; PO 1884; RS 1921–75; school 1880–89; telephone 1891; TX 1913–64; pop. 61 (1901), 42 (1933), 56 (1947), 61 (1961).

Holy Camp (*Co. Forbes*) 33°55'S. 148°06'E., 5 km SW of Grenfell; school 1892–1937.

Holy Dollar (*Co. St Vincent*) see Ulladulla.

Holy Flat (*Co. Macquarie*) see Moorland.

Homeleigh (*Co. Rous*) 28°35'S. 153°03'E., 6 km NE of Kyogle, on Back Ck; school 1930–68; telephone 1926; TX 1926–62; pop. 125 (1933), 117 (1947), 111 (1954), 103 (1961), 151 (2011).

Home Rule (*Co. Phillip*) 32°25'S. 149°38'E., 11 km SE of Gulgong; largely defunct; mining (gold disc. 1872), grazing, farming, dairying, kaolin, yellow ochre; Angl. C. (temporary one) o. 1877 in converted former store, new one (St Alban's) 1898, burnt down; Cong. C. 1872; mines: Christmas 1880–84, Cumbandry (incl. Dog and Cat, Lily May, Britannia) 1872–1909, Periwinkle 1893, Red (incl. Red Streak and Little Cumbandry) <1900–1909, Shallow Rush (incl. Red, White and Blue) 1872–79; PO 1872; quarry (kaolin); Rom. Cath. C.; school (Mobellah till 1913) 1874, new buildings b. 1883 by D. McFarlane, closed 1957; telephone 1914; TX 1928, automatic 1967; pop. 144 (1901), 166 (1911), 100 (1933), 113 (1947), 100 (1954), 84 (1961).

Homestead (*Co. Clive*) 29°00'S. 152°00'E., 6 km NW of Tenterfield, on Tenterfield Ck; quarry; school 1900–48; pop. 47 (1933), 67 (1954).

Homeville (*Co. Northumberland*) see Telarah.

Hominy Point (*Co. Cook*) 33°34'S. 150°53'E., 4 km E. of Wilberforce, on Hawkesbury R.

Honeybugle (*Co. Flinders*) 31°50'S. 146°54'E., 38 km SW of Nyngan; school 1966–71.

Honeysuckle (*Co. Auckland*) 36°56'S. 149°40'E., 19 km W. of Pambula, on Myrtle Ck; agric.; bridge over Myrtle Ck; creamery 1899; eucalyptus oil distillery (Ritchie and

Fineran) 1913, in former rabbit canning works; rabbit canning works (South Coast Canning Co. Ltd) 1911, closed and reused.

Honeysuckle (*Co. Northumberland*) see Newcastle.

Honeysuckle Beach (*Co. St Vincent*) see Callala Beach.

Honeysuckle Corner (*Co. Napier*) 31°41'S. 149°39'E., 17 km N. of Coolah.

Honeysuckle Falls (*Co. Westmoreland*) 33°34'S. 149°56'E., 16 km NE of Oberon, on Fish R.

Honeysuckle Flat (*Co. Cook*) 33°27'S. 150°02'E., 6 km SW of Wallerawang, on Solitary Ck; dam (Rydal) 1957, 52 ft (16 m) high, wall raised 1994.

Honeysuckle Point (*Co. Northumberland*) see Newcastle.

Hongkong Point (*Co. Drake*) 29°09'S. 152°21'E., 35 km E. of Tenterfield, on Timbarra R.

Hoodsville (*Co. Irrara*) see Hungerford.

Hopefield (*Co. Hume*) 35°54'S. 146°26'E., 11 km N. of Corowa; farming; cemetery 1878; horse dip 1936; PO 1913; Presb. C. 1911, destroyed and replaced 1911, closed 1930; RS 1892, station b. by J. Hardy, jun., closed 1975; school 1875, new building b. 1915 by William Murdoch, closed 1952; silo 1920; telephone 1910; TX 1920, automatic 1952; winery (Lindeman's) 1877; pop. 166 (1901), 162 (1911), 106 (1933), 80 (1947), 79 (1954), 75 (1961), 309 (2006).

Hopes Creek (*Co. Westmoreland*) 33°47'S. 149°43'E., 16 km SW of Oberon, on Hopes Ck.

Hopkins Creek (*Co. Rous*) 28°18'S. 153°15'E., 15 km W. of Murwillumbah, on Hopkins Ck; dairying, bananas, beef, vegetables; bridge b. 1929, destroyed 1930, new one 1963; bushfire 1968; flood 1930; sawmill (Thomas Bell & Sons); telephone 1924; pop. 41 (1933), 62 (1961).

Hopping Dick (*Co. Rous*) 28°20'S. 153°14'E., 16 km W. of Murwillumbah, on Hopping Dicks Ck; pop. 76 (1911).

Hopping Jack (*Co. Rous*) see Limpinwood.

Horse Flat (*Co. Wellington*) 32°41'S. 149°40'E., 12 km SE of Mudgee, on Mullamuddy Ck; winery (Optimiste Wines) estab. 1998 and o. 2007 by Steve and Sharlene Dadd.

Horse Lake (*Co. Tandora*) 32°08'S. 142°06'E., 63 km E. of Broken Hill; RS 1923–74; telephone 1920; TX 1939–71.

Horse Lake (*Co. Tandora*) see also Kinalung.

Horse Ridges (*Co. Richmond*) 28°57'S. 153°07'E., 13 km SE of Casino; cheese factory (Charles Oliver); sawmill (Charles Oliver); telephone 1921; TX 1924–60.

Horseshoe (*Co. Hunter*) 32°29'S. 150°38'E., 12 km SW of Denman, on Horseshoe Ck; pop. 53 (1933).

Horseshoe Bend (*Co. Northumberland*) see Maitland.

Horse Shoe Bend (*Co. Wellington*) 32°42'S. 149°11'E., 28 km SE of Wellington, on Macquarie R.

Horseshoe Creek (*Co. Rous*) 28°32'S. 153°02'E., 10 km N. of Kyogle, on Horseshoe Ck; farming; PO 1911; sawmill (E. Hayes); school 1909–69; telephone 1912; TX 1914, automatic 1952; pop. 95 (1911), 166 (1933), 171 (1947), 128 (1954), 127 (1961).

Horse Station Creek (*Co. Rous*) 28°38'S. 152°58'E., 5 km W. of Kyogle, on Horse Station Ck; pop. 69 (1933), 51 (1947), 56 (1954), 53 (1961), 200 (2011).

Horsfield Bay (*Co. Northumberland*) see Woy Woy Bay.

Horsley (*Co. Camden*) see Wongawilli.

Horton (*Co. Murchison*) see Upper Horton.

Horton Valley (*Co. Murchison*) 30°11'S. 150°22'E., 31 km NW of Barraba; TX (automatic); pop. 380 (2006).

Hoskingtown (*Co. Murray*) see Hoskinstown.

Hoskin's Town (*Co. Murray*) see Hoskinstown.

Hoskinstown (*Co. Murray*) 35°25'S. 149°27'E., 18 km S. of Bungendore; Blackheath till 1870 then Hoskin's Town till 1925; farming; Angl. C. (St Mark's) 1872 d. by Alberto Dias Soares, renovated 1913, additions and restoration 1926, also used by Presb. C. since 1936; eucalyptus oil distilleries: E.H. Hopkins and R. White & Sons; PO 1870–1967; Rom. Cath. C. (St Peter and St Paul's) b. 1886 by Beeby, closed 1960, restored and reopened 1992, and graveyard (graves 1884–1966); RS 1940–68; sawmills: Honeysuckle (James Hopkins) and Sandy Creek (Daniel Bros, Ashcroft & Co.); school (Hoskingtown till 1890) 1880–90, 1898–1908, 1957–67; telegraph 1889–91; telephone 1906; TX 1920, automatic 1969; pop. 68 (1901), 92 (1911), 47 (1933), 55 (1947), 58 (1961), 344 (2011).

Houlouhan Point (*Co. Camden*) 34°05'S. 150°26'E., 20 km NW of Picton, on Nattai R.

Hounslow (*Co. Cook*) see Blackheath.

Hovell (*Co. Hume*) 35°52'S. 146°45'E., 17 km NE of Howlong, on Majors Ck; school 1880–1906.

Hovells Creek (*Co. King*) 34°03'S. 148°53'E., 28 km SE of Cowra, on Hovells Ck; Rom. Cath. C. (St Joseph's) 1878, closed, sold 2016, reused, and graveyard; school 1861–66; telephone 1910; pop. 155 (2006).

Howards Grass (*Co. Rous*) see Lismore.

Howell (*Co. Hardinge*) 29°57'S. 151°02'E., 17 km W. of Tingha, on Borah Ck; Bora Creek till 1901; settled 1898, village gaz. 1901, thrived 1912, abandoned 1942; diamonds, silver, stannite, honey, grazing; cemetery 1902; CH 1902, burnt down 1915; dam (mine) 1906; fire 1915; mines: Conrad Mine (orig. Bora Creek mine, incl. sawmill 1900, furnaces and concentrating mill, bought and renamed by John Howell), closed 1913, reopened, and King Conrad (Peter Alwell), man killed 1901; PO 1899, burnt down 1915; PS (incl. lock-up) b. 1901 by John Crimson, closed 1934, moved 1935 by A.R. Bentley to Inverell; Rom. Cath. C. (St Anthony's) 1900, burnt down 1904; school (Conrad till 1901) 1900 b. by W. Morris, closed 1942; telegraph 1901, office burnt down 1915; telephone 1900; TX 1910; Wes. Meth. C. 1901; pop. 452 (1901), 830 (1911), 101 (1933), 199 (2006).

Howes Valley (*Co. Northumberland*) 32°51'S. 150°50'E., 42 km SW of Singleton, on Howes Valley Ck; grazing; cemetery 1875, disused; earth tremor 2008; PO 1873; PS 1877–1907 and 1924–34; quarry; school 1880–95; telephone 1915; TX 1924, automatic 1979; pop. 50 (1911), 124 (1933), 73 (1947), 52 (1954), 69 (1961).

Howlong (*Co. Hume*) 35°59'S. 146°38'E., 21 km E. of Corowa, on Murray R.; disc. 1836 by Major Sir Thomas Livingstone Mitchell, surveyed 1854, town gaz. 1855, lots sold 1856; vineyards, tobacco, oranges, sheep, cattle, grain; Angl. C. (St Thomas's) 1866, rebuilt 1904, and graveyard; Assemblies of God C. (Generation Life Riverina); brewery (Henry Edwards); bridge (Victoria Bridge) 1887, new one (Dare timber-steel truss) b. 1908 by W. Farquharson, 306 ft (93.3 m), new one 2001, over Murray R.; cemetery 1863, expanded 1889, columbarium 1987; CH 1860, demolished, new one (incl. lock-up) b. 1878 by C. Johnson, additions 1883 by W.H. Byrne; Christ. Centre C.; creamery (Corowa & Wahgunyah Dairy Co. Ltd) b. 1894 by J.W. Johnson; customs-house; electricity 1939; experiment farm; FB; fires 1903 and 1912; flour mills: Edwards and William Henry Easterby 1867 (sold 1900 to Thomas Ashford and reused), Russon & Co., Smith's 1869; PO 1861, new one b. 1898 by T.L. Mitchell, closed, sold and reused; pound (stock) 1860; PS 1857, repairs 1930 by R.T. Ball, new building 1960; punt (Thomas Allan) 1857, across Murray R.; 2 reservoirs; Rom. Cath. C. 1877, new one (St Brigid's) 1956 on new site; sale-yards; school 1861, new one b. 1872 by Fuller and Boyce, repairs 1893 by William Haslem & Co., additions 1920 by W. Squires, additions 1922, 1966, 1990; sewerage augmentation 1993; storm 1907; telegraph 1878, new office b. 1898 by T.L. Mitchell; TX 1912, automatic 1969; Unit. C. (St Andrew's, orig. Presb.) 1900; water supply augmentation 1989; Wes. Meth. C. 1887; pop. 107 (1871), 422 (1881), 425 (1891), 479 (1901), *c.*500 (1906), 545 (1911), 515 (1933), 482 (1947), 489 (1954), 410 (1961), 346 (1971), 666 (1976), 1,072 (1981), 1,363 (1986), 1,634 (1991), 1,697 (1996), 1,949 (2001), 2,111 (2006), 2,310 (2011).

Hue Hue (*Co. Northumberland*) see Wyee.

Hughstonia (*Co. Harden*) 34°35'S. 148°40'E., 17 km S. of Boorowa; farming and grazing; PO 1900–44; school (Broughtonsworth till 1925)

1882–96, reopened 1915 in new building b. by L. Herrick, closed 1931; telephone 1924; TX 1924; pop. 56 (1901), 50 (1911), 26 (1933).

Hulong (*Co. Cooper*) see Whitton.

Humbug Bend (*Co. Clarence*) 29°22'S. 153°20'E., 5 km NW of Iluka, on Esk R.

Hume (*Co. Goulburn*) see Albury.

Hume Park (*Co. Murray*) 34°55'S. 148°49'E., 12 km SW of Yass, on Lake Burrinjuck.

Hume Reservoir (*Co. Goulburn*) see Lake Hume Village.

Hume Sawmill (*Co. Cowley*) 35°11'S. 148°49'E., 31 km SW of Murrumbateman, on Sardine Ck.

Hume Weir (*Co. Goulburn*) see Lake Hume Village.

Humula (*Co. Wynyard*) 35°29'S. 147°46'E., 34 km SW of Adelong, on Umbango Ck; also known as American Yards till *c.*1885; village gaz. 1880; gold (disc. 1851), sheep, cattle, logging, dairying, farming; bridges: one b. 1892 by W. Burton, over Umbango Ck and one b. 1892 by Cummings and Bowdren, over Carabost Ck; bushfire 1905; cemetery 1891; FB; flood 1931; hailstorm 1946; PO 1888; Presb. C.; PS 1895, new one b. 1896 by C. Hardy & Co., additions and repairs 1916 by John Burnett, closed 1943; railway coal stage, removed 1941; railway engine shed (removed from Canowindra) 1921; Rom. Cath. C. (St Therese's) b. 1937 by S. Bailey, d. by George William Albert Welch and S. O'Halloran; RS 1917–75; school 1880, new one b. 1882 by W.H. Hilton, new building b. 1918 by C. Hardy & Co.; telephone 1899; TX 1911, automatic 1958; Union C. b. 1888 by T. Meyers; pop. 54 (1891), 137 (1901), 242 (1911), 204 (1933), 228 (1947), 322 (1954), 261 (1961), 213 (2006).

Hungerford (*Co. Irrara*) 29°00'S. 144°25'E., 194 km NW of Bourke; Currawinga till 1870, Hoodsville till 1875, Hungerford since 1876; first lots sold 1880; grazing; cemetery; PO 1870, new one b. 1900 by Spence, burnt down 1901; telegraph 1891; telephone 1890; TX 1914; pop. 90 (1894), 32 (1933), 54 (1961), 22 (1999), 35 (2006).

Hungry Flat (*Co. Northumberland*) 33°13'S. 151°06'E., 31 km W. of Wyong.

Hunter (*Co. Northumberland*) see Broadmeadow, Gateshead and Newcastle.

Hunter River (*Co. Gloucester*) see Heatherbrae.

Hunter Springs (*Co. Durham*) 31°53'S. 151°26'E., 50 km W. of Gloucester; telephone 1939; TX 1939, automatic 1974.

Hunters Vale (*Co. Durham*) 31°47'S. 151°21'E., 50 km E. of Murrurundi, on Hunter R.

Hunterview (*Co. Durham*) see Singleton (*Co. Northumberland*).

Huntingdon (*Co. Macquarie*) 31°28'S. 152°39'E., 7 km W. of Wauchope, on Hastings R.; timber, then farming and dairying; cemetery; creamery and butter factory 1897; PO 1861–1967; Presb. C. 1879, relocated 1926, closed 1971, removed and reused 1974; quarry; school 1880–83, reopened 1915, burnt down 1939, replaced 1940 by F.W. Perkins; telephone 1912; TX 1915–67; pop. 16 (1866), 87 (1901), 92 (1911), 87 (1933), 50 (1947), 58 (1961).

Huntlee (*Co. Northumberland*) see Rothbury North.

Huntley (*Co. Bathurst*) 33°22'S. 149°08'E., 10 km S. of Orange; airport (air force) 1939, became Orange airport in 1961, runway rebuilt 2005, terminal demolished 2013, new one b. 2014 by Momentum Built Pty Ltd; RS 1880–1974; pop. 136 (1901), 79 (1911), 82 (1933), 60 (1947), 56 (1954), 67 (1961), 307 (2011).

Huntley (*Co. Camden*) see Wongawilli.

Huon (*Co. Goulburn*) 35°50'S. 147°00'E., 12 km SE of Walla Walla; village gaz. 1887; bushfire (woman died) 1905; PO 1900–4; Rom. Cath. C. re-erected 1936 (removed from Lake Hume Village); school 1884–1904.

Huonbrook (*Co. Rous*) 28°33'S. 153°21'E., 14 km W. of Mullumbimby; bananas and farming; Meth. C. 1915; PO 1927–61; school 1935–62; telephone 1923; TX 1926, automatic 1961; pop. 92 (1933), 91 (1947), 70 (1954), 305 (2011).

Huon Park (*Co. Goulburn*) 35°54'S. 146°51'E., 15 km S. of Walla Walla.

Hurricane Hill (*Co. Hume*) 35°43'S. 146°58'E.,

8 km SW of Culcairn; quarry (blue granite); RS 1926–54.

Hursley (*Co. Macquarie*) 31°25'S. 152°46'E., 5 km NE of Wauchope, on Hastings R.; settled 1837; agric.; foot-bridge (suspension) 1937, to Rawdon Island, over Hastings R.; PO 1862–73; pop. *c.*30 (1866), 43 (1933).

Hush's (*Co. St Vincent*) see Charleyong.

Huskisson (*Co. St Vincent*) 35°02'S. 150°40'E., 4 km N. of Vincentia, on Jervis Bay; survey by James Charles Burnett approved 1840, settled 1868, subdivided 1870; orig. timber, shipbuilding 1863+, tourism 1945+, fishing; ambulance station; Angl. C. (Holy Trinity) b. 1931 by A.E. Green, d. by Cyril Blacket, re-roofed, closed; bridge to Vincentia over Moona Moona Ck; bushfires 1952 and 2001; electricity 1938; FB 1943; foot-bridge 1931, to Vincentia, over Moona Moona Ck; 2 jetties (incl. one b. 1990); PO 1843; PS 1913–34; reservoir 1955; sawmill; school (Huskisson North till 1918) 1882, new one b. 1884 by William Schadel, alterations 1916, additions 1924 by S.A. Lippman, additions 1970 and 2010; shipyards: A. Conlon, George Dent 1863 (sold to Alfred William Morrow Settree, taken over 1948 by Alfred Raymond Settree, taken over 1977 by John Settree, closed, sold 2014), Thomas M'Call; telephone 1902; TX 1912, automatic 1970; Union C., relocated; Unit. C.; water supply 1960, augmentation 1983; wharf b. 1885 by J.W. Smythe; pop. 94 (1901), 119 (1911), 344 (1933), 320 (1947), 523 (1954), 677 (1961), 641 (1966), 735 (2011).

Huskisson North (*Co. St Vincent*) see Huskisson.

Huskisson South (*Co. St Vincent*) see Vincentia.

Hyams Beach (*Co. St Vincent*) 35°06'S. 150°42'E., 4 km SE of Vincentia, on Jervis Bay; bushfire 2001; FB; PO 1955; reservoir; sewerage augmentation 1985; telephone 1955, automatic 1969; water supply augmentation 1983; pop. 97 (1954), 47 (1961), 122 (2006).

Hyandra (*Co. Narromine*) 32°18'S. 148°28'E., 15 km W. of Dubbo.

Hydes Creek (*Co. Raleigh*) 30°25'S. 152°55'E., 5 km NE of Bellingen, on Hydes Ck; settled 1889 by George and Henry Bennett, thrived 1903–4; timber and dairying; FB (station b. 1993); flood 1950; school 1914–66; telephone 1923; TX 1950–64; pop. 92 (1911), 105 (1933), 118 (1947), 113 (1954), 97 (1961).

Hyland Park (*Co. Raleigh*) 30°38'S. 153°01'E., 2 km N. of Nambucca Heads, on Deep Ck; pop. 296 (1996), 321 (2001), 406 (2006), 441 (2011).

Hylea (*Co. Kennedy*) 32°22'S. 147°12'E., 78 km NW of Trundle.

Hyndman (*Co. Macquarie*) 31°34'S. 152°14'E., 35 km N. of Wingham; dairying; PO 1927–51; sawmills: Erickson Bros and John Wallace; telephone 1916; TX 1926; pop. 21 (1933).

Hyndmans Creek (*Co. Macquarie*) 31°29'S. 152°36'E., 14 km W. of Wauchope; pop. 29 (1933).

I

Iandra (*Co. Monteagle*) 34°05'S. 148°22'E., 27 km N. of Young; orig. sheep, then wheat; Angl. C. (St Saviour's) b. 1886–88 by William Samuel Millard, for George Henry Greene, restored 1916, dilapidated and disused, restored again and reopened 1949, closed 1978, sold 1984 to David and Margaret Morris, and graveyard; PO 1897–1931; pop. 110 (1901), 235 (1911), 75 (1933), 87 (1947).

Iandra (*Co. Monteagle*) see also Greenethorpe.

Iandra Siding (*Co. Monteagle*) see Greenethorpe.

Icely (*Co. Bathurst*) 33°21'S. 149°19'E., 17 km NE of Millthorpe; mines: Icely (Great Western Copper Mining Co.) 1870s, Mount Nicholas (Great Western Copper Mining Co.), Noller Mining Syndicate (nickel) 1931, Ophir (Ophir Gold & Copper Mining Co. and Great Western Copper Mining Co.) 1852, 1875, 1906–7; PO 1866–83; school 1874–80; Wes. Meth. C. 1868.

Idaville (*Co. Bligh*) 31°56'S. 150°13'E., 26 km NW of Merriwa; Craeton till 1882; PO 1875–1909; TX (automatic) 1957; pop. 63 (1911).

Ifield (*Co. Argyle*) see Goulburn.

Ilarwill (*Co. Clarence*) 29°29'S. 153°11'E., 3 km SW of Maclean, on Woodford Island, in Clarence R.; village gaz. 1912, laid out by W.A. Moody; FB; flood 1950; punt across Clarence R.; quarry 1900–3, later reopened; sugar mills: McDonald's and Russell's; pop. 155 (1933), 137 (1947), 132 (1954), 173 (1961), 213 (2011).

Ilford (*Co. Roxburgh*) 32°58'S. 149°51'E., 16 km SW of Kandos, on Crudine R.; Keen's Swamp till 1868; village gaz. 1880; farming, grazing, orchards; Angl. C. (St Paul's) b. 1875 by Robert Martin, repairs 1899 by Oliver; cemetery (143 graves 1871+) 1897; FB; gale 1934; lock-up b. 1876 by Robert Martin; PO 1859, burnt down 1932; PS, closed 1903; 3 quarries; Rom. Cath. C. 1873 d. by Edward Gell, new one (Our Lady Help of Christians) 1895, damaged 1934; sawmill (Ilford Sawmilling Society Ltd) 1926; scarlet fever 1898; school (Keen's Swamp till 1861) 1859–61, reopened 1870, additions 1883 by W. Giles and S. Manell; telephone 1906; TX 1928, automatic 1988; Unit. C. (orig. Wes. Meth.) b. 1867 by George Harris, d. by Thomas Rowe, closed, sold 2010 to Dennis Allard and Sheila Carroll; winery (Mountilford) 1985; pop. *c.*150 (1866), 71 (1901), 191 (1911), 227 (1933), 148 (1947), 149 (1954), 193 (1961), 240 (2006), 306 (2011).

Ilford Railway Station (*Co. Roxburgh*) see Clandulla.

Illabo (*Co. Clarendon*) 34°49'S. 147°45'E., 16 km NE of Junee, on Jeralgambeth Ck; Billabong till 1881; surveyed 1897 by James Ewart Lester, first land sale 1897, village gaz. 1898, second land sale 1900; goldmining and farming; Angl. C. (St John's) 1902–70, demolished 1976; bushfire 1990; cemetery 1901; diphtheria 1926; drought 1944–45; dust storm 1914; electricity 1952; FB 1915; fires 1964 and 2004; Meth. C., removed 1950 from Old Junee, renovated by Wilesmith Bros and reopened 1951; PO 1881, new one b. 1922 by

J.J. Nichols; PS 1911, burnt down 1923, new one, closed 1933; Rom. Cath. C. (All Saints') 1916; RS (Billabong till 1881) 1878, station closed and removed 1984; school 1884 b. by Henry Truelove, additions 1896 by C. Hardy & Co., repairs 1900 by J. Pike and W. Searle, additions 1914 by W.H. Davis; silo 1922; smallpox 1913; storm 1933; telegraph 1890; TX 1914, automatic 1974; Union C. 1898; Unit. C.; Wes. Meth. C. b. 1901 by P. McBeath & Co.; water supply (from Junee) 1969; pop. 95 (1891), 93 (1901), 442 (1911), 186 (1933), 147 (1947), 159 (1954), 167 (1961), 191 (2006).

Illalaung (*Co. Northumberland*) see Morpeth.

Illalong (*Co. Northumberland*) see Greta.

Illalong Creek (*Co. Harden*) 34°43'S. 148°40'E., 27 km NW of Yass, on Illalong Ck; goldmining; 2 bridges (incl. Banjo Paterson Bridge) over Illalong Ck; mine (Mount Mylora or Mount Deigan or Big Lode) 1928, 1932, 1934–37; 4 quarries; railway bridge over Illalong Ck; railway engine house 1914; RS 1916–71.

Illaroo (*Co. Camden*) 34°50'S. 150°27'E., 14 km W. of Nowra; agric.; FB 1944; school 1886–96; pop. 24 (1933), 249 (1947).

Illaroo Road (*Co. Camden*) see Nowra (*Co. St Vincent*).

Illawarra (*Co. Camden*) see Berkeley and Port Kembla.

Illawong (*Co. Gloucester*) see Nelson Bay.

Illawong (*Co. Wallace*) see Anglers Reach.

Illewong (*Co. Robinson*) 31°37'S. 145°57'E., 17 km SE of Cobar; Bee Mountain till 1906; grazing; cemetery 1907; fire 1910; PO 1905; PS 1906–13; school 1905, new one b. 1908 by T. Quiggin, closed 1916; telephone 1905; TX 1917–27; pop. 147 (1911).

Illilliwa (*Co. Waradgery*) 34°26'S. 144°59'E., 15 km NE of Hay; RS 1896–1975, station removed 1984.

Iluka (*Co. Clarence*) 29°25'S. 153°21'E., 3 km N. of Yamba, on Clarence R.; orig. Bang-lo; settled 1862, surveyed 1862 by William Albert Braylesford Greaves, laid out by Patrick R. Donaldson, town gaz. 1875; orig. quarrying then fishing (estab. 1884 by John Wallace), prawns, oysters, farming, tourism; aeroplane crash 1936; Angl. C. 1909, replacement (St Peter's) b. 1977 by Iver Pedersen; Bapt. C.; boat harbour 1972; breakwater, extended 1959 to 2,200 ft (660.6 m); cemetery; cyclone 1913; FB; fish canning works (Clarence River Fresh Fish & Canning Co.) o. 1887 by Robert Harper & Co.; fish processing plant (Clarence River Fishermen's Co-op.) 1973; floods 1890 and 2009; ice works (Iluka Ice Co. Ltd) 1910–68; marina 1970, extended 1978; mineral sand mining plant 1971; PO 1876, new one b. 1969; PS 1884–86, second one 1928–32, third one 1979; 3 reservoirs (incl. one b. 1973, 300,000 gal. or 1,363.8 kl); river training walls: Middle Wall and Moriarty's Wall; Rom. Cath. C. 1880, alterations 1927, closed, replaced (St John's) 1976; school 1880, additions 1915 by T. Champion, additions 1967; sewage works; telephone 1919; tramway (quarry) b. by William Peoples, Grieg and Monday; TX 1928, automatic 1953; water supply 1973; wharves: one b. 1874 by John Strauss and Edward F. Wright, and one b. 1905 by J.J. M'Phillips; pop. *c.*125 (1878), 174 (1881), 125 (1891), 170 (1901), 162 (1911), 162 (1924), 191 (1933), 326 (1947), 353 (1954), 365 (1961), 575 (1971), 789 (1976), 1,362 (1981), 1,484 (1986), 1,795 (1991), 1,863 (1996), 1,855 (2001), 1,739 (2006), 1,701 (2011).

Iluka (*Co. Clarence*) see also Iluka North.

Iluka North (*Co. Clarence*) 29°24'S. 153°21'E., 4 km N. of Yamba, on Clarence R.; Iluka till 1919; telephone 1911; TX 1916.

Imesons (*Co. Rous*) 28°26'S. 152°47'E., 30 km NW of Kyogle, on Richmond R.; telephone 1911; TX 1937–69.

Impimi (*Co. Caira*) 34°47'S. 143°43'E., 22 km SE of Balranald; RS (Victorian railway), closed.

Inches (*Co. Macquarie*) 31°06'S. 152°52'E., 4 km SE of Kempsey, on Pola Ck.

Inchgower (*Co. Ashburnham*) 33°16'S. 147°51'E., 20 km NW of Forbes; telephone 1926; TX 1926, automatic 1964; pop. 54 (1933).

Indi (*Co. Selwyn*) 36°18'S. 148°09'E., 27 km

NW of Perisher Valley, on Back Ck.

Ingalba (*Co. Vernon*) 31°11'S. 151°26'E., 26 km SW of Walcha, on Macdonald R.; Craig Lea till 1905; agric.; flour mill (McIver's) 1854; PO 1900–10; school 1957–68; pop. 87 (1933), 165 (1947), 123 (1954).

Ingar (*Co. Durham*) 32°28'S. 151°20'E., 20 km NE of Singleton, on Reedy Ck; cemetery; school (Merannie till 1921) 1886–1921 and 1957–59; telephone 1921; TX 1921–65.

Ingebirah (*Co. Wallace*) 36°39'S. 148°30'E., 27 km SW of Jindabyne, on Sheep Station Ck; formerly Ingebyra; grazing; bushfire 2003; PO 1899; telephone 1916; TX 1930–72; pop. 42 (1933).

Ingebyra (*Co. Wallace*) see Ingebirah.

Ingleba (*Co. Vernon*) 31°11'S. 151°26'E., 26 km SW of Walcha, on Macdonald R.; manganese and timber; FB; flour mill, burnt down 1901; sawmill (Bob Wall); telephone 1924; TX 1929, automatic 1952; pop. 81 (1911), 70 (1961).

Ingledow (*Co. Murray*) 35°22'S. 149°32'E., 13 km SE of Bungendore; farming and sheep; PO 1927–42; sawmill (George Daniel).

Inglegar (*Co. Gregory*) 31°22'S. 147°52'E., 37 km N. of Warren, on Marthaguy Ck; bridge b. 1893 by Josiah Shakespear, over Marthaguy Ck; PO 1907, burnt down 1918; pop. 80 (1911).

Inglewood (*Co. Bligh*) see Turill.

Ingliswold (*Co. Bathurst*) 33°28'S. 149°09'E., 4 km SW of Millthorpe; school 1888 b. by Thomas Foley, closed 1897, one building removed 1902 by James Murray and another building moved 1904 by Higman and Kirby to Tallwood.

Inner Pocket (*Co. Rous*) 28°29'S. 153°27'E., 8 km NW of Mullumbimby, on Lacks Ck.

Innesvale (*Co. Macquarie*) 31°26'S. 152°46'E., 4 km NE of Wauchope, on Hastings R.

Innes View (*Co. Macquarie*) 31°35'S. 152°23'E., 30 km W. of Kendall, on Tea Kettle Ck; bushfire 2017; PO 1937; school 1957–61; telephone 1924; TX 1928–64; pop. 89 (1954).

Interlaken (*Co. Wallace*) 36°20'S. 148°38'E., 9 km N. of Jindabyne, on Lake Jindabyne.

Inveralochy (*Co. Argyle*) 34°58'S. 149°39'E., 24 km S. of Goulburn, on Reedy Ck; farming; bridge b. 1874 by Webb and Evans, over Mulwaree R.; flour mill (horse powered) estab. by James Macfarlane; hailstorm 1860; PO 1861; RS 1890–1974; pop. 52 (1901), 37 (1933), 214 (1961).

Inverary (*Co. Argyle*) 35°54'S. 149°58'E., 28 km SE of Goulburn; farming; cemetery; lock-up; PO 1927–29; quarry; school 1882–89.

Inverary (*Co. Argyle*) see also Bungonia.

Inverary Park (*Co. Argyle*) 35°54'S. 149°59'E., 29 km SE of Goulburn.

Inverell (*Co. Gough*) 29°47'S. 151°07'E., 97 km NW of Armidale, on Macintyre R.; (incl. Albion Hill subdivision 1884, Belgravia subdivision, North Inverell, Ross Hill subdivision surveyed by Charles Cameron Loxton); Green Swamp till 1856; disc. *c.*1836 by Alexander Campbell, founded 1853 by Colin Ross, surveyed 1855, laid out 1858 by Patrick Heron Henderson, town gaz. and first lots sold 1859, munic. 1872–1979; silver and tin mining, sapphires 1916+, wheat, maize, barley, oats, sorghum, lucerne, sunflowers, sheep, cattle, timber, potatoes, brandy, wine, honey, bacon, butter, cheese, fruit, food processing, smallgoods, dairying till 1960s, tobacco till 1994; agric. implement works (Blake and Collins); airfield (5 km E.) 1937; ambulance station b. 1947 by B.M. Wade Pty Ltd, d. by R.H. Lockwood; Angl. C. (St Augustine's) b. 1876–78 by Moore, d. by John Horbury Hunt; Apostolic C. (Liberty Christ.); Assemblies of God C. (Christ. Life); bacon factories: Inverell Co-op. Butter & Bacon Co. Ltd 1912, and Woods and Reay 1905; Bapt. C. 1969; boot factories: James Adams 1883, Reilly and Morris, A. Roach & Sons, Samuel Rowland; breweries: Inverell Brewery (estab. by Thomas Bros, sold 1909 to Tooths) 1885–1914 and Victoria Brewery (Henry Edmeades) 1884–86; brickworks (removed from Goonoowigal by Benjamin Martin Wade) 1929–74; bridges over Macintyre R.: one b. 1876 by John Strauss and Edward F. Wright, demolished 1894, replacement b. 1896 by Samuel McGill, one of 1906, one (composite truss) 1901, demolished and replaced 1983, O'Connor Bridge, one b. by B.M. Wade Pty Ltd; butter factory (Inverell Co-op. Butter Co. Ltd) 1902, burnt down 1925, replaced, closed 1952; camouflage netting factory 1942; carriage-works: Blake and Collins, Bulluss Bros, Buxton and Ryan (bought 1910 by Henry John Clarke, burnt down 1914, new works b. 1915 by Box, d. by W.M. Goodwin), Central Coach, Buggy & Sulky Factory (N. Gough), Coggan's, Rawle and Cusick, Watling Bros 1873; causeway; cemetery (638 graves) 1863, incl. lawn cemetery, columbarium, memorial garden 2007; CH (incl. lock-up) b. 1861–63 by James Cheadle, second one 1872, additions 1878 by Moor Bros, new one b. 1885–87 by R.T. Harrison, d. by James Johnstone Barnet, repairs 1901 by C.S. Thorley, additions and alterations 1909 by John Devitt, refurbished by New England Constructions Pty Ltd; Chinese joss house; Christ. Life C.; Christ. Outreach C. (Sapphire City); Church of Christ b. 1906 by A. Arnold, new one; cordial factories: J. Brissett & Co. 1903, Central (Henry Turnham, bought 1903 from J.K. Finlayson), Connellan's, Charles Egan 1880 (taken over 1909 by F. and E. Thomas Pty Ltd), Federal Aerated Water Co. (Regan and Thomas, taken over 1907 by George Griffey), F. Harding, McHugh's, Snowclad (damaged 1952); crematorium (Thorley & Sons Pty Ltd); dam 1938; dengue fever 1926; diphtheria 1911, 1912, 1915, 1916, 1917, 1920, 1921; droughts 1864–65, 1875–76, 1877–78, 1888, 1919, 1965, 1979–83; dust storm 1901; electricity 1911; engineering works (Kilminster and Rumble); FB 1904 (station b. 1910, replacement b. 1917 by Kell & Rigby Pty Ltd, d. by Alfred Spain, new ones 1985 and 2013); fibrous plaster works (Allard & Co., renamed Acme Plaster Co. in 1935); fires 1881, 1900, 1901, 1902 (2 died), 1914, 1916, 1954; floods 1864, 1872, 1879, 1890, 1917, 1955, 1976, 1991; flour mills: M'Intyre Steam Flour & Saw Mills (Eastment Bros, sold to William Selby, then William Swanson), Millenium (b. 1914 by John Dunkley for Howard, McIntosh and Gillespie, acquired 1921 by Inverell Milling Co. Pty Ltd, fire 1948, burnt down 1949, reused), Colin Ross 1844 (new one 1863, upgraded 1877, taken over 1881 by T.H. Marks and John P. Pawley, in 1886 Marks was replaced by Thomas Taylor and Alexander McIntyre, bought 1888 by Pawley and Taylor, fire 1897, mill modernised 1890 and 1895, taken over 1900 by Robert Howard and Peter McIntosh, joined 1907 by Gillespie), McIntyre's (estab. 1866 by Swanson, sold 1883, closed 1891, reused as vinegar and cordial factory by Turnham, then a sawmill, demolished), Victoria Mill (o. 1876 by George Woods and Markby, bought 1884 by Henry Edmeades, sold 1886 to Farmers' Milling Co-op. Co. Ltd, sold 1891 to Alfred Oliver and renamed Reform Roller Flour Mills, acquired by Sinclair); foot-bridges (b. 1872 and 1912), over Macintyre R.; foundry estab. 1909 by Robert Gibson, bought 1913 by H. Brown and Franke, acquired 1918 by Campbell and Craig; Free Presb. C. 1859 d. by Colin Ross, closed, bought by T.H. Marks, removed; fruit dehydration plant (Inverell Dehydrated Fruit Co.) 1921; furniture factory (R.W. Johnston), burnt down 1948; gales 1930 and 1952; gaol, repairs 1901 by C.S. Thorley; grasshopper infestation 1937; hailstorm 1907; hospital b. 1874–77 by Alexander M'Ilveen, additions 1882, new one 1935, additions 1966 and 1982, new one b. 2020 by Richard Crookes Constructions, d. by Conrad, Gargett, Riddel, Ancher, Mortlock and Woolley; ice works (Fred and Ernest Thomas); iron foundry (Campbell and Campbell) 1909; joineries: K.L. Clark 1953 and C.S. Thorley; lime-kiln; Meth. C. 1962; milk factory (Norco Co-op. Ltd); mine (tin) 1871; monumental stone works: M.W. Hardy and C.S. Thorley; PO: Inverell 1859 (new one b. 1869, another one b. 1874 by Whitham and Pender, additions 1893 by R.B. Spiers, demolished, replacement b. 1904 by George Frederick Nott, d. by Walter Liberty Vernon, additions 1913–18) and North Inverell 1944; police barracks b.

1879 by Moore Bros; pound (stock) 1859; powerhouse 1911, new chimney b. 1918 by A. Arnold; Presb. C. (St Andrew's) b. 1876–78 by Moore Bros, d. by Alexander Leckie Elphinstone and Ross Hill b. 1909 by B.M. Wade as a hall, additions b. 1927 by George Frederick Nott, d. by Herbert Ross, used as a church, closed, sold 2012; PS b. 1878 by A. Thorley, repairs 1901 by C.S. Thorley, new one 1960; 2 quarries; rabbit freezing works (Garratt Scandrett Freezing Companies Ltd) 1922–31; railway turntable, 60 ft (18.3 m), removed; 2 reservoirs (concrete), reused; rifle range (3 km SE); Rom. Cath. C.: Sacred Heart of Jesus (o. 1872, chancel added 1881, second church b. 1904 by William Noller, d. by Joseph Ignatius Sheerin and John Francis Hennessy, third one 1983) and St Mary's (b. 1953 by Ben Wade & Sons, d. by Hennessy and Hennessy); RS 1902, station b. by J. Bromley and J.N. Holloway, services ceased 1987; sale-yards 1910, new yards 1961; Salv. Army C. 1888, extensions and alterations 1917, new one 1957; sawmills: Paradise, Pioneer (Thomas Hawkins, bought 1903 by Hector Cook & Son, burnt down 1913), Benjamin Martin Wade; scarlet fever 1899 and 1911–21; schools: Inverell primary 1862 (new one 1876, new one b. 1887 by Moore Bros, d. by William Edmund Kemp, additions 1887 and 1902, additions 1910 by C. Harris, additions 1911 by H. Pollock, additions 1962, major upgrade 1996), Inverell HS 1939 (additions 1962, 1966, 1969, fire 2015), Macintyre HS 1974 (d. by Ian McHutchinson, Douglas Anderson and R. Powell), Ross Hill 1894 (b. by George Seagrott, additions 1903 by Thomas Halliday, additions 1910, additions 1922 by Benjamin Martin Wade, further additions 1960, 1963, 1966, 1968, 1971); SD Adventist C.; sewerage 1951, augmentation 1987; silo 1934; snowstorm 1892; soap-works: Furniss's, A.J. Hands, F.R. Hawke & Co. 1916 (in old renovated mill), Thomas Taylor 1878 (sold 1884 to G.H. Wilton); storms 1907 and 1934; streets lit by kerosene 1898, tarred 1907, electric lit 1911; TC, additions 1971, became a campus of New England Institute in 1992; telegraph 1868, new office b. 1874 by Whitham and Pender, additions 1893 by R.B. Spiers, demolished, replacement b. 1904 by George Frederick Nott, d. by Walter Liberty Vernon; telephone (North Inverell) 1944; TX 1903, automatic 1971, closed 1984; typhoid 1897, 1898, 1900, 1902, 1903, 1906, 1913, 1916, 1920, 1953; Unit. C. (Taylor Memorial, orig. Meth.) b. 1904 by George Frederick Nott, d. by Herbert E. Ross; vulcanising works: Harvey Frost, J.E. Giblin, George Mason; water supply 1927, augmentation 1983; weir 1916; Wes. Meth. C. 1874; whooping cough epidemic (Ross Hill) 1934; wool-scour (Samuel Rowland); wool stores: John Bridge & Co., fire 1903, Campbell Bros, R. Delbridge; pop. 177 (1861), *c.*250 (1866), 509 (1871), 1,965 (1881), *c.*2,000 (1887), 2,534 (1891), *c.*3,150 (1895), 3,293 (1901), *c.*4,000 (1905), 5,131 (1911), 5,305 (1933), 6,530 (1947), 7,514 (1954), 8,209 (1961), 8,533 (1966), 9,700 (1971), 9,432 (1976), 9,734 (1981), 9,693 (1986), 9,736 (1991), 9,378 (1996), 9,537 (2001), 9,749 (2006), 9,347 (2011).

Inverella (*Co. Sandon*) see Eversleigh.

Invergordon (*Co. Gloucester*) 32°03'S. 151°45'E., 19 km W. of Gloucester, on Gloucester R.; Presb. C. b. 1907 by Skinner, closed, dismantled and moved; school 1901–16.

Invergowrie (*Co. Sandon*) 30°31'S. 151°31'E., 13 km W. of Armidale; PO 1894; telephone 1906, automatic 1977.

Invermein (*Co. Brisbane*) see Scone.

Inverness (*Co. Denham*) 29°58'S. 148°29'E., 36 km E. of Walgett; RS (Merkadool Tank till 1930) 1922–75.

Iona (*Co. Durham*) see Woodville.

Irish Corner (*Co. St Vincent*) see Reidsdale.

Irish Corner (*Co. Westmoreland*) see Duckmaloi.

Irishtown (*Co. Georgiana*) 34°17'S. 149°33'E., 23 km N. of Crookwell; school 1882–94.

Irishtown (*Co. Murray*) see Queanbeyan.

Irishtown (*Co. Wellington*) see Hill End.

Ironbark Camp (*Co. Vernon*) 30°56'S. 152°13'E., 59 km W. of Kempsey, on Fitzroy Ck.

Ironbarks (*Co. Forbes*) 33°41'S. 147°53'E., 35 km NW of Grenfell; defunct; mining (gold disc. *c.*1880 by William Whitby) 1881–1925; Angl. C. (St James's) 1874, reused; mines: Ironbarks Reef 1896–1910 and Ryries Reef; quarry; school 1909–32; stamper battery (5 head); pop. 30 (1933).

Ironbarks (*Co. Wellington*) see Stuart Town.

Ironbong (*Co. Clarendon*) see Ferndale.

Irondale (*Co. Cook*) 33°23'S. 150°01'E., 6 km NW of Wallerawang, on Gleesons Ck; collieries: Irondale (o. 1883 by John Britty North, strike 1903), Ivanhoe (o. 1893 by George Raffan, sold 1899 to Portland Lime & Cement Co., acquired 1902 by Commonwealth Portland Cement Co. Ltd, strikes 1924, 1926, 1947), Main Range (formerly owned by the estate of J.B. North, strike 1911, acquired 1915 by Main Range Collieries & Estates Ltd, man killed 1917); RS 1889–1945; school (Pipers Flat till 1902) 1881–94 and 1900–11.

Iron Duke (*Co. Kennedy*) 32°21'S. 147°28'E., 60 km SW of Trangie; mine; RS (mine), abandoned.

Iron Gates (*Co. Richmond*) see Evans Head.

Ironmungy (*Co. Wellesley*) 36°36'S. 148°47'E., 27 km SE of Berridale, on Snowy R.; pop. 41 (1933).

Iron Pot Creek (*Co. Rous*) see Ghinni Ghi.

Irrawang (*Co. Gloucester*) see Raymond Terrace.

Irvine (*Co. Cook*) see Mount Irvine and Mount Wilson.

Irvington (*Co. Rous*) 28°52'S. 153°05'E., 4 km E. of Casino, on Richmond R.; farming; Meth. C. 1902 (moved to Clovass); PO 1892–1931; school 1885, additions 1888 by Lane and Cole, new building b. 1924 by Diyal Singh, closed 1933; telephone 1890; Wes. Meth. C. 1884; wharf, enlarged 1907 by G. Lawson; pop. 127 (1911), 84 (1933), 70 (1954), 90 (1961).

Isabella (*Co. Georgiana*) 33°57'S. 149°40'E., 32 km SW of Oberon, on Dairy Station Ck; orig. gold and tobacco, then grazing; bushfire 1929; cemetery (42 graves 1890+); eucalyptus oil distillery; PO 1898–1980; Rom. Cath. C. (St Joseph's) 1897, second one (Holy Angels), third one (Our Lady of Fatima), and graveyard; school 1898–1914; telephone 1925; TX 1925; pop. 103 (1901), 63 (1911), 52 (1933), 65 (1947).

Isis (*Co. Brisbane*) see Isis River.

Isis River (*Co. Brisbane*) 31°53'S. 151°04'E., 26 km NE of Scone, on Isis R.; village gaz. 1897 as Isis; school 1957–70.

Island Bend (*Co. Wallace*) 36°19'S. 148°29'E., 11 NE of Perisher Valley, on Island Bend Pondage; temporary construction camp (1952–68) for Snowy Mountains Hydro-Electric Scheme, resumed by govt 2001; Angl. C. (All Saints'), later moved to Berridale and reused; barracks; PO 1951, burnt down 1962; powerhouse; PS 1961–68; quarry; Rom. Cath. C. (Our Lady of the Snows) b. 1952 by Ralph Mitchell and Ken Palmer; school 1957–68; TX 1952, automatic 1961; pop. 495 (1954), 432 (1961).

Island Holme (*Co. Arrawatta*) 28°58'S. 151°16'E., 44 km N. of Ashford, on Dumaresq R.

Islington (*Co. Northumberland*) see Wickham.

Italia (*Co. Ashburnham*) 33°29'S. 148°23'E., 5 km S. of Eugowra; bushfire (house destroyed) 1914; Meth. C. 1922; school (Meadowbank till 1917) 1904–26.

Itchenstoke (*Co. Camden*) 33°28'S. 150°30'E., 15 km NW of Kurrajong Heights.

Ivanhoe (*Co. Mossgiel*) 32°54'S. 144°18'E., 132 km NW of Hillston; (incl. Railtown); estab. 1870 by George Williamson, village gaz. 1886; wool and gypsum; airfield; cemetery 1888; CH 1887; cyclone 1928; 3 dams 1940; dust storms 1939, 1944, 1989; flood 1923; gale 1895; gaol (Warakirri); heatwave 1938–39; hospital 1938, burnt down 1957, new one 1962; mine (copper) 1965–71; PO 1874, new one b. 1898 by George Huntley Dixon; powerhouse 1936–83; Presb. C. b. 1935 by W. Wilkinson; PS 1885, additions 1931, new one 1962; railway coal stage 1927; railway engine shed 1927; Rom. Cath. C. (St Thomas the Apostle) b. 1940 by Norman Doyle, d. by Gannon; RS 1925; school 1890, additions 1961, 1963, 1985; telegraph 1883; telephone 1917; TX 1911, automatic 1991; water supply augmentation 1959 and 1985; pop. 69 (1901), 221 (1933), 351 (1947), 546 (1954), 473 (1961), 506 (1971), 483 (1976), 517 (1981), 449 (1986), 355 (1991), 322 (1996), 273 (2001), 265 (2006), 200 (2011).

Ivor (*Co. Clarendon*) 34°48'S. 147°37'E., 10 km N. of Junee; school 1902–47; Union C. 1905; pop. 133 (1911), 114 (1933), 60 (1947).

J

Jackadgery (*Co. Gresham*) 29°35'S. 152°33'E., 38 km NW of Grafton, on Mann R.; dairying, grazing, fossicking; bridge (concrete) b. 1961 by Thiess Bros Pty Ltd, d. by G. Maunsell & Partners, 938 ft (285.9 m), over Mann R.; bushfires 1936 and 1951; PO 1927; quarry; sawmill (Northern Sawmills Pty Ltd); school 1915 b. by A.W. Phemister, closed 1932, reopened 1940, additions 1959, closed 2003; telephone 1914; TX 1925, automatic 1979; pop. 92 (1933), 126 (1947), 109 (1954), 108 (1961), 258 (2001).

Jackalass (*Co. Wynyard*) 35°05'S. 148°08'E., 3 km SE of Gundagai; mining (gold) 1895–96; mine (Princess Marina); quarry; pop. 149 (1901), 89 (1911), 164 (1933), 228 (1947), 177 (1954), 162 (1961).

Jacks Creek (*Co. Buckland*) 31°43'S. 150°35'E., 23 km W. of Murrurundi, on Jacks Ck; Angl. C. (St Cuthbert's) 1929–71, sold 1980 to Bob Barwick, sold 2003 to Ray and Judy Hynes; pop. 25 (1933), 88 (1947), 146 (2011).

Jacks Creek (*Co. White*) 30°29'S. 149°44'E., 20 km S. of Narrabri.

Jacks Leap (*Co. Ashburnham*) 33°25'S. 148°23'E., 2 km NE of Eugowra, on Mandagery Ck.

Jacksons Crossing (*Co. Phillip*) 32°20'S. 149°32'E., 4 km NE of Gulgong, on Wialdra Ck; bridge (Winns Bridge) over Wialdra Ck; causeway across Wialdra Ck.

Jacksons Flat (*Co. Buller*) 28°51'S. 152°33'E., 48 km W. of Casino; pop. 33 (1933).

Jacksons Flat (*Co. Cowper*) 30°56'S. 146°51'E., 77 km NW of Nyngan.

Jacksons Waterhole (*Co. Mitchell*) 34°59'S. 146°45'E., 27 km N. of Lockhart; PO 1890; pop. 53 (1911).

Jacky Bulbin Flat (*Co. Richmond*) 29°18'S. 153°08'E., 19 km N. of Maclean; sawmill.

Jacob and Joseph Creek (*Co. Buckland*) 31°29'S. 150°45'E., 8 km E. of Quirindi, on Jacob and Joseph Ck; school (Weybridge Grove till 1887) 1882–1923; pop. 41 (1933).

Jacqua (*Co. Argyle*) 34°55'S. 149°57'E., 27 km SE of Goulburn; bauxite; Angl. C. 1843, closed, later demolished; bushfire 1895; PO 1869; school 1882, burnt down 1895, replaced 1896 on new site by King and Armstrong, closed 1899; telephone 1950; TX 1951–67.

Jaloom (*Co. Fitzroy*) 29°56'S. 152°53'E., 37 km NW of Woolgoolga, on Kangaroo Ck; telephone 1912; TX 1930.

Jamberoo (*Co. Camden*) 34°39'S. 150°47'E., 8 km W. of Kiama, on Hyams Ck; (incl. Woodstock); settled in 1830s, estab. 1838 by Michael Hyam, laid out 1841 by Richard Wright Goodall, village subdivided and sold 1841 to Robert Owen, eastern extension laid out 1881 by John Tate, thrived 1870s–80s, munic. (Kiama) proc. 1859 (changed name in 1892 to Jamberoo); timber, agric. (wheat till 1864), dairying, now hobby farming and tourism; Angl. C. 1842, new one (Resurrection) b. 1865–67 by John Simmons, d. by Edmund Thomas Blacket, extended 1876, tower added 1876, and graves; boot factory (C. Sweeney); brewery (Woodstock, Henry Heathborne) 1844; bridges: William Cole Bridge over Frys Ck, Woodstock Bridge

b. 1904 by Madden Bros, 140 ft (42.7 m), over Minnamurra R., concrete one 1939 over Hyams Ck; bushfires 1862 and 1926; butter factories: Waughope 1887 (Jamberoo Co-op. Dairy Co. Ltd, replaced 1908 by P.C. Davies, cheese-making added 1915, additions 1921 and 1928, new factory b. 1930 by Richard Wildridge & Co. Ltd, closed and reused) and Woodstock Dairy Co. 1888 (became Central Co-op. in 1899 then Woodstock Creamery Co. in 1901, rebuilt 1908); cemeteries: Angl. (44 graves) and general (727 graves), incl. lawn cemetery and columbarium; cheese factories: Jamberoo 1915 and Woodstock 1909–46; coalmine (Olivemount) 1923–27; Cong. C. (Woodstock) and graveyard; FB; flour and timber water-mill (Woodstock) estab. 1838 by Capt. John Gunn Collins, taken over 1844 by Henry Heathborne, closed 1860, reused, demolished; Free Gospel C.; gale 1874; PO 1852; Presb. C. 1842, enlarged 1862, new one (St Stephen's) b. 1876 by John and James Marks, D.L. Dymock and W. Stewart, d. by John Colley, additions 1877, renovated 1892, closed, and graveyard (47 graves 1860–1927); PS (incl. lock-up) b. 1883 by George Osborne, repairs 1907 by J. Collins, closed 1934; rifle range; Rom. Cath. C. (St Matthew's) b. 1875–79 by Daly and Golding, additions 1897, re-roofed 1913, restored 1979, and graveyard (179 graves 1848+); sawmill (Fountaindale, W.B. Campbell), burnt down 1870; schools: Jamberoo 1878 b. by John Simmons, d. by George Allen Mansfield, remodelled and renovated 1923, additions 1983 and 2010, and Woodstock 1873–77; tanneries: J. Chegwyn and Michael Hyam 1838; telegraph 1879; TX 1915, automatic 1964; Unit. C. (orig. Wes. Meth.) b. 1877–79 by George Bigg, d. by William Boles, damaged 1879, upgraded 1888, and graveyard (30 graves 1861–1904); water supply 1939; Wes. Meth. C. 1851; pop. *c.*500 (1866), 2,235 (1891), *c.*2,490 (1895), 1,291 (1901), 775 (1911), 1,095 (1933), 921 (1947), 892 (1954), 574 (1961), 326 (1971), 361 (1976), 462 (1981), 482 (1986), 704 (1991), 883 (1996), 942 (2001), 935 (2006), 905 (2011).

Jamberoo (*Co. Camden*) see also Jerrara.

James Creek (*Co. Clarence*) 29°27'S. 153°14'E., 3 km NE of Maclean; sugar mill (McDonald's); pop. 40 (1933), 92 (1947), 93 (1954), 217 (2011).

Jamieson's Siding (*Co. Inglis*) see Danglemah.

Janina (*Co. Barrona*) 29°58'S. 144°41'E., 121 km W. of Bourke; Rainbar till 1953; telephone 1935; TX 1935.

Jannung (*Co. St Vincent*) 35°05'S. 150°29'E., 9 km W. of St Georges Basin.

Jannung (*Co. St Vincent*) see also Wandandian.

Jasper (*Co. Rous*) see Federal.

Jaspers Brush (*Co. Camden*) 34°48'S. 150°40'E., 5 km SW of Berry, on Jaspers Ck; farming; airfield; bushfire 1895; butter factory (Jaspers Dairy Co. Ltd till 1902 then Jaspers Brush Dairy Co. Ltd) 1889–1938, demolished; caterpillar infestation 1937; FB 1944; PO 1889; RS 1893, station b. by Gerald Dalton Fetherston and Felix Edward Barbat, closed 1988; school 1884, new building b. 1897 by A. Johnston, d. by William Edmund Kemp, closed 1969, sold 1974, restored and reused; telephone 1914; TX 1919–37; wineries: Jasper Valley estab. 1976 by Sidney Mitchell, and The Silos; pop. 180 (1911), 147 (1961), 374 (2011).

Jaunter (*Co. Westmoreland*) 34°00'S. 149°54'E., 31 km S. of Oberon, on Jaunter Ck; grazing; mine (Tuglow Copper Mining Co. Ltd) 1898–1900 and 1906; PO 1927–31; telephone 1923; pop. 28 (1933).

Jawbone (*Co. Bligh*) 32°29'S. 148°59'E., 9 km N. of Wellington; goldmines: Golden Note 1909 and 1934 and Jawbone Lead *c.*1873, 1899–1907, 1910; PO 1900, burnt down 1915; school 1904–7; pop. 204 (1901), 124 (1911), 20 (1933).

Jeerabung (*Co. Ashburnham*) 33°11'S. 148°34'E., 12 km W. of Manildra; quarry; RS 1918, station b. by Frederick Lemm, jun. and Thomas Edward Spencer, closed 1974.

Jeir (*Co. Murray*) 35°03'S. 149°01'E., 9 km S. of Murrumbateman, on Jeir Ck; farming and grazing; Angl. C. (St Nicholas's) b. 1913 by

D.L. Lawrence; cemetery; goldmine (Gooda Creek Prospecting Co. et al.) 1896–1905, 1934, 1936–38; PO 1880; school 1883, new building b. 1884 by J. M'Auliffe, closed 1894; telephone 1908; pop. 230 (1911), 72 (1933), 111 (1947), 91 (1954), 309 (2011).

Jellat Jellat (*Co. Auckland*) 36°43'S. 149°53'E., 6 km SE of Bega; disc. 1797 by George Bass; wheat, timber, maize, dairying, pigs, oats, beans, peas; brick-kiln (F. Peters); bridge, destroyed 1919; bushfire 1952; cheese factory (Robert Ritchie), bought 1918 by D. Gowing, closed and reused; droughts 1885 and 1967–69; electricity 1939; floods 1851, 1857, 1860, 1870, 1871, 1898, 1919, 1928, 1934, 1956, 1959, 1971; flour mill (Daniel Gowing) 1860; sawmill (Daniel A. Gowing); school 1884 b. by A.H. Paulin, additions 1902, new one b. 1925 by M. Johnston, closed 1914, reopened 1931, closed 1974; typhoid 1903; pop. 97 (1911), 61 (1933), 69 (1947), 64 (1954), 54 (1961), 210 (2011).

Jellat South (*Co. Auckland*) 36°43'S. 149°54'E., 7 km SE of Bega, on Whiteleys Waterhole; telephone 1926; TX 1928.

Jellicoe (*Co. Raleigh*) see Tewinga.

Jellingroe (*Co. Wynyard*) 35°05'S. 147°51'E., 23 km W. of Gundagai; school 1884–91; pop. 21 (1933).

Jemalong (*Co. Gipps*) 33°24'S. 147°44'E., 25 km W. of Forbes, on Lachlan R.; FB (station b. 2018); floods 1951 and 1952; school 1955–74, sold and reused; telephone 1954; TX 1954, automatic 1957; pop. 106 (1911), 36 (1933), 56 (1947), 137 (1954), 90 (1961), 186 (2006), 263 (2011).

Jembaicumbene (*Co. St Vincent*) 35°31'S. 149°46'E., 9 km S. of Braidwood, on Jembaicumbene Ck; village gaz. 1867; goldmining, farming, grazing; boiling-down works (Badgery's); bridge b. 1895 by W. McCaffrey, new one 1987, over Jembaicumbene Ck; cheese factory 1921; Chinese joss house 1859; diphtheria 1893 and 1912; flood 1860; flour mill (Charles Edward Dransfield) 1860 d. by C.E. Langley, closed 1885, sold, restored and reused; gold dredges: Bellevue Dredging Co., Elrington Dredging Co., Jembaicumbene Dredging Co., Middle Ground Dredging Co., Morgans Flat Dredging Co.; mines: Bourke's, A.E. Colemane 1929, Matherson's *c.*1935, Stalker's; PO 1861–1971; Rom. Cath. C. b. 1904 by W. and E. Walshe, closed (moved 1949 to Deua River); school 1870–1929; telephone 1903; TX 1915; Union C. 1871; pop. 294 (1901), 208 (1911), 101 (1933).

Jenkins (*Co. Clarendon*) 35°02'S. 147°53'E., 21 km W. of Gundagai; school 1897, new school b. 1904 by W.G. Beaumont, closed 1942.

Jenkin's Siding (*Co. Northumberland*) see Lisarow.

Jennings (*Co. Clive*) 28°56'S. 151°56'E., 15 km NW of Tenterfield, on Tarban Ck; town gaz. 1887; army ammunition depot (World War II); cemetery; PS 1924; school 1890 b. by Saxby and Springborg; pop. 64 (1901), 84 (1911), 185 (1933), 374 (1947), 340 (1954), 299 (1961), 236 (1971), 211 (2011).

Jenolan Caves (*Co. Westmoreland*) 33°49'S. 150°01'E., 20 km SE of Oberon, on Jenolan R.; known as Binda Caves and McKeown's Caves till 1859 then Fish River Caves till 1884; village estab. 1880 by Jeremiah Wilson; tourism (caves disc. 1838 by Charles Whalan, first published reference 1848, 2 caves lit by electricity 1887, connected by road 1896) 1867+; bridge (stone arch) 1896 d. by Ernest Macartney de Burgh, over Jenolan R.; bushfires 1909, 1942, 1957; dam 1889, replaced, on Jenolan R.; fire 1895; PO 1889; power plant (steam) 1886, replaced 1889 with hydro-electric powerhouse, new one 1916, plant upgraded 1953; PS 1914; school 1957–86; sewage works; telegraph 1892; telephone 1886; TX 1917–83; Wes. Meth. C., defunct; pop. 59 (1901), 68 (1911), 83 (1933), 121 (1947), 128 (1954), 114 (1961).

Jeogla (*Co. Clarke*) 30°34'S. 152°07'E., 43 km E. of Armidale, on Jeogla Ck; grazing; FB; PO 1920–74; sawmill (George Frederick Nott); school 1933–68; telephone 1921; TX 1925; pop. 95 (1911), 131 (1933), 64 (1947), 73 (1954), 84 (1961).

Jeogla Warm Corner (*Co. Clarke*) 30°40'S. 152°01'E., 39 km SE of Armidale, on Chandler R.

Jerangle (*Co. Beresford*) 35°52'S. 149°22'E., 46 km NE of Cooma; grazing; Angl. C. (St Andrew's) b. 1875 by David Montgomery; cemetery 1890; FB; fire 1905; PO 1891; PS 1886–1943, reused; Rom. Cath. C. (St Patrick's) 1956; sale-yards (Powell's) 1950; sawmill (Alex. Hawthorne); school 1957; telephone 1907; TX 1921, automatic 1984; pop. 152 (1911), 95 (1933), 83 (1947), 79 (1954), 87 (1961), 227 (2011).

Jerberra (*Co. St Vincent*) 35°03'S. 150°36'E., 6 km W. of Huskisson; subdivided by Henry F. Halloran & Co., but never developed.

Jereelderie (*Co. Urana*) see Jerilderie.

Jeremy (*Co. Georgiana*) 34°01'S. 149°32'E., 45 km SW of Oberon.

Jerilderie (*Co. Urana*) 35°22'S. 145°43'E., 35 km NE of Finley, on Billabong Ck; Jereelderie till 1890; settled 1858 by John Caractacus Powell, surveyed 1863 by James Wood, laid out 1864 by John McCulloch, village gaz. and first lots sold 1865, designated as chief town of the county, thrived 1865–80, munic. 1889–1918; cattle *c.*1842+, sheep 1860+, wheat 1873+, dairying, rice, canola, sorghum, onions, tomatoes, grapes, mung beans; airport; ambulance station; Angl. C. (St Stephen's) b. 1897 by Alex Roe and George Rogerson, repairs 1998 d. by Ruth Daniell, and graveyard; brewery (D. Campbell) 1879–97; 3 brickworks (incl. J.W. Dickson); bridges: one b. by John Caractus Powell over Billabong Ck, one b. 1873 by William Squires over Billabong Ck, Bolton Street Bridge b. 1900 by W.A. White over Billabong Ck, Condigo Bridge b. 1871 over Billabong Ck, one b. by J.H. Galvin over Algudgerie Ck; butter factory (Jerilderie Co-op. & Cool Storage Co. Ltd) 1907–17; cemetery (1,025 graves 1873+) 1876, incl. columbarium; CH 1874 d. by James Johnstone Barnet, extended 1889 by Samuel Stead, closed 1988, reused; cordial factory (McIntyre Lincoln & Co.); diphtheria 1886, 1889, 1909; 2 FB (incl. station b. 1956, new one 2013); fellmongery 1872; fires 1868, 1892, 1894, 1908, 1931; floods 1891, 1931, 1956; flour mill (Thomas and George Wise) 1885, relocated 1894, closed 1917, dismantled 1918–20; 2 foot-bridges 1997, over Billabong Ck; gales 1893 and 1907; gaol 1881; hospital 1886, additions 1942 by J. Burke, new one 1981; lock-up; measles epidemic 1911; Meth. C.; monumental stone works (F. Lindley); mouse plague 1932; PO 1862, new one b. 1879 by P.J. D'Arcy, additions and alterations 1898 by George Boulton, reused; pound (stock) 1864; powerhouse b. 1918 by Edward E. Brett, taken over 1921 by C. Firth, inundated 1931, destroyed; PS 1881, additions 1888 by E.A. Roe, new one b. 1899 by George Boulton, repairs 1931 by Dickson and Vandersluys, additions 1937 by G.H. Dixon & Sons Ltd; punt (John Caractacus Powell) across Billabong Ck; quarry; railway coal stage b. 1884 by Charles Hardy; railway engine shed, burnt down 1925; railway turntable, 51.5 ft (15.7 m); reservoirs (one b. 1893 by A.B. Espley and one b. 1964 d. by W.L. Hurd); Rom. Cath. C. (St Joseph's) b. 1878–82, damaged 1893, enlarged 1898, additions 1928, and graveyard; RS 1884, station b. by Charles Hardy, refreshment room 1920, closed 1988, restored 2011 by Paul Ryan, reused; sale-yards 1955; sawmill (Peasley's) 1947; school 1869, burnt down 1870, (second) b. 1875, (third) b. 1877, reused, (fourth) b. 1895, repairs 1913 by E. Burwood, additions 1965, additions and alterations 2010 by Barker Constructions Pty Ltd; sewerage 1966; streets electric lit 1925; telegraph 1866, new office b. 1879 by P.J. D'Arcy, additions and alterations 1898 by George Boulton; TX 1910, automatic 1968; typhoid 1878 (man died), 1882, 1886, 1914, 1924; Union C.; Unit. C. (St Andrew's, orig. Presb.) 1884, vestry added 1956; waterworks (steam) b. 1894 by A.B. Espley, replaced by electricity 1925, new pump-house 1964 d. by W.L. Hurd, filtration plant 1983; weir 1884, new one 1941, on Billabong Ck; pop. *c.*200 (1866), 170 (1871), 368 (1876), 475 (1878), 353 (1881), *c.*500 (1887), 541 (1891), *c.*705 (1895), 744 (1901), 989 (1911), 835 (1933),

803 (1947), 916 (1954), 931 (1961), 1,038 (1966), 988 (1971), 1,001 (1976), 1,075 (1981), 954 (1986), 898 (1991), 871 (1996), 800 (2001), 768 (2006), 775 (2011).

Jerrabat Gully (*Co. Murray*) see Kain.

Jerrabomberra (*Co. Murray*) see Queanbeyan.

Jerrara (*Co. Camden*) 34°41'S. 150°49'E., 4 km W. of Kiama, on Jerrara Ck; (incl. Saddleback Mountain); farming; cheese factory estab. 1882 by Henry Harding; PO 1892; reservoir; school (Jamberoo till 1875) 1858–1908 and 1918–50; telephone 1923; pop. 61 (1901), 60 (1933), 284 (2011).

Jerrara (*Co. King*) 34°27'S. 149°08'E., 31 km W. of Crookwell; Meth. C. 1904, new one 1955 d. by Bruce Blyton; rifle range 1913.

Jerrawa (*Co. King*) 34°47'S. 149°05'E., 17 km E. of Yass; village mostly defunct; farming; Angl. C. (Emanuel) 1859–90, demolished, (second) 1890–1927, (Christ) 1928; bushfires 1918 and 1979; diphtheria 1861; goldmine (W.A. Allport 1923 and Allport and Davies 1931–32); PO 1883; RS 1876, station b. by D. Williams, closed 1975; school (Catherine Creek till 1882) 1880, new one b. 1885, additions 1936, closed 1963; telegraph 1890; telephone 1916; TX 1929, automatic 1972; pop. 188 (1901), 113 (1933), 157 (1947), 153 (1954), 120 (1961).

Jerrawangala (*Co. St Vincent*) 35°08'S. 150°28'E., 13 km W. of Sussex Inlet, on Wandandian Ck; orig. Jerrawongola; settled by Andrew McKenzie, John Higgins and George Knight, town gaz. 1843 as Farnham; tin (disc. 1911).

Jerrawongola (*Co. St Vincent*) see Jerrawangala.

Jerrong (*Co. Georgiana*) 34°08'S. 149°50'E., 50 km NE of Crookwell; PO 1872–1917; pop. 53 (1911), 33 (1933).

Jerry Bailey (*Co. Camden*) see Shoalhaven Heads.

Jerrys Flat (*Co. Wellesley*) 36°55'S. 148°38'E., 55 km S. of Jindabyne, on Jerrys Flat Ck.

Jerrys Meadows (*Co. Westmoreland*) 33°34'S. 149°59'E., 19 km NE of Oberon, on Annes Ck.

Jerrys Plains (*Co. Hunter*) 32°30'S. 150°55'E., 24 km SE of Denman, on Hunter R.; disc. 1819 by John Howe, settled 1822, laid out 1838 by George Boyle White, town gaz. 1840, lots sold 1842, designated as chief town of the county; grazing, farming, dairying, vineyards, lucerne, citrus; Angl. C. 1847, new one (St James's) b. 1875–79 by Oliver Saunders, d. by John Horbury Hunt; bushfires 1951 and 1994; butter factory (Jerrys Plains Co-op. Butter Co.) 1910; cemeteries: Angl. (79 graves 1842–1925), general (241 graves) 1886, Rom. Cath. (64 graves 1858–1940); creamery (C. Huband-Smith) 1897; drought 1845; FB (station b. 1954); flood 1955; flour mill; grasshopper infestation 1921; hailstorm 1848; PO 1837, new one b. 1881 by William Burnett, d. by James Johnstone Barnet, closed, sold and reused; police barracks; pound (stock), relocated 1842; PS 1850; quarry; Rom. Cath. C. 1847, second one b. 1872 by John M'Mahon, new one (St Matthew's) b. 1900 by Walter Barrett, d. by John Charles Luscombe, closed, sold and reused; sawmill (Archie S. Shearer); school 1881 b. by Nichols and Gervis Parr, d. by John Wiltshire Pender, repairs 1898 by W. Sessions, additions 1959; snowstorm 1900; storm 1862; telegraph 1876, new office b. 1881 by William Burnett, d. by James Johnstone Barnet, restored, reused; telephone 1929; TX 1913, automatic 1975; watch-house b. 1880 by Oliver Saunders, d. by James Johnstone Barnet; pop. 180 (1861), 159 (1871), 295 (1881), 235 (1891), 411 (1901), 433 (1911), 206 (1933), 204 (1947), 269 (1954), 288 (1961), *c.*250 (1987), 560 (2006), 688 (2011).

Jerseyville (*Co. Macquarie*) 30°56'S. 153°02'E., 4 km S. of South West Rocks, on Macleay R.; Spencer's Creek till 1891; fishing, dairying, maize; bridge (concrete) b. 1974–77 by Peter Ver Huel Ltd, 764 ft (233 m), over Macleay R.; creamery 1896; earth tremor 1910; floods 1949 and 1963; foot-bridge over Perrets Ck; ice works (P. Robinson); Meth. C., inundated twice, closed, dismantled by John Gillies, moved 1950 to Yarrahapinni and reused;

PO 1887; PS 1904–24; punt b. 1928 by A.W. Boulton, ceased 1976, to cross Macleay R.; Rom. Cath. C. (Our Lady of Dolours) 1908, moved 1953 to Eungai Rail; school (Pelican Island till *c.*1920) 1883 b. by J.G. Rowe, new building 1892, closed 1971; shipyard; telephone 1890; TX 1891–1963; wharf (Robinson's); pop. 173 (1901), 140 (1911), 92 (1933), 195 (1947), 161 (1954), 180 (1961), 135 (2011).

Jerusalem Creek (*Co. Richmond*) 29°13'S. 153°24'E., 12 km S. of Evans Head, on Tasman Sea; beach mining (gold, tin, platinum) 1895–1909.

Jesmond (*Co. Northumberland*) 32°54'S. 151°42'E., 2 km E. of Wallsend; (incl. Heaton); Dark Creek till 1872; formerly part of the Waratah Coal Co. estate; orig. orchards and vineyards; Angl. C. (St Margaret's) b. 1929 by Way, closed 2016, sold 2018; bridge (Sawmill Bridge) 1876; bushfires 1938 (2 houses destroyed) and 2006; FB (station b. 1926); glass works (Leonora Glass Industries Pty Ltd), bought 1960 by Philips Lighting Industries, closed 1982, site reused by Aust. Commercial Glassblowers, closed 1986; Lay Meth. C. 1890, closed; Meth. C. b. 1923 by J. Simpson, d. by Fred Turner; PO 1909; Prim. Meth. C. 1886, demolished; quarries (stone); sawmill (William Steel & Co.), taken over 1904 by Michael and Robert Steel; schools: Callaghan College (Jesmond HS till 1996, then Jesmond University HS till 2001) 1956, additions 1967 and 1974, Heaton 1958 (additions 1962, 1967, 2010), Jesmond 1887 (b. by Henry Cole, new building 1892, additions 1928 and 2010); soap and tallow factory (Campion's Soaps Pty Ltd) 1881, fires 1900 and 1910, demolished 1949; telephone 1911; Unit. C. (Jesmond Park) 2008; Wes. Meth. C. 1869–72, bought 1872 by William Steel, new one 1872; pop. 154 (1911), 2,442 (2006), 2,607 (2011).

Jettiba (*Co. Wellesley*) see Tea Gardens.

Jewells (*Co. Northumberland*) 33°01'S. 151°41'E., 3 km NE of Belmont, on Jewells Swamp; subdivisions 1916 and 1926; orig. hunting, then rutile in 1960s; Bapt. C. (New Life); bushfire 1951; RS (Jewell's Swamp till 1923) 1917–40; school 1977, additions by R.T. Parker Pty Ltd; pop. 2,570 (2006).

Jewell's Swamp (*Co. Northumberland*) see Jewells.

Jewnee (*Co. Clarendon*) see Old Junee.

Jews Flat (*Co. Beresford*) see Bunyan.

Jiggi (*Co. Rous*) 28°41'S. 153°11'E., 10 km SW of Nimbin, on Jiggi Ck; orig. timber, then dairying, bananas 1945+, beef, passionfruit; Angl. C. (St Luke's) 1912; FB; Meth. C. b. 1905 by James Thompson, d. by Robert Robertson Jack; PO 1886; Rom. Cath. C. (St Patrick's) 1892; sale-yards; sawmill (H.J. Knight & Sons) 1906; school 1901, fire 1921, additions 1923 by Holland and Thorne, additions 2010; telephone 1911; TX 1927, automatic 1960; Wes. Meth. C. 1890; pop. 154 (1901), 295 (1911), 313 (1933), 261 (1947), 212 (1954), 205 (1961), 333 (2011).

Jiguma Beach (*Co. Auckland*) see Pambula Beach.

Jilliby (*Co. Northumberland*) 33°15'S. 151°23'E., 5 km NW of Wyong, on Jilliby Jilliby Ck; (incl. Alison); orig. Gilliby Gilliby; orig. timber, then dairying, now citrus orchards, honey, horses; bridges: Flacks Bridge over Jilliby Jilliby Ck and Woodburys Bridge over Wyong R.; bushfire (house destroyed) 1939; cemetery (1,399 graves 1899+) 1896; flood 1867; hailstorm 2001; Jehovah's Witnesses C.; PO 1909; pottery (Durren), sold 2014; 2 reservoirs; sawmills: Tom Bridge and Jervis, King's, McNaughton's, O'Neill and Goldsmith 1899, Walters, Middleton and Eade; school (Jilliby Jilliby till *c.*1910) 1891, additions 1895 by William Pescud, burnt down, new school 1912; telephone 1913; TX 1938, automatic 1969; pop. 310 (1901), 164 (1911), 270 (1933), 159 (1947), 157 (1954), 139 (1961), 693 (2006), 758 (2011).

Jimaringle (*Co. Wakool*) 35°18'S. 144°15'E., 38 km N. of Barham; village gaz. 1931; RS (Victorian railway); TX (automatic).

Jimenbuen (*Co. Wallace*) 36°43'S. 148°52'E., 39 km S. of Berridale, on Matong Ck; grazing;

PO 1881–1952; school 1884–89; pop. 73 (1901), 80 (1954), 230 (2006).

Jimmys Point (*Co. Dudley*) 30°48'S. 152°27'E., 41 km W. Bowraville, on Macleay R.

Jinabiby (*Co. Clarence*) see Woombah.

Jincumbilly (*Co. Wellesley*) 36°44'S. 149°13'E., 21 km N. of Bombala; RS 1921–75; telephone 1927; TX 1927; pop. 28 (1933).

Jindabyne (*Co. Wallace*) 36°25'S. 148°37'E., 50 km SW of Cooma, on Lake Jindabyne; (incl. Old Jindabyne, abandoned 1967 and submerged under Lake Jindabyne); relocated and rebuilt on present site 1961–67; formerly goldmining then grazing, now gateway to winter snow resorts; airfield (2 km SW); ambulance station; Angl. C.: Christ Church (b. 1845 by A. and D. McDonald, restoration 1936 and 1960), St Andrew's (b. 1890 by Bray and Forster, submerged, new one 1966), St Paul's (b. 1865–69 by James Jackson Mawson, Charles Potter and David Scarlett, d. by Alberto Dias Soares); Assemblies of God C. (Snowy Mountains); brewery (Kosciuszko Brewing Co.) estab. 2009 by Chuck Hahn; bridge b. 1893 by Watson & Co., destroyed 1967 by military, over Snowy R.; bushfire 2003; butter factory (NSW Creamery Butter Co. Ltd) 1895 d. by Charles C. Lance; cemetery (Soldiers' Memorial, 280 graves 1912–59) 1904, human remains exhumed by Luscombe before inundation, new one 1962 on new site, incl. columbarium; CH 1891, new one 1934; FB (station b. 1981); floods 1865 and 1904; flour mills: William Jardine (b. 1847 by Stewart Ryrie, jun., converted 1899 to a butter factory, closed 1900) and one b. 1884 by William Charles Rayner; freezing works (taken over 1924 by Garratt Scandrett Freezing Companies Ltd); gale 2012; PO 1862; pound (stock) 1905; Presb. C. 1913 (submerged); PS 1883, new ones 1934 and 1965, additions and alterations 1976; punt, ceased 1893; quarry (red granite); 2 reservoirs; Rom. Cath. C. (St Columbkille's) b. 1928–30, d. by George Donald Cochran (submerged ruin), new one; sale-yards; sawmills: John W. Adams, Irwin Bros, Ryrie's; school 1884, new building 1966, additions 2006, 2007, 2010; sewerage 1964; telephone 1892; TX 1914, automatic 1965; Unit. C. (St Andrew's, orig. Presb.) b. 1966 by Architon Constructions Pty Ltd, d. by R.J. Magoffin; pop. 15 (1866), 253 (1901), 328 (1911), 308 (1933), 312 (1947), 549 (1954), 428 (1961), 704 (1971), 950 (1976), 1,602 (1981), 1,733 (1986), 4,601 (1991), 4,320 (1996), 4,424 (2001), 1,903 (2006), 1,727 (2011).

Jindabyne Dam (*Co. Wallace*) 36°26'S. 148°38'E., 2 km SE of Jindabyne, on Lake Jindabyne; dam 1967, 236 ft (72 m) high, upgraded 2006 by Belmadar Pty Ltd, on Snowy R.; PO 1950; school 1957–64; telephone 1951.

Jindabyne East (*Co. Wallace*) 36°24'S. 148°39'E., 4 km NE of Jindabyne, on Lake Jindabyne; FB; sewerage augmentation 1994; TX (automatic); water supply augmentation 1991; pop. 560 (1991), 412 (1996), 536 (2001), 418 (2006), 551 (2011).

Jindalee (*Co. Harden*) 34°35'S. 148°05'E., 9 km NE of Cootamundra, on Jindalee Ck; farming; PO 1889; RS 1896–1970; school 1876–1941; telephone 1916; Wes. Meth. C. 1875, reused; pop. 196 (1901), 177 (1911), 138 (1933), 57 (1961).

Jindalee West (*Co. Harden*) 34°34'S. 148°03'E., 8 km N. of Cootamundra; school 1886–1907; pop. 70 (1947), 100 (1954), 69 (1961).

Jinden (*Co. Dampier*) 35°53'S. 149°35'E., 45 km W. of Moruya, on Jinden Ck; pop. 34 (1933).

Jindera (*Co. Goulburn*) 35°57'S. 146°53'E., 14 km N. of Albury, on Bowna Ck; Dight's Forest till 1885; settled by German Lutherans, village gaz. 1869; goldmining (reef), wheat, sheep, cherries; agric. implement works (Harry Haberecht); Angl. C. (St Thomas's) b. 1868–70, demolished, replaced (St Paul's) d. and b. 1878–81 by Haberecht and Yates, renovated 1930, closed 1990 for further renovations, reopened 1992; boiling-down works; brickworks (Albrik, estab. 1975, acquired 1980 by Boral Ltd); bushfires 1901 and 1905; cemetery 1871; cyclone 1971; drought 1967; electricity 1939; FB 1905;

flour mill (Humphrey's) 1877, bought by Johann Carl August Haberecht et al., burnt down, rebuilt 1880; hailstorm 1906; Lutheran C.: Bethlehem 1872–1962, new one 1962 d. by von Schramek, and graveyard, and St John's b. 1880 by Haberecht, d. by Ludwig Briese, renovated 1930, closed 1966, reused, and graveyard (burials 1868+); pleuro-pneumonia epidemic 1888; PO 1870; PS 1890, new one b. 1896 by Smith and Bates, closed 1942; reservoir; Rom. Cath. C. (St Mary's) 2011; school 1876, repairs 1881 by J. Yates, closed, sold and demolished, replaced 1900, new one 1992; sewerage augmentation 1985; snow 1927 and 1966; telegraph 1884; telephone 1886; TX 1914, automatic 1939; water reticulation 1982; works: Cyclone Co. of Aust. (fencing) and Strarch International Ltd (roofing); pop. 130 (1891), 425 (1901), 456 (1911), 216 (1933), 290 (1947), 257 (1954), 394 (1961), *c.*400 (1981), 778 (1991), 906 (1996), 962 (2001), 1,048 (2006), 1,056 (2011).

Jindy Andy (*Co. St Vincent*) 34°54'S. 150°41'E., 8 km E. of Nowra, on Eelwine Ck; butter factory (Jindy Andy Dairy Co.) 1889–1905, bought 1912 by Fresh Food & Ice Co., closed 1927; flood 1870; flour mill (bullock-powered) 1830, restored 1985, reused; granary.

Jingellic (*Co. Goulburn*) 35°56'S. 147°42'E., 33 km SW of Tumbarumba; settled 1837 by Terrance Aubrey Murray; mining (tin), farming, grazing, dairying; bridges: one (timber truss) b. 1887–92, replacement fabricated by Wollongong Engineering Pty Ltd, b. 1956–59 by Brown's Constructional Enterprises Pty Ltd, over Murray R., one (concrete) b. 1934 by Gamble, over Horse Ck, one (concrete) b. 1935 by Hardy & Co., over Jingellic Ck; bushfire 1952; butter factory (West Jingellic) 1919; cemetery 1892; drought 1840; electricity 1962; floods 1931, 1934, 1970; PO 1891, new one b. 1927; Presb. C., destroyed 1923, new one (St John's) 1925; sale-yards (Dalgety & Co.) 1941; school (Jingellic East till 1893) 1884 b. by Metcalf, replaced 1926 by J. Johnson, additions 1930 by A.H. Baglee, renovations 1960 and 1977; storm 1923; telephone 1893; TX 1918–64; pop. 72 (1901), 72 (1911), 135 (1933), 31 (1947), 85 (1954), 24 (2011).

Jingellic East (*Co. Selwyn*) 35°52'S. 147°45'E., 26 km SW of Tumbarumba.

Jingellic East (*Co. Selwyn*) see also Jingellic.

Jingera (*Co. Beresford*) 35°46'S. 149°25'E., 49 km S. of Queanbeyan; Angl. C. (St Andrew the Apostle) 1877; cemetery 1890; pop. 59 (1901), 69 (1911), 57 (1933), 168 (2006).

Jinglemoney (*Co. Murray*) 35°29'S. 149°42'E., 11 km SW of Braidwood, on Shoalhaven R.; airfield; telephone 1914.

Joadja (*Co. Camden*) 34°24'S. 150°14'E., 14 km NW of Berrima, on Joadja Ck; orig. Joadja Creek; estab. 1878 by Aust. Kerosene Oil & Mineral Co., settled mostly by Scots, thrived 1878–85, declined 1892, abandoned 1904, village sold 1911 to Sutherland and Cameron, acquired 1966 by Patricia Lee from Sam Stirling, sold 1993 and 2002, bought 2011 by Valero Jimenez, almost defunct; oil-shale mining (oil-shale disc. *c.*1850 by Edward Carter) 1874–1903, oil-shale retorting and refining till 1903, orchards till 1928 then cabbages and grazing; brickworks; bushfires 1905 and 1911; cemetery (124+ burials, incl. *c.*30 graves 1880–1908); coalmine; dam; distillery (whisky); earth tremor 1973; foot-bridge 1885, burnt down, over Joadja Ck; incline, closed 1924; mines: William Brown and John de Villiers Lamb 1874, Edward Carter, Cosgrove's (all amalgamated 1878 into Aust. Kerosene Oil & Mineral Co. Ltd, mines closed 1903, company went into liquidation 1906, mines reopened 1920 by Shale Petrol Co. and again during World War II by Peters Petroleum Motor Products Pty Ltd); oil-shale works o. 1879, first shale-oil distilled 1879, plant highly mechanised by 1881, fire 1882, acid plant 1883, works closed and dismantled 1903; PO 1878, burnt down 1905; railway (private) to Mittagong 1880, damaged 1893, closed 1903; 3 reservoirs; 66 retorts (horizontal) b. 1878–83 d. by James Fell, closed 1896; school 1879, new one b. 1882 by Gideon Cranston and Phillipson, closed 1905, sold and largely demolished 1930; TX 1882; tramway bridge (private) over Joadja Ck; water supply 1879; pop. *c.*400 (1879), *c.*300 (1880), *c.*450 (1882), *c.*500 (1886), *c.*1,000 (1889–90), *c.*1,200 (1892), *c.*400 (1900–3), 22 (1933).

Joadja Creek (*Co. Camden*) see Joadja.

Joes Box (*Co. Buller*) 28°40'S. 152°35'E., 41 km W. of Kyogle.

Joe's Gully (*Co. Hardinge*) see Old Mill.

Johnsons Creek (*Co. Gloucester*) 32°15'S. 151°57'E., 25 km NE of Dungog, on Mammy Johnsons Ck; farming and dairying; PO 1927–30; school 1882, new one b. 1889 by Walter and John Boots, new building b. 1909 by George Hill, closed 1964, sold 1967; Union C. 1909; pop. 206 (1911), 61 (1933).

Johns River (*Co. Macquarie*) 31°44'S. 152°42'E., 11 km S. of Kendall; village gaz. 1914, bypassed by highway 2010; timber, farming, dairying; Angl. C. o. 1953, removed from Stewarts River, sold 1978, reused; bridge 1880, demolished, new one (4 concrete spans) b. 1930 by Lawson, over Stewarts R.; cemetery 1852; electricity 1953; FB; flood 1929; LDS (Mormon) C.; PO 1899–1995; quarry; railway bridge (steel truss) 1915, 120 ft (36.6 m), over Stewarts R.; RS 1915–74; sawmills; school 1887, new one b. by John Levick, additions 1970 and 2010; telephone 1914; TX 1925–71; pop. 88 (1901), 90 (1911), 228 (1933), 177 (1947), 121 (1954), 122 (1961), 347 (2011).

Jondaryan (*Co. Cooper*) 34°18'S. 146°04'E., 3 km SE of Griffith; pop. 65 (1911).

Jonell Park (*Co. Gloucester*) 32°11'S. 152°29'E., 1 km SW of Tuncurry, on Wallamba Broadwater.

Jones Bridge (*Co. Buccleuch*) 35°23'S. 148°15'E., 9 km S. of Tumut, on Tumut R.; bridge 1885, new one b. 1928 by Herbert Ernest Ibbotson, over Tumut R.; telephone 1926; TX 1928, automatic 1966.

Jones Corner (*Co. Wellesley*) 36°55'S. 149°11'E., 5 km W. of Bombala; airport (Bombala).

Jones Creek (*Co. Clarendon*) 35°03'S. 148°05'E., 3 km NW of Gundagai, on Jones Ck; mining (gold and asbestos); asbestos mine 1880–1921; bushfire 1905; goldmine (Prince of Wales); grasshopper infestations 1911 and 1938; rifle range 1907; school 1898–99; pop. 85 (1901), 72 (1911), 118 (1933), 79 (1961), 194 (2006).

Jones Creek (*Co. Lincoln*) 32°08'S. 148°48'E., 22 km NE of Dubbo, on Jones Ck; pop. 24 (1933).

Jones Island (*Co. Macquarie*) 31°52'S. 152°36'E., 9 km W. of Harrington, on Manning R.; settled 1828 by A.P. Onslow, surveyed 1892; maize, dairying, oysters; butter and cheese factory and ice works (Manning River Co-op. Dairy Co. Ltd) 1918; floods 1857, 1866, 1867, 1875, 1893, 1895, 1929, 1930, 1950, 1978; PO 1868; school (Croki till 1911) 1863, new one 1913, closed 1975; telegraph 1879; telephone 1897; TX 1918–68; Wes. Meth. C. 1858, new one b. 1876 by William John Smith, closed 1899, sold 1899 to A. Perrett, new one b. 1899 by G. and S. Levick; wharf 1938; pop. 15 (1841), 345 (1901), 210 (1911), 242 (1933), 163 (1947), 222 (1961), 235 (2006).

Jones Reserve (*Co. Hunter*) 32°31'S. 150°43'E., 13 km S. of Denman; pop. 34 (1933).

Jonnel Park (*Co. Gloucester*) see Tuncurry.

Joppa Junction (*Co. Argyle*) 34°48'S. 149°41'E., 5 km SW of Goulburn; meat works b. 1947–51 by Howie, Moffat & Co., closed 1979; railway bridge (wrought iron Pratt truss) over Run O Waters Ck.

Jordan's Crossing (*Co. Camden*) see Bundanoon.

Juanbung (*Co. Caira*) 34°12'S. 143°56'E., 89 km W. of Hay.

Jubilee Road (*Co. Northumberland*) see Elermore Vale.

Judds Creek (*Co. Georgiana*) 33°50'S. 149°33'E., 31 km SW of Oberon, on Sawpit Ck; formerly also known as Mount Lawson; farming and sheep; PO 1890, damaged 1928; school (Mount Lawson) 1880, additions and repairs 1882 by C. Stacy & Son, closed 1915; telephone 1906; TX 1924, automatic 1982; pop. 109 (1911), 66 (1933), 55 (1947).

Jugiong (*Co. Harden*) 34°50'S. 148°19'E., 30

km S. of Murrumburrah, on Murrumbidgee R.; estab. 1845 by John Philip Sheahan, town gaz. 1853, first land sale 1854, bypassed by highway 1995; farming, sheep, asparagus; Angl. C. (Christ) b. 1873 by Marshall and M'Kenzie, d. by Edmund Thomas Blacket, sanctuary added 1895, tower added 1913, church repairs 1926 by Hocking, porch added 1970, church closed 2016, and graveyard; bridge 1859 d. by William Henry Downey, destroyed 1870, replacement b. 1870–72, new one b. 1963–65 by Bowas Construction, over Murrumbidgee R.; bushfire 1952; cemetery (316 graves) 1863; CH (incl. police station) 1864, new one 1891, destroyed 1898; fire 1889; floods 1852, 1870, 1950, 1974; hurricane (damaged every building) 1898; lock-up b. by Charles Hardy, destroyed 1898; mine (gold); PO 1856, new one 1949; pound (stock) 1855; 3 quarries; Rom. Cath. C. (St John the Evangelist) 1859, additions 1886 and 1927, and graveyard; school 1883, new one 1927; streets electric lit 1931; telephone 1886; toll-gate; TX 1928, automatic 1956; watch-house 1858; water pumping station 1933, chlorination plant 1960; pop. 98 (1856), 127 (1861), *c.*150 (1866), 247 (1871), 174 (1891), 169 (1901), 358 (1911), 250 (1933), 231 (1947), 251 (1954), 225 (1961), 229 (2006), 303 (2011).

Jump Up (*Co. Clive*) see Bungulla.

Jump-up Creek (*Co. Northumberland*) see Belford.

Junction Hill (*Co. Clarence*) 29°39'S. 152°56'E., 4 km N. of Grafton, on Alumy Ck; (incl. Baileys Estate); Carr's Creek Junction till 1975; foot-bridge over Koolkhan Ck; PO 1927; reservoir b. 1951 by J. Boulton, 1,500,000 gal. (6,819 kl); sale-yards b. 1915 by H. Zietsch; sawmill (Big River Timbers Pty Ltd); telephone 1906, automatic 1953; TX 1915; pop. 107 (1954), 788 (1981), 1,025 (1986), 1,117 (1991), 1,026 (1996), 1,177 (2011).

Junction Hole (*Co. Bland*) 33°51'S. 147°41'E., 46 km E. of West Wyalong, on Caragabal Ck; airfield; silo.

Junction Point (*Co. Georgiana*) 34°08'S. 149°20'E., 39 km N. of Crookwell, on Tuena Ck; defunct, site of former village now privately owned; gold, farming, grazing; cemetery 1884, razed; mines: Caledonian, Carlton, Celestial (Collins & Co.), Golden Dyke (Tennant & Co.), Great Britain (Collins & Co.), Hidden Secret (C. Johnson) 1908–14, Hit or Miss 1875–81, G. Lawrence, No. 1 North Phantom, Old Victoria, Phantom 1875–81, Red Jacket (Maguire & Co.), Royal Alice (Collins & Co.), Royal Standard (closed 1875), Slaughter Yard (Collins & Co.), Staveley & Co., Stockyard Reef (Martin 1895, Reid 1901, A.E. Burnett 1913) 1875–1913, Washington Reef (disc. 1861, estab. by Washington Brown, Towns & Co. 1875, Ford 1898, Joseph Johnson 1906) 1875–1906, Weeks and Lorenz, White Lode (W.G. and T.E. Woodger); PO 1872–1945, sold and reused; 2 stamper batteries; telephone 1914; TX 1928; pop. 78 (1901), 95 (1911), 36 (1933).

Junction Reefs (*Co. Bathurst*) 33°38'S. 149°00'E., 27 km W. of Blayney, on Belubula R.; grazing and mining (gold disc. 1870 by Martin Sheahan) till 1876, some subsequent mining till 1939, mining recommenced 1987; dam (mine) b. 1895–97 by Mount Boppy Mining Co., d. by Carl Oscar Schulze, 347 ft (105.8 m) long, on Belubula R.; flood 1906; mines: Arimes NL and Climax Mining Ltd (open-cut, closed 1996), Bakers Shaft, Belubula (taken over 1895 by Lyndhurst Goldfields Co. Ltd), Climax Mining and Cyprus Minerals 1986, Cornishman's (closed and sold 1876, taken over 1895 by Lyndhurst Goldfields Co. Ltd), Frenchman's (closed and sold 1876 to Martin Sheahan who set up The Sultan Goldmining Co., sold to John Grant & Sons, bought back by Martin Sheahan, taken over 1895 by Lyndhurst Goldfields Co. Ltd), Mandurama Goldmine (taken over 1895 by Lyndhurst Goldfields Co. Ltd), Sulphide, The Junction (closed and sold 1876 by Martin Sheahan to W.H. Binstead & Co., bought back 1885 by Martin Sheahan, closed); PO 1903–30; school 1907 b. by W.R. Gorringe, closed 1917, dismantled 1918–19; stamper battery (10 head) 1910; pop. 85 (1901), 229 (1911), 68 (1933).

Junee (*Co. Clarendon*) 34°52'S. 147°35'E., 34 km NE of Wagga Wagga, on Butlers Gully; Junee Railway Station till 1881, Junee Junction till 1893; first lots sold 1883, munic. proc. 1886, thrived in 1880s, town gaz. 1958; wheat, oats, barley, canola, sheep, beef, egg pulping, wine, railway centre; abattoir (Junee Abattoir Pty Ltd); agric. implement works estab. 1893 by Cohoe and Walster, taken over 1902 by A.J. Walster; ambulance station; Angl. C. 1881, new one (St Luke's) 1889 d. by Arthur Blacket, vestry added 1902, chancel added 1911 by George Mutch; Bapt. C. 1939; brewery (Thomas Edmunds) 1894–95; brickworks: G.H. Mutch & Co. Pty Ltd, and Henry Spence and Robert Irvine McKinney; bushfires 1940 and 2006; carriage-works: Egan Bros and W.J. Beaulock (fire 1923), and J.S. Taylor; cemetery 1881; CH b. 1890 by Bowden and Curtis, d. by James Johnstone Barnet; chocolate and licorice factory (Green Grove Organics, estab. by Neil Druce), in old flour mill; clock tower (war memorial) 1928; clothing factory (Stirling Henry) 1943, taken over by Emstra, closed 1953; cordial factories: Avor (W.E. Haberecht), fire 1937, W. Davoren, W.H.G. Mould 1900, fire 1916; diphtheria 1903 and 1926; dust storm 1915; electricity 1919; FB 1896 (station b. 1915, renovations and repairs 1931 by R.G. Harmon); fires 1893, 1902, 1914, 1915, 1916, 1924, 1933, 1941; floods 1925, 1926, 1928; flour mill (Jeffs Bros NSW Ltd) b. 1936 by M.C. Groat, closed, partly restored and reused; foundry (Pioneer, Cohoe and Walster) 1893, relocated 1928, sold 1994; gaol b. 1991–93 by ADT Aust., Thiess Contractors Pty Ltd and Wackenhut Corrections Corp.; gasworks 1883, demolished 1920; hospital (cottage) 1890 d. by Arthur Blacket, additions 1902, new buildings b. 1919 by George Henry Mutch, new hospital b. 1930 by A.G. Brown, additions 1939 by R.T. Gillies, additions 1943, 1950, 1966, closed, reused 2017, new one b. 2008 by Joss Construction; ice works (Murrumbidgee Dairy Co. Junee Pty Ltd) 1946–56; measles epidemics 1881 and 1939; PO 1878, new one b. 1888 by Gatby and Flock, d. by James Johnstone Barnet, additions and repairs 1899 by Daniel H. Taunton, extended 1909, alterations 1927 and 1960; Presb. C. 1888, new one (St Andrew's) b. 1905 by George Henry Mutch, d. by William John Monks; PS b. 1896 d. by Walter Liberty Vernon; railway barracks 1883, new barracks b. 1890 by Charles Hardy & Co.; railway carriage shed 1891–1985; railway coal stage 1891; railway engine shed b. 1881 by Charles Hardy, additional engine shed (removed from Bomen) 1885, new one b. 1890 by G.F. Fliner, man killed 1925; railway gasworks b. 1882 by John Louis Castner, expanded 1886, closed 1908, replaced 1916; railway round-house (42 bays) b. 1942–47, closed 1993, partly reused 1994; railway turntable 1947, 100 ft (30.5 m); 2 reservoirs (incl. one b. 1937, 500,000 gal. or 2,273 kl); Rom. Cath. C. 1884, new one (St Joseph's) b. 1927–30 by Francis Stenz, d. by William John Monks and Christopher Ernest Jeffs; RS 1878, refreshment room 1880, station burnt down 1882, replacement b. 1883–85 by Justin McSweeney, new refreshment rooms 1885, refreshment rooms fire 1918, station restored 2000; sale-yards 1940; Salv. Army C. 1892, closed and reused; schools: primary (Junee South till 1881, then Junee Junction till 1893) 1880, new buildings b. 1883 by Charles Hardy, additions 1898 by C. Hardy & Co., new building 1913, additions and alterations 1919 by F. Paroz, additions 1928 by Charles Hardy Contracting Co. Ltd, additions 1973 and 1987, and HS 1961 b. by Clarke Constructions Pty Ltd, additions 1966 and 1991; sewerage 1939; snow 1889, 1914, 1938; snowstorm 1913; soap-works (Scrivener Bros); storm 1923; streets were kerosene lit, then acetylene gas lit, then electric lit 1919; straw envelope factory (McCarthy & Co.) 1924, burnt down 1933; telegraph 1878, new office 1907; TX 1906, automatic 1979; typhoid 1889 (man died), 1898 (person died), 1899, 1903, 1909, 1910, 1913; Unit. C. (St Paul's, orig. Meth.) b. 1904 by George Henry Mutch, d. by Adin Parsons; vulcanising works

(Porter's), fire 1927; waterworks b. 1911–13 by Hood Bros, augmentation 1959; Wes. Meth. C. b. 1883 by Patterson and Smith, d. by Henry William Torrington Pincombe, closed, relocated and reused, demolished; winery (Mark View) b. 1904 by John James McWilliam; pop. 538 (1881), 1,682 (1891), *c.*1,730 (1895), 2,190 (1901), 3,606 (1911), 4,213 (1933), 4,010 (1947), 4,064 (1954), 3,980 (1961), 3,906 (1966), 3,765 (1971), 4,005 (1976), 3,993 (1981), 3,720 (1986), 3,673 (1991), 3,681 (1996), 3,592 (2001), 3,744 (2006), 4,400 (2011).

Junee (*Co. Clarendon*) see also Old Junee.

Junee Junction (*Co. Clarendon*) see Junee.

Junee North (*Co. Clarendon*) 34°52'S. 147°35'E., 2 km N. of Junee; mine (Specimen Hill); PO 1926; school 1922; telephone 1926.

Junee Railway Station (*Co. Clarendon*) see Junee.

Junee Reefs (*Co. Clarendon*) 34°44'S. 147°37'E., 16 km N. of Junee, on Wattle Fall Creek; The Reefs till 1917; farming, grazing, mining 1868+; cyanide plant 1901; FB; mines: Just-in-Time, Rockdale, The Doctor's Reefs, The Dust Holes, Wallett's Reefs; PO 1878; Rom. Cath. C. (St John's) b. 1915 by Alec Bowfield; school 1892–1944; stamper battery, moved 1905 to Sebastopol; storm 1933; telephone 1914; TX 1915, automatic 1941; pop. *c.*100 (1869), 221 (1901), 55 (1933), 77 (1947), 96 (1954), 71 (1961), 136 (2006).

Junee South (*Co. Clarendon*) see Junee.

Junee Vale (*Co. Baradine*) 30°47'S. 149°01'E., 18 km N. of Baradine, on Baradine Ck.

Junee Vale (*Co. Baradine*) see also Kenebri.

K

Kadina (*Co. Kennedy*) 32°53'S. 148°17'E., 19 km S. of Peak Hill; cemetery; PO 1890–93; school 1904–14; Wes. Meth. C. 1888; pop. 56 (1954).

Kadina (*Co. Rous*) see Goonellabah.

Kadina Park (*Co. Kennedy*) 32°56'S. 148°19'E., 26 km NE of Parkes, on Kadina Ck.

Kadungle (*Co. Kennedy*) 32°46'S. 147°37'E., 19 km NW of Trundle; farming; PO 1926; RS 1908, station b. by Reid and Castles, closed 1974; silo 1933; telephone 1923; TX 1928–71; pop. 147 (1933), 73 (1947), 77 (1954), 96 (1961).

Kahibah (*Co. Northumberland*) 32°58'S. 151°43'E., 2 km E. of Charlestown, on Flaggy Ck; (incl. Highfields); village gaz. 1864, subdivisions 1889 and 1921; formerly orchards; Angl. C. (St Martin's in the Field); bushfires 1951 and 1953; Meth. C. 1927, new one 1953 d. by W.C. Brown; mine; PO 1923; RS (Kenabah 1913–25) 1889–1971; sawmill (H. Muirhead); school 1938, new school 1955, additions 1966; tannery (William Mills) 1866; telephone 1917; pop. 93 (1911), *c.*400 (1924), 645 (1933), 773 (1947), 8,304 (1971), 8,051 (1976), 7,660 (1981), 3,158 (2006), 2,083 (2011).

Kain (*Co. Murray*) 35°44'S. 149°34'E., 38 km SW of Braidwood; formerly Jerrabat Gully; grazing; airfield; PO 1927–68; telephone 1908; TX 1928; pop. 33 (1933).

Kains Flat (*Co. Phillip*) 32°29'S. 149°51'E., 28 km NE of Mudgee; orig. Keenes Flat; bushfire 2017; pop. 350 (2011).

Kaiser (*Co. Lincoln*) 32°25'S. 149°01'E., 17 km N. of Wellington; defunct; mining (copper and gold); mine 1875–81 and 1916; Rom. Cath. C. (St Joseph's), moved 1899 to Bodangora.

Kalang (*Co. Raleigh*) 30°30'S. 152°46'E., 17 km NW of Bowraville, on Kalang R.; Middle Kalang till 1948; settled 1873 by Tom Brownlee, estab. 1879; timber, farming, dairying; cheese factory (Kalang Co-op. Cheese Co. Ltd), closed and burnt down 1931; FB (station b. 2011); flood 2001; PO 1927–68; sawmill (Penny and Shore); school (Middle Kalang) 1916–35; telephone 1915; TX 1924; pop. 176 (1947), 98 (1961), 174 (1954), 112 (2006), 372 (2011).

Kalangan (*Co. Harden*) 34°30'S. 148°31'E., 14 km E. of Murrumburrah; school (Khalangan) 1885–92.

Kalaru (*Co. Auckland*) 36°44'S. 149°56'E., 4 km W. of Tathra; Tathra Road till 1967; farming; brickworks (William Stafford) 1935, mechanised 1938, modernised 1968 and 1975, disused and derelict, site reused; PO 1927–42; quarry; telephone 1911; pop. 46 (1933), 48 (1947), 214 (1991), 275 (1996), 274 (2001), 307 (2006), 642 (2011).

Kalateenee (*Co. Dudley*) 31°07'S. 152°47'E., 6 km SW of Kempsey; pop. 102 (1933).

Kaleentha Loop (*Co. Livingstone*) 32°37'S. 143°01'E., 119 km S. of Wilcannia; PO 1955; RS 1927; telephone 1952; TX.

Kalkite (*Co. Wallace*) 36°20'S. 148°38'E., 10 km N. of Jindabyne; sawmill (James Broadhead) 1867–84; pop. 164 (2006), 173 (2011).

Kallara (*Co. Killara*) 30°54'S. 144°29'E., 130 km NE of Wilcannia, on Darling R.

Kaludah (*Co. Northumberland*) see Oswald.

Kamandra (*Co. Ashburnham*) 33°08'S. 148°16'E., 9 km E. of Parkes; pop. 30 (1933), 62 (1954).

Kamarah (*Co. Cooper*) 34°19'S. 146°47'E., 12 km W. of Ardlethan; laid out 1907 by Charles John Harnett, first lots sold 1908; wheat; Angl. C. (St Mary's) 1926; PO 1912, burnt down 1986; RS (orig. Bygee) 1908–75; school 1914–74; silo 1923; telephone 1911; TX 1924–85; water supply 1941; pop. 71 (1911), 134 (1933), 125 (1947), 127 (1954), 166 (1961), 130 (2006).

Kamber (*Co. Ewenmar*) 31°38'S. 148°37'E., 10 km NW of Gilgandra; RS (orig. Berida) 1903, station b. by John Allibone and McCarthy, closed 1965.

Kameruka (*Co. Auckland*) 36°45'S. 149°42'E., 14 km SW of Bega; estab. 1834, acquired 1864 by Sir Robert Lucas-Tooth; dairying, wool, beef; airfield; Angl. C. (Holy Trinity) 1869 d. by Edmund Thomas Blacket, re-roofed 1908, and graveyard (burials 1848+); bushfire 1905; butter factory (Home Farm Butter Co.) 1898; cemetery; cheese factories: Bega Co-op. Society Ltd (closed 1971), Lane's XXX, The Island (closed 1971); dried fruit factory; PO 1864–82; school 1880–1962; pop. *c.*130 (1866), 157 (1901), 270 (1911), *c.*260 (1926), 171 (1933), 144 (1947), 118 (1954), 87 (1961).

Kanahooka (*Co. Camden*) 34°29'S. 150°49'E., 3 km E. of Dapto, on Lake Illawarra; (incl. Brooks Terrace and Lakeline Estate); subdivided 1962; dairying 1905–1960s; cemetery (Lakeside, burials 1964+), incl. crematorium 1980; Church of Christ (Dapto); Jehovah's Witnesses C.; jetty b. by A. Mathie, defunct, new one; Presb. Reformed C.; schools: Hayes Park 1969 and Kanahooka HS 1973, additions 1976; smelter (copper, silver, gold, lead, zinc) and sulphide works b. 1897–99 by Smelting Co. of Aust. Ltd, incl. 4 blowers, chimneys 160 ft (48.8 m) and 180 ft (54.9 m), 2 copper furnaces, fusing furnaces, 2 leadblast furnaces, refining plant and zinc oxide plant, closed 1905, moved 1906 to Port Kembla, site razed 1907; pop. 4,540 (2001), 4,938 (2006), 5,167 (2011).

Kandos (*Co. Roxburgh*) 32°52'S. 149°58'E., 46 km SE of Mudgee; Combamolang till 1828, then Combimelong till 1849, then Coombermelon till 1874, then Coomber till 1914, then Candos till 1915; surveyed 1914 by Dawson, subdivided 1915, first land sales 1916; coalmining (started 1910 by W. McKay), cement 1916+, wool, beef, pigs; aerial ropeway 3.75 miles (6 km) b. 1921 by Gibson Battle & Co. Ltd; ambulance station 1945; Angl. C. (St Lawrence's) b. 1921 by Worrall, d. by Harold Robert Hardwick; brick-kiln (J. Owen); bushfires 1929, 1952, 2009; cement works (Aust. Portland Cement Co.) estab. 1914–16, closed 1931, reopened, kiln chimneys demolished 1978; CH b. 1929 by R. Gillies, closed 1975; clock tower; clothing factory 1943; colliery (Kandos No. 3, Kandos Collieries Pty Ltd); copper smelter o. 1918 by CSA Mines Ltd, demolished 1930; cordial factories: William Glynn (sold 1926 to A. Higginson), Beau Sharrock, Jack W. Symonds 1919, Thoms and O'Brien; engineering works; FB (station b. 1954); floods 1921, 1929, 1950; hospital 1917; hurricane 1928; joinery (Gordon Fuller); lock-up 1918; measles epidemic 1935; Meth. C. (United Mission) 1919 d. by Floyd S. Richards, closed 1983; miners' strikes 1938 and 1949; PO 1915, new one b. 1926; Presb. C. b. 1927 by Andy Reid, d. by George Reilly; PS b. 1918 by Country Concrete Constructions, new one 1961; powerhouse; 4 quarries; railway turntable 1928, 75 ft (22.9 m), derelict; 3 reservoirs; Rom. Cath. C. (St Dominic's) 1922 d. by Stanley Jeffrey; RS 1914; sawmills: Harry Franks, O'Brien & Son 1921, George Reilly; school (Coomber till 1914, then Candos till 1915) 1898, new one b. 1924 by John B. Simpkins and Henry Thomas, destroyed 1925, replacement b. 1929 by N.R. Morris, additions 1962, 1967, 1969, 1974, 2008; sewerage 1972; streets electric lit 1920; telephone 1916; TX 1917, automatic 1978; typhoid 1924; Unit. C., closed, sold 2010; water reticulation 1955, augmentation

1963 and 1987; pop. 1,033 (1919), *c.*1,500 (1921), 2,864 (1925), 2,769 (1929), 2,256 (1933), 1,757 (1947), 1,728 (1954), 2,195 (1961), 2,051 (1966), 1,981 (1971), 1,792 (1976), 1,626 (1981), 1,588 (1986), 1,525 (1991), 1,439 (1996), 1,339 (2001), 1,306 (2006), 1,284 (2011).

Kandos Quarries (*Co. Roxburgh*) 32°52'S. 149°55'E., 6 km W. of Kandos, on Carwell Ck; formerly The Quarry; limestone; 2 cemeteries; PO 1927–42; 4 quarries; telephone 1929; pop. 98 (1933).

Kangaloon (*Co. Camden*) 34°33'S. 150°32'E., 13 km SE of Bowral; (incl. West Kangaloon); estab. 1864; orig. timber, wheat, maize, potatoes, then dairying; Angl. C. (St Mark's) b. 1880 by Harrigan Bros, replacement (St Mark's Memorial) b. 1931 by L.G. Price, d. by H. Sheaffe, tower destroyed 1948; butter factory (Kangaloon Dairy Co. Ltd) b. 1889 by W. Rays, closed; cemetery 1877; earth tremor 1961; electricity 1937; flour mill (Roberts); grasshopper infestation 1945; hailstorm 1995; PO 1864; quarry; sawmills: George Cupitt 1887 and James Dorrough; school (Kangaloon West till 1891) 1869; storm 1948; telephone 1910; TX 1921 (equipment installed by McKinley), automatic 1949; Unit. C. (orig. Wes. Meth.) 1883–2016, sold 2016, and graveyard (21 graves); Wes. Meth. C. 1865; pop. *c.*260 (1866), 517 (1871), 539 (1891), 502 (1901), 357 (1911), 230 (1933), 226 (1947), 225 (1954), 209 (1961), 333 (2006), 309 (2011).

Kangaloon (*Co. Camden*)
see also Kangaloon East.

Kangaloon East (*Co. Camden*) 34°34'S. 150°35'E., 17 km SE of Bowral, on Nepean R.; farming; Angl. C. (St Matthew's) b. 1902 by H.W. Dennis, d. by W.J. Simpson, closed, sold to Arthur Horrex, sold again 2019, reused, and graveyard (86 graves 1866–1980); monumental stone works (L.L. Mitchell); PO 1870; quarry; school (Kangaloon till 1887) 1868–1930 and 1957–69; telephone 1924; TX 1925–62; pop. 102 (1933), 66 (1947), 138 (1954), 139 (1961).

Kangaloon West (*Co. Camden*) see Kangaloon.

Kangaroobie (*Co. Wellington*) 33°11'S. 149°02'E., 12 km NW of Orange, on Bell R.; Meth. C. 1934; Wes. Meth. C. 1899; pop. 30 (1933).

Kangarooby (*Co. Forbes*) 33°42'S. 148°26'E., 26 km SW of Canowindra, on Kangarooby Ck.

Kangaroo Camp (*Co. Gough*) 29°56'S. 151°22'E., 15 km E. of Tingha.

Kangaroo Creek (*Co. Fitzroy*) 29°52'S. 152°56'E., 18 km S. of Grafton, on Orara R.; farming and dairying; PO 1874; Presb. C. b. 1907 by William Faulks, d. by Grant; telephone 1929; TX 1930–59; pop. 153 (1901), 179 (1911), 186 (1933), 101 (1947), 96 (1954), 77 (1961).

Kangaroo Flat (*Co. Bathurst*) 33°36'S. 149°03'E., 20 km W. of Blayney.

Kangaroo Flat (*Co. Bathurst*) 33°52'S. 148°48'E., 11 km E. of Cowra; quarry (abandoned).

Kangaroo Flat (*Co. Clive*) 29°23'S. 151°49'E., 40 km N. of Glen Innes, on Kangaroo Ck.

Kangaroo Flat (*Co. Vernon*) 31°08'S. 152°08'E., 52 km E. of Walcha, on Home Ck; airfield; electricity 1969; manganese mine (The Orchid).

Kangaroo Flat (*Co. Wellington*) 33°00'S. 149°35'E., 39 km W. of Kandos.

Kangaroo Hollow (*Co. Vernon*) 31°00'S. 152°04'E., 43 km E. of Walcha, on Green Gully.

Kangaroo Mount (*Co. Buccleuch*) 35°00'S. 148°16'E., 17 km NE of Gundagai, on Murrumbidgee R.; bushfire 1925.

Kangaroo Mountain (*Co. Camden*)
see Bellawongarah.

Kangaroo River (*Co. Camden*)
see Upper Kangaroo River.

Kangaroo Valley (*Co. Camden*) 34°44'S. 150°32'E., 16 km W. of Berry; (incl. Osborne, and Maguire's surveyed 1887); estab. 1867 by Alick Osborne, founded by Charles Wiley, laid out 1876, thrived 1885–95, classified 1977 by National Trust; orig. timber, then dairying and goldmining, now hobby farming and tourism; Angl. C. (Good Shepherd) b.

1870–72 by Frederick Moore and W. Saville, d. by John Horbury Hunt, renovated 1894, re-roofed 1902, renovated 1935, re-roofed again 1942, and graveyard (14 graves); bacon factory (Farmers' Co-op. Co. Ltd) 1899–1901; bridges: one b. 1879 by Kelly and Walsh, 245 ft (74.7 m), destroyed 1898, replacement (Hampden Bridge) b. 1895–98 by Thomas Loveridge and Herbert Charles Hudson, 253 ft (77.1 m), d. by Ernest Macartney de Burgh and Percy Allan, over Kangaroo R. and suspension bridge b. 1931 by George Walker, 206 ft (62.8 m), replaced 1976 in concrete, over Brogers Ck; bushfires 1867–68, 1939 (3 houses destroyed), 1965; butter factory (Kangaroo Valley Dairy Co.) b. 1888 by Paul Ettingshausen, became creamery in 1898, leased 1899 to Farmers' & Settlers' Co-op. Society Ltd, closed 1908; caterpillar infestation 1893; cemetery (693 graves 1864+) 1870, incl. columbarium; CH 1887, new one b. 1902–4 by Daniel H. Taunton, closed 1972, converted 1986 to police station; electricity 1947; FB 1957 (station extensions 2018); fire 1893; floods 1870, 1898, 1951, 1974; foot-bridge (suspension) b. 1919 by Robert Erwin, over Brogers Ck; hailstorm 1908; Meth. C. 1967; PO 1870, new one b. 1909; pound (stock) 1901; Presb. C. (St Andrew's) b. 1879 by Ritchie and Milligan, d. by John Tanner, closed 1925, demolished 1935; PS 1883, new one b. 1902–4 by Daniel H. Taunton; Rom. Cath. C. 1874, replacement (St Joseph's) 1888, restored, and graveyard (7 graves); sawmill (E.M. Davis and J.R. Reid); school 1871 b. by Christopher Binns, new one b. 1884 by Bernard Moss, additions 1898 by W.H. Bebbington, additions 1985, 1995, 2010; telegraph 1884; TX 1912, automatic 1972; Unit. C. (orig. Wes. Meth.) 1886; water reticulation 1955, augmentation 1994; Wes. Meth. C. 1873; winery (Kangaroo Valley Estate); pop. *c.*200 (1861), 1,400 (1881), 552 (1891), 483 (1901), 561 (1911), 281 (1921), 244 (1933), 227 (1947), 216 (1954), 169 (1961), 174 (1966), 135 (1971), 349 (1976), 208 (1986), 247 (1991), 350 (1996), 341 (2001), 319 (2006), 298 (2011).

Kangiara (*Co. King*) 34°36'S. 148°45'E., 18 km S. of Boorowa; Kangiara Mines till 1923; surveyed and village gaz. 1909, thrived 1909–13, largely defunct; gold, silver, copper, lead, zinc (disc. 1901 by Alder), farming, grazing; Bapt. C. 1910, closed, sold and reused 1915; cemetery; concentrating plant 1926; mines: Clan McKenzie 1911–20, Democrat or South Kangiara (Hales, Hall, Besnard) 1907–8, Eclipse, Felicitous, Kangiara (Kangiara Mines Ltd 1907–14, Pyrites Ltd 1914–18, Lake George Mines 1952–58), Mammoth Lode (G. Marsland), Marie Corelli (P. Kennedy and R. Heaslip) 1912–14, Old Kangiara (A.E. Brenton and T.E. Smith) 1937–40, Pierce and Cassia, Stewart Bros, Triangle (Humphreys, Marsland and Price) 1910–18, White Flag (Cliffs); PO 1909; PS 1909–12; 3 quarries; Rom. Cath. C. 1915 (Bapt. C. till 1910); school (Kangiara Mines till 1924) 1910–58; telephone 1923; TX 1928, automatic 1971; pop. 341 (1911), 66 (1933), 87 (1947), 64 (1954), 66 (1961).

Kangiara Mines (*Co. King*) see Kangiara.

Kangy Angy (*Co. Northumberland*) 33°19'S. 151°23'E., 5 km SW of Wyong, on Ourimbah Ck; Meth. C. (removed 1926 from Wyong Creek), closed and reused, moved to Ourimbah and reused; railway bridge (2 steel spans) over Ourimbah Ck; reservoir; school 1878–94, demolished 1895; pop. 73 (1911), 72 (1933), 79 (1961), 301 (2006), 316 (2011).

Kanimbla (*Co. Cook*) see Blackheath.

Kankool (*Co. Buckland*) 31°42'S. 150°46'E., 11 km NW of Murrurundi, on Doughboy Hollow Ck; RS 1909, closed and demolished; pop. 60 (1933), 71 (1954).

Kanoona (*Co. Auckland*) 36°44'S. 149°43'E., 12 km SW of Bega, on Tantawangalo Ck; cheese factory (Charles Schuback); flood 1919; school (Wolumla till 1868, then Wolumla North till 1912) 1865–75 and 1882–92 and 1900–28; pop. 63 (1911), 42 (1933).

Kanwal (*Co. Northumberland*) 33°16'S. 151°29'E., 6 km NE of Wyong, on Tuggerah Lake; (incl. Wyongah); Warnervale till

1915; poultry and orchards; Angl. C. (St Mary's) 1924–81, reused, new one (Holy Spirit); bushfire 1928; FB; flood 1949; jetty (Wyongah) 1931; LDS (Mormon) C.; Meth. C.; PO: Kanwal 1914 and Wyongah 1955; reservoir 1991; Salv. Army C.; school (Warnervale till 1925) 1917, additions 1920, additions 1954 by A.G. Hill, additions 1957, 1962, 1975; SD Adventist C.; sewerage 1975; telephone 1915; TX 1927–66; pop. 220 (1933), 368 (1947), 550 (1954), 812 (1961), 3,873 (2011).

Kapooka (*Co. Mitchell*) 35°09'S. 147°18'E., 9 km SW of Wagga Wagga; army base 1941 (26 soldiers killed 1945 in explosion), additions 1955 by J.D. Clark; RS 1927–75; school 1953, additions 2010 by Burton Constructions Pty Ltd; pop. 340 (2011).

Kara (*Co. Mootwingee*) 30°47'S. 142°15'E., 138 km NW of Wilcannia; pop. 28 (1933).

Karaak Flat (*Co. Gloucester*) 31°56'S. 152°17'E., 10 km SW of Wingham; earth tremor 1886; RS 1913–75; pop. 27 (1933).

Karabar (*Co. Murray*) see Queanbeyan.

Karachi (*Co. Wellesley*) 36°59'S. 148°47'E., 42 km W. of Bombala; PO 1927–30; telephone 1924; TX 1935–58.

Karagi (*Co. Northumberland*) see The Entrance.

Karangi (*Co. Fitzroy*) 30°15'S. 153°03'E., 8 km NW of Coffs Harbour, on Karangi Ck; goldmining, dairying, farming, bananas; bridge, re-decked and renovated 1929, over Karangi Ck; bushfires 1917 and 1946; butter factory (Pioneer) 1899; cemetery (Coffs Harbour, lawn, 2,616 plots *c.*1970+), incl. columbaria and crematorium; copper mine (Lane and Peters); dam 1980, 125 ft (38 m) high, wall raised 1988 to 128 ft (39 m), raised again in 1994 to 161 ft (49 m); electricity 1939; FB; PO 1897, new one 1914, burnt down 1961; Presb. C. b. 1897 by C. Shephard, renovations 1910 by Rennie, further renovations 1934; Rom. Cath. C. (Holy Family) b. 1904 by Philip Landrigan, fire 1919, enlargement and repairs 1937, closed, sold 1991, reused; RS 1922–74; sawmills: William D. Buchanan, H. Hollibone (sold 1911 to Reuben Wood & Wood Ltd), Thomas Johnson, McBean and Walker, Plummer and Ewing 1908, R.E.J. Woods; school 1895, additions 1919 by H. Bull, additions 2010; telephone 1897; TX 1915–72; water treatment plant (Coffs Harbour) 2009; pop. 150 (1901), 195 (1911), 247 (1933), 271 (1947), 261 (1954), 224 (1961), 535 (2011).

Kareela (*Co. Camden*) 34°40'S. 150°14'E., 7 km W. of Bundanoon; Wollondilly till 1891; PO 1902–16; RS 1885–1916.

Karimbla (*Co. Cooper*) 33°58'S. 146°27'E., 52 km NE of Griffith; mining (tin and tungsten).

Kariong (*Co. Northumberland*) 33°26'S. 151°18'E., 4 km W. of Gosford, on Piles Ck; Christ. Revival Crusade C. (Lighthouse); FB (station b. 1999); foot-bridge over Piles Ck; PO 1947; 3 quarries; 2 reservoirs; rifle range; school 1988, additions 1993, 1995, 2010; telephone 1947; TX 1948–59; pop. 82 (1947), 117 (1954), 143 (1961), 6,113 (2006), 6,451 (2011).

Kariong Mountains (*Co. Northumberland*) see Somersby.

Karkatt (*Co. Gloucester*) 32°05'S. 152°13'E., 25 km E. of Gloucester, on Wallamba R.; school 1899–1914, new one b. 1936 by J.A. Butler, closed 1965; pop. 74 (1947).

Karno (*Co. Richmond*) 29°11'S. 153°03'E., 32 km SW of Woodburn, on Myrtle Ck; telephone 1924; TX 1932–33.

Karoola (*Co. Arrawatta*) 29°27'S. 151°03'E., 15 km S. of Ashford, on Macintyre R.

Karrabar (*Co. Cook*) see Warrimoo.

Karraganbah (*Co. Northumberland*) see Tuggerawong.

Kars Springs (*Co. Brisbane*) 31°54'S. 150°34'E., 29 km SW of Murrurundi, on Wybong Ck; grazing; Angl. C. (St Paul's) 1904; hailstorm 1894; PO 1886–1971; school (Upper Wybong till 1907) 1902–70; telephone 1906; TX 1911; pop. 133 (1911), 128 (1933), 83 (1947), 90 (1954), 78 (1961), 252 (2006).

Karuah (*Co. Gloucester*) 32°39'S. 151°58'E., 19 km NW of Nelson Bay, on Karuah R.; Sawyers Point till 1884, then Aliceton till 1892; first land sale 1901, bypassed by highway 2004; dairying, oysters, fishing; Aboriginal Mission C. 1913; Angl. C. (St Columba's) 1913; bridge (steel truss) fabricated by Horseley Bridge & Thomas Piggott Ltd, erected 1957 by Electric Power Transmission Pty Ltd, d. by V. Karmalsky and G.F. Gilbert, 716 ft (218.2 m), over Karuah R.; bushfire 1951; cemetery (365 graves 1907+), incl. columbaria; engineering works (William Dalgleish); FB; jetty and slipway (State Fisheries) b. 1937 by G.A. Zeininger & Sons; Meth. C. b. 1923 by William Frederick Gazzard et al.; PO 1885; PS; punt (manual) 1918–23, new one b. 1923 by Engel Bros, ceased 1957, across Karuah R.; quarry; Rom. Cath. C. (Our Lady of the Rosary) 1950; sawmills: Charles Bate and Muston, closed 1891, and Morten, Waymouth and McCann; school (Aliceton till 1907) 1886 b. by J.C. Watt, closed 1889, reopened 1896, closed 1897, new one b. 1907, additions 1968, 1975, 1981; storm 1927; telephone 1903; TX 1919, automatic 1972; Unit. C.; pop. 184 (1911), 313 (1933), 289 (1947), 374 (1954), 416 (1961), 598 (1971), 673 (1976), 744 (1981), 777 (1986), 838 (1991), 803 (1996), 1,070 (2001), 858 (2006), 1,064 (2011).

Katherine's Landing (*Co. Northumberland*) see Rothbury North.

Kathida (*Co. Gough*) 29°17'S. 151°29'E., 38 km E. of Ashford; 5 mines (tin).

Katoomba (*Co. Cook*) 33°43'S. 150°19'E., 29 km SE of Lithgow, on Kedumba R.; (incl. North Katoomba, North's Siding, South Katoomba, The Gully, Yosemite Park formerly Yosemite Valley); The Crushers till 1877; village gaz. 1883, munic. proc. 1889, city proc. 1946, city (Blue Mountains) proc. 1947; formerly coalmining and oil-shale mining (oil-shale disc. *c.*1870 at Katoomba by Campbell Mitchell and in 1880 at Ruined Castle by John Britty North) till 1903, then leathergoods, furniture, popular (primarily 1920s–30s) mountain resort with magnificent scenery, lookouts and waterfalls; abattoir; Aboriginal Mission C. 1905; aerial ropeway (removed from Leura), for Ruined Castle oil-shale mines, fabricated by Adolf Bleichert & Co., Leipzig, Germany, erected 1888 by Carl Oscar Schulze, collapsed 1889; airfield; ambulance station 1941; Angl. C. 1885, new one (St Hilda's) b. 1914 by F.E. Johnson, d. by John Burcham Clamp and Walter Burley Griffin, tower b. 1928 by Lawrence Pither, d. by John Burcham Clamp and Clifford Horace Finch; Assemblies of God C. (Blue Mountains City); ball-point pen factory (Scripto); Bapt. C. 1917; box factory (Lawrence Pither); brewery (Katoomba Brewing Co.) o. 2016 in former powerhouse; brickworks (Blue Mountains Bricks Pty Ltd); Buddhist C.; bushfires 1905, 1922, 1929, 1940, 1944, 1951, 1952, 1956, 2011, 2014; cemetery (*c.*3,000 graves) 1884, extended 1964, incl. columbarium; CH (incl. lock-up) b. 1895 by Fahey and Ross, d. by Walter Liberty Vernon, additions 1926 by W.J. Bailey, d. by Gorrie McLeish Blair, extensions and restoration 1989 d. by Milton Cameron; chocolate factories: Blue Mountains Chocolate Co. and Zacharias Theodore Simos 1916; Christ. Community C. (Bethany); Christ. Science C. 1939; Church of Christ (Lighthouse); clothing factory (David Jones Ltd) 1944; Cong. C. 1883, relocated and reopened 1888, enlarged twice, reused, new one d. by A.C. Kent, demolished; Contemporary Christ. C. (Blue Mountains); cordial factories: Bronger Bros 1895, George Davies & Co., P. Godfrey, Rowland & Son 1904; 3 dams (on Cascade Ck): 1907, 1926 (b. by Patterson Bros), 1938; earth tremor 1951; electricity 1915; Exclusive Brethren C., d. and b. 1930 by Jack Davies, closed; 4 FB (incl. station b. 1909, new one b. 1914 by Martin Clarence Heraty, d. by Alfred Spain, Thomas Frame Cosh and Robert Smith Dods, extended 1923); fibrous plaster works (E.A. Stanborough & Sons) 1917; fires 1892 (woman died) and 1953; furniture factories: J.S. Henderson Ltd (in former hall) and Andrew Levings 1921; gales 1891, 1898, 1913, 1923 (man killed); gasworks (Katoomba & Leura Gas Co. Ltd) 1906, explosion 1950, taken over 1957 by Aust. Gas Light Co., demolished; hailstorms 1907 and 2014; heatwave 1905; hospital (Anzac Memorial) b. 1925–27 by Thomas Norman Grimsley, alterations 1931 by D.E. Foster, additions 1939, 1946, 1999, damaged 2014; ice works (W.T. Davies); incinerator b. 1891 by John Bustard for night soil and refuse disposal; Jehovah's Witnesses C.; joinery (Katoomba Power Joinery Works, A.M. Duncan), burnt down 1924; landslide (Dogface Rock) at Malaita Point 1931 (nr Daylight Tunnel); measles epidemic 1893; mine haulage tunnel (Daylight Tunnel) b. 1890 for haulage from Glen Shale (Mort's) Mine in Megalong Valley; mines: Katoomba Coal Mine (estab. 1878 by John Britty North and Robert Henry Reynolds in Jamieson Valley, strike 1887, 2 more adits o. 1891, mine closed 1905, acquired and reopened 1925 by Katoomba Colliery Ltd, closed 1945) and Ruined Castle Mine (Katoomba Coal & Shale Co. Ltd, estab. 1889 by John Britty North, closed, acquired 1890 by Aust. Kerosene Oil & Mineral Co., strike 1892, production peaked 1893 from 34 adits, closed 1897, reopened 1903, closed 1903); monumental stone works (R.J. Paterson); moth infestation 1938; Plymouth Brethren C. 1934; PO: Katoomba 1880 (b. 1910 by Alfred Stephens, d. by Walter Liberty Vernon, alterations 1917, additions 1924, reused, new one 1996 on new site), North Katoomba 1964, South Katoomba 1943, Yosemite Park 1928–56; powerhouse (Katoomba Electric Supply Co.) b. 1925 by R.J. Paterson, d. by F. Storer, bought 1926 by local council, closed 1946, chimney dismantled 1949 and sold, powerhouse sold and reused 1985; Presb. C. (St Andrew's) 1913–94, reused; PS 1884, new one 1990; quarry (railway ballast); railway (haulage) b. 1880–82, d. by Norman Selfe for John Britty North's mines, used till 1945, also used for tourists, steam winder (installed 1882) replaced 1935 with electric winder, acquired 1945 by Harry Hammon after mine closed; railway turntable, 60 ft (18.3 m) 1878, moved to Valley Heights; reservoirs: 300,000 gal. (1,363.8 kl) and 1,000,000 gal. (4,546 kl); rifle range 1909; Rom. Cath. C. 1890, reused, new one (St Canice's) b. 1903 by John Hines, d. by Harry Rupert Goyder, sanctuary 1907, steeple 1908, fire 1960; RS (Crushers till 1877) 1868, first station 1874, second station 1877, third station 1881, closed and reused, present station b. 1891 by Quiggin and Kermode, additions 1923, fire 1928; Salv. Army C. 1914, burnt down and replaced 1968; schools: primary 1881 (new one b. 1884 by J. Donald, additions 1891 and 1898, additions 1911 by Arnold Rigby, new building 1915, additions 1924, additions 1926 by Lawrence Pither, replaced 1962, additions 1982), HS 1943 (additions 1962 by Kell & Rigby Pty Ltd, d. by Kenneth Frank Charles Woolley, additions 1967 and 1980, renovations 1987), North Katoomba 1955 (additions 1968, 1973, 1980, 1993); SD Adventist C.; sewerage 1910; shoe factory; snowstorm 1909; storm 1897; streets gas lit 1906; TC; telegraph 1881, new office b. 1910 by Alfred Stephens, d. by Walter Liberty Vernon; telephone: North Katoomba 1964, South Katoomba 1943, Yosemite Park 1928; toy factory (Boomerang); TX 1899, automatic 1973; Unit. C. (orig. Wes. Meth.) 1888, renovated 1894, additions 1907 by W. Brown, d. by Adin Parsons; vulcanising works; waterworks 1907; pop. 1,592 (1891), *c.*1,300 (1895), 2,270 (1901), 3,950 (1911), 6,445 (1933), 8,781 (1947), 6,975 (1954), 7,171 (1961), 8,016 (2011).

Kauthi (*Co. Hawes*) 31°46'S. 151°52'E., 28 km N. of Gloucester; telephone 1917; TX; pop. 51 (1901).

Kaytoun (*Co. Inglis*) 30°54'S. 150°48'E., 17 km SE of Manilla, on Browns Springs Ck; RS 1925–75.

Kayuga (*Co. Brisbane*) 32°12'S. 150°52'E., 5 km SW of Aberdeen, on Hunter R.; surveyed 1858 by John Rogers, plan redesigned 1858 by Bennett, town gaz. 1859 as Kyuga, lots offered for sale 1859; formerly wheat and wool, then mining (coal disc. by Arthur Cox), dairying, vegetables, fruit, oaten hay; Angl. C. (St Andrew's) 1882, renovated 1916, closed, dilapidated, sold and demolished

1936; bridge (continuous lattice iron truss), 253 ft (77 m), fabricated by Butterley Co., Derby, England, erected 1881 by J. Musson & Co., d. by John Alexander McDonald, over Hunter R.; cemetery (50+ burials 1831–1956, incl. 19 graves) 1828; coalmine estab. 1892 by W. Weis, taken over by H. Hironymous, fire 1902; creamery estab. 1893 by Francis Abberton and Robert Gall, became butter factory in 1895 under lease to Alexander Gibson, closed 1898, site sold 1899 to Charles Isaac Guy; PO 1874, burnt down 1941; Prim. Meth. C. 1866, new one 1871; Rom. Cath. C. (St James's); sawmill (William Birk); school 1877, new one b. 1879 by Andrew Bussell, d. by George Allen Mansfield, new school 1929 on new site, closed 1938, reopened 1955–84; telephone 1912; TX 1927; Wes. Meth. C. 1881, new one 1891; pop. 131 (1901), 186 (1911), 147 (1933), 116 (1947), 144 (1954), 116 (1961).

Keajura (*Co. Wynyard*) 35°20'S. 147°39'E., 33 km SE of Wagga Wagga, on Keajura Ck; school (Keajura Creek) 1890–95; TX (automatic); pop. 94 (1933), 78 (1954), 65 (1961).

Keajura Creek (*Co. Wynyard*) see Keajura

Kealys Bight (*Co. Durham*) 32°31'S. 151°31'E., 21 km N. of Bolwarra, on Paterson R.

Kearsley (*Co. Northumberland*) 32°52'S. 151°24'E., 3 km SE of Aberdare, on Swamp Ck; Eddenville till 1916; village gaz. 1913, surveyed and laid out 1915; coalmining; Angl. C. (St Michael's) b. 1923 by L. Hinde, d. by Ernest Tingle, damaged 1937; brickworks estab. by Alexander and A.H. Shedden, acquired 1913 by Caledonian Collieries Ltd; bushfire 1928; collieries: Abermain No. 2 (estab. 1910–12 by Abermain Collieries Ltd, o. 1913, strike 1914, men killed 1914 and 1921, taken over 1922 by Abermain Seaham Collieries Ltd, man killed 1922, strikes 1924 and 1925, man killed 1926, strikes 1927 and 1930, taken over 1930 by J. & A. Brown & Abermain Seaham Collieries Ltd, man killed 1935, closed 1936, damaged 1937, reopened 1938, strike 1939, man killed 1940, strikes 1940, 1943, 1944, 1950, colliery closed, reopened 1959, closed 1963, demolished except for bath-house) and Abermain No. 3 (estab. 1917–23 by Abermain Collieries Ltd, taken over 1922 by Abermain Seaham Collieries Ltd, o. 1924, strike 1924, man killed 1925, taken over 1930 by J. & A. Brown & Abermain Seaham Collieries Ltd, man killed 1934, strikes 1939, 1940, 1942, 1947, men killed 1949 and 1951, taken over and closed 1960 by Coal & Allied Industries Ltd, demolished except for bath-house); earth tremor 1925; FB (station b. 1927 by Skelton and Worth, new one 1990); gales 1928 and 1944; Meth. C. 1921, damaged 1928, destroyed 1937; miners' riot 1929; PO 1916; PS 1926–35; quarry; railway (colliery); Rom. Cath. C., destroyed 1937; school (Abermain Shaft No. 2 till 1915) 1912, new school b. 1915 on new site by Partridge-Wall and Wall, additions 1924 by Drayton and Rowling; storm (nearly every house damaged) 1937; telephone 1917; pop. 450 (1920), 905 (1933), 625 (1947), 584 (1954), 593 (1961), 652 (2006), 740 (2011).

Keenes Flat (*Co. Phillip*) see Kains Flat.

Keen's Swamp (*Co. Roxburgh*) see Ilford.

Keepit (*Co. Darling*) 30°51'S. 150°31'E., 22 km SW of Manilla, on Halla Linga Ck; earth tremor 2012; PO 1875–98; Rom. Cath. C. (St Patrick's) 1877, new one 1910, moved 1951 to Keepit Dam; pop. 258 (1911), 109 (1933).

Keepit (*Co. Darling*) see also Keepit Dam.

Keepit Dam (*Co. Darling*) 30°53'S. 150°30'E., 26 km SW of Manilla, on Lake Keepit; dam first mooted 1896, b. 1938–60, 180 ft (55 m) high, on Namoi R.; earth tremor 2012; flood 1954; PO 1941; power station; PS 1955; Rom. Cath. C. (St Patrick's), removed 1951 from Keepit; school (Keepit till 1928, Keepit Dam till 1966, then Lake Keepit) 1880–89, 1911–14, 1948–73; telephone 1941; TX 1955–76; pop. 237 (1947), 481 (1954), 204 (1961), 318 (2011).

Keera (*Co. Murchison*) 30°00'S. 150°47'E., 24 km SE of Bingara; school 1913–23 and 1957–66; pop. 153 (1911), 100 (1933), 113 (1947), 72 (1954), 60 (1961).

Keerrong (*Co. Rous*) 28°43'S. 153°16'E., 11

km N. of Lismore, on Terania Ck; Angl. C. (St John's) d. and b. 1920–22 by Thomas W. Green; creamery (Foley Bros Ltd) 1899; Meth. C. 1905 (removed from Blakebrook); PO 1905–31; Rom. Cath. C. (St John's) b. 1913 by John Noonan, d. by Frederick Johnson Board; school 1898 b. by R. Gall, closed 1976; telephone 1912; TX (automatic); pop. 69 (1901), 252 (1911), 140 (1933), 155 (1947), 145 (1954), 148 (1961), 348 (2006), 380 (2011).

Keighrans Tank (*Co. Mouramba*) 32°03'S. 146°09'E., 110 km SW of Nyngan; telephone 1923; TX 1930–65.

Keinbah (*Co. Northumberland*) 32°45'S. 151°23'E., 7 km NW of Abermain; South Allandale till 1908; grapes; bushfire (house destroyed) 1929; PO 1902; telephone 1912; TX 1920–32; winery (Majors Lane Wines) 1987; pop. 78 (1911), 64 (1933).

Keira (*Co. Camden*) see Mount Ousley.

Keiraville (*Co. Camden*) see Gwynneville.

Keirson (*Co. Westmoreland*) see Carlwood.

Keith Hall (*Co. Richmond*) 28°53'S. 153°32'E., 4 km SW of Ballina, on Richmond R.; farming and sugar-cane; jetty; PO 1927–79; punt across Richmond R.; telephone 1923; pop. 111 (1933), 89 (1947), 80 (1954), 63 (1961), 175 (2011).

Kellys Creek (*Co. Monteagle*) 33°56'S. 148°24'E., 22 km E. of Grenfell, on Kellys Ck; quarry.

Kelly's Creek (*Co. St Vincent*) see Bimbimbie.

Kellys Gully (*Co. Burnett*) see Warialda Rail.

Kellys Plains (*Co. Sandon*) 30°34'S. 151°39'E., 6 km S. of Armidale; farming; Angl. C. 1896, new one (St John's) 1923, and graveyard (17 burials); PO 1884; Presb. C. 1870; RS 1883–1975; school 1863, repairs 1886 by George Lonsdale, additions 1892 by Thomas Morrissey, additions 2010; telephone 1916; TX 1917; pop. 212 (1901), 195 (1911), 142 (1933), 155 (1947), 126 (1954), 124 (1961).

Kelly's Siding (*Co. Narromine*) see Myall Mundi.

Kelso (*Co. Northumberland*) see Singleton.

Kelso (*Co. Roxburgh*) 33°25'S. 149°36'E., 3 km E. of Bathurst, on Raglan Ck; (incl. Laffing Waters); settled 1818, designated as chief town of the county; farming, orchards, honey; abattoir; Angl. C. (Holy Trinity) b. 1833–35 by John Foster, d. by Thomas Hawkins, tower damaged, tower repaired and church restored 1840, church re-roofed 1874, additions and renovations 1889 by Josiah James Atkins, d. by James Hine, vestry added 1933, church additions 1958, and graveyard (graves 1826+), incl. columbaria; Assemblies of God C. (Christ. Life); brickworks; bridges to Bathurst over Macquarie R.: Denison Bridge 1856, d. by William Christopher Bennett, 256 ft (78 m), destroyed 1867, new one (iron Pratt truss spans), b. 1870–73 by P.N. Russell & Co., d. by Gustavus Alphonse Morell, 474 ft (144.5 m), concrete deck laid 1981, closed 1992 and reused, Evans Bridge 1991, Gordon Edgell Bridge (George Street Falls Bridge till 2006) 1995; carriage-works: Henry E. Pain and Rivett Bros; container terminal (Patrick's Port Link) 2007; engineering works: Avimain Services 1991 and Clyde Engineering Co. Ltd 1970; FB (station b. 1999); fire 1894; floods 1872 and 1899; flour mills: John Ford 1839 and George Innes 1825; food factory (Simplot Australia Pty Ltd) 1979; foot-bridge over Raglan Ck; foundry (Denison) estab. by Denny and Ashworth, bought 1879 by R.R. Blair; house frame and truss factory; ice works (R. and J. McFadden); lock-up b. 1851 by Arnold Rigby, new one b. 1895 by Rigby Bros; PO 1860; pound (stock) 1865; PS, closed 1932; quarry; railway bridge to Bathurst (lattice girder) fabricated by Andrew Handyside & Co., Derby, England, erected 1876 by J.S. Cummings, William Mason, Ellsington and Thomas Smithyman, d. by Sir John Fowler and John Whitton, over Macquarie R.; Rom. Cath. C. (Sacred Heart) d. and b. 1886 by John Wild, closed and reused; RS 1875, station b. by James Stuart Douglas, closed 1975; sausage casing factory (Devro Pty Ltd) 1979; sawmill (R.G. O'Leary), fire 1954; schools: primary 1865–66, reopened 1871, repairs 1894 by Edward Abraham Wright, additions 1959 and 1966, new one 1980, and HS 1976, burnt down 2005, replaced 2008; steel fabrication works (Metalco) 1989; storms 1891 and 1910; tanneries: Great Western (Thompson & Sons, inundated 1899, sold 1914 to J.W. Maguire) and George Hayward; telegraph 1883; toll-gate; typhoid 1893; watch-house 1838; water reticulation 1956; water tank factory (Clark's); weir on Macquarie R.; Wes. Meth. C.; winery (Hamlat Vineyard, Tim and Liz Hamilton); woollen mill, razed; pop. 453 (1841), 464 (1846), 339 (1851), 343 (1856), 357 (1861), *c.*500 (1866), 485 (1871), 546 (1881), 689 (1891), 591 (1901), 553 (1911), 562 (1921), 771 (1933), 745 (1947), 128 (1961), 6,298 (2006), 7,725 (2011).

Kelvin (*Co. Nandewar*) 30°49'S. 150°21'E., 13 km NE of Gunnedah, on Rangira Ck; farming and grazing; Angl. C. b. 1909 by Neville; earth tremor 2012; FB; fire 1907; PO 1902, burnt down 1925; Rom. Cath. C. (St Patrick's) 1923; sawmill (Herbert Jones); school 1901–5, 1913–42, 1953–66; telephone 1914; TX 1915, automatic 1970; pop. 173 (1901), 340 (1911), 373 (1933), 221 (1947), 235 (1954), 306 (1961), 355 (2006).

Kelvin Grove (*Co. Forbes*) 33°36'S. 148°13'E., 30 km SE of Forbes; school 1879–82.

Kember (*Co. King*) 34°00'S. 148°53'E., 26 km SE of Cowra, on Hovells Ck.

Kembla (*Co. Camden*) see Mount Kembla.

Kembla Grange (*Co. Camden*) 34°28'S. 150°49'E., 4 km NE of Dapto, on Dapto Ck; formerly Dunlop Vale; formerly dairying; army camp (World War II); brickworks 1949; cemeteries: general (59 graves 1907–67), lawn (Wollongong, 3,847 plots) 1979, Rom. Cath. (838 graves 1831+), war (12 graves); cheese factory (Thomas Hemming) 1847; clothing factory (Midford Products Pty Ltd); coalmine (Fleming's); FB; gun emplacement (World War II); railway (One Steel); RS 1890; school (West Dapto) 1883–1972; Wes. Meth. C. (Mullet Ck) 1848; pop. 103 (1947), 56 (1954), 65 (1961), 130 (2001), 149 (2006).

Kembla Heights (*Co. Camden*) see Mount Kembla.

Kemblawarra (*Co. Camden*) 34°30'S. 150°54'E., 2 km SW of Port Kembla, on Lake Illawarra; PO 1945; Salv. Army C. 1953; tank traps (World War II); telephone 1945; pop. 853 (1947).

Kemblawarra (*Co. Camden*) see also Warrawong.

Kemmel Hill (*Co. Cooper*) 34°35'S. 146°29'E., 8 km SE of Leeton.

Kempsey (*Co. Dudley*) 31°05'S. 152°50'E., 39 km N. of Port Macquarie, on Macleay R.; formerly Central Kempsey; founded 1856, designated as chief town of the county, munic. 1886–1975, bypassed by highway 2013; orig. timber and shipbuilding, then maize and cattle, then wheat, potatoes, oranges, pumpkins, sugar-cane 1866+, dairying 1890s+, hunting, fishing, pigs, bacon curing, butter, zinc, copper, antimony, furniture, clothing; ambulance station b. 1948 by Foster and Fullick; Angl. C. (All Saints') 1885, demolished 1959, second one b. 1892, spire added 1913 and church refurbished, additions and renovations 1930; bacon factory (Charles Barnes) 1898–1920; brewery (Jonathan Emms) 1872; bridge (Allan timber truss) to East Kempsey, b. 1897–1900 by Taylor, Murphy & Co., demolished 1960, replacement (steel and concrete) b. 1956–59 by Hornibrook McKenzie Clark Pty Ltd, over Macleay R.; bubonic plague 1907 (2 died) and 1908 (girl died); butter and cheese factory, incl. ice works (Foley Bros) 1897, taken over 1905 by Macleay River Co-op. Dairying Co. Ltd, demolished 1922, replacement b. 1923 by L. O'Neill, d. by Richard Wildridge & Co., company changed name in 1925 to Macleay River Dairying Co. Ltd, butter-making ceased 1956, factory sold 1975; carriage-works: H.F. Hand & Co. and Kempsey Coach-building Factory (B. Piggott, W. Munro and J. Arthur Jebb) 1919; cordial factory (George A. Coleman & Co.) b. 1915 by E. Blight, ice works added 1918; earth tremors 1842, 1891, 1910; FB (station b. 1912, new one b. 1922 by G. Lowther); fibrous plaster works (Macleay, Des J. O'Dell); fires 1893, 1907, 1909; floods

1864, 1870, 1890, 1893, 1894, 1921, 1929, 1949, 1950, 1963, 1967, 2001, 2009, 2013; gastroenteritis epidemic 1954; hailstorms 1928 and 1956; ice-cream factory (George A. Coleman Ltd), bought 1938 by Macleay River Dairying Co. Ltd; jetty 1991; joineries: William Harvey 1890 and A. Moore; levee 1964; measles epidemic (boy died) 1910; Meth. C. b. 1908 by J. Ewart & Sons, d. by Alfred Gambier Newman, damaged 1949, inundated and destroyed 1950, replaced; pneumonia epidemic (4 died) 1907; PO 1843, new one b. 1886 by John Gabriel and James McMorrine, d. by James Johnstone Barnet, tower added 1891 by F.W. Hammond, post office alterations 1902, enlargement and repairs 1904 by Hocking Bros and H.P. Morrison, alterations 1915, remodelled and renovated 1927 by John Dunton, restored 1983; powerhouse (Kempsey Electric Light & Power Co. Ltd) 1916, inundated 1921 and 1929; Presb. C. (b. as private school), reused 1884 as church, demolished 1889, replacement (St Andrew's) b. 1890 by H.J. Lancaster, closed 1984, reused, new one 1984; Prim. Meth. C. 1875, reused, demolished 1985; railway bridge to South Kempsey (steel truss spans) 1917, fabricated by State Dockyard (Walsh Island), damaged 1949 and 1950, rebuilt 1967, over Macleay R.; railway round-house 1915; railway turntable, 60 ft (18.3 m); railway viaduct (timber), destroyed 1949 (6 died), rebuilt and destroyed again 1950, replacement (11 steel spans on concrete piers) 1967; RS 1917, refreshment room 1919, station burnt down 1939, rebuilt; Salv. Army C. 1920, closed; sawmills: Jeffrey and Smith, and F.W. Lane; scarlet fever 1876; school 1848–50 and 1883–84; SD Adventist C. b. 1946 by Howard Gill, inundated 1950; sewage works b. by General Constructions Pty Ltd, augmentation 1990; shipyard (Alexander Newton, William Malcolm and John Ferrier) 1836–42; storms 1890 and 1897; streets electric lit 1916; telegraph 1878; TX 1908, automatic 1957; Unit. C. (orig. Meth.) b. 1953 by H. Dudley Blight, d. by Brown and Mowbray; waterworks 1913, water supply augmentation 1969 and 1991; Wes. Meth. C. 1875, burnt down 1907; wharves: one b. 1882 by G. and T. Lawson and Macleay River Co-op. Dairying Co. Ltd 1925; pop. 123 (1851), 112 (1856), 450 (1861), 865 (1871), 1,321 (1881), *c.*1,500 (1887), 2,194 (1891), *c.*2,100 (1895), 2,329 (1901), 2,665 (1908), 2,959 (1911), *c.*3,000 (1924), 4,824 (1933), *c.*5,600 (1941), 6,330 (1947), 7,489 (1954), 8,016 (1961), *c.*8,500 (1965), 8,262 (1966), 8,230 (1968), 8,867 (1971, incl. Greenhill), 8,881 (1976), 9,037 (1981), 9,335 (1986), 9,049 (1991), 8,630 (1996), 8,455 (2001), 8,137 (2006).

Kempsey (*Co. Dudley*)
see also Kempsey West.

Kempsey East (*Co. Macquarie*) 31°05'S. 152°51'E., 2 km E. of Kempsey, on Macleay R.; orig. Rudder's Town; founded 1836 by Enoch William Rudder, laid out 1836 by Henry Fancourt White, first lots sold 1836, bypassed by highway 2013; orig. timber, then maize, potatoes, oranges, pumpkins, sugar-cane; Angl. C. 1859, new one (St Alban's) 1887–1975; bridge (Allan timber truss) to Kempsey, 153 ft (46.6 m), b. 1897–1900 by Taylor, Murphy & Co., demolished 1960, replacement (steel and concrete) b. 1956–59 by Hornibrook McKenzie Clark Pty Ltd, over Macleay R.; creamery 1896; dock and slipway, extended 1889 by G. and T. Lawson; floods 1863, 1864, 1893, 1921, 1929, 1949, 1950, 1963, 2001; furniture factory (Gordon F. Gill) 1931; PO 1860; pound (stock) 1887; Presb. C. 1861; punt (Rudder's) 1842–1900 to Kempsey, across Macleay R.; reservoirs: concrete 250,000 gal. (1,136.5 kl) and steel 250,000 gal. (1,136.5 kl); Rom. Cath. C. (All Saints') 1861; sawmills: East Kempsey Sawmilling & Planing Co., Tilbrook and Davis, George Worthing; scarlet fever 1915; school 1881 b. by Jacob Stayner, d. by William Edmund Kemp, additions 1927 by G.F. Brest, additions 1929 by Thomas Norman Grimsley, additions 1966, 1978, 1995; sugar mill b. 1868 by Neads, Rye & Co.; Wes. Meth. C. 1860; wharves: one b. 1881 by G. and T. Lawson, renovated 1906 by George Parkins, and one b. 1937; pop. 150 (1861), *c.*145 (1866), 240 (1871), 1,117 (2006), 1,320 (2011).

Kempsey Heights (*Co. Dudley*) see Kempsey West.

Kempsey South (*Co. Macquarie*) 31°06'S. 152°50'E., 2 km SW of Kempsey, on Macleay R.; (incl. Commandant Hill); estab. 1926, bypassed by highway 2013; brewery (Bucket) estab. 2015 by Sam and Amanda Preston, and Tim and Peta-Maree Sproule; brickworks; causeway across Gills Bridge Ck; cemetery (5,536 graves), incl. columbarium; floods 1864, 1893, 1921, 1929, 1949, 1950, 1963, 2001; foot-bridge to West Kempsey, over Macleay R.; PO 1947; 2 quarries; railway bridge to Kempsey (steel truss spans) 1917, fabricated by State Dockyard (Walsh Island), damaged 1949 and 1950, rebuilt 1950, new one (viaduct) 1967, over Macleay R.; railway signal control equipment factory (DML) 1980; reservoir 1962; rifle range (3 km SE); sawmills: L. Crispin, S.E. McIllwain (bought 1968 by Allen Taylor & Co. Ltd, taken over by Booral Group, closed), T.A. Miles; schools: primary 1960, additions 1963 and 1990, and Melville HS 1983 b. by E.E. Lahey Constructions, additions 1987; SD Adventist C.; sewage works; telephone 1947; TX (automatic); Unit. C. (Commandant Hill, orig. Meth.) b. 1940 by A.J. Kesby, d. by Brown and Lightfoot, closed, sold and reused; wharf (Commandant Hill) b. 1883 by J. Lawson; pop. 2,466 (2011).

Kempsey West (*Co. Dudley*) 31°05'S. 152°50'E., 1 km W. of Kempsey, on Macleay R.; (incl. Kempsey Heights); surveyed 1856 by William Wedge Darke, land sales 1857, town gaz. 1879; ambulance station 2017; Angl. C. (All Saints') b. 1883–92, spire added 1913 by George Welch, church re-roofed, renovated 1929 by Arthur Partridge-Wall, additions and alterations 2008; Assemblies of God C. (Valley); Bapt. C. b. 1951 by A. Butterfield et al., d. by W.H. Nelson; brickworks (Brenchley Brickworks Pty Ltd) estab. 1888 by John Gabriel, acquired by Perrins, taken over by Welch, bought by Kemp, became Kempsey Brick & Pottery Co., closed 1976; carriage-works (Michael T. Ling) 1903; cemetery (2,377 graves 1860+) 1869; CH (removed from Belgrave Falls) 1859, (second) b. 1864 by Frederick James Chapman, d. by James Johnstone Barnet, reused 1948, remodelled 1983, (third, incl. lock-up) b. 1876 by George A. Worboys, d. by James Johnstone Barnet, additions 1886 and 1888, extended, heightened and re-roofed 1897 by Manning Bros, d. by Walter Liberty Vernon, repairs 1949 by J.R. Mackenzie; Christ. Israelite C. 1977; cordial factory (O.S. Gronvold), bought 1910 by William Graff; FB; fibrous plaster works (D.J. O'Dell); fire 1872; floods 1863, 1864, 1870, 1893, 1894, 1921, 1929, 1949, 1950, 1963, 2001; flour mill estab. 1860 by Samuel Redgate, reused (Alpha sawmill); foot-bridge to South Kempsey, over Macleay R.; gaol, additions 1889 by Henry Manning, demolished 1957; hospital (Macleay Dist.) b. 1881 by Robert Masterman, demolished and replaced 1913, additions, alterations and renovations 1936 by W.P. Mellefont, additions 1955, new one 1963, additions 1964, 1967, 1995, redevelopment 2016; PO: Kempsey Heights 1951 and West Kempsey 1870 (new one b. 1879 by Jacob Stayner, remodelled 1898, additions and alterations 1933 by T. Cook, renovated and restored 1983); police barracks b. 1892 by H. and R. Manning and John Gabriel; Presb. C. 1864; Prim. Meth. C. 1875; PS 1859 (removed from Belgrave Falls), new one b. 1901 by Manning and Morrison, reused, new one o. 1950 (in former house renovated by W. Williams), new one b. 2010 by Lahey Constructions Pty Ltd; reservoir (concrete), 950,000 gal. (4,318.7 kl); Rom. Cath. C. b. 1878–80 by Jacob Stayner, d. by Edward Gell, closed, reused 1922, new one (All Saints') b. 1922 by J.G. Taylor, d. by Austin McKay, grotto 1934, church extended 1958; Salv. Army C. 1994; sawmills: G.F. Brest, Combatine Timber Co., Dangar and Watt (closed and sold 1915), Thomas Hennessy & Sons; schools: primary 1860, demolished, replacement b. 1877 by George A. Worboys, d. by George Allen Mansfield, additions 1884 by H. Leeds, additions 1901 by W. Heffron, additions 1918 and 1969, demolished, new one b. 1972, and HS (Kempsey) b. 1928–30 by Arthur Partridge-Wall, d. by Richard McDonald Seymour Wells, additions 1960, 1963, 1967, 1976, additions 2012 by O'Donnell & Hanlon Pty Ltd; SD Adventist C. 1912; sewage works; sugar mill (steam) estab. 1869 by Sydney Verge; TC 1955, became North Coast Institute, Kempsey Campus, in 1992; telegraph 1870, new office b. 1879 by Jacob Stayner; telephone (Kempsey Heights) 1951; TX b. 1955 by A.E. Davis; Unit. C. (orig. Meth.) b. 1953 by H. Dudley Blight, d. by Brown and Mowbray; Wes. Meth. C. 1866, new one 1901; wharf, destroyed 1864, new one b. 1881 by Thomas Taylor; pop. 212 (1859), *c.*230 (1866), 625 (1871), 4,741 (2006), 4,791 (2011).

Kempston (*Co. Rous*) 28°34'S. 152°58'E., 6 km N. of Kyogle, on Richmond R.; quarry.

Kempton (*Co. Georgiana*) 34°16'S. 149°33'E., 24 km N. of Crookwell; grazing; PO 1899–1945; telephone 1915; TX 1922; pop. 75 (1911), 49 (1933).

Kemsleys (*Co. Cook*) see North Richmond.

Kenabah (*Co. Northumberland*) see Kahibah.

Kendall (*Co. Macquarie*) 31°38'S. 152°42'E., 9 km W. of Laurieton, on Camden Haven R.; Camden Haven till 1891; timber, farming, dairying; Angl. C. (All Saints') b. 1902 by H. Levick, d. by A.G. Smith, closed 2002; brickworks; bridge b. 1898 by G. Lawson, new one b. 1940 by Anderson, new one (concrete) 1969, over Camden Haven R.; butter factory and ice works (Camden Haven Co-op. Dairy Co. Ltd), improvements 1926 by Williams and Sinclair; cemetery (695 graves 1890+) 1878; cheese factory (Tillett's) 1905–12; PO 1875, new one b. 1915; PS 1877, new one 1922, closed 1938; railway bridge (steel truss) 1915, 200 ft (61 m), fabricated by Clyde Engineering Co. Ltd, over Camden Haven R.; reservoir; Rom. Cath. C. (St John the Evangelist) b. 1918–20 by Albert George Smith, sacristy and porch added 1946; RS 1915, station b. by John Allibone, closed 1989; Salv. Army C. 1916; sawmills: Aust. Timber Co. 1897, Hay Bros, Hayden and McInnes, Heron's Creek Timber Mills Ltd, IXL Timber Co., Longworth Ltd, Henry James Perrett (sold 1907), J. Steinmetz and Breckenridge Bros 1907 (additions 1911, sold 1935 to Alf Noone); school (Camden Haven till 1890) 1879, repairs 1900 by A.G. Smith, additions 1924, 1961, 1967, 1971; shoe factory (Crafty Shoes) 1981; telegraph 1915; telephone 1891; tramway (timber) to Lorne 1913–32; TX 1913, automatic 1980; Unit. C. (St Stephen's, orig. Presb.) b. 1916 by Albert George Smith; wharf b. 1896 by T. Wallace, restored 2007; pop. 121 (1901), 287 (1911), 465 (1924), 573 (1933), 533 (1947), 572 (1954), 672 (1961), 533 (1966), 512 (1971), 513 (1976), 522 (1981), 658 (1986), 713 (1991), 715 (1996), 732 (2001), 756 (2006), 834 (2011).

Kendalls Glen (*Co. Northumberland*) see Ourimbah.

Kendall West (*Co. Macquarie*) see Upsalls Creek.

Kenebri (*Co. Baradine*) 30°47'S. 149°00'E., 19 km N. of Baradine, on Baradine Ck; farming and grazing; Angl. C. (St Paul's) 1910, relocated 1958, and graveyard; PO 1929–82; RS 1923–76, station removed 1986; sawmills: Cyprus Sawmills (F.J. Wangmann & Son) and Underwood's; school (Junee Vale till 1927) 1909–72; telephone 1928; TX 1932; Union C. b. 1909 by C. Lyons; pop. 67 (1933), 94 (1947), 153 (1954), 154 (1961), 140 (2006), 170 (2011).

Kenlis (*Co. Westmoreland*) 33°33'S. 149°47'E., 19 km N. of Oberon, on Fish R.; town gaz. 1863, former mining settlement, defunct.

Kenmore (*Co. Argyle*) see Bradfordville.

Kennaicle Creek (*Co. Raleigh*) 30°33'S. 152°49'E., 12 km SW of Bellingen, on Kennaicle Ck; telephone 1930; TX 1946; pop. 49 (1933).

Kennys Creek (*Co. King*) 34°26'S. 148°53'E., 15 km E. of Boorowa, on Kennys Ck.

Kennys Point (*Co. Argyle*) 35°03'S. 149°29'E.,

23 km N. of Bungendore, on Lake George; settled by Francis Kenny, defunct; agric.; PO 1859–67; pop. *c*.83 (1866).

Kentelegraphrove (*Co. Georgiana*) 34°26'S. 149°29'E., 3 km N. of Crookwell, on Crookwell R.

Kent Grove (*Co. Georgiana*) 34°25'S. 149°29'E., 5 km N. of Crookwell; school 1886–93 and 1906–18.

Kentucky (*Co. Sandon*) 30°46'S. 151°27'E., 13 km S. of Uralla; village gaz. 1866; farming, grazing, orchards; Angl. C. (St Mark's) b. 1928 by C.G. Cooper, d. by Frederick James Bishop; cemetery; distillery (gin and whisky) estab. by Stephen and Lyn Dobson; FB; fruit packing house 1933; PO 1882, new one b. 1954; Rom. Cath. C. (St Patrick's) b. 1936 by Moore, d. by Gannon; RS 1882, station b. by C.T. Cook, closed 1983; school 1881, additions 1926 by Ryan and Moore, additions 1929 by J. Wicks, additions 2010; telegraph 1890; TX 1926, automatic 1972; wool-scour (Patrick Griffin and M'Mahon) 1872, tannery added 1888; pop. 40 (1891), 52 (1901), 146 (1911), 289 (1933), 250 (1947), 196 (1954), 217 (1961), 312 (2006), 325 (2011).

Kentucky Soldiers' Settlement (*Co. Sandon*) 30°49'S. 151°26'E., 19 km S. of Uralla; estab. 1918; apples and cherries.

Kentucky South (*Co. Sandon*) 30°48'S. 151°27'E., 18 km S. of Uralla; fruit; PO 1927, new one b. 1952; RS 1926–75; school 1937–71; telephone 1927; TX 1928, automatic 1972; pop. 210 (1933), 219 (1947), 205 (1954), 208 (1961).

Kenyu (*Co. Monteagle*) 34°10'S. 148°47'E., 30 km N. of Boorowa; pop. 73 (1911), 77 (1961).

Keramingly (*Co. Courallie*) 29°46'S. 149°39'E., 40 km S. of Moree; village gaz. 1886; PS, closed 1901

Keranba (*Co. Macquarie*) see Moorland.

Kerein Hills (*Co. Cunningham*) 32°38'S. 146°55'E., 55 km NW of Condobolin; PO 1949–65; telephone 1949; TX 1949.

Kerosene Vale (*Co. Cook*) 33°23'S. 150°06'E., 5 km NE of Wallerawang, on Sawyers Swamp; formerly Bathgate; formerly oil-shale (disc. *c*.1865 by J. Mackenzie) mining 1867+, then coalmining; retort erected 1867 by Mackenzie Bros; mine (Newcom Collieries).

Kerr (*Co. Wellington*) see Kerrs Creek.

Kerrabee (*Co. Phillip*) 32°25'S. 150°19'E., 33 km W. of Denman, on Goulburn R.; grazing; PO 1870–1973; PS 1879–1913; telephone 1908; TX 1916; pop. 66 (1933), 56 (1947), 55 (1961).

Kerrigundi (*Co. Yanda*) 30°54'S. 145°21'E., 83 km NW of Cobar; grazing; PO 1927–59; telephone 1920; TX 1923.

Kerringle (*Co. Pottinger*) 30°55'S. 149°45'E., 35 km SW of Boggabri; farming; FB; sawmills: Eather's (removed from Baan Baa, moved to Gunnedah by Clive and Lindsay Eather), Perseverance (George J. Saunders) 1907, White Bros; telephone 1928; TX 1928–46; pop. 53 (1947).

Kerriwah (*Co. Kennedy*) 32°26'S. 147°23'E., 83 km W. of Narromine.

Kerrs Creek (*Co. Wellington*) 33°03'S. 149°06'E., 22 km E. of Molong, on Kerrs Ck; orig. Carr's Creek; village gaz. 1890 as Kerr; farming and grazing; Angl. C. (All Saints') 1917, (former school) removed from Mumbil and re-erected by Fisher, renovated by Allie Shepherd, closed; electricity 1959; mines: Bonnie Dundee and Lone Pine (Imperial Bushman); PO 1889–1985; railway collision 1891; Rom. Cath. C. (St Therese's) b. 1932 by Allie Shepherd; RS 1882–1974; school 1885, new one b. 1887 by Bennett, new one b. 1929 by A.S. Fairweather, closed 1969, sold and reused; telegraph 1890; TX 1924–85; pop. 126 (1911), 160 (1933), 78 (1947), 90 (1954), 61 (1961).

Keswick (*Co. Lincoln*) see Dubbo South.

Ketaway (*Co. Gloucester*) 32°26'S. 152°25'E., 19 km E. of Bulahdelah, on Myall Lake.

Ketelghay (*Co. Raleigh*) 30°40'S. 152°46'E., 10 km W. of Bowraville, on South Arm; McHugh's Creek till 1921, also formerly known as South Arm; farming, dairying, bananas; PO 1927–31; school 1916–65; telephone 1922; TX 1944–70; pop. 523 (1911), 167 (1947), 131 (1954), 97 (1961).

Kew (*Co. Macquarie*) 31°38'S. 152°43'E., 2 km E. of Kendall; bypassed by highway 2009; timber, farming, dairying; Angl. C., moved 1937 to Kendall; CH (incl. lock-up) b. 1899 by Rudolph George Ochs; Jehovah's Witnesses C.; PO 1892; PS b. 1899 by Rudolph George Ochs; 3 quarries; sawmills: Australasian Timber Co. (leased 1899 to Wright and Muldoon), Bogan and Ellis, McKay and Bibby, J. Rodger, Shipman and Hunter; schools: Camden Haven HS 2000 and Kew 1893–1967; telephone 1891; wood distillation plant (F. Wilson) 1917, incl. 2 iron retorts; pop. *c.*670 (1891), 53 (1901), 98 (1911), *c.*100 (1924), 145 (1933), 153 (1947), 138 (1954), 186 (1961), 649 (2011).

Kewana Siding (*Co. Gipps*) see Pullabooka.

Keybarbin (*Co. Drake*) 29°09'S. 152°36'E., 54 km SW of Casino, on Clarence R.; telephone 1925; TX 1934.

Khalangan (*Co. Harden*) see Kalangan.

Khalassa (*Co. Wellesley*) 36°42'S. 149°08'E., 25 km NW of Bombala.

Khancoban (*Co. Selwyn*) 36°13'S. 148°08'E., 33 km NW of Perisher Valley, on Coldwater Ck; used 1960 as temporary construction camp for Snowy Mountains Hydro-Electric Scheme; cemetery; creamery (Cudgewa Dairy Co.) 1897; PO 1876; PS 1960; quarry; reservoir; Rom. Cath. C. (St Joseph the Worker); school 1960, new buildings 1967; sewage works; telephone 1916; TX 1925, automatic 1959; pop. 53 (1901), 88 (1911), 76 (1933), 75 (1947), 74 (1954), 784 (1961), 1,906 (1966), 480 (1971), 509 (1976), 515 (1981), 481 (1986), 416 (1991), 379 (1996), 308 (2001), 281 (2006), 222 (2011).

Khatabundah (*Co. Macquarie*) 31°51'S. 152°21'E., 3 km NW of Wingham, on Gorman Ck; pop. 41 (1933).

Kiacatoo (*Co. Cunningham*) 33°02'S. 146°49'E., 31 km W. of Condobolin; RS 1919–76; pop. 311 (2006).

Kiah (*Co. Auckland*) 37°09'S. 149°51'E., 10 km S. of Eden, on Towamba R.; farming; bridge, destroyed 1919, replaced 1920, new one (Jack Seiffert Bridge, steel and concrete) fabricated by Arcos Industries Pty Ltd, erected 1965 by Transfield Pty Ltd, 916 ft (279.2 m), over Towamba R.; bushfire 1926; electricity 1961; FB (station b. 2011); floods 1919, 1956, 1972; PO 1892, burnt down 1926; Rom. Cath. C. 1903, burnt down 1926, replacement (Our Lady of the Prince's Highway) 1929; school 1957–68; telephone 1904; TX 1917–71; pop. 169 (1911), 41 (1933), 69 (1947), 73 (1954), 65 (1961), 240 (2011).

Kialla (*Co. Argyle*) 34°33'S. 149°28'E., 10 km S. of Crookwell, on Kialla Ck; farming; Angl. C. (St George's) b. 1904 by Phillip Pinn, d. by Walter Spiers; butter factory (Kialla Butter Factory Co. Ltd) b. 1892 by T.H. Gibson; electricity 1955; hailstorm 1931; PO 1890; school (Gullen till 1889) 1870, alterations and repairs 1932 by Cook and Aspley, closed 1970; telephone 1914; TX 1919–66; Wes. Meth. C. 1871, renovated 1943, and graveyard; pop. 156 (1901), 185 (1911), 105 (1933), 88 (1947), 90 (1954), 54 (1961).

Kiama (*Co. Camden*) 34°40'S. 150°51'E., 28 km S. of Wollongong, on Tasman Sea; (incl. Beachside, Kiama Heights, Primrose Hill); disc. 1797 by George Bass, settled 1821 by David Smith, site reserved 1826, first surveyed 1829 by Edward James Howse Knapp, sen., then in 1830 by Robert Hoddle, then 1831 by William Jaques, and 1837 by P. Elliott, laid out 1838 by James Charles Burnett, town gaz. 1839, first lots sold 1840, harbour surveyed 1857 by A. Bremner, munic. proc. 1859, town laid out again 1868 by E.H. Arnheim, munic. enlarged 1954, bypassed by highway 1987; orig. timber 1821+, cedar port, then grazing, dairying 1842+, wheat till 1864, maize, barley, vegetables (especially potatoes), hides, poultry, pork, iron, coal, blue metal 1871+, basalt 1880+, tourism 1880s+, retirement centre 1945+; ambulance station b. 1937 by J.W. Maynes, d. by H. Longhurst, new ones 1972 and 2018; Angl. C. (Christ) 1843, replacement b. 1856–59 on new site by McDermott, d. by Edmund Thomas Blacket, war memorial tower added 1924 by D. Townend, d. by John Burcham Clamp and Crawford Hutcheson

Mackellar, and graveyard (132 graves 1837+), incl. columbaria; Bapt. C.; beautification plantings estab. 1903–5; breakwater b. 1907 by Hugh S. Carson, repairs 1911 and 1938; breweries: Fitzroy (orig. Gard's, b. 1848 by William Gard, closed 1857) and Illawarra (estab. 1855 by John and Francis Seager, closed 1892, reopened 1893, closed 1895); bridges: Manning Street Bridge b. 1868 by Dinning and one b. 1931 over Spring Ck; bushfire 1926; butter factory (Kiama Pioneer Co-op. Dairy Produce Factory Co. Ltd) 1884, bought 1897 by Fresh Food & Ice Co. and reused as milk depot, demolished 1936; carriage-works (Donald Finlayson) 1864; caterpillar infestation 1893; cemeteries: general 1863 and Sea Cliff (7 burials); CH 1850, new one b. 1861 by Stephen Evangelist Bloomfield, d. by Alexander Dawson, renovated 1879 by W.R. Vaughan, additions 1880 by John Simmons, later additions d. by Walter Liberty Vernon; Christ. Revival Crusade C.; clothing factory (Lightning Button & Pleating Co.) 1944; condensed milk factory 1881, failed; Cong. C. b. 1883 by Galloway and Kirby; cordial factory (Pioneer) estab. by J.T. Stimson, bought 1884 by Lockett and Eyre, Coleman bought out Eyre's interest and later sold it to Lockett, firm taken over 1914 by George and Charles Lockett, closed; droughts 1867 and 1908; electricity 1925; FB 1900 (No. 1 station b. 1901 by Martin Ettingshausen, replaced 1915, reused, No. 2 station 1907, new one 1991, damaged 2013); fires 1888, 1899, 1922; flood 1864; flour mills: Bush Bank 1856, ruined, and one b. 1860 by McDermott for John Sharpe, acquired 1865 by George Bullen, closed, reopened 1878, soon closed again, collapsed 1903; Free Presb. C. 1848, new one (Scots) b. 1860–63 by Thomas Moon, John Simmons and Walker Bros, d. by Thomas Rowe, renovated 1896 by James Walker, vestry added 1897 by Thomas Little, steeple b. 1898 by James Walker, church re-roofed 1952, and 1998 by Manfred Raabe, bell tower restored 2010; gale 1891; gaol 1850; gastroenteritis epidemic 1953; gasworks and tar plant (Kiama Gas Co. Ltd) 1884, renovated 1893, bought 1947 by local council; hailstorm 1887; harbour (Robertson Basin) b. 1871–76 d. by Edward Orpen Moriarty; hospital (cottage) b. 1887 by Anderson and Taylor, additions 1907 and 1910, closed, sold and reused, new one b. 1930 on new site by D.E. Foster, additions 1948, 1950, 1951, 1961, 1963, 1975, largely demolished and redeveloped; ice factory b. 1881 by D.L. Waugh; Jehovah's Witnesses C.; jetty 1849, extended 1852 and 1870, demolished 1876; joinery (C.H. Townend); lighthouse (Blowhole Point) b. 1887 in brick by Anderson and Taylor, d. by Edward Orpen Moriarty, 49 ft (15 m), converted 1908 from oil to coal gas, converted 1920 to acetylene, converted 1969 to electricity; lock-up b. 1855 by Carnell; measles epidemics 1939 and 1948; military barracks 1831; monumental stone works (R. Townend); mooring chains 1848; moth infestation 1905; pilot station b. 1881 by Anton Ettingshausen and Watkins, additions 1902 by S. Stead & Son, closed 1978, reused 1983, renovated and restored 1985; PO 1841, new one b. 1879 by W.R. Vaughan, d. by James Johnstone Barnet, repairs 1907 by N. White, renovated 1978; pound (stock) 1842; PS b. 1863 by Brown, new one 1884 d. by James Johnstone Barnet, additions d. by Walter Liberty Vernon; quarries (blue metal and basalt): Carson's (estab. 1879 by John Carson, taken over 1884 by Blue Metal & Stone Crushing Co., resumed 1912 to become State Metal Quarries, sold 1935 to Quarries Ltd), Larkin and Wakeford (o. 1871 on Pikes Hill, including new crushing works at harbour, resumed 1912 to become State Metal Quarries, sold 1936 to Quarries Ltd), John Leggatt and Douglas Hadkins (partnership dissolved 1880), Salmond's 1899, G.K. Waldron 1881; railway bridge (iron plate web girder) 1893, 107 ft (32.6 m), replacement 1994 d. by Irwin Johnston & Partners; railway coal stage 1897; railway engine shed 1897; railway turntable 1897, 60 ft (18.3 m); railway tunnel 1893, 515 yds (471.2 m); reservoirs: one b. 1899 and one b. 1955 by Construction

Services Pty Ltd; rifle range; Rom. Cath. C. (St Peter's) 1858, additions 1935 d. by Scott, Green and Scott, new one (St Peter and St Paul's) 1963 d. by Sydney George Hirst and David Kennedy; RS 1893, station b. by Charles Coghill; Salv. Army C. b. 1888 by M'Pherson, closed; schools: primary 1861 (new one b. 1871 by W. Brown, d. by George Allen Mansfield, extended 1891–93 by Anton and Paul Ettingshausen, d. by William Edmund Kemp, reused 2006, new buildings 1966 on new site) and HS 1954 (additions 1958, 1962, 1969, 2004, 2007); SD Adventist C.; sea wall, extended by John Ahearn; staithes for loading blue metal b. 1882 by T. Atherden; storm 1968; streets gas lit 1884; 2 tanneries; telegraph 1862; telephone 1905; toll-gate 1844–49; tornado 2013; tramways (quarry): Bombo 1880 (replaced 1914, closed 1961) and Pikes Hill b. 1884–86; TX 1911, automatic 1977; typhoid 1874 and 1887 (3 died); Unit. C. (orig. Meth.) 1969; watch-house b. 1883 by Wilson and Walker; water supply 1900, replaced 1915, augmentation 1955; Wes. Meth. C. 1851, reused, new one b. 1862 by Thomas Moon, d. by Thomas Rowe, damaged 1968, demolished; wharf, extended 2013 by G.P.M. Constructions; pop. 199 (1851), 495 (1856), 741 (1861), *c.*700 (1866), 783 (1871), 1,161 (1881), 2,302 (1891), *c.*2,380 (1895), 1,769 (1901), 1,599 (1911), 2,426 (1933), 2,256 (1947), 2,400 (1954), 2,541 (1961), 3,814 (1966), 4,706 (1971), 6,133 (1976), 7,717 (1981), 6,272 (2011).

Kiama (*Co. King*) see Crookwell.

Kiama Downs (*Co. Camden*) see Minnamurra.

Kiama Heights (*Co. Camden*) see Kiama.

Kiama North (*Co. Camden*) see Bombo.

Kiandool (*Co. White*) 30°18'S. 149°39'E., 12 km W. of Narrabri; RS 1926–75; pop. 53 (1947).

Kiandra (*Co. Wallace*) 35°52'S. 148°30'E., 44 km E. of Tumbarumba, on Eucumbene R.; orig. Spring Creek; estab. 1860, town gaz. 1863, declined *c.*1900+, razed 1974; mining (alluvial gold disc. 1859 by James and Joseph Pollock, gold rush 1859–60, skiing 1861+, large scale hydraulic sluicing 1883+ began by J.M. Lette, sluicing 1900+) till *c.*1904, grazing; Angl. C. (Ascension) 1922, demolished; bushfire 1965; cemetery (14 graves 1860s+) 1864; CH b. 1890 by Lansdown Bros, d. by James Johnstone Barnet, additions 1903 by Witts and Bell, closed, reused 1919–37 as police station, remodelled and reused again 1943, partly restored 2012–14, gutted 2020; Chinese joss house; Christ. (Protestant) Voluntary Mission Church of Aust. b. 1876 by J. Teasdale; dam (mine) b. 1882 by Kiandra Mining Co.; dysentery 1900; earth tremor 1872; hospital 1860; lock-up b. 1890 by Lansdown Bros; PO 1860, repairs 1881 by W. Hoad and R. McCallum, new one b. 1900 by Daniel H. Taunton, closed 1969, bought by William Paterick and reused, demolished; PS (incl. lock-up) 1861, additions 1866, closed and reused 1890, new barracks b. 1890 by Lansdown Bros, relocated 1919–37 to court-house; Rom. Cath. C. d. by George Donald Cochran; school 1864–65, reopened 1880, new one b. 1885, replacement b. 1906, closed 1924 (moved 1948 to Old Adaminaby, then to Adaminaby); stamper battery (water powered, 3 head); telegraph 1860, office repairs 1881 by W. Hoad and R. McCallum, new office b. 1900 by Daniel H. Taunton, closed 1969, demolished; telephone 1909; TX 1910–69; pop. *c.*225 (1861), *c.*300 (1863), 102 (1871), 271 (1881), 234 (1891), 230 (1901), 136 (1911), 41 (1933).

Kianga (*Co. Dampier*) see Narooma.

Kia Ora (*Co. Gloucester*) 31°59'S. 151°58'E., 3 km N. of Gloucester, on Barrington R.

Kiar (*Co. Northumberland*) see Wyee.

Kickabil (*Co. Ewenmar*) 31°50'S. 148°29'E., 21 km SW of Gilgandra; school 1915–36; TX (automatic); pop. 64 (1933), 152 (2006).

Kickabil Junction (*Co. Ewenmar*) 31°54'S. 148°25'E., 26 km SW of Gilgandra, on Kickabil Ck.

Kiel Kiel (*Co. Denham*) 29°57'S. 148°21'E., 25 km E. of Walgett; RS 1952–75.

Kiel Vale (*Co. Rous*) 28°20'S. 153°26'E., 4 km E. of Murwillumbah; sugar-cane; pop. 676 (2006).

Kierstone (*Co. Westmoreland*) see Carlwood.

Kigwegil (*Co. Jamison*) 30°01'S. 148°55'E., 53 km NW of Wee Waa; RS 1939–75.

Kikiamah (*Co. Monteagle*) 34°04'S. 148°08'E., 19 km S. of Grenfell; pop. 61 (1911).

Kikiamah (*Co. Monteagle*) see also Lirambenda.

Kikoira (*Co. Dowling*) 33°39'S. 146°40'E., 47 km SE of Lake Cargelligo; goldmining (reef) and farming; FB; horse dip 1938; PO 1933; RS 1929–75, station removed 1984; school 1939–72; silo 1934; telephone 1934; TX 1934, automatic 1972; pop. 229 (1933), 133 (1947), 153 (1954), 90 (1961), 98 (2006).

Kilaben Bay (*Co. Northumberland*) see Coal Point.

Kilcare (*Co. Northumberland*) see Killcare.

Kilcoy (*Co. Clarke*) 30°26'S. 152°00'E., 34 km E. of Armidale, on Wollomombi R.; goldmine (Della) 1891; Presb. C. b. 1882 by William Neil, renovated 1966 by Noel Williams, and graveyard (131 graves) 1897.

Kildary (*Co. Bourke*) 34°07'S. 147°02'E., 27 km N. of Ardlethan; Bapt. C. b. 1924 by Myers Bros; Rom. Cath. C. (Our Lady of Perpetual Succour) b. 1905 by P.J. Daniel; school (7 km S.) 1915–23; telephone 1925; TX 1926–60; Union C., renovated and rededicated 1954; pop. 155 (1911), 87 (1954), 97 (1961).

Kildary Mines (*Co. Bourke*) 34°13'S. 146°58'E., 17 km N. of Ardlethan; goldmining; mines: Golden Gift, Hit and Miss, Mary Rose, Just the Thing, McGeoch's, Shallow Find, The Mystery, The Shaft, True Blue, Undaunted.

Kilgin (*Co. Rous*) 29°03'S. 153°23'E., 4 km NE of Woodburn, on Richmond R.; farming and sugar-cane; school 1880–1951; PO (Circular Reach till 1884, then Dungarubba till 1893) 1880–1951; sugar mill (Poolman & Co.); pop. 84 (1901), 85 (1933), 102 (1947), 81 (1954), 57 (1961).

Kilgowla (*Co. Jamison*) 29°47'S. 149°47'E., 34 km S. of Moree; RS 1906–74.

Kilgra (*Co. Rous*) 28°33'S. 152°59'E., 8 km N. of Kyogle; cemetery; RS 1930–68, station sold and removed 1976; school (Wyangerie till 1915) 1913, new one b. 1941 by G. Grimsley, closed 1948.

Killabakh (*Co. Macquarie*) 31°44'S. 152°24'E., 15 km N. of Wingham, on Killabakh Ck; timber *c.*1910–1930s, dairying *c.*1918–1975, cattle, farming; Angl. C. (St Saviour's) b. 1915 by E. Crouch, extended 1944, closed 2001; cemetery (249 graves 1910+) 1908, incl. columbarium; Meth. C. 1954; PO 1907; sawmills: James T. Chambers, Henry Machin 1914, Richard H. Worthing 1902; school (Killabakh Creek till 1899) 1891–1980; telephone 1915; TX 1917, automatic 1972; Wes. Meth. C. 1901, renovated 1928; pop. 164 (1901), 223 (1911), 89 (1933), 180 (1947), 186 (1954), 146 (1961), 256 (2011).

Killabakh Creek (*Co. Macquarie*) see Killabakh.

Killare (*Co. Ashburnham*) 33°00'S. 148°16'E., 18 km NE of Parkes; radio telescope (Parkes) 1961.

Killarney (*Co. Nandewar*) 30°16'S. 149°48'E., 6 km N. of Narrabri; wool-scour (Imperial Contract Sheep-Shearing & Wool-Scouring Co.) 1924; pop. 72 (1911).

Killarney (*Co. St Vincent*) 35°15'S. 150°28'E., 6 km NE of Milton, on Lake Conjola.

Killarney (*Co. Wynyard*) see Gilmore.

Killarney Swamp (*Co. Wellesley*) 37°01'S. 149°21'E., 14 km SE of Bombala, on Saucy Ck; peat mine 1984–89; school 1896–1901.

Killarney Vale (*Co. Northumberland*) 33°22'S. 151°27'E., 4 km SW of The Entrance, on Tuggerah Lake; Angl. C. (St Christopher and St Thomas of Canterbury) 1996; FB (station b. 1978); foot-bridge to Berkeley Vale 2014, over Tumbi Umbi Ck; flood 1889; jetty; PO 1953–93; sawmill; schools: Brooke Avenue 1985 and Killarney Vale 1969, new school 1970, additions 1975 and 1979; telephone 1953; pop. 186 (1954), 446 (1961), 6,783 (2006), 6,952 (2011).

Killawarra (*Co. Macquarie*) 31°55'S. 152°19'E., 7 km SW of Wingham, on Killawarra Ck; Angl. C. (St James's) b. 1901 by Silas Brewer, d. by E.H. Wright, closed, sold 1958; bridge (timber truss spans) b. 1901 by Edward William Fitzgerald, d. by Percy Allan, 630 ft (192 m), replaced 1989, over Manning R.; cemetery; droughts 1923, 1927, 1928, 1929; PO 1883; RS 1913, station b. by John Allibone, closed 1975; school 1879, new building b. 1884 by W.J. Smith, closed 1906; telephone 1906; pop. 34 (1841), 72 (1911), 63 (1933), 102 (1947), 78 (1954), 75 (1961).

Killcare (*Co. Northumberland*) 33°32'S. 151°22'E., 6 km SE of Woy Woy, on Tasman Sea; (incl. Box Head, Hardys Bay, Killcare Heights auctioned 1928 by F. Wheeler, Pretty Beach, Wagstaffe estab. 1906 as Wagstaffe Point); formerly Putty Beach, then Kilcare; subdivided by Arthur Rickard & Co., first lots sold 1910, village gaz. 1972; rutile mining 1954+; bushfires 1953 and 2012; Community C. (Hardys Bay); electricity 1937; FB; marina; PO: Hardys Bay 1923 and Wagstaffe Point 1914; reservoir (Killcare Heights); Rom. Cath. C. (Holy Family) 1983; school (Pretty Beach) 1926 b. by H.E. Milligan, additions 1953; sewerage 1993; telephone (Hardys Bay) 1922; TX (Wagstaffe Point) 1949, automatic 1958; Union C.; water reticulation 1980; wharves (Hardys Bay, Pretty Beach, Wagstaffe); pop. 88 (1911), 393 (1933), 489 (1947), 564 (1954), 599 (1961), 614 (1971), 787 (1976), 1,143 (1981), 1,542 (1991), 1,774 (1996), 1,792 (2006).

Killcare Heights (*Co. Northumberland*) see Killcare.

Killimicat (*Co. Buccleuch*) 35°12'S. 148°14'E., 12 km N. of Tumut, on Killimicat Ck; bridge (concrete) 1982; quarry.

Killingworth (*Co. Northumberland*) 32°56'S. 151°34'E., 4 km SW of West Wallsend, on Burkes Ck; (incl. Blacktown and Happy Valley); surveyed 1901 by R.W. Langstaff; bushfires 1929, 1936, 1951, 1991; collieries: West Wallsend Extended (estab. 1888 by Alex McKinnon and John Corbett as the Newcastle New Wallsend Coal Co. Colliery, acquired 1895 by Caledonian Coal Co. which renamed it Killingworth Colliery, o. 1897, changed name 1905 to West Wallsend-Killingworth Colliery till 1915, explosion and fire 1910, closed 1913–20, strikes 1924 and 1928, closed 1929–50, fire 1952, production ceased 1956, closed 1957, demolished and sealed 1962), West Wallsend No. 2 (J. & A. Brown & Abermain Seaham Collieries Ltd) 1971, Westside (Oceanic Coal Aust. Pty Ltd); Cong. C. 1908 d. by Gregory; FB; PO 1900, burnt down 1915; PS 1907–20, demolished; railway (colliery); reservoir (Happy Valley); school 1891–92, new one b. 1902 by George Taylor, closed and demolished 1941; telephone 1906; TX 1928–58; pop. 199 (1901), 372 (1911), 254 (1933), 113 (1947), 119 (1954), 90 (1961), 707 (1991), 734 (1996), 707 (2001), 719 (2006), 700 (2011).

Killoe (*Co. Brisbane*) 32°11'S. 150°14'E., 12 km SW of Merriwa; Angl. C. (St Michael's) and graveyard; FB (station b. 2014); telephone 1929; TX 1930, automatic 1954; pop. 53 (1954).

Killong Butta (*Co. Bathurst*) 33°12'S. 149°25'E., 28 km NW of Bathurst, on Macquarie R.; TX (automatic) 1960.

Kilrush (*Co. Harden*) 34°38'S. 148°07'E., 8 km E. of Cootamundra; school 1881, new one b. 1883 by Woodhouse, Fisher and Holder, closed 1895, reopened 1912–13; pop. 68 (1901).

Kimberley (*Co. Hardinge*) 29°55'S. 151°07'E., 10 km NW of Tingha, on Copes Ck; Middletown till 1875; town gaz. 1873, thrived 1872–76; tin mining; PO 1873–76; pound (stock) 1875.

Kimbriki (*Co. Gloucester*) 31°54'S. 152°15'E., 12 km W. of Wingham, on Stony Ck; farming and dairying; PO 1875–1972; Presb. C. 1888, demolished; school 1876, new one b. 1897 by J.J. Milligan, closed 1940, reopened 1957, closed 1972; sugar mill (I. Allen and A. Kent) 1871; telephone 1906; tobacco kilns; TX 1928–72; pop. 120 (1901), 84 (1911), 116 (1933), 93 (1947), 85 (1954), 77 (1961), 120 (2011).

Kimovale (*Co. Clarendon*) 35°05'S. 148°04'E., 5 km W. of Gundagai, on Back Station Ck; PO 1945; telephone 1947; TX 1950–62; pop. 115 (1954), 55 (1961).

Kinalung (*Co. Tandora*) 32°04'S. 141°58'E., 49

km E. of Broken Hill; PO 1949; RS (Horse Lake till 1923) 1919–74; school 1957–66; storm 1992; telephone 1950; TX 1951–68; water pumping station 1954; pop. 58 (1947), 60 (1954).

Kinchela (*Co. Macquarie*) 30°59'S. 152°59'E., 12 km S. of South West Rocks, on Macleay R.; village gaz. 1869; agric.; Angl. C. (St Andrew's) 1903–80; bridge (bascule) b. 1893 by George Lawson, collapsed 1923, new one (Vincent Bridge) 1925, replaced 1985, over Macleay R.; cheese factory estab. 1910 by Thomas J. Rowe, sold 1918 to McNulty and Drummond; creamery (Excelsior, John James Jackson) 1896; flood 1890; school (Tacking Point till 1884, Summer Island till 1938, then Lower Kinchela till 1976) 1881, repairs 1894 by W.H. Coleman, new school b. 1913 by I.A. Irwin, additions and repairs 1919 by M.A. Irwin; storm (man killed) 1938; sugar mill (Hurrell's); Unit. C. (orig. Meth.) b. 1913 by Archibald Cassie, closed, sold and reused; Wes. Meth. C. 1865, new one 1878–1913; 2 wharves; pop. 205 (1901), 309 (1911), 482 (1933), 191 (1954), 316 (1961), 318 (2011).

Kinchela Creek (*Co. Macquarie*) 31°01'S. 153°00'E., 16 km NE of Kempsey, on Kinchela Ck; farming; PO 1883; school 1874–85, 1904–31, 1957–63; telegraph 1890; telephone 1896; TX 1928, automatic 1957, closed 1988; Wes. Meth. C. 1865; wharf b. 1884 by G. and T. Lawson; pop. 102 (1901), 449 (1947), 146 (1954), 94 (1961).

Kincumber (*Co. Northumberland*) 33°28'S. 151°24'E., 7 km E. of Woy Woy, on Kincumber Broadwater; (incl. Picketts Valley); village gaz. 1881; orig. timber and shipbuilding, later farming and orchards, rutile mining 1954+; Angl. C. (St Paul's) b. 1841–48 by William Hastings and James Taylor, d. by John Bibb, vestry added 2001, and graveyard (963 graves 1810+); brewery (Avoca Beach Brewing Co.) 2015; bushfires 1940 and 1945; cemetery 1876; electricity 1937; foot-bridge over Kincumber Ck; Life C.; PO 1859, closed, sold 2017 to Rianda Barnes; pound (stock) 1846; PS; quarry (Redox); reservoir 1991; sawmills: Frew's and Frost Bros; schools: primary 1904 b. by A. Davis, additions 1915, 1976, 1986, 1993 and HS 1990; sewage works 1976; 4 shipyards (incl. George Frost 1884–1906); telephone 1905; TX 1920–65; Unit. C.; wharf 1923; pop. *c.*400 (1866), 293 (1891), 161 (1901), 302 (1911), 354 (1933), 273 (1947), 337 (1954), 382 (1961), 493 (1976), *c.*2,100 (1987), 7,105 (2011).

Kincumber South (*Co. Northumberland*) see Bensville.

Kindee (*Co. Macquarie*) 31°23'S. 152°26'E., 29 km W. of Wauchope, on Kindee Ck; Free Presb. C. 1939; school 1914–69; telephone 1928; TX 1930; pop. 90 (1933), 134 (1947), 124 (1954), 125 (1961), 293 (2011).

King Creek (*Co. Macquarie*) 31°29'S. 152°45'E., 5 km S. of Wauchope; formerly Kings Creek; FB; SD Adventist C. (Wauchope) 2014; pop. 105 (1933), 1,335 (2011).

Kingfisher Shores (*Co. Northumberland*) see Chain Valley Bay.

Kinghorne Falls (*Co. Westmoreland*) 33°33'S. 149°49'E., 19 km N. of Oberon, on Fish R.

Kingscliff (*Co. Rous*) 28°15'S. 153°34'E., 4 km SE of Banora Point, on Coral Sea; (incl. Cudgen Headland, formerly Sutherland Point); village gaz. 1924; fishing, sugar-cane, sand mining till 1970s, tourism; ambulance station 1936; Angl. C. (St James by the Sea) 1939; beach erosion 2011; bridge over Cudgen Ck; Christ. City C.; FB (station b. 1966); flood 2013; foot-bridge over Cudgen Ck; Meth. C. 1961; PO 1927; PS 1960, new one 1975; reservoir; Rom. Cath. C. (St Anthony's) 1961 d. by J. Toomey, new one 1993; schools: primary 1957 and HS 1986, additions 1995; sewerage 1971; TC (a campus of North Coast Institute), additions 1997; telephone 1940; TX (automatic) 1958; Unit. C.; water supply augmentation 1963; pop. 104 (1933), 370 (1947), 806 (1954), 1,798 (1966), 2,412 (1971), 6,017 (2006), 6,392 (2011).

Kings Corner (*Co. Dampier*) 36°21'S. 150°04'E., 8 km N. of Bermagui, on Wallaga Lake.

Kings Creek (*Co. Clarence*)

see Lower Lawrence.

Kings Creek (*Co. Gloucester*) 32°02'S. 152°19'E., 19 km S. of Wingham; pop. 50 (1933).

Kings Creek (*Co. Macquarie*) see King Creek.

Kings Cross (*Co. Hunter*) 32°43'S. 150°48'E., 39 km SW of Singleton.

Kings Cross (*Co. Selwyn*) 35°56'S. 148°26'E., 41 km SE of Tumbarumba.

Kingsdale (*Co. Argyle*) 34°42'S. 149°42'E., 7 km N. of Goulburn, on Bumana Ck; lime burning 1889–1953, farming, grazing; bridge over Bumana Ck; butter factory (F. Shepherd) 1887; earth tremor 1941; lime-works: L.A. Gray (man killed 1903) and Kingsdale Lime Works Ltd; PO 1903; school 1885, new building b. 1909 by A. Allen, closed 1929; telephone 1905; TX 1936–65; Union C., demolished; pop. 139 (1901), 177 (1911), 154 (1933), 88 (1947), 93 (1954), 99 (1961), 737 (2006).

Kings Flat (*Co. St Vincent*) 35°12'S. 150°03'E., 38 km W. of Milton, on Corang R.

Kings Forest (*Co. Rous*) see Casuarina.

Kingsgate (*Co. Gough*) 29°48'S. 152°00'E., 26 km E. of Glen Innes, on Yarrow R.; village gaz. 1879; formerly bismuth and molybdenite mining (mainly 1885–98), now fossicking; cemetery 1888; mines: Kingsgate Bismuth Co. (sold 1881 to Vickery) and Valentine Sachs (molybdenite mine estab. *c.*1902); pop. 44 (1933).

Kings Head (*Co. Macquarie*) 31°35'S. 152°21'E., 32 km N. of Wingham, on Ellenborough R.

Kings Island (*Co. Durham*) see Largs.

Kingsland (*Co. Arrawatta*) 29°43'S. 151°31'E., 21 km W. of Glen Innes; FB (station b. 2013); school 1957–62; telephone 1952; TX 1952.

Kings Plains (*Co. Arrawatta*) 29°39'S. 151°28'E., 28 km W. of Glen Innes; sheep; mine; pop. 71 (1901), 59 (1933), 157 (1954), 129 (1961).

Kings Plains (*Co. Bathurst*) 33°30'S. 149°20'E., 8 km NE of Blayney; site reserved 1828 by J.B. Richards; mining (gold rush 1881), farming, grazing; airfield; Angl. C. (St John's) 1872, new one 1963–84 (in former Meth. C.); FB 1954; Meth. C. b. 1906 by O'Brien, closed, sold 1963; mines: Last Chance (o. 1889, worked 1892, closed 1897, reopened 1905, closed 1911, demolished by 1914), Letondeurs, McPhillamys Hill 1894, The Confidence Gold Mining Co. 1886–90; PO 1867; school 1879 b. by John Kenny, additions 1882 by W. O'Brien, closed 1955, sold and reused; stamper battery (19 head); telephone 1917; TX 1925–66; pop. 196 (1901), 142 (1911), 135 (1933), 95 (1947), 74 (1954), 78 (1961).

Kings Point (*Co. St Vincent*) see Burrill Lake.

Kings Tableland (*Co. Cook*) see Wentworth Falls.

Kingston (*Co. Mitchell*) see The Rock.

Kingstown (*Co. Ashburnham*) see Nyrang Creek.

Kingstown (*Co. Hardinge*) 30°30'S. 151°07'E., 39 km W. of Uralla, on Stony Batter Ck; tin, grazing, wheat; bridge 1930, destroyed 1976, rebuilt 1977, damaged 1977, over Roumalla Ck; cemetery; FB; floods 1932, 1949, 1955, 1976; foot-bridge, destroyed 1932; mine (Glen), closed; PO 1875–1979; Presb. C.; PS (incl. lock-up) b. 1900 by J. Crimson, closed 1937; school 1906, additions 1908 by Richard Moffatt, additions and repairs 1920 by A.H. Holloway, extended 1922 by H.F. Mitchell, closed 1932, reopened 1954, additions 1960; storm 2008; telephone 1901; TX 1913; Unit. C. (orig. Union) 1893, vestry added 1926, church renovated 1932; pop. 53 (1901), 167 (1911), 180 (1933), 70 (1947), 181 (1954), 137 (1961), 134 (2006).

King's Town (*Co. Northumberland*) see Newcastle.

King Street (*Co. Northumberland*) see Singleton.

Kingsvale (*Co. Harden*) 34°27'S. 148°19'E., 14 km S. of Young; soldiers' settlement 1919, village gaz. 1924; farming, vineyards, orchards (stone fruit); Angl. C. (Ascension) 1938, closed, sold 2017; bushfires 1888 and 1944; earth tremor 2010; electricity 1944; FB; fruit packing house; measles epidemic 1940; prune dehydration plant 1936; prune factory

(J.C. Granger & Sons) estab. 1926 by James Charles Granger, additions 1930; PO 1921; RS 1885–1975, station removed 1984; school (King Vale till 1892) 1883–92, new one b. 1933 by V. Lamotte, closed 1971; telephone 1921; TX 1925, automatic 1941; vegetable dehydration plant 1944; pop. 73 (1911), 330 (1933, incl. 173 at soldiers' settlement), 248 (1947), 257 (1954), 231 (1961), 219 (2011).

Kingswood (*Co. Auckland*) 36°45'S. 149°49'E., 8 km S. of Bega; pop. 61 (1901).

Kingswood (*Co. Parry*) 31°09'S. 150°55'E., 7 km S. of Tamworth; FB; reservoir; pop. 743 (2001), 840 (2006), 905 (2011).

King Vale (*Co. Harden*) see Kingsvale.

Kinross (*Co. Goulburn*) 35°39'S. 147°19'E., 8 km N. of Holbrook; farming; bridge 1938, 143 ft (43.6 m), over Billabong Ck; pop. 81 (1911).

Kinross Gardens (*Co. Gloucester*) see Raymond Terrace.

Kintyre Estate (*Co. Gordon*) see Dubbo West.

Kinvarra (*Co. Kennedy*) 32°36'S. 147°23'E., 47 km NW of Trundle; farming.

Kiola (*Co. St Vincent*) see Kioloa.

Kioloa (*Co. St Vincent*) 35°32'S. 150°23'E., 23 km SW of Ulladulla, on Tasman Sea; village gaz. 1843; timber; FB (station extensions 2018); PO 1912; sawmills: Goodlet and Smith 1884–93, removed 1900, new one o. 1910, burnt down 1928 and H. Mackenzie Ltd 1912, burnt down 1918; school (Redhead till 1885, then Kiola) 1880–93; telephone 1915; TX 1931–73; pop. 22 (1933), 30 (1961), 148 (1996), 207 (2001), 196 (2006), 206 (2011).

Kiora (*Co. St Vincent*) 35°56'S. 150°02'E., 4 km SW of Moruya, on Moruya R.; settled 1830 by John Hawdon, village defunct; mining (gold disc. 1851 by Alexandra Waddell and Henry Hicken), agric., oranges, grapes, maize, dairying; bridge 1893 over Moruya R.; bushfire 1883; cemetery; cheese factory (Kiora Co-op. Dairy Co. Ltd), additions 1909, closed 1951; floods 1863, 1867, 1913, 1914, 1945, 1952, 1974–75, 2015; Meth. C. 1919; PO 1862–1929; school 1868–1928; Wes. Meth. C. 1861, demolished 1918; pop. 54 (1901), 54 (1911), 51 (1933), 51 (1961).

Kiowarrah (*Co. King*) 34°33'S. 149°00'E., 33 km N. of Yass; telephone 1927; TX 1935–59; tin mine (Kiawarra) 1932–63.

Kippaxs (*Co. Macquarie*) 31°39'S. 152°19'E., 25 km N. of Wingham, on Dingo Ck; farming; PO 1927; school (Upper Dingo till 1958) 1957–61; telephone 1922; TX 1927–70; pop. 30 (1933).

Kippenduff (*Co. Richmond*) 29°08'S. 152°52'E., 34 km SW of Casino, on Four Mile Ck; telephone 1921; TX 1945–63; pop. 59 (1933).

Kippilaw (*Co. Argyle*) 34°45'S. 149°36'E., 11 km W. of Goulburn, on Wollondilly R.; Angl. C. (St James's) b. 1860 by Day, d. by H.H. Voss, damaged and repaired 1898, restored 1910 and 1929, and graveyard (graves 1862+); bridge (low-level) 1925 d. by L.M. Ord, over Wollondilly R.; flood 1931; storm 1898.

Kirkconnell (*Co. Roxburgh*) 33°26'S. 149°51'E., 16 km SW of Portland, on Kirkconnell Ck; timber; bushfire 1926; PO 1859–63; pound (stock) 1856; prison camp (afforestation) 1961, additions 1966, 1978, 1980; Rom. Cath. C. (St Mary's) 1863 d. by Edward Gell, additions and renovations 1901 d. by John Job Copeman, renovations 1956, and graveyard (141 graves 1863+); school 1919–2005, sold; pop. 103 (2011).

Kirkconnell (*Co. Roxburgh*) see also Yetholme.

Kirkdale (*Co. Argyle*) 34°59'S. 149°05'E., 22 km SE of Yass; goldmining and grazing; Angl. C. (St Michael and All Angels') b. 1874 by James McKenna, abandoned; mines: Golden Betty 1935 and 1940, P. Millyun and G.A. Paulson, Nanima Creek 1897–99 and 1930, Old Cosmopolitan (C. and J.C. Richens, J. Goodwin and F.C. Hall) 1935–39, Record Reign (Crocker and Butt), Remington and Jordan 1897–99 and 1930, PO 1898; telephone 1925; TX 1928–38.

Kirkdale (*Co. Argyle*) see also Thornford.

Kirkdale (*Co. Northumberland*) see Arcadia Vale.

Kirkton (*Co. Northumberland*) 32°36'S. 151°19'E., 13 km E. of Singleton, on Hunter R.; timber, dairying, vineyards; school

(Lower Belford till 1885) b. 1882 by Robert Sneesby, additions 1888, extended 1894 by Daniel Martin, repairs 1902 by William Hamilton, new one b. 1927 by J. Mitchell & Son, re-roofed 1977, renovated 1979; winery estab. 1830 by James Busby and William Kelman; pop. 41 (1933).

Kitchener (*Co. Northumberland*) 32°53'S. 151°22'E., 5 km S. of Cessnock, on Black Ck; village gaz. 1917; bushfires 1928 and 2016; colliery (Aberdare Central) estab. 1914–17 by Caledonian Collieries Ltd, o. 1918, strikes 1922, 1923, 1924, man killed 1925, strikes 1926, 1928, 1930, 1934, 1936, 1937, 1938, 1939, 1941, 1942, 1943, closed by fire 1943, reopened 1947, strike 1949, taken over 1960 by Coal & Allied Industries Ltd, closed 1961, largely demolished, up-cast shaft headframe restored 1996; dam (colliery); Meth. C. 1948; PO 1915, burnt down 1917; railway (colliery); school 1919, new one b. 1920, additions 1926 by E. Andrews; streets electric lit 1926; telephone 1917; TX 1928–29; water reticulation 1923; pop. 396 (1920), 366 (1933), 259 (1947), 261 (1954), 244 (1961), 209 (1971), 210 (1976), 231 (1981), 267 (1986), 306 (1991), 325 (1996), 309 (2001), 341 (2006), 343 (2011).

Kittegora (*Co. Bourke*) 34°55'S. 147°08'E., 13 km S. of Coolamon; telephone 1910; pop. 70 (1933).

Kiwarric (*Co. Gloucester*) 32°01'S. 152°28'E., 12 km S. of Taree; quarry.

Klimpton (*Co. St Vincent*) 34°59'S. 150°35'E., 9 km NW of Huskisson; PO 1957; telephone 1957.

Klori (*Co. Darling*) 30°50'S. 150°47'E., 11 km SE of Manilla, on Dead Horse Gully; farming; cyclone 1932; PO 1927–43; RS 1907, station b. by John Allibone, closed 1968; telephone 1916; pop. 68 (1901), 75 (1911), 54 (1933).

Knightsdale (*Co. Wallace*) 36°17'S. 148°39'E., 15 km N. of Jindabyne.

Knights Hill (*Co. Camden*) 34°37'S. 150°42'E., 15 km W. of Kiama.

Knockfin (*Co. Durham*) 32°40'S. 151°27'E., 9 km E. of Branxton; farming; school 1879–89; pop. 31 (1933).

Knockrow (*Co. Rous*) 28°46'S. 153°32'E., 7 km NW of Lennox Head; dairying; PO 1907; school 1901, new building b. 1929 by Diyal Singh, closed 1947; telephone 1914; TX 1928–54; pop. 84 (1901), 137 (1911), 157 (1933), 124 (1947), 116 (1954), 100 (1961), 194 (2011).

Knorrit Flat (*Co. Macquarie*) 31°50'S. 152°06'E., 23 km NE of Gloucester, on Rocky Ck; farming; earth tremor 1948; PO 1887; sawmill (Labora & Son); telephone 1911; TX 1924, automatic 1980; pop. 50 (1933), 74 (1947), 56 (1954).

Knoxs Valley (*Co. Wellesley*) 36°47'S. 149°31'E., 28 km NE of Bombala; timber and dairying; PO 1927–31; sawmills: John Taylor, Albert Tulton, Walter E. Williams; telephone 1913; TX 1927.

Kobada (*Co. Murray*) 35°37'S. 149°27'E., 35 km SE of Queanbeyan, on Molonglo R.; village gaz. 1930.

Kockibitoo (*Co. Bourke*) 34°53'S. 146°57'E., 13 km SW of Ganmain; school 1908–23; telephone 1909; TX 1916; pop. 83 (1911), 88 (1933).

Kolkilbertoo (*Co. Cooper*) 34°00'S. 146°36'E., 55 km W. of West Wyalong; telephone 1929; TX 1929; pop. 69 (1933).

Kolodong (*Co. Macquarie*) 31°53'S. 152°25'E., 4 km NW of Taree, on Munghi Ck; Woolla Woolla till 1913; farming; agric. implement works (Agrifarm Engineering); Bapt. C. (Taree); brickworks (Mark Eli Baker); bushfire 1898; cemetery, damaged 1898; fire-hose factory (Aust. Fire Hose) 2006; lime-kiln (Albert Souter Alcorn); PO 1906; rifle range; RS 1913–67; school (Woola Woola till *c.*1866 then Woolla Woolla till 1913) 1859, additions and repairs 1900 by Henry Wilson Alcorn, new school b. 1912 by Stewart Adolphus Levick, closed 1964; storm 1907; telephone 1913; Wes. Meth. C. 1870; pop. 128 (1911), 147 (1933), 85 (1954), 87 (1961).

Koloona (*Co. Murchison*) 29°33'S. 150°46'E., 18 km E. of Warialda; Gragin till 1915; soldiers' settlement 1947; farming; electricity 1953; PO 1913; Presb. C.; RS (Gragin till 1915) 1901, station b. by John Allibone, closed 1971;

school 1920–67, building moved to Warialda, later reused; telephone 1913; TX 1917; pop. 141 (1933), 118 (1947), 103 (1954), 102 (1961).

Kolora Estate (*Co. Clarence*)
see Crystal Waters.

Komungla (*Co. Argyle*) 34°52'S. 149°39'E., 15 km SW of Goulburn, on Mulwaree R.; cemetery; RS (Bangalore till 1916) 1884–1971; telephone 1916; TX 1917, automatic 1970; Wes. Meth. C. b. 1859 by Samuel Taylor, Edwards and Penn, renovated 1883, closed 1920, sold 1929; pop. 142 (1901), 74 (1911), 80 (1933), 66 (1947), 76 (1954), 67 (1961).

Komungla South (*Co. Argyle*) 34°54'S. 149°37'E., 18 km SW of Goulburn; iron; telephone 1926; TX 1928.

Konorigan (*Co. Rous*) 28°40'S. 153°14'E., 8 km S. of Nimbin; school 1919–75; pop. 72 (1911).

Kooba Station (*Co. Cooper*) 34°35'S. 145°03'E., 5 km E. of Darlington Point; pop. 51 (1961).

Koocumbat Flat (*Co. Macquarie*) 31°44'S. 152°17'E., 18 km NW of Wingham, on Dingo Ck.

Kooindah (*Co. Gloucester*)
see Lemon Tree Passage.

Kookabookra (*Co. Gresham*) 30°00'S. 152°01'E., 40 km SE of Glen Innes, on Sara R.; largely defunct; mining (gold disc. by John Drew, rush 1889, and tin), farming, dairying, grazing; bushfire 1927; cemetery (9 burials) 1892; CH, closed, burnt down 1927; earth tremor 1925; lock-up; mine (Sara River); PO 1889; PS 1889–1921; sawmill (W.H. Carr); school 1890–1908; telephone 1924; TX 1936; pop. 147 (1891), *c.*60 (1898), 58 (1901), 67 (1933), 61 (1947).

Kookaburra (*Co. Dudley*) 31°02'S. 152°20'E., 48 km W. of Kempsey; sawmill 1946; school 1957–69; pop. 51 (1954).

Koolbury (*Co. Durham*) 32°13'S. 150°54'E., 6 km S. of Aberdeen, on Hunter R.; RS 1909, defunct.

Koolewong (*Co. Northumberland*) 33°28'S. 151°19'E., 2 km N. of Woy Woy, on Brisbane Water; (incl. Glenrock Estate, surveyed by R.E. Reid & Co. and sold 1927 by Fred Couche); orig. timber and lime; bridge to Woy Woy, b. 1941 by D. and H. Woodward, 265 ft (80.8 m), replacement (concrete) 1985, over Woy Woy Inlet; bushfires 1942, 1944, 1994; electricity 1937; foot-bridge (Spike Milligan Bridge) 2008 d. by Jim Alexander, to Woy Woy, 279 ft (85 m), over Woy Woy Inlet; PO 1945; railway bridge to Woy Woy (3 steel spans on concrete piers) over Woy Woy Inlet; reservoir; RS 1920; telephone 1945; water supply augmentation (Parks Bay) 1979; 3 wharves (incl. Couche Park); pop. 60 (1933), 137 (1954), 153 (1961), 794 (2011).

Koolkhan (*Co. Clarence*) 29°37'S. 152°56'E., 8 km N. of Grafton, on Clarence R.; orig. Solferino Road; gold (disc. 1870); concrete pipe works (Hume Pipe Co. Aust. Ltd); gale 1926; power station (gas turbine) 1952–78, d. by Horace Driver, abandoned and derelict; 2 reservoirs; RS 1905, station b. by H.W. Owen; sawmill (Grafton Sawmill Pty Ltd).

Koonadan (*Co. Cooper*) 34°29'S. 146°22'E., 9 km NW of Leeton; RS (orig. Tuckerbil) 1922–75.

Koonawarra (*Co. Camden*) 34°30'S. 150°49'E., 2 km E. of Dapto, on Koonawarra Bay; dairying 1900–64; Assemblies of God C. (Lakeside); jetty 1995; school 1970; pop. 3,775 (2001), 3,633 (2011).

Koonorigan (*Co. Rous*) 28°40'S. 153°14'E., 7 km S. of Nimbin, on Goolmangar Ck; farming and dairying; FB; landslip 2017; PO 1910; telephone 1910; TX 1927, automatic 1957; pop. 126 (1933), 132 (1947), 128 (1954), 97 (1961), 269 (2011).

Kooragang (*Co. Northumberland*) 32°52'S. 151°44'E., 9 km NW of Newcastle, on Hunter R.; (incl. Ash Island subdivided 1889, Dempsey Island, Moscheto Island or Mosquito Island, Upper Moscheto Island, Walsh Island estab. *c.*1843); estab. in 1950s by PWD from several separate islands; formerly fruit, farming, fishing, oysters, dairying 1845+, industry estab. 1966+ incl. cement, engineering, fertilizer, coal handling; air force radar station (World War II) on Ash Island; Angl. C. (All Saints', Mosquito Island); anti-aircraft batteries (World War

II) on Moscheto Island; breakwater; bridges over Hunter R.: Ash Island Bridge to Hexham Swamp (b. 1909 by J.H. Shedden, new one 1955, 560 ft or 170.7 m), Stockton Bridge 1972, Tourle Street Bridge (steel truss fabricated by Atlas Welding Pty Ltd), b. 1965 by Transfield Pty Ltd, 978 ft (298.1 m); coal loader 1984; dockyard (State) and slipways on Walsh Island 1914, floating dock (630 ft or 192 m) 1929, workshops dismantled and dockyard closed 1933, defunct; drought 1825–28; floods (Ash Island) 1867 and 1893; PO: Ash Island 1891–1955 and Moscheto Island 1927–31; punt 1894–1971, across Hunter R.; railway bridge over Hunter R.; salt-works: Dempsey Island (Port Hunter, W.A. Dixon) 1872 and Moscheto Island (A.W. Humphrey); sawmill; schools: Ash Island 1877, new buildings b. 1881 by W. and J. Turner, closed 1968, and Mosquito Island 1858, new buildings b. 1890 by Robert Savill, closed 1932; telephone: Ash Island 1911 and Moscheto Island 1913; wharves; works: Commonwealth Industrial Gases, Greenleaf Fertilizers (phosphoric acid) 1966, Orica Ltd (chemical plant), sulphuric acid plant; pop. 358 (1871), 328 (1911), 183 (1933), 107 (1947), 111 (1954), 18 (2011).

Koorainghat (*Co. Gloucester*) 31°59'S. 152°28'E., 8 km S. of Taree, on Koorainghat Ck; Sidebottom Creek till 1938; bypassed by highway 1993; farming; Angl. C. (St Paul's) b. 1933 by A. Forster et al., d. by W. Wrigley, defunct; PO 1913, defunct; school (Sidebottom till 1938) 1895–1956, defunct; telephone 1928; TX 1946, automatic 1972; pop. 166 (1933), 75 (1947), 71 (1954), 61 (1961), 208 (2011).

Koorakee (*Co. Taila*) 34°28'S. 142°56'E., 61 km W. of Balranald; RS (Victorian railway), closed.

Koorakine (*Co. Macquarie*) 31°51'S. 152°10'E., 20 km W. of Wingham, on Woolshed Ck.

Koorangal (*Co. Sturt*) see Groongal.

Koorapei Brush (*Co. Macquarie*) 31°50'S. 152°18'E., 8 km NW of Wingham.

Koorawatha (*Co. Monteagle*) 34°02'S. 148°33'E., 26 km SW of Cowra, on Bang Bang Ck; Monica Vale till 1888, also known as Bang Bang; town gaz. 1861 as Koorowatha; farming and prunes; Angl. C. (St Paul's) b. 1902 by Henry Hart, d. by John Job Copeman, refurbished 1911, additions 1915, sold 2007; bushfire 1932; cemetery (282 graves 1900+) 1900; diphtheria 1893; FB; flood 2012; Meth. C.; PO 1887, new one b. 1912 by Hugh Robert Blackett, closed 1997; Presb. C. o. 1919 in reused building removed from Cowra and re-erected by W.J. Waugh; PS b. 1899; reservoir; Rom. Cath. C. (St Joseph's) 1894, new one (St Columba's) b. 1932 by David Larcombe, d. by Hennessy and Hennessy, closed; RS 1886, station b. by William Sharp, alterations 1900, closed 1975, demolished; sawmills: Owen Griffith, and Pease and Munro; school (Monica Vale till 1888) 1884 b. by Henry Ford, additions 1887 by Thomas S. Plunkett, additions 1896 by W. Packett, additions 1910 by Edward Knowles; storm 1893; TX 1914, automatic 1983; Union C.; Unit. C., closed 1983; pop. 117 (1891), 463 (1901), 452 (1911), 561 (1921), 489 (1933), 522 (1947), 393 (1954), 319 (1961), 263 (1971), 264 (1976), 262 (1981), 261 (1986), 296 (1991), 249 (1996), 292 (2001), 258 (2011).

Kooringal (*Co. Wynyard*) see Wagga Wagga.

Kooroongal (*Co. Sturt*) 34°28'S. 145°41'E., 30 km W. of Darlington Point, on Murrumbidgee R.; village gaz. 1878.

Kooroowi (*Co. Raleigh*) 30°29'S. 152°48'E., 9 km W. of Bellingen; telephone 1916; TX.

Koorowatha (*Co. Monteagle*) see Koorawatha.

Koorway (*Co. Drake*) see Fine Flower.

Koothney (*Co. Denham*) 29°58'S. 148°28'E., 33 km E. of Walgett; RS 1941–75.

Kootingal (*Co. Inglis*) 31°03'S. 151°03'E., 12 km E. of Tamworth, on Sandy Ck; Moonbi Railway Station till 1914; village gaz. 1914 first as Ragill then Kootingal; hort., vineyards, wheat, sorghum, maize, tobacco, stone fruit, sheep, pigs, horses, poultry till 1980s; Angl. C. (St Andrew's) b. 1898 by Galbraith, d. by A. Dickson; bridge over Cockburn R.; bushfire 1963; case factory

(A. Raedler) 1944; electricity 1930; FB 1949; flood 1962; lock-up; PO 1883; poultry freezing works 1958–82; PS 1978; railway turntable, 50 ft (15.2 m), replaced 1904, 60 ft (18.3 m); reservoir, 150,000 gal. (681.9 kl), 1964; Rom. Cath. C., burnt down, new one (St Marie Therese's) b. 1932–34 by Harrison, extended 1973; RS (Moonbi till 1914) 1882, station b. by Joseph Conlon, damaged 1932, demolished 1983, replaced; sawmills: one b. 1941 by Charlie Hunt, sold 1950 by A. Raedler to New England Timbers Pty Ltd, Ned Farrell, Harold Norman, Pedler's; school (Cockburn River till 1914) 1878, new buildings 1913, additions 1982, 1993, 2010; sewerage augmentation 1992; storm 1937; telegraph 1882; TX 1916, automatic 1951; Unit. C. (St Luke's, orig. Presb.) b. 1937 by Bill Hopper; water supply filtration and reticulation 1963, augmentation 1987 and 1997; pop. 298 (1933), 607 (1947), 785 (1954), 569 (1961), 437 (1971), 483 (1976), 731 (1981), 903 (1986), 1,007 (1991), 1,400 (1996), 1,442 (2001), 1,593 (2006), 1,596 (2011).

Koppin Yarratt (*Co. Macquarie*) see Central Lansdowne.

Korakoa (*Co. Northumberland*) 33°16'S. 151°27'E., 2 km NE of Wyong.

Koraleigh (*Co. Wakool*) 35°11'S. 143°25'E., 60 km S. of Balranald; dried fruit; FB; footbridge; PO 1926; school (Bungunyah Valley till 1937) 1931–49; telephone 1922; TX 1930, automatic 1951; Unit. C. (orig. Presb.) 1951 d. by Leslie Wilkinson, closed 2015; pop. 211 (1933), 269 (1947), 363 (1954), 427 (1961), 374 (2006), 277 (2011).

Koree (*Co. Northumberland*) see Mangrove Mountain.

Koree Island (*Co. Macquarie*) 31°28'S. 152°40'E., 6 km W. of Wauchope, on Hastings R.; cemetery; pumping station 2003.

Korff's Harbour (*Co. Fitzroy*) see Coffs Harbour.

Koribakh (*Co. Gloucester*) see Koribar.

Koribar (*Co. Gloucester*) 32°06'S. 152°20'E., 18 km NW of Tuncurry, on Nabiac Ck; farming and dairying; Angl. C. (St John's) b. 1882 by John McKay, moved 1923 by James Harris to Dyers Crossing, and graveyard; PO 1908; school (Koribakh till 1906) 1888, closed 1936 and moved to Dyers Crossing; telephone 1913; pop. 57 (1911), 22 (1933).

Koringal Road (*Co. Hume*) 35°48'S. 146°30'E., 24 km NW of Howlong; school 1957–73.

Korora (*Co. Fitzroy*) 30°15'S. 153°08'E., 5 km N. of Coffs Harbour, on Tasman Sea; mineral sand mining and bananas; Assemblies of God C. (Generocity, formerly Blue Cross); bushfires 1951 and 1957; confectionery factory (Carobana Pty Ltd) 1980; FB; hailstorm 1954; sawmills: W.G. Keft and R.E.J. Wood; school (Kororo) 1914, extended 1959, additions by Ware Building Pty Ltd; sugar mill estab. 1886 by James Small, sold to J.B. Hill, sold to E.C. Roberts for scrap, demolished 1913; TX (automatic) 1956; water reticulation 1980; pop. 118 (1933), 352 (1947), 310 (1954), 405 (1976), 661 (1981), 717 (1986), 861 (1991), 1,119 (1996), 1,971 (2006), 2,225 (2011).

Korora Basin (*Co. Fitzroy*) 30°15'S. 153°07'E., 5 km N. of Coffs Harbour; bananas; PO 1950; telephone 1937; TX 1950; pop. 40 (1933).

Korora North (*Co. Fitzroy*) 30°14'S. 153°09'E., 9 km NE of Coffs Harbour; telephone 1923; TX 1930–31; pop. 78 (1954).

Kororo (*Co. Fitzroy*) see Korora.

Kotara (*Co. Northumberland*) 32°56'S. 151°42'E., 5 km SE of Wallsend; (incl. East Kotara, Kotara Fair, South Kotara, Tickhole); once part of the Scottish Aust. Mining Co. estate, estab. 1925 as a garden suburb, some land sales 1925 and 1932, but most building activity 1947+; Angl. C.: Good Shepherd 1960 and St Drostan's b. 1940 by A. Bates, d. by John William Oldham and Robert Godwin Lees; Assemblies of God C. (Hunter City); bushfire 1940; colliery (Crofton No. 2), abandoned 1956; cotton mill (Bradford Cotton Mills Ltd) 1951, became Bradmill Industries Ltd in 1968; fibrous plaster works: F.C. March and F.C. Rich; flood 2008; Meth. C.: Kotara 1947 d. by W.C. Brown and South Kotara 1957 d. by Milo Kanangra Dunphy and Bruce Donald Loder, extended 1962, new one 1969; PO: East Kotara 1963, Kotara 1936, Kotara Fair 1967, South Kotara 1957; Presb. C. 1939, removed from Newcastle; railway tunnel (Tickhole) b. 1883–87, 175 yds (160.3 m), second one o. 1985; Rom. Cath. C. o. 1963 (former colliery bath-house b. 1952), closed and sold 1976, later demolished, replacement (St Philip's) 1976, and columbarium; RS 1924; schools: Kotara 1937, additions 1960, closed 1989 and South Kotara 1959, additions 1965 and 1969; sewerage (South Kotara) 1960; telephone: East Kotara 1963, Kotara 1936, Kotara Fair 1967, South Kotara 1957; water supply (South Kotara) 1928; pop. 5,060 (2011).

Kotara (*Co. Northumberland*) see also Adamstown.

Kotara Fair (*Co. Northumberland*) see Kotara.

Kotara Heights (*Co. Northumberland*) see Garden Suburb.

Koyuna (*Co. Gipps*) 33°20'S. 146°49'E., 41 km SW of Condobolin; telephone 1929; TX 1929.

Krambach (*Co. Gloucester*) 32°03'S. 152°16'E., 23 km SW of Wingham, on Khoribakh Ck; Larry's Flat till 1886; surveyed 1890 by J.J. Tucker; grazing and dairying; cemetery (718 graves 1885+) 1891, incl. columbarium; bushfire 1900; cemetery 1891; creamery (W. Deer) 1897; FB 1959 (new station b. 1992); flour mill (John Wright & Sons); PO 1886, new one b. 1890 by J.J. Gallagher, burnt down; Presb. C. (St Thomas's) b. 1900 by H.W. Murray, now used by Angl. and Unit.; PS 1912–13; quarry; rifle range 1908; Rom. Cath. C. (St Kilian's) 1880, destroyed 1958, replacement (St Bernadette's) 1959, and graveyard (3 graves); sale-yards (J.J. Gallagher) 1907, taken over 1917 by Paterson and Easton, sold 1957 to Dalgetys, closed and demolished; sawmills: K.S. Dee Pty Ltd 1946 (burnt down 1953, replaced on new site) and Wright's; school (Larry's Flat till 1890) 1882, new one b. 1890 on new site by W.B.E. Smith, additions 1898 by J.E. Boan, new building b. 1970 by C. Everingham; storm 1958; telephone 1892; TX 1916, automatic 1980; pop. 357 (1901), 335 (1911), *c.*500 (1925), 179 (1933), 278 (1947), 336 (1954), 245 (1961), 392 (2011).

Krawarree (*Co. Murray*) 35°50'S. 149°38'E., 45 km S. of Braidwood, on Krawarree Ck; molybdenite, farming, grazing; bushfire 1942; cemetery; FB; mine (G.W. and C.E. Cleaver); PO 1867; telephone 1906; TX 1919; pop. 101 (1911), 30 (1933), 57 (1954).

Kubura (*Co. Mitchell*) 35°20'S. 147°05'E., 7 km S. of The Rock; RS 1911–57.

Kudgee (*Co. Menindee*) 32°44'S. 141°41'E., 87 km S. of Broken Hill.

Kulaya (*Co. Monteagle*) 34°16'S. 148°27'E., 14 km E. of Young; telephone 1926; TX 1928.

Kulmurra (*Co. Northumberland*) see Kulnura.

Kulnura (*Co. Northumberland*) 33°14'S. 151°14'E., 20 km W. of Wyong, on Ourimbah Ck; Kulmurra till 1914; passionfruit, citrus, poultry; bottled water plant (Coastal Springs Pty Ltd) 1988; bushfire 1938; FB; fire 1938; fruit juice factory (Eastcoast Foods & Beverages); PO 1916; quarries: Hanson's and Kulnura Quarries Pty Ltd 1962; school 1928 b. by M.B. Smith, additions 1935 by T. Cook, demolished, new school 1986; snow 1965; storm 1936; telephone 1916; TX 1924, automatic 1959; pop. 152 (1933), 254 (1947), 322 (1954), 358 (1961), 390 (2006), 584 (2011).

Kuma (*Co. Beresford*) see Cooma.

Kunama (*Co. Wynyard*) 35°34'S. 148°07'E., 5 km SW of Batlow; soldiers' settlement *c.*1918, failed; orchards; PO 1920, burnt down 1937; RS 1923–57; sawmill (National Box Co.) 1940, boy killed 1946; school 1933–66; telephone 1920; TX 1925, automatic 1954; pop. 156 (1933), 239 (1947), 149 (1954), 101 (1961).

Kundabung (*Co. Macquarie*) 31°13'S. 152°50'E., 14 km S. of Kempsey, on Pipers Ck; farming and dairying; hailstorm 2018; lime-kiln, ruined; PO 1927, burnt down 1931; Presb. C. 1944; railway bridge (steel truss) 1917, fabricated by State Dockyard (Walsh Island), 120 ft (36.6 m), over Pipers Ck; RS 1917–74; sawmills: L. Everson, Macleay Timber Investment, O'Leary Bros, J. Slater;

school (Smiths Creek till *c.*1940) 1920–67; telephone 1924; TX 1951, automatic 1984; pop. 56 (1933), 102 (1947), 123 (1954), 81 (1961), 555 (2011).

Kundibakh (*Co. Gloucester*) 31°58'S. 152°15'E., 16 km SW of Wingham, on Kundibakh Ck; farming; bridge; sawmill; school 1957–69; telephone 1916; Unit. C. (orig. Meth.) 1954, closed, sold and reused; Wes. Meth. C. b. 1901 by C. Hall, demolished 1954; pop. 130 (1933), 55 (1947).

Kundle Kundle (*Co. Macquarie*) 31°51'S. 152°30'E., 8 km NE of Taree; orig. Cundle Cundle; RS 1924–71; pop. 38 (1841), 30 (1933), 323 (2011).

Kungala (*Co. Fitzroy*) 29°57'S. 153°00'E., 22 km NW of Arrawarra, on Orara R.; farming; FB; PO 1927; railway bridge (steel truss) 1915, 120 ft (36.6 m), fabricated by Clyde Engineering Co. Ltd, over Sherwood Ck; RS (Sherwood till 1926) 1915–74; school 1957–77; telephone 1925; TX 1929, automatic 1979; pop. 106 (1933), 62 (1947), 83 (1954), 44 (1961), 205 (2006).

Kunghur (*Co. Rous*) 28°28'S. 153°15'E., 21 km SW of Murwillumbah, on Tweed R.; village gaz. 1913; farming and dairying; Angl. C. (St Paul's) b. 1933 by Hannah Bros; PO 1925; sawmill (Reg Fleming), burnt down 1975, rebuilt by Alf, Barry, Trevor and Paul Harding and sold 1986 to Cut Price Fencing; school 1930–69; telephone 1918; TX 1925, automatic 1971; pop. 82 (1933), 158 (1947), 106 (1954), 94 (1961).

Kunopia (*Co. Benarba*) 28°40'S. 149°33'E., 65 km NE of Mungindi; village gaz. 1878, designated as chief town of the county, defunct; grazing; PO 1862; pound (stock) 1879; PS 1889, new one b. 1900 by Robert Wilson; telegraph 1892; telephone 1896; TX 1911.

Kurmond (*Co. Cook*) 33°33'S. 150°41'E., 2 km E. of Kurrajong, on Howes Ck; orchards; Meth. C. 1936 (moved 1954 to East Kurrajong); PO 1927; school (Longleat till 1926) 1920, additions 1923 by R. Fraser; telephone 1924; winery (Richmond Estate Wines); pop. 240 (1933), 177 (1947), 169 (1954), 186 (1961), 285 (1991), 287 (1996), 284 (2001), 252 (2006), 278 (2011).

Kurrabooma (*Co. Benarba*) 29°31'S. 149°10'E., 66 km W. of Moree; TX (automatic).

Kurraducbidgee (*Co. Murray*) see Larbert.

Kurrajong (*Co. Cook*) 33°33'S. 150°40'E., 6 km NW of North Richmond, on Little Wheeney Ck; Wheeny Creek till 1869, also known as Curryjong; failed as a 1920s soldiers' settlement, village gaz. 1936; former popular health and tourist resort, agric., grazing, oranges, stone fruit; Angl. C. (St Stephen the Martyr) 1869 d. by Edmund Thomas Blacket, restoration 2000, and graveyard; Bapt. C.; bushfires 1862, 1895, 1936 (house destroyed), 2001; caterpillar infestation 1898; cemetery; earth tremor 1919; FB 1939 (station extended 2014); flour mill estab. 1815 by Benjamin Singleton, acquired 1823 by William Leverton, later acquired by John Town; gale 1923; hailstorm 1893; Indep. Church of Christ; lawnmower factory (Grasshopper Lawnmower Co. Pty Ltd), moved 1953; PO 1858; pound (stock) 1865; Presb. C. 1867 d. by Thomas Rowe; PS 1930–34; reservoir; Rom. Cath. C. b. 1834 by John Eggleton and Ireland, removed 1904, new one (St Gregory's) b. 1902–4 by Chambers, and graveyard (258 graves 1845+), incl. columbarium; RS 1926–52; sawmill (George Sydney Rayner); schools: Comleroy Road 1880, repairs 1914 by G. Hutton, additions 1923 by Mellish Bros, additions 1964, new one 1995 and Kurrajong 1929 b. by H.W. Kirton and F. Walker, additions 1981 and 1993; telegraph 1884; telephone 1890; textile mill (B.G. Textiles Pty Ltd); TX 1927, automatic 1947; Wes. Meth. C. 1845 and 1868; winery (Remo & Sons) 1998; pop. 361 (1891), 450 (1901), 550 (1911), 485 (1933), 555 (1947), 525 (1954), 520 (1961), 372 (1971), 536 (1976), 745 (1981), 911 (1986), 1,089 (1991), 1,185 (1996), 1,181 (2001), 1,178 (2006), 1,092 (2011).

Kurrajong East (*Co. Cook*) 33°31'S. 150°47'E., 4 km N. of Glossodia, on Howes Ck; Bull Ridge till 1922; orchards; bushfire 1928; FB;

PO 1927; 2 quarries; school (Bull Ridge till 1899, Morgan till 1901, then Bull Ridge again till 1922) 1898; telephone 1922; TX 1923; Unit. C. (orig. Meth.) 1955 (removed 1954 from Kurmond), closed, sold and reused; pop. 226 (1933), 215 (1947), 219 (1954), 253 (1961), 2,109 (2011).

Kurrajong Heights (*Co. Cook*) 33°32'S. 150°38'E., 5 km NW of Kurrajong; (incl. Bellbird Hill, Northfield, subdivided 1841, Panorama Point, Tabarag); formerly Carmarthen Hills, Douglass's Hill, The Big Hill; settled 1825 by Joseph Douglass; oranges, apples, pears, plums, cherries, raspberries, passionfruit, peas, gooseberries, former resort with magnificent views much favoured by invalids; Angl. C. (St James's) 1888, and graveyard; bushfires 1804, 1936, 2001; FB; PO 1875; Presb. C. 1867; sawmills: Hobby Bros and E.K. Hungerford; telephone 1884; TX 1913, automatic 1968; Unit. C. (St David's, orig. Presb.) b. 1886 by Charles Holdsworth, and graveyard (50 graves); pop. *c.*350 (1903), 146 (1933), 159 (1947), 157 (1954), 161 (1961), 523 (1986), 637 (1991), 742 (1996), 794 (2001), 873 (2011).

Kurrajong Hills (*Co. Cook*) 33°33'S. 150°39'E., 2 km NW of Kurrajong, on Blue Gum Ck; (incl. The Islands); school (Kurrajong North) 1878; pop. 639 (2011).

Kurrajong North (*Co. Cook*) 33°33'S. 150°39'E., 1 km NW of Kurrajong, on Little Wheeney Ck; Netley Hill till 1938; former health and tourist resort, orchards; bushfire 1895; PO 1927–68; telephone 1925; pop. 122 (1933), 119 (1947), 87 (1954), 168 (1961).

Kurrajong North (*Co. Cook*) see also Kurrajong Hills.

Kurrajong South (*Co. Cook*) see Grose Vale.

Kurrara (*Co. Rous*) 28°13'S. 153°33'E., 1 km N. of Banora Point; bananas and sugar-cane.

Kurrara (*Co. Rous*) see also Banora Point.

Kurri Kurri (*Co. Northumberland*) 32°49'S. 151°29'E., 12 km E. of Cessnock; (incl. West Kurri Kurri); surveyed 1902 by T.H. Smith, laid out and town gaz. 1902, first lots sold 1903, further land sales 1906; timber, coalmining, dairying, orchards; abattoir; aluminium re-cycling plant (Weston Aluminium Pty Ltd); ambulance station 1961; Angl. C. (St Paul's) 1964, and columbarium; Bapt. C. b. 1907 by J. Cook; brickworks (Hunter Valley Stoneware & Pipe Co.); bushfires 1904, 1928, 1936, 1944, 1946, 2017, 2018; CH b. 1904 by W. Taylor & Son, additions 1907 also by Taylor, additions 1909 by William Frederick Gazzard, additions and alterations 1989; Church of Christ 1942; clock tower; clothing factory (David Jones Ltd) o. 1946, in former drill hall; Cong. C. b. 1904 by L. and E. Bevan, R.W. Hipwell and J. Hughes-Jones, d. by Thomas James Pepper, renovated 1922, alterations 1954, renovated 1985; cordial factories: Bishop Bros (incl. pickle factory), removed from Hamilton, closed, sold and reused and James Wolstenholme 1904; dust storms 1904 and 1906; earth tremor 1925; FB 1905 (station b. 1906, new one 1929); fires 1914, 1915, 1923, 1957, 1970; floods 1903, 1909, 1924, 1931; gales 1905 and 1944; hailstorm 2017; hospital (temporary one) 1904, new one b. 1910 by S. O'Brien, d. by Walter Liberty Vernon, additions and alterations 1919 by F. and R. Compton, additions 1924, additions 1927 by Leslie Elgin Brander, additions 1938 and 1945, additions 2013 by Ware Building Pty Ltd; ice works (Kurri Kurri Co-op. Society Ltd); Jehovah's Witnesses C.; Meth. C. b. 1904 by D. and W. Watters, closed, reused; PO: Kurri Kurri 1903, new one b. 1907 by William Frederick Gazzard, d. by Walter Liberty Vernon, additions 1909 by Richard Partridge-Wall, closed, sold 1998, reused, new one on new site, and West Kurri Kurri 1955; Presb. C. (St Stephen's) b. 1907 by E.H. Caust, closed, sold 1927 to John Stevenson Ltd, new one b. 1927 also by Caust, d. by Walter Harold Pender, closed, sold 2019, and graveyard; PS 1904, new one b. 1905 by Henry Thomas Hardyman, additions 1909 by W. Taylor & Son, d. by Walter Liberty Vernon, additions 1928, additions 1931 by Bagnall & Son; Rom. Cath. C. b. 1905 by

Waters Bros, burnt down 1928, replacement (St Joseph's) b. 1929 by Price and Avard Bros, d. by Thomas Wilfred Silk, new one (Holy Spirit) b. 1963 by Robert Black, d. by Peter Jerome Gannon, and graveyard; RS (on South Maitland Railway); Salv. Army C. 1908; schools: primary 1904 (b. by Harry Russell, L.E. Sampson and A. Thorley, additions 1906, additions 1909 by Charles Benaud Smith, additions 1917 by George Grace, new building b. 1924, additions 1929 by Leslie Elgin Brander, renovations 1979) and HS 1956, additions 1962, 1966, 1971; SD Adventist C. (damaged during constuction) 1926; sewerage 1941; smallpox 1915; storm 1938; telegraph 1905, new office b. 1907 by William Frederick Gazzard; telephone: Kurri Kurri 1903 and West Kurri Kurri 1955; TX 1910, automatic 1969; Unit. C. (orig. Meth.) o. 1921, after removal from Heddon Greta and extensions by R. Thompson, renovated 1990, closed, sold 2018; water supply 1903; pop. *c.*1,600 (1903), 4,154 (1911), 6,341 (1933), 5,440 (1947), 4,702 (1954), 5,772 (2011).

Kurri Road (*Co. Northumberland*) see Heddon Greta.

Kyalite (*Co. Caira*) 34°57'S. 143°29'E., 35 km S. of Balranald, on Wakool R.; Wakool Crossing till 1927; founded by Henry Talbot; wheat, sheep, citrus fruit, vineyards, nuts; PO 1943; punt (estab. 1848 by Henry Talbot, sold 1889 to Spinks); telephone 1914; TX; pop. 93 (1933), 92 (1947), 81 (1954), 147 (1961), 25 (1982), 107 (2006).

Kyamba (*Co. Wynyard*) see Kyeamba.

Kyarran (*Co. Clarence*) 29°35'S. 152°59'E., 14 km N. of Grafton.

Kybeyan (*Co. Beresford*) 36°21'S. 149°26'E., 30 km SE of Cooma, on Kybeyan R.; relief grazing during droughts; electricity 1958; TX (automatic); pop. 52 (1911), 34 (1933), 87 (1947), 89 (1954), 83 (1961), 179 (2006).

Kydra (*Co. Beresford*) 36°28'S. 149°23'E., 34 km SE of Cooma, on Numeralla R.; school 1898–1906; pop. 74 (1901), 44 (1933).

Kyeamba (*Co. Wynyard*) 35°26'S. 147°37'E., 34 km SE of Forest Hill; Kyamba till 1917; farming and grazing; bushfires 1905 and 1940; PO 1891, burnt down 1916; PS, closed 1895; school 1901–9; telegraph 1861; telephone 1916; TX 1927, automatic 1955; winery (John Smith) 1851; pop. 62 (1891), 133 (1901), 103 (1911), 139 (1933), 96 (1947), 84 (1954), 88 (1961), 213 (2006).

Kyla Park (*Co. Dampier*) 36°02'S. 150°06'E., 5 km NW of Tuross Head; cheese factory (J.E. Hawdon); Presb. C. 1872.

Kyloe (*Co. Wallace*) 36°01'S. 148°40'E., 40 km NW of Cooma, submerged under Lake Eucumbene; copper (disc. 1860 by H. Reynolds); furnace (copper); mine (Kyloe Copper Mines Ltd, shafts sunk 1872, extended 1882 and 1904–7, closed 1913); ore dressing mill (copper) 1907; PO 1910; sawmill; school 1913–18; pop. 183 (1911).

Kynnumboon (*Co. Rous*) 28°19'S. 153°22'E., 4 km W. of Murwillumbah, on Tweed R. (North Arm); Wollumben till 1868; settled 1863 by Joshua Bray and Samuel Gray; timber and maize; boiling-down works (S.A. Masterson); bridge b. 1882–84 by J. Fanning, repairs 1924 by PWD, new one (Allan timber truss) b. 1927 by J.J. McPhillips, 234 ft (71.3 m), over Tweed R. (North Arm); PO 1866; telegraph 1875; pop. 131 (1933), 144 (1947), 84 (1954), 55 (1961).

Kyogle (*Co. Rous*) 28°37'S. 153°00'E., 27 km N. of Casino, on Richmond R.; (incl. Geneva and South Kyogle); formerly Fairy Mount; founded 1901, first lots sold 1901, second land sale 1903, third land sale 1904, surveyed and subdivided 1904, village gaz. 1927; timber, then dairying 1898+, butter, bacon, cattle, lucerne, maize, potatoes; ambulance station b. 1941 by George James Grove; Angl. C. 1905 d. by Albert A. Tayt, new one (St James's) 1961–64; bacon factory (Kyogle Dairy Co.) 1911, taken over 1925 by Norco Co-op. Ltd, closed 1940; Bapt. C.; boiling-down works 1846; brickworks: Merrigan estab. 1909 by A.W. and H.B. Campbell, closed, and Saville's 1905; bridges: one b. 1880, replaced 1909 by Walter Frank Oakes, new one b. 1993 by Dickinson Construction Co. Pty Ltd, over Fawcetts Ck, Walter's Bridge 1907, over Horseshoe Ck, Allan timber truss bridge (324 ft or 98.7 m) b. 1912 by John Andrew Jackson, demolished and replaced 1990, over Richmond R.; butter factory (Kyogle Co-op. Dairy Co. Ltd) b. 1905 by Brown and Jolly, d. by J.G. Popplewell, bought 1925 by North Coast Co-op. Ltd, closed and demolished 1928, new one b. 1928 by Thackeray and Gallagher, closed 1972, sold to Will Larrescy, reused; carriage-works (Brooks'); cemetery; CH (incl. lock-up) b. 1908 by A.E. Beaumont, new one b. 1927 by George James Grove; cheese factories: Burch and Clapp 1912, and H. Prescott Ltd 1919; Christ. Life C. (in former cinema) 1999; Church of Christ; clock tower (Robert John Moore memorial) b. 1941 by A. Beckinsale & Co.; concrete pipe works (Rocla Ltd) 1938; cordial factories: C.E. Leverett (closed 1983, dilapidated) and H. Scullin 1912; creamery 1899; diphtheria 1921 and 1936; drought 1915; dust storm 1933; electricity: Geneva 1945 and Kyogle 1922; FB 1935 (station b. 1953, new one 1973); fibrous plaster works (Thomas Pidcock & Sons Pty Ltd) 1938; fires 1906, 1919, 1926, 1927, 1931, 1935, 1942; floods 1887, 1893, 1921, 1929, 1936, 1945, 1950, 1954, 1956, 1962, 1989, 2001, 2008, 2010; 3 furniture factories (incl. Harry R. Wade, burnt down 1935); gale 1912; hailstorms 1933 and 1937; heatwave 1905; hospital (Soldiers' Memorial) b. 1925 by Holland and Thorn, d. by Frederick Johnson Board, additions 1927, 1935, 1936, 1939, 1946, 1960, 1969, refurbished 1974 and 1978, new buildings 2004; joinery (Holland and Thorne); measles epidemic 1939; Meth. C. 1903, new one b. 1915 by George James Grove, fire 1938; PO: Geneva 1947–76, Kyogle 1903 (new one b. 1908 by James Batten), South Kyogle 1927; pound (stock) 1906; POW control centre (World War II); powerhouse (Kyogle Shire Council Electric Light & Power Station) 1922, additions 1933 by W. Tyrrell; Presb. C. 1903, relocated 1909 by G. Grove, reused, new one (St Andrew's) b. 1939 by G.J. Grove & Sons, d. by Finlay Elgin Munro; PS 1904, demolished 1927, new one (incl. lock-up) b. 1926 by F.S. Small; quarries (gravel); railway bridge 1928, over Fawcetts Ck; railway turntable, 50 ft (15.2 m); reservoir, 250,000 gal. (1,136.5 kl); rifle range 1914; Rom. Cath. C. (St Colman's) b. 1906 by I.J.D. Halcrow, enlarged and renovated 1919, sold, moved and reused 1965, new one (Our Lady of Sorrows) b. 1957 by Frank Bennett, d. by Frank Cullen; RS 1910, station b. by George Albert Leggo and John Allibone; sale-yards 1908; sawmills: H.J. Dennis 1903 (acquired and moved 1907 by Kyogle Sawmilling Co., later sold to Fraser Bros & Co. and moved to Findon Ck) and Munro & Lever Pty Ltd; schools: primary 1897 b. by G. Wilson, new building b. 1906 by S. Ulrick, additions 1914 by George James Grove, additions 1924 by Holland and Thorn, additions and alterations 1935 by W. Tyrrell, additions 1956, 1975, 1993, HS 1955, additions 1960, 1963, 1966, 2013, South Kyogle 1906–19 and 1929–64; SD Adventist C.; sewerage augmentation 1995; silo 1924; storm 1934; telephone: Geneva 1947, Kyogle 1903, South Kyogle 1907; TX 1908, automatic 1976; Unit. C. (orig. Meth.) 1958; veneer factory (Veneer Co. Ltd) estab. 1921 by Munro & Lever Pty Ltd, later moved to Grevillia; water supply 1934; pop. 59 (1901), *c.*600 (1905), 474 (1907), 1,347 (1911), 2,583 (1933), *c.*2,500 (1941), 3,033 (1947), 2,929 (1954), 2,985 (1961), 2,846 (1966), 2,965 (1971), 2,959 (1976), 3,070 (1981), 2,983 (1986), 2,912 (1991), 2,866 (1996), 2,737 (2001), 2,731 (2006), 2,739 (2011).

Kyogle View (*Co. Rous*) 28°23'S. 153°03'E., 27 km N. of Kyogle.

Kyuga (*Co. Brisbane*) see Kayuga.

Kywong (*Co. Mitchell*) 34°59'S. 146°44'E., 27 km N. of Lockhart, on Sandy Ck; electricity 1953; railway coal stage, closed 1942; railway turntable, 50 ft (15.2 m), removed 1974; RS 1929–75; school 1954–85; silo 1936.

L

Lachlan Gold Mine (*Co. Ashburnham*) see Calarie.

Lacmalac (*Co. Buccleuch*) 35°19'S. 148°20'E., 9 km E. of Tumut, on Goobarragandra R.; goldmining (alluvial and reef), farming, grazing, dairying; earth tremor 2001; FB 1939; PO 1908; sawmill (Charles Stokes); scarlet fever 1910; school 1877, additions 1914 by F. Kinred, closed 1972; telephone 1911; TX 1912, automatic 1953; pop. 58 (1901), 115 (1911), 156 (1933), 128 (1947), 160 (1954), 140 (1961), 124 (2011).

Lade Vale (*Co. King*) 34°51'S. 149°08'E., 20 km E. of Yass; school o. 1907 (in building removed from Berebangalo), closed 1939; pop. 70 (1901), 59 (1947).

Ladies Well (*Co. Durham*) 32°09'S. 151°29'E., 38 km NW of Dungog, on Allyn R.

Ladysmith (*Co. Wynyard*) 35°13'S. 147°31'E., 17 km SE of Wagga Wagga; lucerne, barley, lupins, rapeseed, peas, dairying, sheep, cattle, pigs; Angl. C. (St Saviour's) 1910; bushfires 1952 and 1975; FB 1930; flood 2010; PO 1913; Rom. Cath. C. (Our Lady) 1955; RS 1917–75, reused; school (Alfredtown till 1912) 1881, new one b. 1883, additions 1919, new building b. 1926 on new site by M. Johnston; silo 1931; telephone 1915; TX 1926, automatic 1965; Unit. C. (orig. Wes. Meth.), removed 1959 from Forest Hill; pop. 123 (1901), 95 (1911), 90 (1933), 217 (1947), 258 (1954), 261 (1961), 221 (1996), 205 (2006), 197 (2011).

Laffing Waters (*Co. Roxburgh*) see Kelso.

Laggan (*Co. Georgiana*) 34°24'S. 149°32'E., 8 km NE of Crookwell, on Reedy Ck; thrived in 1920s; orig. hunting, then wheat and dairying, now sheep, cattle, potatoes; Angl. C. (All Saints') 1923, and graveyard; brewery (Laggan Brewing Co.); butter factory (Willow Vale) o. 1889 by J. Worrall & Co., new machinery 1892, closed 1904; cemetery (403 graves 1860s+); earth tremor 1872; FB 1939; flour mill (Willow Vale, James Marsden) 1845, taken over by Edward Duffy, burnt down 1883, ruined site bought 1885 by J. Worrall & Co., mill rebuilt 1886, modernised (rollers) 1891, acquired by Walter Adamson Martin, additions 1898, closed 1918, abandoned, damaged 1951, bought, restored and extended for reuse by Graham Liney; lock-up; PO 1861; pound (stock) 1863; Presb. C. b. 1876–78, closed 1943, twice sold and reused; PS; Rom. Cath. C. 1865 d. by John Gordon, closed 1926, bought by Angus McIntosh, demolished 1926, new one on new site (St Andrew's) b. 1925 by R.F. Gillies, d. by Austin McKay, closed 1943, reused, and graveyard (graves 1868+); school 1883 b. by S. Cox, replaced 1914; tannery; telephone 1888; TX 1911, automatic 1957; typhoid 1887 (man died) and 1888 (4 died); pop. *c.*300 (1866), 176 (1901), 276 (1911), 216 (1933), 229 (1947), 256 (1954), 308 (1961), 326 (2011).

Lagoon Grass (*Co. Rous*) 28°47'S. 153°19'E., 4 km NE of Lismore; pop. 47 (1933).

Lagoons (*Co. Bathurst*) see The Lagoon.

Lagoons (*Co. Camden*) see Couridjah.

Lagoon Top (*Co. Durham*) 31°55'S. 151°18'E., 43 km E. of Scone, on Neilds Ck.

Laguna (*Co. Northumberland*) 33°00'S.

151°08'E., 18 km SW of Paxton, on Watagan Ck; farming and grazing; Angl. C. 1856, new one (St Mark's) b. 1882–84 by Thomas Woodbury; bushfires 1929 and 2009; PO 1862–1979; Rom. Cath. C. (St Brendan's) 1886; school 1873, new buildings b. 1882 by J. Pritchard, closed 1910, reopened 1939–41, reopened again 1957; telephone 1915; TX 1925, automatic 1979; pop. 103 (1875), 69 (1911), 52 (1933), 548 (2011).

Laheys Creek (*Co. Lincoln*) 32°11'S. 149°16'E., 22 km SW of Dunedoo; farming and grazing; cemetery (7 graves 1869–1924); PO 1910 b. by Thomas Talbot; sawmill; telephone 1911; TX 1924, automatic 1978; pop. 92 (1933).

Laidley's Ponds (*Co. Menindee*) see Menindee.

Lake Albert (*Co. Wynyard*) 35°10'S. 147°23'E., 5 km S. of Wagga Wagga, on Lake Albert; (incl. Springvale); farming, grazing, dairying; airfield (World War II); Angl. C. (St Peter's) b. 1911 by Charles Hardy & Co., additions 1959; boiling-down works (Halloran Bros) 1892; cemetery (lawn, 6,180 plots) 1971, incl. crematorium; FB 1906; flood 1947; PO 1888, burnt down 1914; school 1868, new one b. 1869, burnt down 1876, replaced 1878, new buildings b. 1892 by Charles Hardy & Co., additions and repairs 1897 by J. M'Intosh, new building 1954, additions 1980; telephone 1906; Union C. 1895; water supply 1945; winery (William Macleay) 1875; pop. 184 (1901), 317 (1911), 100 (1933), 288 (1947), 430 (1966), 268 (1971), 5,918 (1991), 6,054 (1996), 7,571 (2011).

Lake Arthur (*Co. Clarence*) 29°48'S. 153°00'E., 12 km S. of South Grafton, on Glenugie Ck.

Lake Bancannia (*Co. Mootwingee*) 30°48'S. 141°53'E., 134 km N. of Broken Hill; PO 1927, burnt down.

Lake Bathurst (*Co. Argyle*) 35°01'S. 149°39'E., 30 km S. of Goulburn, on Mulwaree Ck; Tarago till 1884; settled 1826, declined 1970+; farming and grazing; Angl. C. (St John's) 1860, chancel added 1920, and graveyard, incl. columbarium; bridge over Bongaralby Ck; fuel bunkers 1943–45; hailstorm 1856; PO 1862; PS b. 1878 by Gideon Cranston, closed 1889; quarry; RS 1884–1975; sale-yards 1953; school (Tarago till 1890) 1869, new one 1881 d. by George Allen Mansfield, closed 1969, sold and reused; telephone 1905; TX 1912–68; pop. 156 (1901), 119 (1911), 113 (1933), 108 (1947), 53 (1954), 107 (1961).

Lake Cargelligo (*Co. Dowling*) 33°18'S. 146°22'E., 102 km NW of West Wyalong, on Lake Cargelligo; Lake Cudgellico till 1915, then Cargelligo till 1919; settled 1841 by Francis Oakes, site reserved 1850 by James Larmer, estab. 1873, laid out 1878 by Menzies, village gaz. 1879 as Cargelligo, founded 1880; mining (gold disc. 1873 by Charlotte Foster, gold rush 1873–81), then wheat *c.*1900+, magnesite *c.*1942–*c.*1955, lucerne, now sheep, wheat, fruit, vegetables; airfield (World War II); ambulance station (Elphick Memorial); Angl. C. 1881, demolished, replaced 1912, new one (Epiphany) 1971 d. by V.E. Twigg; Bapt. C. 1989; brickworks: Bowditch & Son and W. Byrnes; caterpillar infestation 1939; cemetery (*c.*1,000 burials 1887+) 1887; CH 1961; FB 1940 (station b. 1949, replaced 1971); fires 1926 and 1938; flood gates 1892; freezing works (John Davis & Son Ltd) 1931, burnt down 1947; gale 1890; gate works (L.E. and J.M. Fyfe); hospital 1933, additions 1959; joinery (C. Harlow); lock-up; Meth. C. 1923; mine (Foster's Reef, incl. 12 head stamper battery erected 1875 by Foster's Gold Mining Co.); PO 1874, new one b. 1920, replaced 1971; powerhouse b. 1931 by J. Mitchell, d. by Lavert and Mammatt; PS 1881, additions 1892 by J. O'Donnell, additions and alterations 1931, new one 1961; railway coal stage, removed 1970; railway engine shed 1920, removed 1984; railway turntable, 60 ft (18.3 m), closed; reservoir 1902; Rom. Cath. C. (St Collumbkille's) 1897–1958, demolished, replacement (Our Lady of Lourdes) 1957; RS 1917; sale-yards (C.E. Wallder & Co.) 1928; sawmills: Cyprus Pine Co., and T. Turner and W. McFadzean; scarlet fever 1930; school (Lake Cudgellico till 1915, then Cargelligo till 1919) 1880, new one b. 1925 by A.G. Brown, additions 1966, 1972, 1973, 1980; SD

Adventist C.; sewerage 1981; silo 1934; TC (a campus of Riverina Institute), additions 2013; telegraph 1881; TX 1910, automatic 1989; Unit. C. (St Stephen's, orig. Presb.) b. 1927 by Staak; water reticulation 1928, filtration plant 1931; pop. *c.*200 (1873), 166 (1881), 347 (1891), 302 (1901), 415 (1911), 1,039 (1933), *c.*950 (1941), 986 (1947), 988 (1954), 1,118 (1961), 1,129 (1966), 1,095 (1971), 1,171 (1976), 1,240 (1981), 1,206 (1986), 1,256 (1991), 1,218 (1996), 1,204 (2001), 1,146 (2006), 1,152 (2011).

Lake Cathie (*Co. Macquarie*) 31°33'S. 152°51'E., 13 km NE of Laurieton, on Tasman Sea; 2 bridges over Cathie Ck; FB; PO 1958; Rom. Cath. C. (St Mary Star of the Sea), removed from Byabarra, additions 1986; sewerage augmentation 1985; telephone 1956; TX 1956, automatic 1971; pop. 38 (1961), 493 (1976), 941 (1981), 1,153 (1986), 1,474 (1991), 1,774 (1996), 2,098 (2001), 2,736 (2006), 2,872 (2011).

Lake Cathie (*Co. Macquarie*) see also Bonny Hills.

Lake Conjola (*Co. St Vincent*) 35°16'S. 150°29'E., 7 km NE of Milton, on Lake Conjola; settled 1847; silica mining and tourism; FB 1957; floods 2015 and 2020; PO 1962; telephone 1962; pop. 31 (1933), 50 (1954), 41 (1961), 367 (1986), 421 (1991), 403 (1996), 343 (2001), 371 (2006), 395 (2011).

Lake Conjola West (*Co. St Vincent*) 35°16'S. 150°27'E., 6 km N. of Milton, on Lake Conjola; pop. 234 (1996), 269 (2001), 316 (2006).

Lake Cowal (*Co. Gipps*) 33°41'S. 147°21'E., 28 km N. of Wyalong; mines: Billy's Lookout and Smith's; RS 1929–75, station removed 1984; pop. 57 (1901), 88 (1911), 60 (1933), 115 (1947), 52 (1954), 57 (1961), 91 (2006).

Lake Cudgellico (*Co. Dowling*) see Lake Cargelligo.

Lake George (*Co. Murray*) see Gearys Gap.

Lake Haven (*Co. Northumberland*) 33°12'S. 151°29'E., 25 km NE of Gosford, on Budgewoi Lake; (incl. Goobarabah Point); PO (Goobarabah Point) 1965–71; school (Gorokan HS) 1976, new school 1977, additions 1978; telephone (Goobarabah Point) 1965; pop. 3,369 (2011).

Lake Heights (*Co. Camden*) see Warrawong.

Lake Hume Village (*Co. Goulburn*) 36°06'S. 147°02'E., 7 km SE of Thurgoona, on Lake Hume; (incl. Bethanga Bridge); Hume Reservoir 1920–52, and later, Hume Weir; Angl. C. (Ascension) re-erected 1922 (removed from Pine Gully), dismantled 1935; bridge (Bethanga Bridge) b. 1927–30, d. by Percy Allan, 2,467 ft (752 m) incl. 9 Pratt truss spans fabricated by Charles Ruwolt Pty Ltd, erected by W.H. Thompson, timber road deck replaced with concrete and raised 1961, raised again 1966, road deck replaced again 1967 and 2005, over Lake Hume; dam b. 1919–36 d. by Ernest Macartney de Burgh and John Stewart Dethridge, 167 ft (51 m) high, wall raised 1950–61, hydro-electric power station added 1957, dam strengthened 1987, new valve closure gates 1995, on Murray R.; PO: Bethanga Bridge 1929–30 and Lake Hume Village 1920; PS 1927–32; Rom. Cath. C. 1922, badly damaged 1923, moved 1936 to Huon; school 1921–35 and 1955–66; storm 1923; telephone 1921; trout farm; TX 1928–59; pop. 550 (1933), 260 (1954), 251 (1961), *c.*200 (1981).

Lake Illawarra (*Co. Camden*) 34°33'S. 150°52'E., 9 km SE of Dapto, on Lake Illawarra; Lake Illawarra South till 1971; subdivisions 1922, 1925, 1951; formerly fishing; Aboriginal Mission C. 1899; bridge, to Windang, b. 1936–38 by George McIver, 1,050 ft (320 m), new one 1971, over Lake Illawarra; electricity 1928; Meth. C. 1926, closed and reused (acquired by United Pentecostal C.); PO 1927; quarry (Illawarra Harbour & Lands Corp.); Rom. Cath. C. (Sacred Heart) 1973; schools: Lake Illawarra HS 1972, additions 1976, and Lake Illawarra South 1954 b. by G.C. Kirkman, additions 1965; telephone 1925; TX 1929–52; United Pentecostal C. (Faith Point) 1983; water reticulation 1945; pop. 3,087 (2011).

Lake Illawarra (*Co. Camden*)

see also Windang.

Lake Illawarra South (*Co. Camden*) see Lake Illawarra.

Lake Innes (*Co. Macquarie*) 31°30'S. 152°50'E., 10 km SW of Port Macquarie; FB; vineyards.

Lake Keepit (*Co. Darling*) see Keepit Dam.

Lakelands (*Co. Camden*) see Dapto.

Lakelands (*Co. Northumberland*) see Warners Bay.

Lakeline Estate (*Co. Camden*) see Kanahooka.

Lake Macquarie (*Co. Northumberland*) see Booragul.

Lake Macquarie Road (*Co. Northumberland*) see Merewether.

Lake Munmorah (*Co. Northumberland*) 33°12'S. 151°34'E., 5 km N. of Budgewoi, on Lake Munmorah; FB 1966; jetty; PO 1947; Rom. Cath. C. (St Brendan's); schools: primary 1929, additions 1962, 1966, 1970, new one 1993, and HS 2000; sewerage 1986; telephone 1949; TX 1951–70; pop. 228 (1961), 284 (1971), 548 (1976), 954 (1981), 1,417 (1986), 2,228 (1991), 2,623 (1996), 3,240 (2001), 4,445 (2006), 4,802 (2011).

Lake Plain (*Co. Wallace*) 36°15'S. 148°55'E., 19 km W. of Cooma, on Bridle Ck.

Lakeside Village (*Co. Gloucester*) see Raymond Terrace.

Lakesland (*Co. Camden*) 34°10'S. 150°32'E., 7 km W. of Picton, on Cedar Ck; subdivided 1884; orchards (incl. cherries); FB 1940; PO 1896; school 1896–1904, reused; telephone 1926; TX 1944, automatic 1953; pop. 76 (1901), 50 (1911), 56 (1933), 57 (1947), 50 (1954), 77 (1961), 350 (2001), 338 (2006), 407 (2011).

Lake Victoria (*Co. Tara*) 33°47'S. 141°24'E., 59 km NW of Wentworth; PS, closed 1922; pop. 100 (1933).

Lake View (*Co. Cooper*) see Lake Wyangan.

Lakeview (*Co. Northumberland*) see Wangi Wangi.

Lakeview (*Co. Sturt*) 34°16'S. 146°01'E., 3 km NW of Griffith; RS 1923–37; pop. 410 (1933).

Lake View Estate (*Co. Northumberland*) see Wangi Wangi.

Lakewood (*Co. Macquarie*) 31°38'S. 152°46'E., 4 km NW of Laurieton, on Queens Lake; Angl. C. (Christ the Redeemer) 2001; reservoir; SD Adventist C.; pop. 343 (1986), 214 (1996), 224 (2001), 1,203 (2006), 1,318 (2011).

Lake Wyangan (*Co. Cooper*) 34°14'S. 146°02'E., 6 km N. of Griffith; village gaz. 1939; mining, citrus fruit, dairying; mine (gypsum); PO 1925; school (Lake View till 1932) 1925, additions 1965 and 2010; telephone 1924; TX (automatic) 1940–67; pop. 455 (1947), 511 (1954), 559 (1961), *c.*600 (1990), 901 (2011).

Lalalty (*Co. Denison*) 35°48'S. 145°45'E., 17 km E. of Tocumwal; Naranghi till 1900; farming; Meth. C. 1926; PO 1899–1930; school (Berrigan till 1890) 1886–93 and 1946–81; telephone 1922; TX (automatic) 1957; pop. 54 (1954), 87 (1961), 261 (2011).

Lallarook (*Co. Urana*) 35°22'S. 146°49'E., 20 km SE of Lockhart; farming; school (Lalla Rookh) 1897–1902.

Lalla Rookh (*Co. Urana*) see Lallarook.

Lambing Flat (*Co. Monteagle*) see Young.

Lambing Flat (*Co. Roxburgh*) 33°18'S. 149°59'E., 6 km N. of Portland, on Lambing Flat Ck; quarry.

Lambing Hill (*Co. Bligh*) 32°19'S. 149°15'E., 27 km W. of Gulgong; school 1907–43.

Lambs Creek (*Co. Durham*) 32°36'S. 151°26'E., 10 km NE of Branxton, on Lambs Valley Ck; farming; PO 1927–31; telephone 1917; TX 1928; pop. 50 (1901), 29 (1933), 65 (1947).

Lambs Valley (*Co. Durham*) 32°34'S. 151°28'E., 21 km NW of Maitland, on Lambs Valley Ck; FB; school 1901–7; pop. 79 (1911), 38 (1933), 436 (2011).

Lambs Valley (*Co. Gough*) 29°48'S. 151°48'E., 10 km SE of Glen Innes; (incl. Linwood); Angl. C. (All Saints') b. 1906 by G.E. Rowland; school (Beardy till 1918, then Linwood) 1885, new building b. 1900 by M. O'Brien, closed 1957; pop. 71 (1901), 69 (1911), 46 (1933).

Lambton (*Co. Northumberland*) 32°55'S. 151°43'E., 4 km E. of Wallsend; (incl. East Lambton, Grovetown, subdivided 1869 by

Waratah Coal Co., North Lambton); estab. *c.*1861, first land sale 1864, munic. proc. 1871, town gaz. 1875, munic. subsumed 1938 under City of Greater Newcastle; coalmining, sawmilling, orange orchards, vineyards, flower gardens; Angl. C. 1869, defunct, new one (St John's) b. 1907 by W. Timmins, d. by Ernest George Yeomans, extensions 1981; baking powder factory (T. Jones & Co.); Bapt. C. (Parklands Community); blind factory (M. Jenkins & Son) 1953; boot factory (Pioneer, William Bower); bridge (Howe Street, steel and timber) b. by W.H. Hudson; bushfire (man died and house destroyed) 1951; candle factory; cannery (L. Erikson Pty Ltd) 1954; carriage-works (A. Jones); CH (incl. lock-up) b. 1877–79 by Charles Mack, d. by Mortimer William Lewis, jun., additions 1879 by J. Myers, additions 1885 by J.P. Tyler, demolished; Christadelphian C.; collieries: Bayley's Reward, Dog and Rat Pit (o. 1867 by James and Alexander Brown, sold to George R. Gibbs, closed 1884), Lambton Heights, New Lambton (o. 1869 by James and Alexander Brown, later worked in receivership under Edward Combes), North Lambton, Old Lambton (o. 1863 as Lambton, strike 1886, renamed 1924, sold by Scottish Aust. Mining Co. to Hough and Jeffries, closed 1937, defunct), West End; cordial factory (NSW Aerated Water Pty Ltd) b. 1954 by W. Stronach Pty Ltd, d. by F. Stone; electricity 1890; engineering works (A.E.W. Engineering Co.); English Bapt. C. 1871; English Cong. C. 1875–1904, relocated and reused; FB 1875 (station b. 1902, destroyed 1913, replaced 1914 by F. Hickey, new one 2016 on new site); fibrous plaster works (J.D. Watson) 1951; flood 1893; glass works (Leonora Glass Industries Pty Ltd) 1947, burnt down 1957; jam factory (H.R. Williams & Co.); meat-processing plant (Oldham Bros Ltd) 1951; Lay Meth. C. 1891, closed, sold and reused; miners' strikes 1879, 1886, 1939, 1942, 1949; Particular Bapt. C.; pill factory (Northern Drug & Chemical Co. Pty Ltd) 1953; PO: East Lambton 1950, North Lambton 1955, Lambton 1865 (new one b. 1884 by Thomas Bourke, d. by James Johnstone Barnet, repairs 1897 by Gow and Shearman, closed 1994, sold and reused); police barracks, additions 1890 by John Gibson; powerhouse estab. 1890 by Harry Hyde Kingsbury; Presb. C. 1869; Prim. Meth. C. 1864; PS b. 1884–86 by John Shaw, alterations and repairs 1928, closed 1936, derelict, new one; quarries (stone): W. Dawson, Henry Pilkington, T. Russell; reservoir b. 1885 by J.G. Gatty; rifle range 1889; Rom. Cath. C. (St John the Evangelist) b. 1871 by James Ryan, reused, demolished, replacement (Mary Immaculate and St John the Evangelist) b. 1921 by W.G. Sparke, d. by Frederick George and Archer Cox Castleden; Salv. Army C. 1919, remodelled 1952; sawmills; scarlet fever 1933–34; school 1865, additions 1877 by Andrew Burg, new building 1889, repairs 1896 by Southon Bros, additions and alterations 1908 by Joseph Head, new buildings 1956, 1965, 1969, 2011; squall 1913; streets electric lit 1890; telegraph office b. 1884 by Thomas Bourke, d. by James Johnstone Barnet, repairs 1897 by Gow and Shearman, closed 1994, reused; telephone: East Lambton 1950 and Lambton 1955; tobacco factory (L. Erikson Pty Ltd) 1953; tramway (steam) to Newcastle, electrified 1925; Unit. C. (orig. Prim. Meth.) 1869, enlarged 1889, remodelled 1957, closed, sold and reused; Unit. Meth. Free C. 1872; water pumping station b. 1946 by Judd Bros; Welsh Bapt. C. 1868, new one 1877, reused; Welsh Calvinistic Meth. C. 1887; Welsh Cong. C. 1865, new one (Bethel) 1868 on new site, joined 1904 by English Congregationalists, additions and renovations 1935 by R. Owen and A. Cramp, d. by Mervyn A. Smith, closed 1977, sold and reused; Welsh Indep. C. 1864, replaced 1865, new one 1869, closed 1977; Wes. Meth. C. 1874 and 1891; pop. *c.*400 (1866), 550 (1871), 2,903 (1881), *c.*3,000 (1889), 3,434 (1891), *c.*3,600 (1895), 3,159 (1901), 2,796 (1911), *c.*3,700 (1921), 4,390 (1933), *c.*5,400 (1947), *c.*7,400 (1954), *c.*8,400

(1961), *c.*7,900 (1966), *c.*7,600 (1971), *c.*6,900 (1976), 7,700 (2006), 8,119 (2011). (See also New Lambton.)

Landale (*Co. Townsend*) 35°32'S. 145°15'E., 24 km E. of Deniliquin; school 1957–89.

Landervale (*Co. Bourke*) 34°33'S. 146°50'E., 35 km NE of Narrandera; telephone 1925; TX 1928, automatic 1958; pop. 26 (1933).

Langboyd (*Co. Narran*) 29°19'S. 147°04'E., 89 km W. of Lightning Ridge, on Birrie R.

Langdene (*Co. Murray*) see Queanbeyan.

Langley Park (*Co. King*) 34°50'S. 149°17'E., 6 km S. of Guyra, on Meadow Ck; school (Waggalalah till 1908) 1882–94 and 1902–13.

Langley Vale (*Co. Macquarie*) 31°48'S. 152°34'E., 17 km NE of Taree, on Lansdowne R.; sawmilling and farming; bushfire 1948; PO 1907, fire 1921; RS 1916–71; sawmill (William Langley & Sons Ltd) 1897, sold 1933 to Smith & Ellis Pty Ltd, later acquired by Allen Taylor & Co., burnt down 1951, rebuilt, closed 1970; school (Fern Ridge till 1928) 1904–65; telephone 1906; tramway (timber) b. 1897–1902 for William Langley & Sons Ltd, damaged 1923, closed 1939; TX 1928; Union C. (Memorial) 1922; pop. 96 (1911), 157 (1933), 179 (1947), 146 (1954), 77 (1961).

Langs Creek (*Co. King*) 34°30'S. 148°43'E., 7 km S. of Boorowa, on Boorowa R.; gold (disc. 1872 by Morgan); Angl. C. b. 1845 by Munro, d. by William Grant Broughton, destroyed 1849, and graveyard (63 graves); gale 1849; school 1882 b. by William Bundock, closed 1894, removed 1899 by W.A. Brander.

Lang's Crossing Place (*Co. Waradgery*) see Hay.

Langtree (*Co. Nicholson*) 33°40'S. 145°34'E., 22 km S. of Hillston; village gaz. 1923; cemetery; RS 1923–75; pop. 25 (1933).

Langunya (*Co. Denison*) 35°44'S. 145°34'E., 10 km S. of Finley; bushfire 1886; RS 1914–56; sawmill (J.W. Brown); school 1904–41; pop. 50 (1947).

Langworthy's (*Co. Gloucester*) see Weismantels.

Lanitza (*Co. Clarence*) 29°53'S. 153°00'E., 22 km S. of Grafton; RS 1915–74; pop. 24 (1933), 426 (2011).

Lankeys Creek (*Co. Goulburn*) 35°49'S. 147°39'E., 32 km E. of Holbrook; sheep, wheat, tin; FB; PO 1906; Presb. C. 1907; school 1904–9; telephone 1906; TX 1921, burnt down 1952; pop. 74 (1911), 92 (1933), 116 (1954), 158 (1961).

Lansdale (*Co. Flinders*) 32°14'S. 147°11'E., 78 km W. of Trangie; grazing; PO 1893; sawmills: Archibald E. Hutchison, Samuel Lord, William Watkins; telephone 1898; pop. 90 (1901), 83 (1911).

Lansdowne (*Co. Macquarie*) 31°47'S. 152°32'E., 16 km NE of Taree, on Lansdowne R.; formerly Cross Roads; settled by Benjamin Saville, surveyed 1904, village gaz. 1905; farming; Angl. C. (Epiphany) b. 1910 by Parker Bros; bridges: one over Cross Ck, one b. 1883, and one b. 1927, over Lansdowne R., and one b. 1964 over Savilles Ck; broom handle factory (Stanley Atkinson); bushfires 1938, 1939, 1979; cemetery (523 graves) 1870; FB; floods 1978 and 1981; PO 1878; railway bridge (steel truss) 1915, 120 ft (35.6 m), fabricated by Sydney Steel Co., over Lansdowne R.; reservoir 1969; Rom. Cath. C. (St Therese's) 1952; RS 1915–75; sawmills: W.A. Bryan & Sons 1939 (burnt down 1951, rebuilt 1952, closed 1958), Byrnes's (closed), A. Cook & Sons Ltd, Temperley's, H. Walters Pty Ltd (removed from Bundook); school 1904, additions 1952, 1960, 1978; telephone 1907; TX 1927, automatic 1972; Unit. C. (orig. Meth.) 1924; water supply augmentation 1970; weir 1953; wharf b. 1902 by George Lawson; pop. 257 (1891), 121 (1901), 613 (1911), 703 (1933), 561 (1947), 487 (1954), 323 (1961), 243 (1971), 280 (1976), 286 (1981), 347 (1986), 382 (1991), 432 (1996), 416 (2001), 433 (2006), 633 (2011).

Lapstone (*Co. Cook*) 33°47'S. 150°38'E., 2 km E. of Glenbrook, on Nepean R.; bridge 1967, over Tunnel Gully; bushfires 1923, 1936, 1951, 1952, 2001; reservoir; RS 1964, station b. by Arthur Hand; school 1971 d. by Ian McHutchinson, additions 2010; pop. 911

(2011).

Lara (*Co. Cunningham*) 32°50'S. 147°14'E., 48 km W. of Trundle, on Carlisle Ck.

Larbert (*Co. Murray*) 35°18'S. 149°46'E., 16 km N. of Braidwood, on Shoalhaven R.; orig. Kurraducbidgee; town gaz. 1843; farming and grazing; cemetery 1892; flood 1853; PO 1866–1957; telephone 1915; TX 1919; Union C. 1878; pop. 67 (1901), 50 (1911), 35 (1933), 453 (2006).

Largs (*Co. Durham*) 32°42'S. 151°36'E., 6 km NE of Maitland, on Paterson R.; (incl. Kings Island and Phoenix Park); formerly Dunmore; settled by Scots, surveyed *c.*1848; wheat, lucerne, maize, millet, potatoes; Angl. C. (St Andrew's) b. 1862–64, rebuilt 1928 by Arthur Partridge-Wall, d. by Walter Harold Pender, closed and reused; bridge b. 1863–65 by Francis Bell, new one b. 1898 by Samuel McGill, over Paterson R.; Christ. Israelite C.; drought 1827–29; floods 1849, 1864, 1870, 1874, 1893, 1904, 1908, 1950, 1955; flour mills: one b. 1828 by William Lang, and Andrew Lang (b. 1841 by Robert Muir, sold 1843 to A. Blair, demolished); gale (Phoenix Park) 1905; hailstorms 1873 and 1875; military camp b. 1940 by Slazengers Construction Co., closed 1945, razed; paper and flock mill (Andrew Lang, taken over by John Mitchell), burnt down 1876; PO 1858; Presb. C. 1846, renovations and repairs 1883 by Lethbridge, new one (St Andrew's) b. 1900 by Arthur John Keevers, d. by James Warren Scobie; PS, closed 1933; punt (b. by Darke) bought and installed 1859 by John Mitchell, across Paterson R.; reservoir, 43,000 gal. (195.5 kl); Rom. Cath. C. (Holy Family) b. 1910 by William Henry Noad, d. by Thomas Wilfred Silk; school (Dunmore till 1892) 1849 b. by Andrew Lang, new one b. 1873 by James Pritchard, d. by George Allen Mansfield; smallpox 1915; storm 1899; telephone 1886; TX 1928, automatic 1950; typhoid 1908; Wes. Meth. C. 1859, removed, new one b. 1896 by William King, d. by James Warren Scobie, closed, reused; pop. 141 (1861), 172 (1871), 161 (1881), 241 (1891), 552 (1901), 613 (1911), 380 (1933), 414 (1947), 355 (1954), 466 (1961), 340 (1971), 360 (1976), 394 (1981), 381 (1986), 1,135 (2006), 1,350 (2011).

Larmer (*Co. Murray*) see Queanbeyan.

Larnook (*Co. Rous*) 28°39'S. 153°07'E., 11 km E. of Kyogle, on Leycester Ck; dairying; FB; PO 1927; Rom. Cath. C. (St Joseph's); school 1955, additions 1995 and 2010; telephone 1915; TX 1925–56; pop. 96 (1933), 123 (1947), 170 (1954), 152 (1961), 371 (2011).

Larras Lee (*Co. Ashburnham*) 33°00'S. 148°52'E., 10 km N. of Molong, on Molong Ck; Mullylargah till 1923; bridges: one over Bell R. and one over Molong Ck; PO 1920; RS 1925–74; school (Bridgewater till *c.*1960) 1882–89 and 1915–73; telephone 1918; TX 1942, automatic 1954; pop. 46 (1933), 60 (1947), 68 (1954), 68 (1961), 94 (2011).

Larry's Flat (*Co. Gloucester*) see Krambach.

Latins Hole (*Co. Georgiana*) 33°59'S. 149°14'E., 50 km S. of Blayney, on Abercrombie R.

Laura (*Co. Hardinge*) 30°14'S. 151°09'E., 30 km S. of Tingha, on Laura Ck.

Lauradale (*Co. Gunderbooka*) 29°50'S. 145°36'E., 42 km NW of Bourke; telephone 1907.

Laureldale (*Co. Rous*) 28°45'S. 153°25'E., 10 km N. of Alstonville; RS 1913, station b. by Alexander Hamilton Scouller, closed 1972; pop. 68 (1933), 51 (1954).

Laurel Hill (*Co. Selwyn*) 35°37'S. 148°05'E., 12 km SW of Batlow; goldmining and forestry; electricity 1958; FB 1953; fire 1958; mine (Caledonia Two); PO 1901; prison camp (Leslie Nott, afforestation) 1957–95, reused; sawmills: Hansen's Alpine Ash Mill 1908, John Hydes, McDonald & Co., Kopsen & Co. Ltd (incl. oar factory) 1904, burnt down 1946, rebuilt 1947, sold 1980 to Matthews Timber Pty Ltd; school 1949–70; snowstorms 1905 and 1907; telephone 1909; TX 1928, automatic 1954; pop. 95 (1911), 61 (1933), 131 (1947), 173 (1954), 164 (1961).

Laurella (*Co. Parry*) 31°11'S. 150°55'E., 10 km S. of Tamworth; telephone 1916; TX 1922.

Laurieton (*Co. Macquarie*) 31°39'S. 152°48'E., 23 km S. of Wauchope, on Camden Haven

Inlet; orig. Peachgrove; port, sawmilling, fishing, oysters, tourism; ambulance station 1982; Angl. C. (Holy Trinity) 1899, re-roofed, closed, sold 2006, restored 2015, reused; Assemblies of God C.; bridges: one (Hanleys Point) 1966 to Dunbogan over Camden Haven Inlet and one b. 1931 to North Haven, demolished, new one (concrete) 1961, new one 2016, over Stingray Ck; bushfire 1914; cemetery (1,663 graves 1896+) 1886, incl. columbaria; cordial factory (E. Stace), burnt down 1950; FB (station b. 1960); PO 1875, new one b. 1913 by J. and R. Longworth, closed, sold and reused; PS 1901–17, new ones 1959 and 1978; punt to North Haven, across Queens Lake Entrance, ceased 1931; 2 quarries; reservoir; Rom. Cath. C. 1899, reused 1953, demolished, replacement (St Peter's) 1958, extended 1968, new one (St Peter the Fisherman) 1985; sawmills: De Fraine's, Joseph Laurie 1876 (sold to McKay and Bibby, partly destroyed 1891 by boiler explosion, man killed), R. Longworth & Co. (became Longworths Pty Ltd, bought by BHP), John S. Rogers & Co. (burnt down 1897); sawmill strike 1907; school 1877, additions 1898 by Silas Brewer, repairs 1900 by A.G. Smith, additions 1902 by Pead & Sons, additions 1964, 1970, 2010; telegraph 1881; TX 1920, automatic 1970; typhoid 1906; Unit. C. (St Andrew's, orig. Presb.) b. 1907 by Harry Bird, additions and alterations 1995; wharf b. 1901 by Phillip Wotton; pop. 99 (1891), 492 (1901), 587 (1911), *c.*450 (1924), 359 (1933), 549 (1947), 551 (1954), 662 (1961), *c.*1,400 (1987), 1,931 (2011).

Lavadia (*Co. Clarence*) 29°46'S. 153°04'E., 13 km SE of South Grafton; creamery (NSW Fresh Food & Ice Co. Ltd) b. 1896 by R. Cranston, d. by Garratt, moved 1900 to Seelands; school 1885–1913; telephone 1910; pop. 128 (1911), 48 (1933).

Laverstock (*Co. King*) 34°39'S. 148°49'E., 22 km NW of Yass; pop. 26 (1933), 169 (2006).

Lavertys Gap (*Co. Rous*) 28°34'S. 153°25'E., 8 km W. of Mullumbimby; powerhouse (hydro-electric) 1926, extended 1933, improvements 1939 by Higgins & Co. and Dayal Singh, augmented 1951; pop. 28 (1933).

Lavington (*Co. Goulburn*) see Albury.

Lavington East (*Co. Goulburn*) see Albury.

Lawrence (*Co. Clarence*) 29°30'S. 153°06'E., 10 km W. of Maclean, on Clarence R.; orig. Devil's Elbow and The Elbow; first lots sold 1859, laid out 1861 by William Albert Braylesford Greaves, town gaz. 1879, declined 1905+; former river port, sugar-cane 1866+, beef, maize, potatoes, dairying, fishing; Angl. C. 1868, destroyed and rebuilt 1869, rebuilt again 1871, ruined by 1890, new one (All Saints') b. 1904 by F.J. Robertson; Bapt. C. 1882, sold and removed, new one 1907, closed, sold 2010; bridge b. 1883–85 by Denning and Atkinson, re-decked and repaired 1904, rebuilt (Dare truss) 1911 by Oxenford Bros, 301 ft (91.7 m), replaced 2018 by Delaney Civil, over Sportsmans Ck; cemetery (518 graves 1880+) 1880, incl. columbarium; CH 1870, reused, (second) b. 1880 by C. West, (third) 1920–57; coalmine (Lawrence Coal Co.), closed 1886; creamery (Fresh Food & Ice Co.) b. 1896 by R. Cranston; customs-house; cyclone 1869; FB; fires 1908 and 1987; floods 1863, 1876, 1890, 1892, 1893, 1945, 1946, 2001, 2011; Meth. C. b. 1911 by F. Robertson, d. by Alfred Gambier Newman, destroyed 1979; PO 1859, new one b. 1894 by G. Finlay; Presb. C. b. 1885 by E. Hattersley, extended 1907, damaged 1979, replaced 1981; PS 1872; punt 1882; reservoir (steel), 250,000 gal. (1,136.5 kl), 1966; Rom. Cath. C. 1883, new one (St John the Evangelist) b. 1927 by Ebeling, closed, sold 2017; sale-yards 1917, new yards (McPhee and Smith) 1951; sawmill; school 1876, new one b. 1880 by William Kinnear, repairs 1888 by Thomas Moffatt, additions 1895 by Strauss Bros, additions 1899 by Schaeffer; storms 1899, 1946, 1979; sugar mill (horse powered) estab. 1882 by C.N. and George Childs; telegraph 1872; TX 1911, automatic 1969; Unit. C. 1985; water reticulation 1966; wharf b. 1860 by Edward Ogilvie; whooping cough epidemic 1911; pop. 137 (1871), 232 (1881), 354 (1891),

486 (1901), 581 (1911), *c.*500 (1924), 318 (1933), 346 (1947), 353 (1954), 340 (1961), 223 (1971), 269 (1976), 325 (1981), 306 (1986), 328 (1991), 367 (1996), 425 (2001), 740 (2011).

Lawrence Road (*Co. Clarence*) 29°24'S. 153°00'E., 20 km W. of Maclean; RS 1905, station b. by H.W. Owen, closed 1970.

Lawson (*Co. Cook*) 33°43'S. 150°26'E., 5 km E. of Wentworth Falls, on Lawson Ck; known as Wilson's, Christmas Swamp and The Swamp from 1817, Twenty-Four Mile Hollow by *c.*1832, Blue Mountain 1843–79; settled *c.*1828, estab. 1845, laid out 1881 by William Albert Braylesford Greaves, village gaz. 1884; popular summer mountain health and tourist resort 1920s–50s; Angl. C. 1884, reused, new one (Emmanuel) b. 1910 by R.P. Blundell, d. by Charles Rosenthal, renamed Central Villages; Bapt. C. (in former Meth. C.); bushfires 1895, 1897, 1940, 1977; cemetery (372 graves 1901+) 1899; Cong. C. 1888; disability aids factory (Megalong Positioning Service) 2012; electricity 1918; FB (station b. 1961, new one 2001); fires 1923 and 1932; gale (man killed) 1899; Jehovah's Witnesses C.; Meth. C. b. 1908 by Hogbin, additions 1922 by P.J. Gabriel, sold 1975 to Bapt. C., relocated 2009; PO 1885, new one b. 1925 by Lawrence Pither; PS 1902, new one b. 1951 by Ashman and Hart; quarry; railway dam 1867, closed, sold 1907 to Geggie, demolished; reservoir b. 1904 by Gilmore and Connell; Rom. Cath. C. (Our Lady Help of Christians) 1903 d. by H.R. Goyder, relocated and reused, new one (Our Lady of the Nativity) b. 1929 by G. Lambert, d. by Austin McKay, additions 1965, fire 2015; RS (Blue Mountain till 1879) 1867, new station 1879; school 1889, new one 1918, additions 1962, 1966, 1972, 1981, major upgrade 1990, additions 1991; sewerage 1965; streets electric lit 1918; telegraph 1894–1915; TX 1910, automatic 1974; Unit. C., closed, sold and reused; pop. 212 (1891), 502 (1901), 678 (1911), 622 (1933), 953 (1947), 1,188 (1954), 1,256 (1961), 1,122 (1964), 4,791 (1976, incl. Hazelbrook), 6,323 (1981, incl. Hazelbrook), 7,993 (1986, incl. Hazelbrook), 9,092 (1991, incl. Hazelbrook), 9,605 (1996, incl. Hazelbrook), 10,153 (2001, incl. Hazelbrook).

Lawsons Creek (*Co. Phillip*) 32°35'S. 149°39'E., 6 km E. of Mudgee; Angl. C. (St Barnabas's) 1923–50, sold 1954; school 1868, additions 1902, closed 1948; Wes. Meth. C. 1878; pop. 145 (1911), 85 (1933), 64 (1947), 53 (1954).

Leadville (*Co. Bligh*) 32°01'S. 149°33'E., 14 km E. of Dunedoo; orig. Hobbins' Dam, then Mount Stewart till 1891; first lots sold 1913; mining (silver-lead disc. 1887 by Tommy Governor) 1888–98, 1912–27, 1932–37, 1950–51, farming, grazing; Angl. C. (St Matthew's) 1892, moved to Hannahs Bridge 1918 and renamed, new one b. 1914–17 by J. Stoddart & Sons, closed, sold and reused; bridge over Hobbins Gully; bushfire 2017; caterpillar infestation 1922; cemetery (14 graves 1926–2001) 1897; CH; 2 cordial factories; cyclone 1921; dust storm 1909; FB; grasshopper infestation 1924; hospital 1979; measles epidemic 1912; mines (silver-lead-zinc): Mount Scott (Mount Scott Silver Lead Mining Co. Ltd) 1901–14 and Mount Stewart (incl. Grosvenor and Extended, worked by Mt Stewart Silver Mining Co., furnace installed 1892, 2 killed 1893) 1887–98, 1912–27, 1932–37, 1950–51; pound (stock) 1897; PS 1892, demolished and replaced 1908, closed 1937; rifle range 1907; Rom. Cath. C. (St Peter's), enlarged and renovated 1917 by J.J. Cohen, renovated 1939; RS 1920–75; school 1892 b. by John Miller, extended 1893 by Gardiner and Winter, closed 1972; silo; telegraph 1892; TX 1910, automatic 1986; pop. 213 (1901), 265 (1911), 265 (1914), 220 (1933), 145 (1947), 134 (1954), 123 (1961), 185 (2006), 181 (2011).

Leadville (*Co. Yancowinna*) see Purnamoota.

Leamington (*Co. Durham*) see Lemington.

Leaning Oak (*Co. Wellington*) 32°36'S. 149°23'E., 19 km W. of Mudgee, on Merinda Ck; school 1899–1910.

Leconfield (*Co. Northumberland*) 32°39'S. 151°24'E., 5 km E. of Branxton, on Dalwood Ck; North Greta till 1903; colliery estab. 1888 by Greta Coal Co. Ltd, o. 1889 as Leconfield, closed 1892, reopened 1932 by J. Bennett as Leconfield-Greta Colliery, closed 1934, reopened 1944 by W. Mawson as Leconfield Colliery, acquired 1947 by Leconfield Colliery Co., closed and demolished 1957; Presb. C. 1890, closed, reused, sold 1896 to local council, dismantled, moved to Greta and re-erected; pop. 220 (2011).

Ledgerton (*Co. Cowley*) 35°09'S. 148°53'E., 24 km SW of Murrumbateman; farming and grazing; cemetery 1894; PO 1927; pop. 21 (1933), 75 (1947).

Leechey Flat (*Co. St Vincent*) 35°33'S. 150°00'E., 22 km SE of Braidwood, on Currowan Ck.

Leechs Gully (*Co. Clive*) 29°01'S. 152°02'E., 5 km N. of Tenterfield, on Tenterfield Ck; orchards, farming, dairying; PO 1927; school 1882–1957; telephone 1914; pop. 51 (1911), 70 (1933), 114 (1947), 128 (1954), 109 (1961), 202 (2006).

Leefield (*Co. Clive*) 29°03'S. 151°50'E., 18 km W. of Tenterfield; formerly Clifton Gates; farming and sheep; PO 1927–31; telephone 1924; TX 1933; pop. 47 (1933).

Leesville (*Co. Wallace*) 36°26'S. 148°36'E., 3 km SW of Jindabyne, on Lees Ck; PS, moved 1883 to Jindabyne.

Leeton (*Co. Cooper*) 34°33'S. 146°24'E., 44 km SE of Griffith, on Gogeldrie Branch Canal; (incl. Crusher Camp, Gralee, Parkview, Wattle Hill subdivided 1953, Willimbong, Wiradjuri); surveyed by Henry M. Terry, d. 1912 by Walter Burley Griffin as centre of Murrumbidgee Irrigation Area (MIA), founded 1912, irrigation lots sold 1912, town gaz. and lots sold 1913, farming failed till soldiers' settlement 1918+, MIA almost failed 1920, excessive irrigation till 1956; dairying 1912–1920s, fruit (oranges 1917+), rice 1924+, winter cereals, vegetables, cheese, vineyards, sheep, cattle; abattoir; agric. research station 1928; airfield 1931; ambulance station b. 1951–53 by M.A. Churchill, d. by Stephen James O'Halloran; Angl. C. (St Peter, Apostle and Martyr) b. 1913–15 by J. Funnell, d. by G.W.A. Welsh, condemned and demolished 1996, new one (St Peter's) b. 1973 by Siebel Bros, d. by Louis Reginald Williams; bacon factory o. 1915 by WC & IC; Bapt. C. 1913, dismantled 1937 by Davenport and relocated; butter factory and ice works (Ibis) o. 1913 by WC & IC, cheese-making began 1916, sold 1921 to Murrumbidgee Irrigation Dairy Farmers' Co-op. Society Ltd, demolished 1992; cannery o. 1914 by WC & IC, (second) o. 1915 by WC & IC, (third) o. 1918 by WC & IC, strike 1923, cannery extended 1934, taken over 1935 by Leeton Co-op. Cannery Ltd, additions and alterations 1937 by T. Ashton, d. by George William Albert Welch, closed 1994; cemetery (lawn); CH b. 1922–24 by William Charles Hanson, d. by George McRae; cheese factory (Tavella) 1987, now Riverina Cheese; Christ. Revival Crusade C.; clock tower (war memorial) 1965; cordial factories: H. McClellan, McGill and Brown 1915, Murray's 1936; electricity (WC & IC) 1914; engineering works (Leeton Steel & Vehicle Works) estab. 1929 by Arthur James and W. Chandler, became Leeton Steel Works Pty Ltd in 1969; evaporative cooling factory (Celair-Malmet); Crusade Family C.; FB 1913 (station b. 1938 by McDonald and Brown); fibrous plaster works (Tom Ashton) 1933; fires 1923, 1926, 1928, 1930, 1936, 1945; floods 1989 and 2012; fruit packing houses: Attwood's, burnt down 1924, F.J. Lee & Co., Craig Mostyn & Co. 1939, Producers' Co-op. Distributing Society, burnt down 1938; gale 1923; gastroenteritis epidemics 1941, 1946, 1947; hospital (temporary one) 1911, (second) 1912, (third) b. 1917–19 on new site by T. Jones, additions 1938 by Kent and Kent, (fourth) 1942, extended 1951, 1953, 1962; Jehovah's Witnesses C. 1960; joinery (R. Francis), burnt down 1923; juice (citrus) factory estab. 1974 by Leeton Citrus Juices Ltd, joined Southern Farmers Ltd 1987, taken over 1999 by Berri Ltd; Lutheran C.: St John's 1875, new one 1962, and Trinity b. 1924 by Francis Williams Queree; measles epidemic 1935; Meth. C. b. 1913 by George Huntley Dixon and William Godfrey Butterworth, relocated 1937 by Tom

Davenport; plant nursery (WC & IC) 1912–25; Plymouth Brethren C. 1957; PO 1912, burnt down 1915, replaced 1922, new one; pound (stock), closed 1939; Presb. C. (St Andrew's) b. 1916 by Dixon & Co., d. by John Francis Kenny, additions 1947, reused, new one 1958; PS 1913, (second) 1923, new building 1935, additions 1953; punt (Willimbong); quarry; reservoirs 1912, 1937, 1973; rice mill (Ricegrowers' Co-op. Mills Ltd) 1951, rebuilt 1975; Rom. Cath. C. b. 1915 by M'Fadgen and Bland, d. by Thomas Jackson, closed, renovated, reused 1955, new one (St Joseph's) b. 1953–55 by Thomas J. Ashton, d. by Stephen James O'Halloran; RS 1922–89; sale-yards (WC & IC), acquired 1932 by local council, new yards 1939; Salv. Army C. 1915, new one 2014; sawmill (Leeton-Yanco Sawmilling Co.); schools: Gralee 1953 b. by Les Jack, closed 1970, Leeton primary 1912, new building b. 1913 by George Huntley Dixon and William Godfrey Butterworth, new building 1954, additions 1967, Leeton HS 1947, additions 1959 and 1991, Parkview 1971, additions 2010; SD Adventist C. 1934; sewerage 1937, augmentation 1969, 1987, 2000; stockfeed plant (Ricegrowers' Co-op. Ltd); TC 1952, additions 1970 and 1988, became a campus of Riverina Institute in 1992; TX 1914, new building b. 1950, automatic 1972; Unit. C. (orig. Meth.) b. 1937 by W.H. Jones, d. by George William Albert Welch; water reticulation 1913, augmentation 1993; wineries: Lillypilly Estate 1982, Miranda Wines 1939, Toorak Wines 1964; pop. 3,629 (1915), 2,793 (1933), 3,912 (1947), 5,148 (1954), 5,354 (1961), 5,818 (1966), 6,638 (1971), 6,631 (1976), 6,498 (1981), 6,421 (1986), 6,245 (1991), 6,615 (1996), 6,927 (2001), 6,828 (2006), 6,733 (2011).

Leets Vale (*Co. Hunter*) 33°26'S. 150°57'E., 37 km W. of Gosford, on Hawkesbury R.; orchards; cemetery; Meth. C. b. 1937 by Roy and Herbert Eldridge; PO 1887; school (Australian Farm till 1915) 1881–1925 and 1946–54; telephone 1914; TX 1928; Wes. Meth. C. 1875; pop. 70 (1933), 38 (1961).

Leeville (*Co. Richmond*) 28°57'S. 153°00'E., 10 km SW of Casino; farming and dairying; bushfire 1952; hailstorm 1919; PO 1910; RS (Deep Creek till 1908) 1905, station b. by H.W. Owen, closed 1974; school (Deep Creek till 1951) 1902; telephone 1912; TX 1928, automatic 1970; pop. 76 (1911), 169 (1933), 120 (1947), 96 (1954), 107 (1961).

Leewood (*Co. Bathurst*)
see Orange (*Co. Wellington*).

Legume (*Co. Buller*) 28°24'S. 152°18'E., 69 km W. of Kyogle; cattle, farming, dairying; cemetery; Community C.; freezing works (William Frederick Von Harten); PO 1912; sawmill (Lewis Tyler & Co.); school (Acacia Creek till 1900, then Buller till 1912) 1884, additions 1913 by J. Dwyer, closed 1988; telephone 1914; TX 1916, automatic 1978; pop. 162 (1933), 154 (1947), 118 (1954), 128 (1961), 370 (2011).

Leigh (*Co. Fitzroy*) 30°18'S. 152°45'E., 6 km NE of Dorrigo; 3 quarries; RS 1924–57; sawmill 1912; school 1937–67; pop. 137 (1933), 224 (2006).

Leighton Park (*Co. Brisbane*) see Segenhoe.

Leighwood (*Co. Georgiana*) 34°12'S. 149°38'E., 33 km NE of Crookwell; PO 1885–93; school 1882–94; pop. 38 (1933).

Leman's Flat (*Co. Gloucester*) see Gloucester.

Lemington (*Co. Durham*) 32°30'S. 150°59'E., 20 km NW of Singleton, on Hunter R.; orig. Hay, then Leamington; surveyed 1824 by Henry Dangar, village gaz. 1881; flood 1863; school 1957–76; telephone 1949; TX 1951, automatic 1955; pop. 63 (1947), 80 (1954), 69 (1961).

Lemon Tree (*Co. Northumberland*) 33°09'S. 151°22'E., 11 km W. of Wyee, on Jilliby Ck; pop. 59 (1947).

Lemon Tree Passage (*Co. Gloucester*) 32°44'S. 152°02'E., 10 km W. of Nelson Bay, on Port Stephens; Kooindah till 1949; thrived in 1980s; rutile mining, oysters, fishing, tourism, retirement centre; bushfire 1980; coast guard station 1982; FB; jetty; marina; PO 1948; PS 1983; 2 quarries (one abandoned); radar station (weather); reservoir; telephone 1930;

TX 1930–64; wharf b. 1928 by Mansen; pop. 74 (1954), 81 (1961), 253 (1971), 455 (1976), 2,269 (1981), 2,534 (2011).

Lemon Tree Passage (*Co. Gloucester*) see also Tanilba Bay.

Lenaghan (*Co. Northumberland*) see Black Hill.

Leniston (*Co. Denison*) 35°39'S. 145°41'E., 10 km E. of Finley; quarry; RS 1898, station b. by Charles Baker, closed 1975; TX (automatic).

Lennox Head (*Co. Rous*) 28°48'S. 153°36'E., 9 km N. of Ballina, on Coral Sea; subdivided 1922; sand mining and dairying; Angl. C., removed 1947 from North Head but later returned, new one (St John the Baptist) 2004; FB; hailstorm 1951; PO 1935; quarry; 2 reservoirs (incl. one of 50,000 gal. or 227.3 kl); Rom. Cath. C. (Holy Family), removed 1954 from Alstonville; school (North Creek till 1961) 1882, additions 1967, 1986, 1990, 1995, 2010; sewerage augmentation 1996; telephone 1925; tornado 2010; TX 1945, automatic 1957; Unit. C. 1997 (in a hall b. 1951), closed, demolished 2008; water supply augmentation 1969; pop. 74 (1933), 149 (1947), 173 (1954), 201 (1961), 436 (1971), 843 (1976), 1,199 (1981), 1,854 (1986), 3,036 (1991), 4,511 (1996), 5,843 (2001), 6,079 (2011).

Lennoxton (*Co. Durham*) 32°33'S. 151°32'E., 9 km NW of Paterson; surveyed by A. Peters, planned 1842 by F.E. Davis, but village never eventuated.

Leonay (*Co. Cook*) 33°46'S. 150°39'E., 3 km SW of Emu Plains, on Nepean R.; subdivided 1965; floods 1978 and 1990; PO 1977; school 1974; telephone 1977; pop. 2,511 (2001), 2,421 (2011).

Lerida (*Co. King*) 34°52'S. 149°22'E., 35 km SW of Goulburn; school 1891, new building b. 1896 by Arthur Allen, closed 1907; Wes. Meth. C. 1887; pop. 37 (1933).

Letchworth (*Co. Murray*) see Queanbeyan.

Lethero (*Co. Perry*) 33°37'S. 142°27'E., 73 km NE of Wentworth; PO 1907; telephone 1907.

Lette (*Co. Caira*) 34°21'S. 143°11'E., 118 km E. of Wentworth.

Letterewe (*Co. Macquarie*) 31°27'S. 152°43'E., 2 km NW of Wauchope, on Hastings R.; Free Presb. C. 1873.

Leura (*Co. Cook*) 33°43'S. 150°20'E., 2 km E. of Katoomba, on Gordon Ck; subdivided 1881; mountain tourist destination with views and waterfalls; Angl. C. (Mission) 1899, new one (St Alban's) b. 1910 by McIntosh, d. by Waterhouse and Lake, new chancel and vestry 1932, fire 1991, restoration 1993 by Prime Constructions Pty Ltd, d. by Robert Staas; Bapt. C. 1924, relocated and rebuilt 1931, burnt down 1957, replaced 1958; bushfires 1928, 1929, 1936, 1940, 1943, 1944, 1945 (8 houses destroyed), 1947, 1953, 1957, 2011; chocolate factory (Josophan's) estab. 2005 by Jodie Van Der Velden; coalmine (Gladstone Coal Co. Ltd) 1885, incl. aerial ropeway fabricated by Adolf Bleichert & Co., Leipzig, Germany, erected by Carl Oscar Schulze, mine closed 1886 and ropeway moved to Katoomba and reused; crematorium (Leura Crematorium & Memorial Gardens Pty Ltd) 1993; FB (station b. 1971); football factory; gale 1910; jam factory (Princess Pantry) 2002; landslip 2020; LDS (Mormon) C. 1983 d. by Kenneth Frank Charles Woolley; nib factory (Eastwood Pens Pty Ltd) 1947, fire 1952; PO 1896, new one b. 1913 by W.W. Dunk, closed and reused; Presb. C. (St David's) 1901, extended 1906, renovated 1956, burnt down 1957, replaced 1960, reused; PS 1923; 2 quarries; 3 reservoirs (incl. one 500,000 gal. or 2,273 kl); Rom. Cath. C. 1917, new one (St Bonaventure's) 1921 d. by Austin McKay; RS 1890; school 1905 b. by E.P. Frost & Co., additions 1923, burnt down 1957, replaced 1958, additions 1963, alterations 1974 and 1980, additions 1994; sewerage 1910, augmentation 1966 and 1973; storm 1913; telephone 1896; TX (automatic) 1950; Unit. C. (orig. Meth.) 1909 d. by Edward Hewlett Hogben, renovated 1947; water supply 1905; pop. 1,363 (1911), 2,177 (1954), 2,356 (1961), 3,288 (1964), 4,365 (2011).

Levenstrath (*Co. Fitzroy*) 29°49'S. 152°55'E., 14 km S. of Grafton, on Orara R.; pop. 69 (1901).

Leviathan (*Co. Hardinge*) 29°50'S. 151°05'E., 8 km SW of Inverell; 2 mines; 2 quarries; school 1916–47.

Lewers Estate (*Co. Northumberland*) see Belmont.

Lewinsbrook (*Co. Durham*) 32°27'S. 151°35'E., 17 km W. of Dungog, on Lewinsbrook Ck; never developed; agric.; PO 1865; school 1852, additions 1918 by Jones Bros, closed 1964; pop. 56 (1933).

Lewis Ponds (*Co. Bathurst*) 33°16'S. 149°16'E., 15 km E. of Orange; copper mining 1860s–70s, silver-lead-zinc mining 1888–91, farming, grazing; Angl. C. (St Mark's) 1912; Aust. C.; cemetery 1890; mines: Britannia (Great Western Copper Mining Syndicate) 1872, Lady Belmore <1908, Lewis Ponds Silver Mining Co. 1888, Little Bell Mount 1906, Little Gem, Mount Regan 1878 and 1906–7, New Lewis Ponds 1888 (bought 1890 by Great Western Mining Co.), Spicer's 1887–92, Sulphide Corp. 1913–21, Tom's or Gurophian (Great Western Mining Co.) 1887–92 and 1913–15; PO 1888; PS 1890; school 1880, new one b. 1890 by Gartrell, burnt down 1914, replaced 1917 by W. Gow, closed 1949; telephone 1889; TX 1927, automatic 1966; Wes. Meth. C. 1889; pop. 293 (1901), 241 (1911), 159 (1933), 83 (1947), 52 (1954), 80 (1961), 413 (2011).

Leycester (*Co. Rous*) 28°47'S. 153°12'E., 10 km NW of Lismore, on Back Ck; dairying and orchards; gale 1928; landslide 1950; PO 1927; RS 1912–72; school 1957–79; pop. 111 (1933), 144 (1947), 96 (1961).

Liamena (*Co. Lincoln*) 31°58'S. 149°20'E., 7 km NW of Dunedoo; RS 1917, station b. by John Allibone, closed 1972.

Licking Hole (*Co. Georgiana*) 34°05'S. 149°41'E., 46 km NE of Crookwell, on Licking Hole Ck; copper mining.

Liddell (*Co. Durham*) 32°24'S. 151°01'E., 18 km SE of Muswellbrook; village gaz. 1879; agric. and grazing; bridge 1898; coalmine (open-cut); 3 dams: ash 1971, modified 1982, 121 ft (37 m) high, cooling water 1968, 141 ft (43 m) high, water supply 1970, 102 ft (31 m) high; earth tremor 2014; lock-up 1842; mine fatalities (2 died) 1981; PO 1890; power station (Macquarie Generation) b. 1964–73; RS 1879–1966; telephone 1915; TX 1928; pop. 38 (1933), 55 (1954).

Lidsdale (*Co. Cook*) 33°23'S. 150°05'E., 3 km NE of Wallerawang, on Coxs R.; Wallerawang till 1873; mining and agric.; bridge (timber beam), 85 ft (25.9 m), replaced 1945–47 by C. Binns and V. Packer, 230 ft (70.1 m), over Coxs R.; cheese factory (Jannei) estab. 1995 by Neil and Janette Watson; collieries: Folly (H. Maddox) 1888 and Newcom (Newcom Colliery Pty Ltd) 1951, man killed 1952; cordial factory (horse powered) estab. by Everett Summons, taken over by James A. Summons, additions 1909; fire 1887; gale 1909; PO 1870; reservoir, 2,000,000 gal. (9,092 kl), 1957; Rom. Cath. C., damaged 1909, dismantled 1921 and moved to Wallerawang; sawmill; telephone 1921; Unit. C. (orig. Wes. Meth.) 1874, closed, re-roofed and reopened 1921, closed, sold 2016; pop. 123 (1901), 136 (1911), 342 (1933), 405 (1947), 473 (1954), 513 (2011).

Lidsdale (*Co. Cook*) see also Blackmans Flat.

Lidster (*Co. Wellington*) 33°18'S. 148°59'E., 11 km W. of Orange; German's Hill till 1916; grazing, farming, orchards; FB (station b. 2018); PO 1880; Rom. Cath. C. (St Carthage's) 1877, demolished; telephone 1919; TX 1921, automatic 1966; pop. 64 (1901), 87 (1933), 141 (1947), 85 (1954), 112 (1961).

Lidster (*Co. Wellington*) see also Nashdale.

Lightning Ridge (*Co. Finch*) 29°26'S. 147°59'E., 58 km W. of Collarenebri; formerly Wallangulla, was also known as Newtown; estab. 1902, thrived 1980s–90s; mining (opal disc. 1902 by Charles Nettleton, mining began 1902 by Jack Murray, more disc. 1969) and grazing; airport (3 km S.); ambulance station 1984; Angl. C. (St George's) 1912, damaged 1933, replacement b. 1937 by Roy Allport, Jim Denis and Jack Boules, reused 1998, new one (Community); cemetery (690 graves); CH 1960 d. by Edward Herbert

Farmer; cordial factory (Alf Smith); cyclone 1933; electricity 1963; FB (station b. 1982); hailstorm 1922; LDS (Mormon) C.; PO 1906, new one b. 1932 by Jim Alderslade, reused, new one 1961; PS 1908–44, new building 1961 (removed from New Angledool), new one 1984; reservoirs; Rom. Cath. C. (Our Lady of Fatima) 1956; school (Opale till 1910) 1907, new one b. 1911 by D. Scoular, additions 1985 and 1993; SD Adventist C.; Serbian Orthodox C. (St George's, orig. Angl.); sewage works, augmentation 1995; telephone 1911; TX 1924, automatic 1984; water reticulation 1961, augmentation 1985 and 1995; pop. 623 (1911), 225 (1933), 286 (1947), 176 (1954), 261 (1961), 825 (1976), 1,112 (1981), 1,292 (1986), 1,522 (1991), 1,814 (1996), 1,831 (2001), 2,492 (2011).

Lillian Rock (*Co. Rous*) 28°32'S. 153°09'E., 10 km NW of Nimbin, on Websters Ck; farming; bridge (Betteridge Bridge) over Websters Ck; PO 1913; school 1933–73; telephone 1924; TX (automatic) 1956; pop. 149 (1933), 194 (1947), 72 (1954), 64 (1961), 215 (2011).

Lilli Pilli (*Co. St Vincent*) 35°46'S. 150°14'E., 2 km N. of Malua Bay, on Batemans Bay; pop. 613 (2011).

Lilydale (*Co. Auckland*) see Toothdale.

Lilydale (*Co. Clarence*) 29°33'S. 152°40'E., 30 km NW of Grafton, on Clarence R.; bridge 1934, new one (concrete) 1996, over Clarence R.; quarry.

Lilygrove (*Co. Sandon*) 30°19'S. 151°41'E., 11 km S. of Guyra; school 1900 b. by E. Lonsdale, closed 1906.

Limbri (*Co. Inglis*) 31°02'S. 151°09'E., 22 km E. of Tamworth, on Jamiesons Ck; Buri till 1919; goldmining (alluvial) and grazing; Angl. C. (St Barnabas's) 1904, closed, moved 1936 to Moonbi; flood 1962; PO 1902; railway tunnel, 165 yds (150.5 m), 1882; Rom. Cath. C. (Holy Cross) b. 1907 by Galbraith, d. by Philip Ernest Ranclaud; RS (Farquharson till 1893) 1885, closed; school 1900 b. by Robert Williams, closed 1905, reopened 1916–34 and 1949–2007, sold; telephone 1904; TX 1915, automatic 1983; pop. 94 (1911), 88 (1933), 165 (1947), 107 (1954), 121 (1961), 140 (1970), 259 (2006), 244 (2011).

Limeburners Creek (*Co. Gloucester*) 32°36'S. 151°54'E., 9 km NW of Karuah, on Limeburners Ck; orig. timber, boat-building, lime burning, then farming and grazing; PO 1859; 3 quarries; school 1884–90, 1900–18, 1957–66; telephone 1905; TX 1929–72; pop. 90 (1901), 81 (1911), 79 (1933), 90 (1947), 86 (1954), 83 (1961), 520 (2006).

Limeburners Creek (*Co. Macquarie*) 31°20'S. 152°55'E., 13 km NW of Port Macquarie; pop. 34 (1933).

Limeburners Flat (*Co. Macquarie*) 31°36'S. 152°49'E., 3 km W. of Bonny Hills, on Limeburners Ck.

Limekilns (*Co. Gloucester*) see Limestone.

Lime Kilns (*Co. King*) 34°53'S. 149°08'E., 20 km E. of Yass.

Limekilns (*Co. Roxburgh*) 33°16'S. 149°45'E., 24 km NE of Bathurst; formerly The Lime Kilns; agric., grazing, lime burning; goldmine (Blackmans Swamp); marble works (Rosedale, James Tobin) 1894; PO 1861–1930; Rom. Cath. C., moved 1913 to Sofala; school 1860, new one b. 1868 by Thomas McCrane, repairs 1883 by Josiah James Atkins, closed 1893; TX (automatic) 1959; pop. 134 (1901), 131 (1911), 65 (1933), 51 (1947).

Limerick (*Co. Georgiana*) 34°12'S. 149°28'E., 27 km N. of Crookwell, on Deep Ck; farming and sheep; bushfire 1939; PO 1929, burnt down 1939, new one, closed 1975; Rom. Cath. C. (St Fiacre's) b. 1912 by Charles McDonald & Son, closed 1973, renovated 1989; school 1957–73; telephone 1915; TX 1927; pop. 97 (1933), 91 (1947), 94 (1954), 73 (1961).

Limestone (*Co. Arrawatta*) 29°12'S. 151°01'E., 16 km NW of Ashford.

Limestone (*Co. Gloucester*) 32°40'S. 152°08'E., 2 km W. of Tea Gardens, on Pindimar Bay; formerly Holbert's Town and Limekilns.

Limestone (*Co. Wellington*) 32°46'S. 149°45'E., 21 km W. of Rylstone.

Limestone (*Co. Yancowinna*) 31°55'S. 141°20'E., 11 km NW of Broken Hill; Acacia till 1890; PO 1890; quarry (limestone); school (Acacia

Dam till 1904) 1889–1909; pop. *c.*100 (1890).

Limestone Camp (*Co. Wellington*) 32°53'S. 149°02'E., 29 km NE of Molong.

Limestone Creek (*Co. King*) 34°45'S. 148°52'E., 10 km NW of Yass; farming and grazing; mine (Belle Vale Silver Mine) worked by Roche and Minehan; PO 1927; school (Bendenine till 1935) 1883–1948; telephone 1926; TX 1940; pop. 73 (1911).

Limestone Flat (*Co. Roxburgh*) see Portland.

Limestone Flat (*Co. Wellington*) 32°45'S. 149°44'E., 21 km W. of Rylstone, on Limestone Ck; Meth. C. 1902.

Limestone Plains (*Co. Ashburnham*) see Goonumbla.

Limpinwood (*Co. Rous*) 28°18'S. 153°13'E., 17 km W. of Murwillumbah, on Hopping Dicks Ck; formerly Hopping Jack; settled by Dik Keys (also known as Dick Wood), first land sales 1904; timber and dairying; Bapt. C. 1921; bushfires 1936 and 1952; school 1930, additions 1938 by Dayal Singh, closed 1974; telephone 1912; TX 1925; pop. 132 (1933), 130 (1947), 107 (1954), 104 (1961), 223 (2011).

Linburn (*Co. Phillip*) 32°26'S. 149°43'E., 19 km SE of Gulgong; sheep, farming, mining (manganese and umber); mine (N.H. Lambridge) 1908 and 1939–45; PO 1887; school (Cooyal Diggings till 1881) 1880, new buildings b. 1883 by F. Atkinson, closed 1929; telephone 1913; TX 1918; pop. 185 (1901), 107 (1911), 70 (1933), 51 (1947).

Lincoln (*Co. Lincoln*) 32°26'S. 149°02'E., 16 km NE of Wellington; gold, copper, farming, grazing; mines: Geenobby 1900 and 1922 and Kaiser or Belgium 1875–81 and 1916; PO 1875; telephone 1915; TX 1923; pop. 57 (1911), 51 (1933).

Linden (*Co. Cook*) 33°43'S. 150°30'E., 3 km NE of Woodford, on Bulls Ck; Bluff Bridge 1815–26, then Ravine Bridge, then Seventeen Mile Hollow till 1888; bushfires 1880, 1923, 1944, 1968; FB; observatory d. and b. 1938–48 by Ken Beames; PO 1915, burnt down 1926; railway dam 1884, upgraded 1885, new one b. 1927–29, wall 374 ft (113.9 m) long, sold 1935 to local council; reservoir; RS (Henderson's Platform till 1879) 1874, new station b. 1902 by Charles Palmer; telegraph 1890; telephone 1915; toll-house 1849, demolished 1867; TX (automatic) 1977; water supply 1936; pop. 63 (1901), 20 (1933), 45 (1961), 64 (1964), 281 (2011).

Lindendale (*Co. Rous*) 28°50'S. 153°23'E., 6 km W. of Alstonville, on Marom Ck; fruit; broom factory (Alfred Pratt); school 1890–1956; sugar mill (Porch Bros, bought 1879 by Louis Armbruster and named Enterprise Mill); pop. 82 (1911), 71 (1933), 70 (1947), 93 (1954), 64 (1961).

Lindens Flat (*Co. Northumberland*) see Green Point.

Lindesay View (*Co. Rous*) 28°23'S. 152°53'E., 28 km NW of Kyogle, on Findon Ck; formerly Lindsay View; farming; PO 1933; sawmill (Munro and Lever); telephone 1917; TX 1928–68; pop. 47 (1933), 57 (1954), 73 (1961).

Lindsay Creek (*Co. Buller*) 28°27'S. 152°34'E., 47 km NW of Kyogle, on Tooloom Ck; dairying; butter factory (Lindsay Rural Co-op. Society) b. 1927 by Thackeray and Gallagher, taken over 1929 by Norco Co-op. Ltd; telephone 1927; TX 1928; pop. 61 (1954), 51 (1961).

Lindsay Park (*Co. Camden*) see Wollongong.

Lindsay View (*Co. Rous*) see Lindesay View.

Linns Hill (*Co. Camden*) see Werombi.

Linton (*Co. Bourke*) see Pucawan.

Linton (*Co. Darling*) 30°25'S. 150°54'E., 27 km E. of Barraba; grazing; PO 1927; pop. 21 (1933).

Lintonvale (*Co. Bland*) 34°24'S. 147°38'E., 11 km NE of Temora, on Narraburra Ck.

Linwood (*Co. Gough*) see Lambs Valley.

Linwood (*Co. Northumberland*) see Wickham.

Lionsville (*Co. Drake*) 29°12'S. 152°30'E., 48 km E. of Tenterfield; Lion Township till 1872; almost deserted by 1878, yet village gaz. 1881; timber, goldmining (boom 1871), grazing, dairying; cemetery; fire 1946; lock-up; mines: Garibaldi and Lion; PO 1872–1968; PS; telephone 1917; TX 1923; pop. 53 (1933).

Lion Township (*Co. Drake*) see Lionsville.

Lirambenda (*Co. Monteagle*) 34°05'S. 148°10'E., 21 km S. of Grenfell, on Burrangong Ck; Angl. C. (St Thomas's) 1944, sold 2007; school (Kikiamah till 1934) 1899–1951.

Lisarow (*Co. Northumberland*) 33°23'S. 151°22'E., 6 km NE of Gosford, on Cut Rock Ck; formerly Gum Tree Flat; surveyed by J.H. Laycock, subdivided and lots sold by Excelsior Land, Investment, & Building Co. & Bank Ltd; farming, orchards, poultry; Angl. C. 1924, burnt down 1929, replacement (St John's) b. 1932 by T.H. Pryor, and graveyard, closed; camp trailer factory (Complete Campsite); cemetery (275 graves 1865–2009); Church of Christ; electric light factory (Sylvania Lighting A'asia Pty Ltd); electricity 1938; filtration fabric factory (Albany Felt Pty Ltd), became Albany International Pty Ltd, bought by All Filtration Technologies Aust. Pty Ltd, bought 2013 by Gibbens Group, refurbished and reused 2015; frozen food factory (Sara Lee) 1971; Meth. C. b. 1922 by R.E. Midson, d. by Arthur Lanyon Clark; modular building factory (Timberline Built Smart Homes Pty Ltd); office furniture factory (OFD Pty Ltd) 1977; PO 1909; poultry processing plant (Valley View Poultry Pty Ltd, later Chickadee Foods Pty Ltd); RS (Jenkin's Siding till 1902) 1892, new platform 1911 on new site; sawmill (Jackson & Co.); sawmill and case factory (William Hastings Kirkness) 1914–25; schools: primary 1928 b. by H.E. Milligan, additions 1929 by W. Williams, HS 1980, relocated 1982, Narara 1998; SD Adventist C. 1913; telephone 1914; pop. 160 (1911), 488 (1933), 470 (1947), 543 (1954), 494 (1961), 5,038 (2011).

Lismore (*Co. Rous*) 28°49'S. 153°17'E., 337 km NE of Tamworth, on Wilsons R.; (incl. Albert Park, East Lismore, Girards Hill, Howards Grass, Lismore Heights, North Lismore, South Lismore); settled 1844 by William Wilson, surveyed 1855 by Frederick Septimus Peppercorne, laid out 1856 by Peppercorne, village gaz. 1856, first lots sold 1858, resurveyed and laid out again 1866 by Patrick R. Donaldson, first lots on new site auctioned 1870, designated as chief town of the county, munic. proc. 1879, thrived 1867–83, city proc. 1946, thrived 1961–64, munic. enlarged 1977; port till 1954, orig. timber and beef, then sugar-cane 1860s+, then dairying, bananas, maize, potatoes, pigs, bacon, poultry, eggs, fruit, light engineering, textiles, clothing; aeroplane crash 1938; agric. implement works (D. Townley & Son) estab. 1877 by I.W. Lockett, bought 1886 by D. Townley; ambulance station b. 1933 by William Braid, d. by Frederick Johnson Board, additions 1937 also by Braid and d. by Board, extended 1952 by Hampton and Larsson; Angl. C.: All Saints' (South Lismore) rebuilt 1930 by George Hampton & Son, St Andrew's (b. 1871 by John Stephen Lumley, enlarged 1878, relocated 1904, reused, demolished 1970, new one b. 1905 by F.H. Marshall & Sons, d. by Charles Rosenthal, chancel and transepts added 1914, tower and spire b. 1935 by William Braid, d. by George Herbert Godsell, interior finished 1956), St John's (East Lismore) 1954, closed, sold and reused, St Luke's (North Lismore), St Peter's 1872 (demolished 1971), St Silas's (Albert Park) d. by Louis Reginald Williams; Assemblies of God C.: Christ. Family and City; bacon factories: one b. 1896 by Hicks Bros and Foley Bros Ltd 1936 (d. by Richard Wildridge & Co.); Bapt. C.: Central 1926, replaced 1967, East Lismore 1952, South Lismore b. 1915 by T. Bannerman; Bible Meth. C.; boiling-down works; boot factories: Edward & Co. (bought 1896 by Moorhead, Nesbitt and M'Master), W. Sidaway, Thomas and Sidney; brewery (Richmond River Brewery, estab. by Chynoweth & Co.) 1886–88; brickworks (G.F. Knott); bridges: Colemans Bridge (Dare composite timber truss, b. 1906–8 by Walter Frank Oakes, 297 ft or 90.5 m, extensive repairs 2002, over Leycester Ck), Fawcett Bridge (b. 1882–84 by G.H. Royce & Co., d. by J.H. Daniels, 513 ft or 156.4 m, incl. opening span, additions and alterations 1906 by Walter Frank Oakes, re-decked 1940 by

H.W. Stevenson, over Wilsons R.), Keen Street Bridge (b. 1888 by David Rankin, another span added by Rankin in 1900, over Browns Ck), Simes Bridge (over Wilsons R.), Spinks Bridge (d. and b. 1910 by Walter Frank Oakes, over Browns Ck), Robert White Bridge (b. 1926, destroyed 1956, replaced 1963, over Leycester Ck), Wilson Street Bridge (b. 2016, over Hollingworth Ck); broom factory (Jubilee Broom Co.) estab. 1935 by W.R. Brown and W. Crehan; bubonic plague (man died) 1905; bushfire 1905; butter factories: Foley Bros Ltd (b. 1897 at South Lismore by Henry F. Mood, d. by B.W. Foley, additions for cheese-making 1916, taken over 1958 by Norco Co-op. Ltd), NSW Creamery Butter Co. Ltd (b. 1895 at South Lismore by Brown and Jolly), North Coast Fresh Food & Cold Storage Co-op. Co. Ltd 1902 (became North Coast Co-op. Ltd in 1904, then Norco Co-op. Ltd in 1926, new factory b. 1931 by Daniel Gallagher); CAE (Northern Rivers) 1971–89; canvas factory (George Pickers & Co.) 1940; casein factory (Milk Industries Ltd) 1927; carriage-works: J.W. Denny & Son (fire 1925), Frederick & Co., Richmond River Pioneer Coachbuilding Factory (estab. 1877 by William Klein, taken over by B. Klein, taken over by A. Klein); cemetery (pioneer, 368 graves, headstones razed or relocated 1980 by local council) 1880; CH (incl. lock-up) b. 1861 by J. Spithill, (second) b. 1878 by John Perry, additions 1880, (third) b. 1885 by T. and J. Fanning, d. by James Johnstone Barnet, alterations 1888 by Phospical and West, additions, alterations and repairs 1897 by W. Leben, (fourth) 1992, extended 1995, refurbished 2010 by Bennett Constructions Pty Ltd; cheese factory (Norco Co-op. Ltd) 1956–2000; children's home (North Coast) 1921, new building 1936; Christ. City C. (River City); Christadelphian C. (formerly Angl.); Church of Christ b. 1905 by E. and C. Saville and J. and W. Wotherspoon, d. by Robert Robertson Jack, closed 1919, burnt down, replacement b. 1923 by Brown and Jolly, d. by Frederick Johnson Board, closed, sold and reused; clothing factories: Alpha Knitwear Pty Ltd 1944 (extensions b. 1947 by W.J. Harbour, d. by R. Lindsay-Little, closed 1952) and J. Armison & Sons; concrete pipe works (Hume Pipe Co. Aust. Ltd) 1932; concrete plant (M.J. O'Meara); confectionery factory (H. De Montmorency) 1907, new one 1922; cordial factories: Christian Balzer 1875 (damaged 1888), W.E. Bryant, W.M. Glynn (b. by McIntosh and Best), W. Hunter 1947, W.I. Lane 1912, Lismore Cordials Ltd (amalgamation of Balzer's, Bryant's and Glynn's) 1929, Rogers & Co. (taken over 1919 by B. Bushby and W. Balzer), Tickle & Son (bought 1887 by A.C. Lewis); creamery (NSW Creamery Butter Co. Ltd) b. 1897 at South Lismore by Brown and Jolly, taken over by Lismore Co-op. Dairy Co. Ltd, taken over by Norco Co-op. Ltd; dengue fever 1926 and 1942; diphtheria 1918 and 1929; electricity 1912; engineering works: Hope & Co. and McKee Engineering Pty Ltd 1938; FB 1883 (alterations 1907 to old station, demolished 1910, new one b. 1910 by Brown and Jolly, additions 1914 d. by Alfred Spain, Thomas Frame Cosh and Robert Smith Dods); fibrous plaster works: Sam Collins 1924 (in former joinery), A.V. Goldsmith, Granger Bros and Eyears Ltd, New State, Young and Duncan; fires 1901, 1913, 1924, 1930, 1931, 1943, 1952; floods 1861, 1864, 1870, 1887, 1889, 1890, 1892, 1893, 1921, 1929, 1931, 1945, 1948, 1950, 1954, 1956, 1962, 1963, 1965, 1967, 1972, 1974, 1975, 1976, 1978, 1984, 1987, 1989, 2001, 2005, 2009, 2013, 2016, 2017; flour mill (Jeffs Bros Lismore Pty Ltd) 1940, in former sawmill; foundries: McKee's and Richmond Foundry & Engineering Works (J.A. O'Flynn), damaged 1888; furniture factories: Beohm and Barham 1914, Hancock and Hammond, Nesbitt McMaster & Co., burnt down 1899, A.G. Robertson Ltd, burnt down 1914, W.T. Routledge, Carl Small 1946, Francis Strong, fire 1910; gales 1928, 1930, 2015; gaol, additions 1888 by Brown and Jolly, additions and alterations 1896 by Patrick Farrelly; gastroenteritis epidemic

1954; gasworks (incl. 8 retorts) b. 1886–88 by P.M. Ryan, new retorts 1915, works rebuilt 1934 by James Hurll & Co. Ltd; Gospel C. (East Lismore); gristing mill (Norco Co-op. Ltd) 1945; hailstorms 1908, 1943, 2007, 2017; heatwave 1940; home furnishings factory (Jeldi Pty Ltd) 1947, fire 1950; hospital (cottage) b. 1883 by John Stephen Lumley, extended 1886, morgue b. 1916 by Brown and Jolly, hospital additions 1920 also by Brown and Jolly, isolation block b. 1928 by George Hampton & Son, d. by Dominic Victor Ghiggino, additions and alterations 1936 by Stafford Building Co. Ltd, d. by Cobden Parkes, additions 1954 by R. & B. Constructions Pty Ltd, additions 1959, 1967, 1970, 1985, 1988–95, additions 2008 by Bennett Constructions Pty Ltd, additions 2010 by National Buildplan Group, damaged 2015, additions 2016; ice-cream factories: A.A. Hancock, Norco Co-op. Ltd 1950 (upgraded 2003 and 2008), Pioneer (M.A. Newton & Co. Ltd); Islamic C.; Jehovah's Witnesses C.; joineries: A.K. Barnes (fire 1943), Boehm and Barham (incl. mattress factory) 1914, Roy James and Robert A. Campbell 1936, George Hampton & Son, Lardner and James (burnt down 1951), W. Leben 1907, Lismore Steam Sash & Door Factory (Brown & Jolly Ltd, reused 1924), Robb & Brown Pty Ltd, Diyal Singh & Son, W. Taylor (burnt down 1951), W. Wagner 1923; landslips 1927 and 1954; levees: concrete 2005 and South Lismore 1972; Lutheran C. (Good News), in former Angl. C.; mattress factories: Dailhou and Watson, Nicholson and Wilson 1913, Charles Henry Riley 1924, Strong Bros, burnt down 1910, W.E. Wotherspoon; measles epidemics 1931 and 1936; Meth. C. (Lismore Heights) 1959; monumental stone works: A. Beckinsale & Co., H. Edwards, M. Jones 1884, Roberts and Davis; PO: East Lismore 1927, Lismore 1859 (new one b. 1898 by Sanbrook Bros, d. by Walter Liberty Vernon, additions 1900 by Patrick Farrelly), Lismore Heights 1947, South Lismore 1909; police barracks b. 1897 by Patrick Farrelly; pound (stock) 1884; POW control centre 1944; powerhouse b. 1927 by Brown and Jolly, d. by Valentine Lee Miller, new one (South Lismore) b. 1932 by Kennedy and Bird, extended 1936 by Dayal Singh; Presb. C.: St David's (b. 1928 by G.C. Parmenter) and St Paul's (b. 1882 by Robert McKenzie, d. by MacMaster, demolished 1921, new one b. 1908 by George Brown, d. by Frederick Johnson Board, enlargement and renovations 1938 by John Mackinnon, d. by Finlay Munro); PS: Lismore (incl. lock-up) b. 1896 by Patrick Farrelly, additions 1907 by Frank Vernon, renovations and repairs 1918 by A. Montgomery, new one b. 1935 by Percy Albert Nott, renovations 1942, new one 2008, North Lismore 1897–1935, South Lismore b. 1911 by S.K. Farrelly, closed 1935; punt b. 1877 by W. Yabsley, replaced 1885; 5 quarries; railway bridge (steel truss) b. 1892 by Crosbie and Marquand, over Leycester Ck; railway engine shed b. 1893 by Alexander Hamilton Scouller, extended 1895; railway turntable, 40 ft (12.2 m), replaced 1903, 50 ft (15.2 m); reservoirs: 100,000 gal. (454.6 kl), 150,000 gal. (681.9 kl) b. 1936 by A. Hood, 250,000 gal. (1,136.5 kl), 500,000 gal. (2,273 kl), 750,000 gal. (3,409.5 kl), 1,000,000 gal. (4,546 kl) b. 1932 by State Monier Pipe Works, 1,250,000 gal. (5,682.5 kl); rifle range b. 1906 by R. Hood; Rom. Cath. C.: St Carthage's (b. 1877 by John Curtain and Patrick Ryan, new one b. 1904–7 d. by Herbert Edmund Wardell and George Denning, tower added 1911, church altered and modernised 1975–86, damaged 2007, re-roofed 2011), Holy Family (North Lismore) b. 1941 by James Hall Starkey, d. by Austin McKay, Our Lady Help of Christians (South Lismore) b. 1918 by J.J. Moss, d. by Albert Edmund Bates; RS: Lismore 1894, station b. by Alexander Hamilton Scouller, closed 2004 and North Lismore 1907–75; sale-yards estab. 1899 by E.W. Mackay, new yards b. 1927 by J.J. Moss & Son; Salv. Army C. b. 1908 by T.E. Jarman, dismantled, new one b. 1935 by Wilson; sawmills: George Adkins 1902, J.

Breckenridge, Brown & Jolly (Sawmills) Pty Ltd, George Frederick Cottee (boy killed 1891), James Donough 1882 (later bought by Robert Knight), Henry Garrard 1855, John E. Glasgow (b. by Robert Knight, boiler explosion 1880 killed man, sawmill bought 1888 by Cottee and Sharpe, sold 1908 to Alfred R. Knowles), Hurford's, B. Muldoon (man killed 1923), Oxenford's 1905 (taken over by Richmond River Co., burnt down 1909), Pioneer Canadian Sawmills (Charles Dorrough) 1882, burnt down 1905, Joseph Reid (South Lismore), reused, Slade Bros & Co. Pty Ltd, E.J. Smith, Lemuel Griggs Snow 1881, Terania Creek (estab. 1904 by Edwin Roach, dismantled and removed 1911), Twickenham Estate, West and Sharpe; scarlet fever 1913; schools: Albert Park (North Lismore till 1958) 1942, additions 1959 and 2011, East Lismore (Lismore since 1970) b. 1942 by F.C. Powell, Lismore 1862 (new one b. 1868 by Lemuel Griggs Snow, re-roofed and renovated 1879 by Bannantyne and Alexander, new one b. 1885 by Fanning Bros, d. by William Edmund Kemp, additions 1893 by Patrick Farrelly, rebuilt 1901 by Brown and Jolly, additions 1903 by C.B. Smith, extended 1911 by Brown and Jolly, closed 1941, reused as Northern Rivers CAE), Lismore HS 1920 (additions 1961, new HS b. 1969, renamed Rivers Secondary College in 2015), Lismore Heights 1956 (additions 1960 and 1970), Richmond River HS 1958 (additions 1962, 1966, 1972, 1979, fire damage restoration 1983, renamed Rivers Secondary College in 2015), South Lismore 1915 (b. by Christopher W. Griffin, additions 1921, rebuilt 1978 by Alex Roberts Constructions Pty Ltd), Wyrallah Road 1955 b. by Frank Bennett (additions by Bennett Constructions Pty Ltd); SD Adventist C. 1926, new one on new site; sewerage 1905, extended to North and South Lismore 1931, new pumping station b. 1940 by W. Braid, augmentation 1957, 1959, 1961, 1997; soap-works (Magnolia) estab. 1908 by Henry Field, burnt down 1909; spring works (Charles Hope Ltd), relocated 1937; steel fabrication works (Sydney, Hacking & Co.); storms 1888, 1927, 1937, 2002; streets gas lit 1888 and electric lit 1927; sugar mills: Cadzow (James Baillie) 1871, Colonial Sugar Co., Robert McKenzie, Muldoon's, Richmond River Sugar Co.; tannery (Edwards & Co.) b. 1894 by H. Tulk; TC 1928, additions 1964, became a campus of North Coast Institute in 1992; teachers' college 1970; telegraph 1875; telephone: East Lismore 1947, Lismore Heights 1947, North Lismore 1913, South Lismore 1906; TX 1898, new building b. 1939 by Gaskin Bros, automatic 1957; typhoid 1892, 1901, 1953; Unit. C. (orig. Meth.) b. 1909 by R. Hughes, d. by Frederick Johnson Board; univ. (Southern Cross) 1994, previously Northern Rivers Campus of Univ. of New England 1989–93; vulcanising works (Acme, Arthur Walmsley) 1926, enlarged 1927, new works 1930; water supply 1888, augmentation 1900, 1909, 1936, 1956, 1987; Wes. Meth. C. 1877, replaced 1881 by G. Finlay; wharves: one b. 1880 by Taylor and Johnston (shed added 1885 by C. Hodgson), one b. 1887 by John Walsh, one b. 1891 by Kerle and Kerle, one rebuilt 1928 by Walter Frank Oakes; whooping cough epidemics 1934 and 1936; wire fence factory (O.P. Sims), burnt down 1927; wire works (Jasen) estab. 1946 by A.E. Jacobsen; pop. 275 (1870), 93 (1871), *c.*500 (1879), 992 (1881), 2,925 (1891), *c.*3,100 (1895), 4,542 (1901), 7,609 (1911), 7,953 (1913), 8,700 (1921), 11,806 (1933), *c.*14,000 (1941), 15,214 (1947), 17,372 (1954), 18,935 (1961), 19,757 (1966), 20,901 (1971), 22,082 (1976), 24,033 (1981), 24,896 (1986), 27,246 (1991), 28,380 (1996), 27,358 (2001), 27,069 (2006), 27,474 (2011).

Lismore Heights (*Co. Rous*) see Lismore.

Lissington Station (*Co. Culgoa*) 29°30'S. 146°19'E., 74 km NE of Bourke; pop. 22 (1933).

Liston (*Co. Buller*) 28°38'S. 152°06'E., 47 km N. of Tenterfield; village gaz. 1878; mining and grazing; airfield; Angl. C. (St John's) 1910; cheese factories: Tenterfield Dairy Co., and Wilson and Purkiss (removed from

Steinbrook); Chinese joss house; PO 1916; school (Amosfield till 1953) 1876–1968; telephone 1914; TX 1918, automatic 1976; pop. 130 (1933), 122 (1947), 130 (1954), 85 (1961), 350 (2011).

Lithgow (*Co. Cook*) 33°29'S. 150°09'E., 53 km E. of Bathurst, on Farmers Ck; (incl. Bowenfels, Chifley, Cobar Park formerly Cobar Paddock, Cooerwull subdivided 1908–18, Corney Town, Eskbank Estate sold 1880 by Thomas Brown to James Rutherford, sold 1892 to William Sandford, subdivided 1897, Extension Estate orig. Brown's Paddock subdivided 1908, Hermitage Flat subdivided 1895, Littleton, McKellars Park formerly McKellars Paddock, Methven Estate, Morts Estate, North Lithgow, Pottery Estate, Robson, Sheedys Gully, South Littleton, State Mine Gully, Vale of Clwydd); Eskbank till 1879; settled 1824 by Andrew Brown, founded by Thomas Brown, thrived 1870s–80s, surveyed 1888 by William Mylecharane, munic. proc. 1889, city proc. 1945, City of Greater Lithgow proc. 1977; agric., grazing, mining (coal disc. 1841 by Thomas Brown) 1869–1985, coke-making, heavy industry, now limited manufacturing, potatoes, orchards; airfield (3 km E.) d. by J.F. Harrison; ambulance station b. 1921 by N.R. Morris, d. by H.P. Morris, additions 1926 by William Alfred Isley, d. by N.R. Morris, new ones 1942 and 1985; Angl. C. (St Paul's) b. 1880 by W. Ralston, d. by Edmund Thomas Blacket, demolished, new one b. 1924 by Lawrence Pither, d. by Sir Charles Rosenthal and Day; anti-aircraft batteries and command posts (World War II) at Bowenfels and on Scenic Hill; Assemblies of God C. (Christ. Life); Bapt. C. b. 1912 by James Short and Robert Leslie, d. by J.L. Morris & Son; bicycle works (G.H. Yates) 1899; boot factory (A.S. Nicolle); box factory (Lithgow Box Service) 1947; breweries: Burton Brewery (estab. by Richard Jeffrey Inch as Eskbank Brewery) 1878–1917, Louis Stahl, Young's, razed; brickworks: Lithgow Valley Colliery Co. Ltd (Coalex Pty Ltd) 1877–1946, Newbold Silica Fire-Brick Co. Ltd (Sandford's Silica Brickworks till 1912, moved to Mayfield 1918) 1908–18, Scenic Brickworks (or Vale of Clwydd Brickworks, closed 1931, reopened 1937 by Lithgow Brickworks Ltd) 1912–77; bushfires 1905, 1909, 1929, 1936, 1945, 1951, 2013; carriage-works: N. and J. Macarthur and J. Walters & Son, sold 1915 to Leahey Bros; cement tile works (Alfred Norman Wyld and W. Rogers) 1949; cemetery (8,689 graves *c.*1870+); CH (incl. lock-up) b. 1879 by Hardy and Willis, d. by James Johnstone Barnet, additions 1881 by W.C. Drewett, additions and remodelling 1910 by Gerald Dalton Fetherston, d. by Walter Liberty Vernon, alterations and repairs to lock-up 1910 by A. Stephens, court-house renovated 1990; Christ. Brethren Assemblies C. (Bible); clothing factories: Berlei Ltd 1946–52, Jefson's, N. Malouf 1945–52; coke-works (80 ovens) b. 1910–13, later extended to 95 ovens; collieries: Bowenfels 1874, Cobar Tunnel or Great Cobar Copperworks Colliery (bought 1921 from Great Cobar Ltd by Hoskins Iron & Steel Co. Ltd and renamed Smelting Works Colliery, flooded 1928 and 1964) 1899–1964, Cooerwull 1870, Donnybrook 1921–61, Eskbank No. 1 (estab. 1869 by Thomas Brown, closed, reopened by James Rutherford and renamed Ironworks Colliery in 1881, closed 1931), Eskbank No. 2 (Thomas Brown) 1873–1900, Esk Creek (Andrew Brown) 1838, Fairview 1925, Hermitage No. 1 (estab. 1868 by J.J. Poole, Nathaniel Woolley and Robert Anderson, acquired 1873 by Bowenfels Coal Mining & Coppersmelting Co. and renamed Bowenfels Colliery, absorbed 1884 by Hermitage No. 2 Colliery), Hermitage No. 2 (closed 1986, demolished 1987), Ironworks Tunnel (flooded 1928, razed) 1881–1931, Lithgow Valley (estab. 1872 by Patrick Higgins et al., fire killed 3 men and blast killed 5 men in 1886, closed), Methven (Andrew Brown) 1904, State Coal Mine (estab. 1916–21 as Railway Coal Mine, peaked 1929, renamed 1932, fires 1928 and 1941, fire 1953 killed 21 pit ponies, cross measure drift 1953, colliery flooded and closed 1964, largely demolished, partly reused), Steelworks (Charles Hoskins) 1927–57, Tankersley (also known as Bowenfels, estab. 1873 by Campbell Mitchell), Vale of Clwydd (estab. 1874 by John Garsed and Thomas Saywell, fire 1883, man killed 1897, flooded 1899, fire 1899, new screens 1899, man killed 1920, closed 1930–34, major subsidence 1947, flooded 1950, demolished), Zig Zag 1883 (operated by Saywell Collieries Ltd, incl. 20 coke-ovens b. 1885, man killed 1916, 2 killed 1921, bath-house b. 1927 by Lewis and Tyler) 1883–1931; concrete products plant (G. Manners, sold 1953 to E. Maulsbury); copper smelters: Eagle (Constable's) 1876, Emu (Thomas Saywell), Esk Smelting Co. (estab. by Thomas Brown, taken over by Lewis Lloyd, taken over 1912 by Mouramba Copper Co.) 1874–1919, Great Cobar Mining Co. 1896–1911, Vale of Clwydd b. 1876, operated 1878, razed; cordial factories: N. and F. Ashelford, Sharpe Bros (estab. by John Sharpe and Fred Killick) 1917–39, James Summons, S.P. Thornton (bought by Thomas Young & Co., new factory b. 1909 by James Short and Robert Leslie, d. by Kenny); dam b. 1907 by F.J. Carson, 87 ft (26.5 m) high, wall raised 1915 by 3 ft (0.9 m); diphtheria 1896, 1912, 1914, 1924, 1937, 1939 (5 died); dust storms 1909 and 1923; earth tremors 1886, 1902, 1907, 1947; electricity 1922; 2 FB (station b. 1898 by Crowe, demolished 1915, replaced (Cook Street) 1915, Rabaul Street one 1956); fires 1880, 1909, 1912, 1919, 1924, 1926; flood 1842; flour mill (water powered) b. 1837 by William Brown for Andrew Brown at Cooerwull, destroyed and rebuilt 1842, new mill (steam) 1851, enlarged and also used as woollen mill from 1857, largely rebuilt and updated 1869–76, flour milling ceased 1882, new engine and looms 1899, new boiler 1906, woollen mill acquired by Braemar Woollen Mills Pty Ltd, closed 1973, derelict; foundry and engineering works (Great Western) estab. 1907 by George Coleman Morris, closed 1936; Foursquare Gospel C.; gales 1923, 1928, 1935; galvanising and corrugating works 1894; gastroenteritis epidemics 1921 (2 infants died) and 1930 (10 infants died); gasworks b. 1893 by John Meeks for local council, new gasholder b. 1914 by James Hurll & Co. Ltd, fire 1948, new gasholder 1951, site razed; Gospel C.; hailstorms 1932 and 1948; heatwave 1905; home furnishings factories: Gladys Grieve Pty Ltd 1947 and Jeldi Pty Ltd 1947, burnt down 1950; hospital b. 1896 by E. Cook, d. by John Bede Barlow, additions 1908 by James Short and Robert Leslie, additions 1925 by N.R. Morris, additions 1935 by William Lishman Jemison, rebuilt 1944, new one 1998; ice works (M. Lynam) 1917, in old converted stadium; iron and steelworks: blast furnace (Esk Bank Iron Works Co.) b. 1875 by Enoch Hughes, foundry 1876, production began 1878, works bought 1881 by James Rutherford, closed 1882 and blast furnace demolished 1884, site bought 1892 by William Sandford who b. open-hearth steel furnace there in 1900, works acquired 1901 by William Sandford Ltd, second steel furnace 1906, new blast furnace 1907, works closed 1907, taken over 1908 by G. & C. Hoskins Ltd, strike 1911–12, second blast furnace 1913, steelworks rebuilt by 1915, became Hoskins Iron & Steel Co. Ltd in 1920, strike 1927, taken over 1928 by Aust. Iron & Steel Ltd, blast furnaces closed 1928, demolished 1929, steelworks closed 1931, dismantled 1931–33, chimney demolished 1945, site largely razed; Jehovah's Witnesses C.; joinery (Absolute Joinery); measles epidemics 1910, 1925, 1954; meat works (Thomas Sutcliffe Mort) 1873–80, reused as brewery 1880–88, reused as cattle abattoir 1888–89, reused as Inch's Brewery (Lithgow Burton Brewing Co.) 1889, closed, derelict, demolished 1913; 2 Meth. C. (1902 and 1921); mine creep 1921; miners' strikes 1879, 1889, 1890, 1895, 1899, 1908, 1909, 1910, 1911–12, 1917, 1920, 1915, 1930, 1942, 1944, 1947, 1949, 1950; mines rescue station (Western) 1927, new one b. 1978 by J.J. Cordukes, d. by Figgis & Jefferson Pty Ltd, additions 1978 by Kell & Rigby Pty Ltd, d. by Colin Gulson; monumental stone works

(Bowenfels); PO: Bowenfels 1866, Cooerwull 1927, Lithgow 1875, new one b. 1909 by Gerald Dalton Fetherston, Littleton 1941, North Lithgow 1947, Vale of Clwydd 1883–1952; pottery (Lithgow Valley Colliery Co.) 1876–96, reopened 1905 by Edward Arthur Brownfield, closed 1907, though pipes made till works dismantled in 1946, largely demolished 1981, remainder reused by Cameron and Colleen Williams; pound (stock) 1886, at Bowenfels; power station (Department of Railways) b. 1926–29, fire 1932, major fire and explosion 1949, taken over 1953 by Electricity Commission, razed; Presb. C.: Bowenfels 1843, additions 1854, Lithgow (b. 1874 by Andrew Brown as a school, reused as a Union C. 1875–1922, then Presb. C. from 1923), Methven Street b. 1922, St Mary's (Eskbank) b. 1880 by George Donald, closed and reused 1928; Prim. Meth. C. 1880, re-roofed and renovated 1898, closed, reused; PS 1875, new one b. 1911 by A. Stephens, new one 1993; rabbit freezing works (Western) 1916; railway barracks 1881, new barracks b. 1915 by James Short and Robert Leslie, new barracks 1987; railway coal stage 1916; railway engine shed 1869, new one b. 1887 by J.G. Gatty; railway round-house 1924, extended 1927; railway turntable, 60 ft (18.3 m), new one 1924, 75 ft (22.9 m), new one 1929, 90 ft (27.4 m); railway viaducts: 3 arch stone one b. by Patrick Higgins and 7 arch stone one b. 1871 by Patrick Higgins, d. by John Whitton, replaced 1920 with 6 arch brick one, over Farmers Ck; reservoirs (incl. one b. 1939); rifle range (small arms factory); riots 1911 and 1932; Rom. Cath. C.: Our Lady of Fatima (b. 1953, at Littleton, reused 1966), St Patrick's (b. 1878–80 by Everson, d. by Edward Gell, new one b. 1920 by J. Sweetman, d. by William Alfred Isley, damaged 1928, demolished 1976, replaced 1977), St Francis Xavier's (Bowenfels) 1966; RS: Bowenfels 1869 (station b. by W. and G. Wakeford, d. by John Clifton, man killed 1889, closed 1974, station reused), Cooerwull 1941–74, Eskbank 1874 (station b. by W. Newey), Lithgow 1877 (new station b. 1891 by Jack and Slatyer, station relocated 1925); Salv. Army C. 1905, new one 1924; sawmills: Anderson Bros, V.H. Browne, Coates Bros, Eskbank (William Slattery), Lithgow Valley (W. Wilson), J.H. Pippard (incl. joinery); scarlet fever 1912, 1915, 1932, 1939; schools: Cooerwull 1867 (new one b. 1873, Main Camp till 1874, replacement b. 1907 by E. and A.H. Chapman, additions 1916, 1922, 1924, new building b. 1954 by W. Brown, additions 1977 and 2010), Lithgow primary 1875 (Esk Bank till 1895, new one b. 1879, additions 1884, 1885, 1893, repairs 1898 by R. Harper, additions 1908 by W.A. M'Lean, additions 1909 by George William Brewer, additions 1914 by James Short and Robert Leslie, additions 1916 and 1924, additions 1928 by Baglee), Lithgow HS 1938 (additions 1960, 1962, 1972, 1974, 1988, 1994); SD Adventist C. b. 1924 by Mitchell and Behrens; sewerage 1912, augmentation 1987; small arms factory b. 1910–12 by Jones and Allman, d. by George John Oakeshott, enlarged 1916, fire 1920, enlarged 1923–30 and 1938–39, strike 1941, enlarged 1941–43, privatised 1989, now owned by Thales Aust. Ltd; snowstorms 1900 (and avalanche at Hermitage Flat), 1910, 1914; soap-works (Abbey, Joseph Ellis Williams) 1885; spinning mill (Bonds Industries Ltd) 1967–75; squall 1908; stone crushing plant 1923; storms 1905, 1936, 1939, 2018; streets gas lit 1893, electric lit 1922, lights installed by Ramsay Sharpe & Co.; TC 1902 d. by Cyril Blacket, new one 1926 d. by Gorrie McLeish Blair, additions 1985, became a campus of Western Institute in 1992, additions 2000; telegraph: Bowenfels 1877 (office d. by Edward Gell) and Lithgow 1894–1915; telephone: Cooerwull 1928, Littleton 1941, Vale of Clwydd 1914; TX 1897, automatic 1954; typhoid 1889, 1895, 1904, 1905 (boy died), 1907, 1911, 1912, 1920 (3 died), 1924; Unit. C. (Guilford Hoskins Memorial, orig. Presb.) b. 1920–28 by J. Halliwell, d. by John Barr; vulcanising works (Alf Wray); water supply scheme estab. 1890–95 by Kerr and Cronin, augmentation 1986;

Wes. Meth. C. b. 1888 by Mitchell, d. by J.L. Morris; pop. 2,112 (1881), *c*.3,500 (1888), *c*.4,000 (1889), 3,865 (1891), *c*.3,750 (1895), 5,514 (1901), 7,897 (1911), *c*.18,000 (1919–29), 13,444 (1933), 14,461 (1947), 15,128 (1954), 14,286 (1961), 13,165 (1966), 13,135 (1971), 12,703 (1976), 12,793 (1981), 12,369 (1986), 11,968 (1991), 11,441 (1996), 11,033 (2001), 11,298 (2006), 11,143 (2011). (See also South Bowenfels and Oaky Park.)

Little Back Creek (*Co. Rous*) 28°37'S. 153°03'E., 4 km E. of Kyogle.

Little Bago (*Co. Wynyard*) see Lower Bago.

Little Bendigo (*Co. Evelyn*) 29°39'S. 141°54'E., 255 km NW of Wilcannia, PO 1895–96.

Little Billabong (*Co. Goulburn*) 35°35'S. 147°32'E., 24 km NE of Holbrook, on Little Billabong Ck; settled 1848 by Thomas Mitchell; gold, tobacco, farming, grazing; Angl. C. (St Paul's) 1876, ruined, restored 1915 and rededicated as St Thomas's, closed 1929, sold 1948, burnt down 1952; bushfire 1952; cemetery 1872; PO 1874; Presb. C. 1901; TX (automatic); pop. 188 (1901), 209 (1933), 76 (1947), 101 (1954), 84 (1961), 464 (2006), 375 (2011).

Little Bombay (*Co. Murray*) 35°25'S. 149° 42'E., 10 km W. of Braidwood; farming; PO 1927.

Little Burney (*Co. St Vincent*) 35°17'S. 149°53'E., 20 km NE of Braidwood, on Eastlea Ck; mine (Mongarlowe Lead Prospect).

Little Caragabal (*Co. Gipps*) see Caragabal.

Little Dingo (*Co. Macquarie*) see Wherrol Flat.

Little Forest (*Co. Bathurst*) 33°08'S. 149°22'E., 30 km NE of Orange.

Little Forest (*Co. Camden*) 34°23'S. 150°32'E., 9 km NE of Mittagong.

Little Forest (*Co. St Vincent*) 35°17'S. 150°21'E., 8 km W. of Milton; school 1906–14; pop. 60 (1911), 20 (1933), 51 (1961), 325 (2011).

Little Forest (*Co. Wellesley*) 36°56'S. 148°36'E., 56 km W. of Bombala.

Little Hartley (*Co. Cook*) 33°34'S. 150°12'E., 5 km NW of Mount Wilson, on Moyne Ck; farming and orchards; convict stockade (Victoria), dismantled 1833, incl. soldiers' barracks; PO 1857; sawmills: Alfred Harris and W. Grady; school 1861–62; squall 1949; telephone 1898; tool handle factory (Little Hartley Timber Co. Ltd); TX 1924–67; pop. 103 (1901), 146 (1933), 85 (1947), 103 (1954), 171 (1961), 536 (2011).

Little Haystack Creek (*Co. Buller*) 28°43'S. 152°31'E., 48 km W. of Kyogle; telephone 1926; TX 1934.

Little Jilliby (*Co. Northumberland*) 33°14'S. 151°22'E., 8 km NW of Wyong, on Little Jilliby Jilliby Ck; orchards; bridge (timber beam) b. 1906 by James Wellings, over Little Jilliby Jilliby Ck; pop. 62 (1933).

Little Meadow (*Co. Argyle*) 34°58'S. 149°24'E., 24 km SE of Gunning; formerly The Little Meadow.

Little Meadow (*Co. Camden*) see Meroo Meadow.

Little Nymboida (*Co. Fitzroy*) 31°10'S. 152°51'E., 28 km NW of Coffs Harbour; farming; PO 1927–31; telephone 1926; TX 1949–50; pop. 21 (1933).

Little Pelican (*Co. Northumberland*) see Marks Point.

Little Plain (*Co. Buller*) 28°21'S. 152°32'E., 54 km NW of Kyogle.

Little Plain (*Co. Gresham*) 29°56'S. 152°01'E., 34 km SE of Glen Innes.

Little Plain (*Co. King*) 34°36'S. 149°22'E., 16 km S. of Crookwell; airfield.

Little Plain (*Co. Murchison*) 29°44'S. 150°57'E., 16 km W. of Inverell; village gaz. 1911; farming; Angl. C. (St Andrew's) 1896–1971, dismantled, and graveyard (89 graves 1886+); cemetery (26 graves 1907+); dust storm 1952; electricity 1937; fire 1917; PO 1890; telephone 1905; TX 1910, automatic 1952; weir; Wes. Meth. C. 1899, moved 1906 to Myall Creek; pop. 261 (1891), 503 (1901), 319 (1911), 195 (1933), 129 (1947), 92 (1954), 88 (1961).

Little Rawdon Island (*Co. Macquarie*) 31°24'S. 152°47'E., 8 km NE of Wauchope, on Rawdon Channel; (incl. Rawdon Villa, an Irish Cath. settlement); formerly Rawdon Island North; bridge, destroyed 1946; flood 1946; punt; Rom. Cath. C. (St Joseph's) 1869, moved to Rawdon Island; pop. 29 (1947).

Little River (*Co. Buccleuch*) 35°20'S. 148°19'E., 9 km E. of Tumut.

Little River (*Co. Gordon*) 32°36'S. 148°39'E., 28 km W. of Wellington.

Little River (*Co. St Vincent*) see Mongarlowe.

Little Run Creek (*Co. Macquarie*) 31°47'S. 152°12'E., 19 km NW of Wingham, on Little Run Ck; telephone 1928; TX 1949–63; pop. 53 (1933).

Little Thredbo (*Co. Wallace*) 36°27'S. 148°27'E., 6 km SE of Perisher Valley, on Little Thredbo R.

Littleton (*Co. Cook*) see Lithgow.

Littleton (*Co. Roxburgh*) 33°26'S. 149°45'E., 16 km E. of Bathurst, on St Anthonys Ck; goldmining (alluvial and reef); electricity 1924; PO 1865–66; school 1866–67; pop. *c.*150 (1866).

Littleton South (*Co. Cook*) see Lithgow.

Little Topar (*Co. Tandora*) 31°47'S. 142°14'E., 75 km E. of Broken Hill; telephone 1930; TX 1930; pop. *c.*5 (1999).

Little Wobby (*Co. Northumberland*) see Patonga.

Live Bird Lead (*Co. Kennedy*) 32°55'S. 148°15'E., 22 km S. of Peak Hill.

Livingstone (*Co. Camden*) see Mittagong.

Livingstone (*Co. Wynyard*) 35°22'S. 147°27'E., 29 km S. of Wagga Wagga, on Livingstone Ck; formerly Livingstone Gully; school 1959–80.

Livingstone Gully (*Co. Wynyard*) see Livingstone.

Llanarth (*Co. Bathurst*) see Bathurst.

Llangothlin (*Co. Clarke*) 30°08'S. 151°41'E., 10 km N. of Guyra, on Gara R.; farming; cemetery; PO 1890, burnt down 1931; rifle range 1918; RS 1884–1975; school 1910–86; telephone 1913; TX 1914–74; Union C. 1887, new one b. 1935 by A.C. Menzies and Atkins; pop. 129 (1901), 144 (1911), 295 (1933), 196 (1947), 173 (1954), 188 (1961).

Llanillo (*Co. Finch*) 29°38'S. 147°51'E., 26 km SW of Lightning Ridge; pop. 29 (1933), 227 (1961).

Lloyd (*Co. Fitzroy*) 30°14'S. 152°49'E., 15 km NE of Dorrigo, on Morora Ck; PO 1917; RS (Mulhearn's Siding till 1941) 1924–62; sawmill (Mulhearn Bros Ltd); school (Lloyd's Siding) 1956–60; pop. 73 (1947), 60 (1954).

Lloyd (*Co. Wynyard*) see Wagga Wagga.

Lloyd's Siding (*Co. Fitzroy*) see Lloyd.

Loadstone (*Co. Rous*) 28°24'S. 152°59'E., 25 km N. of Kyogle, on Gradys Ck; RS 1930–75; sawmill (Banana Growers' Federation Co-op. Ltd); school (Upper Grady's Creek till 1935) 1933–39 and 1957–67; telephone 1941; TX 1941–68; pop. 62 (1933), 101 (1947), 70 (1954), 57 (1961).

Lobbs Hole (*Co. Selwyn*) see Ravine.

Lobs Hole (*Co. Buccleuch*) 35°46'S. 148°21'E., 33 km SE of Batlow; settled *c.*1860, abandoned *c.*1919, subsequently submerged under Talbingo Reservoir; grazing, agric., gold (disc. 1860), copper (disc. 1860) mining 1874–1919, eucalyptus oil in 1920s; dam (Lobbs Hole Copper-mining Co.); mines (copper): Reeckmann and Forsstrom (taken over 1907 by Lobbs Hole Copper-mining Co.), Alpine or Sonoma (taken over 1907 and renamed Central), Coronation; powerhouse, ruined; smelter (copper) 1908, ruined.

Loch Adair (*Co. Stapylton*) 28°38'S. 149°52'E., 47 km W. of Boggabilla; Rom. Cath. C. (St Dominic's) b. 1940 by B.M. Wade & Co. Ltd.

Loch End (*Co. Sandon*) see Guyra.

Lochiel (*Co. Auckland*) 36°56'S. 149°48'E., 6 km W. of Pambula, on Burtons Ck; dairying; butter factories: Box Range (cheese made from 1913, new factory 1930) and Pambula Co-op. Creamery & Dairy Co. Ltd b. 1898 by S. Turner, upgraded 1905–6, additions and alterations 1912 by James Dowling, upgraded 1914–17, additions 1923, remodelled 1928, new one b. 1930, renovated 1937, closed 1974; cement works; PO 1900; sawmill (Gordon's), boiler explosion 1905; school 1882–1970; telephone 1907; TX 1920, automatic 1953; pop. 168 (1901), 164 (1911), 139 (1933), 80 (1947), 71 (1954), 84 (1961), 314 (2011).

Lochinvar (*Co. Northumberland*) 32°42'S. 151°27'E., 11 km W. of Maitland, on Lochinvar Ck; estab. 1840 by Leslie Duguid and Wentworth, laid out 1840 by Edward

James Howse Knapp, sen., first lots sold 1840; maize, potatoes, barley, oats, vineyards; Angl. C. (Holy Trinity) b. 1890–93 by William Henry Noad and James Richardson, d. by Arthur Coe Lee and James Warren Scobie, and graveyard (240 graves 1855+), incl. columbarium; bridge to Luskintyre, b. 1874 by Thomas Smith, new one (steel Pratt trusses) b. 1902–4 by J.F. Carson, 913 ft (278.3 m), over Hunter R.; bushfire 1944; carriage-works (Henry Crebert) 1882, burnt down 1916; cemetery; dam on Lochinvar Ck; earth tremors 1868, 1909, 1931; FB 1964 (new station b. 2014); flood 1874; gales 1865 and 1899; hailstorms 1875 and 1910; heatwave 1866–67; lock-up b. 1869 by Charles Mack; Meth. C. 1919; PO 1854; pound (stock) 1850; PS (incl. lock-up) b. 1886 by Robert Sneesby; reservoir; Rom. Cath. C. 1858, destroyed 1865, replaced 1866, new one (St Patrick's) b. 1914 by A. Howarth, d. by Thomas Wilfred Silk, and graveyard; RS 1860, station relocated 1914; school 1852, new one b. 1878 by John Sanger Brown, new buildings 1958, 1980, 2011; sheep skin products factory (Frank Mortel) 1978; storms 1873, 1879, 1905 (nearly every building damaged); telegraph 1879–1915; TX 1920, automatic 1953; Wes. Meth. C. b. 1864 by Brown, enlarged 1885; winery (St Helena Vineyard), sold 1883 by Philibert Terrier to Thomas A. Onus; pop. 457 (1861), 320 (1871), 85 (1881), 461 (1891), 484 (1901), 401 (1911), 236 (1933), 435 (1947), 233 (1954), 506 (1961), 436 (1971), 445 (1976), 488 (1981), 507 (1986), 444 (1991), 523 (1996), 553 (2001), 502 (2006), 468 (2011).

Lockerbie (*Co. Cunningham*) 32°55'S. 147°09'E., 18 km N. of Condoblin.

Lockhart (*Co. Urana*) 35°13'S. 146°43'E., 55 km S. of Narrandera, on Brookong Ck; orig. Green's Gunyah, then Ferriers till 1898; surveyed 1895, laid out by Walter Alfred Lipscomb and village gaz. 1896, first lots sold 1897, more lots sold 1901, classified by National Trust; wheat, grazing, mixed farming, poultry; agric. implement works (H. Davies & Sons); ambulance station d. by Don Morrow; Angl. C. (St Aidan's) 1910; brickworks (Maryvale, A. Pridmore) 1915; bridge 1990, over Brookong Ck; bushfires 1886, 1892, 1952 (5 houses destroyed); carriage-works (J. Hafner); cemeteries: general (1,336 graves 1891+) 1898 and lawn (254 plots), incl. columbaria; CH 1902, demolished 1970; Christ. Revival Crusade C.; clock tower; cordial factories: Arthur Edward Mitselburg and William Roy Barraclough (Barraclough left partnership 1950) and Joseph Edward Rankins; diphtheria 1934; droughts 1897 and 1914; dust storms 1900, 1914, 1915, 1922, 1930, 1938; electricity supplied 1937 from Burrinjuck; engineering works (Jim F. Guernier); FB 1926 (station b. 1933 by E. Griffin, new one 1981); floods 1931, 1934, 1939, 2010, 2012; foot-bridge 1924, damaged 1931, replaced, new one b. 2013 by Nelmac Pty Ltd; heatwave 1935; horse dip 1937; hospital 1940 d. by W.L. Hurd, renovations 1961, additions 1972, new one 2014; ice works (Harry Davies) 1915; joinery (J. Nolan & Co.); mouse plagues 1917 and 1918; PO 1883, new one b. 1898, new one b. 1906 by Hocking Bros; pound (stock) 1898; powerhouse (Harry Davies) b. 1912 by Mitchell Bros, sold 1934 to local council; Presb. C. (St John's) b. 1907 by E.W. Sharp, d. by Kernot and Campbell; PS 1897, new one b. 1902, demolished 1970, replacement 1971 d. by Robert Bryant; railway turntable, 50 ft (15.2 m), removed 1966; reservoir, 100,000 gal. (454.6 kl); rifle range 1909; Rom. Cath. C. b. 1899 by James Whittaker, relocated 1908, new one (Our Lady of Perpetual Succour, later known as St Mary's) b. 1935 by Stanley Gordon Lipscombe and Len Price, d. by George William Albert Welch; RS 1901, station b. by C. Hardy & Co., refreshment rooms burnt down 1920, rebuilt 1921, station fire 1944, demolished 1987; sale-yards 1947; sawmill (S.J. Grinter), sold 1948; scarlet fever 1933, 1934, 1944; schools: Green's Gunyah 1893, additions 1897 by T.J. Hastings, closed 1918 and Lockhart 1897, repairs 1913 by J. Nolan & Co., additions 1926 by E. Andrews, new one 1963, additions 1970, major upgrade 1996; sewage works; silo 1920; telegraph office b. 1898, new one b. 1906 by Hocking Bros; TX 1907, automatic 1979; typhoid 1906, 1912, 1917; Union C. b. 1897 by Stephen Thorn Van de Water; Unit. C. (Memorial, orig. Meth.) b. 1953 by Jackson and Jones, d. by William C. Brown; water supply 1944; pop. 329 (1901), 1,406 (1911), 1,096 (1933), 898 (1947), 1,074 (1954), 1,018 (1961), 1,023 (1966), 923 (1971), 913 (1976), 923 (1981), 910 (1986), 887 (1991), 882 (1996), 886 (2001), 837 (2006), 800 (2011).

Locksley (*Co. Roxburgh*) 33°31'S. 149°47'E., 22 km N. of Oberon; Dirty Swamp till 1880; mining (gold disc. 1823 by James McBrien), wheat, oats, maize, barley, potatoes, sheep, cattle; brewery (Fish River Valley Brewing) estab. 2010 by Mick and Deb Hoban, in former school; mines: Acme Copper Mine 1888 and 1898, Eagle (Saywell and Constable), Mount Tennyson Molybdenum Prospect 1918–19, Northumberland (Newton Bros); PO 1869–1970; quarry; RS (Lock's Platform till 1879) 1872, closed; school 1957–69, sold 1974 to Hoban, reused; telegraph 1890; telephone 1915; TX 1936–64; pop. 73 (1901), 77 (1933), 73 (1947), 73 (1954), 74 (1961).

Lock's Platform (*Co. Roxburgh*) see Locksley.

Lockwood (*Co. Ashburnham*) 33°28'S. 148°41'E., 11 km N. of Canowindra; farming; PO 1900; quarry; school 1895, new buildings b. 1896 by Henry Hart, closed 1924; pop. 166 (1911), 55 (1933).

Loftus (*Co. Clarendon*) see Junee.

Loftville (*Co. Rous*) 28°50'S. 153°16'E., 4 km S. of Lismore; hort. and farming; airport (Lismore) 1931; PO 1914; telephone 1910; pop. 147 (1933), 59 (1954), 51 (1961), 246 (2011).

Logans Crossing (*Co. Macquarie*) 31°37'S. 152°42'E., 2 km N. of Kendall, on Camden Haven R.; bridge, destroyed 1950, over Camden Haven R.; pop. 344 (2011).

Logie Brae (*Co. Urana*) 35°28'S. 145°30'E., 24 km SW of Jerilderie; Meth. C. 1957; PO 1957; school 1957–65; telephone 1957; TX (automatic) 1956; pop. 166 (2011).

London Bridge (*Co. Clive*) 29°00'S. 152°04'E., 8 km NE of Tenterfield; airfield; army camp (World War II); tank traps (World War II).

London Bridge (*Co. Gresham*) 29°52'S. 152°11'E., 46 km E. of Glen Innes.

London Bridge (*Co. Murray*) 35°31'S. 149°16'E., 17 km S. of Queanbeyan, on Burra Ck; agric.

Lone Fern (*Co. Raleigh*) 30°23'S. 152°59'E., 10 km W. of Sawtell; telephone 1928.

Long Arm (*Co. Darling*) 30°30'S. 150°32'E., 15 km SW of Barraba, on Long Arm Gully; pop. 29 (1933).

Long Beach (*Co. St Vincent*) 35°42'S. 150°14'E., 5 km E. of Batemans Bay, on Batemans Bay; bushfire 1968; FB; quarry; sawmill (Charlie Croaker); pop. 302 (1986), 581 (1991), 699 (1996), 858 (2001), 1,379 (2011).

Long Bridge (*Co. Auckland*) 36°48'S. 149°49'E., 13 km S. of Bega, on Frogs Hollow Ck; dairying; bridge over Frogs Hollow Ck; school (Wanatta) 1891–1910.

Long Creek (*Co. Rous*) 28°23'S. 152°54'E., 28 km N. of Kyogle, on Long Ck; abandoned 1954; sawmill estab. 1928 by Munro and Lever, closed 1954, destroyed; tramway (timber), closed 1947; pop. 93 (1933).

Long Creek (*Co. Wellington*) 32°48'S. 149°33'E., 23 km S. of Mudgee, on Long Ck; orig. Pure Point; goldmining (alluvial and reef); bridge over Long Ck; goldmine (Crystal Palace Co.) 1878, 1880, 1888, 1935, 1937; PO 1856–59; Rom. Cath. C.; telephone 1898; pop. 123 (1901), 73 (1911), 83 (1933), 76 (1947).

Long Flat (*Co. Buccleuch*) 35°36'S. 148°30'E., 32 km E. Batlow.

Long Flat (*Co. Hawes*) 31°38'S. 151°41'E., 49 km NW of Gloucester, on Barnard R.

Long Flat (*Co. Macquarie*) 31°26'S. 152°29'E., 24 km W. of Wauchope, on Hastings R.; farming and dairying; PO 1892, burnt down 1926, rebuilt, burnt down again 1930; Rom. Cath. C. (St Peter's) b. 1931 by Craig; sawmill (Roy McMillan); school 1940, additions 2010; telephone 1913; TX 1916–71; pop. 123 (1911), 160 (1933), 164 (1947), 193 (1954), 125 (1961), 384 (2011).

Long Flat (*Co. St Vincent*) 35°34'S. 149°42'E., 15 km SW of Braidwood, on Back Ck.

Long Flat (*Co. Vernon*) 30°48'S. 152°00'E., 44 km NE of Walcha.

Longford (*Co. Hardinge*) 30°20'S. 151°26'E., 24 km SW of Guyra, on Wattle Gully.

Longford (*Co. Inglis*) 30°46'S. 151°07'E., 37 km E. of Manilla.

Long Gully (*Co. Hardinge*) 30°03'S. 151°11'E., 10 km S. of Tingha; pop. 123 (1933).

Long Gully (*Co. Hume*) see Orelda.

Long Jetty (*Co. Northumberland*) 33°21'S. 151°29'E., 2 km SW of The Entrance, on Tuggerah Lake; floods 1927 and 2015; jetties: Long Jetty 1915–27, destroyed 1927 and replaced, Parry's, Watkins'; Meth. C. b. 1920 by J. Jennett; closed, relocated and reused, renovated, additions 1981; PO 1923; reservoir; Salv. Army C. 1988; SD Adventist C.; telephone 1922; TX 1925, automatic 1961; Unit. C. (Peace Memorial, now The Entrance Long Jetty, orig. Meth.) b. 1964 by C. Metzke, d. by Viwa M. Turner, additions 1984; pop. 390 (1933), 1,581 (1947), 5,114 (2006), 5,797 (2011).

Longleat (*Co. Cook*) see Kurmond.

Long Park (*Co. Urana*) 35°09'S. 146°39'E., 10 km NW of Lockhart; RS 1910–72.

Long Plain (*Co. Bland*) 34°05'S. 147°53'E., 32 km SW of Grenfell.

Long Plain (*Co. Buccleuch*) 35°39'S. 148°35'E., 41 km E. of Batlow.

Long Plain (*Co. Gough*) 29°46'S. 151°13'E., 12 km E. of Inverell; school (Sinclair) 1914–26; pop. 55 (1901), 70 (1933), 77 (1954), 51 (1961).

Long Point (*Co. Buckland*) 31°11'S. 150°27'E., 18 km SE of Curlewis, on Mooki R.

Long Point (*Co. Macquarie*) 31°48'S. 152°39'E., 8 km N. of Harrington.

Long Point (*Co. Northumberland*) 32°34'S. 151°08'E., 4 km W. of Singleton, on Hunter R.; flood 1893; pop. 70 (1901).

Long Point (*Co. Wellington*) 33°02'S. 149°13'E., 30 km N. of Orange; quarry.

Long Point Crossing (*Co. Pottinger*) 31°10'S. 150°26'E., 10 km E. of Curlewis, on Mooki R.

Long Reach (*Co. Argyle*) see Brayton.

Long Reach (*Co. Dudley*) 30°54'S. 153°01'E., 7 km SW of South West Rocks, on Macleay R.; creamery 1897; flood 1870; Prim. Meth. C. 1880; wharf b. 1885 by G. and T. Lawson; pop. 141 (1911).

Longreach (*Co. St Vincent*) 34°52'S. 150°31'E., 7 km W. of Nowra, on Shoalhaven R.

Long Ridge (*Co. Napier*) 31°21'S. 149°34'E., 30 km E. of Coonabarabran; school 1956–70.

Longs Corner (*Co. Ashburnham*) 33°22'S. 148°36'E., 21 km E. of Eugowra, on Mandagery Ck; bridge.

Long Swamp (*Co. Georgiana*) see Arkell.

Long Tom Point (*Co. Sturt*) 34°11'S. 145°08'E., 44 km NE of Hay.

Loomberah (*Co. Parry*) 31°14'S. 151°01'E., 18 km SE of Tamworth; farming; Angl. C. (St Luke's) 1964; FB; school 1910–29, new one 1931–74; telephone 1925; pop. 326 (1933), 296 (1947), 348 (1954), 325 (1961), 240 (2006), 488 (2011).

Loowee (*Co. Phillip*) see Lue.

Lords Hill (*Co. Wellesley*) 36°58'S. 149°10'E., 8 km SW of Bombala; school 1883–93.

Lorn (*Co. Durham*) 32°44'S. 151°34'E., 1 km N. of Maitland, on Hunter R.; orig. a private town, first lots sold 1850; bridges over Hunter R.: Belmore Bridge to Maitland (iron lattice girders fabricated by Lloyds, Fosters & Co., Wednesbury, England) erected 1866–69 by Francis Bell, d. by Edward Orpen Moriarty, replaced 1964 in steel and concrete, 643 ft (196 m), and Harry Boyle Bridge to Pitnacree (1,148 ft or 350 m) b. 2010 by Daracon Group; FB (temporary station o. 1910, new one 1912–46); floods 1930 and 1955; levee; Lutheran C. (Our Saviour); school (Nillo) 1920; storm 1915; streets gas lit 1902; typhoid 1908; pop. 289 (1901), 879 (1911), 1,512 (1933), 1,297 (2006), 1,264 (2011).

Lorna Doone (*Co. Selwyn*) see Tumut Pond.

Lorne (*Co. Macquarie*) 31°39'S. 152°37'E., 9 km W. of Kendall, on Camden Haven R.; farming and dairying; Angl. C. 1933; bridge (Citizens Bridge) over Camden Haven R.; PO 1906; Presb. C. 1927; sawmills: Heron's Creek

Timber Mills Ltd, and J. and R. Longworth 1937; school (Upper Camden Haven till 1918) 1910–47 and 1957–75; telephone 1914; tramway (timber) to Kendall 1913–32; TX 1923, automatic 1974; Union C.; wharf 1921; pop. 261 (1911), 354 (1933), 328 (1947), 290 (1954), 209 (1961), 395 (2006), 271 (2011).

Lorne (*Co. Macquarie*) see also Upsalls Creek.

Lorraine (*Co. Kennedy*) 32°33'S. 147°20'E., 53 km NW of Trundle.

Lostock (*Co. Durham*) 32°20' S. 151°28'E., 29 km W. of Dungog, on Paterson R., Upper Lostock till 1904; timber, grazing, dairying, butter, cheese, bacon, tobacco, maize, oats, barley, pumpkins; Angl. C. 1847, new one (St John's) b. 1892 by Harry Hailand and William Schmierer, and graveyard (110 graves 1872+); bridge (Spooner Bridge) 1938; bushfire 1952; cheese factory (Herbert Harrington Brown) b. 1897 by B. McKewan; Cong. C.; dam b. 1969–72, 125 ft (38 m), on Paterson R.; PO 1904–71; quarry; school 1880, additions 1908 by J. Head, closed 1978; telephone 1910; TX 1922, automatic 1969; pop. 129 (1901), 169 (1911), 181 (1933), 133 (1947), 116 (1954), 113 (1961), 254 (2006).

Lostock (*Co. Durham*) see also Mount Rivers.

Lost River (*Co. King*) 34°22'S. 149°19'E., 18 km NW of Crookwell, on Stony Ck; diamonds; telephone 1921; TX 1925, automatic 1954.

Lost River (*Co. King*) see also Wheeo North.

Louisa Creek (*Co. Wellington*) see Hargraves.

Louisiana (*Co. Kennedy*) 32°43'S. 147°22'E., 40 km NW of Trundle; telephone 1927; TX 1927, automatic 1955.

Louis Point (*Co. Gresham*) 29°52'S. 152°30'E., 47 km SW of Grafton, on Boyd R.

Louth (*Co. Yanda*) 30°52'S. 145°07'E., 92 km SW of Bourke, on Darling R.; founded by Thomas Andrew Mathews; former river port, wool, fishing; airfield; bond store; bridge (steel and concrete) 1965, 469 ft (143 m), over Darling R.; caterpillar infestation 1890; cemetery 1889; CH 1882, inundated 1890; fire 1956; floods 1890 and 1998; hailstorm 1889; lock-up, inundated 1890; PO 1869, new one b. 1880 by J. Dobbie; Presb. C.; PS 1877, new one b. 1882 by D. Dobbie, new one b. 1890 by L. Cawsey & Sons, closed 1940; punt, ceased 1965, across Darling R.; 2 reservoirs (second one b. 1962); school 1881–1936 and 1958–68, reopened 1978; telegraph 1878, new office b. 1880 by J. Dobbie; TX 1915–89; pop. 140 (1891), 105 (1901), 93 (1911), 61 (1933), 96 (1947), 92 (1954), 213 (1961), 102 (2006).

Louth Park (*Co. Northumberland*) 32°45'S. 151°34'E., 2 km W. of East Maitland, on Wallis Ck; (incl. Dagworth); boiling-down works (Dagworth) estab. by Daniel Burgess, closed and sold 1899; bridges over Wallis Ck: Dagworth Bridge and Yarrabong Bridge; bushfire (Dagworth) 1884; colliery (Maitland Greta, Maitland Mining Co. Pty Ltd); drainage tunnel (agric.) b. 1892 by James Richardson; floods 1864, 1867, 1870, 1876, 1893, 1895, 1904, 1913; hailstorms 1861 and 1875; school (Dagworth) 1853–58; sewerage 1942; storm 1873; tannery (Yarrabong, E. Turner); pop. 195 (1911), 133 (1933), 83 (1947), 62 (1954), 63 (1961), 501 (2011).

Lovedale (*Co. Northumberland*) 32°47'S. 151°21'E., 5 km N. Cessnock, on Black Ck; bridge over Deadmans Ck; cemetery (Glenmore); chocolate factory (Hunter Valley Chocolate Co. Pty Ltd); wineries: Adina Vineyard (Peter and Helen O'Meara), Allandale 1978, Allanmere Wines (estab. 1985 by Newton and Ginny Potter, sold 1996 to Monarch Winemaking Services and renamed First Creek Wines, sold 2001 to Max and Vicki Cooper), Apthorpe Estate (Mark and Sheryl Apthorpe), Bluebush Estate (David McGain), Caldwell Family Vineyards, Capercaillie Wine Co. (estab. 1995 by Alastair and Trish Sutherland when they bought the old Dawson Estate), De Bortoli Wines, Gartelmann Wines Pty Ltd (estab. 1970 by Oliver Shaul, bought 1996 by Jorg and Jan Gartelmann), Lucy's Run Wines (orig. Belbourie) estab. 1998–2002, Saltire Wines 2008, Sandalyn Wilderness Estate 1988 (formerly Lesnik), Tatler Wines (Theo and Spiro Isak) 1998, Wandin Valley Estate (orig. Millstone Vineyard, bought 1991 by James and Philippa Davern); pop. 20 (1933).

Lowanna (*Co. Fitzroy*) 30°13'S. 152°54'E., 20 km NW of Coffs Harbour, on Little Nymboida R.; farming; Angl. C. (St John the Evangelist) 1934; army training centre (World War II) for jungle warfare; bushfire 1936; hailstorm 1937; Meth. C.; PO 1921; RS (3 km W.) 1924–75; sawmills: Lowanna Sawmill Pty Ltd, Mulhearn Bros Ltd, Allen Taylor & Co. Ltd; school 1946, additions 2010; telephone 1917; TX 1917–61; pop. 124 (1933), 174 (1947), 149 (1954), 124 (1961), 323 (2011).

Lower Acacia Creek (*Co. Buller*) 28°25'S. 152°16'E., 74 km N. of Tenterfield, on Acacia Ck; dairying; CH (incl. police station), closed 1936, moved 1938 to Urbenville by J.R. Day; cheese factory 1912; PO 1911–71; school 1957–61; telephone 1914; TX 1923; pop. 60 (1933), 83 (1947).

Lower Araluen (*Co. St Vincent*) 35°42'S. 149°51'E., 28 km S. of Braidwood, on Araluen Ck; flood 1860; mine (Mount Waddell Gold Mine) operated 1915–31 by E.R.E. Mining Co. Ltd; telephone 1938; TX 1948.

Lower Bago (*Co. Wynyard*) 35°34'S. 147°58'E., 23 km N. of Tumbarumba, on Bago Ck; formerly Little Bago; FB; telephone 1925; TX (automatic); pop. 33 (1933), 62 (1947).

Lower Belford (*Co. Northumberland*) 32°37'S. 151°18'E., 7 km NW of Branxton; tobacco and farming; FB 1949 (station b. 1977); PO 1909; telephone 1913; TX 1926–69; Wes. Meth. C., closed, reused; pop. 163 (1933), 72 (1947), 148 (1954), 154 (1961), 384 (2011).

Lower Belford (*Co. Northumberland*) see also Kirkton.

Lower Belmore (*Co. Macquarie*) 31°05'S. 152°59'E., 14 km E. of Kempsey, on Belmore R.; telephone 1914; TX 1924–67; wharf b. 1885 by George Parkins.

Lower Booerie (*Co. Rous*) see Booerie.

Lower Boro (*Co. Argyle*) 35°11'S. 149°47'E., 28 km N. of Braidwood, on Millinded Ck; farming and grazing; bushfire 1926; telephone 1918; TX 1928–65; pop. 82 (1933), 246 (2011).

Lower Botobolar (*Co. Phillip*) 32°31'S. 149°46'E., 19 km NE of Mudgee, on Stony Ck; farming; PO 1927–30; quarry (pyrophyllite); telephone 1925; TX 1928; pop. 55 (1933).

Lower Branch (*Co. Hunter*) see Lower Macdonald.

Lower Bucca (*Co. Fitzroy*) 30°09'S. 153°05'E., 12 km W. of Woolgoolga; goldmining, farming, timber, dairying; bushfire 1946; cemetery 1901; diphtheria (infant died) 1937; PO 1896; sawmill (Williams's), burnt down 1946; school (Bucca Creek till 1919) 1896–1910 and 1916–78; telephone 1905; TX 1924–59; pop. 197 (1933), 195 (1947), 158 (1954), 94 (1961).

Lower Coaldale (*Co. Clarence*) see Coaldale.

Lower Coldstream (*Co. Clarence*) 29°35'S. 153°07'E., 16 km SW of Maclean, on Coldstream R.; flood 1948; school 1879–1937 and 1957–66; pop. 64 (1961).

Lower Corowa (*Co. Hume*) see Corowa South.

Lower Creek (*Co. Clarke*) 30°44'S. 152°15'E., 61 km SE of Armidale, on Dyke R.; grazing and hort.; PO 1927; telephone 1916; TX 1936–82; pop. 54 (1933), 74 (1947), 61 (1954), 189 (2006).

Lower Cudgera (*Co. Rous*) see Pottsville.

Lower Duck Creek (*Co. Buller*) 28°43'S. 152°33'E., 45 km W. of Kyogle; pop. 41 (1933), 59 (1947).

Lower Dungowan (*Co. Parry*) 31°13'S. 151°06'E., 20 km SE of Tamworth, on Peel R.; Angl. C. (St Thomas's), renovated 1911 by W.J. Barber.

Lower Dyraaba (*Co. Rous*) 28°48'S. 152°54'E., 16 km W. of Casino, on Dyraaba Ck; school 1957–66; telephone 1954; TX 1955–67; pop. 131 (2011).

Lower Gloucester River (*Co. Gloucester*) see Heatherdale.

Lower Gumble (*Co. Ashburnham*) 33°06'S. 148°39'E., 11 km NW of Manildra.

Lower Gundaroo (*Co. Murray*) see Gundaroo.

Lower Hexham (*Co. Northumberland*) 32°51'S. 151°41'E., 10 km SW of Raymond Terrace, on Hunter R.; gale 1897; Wes. Meth. C. 1869.

Lower Hickey's (*Co. Dudley*) see Willawarrin.

Lower Kinchela (*Co. Macquarie*) 31°01'S. 153°00'E., 16 km NE of Kempsey, on

Kinchela Ck.

Lower Kinchela (*Co. Macquarie*) see also Kinchela.

Lower Lawrence (*Co. Clarence*) 29°28'S. 153°08'E., 5 km W. of Maclean, on Clarence R.; also known as Kings Creek; dairying and farming; cyclone 1904; flood 1890; PO 1927–62; PS; sawmill (William Kinnear), inundated 1890; school 1883–1955; sugar mill (Kinross) estab. 1880 by Boyle; telephone 1914; whooping cough epidemic 1949; pop. 72 (1901), 65 (1911), 114 (1933), 106 (1947), 52 (1954), 80 (1961).

Lower Lewis Ponds (*Co. Bathurst*) 33°12'S. 149°15'E., 16 km NE of Orange, on Lewis Ponds Ck; grazing; PO 1927; telephone 1921; pop. 43 (1933).

Lower Lila (*Co. Gunderbooka*) 29°38'S. 145°36'E., 55 km NW of Bourke; pop. 38 (1933).

Lower Macdonald (*Co. Hunter*) 33°22'S. 150°58'E., 37 km W. of Ourimbah, on Macdonald R.; formerly Lower Branch; FB; Rom. Cath. C. (St Joseph's) b. 1839–45 by John Watson, abandoned, fire 1898, in ruins for over a century, then bought and reused by Steve Kavanagh, and graveyard (40 graves 1847–1971); school 1865–90; pop. 73 (1891), 60 (1901), 21 (1933), 17 (1961), 2 (1966), 246 (2006), 261 (2011).

Lower McDonald (*Co. Northumberland*) see Upper Macdonald.

Lower Mangrove (*Co. Northumberland*) 33°25'S. 151°09'E., 18 km W. of Gosford, on Mangrove Ck; farming and orchards; Angl. C. (St Peter's) b. by James Everingham, and graveyard; bridges: one over Birdseye Ck and one over Screech Owl Ck; PO 1890; telephone 1913; TX 1934–69; pop. 95 (1933).

Lower Mangrove (*Co. Northumberland*) see also Mangrove Creek.

Lower Mittagong (*Co. Camden*) 34°27'S. 150°29'E., 4 km E. of Mittagong; formerly variously known as Chalker's Flat, Mittagong Flat and Rowes Hill; surveyed 1821, settled 1821 by William Charker (also known as Chalker); airfield 1944; Angl. C. b. 1854 by Lee, replaced 1861, closed 1873, demolished; bushfire 1902; cemetery; flour mill (Hill's), destroyed; Rom. Cath. C. 1861, and graveyard (103 graves 1861+); school 1871, additions 1899 by Alfred Stephens, additions 1908 by E. Cocks, additions 1926 by S.G. McFarlane, closed 1944; wineries: Diamond Creek Estate 1997 and Marist Brothers' Wines 1998.

Lower Mookerawa (*Co. Wellington*) 32°46'S. 149°09'E., 31 km SE of Wellington, on Lake Burrendong; almost deserted by 1951; grazing and goldmining (alluvial) 1881–87; cemetery (Mookerawa) 1858–73; PO 1900; school 1884–90; telephone 1924; TX 1949–55; pop. 113 (1933).

Lower Moore Creek (*Co. Inglis*) 31°01'S. 150°55'E., 10 km N. of Tamworth.

Lower Mount Kembla (*Co. Camden*) see Mount Kembla.

Lower Munmurra (*Co. Bligh*) 32°10'S. 150°01'E., 32 km W. of Merriwa, on Munmurra R.

Lower Nambucca (*Co. Raleigh*) 30°41'S. 152°58'E., 5 km SW of Nambucca Heads; school 1883–1933; pop. 118 (1901), 52 (1947), 57 (1954).

Lower Numba (*Co. St Vincent*) 34°52'S. 150°42'E., 10 km E. of Nowra, on Shoalhaven R.; flood 1891.

Lower Palmers Island (*Co. Clarence*) see Palmers Island.

Lower Pappinbarra (*Co. Macquarie*) 31°25'S. 152°35'E., 14 km W. of Wauchope, on Pappinbarra Ck; pop. 45 (1933), 265 (2011).

Lower Parkes (*Co. Ashburnham*) see Parkes.

Lower Picton (*Co. Camden*) see Picton.

Lower Pindimar (*Co. Gloucester*) 32°41'S. 152°06'E., 6 km W. of Tea Gardens, on Port Stephens; oysters.

Lower Pyramul (*Co. Wellington*) 32°56'S. 149°33'E., 41 km W. of Kandos, on Sweepys Ck; goldmining.

Lower Quipolly (*Co. Buckland*) 31°26'S. 150°36'E., 11 km NW of Quirindi, on Quipolly Ck; Angl. C. (St Chad's) b. 1886 by Amos Davis, closed 1969, abandoned, and graveyard (127 graves); pop. 27 (1933), 50 (1947).

Lower Southgate (*Co. Clarence*) 29°33'S. 153°05'E., 15 km SW of Maclean, on Clarence R.; orig. Southgate; farming; Bapt. C. 1907 d. by E.G. Hockey; bushfire 1936; creamery (Lower Southgate Dairy Co.) 1898; ferry (to Brushgrove) 1902–68, along Clarence R.; flood 1890; PO 1895; school 1877, additions 1927 by A.A. Robertson, closed 1947; telephone 1908; Wes. Meth. C. 1870; wharf; pop. 304 (1901), 134 (1933), 116 (1947), 129 (1954), 99 (1961).

Lower Spring Grove (*Co. Rous*) see Coolaness.

Lower Tarcutta (*Co. Wynyard*) 35°12'S. 147°45'E., 30 km NW of Adelong, on Tarcutta Ck; cemetery (67 burials 1854–1922); PO 1892; telephone 1925; TX 1926; pop. 36 (1933), 60 (1947).

Lower Taylor's Arm (*Co. Raleigh*) see Talarm.

Lower Temora (*Co. Bland*) see Temora.

Lower Tomki (*Co. Rous*) 28°54'S. 153°10'E., 14 km E. of Casino, on Richmond R.; school 1911–36.

Lower Towamba (*Co. Auckland*) 37°07'S. 149°45'E., 16 km SW of Eden, on Towamba R.; farming; PO 1927–71; telephone 1911; TX 1930.

Lower Turon (*Co. Roxburgh*) 33°05'S. 149°23'E., 35 km NE of Orange, on Macquarie R.; mining (reef gold disc. 1852, alluvial gold disc. 1855, gold rush 1855); PO 1872–77.

Lower Ulmarra (*Co. Clarence*) 29°35'S. 153°03'E., 17 km NE of Grafton, on Clarence R.; school 1882 b. by G. Finlay, closed 1893; Wes. Meth. C. 1862.

Lower Wallaby (*Co. Roxburgh*) 33°04'S. 149°36'E., 38 km N. of Bathurst.

Lower Warrell Creek (*Co. Raleigh*) 30°46'S. 152°58'E., 7 km SE of Macksville.

Lower Wyong Creek (*Co. Northumberland*) see Wyong Creek.

Lowesdale (*Co. Hume*) 35°51'S. 146°22'E., 17 km N. of Corowa; agric. and grazing; Angl. C. 1890; fire 1930; PO 1876; school (Burrajaa till 1885) 1882, new one b. 1903 by E.P. Frost & Co.; telephone 1895; TX 1913, automatic 1952; Wes. Meth. C.; pop. 167 (1901), 135 (1911), 91 (1933), 58 (1947), 75 (1954), 125 (1961), 219 (2006), 311 (2011).

Lowes Mount (*Co. Westmoreland*) 33°37'S. 149°51'E., 10 km N. of Oberon, on Deadmans Arm Ck; goldmines: Black Bullock 1899–1902 and 1905, Faugh-A-Ballah Reef <1877, Lucks-All or Golden Horseshoe <1877 and 1911–14, Malloys Reef <1877 and 1883; pop. 57 (1947), 62 (1954).

Lowlands (*Co. Benarba*) 29°19'S. 149°06'E., 39 km S. of Mungindi.

Lowlands (*Co. Blaxland*) 33°11'S. 145°29'E., 33 km N. of Hillston, on Willandra Ck; RS 1931–75.

Lowther (*Co. Westmoreland*) 33°37'S. 150°06'E., 14 km W. of Mount Victoria, on Good Water Ck; farming, incl. potatoes; cemetery (orig. Rom. Cath., 168 graves 1886+) 1881; diphtheria 1912; earth tremors 1999 and 2005; gale 1928; PO 1868, damaged 1928; Rom. Cath. C. 1877 (removed from Mount Victoria), new one (St Matthew's) b. 1906 by James Short and Robert Leslie, closed; school 1868–73, 1882–91, 1900–38; telephone 1905; TX 1928; pop. 101 (1901), 97 (1911), 81 (1933), 71 (1947), 60 (1954), 56 (1961).

Loxford (*Co. Northumberland*) 32°48'S. 151°29'E., 2 km N. of Kurri Kurri, on Swamp Ck; aluminium smelter (Alcan Aust., then Capral Aluminium Ltd in 1995, then VAW Kurri Kurri Pty Ltd in 2000, then Norsk Hydro in 2002) 1969–2014, demolition began 2017; boys' training school (Yawarra) 1969–79, reused; bushfires 1940, 1965, 2002, 2017; colliery (Ayrfield No. 2) o. 1924 by R.W. Miller & Co., strike 1925, man killed 1925, flooded 1926, closed 1931, pit-top fire 1940, man killed 1943, razed 1947; PO 1928; 2 quarries; railway (colliery); sewage works; TC (Kurri Kurri Campus) o. 1983 in former boys' training school, became a campus of Hunter Institute of Technology in 1992, additions by A.C.H. Clifford Pty Ltd, additions 2014 by Richard Crookes Constructions Pty Ltd; telephone 1929; pop. 143 (1933), 72 (1947), 127 (2006).

Luadra (*Co. Wynyard*) 35°10'S. 148°01'E., 15 km SW of Gundagai, on Adelong Ck; RS 1953–75.

Lucan (*Co. Bathurst*) 33°43'S. 148°59'E., 31 km NE of Cowra, on Limestone Ck; RS (orig. Rosegreen) 1907–73.

Lucasville (*Co. Cook*) 33°46'S. 150°38'E., 2 km NE of Glenbrook, on Knapsack Ck; RS 1878–92.

Lucernia (*Co. Hunter*) 32°30'S. 150°52'E., 21 km SE of Denman, on Appletree Ck; telephone 1923; TX 1924; pop. 45 (1933).

Lucknow (*Co. Bathurst*) 33°21'S. 149°10'E., 9 km SE of Orange, on Summerhill Ck; Wentworth Diggings till 1863; estab. 1862, subdivided 1913, largely defunct; agric., mining (gold disc. 1851, boom 1862–67, production peaked 1895) till 1937, orchards; Angl. C. (St John the Evangelist) 1873, chancel added 1896; Aust. C.; cyanide plant (Aust. Gold Mining & Recovery Co.) 1892–1907; dams: Bag Town Dam on Parker's Ck and Boat Dam, Reform Dam and Tangye Dam on Frederick's Valley Ck; foundry; Meth. C. 1904; miners' strike 1897; mines: Aladdin's Lamp 1892 (amalgamated 1899 with Wentworth Goldfields Pty Co., closed 1901), Amana, Bismarck Deeps (incl. battery) 1934, Bismarck Range (New Guinea) Gold Exploration NL (incl. 10 head stamper battery) 1933–37, Crinoline, D'Arcy Estates 1895 (fire 1905, taken over 1907 by Golden Contact Mines Ltd, closed 1912), D'Arcy Wentworth (sold 1902 to J. Gardiner), Golden Contact, Golden Gate, Golden Point (Hans Krause), Homeward Bound, Industry Rewarded, Jackass (Aladdin's Lamp Gold Mining Co. Ltd) 1892–98, Lucknow Extended, Lucknow Pups 1920–29, Lucknow 66, Lucknow Sulphide (orig. part of Wentworth Pty Co., taken over 1934 by Bismarck Group), New Lucknow, New Reform (taken over by Wentworth Pty Co.), North St Aignan, Pascoe's Shaft, Phoenix, Reform, St Aignan (Lucknow) Gold Mines NL (incl. 2 head stamper battery) 1930–34, Shamrock, Snobs, South Lucknow 1920–26, Spicer's Vein, Uncle Tom Co. (estab. 1873, closed, bought and reopened 1878 by Henry Newman), Wentworth Extended, Wentworth Gold-fields Co. Pty Ltd 1891 (amalgamated 1899 with Aladdin's Lamp Gold Mining Co. Ltd), Wentworth Lucknow 1935, Wentworth Main (Great Western), poppet head 1935, bought by Orange City Council; PO 1863, burnt down 1949, rebuilt, burnt down again 1957; PS 1894–1913, sold, moved to Orange and reused; Rom. Cath. C. (St Mary's) b. 1888 by John Walsh, d. by John Hale, demolished; school 1864, destroyed, replaced 1878, additions and repairs 1886 by W. Moulsdale, additions 1900, closed 1971, reused; sewerage augmentation 1990; stamper batteries (incl. Fredericks Valley Gold Mining Co. 10 head and New Gold-Mining Co. Ltd 12 head); telegraph 1877; TX 1915–81; typhoid (2 died) 1900; Wes. Meth. C. 1886, relocated 1892, closed, reused, demolished; wineries: Patina Wines (estab. 1999 by Gerald Naef) and Toogalah Wines (estab. 1995 by Laurence and Susan Mockler); pop. 310 (1891), 1,077 (1901), 459 (1911), 198 (1933), 199 (1947), 229 (1954), 191 (1961), *c.*200 (1975–87), 145 (2006).

Lucky Point (*Co. Roxburgh*) see Sofala.

Lue (*Co. Phillip*) 32°40'S. 149°51'E., 20 km NW of Rylstone, on Lawsons Ck; Loowee till 1884; town gaz. 1887; farming and grazing; Angl. C. (St Luke's) 1925, closed, sold 2019; bushfire 1945; cemetery (90 graves 1902+) 1898; electricity 1957; FB 1946; PO 1891; Rom. Cath. C. 1905, new one (Our Lady of Lourdes) b. 1935 by W. Carmichael & Sons, d. by Harold Robert Hardwick, closed and reused; RS 1884, station b. by Alexander Hamilton Scouller, closed 1992; school (Dungeree till 1913) 1876; telegraph 1896; telephone 1913; TX 1915, automatic 1987; Wes. Meth. C., closed, sold, moved to South Mudgee, reused; pop. 77 (1901), 251 (1911), 194 (1933), 149 (1947), 247 (1954), 210 (1961), 456 (2011).

Lumley (*Co. Argyle*) 34°53'S. 149°55'E., 23 km SE of Goulburn, on Lumley Ck; agric.

Lunatic (*Co. Buller*) 28°49'S. 152°26'E., 46

km NE of Tenterfield, on Lunatic Gully; gold (disc. 1869) and antimony; mines (incl. Dalmorton and Golden Crown); PO 1871; stamper battery (Richard Hooton).

Lunts Vale (*Co. Goulburn*) 35°32'S. 147°32'E., 28 km NE of Holbrook; defunct; cemetery 1873–1924.

Luskintyre (*Co. Durham*) 32°41'S. 151°26'E., 7 km E. of Branxton, on Hunter R.; agric.; aeroplane crash (2 killed) 1994; airfield 1977; bridge to Lochinvar, b. 1874 by Thomas Smith, new one (steel Pratt trusses) b. 1902–4 by J.F. Carson, 913 ft (278.3 m), over Hunter R.; gales 1899 and 1905; school 1896–1904; winery (Tranquil Vale Vineyard) 1996; pop. 75 (1911), 80 (1933), 68 (1947), 73 (1954), 70 (1961), 266 (2011).

Lymington (*Co. Northumberland*) see Cardiff.

Lynchs Creek (*Co. Rous*) 28°27'S. 153°00'E., 19 km N. of Kyogle, on Lynchs Ck; farming; bridge (low-level) b. 1929 by Walsh, over Lynchs Ck; gale 1942; PO 1915; rifle range 1909, upgraded 1922; sawmill (Munro Bros); school 1930–65; telephone 1912; TX 1915; pop. 61 (1911), 147 (1933), 135 (1947), 164 (1954), 107 (1961), 181 (2006), 252 (2011).

Lyndhurst (*Co. Bathurst*) 33°41'S. 149°03'E., 25 km SW of Blayney, on Grubbenbun Ck; town gaz. 1861; goldmining, wheat, lucerne, chaff, hay, oats, peas, cattle, sheep; airfield (1 km E.); Angl. C. (Emmanuel) 1896–1983, sold 1987 to Rodney Swansborough; cemetery 1881; earth tremor 1906; FB; PO 1869; pound (stock) b. 1901 by James Smith; railway turntable, 60 ft (18.3 m), ruined; reservoir 1955; Rom. Cath. C. 1892, rebuilt and enlarged (St Joseph's) 1953, closed, sold 1979 and reused; RS 1888, station b. by John Wadsworth Ashworth; sawmill (W.J. Leabeater); school 1889 b. by Charles Palmer and William Lewis, extended 1914 by William Lishman Jemison; storm 1900; telegraph 1888; TX 1915, automatic 1986; typhoid (girl died) 1901; water reticulation 1956; pop. 161 (1891), 171 (1901), 352 (1911), 344 (1921), 327 (1933), 378 (1947), 375 (1954), 304 (1961), 240 (1971), 223 (1991), 224 (1996), 216 (2001), 219 (2011).

Lyndhurst (*Co. Clarke*) 30°19'S. 152°03'E., 39 km E. of Guyra, on Chandler R.; pop. 66 (1911).

Lyndhurst Vale (*Co. Durham*) 32°27'S. 151°44'E., 5 km S. of Dungog; pop. 37 (1933).

Lynwood (*Co. Caira*) 34°48'S. 143°38'E., 20 km S. of Balranald, on Condoulpe Lake; school 1903–9.

Lynwood (*Co. Rous*) 28°52'S. 153°26'E., 3 km S. of Alstonville; airfield; Meth. C. 1903; pop. 184 (2011).

Lysaghts (*Co. Camden*) see Spring Hill.

Lyttleton (*Co. Auckland*) see Bemboka.

M

McAlister (*Co. Argyle*) 34°27'S. 149°34'E., 8 km E. of Crookwell; village gaz. 1886 as M'Allister, first lots sold 1886; sheep and farming; bushfire 1944; PO 1927, burnt down 1944; RS 1902–75; telephone 1923; TX 1936; pop. 81 (1933), 55 (1947).

Macanally (*Co. Beresford*) 36°05'S. 149°19'E., 24 km NE of Cooma; goldmining; mine; stamper battery (Alf Reed).

Macarthur (*Co. Burnett*) 29°32'S. 150°21'E., 20 km W. of Warialda; school 1912–38.

McCollom's (*Co. Camden*) see Robertson.

McCulloch Park (*Co. Yancowinna*) see Stephens Creek.

McCullys Gap (*Co. Durham*) 32°13'S. 150°59'E., 11 km SE of Aberdeen, on Sandy Ck; dairying and grazing; monumental stone works (Cessnock Memorials); PO 1926; quarry; school 1957–69; telephone 1915; TX 1927–77; Union C. 1911, burnt down 1976; pop. 82 (1933), 82 (1947), 82 (1954), 77 (1961).

Macdonald (*Co. Northumberland*) see St Albans.

MacDonald (*Co. Sandon*) 30°32'S. 151°41'E., 2 km SE of Armidale; sawmill.

McDonald River (*Co. Hunter*) see Central Macdonald

Macdonald River (*Co. Inglis*) see Woolbrook.

McDonald River (*Co. Northumberland*) see Upper Macdonald.

McDonalds Hole (*Co. Roxburgh*) 33°03'S. 149°58'E., 21 km S. of Kandos, on Oaky Ck; PO 1882–3; school 1882–94.

McDonaldtown (*Co. Richmond*) see Broadwater.

Macdonald Valley (*Co. Hunter*) see Central Macdonald.

McDougalls Hill (*Co. Durham*) see Singleton (*Co. Northumberland*).

McGees Flat (*Co. Vernon*) 30°47'S. 152°20'E., 56 km W. of Macksville, on Macleay R.

McGuigans (*Co. Ashburnham*) 33°11'S. 148°06'E., 9 km SW of Parkes; estab. 1874, abandoned 1876; mining (gold disc. 1874 by Peter McGuigan et al., alluvial gold rush 1874) 1874–76; brewery; PO 1874–76; sawmill (W. Maitland).

McHenrys Creek (*Co. Monteagle*) 34°15'S. 148°16'E., 7 km N. of Young; school (Mirrabooka since 1923) 1884, burnt down and replaced 1923 by Hugh Robert Blackett, closed 1949; pop. 33 (1933).

McHugh's Creek (*Co. Raleigh*) see Ketelghay.

Macintyre (*Co. Gough*) see Inverell.

Macintyre (*Co. Murchison*) 30°13'S. 150°46'E., 23 km NE of Barraba; school 1957–68.

McIntyres Corner (*Co. Waradgery*) 34°24'S. 145°00'E., 19 km NE of Hay; rice.

Mackay's (*Co. Buckland*) see Braefield.

McKees Hill (*Co. Rous*) 28°53'S. 153°12'E., 13 km SW of Lismore, on Pelican Ck; farming and dairying; Meth. C. 1917; PO 1907; Rom. Cath. C. (St Joseph's) b. 1935 by J. Watt; school (Tomki till 1923) 1887, additions 1892 by Achilles Step, closed 1976; telephone 1914; TX 1926–69; pop. 129 (1911), 137 (1933), 166 (1947), 137 (1954), 156 (1961).

McKellars Paddock (*Co. Cook*) see Lithgow.

McKellars Park (*Co. Cook*) see Lithgow.

McKenzies Siding (*Co. Gough*)

see Bookoola.

McKeown's Caves (*Co. Westmoreland*) see Jenolan Caves.

McKinley (*Co. Nicholson*) 33°48'S. 145°26'E., 37 km S. of Hillston; flour mill, estab. by Samuel Nixon and John Flanagan, closed 1888.

Macks Flat (*Co. Georgiana*) 34°06'S. 149°37'E., 40 km N. of Crookwell, on Abercrombie R.

Macksville (*Co. Raleigh*) 30°43'S. 152°55'E., 11 km SW of Nambucca Heads, on Nambucca R.; (incl. North Macksville); Nambucca till 1889; settled 1865 by William Hughes, founded by Patrick Macguinness, village gaz. 1870 as Nambucca, bypassed by highway 2017; mining (gold, silver, antimony), timber, fishing, maize, fruit, vegetables, bacon, butter, dairying, paspalum seed; abattoir (Nambucca Meat Co.) 1939; ambulance station; Angl. C. (Holy Trinity) 1910, additions 1935; bridges: one (steel and concrete) 1931, new one 2017 d. and b. by Acciona Ferrovial (Pacifico), over Nambucca R., Wilson Bridge over Taylors Arm, 2 bridges over Tilly Willy Ck; bus body factory (Nambucca River Engineering, became Express Coach Builders Pty Ltd in 1995) estab. 1971 by John Bishop and Geoff Christian; butter factory and ice works (Nambucca Dairy Co. Ltd) b. 1904 by Fred Debenham, moved 1912 to new building, extensions 1929 d. by J. Wildridge & Sinclair Ltd, closed 1954, reused, abandoned; carriage-works (Stewart Bros); cemetery (2,141 graves) 1895, incl. columbarium; CH (incl. lock-up) b. 1892 by Jacob Healey; cordial factory (Hugh McNally); dengue fever 1926; earth tremor 1910; FB (station b. 1953); flood 2009; hailstorm 1996; hospital (Nambucca Dist. Memorial) 1947, new building 1958, additions 1991; Jehovah's Witnesses C.; macadamia nut processing plant (Nambucca Macnuts Pty Ltd); Meth. C. 1909; pneumonia epidemic (boy died) 1921; PO 1868, new one b. 1918; Presb. C. 1894, closed, sold 1907, new one 1930, and columbarium; PS 1876, additions and alterations 1975; punt b. 1914 by George M. Moore, replaced with bridge, to cross Nambucca R.; railway barracks; railway bridges: steel truss 1923, fabricated by State Dockyard (Walsh Island), over Nambucca R. and one over Tilly Willy Ck; railway turntable, 60 ft (18.3 m); 2 reservoirs; Rom. Cath. C. 1886, demolished, replacement 1912 d. by Eaton and Bates, sold and removed, new one (St Patrick's) 1975; RS 1919, man killed 1924; Salv. Army C.; sawmills: J.W.A. Fortescue (incl. box factory), H.I. Lane 1912, F. Mahnken, L. Smith, Haydon Teague, A.G. Whitten (removed 1919 from Warrell Creek, burnt down 1921); schools: primary (Nambucca till 1890) 1876, new buildings b. 1896 by Smart and Jordan, additions 1912 by R. Hibbard, additions 1923 by B.W. Skinner, additions 1962 and 1985, and HS 1950, additions 1959, 1962, 1966, 1970, major upgrade 1996; SD Adventist C. 1952; sewerage 1969, augmentation 1999; smallgoods factory (Midco), in old butter factory, closed and abandoned; TC, now a campus of North Coast Institute; telegraph 1878; TX 1912, automatic 1968; Unit. C. (orig. Meth.) b. 1926 by J. Oliver Jones, d. by Arthur Lanyon Clark; water reticulation 1957, augmentation 1969; wharf b. 1901 by G.R. Moore; pop. 118 (1891), 120 (1897), 165 (1901), 509 (1911), *c.*750 (1924), 1,300 (1933), 1,544 (1947), 2,007 (1954), 2,114 (1961), 2,129 (1966), 2,250 (1971), 2,277 (1976), 2,352 (1981), 2,811 (1986), 2,869 (1991), 2,712 (1996), 2,661 (2001), 2,658 (2006), 2,786 (2011).

Maclaughlin (*Co. Wellesley*) 36°34'S. 149°17'E., 39 km S. of Cooma, on Jettiba Ck; RS 1939–71; school (McLaughlin River) 1910–14.

McLaughlin River (*Co. Wellesley*) see Maclaughlin.

McLaurin (*Co. Goulburn*) see Wantagong.

Maclean (*Co. Clarence*) 29°28'S. 153°12'E., 16 km W. of Yamba, on Clarence R.; Rocky Mouth till 1885; surveyed 1861, laid out 1862 by William Albert Braylesford Greaves, village gaz. 1863, munic. proc. 1887, bypassed by highway 1966; former river port, timber, maize, sugar-cane, agric., dairying, cattle, vegetables, fishing, oysters, some recent tourist development; ambulance station 1946; Angl. C. 1886, enlarged and renovated 1901 by F.J. Robertson, replacement (St James's) b. 1962 by Reginald Joseph Want, d. by A. Manning Richards and MacDonald; Bapt. C. b. 1907 by Till and Robertson, closed 2000, sold and reused; brewery (incl. cordial factory) estab. 1881 by Neil McCarthy as Rocky Mouth Brewery, renamed Clarence River Brewery in 1884, sold 1895, closed 1901, upgraded 1903 by Joseph Gottlieb Kempnich, reopened 1904, closed 1914, reused 1915; brickworks: C. Goddard 1890 and Robert Page, closed 1946; bridge (Macfarlane Bridge, with bascule span) to Woodford Island b. 1903–6 by Mountney & Co. Ltd, bascule span closed 1962, bridge renovated 1979, restored 2011–16, over Clarence R. (South Arm); butter factory (Maclean Refrigerating Works, Ice & Butter Factory) estab. 1901 by Joseph Gottlieb Kempnich, new one (Clarence River Co-op. Butter & Refrigerating Co. Ltd) b. 1907 by Gruer; carriage-works (Kritsch's); cemeteries: old one 1871 and general (2,658 graves); CH (incl. police station and lock-up) b. 1874 by William Kinnear, demolished 1891, new one b. 1892 by Charles Benaud Smith, d. by Walter Liberty Vernon, renovated 1968, re-roofed 1975; Church of Christ; cordial factory estab. 1896 by C.E. Henson, sold 1921 to W.M. Glynn, sold 1924 to Alfred George Harris, sold 1946 to H.G. McPherson, sold 1952 to Rudder and Zeitsch; creamery b. 1896 by Crimson and Pantlin, d. by Garratt; cyclone 1904; FB (station b. 1918); fish canneries: one o. 1890, Clarence River Fish Canning Co. o. 1935 in old butter factory, Taylor Bros 1903–4, demolished 1907; floods 1890, 1892, 1893, 1921, 1945, 1954, 1962, 1988, 2001, 2011; foundry and engineering works (Clarence) estab. 1882 by Boden Bros, sold 1898 by J.S. Boden to David Millar; Free Presb. C. b. 1864 by John Davies; gales 1914 and 1947; hailstorm 1964; hospital b. 1886 by Joseph Walsh and Byron, d. by W. McKenzie, additions 1910, 1914, 1925, 1931, new one 1954, additions by Bennett Constructions Pty Ltd, additions 2017; ice works: Joseph Gottlieb Kempnich 1901 (leased 1926 by C.W. King, extended 1929, ice-cream 1932, sold 1945 to Clarence River Fishermen's Co-op. Ltd) and E.A. and T.A. Powell 1904; measles epidemic 1901; PO 1862, inundated 1890, new one b. 1893 by Patrick Berecry, d. by Walter Liberty Vernon, additions and alterations 1958; Presb. C. b. 1886 by George Fraser, destroyed 1947, new one 1958; PS (incl. lock-up) b. 1896 by Crimson and Pantlin, d. by Walter Liberty Vernon; punt to Ashby till 1985; 3 reservoirs; Rom. Cath. C. 1867, chancel and sacristy added 1880, church demolished 1898, new one (St Mary's) b. 1889–93 by Joseph Walsh, d. by Frederick William Conrad Schaeffer, renovated 1934; sale-yards (Sid Small) 1917; Salv. Army C. 1932; sawmills: George Forrester (sold 1948 to White & Thompson Pty Ltd) and Patrick and Francis Gallagher (partnership dissolved 1902, business carried on by P.H. Gallagher alone in new mill, sold 1910 to W. Deer, rebuilt 1912); scarlet fever 1901; schools: primary (Rocky Mouth till 1888) 1865, additions 1876, 1881, 1884, 1886, 1887, repairs 1894 by Dugald Macdonald, replacement b. 1903 by F.J. Robertson, additions 1909 by Charles Benaud Smith, additions 1923 by Till and Robertson, additions 1928 by H. Walsh, additions 1956, replacement b. 1961 by James Wallace & Co., d. by Wilding, additions 1972 and 1975, and HS 1961, additions 1972, 1976, 1993, 1995, additions 2011 by T.F. Woollam & Son Pty Ltd; SD Adventist C.; sewerage augmentation 1973; shipyard (Francis Schwonberg); storm 2018; sugar mill (William Newby); TC (a campus of North Coast Institute); telegraph 1870; telephone 1905; TX 1908, automatic 1966; typhoid 1905; Unit. C. (orig. Wes. Meth.) b. 1890 by C. Goddard and D. M'Donald, d. by J. Moyes, extended 1908 by Goddard; water reticulation 1964; Wes. Meth. C. 1871, and graveyard; 4 wharves (Criterion demolished 1907); pop. *c.*50 (1866), 139 (1871), 498

(1881), 907 (1891), *c.*900 (1895), 1,333 (1901), 1,592 (1911), 1,670 (1924), 1,588 (1933), 1,665 (1947), 1,698 (1954), 1,804 (1961), 2,231 (1966), 2,325 (1971), 2,488 (1976), 2,593 (1981), 2,681 (1986), 2,890 (1991), 3,157 (1996), 3,254 (2001), 3,245 (2006).

McLeans Ridges (*Co. Rous*) 28°48'S. 153°23'E., 7 km NW of Alstonville, on Marom Ck; PO; school 1882, new building b. 1891 by Edward Knowles, closed 1969; telephone 1913; TX 1925; pop. 137 (1933), 108 (1947), 108 (1954), 94 (1961).

Macleay Entrance (*Co. Macquarie*) see South West Rocks.

Macleay River Steam Works (*Co. Dudley*) see Warneton.

McLeod's Crossing (*Co. Wentworth*) see Wentworth.

McLeods Shoot (*Co. Rous*) 28°39'S. 153°32'E., 4 km N. of Bangalow; pop. 237 (2006).

McMahon (*Co. Harden*) see McMahons Reef.

McMahons Reef (*Co. Harden*) 34°40'S. 148°26'E., 15 km SE of Murrumburrah, on Cunningham Ck; Marshall McMahon Reef till 1933; village gaz. 1898 as McMahon; mining (gold disc. by Patrick Heffernan) 1871–74, 1883–92, 1896–1942, and farming; brickworks; dam (mine); furnaces; 6 mines (incl. New McMahons Reef or Lone Hand and Old McMahons Reef); PO 1886, burnt down 1933; PS, closed 1897; school (Watsons Reef till 1909, then Marshall McMahon Reef till 1921) 1883–1948; smelting and refining works (Cunningar Pty Gold Mining & Chlorination Co.) 1885–92; stamper batteries; telephone 1923; TX 1924, burnt down 1933, reopened 1934, automatic 1958; pop. 104 (1901), 65 (1911), 90 (1933), 91 (1947), 66 (1954), 63 (1961).

MacMasters Beach (*Co. Northumberland*) 33°30'S. 151°25'E., 9 km E. of Woy Woy, on Allagai Bay; tourism; Community C., closed, sold 2013, reused; FB; PO 1961; reservoir; telephone 1947; TX 1948–61; Union C.; water reticulation 1979; pop. 91 (1947), 122 (1954), 133 (1961), 206 (1971), 337 (1976), 536 (1981), 647 (1986), 673 (1991), 764 (1996), 916 (2001), 1,009 (2006), 1,217 (2011).

McPhail (*Co. Narromine*) 32°36'S. 148°13'E., 14 km N. of Peak Hill; defunct; goldmining (reef) 1885–1910, agric., grazing; Angl. C. b. 1903 by Litchfield, d. by Bakes; cyanide plant (Edward Bullock); dust storm 1907; fire 1904; grasshopper infestation 1907; mines: Myall Mine and stamper battery (40 head) operated by Myall United Gold Mining Co., became The Myalls & Peak Hill Gold Mines Ltd in 1904, closed 1908, and Myall United Mine 1883–1913, razed; PO 1897–1913; school 1898–1926; TX; Wes. Meth. C. 1900, closed, moved 1912 to Backwater; pop. 616 (1901), 92 (1911), 68 (1933).

McPhersons Crossing (*Co. Fitzroy*) 29°49'S. 152°55'E., 14 km S. of Grafton, on Orara R.

Macquarie (*Co. Bathurst*) see Neville.

Macquarie (*Co. Macquarie*) see Port Macquarie.

Macquarie Farm Estate (*Co. Camden*) see Picton.

Macquarie Hills (*Co. Northumberland*) see Cardiff.

Macquarie Plains (*Co. Roxburgh*) see Brewongle.

Macquarie Swamp (*Co. Bathurst*) see Neville.

Macquarie Vale (*Co. Roxburgh*) 33°27'S. 149°37'E., 5 km SE of Bathurst; pop. 45 (1933), 56 (1947).

Macqueen (*Co. Durham*) see Moonan Flat.

Macsville (*Co. Northumberland*) see Cardiff.

Madgwick (*Co. Sandon*) see Armidale.

Madron (*Co. Dudley*) 30°59'S. 152°42'E., 18 km NW of Kempsey, on Deep Ck; bridge over Deep Ck; telephone 1915; TX 1928–59; pop. 26 (1933).

Maeranie (*Co. Durham*) see Mirannie.

Maerannie (*Co. Durham*) see Mirannie.

Mafeking (*Co. Forbes*) 33°38'S. 147°52'E., 31 km SW of Forbes, on Back Ck.

Maffra (*Co. Wellesley*) 36°32'S. 148°59'E., 24 km SE of Berridale; Unit. C. (St Andrew's, orig. Presb., then Angl.) b. 1887 by H.T. Foster; pop. 60 (1911).

Magenta (*Co. Kilfera*) 33°52'S. 143°34'E., 86

km N. of Balranald; pop. 116 (1933).

Magenta (*Co. Northumberland*) see The Entrance North.

Magpie Hollow (*Co. Westmoreland*) 33°31'S. 150°03'E., 11 km W. of Lithgow.

Maguire's (*Co. Camden*) see Kangaroo Valley.

Maharatta (*Co. Wellesley*) 37°00'S. 149°14'E., 9 km S. of Bombala, on Saucy Ck; bridge b. 1898 by Arthur Mawson and John M'Arthur, over Saucy Ck; school 1886–96; pop. 64 (1901), 48 (1933).

Mahoneys Corner (*Co. Roxburgh*) 33°05'S. 149°26'E., 38 km NE of Orange, on Clines Ck.

Mahonga (*Co. Hume*) 35°33'S. 146°31'E., 47 km W. of Henty, on Billabong Ck; Mohonga till *c.*1880; bushfires 1883 and 1893; flood 1931; PO 1878, burnt down 1901; pop. 101 (1911), 31 (1933).

Mahonga South (*Co. Hume*) 35°45'S. 146°25'E., 28 km N. of Corowa; school (Mohonga South) 1884–87.

Mahratta Station (*Co. Wellesley*) see Platts.

Mahtle (*Co. Rous*) 28°46'S. 153°24'E., 6 km N. of Wollongbar; dairying; PO 1927–42.

Maida Vale (*Co. Fitzroy*) 30°21'S. 152°24'E., 30 km W. of Dorrigo, on Jocks Water; airfield; cheese factory b. 1924 by Hollingworth and Millikin, merged 1946 with Dorrigo Co-op. Dairy Co. Ltd, closed 1948.

Maidenhead (*Co. Arrawatta*) 29°12'S. 151°21'E., 66 km W. of Tenterfield, on Beardy Ck; sawmill (Henry William Perrin).

Maiden's Punt (*Co. Cadell*) see Moama.

Maids Valley (*Co. Clive*) 29°07'S. 151°39'E., 38 km W. of Tenterfield, on Maids Valley Ck.

Maimuru (*Co. Monteagle*) 34°16'S. 148°16'E., 13 km NW of Young; soldiers' settlement; gold and orchards; airport (Young) 1935; fruit packing house; Meth. C. (Wyndham Memorial) b. 1938 by W.S. Willard Pty Ltd, d. by Claude Symons; mines; PO 1920; prune dehydration plant (W.E. Teggarth) 1936; RS (Scott's Siding till 1921, then Mirrabooka till 1928) 1902–75; school 1931; silo 1927; telephone 1922; TX 1926, automatic 1971; pop. 26 (1921), 275 (1933), 186 (1947), 258 (1954), 210 (1961), 297 (2006).

Main Arm (*Co. Rous*) 28°31'S. 153°26'E., 8 km NW of Mullumbimby, on Brunswick R.; bananas; bushfire (house destroyed) 1946; cyclone 1923; flood (woman died) 2008; Presb. C. 1909; sawmills: King Bros (fire 1912, taken over 1912 by L.Y. King and S. Ellis) and George Law (burnt down 1923); TX (automatic); pop. 239 (1911), 342 (1933), 547 (1947), 517 (1954), 450 (1961).

Main Camp (*Co. Cook*) see Lithgow.

Main Camp (*Co. Gipps*) see Wyalong West.

Main Camp (*Co. Rous*) see Dunbible.

Main Camp Flat (*Co. Clarke*) 30°34'S. 152°09'E., 47 km E. of Armidale, on Rocky Ck.

Main Creek (*Co. Gloucester*) 32°17'S. 151°48'E., 13 km N. of Dungog, on Carowiry Ck; dairying; bridge (Cox's Bridge) 1980, over Carowiry Ck; PO 1912; sawmills: James Croll & Sons (fire 1942) and J.S. Gam 1909 (taken over 1982 by A.S. Nicholas & Sons); school 1954–60; telephone 1915; TX 1925–62; pop. 176 (1911), 139 (1933), 91 (1947), 115 (1954), 82 (1961), 313 (2006).

Mairjimmy (*Co. Urana*) 35°30'S. 145°44'E., 15 km S. of Jerilderie; RS 1897–1975, station removed 1984; telephone 1919; TX 1926, automatic 1954; pop. 101 (1947), 164 (1954).

Maison Dieu (*Co. Durham*) 32°32'S. 151°04'E., 10 km W. of Singleton; quarry; school 1897, additions 1954 by Tuscan Building Co. Ltd, closed 1977; pop. 75 (1901), 83 (1911), 77 (1933), 87 (1947), 86 (1954), 86 (1961), 162 (2011).

Maitland (*Co. Northumberland*) 32°44'S. 151°33'E., 29 km NW of Newcastle, on Hunter R.; (incl. Horseshoe Bend or Port Maitland, North Maitland, South Maitland, Veterans Flat); Schanks's Forest Plains (also known as The Camp) till 1818, Wallis's Plains (also known as Molly Morgan's Plains) till 1835, Maitland till 1852, West Maitland till 1949; disc. 1801 by Lieut. Col. William Paterson et al., settled 1818–21, village estab. 1823–25, surveyed 1830 by George Boyle

White, town gaz. 1833, boundary with East Maitland gaz. 1835, munic. proc. 1863, thrived 1830s–40s and in 1880s, city (incl. East Maitland and Morpeth) proc. 1945, munic. greatly enlarged 1958; wheat, lucerne, maize, millet, barley, oats, potatoes, pumpkins, melons, oranges, grapes, butter, cheese, bacon, tobacco, coal 1870s+, milling, tanning, brewing, clothing; 7 agric. implement works (incl. Capper & Sons and Mark Winter 1876); ambulance station (in former store, converted by George Pilgrim) 1924, demolished 1928, new one b. 1929 by Taylor and Buffier, d. by Walter Harold Pender; Angl. C.: St Barnabas's (Horseshoe Bend) b. 1861 by Graham, demolished 1914, St Mary the Virgin 1843 (d. by James Hume, replacement b. 1860–67 by Black and Hudson, d. by Edmund Thomas Blacket, tower and spire added 1885–87 by Thomas Browne, jun., d. by Blacket Bros, spire restored 2004, and graveyard, incl. columbarium), St Paul's (b. 1856–58 by James Hesp, d. by William White, inundated 1857 during construction, additions 1885, tower b. 1888 by James Richardson, d. by Arthur Coe Lee, church inundated 1913, re-roofed 1928, inundated 1955, renovated 1960, closed 2012, reused 2014); Apostolic C. (Lifehouse Christ.); Assemblies of God C. (Hunter Valley Christ. Life), in reused building; Bapt. C.: one b. 1861 by Phillip Lane, one removed 1943 from Paxton, one o. 1932 in reused bank; beekeeping equipment factory (Pender Bros) 1892, additions 1905 by J. Cook, moved to Rutherford; benevolent asylum (Benhome) b. 1884–86 by William Taylor & Son, d. by John Wiltshire Pender, closed and reused; bicycle works: A.W. Fitness, fire 1903, and L. Prince 1901; boiling-down works (F.J. King) 1844; boot factories: R. Cook, H.J. Payne, J. and R. Monro, John Sawyer 1841; breweries: Burton Brewery (estab. by William Tinson and Clifford) 1846–48, Hunter River Brewery (estab. 1843 by Alexander Berrie and William Tinson, taken over 1844 by Alexander Berrie and Thomas Underwood), Millstream Brewery (estab. by John Edwards and James Stuart in old flour mill, improvements 1880 d. by J.M. White, brewery moved 1887 into another old flour mill and became Maitland Brewery, rebuilt 1891 by Henry Adams and Arthur Wall, acquired by Tooth & Co., closed, sold and reused) 1845–1915, G.M. Milne & Co., Williams and Cohen 1875, in former flour mill; brickworks: Hopkins' and Lowe's; bridges: Belmore Bridge to Lorn (iron lattice girders fabricated by Lloyds, Fosters & Co., Wednesbury, England), erected 1866–69 by Francis Bell, d. by Edward Orpen Moriarty, replaced 1964 in steel and concrete, 643 ft (196 m), over Hunter R., Family Bridge to East Maitland b. 1827 by Alexander McLeod, damaged and rebuilt 1832, tolls removed 1834, replaced by Victoria Bridge (wrought iron girder spans) b. 1852 by William Henry Downey, 170 ft (51.8 m), d. by Edmund Thomas Blacket, major deck repairs 1873 by Thomas Smith, bridge replaced 1875 by Smith, demolished 1895, replaced again 1896 by D. McGill and John McGill, over Wallis Ck, Long Bridge (Veterans Flat) b. 1833, alterations 1890 by John Crimson, destroyed 1893, new one b. 1894 by Samuel McGill, 1,050 ft (320 m), rebuilt 1935–38 and 1955; broom factory (E.B. March), burnt down 1928; butter factory (Forest Hill Creamery) estab. 1896 by George Winkley and J.S. Vindin, from 1910 Winkley was sole proprietor; carriage-works: Freeman and Fullford (b. 1877 by John Clohessy, expanded 1882), H.H. Hall & Co., Great Northern Coach Factory (McNeall and McPherson) 1882, Richard Clement Hammond (fire 1917), James Hazlett, Lord and Scott, Northumberland Buggy Works (o. 1867 in former warehouse b. 1856, sold 1870 by James Woodforth to Miarus Moore, fire 1873, sold 1875 to William Coupland, alterations 1879, closed and sold 1892), H.G. Tuck & Co. (estab. by J.W. Tuck, acquired by C. McNeall, acquired 1854 by C.S. Windover), West End Coach & Buggy Factory (Skinner's), G.M. Winter (damaged 1905, demolished 1924),

James Woodforth 1883–85; CH 1856, one o. 1874 in reused building, new one b. 1897 by William and Charles Taylor, d. by Walter Liberty Vernon, additions 1900, renovated 1991 and 2014; Church of Christ; clothing factories: F.J. Palmer & Sons Ltd 1944–52 and West Maitland Manufacturing Co. 1944; confectionery factory (Davies & Herbert Ltd) 1903; Cong. C. o. 1851 (in renovated Presb. C.), new one b. 1854–57, d. by Goold and Field, closed, sold 1963, reused; cordial factories: William E. Comfort, George Moore (new one b. 1884 on new site by James Richardson), NSW Aerated Water & Cordial Co. Ltd 1903, T.F. Tinson, Volcanic Co. (estab. 1877 by Lewis Morris, relocated 1890, taken over 1902 by James Wolstenholme, burnt down 1922), W.H. Watson & Co.; dengue fever 1926 and 1927; diphtheria 1910 and 1921; earth tremors 1841, 1842, 1868, 1872, 1886, 1902, 1909, 1925; electricity 1922; engineering works (P.W.G. King & Sons Pty Ltd) 1923; FB 1867 (station b. 1878 by James Pritchard, additions 1895 by James Robinson, d. by John Wiltshire Pender, new one b. 1930 by George Pilgrim); fibrous plaster works estab. by Ben Pryor and Arch Pender, who were joined in 1918 by Ken Pryor, becoming Pryor, Pender and Pryor, later became Ben Pryor & Son; fires 1865, 1869, 1870, 1886, 1897, 1901, 1909, 1938; floods 1806, 1819, 1820, 1827, 1830, 1831, 1832, 1857, 1864, 1867, 1870, 1874, 1890, 1893, 1894, 1908, 1913, 1921, 1930, 1931, 1949, 1950, 1951, 1952, 1955 (11 died), 1971, 2007; flour mills: Blackwell's (formerly Gurr's), J.F. Burns (b. 1866 by T. Cooper), Peter Green 1845 (man killed 1847, sold to Joseph Ede Pearce, sold 1861 to Solomon, Vindin & Co., disused, burnt down 1862), Thomas Honeysett (wind powered, sold 1848 to J. Weston), Northumberland 1858 (James Wolstenholme, fire 1922, leased to John Nott, closed and reused), Nott, Crofton and Mitchell (alterations and renovations 1853), Railway (estab. by J.F. Burns, leased to Henry J. Hough, fire 1874, boiler explosion 1877), Henry C. Sempill (b. 1834 by John Dow, later bought by William Nicholson), Samuel Teas (sold 1854 to Solomon, Vindin & Co., closed and reused), J.A. Turner (formerly James Williams's); foundries: Robert Gibson (bought 1907 by D. Sim & Sons), J.T. Pont & Co. 1925 (in old cinema), Frederick Rivett (taken over 1905 by Robert Gibson), Smyth's (damaged 1905); furniture factories: David Cohen & Co. Ltd 1929, fire 1934, Hyndes', burnt down 1865, F. Nicholson, incl. bedding factory; gales 1873, 1894, 1928; gastroenteritis epidemic (6 infants died) 1921; gasworks estab. 1859 by John Warn Tuck, became Maitland Gas Light Co. Ltd in 1873, new retort house 1877, man killed 1918, acquired 1959 by Aberdare County Council, defunct; hailstorms 1861, 1875, 2015; hospital b. 1846–49 by J. Ashton, new wing b. 1903–5 by Andrew Burg, d. by J.J. Clarke, extensions 1916 d. by Walter Harold Pender, additions 1928, extended 1934, additions 1937 by F. and R. Compton, more additions 1940, 1943, 1947, 1960, 1962, 1978, 1996; ice works: Central Ice Depot, Dark-Moore Ice Co. Pty Ltd, Great Northern Ice Co. 1877, J. Wolstenholme Ltd (2 sites) 1897 and 1913; Jewish C. b. 1879 by James Pritchard, d. by John Wiltshire Pender, closed 1898, reused, sold 1926, additions 1946, restoration by Reg Jack, d. by Ian Pender, and graveyard (44 burials); joineries: Albert Dutton 1923, Henry Ikin 1843, Phil James, burnt down 1925, Knox's, James Pritchard; levee, destroyed 1893; lock-up 1851 d. by Edmund Thomas Blacket, demolished, new one b. 1896 by William and Charles Taylor, d. by Walter Liberty Vernon; measles epidemics 1893 (2 died), 1910, 1928; monumental stone works: H.F. Bowd and Thomas Browne Pty Ltd 1875, workshop 1902; PO: Maitland 1829 (new one b. 1879–82 by S. and W. Stanbridge, d. by James Johnstone Barnet, alterations and renovations 1889 by James Pritchard, additions 1900 by Charles Baker, extended 1967) and North Maitland 1938; police barracks o. 1874 in reused building, new barracks b. 1897; Presb. C. (Scots) 1832–49, sold, new one b. 1847–49 on new site; Prim. Meth. C. 1858, renovations and repairs 1872; PS b. 1896 by William and Charles Taylor, d. by Walter Liberty Vernon, new one 1951, redeveloped 1986; quarry (stone); rifle range, additions and alterations 1906 by Robert Hood; Rom. Cath. C.: St John the Baptist b. 1844–46, d. by Mortimer William Lewis, alterations and enlargement 1860 by Scanlan, extended 1866, closed 1933 and reused, reopened as church 1989, closed 2010, restored 2016 and reused and St John's (pro-cathedral) o. 1933 in former hall, converted by Tom Burg, d. by T. Silk, damaged and closed 1989, reused; RS: High Street 1858 and Maitland (West Maitland till 1949) 1858, new station 1880; sale-yards (A.W. Dodd), acquired 1888 by local council, new yards 1915; Salv. Army C. 1883, new one 1890; sawmills: Frederick Brewer (bankrupt 1895), Phil James (burnt down 1936), Pender Bros 1892 (incl. joinery, man killed 1897, fire 1913), Railway Steam Saw & Bone Mills 1842 (estab. by George Tillet Brewer and James Wolstenholm); schools: Maitland (West Maitland till 1949) 1874 b. by James Pritchard, d. by George Allen Mansfield, additions 1877 by Robert James, additions 1883 by J. Robinson, repairs 1892 by James Richardson, extensions 1899 d. by Walter Liberty Vernon, additions 1958, Horseshoe Bend 1885–1982, St Ethels 1882–1986; sewerage 1939; shoe factory (Maitland Shoes Pty Ltd) estab. 1945 by S. Goldberg in former hall, closed 1952; soap-works: Benjamin Cox 1832 (bought 1833 by Phillip Joseph Cohen), Hyland's 1843, Northumberland Soap & Candle Works (J.C. Logan), West Maitland Soap & Candle Manufactory (William Heugh); storms 1899 (most buildings damaged) and 1905; streets gas lit 1878, electric lit 1922; tanneries: Bermondsey (John Sawyer) 1841, relocated 1848, H. Rourke & Co. 1843 (taken over 1848 by James Brackenreg, jun.), Union (Aked and Forster); TC o. 1894 (in former carriage-works), new building b. 1910 by Benjamin George Pearce, d. by Walter Liberty Vernon, inundated 1910, additions and alterations 1911 by W. Holloway, also d. by Vernon, additions 1913, 1915, 1955, closed 1987, sold 2002, renovated, reused 2003–8, extensions 2009 d. by Paul Berkemeier, reopened 2009; telegraph: High Street 1894–1915 and Maitland 1860, new office b. 1879–82 by S. and W. Stanbridge, d. by James Johnstone Barnet; telephone (North Maitland) 1938; tinware factory (Dilly and Hogan); tobacco factories: Clarke and Walthall 1843 (closed, reused 1863 by James E. Wolfe and Jacob Gorrick, strike 1890), Foster's, Fullford's, W. Kelly (burnt down 1881), George Norrie (reused 1883), John Spinks, W.D. & H.O. Wills (Aust.) Ltd 1946–52; toll-gate; tramway (steam) b. by J. Champion, to East Maitland, 1909–26; TX 1887, automatic 1965; typhoid 1883, 1895, 1896, 1897, 1898, 1903 (man died), 1905, 1908, 1909 (man died), 1925; Unit. C. (orig. Wes. Meth.) b. 1859 by John Wright, Mack and Sherwood, extended by Andrew Burg, alterations 1958, renovations 1959, restoration 1997 d. by Barney Collins, and columbarium; water reticulation 1887; watch-house 1858; Wes. Meth. C. b. 1838-40 by William Galway, demolished 1848, and graveyard; pop. 1,456 (1833), 1,746 (1841), 2,409 (1846), 3,131 (1851), 4,441 (1856), 5,694 (1861), 5,079 (1871), *c.*5,000 (1875), 5,300 (1881), 7,295 (1891), *c.*7,700 (1895), 6,789 (1901), 7,395 (1911), 8,700 (1918), 8,191 (1933), 19,151 (1947), 21,331 (1954), 22,917 (1961), 22,440 (1966), 24,530 (1971), 36,030 (1976), 38,865 (1981), 43,247 (1986), 45,209 (1991), 50,108 (1996), 53,470 (2001), 61,431 (2006).

Maitland Bar (*Co. Wellington*) 32°44'S. 149°26'E., 21 km SW of Mudgee; defunct; mining (gold rush 1852); Chinese joss house; pop. 88 (1901), 60 (1911), 55 (1933).

Maitland Camp (*Co. Wellington*) 33°02'S. 149°30'E., 48 km NE of Orange; quarry.

Maitland East (*Co. Northumberland*) 32°45'S. 151°35'E., 3 km SE of Maitland, on Wallis Ck; (incl. Ashtonfield, Eastville, Greenhills,

Metford formerly Enfield, Shamrock Hill); Maitland till 1835; settled 1818, orig. govt town founded 1825, surveyed 1829 by Major Sir Thomas Livingstone Mitchell, laid out 1831 by George Boyle White, town gaz. 1833, boundary with Maitland gaz. 1835, munic. proc. 1862, city (incl. Maitland and Morpeth) proc. 1945, munic. greatly enlarged 1958; coal 1842+, horses, wheat, lucerne, maize, barley, oats, potatoes, pumpkins, melons, orchards, grapes; abattoir; Angl. C.: St Barnabas's 1917, closed, sold 2014 to Simon and Susan O'Rourke and reused, St Mark's (Eastville) 1961–76, in former migrant hostel removed from Greta, St Peter's 1838–40 d. by James Hume, alterations and repairs 1853, closed and reused, new one b. 1884–86 by Oliver Saunders, d. by Blacket Bros, and graveyard (The Glebe, burials 1828+, graves 1841+, disused and desecrated), incl. columbarium; Apostolic C. (Groundlevel); Assemblies of God C. (Christ. Life); Bapt. C. (Metford Community); brickworks: Edmund William Auckett, sold 1890, F. Baker & Sons Pty Ltd, closed 1973, Dawes, Dixon and Sams, John and George Pont, closed 1893, Smith and Dawson (taken over 1882 by Francis Turton, new kiln 1935 d. by Walter Harold Pender, brickworks sold 1965 to Maxwell Porter and David Galbraith, which became PGH Industries, closed 2006, derelict); bridges over Wallis Ck: Family Bridge to Maitland b. 1827 by Alexander McLeod, damaged and rebuilt 1832, tolls removed 1834, replaced by Victoria Bridge (wrought iron girder spans) b. 1852 by William Henry Downey, 170 ft (51.8 m), d. by Edmund Thomas Blacket, major deck repairs 1873 by Thomas Smith, bridge replaced 1875 by Smith, demolished 1895, replaced again 1896 by D. McGill and John McGill, and Trappaud Bridge 1888, replaced 1937 and 2012; carriage-works (J. Riley & Co.) estab. 1885 by James Riley; cemeteries: general (6,909 graves 1854+) and war (6 graves); CH 1831, new one (incl. lock-up) b. 1844 by Mayo, new one b. 1860 by William Cains, d. by Alexander Dawson, additions 1864, 1870, 1884 all d. by James Johnstone Barnet, restored 1979; Chinese joss house, closed, sold and reused; coalmine (Robert Keddie) 1842; collieries: Delta No. 1 (Delta Coals Pty Ltd) and East End; Cong. C. b. 1916 by H.F. Boyle, d. by Thomas James Pepper, and graveyard; concrete plant (Pioneer Concrete Pty Ltd); confectionery factory (Prydes) o. 1934 at Metford, fire 1953, closed 2012, bought 2013 by Rainbow Confectionery, closed 2015; cordial factory (Sharpe Bros) estab. 1908 by John Sharpe, Alex Elliott, Jack Cox, closed 1914; earth tremors 1841, 1868, 1909, 1925; electricity 1923; engineering works: Paul Anderson Engineering Pty Ltd, and Cliff Eyre and Glenn Smith 1988, relocated 1994 to Metford; FB (station b. 1896 by William Henry Noad, new one 1918, closed); fibrous plaster works: A. Betts and A.J. Watters; fire 1871; floods 1826, 1830, 1832, 1857, 1867, 1889, 1890, 1893, 1908, 1955, 2007; flour mills: James Smith 1845 (taken over by Crofton and Mount, which became Mount and Field, additions 1854 and 1857, reused), and James Williams 1844; foundries: John and Robert Ewing, and Richard Marsh; Free Presb. C. b. 1879 by Benjamin Hodgson, d. by John Wiltshire Pender, inundated 1893; gale (damaged much of town) 1905; gaol 1835, new one b. 1844–49 d. by Mortimer William Lewis, additions (incl. new wing and 6 solitary confinement cells) 1861–73 d. by James Johnstone Barnet, chimney 65 ft (19.8 m) b. 1895 by Edges, additions 1899 by A. Burg, additions and alterations 1900 by W.E. Graham, additions 1994, closed 1998, reused; gasworks b. 1887 by Robert S. Dethick, John Grant and Robert James, new gasholder 1896, fire 1930, gasworks acquired by Aberdare County Council; hailstorms 1861, 1873, 1896, 1909, 2015; immigrants' home b. 1840 by John Smith, used 1842 by Caroline Chisholm, reused as hospital till 1843; iron foundry (estab. 1870 by John Ewing, taken over by Richard Francis Marsh and became Washington Machine Supply Co.); joinery estab. 1880 by William Henry Noad; LDS (Mormon) C.; meat works (Shamrock Hill Meat Preserving Co.) estab. 1872 by John B. Christian, acquired by James Ewan and John McElhone; metal fabrication works: Multi-Metal Fabrications and Wayne Peacock Fabrications; PO 1840, new one b. 1876 by Henry Noad, inundated 1893, renovated 1924 by White Bros, closed, sold and reused, new one 1971; police barracks b. 1882 by W. Cains & Son, closed, alterations 1954, reused as police station till 1972, restored 1981 and reused; pottery estab. 1872 by Anthony Hillcoat, closed, sold 1906 to Frederick James Fieldsend, reopened 1908; pound (stock) 1863; Presb. C. (St Stephen's) b. 1858–60, d. by William White, alterations and additions 1886 by W. Taylor & Son, damaged 1893 by flood, demolished 1939, new one b. 1938 by George Pilgrim, d. by John Shedden Adam, jun., and columbarium; Prim. Meth. C. b. 1891 by John Murphy, d. by Pullen; PS b. 1871 by William Cains, closed and reused, new one 1972 on new site, closed; 3 quarries; railway turntable, 50 ft (15.2 m); reservoir, 463,400 gal. (2,106.6 kl); rifle range, additions and alterations 1906 by Robert Hood; Rom. Cath. C. b. 1830–35, damaged 1873, closed and demolished 1933, replacement (St Joseph's) b. 1934 by C. and F. Burg, d. by Peter Joseph Gannon, and graveyard, incl. columbaria; RS: East Maitland (first one) 1857–58, second one 1858–79, third one (Morpeth Junction till 1879) 1864, station b. by Matthew Jamieson, additions 1878, platforms extended 1902, station closed 1914, fourth one 1914, Metford 1995, Victoria Street 1877, station additions 1904; Salv. Army C. 1884, new one 1916, damaged 1928, closed; sawmills: John Paton, jun. (incl. joinery and bone mill), Pender & Foster Ltd 1918, Cornelius Shay (boiler explosion 1883); schools: Ashtonfield 2007 (additions 2011), East Maitland 1858, new one b. 1883 by James Pritchard, d. by William Edmund Kemp, additions 1956, 1961, 1990, Maitland HS (West Maitland Boys HS 1892, East Maitland Boys HS till 1934, Maitland Boys HS till 1986, then Evatt HS till 1989) 1884, new school b. 1894 d. by John Wiltshire Pender, additions 1963 and 1969, Maitland Grossmann HS (West Maitland Girls HS till 1934, Maitland Girls HS till 1986, then Maitland HS till 1989) 1884, additions 1958, 1964, 1969, 1985, Metford 1980, additions 1986; SD Adventist C., fire 1949; sewerage 1938; steel fabrication works (Challen Fabrications); storms 1928 and 2004; streets gas lit 1887; TC (at Metford) 1987, became Hunter Institute of Technology, Maitland Campus, in 1992; telegraph 1862, new office b. 1876 by Henry Noad; tobacco factories: Joseph Cunningham and Godfrey's; tramways: one (steam) to Morpeth 1893–1913 and one (steam) b. by J. Champion, to Maitland, 1909–26; TX (automatic) 1951; typhoid 1908, 1912, 1920 (boy died); Unit. C. (Wesley, orig. Meth.) 1961; water reticulation 1888; Wes. Meth. C. 1845, destroyed 1857, new one b. 1858 on new site, d. by W. White, damaged 1861 and 1873, vestry added 1878, church closed 1937, demolished 1938; pop. 1,022 (1841), 910 (1846), 1,099 (1851), 1,655 (1856), 1,834 (1861), *c.*2,200 (1862), *c.*2,000 (1866), 1,675 (1871), 2,004 (1881), 2,919 (1891), *c.*3,100 (1895), 3,284 (1901), 2,937 (1911), 4,138 (1933), 11,014 (2011).

Maitland North (*Co. Northumberland*) see Maitland.

Maitland Point (*Co. Roxburgh*) see Sofala.

Maitland Point (*Co. Sandon*) 30°35'S. 151°28'E., 8 km NW of Uralla, on Rocky R.; school 1864–66 and 1897–1905; Wes. Meth. C. 1886, demolished; pop. 75 (1933), 63 (1947).

Maitland Vale (*Co. Durham*) 32°41'S. 151°33'E., 6 km N. of Maitland, on Hunter R.; bushfire 1905; pop. 32 (1933), 55 (1961).

Maitland West (*Co. Northumberland*) see Maitland and Maitland East.

Majors Creek (*Co. Dudley*) 30°56'S. 152°35'E., 30 km NW of Kempsey; pop. 23 (1933).

Majors Creek (*Co. St Vincent*) 35°34'S. 149°44'E., 14 km S. of Braidwood, on Majors Ck; Elrington till 1928; settled 1827–31 by

Major William Sandys Elrington, village reserve set aside 1840, laid out 1859 by James Larmer, town gaz. 1860 as Elrington, town gaz. 1928 as Majors Creek; wheat 1840+, mining (alluvial gold disc. 1851 by Baxter, and reef gold 1869+, gold rush finished 1914) till *c.*1940, vegetables (mainly during the gold rush), eucalyptus oil, grazing; Angl. C. (St Stephen's) b. 1870–72 by E. Francis, re-roofed; bridge (Sapling Hill Bridge) b. 1870 by Peter Rusconi, over Majors Ck; cemetery (170 graves) 1863; diphtheria 1911, 1912, 1915 (child died); FB; mines: Camage's (Camage 1907–18 and W.L. Moore 1931–42), Dargue's (Majors Creek Gold Mining Syndicate and Dargue's Reef Gold Mining Co.) 1877–1916, H.J. Dunshea 1935–38, Eureka, Great Star, Homeward Bound, A. Matheson *c.*1887, Mobbs's, Nimrod (G. Cleaver) 1906–10, Perseverance and Hindhaugh's Shoot 1896–1919, Rigby's, Rise and Shine No. 1 1882–88, Rise and Shine No. 2 1909, Scotsmans Gully Reef North (A. Hay), Scotsmans Gully Reef South (A. Hay), Snobs or Mount Hope (S. Holmes and Eureka Gold Mining Co.) 1895–1908, Spencer's, Sperantum Gold Mining Co. 1931–35, United Miners (Stewart and Merton, and United Gold Miners' Gold Mining Co.) 1876–1910, Whiteman and Merton, Young Australia; PO 1858, new one b. 1898 by Charles Baker; pound (stock) 1862; Presb. C. 1907; PS b. 1900 by Lansdown and Murray, closed 1939, reused; quarry; Rom. Cath. C., burnt down 1868, rebuilt 1869 by Michael Costello, defunct, new one (St Mary's) b. 1937 by Jack Hall et al., d. by Devine, closed, sold 2016 and reused; Salv. Army C. 1889; school 1857, new building b. 1889 by Knowles, closed 1967, sold and reused; telegraph 1882, new office b. 1898 by Charles Baker; TX 1928–79; typhoid 1873 (boy died), 1897 (girl died), 1899, 1902, 1919 (man died); Union C.; pop. *c.*200 (1866), 1,074 (1871), 966 (1891), 611 (1901), 337 (1911), 224 (1933), 175 (1947), 114 (1954), 130 (1961), 220 (2011).

Majors Flat (*Co. Gloucester*) 32°47'S. 151°56'E., 12 km SW of Lemon Tree Passage.

Majors Plains (*Co. Hume*) 35°55'S. 146°43'E., 11 km NE of Howlong, on Majors Ck; school 1884, additions 1889 by J.W. Johnson, closed 1899, reopened 1915, closed 1918.

Malabar (*Co. Bathurst*)
see Orange (*Co. Wellington*).

Malabugilmah (*Co. Drake*) 29°11'S. 152°38'E., 54 km SW of Casino, on Bugilbar Ck.

Malara (*Co. Drake*) see Millera.

Maldon (*Co. Camden*) 34°11'S. 150°38'E., 3 km SE of Picton, on Stonequarry Ck; farming; bridge (suspension) b. 1903 by James McCall, d. by Ernest Macartney de Burgh and Harvey Dare, 618 ft (188.5 m), largely destroyed 1939, rebuilt 1940, closed to vehicular traffic 1980, new one downstream (pre-stressed concrete box girder) d. and b. 1977–80 by John Holland (Constructions) Pty Ltd, 610 ft (186 m); bushfire 1939; cement works (Metrop. Portland Cement Ltd) b. 1949–51; PO 1927–42; RS (Wilton till 1890) 1889, new station 1892, closed 1973; pop. 63 (1933), 115 (1954), 96 (1961), 131 (2001).

Malebo (*Co. Bourke*) 35°04'S. 147°16'E., 11 km NW of Wagga Wagga; Meth. C. 1910; PO 1888–1912; school 1882, new one b. 1883 by Charles Hardy, repairs 1891 by M.J. M'Mullen, repairs 1918 by G. Broadfoot, destroyed 1927, replacement b. 1928 by Roebuck and Mueller, closed 1968; Wes. Meth. C. 1873; pop. 57 (1901), 145 (1911), 145 (1933), 121 (1947), 124 (1954), 68 (1961).

Malgarai (*Co. Stapylton*) see Wearne.

Mallabula (*Co. Gloucester*) 32°44'S. 152°01'E., 12 km W. of Nelson Bay, on Port Stephens; mining (rutile and zircon); Angl. C. (Holy Name) 1983; mine (Assoc. Minerals Consolidated Ltd) 1965; Rom. Cath. C. (Our Lady Help of Christians) b. 1982 by Dick Harding; sewage works (Tanilba Bay); water supply 1969; pop. 13 (1961), 851 (2011).

Mallan (*Co. Wakool*) 35°11'S. 143°41'E., 58 km S. of Balranald, on Niemur R.; PO 1896–1917; school 1957–2013, sold; TX (automatic) 1961; pop. 81 (1911), 118 (1933), 191 (2006).

Mallanganee (*Co. Drake*) 28°54'S. 152°43'E., 32 km W. of Casino; Sandilands till 1906; village gaz. 1917; timber, cattle, dairying; Angl. C. (St Ambrose's) 1920, moved to Queensland; butter factory and ice works (Casino Co-op. Dairy Co. Ltd) b. 1916 by Gibbons and Hogg, d. by J.G. Popplewell, burnt down 1938; cemetery; hailstorm 1936; PO 1909, new one b. 1913; quarry; Rom. Cath. C. (Our Lady of Perpetual Succour) b. 1919–22 by John A. Connolly; sawmills: Hugh Emmanuel Alvos, Duncan's Holdings Ltd 1969, T.W. Hewetson (b. 1897 by Thomas and John Hewetson, John Sexton joined the business, firm acquired by Duncan's Holdings Ltd, burnt down 1946); school (Sandilands Range till 1914) 1907, new one b. 1924, closed 2010; telephone 1911; TX 1914, automatic 1973; pop. 111 (1911), 436 (1933), 483 (1947), 466 (1954), 396 (1961), *c.*140 (2001), 120 (2006), 197 (2011).

Mallawa (*Co. Benarba*) see Mallowa.

Mallee Cliffs (*Co. Wentworth*) 34°18'S. 142°17'E., 40 km SE of Wentworth, on Murray R.

Mallee Plains (*Co. Bland*) 33°53'S. 147°19'E., 11 km E. of West Wyalong; school 1908–34.

Malleevale (*Co. Bourke*) 34°13'S. 146°54'E., 16 km N. of Ardlethan; telephone 1925; TX 1926–38.

Mallowa (*Co. Benarba*) 29°39'S. 149°22'E., 50 km SW of Moree; school (Mallawa) 1960, additions 1964 and 2010; pop. 284 (2011).

Mallowgrove (*Co. Bathurst*) 33°37'S. 149°13'E., 9 km S. of Blayney, on Carcoar Lake; airfield; school 1924 b. by J. Bridgman, closed 1929, sold and moved 1936.

Malmsbury (*Co. Bathurst*) see Dunkeld.

Maloneys Beach (*Co. St Vincent*) 35°42'S. 150°15'E., 6 km E. of Batemans Bay, on Chain Bay; pop. 369 (2011).

Malongulli (*Co. Bathurst*) 33°35'S. 148°50'E., 15 km E. of Canowindra, on Belubula R.; village gaz. 1882.

Malua Bay (*Co. St Vincent*) 35°47'S. 150°14'E., 10 km SE of Batemans Bay, on Tasman Sea; (incl. Mosquito Bay and North Burrewarra); formerly timber, then wattle-bark, farming, dairying, passionfruit (industry founded by C. Neilsen); cheese factory 1923, burnt down 1929; FB; PO: Malua Bay 1970 and Mosquito Bay 1928–31; reservoir; sewerage 1980; telephone: Malua Bay 1970 and Mosquito Bay 1930; TX: Malua Bay (automatic) 1978, Mosquito Bay 1934, North Burrewarra 1947–54; pop. 25 (1933), 503 (1981), 694 (1986), 1,361 (1991), 1,494 (1996), 1,676 (2001), 1,907 (2006), 2,051 (2011).

Maluerindi (*Co. Inglis*) see Woolbrook.

Mambo Island (*Co. Macquarie*) see Mamboo Island.

Mamboo Island (*Co. Macquarie*) 31°51'S. 152°37'E., 7 km W. of Harrington, on Manning R.; formerly Mambo Island; Angl. C. 1862; flood 1929; pop. 55 (1901), 60 (1911), 48 (1933).

Manar (*Co. Murray*) 35°18'S. 149°40'E., 19 km NW of Braidwood; PO 1867; telephone 1937; TX (automatic) 1972; pop. 60 (1901), 39 (1933).

Manara (*Co. Manara*) 32°28'S. 143°57'E., 116 km SE of Wilcannia; RS 1949–74; school 1957–72.

Manchester Square (*Co. Camden*) 34°37'S. 150°24'E., 7 km SE of Moss Vale; bushfire 1905; butter factory 1891, closed; school 1884–1911; telephone 1947; TX 1948–68; pop. 30 (1933).

Mandagery (*Co. Ashburnham*) 33°14'S. 148°24'E., 24 km SE of Parkes; formerly Goambeen; wheat, farming, grazing; FB; Meth. C. b. 1902 by Watts; PO 1927; RS (Moura till 1921) 1893, station b. by Frederick Lemm, jun. and Thomas Edward Spencer, closed 1974; school 1957–88; telephone 1922; TX 1927, automatic 1965; pop. 95 (1933), 128 (1947), 115 (1961).

Mandalong (*Co. Northumberland*) 33°08'S. 151°25'E., 7 km SW of Morisset, on Morans Ck; settled 1852 by Carl Frederick Solling; orig. timber, then agric., dairying, citrus orchards, now hobby farming; bushfire 1927; cemetery 1889, defunct; coalmine (Centennial Coal Co. Ltd) 2005; FB; PO 1884, burnt down 1892; Rom. Cath. C. 1877; sawmill (Archibald O'Neill); school 1910–25; telephone 1916; TX 1925–62; pop. 70 (1901),

87 (1933), 60 (1961), 388 (2011).

Mandamah (*Co. Bland*) 34°14'S. 147°16'E., 34 km S. of Wyalong; surveyed 1884 by Arthur Hulance Bray, village gaz. 1885, never developed; FB 1948 (station b. 2013); Rom. Cath. C. 1906; school 1910–16; pop. 33 (1891).

Mandemar (*Co. Camden*) 34°26'S. 150°18'E., 8 km NW of Berrima; eucalyptus oil distillery (Bosisto Co. Ltd) 1925, extended 1926; school (Mangellore) 1896–98; pop. 93 (1901).

Mandle (*Co. Buller*) 28°29'S. 152°18'E., 69 km W. of Kyogle; school 1913–20.

Mandurama (*Co. Bathurst*) 33°39'S. 149°05'E., 21 km SW of Blayney, on Mandurama Ponds; estab. 1875 as a private village by Thomas Icely, surveyed 1875 by Alfred John Pechey, every house acquired 1881 by Cobb & Co., declined 1890s+; formerly goldmining, then wheat, fruit, peas, now livestock breeding; Angl. C. (St Stephen the Martyr) b. 1912 by Walter Goodacre, d. by John Job Copeman, closed, and graveyard (3 graves); butter factory (Thomas Icely), burnt down; diphtheria 1914; earth tremor 1919; FB; fire 1925; gale 1947; hailstorm 1989; PO 1876, inundated 1913, damaged 1932, new one 1953; Presb. C. 1925; PS 1875, new one b. 1934 by Frederick Joseph Hokin and John Devereaux Boon; reservoir 1955; Rom. Cath. C. (St Laurence O'Toole's) b. 1936 by Peter Beddie and J.W. Brown, d. by Edward Rodwell Green; RS 1888, station b. by John Wadsworth Ashworth, relocated 1892, closed 1979; school 1878, new one b. 1882 by John Cody, d. by William Edmund Kemp, additions 1887 by Henry Ford, new one b. 1923 by L.H. Ralph; SD Adventist C. 1935; storm 1932; telegraph 1894; telephone 1887; TX 1914–86; water reticulation 1956; Wes. Meth. C. 1875, new one 1895; pop. 20 (1891), 299 (1901), 299 (1911), 379 (1921), 270 (1933), 283 (1947), 274 (1954), 165 (1961), *c.*200 (1975), 379 (2006), 496 (2011).

Mandurama Ponds (*Co. Bathurst*) see Gallymont.

Manera Heights (*Co. Lincoln*) see Dubbo.

Manfred (*Co. Manara*) 33°19'S. 143°47'E., 150 km N. of Balranald; telephone 1931; TX 1932–49; pop. 30 (1933).

Mangain (*Co. Bourke*) 34°55'S. 147°02'E., 14 km S. of Ganmain; school 1899–1924; telephone 1909; pop. 128 (1911), 93 (1933), 73 (1947).

Mangamore (*Co. Argyle*) see Springfield.

Mangellore (*Co. Camden*) see Mandemar.

Mangerton (*Co. Camden*) see Coniston.

Mangoola (*Co. Brisbane*) 32°20'S. 150°44'E., 7 km NE of Denman, on Sandy Ck; RS 1930–70; school 1957–68; telephone 1934; TX 1935–53; pop. 63 (1947).

Mangoplah (*Co. Mitchell*) 35°23'S. 147°15'E., 17 km SE of The Rock, on Burkes Ck; settled by German immigrants, village gaz. 1863; farming; aeroplane crash (2 killed) 1941; bridge (timber) 1909, additional span 1916, replacement (concrete) b. 1954 by Central Construction Co., 123 ft (37.5 m), over Burkes Ck; bushfires 1904 and 1952; Lutheran C. b. 1914 by H. Haycroft, closed 1983, and graveyard; Meth. C. 1938 d. by R.N. Gledhill, closed, moved 1951 to Bidgeemia and reused; PO 1911; reservoir (elevated, steel); Rom. Cath. C. (St Michael the Archangel) 1955; RS 1925–56, reused; school 1916–2012; silo 1928; telephone 1915; TX 1916, automatic 1981; Unit. C. (Scots, orig. Presb.) 1953; water supply 1963; pop. 265 (1911), 313 (1933), 303 (1947), 278 (1954), 311 (1961), 516 (2011).

Mangoplah North (*Co. Mitchell*) see Birdlip.

Mangrove (*Co. Northumberland*) see Mangrove Creek.

Mangrove Creek (*Co. Northumberland*) 33°21'S. 151°09'E., 21 km W. of Ourimbah, on Mangrove Ck; timber till *c.*1897, then farming (mainly maize) and grazing; hailstorm 1848; PO 1857, burnt down 1940; pumping station; sawmill (Walker Bros) 1935; school (Mangrove till 1872 and Lower Mangrove till 1889) 1861–77, new one 1880–1902 and 1909–38; telephone 1913; TX 1926; wharf (Bullock Wharf); pop. *c.*250 (1866), 342 (1901), 252 (1911), 110 (1933), 58 (1947), 531 (1961).

Mangrove Mountain (*Co. Northumberland*)

33°18'S. 151°12'E., 18 km W. of Ourimbah, on Popran Ck; (incl. Shakeshaft); citrus orchards and poultry farms (quarantined 1999); bushfire 1944; cemetery; FB; fruit packing house, burnt down 1941; hailstorm 2015; PO 1951; poultry processing plant (Inghams Enterprises, bought 2014 by Supreme Poultry & Chickens Pty Ltd); 2 quarries; school (Koree till 1937) 1918, additions 1967, closed 1978; telephone (Shakeshaft) 1913; TX (automatic) 1965; Union C. b. 1912 by Gibson, Greentree and Benson; pop. 94 (1911), 270 (1933), 361 (1947), 467 (1954), 725 (2011).

Mangrove Point (*Co. Northumberland*) see Mount White.

Manies Creek (*Co. Vernon*) 31°02'S. 151°40'E., 9 km SE of Walcha, on Maineys Ck; school 1880–1900.

Manifold (*Co. Rous*) 28°45'S. 153°05'E., 13 km N. of Casino, on Back Ck; school 1930, additions 2010.

Manildra (*Co. Ashburnham*) 33°11'S. 148°42'E., 40 km W. of Orange, on Mandagery Ck; formerly known as Flash Jack Creek and Flash Jack's Flat; village gaz. 1881; wheat, rye, lucerne, pigs, stock feed, flour; 2 airfields; Angl. C. (St Luke's) b. 1909 by Joseph J. Wells, d. by John Holderness Bates; Bapt. C. b. 1909 by Joseph J. Wells, d. by Augustus Dixon Chater; bridges 1879, 1900, 1930, over Mandagery Ck; carriage-works (James Jones) 1908; cemetery (*c.*410 burials) 1881; creamery (Molong Dist. Dairying Co.) 1900; earth tremors 1936 and 1950; FB; fire 1925; flour mill (Gem of the West), removed 1904 from Cargo by Worrall Bros, new one 1907, overhauled 1909, taken over 1921 by Hamilton Bros, burnt down 1936, rebuilt 1938, converted 1946 from steam to electricity, sold 1952 to Jack Honan and Bill Anderson and became Manildra Flour Milling Co. Pty Ltd, expanded 1996–2001, damaged by explosion 2018; foot-bridge over Mandagery Ck; 4 piggeries; PO 1891, new one b. 1911 by Maudsley and Hainwright, closed 2007; pound (stock) 1903; PS (in rented premises) 1890, new one b. 1934 by Peter Beddie and J.W. Brown; 5 quarries; railway bridge over Mandagery Ck; reservoir 1959; Rom. Cath. C. (St Michael's) b. 1940 by A.E. Rauch, d. by Edward Rodwell Green; RS 1893, station b. by Frederick Lemm, jun. and Thomas Edward Spencer, demolished 1985; sale-yards (A.H. Oldham & Co.); sawmill (Cochram's) 1878; school 1882, repairs 1891 and 1893 by James Price, new buildings b. 1908 by Joseph Wells, additions 1961 and 1966; silo 1920; telegraph 1894; TX 1910, automatic 1980; typhoid 1902; Unit. C. (orig. Meth.) b. 1913 by R.A. Allum, d. by Alfred Gambier Newman; water reticulation 1959, augmentation 1995; pop. 379 (1901), 653 (1911), 615 (1933), 743 (1947), 787 (1954), 591 (1961), 399 (1966), 451 (1971), 557 (1976), 520 (1981), 520 (1986), 498 (1991), 533 (1996), 517 (2001), 503 (2006), 464 (2011).

Manilla (*Co. Darling*) 30°45'S. 150°43'E., 43 km NW of Tamworth, on Namoi R.; The Junction till 1856; settled and founded 1853 by George Veness, surveyed 1861 by Arthur Dewhurst, town gaz. and first lots sold 1862, designated as chief town of the county, thrived 1894–1900, munic. 1901–59; wheat 1872+, surpassed by wool 1880, later cattle, tobacco (peaked 1923), sorghum, mixed farming, eggs, lime; abattoir; agric. implement works: H. Baker and W. Bluett (incl. engineering works); ambulance station; Angl. C. b. 1893 by Thomas John Bowen, d. by H.S. Turner, replacement (Holy Trinity) b. 1914 by Walter Jackson, d. by Charles Rosenthal, additions 1939 by W.C. Grantham; brickworks (S.G. Hartley); bridges: one (metal lattice truss) b. 1884–86 by Royce Bros & Co., 1,001 ft (305 m), over Namoi R., one b. 1908, one (low-level) b. 1938, Mandowa Bridge over Manilla R.; bushfire 1884; carriage-works: A.E. Bailey 1893 (sold 1933 to A.C. Blanch), and H.M. Baker 1906 (sold 1928, demolished); caterpillar infestations 1936, 1940, 1945; causeway b. 1878 by Joseph Conlon, destroyed 1879; cemetery (1,988 graves), incl. columbaria; CH b. 1886 by Thomas John Bowen, alterations 1911 by T.N. Josephson, damaged 1937, larger porch added 1958; clock tower 1938; cordial factories: Manilla Steam Aerated & Cordial Manufactory (William Henry O'Dell) 1894, sold 1912 to North, sold again 1928, and North and Macdonald (acquired 1910 from Evans); diphtheria 1910, 1911, 1912, 1917; drought 1946; earth tremors 1923 and 2012; electricity 1915; FB (station b. 1935 by W.C. Grantham); fire-hose factory 1981, upgraded 1991, closed 2006; fires 1913, 1914, 1927; fish hatchery; floods 1840, 1864 (8+ died), 1910, 1952 (8 died), 1955, 1964; flour mill (Clark and Crocker) b. 1899 by Thomas John Bowen, bought 1902 by Wilson Bros and Oram and named Snowcloud Flour Mill, rebuilt 1912 on new site, taken over 1920 by M.C. Mackenzie & Sons, burnt down 1929; foundry (H.M. Baker) 1906; grasshopper infestation 1928; hailstorm 1937; honey processing plant; hospital b. 1905 by Richard Allright Stanfield, d. by Philip Ernest Ranclaud, additions 1905 by W. Mitchell, additions 1922, 1935, 1937, fire (nurse died) 1948, additions 1952, 1956, 1962, 1967, 2012; lock-up b. 1875 by Thomas John Bowen; meadery (Dutton's); measles epidemic 1894; PO 1854, new one b. 1899 by Thomas John Bowen, additions 1908 and 1923, new one b. 1926 by Jones, damaged 1937; pound (stock) 1865; powerhouse (Falkner Electric Co.) 1915, taken over 1925 by Aust. Electric Light Co.; Presb. C. (St Andrew's) b. 1904 by Chapman and Byron, replacement b. 1968 by Sweeney Constructions Pty Ltd, d. by Ian McKay; PS (incl. lock-up) 1898, new one b. 1909 by William Robert Ibbotson, new one 1980; rabbit freezing works b. 1916 by McKay; railway bridge (steel Pratt truss) 1906, fabricated by Clyde Engineering Co. Ltd, over Namoi R.; railway engine shed 1901; railway turntable, 50 ft (15.2 m), ruined; railway viaduct 1906, over Namoi R.; reservoir 1933; rifle range 1906; Rom. Cath. C. b. 1895 by Thomas John Bowen, d. by French, additions 1902, reused 1938, new one (St Michael's) b. 1938 by C. Davis & Sons Pty Ltd, d. by Peter Jerome Gannon, burnt down 1971, replacement b. 1972 by F.S. and P.O. Meere, d. by K. Bonner; RS: Manilla 1899, station burnt down 1899, rebuilt 1900, closed 1978 and Rowan Street 1923, closed; sale-yards: 1908 and 1935 (estab. by V.J. Byrnes, modernised 1973 by V.J. Byrnes Pty Ltd); sawmills: Victoria (J.F. Wearne) and T.A. Wilson & Co. (burnt down 1905); scarlet fever 1920; school 1878, new one b. 1879, new one b. 1901 on new site by C. Harris, additions 1923 by G.W. Barnard, additions 1926, 1933, 1966, 1983, 1993; sewerage 1951; silo 1934; streets electric lit 1915; telegraph 1878, new office b. 1889; telephone 1899; TX 1907, new building b. 1926 by Jones, automatic 1980; Union C. b. 1877 by P. and J. McGauley; Unit. C. (orig. Meth.) b. 1911 by T.F. Rowe, d. by Alfred Gambier Newman; water supply 1933, augmentation 1990; 2 weirs on Namoi R.; Wes. Meth. C. b. 1890 by Thomas John Bowen; pop. 12 (1864), *c.*50 (1866), 275 (1891), 650 (1896), 888 (1901), 2,374 (1911), 1,774 (1933), *c.*1,850 (1941), 1,919 (1947), 1,972 (1954), 1,914 (1961), 1,761 (1966), 1,660 (1971), 1,849 (1976), 1,884 (1981), 2,017 (1986), 2,110 (1991), 2,073 (1996), 2,041 (2001), 2,081 (2006), 2,107 (2011).

Manilla Road (*Co. Inglis*) see Tamworth.

Mannafield (*Co. Argyle*) see Towrang.

Mannering Park (*Co. Northumberland*) 33°09'S. 151°32'E., 5 km W. of Gwandalan, on Lake Macquarie; (incl. Vales Point); founded by James Vinrace Vale; Angl. C. (St Andrew's) 1961; collieries: Chain Valley (Coal & Allied Operations Pty Ltd, acquired by Lake Coal, acquired 2006 by Peabody Energy Aust.) 1961, Newvale No. 1 (formerly Elcom Collieries Pty Ltd), Wyee (Powercoal, formerly Elcom Collieries Pty Ltd) 1962; colliery accident (5 died) 1966; electricity 1959; FB; jetty; Meth. C. 1965; mines rescue station; PO 1947; power station (Vales Point) 1964, augmented 1978–80, bought 2015 by Sunset Power International Pty Ltd; 2 reservoirs; 2 sawmills estab. by James Vinrace Vale, one steam, and a later diesel powered one; school 1961 in rented premises, new school b. 1964 by W.A. Wenham, additions 1977, 1981, 1982, 1991, 1994; sewerage 1985; telephone 1948; TX 1949–60; Unit. C. (St Mark's); water reticulation 1962; pop. 71 (1947), 64 (1954), 262 (1961), 772 (1971), 1,067 (1976), 1,401 (1981), 1,728 (1986), 2,261 (1991), 2,344 (1996), 2,445 (2001), 2,409 (2006), 2,398 (2011).

Manning Gardens (*Co. Macquarie*) see Taree.

Manning Point (*Co. Macquarie*) 31°54'S. 152°40'E., 3 km SW of Harrington, on Mitchells Island; formerly Brighton; oysters, fishing, tourism; coaling station; FB; jetties; sewage works; telephone 1949; TX 1949–67; water reticulation 1986; pop. 284 (1986), 301 (1991), 276 (1996), 242 (2001), 227 (2006), 206 (2011).

Manning River Heads (*Co. Macquarie*) see Harrington.

Mannus (*Co. Selwyn*) 35°48'S. 147°56'E., 7 km SW of Tumbarumba; soldiers' settlement; farming; Angl. C. (St Michael and All Angels') b. 1918 by George Armstrong, damaged 1923; cemetery; cheese and bacon factory (McMicking & Co.) 1905, reused and burnt down; creamery; hurricane 1923; PO 1918, closed, removed and reused; prison camp (Brookfield, afforestation) 1930–93; school 1934–46; telephone 1918; TX 1935, automatic 1954; wool-scour; pop. 82 (1911), 200 (1933), 186 (1947), 122 (1954), 137 (1961).

Manoa (*Co. Narromine*) see Minore.

Manobalai (*Co. Brisbane*) 32°12'S. 150°40'E., 21 km W. of Aberdeen, on Wybong Ck; school 1957–78; telephone 1930; TX 1942, automatic 1977.

Manton (*Co. King*) 34°52'S. 149°00'E., 9 km SE of Yass; school 1882–1940, reused; pop. 66 (1933), 79 (1947).

Manyana (*Co. St Vincent*) see Cunjurong Point.

Maragle (*Co. Selwyn*) 35°56'S. 148°07'E., 18 km SE of Tumbarumba, on Maragle Ck; formerly Old Maragle; goldmining, then grazing; FB; TX (automatic); pop. 86 (2006). (See also New Maragle.)

Marambir (*Co. Courallie*) 29°32'S. 150°04'E., 22 km E. of Moree; RS (Bogamildie till 1901, then Weetah till 1917) 1900, station b. by E.W. Rowland, closed 1975; sawmill (Methven, Hector Cook & Son), burnt down 1904.

Marangaroo (*Co. Cook*) see Marrangaroo.

Marangulla (*Co. Bathurst*) 33°41'S. 149°00'E., 15 km SW of Carcoar, on Marangulla Ck; Angl. C. (St John's), closed; school 1879 b. by John Wadsworth Ashworth, additions and repairs 1882 by C. Shandley, closed 1911; pop. 66 (1901).

March (*Co. Wellington*) 33°13'S. 149°05'E., 7 km N. of Orange; mining (gold disc. *c.*1888 and more in 1899, and silver and lead), agric., orchards; airfield; Angl. C. (St Philip's) 1875, and graveyard; flour mill; mine (Rosedale Mining Co. Ltd), incl. 20 head stamper battery and cyanide plant; PO 1877; school (Marchvale till 1873) 1866–1976; telephone 1913; TX 1928, automatic 1970; Unit. C. (orig. Meth.) b. 1921 by W. Johnstone, and graveyard; Wes. Meth. C. 1875; winery (Woodhouse Wines); pop. 278 (1901), 181 (1911), 216 (1933), 197 (1947), 150 (1954), 234 (1961), 708 (2006).

March (*Co. Wellington*) see also Clergate.

Marchvale (*Co. Wellington*) see March.

Mardi (*Co. Northumberland*) 33°18'S. 151°25'E., 2 km S. of Wyong, on Deep Ck; formerly Yangy Angy; farming; bridges: one over Deep Ck and Woodburys Bridge over Wyong R.; dam b. 1963 by Hirst Bros, 85 ft (26 m) high; PO 1927–62; reservoir; telephone 1923; water supply augmentation 1994; pop. 191 (1933), 91 (1947), 2,935 (2006), 3,439 (2011).

Marengo (*Co. Gresham*) 30°10'S. 152°22'E., 39 km NW of Dorrigo, on Dangars Ck; airfield.

Marengo (*Co. Monteagle*) see Bendick Murrell and Murringo.

Mares Flat (*Co. Bathurst*) 33°41'S. 149°13'E., 17 km S. of Blayney, on Number One Swamp; quarry.

Mares Nest (*Co. Roxburgh*) 33°05'S. 149°24'E., 36 km NE of Orange; mines.

Marfield (*Co. Woore*) 32°33'S. 144°13'E., 128 km SE of Wilcannia; pop. 52 (1933).

Margules (*Co. Buccleuch*) see Tumorrama.

Maria River (*Co. Macquarie*) 31°14'S. 152°53'E., 10 km SW of Crescent Head, on Maria R.; sawmill (S.W. Baker); pop. 71 (1911), 226 (1933), 230 (1947), 178 (1954), 83 (1961).

Mariaville (*Co. Macquarie*) 31°10'S. 152°53'E., 10 km S. of Kempsey, on Maria R.; known as Boat Harbour by 1870; laid out *c.*1836, first lots sold *c.*1838, never developed; agric. and tin.

Marilba (*Co. Harden*) 34°48'S. 148°42'E., 20 km W. of Yass; mine (Winooka Reef).

Marinna (*Co. Clarendon*) 34°51'S. 147°39'E., 7 km NE of Junee; farming; flood 1928; PO 1925; RS (Boree Siding till 1910) 1897, new station 1916, closed 1975, removed 1984; silo 1925; telephone 1926; TX 1926, automatic 1952; pop. 58 (1933).

Marka Point (*Co. Dampier*) see Potato Point.

Markdale (*Co. Georgiana*) 34°15'S. 149°15'E., 32 km NW of Crookwell; goldmining; Angl. C. (St Andrew's) b. 1938 by George Bradney; cemetery (burials 1830–1910, 3 graves 1883+); earth tremor 1870; mines: Homeward Bound (Macauley et al.), Peep o' Day, Pine Hill, Rise and Shine, Wheel of Fortune, Young Australian; stamper battery 1889; telephone 1913; pop. 57 (1901), 60 (1911), 42 (1933), 53 (1947).

Marks Point (*Co. Northumberland*) 33°04'S. 151°39'E., 3 km S. of Belmont, on Lake Macquarie; (incl. Little Pelican, and Pelican, formerly Pelican Flat); settled by Henry and Charles Marks; subdivisions 1902, 1909, 1915; fruit in 1880s and hort.; airport (Belmont); Assemblies of God C. (Gateway); Bapt. C. 1933, renovated 1937; bridge (sliding opening span) to Swansea, 606 ft (184.7 m), b. 1881 by A. and R. Amos, o. 1895 as public road bridge, replacement (bascule span) b. 1909 by Peter Callen & Sons, d. by Henry Harvey Dare, 409 ft 6 in. (124.8 m), dismantled 1956, new one (steel and concrete, with double-leaf bascule span), 570 ft (173.7 m), fabricated by Maschinenfabrik-Augsburg-Nurnberg AG, Germany, b. 1952–55, fourth one b. 1989 by Transfield Pty Ltd, over Swansea Channel; flood 2015; Interdenominational C.; Jehovah's Witnesses C.; jetty 1992; marina 1980; Mission Community C.; PO: Marks Point 1927 and Pelican Flat 1927; schools: Marks Point 1954 b. by T. Simpson, additions 1960, additions 1965 and 2010 by R.T. Parker Pty Ltd, and Pelican Flat (Marks Point till 1950) 1938; slipway (Charlie Hollis) 1954–80; telephone: Marks Point 1923 and Pelican Flat 1925; water supply 1947; wharf b. 1885 by W. Castor; pop. 598 (1933), 1,051 (1947), 1,121 (2006), 2,572 (2011).

Markwell (*Co. Gloucester*) 32°20°S. 152°11'E., 10 km N. of Bulahdelah, on Myall R.; farming and dairying; PO 1909; Rom. Cath. C. (Our Lady) 1870–1940; sawmill (Newells Creek Sawmill Co.) estab. 1936 by Albert John Bartee Shoobridge, Harold Dorney and Arthur Samuel Harvey; school 1874–1962; telephone 1912; TX 1944, automatic 1975; pop. 162 (1911), 121 (1933), 185 (1947), 187 (1954), 187 (1961), 270 (2011).

Marlee (*Co. Macquarie*) 31°48'S. 152°19'E., 9 km NW of Wingham; farming and dairying; Angl. C. (St Mark's) 1875, re-roofed; bridge (Duff Bridge) 1882, destroyed 1898, replaced 1900 by R.H. Worthing, new one (James Campbell Duff Bridge) b. 1926 by J.J. McPhillips, over Dingo Ck; cemetery (533 graves 1861+) 1863; PO 1876; school 1869, additions 1884 by J.M. Gillogby, damaged 1901, closed 1974; storm 1901; telephone 1908; TX 1926, automatic 1972; pop. 204 (1911), 199 (1933), 191 (1947), 154 (1954), 154 (1961), 323 (2006), 340 (2011).

Marlee Flat (*Co. Macquarie*) 31°46'S. 152°19'E., 13 km NW of Wingham; bridge (Allan timber truss) 1902, 233 ft (71 m), over Dingo Ck.

Marlow (*Co. Northumberland*) see Mount White.

Marlow (*Co. St Vincent*) see Marlowe.

Marlowe (*Co. St Vincent*) 35°17'S. 149°53'E., 20 km NE of Braidwood; Charleyong till 1892; town gaz. 1843 as Marlow; agric. and grazing; PO 1871–1942; Presb. C.; school (Charleyong till 1893) 1873–74 and 1882–96;

Union C., relocated and renovated 1899 by G. Brooks; pop. 71 (1911), 71 (1933).

Marmong (*Co. Northumberland*) see Booragul.

Marmong Point (*Co. Northumberland*) see Booragul.

Marne (*Co. Inglis*) 30°41'S. 151°09'E., 33 km W. of Uralla; Bells Swamp till 1915; grazing; Wes. Meth. C. 1893; pop. 89 (1911).

Marom Creek (*Co. Rous*) 28°54'S. 153°22'E., 10 km SW of Alstonville, on Marom Ck; farming; cheese factory (Foley Bros Ltd) 1916; PO 1928; school 1928–75; telephone 1925; TX 1925; pop. 102 (1933), 84 (1947), 88 (1954), 88 (1961).

Maroona (*Co. Cowper*) 30°18'S. 146°07'E., 29 km SE of Bourke; RS (Goondabooka till 1893, then Gundabooka till 1900) 1891–1957.

Marra Creek (*Co. Gregory*) 30°53'S. 147°21'E., 74 km N. of Nyngan; wool; Angl. C. (St Mary the Virgin) 1913, and graveyard; school (Marra Hall till 1972) 1971; pop. 118 (1947).

Marra Hall (*Co. Gregory*) see Marra Creek.

Marrana Creek (*Co. Durham*) see Mirannie.

Marrangaroo (*Co. Cook*) 33°26'S. 150°07'E., 6 km SE of Wallerawang, on Marrangaroo Ck; clay, quartzite, oil-shale mining (disc. 1867 by Mackenzie Bros), dairying; brickworks (Newbold Silica Firebrick Co. Ltd) 1912; earth tremor 1903; FB; gaol (Lithgow) 1990 d. by Perumal Pedavoli; hailstorm 1895; oil-shale works (Lithgow Oil Shale Pty Ltd) 1940–45; PO 1889–1960; quarry; railway dam 1922; railway tunnel 1870–1923, 267 yds (243.8 m), abandoned, new one 1923, 1,064 yds (972.9 m); railway viaduct (8 stone arches) 1871–1921, b. by Patrick Higgins, replaced 1920 in brick, over Middle R.; retort (NTU) 1941, 2 more b. 1942, closed 1945; RS (relocated 1923) 1878–1972; school (Morangaroo till 1860, then Marangaroo till *c.*1890) 1859–60, reopened 1881, additions 1966, closed 1983; telephone 1921; TX 1929–60; Union C. b. 1898 by Kirkwood, d. by Morris, ceded 1979 to Angl. C., closed 1980, reused 1983, reopened 1989 as church, closed again 1997, sold 2002 and 2017; pop. 131 (1901), 128 (1911), 241 (1933), 310 (1947), 249 (1954), 250 (1961), 297 (2011).

Marrar (*Co. Bourke*) 34°50'S. 147°21'E., 14 km E. of Coolamon; estab. 1881, surveyed 1904, village gaz. 1904 as Marror, thrived 1905–14, soldiers' settlement; wool and hay; Bapt. C. 1912–40, became Angl. C. (St Francis's) 1940, closed; brick-kiln 1908; cemetery 1902; chaff mill (Prescott's Ltd) 1919, fire 1927, reused, demolished; fire 1913; gale 1923; lock-up 1917; PO 1902, new one b. 1908, damaged 1923; PS 1911, burnt down 1930, replaced 1931, new one 1942; reservoir (elevated), 50,000 gal. (227.3 kl); Rom. Cath. C. (St Patrick's) 1913; RS 1882, new station 1913, relocated 1913, demolished 1985; school 1909 b. by J. Gray; silo 1922; telephone 1906; TX 1910, automatic 1979; Unit. C. (orig. Meth.) b. 1910 by Beaumont and White; water supply 1941; pop. 432 (1911), 510 (1933), 331 (1947), 426 (1954), 224 (1961), 169 (2011).

Marror (*Co. Bourke*) see Marrar.

Marsden (*Co. Bland*) 33°46'S. 147°31'E., 35 km NE of West Wyalong, on Bland Ck; orig. Bland Billabong then Marsdens till 1912; first site estab. *c.*1860, laid out 1866, surveyed 1875, village gaz. 1877; grazing; Angl. C. (St Andrew's) d. an b. 1891 by William Heares, new one (St Peter and St Paul's) 1919, destroyed 1951; bridge 1934; cemetery (burials 1871–1913); CH (incl. lock-up) 1897; gales 1885 (houses unroofed) and 1951; PO 1866; pound (stock) 1899; PS 1875–1931; sawmill (Robert Brennen); school 1888–1927; silo; telegraph 1879; TX 1911; weir on Bland Ck; pop. 125 (1891), 100 (1901), 210 (1911), 57 (1933).

Marsdens (*Co. Bland*) see Marsden.

Marsdens Swamp (*Co. Westmoreland*) see Ganbenang.

Marshall McMahon Reef (*Co. Harden*) see McMahons Reef.

Marshall Mount (*Co. Camden*) 34°33'S. 150°45'E., 6 km SW of Dapto, on Duck Ck; settled 1829 by Henry Osborne, subdivided 1890; farming and dairying; electricity 1928; PO 1881; school 1859–1972; telephone 1924; TX 1926–46; Wes. Meth. C. 1856, burnt down

1879, replacement 1879–1959, and graveyard (305 graves 1881+), incl. columbarium; pop. 141 (1911), 102 (1947), 120 (1961).

Marshalls Flat (*Co. Gough*) 29°37'S. 151°48'E., 15 km NE of Glen Innes, on Seven Hills Ck.

Marshdale (*Co. Gloucester*) 32°27'S. 151°47'E., 6 km SE of Dungog, on Thalaba Ck; dairying; PO 1927; quarry; telephone 1919; TX 1920–70; pop. 72 (1933), 72 (1947), 91 (1954), 92 (1961).

Marshwood (*Co. Northumberland*) see Dalwood.

Martell (*Co. Raleigh*) 30°32'S. 152°56'E., 8 km SE of Bellingen; telephone 1929.

Marthaguy (*Co. Ewenmar*) 31°46'S. 148°39'E., 7 km S. of Gilgandra; RS 1912–53, station defunct; pop. 166 (2006), 253 (2011).

Martin (*Co. Ashburnham*) see Tichborne.

Martindale (*Co. Hunter*) 32°28'S. 150°40'E., 8 km S. of Denman, on Martindale Ck; Angl. C. (St Martin's) 1924; bushfire 1909; flood 1950; grasshopper infestation 1924; school 1927; telephone 1954; TX 1954, automatic 1969; pop. 63 (1911), 193 (1933), 132 (1947), 158 (1954), 169 (1961), 434 (2011).

Martins Creek (*Co. Durham*) 32°34'S. 151°37'E., 21 km N. of Maitland, on Martins Ck; blue metal, vegetables, fruit, dairying; Angl. C. 1899, replacement (St James's) b. 1928 by Vince Hall, d. by J.W. Scobie & Sons, closed 2017, sold 2018; bridge over Martins Ck; FB; PO 1915–78; quarries: BHP, Hamilton Hill (estab. 1915 by W.B. Wilson, acquired 1916 by govt), Martin's Creek Metal Quarries Ltd (boiler explosion 1923), Railways 1914; RS 1911; sawmill (Grahame's); school 1893 b. by Augustus Vogele, additions 1909 by J. Head, replaced 1913, removal and additions 1923 by F. and R. Compton; telephone 1915; TX 1924, automatic 1970; water supply 1980; pop. 154 (1911), 426 (1933), 197 (1947), 306 (1954), 272 (1961), 341 (2011).

Martin's Creek Metal Quarry (*Co. Durham*) see Barokee.

Martins Crossing (*Co. Phillip*) 32°20'S. 149°34'E., 4 km NE of Gulgong, on Wialdra Ck.

Martins Flat (*Co. Sandon*) 30°48'S. 151°40'E., 22 km N. of Walcha, on Bough Yard Ck.

Martins Gully (*Co. Sandon*) 30°31'S. 151°38'E., 3 km W. of Armidale, on Martins Gully; school 1923 b. by G.W. Barnard, additions 1995; pop. 59 (1954).

Martinsville (*Co. Northumberland*) 33°04'S. 151°25'E., 5 km W. of Cooranbong, on Dora Ck; orig. Deep Creek, then Dora Creek till 1892 and Brush till 1894; thrived 1900–*c.*1928; timber, farming, dairying, orchards; cemetery (pioneer, 206 graves 1886+) 1875; creamery; electricity 1946; meat works (Oak Bank) estab. by William Mathews, demolished; PO 1889, burnt down 1969; sawmills: Browne's 1948–83, A.B. Espley, closed 1921 (following boiler explosion), Herbert Bradley Mullard 1890, Sylvester's 1950, Walters, Middleton & Eades Ltd, fire 1920, Whirley Timber Co.; school (Deep Creek till 1883, Dora Creek till 1894) 1879, new buildings b. 1895 by Norbert A. O'Leary, additions 1923 by T.C. Southon, closed 1974, sold; storm 1907; telephone 1907; TX 1925–62; Union C. (United Indep.) 1893, extended and re-roofed 1901, extended 1905, removed and replaced 1924; pop. 192 (1901), 307 (1911), 227 (1933), 177 (1947), 181 (1954), 169 (1961), 365 (2011).

Martins Wharf (*Co. Northumberland*) see Millers Forest.

Martin Town (*Co. Lincoln*) see Cobbora.

Marulan (*Co. Argyle*) 34°43'S. 150°00'E., 27 km E. of Goulburn, on Jaorimin Ck; Mooroowoolen till 1878; first lots sold 1867, founded 1868 by John Morrice, bypassed by highway 1986; grazing, agric. (mostly wheat and hay), now tourist craft village; Angl. C. (All Saints') b. 1878 by William Duncan, d. by Alberto Dias Soares; bushfire 1926; cemetery; CH 1884; clock tower 1991; earth tremor 1930; electricity 1940; engineering works (T & C Services Pty Ltd); FB 1946; heavy vehicle inspection station 1931, (second) 1958, (third) 1971; pavlova factory (Moccador) estab. 1984 by Peter Jackson-Calway, closed 1991; PO 1868, new one b. 1886 by Louis Le Breton and Donohue, additions 1895 by Northwood and Venteman, closed 2010, reused, new one on new site; PS (incl. lock-up) b. 1877 by W.R. Farrow and J. Ward, new one adjacent; rifle range 1906, new one 1920; Rom. Cath. C. (St Patrick's) 1930; RS 1868, station b. by Frederick Horn; sawmill (Eddie Murphy); school (Mooroowoollen till 1880) 1871; storm 1940; telegraph 1869–71; TX 1915, automatic 1963; Unit. C. (St Stephen's, orig. Presb.) 1873; wattle-bark mill (Craig, Mostyn & Co.); pop. 112 (1871), 250 (1891), 244 (1901), 297 (1911), 368 (1933), 322 (1947), 440 (1954), 481 (1961), 411 (1966), 420 (1971), 380 (1976), 330 (1981), 343 (1986), 360 (1991), 411 (1996), 442 (2001), 540 (2006), 587 (2011). (See also Old Marulan.)

Marulan South (*Co. Argyle*) 34°46'S. 150°02'E., 29 km E. of Goulburn; estab. in 1920s by Blue Circle Southern Cement; marble, lime, sandstone; FB (station b. 1997); lime-kiln (Marulan Marble Lime Co.) 1879; PO 1929; quarry (Southern Portland Cement Co. Ltd); railway (cement works) 1928; school 1944–95; strike 1946; telephone 1934; TX 1934–66; pop. 54 (1933), 131 (1947), 212 (1954), 226 (1961).

Maryamma (*Co. King*) 34°01'S. 148°56'E., 30 km SE of Cowra, on Newhams Ck; telephone 1911.

Maryland (*Co. Buller*) see Maryland Creek.

Maryland (*Co. Northumberland*) 32°53'S. 151°40'E., 3 km N. of Wallsend, on Hexham Swamp; (incl. Fletcher); formerly Merrylands; Bapt. C. (New Vine); cemetery (Allendor); flood 2016; foot-bridge over Wentworth Ck; schools: Glendore 1997 and Maryland 1992, new building b. by R.T. Parker Pty Ltd; pop. 52 (1947), 70 (1954), 7,787 (2011).

Maryland Creek (*Co. Buller*) 28°33'S. 152°00'E., 55 km N. of Tenterfield, on Maryland Ck; village gaz. 1866 as Maryland, designated as chief town of the county; tin (disc. by Thomas Funnell) and grazing; airfield; cemetery; PO 1859; school (Maryland) 1875–1926; telephone 1923; pop. 144 (1901), 164 (1911), 71 (1933), 84 (1947), 110 (1954), 140 (1961), 216 (2006).

Marys Mount (*Co. Argyle*) 34°44'S. 149°44'E., 4 km NE of Goulburn; school 1957–65; pop. 62 (1933), 63 (1947), 64 (1961).

Marys Mount (*Co. Pottinger*) 30°59'S. 149°58'E., 28 km W. of Gunnedah; FB; TX (automatic); pop. 51 (1947), 224 (2011).

Maryvale (*Co. Argyle*) 34°29'S. 149°36'E., 11 km E. of Crookwell.

Maryvale (*Co. Lincoln*) 32°29'S. 148°54'E., 10 km N. of Wellington, on Three Mile Flat Ck; wheat and grazing; Angl. C. 1884, moved 1901 to Bodangora; Bapt. C. 1902, relocated and renovated 1933; copper mine (Petley's Shaft) 1958; cyclone 1907; PO 1875; RS 1881–1974; school 1879, additions 1892 by James Prior Hull, closed 1970; telegraph 1883; telephone 1917; TX 1938–72; pop. 247 (1901), 253 (1911), 76 (1933), 121 (1947), 83 (1954), 85 (1961).

Maryville (*Co. Northumberland*) see Wickham.

Masseys Creek (*Co. Durham*) 32°20'S. 151°33'E., 21 km W. of Dungog; pop. 22 (1933).

Matakana (*Co. Blaxland*) 33°00'S. 145°45'E., 63 km NE of Hillston; sheep; bushfire 1957; PO 1951; railway (mineral) to Mount Hope 1919–24; RS 1919; telephone 1950.

Matcham (*Co. Northumberland*) 33°25'S. 151°25'E., 8 km E. of Gosford, on Erina Ck; subdivision surveyed 1912 by Cowdery; farming; Angl. C. (St George's) 1926, closed and sold 2017; bushfires 1930 and 1994; dam; PO 1911–86; sawmill (estab. by A.Y.H. Smith, acquired 1912 by Matcham Sawmills Ltd, in liquidation 1917), closed; streets electric lit 1939; telephone 1912; pop. 88 (1911), 307 (1933), 296 (1947), 323 (1954), 335 (1961), 582 (2006), 974 (2011).

Mate (*Co. Wynyard*) see Oberne.

Matheson (*Co. Gough*) 29°44'S. 151°34'E., 15 km W. of Glen Innes, on Wellingrove Ck; grazing; bridge 1951, over Wellingrove Ck; FB; 2 mines; PO 1889, new one 1953; telephone 1916; TX 1953–80; Unit. C. (orig. Presb.) 1925; pop. 52 (1933), 56 (1947), 109 (1954), 109 (1961).

Mathews Creek (*Co. Fitzroy*) 30°19'S. 152°47'E., 7 km E. of Dorrigo; dairying; PO 1923; sawmill (Bellingen Timber Co. Ltd); telephone 1923; TX 1927–63; pop. 74 (1954), 81 (1961).

Mathoura (*Co. Cadell*) 35°49'S. 144°54'E., 33 km S. of Deniliquin, on Gulpa Ck; orig. Redbank; settled 1846 by William Moore Carter, site reserved 1848 by Thomas Scott Townsend, laid out 1860 by John McCulloch, lots sold 1864 (John Taylor bought village); fodder, wheat, butter, timber, livestock, wool; Angl. C. (Holy Cross) b. 1930–35, d. by Louis Reginald Williams; bridge (Pollys Bridge) over Gulpa Ck; cemetery 1882; CH (incl. lock-up) b. 1896 by R.T. Hill; charcoal works: Crane Bros and E. Stockdale; electricity 1938; FB (station b. 1988); flour mill b. 1882 by Hood and Birrell; foot-bridges over Gulpa Ck: Cranes Bridge and Liston Bridge; grasshopper infestation 1931; PO 1867; PS 1878; reservoir; Rom. Cath. C. (St Brigid's) d. and b. 1915 by H. Gamble; RS (Victorian railway), closed, station defunct; sawmills: Edwards', A.H. Parry & Co., M.V. Quiggen (acquired by C.B. Opitz, sold to Douglas Bros, burnt down 1923, rebuilt); school 1879, repairs 1881 by W. Clark, additions 1911 by H.C. Bruce, additions 1968; sewerage augmentation 1994; silo; telegraph 1884; TX 1910, automatic 1959; Union C.; Unit. C. (St Andrew's, orig. Presb.) b. 1918 by W.W. Moore & Sons, d. by Louis Harrison; waterworks 1965; pop. 174 (1891), 218 (1901), 491 (1911), 567 (1933), 472 (1947), 577 (1954), 570 (1961), 595 (1966), 616 (1971), 547 (1976), 582 (1981), 622 (1986), 666 (1991), 653 (1996), 645 (2001), 653 (2006), 650 (2011).

Matong (*Co. Bourke*) 34°46'S. 146°55'E., 12 km W. of Ganmain; Devlins Siding till 1900; village gaz. 1900; wheat, hay, chaff cutting; FB; Meth. C. 1927; PO 1886; PS 1917–33; reservoir (elevated), 50,000 gal. (227.3 kl); Rom. Cath. C. (St Patrick's) b. 1916–18 by A.C. Witts, d. by John Hill Robertson; RS (Devlins Siding till 1900) 1882, new station 1907, closed and removed 1985; school (Devlins Siding till 1901) 1899, additions and repairs 1913 by C.P. Bundock, new school b. 1919 by Haynes and Dixon; silo 1922; telephone 1898; TX 1913, automatic 1983; Unit. C.; water supply 1941; pop. 396 (1911), 225 (1933), 203 (1947), 260 (1954), 254 (1961), 305 (2011).

Matong (*Co. Wallace*) 36°40'S. 148°51'E., 32 km S. of Berridale, on Numbla Ck; pop. 53 (1954).

Maude (*Co. Waradgery*) 34°29'S. 144°18'E., 50 km W. of Hay, on Murrumbidgee R.; village reserve surveyed 1861, laid out by Wood, first land sale 1865; former river port then grazing; bridge b. 1955 by McDonald Constructions Pty Ltd, over Murrumbidgee R.; cemetery 1891; fire 1901; lock-up b. 1900 by George Huntley Dixon; PO 1863, burnt down 1928; pound (stock) 1865; PS 1876, burnt down 1911, new one b. 1920 by Alfred Ede, closed 1934; punt (manual), new one 1941–55, across Murrumbidgee R.; school 1887, new one b. 1941 by E. Fayle, closed 1983; telephone 1894; TX 1914, automatic 1982; weir 1940 on Murrumbidgee R.; wharf; wool store (Murphy's), demolished; wool-scour (W. Honeyman & Son) estab. 1878 by Thomas Honeyman; pop. *c.*30 (1866), 92 (1901), 99 (1911), 48 (1933), 61 (1947), 91 (1954), 73 (1961), 159 (2006).

Maudville (*Co. Gloucester*) 32°03'S. 151°44'E., 22 km W. of Gloucester, on Gloucester R.; telephone 1914; TX 1938–70.

Maules Creek (*Co. Nandewar*) 30°30'S. 150°08'E., 26 km NE of Boggabri, on Horsearm Ck; cattle; FB (station b. 2017); cemetery; Presb. C. (St David's); Rom. Cath. C. (Our Lady Help of Christians) 1964; telephone 1927; TX 1928, automatic 1953; pop. 284 (1933), 203 (1947), 227 (1954), 232 (1961), 181 (2006).

Mawson (*Co. Northumberland*)
see Caves Beach.

Maxton (*Co. Bourke*) 34°40'S. 147°16'E., 17 km N. of Coolamon; Rannock till 1912; farming; PO 1908, burnt down 1922; telephone 1907; TX 1917–22.

Maxton (*Co. Bourke*) see also Rannock.

Maxwell (*Co. Mitchell*) 35°18'S. 147°18'E., 22 km S. of Wagga Wagga; telephone 1925; TX 1925, automatic 1951.

Maybole (*Co. Gough*) 29°54'S. 151°35'E., 23 km SW of Glen Innes; cemetery 1891; school 1888–95; telephone 1925; TX 1926–63; pop. 70 (1911), 63 (1933), 63 (1947), 53 (1954), 50 (1961).

Mayers Flat (*Co. Gloucester*) 32°23'S. 152°21'E., 13 km E. of Bulahdelah, on Myall Lake; dairying; PO 1927; Rom. Cath. C. b. 1931 by C. Moran, closed and reused; telephone 1922; TX 1928–67; wharf; pop. 73 (1933).

Mayers Point (*Co. Gloucester*) 32°25'S. 152°25'E., 19 km E. of Bulahdelah, on Myall Lake; sawmills: Beresford (Allen Taylor & Co. Ltd) 1915, closed, reopened 1926, sold 1940 and moved, and George Wilton Mitchell; tramway (Aust. Timber Exporting Co.) 1900, extended 1912, closed 1944; pop. 44 (1933).

Mayfair (*Co. Cooper*) see Griffith.

Mayfair (*Co. Dowling*) 33°23'S. 146°28'E., 13 km SE of Lake Cargelligo; telephone 1928; TX 1928–36.

Mayfield (*Co. Argyle*) 35°13'S. 149°48'E., 25 km N. of Braidwood; Angl. C. (St Luke's) 1899, additions 1906, defunct; PO 1879.

Mayfield (*Co. Northumberland*) 32°54'S. 151°44'E., 5 km NW of Newcastle, on Throsby Ck; (incl. East Mayfield, Tirrikiba till 1952); subdivision (The Highlands) 1888; orig. wheat and grapes, then heavy industry; Angl. C. 1861, reused 1924, damaged 1928, demolished 1950, replacement (St Andrew's) b. 1924 by H. Crane and H. Campbell, d. by Louis Reginald Williams, and graveyard (headstones removed 1957), and St Michael and All Angels' (East Mayfield) 1927; Bapt. C. 1926–54, sold, replaced 1954; brickworks (Newbold Silica Fire-Brick Co. Ltd, removed from Lithgow 1918, renamed Newbold General Refractories Ltd in 1940); chemical works (Newcastle Chemical Co. Pty Ltd) 1940; Church of Christ 1937; cistern factory (T.V. Richards & Son Pty Ltd); engineering works (Dan Mott & Co. Pty Ltd); FB (No. 2 station b. 1898); fire 1972; fireworks factory (S. Howard); flood 1928; foot-bridge over Throsby Ck; foundry (A.N. Hales); furniture factories: Bridgebuilt Tubular Products Pty Ltd, Carpenter and Caldwell, R.B. Woodward; gasworks 1889; gate works (William C. Lynch & Co.); ice works: Northern (B. and S. Searl) 1923 and Swan Bros; Islamic C. (Sultan Fatih) 2007, in former Salv. Army C.; joineries: George William Hipwell and W.J. Sandall & Sons; measles epidemic 1948; Meth. C. (East Mayfield) 1916; PO 1910, new one b. 1925 by Southon and Wallen; Presb. C. (St John's) b. 1915 by Pearce and Southon, d. by Ernest George Yeomans; PS (in rented premises), new one b. 1936 by A.E. Young, renovated 1986; quarry (stone) 1914; Rom. Cath. C. (St Columban's) b. 1940 by Thomas C. Whittle, d. by John Patrick Gannon, refurbished 1971, closed 2017, new one (Christ the King); Salv. Army C. 1922, closed, sold and reused 2007; school (The Folly or Waratah till 1912, Mayfield till 1923, then East Mayfield) 1858, additions 1883 by J. Fawcett, new building b. 1920 by G. Grace, additions 1937 by William Stronach; shirt factory (Sportsmaster Pty Ltd); shoe factory (Ilford Shoe Pty Ltd) 1945; smelter (antimony) 1911; soap and candle factory (Sydney Soap & Candle Co. Ltd) estab. 1886 by Charles Upfold and A.W. Gillies, d. by Peter Bennett and Ernest George Yeomans, became J. Kitchen & Sons Pty Ltd in 1912, fires 1916, 1919, 1928, 1933, chimney (b. by R. King) demolished 1933; squall 1950; steel appliance and equipment factory (John C.W. Bridge & Co. Newcastle Pty Ltd) 1947; storm 1928; telegraph office b. 1925 by Southon and Wallen; telephone 1910; tramway (steam) to Newcastle 1901, electrified 1923; TX (automatic) 1948; Unit. C. (Jubilee, orig. Meth.) b. 1937 by S.W. and R.C. Potter, d. by Norman Welland McPherson, renovations 1954; Wes. Meth. C. b. 1890 by Thomas New, d. by Peter Bennett and Ernest George Yeomans, demolished 1936; works:

Commonwealth Oxygen & Acetylene Pty Ltd (extended 1944 by J.C. Davis & Son) and The Aust. Wire Rope Works Pty Ltd 1925–80; pop. 631 (1911), *c.*9,000 (1921), 10,492 (2006), 10,780 (2011).

Mayfield (*Co. Rous*) see Eltham.

Mayfield (*Co. Westmoreland*) see Sweetbriar.

Mayfield North (*Co. Northumberland*) 32°53'S. 151°44'E., 6 km NW of Newcastle, on Hunter R.; (incl. Port Waratah); heavy industry; ambulance station; copper and tin smelter (Hunter River Smelting Co.) 1868–93; quarry; railway round-house (Port Waratah) 1908, closed; steelworks estab. 1915 by BHP (incl. first battery of 66 Semet-Solvay recuperative coke-ovens operated 1915–55, second battery of 95 Semet-Solvay ovens, third battery of 63 Semet-Solvay ovens operated 1921–71, fourth battery of 53 ovens operated 1929–79 and demolished 1986, fifth battery of 53 ovens 1934, sixth battery of ovens 1939, seventh battery of 68 Wilputte ovens 1954, eighth battery of 57 ovens rebuilt 1957, ninth battery of ovens 1971, tenth battery of ovens 1979, No. 1 blast furnace 1915–82, No. 2 blast furnace 1918–85, No. 3 blast furnace 1920–82 but reopened and enlarged 1985, No. 4 blast furnace 1963–99), acquired 2000 by Onesteel Ltd, demolished 2001; tramway (steam, Port Waratah to Newcastle) 1916, electrified 1926; wharf (BHP), 1,800 ft (548.6 m); works: Bullivants' Aust. Co. Pty Ltd (liquidated 1993), Buttweld Pty Ltd 1929 (became Stewarts & Lloyds Aust. Pty Ltd in 1935, then Tubemakers of Aust. Pty Ltd in 1946, then BHP Structural & Pipeline Products), CSR, Koppers Aust. Pty Ltd (chemicals), John Lysaght Aust. Pty Ltd (sheet iron) 1921, Rylands Bros (Aust.) Pty Ltd (estab. 1919 as Austral Nail Co. Pty Ltd, making wire, nails, star pickets, amalgamated 1923 with Rylands, became Aust. Wire Industries Pty Ltd in 1980, renamed BHP Steel AWI Pty Ltd in 1994), Titan Nail & Wire Pty Ltd (incorp. 1927, acquired 1933 by BHP and became Titan Manufacturing Co. Pty Ltd in 1951).

Mayfield West (*Co. Northumberland*) 32°53'S. 151°44'E., 7 km NW of Newcastle, on Hunter R.; formerly Mill Paddock; settled 1823 by John Laurie Platt; heavy industry; abattoir 1916; Angl. C. (St Nicholas's) 1928; brickworks (Newcastle Brick & Tile Co. Ltd) 1913–18, reused; bridge (Tourle Street Bridge, steel and concrete) to Kooragang, fabricated by Atlas Welding Pty Ltd, erected 1965 by Transfield Pty Ltd, 978 ft (298.1 m), new one 2009, over Hunter R.; Church of Christ; Cong. C. 1929, closed, sold, reused; FB (station b. 1995); flood 1946; iron foundry (Commonwealth Steel Co. Ltd) 1919, at former brickworks, became Vickers Commonwealth Steel Products Ltd in 1923, taken over 1935 by BHP; migrant hostel; PO 1970–78; quarry; Rom. Cath. C. (Santa Maria) 1952; Russian Orthodox C. (Theophany), in former Cong. C.; school 1925, new building 1933, additions 1977; works (Delta EMD); pop. 1,449 (1933), 1,650 (2006), 1,771 (2011).

Maynards Plains (*Co. Fitzroy*) 30°24'S. 152°41'E., 6 km S. of Dorrigo; school 1922–33; telephone 1927; TX 1952–61; pop. 31 (1933).

Mayrung (*Co. Townsend*) 35°28'S. 145°18'E., 32 km E. of Deniliquin; settled 1912; FB 1931; Meth. C. 1961; school (Narrama till 1930) 1915–42, reopened 1957, additions 1963; telephone 1924; TX 1925, automatic 1956; pop. 64 (1933), 101 (1947), 159 (1954), 254 (1961).

Mayvale (*Co. Darling*) 30°24'S. 150°25'E., 19 km W. of Barraba, on Tareela Ck; pop. 35 (1933).

Meadowbank (*Co. Ashburnham*) see Italia.

Meadowfield Estate (*Co. Northumberland*) see New Lambton.

Meadow Flat (*Co. Roxburgh*) 33°26'S. 149°55'E., 10 km SW of Portland, on Scotts Ck; village gaz. 1858 as Meadow Lee; wheat, oats, potatoes, fruit; Angl. C. (St Luke's) 1882; bushfires 1926 and 1944; cemetery (132 graves 1859+) 1880; FB; hailstorm 1852; mine (tin) 1905; PO 1957; pound (stock) 1841; Presb. C. 1862; 2 quarries; scarlet fever 1876; school 1856–1939, reopened 1952; telephone

1915; toll-gate (toll abolished 1874); TX 1928, automatic 1978; Wes. Meth. C. 1857, new one 1896; pop. 160 (1871), 167 (1911), 128 (1933), 150 (1947), 116 (1954), 165 (1961), 354 (2011).

Meadow Glen (*Co. Booroondarra*) 31°32'S. 145°17'E., 53 km W. of Cobar; Meadows Hotel till 1960; grazing; PO 1927–42; telephone 1924; TX 1937.

Meadow Lee (*Co. Roxburgh*) see Meadow Flat.

Meadows Hotel (*Co. Booroondarra*) see Meadow Glen.

Mebbin (*Co. Rous*) 28°26'S. 153°13'E., 21 km SW of Murwillumbah, on Byrrill Ck; telephone 1925; TX 1947–63.

Mebul (*Co. Bligh*) 32°22'S. 149°19'E., 20 km W. of Gulgong; Cudgebegong Creek till 1917; farming and grazing; goldmine worked *c.*1900, in 1920s, 1935–36, 1962–63; PO 1886–1962; school (Cudgebegong till 1917) 1882, new buildings b. 1884 by J. Cottrell, closed 1922; telephone 1917; TX 1920; pop. 171 (1901), 145 (1911), 49 (1933), 67 (1954).

Medgun Creek (*Co. Courallie*) see Ashley.

Medina (*Co. Ashburnham*) 33°20'S. 148°54'E., 18 km W. of Orange; farming; PO 1901, burnt down 1903; telephone 1919.

Medlow (*Co. Cook*) see Medlow Bath.

Medlow (*Co. Raleigh*) 30°47'S. 152°41'E., 23 km W. of Macksville, on Taylors Arm; school 1907, additions 2010.

Medlow Bath (*Co. Cook*) 33°41'S. 150°17'E., 5 km N. of Katoomba, on Adam Ck; Pulpit Hill till 1891, Medlow till 1903; former mountain health resort; airfield (Katoomba); Angl. C. (St Luke's) 1902, additions 1913 by Whiting Bros, d. by P.V. Tabrett, damaged 1928, rebuilt 1929 by F.J. Peatfield, d. by L.W. Hodgkinson, closed 2004, sold 2008 to De Zign Pty Ltd, sold again 2011; bushfires 1922, 1947, 1952; dam (Lake Medlow) 1907, 65 ft high (19.8 m), d. by Leslie Augustus Burton Wade; FB; fire 1922; PO 1891; PS 1863; RS (orig. Brown's Sawmill Siding then Pulpit Hill in 1883, then Medlow in 1883, then Medlow Bath in 1903) 1883, new station 1903; sawmills: Valentine Harding Brown and Snell Bros; storm 1928; telegraph 1894; telephone 1897; TX (automatic) 1978; watch-house b. 1861 by William Petttit; waterworks (Greaves Ck) 1891; pop. 270 (1911), 266 (1954), 292 (1961), 250 (1964), 210 (1976), 270 (1981), 340 (1986), 377 (1991), 448 (1996), 504 (2001), 517 (2011).

Medowie (*Co. Gloucester*) 32°44'S. 151°52'E., 12 km E. of Raymond Terrace, on Moffats Swamp; settled 1888 by Daniel James; sheep then forestry, peaches, poultry, dairying, macadamia nuts; Angl. C. (St Francis's) 1984; Bapt. C. (Overflow); bushfire 2018; cyclone 1946; FB 1946; PO 1927; reservoir; Rom. Cath. C. (St Christopher's) 1957; sawmill (William H. James); schools: Medowie (New Glanmorgan till 1895) 1894 b. by William Mitchell, closed 1912, reopened 1940, additions 1956 and 1985 and Wirreanda 1985; telephone 1922; TX 1942, automatic 1963; Unit. C.; waterworks; winery (Pioneer Ridge Estate); pop. 83 (1901), 78 (1933), 250 (1947), 424 (1954), 485 (1961), 966 (1981), 1,428 (1986), 3,256 (1991), 5,294 (1996), 6,290 (2001), 7,828 (2006), 8,342 (2011).

Medway (*Co. Camden*) 34°30'S. 150°16'E., 6 km W. of Berrima, on Wingecarribee R.; estab. 1926, village gaz. 1932; mining (coal disc. 1923 by T.W. Foley); bushfire 1953; coalmines: Berrima 1874 (acquired 1889 by Ebenezer Vickery, closed, reopened 1928, acquired by Southern Portland Cement Ltd, bought 1988 by Boral, leased 1994 to Centennial Coal Co. Ltd), Cataract or Medway (estab. 1867 by John Le Gay Brereton and Alfred Reynolds Huntley, closed 1870, reopened 1874, closed *c.*1877), Loch Catherine (estab. 1923 by W.E. Marsh, taken over 1926 by Southern Portland Cement & Coal Co., closed 1959); electricity 1946; school (Berrima Colliery till 1898) 1883, new building b. 1884 by W.J. Barnsley, closed 1898 and 1957–68; water treatment plant (Berrima) 1980; pop. 386 (2011).

Medway (*Co. Lincoln*) 32°06'S. 149°12'E., 21 km SW of Dunedoo, on Sandy Ck; school 1881–87.

Medway Junction (*Co. Argyle*) 34°43'S. 150°02'E., 25 km W. of Bundanoon.

Meehan Street (*Co. King*) see Yass.

Meemar (*Co. Bland*) 34°33'S. 147°59'E., 10 km NW of Cootamundra, on Deep Ck; mine (Baldooran).

Meermaul (*Co. Pottinger*) 31°02'S. 150°14'E., 7 km SW of Gunnedah; farming; FB; school 1884–96 and 1909–40; telephone 1930; TX 1930; pop. 521 (2006).

Meerschaum (*Co. Rous*) 28°53'S. 153°26'E., 6 km S. of Alstonville.

Meerschaum Vale (*Co. Rous*) 28°55'S. 153°26'E., 8 km S. of Alstonville, on Yellow Ck; farming; Angl. C. (St Thomas's), removed from Dalwood and re-erected 1945 by G. Wright; FB; PO 1906; sawmill (Robert J. Randle) 1883; school 1886, additions 1909, closed 1975, building removed; telephone 1908; TX 1928–63; pop. 188 (1901), 210 (1933), 205 (1947), 239 (1954), 238 (1961), 357 (2011).

Meeting Ridge (*Co. Gloucester*) 32°14'S. 152°26'E., 10 km SW of Tuncurry; dairying; PO 1927; school 1908–28.

Megalong (*Co. Cook*) 33°43'S. 150°14'E., 7 km W. of Katoomba, on Pulpit Hill Ck; (incl. Megalong Junction and Megalong Valley); orig. Nellies Glen; estab. 1891, thrived 1893, largely dismantled and removed 1903, and remainder burnt down 1905; mining (oil-shale disc. 1870 by Campbell Mitchell), farming, grazing; aeroplane crashes: 1939 (2 killed) and 1940; bushfires 1905, 1940, 1952, 1956, 1957; cemetery 1898; FB (equipment shed b. 1953); mine haulage tunnel (Mt Rennie or Narrow Neck Tunnel) b. 1891 by Aust. Kerosene Oil & Mineral Co. for haulage to Katoomba from Glen Shale (Mort's) Mine; mines: Blackheath Glen (operated by Blackheath Coal Mining Co.), Glen Shale Mine (16 adits) estab. by Campbell Mitchell, taken over by Thomas Sutcliffe Mort and P. Finn, bought 1890 by Aust. Kerosene Oil & Mineral Co. and worked 1891–97 and 1921, reworked 1941–44, The Sugarloaf (estab. 1867 by John Cripps), Wall's Tunnel; PO 1892; Rom. Cath. C. (St Joseph's) 1905, burnt down 1915, replacement b. 1918 by Steve Gibbons, moved 1952, restored 1988; sawmills: Fred Brooks and Joseph Ives; school 1892–97, reopened 1957; telephone 1915; TX (automatic) 1956; Unit. C. (orig. Cong.) b. 1943 by Ben Esgate, and graveyard; pop. 57 (1911), 84 (1933), 89 (1947), 108 (1954), 53 (1961), 165 (2006).

Megalong Junction (*Co. Cook*) see Megalong.

Megalong Valley (*Co. Cook*) see Megalong.

Megan (*Co. Fitzroy*) 30°17'S. 152°46'E., 8 km NE of Dorrigo, on Wild Cattle Ck; village gaz. 1925; timber and dairying; PO 1913, burnt down 1924; PS, closed 1924; RS 1924–75; sawmills: Backhouse and Roebuck, G.L. Briggs & Sons (burnt down 1922), F.W. Brim & Co., Cockburn's, Cypress Pine Co., Earp, Woodcock, Beveridge & Co. Pty Ltd, Megan Sawmills, Melviney's, Arthur Morris; school 1949–71; telephone 1923; TX 1927, automatic 1971; pop. 142 (1933), 172 (1947), 171 (1954), 108 (1961), 193 (2011).

Meglo (*Co. Georgiana*) 34°01'S. 149°16'E., 53 km N. of Crookwell, on Meglo Ck; farming and mining; mines: Bonanza (Robert and Montgomery Clarke), G.F. Campbell, Meglo Silver Mining Co. NL, H.B. Thomas.

Melbergen (*Co. Nicholson*) 33°42'S. 146°03'E., 65 km N. of Griffith; PO 1927, burnt down 1929; telephone 1926; TX 1934–80; pop. 39 (1933).

Melbury (*Co. Durham*) 32°14'S. 151°36'E., 24 km NW of Dungog, on Williams R.; Angl. C. (St Matthew's) b. 1905 by Ben Bosworth and Herb Deards, closed 1998, later burnt down, and graveyard, incl. columbarium 2004.

Meldrum (*Co. Fitzroy*) 30°22'S. 152°29'E., 21 km W. of Dorrigo; Deer Vale till 1913; farming; PO 1913–59; telephone 1913; TX 1919; pop. 35 (1933).

Melinga (*Co. Macquarie*) 31°49'S. 152°31'E., 12 km NE of Taree; quarry; RS (Comboyne Road till 1917) 1915–74; sawmill estab. by Alf Collins, taken over 1934 by Andrew Cook & Sons Pty Ltd; pop. 55 (1933).

Mellong (*Co. Hunter*) 33°12'S. 150°41'E., 67 km W. of Ourimbah.

Mellool (*Co. Wakool*) 35°24'S. 143°47'E., 40 km NW of Barham; PO 1897–1914; school 1960–

85; TX (automatic) 1962; pop. 100 (1911), 64 (1933), 80 (1961).

Meloola (*Co. Cunningham*) 32°47'S. 147°15'E., 46 km W. of Trundle, on Murda Ck.

Melrose (*Co. Cunningham*) 32°41'S. 146°57'E., 48 km N. of Condobolin; defunct; mining (copper, disc. 1885, and gold); bushfires 1891 and 1898; mines: Anaconda and Melrose; school (Three Peaks) 1957–67; pop. 95 (1911), 94 (1954).

Melrose (*Co. Sandon*) see Enmore.

Melville (*Co. Durham*) 32°41'S. 151°31'E., 7 km NW of Maitland, on Hunter R.; Angl. C. (St Mark's), inundated 1893; bridge (Melville Ford Bridge) b. 1897 by Taylor and Littleproud, destroyed 1904, replaced 1905 by Walter Frank Oakes, new one b. 1939 by Jackson's Bridge Building Co. Pty Ltd, over Hunter R.; bushfire 1905; floods 1893 and 1904; gale 1899; pop. 28 (1933).

Melville (*Co. Macquarie*) see Kempsey South.

Melyra (*Co. Forbes*) see Warraderry.

Memagong (*Co. Bland*) 34°15'S. 148°02'E., 24 km W. of Young; pop. 64 (1911), 21 (1933), 495 (2011).

Memorial (*Co. Fitzroy*) 29°52'S. 152°50'E., 21 km SW of South Grafton.

Memundie (*Co. Georgiana*) see Blanket Flat.

Menah (*Co. Wellington*) 32°33'S. 149°33'E., 6 km NW of Mudgee; flood 1870; tanneries: William Burgess, demolished 1905 and Langbridge's, inundated 1870; pop. 422 (2011).

Menah (*Co. Wellington*) see also Wilbetree Flat.

Mena Murtee (*Co. Young*) 31°25'S. 143°10'E., 26 km NW of Wilcannia; pop. 30 (1933), 57 (1947).

Menangle (*Co. Camden*) 34°07'S. 150°44'E., 9 km SE of Camden, on Foot Onslow Ck; Riversford till 1865; farming, grazing, dairying; agric. institute (Elizabeth Macarthur) 1990, additions 2012; Angl. C. (St James's) b. 1876 by Thomas McBeath, d. by John Horbury Hunt, tower and chancel added 1897, d. by Sir John Sulman and Joseph Porter Power, church re-roofed 1962, and columbarium; bridges: Macarthur Bridge over Foot Onslow Ck and Menangle Bridge b. 1856, new one 1929, over Nepean R.; creamery (Camden Park Estate) 1892, new one 1898; electricity 1937; FB; floods 1860, 1863, 1875; hailstorm 1932; milk factory; milking machine (Rotolactor) b. 1952 by E.V. Campbell Pty Ltd, d. by T.M. Moloney, closed 1977, bought by Halfpenny Hobbs Pty Ltd, renovated and modified, closed 1982, abandoned and derelict; PO 1856; pound (stock) 1861; railway bridge (wrought iron cellular girders fabricated 1861 at The Canada Works, Birkenhead, England) erected 1863 by Peto, Brassey and Betts, d. by John Whitton, 486 ft (148.1 m), track duplicated 1892, intermediate piers added 1907, bridge strengthened 1923 and 1930, damaged 1975, over Nepean R.; refrigerating works b. 1898 by William Noller; Rom. Cath. C. (St Patrick's) 1895 d. by Richard Joseph Dennehy; RS 1863, station b. by Thomas Parkinson; school 1871, new building b. 1906 by Hindes and Farmdon, closed 1976; telegraph 1869; telephone 1899; TX 1922, automatic 1965; water pumping station 1903; weir 1903, on Nepean R.; winery (Razorback Ridge); pop. *c.*100 (1866), 253 (1891), 255 (1901), 258 (1911), 404 (1933), 362 (1947), 242 (1954), 208 (1961), 206 (1971), 236 (1996), 302 (2001), 327 (2006), 507 (2011).

Mendooran (*Co. Napier*) 31°49'S. 149°07'E., 34 km NW of Dunedoo, on Castlereagh R.; Mundooran till 1918; laid out 1851 by George Boyle White, village gaz. 1852, first lots sold 1853, thrived 1915; orig. grazing, then farming; airport 1938; Angl. C. (St Chad's) b. 1886 by Samuel Hatton, dismantled, replacement b. 1914–16 by Collyer Bros and Stoddart & Sons, d. by Harold Robert Hardwick, destroyed 1950, new one 1959; brickworks (Miller Bros) 1916; bridges: one b. 1959, over Castlereagh R. and Manusu Bridge 1979, over Merrygoen Ck; cemetery (428 graves 1894+) 1880; distillery (Black Gate) estab. 2009 by Brian and Genise

Hollingworth; FB; fires 1915 and 1936; floods 1874 (almost destroyed town) and 1955; flour mill estab. by Marchant, reused 1912, burnt down 1924; grasshopper infestation 1907; lock-up 1862; Meth. C. 1959; PO 1851, new one b. 1900 by Espley and Morgan, enlargement and alterations 1926 by A. Clarke; pound (stock) 1861; Presb. C. (St Andrew's) b. 1924 by T. Jones, additions 1963; PS b. 1878 by A. English, repairs 1896 by G.G. Martin, repairs 1908 by J.T. Andrews, new one 1925, additions 1935, new one (incl. court room and lock-up) 1958; rabbit freezing works 1917, acquired 1927 by Amalgamated Rabbit & Skin Export Co. Ltd, burnt down 1929; reservoir (steel tower); rifle range 1954; Rom. Cath. C. (St Mary's) b. 1914–17 by Albert Murphy, d. by F. Kenny; RS (2 km S.) 1916–72, station removed 1979; sawmills: Kelly and Stevens, Hatton and Copelin 1916, Fred G. Jones, J. Lalor & Sons (taken over 1912 by Naseby & Co.), Marchant's, F.S. Spies; school (Mundooran till 1918) 1869–71, 1881–83, additions 1887 by Thomas Pericles Manusu, repairs 1910 by Brown, additions 1913 by D.J. O'Brien, additions 1916 by W. Murphy, additions 1956, 1963, 1965, 1972, 2010; silo 1935; squall 1925; storm 1950; telegraph 1882; TX 1910, automatic 1984; Wes. Meth. C. 1863; pop. *c.*30 (1866), 185 (1891), 183 (1901), 327 (1911), 462 (1921), 477 (1933), 552 (1947), 650 (1954), 477 (1961), 344 (1971), 388 (1976), 325 (1981), 366 (1986), 362 (1991), 325 (1996), 322 (2001), 319 (2006), 302 (2011).

Mengello (*Co. Narromine*) see Mingelo.

Menindee (*Co. Menindee*) 32°24'S. 142°25'E., 102 km SE of Broken Hill, on Darling R.; Laidley's Ponds from 1835, Perry 1861–66, Menindie till 1918; first lots sold 1862, town gaz. 1862 as Perry, designated as chief town of the county; orig. river port and grazing, then irrigated cropping, grapes, oranges, rockmelons, apricots, tomatoes, vegetables; airfield (4 km N.) 1940; Angl. C. (Holy Trinity) 1893; astronomical station; brewery (Charles Medlicott) 1870–74; bridge (steel, with Strauss bascule span) 1927, fabricated by Poole & Steele Ltd, over Darling R.; cemetery 1864; CH b. 1874 by E. White, new one 1934; FB; flood 1890; heatwave 2016; hospital 2007; Meth. C. 1956, new one 1975; PO 1861, new one b. 1879 by Z. and S. Burton, additions 1896 by H. Faust, d. by L. Robertson; police barracks b. 1891 by L. Cawsey & Sons; pound (stock) 1865; PS 1866, new one b. 1933–35 by Charles Alexander Stewart Boag, additions and alterations 1973; punt, ceased, removed, sold and dismantled 1931; railway bridge (steel bascule on concrete piers) 1927, closed 1947, replaced by 8 span concrete and steel viaduct, over Darling R.; Rom. Cath. C. (St Patrick's) 1924; RS 1919, closed; sawmill (A.B. Rowe & Son); school (Menindie till 1918) 1868, new buildings b. 1903 by Albert Sumsion, additions 1956, 1959, 1967, new one 1990; spider infestation 2016; telegraph 1877, new office b. 1879 by Z. and S. Burton, additions 1896 by H. Faust, d. by L. Robertson; TX 1911, automatic 1989; typhoid 1889; water pumping station b. 1953 by Constructions (B.H. Ltd, damaged 1953; weir 1960 on Darling R.; wharf 1915; pop. 201 (1871), 261 (1881), 194 (1891), 245 (1901), 177 (1911), 509 (1933), 511 (1947), 644 (1954), 629 (1961), 493 (1966), 474 (1971), 424 (1976), 455 (1981), 406 (1986), 467 (1991), 385 (1996), 392 (2001), 332 (2006), 449 (2011).

Menindie (*Co. Menindee*) see Menindee.

Meragle (*Co. Selwyn*) 35°51'S. 148°15'E., 22 km E. of Tumbarumba; PO 1905; snowstorm 1907; pop. 32 (1933).

Merah North (*Co. Jamison*) 30°11'S. 149°18'E., 15 km W. of Wee Waa, on Pian Ck; grazing; cotton gin (Namoi Cotton Co-op. Ltd); PO 1904; RS 1903–76; telephone 1898; TX 1928, automatic 1966; pop. 83 (1911), 111 (1933), 97 (1947), 164 (1954), 152 (1961), 207 (2006), 386 (2011).

Meranburn (*Co. Ashburnham*) 33°12'S. 148°38'E., 6 km W. of Manildra, on Manildra Ck; farming; cemetery (659 graves) 1879, incl. columbarium 1996; PO 1895–1932; PS (in rented premises) 1885, burnt down 1889; RS 1893, station b. by Frederick Lemm, jun. and Thomas Edward Spencer, closed 1974;

school 1880–1921; telephone 1907; Wes. Meth. C. 1879; pop. 151 (1901), 102 (1911), 29 (1933), 87 (1947).

Merannie (*Co. Durham*) see Ingar.

Merebene (*Co. Baradine*) 30°41'S. 148°59'E., 29 km N. of Baradine; RS 1925–71.

Merewether (*Co. Northumberland*) 32°57'S. 151°45'E., 3 km SW of Newcastle, on Tasman Sea; (incl. Burwood, Lake Macquarie Road, Merewether Heights, Ocean Park Estate 1927, The Glebe, The Junction, The Pottery); estab. 1836 by James Mitchell, munic. 1885–1938 but became part of City of Greater Newcastle; mining (coal disc. 1791 by William Bryant et al.); Angl. C. (St Augustine's) b. 1889 by John Frogley; Aust. C. 1899, closed, reused 1894; Bapt. C. b. 1936 by Charles Waugh; brickworks: Beehive (estab. 1868 by John Gulliver), Newcastle Burwood Fire-clay & Brick Works (estab. 1866 by Moses Hughes and Drury, enlarged 1879 by Samuel Hughes), Giddey's, Mills', Steam Brick & Tile Works (estab. by Joseph Bowtell), razed, Robert Turton (moved 1855 to Waratah), James Wood; Christ. City C.; Church of Christ; collieries: A Pit (Newcastle Coal Mining Co.) 1876–1921, B Pit (Newcastle Coal Mining Co.) 1886–1909, Beach Tunnel (taken over 1853 by Newcastle Coal & Copper Co.), J. & A. Brown's Tunnel (o. 1852, taken over 1856 by Newcastle Coal & Copper Co.), Glenrock (estab. *c.*1904 by Howley and Foreshaw, closed 1944), Happy Valley (estab. *c.*1844 by William Donaldson, taken over 1853 by Newcastle Coal & Copper Co., closed 1863), Hillside (estab. 1885 by Allen Wilde), Howley's, Nott's Tunnel (taken over 1853 by Newcastle Coal & Copper Co.), Victoria Gully (James Brown) *c.*1848, Victoria Tunnel (Morgan's); Cong. C. (in former Lay Meth. C.) o. 1921; dengue fever 1926; FB 1891 (station b. 1893 by Somers, d. by Thomas Robson, closed and removed 1933 by Moran, replaced 1933, closed 1945); fibrous plaster works (James H. Duncanson); fire 1893; floods 1893 and 2008; gale 1899; joinery (E. Dann & Sons Ltd); furniture factory (J. Jefferson); Lay Meth. C. (The Junction) 1894, closed and reused; measles epidemic 1948; Meth. C. 1922; mine subsidence 1893, 1904, 1916, 1925, 1926, 1927; PO: Lake Macquarie Road 1860–66, Merewether 1888 (new one b. 1927 by J.C. Davies & Sons), The Junction 1860 (new one b. 1938 by McGrorey and Keenan, d. by Jeater, Rodd and Hay); potteries: Hughes Potteries Pty Ltd (founded 1865 by Moses Hughes, closed 1981), Page's (taken over 1848 by Samuel Welham) 1846–50, Nathan Welham 1849–68; Presb. C. o. 1904 in former Aust. C.; Prim. Meth. C.: Burwood 1859, demolished 1879, new one b. 1879 by William Dart and H. Chandler, d. by J. Cropley, extended 1904, closed 1927 and Merewether 1887, new one 1922; PS: Merewether 1927–36 and The Glebe 1886; quarry; railway (Newcastle Coal & Copper Co.); 2 reservoirs; Rom. Cath. C.: Holy Family (South Merewether) b. 1939 by McGrorey and Keenan, d. by Peter Joseph Gannon, and columbarium, new one (Merewether Beach) 1952–2007 and St Joseph's (The Junction) 1876, extended 1912, demolished 1962, replaced; salt-works estab. by William Donaldson (taken over by James Mitchell and reused as a copper smelter); Salv. Army C. 1888; schools: Merewether 1891 (additions 1966, 1977, 2010), Merewether Heights 1970 (additions 1972 and 1975), South Hamilton 1933 (additions 1966 and 1977), The Junction (South Newcastle till 1926) 1872, additions 1883 by John Rollo Rodgers, additions 1909 by C. Davis, additions 1939 and 1962, damaged 1989; sewerage 1908, amplification 1935; smelter (copper) estab. 1851 by James Mitchell and J. Llewellyn Morgan, closed 1853, reopened 1864 by Newcastle Coal & Copper Co., taken over 1866 by Burwood & Newcastle Smelting Co., taken over 1871 by Ebenezer Vickery, closed 1872; storms 1936 and 2007; streets gas lit 1911, electric lit 1928; telegraph 1888; telephone (The Junction) 1904; tramway (steam) to Newcastle 1894 (plagued by subsidence during construction), electrified 1924; TX (automatic) 1953; Unit. C. (orig. Meth.) b. 1927 by Percy Albert Nott, d.

by Arthur Lanyon Clark and Harry Wardle; United Meth. Free C. (The Glebe) 1880–1926, sold; Welsh Bapt. C. (Cave Adullam), closed, sold 1887, replacement (Noddfa) 1888; Welsh Cong. C. 1899; Wes. Meth. C.: Merewether 1887 and The Glebe 1856, demolished; pop. 970 (1871), *c.*2,100 (1881), 4,340 (1891), *c.*4,350 (1895), 4,547 (1901), 4,234 (1911), *c.*5,900 (1921), 8,432 (1928), 8,091 (1933), *c.*8,600 (1947), *c.*11,000 (1954), *c.*8,500 (1961), *c.*8,800 (1966), *c.*11,200 (1971), *c.*11,400 (1976), 13,036 (2006), 13,397 (2011).

Merewether (*Co. Northumberland*) see also Broadmeadow.

Merewether Heights (*Co. Northumberland*) see Merewether.

Meri Angles (*Co. Roxburgh*) 32°54'S. 150°03'E., 13 km SE of Rylstone; telephone 1921; TX 1937.

Merihula (*Co. Jamison*) 30°13'S. 149°40'E., 17 km NW of Narrabri; pop. 55 (1961).

Merima (*Co. Wellesley*) 36°54'S. 149°10'E., 7 km W. of Bombala; telephone 1918; TX.

Merimborough (*Co. Baradine*) 30°27'S. 149°12'E., 58 km W. of Narrabri; pop. 55 (1911).

Merimbula (*Co. Auckland*) 36°53'S. 149°55'E., 25 km S. of Bega, on Merimbula Lake; (incl. Berrambool and Mirador); formerly also spelt as Merrimbula; estab. 1855 as private village by Twofold Bay Pastoral Assoc., first lots sold 1860 after Assoc. dissolved, bypassed by highway 1992; former seaport 1855+, timber, maize, sheep, cattle, pigs, butter, cornflour, tourism 1950s+, fishing, oysters, retirement centre; airport (2 km S.) b. 1956 by McKenna and Armistead Pty Ltd, terminal b. 1956 by P.J. Rimington Pty Ltd; ambulance station; Angl. C. (St Clement's) 1962; Assemblies of God C. (Sapphire Coast Community); bacon factory o. 1922 by Merimbula Co-op. Bacon Society Ltd in old Maizena Works, burnt down 1944; bark crushing works (Bate's); bridge b. 1909 by Phillips, replaced 1982, over Merimbula Lake; bushfires 1926 and 2006; 2 FB (incl. station b. 1984); flour mill (operated by James Kirkwood for Twofold Bay Pastoral Assoc.) 1858, abandoned, reused 1868–1913 by Matthew Adam Munn as cornflower mill, known as the Maizena Works, acquired 1913 by James Channon, reused 1920, burnt down 1944; jetties: one b. 1855 by Twofold Bay Pastoral Assoc., one b. 1865, one b. 1991; marina; Meth. C. 1958; observatory 1898; PO 1857; Presb. C.; PS, closed 1917, new ones 1962 and 1978; punt (Spencer Lasinby Bransby) 1857, across Merimbula Lake; rabbit freezing works 1916; 4 reservoirs; Rom. Cath. C. (St Joseph's) 1963; sawmill; school 1872 b. by James Fowler, rebuilt 1898, additions 1905, relocated 1946, additions 1962, 1966, 1970; sewerage augmentation 1971 and 1992; telegraph 1868; telephone 1875; tornado 1995; TX 1910, automatic 1950; Union C.; Unit. C.; wharf 1902, closed to shipping 1952, demolished 1979, replaced 1983; pop. *c.*90 (1866–68), 115 (1871), 184 (1891), 192 (1901), 113 (1911), 250 (1933), 335 (1947), 524 (1954), 704 (1961), 841 (1966), 1,434 (1971), 1,956 (1976), 2,899 (1981), 3,278 (1986), 4,259 (1991), 4,383 (1996), 4,883 (2001), 3,851 (2006), 3,952 (2011).

Merindee (*Co. Wellington*) see Yarrabin.

Meringlo (*Co. Auckland*) see Numbugga.

Meringo (*Co. Dampier*) 35°59'S. 150°09'E., 10 km SE of Moruya, on Tasman Sea.

Meringo (*Co. Narromine*) 32°05'S. 147°44'E., 25 km W. of Trangie.

Meringola (*Co. Auckland*) 36°40'S. 149°42'E., 13 km W. of Bega; cheese factory (Catherine Rheinberger); pop. 80 (1901), 107 (1911), 31 (1933).

Meringullalong (*Co. King*) 34°23'S. 148°49'E., 10 km NE of Boorowa.

Meriti (*Co. Arrawatta*) 29°05'S. 150°45'E., 43 km NW of Ashford.

Merkadool Station (*Co. Denham*) 29°50'S. 148°23'E., 37 km SW of Collarenebri.

Merkadool Tank (*Co. Denham*) see Inverness.

Merleigh (*Co. White*) 30°23'S. 149°26'E., 17 km S. of Wee Waa; telephone 1925; TX 1928–44.

Meroe (*Co. Benarba*) see Bullarah.

Merom (*Co. Kennedy*) 32°55'S. 148°04'E., 24 km S. of Peak Hill.

Meroo (*Co. Camden*) see Meroo Meadow.

Meroo (*Co. Wellington*) 32°46'S. 149°33'E., 18 km S. of Mudgee; pop. 187 (1911).

Meroo Creek (*Co. Wellington*) see Avisford.

Meroo Flat (*Co. St Vincent*) 35°26'S. 149°53'E., 8 km E. of Braidwood; school 1883–88.

Meroo Meadow (*Co. Camden*) 34°49'S. 150°36'E., 7 km N. of Nowra, on Tandingulla Ck; formerly Meroo; farming; caterpillar infestation 1937; creamery (Meroo Meadow Dairy Co.) b. 1899 by George and Martin Muller, closed 1906; FB 1944; PO 1899; school (Meroo till 1882, Little Meadow till 1884, then Meroo till 1923) 1867, new building 1885, demolished, new building 1898 d. by William Edmund Kemp, closed 1971, bought 1987 by Ted and Glenda North; telephone 1914; TX 1930, automatic 1966; Union C. d. and b. 1890 by William A. Isley & Sons, re-roofed; pop. 265 (1911), 122 (1954), 159 (1961).

Merotherie (*Co. Bligh*) 32°07'S. 149°33'E., 18 km SE of Dunedoo; airfield.

Merotherie Crossing (*Co. Bligh*) 32°06'S. 149°34'E., 18 km SE of Dunedoo, on Talbragar R.; bridge (Leo Nott Bridge) over Talbragar R.

Merrendee (*Co. Wellington*) see Yarrabin.

Merricumbene (*Co. St Vincent*) 35°44'S. 149°54'E., 33 km S. of Braidwood, on Deua R.; settled 1828; gold (disc. 1859); bushfire 1883; cemetery 1895; goldmine (Merricumbene Reef) 1912–19.

Merrigal (*Co. Ewenmar*) 31°29'S. 148°15'E., 38 km NW of Gilgandra, on Merrigal Ck.

Merriganowry (*Co. Forbes*) 33°41'S. 148°32'E., 18 km SW of Canowindra, on Stockyard Ck; bridge over Lachlan R.; goldmine (Shannons Reef) 1885; TX (automatic); pop. 67 (1911), 105 (1933).

Merrill (*Co. King*) 34°41'S. 149°16'E., 35 km NE of Yass; school (Merrill Creek) 1880–91; pop. 29 (1933).

Merrilla (*Co. Argyle*) 34°43'S. 149°33'E., 16 km W. of Goulburn, on Wollondilly R.; farming, grazing, orchards; PO 1875; school (Mummell till 1876) 1870–1927; TX; Unit. C. (orig. Wes. Meth.) b. 1859 by George Bool, and graveyard (graves 1861+); telephone 1922; TX 1928; pop. 83 (1901), 87 (1911), 60 (1933), 57 (1947).

Merrill Creek (*Co. King*) see Merrill.

Merrimboolla (*Co. Harden*) see Murrumburrah.

Merrimbula (*Co. Auckland*) see Merimbula.

Merri Merri (*Co. Gregory*) 31°15'S. 148°15'E., 23 km W. of Gulargambone, on Merri Merri Ck; designated as chief town of the county; flood 1862.

Merriong Estate (*Co. Narromine*) see Narromine.

Merritts Wharf (*Co. Northumberland*) see Empire Bay.

Merriwa (*Co. Brisbane*) 32°08'S. 150°21'E., 49 km W. of Scone, on Witneys Ck; laid out 1839 by J.S. Rusden, town site reserved 1840, first lots (13) sold 1840, village gaz. 1880; orig. wool, then vineyards, dairying, cattle, horses, wheat, maize, barley, sorghum, potatoes, pork, hort.; airfield; ambulance station; Angl. C. 1851 d. by R.G. Boodle, transepts and chancel added 1869, replacement (Holy Trinity) b. 1900 by W. Barrett, d. by George Sanders & Son, and graveyard (77 graves), incl. columbarium; bridges: one destroyed 1889, replaced 1890 by J.E. McDonald, new one 1961, over Merriwa R. and 2 bridges over Witneys Ck; cemeteries: Angl. (21 graves 1900–24) and general (729 graves) 1849, incl. lawn cemetery; CH (incl. police station and lock-up) 1858, new one b. 1867 by William Cains, additions 1885, repairs 1899 by John S. Nutt, additions 1908, alterations 1958; cordial factories: George H. Bridger and C. Nebauer; diphtheria 1933; drought 1877; electricity 1936; 2 FB (station b. 1973, refurbished 2013); floods 1889, 1893, 1920, 1950, 1955; flour mill (Merriwa Flour Milling & Farming Produce Co. Ltd) 1892; hailstorm 1880; heatwaves 1896 and 1940; hospital b. 1892 by John Leard, d. by Pender and Thomas Wilfred Silk, additions 1902, 1922, 1954, 1958, 1962, 1979, alterations 1994, additions 2008; mouse plagues 1905 and 1943; police barracks b. 1878 by Thompson and Turner; PO 1845, new one b. 1879 by Thompson and Turner, d. by James Johnstone Barnet, new one b. 1924 by F. and R. Compton; pound (stock) 1865; powerhouse (M. Campbell & Co. Pty Ltd); quarry (stone); rabbit freezing works (Merriwa Freezing & Canning Co. Ltd) 1915, additions 1918, company wound up 1929; railway engine shed (removed from Denman), re-erected 1917 by Robert Daniel Quiggin; railway turntable, 60 ft (18.3 m), removed from Denman and reinstalled 1917, closed; reservoir; Rom. Cath. C. (St Matthias's) 1858, demolished, new one (St Anne's) b. 1878–81, d. by John Wiltshire Pender, rebuilt 1939 by F. and R. Compton and W.B. Armitage & Co., d. by John Patrick Gannon, and graveyard (143 graves); RS 1917, station b. by John Allibone, closed, reused; sale-yards 1955; school 1850, replaced 1878, new building b. 1919 by A. Quiggin, additions 1954 by E.J. Thacker, additions 1960, 1962, 1964, 1971; sewerage augmentation 1971; silo; storm 1918; telegraph 1865, new office b. 1879 by Thompson and Turner, d. by James Johnstone Barnet; TX 1912, automatic 1980; Unit. C. (St David's, orig. Meth., then Presb. since 1949) b. 1910 by J.W. Colless; water supply augmentation 1959; pop. 42 (1846), 123 (1851), 205 (1856), 170 (1861), *c.*200 (1866), 287 (1871), 342 (1881), 437 (1891), 565 (1901), 1,019 (1911), 1,093 (1933), 904 (1947), 910 (1954), 1,075 (1961), 923 (1966), 971 (1971), 925 (1976), 943 (1981), 961 (1986), 962 (1991), 937 (1996), 987 (2001), 946 (2006), 973 (2011).

Merriwagga (*Co. Nicholson*) 33°49'S. 145°38'E., 39 km S. of Hillston; village surveyed and gaz. 1924; wheat; cemetery (Black Stump); dam b. by R.A. Green; drought 1967–68; lock-up 1930 (removed from Gunbar), closed, sold 1944 to Jack and Mollie Cantwell, moved 1972 to Griffith and reused; PO 1924; PS 1927, closed, sold 1944 to Jack and Mollie Cantwell; Rom. Cath. C. (St Therese's) 1928; RS 1923, closed, station removed 1984; sale-yards 1935; sawmills: B.W. Coates 1935 and W.J. Turner; school 1937–2001, sold; silo; telephone 1925; TX 1926, automatic 1985; Unit. C. (Soldiers' Memorial, orig. Presb.) b. 1929 by W.J. Bacon, d. by George William Albert Welch; water supply 1936, augmentation 1955, 1966, 1968, 1995; pop. 325 (1933), 102 (1947), 178 (1954), 99 (1961), *c.*100 (1999), 169 (2011).

Merry Beach (*Co. St Vincent*) 35°34'S. 150°22'E., 24 km NE of Batemans Bay, on Tasman Sea.

Merrygoen (*Co. Napier*) 31°49'S. 149°14'E., 26 km NW of Dunedoo; orig. Richardson's Corner; pipeclay, silica, wheat, wool; Angl. C. (St Augustine's) 1935; cemetery (17 graves 1851–1920); fire 1934; open-cut mine (silica); PO 1879, closed and reused; railway coal stage 1914; railway turntable 1919, 60 ft (18.3 m), derelict; RS 1917, station b. by John Allibone; sawmill (James Lalor); school 1917 b. by Albert Murphy, new building b. 1935 by J.M. Johnson, closed 1969; silo 1935; telephone 1904; TX 1916–84; water supply 1952; pop. 72 (1911), 215 (1933), 170 (1947), 271 (1954), 95 (1961), 149 (2011).

Merrylands (*Co. Northumberland*) see Maryland.

Merrymeric (*Co. Hume*) 35°34'S. 147°06'E., 19 km SE of Henty; school 1957–60.

Merrywinebone (*Co. Denham*) 29°38'S. 148°49'E., 24 km SE of Collarenebri; grazing; cotton gin (Namoi Cotton Co-op. Ltd); RS (6 km S.) 1906, station b. by John Allibone and Augustus Ringholme, closed 1974; TX, closed 1960; pop. 69 (1911), 20 (1933), 82 (1947), 43 (1954), 51 (1961).

Merton (*Co. Brisbane*) see Denman.

Merton (*Co. Denison*) 35°55'S. 146°12'E., 20 km NW of Corowa; pop. 41 (1933).

Merton (*Co. Forbes*) see Noonbinna East.

Merton Vale (*Co. Hume*) 35°55'S. 146°12'E., 19 km NE of Mulwala.

Merungle Hill (*Co. Cooper*) 34°36'S. 146°26'E., 6 km SE of Leeton; bridge over canal; school 1929–74; water (irrigation) pumping station; pop. 232 (1933), 229 (1947), 207 (1954), 139 (1961), 237 (2011).

Meryla (*Co. Camden*) 34°41'S. 150°23'E., 8 km SE of Bundanoon; bushfires 1905 and 1909; pop. 26 (1933), 10 (2011).

Meryla (*Co. Camden*) see also Werai.

Meryula (*Co. Kennedy*) 32°20'S. 147°16'E., 86 km S. of Nyngan, on Bulbodney Ck.

Meryula (*Co. Robinson*) 31°31'S. 146°04'E., 21 km E. of Cobar; RS 1892, closed; school (Meryula Siding) 1912–14; pop. 67 (1911).

Meryula Siding (*Co. Robinson*) see Meryula.

Metford (*Co. Northumberland*) see Maitland East.

Methul (*Co. Bourke*) 34°36'S. 147°10'E., 24 km N. of Coolamon; PO 1907–13; Presb. C. b. 1938 by W.J. Macauley; school 1913–48; storm 1935; telephone 1906; TX 1918, automatic 1961; pop. 204 (1911), 271 (1933), 212 (1947), 173 (1954), 148 (1961), 306 (2011).

Methven Estate (*Co. Cook*) see Lithgow.

Metz (*Co. Sandon*) 30°35'S. 151°52'E., 21 km E. of Armidale; formerly Sunlight; estab. 1889, village gaz. 1898, thrived 1898, declined *c.*1904+, defunct; farming and mining; airfield; Angl. C. (St Paul's); bushfire 1905; cemetery 1894; 5 mines; PO 1890–1928; PS 1891–1910; Rom. Cath. C. (St Patrick's), moved 1914 to Ebor; school (Hillgrove West till 1896) 1890–1923; telephone 1890; Wes. Meth. C. 1893; pop. *c.*750 (1898), 169 (1911), 81 (1933), 74 (1947), 77 (1954), 90 (1961).

Mewburn (*Co. King*) see Rugby.

Mia Creek (*Co. Courallie*) 29°30'S. 150°00'E., 15 km E. of Moree; RS 1899–1983.

Miamley (*Co. Flinders*) 32°21'S. 146°55'E., 90 km S. of Nyngan; pop. 54 (1947).

Miandetta (*Co. Flinders*) 31°34'S. 146°59'E., 20 km W. of Nyngan; grazing; PO 1906; RS (Pangee till 1893) 1892–1975; telephone 1906; TX 1936; pop. 78 (1911), 157 (1933), 205 (1961).

Mianga Creek (*Co. Georgiana*) 34°23'S. 149°36'E., 14 km NE of Crookwell, on Mianga Ck; also known as Myanga Creek; farming and grazing; school 1957–64.

Micabil (*Co. Cunningham*) 33°03'S. 146°58'E., 18 km W. of Condobolin; RS 1919–73.

Micalo Island (*Co. Clarence*) 29°27'S. 153°19'E., 5 km W. of Yamba, in Clarence R.; sugar mill; pop. 20 (1881).

Micalong (*Co. Buccleuch*) 35°17'S. 148°35'E., 32 km E. of Tumut; sawmill estab. 1921 by Edward John Lees Hallstrom, bought 1922 by A.W. Railton and H. Stokes, bought 1927 by George Brown and moved to Yellowin Creek.

Michelago (*Co. Murray*) 35°43'S. 149°10'E., 40 km S. of Queanbeyan, on Micaligo Ck; formerly Micilago; surveyed 1886 by William Henry O'Malley Wood; goldmining (reef) 1872–92, iron ore, grazing, farming; Angl. C. (St Thomas's) 1902; bushfires 2003 and 2009 (3 houses destroyed); cemetery 1865; CH (incl. police station) b. 1861 by J.J. Wright, new one (incl. lock-up) b. 1892 by John M'Kie; mines: Golden Crown Reef (incl. 5 head and 10 head stamper batteries) *c.*1887 and D. Murray; PO 1860, new one b. 1887; pound (stock) 1861; quarry (Aust. Iron & Smelting Co. and Hoskins Iron & Steel Co. Ltd) 1921–31 and 1941–45; railway turntable, 50 ft (15.2 m), removed from The Rock; rifle range; Rom. Cath. C. (St Patrick's) b. 1865 by Thomas Kennedy, ruined, new one (Father O'Gorman Memorial) b. 1907 by J. Taylor, d. by James Nangle; RS 1887, station b. by Pooley and Harris, closed 1976, reused; school 1880, new buildings b. 1883 by Sanders Helman; telegraph 1878; TX 1915, automatic 1969; pop. 80 (1901), 219 (1911), 221 (1933), 207 (1947), 204 (1954), 179 (1961), 648 (2011).

Micilago (*Co. Murray*) see Michelago.

Micketymulga (*Co. Gordon*) 32°31'S. 148°51'E., 10 km NW of Wellington; farming; Rom. Cath. C. (Our Lady of Mount Carmel) b. 1908–10, closed and demolished; pop. 77 (1901).

Mickibri (*Co. Kennedy*) 32°52'S. 148°12'E., 15 km S. of Peak Hill; bushfire 1905; RS 1914–74; silo 1933.

Middle Adelong (*Co. Wynyard*) see Wondalga.

Middle Arm (*Co. Argyle*) 34°33'S. 149°45'E., 18 km E. of Crookwell, on Tarlo R.; (incl. Slate Vale, also known as Slateland); farming and grazing; bushfire 1918; hailstorm (every house damaged) 1901; mine; PO 1873–1930;

quarry (Chatsbury Slate Quarries), taken over by F.G. White and A.F. Carr, became the NSW Slate Co., closed 1934; Rom. Cath. C. (St Francis's) b. 1911 by George Wright; telephone: Middle Arm 1925 and Slateland 1916; TX 1950–66; pop. 116 (1901), 87 (1911), 54 (1933), 63 (1947), 498 (2011).

Middle Brook (*Co. Brisbane*) 31°57'S. 150°49'E., 13 km NW of Scone, on Middle Brook; telephone 1926; TX 1934–53; pop. 91 (1933), 102 (1947), 81 (1961), 264 (2006), 405 (2011).

Middle Camp (*Co. Gloucester*) 32°28'S. 152°27'E., 24 km E. of Bulahdelah, on Tasman Sea.

Middle Camp (*Co. Northumberland*) see Catherine Hill Bay.

Middle Creek (*Co. Brisbane*) 31°56'S. 150°48'E., 19 km S. of Murrurundi, on Middle Brook; school 1880–92.

Middle Creek (*Co. Gough*) see Stannifer.

Middle Falbrook (*Co. Durham*) 32°26'S. 151°09'E., 15 km N. of Singleton; bridge (de Burgh timber truss) b. 1904 by Murphy and Taylor, 247 ft (75.3 m), over Glennies Ck; creamery (John Lethbridge) 1892; FB.

Middle Falbrook (*Co. Durham*) see also Glennies Creek.

Middlefield (*Co. Kennedy*) 32°26'S. 147°34'E., 65 km NW of Peak Hill; RS 1916, station b. by T.E. Quiggin, closed 1974; pop. 33 (1933).

Middle Flat (*Co. Beresford*) 36°14'S. 149°11'E., 5 km E. of Cooma; pop. 21 (1933).

Middle Kalang (*Co. Raleigh*) see Kalang.

Middle Pocket (*Co. Rous*) 28°30'S. 153°29'E., 7 km N. of Mullumbimby, on Lacks Ck; school 1954–68; telephone 1924; pop. 117 (1933), 179 (1947), 176 (1954), 133 (1961).

Middle Temora (*Co. Bland*) see Temora.

Middleton (*Co. Ashburnham*) see Parkes.

Middletown (*Co. Hardinge*) see Kimberley.

Middlingbank (*Co. Wallace*) 36°13'S. 148°48'E., 30 km W. of Cooma, on Lake Eucumbene; airfield; Angl. C. (St Thomas's), removed from Rocky Plain, re-erected 1900, renovated 1935, closed, sold and reused; earth tremors 2002 and 2011; flour mill and sawmill (Alpine, James Broadhead), water powered, girl killed 1894; school 1885–96; pop. 77 (1911), 28 (1933).

Midgen Flat (*Co. Rous*) 28°43'S. 153°35'E., 7 km SE of Bangalow; formerly Mignon Flat.

Midginbil (*Co. Rous*) 28°29'S. 153°16'E., 21 km SW of Murwillumbah, on Perch Ck; farming; PO 1910–43; school 1914–69; telephone 1912; pop. 109 (1933), 62 (1947), 87 (1954), 87 (1961).

Midkin Station (*Co. Courallie*) 29°18'S. 149°44'E., 20 km NW of Moree; pop. 122 (1933), 82 (1947).

Midway (*Co. Wynyard*) see Minjary.

Mignon Flat (*Co. Rous*) see Midgen Flat.

Mihi (*Co. Sandon*) 30°43'S. 151°42'E., 19 km SE of Uralla; sawmill (Donald MacDonald) 1909; pop. 55 (1933).

Mila (*Co. Wellesley*) 37°03'S. 149°10'E., 16 km S. of Bombala, on Tombola Ck; farming and grazing; bushfire 1939; creamery (Bombala Co-op. Dairy Co. Ltd); PO 1896; school 1884–1909; telephone 1914; TX 1917, automatic 1954; pop. 106 (1901), 106 (1911), 106 (1933), 64 (1947), 84 (1954), 59 (1961), 100 (2006), 240 (2011).

Milbang (*Co. Argyle*) 34°50'S. 149°27'E., 26 km W. of Goulburn; bridge (Maryfield Bridge); school (Millbang) 1866–72; pop. 57 (1911).

Milbrodale (*Co. Northumberland*) 32°42'S. 151°00'E., 20 km SW of Singleton, on Darkey Ck; settled 1822–24; agric.; 4 quarries; school 1930 b. by A. Peterson, renovated 1960; pop. 114 (1933), 54 (1947).

Milbrulong (*Co. Urana*) 35°15'S. 146°51'E., 11 km E. of Lockhart; village gaz. and lots sold 1902; wheat; cemetery; electricity 1937; FB (station b. 1982); Lutheran C. (Bethlehem) 1901, and graveyard; PO 1899; reservoir, 50,000 gal. (227.3 kl); RS 1901, station b. by C. Hardy & Co., closed 1975, removed 1983; school 1895, additions 1897, closed 2014, sold 2016; silo 1919; telephone 1913; TX 1913, automatic 1940; pop. 63 (1901), 258 (1911), 76 (1933), 174 (1947), 154 (1954), 148 (1961), 364 (2006).

Milburn Creek (*Co. Bathurst*) 33°52'S.

148°53'E., 18 km E. of Cowra, on Milburn Ck; Green Gully till 1876; mining (copper disc. 1872) and grazing; airfield; mine 1873; PO 1876–1931; school 1877–1904; pop. 46 (1933).

Milby (*Co. Gipps*) 33°22'S. 146°54'E., 39 km SW of Condobolin; pop. 78 (1933).

Milchoni (*Co. Baradine*) 30°22'S. 148°40'E., 74 km W. of Wee Waa, on Baradine Ck.

Mildil (*Co. Gipps*) 33°53'S. 147°01'E., 19 km W. of West Wyalong; horse dip 1937; school 1957–69; pop. 48 (1933), 85 (1947), 91 (1954), 127 (1961).

Mildura Bridge (*Co. Wentworth*) see Buronga.

Mile Ridge (*Co. Hunter*) see Colo Heights.

Milgadara (*Co. St Vincent*) 35°17'S. 149°54'E., 8 km NE of Braidwood; telephone 1917; TX 1920–30.

Milguy (*Co. Courallie*) 29°21'S. 150°12'E., 36 km E. of Moree; Lutheran C. (St John's); PO 1955; RS 1932–83; school 1956, extended 1964, closed 1967; silo 1955; telephone 1955; TX 1956–69.

Milkers Flat (*Co. Roxburgh*) 33°17'S. 149°24'E., 23 km NE of Bathurst, on Macquarie R.; settled 1855 by Hugh and Janet Smith; Union C. 1896.

Millah Murrah (*Co. Roxburgh*) 33°11'S. 149°35'E., 26 km N. of Bathurst, on Millah Murrah Ck; wheat; PO 1865–1901; school (Millamurra) 1876–83; slate quarry (New Bangor) 1880–84; pop. 23 (1933).

Millamolong (*Co. Bathurst*) 33°36'S. 148°57'E., 25 km SW of Millthorpe, on Merrimalong Ck; farming and grazing; PO 1914–47; pop. 40 (1933).

Millamurra (*Co. Roxburgh*) see Millah Murrah.

Mill Angle (*Co. Wynyard*) see Tumut.

Millbang (*Co. Argyle*) see Milbang.

Millbank (*Co. Dudley*) 30°52'S. 152°38'E., 30 km NW of Kempsey, on Hickeys Ck; farming; flood 1963; PO 1927; school (Urulgurra till 1895, then Hickeys Creek till 1912) 1893, additions 1923 by Landers and Furnifull, additions 2010, closed 2017; telephone 1914; TX 1928–79; pop. 161 (1933), 165 (1947), 128 (1954), 90 (1961).

Millbank North (*Co. Dudley*) 30°49'S. 152°37'E., 38 km NW of Kempsey, on Hickeys Ck; telephone 1926; TX 1938–65.

Millbrook (*Co. Camden*) see Wollongong.

Mill Creek (*Co. Gloucester*) 32°21'S. 151°58'E., 5 km N. of Stroud, on Mill Ck; pop. 80 (1947).

Mill Crossing (*Co. Clarke*) 30°32'S. 152°08'E., 47 km E. of Armidale, on Oaky R.

Milleara (*Co. Clarence*) 29°52'S. 153°07'E., 28 km N. of Woolgoolga, on Halfway Ck; bushfire (house destroyed) 1936; sawmill (Northern Sawmills Pty Ltd); telephone 1933; TX 1933–41; pop. 41 (1933).

Millera (*Co. Drake*) 29°09'S. 152°21'E., 35 km E. of Tenterfield, on Rocky R.; formerly Malara; goldmining; cemetery.

Millers Creek (*Co. Buckland*) 31°49'S. 150°31'E., 29 km W. of Murrurundi, on Millers Ck; TX (automatic); pop. 55 (1933), 51 (1947).

Millers Forest (*Co. Northumberland*) 32°45'S. 151°42'E., 4 km W. of Raymond Terrace, on Hunter R.; (incl. Alnwick gaz. 1849, and Dockyard); also known as Martins Wharf till 1912; wheat, tobacco, maize, millet, broom-making; Angl. C. (St Saviour's) 1877; bridge (Irrawang Bridge) 1970, to Nelsons Plains, over Hunter R.; caterpillar infestation 1926; creamery (Millers Forest Co-op. Creamery Co. Ltd) 1892–1915; dockyard; floods 1857, 1867, 1870, 1890, 1893, 1895, 1913, 1930, 1946, 1949, 1955; gale (nearly every house damaged) 1905; levee banks 1969; PO 1859; Prim. Meth. C. 1866, new one b. 1876 by William Gilbert, renovated and porch added 1882–84, inundated 1893, extended 1897, re-roofed and new porch added 1915, church inundated 1949, demolished 1953; school 1883, new one b. 1884 by John Rollo Rodgers, repairs 1893 by D.L. Garred, alterations and repairs 1915 by R. Harper, additions 1918 by W. M'Pherson; sugar mill (Hugh Fraser), upgraded 1873; telephone 1912; Unit. C. (orig. Meth.) b. 1953 by M.R. Myers; wharf 1890; pop. 616 (1911), 477 (1933), 435 (1947), 393 (1954), 331 (1961), 321 (2011).

Millers Waterholes (*Co. Clarence*) see Trenayr.

Mill Farm (*Co. Rous*) 28°33'S. 152°56'E., 11 km NW of Kyogle, on Eden Ck.

Millfield (*Co. Northumberland*) 32°54'S. 151°16'E., 2 km NW of Paxton, on Congewai Ck; (incl. Crawfordville); wheat, tobacco, maize, then oats, potatoes, wine, coalmining; Angl. C. b. 1880 by George Brown, new one (St Luke's) 1956; bridges: first one b. 1867, demolished, replaced 1935 by James and Reuben Shedden, 543 ft (165.5 m), over Congewai Ck, and one b. 2003 over Wollombi Brook; bushfires 1968–69; cemetery (271 graves) 1863; collieries: Millfield Greta (estab. 1921–24 by Millfield Coal Mining Co. and Millfield Greta Coal Mining Co., acquired and o. 1929 by R.W. Miller & Co., 2 killed 1929, strikes 1932, 1942, 1943, 1949, 1950, closed and abandoned 1955, surface works fires 1968 and 1969, acquired and reopened 1976 by Hetton-Bellbird Co., closed and razed 1978) and Millfield North (estab. 1945 by R.W. Miller & Co. as Millfield No. 2 Tunnel, o. 1946 as Millfield North, closed, razed); diphtheria 1921; flour mills: Alex Crothers (burnt down 1867, new one 1872), Hinchcliffe's (also used for sawmilling) 1850, George Smyth; ice works (Craft Bros); PO 1854; pound (stock) 1876; sawmills: Craft Bros (removed from Greta Main) 1926, Richard Andrew Sweetman (removed from Sweetmans Creek), Wolstenholme's 1906; scarlet fever 1909; schools: Crawfordville 1929 b. by W. Williams, closed 1969 and Millfield 1871, additions 1929; storm (man killed) 1895; telephone 1892; TX 1927–60; winery (Millbrook Estate) 1999; pop. 114 (1901), 138 (1911), 193 (1933), 214 (1947), 434 (1954), 430 (1961), 280 (1971), 259 (1976), 245 (1981), 294 (1986), 389 (1991), 468 (1996), 486 (2001), 559 (2006), 586 (2011).

Millie (*Co. Jamison*) 29°49'S. 149°33'E., 46 km N. of Wee Waa, on Millie Ck; agric. and grazing; PO 1874; pound (stock) 1868; PS 1882; telegraph 1877; TX 1910, automatic 1980; pop. *c.*400 (1903), 153 (1911), 50 (1933), 147 (2006).

Millingandi (*Co. Auckland*) 36°53'S. 149°51'E., 5 km W. of Merimbula, on Boggy Ck; farming; bushfire 2013; creamery (Boggy Creek) b. by S. Turner, closed 1901; school 1887–1921 and 1933–36; TX; pop. 59 (1933), 389 (2001), 61 (1911), 77 (1954), 53 (1961), 385 (2011).

Millingarie (*Co. Macquarie*) 31°45'S. 152°18'E., 15 km NW of Wingham, on Dingo Ck; school 1907–73.

Milliwindi (*Co. Darling*) 30°49'S. 150°33'E., 19 km SW of Manilla, on Lake Keepit; village gaz. 1880; Angl. C. (St Matthew's) 1901; sawmills: Miller and Roach, burnt down 1931, and Pincham Bros; school 1886–88.

Mill Paddock (*Co. Northumberland*) see Mayfield West.

Millpost (*Co. Bathurst*) 33°43'S. 149°04'E., 27 km SW of Blayney, on Mandurama Ponds; earth tremor 1919; school 1906–17.

Mills Mews (*Co. Rous*) 28°25'S. 153°01'E., 23 km N. of Kyogle, on Sheepstation Ck.

Millsville (*Co. Wellington*) 32°41'S. 149°40'E., 13 km SE of Mudgee, on Mullamuddy Ck; school 1881, new buildings b. 1883 by R. Martin, closed 1913; telephone 1925; whooping cough epidemic 1907.

Millthorpe (*Co. Bathurst*) 33°27'S. 149°11'E., 12 km NW of Blayney; Cross Roads till 1840s then Spring Grove till 1884; settled 1823, thrived in 1870s, declined *c.*1920+, classified by National Trust; orig. wheat and vegetables, then oats, barley, flour, wool, rabbits, dairying, chaff, hay, lambs, beef, fruit, potatoes, peas; Angl. C. 1879, reused, new one (St Mark the Evangelist) b. 1909 by Joseph Wells and William Murray, d. by John Francis Kenny; Bapt. C. b. 1903 by William Murray, closed, sold 2002, reused; boot factory (A. Evans & Co.) 1902; butter factory 1894; butter and bacon factory (Millthorpe Butter & Bacon Co-op. Co. Ltd) 1906; carriage-works (J. Nicholis), bought 1900 by J. Murphy, damaged 1900; cemetery (burials 1867+) 1874, incl. columbarium 1993; CH b. 1902 by John Burnett; chaff mill estab. 1914 by Gus. R. Kleinig, J.E. Kleinig and Arthur Stockman, burnt down 1931; electricity 1934; FB; fires 1902, 1923, 1934; floods 1900, 1902, 1916 (2 died); flour mill (Great Western Milling Co. Ltd) b. 1885 by F. Seibert, converted to roller mill 1890, enlarged 1906, modernised 1907, closed 1962, reused by Algie Masters as potato processing plant, reused by Jim Cheney as house frame and truss factory, demolished 1974; gale 1900; hailstorm 1918; jam factory (Millthorpe Jam & Preserving Co.) estab. 1922 by W.O. Moad (in former rabbit freezing works), burnt down 1922; joinery (Wells), burnt down 1915; measles epidemic 1893; pea vining plant (R. Gordon Edgell & Sons Ltd) 1943; PO 1874, new one b. 1895 by T.W. Chalmers, extended 1899 and 1902, replaced 1927; pound (stock) 1893; PS 1894, new one b. 1902 by John Burnett; rabbit freezing works (in former butter factory) 1910, fire 1915, reused 1921; reservoir 1955; Rom. Cath. C. (St Canice's) 1904, renovated 2003; RS (Spring Grove till 1884) 1877, new station b. 1886 by James Stuart Douglas; Salv. Army C. 1925; school (Spring Grove till 1883) 1867, new one b. 1876 by William Chambers, additions 1878 by William O'Brien, additions 1888 by James Prior Hull, re-roofed 1897 by R.C. Millar, additions 1900 by H.T. Seymour, renovated 1911, additions 1981 by E. Tilston & Sons; silo; snowstorms 1896, 1920, 1921; telegraph 1879, new office b. 1895 by T.W. Chalmers; telephone 1905; TX 1910, automatic 1980; Unit. C. (orig. Wes. Meth.) 1885; water reticulation 1956; wooden blind factory; pop. 498 (1891), 994 (1901), 1,390 (1911), 1,102 (1921), 864 (1933), 899 (1947), 853 (1954), 752 (1961), 656 (1966), 608 (1971), 640 (1976), 607 (1981), 638 (1986), 628 (1991), 625 (1996), 711 (2001), 725 (2006), 737 (2011).

Milltown (*Co. Bathurst*) see Bathurst.

Millwood (*Co. Bourke*) 35°01'S. 147°09'E., 23 km NW of Wagga Wagga; Meth. C. 1909–55; PO 1898–1918; quarry; Rom. Cath. C. b. 1908 by J. Bance; school (Notherwono till 1899) 1895–1966; pop. 125 (1911), 76 (1933), 56 (1954).

Milong (*Co. Bland*) 34°19'S. 148°08'E., 15 km W. of Young; earth tremor 1918; Rom. Cath. C. (St Eugene's) 1910; school 1885–1930; pop. 66 (1911).

Milparinka (*Co. Evelyn*) 29°44'S. 141°53'E., 248 km NW of Wilcannia, on Evelyn Ck; orig. Evelyn Creek, then Milperinka 1881–1925; surveyed 1881, town gaz. 1883, thrived in 1880s, now largely ruinous and almost defunct; goldmining and stock breeding; cemetery 1886; CH 1886 d. by James Johnstone Barnet, new one b. 1896 by A. Reid, d. by Walter Liberty Vernon, closed 1929, restored and reused; dust storms 1944 and 2018; earth tremor 1953; hospital 1889; lock-up, derelict, restored and reused; PO 1881, new one b. 1901 by Michael Kenna Power, damaged 1944, closed, ruined; pound (stock) 1882; PS 1881–1930, restored and reused 2005; school 1884–1926; telegraph 1890; telephone 1907; TX 1915–84; typhoid 1894; pop. 143 (1891), 70 (1901), 87 (1911), 252 (1922), 102 (1933), 83 (1947), 38 (1954), 149 (1961), *c.*100 (1987), 53 (2006).

Milpose (*Co. Ashburnham*) 32°57'S. 147°54'E., 17 km E. of Trundle; pop. 146 (1911), 93 (1933), 118 (1947).

Milpost (*Co. Bathurst*) see Gallymont.

Milray Estate (*Co. Northumberland*) see Swansea.

Milroy (*Co. Narran*) 29°36'S. 146°42'E., 43 km N. of Brewarrina; pop. 22 (1933).

Milroy (*Co. Phillip*) 32°35'S. 149°37'E., 3 km E. of Mudgee.

Milroy (*Co. Pottinger*) 31°08'S. 150°04'E., 26 km SW of Gunnedah; FB; sawmill (Martin Bros); school 1909–35 and 1959–64; pop. 33 (1933), 74 (1961).

Milton (*Co. St Vincent*) 35°19'S. 150°26'E., 6 km NW of Ulladulla, on Pettys Ck; The Settlement till 1859; settled by Joseph Whatman, surveyed 1859 by Henry G. Morton, founded 1859 by John Booth, first lots sold 1860, thrived 1870s–80s, classified 1986 by National Trust; orig. timber, then wheat, maize, pigs, vegetables, later dairying, cattle, horses; Angl. C. (St Paul's) 1860, became St Peter and St Paul's, additions 1907, and graveyard (97 graves); bushfires 1868, 1869, 1896, 1948 (2 houses destroyed), 1952 (4 houses destroyed); butter factory (Ulladulla Refrigerating Butter Co. Ltd) 1896–1942, reused 1962; CH (incl. lock-up) 1877, additions 1878 by Moore Bros; Christ. Ministry Pentecostal C.; condensed milk factory 1873, failed; cordial factories: J. Buchan, Cork's (reused), Johann M. Faust 1887, M.J. Mudge, W. Nelson; FB 1961; flour mill (George Knight, sen.) 1860; gales 1947 and 1951; hailstorm 1887; heatwave 1896; hospital (cottage) 1908, taken over 1936 by govt, renamed Milton Ulladulla hospital in 1938, new one 1967, fire 2005; Jehovah's Witnesses C.; pneumonia epidemic (15 died) 1901; PO 1860, new one b. 1878–80 by James Poole, additions and alterations 1894 and 1904; PS 1881; Rom. Cath. C. (St Mary Star of the Sea) b. 1891 by William Riley, fire 1902; Salv. Army C. b. 1900 by William Samuel Garrad, closed, sold and reused; sawmills: A. Calegroes 1951 and Fenning's; school 1878, additions 1906, repairs 1913 by M. Mudge, renovated 1925 by E.R.S. Potter, additions 1958, 1963, 1966, 2008; SD Adventist C. (Woods Cottage) 2014; silica quarry (Pattimore's) 1918–39; snow 1932; storm 1899; telegraph 1875, new office b. 1878–80 by James Poole, additions and alterations 1904; TX 1914, automatic 1962; Unit. C. (orig. Cong.) b. 1872 by James Poole and J.B. Moore, extended 1885, rebuilt 1922 by William Poole, damaged 1947, restored 1948 by George Poole, closed, sold 2017, and graveyard; Wes. Meth. C. 1857, additions 1861, new one b. 1883 by Thomas W. Carwardine, damaged 1899, repaired by Hamon, renovated by Riley and Poole, sold 1982, reused, and graveyard 1856–1905; pop. *c.*80 (1866), *c.*250 (1871), *c.*1,000 (1891), 1,084 (1911), 744 (1954), 764 (1961), 717 (1966), 691 (1971), 729 (1976), 740 (1981), 897 (1986), 980 (1991), 1,030 (1996), 1,132 (2001), 1,106 (2006), 1,204 (2011).

Milton East (*Co. St Vincent*) see Mollymook.

Milton Estate (*Co. Bathurst*) see Westville.

Milton Park (*Co. Camden*) 34°30'S. 150°29'E., 11 km NE of Moss Vale; pop. 35 (1933).

Milvale (*Co. Bland*) 34°19'S. 147°55'E., 35 km W. of Young, on Tumbleton Ck; soldiers' settlement; grazing, wheat, orchards; mouse plague 1917; PO 1916; Rom. Cath. C. (St Brendan's) 1922; RS 1916, station b. by W.S. Millard & Sons Ltd, closed 1975; school 1957–70; silo 1922; telephone 1916; TX 1918, automatic 1977; pop. 99 (1921), 113 (1933), 103 (1947), 135 (1954), 134 (1961), 98 (2006).

Mimosa (*Co. Bourke*) 34°35'S. 147°21'E., 22 km SW of Temora; farming; Bapt. C. 1908; school (Big Mimosa 1913–21) 1909, new school 1913, closed 1948; TX (automatic) 1954; pop. 242 (1911), 244 (1933), 115 (1947), 147 (1954), 119 (1961).

Mimosa (*Co. Bourke*)
see also Boundary Villa.

Mimosa Dell (*Co. Westmoreland*)
see Black Springs.

Mimosa Park (*Co. St Vincent*) 35°25'S. 150°21'E., 13 km SW of Ulladulla; school 1882–1926.

Mindaribba (*Co. Durham*) 32°40'S. 151°35'E., 8 km N. of Maitland, on Paterson R.; Belle Vue till 1912; farming and dairying; mine; quarry; RS (Dunmore till 1912) 1911, station closed and removed 1985; pop. 29 (1933).

Mine Camp (*Co. Northumberland*) 33°08'S. 151°38'E., 3 km E. of Nords Wharf; founded by Thomas Parton, defunct; coalmining; PO 1903; Prim. Meth. C.; quarry; railway (Wallarah Coal Co. Ltd) to Catherine Hill Bay 1890; sawmill; telephone 1950; pop. 165 (1911).

Minemoorong (*Co. Kennedy*) 32°17'S. 147°27'E., 74 km W. of Narromine; RS 1916–74.

Mineral Hill (*Co. Cunningham*) 32°36'S. 146°59'E., 57 km N. of Condobolin; mining (gold, and silver-lead disc. 1911 by McClure and C.J.S. McPhillamay) and grazing; mine (bought 1912 by Iodide Mineral Hill Ltd), closed 1917; PO 1912; school 1914–20;

telephone 1916; TX 1927–45; pop. 29 (1933).

Mingaletta (*Co. Macquarie*) 31°15'S. 152°50'E., 19 km S. of Kempsey; RS 1926–66.

Mingay (*Co. Harden*) 34°58'S. 148°09'E., 11 km N. of Gundagai, on Muttama Ck; gold (alluvial and reef); RS 1890–1971; wool-scour (James Ah Chuey) 1896.

Mingelo (*Co. Narromine*) 32°44'S. 148°09'E., 4 km W. of Peak Hill; Mengello till 1889; village gaz. 1889; cyanide plant (A.G. Litchfield and Brodie) 1903, sold 1906 to C. Richards and Curtis and dismantled by Steve Kelly and Jack Meadows, for removal to Euabalong; goldmine (Matson and Wooden); PO 1889, burnt down 1906; pop. 110 (1911).

Mingelo (*Co. Narromine*) see also Trewilga.

Mingerong (*Co. Kennedy*) 32°40'S. 148°03'E., 15 km NW of Peak Hill; school 1957–65; pop. 165 (1933), 58 (1947).

Mingoola (*Co. Clive*) 29°00'S. 151°33'E., 46 km W. of Tenterfield, on Mole R.; tobacco; freezing works (Wade Bros), acquired 1927 by Amalgamated Rabbit & Skin Export Co. Ltd; school 1957; pop. 96 (1911), 32 (1933), 18 (2016).

Minimbah (*Co. Gloucester*) 32°10'S. 152°23'E., 11 km W. of Tuncurry; Bapt. C. 1933, closed, later demolished; PO 1927–42; school 1957–64; telephone 1929; TX 1957–65.

Minimbah (*Co. Gloucester*) see also Forster.

Minimbah (*Co. Northumberland*) 32°40'S. 151°15'E., 10 km W. of Branxton; dairying; Aboriginal mission 1946; RS 1898–1976.

Minjary (*Co. Wynyard*) 35°12'S. 148°08'E., 14 km NW of Tumut, on Stuckeys Ck; formerly Midway; village gaz. 1863; PO 1927; quarry; telephone 1926; TX 1928–31; pop. 50 (1911), 44 (1933).

Minmi (*Co. Northumberland*) 32°53'S. 151°37'E., 4 km NE of West Wallsend, on Minmi Ck; estab. 1855 by John Brown as a private town, declined 1913+; coalmining till 1924 and oranges; Angl. C. (St John's) 1882–1984, sold and reused; brickworks (J. and A. Brown); bushfire 2013; cemetery (642 graves 1863+); CH b. 1896 by W.B. Chessell, closed, sold and reused; Christ. Brethren C.; 33 coke-ovens (beehive type) estab. 1861 by John Eales, acquired by J. and A. Brown, closed 1898, demolished; collieries: Minmi (estab. 1857 by John Eales and John Christian, sold 1859 to James and Alexander Brown, acquired 1861 by Melbourne, Newcastle, Minmi Coal Mining Co., transferred 1863 to Rolfe, Nuttall and De Little, flooded 1864, taken over again by J. and A. Brown, new foundry 1879, colliery closed 1893, reopened, closed 1924–35), Minmi New Tunnel, Minmi Open-Cut, Turner Bros (acquired by John Eales); Cong. C.; Coptic Orthodox C. (St Mary and St George's), in former Presb. C.; electricity 1949; engineering works estab. 1861 by J. and A. Brown, expanded 1865; FB (old station renovated 1929, new one 1995); fire 1893; lock-up (3 cells) 1892, additions 1895 by Southon Bros; miners' strike 1861; PO 1860, new one b. 1896 by Andrew Burg, d. by Walter Liberty Vernon, closed, sold and reused; Presb. C. (St Andrew's) 1885, closed, sold and reused; Prim. Meth. C. 1863, reused; PS 1879–1933, reused, sold 1955, reused again; quarry (J. and A. Brown); railway (coal) to Hexham 1856; reservoir, 69,200 gal. (314.6 kl); Rom. Cath. C. (St Joseph's) 1888, demolished 1941; Salv. Army C. 1902; school 1861, new one b. 1878 by James and Humphrey, repairs 1902 by G. Taylor, new buildings b. 1906 by Southon Bros; telegraph 1881; telephone 1911; United Meth. Free C. 1878; Welsh Indep. C. 1863; pop. *c.*150 (1866), *c.*250 (1870), 1,936 (1881), 2,357 (1891), 2,595 (1901), 1,708 (1911), *c.*1,000 (1921), 533 (1933), 362 (1947), 342 (1954), 298 (1971), 332 (1976), 284 (1981), 273 (1986), 318 (1991), 505 (1996), 683 (2011).

Minnalong (*Co. Kennedy*) 32°32'S. 147°11'E., 61 km N. of Condobolin.

Minnamurra (*Co. Camden*) 34°38'S. 150°51'E., 5 km N. of Kiama, on Minnamurra R.; (incl. Kiama Downs); formerly Peterborough and Bustle Hill; bypassed by highway 2005; Angl. C. (St Paul's) 1936, extensions and alterations 1949; bacon factory (Charles Barns); bridge 1872, (second) b. 1891 by H. Reid, (third)

1965, over Minnamurra R.; bushfire 1940; electricity 1948; Mission C. 1936; PO 1927; punt 1861–72, across Minnamurra R.; quarries: Federal Blue Metal Quarries Ltd 1923–43 and NSW Assoc. Blue Metal Quarries Ltd; railway bridge 1887, new one 1924, over Minnamurra R.; RS 1891, station relocated 1943; school 1976; telephone 1922; TX (automatic) 1963; pop. 247 (1961), 5,703 (2011).

Minnamurra (*Co. Camden*) see also Dunmore.

Minnie Water (*Co. Clarence*) 29°47'S. 153°17'E., 36 km E. of Grafton, on Coral Sea; sand mining 1939; FB; telephone 1954; TX 1954–78; water supply augmentation 1996; pop. 38 (1961), 212 (2006), 189 (2011).

Minore (*Co. Narromine*) 32°16'S. 148°27'E., 14 km W. of Dubbo; village gaz. 1903; farming and grazing; butter factory (Edwin Henry Utley and Thomas Duggan) 1892; mines (chalk), abandoned; PO 1875; RS (Manoa till 1908) 1887, additions to station 1903, closed 1975; schools: Minore 1881–98 and Minore Siding (Manoa till 1903) 1900–8; silo 1935; telephone 1916; TX 1928, automatic 1965; pop. 127 (1901), 105 (1933), 64 (1947), 58 (1954), 62 (1961), 302 (2006).

Minore (*Co. Narromine*)
see also Dickygundi.

Minore Falls (*Co. Narromine*) 32°12'S. 148°24'E., 15 km E. of Narromine.

Minore Siding (*Co. Narromine*) see Minore.

Minyon (*Co. Rous*) 28°38'S. 153°24'E., 12 km SW of Mullumbimby, on Coopers Ck; telephone 1922; TX 1923, automatic 1966.

Miowera (*Co. Oxley*) 31°37'S. 147°19'E., 13 km SE of Nyngan, on Belar Ck; RS (Allison's Siding till 1895) 1889, station rebuilt 1910 after fire, closed 1975.

Mirador (*Co. Auckland*) see Merimbula.

Mirannie (*Co. Durham*) 32°24'S. 151°23'E., 28 km NE of Singleton, on Glendon Brook; Marrana Creek till 1905 then Maeranie till 1906; dairying; Angl. C. 1874; bridge (Brookers Bridge) over Glendon Brook; butter factory and creamery (Richard Binnie); cemetery 1874; PO 1896; school (Maerannie till 1966) 1957–70; telephone 1921; TX 1921, automatic 1979; pop. 67 (1901), 134 (1911), 122 (1933), 87 (1947), 88 (1954), 69 (1961).

Miroma (*Co. Rous*) 28°50'S. 153°30'E., 6 km E. of Alstonville, on Maguires Ck; quarry; RS 1940–49.

Mirrabooka (*Co. Monteagle*)
see McHenrys Creek and Maimuru.

Mirrabooka (*Co. Northumberland*)
see Brightwaters.

Mirra View (*Co. Northumberland*) 33°06'S. 151°34'E., 2 km NE of Brightwaters, on Lake Macquarie; PO 1936; school 1936–72; telephone 1936; TX 1952–62.

Mirriadool (*Co. Courallie*) 29°38'S. 149°27'E., 44 km SW of Moree; TX (automatic).

Mirrool (*Co. Bourke*) 34°19'S. 147°05'E., 18 km E. of Ardlethan, on Mirrool Ck; laid out 1909 by Eugene Ernest William Herborn, first lots sold 1909, soldiers' settlement; rice and farming; bridge (timber beam spans) b. by H.E. Ibbotson & Son, over Mirrool Ck; cheese factory 1916–22, reused; fire 1950; Meth. C. 1914; reservoir (elevated), 50,000 gal. (227.3 kl); PO 1911; RS 1908, station b. by Frank Vernon, closed; school 1910–74; silo 1922; telephone 1910; TX 1912; water supply 1941; pop. 202 (1911), 128 (1933), 40 (1947), 56 (1954), 164 (1961), 211 (2006), 234 (2011).

Missabotti (*Co. Raleigh*) 30°34'S. 152°48'E., 10 km N. of Bowraville, on Missabotti Ck; farming, dairying, bananas; bridge 1932; bushfires 1951 and 2017; PO 1918–72; Rom. Cath. C. (Holy Cross) 1937, closed, sold 1980 and reused; sawmill; school 1893, new building b. 1919, begun by T.W. Morris but completed by Thomas Norman Grimsley, closed 1963; telephone 1918; TX 1925; pop. 160 (1911), 241 (1933), 234 (1947), 146 (1954), 102 (1961), 310 (2011).

Missingham (*Co. Rous*) 28°42'S. 153°03'E., 9 km S. of Kyogle, on Boorabee Ck; quarry; telephone 1925; TX 1929, automatic 1955.

Mistletoe Farm (*Co. Northumberland*)
see Pokolbin.

Mitchell (*Co. Bathurst*) see Bathurst.

Mitchell (*Co. Gough*) 29°41'S. 152°07'E., 37 km

E. of Glen Innes, on Mitchell R.; town gaz. 1871.

Mitchell (*Co. Roxburgh*) see Sunny Corner.

Mitchell's Creek (*Co. Bligh*) see Bodangora.

Mitchell's Creek (*Co. Roxburgh*) see Mitchell West and Sunny Corner.

Mitchells Flat (*Co. Durham*) 32°34'S. 151°17'E., 11 km E. of Singleton, on Glendon Brook; tobacco, farming, dairying; bridge (Griffiths Crossing) over Glendon Brook; flood 1893; PO 1893; school 1882 b. by Moran Bros, closed 1956; telephone 1914; TX 1923–69; pop. 245 (1901), 207 (1911), 129 (1933), 134 (1947), 136 (1954), 85 (1961).

Mitchells Flat (*Co. Sandon*) 30°28'S. 151°35'E., 8 km NW of Armidale; cemetery.

Mitchells Island (*Co. Macquarie*) 31°54'S. 152°37'E., 7 km SW of Harrington, in Manning R.; (incl. Booth Town, Pelican Point, Scott's Creek); disc. 1818; orig. sawmilling and shipbuilding, later farming, grapes, oysters, dairying; Angl. C. (St Mark's) b. 1872 by William Albury, re-roofed 1902, and graveyard (197 graves *c.*1872+), incl. columbarium; bridge to Oxley Island over Scotts Ck; bushfire 1900; butter factory (Lower Manning Co-op. Dairy Co. Ltd) 1893, name changed in 1899 to Manning River Dairy Co-op. Co. Ltd, factory replaced (Manning River Co-op. Dairy Co. Ltd) 1918, cheese-making and ice-making plants installed 1919, closed, sold and reused; cemetery (344 graves 1866+) 1866; creameries: Redbank (removed 1899 from Pampoolah) and Luthrie Bay 1900–4; FB; PO 1881; punts: one to Croki (4 car capacity) across Manning R. and one to Oxley Island (2 car capacity) across Scotts Ck; sawmills: John Booth & Co. (Summer-Hill) 1864–1902, MacMurrell's 1951, George Scott; schools: Mitchells Island 1869, additions 1898 by Stewart Adolphus Levick, additions 1924 by Levick and Mudford, additions 2010, and Pelican Point 1866–69; shipyard (Alexander Newton and William Malcolm) 1847–78; storm 1907; telephone 1914; TX (automatic) 1969; wharf (butter factory); pop. 6 (1841), 361 (1901), 399 (1911), 406 (1933), 373 (1947), 358 (1954), 300 (1961), 411 (2006), 445 (2011).

Mitchell West (*Co. Roxburgh*) 33°23'S. 149°52'E., 10 km W. of Portland, on Bobs Ck; Mitchell's Creek till 1885; farming and mining (gold disc. 1851); kilns (gold quartz); mines: Big Hill 1886–92 and 1897–1911, Bobs Creek 1887–1908 and 1933, Little Hill (Band & Albion Co.) 1889–1906, Mitchells Creek; PO 1862–1930; PS; stamper batteries; Union C. 1897; pop. *c.*150 (1875), 93 (1911), 36 (1933).

Mittagong (*Co. Camden*) 34°27'S. 150°27'E., 4 km NE of Bowral, on Nattai R.; (incl. Gainsborough subdivision 1841, Livingstone subdivision 1842, New Sheffield subdivision 1865, Oaklands subdivision 1888, Renwick subdivision); Nattai till 1875; settled by George Cutter, laid out 1884 by Mittagong Land Co. Ltd (encompassing New Sheffield), first lots sold 1884, munic. proc. 1889, thrived 1890, 1910, 1921, 1926, bypassed by highway 1992; orig. coal and iron ore (disc. 1833 by William Jaques), later popular health resort, then grazing, hort., mushrooms, dairying, poultry, manufacturing; Angl. C. 1871, new one (St Stephen's) b. 1876–78 by Frederick Draper, d. by Edmund Thomas Blacket, additions 1892–94 d. by Arthur Blacket, extended 1928 by T.E. Farrar, d. by W.A. Nelson; Bapt. C. (Highlands); Bethesda Ministries International C. (Highlands Christ.) o. 1983 in reused building; bottled water plant (Spring Alive); brewery (Jacob and Deb Newman) 2017; brickworks: A. Bennett and Cupitt's; bushfires 1904–5, 1928, 1939 (many buildings burnt down), 1951, 2002; butter factory (Fresh Food & Ice Co.) b. 1882 by Matthew Forde, closed, acquired 1895 by Berrima Dist. Farm & Dairy Co., rabbit freezing facilities added 1912, closed 1924, operations moved to Bowral; carriage-works estab. 1866 by John McCallum, taken over by Hector McCallum and Archibald Duncan McCallum, burnt down 1897, rebuilt, bought 1908 by Alfred Lippiatt and John Roberts, partnership dissolved 1928; CH b. 1886 by John Kealman, renovated 1902 by A.E. Lees, reused 1962; Christ. Brethren Assemblies C. (Southern Highlands Community); clock tower b. 1920 by Benjamin Bourne, d. by W.B. Hudson; colliery (Mount Alexander, McDonald Bros Pty Ltd) 1956–72; cordial factories: Fraser and Connell, and John Mealing (relocated 1887, later sold to E.A. Dobson); electricity 1924; eucalyptus oil distillery (Daniel Chalker), moved to Glenquarry; farm (or industrial) school for convicted boys 1906, renamed a training school in 1947, additions 1956 and 1968, reused 1976, closed 1994; FB 1916 (station b. 1918 by S. Box, d. by William Hull McNiven); fires 1897 and 1905; flood 1893; flour mill (George Cutter); foundry (William Brazenall & Sons); Foursquare Gospel C.; gales 1890, 1891 (boy killed), 1898; gasworks 1959, sold to Aust. Gaslight Co.; hailstorms 1904 and 1907; iron smelter (Nattai Bridge) estab. 1848 by John Thomas Neale, Thomas Holmes, Thomas Tipple Smith and William Tipple Smith, became Fitz Roy Iron-mining Co. in 1851, new company estab. 1854 as Fitz Roy Iron & Coal Mining Co., closed 1856, works taken over 1857 by Henry William Johnson who erected rolling mills, taken over 1859 by Fitz Roy Ironworks Co., leased 1863 by Benjamin Wright Lattin, blast furnace d. by Enoch Hughes and Joseph Kaye Hampshire o. 1864 and partly rebuilt, works closed 1866, ironworks expanded by Ebenezer Vickery, works leased 1868 by Enoch and William Hughes and later that year by Bladen & Co., furnace modified 1869 by Thomas Levick, works closed 1869, sold 1870 to John Frazer, John Keep, Ebenezer Vickery and Simon Zollner, sold 1873 to Bessemer Steel, Hematite, Iron & Coal Co. Ltd, reopened 1874 by David Smith, smelting 1876 by David Lawson, closed 1877, rolling mill reopened 1877 by E.G. Larkin, Hunter and Henshaw, blast furnace closed and company went into liquidation 1878, site sold 1884 to Mittagong Land Co. Ltd, rolling mills reopened, remodelled and reused 1886 by William Sandford, Lambert Bros attempted to reopen ironworks in 1886, rebuilt 1906 by Daniel Flood and reopened 1910, closed 1911, dismantled and removed, site razed 1927; LDS (Mormon) C.; maltings (Malting Co. of NSW Ltd) b. 1899 by Stuart Bros, sold 1905 to Tooth & Co. Ltd which b. second malt-house 1905–7 d. by Frederick Herbert Broughton Wilton and Maurice Bernard Halligan, burnt down 1942, rebuilt 1953, and third malt-house 1916 also d. by Wilton and Halligan, fire, maltings closed 1980, bought 1981 by The Maltings Pty Ltd, fire 2016, abandoned and derelict; mine (iron ore) 1941, operated by BHP; oil-shale retorts (Gotting, replaced by Dye type) 1930 and 1941; PO 1862, new one b. 1891 by G. Gatty and Richard Flook, reused, new one b. 1964; pound (stock) 1883; Presb. C. (St Paul's) b. 1885 by James Linklater; PS 1868, new one 1885; quarry (Frederick Lemm); railway turntable 1898, 40 ft (12.2 m); reservoirs: Barkers Creek b. 1909 by A.W. Tooth, collapsed 1909, replaced 1910, new ones 1931 and 1958; Rom. Cath. C. (St Michael's) 1889, additions d. 1904 by James Nangle, additions 1914 d. by Buchanan and M'Kay, alterations 1925; RS 1867, station b. by J.B. Elphinstone, refreshment rooms 1873–91, station additions 1887, alterations 1891 by W. Richards; sawmills: Eastley Bros, Edward Selems (removed 1911), Stenner's; school (New Sheffield till 1880) 1865, additions 1888 by Charles Palmer and William Lewis, additions and repairs 1897 by W. Richards, additions 1924 by F. Walker, new building b. 1954 by J.P. Stegga, additions 1956 and 1985; sewage works 1939 d. by Harding, Frew and Joyce; shale-oil refinery (Peters Petroleum Products Ltd) 1941, burnt down 1944; shoe factory (Watkins Footwear Mittagong Pty Ltd); snowstorm 1899; streets kerosene lit 1891, electric lit 1924; telegraph 1883, new office b. 1891 by G. Gatty and Richard Flook, reused; telephone 1906; TX 1914, automatic 1971; Unit. C. (orig. Wes. Meth.) b. 1866 by R. Snowden, d. by J.K. Hampshire, additions and alterations 2005; watch-house, additions

1886 by John Kealman; waterworks b. 1909 (and pumping machinery erected) by Gilliver, Gilmore and Connell, machinery repaired and overhauled 1914 by Charles Hughes (PWD), filtration plant 1935, augmentation 1964; pop. 291 (1871), 499 (1881), 1,468 (1891), *c.*1,100 (1895), 1,210 (1901), 1,488 (1911), 1,435 (1921), 1,747 (1933), *c.*2,000 (1941), 2,094 (1947), 2,372 (1954), 2,621 (1961), 2,837 (1966), 3,865 (1976), 4,266 (1981), 4,828 (1986), 5,666 (1991), 6,088 (1996), 6,270 (2001), 5,722 (2011). (See also Lower Mittagong and Welby.)

Mittagong (*Co. Mitchell*) 35°21'S. 146°57'E., 26 km SE of Lockhart, on Mittagong Ck; wheat; Union C. 1889.

Mittagong Flat (*Co. Camden*) see Lower Mittagong.

Mitta Mitta (*Co. Clarendon*) 34°54'S. 147°51'E., 22 km E. of Junee, on Mitta Mitta Ck; farming and grazing; Angl. C. (St Stephen's) b. 1898 by Taunton Bros; butter factory (J. Beveridge) 1893; cemetery; PO 1888–1931; school 1882–1905; telephone 1925; TX 1931, automatic 1964; pop. 100 (1911), 40 (1933).

Moama (*Co. Cadell*) 36°07'S. 144°46'E., 67 km S. of Deniliquin, on Murray R.; Maiden's Punt till *c.*1857; settled 1845, surveyed 1848 by Thomas Scott Townsend, site of Moama fixed upon and lots sold 1851 (village bought by James Maiden), thrived 1853, town gaz. 1869, designated as chief town of the county, munic. 1890–1952; cattle market 1851–56, boat-building, oats, citrus fruit 1911+, now sheep, cattle, wheat, rice; Angl. C. (St James's) b. 1883 by Walter William Moore, and graveyard; Bible Christ. C. b. 1893 by A. Chanter; boiling-down works: George Gregson Claughten 1893 and Echuca Meat Preserving Co. (estab. 1868 by Henry Leonard and James Symington, sold 1869, inundated 1870); bond store (in Watt's store) 1864; bridge (Hopwood's Pontoon Bridge) 1857–73, 350 ft (106.7 m), replaced; carriage-works (F.E. Calloway), burnt down 1895; cemetery (747 graves) 1874; CH 1860, (second) 1876, (third) b. 1881–84 by Moore & Co., d. by James Johnstone Barnet, repairs 1891 by Duckett and M'Bride; clock tower (war memorial) 2007; customs-house 1864, new one 1876, new one b. 1888 by Symons & Sons; dock b. 1879 by John Dunlea; electricity 1931; engineering works (R. and K. Brown); 2 FB (one station moved 1949 by J.F. Hand & Son, one b. 1970, renovated 2008); fellmongery (Marshall's) 1863; fire 1862; floods 1851, 1852, 1867, 1870, 1905, 1916, 1917, 1956, 1974, 1975, 1993; flour mill (Palmer's) 1880, bought 1893 by D. Stratton & Co.; Jehovah's Witnesses C.; lock-up 1860, new one b. 1888 by Cawsey Bros; marina; Meth. C.; mouse plague 1917; PO (Port Phillip) 1848, transferred from Victoria 1855, burnt down 1861, new one b. 1876, (third) b. 1883 by M'Bride and Robertson, d. by James Johnstone Barnet; pound (stock) 1861; PS b. 1878 by M'Bride and Robertson; punts: Henry Hopwood 1853, James Maiden (removed from Perricoota, replacement b. 1857 by Henry Leonard), Watts' 1864; quarantine station; railway (from Deniliquin) 1876; railway and road bridge (plate girder) b. 1875–79 by Halliday, Walker & Co., d. by William Henry Greene, 1,452 ft (442.6 m), railway use ceased in 1989, new railway bridge 1989, over Murray R.; reservoir (concrete tower), 33,000 gal. (150 kl); Rom. Cath. C. (St Aloysius's) b. 1999 by S.D. & E.M. Bourke Pty Ltd, d. by Barry Adams & Associates; RS (Victorian railway), closed, station demolished; sale-yards (John McNamara & Co. Pty Ltd) 1932; sawmill 1856; school 1866, new one b. 1877, additions and renovations 1890 by W.W. Moore, additions, alterations and renovations 1951, additions 1958 and 1967; sewerage 1968, augmentation 1996; shipyard and slipway (Air and Westergard), slipway enlarged 1877; telegraph 1864, new office b. 1883 by M'Bride and Robertson, d. by James Johnstone Barnet; telephone 1905; waterworks 1894, reticulation 1957, augmentation 1969 and 1985; wharf b. 1879 by James Dunlea, new ones 1893 and 1995; wineries: Chanter Estate 1996, Morrisons

Riverview, St Anne's Vineyards 1994; wool stores; pop. 30 (1851), 144 (1861), *c.*200 (1866), 281 (1871), *c.*300 (1876), 1,204 (1881), 716 (1891), 850 (1895), 928 (1901), 778 (1911), 779 (1933), 662 (1947), 836 (1954), 885 (1961), 967 (1966), 1,126 (1971), 1,202 (1976), 1,507 (1981), 1,924 (1986), 2,263 (1991), 2,469 (1996), 2,823 (2001), 3,331 (2006), 5,559 (2011).

Moatefield (*Co. Harden*) see Frampton.

Mobellah (*Co. Phillip*) see Home Rule.

Mobinbry (*Co. Stapylton*) 28°49'S. 150°24'E., 23 km S. of Boggabilla; pop. 54 (1911), 37 (1933).

Modanville (*Co. Rous*) 28°44'S. 153°18'E., 10 km N. of Lismore; school 1928, additions 2011; telephone 1922; TX 1925, automatic 1958; pop. 82 (1933), 83 (1954), 117 (1961), 307 (1996), 467 (2001), 515 (2006), 566 (2011).

Modanville (*Co. Rous*) see also Tullera.

Mogareeka (*Co. Auckland*) 36°42'S. 149°59'E., 4 km N. of Tathra, on Bega R.; bridge (Handcock Bridge) 1959, damaged 1971; floods 1928 and 1971; punt till 1959; sawmill (McMillan and Innes) 1908; pop. 82 (1991).

Mogendoura (*Co. St Vincent*) 35°52'S. 150°03'E., 5 km NW of Moruya, on Mogendoura Ck; bushfires 1883 and 1919; cheese factory 1906–36; sawmills: Graham's, Lynch Bros (burnt down 1904), Mitchell's 1920; telephone 1927; TX 1950–63; pop. 55 (1911), 56 (1933), 234 (2011).

Moggs Swamp (*Co. Gresham*) 29°58'S. 152°01'E., 37 km SE of Glen Innes, on Moggs Swamp; school 1957–69; telephone 1923; TX 1928–65; pop. 60 (1933), 53 (1954).

Mogila (*Co. Narran*) 29°03'S. 147°31'E., 115 km NW of Collarenebri; pop. 53 (1933).

Mogilla (*Co. Auckland*) 36°42'S. 149°35'E., 23 km W. of Bega, on Sandy Ck; dairying and farming; Angl. C. (St Mark's) 1891, demolished 1915; butter factory (NSW Creamery Butter Co. Ltd) 1896–1903; PO 1879–1961; school 1877 b. by N.W. Isley, burnt down 1915, reopened 1957–59; telephone 1913; TX 1924; pop. 229 (1901), 156 (1911), 90 (1933), 80 (1947), 87 (1954), 83 (1961).

Mogil Mogil (*Co. Finch*) 29°21'S. 148°41'E., 23 km NE of Collarenebri, on Barwon R.; surveyed and town gaz. 1869 as Mogil Mogul; grazing; CH 1881; lock-up; PO 1871; pound (stock) 1865; PS 1876, additions and repairs 1909 by B.B. Kinnear, closed 1923; telegraph 1881; TX 1919; pop. 37 (1891), 65 (1911), 58 (1954).

Mogil Mogul (*Co. Finch*) see Mogil Mogil.

Mogo (*Co. Phillip*) 32°16'S. 150°01'E., 35 km W. of Merriwa.

Mogo (*Co. St Vincent*) 35°47'S. 150°09'E., 9 km S. of Batemans Bay, on Mogo Ck; estab. 1859, town gaz. 1873; mining (gold disc. 1857) mainly 1857–1913, sawmilling, dairying, agric., now tourist craft village; Angl. C. (St Mark's) 1889, restored 1915; bushfire 1953; cemetery (200 graves 1858+); cheese factory (Mogo Co-op. Dairy Society) 1933; Chinese joss house; FB 1968 (new station b. 2012); flood 1974–75; mines: Mogo Alluvial Gold Mining Co. 1891, Ryan's Hill Mine 1877–1940, Shamrock Gold Mine 1904–9 and 1935; PO 1869; Rom. Cath. C. 1875, new one (St Mary's) 1906, closed, sold 1980 and reused; sawmills: Barling Bros 1908, Guy Sawmilling Co. Ltd (estab. 1868 by Francis Guy, sold to John Perry), Lynch's, Mitchell & Sons; school 1877, new buildings b. 1910 by E. Gould, additions and alterations 1912 by A. Allen; sewerage augmentation 1996; telephone 1885; TX 1937–68; Union C.; Wes. Meth. C. 1872, new one 1888; pop. 242 (1891), 240 (1901), 235 (1911), 207 (1933), 175 (1947), 168 (1954), 192 (1961), 230 (1996), 223 (2001), 257 (2006), 263 (2011).

Mogo Creek (*Co. Northumberland*) 33°10'S. 151°04'E., 39 km W. of Wyee, on Mogo Ck; Meth. C. 1904; quarry; pop. 22 (1933).

Mogong (*Co. Ashburnham*) 33°29'S. 148°37'E., 12 km N. of Canowindra, on Mogong Ck; settled *c.* 1846 by Clements; agric.; school 1910–19.

Mogong Creek (*Co. Ashburnham*) 33°31'S. 148°38'E., 6 km NW of Canowindra, on Mogong Ck; school 1957–59.

Mogongong (*Co. Monteagle*) 33°56'S. 148°16'E.,

11 km E. of Grenfell, on Brundah Ck; gold; mine (Surprise) *c.*1900 and 1936; RS 1901, station b. by F.W. Kinch, closed 1974.

Mograni Creek (*Co. Gloucester*) 32°02'S. 152°02'E., 8 km E. of Gloucester, on Mograni Ck; winery (Tugwood) 1999; pop. 36 (1933).

Mogriguy (*Co. Lincoln*) 32°04'S. 148°40'E., 22 km N. of Dubbo, on Mogriguy Ck; village gaz. 1913; wheat and oats; Angl. C., removed 1924 from Brocklehurst and renovated, new one (St John's) 1963; drought 1918–20; mine (ochre); PO 1909; RS (Goonoo till 1908) 1903, station b. by W.H. Hudson, closed 1974; school (Goonoo Railway Station till 1908, then Bickan till 1909) 1907, additions 1911 by W.J. Brown, closed 1984; telephone 1911; TX 1934, automatic 1968; pop. 209 (1911), 183 (1933), 111 (1947), 59 (1954), 153 (1961), 416 (2006).

Mogul (*Co. Finch*) 29°22'S. 148°42'E., 22 km NE of Collarenebri, on Barwon R.

Mohonga (*Co. Hume*) see Mahonga.

Mohonga South (*Co. Hume*) see Mahonga South.

Moira (*Co. Cadell*) 35°56'S. 144°51'E., 15 km S. of Mathoura; village gaz. 1887; farming; PO 1879; RS (Victorian railway), closed; school 1880–91; telephone 1916; TX 1933–70; pop. 90 (1891), 61 (1911), 74 (1933), 51 (1954), 50 (1961).

Molarban (*Co. Phillip*) see Moolarben.

Mole Creek Tank (*Co. Fitzroy*) 30°11'S. 152°54'E., 24 km NW of Coffs Harbour, on Mole Ck.

Mole River (*Co. Clive*) see The Mole.

Moleton (*Co. Fitzroy*) 30°10'S. 152°54'E., 27 km NW of Coffs Harbour, on Mole Ck; goldmining and farming; bushfire 1928; mine (Bayfield Mine, renamed George's Goldmine), reused; PO 1927; RS (6 km N.) 1924–72; sawmill (Enterprise Sawmills, Joseph Reid Pty Ltd) 1926, burnt down 1953; school 1932–55; telephone 1925; TX 1928; water supply installed 1927 by Joseph Reid Pty Ltd; pop. 138 (1933), 164 (1947).

Mollee Crossing (*Co. White*) 30°15'S. 149°41'E., 13 km NW of Narrabri, on Namoi R.; school (Molley) 1884–87.

Molley (*Co. White*) see Mollee Crossing.

Mollymoke (*Co. St Vincent*) see Mollymook.

Mollymook (*Co. St Vincent*) 35°20'S. 150°28'E., 3 km N. of Ulladulla, on Tasman Sea; (incl. Mollymook Beach and Narrawallee, formerly East Milton); Mollymoke till 1931; settled 1859 by Uriah Coller and Henry Mitchell; silica mining *c.*1925+, tourism 1945+; Bapt. C. (Milton-Ulladulla) 1988; bridge 1958, over Blackwater Ck; cemetery (Sandridge), laid out 1863, dedicated 1869, rededicated 1893; PO 1961–77; 2 quarries; reservoir; Salv. Army C. b. 1900 by W. Garrad; 2 sawmills (incl. Frank Higgins); sea wall; TX; wharf 1921–61; pop. 55 (1954), 142 (1961), 550 (1971), 1,373 (1976), 4,526 (2011).

Mollymook Beach (*Co. St Vincent*) see Mollymook.

Molly Morgan's Plains (*Co. Northumberland*) see Maitland.

Molong (*Co. Ashburnham*) 33°06'S. 148°52'E., 31 km NW of Orange, on Molong Ck; formerly also known as Bell River City; disc. by Major Sir Thomas Livingstone Mitchell, village gaz. 1849, laid out 1850 by Nicholson, first land sales 1854, munic. proc. 1878, munic. reduced in size 1921, town thrived 1886–93 and 1927, munic. abolished 1951; gold, copper (disc. 1824, mined *c.*1845+), wheat, maize, oats, barley, potatoes, fruit, vineyards, beef, sheep; agric. implement works (Davimac Manufacturing) 1982; ambulance station 1989; Angl. C. b. 1860 by James Prior Hull, closed 1906, reused, new one (St John's) b. 1906 by J.W. Chalmers, d. by William Lamrock, jun., and graveyard; Assemblies of God C. (Community); Bapt. C. (former school) 1879, new ones 1947 and 2006; brewery (Swan Brewery, estab. by Hirons, Clifton and Hughes) 1892–98, demolished 1921; bridges: one b. 1905 over Molong Ck and one b. 1984 over Bell R.; butter factory (Molong Dist. Dairying Co.) b. 1901 by William J. Harding, additions 1913 by William Gadd, d. by Richard Wildridge & Co., closed 1919, reused; carton factory

(Centa-Pak Enterprises) 2000, new factory 2013; cemetery (1,947 graves) 1863, extension 1920, incl. lawn cemetery and columbarium; CH 1847, new one (incl. lock-up) b. 1862 by Arundel Everett and William Stephens, d. by James Johnstone Barnet, major additions 1883 by J.B. Fitzgerald, also d. by Barnet, additions and repairs 1911 by A.A. Folkhard, reused; Christ. Army C. 1888; cordial factories: W.C. Bennett 1878, McGroder's, sold 1921, G.L. Turley, William Joseph Windred, sold 1883; dam 1927; drought 1866; dust storm 1913; earth tremor 1934; electricity 1930; engineering works (Neatfit Products) 1948; FB 1910 (station b. 1934 by Harry Midgley, reused, replaced); fires 1888 and 1927; floods 1862, 1870, 1928, 1956, 2005; flour mills: Britannia (b. 1878 by John Black, extended 1888 for conversion to rollers, new one 1901, taken over 1911 by Hector and Rod Black, upgraded 1933 by Van Gelder, bought by Sydney Milling Co., fire 1945, sold 1950 to White Rose Flour Mills Pty Ltd), James Hamilton (burnt down 1936, replaced 1937 by J.M. Groat), Haslem's 1862 (acquired 1868 by Charles Blakefield from Walter Samson & Co., acquired 1875 by John and Henry Langdon, acquired 1876 by James Haslam, closed and reused); gale 1907; gasworks b. 1893 by Henley and Wise, new retorts 1947; German measles epidemic (2 children died) 1893; hailstorms 1896 and 1967; hospital (Queen's) 1888 d. by John Hale, additions 1898 by James Stuart Douglas, d. by William Lamrock, jun., additions 1902 and 1905 also d. by Lamrock, fire 1907, additions 1912 by William Henry Lewis, also d. by Lamrock, renovated 1925 by R. Prideaux, additions 1939 by Peter Beddie and J.W. Brown; ice works (John Grace) 1947; lime-kilns (T.E.A. Cupitt), taken over 1918 by T.F. Walker; metal fabrication works (John Wythes Bros & Co.) 1946; military stockade; mine (Vale Head Phosphate Mine); pneumonia epidemic (2 died) 1901; PO 1845, new one b. 1880 by Gadd, Neville and James, enlarged 1890, new one b. 1901 by J.W. Hull; pottery (Dowling); pound (stock) 1865; powerhouse b. 1930 by Charles W. Evans, closed; Presb. C. (St Andrew's) b. 1888 by Mitchell, closed, sold 2000, reused; PS b. 1876–78 by Robert Barlow, Flynn and Melville, d. by James Johnstone Barnet, additions 1884 by J. Mitchell, additions and repairs 1907 by William Gadd, renovated 1914 by M. Mullins, new one b. 1934 by Peter Beddie and J.W. Brown, additions and repairs 1963; 3 quarries; rabbit freezing works (in former butter factory) 1919, burnt down; railway bridge over Molong Ck; railway turntable, 50 ft (15.2 m), replaced 1901, 60 ft (18.3 m); reservoir, 338,250 gal. (1,537.7 kl); rifle range 1909; Rom. Cath. C. b. 1874–77 by James Prior Hull, d. by John Hale, reused, new one (Sacred Heart and St Laurence O'Toole's) b. 1916–18 by G.R. Wright, d. by Albert Edmund Bates; RS 1885, station b. by Alexander Hamilton Scouller, refreshment rooms 1916–56, station closed 1989, reused; sale-yards (S.D. Bennett & Co.) 1900, new yards b. 1920 by Bert Goodwin, new yards 1966 d. by C.D. Williamson; Salv. Army C. (in rented premises) 1889, new one b. 1905 by J.W. Hull and R. Jaye; sawmill (A.E. Anlezark); scarlet fever 1908; school 1859, reused, new one b. 1880 by Gadd, Neville and James, additions 1909 by Steel Bros, reused, new buildings 1948 on new site, additions 1958, 1962, 1969, 1975, major upgrade 1994; shed factories: Colorpanel Industries Co., Tilmac 2011, Tri-Steel; silo 1920; snowstorms 1888 and 1896; stamper battery (3 head) estab. 1897 by John Black; storms 1860, 1878, 1902, 1932; straw insulation factory (Solomit SA Ltd) 1945, in old flour mill; streets kerosene lit 1884, gas lit 1893, electric lit 1930; telegraph 1876; TX 1909, automatic 1980; typhoid 1902–3 (man died), 1904, 1909; Unit. C. (orig. Meth.) 1957; water supply 1928, filtration plant 1963, augmentation 1986; Wes. Meth. C. 1858, porch added by Gadd, church re-roofed by James Prior Hull, transcept and vestry added 1904, church renovated 1933 by C. Griffen, Moses Brooks and J.H. Caldwell; pop. 32 (1851), 263 (1861), 277 (1866), 360

(1871), 755 (1881), *c*.800 (1887), 1,112 (1891), *c*.1,275 (1895), 1,254 (1901), 1,448 (1911), *c*.1,500 (1927), 1,531 (1933), 1,662 (1947), 1,791 (1954), 1,655 (1961), 1,430 (1966), 1,357 (1971), 1,504 (1976), 1,374 (1981), 1,400 (1986), 1,563 (1991), 1,604 (1996), 1,563 (2001), 1,569 (2006), 1,629 (2011).

Molonglo (*Co. Murray*) 35°27'S. 149°23'E., 17 km SE of Queanbeyan, on Primrose Valley Ck; farming and grazing; Angl. C. (St Thomas's) b. 1865–74, d. by Alberto Dias Soares; PO 1860–1916; PS 1922; Rom. Cath. C. 1904; pop. 66 (1911).

Molonglo (*Co. Murray*) see also Burbong.

Molroy (*Co. Murchison*) 29°48'S. 150°36'E., 7 km N. of Bingara, on Myall Ck; school 1903–12.

Momba (*Co. Killara*) 30°59'S. 143°29'E., 65 km N. of Wilcannia.

Momolong (*Co. Urana*) 35°36'S. 146°00'E., 17 km NE of Berrigan; pop. 63 (1933).

Monak (*Co. Wentworth*) 34°17'S. 142°16'E., 12 km S. of Gol Gol, on Murray R.; estab. 1937; grapes and oranges; fruit packing house; TX (automatic); pop. 135 (1954), 142 (1961).

Monaltrie (*Co. Rous*) 28°51'S. 153°17'E., 5 km S. of Lismore; FB; sewage works (Lismore); pop. 25 (1933), 207 (2011).

Monaro (*Co. Beresford*) see Cooma.

Monaro Vale (*Co. Denison*) 35°44'S. 145°50'E., 9 km S. of Berrigan; TX (automatic).

Mondrook (*Co. Gloucester*) 31°55'S. 152°24'E., 5 km W. of Taree; formerly also known as Monrook; flood 1929; school 1882–1970; pop. 15 (1841), 58 (1911), 67 (1933), 87 (1947), 94 (1954), 115 (1961), 194 (2006).

Monga (*Co. St Vincent*) 35°35'S. 149°55'E., 18 km SE of Braidwood, on Mongarlowe R.; sawmilling and eucalyptus oil; bushfire 1940; eucalyptus oil distillery (Charles Coleman) 1906; PO 1951–71; sawmills: Jackson's (fire 1940), George and Donald McRae (water powered), defunct, Monga Sawmill Pty Ltd 1948 d. by Reginald Cornish; school 1955–71; telephone 1925; TX 1948; pop. 23 (1933), 63 (1947), 153 (1954), 85 (1961).

Monga (*Co. St Vincent*) see also Mongarlowe.

Mongarlowe (*Co. St Vincent*) 35°25'S. 149°57'E., 13 km E. of Braidwood, on Mongarlowe R.; orig. Little River, then Monga till 1891; gold (disc. 1852), then eucalyptus oil, farming, grazing, fishing; Angl. C., burnt down 1919; bridge 1894, collapsed and replaced 1930, over Mongarlowe R.; bushfires 1919 and 1929; cemetery (53 burials, incl. 21 graves) 1878; Chinese joss house, burnt down 1919; eucalyptus oil distilleries: Arthur Jonas and T. Nolan; FB; fire 1907; flood 1860; foot-bridge over Mongarlowe R.; lock-up 1866; mines: Alma or Mary Louise (Wisbey and Steele 1908–13, Dadley 1931, Franks and Harris 1932), H.R. Conroy, Day Dawn (Day Dawn Gold Mining Co.) 1884–91, and 1900–5, Dogs Head (Burnes and Buckley), Earl of Granville, Golden Streak (J. Warren), Great Britain (Norton and Mair), Homeward Bound (Norton, Mair and J. Kingsland) <1884, Nomchong & Co., Pride of Mongarlowe (C. Martin), Red, White and Blue (Norton and Mair), Scotch Lassie (T. O'Brien and Meredith), F. Stagg *c*.1931; PO 1861; Presb. C. 1853, porch added 1896, church burnt down 1919; PS, closed 1916, burnt down 1919; Rom. Cath. C. 1886, burnt down 1919, new one (St Joseph's) b. 1937 by J. McGrath and W. Kelly, d. by Devine, demolished; sawmill (Reuben Bourke); school (Little River till 1892) 1863, new one b. 1868, renovated 1879 by Michael Bowe, additions and repairs 1898 by M. Bowe, closed 1963; stamper battery erected by William Radburn, destroyed 1919; telephone 1907; TX 1927; Wes. Meth. C. 1872; pop. *c*.300 (1866), 120 (1901), 237 (1911), 116 (1933), 85 (1947), 92 (1954), 63 (1961).

Mongogarie (*Co. Richmond*) 28°57'S. 152°55'E., 16 km SW of Casino, on Middle Ck; bridge (Hildebrand's Bridge) 1907, over Middle Ck; bushfire 1926; caterpillar infestation 1936; kilns; school 1923–42; telephone 1926; TX 1926–70; pop. 125 (1911), 120 (1933), 78 (1947).

Monia Gap (*Co. Nicholson*) 33°36'S. 145°58'E., 42 km E. of Hillston; village gaz. 1927; cemetery 1928; drought 1967–68; school

1958, additions 1965, closed 1971; pop. 72 (1933).

Monica Vale (*Co. Monteagle*) see Koorawatha.

Monkerai (*Co. Gloucester*) 32°16'S. 151°51'E., 18 km NE of Dungog, on Karuah R.; goldmining (reef) 1894–1916 and 1925–29, farming, dairying; bridge (queen post timber truss) b. 1882 by Matthew Murphy, 323 ft (98.5 m), new one 1931, over Karuah R.; cemetery, defunct; PO 1864–1967; sawmills: Croll & Sons, Edward Stewart, W.D. Woods Ltd, burnt down 1926; school 1861–1974; telephone 1906; TX 1924, automatic 1968; Union C. 1887; pop. *c.*150 (1866), 170 (1901), 162 (1911), 105 (1933), 125 (1947), 109 (1954), 77 (1961).

Monkey Jacket (*Co. Gloucester*) 32°38'S. 150°10'E., 3 km N. of Tea Gardens, on Myall R.; reservoir; quarry.

Monkittee (*Co. St Vincent*) 35°27'S. 149°50'E., 4 km SE of Braidwood; school 1866–85; pop. 35 (1933).

Monks (*Co. Gowen*) 31°41'S. 149°04'E., 32 km SW of Binnaway; farming and grazing; PO 1927–31.

Monolon (*Co. Fitzgerald*) 30°14'S. 143°13'E., 150 km N. of Wilcannia.

Monomie (*Co. Cunningham*) 33°07'S. 147°41'E., 22 km S. of Trundle; bushfire 1926; RS 1902–73; sawmill (A.C. Hood); pop. 25 (1933).

Monrook (*Co. Gloucester*) see Mondrook.

Montavella (*Co. Bathurst*) 33°28'S. 149°37'E., 6 km SE of Bathurst, on Macquarie R.; soldiers' settlement 1916, abandoned 1927; orchards; hailstorms 1919 and 1923.

Monteagle (*Co. Monteagle*) 34°12'S. 148°21'E., 14 km N. of Young; farming and orchards; village gaz. 1878 as Bulla, also known as Bulla Creek, laid out by H.C. Hosie, gaz. 1916 as Monteagle; Angl. C. 1872–98, moved 1898 to Woodonga and reused, new one (St Mark's) b. 1898 by Coutts, tower and spire added 1909, church renovated 1927, closed, sold 2007 and reused; cemetery (159 graves 1904+) 1878; creamery (Young Butter & Dairy Products Co-op. Factory Co. Ltd) 1894; cyclone 1909; FB; PO 1881; Rom. Cath. C. (Sacred Heart) 1904, destroyed and replaced 1909, new one (St James's) 1940; RS (4 km SE) 1886, station b. by William Sharp, closed 1975; school (Bulla Creek till 1883) 1882, new school b. 1908 by Hugh Robert Blackett, new building b. 1910 also by Blackett; storm 1900; telephone 1908; TX 1911, automatic 1950; Wes. Meth. C. b. 1880 by J.S. Bell, d. by J.H. Bryant; pop. 214 (1891), 223 (1901), 391 (1911), 327 (1921), 344 (1933), 240 (1947), 240 (1954), 120 (1961), 184 (2006), 415 (2011).

Montecollum (*Co. Rous*) 28°35'S. 153°28'E., 5 km SW of Mullumbimby, on Beatties Ck; bridge (Donaghy's Bridge) over Wilsons R.; FB 1951; school 1915–21; pop. 68 (1911), 50 (1947), 73 (1954), 52 (1961).

Montefiores (*Co. Bligh*) 32°32'S. 148°56'E., 2 km N. of Wellington, on Macquarie R.; orig. Strathfieldsaye; private village founded 1841 by Joseph Barrow Montefiore, laid out 1841 by Edward James Howse Knapp, sen., first lots sold 1841, declined 1854+, largely abandoned by 1858; farming and grazing; Angl. C. (Holy Trinity); bridges (to Wellington) over Macquarie R.: Duke of Wellington Bridge and Macquarie Bridge (b. 1871 by Joseph Sorrie, removed 1920, new one b. 1920 by State Monier Pipe Co., collapsed 1989, new one 1991); dust storm 1938; earth tremor 1928; floods 1867 and 1870; lock-up 1843; PO 1861; pound (stock) 1849; PS; punt to Wellington 1866, across Macquarie R.; telephone 1923; typhoid (2 children died) 1900; pop. 129 (1846), 182 (1851), 159 (1861), 115 (1871), 241 (1901), 206 (1911), 261 (1933), 305 (1947), 262 (1954), 330 (1961), 471 (2011).

Montreal (*Co. Dampier*) 36°23'S. 150°04'E., 6 km N. of Bermagui, on Wallaga Lake; gold (disc. 1880 by Henry Williams, gold rush 1880); PO 1880; PS, moved 1883 to Eurobodalla; 3 quarries; school 1882–83.

Mooball (*Co. Rous*) 28°27'S. 153°29'E., 10 km SW of Pottsville, on Burringbar Ck; dairying, bananas, sugar-cane; cemetery; floods 1931 and 1945; PO 1927; RS 1895, station b. by Frederick Lemm, closed 1974; sawmills: H. Bashforth 1920, burnt down 1921, Enterprise

(Charles Sumner Snow), damaged 1914, burnt down, R.C. Ewing & Co., Percy Henry Watterson and Eric Clarence Hall, burnt down 1948; school 1913–73; telephone 1927; TX 1928, automatic 1954; pop. 197 (1911), 269 (1933), 323 (1947), 319 (1954), 396 (1961).

Mooball (*Co. Rous*) see also Crabbes Creek.

Moobi (*Co. Brisbane*) 32°04'S. 150°48'E., 7 km W. of Scone; pop. 127 (1901), 137 (1911), 98 (1947), 93 (1954), 56 (1961), 188 (2006), 256 (2011).

Mooculta Siding (*Co. Cowper*) see Boorindal.

Moogem Camp (*Co. Clive*) 29°21'S. 152°15'E., 40 km SE of Tenterfield, on Timbarra R.

Mookerawa (*Co. Wellington*) 32°47'S. 149°10'E., 32 km SE of Wellington; village now submerged under Lake Burrendong; pop. 106 (1911), 72 (1933).

Mookerawa Park (*Co. Wellington*) 32°47'S. 149°07'E., 33 km SE of Wellington; telephone 1955; TX 1955.

Mooki Springs (*Co. Buckland*) 31°30'S. 150°26'E., 22 km W. of Quirindi, on Mooki R.

Moolah (*Co. Mossgiel*) 32°39'S. 145°00'E., 105 km NW of Hillston.

Moolarben (*Co. Phillip*) 32°20'S. 149°47'E., 24 km E. of Gulgong, on Moolarban Ck; airfield; Rom. Cath. C. (St Philomena's) b. 1911 by Allen Bros, moved 1959 to Ulan; school (Molarban) 1882–85; pop. 111 (1911), 42 (1933), 188 (2006).

Moolpa (*Co. Wakool*) 34°52'S. 143°48'E., 33 km SE of Balranald; RS (Victorian railway), closed.

Moomaga (*Co. Auckland*) see Wonboyn Lake.

Moombooldool (*Co. Cooper*) 34°18'S. 146°41'E., 22 km W. of Ardlethan; wheat; PO 1914; Presb. C., removed from Bimbi and reopened 1951; RS (Erin till 1912) 1908, station b. by Frank Vernon, new station 1913, closed 1975, demolished 1982; school 1919–72; silo 1923; telephone 1912; TX 1924; water supply 1941; pop. 54 (1911), 179 (1933), 67 (1947), 119 (1954), 165 (1961).

Moonahcullah (*Co. Townsend*) 35°24'S. 144°39'E., 33 km NW of Deniliquin, on Edward R.; cemetery; typhoid 1932; pop. 85 (1947), 82 (1954), 71 (1961).

Moonan Brook (*Co. Durham*) 31°57'S. 151°17'E., 40 km E. of Scone, on Moonan Brook; estab. in 1880s; mining, agric., grazing; bridge over Moonan Brook; cemetery (100 graves 1875+) 1874; PO 1862; school 1879–1970; stamper battery (water powered); telephone 1891; TX 1923–64; Union C. 1912; pop.151 (1901), 106 (1933), 79 (1947), 78 (1954), 73 (1961).

Moonan Flat (*Co. Durham*) 31°55'S. 151°14'E., 37 km E. of Scone, on Hunter R.; town gaz. 1871 as Macqueen; grazing and dairying; bridge b. 1958 by Central Constructions, 105 ft (32 m), destroyed 1984, replacement (Rex Collison Bridge) b. 1986 by Brick Civil Construction, over Hunter R.; FB; flood 1984; foot-bridge (suspension), over Hunter R.; PO 1896; PS; Rom. Cath. C. (Immaculate Heart of Mary) o. 1947 in former court-house (removed from Stewarts Brook); school 1881, new one b. 1883 by James A. Finch, closed 2007, sold 2010; telephone 1900; TX 1913, automatic 1964; Union C. b. 1889 by Richard Whitsitt, vestry and porch added 1905, church extended 1921, and graveyard; Unit. C.; pop. 85 (1911), 163 (1933), 159 (1947), 245 (1954), 172 (1961), 185 (2006), 274 (2011).

Moona Plains (*Co. Vernon*) 31°01'S. 151°55'E., 27 km E. of Walcha; TX (automatic) 1970; pop. 20 (1933).

Moonaran (*Co. Darling*) 30°48'S. 150°45'E., 6 km S. of Manilla, on Greenhatch Ck; RS (Somerton Road till 1927) 1899, station b. by John Allibone, closed 1964.

Moonbah (*Co. Wallace*) 36°30'S. 148°33'E., 11 km SW of Jindabyne, on Grosses Plain Ck; sheep; airfield; bushfire 2003; cemetery; creamery (NSW Creamery Butter Co. Ltd) 1895; PO 1891; quarry (abandoned); Rom. Cath. C. (St Thomas's) 1890, enlarged 1901, and graveyard (425 graves 1862+); school 1895–1971; telephone 1907; TX 1917–24; pop. 221 (1901), 108 (1911), 105 (1933), 144 (1947), 162 (1954), 110 (1961), 736 (2006), 935 (2011).

Moonbi (*Co. Gipps*) 33°16'S. 147°19'E., 25 km

SE of Condobolin, on Bogandillon Ck; pop. 38 (1933).

Moonbi (*Co. Inglis*) 31°01'S. 151°04'E., 15 km NE of Tamworth, on Moonbi Ck; town gaz. 1879; molybdenite, grazing, farming, poultry 1918+; Angl. C. (St Peter's) 1898 d. by A.A. Dickson; bridges: one b. 1900, new one 1963, over Moonbi Ck and Mick Maher's Bridge over Gaol Ck; bushfire 2002; cemetery (544 burials 1872+) 1869, incl. lawn cemetery 2012; FB (station reused); hailstorm 1914; mine (Betts); PO 1859; Presb. C. (Scots, orig. Union) b. 1936 by R. Hunt and J. Streeting; PS b. 1898 by J. Lonsdale; reservoir; Rom. Cath. C. (St Gerard Majella) 1936, closed, and graveyard; school (Old Moonbi 1907–14) 1882, new one b. 1914 by Thomas John Bowen, additions 2010; steel sling and rubber belt factory (Andromeda Industries Pty Ltd) estab. by Raymond J. McLaren; telegraph 1880–82; telephone 1914; TX, closed 1967; water supply filtration and reticulation 1963, augmentation 1987 and 1997; pop. 35 (1866), 261 (1891), 163 (1901), 503 (1911), 232 (1933), 285 (1947), 290 (1954), 435 (1961), 273 (1986), 266 (1991), 326 (1996), 330 (2001), 324 (2011).

Moonbi (*Co. Inglis*) see also Kootingal.

Moonbi Railway Station (*Co. Inglis*) see Kootingal.

Moonbria (*Co. Townsend*) 35°07'S. 145°28'E., 65 km NE of Deniliquin; pop. 30 (1933).

Mooneba (*Co. Dudley*) 31°03'S. 152°42'E., 14 km W. of Kempsey, on Macleay R.; telephone 1927; TX 1955, automatic 1974; pop. 68 (1933), 52 (1947), 264 (2011).

Moonee (*Co. Fitzroy*) 29°59'S. 153°00'E., 12 km NW of Coffs Harbour; hailstorm 1954; sawmill; pop. 62 (1901), 66 (1911), 166 (1933), 241 (1954), 269 (1961), 122 (1947).

Moonee (*Co. Northumberland*) see Frazer Park.

Moonee Beach (*Co. Fitzroy*) 30°13'S. 153°09'E., 12 km S. of Woolgoolga, on Moonee Ck; mineral sand mining and bananas; FB; PO 1958; reservoir; telephone 1932; TX 1932–70; water reticulation 1980; pop. 358 (1986), 470 (1991), 505 (1996), 534 (2001), 439 (2006), 556 (2011).

Mooney Mooney (*Co. Harden*) see Wambidgee.

Mooney Mooney (*Co. Northumberland*) 33°31'S. 151°12'E., 12 km SW of Woy Woy, on Mooney Mooney Ck; (incl. Cheero Point subdivided 1918, Mooney Mooney Creek, Peat Island formerly Rabbit Island till 1934); subdivided 1911; farming; ambulance station; asylum for habitual female drunkards (Peat Island) b. 1902–4, closed 1907, reopened 1911 as hospital for insane men and boys, renamed a mental hospital, renamed a hospital in 1973, women admitted in 1976, renamed Peat Island Centre in 1989, closed 2010, abandoned; bridges: Mooney Mooney Creek Bridge (Warren steel truss) 1930, new one b. 1986 by Enpro Constructions, d. by Bruce Judd, 1,575 ft (480 m), and Peats Ferry Bridge, 2,006 ft or 611.7 m (incl. 2 welded steel K-trusses fabricated by Clyde Engineering Co. Ltd), erected 1939–45 by Balgue Constructions Pty Ltd, new steel girder one beside it, 2,014 ft (614 m), b. 1965–73, over Hawkesbury R.; Community C.; FB; ferry (George Peat) 1844, 2 new govt ones 1930, across Hawkesbury R.; PO 1926; PS, closed 1927; reservoirs: 10,000 gal. (45.5 kl) 1968 and 200,000 gal. (909.2 kl) 1973; school 1941, additions 1963, closed 2006; telephone 1924; toll-gate 1965–88; TX 1925, automatic 1959; water reticulation 1973; pop. 171 (1933), 163 (1947), 186 (1954), 312 (1961), 292 (1971), 341 (1976), 505 (1981), 506 (1986), 513 (1991), 535 (1996), 529 (2001), 488 (2006), 424 (2011).

Mooney Mooney Creek (*Co. Northumberland*) see Mooney Mooney.

Moongulla (*Co. Finch*) 29°18'S. 148°20'E., 35 km NW of Collarenebri; grazing; experiment farm; PO 1898; sawmill (J. Rolls); telephone 1897; TX 1915–60; pop. 50 (1911), 65 (1933).

Mooni Mooni (*Co. Harden*) see Wambidgee.

Moonoon (*Co. Bland*) see Alleena.

Moorabin (*Co. Young*) 31°36'S. 143°21'E., 5 km SW of Wilcannia, on Darling R.; boiling-down works (Menindee Boiling Down, Freezing & Meat Preserving Co. Ltd) 1896.

Mooral Creek (*Co. Macquarie*) 31°43'S. 152°21'E., 17 km N. of Wingham, on Mooral

Ck; grazing and dairying; FB; PO 1927; sawmill (James Andrews); school 1933–62; telephone 1925; TX 1928–72; pop. 114 (1933), 73 (1947), 63 (1954), 55 (1961), 217 (2006).

Mooral Creek (*Co. Macquarie*) see also Strathcedar.

Moorbel (*Co. Ashburnham*) 33°34'S. 148°42'E., 3 km E. of Canowindra, on Belubula R.; formerly Belmore; mining (copper 1867 and gold, rush 1868), then grapes; flour mill estab. 1879 by Kenworthy, sold to F.W. Smith, disused for years, sold 1903 to John H. Tee, renovated and reopened as the Belmore Roller Flour Mills; hurricane (destroyed town) 1902; mines: Belmore or Blue Jacket 1870–76, 1885–92, 1897, 1902–3, 1910–14, Blue Maxwell (Reynolds) 1936, Boyds, Gospel Oak 1889, 1905, 1909, 1911, Grants Reef, Hayes, McCloskys, No. 1 South, Perseverance, Red Jacket, The Never Sweat; PO 1927; quarry; reservoir 1955; Rom. Cath. C. (St Therese of Lisieux) 1923–65, sold 1969, reused; school 1920–62; telephone 1922; water reticulation 1956; winery (The Falls) 1997; pop. 103 (1901), 99 (1911), 322 (1933), 164 (1947), 199 (1954), 241 (1961), 236 (2006), 243 (2011).

Moor Creek (*Co. Inglis*) see Moore Creek.

Moore (*Co. Inglis*) 30°58'S. 150°52'E., 15 km NW of Tamworth, on Moore Ck.

Moore Creek (*Co. Inglis*) 31°00'S. 150°54'E., 10 km N. of Tamworth; Angl. C. (St Luke's) 1881; diphtheria 1896 (boy died); FB; PO 1879; school (Moor Creek) 1878–1928 and 1934–69; telephone 1949; TX 1949, automatic 1967; pop. 267 (1901), 187 (1911), 212 (1933), 217 (1947), 177 (1954), 862 (2006), 1,541 (2011).

Moorefield (*Co. Cunningham*) 32°47'S. 147°17'E., 33 km N. of Condobolin; school 1957–62.

Mooren (*Co. Napier*) 31°42'S. 149°20'E., 16 km S. of Binnaway; RS 1917, station b. by John Allibone, closed 1974; pop. 25 (1933).

Moores Flats (*Co. Camden*) 34°37'S. 150°16'E., 5 km NW of Bundanoon, on Black Bobs Ck; winery (St Maur Estate) 1998.

Mooreville (*Co. Cooper*) see Griffith.

Moorilda (*Co. Bathurst*) 33°37'S. 149°20'E., 12 km SE of Blayney; Tea Pot Swamp till 1878; agric.; Angl. C. (St Andrew's) 1875 d. by Edward Gell, closed and abandoned, sold 1998, and graveyard (31 burials 1879–1984); cemetery; flour mill estab. by David Gordon and Michael Hamer, man killed 1879, ruined, though part reused; goldmine (Craig Lea) 1899–1900; PO 1869–1920; Presb. C. (St David's) b. 1877–83 by Thomas Wardman, d. by Edward Gell, additions 1937 by James H. Newton, and graveyard; Rom. Cath. C. (St Thomas's) b. 1871–75 by John Cody, d. by Edward Gell, renamed St Brigid's, renovated 1927 by Flood, closed, sold and reused; school (Tea Pot Swamp till 1876) 1867 b. by Thomas McGraw, renovated 1883 by Andrew Graham, additions 1884 by J.E. M'Donald, d. by William Edmund Kemp, renovated 1935, closed 1943, reopened 1957–67, sold and reused; telephone 1907; pop. 157 (1901), 134 (1911), 67 (1933), 84 (1947), 64 (1954).

Moorilla (*Co. Monteagle*) 34°05'S. 148°15'E., 21 km S. of Grenfell; pop. 23 (1933).

Moorland (*Co. Macquarie*) 31°48'S. 152°39'E., 9 km N. of Harrington, on Pipeclay Ck; Holy Flat till 1889; timber 1910–20, orchards 1920–54, farming, dairying; cemetery (622 graves 1894+) 1886, incl. columbarium; Cong. C.; FB; PO 1886, burnt down 1998; RS (3 km S.) 1915–73; sawmills: C. Bignell (incl. case factory), burnt down 1946, and Solomon Staples 1926; school (Holey Flat till 1890, Moorland till 1914 then Keranba till 1915) 1883, additions 1918 by Thomas Norman Grimsley, additions 1969 and 2010; telephone 1890; TX 1917, automatic 1971; Union C., renovated 1913; Unit. C. (orig. Meth.) 1963; pop. 119 (1901), 235 (1911), 223 (1933), 417 (1947), 194 (1954), 248 (1961), 286 (2006), 566 (2011).

Moorna (*Co. Tara*) 34°07'S. 141°37'E., 27 km W. of Wentworth, on Murray R.; town gaz. 1860; airfield; bridge b. 2002–4; cemetery 1860; PO 1855–60; wharf; pop. 40 (1933).

Moorong (*Co. Wynyard*) see Wagga Wagga.

Mooroowoolen (*Co. Argyle*) see Marulan.

Mooroowoollen (*Co. Argyle*) see Marulan.

Moorwatha (*Co. Hume*) 35°56'S. 146°42'E., 8 km NE of Howlong; agric., wheat, vineyards; Angl. C. (St Mary's), ruined; cemetery (3 km SE) 1870; earth tremor 1869; electricity 1948; hailstorm 1877; PO 1869–1902; school 1866 and 1868, reopened 1880, additions 1883 by J. Yates, closed 1890, old school building sold 1891 to August Just, burnt down 1891 before removal, new school 1892, closed 1923; storms 1914 and 1923; Union C. (Reid Memorial) b. 1907 by E. Sharp, d. by A.C. Frew and S.M. Logan; pop. 99 (1891), 407 (1901), 137 (1911), 92 (1933), 83 (1947), 396 (2006).

Mootai (*Co. Northumberland*) see Congewai.

Mootwingee (*Co. Mootwingee*) 31°17'S. 142°18'E., 106 km W. of Wilcannia.

Mooyabil (*Co. Rous*) 28°33'S. 153°27'E., 5 km W. of Mullumbimby, on Mullumbimby Ck.

Mooyabil (*Co. Rous*) see also Mullumbimby Creek.

Moparrabah (*Co. Dudley*) 30°58'S. 152°32'E., 30 km W. of Kempsey; Glen Rock till 1894; quarrying (marble) and farming; Angl. C. (St Paul's) 1906, closed, moved 1918 to Comara; creamery 1899; flood 1891; PO 1927–29; telephone 1924; pop. 66 (1901), 32 (1933).

Moppin (*Co. Stapylton*) 29°12'S. 149°45'E., 30 km N. of Moree, on Wallon Ck; Wallon till 1913; grazing; PO 1897–1950; RS (1 km S.) 1913–75; telephone 1905; TX 1920, automatic 1967; pop. 32 (1933).

Moppity (*Co. Harden*) 34°22'S. 148°22'E., 9 km SE of Young; bushfires 1888 and 1905; heatwave 1905; school 1884–94; pop. 143 (1911).

Moppity Gap (*Co. Harden*) 34°22'S. 148°25'E., 12 km SE of Young; quarry.

Moppy (*Co. Gloucester*) 31°59'S. 151°38'E., 31 km W. of Gloucester, on Barrington R.; quarry; pop. 149 (2006).

Morago (*Co. Townsend*) 35°22'S. 144°42'E., 29 km NW of Deniliquin; grazing; PO 1904; telephone 1905; TX 1929, automatic 1954; pop. 90 (1911), 71 (1933), 56 (1947), 56 (1954), 74 (1961), 148 (2006).

Morangarell (*Co. Bland*) 34°09'S. 147°42'E., 37 km NE of Temora, on Bland Ck; town gaz. 1884; farming; Angl. C. (Denison) 1860; bridge (timber beam spans) b. 1958 by J.W. Bailey, over Bland Ck; cemetery (14–18 burials 1872+, incl. 4 graves) 1891; CH 1876; FB; fire 1898; PO 1858; pound (stock) 1866; Presb. C. 1903, renovations 1939; PS 1870–1929; quarry (sand); telegraph 1877; telephone 1899; TX 1917; Union C.; pop. *c.*50 (1903), 260 (1911), 103 (1933), 85 (1961).

Morangaroo (*Co. Cook*) see Marrangaroo.

Morans Crossing (*Co. Auckland*) 36°40'S. 149°39'E., 17 km W. of Bega, on Bemboka R.; dairying; bridge 1891, destroyed 1934, temporary low-level bridge 1934, new one (reinforced concrete girder) b. 1937 by W.D. McDonald, 302 ft (92.2 m), new adjacent one b. 2016 by Nelmac Pty Ltd, 308 ft (94 m), over Bemboka R.; butter factory (West End Creamery Co-op. Co. Ltd) 1898–1921, removed 1927; flood 1934; PO 1909; telephone 1910; TX 1923, automatic 1971; pop. 54 (1933).

Morden (*Co. Mootwingee*) 30°29'S. 142°25'E., 151 km NW of Wilcannia, on Yandenberry Ck.

Morebringer (*Co. Hume*) 35°53'S. 146°35'E., 12 km N. of Howlong, on Long Plain Ck; school 1875–80 and 1912–36; pop. 103 (1911).

Moredun (*Co. Hardinge*) 30°00'S. 151°32'E., 28 km NW of Guyra, on Moredun Ck; cemetery (45 graves).

Moree (*Co. Courallie*) 29°28'S. 149°51'E., 126 km W. of Inverell, on Mehi R.; settled 1852 by James and Mary Brand, surveyed 1859 by Thomas J. Oliver, laid out 1861 by Gordon, town gaz. and first land sales 1862, designated as chief town of the county, munic. proc. 1890; formerly farming, grazing, maize, potatoes, butter, cheese, bacon, fruit, then wheat, lucerne, oats, barley, sorghum, sunflowers, oilseeds, cotton 1960s+, pecan nuts 1966+, olives; abattoir 1964; aeroplane crash (4 killed) 2011; airfield 1937; ambulance station b. 1939 by Benjamin Martin Wade, inundated 1950; Angl. C. 1891, dismantled and moved 1936 to

Croppa Creek, replacement (All Saints') 1936, damaged 1948, additions (Warriors' Chapel) 1951, repairs 1998 by F.A. & C.K. Edwards Pty Ltd, d. by Robert Moore and Fred Kelley; artesian water struck 1895 by Crawford and M'Cray; Assemblies of God C. (Life House); Bapt. C.; brewery (Gwydir Brewery, Charles Collins) 1889–1907; brickworks: R.F. Child and N.E. Smith; bridges: Broadwater Bridge b. 1874–77 by T.B. Kelly, repairs 1886 by John Gray, replaced 1896 with timber beam bridge b. by Bingley, replacement (Elizabeth Bridge or Mahaffey Bridge) 1956, over Broadwater Ck, one b. 1880 by G.D. Light over Mehi R., one b. 1898–1901 by A. and L. Moscatt, replacement (Dr Geoffrey Hunter Bridge) 1960, over Mehi R., one (Dr Hollingworth Bridge) over Mehi R., one (Greg Jones Bridge) over Mehi R.; Calvary Christ. C.; carriage-works (Gwydir Coach, Buggy & Wagon Factory) estab. by Ritter and Dorrington, new factory 1906, taken over 1933 by Ritter Bros; caterpillar infestation 1939; cement works (McDonald Ready Mix Concrete & Earthmoving); cemetery 1870; CH b. 1878 by Cross, additions 1885 by S. Seinor, new one b. 1900–2 by Charles Grant, d. by Walter Liberty Vernon; Chinese joss house; Church of Christ, sold to Salv. Army; Church of God; cordial factory (Artesian) estab. 1898 by Joseph Leonard Lillyman, explosion 1909, taken over 1921 by Leslie M. Lillyman and Norman E. Lillyman; dengue fever 1926; diphtheria 1894; electricity 1911; experimental (irrigation) farm 1900–10; FB 1902 (station b. 1916 by Robert Wilson & Sons); fibrous plaster works (Fraser Bros); fires 1908, 1917, 1919, 1928; floods 1864, 1872, 1890, 1910, 1920, 1946, 1949, 1950, 1955, 2012; flour mill (F. Crago & Sons) b. 1955 by Kell & Rigby Pty Ltd, bought by B. & W. Rural Pty Ltd, reused; 2 footbridges over Mehi R.; Foursquare Gospel C. (Impact); furniture factories: Logan & Co. 1922, burnt down 1930 and W.J. Trenchard 1922; gale 1901; gastroenteritis epidemic 1943; hailstorms 1959 and 1996; hospital 1889 d. by C.J. McMaster, additions 1896 also d. by McMaster, new building 1914, additions 1917, 1942, 1946, 1947, 1959, 1961, upgraded 2016; ice works: J.A. Gall and Parker Bros; Jehovah's Witnesses C.; jetty; lock-up b. 1882 by S. Senior, additions 1894 by G.W. Brewer; Lutheran C. (Grace); measles epidemics 1894 and 1930; PO: East Moree 1912 and Moree 1853 (new one b. 1880 by T. Avey, demolished, replaced 1899, additions and alterations 1914 by A.J. Hulbert); police barracks b. 1889 by William Wilson; pound (stock); powerhouse (Moree Electric Light Co. Ltd) 1911, inundated 1946; Presb. C. b. 1885 by James Cornell, porch added 1932 by W. Sinton, d. by Hugh Henry McCourt, church renovated 1939, damaged 1948, demolished 1949, replaced (St Andrew's War Memorial) 1957; PS 1879, new one b. 1922 by Philip James Killey, replaced 1959, demolished, new one b. 2014 by Lahey Constructions Pty Ltd; quarry; railway bridge (steel truss) 1913, 120 ft (36.6 m), over Mehi R.; railway coal stage b. 1895 by William Mitchell, enlarged 1904; railway depot 1897; railway engine shed b. by William Mitchell, extended 1903; railway turntable, 60 ft (18.3 m); reservoirs: one b. 1900 by Mountney & Co., one b. 1930, one b. 1954 by A.E. Goodwin Ltd; Rom. Cath. C.: St Francis Xavier's (b. 1913 at West Moree, d. by Harold Robert Hardwick, rebuilt 1959) and St Henry's (b. 1885 at East Moree, closed and reused 1930, new one, St John and St Henry's, b. 1930 by Ryan and Hoyle, d. by Peter Joseph Gannon, closed, sold 1998, demolished 2002); RS 1897, station b. by William Mitchell, new one 1904; Salv. Army C.; sawmill (Theo O. Humphreys); schools: East Moree 1959, additions 1961, 1963, 1965, 1968, 1972, 2016, Moree 1877 (new school b. 1880 by James Cornell, additions 1884 and 1888, additions 1923 by Benjamin Martin Wade, new building 1957 on new site d. by Edward Henry Rembert, new one b. 1965, additions 1967 and 1969), Moree HS (Albert Street Campus) 1961, additions by O'Donnell & Hanlon Pty Ltd,

Moree HS (Carol Avenue Campus, Courallie HS till 2002) 1972 d. by Charles Carter, additions 1976, Wirajarai (Moree Aboriginal till 1968) 1944–71; SD Adventist C.; sewage works b. 1948–53, augmentation 1986; silo; smallpox 1914; soap-works: Hille & Co. 1878 and Arthur Thompson & Co. 1894; storm 1948; streets electric lit 1911; TC (in former council chambers), became a campus of New England Institute in 1992; telegraph 1877, new office b. 1880 by T. Avey; telephone (East Moree) 1912; TX 1904, automatic 1969; Unit. C. (orig. Meth.) b. 1938 by Hetherington and Pritchard, d. by Hugh Henry McCourt; vulcanising works: H. Hoffman, burnt down 1930 and Nell's, burnt down and man died 1928; waterworks 1901, water supply augmentation 1988; weir on Mehi R.; Wes. Meth. C. b. 1867–69 by James Greenaway, new one b. 1895 by E. Markham (dismantled and moved 1938 to Gravesend by Ephraim Tomkins and reused), and graveyard; wool-scour and store (Arthur Thompson & Co. Ltd, East Moree), burnt down 1932; wool store (Kirkby's, leased to T.H. Plante), burnt down 1911; pop. 43 (1861), 43 (1866), 57 (1868), 107 (1871), 295 (1881), 1,143 (1891), *c.*1,600 (1895), 2,298 (1901), 3,161 (1911), 4,355 (1933), *c.*5,000 (1941), 5,106 (1947), 5,502 (1954), 6,795 (1961), 8,094 (1966), 9,114 (1971), 9,359 (1976), 10,459 (1981), 10,215 (1986), 10,062 (1991), 9,270 (1996), 9,273 (2001), 8,083 (2006), 7,720 (2011), *c.*9,346 (2017).

Moreton Bay Flat (*Co. Bligh*) 32°05'S. 149°36'E., 20 km E. of Dunedoo, on Moreton Bay Ck.

Morgan (*Co. Cook*) see Kurrajong East.

Morgans Gully (*Co. Vernon*) see Dungate.

Morgan Street (*Co. Yancowinna*) see Broken Hill.

Morisset (*Co. Northumberland*) 33°07'S. 151°29'E., 6 km NW of Mannering Park, on Stockton Ck; (incl. Beauty Point); town gaz. 1887 as Morrisset, subdivided and lots sold 1888; sawmilling and vegetables; ambulance station; Angl. C. (St Laurence's) 1902, destroyed 1913, new one (All Saints') b. 1976 by R.A. Wenham Pty Ltd, d. by R. Donaldson, and graveyard; asylum (orig. for the insane, later for lunatics, became mental hospital in 1958, later became psychiatric hospital) b. 1907–9 by John Howie & Son, additions 1911 by Benjamin George Pearce, additions 1920 and 1932, maximum security wards No. 21 and No. 22 for the criminally insane b. 1933 on separate site (closed 1990, abandoned, derelict and partly demolished), female patients admitted 1934, further hospital additions 1934–36 by Richard Seed, additions 1953–54, chapel b. 1954–57, hospital additions and alterations 1960, 2 wards demolished 1991, additions 1992; Bapt. C.; box factory (Avondale Industries); bridge over Pourmalong Ck; Buddhist C.; cemetery (573 graves 1911+); CH b. 1920 by Herbert Bradley Mullard, closed 1933; chilli sauce factory estab. by Marcel, Connie and Alex de Wit; Christadelphian C. (Eden); dam; electricity 1930; FB (station b. 1962, new one 1987); gale 1913; house frame and truss factory (Newcastle Steel Frames & Trusses Pty Ltd); Jehovah's Witnesses C.; jetty; Meth. C. b. 1912 by Benjamin George Pearce; PO 1898, new one b. 1960 by Charles A. Lonergan; PS b. 1920 by Herbert Bradley Mullard, new one b. 1935 by Richard Seed, closed and demolished 2015, replaced 2016; 4 reservoirs; Rom. Cath. C. (St John Vianney) 1930, renovated 1977 by Charles A. Lonergan, and graveyard; RS 1887, station b. by G.R. and F.H. Harrison, new one 1938; sawmill, incl. spoke and tool handle factory (C. & H. Mullard Ltd), fire 1927, closed 1968; schools: Morisset 1891 (b. by Thomas Smith, additions 1913 and 1916, extended 1928 by Herman Brandstater, new building b. 1954 by W.E. and F.L. Galbraith and A. Blundell, additions 1956, new building 1961, reused as high school, new one b. 1984) and HS 1965, additions 1979, 1986, 1988, 1991, additions 2010 by R.T. Parker Pty Ltd; SD Adventist C.; sewage works; telegraph 1890; TX 1910–62; Unit. C. (orig. Meth.) b. 1965 as a hall, converted 1976 to a church, sold and reused, replaced; water supply 1941; pop. 221 (1901), 640 (1911), 1,125 (1921), 1,409 (1933), 2,008 (1947), 2,201 (1954), 969 (1961), 2,152 (1966), 1,740 (1971), 1,595 (1976), 1,593 (1981), 1,425 (1986), 1,046 (1991), 1,050 (1996), 1,041 (2001), 2,583 (2006), 2,857 (2011).

Morisset East (*Co. Northumberland*) see Bonnells Bay.

Morisset Park (*Co. Northumberland*) see Bonnells Bay.

Mornington (*Co. Roxburgh*) see Clandulla.

Moroco (*Co. Townsend*) 35°46'S. 145°09'E., 31 km SE of Deniliquin, on Bulltale Ck; pop. 60 (1901).

Moroco East Station (*Co. Townsend*) 35°47'S. 145°14'E., 35 km SE of Deniliquin; pop. 26 (1933).

Moroko (*Co. Macquarie*) see Pembrooke.

Morongla Creek (*Co. Forbes*) 33°57'S. 148°41'E., 13 km S. of Cowra, on Morongla Ck; agric.; Angl. C. 1901, new one (St Peter's) 1926; cemetery (graves 1916+) 1903; copper mine (Pope of Rome) *c.*1900–5; PO 1890, burnt down 1922; Presb. C. (St Andrew's) 1915, closed, sold 2016; Rom. Cath. C. (St Daniel's) 1904 d. by Jack M'Donald, burnt down 1970; school 1882–1948; telephone 1906; TX 1921–71; pop. 374 (1901), 239 (1933), 180 (1947), 165 (1954), 116 (1961).

Mororo (*Co. Clarence*) 29°20'S. 153°14'E., 15 km N. of Maclean; farming and sugar-cane; Meth. C. b. 1907 by Smith and Payne; PO 1909; school 1886–1939; telephone 1907; pop. 64 (1911), 78 (1933), 77 (1947), 51 (1954), 53 (1961).

Morpeth (*Co. Northumberland*) 32°44'S. 151°38'E., 7 km E. of Maitland, on Hunter R.; Green Hills (and also known as Illalaung) 1801–34; disc. 1801 by Lieut. Col. William Paterson, settled and founded 1821 by Lieut. Edward Charles Close, town laid out 1832, first lots sold 1834, later land sales 1840, 1841, 1842, munic. proc. 1865, town declined 1889+, city (incl. Maitland and East Maitland) proc. 1945, classified by National Trust; river port 1828–1946, wool, wheat, tallow, hides, barley, then maize, lucerne, rye, millet, vegetables, wine, butter, cheese, ham, bacon, now tourist craft village; agric. implement works, foundry and engineering works (Duncan Sim) 1849, later also built rolling stock, sold 1926 to James Douglas Couston, demolished 1936; Angl. C. (St James's) d. and b. 1837–40 by Lieut. Edward Charles Close, chancel and vestry b. 1864 by D. Yeates, d. by Edmund Thomas Blacket, fire damaged 1874, nave rebuilt and re-roofed 1875 by James Sherwood, d. by John Horbury Hunt, church damaged 1989, repairs 1993, and graveyard (204 graves), incl. columbarium 1972; Bapt. C. 1858; boiling-down works (F.J. King) 1844; bond stores: James Campbell, Capt. Patterson, sold 1855, James Taylor 1855, closed, sold and reused; breweries: Johnson and McClelland 1863 and Morpeth Brewery & Beer Co. (Dave Allen) 2012; bridge (timber truss) b. 1896–98 by Samuel McGill, d. by Percy Allan, 924 ft (281.6 m), over Hunter R.; butter factory (Duckenfield Park Central Creamery & Butter Factory) removed 1906 from Duckenfield, sold 1908 to Bowthorne Co-op. Butter Factory Ltd, new one b. 1918 by Montague Audet, d. by Walter Harold Pender, closed 1951, reused; cemetery (2,133 graves 1839+), incl. columbarium; CH b. 1862 by William Cains, d. by Mortimer William Lewis, jun., damaged 1868, repairs 1869 by James Hesp, refurbished 1870, repairs 1876 by M. Newton, additions 1880 by William Cains, d. by James Johnstone Barnet, closed and reused 1942, taken over 1968 by local council, restored 1970, damaged 1989; Church of Scotland 1854; coalmine (Close's) 1847; convict stockade 1837; cordial factory (Ma Beattie's Ginger Beer); customs-house, closed 1917; earth tremors 1841 and 1868; earthquake 1989; electricity 1924; engineering works: Argo Engineering Pty Ltd, K. and C. Harris, D. Sim & Sons (taken over by James Douglas Couston, additions 1883); fastener factory (K. and C. Harris); FB (station b. 1970, fire 1990, replaced 2000); floods 1857, 1867, 1870, 1874, 1893, 1913, 1955; flour mill (John Portus, sen.) 1837, taken over 1855 by Portus Bros, taken over by Rundle, closed, machinery sold 1874 to Blair and Oxley, mill reused, later demolished; furniture factory and joinery (Joseph George White), restored 1988 by C.A. Richards, reused; gale 1928; grasshopper infestation 1907; hailstorms 1861 and 1875; metal fabrication works (Hunter Stainless Steel) 1994, moved to Beresfield; milk bottling plant (Hunter Valley Co-op. Dairy Co. Ltd) o. 1953, in old butter factory, moved 1960 to Hexham; pipe (steel) fabrication works (Pope, Maher & Co.) 1896, closed; PO 1838, first one b. 1839, second one in court-house 1862–81, third one b. 1881 by John Frogley, repairs 1897 by J.B. Rooney, alterations 1906, closed 2010, sold 2013 and reused, new one on new site; pound (stock) 1854; Presb. C., repairs 1880, closed 1898, reopened 1902, closed 1972, and graveyard; Prim. Meth. C. b. 1855 by Thomas Hallett, closed, sold and reused; PS (incl. lock-up) b. 1879 by J. Pritchard, d. by James Johnstone Barnet, additions to lock-up 1884 by R. James, police station closed and reused, and lock-up reused as police station; punt to Hinton till 1896, across Hunter R.; railway coal stage 1877; railway engine shed 1877, demolished; Rom. Cath. C. (St Bede's) b. 1862 by Thomas Purcell, d. by William Munro, additions 1870 d. by Edward Gell, closed and reused, sold 1994 and reused, new one (Immaculate Conception) b. 1898 by J.B. and George J. Burg, d. by Pender and Silk, renovations 1971, and graveyard; RS 1864, station b. by M. Jamison and David Forrest, second one (Edward Street) b. 1870 by J. Bunker and William Cains, third one (Northumberland Street) 1876, fourth one (Robert Street) b. 1889 by Thomas Leggo, closed 1953, reused; sawmills: Thomas Adam (in former flour mill), Jaques's, R.L. Pattison; school 1862, new one b. 1866 by Peter Canavan, repairs 1884 by B. Hodgson, repairs 1892 by Burg Bros, repairs 1898 by J.W. Harradine, renovations 1912, additions 1965, extensions 1971 and 1981; sewerage 1939; soap and candle factories: Frederic Nainby 1844 and Thomas Tyrrell 1855, bought 1857 by William Heugh, inundated 1857; staithes for loading coal 1866, little used; storms 1873 and 1905; telegraph 1860, office in court-house 1862–81, new one b. 1881 by R. James, repairs 1897 by J.B. Rooney; tobacco factory (W.D. & H.O. Wills Aust. Ltd) 1946–52, in former vegetable dehydration plant; toll-gate; tramway (steam) to East Maitland 1893–1913; TX 1910–63; typhoid 1889, 1908, 1928 (woman died); Unit. C. (orig. Meth.) 1971; vegetable dehydration plant 1944–46, reused; watch-house 1857, repairs 1867 by W.H. Galbraith, closed, sold 1910 to M. Murphy and dismantled; water reticulation 1888; Wes. Meth. C. 1847, replaced 1865 on new site, damaged 1905, demolished 1970; wharves: Argo Engineering Pty Ltd 1988, Canvin's (bought from Griffin, enlarged 1855, sold to A'sian Steam Navigation Co.), Newcastle & Hunter River Steam Navigation Co., Pattison's, Pope, Maher & Co., Queen's (rebuilt 1870 by Matthew Murphy); wool stores; pop. 635 (1846), 734 (1851), 1,472 (1856), 1,175 (1861), 1,159 (1865), 1,450 (1866), 1,236 (1871), *c.*1,700 (1872), 1,372 (1881), 1,130 (1891), *c.*1,100 (1895), 1,288 (1901), 1,159 (1911), 1,045 (1933), 1,110 (1966), *c.*550 (1987), *c.*1,100 (1999), 892 (2006), 1,260 (2011).

Morpeth Junction (*Co. Northumberland*) see Maitland East.

Morrisons Hill (*Co. Harden*) 34°32'S. 148°07'E., 14 km NE of Cootamundra; RS (relocated 1915) 1908–75.

Morris Point (*Co. Georgiana*) 33°58'S. 149°15'E., 49 km S. of Blayney, on Abercrombie R.

Morrisset (*Co. Northumberland*) see Morisset.

Morton (*Co. St Vincent*) 35°24'S. 150°21'E., 12 km W. of Ulladulla, on Boyne Ck; ostrich farming 1889–1914; PO 1927–34; school 1957–73; telephone 1922; TX 1928–70; pop. 77 (1911), 59 (1933), 197 (2011).

Mortonmain (*Co. Phillip*) 32°44'S. 149°55'E., 9 km NW of Rylstone; colliery 1917, closed; RS 1917–62.

Mortons Creek (*Co. Macquarie*) 31°23'S. 152°39'E., 11 km NW of Wauchope, on Mortons Ck; telephone 1929; TX 1937–72;

pop. 218 (1911), 155 (1933), 82 (1954), 52 (1961), 382 (2006).

Mortons Creek (*Co. Macquarie*) see also Beechwood.

Mortray (*Co. Forbes*) see Pinnacle South.

Morts Estate (*Co. Cook*) see Lithgow.

Morundah (*Co. Urana*) 34°56'S. 146°18'E., 30 km SW of Narrandera, on Columbo Ck; Colombo Creek till 1889, then Murundah till 1895; subdivided 1911, thrived in 1920s and 1960s; farming and grazing; Angl. C. (St Philip's) 1912, new one (All Souls') 1939; cemetery; dam (Colombo); FB; floods 1931 and 1950; PO 1877; reservoir; Rom. Cath. C. (St Columba's) b. 1897 by P. Hughes; RS (Colombo till 1889) 1884, station b. by George Alfred Bright, closed 1975, removed 1984; school 1897, repairs 1901 by E.P. Bundock, closed 1910, reopened 1918, extended 1923, closed 1977; telegraph 1885; telephone 1912; TX 1914, automatic 1974; water reticulation 1967; pop. 60 (1901), 92 (1911), 179 (1933), 150 (1947), 117 (1954), 101 (1961), 76 (2006).

Morungulan (*Co. Wellington*) see Dripstone.

Moruya (*Co. Dampier*) 35°55'S. 150°05'E., 24 km S. of Batemans Bay, on Moruya R.; (incl. Gundary, Mynora, North Moruya); founded by Edward Kirby, surveyed 1850 by Samuel Parkinson, village laid out and gaz. 1851, first lots sold 1853, thrived 1850s–80s, town gaz. 1880, designated as chief town of the county, munic. 1891–1913, town declined 1890–1960; wattle-bark, eucalyptus oil, maize, wheat till 1900, tourism 1913+, shipping freight till 1952, dairying, barley, oats, potatoes, fruit, fish, oysters, timber; abattoir (D. and S. Afflick); ambulance station 1953, new one b. 1966 by P.J. and D.F. Tober; Angl. C. d. and b. 1858–63 by Reginald Herbert Barlow, demolished 1890, replacement (St John the Evangelist) b. 1891 by H.T. Reeves and F.W. Peplow, d. by Arthur Blacket, re-roofed 1915, restored 1915 and 1928, renovated 1990; Bapt. C. 1981; Bethesda Ministries International C. (Southern Life); brickworks (Averill's); bridge b. 1876 by Kingdom, Turner and Waddell, 17 spans, 900 ft (274.3 m), demolished, replaced 1900, destroyed and replaced 1945, demolished 1967, new one (steel and concrete) b. 1966 by Transbridge Pty Ltd, 892 ft (271.9 m), over Moruya R.; bushfires 1884, 1926, 1928, 1929, 1968; camper trailer factory (Ultimate); cemetery 1863; CH (incl. lock-up) b. 1859 by Reginald Herbert Barlow and Mooney, d. by Reginald Herbert Barlow, new one b. 1879–81 by William Duncan, d. by James Johnstone Barnet, alterations 1926; cheese factories: one b. 1886 by Roger Heffernan, modernised 1954 and 1956, Moruya Co-op. Cheese Society Ltd (b. 1892 by Ziegler Bros, new one 1930, closed, sold and reused), Charles Parbery 1933; Christ. Family C.; clock tower (Olive A. Clarke memorial) 1967; cordial factories: A. Lavis, Moruya Cordials Pty Ltd, Nelson's (bought 1912 by Johan Hansen), W. Pollock (moved 1904 to Nowra), O.S. Veitch; diphtheria (2 children died) 1897; earth tremors 1885, 1892, 1895; electricity 1924; 2 FB (incl. station b. 1974); fire 1890; floods 1860, 1863, 1867, 1873, 1891, 1897, 1898, 1899, 1900, 1906, 1911, 1922, 1925, 1934, 1942, 1943, 1944, 1945, 1974–75, 1978; flour mill (Gundary) estab. 1860 by William Ellison, taken over by Josiah Taylor, closed 1898; foot-bridge; freezing and ice works (Moruya Refrigerating Co. Ltd) 1917, bought 1945 by Fred Wood; gale 1928; hailstorms 1922, 1936, 1969; hospital (cottage) b. 1889–91 by Shottin and Stubbs, d. by Reginald Herbert Barlow, additions and alterations 1937 by J.S. Brogan, sold and removed 1954, new one b. 1950–54, modernised 1972 by Hughes Bros, additions 1992, additions 2014 by Edwards Constructions (NSW) Pty Ltd; house frame and truss factory (South Pacific Roof Trusses); ice-cream factory (Streets Ice Cream Pty Ltd) 1951–54, abandoned, later demolished; jetty; lock-up b. 1896 by Holloway Bros; mine (silver) o. 1860 by Want and Sir Samuel Saul, abandoned, reopened by F. Guy, with a 10 head stamper battery; PO 1855, new one b. 1887, extended 1926 and 1984; pound (stock) 1856; powerhouse (Moruya Electrical Supply

Co.) 1931–49; Presb. C. (St Stephen's) b. 1863 by George Wright; PS (incl. lock-up) b. 1880 by William Duncan, new one (in rented premises) 1986; punt 1840, new one (Sam Barr) 1850, new one (Christopher Brown) 1861, across Moruya R.; 2 reservoirs (incl. concrete one b. 1954, 150,000 gal. or 681.9 kl); Rom. Cath. C. (Immaculate Conception) b. 1856, altered and re-roofed 1882 by Walters, reused 1883, replacement (Sacred Heart) b. 1887–89 by G. Chidgey, d. by John Francis Hennessy and Joseph Ignatius Sheerin, re-roofed 1963, gallery added 1969 by Jack Brown, church renovated 1977–79 by Joseph Herman Gschwend; roof truss plant (South Pacific) 1975; sale-yards 1917, relocated 1960, demolished and replaced 1987 on new site; Sanctuary C.; sand-paper factory 1881; sawmills: Ball and Wilson, Graham and Sly, Lynch's (fire 1904), H. Preddy, George Sydney Rayner, Ryan Bros (bankrupt 1951), White Bros (sold 1919 to Clyde Sawmill & Shipping Co.); schools: primary 1879 b. by Christian Bohm and William Harkus, additions 1947–52, 1966, 1988, and HS 1966, new one b. 1970 by Hughes Bros, additions 1979, 1988, 1995; sewerage 1972; shipyard (South Coast Co-op. Shipbuilding, Canning & Development Society) 1941, damaged 1945; TC, became a campus of Illawarra Institute of Technology in 1992; telegraph 1863; tobacco factory (James Mooney); TX 1911, automatic 1975; typhoid 1911; Unit. C. (orig. Wes. Meth.) b. 1864 by Edward Walters and Peter Small, d. by Thomas Rowe; water reticulation (incl. pumping station) 1954; wattle-bark mill (Craig, Mostyn & Co.); Wes. Meth. C. 1854, demolished 1863; wharves: one b. 1844, one b. 1860 (south bank), one b. 1869 by Joseph Mather, one b. 1884 (replaced 1901), one b. 1899 by J.P. Madden, new one 1960; pop. 148 (1856), 250 (1861), 547 (1871), 829 (1881), *c.*850 (1883), *c.*1,000 (1887), 1,236 (1891), *c.*1,200 (1895–98), 1,099 (1901), 1,001 (1911), 1,078 (1933), 998 (1947), 1,201 (1954), 1,280 (1961), 1,449 (1966), 1,656 (1971), 1,869 (1976), 2,003 (1981), 2,386 (1986), 2,520 (1991), 2,602 (1996), 2,549 (2001), 2,432 (2006), 2,531 (2011).

Moruya Heads (*Co. Dampier*) 35°55'S. 150°10'E., 7 km E. of Moruya, on Moruya R.; settled 1834 by Archibald McLean; breakwater; cemetery; flood 1925; gale 1920; pilot station 1861, additions 1863 by Edward Walters and Peter Small, reused; PO (Moruya Quarry) 1926; powerhouse; quarry (sandstone) 1863; reservoir; telephone: Moruya Heads 1887 and Moruya Quarry 1926; training wall b. 1897–1901, later extended, completed 1954; TX 1927–60; wharves 1869 and 1925; pop. 39 (1933), 52 (1947), 79 (1954), 84 (1961), 648 (1991), 710 (1996), 730 (2001), 800 (2006), 921 (2011).

Morven (*Co. Hume*) 35°40'S. 147°07'E., 8 km E. of Culcairn, on Billabong Ck; surveyed 1860 by Philip Francis Adams, village gaz. and lots sold 1861; farming and grazing; Angl. C. (St Peter's) 1874, restored; bridge b. 1876 by Kennedy and Holimuth, new one b. 1913 by John Comyns, over Billabong Ck; FB; flood 1931; PO 1880; Presb. C. b. 1940 by John Watson; RS (3 km SW) 1902, station b. by John Allibone, closed 1975; school 1908, new one b. 1923 by J.S. Gamble, burnt down 1925, replaced 1928 by A.H. Baglee, closed 1967, sold, moved and reused; telephone 1909; TX 1912, automatic 1959; water supply 1950; pop. 129 (1901), 114 (1911), 126 (1933), 165 (1947), 143 (1954), 177 (1961), 465 (2006).

Moscheto Island (*Co. Northumberland*) see Kooragang.

Moses Lambing (*Co. Clarke*) 30°12'S. 152°03'E., 36 km E. of Guyra, on Aberfoyle R.

Mosquito Bay (*Co. St Vincent*) see Malua Bay.

Mosquito Creek (*Co. Burnett*) 29°26'S. 150°22'E., 24 km NW of Warialda, on Mosquito Ck; sawmills: G.H. Maidens 1935 and Ephraim Tomkins 1924; school 1917 b. by R. Wilson, closed 1932; Union C. b. 1929 by Ephraim Tomkins, d. by Hugh Henry McCourt; pop. 107 (1933).

Mosquito Island (*Co. Northumberland*) see Kooragang.

Mossgiel (*Co. Waljeers*) 33°15'S. 144°34'E., 93 km W. of Hillston; village gaz. 1888; grazing; Angl. C. b. 1900 by W. Silk; cemetery 1889; CH 1879; grasshopper infestation 1955; fire 1882; hospital (cottage) b. 1898 by R. Massie, d. by Ernest Rees Laver; PO 1870, new one b. 1898 by George Huntley Dixon, closed and sold; PS 1876–1924; sand storm 1899; school 1890–1916; telegraph 1882, new office b. 1898 by George Huntley Dixon; TX 1911; pop. 114 (1891), 152 (1901), 195 (1911), 35 (1933), 86 (1961), 1 (2008).

Moss Vale (*Co. Camden*) 34°33'S. 150°22'E., 9 km SW of Bowral, on Whites Ck; formerly also known as Sutton Forest North; settled 1853, surveyed and subdivided 1864, thrived in 1880s, munic. 1888–1933; orig. wheat and potatoes, former highland resort 1870+, timber, fruit, vegetables, sheep, cattle, hort., goats, horses, dairying, educational centre, retirement centre 1960s+; abattoir (Berrima Dist. Meats Pty Ltd) 1963, closed; Angl. C. b. 1881 by James Nutman, new one (St John's Memorial) b. 1930 by Alfred Stephens & Sons, d. by William A. Nelson; Assemblies of God C. (Connect); bicycle works (Yabsley Bros); brickworks (H.C. McDonald & Sons); bushfires 1898 and 1899; butter factory (Dairy Farmers' Co-op. Milk Co. Ltd) b. 1922 by J. Grainger, d. by H.W. May & Co., closed; carriage-works: Thomas Brownlow and Richard Oscar Albert Mirow 1885, J. McLeery 1883, Phillips and White (Norman L. Cross replaced White in 1925), Yabsley Bros; caterpillar infestation 1893; cemetery 1897; CH b. 1880 by Jones and M'Intyre, additions 1894 by A. M'Cann, new one 1924 d. by George McRae; clock tower (J.M. Alcorn memorial) 1938 d. by Harry Sheaffe; cordial factories: E.H. Bendall (sold 1912 to R.G. Thomas), A.J. Colless, Cullen and Grogin 1886 (bought 1893 by Robert Ritchie), Irving Bros, M.A. Mealing 1896, Robert Ritchie 1880, T.J. Winner; dust storm 1901; earth tremors 1897 and 1961; electricity supplied 1890–1911 by Electric Lighting Co., then local council till 1924, then from Port Kembla; engineering works: Joy Manufacturing Co. Pty Ltd 1944, McLeery's 1883, Neil Moxon Pty Ltd 1966, Vale Engineering Pty Ltd 1967; eucalyptus oil distillery (Aust. Eucalyptus Oil Co.); FB 1884 (station b. 1898 by William Jones, d. by E. Vennard, new one 1971); floods 1893 and 1898; gasworks 1889; hailstorm (nearly every building damaged) 1907; Jehovah's Witnesses C.; monumental stone works (R. Metz); PO 1867, new one b. 1891, additions and alterations 1910 by W. Jones, alterations 1932; pound (stock) 1870; Presb. C. (St Andrew's) b. 1879 by James Linklater; Prim. Meth. C. 1880; PS 1877, new one b. 1922 by Alfred Stephens & Sons, new one 2018; quarry; railway to Port Kembla 1932; railway bridge (timber beam) 1868 d. by John Whitton, replacement (wrought iron Schweidler pony truss) 1885, 98 ft (29.9 m), new one (steel Pratt truss) 1915, 133 ft (40.5 m); railway turntable, 60 ft (18.3 m), strengthened 1917, new one 75 ft (22.9 m), defunct; 2 reservoirs; Rom. Cath. C. (St Paul's) b. 1888 by James Cashman, additions 1896, additions 1916 by A.M. Sweetnam, d. by Austin McKay; RS (Sutton Forest North till 1877) 1867, station b. by W. and A. Elphinstone, additions and alterations 1890 by T. and G. Brown, refreshment rooms b. 1890 by Dean & Sons, additions and alterations 1905, closed 1962; sale-yards 1904, replaced 1952; Salv. Army C. 1889, inundated 1893, closed 1905; sawmills: S.E. Browne & Co., burnt down 1941, McCleery's Ltd 1915, Moss Vale Case & Timber Mill, F.C. Webb & Co. 1922, Frederick and William Yabsley (Frederick killed 1900); schools: primary (Sutton Forest North till 1872) 1868, additions 1884 by James Linklater, additions 1890, 1897, 1909, new building b. 1918 by J. Burnett, additions and alterations 1928 also by Burnett, additions 1940, 1954, 1958, 1974, and HS 1964, additions 1974, 1977, 1989, 1991; sewerage 1937, augmentation 1995; smallpox 1884; streets electric lit 1890; TC, additions 1976 and 1986, became a campus of Illawarra Institute of Technology in 1992;

telegraph 1871, additions and alterations to office 1910 by W. Jones; TX 1908, automatic 1971; Unit. C. (orig. Meth.) 1937; water reticulation 1894, water supply filtration 1963, augmentation 1966 and 1988; Wes. Meth. C. 1888, additions 1914, closed and reused; winery (Southern Highlands); pop. 134 (1871), 570 (1881), *c.*1,200 (1886), 1,240 (1891), 1,385 (1901), 1,555 (1911), 1,947 (1921), 2,359 (1933), *c.*3,000 (1941), 3,096 (1947), 2,890 (1954), 3,040 (1961), 3,144 (1966), 3,233 (1971), 3,638 (1976), 4,415 (1981), 5,016 (1986), 5,690 (1991), 6,108 (1996), 6,623 (2001), 6,723 (2006), 7,305 (2011).

Mossy Point (*Co. St Vincent*) 35°50'S. 150°11'E., 12 km NE. of Moruya, on Broulee Bay; Connell's Point till 1941, then Rendezvous Point till 1942; bridges: one b. 1966 to Broulee, closed and demolished 2015, replaced 2015 by Nelmac Pty Ltd, over Candlagan Ck and one b. 1974, to Tomakin, over Tomaga R.; bushfires 1952, 1965, 1994; FB; foot-bridge to Broulee, over Candlagan Ck; jetty; mine; PO 1953; PS; reservoir; 3 sawmills (incl. Cook's, burnt down 1924); sewerage 1984; telephone 1941; TX 1942, automatic 1968; pop. 57 (1954), 57 (1961).

Mother Moores Crossing (*Co. Wellesley*) 36°57'S. 149°02'E., 18 km W. of Bombala, on Mother Moores Ck; airfield.

Mother of Ducks (*Co. Sandon*) see Guyra.

Moto (*Co. Macquarie*) 31°51'S. 152°35'E., 9 km W. of Harrington, on Ghinni Ghinni Ck; FB; flood 1929; Meth. C. b. 1928 by C.J. Mathers; pop. 84 (1901), 162 (1947), 144 (1954), 82 (1961), 290 (2011).

Motto Farm (*Co. Gloucester*) see Heatherbrae.

Mottram (*Co. Macquarie*) 31°51'S. 152°35'E., 10 km W. of Harrington, on Ghinni Ghinni Ck; telephone 1927; TX 1927.

Moulamein (*Co. Wakool*) 35°05'S. 144°02'E., 60 km N. of Barham, on Edward R.; settled 1830, surveyed 1849, laid out 1851 by Thomas Scott Townsend, first lots sold 1851, town gaz. 1879, designated as chief town of the county; former river port 1864+, formerly oats, then grazing, wheat, rice; airfield; ambulance station; Angl. C. (St Martin's) 1971; bridges: one b. 1864, second one b. 1925 by A. Burdett and W. Hudson, d. by J.J. Gardiner, third one 1970, fourth one 2003 over Edward R., and one over Billabong Ck; cemetery 1881; CH 1848, demolished 1860, new one b. 1900 by George Huntley Dixon, d. by Walter Liberty Vernon, closed 1968, restored and reused, new one 1969; FB; fire 1926; flood 1870; foot-bridge 1927, replaced, over Billabong Ck; lake (artificial), deepened 2009; lock-up 1848; PO 1849, new one b. 1871; pound (stock) 1865; powerhouse 1948; PS b. 1908 by George Huntley Dixon and William Godfrey Butterworth, new one 1969; punt b. 1883 by J. Lawrence; railway bridges 1925 over Billabong Ck and Edward R.; Rom. Cath. C. (St Mary's) 1961; RS (Victorian railway) 1926, station demolished; sawmill (Charles E. Burdett and W. Hudson) 1925; school 1867, inundated 1867, new buildings b. 1893 by Henry Quin, repairs 1900 by C.N.H. Woolfrey, new school 1937, additions 1961, 1963, 1966, 1969, 1973; silo; telegraph 1866; TX 1910, automatic 1989; Unit. C. (orig. Presb.) 1879, renovated 1925 by H. Downe; weir on Billabong Ck; wharf 1908; pop. 72 (1861), *c.*100 (1866), 81 (1871), 120 (1881), 131 (1891), 121 (1901), 393 (1911), 372 (1933), 395 (1947), 514 (1954), 502 (1961), 450 (1966), 492 (1971), 424 (1976), 396 (1981), 425 (1986), 459 (1991), 459 (1996), 423 (2001), 349 (2006), 330 (2011).

Mount Adrah (*Co. Wynyard*) 35°13'S. 147°54'E., 25 km SW of Gundagai, on Yaven Yaven Ck; farming and grazing; Angl. C. (St John's, also known as St Paul's) 1902, restored 1914, closed and reused; bushfire 1905; PO 1879; school 1875–89 and 1899–1906; telephone 1926; TX 1929; pop. 82 (1901), 53 (1911), 61 (1933), 78 (1947), 66 (1954), 84 (1961).

Mountain Creek (*Co. Goulburn*) 35°48'S. 147°10'E., 16 km SW of Holbrook, on Mountain Ck; TX (automatic); pop. 96 (1911), 85 (1933), 66 (1947), 72 (1961), 260 (2006).

Mountain Creek (*Co. Narromine*) 32°26'S. 148°28'E., 23 km SW of Dubbo.

Mountain Home (*Co. Westmoreland*) 33°35'S. 149°57'E., 16 km NE of Oberon; Angl. C. 1885; PO 1897–1901; school 1881–89 and 1894–1903.

Mountain Lagoon (*Co. Cook*) 33°27'S. 150°38'E., 8 km N. of Kurrajong Heights, on Lagoon Ck; settled by John Stewart; timber; bushfire 1909; electricity 1968; FB 1968 (station b. 1984); sawmill; pop. 23 (1933), 327 (2011).

Mountain Maid (*Co. Gloucester*) 32°00'S. 151°50'E., 13 km W. of Gloucester.

Mountain Top (*Co. Auckland*) 36°35'S. 149°24'E., 40 km W. of Bega.

Mountain Top (*Co. Raleigh*) 30°23'S. 152°43'E., 4 km S. of Dorrigo; pop. 65 (1933).

Mountain Top (*Co. Rous*) 28°37'S. 153°10'E., 6 km SW of Nimbin, on Jiggi Ck; airfield.

Mountain View (*Co. Bourke*) 34°28'S. 146°52'E., 12 km S. of Ardlethan.

Mountain View (*Co. Clarence*) 29°36'S. 152°56'E., 10 km N. of Grafton, on Clarence R.; reservoir, 20,000 gal. (90.9 kl), 1967; sawmill (Henson Sawmilling Pty Ltd) 1986; water reticulation 1966; pop. 39 (1933), 89 (1961), 187 (2011).

Mountain View (*Co. Darling*) see New Mexico.

Mount Airy (*Co. Wynyard*) 35°32'S. 147°44'E., 38 km SW of Adelong, on Carabost Ck; farming and dairying.

Mount Allen (*Co. Blaxland*) 32°42'S. 145°52'E., 92 km N. of Hillston; abandoned *c.*1902; formerly mining (gold disc. 1892 and copper); cemetery 1897; mines: Double Peak Southeast, Double Peak Southwest, Mount Allen, Mount Dromedary Line.

Mount Andrew (*Co. Hunter*) 33°26'S. 150°53'E., 22 km NE of North Richmond, on Colo R.; orchards.

Mount Arthur (*Co. Gordon*) 32°34'S. 148°55'E., 3 km W. of Wellington, on Curra Ck; FB (station b. 2012); sewage works; pop. 481 (2011).

Mount Austin (*Co. Wynyard*) see Wagga Wagga.

Mount Baltimore (*Co. Lincoln*) see Ballimore.

Mount Billagoe (*Co. Robinson*) see Mount Drysdale.

Mount Boppy Mine (*Co. Canbelego*) see Canbelego.

Mount Brandon (*Co. Camden*) 34°41'S. 150°47'E., 7 km W. of Kiama; Angl. C. 1890; school (Brandon Hill) 1872–91.

Mount Brown (*Co. Camden*) see Dapto.

Mount Browne (*Co. Evelyn*) 29°47'S. 141°47'E., 248 km NW of Wilcannia; almost deserted by 1903, defunct; gold (disc. 1881 by James Evans, gold rush 1881); cemetery; earth tremor 1953; mines: Billygoat Hill and The Four Mile; PO 1890; school 1891–95; pop. 134 (1891).

Mount Burrell (*Co. Rous*) 28°30'S. 153°13'E., 10 km N. of Nimbin, on Snake Ck; farming and dairying; cemetery; PO 1927; school 1937–63; telephone 1923; TX 1945–65; pop. 203 (1933), 88 (1947), 87 (1954), 80 (1961), 290 (2006).

Mount Collins (*Co. Monteagle*) 34°00'S. 148°46'E., 19 km S. of Cowra; gold (alluvial); pop. 77 (1933), 68 (1947), 68 (1961).

Mount Cooper (*Co. Wellesely*) 36°40'S. 149°14'E., 28 km N. of Bombala, on Mount Cooper Ck; cemetery.

Mount Costigan (*Co. Georgiana*) 34°01'S. 149°22'E., 49 km N. of Crookwell, on Tuena Ck; surveyed 1887 by Charles Thurburn, village gaz. 1888; mining (silver-lead disc. 1887 by J. Maguire and another lode 1888 by Richard Reynolds, also copper and zinc) and grazing; earth tremor 1890; mines: Beetson Co. and Mount Costigan Silver & Lead Mining Co. 1887–88, 1892–93, 1911–15; PO 1888; 3 quarries; Rom. Cath. C. 1888 d. by Ferguson, destroyed 1895; school 1888 b. by John Howard, closed 1915; smelters b. 1887 by J. Kee; storm 1895; pop. 160 (1887), *c.*550 (1889), 136 (1891), *c.*150 (1903), 40 (1912), 64 (1933).

Mount Crystal (*Co. Cooper*) 34°31'S. 146°41'E., 26 km SW of Ardlethan; school 1918–35; pop. 117 (1911), 52 (1933), 59 (1961).

Mount Dangar (*Co. Hunter*) 32°23'S. 150°27'E., 21 km W. of Denman; Angl. C. (St Matthew's) 1864, demolished and replaced

1891, and graveyard; school (Baerami till 1902) 1882–86, 1898–1907, 1919–64.

Mount Darragh (*Co. Auckland*) 36°50'S. 149°31'E., 27 km E. of Bombala, on New Station Ck; vegetables; PO 1927–60; sawmills: Bourke's (bought by George Sydney Rayner) and O.L. Harrison (removed 1924 from Eden); telephone 1915; TX 1928–48; pop. 42 (1933).

Mount David (*Co. Georgiana*) 33°49'S. 149°36'E., 28 km SW of Oberon, on Poison Ck; mining (gold disc. 1891 by David Crozier) *c.*1896+, farming, grazing; airfield; fire 1906; mines: Little Marvel (estab. by Mick Lannigan, sold to Butler Boyd & Co., sold to Mount David Mining Co.) and Mount David or Mount Maude (incl. Crozier's and Little Marvel) 1894, 1897–1910, 1915, 1931–34, 1938, 1941; PO 1897; quarry; Rom. Cath. C. (St Francis Xavier's) 1920 d. by William Dryden, closed and reused; school 1899 b. by Rigby Bros, closed 1968; stamper batteries: 10 head (Mount David Mining Co. Ltd), 20 head, 25 head; telephone 1906; TX 1935, automatic 1982; pop. 181 (1901), 210 (1911), 77 (1933), 66 (1947), 59 (1954), 133 (1961).

Mount Dee (*Co. Northumberland*) see Telarah.

Mount Defiance (*Co. Georgiana*) 34°09'S. 149°45'E., 42 km NE of Crookwell; silver (disc. 1910) and grazing; mine 1910; PO 1927–30; telephone 1926; TX 1936–85.

Mount Dromedary (*Co. Dampier*) 36°19'S. 150°02'E., 13 km SW of Narooma, on Dromedary Ck; estab. 1881; mining (gold disc. 1853 by William Branwhite Clarke, silver disc. 1861, more gold disc. 1877 by Cowdroy Bros) *c.*1860+; miners' strike 1898; mines: Enterprise, Mount Dromedary Gold Mining Co. (incl. battery) 1878–1910, Star of the South (Latimer and Read) 1882.

Mount Drummond (*Co. Camden*) see Coniston.

Mount Drummond (*Co. Hardinge*) 30°10'S. 151°00'E., 29 km SW of Tingha; school 1908–39 and 1957–66; pop. 70 (1911).

Mount Drysdale (*Co. Robinson*) 31°10'S. 145°53'E., 36 km N. of Cobar; Mount Billagoe till 1895; disc. by David Drysdale, thrived 1880–1910, village gaz. 1893, laid out 1895, abandoned; mining (alluvial gold disc. 1892 by R. McPherson and reef disc. 1892 by David Drysdale) mainly 1892–1909; cemetery (*c.*35 burials) 1895; mine fatality 1893; mines: El Dorado and Mount Drysdale (fire 1909), both disc. by David Drysdale; PO 1895–1942; powder magazine; PS 1894, additions 1907 by Arnold Rigby, closed 1914; school 1895 b. by James Prior Hull, closed 1913, building removed 1929; stamper battery 1922; telegraph 1901; telephone 1898; TX 1924; pop. *c.*1,000 (1892), *c.*600 (1895), *c.*5,000 (1900), 209 (1901), 92 (1911), 57 (1933). (See also West Drysdale.)

Mount Elliot (*Co. Northumberland*) see Holgate.

Mount Fairy (*Co. Murray*) 35°10'S. 149°36'E., 18 km NE of Bungendore, on Fairy Meadow Ck; mining (copper, limestone, dolomite) and grazing; 2 mines; PO 1904; RS (Fairy Mount till 1903) 1886–1975; telephone 1914; TX 1934, automatic 1970; pop. 75 (1911), 36 (1933), 61 (1947), 184 (2011).

Mount Frome (*Co. Phillip*) 32°36'S. 149°39'E., 6 km E. of Mudgee, on Lawsons Ck; limestone, farming, grazing; bushfire 1875; lime-kilns; PO 1927; 6 quarries (limestone); RS (Bumberra till 1894) 1884, station b. by Duncan McFarlane, closed 1974; telephone 1914; TX 1925; wineries: Moothi Estate 2006 and Mount Frome Vineyard Pty Ltd estab. 1990 by Bruce Browne; pop. 69 (1911), 77 (1933), 55 (1947), 50 (1954).

Mount George (*Co. Macquarie*) 31°53'S. 152°11'E., 18 km W. of Wingham, on Manning R.; gold (disc. 1899), farming, orchards; FB; PO 1916; Presb. C. 1872; PS 1924 (closed during World War II); rifle range 1924; RS 1913, station demolished 1985; sawmills: A.M. Hawkins & Sons, burnt down 1937 and Rhodes Timber Co. (Tulloch's) 1920, burnt down 1923, replaced 1924, taken over 1993 by Booral Timber, closed 1995; school 1882, new one b. 1885 by Francis John Dennes, repairs 1898 by J. Small, repairs 1900 by

Silas Brewer, additions 1916 by W. Sellick; telephone 1914; TX 1916, automatic 1980; pop. 21 (1841), 271 (1933), 321 (1947), 253 (1954), 270 (1961), 339 (2011).

Mount Gipps (*Co. Yancowinna*) 31°54'S. 141°36'E., 14 km NE of Broken Hill; PO 1870–93; RS 1919–74; school (Eaglehawk till 1891) 1889–99; telephone 1954; TX; pop. 106 (1891).

Mount Gwynne (*Co. Denison*) 35°55'S. 145°54'E., 19 km E. of Barooga; farming and grazing; PO 1927–30; 2 quarries; school 1898–1967; telephone 1919; TX (automatic) 1958; pop. 68 (1911), 50 (1933), 105 (1947), 107 (1954), 63 (1961).

Mount Harris (*Co. Gregory*) 31°19'S. 147°38'E., 46 km NW of Warren, on Marra Ck; PO 1867, burnt down 1915.

Mount Hope (*Co. Blaxland*) 32°52'S. 145°52'E., 79 km NE of Hillston; laid out 1888, largely defunct; formerly mining (copper disc. 1878 by McDowall) 1878–*c.*1919 and smelting 1880+, then grazing; airfield; brewery (Edward Evans) 1883–86; CH 1886; fire 1884; Meth. C. 1905; mine 1878, man killed 1888, closed 1902, reopened 1906; PO 1881; PS (incl. lock-up) 1882, abandoned; railway (mineral) to Matakana 1919–24; Rom. Cath. C., closed; RS 1919–24; school 1884, new buildings b. 1885, closed 1945; 4 smelters; telegraph 1884; telephone 1904; TX 1910; pop. *c.*800 (1882), *c.*160 (1888), 250 (1891), 337 (1901), 107 (1911), 102 (1933), 129 (1947), 153 (1954), 138 (1961), 54 (2006).

Mount Hope South (*Co. Blaxland*) 32°53'S. 145°51'E., 77 km NE of Hillston; (incl. Nombinnie); laid out 1888, defunct; copper mining till 1902; cemetery (Nombinnie) 1886; mines: Great Central (McDowall's) 1882–98, South Mount Hope (Brown's), The Comet; PO 1883–1913; school (Great Central) 1884–1904; 2 smelters; pop. *c.*400 (1888).

Mount Horeb (*Co. Wynyard*) 35°13'S. 148°02'E., 12 km N. of Adelong, on Adelong Ck; goldmining (alluvial and dredging); FB 1955; gold dredging companies: Adelong Creek Dredging Co. NL 1911–28 and Golden Valley Mining Co. NL 1932–42; gale 1914; PO 1926–72; RS 1903, station b. by F.G. Filmer, removed 1984; school 1913–29; telephone 1905; TX; pop. 64 (1911), 64 (1933), 81 (1947), 73 (1954), 55 (1961).

Mount Horrible (*Co. Roxburgh*) 33°13'S. 149°51'E., 19 km NW of Portland, on Palmers Oaky Ck; quarry.

Mount Hunter (*Co. Camden*) 34°04'S. 150°38'E., 6 km W. of Camden, on Mount Hunter Rivulet; (incl. Westbrook); disc. 1796 by John Hunter; dairying; Angl. C. (St Paul's) 1878, chancel added 1893; bridge (Westbrook Bridge) 1897, over Mount Hunter Rivulet; butter factory (Camden Dairy Co. Ltd) 1888, taken over 1896 by Camden Park Estate and converted into a creamery, burnt down 1902, rebuilt, closed 1907, bought by Edward Lavercombe and reused, sold 2001; FB 1952; PO 1888–1948; quarry (disused); school (Westbrook till 1888) 1859, new one b. 1884 by Wheatley, extended 1900, new building b. 1912 by W.W. Dunk, new building 1983; telephone 1911; TX (automatic) 1959; Unit. C. (orig. Wes. Meth.) 1900–74, sold 2000; weir on Mount Hunter Rivulet; Wes. Meth. C. 1858; pop. 165 (1911), 114 (1933), 78 (1947), 89 (1954), 191 (1961), 224 (1996), 246 (2001), 202 (2006), 807 (2011).

Mount Hutton (*Co. Northumberland*) 32°59'S. 151°40'E., 3 km SW of Charlestown, on Scrubby Ck; (incl. Hillsborough, estab. 1874 as Winding Creek by John James Hill for miners, subdivided 1876, renamed Higham Road in 1877); subdivisions 1921 and 1932; Bapt. Reformed C. 1994; bushfires 1905 and 1953; mine (Australasian Coal Mining Co.) 1874–79; PO: Higham Road 1876–80 and Mount Hutton 1941–79; reservoir (concrete), 750,000 gal. (3,409.5 kl), b. 1953 by Monier Construction Pty Ltd; schools: Hillsborough 1878–81, new one o. 1963, additions 1966, 1970, 1978, re-roofed 2013, and Mount Hutton 1955, additions 2010 by R.T. Parker Pty Ltd; sewerage: Hillsborough 1960 and Mount Hutton 1964; storm 2007; telephone 1945; TX 1950, automatic 1958; United Meth.

Free C. (Hillsborough) 1878; water supply 1948; Wes. Meth. C. 1900; pop. 53 (1933), 306 (1947), 3,772 (2006), 3,848 (2011).

Mount Irvine (*Co. Cook*) 33°29'S. 150°28'E., 15 km W. of Kurrajong Heights; Irvine till 1948; settled 1897; bushfire 1957; cemetery (9 graves 1934–92) 1935; PO 1933, burnt down 1940; quarry (iron ore); sawmill (Scrivener's), burnt down 1926, rebuilt, burnt down 1931; telephone 1925; TX 1925; pop. 46 (1933).

Mount Kanwary (*Co. Durham*) see Osterley.

Mount Keira (*Co. Camden*) 34°25'S. 150°52'E., 3 km W. of Wollongong, on Byarong Ck; formerly Paulsgrove; coalmining; Angl. C. (St John's) 1906, damaged 1940, and graveyard; caterpillar infestation 1898; colliery (Albert or Shoobert's Mine) estab. 1849 by James Shoobert, taken over 1853 by William Robson, sold 1856 to Henry Osborne, renamed Osborne-Wallsend Colliery in 1857, leased 1859 to Robson & Co., renamed Mount Keira Colliery in 1884, sold 1899 to Ebenezer Vickery & Sons, new tunnel and ventilation shaft 1913, acquired 1937 by Aust. Iron & Steel Ltd, mechanisation introduced 1938, renamed Kemira Colliery in 1955, new shaft 1957, long-wall mining 1965, closed 1991, 2 shafts and 4 tunnels sealed 1995); electricity 1924; FB; flour mills: James Staires Spearing, water powered, destroyed 1832, and wind powered one; gale 1939; mine fatalities 1870 (boy killed), 1871 (2 killed), 1879, 1885, 1887, 1896, 1897, 1906 (2 killed), 1908, 1910 (2 killed), 1912, 1915, 1930, 1939, 1949, 1951; miners' strikes 1886–87, 1909–10, 1951, 1954, 1982; PO 1882, burnt down 1929, reopened, closed 1993; Prim. Meth. C. 1862–82; reservoirs: first one (concrete), 100,000 gal. (454.6 kl), 1915 and second one 1948; sawmill (William Henry Hurt); school 1861, new building b. 1877 by George Osborne, d. by George Allen Mansfield, additions 1886 by A. M'Donald & Co.; storms 1832 and 1940; telephone 1906; tramway (horse drawn) b. 1859–61 for Robson & Co. from colliery to Belmore Basin, Wollongong; water supply 1915; Wes. Meth. C. 1862, new one 1889, destroyed 1939; pop. 520 (1911), 401 (1954), 500 (1961), 1,389 (2001), 1,444 (2006), 1,522 (2011).

Mount Kembla (*Co. Camden*) 34°26'S. 150°49'E., 4 km NW of Unanderra, on American Ck; (incl. Kembla, Kembla Heights, Lower Mount Kembla); orig. American Creek; oil-shale (disc. 1849 by William Branwhite Clarke) 1865–80, coalmining, farming, dairying, orchards; Angl. C. 1858, new one (Soldiers and Miners' Memorial) 1932, and graveyard (354 graves), incl. columbarium 1976; bushfires 1936, 1940, 1968; cemetery (Windy Gully, 58 graves) 1902; collieries: Bushells Hill Tunnel, Illawarra (o. 1920 by Illawarra Coal Co., renamed Port Kembla No. 2, closed 1960, acquired 1964 by Aust. Iron & Steel Ltd and became part of Nebo Colliery), Mount Kembla (d. by William Burrell, operated 1883–1913 by Mount Kembla Coal & Oil Co. Ltd, explosion 1902 killed 96, operated 1913–41 by Mount Kembla Collieries Ltd, acquired 1945 by Aust. Iron & Steel Ltd, closed 1970, razed except for pit pony stables), Nebo (estab. 1946–49 by BHP, creep 1951, mining ceased and underground workings connected 1993 to form portal of Eloura colliery, pit-top reused 2001 for Dendrobium Colliery) Port Kembla No. 2 (mined 1929–33 by Illawarra Coke Co., sold 1933 to Port Kembla Coal Co., closed 1936, acquired 1941 by Broken Hill Associated Smelters Co., fire 1960), Tom Thumb (Aust. Iron & Steel Ltd) 1967–71; dam (colliery) 1908; FB; miners' strikes 1885, 1889, 1893–94, 1924, 1943, 1951, 1952; oil-shale works (Grahams' Pioneer Kerosene Works) incl. 23 horizontal retorts, b. 1865 by Robert Longmore for John, Edward and Neville Graham, d. by W.J. Hammill, first oil-shale retorted 1865, works sold 1874 to Mount Kembla Coal & Oil Co. Ltd, fire 1874, closed 1875, reopened 1876, fire 1877, closed 1878 and abandoned, reworked 1943 by Madden & Co., razed; PO: Kembla 1857–66, Kembla Heights 1892, Mount Kembla 1883; Presb. C. 1888, burnt down 1914, replaced 1915, closed 1971, dismantled 1975; Prim. Meth. C. 1885 (used as Angl. C. 1940–56); railway (Mount Kembla Coal & Oil Co. Ltd) 1882; 2 reservoirs (incl. steel one b. 1915, 62,000 gal. or 281.9 kl); Rom. Cath. C. (St Clement's) b. 1894 by Moran and Pleus, closed 1981; school (Violet Hill till 1884) 1859, additions 1886 by P. Gavine, new one b. 1896 by Alexander David Henry Scouller, d. by William Edmund Kemp, extended 1973; telephone: Kembla Heights 1905 and Mount Kembla 1905; water supply 1915; Wes. Meth. C. 1892; pop. *c.*1,000 (1903), 332 (1911), 701 (1947), 746 (1954), 888 (1961), 611 (1966), 848 (1971), *c.*500 (1987), 909 (2006), 1,028 (2011).

Mount Knowles (*Co. Phillip*) 32°37'S. 149°43'E., 13 km E. of Mudgee, on Lawsons Ck; Walls Siding till 1918; lime-kilns; PO 1918; quarries (limestone and dolomite): BHP and Metrop. Lime & Cement Co.; RS 1918–74; telephone 1916; TX 1922, automatic 1977; pop. 66 (1933), 50 (1947).

Mount Lambie (*Co. Roxburgh*) 33°27'S. 149°59'E., 10 km SW of Wallerawang, on Thompsons Ck; bushfire 1940; Presb. C. 1865, now seldom used, and graveyard; quarry (stone); school (Thorps Pinch till 1904 then Warrawang) 1880, new one b. 1882 by W. Moulsdale, closed 1911; pop. 44 (1933).

Mount Lawson (*Co. Georgiana*)
see Judds Creek.

Mount Lion (*Co. Rous*) 28°26'S. 152°57'E., 21 km N. of Kyogle, on Gradys Ck; RS 1930–75; school 1957–75; pop. 95 (1933), 76 (1947), 62 (1954), 51 (1961).

Mount McDonald (*Co. Bathurst*) 33°56'S. 148°57'E., 26 km E. of Cowra; estab. 1881, largely defunct by *c.*1920; mining (gold disc. 1880 by John, James and Donald McDonald) till 1920, farming, grazing; cemetery; CH 1900; cyclone (unroofed nearly every house) 1893; diphtheria 1884 and 1893; earth tremor 1889; FB 1932; mines: Balmoral group (Australasian Mining Investment Assoc., incl. Balmoral West, Bobby Burns, Webb) 1881–91 and 1903–5, Caledonian group (incl. Caledonia Reform, Fergusson's, Great Eastern, Long, Shamrock, Woolston & Co., Zulu) 1882, 1886–87, 1890–92, 1896, 1902–3, 1906, 1937, 1939–41, Eureka group (incl. Cash, Dominish and Frazer, Fifield and Mullen, Fitzgibbons) 1884–86, 1890, 1897–98, 1902, 1906–9, 1924, Grants Amalgamated group (incl. Franklin, J. and A. Kennedy, Kennedy and Cash, Queen of the Mount, Te Kooti) 1881–82, 1885–91, 1903, 1910–17, Milburn Creek (incl. Eldorado) 1873–78, 1888, 1919–21, Olivers Freehold (Australasian Mining Investment Assoc.) 1883; PO b. 1881 by Collins, burnt down 1892; pound (stock) 1890; PS b. 1881 by E. Coady, closed 1926, later demolished; Rom. Cath. C. (St Patrick's) 1885, demolished 1927; sawmill; school 1882, demolished 1893, replaced, closed 1924; telegraph 1882, office burnt down 1892; TX 1914, automatic 1954; Union C. 1883, demolished; pop. *c.*700 (1881), 334 (1891), 470 (1901), 96 (1911), 52 (1933).

Mount Mackenzie (*Co. Clive*) 29°06'S. 151°57'E., 8 km SW of Tenterfield, on Eagle Ck; pop. 51 (1933), 231 (2006).

Mount Macquarie (*Co. Bathurst*)
see Neville.

Mount Manara (*Co. Manara*) 32°28'S. 143°55'E., 113 km SE of Wilcannia; telephone 1923; TX 1935; pop. 17 (1933).

Mount Mitchell (*Co. Gough*) 29°57'S. 151°49'E., 24 km S. of Glen Innes; grazing; cemetery (14 graves); flour mill (water powered), closed 1875; PO 1887; sawmill (J. Crampton); school 1887, new one b. 1890 by Martin O'Brien, closed 1937; telephone 1923; TX 1924; pop. 118 (1901), 128 (1911), 104 (1933).

Mount Moobi (*Co. Brisbane*) 32°05'S. 150°46'E., 10 km SW of Scone; school 1882–1909 and 1957–58; pop. 60 (1933).

Mount Murchison (*Co. Young*) 31°27'S. 143°39'E., 29 km NE of Wilcannia, on Darling R.; airfield.

Mount Murchison (*Co. Young*)
see also Wilcannia.

Mount Murray (*Co. Camden*) 34°33'S. 150°38'E., 16 km W. of Dapto; bushfire 1905; PO 1879; RS 1932, closed; sawmill (Seery and Hayter) 1887, burnt down 1905; school 1880–97, 1900–21, 1929–43; pop. 40 (1933).

Mount Oldry (*Co. St Vincent*) 35°51'S. 150°08'E., 8 km NE of Moruya; pop. 40 (1841).

Mount Olive (*Co. Durham*) 32°24'S. 151°13'E., 20 km N. of Singleton, on Glennies Ck; farming, grazing, dairying; electricity 1960; PO 1872–1973; sawmill; telephone 1909; TX 1915, automatic 1980; Wes. Meth. C. 1872, demolished, and graveyard; pop. 43 (1933), 77 (1947), 63 (1961), 238 (2011).

Mount Olive (*Co. Durham*) see also Mount Pleasant.

Mount Olive (*Co. Westmoreland*) 33°36'S. 149°56'E., 14 km NE of Oberon; Wes. Meth. C., replaced, moved to Edith, and graveyard (14 burials); pop. 160 (2006).

Mount Oriel (*Co. Monteagle*) 34°05'S. 148°22'E., 25 km N. of Young; school 1912–63.

Mount Ousley (*Co. Camden*) 34°24'S. 150°53'E., 1 km S. of Balgownie; Assemblies of God C.; blast furnace (Mount Pleasant Iron & Coal Mining Co.); brickworks (W.K. Bates) 1883; flood 1974; Meth. C. (Chinese); schools: Keira HS (Wollongong Junior Technical HS till 1959) 1944, additions 1971 and 1985, Pleasant Heights 1969, additions 1974, Wollongong HS (High School of Performing Arts since 1993) 1917 d. by John Hingston Buckeridge, additions 2011; univ. college (NSW) 1962, became univ. (Wollongong) in 1975, four additions in 2000, 2001, 2006, 2008 by Manteena Pty Ltd, d. by Graham, Bell and Bowman, further additions 2011 d. by Graham, Bell and Bowman; pop. 1,481 (1954), 1,530 (2011).

Mount Ousley (*Co. Camden*) see also Fairy Meadow.

Mount Panorama (*Co. Bathurst*) see Bathurst.

Mount Parry (*Co. Parry*) 31°45'S. 150°18'E., 43 km N. of Merriwa; school 1957, additions 1966, closed 2002; TX.

Mount Peerless (*Co. Gloucester*) 31°57'S. 151°47'E., 17 km W. of Gloucester, on Bowman R.; telephone 1916; TX 1951–63.

Mount Pleasant (*Co. Ashburnham*) 32°59'S. 147°58'E., 26 km NW of Parkes.

Mount Pleasant (*Co. Auckland*) 36°40'S. 149°48'E., 4 km W. of Bega.

Mount Pleasant (*Co. Bathurst*) see Evans Plains.

Mount Pleasant (*Co. Camden*) 34°24'S. 150°52'E., 1 km SW of Balgownie; coalmining; iron smelter (Patrick Lahiff) 1863; milk factory (Fresh Food & Ice Co.) 1898; Prim. Meth. C. (St Aidan's) 1890; pop. 200 (1911), 151 (1954), 470 (1961), 907 (2006), 1,194 (2011).

Mount Pleasant (*Co. Camden*) see also Burrawang.

Mount Pleasant (*Co. Durham*) 32°25'S. 151°11'E., 18 km N. of Singleton, on Goorangoola Ck; school (Mount Olive 1909–11) 1880, new one b. 1889 by Henry Sherwood, replaced 1964; Wes. Meth. C. b. 1888 by Robert Sneesby.

Mount Pleasant (*Co. Killara*) 31°00'S. 143°46'E., 73 km NE of Wilcannia.

Mount Pleasant (*Co. King*) 34°41'S. 149°10'E., 28 km NE of Yass; cemetery; Wes. Meth. C. 1881.

Mount Pleasant (*Co. Northumberland*) see Saratoga.

Mount Pleasant (*Co. Wynyard*) 35°16'S. 147°56'E., 11 km W. of Adelong.

Mount Poole (*Co. Evelyn*) 29°40'S. 141°46'E., 259 km NW of Wilcannia; gold (disc. 1880 by John Thompson); mines: Mount Poole and Sturt's Depot Glen; PO 1879–81.

Mount Rae (*Co. Georgiana*) 34°27'S. 149°43'E., 23 km E. of Crookwell; RS 1926–57.

Mount Rankin (*Co. Roxburgh*) 33°20'S. 149°31'E., 11 km NW of Bathurst, on Sandy Ck; school 1885–95 and 1957–63; pop. 41 (1933), 340 (2011).

Mount Rivers (*Co. Durham*) 32°22'S. 151°29'E., 26 km W. Dungog, on Paterson R.; Lostock till 1904; mining (antimony), wheat, tobacco, grapes, dairying; cheese factory (Holden's); mine (T.R. Hancock); PO 1861; quarry; school 1882–1924 and 1957–81; telephone

1910; TX 1917–67; pop. 75 (1911), 78 (1933), 82 (1947), 76 (1954), 65 (1961).

Mount Riverview (*Co. Cook*) 33°44'S. 150°38'E., 2 km NE of Blaxland, on Cripple Ck; Angl. C. (St Martin's) 1967; Assemblies of God C. (Blue Mountains City); bushfire 2001; FB 1968 (station b. 1971, additions 1978 and 1981); Gospel C.; 2 reservoirs; school 1971, re-roofed 2012; sewage works 1976; pop. 2,968 (2011).

Mount Russell (*Co. Murchison*) 29°41'S. 150°56'E., 20 km NW of Inverell; farming; Angl. C. (St Matthew's) b. 1925 by Ernest Malcolm Baker, repaired and refurbished, reopened 2007 as Angl. Cath. C. (Our Lady of Walsingham); PO 1911, new one b. 1971, closed 1979; RS 1902, station b. by John Allibone, closed 1980; school 1882–96, new one b. 1920, closed 1969; silo 1934; storm 1957; telephone 1913; TX 1927, closed 1987; pop. 90 (1911), 204 (1933), 161 (1947), 167 (1954), 151 (1961), 239 (2006), 308 (2011).

Mount St Thomas (*Co. Camden*) see Coniston.

Mount Seaview (*Co. Hawes*) 31°24'S. 152°05'E., 61 km W. of Wauchope; school 1955–71; pop. 98 (2006).

Mount Slow (*Co. Gough*) 29°56'S. 151°53'E., 26 km SE of Glen Innes; farming; PO 1927; sawmill (Wetherspoon Bros); telephone 1924; pop. 22 (1933).

Mount Speribo (*Co. Clive*) 29°19'S. 152°08'E., 30 km S. of Tenterfield; timber and grazing; sawmills: Armstrong Bros and Rand, Walter W. Edwards, James Mangleson (sold to Jim McLeod).

Mount Stewart (*Co. Bathurst*) 33°24'S. 149°30'E., 7 km W. of Bathurst; quarry.

Mount Stewart (*Co. Bligh*) see Leadville.

Mount Tallebong (*Co. Blaxland*) 32°49'S. 146°25'E., 73 km W. of Condobolin; mining; PO 1927–29.

Mount Tamar (*Co. Bathurst*) 33°28'S. 149°36'E., 6 km S. of Bathurst; school 1882–1901.

Mount Tarana (*Co. Roxburgh*) see Tarana.

Mount Tenandra (*Co. Leichhardt*) see Tenandra.

Mount Tennyson (*Co. Roxburgh*) 33°30'S. 149°49'E., 22 km SW of Portland, on Stony Ck; molybdenum (disc. 1914 by Kirk and Wade).

Mount Terry (*Co. Camden*) see Albion Park.

Mount Thorley (*Co. Northumberland*) 32°37'S. 151°06'E., 9 km SW of Singleton, on Nine Mile Ck; Angl. C. 1874, extended and vestry added 1884 by I. Thorley, church demolished, replaced 1913; cemetery (31 graves 1929+); colliery (R.W. Miller & Co. Pty Ltd); engineering works (Hedweld Engineering Pty Ltd) estab. 1980 by Ian Hedley; flour mill (wind powered, Philip Thorley) 1841; 2 quarries; school 1880, new one b. 1912, closed 1945; telephone 1929; TX 1929, automatic 1972; pop. 65 (1911), 80 (1933), 62 (1947), 95 (1954), 69 (1961), 181 (2011).

Mount Tomah (*Co. Cook*) 33°33'S. 150°26'E., 17 km E. of Mount Victoria, on Mill Ck; bushfires 1909, 1968, 1979, 1994; electricity 1967; FB 1961 (station b. 1970); sawmill (John Anderson).

Mount Victoria (*Co. Cook*) 33°35'S. 150°15'E., 6 km NW of Blackheath; (incl. Brown Town, estab. *c.*1887); One Tree Hill till 1876; former mountain summer tourist resort; Angl. C. (St Peter's) b. 1875 by Alexander Armstrong, d. by David Macbeath, enlarged 1890 by John McCausland; bushfires 1895, 1919, 1928, 2013; cemetery (77 graves 1891–1991) 1881; Christ. C. (Trinity); coalmine (Blair Athol Coal & Timber Co. Ltd) 1920–23; FB (station b. 1959, new one 2003); hailstorm 1904; PO 1866, closed, bought by L.H. Howell, demolished 1914, new one b. 1897 by W.B. Chessell, d. by Walter Liberty Vernon, reused; police barracks (incl. lock-up) b. 1868 by E. Poulton and Thomas Binks; Presb. C. 1909, reused; PS 1884, new one (incl. lock-up) b. 1887; railway barracks b. 1911–13; railway engine shed 1897; railway turntable, 40 ft (12.2 m), replaced 1885, 50 ft (15.2 m), replaced 1902, 60 ft (18.3 m), new one 75 ft (22.9 m), defunct; reservoirs (incl. concrete one of 100,000 gal. or 454.6 kl); Rom. Cath.

C. (St Paul's) 1895, additions 1907; RS 1868, station b. by Allan Maclean, replaced 1874, extended 1884, 1891, 1898, 1910, refreshment rooms 1912, additional refreshment room 1921; school (usually Mount Vittoria till *c.*1880) 1868, repairs 1900 by W. Field, additions 1906 by James Short and Robert Leslie, d. by Walter Liberty Vernon, new building b. 1913 by W.W. Dunk, additions 1989; sewage works; storm 1898; telegraph 1868, new office b. 1897 by W.B. Chessell, d. by Walter Liberty Vernon, closed 1960; toll-house 1849–76, sold, restoration d. by Peter Buckwell, reused, abandoned; Trinity Christ. C.; TX 1910, automatic 1938; typhoid (woman died) 1898; water supply 1940; Wes. Meth. C. b. 1898 by McCausland; pop. 664 (1891), 556 (1901), 476 (1911), 422 (1933), 435 (1947), 481 (1954), 425 (1961), 406 (1964), 334 (1971–76), 410 (1981), 601 (1986), 718 (1991), 769 (1996), 869 (2001), 828 (2006), 823 (2011).

Mount View (*Co. Northumberland*) 32°51'S. 151°17'E., 8 km W. of Cessnock, on Limestone Ck; farming; bridge (Kings Bridge) over Cedar Ck; PO 1911; school 1881, additions and repairs 1910 by W.J. Brown, closed 1953; telephone 1924; TX 1950; wineries: Bimbadeen Estate 1998, Briar Ridge Vineyard (estab. 1972 by Murray Robson, bought 1989 by John Davis), Farrell's Limestone Creek Vineyard 1980, Jackson's Hill Vineyard 1983, Mount View Estate 1971, Savannah Estate Vineyards (Peterson's) 1982, Tallavera Grove (Davis's) 2000; pop. 158 (1901), 327 (1911), 161 (1933), 152 (1947), 119 (1954), 56 (1961).

Mount View (*Co. Northumberland*) see also Cessnock.

Mount Vincent (*Co. Northumberland*) 32°55'S. 151°29'E., 10 km W. of West Wallsend, on Wallis Ck; agric. and grazing, then dairying; Angl. C. (Christ) b. 1848 by W. Knox Child and Daniel Murrell, closed 1870, (second) b. 1870 also by Child, closed 1909, (third) b. 1910 by Charles Taylor, d. by James Warren Scobie, and graveyard (292 graves 1856+), incl. columbarium; bushfire 1902; cyclone 1902; PO 1859; sawmills: Forbes and Whiting, Henry Hector (boiler explosion 1887), Lister & Co., Monnox Foster & Co. (unroofed 1902), Wyborn & Co.; telephone 1898; pop. 85 (1911), 77 (1933), 102 (1947), 101 (1954), 95 (1961).

Mount Vincent (*Co. Roxburgh*) 33°01'S. 149°55'E., 25 km S. of Rylstone; sawmill; pop. 51 (1933).

Mount Vittoria (*Co. Cook*) see Mount Victoria.

Mount Warning (*Co. Rous*) 28°23'S. 153°17'E., 13 km SW of Murwillumbah.

Mount Warrigal (*Co. Camden*) 34°33'S. 150°51'E., 7 km SE of Dapto, on Lake Illawarra; subdivisions 1964, 1965, 1966, 1969; reservoir; school 1967, damaged 2011; pop. 4,543 (2011).

Mount Werong (*Co. Westmoreland*) 34°05'S. 149°55'E., 42 km S. of Oberon, on Ruby Ck; thrived 1880, now abandoned; mining (gold rush 1880, silver-lead-zinc), farming, grazing; airfield; bushfire 1957; cemetery; dam (mine) on Ruby Ck; foot-bridge (mine) over Ruby Ck; mines: Hell Hole (Blue Mountain), J.D. Inglis 1930–33, Ruby Creek estab. 1898 by J.E. Clarke and F.M. Bartlett, worked 1903, 1908–12, 1919, 1929, The Flat Lode 1911 and 1930–34; PO 1928–38; quarry; tramway (mine); pop. 53 (1933).

Mount White (*Co. Northumberland*) 33°27'S. 151°12'E., 13 km W. of Woy Woy, on Calverts Ck; (incl. Marlow, Wendoree Park, Mangrove Point private village estab. 1952 by A.L. Spring); orchards; bushfire 2006; 2 FB (Mount White and Wendoree Park); PO 1944, burnt down 1992; quarry; school 1953–89; telephone 1940; TX 1940, automatic 1953; wharf b. 1952 by A.L. Spring; pop. 52 (1933), 78 (1947), 97 (1954), 120 (1961).

Mount Wiagdon (*Co. Roxburgh*) 33°11'S. 149°41'E., 27 km N. of Bathurst; goldmines: Bald Hill (Neary and Carmichael) and Mount Wiagdon; quarry.

Mount Wills (*Co. Northumberland*) see Rothbury.

Mount Wilson (*Co. Cook*) 33°30'S. 150°23'E., 15 km NE of Mount Victoria, on Waterfall Ck; Irvine till 1889; orig. disc. 1833 by

William Romaine Govett, rediscovered 1867 by George Bartley Bowen, surveyed and subdivided 1868 by Edward Sanford Wyndham, one lot sold 1870, most lots sold 1875; orig. timber then orchards and mountain retreat for the wealthy; Angl. C. (St George's) 1915, and graveyard (31 graves); bushfires 1952 and 1957; FB (station 1998 d. by Owen Haviland); gale 2011; PO 1896, new one 1922 d. by John D. Moore, closed 1986, sold to Mark and Sue Austin and reused, sold to Colleen Jones; pottery (Cherry Cottage) estab. by Frederick Farrell Mann, bought 1964 by Richard and Jim Prentice; RS 1875, renamed Bell in 1889, relocated 1910; sawmills (incl. Kirk Bros, derelict); school 1957–83; telephone 1915; TX 1916, automatic 1986; pop. 64 (1901), 66 (1933), 80 (1947), 66 (1954), 64 (1961), 220 (2006).

Moura (*Co. Ashburnham*) see Mandagery.

Mourgoung (*Co. Wentworth*) see Mourquong.

Mourquong (*Co. Wentworth*) 34°08'S. 142°10'E., 4 km W. of Gol Gol, on Murray R.; also known as Mourgoung; town gaz. 1851; grapes and oranges; fibrous plaster works (Hycal) estab. 1947 by Tom Phillips and Jack Mathers, bought by CSR and Aust. Gypsum, sold to Boral; fruit packing house; wineries: Hungerford Hill (Aust. Vintage Ltd) and Stanley Wines (formerly part of Hardy Wine Co., now part of Constellation Wines).

Mowabla (*Co. Cunningham*) 32°55'S. 147°05'E., 20 km N. of Condobolin; goldmining; mines: Aulde's, Hutchinson's, Mount Alma (Sam Sperry) 1895, Mysterious or Seberry's Reef 1897 and 1903, Roberts 1903 and 1911; PO 1900; stamper battery 1903; telephone 1916; TX 1928.

Mowbray Park (*Co. Camden*) 34°09'S. 150°33'E., 5 km W. of Picton, on Long Gully; ice works (Wellington Park); school 1907–12 and 1929–48; winery (Nangarin Vineyard Estate); pop. 91 (1954), 47 (2001).

Mowenbah (*Co. Wallace*) 36°28'S. 148°38'E., 6 km S. of Jindabyne, on Mowamba R.; tin mining; pop. 75 (1911).

Mozart (*Co. Westmoreland*) 33°49'S. 149°50'E., 12 km S. of Oberon; school 1945–69.

Mucra (*Co. Urana*) 35°10'S. 146°26'E., 26 km W. of Lockhart.

Mucra (*Co. Urana*) see also Yuluma.

Mudgee (*Co. Wellington*) 32°36'S. 149°35'E., 88 km NE of Orange, on Cudgegong R.; (incl. South Mudgee); disc. 1821 by Lieut. William Lawson and John Blackman, settled by George and Henry Cox, surveyed 1836 by Richard Lewis, estab. 1837 by James Blackman, resurveyed 1837 by Peter Grant Ogilvie, laid out 1837 by N.H. Lewis, jun., village gaz. and first lots sold 1838, thrived 1851–65, munic. 1860–1975; orig. wool, lucerne, maize, then goldmining (alluvial and reef, gold rush 1851), wheat, barley, oats, beef, hort., potatoes, tobacco, wine *c.*1858+, butter, cheese, ham, bacon, poultry, honey, fruit, textiles; abattoir 1965, extended 1971, 1975, 1978, closed, bought 2003 by Fletcher International Exports Pty Ltd; ambulance station b. 1944 by P.G. Flack; Angl. C. (St John the Baptist) b. 1839–41, d. by James Hume, demolished 1860, replacement b. 1858–60 by James Atkinson, d. by William Weaver and William Edmund Kemp, tower added 1870, church altered and re-roofed 1877 by Duncan McFarlane, re-roofed again 1912, additions 1938, re-roofed again 1956, upgraded 1991; Assemblies of God C. (Frontline Christ.) 1973, in former Rom. Cath. C., closed, sold, removed and reused 1996; Baha'i C.; baking powder factory (Champion's); Bapt. C. 1951; bicycle works (Byrnes Bros); biscuit factory (William Lang Nicholson), closed, reused 1901, sold 1908; boot factories: Cohen Sons and H. Schipp, McCamely and Burgess, Nelson and Stephens 1923, A.E. Thomas & Co.; breweries: Broombee, Crossen's 1857 (taken over 1864 by J.K. McArdill and renamed Tipperary Brewery), Mudgee Brewing Co. (estab. 2007 by Garry Leonard), Victoria (estab. 1871 by George John Southward, closed 1888, bought 1891 by George Douglas Young and Robert Heather Ferrier and renamed Federal Brewery, fire 1892, sold 1901 to George

Henry O'Connor, bought back from O'Connor 1904 by George Douglas Young and Robert Heather Ferrier, sold 1916 to Henry Smith, Alfred Cornelius Wade and Jack Birtles, sold 1946 to Federal Brewery Pty Ltd, taken over by Hungerford, Spooner & Co., sold to Robert Thomas Hook and Robert Mitchell, taken over 1953 by Dressler Aust. Pty Ltd and renamed Dressler's Brewery, closed 1956, sold 1958); bridges: first one b. 1859 by James Atkinson, second one b. 1876 by John Ahearn, third one (Holyoake Bridge, timber beam spans) 1913, replacement (concrete girder spans) 1954, 191 ft (58.2 m), over Cudgegong R., and Neville H. Paine Bridge over Lawson Ck; butter factory (Mudgee Dairy Co. Ltd) b. 1876, new one b. 1890 on new site by Adam Spies, ice-making plant added 1899, extended 1961, butter production ceased 1965, chimney demolished 1972; carriage-works: A. Hartcher (burnt down 1918, rebuilt), E.H. Deane 1888 (additions 1899 by G. Collyer and W. Carmichael, fire 1901, Frederick Leslie became a partner 1902, taken over 1917 by P.G. Keighran, taken over and remodelled 1919 by C. Collier & Co.), J.G. Gallatley, Keegan and Casimir (Keegan left partnership in 1912, taken over 1917 by W. Bowen, jun.), Kelly and Milton, Premier (J.F. Bax, additions and alterations 1899, acquired 1901 by H. Hoyle), W. Rope (taken over 1921 by Alfred Singleton), West End Coach Factory (taken over 1917 by Kelly and Milton); cemeteries: general (7,829 graves 1850s+) 1863, incl. columbarium, lawn (800 plots) 1993, memorial park; CH 1845, new one b. 1860–62 by Andrew McCauley, d. by Alexander Dawson, additions 1874 by Silas Winter, additions 1875 by A. M'Lean, additions and alterations 1877 by D. McFarlane and G. Henry, d. by James Johnstone Barnet, additions 1896 by John Dunkley, d. by Walter Liberty Vernon; Christ. Outreach C.; clock tower (war memorial) 1952; confectionary factory (McFarlane Bros) b. 1910 by G. Collyer and W. Carmichael, d. by Harold Robert Hardwick; cordial factories: E.A Brigden, H.O. Butler 1928 (acquired 1938 by R. Lord), Byrne and Stevens, Allan Fitzgerald Cameron, sen. 1881 (brewery added 1901, acquired 1913 by A.J. Lunt, ice-making plant added 1915, taken over 1925 by E.T. Webster), H.J. Collins, Crystal Fountain (Henry Meers, bought 1899 by Charles Gentle), J. Curran 1904 (in former store), Great Western (bought 1899 by Thomas H. Brady, bought 1904 by Charles Gentle, taken over 1905 by George Beckton, sold 1913 to Alan Fitzgerald Cameron, jun.), Robert F. Milne (fire 1863); diphtheria 1887, 1909, 1935; dust storms 1882, 1893, 1902; earth tremors 1862, 1866, 1937; 2 FB (stations b. 1901 and 1974); fibrous plaster works (L.J. Lawsen); fires 1895 and 1897 (2 boys died); floods 2000 and 2003; flour mills: Thomas Chappell 1857 (acquired 1865 by Dickson and Burrows, sold 1885 to George Rouse, substantially rebuilt 1885, modernised 1890, sold 1899, moved to Gulgong and operated by James Loneragan & Co.), Henry Dare (taken over by Arnold, man killed 1857, known as Wilton's 1857–59, closed, bought by James Loneragan & Co. and reused), Great Western Steam Flour Mill (b. 1865 by R. Crossing, modernised 1898), Mudgee Farmers' Co-op. Patent Steam Flour Mills (b. 1893 by James Stodard Casimir and Collier, taken over by James Loneragan & Co., bought 1911 by Great Western Milling Co. Ltd, burnt down 1913); foot-bridges over Cudgegong R.: Glen Willow (suspension) 2014 and Holyoake 2018; foundries: Spies', Stearn's, West End (C.N. Hanson, taken over 1902 by Tom Laing and renamed Phoenix); freezing works: Currabubula Freezing Works Co. 1933 (bought 1934 by Thomas Borthwick A'sia Ltd, demolished 1937) and Mudgee Freezing & Dairying Co. (b. 1907 by Thomas Borthwick & Sons Ltd, closed 1915, reopened, closed 1920, reopened 1921, burnt down 1931, demolished 1932); furniture factories: Dickson & Sons, sold 1890, and William Schnalke, closed and sold 1905; gale 1877; gaol b. 1862 by Arundel Everett and William Stephens, d. by Alexander Dawson, wall b.

1862 by Alan Scot, additions 1873 by J. Dwane, additions 1875 by A. M'Lean, additions and alterations 1877 by D. McFarlane and G. Henry, additions 1896 by Rigby Bros, closed 1904, reused, demolished 1936; gastroenteritis epidemic 1952; gasworks estab. 1885 by Mudgee Gaslight & Coke Co. Ltd, closed 1930, sold 1937; German measles epidemic 1936; hailstorm 1892; heatwave 1882; home furnishings and clothing factory (Jeldi Pty Ltd) o. 1945 in former munitions factory; hospital 1840, (second) 1852, (third) 1858, (fourth) b. 1875 by Silas Winter, d. by Edmund Thomas Blacket, re-roofed 1895 by John Miller, additions 1910 by G. Collyer and W. Carmichael, d. by Harold Robert Hardwick, alterations 1913 also by Collyer and Carmichael, additions 1946 by Fuller, closed 1955, demolished, (fifth) 1955, extended 1967, additions 2010; Jehovah's Witnesses C.; joineries: George Knight 1917, R. Piper, Silas Winter; lock-up b. 1883 by M'Farlane and Stoddart, demolished; meadery (Mount Vincent) estab. 1972 by Jane Nevell, closed; measles epidemic 1928; meat works (Bourke Meat Preserving Co.) 1892, new works 1938; monumental stone works: T.W. Collier & Son and W.M. Reynolds 1932; PO: Mudgee 1840 (new one 1862 d. by Alexander Dawson, new one b. 1875 by Silas Winter, alterations 1887 by John Miller, sen., d. by James Johnstone Barnet, additions 1888 by John Miller, jun., additions and alterations 1902 by Alfred Stephens, d. by Alfred Moser, repairs 1907 by Albert Murphy) and South Mudgee 1936; police barracks 1867, new barracks b. 1893 by C.B. Smith, additions and alterations 1897 by John Miller, sen., alterations 1899 by Stoddart and Casimir; pound (stock) 1842; POW control centre 1944; powerhouse (A.E. Grace, taken over 1928 by local council) 1912; Presb. C.: St Luke's (b. 1951, sold 1962 to Anglicans), St Paul's (b. 1858 by Andrew McCauley, reused, demolished 1991, replacement b. 1875–78 by John Webb, d. by Thomas Rowe, restored and re-roofed 1942); Prim. Meth. C. 1874, sold 1902; PS (incl. lock-up) b. by Thomas Purdy, demolished, replacement b. by Silas Winter, d. by James Johnstone Barnet, additions 1868 by James Atkinson, repairs 1916 by John Belford, new one b. 1925 by Manuel, additions and alterations 1931; railway barracks 1883, new barracks 1987; railway coal stage b. 1883 by John Ahearn; railway engine shed b. 1883 by John Ahearn; railway locomotive depot 1891, demolished 1987; railway turntable, 50 ft (15.2 m), replaced (William Sellers & Co.) 1903, 60 ft (18.3 m), derelict; reservoirs (incl. The Malakoff b. 1870 by Thomas Chappell, 300,000 gal. or 1,363.8 kl, demolished 1970, and one b. 1932); rifle range (3 km SW); Rom. Cath. C.: St Mary's 1843 (demolished), Presentation of the Blessed Virgin Mary (b. 1860 by Trier and Anderson, d. by William Munro, rebuilding and enlargement 1876 begun by John Webb but completed by Henry Donaldson, d. by Edward Gell, alterations 1903, steeple 1911 d. by Arthur John Paul Watson, restored 1989), St Martin de Tours (removed from Dungeree, rebuilt by James Hoctor and reopened 1936, closed, sold 1973); RS 1884, station b. by John Ahearn and John Miller, sen., d. by John Whitton, refreshment room 1911, services ceased 1985, station closed 1992, reused; sale-yards b. 1899 by John Bedford, d. by Harold Robert Hardwick, extended 1905 and 1906, new yards (H.A. Chick) 1937; Salv. Army C. b. 1889 by Collier and Cassimer; sawmills: W. Watterson (sold 1929) and Woolpack (William Smith); scarlet fever 1876 and 1927; schools: Cudgegong Valley 1984 (b. by White Industries Ltd), Mudgee 1855 (new one b. 1857, replacement 1878 d. by George Allen Mansfield, additions 1896 and 1903, alterations and repairs 1907 by Albert Murphy, repairs 1908 by G. Collyer and W. Carmichael, additions and alterations 1910 by Arnold Rigby, additions 1914 by G. Collyer and W. Carmichael, additions 1929, 1956, 1960, 1965, 1967, 1986, 1989), Mudgee HS 1916 (additions 1956, 1966, 1973, 1976, major upgrade 1996), South Mudgee (Redbank till 1885) 1884, repairs 1898 by G.

Collyer and W. Carmichael, enlarged 1912, closed 1964; SD Adventist C. b. 1924 by Michell and Behrens; sewage works b. 1931–35 d. by Fleming, new treatment plant 2013; small arms factory (World War II); soap-works estab. by Samuel Henry Wilton, leased 1900 to William Selff, bought 1914 by Blundell and William Selff, Selff later bought out Blundell's share, taken over by Henry Thomas Selff, sold 1918; storms 1880, 1903, 1916, 1933, 1939, 1946, 1951, 2017; streets gas lit 1886; tanneries: Crossing's and A.E. Thomas & Co.; TC, erection of building 1954 by Carmichael and Rickwood, additions 1958 and 1969, became a campus of Western Institute in 1992; telegraph 1861, new office 1862 d. by Alexander Dawson, new one b. 1875 by Silas Winter, alterations 1887 d. by James Johnstone Barnet, additions 1888 by John Miller, sen., additions and alterations 1902 by Alfred Stephens, d. by Alfred Moser, repairs 1907 by Albert Murphy; telephone (South Mudgee) 1937; TX 1900, new one 1948, automatic 1964; typhoid 1901, 1902, 1903; Unit. C. (orig. Wes. Meth.) b. 1863–66 by Silas Winter, d. by George Allen Mansfield, renovated 1918, extensions 1927 d. by Harold Robert Hardwick, renovated 1946, re-roofed 1975, later extended; waterworks b. 1886 by Adam Spies, new works 1899, water supply augmentation 1986; weir on Cudgegong R.; Wes. Meth. C. 1853, closed, reused 1927; whooping cough epidemics 1907, 1928, 1945; winery (Elliot Rocke Estate) estab. 1987 as Seldom Seen Wines; wool-scour (Bruce, Rouse and Sykes) 1902; wool stores: Blackman and Conway, Crossing and Cox (fire 1878), C.F. Saunders; pop. 131 (1846), 292 (1851), 803 (1856), 1,507 (1861), 1,786 (1871), 2,492 (1881), 2,410 (1891), *c.*2,840 (1895), 2,789 (1901), 3,621 (1911), 3,993 (1933), 4,160 (1941), 4,178 (1947), 5,294 (1954), 5,312 (1961), 5,372 (1966), 5,583 (1971), 5,724 (1976), 6,015 (1981), 6,576 (1986), 7,447 (1991), 8,195 (1996), 8,619 (2001), 8,249 (2006), 9,830 (2011). (See also Bombira Hill and Redbank.)

Mudgee River (*Co. Wellington*) 32°37'S. 149°15'E., 30 km E. of Wellington, on Cudgegong R.; pop. 43 (1933).

Mudmelong (*Co. St Vincent*) see Araluen.

Mugabeen (*Co. Nicholson*) 33°24'S. 145°47'E., 24 km E. of Hillston; telephone 1929; TX 1933–40.

Mugincoble (*Co. Ashburnham*) 33°11'S. 148°13'E., 8 km SE of Parkes; army stores depot 1942, reused; RS (Bartley's Creek till 1911) 1901, station b. by Frederick Lemm, jun. and Thomas Edward Spencer, closed 1974; school 1897–1907; pop. 39 (1933), 64 (1954).

Mugwill (*Co. Murray*) 35°41'S. 149°12'E., 32 km N. of Queanbeyan; school 1881, new one b. 1884 by Sanders Helman, closed 1894, demolished.

Muirbank (*Co. Raleigh*) 30°46'S. 152°40'E., 24 km W. of Macksville, on Taylors Arm; bananas; school 1958–67; telephone 1926; TX 1943.

Mulberrygong (*Co. Waradgery*) 34°30'S. 145°15'E., 38 km E. of Hay, on Murrumbidgee R.

Mulbring (*Co. Northumberland*) 32°54'S. 151°29'E., 9 km W. of West Wallsend, on Wallis Ck; village gaz. 1880; timber, dairying, fruit; bridges: one b. 1895 over Church Ck, one over Wallis Ck, Lister Bridge over Brunkerville Ck; FB; foot-bridge over Church Ck; measles epidemic 1934; PO 1900; PS 1860, new one (incl. lock-up) b. 1909 by Richard Partridge-Wall, closed 1934; quarry; reservoir; sawmill (Thomas Chappell Hector) 1871; school (Sugarloaf till 1883) 1849, new buildings b. 1884 by Thomas Humphries Cooper; telephone 1908; TX (automatic) 1955; Unit. C. (orig. Meth.) 1915, and graveyard (224 graves 1871+), incl. columbarium; Wes. Meth. C. 1842, (second) 1853, (third) 1872; pop. 122 (1871), 264 (1891), 322 (1901), 228 (1911), 295 (1933), 242 (1947), 241 (1954), 223 (1961), 223 (1976), 258 (1981), 291 (1986), 301 (1991), 298 (1996), 291 (2001), 316 (2006), 356 (2011).

Mulchacera (*Co. Barrona*) 29°46'S. 145°17'E.,

75 km NW of Bourke.

Muldiva (*Co. Fitzroy*) 30°18'S. 152°34'E., 14 km W. of Dorrigo, on Muldiva Ck; sawmills: Davidson's and Mulhearn Bros 1935; telephone 1930; TX 1930–44.

Mulga Valley (*Co. Fitzgerald*) 30°26'S. 143°04'E., 125 km N. of Wilcannia; TX.

Mulgawarrina (*Co. Cowper*) 30°44'S. 147°00'E., 134 km W. of Coonamble, on Bogan R.; pop. 22 (1933).

Mulgoa Forest (*Co. Camden*) see Orangeville.

Mulgoa Forest Mountain (*Co. Camden*) see Silverdale.

Mulgowrie (*Co. Georgiana*) 34°14'S. 149°11'E., 36 km NW of Crookwell, on Mulgowrie Ck; school 1959–72.

Mulguthrie (*Co. Cunningham*) 33°12'S. 147°26'E., 29 km SE of Condobolin; PO 1884–87; pop. 21 (1933).

Mulhearn's Siding (*Co. Fitzroy*) see Lloyd.

Mulla Creek (*Co. Parry*) 31°11'S. 151°13'E., 28 km SE of Tamworth, on Mulla Ck; pop. 95 (1911), 89 (1933), 51 (1947), 61 (1954).

Mullaley (*Co. Pottinger*) 31°06'S. 149°55'E., 36 km W. of Gunnedah, on Coxs Ck; village gaz. 1882; sheep and cattle then wheat, sorghum, sunflowers, barley, oats, beans; Angl. C. (St Phillip's) 1914–60, replaced on new site; cemetery; artesian bore sunk 1903 by Donovan and M'Cray; cyclones 1900 (man killed and most buildings destroyed) and 1996; drought 1964; engineering works estab. 1993 by David and Vicki Isbester; FB 1952; Meth. C. 1909; mouse plague 1984; PO 1881, destroyed 1900; PS 1902, new one b. 1938 by Rose and French; reservoir, 50,000 gal. (227.3 kl), 1972; Rom. Cath. C. (St Teresa a Jesu Infante) 1937, extended; school 1910, additions 1959 and 1961, additional (reused) building 1973; telephone 1894; TX 1910, automatic 1986; water reticulation 1972; pop. 57 (1901), 359 (1911), 63 (1933), 84 (1947), 147 (1954), 94 (1961), 217 (2006).

Mullamuddy (*Co. Wellington*) 32°39'S. 149°40'E., 11 km SE of Mudgee, on Cudgegong R.; goldmining; butter factory (T.H. Foyster), closed 1914; earth tremor 2010; FB (station b. 2014); school 1880, repairs 1883 by W. Newton, reused, replacement b. 1911 by J. Bartlett, closed 1960; snow 1899; TX (automatic); Union C., dismantled and rebuilt 1941, closed and dismantled in 1961; Wes. Meth. C. 1873; winery (Optimiste) estab. 1998 by Steve and Sharlene Dadd; pop. 120 (1911), 118 (1933), 77 (1947).

Mullanjandra (*Co. Goulburn*) see Mullengandra.

Mullaway (*Co. Fitzroy*) 30°05'S. 153°12'E., 4 km N. of Woolgoolga, on Tasman Sea; school 1994; pop. 414 (2006), 523 (2011).

Mullenderee (*Co. St Vincent*) 35°53'S. 150°05'E., 3 km N. of Moruya; settled 1828 by Francis Flanagan; agric.; aeroplane crash (6 killed) 1945; cordial factory (Howard's), bought by Pollock Bros; floods 1860, 1863, 1952; PO 1857; pound (stock); typhoid 1907; pop. 156 (1911), 95 (1933), 161 (1947), 51 (1954).

Mullengandra (*Co. Goulburn*) 35°54'S. 147°10'E., 31 km NE of Albury, on Mullanjandra Ck; formerly Dixson's Swamp; village gaz. 1871 as Mullanjandra; mining (tin), grazing, agric., dairying, wine, fruit; Angl. C. (St Luke's) 1876, demolished 1927, replaced (St James's) 1927, rededicated (St Luke's) 1934, closed, sold 2014; cemetery 1884; FB 1932; PO 1888; Presb. C. (St John's) b. 1888 by P.H. Stewart & Son; quarry; school (Mullenjandra till *c.*1880) 1871–1921, reopened 1952, new building 1962, closed 2017; stamper battery; telephone 1905; TX 1925, automatic 1956; pop. 172 (1901), 110 (1911), 131 (1933), 117 (1947), 137 (1954), 111 (1961), 320 (2011).

Mullengrove (*Co. King*) 34°29'S. 149°10'E., 28 km W. of Crookwell, on Jerrara Ck; quarry; school 1887, new building b. 1911 by W. Fielding, closed 1933, reopened 1957, closed 1964.

Mullengudgery (*Co. Oxley*) 31°41'S. 147°26'E., 26 km SE of Nyngan; grazing; bushfire 1951; PO 1883; RS 1883–1975, station demolished 1978; telegraph 1890–93; telephone 1910; TX 1914, automatic 1986; pop. 107 (1911), 144

(1933), 46 (1947), 34 (1954), 70 (1961).

Mullengullenga (*Co. Argyle*) see Bronti.

Mullenjandra (*Co. Goulburn*) see Mullengandra.

Mullens Crossing (*Co. Clarke*) 30°34'S. 152°14'E., 55 km E. of Armidale, on Styx R.

Mullet Creek (*Co. Northumberland*) 33°29'S. 151°16'E., 6 km W. of Woy Woy, on Mullet Ck; PO 1885–89; PS 1888; RS 1888–97; school 1884–89.

Mullet Creek Junction (*Co. Northumberland*) see Wondabyne.

Mulligans Plain (*Co. Wakool*) 35°20'S. 143°53'E., 39 km NW of Barham.

Mulli Mulli (*Co. Buller*) 28°25'S. 152°35'E., 47 km NW of Kyogle, on Tooloom Ck.

Mullion (*Co. Cowley*) 35°08'S. 148°53'E., 33 km S. of Yass; pop. 56 (1933), 80 (1961).

Mullion Creek (*Co. Wellington*) 33°08'S. 149°07'E., 17 km N. of Orange, on Mulyan Ck; estab. *c.*1864; gold (alluvial), wool, orchards; Angl. C. (St Paul's) 1920; electricity 1954; FB; fire 1909; fruit cool store 1956; PO 1880; railway turntable 1898, 50 ft (15.2 m); rifle range 1910; Rom. Cath. C. 1916 (former engine driver's shed), new one (St Brendan's), and graveyard 2006, incl. columbarium; RS 1880–1976, station sold 1987; school 1881, new building b. 1895 by William Bailey Hurrell, new building 1968 (removed from Farnham); stamper battery (5 head) erected 1905 by James Spratt; telegraph 1880; telephone 1913; TX 1921–71; Wes. Meth. C. 1877; pop. 149 (1901), 165 (1911), 239 (1933), 159 (1947), 98 (1954), 194 (1961), 576 (2011).

Mulloon (*Co. Murray*) 35°16'S. 149°36'E., 15 km E. of Bungendore, on Mulloon Ck; mining and grazing; airfield; brick-kiln; copper smelter 1874; FB; mines (Scotsdale Copper Mining Co. NL): Mulloon Copper Mine 1921–24, New Griffin Shaft 1873–1924, Old Griffin Shaft and Mount Fisher Mine 1873, 1898–1924, 1952, Scotts 1921–24, Scotts North Boundary 1921–24; PO 1873–1930; telephone 1907; TX 1917–56; pop. 112 (2011).

Mullumbimby (*Co. Rous*) 28°33'S. 153°30'E., 27 km S. of Murwillumbah, on Brunswick R.; site reserved 1872, reserve surveyed 1881 by James Anderson, village surveyed 1887, first land sales 1888, thrived *c.*1900, munic. 1908–79; timber, dairying 1894+, agric. 1894+, cattle, pigs, maize, fruit (incl. bananas), nuts, alternative lifestyle centre; ambulance station (in converted house) 1937; Angl. C. (St John's) 1905, new one (St Martin's War Memorial) b. 1921–25 by W.B. King, d. by Louis Reginald Williams; Bapt. C. 1963; brickworks: Fred Bartlett Frost, closed 1947, and Mullumbimby Brick, Tile & Pipe Co., closed; bridge (Federation Bridge) b. 1901 by David Rankin, demolished, replaced 1930 by Concrete General Constructions Ltd, over Brunswick R.; bushfire 1936; butter factories: Foley Bros Pty Ltd (b. 1937 by D. Gallagher, d. by Richard Wildridge & Co. Ltd) and J. Ford; carriage-works (E.C. Uhr) 1909; cemetery (3,370 graves) 1892, incl. columbaria; CH b. 1908 by Charles Benaud Smith, d. by Walter Liberty Vernon, additions and alterations 1989; cordial factories: William David Bryant (sold 1930 to Earl Starr) and F.A. Row (sold 1915); dengue fever 1916 and 1926; electricity 1926; 2 FB (incl. station b. 1956); fires 1911, 1963, 1983; floods 1921, 2001, 2003; gale 1950; hospital (War Memorial) 1949, burnt down and replaced 1968, closed 2016; Jehovah's Witnesses C. 1974, extended 1985; measles epidemic 1946; Meth. C. b. 1908 by H.T. Blanch, new one 1963; monumental stone works (A. Beckinsale & Co.); PO 1891, new one b. 1907 by George Edward Moore, closed and reused; Presb. C. (St Andrew's) 1903, closed, sold, relocated and reused; PS 1897, new one b. 1908 by Charles Benaud Smith, d. by Walter Liberty Vernon, upgraded 2006 by T.F. Woollam & Son Pty Ltd; reservoir (concrete), 200,000 gal. (909.2 kl); Rom. Cath. C. b. 1900 by John Godding, second one b. 1905–7 by O'Shea, d. by Barr and Pullinger, third one (St John's) 1974; RS 1894, station b. by William Mitchell, closed 2004, reused; sale-yards (Enterprize, Robert Raymond Mallett) 1917; Salv. Army C. 1905, sold and removed; sawmills: John

E. Glasgow (removed 1897 from Byron Bay, bought 1902 by J.N. Hollingworth & Co., Robert Raymond Mallett joined 1903 as partner and firm became Hollingworth and Mallett till 1916 when the latter left, sold 1964 to Standard Sawmilling, closed 1964) and D.E. Mann; schools: primary 1888, new one b. 1891 by W.J. Gillies, additions 1903 by A. Kendrick, additions 1935, 1956, 1991, and HS 1955, additions 1959, 1964, 1967, 1970, 1985, 2007; SD Adventist C. 1945, new one 1961; sewerage 1964; storms 1927 and 2000; streets lit by hydro-electricity 1925; telegraph 1898; telephone 1892; TX 1909, automatic 1976; Unit. C.; water supply 1939, filtration plant 1941, augmentation 1991; whooping cough epidemic 1946; pop. 428 (1901), 1,509 (1911), *c.*1,500 (1924), 1,362 (1933), *c.*1,500 (1941), 1,609 (1947), 2,017 (1954), 1,966 (1961), 1,981 (1966), 1,889 (1971), 2,028 (1976), 2,234 (1981), 2,453 (1986), 2,612 (1991), 2,870 (1996), 3,000 (2001), 3,129 (2006), 3,164 (2011).

Mullumbimby Creek (*Co. Rous*) 28°33'S. 153°28'E., 3 km W. of Mullumbimby, on Mullumbimby Ck; sawmill (Alf Wallace), burnt down 1923; school (Mooyabil till 1945) 1904, new building b. 1923 by John P. Slapp, closed 1964; pop. 131 (1933), 164 (1947), 204 (1954), 178 (1961), 338 (2006), 630 (2011).

Mullylargah (*Co. Ashburnham*) see Larras Lee.

Mulwala (*Co. Denison*) 35°59'S. 146°00'E., 35 km W. of Corowa, on Lake Mulwala (created 1939); laid out 1858 by Philip Francis Adams, thrived 1860s–70s; agric., rice, grazing; Angl. C. 1863, replacement (St Andrew's) 1927, and graveyard; bridge (steel, with lift span) b. 1890–92, approaches re-decked 1902 by Barry Christian, replacement bridge (steel Pratt trusses) 1925 d. by Percy Allan, over Murray R.; cemetery 1877; CH (incl. lock-up) 1887 d. by James Johnstone Barnet, extended 1985; customs-house; diphtheria 1904; electricity 1937; FB (station b. 1984); munitions factory (Commonwealth) 1943; PO 1864; PS 1868; punts: James McRae 1855, new one 1857 and E. Pettier, sunk 1870, refloated, damaged 1890, across Murray R.; 3 reservoirs; Rom. Cath. C. (St Brigid's); RS (Victorian railway); sawmills: W.B. Cairnes 1886, and King and Jones; school 1874, new one b. 1877 by C. Johnson, new building b. 1891 by E.J. Crocker, alterations 1897 by Andrew Jepson, additions and alterations 1902 by William James Mason, remodelled 1930, additions 1964 and 1968; sewerage 1969; snowstorm 1882; telegraph 1881; tornado 2013; TX 1910–21; water reticulation 1944, augmentation 1990; weir (Yarrawonga) b. 1935–39, 23 ft (7 m) high, hydro-electric power station added 1994, wall strengthened 2002, on Murray R.; pop. 206 (1891), 417 (1901), 636 (1911), 723 (1933), 617 (1947), 892 (1954), 830 (1961), 827 (1966), 862 (1971), 840 (1976), 1,034 (1981), 1,330 (1986), 1,701 (1991), 1,593 (1996), 1,677 (2001), 1,624 (2006), 1,904 (2011).

Mulwaree (*Co. Argyle*) see Goulburn.

Mulwee (*Co. Gloucester*) 32°43'S. 151°57'E., 6 km S. of Karuah, on Big Swan Bay; brickworks; 2 quarries; school 1905–22 and 1948–92; telephone 1955; TX 1955–80.

Mulyan (*Co. Bathurst*) see Cowra.

Mulyan (*Co. Wellington*) see Clergate.

Mulyandry (*Co. Forbes*) 33°32'S. 148°08'E., 20 km SE of Forbes; school 1902–7; quarry; TX (automatic); pop. 73 (1947), 87 (1954), 103 (1961), 124 (2006).

Mumbil (*Co. Wellington*) 32°44'S. 149°03'E., 21 km SE of Wellington, on Long Gully; estab. 1879, thrived 1950+; farming and grazing; Angl. C. (St Mary's) 1906, destroyed 1925, replaced 1926 by B.T. Male, renovated 1937, new one 1951; grasshopper infestation 1925; PO 1888; PS 1951–66; Rom. Cath. C. (St Therese's) 1950 (removed from Fashions Mount), closed, sold and reused; RS (orig. Burrendong) 1885–1976; school 1881, new building b. 1884 by Frederick H. Kennard, sold 1917 to Charles Stein, acquired by T.W. Barry and moved to Kerrs Creek, new school 1917; storms 1902 and 1925; telegraph 1890; TX 1915, automatic 1979; pop. 167 (1911), 163 (1933), 133 (1947), 436 (1954), 975 (1961), 227 (1986), 421 (2011).

Mummel (*Co. Argyle*) 34°41'S. 149°36'E., 14 km NW of Goulburn, on Dixons Ck; formerly Mummell; estab. 1854; grazing and orchards; bushfire 1953; flood 1860; mine (copper); PO 1865; pound (stock) 1854; Rom. Cath. C. (St Patrick's) 1855, reused, new one (Sacred Heart) b. 1878–80 by John Murphy, and graveyard (burials 1898+); school (East Mummell till 1876) 1870–1906, reopened 1907, closed 1911; slate works (Wilkins and Bool); storm 1908; telephone 1922; TX 1922–60; Wes. Meth. C. b. 1859 by George Bool and Adams; pop. 127 (1901), 105 (1911), 58 (1933), 54 (1947).

Mummell (*Co. Argyle*) see Merrilla and Mummel.

Mummell East (*Co. Argyle*) see Mummel.

Mummulgum (*Co. Rous*) 28°51'S. 152°48'E., 24 km W. of Casino, on Deep Ck; farming and dairying; land sale 1854; Angl. C. (St Mary's) b. 1907 by W.G. Mackney, d. by William Gill, renovated 1951, closed, sold 2015, reused; bushfire 1926; PO 1913; quarry; Rom. Cath. C. (St Patrick's) b. 1878–80, new one (Our Lady of Fatima) b. 1952 by Jordan Bros, d. by A.E. Surtees, closed, sold 2001, 2010, 2011, 2015, reused; sawmill (Pidcock Bros Ltd); school (2 km NE) 1917 b. by G. Pidcock, sold and removed 1926, new one b. 1925 on new site by Mark T. Edwards, extended 1934 by Diyal Singh, additions 2010; telephone 1911; TX 1916, automatic 1973; pop. 65 (1901), 130 (1911), 244 (1933), 329 (1947), 199 (1954), 162 (1961), 90 (2001), 259 (2011).

Munanbang (*Co. Macquarie*) see Pembrooke.

Mundamia (*Co. St Vincent*) see Nowra.

Mundarlo (*Co. Wynyard*) 35°05'S. 147°50'E., 26 km W. of Gundagai, on Murrumbidgee R.; village gaz. 1878, bypassed by highway 1938; Angl. C. (St Peter's) b. 1877 by James Tilsley, rebuilt and restored 1921; bushfire 1904; cemetery 1886; PO 1872–73; school (6 km N.) 1880–84 (Hillas Creek) and 1955–71; TX (automatic) 1966; pop. 52 (1901), 91 (1911), 74 (1933), 217 (2006).

Mundarragong (*Co. Wellesley*) 36°55'S. 149°03'E., 16 km W. of Bombala, on Bombala R.; airfield.

Mundawa (*Co. Durham*) 32°29'S. 151°14'E., 10 km NE of Singleton; school (Tanilba till 1888) 1882–1904.

Mundawaddery (*Co. Mitchell*) 35°24'S. 146°58'E., 15 km N. of Henty; formerly Mundawaddra; cemetery 1888; Presb. C. 1925; school 1891–93 and 1905–39; TX (automatic) 1966; pop. 105 (1911), 54 (1933), 53 (1947).

Mundawaddra (*Co. Mitchell*) see Mundawaddery.

Munderoo (*Co. Selwyn*) 35°51'S. 147°53'E., 15 km SW of Tumbarumba, on Munderoo Ck; Angl. C. (St James's) 1901, chancel added 1915, closed, sold 2019; bridge (The Glen Bridge) b. 1941 by D. Embery, over Munderoo Ck; pop. 26 (1933).

Mundiwa (*Co. Townsend*) 35°34'S. 145°01'E., 5 km SE of Deniliquin; TX (automatic).

Mundongo (*Co. Buccleuch*) 35°17'S. 148°15'E., 3 km N. of Tumut; school 1883–1983; pop. 101 (1911), 50 (1961), 215 (2011).

Mundoonan (*Co. Murray*) 34°54'S. 149°05'E., 16 km SE of Yass; Angl. C. (St Luke's) 1901, new one (St Mary Magdalene) b. 1912 by E.A. Bowden; school 1862–66 and 1885–93; Unit. C. (orig. Wes. Meth.) 1863, re-roofed and repaired 1912, closed 1986, and graveyard (14 graves); pop. 55 (1911).

Mundooran (*Co. Napier*) see Mendooran.

Mundowey (*Co. Darling*) 30°47'S. 150°55'E., 18 km E. of Manilla, on Halls Ck; Presb. C. 1927.

Mungay Creek (*Co. Dudley*) 30°55'S. 152°41'E., 25 km NW of Kempsey, on Mungay Ck; antimony (disc. 1877), farming, dairying; mine (Corangula Antimony Co.), closed 1893; PO 1927; PS; school 1907–65; smelter; telephone 1923; TX 1952–61; pop. 119 (1933), 78 (1947), 81 (1954).

Mungeribar (*Co. Narromine*) 32°08'S. 148°07'E., 16 km NW of Narromine; farming and grazing; FB; RS (Bragg's Siding till 1895) 1892–1974; silo 1935; TX (automatic) 1972; pop. 24 (1933).

Mungery (*Co. Kennedy*) 32°34'S. 148°01'E., 23

km NW of Peak Hill, on Bogan R.; bushfire 1926; FB; PO 1910; school 1957–71; storm 1926; TX (automatic) 1972; Union C. 1927; pop. 79 (1911), 160 (1933), 228 (1947), 67 (1954), 88 (1961).

Munghorn (*Co. Phillip*) 32°26'S. 149°48'E., 26 km E. of Gulgong, on Cooyal Ck; school 1880–1909.

Mungie Bundie (*Co. Courallie*) 29°30'S. 149°58'E., 11 km E. of Moree; RS 1901, station b. by E.W. Rowland, relocated 1909, closed 1975.

Mungindi (*Co. Benarba*) 28°59'S. 148°59'E., 99 km NW of Moree, on Barwon R.; surveyed 1881, village gaz. 1886, first lots sold 1888; river port 1893+, grazing, cattle, wheat, cotton; airport 1963; ambulance station 1939; Angl. C. (St James's) b. 1901–4; brick-kiln (W. Kelly); bridge b. 1878–80 by Scott Bros, new one (Dare timber truss) b. 1914 by Lawson and Waldron, 202 ft (61.6 m), replaced 2010, over Barwon R.; bushfire 1951; cemeteries: general (507 graves 1895+) 1896 and lawn; CH (incl. lock-up) b. 1899 by Roland; cordial factories: James Charles Matthews, H.E. Mortimer, Richard William and Margaret Valentine Passmore, George Tillman; cotton gin (Namoi Cotton Co-op. Ltd) 1992; droughts 1965 and 1980; electricity 1939; FB; fires 1912 (most buildings destroyed), 1917, 1929, 1935, 1936, 1966, 1968; floods 1890, 1921, 1950, 1956, 1974, 1976, 1998; ice works (acquired 1931 by George Tillman); levee 1981; measles epidemic 1930; PO 1867, new one b. 1901 by W. Robert Wilson; powerhouse (L.J. Bingham); PS 1882, new one b. 1899 by Roland; railway turntable, 60 ft (18.3 m); 2 reservoirs (incl. tower); Rom. Cath. C. (St Joseph's) 1911; RS 1914–73, reused; sawmill; school 1894 b. by Harris, additions 1913 by D. M'Cune, new building b. 1939 by A.E. Yard Pty Ltd, additions 1960, 1966, 1973, 2010; sewerage 1973; storm 1954; streets electric lit 1937; telegraph 1881; TX 1910, automatic 1987; water supply 1939, augmentation 1987; weir 1937; Wes. Meth. C. 1899; pop. 62 (1891), 330 (1901), 601 (1911), 669 (1933), 813 (1947), 789 (1954), 773 (1961), 834 (1966), 735 (1971), 606 (1976), 707 (1981), 682 (1986), 660 (1991), 648 (1996), 645 (2001), 545 (2006), 485 (2011), 601 (2016).

Mungle (*Co. Stapylton*) 28°50'S. 150°24'E., 26 km S. of Boggabilla; RS 1932–74.

Mungo Brush (*Co. Gloucester*) 32°33'S. 152°19'E., 18 km SE of Bulahdelah, on Tasman Sea; gale 1948; wharf, destroyed 1948, rebuilt, destroyed again.

Munmurra (*Co. Bligh*) 32°11'S. 149°58'E., 37 km W. of Merriwa; farming and grazing; PO 1927; telephone 1921; TX 1928; pop. 43 (1933).

Munna (*Co. Wellington*) 32°32'S. 149°34'E., 7 km N. of Mudgee on Cudgegong R.; goldmine (Crossing Reef or Town View) <1934 and 1934–38; railway bridge (timber truss) 1909, over Cudgegong R.; RS 1909, station b. by Reid and Castles, closed 1974.

Munni (*Co. Gloucester*) 32°18'S. 151°41'E., 13 km NW of Dungog, on Williams R.; dairying; bridge over Williams R.; cemetery; FB; school 1883–1939; telephone 1911; Union C. b. 1900 by Rumbel Bros, d. by Charles Herbert Davy Button, closed 1951, sold 1955 to Smith and dismantled; pop. 101 (1901), 40 (1933), 51 (1947), 90 (1954), 64 (1961).

Munns Crossing (*Co. Wellington*) 32°35'S. 149°15'E., 29 km E. of Wellington, on Cudgegong R.

Munyabla (*Co. Urana*) 35°30'S. 146°52'E., 15 km W. of Henty; settled by German immigrants, surveyed 1881; wheat; cemetery (4 km E.); Lutheran C. (St John's) 1888–1913, new one 1913 on new site; RS 1920–75; school (Eulenstein till 1894) 1893–1935; silo 1928; telephone 1915; TX 1923; pop. 62 (1911), 55 (1933), 68 (1947).

Munyabla (*Co. Urana*) see also Pleasant Hills.

Munyang (*Co. Wallace*) 36°21'S. 148°25'E., 6 km N. of Perisher Valley, on Snowy R.; laid out 1950 as temporary construction camp for Snowy Mountains Hydro-Electric Scheme; power station (Guthega) b. 1951–55 by Selmer Engineering Pty Ltd; pop. 570 (1954).

Munyaree Flat (*Co. Macquarie*) 31°51'S.

152°18'E., 8 km NW of Wingham, on Dingo Ck.

Murabah (*Co. Phillip*) 32°27'S. 149°42'E., 17 km SE of Gulgong, on Cooyal Ck.

Murga (*Co. Ashburnham*) 33°22'S. 148°33'E., 17 km NE of Eugowra, on Mandagery Ck; estab. 1862; timber, tobacco, farming, grazing; bridge, destroyed 1950, replacement (O'Neils Bridge) b. 1953 by Clarrie Howarth and John and Frank Tracey, over Mandagery Ck; flood 1950; goldmine (Claytons or Nangar Range); hailstorm 1863; PO 1862; pound (stock) 1863; quarry, abandoned; sawmill, abandoned and derelict; school 1954, closed 1966, building moved to Canowindra and reused; tobacco factory (Campbell's); telephone 1907; TX 1914, automatic 1976; pop. *c.*50 (1866), 102 (1911), 123 (1933), 89 (1947), 111 (1954), 92 (1961), 201 (2006).

Muriel (*Co. Canbelego*) 31°33'S. 146°32'E., 62 km W. of Nyngan; never developed; goldmining; mines: Butler's, Fettler's, Golden Horseshoe, Mitchell's, Russel's, Toomey's, True Blue; RS (Muriel Tank Platform) 1899–1974.

Muriel Tank Platform (*Co. Canbelego*) see Muriel.

Murlingbung (*Co. Wallace*) 36°14'S. 148°45'E., 16 km NW of Berridale; farming and grazing; flour mill; PO 1927; telephone 1924; TX 1925.

Muronbung (*Co. Lincoln*) 32°11'S. 148°58'E., 33 km E. of Dubbo, on Spicers Ck; farming; PO 1920; RS 1918–75, station removed 1980; silo; telephone 1923; TX 1923–73; pop. 35 (1933).

Murphys Flat (*Co. Clarence*) 29°30'S. 153°02'E., 17 km W. of Maclean, on Sportsmans Ck.

Murra (*Co. Wakool*) 35°25'S. 143°48'E., 39 km NW of Barham; airfield.

Murragamba (*Co. Phillip*) 32°18'S. 149°48'E., 26 km E. of Gulgong; farming and grazing; PO 1927–38; telephone 1921; TX 1943–63; pop. 33 (1933).

Murraguldrie (*Co. Wynyard*) 35°30'S. 147°37'E., 37 km NE of Holbrook; soldiers' settlement; PO 1874–87.

Murrah (*Co. Dampier*) 36°32'S. 150°02'E., 12 km S. of Bermagui; cheese factory (Edgar O. Gowing); PO 1907–19; school 1957–63; telephone 1906; pop. 78 (1901), 81 (1911), 68 (1933), 64 (1947), 61 (1954).

Murramarang (*Co. St Vincent*) 35°32'S. 150°23'E., 20 km S. of Ulladulla; bushfire 1868; school (Murramurrang) 1931, closed.

Murrami (*Co. Cooper*) 34°25'S. 146°19'E., 17 km NW of Leeton; village gaz. 1924; Bapt. C. 1928; FB (Bob Robertson station); PO 1922; Presb. C. 1935; rice mill (Wilfred T. Henham) 1932; RS 1922–75; school 1933–2014; silo; telephone 1926; TX 1926, automatic 1953; water supply augmentation 1993; pop. 447 (1933), 326 (1947), 331 (1954), 373 (1961), 327 (2006), 271 (2011).

Murramurrang (*Co. St Vincent*) see Murramarang.

Murrawal (*Co. Napier*) 31°28'S. 149°20'E., 22 km S. of Coonabarabran, on Castlereagh R., RS 1917, station b. by John Allibone, closed 1972.

Murrawombie (*Co. Gregory*) 31°06'S. 147°08'E., 52 km N. of Nyngan, on Duck Ck; telephone 1911.

Murray (*Co. Goulburn*) see Albury.

Murray Downs (*Co. Wakool*) 35°18'S. 143°37'E., 58 km NW of Barham; sheep; pop. 36 (1933), 80 (1947), 96 (1954), 106 (1961), 145 (2011).

Murray Flat (*Co. Auckland*) 36°39'S. 149°53'E., 5 km NE of Bega, on Brogo R.

Murray Hut (*Co. Denison*) see Finley.

Murrays Beach (*Co. Northumberland*) see Nords Wharf.

Murrays Break (*Co. Oxley*) 31°47'S. 147°54'E., 11 km SE of Warren, on Macquarie R.

Murrays Flats (*Co. Argyle*) 34°44'S. 149°47'E., 8 km NE of Goulburn, on Wollondilly R.; agric.; quarry; RS 1888–1975; school (Towrang till 1890) 1859–1910; silo; Wes. Meth. C. b. 1858 by H. Lord, closed 1911, sold 1929; pop. 37 (1933).

Murrays Run (*Co. Northumberland*) 33°05'S. 151°09'E., 24 km SW of Paxton, on Wollombi Brook; school 1883–93; pop. 36 (1933).

Murray's Siding (*Co. Richmond*) see Rappville.

Murrayville (*Co. Clarence*) 29°24'S. 153°13'E., 7 km N. of Maclean, on Mangrove Ck; private village founded 1895 by W. Murray & Co.; timber and sawmilling; sawmill (W. Murray & Co.) 1895; school 1895–99; storm 1902; telephone 1895–1905; tramway (timber); pop. *c.*250 (1897).

Murrells Crossing (*Co. Beresford*) 36°07'S. 149°07'E., 14 km N. of Cooma, on Murrumbidgee R.

Murrimba (*Co. Camden*) see Paddys River.

Murrimboola (*Co. Harden*) see Murrumburrah.

Murrin (*Co. Blaxland*) 33°10'S. 146°16'E., 18 km NW of Lake Cargelligo, on Booberoi Ck.

Murrin Bridge (*Co. Blaxland*) 33°13'S. 146°22'E., 9 km N. of Lake Cargelligo, on Lachlan R.; Aboriginal mission; bridge b. 1883 by T. Brookes, new one (Allan timber truss) 1920, 178 ft (54.3 m), over Lachlan R.; pop. 167 (1954), 251 (1981), 99 (2011).

Murringo (*Co. Monteagle*) 34°18'S. 148°31'E., 20 km E. of Young, on Murringo Ck; also known as Marengo till 1926; settled 1827, surveyed 1849 by James Larmer, laid out and village gaz. 1850, thrived in 1860s; orig. flour milling and mining, then farming and sheep; Angl. C. (Christ) b. 1866 by Gunner and Wilson, d. by Alberto Dias Soares; bridges: one b. 1875 by Johnston over Murringo Ck and one b. 1953 over Willawong Ck; bushfires 1900 and 1932; cemetery (588 graves 1859+); CH 1887; cheese factory (W.H. Corkhill); diphtheria 1893; FB; floods 1870, 1878, 1920 (girl died); PO 1857; pound (stock) 1862; PS (incl. lock-up) 1880, additions and repairs 1914 by J.J. Cummins, closed; Rom. Cath. C. (Sacred Heart of Jesus) b. 1875 by Cranston Bros, sanctuary and sacristy 1883 d. by Lynch, church extended 1907 by Blackett, alterations 1922; school (Marengo till 1926) 1860, new one b. 1870, extended 1887; telegraph 1880; TX 1910, automatic 1972; pop. 128 (1861), 119 (1871), 1,003 (1881), 139 (1891), *c.*80 (1903), 603 (1911), 544 (1921), 219 (1933), 285 (1947), 344 (1954), 186 (1961), *c.*100 (1987), 165 (2006), 322 (2011).

Murringo Flats (*Co. Monteagle*) 34°13'S. 148°33'E., 25 km NE of Young, on Top Ck; creamery (Young Butter & Dairy Products Co-op. Factory Co. Ltd) 1894, burnt down 1897; telephone 1927; TX 1927–51; pop. 43 (1933), 61 (1947).

Murrobo (*Co. Bathurst*) 33°33'S. 149°17'E., 3 km E. of Blayney; container terminal; copper mine (Athol-Blayney Syndicate NL) <1908; flour mill (post mill estab. by Robert Lambert, taken over by John Louden); lime-kiln; quarry (abandoned).

Murroo (*Co. Wallace*) 36°08'S. 148°57'E., 25 km NW of Cooma; school 1883–1916, sold and reused.

Murroon (*Co. Parry*) see Bithramere.

Murrulebale (*Co. Bourke*) 34°44'S. 147°24'E., 21 km NW of Junee; Presb. C.; school 1889–1906; telephone 1925; TX 1928–31; pop. 182 (1911), 108 (1933).

Murrumbah (*Co. Camden*) 34°39'S. 150°07'E., 17 km W. of Bundanoon, on Paddys R.; agric. and grazing; PO 1861; pop. *c.*100 (1866).

Murrumbah (*Co. Narromine*) 32°09'S. 147°50'E., 20 km SW of Trangie.

Murrumbateman (*Co. Murray*) 34°58'S. 149°02'E., 18 km SE of Yass; settled in 1820s, first lots sold 1876, developed 1960s+; mining (gold rush 1872) mainly 1896, agric., wool, then hobby farming and wine; Angl. C. (All Saints Soldiers' Memorial) b. 1912–19 by D.L. Lawrence, d. by T.L. Thompson; bushfires 1902 and 1964; cemetery 1879; Community C. (former Unit. C.); earth tremor 1924; electricity 1956; FB (Lloyd Connor Memorial); foot-bridge; mines: Caledon or Caledonian 1935–39 and Edith-May (Ryan and Watson) 1910–11; PO 1873, new one b. 1909 by William McClung; school 1872 b. by David Howell, new one b. 1954, closed 1973, reused 1983; telephone 1905; TX 1921, automatic 1967; typhoid 1894; Unit. C. (Scots, Union till 1926, then Presb.) b. 1876 by William McClung, closed 1982, renovated and reused 1995; water supply augmentation

1985; wineries: Clonakilla Wines (estab. 1971 by John Kirk), Doonkuna Estate (estab. 1973 by Harvey Smith, sold 1978 to Sir Brian and Lady Jane Murray who built a winery in 1980, sold 1996 to Barry and Maureen Moran who built a new winery, bought 2011 by Chris Coffman), Four Winds Vineyard 1998, Helm Wines (estab. 1973 by Ken and Judith Helm), Murrumbateman Winery (Geoffrey and Trish Middleton) 1973, Yass Valley Wines (estab. 1978 by Peter Griffiths, bought 1991 by Michael Withers and Anne Hillier, sold 2014); pop. 17 (1881), 166 (1891), 92 (1901), 198 (1911), 164 (1933), 170 (1947), 213 (1954), 238 (1961), 525 (1986), 774 (1991), 1,087 (1996), 1,272 (2001), 1,542 (2011).

Murrumbidgee (*Co. Cooper*) see Griffith.

Murrumbidgerie (*Co. Lincoln*) 32°24'S. 148°43'E., 19 km SE of Dubbo.

Murrumbidgerie (*Co. Lincoln*) see also Wongarbon.

Murrumbo (*Co. Phillip*) 32°25'S. 150°13'E., 33 km S. of Merriwa; school 1941–49.

Murrumbo Valley (*Co. Phillip*) 32°24'S. 150°14'E., 31 km S. of Merriwa.

Murrumbucca (*Co. Beresford*) 36°07'S. 149°03'E., 14 km NW of Cooma, on The Green Gully; pop. 59 (1947).

Murrumburrah (*Co. Harden*) 34°33'S. 148°21'E., 27 km S. of Young, on Murrimboola Ck; Merrimboolla till 1860 then Murrimboola till 1882; settled 1848, town gaz. 1858 as Murrimboola, laid out 1858 by Francis Benson William Woolrych, first lots sold 1858, thrived in 1870s, munic. proc. 1890, town gaz. 1892, more lots sold 1892, munc. abolished 1975, decl. historic town 1990; mining (gold disc. 1856) till 1941, cereal crops, sheep, cattle, pigs, poultry, orchards, lime; Angl. C. (St Paul's) b. 1875–84, chancel added 1892, church re-roofing and renovations 1923 by Henry Spence and Robert Irvine McKinney, d. by Purvis and Sowter; bridge b. 1899 by Walter Frank Oakes, new one 1967, over Murrimboola Ck; bushfire 1944; butter factory 1892; carriage-works (David Reid) 1884, new building 1888, became David Reid & Sons in 1916, demolished; cemetery 1870; CH b. 1879–81 by C. Hardy, d. by James Johnstone Barnet, additions and alterations 1896 by G. M'Gee, closed 1988; clothing factory (Rutco Pty Ltd) 1944, owned by Rutgovich, Bourke and Carr, became Carr Clothing Co.; cordial factories: E. Chalker and John Haughey (acquired by Phil Haughey, fire 1898, acquired by Charles E. Sutton); earth tremor 1940; electricity 1920; FB 1934; fires 1911, 1918, 1929; floods 1893 and 1909; flour mills: Miles Murphy 1866 and Silver Spray Flour Mills Ltd (estab. 1871 by Murphy Bros, acquired 1878 by Thomas Allsopp & Sons Ltd, converted 1896 to a roller mill, burnt down 1919, replaced 1921, sold 1947 to Bunge Aust. Pty Ltd, closed); gales 1892 and 1922; hailstorms 1867, 1909, 1918; heatwave 1904; honey factory (Ken Tanson) 2009, in former post office, relocated 2016; hospital (Murrumburrah-Harden Dist.) b. 1927 by Spence and McKinney, additions 1928, 1959, 1962; lock-up b. 1884 by Thomas McBeath; mine (Blind Ck); PO 1860, new one b. 1879 by Thomas McBeath, repairs 1891 by E. Quartly, burnt down 1913, rebuilt 1915 by Joseph Burnett, reused; Presb. C. b. 1883–85 by Thomas McBeath, d. by Robert Young, tower demolished; PS b. 1897 by A. Stephens; quarry; rifle range b. 1907 by George Hurford; Rom. Cath. C. (St Mary's) b. 1868–71, additions 1896; RS 1879, station b. by Langley and Thompson, second station 1897, third station 1900, fourth station 1918, closed 1976, demolished 1986; school 1862–70, reopened 1877, new one b. 1884 on new site by Charles Hardy, d. by William Edmund Kemp, additions 1913 by Allen, additions 1923 by John Waugh, additions 1956, 1961, 1965, 1967, additions 2010 by Barker Constructions Pty Ltd; sewage works b. 1938–40; silo; snow 1899 and 1900; storms 1900, 1908, 1937; streets electric lit 1912, extended 1920; telegraph 1876, new office b. 1879 by Thomas McBeath; typhoid 1877 (man died), 1892, 1902 (woman died), 1906, 1907, 1910 (man died); Unit. C. (orig. Presb.)

b. 1915 by Brown and Haynes, d. by John Reid & Son; watch-house b. 1862 by William Henry Downey, additions 1874 by John Hammond; water supply 1929; Wes. Meth. C. 1870, destroyed 1883, new one 1890; pop. 100 (1861), *c.*150 (1866), 182 (1871), 1,620 (1881), 1,226 (1891), *c.*1,800 (1895), 1,448 (1901), 1,951 (1911), 2,960 (1921), 2,851 (1933), 2,595 (1947, incl. Harden), 2,727 (1954), 2,634 (1961), 2,435 (1966), 2,268 (1971, incl. Harden), 2,112 (1976, incl. Harden), 2,070 (1981, incl. Harden), 2,045 (1986, incl. Harden), 2,016 (1991, incl. Harden), 1,700 (1996, incl. Harden), 1,911 (2001, incl. Harden), 1,996 (2006, incl. Harden), 1,925 (2011, incl. Harden).

Murrumburrah (*Co. Harden*) see also Harden.

Murrumburrah North (*Co. Harden*) see Harden.

Murrurundi (*Co. Brisbane*) 31°46'S. 150°50'E., 33 km SE of Quirindi, on Pages R.; (incl. Haydonton founded 1840 by Thomas Haydon, Paradise Rocks, Stuarts Rocks, Temple Court); formerly The Page and Pages River; settled by Abbott, founded 1836, surveyed and laid out 1840 by J.S. Rusden, first lots sold 1840, munic. proc. 1890, town thrived 1860–1900 and 1914, then declined, munic. abolished 1948; mining (oil-shale disc. 1862 by Andrew Loder at Colley Ck), cattle, sheep, horses; aerial ropeway (Adolf Bleichert & Co.) b. 1911 by Gorski and Braunig from Temi oil-shale mine; airfield; ambulance station; Angl. C. b. 1855 by A. and W.J. Mackay, bell tower added 1868, new one (St Paul's) b. 1872–74 by John Sherwood, sen., d. by John Horbury Hunt, re-roofed 1908, tower (Frederick R. White Memorial Tower) b. 1913 by Myers, d. by Frederick George Castleden; benevolent asylum 1860; brick-kilns; bridge (Arnold Bridge) b. 1861 by Joseph Martindale, d. by William Christopher Bennett, destroyed 1864, rebuilt 1866 by R.S. Simms, over Pages R.; cemeteries: family (1 km NE), general 1869, north (3 km NW); CH 1843, new one 1862 d. by Alexander Dawson, repairs 1879 by W. Shaw, extended 1888, additions 1958; Cong. C.; cordial factory (F. Hayne); dengue fever 1926; diphtheria 1907; dust storm 1899; electricity 1930; FB (stations b. 1934, 1966, 2018); fires 1889, 1917, 1938; floods 1864, 1870, 1949; flour mills: A. Brodie, T.S. Grehan, Murrurundi Steam Flour Mill Co. 1860, Pages River Steam Mill (sold 1853), J.L. Tebbutt (b. by Bossley); foot-bridge 1911, over Pages R.; gaol (with stocks in front) 1861 d. by Alexander Dawson; hospital 1862, damaged 1865, additions and alterations 1881 by William M'Nair, d. by John Wiltshire Pender, new one (Wilson Memorial) b. 1917–19 by Fred Dinham; hurricane 1865; PO: Haydonton 1873, burnt down 1917, and Murrurundi 1837, new one b. 1863 by Josiah Barlow, alterations 1889 by William M'Nair, additions and alterations 1900 by Wooden and Frost, new one b. 1912 by Ellis & Sons; police barracks b. 1869 by Charles Mack, new barracks b. 1899 by Wooden and Frost; pound (stock) 1839; powerhouse (Murrurundi Electric Supply Co. Ltd); Presb. C. 1856, closed, sold and removed to Quirindi, reused, new one b. 1888 by William M'Nair, closed, sold and reused; PS 1840, new one 1860 d. by Alexander Dawson, additions and alterations 1973; quarry (stone); rabbit freezing works and ice works (Murrurundi Electric Supply Co.) 1931; railway (to oil-shale retorts) b. 1910 by Champion and Dunbar for the Aust. Shale Syndicate, which was acquired 1910 by British-Aust. Oil Co. Ltd, closed 1931; railway barracks b. 1891 by William M'Nair; railway coal stage 1891, new one b. 1899 by W. Taylor & Sons; railway engine shed b. 1871 by Stephen and Smith, new one b. 1899 by W. Taylor & Sons; railway turntable 1899, 60 ft (18.3 m); railway workshops, closed 1896; 2 reservoirs (incl. one b. 1939 by Archie F. Hood); retorts (first bench of 48 d. by Young and Fyfe), mechanical vertical type b. 1910 by British-Aust. Oil Co. for oil-shale from Temi, second bench of 48 retorts b. 1913, works demolished 1929; Rom. Cath. C. 1841, demolished, replacement (St Joseph's) b. 1855–60, additions 1875, fire 1893, additions 1894, re-floored and re-roofed 1900, rebuilding d. by J.T. McCarthy, and graveyard (551 graves 1842+); RS: Murrurundi 1872, station b. by Stephens and Smith, alterations 1891 by Charles Baker, closed 1989, and Temple Court 1878–1975; sawmill (David G. Teys); schools: Murrurundi 1849, new one b. 1851, reused, new one b. 1877 by William M'Nair, d. by James Donaldson, additions and repairs 1889 by William Price, repairs 1891 by S. Gossling, additions and repairs 1898 by Charles Joseph Skinner, renovations and repairs 1908 by E.F. Archer, additions 1959, and Pages River 1895–1906; sewage works; storm (man killed) 1935; streets first lit by naphtha gas; telegraph 1861, new office b. 1864 by Josiah Barlow, alterations 1889 also by William M'Nair, additions and alterations 1900 by Wooden and Frost, closed 1913, reused; TX 1910, automatic 1979; Unit. C. (orig. Wes. Meth.) 1891, closed, sold and reused; water reticulation 1937, water supply augmentation 1990; weir 1936; Wes. Meth. C. b. 1865 by Lee, new one 1885; pop. 169 (1846), 228 (1851), 310 (1856), 579 (1861), 350 (1867), 568 (1871), 652 (1881), *c.*1,000 (1887), 1,254 (1891), *c.*1,200 (1895), 1,235 (1901), 1,791 (1911), 1,434 (1921), 1,253 (1933), *c.*1,200 (1941), 1,039 (1947), 1,041 (1961), 969 (1966), 925 (1971), 930 (1976), 861 (1981), 878 (1986), 983 (1991), 902 (1996), 791 (2001), 805 (2006), 847 (2011).

Murrwillumbah (*Co. Rous*) see Murwillumbah.

Murrybong (*Co. Dowling*) 33°44'S. 146°24'E., 48 km S. of Lake Cargelligo; telephone 1927; TX 1939–50.

Murtee (*Co. Werunda*) 31°35'S. 143°29'E., 11 km E. of Wilcannia.

Murulla (*Co. Brisbane*) 31°50'S. 150°55'E., 11 km SE of Murrurundi; 8 mines (flint clay); railway accident (27 passengers died) 1926.

Murulla (*Co. Brisbane*) see also Blandford.

Murundah (*Co. Urana*) see Morundah.

Murwillumbah (*Co. Rous*) 28°20'S. 153°24'E., 22 km SW of Tweed Heads, on Tweed R.; (incl. Bray Park, East Murwillumbah, South Murwillumbah); surveyed 1868 by John Barling, laid out 1872 also by Barling, designed 1878 by Patrick R. Donaldson, village gaz. 1879 as Murrwillumbah, thrived 1894+, munic. 1902–46; timber, cattle, pigs, dairying, butter, sugar-cane 1869+, bananas, hort., tourism 1960s+; airport (South Murwillumbah); ambulance station b. 1936 by E. Erikson, d. by Ashe and Gilbert; Angl. C. 1882, replaced 1909, new one (All Saints') b. 1960 by Geo. Hanna Pty Ltd, d. by Conrad and Gargett; bacon factory (Tweed River Butchering & Bacon Factory Co. Ltd); Bapt. C. 1923, new one on new site, closed 2017; brewery (Murbah) estab. 2014 by Stone & Wood Brewing Co.; bridge (lift span) b. 1899–1901 by H. Reid & Co., 520 ft (158.5 m), re-decked 1944 by PWD, replaced 1968, over Tweed R.; butter factory (Tweed River Co-op. Butter Factory Co. Ltd) estab. 1897 by Isaac McIlrath, new factory 1906, taken over 1929 by Norco Co-op. Ltd, enlargement and remodelling (Southside) 1932 by D. Gallagher, d. by J.R. Hunter, closed 1996, demolished 2006; carriage-works: Jacob Abel Berthelsen (bought 1918 by A.E. Hayes, fire 1919) and A.H. Newlyn (bought 1915 from Alf Riley); casein factory (Milk Industries Ltd) 1921, boy killed 1936; caterpillar infestation 1954; cemeteries: general (2,348 burials 1877–1977) 1881 and lawn cemetery; CH (incl. lock-up) b. 1876–79 by Henry John Van der Waerden, additions 1888 by James McMorrine, additions 1893, additions 1906 by Charles Benaud Smith, court-house burnt down 1907, replacement b. 1909 by D.M. Mitchell, d. by Walter Liberty Vernon; Christ. Outreach C. (Conxions); Church of Christ 1957; clock tower 1952; clothing factory (Keren Clothing Co.) 1944; cordial factories: E.J. Fackerell 1902 (sold to H.W. Dunn, sold 1926 to P. Clifford, sold 1958 to Linsay Munro) and G. Skinner & Co. 1891 (removed from North Tumbulgum, became Skinner, Lowes & Co. in 1913, then Skinner, Lowes & Co. Pty Ltd in 1920, new factory b. 1925); dengue fever 1916, 1926,

1942; drought 1912; electricity 1919; FB (station b. 1919, additions 1935, new one 1972); fires 1907 (largely destroyed town), 1914, 1919, 1929, 1935; floods 1898, 1906, 1917, 1919, 1928, 1929, 1931, 1933, 1948, 1954, 2001, 2008, 2012, 2013, 2017; gales 1898, 1930, 1953; hospital b. 1904 by Gilbert and Doyle, d. by Frederick Johnson Board, additions 1906, renamed Tweed Dist. in 1910, additions 1925, new one b. 1937–39 by John Hutchinson, d. by Cobden Parkes, renamed Murwillumbah Dist. in 1972, upgraded by Bennett Constructions Pty Ltd; iceblock factory (Flyin' Fox Ice Blox) 2009; ice-cream cone factory (Scandinavian Cone Co.) 1981; joineries: W. Carew and R.P. Stevens, bought 1923 by F.P. Cuthbert; levee 1948; measles epidemics 1908, 1935, 1953; monumental stone works (H.J. Edwards Pty Ltd); PO: Bray Park 1951, Murwillumbah 1866 (new one b. 1910 by M. Mitchell, new one b. 1954 by Jennings & Co.), South Murwillumbah 1894; pound (stock); POW control centre (World War II); powerhouse 1919, enlarged 1923, chimney repairs 1946; Presb. C. 1889, new one (St Andrew's) b. 1912 by S. Lewis; PS: Murwillumbah, additions 1892 by W.J. Gillies, new one b. 1909 by D.M. Mitchell, d. by Walter Liberty Vernon, additions and alterations 1985, and South Murwillumbah 1919, closed, reopened 1929–35; punt 1882, across Tweed R.; quarry; railway coal stage, extended 1923; railway turntable, 60 ft (18.3 m), closed; reservoirs: 250,000 gal. (1,136.5 kl) and 600,000 gal. (2,727.6 kl); rifle range; Rom. Cath. C.: Our Lady of Perpetual Succour (South Murwillumbah) 1959, St Francis's 1883 (moved 1896 to Stotts Creek), St Mary's b. 1896 by W.J. Gillies, d. by James Fanning, additions 1907, reused, new one (Sacred Heart of Jesus) b. 1938 by John Sutton, d. by Austin McKay, Lourdes grotto added 1947; RS 1894, station b. by Frederick Lemm, new one 1922, closed 2004; sale-yards, inundated 1919; Salv. Army C. b. 1920 by J. Liscombe, closed 1980, sold 1991, reused; sawmills: Sly's and Standard Sawmilling Co. (fires 1922 and 1939); schools: East Murwillumbah 1958 (additions 1965 and 1995), Murwillumbah (Tweed River Junction till 1874) 1872 (additions 1892 by Hugh Mimnow, new building b. 1911 by D.M. Mitchell, d. by Walter Liberty Vernon, additions 1922, 1965, 1978), Murwillumbah HS b. 1930 by A.S. Webb (additions 1958, 1962, 1971, 1992, 2012), South Murwillumbah 1954 (additions 2010, closed 2017), Wollumbin HS 1995; SD Adventist C. 1920; sewerage 1957; Sikh C. 2001; storms 1892, 1913, 1998; TC, additions 1962 and 1970, became a campus of North Coast Institute in 1992; telephone: Bray Park 1951, Murwillumbah 1905, South Murwillumbah 1897; TX 1907, inundated 1931, new building b. 1952, automatic 1968; Unit. C. (Tweed Valley, orig. Meth.) 1905 d. by Frederick Johnson Board; vulcanising works (Besson Bros), taken over 1924 by Walmsley & Co.; water supply 1918, augmentation 1963; weir on Tweed R.; Wes. Meth. C. 1895; wharves: one b. 1885 by David Rankin and North Coast Steam Navigation Co. 1933; pop. 492 (1891), 953 (1901), 2,676 (1911), 3,895 (1933), 5,010 (1947), 7,151 (1961), 7,311 (1966), 7,294 (1976), 7,807 (1981), 7,678 (1986), 8,003 (1991), 7,657 (1996), 7,596 (2001), 7,952 (2006), 10,418 (2011).

Musclebrook (*Co. Durham*) see Muswellbrook.

Muscle Creek (*Co. Durham*) 32°17'S. 150°59'E., 10 km E. of Muswellbrook, on Muscle Ck; sheep, farming, dairying; airfield; Angl. C. (Holy Trinity) 1875; bushfire 1944; footbridge over Muscle Ck; PO 1892; Presb. C. 1891, burnt down 1944; school 1873–88 and 1897–1920; storm 1918; telephone 1915; TX 1926, automatic 1953; pop. 151 (1901), 92 (1911), 128 (1933), 73 (1947), 56 (1954), 58 (1961), 373 (2006), 522 (2011).

Muskgrove (*Co. St Vincent*) see Wog Wog.

Musk Valley (*Co. Clarence*) see Grafton South.

Muswellbrook (*Co. Durham*) 32°16'S. 150°53'E., 42 km NW of Singleton, on Hunter R.; (incl. Balmoral Corner, Edinglassie, Forbestown laid out 1842 by Francis and David Forbes and incl. in Muswellbrook in 1845, South

Muswellbrook); Musclebrook till 1838; disc. and settled 1824 by Henry Dangar, founded 1827, surveyed 1833 by Robert Dixon, laid out 1833 by George Boyle White, estab. and first lots sold 1834, second auction 1835, munic. proc. 1870 as Musclebrook, thrived 1960s–70s, munic. abolished 1979; wool, wheat, maize, tobacco, wine, sugar-cane, then cattle, horses, mining (coal disc. 1908 by Harry J. Jeans), vegetables, lucerne, hay, fruit, dairying, manufacturing, clothing; abattoir; ambulance station (temporary one) 1951, new one b. 1953 by V. Garlick & Sons, d. by J.H. Cunningham; Angl. C. (St Alban's) b. 1839–45 by Capt. David Charles Frederick Scott, tower added 1846, chancel added 1850 by Joseph Stafford and James Blackman, tower demolished 1938, second church b. 1864–69 by James Black, J. Black and W. Black, d. by Sir George Gilbert Scott, bell tower added 1880 d. by John Horbury Hunt, clock added 1914, and graveyard (incl. memorial chapel d. by John Burcham Clamp); Assemblies of God C. (Hope City), in former Presb. C.; Bapt. C. (Brookside) 1968, new one in building removed 1974 from Warabrook, extended 1986; boiling-down works and soap-works (Kerr's) 1844; brewery (Eli Allen) 1868–70; brickworks: Alfred Newman & Sons 1878, Muswellbrook Brick & Tile Co. 1957, Edwin Smithers; bridges: Kayuga Bridge (metal lattice truss) fabricated by Head, Wrightson & Co., Stockton-on-Tees, England, erected 1881 by J. Musson & Co., d. by Sir John Fowler, 531 ft (161.8 m), over Hunter R., bridges over Muscle Ck (1843, 1892, 1949, 1967, 1972), one over Ramrod Ck; bushfire 1944; butter factories: Millgrove (estab. 1895 by James Withycombe in old flour mill, fire 1899, closed, reused as freezing works) and Muswellbrook Co-op. Dairy Co. Ltd (d. and b. 1919 by Bell & Co., ice-making plant added 1922, factory extended 1926, amalgamated 1932 with Raymond Terrace Dairy & Produce Co. Ltd, closed 1935, reopened 1941, milk collection 1942, closed, sold 1952 to Gordon Murray and S. Hatton, reused); carriage-works: James Jennison (inundated 1913) and H.E. Sternbeck (bought 1907 by H.J. Clarke & Co.); caterpillar infestation 1930; cemeteries: general 1863 and lawn 1983; CH 1840, new one b. 1851 by Henry Howland, repairs 1874 by J.B. Cross, additions 1878 by J. Pritchard, repairs 1898 by D. M'Donald, additions 1934, demolished 1978, replacement 1980 d. by John Whyte Ian Thomson; cheese factory (Hunter Belle) 2004; Christ. Outreach C.; clothing factory (Berelle Clothing Co.) 1948; collieries: Muswellbrook No. 1 (Muswellbrook Coal Co. Ltd) 1909, Muswellbrook No. 2 Open-Cut (Bayswater Colliery Co. Pty Ltd), No. 3 Open-Cut 1944; Community C. (The Vines), in former shop; cordial factories: Frederick George Dunn, Krantz Bros 1923, G. Margin, closed 1906, Thomas James Purvis 1910–13, Albert G. Saunders (later Hunter Valley Cordials), new factory b. 1939 by J.S. Cook; droughts 1836–39, 1851, 1979, 1980; earth tremors 2016 and 2019; electricity 1923; FB 1910 (station b. 1917 by Thorne, closed, sold and reused, new one 1975); fires 1894 and 1984; floods 1857 (person died), 1870, 1874, 1890, 1893, 1913, 1935, 1955, 1971, 1976; flour mill (George Chivers) 1841, tweed mill added 1844, flour mill taken over by Frederick William Thrum, leased 1887 to Edward Franz, closed 1889, bought 1895 by James Withycombe and converted to a butter factory; furniture factory (Muswellbrook Furniture Manufacturing Co.); gaol (4 cells) b. 1860 by William Puxley, additions 1885 by Thomas A. Bourke; gasworks 1894, explosion 1929, extended 1950 by Woodall-Duckham Pty Ltd, demolished 1979; grasshopper infestation 1918; hailstorms 1859, 1970, 2004; heatwaves 1938, 1940, 1946; hospital b. 1862–64, alterations 1880 by Alex. Robertson Lang, d. by John Horbury Hunt, closed and reused 1914, new one 1971, redeveloped 2015; ice works: Barrett & Son Ltd 1915 and J.C. Hilder; Jehovah's Witnesses C. 1991; joinery estab. 1906 by Walter Barrett, taken over 1923 by Rixon, Hastie & Baker Pty Ltd; levee; lock-up (12 cells) 1834, replaced, demolished and replaced 1926; machinery workshops (Thiess

Bros Ltd) 1945; measles epidemic 1946; milk factory (Hunter Valley Co-op. Dairy Co. Ltd) b. 1945–53 by Frank Burg, d. by Richard Wildridge & Co., reused 1987, closed 1994, reused; miners' strikes 1916, 1947, 1949; monumental stone works: W.B. Armitage and Hunter Valley Memorials; PO 1837, new one b. 1883–85, d. by James Johnstone Barnet; pound (stock) 1840; powerhouse (Muswellbrook Coal Co. Ltd); Presb. C. (St John's) 1843, enlarged 1866, reused, new one b. 1913–15 by Walter Barrett & Son Ltd and J.E. Lowe, d. by Walter Harold and John Wiltshire Pender, reused; prickly pear poison factory (McLeod's) 1925; PS 1839, new one b. 1868 by Alexander Watt, additions and repairs 1903 by Walter Barrett, extended 1926 by Rixon, Hastie & Baker Pty Ltd, additions 1961, new building 2007; railway barracks 1945; railway bridge (steel truss) 1913, 157 ft (47.9 m), over Hunter R.; railway depot 1943; railway round-house (5 bays) 1943, dismantled 2006; railway turntable 1869, 40 ft (12.2 m), new one 1890, new one 1943–89, 75 ft (22.9 m); 6 reservoirs (incl. one b. 1973–76 and later one b. by Saunders International); rifle range 1904; Rom. Cath. C. 1861, additions 1883 by John Saunders, d. by John Wiltshire Pender, demolished, new one (St James the Apostle) b. 1912 by David Jordan and William Armitage, d. by James Hicks, additions 1978, and 6 graves; RS 1869, station b. by Thomas Hyndes, refreshment room 1922–64, station restored; sale-yards 1886, new yards 1934; sawmills: Walter Barrett (incl. joinery, sold 1925 to W. Turner and C. Leahey, dismantled 1925 and moved to Denman), Ted Bromley 1965, Thomas Bros 1882; scarlet fever 1915; schools: Muswellbrook 1852, 1862–63, reopened 1876, new one 1879 d. by George Allen Mansfield (extended 1883 by S. Dumbrell, additions 1908 by Walter Barrett, additions 1924 by T. Simpson & Son, new one b. 1947 by Charles Alexander Stewart Boag, additions 1963, 1970, 1993), Muswellbrook HS 1952 (additions 1967, 1987, 1991, 1993), South Muswellbrook 1952 (additions by R.T. Parker Pty Ltd); SD Adventist C. 1971; sewerage 1937, augmentation 1956 and 1986; soap and candle factory 1856; storms 1863 and 1918; streets gas lit 1894 (installed by Kirk), electric lit 1923; tannery (Lyngarra) estab. 1871 by E. Gerson; TC 1955, additions 1979, 1981, 1984, 1989, became a campus of Hunter Institute of Technology in 1992; telegraph 1861, new office b. 1862 by Henry Nowland, additions 1869; trees planted in streets 1888+; TX 1908, automatic 1977; typhoid 1894 and 1913; Unit. C. (Trinity, orig. Meth.) b. 1913 by Walter Barrett & Son Ltd, d. by James Hicks, vestry added 1954; waterworks 1914, filtration plant 1937, rebuilt 1974; weir on Hunter R.; Wes. Meth. C. 1862, demolished 1912; wineries: Simon Gilbert (in former milk factory) 1995 and (Queldinberg) estab. 1974 by Kevin and Margaret Sobels, moved 1986 to Pokolbin; wool-scours: Muswellbrook Woolwashing & Fellmongery Establishment (Joseph Chivers) 1848 and Lyngarra (Philip Wentworth Wright) 1867–76; pop. 215 (1836), 108 (1839), 215 (1841), 208 (1846), 204 (1851), 450 (1856), 625 (1861), *c.*600 (1866), 1,445 (1871), 1,074 (1881), 1,298 (1891), *c.*1,600 (1897), 1,710 (1901), 2,403 (1911), 2,141 (1921), 2,640 (1931), 3,287 (1933), *c.*3,500 (1941), 3,939 (1947), 5,635 (1954), 5,717 (1961), 6,371 (1966), 6,780 (1969), 8,082 (1971), 7,805 (1976), 8,548 (1981), 9,988 (1986), 10,140 (1991), 10,541 (1996), 10,036 (2001), 10,222 (2006), 11,042 (2011), *c.*11,791 (2018).

Muttama (*Co. Harden*) 34°48'S. 148°07'E., 20 km SE of Cootamundra, on Muttama Ck; Muttama Reef till 1889; village gaz. 1879; mining (gold reef disc. 1862 by Guy), farming, grazing; bridge (concrete) 1938; bushfires 1908, 1952, 1987, 1990; cemetery; dam (mine); FB; hailstorm 1935; mine estab. by Guy Bros, taken over by Traverse Jones; PO 1876, new one b. 1928, burnt down 1978; Rom. Cath. C. (St Mark's) 1902; RS 1886, station b. by John Miller, closed 1975; sale-yards 1937; school 1883, additions 1897 by C. Harrington, closed 1968, reused; stamper battery (10 head); telephone 1904; TX 1916, automatic 1941; Unit. C. (orig. Presb.) b. 1904 by George I. Armstrong, closed, sold 2012; pop. 98 (1891), 214 (1901), 240 (1911), 312 (1933), 262 (1947), 208 (1954), 262 (1961).

Muttama Reef (*Co. Harden*) see Muttama.

Mutt Billy (*Co. Argyle*) see Breadalbane.

Mutton Falls (*Co. Westmoreland*) 33°33'S. 149°52'E., 18 km N. of Oberon, on Fish R.; agric.; Angl. C. (Christ Church), new one (St Peter's) 1890 (in former Union C.), now seldom used, and graveyard (222 graves 1869+), incl. columbarium; flour mill (Rowe's); hailstorm 1864; PO 1861–84; Rom. Cath. C. 1869; school 1869–87; Union C., reused 1890; pop. 52 (1891).

Myalla (*Co. Bathurst*) see Waugoola.

Myalla (*Co. Beresford*) 36°25'S. 149°07'E., 21 km S. of Cooma, on Myalla Ck; farming and grazing; PO 1927; school 1883–1920; pop. 64 (1911), 53 (1933).

Myall Camp (*Co. Narromine*) 32°25'S. 148°05'E., 25 km SW of Narromine.

Myall Cowal (*Co. Flinders*) 32°01'S. 147°07'E., 49 km S. of Nyngan.

Myall Creek (*Co. Murchison*) 29°46'S. 150°43'E., 17 km NE of Bingara, on Myall Ck; subdivided 1905; Angl. C. (St Faith's) 1935; Meth. C. (removed 1906 from Little Plain); pop. 271 (1911), 93 (1947), 69 (1954), 230 (2006).

Myall Creek (*Co. Richmond*) see Whiporie.

Myall Lake (*Co. Gloucester*) 32°26'S. 152°23'E., 18 km E. of Bulahdelah, on Myall Lake; pop. 34 (1933).

Myall Mundi (*Co. Narromine*) 31°59'S. 147°55'E., 9 km NW of Trangie; RS (Kelly's Siding till 1895) 1889–1974.

Myall Park (*Co. Cooper*) 34°08'S. 146°06'E., 17 km N. of Griffith; dust storm 1944; flood 1939; heatwave 1937; school (Climsland till 1967) 1957–71; pop. 136 (2011).

Myall Park (*Co. Ewenmar*) 31°31'S. 148°24'E., 23 km S. of Gulargambone.

Myall Plain (*Co. Narromine*) 32°11'S. 148°13'E., 7 km NW of Narromine.

Myall Plains (*Co. Urana*) 35°31'S. 145°56'E., 18 km NE of Berrigan, on Wangamong Ck.

Myall River (*Co. Gloucester*) see Bulahdelah.

Myall Vale (*Co. Jamison*) 30°12'S. 149°33'E., 11 km E. of Wee Waa, on Namoi R.

Myambat (*Co. Brisbane*) 32°23'S. 150°37'E., 7 km W. of Denman; POW camp (World War II), reused as military camp, 2 killed 1946, additions and alterations 1954 by A. Schoderboeck, reused again as ammunition depot, 34 new magazines b. 1994 by Spantech Pty Ltd; RS 1917–75; winery.

Myanga Creek (*Co. Georgiana*) see Mianga Creek.

Myhill Flat (*Co. Clarke*) 30°46'S. 152°19'E., 58 km W. of Macksville.

Mylandra Creek (*Co. Forbes*) 33°36'S. 148°18'E., 20 km S. of Eugowra; goldmining; mines: Goonigal (J. Lovell 1903–5, Collinton 1905, J. Gibson 1906, Beath 1909) and Nuggetty Gully (C. Petersen 1907–9 and J. Gibson 1936).

Mylatchie (*Co. Caira*) 34°22'S. 143°04'E., 80 km W. of Gol Gol.

Mylestom (*Co. Raleigh*) 30°28'S. 153°03'E., 4 km NE of Urunga, on Bellinger R.; formerly also known as North Arm; FB; flood 2015; mineral sand mining plant (Bellingen Titanium Pty Ltd) 1956–58; PO 1938; telephone 1924; pop. 91 (1911), 73 (1933), 139 (1947), 148 (1954), 191 (1961), 265 (1976), 388 (1981), 428 (1986), 436 (1991), 384 (1996), 382 (2001), 338 (2006), 339 (2011).

Mylneford (*Co. Clarence*) 29°38'S. 152°51'E., 12 km NW of Grafton, on Clarence R.; farming; cemetery (31 graves 1841+) 1893; PO 1927–31; punt, ceased 1960, across Clarence R.; storms 1935 and 1937; telephone 1914; pop. 45 (1933).

Mynora (*Co. Dampier*) see Moruya.

Myocum (*Co. Rous*) 28°35'S. 153°31'E., 6 km S. of Mullumbimby; creamery 1894; RS (3 km N.) 1897–1975; school 1903–73; Wes. Meth. C. 1890; pop. 211 (1911), 282 (1933), 198 (1947), 204 (1954), 168 (1961), 941 (2011).

Myola (*Co. St Vincent*) 35°01'S. 150°40'E., 2 km N. of Huskisson, on Currambene Ck; cemetery (4 burials).

Myrangle (*Co. Gordon*) 32°53'S. 148°45'E.,

26 km NW of Molong; village gaz. 1886; grasshopper infestation 1907; school 1893, new one b. 1895 by William Gadd, closed 1908.

Myra Vale (*Co. Camden*) 34°38'S. 150°32'E., 17 km SE of Moss Vale, on Fitzroy Falls Reservoir; school (Burrawang East till 1885, then Wildes Meadow till 1893) 1877–1968; Wes. Meth. C. 1874, renovated and reopened 1953, closed, sold, renovated 2003, reused, and graveyard (25 graves 1847–2004).

Myroolia Plain (*Co. Barrona*) 29°50'S. 145°00'E., 98 km W. of Bourke.

Myrourlie (*Co. King*) 34°29'S. 149°01'E., 28 km E. of Boorowa, on Old Man Gunyah Ck; TX 1935–58.

Myrtle (*Co. Richmond*) see Myrtle Creek.

Myrtle Creek (*Co. Richmond*) 29°07'S. 152°57'E., 31 km S. of Casino; village gaz. 1904 as Myrtle; farming and dairying; airfield; Bapt. C. 1907; hailstorm 1900; PO 1893; Presb. C. 1909; Rom. Cath. C. (St Patrick's) 1913; RS 1905, station b. by H.W. Owen, closed 1970; sawmill (Murray Bros) 1905; school (Nandabah) 1906–11; telegraph 1891; telephone 1897; TX 1921–62; pop. 284 (1911), 131 (1933), 236 (2011).

Myrtle Gully (*Co. St Vincent*) 35°14'S. 150°26'E., 9 km N. of Milton.

Myrtle Park (*Co. Townsend*) 35°34'S. 145°27'E., 15 km NW of Finley; school 1904–6; TX (automatic).

Myrtle Scrub (*Co. Hawes*) 31°21'S. 152°02'E., 58 km SE of Walcha.

Myrtleville (*Co. Argyle*) 34°28'S. 149°49'E., 32 km E. of Crookwell; dairying and grazing; butter factory b. 1889 by John Boardman & Son, reused, demolished 1975; flour mill (George Charles Blay) 1868; PO 1861–1979; sawmill; school 1860 b. by Dunbar and McIvor, new one b. 1892 by Taunton Bros, closed 1909, reopened 1956, closed 1970; telephone 1907; TX 1926, automatic 1979; pop. *c.*100 (1860–66), 51 (1901), 77 (1911), 103 (1933), 88 (1947), 75 (1954), 121 (1961), 377 (2011).

Mystery Bay (*Co. Dampier*) 36°18'S. 150°08'E., 9 km S. of Narooma, on Mystery Bay; pop. 168 (2006), 248 (2011).

Myuna (*Co. Wellesley*) 37°07'S. 149°09'E., 23 km S. of Bombala; telephone 1921; TX 1928–51.

Myuna Bay (*Co. Northumberland*) see Wangi Wangi.

N

Nabiac (*Co. Gloucester*) 32°06'S. 152°23'E., 15 km NW of Tuncurry, on Wallamba R.; (incl. Bullocks Wharf); orig. Wollomba, then Cape Hawke till 1880, then Clarkson's Crossing till 1894; first land sale 1855, further lots offered unsuccessfully in 1857, surveyed 1885 by Joseph Andrews, village gaz. 1886; former shipping terminus, then timber, dairying, cattle, fern gathering, farming; airfield b. 1942 by PWD, closed and reused; Angl. C. (St Paul's) 1904; botanical products works (Aust. Botanical Products Ltd) 1913; bridge (Leslie Mick Weller Bridge) fabricated by G.H. & J.A. Watson Pty Ltd, erected 1956–58 by Brown's Constructional Enterprises Pty Ltd, replaced 2006, over Wallamba R.; causeway (Clarkson's Crossing) across Wallamba R.; cemetery (Failford, 698 graves) 1897; CH b. 1911 by E.W. Milligan, reused; creamery (Aust. Dairy Co.); electricity 1928; FB; foot-bridge; gale 1942; ice works (Great Lakes Ice Pty Ltd), removed from Tuncurry; PO 1876, new one b. 1898; PS (incl. lock-up) b. 1899 by J. Breckenridge, new one b. 1911 by E.W. Milligan; Rom. Cath. C. (St Isidore's) b. 1889 by Andrew Smith and James McKeough, renovated; sawmills: Fred Phillips 1901 (burnt down 1907, acquired by E.L. Everingham, burnt down 1930) and Miles's; school (Cape Hawke till 1884, then Clarkson's Crossing till 1900) 1876, new one b. 1884 by Henry Miles, additions and repairs 1898 by W. Avery, additions 1960 and 2010; sewage works; telephone: Nabiac 1900 and Bullocks Wharf 1913; TX 1913, automatic 1973; Unit. C. (orig. Meth.) b. 1905 by J.P. Maybury, extended 1971; water reticulation 1969; wharf b. 1897 by W. Avery; pop. 82 (1891), 177 (1901), 407 (1911), 345 (1933), 443 (1947), 411 (1954), 359 (1961), 259 (1971), 323 (1976), 363 (1981), 460 (1986), 510 (1991), 536 (1996), 568 (2001), 590 (2006), 637 (2011).

Nacurrie (*Co. Wakool*) 35°24'S. 143°54'E., 32 km NW of Barham, on Little Merran Ck; RS (Victorian railway) 1928, closed.

Nambucca (*Co. Raleigh*)
see Macksville and Nambucca Heads.

Nambucca Heads (*Co. Raleigh*) 30°39'S. 153°00'E., 38 km S. of Coffs Harbour, on Nambucca R.; (incl. Bellwood); reserve for village gaz. 1861, settled by Lane 1867, town gaz. 1870, surveyed 1874 by Ernest William Lewis Herborn, first lots offered for sale 1874, first lots sold 1879, bypassed by highway 1980; shipbuilding, sawmilling, maize, dairying, hort., pigs, cattle, bananas, vegetables, fish, oysters, retirement centre; ambulance station; Angl. C. 1903, new one (St John the Baptist) 1960 d. by E.L. Skinner; Assemblies of God C. (Christ. Life); Bapt. C.; breakwater b. 1896 by Wooden, Frost and Rogers, vee wall added 1930, in Nambucca R.; causeway, to Stuart Island, across Nambucca R.; cemetery (1,446 graves) 1888; FB (station b. 1910, (second) b. 1976, (third) b. by O'Donnell & Hanlon Pty Ltd); fire 1893; flood 2009; ice works (Piggott's); Meth. C. 1955; pilot station 1874; PO 1881; Presb. C. 1902, renovated 1911; PS 1891, new one b. 1910 by George Parkins, new one 1938 on new site, additions and alterations 1973; punt (Lane's) across Nambucca R.; quarry (man killed 1901); reservoir, 600,000 gal. (2,727.6 kl), 1968; Rom. Cath. C. b. 1917 by Charles Pickett, d. by Albert Edmund Bates, demolished 1954, replacement (Our Lady Star of the Sea) b. 1954 for Aborigines by R. & B. Constructions Pty Ltd, d. by Francis Leo Cullen, additions 1981; RS (3 km NW, Nambucca 1925–64) 1923, station burnt down 1942, replaced 1945, closed 1989, reused; sawmills: James Butler (man killed 1911, burnt down 1914), Copenhagen (William Buckman and Nicolai Christensen) 1892, Dalley and McMorrine, A. and E. Ellis (burnt down 1908), Enterprise (John Eichmann), Axel Englebert Jansen (Bellwood), Leonard's 1910, Newman's 1910; schools: Frank Partridge VC 1989, Nambucca Heads primary 1884, new buildings b. 1912 by George Parkins, additions 1959, 1988, 1995, 2010, Nambucca Heads HS 1992, additions by O'Donnell & Hanlon Pty Ltd; SD Adventist C.; sewerage 1972, augmentation 1994; streets electric lit 1934; telegraph 1881; telephone 1903; TX 1914, automatic 1973; Unit. C. 1990; water reticulation 1957, augmentation 1969; wharves: govt and Axel Englebert Jansen; pop. 276 (1891), 335 (1901), 555 (1911), 774 (1933), 1,364 (1947), 1,998 (1954), 2,252 (1961), 2,385 (1966), 2,712 (1971), 3,217 (1976), 4,053 (1981), 4,923 (1986), 5,683 (1991), 6,253 (1996), 6,146 (2001), 5,873 (2006), 6,220 (2011).

Nammoona (*Co. Rous*) 28°50'S. 153°01'E., 4 km NW of Casino; cemetery (lawn); RS 1910, station b. by George Albert Leggo and John Allibone, closed 1969.

Nana (*Co. Fitzroy*) see Nana Glen.

Nana Glen (*Co. Fitzroy*) 30°08'S. 153°00'E., 19 km W. of Woolgoolga, on Nana Ck; village gaz. 1885 as Nana; mining (gold disc. 1881 by Henry and Fairfax Sharpe), timber, farming, dairying, beef; Angl. C. (St Peter's) b. 1904 by Charlie and Clarrie Shephard, additions 1911; bridges: one b. 1899 over Nana Ck, one b. 1900 by Boulton over Orara R., Edward Sharpe Bridge over Orara R.; bushfire 1936; cemetery 1886; drought 1935–36; FB 1946; fires 1921 and 1941; floods 1945, 1950, 2020; mines: Beacon, Bella, Black Prince, Coronation, Fifteen Acre, Illabo, Jubilee, Lady Matilda, Surprise; PO 1892; quarry (Ellem's); rifle range; RS (1 km NE) 1922–74; sawmills: Enterprise (Joseph Reid) 1907, James Porter (sold 1912 to British Aust. Timber Co., burnt down 1928, rebuilt by A.H. Thompson, became Thomas Smith & Ellis Pty Ltd, amalgamated with Allen Taylor & Co. Ltd, moved 1953 to Coffs Harbour), C.W. and T.A. Ritchie (estab. 1945, sold 1960 to Max Swadling, burnt down 1961); school (Bagawa till 1911) 1899, new one b. 1903, enlarged 1911, replaced 1934 on new site by G.W. and L.E. Shephard, additions 1991 and 1995; 4 stamper batteries (incl. one erected 1882 for Dargue and one for Matilda Co.); telephone 1905; TX 1916, automatic 1959; Unit. C. (Community, orig. Meth.) 1906, fire 1964; water supply augmentation 1996; wineries: Kia-Ora and Two Tails (Maher's); pop. 30 (1893), 344 (1911), 352 (1933), 388 (1947), 310 (1954), 311 (1961), 238 (2011).

Nanama (*Co. Murray*) 35°01'S. 149°07'E., 27 km SE of Yass; farming; earth tremor 2012; PO 1927–31; Wes. Meth. C. 1901.

Nanami (*Co. Ashburnham*) 33°32'S. 148°24'E., 12 km S. of Eugowra, on Lachlan R.; lucerne mill; RS 1933–71; pop. 127 (1933), 55 (1954).

Nanangroe (*Co. Buccleuch*) 34°58'S. 148°29'E., 35 km E. of Gundagai; Chidowla till 1895; grazing; TX (automatic) 1970; pop. 32 (1933).

Nanardine (*Co. Ashburnham*) 33°04'S. 148°07'E., 10 km NW of Parkes; gold and copper; mines: Black Ridge or Limestone Reserve (Willacy 1872 and others 1882–83), Secret 1901, The Secrets or Goobang *c.*1882; RS 1914–76.

Nandabah (*Co. Richmond*) see Myrtle Creek.

Nandewar (*Co. Nandewar*) 30°48'S. 150°16'E., 22 km N. of Gunnedah; pop. 25 (1933).

Nangar (*Co. Ashburnham*) 33°27'S. 148°34'E., 17 km NW of Canowindra; PO 1891–95.

Nangerybone (*Co. Flinders*) 32°20'S. 146°33'E., 103 km SW of Nyngan; copper mining.

Nangus (*Co. Clarendon*) 35°03'S. 147°54'E., 18 km W. of Gundagai; village gaz. 1925, soldiers' settlement 1948; farming, grazing, dairying; Angl. C. (St Paul's) b. 1878 by James Tilsley, renovated 1955, additions 1958 by J. Freestone; bridge 1981, over Nangus Ck; bushfire 1904; butter factory (J. and W.J. McKinney); cemetery (318 graves 1884+); FB; PO 1897; school 1935; telephone 1907; TX 1910, automatic 1955; Union C.; pop. 173 (1901), 303 (1911), 270 (1933), 286 (1947), 282 (1954), 330 (1961), 410 (2011).

Nangus Creek (*Co. Clarendon*) 35°01'S. 147°57'E., 15 km W. of Gundagai; school 1880–94, 1902–4, 1911–15.

Nanima (*Co. Murray*) 35°01'S. 149°06'E., 9 km SE of Murrumbateman, on Murrumbateman Ck; gold; mine (Praetorite Mining Co.) 1908–10 and 1919; Wes. Meth. C., destroyed, replaced 1901, reused; pop. 82 (1911), 35 (1933), 149 (2011).

Nanima (*Co. Wellington*) 32°35'S. 148°59'E., 5 km SE of Wellington, on Macquarie R.; flour mill estab. 1859 by David T. Dunlop, burnt down, new one estab. by John Andrew Gardiner, leased to Henry Edward Kater, taken over by Matthews, leased to Backs, demolished 1908.

Nannong (*Co. Harden*) 34°32'S. 148°34'E., 18 km SW of Boorowa, on Spring Ck; RS 1929–74.

Napier (*Co. Urana*) 35°15'S. 146°46'E., 6 km SE of Lockhart; RS 1901, station b. by Charles Hardy & Co., closed 1967.

Nap Nap (*Co. Caira*) 34°27'S. 144°11'E., 58 km W. of Hay, on Murrumbidgee R.

Napoleon Reef (*Co. Roxburgh*) 33°26'S. 149°45'E., 16 km E. of Bathurst, on St Anthonys Ck; mining (gold disc. 1863 by Pierre Pourot); mine (Peter's); miners' strike 1911; stamper battery (5 head).

Naradhan (*Co. Dowling*) 33°37'S. 146°20'E., 35 km S. of Lake Cargelligo; village gaz. 1930; wheat and sheep; bushfire 1905; cemetery; FB (station b. 2017); PO 1930; railway coal stage; railway dam b. 1928 by E.J. O'Kane; railway turntable 1929, removed from Picton, 60 ft (18.3 m), derelict; RS 1929–75, station removed 1984; school 1940–47, reopened 1955; silo 1936; telephone 1929; TX 1930; water supply augmentation 1988; pop. 181 (1933), 26 (1947), 85 (1954), 131 (1961), 166 (2011).

Naradhun (*Co. Cooper*) see Erigolia.

Naradhun (*Co. Nicholson*) 33°35'S. 145°31'E., 13 km S. of Hillston.

Naranghi (*Co. Denison*) see Lalalty.

Narani (*Co. Gloucester*) see Bungwahl.

Narara (*Co. Northumberland*) 33°24'S. 151°21'E., 4 km N. of Gosford, on Narara Ck; orig. Hogan's Brush, then Narrara; settled 1825 by Frederick Augustus Hely, subdivided 1887 by The Hogan's Brush Land Co. Ltd; orchards 1824+, timber 1830s+, shipping, poultry; aeroplane crash 1970; agric. research station (hort.) 1912; airfield; Angl. C. (All Saints') b. 1926 by A. Schwartz, closed; Bapt. C. (Narara Valley) 1978, collapsed 2007; bridge 1892, over Narara Ck; bushfire 1951; Christ. Brethren Assemblies C. (Gospel); Christ. City C. 2015; cordial factory (Cadell's); electricity 1938; flood 1953; forestry school 1920–21, became training farm 1927–34; Jehovah's Witnesses C.; Meth. C. 1906; PO 1888; railway dams, 1901 and 1925, on Fountain Ck; RS 1887; sawmills: Anderson and Olsen, and Fountain and Allison; schools: primary 1889, additions and alterations 1911 by Charles Benaud Smith, additions 1961, new one 1998, and HS (Narara Valley) 1991; SD Adventist C.; telephone 1904; TX (automatic) 1977; Union C., acquired 1948 by Meth. C. and renovated, reopened 1949; wharf; pop. 234 (1901), 364 (1911), 455 (1933), 548 (1947), 595 (1954), 722 (1961), 7,767 (2011).

Narara (*Co. Northumberland*) see also Lisarow.

Narara Valley (*Co. Northumberland*) see Narara.

Nardu (*Co. Buckland*) 31°22'S. 150°29'E., 16 km W. of Werris Ck; RS 1932–73.

Nareena Hills (*Co. Camden*) see Figtree.

Nargong (*Co. Bathurst*) 33°44'S. 148°56'E., 26 km NE of Cowra; grazing; PO 1927; railway navvy strike 1891; RS (Swan Ponds till 1895, then Watervale till 1923) 1892–1974; school (Swan Ponds) 1891–1902; telephone 1924; TX 1941–59; pop. 36 (1933).

Nariah (*Co. Cooper*) see Narriah.

Narira (*Co. Dampier*) 36°23'S. 149°58'E., 9 km NW of Bermagui, on Narira Ck; pop. 52 (1911), 50 (1933).

Narone Creek (*Co. Northumberland*) 32°57'S. 151°09'E., 2 km S. of Wollombi; pop. 26 (1933).

Narooma (*Co. Dampier*) 36°13'S. 150°08'E., 57 km S. of Batemans Bay, on Wagonga Inlet; (incl. Kianga and North Narooma); orig. Noorooma, then South Wagonga Heads till 1884; settled 1882 by Field, surveyed 1883, port proc. 1884, village gaz. 1886 as Noorooma, thrived 1910–20; orig. sawmilling and shipbuilding, then goldmining, prawns, oysters *c.*1900+, fishing 1930s+, dairying, tourism (whale watching 1991+), retirement centre; ambulance station 1956; Angl. C. (St Paul's) 1900, replaced 1978; bacon factory b. 1885 by John Forster; breakwaters (Mill Bay) b. 1972–78 by Cleary Bros; bridge (with Strauss bascule span fabricated by Morison & Bearby Ltd) erected 1931 by State Monier Pipe & Reinforced Concrete Works, over Wagonga Inlet; bushfire 1928; cemetery 1886; CH, demolished, new one b. 1935 by Ernest Millican, d. by Cobden Parkes; cheese factory (Narooma Rural Co-op. Society) b. 1915 by John McMillan, closed 1944, bought by Richardson and reused; clock tower (war memorial) 1975; electricity 1936; FB 1939 (station b. 1982); fish cannery (Narooma Fish Canning Pty Ltd) b. 1937–39, extended 1940, rabbits canned instead from 1951 by Green's Products, acquired 1960 by Kraft Foods Ltd, acquired by H.J. Heinz Co. (Aust.) Ltd, closed 1974, sold 1976, razed; foot-bridge, to Lewis Island, over Wagonga Inlet; jetty (Withers') b. by George Fuller, demolished 1964; 2 marinas; pilot station 1902; PO: Narooma 1889 and North Narooma 1927; powerhouse b. 1935 by Harold Koerber; Presb. C.; PS 1895–97, reopened 1903, new one b. 1935 by Ernest Millican, new one 1978; punt 1894, converted 1927 from hand to engine power, replacement (from Batemans Bay) 1929, returned 1931 with opening of bridge, across Wagonga Inlet; quarry; reservoir 1935 and another one (North Narooma) 1952; Rom. Cath. C. 1895, closed, demolished 1984, replaced (Our Lady Star of the Sea) 1984; sawmills: Clyde Sawmilling & Shipping Co. Ltd 1906, Fred Cox (b. by George Fuller, sold to W.S. Preddey, leased 1905 by George Wilton Mitchell, renovated 1915, operated by Mitchell & Sons then Mitchell Bros from 1916, fire 1937, closed 1960), R.H. Face, William Joseph Lynch 1884–94, John McMillan, jun., Henry Withers 1877 (sold 1881 to Curtis); schools: Kianga 1904–38, Narooma (Noorooma till 1944) 1889, new building b. 1906 by Jacob John Shottin, additions 1936, 1960, 1966, 1982, 2010, Narooma HS 1979, relocated 1981, additions 1991; SD Adventist C.; sewerage augmentation 1986; shipyard (Henry Dent); telegraph office 1890; telephone: Narooma 1890 and North Narooma 1952; 2 training walls 1919–36; tramway (horse drawn, on wooden rails, 11 m. or 17.7 km) b. for bacon and cheese transport from Bodalla; TX 1912, automatic 1978; Unit. C. (orig. Meth.) b. 1914 by H. Trapp, bell tower b. 1934 by Les Ralph, d. by Norman Welland McPherson, church restored 1982; water reticulation 1935, augmentation 1952, 1987, 1990; wattle-bark mill (Craig, Mostyn & Co.); wharves (incl. one b. 1893 by M'Hugh and Lynch, one b. 1900 by James Lynch and M. O'Connor, one b. 1930); pop. 401 (1911), 613 (1933), *c.*800 (1941), 1,021 (1947), 1,142 (1954), 1,185 (1961), 1,295 (1966), 1,551 (1971), 1,945 (1973), 2,038 (1976), 2,758 (1981), 2,864 (1986), 3,443 (1991), 3,389 (1996), 3,412 (2001), 3,100 (2006), 3,127 (2011).

Narrabarba (*Co. Auckland*) 37°15'S. 149°51'E., 21 km S. of Eden, on Old Road Ck; grazing; PO 1927; sawmill; telephone 1916; pop. 20 (1933).

Narrabri (*Co. Nandewar*) 30°20'S. 149°47'E.,

86 km NW of Gunnedah, on Narrabri Ck; (incl. Dangar Village and West Narrabri, Narrabri Railway Station till 1890); settled 1834, land reserved for town 1858, surveyed 1859 by John Valentine Gorman, laid out by Arthur Dewhurst, town gaz. and first lots sold 1860, munic. proc. 1883 (West Narrabri munic. proc. 1895), town thrived in 1880s (West Narrabri thrived 1882–97); grazing, later wheat 1873+, maize, potatoes, butter, cheese, ham, bacon, now oilseeds, safflower, sorghum, cotton, sawmilling, cattle, hort.; airport (5 km E.) 1937, new terminal 1962; ambulance station b. 1953 by T.G. Foxe, d. by R.H. Lockwood, sold 2012, new one 2012; Angl. C.: one b. 1863, destroyed 1865, St Matthew's 1883, destroyed, St Cyprian's 1895 d. by John Horbury Hunt, St Lawrence's (West Narrabri) 1894; artesian bore 1901; Assemblies of God C. (Christ. Fellowship); Bapt. C.; brewery (estab. by Thomas Usher, sold to P. Simpson) 1881–96; brick-kiln (T. Avery); brickworks (John Thomas Gleeson); bridges: two over Horsearm Ck, two over Narrabri Ck (incl. one b. by Wright), one b. 1863 over Namoi R., new one b. 1880 by J.A. Jones over Namoi R.; bushfire 1893; butter factory and rabbit freezing works (Narrabri Co-op. Dairy Co. Ltd) b. 1906 by C.A. McDonald; carriage-works (Shaw and Lamb); caterpillar infestations 1899 and 1951; cemeteries: old one (3,349 graves 1871+) 1863, damaged 1955, and lawn (1,719 plots); CH (incl. lock-up) 1865 d. by James Johnstone Barnet, reused, new one b. 1886–88 also d. by Barnet, additions and alterations 1911 by A.J. Hulbert, d. by Walter Liberty Vernon, additions 1962, upgraded 2011; Christ. Fellowship C. (New Life); Christ. Outreach C.; Church of Christ 1913, additions 1916, closed 1919, sold 1921; clock tower (war memorial) 1980; concrete pipe works; container terminal (IPS Logistics) 1997, sold 2012 to Viterra; cordial factories: James Herbert Clarke, Edmund Fuss (bought by John Lillyman, bought 1891 by Septimus Faulkner & Co., new factory on new site 1912–80, reused), McNamara and Scanlon 1888, H. Trim; cotton gin 1968; cyclone (man killed) 1902; dengue fever 1926; diphtheria 1902 and 1903; dust storm 1902; electricity (Narrabri) 1922, and West Narrabri 1934; engineering works (BNB Engineering Pty Ltd); FB 1917 (station b. 1921 by Mitchell Bros, d. by William Hull McNiven); fibrous plaster works (Fraser Bros); fires 1884, 1889, 1897, 1900, 1906, 1911, 1912, 1917, 1924, 1926, 1942, 1972, 1994; floods 1841, 1864, 1873, 1890 (5 died), 1908, 1910, 1955, 1971, 1998, 2000; flour mills: Excelsior (Keys & Co. Pty Ltd 1911, silo b. 1933 by Thomas Robinson & Son, mill taken over by Allied Mills Ltd, new one 1952, closed 1985, fire 2005, demolished) and Narrabri Steam Flour Works (b. 1880 by H.J. Wyatt, d. by Thomas Rowe, for A. Goldman & Co., closed 1885, acquired by Charles A. Ross, acquired, refurbished and reopened 1900 by Barry and Stafford, sold 1907 to W.H. Short & Co., moved 1911, reused); furniture factory (M. Lewis and McNamara) 1888; gaol (lock-up proc. a gaol 1871), additions 1877 by Philip Wolledge, new one (incl. lock-up) b. 1880–82 by Joseph Conlon, d. by James Johnstone Barnet, closed 1982, restored and reused 1988; grasshopper infestations 1883, 1893, 1908, 1934; hailstorms 1890, 1892, 1933, 1948; hospital 1865, re-roofed and renovated 1874, razed 1912, (second) b. 1897 by Louis C. Young, d. by George Sanders & Son, improvements 1933, (third) 1944, (fourth) b. 2012 by Richard Crookes Pty Ltd, d. by Thomson Adsett; hurricane 1865; ice works (Narrabri Ice Co.), burnt down 1926, replaced 1927; Jehovah's Witnesses C.; joineries: A.J. Hulbert and Logan & Co. Pty Ltd; Meth. C., renovated 1947, destroyed 1948; monumental stone works: M.W. Hardy, and Smith and Gamble; oilseed refinery (Cargill Processing Ltd) 1967; PO: Narrabri 1861, new one b. 1877–79 by T. Avery, d. by James Johnstone Barnet, additions 1888 by F.A. King, also d. by Barnet, additions 1910, alterations 1913 by A.J. Hulbert, alterations 1916 and 1955,

and West Narrabri 1883, new one b. 1905 by George Grace; police barracks b. 1878 by R. Terbutt; pound (stock) 1861; powerhouse; Presb. C. (St Stephen's) b. 1893–96; PS: Narrabri (b. 1879 by George Barnes, additions 1890 by M. Mackie, additions, alterations and repairs 1909 by J. Waugh, new one 1973) and West Narrabri (closed 1935); 2 quarries; railway barracks 1882; railway bridges: one over Horsearm Ck, one over Narrabri Ck (Howe timber truss 1896, replaced 1980), one over Namoi R. (Howe timber truss 1896, replaced 1978); railway coal stage b. 1882 by Alexander Hamilton Scouller; railway engine shed b. 1882 by Alexander Hamilton Scouller, extended 1907, damaged 1933, demolished 1980; railway turntable, 50 ft (15.2 m), replaced 1903 (William Sellers & Co.), 60 ft (18.3 m); reservoirs (steel): one 250,000 gal. (1,136.5 kl) and one 660,000 gal. (3,000.4 kl); rifle range 1914; Rom. Cath. C. 1881, additions and alterations 1897 by Montague Audet, d. by William H. Lee, new one (St Francis Xavier's) b. by Reg J. Want Pty Ltd, d. by Fowell, Mansfield and Maclurcan, and one at West Narrabri (St Patrick's) 1935; RS: Narrabri 1897, refreshment room 1902, station destroyed 1907, rebuilt 1908, refreshment room closed 1986 and demolished 1988, Narrabri Junction 1897, new station 1900, closed, West Narrabri 1882, station b. by Alexander Hamilton Scouller, demolished 1987; sale-yards 1949; Salv. Army C. b. 1896 by William Hayes; sawmills: Albion (Johnson and Coventry), Hector Cook, Davis and Johnstone, Gately's, A.J. Hulbert 1914 (fire 1924), Ireland Bros, Theodore Morath 1876, destroyed 1900, Premier (Bradley and Wightman) 1914, burnt down, rebuilt 1930, A.R. Stafford, burnt down 1899; schools: Narrabri primary 1868 (new one 1884, repairs 1892 by Reece Lewis, additions 1897 by Montague Audet, additions 1927 by Gleeson and Wright, additions 1963, 1968, 1988), Narrabri HS 1956 (additions 1962, 1967, 1969, 1972, 1975, 1985), West Narrabri (Narrabri Railway Station till 1890) 1884 (extended 1887, additions 1899 and 1902, extended 1908, additions 1962, 1965, 1970, 1972); SD Adventist C.; sewerage (West Narrabri) 1970; silos 1934 and 1955; soap and candle factory estab. by Charles Reubens, sold to Alfred Thirkettle, sold 1882 to J.J. Piper who built new factory, explosion killed man 1901, burnt down 1910; straw envelope factory (Aust. Straw Envelope Co.) 1948–51, reused; TC, additions 1970 and 1986, became a campus of New England Institute in 1992; telegraph: Narrabri 1869, new office b. 1877–79 by T. Avery, d. by James Johnstone Barnet, additions 1888 by F.A. King, and West Narrabri 1883, new office b. 1905 by George Grace; telephone (West Narrabri) 1909; toolbox factory (Faber) 1984; tornadoes 1891 and 1900 (every building damaged); TX 1907, new building b. 1951, automatic 1974; typhoid 1898–1900 (5 died) and 1903; Unit. C. (Peace Memorial, orig. Meth.) 1973 d. by James Hicks, extended 1993 by Les Gardoll; vulcanising works (Miller & Sons) 1928; water supply (Narrabri) 1941 and (West Narrabri) 1937; Wes. Meth. C. 1876, reused, replaced 1896, burnt down 1972; wool-scours: Hall Bros 1895, burnt down 1903, Sydney Jones, Lloyd & Co., Swinbourne & Sons, A. Thompson & Co.; wool stores: E.W. Burns and Hall Bros 1895, burnt down 1903; pop. *c.*95 (1866), *c.*220 (1868), 313 (1871), 832 (1881), *c.*1,200 (1885), 1,825 (1889), 2,361 (1891), *c.*2,450 (1895), 3,120 (1900), 2,963 (1901), 4,689 (1911), 2,358 (1921), 3,946 (1933), 4,430 (1947), 4,957 (1954), 5,423 (1961), 6,037 (1966), 6,875 (1971), 6,951 (1976), 7,296 (1981), 7,246 (1986), 6,694 (1991), 6,419 (1996), 6,245 (2001), 6,102 (2006), 5,890 (2011), *c.*7,392 (2017).

Narrabri Railway Station (*Co. Nandewar*) see Narrabri.

Narraburra (*Co. Bland*) 34°20'S. 147°39'E., 17 km NE of Temora, on Narraburra Ck; Temora till 1880, then West Temora till 1897; farming; Angl. C. (St George's) d. and b. 1955 by Neville Thomas, re-roofed 1999, closed 2009; cemetery; PO 1874, relocated 1889;

telephone 1906; TX 1923, automatic 1973; pop. 204 (1911), 134 (1933), 120 (1947), 113 (1954), 84 (1961), 274 (2011).

Narrallen (*Co. Monteagle*) 34°17'S. 148°40'E., 20 km N. of Boorowa, on Narrallen Ck.

Narrama (*Co. Townsend*) see Mayrung.

Narrambla (*Co. Wellington*) see Orange.

Narramine (*Co. Narromine*) see Narromine.

Narrandera (*Co. Cooper*) 34°45'S. 146°33'E., 26 km E. of Leeton, on Murrumbidgee R.; Gillinbah till 1861; surveyed 1850 by James Larmer, laid out 1859 by Edward Twynam, first lots sold 1860, town gaz. 1863, designated as chief town of the county, more lots sold 1880, munic. proc. 1885, town thrived 1886 and 1908–13, munic. abolished 1960; former river port, goldmining, timber 1870s–80s, maize, oats, barley, wheat, hay, lucerne, fruit, vegetables, poultry, sheep, cattle, rice, manufacturing; aeroplane crashes: 4 killed 1943 and 7 killed 1945; air force training school (World War II) 1940; airport (5 km NW) 1938; ambulance station b. 1952 by H.M. Dixon, d. by J.H. Robertson; Angl. C.: Chinese 1894 and St Thomas's 1880 d. by Charles Mayes, damaged 1923, and graveyard; Bapt. C., closed and reused; bicycle works (William Hanson) 1897; brewery estab. 1879 by George Wildman, bought 1882 by William Jones, became Jones, Lincoln & Co. in 1884, renamed Oakbank Brewery, flood damaged 1891, became McIntyre, Lincoln & Co. in 1893, burnt down and rebuilt 1894, major improvements 1906, tower 1912 d. by John Hill Robinson, brewery sold 1923 to Mahon and Hedley, sold 1924 to P.M.G. Terry, reused, abandoned and derelict; brickworks: Dixons Pty Ltd and George Eden (estab. 1875, acquired by William Jones); bridges: Larmer Street Bridge b. 1882 by M'Evoy and Keefe and one b. 1892 by Kerr and Cronin, 310 ft (94.5 m), replacement (Allan timber truss), 330 ft (100.6 m), b. 1920 by Walter Frank Oakes, over Murrumbidgee R.; carriage-works (T.P. Dunne & Co., later became Riverina Carriage Factory, taken over by Clark); cemetery (graves 1886+) 1863; CH b. 1879 by W.E. Barry, d. by James Johnstone Barnet, additions 1881 by Charles Stewart, new one 1902 in old post and telegraph office, additions and alterations 1906 d. by Walter Liberty Vernon; Chinese joss house; Christ. Revival Crusade C. (in former theatre); concrete pipe works (Rocla) 1953; cordial factories: W. Graff 1925 (acquired 1932 by Erwin and Rheinberger) and N.G. Maguire (in former brewery), sold 1933 by J.J. Howell & Sons, new plant 1951; dust storms 1892, 1900, 1902, 1915; electricity supplied 1912–21 by Wise Bros, supplied from 1922 by local council; FB 1893 (station b. 1902, burnt down, new one b. 1927 by Haynes and Dixon, d. by William Hull McNiven); fellmongery (Joseph Francis Ragless); fibrous plaster works (Dixons Ltd); fires 1890, 1896, 1926, 1937; floods 1852, 1870, 1891, 1896, 1899, 1900, 1925, 1956, 1989; flour mill estab. 1889 by Thomas and George Wise, upgraded 1912, new mill b. 1924 on new site by Haynes and Dixon, d. by Robinson & Sons, silo b. by J. Laverick, mill burnt down 1944, rebuilt 1947 by H.M. Dixon, d. by Stephenson and Turner; grasshopper infestations 1899 and 1900; hospital 1883, new one 1885, additions 1902, 1907, 1911, 1929, 1936, 1940; ice works: W. Clark, and Hamilton and Dickson 1914; joinery (Dixons Ltd); lock-up b. 1881 by Charles Stewart, upgraded 1898 to a gaol; meat-chilling works (Riverina Chilled-Meat Co. Ltd) b. 1891 by Hudson Bros, leased 1892 to J.H. Geddes & Co., sold 1894, closed 1896, reopened 1902, leased 1905 to George Julius Rohr, closed 1910; monumental stone works: F. Lindley and Watkins Bros; Pentecostal C.; PO 1859, new one b. 1881 by Charles Stewart, additions 1892, closed, converted 1902 by Hocking Bros for reuse, new one b. 1900 by R.L. Thompson; pound (stock) 1861; powerhouse 1923; Presb. C. 1882–1907, reused; PS b. 1877 by C.R. Stewart, reused, new one 1902; punt 1872, new one b. 1880 by Davy & Co.; quarry; railway barracks, removed 1966; railway bridge (lattice girder) fabricated by Westwood, Baillie & Co.,

London, England, erected 1885 by Halliday and Owen, d. by Sir John Fowler and John Whitton, over Murrumbidgee R.; railway coal stage 1881, additional ones 1900, 1913, 1942; railway depot 1881; railway engine shed 1913 (destroyed during construction), rebuilt, additional one (removed from Dunedoo) re-erected 1926, relocated 1942; railway turntable 1881, 50 ft (15.2 m), new one 1910, 60 ft (18.3 m), closed; 4 reservoirs (incl. elevated steel one b. 1891, 100,000 gal. or 454.6 kl); Rom. Cath. C. (St Brigid's) 1883, new one (St Mel's) b. 1909 by W.G. Ireland, d. by Kempson and Conolly; RS 1881, station b. by Charles Hardy & Co., d. by John Whitton, refreshment rooms 1917, station closed 1989, reused; sale-yards (Culley & Co.), new ones 1932; Salv. Army C., burnt down 1890, new one 1924, closed; sawmills: Beecher Bros, George Huntley Dixon and Joe Hansell 1914 (became Dixons Pty Ltd), William McFadzean and Charles Frederick Bland, Narrandera Steam Saw Moulding and Planing Mills (estab. by George H. Risby, sold to W. Plant and Sam Langham, sold to James and E. Roach, burnt down and man died 1924), Sweeting and Fyfe; schools: East Narrandera 1960, additions 2010, Narrandera 1873 (b. 1883 by A.J. King, additions 1891 by Bundock and Hosking, additions 1926, new school 1934 d. by Edwin Evan Smith), Narrandera HS 1947, additions 1965 and 1977; SD Adventist C. 1937; sewage treatment works b. 1954 by Fraser Bros Constructions Ltd, augmentation 1958 and 1976; sheep-nut factory (Riverina Sheep Nuts Pty Ltd) 1929, burnt down 1944, rebuilt 1947; silo 1964; smallpox 1881; snail infestation 1950; soap and vinegar works (McIntyre, Lincoln & Co.) 1889, in former brewery; steel fabrication works (Hutchins Bros) estab. 1982 by Stewart and Graham Hutchins; storms 1913 and 1923; streets lit by kerosene 1888, then electricity 1912 (generated by Wise Bros at their flour mill till 1923); TC 1944, became a campus of Riverina Institute in 1992; telegraph 1882, new office b. 1881 by Charles Stewart, closed, converted 1902 by Hocking Bros for reuse, new one b. 1900 by R.L. Thompson; TX 1902; typhoid 1889 and 1901; Unit. C. (St John's, orig. Presb.) b. 1908 by William Bundock, d. by Campbell and Kernot, vestry 1954 also d. by Campbell and Kernot, and graveyard; vulcanising works; watch-house b. 1864 by Charles Hardy and Thomas Hodson; waterworks 1889, augmented 1921, new pumping station (electric) 1923; weir on Main Canal; Wes. Meth. C. b. 1891 by S. Bundock; wool-scours: Federal (Joseph Francis Ragless) 1890, George T. Spencer, George Frederick Sugden 1886; pop. *c.*100 (1866), 142 (1871), *c.*200 (1872), 1,142 (1881), 1,815 (1891), *c.*1,700 (1895), 2,255 (1901), 2,888 (1911), 2,985 (1921), 4,119 (1933), 4,186 (1947), 4,418 (1954), 4,718 (1961), 4,914 (1966), 4,825 (1971), 4,984 (1976), 5,013 (1981), 4,835 (1986), 4,649 (1991), 4,678 (1996), 4,119 (2001), 3,961 (2006), 3,871 (2011). (See also Gillenbah.)

Narrandera East (*Co. Cooper*) see Narrandera.

Narranga (*Co. Fitzroy*) see Coffs Harbour.

Narrango (*Co. Phillip*) 32°50'S. 150°09'E., 15 km E. of Kandos, on Cudgegong R.; school 1884–1905; pop. 29 (1933).

Narrara (*Co. Northumberland*) see Narara.

Narrawa (*Co. King*) 34°26'S. 149°10'E., 29 km W. of Crookwell, on Narrawa Ck; farming and grazing; Angl. C. b. 1898 by J.P. Pinn, new one (St Barnabas's) 1949, and graveyard, incl. columbarium; FB; Meth. C. b. by James Spring; PO 1888; quarry; school 1884–97 and 1963–70; telephone 1914; TX 1918–37; pop. 93 (1901), 125 (1911), 67 (1933), 138 (1947), 65 (1954), 60 (1961), 247 (2006).

Narrawa East (*Co. King*) 34°25'S. 149°13'E., 25 km W. of Crookwell.

Narrawallee (*Co. St Vincent*) see Mollymook.

Narrawa North (*Co. King*) 34°21'S. 149°10'E., 31 km W. of Crookwell, on Burrawinda Ck; school 1957–59; telephone 1927; TX 1927–75.

Narrawa West (*Co. King*) 34°18'S. 149°05'E., 39 km W. of Crookwell, on Lachlan R.; telephone 1929; TX 1929–68.

Narriah (*Co. Cooper*) 33°56'S. 146°43'E., 46 km

W. of West Wyalong; Nariah till 1929; village gaz. as Nariah and lots sold 1925, abandoned; gold (disc. 1894) and tin (alluvial); PO 1929; RS 1923–75; sawmill (Macpherson Bros); telephone 1930; TX, closed 1973; pop. 38 (1933).

Narromine (*Co. Narromine*) 32°14'S. 148°15'E., 34 km W. of Dubbo, on Macquarie R.; Narramine till 1900; site reserved 1849, founded by William O'Neill, surveyed 1883 by Henry Adam Torry, village gaz. 1883, first lots sold 1884, munic. proc. 1898, subdivisions: Bulgandramine Estate 1948, Cornucopia Estate 1947, Dapto Estate 1948, Fairview Estate 1914, Merriong Estate 1954, Tyrie Estate 1961; wheat 1880+, citrus 1913+, sheep, cattle, pigs, oats, barley, linseed, sorghum, apples, vegetables, tomatoes, cotton; air force training school (World War II) 1940; airport 1930, new hangar 1937, new terminal 1954; ambulance station b. 1949 by Richard Davis; Angl. C. 1894 d. by John Hingston Buckeridge, new one (St Mary's) 1929, extended 1959; Apostolic C.; Assemblies of God C. (Generocity); Bapt. C. 1991; bridge 1897, destroyed 1903, new one (Dare timber truss) b. 1907 by J.H. Shedden, 524 ft (159.7 m), replaced, over Macquarie R.; Calvary Life Assemblies Pentecostal C. (Oasis) 1968; cemeteries: general (2,537 graves) 1884, incl. columbaria, and war (12 graves) 1957; CH 1898, new one 1962 d. by Edward Herbert Farmer, upgraded 2011; citrus juice factory 1971; clock tower 1970 d. by W. Baker; Combined Protestant C. 1890, later used as Meth. C. till 1926; cordial factories: W.E. Clancey (b. 1929 by A.G. Chandler) and John Hives & Son (burnt down 1917); cyclone (damaged much of town) 1932; diphtheria 1928; droughts 1875, 1878, 1884, 1888, 1912, 1918, 1919, 1922, 1923, 1929, 1935, 1937, 1940, 1946, 1957, 1965, 1967, 1994; earth tremors 1930, 1932, 1933, 1936; electricity 1928; engineering works (Geoff Parker); FB 1929 (station b. 1932 by W.F. Fuller, extended 2004); fires 1899, 1921, 1923, 1925, 1928, 1938, 1939, 1967, 1996; floods 1867, 1870, 1892, 1920, 1926, 1950, 1952, 1955, 1956, 1971, 1990; flour mill b. 1900 by John Dunkley for Chandler, acquired 1904 by R. Gillespie and M. McLeod, converted 1928 from steam to electricity, closed 1941, reused 1962, burnt down 1964; freezing and ice works (rabbits and poultry); fruit packing house (Sungift, G.H.R. Barlow & Sons) 1945, reused; Full Gospel C.; gale 1994; grasshopper infestations 1907 and 1921; hospital 1949, additions 1975; lock-up 1898; Meth. C. b. 1926 by Edward Martin Wright, damaged 1932, repaired 1932 by Wright, extended 1967, reused; mouse plague 1922; PO 1882, new one b. 1904 by A.G. Litchfield, replaced 1959; powerhouse b. 1928 by W. Fuller; PS 1890, additions and alterations 1898 by John Dunkley, new one b. 1908 by W.W. Sutton & Son; railway turntable, 60 ft (18.3 m) 1910, closed and relocated; reservoir (concrete), 127,000 gal. (577.3 kl), b. 1929 by State Monier Pipe Works; Rom. Cath. C. b. 1912 by Hill, d. by John Francis Kenny, destroyed 1932, replacement (St Augustine's) b. 1933 by Wallace and McGee, d. by Peter Joseph Gannon; RS 1883, station b. by D. Ralston and Nicholas Martin, alterations and repairs 1949; sale-yards 1932, renovated 1952 by N. Walsh; sawmills: R.E. Locks, James Millar, W.J. Treseder (incl. joinery), burnt down 1953, rebuilt 1954, burnt down 1981; schools: primary 1883, new buildings b. 1892 by James Prior Hull, additions 1896, 1911, 1928, damaged 1932, additions 1937, 1943, 1952, 1956, 1965, 1966, 1970, 1972, damaged 1976 and HS 1969, additions 1973 and 1975, damaged 1976, fire 2009; SD Adventist C. 1961; seed cleaning plant (M.E. Herman & Sons Pty Ltd); sewerage 1959; silos 1920, 1927, 1955; stock feed mill (Narromine Stock Foods Pty Ltd) o. 1962 in former flour mill, burnt down 1964, rebuilt; storm 1976; telegraph 1890; TX 1907, automatic 1968; typhoid 1903; Union C.; Unit. C. (St Andrew's, orig. Presb.) b. 1906 by P. Herbert, d. by Nixon and Adams; vulcanising works 1932; waterworks b. 1929 by R. Hood, extended 1960, 1966, 1976, augmentation 1991; Wes. Meth. C. 1889; pop. 236 (1891), 931 (1901), 2,228 (1911), 1,617 (1933), *c.*1,800 (1941), 1,816 (1947), 1,975 (1954), 2,282 (1961), 2,466 (1966), 2,724 (1971), 2,802 (1976), 2,994 (1981), 3,205 (1986), 3,378 (1991), 3,486 (1996), 3,548 (2001), 3,599 (2006), 3,789 (2011).

Narrowgut (*Co. Northumberland*) 32°43'S. 151°37'E., 2 km W. of Morpeth, on Hunter R.; earth tremor 1868; floods 1867, 1870, 1895, 1898; pop. 74 (1901), 27 (1933).

Narwonah (*Co. Narromine*) 32°19'S. 148°11'E., 9 km SW of Narromine, on Yellow Ck; FB; RS 1910, station b. by T.E. Quiggin, closed 1974; silo.

Nashdale (*Co. Wellington*) 33°18'S. 149°01'E., 8 km W. of Orange, on Colemans Ck; apples, pears, stone fruit, wine; PO 1927; RS (Cargo Road till 1930) 1885, station b. by James Stuart Douglas, services ceased 1987; school (German's Hill till 1916, then Lidster till 1927) 1889 b. by Job and Harding, burnt down 1923, new one b. 1924 by W. Fuller, additions 1961, 1969, 1986; telephone 1927; wineries: Dindima Wines (bought 2002 by James and Michelle Bell), Ku-ring-gai Vineyard, Orange Highland Wines (Ross and Helen Harrison) 2004, Osmond Wines; pop. 168 (1933), 208 (1947), 218 (1954), 219 (1961), 367 (2011).

Nashua (*Co. Rous*) 28°44'S. 153°28'E., 8 km SW of Bangalow, on Byron Ck; (incl. Spring Vale); logging, then farming and dairying; bridge b. 1901 by John Finn, new one (concrete) b. 1941 by W. Braid, over Wilsons Ck; cheese factory 1905; PO 1891; Presb. C. (Immanuel) b. 1898 by John Duncan, enlarged and renovated 1907, damaged 1927, restored and renovated 1928 by James Muirhead; RS 1896–1972; school (Gays Hill till *c.*1910) 1899–1976; storms 1927 and 1942; sugar mill (Toohey's); telephone 1907; TX 1917–64; pop. 179 (1933), 145 (1947), 125 (1954), 107 (1961), 243 (2011).

Native Dog Flat (*Co. King*) 34°29'S. 149°22'E., 11 km W. of Crookwell.

Nattai (*Co. Camden*) 34°04'S. 150°27'E., 24 km W. of Camden; coal washery; collieries: Nattai Bulli (o. 1930 as Camden Colliery by Knutsen, Kemp and Clinton Bros, renamed 1935, acquired by Clutha Development Pty Ltd), Wollondilly (orig. Oakleigh, Burragorang Collieries Pty Ltd), Wollondilly Extended, abandoned; 3 pumping stations; waterworks (Oakdale).

Nattai (*Co. Camden*)
see also Mittagong and Nattai River.

Nattai River (*Co. Camden*) 34°04'S. 150°26'E., 26 km W. of Camden, on Nattai R. (now Lake Burragorang); defunct, village moved east to new site (Nattai); timber, maize, oats, wheat, hort., pigs; Angl. C. (St Stephen's) b. 1876–78; fire 1869; PO 1907; Presb. C. 1885; sawmill (Holdsworth, Ward and Irwin); school 1952–73; telephone 1905; TX 1926–69; pop. 291 (1871), 114 (1933), 123 (1947), 308 (1954), 193 (1961).

Naughtons Gap (*Co. Rous*) 28°48'S. 153°06'E., 8 km NE of Casino; farming and dairying; PO 1901; quarry; RS 1903–75; school (Nortons Gap till 1921) 1897, new building b. 1926 by Diyal Singh, closed 1967; telephone 1926; TX 1928–63; pop. 91 (1911), 72 (1933), 67 (1947), 111 (1954), 88 (1961).

Nea (*Co. Pottinger*) 31°10'S. 150°20'E., 22 km S. of Gunnedah; FB; RS (3 km NE) 1911–66; school 1957–68; silo 1934; pop. 21 (1933).

Neath (*Co. Northumberland*) 32°50'S. 151°25'E., 2 km SW of Abermain, on Swamp Ck; village gaz. 1913; brickworks (Cessnock Neath Brickworks Ltd) 1925; colliery estab. 1903–6 by Wickham & Bullock Island Coal Co., o. 1907, closed by fire 1914, reopened 1915, flooded 1926, taken over 1927 by Cessnock Collieries Ltd, third tunnel o. 1930, man killed 1939, old tunnel closed 1942, strikes 1943, 1944, 1946–47, colliery closed 1951, washery installed 1957, taken over 1959 by Caledonian Collieries Ltd, taken over 1960 by Coal & Allied Industries Ltd, washery closed 1988, colliery demolished 1988, razed; earth tremors 1925 and 2011; FB; Meth. C. 1908; PO 1911; 2 quarries; railway (colliery); reservoir (concrete), 303,100 gal. (1,377.9 kl),

1909; school 1913, new building b. 1916 by F. Morgan, closed 1971; telephone 1912; water pumping station (steam) 1908, demolished and replaced 1927; pop. 602 (1911), 557 (1933), 466 (1947), 452 (1954), 415 (1961), 294 (1971), 307 (1976), 272 (1981), 318 (1986), 454 (1991), 377 (1996), 362 (2001), 387 (2006), 431 (2011).

Neckarboo (*Co. Woore*) 32°04'S. 144°36'E., 133 km SW of Cobar.

Neeambah (*Co. Cooper*) 34°23'S. 146°15'E., 22 km SE of Griffith; RS 1925–61.

Neerealleroi (*Co. Nandewar*) 30°17'S. 149°49'E., 5 km NE of Narrabri, on Mulgate Ck.

Neeworra (*Co. Benarba*) 29°02'S. 149°04'E., 11 km SE of Mungindi; grazing; declined 1938+, defunct; earth tremor 2013; flood 1890; PO 1927, burnt down 1962; railway bridge (steel truss) 1914, 120 ft (36.6 m), over Boomi R.; RS 1914, station b. by Roberts, closed 1975; telephone 1916; pop. 58 (1933).

Neible (*Co. Napier*) 31°39'S. 149°38'E., 30 km NW of Coolah, on Oakey Ck; RS 1941–75.

Neila Creek (*Co. Forbes*) 33°55'S. 148°43'E., 9 km S. of Cowra, on Neila Ck; 2 quarries; school 1893–1949; pop. 133 (1911), 30 (1933), 94 (1947).

Neiles Creek (*Co. Murray*) 35°23'S. 149°29'E., 15 km S. of Bungendore.

Neilpo (*Co. Wentworth*) see Pomona.

Neilrex (*Co. Napier*) 31°44'S. 149°18'E., 20 km S. of Binnaway, on Butheroo Ck; village gaz. 1917; farming; Angl. C. (St Laurence's), removed 1968 from Hannahs Bridge; PO 1918; RS 1917, station b. by John Allibone, closed 1974; school 1957–68; telephone 1924; TX 1925, automatic 1984; pop. 140 (1933), 69 (1947), 78 (1954), 103 (1961).

Neilsons Creek (*Co. Hunter*) 32°31'S. 150°51'E., 21 km SE of Denman.

Nelanglo (*Co. King*) 34°59'S. 149°14'E., 35 km NW of Bungendore; school 1882 b. by W. Affleck, closed 1932.

Nelbothery (*Co. Wellesley*) 36°58'S. 149°02'E., 20 km W. of Bombala, on Delegate R.; gold; dam (Delegate River Hydraulic Sluicing Co.), 4,000,000 gal. (18,184 kl), 1892; hydraulic sluicing works: Delegate River Hydraulic Sluicing Co. 1892 d. by Otway, and Eureka & Sluicing Water Co. 1861, waterwheel erected 1861 by Minet; school 1884–91.

Nelia Gaari (*Co. Young*) 32°06'S. 142°51'E., 51 km NE of Menindee, on Darling R.; telephone 1924; TX 1929–63.

Nellies Glen (*Co. Cook*) see Megalong.

Nelligen (*Co. St Vincent*) 35°39'S. 150°08'E., 8 km NW of Batemans Bay, on Clyde R.; town gaz. and laid out 1854, surveyed 1858 by James Ferrier Cuthill and again in 1859 by Isaiah Rowland, village gaz. 1859, land sales 1860; early alluvial gold workings, river port, timber, grazing, farming, dairying, orchards, oysters; Angl. C. (St Nicholas's) b. 1873–76 by G. Eckley, burnt down 1939, and graveyard, church later reopened in the former court-house; bridge (concrete, 7 spans) b. 1960–64 by E.S. Clemenson (NSW) Pty Ltd, d. by Macdonald, Wagner and Priddle, 827 ft (252.1 m), over Clyde R.; bushfires 1905, 1939 (destroyed most of town), 2006; carriage-works (George Webber); cemetery (222 graves 1865+) 1881, incl. columbaria; CH b. 1893 by John M'Donald, d. by Walter Liberty Vernon, closed 1940, sold and reused 1955; cheese factory (Clyde River Co-op. Dairy Co.) 1906, closed and reused; electricity 1961; floods 1860, 1914, 1924, 1945, 1963; lock-up b. 1860 by Morris and Francis; Meth. C. 1923; PO 1859, condemned 1899, new one b. 1900, restored and reused, new one 1958–82, sold to Eldridge, reused; PS 1860, additions 1884 by Peak, new one 1916, closed 1940, sold and reused; punt b. 1857 by Dawson for Wilson and Bush, new one (Templeman's) 1878, sunk 1884, refloated, boiler exploded 1903, sunk 1945, refloated, new one 1962, service ceased 1964, across Clyde R.; Rom. Cath. C. (St Mary's) b. 1872 by Guy and Gloscoe, new one (St Joseph's) b. 1896 by William Alfred Isley, closed 1976, later reused; sawmills: James E. Anderson, H.G. Manning, George Webber (orig. horse powered); school 1865, new one b. 1869 by George Eckley, enlarged 1892 by

W.R. Kirby, repairs 1898 by George Hunter, new building 1962 (removed from Stony Ck), closed 1969, building moved to Batemans Bay and reused; telegraph 1878; telephone 1908; TX 1915, automatic 1983; Union C. b. 1893 by Webber; watch-house 1860, closed and demolished 1920; wattle-bark mills: Craig, Mostyn & Co., burnt down 1939 and Henry Manning 1865, burnt down 1939; Wes. Meth. C. 1894; wharves: Illawarra Steam Navigation Co. (126 ft or 38.4 m) and public 1876 (crane erected 1897 by Taylor); pop. *c.*100 (1859), *c.*150 (1866), 127 (1871), *c.*200 (1876), 188 (1891), 150 (1901), 185 (1911), 94 (1933), 97 (1947), 115 (1954), 127 (1961), 195 (1996), 219 (2001), 228 (2006), 253 (2011).

Nelson (*Co. Dampier*) 36°37'S. 149°58'E., 13 km NE of Bega; gold (disc. 1873 and more in 1888).

Nelson Bay (*Co. Gloucester*) 32°43'S. 152°09'E., 40 km NE of Newcastle, on Port Stephens; (incl. Corlette formerly Illawong till 1968, Dutchmans Bay, Gan Gan, Redpatch Point, Sandy Point); settled by Glover, surveyed 1874; fishing, lobsters, oysters, retirement centre, tourism; ambulance station; Angl. C. (All Saints') 1923, replaced 1959; army camp (Gan Gan); Bapt. C. (Lighthouse) 1978; bushfire 1898; cemetery (394 graves 1897+) 1882; 2 FB (incl. station b. 1956); hailstorm 2018; Jehovah's Witnesses C.; jetties: 1976 and 1987; lighthouse (Nelson Head) 1872, replaced 1876, converted 1948 from kerosene to electricity, restored 1988–90; marinas (Anchorage and d'Albora); Meth. C. (orig. Union) 1909, enlarged 1953 and reused, new one 1954, extended 1968; military camp (Gan Gan) 1941; naval base (HMAS Assault) in World War II, reused 1949–53 as migrant hostel, sick bay reused 1956–81 as hospital, base incl. jetty on Fly Point; PO: Corlette 1963 and Nelson Bay 1883, repairs 1901 by Head, new one b. 1960; Presb. C. (St Stephen's); PS 1942, new one 1966; quarry; 3 reservoirs; Rom. Cath. C. 1962, replaced (St Michael's) 1978; squall 1905; TC, moved to Tomaree; telegraph 1869; telephone (Corlette) 1963; tornado 2001; TX 1917, automatic 1959; wharves: one b. 1910 by Andrew Dahl and NSW Fish Co.; pop. *c.*30 (1886), 88 (1891), 150 (1901), 136 (1911), 353 (1933), 525 (1947), 1,249 (1954), 1,867 (1961), 2,272 (1966), 4,186 (1971), 5,376 (1976), 7,931 (1981), 9,376 (1986), 8,219 (1991), 9,220 (1996), 10,733 (2001), 10,974 (2006), 11,650 (2011).

Nelson Bay (*Co. Gloucester*)
see also Salamander Bay.

Nelsons Plains (*Co. Durham*) 32°44'S. 151°44'E., 5 km NW of Raymond Terrace, on Hunter R.; farming; bridges: Fitzgerald Bridge (concrete) to Raymond Terrace, b. 1965 by John Holland (Constructions) Pty Ltd, d. by Macdonald, Wagner and Priddle, 864 ft (263.3 m), over Williams R. and Irrawang Bridge 1970, to Millers Forest, over Hunter R.; bushfires 1914 and 1926; floods 1857 and 1867; military depot; PO 1877–1932; punt (diesel) to Raymond Terrace, replaced by bridge across Williams R.; school 1852–1918; telephone 1899; TX 1916; wharf b. 1901 by J.S. Gain; pop. 177 (1901), 185 (1911), 162 (1933), 201 (1947), 148 (1954), 143 (1961), 324 (2011).

Nelungaloo (*Co. Ashburnham*) 33°09'S. 148°00'E., 17 km W. of Parkes, on Brolgan Ck; farming; PO 1915; RS 1896, station b. by John Allibone, closed 1974; school 1957–61, sold and reused; silo 1930; telephone 1915; TX 1915, automatic 1956; pop. 136 (1933), 117 (1947), 93 (1954), 91 (1961).

Nelyambo (*Co. Rankin*) 31°13'S. 144°06'E., 82 km NE of Wilcannia; pop. 25 (1933).

Nemingha (*Co. Inglis*) 31°07'S. 150°59'E., 7 km SE of Tamworth, on Cockburn R.; lucerne, hay, chaff, maize, oats, millet, vegetables, hort., tobacco, wheat, dairying; agric. research station 1950, became a campus of Tamworth Agric. Institute; Angl. C. (All Saints') 1899; bridge (Johnston Bridge) b. 1939 by Gam and Jenkins, damaged 2002, new one 2007, over Cockburn R.; creamery and butter factory (Tamworth Farmers' Union) 1893, burnt down 1895, rebuilt, taken over 1901 by Tamworth Co-op. Dairy Co. Ltd, merged in 1925 with

Tamworth & Dist. Primary Producers' Co-op. Co. to become Tamworth Co-op. Dairy Society Ltd and a new factory followed; cyclone 1914; electricity 1930; floods 1874 and 1910; hailstorm 1909; PO 1897; Presb. C. 1905; reservoir; RS 1896, closed; school 1878, new one b. 1882 by F. Wilson, additions 1924 by H.M. Powell, additions 1956, new one 1995; sewerage augmentation 1994; silo 1934; telephone 1905; TX (automatic) 1949; water reticulation 1967; pop. 381 (1911), 305 (1933), 300 (1947), 376 (1954), 649 (1961), 307 (1976), 337 (1981), 332 (1986), 325 (1991), 301 (1996), 301 (2001), 287 (2006), 232 (2011).

Neotsfield (*Co. Northumberland*) 32°36'S. 151°13'E., 6 km SE of Singleton, on Hunter R.; flood 1867; gale 1899; hailstorm 1912.

Nepean (*Co. Cook*) see Emu Plains.

Nepean Dam (*Co. Camden*) 34°20'S. 150°37'E., 6 km SE of Bargo, on Lake Nepean; dam (cyclopean masonry), b. 1925–30 and 1933–35, on Nepean R.; PO 1926; PS 1926–33; school 1926–36; telephone 1926; TX 1926; pop. 516 (1933), 78 (1947).

Neranie (*Co. Gloucester*) see Bungwahl.

Nericon (*Co. Cooper*) 34°13'S. 146°03'E., 9 km N. of Griffith; village gaz. 1924; dairying, rice, hort.; TX (automatic); pop. *c.*70 (1990), 115 (2006), 309 (2011).

Neringla (*Co. St Vincent*) 35°44'S. 149°48'E., 31 km NW of Moruya; pop. 128 (2006).

Nerong (*Co. Gloucester*) 32°31'S. 152°12'E., 11 km S. of Bulahdelah, on Bombah Broadwater; village estab. 1883, burnt down 1916; timber; sawmill: W.H. Masters 1900 and Port Stephens Hardwood Co.; wharf, defunct; pop. 349 (2011).

Nerong Waterholes (*Co. Gloucester*) 32°33'S. 152°09'E., 13 km N. of Tea Gardens.

Nerriga (*Co. St Vincent*) 35°07'S. 150°05'E., 39 km NW of Milton, on Bindi Brook; settled by George Galbraith; wattle-bark, goldmining (alluvial) till 1960, farming, wool, beef, honey, eucalyptus oil; Angl. C. (Good Shepherd) 1936; bushfire 1965; cemeteries: general (46 graves 1858–2001) and Rom. Cath. (37 graves 1897+); electricity 1961; FB (station b. 1978); foot-bridge over Bindi Brook; lock-up 1905; PO 1865; PS 1901; Rom. Cath. C. (Our Lady Help of Christians) b. 1957 by F. Brown, and graveyard (37 graves 1897+); sawmill (Nerriga Sawmilling Co. Pty Ltd) 1951, burnt down 1952, rebuilt by Lewis Rolfe, sold 1956 to Irvine & Son; school 1880, re-roofed 1882, new one b. 1897, closed 1917, reopened 1950, new one b. 1952 by Roy Lamont, closed 1975, reused 1984; telephone 1912; TX 1928–81; Union C.; Wes. Meth. C. 1871; pop. 12 (1841), 59 (1901), 133 (1911), 147 (1933), 128 (1947), 142 (1954), 125 (1961), *c.*50 (1990), 367 (2011).

Nerriga (*Co. St Vincent*) see also Corang.

Nerrigundah (*Co. Dampier*) 36°07'S. 149°54'E., 21 km W. of Tuross Head, on Gulph Ck; orig. The Gulph; estab. 1861, surveyed 1867 by Alexander Pacifico Lindo, village gaz. 1868, lots sold 1870; mining (gold disc. 1861 by George Cook, Joseph Goodenough and William Crouch, gold rush 1861), eucalyptus oil distillation 1920, sawmilling, farming; Angl. C. (Christ) 1913; brewery (Thomas Auld, T.H. Saunders and George Hopkins) 1863; bushfires 1875, 1909, 1953; cemetery (burials 1861+) 1870; CH (incl. police station) 1862, closed 1881, reopened 1888, new one (incl. lock-up) b. 1904 by Hocking Bros, closed 1926, moved 1928 to Bodalla; Chinese joss house, demolished; FB; mines (incl. Mount Pleasant); PO 1861; Presb. C. 1870–1953, dismantled and moved 1953 to Tuross Head; PS, closed, reopened 1888–1926, moved to Bodalla; Rom. Cath. C. (St Patrick's) 1862, new one (St Philip and St James's) b. 1898 by Brogan, and graveyard; sawmill; school 1863, new buildings b. 1883 by G. Dawson, closed 1922, reopened 1959, additions 1963, closed 1972; stamper batteries: 10 head, Community, Fraser's (re-erected 1911); telephone 1899; TX 1948–77; pop. *c.*500 (1861), *c.*500 (1866), 483 (1871), *c.*200 (1891), 266 (1901), 169 (1911), 105 (1933), 104 (1961), 99 (2006), 55 (2011).

Nesca (*Co. Northumberland*) 33°06'S. 151°37'E., 2 km SW of Swansea, on Lake Macquarie; colliery (North Wallard).

Nethercote (*Co. Auckland*) 37°01'S. 149°50'E.,

9 km NW of Eden, on Old Hut Ck; farming; bridge, destroyed 1919; flood 1919; PO 1908, burnt down 1917, replacement burnt down 1927; school 1894–1963; telephone 1910; TX 1918–73; pop. 77 (1901), 142 (1911), 125 (1933), 128 (1947), 89 (1954), 90 (1961), 366 (2011).

Netley (*Co. Menindee*) 32°36'S. 141°29'E., 71 km S. of Broken Hill; pop. 83 (1911), 59 (1933).

Netley Hill (*Co. Cook*) see Kurrajong North.

Nettley Corner (*Co. Bathurst*) 33°49'S. 148°39'E., 5 km NW of Cowra, on Lachlan R.

Nettley Flat (*Co. Bathurst*) 33°49'S. 148°38'E., 5 km NW of Cowra, on Lachlan R.

Neurea (*Co. Gordon*) 32°41'S. 148°57'E., 15 km S. of Wellington; surveyed 1839 by Peter Grant Ogilvie, laid out 1840 by Walker Rannie Davidson, village gaz. 1880 as Newrea, designated as chief town of the county, but never fully developed; farming and grazing; cemetery (6 graves) 1879; mines: Bell's and Eagle Plateau 1932; school 1881–84, 1892–1913, 1957–66; telephone 1907; TX 1923, automatic 1982; Union C. 1911, new one 1956; winery (Markeita Cellars) estab. 1974 by K. and M. Reinhard; pop. 44 (1847), 75 (1851), 71 (1891), 66 (1901), 90 (1911), 105 (1933), 53 (1947), 74 (1954), 95 (1961), 144 (2006), 369 (2011).

Nevada (*Co. Yancowinna*) 31°48'S. 141°20'E., 21 km NW of Broken Hill, on Lakes Ck; village gaz. 1886, defunct.

Never Never (*Co. Raleigh*) see Thora.

Nevertire (*Co. Oxley*) 31°50'S. 147°43'E., 19 km SW of Warren; laid out 1883 by Tretton, town gaz. 1884, first lots sold 1885; sheep and agric.; Angl. C., destroyed 1896, new one (St Thomas's) 1898; carriage-works (Walter John Parker and Patrick Lyons) 1888; cemetery (156 graves 1891+) 1886; CH 1893, damaged 1896; dust storms 1929, 1935, 1960 (numerous houses unroofed), 2020; earth tremor 1935; 2 FB; fire 1903; lock-up; PO 1883, unroofed 1960; PS 1883, damaged 1896; railway barracks; railway turntable, 40 ft (12.2 m), replaced 1895, 50 ft (15.2 m); reservoir; rifle range 1913; Rom. Cath. C., destroyed 1896, replacement (St Brigid's) 1954, closed; RS 1882, station b. by D.S. Ralston, destroyed 1896, replaced; school 1883, damaged 1896, new one b. 1905 by Alfred Stephens, extended 1960 and 1970, provisionally closed 2005, finally closed 2008, sold; sewage works; telegraph 1883; tornadoes 1896 (destroyed most of town) and 1902; TX 1910, automatic 1984; water reticulation 1955; pop. 134 (1891), 250 (1901), 400 (1911), 170 (1933), 224 (1947), 364 (1954), 158 (1961), 225 (2011).

Nevertyre (*Co. Northumberland*) 33°14'S. 151°11'E., 24 km W. of Wyong, on Warre Warren Ck.

Neville (*Co. Bathurst*) 33°43'S. 149°13'E., 20 km S. of Blayney, on Number One Swamp; Number One Swamp and Macquarie Swamp till 1859, Macquarie and Mount Macquarie till 1892; village gaz. 1890 as Macquarie, thrived in 1890s; farming and grazing; airfield (2 km E.); Angl. C. (St Luke's) b. 1872 by Arthur Shakespear, closed 1983, sold and reused; bushfire 1939; butter factory 1892, burnt down 1901; carriage-works (R. Oats & Son); cemetery (1 km S.) 1880; cyclone 1913; diphtheria (child died) 1890; earth tremor 1906; FB; fire 1926; PO 1870; Presb. C. 1866, and graveyard; Rom. Cath. C. (St Thomas the Apostle) 1897, closed, reopened 1931, closed again 1970, sold and demolished; sawmills: Samuel L. Bird and Hargans & Sons; scarlet fever 1898; school (Macquarie Swamp till 1859, then Mount Macquarie till 1892) 1858, new one b. 1861, new building b. 1880 by Josiah Shakespear, d. by Robertson, additions 1892 by J. Donald, repairs 1898 by G. Ford, new building 1925; telephone 1892; TX 1917, automatic 1984; Unit. C. (orig. Wes. Meth.) 1878 and graveyard; pop. 500 (1901), 376 (1911), 269 (1921), 162 (1933), 214 (1947), 219 (1954), 148 (1961), *c.*150 (1975), 222 (2011).

New Angledool (*Co. Narran*) see Angledool.

New Ballarat (*Co. Northumberland*) see Wallsend.

New Bendigo (*Co. Evelyn*) 29°39'S. 141°54'E.,

253 km NW of Wilcannia; village gaz. 1895; gold.

New Berrima (*Co. Camden*) 34°30'S. 150°20'E., 2 km S. of Berrima, on Stony Ck; estab. and first lots sold 1928; cement works (Southern Portland Cement & Coal Co.) b. 1927–29; cemetery; PO 1952; quarry; reservoir; rifle range 1932; sewerage augmentation 1990; telephone 1952; water tower; pop. 55 (1947), 542 (2011).

Newbold Grange (*Co. Gresham*) 29°30'S. 152°40'E., 32 km NE of Grafton, on Clarence R.; grazing; airfield; boiling-down works.

Newbridge (*Co. Bathurst*) 33°35'S. 149°22'E., 12 km SE of Blayney, on Back Ck; Back Creek till 1876, then Duramana 1877–78; iron ore (disc. 1877 by George Hayton), gold (alluvial and reef), wheat, oats, vegetables, fruit, lambs, pottery clay; airfield (2 km S.); Angl. C. (St Bartholomew the Apostle) 1938–2009; cemetery (2 km E.) 1886; Cong. C.; drought 1913; FB; fire 1935; freezing works, taken over 1921 by Garratt Scandrett Freezing Companies Ltd; mines: Bright Star (estab. by Joseph Collins) 1910–12 and 1933–36, Davis 1915 and 1933–38, Foy's or Lady Tindall 1937–41 and 1946–47, Lowe and Duffields Shaft <1938, Pullens 1935–36 and 1938; PO (in rented premises) 1877, burnt down 1905, new one b. 1905 by Albert Emanuel Ennis, closed 1943, sold and reused; Presb. C. and graveyard; PS (in rented premises) 1892; quarry (The Great Gulf Iron Co.) 1877; railway embankment collapsed 1903; Rom. Cath. C. (Blessed Sacrament) b. 1919–22, d. by William Dryden, closed, sold and reused; RS (Back Creek till 1878) 1876–1989; school 1878 b. by S.F. Smith, additions 1881 also by Smith, additions and repairs 1892 by John Dunkley, additions 1913, closed 2010, sold; telegraph 1877, new office b. 1905 by Albert Emanuel Ennis; TX 1915, automatic 1986; Wes. Meth. C.; pop. 401 (1901), 365 (1911), 298 (1921), 298 (1933), 242 (1947), 274 (1954), 200 (1961), *c.*150 (1975), 183 (2011).

New Brighton (*Co. Rous*) 28°31'S. 153°33'E., 4 km N. of Brunswick Heads, on Coral Sea; land sales 1906; sand mining 1934+; PO 1927; storm 1921; telephone 1925; TX 1941–63; pop. 69 (1933), 126 (1947), 73 (1954), 120 (1961), 274 (2006), 293 (2011).

New Buildings (*Co. Auckland*) 36°58'S. 149°33'E., 28 km W. of Pambula, on Towamba R.; orig. Yuglamah; bridge (Pioneer Bridge) b. 1884 by Sims & Co., 244 ft (74.4 m), destroyed 1919, new one (Dare timber truss) 1921, 332 ft (101.2 m), repairs 2017, over Towamba R.; flood 1919.

Newburn (*Co. Rous*) 28°29'S. 153°33'E., 7 km N. of Brunswick Heads, on Coral Sea.

Newcastle (*Co. Northumberland*) 32°56'S. 151°47'E., 117 km NE of Sydney, on Hunter R.; (incl. Bank Corner, Bar Beach, Civic, Cooks Hill was Darby Street till 1944, East Newcastle orig. The Sandhills, Honeysuckle Point, The Hill, West Newcastle); Coal River till 1804, then Newcastle, but known also as King's Town till 1830; disc. 1797 by Lieut. John Shortland, penal settlement founded 1801 by Lieut. Col. William Patterson under command of Cpl Wixtead, abandoned 1802, penal settlement re-estab. 1804 under Lieut. Charles Menzies, consolidated 1816–19 under Capt. James Wallis, penal settlement closed and free settlement gaz. 1823, surveyed 1823 by Henry Dangar, decl. a free port 1846, town gaz. 1848, British military forces withdrawn 1851, munic. proc. 1859, designated as chief town of the county, thrived 1850s–1880s and 1915–20, city (Greater Newcastle) proc. 1938; timber till 1827, mining (coal disc. 1797 by Lieut. John Shortland) 1804–1912, lime burning 1809–22, maize 1812+, wheat 1812+, barley 1812+, shipbuilding 1818+, rope-making, seaport, salt-making 1820s–30s, tobacco 1830s–40s, hides, biscuits, dairying, brickmaking, heavy industry; air-conditioning factory (Vincent Ventilating & Air Conditioning Co.) 1935; ambulance station 1921; Angl. C.: first one (b. 1812, demolished 1816), Christ C. (b. 1818, d. by Capt. James Wallace, James Clohasy and Joseph Lycett, repairs 1827 by Mackay, spire dismantled 1868, church closed 1884, new one 1884–1904 b. by James Russell, d. by John Horbury Hunt, reused, replacement 1885–1979, first stage b. by John Straub, also d. by Hunt, later stage d. by Frederick George Castleden and John Hingston Buckeridge, and after World War II d. by Edwin Clarence Sara and then John Sara, damaged 1989, restored 1995–97, and graveyard, burials 1802–81), St John's (b. 1857–60 by James Hesp, d. by Edmund Thomas Blacket, belfry 1865, church alterations 1920, re-floored 1953); Assemblies of God C. (City); bacon factories: Barnes Bacon Co. Pty Ltd 1935 and Foggitt Jones Pty Ltd (b. 1919 by Young and Parry, d. by Wallace L. Porter); baking powder and condiment factory (J. Griffiths Pty Ltd); Bapt. C. 1865, new one b. 1890 by John Rollo Rodgers, d. by Frederick Burnhardt Menkens; beacon (Flagstaff Hill) 1813–57; benevolent asylum 1897; bicycle works (J.D. Smith) 1880; biscuit factory (William Arnott) estab. 1865, relocated 1877, extended 1884 and 1885, boy killed 1898, closed 1942, demolished 1949; blind factory (Great Northern Venetian Blind Works) o. 1889 by A. Scorer & Co.; boat harbour b. 1866–73; bond stores: Bingle & Son 1855, David Cohen & Co. (b. 1901 by F.J. Thorby, d. by Frederick Burnhardt Menkens, burnt down 1907, replacement 1908 d. by Menkens and Castleden, adaptive reuse 1993 d. by Cornucopia Aust. Pty Ltd), Earp Gillam & Co. (b. 1888 by John Straub, d. by Frederick Burnhardt Menkens, disused and derelict, bought by Lahey Constructions Pty Ltd, restoration 1987–93 d. by Suters Snell, reused), Francis Gardner 1872, R. Hall & Son (b. 1899, d. by Frederick Burnhardt Menkens, reused by Rundles as clothing factory), Jesse Ireland (b. 1885, d. by James Henderson, reused), Stanton Catchlove & Co., C.M.B. Wood Bros & Co. Ltd 1865 (burnt down 1874, new one 1875 d. by Mansfield); boot factories: John Kidd & Co. 1878 (moved 1884 to Islington) and Walter A. Pike 1879; breakwaters: Macquarie Pier, linking Nobby's Island, b. 1818–46, rebuilt 1864, enlarged and strengthened, and southern one 4,535 ft (1,382.3 m), light tower erected 1880 by H. Burrow; breweries: Castlemaine Brewery (b. 1874–76 by Laing and Wylie for Prendergast and Fitzgerald and Wood Bros & Co., d. by Oswald H. Lewis, additions 1878 by George Yeomans, company name changed 1883 from Castlemaine Brewery & Malting Co. Ltd to Castlemaine Brewery Maltings & Wine & Spirit Co. Ltd, alterations and renovations 1898, alterations 1910–14 d. by Frederick George Castleden, taken over 1921 by Tooth & Co. Ltd, closed 1931, alterations and modifications 1938 by Elliott and Beck, d. by Pitt and Merewether, reused as depot 1938–74, additions 1960, sold 1974, adaptive reuse 1988 d. by D.W.P. Suters), Fog Horn Brewhouse 2015, Great Northern Brewery (b. 1888 by Thomas, Perry and Rowledge, d. by Peter Bennett and Ernest George Yeomans, closed 1889, acquired 1891 by Castlemaine Brewery, reused 1919), Scarr's Brewery (Thomas Scarr); broom factories: Emery & Co., fire 1922 and NSW Co-op. Wholesale Society, fire 1929, extensions 1941 by J.C. Davis & Son, d. by John William Oldham and Robert Godwin Lees; bubonic plague 1902 (man died) and 1905 (boy died); cardboard box and paper bag factory (P.J. Firth Pty Ltd); carriage-works: City Coach Factory (John Rees) 1877 and John and George Gilbert 1881 (replaced 1885 by Frank B. Gilbert, and John and Herbert Pearse, fire 1909); cemetery (Honeysuckle, 375 graves *c.*1840–81), closed 1883; CH 1822, reused, replacement (incl. lock-up) b. 1837–41, d. by Mortimer William Lewis, alterations 1866 also d. by Lewis, rebuilt 1878, demolished 1899, new one b. 1890–92 by Charles Coghill, d. by James Johnstone Barnet, additions and alterations 1938 by J.C. Pickles, extensions 1949, extensions 1966 d. by M. Stanley, additions 1981, restored 1985, damaged 1989, repaired 1991, closed, sold 2016 to Nihon University (Japan), new one b. 2013–16 on new site by John Holland (Constructions) Pty Ltd, d. by Cox Architecture; chemical factory

(W.H. Sproull & Co., became Sproull's Neuron Pty Ltd); chenille factory (Pacific Chenille Craft Pty Ltd) 1945; Chinese Presb. C. 1898, closed, moved 1939 to Kotara and reused; cholera 1883; Christ. Fellowship Ministries C. (Potter's House), in reused building; Christ. Revival Crusade C.; Christadelphian C.; Church of God; cistern factory (T.V. Richards & Son), new one 1939; clothing factories: David Cohen & Co. 1911 (in old bond store), H.R. Hayman Pty Ltd, McLaren Johnson & Co., Rundles' (in old bond store), Sutcliffe Manufacturing Pty Ltd (b. 1940 by A. McIlroy, d. by Jeater, Rodd and Hay); coke-ovens b. 1853 by Coal & Copper Co.; collieries: A Pit (Aust. Agric. Co.) 1831, B Pit (Aust. Agric. Co.) 1837, C Pit (Aust. Agric. Co.), Ironbark (John Laurio Platt), New Discovery estab. by Lieut. Charles Menzies, Sea Pit or New Winning 1888–1916; commissariat store 1812–49; confectionery factories: Great Northern Confectionery Works (estab. 1896 by Llewellyn Davies in a factory b. by George Galton) and Niagara Ltd; Cong. C. (Brown Street) 1856, gallery added 1865, church extended 1879, renovated, demolished 1974; convict barracks 1820; convict stockade, reused, burnt down 1851; cordial factories: F. Bradford, B. Burlinson 1886, G. Elands, S.C. Mears, Augustus Frederick Moore 1876 (became National Bottling Co. Newcastle Ltd in 1968, taken over by Coca-Cola), Newcastle Ice & Cordial Works (estab. 1884 by J.C. Palmer, bought 1887 by R. Wilson and moved to Wickham), NSW Aerated Water & Confectionery Co. Ltd (estab. 1865 by George Edward Redman, acquired businesses of J.T. Atkinson of Wallsend, Coleman Bros of Wickham, George Edward Redman of Wickham, and E. Rowlands of Newcastle, in 1896, new factory b. 1916 by A.E. Young, d. by E.G. Yeomans & Son, factory sold 1954 to McLeod, Kelso and Lee, business moved to Lambton), Wood and Clifton; creamery and butter factory (J. Ireland Ltd) 1892; customs-house b. 1874–77 by Jennings and Pallister, d. by James Johnstone Barnet and Edmund S.V. Spencer, damaged 1895, additions 1899 d. by Walter Liberty Vernon, repairs 1901 by I. Banks & Sons, refurbished 1956, fire damaged 1959, re-roofed 1963, restored 1968 and 1981, damaged 1989, repaired 1990–94, substantially altered and reused 1995; dengue fever 1942; diphtheria 1921, 1925 (3 died), 1926, 1929, 1934, 1941; droughts 1875, 1876, 1877, 1885, 1962; earthquake (9 died and buildings damaged) 1989; earth tremors 1837, 1842, 1868, 1872, 1886, 1907, 1925, 1951; electricity 1891; electricity substation b. 1939 by Orrett Bros, d. by Castleden and Sara; electroplating works: Barnard Electro Plating Co. Pty Ltd and Hamilton Chrome; engineering works: Acme Oil Engine Co. Pty Ltd, Brent and Warburton, J. and A. Dick, K. Henderson, John Moyes and Andrew Donald 1868 (moved 1879 to Wickham), G.H. Varley Pty Ltd; FB: Honeysuckle 1882 and Newcastle 1856, new station b. 1913 by Frank Hickey, d. by Alfred Spain and Thomas Frame Cosh, new one b. 1931 by D. Hobbs, new one 1993; ferry (steam) to Stockton, across Hunter R., estab. 1869 by Hugh and Robert Boyce; fire 1902; fibrous plaster works (Newcastle Fibrous Manufacturing Co. Ltd) 1920; fires 1851, 1859, 1866, 1867, 1872, 1873, 1877, 1879, 1880, 1881, 1882, 1884, 1891, 1895, 1947; floods 1871, 1893, 1908, 1946, 1949; flour mills: Stephen Durrant Lott 1868–77, Major James Thomas Morisset (wind) 1820–47, James Steele (steam) 1844 (leased 1856 to J.B. North); foodstuff factories: J.A. Bull & Co. Pty Ltd and J. Ireland Ltd; forts: Flagstaff Hill (first 1822, second 1878), Fort Scratchley (b. 1881–86 by James Russell and George A. Smith, d. by Major Gen. Sir William Francis Drummond Jervois, Lieut. Col. Sir Peter Henry Scratchley and Gustavus Alphonse Morell, barracks b. 1886 by John Frogley, fort remodelled and expanded 1889–92 by James Russell, repairs 1903 by Southon Bros, altered and modernised 1911 and 1939–40, closed 1962, abandoned 1972, restored 1977+, reused 1982, restored again 2008), Shepherds Hill

(b. 1890–94 by James Russell, repairs 1903 by Southon Bros, upgraded 1938–43); foundries: British Iron Foundry (estab. 1872 by John Gibson, taken over 1883 by Robert Gibson, moved 1885), Alexander Campbell (Honeysuckle Point), fire 1897, V. & H. Horley Ltd, E.E. Robbins 1885, Archibald Rodgers 1854 (new works 1862, taken over 1871 by James S. and Alexander Rodgers, explosion 1876), G.H. Varley Ltd 1886, new works b. 1918 on new site by W. Warland, d. by W.L. Porter; freezing works: P.H. Evans and F. Tickle; furniture factories: Federal Furnishing Warehouse (J. Mackie & Co. Pty Ltd) 1897, fire 1927, Great Northern Furniture Bazaar (Walter Neve) 1866, M. Light & Son Ltd (b. 1938 by H.C. Owen, d. by Jeater, Rodd and Hay), A. Macrow & Sons Pty Ltd, D. Murray 1898, S.C. Nevill & Co., William F. Nicolson, O'Connor Bros, Pearson's Furnishing Warehouse 1877, H. Prentice & Co. Ltd, burnt down 1934, Henry James Pullin and Aldis, fire 1922; gales 1866, 1867, 1897 (Cooks Hill), 1951; galvanised iron works (Tinning Products Co.); gaol 1817, reused 1822 as hospital, second one d. by Capt. James Wallis, closed 1845, abandoned 1855, demolished; gastroenteritis epidemics 1940 (child died) and 1951; gasworks (The City of Newcastle Gas & Coke Co. Ltd) 1867, explosion (killed man) 1892, inundated 1893; govt house 1804, enlarged, burnt down 1823; hailstorms 1886 and 1895; harbour dredging 1859+; hat factory (W.R. Denton); Hillsong C. (in former cinema); hosiery factory (Lustre Hosiery Pty Ltd) 1941; hospital (Royal Newcastle) b. 1866 by George Henry Cox, d. by Mortimer William Lewis, jun., new wing (Hannell Wing) b. 1885 by John Frogley, d. by Frederick Bernhardt Menkens, additions 1887, additions and alterations 1891 by John Rollo Rodgers, also d. by Menkens, additions 1897 also d. by Menkens, damaged 1898, additions 1902 by Banks & Son, extensions 1913, 1915, 1917 d. by George McRae, further extended 1924, 1927, 1934, 1938, 1951, extensions 1953 by James Mullan Pty Ltd, d. by Stephenson and Turner, demolished 2008 (except for north wing which was restored and reused); hurricane 1898; ice-cream factories: Newcastle Milk & Delicacy Co. Pty Ltd 1918, additions 1939 by C.L. Saxby, d. by Ashton and Peters American Delicacy Co. Ltd 1927, additions and alterations 1938, demolished 1974; ice works: P. Callen & Sons 1899, Dark's Ice & Cold Storage Ltd 1912 (fire 1928, extended 1934 and 1940 by E. Wilson, additions 1942 by C.A. Hutcherson, d. by M. Sproull, explosion killed man 1944, demolished), C.J. Kirchner 1884–90; incinerator b. 1938 by Baker and Lamb, d. by Frederick Abraham Scorer, chimney 117 ft (35.7 m) b. by J. Jamieson & Son, furnaces by Reverberatory Incinerator & Engineering Co. Pty Ltd, closed 1946, reused, damaged 1989, demolished; ink factory (Arthur Simpson); jetty 1994; Jewish C. b. 1927 by Frewin & Cook Pty Ltd, d. by Thomas James Pepper and Bill Jeater; joineries: Andrew Cook & Sons Ltd, extensions 1935 d. by Andrew Cook, sen., G. Dixon & Co., fire 1939, Hay's, burnt down 1866, Johnston's 1921, relocated 1924, Manning & Co., burnt down 1922, new one burnt down 1926, A.L. Peterson; 2 leading light navigation towers 1866, 23 ft (7 m), d. by James Johnstone Barnet, one rebuilt 1877 and heightened to 66 ft (20 m) by William Dart, the other one demolished; leadlight works (H.T. Dooley), fire 1929; lighthouses: Flagstaff Hill 1822, new one 1836, and Nobby's Head 1858, 33 ft (10 m), converted 1935 to electricity; lock-up b. 1886 by E. Young & Co.; lunatic asylum for imbeciles o. 1872 (in old military barracks), repairs 1874 by John Ash, additions and repairs 1876 by Smith and Laurenson, additions 1877 by William Dart, became institution for idiots in 1879, female ward b. 1892 by John Ash & Sons, damaged 1893, became hospital for the insane in 1896, became mental hospital in 1917, additions 1925 by Kent and Kent, became psychiatric centre in 1963, additions 1971, became Hunter Hospital in 1983, became James Fletcher

Hospital in 1989, additions 2009; mattress factory (L. Joseph Pty Ltd) 1921; meat canning works (Newcastle Meat Preserving Co.) estab. 1849 by Henry, Richard and William Dangar, closed 1855; Meth. C. 1903 d. by T. Dixon Chater and Augustus D. Chater, closed, sold and reused; military barracks b. 1841–43 by Hudson and Richardson, closed 1855, reused 1867 as female reformatory, reused 1872 as lunatic asylum; military hospital 1841; milk factory (Dairy Farmers' Co-op. Milk Co. Ltd) 1938 d. by Alva Charles Likely, demolished 1997; miners' strikes 1850, 1861, 1862, 1888, 1896, 1909–10, 1916, 1949; morgue b. 1886 by James Russell, new one 1932; navigation obelisk 1850, damaged 1985 and 1989; peanut processing plant (Nut Foods Pty Ltd) 1946; pilot station 1866; PO: Cooks Hill 1909–95, Honeysuckle Point 1866, Newcastle 1828 (new one b. 1873 by Laing and Wylie, additions and alterations, incl. portico, b. 1883–86 by M. Parkhill, d. by Mortimer William Lewis, jun., reused, third one b. 1900–3 d. by Walter Liberty Vernon, additions 1913, repairs 1936 by W.H. Ashmore, extended 1938, partly restored 1999, closed, sold 2002 to Sean Ngu, bought 2010 by NSW govt, acquired 2014 by Aboriginal land council, disused and in disrepair), Newcastle Hill 1957, West Newcastle 1889, new one b. 1898 by Wooden and Frost; pound (stock) 1861; powerhouses: munic. 1928 and tramway 1923; power station (Zaara Street) b. 1915, upgraded 1920, 1921, 1923, 1928, 1930, 1936, 1942, 1944, man killed 1941, explosion 1951, taken over 1953 by Electricity Commission, closed 1975, demolished 1978; Presb. C.: St Andrew's b. 1847–54 (enlarged 1874, demolished 1893, new one b. 1890 on new site by Raymond Dumbrell, d. by Frederick Burnhardt Menkens, damaged 1989) and St Philip's (b. 1863 by Laing and McLaughlin, replacement b. 1905 on new site by D. McRae & Son, d. by William Mark Nixon and John Shedden Adam, jun., re-roofed 1959, closed, sold and reused); Prim. Meth. C.: one b. 1855 (enlarged 1866, demolished 1974) and Maitland Road (b. 1889 by Myers and Thompson, d. by Peter Bennett and Ernest George Yeomans, closed, reused); PS: East Newcastle (b. 1876 by W.R. Vaughan, closed 1982, reused), Honeysuckle Point (damaged 1902, new one b. 1908 by W.F. Foster & Co., renamed West Newcastle in 1926, closed and reused 1936), Newcastle 1828 (replacement 1849 d. by Mortimer William Lewis, new one b. 1859–61 by John Scanlon, d. by Alexander Dawson, modified 1867, perimeter wall 1882, second storey added 1890, additions 1893, extensions 1956, closed 1982, reused, new one 1982 d. by J.W. Thompson); railway engine shed (Honeysuckle) b. 1871 by Thomas Smith; railway gasworks b. by John Louis Castner, reused; railway workshops (Honeysuckle, later Civic) 1856, incl. locomotive machine shop 1874, closed, restored and reused, blacksmiths and wheel shop 1880–1937, closed, restored and reused, perway store 1882, closed, restored and reused, locomotive boiler shop b. 1882–87, reused 1951–57 as powerhouse, closed, restored 1996 and reused, erecting shop 1920, closed, restored and reused, remainder of site razed; 4 reservoirs (incl. 1882, 1918, 1929); Rom. Cath. C.: first one (temporary chapel) b. 1852, Sacred Heart 1875 (additions 1895, extended 1899 by M. Crosby, closed 1930, reused, demolished 1974, new one b. 1928–30 by Elliott and Beck, d. by Peter Joseph Gannon, damaged 1989, became cathedral in 1995, and columbaria 2015), St Luke's (Cooks Hill) 1962 d. by Peter Jerome Gannon, closed 2003, St Mark's (chapel) 1970–2007, sold, St Mary Star of the Sea (b. 1864–66 by Thomas Purcell, d. by William Munro, alterations d. by Peter Joseph Gannon); RS: Civic (o. 1857 as Newcastle, became Honeysuckle 1858, changed to Honeysuckle Point 1866, second station b. 1872 by J. Dart, closed 1936, demolished, new one o. 1935 as Civic, closed 2014) and Newcastle 1858 (station rebuilt 1872, new one b. 1878 by William Cains, d.

by John Whitton, additions and alterations 1897 by Mitchell, restored 1985, upgraded 2007, closed 2014); sale-yards 1889; salt-works: Aust. Agric. Co. (J.S. Brickwood) and Gregory Blaxland 1826–28; Salv. Army C. 1885, new one b. 1912 by L. Fox, new one 1926; sawmills: Robert Breckenridge (incl. joinery), fire 1908, Andrew Cook & Sons Pty Ltd, fire 1908, Laing and Wylie, fire 1886, Hugh Meehan (removed from Stockton); scale factories: Australasian Scale Co. Pty Ltd, Henry William Frost & Son, Toledo-Berkel Pty Ltd; schools: Cooks Hill 1885 (b. by William Dart, new buildings b. 1899–1903 by A. Cook, d. by Walter Liberty Vernon, additions 1966, closed 1984), Cooks Hill Girls HS 1963–76, East Newcastle 1883 (repairs 1900 by J. Hestelow, new one b. 1909 on new site by E.M. Banks, additions 1911 by W.F. Gazzard & Son, closed and reused), Hunter Girls HS 1923–75, Newcastle 1858 (new one b. 1879 by Yeomans, d. by George Allen Mansfield, closed 1911), Newcastle HS 1906–29 (new one 1976, additions 1979, new one 2014), Newcastle Girls HS 1929 b. by Baker and Lamb, d. by Edwin Evan Smith, closed 1975, Newcastle Hill Boys HS 1934–73; sessions house (first used as court-house, then post office 1828+, then customs-house 1839+, then Presb. manse 1859+) 1822–90; shipyard (John W. Scott), closed 1869; shoe polish factory (Supreem Polish Co.); signal station (Flagstaff Hill) b. 1822 by Lieut. Edward Charles Close, replaced 1869; smallpox 1915; soap and candle factory o. 1866 by Frederic Nainby but by 1869 taken over by Charles Upfold and became the Great Northern Soap & Candle Co.; soap-works (Lever Bros Ltd); Spiritualist C.; squalls 1897, 1913, 1945, 1946; storms 1864, 1899, 1902, 1921, 2007 (man died); streets gas lit 1875, then electric lit 1891; submarine attack by Japanese 1942; tank traps (World War II); TC: Parry Street, o. 1920 in former brewery, C Block 1934, B Block (former brewery) restored and renovated 1984 by M/W Building Pty Ltd, A Block b. 1986 by Citra Constructions Ltd, damaged 1989, became Hunter Institute of Technology, Hamilton Campus, in 1992, and West Newcastle b. 1894–96, d. by William Edmund Kemp, additions 1902 by T. and W. Cowan, additions 1910, 1911, 1913, 1917, 1918, 1919, became Hunter Institute of Technology, Hunter Street Campus, in 1992; teachers' college 1951 (formerly at Broadmeadow), additions 1963 and 1970, moved 1974 to Callaghan; telegraph: Honeysuckle Point 1894, Newcastle 1860 (new office b. 1861, d. by Alexander Dawson, additions 1877 d. by James Johnstone Barnet, additions 1882 by John Rollo Rodgers, reused 1886, new one b. 1903, d. by Walter Liberty Vernon), West Newcastle 1889 (new office b. 1898 by Wooden and Frost); telephone: Cooks Hill 1911 and Newcastle Hill 1957; tidal waves 1895 and 1960 (sunk 3 fishing boats); tinware factory (Hewitt Bros) 1877; tramway (steam) 1894, electrified 1923, closed 1950; tramway substation 1923–50, reused; TX 1893, new building b. 1938–41 by J.E. Parry; typhoid 1876 (54 died), 1886, 1914, 1940, 1953; United Meth. Free C.: Cooks Hill 1881 and Newcastle 1884; univ. (Newcastle, City Campus) 2018 d. by Lyons Architecture and EJE Architecture; 3 vehicular ferries (steam) to Stockton across Hunter R., sold 1971 to Stuart Allen White (Goldfields Metal Traders), wrecked 1972; vulcanising works: Apex Tyre Service Co. 1926, H.A. Douglas, J.A. Merton & Co. Ltd 1925, fire 1927; water supply 1877; Wes. Meth. C. 1845, demolished, new one b. 1863 by William Black and Alexander Leckie Elphinstone, d. by George Allen Mansfield, damaged 1864, re-roofed, sold 1903, demolished; wharves: first 1804 (186 ft or 56.7 m), Aust. Agric. Co. 1831 (new one b. 1888 by John Russell), coal wharf (704 ft or 214.6 m) 1964, Lee (b. 1907–10, extended 1927–30, extended 1937 by Court and Braithwaite), Market (wharf sheds added 1882), Merewether Street 1957, Queens (b. 1852 by J.D. Davies, fire 1872, renamed Kings in 1901, damaged and repaired 1910),

Stockton (passenger ferry) 1955; wool exchange, building remodelled 1953 by T.E. Taylor, d. by Stephenson and Turner, closed and reused; wool store (Pitt, Son & Badgery) b. 1940 by John Grant & Sons Pty Ltd, d. by John Reid & Son, closed, sold and reused; pop. (figures since World War II relate to Greater Newcastle and include many places outside Newcastle as delineated above and are therefore not comparable with earlier figures), 133 (1808), 120 (1810), 196 (1812), 272 (1814), 846 (1819), 1,169 (1821), 708 (1823), *c.*400 (1829), 536 (1833), 704 (1836), 1,377 (1841), 1,471 (1846), 1,340 (1851), 1,404 (1856), 1,462 (1861), 7,581 (1871), 8,986 (1881), *c.*9,000 (1886), 12,914 (1891), *c.*13,500 (1895), 14,238 (1901), 12,816 (1911), 13,657 (1933), 127,138 (1947), 134,079 (1954), 208,630 (1961), 234,005 (1966), 249,962 (1971), 363,011 (1976), 258,972 (1981), 255,787 (1986), 262,331 (1991), 270,324 (1996), 279,975 (2001), 288,732 (2006), 308,308 (2011). (See separate entries for surrounding suburbs.)

Newcastle (*Co. Northumberland*) see also Broadmeadow.

Newcastle South (*Co. Northumberland*) see Merewether.

Newdell Junction (*Co. Durham*) 32°25'S. 151°03'E., 21 km SE of Muswellbrook.

Newee Creek (*Co. Raleigh*) 30°40'S. 152°57'E., 6 km W. of Nambucca Heads; RS 1923–74; sawmill (Allen Taylor & Co. Ltd); school 1957–66; pop. 55 (1911), 139 (1933), 156 (1947), 199 (1954), 145 (1961), 384 (2011).

Newfreugh (*Co. Northumberland*) 32°37'S. 151°14'E., 8 km SE of Singleton; pound (stock).

New Glanmorgan (*Co. Gloucester*) see Medowie.

New Hartley (*Co. Roxburgh*) see Torbane.

Newhaven (*Co. Rous*) see Wooyung.

Newington (*Co. Murray*) 35°12'S. 149°18'E., 15 km NW of Bungendore; estab. 1865, deserted and razed 1866; mining (gold disc. 1865 by John M'Enally) 1865–66, 1880–88, 1894; mine (Mac's Reef); stamper battery 1866; Wes. Meth. C. 1867 (moved to Sutton).

New Italy (*Co. Richmond*) 29°09'S. 153°17'E., 10 km SW of Woodburn; founded 1882 by Rocco Caminiti and Antonio Pezzutti and settled 1882–88 by Italian immigrants, declined 1942+, abandoned 1955, largely defunct; timber till 1918, fruit, agric., silk, dairying; cemetery; cyclone 1945; flood 1917; PO 1892; Rom. Cath. C. 1887, destroyed 1907, replacement (St Peter's) 1907, damaged 1945, demolished; sawmill (Giacomo Rosolen) 1900, leased 1910 to Hodge and De Hayr, closed 1918; school 1885 b. by John Burke, closed 1933; storm 1907; telephone 1905; pop. 253 (1901), 187 (1911), 37 (1933), 295 (2011).

New Koreelah (*Co. Buller*) 28°29'S. 152°20'E., 65 km W. of Kyogle, on Koreelah Ck; farming, grazing, dairying; cheese factory (Tenterfield Dairy Co.) 1914; PO 1916–56; telephone 1914; TX 1916; pop. 77 (1933), 73 (1947), 76 (1954), 55 (1961). (See also Old Koreelah.)

New Lambton (*Co. Northumberland*) 32°56'S. 151°43'E., 5 km SE of Wallsend, on Styx Ck; (incl. New Lambton Heights and South New Lambton); estab. 1868, formerly part of the Scottish Aust. Mining Co. estate, munic. proc. 1889, subdivision (Meadowfield Estate) 1925, munic. subsumed 1938 under City of Greater Newcastle; coalmining; Angl. C.: All Saints' b. 1924 by Sowerby, new one 1959 and St Chad on the Hill 1961, closed, sold and reused; Bapt. C. 1928, reused, new one 1993; blind factory (M. Jenkins & Son); brickworks: Thomas Cottrell, William Hammon, James Wood; bushfires 1928, 1933, 1936, 1940; Church of Christ (The Heights Family); collieries: Buchanan Borehole 1969–79, Dog and Rat or A Pit, closed 1884, Hartley Vale (John and Alexander Brown); copper works (English & Aust. Copper Co. Ltd); FB (station b. 1897, new one 1934, closed); flood 1893; 2 foot-bridges over Styx Ck; hailstorm 2004; hospitals: John Hunter 1991 d. by J.W. Thompson and Lindsay Kelly, additions 2014 by North Construction & Building Pty Ltd, and Royal Newcastle Centre 2006; ice works (W.H. Llewellyn); landslip 1951; Lay Meth. C.

b. 1892 by Hardyman and Holmes, additions and alterations 1902 by Charles Byron, closed 1951, reused; measles epidemic 1954; miners' strike 1888; monumental stone works (Lock and Myers); PO: New Lambton 1872, new one b. 1939, additions and alterations 1945 by R.A. Keevers and South New Lambton 1950; Presb. C. (St James's) 1933, new one (now Samoan) b. 1963–66 d. by Stan Smith; Prim. Meth. C. 1869, rebuilt 1892, closed 1923; PS 1876–1936; 4 reservoirs; Rom. Cath. C. b. 1926 by R.L. Painter, d. by Peter Joseph Gannon, reused 1956, new one (St Therese's) b. 1956 by F.H. Compton & Sons, d. by Sydney George Hirst and David Kennedy; schools: Lambton HS 1974, additions by R.T. Parker Pty Ltd, New Lambton 1880 b. by Edward Constable, additions 1898 by Davis, Hardyman and Davis, additions and alterations 1909 by J. Head, Block B (infants) 1922, remodelled 1924 by Leslie Elgin Brander, Block C (girls) 1931, school reused by RAAF 1942–45, temporary infants school b. 1944 on new site by R.A. Keevers, Block D 1956, additions 1978, New Lambton Heights 1951, South New Lambton 1950, additions 2010; storm 2007; streets electric lit 1916; telegraph 1892, additions and alterations to office 1945 by R.A. Keevers; telephone: New Lambton 1903 and South New Lambton 1950; tramway (steam); TX 1937, automatic 1947; Unit. C. (Trinity, orig. Meth.) b. 1955 by R.A. Keevers, d. by C.H. Smith and Johnson, extended 2008; Wes. Meth. C. 1869, closed 1884, renovated and reopened 1892; pop. 403 (1871), *c.*800 (1881), 1,548 (1891), *c.*1,500 (1895), 1,464 (1900), 1,578 (1901), 1,872 (1911), *c.*3,600 (1921), 6,323 (1933), *c.*9,600 (1947), *c.*12,600 (1954), *c.*15,500 (1961), *c.*16,200 (1966–71), *c.*15,700 (1976), 11,026 (2006), 11,913 (2011).

New Lambton Heights (*Co. Northumberland*) see New Lambton.

Newlands (*Co. Gipps*) 33°14'S. 147°20'E., 23 km SE of Condobolin; farming and grazing; PO 1907; telephone 1924.

New Line Farm (*Co. King*) 34°48'S. 149°11'E., 8 km W. of Gunning, on Oolong Ck; settled by Benjamin Granger; Wes. Meth. C. b. 1880 by W.A. Preston.

Newling (*Co. Sandon*) see Armidale.

New Maragle (*Co. Selwyn*) 35°50'S. 148°15'E., 22 km E. of Tumbarumba, on Sparkes Ck; goldmining.

New Mexico (*Co. Darling*) 30°44'S. 150°37'E., 11 km W. of Manilla; formerly Mountain View; wheat and grazing; cemetery; Meth. C. 1909; PO 1912–41; school (Mountain View till 1902) 1901–38; pop. 105 (1901), 95 (1911), 117 (1933), 93 (1947), 281 (2006).

New Mollyan (*Co. Gowen*) 31°36'S. 149°13'E., 16 km W. of Binnaway; farming and grazing; PO 1898; telephone 1925; TX 1928, automatic 1982; pop. 56 (1933), 55 (1947).

Newnes (*Co. Cook*) 33°11'S. 150°14'E., 30 km NE of Wallerawang, on Wolgan R.; (incl. South Newnes); formerly also known as Wolgan; disc. 1823 by Robert Hoddle, settled by Edwin Barton, surveyed 1906, estab. 1906 by Commonwealth Oil Corp. Ltd, village gaz. 1907 as Wolgan, same village gaz. 1908 as Newnes, dismantled and removed 1932–46 (some of the works going to Glen Davis); oil-shale (disc. *c.*1863 by Campbell Mitchell, who mined it in 1873) and coal; Angl. C. 1908; brickworks (incl. 5 kilns) b. by Commonwealth Oil Corp. Ltd; bridge, destroyed 1910, over Wolgan R.; bushfires 1944 and 1953; candle factory b. by Commonwealth Oil Corp. Ltd; colliery (Wolgan) and 88 coke-ovens 1909–11, ruined, colliery reopened 1916, demolished; floods 1910, 1952, 1986; foot-bridge, destroyed 1910, over Wolgan R.; miners' strikes 1908–9, 1910, 1911–12, 1917, 1919–20; 2 oil-shale mines, 64 retorts and refinery estab. 1906–11 by Commonwealth Oil Corp. Ltd, retorting began 1911, company went into liquidation 1911, works sold 1912 to John Fell & Co. Ltd, 32 retorts modified 1913, works reopened 1915, taken over 1919 by Commonwealth Oil Corp. Ltd, closed and reopened 1923, closed 1926, partly dismantled 1927, taken over and reopened 1931 by Shale Oil Development

Committee Ltd, closed 1932 and acquired by R.A. Treganowan and C.O. Chambers, acquired 1937 by National Oil Co., demolished 1938, remains scrapped 1946, site resumed 1978; PO 1906; powerhouse b. 1908–10 (incl. chimney, 200 ft or 61 m, b. by J. Collins); PS 1906–1913, 1915–27, 1931–33; quarry; railway (private) to Newnes Junction, surveyed by John Haydon Cardew, b. 1907 by J.D. Simpson, d. by Henry Deane, closed, track removed 1943 by Dickson Primer Co.; reservoir; Rom. Cath. C. (St James's) 1910, closed, burnt down 1944, shortly before its proposed relocation to Glen Davis; school (South Newnes till *c.*1912) 1907, new one b. 1910, closed 1940; storm 1910; telephone 1909; tin can factory b. by Commonwealth Oil Corp. Ltd; TX; typhoid 1908; Union C. 1908, sold, dismantled, removed; whooping cough epidemic 1936; pop. *c.*100 (1906), 1,652 (1911), *c.*1,500 (1913), *c.*800 (1917), 820 (1921), *c.*200 (1924), 339 (1933), *c.*12 (1940), *c.*5 (1948).

Newnes Junction (*Co. Cook*) 33°28'S. 150°15'E., 8 km E. of Lithgow, on Dargans Ck; box factory; colliery (Clarence Colliery Pty Ltd) 1979; PO 1911; quarry (sand); RS 1906, station relocated 1910, closed 1975; sawmills: Richard Richards and W. McKenzie; telephone 1915; TX 1928–50; pop. 33 (1933), 70 (1947).

New Park (*Co. Gloucester*) 32°15'S. 151°42'E., 18 km N. of Dungog; PO 1879–90; Union C. 1910, defunct.

New Park (*Co. Rous*) 28°36'S. 152°59'E., 3 km NW of Kyogle; estab. by Robert Walters; creamery (NSW Creamery Butter Co. Ltd) 1898; gale 1933; PO 1897; telephone 1898; pop. 528 (2006).

New Park (*Co. Urana*) 34°55'S. 146°22'E., 26 km SW of Narrandera; RS (orig. Brown's Siding) 1895–1975; sawmill (J. and E. Roach), burnt down 1900; pop. 40 (1933).

New Pipe Clay (*Co. Phillip*) see Eurunderee.

Newport (*Co. Northumberland*) see Dora Creek and Swansea.

Newrea (*Co. Gordon*) see Neurea.

Newrybar (*Co. Rous*) 28°43'S. 153°32'E., 4 km S. of Bangalow; bypassed by highway 1968; dairying till 1970s, now fruit, nuts, coffee, sugar-cane; butter factory (Newrybar Co-op. Dairy Co. Ltd) b. 1891 by Hawkins and Semgreen; caterpillar infestations 1896 and 1924; cyclones 1921, 1940, 1942, 1963; electricity 1934; FB (station b. 1985); gale 1928; Meth. C. b. 1909 by W.J. Lawson, destroyed and rebuilt 1940 by Alcorn Bros, closed 1981; PO 1892; Presb. C. 1911 d. by Alexander Stewart Jolly, damaged 1942, closed 1973, later sold and reused; school 1890, relocated 1903; telephone 1899; water reticulation 1969; Wes. Meth. C. 1894; pop. 256 (1901), 426 (1911), 265 (1933), 186 (1947), 212 (1954), 186 (1961), 460 (2011).

Newry Island (*Co. Raleigh*) 30°30'S. 153°00'E., 1 km W. of Urunga, on Kalang R.; settled by Kerr; pop. 26 (1933), 768 (2006).

New Sheffield (*Co. Camden*) see Mittagong.

Newstead (*Co. Dampier*) 35°55'S. 150°08'E., 6 km E. of Moruya, on Moruya R.; flood 1863; PO 1892–93; school 1881–1914 and 1920–34.

Newstead (*Co. Gough*) 29°49'S. 151°21'E., 23 km E. of Inverell, on Kings Ck; tin (disc. 1866 by Joseph Wills) and lime; flood 1870; lime-kilns; 2 mines; Presb. C. b. 1861 by Colin Anderson, repairs 1903 by D.S. Anderson, burnt down 1909, and graveyard; pop. 74 (1911).

Newstead Mines (*Co. Gough*) 29°50'S. 151°20'E., 22 km E. of Inverell, on Kings Ck; mine.

Newstead North (*Co. Gough*) 29°50'S. 151°21'E., 24 km E. of Inverell, on Kings Ck.

Newstead South (*Co. Gough*) 29°49'S. 151°22'E., 25 km E. of Inverell.

Newton Boyd (*Co. Gresham*) 29°46'S. 152°15'E., 51 km E. of Glen Innes, on Bruisers Ck; Barney's Hill till 1949; designated as chief town of the county; farming and grazing; bushfire 1953; cheese factory (Newton Boyd Co-op. Cheese Co.) 1923 d. by Frederick John Madigan and Sydney Theo Cusick; flood (man died) 1962; PO 1900, burnt down 1941; pound (stock) 1879; school 1957, additions

1963, closed 1974; telephone 1914; TX 1930, automatic 1968; pop. 75 (1901), 53 (1911), 50 (1933), 62 (1947), 61 (1961), 217 (2006).

Newtown (*Co. Argyle*) see Goulburn.

Newtown (*Co. Finch*) see Lightning Ridge.

Newtown (*Co. Lincoln*) see Dubbo South.

Newtown (*Co. Murray*) see Captains Flat.

Newtown (*Co. Northumberland*) see Hamilton.

Newtown (*Co. St Vincent*) see Araluen North.

Newtown (*Co. Wellington*) see Hill End and Ophir.

Newtown (*Co. Westmoreland*) see Yerranderie.

Newtown (*Co. Wynyard*) see Wagga Wagga.

New Vale (*Co. Cook*) see Oakey Park.

New Valley (*Co. Hardinge*) 30°03'S. 151°20'E., 32 km NW of Guyra; school 1887–90.

New Wallsend (*Co. Northumberland*) see Catherine Hill Bay.

New Wharf (*Co. Gloucester*) see Allworth.

New Yard (*Co. Hunter*) 33°20'S. 150°42'E., 23 km N. of Kurrajong Heights.

New Yards (*Co. Westmoreland*) 33°56'S. 150°18'E., 24 km S. of Katoomba, on New Yards Ck; formerly The New Yards.

Ngarigo (*Co. Wallace*) 36°27'S. 148°23'E., 6 km S. of Perisher Valley, on Thredbo R.

Niagara (*Co. Auckland*) 36°42'S. 149°40'E., 15 km W. of Bega; cheese factory (Kameruka Estate), closed; school 1957–58; pop. 25 (1933), 74 (1947).

Niagara Park (*Co. Northumberland*) 33°23'S. 151°21'E., 5 km N. of Gosford, on Narara Ck; subdivided by Frank Joseph Lappen Measures; farming and orchards; bushfire (3 houses destroyed) 1944; fruit packing house (Niagara Park Growers Ltd) 1933; PO 1927; reservoir; RS 1902; sawmill (Edward Patrick Michael Sheedy); school 1974, additions 1982; telephone 1953; pop. 51 (1933), 120 (1954), 169 (1961), 2,288 (2006), 2,815 (2011).

Niangala (*Co. Parry*) 31°18'S. 151°24'E., 39 km SW of Walcha, on Bungendore Ck; (incl. South Niangala); Bungadore till 1890; village gaz. 1893; gold (disc. 1890 by William Patrick Sullivan), manganese, timber, grazing, berries, potatoes (South Niangala); Angl. C. (Sacred Advent) b. 1964 by Cyril Cross; cemetery (burials 1892–1977) 1901; electricity: Niangala 1966 and South Niangala 1963; eucalyptus oil distillery (A.A. Stevenson) 1939–40; FB (station b. 2011); flood 2008; mines: Aurora, Aust. Republic, Democrat, Evening Star, Gem, GFM (Waratah Gold Mining Co. NL), Golden Spur, Jersey Lily, Jewel, Joker, Just-in-Time (Bungadore Gold Mining Co., incl. 5 head stamper battery removed from Weabonga and re-erected 1892), Lady Jersey (estab. 1890 by Scott and Kermode, taken over 1891 by Jersey Gold Mining Co., sold 1892, acquired 1896 by NSW Goldfields Ltd, closed 1900, reworked 1915+ by Fred Rollo and James Butler who erected 2 head stamper battery in 1916), Little Klondyke, Morning Star, Starlight, Twicer; PO 1890–1977; sawmills: James Burton, Billy Clark, Harry and Tom Newman, Ellis Wall; school 1891 b. by Robert Williams, renovated 1924 by W.J. Sibley and M. Peterson, replacement b. 1955, renovated 1961 and 1965, additions 2010; stamper battery (5 head) erected 1891 by Harle; telephone 1901; tornado 2002; TX 1926–70; pop. 117 (1901), 147 (1911), 240 (1933), 190 (1947), 116 (1954), 161 (1961), 164 (2006), 142 (2011).

Nicholsons Lagoon (*Co. Buckland*) 31°26'S. 150°33'E., 13 km NW of Quirindi; school 1899–1931.

Nickelville (*Co. Yancowinna*) 31°44'S. 141°31'E., 26 km N. of Broken Hill; mine (Maybell).

Niemur (*Co. Wakool*) 35°15'S. 144°13'E., 43 km N. of Barham; RS (Victorian railway); school 1957–69; TX (automatic); pop. 55 (1933).

Nillo (*Co. Durham*) see Lorn.

Nimbin (*Co. Rous*) 28°36'S. 153°13'E., 22 km E. of Kyogle, on Mulgum Ck; subdivided 1903; dairying, cattle, pigs, tropical fruit, centre of hippie culture and alternative lifestyles since Aquarius festival 1973; Angl. C. (St Mark's) b. 1909 by Arthur J. West; bridges: Green Bridge, Cullen Bridge b. 1930 by Lawson Bros over Mulgum Ck, Rann Bridge, Sinclair Bridge, Southwell Bridge 1930 over Goolmangar Ck; butter factory (Nimbin Co-op. Dairy Co. Ltd) b. 1908 by George Hardy, additions 1913 by G.H. Jarrett, extensions and alterations 1916 d. by Kay Macnicol Co., taken over 1921 by North Coast Co-op. Ltd, new factory b. 1932 by Daniel Gallagher, closed 1961, reused; candle factory; cemetery 1891; Church of Christ; electricity 1933; FB 1953; fires 1924 and 2014; hailstorm 2000; PO 1886; pound (stock) 1924; Presb. C. (St Stephen's) b. 1909 by Brander Bros, d. by Robert Robertson Jack; PS 1920, new one b. 1934 by Campbell and Rodgers, new one 1989; reservoir; rifle range, upgraded 1947; Rom. Cath. C. (St Patrick's) b. 1913 by J. Fitzgerald, d. by Carroll and McGuire, additions 1925 by J.J. Moss & Sons, closed, sold and reused; sawmill (West and Sharpe) 1904; school 1905, new building 1910, additions 1916 by V.H. Gaggin, additions 1927 and 1966, replacement 1995, additions 2010; sewerage augmentation 1993; telephone 1908; TX 1914, automatic 1956; Unit. C. (orig. Meth.) 1912, additions 1933; water supply 1952, augmentation 1970 and 1993; pop. 64 (1901), 666 (1911), 847 (1933), 685 (1947), 698 (1954), 523 (1961), 310 (1971), 328 (1976), 331 (1981), 282 (1986), 274 (1991), 319 (1996), 400 (2001), 352 (2006), 468 (2011).

Nimitybelle (*Co. Wellesley*) see Nimmitabel.

Nimmitabel (*Co. Wellesley*) 36°31'S. 149°17'E., 34 km SE of Cooma, on Bobundara Ck; Nimitybelle till 1912; founded and surveyed 1840, laid out 1857 by E.H. Arnheim, first lots sold 1858, thrived in 1860s, town gaz. 1880; sawmilling 1921+, farming, sheep, cattle; Angl. C. (St Peter's) b. 1878–82 by Joseph McKee, d. by Richard Leigh, roof replaced 1996; butter factories: NSW Creamery Butter Co. Ltd 1895 d. by Charles C. Lance and Southern Monaro Co-op. Butter Co. Ltd; cemeteries: pioneer (graves 1842+) and new one; CH (incl. lock-up) b. 1863 by John Malcolm, repairs 1878 by M.C. Hayes, repairs 1890 by John Harris; earth tremor 1912; electricity 1952; fire 1949; flour mill b. 1865–72 by John Geldmacher as a stone tower windmill but powered instead by horses, operated 1872–1885 and then as a sawmill, closed, sold, restored 1961 by local council, reused; measles epidemic 1912; meat works (Monaro & South Coast Meat Co.), closed; PO 1858, new one b. 1883–85 by John Harris, additions and repairs 1911 by Alfred Ede; pound (stock) 1862; Presb. C.; PS 1863, additions 1893 by John Harris; rabbit freezing works 1915, burnt down 1933; railway barracks 1938, sold and demolished 1986; railway bridge over Bobundara Ck; railway turntable, defunct; Rom. Cath. C. 1856, new one (St Andrew's) b. 1863–65 by John Geldmacher and Beileiter, d. by P. Newman, renovated 1916, extended 1918 by Arthur Mawson, re-roofed; RS 1912, station b. by D.L. Reid, closed 1986, reused; sawmills: Crabtree Bros, Charles Hoore (leased 1914 to James Butler), G.S. Rayner 1948 (burnt down, replaced by Rayner Bros, taken over by Ray Richards, taken over 1974 by Tableland Sawmills Pty Ltd, closed 1992); school (Nimitybelle till 1912) 1880, new building b. 1882 on new site by J. M'Kee, extended 1928; snowstorms 1932 and 2005; telegraph 1871; TX 1911, automatic 1986; Unit. C. (orig. Meth.) 1904, extended and renovated 1958, closed 2004; water supply 1963, augmentation 1995; Wes. Meth. C. 1885; pop. *c.*100 (1866), 122 (1871), 91 (1881), 254 (1891), 422 (1901), 892 (1911), 449 (1933), 376 (1947), 389 (1954), 345 (1961), 336 (1971), 311 (1976), 257 (1981), 265 (1986), 256 (1991), 268 (1996), 235 (2001), 237 (2006), 224 (2011).

Nimmo (*Co. Wallace*) 36°11'S. 148°38'E., 31 km SW of Perisher Valley, on Eucumbene R.; bridge over Eucumbene R.; earth tremor 2009; pop. 24 (1933).

Nine Mile (*Co. Gough*) see Stannum.

Nine Mile (*Co. Wentworth*) see Dareton.

Nine Mile Cowal (*Co. Narromine*) 32°07'S. 147°52'E., 14 km SW of Trangie, on The Boggy Cowal.

Nirrim (*Co. Macquarie*) 31°55'S. 152°30'E., 4 km E. of Taree, on Dumaresq Island, in Manning R.; farming; PO 1927–59; telephone 1915.

Nithsdale (*Co. St Vincent*) 35°35'S. 149°38'E., 21 km SW of Braidwood; airfield (2 km E.); earth tremor 1859.

Nithsdale (*Co. St Vincent*) see also Ballalaba.

Noah Bank (*Co. Raleigh*) 30°45'S. 152°46'E., 16 km W. of Macksville, on Taylors Arm.

Nobbys Creek (*Co. Rous*) 28°17'S. 153°20'E., 8 km NW of Murwillumbah, on Nobbys Ck; school 1957–75; telephone 1914; TX 1926–62; pop. 80 (1911), 144 (1933), 155 (1947), 166 (1954), 169 (1961), 274 (2011).

Nocoleche (*Co. Barrona*) 29°51'S. 144°07'E., 174 km W. of Bourke.

Noggabri (*Co. Buckland*) 31°00'S. 150°19'E., 7 km E. of Gunnedah; FB.

Noisy Point (*Co. Hunter*) 32°50'S. 150°47'E., 45 km SW of Singleton, on MacDonald R.; cemetery (6 graves).

Nombinnie (*Co. Blaxland*)
see Mount Hope South.

No Mistake (*Co. Ashburnham*) 33°02'S. 148°12'E., 11 km N. of Parkes; quarry.

Noonbinna (*Co. Forbes*) 33°53'S. 148°38'E., 7 km SW of Cowra; goldmine (Fairview) 1935–36; PO 1942; RS 1909–70; school 1914–17 and 1940–72, reused; silo 1935; telephone 1942; TX (automatic) 1952; pop. 43 (1933), 132 (1947), 145 (1954), 121 (1961).

Noonbinna East (*Co. Forbes*) 33°53'S. 148°40'E., 6 km S. of Cowra; school (Merton) 1900–11.

Noorong (*Co. Wakool*) 35°20'S. 143°59'E., 31 km N. of Barham; sheep; school 1955, additions 1961, closed 1983; pop. 70 (1933), 96 (1947), 90 (1954), 104 (1961).

Nooroo (*Co. Gloucester*) 32°22'S. 151°54'E., 14 km E. of Dungog, on Ramstation Ck; RS 1913, station b. by Robert Daniel Quiggin, closed 1975; pop. 55 (1947), 243 (2006).

Noorooma (*Co. Dampier*)
see Central Tilba, Corunna and Narooma.

Nora Creek (*Co. Ashburnham*) 33°02'S. 148°48'E., 9 km NW of Molong; bushfire 1909; school 1884–1910.

Norah (*Co. Northumberland*) see Norah Head.

Norah Head (*Co. Northumberland*) 33°17'S. 151°34'E., 4 km SE of Toukley, on Tasman Sea; formerly also known as Bungaree Norah; village gaz. 1864 as Norah; lighthouse (concrete) b. 1901–3 by P. and W.E. Graham, d. by Charles Assinder Harding, 90 ft (27.5 m), converted 1961 from kerosene to electricity, automated 1994; PO 1955; sewerage 1976; telephone 1955; pop. 42 (1933), 75 (1954), 152 (1961), 1,086 (2011).

Norahville (*Co. Northumberland*) see Wyee.

Noraville (*Co. Northumberland*) 33°16'S. 151°34'E., 3 km E. of Toukley, on Tasman Sea; surveyed 1829; farming and fishing; cemetery, incl. lawn cemetery and columbaria; PO 1927; Rom. Cath. C. (St Mary's) 1969; school 1901–20, reopened (Toukley) 1944, additions 1956, 1962, 1964, 1968, 1971, 1984, 1988; sewage works; telephone 1914; TX 1926–35; pop. 51 (1911), 59 (1947), 69 (1954), 269 (1961), 2,250 (2006), 2,698 (2011).

Nords Wharf (*Co. Northumberland*) 33°08'S. 151°36'E., 2 km E. of Gwandalan, on Crangan Bay; (incl. Cams Wharf, Crangan Bay, Murrays Beach, Shellsea Estate); subdivided 1924; colliery (Wallarah), new access o. 1957 by J. & A. Brown & Abermain Seaham Collieries Ltd, taken over 1960 by Coal & Allied Industries Ltd, closed; FB; jetty; Meth. C. 1925, closed, sold and reused; PO 1916; reservoir (Crangan Bay); school (Wallarah till 1919) 1902, new one 1954 on new site; telephone 1914; TX (automatic) 1955; water supply 1958; pop. 92 (1911), 187 (1933), 148 (1947), 391 (1971), 490 (1976), 620 (1981), 683 (1986), 778 (1991), 840 (1996), 880 (2001), 820 (2011).

Norongo (*Co. Murray*) 35°42'S. 149°24'E., 41 km S. of Queanbeyan, on Queanbeyan R.; telephone 1916; TX 1922; pop. 29 (1933).

Norries Head (*Co. Rous*) 28°20'S. 153°34'E., 1 km S. of Bogangar, on Coral Sea; rutile mining.

Norrong (*Co. Argyle*) 34°37'S. 149°50'E., 19 km NE of Goulburn, on Tarlo R.; Rom. Cath. C. (St Finbar's) b. 1901 by W. Fielding.

Northangera (*Co. St Vincent*) 35°28'S. 149°56'E., 12 km E. of Braidwood, on Mongarlowe R.; formerly Warrambucca or Warrumbucca; bushfires 1888, 1896, 1917;

telephone 1917; TX 1952; typhoid 1907 (man died); pop. 50 (1901).

North Arm (*Co. Raleigh*) see Mylestom and Upper Nambucca.

North Arm (*Co. Rous*) 28°20'S. 153°20'E., 7 km W. of Murwillumbah; Angl. C. 1883; bushfire 1936; Meth. C. 1907 (moved 1925 to Burringbar); pop. 202 (1911), 25 (1933), 173 (1947), 213 (1954), 140 (1961).

North Arm Cove (*Co. Gloucester*) 32°40'S. 152°02'E., 7 km E. of Karuah, on North Arm Cove; orig. Port Stephens City; laid out 1918 by Walter Burley Griffin, taken over 1920 by Henry Ferdinand Halloran, but city never developed; FB (station b. 1993); pop. 226 (1991), 274 (1996), 292 (2001), 364 (2006), 422 (2011).

North Arm Junction (*Co. Rous*) 28°19'S. 153°20'E., 5 km W. of Murwillumbah; telephone 1925; TX 1940–47.

North Bank (*Co. Raleigh*) 30°44'S. 152°46'E., 16 km W. of Macksville, on Taylors Arm; bananas; telephone 1916; TX 1925–54; pop. 66 (1933), 581 (2006).

North Beach (*Co. Raleigh*) 30°29'S. 153°02'E., 3 km NE of Urunga; pop. 71 (1933).

North Berembed (*Co. Bourke*) 34°39'S. 146°53'E., 23 km NW of Ganmain; pop. 36 (1933).

North Burrewarra (*Co. St Vincent*) see Malua Bay.

North Creek (*Co. Rous*) 28°49'S. 153°36'E., 2 km S. of Lennox Head; dairying and rutile mining; Angl. C. (St John the Baptist) 1898, moved 1947 to Lennox Head but later returned; cheese factory estab. 1908 by J. Ainsworth, jun.; sugar mills: W. Clement, Prospect (McKinnon and Sharpe), John Skennar; wharf; pop. 160 (1901), 206 (1911), 80 (1933), 124 (1947), 93 (1954), 62 (1961).

North Creek (*Co. Rous*) see also Lennox Head.

North Cuerindi (*Co. Darling*) 30°39'S. 150°47'E., 11 km N. of Manilla; school 1892–96.

Northfield (*Co. Cook*) see Kurrajong Heights.

North Haven (*Co. Macquarie*) 31°38'S. 152°49'E., 3 km NE of Laurieton, on Camden Haven Inlet; fishing and tourism; Bapt. C. 1987; breakwater, remedial works 2013; bridge (to Laurieton) 1931, demolished, new one (concrete) 1961, new one 2016, over Stingray Ck; PO 1951; punt, to Laurieton, ceased 1931, across Queens Lake Entrance; school 1957, additions 1960 and 1994; telephone 1951; pop. 207 (1947), 438 (1954), 526 (1961), 1,596 (2011).

North Hill (*Co. Sandon*) see Armidale.

Northlakes (*Co. Northumberland*) see San Remo.

North Logan (*Co. Bathurst*) 33°42'S. 148°34'E., 17 km SW of Canowindra; pop. 29 (1933).

North Macquarie (*Co. Camden*) 34°34'S. 150°44'E., 3 km W. of Albion Park; church b. 1879 by Mood Bros, and graveyard.

Northmeadow (*Co. Clarence*) see Grafton.

North Richmond (*Co. Cook*) 33°35'S. 150°43'E., 20 km NE of Springwood, on Hawkesbury R.; orig. Enfield; surveyed and laid out 1840 as private village by Charles Whitaker; grazing, orchards, farming, dairying; Angl. C. (St Philip's) 1861, closed, sold and reused, and graveyard (149 graves, 1864+); Bapt. C. (Hawkesbury Valley); bridges: Richmond Bridge (b. 1860 by Richmond Bridge Co., 537 ft or 163.7 m, damaged 1867, 1870, 1900, replacement, with 13 reinforced concrete spans, b. 1903–5 by J.F. Carson, d. by James Waller Roberts, 705 ft or 215 m, widened to carry railway, track replaced by road deck 1966, damaged 1975) over Hawkesbury R. and 2 bridges over Redbank Ck; bushfires 1905 and 1951; distillery (Ironbark) estab. 2013 by Reg and Greta Papps; floods 1867, 1897, 1900, 1925, 1927, 1949, 1950, 1952; foot-bridge over Redbank Ck; gale 1928; Jehovah's Witnesses C.; match factory (Hanna Match Aust. Pty Ltd); Plymouth Brethren C.; PO 1858; PS (incl. lock-up) b. 1911 by Frank Vernon, closed 1933; punt across Hawkesbury R.; 2 reservoirs (incl. one b. 1892); RS: Kemsleys 1928–52 and North Richmond 1926–52; schools: Colo HS 1978, additions

1982, and North Richmond 1871, additions 1882 by Crisford and Boughton, additions 1982 and 2010; SD Adventist C.; sewage works; storms 1956 and 1971; telegraph 1884; telephone 1890; TX (automatic) 1980; water reticulation 1892; Wes. Meth. C. 1857, reused, new one 1893, damaged 1928; wharf; winery (Richmond Estate) 1967; pop. *c.*150 (1866), 231 (1871), 158 (1901), 344 (1911), 278 (1933), 504 (1947), 588 (1954), 746 (1961), 1,082 (1971), 1,768 (1976), 2,462 (1981), 2,787 (1986), 3,095 (1991), 3,390 (1996), 3,553 (2001), 3,635 (2006), 4,601 (2011).

North Shore (*Co. Gloucester*) see Tuncurry.

North Shore (*Co. Macquarie*) 31°24'S. 152°54'E., 3 km N. of Port Macquarie, on Hastings R.; quarry; pop. 380 (2011).

North's Siding (*Co. Cook*) see Katoomba.

North Star (*Co. Stapylton*) 28°56'S. 150°24'E., 36 km S. of Boggabilla; wheat; Angl. C. (St Peter's) 1939; FB; PO 1937; reservoir; Rom. Cath. C. (Our Lady of Fatima) 1955; RS 1932–79; school 1955, additions 1963, 1966, 2010; silo 1955; telephone 1916; TX 1921; pop. 90 (1947), 236 (1954), 118 (1961), 327 (2006), 423 (2011).

Northumberland Colliery (*Co. Northumberland*) see Fassifern.

Northville (*Co. Northumberland*) see Barnsley.

North Wahgunyah (*Co. Hume*) see Corowa.

North Wyrrabalong (*Co. Northumberland*) see The Entrance North.

North Yathong (*Co. Urana*) 35°15'S. 145°54'E., 20 km NE of Jerilderie; RS (Yathong till 1890) 1884–1971.

Norton (*Co. Bathurst*) 33°34'S. 149°16'E., 4 km S. of Blayney; farming; copper mine (Osborns or Quigleys Hill); goldmine (Blue Bird) worked 1936 by Maling; school 1882, new building b. 1884 by Josiah Shakespear, closed 1994; Wes. Meth. C. 1869, sold 1909 for removal.

Nortons Gap (*Co. Rous*) see Naughtons Gap.

Norway (*Co. Westmoreland*) 33°46'S. 149°49'E., 7 km SW of Oberon; farming and grazing; PO 1915; school 1883–1989; telephone 1914; TX (automatic) 1964; pop. 77 (1901), 91 (1933), 65 (1947), 46 (1954), 140 (1961).

Norwood (*Co. Argyle*) 34°41'S. 149°44'E., 8 km N. of Goulburn; earth tremor 2000; RS 1902–43; school 1863–99; Wes. Meth. C. 1876; pop. 62 (1901), 88 (1911), 64 (1933).

Norwood (*Co. Cook*) see Bilpin.

Notherwono (*Co. Bourke*) see Millwood.

Nottingham (*Co. Buccleuch*) 35°14'S. 148°37'E., 36 km E. of Tumut; telephone 1926; pop. 20 (1933).

Noucome (*Co. Richmond*) see Swan Bay.

Nowendoc (*Co. Hawes*) 31°31'S. 151°43'E., 60 km S. of Walcha, on Nowendoc R.; estab. 1837 by Aust. Agric. Co., laid out 1857 by John Hall, town gaz. and lots sold 1859, designated as chief town of the county; gold (disc. 1872 by Thomas Laurie) mining mainly 1872–90, sheep, cattle, pigs from *c.*1895, dairying till 1960; bridge 1930, new one (Laurie Bridge) b. 1971 by M.R. and E.M. Firth, 212 ft (64.6 m), over Nowendoc R.; cemetery (69 graves 1885+) 1870, incl. columbarium; dairy factory (New England) estab. by John and Lia Christensen; electricity 1964; FB 1970; footbridge over Nowendoc R.; PO 1862–1979; Presb. C.; PS b. 1896 by W.J. Goman; quarry; sawmill (Gulliver, Gleeson Pty Ltd) 1952; school 1954, additions 1963, renovated 1977, additions 2010; snow 1911; telephone 1917; TX 1920, automatic 1983; Union C. b. 1915 by Waller & Sons, closed 1970; United C. d. and b. 1976 by S.J. Partridge; pop. 101 (1911), 137 (1933), 108 (1947), 162 (1954), 149 (1961), 139 (2011).

Nowlanville (*Co. Rous*) see Spring Grove.

Nowley (*Co. Jamison*) 30°00'S. 149°10'E., 34 km NW of Wee Waa; PO 1902.

Nowra (*Co. St Vincent*) 34°53'S. 150°36'E., 57 km SW of Wollongong, on Shoalhaven R.; (incl. Bangalee, East Nowra, Mundamia, North Nowra, South Nowra, West Nowra, Worrigee, formerly Boston); site reserved 1850, laid out 1852 by John Frederick Mann, first lots sold 1855, founded 1862 by Henry Moss, developed 1870+, munic. proc. 1871, town gaz. 1879, munic. abolished 1948, city proc. (Shoalhaven) 1979; orig. timber, maize, wheat then dairying 1860s+, potatoes, oats, millet, lucerne, fruit, shipbuilding, pigs, cattle, fishing, manufacturing, tourism 1920s+; abattoir (A.K. Schofield); ambulance station b. 1938 by J.W. Maynes, d. by C. Parkes; Angl. C. 1857, (second) 1880, new one (All Saints') b. 1900 by Alexander Johnson; Assemblies of God C. (Mannahouse); Bapt. C. 1909 (Wes. Meth. C. removed from Terara), closed, reused, new one 1938; brewery (Hop Dog) estab. 2011 by Tim and Tess Thomas; brickworks estab. 1946 by Claude Downes, expanded 1951; bridge (steel Whipple truss), fabricated by Edgemoor Iron Co., Delaware, USA, erected 1881 by Onward Bates, d. by C. Shaler Smith, 1,115 ft (340 m), re-decked 1981, new one adjacent (pre-stressed concrete box girders) b. 1980 by Codelfa Construction Pty Ltd and Cogefar Construction Pty Ltd, 1,181 ft (360 m), over Shoalhaven R.; bushfires 1888, 1919, 1939 (15 houses destroyed), 1952 (10 houses destroyed), 1965, 2002, 2017; butter factories: Nowra Co-op. Dairy Co. Ltd (b. 1902 by Alick Johnston, additions 1918) and Worrigee Dairy Co. 1889 (converted to cheese factory 1899, closed 1904); carriage-works: O'Heir & Son, Frank Taylor, H. Weigand; catamaran factory (Seawind Group Holdings Pty Ltd); cemeteries: lawn cemetery and crematorium 1987, Nowra (6,607 graves) 1875, Rom. Cath. (239+ burials 1845–1948), Worrigee (22 graves); CH (incl. lock-up) 1858, repairs 1870 by John Schadel, additions 1883 also by Schadel, reused 1905, new one b. 1896 by George William Brewer, d. by Walter Liberty Vernon, repairs 1906 by H.A. Baglee, extended 1985, additions 2007 by Project Coordination (Aust.) Pty Ltd; cheese factory (Unicorn) o. 1980 by Piam Pty Ltd, sold 1990 to Snow Brand Milk Products Co. Ltd, merged 1999 into Snow Brand Aust. Pty Ltd; Christ. Brethren Assemblies C. (Gospel); Christ. Fellowship C.; Christ. Outreach C. (Shoalhaven City), additions and alterations 2007; Christ. Revival Crusade C.; Church of Christ; clothing factory (South Coast Clothing Manufacturing Co.); cordial factories: Nowra Cordial & Ice Co., Pollock Bros 1883 (taken over 1910 by Reginald G. Thomas, fire 1911, acquired 1912 by William Kelly and later James Kelly, burnt down 1968), Steam Lemonade & Cordial Factory & Vinegar Works (A.W. Garth) 1902; dam (Flat Rock); drought 1888; electricity 1928; FB: town fire brigade 1896 (station b. 1896, new one 1909, replaced 1978) and bushfire brigade (station b. 2016); fibrous plaster works (H. Chamberlain); fire 1894; floods 1860, 1867, 1870, 1903, 1916, 1951, 1959, 2015; flour mill b. 1857 by Owen Hewitt, sold 1858 to Mort & Co.; foot-bridges: two over Flatrock Ck and one b. 1887, rebuilt 1922, over Nowra Ck; gale 1951; gasworks b. 1905 by Kennedy and Halmarick; hailstorm 1893; hospital (Shoalhaven Dist. Memorial) b. 1951 by Eldwell, additions 1958, 1972, 1980, 2013, additions 2014 by Edwards Constructions (NSW) Pty Ltd; Jehovah's Witnesses C. (Currambene); jetty 1986; joinery and cabinet works (G. Muller); LDS (Mormon) C.; milk factory 1939; monumental stone works: T. Dudgeon and J.W. Oliver; New Life Covenant C.; PO: East Nowra 1969, North Nowra 1951, Nowra 1861 (additions and alterations 1899 by J. Kermode, repairs 1908 by T. Hermann), South Nowra 1951; pound (stock) 1857, relocated 1881; Presb. C. 1857, new one (St Andrew's) b. 1873–75 by Charles Moore and R. Savill, d. by John Horbury Hunt, alterations and renovations 1918, tower (War Memorial) added 1926 by H. Goldsborough, d. by Power, Adam and Munnings; PS (incl. lock-up) b. 1901 by Alexander Johnston, d. by Walter Liberty Vernon, repairs 1908 by E. Kennedy, closed, restored and reused 1980, new one 1977; punt 1866, across Shoalhaven R.; quarry; reservoir 1957; rifle range (2 km W.) 1899, new one (6 km SE) 1909; Rom. Cath. C. 1849, new one (St Michael's) b. 1875–77 by Alex McArthur, d. by George Osborne, extensions and re-roofing 1921 by J. Farrell, d. by Albert Edmund Bates, additions 1958, renovated 1969, and graveyard (burials 1845+); sale-yards (Hunt and Yeo) b. 1905 by

William Harvey; Salv. Army C. 1885, burnt down 1944, replaced 1946, new one 1988 (in former Bapt. C.); sawmills: Kimpton & Sons and Perseverance (taken over 1895 by G. and W. Duncombe); schools: East Nowra 1964 (additions 1965, 1967, 1982), Illaroo Road 1969 (additions 1981, additions 2002 by R.A. Baxter & Co. Ltd), North Nowra 1998, Nowra 1862 b. by Willet Burry (additions 1892 by Frederick Moore, additions 1908, new building b. 1954 by Hughes Bros, additions 1960 and 1966), Nowra HS 1956 (additions 1965, 1967, 1972, 1976, fire 1987, additions 1989, rebuilt 1992), Shoalhaven HS 1983, Worrigee (Worragee) 1855, new building b. 1880 by Thomas W. Carwardine, closed 1906; SD Adventist C.; sewerage 1935, augmentation 1992; shipyards; streets gas lit 1904, electric lit 1928; TC, additions 1945, additions 1954 by Bristol Construction Pty Ltd, additions 1962, 1967, 1985, became a campus of Illawarra Institute of Technology in 1992, additions 1997, 2000, 2011; telegraph 1879; telephone: East Nowra 1969, North Nowra 1951, South Nowra 1951; tornado 1921; TX 1908, automatic 1960; typhoid 1902; Union C. 1897; Unit. C. (orig. Wes. Meth.) b. 1878 by Alexander McArthur, d. by Thomas Rowe, vestry added 1919; univ. (Wollongong, Shoalhaven Campus); water supply 1894, improved 1911, completed 1934, augmentation 1955; wharves: one b. 1881 by Henry Bryce, one b. 1906 by R.W. Henry, one b. 1937 by W.G. Bailey, one b. 1991; winery (Cambewarra Estate); pop. *c.*350 (1866), 243 (1871), 120 (1875), 886 (1881), *c.*1,000 (1887), 1,705 (1891), 1,904 (1901), 1,887 (1911), 2,978 (1933), *c.*3,000 (1941), 3,190 (1944), 3,551 (1947), 6,243 (1954), 6,304 (1961), 9,641 (1966), 12,866 (1971, incl. Bombaderry), 15,496 (1976, incl. Bomaderry), 17,887 (1981, incl. Bomaderry), 19,553 (1986, incl. Bomaderry), 21,942 (1991, incl. Bomaderry), 23,823 (1996, incl. Bomaderry), 24,765 (2001, incl. Bomaderry), 27,478 (2006, incl. Bomaderry), 28,795 (2011, incl. Bomaderry).

Nowra Hill (*Co. St Vincent*) 34°56'S. 150°34'E., 7 km SW of Nowra; airport (Nowra) 1935, taken over 1942 by RAAF, reused 1944–46 as fleet air arm base (HMS Nabbington, Royal Navy), reused 1948 as Royal Aust. Navy air station (HMAS Albatross), 2 hangars b. 1954 by Eldweld Pty Ltd, new control tower 1958, fire 1976, additions 2013 by Richard Crookes Constructions, d. by Woods Bagot, major upgrade 2015; Angl. C. (Falls); bushfires 1919 and 1939; butter factory (Nowra Hill Creamery Co.) 1896–1904; gale 1951; gaol b. 2008–10 by Richard Crookes Constructions, d. by Perumal Pedavoli; PO 1954–85; sawmill (Davis & Herbert Pty Ltd); school 1877–1926, reopened 1956; telephone 1924; torpedo storage bunker (World War II); Wes. Meth. C. b. 1883 by T. Jerrett & Sons, closed, dismantled 1928 and moved to Bolong; pop. 797 (2006), 846 (2011).

Nowranie (*Co. Urana*) 35°26'S. 146°05'E., 33 km E. of Jerilderie; pop. 92 (1911).

Noyeau (*Co. Bathurst*) see Woodstock.

Nubba (*Co. Harden*) 34°32'S. 148°14'E., 12 km W. of Murrumburrah, on Two Mile Ck; farming; PO 1887; RS (o. as Two Mile Creek, relocated and renamed Nubba in 1885) 1882–1975; school (Two Mile Creek till 1884) 1876–1954; telephone 1915; TX 1924, automatic 1951; Union C.; Wes. Meth. C. b. 1887 by W. Richards; pop. 179 (1901), 162 (1911), 113 (1947), 69 (1954), 282 (2006).

Nubingerie (*Co. Gordon*) 32°31'S. 148°40'E., 25 km W. of Wellington, on Box Ck; airfield; RS 1925–74; pop. 33 (1933), 23 (1947).

Nugal (*Co. Leichhardt*) 30°21'S. 148°04'E., 36 km S. of Walgett.

Nuggety Gully (*Co. Hawes*) 31°27'S. 151°47'E., 55 km S. of Walcha, on Cooplacurripa R.

Nugra (*Co. Gloucester*) 32°32'S. 152°05'E., 17 km NW of Tea Gardens, on Kellys Ck; quarry; sawmill (James Croll) 1906; telephone 1915.

Nulabor (*Co. Waradgery*) 34°26'S. 145°06'E., 25 km E. of Hay; rice; RS (Beabula till 1896 then Old Beabula till 1901) 1883–1961; pop. 20 (1933).

Nulkaba (*Co. Northumberland*) 32°49'S. 151°21'E., 3 km N. of Cessnock, on Black

Ck; Pokolbin 1885–1927; laid out 1884–85; brewery (Hunter Beer Co.) estab. 2003 by Colismo, at old pottery, new building 2006, sold 2008 to Hamish and Prue Ord, refurbished 2011; crematorium (St Patrick's) 2002; Jehovah's Witnesses C.; PO 1950–93; pottery (incl. 5 beehive kilns and 7 down draught kilns) estab. 1922 by Mark Robinson and Stephen Arthur Henery, became Robinson & Henery Ltd in 1928, became Cessnock Potteries Ltd in 1929, closed 1975, reused 1989, one beehive kiln demolished 2004; Rom. Cath. C. b. 1872 by James Love and John Melville, new one (St Patrick's) b. 1893 by Burg Bros, d. by Frederick Burnhardt Menkens, closed and reused; school 1922, additions 1995; telephone 1950; wineries: Andahlasia Vineyard, Ernest Hill Wines (estab. by Harry Tulloch for Seppelts Wines), Tocamber Vineyard, Wirral Grange Vineyard (Terry and Carol Hughes); pop. 137 (1933), 158 (1947), 160 (1954), 171 (1961), 552 (2011).

Nullabong (*Co. Gowen*) 31°17'S. 149°12'E., 8 km W. of Coonabarabran, on Castlereagh R.; school 1881–1918.

Nullamanna (*Co. Arrawatta*) 29°39'S. 151°13'E., 17 km NE of Inverell; dairying, wheat, tobacco, mining; Angl. C. 1884, new one (St Peter's) 1896, burnt down and rebuilt, closed, and graveyard; bridge (D.G. Mather Bridge) 1957, over Frazer Ck; cemetery (18 graves 1894–1961) 1902; gale 1883; grasshopper infestation 1935; 3 mines; PO 1883–1979; Presb. C. 1879, new one 1910, removed from Airlie Brake; quarry; sawmill; school o. and destroyed 1883, new one b. 1884, extended 1924, closed 1973, reused; storm 1889; telephone 1908; TX 1910, automatic 1984; Wes. Meth. C. 1901, closed, moved 1971 to Inverell, reused; pop. 240 (1901), 231 (1911), 253 (1933), 206 (1947), 166 (1954), 196 (1961), 352 (2006), 415 (2011).

Nulla Nulla (*Co. Dudley*) 30°45'S. 152°30'E., 34 km W. of Bowraville, on Nulla Nulla Ck; farming; PS; school 1957–66; pop. 68 (1911), 105 (1933), 153 (1947), 202 (1954), 126 (1961).

Nullawa (*Co. Narran*) 29°06'S. 147°53'E., 38 km N. of Lightning Ridge.

Nullica (*Co. Auckland*) 37°06'S. 149°50'E., 8 km SW of Eden, on Leos Ck; pop. 57 (1933).

Numalla (*Co. Kennedy*) 32°43'S. 147°46'E., 24 km N. of Trundle, on Sandy Ck; Meth. C. 1953 d. by W. Brown; pop. 124 (1947).

Numantia (*Co. Cook*) 33°43'S. 150°32'E., 4 km W. of Springwood, on Numantia Ck; bushfire 1895; RS 1876, relocated 1896, closed 1897, demolished.

Numba (*Co. St Vincent*) see Numbaa.

Numbaa (*Co. St Vincent*) 34°52'S. 150°41'E., 7 km E. of Nowra; Shoalhaven till 1869; munc. proc. 1868 as Numba; farming and dairying; carriage-works; cemetery (orig. Riverbank, later Cook's Wharf, 322 graves 1853+); CH 1852, inundated 1860, closed, bought by George Coulthart, reused, demolished 1931; floods 1860, 1865, 1867, 1870, 1873, 1874, 1898; flour mill (Alexander Berry); lock-up; PO 1840; pound (stock) 1856; Presb. C. 1856; punt 1858, across Shoalhaven R.; Rom. Cath. C. 1870; school (Shoalhaven till 1884, then Numba till 1938) 1883–1953, reused; water reticulation 1959; pop. 61 (1841), 1,042 (1861), *c.*200 (1866), 646 (1871), 40 (1875), 50 (1877), 688 (1891), *c.*650 (1895), 216 (1911), 121 (1954), 190 (1961).

Number One (*Co. Macquarie*) 31°44'S. 152°04'E., 33 km N. of Gloucester, on Rowleys R.; Cooplacurripa till 1893; farming, grazing, dairying; PO 1891; telephone 1923; TX 1929–78; pop. 37 (1933).

Number One Swamp (*Co. Bathurst*) see Neville.

Numbla Vale (*Co. Wallace*) 36°38'S. 148°49'E., 29 km S. of Berridale, on Numbla Ck; PO 1940–74; school 1881–89 and 1904–72; telephone 1926; TX 1929, automatic 1981; pop. 121 (1947), 61 (1961).

Numbugga (*Co. Auckland*) 36°39'S. 149°42'E., 12 km W. of Bega; farming; FB (station b. 2017); fire 1907; flood 1919; gale 1895; PO 1888, burnt down 1929; sawmill (John Alcorn & Sons); school (Meringlo till 1912) 1877, new buildings b. 1883 by J. Malcolm, new building b. 1911 by J. Phillips, closed 1923, burnt down 1929; telephone 1905; TX 1928; pop. 148 (1901), 127 (1911), 140 (1933), 116 (1947), 93 (1954), 104 (1961), 178 (2011).

Numby (*Co. King*) see Reids Flat.

Numeralla (*Co. Beresford*) 36°11'S. 149°21'E., 21 km E. of Cooma, on Numeralla R.; Umaralla till 1921; village gaz. 1863 as Umaralla; sawmilling 1850s+, goldmining 1858+, eucalyptus oil 1900–40, grazing, farming, potatoes; Angl. C. b. 1872 by Denny Roche, (St Aidan's) 1898, (St John's) b. 1914–17 by Ted Thomas; bridge 1913, over Numeralla R.; cemetery 1866; electricity 1958; flood 1922; PO 1863; punt till 1913, across Numeralla R.; Rom. Cath. C. b. 1894 by Henry Brae, sold 1927, demolished, new one (All Saints') b. 1915 by Arthur Mawson, d. by George Donald Cochran; school (Umaralla till 1890) 1880–90, reopened 1902–2016; telephone 1909; TX 1925, automatic 1982; pop. 55 (1901), 338 (1911), 171 (1933), 130 (1947), 102 (1954), 142 (1961), 325 (2006), 362 (2011).

Numinbah (*Co. Rous*) 28°17'S. 153°15'E., 15 km W. of Murwillumbah, on Rous R.; bananas; flood 1928; sawmill (Cavanaugh and Boorman); school 1914–45 and 1957–62; telephone 1923; TX 1949–61; pop. 99 (1933), 104 (1947), 103 (1954), 117 (1961).

Numulgi (*Co. Rous*) 28°45'S. 153°20'E., 9 km NE of Lismore, on Numulgi Ck; farming and dairying; dairy factory (Foley Bros); PO 1927; school 1895–1941 and 1948–2005, sold; telephone 1920; TX 1928–58; pop. 86 (1901), 144 (1911), 135 (1933), 116 (1947), 128 (1954), 118 (1961), 260 (2011).

Nundah (*Co. Durham*) 32°29'S. 151°08'E., 10 km N. of Singleton; colliery (Elsmere) o. 1879 by William and Thomas Longworth, renamed Rosedale; RS 1891–1975; telegraph 1894–95; pop. 77 (1911).

Nunderi (*Co. Rous*) 28°19'S. 153°28'E., 6 km E. of Murwillumbah; formerly Boydsville.

Nundle (*Co. Parry*) 31°28'S. 151°08'E., 42 km E. of Quirindi, on Peel R.; estab. 1852, laid out 1853 by John Valentine Gorman, first lots sold 1855, town gaz. 1880; formerly goldmining (reef disc. 1852), then dairying, timber, scheelite (disc. 1907), maize (production peaked in 1910), sheep, cattle, wheat, poultry, fossicking; Angl. C. (All Saints') 1907; brickworks (Alex McClelland); bridge 1924, new one 2008, over Peel R.; cemetery (479 graves 1852+) 1863, incl. columbarium; CH 1853, demolished 1889, new one b. 1880 by George Davidson, repairs 1885 also by Davidson, repairs 1900 by Davidson and Partridge, reused; coffin factory, restored and reused; electricity 1941; FB; flood 1874; flour mill (William McIlveen) 1859; gale 1884; lock-up; PO 1853, new one b. 1904 by Henry Partridge, additions 1911 by Robert Hamilton Gillies; pound (stock) 1856; Presb. C. 1860, dismantled, new one b. 1892 by George Davidson, closed, sold 2005 and reused; PS 1853, new ones 1895 and 1981; Rom. Cath. C. b. 1885 by Fitzsimmons, new one (St Peter's) b. 1938 by R. Lane, d. by Lovett; sawmill; school 1872 b. by Samuel Lambert, extended 1877, additions 1884 also by Lambert, additions and repairs 1897 by C. Waters, repairs 1900 by J. Lorenz, new school 1907, additions 1915 and 2010; snowstorm 1857; streets electric lit 1941; telegraph 1881, new office b. 1904 by Henry Partridge, additions 1911 by Robert Hamilton Gillies; telephone 1902; TX 1910, automatic 1983; Unit. C. (orig. Prim. Meth.) 1882, sold 1966 to local council, reused; watch-house b. 1863 by Amos Davies; water reticulation 1969, augmentation 1995; woollen mill estab. 2001 by Peter Howarth, Judy Howarth and Carol Olde; pop. *c.*500 (1866), 132 (1871), 170 (1881), 260 (1891), 496 (1901), 602 (1911), 1,442 (1921), 391 (1933), 388 (1947), 329 (1954), 319 (1961), 257 (1971), 268 (1976), 235 (1981), 265 (1986), 261 (1991), 270 (1996), 261 (2001), 289 (2006), 270 (2011).

Nundora (*Co. Mootwingee*) 30°43'S. 142°05'E., 149 km N. of Broken Hill.

Nungatta (*Co. Auckland*) 37°13'S. 149°24'E., 37 km SE of Bombala, on Nungatta Ck; airfield (2 km S.); pop. 22 (1933).

Nuntherungie (*Co. Mootwingee*) 30°48'S. 142°29'E., 160 km NE of Broken Hill, on Noonthorangee Ck; village gaz. 1891, abandoned *c.*1892; silver mining.

Nurenmerenmong (*Co. Selwyn*) 35°49'S. 148°17'E., 24 km E. of Tumbarumba.

Nurri (*Co. Cook*) 33°34'S. 150°41'E., 2 km SE of Kurrajong; RS 1928–52.

Nurung (*Co. Harden*) 34°29'S. 148°34'E., 13 km SW of Boorowa; school 1885, new building b. 1896 by G. Patterson, closed 1901.

Nutleys Creek (*Co. Dampier*) 36°25'S. 150°01'E., 5 km W. of Bermagui; pop. 20 (1933).

Nymagee (*Co. Mouramba*) 32°04'S. 146°19'E., 77 km SE of Cobar; village gaz. 1883; mining (copper disc. 1880 by Henry Manley) mainly 1881–94 and grazing; airfield 1924; Angl. C. (Resurrection), damaged 1922, new one 1960; brewery (Samuel Williams) 1881–89; cemetery; CH b. 1902 by George W. Brewer; cordial factory (Henry Green); cyclone 1922; drought 1882–3; fire 1916; hospital (cottage) b. 1886 by Maliphant and Tay, d. by H.E.A. Miller, reused; mine 1880 (incl. brick-kilns, powder magazine, reverberatory furnaces), closed 1893, acquired 1896 by Great Cobar Mining Syndicate who replaced it with new blast furnaces, sold 1906 to Nymagee Copper Ltd, extensive additions and alterations to plant 1907, sold 1910 to Mouramba Copper Mining Co., reopened 1912, closed 1914, reopened 1915, closed 1917; PO 1880, new one b. 1887 by Thomas Maugher, additions 1899, sold 1966 to Schilt; pound (stock) 1881; PS (incl. lock-up) 1889, new one b. 1902 by George W. Brewer; Rom. Cath. C. (St Mary's) 1885, burnt down 1919, new one (Our Lady of Victories) 1922, destroyed 1922, new one 1924; sawmill; school 1881–1926 and 1957–2003, sold; telegraph 1881, new office b. 1887 by Thomas Maugher; TX 1911; water supply 1964, augmentation 1986 and 1992; Wes. Meth. C. 1884, closed; pop. *c.*2,000 (1882), 1,321 (1891), 881 (1901), 379 (1911), 160 (1933), 197 (1947), 243 (1954), 75 (1961), *c.*50 (1999), 102 (2006).

Nymboida (*Co. Fitzroy*) 29°57'S. 152°44'E., 35 km SW of Grafton, on Nymboida R.; village gaz. 1870; timber, coal 1909–79, gold, farming, canoeing 1973+; Angl. C. 1900; cemetery (117 graves 1930+) 1900; PO 1892; powerhouse (hydro-electric) 1924; Presb. C. (St John's) 1910, rebuilt 1948 by Kitcher, closed, sold 2006 and 2008, reused; PS 1895, new one b. 1911 by T.E. Jarman; punt b. 1891 by J. Mudford to cross Nymboida R.; rifle range 1914; sawmill (Pidcock Bros Ltd, hydro-electric powered) 1928; school 1880, additions 1935 by Jordon and Barnier, additions 2010; telephone 1909; TX 1916, automatic 1959; weir; pop. 56 (1901), 255 (1911), 377 (1933), 209 (1947), 235 (1954), 241 (1961), 301 (2011).

Nyngan (*Co. Oxley*) 31°34'S. 147°12'E., 128 km E. of Cobar, on Bogan R.; disc. 1835 by Major Sir Thomas Livingstone Mitchell, founded 1880, surveyed 1882 by Arthur Burgess, village gaz. 1882, munic. 1891–1971; orig. cattle, later sheep and wheat; aeroplane crash (man killed) 1930; airport (1 km N.), new terminal o. 1960; ambulance station; Angl. C. 1883, new one (St Paul's) 1897, replacement (St Mark's) b. 1920–26, d. by Louis Reginald Williams; Assemblies of God C.; Bible Christ. C.; 2 boiling-down works; brewery (Peter Crane) 1892–97; bridge b. 1884 by A. M'Fadyen, new one b. 1930 by H. Woodward, new one (Peter Sinclair Bridge) 1993, over Bogan R.; carriage-works (orig. operated by George Kelly and Edward Scully, later by Don Burns); cemetery (2,044 graves) 1886, incl. lawn cemetery and columbarium; CH 1885, alterations 1896 by F. Putensen, damaged 1904, new one 1902 d. by Walter Liberty Vernon, additions and alterations 1936 by G.A. Palmer, d. by C. Parkes; cordial factories: Walter E. Clancy and J. McMillan (later Sloane's); cyclone 1904; droughts 1964, 1965, 1966, 1982, 1983; dust storms 1902, 1923, 2020; earth tremor 1887; electricity 1926; experiment farm 1910–33; 2 FB (incl. station b. 1935, renovated 1982, new one 2017); fires 1901 (destroyed much of town) and 1903; floods 1890, 1905, 1925, 1928, 1950,

1955, 1956, 1972, 1975, 1990; foundry (The Far Western Motor & Engineering Works Ltd); hailstorm 1998; hospital 1897, additions and alterations 1935 by H. Janes, extended 1943, new one 1951, closed 2008; levee, rebuilt 1991; Lutheran C.; meat-chilling works (Graziers' Meat Export Co.); monumental stone works (C.J. Shakespeare); PO b. 1880 by Sullivan, Willis & Co., replacement b. 1889 by D. McDonald, additions 1900 by George William Brewer, additions and alterations 1913 by J.J. Lyle; powerhouse 1926; Presb. C. 1901; PS 1882, new one b. 1909 by A.E. Beaumont, renovations 1931 by G.A. Jacobs, new one 1975; railway barracks b. 1882 by James Stuart Douglas; railway bridge (timber truss) 1884, replaced 1934, over Bogan R.; railway coal stage, enlarged 1902; railway engine shed b. 1882 by James Stuart Douglas, fire 1895, enlarged 1902; railway turntable (William Sellers & Co.) 1904, 60 ft (18.3 m); 2 reservoirs (incl. an elevated steel tank on piles, 33,330 gal. or 151.5 kl); Rom. Cath. C. 1883, new one (St Patrick's) b. 1900–2 by John Hines, d. by William Lamrock, jun., extended 1955; RS 1883, station b. by James Stuart Douglas, refreshment rooms b. by Alexander Hamilton Scouller, station closed 1975, restored and reused; sale-yards (A. Lyn & Co.) 1936, new yards b. 1960 by Mid-Western Engineering; sawmill (D. Priest & Co.); schools: primary b. 1883 by Dennis Phelan, new building 1889, additions and alterations 1907 by E.P. Frost & Co., new building 1916, alterations and repairs 1919 by R. Harper, additions 1956, 1958, 1960, 1967, 1978, and HS 1974, additions 1994; SD Adventist C.; sewerage 1959, augmentation 1991; TC (a campus of Western Institute); telegraph 1883, new office b. 1889; TX 1910, automatic 1983; Unit. C. (orig. Meth.) 1958; water reticulation 1895, secure supply 1942, augmentation 1988; Wes. Meth. C. b. 1898 by Gordon Bros, renovated 1910; pop. *c.*1,000 (1888), 1,355 (1891), *c.*1,150 (1895), 1,455 (1901), 1,499 (1911), 1,375 (1921), 1,545 (1933), *c.*1,800 (1941), 1,802 (1947), 2,257 (1954), 2,360 (1956), 2,414 (1961), 2,591 (1966), 2,478 (1971), 2,359 (1976), 2,485 (1981), 2,502 (1986), 2,311 (1991), 2,240 (1996), 2,068 (2001), 1,975 (2006), 2,073 (2011), *c.*2,389 (2018).

Nyora (*Co. Urana*) 35°32'S. 145°59'E., 21 km NE of Berrigan; surveyed 1904, settled 1906; school 1910–22 and 1957–66; pop. 66 (1947).

Nyrang (*Co. Ashburnham*) 33°13'S. 148°51'E., 14 km S. of Molong, on Walkers Ck; PO 1880–85; pop. 22 (1933).

Nyrang (*Co. Ashburnham*) see also Cranbury.

Nyrang Creek (*Co. Ashburnham*) 33°33'S. 148°33'E., 10 km W. of Canowindra, on Nyrang Ck; farming; cemetery (39 graves) 1886; FB 1938; PO 1927; RS 1922–75; school (Kingstown till 1885) 1884–1932 and 1957–60; silo 1941; telephone 1911; TX (automatic) 1967; Wes. Meth. C. 1884–1939, sold to Charlie Loomes and dismantled; pop. 155 (1911), 88 (1933), 83 (1947), 106 (1954).

O

Oakburn (*Co. Rous*) 28°39'S. 152°51'E., 15 km W. of Kyogle, on Iron Pot Ck.

Oakburn (*Co. Rous*) see also Ghinni Ghi.

Oakdale (*Co. Camden*) 34°05'S. 150°30'E., 17 km W. of Camden, on Back Ck; settled by Henry Longhurst and Robert and Patrick Martin, surveyed 1863; orig. timber and orchards, then coal till 1990s, now hobby farming; bushfires 1888, 1936, 2001; colliery (Clutha Development Pty Ltd), closed; FB; PO 1912, burnt down 1922; Rom. Cath. C. (St Joseph the Worker) b. 1963 by M.J. Williams; sawmill; school 1882–1914, reopened 1929, additions 1994; telephone 1911; TX 1936, automatic 1954; Unit. C. (orig. Meth.) 1906, renovated 1935 by P.E. and Gordon Butler; water supply 1985; pop. 153 (1933), 262 (1947), 452 (1954), 508 (1961), 274 (1971), 368 (1976), 398 (1981), 530 (1986), 780 (1991), 882 (1996), 1,030 (2001), 1,006 (2006), 1,138 (2011).

Oak Dale (*Co. Northumberland*) see Gateshead.

Oakdene (*Co. Hume*) 35°34'S. 146°46'E., 25 km W. of Henty.

Oakdene (*Co. Narromine*) 32°18'S. 148°28'E., 15 km W. of Dubbo.

Oakendale (*Co. Durham*) see Glen Oak.

Oakey Creek (*Co. Burnett*) 29°39'S. 150°33'E., 13 km S. of Warialda; farming and grazing; PO 1927–31; telephone 1918; TX 1951, automatic 1972; pop. 31 (1933).

Oakey Creek (*Co. Napier*) 31°38'S. 149°42'E., 23 km N. of Coolah; grazing; PO 1859–71; RS 1923–75; pop. *c.*40 (1866), 73 (1911), 53 (1933).

Oakey Park (*Co. Cook*) 33°28'S. 150°11'E., 3 km NE of Lithgow, on Farmers Ck; formerly also spelt as Oaky Park; brewery o. 1888 by Henry Philip Corbett and Alfred Goodare as Zig Zag Brewery, partnership dissolved 1890, taken over 1896 by J.A.S. Jones, bought 1928 by Lithgow Brewery Ltd, closed and reopened five times 1928–35, renamed Terry's Brewery in 1935, sold 1941 to Alfred Norman Wyld, renamed Blue Mountains Brewery in 1955, closed 1958, reused by Dale's Brewed Beverages Pty Ltd as cordial factory till 1978, bought 1981 by Schindler and brewing resumed; bushfires 1936, 1940, 1997, 2013; coke-works (Oakey Park Coal & Coke Co.) incl. 8 beehive ovens b. 1899, 40 McLanahan-type ovens b. 1906, closed 1919 and demolished; collieries: Oakey Park Coal Mining & Coke Co. Ltd o. 1890 (man killed 1890, strike 1899, fire 1920, closed 1941, flooded 1964) and The Vale or New Vale (incl. coke-ovens and washery) 1888–1900; dams: Lithgow No. 1, b. 1896, d. by Cecil West Darley, 36 ft (11 m) high and Lithgow No. 2, b. 1907, 89 ft (27 m) high; foot-bridge over Farmers Ck; gastroenteritis epidemic 1939; Meth. C. 1915; PO 1910; Presb. C. 1924 d. by David Owen; railway (Great Zig Zag), incl. tunnel 75 yds (68.6 m), and 3 stone viaducts: No. 1 has 7 arches, No. 2 has 11 arches, No. 3 has 8 arches, b. 1866–69 by William Watkins and Patrick Higgins, d. by John Whitton, track duplicated 1880, bypassed 1910 by 10 tunnel deviation, reopened 1975 as narrow gauge tourist railway, collision 2011, closed

2012; railway accidents: 1883 (person killed) and 1908 (person killed); RS (Zig Zag) 1875–1910; school (New Vale till 1910, then Zig Zag) 1892, additions and alterations 1910 by A. Stephens, new one b. 1920 by T.E. Quiggin; telephone 1911; pop. 443 (1911), 31 (1933), 330 (2011).

Oak Flats (*Co. Camden*) 34°34'S. 150°49'E., 7 km S. of Dapto, on Lake Illawarra; (incl. Balarang and East Oak Flats); subdivisions 1925, 1926, 1928; Angl. C. (St Andrew's) 1951, belfry 1956, church extensions 1989 d. by Mark Jones; bushfire (3 houses destroyed) 1939; FB; 2 foot-bridges (incl. Slaters Bridge to Albion Park Rail, over Horsley Ck); hospital (Shellharbour) 1986, extended 2005; 2 jetties; Lutheran C. 1964, new one (Holy Cross) 1982; Meth. C. 1962; PO 1936; PS: Lake Illawarra b. 2011 by Richard Crookes Constructions and Oak Flats 1962–69; RS 1925; schools: Balarang (East Oak Flats till 1969) 1968, additions 1969 and 1979, Oak Flats 1952 (additions 1958, 1960, 1962, 1985), Oak Flats HS 1962 (additions 1963, 1965, 1972, 1975); SD Adventist C. 1968; sewerage 1978; telephone 1939; TC (Illawarra Institute of Technology, Shellharbour Campus); Unit. C.; water supply 1955; pop. *c.*200 (1937), 6,310 (2011).

Oakhampton (*Co. Northumberland*) 32°42'S. 151°34'E., 2 km N. of Maitland, on Hunter R.; (incl. Oakhampton Heights and Walka); bridge (steel truss) to Bolwarra Heights, fabricated by Clyde Engineering Co. Ltd, erected 1911 by Carson, Carey and Simpson, d. by James Waller Roberts, over Hunter R.; bushfire (Walka) 1884; cemetery (149 graves 1841–94); cordial factory estab. 1849 by William Tinson, taken over by Thomas F. Tinson, sold 1918; diphtheria 1921; floods 1870, 1893, 2007; grasshopper infestation 1921; hailstorm 1937; levee, destroyed 1893; reservoir (Walka) b. 1885 by George Blunt; rifle range (Walka) 1900; RS 1911–75; school 1879, new one b. 1882 by Bertles and Walker, closed 1955; storm 1928; tannery (Walka) estab. by George Turner, bought 1882 by George James Taylor; telephone 1917; TX 1955–59; waterworks (Walka) b. 1885–87 by M. Parkhill, d. by William Clark, 3 beam engines supplied by James Watt & Co., Birmingham, England, fed by 5 boilers, chimney 125 ft (38.1 m), waterworks on stand-by from 1925, closed 1945, beam engines scrapped 1949, pumping station reused 1953–78 as temporary powerhouse, reused again; wool-scour (Northern Wool Scouring Co.) estab. 1886 by Edward Lee, taken over 1893 by W.B. Sharp; pop. 157 (1901), 439 (1911), 320 (1933), 97 (1954), 87 (1961), 591 (2011).

Oakhampton Heights (*Co. Northumberland*) see Oakhampton.

Oak Hill (*Co. Bland*) 33°47'S. 147°54'E., 26 km NW of Grenfell; telephone 1926; TX 1927–40.

Oakhill Crossing (*Co. King*) 34°49'S. 147°54'E., 2 km N. of Yass; RS 1903–58.

Oakland (*Co. Rous*) see Yeagerton.

Oaklands (*Co. Auckland*) 36°37'S. 149°53'E., 8 km N. of Bega; cheese factory (James Jauncey).

Oaklands (*Co. Camden*) see Mittagong.

Oaklands (*Co. Rous*) see Yeagerton.

Oaklands (*Co. Urana*) 35°33'S. 146°10'E., 34 km E. of Berrigan; formerly Clear Hills; site reserved 1899, village gaz. 1900, first lots sold 1901; wheat, barley, oats, sheep, cattle; Angl. C. (St Mary Magdalene) 1959 (removed from Uranquinty), closed, sold 2017; army camp (incl. supply depot) 1942–46; brick-kilns: Ernie Barratt (inundated 1931) and Samuel Wilson; cemetery 1903; drought 1914; electricity 1946; FB; flood 1931; lock-up (removed from Daysdale); PO 1890, new ones b. 1909 and 1925; PS 1908–48, reopened 1952, new one 1963; railway turntable, 50 ft (15.2 m), derelict; railway coal stage 1911; reservoir (elevated, concrete), 100,000 gal. (454.6 kl), b. 1954 by William F. Stephenson Pty Ltd; rifle range 1916; Rom. Cath. C. (St Columba's) b. 1915–17, d. by Louis Harrison; RS 1912, station b. by Ernest Frederick Leggo, services suspended 1977; sale-yards 1951; 3 sawmills (incl. Whiteman's and William Tudor Yeager);

school (Clear Hills till 1914) 1895, new building b. 1911 by J. Devitt, new building b. 1935 by Dixon & Sons, additions 1963, 1966, 1983, additions 2010 by Barker Constructions Pty Ltd; silo 1920; storm 1911; telegraph 1913; telephone 1906; TX 1913, automatic 1982; Unit. C. (orig. Union) b. 1911 by A. Alston and Lionel Johnson, damaged 1911; water supply 1956; pop. 560 (1911), 363 (1933), 370 (1947), 369 (1954), 399 (1961), 355 (1971), 322 (1976), 283 (1981), 263 (1986), 238 (1991), 282 (1996), 249 (2001), 239 (2006), 238 (2011).

Oaklyn (*Co. Arrawatta*) 29°23'S. 151°10'E., 9 km SE of Ashford; farming and grazing; telephone 1913; TX 1916–20.

Oak Park (*Co. Durham*) 32°28'S. 151°08'E., 12 km N. of Singleton; school 1880–1925 and 1957–77.

Oaks (*Co. Camden*) see The Oaks.

Oakvale (*Co. Murray*) see Captains Flat.

Oakvale (*Co. Parry*) 31°18'S. 151°13'E., 36 km SE of Tamworth, on Oaky Ck; school 1906–19.

Oakwood (*Co. Arrawatta*) 29°39'S. 151°03'E., 16 km NW of Inverell; estab. 1870; goldmining, wool, wheat, beef; Angl. C. (St Cuthbert's) 1909, closed; drought 1965; electricity 1955; hailstorm 1966; Meth. C.; PO 1883–1961; Presb. C. 1883, closed, renovated and reopened 1912; school 1877, burnt down 1878, rebuilt, new buildings b. 1908 by B.M. Wade, additions 1960, closed 1966; telephone 1905; TX 1910, automatic 1971; pop. 69 (1901), 270 (1911), 220 (1933), 198 (1947), 154 (1954), 126 (1961), 694 (2006).

Oaky Flat (*Co. Macquarie*) 31°48'S. 152°30'E., 14 km N. of Taree.

Oaky Park (*Co. Cook*) see Oakey Park.

Oallen (*Co. St Vincent*) 35°10'S. 149°57'E., 34 km NE of Braidwood; gold dredging, farming, grazing; airfield; PO 1927; sawmill; telephone 1927; TX 1934–57; pop. 57 (1901), 81 (1933).

Oallen Ford (*Co. St Vincent*) 35°09'S. 149°57'E., 35 km NE of Braidwood, on Shoalhaven R.; bridge 1935, 125 ft (38.1 m), over Shoalhaven R.

Oban (*Co. Clarke*) 30°07'S. 151°52'E., 21 km NE of Guyra, on Oban R.; goldfield (disc. 1855 by James Rutherford), tin dredging and sluicing, agric., cattle; PO 1869–1913; storm (man killed) 1908; TX (automatic) 1974; pop. 57 (1933).

Oban Soldiers' Settlement (*Co. Napier*) see Coolah.

Obanvale (*Co. Durham*) 32°30'S. 151°10'E., 6 km N. of Singleton; hailstorm 1913; school 1901–25.

Oberne (*Co. Wynyard*) 35°23'S. 147°50'E., 23 km SW of Adelong, on Tarcutta Ck; formerly Mate; farming; FB 1940; flour mill (Moon's, water powered) 1850; school 1879–93, 1926–39, 1957–66; telephone 1922; TX 1925, automatic 1955; pop. 121 (1911), 103 (1933), 121 (1947), 152 (1954).

Oberne Creek (*Co. Wynyard*) see Westbrook.

Oberon (*Co. Westmoreland*) 33°42'S. 149°51'E., 40 km W. of Katoomba, on Lake Oberon; Bullock Flats till 1855, then Fish River Creek till 1866; settled 1837 by Charles Whalan, surveyed by Horace Charlton and John Frederick Mann, village gaz. 1863; mining, oats, rye, corn, peas 1906+, sheep 1910+, cattle, timber (pine) 1931+, mushrooms 1940s+, eucalyptus oil, potatoes, turnips; abattoir; airfield; ambulance station 1987; Angl. C. (St Barnabas's) b. 1868 by Billy Robertson, and graveyard (10 graves 1871–87); cemeteries: general (1,205 graves 1876+) 1886, incl. lawn cemetery and columbarium, and Meth. (166 graves 1859+); CH (incl. lock-up) b. 1872 by Nugent and Moore, d. by James Johnstone Barnet, new one 1963; dam (first stage) b. 1943–49, wall raised 1954, second stage o. 1958, wall raised again 1996, now 110 ft (33.5 m) high, on Fish R.; dust storm 1925; earth tremors 1934 and 1949; engineering works: Moorhead Engineering (estab. 1988 by Shane Moorhead), Oberon Engineering (estab. 1953 by Zika Tosic), MRD Engineering; FB (station b. 1958); flour mills: G.A. Batcheldor and Glyndwr (Alfred Whalan, orig. water powered) 1851; foot-bridge; hailstorms 1895 and 1901; hospital 1918, new buildings 1927 and 1944, additions 1946, alterations 1949 by H. Jackson, additions 1960, upgraded 1999; house frame and truss factory (Dark Red Frames & Trusses Pty Ltd); measles epidemics 1899 and 1952; pea vining plant (R. Gordon Edgell & Sons Ltd); PO 1855, new one b. 1885 by John Dunkley and Richard Clifford Bartlett, additions and alterations 1913 by W.J. Bailey; pound (stock) 1869; powerhouse estab. 1936 by Les Anstiss and Herb David, acquired 1946 from L.A. Anstiss by local council; PS, renovated 1930 by Jim Rogers, new one 1963; rabbit freezing works b. by McKay; railway turntable, 60 ft (18.3 m), moved 1927 to Bourke, new one 1963, 60 ft (18.3 m); 2 reservoirs; Rom. Cath. C. 1902 d. by John Job Copeman, closed, reused 1937, demolished, new one (St Ignatius's) b. 1938 by Sweetnam, d. by Hamleto Agabiti and R. Millane, demolished and rebuilt 1987; RS 1923, closed, station reused; sawmills: Arthur Cunynghame (bought by Bert Cunynghame and David Watson, moved) and T. Luxton 1885; schools: primary 1876, repairs 1881 by C. Stewart, repairs 1895 by T.E. Quiggin, new building b. 1912 by W.J. Bailey, additions 1956, 1959, 1965, and HS 1993; SD Adventist C. 1954; sewerage 1965, augmentation 1988; snowstorm 1894; storms 1909 and 1941; timber product factories: Boral Ltd (estab. 1944 as Timber Industries Pty Ltd by H.L.C. Cotton), Carter Holt Harvey (acquired 2010 by Borg Manufacturing), Pyneboard Pty Ltd 1961 (taken over 1964 by CSR and APM, taken over wholly by CSR 1978); telegraph 1881, new office b. 1885 by John Dunkley and Richard Clifford Bartlett, additions and alterations 1913 by W.J. Bailey; TX 1914, automatic 1978; Unit. C. (orig. Wes. Meth.) b. 1871–74 by Cardine; water supply augmentation 1956; Wes. Meth. C. (Glyndwr) b. 1845 by Charles Whalan; pop. *c.*30 (1866), 102 (1881), *c.*80 (1886), 245 (1891), 353 (1901), 586 (1911), 579 (1933), 834 (1947), 1,354 (1954), 1,489 (1961), 1,774 (1966), 1,868 (1971), 1,892 (1976), 1,937 (1981), 1,840 (1986), 2,236 (1991), 2,545 (1996), 2,523 (2001), 2,473 (2006), 2,459 (2011).

Obley (*Co. Gordon*) 32°42'S. 148°33'E., 34 km E. of Peak Hill, on Little R.; village gaz. and first lots sold 1863; mining, farming, grazing; agric. implement works (David Kerin); bridge b. 1881 by R. Bishop, over Little R.; cemetery 1884; CH 1870, new one (incl. lock-up) 1891; flood 1892; lock-up 1866; Lutheran C.; PO 1858–1948; pound (stock) 1865; Presb. C., closed, renovated 1910 by T. Bain, reopened 1910; PS, closed 1924, sold 1925 to John Coady; Rom. Cath. C. (St John the Baptist) b. 1906 by James Murray, closed, later demolished; school 1882, new buildings b. 1884 by James Prior Hull, closed 1886, reopened 1892, closed 1937; telegraph 1882; telephone 1897; TX 1915–39; pop. *c.*30 (1866), 80 (1901), 194 (1933), 76 (1947), 63 (1954), 110 (1961), 304 (2006), 354 (2011).

Obley Road (*Co. Gordon*) 32°23'S. 148°35'E., 14 km S. of Dubbo; pop. 181 (1911).

OBX Creek (*Co. Fitzroy*) 29°48'S. 152°43'E., 22 km SW of Grafton, on OBX Ck; farming and grazing; PO 1927–31; school 1891–1905 and 1914–22; telephone 1916; TX 1930; pop. 25 (1933).

Ocean Beach (*Co. Northumberland*) see Umina Beach.

Ocean Beach City Estate (*Co. Northumberland*) see Umina Beach.

Ocean Park Estate (*Co. Northumberland*) see Merewether.

Ocean Shores (*Co. Rous*) 28°31'S. 153°32'E., 5 km NE of Mullumbimby, on Coral Sea; founded 1969 by Wendell West Development Co.; Angl. C. (St Anselm's) 1995; Bapt. C. (The Hub) 1984; bridges: one over Brunswick R. and Orana Bridge over Marshalls Ck; 7 quarries; 2 reservoirs; sewerage augmentation 1996; pop. 255 (1976), 1,018 (1981), 1,826 (1986), 2,797 (1991), 3,361 (1996), 3,466 (2001), 3,739 (2011).

Ocean Shores (*Co. Rous*) see also South Golden Beach.

Ocean Shores North (*Co. Rous*) see South Golden Beach.

Ocean View (*Co. Camden*) 34°34'S. 150°38'E.,

18 km SW of Dapto; RS 1936–68.

Ocean View Beach (*Co. Fitzroy*) 30°04'S. 153°12'E., 5 km N. of Woolgoolga, on Tasman Sea.

O'Connell (*Co. Westmoreland*) 33°32'S. 149°43'E., 19 km SE of Bathurst, on Fish R.; (incl. O'Connell Plains); settled *c.*1822, designated as chief town of the county, classified 1974 by National Trust; mining (gold disc. and gold rush 1851), grazing, agric.; Angl. C. (Salem) b. 1832 by Thomas Hassall, defunct, replacement (St Thomas's) b. 1866 by Edward Foote, additions 1877, belfry demolished 1955, and graveyard (83 graves 1835+); bridge b. 1881 by Alfred Bowden, damaged 1952, replaced 1984, over Fish R.; butter factory (O'Connell Dairying Co.); cemetery (216 graves) 1898; earth tremor 1876; FB (new station b. 2018); flood 1952; flour mill (Daniel Roberts) estab. 1826 as a water-mill, converted to steam 1858, acquired 1862 by Joseph Golsby, then John Black, alterations 1881, converted to roller mill 1891; foot-bridge (iron, fabricated at Bloomfield Ironworks, Tipton, England) erected 1869–71 by Thomas M'Arthur & Co., moved 1882 by J.K. Mackenzie to Sofala, over Fish R.; gale 1909; mine (Breakfast Ck); PO 1834, new ones 1840 and 1925; pound (stock) 1844; PS, burnt down 1916, new one, damaged 1924, closed 1939; rabbit freezing works (Bryant & Co.) b. 1916 by H. Bridge; Rom. Cath. C. (St Francis of Assisi) b. 1864–67, d. by Edward Gell, closed, sold and reused, and graveyard (79 graves 1868–1900); sale-yards; school 1869, new one b. 1876 by John Stanford, additions and repairs 1883 by T.G. Morgan, closed 1949, reopened 1957, additions 1967; telephone 1890; TX 1925, automatic 1970; pop. 200 (1891), 206 (1901), 278 (1911), 218 (1933), 111 (1947), 145 (1954), 137 (1961), *c.*250 (1987), 356 (2006), 648 (2011).

O'Connell Plains (*Co. Westmoreland*) see O'Connell.

O'Connells Paddock (*Co. Urana*) 35°10'S. 146°40'E., 8 km NW of Lockhart.

Oddfield (*Co. Wellington*) 32°37'S. 148°58'E., 7 km S. of Wellington; RS 1893–1956.

O'Donnelltown (*Co. Northumberland*) see Wallsend West.

Off Flat (*Co. Westmoreland*) see Hampton.

Ogles Gap (*Co. Narromine*) 32°12'S. 147°57'E., 18 km S. of Trangie.

Ogunbil (*Co. Parry*) 31°21'S. 151°17'E., 40 km SE of Kootingal, on Dungowan Ck; farming and grazing; PO 1909–54; telephone 1924; TX 1924, automatic 1961; Union C.; pop. 147 (1911), 71 (1933), 66 (1947), 152 (1954), 87 (1961).

O'Hares (*Co. Selwyn*) 35°49'S. 148°22'E., 32 km E. of Tumbarumba, on Tumut R.

Ohio (*Co. Vernon*) 30°58'S. 151°37'E., 3 km NE of Walcha, on Ohio Ck; pound (stock) 1856.

Old Adaminaby (*Co. Wallace*) see Adaminaby.

Old Banks (*Co. Durham*) 32°39'S. 151°36'E., 6 km S. of Paterson, on Paterson R.; timber; CH (incl. lock-up) b. 1827 by Michael Hearne, dilapidated by 1832; military barracks 1820; pound (stock), moved 1841 to Paterson; punt across Paterson R.

Old Bar (*Co. Gloucester*) 31°58'S. 152°35'E., 13 km SE of Taree, on Tasman Sea; disc. 1818, subdivisions: one in 1912, Waterman's Estate 1947, Hall's Estate 1950, Bella Vista 1961; farming then tourism; airfield b. 1930 by George Bunyan, licensed 1931, closed 1989, reopened 1991; Church of Christ; FB; gales 1866 and 1921; flood 1866; PO 1927, new one b. 1996; quarry; Rom. Cath. C. (Our Lady of Fatima) b. 1952 by Schmitzer and Burg, (shared with Angl.), extended 1978; sawmill (Souter, Aldous and Southwell) 1947, burnt down 1949; school 1949, additions 1991; sewerage augmentation 1985; telephone 1913, automatic 1972; TX 1926; Unit. C. (orig. Meth.) 1940, refurbished 1978; water reticulation 1969; pop. 58 (1933), 174 (1947), 339 (1954), 319 (1961), 666 (1976), 970 (1981), 1,295 (1986), 1,992 (1991), 2,650 (1996), 2,853 (2001), 3,358 (2006), 3,650 (2011).

Old Beabula (*Co. Waradgery*) see Nulabor.

Old Bemboka (*Co. Auckland*) 36°40'S. 149°37'E., 20 km W. of Bega, on Bemboka R.

Old Bonalbo (*Co. Buller*) 28°39'S. 152°36'E., 40

km W. of Kyogle; farming and grazing; Angl. C. (All Saints') 1959; bridge (Dare timber truss) 1934, 123 ft (37.5 m), over Bonalbo Ck; bushfire 1926; cemetery (145 graves), incl. columbarium; cheese factory (Charles Waller) 1926; FB; floods 1934 and 2011; PO 1912; sawmill (McKee Bros); school 1920, additions 1924 by F. Spencer, additions 2010; TX 1921, automatic 1975; pop. 116 (1933), 163 (1947), 212 (1954), 240 (1961), 240 (2006), 273 (2011).

Old Bowenfels (*Co. Cook*) see Bowenfels South.

Old Burren (*Co. Jamison*) 29°57'S. 148°53'E., 54 km SE of Collarenebri, on Pian Ck; settled 1861; wheat 1956+; cemetery; RS 1906–75; pop. 21 (1933).

Oldbury (*Co. Camden*) 34°32'S. 150°19'E., 6 km W. of Moss Vale, on Medway Rivulet; agric.; flour mills: James Atkinson (post mill) 1827, demolished, and George Bruce Barton (steam mill) 1837.

Old Casino (*Co. Rous*) 28°52'S. 153°03'E., 1 km N. of Casino; RS (Casino till 1930) 1903–86, station reused; sawmill; sewage works.

Old Erowal Bay (*Co. St Vincent*) see Erowal Bay.

Old Grevillia (*Co. Rous*) 28°27'S. 152°53'E., 23 km NW of Kyogle, on Richmond R.; pop. 64 (1954), 50 (1961), 283 (2006), 213 (2011).

Old Gunyerwarildi (*Co. Burnett*) 29°11'S. 150°23'E., 42 km NW of Warialda, on Croppa Ck.

Old Jeremiah Creek (*Co. Buccleuch*) 35°04'S. 148°30'E., 37 km E. of Gundagai, on Old Jeremiah Ck; school 1899–1902.

Old Jindabyne (*Co. Wallace*) see Jindabyne.

Old Junee (*Co. Clarendon*) 34°50'S. 147°31'E., 7 km NW of Junee, on Houlaghans Ck; village gaz. 1863 as Jewnee, gaz. 1958 as Old Junee; goldmining 1869–81, grazing, then agric.; Angl. C. (St Thomas's) 1891, restored 1911, rebuilt 1958, demolished 1979; cemetery, restored 1985; chaff mill estab. 1919 by Gus. R. Kleinig, J.E. Kleinig and Arthur Stockman; diphtheria 1926; FB; hospital (cottage) 1890; Meth. C. 1905, closed, moved 1950 to Illabo, new one 1956; PO 1862; RS (2 km SW) 1881, station b. by Charles Hardy; school (Junee till 1893) 1881 b. by W.A. Crawley, additions and alterations 1913 by W. Davis; silo 1922; telephone 1909; TX 1924–79; Wes. Meth. C. b. 1879 by J. Maclean, d. by D. Robertson; pop. *c.*12 (1866), 20 (1876), 320 (1901), 467 (1933), 194 (1947), 268 (1954), 233 (1961), 530 (2011).

Old Koreelah (*Co. Buller*) 28°24'S. 152°25'E., 59 km NW of Kyogle, on Hoffmans Ck; farming and grazing; Angl. C. (St Peter's); PO 1916; sawmills: Cossart & Sons and Allan Foster; telephone 1916; TX 1925, automatic 1978; pop. 392 (1933), 106 (1947), 97 (1954), 101 (1961). (See also New Koreelah.)

Old Maragle (*Co. Selwyn*) see Maragle.

Old Marulan (*Co. Argyle*) 34°44'S. 149°59'E., 24 km E. of Goulburn; disc. 1798 by Wilson, Price, Hocking and Collins, surveyed 1834 by Robert Hoddle, laid out by Major Sir Thomas Livingstone Mitchell, village gaz. 1835, estab. 1836, declined 1867+, defunct; agric.; Angl. C. (St Jude's) 1847, and graveyard (burials 1841+); cemetery 1863; CH, closed 1850; PO 1838; PS (removed from Bungonia) 1847; pound (stock) 1842; rifle range 1913; Rom. Cath. C. (St Patrick's) b. 1859–63 by Boulster and Kelly, closed 1930, dismantled 1936, moved 1937 to Kenmore, and graveyard (burials 1865+); school 1860; pop. *c.*500 (1866), 31 (1933).

Old Mill (*Co. Hardinge*) 29°54'S. 151°12'E., 6 km N. of Tingha, on Jones Ck; orig. Joe's Gully, then Old Saw Mill; tin mining; 6 mines; PO 1927; school 1913, new one b. 1917 by Newetson and Hickey & Co., closed 1942; telephone 1920; TX 1952–61; pop. 73 (1933), 62 (1947).

Old Moonbi (*Co. Inglis*) see Moonbi.

Old Saw Mill (*Co. Hardinge*) see Old Mill.

Old Ulan (*Co. Bligh*) 32°14'S. 149°43'E., 24 km NE of Gulgong, on Ulan Ck; settled by William Robinson, defunct; wheat, oats, grazing.

Old Warrah (*Co. Buckland*) 31°40'S. 150°40'E., 18 km S. of Quirindi, on Warrah Ck; electricity 1937; pop. 83 (1901), 36 (1933).

Old Womans Creek (*Co. Bathurst*) 33°49'S. 149°01'E., 31 km E. of Cowra.

Old Yaminba (*Co. White*) 31°06'S. 149°27'E., 26 km NE of Coonabarabran, on Yaminba Ck.

Old Yarrawa (*Co. Hunter*) 32°24'S. 150°36'E., 8 km W. of Denman; farming; PO 1928–58; telephone 1929.

Olinda (*Co. Phillip*) 32°50'S. 150°09'E., 15 km E. of Kandos, on Cudgegong R.; farming and grazing; PO 1894; telephone 1918; TX 1918, automatic 1959; pop. 52 (1933), 71 (1954), 53 (1961).

Olive Downs (*Co. Tongowoko*) 29°04'S. 141°52'E., 311 km NW of Wilcannia; dust storm 1945.

Ollera (*Co. Hardinge*) 30°07'S. 151°31'E., 19 km NW of Guyra, on Georges Ck; founded *c.*1837 by Everett Bros; Angl. C. (St Bartholomew's) b. 1877 by Hugh McKay, d. by John Horbury Hunt; cemetery (394 graves 1843+) 1887; PO 1870; school 1888–94; wool-scour (Everett and Mackenzie) 1895; pop. 62 (1911), 33 (1933), 56 (1947).

Omadale Brook (*Co. Durham*) 31°53'S. 151°19'E., 46 km E. of Scone, on Omadale Brook; telephone 1909; TX 1928–72; pop. 62 (1933).

Omega (*Co. Camden*) 34°44'S. 150°50'E., 2 km N. of Gerringong, on Werri Ck; farming; milk factory 1881, taken over 1886 by NSW Fresh Food & Ice Co. and reused as butter factory, closed; PO 1891–1931; RS 1893, station b. by Gerald Dalton Fetherston and Felix Edward Barbat, replaced 1952; school (Omega Retreat till 1908) 1860, repairs 1892 by Anton Ettingshausen, closed 1941, building reused; tannery (Camps'), taken over 1901 by James Missingham; telephone 1925; pop. 59 (1911).

Omega Retreat (*Co. Camden*) see Omega.

Omeo Flat (*Co. Wellesley*) 36°48'S. 148°16'E., 32 km S. of Thredbo.

Omigal (*Co. Wellington*) 32°44'S. 149°01'E., 20 km S. of Wellington; town gaz. 1869, never developed.

Onebygamba (*Co. Northumberland*) see Carrington.

One Eye (*Co. Georgiana*) 33°48'S. 149°21'E., 31 km S. of Blayney, on Mulgunnia Ck.

One Mile (*Co. Gloucester*) see Boat Harbour.

One Tree (*Co. Waradgery*) 34°11'S. 144°43'E., 36 km N. of Hay; village laid out and gaz. 1869; PO 1895.

One Tree Farm (*Co. Rous*) see Casino North.

One Tree Hill (*Co. Cook*) see Mount Victoria.

Onybigambah (*Co. Northumberland*) see Carrington.

Oolong (*Co. King*) 34°47'S. 149°11'E., 25 km E. of Yass; farming and grazing; earth tremors 1998 and 1999; PO 1927–31; Prim. Meth. C. 1868; RS 1890–1972; telephone 1920; typhoid 1914; pop. 75 (1911), 27 (1933), 246 (2006).

Ooma (*Co. Forbes*) 33°39'S. 148°06'E., 27 km N. of Grenfell, on Ooma Ck; pop. 126 (1933), 165 (1947), 75 (1961).

Ooma Creek (*Co. Forbes*) 33°42'S. 148°05'E., 23 km N. of Grenfell, on Ooma Ck; farming; bushfire 1884; PO 1927–28; quarry; TX (automatic); pop. 23 (1933).

Ooma North (*Co. Forbes*) 33°37'S. 148°04'E., 26 km S. of Forbes; school 1957–69.

Oorin (*Co. Buller*) see Capeen.

Oorundunby (*Co. Vernon*) 31°09'S. 151°36'E., 17 km S. of Walcha.

Ootha (*Co. Cunningham*) 33°07'S. 147°27'E., 28 km E. of Condobolin; farming; FB (new station b. 2011); PO 1914, burnt down 1922; Presb. C. 1939, closed, sold 2014; quarry (gravel); RS (Ringwood Siding till 1910) 1899–1989; school 1957, additions 1966, closed 1984; silo 1932; telephone 1915; TX 1917, automatic 1976; pop. 70 (1911), 175 (1933), 144 (1947), 167 (1954), 177 (1961), 94 (2006), 92 (2011).

Opale (*Co. Finch*) see Lightning Ridge.

Ophir (*Co. Wellington*) 33°10'S. 149°15'E., 20 km NE of Orange, on Lewis Ponds Ck; (incl. Newtown); orig. Yorkey's Corner; laid out 1851 by Major Sir Thomas Livingstone Mitchell, first lots sold 1852, defunct; orig. mining (alluvial gold disc. 1851 by William Tom, jun. and John Hardman Australia Lister, gold rush 1851–52, reef gold disc. 1868 by Joseph Christopherson), copper 1851–65, then sheep and cattle; Angl. C. (St George's) 1851, defunct, and graveyard (25+ burials 1861–1913, 4 graves 1870–1913); causeway across Lewis Ponds Ck; cemetery (4 graves); mines: Bentley's Tunnel, Bismarck Tunnel, Bluff Tunnels, Boulton and Byrnes's Tunnel, Coote's Find 1917, Gunnado, Kurrajong Hill, Lucas Gully (William McConnell), Murray's Hill, Nelson's, Queen of the Ranges, Salvation Bob (Bob McConnell), Say's Tunnel, Slater's Tunnel, Spencer's Cut *c.*1875, The Belmore Reef (Joseph Christopherson and later Richard Spencer) 1866, The Drift Gold Mining Co. Tunnel, The Jeweller's Shop, The Lady Belmore, The Lady Mary, The Little Belmore, Uren's Tunnel, Wet Tunnel, Wright's Tunnel, Young Australia (Robert McConnell); PO 1851; PS (incl. lock-up); school 1884–1923, sold and removed 1930; stamper batteries (incl. a 7 head and a 10 head); TX 1969; weir on Lewis Ponds Ck; pop. *c.*350 (1866), 50 (1889), 73 (1911), 26 (1933), 127 (1954), 106 (1961), 150 (2011).

Ophir Glen (*Co. Rous*) 28°28'S. 153°26'E., 11 km NW of Mullumbimby.

Opossum Creek (*Co. Rous*) 28°40'S. 153°30'E., 3 km W. of Bangalow, on Wilsons Ck; foot-bridge 1905; school 1901, new building b. 1910 by Wilson and Sanson, closed 1963, sold and reused; pop. 74 (1911), 85 (1933), 121 (1947), 115 (1954), 84 (1961).

Orama (*Co. Raleigh*) 30°26'S. 152°41'E., 10 km S. of Dorrigo, on Bellinger R.; farming; Angl. C. 1924; PO 1912, burnt down 1915, reopened 1927, closed 1961; school (Cavan till 1922) 1919–30, 1942–53, reopened 1981; telephone 1911; TX 1928; pop. 45 (1933), 56 (1947).

Orana (*Co. Manara*) 32°45'S. 144°02'E., 158 km NW of Hillston.

Orana Heights (*Co. Lincoln*) see Dubbo.

Orandelbinnia (*Co. Gowen*) 31°34'S. 149°11'E., 19 km W. of Binnaway; school 1882–93.

Orandumbie (*Co. Vernon*) 31°08'S. 151°36'E., 17 km S. of Walcha; electricity 1960; school (Orundumbie) 1883–93; pop. 33 (1933).

Orange (*Co. Wellington*) 33°17'S. 149°06'E., 204 km W. of Sydney, on Blackmans Swamp Ck; (incl. Avondale, Bel Air, Bletchington, Bloomfield, Bowen, Calare, Clinton, Clover Hill, East Orange, Endsleigh, Glenroi, Leewood, Malabar, Narrambla, North Orange, South Orange, Suma Park, Warrendine, West Orange); Blackman's Swamp till *c.*1828; disc. 1820 by James Meehan, estab. 1823 by Lieut. Percy Simpson, settled 1827 by George Blackett, surveyed 1828, planned 1829 by James B. Richards, estab. *c.*1843, laid out by Walker Rannie Davidson and village gaz. 1846, first lots sold 1849, munic. proc. 1860 (East Orange 1888, amalgamated 1912), designated as chief town of the county, thrived 1850s–70s, 1884, 1920s–30s, city proc. 1946 (area enlarged 1977), designated part of growth centre 1972 but short-lived; wheat 1850s+, vegetables 1870s+, fruit (specially apples, pears, cherries) *c.*1886+, maize, barley, oats, timber, dairying, ham, bacon, tourism in 1920s, now also olives, grapes, berries, sheep, cattle, manufacturing; abattoir (Graziers' Assoc.) 1927; aeroplane crash (2 killed) 1925; agric. college 1973 d. by Donald Coleman, closed 2000; airport 1938, new hangars 1946, closed 1966; ambulance station b. 1932 by Lawrence Pither; Angl. C.: Holy Trinity (b. 1857–59 by Dennis Hanrahan, enlarged 1864, reused, new one b. 1877–79 by Thomas Taylor, d. by Thomas Rowe, steeple 1924 d. by William Lamrock, jun. and John Holderness Bates, church additions 1938) and St Barnabas's 1888 (new one 1940, demolished and replaced 1970); Apostolic C. (Ever Upward) o. 2000 in former Rom. Cath. C.; Assemblies of God C. (Christ. Ministry); bacon factory (Country Freezing Co. Ltd); Baha'i C.; Bapt. C. 1873, demolished 1913, new one b. 1913 by F.A. Collins, d. by Augustus Dixon Chater; bicycle works (Fred O'Brien & Son); boiling-down works (James Arthur Templer) 1847; boot factories: Maurice Bebb Bowen 1861, fire 1877 and J. Johnstone; breweries: Badlands Brewery, Henry W. Boxall, Burton Brewery (S. Irwin) 1880, John Chynoweth 1875–82, Hopping Mad Brewery 2003–7, Macquarie

Brewery (McCallum & Co.), Red Lion Brewery (sold 1884 to Lindsay's Brewing Co. Ltd, taken over by James Walker & Co., closed 1903), Standard Brewery (b. 1877 by E.J. Heap, acquired 1880 by W.H. Elwin & Co., extended and upgraded 1881, taken over 1903 by Walker & Co. Ltd, bought 1926 by Toohey's Ltd, closed, demolished); brickworks: Central Western Dry Press Brick Co., Samuel Frost 1865, Great Western Brick Co. Ltd, J. and C. Leigh; bridges over Blackmans Swamp Ck: one b. 1859 and one b. 2010; butter factories: Orange Co-op. Central Dairy Co. Ltd 1902 (bacon curing began 1906) and W.R. Brown; carriage-works: Great Eastern (became Dorman and Pike, acquired by W.T. Gardiner & Sons), Great Western (estab. 1865 by Michael Keneally, remodelled and reopened by C. Collier & Co.), Great Western Sulky & Carriage Factory (S.J. Greer), M'Keon and Lohan, fire 1901, George Nichols, Richard Venables, D.J. Wenban; case-making factories: Loughnane Bros and Orange Box Co.; cemetery (graves 1854+); CH 1851 (in former watch-house), new one 1854, replacement b. 1860–62 by Kennard and Snow, d. by Alexander Dawson, additions 1870 by James Stuart Douglas, demolished 1881, new one b. 1881–83 by Frederick Steinan, d. by James Johnstone Barnet, repairs 1899 by F. Archer, additions and alterations 1909 by James Stuart Douglas, extended 1965 and 2001, restoration and additions d. by Peter Armstrong Architecture and GHD Group; cheese factory (Second Mouse Cheese Co.) estab. 2011 by Kai and Annie Woltmann; cherry brining works (Orange Producers' Rural Co-op. Society) 1938; Christ. Brethren Assemblies C.; Church of Christ; clothing factory (W.E. Gardiner); Cong. C. 1878, additions 1926; cordial factories: W.E. Barrett (acquired 1915 by A.T. Cartwright, sold 1916 to Frederick George Augustus Williams), Fred H. Brown (burnt down 1918), Great Western, H.L. Lindsay, Sharpe Bros (estab. 1922 by John Sharpe, rebuilt 1931, closed 1939), W.S. Stabback, George Weily 1885, W. Yeo; creamery (Dalton Estate Ltd); crematorium (Canobolas Gardens); dams: Gosling Creek (Bloomfield), Spring Creek (Bloomfield, b. 1929–31, wall raised 1947, upgraded 2007), Suma Park; Dutch Reformed C.; diphtheria 1919 and 1935; dust storms 1910 and 1911; earth tremors 1886, 1934, 1936, 1952, 1956; electricity 1923; engineering works: Tom Edwards and Robinson & Co.; FB 1870 (station 1904 d. by John Hale, alterations and repairs 1912 by James Stuart Douglas, renovations 1914 also by Douglas); fibrous plaster works: F.H. Brown and Waratah Fibrous Plaster & Reinforced Concrete Works; fires 1868, 1881, 1897, 1909, 1913, 1928, 1949; floods 1861, 1916, 1928, 1935, 2010; flour mills: Henry Curran 1855 (acquired by W.T. Trappitt, later acquired by M.B. Bowen, closed 1890), James Dalton 1866 (new one b. 1892 by John Henry Gain, d. by A.D. Nelson & Co., became Dalton Bros Ltd, demolished 1907, replaced 1908 on new site by William Mitchell, known as Lily of the West Roller Mills, closed, largely demolished 1965), Great Western (Benjamin Nelson) b. 1863–65, demolished, Narrambla Steam Mills (estab. 1848 by James Arthur Templer, horse powered till 1851, then steam, closed, demolished 1971), B. Nelson 1860; foundries: Atlas (T.J. Robinson Orange Pty Ltd), J. Godwin, Groub and Sattler, Richard Venables; Foursquare Gospel C.; freezing works (Gosling Creek) 1881 d. by John Hale; fruit pulp factory (Fruit Packing & Distributing Co. Orange NSW Ltd) 1932; furniture factories: Dalton Bros Ltd 1913 and Smith Bros; gales 1880 and 1941; galvanised iron works (J. Withers); gaol (orig. a lock-up) 1859, extended 1876, closed 1909, demolished 1912; gasworks (Orange Gaslight Co. Ltd) 1877, modernised 1885, explosion 1911, new gasholder b. 1912 by James Hurll & Co. Ltd, expanded 1926, 1952, 1957, razed 1976, (gas connected to East Orange 1914); goldmines: Surprise *c.*1939 and Wellwood 1925 and

1939; hailstorms 1890, 1896, 1927; hospital 1867 d. by John Hale, new wing added 1886, additions 1905 by Oliver and Arthur, d. by Thomas Tidswell, demolished 1959, new one 1933, extended 1937 by Robert Daniel Quiggin, additions 1946 and 1966, additions 1971 d. by I. Roberts and E. Mack, additions 1986, new one (Bloomfield) 2011; ice-cream factory (F. Lippold); ice works: W.E. Barrett, W.J. Gifford 1901, Perry & Co.; incinerator b. 1893 by John Bustard for night soil and refuse disposal, closed 1896; Indep. Bapt. C.; jam factory (William Hood, jun.) 1921; Jehovah's Witnesses C.; joineries: F. Bates and Eslick's; knitting mill (Leonard Needham, became Orange Knitting Mills Pty Ltd in 1936); LDS (Mormon) C. 1966; lingerie factory (Emstra Pty Ltd); lock-up, additions 1861; Lutheran C. (St Peter's); mattress factory (Moonrise Pty Ltd) 1947; measles epidemic 1875; mental hospital (Bloomfield) b. 1923–31, additions 1931, 1956, 1961; migrant hostel 1952; military detention barracks (World War II); milk factories: Allowrie Foods Aust. Ltd and T.A. Barrett Pty Ltd; monumental stone works: L.G. King, McMurtrie Bros, A.H. Pady, Arthur William Wright; New Life City C.; optical goods factory (Western Optical Pty Ltd); plastics factories: Allmould Plastics 1995, Blackpoly Pipelines 2001, fire 2013, Plaztech Industries; Plymouth Brethren C.; pneumonia epidemics 1902 (many died) and 1929 (2 boys died); PO: Boomfield 1909, East Orange 1901, Endsleigh 1942–79, North Orange 1949–82, Orange 1849 (new one b. 1864 by William and John Hale, d. by James Johnstone Barnet, demolished 1878, replacement b. 1878–80 by James Stuart Douglas, also d. by Barnet, additions 1892, repairs 1897 by Withers Bros, additions and alterations 1903 by John Gain, additions 1913 and 1979), South Orange 1935–94, West Orange 1946; police barracks b. 1908 by J.H. Burns, repairs 1909 by E.P. Frost & Co.; pound (stock), relocated 1878; POW control centre 1943; powerhouse 1923, additions 1926; Presb. C. (St John's) b. 1860–63, demolished 1898, new one (St James's); PS: East Orange 1890–1930 and Orange 1848, new one 1850, additions 1878 by T. Taylor, additions and repairs 1899 by James Stuart Douglas, additions 1935 by William Lishman Jemison, new ones 1954 and 2009; quarry (Orange Blue Metal Quarries); railway coal stage 1877; railway engine shed 1893, repairs 1923 following fire; railway round-house 1937; railway turntable, 60 ft (18.3 m), strengthened 1928, new one, 75 ft (22.9 m), closed; refrigerator factory (Electricity Meter Manufacturing Co., became Email Ltd, taken over by Electrolux) 1946–2016; reservoirs: 500,000 gal. (2,273 kl) and 1,000,000 gal. (4,546 kl); rifle range 1911; Rom. Cath. C.: Holy Family (Glenroi) 1964, sold 1999, renovated and reused 2000, St Joseph's 1859 (replacement b. 1869–71 by David Jones, d. by Edward Gell, major additions 1897–99 by J.M. Pringle, d. by Herbert Edmund Wardell), Mary Immaculate (East Orange) b. 1926 by A. Butcher, d. by William James Gilroy, demolished and replaced 1988; RS: Bloomfield (Orange Meat Co. Siding till 1891) 1890–1974, Orange 1877 (station b. by James Stuart Douglas, refreshment rooms, station alterations 1918), Orange East Fork (for Indian-Pacific) 1970, Orange Exchange (for Broken Hill Express) 1932–37; rubber works (Orco, J.T. Rossiter & Sons); sale-yards 1878–1936, replaced 1936, upgraded 1954, enlarged 1963; Salv. Army C. b. 1921 by J. Liscombe; sawmills (incl. John Henry Gain's Steam Joinery and Wangarrie Sawmill Pty Ltd); schools: Bletchington 1957, additions 1962, 1966, 2011, Bloomfield 1900 b. by Frederick J. Lewis, closed 1962, Bowen 1982, Calare 1967 (d. by John Moran and R. Scott, West Orange till 1968, additions 1980), Canobolas Rural Technology HS 1967 (Canobolas HS till 1996, additions 1976 and 1991), East Orange 1890 (repairs 1900 by F.F. Archer, additions 1909 by Peter Beddie, additions 1929 by A.E. Rauch, additions 1960, 1962, 1971), Glenroi Heights 1952 (additions 1977), Gosling Creek 1874–1910,

Orange 1852 (additions 1875, 1876, 1878, 1881, 1907, 1910, 1916, 1925, 1967, 1972, 1975), Orange HS 1912 (new building b. 1913, new one 1959 on new site, additions 1975 and 1996); SD Adventist C.; sewerage: Orange 1918 and East Orange 1922; Slavic Pentecostal C.; small arms factory 1941–45, later acquired by Electricity Meter Manufacturing Co. (Emmco); snowstorms 1878, 1900, 1901, 1914, 1921; soap and candle factories: Alberto Charles Oram Lane, burnt down 1871, rebuilt and Patrick Mulholland; streets gas lit 1877 (East Orange 1902), electric lit 1923; street tree plantings 1886+; strike (rabbit trappers) 1914; tanneries: Maurice Bebb Bowen 1861 (sold 1912 to Anzelark Bros), C. Christopherson, W. Johnstone, Parkes (J. Wooden); TC, additions 1972 and 1988, became Western Institute in 1992; telegraph 1860, new office b. 1878–80, d. by James Johnstone Barnet, repairs 1897 by Withers Bros; telephone: Bloomfield 1912, East Orange 1911, Endsleigh 1942, North Orange 1949, South Orange 1935, West Orange 1946; toll-gate 1863–75; tornado 1914; TX 1899, automatic 1956; typhoid 1900, 1904, 1913; Unit. C.: Five Ways (orig. Cong.) b. 1904 by H. Richardson, d. by Harry Chambers Kent and Henry Ebenezer Budden, tower and porch added 1949 by Tom Davies, d. by Eric Thomas, closed 2018, sold 2019, St John's (orig. Presb.) b. 1910–13 by James Stuart Douglas, d. by Joseph Power and John Adam, Wesley (orig. Wes. Meth.) b. 1863 by Mugridge Bros and John Hale, d. by Thomas Rowe, enlarged and spire added 1876, church additions 1921 by Black Bros, d. by William Lamrock, jun. and John Holderness Bates, porch 1953 d. by E. Thomas; univ. (Charles Sturt) 2006, new buildings 2009; vehicle body fabrication works (Almighty Industries); watch-house 1849, reused 1851; water supply (from Gosling Ck) 1890, upgraded 1911, reticulation to East Orange 1917, filtration plant b. 1931 by State Monier Pipe Works; Wes. Meth. C. 1849; winery (Harold Borrodell Gartrell); woollen mills: Amalgamated Textiles Aust. Ltd (became Macquarie Worsteds Ltd) 1925–89 and H.J. Griffith (removed 1915 from Clergate); wool-scour; wool stores (East Orange); pop. 28 (1851), 236 (1856), 581 (1861), *c.*600 (1866), 1,456 (1871), 2,701 (1881), 5,064 (1891), 4,178 (1901), 7,799 (1911), 7,398 (1921), *c.*8,000 (1923), 11,544 (1933, incl. 1,391 in Bloomfield mental hospital), 15,450 (1947, incl. 1,556 in Bloomfield mental hospital), 19,842 (1954, incl. 1,510 in Bloomfield mental hospital), 19,250 (1959), 19,045 (1961), 22,208 (1966), 24,154 (1971), 26,254 (1976), 27,626 (1981), 28,935 (1986), 29,635 (1991), 30,705 (1996), 31,970 (2001), 31,544 (2006), 34,992 (2011).

Orange East Fork (*Co. Wellington*) see Orange.

Orange Exchange (*Co. Wellington*) see Orange.

Orange Grove (*Co. Nandewar*) 30°58'S. 150°23'E., 12 km E. of Gunnedah; earth tremor 2012; FB.

Orange Grove (*Co. Northumberland*) see Blackwall.

Orange Meat Co. Siding (*Co. Wellington*) see Orange.

Orange Racecourse (*Co. Wellington*) see Canobolas.

Orange Tree Flat (*Co. Clarke*) 30°43'S. 152°12'E., 53 km E. of Armidale, on Georges Ck.

Orangeville (*Co. Camden*) 34°02'S. 150°35'E., 11 km W. of Camden, on Th Big Gully; Bob's Range till 1916; oranges 1880s–1960s, cattle, horses, deer; FB; PO 1912; Prim. Meth. C. 1875; quarry; sawmill; school (Mulgoa Forest till 1916) 1866, burnt down 1964; telephone 1914; TX 1929–64; Unit. C. (orig. Meth.) b. 1905 by William Dunk, rebuilt 1981 by L.G. Young Pty Ltd; pop. 99 (1901), 142 (1933), 97 (1947), 69 (1954), 145 (1961), 598 (2001), 1,182 (2006), 1,102 (2011).

Orangies Point (*Co. Wellington*) 32°47'S. 149°09'E., 32 km SE of Wellington, on Muckerwa Ck.

Oranmeir (*Co. Murray*) 35°41'S. 149°38'E., 31 km SW of Braidwood, on Shoalhaven R.;

agric., grazing, alluvial mining; PO 1859–1971; PS, closed 1930; telephone 1906; TX 1924; pop. 26 (1933), 78 (1947).

Orara (*Co. Fitzroy*) see Coffs Harbour.

Orara East (*Co. Fitzroy*) 30°10'S. 153°01'E., 19 km W. of Woolgoolga, on Orara R.; telephone 1923.

Orchard Flat (*Co. Vernon*) 31°03'S. 152°03'E., 42 km E. of Walcha, on Apsley R.

Orelda (*Co. Hume*) 35°48'S. 146°45'E., 15 km W. of Walla Walla; RS (Long Gully till 1902) 1893–1972.

Oreston (*Co. Harden*) 34°31'S. 148°36'E., 14 km SW of Boorowa; RS 1931–69.

Orient Point (*Co. St Vincent*) 34°55'S. 150°45'E., 1 km E. of Greenwell Point, on Crookhaven R.; subdivided *c.*1928 by Henry Ferdinand Halloran; orig. farming, now tourism; FB 1942; pilot station; PO 1954; sewerage augmentation 1985; telephone 1954; wharf; pop. 82 (1961), 1,416 (1976, incl. Culburra Beach), 2,068 (1981, incl. Culburra Beach), 2,525 (1986, incl. Culburra Beach), 3,145 (1991, incl. Culburra Beach), 3,533 (1996, incl. Culburra Beach), 3,622 (2001, incl. Culburra Beach), 3,416 (2006, incl. Culburra Beach), 3,289 (2011, incl. Culburra Beach).

Orita (*Co. Vernon*) 31°07'S. 151°40'E., 17 km SE of Walcha; telephone 1934; TX 1934, automatic 1954.

Orton Park (*Co. Bathurst*) 33°28'S. 149°34'E., 5 km S. of Bathurst, on Queen Charlottes Ck; farming and dairying; floods 1906 and 1928; hailstorm 1856; PO 1892–1931; 2 quarries; RS 1880–1963; telephone 1913; pop. 51 (1911), 60 (1933), 106 (1947), 55 (1954), 65 (1961).

Orundumbi (*Co. Vernon*) see Brackendale.

Orundumbie (*Co. Vernon*) see Orandumbie.

Osborne (*Co. Bathurst*) see Osborneville.

Osborne (*Co. Camden*) see Kangaroo Valley.

Osborne (*Co. Urana*) 35°21'S. 146°43'E., 15 km S. of Lockhart; farming; PO 1903; school (Gum Holes till 1915) 1913–71; telephone 1914; TX 1918, automatic 1951; Union C.; pop. 103 (1911), 129 (1933), 111 (1947), 103 (1954), 110 (1961).

Osborneville (*Co. Bathurst*) 33°38'S. 149°17'E., 11 km S. of Blayney; flood 1920; school (Evans Swamp till 1883, then Osborne till 1915) 1882–1923.

Osborne Well (*Co. Denison*) 35°37'S. 145°54'E., 10 km NE of Berrigan; school 1957–74.

Osterley (*Co. Durham*) 32°44'S. 151°42'E., 6 km NW of Raymond Terrace, on Hunter R.; (incl. Mount Kanwary); orig. wheat and wool, then farming and dairying; creamery (Hunter River Pioneer Co-op. Creamery Co.) 1892–1903; electricity 1940; flour mill, unused, demolished 1939; PO (Mount Kanwary) 1927–31; pound (stock) 1861; school (Mount Kanwary) 1929 b. by Arthur Partridge-Wall; telephone 1926; TX 1928–36; wharf; pop. 34 (1933), 243 (2011).

Oswald (*Co. Northumberland*) 32°42'S. 151°25'E., 7 km SE of Branxton, on Hunter R.; (incl. Kaludah); agric.; bushfire (woman died) 1944; flood 1867; school 1859–82; storm 1905; Wes. Meth. C. 1855, new one b. 1901 by Russell, and graveyard (89 graves 1851+); pop. 55 (1911), 50 (1933), 50 (1947), 62 (1954), 50 (1961).

Oura (*Co. Clarendon*) 35°07'S. 147°32'E., 15 km E. of Wagga Wagga, on Murrumbidgee R.; village gaz. 1868; Angl. C. (St Mark's) 1931, renovated 1935 by George Hoskinson, restored 1943 by George Hoskinson, Boyton et al., closed, sold; FB; hailstorm 1946; Presb. C. (Church of the Pioneers) b. 1933 by J. Waters, d. by John Donald Morrow, rededicated (Scots Church of the Pioneers) 1948; sawmill (Campbell's); school 1882–85, 1908–20, 1931–70; telephone 1923; TX 1930, automatic 1959; Union C.; winery (Wagga Wagga) 1987; pop. 126 (1911), 188 (1933), 85 (1947), 99 (1954), 148 (1961), 382 (2006), 476 (2011).

Ourimbah (*Co. Northumberland*) 33°22'S. 151°22'E., 8 km N. of Gosford, on Bangalow Ck; (incl. Kendalls Glen); Blue Gum Flat till 1888; estab. *c.*1855, subdivided 1887 and 1896; orig. timber, then farming and citrus fruit; Angl. C. 1859, second one b. 1879 by Robert Coulter, new one (St Peter's), renovated 1911, closed 1975; bushfire 1944;

Christadelphian C.; cordial factory (E. Mundy) 1920; crematorium (Mackay's); dam; diphtheria 1910; electricity 1938; FB; fibro cement factory (A.M. Wilson); fire 1950; fruit case factories: Brownlee and Scarvell, and H.L. Taylor; moth infestation 1905; PO 1871, new one b. 1933 by Montague Audet; pound (stock) 1908; Presb. C. 1910; PS 1910–16; reservoir; RS 1887, station b. by G.R. and F.H. Harrison; sawmills: R. Brownlee & Co. Ltd (later acquired by R. Love), Denton and Callcott, Eglington (H.E. Pratten, leased 1911 from him by Brown and Tooby), William G. Goldie, Stan Luke, H. McKenzie Pty Ltd 1907, Lyall Scott, closed 1888, J.L. Travers, Edward West; school (Blue Gum Flat till 1887) 1863, relocated 1886, repairs 1892 by James Ditolerjson, additions 1918 by E. Hewson, additions 1922, 1969, 1995; sewerage 1987; storm 1889; TC (Hunter Institute of Technology, Central Coast Campus) 1995; telegraph 1888; TX 1910, automatic 1970; Unit. C. (orig. Meth.) b. 1927 by Walter A. Buscombe, d. by A.W. Anderson; univ. (Newcastle, Central Coast Campus) 1995, new building 2010; water reticulation 1966, augmentation 1974; Wes. Meth. C. (orig. Free Meth.) 1894, new premises bought 1897, extended 1898; pop. 354 (1901), 964 (1911), 604 (1933), 716 (1947), 962 (1954), 792 (1961), 540 (1966), 522 (1971), 692 (1976), 711 (1981), 675 (1986), 3,076 (2006), 4,162 (2011).

Ourimbah Creek (*Co. Northumberland*) 33°21'S. 151°20'E., 3 km W. of Ourimbah, on Ourimbah Ck; timber, dairying, citrus; flood 1927; sawmills: Beckford, Keft's, A.S. Jaques, William Jolly, Scott's, T.C. White; pop. 239 (1933), 51 (1947).

Ournie (*Co. Selwyn*) 35°55'S. 147°51'E., 22 km SW of Tumbarumba; goldmining (reef) and grazing; bushfire 2009; mines: Isabella (ceased 1901) and Peep-O-Day (ceased 1881); PO 1872; PS 1883; school 1880–91, 1897–1927, 1958–69; telephone 1915; TX 1916, automatic 1969; pop. *c.*80 (1903), 95 (1911), 60 (1933), 85 (1947), 89 (1954), 75 (1961).

Overton (*Co. Brisbane*) 32°17'S. 150°51'E., 4 km W. of Muswellbrook, on Hunter R.; subdivided 1912; sheep, dairying, coal; butter factory (Thomas Blunt) b. 1904 by Walter Barrett, sold 1918; cemetery (Bengalla, 18 graves); colliery 1922.

Overton (*Co. Urana*) 35°30'S. 146°16'E., 45 km E. of Berrigan, on Billabong Ck; surveyed and village gaz. 1889, soldiers' settlement 1920; agric.; cemetery (2 graves) 1890; mine (kaolin); PO, closed 1910; pop. 70 (1901).

Owendale (*Co. Northumberland*) 32°48'S. 151°04'E., 23 km NW of Paxton, on Wollombi Brook; grazing, farming, dairying; school 1896–99; telephone 1916.

Owens Gap (*Co. Brisbane*) 32°02'S. 150°43'E., 15 km W. of Scone, on Sophia Ck; farming and grazing; PO 1900–71; Rom. Cath. C. (Most Precious Blood) 1898, new one 1918, closed, defunct, and graveyard (11 graves); school 1886–1928; telephone 1900; TX 1921, automatic 1977; pop. 86 (1911), 88 (1933), 55 (1947), 85 (1954), 79 (1961).

Oxley (*Co. Gregory*) 31°01'S. 147°41'E., 67 km W. of Coonamble.

Oxley (*Co. Inglis*) see Tamworth.

Oxley (*Co. Waljeers*) 34°12'S. 144°06'E., 71 km NE of Balranald, on Lachlan R.; surveyed 1850 by F.P. McCabe, town gaz. 1880; grazing; Angl. C. (St Barnabas's) b. 1900 by C. Southion & Son, d. by Laver, and graveyard; bridge b. 1881 by G.H. Royce & Co., over Lachlan R.; fire 1888; PO 1884, burnt down 1920; PS b. 1886 by H.B. Broughton, closed 1933; school 1887–1919 and 1963–68; telegraph 1891; telephone 1905; TX 1913; pop. 190 (1891), 138 (1901), 105 (1911), 25 (1933), 128 (1947), 158 (1961), 159 (2006).

Oxley Hill (*Co. Camden*) 34°29'S. 150°24'E., 2 km W. of Bowral.

Oxley Island (*Co. Macquarie*) 31°55'S. 152°34'E., 6 km N. of Old Bar, on Manning R.; settled 1852 by Robert, Hector and Archibald MacLean, first land sale 1852, village estab. *c.*1870; former river port, shipbuilding, maize, millet, farming, dairying, oysters; Angl. C., demolished 1908, new one (St Barnabas's)

b. 1923 by F.C. Sweeney, d. by H. Wilfred Webster, renovated 1953 by A.J. Hayter, closed 1983, sold and reused, and graveyard; brick-kiln (W. Sharp); bridges: Neville Weiley Bridge 1958, to Bohnock, over South Passage of Manning R. and bridge to Mitchells Island over Scotts Ck; butter factory 1893; caterpillar infestation 1947; cemetery (296 graves 1884+) 1879; floods 1918 and 1929; hailstorm 1877; oar factory (Howard Croker) 1977; PO 1878, defunct; punts: one to Cundletown (4 car capacity) across Manning R. and one to Mitchells Island (2 car capacity) across Scotts Ck; quarry; Rom. Cath. C. 1892, burnt down, replaced (St Brigid's) 1952, closed, sold and moved 1978 to Tinonee, reused; school 1862 b. by John Levick, new one 1878, repairs 1884 by H. Moscatt, additions 1886, additions 1889 by Frederick Rye, repairs 1902 by Silas Brewer, additions 1928 and 1961; slipway (W. Ryan & Sons); sugar mills: William Allan 1867 and Baird's 1869; telephone 1914; TX 1918, automatic 1967; Union C. b. 1878 by Neil McKinnon, new one b. 1903 by E. Greenaway, dismantled 1926 by Greenaway, replaced 1927, closed; water supply 1943; wharf b. 1883 by H. Moscatt, on Manning R.; wineries: Schmitzer's and Wolf's; pop. 307 (1891), 399 (1901), 380 (1933), 312 (1947), 308 (1954), 277 (1961), 284 (2006), 301 (2011).

Oxley Vale (*Co. Inglis*) see Tamworth.

Oxton (*Co. Goulburn*) 35°46'S. 147°10'E., 15 km W. of Holbrook.

Oyster Cove (*Co. Gloucester*) 32°44'S. 151°57'E., 5 km W. of Lemon Tree Passage, on Big Swan Bay; pop. 80 (1961).

P

Pabbinbarra (*Co. Macquarie*) see Brombin.

Pacific City (*Co. St Vincent*) 35°05'S. 150°40'E., 2 km NE of Erowal Bay; subdivided by Henry F. Halloran & Co., but never developed.

Pacific Palms (*Co. Gloucester*) 32°21'S. 152°31'E., 18 km S. of Forster, on Wallis Lake; Charlotte Bay till 1962; timber then fishing; FB; PO 1945; school (Charlotte Bay till 1966) 1957, additions 1993 and 2010; sewerage 1996, augmentation 1999; telephone 1928; TX 1928, automatic 1972; water supply augmentation 1991; pop. 141 (1947), 53 (1954), 72 (1961), 444 (1986), 436 (1991, incl. Blueys Beach), 542 (1996, incl. Blueys Beach), 655 (2001, incl. Blueys Beach), 673 (2006, incl. Blueys Beach).

Pacific Palms (*Co. Gloucester*) see also Boomerang Beach.

Pack Saddle (*Co. Clarke*) 30°06'S. 152°04'E., 41 km E. of Guyra.

Packsaddle (*Co. Mootwingee*) 30°37'S. 141°58'E., 159 km N. of Broken Hill; telephone 1965; TX 1965; pop. *c*.5 (1999).

Paddys Flat (*Co. Buller*) 28°43'S. 152°25'E., 48 km NE of Tenterfield, on Clarence R.; goldmining (alluvial) and grazing; cemetery; PO 1927; tank traps (World War II); telephone 1924; TX 1939–54.

Paddys Flat (*Co. Wellesley*) 37°01'S. 149°20'E., 15 km SE of Bombala.

Paddys Gully (*Co. Clarke*) 30°05'S. 151°55'E., 29 km NE of Guyra; cemetery 1904; PO 1872–76.

Paddys Plain (*Co. Fitzroy*) 30°15'S. 152°41'E., 13 km N. of Dorrigo; school 1957–59; pop. 68 (1933), 77 (1961).

Paddys River (*Co. Camden*) 34°38'S. 150°08'E., 15 km W. of Bundanoon, on Paddys R.; estab. 1833, village gaz. 1835 as Murrimba, defunct; bridge b. 1833 by James Murray, destroyed, 2 new bridges 1974, over Paddys R.

Paddys River (*Co. Selwyn*) 35°47'S. 148°11'E., 14 km E. of Tumbarumba; snowstorm 1907.

Paff Hill (*Co. Gloucester*) 32°04'S. 152°17'E., 24 km SW of Taree, on Kings Flat Ck; Fairview till 1909, Avalon till 1950; estab. *c*.1898 as private village by John Wright; dairying and grazing; flour mill b. 1898 by John Wright, demolished and rebuilt at Tuncurry; PO 1907; sawmill (John Wright, taken over by S.G. Wright), closed 1918; telephone 1907; TX 1925; pop. 110 (1911).

Pages Creek (*Co. Brisbane*) 31°44'S. 151°14'E., 39 km E. of Murrurundi, on Pages Ck; grazing; pop. 61 (1911).

Pages River (*Co. Brisbane*) see Murrurundi.

Pageville (*Co. Richmond*) 29°18'S. 152°42'E., 49 km NW of Grafton, on Dome Mountain Ck; telephone 1925; TX 1966–69.

Paika (*Co. Caira*) 34°29'S. 143°35'E., 17 km N. of Balranald; school 1882–91; pop. 59 (1901), 81 (1911).

Painters Bore Camp (*Co. Burnett*) 29°12'S. 150°14'E., 48 km NE of Moree.

Paisley Park (*Co. Flinders*) see Peisley Park.

Palamba (*Co. Camden*) see Bellambi.

Paleroo (*Co. Murchison*) 30°07'S. 150°09'E., 43 km NE of Narrabri, on Rocky Ck; school 1910–27 and 1957–68; telephone 1925; TX 1926; pop. 38 (1933), 63 (1947).

Palestine Creek (*Co. Auckland*) 37°02'S. 149°53'E., 3 km N. of Eden; flood 1956; school 1956–68; telephone 1914; pop. 80 (1954), 135 (1961).

Paling Yards (*Co. Georgiana*) see Wallangrive.

Paling Yards (*Co. Roxburgh*) 33°11'S. 149°45'E., 30 km NE of Bathurst; goldmining; mine (Bullock Flat); pop. 20 (1933).

Palinyewah (*Co. Wentworth*) 33°50'S. 142°01'E., 32 km N. of Wentworth; PO 1957; school 1957; telephone 1953; TX 1957–73.

Palisthan (*Co. Cunningham*) 32°47'S. 146°43'E., 50 km NW of Condobolin; pop. 22 (1933).

Pallamallawa (*Co. Courallie*) 29°28'S. 150°08'E., 28 km E. of Moree, on Gwydir R.; village gaz. 1867 as Paramellowa; grazing and wheat; Angl. C. b. 1893–95, new one (St Mark's) b. 1925 by R. Wilson & Son, d. by Robert Newburgh Hickson; bridge (Allan timber truss) 1908, 305 ft (93 m), new one (Agnes Hutton Bridge), over Gwydir R.; cemetery (224 graves 1870+) 1884; diphtheria 1914; flood 1946; gale 1932; PO 1875, burnt down 1925; pound (stock) 1869; PS 1890, new one b. 1908 by A.J. Hulbert, closed during World War II, reopened 1946, new one 1984; Rom. Cath. C. (St Peter Julian Eymard) 1915; sawmills: James Matthews, James Ambrose Taylor (fires 1925 and 1932), Tomkins's; school 1884 b. by William Lee, d. by William Edmund Kemp, new building b. 1910 by A.J. Hulbert, new one b. 1928, old one removed 1956, additions 1972; telephone 1898; TX 1912, automatic 1940; Union C. 1923, later became Meth. C.; Unit. C., closed, sold and reused; pop. 88 (1901), 320 (1911), 308 (1933), 289 (1947), 348 (1954), 309 (1961), 268 (1971), 280 (1976), 340 (1981), 325 (1986), 336 (1991), 309 (1996), 307 (2001), 286 (2006), 253 (2011).

Pallamallawa (*Co. Courallie*) see also Wubbera.

Palmdale (*Co. Northumberland*) 33°20'S. 151°22'E., 4 km N. of Ourimbah, on Canada Drop Down Ck; orchards; bridge over Canada Drop Down Ck; cemetery (lawn), incl. columbaria and crematorium, additions and alterations 2009; electricity 1938; quarry; pop. 51 (1933).

Palmer (*Co. Murray*) 35°23'S. 149°12'E., 4 km SW of Queanbeyan.

Palmers Channel (*Co. Clarence*) 29°28'S. 153°16'E., 7 km E. of Maclean, on Palmers Channel; sugar-cane; electricity 1935; flood 1954; PO 1914; school (Taloumbi till 1907) 1872–1975; sugar mills: Atkins's, Cameron's, Elder's, Marsh's; telephone 1914; TX 1925, automatic 1953; Union C. 1885, destroyed 1907; pop. 300 (1911), 180 (1933), 174 (1947), 138 (1954), 136 (1961).

Palmers Island (*Co. Clarence*) 29°25'S. 153°17'E., 6 km W. of Iluka, on Clarence R.; settled 1864; cedar 1861–67, maize till 1874, sugar-cane, dairying, fishing, oysters, poultry, ducks, fruit; airfield; Angl. C. (All Saints') 1903, damaged 1904; butter and cheese factory (Palmers Island Dairy Co. Ltd) 1903, damaged 1916; cyclones 1904 and 1916; erosion 1950; floods 1890, 1928 (man died), 1945, 1948, 1950; gale 1948; landslip 1894, additions 1899; Meth. C. b. 1908 by Smith and Payne; PO 1864, new one b. 1939; Presb. C.; PS 1878–1918; Rom. Cath. C. (St Francis's) 1880, dismantled 1931; schools: Lower Palmers Island 1888–94 and Palmers Island 1866, new one b. 1873, relocated 1951; sugar mills: Abraham Carr 1879, Edmondson's, Lowe's, Alexander Ross (orig. a sawmill); telegraph 1874, office inundated 1890; telephone 1904; TX (automatic) 1966; Union C., damaged 1904; water reticulation 1966; wharves: one b. 1884 by Joseph Walsh and one (for butter factory) 1908; pop. 445 (1881), 460 (1891), 452 (1901), 403 (1911), 359 (1933), 284 (1947), 318 (1954), 296 (1961).

Palmers Oaky (*Co. Roxburgh*) 33°12'S. 149°52'E., 21 km NW of Portland, on Palmers Oaky Ck; mining (gold disc. 1853), farming, agric., apiculture; cemetery (67 graves) 1869; diphtheria 1891; FB 1940; lock-up; mines: British Lion, Golden Lion, Lucky Hit, Queen of the Ranges; PO 1868–1925; PS; pop. 94 (1901), 80 (1911), 60 (1921), 63 (1933).

Palmers Oaky Junction (*Co. Roxburgh*) see Upper Turon.

Palm Grove (*Co. Northumberland*) 33°20'S. 151°19'E., 6 km NW of Ourimbah, on Bangalow Ck; dairying and orchards; PO 1927; sawmills: John Bradley & Co., Kennedy Bros, J. Preston; telephone 1923; TX 1923.

Palmvale (*Co. Rous*) 28°22'S. 153°29'E., 6 km W. of Pottsville, on Christies Ck; farming; PO 1912; telephone 1922; TX 1928–68; pop. 62 (1933), 59 (1947), 54 (1954), 50 (1961).

Palm Valley (*Co. Rous*) see Byron Bay.

Palmwood (*Co. Rous*) see Palmwoods.

Palmwoods (*Co. Rous*) 28°31'S. 153°24'E., 9 km NW of Mullumbimby, on Wilsons R.; formerly Palmwood; bushfire 1946; pop. 156 (1947), 75 (1954).

Paloma Siding (*Co. Bathurst*) 33°30'S. 149°12'E., 6 km S. of Millthorpe.

Pamandi (*Co. Bourke*) 34°45'S. 146°52'E., 18 km W. of Ganmain; RS 1912–59.

Pambula (*Co. Auckland*) 36°56'S. 149°52'E., 6 km SW of Merimbula, on Pambula R.; laid out 1843 by Thomas Scott Townsend but relocated due to flooding, village gaz. 1847 as Panbula, land sales 1851 and 1853, subdivision 1883; wattle-bark, mining (gold disc. 1888) 1889, oysters 1891+, maize, potatoes, butter, cheese, ham, bacon, dairying, cattle, forestry, fishing; Angl. C. 1856–1865, new one b. 1864–66, d. by Lieut. Woore, strengthened 1912, renovated 1916, replacement (Christ) d. and b. 1953–56 by David Larcombe; bacon factory 1922; Bapt. C. 1988; boiling-down works; brewery (Long Stocking) estab. 2016 by Rob Barber; bridge b. 1896 by McHugh, 105 ft (32 m), demolished, replaced 2008, over Pambula R.; bushfires 1862 (houses destroyed), 1869, 1929; cemetery 1863, incl. lawn cemetery and columbarium; CH b. 1861 by Lloyd & Co., additions and alterations 1898 by Underhill and Thatcher, repairs 1910 by Olaf Rye Lassen, enlarged 1934, closed 1984, reused 1992, transferred 1994 to local council; cordial factory (P.J. Robinson); diphtheria 1895; dust storm 1898; earth tremor 1912; fires 1862 and 1924; floods 1851, 1860, 1870, 1893; gale 1895; hospital 1899, additions 1907 by Job Koerber, closed 1916, new one b. 1917 also by Koerber, demolished, replaced 1980 by K.B. Hutchinson; meat works (West Pambula Meat Preserving Co.) 1868; Meth. C., closed, reopened 1922; PO 1853, new one b. 1905 by A.E. Beaumont, new one b. 1937; pound (stock) 1848; powerhouse (Murrell Bros); Presb. C.; PS, repairs 1910 by Olaf Rye Lassen, closed 1979; Rom. Cath. C. (St Mark's) 1855, burnt down 1862, replacement (St Peter's) d. and b. 1868 by Patrick O'Connor, rebuilt 1900 by Job Koerber; sawmills: Gordon Bros and Tableland Sawmills Pty Ltd; school (Panbula till *c.*1890) 1849, destroyed, replaced 1872, new one b. 1907 by Olaf Rye Lassen, additions 1978; sewerage 1971; streets electric lit 1927 by Godfrey Bros; tannery (Charles Henry Baddeley) 1866, closed; telegraph 1880, new office b. 1905 by A.E. Beaumont; telephone 1893; TX 1910, automatic 1978; Unit. C. (St Columba's); watch-house b. 1861 by Lloyd & Co., new one 1893, closed; Wes. Meth. C. 1893; pop. 24 (1848), 203 (1856), 186 (1861), 293 (1871), 128 (1881), 422 (1891), 543 (1901), 532 (1911), 313 (1933), 349 (1947), 294 (1954), 319 (1961), 293 (1971), 416 (1976), 604 (1981), 731 (1986), 790 (1991), 765 (1996), 1,109 (2001), 1,146 (2006), 867 (2011).

Pambula Beach (*Co. Auckland*) 36°57'S. 149°55'E., 4 km SE of Pambula, on Tasman Sea; (incl. Jiguma Beach); PO 1958–84; 2 reservoirs; telephone 1958; pop. 49 (1961), 690 (1986), 726 (1991), 701 (1996), 728 (2001), 655 (2006), 665 (2011).

Pambula South (*Co. Auckland*) 36°57'S. 149°52'E., 2 km SW of Pambula; fire 1900; PO 1914–68; 2 quarries; sawmill; telephone 1906; pop. 89 (1933), 69 (1947), 70 (1954), 53 (1961), 198 (1991), 280 (1996), 333 (2001), 382 (2006), 418 (2011).

Pampoolah (*Co. Gloucester*) 31°56'S. 152°32'E., 7 km E. of Taree, on Manning R. (South Passage); Redbank till 1890; maize, farming, dairying; bridge (Ella Simon Bridge) to Dumaresq Island, over South Passage of Manning R.; cemeteries: Manning Great Lakes Memorial Gardens (2,828 graves and plots) 1999 and Redbank (805 graves 1864+); creamery (George Murray), closed 1899 and moved to Mitchells Island; floods 1866 and 1929; Free Presb. C. 1859; PO 1859; punt to Cundletown (4 car capacity), across South Passage of Manning R.; sawmills: John Allan, William Owen McMahon, John M'Cleer (man killed 1886), Street Bros; school (Redbank till 1890) 1852 b. by John Levick, repairs 1895 by W.C. Wilson, additions 1899 by Rudolph George Ochs, closed 1973, reused; sugar mill; telephone 1914; TX 1917–55; Union C. (McCartney Memorial) b. 1937–40 by Sam Bird; wharf; pop. 86 (1901), 118 (1911), 122 (1933), 96 (1947), 98 (1954), 84 (1961), 365 (2011).

Panbula (*Co. Auckland*) see Pambula.

Pandora (*Co. Pottinger*) 31°41'S. 149°55'E., 24 km NE of Coolah; grazing.

Pangee (*Co. Flinders*) 32°00'S. 146°46'E., 63 km SW of Nyngan, on Grahway Ck.

Pangee (*Co. Flinders*) see also Miandetta.

Pangela (*Co. Brisbane*) 31°46'S. 150°48'E., 4 km W. of Murrurundi; landslip 1926.

Panorama Point (*Co. Cook*) see Kurrajong Heights.

Panpong (*Co. Wallace*) see Paupong.

Panuara (*Co. Bathurst*) 33°30'S. 148°57'E., 29 km E. of Canowindra, on Swallow Ck; soldiers' settlement 1953; earth tremor 2017; school 1957–70; winery (Angullong) estab. 1998, wine produced 2003; pop. 90 (1961).

Paper Forest (*Co. Mitchell*) 35°27'S. 147°16'E., 23 km E. of Henty, on Paper Forest Ck.

Pappinbarra (*Co. Macquarie*) 31°22'S. 152°30'E., 24 km W. of Wauchope, on Pappinbarra R.; farming; Angl. C. (All Saints') 1931, restored 1988; bushfire 2017; FB 2014; PO 1914; sawmill (Charles Everett); telephone 1914; TX 1928, automatic 1980; pop. 118 (1933), 207 (1947), 83 (1954), 98 (1961).

Pappinbarra Junction (*Co. Macquarie*) 31°19'S. 152°27'E., 31 km NW of Wauchope, on Pappinbarra Ck; school 1957–67; telephone 1933; TX 1944–65.

Parading Ground (*Co. Gloucester*) see The Parading Ground.

Paradise (*Co. Gough*) 29°53'S. 151°26'E., 31 km SW of Glen Innes, on Paradise Ck; quarry (abandoned); school (Paradise Creek till 1889) 1888–94; pop. 26 (1933).

Paradise Creek (*Co. Gough*) see Paradise.

Paradise Rocks (*Co. Brisbane*) see Murrurundi.

Paragon (*Co. Hume*) 35°45'S. 146°30'E., 39 km N. of Corowa; telephone 1926; TX 1927, automatic 1969.

Para Meadow (*Co. Camden*) see Balgownie and Fairy Meadow.

Paramellowa (*Co. Courallie*) see Pallamallawa.

Paringi (*Co. Wentworth*) 34°20'S. 142°21'E., 20 km SE of Gol Gol.

Park (*Co. Brisbane*) see Parkville.

Park Beach (*Co. Fitzroy*) see Coffs Harbour.

Parkers Gap (*Co. Murray*) 35°38'S. 149°31'E., 33 km SW of Braidwood, on Witts Ck; cemetery; sawmill (Thompson's).

Parkes (*Co. Ashburnham*) 33°08'S. 148°10'E., 87 km W. of Orange, on Goobang Ck; (incl. East Parkes, Lower Parkes, Middleton, North Parkes, South Parkes); estab. 1862 as Currajong (nearby), moved 1871 and became Bushmans Lead till 1873, town gaz. 1874 as Parkes, munic. proc. 1883, subdivided 1912, thrived 1923; mining (gold disc. 1862 by James Pugh at Currajong, gold rush 1862 at Currajong, declined 1867+, more gold disc. 1871 by Thomas Hall Brogden and George Bush nearby at Bushman's Hill) 1862–67 and 1871–73, wheat 1865+, flour milling 1870s+, orchards, vineyards, maize, barley, wool, lucerne 1926+, dairying 1930+, linseed, oats, potatoes, butter, pigs, turkeys; agric. implement works: Mitchell & Co. Pty Ltd 1925 and Parkes Steel Products 1978; air force training school (World War II) 1940, reused 1950; airport (6 km E.), upgaded 2016; ambulance station b. 1938 by A. Davis, d. by Harry Helman; Angl. C. b. 1889–95 by Bligh and M'Glynn, d. by William Lamrock, jun., reused, new one (St George's) b. 1927 by Lawrence Pither, d. by Louis Reginald Williams; apple and tomato pulping plant

(Cerebos Aust. Ltd); Assemblies of God C. (Generocity); Bapt. C. 1950, rebuilt 1964 by Garry Hayes; breweries: Bothwell and Crawford 1874, and Norfolk (Rippendale's) 1874–79; brickworks: F. Baker & Sons (b. 1925 by S.G. Lipscombe, with 6 kilns, later taken over by Balwin Investments, closed 1980), Ed Lewis, C.W. Morgan, Parkes Steam Brickworks; bushfires 1926, 1994, 1998, 2004; butter factory (Parkes Dairy Co. Ltd, leased 1916 to Country Freezing Co. Ltd, then sold to it in 1924) 1901, extensive additions 1915 to accommodate ice-making and rabbit chilling; carriage-works: C. Jarrett (bought 1893 by John Westcott), Miller and Cheney, Charles Smart 1884; causeway across Goobang Ck; cemetery (9,017 graves) 1875; CH b. 1875 by Pickering and Hilton, additions 1875 also by Pickering and Hilton, replacement b. 1895–98 by F.G. Goodwin and W. Mitchell, d. by Walter Liberty Vernon, additions 1899 also d. by Vernon; Community Bapt. C. (Middleton); cordial factories: Alliance (Surrey and Myers), S. Alsop, A.T. Cartwright (acquired 1910 by J.G. Derwin), W.H. Coleman, C.M. Cordaiy and R.M. Ashcroft 1929 (acquired by Orbells), Mealing, Mullins & Sons, George Pear; 5 cyanide plants (incl. C.T. Woodward); dam (Bushman's) b. 1876 by Heraghty; diphtheria 1891 and 1894; droughts 1944, 1965, 1980, 1982, 1986, 1994–95; dust storms 1924 and 2020; engineering works: Bosmac Pty Ltd 1981, W.J. Leaney 1906, E. McPherson; FB 1892 (station b. 1909 by W. Bligh, new one b. 1924 by Lowther and Horrocks, d. by William Hull McNiven, new one 1994); fibrous plaster works (Veness and Cowle) 1925; fires 1896, 1900, 1903, 1915, 1917, 1932, 1973, 1983; flood 1878; flour mills: Buckwheat Enterprises Pty Ltd 1992 and Guigni and Mulholland (b. 1877 by Iram Nash, sold 1878 to Edward McGee and Charles Quinn, Quinn replaced 1895 in partnership by Jerry Perry, sold 1905 to Frank McGee & Co., closed, dismantled 1909, new one b. 1910 on new site, silo added 1925, closed and demolished 1963); foundries: R.H. Kenyon 1945 (taken over 1974 by E.G. Bishop Pty Ltd, closed 1976) and Richard Venables 1895 (fire 1916); freight interchange 1989; gale 1913; gasworks b. 1911 by William Terry, new gasholder b. 1931 by James Hurll & Co. Ltd, new retorts 1923, 1932, 1936, 1958, closed and replaced 1963, coal gas production ceased 1970; glove factory o. 1946 by A.S. Horne Ltd, in former small arms factory; glue and sealant factory (G.H. Matthews); Gospel C. (Middleton); gunnery range (World War II); hailstorm 2016; heatwaves 1929 and 1982; hospital b. 1876 by Pepper and Elliott, additions 1887, additions and alterations 1905 by W.A. M'Lean, additions 1947, 1956, 1970, 1973, 1979, 1982, 1985, 1990, closed 2015, demolished 2016, replaced 2016 on new site by Richard Crookes Constructions, d. by H.D.R. Rice Daubney; Jehovah's Witnesses C.; joineries: Les Carrett, F. Dodd & Co., burnt down 1915, R. Shaw, Vanderfield and Reid; Lutheran C. (St Paul's) 1953, vestry added 1986, church extended 1992–97; migrant hostel 1950–52; mines: Band of Hope *c.*1890, Bonnie Dundee (T. Mitchell 1870, Ehlers 1876, Bonnie Dundee Gold Mining Co. 1879–85), Bread and Dripping, Buchanan and Phoenix (Phoenix Reform Gold Mining Co. NL) 1867–1910, Bushmans Hill (Bushmans Hill Gold Mining Syndicate 1877–*c.*1902 and Vickery 1936), Bushman's Lead (incl. 30 head stamper battery) 1871–1914 (reopening attempted 1934 by John Warne), Dayspring 1862–66, 1872–73, 1885–1908, Federal 1901–9, Gladstone, Kable's 1931–33, London Victoria 1874–1996 (incl. tailings dam b. 1988 by BHP), Mount Morgan 1905 and 1930, New Haven, Pioneer (disc. by James Pugh et al.) 1862–1908, Quayle & Co.; monumental stone works: J.T. Cocks and Christopher J. Shakespeare & Sons 1923; Pentecostal C. b. 1926 by A.G. Souter, d. by William George Dodd; PO: East Parkes 1965, Lower Parkes 1948, North Parkes 1948, Parkes 1872 (new one b. 1878–80 by H. Sutherland, d. by James Johnstone Barnet, additions 1895 by Gardiner and Whitehurst, d. by Walter Liberty Vernon, alterations 1901–3 also d. by Vernon, alterations 1914 by James Frizelle, closed 1990, bought 1990 by Peter and Maddalena Sgarlata, restored and reused, new one 1990 on new site), South Parkes 1954; pound (stock); POW control centre 1943; powerhouse b. 1924 by Arthur Davis, replaced 1953; Presb. C. (Scots) 1890, reused; PS: Currajong 1872 and Parkes 1875 d. by James Johnstone Barnet, new one b. 2014 by Richard Crookes Constructions; puddling machines: George Draper, Robert Lowe, James McIntyre, Jerry Perry; railway barracks 1912, new barracks 1987; railway coal stage, 80 ft (24.4 m) long, 1893, extended 1903; railway locomotive depot 1896, second one 1927, third one 1942; railway parts factory (Fessl Pty Ltd); railway round-house 1928, enlarged 1944; railway turntable, 50 ft (15.2 m), replaced 1902, 60 ft (18.3 m), new one 1944, 75 ft (22.9 m); 7 reservoirs (incl. ones b. 1894, 1930, 1945, 1968); rifle range (2 km N.) 1905–87; Rom. Cath. C. (St Jarlath's) 1890, demolished 1941, replacement (Holy Family) b. 1942 by Gaskin Bros, d. by Fowell, McConnel and Mansfield; RS 1893, station b. by Frederick Lemm, jun. and Thomas Edward Spencer, alterations 1926, refreshment rooms 1928, station alterations 1947; sale-yards b. 1911 by William Catling, new yards (munic.) 1930; Salv. Army C. 1896, alterations 1928, new one 1992; sawmills: A.C. Hood, Slater and Hughes, Vanderfield and Reid 1923; schools: East Parkes 1962, Middleton 1957 b. by Tom Cole, fire 1977, rebuilt 1985, additions 1995, Parkes primary (Currajong till 1874) 1868, new building b. 1876 by Pepper and Elliott, new building b. 1908 by Peter Beddie, additions 1909 also by Beddie, alterations and repairs 1909 by Lewis Myers, additions 1918, new building 1931, new building b. 1935 by Kent and Kent, additions 1969 and 1995, Parkes HS 1941 b. by A. Davis, additions 1964, 1968, 1973, Trelowarren 1881–1916; SD Adventist C., enlarged 1961, reused 1967, new one 1992; sewage works 1933, augmentation 1969 and 1996; silo 1921; small arms factory (World War II), reused; soap-works: John Mulholland and H. Unger; 5 stamper batteries; steel fabrication works (Parkes Industries) estab. by Rex Ruwoldt, Alf Knowles and Tom Shearwood; storage tank works (Transtank Pty Ltd, became Western Global) 2004; storms 1923, 1928, 1990, 2019; streets oil lit 1892, vapour lit 1902, electric lit 1924; tanneries: Herbert Barnes (leased from Thomas Denning), burnt down 1924, and J. and O. Wooden; TC, additions 1960, 1965, 1975, 1977, 1983, became a campus of Western Institute in 1992; telegraph 1875; telephone: East Parkes 1965, Lower Parkes 1948, North Parkes 1948, South Parkes 1954; trees (ornamental) planted in streets 1920; TX 1906, automated and relocated 1965; typhoid 1895–96 and 1901; Union C. 1873; Unit. C.: St Andrew's (orig. Presb.) b. 1919 by Arthur Davis, d. by William George Dodd and Wesley (orig. Wes. Meth.) b. 1897 by R.B. Keast, d. by J. Rigelsford; watch-house b. 1883 by William H. Bligh and Matthew McGlynn, additions and repairs 1910 by Charles Burns; water supply 1897, new waterworks b. 1958 by Filtration & Water Softening Pty Ltd, augmentation 1968, 1988, 1995; Wes. Meth. C. 1863 (Currajong), demolished; wool processing plant (Aus Top); pop. *c.*1,500 (1872), 1,961 (1881), *c.*1,900 (1887), 2,449 (1891), *c.*3,500 (1895), 3,181 (1901), 3,411 (1911), 3,941 (1921), 4,813 (1925), 5,846 (1933), 6,897 (1947), 7,973 (1954), 8,223 (1961), 8,442 (1966), 8,849 (1971), 8,905 (1976), 9,047 (1981), 8,739 (1986), 8,784 (1991), 10,094 (1996), 9,805 (2001), 9,826 (2006), 10,026 (2011).

Parkesborough (*Co. Ashburnham*) 33°11'S. 148°10'E., 5 km S. of Parkes, on Goobang Ck; goldmining and farming; cyanide plant (Avoca Reefs Gold Mining Co.) 1898; flour mill (Welcome), transferred by Simms to Guigni and Mulholland who moved it to Parkes in 1877; mines: Baden-Powell 1901–2, 1904, 1932–35, Ben Nevis 1894–1904, Birthday (Avoca Reefs Gold Mining Co.)

<1896–1900, Koh-i-noor 1879–1907, London 1870–1909, 1935–38, 1940–47, 1949–52, Mount Pleasant 1897, Nibblers 1874, Nibblers Hill (The Nibblers Hill Gold Mining Syndicate and Hocking) *c.*1880–1924, Ramsay's 1894+, Victoria (Wright) 1876, Welcome 1872–91, Welcome (Wild Cat lode) 1900–4 and 1928; PO 1910; school 1880–1964; telephone 1950; TX 1951–60; pop. 133 (1933), 76 (1947), 66 (1954), 60 (1961).

Parkesbourne (*Co. Argyle*) 34°46'S. 149°32'E., 18 km W. of Goulburn; sheep and orchards; bushfires 1905 and 1986; PO 1918; school 1872 b. by George Bool, re-roofed 1901, closed 1969, sold and reused; telephone 1915; TX 1922–49; Unit. C. (orig. Prim. Meth.) b. 1866 by George Bool, porch added 1921, church re-roofed 1922, alterations 1966, and graveyard; pop. 139 (1901), 106 (1911), 94 (1933), 85 (1947), 73 (1954), 74 (1961), 350 (2011).

Park Valley (*Co. Rous*) 28°44'S. 153°10'E., 14 km NW of Lismore, on Leycester Ck.

Parkview (*Co. Cooper*) see Leeton.

Park Village (*Co. Brisbane*) see Parkville.

Parkville (*Co. Brisbane*) 31°59'S. 150°52'E., 7 km N. of Scone, on Kingdon Ponds; Park Village till May 1888, then St Aubyn's till June 1888; village gaz. 1881; farming; Angl. C. 1874, new one (St John's) 1927 d. by Louis Reginald Williams, renamed St Christian's in 2001, closed, sold and reused; cemetery 1886; FB 1944; gale 1892; PO 1879; RS (Park till 1899) 1877, station closed and demolished 1987; school (Park till 1888) 1880, new building b. 1917 by G.H. Cavanagh, closed 1944; telephone 1914; TX 1916, automatic 1974; pop. 103 (1846), 90 (1851), 118 (1871), 160 (1901), 241 (1911), 247 (1933), 200 (1947), 221 (1954), 249 (1961), 323 (2011).

Parkwood Village (*Co. Northumberland*) see Thornton.

Parma (*Co. St Vincent*) 34°58'S. 150°32'E., 12 km SW of Nowra, on Yerriyong Gully; bushfires 1919 and 1939 (3 houses destroyed); FB.

Parragundy Gate (*Co. Irrara*) 29°00'S. 144°44'E., 167 km NW of Bourke; grazing; PO 1904; telephone 1896; TX 1914–46.

Parrots Nest (*Co. Rous*) 28°51'S. 153°14'E., 7 km SW of Lismore.

Parrs Brush (*Co. Hunter*) 33°22'S. 150°44'E., 20 km NE of Kurrajong Heights; quarry.

Parsons Forest (*Co. Hunter*) 33°22'S. 150°43'E., 20 km NE of Kurrajong Heights.

Paterson (*Co. Durham*) 32°36'S. 151°37'E., 16 km N. of Maitland, on Paterson R.; surveyed 1832 by George Boyle White, laid out 1833 by Henry Dangar, first lots sold 1833, town gaz. 1880, designated as chief town of the county, declined 1911+; orig. timber, former river port, shipbuilding, then maize, millet, root crops, oranges, grapes, tobacco, oaten hay, lucerne hay, poultry, eggs, dairying, butter, cheese, bacon; abattoir (1 km W.); Angl. C. (St Paul's) b. 1837–45, renovated 1911 by Taylor Bros, restored 1974, and graveyard (734 graves); brickworks; bridge (metal lattice truss) fabricated by D. and W. Robertson, erected 1886–88 by M'Kenzie and Burley, d. by John Alexander McDonald, 301 ft (91.7 m), over Paterson R.; cemetery (978 graves) 1882, incl. columbarium; CH (incl. lock-up) 1835, lock-up demolished 1876, new court-house b. 1858 by Stephen Stanbridge, d. by Alexander Dawson, additions and alterations 1863 by Charles Mack, d. by Mortimer William Lewis, jun., closed 1967, reused 1974; drought 1843; earth tremor 1868; electricity 1930; FB 1974; fires 1868 and 1931; floods 1851, 1875, 1946, 1962, 2001, 2015; flour mills: A. Hough 1875, James Keppie, Menzies', damaged 1857, James Sewell (sold 1846 to John Richard Houlding); fruit packing house (oranges) 1917; gale 1884; hailstorm 1867; milk factory (Hunter Valley Co-op. Dairy & Produce Co. Ltd) 1962–75; PO 1832, new one b. 1885 by Alexander McLaren, sold 1976; pound (stock) 1865; Presb. C. (St Ann's) b. 1840–42, renovated and restored 1878 by Stanbridge, re-roofing and renovations 1906 by J. Thompson, d. by James Warren Scobie, closed, sold, and graveyard (defunct); PS 1834, new one b. 1883 by Dobbin & Co., new one 1983; punt, till

1887, across Paterson R.; 2 quarries; railway bridge (steel truss), 200 ft (61 m), fabricated by Clyde Engineering Co. Ltd, erected 1911 by Carson, Carey and Simpson, over Paterson R.; Rom. Cath. C. (St Columba's) b. 1884 by Edward Coleman and Isaac Morris, d. by John Wiltshire Pender, porch and sacristy added 1926, renovated 1984; RS 1911–90; sawmills: Andrew and John Keppie (burnt down 1908, rebuilt, burnt down 1911, rebuilt, closed 1914) and Maunder Bros 1892; school 1875, new one b. 1878 by Stephen and William Stanbridge, d. by George Allen Mansfield, additions 1909 by Richard Partridge-Wall, closed, sold and reused, new one 1970; storms 1873, 1878, 1899; tannery; telegraph 1874; tobacco factory (Long's), sold 1871 to James Arthur; TX 1911, automatic 1970; watch-house b. 1883 by Dobbin & Co.; water reticulation 1980; Wes. Meth. C. 1846, new one 1862, destroyed 1875; wharves (one b. 1877 and one b. 1920 by Peter Callen); pop. 90 (1841), 141 (1846), 86 (1851), 309 (1856), 241 (1861), 288 (1871), 293 (1881), 327 (1891), 506 (1901), 708 (1911), 416 (1933), 463 (1947), 384 (1954), 327 (1961), 272 (1971), 259 (1976), 268 (1981), 313 (1986), 312 (1991), 347 (1996), 344 (2001), 345 (2006), 372 (2011).

Patonga (*Co. Northumberland*) 33°33'S. 151°16'E., 8 km SW of Woy Woy, on Hawkesbury R.; (incl. Little Wobby); subdivision surveyed by R.F. Reid, further subdivion 1918, village gaz. 1929, road access 1937; fishing and oysters; Angl. C.; electricity 1929; FB; jetty (steel and concrete) 1990; PO 1926; Rom. Cath. C. (St Anthony's), closed 1994, dilapidated and disused, bought 2004 by Tony and Adrienne Ryan, renovated and reused; sewerage 1993; telephone 1923; TX 1928, automatic 1971; 3 wharves (incl. one b. 1930 by W. Woodward); pop. 123 (1933), 192 (1947), 201 (1954), 211 (1961), 232 (1971), 280 (1976), 256 (1981), 247 (1986), 257 (1991), 420 (2011).

Patons (*Co. Selwyn*) 35°54'S. 148°13'E., 23 km SE of Tumbarumba, on Reedy Ck.

Patrick's Plains (*Co. Northumberland*) see Singleton.

Paulsgrove (*Co. Camden*) see Mount Keira.

Paupong (*Co. Wallace*) 36°35'S. 148°41'E., 19 km S. of Jindabyne, on Beloka Ck; Panpong till 1899; grazing; PO 1926–43; school 1887–96; telephone 1913; TX 1915; pop. 51 (1901), 50 (1911), 40 (1933).

Paxton (*Co. Northumberland*) 32°54'S. 151°17'E., 7 km SW of Bellbird, on Congewai Ck; surveyed and subdivided 1922 by East Greta Coal Mining Co. and first lots sold 1922; Angl. C. (St Ambrose's) b. 1923 by Charles Waugh, reused; Bapt. C. 1928 (moved 1943 to Maitland); colliery estab. 1921–23 by East Greta Coal Mining Co. and o. 1923 as Stanford Merthyr No. 2, acquired 1931 by J. & A. Brown & Abermain Seaham Collieries Ltd and renamed Stanford Main No. 2, strikes 1932, 1933, 1936, 1938, 1939, man killed 1939, strikes 1940, 1941, 1942, 1943, 1944, 1948, 1949, 1950, taken over and closed 1961 by Coal & Allied Industries Ltd, later bought by Hardie Holdings Pty Ltd; Cong. C. 1925, moved to Cessnock and reused; electricity orig. supplied by J. & A. Brown & Abermain Seaham Collieries Ltd from Richmond Main Colliery; FB (station b. 1930, demolished 1988, new one 1990); Meth. C. 1924; PO 1923; PS 1925–35; railway (colliery); sawmills: Graham's (taken over by Hop James) and Joseph William Whiting; school 1923 b. by E.R. Potter, extended 1927; streets electric lit 1927; telephone 1923; TX 1926, automatic 1953; pop. 680 (1933), 590 (1947), 638 (1954), 584 (1961), 496 (1971), 496 (1976), 524 (1981), 561 (1986), 566 (1991), 580 (1996), 555 (2001), 667 (2006), 852 (2011).

Paynes Crossing (*Co. Northumberland*) 32°52'S. 151°05'E., 18 km W. of Paxton, on Wollombi Brook; settled *c.*1825; farming; Angl. C. (St Matthew's) 1888, new one 1935; bridge, damaged 1949, rebuilt, over Wollombi Brook; flood 1949; grasshopper infestation 1921; PO 1906; Rom. Cath. C. (Our Lady of Lourdes) 1901; school 1880–1932, sold 1955; telephone 1914; TX 1925–67; pop. 117 (1911), 70 (1933), 64 (1947).

Paynters Siding (*Co. Cooper*) 34°41'S.

146°31'E., 7 km N. of Narrandera; RS 1930–75.

Paytens Bridge (*Co. Forbes*) see Bandon.

Peachgrove (*Co. Macquarie*) see Laurieton.

Peach Tree Crossing (*Co. Vernon*) 30°49'S. 152°09'E., 55 km E. of Walcha, on Macleay R.

Peach Tree Cutting (*Co. Hawes*) 31°44'S. 151°51'E., 32 km N. of Gloucester, on Barnard R.

Peacock Creek (*Co. Buller*) 28°46'S. 152°36'E., 42 km W. of Kyogle, on Peacock Ck; droughts 1915 and 1986; flood 1954; sawmill (Sam Priest) 1919, sold 1921 to Bonalbo Sawmilling Co.; pop. 23 (1933), 61 (1947), 52 (1954).

Peak Hill (*Co. Narromine*) 32°43'S. 148°11'E., 45 km N. of Parkes; surveyed 1889 by Roderick Baylis Mackenzie, town laid out and gaz. 1889, munic. 1894–1971; mining (gold disc. 1889 by Dennis Madden, gold rushes 1889 and 1890) till 1917, agric. (wheat 1897+), lucerne, sheep, cattle; ambulance station, closed, new one at hospital; Angl. C. 1896, new one (St Stephen's) b. 1928–30, d. by Louis Reginald Williams, extended 1959; Assemblies of God C. b. 1952 by McIlvogue; boomerang factory (Harold Keed and Fred Powell) 1966; brickworks: Harry Bramley, W.G. Chandler, J. Waser; bushfires 1926 and 1951; cemetery (1,554 graves 1890+) 1891, incl. columbarium; CH (incl. lock-up) b. 1898 by C. Grant, d. by Walter Liberty Vernon; cordial factories: W. M'Casand and H.A. Wooden; FB (station b. 1942 by W. Fuller, d. by H. Kelly), reused, new one; fires 1891, 1897, 1900, 1904, 1905; freezing and ice works (A.J. Mackie); furnace (gold) 1900; gale 1902; gastroenteritis epidemic 1954; grasshopper infestations 1907 and 1921; hailstorm 1890; hospital 1891, sold 1905, burnt down 1926, new one b. 1905 by A.J. Litchfield, d. by John Holderness Bates, additions 1938, 1962, 2016; mines: Alkane Exploration NL 1996, Bobby Burns *c.*1894–1911, Cemetery Reef 1908–17, Crown of Peak Hill (or Golden Crown) 1891–1910, Garnsey *c.*1900 and 1935, Golden Hole (or Golden Hollow) 1890, Great Eastern 1891–98, Lambert's 1895–98, Paddy's Flat (alluvial) 1889–93 and 1939–41, Peak Hill Pty 1889–1917 and 1996–2002, Smith and Wooden 1915–18, Wythes and Mooney *c.*1893–1900; PO 1889, new one b. 1899 by John Dunkley; powerhouse b. 1928 by Wallace and McGee; Presb. C. (St Andrew's) 1957; PS 1889, additions 1961; railway engine shed 1910, moved 1915 to Tullamore; railway turntable, 60 ft (18.3 m); reservoir, 238,600 gal. (1,084.7 kl); Rom. Cath. C. 1894, new one (St James's) 1936 d. by M. Heath; RS 1910, station b. by T.E. Quiggin, closed; sale-yards 1932; Salv. Army C.; sawmill (Samuels); school 1890 b. by Sutton and Nightingale, demolished 1910, replaced, additions 1958, additions 1966 by J. McCabe, additions 1985; sewerage 1968; silo 1918; stamper battery (Alfred Bennett's 15 head, removed from Tambaroora) 1891; streets were once lit by acetylene gas; telegraph 1890, new office b. 1899 by John Dunkley; TX 1910, automatic 1979; Unit. C. (orig. Meth.) 1953 d. by William C. Brown; water supply 1921, augmentation 1969, 1988, 1995; Wes. Meth. C. b. 1900 by J.M. Job, extended 1911, enlarged 1926; pop. 1,557 (1891), *c.*1,100 (1895), 1,107 (1901), 1,734 (1911), 1,078 (1921), 1,224 (1933), *c.*1,200 (1941), 1,144 (1947), 1,409 (1954), 1,451 (1961), 1,387 (1966), 1,258 (1971), 994 (1976), 1,037 (1981), 1,097 (1986), 981 (1991), 1,061 (1996), 969 (2001), 946 (2006), 755 (2011).

Peak Top (*Co. Cooper*) 34°00'S. 146°19'E., 40 km NE of Griffith; telephone 1928; TX 1928; pop. 20 (1933).

Peak Vale (*Co. Auckland*) 36°55'S. 149°48'E., 8 km W. of Pambula; telephone 1921; TX 1930–67.

Peak View (*Co. Beresford*) 36°04'S. 149°23'E., 30 km NE of Cooma, on Murphys Ck; grazing; PO 1905–71; school (Good Good till 1890) 1887–90 and 1958–60; telephone 1914; TX 1928–85; pop. 52 (1911), 75 (1933), 111 (1947), 97 (1954), 71 (1961).

Pearces Corner (*Co. Rous*) 28°49'S. 153°20'E., 6 km E. of Lismore, on Tucki Tucki Ck.

Pearces Creek (*Co. Rous*) 28°46'S. 153°27'E.,

7 km N. of Alstonville, on Pearces Ck; settled *c.*1880; orig. timber, then dairying; butter factory (Union Dairy Co. Ltd) b. 1890 by J. Dorough; measles epidemic 1912; PO 1886–1903; Presb. C.; school 1898, new one b. 1902, additions 1914 by Edwards, closed 2014, sold 2015; Wes. Meth. C.; pop. 153 (1901), 169 (1911), 86 (1933), 129 (1947), 84 (1954), 89 (1961).

Pearl Beach (*Co. Northumberland*) 33°33'S. 151°18'E., 7 km S. of Woy Woy, on Broken Bay; also formerly known as Green Point Beach; disc. 1788 by Capt. Arthur Phillip, road access 1925, subdivided 1925 and 1927 by C.R. Staples & Co. Ltd, first lots sold 1927; orig. timber, then fishing, now exclusive waterfront retreat for the wealthy; bushfires 1948, 1990, 2006; electricity 1929; FB; PO 1945; reservoir; sewerage 1988; storm 1974; telephone 1938; TX; Union C.; water supply 1967; pop. 127 (1947), 128 (1954), 227 (1961), 128 (1954), 479 (2006), 513 (2011).

Pearson (*Co. Mitchell*) 35°16'S. 147°12'E., 8 km E. of The Rock; quarry; school 1911–27 and 1957–69.

Pearsons Selection (*Co. Camden*) 34°30'S. 150°33'E., 11 km SE of Mittagong.

Peat Island (*Co. Northumberland*) see Mooney Mooney.

Peats Ridge (*Co. Northumberland*) 33°20'S. 151°14'E., 14 km W. of Ourimbah; citrus orchards and poultry; bushfire 2009; fruit packing house (Central Mangrove Citrus Packing House Ltd); PO 1927; 3 quarries (incl. Boral Concrete); sawmill (Bushell Bros); school 1946, additions 1956 and 1963; telephone 1917; TX 1924, automatic 1965; pop. 85 (1933), 185 (1947), 236 (1954), 341 (1961), 247 (2006), 330 (2011).

Pebbly Beach (*Co. St Vincent*) 35°37'S. 150°19'E., 17 km NE of Batemans Bay, on Tasman Sea; sawmill (Francis Guy) 1901.

Pee Dee (*Co. Dudley*) 30°49'S. 152°27'E., 46 km W. of Macksville, on Macleay R.; farming; airfield; bushfire 1927; flood 1893; PO 1909; school 1896–1906; telephone 1914; TX 1921–55.

Peel (*Co. Parry*) see Tamworth.

Peel (*Co. Roxburgh*) 33°19'S. 149°38'E., 13 km NE of Bathurst, on Clear Ck; village gaz. 1849, estab. 1850 by John Howard, lots sold 1851; grazing, honey, agric.; Angl. C. (St John the Evangelist) b. 1860–66 by William Nixon, d. by Matthew Henry Sadlier, re-roofed 1888; 2 bridges (incl. one b. 1991), over Clear Ck; cemetery (99 graves) 1878; flood 1857; flour mills: Cummins's, Dennis Dunnolly, Grosvenor Francis 1856; goldmines: Blue Lode (Machattie and Blackman) 1903–7, Last Chance (Sinclair) 1879–1910, Mount Conqueror Gold Recovery Co. 1901–14, A.W. Reakes 1935; hailstorm 1876; PO 1856–1965; pound (stock) 1865; quarry; Rom. Cath. C. (Immaculate Conception of the Blessed Virgin Mary) b. 1861 by William Timothy Atkins, d. by Edward Gell, closed, sold and reused; school 1856 b. by John Howard, d. by Henry Robertson, repairs 1898 by John Wadsworth Ashworth, closed 1969, reused; snowstorm 1900; stamper battery (5 head) erected by Sinclair; telephone 1907; TX 1926, automatic 1968; pop. 15 (1851), 130 (1861), 155 (1871), 116 (1891), 89 (1901), 122 (1911), 152 (1933), 102 (1947), 59 (1954), 96 (1961), 177 (2006), 552 (2011).

Peel River (*Co. Parry*) see Bowling Alley Point.

Peels Creek (*Co. Wynyard*) 35°30'S. 148°06'E., 21 km S. of Adelong; school 1919–26 and 1957–69.

Peelwood (*Co. Georgiana*) 34°07'S. 149°26'E., 39 km N. of Crookwell, on Peelwood R.; orig. Five Mile Flat; settled 1854 by William Ford, defunct; mining (lead-zinc-copper disc. *c.*1874 by William Ford and William Montague), farming, grazing; Angl. C. b. 1879 by William Ford, abandoned, new one (St Paul's) b. 1898–1900, renovated 1929, restored 1936, closed 1961, demolished, replacement (St Paul's War Memorial) b. 1962 by R.A. Rodgers and D.B. and G. Blyton; cemetery; mine estab. by William Ford and William Montague, sold to Peelwood Hill Silver Mining & Smelting Co. NL which operated it 1874–83 with 4 reverberatory furnaces, sold 1886, reopened 1888 by Beetson Co. with new furnace, mine and smelting plant dismantled 1889, surface works successively destroyed by rehabilitation activity 1988, 1994, 1996; PO 1871; quarry; Rom. Cath. C. 1877, new one (Sacred Heart) b. 1940 by John A. Walton, d. by Burns; school 1874, burnt down 1937, rebuilt 1938, closed 1967; telephone 1915; TX 1918, automatic 1974; Wes. Meth. C. 1871; pop. 63 (1891), 198 (1911), 179 (1933), 48 (1947), 20 (1954), 133 (1961).

Peeroo (*Co. Cadell*) 35°41'S. 144°42'E., 23 km NW of Mathoura; TX 1927, automatic 1967.

Peisley Park (*Co. Flinders*) 32°00'S. 146°56'E., 54 km SW of Nyngan; school (Paisley Park) 1959–71.

Pejar (*Co. Argyle*) 34°35'S. 149°35'E., 17 km SE of Crookwell, on Wollondilly R.; farming; Angl. C. 1866, new one (St Stephen's) b. 1883 by John Campbell and R. Albon, d. by Edmund Cooper Manfred, derelict, restored, and graveyard (graves 1889–1994); dam 1979, 75 ft (23 m) high; PO 1875; pound (stock) 1869; school 1881–1909; telephone 1925; TX 1935–38; pop. *c.*20 (1866), 149 (1901), 136 (1911), 75 (1933).

Pelaw Main (*Co. Northumberland*) 32°50'S. 151°29'E., 1 km S. of Kurri Kurri; estab. 1903, village gaz. 1916; coalmining; Angl. C. (St Michael and All Angels') 1906; brickworks; bushfires 1909, 2001, 2018; colliery estab. by Henry Trenchard, Samuel Clift, Henry John Adams, et al., as Stanford Greta No. 2 Tunnel, acquired 1900 by East Greta Coal Mining Co. Ltd and J. & A. Brown, o. 1901 as Pelaw Main Colliery, strike 1903, man killed 1905, boy killed 1906, strikes 1906 and 1908, explosion 1909, strikes 1909 and 1910, man killed 1911, fire 1912, strikes 1914, 1915, 1925, 1926, acquired 1931 by J. & A. Brown & Abermain Seaham Collieries Ltd, pit-top burnt down 1931 and rebuilt by Baker and Lamb, strike 1935, man killed 1939, strikes 1939, 1942, 1944, 1945, 1950, taken over 1960 by Coal & Allied Industries Ltd, closed 1961; Cong. C. 1903–17, sold to Roderick, then sold to Angl. C.; diphtheria 1902; Foursquare Gospel C.; Meth. C. 1903, enlarged 1904, fire 1927, new one 1963; PO 1902; 2 quarries; railway (colliery); reservoir (concrete), 501,000 gal. (2,277.5 kl), 1908; school 1903 b. by James Robinson, d. by J. Wigram, improvements 1910, 1916, 1918, 1927; telephone 1904; pop. 730 (1911), 1,121 (1933), 806 (1947), 1,424 (1954), 1,027 (2011).

Pelican (*Co. Northumberland*) see Marks Point.

Pelican Creek (*Co. Rous*) see Gundurimba South.

Pelican Flat (*Co. Northumberland*) see Marks Point.

Pelican Flats (*Co. Northumberland*) see Swansea.

Pelican Island (*Co. Dudley*) 30°57'S. 153°00'E., 8 km SW of South West Rocks, on Macleay R.; farming; PO 1892; telephone 1912; TX 1929–68; Wes. Meth. C. 1890; wharf b. 1884 by George Parkins; pop. 14 (1841), 67 (1901), 58 (1911), 113 (1933), 144 (1947), 84 (1954), 53 (1961).

Pelican Island (*Co. Macquarie*) see Jerseyville.

Pelican Point (*Co. Macquarie*) see Mitchells Island.

Pelton (*Co. Northumberland*) 32°53'S. 151°19'E., 3 km S. of Bellbird; coalmining; collieries: Hilldale (estab. by George Crawford and John Thomas Flarty, o. 1928, closed 1930) and Pelton (estab. 1916 by Newcastle Wallsend Coal Co. Pty Ltd, o. 1918, strikes 1927 and 1936, man killed 1941, strikes 1942, 1943, 1944, 1948, 1950, acquired 1968 by Peko-Wallsend Ltd, acquired 1988 by Elders Resources, taken over 1990 by a consortium, underground mining finished 1992, open-cut mining 1995–98); railway (colliery); reservoir, 1,205,750 gal. (5,481.3 kl); telephone 1934; pop. 111 (1933), 74 (1947), 72 (1954), 81 (1961).

Pembrooke (*Co. Macquarie*) 31°24'S. 152°45'E., 7 km N. of Wauchope, on Stony Ck; farming and dairying; Angl. C. (St Matthew's) b. 1922 by T. and H. Fowler; PO 1921; RS (Munanbang till 1921) 1917–75; school (Moroko till 1921) 1915–75; telephone 1914; TX 1926, automatic

1969; pop. 133 (1933), 110 (1947), 112 (1954), 103 (1961), 147 (2011).

Penarie (*Co. Caira*) 34°25'S. 143°37'E., 25 km N. of Balranald, on Lake Dundomallee; telephone 1923; TX 1936, automatic 1972.

Penderlea (*Co. Wallace*) 36°27'S. 148°30'E., 9 km SE of Perisher Valley, on Wollindibby Ck; farming and grazing; PO 1927–42; quarry (Deerson); telephone 1924; TX 1938.

Penrose (*Co. Camden*) 34°40'S. 150°13'E., 8 km W. of Bundanoon; Cable's Siding till 1897; surveyed 1895, declined 1945+; orchards; bushfires 1939 (largely destroyed village) and 1965; cemetery 1895; FB; fruit packing houses: Fruitgrowers' Co-op. Society Ltd) 1923, burnt down 1939, replaced 1939 by J.H. Counsell, Rose's, burnt down 1939, Watson's, burnt down 1939; Meth. C. b. 1911 by G.E. Rush, d. by T. Hewson, relocated 1924 by Cook Bros, burnt down 1939, replaced 1939 by G. Parry, d. by Brown, closed, sold 1997, 2001, 2018, reused; PO 1894, burnt down 1939; Prim. Meth. C. 1893 (removed from Bowral); rifle range 1914; RS (Cable's Siding till 1897) 1869, station relocated 1916; sawmills: H.H. Cush & Co. and Hardwoods Ltd; school 1927; telephone 1915; TX 1920, automatic 1949; pop. 70 (1911), 135 (1933), 209 (1947), 228 (1954), 221 (1961), 223 (2006), 282 (2011).

Penrose (*Co. Camden*) see also Dapto West.

Penshurst (*Co. Durham*) 32°22'S. 151°29'E., 26 km W. of Dungog, on Paterson R.; pop. 55 (1901).

Penuca (*Co. Auckland*) 36°44'S. 149°53'E., 8 km S. of Bega; cheese factory (H.B. Ritchie); pop. 21 (1933).

Pera Bore (*Co. Gunderbooka*) 30°01'S. 145°49'E., 14 km NW of Bourke; irrigation settlement estab. 1896; 2 bores; PO 1898–1915; telephone 1898.

Perch Creek (*Co. Rous*) 28°29'S. 153°16'E., 21 km SW of Murwillumbah, on Perch Ck.

Perch Ponds (*Co. Cook*) 33°44'S. 150°34'E., 4 km W. of Blaxland, on Glenbrook Ck.

Perekerten (*Co. Wakool*) 34°55'S. 143°52'E., 41 km SE of Balranald; village gaz. 1935; grazing; PO 1927; RS (3 km W., on Victorian railway), closed; telephone 1928; TX 1928; pop. 81 (1933).

Pericoe (*Co. Auckland*) 37°06'S. 149°36'E., 28 km W. of Eden, on Pericoe Ck; farming and dairying, then outpost of hippie culture and alternative lifestyles; diphtheria 1909; PO 1889–1963; sawmill (E.P. Legge), fire 1911; school 1888–89; telephone 1906; TX 1928; pop. 68 (1901), 114 (1911), 74 (1933).

Perisher Valley (*Co. Wallace*) 36°24'S. 148°24'E., 14 km NE of Thredbo, on Perisher Ck; trout fishing and winter snow resort; bushfire 2003; FB (station b. 1984); Interdenominational C. (Alpine) 1976; PO 1971; PS; quarry; 4 reservoirs; Rom. Cath. C. (St John the Apostle) b. 1964 by Freddie Moser, d. by H.R. Zimmermann; RS (ski-tube to Bullocks Flat) 1987; sewage works; TX; pop. 149 (2011).

Perkins Flat (*Co. Buccleuch*) 35°28'S. 148°43'E., 49 km W. of Queanbeyan, on Goodradigbee R.; mine (disused).

Perricoota (*Co. Cadell*) 36°01'S. 144°36'E., 18 km NW of Moama; PO 1879–1910; punt (James Maiden) 1844, moved 1846 to Moama; school 1957–67; pop. 39 (1933), 55 (1954).

Perry (*Co. Menindee*) see Menindee.

Perrys Crossing (*Co. Northumberland*) 33°12'S. 150°58'E., 39 km NW of Ourimbah, on Broad Arm.

Perrys Hill (*Co. Rous*) 28°51'S. 153°27'E., 2 km SE of Alstonville, on Duck Ck; cemetery.

Perth (*Co. Bathurst*) see Perthville.

Perthville (*Co. Bathurst*) 33°29'S. 149°33'E., 9 km S. of Bathurst, on Queen Charlottes Ck; Queen Charlotte's Vale till July 1880, Apsley till Sept. 1880, Perth till 1908; village gaz. 1864 as Perth; goldmining, farming, orchards; Angl. C. (St Martin's) b. 1925 by Edward Abraham Wright, d. by Louis Reginald Williams; Bapt. C., closed 1910, reopened 1913; cemetery (1 km NE); floods 1950 and 1955; goldmine (Bald Hills) operated 1879–96 by Bathurst Gold Mining & Prospecting Assoc.; grasshopper infestation 1925; PO 1875; PS 1903–40; Rom. Cath. C. (St Joseph's)

1886, extended 1912 by Frederick R. Jones, d. by John Francis Kenny, closed, disused, renovated and reused 2000, and graveyard; RS 1878, station closed and demolished 1986; school (Charlottes Vale) 1865–66, reopened (as Perth) 1873 in new building b. by William Timothy Atkins, repairs 1883 by W. Whitemore, alterations 1884 by S.F. Smith, repairs 1895 by John Wadsworth Ashworth, renamed Perthville in 1908, new building b. 1911 by Albert Emanuel Ennis; sewerage augmentation 1995; telephone 1889; TX 1914, automatic 1982; Unit. C. (orig. Wes. Meth.) 1863, additions and alterations 1892 by Josiah James Atkins, re-roofed 1892 and 1922, fire 1926, closed 2018, and graveyard (56 graves); water supply augmentation 1994; Wes. Meth. C. 1860; pop. 165 (1871), 231 (1881), 369 (1891), 398 (1901), 421 (1911), 432 (1933), 414 (1947), 477 (1954), 423 (1961), 294 (1971), 282 (1976), 639 (1981), 392 (1986), 392 (1991), 388 (1996), 422 (2001), 450 (2006), 471 (2011).

Peterborough (*Co. Camden*) see Dunmore and Minnamurra.

Petrolea Vale (*Co. Cook*) see Hartley Vale.

Pettit (*Co. Harden*) 34°57'S. 148°10'E., 14 km N. of Gundagai, on Muttama Ck; RS 1946–75.

Peugeot Point (*Co. Durham*) 32°10'S. 151°25'E., 42 km NW of Dungog, on Paterson R.

Pheasant Ground (*Co. Camden*) 34°37'S. 150°40'E., 17 km SW of Dapto, on Kangaroo Ck; farming; bushfire 1940; butter factory 1892, closed; 2 quarries; sawmill (J. Missingham & Sons); pop. 40 (1933).

Pheasants Nest (*Co. Camden*) 34°15'S. 150°39'E., 9 km NE of Bargo; bridges: one b. 1980, 1,000 ft (305 m), over Nepean R. and one over Dry Ck; FB 1969; TX (automatic); pop. 57 (1933), 461 (2001), 592 (2011).

Phegans Bay (*Co. Northumberland*) see Woy Woy Bay.

Phillip (*Co. Parry*) 31°08'S. 150°51'E., 10 km SW of Tamworth; Bapt. C. 1910; school 1910–40.

Phils Creek (*Co. King*) 34°22'S. 148°55'E., 19 km NE of Boorowa, on Phils Ck; school 1914, new one b. 1926 by Oliver John Stuart, closed 1943; telephone 1911; TX 1925, automatic 1957; pop. 60 (1911), 77 (1933).

Phils Falls (*Co. Westmoreland*) 33°35'S. 149°56'E., 15 km NE of Oberon, on Fish R.

Phoenix Park (*Co. Durham*) see Largs.

Piallamore (*Co. Parry*) 31°10'S. 151°03'E., 15 km SE of Tamworth; Upper Nemingha till 1911; village gaz. 1876; farming and grazing; Angl. C. (St Martin's) 1906; broom factory (B. Long & Son); PO 1910; Presb. C. 1904, closed, damaged 1946, demolished; school (Upper Nemingha till 1912) 1906–65; telephone 1910; TX 1928–64; pop. 119 (1911), 226 (1933), 185 (1947), 141 (1954), 141 (1961), 370 (2006), 219 (2011).

Piallaway (*Co. Buckland*) 31°09'S. 150°34'E., 22 km N. of Werris Creek, on Currabubula Ck; FB; school (Piallaway Closer Settlement since 1947) 1910–70; TX (automatic); pop. 131 (1911), 131 (1933), 97 (1947), 75 (1961), 238 (2011).

Piallaway Closer Settlement (*Co. Buckland*) see Piallaway.

Piambong (*Co. Wellington*) 32°30'S. 149°24'E., 20 km NW of Mudgee; grazing; FB; PO 1927–30; telephone 1922; TX (automatic) 1954; pop. 59 (1911), 52 (1933), 52 (1954), 68 (1961), 239 (2006), 382 (2011).

Piambra (*Co. Napier*) 31°38'S. 149°23'E., 9 km S. of Binnaway; farming and grazing; PO 1927–48; RS 1917, station b. by John Allibone, closed 1974; telephone 1924; TX 1924; pop. 42 (1933).

Pian Creek (*Co. Denham*) see Bugilbone.

Pibbon (*Co. Gowen*) 31°36'S. 149°04'E., 31 km W. of Binnaway.

Piccabeen (*Co. Rous*) see Piggabeen.

Pickering (*Co. Brisbane*) 32°22'S. 150°41'E., 3 km N. of Denman; pop. 52 (1911), 65 (1933).

Picketts Valley (*Co. Northumberland*) see Kincumber.

Picton (*Co. Camden*) 34°10'S. 150°37'E., 15 km SW of Camden, on Stonequarry Ck; (incl. Lower Picton, Macquarie Farm Estate, Stargard Estate, Stonequarry Estate, Upper Picton formerly Redbank); Stonequarry till

1841; surveyed 1821 by G. Harper, laid out by John James Galloway and village gaz. 1845, first lots sold 1847, more lots sold 1854, munic. proc. 1895; orig. wheat, former tourist destination, dairying, farming, fruit; abattoir (Wollondilly Abattoir Pty Ltd); ambulance station; Angl. C.: St Mark's (b. 1850–57, begun by Thomas Smith but completed by G. Wandess and Ramsdale, d. by Edmund Thomas Blacket, extensions 1872 also d. by Blacket, transepts 1886 d. by Blacket Bros, re-roofed 1904, re-roofed again 1930, inundated 2016, and graveyard with burials 1858+) and St Paul's (b. 1886 by George William Sell, closed 1914, moved to Bargo); Bethesda Ministries International C. (Hishouse); brewery (Geoff Scharer); brickworks (J.T. Ashcroft); bridges: Abbotsford Bridge, Brookside Bridge over Racecourse Ck, Cedar Creek Bridge, Chiddys Bridge over Cedar Ck, Evelyn Bridge, Stonequarry Creek Bridge (first one b. 1834, destroyed 1860, second one b. 1861 by J. Sorrie & Co., third one b. 1899, 124 ft or 37.8 m, widened 1962 and 1979), Victoria Bridge (Allan timber truss), 273 ft (83.4 m), b. 1897 by Charles John Foord, over Stonequarry Ck; bushfires 1928, 1939, 2006; carpet factory (Interface Aust. Pty Ltd), burnt down 2012; cemetery (432 graves) 1834; CH 1829, replacement (incl. lock-up) b. 1864 by Peters and Coates, d. by James Johnstone Barnet, repairs 1870 by E.G. Larkin; Christ. Brethren C. 1995; cordial factory (Alfred E. Dowse), sold 1893, relocated 3 times; creamery b. 1899 by William Pritchard for Farmers & Dairymen's Milk Co. Ltd, reused 1945; electricity 1922; FB (station b. 1963, new one 2014); floods 1860, 1890, 2016; flour mills: Allied Mills Aust. Pty Ltd 2009 and post mill estab. 1842 by Thomas Larkin, who also estab. a steam mill 1847, demolished 1913; fur and feather factory (William Kutnewsky) 1920–28, bought by Tonnesen & Sons and reused as cheese factory, sold 1937 to Joe Attanasio and used as cheese factory by him and George Ray, closed 1939, reused briefly as ice works, abandoned, bought by Pierre, sold to Stewart Laynor, reused; heatwave 1939; Indep. Bapt. C. (Bible) 1924, in former school hall; lock-up (Stonequarry gaol) 1829, new one b. 1847 by Munro, demolished 1863; Meth. C. (Lower Picton) 1910, relocated 1912, sold 1964; monumental stone works (A. Speers); PO 1840, new one b. 1892 by Peter Graham, d. by Walter Liberty Vernon, clock tower added 1893, office repairs 1905 by Edward Cocks, closed 1994, sold and reused; pound (stock) 1844; PS 1864, new one b. 1878 by W. Duncan, alterations 1908 by J.G. Taylor; quarry (sandstone); railway barracks b. 1890 by R. Flood; railway coal stage, extended 1890, additional one 1892, new one 1912, extended 1963; railway engine shed b. 1876 by Frederick Horn, extended 1912; railway tunnel 1867–1919, 197 yds (180.4 m), reused, new one 1919, 200 yds (182.8 m); railway turntable (William Sellers & Co.), 60 ft (18.3 m); railway viaduct (5 stone arches) b. 1863–67 by Murnin and Brown, d. by John Whitton, 276 ft (84.1 m), over Stonequarry Ck; reservoir, 400,000 gal. (1,818.4 kl); rifle range 1889, man killed 1905, additions 1909 by R. Hood, jun.; Rom. Cath. C. (St Patrick's) b. 1845–47 by John Bollard, demolished 1947, new one b. 1880, repairs 1901 by W. Pritchard, closed 1901, reused 1902, demolished 2007, replacement (St Anthony's, also known as Sheil Memorial) b. 1901 by Thomas Fanning, d. by T.J. Moloney; RS 1863, station b. by Matthew Jamieson and Andrew Eaton, man killed 1884; sale-yards 1937, new yards 1954; sawmills: Buckley and Oprey 1924, L. Stan Rutter (Redbank) 1941, Shelley's (Redbank), Sweet's; schools: Picton (Lower Picton till 1875) 1868 b. by Larkin, replaced 1910 by M. Christiansen & Co., additions 1948 and 1995, Picton HS 1958, additions 1969, 1985, 1990, 1993, Upper Picton (Picton till 1868) 1856–75; sewerage augmentation 1995; telegraph 1866; toll-house 1867, closed, sold and reused; TX 1917, automatic 1957; Unit. C.: one orig. Presb. 1887 and one orig. Wes. Meth. (Redbank) b. 1850 by James Rogers, extended 1865 also by Rogers, floored and re-roofed 1894, closed, sold and reused 1997, and graveyard (graves 1851+); water supply 1898; pop. 120 (1846), 142 (1851), 226 (1856), 384 (1861), *c.*400 (1864), 452 (1871), 667 (1881), 1,176 (1891), 1,053 (1901), 1,244 (1911), 1,079 (1933), 1,091 (1947), 1,234 (1954), 1,314 (1961), 1,327 (1966), 1,512 (1971), 1,715 (1976), 1,817 (1981), 1,975 (1986), 2,116 (1991), 2,668 (1996), 2,930 (2001), 3,027 (2006), 3,146 (2011).

Picton Lagoons Tank (*Co. Camden*) see Couridjah.

Picton Lakes Village (*Co. Camden*) 34°15'S. 150°33'E., 5 km SW of Tahmoor; pop. 64 (1901).

Pidcocks Lane (*Co. Richmond*) 28°56'S. 153°12'E., 11 km NW of Coraki, on Richmond R.; school 1909, dismantled 1920 by F. Bolton and moved to Evans Head, building replaced by T. Bevan, closed 1934.

Piedmont (*Co. Murchison*) 30°14'S. 150°38'E., 16 km N. of Barraba, on Cobbadah Ck; pop. 32 (1933).

Pigeon Point (*Co. Northumberland*) see Singleton.

Piggabeen (*Co. Rous*) 28°11'S. 153°28'E., 8 km W. of Tweed Heads, on Piggabeen Ck; farming and dairying; gale 1929; PO 1910, burnt down 1915; school (Piccabeen till 1916) 1913–74; telephone 1913; TX 1924, automatic 1952; pop. 103 (1911), 187 (1933), 99 (1947), 99 (1954), 104 (1961), 226 (2006), 327 (2011).

Pigman Creek (*Co. Rous*) see Dyraaba Creek.

Pikedale (*Co. Clarendon*) 34°45'S. 147°29'E., 16 km NW of Junee; Angl. C. (St Matthew's) 1905–71.

Pikes (*Co. Vernon*) 31°07'S. 152°11'E., 56 km E. of Walcha, on Camp Ck.

Pile Flat (*Co. Clarence*) 29°36'S. 153°14'E., 15 km S. of Maclean, on Boundary Ck.

Pilgoorie (*Co. Parry*) 31°17'S. 150°53'E., 21 km S. of Tamworth; telephone 1926; TX 1934–68.

Pillar Valley (*Co. Clarence*) 29°46'S. 153°07'E., 18 km E. of South Grafton, on Pillar Valley Ck; farming, dairying, fishing; bridge over Pillar Valley Ck; cheese factory (W. Goodger) 1884, closed; FB; PO 1927–69; 2 quarries; sawmill (James Saye); school 1909–18; telephone 1913; pop. 121 (1901), 62 (1911), 85 (1933), 65 (1947), 54 (1961), 347 (2011).

Pilliga (*Co. Baradine*) 30°21'S. 148°53'E., 54 km W. of Wee Waa; hunting, timber, grazing, agric.; Angl. C. (St John's) b. 1899 by Mooy Bros; caterpillar infestation 1939; cemetery (283 graves) 1883; CH 1875, new one b. 1879 by John Thomas Coleman, repairs 1896 also by Coleman; cordial and vinegar factory (Harry Drew); FB; fire 1960; floods 1904, 1974, 1976, 1978, 2010; lock-up; PO 1867, repairs 1896 by F.G. Williams, renovations 1936, new one 1962; pound (stock) 1866; PS 1875, new one 1887, repairs 1937 by J.T. Henry; Rom. Cath. C. (St Patrick's) b. 1911 by James William Doherty, renamed St Brigid's in 1939, new one b. 1981 by Ted Ginty, d. by Bernard Frize; sawmills: A. Bleakley, T.L. Brown, Colwell and Holcombe, Pat Kelly, Robert Morrow, G.J. Saunders (burnt down 1913), George Wilkins & Son; school 1883, additions 2010; telegraph 1872; TX 1910, automatic 1990; whooping cough epidemic 1937; pop. 280 (1901), 305 (1911), 431 (1933), 261 (1947), 279 (1954), 289 (1961), 251 (1971), 238 (1976), 206 (1981), 217 (1986), 210 (2006).

Pilot Hill (*Co. Wynyard*) 35°37'S. 148°09'E., 10 km S. of Batlow; sawmill (water powered, John Hides), man killed 1901.

Pilot Wilderness (*Co. Wallace*) 36°49'S. 148°18'E., 35 km S. of Thredbo.

Pimlico (*Co. Richmond*) see Empire Vale.

Pimlico (*Co. Rous*) 28°55'S. 153°30'E., 9 km SW of Ballina, on Richmond R.; North Pimlico till 1904; sugar-cane, farming, dairying; PO 1890; school (North Pimlico till 1911) 1887–1967; storm 1907; telephone 1907; Wes. Meth. C. 1884; pop. 167 (1911), 198 (1933), 196 (1947), 179 (1954), 176 (1961), 363 (2006), 458 (2011).

Pinch Flat (*Co. Sandon*) 30°23'S. 151°41'E., 15 km N. of Armidale, on Commissioners Waters; school 1889–95.

Pindari (*Co. Arrawatta*) 29°31'S. 151°17'E., 29 km SE of Ashford, on Mordington Ck; PO

1968–69.

Pindemar (*Co. Gloucester*) see Pindimar.

Pindimar (*Co. Gloucester*) 32°40'S. 152°07'E., 4 km W. of Tea Gardens, on Pindimar Bay; (incl. North Pindimar and South Pindimar); Pindimar City surveyed by H. Sheaffe, d. 1913 by Walter Scott-Griffiths, for Pindimar Port Stephens Ltd, but never eventuated; FB; fish receiving and refrigeration depot o. 1917, closed, reused as shark processing station (Marine Industries Ltd) 1927–33, reused as fish canning and oyster factory (Port Stephens Canning Co. Ltd), burnt down 1938; jetty; PO 1923; school (Pindemar) 1927–38; telephone 1924; TX 1924–66; pop. 109 (1933), 157 (1996), 215 (2006), 230 (2011).

Pindjera (*Co. Beresford*) see Bunyan.

Pine Cliff (*Co. Ashburnham*) see Pinecliffe.

Pinecliffe (*Co. Ashburnham*) 33°09'S. 148°48'E., 9 km SW of Molong; farming; Pine Cliff till 1923; Bapt. C. 1890–1964; bushfire 1909; PO 1907; RS (Brockoble till 1902) 1897, station b. by Frederick Lemm, jun. and Thomas Edward Spencer, closed 1974; school (Buckhobble till 1903) 1890–1946; telephone 1906; TX 1915; pop. 131 (1911), 139 (1933), 67 (1947), 50 (1961).

Pine Clump (*Co. Ewenmar*) 31°23'S. 148°09'E., 32 km W. of Gulargambone; school 1957–76.

Pine Field (*Co. Kennedy*) 32°28'S. 147°24'E., 71 km SW of Trangie; school 1957–67.

Pinegobla (*Co. Finch*) 29°19'S. 148°18'E., 32 km NE of Lighning Ridge.

Pine Grove (*Co. Flinders*) 31°38'S. 146°53'E., 30 km W. of Nyngan.

Pine Grove (*Co. Hume*) 35°56'S. 146°17'E., 13 km NW of Corowa.

Pine Grove (*Co. Leichhardt*) 30°54'S. 148°41'E., 30 km E. of Coonamble.

Pine Hills (*Co. Townsend*) 35°34'S. 145°22'E., 21 km NW of Finley; PO 1899–1916; pop. 30 (1933).

Pine Mount (*Co. Bathurst*) 33°52'S. 148°53'E., 16 km E. of Cowra; farming and grazing; telephone 1912; TX 1928.

Pine Park (*Co. Bligh*) 32°57'S. 149°09'E., 21 km E. of Wellington, on Lake Burrandong.

Pine Ridge (*Co. Blaxland*) 32°39'S. 146°13'E., 97 km NW of Condobolin, on Marobee Ck.

Pine Ridge (*Co. Buckland*) 31°30'S. 150°27'E., 21 km W. of Quirindi, on Mooki R.; estab. as private village; grazing; Angl. C. (St John's) 1927, closed, reused, sold 2019; bridges: one b. 1883, 164 ft (50 m), over Warrah Ck, replaced 1968 and one b. 1933 by C.A. Leahy, 133 ft (40.5 m), over Mooki R.; PO 1868, new one 1930; sawmills: Reuben Austin, R.H. Jensen, Pike's; school 1934–48 and 1955–86; telegraph 1892; TX 1910, automatic 1985; pop. 127 (1911), 89 (1933), 67 (1947), 82 (1954), 292 (2011).

Pine Ridge (*Co. Farnell*) 30°41'S. 141°21'E., 144 km N. of Broken Hill.

Pine Ridge (*Co. Napier*) 31°59'S. 149°33'E., 14 km E. of Dunedoo; mining (silver-lead); pop. 98 (1933).

Pine Ridge (*Co. Nicholson*) 33°29'S. 145°49'E., 25 km E. of Hillston.

Pine Rocks (*Co. Bathurst*) 33°24'S. 149°02'E., 14 km SW of Orange; school 1891–1901; telephone 1924; TX 1925–45; pop. 55 (1933).

Pines (*Co. Macquarie*) 31°08'S. 152°21'E., 46 km W. of Kempsey.

Pine Vale (*Co. Ewenmar*) 31°33'S. 148°35'E., 20 km N. of Gilgandra.

Pine Vale (*Co. Pottinger*) 31°08'S. 149°43'E., 44 km E. of Coonabarabran; PO 1900–2; pop. 26 (1933).

Pine Valley (*Co. Beresford*) 36°15'S. 149°04'E., 6 km W. of Cooma; brewery (Catcher & Co.).

Piney Range (*Co. Bland*) 33°49'S. 147°58'E., 21 km NW of Grenfell; farming; FB; PO 1927; Rom. Cath. C. 1897, new one (St Brigid's) 1939; sawmill (J. Huckel); telephone 1926; TX 1939, automatic 1955; pop. 314 (1911), 163 (1933), 139 (1947), 145 (1954), 95 (1961).

Piney Range (*Co. Hume*) see Walbundrie.

Pinkerton (*Co. Harden*) 34°39'S. 148°03'E., 2 km SE of Cootamundra; PO 1927–30; 2 quarries; pop. 140 (1901), 95 (1933), 94 (1947).

Pinkett (*Co. Gough*) 29°53'S. 151°57'E., 26 km SE of Glen Innes, on Swamp Ck; farming and dairying; Angl. C. (St Michael's) 1903–98, moved to Glen Innes gaol by Jeff Paul and reused 1998; mine (sapphires); PO 1913–65; Rom. Cath. C. (St Joseph's), closed, and graveyard (9 graves); sawmill; school 1957–60; telephone 1914; TX 1918, automatic 1967; pop. 69 (1933), 103 (1947), 72 (1954), 109 (1961).

Pinnacle (*Co. Forbes*) 33°42'S. 147°59'E., 28 km NW of Grenfell, on Pinnacle Ck; PO 1865; telephone 1909, automatic 1951; pop. 100 (1933), 126 (1947), 70 (1954), 88 (1961).

Pinnacle Reefs (*Co. Forbes*) 33°38'S. 147°55'E., 29 km S. of Forbes; goldmining; mines: Haley's Reef (C.A. Haley) 1900–1, Kirkpatrick's Reef 1895–1938, Pinnacle Reef (Gold Hill Mine, Ward's Mine, Ben Hall's Mine) 1883–1910, Soldiers Reef 1896–1937, Young Australia (A. Morrison) 1897; quarry.

Pinnacle Reefs (*Co. Forbes*) see also Boyd.

Pinnacle Road (*Co. Bathurst*) 33°21'S. 149°03'E., 8 km S. of Orange; school 1933–63, sold and reused; TX (automatic).

Pinnacles (*Co. Yancowinna*) see The Pinnacles.

Pinnacle South (*Co. Forbes*) 33°42'S. 147°58'E., 27 km NW of Grenfell; Mortray till 1943; telephone 1923; TX 1924, automatic 1966.

Pinnacle Swamp (*Co. Phillip*) 32°46'S. 149°55'E., 5 km NW of Rylstone, on Pinnacle Swamp Ck; bushfire 2009; school 1897–1904; pop. 20 (1933).

Pinny Beach (*Co. Northumberland*) see Caves Beach.

Pioneer (*Co. Cooper*) see Griffith.

Piora (*Co. Richmond*) 28°51'S. 152°55'E., 14 km W. of Casino, on Shannon Brook; farming and dairying; PO 1927; school 1909–63; telephone 1911; TX 1949, automatic 1957; pop. 133 (1933), 107 (1947), 84 (1954), 79 (1961).

Pipeclay (*Co. Macquarie*) 31°26'S. 152°33'E., 13 km W. of Wauchope, on Hastings R.

Pipeclay Creek (*Co. Auckland*) 36°58'S. 149°52'E., 4 km S. of Pambula; gold; fire 1899; mine (Faulkner); PO 1896, burnt down 1899; telephone 1893.

Pipeclay Creek (*Co. Phillip*) see Buckaroo.

Pipeclay Springs (*Co. Wellesley*) 36°53'S. 149°17'E., 6 km NE of Bombala; school 1886, enlarged 1897 by Oliver & Co., new building b. 1915 by D. Livingstone, closed 1932.

Pipers Bay (*Co. Gloucester*) see Forster Keys.

Pipers Creek (*Co. Macquarie*) 31°10'S. 152°44'E., 14 km SW of Kempsey, on Pipers Ck; lime-kilns 1834, ruined; pop. 107 (1933), 61 (1947).

Pipers Flat (*Co. Cook*) 33°22'S. 150°00'E., 3 km SE of Portland, on Pipers Flat Ck; colliery 1903; dam 1920, 33 ft (10 m) high, on Pipers Flat Ck; earth tremor 1903; mine (Portland Iron Ore) <1880; PO 1883; RS 1882, station b. by William Cameron and John Briton, closed 1974; pop. 196 (1901), 181 (1911), 125 (1933), 69 (1947).

Pipers Flat (*Co. Cook*) see also Irondale.

Pipers Flat (*Co. Roxburgh*) see Wattle Flat.

Pirate Point (*Co. Gloucester*) see Stockton.

Pise (*Co. Manara*) 32°42'S. 144°06'E., 147 km SE of Wilcannia; telephone 1925.

Pitlochry (*Co. Gloucester*) 31°57'S. 152°01'E., 8 km NE of Gloucester; RS 1929–64; school (Bulliac till 1933) 1916–65, abandoned.

Pitnacree (*Co. Northumberland*) see Raworth.

Pitstone (*Co. Monteagle*) 34°21'S. 148°19'E., 4 km SE of Young, on Sawpit Gully; farming; PO 1927–31; railway dam; school (Sawpit Gully till 1922) 1884–1952; telephone 1914; pop. 58 (1947).

Pit Town (*Co. Northumberland*) see Hamilton

Pittown (*Co. Northumberland*) see Wallsend.

Pitts Corner (*Co. Westmoreland*) 33°36'S. 150°00'E., 18 km NE of Oberon; airfield.

Plahgoman (*Co. Mitchell*) see Birdlip.

Plains Station (*Co. Drake*) see Tabulam South.

Planters Flat (*Co. Phillip*) 32°19'S. 149°50'E., 29 km E. of Gulgong; quarry.

Plashette (*Co. Hunter*) 32°27'S. 150°52'E., 18 km E. of Denman; dam 1987, 151 ft (46 m) high, on Saltwater Ck.

Platform (*Co. Bathurst*) 33°32'S. 149°07'E., 13 km W. of Blayney.

Platina (*Co. Cunningham*) 32°50'S. 147°28'E., 23 km W. of Trundle; defunct; mining (platinum and gold) and farming; mine (Platina or Simmons Rush) 1893–1964; pop. 56 (1933).

Platts (*Co. Wellesley*) 37°05'S. 149°18'E., 20 km S. of Bombala; Mahratta Station till 1903; farming; PO 1916–59; sawmill (Thomas Hite & Sons); telephone 1907; TX 1927.

Plattsburg (*Co. Northumberland*) see Wallsend.

Pleasant Heights (*Co. Camden*) see Mount Ousley.

Pleasant Hills (*Co. Urana*) 35°28'S. 146°48'E., 23 km W. of Henty; settled by German immigrants; wheat; chaff mill (J.S. Lewington) 1946; Lutheran C. (St John's) 1888, and graveyard (1883–1907); PO 1890; Presb. C. (War Memorial) b. 1951–53 by W.W. Holt, closed, sold 2008; PS 1919–40; RS 1920–75; school (Munyabla till 1894) 1893, extended 1900 by C. Hardy & Co.; silo 1932; telephone 1908; TX 1911, automatic 1940; water supply 1892, augmentation 1989; pop. 350 (1911), 225 (1933), 188 (1947), 189 (1954), 231 (1961), 305 (2011).

Pleasure Point (*Co. Goulburn*) 36°00'S. 147°08'E., 27 km NE of Albury, on Lake Hume.

Plevna (*Co. Cunningham*) 32°49'S. 147°44'E., 10 km N. of Trundle.

Plumthorpe (*Co. Darling*) 30°21'S. 150°28'E., 13 km W. of Barraba; school 1957–65; pop. 29 (1933).

Poddy Hut (*Co. Wellesley*) 36°46'S. 149°18'E., 17 km NE of Bombala.

Point Clare (*Co. Northumberland*) 33°27'S. 151°20'E., 2 km SW of Gosford, on The Broad Water; surveyed 1907; model sugar-cane plantation estab. in 1830s by Thomas Alison Scott, later farming, fishing, tourism; ambulance station; Angl. C. (St John's) 1939, and graveyard; bushfire 1994; cemetery (Coorumbine); electricity 1937; foot-bridge over Fagans Bay; PO 1905; rifle range; RS 1891; school 1955, additions 1963, 1970, 1974; sugar mill; telephone 1905; wharf (Goodaywang) 1841, defunct; pop. 118 (1911), 245 (1933), 414 (1954), 669 (1961), 2,973 (2006), 3,810 (2011).

Point Danger (*Co. Rous*) see Tweed Heads.

Point Frederick (*Co. Northumberland*) see Gosford.

Point Plomer (*Co. Macquarie*) 31°19'S. 152°58'E., 14 km N. of Port Macquarie.

Point Wolstoncroft (*Co. Northumberland*) see Gwandalan.

Poison Gate (*Co. Benarba*) 29°38'S. 149°09'E., 56 km E. of Collarenebri.

Poison Point Plain (*Co. Barrona*) 29°59'S. 145°17'E., 66 km W. of Bourke.

Pokataroo (*Co. Benarba*) 29°35'S. 148°41'E., 13 km SE of Collarenebri; East Collarenebri till 1913; village gaz. 1918; grazing; PO 1909; PS 1924; RS (o. as Collarendabri, then Collarenebri East till 1919) 1906, station b. by John Allibone and Augustus Ringholm, closed 1975; school 1919–36 and 1955–65; telephone 1908; TX 1914; pop. 74 (1933), 52 (1947), 91 (1954), 172 (1961).

Pokolbin (*Co. Northumberland*) 32°48'S. 151°17'E., 8 km NW of Cessnock, on Pokolbin Ck; (incl. Mistletoe Farm); village gaz. 1885; farming, dairying, wine; airport (Cessnock) 1935; Angl. C. (St Mark's) 1910; brewery (Matilda Bay Brewhouse); bushfires 1942, 1961, 1968; cheese factory (Hunter Valley) 1995; cyclone 1899; 2 FB; measles epidemic 1907; FB (Rothbury, station b. 1984); PO: Mistletoe Farm 1927–30 and Pokolbin 1877; school 1880, new school b. 1902 by G. and T. Russell, closed 1973; telephone 1900; TX 1916, automatic 1963; Wes. Meth. C. 1886; wineries: Ablington Vineyard Estate (bought 1995 by Bekker, estab. 1996, expanded 2008 to include the old Stevens Vineyard), Arrowfield Estate 1970, Blaxlands, Blueberry Hill Vineyard 1973, Broken Ridge Estate, Brokenwood (estab. 1970–73 by Tony Albert, John Beeston and James Halliday, new winery 1975, new barrel shed 2004), Calais Estate 1987 (bought 2000 by Richard and Susan Bradley), Centurion Wines, Chateau Francois, Christies Wines, Cockfighter's Ghost Wines, Constable Estate Vineyards, De Iuliis Wines 1999 (Joss and Anna De Iuliis, winery 2001 d. by Lionel Glendenning), DenMar Estate (Dennis and Marie Eldridge), Reg Drayton's Wines,

Drayton's Family Wines (W. Drayton & Sons Pty Ltd, formerly Bellevue) 1877, Eagles Rest Winery Pty Ltd (Hill's) 2007, Echo Ridge Wines (Greg and Anthony Ward), First Creek Wines 1984, Ghost Riders Vineyard, Glandore Estate Wines, Golden Grape Estate (closed 2010), Gundog Estate 2006, Hanging Tree Wines, Harrigan's Cellars, Hermitage Road Cellars, Hillside Vineyard (acquired 2010 by Matt Cowley), Honeytree Estate, Hungerford Hill Wines Pty Ltd 1967 (bought 2016 by Sam and Christie Arnaout), Hunter Cellars, Ironbark Hill Vineyard (Peter Drayton), Iron Gate Winery Pty Ltd (estab. 1996 by Roger Lilliott, o. 2000), Ivanhoe Wines (Lionel V.H. Stephen), James Estate Winery Pty Ltd, J.Y.T. Wine Co., Kindred's Lochleven Estate, Lake's Folly Vineyard (estab. 1963 by Max Lake), Lambloch Estate, Leogate Estate Wines 2009, Lindemans Wines, Littles 1984, Lowes Family Wines, McGuigan Cellars, McLeish Estate, Marshalls Vineyard, Meerea Park Wines (Rhys and Garth Eather) 1991, Mistletoe Wines, Montagne View Estate, Moon Mountain Vineyard (bought 2009 by Steve Allen and Craig Brown-Thomas), Mount Eyre Vineyard, Mount Pleasant Estate of McWilliam's Wines Pty Ltd (estab. by Charles King, taken over 1921 by Maurice O'Shea, later joined with McWilliam's family), Oakvale 1893, Pendarves Estate (estab. 1988 by Phil Norrie, now owned by Graham Burns), Pepper Tree Wines 1991, Peppers Creek, Peterson House Ltd, Pigs Peake, Pokolbin Bros Wines, Pokolbin Estate (formerly MacDougall's Estate), Polin & Polin Hunter Wines 1996, Poole's Rock Winery (estab. 1988 by David Clarke), Potters Inn (became Windarra, bought 2005 by Terry, Efrem and Richard Harkam and became Harkam Wines), Racecourse Lane Wines (estab. 1998 by Mike and Helen McGorman), Murray Robson Wines, Rosemount Estate 1974, Rothbury Estate (acquired 2006 by Michael Hope from the Fosters Group), Saddler's Creek Wines 1990, Scarborough Wine Co. 1987, Kevin Sobels Wines 1986 (formerly at Muswellbrook), Tamburlaine Wines estab. 1967–76, Tempus Two (estab. 1999 by Lisa McGuigan, bought 2009 from Australian Vintage by the Roche Group and renamed Roche Estate), Thalgara Estate 1985, The Little Wine Co. (Ian and Suzanne Little), The Vintry, Thomas Wines 1997, Tinklers Vineyard (estab. by Usher Gordon Tinkler, Usher William Tinkler and Ian Geoffrey Tinkler), Tintilla Estate 1994, Tower Estate (founded 1999 by Len Evans, sold 2013 by Cowley to Michael Hope), Tulloch Wines, Keith Tulloch Wine (founded 1997 by Keith and Amanda Tulloch), Tyrell's Vineyards Pty Ltd (estab. 1864 by Edward Tyrell), Van de Scheur Wines, Vanesa Vale Vineyard, Verona Vineyard, Vinden Estate 1990, Audrey Wilkinson Vineyard 1866, Windsors Edge Wines estab. 1996 by Tim and Jessie Windsor, Wollundry Wines (estab. 1971 by Ron Hansen), Wombat Crossing Vineyard (estab. 1994, first wine 2005), Wynwood Estate; pop. 329 (1891), 655 (1901), 354 (1911), 300 (1933), 236 (1947), 236 (1954), 222 (1961), 624 (2006), 694 (2011).

Pokolbin (*Co. Northumberland*) see also Nulkaba.

Pola Creek (*Co. Macquarie*) 31°03'S. 152°53'E., 6 km NE of Kempsey; pop. 72 (1911), 40 (1933).

Police Point (*Co. Waradgery*) see Hay.

Polo Flat (*Co. Beresfield*) 36°14'S. 149°09'E., 3 km E. of Cooma; airport (Cooma-Polo Flat) 1921; FB; metal fabrication works (Allenspach Steel Pty Ltd) 1965; pop. 12 (2011).

Polona Loop (*Co. Bathurst*) 33°30'S. 149°12'E., 5 km S. of Millthorpe.

Pomeroy (*Co. Argyle*) 34°40'S. 149°30'E., 22 km S. of Crookwell, on Wollondilly R.; copper; earth tremor 1860; flour mill (orig. water powered) estab. 1870 by Lieut. Thomas Woore; mines: Chisolm's, Costley's, Donnelly's, Gurrunda (W.J. O'Neill 1946–50, Glenburn Tributes 1954–56, J.H. Tyreman 1956–58), Heffrons Creek (Heffron, P. Nosworthy, Le Champ), Lucky Hit (H. Gillett, E.T. McCabe, C.A.M. and J.F. Betts)

1906–19, Merrilla 1907 and 1918, Taunton's (D.H. Taunton, Betts, W. Wilson, E. Rigley) 1912; pound (stock) 1863; school 1880–94; squall 1867; TX; pop. 88 (1901), 84 (1911), 36 (1933), 103 (1954), 63 (1961).

Pomeroy West (*Co. Argyle*) 34°37'S. 149°31'E., 18 km S. of Crookwell, on Howey Ck.

Pomona (*Co. Wentworth*) 34°01'S. 141°53'E., 11 km N. of Wentworth; orig. Seven Mile Point; settled by John Dunn, founded 1908; irrigation settlement; grapes and oranges; drought 1922; electricity 1941; FB 1992; flood 1956; fruit packing house (Robern); PO (Neilpo) 1927–41; sawmill (McCauley Bros); school 1923–29, reopened 1952; telephone 1925; TX 1926, automatic 1950; pop. 77 (1933), 125 (1947), 181 (1954), 77 (1961), 136 (2011).

Ponds Creek (*Co. Gough*) 29°53'S. 151°11'E., 8 km N. of Tingha, on Ponds Ck; school 1883, new one b. 1884, closed 1910, building moved 1912 to Old Mill; typhoid 1898; pop. 91 (1901).

Ponds Flat (*Co. Harden*) 34°52'S. 148°32'E., 35 km W. of Yass.

Ponto (*Co. Gordon*) 32°28'S. 148°48'E., 16 km NW of Wellington; farming; lots sold 1905; Angl. C. b. by Septimus Haddock and Sam Jackson, demolished 1908; cemetery 1879; PO 1875–1931; school 1874–91 and 1957–68; telephone 1913; Union C.; pop. 492 (1911), 112 (1933), 64 (1947), 73 (1954), 69 (1961).

Ponto Railway Station (*Co. Lincoln*) see Geurie.

Poolbrook (*Co. Arrawatta*) 29°39'S. 151°17'E., 21 km NE of Inverell, on Chain of Ponds; mining; school 1902–12.

Poonboon (*Co. Wakool*) 35°04'S. 143°35'E., 47 km S. of Balranald; pop. 38 (1933).

Poonboon (*Co. Wakool*) see also Stony Crossing.

Pooncaira (*Co. Perry*) see Pooncarie.

Pooncarie (*Co. Perry*) 33°23'S. 142°34'E., 93 km NE of Dareton, on Darling R.; Pooncaira till 1869; surveyed 1862 by James H. Wood, village gaz. as Pooncaira and first lots sold 1863; former river port, then grazing; airfield; astronomical station; bridge (Callender-Hamilton truss span) b. 1963 by McMillan Constructions Ltd, 314 ft (95.7 m), over Darling R.; bushfire 1974–75; cemetery (graves 1870+); CH (incl. lock-up) 1875, reused, new one 1906–44, reopened 1947, closed, reused; diphtheria 1898–99; drought 1939; dust storm 1944; electricity 1974; FB 1966 (station b. 1979); floods 1950–51 and 1956; PO 1869, new one b. 1877, replaced 1886, new one 1928, extended 1952; pound (stock) 1899; PS 1868, new one b. 1906 by George Edward Moore, closed, renovated and reused; punt (manual) 1941–63, across Darling R.; school 1895–2013, reopened 2019; telegraph 1877; TX 1910, automatic 1984; typhoid 1903; water supply 1970; weir; wharf; pop. 45 (1891), 91 (1901), 84 (1911), 127 (1933), 66 (1947), 157 (1954), 97 (1961), *c.*50 (1987–99), 152 (2006), 328 (2011).

Pooraka (*Co. Canbelego*) 31°32'S. 146°26'E., 56 km E. of Cobar; RS 1911–51.

Popran (*Co. Northumberland*) 33°16'S. 151°13'E., 18 km NW of Ourimbah; orig. maize and timber, then orchards; fruit packing house; quarry; Rom. Cath. C. 1860; sawmill (Marshall Saw Milling Co.); telephone 1913; TX 1923.

Porcupine Gap (*Co. Ashburnham*) 33°12'S. 148°29'E., 19 km W. of Manildra; railway camp; PO 1892–93; railway ballast pits; school 1892 b. by Matthew M'Glynn, closed 1894.

Port Erringhi (*Co. Cook*) 33°31'S. 150°54'E., 7 km NE of Wilberforce, on Hawkesbury R.; quarry.

Porters Mount (*Co. Bathurst*) 33°52'S. 148°45'E., 6 km SE of Cowra; school 1916–23; pop. 20 (1933).

Porters Retreat (*Co. Georgiana*) 33°59'S. 149°46'E., 31 km S. of Oberon; formerly Glencoe; mining (gold and copper), farming, grazing; bushfire 1929; cemetery (79 graves 1898+) 1888; mines: Porters Retreat *c.*1860s–1910, Retreat River, Wrens Nest; PO 1898, burnt down 1930; PS 1903–14; Rom. Cath. C. 1909 d. by John Francis Kenny, closed, sold and reused; telephone 1906; TX

1939, automatic 1969; pop. 92 (1901), 153 (1911), 121 (1933), 139 (1947), 102 (1954), 178 (1961), 255 (2011).

Port Kembla (*Co. Camden*) 34°29'S. 150°54'E., 6 km S. of Wollongong, on Tasman Sea; (incl. Cringila, North Port Kembla, Port Kembla Steelworks); Red Point till 1892; disc. 1770 by Capt. James Cook, estab. 1817, garrison estab. 1826 under Capt. Peter Bishop, founded 1883, first subdivided (Five Islands Estate) 1909, further subdivision (Steeltown Estate) 1929; seaport 1883+ and heavy industry; Angl. C. 1903, alterations 1916, replacement (St Stephen's) 1925; Bapt. C. 1944, new one 1972; bomb shelter (World War II); breakwaters: eastern one b. 1901–8, 3,750 ft (1,143 m), damaged 1960, and northern one b. 1912–25, 3,263 ft (994.6 m), damaged 1960; brickworks (Ulladulla Silica & Firebrick Co., became Newbold Silica Fire-Brick Co. Ltd, renamed Newbold General Refractories Ltd in 1940); bridges: 2 bridges over Allan's Ck and one b. 1900 by Lawson, demolished, over Tom Thumb Lagoon; CH, new building 1967 d. by John Whyte Ian Thomson; clothing factory (Bonds Industries Ltd) 1961–1992; coal loaders 1898, 1910, 1915, 1964, 1982; coke-works: Aust. Iron & Steel Ltd (48 ovens o. 1950 and 96 ovens b. 1957–60 by Simon Carves Aust. Pty Ltd) and Mt Lyell Co. (36 rectangular beehive ovens) 1899–1926; Cong. C., sold 1907 to Meth. C.; customs-house 1937; electricity 1920; engineering works (Garnock Engineering Co. Pty Ltd); FB (station b. 1928 by Lowther and Horrocks); fibrous plaster works: Setzard Plasters Pty Ltd and Tolhurst Bros; foot-bridge (Trimmers' Bridge) d. and. b. 1898 by P.L. Tighe, 460 ft (140.2 m), over Tom Thumb Lagoon; forts: Breakwater Battery b. 1939–42, dismantled 1946 and Illowra Battery (Hill 60) 1943, dismantled 1946; gale 1928; harbour (inner) b. 1956–60; hospital 1965 d. by John Kinstler and W. Turner, additions 1990 and 2006; Islamic C. (Bilal); jetties: No. 1 (b. 1912–15, 1,343 ft or 409.3 m, demolished 1968), No. 2 (Southern Coal Co., 1887–1916, 1,400 ft or 426.7 m, demolished 1925, replaced 1929 for Aust. Iron & Steel Ltd, 834 ft or 254.2 m), No. 3 (Red Point, b. 1883 by Mount Kembla Coal & Oil Co. Ltd, 900 ft or 274.3 m, d. by William Burall, second one 1889, third one 1914, condemned and replaced 1940, damaged 1960), No. 4 (b. 1909, 400 ft or 152.4 m, extended 1930 to 800 ft or 243.8 m, damaged 1960, re-decked 1964), No. 6 (b. 1959, damaged 1960), police jetty 1990; Macedonian Orthodox C. (St Kliment Ohridski's), in former Presb. C.; Meth. C. 1911, (second) 1921, burnt down 1931, (third) 1932, (fourth) 1961; migrant hostel (Karingal) 1948–84; oil terminal (Vacuum Oil Co.) 1952; pilot station; PO: Cringila 1938–93 and Port Kembla 1901, new ones 1913 and 1926; powerhouse 1914, upgraded 1921 and 1929, explosion 1952, closed; Presb. C. 1924, closed and reused, new one (St Andrew's) 1940, closed, sold 1982 and reused; PS 1912, new one (incl. lock-up) 1933, additions 1961; quarries (stone): Gillian's Hill, Reid's Hill 1906, State Metal Quarries; railway to Moss Vale 1932; 2 railway bridges over Allan's Ck; 3 reservoirs (incl. concrete one, 501,200 gal. or 2,278.5 kl, 1909); rifle range; Rom. Cath. C. b. 1919 by W.J. Cooney, d. by Austin McKay, additions 1928, new one (St Patrick's) 1951; RS: Cringila 1926, North Port Kembla 1936, Port Kembla 1920; Salv. Army C. 1953, burnt down 1973, new one 1975; schools: Cringila 1957, additions 1961 and 1978, Five Islands Secondary College (Port Kembla HS till 1992, Illawarra Senior College till 2014) 1961, additions 1968, Port Kembla 1890–92, reopened 1901 in new building b. by A. Rankin, new building 1917, additions 1931, additions 1952 by A.F. Little & Co. Pty Ltd, additions 1956 and 2000, Steeltown moved 1944 to Warrawong; sewage works; shoe factory (Robin Bros) 1968; steelworks b. 1927–31 by Aust. Iron & Steel Ltd (acquired 1935 by BHP), incl. No. 1 blast furnace 1928, No. 2 blast furnace 1938, mill 1949, No. 3 blast furnace 1952, mills 1955, 1957, 1958, No. 4 blast furnace 1959, No. 5 blast furnace

1972, No. 6 blast furnace 1996, steelworks acquired 2003 by Bluescope Steel Ltd, fire 2014; storms 1902, 1904, 1910, 1960; strikes 1907, 1908, 1909, 1911, 1919, 1920, 1924, 1935, 1936, 1937, 1938, 1939, 1940, 1941, 1943, 1944, 1945, 1949, 1952, 1953; tank traps (World War II); telephone: Cringila 1938 and Port Kembla 1906; TX 1917, automatic 1956; Unit. C.: one orig. Presb. and one Tongan; water reticulation 1902; works: Armco Aust. Pty Ltd, Aust. Fertilizers Ltd 1921 (company became Incitec), Aust. Scale Co. Pty Ltd, Aust. Smelting Corp. Ltd, British Aust. Power Cables Pty Ltd (b. 1952 by Elweld Pty Ltd), Commonwealth Oil Refineries Ltd 1937, Commonwealth Oxygen & Acetylene Co. Ltd, Commonwealth Steel Rolling Mills Pty Ltd 1939 (taken over 1947 by John Lysaght Aust. Ltd), Electrolytic Refining & Smelting Co. of Aust. Ltd 1909 (damaged 1928, new chimney b. 1965 by Tileman & Co., works sold 1990 to CRA, Furukawa Co. and Nissho Iwai and works renamed Southern Copper, major refurbishment 1991, closed 1995, reopened 2000 by Port Kembla Copper Pty Ltd, closed 2003, chimney demolished 2014), Industrial Galvanizers Corp., Lysaghts Works Pty Ltd 1936, Metal Manufactures Ltd (rolling mill) 1917, with tube factory added 1920 and telephone cable factory added 1923, Monier Industries Ltd; pop. 123 (1901), 844 (1911), 1,622 (1921), *c.*3,700 (1936), 4,780 (1937), 5,733 (1947), 7,216 (1951), 8,498 (1954), 6,548 (2006), 6,998 (2011).

Port Kembla Steelworks (*Co. Camden*) see Port Kembla.

Portland (*Co. Roxburgh*) 33°21'S. 149°59'E., 22 km NW of Lithgow, on Dulhuntys Ck; (incl. East Portland); orig. Limestone Flat; settled 1863 by Thomas Murray, estab. 1886, village gaz. 1894, lots auctioned 1901, subdivided 1904; limestone (disc. 1863 by Thomas Murray) quarrying 1869+ and cement production; abattoir; Angl. C. (St Stephen's) 1903 d. by H. Kenway; carriage-works (James Oglethorpe), sold 1913; caterpillar infestation 1933; cement works estab. 1887 by Cullen Bullen Lime & Marble Works by Alexander Currie and George Raffan, became the Cullen Bullen Lime & Cement Co., failed 1895, site and plant bought 1899 by August Scheidel, taken over 1900 by Commonwealth Portland Cement Co., plant replaced 1901, works reopened 1902, new plant installed 1951, closed 1991; cemetery (1,579 graves 1909+), incl. lawn cemetery and columbarium; CH b. 1910 by A.E. Beaumont, extended 1986; colliery 1905; diphtheria 1913 and 1917; FB (station b. 1955, new one 2001); fire 1914; gastroenteritis epidemic 1929; hospital b. 1913 by Crisp and Ladkin, additions 1955, new one 2007; landslide 1924; 8 lime-kilns (static charge, bottle shape) b. 1869+ by Thomas Murray, 6 demolished; measles epidemic (boy died) 1928; miners' strikes 1915, 1917, 1925; PO: East Portland 1935–59 and Portland 1891, closed and reused 1913, new one b. 1913 by Albert Emanuel Ennis; powerhouse (cement works); Presb. C. re-erected 1908 by Thew and Cale (removed from Sunny Corner), burnt down 1914, replaced (St Andrew's) 1915; PS 1903, new one b. 1910 by A.E. Beaumont; 7 quarries (Commonwealth Portland Cement Co. Ltd), last one closed 1998; reservoir; rifle range 1906, new one 1913; Rom. Cath. C. (St Vincent's) b. 1905 by William Alfred McLean, d. by John Job Copeman; RS (Cullen Siding till 1889) 1887, relocated 1911, closed; Salv. Army C. 1928; school (Cullen till 1899) 1884, new building b. 1895 on new site by Robert Maders, additions 1906 by James Short and Robert Leslie, additions 1923 by Albert Emanuel Ennis, additions 1963; sewerage 1961; small arms factory (World War II), reused; streets electric lit 1911; strike (general) 1944; telegraph 1903; telephone: East Portland 1935 and Portland 1899; TX 1912, automatic 1972; Unit. C.; water supply 1903; Wes. Meth. C. 1901, enlarged 1906 by James Short and Robert Leslie; window frame factory (J. Connolly Ltd) 1946, in former small arms factory; pop. *c.*400 (1897), 543 (1901), 2,370 (1911), 3,082

(1933), *c.*3,000 (1941), 2,635 (1947), 2,558 (1954), 2,442 (1961), 2,221 (1966), 1,940 (1971), 1,883 (1976), 1,980 (1981), 2,002 (1986), 2,055 (1991), 1,888 (1996), 1,817 (2001), 1,881 (2006), 1,829 (2011).

Portland Head (*Co. Cook*) see Ebenezer.

Port Macquarie (*Co. Macquarie*) 31°26'S. 152°55'E., 196 km NE of Newcastle, on Tasman Sea; (incl. Hibbard formerly Hamilton, Settlement City, Tacking Point); also formerly known as Macquarie; disc. 1818 by John Joseph William Molesworth Oxley, penal settlement estab. 1821 by Capt. Francis Allman, proc. free settlement 1830, surveyed 1831 by James Meehan, land available 1831+, penal status ended 1847, town gaz. 1878, designated as chief town of the county, munic. proc. 1887 (amalgamated with and became Hastings in 1981); orig. logging and sugar-cane (1821–80), then maize, tallow, barley, oats, potatoes, vineyards, dairying, pigs, cobalt (disc. 1886, mined 1898–1904), tin mining, shipping port till 1915, now manufacturing, fish, oysters, fruit, retirement centre 1960s+; airport (4 km W.), terminal upgraded 2019; ambulance station 1953; Angl. C. (St Thomas the Apostle) b. 1824–28, d. by Lieut. T.H. Owen, damaged 1839, repairs 1841, gallery and vestry added 1844, church damaged 1854, re-roofed 1855 and 1883, restoration 1923 by Hutcherson Bros, d. by Rhoderic Welch, renovated 1952, damaged and re-roofed 1984; Assemblies of God C.: City and Honour; asylum for infirm and destitute (in old convict barracks) 1866, demolished 1891; Bapt. C. 1964; boiling-down works; breakwaters: southern one b. 1897–1938, 2,700 ft (822.9 m) and northern one b. 1939–42, new one b. 1977; breweries: Black Duck estab. 2010 by Al and Kate Owen and The Little Brewing Co. estab. 2007 by Warwick and Kylie Little; bridges: ones b. 1932 and 1968 over Kooloonbung Ck, Edmund Barton Bridge over The Broadwater, Newport Bridge, one over The Governors Way; broom and brush factory (K. & D. Thompson Pty Ltd); butter factories: Aust. Dairying Co. Ltd 1897 and Hastings Dist. Co-op. Dairy Co. Ltd 1903–34; carriage-works: Latham and Dick, and Otto Charles Ochs; caterpillar infestation 1886; causeway across The Governors Way; cemeteries: historic (93 graves) 1821 and general (3,419 graves) 1863; CH b. 1870 by Butler and Bourne, d. by James Johnstone Barnet, extensions 1890 also d. by Barnet, repairs 1953 by John R. Mackenzie, re-floored 1974, closed 1986, restored 1993, reused, new one 1986; Church of Christ; clock tower 1963; convict barracks 1840, reused as asylum; cordial factory (W.J. Ross), acquired 1920 by W.H. Marshall; dam (Rosendahl reservoir), 79 ft (24 m) high, 1980; earth tremor 1842; electricity 1927 estab. by G.P.C. Quast, taken over 1938 by local council; FB (station b. 1958); female factory 1825; fire 1886; floods 1954, 1995, 2009, 2013; flour mill (wind) b. by Robert Peebles for A.C. Innes; foot-bridge over Kooloonbung Ck; gaol 1824–46, new one b. 1837–40, damaged 1848, alterations and repairs 1866 by James Butler, fire 1869, damaged 1881, closed 1905, reused 1907–13, demolished 1917–20; Grace C.; granary 1830; hailstorms 1886, 1891, 1984; hospital 1825, replaced 1848, new one (cottage) 1901, morgue burnt down 1935 and replaced by H. Bourne, new hospital b. 1947–51, new one (Base Hospital) 1994, extended 2014, new mental health unit o. 2019; hurricanes 1839, 1854, 1897; ice works and ice-cream factory (Port Macquarie Ice & Ice Cream Supply); immigrant depot estab. 1841–42 by Caroline Chisholm; Jehovah's Witnesses C.; LDS (Mormon) C.; lighthouse (Tacking Point) b. 1878 by Shepherd and Mortley, 26 ft (8 m), converted to acetylene 1919 then to electricity 1974; lock-up b. 1899 by T.L. Mitchell, repairs 1953 by John R. Mackenzie; Lutheran C. (St Peter's) 1988; military barracks; mill (tide); pilot station, reused 1990; PO: Hibbard 1912 and Port Macquarie 1832 (new one b. 1880 by W.J. Smith, additions and repairs 1913 by E.G. Fenn, replacement b. 1969 by E.E. Lahey Co. Pty Ltd); pound (stock) 1875; powerhouse (G. Quast) 1926; Presb. C. b. 1840–43 by Jean

Baptiste Charles Lamonnerie Dit Fattorini, rebuilt, replaced 1969; PS b. 1892 by Edward Knowles, new ones 1976 and 1991; punts across Hastings R.; reservoirs; rifle range; Rom. Cath. C. (Immaculate Conception) 1862, replacement b. 1878 by Craig and Walsh, extended 1889, demolished 1940, new one (St Agnes's) b. 1941 by P.J. Knudson, d. by Austin McKay; Salv. Army C.; sawmills: British Aust. Timber Co. Ltd, Hamilton Mills (estab. 1875 by J.J. Hibbard, man killed 1901, sold 1911 to Dalgety), Hastings River Sawmills Ltd, Frederick Hayward (closed and moved 1902), Jennings Pickering & Co. 1885, J. Rodger; schools: Hastings 1982, Hibbard 1893–1970, Port Macquarie primary 1852, additions 1926 by Thomas Norman Grimsley, additions 1968 and 1978, re-roofed 2013, Port Macquarie HS 1962, additions 1966, 1972, 1985, 2012, renamed Hastings Secondary College in 2015, Tacking Point 1996, Westport primary 1970, additions 1975 and 1978, Westport HS 1981, renamed Hastings Secondary College in 2015; SD Adventist C. b. 1941 by A.H. Godfrey, d. by V. Warden; sewage works b. 1963–68, sewerage completion 1971, augmentation 1990, 1992, 1997, 1999; slipway; soap and candle factory; storms 1923 and 2016; streets lit by acetylene gas 1911, electric lit 1927; sugar mill (E. Holland, horse powered), new one nearby estab. 1868 by Davis and Somerville; tanneries (incl. Blair's, replaced by John S. Dick); TC, additions 1987, became North Coast Institute in 1992, additions 1995; telegraph: Port Macquarie 1869, new office b. 1880 by W.J. Smith, and Tacking Point 1897; telephone (Hibbard) 1912; TX 1910, automatic 1967; Unit. C. (Sherwood Road) b. 1995 by Gary Bannister; univ. (Charles Sturt) 2012, new building b. 2016 by Watpac Construction (NSW) Pty Ltd; water supply 1957, augmentation 1980; weirs: one on Kooloonbung Ck, demolished 1955 and one on The Broadwater; Wes. Meth. C. 1837, new one b. 1840–46, extended 1869–71, re-roofed and re-floored 1918, new porch, church remodelling and renovations 1928 by A.G. Smith, d. by J.C.R. Mills, additions 1930, extended 1936, renovated 1955, reused 1995, restoration 1997 d. by David Boram; wharves: govt wharf b. 1904 by John Lawson, Lady Nelson, one b. 1921 by S. Anderson, one b. 2001; pop. 536 (1833), 820 (1836), 1,053 (1841), 819 (1846), 519 (1851), 495 (1856), 514 (1861), 691 (1871), 773 (1881), *c.*900 (1886), 961 (1891), *c.*920 (1895), 1,160 (1901), 1,058 (1911), 1,563 (1921), *c.*1,200 (1924), 1,824 (1933), 2,905 (1947), 4,408 (1954), 5,952 (1961), 7,072 (1966), *c.*7,500 (1968), 9,362 (1971), 13,362 (1976), 19,581 (1981), 22,884 (1986), 26,798 (1991), 33,709 (1996), 37,982 (2001), 39,219 (2006), 41,491 (2011).

Port Maitland (*Co. Northumberland*) see Maitland.

Port Phillip (*Co. Cadell*) see Moama.

Port Phillip (*Co. Selwyn*) see Wolseleys Gap.

Portree (*Co. Gloucester*) see Eagleton.

Port Stephens City (*Co. Gloucester*) see North Arm Cove.

Port Waratah (*Co. Northumberland*) see Mayfield North.

Possum Brush (*Co. Gloucester*) 32°04'S. 152°26'E., 13 km NW of Tuncurry; quarry (Jandra, Holkim Aust. Pty Ltd); pop. 10 (2011).

Possum Power Tank (*Co. Bland*) see Springdale.

Potato Point (*Co. Dampier*) 36°06'S. 150°08'E., 4 km S. of Tuross Head, on Tasman Sea; orig. Marka Point; disc. 1797 by George Bass, subdivided 1961; FB 1981; jetty 1912; sawmills: Ironbark Timber Co. 1914 and McMillan Bros 1917, closed 1933; water supply augmentation 1994; pop. 134 (2006), 270 (2011).

Pothana (*Co. Northumberland*) see Belford.

Pottery Estate (*Co. Cook*) see Lithgow.

Pottsville (*Co. Rous*) 28°23'S. 153°34'E., 7 km S. of Bogangar, on Coral Sea; Lower Cudgera till 1945; ambulance station b. 2019 by Hutchinson Builders; Angl. C. (St Mark's) 1964; bridges: 2 over Cudgera Ck and 2 over Mooball Ck; 2 foot-bridges; PO 1941; Rom.

Cath. C. (St Mary and St Ambrose's) 1983; school (Pottsville Beach) 1948, new one 1996; sewerage augmentation 1985; telephone 1941; TX 1941–63; pop. 136 (1947), 164 (1954), 248 (1961), 240 (1971), 332 (1976), 673 (1981), 621 (1986), 1,293 (1991), 1,987 (1996), 2,585 (2001), 3,298 (2006), 5,735 (2011).

Pottsville Beach (*Co. Rous*) see Pottsville.

Poverty Point (*Co. Bligh*) 32°33'S. 149°15'E., 28 km E. of Wellington.

Poverty Point (*Co. Cadell*) 35°52'S. 144°58'E., 8 km SE of Mathoura.

Poverty Point (*Co. Clive*) 29°08'S. 152°19'E., 30 km E. of Tenterfield; mining (gold disc. by Paulo Marcolini, gold rush 1859).

Prairie Oak (*Co. Argyle*) 34°47'S. 149°58'E., 23 km E. of Goulburn, on Stony Ck; 2 quarries (Newbold).

Premer (*Co. Pottinger*) 31°27'S. 149°54'E., 45 km NE of Coolah; subdivided 1924 by H. McMaster, laid out by William Rhodes, first lots sold 1924, village gaz. 1926, further subdivided 1928, 1929, 1959, 1963; timber, sheep, cattle, wheat, lucerne hay; Angl. C. (St Andrew's) 1955; drought 1965; flood 1920; PO 1927; Rom. Cath. C. (Sacred Heart) 1936; RS 1923–78; school (Weetalaba till 1898) 1881, new one b. 1884 by Thomas Davison, closed 1898, reopened 1929, new one b. 1947 on new site by Ronald Savage, additions 1956 and 2010; silo 1941; telephone 1925; TX 1925, automatic *c.*1965; waterworks 1968; pop. 46 (1926), 80 (1929), 133 (1933), 220 (1947), 151 (1954), 114 (1961), *c.*85 (1981), 224 (2006), 234 (2011).

Pretty Beach (*Co. Northumberland*) see Killcare.

Pretty Gully (*Co. Buller*) 28°47'S. 152°27'E., 50 km NE of Tenterfield; goldmining till *c.*1900; cemetery 1894; mine (abandoned); telephone 1933; TX 1938; pop. *c.*50 (1866), 64 (1901), 66 (1933).

Pretty Pine (*Co. Townsend*) 35°25'S. 144°53'E., 15 km NW of Deniliquin; farming and grazing; fire 1916; PO 1903–42; sawmill; telephone 1907; TX 1949, automatic 1954; pop. 57 (1911), 53 (1933), 51 (1961).

Pretty Valley (*Co. Gough*) 29°52'S. 152°01'E., 31 km SE of Glen Innes, on Pretty Valley Ck.

Primbee (*Co. Camden*) 34°30'S. 150°53'E., 4 km SW of Port Kembla, on Lake Illawarra; Angl. C. (St Matthew's) 1956; flood 1952; jetty (Purry Burry Point); Meth. C. 1924; PO 1942; school 1938, additions 1958 and 1963, additions 2010 by Patterson Building Group Pty Ltd; steel fabrication works (Garnock Engineering Co. Pty Ltd); telephone 1942; pop. 551 (1947), 1,184 (1954), 1,751 (1961), 1,646 (2006), 1,579 (2011).

Primrose Hill (*Co. Camden*) see Kiama.

Promised Land (*Co. Raleigh*) 30°22'S. 152°53'E., 10 km N. of Bellingen; cheese factory.

Prossers Crossing (*Co. King*) 34°09'S. 148°48'E., 36 km S. of Cowra, on Boorowa R.; TX 1914–38.

Providence Portal (*Co. Wallace*) 35°57'S. 148°38'E., 52 km N. of Jindabyne, on Providence Arm; quarry; sawmills: Alpine Creek (James Broadhead, water powered) 1884–1901, Belcher's, Kelly's 1936–46.

Providential Cove (*Co. Camden*) see Wattamolla.

Prunevale (*Co. Harden*) 34°24'S. 148°20'E., 10 km S. of Young; soldiers' settlement; orchards (stone fruit); quarry; RS 1928–75; pop. 38 (1933).

Pucawan (*Co. Bourke*) 34°24'S. 147°21'E., 16 km W. of Temora, on Mirrool Ck; farming, charcoal burning 1939–45; airfield (World War II); PO 1929; RS (Linton till 1914) 1906, station b. by Allibone and Ringholme, closed 1975; school 1915–55; silo 1927; telephone 1919; TX 1949–68; pop. 120 (1933), 103 (1947), 71 (1954), 72 (1961), 184 (2006).

Puddledock (*Co. Sandon*) 30°23'S. 151°45'E., 16 km NE of Armidale; cemetery (3 graves); dam 1928; PO 1877; school 1882–89 and 1907–26; telephone 1925; TX 1926–36; pop. 61 (1901), 102 (1911), 66 (1933), 73 (1947), 75 (1961).

Pudman Creek (*Co. King*) 34°36'S. 148°56'E., 27 km N. of Yass, on Pudman Ck; farming and grazing; CH 1879; flood 1947; PO

1927–54; PS 1877–1900; school 1885–1952; telephone 1919; TX 1925; pop. 96 (1911), 93 (1933), 67 (1947).

Puen Buen (*Co. Auckland*) 36°27'S. 149°43'E., 31 km W. of Bermagui.

Puggoon (*Co. Bligh*) 32°16'S. 149°29'E., 13 km N. of Gulgong; iron ore; mines: Tallawang (Aust. Magnetite Pty Ltd 1901–3 and G. & C. Hoskins Ltd 1902–27) and Tallawang South; RS 1910, station b. by George Albert Leggo and John Allibone, closed 1975; pop. 27 (1933).

Pullabooka (*Co. Gipps*) 33°45'S. 147°46'E., 41 km W. of Grenfell; farming; bushfire 1926; PO 1925; Rom. Cath. C. (Sacred Heart) 1906, burnt down 1926; RS (Kewana Siding till 1919) 1918–74; school 1905–11; silo; telephone 1923; TX 1928, automatic 1987; pop. 193 (1933), 108 (1947), 58 (1954), 71 (1961).

Pullaming (*Co. Pottinger*) 31°03'S. 150°20'E., 11 km SE of Gunnedah; FB.

Pulletop (*Co. Mitchell*) 35°26'S. 147°23'E., 31 km SE of The Rock, on Burkes Ck; Duneba till 1950; gold and tin; RS (Pullitop till 1932) 1925–52; telephone 1923; TX 1950, automatic 1959; Union C. (Knox, orig. Presb.) 1932; pop. 160 (1911), 77 (1933), 54 (1947), 68 (1954), 58 (1961).

Pullitop (*Co. Mitchell*) see Pulletop.

Pulpit Hill (*Co. Cook*) see Medlow Bath.

Pumpenbil (*Co. Rous*) 28°22'S. 153°10'E., 24 km W. of Murwillumbah, on South Pumpenbill Ck; colliery (Tyalgum) 1936; sawmill; school 1957, damaged 1961, closed 1977; storm 1961; pop. 122 (1933), 109 (1947), 116 (1954), 70 (1961), 441 (2011).

Punchbowl (*Co. Clarence*) 29°27'S. 152°46'E., 31 km NW of Grafton; pop. 50 (1911).

Punkalla (*Co. Dampier*) see Wagonga.

Pure Point (*Co. Wellington*) see Long Creek.

Purfleet (*Co. Gloucester*) 31°56'S. 152°28'E., 3 km S. of Taree; bypassed by highway 1997; agric.; Aboriginal mission station 1900, incl. church 1927; Assemblies of God C. (Community); brick-kiln; butter factory (Aust. Dairying Co.) 1897, taken over 1906 by Upper Manning Co-op. Dairy Co. Ltd, relocated 1918; cemetery; cordial factory (Saxby & Coleman Ltd) 1976, d. by Newton Jones; droughts 1923, 1927, 1928, 1929; measles epidemic 1898; PO 1966–88; 3 quarries; sale-yards (Roy Smith) 1953; school 1857–71; storm 1907; telephone 1966; pop. 110 (1901), 161 (1911), 228 (1933, incl. 65 at the Aboriginal mission station), 229 (1947, incl. 153 at the Aboriginal mission station), 314 (1954, incl. 235 at the Aboriginal mission station), 291 (1961, incl. 211 at the Aboriginal mission station).

Purgatory (*Co. Gloucester*) 32°23'S. 152°06'E., 10 km W. of Bulahdelah; sawmill (Port Stephens Hardwood Co.) 1903.

Purlewaugh (*Co. Napier*) 31°20'S. 149°31'E., 23 km E. of Coonabarabran, on Baby Ck; farming and grazing; PO 1907–79; Presb. C.; Rom. Cath. C. (St Michael the Archangel) b. 1922 by B. Robertson, closed, sold and reused; sawmill (J.T. Paul); school 1957–68; telephone 1908; TX 1914, automatic 1984; pop. 82 (1911), 137 (1933), 79 (1954), 117 (1961).

Purnamoota (*Co. Yancowinna*) 31°42'S. 141°23'E., 29 km N. of Broken Hill, on Purnamoota Ck; orig. Leadville, also known as The Soakage; village gaz. 1884, declined 1887+, defunct; mining (silver-lead disc. 1887 by Tommy Governor); Bible Christ. C.; brewery (Falcon) estab. 1884 by John Cocks, Alfred Martin and Charles Kite, closed 1886; cemetery 1887; CH 1887; cordial factory (J.W. Fairchild); mines (within 5 km): Atlas, Blackbird, Black Prince, Constellation, Eclipse, Ethel, Great Northern, Lubra, Lubra South, Lubra West, Maori Chief, Orient, Red Hill, Terrible Dick, The Lily, Uncle Tom, War Dance, War Dance Extended (formerly Pluck-Up); PO 1885; PS 1885–94; school 1889–93; smelter 1885; telegraph 1888–94; pop. 365 (1888), 127 (1891), 73 (1901).

Purnanga (*Co. Fitzgerald*) 30°26'S. 143°19'E., 121 km N. of Wilcannia; opals.

Purreah (*Co. St Vincent*) see Burrier.

Putta Bucca (*Co. Phillip*) 32°34'S. 149°35'E., 4 km N. of Mudgee; sewage works, closed 2013; storm 1938; pop. 63 (1933), 60 (1954),

291 (2011).

Putty (*Co. Hunter*) 32°58'S. 150°40'E., 57 km W. of Paxton, on Wollemi Ck; grazing, farming, dairying; PO 1877, burnt down 1905, reopened 1927, closed 1979; sawmill; school 1898 b. by T.H. and J.W.P. Blick, closed 1946; telephone 1915; TX 1946, automatic 1984; pop. 71 (1901), 84 (1911), 99 (1933), 68 (1947), 52 (1954), 55 (1961), 183 (2006), 321 (2011).

Putty Beach (*Co. Northumberland*) see Killcare.

Puxtys Hollow (*Co. Durham*) 32°32'S. 151°36'E., 20 km SW of Dungog.

Pyangle (*Co. Phillip*) 32°39'S. 149°55'E., 17 km N. of Rylstone; school 1882–1916.

Pyes Creek (*Co. Clive*) 29°15'S. 151°50'E., 29 km SW of Tenterfield, on Pyes Ck; PO 1927–31; arsenic mine *c.*1924; tin mine (Heffernan's), incl. 4 buddles.

Pyes Gap (*Co. Ashburnham*) 33°29'S. 148°26'E., 2 km SE of Eugowra.

Pyramul (*Co. Wellington*) 32°53'S. 149°37'E., 33 km W. of Kandos, on Pyramul Ck; Upper Pyramul till 1938; goldmining and grazing; Angl. C. (St James's) b. 1875 by Foster, and graveyard (59 graves 1864–2003); butter and cheese factory (William Price) 1890; cemetery; fire 1902; PO 1870–1979; quarry; Rom. Cath. C. (St Patrick's) 1873–2005, defunct, and graveyard (84 graves 1859+); school (Upper Pyramul 1884–1925) 1874–1925 and 1957–97, sold; telephone 1899; TX 1930; pop. 94 (1933), 87 (1947), 100 (1954), 91 (1961).

Pyree (*Co. St Vincent*) 34°55'S. 150°41'E., 4 km W. of Greenwell Point, on Saltpan Ck; orig. Swamp Paddock; farming and dairying; bridge 1894, over Crookhaven R.; FB 1944; floods 1860, 1865, 1870; PO 1869; school 1860, new one b. 1877 by Bartholomew Carey, additions and repairs 1908 by E. Kennedy, closed 1976, reused; telephone 1915; TX 1923–61; pop. 117 (1911), 146 (1954), 152 (1961).

Q

Quaama (*Co. Dampier*) 36°28'S. 149°52'E., 18 km W. of Bermagui, on Dry R.; Dry River till 1893; wattle-bark, farming, dairying; Angl. C. (St Saviour's) b. 1907 by George Hyland; bridge, destroyed 1893, replaced 1894 (Allan truss), over Dry R.; bushfires 1912 and 1952 (man died); cemetery 1888; cheese factories: Fairfield (J.J. Browne) and Pidgeondale (T. Wilson) b. 1909 by Olaf Rye Lassen; fire 1914; PO 1889; reservoir (concrete) 1955; rifle range; Rom. Cath. C. (St Patrick's) b. 1913 by John Eden Stapleton, demolished; school 1884, new building b. 1907 by C. Gough, additions 1993; telephone 1891; TX 1923, automatic 1957; pop. 149 (1901), 225 (1911), 149 (1921), 204 (1933), 183 (1947), 162 (1954), 171 (1961), 126 (1991), 165 (1996), 158 (2001), 141 (2006), 161 (2011).

Quambone (*Co. Gregory*) 30°56'S. 147°52'E., 49 km W. of Coonamble, on Merri Merri Ck; village site reserved 1888; grazing; Angl. C. (St Paul's) 1899; cemetery (116 graves 1902+) 1894; cordial factories: Ferguson's and Walter Jones; electricity 1959; FB; flood 1955; PO b. 1900 by William Robert Ibbotson; PS 1876, additions 1905 by John O'Reilly; reservoir; Rom. Cath. C. (Sacred Heart) 1906, additions 1937; sawmills: Stan Parker (bought by Wallace and McGee, sold to Roy Wangmann), Charles Rankmore, Rose and Walden, Turner's; school 1898, additions 1900 by A. Cormack, new one b. 1908 by J.E. M'Donald, additions 1914 by J.A. Wise; telegraph 1899; telephone 1898; TX 1910, automatic 1987; water supply (No. 1 town bore 1938–69 and No. 2 town bore 1969); whooping cough epidemic 1934; pop. 58 (1891), 115 (1901), 382 (1911), 154 (1933), 189 (1947), 260 (1954), 214 (1961), 197 (2006), 247 (2011).

Quandary (*Co. Bourke*) 34°23'S. 147°19'E., 21 km W. of Temora; farming; Angl. C. (St James's) 1934 d. by L. Wilkinson; bushfire 1951; PO 1913, burnt down 1915, rebuilt, burnt down again 1917, rebuilt, burnt down again 1926, rebuilt, closed 1968; RS (Beaconsfield till 1907) 1906, station b. by John Allibone and Augustus Ringholm, closed 1975, demolished 1985; school 1920–36; silo 1931; telephone 1907; TX 1914–68; Union C. 1912, renovations and repairs 1927 by Berry Bros, demolished; pop. 138 (1911), 129 (1933), 77 (1947), 62 (1954).

Quandialla (*Co. Bland*) 34°01'S. 147°48'E., 36 km W. of Grenfell; orig. Euroka Siding then Bland Road Siding till 1916; farming and sheep; Angl. C. (Ascension) b. 1919–21 by H.R. Davidge, additions 1937, new one (St Mark's) 1963; candle factory (Sarah Ryan) 2011; electricity 1949; fires 1938 and 1951; Meth. C. b. 1913 by H.F. Pearse; PO 1916, new one b. 1924 by H.N. Conn; powerhouse (M.L. Fisher); PS 1930, new one 1961; reservoir (elevated); Rom. Cath. C. (St Brigid's) b. 1924 by Len Prendergast; RS 1916, station demolished 1985; sawmill (John Jessup); school 1918, new one 1928, additions 1934 by H.H. Collingridge, additions 1963; silo 1928; telephone 1918; TX 1921, automatic 1987; Unit. C. (orig. Meth.) 1929, became Community C., closed, sold 2017; whooping cough epidemic 1937; pop. *c.*320 (1928), 244 (1933), 341 (1947), 362 (1954), 237 (1961), 311 (2006), 349 (2011).

Quandong (*Co. Monteagle*) 33°55'S. 148°10'E., 3 km SE of Grenfell; goldmining; bushfire 1900; cemetery; mines: Enterprise 1867–97, 1913, *c.*1935, Four Mile *c.*1875–1880, Lawsons Hill 1878–92, Milkman's *c.*1875–1876, Quondong 1875–80, Stuart's Gully *c.*1875–1890, Two Mile *c.*1879; quarry; RS (Quondong) 1901, station b. by F.W. Kinch, closed; pop. 73 (1911).

Quarantine Bay (*Co. Auckland*) 37°04'S. 149°53'E., 3 km SW of Eden, on Twofold Bay; breakwater, 394 ft (120 m), 1979.

Quarry Siding (*Co. Hume*) 35°57'S. 146°35'E., 5 km NW of Howlong.

Quart Pot (*Co. Bathurst*) 33°55'S. 149°01'E., 28 km E. of Cowra, on Lake Wyangala; pop. 46 (1933).

Quartz Ridge (*Co. Roxburgh*) see The Reefs.

Quartzville (*Co. Selwyn*) 35°41'S. 148°09'E., 15 km NE of Tumbarumba; goldmining; mine (Storey's Reef) 1860s; snowstorms 1901 and 1907.

Quat Quatta (*Co. Hume*) 35°57'S. 146°35'E., 5 km NW of Howlong; FB 1936; pound (stock) 1871; storm 1901; pop. 77 (1911), 69 (1947).

Queanbeyan (*Co. Murray*) 35°21'S. 149°14'E., 170 km E. of Wagga Wagga, on Queanbeyan R.; (incl. Crestwood, De Salis, Dodsworth, East Queanbeyan, Gale, Greenleigh, Irishtown, Jerrabomberra, Karabar, Langdene, Larmer, Letchworth, South Queanbeyan, West Queanbeyan, White Rocks); disc. 1820 by Charles Throsby, James Vaughan and Joseph Wild, settled 1828 by Timothy Beard, surveyed 1828 by Robert Dixon, estab. 1836, laid out 1838 by James Larmer, first lots sold 1839, munic. proc. 1885, subdivided (Garryowen Estate) 1885 by William Henry O'Malley Wood, thrived in 1920s and 1948–73, city proc. 1972; sheep, cattle, wheat, maize, barley, oats, rye, potatoes, honey, wine, olives, nurseries, mining; aluminium prefabrication plant (Dowell Aust. Ltd) 1968; ambulance station 1942; Angl. C.: Christ (b. 1844 by McLean and Ross, razed 1859, replacement b. 1860 by Daniel Jordan, d. by Alberto Dias Soares, spire added 1861 by Allan McLean and Donald Ross, church re-roofed, renovated 1960) and St Matthew's (Karabar) 1988 (built as a pre-school); Assemblies of God C. (Slavic Christ. Fellowship); Baha'i C.; Bapt. C. (in renovated house) 1968–78, reused, new one (in hall) 1978, extensions and renovations 1986; Bible Bapt. C.; brewery estab. 1845 by Alfred Bradbury, closed 1862, reopened 1884 by George Billson and John Farrell, closed again 1885; brickworks: Mason Brick, Tile & Pottery Works 1926 and Multibricks Pty Ltd 1965; bridge (Queens Bridge) d. and b. 1858 by William Henry Downey, 342 ft (104.2 m), damaged 1861, repairs 1867 by Edward Oswald Evans, rebuilt 1874 by Webb and Evans, closed 1899, replacement b. 1898–1900 by Hungerford & Sons, d. by Ernest Macartney de Burgh, replaced again 1975, over Queanbeyan R.; bushfires 1926 and 1952; carriage-works: R. Kay and J. McGiven (gutted 1926), Noldt and Watson, William Snow (relocated 1904 to former brewery); cemeteries: Riverside 1844, Tharwa Road 1885, Lanyon Drive (lawn) 1969; central heating factory (Bishop Engineering) estab. 1972 by Ken Bishop; CH 1850, new one (incl. lock-up) b. 1861 by Allan M'Lean and Donald Ross, d. by William Henry Downey, additions 1881 by John Kealman, repairs 1890 by Charles Brown, demolished 1976, replacement b. 1976–78; Church of Christ; concrete floor slab plant (Ultrafloor Southern Pty Ltd); cordial factories: Commonwealth Cordial Co. Ltd (incl. ice works), W. Martin, George N. Morton 1906, Myers and Goodhew (partnership dissolved and factory sold 1886), Abraham Myers and William Emley (Emley left partnership in 1876), John J. O'Rourke, O'Sullivan's, W. Pike & Son; dairy factory (Bega Co-op. Creamery Co. Ltd) 1975; diphtheria 1861, 1894, 1934; earth tremors 1860, 1872, 1883, 1898; electricity 1921; engineering works (ARC Engineering

Pty Ltd); FB 1891 (station b. 1925, reused, new one 1982); fibrous plaster works: Beazley and Bruce, and The Victoree (Vic Sacagio) 1937; floods 1852, 1861, 1870, 1891, 1910, 1916, 1922, 1924, 1925, 1956, 1974, 1976, 1988, 1989, 1991, 1995, 1998, 2010, 2012; flour mills: Martin Byrne (b. 1883 by Thomas Jordan and Thomas McCauley, d. by William Crispin, closed 1889, sold, reused, restored 1978), Dodsworth 1863, Alfred Tasker Faunce (water powered, destroyed 1853), James Hutchinson & Sons (Queanbeyan Steam Mills, estab. 1855, acquired by Edward Severne, taken over 1857 by H.S. Hayes, bought 1858 by J.J. Wright, damaged 1890, closed, partly demolished 1933, razed 1948), John Knox (transferred 1915 to C.H. Bowers, closed and demolished 1921), Stephen Nutter (horse powered, estab. 1850, sold 1852 to John William Wiseman Wishart and moved to Gundaroo), Queanbeyan Roller Flour Mill Co. b. 1890 by G.H. Rhodes & Co.; foot-bridge (suspension) 1901, destroyed 1925, replacement 1938 d. by James and William Pike and Henry Hungerford, over Queanbeyan R.; furniture factories: H. Brown 1915, and Livingstone and Douglas, fire 1926; Greek Orthodox C. (St Dimitrios's); hailstorms 1861, 1865, 1884, 1928; hospital (benevolent asylum) 1847, replacement b. 1859–62 by Daniel Jordan and Gibson, d. by William Henry Downey, repairs 1898 by M. O'Rourke, new one 1933, additions 1952, replacement b. 2009 by Reed Constructions Aust. Pty Ltd, d. by D.W.P. Suters; ice works: Edwin Nelson Bell (till 1950) and W.E. Oldfield & Son; Jehovah's Witnesses C.; LDS (Mormon) C.; Liberal Catholic C.; lime-kilns; lock-up, proc. a gaol 1862, additions 1869, additions 1878 by John Kealman, re-roofed 1893 by H.N. Lander, additions and repairs 1896 by J. Jordan, demolished 1976; Lutheran C. (St John the Baptist) b. 1957–59; Macedonian Orthodox C. (St Ilija's) b. 1877 by Thomas Jordan as a Protestant hall, used by Salv. Army from 1884, bought 1966 by Macedonian community and o. 1969 as their church, demolished 1994, rebuilt 1996; mine (Valley Creek); monumental stone works (J.A. Bryant); PO: South Queanbeyan 1964, Queanbeyan 1836 (new one b. 1880 by John Kealman, repairs 1904 by Arthur Allen, additions and alterations 1907 by John Jordan, demolished and replaced 1972), West Queanbeyan 1947; police barracks 1838, replaced, new barracks b. 1876 by John Kealman, reused; pound (stock) 1839; Presb. C. (St Stephen's) b. 1872–74 by T. Priest and T. Jordan, d. by Alberto Dias Soares, re-roofed 1905 by Henry Lazarus; PS 1853, new one b. 1876 by John Kealman, closed and reused, demolished 1976, replacement b. 1976–78; quarry (CSR Readymix); rabbit freezing works (Curtis's); railway coal stage; railway engine shed 1896; railway turntable, 60 ft (18.3 m), removed from Nimmitabel; railway viaduct (laminated timber spandrel arch) 1887, steel Warren deck trusses substituted 1926, over Queanbeyan R.; 4 reservoirs; rifle range, rebuilt 1913; Rom. Cath. C.: St Gregory's (b. 1850 by Daniel McCloskey, d. by John Bell, extensions 1874, alterations 1897, renovated 1957, restored), St Raphael's 1956, fire 2012, Sacred Heart (Crestwood) 1957, new one 1981; RS: Letchworth 1926–56 and Queanbeyan 1887 (station b. by Joseph Jordan and G. Williams, refreshment rooms closed 1956, station restored 1994); sale-yards; Salv. Army C. 1887–1902, new ones 1927 and 1963; sawmills: Bill Hopkins and Len Donoghoe 1936 (burnt down and rebuilt 1951) and M.J. Goldsmith (fire 1953); schools: East Queanbeyan 1967, additions 1972, Jerrabomberra 2001, additions 2011, Karabar HS 1977, Queanbeyan primary 1864 (new one b. 1877 by Sanders Helman and Thomas Priest, additions 1891 by John Jordan, additions 1918, 1933, 1936, 1956, 1970, additions 1973 d. by Christopher Richard Johnson), Queanbeyan HS 1958, additions 1963, 1966, 1972, South Queanbeyan 1969, additions 1973 and 1976, West Queanbeyan 1958, additions 1964, 1967, 1975; sewerage 1938, augmentation 1986; snowstorms

1869, 1881, 1899; TC (a campus of Illawarra Institute of Technology), additions 2008 and 2012; tannery (Thomas Buttle); telegraph 1864; telephone: South Queanbeyan 1964 and West Queanbeyan 1927; TX 1906, automatic 1969; typhoid 1900; Ukrainian Catholic C. (St Michael's) b. 1963–67; Unit. C. 1994; water supply 1925; weir 1901, on Queanbeyan R.; Wes. Meth. C. 1860, renovations and repairs 1865, extended 1867 by Edward Oswald Evans and Thomas Bryant, reused; winery (Madew Wines) 1984; wool-scour and fellmongery (Oaks Fellmongery and Wool-Washing Works) estab. 1877 by John Bull, sold 1885 to George Tompsitt who expanded it into the Hazellbrook Wool-Scouring Works, Tannery and Wholesale Produce Warehouses, closed 1896; pop. *c.*50 (1838), 72 (1841), 208 (1846), 372 (1851), 504 (1856), 526 (1861), *c.*550 (1866), 682 (1871), 939 (1881), *c.*1,000 (1887), 1,262 (1891), *c.*1,425 (1895), 1,219 (1901), 1,408 (1911), 1,825 (1921), 4,019 (1933), 4,130 (1935), 4,150 (1938), *c.*4,500 (1941), 5,033 (1947), 7,310, (1954), 9,448 (1961), 12,515 (1966), 16,058 (1971), 18,538 (1976), 19,056 (1981), 21,850 (1986), 23,714 (1991), 25,689 (1996), 29,928 (2001), 34,084 (2006), 37,991 (2011). (See also Googong.)

Queen Charlotte's Vale (*Co. Bathurst*) see Perthville.

Queens Pinch (*Co. Wellington*) 32°44'S. 149°41'E., 17 km SE of Mudgee, on Meroo Ck; pop. 33 (1933).

Quialigo (*Co. Argyle*) 34°47'S. 149°45'E., 21 km S. of Goulburn; telephone 1918, TX (automatic) 1954.

Quiera (*Co. St Vincent*) 34°58'S. 150°10'E., 38 km S. of Bundanoon.

Quigley Estate (*Co. Northumberland*) see Teralba.

Quigtown (*Co. Westmoreland*) see Yerranderie.

Quinburra (*Co. Wellesley*) 37°08'S. 149°04'E., 29 km SW of Bombala; creamery (Bombala Co-op. Dairy Co.) b. 1897 by Thomas Moore, closed 1903; school (Upper Quinburra till *c.*1890) 1887–93 and reopened 1899 in new building b. by T. Stewart, closed 1908.

Quinine Park (*Co. Gregory*) 31°12'S. 147°11'E., 41 km N. of Nyngan, on Duck Ck; telephone 1907.

Quipolly (*Co. Buckland*) 31°25'S. 150°40'E., 8 km S. of Werris Creek; farming; Angl. C. (St Chad's); creamery (McLean's) 1897, closed 1898, bought 1899 by J.W. Croker; PO 1874; Rom. Cath. C. (St Michael's) 1885, new ones 1919 and 1928, defunct; RS 1879–1974; school 1880, new one b. 1881 by J. Clarke, closed 1930; storm 1899; telephone 1923; TX 1925, automatic 1954; pop. 262 (1901), 347 (1911), 165 (1933), 139 (1947), 111 (1954), 326 (2006).

Quipolly Creek (*Co. Buckland*) 31°26'S. 150°39'E., 9 km N. of Quirindi; farming; PO 1884; school 1881, buildings (removed from Temi) re-erected 1886 by Joseph P. Clarke, additions and repairs 1892 by W. Bryant, closed 1963; telephone 1916; TX 1925–74; pop. 53 (1933), 66 (1954), 69 (1961).

Quirindi (*Co. Buckland*) 31°30'S. 150°41'E., 52 km SW of Tamworth, on Jacob and Joseph Ck; settled *c.*1830 by George Loder, surveyed 1856 by Benjamin Charles Flide, town gaz. and first land sale 1856, thrived in 1880s, munic. proc. 1890; wheat in 1890s, dairying (declined in 1930s), maize, sorghum, lucerne, oats, soybeans, sunflowers, vegetables, fruit, cotton, sheep, cattle, pigs, poultry, honey; ambulance station (in remodelled council chambers) 1938; Angl. C. b. 1886 by Joseph P. Clarke, relocated 1915, reused, condemned 1938, new one (St Alban's) 1925 d. by Ronald Richardson; Assemblies of God C. (Harvest Christ.); bicycle works (Everett's) 1906; brickworks (Price's); bridges: one 1901 and one 1929 over Jacob and Joseph Ck, and one b. 1936 by Concreters Ltd, 129 ft (39.3 m), over Quirindi Ck; bushfire 1904; butter factories: Central (b. by I.J. Hill for William Pollock, bought 1906 by Hamilton York, bought 1911 by Charles Waters Lynch, bought 1913 by Thomas Blunt, bought 1917 by J.W. Moss, Scott and Garrard) and Quirindi Co-op. Dairy Co. Ltd 1894–1956; carriage-works: Cogan and Coleman, Federal (estab.

1882 by Cullen Bros, sold 1916 to Les Turner and became L.H. Turner & Co.), John Johns (taken over 1907 by David Moffat); caterpillar infestation 1940; cemeteries: general (1,904 graves 1870+) 1878 and lawn (1,098 plots), incl. columbarium; CH b. 1883 by Joseph P. Clarke, burnt down 1929, replacement b. 1931 by George Kidney, d. by Edward Henry Rembert; clock tower (war memorial) b. 1925–35, d. by P. Ranclaud; clothing factory 1946; cordial factories: W. Brierer (taken over 1904 by Walter G. Denham, sold 1910 to R.J. Harrison, operated as Harrison and Lunt, taken over 1914 by T.P. Tinson), George Chapple, Timothy Flanagan 1879 (sold 1914 to A.L. Weary, closed 1920); dengue fever 1926; droughts 1877, 1886, 1965; earth tremor 1950; FB 1913 (station b. 1922); fires 1901, 1910, 1927; floods 1883, 1889, 1890, 1910, 1920, 1941, 1949, 1955, 1984, 2000; flour mills: Darlington (o. 1875 by J.L. Tebbutt & Co., taken over 1887 by J.W. Tebbutt, bought 1895 by Thomas Meden, burnt down 1905), R. Gillespie, David Lawrence 1883, Quirindi Roller Flour Mills (estab. 1897 by Alexander McIntyre and Peter McIntosh, became McIntyre & Sons); 2 foot-bridges (incl. suspension one b. 1902, rebuilt 1955) over Quirindi Ck; freezing works: Curtis and Curtis 1913, John Davis & Sons 1926, Woolbrook Freezing Co. (taken over 1921 by Garratt Scandrett Freezing Companies Ltd); hospital (cottage) b. 1900 by G. Cole, d. by Charles Edward Kemmis, additions 1902, 1912, 1923, 1929, additions and alterations 1936 by John Jamieson, additions 1956, 1970, 1974, 1983; ice works (Quirindi Co-op. Dairy Co. Pty Ltd); Jehovah's Witnesses C. 1978; lock-up b. 1877 and 1898; monumental stone works; mouse plague 1888; PO 1858, new one b. 1884 by Joseph P. Clarke; pound (stock) 1858; powerhouse 1920–40; PS 1877, new ones b. 1885, 1898, 1963; reservoirs 1912, 1929, 1955; rifle range 1899; Rom. Cath. C. b. 1898 by William Price, d. by Alexander Leis, chancel and vestry added 1899, church demolished, new one (St Brigid's) b. 1935 by F. and R. Compton, d. by Peter Joseph Gannon; RS 1877, station b. by William and Charles Cains, closed, reused; sale-yards 1915; sawmills: Reuben Austin, George Dawson (taken over 1904 by Winson and English, fire 1910), Quirindi Timber Co. (estab. by Dave Lawrence, taken over by Robert Gillespie then Thomas Wyburn, George Winsor and Cecil Marshall); scarlet fever 1884; schools: primary 1877 (b. by Michael Burke, additions 1883 by J. Rixon, additions 1890 by G. Parr, additions 1899 by G.F. Cole, remodelled 1923 by A. Ede, new building b. 1935 by Wallace and McGee, additions 1966, 1979, 1982, major upgrade 1996) and HS 1954 (new one b. 1956 by A. Pinfold, additions 1962, 1969, 1973, 1979, additions 2013 by O'Donnell & Hanlon Pty Ltd); SD Adventist C. 1916, additions 1961; seed-cleaning works (R.J. Webster); sewage works b. 1937 by Charles Harris; silo 1933; tank works (W.J. Saunders); TC, became a campus of New England Institute in 1992, new one 2017 on new site d. by Brewster Hjorth Architects; telegraph 1877, new office b. 1884 by Joseph P. Clarke; trees (ornamental) planted in streets 1927; TX 1908, new one b. 1911 by W.J. Wooden, automatic 1982; typhoid 1884; Union C. 1876; Unit. C. (orig. Presb.) b. 1921 by D. M'Naughton & Sons, d. by Power and Adam, re-roofed 1955; waterworks b. 1911 by William Murdock, augmentation 1987; Wes. Meth. C. 1882, reused; wool-scours: Henshaw Jackson 1900 and Quirindi Wool Scouring Co. 1943 (became Quirindi Lucerne Mills, burnt down 1957); pop. *c.*250 (1866), 278 (1881), 1,139 (1891), *c.*1,500 (1895), 1,676 (1901), 2,752 (1911), 2,589 (1933), 2,628 (1947), 2,735 (1954), 2,790 (1961), 2,732 (1966), 2,876 (1971), 2,955 (1976), 2,851 (1981), 2,812 (1986), 2,830 (1991), 2,671 (1996), 2,540 (2001), 2,609 (2006), 2,580 (2011).

Quondong (*Co. Monteagle*) see Quandong.

Quondong (*Co. Yancowinna*) 32°09'S. 141°55'E., 46 km SE of Broken Hill; dust storm 1946; PO 1949–67; telephone 1947; TX 1963; pop. 31 (1933).

Quorrobolong (*Co. Northumberland*) 32°55'S. 151°22'E., 9 km E. of Paxton, on Cony Ck; farming; Angl. C. (Holy Advent) 1924; bridges: bridge over Sandy Ck and Forbes Bridge over Quorrobolong Ck; FB; hailstorm 1872; PO 1927; pound (stock) 1864; sawmills: Jack Graham (removed from Cedar Creek) and Forbes and Whiting; school 1865–68, reopened 1882, new building b. 1900 by T. and W. Cowan, repairs 1902 by C. Chapman, new school b. 1929 by C.M. Wallis, closed 1961; telephone 1922; TX 1927, automatic 1953; pop. 60 (1911), 156 (1933), 123 (1947), 106 (1954), 73 (1961), 545 (2006), 750 (2011).

R

Rabbit Flat (*Co. Vernon*) 31°01'S. 152°03'E., 41 km E. of Walcha, on Apsley R.

Rabbit Island (*Co. Northumberland*) see Mooney Mooney.

Raby (*Co. Oxley*) 31°35'S. 147°42'E., 18 km NW of Warren, on Crooked Ck; pop. 24 (1933).

Radnor (*Co. King*) 34°30'S. 149°04'E., 33 km E. of Boorowa; telephone 1925.

Ragill (*Co. Inglis*) see Kootingal.

Raglan (*Co. Roxburgh*) 33°26'S. 149°39'E., 7 km E. of Bathurst; village gaz. 1881; grazing and agric.; airport (Bathurst) o. 1942 as military airfield, o. 1946 as civil airfield, new buildings 1952 and 1964, runway rebuilt 1967; Angl. C. (St James's) 1873; Bapt. C. o. 1899 (in renovated building); brickworks; FB; pet food factory (Uncle Ben's of Aust.) 1977, new plant (Mars Petcare) 2015; PO 1873; Rom. Cath. C. (St Anthony's), closed and sold; RS 1873, new station b. 1890 on new site by Charles Palmer, closed; school 1874, new building b. 1889 by Payne and Milligan, d. by William Edmund Kemp, new school 1989; sewerage augmentation 1985; telegraph 1873; TX 1926, automatic 1967; water supply augmentation 1985; pop. 164 (1901), 103 (1911), 135 (1933), 110 (1947), 138 (1954), 136 (1961), 1,071 (2006), 1,081 (2011).

Railtown (*Co. Mossgiel*) see Ivanhoe.

Railway Camp (*Co. Northumberland*) see Woy Woy.

Railway Crossing (*Co. Inglis*) see Woolbrook.

Railway End (*Co. Wynyard*) see Tumut.

Railway Town (*Co. Yancowinna*) see Broken Hill.

Rainbar (*Co. Barrona*) see Janina.

Rainbow Flat (*Co. Gloucester*) 32°02'S. 152°29'E., 11 km S. of Taree, on Khappinghat Ck; also known as Stony Creek; bypassed by highway 1993; FB; quarry; telephone 1928; TX 1949–72; pop. 212 (2011).

Rainbow Reach (*Co. Dudley*) 30°55'S. 153°00'E., 5 km SW of South West Rocks, on Macleay R.; cheese factory 1916; flood 1870; PO 1871–1919; school 1869–1967; pop. 73 (1901), 117 (1911), 86 (1933), 61 (1954).

Rainville (*Co. Westmoreland*) 33°33'S. 149°48'E., 18 km N. of Oberon, on Sidmouth Valley Ck; flour mill (water-mill, St Boswell's) estab. 1836 by Alexander Kinghorne, jun., destroyed 1857, rebuilt, burnt down 1861; flood 1857.

Raleigh (*Co. Raleigh*) 30°27'S. 153°01'E., 5 km N. of Urunga, on Bellinger R.; Central Raleigh till 1911; village gaz. 1867, thrived 1911–15, bypassed by highway 1998; farming and dairying; Angl. C. (Prince of Peace) 1922; bridge (steel and concrete) b. 1933–35 by A. Goninan & Co., State Monier Pipe & Reinforced Concrete Works, and Gam and Jenkins, over Bellinger R.; butter factory and ice works (Raleigh Co-op. Butter Society Ltd) 1899, new one b. 1925 by John Dunton, taken over 1949 by Cow & Gate Pty Ltd, sold 1952 to Co-op. Dairy Assoc., taken over 1981 by Norco Co-op. Ltd; cemetery 1889; floods 1950 and 2009; PO 1899; punt 1907 (transferred from Repton), new one 1921, replaced with bridge 1935, across Bellinger R.; railway turntable, 60 ft (18.3 m); Rom. Cath. C. (St

Brigid's) 1884, replacement (St Joseph's) 1889, closed 1956, sold and demolished; RS 1915, station b. by Ernest Frederick Leggo; sale-yards 1975; sawmills: E.D. Pike & Co. Ltd 1910 and Smith and Allan (bought from Hudson); school (Central Raleigh till 1889) 1887; telephone 1905; winery 1983, taken over 1989 by Lavinia Dingle; pop. 139 (1901), 541 (1911), 217 (1933), 242 (1947), 307 (1954), 282 (1961), 550 (2011).

Raleigh East (*Co. Raleigh*) see Repton.

Ralvona (*Co. Goulburn*) 35°41'S. 147°14'E., 9 km NW of Holbrook, on Willow Bend Ck; RS 1902–61.

Ramornie (*Co. Fitzroy*) 29°39'S. 152°48'E., 14 km W. of Grafton, on Orara R.; settled 1839 by John Dobie; boiling-down works (Charles Grant Tindal); bridge (low-level timber) 1937, replacement (Tindal Bridge, steel and concrete) fabricated by Arcos Industries Pty Ltd, erected 1966 by John Holland (Constructions) Pty Ltd, d. by Gordon Bull & Associates, 735 ft (224 m), over Orara R.; cemetery (burials 1871–1931); meat works (Aust. Meat Preserving Co. Ltd, produced meat, tallow, beef extract, hides, butterine, horns, bones, bone dust) estab. 1866 by Charles Grant Tindal, plant enlarged 1894, closed 1914, sold 1915 to Kensington Meat Preserving Co., closed 1923, demolished; PO 1892–1927; punt across Orara R.; school 1872–1927; telephone 1894; TX 1917–32; pop. 337 (1901), 250 (1911), 39 (1933), 53 (1947), 233 (2006), 332 (2011).

Rampsbeck (*Co. Clarke*) 30°17'S. 152°08'E., 45 km E. of Guyra, on Copes Ck.

Ramsgate (*Co. Northumberland*) see Wyee Point.

Rand (*Co. Hume*) 35°36'S. 146°35'E., 42 km W. of Henty, on Billabong Ck; wheat; airfield; Angl. C. (St Matthew's) 1960; bridge (Townsend Bridge) 1953, over Billabong Ck; flood 2010; PO 1926; Presb. C. (Scots) 1969; PS 1928, new one 1969; quarry; 2 reservoirs (elevated, steel); Rom. Cath. C. (St Francis Xavier's) b. 1936 by Jack Barrie, jun., d. by H.L. Hanlon, closed, sold 2017, reused; RS 1920–75; sale-yards (Younghusband Ltd) 1934; sawmill; school 1912, new school b. 1926 by Haynes and Dixon, additions 1960; silo 1928; telephone 1925; TX 1925, automatic 1952; Union C. b. 1926 by Chitts; Unit. C., closed, sold and reused; water reticulation 1969; pop. 210 (1933), 207 (1947), 296 (1954), 106 (1961), 208 (2006).

Ranelagh (*Co. Camden*) see St Anthonys.

Rangari (*Co. Nandewar*) 30°41'S. 150°23'E., 33 km E. of Boggabri; FB; school 1957–65; pop. 85 (1911), 22 (1933).

Rangemore (*Co. Wakool*) 35°19'S. 144°19'E., 38 km NE of Barham; farming and grazing; PO 1907; telephone 1909; TX 1910–45.

Rangers Valley (*Co. Gough*) 29°31'S. 151°44'E., 23 km N. of Glen Innes, on Severn R.

Rankin Park (*Co. Northumberland*) see Elermore Vale.

Rankins Springs (*Co. Cooper*) 33°50'S. 146°16'E., 54 km N. of Griffith; estab. *c.*1870, moved *c.*1923 about 10 km to new site, village gaz. and first land sale 1925; gold, tin (alluvial), wheat, oats, beef, wool; Angl. C. (St Luke's) 1956; brickworks (W. Mannering); cemetery; drought 1967–68; electricity 1965; FB; fires 1880 and 1939; mouse plague 1970; PO 1875; Presb. C.; PS 1928–44; railway coal stage, removed 1983; railway engine shed 1922, removed from Tullamore; railway turntable 1923, 60 ft (18.3 m), closed; Rom. Cath. C. (St Kevin of Glendalough) 1955; RS 1923, station removed 1986; sale-yards 1937; sawmill (M. Michelson); school 1931 b. by A.S. Fairweather, additions 1940 and 1966; silo 1964; telephone 1925; TX 1926; Unit. C. 1965; water reticulation 1969, augmentation 1981; pop. 260 (1933), 206 (1947), 259 (1954), 155 (1961), *c.*300 (1987), 112 (2001), 230 (2006), 299 (2011).

Rannock (*Co. Bourke*) 34°38'S. 147°15'E., 21 km N. of Coolamon; Maxton till 1912; farming; cemetery; PO 1913; school 1900 b. by Pike and Searle, closed 1968; TX 1922, automatic 1970; Union C.; water supply augmentation 1989; pop. 203 (1911), 235 (1933), 142 (1947), 145 (1954), 133 (1961), 105 (2006).

Rannock (*Co. Bourke*) see also Maxton.

Rappville (*Co. Richmond*) 29°05'S. 152°57'E., 27 km S. of Casino, on Nandabah Ck; village gaz. 1911, lots auctioned 1912; timber, tea-tree oil, cattle, farming, dairying; Angl. C. (St John the Evangelist) 1910, remodelled 1913; boiling-down works (C.T. White) 1910; bridge over Nandabah Ck; bushfire 1936; PO 1908, burnt down 1918; Presb. C. 1910; PS 1908; railway bridge (timber truss) 1905, replaced 1926, destroyed 2019, over Myrtle Ck; RS (Murray's Siding till 1907) 1905–76; sawmills: Murray Bros 1905, Rappville Timber Co. Ltd (acquired 1914 by Noble Bros Ltd), Tarmac Sawmilling Pty Ltd, burnt down 2019; school 1908, additions 1966 and 2009; tea-tree oil still, derelict; telephone 1907; trees (ornamental) planted in streets 1938; TX 1916, automatic 1975; pop. 288 (1911), 162 (1933), 200 (1947), 241 (1954), 208 (1961), 115 (2001), 261 (2006), 309 (2011).

Raspberry Gully (*Co. Northumberland*) see Charlestown.

Raspberry Junction (*Co. Hunter*) 32°42'S. 150°41'E., 46 km W. of Singleton.

Rathbones Point (*Co. Sandon*) 30°42'S. 152°02'E., 41 km SE of Armidale, on Chandler R.; mine (Blue Slate).

Rathmines (*Co. Northumberland*) 33°03'S. 151°36'E., 3 km S. of Toronto, on Kilaben Bay; (incl. Balmoral estab. 1882 and Fishing Point); settled *c.*1840 by Edward Norton Hely, subdivisions 1882 and 1920; bushfire 1940; flying-boat base 1939, additions 1940 by John Grant & Sons Pty Ltd, closed and abandoned 1952, sold 1963; 3 jetties; Meth. C. 1940; PO: Fishing Point 1953 and Rathmines 1940, burnt down 1957; quarry; school 1951, additions 1960, 1995, 2010; telephone: Fishing Point 1952 and Rathmines 1940; TX 1940, automatic 1955; pop. 45 (1933), 235 (1947), 314 (1954), 1,940 (2011).

Rats Castle (*Co. Wellington*) 32°29'S. 149°27'E., 15 km S. of Gulgong; goldmining (alluvial).

Rattly Ground (*Co. Durham*) 32°12'S. 151°16'E., 51 km NW of Dungog.

Ravensdale (*Co. Northumberland*) 33°10'S. 151°19'E., 17 km W. of Wyee, on Wyong R.; farming; PO 1927; school 1896, demolished and replaced 1919, burnt down and replaced, new one 1953, closed 1956; telephone 1921; pop. 79 (1901), 108 (1933), 66 (1947).

Ravensfield (*Co. Northumberland*) 32°45'S. 151°30'E., 5 km W. of Maitland; flood 1867; quarry (Thomas Browne).

Ravensworth (*Co. Durham*) 32°27'S. 151°04'E., 17 km NW of Singleton, on Bowmans Ck; Camberwell Railway Station till 1876; subdivided 1889 and 1953+; farming and dairying; coalmines: Foybrook No. 1 (Clutha Development Pty Ltd), Foybrook Open-Cut (Clutha Development Pty Ltd), Howick Open-Cut (Clutha Development Pty Ltd), Liddell (Coal & Allied Industries Ltd, now Glencore Coal Pty Ltd), Ravensworth No. 2 Open-Cut (Costain Aust. Ltd); landslip 1951; PO 1876, damaged 1916; Rom. Cath. C. (St Francis of Assisi) 1926, closed 1976, sold, derelict; RS (Camberwell till 1876) 1869–1975; school 1880 b. by J. Pritchard, additions 1883 by D. Gardiner, re-roofed and renovated 1913, derelict, new one 1971, closed 1986; storm 1916; telegraph 1879; telephone 1914; TX 1918, automatic 1953; pop. *c.*100 (1866), 150 (1901), 138 (1911), 158 (1933), 113 (1947), 191 (1954), 185 (1961), 200 (2006).

Ravine (*Co. Selwyn*) 35°48'S. 148°23'E., 38 km SE of Batlow, on Yarrangobilly R.; estab. 1900–1 to service Lobs Hole mines; grazing; cemetery; PO 1907; PS 1909–16; school (Lobbs Hole till 1910) 1909–21; telephone 1907; pop. 127 (1911).

Ravine Bridge (*Co. Cook*) see Linden.

Rawden Vale (*Co. Macquarie*) see Rawdon Vale.

Rawdon (*Co. Phillip*) 32°46'S. 150°03'E., 8 km E. of Rylstone, on Coxs Ck.

Rawdon Island (*Co. Macquarie*) 31°25'S. 152°47'E., 6 km NE of Wauchope, in Hastings R.; farming; Angl. C. (St Paul's) b. 1906 by T. Fowler and W. Freeman, closed, derelict, sold 2015, restored and reused; floods 1864 and 1870; foot-bridge (suspension) 1937, to Hursley, over Hastings R.; PO 1881, new one

b. 1915; punt across Hastings R.; Rom. Cath. C. (St Joseph's) 1869, removed from Little Rawdon Island, renovations 1902, additions and renovations 1937, and graveyard, church moved 1976 to Wauchope; school 1880, new buildings 1882, additions and repairs 1898 by G. Waring, closed 1976, moved and reused; telephone 1901; TX 1949–69; Wes. Meth. C. 1880; wharf 1897; pop. 143 (1901), 140 (1911), 140 (1933), 117 (1947), 126 (1954), 88 (1961).

Rawdon Island North (*Co. Macquarie*) see Little Rawdon Island.

Rawdon Vale (*Co. Gloucester*) 32°00'S. 151°42'E., 25 km W. of Gloucester, on Kerripit R.; Rawden Vale till 1909; estab. 1855; mining (gold rush 1897), livestock, wheat, maize, arrowroot meal; PO 1877; quarry; telephone 1913; TX 1914, automatic 1973; pop. 60 (1911), 53 (1933), 58 (1961).

Rawdon Villa (*Co. Macquarie*) see Little Rawdon Island.

Rawleys Lake (*Co. Wakool*) 34°53'S. 144°04'E., 81 km SW of Hay.

Raworth (*Co. Northumberland*) 32°44'S. 151°37'E., 5 km E. of Maitland, on Hunter R.; (incl. Pitnacree); agric.; bridge b. 1863–66 by Francis Bell, between Pitnacree and Lorn, demolished 1962, new one (Harry Boyle Bridge) 2010, over Hunter R.; earth tremor 1868; floods 1870, 1874, 1893, 1895, 1898, 1951 (changed course of River); gale 1905; RS, closed 1953; toll-gate; pop. 64 (1901), 64 (1911), 163 (1933), 166 (1947), 1,225 (2011).

Rawson (*Co. Macquarie*) 31°52'S. 152°38'E., 6 km W. of Harrington, on Cattai Ck; formerly Rawson River; school (Cattai Creek till 1910) 1886–1925 and 1957–72; pop. 27 (1933).

Rawson River (*Co. Macquarie*) see Rawson.

Rawsonville (*Co. Lincoln*) 32°10'S. 148°29'E., 17 km NW of Dubbo; Belarbigill till 1903; farming; Angl. C. 1875, new one (St James's) 1911; cemetery 1881; mouse plague 1922; PO 1883; school (Belarbigill till 1906) 1880–85 and 1895–1921; TX (automatic) 1965; pop. 200 (1901), 235 (1911), 93 (1933), 64 (1961).

Raymond Terrace (*Co. Gloucester*) 32°46'S. 151°45'E., 19 km N. of Newcastle, on Hunter R.; (incl. East Raymond Terrace, Ferodale submerged under Grahamstown Lake, Irrawang, Kinross Gardens, Lakeside Village); disc. 1801 by Lieut. Col. William Paterson et al., surveyed 1835 by George Boyle White, site reserved by Henry Dangar, village gaz. 1837, first land sales 1838, designated as chief town of the county, munic. proc. 1884, bypassed by highway 1998; river port 1840s–1920s, shipbuilding 1840s+, olives 1848+, wine *c.*1828–*c.*1900, wheat till 1860s, ironstone till 1914, maize, millet, lucerne, fruit, onions, dairying, cattle, prawns, particle board 1939+, mineral sand mining 1967+; ambulance station; Angl. C. (temporary one) 1841, reused, new one (St John the Evangelist) b. 1862 by Robert Carnell, d. by Edmund Thomas Blacket, bell-cote added later, church partly demolished 1965, extensions and alterations 1975 by N. Adamthwaite, d. by Brian Suters, chancel rebuilt, and lawn cemetery (263 plots 1958+); Apostolic C. (Port Stephens); Assemblies of God C. (Hunter Christ. Life); Bapt. C., closed, sold 2002, reused; brewery (Francis Haviland) 1860–62; bridge (Fitzgerald Bridge) to Nelsons Plains, b. 1965 by John Holland (Constructions) Pty Ltd, d. by Macdonald, Wagner and Priddle, concrete, 864 ft (263.3 m), over Williams R.; broom factory (Alfred Charles Pratt) 1882, burnt down 1889; bushfires 1939 and 1951; butter factory (Raymond Terrace Co-op. Dairy & Produce Co. Ltd, became Hunter Valley Co-op. Dairy Co. Ltd) b. 1903 by Andrew Burg, d. by James Warren Scobie, (produced milk and cheese 1916+), moved 1927 to Hexham, amalgamated with Muswellbrook Co-op. Dairy Co. Ltd 1932; cannery (fish) 1931; carriage-works: Federal Coach Factory (J.M. Feeney) and Smith's, destroyed 1905; caterpillar infestation 1899; cemeteries: Pioneer Hill (1,099 graves 1840+) 1863 and general (1,522 graves 1917+), incl. columbarium; CH b. 1839–41, d. by Mortimer William Lewis, extended 1984, renovated 2015; Christ. Brethren Assemblies C. (Community) 2003; clock tower 1955; earth tremor 1842; FB 1937 (station b. 1959, new one b. 2008 by R.T. Parker Pty Ltd); floods 1851, 1857, 1864, 1867, 1874, 1875, 1893, 1913, 1946, 1949, 1955, 2005, 2007, 2015, 2016; flour mills: Houlding's 1840, demolished, John Portus, sen. 1854 (closed 1867, acquired 1874 by Thomas Adam & Son and converted to steam sawmill), Simpson's 1848; Free Presb. C. b. 1865 by Frank Bowden, replaced (St Andrew's) 1905; gale 1905; grasshopper infestation 1953; hailstorms 1868, 2004, 2005; hurricane 1928; Jehovah's Witnesses C.; joinery (Joseph George White); lock-up 1846, (second) b. 1877 by William Dart, (third) b. 1907 by Richard Partridge-Wall; monumental stone works (Joseph John Edstein) 1896; PO: East Raymond Terrace 1961, Ferodale 1927, Raymond Terrace 1834 (new one b. 1880 by W.H. Galbraith, d. by James Johnstone Barnet, closed 1995, reused); pottery (James King, Irrawang) 1833–38 and 1843–56; pound (stock) 1865; powder magazine b. by Muirhead; Presb. C. (Hunter); PS 1840, new one b. 1877 by William Dart, repairs 1878 by P. Larson, unroofed 1905, cell block attached 1949, police station alterations and renovation 1971, new one b. 2011 by Lahey Constructions Pty Ltd; punts: one 1871 across Hunter R. and one to Nelsons Plains across Williams R.; reservoir, 306,000 gal. (1,391.1 kl); Rom. Cath. C. (St Brigid's) b. 1862 by Mair, M'Leod and M'Kenzie, d. by William Munro, renovated 1981; sawmills: Henry Berry & Sons, Blackbrook Steam Sawmill (o. 1874 by Thomas Adam & Son in converted flour mill, reused 1887), James Buckman 1876, Eldon Sawmills Pty Ltd, John Shadrach Hart (boiler explosion 1882 killed man, closed 1886), N. McLellan; scarlet fever 1878; schools: Grahamstown 1994, Irrawang primary 1968, new school 1969, additions 1976 and 2010, Irrawang HS 1983, additions 1987, Raymond Terrace primary 1858, additions 1883 by G. Dobbins, new buildings b. 1936 by Pickles and McIlroy, new building b. 1955 by Tuscan Building Co. Pty Ltd, additions 1966 and 2007; swamp drainage works (Grahamstown) completed 1911 by Pepper and Moy; tannery (W.E. Shaw); telegraph 1868, new office b. 1880 by W.H. Galbraith, d. by James Johnstone Barnet, closed 1995; telephone: East Raymond Terrace 1961 and Ferodale 1927; TX: Ferodale 1935 and Raymond Terrace 1910, automatic 1961; typhoid 1908; Unit. C. (Peace Memorial, orig. Meth.) b. 1921 by G.W. Vallender, d. by Benjamin George Pearce; water reticulation 1928; Wes. Meth. C. b. 1851–54, replaced 1877 by Thomas Adams; wharves; winery (Irrawang) estab. 1832 by James King, o. 1836, demolished; pop. 364 (1841), 262 (1846), 313 (1851), 551 (1856), 535 (1861), 535 (1871), 694 (1881), 899 (1891), *c.*900 (1895), 823 (1901), 1,061 (1911), 1,004 (1933), 1,450 (1947), 2,830 (1954), 3,962 (1961), 4,955 (1966), 6,001 (1971), 6,989 (1976), 7,548 (1981), 8,793 (1986), 11,159 (1991), 12,332 (1996), 12,514 (2001), 12,700 (2006), 13,217 (2011).

Raymond Terrace (*Co. Gloucester*) see also Heatherbrae.

Razorback (*Co. Camden*) 34°09'S. 150°40'E., 5 km NE of Picton; (incl. Rofe Estate); bridges: one over Apps Ck and one over Racecourse Ck; cemetery; pop. 90 (1901), 36 (1933), 105 (1947), 94 (1954), 79 (1961), 536 (2001), 638 (2006), 964 (2011).

Razorback (*Co. Rous*) 28°42'S. 153°36'E., 8 km E. of Bangalow.

Razorback (*Co. Roxburgh*) 33°02'S. 149°47'E., 27 km SW of Kandos, on Oaky Ck; pop. 31 (1933).

Redbank (*Co. Arrawatta*) 29°25'S. 150°58'E., 16 km SW of Ashford.

Redbank (*Co. Bligh*) 32°01'S. 149°25'E., 2 km NE of Dunedoo.

Redbank (*Co. Brisbane*) 32°04'S. 150°49'E., 4 km SW of Scone, on Dart Brook; surveyed 1826, largely abandoned by 1840; CH 1832; hospital 1834.

Redbank (*Co. Burnett*) 29°04'S. 150°20'E., 50 km S. of Boggabilla.

Redbank (*Co. Cadell*) see Mathoura.

Redbank (*Co. Camden*) see Picton and Thirlmere.

Redbank (*Co. Georgiana*) 34°25'S. 149°35'E., 11 km NE of Crookwell, on Cliffords Ck; pop. 24 (1933).

Redbank (*Co. Gloucester*) see Pampoolah.

Redbank (*Co. Macquarie*) 31°26'S. 152°44'E., 2 km N. of Wauchope; agric.; Wes. Meth. C.; pop. *c.*170 (1866), 53 (1933), 62 (1947), 66 (1954), 55 (1961), 393 (2011).

Redbank (*Co. Nicholson*) see Hillston.

Redbank (*Co. St Vincent*) see Araluen.

Redbank (*Co. Wellington*) 32°37'S. 149°35'E., 4 km S. of Mudgee, on Redbank Ck; brickworks (Kenny's, incl. 2 Scotch kilns), closed; dam 1898, failed, disused 1902, on Redbank Ck; 3 quarries; sawmill 1959; pop. 189 (1911), 118 (1954).

Redbank (*Co. Wellington*) see also Mudgee.

Red Bend (*Co. Forbes*) 33°25'S. 148°02'E., 5 km SE of Forbes; RS 1918–74; silo.

Redbournberry (*Co. Northumberland*) see Singleton.

Redbridge (*Co. Harden*) 34°29'S. 148°16'E., 11 km NW of Murrumburrah, on Demondrille Ck; Demondrille till 1900; farming and grazing; mines: Archdeacon, Demondrille Creek, Rocky Hill, Wombat Creek, Whybrow's; PO 1885; school (Demondrille till 1902) 1880–1950; telephone 1924; TX 1939–64; pop. 117 (1911), 96 (1933).

Red Cutting (*Co. Cook*) 33°35'S. 150°42'E., 2 km W. of North Richmond, on Redbank Ck; RS 1928–52.

Red Cutting (*Co. Rous*) 28°21'S. 153°20'E., 7 km W. of Murwillumbah, on Oxley R.

Reddalls Valley (*Co. Goulburn*) 35°49'S. 147°21'E., 12 km S. of Holbrook, on Reddall Ck; earth tremor 2003.

Reddestone (*Co. Gough*) 29°38'S. 151°41'E., 12 km NW of Glen Innes, on Reddestone Ck; farming and grazing; FB; 7 mines (sapphires); school (Clairvaulx till 1896) 1881–1916 and 1922–27; telephone 1925; TX 1925, automatic 1952; pop. 64 (1901), 71 (1911), 128 (1933), 111 (1947), 87 (1954), 69 (1961).

Redground (*Co. Georgiana*) 34°23'S. 149°28'E., 9 km N. of Crookwell; mining (iron) and potatoes; bushfire 1914; mine (Aust. Iron & Steel Ltd) 1941–45; school 1884–87; telephone 1923; TX 1932–66; pop. 59 (1901), 68 (1911), 60 (1947).

Red Gums (*Co. Gloucester*) 32°30'S. 151°58'E., 23 km SE of Dungog, on Karuah R. aeroplane crash (pilot killed) 1952.

Red Head (*Co. Gloucester*) see Hallidays Point.

Redhead (*Co. Northumberland*) 33°01'S. 151°43'E., 6 km NE of Belmont, on Tasman Sea; settled *c.*1865 by James Parker, village gaz. 1881, subdivided 1894, thrived 1949; orig. orchards, then coalmining, mineral sand mining in 1960s; Angl. C. (Holy Name); bushfires 1946, 1949, 1951, 1952, 2013; collieries: Lambton (o. 1887 as Ryhope by Scottish Aust. Mining Co., renamed Durham in 1888, renamed Lambton No. 2 in 1898, renamed Lambton B in 1898, fire 1907 killed 19 horses, strike 1916–19, renamed 1924, closed 1928, acquired 1932 by BHP, reopened 1935, strikes 1944, 1949, 1950, man killed 1951, modernised 1961, sold 1989 to Pacific Copper, taken over 1990 by FAI Mining Group, closed 1991, largely razed 1993, upcast pit-head restored 1995) and Redhead (o. 1889 by Redhead Coal Co., closed 1891, reopened 1903 as Ocean Colliery, bought 1904 by T. Cowlishaw and renamed Burwood Extended, strikes 1908 and 1917, taken over 1920 by Redhead Colliery Co. Ltd and renamed, strike 1925, explosion 1926 killed 5, closed 1928, bought 1932 by BHP from Scottish Aust. Mining Co.); earth tremor 1939; Meth. C. 1906; mineral sand mining plant (removed from Coffs Harbour) 1958; PO 1907; Presb. C. (St Philip's) 1923; railway (colliery); Rom. Cath. C. (St John Vianney) b. 1938 by Stan Ross; RS: Redhead 1916, station relocated 1925, closed 1971 and South Redhead 1925–28; school 1908, new one b. 1911 by E. Knowles, additions 1956, 1961, 1966, additions 2010 by RTC Group; sewerage 1964, augmentation 1988; telephone 1911; water supply 1929; pop. 119 (1911), 331 (1933), 424 (1947), 3,337 (2006), 3,453 (2011).

Red Head (*Co. St Vincent*) see Bendalong.

Redhead (*Co. St Vincent*) see Kioloa.

Red Hill (*Co. Ashburnham*) 33°11'S. 148°34'E., 13 km W. of Manildra; quarry; Wes. Meth. C. 1895; pop. 63 (1911), 20 (1933).

Red Hill (*Co. Buccleuch*) 35°05'S. 148°23'E., 25 km E. of Gundagai, on Adjungbilly Ck; pop. 20 (1933).

Red Hill (*Co. Camden*) 34°40'S. 150°26'E., 13 km E. of Bundanoon.

Red Hill (*Co. Darling*) 30°30'S. 150°39'E., 14 km S. of Barraba.

Red Hill (*Co. Fitzroy*) 30°17'S. 153°04'E., 4 km W. of Coffs Harbour; reservoirs; pop. 288 (1947), 68 (1961).

Red Hill (*Co. Gloucester*) 32°23'S. 152°21'E., 14 km E. of Bulahdelah.

Red Hill (*Co. Macquarie*) 31°03'S. 152°54'E., 8 km NE of Kempsey; pop. 27 (1933), 50 (1954).

Red Hill (*Co. Murray*) 35°10'S. 149°40'E., 22 km NE of Bungendore.

Red Hill (*Co. Oxley*) 31°43'S. 147°46'E., 7 km W. of Warren.

Red Hill (*Co. Wellington*) 32°39'S. 149°00'E., 11 km SE of Wellington; estab. as railway construction camp; gold and silver; mine (McDowells or Old Paint) 1936–37; PO 1878–80; pop. 288 (1947).

Red Hill (*Co. Wellington*) see also Dripstone.

Red Hill (*Co. Wynyard*) see Wagga Wagga.

Redlands (*Co. Hume*) 35°55'S. 146°19'E., 11 km NW of Corowa; goldmining 1861+ and farming; FB; PO 1927–30; school 1878–90 and 1898–1927; stamper battery (8 head); pop. 112 (1901), 170 (1911), 70 (1933), 81 (1947).

Redlands Hills (*Co. Hume*) 35°56'S. 146°20'E., 9 km NW of Corowa.

Redman Vale (*Co. Hunter*) 32°32'S. 150°55'E., 26 km SE of Denman; Rom. Cath. C. and graveyard.

Redpatch Point (*Co. Gloucester*) see Nelson Bay.

Red Point (*Co. Camden*) see Port Kembla.

Red Range (*Co. Gough*) 29°46'S. 151°54'E., 16 km E. of Glen Innes, on Rocky Ck; maize, oats, dairying, grazing; butter factory (Red Range Co-op. Dairy Co. Ltd) 1910 d. by Wildridge and Sinclair; cemetery (143 graves 1890+); electricity 1955; hailstorms 1895 and 1928; PO 1881; rifle range, repairs 1914; sawmills: Marshall Bros 1905 and E.A. Potter; school 1880, new one b. 1886 by George Arnall, extensions 1914, additions 2010; telephone 1910; TX 1915, automatic 1952; Union C. 1887; pop. 391 (1901), 342 (1911), 363 (1933), 442 (1947), 297 (1954), 194 (1961), 249 (2006), 606 (2011).

Red Ridge (*Co. Richmond*) 29°00'S. 153°06'E., 16 km SE of Casino.

Red Rock (*Co. Arrawatta*) 29°17'S. 151°13'E., 14 km E. of Ashford.

Red Rock (*Co. Buller*) 28°50'S. 152°19'E., 37 km NE of Tenterfield, on Crooked Ck; mines (copper and gold); PO 1887–1910.

Red Rock (*Co. Fitzroy*) 29°59'S. 153°14'E., 9 km N. of Arrawarra, on Coral Sea; hailstorm 2015; PO 1947; telephone 1927; tornado 2011; TX 1948, automatic 1971; pop. 89 (1947), 65 (1954), 58 (1961), 262 (1991), 298 (1996), 291 (2001), 274 (2006), 310 (2011).

Red Rocks (*Co. Camden*) 34°46'S. 150°31'E., 15 km NW of Nowra.

Reedy Camp Hole (*Co. Arrawatta*) 29°23'S. 151°17'E., 20 km E. of Ashford, on Pindari Dam.

Reedy Creek (*Co. Ashburnham*) 33°15'S. 148°30'E., 24 km NE of Eugowra, on Reedy Ck; drought 1981–82; FB 1959; Meth. C. b. 1902 by Watts (became Presb., then Angl.); pop. 103 (1933).

Reedy Creek (*Co. Burnett*) see Delungra.

Reedy Creek (*Co. Durham*) 32°29'S. 151°20'E., 18 km NE of Singleton, on Reedy Ck; Angl. C. 1871, demolished, replacement (St John the Baptist) 1908 d. by J.W. Manson; cemetery; Wes. Meth. C. 1880; pop. 108 (1901), 84 (1911), 74 (1933), 74 (1947), 69 (1954), 62 (1961), 397 (2011).

Reedy Creek (*Co. Phillip*) 32°42'S. 150°02'E., 11 km N. of Rylstone; pop. 62 (1911).

Reedy Flat (*Co. Wynyard*) see Batlow.

Reedy Swamp (*Co. Auckland*) 36°41'S. 149°52'E., 3 km SE of Bega, on Bega R.

Reefton (*Co. Bland*) 34°15'S. 147°26'E., 24 km N. of Temora; estab. 1894; goldmining 1894+ and farming; cyanide plants; mines: Pioneer or Enterprise (Storm and Lauder 1894 and S. Shepherd 1934–35) and Pride of Reefton or Sydney 1928–41; PO 1894, burnt down 1906, rebuilt, burnt down again 1914, rebuilt, burnt down again 1968; PS 1895–1905; RS 1903–75; school 1894–1971; silo 1920; stamper battery (10 head) 1896; TX 1921–78; pop. *c.*60 (1903), 162 (1911), 146 (1933), 124 (1947), 89 (1954), 86 (1961), 132 (2006).

Regatta Point (*Co. Dampier*) 36°22'S. 150°04'E., 7 km N. of Bermagui, on Wallaga Lake.

Reidsdale (*Co. St Vincent*) 35°34'S. 149°51'E., 15 km S. of Braidwood; also formerly known as Irish Corner or The Corner; goldmining (alluvial, disc. 1851), grazing, farming; Angl. C., damaged 1874; bridge (M'Mahon's Bridge) b. 1901 by Thomas Lee, jun. and R. Scarff, over Reidsdale Ck; bushfires 1918 and 1933; butter factories: J.J. Barrett 1894, Feehan and Gilligan, W.J. Maher; cemetery (*c.*60 burials 1852+, incl. 11 graves); cheese factory estab. 1913 by J.M. Hyndes, new one (Reidsdale Co-op. Dairy Co. Ltd) 1920, condemned, replaced 1927; fire 1938; hailstorms 1874 and 1917; PO 1867–1971; Rom. Cath. C. (St Bernard's) 1851, damaged 1874, new one 1875, closed, sold 2007; sawmills: Federal (bought by Wilder and Daniels from George Crandell) and Tippet's (bought by Donald McDonald); school 1883–1921; telephone 1907; TX 1916, automatic 1979; Union C. 1847, demolished; pop. 148 (1901), 151 (1911), 92 (1933), 50 (1947), 63 (1954), 51 (1961).

Reid's Flat (*Co. Beresford*) see Bunyan.

Reids Flat (*Co. King*) 34°08'S. 149°01'E., 43 km NE of Boorowa, on Grahams Ck; surveyed 1869, village gaz. 1871 as Numby, subdivided by Joseph Witter Allworth and first lots sold 1872; mining, wool, wheat, maize, oats, hay, hort., orchards; bridge b. 1936 by E. Selmes, d. by Dowden, 132 ft (40.2 m), damaged 1961, replaced 1965 by Pearson Bridge Pty Ltd, over Lachlan R.; bushfires 1929, 1944, 1964, 1975; cemetery 1899; electricity 1956; FB 1930; floods 1852, 1853, 1864, 1870, 1896, 1900, 1911, 1916, 1922, 1931, 1952, 1961, 1974, 1984; mines: James Marks (estab. 1911, closed, reopened 1937 by Marks Wolfram Ltd, closed 1943, reopened 1952 by Max Jezernick and Joe Adams) and Taylor and Sligar; PO 1859, destroyed 1870; pound (stock) 1871; PS 1886–1921 and 1929–36; Rom. Cath. C. (St John's) b. 1913 by Gerald Francis Murphy, d. by William John Monks, closed 1968, reopened, closed again, sold, demolished 1987; sale-yards; school 1930–2014, sold 2016; snow 1948; telephone 1907; TX 1912, new switchboard 1927, automatic 1979; Union C. b. 1907 by Garry Murphy & Sons, restored 2011; pop. 74 (1891), 59 (1901), 145 (1911), 117 (1933), 157 (1947), 185 (1954), 175 (1961).

Reidtown (*Co. Camden*) see Fairy Meadow.

Reka (*Co. Wynyard*) 35°17'S. 148°07'E., 11 km W. of Tumut; RS 1906–71.

Remep (*Co. Pottinger*) 31°30'S. 149°54'E., 38 km N. of Coolah; RS 1934–64.

Rendezvous Point (*Co. St Vincent*) see Mossy Point.

Rennie (*Co. Denison*) 35°49'S. 146°08'E., 23 km NE of Mulwala; village gaz. 1933; electricity 1952; PO 1937, burnt down 1938; RS (Victorian railway); school 1957–72; telephone 1938; TX 1938, automatic 1967; pop. 89 (1947), 106 (1954), 86 (1961).

Reno (*Co. Clarendon*) 35°01'S. 148°02'E., 9 km NW of Gundagai, on Back Station Ck; village gaz. 1900, abandoned *c.*1903; mining (gold disc. 1894 by Edward Battye) till *c.*1903; mines: Bushman's Daughter, Kangaroo Reef, Prince of Wales (sold 1896 by Edward Battye to Howell and Davis), Rice and Robinson; PO 1898–1930; PS 1899–1906; Rom. Cath. C. (Sacred Heart) b. 1899 by Egan; school 1900–14; stamper batteries: 10 head 1898 and 30 head (Prince of Wales); telegraph 1900; Union C. 1900 (building removed from Gundagai and reused), demolished; pop. 410 (1901), 53 (1933).

Renwick (*Co. Camden*) see Mittagong.

Repentance Creek (*Co. Rous*) 28°39'S. 153°25'E., 13 km SW of Mullumbimby, on Coopers Ck; school 1905 b. by H.H. Hicks, closed 1964; pop. 52 (1947).

Repton (*Co. Raleigh*) 30°26'S. 153°01'E., 6 km N. of Urunga, on Bellinger R.; Raleigh East till 1911; thrived 1911–15, bypassed by highway 1950; timber and farming; abattoir (Perry's); bushfire 1952; cemetery; FB; PO 1877; punt (manual) 1877–1907, across Bellinger R.; railway bridge (steel truss) 1915, fabricated by American Bridge Co., over Bellinger R.; RS 1916–75; sawmills: William Caine (burnt down 1932), Henry Bligh Moran, E.D. Pike & Co. Ltd (b. by Smith and Moran, burnt down 1922, rebuilt, fire 1947), Smith and Allen; schools: East Raleigh 1880–87 and Repton 1915, additions 1994; telephone 1896; TX 1913, automatic 1941; Union C.; winery; pop. 250 (1933), 224 (1947), 190 (1954), 176 (1961), 620 (2006), 631 (2011).

Reserve Creek (*Co. Rous*) 28°21'S. 153°29'E., 8 km NW of Pottsville, on Reserve Ck; beans, fruit, dairying; school 1930–73; pop. 108 (1933), 174 (1947), 176 (1954), 127 (1961).

Retreat (*Co. Inglis*) 30°37'S. 151°07'E., 40 km E. of Manilla, on Muluerindie R.; PO 1927; telephone 1924; TX 1928–65; pop. 29 (1933), 145 (2006).

Rhine Falls (*Co. Wallace*) 36°11'S. 148°53'E., 23 km W. of Cooma; farming; fire 1906; flour mill (Hassell's); PO 1911; school 1893–1904; telephone 1905; TX 1929–56; pop. 66 (1911), 28 (1933).

Rhondda (*Co. Northumberland*) see Wakefield.

Rhones Creek (*Co. Raleigh*) 30°42'S. 152°51'E., 7 km W. of Macksville, on Rhones Ck.

Rhyanna (*Co. Argyle*) 34°36'S. 149°46'E., 18 km N. of Goulburn; school 1903–37 and 1957–62; pop. 30 (1933).

Riamukka (*Co. Hawes*) 31°25'S. 151°41'E., 49 km S. of Walcha; airfield; quarry; sawmill (Margery Bros and Patrick Grace) 1927, sold 1941 to Reuben J. Goldsmith, fire 1954, taken over 1955 by Rex Thomas Goldsmith and Max Charlie Goldsmith, closed 1982; telephone 1923; TX 1929–72; pop. 71 (1954), 42 (1961), 188 (2006).

Richardson's Corner (*Co. Napier*) see Merrygoen.

Richardsons Crossing (*Co. Macquarie*) 31°09'S. 152°58'E., 4 km N. of Crescent Head.

Richardson's Point (*Co. Wellington*) see Windeyer.

Richlands (*Co. Argyle*) 34°19'S. 149°48'E., 34 km NE of Crookwell; creamery (Camden Park Estate Pty Ltd) b. 1896 by G.F. Furner; PO 1946–62; school 1901–12; telephone 1940; TX 1943, automatic 1981; pop. 116 (1911), 115 (1933), 87 (1947).

Richmond (*Co. Hume*) see Carnsdale.

Richmond Hill (*Co. Cook*) 33°36'S. 150°42'E., 2 km SW of North Richmond, on Hawkesbury R.

Richmond Hill (*Co. Rous*) 28°47'S. 153°20'E., 7 km E. of Lismore, on Lagoon Ck; school 1906 b. by J. Thompson, closed 1969; pop. 34 (1933), 820 (2011).

Richmond River (*Co. Rous*) see Casino and Lismore.

Richmond River Heads (*Co. Rous*) see Ballina.

Richmond Vale (*Co. Northumberland*) 32°52'S. 151°30'E., 6 km S. of Kurri Kurri, on Wallis Ck; settled 1840 by Charles William Roemer, estab. 1889 by Trenchard, Adams & Co., laid out by Alfred Francis Hall, subdivided and lots auctioned 1890, never fully developed; orig. timber and farming, then coalmining; brickworks; bushfires 1994 and 2017; causeway; colliery (Richmond Vale) estab. 1888–90 by Trenchard, Adams & Co., o. 1891 by Richmond Vale Coal Co., closed 1892, acquired and closed 1897 by John Brown, renamed Richmond Main in 1911, powerhouse 1912, colliery reopened 1914, strikes 1917, 1923, 1924, 1925, man killed 1924, colliery redeveloped 1926–28, strikes 1928 and 1929–30, acquired 1931 by J. & A. Brown & Abermain Seaham Collieries Ltd, strikes 1935, 1939, 1942, 1943, 1944, colliery damaged 1944, strikes 1945, 1946, 1949, man killed 1949, strike 1950, colliery acquired 1960 by Coal & Allied Industries Ltd, closed 1967, powerhouse operated till 1976, colliery partly reused; dam (colliery); gale 1944;

quarry; railway (colliery) b. 1901–6, closed 1972, partly reused; school 1882–1932; storm 1946; pop. 97 (1911), 27 (1933).

Ridgeway (*Co. Murray*) 35°20'S. 149°15'E., 3 km NE of Queanbeyan, on Molonglo R.; formerly The Ridgeway; FB.

Rifle Butts Corner (*Co. Wakool*) 35°20'S. 143°36'E., 57 km NW of Barham.

Riley (*Co. Richmond*) see Brickella.

Rileys Hill (*Co. Richmond*) 29°01'S. 153°24'E., 8 km NE of Woodburn, on Richmond R.; farming, dairying, sugar-cane; dry dock (govt) b. 1899–1902 by PWD, 210 ft (64 m), extended 1930 and 1984, closed 1991; PO 1893; Rom. Cath. C. (St John's) 1903, dismantled and moved 1934 to Dungarubba; quarry (stone) 1889–1911; school 1893 b. by Frank Pospichal, additions 1900 by T.W. Keith, closed 1931, reopened 1957, closed 1975; telephone 1899; TX 1928–58; Union C. 1901; wharf b. 1892 by Josiah Mudford, new one 1931; pop. 384 (1901), 197 (1911), 92 (1933), 65 (1947), 80 (1954), 72 (1961), 227 (2011).

Rimbanda (*Co. Inglis*) 30°48'S. 151°21'E., 22 km SW of Uralla.

Ringstone (*Co. Bathurst*) 33°51'S. 148°47'E., 7 km E. of Cowra; telephone 1926; TX 1927–40.

Ringwood (*Co. Brisbane*) 32°09'S. 150°13'E., 14 km W. of Merriwa, on Killoe Ck; soldiers' settlement (5 km SW).

Ringwood (*Co. Camden*) 34°38'S. 150°21'E., 4 km NE of Bundanoon, on Indigo Ck; bushfire 1905; coalmine (Ringwood or Trood's Cut or Christmas Creek) estab. 1884 by Thomas Saywell & Sons, closed 1885, reopened 1896 by James Collins, closed 1911; tramway (mine) 1883.

Ringwood (*Co. Hume*) 35°52'S. 146°15'E., 20 km NW of Corowa; pop. 53 (1911), 109 (1961).

Ringwood Siding (*Co. Cunningham*) see Ootha.

Riplevale (*Co. Nicholson*) 33°54'S. 145°48'E., 48 km NW of Griffith; PO 1927–39; telephone 1926; TX 1927.

Riverbyn (*Co. Fitzroy*) 30°11'S. 153°00'E., 16 km NW of Coffs Harbour; telephone 1915.

Riverdale (*Co. Rous*) 28°34'S. 152°58'E., 8 km NW of Kyogle, on Richmond R.

River Heights (*Co. Argyle*) see Goulburn.

Rivers (*Co. Rous*) see Goonellabah and Lismore.

Riversdale (*Co. Roxburgh*) 32°49'S. 149°52'E., 10 km W. of Rylstone, on Cudgegong R.; Meth. C. 1904.

Riversford (*Co. Camden*) see Menangle.

Riverside (*Co. Leichhardt*) 31°01'S. 148°23'E., 7 km S. of Coonamble, on Castlereagh R.; school 1886–90.

Rivertree (*Co. Buller*) 28°37'S. 152°18'E., 54 km NE of Tenterfield, on Clarence R.; silver-lead-zinc; telephone 1952; TX 1952; pop. 66 (1901), 59 (1911), 77 (1933), 58 (1947), 61 (1954), 70 (2006).

Rixs Creek (*Co. Durham*) 32°32'S. 151°08'E., 5 km NW of Singleton, on Rixs Ck; coalmining *c.*1860–1928 and coke-making 1869–1919; coalmines: Bloomfield Open-Cut 1990 (man killed 2013), Cunneen's *c.*1885, Ellesmere (estab. 1878 by Thomas Longworth, killed 1884 in mine, taken over by Thomas, jun. and William Longworth, sold 1900), New Park (estab. 1881 by Richard Read et al., joined 1885 by Thomas, jun. and William Longworth, later sold to them, closed 1921), Nowland's *c.*1885, Rixs Creek (renamed Elliott's *c.*1890, boy killed 1893, renamed Granbalang *c.*1897); coke-works: old bench of ovens, closed and new bench (Great Cobar Copper Co., 26 beehive ovens), closed; flood 1893; hailstorm 1913; measles epidemic 1888; miners' strike 1907; PO 1883–1930; RS 1885–1938; school 1882, repairs 1909 by T. Ellis & Sons, closed 1923; Union C. b. 1899 by G. Partridge; pop. 327 (1901), 272 (1911), 66 (1933).

Roach (*Co. Cooper*) 34°39'S. 146°28'E., 12 km SE of Leeton; RS 1930, closed.

Roachs Saw Mills (*Co. Cooper*) see Genista.

Road View (*Co. Gloucester*) see Rookhurst.

Roberton Park (*Co. Camden*) see Glenquarry.

Roberts Creek (*Co. Clarence*) 29°33'S. 153°08'E., 10 km SW of Maclean; farming;

PO 1927–30; telephone 1914; TX 1948–59; pop. 102 (1911), 59 (1933), 137 (1947), 90 (1954), 90 (1961).

Robertson (*Co. Camden*) 34°35'S. 150°35'E., 20 km SE of Bowral, on Caalang Ck; orig. Three Creeks, then Yarrawah till Jan. 1869, then McCollom's till Feb. 1869; estab. 1862, surveyed 1863 by Campbell, village gaz. 1865, laid out 1865 by Campbell, first lots sold 1865; former highland resort (incl. fishing and hunting), beef, dairying, vegetables (specially potatoes), blackberries; Angl. C. (St John the Evangelist) 1876, additions 1887, extended 1940, tower destroyed 1961, later rebuilt, and columbarium; bacon factory (Gilroy and W.R. Hindmarsh) 1891; bridge (concrete) b. 2015 by Kenpass Pty Ltd, over Caalang Ck; bushfire 1928; butter factories: Berrima Dist. F. and D. Co. Ltd and Fresh Food & Ice Co. 1889–1922; carriage-works (A. Harrigan); caterpillar infestation 1893; cemetery (265 graves); CH (incl. lock-up) b. 1891 by Holloway Bros, repairs 1892 by W. Jones, reused; cheese factory (Robertson Co-op. Dairy Society Ltd) b. 1936 by E. Bursill, taken over 1951 by Dairy Farmers' Co-op. Milk Co. Ltd, closed 1989, reused; drought 1867–69; earth tremor 1961; electricity 1930; FB (station b. 1973, new one 2009); grasshopper infestation 1945; PO 1869, new one b. 1884, replacement 1896, damaged 1961, restored and reopened 1966, closed 1994, reused, new one; pound (stock) 1880; PS 1881; railway accidents: 1962 (person killed), 1966 (person killed), 1972 (person killed); Rom. Cath. C. (St Anthony's) 1968, closed; RS 1932–85, reused; sale-yards (R.M. Graham); sawmills: Pearson Sandsoap Co. (b. 1917 by John Missingham, burnt down 1921) and William Todd 1905 (taken over 1906 by John Missingham & Sons); schools: Robertson 1872 b. by John Staggs, additions 1887, alterations 1891, additions 1993, and Yarrawah 1889–1911; snowstorm 1898; tannery (Haines's); telegraph 1879; telephone 1917; TX 1917, automatic 1962; Unit. C. (orig. Meth.) b. 1902 by T.E. Bursill, additions 1932, closed and reused; water supply augmentation 1995; Wes. Meth. C. 1870, replaced 1888, closed 1902; pop. 460 (1891), 574 (1901), 510 (1911), 314 (1933), 455 (1947), 274 (1954), 532 (1961), 212 (1971), 226 (1976), 269 (1981), 273 (1986), 252 (1991), 922 (1996), 1,023 (2001), 1,206 (2006), 1,355 (2011), 1,338 (2016).

Robertsons Point (*Co. Roxburgh*) 33°18'S. 149°58'E., 7 km N. of Portland, on Williwa Ck.

Roberts Plain (*Co. Macquarie*) 31°22'S. 152°49'E., 11 km NW of Port Macquarie.

Robin Hill (*Co. Bathurst*) see Bathurst.

Rob Roy (*Co. Arrawatta*) 29°45'S. 151°00'E., 11 km W. of Inverell; farming and orchards; PO 1881–1961; school 1880–1918 and 1957–66, burnt down; telephone 1905; TX 1914, automatic 1971; pop. 102 (1911), 222 (1933), 97 (1947), 129 (1954), 133 (1961).

Rob Roy (*Co. Murray*) see Royalla.

Robson (*Co. Cook*) see Lithgow.

Roche (*Co. King*) 34°14'S. 149°03'E., 39 km NE of Boorowa, on Callaba Ck; farming and grazing; PO 1914; telephone 1927; TX 1928; pop. 31 (1933).

Rock Abbey (*Co. Clarke*) 30°17'S. 152°04'E., 37 km E. of Guyra; school 1900–11 and 1957–76.

Rock Flat (*Co. Beresford*) 36°21'S. 149°12'E., 15 km SE of Cooma, on Spring Ck; orig. Soda Water Spring; village gaz. 1886; grazing; bridge over Rock Flat Ck; PO 1890; RS 1912, station b. by D.L. Reid, closed 1984; school 1884–91; silica mine (Newbold General Refractories Ltd), closed 1985; spa water plant (Koomah), incl. pumping station; telephone 1904; TX 1938–40; pop. 53 (1901), 125 (1911), 38 (1933), 66 (1947), 109 (2011).

Rock Forest (*Co. Bathurst*) 33°21'S. 149°22'E., 21 km NE of Millthorpe, on Oaky Ck; pop. 54 (1933), 342 (2011).

Rockley (*Co. Georgiana*) 33°42'S. 149°34'E., 28 km W. of Oberon, on Peppers Ck; settled 1829 by Capt. W.A. Steele, surveyed 1833 by Nicholson, village laid out by John Nelson and gaz. 1851, first lots sold 1853, settled by Daniel Nightingale, declined 1901+, classified by

National Trust; farming, grazing, copper (disc. 1847) 1847–58 and 1897–1901, gold (alluvial and reef); Angl. C. (St Peter's) b. 1868 by David Jones and Louis Gronin, d. by Edward Gell, spire, chancel and vestry added 1872; bushfire 1939; cemetery (Jumpers Flat, 223 graves); CH 1867; clock tower (war memorial); FB 1938; fire 1869; flour mill (Arthur Budden and Alfred George Stanger) 1862, acquired 1878 by Cox and Worrall, acquired by Christopher Armstrong, acquired 1891 by Henry Hunt Hackney, closed, acquired 1920 by William Horace Stevens, chimney demolished 1921, steam engine and boiler sold 1922 to Carter's Hill Gold Mining Co., mill reused 1976; gale 1923; PO 1851, new one b. 1878–80 by Alfred George Stanger; Presb. C. 1863; PS (incl. lock-up) 1867, additions and alterations 1897 by James Inseal; quarry (Edwards Marble Co.); rabbit freezing works 1917; rifle range 1900; Rom. Cath. C. (St Patrick's) b. 1869–73 d. by Edward Gell, additions 1900 by Rigby Bros, d. by John Job Copeman, new one 1941; school 1860, new one b. 1862, repairs 1883 by Moore and Whitmore, additions 1891, repairs 1894 by W.G. Hezlet, repairs 1918 by J. Bartlett, additions 1956; storm 1901; telegraph 1879, new office b. 1878–80 by Alfred George Stanger; TX 1914; Wes. Meth. C. 1860; pop. *c.*130 (1866), 135 (1871), *c.*125 (1886), 219 (1891), 293 (1901), 378 (1911), 227 (1933), 213 (1947), 267 (1954), 186 (1961), 225 (2011).

Rock Lodge (*Co. Wellesley*) 36°31'S. 149°06'E., 30 km S. of Cooma.

Rockmore (*Co. Darling*) 30°26'S. 150°41'E., 8 km SE of Barraba, on Manilla R.; farming and grazing; PO 1927; school 1897–1902; telephone 1923; TX 1928–60; pop. 67 (1901), 22 (1933).

Rocks Crossing (*Co. Burnett*) 29°09'S. 150°45'E., 38 km NW of Ashford, on Ottleys Ck; quarry.

Rocks Crossing (*Co. Macquarie*) 31°46'S. 152°05'E., 29 km N. of Gloucester, on Nowendoc R.; sawmill (Eric William Hawkins); school 1957–76; pop. 39 (1933), 62 (1947), 56 (1954).

Rockton (*Co. Auckland*) 37°09'S. 149°19'E., 26 km S. of Bombala, on Genoa R.; farming and grazing; PO 1905; sawmill (Thomas Hite & Sons); telephone 1907; TX 1923; pop. 80 (1911), 40 (1933).

Rockvale (*Co. Sandon*) 30°23'S. 151°56'E., 31 km NE of Armidale, on Wollomombi R.; mining and grazing; goldmine (Phoenix); silver mines: Ruby Mine (estab. 1895 by Baker and Wade, closed, reopened 1968 by Silver Valley Minerals) and Tulloch Mine (Wade and Lawrence); PO 1897–1964; school 1892–1913 and 1925–67; storm 2004; telephone 1906; TX 1922, automatic 1972; pop. 237 (1901), 135 (1911), 131 (1933), 105 (1947), 100 (1954), 67 (1961).

Rock Valley (*Co. Rous*) 28°45'S. 153°10'E., 13 km NW of Lismore, on Leycester Ck; dairying and bananas; bridge (Thorne Bridge) 1911, destroyed and replaced 1931, new one 1999, over Richmond R.; bushfire 1936; floods 1931 and 1962; gale 1958; PO 1927, destroyed 1958, replaced, relocated 2009, burnt down 2012; school 1914–75; storm 1958; telephone 1922; TX 1929, automatic 1953; pop. 180 (1933), 227 (1947), 241 (1954), 252 (1961), 272 (2011).

Rockview (*Co. Clarendon*) 34°50'S. 147°25'E., 15 km W. of Junee; earth tremor 1998; RS 1897–1975; flood 1928; pop. 50 (1933).

Rockwell (*Co. Yancowinna*) 32°02'S. 141°35'E., 14 km SE of Broken Hill; PO 1888–1901.

Rockwood (*Co. Sandon*) 30°44'S. 151°41'E., 18 km SW of Uralla, on Mihi Ck; pop. 64 (1901), 142 (1911).

Rocky Creek (*Co. Arrawatta*) 29°18'S. 151°22'E., 26 km E. of Ashford, on Rocky Ck; pop. 54 (1911).

Rocky Creek (*Co. Fitzroy*) 30°23'S. 152°42'E., 4 km S. of Dorrigo; pop. 42 (1933).

Rocky Creek (*Co. Murchison*) 30°02'S. 150°17'E., 33 km SW of Bingara; aeroplane crash 1951; Angl. C. (St James's War Memorial); school 1957–67; pop. 163 (1911), 83 (1947).

Rocky Creek (*Co. Rous*) see Whian Whian.

Rocky Crossing (*Co. Roxburgh*) 32°02'S.

151°52'E., 9 km SW of Gloucester, on Barrington R.

Rocky Dam (*Co. Burnett*) 29°05'S. 150°44'E., 43 km NW of Ashford; Presb. C. 1907, renovated 1926, closed 1965, collapsed; cemetery.

Rocky Glen (*Co. White*) 31°07'S. 149°34'E., 33 km NE of Coonabarabran, on Borah Ck; village gaz. 1884; farming and grazing; cemetery (20 graves) 1886; PO 1875, burnt down 1917; school 1884–94; telephone 1925; TX 1928, automatic 1981; pop. 84 (1911), 123 (1933), 65 (1947), 62 (1961).

Rocky Gully (*Co. Inglis*) 30°50'S. 151°14'E., 40 km NE of Tamworth; hurricane 1864.

Rocky Hall (*Co. Auckland*) 36°56'S. 149°30'E., 24 km E. of Bombala, on Towamba R.; gold, maize, dairying, now centre of alternative lifestyles; butter factory (Rocky Hall Co-op. Dairy Co. Ltd) 1896–1923, reused, destroyed 2005; cemetery (graves 1894+) 1880; drought 1923; hailstorm 1904; PO 1883–1975; school 1883, new one b. 1887, closed 1924, reused; squall 2005; telephone 1896; TX 1926; pop. 243 (1901), 152 (1911), 118 (1933), 100 (1947), 79 (1954), 66 (1961), 123 (2001).

Rocky Mouth (*Co. Clarence*) see Maclean.

Rocky Plain (*Co. Wallace*) 36°14'S. 148°41'E., 21 km N. of Jindabyne, on Biggam Ck; formerly Rocky Plains; Angl. C. b. 1890 by Muggridge and Hedger (moved 1900 to Middlingbank); earth tremor 2001; PO 1883–97; school 1884–91 and 1968–69; TX (automatic) 1958; Wes. Meth. C.; pop. 55 (1961).

Rocky Plains (*Co. Wallace*) see Rocky Plain.

Rocky Point (*Co. Ewenmar*) 32°02'S. 148°14'E., 23 km E. of Trangie, on Macquarie R.

Rocky Point (*Co. Northumberland*) see Tacoma.

Rocky Ponds (*Co. Gordon*) 32°54'S. 148°28'E., 32 km SE of Peak Hill, on Balrudgery Ck; cemetery 1892; school 1884–1914.

Rocky Ponds (*Co. Harden*) 34°35'S. 148°30'E., 12 km E. of Murrumburrah; railway derailment (4 killed) 1948; RS 1877, station relocated 1916, closed 1975.

Rocky River (*Co. Drake*) 29°06'S. 152°22'E., 33 km E. of Tenterfield; pop. 39 (1933).

Rocky River (*Co. Sandon*) 30°37'S. 151°29'E., 3 km N. of Uralla, on Post Office Gully; declined 1857+; mining (gold disc. 1851 by W.F. Buchanan and J. Lucas, and more in 1856 by Jones), later farming and fruit growing; Angl. C. 1854; Chinese joss house 1857, (second) 1866, (third) 1877, burnt down 1912; PO 1854; Presb. C. 1854; Rom. Cath. C. 1856; sawmill (Frederick Vickery); school 1861, additions 1885 by G. Lonsdale, additions and repairs 1891 by James Ford, additions and repairs 1904 by J.P. Henry, additions 2010; telephone 1913; pop. *c.*4,500 (1856), *c.*300 (1860), 437 (1911), 431 (1933), 278 (1947), 261 (1954), 251 (1961), 258 (2011).

Rocky Waterhole (*Co. Parry*) 31°11'S. 150°52'E., 12 km SW of Tamworth, on Tinbumburi Ck.

Rodney (*Co. Wellesley*) 36°51'S. 148°57'E., 26 km W. of Bombala, on Delegate R.; Burnt Hut Crossing till 1926; telephone 1926; TX 1939–53.

Rofe Estate (*Co. Camden*) see Razorback.

Rollands Plains (*Co. Macquarie*) 31°17'S. 152°41'E., 20 km N. of Wauchope, on Bril Bril Ck; sugar-cane estab. 1824 by Thomas Alison Scott, then wheat and dairying; Angl. C. 1862, new one (St John the Baptist) 1901 d. by Thomas, extended 1915 by S. Thurling and T. and R. Rosenbaum, renovated 1935 by Vogele; cemetery 1881; diphtheria 1915; floods 1833, 1853, 1864, 1870, 1873; flour mill (Frank Little); hailstorm 2018; mill (horse powered, W.H. Geary); PO 1856; Presb. C. 1883; sawmill (John Jeremiah Walsh); school 1852, new one 1882, additions and repairs 1916 by A.W.S. Mackay, new building b. 1933 by J. Poulton, closed 1965; stockade; sugar and grist mill (Thomas Alison Scott) 1825–30; telephone 1888; TX 1927, automatic 1969; Union C.; pop. 318 (1901), 314 (1911), 135 (1933), 123 (1947), 69 (1954), 63 (1961).

Rollies Grass (*Co. Rous*) 28°40'S. 153°13'E., 9 km S. of Nimbin, on Goolmangar Ck.

Ronavis (*Co. Nicholson*) 33°37'S. 145°36'E., 16 km S. of Hillston; telephone 1929; TX 1929–

50.

Rookhurst (*Co. Gloucester*) 31°54'S. 151°53'E., 15 km NW of Gloucester, on Chinamans Ck; formerly Craven Creek; bridge over Craven Ck; Cong. C. 1916, bought 1953 by Presb. C.; FB (station b. 1995); school (Road View till 1939) 1916, closed, sold 2016; telephone 1916; TX 1920, automatic 1957; pop. 23 (1933).

Root Hog (*Co. Roxburgh*) 33°06'S. 149°24'E., 35 km NE of Orange, on Macquarie R.

Rooty Flat (*Co. Northumberland*) see Wakefield.

Rosebank (*Co. Bourke*) see Ardlethan.

Rosebank (*Co. Rous*) 28°40'S. 153°24'E., 16 km SW of Mullumbimby, on Yankey Ck; settled 1879 by Alfred Slade; dairying, farming, cattle, now coffee and macadamia nuts; bushfire 1902; creamery 1896–1902; cyclone 1903; diphtheria 1890; electricity 1938; FB; Meth. C. 1905 d. by Robert Robertson Jack, closed, sold 2017, reused; PO 1889; rifle range 1916; Rom. Cath. C. 1879, new one (St Patrick's) b. 1935 by J. Watt, d. by Frederick Leben, closed, sold and reused; sawmill b. 1898 by Duncan and William Campbell, sold 1904 to Alexander Duncan, sold 1908 and moved to Dorrigo; school 1897 b. by Thomas Loft, new building b. 1951 by Harry Cave, additions 2010; telephone 1905; TX 1923, automatic 1966; pop. 191 (1901), 453 (1911), 120 (1933), 295 (1947), 315 (1954), 263 (1961), 509 (2011).

Roseberry (*Co. Bathurst*) 33°28'S. 149°05'E., 10 km W. of Millthorpe.

Roseberry (*Co. Rous*) 28°29'S. 152°55'E., 18 km NW of Kyogle, on Richmond R.; cemetery; gale 1933; sawmills: Dennis's and Hancock & Gore Ltd, damaged 1933, closed 1967; pop. 125 (1911), 92 (1933), 79 (1947), 79 (1954), 69 (1961).

Roseberry Creek (*Co. Rous*) 28°28'S. 152°50'E., 23 km NW of Kyogle, on Roseberry Ck; pop. 47 (1933), 79 (1947), 61 (1961), 182 (2011).

Rosebrook (*Co. Durham*) 32°39'S. 151°31'E., 10 km NW of Maitland, on Hunter R.; farming and dairying; flood 1867; FB; gale 1899; PO 1927–56; school 1957–84; telephone 1916; TX 1945; pop. 57 (1901), 61 (1933), 51 (1961), 174 (2011).

Rosedale (*Co. Beresford*) 35°59'S. 148°50'E., 38 km NW of Cooma, on Murrumbidgee R.; PO 1880; telephone 1906; pop. 127 (1901).

Rosedale (*Co. Dowling*) 33°28'S. 146°01'E., 45 km E. of Hillston.

Rosedale (*Co. Durham*) 32°29'S. 151°08'E., 10 km N. of Singleton; mine 1885–1931; storm 1913; Wes. Meth. C. 1899; pop. 79 (1911).

Rosedale (*Co. St Vincent*) 35°49'S. 150°14'E., 3 km S. of Malua Bay, on Tasman Sea; (incl. North Rosedale and South Rosedale); Jehovah's Witnesses C. (Rosedale and Batemans Bay, at South Rosedale); pop. 231 (2011).

Rosegreen (*Co. Bathurst*) see Lucan.

Rose Hill (*Co. Gough*) 29°41'S. 151°39'E., 10 km NW of Glen Innes, on Reddestone Ck.

Rose Hill (*Co. Harden*) 34°45'S. 148°12'E., 20 km SE of Cootamundra; farming and grazing; goldmine (Stringy Bark Reef); pop. 70 (1911), 22 (1933).

Rose Hill (*Co. Sandon*) 30°33'S. 151°33'E., 10 km SW of Armidale.

Rose Hill (*Co. Sandon*) see also Arding.

Rosemeath (*Co. Wellesley*) 36°57'S. 149°15'E., 5 km S. of Bombala; school 1902–63; pop. 73 (1933), 59 (1961), 138 (2006).

Rosemonder (*Co. Bourke*) 34°26'S. 146°48'E., 15 km SW of Ardlethan; telephone 1925; TX 1926–39.

Rosemonte (*Co. Argyle*) 34°47'S. 149°47'E., 7 km SE of Goulburn, on Boxers Ck; Angl. C. (St Barnabas's) 1901; electricity 1949; pop. 58 (1911), 62 (1933).

Rosemount (*Co. Buccleuch*) 35°10'S. 148°19'E., 18 km NE of Tumut, on Bringle Ck; dairying and grazing; PO 1927–42; telegraph, closed 1917; telephone 1916; TX 1936; pop. 53 (1933).

Roseneath (*Co. Wellesley*) 36°56'S. 149°14'E., 2 km S. of Bombala; sawmill.

Rosenthal (*Co. Gloucester*) 32°22'S. 152°11'E., 5 km NW of Bulahdelah; Meth. C. 1905; school 1884–1947; storm 1954; pop. 72 (1911), 23 (1933), 76 (1961).

Rose Point (*Co. Northumberland*) see Singleton.

Rose Vale (*Co. Argyle*) 34°57'S. 149°53'E., 27 km SE of Goulburn, on Mitchells Waterholes; airfield; school 1880–95.

Rose Valley (*Co. Beresford*) 36°08'S. 149°15'E., 16 km NE of Cooma.

Rose Valley (*Co. Camden*) 34°43'S. 150°48'E., 3 km NW of Gerringong, on Rose Valley Ck; farming; PO 1890–1930; school 1868–77 and 1890–96, burnt down 1901; pop. 55 (1954), 308 (2006).

Rose Valley (*Co. Gough*) 29°24'S. 151°33'E., 41 km NW of Glen Innes; mine; pop. 179 (1901), 161 (1933), 149 (1947).

Rosewarne (*Co. Pottinger*) 30°57'S. 150°12'E., 6 km NW of Gunnedah; FB; school (Burburgate till 1904) 1902–44.

Rosewood (*Co. Macquarie*) 31°27'S. 152°41'E., 4 km W. of Wauchope, on Hastings R.; pop. 24 (1933), 345 (2011).

Rosewood (*Co. Selwyn*) 35°40'S. 147°52'E., 17 km NW of Tumbarumba, on Mannus Ck; farming and eucalyptus oil; cemetery 1892; FB; PO 1885; RS 1921–75; school 1883–1906, reopened 1918, new building b. 1941 by O. Lyons; telephone 1913; TX 1919, automatic 1958; Union C., repairs 1890 by Penhorn, re-roofed and repaired 1897 by T.K. M'Guchem, new one b. 1902 by Sam Thompson, new one (Good Shepherd) 1981; pop. 193 (1901), 162 (1911), 91 (1933), 277 (1947), 280 (1954), 190 (1961), 224 (2011).

Rosewood Camp (*Co. Stapylton*) 28°34'S. 150°18'E., 7 km NW of Boggabilla.

Roslyn (*Co. Argyle*) 34°30'S. 149°36'E., 13 km E. of Crookwell; farming and grazing; Roslyn Railway Station till 1913; Meth. C. 1914; PO 1909; RS 1902, new station 1926, closed 1974; school 1865–79 and 1957–75; snowstorms 1901 and 1925; telephone 1914; TX 1918, automatic 1973; pop. 62 (1901), 85 (1911), 94 (1933), 105 (1947), 100 (1954), 96 (1961).

Roslyn Railway Station (*Co. Argyle*) see Roslyn.

Ross (*Co. Selwyn*) 36°10'S. 148°21'E., 27 km N. of Perisher Valley, on Bogong Swamp.

Ross Crossing (*Co. Bligh*) 32°05'S. 149°42'E., 29 km E. of Dunedoo, on Talbragar R.; bridge over Talbragar R.

Rossglen (*Co. Macquarie*) 31°40'S. 152°44'E., 4 km SE of Kendall, on Camden Haven R.; Camden Haven Punt till 1891, Camden Haven till 1921; dairying; airfield (Camden Haven); bridge b. 1940 by A.T.B. Anderson, replaced 1986, over Camden Haven R.; PO 1878; 2 quarries; Rom. Cath. C. (St John the Evangelist) 1880, closed and sold; RS (Camden Haven River till 1921) 1915–73; sawmills: Haydon and McInnes 1921, IXL, Steiman's; telephone 1914; TX 1937–64; pop. 128 (1933), 94 (1947), 85 (1954).

Ross Hill (*Co. Gough*) see Inverell.

Rossi (*Co. Murray*) 35°28'S. 149°30'E., 24 km S. of Bungendore, on Yandyguinula Ck; grazing; Meth. C. 1922; sawmill (Pioneer); school 1883–90, 1898–1933, 1957–72; telephone 1922; TX 1924–69; pop. 105 (1901), 79 (1911), 62 (1933), 52 (1947), 70 (1954), 73 (1961).

Rossi Street (*Co. Murray*) see Yass.

Rothbury (*Co. Northumberland*) 32°45'S. 151°20'E., 10 km S. of Branxton, on Black Ck; farming, dairying, vineyards; Angl. C. (St Paul's) b. 1867 by Holmes, re-roofed, demolished 1961, timber reused by Errol Mears; bridge (Coronation Bridge, composite steel and timber truss) b. 1902 by Walter Frank Oakes, d. by Ernest Macartney de Burgh, over Black Ck; bushfires 1895, 1964, 1968; cemetery (orig. Angl. graveyard, 187 graves 1851+) 1882; collieries: Ayrfield No. 3 Open-Cut No. 2 (o. 1946 by Maitland Extended Collieries Ltd), Maitland Extended No. 6 (o. 1952 by R.W. Miller & Co., closed 1962, demolished), Mary Anne Open-Cut; cyclone 1899; Meth. C. 1917; PO 1876; school (Mount Wills till 1883) 1880, new one b. 1882 by J.S. Brown, additions 1956, closed 1964; telephone 1912; Wes. Meth. C. 1866; wineries: Ballabourneen Wine Co. (Alex and Di Stuart) 1994, Bimbadgen Estate, Calais Estate, Carindale Wines, Cottage Grove, Daisy Hill 1917–68, Emma's Cottage Vineyard, First Creek (Greg Silkman), Fraser Winery,

Gabriel's Paddocks Vineyard & Pomegranate Wine Co., Gemelli Estate, Hope Estate (orig. Rothbury Estate, acquired by Michael Hope), James Hunter Estate, Latara Wines, Lee Hunter Estate, Madigan Vineyard, Maling Family Estate, Marsh Estate (estab. 1971 by Quentin Taperell as Quentin Estate, sold 1976 to Peter and Robyn Marsh and renamed), Misty Glen Wines, Molin & Fils, Monahan Estate, Moorebank Vineyard, Molly Morgan Vineyard, Noonji Estate 1996, Parker Wines, Parrot Stump Farm & Midnight's Promise Wines, Peacock Hill Vineyard, Murray Robson Wines, Petersons Champagne House, Rothbury Ridge Vineyard, Rothvale Vineyard and Winery, Sabor on the Hunter, St Clements Estate, Sandalyn Estate, Sovereign Hill Vineyard, Swish Wine 1970, Tamalee Vineyard Estate, Terrace Vale, Warraroong Estate (bought by Swish Wine), Waverley Estate Aged Wines; pop. 54 (1901), 310 (1911), 240 (1933), 92 (1947), 64 (1954), 452 (2011).

Rothbury North (*Co. Northumberland*) 32°41'S. 151°21'E., 2 km S. of Branxton; estab., subdivided and first lots sold 1912, new subdivisions (Huntlee and Katherine's Landing); coalmining; bushfire 1938; cemetery; collieries: Ayrfield No. 3 (estab. 1910–14 as Rothbury by Edward Alworth Mitchell Merewether and Henry Alfred Mitchell Merewether, strikes 1924 and 1926, man killed 1929 in miners' riot, strike 1929–30, closed 1931, taken over 1932 by James Ruttley and renamed Branxton, closed 1935, acquired 1936 by R.W. Miller & Co. and renamed, strike 1938, acquired 1940 by Maitland Extended Collieries Pty Ltd, men died 1940 and 1943, strike 1944, fire 1949 killed 5 pit ponies, reopened 1960 after being flooded for years, surface works fire 1972, closed 1974 except for washery which closed 1985 and was sold and reused 1990, colliery derelict), Ayrfield No. 3 Open-Cut No. 1 (Maitland Extended Collieries Ltd) 1943–46, Cwmdu (estab. 1934 by Richard Thomas, Adam North, H.M. Hughes and James Morgan, closed 1940, reopened 1948 by Maitland Extended Collieries Pty Ltd, closed 1956, reopened, closed 1973, demolished), Maitland Extended No. 1 (estab. 1935 by Alexander Francis, taken over 1940 by Maitland Extended Collieries Ltd, closed 1968, razed 1990), Maitland Extended No. 2 (estab. 1935 by Peter C. Sattler, taken over 1939 by R.W. Miller & Co., acquired 1940 by Maitland Extended Collieries Pty Ltd, fire 1949 and closed, razed 1990), Maitland Extended No. 3 (estab. 1935 as Back Creek by George A. Randall, renamed 1935, taken over 1939 by R.W. Miller & Co., transferred 1940 to Maitland Extended Collieries Pty Ltd, closed 1950), Maitland Extended No. 4 (estab. 1935 by R. Robinson, acquired 1937 by N.E. Smith, acquired 1938 by J.R. Clark, transferred 1939 to R.W. Miller & Co., transferred 1940 to Maitland Extended Collieries Pty Ltd, closed 1944, reopened 1949, closed 1955), Maitland Extended No. 5 (o. 1936 by R.W. Miller & Co., closed 1938); FB; Meth. C. 1917; PO 1914; 2 quarries; railway (colliery); rifle range; school 1916–84, building moved 1987 to Kirkton; telephone 1915; TX; pop. 227 (1933), 238 (1947), 253 (1954), 206 (1961), 250 (1986), 300 (1991), 447 (1996), 480 (2001), 502 (2006), 510 (2011).

Rothdene (*Co. Sturt*) 33°57'S. 146°08'E., 38 km N. of Griffith; telephone 1927; TX 1937–80.

Rotherwood (*Co. Bligh*) 31°52'S. 149°55'E., 19 km E. of Coolah, on Norfolk Island Ck; TX (automatic); pop. 27 (1933).

Roto (*Co. Blaxland*) 33°03'S. 145°28'E., 47 km N. of Hillston; village gaz. 1932; grazing; bushfires 1960 and 1969–70; fire 1889; PO 1900, burnt down 1943, rebuilt, burnt down again 1969; RS 1919, closed; school 1954–72; telephone 1934; TX 1934; pop. 91 (1933), 127 (1947), 158 (1954), 68 (1961), 47 (2006).

Rouchel (*Co. Durham*) 32°09'S. 151°04'E., 17 km E. of Aberdeen, on Stony Ck; formerly Rouchel Brook; wool, wheat, maize, then lucerne, oats, cattle; Angl. C. (St John's) 1875; bridge (Kennedy Bridge), over Stony Ck; bushfires 1965, 1978, 1979, 1990, 1991, 2002; cemetery (138 graves 1870+) 1870; FB 1951;

PO 1872, burnt down 1944; Presb. C. 1873; rifle range 1907; school 1880–1910, reopened 1915, additions 1967, closed 2014; telephone 1900; TX 1915, automatic 1969; Unit. C. (St Phillip's, orig. Presb.) b. 1908 by J.A. Rae, d. by John Reid; pop. 224 (1901), 267 (1911), 84 (1933), 91 (1947), 78 (1954), 72 (1961), 260 (2006), 298 (2011).

Rouchel Brook (*Co. Durham*) see Rouchel.

Roughit (*Co. Durham*) 32°35'S. 151°15'E., 7 km E. of Singleton, on Hunter R.; bridge (Pankhurst Bridge) 1974; bushfire 1965; FB; school (Scotts Flat till 1871) 1864, new one b. 1872 by William Gellatly, replacement b. 1889 by Thomas Burton, d. by E.B. Cragg, renovated 1972, closed 1980.

Round Camp (*Co. Dudley*) 30°42'S. 152°24'E., 45 km W. of Bowraville, on Five Day Ck.

Round Flat (*Co. Hunter*) 32°29'S. 150°23'E., 30 km SW of Denman, on Widden Brook.

Round Hill (*Co. Clarence*) 29°32'S. 153°04'E., 16 km SW of Maclean.

Round Hill (*Co. Cooper*) 34°34'S. 146°40'E., 20 km NE of Narrandera; school 1903–4 and Apr.-Dec. 1910.

Round Hill (*Co. Hume*) 35°39'S. 147°05'E., 4 km E. of Culcairn; pop. 113 (1901), 20 (1933).

Round Hill (*Co. Yancowinna*) see Taltingan.

Round Mount (*Co. Hardinge*) see Copeton.

Round Mountain (*Co. Rous*) 28°22'S. 153°33'E., 3 km NW of Pottsville; farming, dairying, fruit; bushfire 1936; PO 1927–46; reservoir; sawmill; school 1919 b. by Alfred John Modini, closed 1975; TX 1926; pop. 151 (1933), 52 (1961), 262 (2011).

Round Plain (*Co. Wallace*) 36°15'S. 148°42'E., 16 km NW of Berridale; formerly The Round Flat; Unit. C. (orig. Presb.) b. 1870 by William Wilson Beattie, restored 1960, and graveyard.

Round Swamp (*Co. Roxburgh*) 33°04'S. 149°56'E., 25 km S. of Kandos, on Jack Halls Ck; farming; cemetery; PO 1897, burnt down 1926; school 1877–1916, demolished and bought 1928 by Chadwick Bros; telephone 1913; pop. 70 (1911).

Round Swamp (*Co. Vernon*) 31°13'S. 151°42'E., 27 km S. of Walcha.

Round Swamp (*Co. White*) see Culgoora.

Round Water Hole (*Co. Georgiana*) 34°00'S. 149°24'E., 52 km N. of Crookwell, on Abercrombie R.

Rous (*Co. Rous*) 28°52'S. 153°25'E., 4 km SW of Alstonville, on Gum Ck; Dalwood Richmond River till 1882; farming and sugar-cane; Angl. C. (St John the Evangelist) b. 1896 by Arthur J. West, closed; butter factory (Rous Co-op. Dairy Co. Ltd) 1889; cemetery (345 graves 1895+) 1889; PO 1879–1950; Presb. C. (St John's) 1882; PS 1897–1903; sawmill (West's), burnt down 1894; school (Dalwood till 1884) 1881, new one b. 1884 by Charles West; sugar mill (Bryant's); telephone 1899; pop. 349 (1901), 430 (1911), 170 (1933), 152 (1947), 137 (1954), 55 (1961).

Rous Mill (*Co. Rous*) 28°53'S. 153°23'E., 6 km SW of Alstonville, on Youngman Ck; largely defunct; sugar-cane then dairying; broom factory; cheese factory (Jens Christian Frederiksen) b. 1901 by Frederiksen Bros; creamery (NSW Creamery Butter Co. Ltd) 1901; hydro-electric plant (Jens Christian Frederiksen) b. 1931 by Frederiksen Bros, destroyed 1945; Meth. C. b. 1904 by George and Edward Towner, d. by Frederick Johnson Board, renovated 1939; PO 1890; sawmill (Arthur J. West); school 1892, new building b. 1895 by Brown and Jolly, remodelled 1924, closed 1960; sugar mill b. 1883 by Samuel and W.J. Staines, taken over 1884 by Richmond River Sugar Co., taken over 1900 by Union Bank, closed and dismantled 1901; telephone 1890; tramway (sugar-cane); TX 1910–63; Wes. Meth. C. 1881, closed, sold; whooping cough epidemic 1925; pop. 336 (1901), 218 (1933), 234 (1947), 195 (1954), 170 (1961), 194 (2011).

Rowan (*Co. Wynyard*) 35°12'S. 147°20'E., 11 km S. of Wagga Wagga; Angl. C. 1906; school 1880–88; telephone 1923; pop. 86 (1961).

Rowans Hole (*Co. Cook*) 33°13'S. 150°04'E., 17 km NE of Portland, on Coco Ck.

Rowan Street (*Co. Darling*) see Manilla.

Rowena (*Co. Jamison*) 29°49'S. 148°54'E., 44 km SE of Collarenebri; Eaton till 1907;

estab. 1906; grazing; Angl. C. (St Mark's); fire 1927; gale 1927; PO 1908; PS 1920–42; Rom. Cath. C. (St Mary of the Angels), removed from Bulyeroi and re-erected 1927, destroyed 1979, replaced; RS (Eton till 1908) 1906, station b. by John Allibone and Augustus Ringholm, station relocated 1912, closed 1974, demolished 1980; school 1955, additions 1994; telegraph 1908; TX 1911, automatic 1983; water supply (bore) 1924, augmentation 1955; pop. 61 (1911), 102 (1933), 96 (1947), 158 (1954), 66 (1961), 200 (2006).

Rowes (*Co. Wellesley*) 37°00'S. 149°06'E., 16 km SW of Bombala, on Little Plains R.; Wellesley till 1931; village gaz. 1867 as Wellesley; grazing; bridge b. 1895 by Arthur Mawson and John M'Arthur, over Little Plains R.; PO 1927–36; school (Wellesley) 1893–1905; telephone 1916; TX 1928.

Rowes Hill (*Co. Camden*) see Lower Mittagong.

Rowlands Creek (*Co. Rous*) 28°27'S. 153°22'E., 13 km S. of Murwillumbah; PO 1909–10; pop. 38 (1933), 247 (2011).

Roxburgh (*Co. Brisbane*) 32°19'S. 150°45'E., 11 km NE of Denman, on Hunter R.; RS 1915–75; pop. 40 (1933), 67 (1954), 67 (1961).

Royalla (*Co. Murray*) 35°31'S. 149°09'E., 19 km S. of Queanbeyan; RS (Rob Roy till 1905) 1887–1975; school 1904–25; pop. 28 (1933), 835 (2006), 879 (2011).

Royston (*Co. Westmoreland*) 33°40'S. 149°47'E., 9 km NW of Oberon, on Muggletons Ck.

Ruby Creek (*Co. Buller*) 28°38'S. 152°01'E., 46 km N. of Tenterfield; cemetery; PO 1872–75; PS b. 1874 by Ralph Kerr Butt.

Rudder's Town (*Co. Macquarie*) see Kempsey East.

Rufus River (*Co. Tara*) 34°03'S. 141°16'E., 60 km W. of Wentworth, on Lake Victoria; PO 1927; school 1957–69; telephone 1923; TX 1928; pop. 95 (1933), 52 (1954), 81 (2006).

Rugby (*Co. King*) 34°24'S. 149°00'E., 26 km E. of Boorowa, on Five Mile Ck; Five Mile Creek till 1891, then Mewburn till 1899; subdivided 1886; farming and grazing; Angl. C. (St Aidan's) 1924 d. by John Burcham Clamp and Crawford Hutcheson Mackellar; brick-kiln (Fred Willis); bushfires 1952, 1975, 1979; cemetery; electricity 1954; FB 1909 (station b. 2011); flood 1956; goldmine (S. Pearsall) 1916; PO 1888; PS 1896; Rom. Cath. C. (St Virgil's) 1905, extended, closed; sawmill (A. Paget); school 1922–2017; snow 1948; storm 1956; telephone 1890; TX 1917, automatic 1972; pop. 149 (1911), 90 (1933), 99 (1947), 154 (1954), 200 (1961).

Rugby (*Co. Northumberland*) 33°10'S. 151°08'E., 32 km W. of Wyee, on Mangrove Ck; site now largely submerged under Mangrove Creek dam; town site surveyed 1885, subdivided and sold by Phillips & Co., but never developed.

Rukenvale (*Co. Rous*) 28°28'S. 152°54'E., 20 km NW of Kyogle, on Roseberry Ck; farming; PO 1928; rifle range 1934; school 1931, additions 2010; telephone 1928; TX 1934–68; pop. 98 (1933), 84 (1947), 136 (1954), 72 (1961).

Rules Point (*Co. Buccleuch*) 35°43'S. 148°32'E., 41 km SE of Batlow; bushfire 1965; goldmine (W. Cahill and A. Pether) 1898–1908; telephone 1961; TX 1961.

Runnimede Estate (*Co. Northumberland*) see Erina.

Running Stream (*Co. Roxburgh*) 33°02'S. 149°54'E., 21 km S. of Kandos, on Running Stream; farming, grazing, orchards; FB; PO 1856; Presb. C. b. by David Leighton, closed 1905, demolished; 4 quarries; school 1921–43 and 1957–78; telephone 1913; TX 1924, automatic 1988; Unit. C. (St John's, orig. Union) b. 1906 by Thomas Gunn and George Harris, and graveyard (31 graves 1859–1983); pop. 70 (1933), 77 (1947), 101 (1954), 123 (1961).

Runnyford (*Co. St Vincent*) 35°42'S. 150°06'E., 7 km W. of Batemans Bay, on Buckenbowra R.; formerly Austin's Crossing and Runnymede; farming; bridge over Buckenbowra R.; bushfire 1905; cheese factory (Runnymede) 1887, fire 1905; PO 1909–31; sawmills: Harden and Green, and Oakley & Co. 1951; TX 1929; pop. 21 (1933).

Runnymede (*Co. Rous*) see Backmede.

Runnymede (*Co. St Vincent*) see Runnyford.

Run of Water (*Co. Argyle*) see Yarra.

Rushford (*Co. Clarence*) see Rushforth.

Rushforth (*Co. Clarence*) 29°46'S. 152°52'E., 12 km SW of Grafton, on Orara R.; school (Rushford) 1882–1908; pop. 354 (2006).

Rushs Creek (*Co. Darling*) 30°48'S. 150°35'E., 14 km SW of Manilla; earth tremor 2012; pop. 75 (1911), 103 (1933), 100 (1947), 94 (1954), 196 (2006).

Rush's Platform (*Co. Camden*) see Braemar.

Russell Vale (*Co. Camden*) see Woonona.

Rutherford (*Co. Northumberland*) 32°43'S. 151°32'E., 3 km NW of Maitland, on Stony Ck; (incl. Campbells Hill); abattoir (Maitland) 1943; airfield (Maitland) 1963; ambulance station 2019; Angl. C. (St Christopher's) 1980, and graveyard; asphalt plant (Pioneer Road Services); bacon factory and meat works (Foggitt Jones Ltd) 1923 d. by Wallace Lintott Porter; Bapt. C. (Maitland); beekeeping equipment factory (Pender Beekeeping), burnt down 1998; blind factory (Cedar Venetians); boiling-down works: Isaac Gorrick and Joseph Passfield (Oliver replaced Joseph in 1930), and Robert Lindsay; bushfire 1905; cemetery (735 burials); concrete floor slab plant (Aust. Ultra Concrete Floors Pty Ltd) 1990; concrete plants: Boral, Maitland Ready Mixed Concrete and Block Co. (estab. 1965 by Bernard and Nona Kauter), Rutherford Concrete Products; earth tremor 1868; engineering works: J. and S. Engineering and Transfield Pty Ltd; FB (station b. 2016); fire 1895; flood 2016; foundry (Treloar Enterprises Ltd) 1975–2013; furniture factory (Furnstyle Products); gale 1899; hailstorms 1861 and 1938; military staging camp (incl. hospital o. 1916); metal fabrication works: BMCH Constructions Pty Ltd, Gibbs, Hunter Valley Constructions Pty Ltd, Industrial Maintenance and Fabrication 1994, Maitland Sheet Metal, Metal Fabrications Pty Ltd, Transarte Pty Ltd; munitions factory 1941–45, reused; oilseed refinery (William C. Caines); PO 1925; Presb. C. (Mackay Memorial) b. 1929 by Taylor and Buffers, new one 1964; PS (Campbells Hill) 1901–19; quarry (William Taylor) 1843; reservoir, 502,600 gal. (2,284.8 kl); Rom. Cath. C. (Sacred Heart of Jesus) b. 1918 by Andrew Burg, d. by Thomas Wilfred Silk, and graveyard, new one (St Paul's) and columbarium; RS (Rutherford Junction) 1886–1974; sale-yards (Campbells Hill); Salv. Army C. (Maitland City); schools: primary 1985, additions 2010 by RTC Group, and HS 1985; sewerage 1957; storm 1928; tank factories: Biocycle Waste Water Treatment Systems and Dennis Edwards; telephone 1923; textile mills: Burlington Mills Aust. Pty Ltd 1945, in former munitions factory, taken over 1956 by Bradmill Cotton Mills Ltd, became National Textiles, closed 2000, and Wax Converters Textiles Aust. Pty Ltd 1991; toll-gate (Campbells Hill); TX (Campbells Hill) 1954; typhoid (man died) 1914; Unit. C.; Wes. Meth. C. (Living Light); pop. 306 (1911), 814 (1933), 8,700 (2006), 10,182 (2011).

Rutherford Junction (*Co. Northumberland*) see Rutherford.

Ruthven (*Co. Rous*) 28°56'S. 153°17'E., 6 km N. of Coraki, on Pelican Ck; farming; creamery (NSW Creamery Butter Co. Ltd) 1897; PO 1910; quarry; school (Codrington North till 1914) 1884–1974; storm 1937; sugar mill (horse powered, Joseph Rathborne) b. 1870 by Francis Black for; telephone 1924; TX 1924–58; pop. 149 (1933), 89 (1947), 129 (1954), 108 (1961).

Ryalstone (*Co. Roxburgh*) see Rylstone.

Ryan (*Co. Urana*) 35°34'S. 146°52'E., 15 km W. of Henty; farming; PO 1916–22; Presb. C. b. 1917 by J. Barrie; RS (6 km NE) 1920–75; school 1913–69; TX (automatic) 1966; pop. 177 (1933), 144 (1947), 123 (1954), 118 (1961).

Ryanda (*Co. Clarke*) 30°06'S. 151°41'E., 12 km N. of Guyra, on Ryanda Ck; school 1885–1909.

Ryans Crossing (*Co. Auckland*) 36°39'S. 149°39'E., 17 km W. of Bega.

Ryansvale (*Co. Argyle*) see Springfield.

Rydal (*Co. Cook*) 33°29'S. 150°02'E., 9 km S.

of Wallerawang, on Solitary Ck; village gaz. 1843, thrived 1870–76; farming and grazing; bushfires 1940 and 1952; cemetery (148 graves 1869+) 1871; FB; flour mill (Frederick Poncet), moved to Nowra; PO 1859; Presb. C. 1869; PS 1869, additions 1903 by E.P. Frost & Co., renovations and repairs 1916 by Wilson, closed 1942, reused; Rom. Cath. C. (St Matthew's) 1870 d. by Edward Gell, and graveyard (2 graves 1870 and 1873); RS 1870, station b. by Robert McIntosh, d. by John Whitton, closed 1989; school 1869–1985, reused; telegraph 1869; TX 1924, automatic 1953; Union C. b. 1899 by Brown Bros and Parker; pop. *c.*200 (1866), 310 (1871), 158 (1891), 177 (1901), 159 (1911), 158 (1933), 162 (1947), 184 (1954), 212 (1961), 188 (2011).

Rye Park (*Co. King*) 34°31'S. 148°54'E., 19 km SE of Boorowa, on Pudman Ck; settled 1836, subdivision 1886; bismuth, scheelite, tin 1952+, wool, farming; Angl. C. (St Matthew's) b. 1909 by Oliver John Stuart, closed, sold 2011; bridge b. 1887 by W.A. Brander, over Pudman Ck; bushfires 1944, 1952, 1956; cemetery (283 graves) 1900, incl. columbarium 1996; electricity 1952; mines: Clifton's, Just in Time (estab. 1914 by J.B. Hardiman, J.A. Hardiman, Wilson and O'Hara, reopened 1951 by H. Gordon and Edgerton Bros for scheelite, reworked 1952 by Scheelite NL), Mt Merton, Wallah Wallah Silver Mine (incl. smelter) 1891–1919, White Rock Tungsten Mine (Rye Park Scheelite NL and Tungsten Consolidated Ltd) 1915–19 and 1951–52; PO 1870; pound (stock) 1886; powder magazine; PS 1900, new one b. 1924 by J.J. Cummins; quarry; rifle range 1931; Rom. Cath. C. (St Joseph's) 1917; Salv. Army C. 1914; sawmills: George Noakes, A. Southwell, George Wilson & Son 1896, fire 1898, rebuilt 1899; school 1877, repairs 1896 by T. Telford, additions 1906 by G. Patterson; snow 1956; telephone 1901; TX (automatic) 1957; typhoid 1927; Unit. C. (orig. Meth.) b. 1927 by W.J. Irvine, and graveyard; Wes. Meth. C. 1866, reused, demolished, new one 1878; winery (G. Wilson); pop. 171 (1901), 318 (1911), 156 (1933), 323 (1947), 228 (1954), 283 (1961), 237 (2011).

Ryhope (*Co. Northumberland*) 32°59'S. 151°31'E., 7 km W. of Toronto, on Palmers Ck; cemetery (Lake Macquarie Memorial Park), incl. lawn cemetery, columbaria and crematorium; quarry; pop. 103 (2011).

Rylstone (*Co. Roxburgh*) 32°48'S. 149°58'E., 7 km N. of Kandos, on Cudgegong R.; Ryalstone till *c.*1856; surveyed and laid out 1842 by Walker Rannie Davidson, village gaz. 1843; mining, wool, cattle, olives, agric.; airfield (4 km NE); ambulance station; Angl. C. (St James's) b. 1858 by William Highfield, additions 1870; bridges over Cudgegong R.: one b. 1861, destroyed 1867, one b. 1899 by Edward William Fitzgerald, one b. 1948; bushfire 2009; butter factory (Rylstone Co-op. Dairy Co. Ltd) 1906 d. by A.H. Hardwick, reused; carriage-works: George H. Johnston and John H. Neil; cemetery (2,585 graves 1854+) 1868, incl. columbarium; CH 1856, reused, new one 1873, additions 1901 by Rigby Bros; concrete products plant (Jackson's); cordial factories: Alan Fitzgerald Cameron, sen. 1913 and J.N. Collins 1880; dam 1953, 49 ft (15 m) high, on Cudgegong R.; diphtheria (13 died) 1880; electricity 1926; FB; fire 1927; flour mills: Andrews', John Elgar and Skelton 1904, William Purvis 1872 (acquired and reused by E.H. Nash, fire 1922), J.H. Tee 1896–1901; freezing works (Sidney Phillip Paddison and Booth) 1913, leased 1922 to Francis Joseph Staff; granary; hailstorm 1897; hospital b. 1915–17, additions 1918 and 1928, additions and alterations 1935 by J.B. Simpkins; lock-up b. 1895 by Kidney and Corfield, closed; measles epidemic 1893; PO 1849, new one b. 1881 by Robert Thompson Highfield, closed 2007; police barracks b. 1885 by John Miller, jun.; pound (stock) 1860; Presb. C. (St Andrew's) b. 1902 by Robert Thompson Highfield, closed, sold and reused; PS 1866, new one b. 1887 by J.F. Hill; rabbit boning works (Quinnell Bros) 1934; railway bridge (timber truss) 1884 d. by John Whitton, replaced 1924, over Cudgegong R.;

reservoir; rifle range 1909; Rom. Cath. C. (St Malachy's) b. 1873–76 by Michael Mealey, d. by Edward Gell, extended 1960; RS 1884, station b. by White and Coghill, closed 1992; sale-yards 1954; school 1857–62, reopened 1869, new one b. by Alf Doorey, d. by George Allen Mansfield, additions and renovations 1883, modernised 1909, repairs 1918 by F.L. Wurth, burnt down 1925, replaced 1926 by Philip James Killey, new one 1980; sewerage 1973; tanneries: Michael Allen Hayes and William Henry Hawkins; telegraph 1875, new office b. 1881 by Robert Thompson Highfield; TX 1914, automatic 1983; Unit. C. (orig. Wes. Meth.) b. 1884 by Billie Smith, demolished; watch-house 1871; water reticulation 1955, treatment plant, augmentation 1963 and 1987; Wes. Meth. C. (Zion) 1853, closed, sold and reused, later demolished; pop. 135 (1861), *c.*130 (1866), 239 (1871), 333 (1881), *c.*400 (1884), 592 (1891), 499 (1901), 765 (1911), 756 (1933), 740 (1947), 761 (1954), 799 (1961), 716 (1966), 695 (1971), 691 (1976), 651 (1981), 654 (1986), 721 (1991), 723 (1996), 654 (2001), 615 (2006), 624 (2011).

Rywung (*Co. Parry*) see Weabonga.

S

Sackville (*Co. Cook*) 33°30'S. 150°53'E., 19 km E. of North Richmond, on Hawkesbury R.; formerly Sackville Reach; settled 1803; farming and orchards; Angl. C. (St Thomas's) 1833, destroyed 1867, replaced 1871 on new site, fire 1959, restored 1960, closed, sold and reused, and graveyard (85 graves 1827–1987); bridge 1880; church (Aboriginal) b. 1900 by Tommy Toloman, d. by Billy Buckambee; floods 1867, 1899, 1920; PO 1858; punt (diesel) b. 1948 by Morison & Bearby Pty Ltd, new one 2009, across Hawkesbury R.; telephone 1895; TX 1913, automatic 1967; Wes. Meth. C. 1825, new one 1838, destroyed 1867; wharf b. 1898 by W.B. Woodbury; pop. 51 (1947), 251 (2011).

Sackville Reach (*Co. Cook*) see Sackville.

Saddleback Mountain (*Co. Camden*) see Jerrara.

Saddle Camp (*Co. Murchison*) 30°07'S. 150°47'E., 34 km NE of Barraba, on Gundamulda Ck.

Saddle Camp (*Co. Selwyn*) see Cabramurra.

Safety Beach (*Co. Fitzroy*) 30°06'S. 153°12'E., 2 km N. of Woolgoolga, on Tasman Sea; FB; pop. 568 (1986), 530 (1991), 565 (1996), 590 (2001), 653 (2006), 769 (2011).

Sailors Flat (*Co. Inglis*) 30°43'S. 151°15'E., 25 km W. of Uralla.

St Albans (*Co. Northumberland*) 33°18'S. 150°58'E., 38 km W. of Ourimbah, on Macdonald R.; orig. Bullock Wharf, then Macdonald till 1840; surveyed 1837 by Butler, first lots sold 1842, town gaz. 1880, surveyed again by Felton Mathew; former river port, orig. wheat, then maize, fruit, vegetables, poultry, dairying, now tourism; Angl. C. (St Alban the Martyr) 1843, new one 1863, rebuilt 1897 by J.B. Stephens, d. by S. Rigg; bridges: one b. 1883–85 by Richard Jurd, destroyed 1889, and Norton Bridge (composite truss) b. 1901–3 by John Ahearn & Son, d. by Ernest Macartney de Burgh, 381 ft (116.1 m), over Macdonald R.; cemeteries: old (85 graves 1833+) and new (266 graves 1887+); CH 1876, destroyed 1889, new one (incl. lock-up) b. 1890–92 on new site by L. Pickup and W. Cummins, reused; electricity 1961; FB (station b. 1995, additions 2005); floods 1867, 1889 (man died and all houses destroyed), 1890, 1895, 1913, 1949, 1952, 1978; PO 1854–1979; police barracks 1883, destroyed 1889; school 1868, repairs 1900 by Laughton Bros, alterations 1901 by P. Morris, additions and repairs 1908 by Mellish Bros, closed 1946; telegraph 1879–85; telephone 1885; TX 1924, automatic 1979; Unit. C. (orig. Meth.) 1902, reused; watch-house b. 1848–52, destroyed 1889; Wes. Meth. C. 1858, new one 1862, damaged 1889, closed; pop. 21 (1846), 60 (1851), 91 (1856), 97 (1861), *c.*80 (1866), 57 (1871), 93 (1891), 170 (1901), 236 (1911), 174 (1933), 143 (1947), 86 (1954), 81 (1961), 50 (1966), 73 (2006).

St Anthonys (*Co. Camden*) 34°35'S. 150°37'E., 20 km SW of Dapto; RS (Ranelagh till 1948) 1932–70.

St Aubyn's (*Co. Brisbane*) see Parkville.

St Clair (*Co. Durham*) 32°22'S. 151°16'E., 25 km N. of Singleton, on Lake St Clair;

dairying and grazing; cemetery (submerged under Glennies Creek Dam); PO 1874–1947; telephone 1914; tin works (Larry M'Gowen); TX 1914; pop. 97 (1911), 79 (1933).

St Clements (*Co. Harden*) 34°34'S. 148°34'E., 20 km E. of Murrumburrah; RS 1927–75.

St Elmo (*Co. Hunter*) see Baerami Creek.

St Ethels (*Co. Northumberland*) see Maitland.

St Georges Basin (*Co. St Vincent*) 35°05'S. 150°36'E., 4 km NW of Sanctuary Point, on St Georges Basin; fishing, farming, tourism 1945+; Bapt. C.; bushfire 1952; FB; flood 2015; flying-boat base (World War II); Jehovah's Witnesses C.; PO 1927; salt-works (Cyril Blacket, became Tasman Salt Works Ltd in 1922); telephone 1914; TX 1926–69; Unit. C. (Bay and Basin) 1999; water supply augmentation 1983; pop. 20 (1933), 126 (1947), 207 (1954), 148 (1961), 1,129 (1976, incl. Sanctuary Point), 1,881 (1981, incl. Sanctuary Point), 3,126 (1986, incl. Sanctuary Point), 4,610 (1991, incl. Sanctuary Point), 5,988 (1996, incl. Sanctuary Point), 7,622 (2001, incl. Sanctuary Point), 8,343 (2006, incl. Sanctuary Point), 9,242 (2011, incl. Sanctuary Point).

St Georges Basin (*Co. St Vincent*) see also Basin View.

St Georges Basin East (*Co. St Vincent*) 35°06'S. 150°37'E., 2 km NW of Sanctuary Point, on St Georges Basin; PO 1959–84.

St Helena (*Co. Rous*) 28°40'S. 153°35'E., 4 km SW of Byron Bay, on Tinderbox Ck; RS, closed 1974; pop. 58 (1933), 53 (1954).

St Heliers (*Co. Durham*) 32°14'S. 150°55'E., 4 km N. of Muswellbrook, on St Hilliers Brook; orig. private village founded *c.*1836 by Lieut. Col. Henry Dumaresq, largely deserted by 1870; mining (coal disc. 1923 by John Loader); airfield; coalmine (St Heliers Coal Co.) 1923; flour mill (powered by horses or bullocks), bought by Lieut. Col. Henry Dumaresq and removed from Black Creek, re-erected 1833 by John Portus; training farm 1945–86, reused 1989 as gaol; pop. 70 (1911), 57 (1954), 82 (1961).

St Hilaire (*Co. Goulburn*) see Thurgoona.

St Huberts Island (*Co. Northumberland*) 33°30'S. 151°21'E., 2 km SE of Woy Woy, in Brisbane Water; orig. Bird Island; bought and subdivided by Kinnane, canal system subdivision by Hooker Rex Pty Ltd; oysters; sewerage 1993; pop. 1,032 (2011).

St Johns Hill (*Co. Goulburn*) 36°03'S. 147°00'E., 8 km NE of Albury, on Eight Mile Ck.

St Leonards (*Co. Vernon*) 31°14'S. 151°36'E., 27 km S. of Walcha, on Cobrabald R.; farming and grazing; PO 1890; telephone 1923; TX 1924; pop. 73 (1901), 65 (1933).

St Michaels (*Co. Harden*) 34°35'S. 148°33'E., 18 km E. of Murrumburrah; RS 1946–69.

St Patricks (*Co. Sandon*) see Armidale.

St Patrick's Plains (*Co. Northumberland*) see Singleton.

St Rocks (*Co. Macquarie*) see Sancrox.

St Vincent City (*Co. St Vincent*) 34°58'S. 150°44'E., 4 km N. of Callala Bay; subdivided by Henry F. Halloran & Co., but never developed.

Salamander Bay (*Co. Gloucester*) 32°44'S. 152°05'E., 5 km W. of Nelson Bay, on Salamander Bay; formerly rutile mining and oysters; aircraft parts factory (Aerospace Plastic Components Pty Ltd); ambulance station 2011; bushfires 1951 and 2018; Christ. Outreach C. (The Rock) 2001; Christ. Revival Crusade C. (Beachside); FB (station b. 2014); naval base 1916–22, sold and dismantled 1922; PO 1956; quarry (Diemars); research station (brackish water fish culture) 1968; Salv. Army C.; schools: primary (Nelson Bay till 1998 then Tomaree) 1892, new buildings b. 1893 by Norbert A. O'Leary, new school b. 1929 by W. Williams, extended 1910, additions 1958, 1960, 1964, 1967, 1974, and HS (Nelson Bay till 1998 then Tomaree) 1975, additions 1981; SD Adventist C. (Nelson Bay); TC (Hunter Institute of Technology, Tomaree Campus) 1998; telephone 1956; Unit. C. (Port Stephens) 1990; pop. 124 (1961), 97 (1954), 4,087 (1996, incl. Soldiers Point), 4,968 (2001, incl. Soldiers Point), 5,232 (2006, incl. Soldiers Point), 5,101 (2011, incl. Soldiers Point).

Salisbury (*Co. Durham*) 32°13'S. 151°34'E., 28 km NW of Dungog, on Williams R.; dairying; cemetery 1904, incl. columbarium; Cong. C. b. 1903 by James Rumbel; diphtheria 1918; PO 1916; sawmills: Pender & Foster Ltd and C.A. Tiedeman; school 1882–1972; telephone 1914; TX 1915–61; typhoid 1907; Union C. 1884; pop. 104 (1901), 94 (1911), 94 (1933), 114 (1947), 106 (1954), 113 (1961), 85 (2006).

Salisbury Court (*Co. Sandon*) 30°44'S. 151°31'E., 10 km S. of Uralla.

Salisbury Plains (*Co. Sandon*) 30°46'S. 151°32'E., 13 km S. of Uralla; farming; earth tremor 1935; PO 1892–1931; school 1881–1926; pop. 73 (1901), 100 (1933), 61 (1947), 57 (1954), 54 (1961), 220 (2011).

Salis Flats (*Co. Cook*) see The Slopes.

Sallys Corner (*Co. Camden*) 34°37'S. 150°14'E., 9 km NW of Bundanoon; winery (Sutton Forest Estate) estab. 2002 by Nick and Santina Lo Russo.

Sallys Flat (*Co. Wellington*) 33°00'S. 149°34'E., 41 km W. of Kandos, on Slatterys Ck; gold, farming, grazing; mine (Monkey Hill Deep Lead operated by Turon Ancient Leads Mining Co.) <1910; PO 1899; 2 quarries; Rom. Cath. C. (St Columba's) 1895, additions 1931 by P. Guthrie, demolished 1997, replacement (St Brigid's) 1997, and graveyard (93 graves 1864+); school 1884, closed 1888, new school b. 1914 by Alfred Ede, closed 1932; telephone 1914; TX 1928–81; pop. 51 (1901), 71 (1911), 67 (1933), 54 (1947), 51 (1954), 54 (1961).

Sallys Flats (*Co. Cook*) see The Slopes.

Salt Ash (*Co. Gloucester*) 32°47'S. 151°56'E., 18 km E. of Raymond Terrace, on Tilligerry Ck; settled 1837; oysters, farming, sand mining; bushfire 2018; Church of Christ (Port Stephens); electricity 1942; FB; gunnery range (World War II); PO 1890, burnt down 1964; sawmill (A.C. Brown) 1929, burnt down 1935; school 1884 b. by Blanch, additions 1954 by A.H. McKenzie & Sons, additions by R.T. Parker Pty Ltd; storm 2015; tank traps (World War II); telegraph 1906; telephone 1906; TX 1926, automatic 1963; wharf (Thurlow's, opened to public 1933); pop. 147 (1901), 120 (1911), 206 (1933), 276 (1947), 313 (1954), 280 (1961), 621 (2006), 1,098 (2011).

Saltbush Plain (*Co. Barrona*) 29°56'S. 144°38'E., 127 km W. of Bourke.

Salt Creek (*Co. Tara*) see Tareena.

Salt Village (*Co. Rous*) see Casuarina.

Saltwater (*Co. Gloucester*) 32°00'S. 152°34'E., 3 km SW of Old Bar, on Tasman Sea; (incl. Saltwater Beach Estate).

Saltwater Beach Estate (*Co. Gloucester*) see Saltwater.

Salty Creek (*Co. Northumberland*) see Edgeworth.

Sams Corner (*Co. Auckland*) 36°38'S. 149°31'E., 30 km W. of Bega; school 1903 b. by Robert Wilson, new one b. 1910 by H.J. Wilton, d. by H. Henry, closed 1919; pop. 85 (1933).

Sams Creek (*Co. Dampier*) 36°22'S. 149°57'E., 10 km W. of Bermagui; school 1900 b. by E.J. Martin, closed 1903.

Sams Flat (*Co. Vernon*) 31°15'S. 151°47'E., 34 km SE of Walcha, on Tia R.; school 1897–1912.

Sancrox (*Co. Macquarie*) 31°26'S. 152°47'E., 6 km NE of Wauchope, on Hastings R.; formerly St Rocks; village laid out and gaz. 1869, but never developed; cemetery 1892; Meth. C. 1902; sawmill b. by George Allan Johnson, burnt down 1906.

Sanctuary Point (*Co. St Vincent*) 35°07'S. 150°38'E., 26 km S. of Nowra, on St Georges Basin; Angl. C. (St Peter's); bridge over Cockrow Ck; bushfire 1965; FB; PO 1957; school 1976, additions 1993; sewage works; telephone 1956; TX (automatic) 1969; water supply augmentation 1983; pop. 38 (1961), 272 (1971), 1,129 (1976, incl. St Georges Basin), 1,881 (1981, incl. St Georges Basin), 3,126 (1986, incl. St Georges Basin), 4,610 (1991, incl. St Georges Basin), 5,988 (1996, incl. St Georges Basin), 7,622 (2001, incl. St Georges Basin), 8,343 (2006, incl. St Georges Basin), 9,242 (2011, incl. St Georges Basin).

Sandbar (*Co. Gloucester*) 32°23'S. 152°31'E., 22 km S. of Forster, on Smiths Lake.

Sandgate (*Co. Northumberland*) 32°52'S. 151°42'E., 5 km NE of Wallsend, on Hunter

R.; formerly Sand Hills Crossing; bridge 1938 to Hexham, destroyed 1956, replaced 1962 (with Bailey bridge being used in the interim), over Ironbark Ck; cemetery (85,000+ burials) 1887, damaged 1989, lawn cemetery added 1998; container terminal (Crawfords Freight Lines) 2009; Meth. C. 1927; monumental stone works: B. Barnes, D. Davies, N. Eggleston, Charles Gaites, F. Jordon, V.J. Palmer, Russell Bros, A. Smith, Thomas Tonks & Son, Edward Young; PO 1923; railway bridge (steel truss) 1898 to Hexham, 110 ft (33.5 m), new one (steel truss) 1912, 126 ft (38.4 m), over Ironbark Ck; RS: Sandgate 1881–1985, station demolished 1987 and Sandgate Cemetery 1881–1985; school 1942 b. by J.C. Pickles, closed 1969; telephone 1923; TX (automatic) 1953–62; pop. 57 (1911), 287 (1933), 309 (2011).

Sandgate (*Co. Northumberland*) see also Shortland.

Sandgate Cemetery (*Co. Northumberland*) see Sandgate.

Sand Hills Crossing (*Co. Northumberland*) see Sandgate.

Sand Holes (*Co. Benarba*) 28°57'S. 149°39'E., 65 km E. of Mungindi.

Sandigo (*Co. Mitchell*) 34°55'S. 146°39'E., 21 km S. of Narrandera, on Sandy Ck; farming; PO 1925; 2 quarries; school 1896–1903 and 1914–55; telephone 1923; TX 1924, automatic 1951; pop. 120 (1933), 103 (1947), 114 (1954), 62 (1961), 175 (2006).

Sandilands (*Co. Drake*) see Mallanganee.

Sandilands Range (*Co. Drake*) see Mallanganee.

Sandon (*Co. Clarence*) 29°40'S. 153°19'E., 26 km S. of Yamba, on Coral Sea; site reserved 1885, settled *c.*1901 by S.W. Dowling; isolated fishing and holiday retreat, oysters 1906+, then timber, later cattle; aeroplane crash 1948; bushfire 1994; cyclones 1955 and 1977; electricity 1964; jetty 2001; school 1957–59; pop. 29 (1961).

Sandy Beach (*Co. Fitzroy*) 30°09'S. 153°12'E., 5 km S. of Woolgoolga, on Tasman Sea; also known as Diamond Head; bananas; Bapt. C. 1994; FB; Jehovah's Witnesses C. 1989; reservoir; 2 sawmills; school 1985; water reticulation 1980; pop. 933 (1986), 1,431 (1991), 1,685 (1996), 1,804 (2001), 1,828 (2006), 2,125 (2011).

Sandy Camp (*Co. Clarence*) 29°32'S. 153°02'E., 18 km SW of Maclean, on Rush Gully.

Sandy Creek (*Co. Ashburnham*) 33°12'S. 148°48'E., 13 km S. of Molong; school 1883–94.

Sandy Creek (*Co. Bland*) 33°49'S. 147°59'E., 19 km W. of Grenfell.

Sandy Creek (*Co. Booroondarra*) 31°54'S. 145°23'E., 61 km SW of Cobar.

Sandy Creek (*Co. Brisbane*) 31°50'S. 150°59'E., 14 km E. of Murrurundi.

Sandy Creek (*Co. Brisbane*) 32°16'S. 150°46'E., 12 km W. of Muswellbrook; toll-gate; Union C. b. 1911 by D. Jordan, d. by James Hicks; pop. 94 (1911), 66 (1933).

Sandy Creek (*Co. Clarke*) 30°30'S. 152°12'E., 51 km E. of Armidale; pop. 51 (1933).

Sandy Creek (*Co. Cooper*) 34°11'S. 146°39'E., 30 km NW of Ardlethan; Meth. C. 1923.

Sandy Creek (*Co. Lincoln*) 32°13'S. 149°14'E., 28 km SW of Dunedoo, on Sandy Ck; school 1957–58; pop. 77 (1911).

Sandy Creek (*Co. Mitchell*) 35°19'S. 147°19'E., 24 km S. of Wagga Wagga; pop. 58 (1911).

Sandy Creek (*Co. Mitchell*) see also Uranquinty.

Sandy Creek (*Co. Oxley*) see Egelabra.

Sandy Crossing (*Co. Clarence*) 29°46'S. 153°06'E., 16 km SE of South Grafton.

Sandy Crossing (*Co. Richmond*) 29°10'S. 153°11'E., 20 km SW of Woodburn.

Sandy Falls (*Co. Harden*) 34°59'S. 148°12'E., 12 km NE of Gundagai, on Murrumbidgee R.; pop. 20 (1933).

Sandy Flat (*Co. Camden*) 34°28'S. 150°09'E., 17 km W. of Berrima.

Sandy Flat (*Co. Clive*) 29°14'S. 152°01'E., 20 km S. of Tenterfield; formerly Cottesbrook; farming and grazing; butter factory (J.H. Reid); cemetery; FB; PO 1887–1980; RS 1886–1975; sawmills: T.W. Hewetson, James Mangleson, Harry Perrin; school (Bluff River till 1911) 1886–1911 and 1957–65; telephone 1906; TX 1928; pop. 242 (1901), 151 (1911), 125 (1933), 100 (1947), 99 (1954), 70 (1961), 193 (2006), 209 (2011).

Sandy Flat (*Co. Rous*) 28°48'S. 153°32'E., 6 km W. of Lennox Head.

Sandy Flat (*Co. Roxburgh*) 33°01'S. 149°47'E., 30 km SW of Rylstone.

Sandy Gully (*Co. Wynyard*) 35°19'S. 148°02'E., 2 km W. of Adelong; pop. 81 (1911), 44 (1933).

Sandy Hill (*Co. Clive*) 28°55'S. 152°15'E., 26 km NE of Tenterfield, on Cataract R.; formerly Sandy Hills; timber and grazing; cemetery; PO 1888, burnt down 1940; sawmill (Julius Imberger, later sold to Armstrong Bros & Rand, closed 1922); school 1888–92; telephone 1914; TX 1928; pop. 27 (1933).

Sandy Hills (*Co. Clive*) see Sandy Hill.

Sandy Hollow (*Co. Brisbane*) 32°20'S. 150°34'E., 13 km NW of Denman; dairying and farming; bridge 1893, new one (steel truss) 1961, over Goulburn R.; bushfire 1957; caterpillar infestation 1937; FB; flood 1955; 40 oil-shale retorts (Gotting) operated by Shale & Oil Products Co-op. Ltd 1942–45, site ruinous; PO 1937; RS 1917–73; sawmill (James Gageler); school (Giants Creek till 1970) 1877, new one 1971, additions 1975; telephone 1927; TX (automatic) 1974; pop. 71 (1933), 196 (1947), 109 (1954), 88 (1961), 263 (2006), 401 (2011).

Sandy Hook (*Co. Cook*) 33°41'S. 150°10'E., 13 km SW of Blackheath, on Coxs R.

Sandy Point (*Co. Argyle*) 35°04'S. 149°52'E., 37 km S. of Goulburn.

Sandy Point (*Co. Gloucester*) see Nelson Bay.

Sandy Point (*Co. Northumberland*) see Woy Woy.

Sandy's Middle Station (*Co. Wellington*) see Stuart Town.

Sangar (*Co. Denison*) 35°42'S. 146°10'E., 32 km E. of Berrigan; RS (Victorian railway); silo.

San Isidore (*Co. Mitchell*) 35°08'S. 147°18'E., 8 km W. of Wagga Wagga; PO 1964–78; Rom. Cath. C. (Our Lady of the Blessed Eucharist); school 1958–83; pop. 125 (1961), 323 (2001), 308 (2006), 339 (2011).

San Remo (*Co. Northumberland*) 33°13'S. 151°31'E., 2 km NE of Charmhaven, on Budgewoi Lake; bridge 1916, replaced 1933, to Charmhaven, over Wallarah Ck; schools: Northlakes primary 1991, additions by R.T. Parker Pty Ltd and Northlakes HS 1981; sewerage 1990; pop. 4,304 (2011).

Sapling Flat (*Co. Cook*) 33°11'S. 150°09'E., 27 km N. of Wallerawang.

Sapphire (*Co. Arrawatta*) 29°41'S. 151°20'E., 24 km NE of Inverell; mining, farming, grazing; airfield; mines; PO 1927–61; school 1886–1928; telephone 1924; TX 1925; pop. 77 (1933), 76 (1954), 70 (1961).

Sapphire Beach (*Co. Fitzroy*) 30°14'S. 153°09'E., 8 km NE of Coffs Harbour; water reticulation 1980; pop. 917 (1991), 994 (1996), 1,765 (2011).

Sapphire Gardens (*Co. Fitzroy*) 30°15'S. 153°09'E., 6 km NE of Coffs Harbour, on Tasman Sea; bananas; reservoir.

Saratoga (*Co. Northumberland*) 33°28'S. 151°21'E., 3 km NE of Woy Woy, on Brisbane Water; (incl. Veteran Hall and Yattalunga); Mount Pleasant till 1910; subdivided 1906 by Arthur Rickard & Co.; oranges, fishing, boating, tourism; Angl. C. (St Bede's); cemetery (Veteran Hall, 15 burials 1827–1934); electricity 1938; FB (station b. 1988); fire 1924; New Apostolic C.; PO 1915; Presb. C.; school (Brisbania) 1941, additions 1973 and 1988; telephone: Saratoga 1914 and Yattalunga 1951; TX 1919–28; Unit. C. (orig. Meth.) 1921, extended 1951, closed 1983, sold 1985, removed and reused; Wes. Meth. C. 1889; wharves (incl. Bayview, Byalla Lane, Newton, Saratoga, Veteran Hall, Yattalunga); pop. 222 (1933), 361 (1947), 523 (1954), 709 (1961), 3,715 (2011).

Sassafras (*Co. St Vincent*) 35°06'S. 150°15'E., 29 km NW of Milton; surveyed by George Legg, laid out 1856, largely deserted; nuts; bushfire 1923; FB 1942; PO 1861–1931; sawmill (Sassafras Timber Co.), burnt down 1923; school 1890–1903; snowstorm 1919; pop. 66 (1901), 38 (2011).

Satur (*Co. Brisbane*) see Scone.

Saucy Creek (*Co. Wellesley*) 36°58'S. 149°12'E., 7 km S. of Bombala, on Saucy Ck; school 1882–1901; Union C. 1890 (moved to Ando).

Saumarez (*Co. Sandon*) 30°33'S. 151°35'E., 7 km SW of Armidale; school 1862–1927; pop. 29 (1933).

Saumarez Ponds (*Co. Sandon*) 30°29'S. 151°34'E., 10 km W. of Armidale, on Saumarez Ck; Angl. C. (St Nicholas's) b. 1864 by Henry Lane, vestry added 1871, church renovated 1973–74; Bapt. C. 1884; cemetery; PO 1863–64; Wes. Meth. C. 1872; pop. 153 (1911), 60 (1933), 69 (1947), 52 (1954), 422 (2011).

Savernake (*Co. Denison*) 35°44'S. 146°03'E., 24 km E. of Berrigan; surveyed 1889; East Savernake till 1892; wheat, sheep, cattle; cemetery (burials 1897+) 1890; FB 1977 (station b. 2009); fire 1980; flood 1939; gale 1923; PO 1895, new one b. 1908, burnt down 1912; Rom. Cath. C. (St Brendan's) b. 1912 by E. Burwood, d. by Louis Harrison; sale-yards 1918–39; sawmill (J.W. Brown) 1886; school 1906–41, reopened 1954, burnt down 1980; telephone 1899; TX 1911, automatic 1975; Unit. C. (orig. Presb.) b. 1924 by Henshaw, d. by Andrew G. Sloane; pop. 156 (1911), 154 (1933), 100 (1947), 96 (1954), 98 (1961).

Savernake (*Co. Denison*) see also Warmatta.

Sawpit Creek (*Co. Wallace*) 36°21'S. 148°34'E., 9 km NW of Jindabyne, on Sawpit Ck; quarry.

Sawpit Gully (*Co. Monteagle*) 34°21'S. 148°19'E., 4 km SE of Young; pop. 59 (1901), 53 (1911), 76 (1933).

Sawpit Gully (*Co. Monteagle*) see also Pitstone.

Sawtell (*Co. Raleigh*) 30°22'S. 153°06'E., 8 km S. of Coffs Harbour, on Tasman Sea; Bonville Reserve till 1928; reserve surveyed 1861 by William Albert Braylesford Greaves, settled 1863 by Walter Harvey, subdivided 1923 by Oswald Sawtell, village gaz. 1927; fruit, tourism, retirement centre; Angl. C. (St Nicholas's) o. 1978 in former Union C.; clock tower fabricated 2008 by W.E. Smith Engineering; drought 1960–61; FB 1950 (old station closed 1971, relocated and reused, new one b. 1972 by Keith Johnston); floods 1954, 2001, 2017; hailstorm 2013; PO 1927; PS (in rented premises) 1951; railway bridge (Walter Harvie Bridge) over Boambee Ck; 2 reservoirs; Rom. Cath. C. (Mary Help of Christians) o. 1983 in former church hall; RS (1 km N.) 1925–89; school 1928, additions 1953, 1956, 1970, new buildings b. 1974 by R. & B. Constructions Pty Ltd; sewerage 1973, augmentation 1992; telephone 1923; TX 1926, automatic 1950; Union C. b. 1934 by Jack Scheef, d. by O.C. Sawtell, sold 1978 to Angl. C.; Unit. C. 1998; water reticulation 1956, augmentation 1980; pop. 349 (1933), 823 (1947), 1,440 (1954), 1,440 (1954), 1,596 (1961), 1,558 (1966), 3,711 (1976), 5,970 (1981), 7,905 (1986), 10,809 (1991), 13,240 (1996), 13,831 (2001), 15,009 (2006).

Sawyers Creek (*Co. Gloucester*) see Willina.

Sawyers Gully (*Co. Burnett*) 29°33'S. 150°32'E., 4 km W. of Warialda.

Sawyers Gully (*Co. Northumberland*) 32°47'S. 151°26'E., 4 km N. of Abermain, on Sawyers Gully; farming; abattoir 1915; bridge b. 1910 by C.E. Mitchell, over Black Waterholes Ck; colliery (Glen Greta) o. 1930 by Glen Greta Colliery Co. Ltd, flooded 1930, closed 1931, sold 1933 by James Fallins to E.M. Robbins and reopened and renamed Glen Main Colliery, sold 1936 to Alfred Osland, closed 1939, razed; diphtheria 1910; measles epidemic 1910; Meth. C. 1907; PO 1898; railway (colliery); school (Heddon till 1904) 1903–65; telephone 1910; TX, closed 1943; typhoid 1916; pop. 305 (1911), 337 (1933), 189 (1947), 61 (1954), 58 (1961), 261 (2006).

Sawyers Point (*Co. Gloucester*) see Karuah.

Saxa (*Co. Lincoln*) 32°13'S. 149°01'E., 40 km E. of Dubbo, on Spicers Ck.

Sayers Lake (*Co. Livingstone*) 32°44'S. 143°16'E., 128 km S. of Wilcannia; RS 1936, closed.

Scabben Flat (*Co. Georgiana*) 33°47'S. 149°17'E., 27 km S. of Blayney, on Rocky Bridge Ck; formerly also known as Colo Creek; gold rush 1881; barytes mine (Kempfield) 1918 and 1923–67; goldmines: Colossal Reef 1918, Gully Swamp (Lane and

Lyndhurst Railways & Mines Ltd) <1903, Mastodon 1918–20, The Sugar Loaf; PO 1895.

Scarborough (*Co. Northumberland*) see Bonnells Bay.

Schanks's Forest Plains (*Co. Northumberland*) see Maitland.

School Gates (*Co. Murray*) see Yass.

Scone (*Co. Brisbane*) 32°03'S. 150°52'E., 23 km N. of Muswellbrook, on Figtree Ck; (incl. Satur); orig. Invermein; disc. 1824 by Henry Dangar, settled 1825 by Francis Little, site reserved 1826, surveyed 1836 by Robert Dixon, laid out 1837 by James Ralfe, town gaz. 1837, first lots sold 1838, designated as chief town of the county, munic. 1888–1957; orig. wheat, then grazing, tobacco, maize, oats, lucerne, grapes, fruit, vegetables, dairying, horses, mining; abattoir; airfield (Nandowra) 1936; airport (4 km NW) b. 1961 by R.G. Wakefield and Shorncliffe Pty Ltd, upgraded 1983, runway extended 2011; ambulance station b. 1936 by Frank Treasure, d. by Robert Newburgh Hickson; Angl. C. 1841, new one 1859, demolished 1883, replacement (St Luke's) b. 1884 by M. Parkhill, d. by John Wiltshire Pender, and graveyard (182 graves 1840+), incl. columbarium; Bapt. C. o. 1981 (in former Wes. Meth. C.); benevolent asylum 1872, closed, reused, restored; boot factory (Harper's) 1867–78, reused; 4 brickworks (incl. Newman Bros and Edwin Smithers 1884); bridges: one over Kingdon Ponds and one over Middle Brook; butter factory (Scone Dairy Co-op. Co. Ltd) b. 1910 by Hardy, rebuilt 1926, acquired 1933 by Raymond Terrace Co-op. Dairy Co. Ltd; carriage-works (Scone Coach Works); cemetery 1878, incl. lawn cemetery; CH (Invermein) 1838, new one 1849 d. by Mortimer William Lewis, additions 1862 d. by Alexander Dawson, repairs 1867 by Thomas W. Brown, additions 1883 d. by James Johnstone Barnet, closed, reused, third one b. 1937 on new site by H.T. Brown, d. by Edwin Evan Smith; concrete pipe works (Monier) 1937; cordial factories: John T. Aisbett, Charles Waterland Satchell, R.E. and E.M. Bragg, J. and J. Hayne; creamery (Scone Dairy Co-op. Co. Ltd) b. 1893 by Whitehead and Boyd, closed, sold 1899; dengue fever 1926; earth tremor 1868; electricity 1920; FB 1925 (station b. 1956, new one 1968); fires 1909, 1924, 1926; floods 1879 and 1955; flour mill b. 1860 by John Boorer, enlarged 1870, bought 1872 by James Little, bought 1880 by Malcolm Campbell & Co., taken over and reused by M. Campbell & Co. Pty Ltd, chimney demolished 1949, and mill reused again; foot-bridge over Figtree Gully; grasshopper infestations 1875 and 1937; hailstorm 1948; heatwave 1946; hospital (Scott Memorial) b. 1913 by H.A. Whittle, d. by Walter Liberty Vernon, additions 1934, additions 1937 by Robert Daniel Quiggin, additions 1939 by F. and R. Compton, additions 1962; kerbing and guttering commenced 1892; PO 1833, new one b. 1879 by J. Pritchard, additions 1898 by D. M'Donald, additions and alterations 1909 by Charles Benaud Smith; pounds (stock): Satur 1840 and Scone 1849; powerhouse (Scone Electric Light & Power Co.) 1921; Presb. C. 1861, alterations and renovations 1875, additions 1886, reused, new one, and graveyard; PS (incl. lock-up) b. 1874 by John Hudson, repairs 1897 by J.G. Imrie, additions and alterations 1910 by A. Folkhard, reused, new one b. 1947 by J.C. Pickles; reservoir 1931; rifle range, man killed 1903, new range 1912; Rom. Cath. C. 1861, porch added 1886, church closed 1925, reused, new one on new site (Our Lady, Queen of Peace) b. 1925 by J.E. Smith, d. by Peter Joseph Gannon, and graveyard (106 graves 1863+); RS 1871, station b. by William and Charles Cains; sale-yards 1905, rebuilt 1973; sawmill (M. Campbell & Co.), fire 1922; schools: primary 1863, new one b. 1876 by John Hudson, additions 1881, additions and repairs 1898 by Mantova and Brown, additions and alterations 1909 by Charles Benaud Smith, additions 1922 and 1927, additions 1929 by W.H. Mitchell, additions 1934 by William Stronach, additions 1957, and HS 1964 b.

by William Hughes & Co., additions 1972; sewerage: Scone 1939, augmentation 1987, and Satur 1981; storms 1932 and 2007; streets kerosene lit 1896, gas lit 1902; TC (a campus of Hunter Institute of Technology); telegraph 1862, new office b. 1879 by J. Pritchard, additions 1898 by D. M'Donald; toll-gate (toll abolished 1874); tornado 1892; TX 1908, automatic 1974; typhoid 1883 and 1894; Unit. C. (St Andrew's, orig. Presb.) b. 1911 by D. McNaughton & Son, d. by Power and Adam, and columbaria (1963 and 1982); watch-house b. 1869 by Thomas Pillow; waterworks b. 1931 by G.W. and H.R. Gilmore, water supply augmentation 1956, 1970, 1984, (water supply to Satur 1951); Wes. Meth. C. b. 1892 by Miller and Wilson, damaged 1892, additions, reopened 1930, damaged 1948, reused; pop. 63 (1841), 117 (1846), 180 (1851), 244 (1856), 343 (1861), *c.*400 (1866), 574 (1871), 600 (1881), 876 (1891), *c.*1,200 (1895), 1,290 (1901), 1,548 (1911), 2,261 (1933), *c.*2,300 (1941), 2,391 (1947), 3,504 (1954), 2,813 (1961), 2,915 (1966), 3,259 (1971), 3,424 (1976), 3,949 (1981), 4,272 (1986), 4,290 (1991), 4,581 (1996), 4,565 (2001), 4,624 (2006), 5,079 (2011).

Scotchman (*Co. Raleigh*) 30°28'S. 152°50'E., 6 km W. of Bellingen, on Bellinger R.; school 1919–36; telephone 1928; TX 1929–73; pop. 29 (1933).

Scotts Creek (*Co. Brisbane*) 31°45'S. 150°58'E., 12 km E. of Murrurundi; pop. 58 (1954).

Scott's Creek (*Co. Macquarie*) see Mitchells Island.

Scotts Flat (*Co. Durham*) 32°36'S. 151°14'E., 8 km SE of Singleton, on Hunter R.; farming and dairying; floods 1867 and 1893; PO 1868; telephone 1914; TX 1915, automatic 1953; pop. 158 (1901), 89 (1911), 228 (1933), 180 (1947), 160 (1954), 213 (1961).

Scotts Flat (*Co. Durham*) see also Roughit.

Scotts Flat (*Co. Wellesley*) 37°02'S. 149°09'E., 15 km SW of Bombala, on Boggy Ck.

Scotts Head (*Co. Raleigh*) 30°45'S. 153°00'E., 9 km SE of Macksville, on Tasman Sea; Angl. C. (Church of the Ascension) 1985; FB; PO 1938; 2 reservoirs (towers); rifle range; school 1948, additions 1991; telephone 1939; TX 1939, automatic 1956; water reticulation 1967; pop. 34 (1933), 124 (1947), 190 (1954), 150 (1961), 209 (1971), 332 (1976), 517 (1981), 649 (1986), 840 (1991), 821 (1996), 793 (2001), 789 (2006), 820 (2011).

Scotts Hill (*Co. Camden*) see Theresa Park.

Scott's Siding (*Co. Monteagle*) see Maimuru.

Scott's Town (*Co. Gloucester*) see Stockton.

Scouts Alley (*Co. Durham*) 32°05'S. 151°28'E., 44 km NW of Dungog.

Seaham (*Co. Durham*) 32°40'S. 151°44'E., 11 km N. of Raymond Terrace, on Williams R.; (incl. Brandy Hill); surveyed and laid out by George Boyle White, village gaz. 1838, declined 1939+, partly recovered *c.*1970+; farming and dairying; Angl. C. (St Andrew's) 1861, closed, sold 2019; bridge (Jimmy Scott Bridge) 1973, to East Seaham, over Williams R.; bushfires 1939 (3 houses destroyed) and 1951; cemetery (130 graves 1851+) 1886; FB; fires 1928 and 1935; floods 1893, 1895, 1913; furniture factory (Wallace's); PO 1853; Presb. C. b. 1878 by James Wallace, burnt down 1939, replacement b. 1941 by Robards, d. by Walter Harold Pender; punt 1830, sunk, second one (manual) b. 1862 by Cameron, Ritchie and Hay, third one (4 car capacity) b. 1927 by Hackett Bros, ceased 1971, across Williams R.; quarry (shale), disused; Rom. Cath. C. (St Ita's) 1893, demolished; school 1852, new one 1885 on new site, burnt down 1939, reopened 1939 in building removed from Greswick, new building b. 1968, additions 2002 by R.T. Parker Pty Ltd; telephone 1889; TX 1918, automatic 1958; weir on Williams R.; Wes. Meth. C. 1850, abandoned and collapsed; wharves; winery (Porphyry Point) estab. 1838 by Henry Carmichael, inundated 1895; pop. 18 (1851), *c.*50 (1866), 71 (1891), 325 (1901), 240 (1911), 98 (1933), 78 (1947), 141 (1954), 146 (1961), 977 (1996), 1,149 (2001), 1,284 (2011).

Seaham East (*Co. Gloucester*) 32°39'S. 151°45'E., 14 km N. of Raymond Terrace; bridge (Jimmy Scott Bridge) 1973, to Seaham, over Williams R.; FB; pop. 58 (1947), 359

(2011).

Seahampton (*Co. Northumberland*) 32°54'S. 151°35'E., 2 km N. of West Wallsend, on Minmi Ck; surveyed 1889; collieries: Blue Gum and Seaham No. 1 (o. 1890 as Monkwearmouth, renamed 1892, fire 1895 and sealed, reopened 1898, strike 1924, closed); FB; pop. 166 (1911), 136 (1933), 80 (1947), 97 (1954), 94 (1961), 229 (1991), 268 (1996), 354 (2006), 311 (2011).

Seal Rocks (*Co. Gloucester*) 32°26'S. 152°32'E., 28 km S. of Forster, on Tasman Sea; tourism; lighthouse (Sugarloaf Point) b. 1875 of brick by John McLeod, d. by James Johnstone Barnet, 49 ft (15 m), converted to electricity 1966, automated 1987; PO 1957; telephone 1911; TX 1955–75; water supply augmentation 1991; pop. 44 (1961), 129 (2006).

Sebastopol (*Co. Clarendon*) 34°35'S. 147°32'E., 15 km S. of Temora; mining (gold disc. 1869, rush 1880–84) and farming; mines: Barron Syndicate, Evening Star, Homeward Bound, La Mascotte, Maid of Judah, Morning Star, The Cameron; PO 1870–1973; Presb. C. (St Stephen's); school 1871–73 and 1884–1949; stamper battery 1906 (removed from Junee Reefs); telephone 1906; TX 1911, automatic 1973; pop. 153 (1901), 151 (1911), 124 (1933), 78 (1947), 73 (1961), 359 (2011).

Second Flat (*Co. Dudley*) 30°49'S. 152°26'E., 48 km W. of Macksville, on Macleay R.

Second Moonbi (*Co. Inglis*) 30°56'S. 151°07'E., 24 km NE of Tamworth.

Secret Bay (*Co. Northumberland*) 33°03'S. 151°35'E., 2 km N. of Wangi Wangi, on Eraring Bay.

Sedgefield (*Co. Durham*) 32°33'S. 151°15'E., 7 km E. of Singleton, on Stinking Gully; farming and dairying; 4 bridges; cemetery (1,261 graves 1898+), incl. columbaria; Faith Walk C.; PO 1876; school 1859, new building b. 1897 by T.H. and J.W.P. Blick, closed 1920, moved 1927 to Mirannie; telephone 1914; TX 1915; pop. 80 (1901), 106 (1911), 57 (1933), 489 (2011).

Seelands (*Co. Clarence*) 29°37'S. 152°54'E., 8 km NW of Grafton, on Clarence R.; dairying; bushfire 1936; creamery (NSW Fresh Food & Ice Co. Ltd) removed 1900 from Lavadia; PO 1927–44; punt, to The Whiteman, across Clarence R.; school 1889–1901, reopened 1918, new school b. 1929 on new site by E.C. Bragg, closed 1967; telephone 1914; TX 1928, automatic 1952; water supply augmentation 1986; pop. 83 (1901), 96 (1933), 96 (1947), 90 (1954), 96 (1961), 211 (2011).

Segenhoe (*Co. Brisbane*) 32°07'S. 150°56'E., 8 km NE of Aberdeen, on Pages R.; estab. 1827+ by Peter McIntyre for settlement in 1834 by Thomas Potter Macqueen; horses; Angl. C. (St Paul's) o. 1952, removed from Brushy Hill; drought 1867; school (Leighton Park till 1936) 1912–74; telephone 1912; TX 1949, automatic 1958; pop. 114 (1911), 204 (1933), 154 (1947), 122 (1954), 187 (1961), 317 (2011).

Segenhoe (*Co. Durham*) see Dangarfield.

Selection Flat (*Co. Richmond*) 29°11'S. 152°57'E., 36 km S. of Casino.

Selmes (*Co. King*) see Winduella.

Settlement City (*Co. Macquarie*) see Port Macquarie.

Seven Mile (*Co. Monteagle*) see Weddin.

Seven Mile Junction (*Co. Napier*) 31°44'S. 149°42'E., 10 km N. of Coolah.

Seven Mile Point (*Co. Wentworth*) see Pomona.

Seven Oaks (*Co. Dudley*) 31°00'S. 152°57'E., 15 km NE of Kempsey, on Macleay R.; agric.; bushfire 1895; cheese factory (A. Jackson) 1916, taken over and closed down 1930 by Macleay River Dairying Co. Ltd; creamery (Victoria) b. 1897 by E. Debenham; floods 1863 and 1893; heatwave 1902–3; wharf b. 1884 by Thomas Lawson, damaged 1890; pop. 127 (1901), 156 (1911).

Seven Oaks (*Co. Dudley*) see also Bellimbopinni.

Seventeen Mile Hollow (*Co. Cook*) see Linden.

Seventeen Mile Plain (*Co. Gunderbooka*) 29°58'S. 145°51'E., 22 km NW of Bourke.

Severn (*Co. Gough*) see Dundee.

Sevington (*Co. Arrawatta*) 29°32'S. 151°22'E.,

34 km SE of Ashford; grazing; PO 1927–31; telephone 1927; TX 1928–31.

Sewells Creek (*Co. Westmoreland*) 33°46'S. 149°39'E., 21 km W. of Oberon, on Sewells Ck; goldmining; mines: Carters Hill 1923–32 and Main Ridge group 1907–17 and 1935–38; pop. 48 (1933).

Sexton Hill (*Co. Rous*) see Banora Point.

Sextonville (*Co. Rous*) 28°40'S. 152°49'E., 19 km W. of Kyogle, on Doubtful Ck; soldiers' settlement 1922–23; sawmilling, farming, dairying; bushfire 1926; PO 1927–42; sawmills: Gloucester Estate Timber Co., sold 1923, and John Thomas Sexton, bought 1918 by NSW Box Co. Ltd; telephone 1924; weir on Doubtful Ck; pop. 28 (1933), 52 (1954).

Seymour (*Co. Wallace*) see Adaminaby.

Shadforth (*Co. Bathurst*) 33°23'S. 149°12'E., 8 km N. of Millthorpe; orig. also known as Frederick's Valley; farming and orchards; Angl. C. (St Paul's) 1873, chancel added 1896, closed 1977, moved to Orange; flour mill (Phoenix), wind powered, estab. 1843 by Thomas Raine, d. by Henry Hough, steam engine added 1844, taken over 1860 by Edmund Raine; PO: Frederick (or Frederick's Valley) 1861–67 and Shadforth 1927; school (Guyong West till 1884) 1881 d. by William Edmund Kemp, closed 1976; telephone 1923; TX 1937–65; pop. 199 (1911), 82 (1933), 71 (1947), 67 (1954), 85 (1961), 247 (2011).

Shakeshaft (*Co. Northumberland*) see Mangrove Mountain.

Shaking Bog (*Co. Buccleuch*) 35°13'S. 148°26'E., 22 km NE of Tumut, on Shaking Bog Ck.

Shallow Bay (*Co. Gloucester*) 32°13'S. 152°26'E., 9 km SW of Forster, on Shallow Bay; bushfire 2013; pop. 33 (1933).

Shallow Crossing (*Co. St Vincent*) 35°32'S. 150°12'E., 20 km N. of Batemans Bay, on Clyde R.; Angl. C. (St Peter and St Paul's) 1914–36, sold 1936 to W.J. Meyers, sold 1994 to A. Ryan who moved it to Runnyford and reused it; causeway across Clyde R.; footbridge 1937; PO 1927, burnt down 1957; sawmill (A.S. Veitch); school 1916–42; telephone 1916; TX 1921; pop. 81 (1933).

Shallow Rush (*Co. Ashburnham*) 33°07'S. 148°09'E., 3 km NW of Parkes.

Shamrock Hill (*Co. Northumberland*) see Maitland East.

Shannon Brook (*Co. Richmond*) 28°55'S. 152°57'E., 11 km SW of Casino, on Serpentine Lagoon; Angl. C. (St James's) 1914; broom factory (D. Attrill); bushfire 1926; hailstorm 1919; RS (5 km E.) 1927–75; school 1883–87 and 1907–75; telephone 1923; TX 1923–65; pop. 194 (1911), 249 (1933), 286 (1947), 204 (1954), 199 (1961), 245 (2011).

Shannons Flat (*Co. Beresford*) 35°56'S. 148°57'E., 37 km NW of Cooma; bushfire 2014; school 1957, additions 1960, closed 1965, moved to Peak View; TX (automatic); pop. 51 (1933), 56 (1961), 208 (2011).

Shannon Vale (*Co. Gough*) 29°42'S. 151°53'E., 15 km E. of Glen Innes, on Mann R.; grazing, farming, dairying; caterpillar infestation 1947; gale 1907; PO 1927–46; Presb. C. 1914; school 1881, repairs 1892 by G.B. Clark, closed 1940; telephone 1925; TX 1949, automatic 1966; pop. 39 (1841), 61 (1901), 131 (1911), 76 (1933), 60 (1947), 54 (1954), 58 (1961), 177 (2006).

Shark Creek (*Co. Clarence*) see Central Tyndale.

Shark Hole (*Co. Auckland*) 36°58'S. 149°53'E., 3 km SW of Pambula Beach, on Pambula R.

Shark Island (*Co. Macquarie*) 30°52'S. 153°01'E., 3 km NW of South West Rocks, in Tasman Sea; pop. 37 (1933).

Shark's Creek (*Co. Clarence*) see Upper Shark Creek.

Sharps Creek (*Co. Wynyard*) 35°24'S. 148°03'E., 10 km S. of Adelong; farming and grazing; Angl. C. (St Andrew's) 1913–28, reopened 1933; bushfire 1940; school (Greenhills till 1890) 1881–1913; pop. 117 (1901), 72 (1911), 61 (1954).

Shaw (*Co. Bathurst*) 33°40'S. 149°12'E., 15 km S. of Blayney; farming and grazing; Angl. C. (St Peter's), closed, sold for demolition 1952; cemetery (graves 1880–1929); PO 1888; school 1879 b. by S.F. Smith, closed 1905, reopened 1913, closed 1922; telephone 1919; TX 1920–60; pop. 119 (1901), 67 (1911), 78 (1933), 53 (1947).

Shaws (*Co. Wynyard*) 35°27'S. 148°11'E., 8 km NE of Batlow; RS 1940–75.

Shaws Bay (*Co. Rous*) see Ballina East.

Shaws Creek (*Co. Argyle*) 34°47'S. 149°47'E., 7 km E. of Goulburn; school 1882, new building b. 1884 by J. Cahir, closed 1934, reopened 1957, closed 1961.

Sheahan (*Co. Wynyard*) 35°27'S. 147°46'E., 30 km SW of Adelong, on Umbango Ck; RS 1951, closed.

Shearlegs (*Co. Robinson*) 31°53'S. 145°58'E., 44 km S. of Cobar; telephone 1928; TX 1929–64.

Sheedys Gully (*Co. Cook*) see Lithgow.

Sheep Station Point (*Co. Roxburgh*) see Sofala.

Sheet of Bark (*Co. Bathurst*) 33°43'S. 148°50'E., 17 km NE of Cowra, on Sheet of Bark Ck; PO 1874–88.

Shell Cove (*Co. Camden*) see Albion Park and Shellharbour.

Shellharbour (*Co. Camden*) 34°35'S. 150°52'E., 11 km SE of Dapto, on Tasman Sea; (incl. Bass Point, Blackbutt, Flinders, Shell Cove); estab. and laid out 1851, munic. proc. 1859, subdivisions 1923 and 1966, city proc. 1996; orig. timber, then maize, wheat, potatoes, hort., dairying, beach goldmining 1868+, basalt 1880+, cattle and pigs 1882+, shipping till 1887, fishing, tourism; Angl. C.: Lakeview and St Paul's (b. 1859 by William James, demolished, replacement d. and b. 1884–86 by John Simmons); bacon factory (Hicks Bros) 1878–1904, demolished 1905; Bapt. C. 1861; breakwater b. 1877–79; carriage-works (Mood Bros, moved 1895 to Albion Park); cemetery (3,391 graves) 1895; CH (incl. lock-up) 1877–1908, acquired 1938 by E. Thomas and reused; Christ. Outreach C.; dam (Blackbutt) 1957, 20 ft (6 m) high; droughts 1862 and 1908; electricity 1928; flood 1873; flour mill estab. 1857 by Robert Wilson, demolished 1922; harbour b. 1859–79; Jehovah's Witnesses C. (Blackbutt); jetty b. 1859 by Groat and Martin, (second) 1864, (third) 1874, (fourth) b. 1880 by Chambers & Co., (fifth) 1909; lime and cement works (Exploratory Construction Products Ltd) 1931; Lutheran C. (Holy Cross); PO 1857, new one b. 1949; Presb. C. 1859; PS 1877, new one (in rented premises) 1952; quarries: Bass Point (Chambers & Co.) 1880, man killed 1928, closed 1938, new one 1968, and Fuller's; reservoirs (Blackbutt and Shellharbour); Rom. Cath. C. (Our Lady Star of the Sea) 1861, extensions b. 1906 by Jones and Thorn, d. by John Francis Hennessy and Joseph Ignatius Sheerin, renamed Stella Maris in 1953, new one (All Saints') b. 2012 by Manteena Pty Ltd, d. by Darnall Holdings; schools: Flinders 2003, Shell Cove 2005, Shellharbour 1859 (new building b. 1928 by A. Stephens & Son, additions 1962, 1964, 1966); streets lit by oil 1899, then electricity 1928; TC 1978, additions 1985 and 1997; telegraph 1879; TX 1920, automatic 1938; typhoid (man died) 1896; Unit. C. (orig. Wes. Meth.) b. 1863–66 by James and I. Dinning, renovated 1901, extended 1979; watch-house 1861–77; waterfront beautification 1895; water supply 1955; wharf b. 1908 by T. Whitfield; pop. 1,732 (1871), 1,400 (1881), 1,587 (1891), *c.*1,600 (1895), 1,929 (1901), 474 (1911), *c.*1,400 (1916), 1,527 (1921), 1,670 (1926), 1,660 (1931), 1,877 (1933), 1,990 (1936), 2,300 (1941), 2,390 (1946), 3,117 (1947), 5,523 (1954), 13,394 (1961), 22,062 (1966), 31,137 (1971), 37,316 (1976), 41,790 (1981), 57,071 (2001).

Shellharbour (*Co. Camden*) see also Dunmore.

Shellharbour Junction (*Co. Camden*) see Dunmore.

Shellharbour Railway Station (*Co. Camden*) see Dunmore.

Shellsea Estate (*Co. Northumberland*) see Nords Wharf.

Shelly Beach (*Co. Macquarie*) 31°27'S. 152°56'E., 3 km SE of Port Macquarie, on Tasman Sea.

Shelly Beach (*Co. Northumberland*) 33°22'S. 151°30'E., 3 km S. of The Entrance, on Tasman Sea; Bapt. C.; PO 1969–93; school

(Tuggerah Lakes Secondary College, The Entrance HS till 2002) 1970, additions 1972, 1975, 1977; telephone 1969; pop. 1,266 (2011).

Shellys Flat (*Co. Argyle*) 34°44'S. 149°55'E., 19 km E. of Goulburn; mine (Argyle or Carrington Iron Mine).

Shepardstown (*Co. Wynyard*) 35°17'S. 148°03'E., 4 km NW of Adelong, on Adelong Ck; founded 1871 by Amos Shepard, declined 1916+; goldmining; Angl. C. (St Luke's), enlarged and re-roofed 1899, refurbished 1910; bridge b. 1921 by H. Bailey, over Adelong Ck; fire 1912; flood 1879; footbridge over Adelong Ck; mines: Donkey Hill, Gibraltar Consolidated 1857, strike 1898, closed 1916, reworked 1928–42, Great Victoria, O'Brien's, Perkins's, Radcliffe's; PO 1872, burnt down 1944; school 1879 b. by William Balman, repairs 1881 by William M. Hotten, additions and alterations 1883 by D. Boston, repairs 1906 by W.J. Ritchie, closed 1969; stamper batteries: Lane's and Perkins's; telephone 1946; pop. 150+ (1872), 430 (1901), 332 (1911), 191 (1933), 92 (1947), 62 (1954).

Shepherds (*Co. Clarendon*) 35°00'S. 147°28'E., 15 km NE of Wagga Wagga; RS 1893–1975; silo 1932.

Shepherds Creek (*Co. Wellington*) 32°58'S. 149°06'E., 27 km NE of Molong, on Shepherd Ck; PO 1870–79.

Shepherds Flat (*Co. Clarke*) 30°32'S. 152°09'E., 47 km E. of Armidale, on Shepherds Flat Ck.

Shepherds Gully (*Co. Argyle*) 34°42'S. 150°02'E., 30 km E. of Goulburn.

Shepherds Siding (*Co. Clarendon*) 35°01'S. 147°28'E., 14 km NE of Wagga Wagga; farming; PO 1927–43; silo 1932; pop. 57 (1933).

Sheraton Meadows (*Co. Lincoln*) see Dubbo.

Sherwins Flat (*Co. Argyle*) see Tarago.

Sherwood (*Co. Dudley*) 31°04'S. 152°44'E., 11 km W. of Kempsey, on Macleay R.; farming; Angl. C. (St John's) 1903, sanctuary 1929; bridge b. 1892 by Lawson Bros, over Macleay R.; cheese factory (P. McCabe) 1917; diphtheria 1915; floods 1891 and 1894; PO 1883; Rom. Cath. C. (Sacred Heart) 1910, closed, reused; sawmill; school 1882–1968; telephone 1913; TX 1949, automatic 1959; pop. 101 (1901), 104 (1911), 167 (1933), 126 (1947), 123 (1954), 134 (1961), 261 (2011).

Sherwood (*Co. Fitzroy*) see Kungala.

Sherwood (*Co. Rous*) 28°26'S. 152°46'E., 31 km NW of Kyogle; pop. 59 (1947), 75 (1954), 61 (1961).

Sherwyn (*Co. Hume*) 35°37'S. 146°49'E., 18 km W. of Culcairn; school 1911–40.

Shipley (*Co. Cook*) see Blackheath.

Shirrenden Hill (*Co. Monteagle*) 34°17'S. 148°22'E., 8 km NE of Young; Yatnaville till 1927; PO 1927; quarry; school (Woodonga till 1927) 1881–1929; telephone 1921; TX 1926.

Shoal Bay (*Co. Gloucester*) 32°43'S. 152°11'E., 3 km E. of Nelson Bay, on Shoal Bay; (incl. Tomaree Head); army garrison camp 1942–45, reused 1947 as hospital; fort (World War II) on Tomaree Head, abandoned and derelict; jetty, closed 2011, replaced 2013; PO 1952; quarry (abandoned); school 1991; telephone 1952; pop. 142 (1954), 2,090 (1997), 1,749 (2006), 1,837 (2011).

Shoalhaven (*Co. St Vincent*) see Nowra and Numbaa.

Shoalhaven Heads (*Co. Camden*) 34°51'S. 150°45'E., 13 km E. of Nowra, on Shoalhaven R.; Jerry Bailey till 1953; tourism; Angl. C. (St Peter's) o. 1961 in reused building removed from Coolangatta, relocated 1991, fire 1998, extended 1999; cemetery, defunct; FB (station b. 1961); flood 2015; jetty 1991; PO 1937; Presb. C.; reservoir 1955; school (Coolangatta till 1958) 1861, additions 1960, 1978, 2010; sewage works; telephone 1937; TX (automatic) 1954; pop. 175 (1954), 220 (1961), 486 (1971), 718 (1976), 1,542 (1981), 1,999 (1986), 2,351 (1991), 2,486 (1996), 2,738 (2001), 2,910 (2006), 2,995 (2011).

Shooters Hill (*Co. Westmoreland*) 33°54'S. 149°52'E., 21 km S. of Oberon; orig. hunting, later farming and grazing; cemetery (104 graves) 1888; gaol (Oberon afforestation camp) 1931, additions 1990, renamed 1993; mine (gold and silver); PO 1889; Rom. Cath.

C. (St Michael's) 1909 d. by John Francis Kenny, closed, sold and reused; school 1882–95 and 1957–70; telephone 1906; TX 1915–78; pop. 60 (1901), 59 (1911), 52 (1933), 53 (1954), 71 (1961).

Shortland (*Co. Northumberland*) 32°53'S. 151°41'E., 3 km NE of Wallsend, on Ironbark Ck; cemetery; Christ. Brethren Assemblies C. (Gospel); flood (girl died) 1951; Meth. C. 1963; PO 1934; Rom. Cath. C. (Our Lady of Victories) b. 1964 by R.J. Avard & Son, d. by John Kevin Gannon; Salv. Army C. 1938; school (Sandgate till 1932) 1929, additions 1956, 1960, 1966, 1974, additions 2010 by RTC Group; sewage works; telephone 1931; Unit. C.; pop. 304 (1933), 3,705 (2011).

Shuttleton (*Co. Mouramba*) 32°08'S. 146°04'E., 74 km S. of Cobar; village gaz. 1902, thrived 1902, defunct; mining (copper disc. 1900 by Jacky Owen) till 1907 and grazing; cemetery 1904; fire 1905; mine (W. Longworth & Co.), incl. furnaces and refinery b. 1903, strike 1904, sold 1908 to Nymagee Copper Co.; PO 1903; PS 1902–10; sawmill; school 1903–20; telephone 1905; TX 1916–65; pop. *c.*500 (1902), 98 (1911).

Sidebottom (*Co. Gloucester*) see Koorainghat.

Sidebottom Creek (*Co. Gloucester*) see Koorainghat.

Sidebrook (*Co. Hardinge*) see Ben Lomond.

Sidmouth Valley (*Co. Westmoreland*) 33°35'S. 149°50'E., 14 km N. of Oberon, on Sidmouth Valley Ck; also formerly known as Sydmouth Valley; Wes. Meth. C. 1859, new one 1885–1905, dismantled 1934 by K.M. Hunt, and graveyard.

Silent Grove (*Co. Clive*) 29°09'S. 151°40'E., 34 km W. of Tenterfield, on Silent Grove Ck; 2 mines (tin); PO 1878–82; pop. 32 (1933).

Silverdale (*Co. Camden*) 33°56'S. 150°35'E., 17 km S. of Glenbrook, on Scotcheys Ck; orig. Mulgoa Forest Mountain; Angl. C. (All Saints') 1906, closed, sold 2016 and 2019, reused; bridge (James Beres Bridge) over Beres Ck; bushfires 1957 and 2001; FB; PO 1945; reservoir; rifle range; school 1891–96 and 1942–68; telephone 1945; pop. 60 (1911), 149 (1933), 159 (1947), 194 (1954), 241 (1961), 1,406 (1981, incl. Warragamba), 2,666 (1986, incl. Warragamba), 3,509 (1991, incl. Warragamba), 3,873 (1996, incl. Warragamba), 4,175 (2001, incl. Warragamba), 4,466 (2006, incl. Warragamba), 4,365 (2011, incl. Warragamba).

Silver Hill (*Co. Murray*) 35°32'S. 149°27'E., 30 km SE of Queanbeyan, on Molonglo R.; airfield; school 1892, additions and repairs 1895 by H.C. Bruce, closed 1906.

Silverton (*Co. Yancowinna*) 31°53'S. 141°13'E., 24 km W. of Broken Hill, on Umberumberka Ck; Umberumberka till 1883; founded 1876 by John Stokie, surveyed and laid out 1884 by Barlow, town gaz. 1884, thrived 1884–85, munic. proc. 1886 (council disbanded 1899, munic. status removed 1907), town declined 1886+, now virtually abandoned; mining (silver-lead disc. 1882 by John Stokie) 1882–94, then poultry, now limited tourism; Angl. C. (St Stephen's) 1887–97; Bible Christ. C. 1885; bond store; breweries: Lion Brewery (o. 1885 by Edmund Resch, Richard Frederick Edward Nicolas Resch and John Penrose, taken over 1885 by Emil Karl Resch, inundated 1898, closed 1901), Topman's Brewery (T. Bock) 1891, Unicorn Brewery (A. Gillett and E. Phillips), Union Brewery (estab. 1886 by John Crossing as Nectar Brewery, acquired 1888 by Union Barrier Brewing Co. Ltd, in liquidation 1890, renamed, closed, ruined); cemetery 1887; CH b. 1887–89 by Sara and Dunstan, d. by James Johnstone Barnet, closed, reused 1948; cordial factories: J.W. Fairchild and Melbourne (o. 1886 by E. Carlisle & Co.); customs-house; dam (Rathole) 1885; electricity 1967; floods 1884, 1898, 1904, 1911, 1972; gale 1891; gaol b. 1888 by Walter and Morris, additions 1891 by John Colmer, closed 1892, reused, closed 1943, restored 1968, reused; hospital 1884, new one 1887, reused, demolished 1914; mines (within 5 km): Little Bonanza, Lucky Hit, Nadbuck Copper Mine, Silverton Proprietary, Umberumberka (John Stokie) 1882–92, Umberumberka East, Umberumberka North;

PO 1883; powder magazine b. by Ground and Snowball; Presb. C. 1885, sold to Wes. Meth. C. and reused; PS 1884–1945; Rom. Cath. C. (St Carthage's) 1886, restored, disused; RS 1888; Salv. Army C.; schools: Silverton 1884, new one b. 1888 by Sara and Dunstan, closed 1970, reused, and Umberumberka 1889–94; telegraph 1885; telephone 1902; tramway (to Broken Hill), 3 ft 6 in. (1,067 mm) gauge, b. 1888 by Millar Bros for Silverton Tramway Co. Ltd, closed 1970; TX 1912; typhoid 1885; Wes. Meth. C. 1886, destroyed 1891, new one o. in former Presb. C., closed and disused; pop. *c.*150 (1882), *c.*250 (Sept. 1883), *c.*500 (Dec. 1883), 1,745 (Dec. 1884), *c.*3,000 (1886), 1,695 (1888), 1,397 (1891), *c.*600 (1895–1900), 286 (1901), 252 (1911), 403 (1922), 131 (1933), 103 (1947), 141 (1954), 137 (1961), *c.*60 (1983), *c.*85 (1987), *c.*50 (1999), 87 (2006).

Silverwater (*Co. Northumberland*) see Balcolyn.

Simpkins Creek (*Co. Rous*) 28°50'S. 152°47'E., 28 km W. of Casino; pop. 60 (1933).

Simpsons Ridge (*Co. Raleigh*) 30°39'S. 152°48'E., 5 km W. of Bowraville, on Bendinni Ck; school 1887, new building b. 1888 by George Parkins, closed 1947; pop. 50 (1947).

Simsville (*Co. Gloucester*) 32°24'S. 152°02'E., 16 km W. of Bulahdelah, on Alderley Ck; estab. 1914; timber; PO 1936–47; sawmill (Millars Timber & Trading Co. 1911–22, Pines & Hardwoods of Aust. Ltd 1922–28, Smith & Ellis Ltd 1934–42, Allen Taylor & Co. Ltd 1942, burnt down 1947); tramway (timber), closed 1940; pop. 46 (1933).

Sinclair (*Co. Gough*) see Long Plain.

Singleton (*Co. Northumberland*) 32°34'S. 151°10'E., 41 km NW of Maitland, on Hunter R.; (incl. Combo, Darlington, Dunolly, Glenridding, Gowrie, Hunterview, Kelso, McDougalls Hill, Pigeon Point, Redbournberry, Rose Point, Singleton Heights, South Singleton, The Retreat, Wattle Ponds); orig. St Patrick's Plains then Patrick's Plains till 1829, Darlington till 1841; disc. 1820 by John Howe, estab. 1827 by Benjamin Singleton, surveyed and founded 1835, first lots sold 1836, munic. proc. 1866, thrived 1863–69, munic. abolished 1976; orig. wheat (declined 1890–1900), maize, grapes, then tobacco till 1890s, dairying 1860+, oats, barley, vegetables, wine, fruit, sheep, cattle, coalmining, engineering; ambulance station (in former house) 1936, new one b. 1952 by H.J. Bartrop & Son; Angl. C.: All Saints' (b. 1845–51, original building work condemned and demolished, rebuilt from 1849 by Thomas Turner, d. by Edmund Thomas Blacket, extensions 1865 also d. by Blacket, extensions 1881–83 by G.B. Lloyd, d. by Blacket Bros, deteriorated by 1907, demolished 1911 as unsound, replacement b. 1911–13 by H.P. Conolly, d. by Frederick George Castleden, enlarged and renovated 1924, rebuilt 1969, renovated again, and columbarium) and St Luke's (South Singleton) 1888, enlarged 1906; army camp 1941; Assemblies of God C. (Christ.); Bapt. C. 1963, sold 1988, new one 1989; benevolent asylum 1862 d. by Thomas Rowe, closed, sold to Loder and reused; bicycle works (Oscar Burleigh Hatherly); 2 boiling-down works (incl. J.B. Bossley); boot factory (Jarman's); breweries: first one 1845, second one 1849, William Tinson 1867–68; 2 brickworks (Darlington); bridges over Hunter R: first one b. 1866 by Goddard, Dunolly (steel Pratt truss) b. 1905 by Gummow, Forrest & Co., 611 ft (186.2 m), closed 1986, reopened 1992, Redbourneberry 1870, destroyed 1877, replacement (3 iron lattice truss continuous spans fabricated in Belgium) erected 1889–91 by A.C. Shadler & Co., d. by John Alexander McDonald, 1,230 ft (375 m), reused, new adjacent one (continuous steel composite trough girder spans) b. 2003 by John Holland (Constructions) Pty Ltd, The Crossing 1986; butter factories: Singleton Central Co-op. Dairy Co. Ltd (incl. cheese factory and ice works), rebuilt 1916, Singleton Creamery & Butter Factory (James Moore & Co. Ltd) 1897, Singleton Farmers & Dairying Co. Ltd, sold 1912 to Thomas Blunt; carriage-works: Diedrich Buchtmann, J.S. Hayes 1907 (sold 1919 to Albert Partridge), H. McFadden, jun. 1883, Edward Gates (taken over 1881 by John T. Gates), Peter Naylor 1897; cemeteries: general (1,257 graves) 1889, Glenridding (orig. Presb., now Unit., 525 graves 1843+), Windmill Hill 1844; CH 1841 d. by Mortimer William Lewis, reused, demolished, replacement b. 1868 by William Cains, d. by James Johnstone Barnet, repairs 1879 by Melville, Anderson & Son, reused 1899, additions 1899, renovated 1929, re-roofed 1972; Christ. Israelite C. 1862, closed, relocated and reused, new one b. 1934 by J. Cann and E. Gould; clothing factory (H. Henry & Co.) 1944; cordial factories: George Achurch (bought by Jules Hopkins), George Coe, A.J. Foster and Moroney (bought by Coleman Bros), Harry Pinchin 1877 (taken over by Alexander Mather, taken over 1938 by Alexander Mather, jun. and James C. Mather); cyclone (houses unroofed) 1899; dengue fever 1926 and 1943; diphtheria 1907; droughts 1837–39 and 1906; earth tremors 1841, 1842, 1868, 1872; FB: McDougalls Hill, Singleton 1886 (station b. 1916 by E.L. Thorne, repairs 1933 by E.C. Partridge), Wattle Ponds; fires 1888, 1897, 1900, 1902, 1903, 1914, 1918, 1929, 1933; floods 1840, 1857, 1867, 1870, 1874, 1877, 1890, 1893, 1913, 1949, 1952, 1955, 2007; flour mills: J.D. Bower, Larkins', J. Martin, Phoenix (estab. 1829 by Benjamin Singleton, burnt down, rebuilt 1860, acquired 1885 by Charles H. Martin, bought by James Moore & Co. Ltd and converted to butter factory 1897, destroyed 1955), Railway (estab. by William Kingston, burnt down 1852, new one 1877, taken over 1879 by John Atkin and E. Horder, burnt down 1907), E.B. Sawkins, F. Williams; foundry (Silver's); Free Presb. C. 1860, and graveyard; 4 furniture factories; gales 1902, 1905, 1918, 1925; gasworks estab. 1881 by Alexander Munro; grasshopper infestations 1918, 1922, 1937; hailstorms 1895 and 1996; hospital (Dangar) b. 1907 by H.P. Conolly, d. by Alfred Spain and Thomas Frame Cosh, additions 1909, 1961, 2012, extended 2013 by Ware Building Pty Ltd; jam and pickle factory (Berry's) 1938; Jehovah's Witnesses C.; joineries: C. Fellowes & Sons 1952, and Charles Gould and Frederick King 1874, relocated 1882, burnt down 1888, partnership dissolved, reopened 1914 by Gould Bros & Co.; lock-up 1840, additions 1861 by George Kain, additions 1874, closed, reused 1899; milk factory (Singleton Dist. Co-op. Society Ltd), additions 1948; mines rescue station (Hunter Valley) 1983; monumental stone works (H.J. Bartrop); PO: Darlington 1864–71, Singleton 1829 (new one b. 1878 by William Dart, d. by James Johnstone Barnet, additions d. by Walter Liberty Vernon, reused, replacement b. 1973–75), South Singleton 1901 (additions and alterations 1923 by T. Simpson & Son, additions and alterations 1939 also by Simpson, d. by Hoskings and Pilgrim); police barracks b. 1879 by W.H. Galbraith; pounds (stock): Darlington 1865 and Singleton 1864; Presb. C. (St Andrew's) 1838, renovated 1867 by Christian; PS (incl. lock-up) b. 1897 by James Richardson, d. by Walter Liberty Vernon, new one b. 1926 by Thomas Ellis, additions and alterations 1976; punt estab. by Benjamin Singleton; railway bridge (laminated timber arch) b. 1862–66 by Hughes and Goddard, 523 ft (159.4 m), reused 1924 as road bridge, railway bridge replaced 1902 with steel Pratt truss, replaced again 1974, over Hunter R.; railway engine shed 1875, extended 1897 and 1899; railway round-house (6 bays) 1905, enlarged 1923; railway turntable, 50 ft (15.2 m), replaced 1901, 60 ft (18.3 m); reservoirs (on Gowrie Hill): No. 1 (500,000 gal. or 2,273 kl) b. 1909 by T. Connell & Sons, and No. 2 (750,000 gal. or 3,409.5 kl) b. 1930 by T. Connell & Sons; rifle range (Combo) b. 1908 by David Hooker; Rom. Cath. C.: St Augustine's 1845 (replaced by St Patrick's, b. 1860 by Alexander C. Anderson and Christopher Trier, d. by William Munro, additions 1875 by Richard Southon, d. by William Morrison, extensions 1881 by Gervis Parr, d. by John Wiltshire Pender, extensions

1894 d. by Frederick Burnhardt Menkens, damaged 1915, additions, twin towers and chapel 1921 d. by Thomas Wilfred Silk, and columbarium) and Sacred Heart of Jesus; RS 1863, station b. by Matthew and Walter Jamieson, additions and alterations 1885 by T.A. King, additions and alterations 1896, refreshment room closed 1961; sale-yards: Darlington (Thomas Cadell) 1863, Dunolly (b. by M'Cosker), Redbournberry 1909, Singleton (William Foster); Salv. Army C. 1888; sawmills: Excelsior Steam Saw & Joinery Works (estab. 1874 by Charles Gould and Fred King, relocated 1882, boiler explosion 1886, burnt down 1888 and King left firm, mill rebuilt, became Gould Bros & Co., boy killed 1902, steam powered till 1943), Kelso Steam Saw Mill (Spinks Bros), Singleton Sawmill Co. 1892; schools: Darlington 1864–65, Dunolly 1883–1940, King Street 1979, additions 1982, Singleton primary 1852 (new building 1858, demolished, new school b. 1876 by James Pritchard, d. by John Wiltshire Pender, repairs 1884 by D. Gardiner, additions 1909 by E.P. Frost & Co., additions 1940 by Short Bros, d. by Cobden Parkes, additions 1961, 1965, 1970), Singleton HS 1956 (additions 1965, 1968, 1978, major upgrade 1995), Singleton Heights 1978 (additions 1990), South Singleton 1906 (b. by Thomas Ellis, additions and alterations 1923 by T. Simpson & Son, closed 1928, reopened 1949, closed 1978); SD Adventist C.; sewerage 1940, augmentation 1987; smallpox 1914; soap and candle factory (John Campbell) 1860; squalls 1926 and 1932; streets gas lit 1881, electric lit 1922; tannery (Darlington); TC 1955, became a campus of Hunter Institute of Technology in 1992, additions by R.T. Parker Pty Ltd, additions 2018 d. by Brewster Hjorth Architects; telegraph 1861, new office b. 1878 by William Dart, d. by James Johnstone Barnet; telephone (South Singleton) 1901; tin works (George Adams); tobacco factories: James Hutchison 1884 and Smith's; tornado 1899; toy factory (Alan Glass) 1939; TX 1899, automatic 1975; typhoid 1896, 1901, 1904, 1910; Unit. C.: Wesley (orig. Wes. Meth.) b. 1882 by Edmund Gould, d. by James Henry Bolster and James Edward Justelius, alterations 1949, re-roofed 1957 and St Andrew's (orig. Presb.) b. 1904–6 by George Broomfield, d. by William Mark Nixon and John Shedden Adam, jun.; waterworks b. 1910 by Gilliver, Gilmore and Connell (machinery supplied by Gibson, Battle & Co.), augmentation 1988 and 1994; Wes. Meth. C.: Dunolly 1898 and Singleton 1845, new one 1857, reused; pop. 500+ (1828), 431 (1841), 565 (1846), 630 (1851), 739 (1856), 1,000 (1861), 1,187 (1871), 1,951 (1881), 2,595 (1891), 3,001 (1901), 3,985 (1911), 4,402 (1933), *c.*4,500 (1941), 4,683 (1947), 5,265 (1954), 5,223 (1961), 6,188 (1966), 7,181 (1971), 7,917 (1976), 9,572 (1981), 10,990 (1986), 11,861 (1991), 12,519 (1996), 12,531 (2001), 13,665 (2006), 13,962 (2011).

Singleton Heights (*Co. Northumberland*) see Singleton.

Six Mile Creek (*Co. Auckland*) 36°55'S. 149°48'E., 7 km W. of Pambula; pop. 20 (1933).

Six Mile Flat (*Co. St Vincent*) 35°22'S. 149°46'E., 9 km N. of Braidwood; farming and grazing; PO 1927–30; telephone 1915; TX 1928–59; pop. 58 (1911).

Sixteen Mile Gums (*Co. Waradgery*) 34°44'S. 144°47'E., 26 km S. of Hay.

Sixteen Mile Tank (*Co. Bland*) 33°56'S. 147°15'E., 5 km E. of West Wyalong; PO 1894–95.

Skeleton Creek (*Co. Gough*) 29°43'S. 151°52'E., 12 km E. of Glen Innes; mining (tin); Chinese joss house; pop. 150 (1933), 52 (1947).

Skennars Head (*Co. Rous*) 28°50'S. 153°36'E., 4 km S. of Lennox Head, on Coral Sea; pop. 23 (1933), 1,032 (2006), 1,104 (2011).

Skillion Flat (*Co. Dudley*) 31°01'S. 152°44'E., 13 km NW of Kempsey; farming; cemetery 1899; creamery (W.G. Trees, jun. and C. Sutherland, jun.) o. in Apr. 1897, moved in Sept. 1897 to Turners Flat; PO 1886; school 1897–1902; telephone 1907; TX 1928–64; pop. 54 (1901), 32 (1933).

Skinners Shoot (*Co. Rous*) 28°39'S. 153°35'E., 2 km SW of Byron Bay, on Cumbebine Swamp; pop. 62 (1933), 51 (1947), 54 (1954), 239 (2011).

Slamannon (*Co. Livingstone*) 32°02'S. 143°39'E., 59 km SE of Wilcannia; telephone 1923; TX 1939–51.

Slashers Flat (*Co. Wellington*) see Cullenbone.

Slateland (*Co. Argyle*) see Middle Arm.

Slate Vale (*Co. Argyle*) see Middle Arm.

Sleepy Hollow (*Co. Goulburn*) see Albury.

Sleepy Hollow (*Co. Rous*) 28°25'S. 153°30'E., 6 km SW of Pottsville, on Sheens Ck; telephone 1926; TX 1949–59; pop. 103 (1933), 52 (1954), 190 (2006).

Slippery Creek (*Co. Westmoreland*) see Hazelgrove.

Sloane (*Co. Denison*) 35°55'S. 146°01'E., 8 km N. of Mulwala; horse dip 1936; RS (Victorian railway); silo.

Smalls Forest (*Co. Clarence*) 29°40'S. 153°03'E., 12 km E. of Grafton; school 1885–1911 and 1919–71.

Smedmore (*Co. Northumberland*) see Wickham.

Smelleys Lagoon (*Co. Harden*) 34°30'S. 148°41'E., 8 km S. of Boorowa; school 1902–13, sold and removed 1916.

Smiggin Holes (*Co. Wallace*) 36°24'S. 148°26'E., 2 km NE of Perisher Valley, on Pipers Ck; winter snow resort; PO 1963; 3 reservoirs; sewage works; TX (automatic) 1960.

Smiths Creek (*Co. Clarence*) 29°31'S. 152°44'E., 26 km NW of Grafton, on Smiths Ck; pop. 34 (1933).

Smiths Creek (*Co. Macquarie*) 31°13'S. 152°47'E., 15 km S. of Kempsey; pop. 61 (1911), 55 (1933).

Smiths Creek (*Co. Macquarie*) see also Kundabung.

Smiths Creek (*Co. Rous*) 28°26'S. 153°23'E., 10 km S. of Murwillumbah; pop. 83 (1911), 81 (1947), 88 (1954), 75 (1961), 319 (2011).

Smiths Creek (*Co. Vernon*) 31°18'S. 151°30'E., 35 km S. of Walcha, on Smiths Ck.

Smiths Flat (*Co. Clarence*) 29°33'S. 152°44'E., 27 km NW of Grafton, on Eaton Ck; cemetery (Copmanhurst, 233 graves 1856+).

Smiths Flat (*Co. Clarence*) see also Upper Copmanhurst.

Smiths Flat (*Co. Clarke*) 30°46'S. 152°18'E., 59 km W. of Macksville, on Macleay R.

Smiths Gap (*Co. Murray*) see Bungendore.

Smiths Hill (*Co. Camden*) see Wollongong.

Smiths Lake (*Co. Gloucester*) 32°23'S. 152°30'E., 22 km S. of Forster, on Smiths Lake; FB; jetty; reservoir; tank traps (World War II); pop. 425 (1986), 652 (1991), 849 (1996), 907 (2001), 1,036 (2006), 1,076 (2011).

Smithtown (*Co. Dudley*) 31°01'S. 152°57'E., 12 km NE of Kempsey, on Macleay R.; West Gladstone till 1877; subdivided *c.*1861 by Peter and James Hoy; agric., maize, dairying; Angl. C. (St John the Divine) b. 1879 by James Patrick Sullivan, enlarged 1885, renovations 1901, additions 1969, closed, sold and reused; Assemblies of God C.; bridge to Gladstone b. 1929 by Lawson Bros, new one (Major Oakes Bridge), 1,125 ft (342.9 m), b. 1971–73 by John Holland (Constructions) Pty Ltd, over Macleay R.; earth tremor 1889; fire 1893; floods 1879, 1890, 1893, 1894, 1921, 1929, 1949, 1950, 1963, 1964, 1967, 2001, 2009, 2011; milk factory (Smithtown Dairy Co.) 1891, taken over by Smithtown Dairy Produce Co. Ltd, acquired by Bacchus Marsh Concentrated Milk Co. Ltd, new factory b. 1917 by J.G. Taylor, acquired 1921 by Nestle & Anglo-Swiss Condensed Milk Co. (A'asia) Ltd, fire 2012; PO 1877, new one b. 1927 by J.C. Davis & Son; Prim. Meth. C. 1874; PS 1885; punt 1842, new one (diesel) b. 1913 by L.A. Davis, replaced, ceased 1973, across Macleay R.; reservoir (steel), 1,000,000 gal. (4,546 kl), 1968; Rom. Cath. C. 1867, demolished and replaced 1886 by W. Neal, demolished 1974, new one (St Patrick's) b. 1974 by E.E. Lahey Constructions, d. by J.L. Toomey; school 1891 b. by Edward Knowles, new one b. 1952 on new site by Gill Bros; sewerage 1985; telegraph 1878; TX 1919, automatic 1977; Unit. C. (orig. Meth.) 1910, closed, sold 2013, reused; water reticulation

1969; wharves: one b. 1879 by Taylor and Johnstone, one b. 1890 by G. and T. Lawson, Nestle's 1941; pop. 221 (1891), 255 (1901), 491 (1908), 365 (1911), 647 (1933), 901 (1947), 879 (1954), 1,148 (1961, incl. Gladstone), 1,101 (1966, incl. Gladstone), 1,007 (1971, incl. Gladstone), 977 (1976, incl. Gladstone), 953 (1981, incl. Gladstone), 979 (1986, incl. Gladstone), 965 (1991, incl. Gladstone), 960 (1996, incl. Gladstone), 973 (2001, incl. Gladstone), 958 (2006, incl. Gladstone), 995 (2011, incl. Gladstone).

Smithtown (*Co. Monteagle*) see Weddin.

Smoky Camp (*Co. Gordon*) 32°40'S. 148°46'E., 19 km SW of Wellington.

Smoky Cape (*Co. Macquarie*) 30°55'S. 153°05'E., 6 km SE of South West Rocks, on Tasman Sea; lighthouse b. 1889–91 of concrete, begun by William Frank Oakes but completed by Walter Frank Oakes, Percy George Oakes, Medcalf and Williams, 57 ft (17.4 m), d. by James Johnstone Barnet and Cecil Darley, converted 1962 from kerosene to electricity; telephone 1903; pop. 21 (1933).

Smoky Valley (*Co. Rous*) 28°32'S. 153°32'E., 2 km NW of Brunswick Heads, on Brunswick R.; quarry; water treatment works.

Snake Avenue (*Co. Wakool*) 35°20'S. 143°40'E., 52 km NW of Barham.

Snarebrook (*Co. Raleigh*) see Valery.

Snodgrass Plain (*Co. Wellesley*) 36°52'S. 148°46'E., 42 km W. of Bombala.

Snodgrass Valley (*Co. Northumberland*) 33°20'S. 151°05'E., 27 km W. of Ourimbah; orig. Twelve Mile Hollow, later Ten Mile Hollow; surveyed 1836 by Henry Fancourt White, village gaz. 1836, never developed; bridge 1830.

Snowball (*Co. Dampier*) 35°57'S. 149°35'E., 45 km W. of Moruya, on Currambene Ck; gold.

Snowball (*Co. Wynyard*) 35°08'S. 148°02'E., 11 km SW of Gundagai; The Snowball till 1880; grazing and mining (copper disc. 1873 by James Clayton) mainly in 1870s; mine *c.*1876, closed, reopened 1906 by J.M. Dodd, closed; school 1879–81; smelter (copper), closed 1880.

Snowview (*Co. Wallace*) 36°21'S. 148°41'E., 11 km NE of Jindabyne; telephone 1925.

Soapy Flat (*Co. Camden*) 34°25'S. 150°20'E., 9 km N. of Berrima, on Joadja Ck; quarries (sand); TX; winery (Joadja Vineyards & Winery) estab. 1983 by Kim and Frances Moginie, sold 2016 to Matt Toomey and Siobhan Maloy.

Soda Water Spring (*Co. Beresford*) see Rock Flat.

Sodwalls (*Co. Westmoreland*) 33°31'S. 150°00'E., 13 km SW of Wallerawang, on Solitary Ck; formerly peas and potatoes, now sheep and cattle; cemetery; PO 1869; quarries (granite and gravel, incl. a granite one worked 1926–37); RS 1872–1974; school 1955, additions 1958, closed 1982; telephone 1907; TX 1938; pop. 101 (1911), 145 (1933), 70 (1947), 107 (1954), 111 (1961).

Sofala (*Co. Roxburgh*) 33°05'S. 149°41'E., 36 km SW of Kandos, on Turon R.; (incl. Bathurst Point, Erskine Flat, Erskine Island, Golden Point, Lucky Point, Maitland Point, Sheep Station Point); estab. 1851, laid out 1851 by John Nicholson, first lots sold 1851, resurveyed 1859 by John Alexander Horatio Price, town gaz. 1880; formerly goldmining (alluvial, disc. 1851), then grazing and honey, now tourism; Angl. C. (Christ) 1851, new one d. and b. 1887 by Charles Taylor, and graveyard (69 graves 1851–1903); bridge 1897, new one (Crossley Bridge) 1930, over Turon R.; cemeteries: general (184 graves 1869+) and Rom. Cath. (102 graves 1862–1947); CH b. 1857–66, new one 1874, re-roofed 1904 by Rigby Bros, reused 1934 as hospital, reused again; Chinese joss house; drought 1862; earth tremors 1862 and 1872; floods 1852, 1986, 2012; foot-bridge, removed 1882 by J.K. Mackenzie from O'Connell, re-erected, condemned 1958, restored 1974, destroyed 1986, retrieved from riverbed, restored and displayed adjacent to Turon R.; hailstorm 1916; hospital b. 1852 by Brady, new one o. 1934 in old court-house; lock-up b. 1897 by G.F. Cole and W. Frost, renovations and repairs 1912 by George Taylor; miners' strike 1853; mines: Big Oakey or Surface Hill 1877–1919, 1922, 1934–37, Nuggetty Hill 1891, Queenslander or King 1888–1916 and 1935–39, Red Hill 1879–82; PO 1851, new one b. 1880 by Charles Taylor, d. by James Johnstone Barnet, repairs 1888 by J. Steddat, closed and reused 1988; pound (stock) 1852; PS, renovations and repairs 1912 by George Taylor, additions and renovations 1937 by William Pittendrigh; 2 quarries; Rom. Cath. C. b. 1892 by George Taylor, demolished 1922; school 1878, new one b. 1881 by Mannell and Harris, additions 1883 by H. Clifford, additions and repairs 1897 by Albert Emanuel Ennis, new building b. 1912 by George Taylor, fire 1952, abandoned and derelict, new one; 6 stamper batteries; tanneries: Ashe's and Pickering's; telegraph 1861, office burnt down 1875, replaced, repairs 1888 by J. Steddat; TX 1925, automatic 1985; watch-house b. 1861 by Arundel Everett and William Stephens; Wes. Meth. C. 1852; pop. 528 (1856), *c.*700 (1858), 1,646 (1861), *c.*1,000 (1866), 644 (1871), 622 (1881), *c.*650 (1886), 307 (1891), 334 (1901), 247 (1911), 129 (1921), 227 (1933), 153 (1947), 137 (1954), 93 (1961), *c.*180 (1965), *c.*250 (1987), 207 (2006).

Soldiers Flat (*Co. Bathurst*) see Billimari.

Soldiers Point (*Co. Gloucester*) 32°42'S. 152°04'E., 8 km W. of Nelson Bay, on Port Stephens; orig. Friendship Point; estab. 1922; fishing, oysters, hort., tourism; marina; PO 1945; quarry; reservoir; sawmill (Alan Vitnell and Alex Brown); school 1952, additions 1979 and 1988, later additions by R.T. Parker Pty Ltd; TX 1948, automatic 1968; Unit. C. (orig. Meth.) b. 1954 by M.R. Myers, d. by William C. Brown, closed; wharves; pop. 87 (1933), 167 (1947), 222 (1954), 228 (1961), 4,087 (1996, incl. Salamander Bay), 4,968 (2001, incl. Salamander Bay), 5,101 (2011, incl. Salamander Bay).

Solferino (*Co. Drake*) 29°10'S. 152°30'E., 47 km E. of Tenterfield, on Gnarcoco Ck; thrived 1872, almost deserted by 1878, village gaz. 1882, defunct; gold (disc. 1871 by Paulo Marcolino, followed by gold rush); PO 1872; school 1875–76; stamper battery (Thomas Wilkinson).

Solferino (*Co. Monteagle*) 34°16'S. 148°21'E., 7 km NE of Young, on Five Mile Ck; school 1886–1909.

Solferino Road (*Co. Clarence*) see Koolkhan.

Solitary Creek (*Co. Westmoreland*) 33°31'S. 149°58'E., 24 km NE of Oberon, on Solitary Ck; gold 1882; RS 1900, station relocated 1903, closed 1910.

Solomons Temple (*Co. Narromine*) 32°10'S. 147°50'E., 21 km SW of Trangie.

Somers (*Co. Bathurst*) 33°41'S. 149°06'E., 22 km SW of Blayney, on Mandurama Ponds; town gaz. 1861, status downgraded 1881 to village; earth tremor 1919; quarry; water reticulation 1957.

Somersby (*Co. Northumberland*) 33°22'S. 151°18'E., 7 km W. of Ourimbah, on Floods Ck; citrus orchards 1888+; agric. research station 1953; airfield (abandoned), new one; aluminium extrusion factory (AluShapes) 1998; bottled water plant (Laing-Peach's Somersby Springs Pty Ltd); bridge over Little Mooney Mooney Ck; conveyor equipment factory (Aust. Conveyor Engineering Pty Ltd, acquired 2012 by Fenner Dunlop Aust. Pty Ltd); cosmetics factory (Delta Laboratories Pty Ltd) 2000; dam (Mooney); evaporative equipment factory (Baltimore Aircoil Aust. Pty Ltd); farm home (Gosford) for boys o. 1913, d. by James Nangle, though building work continued till 1922, renamed Mount Penang training school for boys in 1946, additions 1956, renamed Mount Penang detention centre in 1988, renamed Mount Penang juvenile justice centre in 1991, reused; FB; fibreboard plant (Borg Manufacturing); flood (5 died) 2007; foam factory (Thermoplastic Foam Industries Pty Ltd); foot-bridge; house frame and truss factory (Trussmaster NSW Pty Ltd) 2006; juvenile justice centres: Frank Baxter 1999, riot 2019 and Kariong 1991–2015; laminate products factory (Aust. Panel Products Pty Ltd); lighting factory (3S Lighting Pty Ltd); 6 quarries (incl. Gosford Quarries Pty Ltd,

Pioneer Concrete, Rindean Sands); railway dam on Fountain Ck; 3 reservoirs; schools: Kariong Mountains HS 2010 and Somersby 1928, new building 1970; telephone 1913; TX 1922, automatic 1963; waterworks; pop. 490 (1933, incl. 257 at Mount Penang training school for boys), 549 (1947, incl. 197 at Mount Penang training school for boys), 693 (1954, incl. 271 at Mount Penang training school for boys), 567 (1961), 981 (2011).

Somerset (*Co. Gloucester*) 31°53'S. 152°09'E., 21 km W. of Wingham, on Belbora Ck; railway bridge (steel truss) fabricated by R. Tulloch, erected 1913 by Smith, Timms & Co., over Manning R.; RS 1913–73.

Somerton (*Co. Parry*) 30°56'S. 150°39'E., 23 km S. of Manilla, on Peel R.; formerly Summer Hill; surveyed 1852 by John Valentine Gorman, town gaz. 1856; farming and grazing; airfield; Angl. C. 1898, destroyed 1902, new one (St Mark's) 1903; bridge 1911, 260 ft (79.2 m), new one (timber beam) 1949, 340 ft (103.6 m), over Peel R.; cemetery (23 graves 1885+) 1875; earth tremor 2012; FB; flood 1910; PO 1869; Presb. C. (St Matthew's) 1905; PS 1879, new one b. 1908 by Charles Benaud Smith, closed 1955; school 1880; storm 1902; telephone 1907; TX 1913, automatic 1953; pop. *c.*120 (1903), 298 (1911), 124 (1933), 334 (1947), 328 (1954), 124 (1961), 279 (2006), 573 (2011).

Somerton Road (*Co. Darling*) see Moonaran.

Som Valley (*Co. Wallace*) 36°05'S. 148°48'E., 18 km NW of Cooma, on Lake Eucumbene.

Sorrento (*Co. Northumberland*) see Empire Bay.

Soudan Heights (*Co. Sandon*) see Armidale.

South Arm (*Co. Clarence*) 29°33'S. 153°09'E., 11 km S. of Maclean, on Clarence R.; sugar-cane; Bapt. C.; caterpillar infestation 1919; sawmill (Shore's), burnt down 1915; school 1875–1967; sugar mills: E. Kennedy 1872 and Duncan Robertson; pop. 135 (1911), 179 (1933), 156 (1947), 174 (1954), 149 (1961), 307 (2006).

South Arm (*Co. Raleigh*) see Ketelghay.

South Bank (*Co. Raleigh*) 30°44'S. 152°48'E., 12 km W. of Macksville; telephone 1913; TX 1926, automatic 1968.

South Beach (*Co. Northumberland*) 33°08'S. 151°36'E., 1 km S. of Nords Wharf, on Crangan Bay.

South Camira (*Co. Richmond*) see Whiporie.

Southdown (*Co. Townsend*) 35°37'S. 144°54'E., 11 km SW of Deniliquin; PO 1895–1903; RS (Victorian railway) 1926–56, defunct.

Southern Cross (*Co. Rous*) see Ballina East.

Southgate (*Co. Clarence*) 29°37'S. 153°00'E., 10 km NE of Grafton, on Alumy Ck; estab. as private village, gaz. 1871; farming, dairying, maize, sugar-cane; bridge (Tarrant Bridge) over Alumy Ck; creamery (Southgate Dairy Co. Ltd) b. 1898 by John Mackay; floods 1893 and 1945; PO 1879; punt b. 1901 by John Bichmann, to Ulmarra, across Clarence R.; reservoir (steel), 250,000 gal. (1,136.5 kl), 1968; Rom. Cath. C. (St Patrick's) b. 1935 by R.B. Grainger, d. by Frederick Leben; sawmill (G. Finlay); school 1867, new building b. 1882 on new site by William Kinnear, closed 1975, disused; storm 1912; sugar mills: Edward Arnold 1876, Boothby's 1872, CSR 1870–79, dismantled 1885, G. Finlay 1882; telephone 1890; TX 1916, automatic 1952; Union C. 1872, new one d. and b. 1906 by F. Sault, damaged 1912; water reticulation 1966; wharf; whooping cough epidemic 1938; pop. 673 (1881), 178 (1891), 316 (1901), 656 (1911), 190 (1933), 244 (1947), 207 (1954), 151 (1961), *c.*100 (2001), 176 (2011).

Southgate (*Co. Clarence*) see also Lower Southgate.

South Golden Beach (*Co. Rous*) 28°30'S. 153°33'E., 4 km N. of Ocean Shores, on Coral Sea; (incl. North Ocean Shores); foot-bridge 2010 d. by Tony Baggio, over Capricornia Canal; school (Tuckaburra till 1899, then Billinudgel till 1993, then Ocean Shores) 1893, new one b. 1912 by Alfred John Modini, new one 1993; SD Adventist C.; pop. 383 (1986), 782 (1991), 1,327 (1996), 1,486 (2001), 1,729 (2006), 1,876 (2011).

Southampton (*Co. Clarence*) 29°43'S. 152°54'E., 4 km W. of South Grafton;

butter factory (G.A.E. Blanch) b. 1892 by G. Wunderlich, closed 1904; Christ. Outreach C.

South Hill (*Co. Sandon*) see Armidale.

South Lambton (*Co. Camden*) 34°40'S. 150°15'E., 3 km SW of Bundanoon.

South Marowie (*Co. Nicholson*) 33°26'S. 145°34'E., 5 km N. of Hillston, on Lachlan R.; school 1884–91.

South Pacific (*Co. St Vincent*) 35°23'S. 150°28'E., 2 km S. of Ulladulla.

South Side (*Co. Gough*) 29°47'S. 151°06'E., 1 km S. of Inverell, on Macintyre R.

South West Rocks (*Co. Macquarie*) 30°53'S. 153°02'E., 23 km SE of Macksville, on Trial Bay; settled 1886, estab. 1896; fishing and tourism; ambulance station; Angl. C. 1916, closed, removed and reused, new one (Holy Trinity) 1992; Assemblies of God C. (Christ. New Life); bridge (German Bridge) to Arakoon, over Saltwater Ck; bushfire 2001; dengue fever 1942; earth tremor 2018; FB (station b. 1976); floods 1893 and 2009; foot-bridges: one over Saltwater Ck and one over South West Rocks Ck; gale 1893; gun battery (World War II); oil terminal 1961; pilot station b. 1902 by C.B. Smith, reused; PO 1903; Presb. C.; PS 1924, alterations and repairs 1937 by G.F. Brest; quarry; reservoir (concrete), 750,000 gal. (3,409.5 kl), 1968; Rom. Cath. C. (Our Lady Star of the Sea) 1926; school (Macleay Entrance till 1910) 1897, relocated 1909, additions 1956, 1966, 1994, 2010; sewerage augmentation 1985; streets electric lit 1939; telephone 1903; trees (ornamental) 1914+; TX 1915, automatic 1961; Unit. C. (orig. Meth.) 1915, closed, sold, removed 1988 and reused, new one 1989; water reticulation 1969; pop. 105 (1911), 306 (1933), 519 (1947), 486 (1954), 595 (1961), 636 (1966), 836 (1971), 1,176 (1976), 1,314 (1981), 1,947 (1986), 2,886 (1991), 3,514 (1996), 4,116 (2001), 4,069 (2006).

Spa (*Co. Argyle*) 35°03'S. 150°01'E., 43 km SE of Goulburn, on Shoalhaven R.; goldmining; mines; stamper battery (Mason and Flook) 1869.

Spaniards Hill (*Co. Camden*) see Douglas Park.

Sparkes Creek (*Co. Brisbane*) 31°56'S. 150°42'E., 20 km NW of Scone, on Dart Brook; Woodlands till 1907; cemetery 1881; PO 1879; school 1880–98; pop. 66 (1911), 32 (1933).

Sparling Swamp (*Co. Ashburnham*) 33°03'S. 148°13'E., 10 km NE of Parkes; bushfire 1918; school 1895 b. by W.H. Bligh, closed 1912.

Speers Point (*Co. Northumberland*) 32°58'S. 151°38'E., 2 km NW of Warners Bay, on Cockle Bay; formerly Batten's Point; subdivisions 1902 and 1912; Angl. C. 1918, new one (All Saints') 1957 d. by Louis Reginald Williams; bridge (Watkins Bridge) 1973 to Teralba, over The Five Islands; colliery (Lochend) estab. 1843 by William Brooks, closed 1847; Cong. C. (Bethany) 1925; earthquake 1989; earth tremor 1925; foot-bridge 1928 over Cockle Ck; Full Gospel C.; jetty, destroyed 1920, replacement d. by Lowry; mine (Speers Point Gully) estab. 1916 by T.D.H. Rhodes; PO 1916; pound (stock) b. 1926 by George Irwin; PS; quarry; reservoir; Rom. Cath. C. (Our Lady Help of Christians) 1961; school 1957 d. by R. Evans, additions 1962 and 1966; SD Adventist C. (Boolaroo) 1923; sewerage 1945; telephone 1916; tramway (steam) to Newcastle 1912–30; wharf; pop. 225 (1911), 1,285 (1933), 2,021 (1947), 3,104 (2006), 3,230 (2011).

Speers Point East (*Co. Northumberland*) see Warners Bay.

Speewa (*Co. Wakool*) 35°12'S. 143°34'E., 61 km S. of Balranald, on Murray R.; PO 1965–73; punt (manual) across Murray R.; pop. 74 (1933), 58 (1947), 63 (1954), 63 (1961), 374 (2011).

Spencer (*Co. Northumberland*) 33°28'S. 151°09'E., 19 km W. of Gosford, on Hawkesbury R.; Fernleigh till 1914; settled 1860 by Major Sampson, subdivided 1919 by Stephen Collier; orchards, oysters, fishing; bridge d. and b. 2006 by Civilbuild, over Allens Ck; bushfires 1994 and 2001; cemetery; FB; PO 1899; Rom. Cath. C. 1861, new one (Holy Trinity) b. 1909 by Greentree

Bros, and graveyard (155 graves 1873+); school 1902 b. by George Byrnes, relocated 1921 to new site in rented premises, new school 1922, additions by Robert Frazer, school closed 2015, sold 2016; telephone 1915; TX 1922, automatic 1969; wharf b. 1916 by A. Andrews; pop. 79 (1911), 167 (1933), 90 (1947), 122 (1954), 97 (1961), 297 (2006), 515 (2011).

Spencer's Creek (*Co. Macquarie*) see Jerseyville.

Spicers Creek (*Co. Lincoln*) 32°23'S. 149°09'E., 28 km NE of Wellington; gold, farming, grazing; Angl. C. (All Souls') b. 1956 by Malcolm Cunnynghame, d. by Barry King, closed; cemetery (41 graves 1891+) 1888; PO 1880, burnt down 1977; Presb. C. 1905; school 1881, new one b. 1882 by G.G. Payne, closed 1901, reopened 1908–27 and 1957–84; telephone 1914; TX 1918; Union C., demolished; whooping cough epidemic 1921; pop. 363 (1901), 235 (1911), 153 (1921), 150 (1933), 119 (1947), 103 (1954), 128 (1961).

Spicers Diggings (*Co. Wellington*) 32°46'S. 149°38'E., 19 km S. of Mudgee, on Redbank Ck; gold.

Spicketts Creek (*Co. Raleigh*) 30°33'S. 152°52'E., 11 km S. of Bellingen; telephone 1924; TX 1929; pop. 65 (1911), 32 (1933).

Spion Kop (*Co. Northumberland*) 33°28'S. 151°18'E., 2 km NW of Woy Woy, on Woy Woy Bay; pop. 203 (1933), 292 (1947).

Splashers Flat (*Co. Wellington*) see Cullenbone.

Splitters Creek (*Co. Hume*) 36°03'S. 146°50'E., 8 km NW of Albury; pop. 28 (1933), 268 (2011).

Spoonerville (*Co. Camden*) see Warrawong.

Sportsmans Creek (*Co. Clarence*) 29°30'S. 153°01'E., 19 km W. of Maclean, on Sportsmans Ck; telephone 1910.

Sportsmans Creek (*Co. Clarence*) see also Gurranang.

Springbrook (*Gresham*) 29°51'S. 152°23'E., 54 km W. of Grafton, on Boyd R.; village gaz. 1892; PO 1891–99.

Spring Creek (*Co. Argyle*) 35°00'S. 150°00'E., 37 km SE of Goulburn; goldmining (incl. Mantons' Reef) 1869–75, 1895–96, 1908–14; stamper battery (Manton Bros) 1869.

Spring Creek (*Co. Arrawatta*) 29°41'S. 151°24'E., 28 km E. of Inverell.

Spring Creek (*Co. Auckland*) 36°40'S. 149°48'E., 4 km W. of Bega.

Spring Creek (*Co. Bathurst*) 33°52'S. 148°48'E., 10 km E. of Cowra; pop. 55 (1933), 54 (1947).

Spring Creek (*Co. Brisbane*) 32°16'S. 150°44'E., 16 km W. of Muswellbrook; lucerne and dairying; Angl. C. 1878, new one (St Paul's) b. 1921 by David Jordan; PO 1927–30; telephone 1915; TX 1917–28; pop. 69 (1911), 68 (1933), 50 (1947), 51 (1954), 53 (1961).

Spring Creek (*Co. Buccleuch*) 35°12'S. 148°21'E., 17 km NE of Tumut, on Brungle Ck.

Spring Creek (*Co. Camden*) 34°06'S. 150°37'E., 8 km SW of Camden; pop. 110 (1933), 85 (1947), 94 (1954), 75 (1961).

Spring Creek (*Co. King*) 34°38'S. 149°11'E., 32 km NE of Yass.

Spring Creek (*Co. Murray*) see Euralie.

Spring Creek (*Co. Narromine*) 32°27'S. 148°18'E., 24 km S. of Narromine; FB; bushfire 1905.

Spring Creek (*Co. Phillip*) 32°27'S. 149°56'E., 36 km NE of Mudgee.

Spring Creek (*Co. Wallace*) see Kiandra.

Springdale (*Co. Bland*) 34°28'S. 147°43'E., 18 km E. of Temora; Possum Power Tank till 1897; village gaz. 1899; mining (gold disc. 1864) and farming; Angl. C. (All Saints') b. 1918 by Houston, d. by Henry Laker, restoration 1937; cemetery; charcoal plant 1941; FB; mines: Bristol Reef, Emu Reef, Haeusler's 1879–1907, Halls Reward, Little Wonder, Opossum Power, Victoria; PO 1897–1977; Rom. Cath. C. (St Mary's) b. 1914 by Arthur Pettit, demolished 1974; RS (Possum Power Tank till 1895) 1893–1975; school 1896, additions 1911 by J.P. Gibson, closed 1974; stamper battery (single head) erected 1868 by Harry Woods; telephone 1901; TX 1917, automatic 1973; pop. 184 (1911), 179 (1933), 182 (1947), 177 (1954), 172 (1961).

Springdale Heights (*Co. Goulburn*)

see Albury.

Springfield (*Co. Argyle*) 34°54'S. 149°40'E., 18 km S. of Goulburn, on Mulwaree R.; orig. Ryansvale; cemetery; flour mill (horse powered) estab. by William Pitt Faithfull; Rom. Cath. C. (St Michael's) b. 1848 by Michael Ryan; school (Mangamore till 1899) 1882–1971; pop. 55 (1901), 70 (1911), 97 (1933), 93 (1947), 83 (1954), 75 (1961).

Springfield (*Co. Bathurst*) see Byng.

Springfield (*Co. Murray*) 35°04'S. 149°11'E., 31 km NW of Bungendore.

Springfield (*Co. Northumberland*) 33°26'S. 151°22'E., 2 km E. of Gosford, on Erina Ck; Angl. C. (St Peter's) 1927; bridge (Yerin Bridge) 1998, to Erina, over Erina Ck; bushfires 1928, 1937, 1953; electricity 1938; PO 1968–71; quarry; school (Chertsey) 1969 d. by C. Carter, additions 1972 and 2010; pop. 83 (1933), 258 (1947), 141 (1954), 4,108 (2011).

Springfield (*Co. Phillip*) 32°26'S. 149°34'E., 8 km S. of Gulgong.

Springfield (*Co. Phillip*) see also Galambine.

Springfield (*Co. Wellesley*) 36°33'S. 149°06'E., 34 km S. of Cooma, on Lower Dog Kennel Ck; pop. 123 (2006).

Springfield (*Co. Wynyard*) 35°21'S. 148°15'E., 5 km S. of Tumut; airfield.

Spring Flat (*Co. Clarendon*) 35°03'S. 148°07'E., 2 km N. of Gundagai; gold (disc. 1861, gold rushes 1861 and 1864); earth tremor 1871; flour mill (George F. Hayes), burnt down 1878; pop. 139 (1901), 36 (1933).

Spring Flat (*Co. Georgiana*) 34°08'S. 149°27'E., 36 km N. of Crookwell, on Spring Ck.

Spring Flat (*Co. Wellington*) 32°39'S. 149°36'E., 7 km S. of Mudgee, on Oaky Ck; school 1871–93; winery (Mongrel Vineyard) estab. 1998 by David and Sue Fairlie-Cuninghame; pop. 115 (1911), 114 (1933), 70 (1947), 69 (1954), 93 (1961), 424 (2011).

Spring Grove (*Co. Bathurst*) see Millthorpe.

Spring Grove (*Co. Rous*) 28°50'S. 153°11'E., 10 km W. of Lismore, on Pelican Ck; Nowlanville till 1923; farming; bridge b. 1912 by Walter Frank Oakes, d. by Kirkpatrick, over Pelican Ck; Meth. C. 1910; PO 1927; school 1909–58; telephone 1923; TX 1923–69; pop. 143 (1933), 159 (1947), 105 (1954), 123 (1961), 345 (2011).

Spring Hill (*Co. Bathurst*) 33°24'S. 149°09'E., 6 km NW of Millthorpe; surveyed, laid out and village gaz. 1877, lots sold 1878; wheat, oats, rye, hay, barley, potatoes, peas, fruit, dairying; Angl. C. (All Saints') 1904–83, reopened 1987, closed again 1992, sold 1999; Bapt. C.; cemetery (87 graves 1881–1977) 1882; chaff mill (Goulburn Produce Co. Pty Ltd); foundry (H.D. Melhuish & Son) estab. by Henry Dutton Melhuish, taken over 1910 by Arthur Moad, jun.; PO 1879; pound (stock), closed 1893; PS 1913, new one (incl. lock-up) 1925, closed during World War II, reopened 1950–79, sold and reused; railway (iron ore) to Cadia 1919–29 (G. & C. Hoskins Ltd) and 1941–45 (Aust. Iron & Steel Ltd); Rom. Cath. C., removed from Cadia, closed, moved to Orange and reused; RS 1877, station b. 1884, demolished 1988; school 1878, additions 1883 by W.H. Lewis, repairs 1891 by W. Jones & Son, additions and alterations 1910 by Peter Beddie; sewerage augmentation 1990; telegraph 1881; TX 1915, automatic 1951; Unit. C. (orig. Wes. Meth.) 1874, renovated 1892 by R. Ainsworth; Wes. Meth. C. 1863, renovated 1892 by R. Ainsworth; pop. 389 (1901), 426 (1911), 273 (1933), 295 (1947), 281 (1954), 281 (1961), *c.*200 (1975), 238 (1986), 237 (1991), 304 (1996), 285 (2001), 276 (2006), 281 (2011).

Spring Hill (*Co. Camden*) 34°27'S. 150°52'E., 3 km E. of Unanderra, on Allan's Ck; RS (Lysaght's) 1938; works (John Lysaght Aust. Ltd).

Spring Mount (*Co. Bathurst*) 33°27'S. 149°18'E., 11 km E. of Millthorpe; school 1878 b. by W. O'Brien, repairs 1895 by J. Bromfield, repairs 1911 by W.W. Nixon, closed 1924, reopened 1952–72; pop. 57 (1901).

Spring Plains (*Co. Jamison*) 29°56'S. 149°18'E., 33 km N. of Wee Waa; pop. 88 (2006).

Spring Ridge (*Co. Bligh*) 32°17'S. 149°22'E., 19 km NW of Gulgong.

Spring Ridge (*Co. Pottinger*) 31°24'S. 150°15'E., 38 km W. of Werris Creek; village gaz. 1926;

farming and grazing; Angl. C. 1884, new one (St Matthias's) 1963; cemetery (71 graves 1891–1999); FB; floods 1950, 1970, 1974; PO 1879; PS 1934; Rom. Cath. C. (Our Lady of Dolours) 1936; RS 1923–78; sawmill (Togo, Lawrence's), new mill o. 1906; school 1892, additions 2010; silo 1959; telephone 1906; TX 1921, automatic 1984; water reticulation 1968; Wes. Meth. C. 1883; pop. 72 (1901), 226 (1911), 208 (1933), 180 (1947), 339 (1954), 232 (1961), 389 (2011).

Springs (*Co. Wellington*) see Dripstone.

Springside (*Co. Bathurst*) 33°23'S. 149°03'E., 12 km S. of Orange, on Spring Ck; farming; FB (station b. 2017); PO 1869; school 1879, additions 1891 by G.G. Payne, closed 1972, sold and reused; telephone 1915; TX 1917, automatic 1951; Wes. Meth. C. 1897; pop. 234 (1901), 219 (1911), 212 (1933), 255 (1947), 165 (1954), 162 (1961), 230 (2011).

Spring Terrace (*Co. Bathurst*) 33°24'S. 149°06'E., 10 km NW of Millthorpe, on Cowriga Ck; farming; pea vining plant (R. Gordon Edgell & Sons Ltd), closed 1947; PO 1898; school 1899 b. by Rigby Bros, additions 1966; telephone 1911; TX 1911–51; Wes. Meth. C. 1872; pop. 58 (1901), 143 (1911), 142 (1933), 96 (1947), 119 (1954), 130 (1961), 280 (2011).

Springvale (*Co. Auckland*) 36°41'S. 149°46'E., 6 km W. of Bega, on Spring Ck; school 1881, additions 1910 by John Hines, closed 1962; telephone 1946; TX (automatic) 1952; pop. 70 (1933), 101 (1947), 111 (1954), 124 (1961).

Spring Vale (*Co. Cook*) 33°25'S. 150°07'E., 5 km E. of Wallerawang; colliery 1926, man killed 1930, strike and closed 1931, acquired and reopened 1941 by Western Collieries Pty Ltd and renamed Renown Extended, strike 1943, man killed 1949, closed 1958, abandoned.

Spring Vale (*Co. King*) 34°08'S. 148°49'E., 34 km N. of Boorowa, on Boorowa R.; bridge 1930, replaced 1973, over Boorowa R.

Spring Vale (*Co. Rous*) see Nashua.

Springvale (*Co. Wallace*) 36°41'S. 148°52'E., 35 km S. of Berridale, on Numbla Ck.

Springvale (*Co. Wynyard*) see Lake Albert.

Spring Valley (*Co. Argyle*) 34°56'S. 149°33'E., 25 km SW of Goulburn, on Wollogorang Ck; agric., dairying, sheep; airfield; PO 1865–67; Rom. Cath. C. 1862, replacement (St Laurence O'Toole's) b. 1883–88, and graveyard; school 1863–66 and 1880–1905; pop. *c.*200 (1866), 108 (1901).

Springview (*Co. Hume*) 35°29'S. 147°06'E., 7 km NE of Henty; school 1920–31.

Springwell (*Co. Beresford*) 36°23'S. 149°03'E., 17 km S. of Cooma.

Springwood (*Co. Cook*) 33°42'S. 150°34'E., 23 km E. of Katoomba, on Springwood Ck; disc. 1813 by Gregory Blaxland, William Lawson and William Charles Wentworth, estab. 1816 as military depot, first land grant 1834; former popular mountain destination (1880s+), dairying, apiculture, orchards; Angl. C. (Christ) b. 1889 by Alfred Buckley and Mitchell, d. by Sir John Sulman, additions 1961; Assemblies of God C. (Christ. Life); Bapt. C. o. 1957 (in church removed from Sydney), replaced 1965, extended 1976 by G.E. Bailey; brickworks (Springwood Brick & Tile Co.) 1914; bushfires 1905, 1936, 1944, 1951 (4 houses destroyed), 1956, 1968, 1976, 1977, 2001, 2013; cemetery (*c.*1,100 graves) 1886, incl. columbaria 1975; concrete products plant 1964; electricity 1924; FB (station b. 1937, renovations 1951, new one on new site o. 1958 in house converted by Manktelow and McGraw, demolished 1986, new one b. 1987 by Welch Bros, d. by Davey, Brindley & Vickers Pty Ltd, additions and alterations 2014); fires 1913, 1921, 1924, 1975; gales 1895 and 1896; hospital 1976; joinery (Blue Mountains Pty Ltd) 1994; Lutheran C. (Our Saviour); Meth. C. b. 1923 by Watson, replaced 1959; military barracks b. 1816 by William Cox, rebuilt 1833 on new site, closed 1845; plastics factory 1964; PO 1880, new one b. 1901 by J. Beaumont, alterations 1903, repairs 1912 by Hewson, extended 1955 by R. Price; pound (stock) 1891; Presb. C. (Frazer Memorial) b. 1895 by Neil Livingston, d. by Charles Slayter and Thomas Frame Cosh, additions 1896 also by Livingston, also d. by Slayter and Cosh; PS (incl. lock-up) b. 1881 by Frederick Staveley, demolished 1954, second one 1952 on new site, closed and reused, third one 1982 on new site; railway accidents 1895 and 1923; reservoir; Rom. Cath. C. b. 1892 by Frederick Lawrence, relocated and reused 1921, demolished, new one on new site (St Thomas Aquinas and the Angels' Guardian) b. 1919 by James Smith, d. by Bartholomew Stephen Moriarty, reused, third one 1995; RS 1867, new station b. 1884 by John White and Charles Coghill, modernised 1998; sawmill (Turnbull and Murray); schools: Ellison 1986 and Springwood 1878 d. by George Allen Mansfield (additions 1915 by H.A. Donald, additions 1928, new school 1954 on new site, additions 1995); sewerage 1960; streets lit by carbide gas 1906; telegraph 1879, repairs to office 1912 by Hewson; TX 1912, automatic 1965; Unit. C. 1978; water supply 1936; pop. *c.*200 (1878), 69 (1891), *c.*400 (1895), 618 (1901), 724 (1911), 1,336 (1933), 1,921 (1947), 2,436 (1954, incl. Winmalee), 3,117 (1964), *c.*4,000 (1987), 8,437 (2011).

Springwood (*Co. Cook*)
see also Faulconbridge.

Springwood North (*Co. Cook*)
see Winmalee.

Sproules Lagoon (*Co. Bland*) 34°23'S. 147°30'E., 8 km NW of Temora; RS 1903–59.

Sputters Hollow (*Co. Hunter*) 32°33'S. 150°56'E., 22 km W. of Singleton, on North Wambo Ck.

Square Bush (*Co. Buckland*) 31°18'S. 150°29'E., 28 km SE of Curlewis.

Square Place (*Co. Hunter*) 33°00'S. 150°39'E., 60 km W. of Paxton, on Putty Ck.

Square Range (*Co. Wellesley*) 36°34'S. 149°15'E., 38 km N. of Bombala; school 1883–1901.

Stackpoole (*Co. Nicholson*) 33°56'S. 145°56'E., 41 km N. of Griffith; PO 1929–31; telephone 1929; TX 1930; pop. 20 (1933).

Stafford (*Co. Nandewar*) 30°22'S. 149°50'E., 7 km SE of Narrabri, on Deep Ck; school (Tippereenah till 1894) 1885–94 and 1920–40.

Staggy Creek (*Co. Murchison*) 29°47'S. 150°51'E., 26 km W. of Inverell, on Staggy Ck; diamonds; grasshopper infestation 1934; mine; sawmill (Paradise, J.R. Noble), burnt down 1936; school 1894–1908; pop. 99 (1901), 25 (1933), 75 (1954), 62 (1961).

Stamford (*Co. Northumberland*) 32°38'S. 151°20'E., 4 km NW of Branxton.

Stanborough (*Co. Hardinge*) 29°58'S. 151°07'E., 9 km W. of Tingha; surveyed 1872; tin (alluvial) and grazing; PO 1872–1961; sawmill (Hawkins'); school 1884–91 and 1907–67; telephone 1918; TX 1949; pop. 52 (1933), 60 (1947), 54 (1954).

Stanbridge (*Co. Cooper*) 34°31'S. 146°14'E., 16 km W. of Leeton; village gaz. 1924; food factory (Freedom Foods Group Ltd) 2009; Meth. C. 1927, sold 1938; school 1917, additions 1927 by A.T. McKay, closed 1987; telephone 1923; TX (automatic) 1957; pop. 171 (1933), 292 (1947), 392 (1954), 333 (1961), 414 (2011).

Stanfield (*Co. Bathurst*) 33°34'S. 149°10'E., 9 km SW of Blayney, on Mackenzies Waterholes Ck; RS 1907–68.

Stanford Merthyr (*Co. Northumberland*) 32°50'S. 151°30'E., 1 km SE of Kurri Kurri; village gaz. 1918; bushfire 1940; colliery estab. 1891 by Henry Trenchard, Samuel Clifts, Henry John Adams et al. as Stanford Greta No. 1 Tunnel, acquired 1900 by East Greta Coal Mining Co., o. 1901 as Stanford Merthyr, strike 1904, explosion and fire (killed 6) 1905, closed and sealed 1905, reopened, strike 1914, flooded 1918, strike 1925, closed 1927, reopened 1928, strike 1929, flooded 1930, acquired 1931 by J. & A. Brown & Abermain Seaham Collieries Ltd and renamed Stanford Main No. 1, strikes 1931 and 1932, closed 1935, reopened 1937, strikes 1938, 1939, 1940, 1942, 1943, 1945, 1947, closed 1957, razed 1968; columbarium (at Kurri Kurri bowling club); fire 1903; PO 1914; PS 1903–4; quarry; railway (colliery) b. 1901 by East Greta Coal Mining Co., new station b. 1912, closed 1955; school 1903 b.

by Frederick Brewer, new one b. 1926 by Bagnall & Son; telephone 1920; TX; pop. 345 (1911), 509 (1933), 415 (1947), 563 (2011).

Stanhope (*Co. Durham*) 32°36'S. 151°23'E., 7 km NE of Branxton, on Hunter R.; farming; 3 bridges over Stanhope Ck; bushfire 1905; creamery (Reginald Wyndham, jun.) 1896; FB; PO 1927–31; school 1850, new one b. 1878 by James Pritchard, repairs 1900 by J. Libby, burnt down 1905, replaced 1906, closed 1943, reopened 1957, closed 1958; telephone 1919; pop. 78 (1901), 74 (1911), 77 (1933), 55 (1947), 51 (1954).

Stanley Park (*Co. Cook*) 33°30'S. 150°48'E., 4 km N. of Glossodia; quarry.

Stannifer (*Co. Gough*) 29°53'S. 151°13'E., 8 km N. of Tingha, on Middle Ck; Middle Creek till 1882; settled largely by Cornishmen, founded 1880, village gaz. 1887; tin (alluvial), grazing, now hobby farming; cemetery 1884; mines: Gem, Bischoff, Wheal Herbert, Wheal Victoria; PO b. 1880 by Warland; PS 1880; Rom. Cath. C. (Sacred Heart) 1881; sawmill (Woodford's) 1923; school 1881, new buildings b. 1883 by J.F. Ross, closed 1966; smelter estab. 1888 by E.W. Bathurst, closed 1889; telegraph 1881–92; telephone 1905; TX 1928–72; Union C. 1913; pop. 181 (1901), 250 (1911), 158 (1933), 80 (1947), 53 (1954), 50 (1961).

Stannum (*Co. Gough*) 29°20'S. 151°47'E., 38 km SW of Tenterfield; Nine Mile till 1905; tin (alluvial), farming, grazing; Angl. C. (St Mark's) 1905–50, reopened 1954; cemetery (105 graves) 1895; mines; PO 1890–1972; PS 1894; 5 quarries; school (Nine Mile till 1907) 1888–1961; telephone 1891; TX 1923; pop. 273 (1901), 295 (1911), 241 (1933), 159 (1947), 118 (1954), 81 (1961), 196 (2006).

Stargard Estate (*Co. Camden*) see Picton.

State Mine Gully (*Co. Cook*) see Lithgow.

Station Point (*Co. Wellington*) see Walters.

Steeltown (*Co. Camden*) see Port Kembla and Warrawong.

Steeltown Estate (*Co. Camden*) see Port Kembla.

Steeple Flat (*Co. Wellesley*) 36°34'S. 149°23'E., 43 km SE of Cooma; farming; PO 1927–42; telephone 1921; TX 1938–75; pop. 44 (1933).

Steinbrook (*Co. Clive*) 29°05'S. 152°06'E., 8 km E. of Tenterfield, on Barney Downs Ck; timber; cheese factory (A. Purkiss and S. Wilson) b. 1905 by Gottleib Kyburz, moved to Liston; PO 1886, burnt down 1895; sawmills: Clark Bros (taken over 1910 by A.D. Clark) and James Mangelson, later removed; school 1881–95, 1908–39, 1957–58; telephone 1922; TX 1923, automatic 1953; pop. 103 (1901), 110 (1911), 99 (1933), 69 (1947), 66 (1954), 52 (1961), 137 (2006).

Stephens Creek (*Co. Yancowinna*) 31°50'S. 141°30'E., 14 km N. of Broken Hill, on Stephens Ck; fire 1891; Meth. C. 1912; PO 1927; RS (railway to take limestone to Broken Hill) 1891; school (McCulloch Park) 1901–5 and 1915–34; telephone 1911; TX 1948; waterworks b. 1893 by Lewis and Davis; pop. 84 (1911), 35 (1933), 52 (1947), 89 (1954).

Steve Kings Plains (*Co. Rous*) 28°55'S. 153°18'E., 8 km N. of Coraki, on Wilsons R.; farming and dairying; PO 1901–31; sugar mill (J. Thompson); telephone 1916; pop. 27 (1933).

Stevys Forest (*Co. Camden*) 34°03'S. 150°32'E., 4 km N. of Oakdale.

Stewarts Brook (*Co. Durham*) 32°00'S. 151°19'E., 41 km E. of Scone, on Stewarts Brook; mining (gold disc.1881) and grazing; cemetery (19 graves 1923–2003) 1900; CH b. 1900 by Hocking Bros, closed, used by the military during World War II, sold 1945, moved to Moonan Flat and reused 1947; mines: Bluey Reef (Imperial Standard Co.) 1888–1900 and 1936–39, Lady Maude 1888–98 and 1934, Maid O'Galla (Frame's) 1889–91, New Royal Standard 1886–1904, Terry (Terry Gold-Mining Co.) 1888–91; PO 1887, burnt down; PS, closed 1905, moved to Moonan Flat; school 1889, new building b. 1899 by J. Finch, closed 1958; storm 1940; telephone 1891; TX 1914, automatic 1968; Union C. b. 1912 by Gregory Carter; pop. 254 (1901), 265 (1911), 142 (1933), 75 (1947), 74 (1954).

Stewarts Mount (*Co. Bathurst*) see Bathurst.

Stewarts River (*Co. Macquarie*) 31°44'S. 152°38'E., 12 km SW of Kendall, on Stewarts R.; timber, farming, grazing, dairying; Angl. C. (St Peter's) 1913, moved 1953 to John's River; bridge (Crossingham Bridge) b. 1907 by C. Henderson, over Stewarts R.; creamery (Aust. Dairying Co.); LDS (Mormon) C. b. 1914 by Fred Unicomb; Meth. C. 1904; PO 1927; Rom. Cath. C. b. 1899 by Peter McGovern and James Royan, sold and demolished, new one (St James's) d. and b. 1964 by P.J. Smyth, closed 1989, reopened; school 1902, additions 1930 by A.J. Ivers, closed 1951, reopened 1957–69; telephone 1914; TX, closed 1969; pop. 203 (1911), 51 (1933), 103 (1947), 87 (1954), 128 (1961).

Stingaree (*Co. Northumberland*) see Dora Creek.

Stockinbingal (*Co. Bland*) 34°30'S. 147°53'E., 21 km NW of Cootamundra, on Bland Ck; village gaz. 1881; wheat, canola, cereal crops, sheep, cattle; Angl. C. (St James's) b. 1911 by Hermann Ernest Hellner, d. by Ernest Rees Laver; bridge b. 1880 by Davies and Edwards, new one 1973, over Bland Ck; cemetery (graves 1898+) 1893; CH (in former Rom. Cath. C.) 1920, closed, sold 1940 to Hicks Bros and demolished, new one b. 1940 by A.J. Collingridge, closed 1984; FB; floods 1949 and 2016; hospital (Soldiers' Memorial) b. 1927 by Fred Smith, d. by Frederick James Purvis, closed, reused; lock-up b. 1900 by Williams and Bruce; Meth. C. b. 1918 by Mitchell Bros, damaged 1973, demolished; PO 1891, new one b. 1914 by E.V. Begley, new one b. 1924, closed, sold 1982, disused; Presb. C.; PS 1892, new one 1940; reservoir; Rom. Cath. C. (St Joseph's) b. 1902 by McBeath, sold 1913, reused 1920; RS 1893, station b. by Franklin and Finlay; school 1894 b. by William Wood, new one b. 1911 by Smith and Smith; sewage works; silo 1922; storm 1973; streets electric lit 1931; telephone 1900; TX 1910, automatic 1981; water supply 1929; Wes. Meth. C. b. 1894 by O. Robinson and G. Russell, d. by Robinson and Kenyon, demolished; pop. 144 (1901), 508 (1911), 438 (1933), 435 (1947), 363 (1954), 327 (1961), 262 (1991), 255 (1996), 242 (2001), 221 (2006), 244 (2011).

Stockrington (*Co. Northumberland*) 32°52'S. 151°36'E., 5 km N. of West Wallsend, on Blue Gum Ck; collieries operated by J. & A. Brown & Abermain Seaham Collieries Ltd: Duckenfield No. 2, o. 1877, strike 1923–25, Rosewood Borehole (strikes 1949, 1950, 1951), Stockrington No. 1 (strikes 1944 and 1951, closed 1956), Stockrington No. 2, o. 1940, strikes 1943, 1944, 1947, 1950, 1951; pop. 59 (1933), 63 (1947).

Stockrington (*Co. Northumberland*) see also Buttai.

Stockton (*Co. Gloucester*) 32°55'S. 151°47'E., 1 km N. of Newcastle, on Hunter R.; (incl. Corroba); orig. Pirate Point, then Scott's Town; disc. 1797 by Lieut. John Shortland, settled *c.*1800, estab. 1835, town gaz. 1887, munic. 1889–1938 but became part of City of Greater Newcastle; sawmilling 1799+, lime burning 1801+, salt making 1838+, shipbuilding 1847+, fishing till 1882, coalmining; Angl. C. (St Andrew's) 1846 d. by Henry Ginn, new one b. 1870 by Cookson and Joseph Taylor, d. by Joseph Backhouse, third one (St Paul's) b. 1890 by P. Price, d. by George Sanders & Son, and graveyard; breakwater (northern) b. 1866–1914, 3,400 ft (1,036.3 m); bridge (concrete) 1972 d. by Albert Fried, 3,360 ft (1,024 m), to Kooragang, over Hunter R.; bushfires 1911, 1928, 1933, 1951, 2018; cemetery (2,036 graves) 1887; chemical works (Stockton-on-Hunter) estab. 1855 by William Norton, taken over 1855 by J. Elliot Blake, closed 1861, reopened 1863 by James Tennant; collieries: Stockton (11 killed in 1896) 1885–1908 and Stockton No. 3 Shaft 1893; Cong. C. 1887 d. by George C. Sanders, and graveyard; dengue fever 1926; FB (station b. 1930 by McGrorey and Keenan); ferry (steam) to Newcastle, across Hunter R., estab. 1869 by Hugh and Robert Boyce; fire 1902; flood 1955; fort (Fort Wallace) 1913, upgraded 1940, largely closed 1945, fully closed 1951, guns removed 1963, fort reused 1967–93, acquired 2015 by Defence Housing Aust. for future redevelopment; foundry (iron) estab. 1842 by Alexander Walker Scott, taken over by James Mitchell, and later by Robert Fisher and William Donaldson; gales 1851, 1898, 1899; hospital for the insane 1910–17, became mental hospital in 1917, additions 1917, 1925, 1934, 1938, nursery wards b. 1941 by Baker and Lamb, hospital additions 1955, 1958, 1960, 1962, 1968, 1981, closed 1989, reused; joineries: Callen Bros and J.H. Priestley; lime-works (Constitutional) estab. 1870 by John Donovan (4 kilns); lock-up b. 1880 by M. Parkhill; Meth. C. b. 1902 by Bevan & Son, d. by Augustus Dixon Chater; miners' strikes 1888 and 1894; PO: Corroba 1927–78 and Stockton 1862, new one b. 1901 by Benjamin George Pearce, new one b. 1942 on new site by R. Keevers; pound (stock) 1891; Presb. C. (St Giles's) 1920, closed, reused, new one (Surfside); Prim. Meth. C. 1886, new one b. 1892 by H. Bevan, burnt down 1902; PS 1876, renovated 1900 by Joseph Head, additions and alterations 1909 by Montague Audet, reused, new one 1978; punt (horse) estab. 1889 by Peter Callen; quarantine station 1900; reservoir (steel tank), 1,000,000 gal. (4,546 kl), b. 1954 by Steel Tank & Pipe Constructions; Rom. Cath. C. 1887 d. by Frederick Burnhardt Menkens, additions 1937 by Vincent Doran, d. by Gannon, new one (St Peter-in-Chains) 1961; salt-works estab. 1836 by Alexander Walker Scott, closed; Salv. Army C.; sawmills: Avery and Davies, Callen Bros, John Hay, Hugh Meehan 1800, later moved to Newcastle, Mitchell and Tully, burnt down 1851; school 1861, new building b. 1882 by John Rollo Rodgers, additions 1887, additions 1891 by William L. Bevan, repairs 1895 by Whitehead and Stott, additions 1923, 1928, 1934, 1952, 1996; SD Adventist C.; sewerage 1936; shipwrecks: Adolphe 1904, Cawarra 1886, Colonist 1894, Lindus 1899, Sygna 1974, Wendouree 1898; shipyards and slipways: Callen Bros (taken over by Edward Beattie, later joined by Ellis Davis), Phoenix, Ritchie and Hay (acquired by Callen Bros) 1858–1928, James Scott 1860 (taken over 1869 by Daniel Macquarie, largely rebuilt, taken over 1876 by Timothy D. O'Sullivan and Burns, became O'Sullivan & Co., acquired 1905 by Thomas Warland, sold 1920 to Albert Hough and became Newcastle Patent Slip & Engineering Co., closed and sold 1932), Slazenger Construction Co. (bought 1948 by Wynne Breden, closed, bought by Steel Pipe & Tank Constructions), Stockton Ferries Pty Ltd (Thomas Walter); smelter (tin) estab. 1872 by C.T. Stephens (at Scott's old salt-works), closed 1876; storms 1942 and 1974; tank traps 1942; tannery 1866; telegraph 1887, new office b. 1900 by Benjamin George Pearce; telephone (Corroba) 1945; tweed mill (Stockton Tweed Cloth Manufactory, James Mitchell) b. 1840–43, taken over 1843 by Fisher and Donaldson, expanded 1844, 1845, 1846, burnt down 1851; TX 1904, new one 1955, automatic 1963; Unit. C. (orig. Meth.) 1967; 3 vehicular ferries (steam) 1916, to Newcastle, across Hunter R., sold 1971 to Goldfields Metal Traders (Stuart Allen White), wrecked 1972; water reticulation 1927; wharf b. 1888 by Callen Bros, 2 steam cranes supplied and erected 1885 by Appleby Bros, wharf extended 1897 by Peter Callen; pop. 112 (1846), 166 (1851), 130 (1856), 159 (1861), 341 (1871), 666 (1881), 2,416 (1891), *c.*2,500 (1895), 2,549 (1901), 2,106 (1911), *c.*4,600 (1921), *c.*6,000 (1929), 5,700 (1933), *c.*6,000 (1940), *c.*6,600 (1947), *c.*6,800 (1954), *c.*7,000 (1961), *c.*6,600 (1966), *c.*5,900 (1971), *c.*5,600 (1976), 4,208 (2006), 4,195 (2011).

Stockton North (*Co. Gloucester*) see Fern Bay.

Stockyard Creek (*Co. Clarence*) 29°31'S. 152°48'E., 22 km NW of Grafton, on Stockyard Ck; grazing, farming, dairying; cheese factory (George Chevalley) 1896; PO 1886; sawmill (R. & L. Burrows Pty Ltd), burnt down 1951; school (Fern Glen) 1882, new buildings b. 1883 by R. and J. Jurd, closed 1895, reopened 1904, closed 1907; telephone 1915; TX 1953–61; pop. 70 (1933).

Stockyard Flat (*Co. Macquarie*) 31°46'S. 152°18'E., 13 km NW of Wingham, on Dingo Ck.

Stockyard Flat (*Co. Vernon*) 31°09'S. 152°03'E., 45 km SE of Walcha, on Yarrowitch R.

Stoker (*Co. Rous*) see Stokers Siding.

Stokers (*Co. Rous*) see Stokers Siding.

Stokers Siding (*Co. Rous*) 28°24'S. 153°24'E., 8 km S. of Murwillumbah, on Smiths Ck; formerly Stoker; farming, dairying, fruit; Angl. C. (St John the Baptist) b. 1912 by A.A. Gaggin, Meth. till 1936, closed 1982, bought 1983 by Laine Langridge and reused; caterpillar infestation 1914; PO 1912; pottery estab. 1978 by Bob Connery and Laine Langridge; RS (Dunbible Siding till 1925, then Stokers) 1896–1974, station reused; sawmills: Byrnes & Co. and A.J. Waters 1908; school 1917; telephone 1911; TX 1926, automatic 1954; pop. 140 (1911), 373 (1933), 304 (1947), 289 (1954), 172 (1961), 446 (2006), 655 (2011).

Stonefield (*Co. Burnett*) 29°36'S. 150°31'E., 8 km SW of Warialda; FB (station b. 2017); school 1885–1903; Union C.

Stonehenge (*Co. Gough*) 29°48'S. 151°44'E., 9 km S. of Glen Innes; orig. Boyd's Plains; settled 1838 by Archibald Boyd, surveyed 1851 by John James Galloway, town gaz. 1852; farming; flour mill (wind) b. 1845 by Archibald Boyd; PO 1885; RS 1884–1975; school 1881 b. by Edward Grover, repairs 1892 by Nicholas Josephson, closed 1956; telephone 1914; TX 1938, automatic 1953; pop. 73 (1901), 211 (1911), 219 (1933), 233 (1947), 198 (1954), 143 (1961), 219 (2011).

Stonehenge (*Co. Wallace*) 36°21'S. 148°29'E., 9 km NE of Perisher Valley, on Diggers Ck.

Stonequarry (*Co. Argyle*) 34°22'S. 149°46'E., 29 km NE of Crookwell; cemetery (600 graves 1865+); telephone 1926; TX 1926–69; pop. 50 (1901), 39 (1933).

Stonequarry (*Co. Camden*) see Picton.

Stonequarry Estate (*Co. Camden*) see Picton.

Stoney Creek (*Co. Dudley*) 30°58'S. 152°40'E., 22 km NW of Kempsey; Presb. C. 1901.

Stoney Creek (*Co. Wellington*) see Stuart Town.

Stoney Creek Loop (*Co. Roxburgh*) see Gemalla.

Stony Chute (*Co. Rous*) 28°35'S. 153°10'E., 7 km W. of Nimbin; dairying; FB; school 1928–71; pop. 138 (1933), 114 (1947), 105 (1954), 87 (1961), 235.

Stony Creek (*Co. Auckland*) 36°37'S. 149°49'E., 7 km N. of Bega; cheese factory 1914; school 1879–96, 1910–37, 1957–60; pop. 57 (1933), 63 (1947), 61 (1961).

Stony Creek (*Co. Dampier*) 36°01'S. 150°01'E., 12 km SW of Moruya.

Stony Creek (*Co. Georgiana*) 34°11'S. 149°28'E., 32 km N. of Crookwell, on Stony Ck.

Stony Creek (*Co. Gloucester*) see Rainbow Flat.

Stony Creek (*Co. Phillip*) 32°29'S. 149°44'E., 20 km NE of Mudgee; Cooyal till 1882; farming, specially cereal crops; PO 1872–1961; Rom. Cath. C. (St John's) 1888; school (Welshville) 1927–38; telephone 1926; TX 1928; winery (Blue Wren Wines); pop. 65 (1911), 78 (1933).

Stony Creek (*Co. Westmoreland*) 33°42'S. 149°40'E., 19 km W. of Oberon, on Sewells Ck; Meth. C. 1946–68; mine; Wes. Meth. C. 1874, demolished 1947; pop. 67 (1901).

Stony Crossing (*Co. Richmond*) 29°12'S. 153°06'E., 27 km SW of Woodburn, on Bungawalbin Ck; tea-tree still.

Stony Crossing (*Co. Wakool*) 35°04'S. 143°34'E., 47 km S. of Balranald; village gaz. 1931; farming and grazing; cemetery; PO 1890, burnt down 1930; RS (Victorian railway, Poonboon till 1929) 1928, closed; TX 1929–56; pop. 96 (1911), 98 (1933), 55 (1954), 52 (1961).

Stony Pinch (*Co. Wellington*) 32°44'S. 149°46'E., 20 km W. of Rylstone, on Windamere Dam.

Stony Point (*Co. Cooper*) 34°29'S. 146°25'E., 8 km N. of Leeton; Bapt. C. 1915, closed, reopened 1935; school (Brobenah till 1927) 1895–1906 and 1915–78; pop. 237 (1933), 186 (1947), 160 (1954), 145 (1961).

Store Creek (*Co. Wellington*) 32°53'S.

149°05'E., 31 km NE of Molong, on Store Ck; farming and grazing; PO 1901; Rom. Cath. C. (St Thomas More's) b. 1936 by H. Shepherd, demolished; RS (Watertank till 1885) 1880–1974; school 1905–42; telegraph 1890; telephone 1915; TX 1922–61; typhoid 1908; pop. 76 (1901), 112 (1911), 111 (1933), 58 (1947).

Stotts Creek (*Co. Rous*) 28°17'S. 153°31'E., 6 km SW of Kingscliff, on Tweed R.; farming, dairying, sugar-cane; PO 1911; Rom. Cath. C. 1895, removed from Murwillumbah, damaged 1925, moved to and re-erected 1926 at Duranbah; storms 1913 and 1925; telephone 1926; wharf b. 1892 by Alex Clarke; pop. 52 (1911), 77 (1933), 92 (1947).

Strangers Corner (*Co. Gloucester*) 32°14'S. 152°03'E., 23 km NE of Stroud, on Terreel Ck.

Stratford (*Co. Gloucester*) 32°07'S. 151°56'E., 13 km S. of Gloucester, on Avon R.; orig. the Aust. Agric. Co.'s horse station, then timber, dairying, cattle, farming; Angl. C. (St John's) 1958; bridge b. by J. Burley, new one 1981, over Avon R.; cemetery (207 graves 1925+); FB 1967, renamed Avon; PO 1908; railway bridge (steel truss) fabricated by R.L. Scrutton & Co., erected 1913 by Smith, Timms & Co., over Avon R.; RS 1913, station b. by Robert Daniel Quiggin, closed 1978; school 1912, new building b. 1913 by Germon and Wright, additions 1928 by White Bros, additions 2010; telephone 1910; TX 1918, automatic 1952; Union C. 1918, new one 1929; pop. 182 (1911), 204 (1933), 312 (1947), 294 (1954), 226 (1961), 110 (2006).

Strathaird (*Co. Argyle*) 34°25'S. 149°44'E., 25 km E. of Crookwell, on Woolshed Ck; RS 1926–57, reused; school (Wowagin till 1939) 1882–1965; pop. 51 (1901).

Strathallan (*Co. St Vincent*) see Braidwood.

Strathallyn (*Co. Narromine*) 32°27'S. 147°52'E., 43 km SW of Narromine; school 1959–66.

Strathbogie (*Co. Arrawatta*) 29°28'S. 151°29'E., 40 km E. of Ashford, on Severn R.; hailstorm 1864; pop. 61 (1901), 67 (1911), 35 (1933).

Strathcedar (*Co. Macquarie*) 31°46'S. 152°22'E., 11 km N. of Wingham, on Cedar Party Ck; Mooral Creek till 1910; farming; PO 1927–40; telephone 1924; TX 1925; pop. 76 (1933), 67 (1947), 65 (1954).

Stratheden (*Co. Rous*) 28°48'S. 152°58'E., 11 km NW of Casino, on Eden Ck; dairying; gale 1916; PO 1927; school 1918, additions 2010; storms 1927 and 1936; telephone 1914; TX 1928, automatic 1954; pop. 190 (1933), 146 (1947), 183 (1954), 124 (1961), 232 (2011).

Strathfieldsaye (*Co. Bligh*) see Montefiores.

Strathisla (*Co. Durham*) 32°18'S. 151°25'E., 37 km NE of Singleton, on Paterson R.; pound (stock) 1850.

Strathlone (*Co. Cook*) see Bowenfels South.

Strathmore (*Co. Clarendon*) 34°54'S. 147°26'E., 11 km W. of Junee; Angl. C. (St Margaret's) 1930 d. by John Donald Morrow.

Strathvale (*Co. King*) 34°09'S. 148°49'E., 33 km N. of Boorowa, on Boorowa R.; school 1957–66.

Streamville (*Co. Georgiana*) 33°58'S. 149°02'E., 34 km SE of Cowra.

Stringybark Flat (*Co. Monteagle*) 34°21'S. 148°35'E., 15 km NW of Boorowa, on Shanty Ck.

Strontian Park (*Co. Clarence*) 29°38'S. 152°59'E., 7 km NE of Grafton; settled by Angus Cameron; school 1859, repairs 1883 by G. Hattersley, additions and repairs 1890 by George Wunderlich, closed 1902; wharf.

Stroud (*Co. Gloucester*) 32°24'S. 151°58'E., 20 km E. of Dungog, on Mill Ck; laid out 1829 as second headquarters of Aust. Agric. Co., estab. 1832, thrived 1830s–40s, subdivided 1849, town lots sold 1850–56, declined *c.*1857+, Aust. Agric. Co. departed 1873; wheat and maize *c.*1830+, then beef, dairying, timber, poultry; ambulance station 1946; Angl. C. (St John the Evangelist) 1833 d. by Thomas Laman for Aust. Agric. Co., upgraded 1851 from chapel to church, repairs 1874 and 1883, restoration 1983, repairs 1997 d. by Barney Collins, renovation 2004, and graveyard (185 graves 1836+), incl. columbarium 1979; Bapt. C. b. 1912 by W. March, vestry added 1942; brewery (Australia Inn and Brewery); brick-kilns; bridges: one b. 1871 by Thomas Smith over Mill Ck and one b. 1986 over Lamans Ck; butter factory (Gloucester Dist. Co-op. Butter Factory Co. Ltd) 1902; carriage-works: P.W. Casey 1901 and P. Krohn; cemetery; CH (incl. lock-up) 1860, new one b. 1876–78 by S. and W. Stainbridge, d. by James Johnstone Barnet, closed 1974, restored and reused 1988; clock tower; diphtheria 1934; earth tremor 1842; electricity 1937; FB; floods 1955 and 2015; flour mill and sawmill (Aust. Agric. Co.) 1834, converted to steam 1859, demolished; gale 1909; grain drying kiln 1835; granary 1831; hospital (cottage, Aust. Agric. Co.); measles epidemic 1910; PO 1851, new one b. 1884 by Bretnall and Poulton, restored 1984; pound (stock) 1853; Presb. C. (St James's) 1887, and graveyard; PS 1953; punt b. 1864 by George Darwood for Philip Snape; reservoir 1959; Rom. Cath. C. (St Malachy's) b. 1861 by Robert Connell and Coleman, later rededicated to St Columbanus; sale-yards (Alison and Jones) 1907; sawmills: Armstrong & Royse Pty Ltd 1937, R.W. Brown, Smith & Ellis Ltd, Yates Bros; school 1882, new one b. 1885 by William Humphries, d. by William Edmund Kemp, alterations 1907 by Charles Coleman, additions 1920 by Quiggin, additions 1926 by J. Mitchell, additions 1953, 1957, 1969; sewerage 1981; 8 silos (underground) 1841, disused; telegraph 1877, new office b. 1884 by Bretnall and Poulton; telephone 1911; TX 1915, automatic 1982; typhoid 1902 (person died) and 1903; Unit. C. (orig. Meth.) 1904; water reticulation 1961, augmentation 1996; Wes. Meth. C. (Jubilee) 1865, rebuilt; wharf (Karuah R.) b. 1880 by R.H. Worthing; whooping cough epidemic 1936; pop. 368 (1856), 398 (1861), 380 (1866), 289 (1871), 344 (1881), *c.*300 (1886), 259 (1891), 307 (1901), 1,098 (1911), 545 (1933), 686 (1947), 769 (1954), 655 (1961), 535 (1966), 563 (1971), 541 (1976), 522 (1981), 484 (1986), 556 (1991), 598 (1996), 672 (2001), 669 (2006), 701 (2011).

Stroud Hill (*Co. Gloucester*) see Dingadee.

Stroud Road (*Co. Gloucester*) 32°21'S. 151°56'E., 17 km E. of Dungog, on Mammy Johnsons R.; timber, dairying, farming, chickens 1960s+; bridge 1984 over Mammy Johnsons R.; butter factory (Gloucester Dist. Co-op. Butter Factory Co. Ltd) b. 1920 by Thackray and Gallagher, d. by Richard Wildridge & Co., closed 1928, abandoned, reopened 1933 by Bowthorne Co-op. Butter Factory Ltd, closed; CH 1876–1974; colliery (Duralie Coal Pty Ltd) 2003; creamery (Gloucester Dist. Factory) 1904; FB; PO 1916; quarry; railway bridge (steel truss), 120 ft (36.6 m), fabricated by H. Vale & Sons, erected 1913 by G. Wilcocks, over Karuah R.; RS 1913, station b. by Robert Daniel Quiggin; sawmills: E.D. Pike & Co. Ltd (burnt down 1984), Turner and Ebbeck, White and Sweeney, W.D. Wood Ltd (b. 1927 by Saville and Goodwin), burnt down 1931, Young and Jackson; school 1919, additions 2010; telephone 1914; TX 1922; Unit. C. (orig. Meth.) b. 1915 by G. Wenham, d. by R.S. Rutledge; Wes. Meth. C. 1883; pop. 226 (1933), 219 (1947), 282 (1954), 212 (1961), 249 (2006), 280 (2011).

Stuart (*Co. Wellington*) see Stuart Town.

Stuarts Point (*Co. Dudley*) 30°49'S. 153°00'E., 9 km NW of South West Rocks, on Macleay Arm; farming, fruit, tourism; Angl. C. (All Saints') 1959; bushfire 1895; cemetery (Kinki, 205 graves 1880+), incl. columbarium; earth tremor 2018; FB; flood 1893; foot-bridge over Macleay Arm; PO 1891; sawmills: Walter G. Conn, Thomas Hennessy & Sons, Parrisotto's, Allen Taylor & Co. Ltd, H. Tessier; school 1899 b. by A.H. Scand, closed 1917, reopened 1954, additions 1991; shipyard (John Stuart); telegraph 1884; TX 1928, automatic 1969; water supply augmentation 1985 and 2000; Wes. Meth. C. 1900; wharf, additions 1901 by W.G. Boulton; pop. 92 (1901), 66 (1911), 82 (1933), 191 (1947), 237 (1954), 235 (1961), 206 (1971), 296 (1976), 439 (1981), 591 (1986), 685 (1991), 751 (1996), 781 (2001), 724 (2006), 677 (2011).

Stuarts Rocks (*Co. Brisbane*) see Murrurundi.

Stuart Town (*Co. Wellington*) 32°48'S.

149°05'E., 30 km SE of Wellington, on Oaky Ck; orig. Sandy's Middle Station, then Stoney Creek till 1858, then Ironbarks till 1889; town gaz. 1886 as Stuart; formerly mining (gold disc. 1849 by Wallace, gold rush 1856, dredging 1899–1958, production peaked 1905), now grazing and fruit; Angl. C. (St James's) 1874, new one (St Michael and All Angels') b. 1909–13 by Kennard Bros, closed 1969; cemetery (597 graves 1874+) 1870; CH 1865, new one 1887, burnt down 1943; cyanide plant; FB 1939; fire 1913; lock-up, repairs 1897 by F.F. Archer; mines: Bell's, Burthundra, Caledonian, Canadian 1866–70, Chinaman's <1870s, Company or Mookerawa 1877–84, German Hill (Excelsior), German Jack (Hanley) 1870s, Ginger 1857, Hanlon, Happy-Go-Lucky, Horseshoe (Boehme), Knockout, Macatanamy's, Madman's <1885, Manna Hill 1912–38, Old Canadian, Perseverance, Poor Man's (Poor Man's Reef Co., Liddell, Grimley and Reid) 1858 and 1876–98, Post Office (Emma Co., Turn of Century, Boehme Bros) 1858–1916, Princess Alexandra 1880s, Princess Alexandra Extended 1880s, Prince William, Quartz Hill (Ron Halliday) 1965+, Rockdale 1890s, Specimen Hill (Sundowners, Specimen Hill Gold Mining Co., J.A. Halliday) 1887–88 and 1931–35, Trickett's (disc. 1876 by Numa Chadeysson, worked by Marshall & Co. and Houstan & Co.) 1877–82, Water Lily, Welcome Stranger, Widow's Mite <1890; PO 1856, new one b. 1891 by Joseph Cottrell, additions and alterations 1907 by Frank J. Stanford, repairs 1930 by J.T. Butterworth and V. Miller; PS b. 1884 by William Gadd, repairs 1897 by F.F. Archer, additions 1912 by F.H. Kennard, burnt down 1943; Rom. Cath. C. (St John the Baptist) b. 1898 by James Connor, d. by John Job Copeman; RS 1880, station b. by James Stuart Douglas, closed 1976; school (Ironbarks till 1889) 1858–60, reopened 1870, new building b. 1898 by John Dunkley; stamper battery (12 head) 1860; telegraph 1880, additions and repairs to office 1907 by Frank J. Stanford; TX 1915, automatic 1939; typhoid 1905 and 1920; pop. *c.*300 (1866), *c.*250 (1886), 563 (1891), 587 (1901), 547 (1911), 370 (1933), 388 (1947), 257 (1954), 264 (1961), 256 (1966), *c.*200 (1987), 487 (2011).

Stubbo (*Co. Bligh*) 32°18'S. 149°32'E., 7 km N. of Gulgong, on Stubbo Ck; Angl. C. (St Bede's) 1899; school 1881–1927; pop. 64 (1911), 32 (1933), 61 (1954), 236 (2011).

Sturt (*Co. Auckland*) see Towamba.

Sturt (*Co. Wynyard*) see Wagga Wagga.

Sue City (*Co. Selwyn*) 35°49'S. 148°21'E., 32 km E. of Tumbarumba, on Tumut R.; temporary construction camp estab. by Kaiser-Walsh-Perini-Raymond for Snowy Mountains Hydro-Electric Scheme, dismantled and removed 1962; bridge over Tumut R.; PS (in rented premises) 1958–61; school 1959–62.

Suffolk Beach (*Co. Rous*) see Suffolk Park.

Suffolk Park (*Co. Rous*) 28°41'S. 153°37'E., 4 km S. of Byron Bay, on Tallow Ck; (incl. Baywood Chase and Byron Hills); formerly Suffolk Beach; laid out 1922 by Frank Wearne; FB; foot-bridge (Wilkinson Bridge) over Tallow Ck; quarries; 2 reservoirs; pop. 239 (1976), 681 (1981), 895 (1986), 1,221 (1991), 2,528 (1996), 3,318 (2001), 3,291 (2006), 3,467 (2011).

Sugar Bay (*Co. Northumberland*)
see Brightwaters.

Sugarloaf (*Co. Durham*) 32°23'S. 151°43'E., 4 km W. of Dungog, on Sugarloaf Ck; pop. 68 (1933), 304 (2006).

Sugarloaf (*Co. Northumberland*) see Mulbring.

Sulcor (*Co. Inglis*) 30°52'S. 150°48'E., 16 km SE of Manilla; lime and cement plant; limestone quarry 1924 (worked by Sulphide Corp. Ltd, acquired by Newcastle Lime & Cement Co., bought 2001 by Unimin Aust. Ltd); RS 1924–75; school (Brown Springs till 1945) 1931–46; pop. 98 (1933), 84 (1947), 63 (1961).

Sulphide Junction (*Co. Northumberland*)
see Cardiff.

Suma Park (*Co. Bathurst*)
see Orange (*Co. Wellington*).

Summer Hill (*Co. Bathurst*) 33°20'S. 149°09'E., 7 km SE of Orange, on Summer Hill Ck;

school 1861–62.

Summer Hill (*Co. Durham*) 32°31'S. 151°32'E., 24 km N. of Maitland, on Paterson R.; formerly Bunnabunoo; bridge (Bruxner Bridge) b. 1930 by J. McNulty, d. by W.R. Lindsay, 95 ft (29 m), over Paterson R.; Rom. Cath. C. (Guardian Angels) b. 1840 by John Dobson, new one (Sacred Heart) b. 1913 by A. Howarth, d. by Thomas Wilfred Silk, renovated 1985, now seldom used, and graveyard (23 burials and 96 graves); TX, closed 1964.

Summer Hill (*Co. Durham*) see also Fishers Hill.

Summer Hill (*Co. Parry*) see Somerton.

Summer Hill Creek (*Co. Wellington*) 33°13'S. 149°08'E., 7 km N. of Orange, on Summer Hill Ck; Angl. C. (St James's); Meth. C. 1905; mines: Mount Lindsay Copper Mine (Mount Lindsay Mining Syndicate), Mount Shorter (Mount Lindsay Mining Syndicate) 1899–1905 and 1931–33, Pride of the Hills (Mount Lindsay Mining Syndicate, incl. stamper battery and cyanide plant) 1901–7; school 1902–94; pop. 72 (1911), 40 (1933).

Summer Island (*Co. Dudley*) 30°59'S. 152°59'E., 12 km SW of South West Rocks, on Macleay R.; agric. and dairying; cheese factory (Martin McCabe); floods 1863 and 1870; PO 1863; punt; sugar mills: Samuel Jackson (horse powered) and Henry Woods (steam powered); telephone 1912; TX 1918–26; wharves: one b. 1883 and one b. 1897 by G. Lawson; pop. 53 (1866), 56 (1901), 117 (1911), 82 (1933), 63 (1961).

Summer Island (*Co. Macquarie*) see Kinchela.

Summerland Point (*Co. Northumberland*) 33°08'S. 151°34'E., 2 km W. of Gwandalan, on Lake Macquarie; jetty; PO 1970; sewerage 1987; pop. 2,358 (2011).

Summervale (*Co. Canbelego*) 31°25'S. 147°04'E., 20 km NW of Nyngan; PO 1899–1913; RS 1894–1977.

Summer Vale (*Co. Vernon*) 30°58'S. 151°39'E., 5 km E. of Walcha, on Ohio Ck; Aboriginal reserve; school 1887–1929; pop. *c.*35 (2009).

Summit Tank (*Co. Camden*) 34°31'S. 150°42'E., 8 km W. of Dapto; railway turntable, 60 ft (18.3 m), ruined; RS 1932.

Sunlight (*Co. Sandon*) see Metz.

Sunny Corner (*Co. Raleigh*) 30°29'S. 152°52'E., 4 km SW of Bellingen; bridges: one over Kalang R. and one over Woods Ck; pop. 30 (1933).

Sunny Corner (*Co. Roxburgh*) 33°23'S. 149°53'E., 9 km W. of Portland; Mitchell 1885–87 (though PO did not change till 1888); surveyed 1884, village gaz. 1885, thrived 1884–91, virtually deserted by 1925; copper, gold (disc. 1865) mining 1865–81 and silver (disc. 1876) mining 1876–1922, silver smelting 1884+, then potatoes and peas, forestry 1946+, eucalyptus oil; Angl. C. (Holy Trinity) 1886, dismantled, new one 1902; bushfires 1902, 1908, 1909, 1932, 1940; caterpillar infestation 1900; cemetery (156 burials 1885–1950) 1887; cordial factory (Thomas J. Eather); dam (mine) 1885; drought 1876; FB; gale 1909; hospital 1892 d. by Clarence Backhouse and Reginald William Laidley, never used as such; measles epidemic 1898; miners' strikes 1885 and 1886; 27 mines: incl. Banna and Allison, Bighill, Bulldog, Central, Cornstalk, Garlands, General Gordon, Great Western 1884–87, Honest John, Montana, New Find, Phoenix (formerly Nevada) *c.*1884–92, St George, Silver Hill, Silver King 1882–90, Silver Prince, Silver Queen, Silver Star, Sunny Corner (incl. 6 Pacific furnaces) 1865–92, Taskers Lode, Tompkins 1884 (abandoned and later reworked as Montana Copper Mine 1906–10), Winterton; pneumonia epidemic 1902; PO 1885, repairs 1896 by F.F. Archer, alterations 1909, renovations 1950, burnt down 1970; Presb. C. (Scotch) 1886, closed, moved 1918 to Portland and reused; PS (incl. court room and lock-up) 1884, rebuilt 1885, additions 1896 by Rigby Bros, fire 1910, closed and removed 1925; reservoir b. 1891 by George Francis; Rom. Cath. C. (St Matthias's) b. 1885 by Muggridge, closed, new one 1891, moved 1943 to Cullen Bullen; sawmills: John Hurley 1885 and Thomas Augustine Sparks; scarlet fever 1898; school (Mitchell's Creek till 1886 then Mitchell till 1899) 1864, repairs 1883 by John Cook, new one b. 1886 by James Donald, alterations 1916, closed 1979; 11 smelters, operated mainly 1884–90; snowstorms 1893, 1910, 1914, 1917; 14 stamper batteries; storms 1887 and 1906; telegraph 1885, repairs to office 1896 by F.F. Archer; telephone 1914; tramway (mine) 1885; TX (automatic) 1984; typhoid (girl died) 1900; Union C. b. 1886 by R. Clarke, relocated, enlarged and renovated 1897 by Frank Cook and G. Shumack, closed; water reticulation 1891; Wes. Meth. C. 1886, relocated and re-erected 1896; pop. *c.*2,000 (1884), *c.*4,000 (1885), *c.*1,700 (1887), 1,677 (1891), 515 (1901), 260 (1911), 117 (1933), 106 (1947), 121 (1954), 120 (1961), 269 (2011).

Sunny Ridge (*Co. Bathurst*) 33°38'S. 148°45'E., 11 km SE of Canowindra, on Tenandra Ck; pop. 22 (1933), 65 (1947).

Sunnyside (*Co. Clive*) 29°00'S. 151°57'E., 9 km NW of Tenterfield, on Tenterfield Ck; farming and grazing; airfield 1968; cemetery; gale 1884; PO 1891–1971; quarries; railway viaduct (timber truss) 1888 d. by John Whitton, over Tenterfield Ck; RS 1888–1973; school 1884–1966; telephone 1915; TX 1951; Union C. 1883, damaged 1884, removed 1975; pop. 114 (1901), 128 (1911), 173 (1933), 83 (1947), 91 (1954), 54 (1961).

Sunnyside (*Co. Jamison*) 29°56'S. 149°14'E., 38 km NW of Wee Waa.

Sunnyside (*Co. Murchison*) 30°01'S. 150°35'E., 16 km S. of Bingara.

Sunnywood (*Co. Northumberland*) 33°02'S. 151°29'E., 12 km W. of Toronto, on Jigadee Ck; school 1957–80.

Sunpatch (*Co. St Vincent*) see Tomakin.

Sunrise (*Co. Hume*) 35°39'S. 146°55'E., 11 km W. of Culcairn; airfield; school 1918–36.

Sunset Strip (*Co. Menindee*) 32°16'S. 142°20'E., 88 km SE of Broken Hill, on Lake Menindee; outback holiday hamlet; spider infestation 2016; pop. *c.*50 (2013).

Sunshine (*Co. Northumberland*) see Brightwaters.

Sunshine Bay (*Co. St Vincent*) see Denhams Beach.

Suntop (*Co. Gordon*) 32°35'S. 148°51'E., 10 km W. of Wellington; Bloomsdale till 1890; Bapt. C.; gale 1928; PO 1899; Rom. Cath. C. (St John the Baptist) 1907, closed, sold and reused; school 1892–1969; telephone 1912; TX 1912–20; Union C., damaged 1928, repairs 1930; pop. 280 (1901), 195 (1911), 166 (1933), 85 (1947), 90 (1954), 116 (1961).

Sun Valley (*Co. Cook*) 33°43'S. 150°36'E., 3 km E. of Springwood, on Fitzgeralds Ck.

Surface Hill (*Co. Clive*) 29°07'S. 152°17'E., 27 km E. of Tenterfield, on Rocky Ck; cemetery.

Surf Beach (*Co. St Vincent*) see Denhams Beach.

Surfside (*St Vincent*) see Batemans Bay North.

Surprise Town (*Co. Northumberland*) see Windale.

Surprise Township (*Co. Northumberland*) see Windale.

Surveyors Creek (*Co. Inglis*) 30°59'S. 151°24'E., 19 km W. of Walcha, on Surveyors Ck; PO 1880–82; school 1881–82.

Surveyors Flat (*Co. Georgiana*) see Apple Tree Flat.

Sussex Inlet (*Co. St Vincent*) 35°10'S. 150°36'E., 6 km SW of Sanctuary Point, on Sussex Inlet; (incl. South Sussex Inlet); formerly fishing and tourism; ambulance station; Angl. C. (St Mark's); 3 bridges; bushfires 1965, 1968, 2001; canal system began 1950 by James Cater, later completed by Lucas and Tait; cordial factory and ice works, sold 1950; electricity 1947; FB; floods 1920, 1942, 1959, 1971, 2015; Meth. C. 1940; PO: South Sussex Inlet 1952 and Sussex Inlet 1927; PS 1981; reservoir; Rom. Cath. C. (St Patrick's) 1972; sawmill estab. by Abe Jennings, taken over 1909 by Watt and Mathie, and became William Watt & Son in 1921; school 1954, additions 1993 and 2010; sewerage augmentation 1990; telephone: South Sussex Inlet 1952 and Sussex Inlet 1906; TX 1938, automatic 1970; Union C.; Unit. C. (Community) 1897; 2 wharves; pop. 34 (1933), 131 (1947), 222 (1954), 322 (1961), 386

(1966), 534 (1971), 933 (1976), 1,293 (1981), 1,705 (1986), 2,324 (1991), 2,651 (1996), 3,033 (2001), 3,167 (2006), 3,193 (2011).

Suterville (*Co. Macquarie*) see Bonny Hills.

Sutherland Point (*Co. Rous*) see Kingscliff.

Sutton (*Co. Murray*) 35°10'S. 149°15'E., 21 km N. of Queanbeyan, on Yass R.; village gaz. 1867; farming and grazing; Angl. C. 1907, additions 1911 by G.A. McInnes, new one (St Peter's) 1926; bushfire 2017; electricity 1951; mine (Goorooyarroo Gold Prospect) 1917–19; PO 1875; school 1881, new buildings b. 1883 by J. Kealman, d. by William Edmund Kemp, closed 1896, reopened 1903, additions 2010; telephone 1915; TX 1915, automatic 1961; Wes. Meth. C. 1867 (removed from Newington), closed 1888; pop. 59 (1891), 91 (1901), 156 (1911), 68 (1933), 73 (1947), 61 (1954), 160 (1961), 221 (1996), 257 (2001), 220 (2006), 229 (2011).

Sutton Forest (*Co. Camden*) 34°34'S. 150°19'E., 6 km SW of Moss Vale, on Paynes Ck; founded 1854; orig. potatoes, orchards 1870s, former highland retreat for the wealthy (incl. State Governors 1882–1958) 1876+, wheat, cattle, dairying, horses; Angl. C. 1830, new one (All Saints') 1861 d. by Edmund Thomas Blacket, and graveyard (burials 1829+, 800 graves); gale 1899; hailstorm 1907; lock-up 1864; PO 1857; pound (stock) 1856; Presb. C. 1866, closed, reopened 1892, closed again, sold 1935; Rom. Cath. C. 1854, new one (St Patrick's) b. 1879 by R. Metz, and graveyard (graves 1854+); sale-yards; sawmill (Amos Bros); school 1880 b. by Murphy and Jones, d. by George Allen Mansfield, additions 2009, closed 2014, sold 2016; telegraph 1881; telephone 1910; TX 1916; pop. 621 (1871), 436 (1891), 375 (1901), 297 (1911), 178 (1933), 209 (1947), 187 (1954), 154 (1961), 253 (2006), 579 (2011).

Sutton Forest (*Co. Camden*) see also Moss Vale.

Sutton Forest North (*Co. Camden*) see Moss Vale.

Swallows Nest (*Co. Westmoreland*) 33°46'S. 149°37'E., 23 km W. of Oberon; defunct; gold (disc. 1868); drought 1880; mines: Crosiers Reef 1877, L. Edgley <1877 and 1903–5, Long Ridge Deep Lead; PO 1868–93.

Swamp Oak (*Co. Arrawatta*) 29°42'S. 151°19'E., 21 km E. of Inverell; pop. 89 (1901), 121 (1911).

Swamp Oak (*Co. Inglis*) see Tanglewood.

Swamp Oak (*Co. Parry*) see Weabonga.

Swamp Oak Creek (*Co. Clive*) 29°02'S. 152°09'E., 12 km E. of Tenterfield; school 1912–36.

Swamp Paddock (*Co. St Vincent*) see Pyree.

Swan Bay (*Co. Gloucester*) 32°42'S. 151°58'E., 5 km S. of Karuah, on Port Stephens; oysters; brickworks (Port Stephens Fire Brick Co. Ltd) 1916, defunct except for chimney; bushfires 1914 and 2016; electricity 1954; jetty; pop. 51 (1911), 41 (1933), 96 (1947), 83 (1954), 72 (1961), 437 (2011).

Swan Bay (*Co. Richmond*) 29°03'S. 153°19'E., 3 km NW of Woodburn, on Richmond R.; Noucome till 1876; farming, millet, oysters; broom factory (Maloney Bros) 1901; caterpillar infestations 1919, 1921, 1928, 1929, 1931, 1948; creamery (NSW Creamery Butter Co. Ltd) 1897; electricity 1954; flood 2008; levee 1932; PO 1875; Rom. Cath. C. (St Bridget's) 1873–1933; school 1879, repairs 1900 by T.A. West, closed 1942; shipyards: Conroy Bros (new slipway b. 1889) and York's; sugar mills: Gairloch (Alexander M'Pherson) 1873, P.J. and C. McLaren 1873, John Robinson 1873; telephone 1890; TX 1916–65; wharf b. 1888 by D. Rankin; whooping cough epidemic (child died) 1890; pop. 283 (1901), 290 (1911), 306 (1933), 207 (1947), 176 (1954), 176 (1961), 286 (2011).

Swanbrook (*Co. Gough*) 29°43'S. 151°13'E., 12 km NE of Inverell, on Swan Brook; PO 1878; school 1880, new building b. 1883 by A. Thorley, closed 1887; sugar mill (Young's); pop. 94 (1911), 44 (1933).

Swan Creek (*Co. Clarence*) 29°40'S. 152°59'E., 5 km NE of Grafton, on Swan Ck; cattle, farming, dairying; Angl. C. (St Mark's) 1907; bridge 1935; creameries: Clarence River Pioneer Dairy Co. (b. 1899 by S. M'Phee, closed 1909) and Fresh Food & Ice Co. 1899–1904; floods 1863 and 1928; PO 1927–31; school 1870, new buildings b. 1895 by Hermann Schaeffer, closed 1994; telephone 1910; pop. 82 (1961).

Swanhaven (*Co. St Vincent*) 35°11'S. 150°34'E., 4 km SW of Sussex Inlet, on Swan Lake; estab. 1955.

Swan Ponds (*Co. Bathurst*) 33°44'S. 148°57'E., 27 km NE of Cowra; RS 1918–74; strike (railway navvies) 1891.

Swan Ponds (*Co. Bathurst*) see also Nargong.

Swans Crossing (*Co. Macquarie*) 31°36'S. 152°35'E., 12 km W. of Kendall, on Upsalls Ck.

Swansea (*Co. Northumberland*) 33°05'S. 151°38'E., 7 km S. of Belmont, on Lake Macquarie; (incl. East Swansea and Swansea Heads); formerly Black Margaret Swamp and Newport, then Pelican Flats 1879–87; lots sold 1863, subdivided 1889, village gaz. 1906, further subdivided 1909, developed 1909+, further subdivided (Milray Estate) 1913; fish curing, hort., hat making, shipbuilding, sand mining, tourism; Angl. C. 1884, second one 1919, new one (St Peter's) 1958; Assemblies of God C. (Gateway), closed, sold 2018; breakwaters b. by A. and R. Amos, rebuilt 1994; bridge (sliding opening span), 606 ft (184.7 m), b. 1881 by A. and R. Amos, o. as public road bridge 1895, replacement (with bascule span) b. 1909 by Peter Callen & Sons, d. by Henry Harvey Dare, 409 ft 6 in. (124.8 m), dismantled 1956, new one (steel and concrete, with double-leaf bascule span), 570 ft (173.7 m), fabricated by Maschinenfabrik-Augsburg-Nurnberg AG, Germany, b. 1952–55, fourth one b. 1989 by Transfield Pty Ltd, over Swansea Channel; cemetery, defunct; CH 1891; collieries: one estab. 1863 by Murray Bros, one estab. 1879 by Lamb, Robert Vernon Saddington and Charles Parbury, North Wallarah (strikes 1917, 1918, 1937, man killed 1937, strikes 1938, 1940, 1943, 2 killed 1944, flooded 1946); FB (station b. 1937 by A. Mills, new one 1973); floods 1946 and 1990; Foursquare Gospel C. (New Hope); jetty; measles epidemic 1940; Meth. C. 1930; pilot and signal station; PO: East Swansea 1956 and Swansea 1879; police barracks (incl. lock-up) 1885; Presb. C. (St Stephen's) 1937; PS, closed 1906, reopened, closed during World War II, reopened 1948; quarry; Rom. Cath. C. (St Patrick's) 1939; salt-works (John Herring Boughton) 1834–35; school (Galgabba till 1889) 1882, additions 1924 by William Venor Southon, additions 1981 and 1995; SD Adventist C. (Community); sewerage 1964; shipyard (Woodward's); telegraph 1883; telephone: East Swansea 1956 and Swansea 1888; TX 1915, automatic 1935; water supply 1937; wharf (govt) b. 1885 by W. Castor; pop. *c.*65 (1860), 120 (1877), 155 (1901), 279 (1911), 539 (1921), 1,632 (1933), 3,174 (1947), 5,242 (2006), 5,541 (2011).

Swansea (*Co. Northumberland*) see also Caves Beach.

Swansea Heads (*Co. Northumberland*) see Swansea.

Swan Vale (*Co. Gough*) 29°46'S. 151°27'E., 27 km W. of Glen Innes, on Swan Brook; farming and grazing; cemetery 1901; creamery 1897; 3 quarries; school 1895–1916; telephone 1916; TX 1916–81; pop. 65 (1901), 123 (1911), 47 (1933), 79 (1954), 93 (1961), 240 (2006).

Swashfield (*Co. Georgiana*) see Swatchfield.

Swatchfield (*Co. Georgiana*) 33°54'S. 149°45'E., 24 km SW of Oberon; village gaz. 1954; PO 1860–71; school (Swashfield) 1882–1957.

Sweetbriar (*Co. Westmoreland*) 33°40'S. 149°47'E., 9 km NW of Oberon, on Dicks Ck; formerly Mayfield; farming; PO 1927–30; school (Mayfield) 1881–92; telephone 1915; TX 1955–60; pop. 24 (1933), 50 (1954), 61 (1947).

Sweetmans Creek (*Co. Northumberland*) 32°53'S. 151°12'E., 9 km W. of Paxton, on Sweetmans Ck; farming; bridge b. 1875 by Richard Jurd, new one b. 1891 by Leonard Burgess, over Sweetmans Ck; PO 1906; sawmill (Richard A. Sweetman), moved to Millfield; school 1883–1937; telephone 1913; TX 1925–72; winery (Stonehurst Wines);

pop. 50 (1911), 59 (1933).

Sweetwater (*Co. Dampier*) 35°51'S. 149°33'E., 49 km W. of Moruya, on Jerrabattgulla Ck; sawmill (ruin).

Sydmouth Valley (*Co. Westmoreland*) see Sidmouth Valley.

Sydney Plain (*Co. Gresham*) 29°55'S. 152°07'E., 43 km SE of Glen Innes, on House Ck.

Syfield (*Co. Burnett*) 29°35'S. 150°23'E., 19 km W. of Warialda; RS 1901, station b. by John Allibone, closed 1983.

Sylvia Vale (*Co. Georgiana*) 34°16'S. 149°17'E., 27 km NW of Crookwell, on Sylvia Ck; school 1960–64.

T

Tabarag (*Co. Cook*) see Kurrajong Heights.

Tabbil Creek (*Co. Durham*) 32°25'S. 151°14'E., 18 km N. of Singleton; cemetery.

Tabbimoble (*Co. Richmond*) 29°12'S. 153°16'E., 18 km SW of Evans Head; sawmill (Sly Bros); telephone 1923; TX 1937–69.

Tabbita (*Co. Sturt*) 34°06'S. 145°51'E., 27 km NW of Griffith; village gaz. 1926; PO 1927; RS 1923–75, station demolished 1979; school 1957–69; silo; telephone 1926; TX; pop. 285 (1933), 129 (1947), 137 (1954), 76 (1961).

Tableland (*Co. Clive*) see Timbarra.

Table Top (*Co. Goulburn*) 35°58'S. 147°00'E., 14 km NE of Albury; Bowna Railway Station till 1883 then Yambla till 1895; soldiers' settlement; wheat and grazing, now mostly hobby farms; Angl. C., closed 1971; bushfires 1905 and 1909; electricity 1948; FB; PO 1886–1968; Presb. C. b. 1933 by Andrew M'Donald, closed 1979; RS (Bowna till 1883, then Yambla till 1895) 1881, station b. by Alex Johnson and John Walton, closed and removed 1984 by Peter Rue; school (Yambla till 1944) 1884 b. by Charles Jackson and James Neill, closed 1908, reopened 1936, relocated 1986, additions 2010 by Barker Constructions Pty Ltd; TX 1914, automatic 1953; Union C. 1886, moved 1940 to West Albury and reused; water reticulation 1983; pop. 155 (1901), 83 (1911), 110 (1933), 129 (1947), 118 (1954), 177 (1961), 1,179 (2006), 1,253 (2011).

Tabourie Lake (*Co. St Vincent*) 35°27'S. 150°24'E., 12 km SW of Ulladulla, on Tabourie Ck; Toubouree Lake till 1970; bridge over Tabourie Ck; FB; PO 1958; sawmill; telephone 1951; TX (automatic) 1974; pop. 28 (1933), 30 (1961), 147 (1971), 249 (1976), 406 (1991), 462 (1996), 531 (2001), 575 (2006), 600 (2011).

Tabrabucca (*Co. Roxburgh*) see Warrangunia.

Tabratong (*Co. Oxley*) 32°10'S. 147°30'E., 49 km W. of Trangie, on Bogan R.

Tabulam (*Co. Drake*) 28°54'S. 152°34'E., 48 km W. of Casino, on Clarence R.; settled by Peter Cunningham Pagan and William Evans, first land sales 1858; grazing (mainly cattle), dairying, horses, mining, fossicking; airfield (2 km N.); Angl. C. (St John the Evangelist) 1901, closed, sold 2014, reused; bridge (de Burgh composite truss) b. 1900–3, ironwork supplied by Pope, Maher & Co., 976 ft (297.5 m), over Clarence R.; bushfires 1926 and 2018; cemeteries: old (20 graves) 1862–1903 and new (98 graves); CH 1849, destroyed 1863; Christ. C.; floods 1863 (4 died), 1864, 1876, 1890, 1893, 1948, 1976, 2011; lock-up, destroyed 1863; PO 1849, destroyed 1863, new one b. 1897; pound (stock) 1925; PS 1900, new one b. 1910 by Arthur Roberts; punt 1863, new one b. 1894 by J. M'Geary; Rom. Cath. C. (St Pius X), removed 1960 from Drake, rebuilt and renovated by M.F. Eastoe, reopened 1960; sawmill (Thomas and John Hewetson, and John Sexton), burnt down 1904, rebuilt, burnt down 1917; school 1901–9, reopened 1930, rebuilt 1955, additions 1994; telegraph 1875; timber factory (Yabbra Timber Co. Ltd); TX 1917, automatic 1960; pop. 1,233 (1856), 29 (1866), 64 (1891), 105

(1901), 106 (1911), 205 (1933), 322 (1947), 199 (1954), 109 (1961), *c*.150 (2001), 575 (2006), 644 (2011).

Tabulam South (*Co. Drake*) 28°59'S. 152°33'E., 50 km W. of Casino, on Cornelian Ck; Plains Station till 1960; telephone 1925; TX 1926, automatic 1960; pop. 25 (1933).

Tacking Point (*Co. Macquarie*) see Kinchela and Port Macquarie.

Tacoma (*Co. Northumberland*) 33°17'S. 151°28'E., 3 km E. of Wyong, on Tuggerah Lake; (incl. Rocky Point and South Tacoma); orig. East Wyong; fishing; flood 1946; Jehovah's Witnesses C.; PO 1927–79; school 1905, new one 1969 on new site, additions 1994 and 2010; sewerage 1990; telephone 1922; TX, closed 1964; wharf; pop. 68 (1911), 209 (1933), 168 (1947), 191 (1954), 311 (1961), 1,247 (2006), 1,290 (2011).

Taemas (*Co. Cowley*) 35°00'S. 148°50'E., 18 km S. of Yass, on Murrumbidgee R. (now Lake Burrinjuck); bridge (lattice girder) fabricated by Lecoq's Works, Belgium, erected 1888 by G.H. Royce & Co., d. by John Alexander McDonald, raised and extended 1924, destroyed 1925, new one (steel truss) fabricated by Dorman Long & Co. Ltd, Middlesborough, England, erected 1931 on new site by State Monier Pipe & Reinforced Concrete Works, over Murrumbidgee R.; floods 1925 and 1929; PO 1869–76; punt 1924, destroyed and replaced 1929.

Tahlee (*Co. Gloucester*) 32°40'S. 152°00'E., 4 km SE of Karuah, on Port Stephens; estab. 1826 by Robert Dawson for Aust. Agric. Co.; boat harbour; telephone 1891; wharf, destroyed 1928.

Tahmoor (*Co. Camden*) 34°13'S. 150°35'E., 21 km SW of Camden, on Myrtle Ck; also formerly known as Cordeaux; subdivided by Samuel Emmett, thrived 1950s–70s; timber, fruit, cattle, horses, pigs, poultry; Angl. C. (Holy Trinity) b. 1931 by A.G. Miller, d. by John Burcham Clamp & Son; Bapt. C. 1952; bridge (concrete) b. 1967 by Transbridge Pty Ltd, d. by Maunsell & Partners, 627 ft (191.1 m), over Bargo R.; bushfires 1936, 1952, 1972; Christ. Revival Crusade C. (Lighthouse); colliery 1977; FB; Meth. C. o. 1935 in former Angl. rectory converted by A.G. Miller; PO 1916; poultry processing plant (Inghams Enterprises); Presb. C. b. 1921 by F. Wherritt, new one 2001; quarry; Rom. Cath. C. (St Anthony's) 1963; RS 1919; sawmill (Rudd and Hymen); school 1917, additions 1959, 1963, 1976, 1982; SD Adventist C.; sewerage 1996; telephone 1916; TX 1924, automatic 1968; Unit. C.; winery (Johannes Knauer); pop. 318 (1933), 476 (1947), 679 (1954), 852 (1961), 483 (1966), 792 (1971), 1,346 (1976), 1,996 (1981), 2,350 (1986), 3,409 (1991), 3,874 (1996), 4,395 (2001), 4,138 (2001), 4,236 (2006), 4,126 (2011).

Tahpit (*Co. Gloucester*) 32°05'S. 152°08'E., 18 km SE of Gloucester, on Wallamba R.; telephone 1924; TX 1926.

Tahrone (*Co. Leichhardt*) see Tyrone.

Tailing Flat (*Co. Buccleuch*) 35°12'S. 148°41'E., 40 km SW of Murrumbateman.

Talarm (*Co. Raleigh*) 30°43'S. 152°51'E., 7 km W. of Macksville, on Taylors Arm; Lower Taylor's Arm till 1919; dairying and bananas; FB; PO 1913–44; Presb. C. 1927; Rom. Cath. C. (Christ the King) 1928, closed, moved 2001 to Taylors Arm and reused; school 1914–60; telephone 1913; TX 1928–41; pop. 129 (1933), 100 (1947), 99 (1954), 104 (1961).

Talawanta (*Co. Narran*) 29°32'S. 146°58'E., 50 km N. of Brewarrina, on Culgoa R.; PO 1870–83; pound (stock) 1868; pop. 30 (1933), 71 (2006).

Talbingo (*Co. Buccleuch*) 35°34'S. 148°18'E., 16 km E. of Batlow, on Lake Jounama; settled 1848 by William Bridle, village gaz. 1885, revoked 1906, old village submerged 1968 by filling of Lake Jounama; farming and dairying, now tourism; dam b. 1971 by Thiess Bros Ltd, 531 ft (162 m) high, on Tumut R.; Interdenominational C. (St Paul's) b. 1967 by D. & D. Constructions Pty Ltd, d. by Fowell, Mansfield, Jarvis and Maclurcan; PO 1913–31; power station (Tumut 3, hydro-electric) b. 1972 by Thiess Bros Ltd; PS 1966; school 1965; telephone 1916; TX 1928; pop. 25 (1933), 56 (1961), 1,494 (1971), 479 (1976),

481 (1981), 460 (1986), 376 (1991), 297 (1996), 297 (2001), 241 (2006), 199 (2011).

Talbragar (*Co. Lincoln*) 32°11'S. 148°38'E., 7 km N. of Dubbo, on Talbragar R.; bridge 1866, demolished 1900, replaced 1900 by C.O. Bagge; cemetery (lawn); container terminal (Fletcher International Exports) 2008; pound (stock) 1859; railway bridge (timber truss) b. 1903 by William Hutchins, replaced 1981, over Talbragar R.; RS 1903, station b. by W.H. Hudson, closed 1974; school (Talbragar River) 1942–50; silos 1935 and 1955; pop. 93 (1911), 235 (1933), 69 (1947).

Talbragar River (*Co. Lincoln*) see Talbragar.

Taleeban (*Co. Cooper*) 33°52'S. 146°28'E., 60 km NE of Griffith; village gaz. 1929; PO 1927–44; RS (Conapaira Jan.-July 1923) 1923–75; telephone 1927; pop. 69 (1933).

Tallabung (*Co. Forbes*) 33°40'S. 147°43'E., 42 km SW of Forbes; pop. 37 (1933).

Tallaganda (*Co. St Vincent*) 35°39'S. 149°39'E., 27 km SW of Braidwood, on Shoalhaven R.; quarry.

Tallagandra (*Co. Murray*) 35°04'S. 149°09'E., 34 km SE of Yass; PO 1896–1931; school 1877, new one b. 1883 by Sanders Helman, closed 1915; pop. 142 (1911), 30 (1933).

Tallama (*Co. Baradine*) 30°49'S. 149°07'E., 14 km N. of Baradine.

Tallawang (*Co. Bligh*) 32°12'S. 149°26'E., 19 km N. of Gulgong; farming; bushfire 1952; FB; iron mine (G. & C. Hoskins Ltd) 1911–27; PO 1880–1922; Rom. Cath. C. 1888, additions 1906, new one (St Joseph's) b. 1914 by S. Maudsley, d. by John Francis Kenny, closed 1972, demolished; RS 1910, station b. by George Albert Leggo and John Allibone, closed 1975; sawmill (Lincoln's); school (Upper Tallawang 1884–92) 1881–1941; Union C. 1908; pop. 101 (1901), 313 (1911), 164 (1933), 103 (1947), 114 (1954), 80 (1961), 366 (2011).

Tallawang Road (*Co. Bligh*) 32°17'S. 149°27'E., 12 km NW of Gulgong; goldmines: Scabby Gully 1899 and Tallawang Lead *c.*1875; school 1913–21.

Tallawudjah (*Co. Fitzroy*) 30°05'S. 152°57'E., 24 km W. of Woolgoolga, on Tallawudjah Ck; pop. 70 (1901), 24 (1933), 50 (1947).

Tallebung (*Co. Blaxland*) 32°46'S. 146°37'E., 67 km NW of Condobolin; mine (tin) 1897, shortlived, reworked 1938 by David Thistleton, reopened 1955, reworked 1963; PO 1941–62; school 1963–72; telephone 1963; TX 1964; pop. 50 (1954).

Tallimba (*Co. Bourke*) 33°59'S. 146°53'E., 31 km W. of West Wyalong; village gaz. 1927; formerly goldmining, now wheat and sheep; Angl. C. (St John the Divine) 1959, closed; Bapt. C. 1924; cemetery; CH (incl. police station) 1927 (removed from Yalgogrin), new one b. 1937 by C.L. Meakin & Son; fire 1939; PO 1924; powerhouse 1939; Presb. C. (Scots Memorial) 1966, closed; Rom. Cath. C. (St Bernadette Soubirous) 1953; RS 1923–85, station demolished 1986; sale-yards 1941; school 1935 b. by Williamson Bros, d. by Harry Helman; silo 1928; TX 1925; water supply augmentation 1988; whooping cough epidemic 1941; pop. 317 (1933), 263 (1947), 248 (1954), 279 (1961), 335 (2011).

Tallong (*Co. Camden*) 34°43'S. 150°05'E., 21 km W. of Bundanoon, on Barbers Ck; (incl. Tallong Park Estate); Barbers Creek till 1905; apples and pears *c.*1900+, grazing, timber, former highland holiday destination; Angl. C. (St Stephen's) 1893; bushfires 1942 (2 houses destroyed) and 1965 (28 houses destroyed); cemetery 1904; FB; fruit packing house 1941; hailstorm 1896; Meth. C. 1918; PO 1892–1987; railway dam 1883, wall raised 1917, modified 1975, on Barbers Ck; RS (Barbers Creek till 1905) 1869, fire 1939; sawmill (W.G. James) 1882; school (Barbers Creek till 1906) 1865–66, reopened 1885; telegraph 1890; TX 1921, automatic 1922; pop. 161 (1901), 219 (1911), 220 (1933), 187 (1947), 200 (1954), 246 (1961), 703 (2006), 715 (2011).

Tallong Park Estate (*Co. Camden*) see Tallong.

Talloweena (*Co. Westmoreland*) see Barrallier.

Tallowood Point (*Co. Raleigh*) 30°21'S. 152°54'E., 11 km N. of Bellingen, on North Ck; flood 1950; telephone 1929; TX 1930;

pop. 37 (1933).

Tallwood (*Co. Bathurst*) 33°30'S. 149°07'E., 8 km SW of Millthorpe; farming; PO 1903–68; quarry; school 1902, conducted from *c.*1904 in a building removed from Ingliswold by Higman and Kirby, closed 1933, reopened 1955–72; telephone 1914; TX 1936; Union C.; pop. 58 (1901), 180 (1911), 98 (1933), 69 (1947), 55 (1954), 61 (1961).

Tallwoods Village (*Co. Gloucester*) 32°03'S. 152°31'E., 13 km N. of Tuncurry, on Moor Ck; pop. 323 (2006), 546 (2011).

Tally Ho (*Co. Dampier*) 36°11'S. 149°58'E., 14 km W. of Dalmeny, on Tuross R.

Talmalmo (*Co. Goulburn*) 35°57'S. 147°30'E., 30 km SE of Holbrook; sheep; PO 1904–71; school 1890–1907 and 1957–69; TX 1928; pop. 54 (1911), 48 (1933), 70 (1947), 86 (1954), 56 (1961).

Talmo (*Co. Harden*) 34°53'S. 148°36'E., 28 km W. of Yass, on Jugiong Ck; goldmine (Last Hope) 1931.

Talofa (*Co. Rous*) 28°40'S. 153°34'E., 4 km NE of Bangalow, on Tinderbox Ck; RS 1908–74; pop. 36 (1933).

Taloumbi (*Co. Clarence*) 29°32'S. 153°16'E., 12 km SE of Maclean; sugar mill (Thomas Plater); pop. 271 (1881), 102 (1911), 102 (1933), 61 (1947), 57 (1954), 58 (1961).

Taloumbi (*Co. Clarence*)
see also Palmers Channel.

Taltingan (*Co. Yancowinna*) 31°56'S. 141°32'E., 9 km NE of Broken Hill, on Willa Willyong Ck; Round Hill till 1888; surveyed 1885 by T.H. Goodwin, town gaz. 1887, abandoned 1924; cemetery (63 burials 1887–1904) 1890, restored 1997; cordial factory (Carlisle & Co.), sold 1890; fires 1889 and 1892; mine (Round Hill Silver Mining Co. Ltd); PO 1886–97; PS 1889; school (Round Hill till 1905, then Gossan Hill) 1887–98 and 1909–20; pop. *c.*100 (1886), 345 (1891).

Tamarang (*Co. Pottinger*) 31°28'S. 150°06'E., 54 km W. of Quirindi; RS 1923–75.

Tamaroora (*Co. Wellington*) see Tambaroora.

Tamban (*Co. Raleigh*) 30°52'S. 152°50'E., 20 km SW of Macksville, on Eungai Ck; formerly Upper Eungai; orig. timber then farming and dairying; PO 1927–61; RS (9 km S.) 1934, closed; school 1904, new building b. 1918 by Thomas Norman Grimsley, closed 1950; telephone 1915; TX; pop. 64 (1933), 54 (1947), 51 (1961).

Tambaroora (*Co. Wellington*) 33°00'S. 149°25'E., 43 km NE of Orange, on Golden Gully; orig. Tamaroora; settled 1851, surveyed by John Alexander Horatio Price and town gaz. 1859, thrived in 1850s and 1871–72, defunct; orig. grazing then mining (gold disc. 1851, gold rush 1852, alluvial mining till 1870, hydraulic mining 1937), now fossicking; Angl. C. 1854, new one (St Saviour's) 1872; boiling-down works (Treweeke's); bushfire 1910; cemeteries: general (459 graves 1850s+) 1863 and Rom. Cath. (76 graves 1859–1991); Chinese joss house 1874; dam 1936; droughts 1854–55, 1880, 1888; earth tremor 1862; mines: Colonial Gold Mining Co. 1855 (incl. roasting pits 1858), Dirt Hole 1852, 1884–85, 1889–90, 1937–39, Valentine (Alpha Mining Co.) 1856–61, 1877, 1907, 1910–12, 1914–15, 1922–23, 1933–35; PO 1852–1923; pound (stock) 1865; Presb. C.; PS; Rom. Cath. C. (St Agatha's) b. 1873–76 by John Webb, d. by Edward Gell; school 1858–1928; stamper batteries: Alpha Mining Co. 1871, Harriet Beard 1860, Colonial Gold Mining Co. 12 head, sold, J.G. Reneteau 1859, which became Beattie's; telegraph 1870; telephone 1914; watch-house b. 1861 by Arundel Everett and William Stephens; Wes. Meth. C. 1852; pop. *c.*800 (1853), 259 (1861), *c.*400 (1866), 409 (1871), 2,683 (1881), 257 (1891), 201 (1901), 167 (1911), 37 (1933).

Tambar Springs (*Co. Pottinger*) 31°21'S. 149°50'E., 48 km NE of Binnaway; village gaz. 1888; farming and grazing; Angl. C. (St Mark's) 1909; cemetery (197 graves 1901+) 1884, incl. columbarium; CH 1909; FB; flood 1904; PO 1867; pound (stock) 1878; PS 1876, new one (incl. lock-up) b. 1909 by Thomas John Bowen; Rom. Cath. C. (Immaculate Heart of Mary) 1905; sawmills: George Bowen, George A. Dawson, C. and

V. Lovegrove; school 1881, new one b. 1882 by J. Neate, additions 1912 by Thomas John Bowen, additions 1963 and 2010; telegraph 1891; telephone 1900; TX 1910; water supply augmentation 1992; pop. 114 (1901), 491 (1911), 301 (1933), 259 (1947), 271 (1954), 241 (1961), 540 (2011).

Tamboolba (*Co. Wynyard*) 35°14'S. 147°34'E., 21 km SE of Wagga Wagga; RS (Tywong till 1928) 1917–75.

Tamboy (*Co. Gloucester*) 32°33'S. 152°17'E., 17 km NE of Hawks Nest, on The Broadwater; fishing; telephone 1947.

Taminda (*Co. Inglis*) see Tamworth.

Tamworth (*Co. Inglis*) 31°06'S. 150°55'E., 192 km N. of Maitland, on Peel R.; (incl. Calala, Coledale, East Tamworth, Hillvue, North Tamworth, Oxley Vale formerly Woolomol, South Tamworth, Taminda, Westdale, West Tamworth); disc. 1818 by John Joseph William Molesworth Oxley, settlement on western side of Peel River estab. 1834 by Aust. Agric. Co., settlement on eastern side of Peel River estab. 1835 by James Charles White, surveyed 1849 by John Valentine Gorman, town gaz. 1849, laid out by Major Sir Thomas Livingstone Mitchell, first lots sold 1851, munic. proc. 1876, city proc. 1946, thrived 1960s–70s; sheep, cattle, horses, pigs, wheat, lucerne, maize, millet, barley, oats, fruit, vegetables, tobacco, honey, wine, poultry, dairying, brewing, mining, building supplies, agric. engineering, manufacturing; abattoir (munic.) b. 1938 by C. Davis & Sons Pty Ltd, d. by H. Cunningham, additions 1964, new one (Westdale) 1991; aeroplane crash (2 killed) 1930; agric. implement works: John Bluett 1886 and William Silver; airfield (Taminda) 1932; air force training school (World War II) 1940, reused; airport (Westdale) 1956, upgraded 1982, terminal expanded 2012, 2014, 2019; ambulance station b. 1927 by E.D. Moore, d. by Frederick James Bishop, second one 1983 (at hospital); Angl. C.: St Paul's (West Tamworth) b. 1857–59 by James Hesp, new one 1959, St Peter's (South Tamworth), extended 1974, St John the Evangelist (East Tamworth) b. 1881 by William Springthorpe Dowel, d. by Albert Bond, restored, St Michael and All Angels' (Westdale) 1913 d. by William Powell; army camp 1942–62; Assemblies of God C.: Liberty, fire 2004, and Northwest; Bapt. C.: one o. 1893, reused as Harvest Bible C., Bible (Taminda), one at Hillvue; boot factory (W. and A. Smith) 1879; breweries: Rebel Ant Brewing Co. (Anthony Fitzgerald), Royal Standard Brewery (estab. 1879 by Joseph S. Oddy, closed, additions 1881, taken over 1885 by Charles Jeffries Britten, maltings added 1897, fire 1900 destroyed malting kiln, extensions 1903 d. by Philip Ernest Ranclaud, closed 1922, occupied 1923 by Tamworth Products, bought 1926 by N.E. Lillyman), Tamworth Brewery (estab. 1877 by John Milne and James Graham, closed 1879, reopened 1881 by Ross Bros, renamed Tiger Brewery in 1882, closed 1885, demolished); brickworks: W. Budge and John Frederick Peterson 1877, John Cannon 1874, Coutman & Sons, E.D. Moore, Edwin Smithers, Tamworth Machine Brick & Tile Co. 1900–16; bridges: one b. 1859, destroyed 1864, replaced 1864 by Amos Davis, over Goonoo Goonoo Ck, one b. 1863 and one b. 1919 over Barnes Gully, Dray Bridge (b. 1861 by Thomas William Chowne, 128 ft or 39 m, over Peel R.), Iron Bridge (b. 1882 by George Royce, replaced with concrete bridge 1965, over Peel R.), George Fielder Bridge over Peel R., Jewry Street Bridge (b. 1922, closed 1968, replaced 1971, over Peel R.), Paradise Bridge (orig. Cockburn Bridge, b. 1862, over Peel R.); broom factories: W.A. Cramp 1876–1905, B. Long & Son 1912, burnt down 1914, Robert G. Jones 1909; bus body factory (Ansair) 1993, bought 1995 by Clifford Corp., taken over 1998 by Jakab Industries Pty Ltd, in liquidation 2002; butter factories: Tamworth Co-op. Dairy Co. Ltd 1901, additions 1913, and Tamworth & Dist. Primary Producers' Co-op. Society 1924 d. by Richard Wildridge & Co., companies merged 1925 and became Tamworth Co-op. Dairy Society Ltd, enlarged 1960, taken over 1986 by Hunter Valley Co-op., closed 2002; carriage-works: Hughes Bros (taken over 1911 by W. Moffat), Lye and Bizant (fire 1897, burnt down 1905), New State (Markham and Hinkelbein) 1920, Reilly and Quinton 1877 (burnt down 1884, re-established in new premises), Steam Coach & Buggy Factory (William Silver), Wade and Warbrook; cemeteries: general (10,161 graves) 1863, incl. columbarium and lawn cemetery 1972, Jewish (7 graves), war (28 graves); CH 1848, (second) 1862 d. by Alexander Dawson, additions 1875 by M. Bourke, reused, (third) b. 1938 by F.C.W. Powell, (fourth) 1995; Christ. City C. (Hillvue); Church of Christ (Aboriginal); clock tower (war memorial) 1959; concrete pipe works (Hume Pipe Co. Aust. Ltd); cordial factories: Bryant Bros, Thomas Joseph Butler, O. Jeffries Butler & Co., Lillyman Bros (orig. a brewery, later Coca Cola) 1926, Morris's, Sharpe Bros (estab. by John Sharpe in former flour mill), closed 1928; crematorium (Lincoln Grove Memorial Gardens); cyclone 1914; dengue fever 1926; diphtheria 1871 (girl died), 1908, 1934; droughts 1875–77, 1919, 1965; dust storm 1923; egg pulping and handling factory (West Tamworth) 1946; engineering works: T.B. Goddard and N.A. Hodges; FB 1878 (stations b. 1878, 1908, 1929, 1969, 1981); fibrous plaster works: E. Mackie, and Pearson and Kemp; fires 1860, 1873, 1894, 1897, 1913, 1916; floods 1840, 1852, 1857, 1861, 1863–64, 1866, 1870, 1872, 1874, 1908, 1910, 1942, 1955, 1984, 1989, 1998, 2000, 2008; flour mills: Allied Mills Pty Ltd 1924 (owned by Goodman Fielder, sold 2002 to GrainCorp Ltd and Cargill Aust. Ltd, in 2017 GrainCorp sold its share to Pacific Equity Partners), Charles Armstrong 1859, Patrick J. Coghlan 1869 (acquired 1874 by Lewis Bros, new one b. by Charles Grace, d. by John Frederick Hilly, and named Phoenix, acquired 1886 by Farmers Co-op., bought 1901 by George Fielder, sold 1912 to Charles Regan and Harry Rawson), Cohen and Levy 1867 (bought 1896 by Lewis H. Hyman, acquired by Hugo S. Reid, acquired 1906 by Charles Regan and Harry Rawson and incorp. 1909 as Regan Palace Roller Flour Mills Ltd, acquired by S.G. and P.G. Smith, demolished 1932), FPM Cereal Milling Systems Pty Ltd 2004, Donald Munro (b. 1864 by William Springthorpe Dowel, acquired 1869 by William Cohen, became Cohen and Levy in 1870, acquired and modernised 1877 by W. and C. Hayes, acquired 1877 by Aiken Bros, became Aiken and Fielder in 1884, became Fielder and Maxwell in 1890, became Fielder & Son in 1898, closed 1901, reused), Tamworth Steam Flour Mill (estab. by Aiken and George Fielder, taken over 1913 by Regan Palace Roller Flour Mills Ltd, became Geo. Fielder Co. Ltd in 1929), West Tamworth Milling Co. Pty Ltd 1908 (burnt down 1943, rebuilt, closed 1958); foot-bridge (suspension) b. 1857 by William Springthorpe Dowel; freezing works (West Tamworth); furniture factories: A.A. Bussel and R. Taylor; gales 1905 and 1914; galvanised iron works (Turton & Co.); gaol b. 1878–80 by William Cains, extended 1898, closed 1943, reused 1943–46 as military prison, renovated 1947, reused 1948–89 as boys' reformatory, reverted to gaol 1990; gastroenteritis epidemic 1954; gasworks (Tamworth Gas & Coke Co. Ltd) b. 1882 by J.A. Wark; grasshopper infestation 1937; Greek Orthodox C. (St Dimitrios's) 1961; hailstorms 1920, 1959, 1996; hospital 1840, second one 1856, new one b. 1884 by Bourke and Wilson, d. by John Wiltshire Pender, additions and alterations 1910 by Henry Prince, extensions 1921, 1928, 1934, additons 1936 by J.H. Shaw, additions 1954 by E.D. Moore & Son, additions 1964, additions 1973 d. by R. Forster, additions 1975 and 1978, additions 2015 by Richard Crookes Constructions, d. by McConnel Smith & Johnson Pty Ltd; house frame and truss factory (Trussted Frames & Trusses); ice works (Tamworth & Dist. Primary Produce Co-op. Co. Ltd); ink factory 1901; Jehovah's Witnesses C.; joineries: L.C. Jeans, C.A.

Skinner 1929, fire 1930, Richard Allright Stanfield; LDS (Mormon) C.; Life C. 1960; lime-kiln (John Frederick Peterson) 1877; livestock-handling equipment factory (Arrow Farmquip) estab. 1988 by Philip Firth; maltings (Joe White Maltings Ltd) 1968, acquired 2013 by Cargill Aust. Ltd; Meth. C. (South Tamworth) 1962; military camp and hospital (World War II); milk factory (Aust. Co-op. Foods Ltd); milk and ice-cream factory (G. Quast) 1938; monumental stone works: G. Branson, Frederick A. Calcott Ltd, Gibney & Son, Lincoln Grove; munitions factory 1941, reused; PO: East Tamworth 1968–71, North Tamworth 1942, South Tamworth 1962, Tamworth 1840 (new one b. 1866 by Brown and Grace, demolished, replacement b. 1886 by William Charles Cains, d. by James Johnstone Barnet, additions 1911 by Robert Hamilton Gillies, alterations 1913, extensions 1966, alterations and renovations 1986), Westdale 1917, West Tamworth 1879; police barracks 1862–75, bought by Lambert and reused; poultry processing plant (Baiada Poultry Pty Ltd) 1964; pound (stock) 1847; powerhouse b. 1889 by George Harrison and Alfred Whiffen, demolished, second one 1911, relocated 1922, third one 1931, fourth one 1956, closed; Presb. C.: St Andrew's b. 1863–67 by Charles Grace, closed, sold, reused, and St Stephen's (West Tamworth) 1970; PS: South Tamworth 1879 and Tamworth b. 1874 by Charles Grace, additions 1878 by Ockleshaw and Cook, additions and repairs 1898 by Robert Hamilton Gillies, new one b. 1938 by F.C.W. Powell, additions 1973 and 1981, new one 1995; railway bridge (lattice girder) fabricated by J.O. and C.E. Brettell, Worcester, England, erected 1882 by A. and R. Amos and J.S. Bennett, d. by Sir John Fowler and John Whitton, rebuilt 1913–28, over Peel R.; railway coal stage (120 ft or 36.6 m) b. 1877 by George Brown; railway engine shed b. 1877 by George Brown, demolished; railway turntable, 40 ft (12.2 m), replaced 1891, 50 ft (15.2 m), replaced 1902, 60 ft (18.3 m); Reformed C.; 10 reservoirs (incl.): East Tamworth 1,250,000 gal. (5,682.5 kl), North Tamworth 500,000 gal. (2,273 kl), West Tamworth 300,000 gal. (1,363.8 kl); Rom. Cath. C.: Mary Help of Christians (South Tamworth, b. 1983 by Groenneau Constructions, d. by Michael Nelson), Our Lady of Victories (North Tamworth, b. 1939 by R. Lane, d. by Frederick James Bishop), St Edward's (South Tamworth), St Nicholas's (b. 1859, closed, reused 1879, new one b. 1878 by William Springthorpe Dowel, d. by W. Vett, extensions 1914 by A. Moore, d. by Philip Ernest Ranclaud), St Patrick's (West Tamworth) b. 1930 by H.C. Jones, d. by Peter Joseph Gannon; RS: Tamworth 1882, station b. by Alexander Hamilton Scouller, refreshment rooms 1917–56, West Tamworth 1878, station b. by George Brown, Westdale 1915–57; sale-yards: Nathan Cohen & Co., Regional Livestock Exchange Investment Co. 2013, Westdale 1976; Salv. Army C. 1887, new one 1948, closed, sold and reused; sawmills: J.T. Frazer & Co. 1953, Gould Bros & Co. Pty Ltd 1929, Great Northern Saw Mills (Richard Allright Stanfield), William Pitfield 1876, West Tamworth Steam Saw Mills (W. Budge & Co.), William Silver & Co., Thorsbys Ltd (in liquidation 1912); schools: Calala 1920 b. by Robert Hamilton Gillies, closed 1954, Farrer Memorial Agric. HS (Calala) 1939 b. by F.C.W. Powell, additions 1955, 1960, 1970, 1994, 1996, Hillvue 1970, re-roofed 2013, Oxley HS 1968, new school 1969, additions 1973 and 2014, fire 2018, Oxley Vale (Manilla Road till 1956) 1947, additions 1982, Peel HS 1977, South Tamworth 1952 b. by N. Watson, additions 1960, Tamworth 1855 (b. by W. Ayre, closed 1877, reused, demolished, new one b. 1877 by William Springthorpe Dowel, additions 1885, additions and repairs 1900 by T.E. Nott, additions 1909 by John Allibone, additions and alterations 1911 by W.H. Bryant, new building b. 1918 by E.D. Moore), Tamworth HS 1919, damaged 1950, new one 1961, additions 1965 and 1976, Westdale 1913, additions 1991, West Tamworth 1883 b. by William Springthorpe Dowel, additions 1888 by Hume and Galbraith, new building b. 1918 by M. Cooper, additions 1970; SD Adventist C. 1948; sewerage 1927, augmentation 1995; silo 1934; slipper factory; soap and candle factories: Nathan Cohen & Co. (bought 1873 by James Piper, new factory 1896) and D. Regan 1870; soap-works (J. Kitchen & Sons Pty Ltd); starch factory (Fielders General Products Pty Ltd), man killed 1941, sold 2000 to Penford A'sia; steel fabrication works (Belmore Engineering); storm 2018; streets oil lit (2 lamps) 1877, gas lit (25 lights) 1882, electric lit (89 lights) 1888; street tree plantings 1936; Surefire C.; tanneries: Bignell Bros 1872 and W. and A. Smith 1875, fire 1893; TC 1963, additions 1969, 1978, 1982, 1990, became New England Institute in 1992, additions 2015 d. by Perumal Pedavoli; telegraph: Tamworth 1866, office b. by Brown and Grace, demolished and replaced 1886 by William Charles Cains, and West Tamworth 1879; telephone: East Tamworth 1968, North Tamworth 1942, South Tamworth 1962, Westdale 1913, West Tamworth 1901; tornado 1950; TX: Tamworth 1900, automatic 1939, and Westdale 1929, automatic 1955; typhoid 1882, 1885 (girl died), 1895 (man died), 1896 (man died), 1898, 1903, 1908, 1910, 1912 (man died); Unit. C.: City (orig. Wes. Meth.) b. 1872 by Charles Grace, d. by Thomas Rowe, enlarged 1885, re-roofed and renovated, St Andrew's (orig. Presb.) b. 1909 by Robert Hamilton Gillies, alterations 1911 by Gillies, closed, sold and reused, Southside (Hillvue); vegetable dehydration plant (Tamworth Co-op. Dairy Society Ltd) o. 1945, in former munitions factory; watch-house (Aust. Agric. Co.) 1842, new one 1859, additions 1862 by John Heritage, new one 1893; water supply 1880, reticulation 1898, augmentation 1957, 1959, 1980, 1987, 1994; waterworks 1898; woollen mill (Fibres and Beyond); wool-scour (W. and A. Smith) 1883; pop. 254 (1851), 448 (1856), 654 (1861), 1,511 (1871), *c.*3,000 (1876), *c.*3,500 (1878), 3,612 (1881), *c.*4,000 (1887), 4,602 (1891), *c.*5,100 (1895), 5,898 (1901), 6,150 (1906), 8,214 (1911), 7,264 (1921), 10,506 (1933), *c.*11,000 (1941), 13,371 (1947), 16,516 (1954), 19,572 (1961), 20,588 (1966), 24,649 (1971), 27,273 (1976), 29,657 (1981), 30,729 (1986), 31,716 (1991), 31,865 (1996), 32,543 (2001), 33,475 (2006), 36,131 (2011).

Tangaratta (*Co. Parry*) 31°04'S. 150°50'E., 11 km W. of Tamworth; winery 1998; pop. 126 (1933).

Tanglewood (*Co. Inglis*) 31°03'S. 151°06'E., 5 km E. of Kootingal, on Cockburn R.; school (Swamp Oak till 1906) 1880–1914.

Tanglewood (*Co. Rous*) 28°20'S. 153°32'E., 4 km W. of Bogangar, on Reserve Ck.

Tangmangaroo (*Co. King*) 34°38'S. 148°48'E., 23 km S. of Boorowa; Angl. C. (All Saints') b. 1887–89 by Lansdown Bros, rebuilt 1904 by Oliver John Stuart, chancel added 1926, and graveyard (44 graves 1897+); Bapt. C. 1910; bridge b. 1892 by R. Hughes, over Boorowa R.; PO 1870–1912; school 1881–1900 and 1957–69; pop. 179 (1901), 170 (1911), 80 (1933), 50 (1954).

Tangulla (*Co. Fitzroy*) see Fernbrook.

Tanilba (*Co. Durham*) see Mundawa.

Tanilba Bay (*Co. Gloucester*) 32°44'S. 152°00'E., 4 km W. of Lemon Tree Passage, on Tanilba Bay; settled 1831 by Lieut. William Caswell, subdivided by Henry Ferdinand Halloran; rutile mining till 1972, oysters; ambulance station; Bapt. C. 1989; Christ. Reformed C.; FB (station b. 1981, new one 2017); mineral sand mine (Associated Minerals Consolidated Ltd) 1965; PO 1964; school (Lemon Tree Passage till 1982) 1957, new one 1982, additions 1994; sewage works 1993; TX (automatic); Unit. C. (Tilligerry); water supply 1969; pop. 54 (1961), 2,330 (1997), 2,332 (2006), 3,757 (2011).

Tanja (*Co. Dampier*) 36°39'S. 149°58'E., 12 km E. of Bega, on Sandy Ck; sawmilling, farming, dairying; Angl. C. (St Paul's) 1899, closed, sold 1993, reused; bridge 1915, over Sandy Ck; bushfire 1882; caterpillar infestation 1911; cheese factories: Barrabooka

(J. Russell) 1910, Distant View (D. Sercombe), Essex Hill, Hillside (H.B. Ritchie), Limegrove (H.B. Ritchie), T.W. Taylor 1916; drought 1884–85; FB 1943; floods 1919, 1934, 1950; PO 1878–1980; sawmills: Alexander Percival Beare (burnt down 1925), Daniel A. Gowing and T.J. Kelly 1877 (bought 1903 by L.V. Harrison, sold 1911 to C. Innes), Isaac Innes 1915 (moved 1936 to Bega), T.W. Taylor 1916, Charles Thomas; school 1880 b. by Braine, renovated 1905 by Olaf Rye Lassen; telephone 1905; TX 1923; Union C. 1878, burnt down 1888; wharf 1911; pop. 193 (1901), 144 (1911), 184 (1933), 136 (1947), 116 (1954), 105 (1961), 381 (2011).

Tank (*Co. King*) see Fish River.

Tank (*Co. Roxburgh*) see Brogans Creek.

Tankerooka (*Co. Rankin*) 31°06'S. 144°17'E., 101 km NE of Wilcannia; grazing; PO 1869–83.

Tannabutta (*Co. Wellington*) 32°43'S. 149°44'E., 19 km SE of Mudgee; goldmining; cemetery (50 graves 1880s+) 1894; quarry.

Tannawanda (*Co. White*) 31°01'S. 149°26'E., 33 km NE of Coonabarabran, on Yaminba Ck.

Tanners Mount (*Co. Bathurst*) 33°36'S. 149°39'E., 21 km S. of Bathurst, on Campbells R.; farming and grazing; PO 1927–29; school 1880–90; pop. 41 (1933).

Tanners Spring (*Co. Gordon*) 32°33'S. 148°25'E., 28 km NE of Peak Hill.

Tantangara (*Co. Wallace*) 35°52'S. 148°38'E., 58 km SE of Batlow, on Nungar Ck; estab. as temporary construction camp (1958–61) for Snowy Mountains Hydro-Electric Scheme.

Tantawangalo (*Co. Auckland*) 36°46'S. 149°37'E., 21 km SW of Bega, on Tantawangalo Ck; first lots advertised 1882, town planned 1883; mining (gold disc. 1903) and dairying; Angl. C. 1877, demolished 1905, new one (St John's) b. 1905–8, d. by F.W.E. Wilkinson, closed, sold 2018; bushfire 1904; cemetery; cheese factory (Deep Dene, A. Targett); creamery (NSW Creamery Butter Co.); flood 1971; PO 1892; school 1871–1960; telephone 1957; Union C.; water supply augmentation 1955 and 1987; Wes. Meth. C. 1872; pop. 189 (1901), 187 (1911), 84 (1933), 69 (1947), 225 (2011).

Tantonan (*Co. Cadell*) 35°42'S. 144°32'E., 34 km W. of Mathoura; farming; earth tremor 2008; PO 1926–39; RS (6 km S., on Victorian railway); telephone 1939; pop. 73 (1911), 42 (1933).

Tapio (*Co. Wentworth*) 33°57'S. 141°58'E., 17 km N. of Wentworth, on Darling R.; pop. 114 (1911).

Tapitallee (*Co. Camden*) 34°50'S. 150°32'E., 8 km NW of Nowra, on Tapitallee Ck; farming; bushfire 1968; cemetery (West Cambewarra); FB 1947–65; PO 1927–31; telephone 1917; pop. 35 (1933), 242 (1996), 358 (2001), 315 (2006), 340 (2011).

Tara (*Co. Bourke*) 34°30'S. 147°10'E., 31 km SE of Ardlethan; FB 1948; school 1918–49; pop. 116 (1911), 54 (1947), 52 (1954).

Tara (*Co. Roxburgh*) 32°59'S. 149°49'E., 5 km SW of Ilford, on Tara Ck; school 1881–96; pop. 81 (1933).

Taradale (*Co. Wynyard*) 35°35'S. 147°57'E., 19 km SW of Batlow, on Tarcutta Ck; pop. 51 (1901), 61 (1911), 70 (1947).

Tarago (*Co. Argyle*) 35°04'S. 149°39'E., 29 km NE of Bungendore, on Mulwaree R.; orig. Sherwins Flat, then Upper Tarago till 1884; agric., grazing, barytes; Angl. C. 1893, replaced (St Andrew's) 1932 on new site; bushfires 1905, 1927, 2017; cemetery 1895; container terminal; FB; PO 1883, burnt down 1918; pound (stock) 1862; PS 1889, new one (incl. lock-up) b. 1895 by William R. Trotter; Rom. Cath. C. (St Joseph's) b. 1902–4; RS 1884, station b. by George J. Horn, closed 1989; school (Sherwins Flat till 1890) 1880, new buildings b. 1881 by G.J. Clarke; TX; pop. 59 (1891), 191 (1901), 250 (1911), 169 (1933), 217 (1947), 223 (1954), 101 (1961), 351 (2011).

Tarago (*Co. Argyle*) see also Lake Bathurst.

Taralga (*Co. Argyle*) 34°24'S. 149°49'E., 32 km E. of Crookwell; settled 1825, private village estab. *c.*1843, town estab. 1858, declined 1960+; sheep, beef, dairying, potatoes, berries, vineyards, marble; Angl. C. b. 1867 by Thomas and William Davies, d. by R. Leigh, demolished, new one (St Luke's) b. 1906 by Arthur Allen, d. by Edmund Cooper Manfred, restoration 1930, and columbarium; brickworks estab. 1921 by C.S. Bradbury; butter factories: Lyre Bird (b. 1890 by E. Hawkens, d. by Waugh and Josephson, closed) and Taralga Co-op. Dairy Co. Ltd 1923 (taken over 1950 by Dairy Farmers' Co-op. Milk Co. Ltd); cemetery 1863; CH b. 1878 by Henry William Horn, new one b. 1887 by J.P. Pinn and William Thomas, repairs 1900 by H.J. Maynard, reused as police station; cordial factory (Fred Baxter); diphtheria 1933; drought 1885; electricity 1935; FB; flour mill (George Charles Blay) 1865–75, demolished; freezing works 1916–22, demolished; lock-up 1886; PO 1856, new one b. 1897, sold, renovated and reused 2007; pound (stock) 1865; powerhouse (Sidney Holt) 1935–55; Presb. C. 1862, reused, new one (St Stephen's) b. 1954 by J.P. Cordukes, d. by George B. Gray; PS b. 1863 by Edward Simon Arnett, new one b. 1886 by Richard Benjamin Clewett; railway turntable, 60 ft (18.3 m), ruined; Rom. Cath. C. (St Ignatius's) 1864, sold and reused, new one (Christ the King) b. 1934 by R.M. Bowcock, d. by Sydney Smith and Clement Glancey; RS 1926–57, defunct; sale-yards 1947; sawmill; school 1858 (began in former house b. 1832), new building 1867, repairs 1891 by Charles Munn; sewage works b. 2010 by Ted Wilson & Sons Pty Ltd; snowstorm 1935; tannery (Denning & Son) 1872; TX 1911; Wes. Meth. C. b. 1868 by Edward Denning and Davis Bros, closed, reopened 1895, restored 1950, reused 1972; pop. 110 (1862), *c.*110 (1866), 165 (1871), 326 (1881), 723 (1891), 359 (1901), 468 (1911), 468 (1933), 483 (1947), 536 (1954), 408 (1961), 278 (1971), 293 (1976), 272 (1981), 301 (1986), 393 (1991), 341 (1996), 318 (2001), 312 (2006), 285 (2011).

Tarana (*Co. Roxburgh*) 33°32'S. 149°54'E., 20 km N. of Oberon, on Solitary Ck; farming; Angl. C. (St Stephen's) 1885; bushfire 1929; causeway; diphtheria 1912; FB; measles epidemic 1940; PO 1873–1985; PS, closed 1916, reopened 1921–23, reopened 1925; railway bridge (plate girder) d. by John Whitton; railway coal stage 1924; rifle range 1916; RS 1872, station b. by Frederick Horn, alterations 1923, closed 1989; school (Mount Tarana till 1895) 1869, new one 1879 d. by George Allen Mansfield, new buildings b. 1913 by John Bartlett, closed 1979, sold and reused; TX 1914, automatic 1981; typhoid (woman died) 1923; Unit. C. (orig. Meth.) b. 1913 by G.A. Heaydon, d. by C.E. Richards, closed, sold 2010 and 2019, reused; Wes. Meth. C. 1875, sold 1913 to R.W. Webb; pop. 69 (1891), 174 (1901), 276 (1911), 327 (1933), 197 (1947), 171 (1954), 90 (1961).

Tarana Quarry (*Co. Roxburgh*) 33°31'S. 149°52'E., 21 km N. of Oberon, on Fish R.; PO 1915–41; quarry; RS, closed 1974; telephone 1916; pop. 66 (1933).

Taranora (*Co. Rous*) see Terranora.

Tarban (*Co. Clive*) 28°59'S. 151°54'E., 12 km NW of Tenterfield, on Tenterfield Ck; dairying and sheep; PO 1927–31; school 1897–1912; pop. 90 (1911), 54 (1933), 51 (1947), 172 (2006).

Tarbuck Bay (*Co. Gloucester*) 32°22'S. 152°29'E., 21 km S. of Forster, on Smiths Lake.

Tarcoon (*Co. Cowper*) 30°15'S. 146°43'E., 35 km S. of Brewarrina; grazing; PO 1901–70; RS 1901, station b. by Charles Baker, closed 1974; telephone 1903; TX 1923; pop. 103 (1933).

Tarcutta (*Co. Wynyard*) 35°17'S. 147°44'E., 29 km SE of Forest Hill; settled 1836 by Thomas Hodges Mate, village gaz. 1890, soldiers' settlement, bypassed by highway 2011; gold prospecting 1879–84, grazing, dairying, some tobacco; Angl. C. (St Mark's, also known as Mate Memorial) b. 1902 by John Gray, d. by William John Monks, and graveyard; bridge 1861, new one b. 1906 by George Burt and J. M'Arthur, new one 1954, over Tarcutta Ck; bushfire 1940; cemetery (302 graves 1893+) 1880; earth tremor 1871; FB 1905 (new station b. 2018); floods 1956 and 2010; PO

1849, repairs 1897 by Charles Hardy & Co., additions and alterations 1905 by William Silk; Presb. C. 1889, closed, dismantled and moved 1920 to Uranquinty, new one (St Columba's) b. 1932 by L. Beattie, closed and sold 2013; PS b. 1885 by Charles Hardy, new one b. 1896, additions 1902 by John Gray; Rom. Cath. C. (St Francis Xavier's) b. 1906 by J. M'Fadgean, d. by William John Monks; RS (Upper Tarcutta till 1925) 1917–74; school (Upper Tarcutta till *c.*1912) 1881, new one b. 1884 by Charles Hardy, additions 1902 by John Gray, burnt down 1949, new one 1953, additions 1958; sewerage 1991; telephone 1910; TX 1914, automatic 1972; Union C.; watch-house; pop. *c.*80 (1866), 196 (1891), 302 (1901), 520 (1911), 318 (1933), 372 (1947), 445 (1954), 365 (1961), 279 (1971), 248 (1976), 263 (1981), 249 (1986), 237 (1991), 255 (1996), 263 (2001), 243 (2006), 224 (2011).

Taree (*Co. Macquarie*) 31°55'S. 152°27'E., 68 km SW of Port Macquarie, on Manning R.; (incl. Browns Creek, Chatham estab. 1841, The Basin); settled 1829 by William Wynter, subdivided and laid out 1854 by Henry Flett, first lots sold 1854, munic. proc. 1885, city proc. (Greater Taree) 1981, bypassed by highway 1997; former river port, limestone (disc. 1866), goldmining, wheat, maize, timber, barley, oats, millet, lucerne, potatoes, wine, tobacco, oranges, fishing, oysters, cattle, pigs, dairying, manufacturing; ambulance station b. 1947 by T. Taylor, d. by Jeater, Rodd and Hay; Angl. C.: St John's 1856, new one b. 1954–58 by A.J. Hayter Pty Ltd, d. by Hubert Ollyett Woodhouse, alterations and renovations 2008, and columbaria, and St Mark the Evangelist 1991; Assemblies of God C. (One in Christ Fellowship); Bapt. C. b. 1936 by A.H. Nelson; boat-building factory (Stebercraft Pty Ltd) 1974; brickworks: Beeton's 1921 and H.E. Strange; bridges: Burdett-Smith Bridge 1879, replaced 1933, to Cundletown, over Dawson R., Martin Bridge to Glenthorne, 1,518 ft (462.7 m), incl. lift span fabricated by Clyde Engineering Co. Ltd, erected 1938–40 by Monier Industries Ltd, over Manning R., Victoria Street Bridge (5 spans) b. 1925 by Taree Timber & Trading Co., over Browns Ck; broom factory (Stan Wallace) 1953; butter factories: one at Chatham b. 1918 by Standard Waygood Hercules Ltd and C. Sander 1927 (butter, cheese and ice-cream factory and ice works, became Sander's Dairies Ltd in 1932, additions 1934 by Dunn); bicycle works (Harold Staples) 1905; carriage-works (S.T. Lean); cement tile works (Arnold Robinson) 1950; cemeteries: old (Woola, 199 graves 1863+), new (3,757 graves), lawn (2,997 plots); CH 1866, new one b. 1882 by W.J. Smith, d. by James Johnstone Barnet, additions and repairs 1897 by Rudolph George Ochs, renovations 1949 by F.E. Foster, additions 1982, extensions 2011 by Ware Building, d. by D.W.P. Suters; Christ. Outreach C. (Rivercity); Church of Christ (Chatham) 1887, sold 1907, replacement (Taree) b. 1907 by A.M. Wynter, G. Bradley and W. Clinch, relocated 1934; clock tower (war memorial) 1925 d. by Purnell and Fizelle; clothing factory (Loomlock Lingerie Pty Ltd) b. 1945 by Levido & Sons; cordial factories: Northcoast Beverage Co., George Coleman (estab. 1864 at Chatham, factory moved into Taree, relocated again, joined 1914 with George Saxby, Coleman withdrew 1917, additions 1924 d. by Patrick John Moran, defunct), W. Sloman 1900; Covenant Ministries C. (Manning Valley) 2008 (in converted warehouse); droughts 1923, 1927, 1928, 1929; electroplating works (T. Mitchison); FB (station demolished 1913, new one b. 1925 by S.W. and R.C. Potter); fibrous plaster works: D.S. Davies and John Ashley Dunn; fires 1905, 1907, 1913, 1924, 1925, 1954; floods 1858, 1866, 1890, 1929, 1950, 1978, 2011; flour mill (Thomas Avery); Free Presb. C. b. 1907 by W. George Bradley, destroyed 1907 before completion, rebuilt 1907; gale 1880; hailstorm 1928; hospital b. 1887–89 by John Rye, d. by James Henry Bolster and James Edward Justelius, additions 1897 by Rudolph George Ochs, additions 1922 by Hutcherson Bros, new wing 1934, additions 1941, partly demolished 1949, new one (Manning Base) b. 1950–53 by A.J. Hayter Pty Ltd, additions 1955 and 1958; ice-cream factory (Peters Creameries Pty Ltd) b. 1939 by D. Gallagher, additions by A.J. Hayter Pty Ltd, closed, abandoned and derelict; iron foundry (Manning River Plumbing Co.); Jehovah's Witnesses C.; 2 joineries; LDS (Mormon) C. (Community of Christ); lime-works (Manning River Lime Co.) 1868; measles epidemic 1901; milk factories: Allowrie Foods Aust. Ltd, Aust. Co-op. Foods Ltd, Manning River Co-op. Dairy Society Ltd (additions b. 1937 for ice-cream manufacture); monumental stone works: Tom L. Dudgeon and Joseph John Edstein (became J.J. Edstein & Sons) 1896; PO: Chatham 1927 and Taree 1861, new one b. 1874 by William John Smith, new one b. 1899 by Sanbrook Bros; pound (stock) 1893; POW control centre (World War II); powerhouse (Taree Electric Supply Co.) b. 1918 by J.H. Stewart, fire 1921, upgraded 1925, closed 1937, reused 1953; Presb. C.: St Paul's b. 1869 by Hezekiah Edwards, alterations and repairs 1892, restored, new one 1966 and High Street 1977; PS b. by Schmitzer, additions and renovations 1972, new one 2020; punt (steam) b. 1902 by E.W. Fitzgerald, ceased 1937, across Manning R.; quarries (limestone): BHP and Manning River Lime Co.; railway barracks; railway locomotive depot b. 1913 by John Allibone; railway round-house (8 bays) b. 1911 by W. Boulton, closed and demolished; railway turntable 1913, 60 ft (18.3 m), new one 1934, 75 ft (22.9 m), new one (electric) 1951, 75 ft (22.9 m); 4 reservoirs (incl. one on Browns Hill of 400,000 gal. or 1,818.4 kl b. 1953 by A.J. Hayter Pty Ltd); rifle range (3 km NW); Rom. Cath. C. b. 1870–73 by Lowe, reused 1931, new one (Our Lady of the Rosary) b. 1930 by Vincent Doran, d. by Peter Joseph Gannon; RS 1913, station b. by John Allibone, replaced 1929, refreshment room 1929; sale-yards b. 1936 by Richard George Lansdowne for local council; Salv. Army C. 1907 d. by Saunders, damaged 1923, new one 1966; sawmills: Barrett and Williams, James Bullock 1945 (burnt down 1947), Campbell and Jones, Pen Manufacturers Pty Ltd (incl. pen factory) 1954, William Smith and William Basham 1905 (sold 1919 to Charles Palmer, sold to C.S. McLaren, sold to Taree Timber & Trading Co.), S. Spence; schools: Chatham 1952 (additions 1956, 1958, 1962, 1971, re-roofed 2013), Chatham HS 1965 (additions 1968, 1978, 1990, 1992, additions 2010 by O'Donnell & Hanlon Pty Ltd, re-roofed 2013), Manning Gardens 1984, Taree (Tarree till 1866) 1864 (additions 1902 by Stewart Adolphus Levick, extended 1907 by Henry Wilson Alcorn, new building 1917, additions 1972), Taree HS 1925 (b. by William Lishman Jemison, additions 1949 by A.E. Davis, additions 1955 and 1960, fire 1971, additions 1975, 1990, 1993), West Taree 1953 (additions 1957, 1963, 1967, 1971); SD Adventist C.: Chatham and Commerce Street 1954; sewerage 1937, augmentation 1986 and 1989; shipyards: John Nicholson and W. Ryan & Sons 1943; storms 1907 and 1932; streets lit 1900 by acetylene gas, electric lit 1918; TC b. 1964 by A.J. Hayter Pty Ltd, d. by Michael John Dysart, additions 1987, became a campus of North Coast Institute in 1992, additions 1995; telegraph office b. 1875 by William John Smith; telephone (Chatham) 1929; textile mill (Speedo Knitting Mills Pty Ltd) 1971; tobacco factory (Butt's); toy factory (Bimbo Rubber Works, A.W. Eysma and G.A. Vittali) 1953; TX 1909, automatic 1972; Unit. C.: Chatham (orig. Meth.) 1942, enlarged 1950 and Taree (orig. Wes. Meth.) b. 1881 by William John Smith, d. by William Boles, extensions 1952 by A.E. Davies, d. by William C. Brown, renovated 1954 by Cornish and Humphries; watch-house 1865, proc. a gaol 1884, additions 1916 by Ernest Bacon; water reticulation 1928, augmentation 1969; Wes. Meth. C. 1857, new one 1866, damaged 1880; wharves: North Coast Steam Navigation Co. wharf, Market wharf at Chatham b. by John Newby, Peters Creameries Pty Ltd wharf 1939, public wharf

b. 1879 by H.W. Flett, Pulteney Street wharf b. 1954 by Milligan, Smith and Basham's sawmill wharf 1903; pop. 46 (1841), 118 (1861), 150 (1866), 339 (1871), 488 (1881), 716 (1891), *c.*800 (1895), 871 (1901), *c.*1,300 (1909), 1,631 (1911), *c.*1,700 (1921), *c.*2,800 (1924), 4,950 (1933), 4,850 (1935), *c.*5,200 (1941), 5,475 (1947), 7,462 (1954), 10,050 (1961), 10,594 (1966), 13,440 (1976), 14,697 (1981), 15,994 (1986), 16,303 (1991), 16,702 (1996), 16,658 (2001), 16,517 (2006), 17,820 (2011).

Taree Estate (*Co. Macquarie*) 31°56'S. 152°25'E., 3 km SW of Taree, on Manning R.; flood 1929; pop. 147 (1933), 141 (1947), 144 (1954).

Tareena (*Co. Tara*) 34°01'S. 141°01'E., 84 km W. of Wentworth, on Murray R.; Salt Creek till 1886; farming and grazing; cemetery 1901; PO 1881–1906; telegraph 1881; telephone 1906.

Tarkeeth (*Co. Raleigh*) 30°30'S. 152°57'E., 6 km W. of Urunga, on Kalang R.; farming; PO 1927–40; quarry; school 1929 b. by Frank McCristal; telephone 1926; pop. 97 (1933), 50 (1947).

Tarlee (*Co. Darling*) see Tarpoly.

Tarlo (*Co. Argyle*) 34°36'S. 149°48'E., 18 km NE of Goulburn, on Tarlo R.; laid out 1856 by E.G. Bennett; grazing, farming, dairying; Angl. C. 1872, reused; bridge b. 1877 by E. Turner, destroyed, replaced, over Tarlo R.; butter and cheese factory (E. Cunningham), closed; diphtheria 1859; FB; PO 1860–1954; pound (stock) 1864; Presb. C. b. 1860 by Battye, new one 1874, closed, later reused; Rom. Cath. C. o. 1921 in former Presb. C. after additions, alterations and renovations by J. Murray; school 1858–66; TX 1918; pop. *c.*400 (1860), 118 (1901), 111 (1911), 64 (1933).

Tarlo Gap (*Co. Argyle*) 34°36'S. 149°52'E., 21 km NE of Goulburn, on Tarlo R.; Bapt. C. 1919–22, moved to Goulburn and reused; school 1896–1922.

Tarpoly (*Co. Darling*) 30°36'S. 150°39'E., 19 km NW of Manilla; grazing; RS (Tarlee till 1912) 1908, station b. by W. Gawne & Sons, closed 1963.

Tarrabandra (*Co. Wynyard*) 35°07'S. 148°11'E., 10 km SE of Gundagai; soldiers' settlement; quarry; school 1883–98 and 1937–72; pop. 196 (1933), 126 (1947), 114 (1954), 80 (1961).

Tarraganda (*Co. Auckland*) 36°40'S. 149°52'E., 3 km NE of Bega; hort.; boiling-down works; brickworks (Stafford Bros) estab. 1913 by S.H. Pearce; bridge (McDonald timber truss) b. 1890–94, begun by W.J. Lansdown but completed by John M'Donald, 1,101 ft (335.6 m), demolished 1987, over Bega R.; bushfire 2018; cemetery; flood 1914; school 1891–1932; pop. 112 (1901), 103 (1933), 102 (1947), 116 (1954), 93 (1961), 214 (1991), 238 (1996), 245 (2001), 269 (2006), 246 (2011).

Tarramia (*Co. Denison*) 35°59'S. 146°06'E., 8 km E. of Mulwala; FB; pop. 167 (1901), 138 (1911).

Tarramia North (*Co. Denison*) 35°58'S. 146°05'E., 7 km E. of Mulwala.

Tarrawanna (*Co. Camden*) see Corrimal.

Tarrawingee (*Co. Farnell*) see Torrowangee.

Tarrawingie (*Co. Farnell*) see Torrowangee.

Tarree (*Co. Macquarie*) see Taree.

Tarriaro (*Co. Nandewar*) 30°24'S. 149°54'E., 13 km SE of Narrabri, on Namoi R.; agric.; bridge 1862; school 1957–67; pop. 52 (1933), 57 (1954).

Tarrion (*Co. Clyde*) 30°04'S. 146°52'E., 12 km S. of Brewarrina; RS 1901, station b. by Charles Baker, closed 1974.

Tarro (*Co. Northumberland*) 32°49'S. 151°40'E., 9 km SW of Raymond Terrace, on Purgatory Ck; formerly Upper Hexham; limited development till 1945; farming; Angl. C. 1849, demolished, replacement (St Stephen's) b. 1905 by James Tate, d. by Peter Bennett; Bapt. C.; cemetery (141 graves 1840s–1971); FB (station b. 1962); flood 1856; PO 1883; PS 1962; Rom. Cath. C. b. 1923 by Holmes, d. by Thomas Wilfred Silk, new one (Our Lady of Lourdes) 1944; RS (Hexham till 1883) 1857, station b. by John Paton, station relocated 1913; school 1961; TX 1923, automatic 1957; Unit. C. (orig. Meth.) 1954; water pumping station b. 1930 by J. Jamieson; Wes. Meth.

C. b. 1867 by John Coulton; pop. 194 (1901), 247 (1911), 160 (1933), 403 (1947), 644 (1954), 1,558 (2006), 1,641 (2011).

Tarro (*Co. Northumberland*) see also Beresfield.

Tartna Point (*Co. Perry*) 32°58'S. 142°25'E., 63 km S. of Menindee; PO 1897–1951; telephone 1900; TX 1923.

Tascott (*Co. Northumberland*) 33°27'S. 151°19'E., 3 km SW of Gosford, on Brisbane Water; fishing; bushfire 1994; RS 1905; pop. 21 (1933), 127 (1954), 141 (1961), 1,706 (2011).

Tataila (*Co. Cadell*) 36°03'S. 144°39'E., 12 km NW of Moama; PO 1890–1911; school (Tattaila till *c.*1930) 1874–1901 and 1908–34; Wes. Meth. C. 1870; pop. 119 (1911).

Tatham (*Co. Richmond*) 28°56'S. 153°09'E., 13 km SE of Casino, on Spring Ck; timber, farming, dairying; boiling-down works estab. by Edward Hamilton; bridges: one over Richmond R., one over Shannon Brook, one over Spring Ck, one over Walshs Ck, Willox Bridge; broom factory (T. Johnston & Sons) 1903; cemetery 1883; creamery (NSW Creamery Butter Co. Ltd) 1896; gale 1886; hailstorm 1895; PO 1878, new one b. 1905 by Askew and Ramsay, closed 1977; Presb. C., destroyed 1886, new one b. 1906 by W.G. Mackney; punt, sunk 1890, new one b. 1909 by A. Conroy, for local council, across Richmond R.; Rom. Cath. C. 1893, new one b. 1924 by Turner Bros, burnt down 1931, replacement (St Patrick's) b. 1932 by Wulff Bros, d. by Frederick Johnson Board, closed, sold and reused; sawmills: Lebon's, damaged 1895 and Pidcock Bros Ltd, burnt down 1906, rebuilt, sold 1909 to James and Eaton; school (Wooram till 1886) 1883, new building b. 1886 by G. Hughes, closed 1906; telephone 1894; TX 1926–69; Wes. Meth. C., damaged 1895; wharf b. 1887 by David Rankin, cargo shed added 1890 by Arthur Davis; whooping cough epidemic 1891; pop. 203 (1901), 333 (1911), 286 (1933), 241 (1947), 206 (1954), 194 (1961), 174 (2011).

Tathra (*Co. Auckland*) 36°44'S. 149°59'E., 14 km SE of Bega, on Tasman Sea; town gaz. 1864; shipping port 1862–1954, now oysters and tourism; Angl. C. (St Martin by the Sea) 1977; bridge (Handcock Bridge) 1960, damaged 1971, rebuilt and strengthened 1976; bushfires 1940 (5 houses destroyed) and 2018 (69 houses destroyed); cheese factory (Wattalia, Walter Dalton); dried fruit factory (Bega Dried Foods Pty Ltd); earth tremor 1945; FB; fire 1880; flood 1971; PO 1882; PS 1912–20, new one 1989; reservoir; Rom. Cath. C. (Star of the Sea) 1939, additions and alterations 2004; sawmill (Gowing's), man killed 1899; school 1912, additions 1964 and 1983, major upgrade 1996; storm 1889; telegraph 1882; telephone 1905; TX (automatic) 1949; Unit. C. (orig. Meth.) 1909 d. by Adin Parsons, relocated, new one 1994; water supply 1958, augmentation 1984 and 1987; wharf (Farmer's Sea) b. 1862 by Robert Mowatt, damaged 1864, enlarged 1873 by George Michael, extended 1878, 1886, 1889, damaged and repaired 1889, modified 1900 and 1905, extended 1907–12, cargo shed added 1910, modified 1913 by Oakes and Oakes, second shed added 1918, decking renewed 1935, closed 1954, restored 1986–87, reused; pop. 56 (1891), 80 (1909), 81 (1911), 83 (1921), 184 (1933), 402 (1947), 371 (1954), 435 (1961), 648 (1971), 847 (1976), 1,077 (1981), 1,249 (1986), 1,571 (1991), 1,684 (1996), 1,646 (2001), 1,622 (2006), 1,526 (2011).

Tathra Road (*Co. Auckland*) see Kalaru.

Tattaila (*Co. Cadell*) see Tataila.

Tattersals (*Co. Gloucester*) 32°36'S. 151°57'E., 7 km N. of Karuah.

Tatton (*Co. Wynyard*) see Wagga Wagga.

Tayfield (*Co. Wellesley*) 36°58'S. 149°19'E., 8 km SE of Bombala, on Warburton Ck; telephone 1926; TX 1935–56.

Taylors Arm (*Co. Raleigh*) 30°46'S. 152°43'E., 20 km W. of Macksville, on Taylors Arm; timber, antimony, maize, bananas, vegetables, dairying; Angl. C. (St Mary's) b. 1935 by L. Baker, d. by J. Ashton, closed, sold 2009 and 2017, reused; butter factory (Nambucca Co-op. Society Ltd) 1918; cheese factory (Charles Johnson) b. 1909 by Ford; hailstorm 1959;

landing stage b. 1891 by Thomas Boulton; PO 1891; Presb. C. 1904, new one 1930; Rom. Cath. C. (St Finbar's) b. 1901 by W. Taylor, burnt down 1925, replacement (Christ the King) 1927; school (Upper Taylors Arm till 1916) 1900–75; telephone 1908; TX 1920, automatic 1920; Union C., burnt down 1915; wharf b. 1903 by G. Lawson; pop. 588 (1911), 351 (1933), 583 (1947), 599 (1954), 475 (1961), 341 (2011).

Taylors Beach (*Co. Gloucester*) 32°44'S. 152°03'E., 8 km W. of Nelson Bay, on Tilligery Ck; (incl. Cromartys Bay); oysters; aquaculture research station 1970; jetty; salt pans (disused); salt-works (abandoned); pop. 5 (1961), 99 (2011).

Taylors Flat (*Co. King*) 34°16'S. 149°02'E., 33 km NE of Boorowa, on Callabah Ck; farming, grazing, wolfram; Beachside Christ. Fellowship C.; bushfire 1975; mine (Marks Hill) 1917–18 and 1942; PO 1927–49; telephone 1925; TX 1927; pop. 30 (1933), 216 (2006).

Taylors Flat (*Co. Wallace*) 36°21'S. 148°41'E., 10 km NE of Jindabyne.

Taylors Flat (*Co. Wellesley*) see Cathcart.

Taylors Settlement (*Co. St Vincent*) 35°16'S. 149°54'E., 22 km NE of Braidwood, on Mongarlowe R.; defunct; cemetery.

Taylors Vale (*Co. Clarke*) 30°06'S. 152°13'E., 55 km E. of Guyra, on Boban Ck.

Tea Gardens (*Co. Gloucester*) 32°40'S. 152°10'E., 2 km W. of Hawks Nest, on Myall R.; orig. Coweambah; former timber port, fishing, oysters, pine plantations *c.*1935+, rutile mining 1957+, tourism, retirement centre; abattoir (George Adolph Engel); ambulance station (in rented premises) 1968, new one 1972; Angl. C. (St Andrew's) b. 1909 by Edward and Aaron Yates, sold, moved and reused 1998, new one 2000; Bapt. C. 2006; brickworks (John Witt), closed 1915; bridge (Singing Bridge) to Hawks Nest, b. 1974 by Central Constructions Ltd, over Myall R.; bushfire 1969; cemetery 1906, incl. columbarium; CH 1910, new one b. 1933 by G.A. Zeininger & Sons; earth tremor 1949; electricity 1939; FB 1960 (new station 2007, refurbished 2013 by R.T. Parker Pty Ltd); jetty (police), 60 ft (18.3 m), 1955; PO 1889; pound (stock) 1938; PS (incl. lock-up) 1912, demolished and replaced 1921, additions 1987; punt to Hawks Nest 1930–74, across Myall R.; Rom. Cath. C. b. 1889 by Hammond, extended 1926–27, renovated 1949, demolished 1993, new one (St Stephen's) b. 1994 by Graham Lawler; sawmills: Andrew Cook & Sons Pty Ltd 1913, burnt down 1928, Allen Taylor & Co. Ltd, Witt's, closed 1889; school (Hawks Nest till 1888) 1877, additions 1902 by Southon Bros, additions 1924 by J. Worth, additions 1975; shipyard (G.A. Engle & Sons Ltd); telegraph 1892; telephone 1904; TX 1915, automatic 1959; Unit. C. (orig. Meth.) b. 1929 by Zeininger Bros, redesigned 1987; water reticulation 1966, augmentation 1985; wharves: one b. 1896 by P. Grey and Armstrong's 1948; pop. 129 (1901), 335 (1911), 536 (1933), 471 (1947), 470 (1954), 421 (1961), 500 (1971), 567 (1976), 601 (1981), 572 (1986), 679 (1991), 996 (1996), 1,372 (2001), 1,978 (2006), 2,100 (2011).

Tea Gardens (*Co. Wellesley*) 36°36'S. 149°18'E., 35 km N. of Bombala, on Tea Gardens Ck; school (Jettiba after 1888) 1887–90.

Teamsters Flat (*Co. Camden*) 34°46'S. 150°19'E., 13 km S. of Bundanoon, on Shoalhaven R.

Tea Pot Swamp (*Co. Bathurst*) see Moorilda.

Teatree Flat (*Co. Vernon*) 30°51'S. 152°06'E., 50 km E. of Walcha, on Macleay R.

Teesdale (*Co. Bathurst*) 33°40'S. 149°18'E., 16 km S. of Blayney; agric. and grazing; PO 1862–79; pop. *c.*300 (1866).

Tegerin (*Co. Northumberland*) 33°16'S. 151°30'E., 8 km E. of Wyong, on Tuggerah Lake.

Telarah (*Co. Northumberland*) 32°44'S. 151°32'E., 2 km W. of Maitland, on Telarah Lagoon; (incl. Mount Dee); formerly Homeville; subdivided 1888; Angl. C. (St Luke's) 1912; bushfire 1939; 3 cemeteries (incl. Campbells Hill, 12,386 graves); colliery (Homeville 1887, taken over by Austral Main

Co., renamed South Greta), strikes 1890, 1900, 1902, 1908, 1909, 1914, men killed 1917, 1919, 1920, strike 1921; diphtheria 1921; FB (station b. 1917 by S. Box, new one 1977); floods 1875 and 2015; Meth. C. 1915; monumental stone works (S.R. Horder & Son Pty Ltd); PO 1913; Prim. Meth. C. b. 1890 by George Hill, d. by Frederick Burnhardt Menkens; 3 quarries; railway workshops (South Maitland Railway Co.) 1912, many additions and alterations till 1960; RS (West Maitland Marshalling Yard till 1922) 1911; school (Homeville till 1950) 1890, new one b. 1895 by J. Richardson, additions 1929 by Thomas Norman Grimsley, additions 1965, 1973, 1983, 1994, additions 2010 by RTC Group; telephone 1914; typhoid (man died) 1914; pop. 316 (1911), 828 (1933), 2,143 (2006), 2,227 (2011).

Telararee (*Co. Gloucester*) see Teleraree.

Telegherry (*Co. Gloucester*) 32°22'S. 151°56'E., 18 km E. of Dungog; founded by Aust. Agric. Co., declined 1913+; PO 1911–16; Presb. C. d. and b. 1902 by Isaac Allen; school 1860–1919; storm 1909; Wes. Meth. C. 1882; winery (Telegherry Estate); pop. 63 (1911).

Telegraph Point (*Co. Macquarie*) 31°20'S. 152°48'E., 16 km NW of Port Macquarie, on Wilson R.; bypassed by highway 1974; timber, farming, hort., dairying; Angl. C. (St James's) b. 1897–99; bridge (timber beam with steel bascule span) b. 1900–2 d. by Henry Harvey Dare, demolished 1975, new one, 1,821 ft (555 m), 1974, over Wilson R.; butter factory (Hastings Dairy Co. Ltd) 1934, taken over 1946 by Macleay River Dairying Co. Ltd, sold 1948 to Hastings Valley Food Processing Co-op. Society, reused; cemetery (30 graves 1898–1982) 1886; floods 1929, 1949, 1963, 1968, 1974; hailstorm 1949; passionfruit pulping plant (Hastings Valley Food Processing Co-op. Society) 1948; PO 1872; Presb. C. b. 1920 by William Nicholls, demolished; PS (in rented premises) 1918, closed 1921; punt b. 1876 by D. Anderson; quarry; railway bridge (steel truss) 1917, fabricated by State Dockyard (Walsh Island), over Wilson R.; Rom. Cath. C. 1904, new one (St Bernard of Clairvaux) 1924, burnt down 1993, replaced; RS (2 km N.) 1917, station closed and removed 1984; sawmills: Hungerford's, Lindsay and Love's, Munday's, J.D. Rowsell and Jack Kirkwood; school (Cornbury Park till 1883) 1881–86, reopened 1895, new building b. 1897 by Stanford and Graham, additions 1918, 1954, 1962; SD Adventist C.; storm 2012; telephone 1900; TX (automatic) 1972; wharf; pop. 72 (1901), 242 (1911), 215 (1933), 383 (1947), 402 (1954), 415 (1961), 221 (2011).

Teleraree (*Co. Gloucester*) 32°14'S. 152°18'E., 20 km W. of Tuncurry, on Curreeki Ck; surveyed 1879, village gaz. 1881 as Telararee, deserted by 1888; goldmining.

Telleraga (*Co. Benarba*) 29°34'S. 149°24'E., 43 km W. of Moree, on Gwydir R.

Temagog (*Co. Dudley*) 30°59'S. 152°39'E., 21 km NW of Kempsey, on Macleay R.; farming; bridge 1931, destroyed 1963, replacement (Berthold Bridge) 1966 d. by Ray Berthold, over Macleay R.; FB (station b. 2015); flood 1963; PO 1927–54; telephone 1923; TX 1946; pop. 48 (1933), 359 (2011).

Temi Shale Mine (*Co. Buckland*) 31°42'S. 150°50'E., 5 km N. of Murrurundi, on Back Ck; oil-shale disc. 1862; aerial ropeway to Murrurundi (Adolf Bleichert & Co.) b. 1911 by Gorski and Braunig; mine (Harper's Kerosene Shale Mine) 1871, developed 1886 by Murrurundi Petroleum Oil Cannel Co., taken over by Aust. Shale Syndicate, acquired 1910 by British Aust. Oil Co., which suspended operations, mining resumed 1913, production peaked 1914, mining ceased 1915.

Temora (*Co. Bland*) 34°27'S. 147°32'E., 50 km NW of Cootamundra; (incl. Lower Temora and Upper Temora); orig. Watsonford, also known as Middle Temora, then East Temora till 1880; surveyed and town gaz. 1880, laid out by Adelbert Theophilus Schleicher, thrived 1881–83, munic. proc. 1891; mining (gold disc. 1879, rush 1880) mainly 1881–84, wheat, oats, barley, hort., poultry, eggs, cattle, sheep, pigs, horses, honey, canola, clothing, manufacturing; aeroplane crash 1947; agric.

research station (4 km N.) 1912; airport (3 km NW) 1940, air force training school (World War II) 1941, buildings sold 1947, site upgraded 2004; ambulance station b. 1950 by N.W. Bland, d. by Norman Leslie Lipman; Angl. C. (St Paul's) b. 1907 by Falconer Bros, d. by Henry Laker, additions and alterations 1936 by N.W. Bland, d. by Louis Reginald Williams; Assemblies of God C. (Generocity, formerly Kings Christ.); Bapt. C. b. 1909 by Hermann Ernest Hellner; bicycle works (Byrnes Bros), burnt down 1903; boot and shoe factory; breweries: Jones, Lincoln & Co. 1892–1900, Lion Brewery (estab. by James Howison) 1881–84, Temora Brewery (estab. by Robert Ecclestone and P. Lugton) 1884–94, burnt down 1896, Upper Temora Brewery (estab. by W.S. Eaton and Alphonso R. Tewkesbury) 1891–1918; brick-kiln (Hermann Ernest Hellner); brickworks: N.W. Bland and Temora Pressed Brickworks Co. (estab. by James Edwin James, Oscar Adolf Hauenstein and John Walter Denyer, both James and Denyer were replaced in 1936 by Samual Thomas Batley); bushfire 1905; butter factory (Temora Co-op. Butter Factory Co. Ltd) 1907–14, disused, burnt down 1914; carriage-works (A.G. Reid Ltd); cemetery 1881, incl. lawn cemetery; CH 1880 d. by James Johnstone Barnet, closed and reused, new one b. 1902 by Alfred Stephens, d. by Walter Liberty Vernon; chaff mills: John Dolden & Co., burnt down 1933 and Gus R. Kleinig, J.E. Kleinig and Arthur Stockman, fire 1917; clothing factory 1948; cordial factories: M. Lazarus, Lincoln's, Moglia and Smith, Alphonso R. Tewkesbury, T.J. Webser 1880; cyclone (woman killed) 1904; dam; dust storms 1923 and 2019; electricity 1913; FB 1881 (station b. 1915, extended 1997); fibrous plaster works (A.C. Melzer); fires 1882, 1891, 1897, 1901, 1910, 1929, 1931; floods 1964 and 1974; flour mills: Edwin Gardener and Richard James 1885, May and East (burnt down 1895, rebuilt, bought 1899 by John Knowlman), Pardey & Co. Ltd (b. 1907 by John Dunkley, silo added 1941, mill bought 1973 by Allied Mills, closed); foundry and engineering works (Pratt and Macauley); freezing works (T. Lawrence & Sons); furniture factory (C. Murphy); gales 1882 and 1941; grasshopper infestation 1899; hailstorm 1973; heatwave 1904; hospital b. 1883 by C.S. Smith, new one 1908 d. by Henry Laker, additions 1915, demolished, new one b. 1940 by R.T. Gillies, additions 2018 by Fugen Pty Ltd; Jehovah's Witnesses C.; joinery (Oscar Adolf Hauenstein); Lutheran C.: Chapel on the Hill b. 1909 by Hermann Ernest Hellner, d. by Richard Rahnenfuehrer, Evangelical 1936, Trinity 1955; mine (Mother Shipton); monumental stone works (G. Aslin); PO: Lower Temora 1880–87 and Temora 1880 (additions and alterations 1901 by Herbert Butler, post office burnt down 1902, replacement b. 1904 by Rigby Bros); police barracks b. 1909 by H. Butler; pound (stock) 1880; powerhouse 1924, chimney (81 ft or 24.7 m) demolished 1933; Presb. C. (St Andrew's) 1881, reused, new one b. 1930 by Frank Mitchell, d. by A. McDonald; PS 1880, cells added 1895 by R.L. Thompson; puddling machine (Upper Temora) erected 1933; railway coal stage 1903; railway engine shed 1896, new one 1903; railway round-house (3 bays), demolished 1969; railway turntable 1903, 50 ft (18.2 m), replaced 1912, 60 ft (18.3 m), replaced 1918, defunct; reservoirs: one b. 1935 by Hood and steel one (500,000 gal. or 2,273 kl) 1969; rifle range (2 km S.); Rom. Cath. C. (St Patrick's) 1881 d. by Gordon and Shepherd, new one (Most Sacred Heart of Jesus) b. 1908 by C.O. Lough, d. by Kempson and Conolly; RS 1893, station b. by Eaton Bros, refreshment room wrecked 1902 by railway accident, rebuilt 1914, station closed 1989; sale-yards 1912, new yards 1953; Salv. Army C. 1923, new one 1948; sawmill (Roderick Joseph King); schools: Temora 1880, new one b. 1883 by Charles Hardy, additions 1910 by Hermann Ernest Hellner, additions 1967, HS 1953, additions 1962, 1966, 1972, major upgrade 1996, West Temora 1956, additions 1960; SD Adventist

C.; sewerage 1939; silo 1921; storm 1935; TC 1956, additions 1958, became a campus of Riverina Institute in 1992, new one 2010 on new site d. by Perumal Pedavoli; telegraph 1880, additions and alterations to office 1901 by Herbert Butler, telegraph office burnt down 1902, replacement b. 1904 by Rigby Bros; TX 1902, automatic 1973; typhoid 1880 and 1909; Unit. C. (orig. Meth.) b. 1908 by A.J. Butler, d. by Augustus Dixon Chater, extensions 1927; vulcanising works (E.J. Wood), burnt down 1929; watch-house 1880; water supply 1935, augmentation 1958 and 1969; Wes. Meth. C. 1885; pop. 3,254 (1881), 915 (1891), *c.*1,800 (1895), 1,603 (1901), 3,561 (1911), 3,823 (1933), 4,179 (1947), 4,567 (1954), 4,469 (1961), 4,536 (1966), 4,462 (1971), 4,324 (1976), 4,350 (1981), 4,295 (1986), 4,279 (1991), 4,125 (1996), 4,146 (2001), 4,086 (2006), 4,417 (2011).

Temora (*Co. Bland*) see also Narraburra.

Temora West (*Co. Bland*) see Narraburra.

Temple Court (*Co. Brisbane*) see Murrurundi.

Tenambit (*Co. Northumberland*) 32°45'S. 151°36'E., 2 km NE of East Maitland, on Howes Lagoon; Angl. C. (St Egwin's) b. 1895 by Albert Avard; cemetery (499 graves 1841+); Jehovah's Witnesses C.; quarry; reservoir, 1,398,500 gal. (6,357.6 kl), 1928; sawmill; school 1902 b. by William Henry Noad, additions 1903 by Andrew Burg, additions 1956, 1961, 1963, 1968, 1975; typhoid 1919; pop. 99 (1901), 150 (1911), 207 (1933), 2,302 (2006), 3,008 (2011).

Tenandra (*Co. Bathurst*) 33°39'S. 148°45'E., 12 km SE of Canowindra, on Tenandra Ck; pop. 60 (1933).

Tenandra (*Co. Clarendon*) 35°04'S. 147°50'E., 25 km W. of Gundagai, pop. 38 (1933).

Tenandra (*Co. Ewenmar*) 31°34'S. 147°57'E., 19 km NE of Warren, on Marthaguy Ck; sheep; PO 1874; pop. 89 (2006).

Tenandra (*Co. Leichhardt*) 31°13'S. 148°46'E., 30 km NE of Gulargambone, on Tenandra Ck; formerly Mount Tenandra.

Tenandra Plain (*Co. Kennedy*) 32°58'S. 148°04'E., 22 km NW of Parkes; mine.

Tenango (*Co. Napier*) 31°53'S. 149°42'E., 7 km S. of Coolah; RS 1943–70.

Tenby (*Co. Rous*) see Casino North.

Ten Mile (*Co. Gough*) 29°27'S. 152°00'E., 41 km NE of Glen Innes, on Deepwater R.; tin mining; pop. 55 (1933).

Ten Mile Creek (*Co. Goulburn*) see Holbrook.

Ten Mile Hollow (*Co. Northumberland*) see Snodgrass Valley.

Ten Mile Mulla (*Co. Parry*) 31°10'S. 151°11'E., 16 km SE of Kootingal, on Mulla Mulla Ck.

Ten Mile Waterholes (*Co. Townsend*) see Barratta.

Tennessee (*Co. Dudley*) 31°03'S. 152°51'E., 6 km N. of Kempsey; pop. 28 (1933).

Tennyson (*Co. Cook*) 33°32'S. 150°44'E., 4 km W. of Glossodia; orchards and poultry; bushfire 1944; FB; PO 1927–67; reservoir; school 1900–51; telephone 1917; TX 1918; pop. 76 (1901), 83 (1911), 130 (1933), 115 (1947), 81 (1954), 88 (1961), 431 (2011).

Tenterden (*Co. Hardinge*) 30°08'S. 151°26'E., 24 km NW of Guyra, on Georges Ck; grazing; Angl. C. (St Thomas's) 1898; cemetery; earth tremor 1938; rifle range 1921; PO 1911–52; school 1887–93 and 1957–75; TX 1925, automatic 1952; pop. 90 (1901), 155 (1911), 77 (1933), 98 (1947), 121 (1954).

Tenterfield (*Co. Clive*) 29°03'S. 152°01'E., 80 km N. of Glen Innes, on Tenterfield Ck; disc. by Charles Tuckwood, settled 1840 by J.A. Templer, surveyed and laid out 1850 by John James Galloway, town gaz. 1851, first lots sold 1854, further land sales 1859, designated as chief town of the county, munic. proc. 1871; orig. sheep, cattle, wheat, then mining (tin disc. 1872), hunting, timber, dairying, maize, fruit, tobacco, honey, vineyards; aeroplane crash (2 killed) 1948; agricultural implement works (Ernst Kuskey) 1867; airport 1933–49; ambulance station 1942; Angl. C. (Christ) b. 1860 by Erasmus Styles and George Fagg, additions 1893, replacement 1956 d. by Bruce Woolnough; Assemblies of God C. (Community); bond store; boot factory (E.R. Whereat & Co.) 1889, fire 1903; brickworks: H. Cannon and John Willis; bridge b. 1881 by John Strauss, over Tenterfield Ck; butter factory (Tenterfield Co-op. Butter Factory Co. Ltd) 1893, closed, reopened 1896, leased 1897 by Roper and Walker, closed, reopened 1905, extended 1907 by Wildridge and Sinclair, burnt down 1926, replacement b. 1926 by George Hardy, d. by J. Wildridge & Sinclair Ltd, closed 1970, sold 1985 to Norco Co-op. Ltd; carriage-works estab. 1867 by Frederick Kuskey, taken over 1917 by Walter Kuskey; cemeteries: Stoney Creek and Tenterfield 1863; CH b. 1860 by Erasmus Styles and George Fagg, repairs 1864 and 1869, new one (incl. lock-up) b. 1879–82, begun by Thomas and John McGauran but completed by Thomas Ardern Lewis, d. by James Johnstone Barnet, additions and alterations 1911 by T.L. Mitchell, d. by Walter Liberty Vernon, restored; cheese factory (Tenterfield Cheese Co. Pty Ltd) estab. 1904 by A. Purkiss and S. Wilson, closed 1919; creamery (Sunnyside) 1894; cyclone 1907; dam (Glen Lyon) b. 1974–76; drought 1865; FB 1896 (station b. 1924 by Bowden); floods 1918 and 2011; flour mills: Stuart Alexander Donaldson (estab. 1854, sold 1866 by James Arbouin to Eugene O'Connell and Samuel Davison, O'Connell bought out Davison 1867, acquired 1870 by Edward Reaves Whereat, demolished), Charles Geldart (removed from Bryans Gap, burnt down 1882, new one 1899), Irby Bros, T. Peberdy & Co. (taken over by Reid, reused), Pride of the North (o. 1881 by W. Reid & Co., upgraded and renovated 1904), Riley and Cowper, Roland John Traill 1854; freezing works: Central (Coward Bros) 1945, A.G. Nelmes, Lloyd's Freezing & Export Co. 1917; hospital (Prince Albert Memorial) b. 1863–65, d. by George Wilson, improvements 1871, damaged 1879, additions 1880 by T. Clark, new one b. 1907 by James Lonsdale, additions 1919 by Benjamin Martin Wade, additions 1924 by Kyburz & Son, additions 1927, additions and alterations 1937 by Kent and Kent, extended 1972; Jehovah's Witnesses C. 1973; measles epidemic 1883; meat-chilling works estab. 1892 by W.H. Walker, taken over 1896 by Geddes, Birt & Co., taken over 1941 by Tancred Bros, sold 1960 to Riverstone Meat Co. Pty Ltd, closed 1981; military barracks 1942; mine (silica) 1936; monumental stone works (J. and J.P. Flynn); PO 1849, new one b. 1878–81, begun by Thomas and John McGauran but completed by Thomas Ardern Lewis, d. by James Johnstone Barnet, extensive repairs 1895, re-roofed 1897; pound (stock) 1851; powerhouse 1917, new one 1930–70; Presb. C. (St Stephen's) 1884, renovations 2019; PS b. 1863 by John Brown, new one b. 1884 by John Strauss, additions and alterations 1916 by James R. Day, sen., major upgrade 2011; quarry; railway coal stage b. 1886 by William Murray, additional one 1891; railway engine shed b. 1886 by William Murray, 111 ft (33.8 m), destroyed 1907; railway turntable, 50 ft (15.2 m), replaced 1899 (William Sellers & Co.), 60 ft (18.3 m), closed; 3 reservoirs (incl. one b. 1944 by Diyal Singh & Son); rifle range; Rom. Cath. C. (St Mary's) b. 1867 by Thomas and John McGauran, reused, new one (Our Lady of Perpetual Succour) b. 1940 by Peter Knudson, d. by John Patrick Donoghue; RS 1886, station b. by William Murray, d. by John Whitton, closed 1990, restored and reused; sale-yards 1980; Salv. Army C.; sawmills: J. Drury, Imberger's (sold to Armstrong Bros and Rand), J. Mengleson, Robb and Brown 1975, P. Ryan (incl. joinery), burnt down 1929; scarlet fever 1910; schools: Sir Henry Parkes Memorial (Tenterfield till 1960) 1864, new one b. 1867 by Erasmus Styles, new one b. 1888 by O'Connor and Lonsdale, additions 1890 by J.C. Springbord and John Saxby, remodelled 1912 by J.R. Day, extended 1928 by W.J. Brown, additions 1960 and 1967, and HS 1962, additions 1970, 1985, 1988, 1990, 1992; SD Adventist C. 1948; sewerage 1957; snow 1889 and 1901; soap-works: William Henry Evenis 1891, Janityky's, A.F. Martin, Ross's; storms 1876, 1879, 1890, 1928; streets electric lit 1917; tanneries: Charles Pavel (Stoney Creek) 1861 and Edward Reaves Whereat 1887, fire 1895, closed 1897; TC

1870, became a campus of New England Institute in 1992, additions 2017 d. by Brewster Hjorth Architects; telegraph 1862, new office b. 1865, replacement b. 1879–81, begun by Thomas and John McGauran but completed by Thomas Ardern Lewis, d. by James Johnstone Barnet, extensive repairs 1895, re-roofed 1897; trees (ornamental) planted in streets by Robert Brush; TX 1906, automatic 1973; typhoid 1887; Unit. C. (orig. Meth.) b. 1930 by S.W. and R.C. Potter, d. by Arthur Lanyon Clark, closed 2012, reused; vulcanising works (Acme); watch-house 1861, bought and removed by Patrick Finn; water supply 1930; Wes. Meth. C. b. 1867 by John Brown, enlarged 1878, burnt down 1928; pop. 133 (1856), 676 (1861), *c.*700 (1866), 911 (1871), 1,816 (1881), *c.*2,000 (1886), 2,477 (1891), 2,604 (1901), 2,724 (1911), 2,622 (1933), *c.*2,700 (1941), 3,046 (1947), 3,690 (1949), 3,268 (1954), 3,105 (1961), 3,270 (1966), 3,232 (1971), 3,563 (1976), 3,402 (1981), 3,370 (1986), 3,310 (1991), 3,205 (1996), 3,191 (2001), 3,130 (2006), 2,997 (2011).

Tent Hill (*Co. Gough*) 29°26'S. 151°39'E., 35 km N. of Glen Innes, on Tent Hill Swamp; village gaz. 1874; mining (tin, disc. 1881 by Alexander Ottery, worked 1882–1905, and arsenic); arsenic treatment works estab. 1920–22 by William Cooper & Nephews (Aust.) Pty Ltd, dismantled 1940, derelict, site rehabilitated 1993 and 2003; dams 1927 and 1939; mine (The Ottery) estab. 1882 for tin by Glen Smelting Co., closed 1905, acquired 1920 by William Cooper & Nephews (Aust.) Pty Ltd and reopened 1921 for arsenic, closed 1936; PO 1874–1961; PS b. 1874 by Ralph Kerr Butt; quarry; school (The Glen till 1943) 1881–1958; smelter (Glen Smelting Co.) estab. 1875 by John Moffat and John H. Reid, then joined by George Young; stamper battery (10 head) 1927, operated by Glen Smelting Co.; telephone 1914; tin treatment works 1927, closed 1936, bought and reopened 1938 by Burma Malaya Tin Mining Co., closed and largely dismantled 1940, mill reopened and worked 1956–57 by Guardian Trading & Investment Co. Pty Ltd, derelict; TX 1924; pop. 319 (1891), 356 (1901), 311 (1911), 156 (1933), 120 (1947), 64 (1954), 56 (1961).

Tenundra (*Co. Lincoln*) see Comobella.

Teralba (*Co. Northumberland*) 32°58'S. 151°36'E., 2 km SW of Speers Point, on Cockle Bay; orig. Freshwater Creek and The Gravel Pits, then Winding Creek 1885–88; settled 1829 by James St John, estab. 1884, laid out *c.*1886, subdivision (Glen Mitchell) 1886, subdivision (Quigley Estate) 1909; coalmining; Angl. C. (St David's) b. 1915 by T. Coventry, d. by Frederick George Castleden, closed, sold 2019; bridge (Watkins Bridge) 1899 to Boolaroo, demolished, over Cockle Ck, replaced 1973 to Speers Point, over The Five Islands; bushfire 1940; causeway across Cockle Ck; cemetery 1894–1975; coke-ovens (Pacific Colliery); collieries: Northern Extended (estab. 1890 as Gartlee by Andrew Sneddon, renamed 1892, closed 1964), Pacific (o. 1887 as Great Northern Colliery by Great Northern Coal Mining Co., renamed Northern in 1890, renamed Pacific Co-operative in 1893, men killed 1900 and 1908, renamed 1914, men killed 1919, 1941, 1942, bought and closed by BHP which o. Macquarie coal preparation plant on same site), Stockton Borehole (estab. 1886–1901 as Teralba Colliery by Teralba Co-op. Coal Co., also known as Black's Colliery, taken over 1906 by Borehole Colliery Ltd and renamed Borehole Colliery, man killed 1906, renamed 1908, men killed 1911, 1913, 1917, 1920, 1925, 1926, strike 1929, men killed 1927, 1929, 1933, 1937, 1938, 1949, acquired 1949 by BHP, man killed 1950); earthquake 1989; FB (station b. 1966); flood 2007; jetty b. 1901 by Keenan; Lay Meth. C. b. 1928 by G. Wood, jun., closed, reused; miners' strikes 1892, 1895, 1899, 1923, 1924, 1925, 1928, 1943, 1944, 1946, 1947, 1949, 1950, 1954; Pentecostal Family C.; PO 1885, new one b. 1904 by J.W. Finlay; power plant (Glencore Aust.) 2004; Prim. Meth. C. 1889, closed, sold and reused; PS (Ballast Pit) 1886; quarries: Amos & Co. 1884, Gardener and McNulty (taken over 1922 by Teralba Gravel Quarries Ltd, closed, reopened by Readymix), Hodge's (taken over 1922 by Teralba Gravel Quarries Ltd, closed, reopened by Readymix); railway (colliery); railway bridge (Pratt truss) 1957 to Boolaroo, 147 ft (44.8 m), over Cockle Ck; Rom. Cath. C. (St Michael's) 1902, closed and sold 1963; RS 1887, station b. by John M'Donald; sawmill (Turner Bros); school (Hillsborough till 1886, Gravel Pits till 1889, then Glen Mitchell till 1891) 1884, additions 1918 by William Venor Southon, additions 1953; sewerage 1963; telegraph office b. 1904 by J.W. Finlay; water supply 1916, booster station b. 1954 by Noel F. Mitchell; pop. 240 (1891), 1,051 (1901), 676 (1911), 925 (1933), 986 (1947), 2,721 (1961), 1,460 (2006), 1,558 (2011).

Teralba (*Co. Northumberland*) see also Barnsley.

Terania (*Co. Rous*) see The Channon.

Terania Creek (*Co. Rous*) 28°37'S. 153°18'E., 8 km E. of Nimbin, on Terania Ck; popular area for communal living on small holdings in 1970s; Meth. C. 1908–41, sold 1968; school 1957–65; telephone 1925; TX 1956–61; pop. 170 (1933), 138 (1947), 82 (1954), 99 (1961), 201 (2006), 228 (2011).

Terara (*Co. St Vincent*) 34°52'S. 150°38'E., 3 km E. of Nowra, on Shoalhaven R.; founded 1847 by Michael Hyam, surveyed by H.G. Morton, land sale 1860, thrived in 1860s, destroyed 1870; farming and dairying; Angl. C. (St John's) b. 1856 by Tom Wright, closed 1890, reopened 1893; floods 1842, 1860, 1867, 1870, 1871, 1873, 1874, 1891, 1898, 1975; flour mill (De Mestre's) 1855, converted 1867 to sawmill, closed 1873; iron foundry; PO 1865, destroyed 1870, new one b. 1880; Presb. C. 1850, reused 1875; punt (Pig Island) across Shoalhaven R.; Rom. Cath. C. 1877; sand treatment works; school (Terrara till 1935) 1878, new one b. 1883 by John Schadel, d. by George Allen Mansfield and William Edmund Kemp, closed 1906, reopened 1920; streets acetylene gas lit 1902, coal gas lit 1905, electric lit 1928; telegraph 1880; Wes. Meth. C. 1857–85, sold to Bapt. C., moved to Nowra and reused; wharves: Adam's (destroyed 1860), Illawarra Co. (destroyed 1891), 3 wharves b. 1854 for De Mestre, one b. 1881 by Henry Bryce; pop. 218 (1871), 621 (1891), 110 (1911), 104 (1954), 278 (2006), 237 (2011).

Terembone (*Co. Leichhardt*) 30°39'S. 148°31'E., 35 km N. of Coonamble, on Terembone Ck; Meth. C. 1908, moved 1958 to Gilgooma.

Teridgerie (*Co. Leichhardt*) 30°53'S. 148°50'E., 22 km W. of Baradine, on Teridgerie Ck; farming and grazing; PO 1909–67; Rom. Cath. C. (St Therese's) 1936; telephone 1913; TX 1914, automatic 1967; Union C.; pop. 114 (1933), 62 (1947), 52 (1954).

Termeil (*Co. St Vincent*) 35°29'S. 150°20'E., 19 km SW of Ulladulla, on Reedy Ck; farming; bushfire (largely destroyed village) 1948; cemetery 1901; cheese factory (E. Evans); FB 1942; fire 1917; PO 1889; sawmills: A. & E. Ellis Ltd, H. Mackenzie Ltd, Rixon and Drury; school 1893–1941; telephone 1908; tramway (timber) to Bawley Point; TX 1933–73; Wes. Meth. C. 1897, dismantled 1940; winery (Fern Gully) 1998; pop. 222 (1901), 138 (1911), 89 (1933), 121 (1947), 75 (1954), 50 (1961), 250 (2011).

Terowie (*Co. Kennedy*) 32°28'S. 147°53'E., 42 km SW of Narromine; school 1957–83.

Terrabella (*Co. Gordon*) 32°26'S. 148°43'E., 22 km SE of Dubbo, on Little R.; PO 1896–1912; school 1884–1905; pop. 68 (1911), 44 (1933).

Terrabile (*Co. Gowen*) 31°32'S. 148°36'E., 41 km N. of Gilgandra; village gaz. 1866.

Terrace Creek (*Co. Rous*) 28°26'S. 152°53'E., 24 km NW of Kyogle, on Terrace Ck; sawmill (Piddcock's, acquired by Walter Lever), fire 1912, largely burnt down 1928.

Terrace Creek (*Co. Rous*) see also Bundgeam.

Terragon (*Co. Rous*) 28°26'S. 153°17'E., 17 km SW of Murwillumbah, on Tweed R.; bushfire 1926; sawmill estab. 1901 by Joseph Charles Priest, sen., sold 1935 to Withys (Standard Sawmill); pop. 121 (1933), 89 (1947), 78 (1954), 68 (1961).

Terragong (*Co. Brisbane*) 32°06'S. 150°22'E., 5

km N. of Merriwa, on Merriwa R.; caterpillar infestation 1931; pop. 20 (1933).

Terramungamine (*Co. Lincoln*) 32°09'S. 148°34'E., 11 km N. of Dubbo; subdivided 1905; Presb. C. (St Andrew's), renovations and repairs 1954; sawmill; pop. 82 (1947), 247 (2011).

Terranna (*Co. Argyle*) see Tirrannaville.

Terranora (*Co. Rous*) 28°14'S. 153°30'E., 5 km SW of Banora Point, on Tweed R.; formerly Taranora; estab. 1844; dairying and bananas; PO 1917; PS; 2 quarries; reservoir; school (Bungalora till 1920) 1906, additions 1962 and 1994; telephone 1916; TX 1928–64; pop. 270 (1911), 236 (1933), 257 (1947), 272 (1954), 330 (1961), 2,796 (2011).

Terranora (*Co. Rous*) see also Tweed Heads South.

Terranora Heights (*Co. Rous*) 28°12'S. 153°30'E., 5 km SW of Tweed Heads, on Terranora Ck.

Terrara (*Co. St Vincent*) see Terara.

Terrible Billy (*Co. Parry*) 31°21'S. 151°24'E., 43 km SW of Walcha, on Mulla Ck; pop. 33 (1933).

Terrible Vale (*Co. Buckland*) see Warrigundi.

Terrible Vale (*Co. Sandon*) 30°47'S. 151°29'E., 16 km S. of Uralla, on Salisbury Waters; pop. 26 (1933).

Terrigal (*Co. Northumberland*) 33°27'S. 151°27'E., 10 km E. of Gosford, on Terrigal Lagoon; settled 1826 by John Gray, first lots sold 1900; orig. timber and shipbuilding, later dairying, farming, orchards, fishing, popular coastal holiday destination, now retirement centre; ambulance station; Angl. C. (St Mark's) 1916, relocated 1926 by A.E. Caldwell, closed 2010, new one (Holy Trinity) b. 2010 by North, d. by Thrum; 2 bridges (1927 and 1970) over Terrigal Lagoon; bushfire 1957; cemetery 1881; Christ. Israelite C. 1989; FB (station b. 1965, demolished, replaced 2013); foot-bridge over Terrigal Lagoon; Maronite Meth. C. b. 1934 by T.H. Pryor; PO 1904, new one b. 1929 by J.C. Davis & Sons; Presb. C. 1931, new one (Scots) b. 1963 by W. Sanson, d. by Stanley Smith, additions 2003; PS 1957, new one 1976; Rom. Cath. C. 1961, extended 1979, sold 2002, demolished, replaced (Our Lady Star of the Sea) 2002; sawmill (Thomas Davis) 1870; schools: primary 1930 b. by T.C. Hammond, new school b. 1937 on new site by A. Mills, additions 1958, 1962, 1969, 1978, 2011 and HS 1978 (located temporarily till 1981 at Bateau Bay), new school 1981 at Terrigal; SD Adventist C.; shipyard (Thomas Davis); storms 1974 and 2016; telephone 1905; TX 1912, automatic 1966; Unit. C. 2000; pop. 163 (1911), 473 (1933), 979 (1947), 1,105 (1954), 9,749 (2006), 10,614 (2011).

Terry Hie Hie (*Co. Courallie*) 29°47'S. 150°09'E., 46 km SE of Moree, on Weah Waa Ck; grazing; Angl. C. (St John's); cemetery; cyclone 1932; earth tremor 2000; PO 1901–81; PS 1903, new one b. 1910 by W.H. Bryant, closed 1934; sawmills: Taylor Bros, and Wiggin and Whitton, boy killed 1935, burnt down 1946; school 1897–99 and 1931–73; telephone 1907; TX 1910, automatic 1981; pop. 306 (1911), 150 (1933), 216 (1947), 144 (1954), 130 (1961).

Terry's Meadows (*Co. Camden*) see Albion Park.

Testers Hollow (*Co. Northumberland*) see Cliftleigh.

Teven (*Co. Rous*) 28°49'S. 153°30'E., 6 km NE of Alstonville, on Maguires Ck; sugar-cane 1878+, dairying, cattle, pigs, hort., bananas; bridge (Rattan Singh Bridge) over Houghlahans Ck; floods 1948, 1976, 1985; PO 1904; 2 quarries; rifle range; RS 1930–49; school (Teven Creek till 1906) 1888, relocated 1895, additions 1898 by John McVicar, extended 1901, new building b. 1916 by V.H. Gaggin, closed 1988; telephone 1906; TX 1952–61; Wes. Meth. C. 1889, removed; pop. 167 (1901), 278 (1911), 144 (1933), 193 (1947), 159 (1954), 158 (1961), 250 (2011).

Teven Creek (*Co. Rous*) see Teven.

Teven-Tintenbar (*Co. Rous*) see Tintenbar.

Tewinga (*Co. Raleigh*) 30°39'S. 152°54'E., 10 km W. of Nambucca Heads, on Nambucca R.; farming; PO 1918–69; school (Jellicoe till 1917) 1915–75; telephone 1917; TX 1928–61;

pop. 105 (1933), 63 (1947), 92 (1954), 68 (1961).

Thackaringa (*Co. Yancowinna*) 32°02'S. 141°03'E., 38 km W. of Broken Hill; Thackaringa Mines till 1889; founded by Patrick Green; mining (silver-lead disc. 1875 by Julius Charles Nickel and Dan McLean) till 1897; Bible Christ. C.; cemetery 1891; CH 1890; mines: Alberta, Bonanza, Comstock, Devlins, Exhibition Lode, Goat Hill, Goat Hill Extended, Gipsy Boy, Gipsy Girl, Gipsy Queen, Hercules, Homeward Bound, Lady Brassey, Lily, McGrath and Kingston, Maggies Secret, Dan O'Connell, Outward Bound, Pioneer (estab. 1876 by Patrick Green, taken over 1877 by Richard Green and A.L. Garot), Pioneer Extended; PO 1882–1929; PS 1888–1907; quarry (sillimanite); school 1889–1907; telegraph 1889; TX 1921; pop. *c.*2,000 (1883), *c.*250 (1888), 257 (1891), 290 (1899), 103 (1901), 55 (1911), 23 (1933).

Thackaringa Mines (*Co. Yancowinna*) see Thackaringa.

Thalaba (*Co. Georgiana*) 34°16'S. 149°31'E., 23 km N. of Crookwell; farming and grazing; PO 1910; school (Greenwattle) 1900–3; telephone 1915; TX 1928; pop. 90 (1911), 26 (1933).

Thalaba (*Co. Jamison*) 29°47'S. 149°17'E., 46 km N. of Wee Waa, on Thalaba Ck.

Thalaba Bridge (*Co. Gloucester*) 32°28'S. 151°46'E., 8 km S. of Dungog, on Williams R.; settled by Baptists; Bapt. C. b. 1881 by Robson, new one b. 1913 by G. Baker, extended 1950, and graveyard (209 graves 1862+), incl. columbarium; bridge (low-level) b. 1872 by Marsh Bros, d. by Capt. H. Ross, destroyed 1955, new one 1972, over Williams R.; diphtheria 1910; flood 1955.

Thalgarrah (*Co. Sandon*) 30°27'S. 151°49'E., 17 km NE of Armidale, on Gara R.; Angl. C. (All Saints') 1897; bridge over Gara R.; school 1908–27 and 1962–72; TX (automatic); pop. 158 (2006), 228 (2011).

Thanowring (*Co. Bland*) 34°24'S. 147°27'E., 10 km NW of Temora; school 1889–94.

Tharbogang (*Co. Sturt*) 34°15'S. 145°59'E., 6 km NW of Griffith; village gaz. 1933; wheat, oranges, grapes; fruit juice factory (Summertime Fruit Juices Pty Ltd) estab. by Tony Sergi, in liquidation 2014, fire 2014; fruit packing house; heatwave 1936; plastics factory (Celluform Plastics); PO 1955–90; RS 1923–75; sale-yards; school 1932; silo; storm 1947; telephone 1955; TX 1951; pop. 110 (1947), 203 (1954), 676 (2011).

The Alberts (*Co. Kennedy*) see Albert.

The Anchorage (*Co. Dampier*) 35°55'S. 150°08'E., 4 km E. of Moruya, on Moruya R.

The Avenue (*Co. Clarence*) 29°42'S. 153°04'E., 11 km E. of South Grafton.

The Avenue (*Co. Yungnulgra*) 31°05'S. 143°12'E., 55 km N. of Wilcannia; telephone 1923; TX.

The Barbs (*Co. Arrawatta*) 29°24'S. 151°16'E., 19 km SE of Ashford, on Pindari Dam; quarry.

The Basin (*Co. Darling*) 30°22'S. 150°38'E., 2 km NE of Barraba.

The Basin (*Co. Hardinge*) 30°12'S. 151°17'E., 38 km W. of Guyra, on Georges Ck.

The Basin (*Co. Hawes*) 31°30'S. 151°23'E., 61 km S. of Walcha, on Tomalla Ck.

The Basin (*Co. Macquarie*) see Taree.

The Bend (*Co. Richmond*) see Wooroowoolgan.

The Big Flat (*Co. Ashburnham*) see Bowan Park.

The Big Flat (*Co. Brisbane*) 31°44'S. 150°58'E., 12 km E. of Murrurundi, on Scotts Ck.

The Big Hill (*Co. Cook*) see Kurrajong Heights.

The Bight (*Co. Gloucester*) 31°53'S. 152°22'E., 2 km S. of Wingham, on Manning R.; orig. Yaypo Brush; bridge to Wingham, over Manning R.; cemetery (316 graves 1859+) 1863; pop. 69 (1933), 54 (1947), 51 (1954), 65 (1961).

The Bluff (*Co. Roxburgh*) 33°16'S. 149°24'E., 23 km NW of Bathurst, on Macquarie R.

The Branch (*Co. Gloucester*) 32°32'S. 152°01'E., 13 km N. of Bulahdelah, on The Branch R.; estab. 1914; timber and grazing; PO 1916; sawmills: Armstrong & Royse Pty Ltd (closed and dismantled 1936, moved to Stroud) and Port Stephens Timber Co.;

school (Branch River till 1906) 1900 b. by Neil M'Lellan, closed 1939; telephone 1906; TX 1933–36; Union C., rebuilt 1931; pop. 77 (1901), 113 (1911), 52 (1933), 256 (2006).

The Bulga (*Co. Hunter*) see Bulga.

The Bulls Nest (*Co. Drake*) see Bulls Nest.

The Camp (*Co. Gipps*) see Wyalong West.

The Camp (*Co. Northumberland*) see Maitland.

The Cape (*Co. Rous*) 28°30'S. 152°57'E., 14 km N. of Kyogle, on Richmond R.; RS 1936–68.

The Channon (*Co. Rous*) 28°40'S. 153°17'E., 10 km SE of Nimbin, on Terania Ck; orig. Channon Grass then Terania till 1908; settled 1882 by Don and Jim Thorburn, first lots sold 1908; timber, farming, bananas 1927+, dairying till 1960s then popular commune area in 1970s; bridges: Ford's Bridge 1949, replaced 1970 (at Funnell's Crossing), over Terania Ck, Osborne's Bridge 1929 d. by Newton, replaced 1973, over Tuntable Ck, Rocky Creek Bridge b. 1907 by Kennedy and Ward, collapsed and replaced 1921, replaced again 1996 with R.A. Robertson Bridge, Skaines's Bridge 1929, over Tuntable Ck, The Channon Bridge b. 1912 by Walter Frank Oakes, d. by C. Burrows, replaced 1970 with H.E. King Bridge, over Terania Ck, nr Tuntable Ck junction; butter factory (North Coast Co-op. Ltd) 1913, rebuilt 1938 by Daniel Gallagher, closed 1946, sold, reused 1991; electricity 1934; FB; hailstorm 1990; PO 1910; rifle range 1916; sawmill (Edward Roach) 1904–11; school (Tuntable Creek till 1922) 1909 b. by C. Johnson; telephone 1910; TX 1924, automatic 1953; water reticulation 1949, second scheme 1971; pop. 119 (1901), 299 (1911), 130 (1933), 190 (1947), 301 (1954), 480 (2011).

The Chips (*Co. Gowen*) 31°20'S. 149°05'E., 19 km W. of Coonabarabran, on Belar Ck.

The Commonage (*Co. Northumberland*) see Hamilton.

The Corals (*Co. Rous*) 28°47'S. 153°21'E., 7 km E. of Lismore; telephone 1924.

The Corner (*Co. Auckland*) 36°38'S. 149°53'E., 6 km NE of Bega.

The Corner (*Co. St Vincent*) see Reidsdale.

The Cowpastures (*Co. Camden*) see Camden.

The Creel (*Co. Wallace*) 36°21'S. 148°38'E., 7 km N. of Jindabyne.

The Crossing (*Co. Rous*) see Casino.

The Crossing Place (*Co. Clarendon*) see Gundagai.

The Crossing Place (*Co. Goulburn*) see Albury.

The Cross Roads (*Co. Camden*) see Hoddles Cross Roads.

The Crushers (*Co. Cook*) see Katoomba.

The Downs (*Co. Brisbane*) 32°03'S. 150°50'E., 3 km W. of Scone.

The Drop (*Co. Denison*) 35°46'S. 145°45'E., 14 km S. of Berrigan.

The Duckbill (*Co. Macquarie*) 31°48'S. 152°18'E., 9 km NW of Wingham, on Dingo Ck.

The Dungeons (*Co. Ashburnham*) 33°10'S. 148°24'E., 21 km E. of Parkes.

The East Pines (*Co. Townsend*) 35°15'S. 145°16'E., 43 km NE of Deniliquin.

The Elbow (*Co. Clarence*) see Lawrence.

The Elms (*Co. Georgiana*) 34°20'S. 149°33'E., 16 km NE of Crookwell; telephone 1925; TX 1929.

The Entrance (*Co. Northumberland*) 33°21'S. 151°30'E., 18 km NE of Gosford, on Tasman Sea; Karagi till 1911; settled 1823 by James Webb, subdivided 1920, foreshore redeveloped 1995; fishing, prawning, tourism 1920+, retirement centre 1960s+; ambulance station 1954; Angl. C. 1923, moved to Tumbi Umbi, new one (All Saints') 1972, tower removed 2012; Bapt. C. 1940; brick-kiln (Taylor's) 1920–1922; bridge to The Entrance North b. 1934 by Beattie and Frost, 1,200 ft (365.8 m), demolished 1969, replacement (concrete) b. 1967–69 by Transbridge Pty Ltd, 1,532 ft (467 m), over The Entrance Channel; bushfire 1955; FB 1947 (station b. 1969); fire 1934; floods 1889, 1927, 1939, 1949; ice works (Cecil F. Gall); Meth. C. b. 1920 by Jennett; PO 1911, new one b. 1934; Presb. C. (St Andrew's) 1949; PS 1926, new one 1948, additions and alterations 1974; Rom. Cath. C.

b. 1925 by Gilbert Dixon and William Daniel Ponton, d. by S. Roarty, extensions 1936 by Gilbert Dixon, d. by Roarty and Roarty, demolished 1962, replacement (Our Lady of the Rosary) 1962 d. by Sydney George Hirst and David Kennedy; school (Tuggerah Entrance till 1935) 1917, additions 1924, additions 1927 by J.M. Thom, additions 1959, 1962, 1964, 1966, 1968, 1970, additions by A.C.H. Clifford Pty Ltd; SD Adventist C. 1954; sewerage 1971; telephone 1913; TX 1949–69; water reticulation 1966; wharf; pop. 58 (1915), 569 (1933), 1,672 (1947), 2,635 (2006), 3,873 (2011).

The Entrance (*Co. Northumberland*) see also Shelly Beach.

The Entrance North (*Co. Northumberland*) 33°20'S. 151°30'E., 1 km NE of The Entrance, on Tasman Sea; (incl. Magenta and North Wyrrabalong); bridge to The Entrance b. 1934 by Beattie and Frost, 1,200 ft (365.8 m), b. 1934 by Beattie and Frost, 1,200 ft (365.8 m), demolished 1969, replacement (concrete) b. 1967–69 by Transbridge Pty Ltd, 1,532 ft (467 m), over The Entrance Channel; flood 2015; PO 1927–35; school 1930, new building b. 1982, closed 1989; sewerage 1971; telephone 1923; wharf; pop. 108 (1933), 220 (1947), 1,105 (2006), 1,392 (2011).

The Falls (*Co. Rous*) see Casino.

The Falls (*Co. St Vincent*) see Falls Creek.

The Fishing Village (*Co. Clyde*) see Brewarrina.

The Five Corners (*Co. Townsend*) see Five Corners.

The Flags (*Co. Vernon*) 31°21'S. 151°32'E., 41 km S. of Walcha, on Macdonald R.; FB; telephone 1928; TX 1929; pop. 48 (1933).

The Flats (*Co. Clarke*) 29°59'S. 152°13'E., 53 km SE of Glen Innes, on Sara R.; mine (gold).

The Folly (*Co. Northumberland*) see Mayfield.

The Forest (*Co. Argyle*) 34°38'S. 149°44'E., 15 km N. of Goulburn; airfield; Angl. C. (St Columba's, orig. Meth.) 1930 d. by Bertram Chisholm, new one 1940; RS 1902–75; TX (automatic); pop. 61 (1911), 63 (1933).

The Forest (*Co. Inglis*) 31°02'S. 150°56'E., 7 km N. of Tamworth; school 1905–46; pop. 146 (1901), 56 (1933).

The Forest (*Co. Phillip*) 32°27'S. 149°52'E., 30 km NE of Mudgee.

The Four Mile (*Co. Beresford*) 36°15'S. 149°03'E., 7 km W. of Cooma.

The Gap (*Co. Arrawatta*) 28°58'S. 150°54'E., 65 km SE of Boggabilla.

The Gap (*Co. Clarendon*) 35°00'S. 147°16'E., 15 km NW of Wagga Wagga; Angl. C. (St Edward's) 1922, closed, sold 2013 to Josh and Sophie Walsh and reused; TX (automatic); pop. 78 (1933), 72 (1947), 99 (1954), 86 (1961).

The Gap (*Co. Gipps*) 33°32'S. 147°43'E., 31 km SW of Forbes.

The Gap (*Co. Gordon*) 32°59'S. 148°49'E., 14 km N. of Molong, on Gap Ck.

The Gap (*Co. King*) 34°29'S. 149°26'E., 5 km SW of Crookwell.

The Gap (*Co. Richmond*) 29°08'S. 153°23'E., 8 km S. of Woodburn.

The Gardens (*Co. Jamison*) 30°16'S. 149°19'E., 14 km W. of Wee Waa.

The Geebung Ground (*Co. Hunter*) see Geebung Ground.

The German's (*Co. Goulburn*) see Holbrook.

The Glade (*Co. Raleigh*) 30°22'S. 152°43'E., 4 km S. of Dorrigo.

The Glebe (*Co. Northumberland*) see Merewether.

The Glen (*Co. Gloucester*) 32°10'S. 152°00'E., 18 km S. of Gloucester, on Wards R.

The Glen (*Co. Gough*) see Tent Hill.

The Glen (*Co. Selwyn*) 35°50'S. 147°52'E., 14 km SW of Tumbarumba; farming; PO 1927–54; telephone 1913; TX 1925, automatic 1954; pop. 28 (1933), 69 (1954).

The Glen (*Co. Vernon*) 30°57'S. 151°36'E., 5 km N. of Walcha, on Ohio Ck.

The Gorge (*Co. Yancowinna*) 31°55'S. 141°41'E., 22 km E. of Broken Hill; RS 1919–76.

The Granite (*Co. Tongowoko*) see Tibooburra.

The Gravel Pits (*Co. Northumberland*) see Teralba.

The Grove (*Co. Hardinge*) 30°01'S. 151°10'E., 5 km SW of Tingha.

The Grove (*Co. Wynyard*) 35°22'S. 148°05'E., 6

km S. of Adelong, on Adelong Ck; farming; PO 1927–30; pop. 23 (1933).

The Gulf (*Co. Gough*) 29°18'S. 151°27'E., 34 km E. of Ashford; thrived 1912 and 1932–42; mining (tin and wolfram); cemetery; mines: Carr's Reef (later Wilson Bros), Garth's Reef, Gulf Stream Mining Co., Kathida, Rumsey's Wolfram Mine; PO 1878–1928; school 1915–16, demolished; pop. 138 (1911).

The Gully (*Co. Cook*) see Katoomba.

The Gulph (*Co. Dampier*) see Nerrigundah.

The Hatch (*Co. Macquarie*) 31°22'S. 152°51'E., 9 km NW of Port Macquarie, on Maria R.; school 1901–21 and 1957–67; telephone 1929; TX 1955; pop. 30 (1933).

The Heath (*Co. Rous*) 28°35'S. 153°33'E., 6 km SE of Mullumbimby, on Simpsons Ck; 3 quarries.

The Highlands (*Co. Northumberland*) see Mayfield.

The Hill (*Co. Northumberland*) see Newcastle.

The Holes (*Co. Hunter*) 33°00'S. 150°42'E., 55 km W. of Paxton.

The Ironbarks (*Co. Cook*) 33°48'S. 150°37'E., 3 km S. of Glenbrook.

The Island (*Co. Richmond*) 29°03'S. 152°51'E., 28 km SW of Casino, on Busbys Ck; sawmill.

The Islands (*Co. Cook*) see Kurrajong Hills.

The Junction (*Co. Dampier*) see Cobargo.

The Junction (*Co. Darling*) see Manilla.

The Junction (*Co. Georgiana*) see Abercrombie.

The Junction (*Co. Gordon*) 32°46'S. 148°41'E., 47 km E. of Peak Hill, on Buckinbah Ck.

The Junction (*Co. Northumberland*) see Merewether.

The Junction (*Co. Richmond*) see Coraki.

The Junction (*Co. Roxburgh*) 33°18'S. 149°32'E., 14 km N. of Bathurst, on Dicks Ck.

The Junction (*Co. Wentworth*) see Wentworth.

The Junction (*Co. Wynyard*) 35°01'S. 148°11'E., 8 km NE of Gundagai, on Murrumbidgee R.

The Jungle (*Co. Gregory*) 31°21'S. 147°46'E., 40 km N. of Warren.

The Lagoon (*Co. Bathurst*) 33°33'S. 149°36'E., 14 km S. of Bathurst, on The Lagoon; Lagoons till 1877; copper mining, farming, grazing, horses; Angl. C. 1893, demolished, replaced 1931; mine (Mount Morris); PO 1860; Rom. Cath. C. (St Mary's) 1955, closed; school (Campbells River till 1870) 1858–62, reopened 1880, repairs 1905 by John Wild, closed 2010, sold; TX 1923, automatic 1981; Wes. Meth. C. 1850; pop. 270 (1901), 227 (1911), 229 (1933), 210 (1947), 183 (1954), 162 (1961), 246 (2011).

The Letter "A" (*Co. Northumberland*) 33°08'S. 151°12'E., 27 km W. of Morisset.

The Lime Kilns (*Co. Roxburgh*) see Limekilns.

The Little Meadow (*Co. Argyle*) see Little Meadow.

The Little Plain (*Co. Wellington*) 32°47'S. 149°46'E., 19 km W. of Rylstone.

The Little Point (*Co. Monteagle*) 34°12'S. 148°44'E., 27 km N. of Boorowa, on Narrallen Ck; mining (copper); mines: Bell View 1907, Right Hand Creek, Sapling Gully, Stewart 1905–7, Yundoo Lode <1908.

The Long Plain (*Co. Narromine*) 32°03'S. 148°02'E., 5 km SE of Trangie.

The Meadows (*Co. Gordon*) 32°35'S. 148°32'E., 35 km NE of Peak Hill; mine (Beehive) worked by K. Barker; typhoid 1884.

The Meadows (*Co. Wallace*) 36°18'S. 148°40'E., 13 km N. of Jindabyne.

The Meadows (*Co. Wallace*) 36°38'S. 148°54'E., 32 km S. of Berridale, on Meadow Ck.

The Meadows (*Co. Wellington*) 33°17'S. 149°02'E., 6 km W. of Orange, on Molong Ck; agric.; PO 1865–69; pop. *c.*180 (1866).

The Meadows (*Co. Westmoreland*) 33°38'S. 149°56'E., 10 km NE of Oberon, on Meadow Ck; quarry; pop. 52 (1901), 55 (1911).

The Mission (*Co. Arrawatta*) 29°27'S. 151°20'E., 28 km SE of Ashford; Aboriginal mission (abandoned); cemetery (Aboriginal).

The Mole (*Co. Clive*) 29°06'S. 151°46'E., 28 km W. of Tenterfield, on Mole R.; formerly Mole River; arsenic (disc. 1923); arsenic mine (Mole River) o. 1924 by Archie Nelmes and Dick Patching, taken over 1924 by Oliver Cromwell Roberts, rotary furnace added 1928, mine closed, derelict; PO 1935–55; school 1961–71; telephone 1938; TX 1938, automatic 1983; pop. 75 (1911), 101 (1933), 91 (1947), 82 (1954), 87 (1961).

The Mole (*Co. Clive*) see also Torrington.

The Moor (*Co. Gloucester*) 32°00'S. 152°34'E., 4 km SW of Old Bar, on Tasman Sea.

The Mount (*Co. Bathurst*) 33°34'S. 149°33'E., 18 km S. of Bathurst.

The Mullion (*Co. Cowley*) 35°08'S. 148°52'E., 33 km S. of Yass; school 1959–72; TX (automatic).

The New Yards (*Co. Westmoreland*) see New Yards.

The Nine Mile (*Co. Selwyn*) 35°51'S. 148°06'E., 11 km SE of Tumbarumba; estab. 1860; goldmining; bridge b. 1887 by John Wilson, over Stony Ck; lock-up; pop. 51 (1901).

The Oaks (*Co. Camden*) 34°05'S. 150°34'E., 12 km W. of Camden, on Werriberri Ck; orig. Vanderville, then Oaks 1858–95; settled 1823 by John Wild, subdivided and lots offered for sale 1858, relocated 1863+; cattle till 1826, wheat till 1890s, then dairying, hort., orchards, poultry; airfield (RAAF) 1942, bought 1975 by Grahame Onus; Angl. C.: St Matthew's (b. 1839 for John Benton Wild and Major William Russell, rebuilt 1923, restored 1983, and graveyard) and St Luke's 1892, additions 1961, and graveyard; brickworks; bushfires 1889, 1929, 1939, 2001; cemetery; electricity 1946; FB; fire 1911; flour mill (John Roberts); foot-bridge over Monkey Ck; PO 1858; pound (stock) 1847; PS 1900, additions and repairs 1909 by John M'Donald, closed 1934, new one; quarry (disused); Rom. Cath. C. (St Aloysius's) b. 1865 by Stokes and Kealy, and graveyard; sawmill; school 1862–63, reopened 1883, burnt down and replaced 1929, additions 1963 and 1994; telephone 1892; TX 1911, automatic 1970; water supply 1985; pop. 248 (1901), 319 (1911), 345 (1933), 339 (1947), 503 (1954), 590 (1961), 399 (1966), 468 (1971), 531 (1976), 931 (1981), 1,095 (1986), 1,367 (1991), 1,500 (1996), 1,591 (2001), 1,586 (2006), 1,706 (2011).

The Old Wharf (*Co. Gloucester*) see Tinonee.

The Page (*Co. Brisbane*) see Murrurundi.

The Parading Ground (*Co. Gloucester*) 32°49'S. 151°53'E., 13 km E. of Raymond Terrace; school (Parading Ground) 1857–78; Wes. Meth. C. 1878; pop. *c.*120 (1887).

The Park (*Co. Gordon*) 32°44'S. 148°38'E., 2 km NW of Yeoval.

The Peak (*Co. Mouramba*) 32°06'S. 146°18'E., 103 km SW of Nyngan.

The Peaks (*Co. Westmoreland*) see Yerranderie.

The Pig Farm (*Co. Drake*) 29°09'S. 152°36'E., 56 km E. of Tenterfield, on Clarence R.

The Pilgrim (*Co. Cook*) see Blaxland.

The Pinnacles (*Co. Clarence*) 29°33'S. 152°55'E., 16 km N. of Grafton; cemetery; pop. 291 (2011).

The Pinnacles (*Co. Yancowinna*) 32°03'S. 141°19'E., 16 km SW of Broken Hill, on Pine Ck; orig. Pinnacles; village gaz. 1891; mining; fire 1933; mines: Bewick Moreing, Consols, Kinchega, Lady Bevys, Marshalls Monarch, Pinnacles, South Kinchega; PO 1888–1930; PS 1890–95; school 1891–1912; smelter 1885, soon abandoned; telephone 1909; TX 1913; pop. *c.*450 (1891), 157 (1901), 77 (1911), 30 (1933).

The Plains (*Co. Northumberland*) see Caves Beach.

The Plains Beach (*Co. Northumberland*) see Caves Beach.

The Platforms (*Co. Gowen*) 31°17'S. 149°02'E., 23 km W. of Coonabarabran.

The Pocket (*Co. Rous*) 28°30'S. 153°29'E., 5 km N. of Mullumbimby, on Marshalls Ck; cheese factory (Foley Bros) 1920, casein later made instead, closed; Meth. C. 1960; PO 1893–95; school (Upper Pocket till 1915) 1907, new one b. 1918 by Alfred John Modini; telephone 1914; TX 1915, automatic 1954; pop. 206 (1947), 172 (1954), 174 (1961).

The Ponds (*Co. Wellington*) 32°46'S. 149°23'E., 28 km SW of Mudgee, on Gundowda Ck.

The Pottery (*Co. Northumberland*) see Merewether.

The Quarries (*Co. Cooper*) see Yanco.

The Quarry (*Co. Roxburgh*) see Kandos Quarries.

The Quiet Corner (*Co. Gregory*) 31°22'S.

148°06'E., 35 km W. of Gulargambone.

The Racecourse (*Co. Camden*) 34°27'S. 150°33'E., 10 km E. of Mittagong.

The Racecourse (*Co. Hawes*) 31°35'S. 151°38'E., 66 km S. of Walcha, on Myall R.

The Racecourse (*Co. Selwyn*) 35°51'S. 148°06'E., 12 km SE of Tumbarumba, on Paddys R.

The Racecourse (*Co. Vernon*) 31°08'S. 152°17'E., 53 km W. of Kempsey.

The Reeds (*Co. Georgiana*) 33°55'S. 149°16'E., 42 km S. of Blayney; mines: Mount Nicholls (gold) 1906–7, South Vanderbilt (gold), The Reeds (iron).

The Reef (*Co. Westmoreland*) 33°43'S. 149°50'E., 2 km W. of Oberon, on Diamond Gully; goldmine (Homeward Bound or Blackman's Reef) 1875, 1883, 1885–86, 1889; pop. 77 (1954), 54 (1961).

The Reefs (*Co. Clarendon*) see Junee Reefs.

The Reefs (*Co. Roxburgh*) 33°04'S. 149°33'E., 39 km N. of Bathurst, on Turon R.; also known as Quartz Ridge; grazing and goldmining (alluvial and quartz); 4 mines (abandoned); PO 1865–83; pop. *c.*90 (1866).

Theresa Creek (*Co. Rous*) 28°46'S. 152°47'E., 27 km W. of Casino, on Theresa Ck; school 1957–69; telephone 1948; TX 1948, automatic 1953; Wes. Meth. C. 1901; pop. 23 (1933), 162 (1947), 152 (1954), 127 (1961).

Theresa Park (*Co. Camden*) 34°01'S. 150°38'E., 7 km NW of Camden, on Nepean R.; (incl. Scotts Hill); Angl. C. 1854, new one (St Peter's) 1886; FB; Prim. Meth. C. 1857; school 1879, new one b. 1882 by W. Packenham, closed 1958; telephone 1925; TX 1932; weirs (Brownlow Hill and Mount Hunter Rivulet) b. 1910 by F.J. Cornwell, on Nepean R.; pop. 55 (1901), 64 (1933), 77 (1954), 87 (1961), 341 (2001), 551 (2011).

The Retreat (*Co. Denison*) 35°37'S. 145°29'E., 10 km W. of Finley; school 1913–67.

The Retreat (*Co. Durham*) see Singleton (*Co. Northumberland*).

The Ridgeway (*Co. Murray*) see Ridgeway.

The Risk (*Co. Rous*) 28°29'S. 152°56'E., 17 km N. of Kyogle, on Richmond R.; settled 1869 by John Wilson, subdivided 1912; farming and dairying; bridge (Dourigan Bridge) 1912; gale 1942; PO 1908–72; RS 1930–74, station demolished; school (Gradys Creek till 1924) 1912, relocated 1915, dismantled and removed 1919, new one b. 1919 by W. Tyrell, additions 1928 also by Tyrell, additions 2010; telephone 1911; TX 1924; pop. 129 (1933), 130 (1947), 117 (1954), 109 (1961), 203 (2006).

The Rock (*Co. Mitchell*) 35°16'S. 147°07'E., 29 km SW of Wagga Wagga, on Burkes Ck; surveyed and village gaz. 1880 as Kingston, resurveyed 1881 by Walter Alfred Lipscomb, declined 1950s+; ostrich farming 1906–26, wheat, oats, barley, lupins, rape, peas, sorghum, sheep, cattle; Angl. C. (St Peter's) b. 1920 by C. Hardy & Co., d. by E.E. Giles; 2 brick-kilns 1910; bridge, rebuilt 1954 by E. Selmes, new one (concrete) b. by H. Mueller & Co. Pty Ltd, new one 1980, over Burkes Ck; broom factory (Doug Pratt); bushfires 1961 and 1975; cemetery (700 graves 1902+) 1897, incl. lawn cemetery and columbaria; drought 1944; dust storm 1914; electricity (Hugh Milne) 1926, upgraded 1937; FB; fire 1901; floods 1891, 1916, 1931, 1939, 2010, 2012; hospital 1923, new one b. 1958 by Neil Martin and Norm Donkin; ice works: W.B. Davies (bought by Murrumbidgee Dairy Co.) and Hugh Milne; PO 1880, new one b. 1905, additions 1914 by H.B. Russ; Presb. C. 1887, relocated 1911; PS 1880, new one b. 1911 by C. Hardy & Co.; railway coal stage 1901, sold 1966; railway engine shed 1901, demolished 1976; railway turntable, 50 ft (15.2 m), sold and removed 1985; reservoir 250,000 gal. (1,136.5 kl); Rom. Cath. C. (St Mary's) b. 1931 by H.G. Webb, d. by Harrison and Glaskin; RS (Hanging Rock till 1882, then Kingston till 1883), station b. 1880 by Joseph Oats, closed 1989, reused; sawmill (T.S. Carson); scarlet fever 1928 and 1944; school 1887, additions 1913, 1960, 1966, 1993; SD Adventist C.; sewerage 1981, augmentation 1995; silo 1918; snow 1899; storms 1911 and 1923; street tree plantings 1912, 1918, 1920; telegraph 1882, additions to office 1914 by H.B. Russ; TX

1912, automatic 1984; Union C. b. 1897 by Van der Water; Unit. C.: one (orig. Meth.) b. 1914 by Webb and Lodge, d. by A. Newman and St Stephen's (orig. Presb.) b. 1930 by Webb and Lodge, d. by Eric Clarke Pitt and John Donald Morrow, closed, sold 2014 and 2016, reused; water supply 1942; pop. 117 (1901), 672 (1911), 848 (1933), 861 (1947), 837 (1954), 766 (1961), 563 (1966), 545 (1971), 656 (1976), 693 (1981), 768 (1986), 809 (1991), 859 (1996), 872 (2001), 860 (2006), 862 (2011).

The Rocks (*Co. Bathurst*) 33°25'S. 149°25'E., 15 km W. of Bathurst, on Rocks Ck; 2 quarries; pop. 20 (1933).

The Round Flat (*Co. Wallace*) see Round Plain.

The Round Hole (*Co. Roxburgh*) 33°15'S. 149°25'E., 24 km NW of Bathurst, on Macquarie R.

The Sandhills (*Co. Northumberland*) see Newcastle.

The Sandhills (*Co. Townsend*) see Deniliquin.

The Sands (*Co. Georgiana*) 33°51'S. 149°18'E., 36 km S. of Blayney, on Copperhannia Ck; goldmines: Betsys Flat 1911 and 1913, Mountain Run 1891–94, 1905, 1917, 1931–32, Rose of Australia 1926; pop. 21 (1933).

The Sandspit (*Co. Clarence*) see Ulmarra.

The Scrub (*Co. Clive*) 29°08'S. 152°04'E., 10 km SE of Tenterfield; Meth. C. 1916, demolished 1941; sawmill (Riding Bros); school 1891–1918; telephone 1925; TX 1928; pop. 81 (1933).

The Settlement (*Co. Clarence*) see Grafton.

The Settlement (*Co. St Vincent*) see Milton.

The Shades (*Co. Wellington*) 33°03'S. 148°54'E., 6 km NE of Molong; school 1882–86 and 1906–27; Union C. b. by D. Ball, new one 1906; pop. 57 (1911), 37 (1933).

The Silver City (*Co. Yancowinna*) see Broken Hill.

The Slopes (*Co. Cook*) 33°32'S. 150°43'E., 4 km NE of Kurrajong; formerly Salis Flats, also known as Sallys Flats; farming and orchards; Angl. C. (St John the Evangelist) b. 1894 by Hind; bushfires 1895, 1936, 1944 (7 houses destroyed); PO 1909–67; telephone 1911; TX 1916; pop. 79 (1911), 63 (1933), 54 (1947), 247 (2011).

The Snowball (*Co. Wynyard*) see Snowball.

The Soakage (*Co. Yancowinna*) see Purnamoota.

The Springs (*Co. Bligh*) 32°05'S. 149°42'E., 29 km E. of Dunedoo.

The Springs (*Co. Georgiana*) 33°59'S. 149°18'E., 51 km S. of Blayney.

The Springs (*Co. Georgiana*) 34°16'S. 149°49'E., 38 km NE of Crookwell.

The Springs (*Co. Gordon*) 32°33'S. 148°35'E., 41 km NE of Peak Hill; pop. 50 (1961).

The Springs (*Co. Narromine*) 32°18'S. 148°28'E., 15 km W. of Dubbo.

The Springs (*Co. Raleigh*) 30°39'S. 152°38'E., 22 km W. of Bowraville.

The Springs (*Co. St Vincent*) 35°39'S. 149°45'E., 23 km S. of Braidwood.

The Stables (*Co. Georgiana*) 34°11'S. 149°34'E., 32 km N. of Crookwell.

The Swamp (*Co. Cook*) see Lawson.

The Terrace (*Co. Cook*) 33°34'S. 150°46'E., 3 km W. of Freemans Reach, on Hawkesbury R.

The Township (*Co. Bland*) see Wyalong.

The Troffs (*Co. Cunningham*) 32°50'S. 147°39'E., 12 km NW of Trundle; RS 1908, station b. by Reid and Castles, closed 1974; silo 1933; pop. 26 (1933).

The Vale (*Co. Kilfera*) 33°48'S. 143°47'E., 95 km N. of Balranald; telephone 1924; TX 1927.

The Valley (*Co. Cook*) see Valley Heights.

The Village (*Co. Bathurst*) 33°32'S. 149°20'E., 8 km E. of Blayney.

The Vines (*Co. St Vincent*) 35°12'S. 150°13'E., 24 km NW of Milton, on Vines Ck; bushfire 1949; sawmills: Nomchong's and White Cat (estab. 1950 by Whitlam Catts, burnt down 1957).

The Waterhole Flats (*Co. King*) see Waterhole Flats.

The Waterholes (*Co. Auckland*) see Wolumla.

The Well Corner (*Co. Gordon*) 32°53'S. 148°49'E., 24 km N. of Molong.

The Whiteman (*Co. Clarence*) 29°37'S. 152°53'E., 11 km NW of Grafton; bridge (Rogan Bridge) 1960, over Clarence R.; punt, to Seelands, ceased 1960, across Clarence R.; telephone 1924; TX 1928–52.

The Willows (*Co. Cooper*) 34°25'S. 146°43'E., 33 km NE of Leeton, on Mirrool Ck; pop. 47 (1933).

The Woolshed (*Co. Pottinger*) see Gunnedah.

Thiess Village (*Co. Selwyn*) 36°03'S. 148°17'E., 39 km SE of Tumbarumba, on Tooma R.; estab. by Thiess Bros Ltd as temporary construction camp for Snowy Mountains Hydro-Electric Scheme, defunct; PS; reservoir (Tooma); school 1959–61.

Third Angle Flat (*Co. King*) 34°00'S. 148°52'E., 24 km SE of Cowra, on Hovells Ck.

Third Creek (*Co. Argyle*) 34°31'S. 149°31'E., 9 km SE of Crookwell, on Third Ck; school 1881, new building b. 1900 by A. Allen, closed 1912.

Thirlmere (*Co. Camden*) 34°12'S. 150°34'E., 3 km NW of Tahmoor, on Matthews Ck; village gaz. 1889; orig. timber, then agric., orchards, poultry; Angl. C. (St Stephen's) 1888, renovated 1929 by Turner, new one 1991; bridge (Scroggies Bridge) over Cedar Ck; bushfires 1936, 1939, 2001; cemetery 1886; Estonian Bapt./Lutheran C. b. 1952 by Elmar Pilt, closed 1997; FB 1940; Jehovah's Witnesses C.; PO 1886; railway turntable, 105 ft (32 m); railway workshops; reservoir; Rom. Cath. C. (Queen of the Rosary) b. 1954 by S. McFarlane & Sons, d. by Fowell, Mansfield and Maclurcan, extended 1986, closed 1995, reused; RS (Redbank till 1886) 1885–1975, reused; sawmills: Chalker Bros, George J. Davis, S.W.J. Edwards, Herbert Hesse; school 1888, additions 1990; sewerage 1996; TX 1924–68; Unit. C. (orig. Presb.) 1936, reused; pop. 279 (1901), 477 (1911), 570 (1933), 689 (1947), 752 (1954), 789 (1961), 519 (1966), 547 (1971), 683 (1976), 914 (1981), 1,337 (1986), 1,586 (1991), 2,417 (1996), 2,753 (2001), 2,806 (2011).

Thirty Mile Gums (*Co. Sturt*) 34°13'S. 145°09'E., 43 km NE of Hay.

Thoko (*Co. Wellesley*) 36°39'S. 149°19'E., 31 km N. of Bombala, on Native Dog Ck; telephone 1923; TX 1928; pop. 50 (1911), 25 (1933).

Thommond (*Co. Bathurst*) 33°42'S. 149°08'E., 21 km SW of Blayney; school 1881, new one b. 1884 by J.T. Lodge, closed 1889.

Thompsons Creek (*Co. Georgiana*) 33°56'S. 149°36'E., 35 km SW of Oberon; Wes. Meth. C. 1883.

Thompsons Hole (*Co. Phillip*) 32°43'S. 150°12'E., 23 km NE of Rylstone, on Lee Ck.

Thompsons Ridge (*Co. Cook*) 33°35'S. 150°42'E., 2 km W. of North Richmond, on Redbank Ck; RS 1928–52.

Thoomee (*Co. Dowling*) 33°32'S. 146°01'E., 44 km E. of Hillston, on Lake Brewster; telephone 1926; TX 1928.

Thora (*Co. Raleigh*) 30°26'S. 152°46'E., 11 km SE of Dorrigo, on Bellinger R.; Never Never till 1912; settled 1860; orig. timber, maize, pigs, poultry, cattle, later dairying; floods 1950 and 2009; Meth. C. b. 1904 by A. Anderson; PO 1883; sawmill, man killed 1921; school (Never Never till 1912) 1898–1947; telephone 1909; TX 1923, automatic 1972; Union C.; pop. 231 (1911), 210 (1933), 80 (1947), 132 (1954), 128 (1961), 292 (2011).

Thorndale (*Co. Flinders*) 31°34'S. 146°54'E., 27 km W. of Nyngan; RS 1892, closed.

Thornes Bridge (*Co. Rous*) 28°46'S. 153°13'E., 9 km NW of Lismore; PO 1927; TX 1929.

Thornford (*Co. Argyle*) 34°53'S. 149°35'E., 18 km SW of Goulburn, on Wollogorang Ck; farming and grazing; Angl. C. (St Michael and All Angels') 1873, ruined; butter factory 1890; PO 1927; school (Kirkdale till 1889) 1882–1925; telephone 1914; TX 1946; Wes. Meth. C. 1884–1920, sold, dismantled and moved 1925 to Yarra; pop. 57 (1901), 20 (1933).

Thornthwaite (*Co. Brisbane*) 31°58'S. 150°43'E., 16 km NW of Scone; private village; farming and grazing; Angl. C. (St Stephen's) b. 1882 by Newcombe, replacement b. 1930 by H.R. Welsh, closed; cemetery; PO 1862–72; pop. 46 (1933).

Thornton (*Co. Northumberland*) 32°47'S. 151°39'E., 6 km SE of East Maitland; (incl. Berry Park, Brisbanefields, Chisholm, Parkwood Village); Woodford till 1888;

farming; Angl. C. 1922, new one (St Michael's) b. 1939 by Arthur Partridge-Wall, d. by John William Oldham and Robert Godwin Lees; brickworks: Thornton Fire & Building Brick Co. Ltd 1923, defunct, United Coke & Brick Co. Ltd, Longworth's Ashtonfield Colliery Brickworks (taken over by Waterloo Fire Brick Co. Ltd) 1913; bushfire 1952; FB 1968 (new station b. 2014, inundated 2015); flood 1893; hailstorm 2015; handle factory (W. Miller); house frame and truss factory (Hunter Frame & Truss); metal fabrication works (Hawl Fabrications Pty Ltd); Meth. C. 1922; PO 1883; 2 quarries; RS (Woodford till 1887) 1871, station relocated 1913; sawmill: Ellesmere and Longworth's Ashtonfield Colliery; school 1919 o. in building removed from Four Mile Creek by Arthur Partridge-Wall, new building 1928, additions 1985, additions by R.T. Parker Pty Ltd; sheep skin products factory (Frank Mortel); storm 2004; TX 1926–60; United Free Meth. C. b. 1893 by Somers, d. by Watson, enlarged 1899; pop. 276 (1911), 501 (1933), 507 (1947), 621 (1954), 730 (1961), 7,862 (2011).

Thorps Pinch (*Co. Roxburgh*) see Mount Lambie.

Thredbo (*Co. Wallace*) 36°30'S. 148°18'E., 29 km W. of Jindabyne, on Thredbo R.; (incl. Friday Flat Camp); estab. 1957, designed and laid out by E.M. Nicholls; winter snow resort 1950s+; bushfire 2003; Ecumenical C. 1996; FB (station b. 1982); foot-bridge over Thredbo R.; landslide (18 died) 1997; PO 1963; PS 1983; sewage works; TX (automatic) 1961; pop. 162 (1961), 506 (1971), 719 (1976), 1,059 (1981), 471 (2011).

Three Creeks (*Co. Camden*) see Robertson.

Three Mile Camp (*Co. Forbes*) 33°51'S. 148°01'E., 15 km NW of Grenfell; Prim. Meth. C.; quarry.

Three Mile Waterhole (*Co. Auckland*) see Wolumla.

Three Peaks (*Co. Cunningham*) see Melrose.

Three Rivers (*Co. Wellington*) 32°58'S. 148°55'E., 16 km N. of Molong; bridge; bushfire 1881; watch-house b. 1860 by Kennard and Snow.

Thrumster (*Co. Macquarie*) 31°28'S. 152°50'E., 8 km W. of Port Macquarie, on Partridge Ck; crematorium and lawn cemetery (Innes Gardens Memorial Park) 1984 (7,506+ plots).

Thubergal Lake (*Co. Beresford*) see Dartmoor.

Thuddungra (*Co. Monteagle*) 34°08'S. 148°06'E., 27 km NW of Young, on Bribbaree Ck; farming and grazing; Angl. C. (St Luke's) b. 1911–17, d. by Walter W. List, closed; cemetery 1892; mine (magnesite) 1931, acquired 1952 by Young Mining Co.; PO 1886–1978; Presb. C. (orig. Union) 1893; Rom. Cath. C. (St Patrick's) 1905, renovated 1929; school 1883, additions 1920 by W.S. Millard & Sons, closed 1971; telephone 1908; TX 1913, automatic 1978; pop. 131 (1901), 334 (1911), 209 (1921), 117 (1933), 238 (1947), 118 (1954), 207 (1961).

Thugga Plain (*Co. Goulburn*) 35°38'S. 147°14'E., 18 km E. of Culcairn, on Jerra Jerra Ck.

Thule (*Co. Cadell*) 35°40'S. 144°21'E., 21 km E. of Barham; TX (automatic); pop. 116 (1933), 95 (1947), 59 (1954), 85 (1961).

Thulloo (*Co. Gipps*) 33°39'S. 146°46'E., 50 km NW of West Wyalong; PO 1935–66; RS 1929–75, station removed 1984; telephone 1927; TX 1928; pop. 84 (1933), 77 (1947).

Thumb Creek (*Co. Raleigh*) 30°41'S. 152°36'E., 23 km W. of Bowraville, on Thumb Ck; farming; bushfire 1951; 2 mines (antimony); PO 1927–70; sawmill (G. Ballard), burnt down 1951; school 1957–60; telephone 1924; TX; pop. 74 (1933), 89 (1947), 74 (1954).

Thurgoona (*Co. Goulburn*) 36°02'S. 147°00'E., 9 km NE of Albury, on Eight Mile Ck; (incl. St Hilaire); farming, grazing, vineyards; Angl. C. 1860, demolished, new one (St John's) b. 1873 by A. Jackson; Apostolic C. (Go) 2000; FB 1910; metal fabrication works (D.T.D. Engineering Pty Ltd) 1980; PO 1874–1961; Rom. Cath. C. (Immaculate Heart of Mary) b. 2002 by Riverina Rammed Earth Constructions; school 1862, new one b. 1868 by R. Owen, additions 1895 by William Haslem, repairs 1915 by P. Phillips, additions 1952 and 1987, major upgrade 1996; telephone 1896; TX 1914–59; univ. (Charles Sturt) 1997, additions 2000; pop. 72 (1901), 218 (1911), 240 (1933), 297 (1947), 214 (1954), 4,855 (2006), 6,160 (2011).

Thurlow (*Co. Argyle*) 34°43'S. 149°37'E., 10 km NW of Goulburn; cemetery; Prim. Meth. C. b. 1875 by Everett Bros and John Lansdown, closed 1949.

Thurrowa (*Co. Urana*) 35°09'S. 145°56'E., 29 km NE of Jerilderie, on Yanko Ck; village gaz. 1867, but never developed.

Thurungle (*Co. Forbes*) 33°37'S. 148°01'E., 27 km S. of Forbes.

Thyra (*Co. Cadell*) 35°51'S. 144°38'E., 25 km W. of Mathoura; village gaz. 1928; PO 1904; rifle range 1907; RS (Victorian railway); school (Bunaloo till 1927, Bunaloo East till 1935, then Bunnaloo East till 1978) 1880–93, 1904–46, 1959–85; pop. 128 (1933), 68 (1947), 59 (1954).

Tia (*Co. Vernon*) 31°13'S. 151°48'E., 31 km SE of Walcha, on Tia R.; formerly goldmining, then farming and grazing; cemetery; PO 1902; school (Tia Common till 1936) 1912–66; TX 1924–67; Union C. b. 1920 by Waller & Son; pop. 121 (1901), 197 (1911), 180 (1933), 138 (1947), 173 (1954), 132 (1961), 378 (2006).

Tia (*Co. Vernon*) see also Brackendale.

Tia Common (*Co. Vernon*) see Tia.

Tianjara (*Co. St Vincent*) 35°07'S. 150°20'E., 25 km N. of Milton; town gaz. 1842, laid out 1883, never developed; agric.; airfield.

Tibbereena (*Co. White*) 30°22'S. 149°46'E., 4 km S. of Narrabri; sheep and wheat; FB (station b. 2012); boiling-down and freezing works (Narrabri Refigerating, Preserving & Boiling-down Co. Ltd) 1895, company wound up 1904, man killed 1906, works dismantled and rebuilt 1918, burnt down 1924; PO 1919–40; RS 1909–55; telephone 1926; TX 1928; pop. 87 (1911), 45 (1933).

Tibbuc (*Co. Hawes*) 31°49'S. 151°54'E., 21 km N. of Gloucester, on Manning R.; FB; telephone 1917; TX 1927.

Tibeaudo (*Co. Dowling*) 33°28'S. 146°34'E., 25 km SE of Lake Cargelligo; school 1934–48.

Tibooburra (*Co. Tongowoko*) 29°26'S. 142°01'E., 270 km NW of Wilcannia; orig. The Granite, Granite Rush and Granite Diggings; village gaz. 1886, surveyed 1887; formerly gold (disc. 1881), then wool; airfield 1940; airport (5 km E.); Angl. C. (St Barnabas's); brewery (Wittabrinna, Michael Nolan and David Scott) 1889; cemetery (140 burials 1882+) 1888; CH 1888, additions 1901 by Michael Kenna Power, d. by Walter Liberty Vernon, reused; cordial factory (James Blair); cyclone 1941; diphtheria 1890; dust storms 1941 and 1944; electricity 1977; fire 1895; floods 1974 and 1976; hospital 1901, additions 1965 and 1973; mines: Easter Monday, Granite Diggings, Tipperary Gully; PO 1881, new one b. 1901 by Michael Kenna Power; PS 1888, additions 1958, additions and alterations 1973; school 1888; telegraph 1890; telephone 1917; TX 1923; Unit. C. (orig. Church of the Corner); water reticulation 1961, filtration plant 1963; pop. 296 (1891), 222 (1901), 172 (1911), 240 (1922), 210 (1933), 135 (1947), 138 (1954), 154 (1961), 211 (1976), *c.*100 (1987), 214 (1996), 161 (2006), 262 (2011).

Tichborne (*Co. Ashburnham*) 33°14'S. 148°07'E., 11 km S. of Parkes; Martin till 1896; village gaz. 1879 as Martin; gold (disc. 1875), kaolin 1877–1907, 1958–59, 1968–71, farming; Angl. C. (St Paul's) 1912–71, sold to Rusden, sold 1979 to Quinlan, demolished; bridge b. 1880 by R. Bishop; bushfire 1926; dust storm 1930; fire 1920; flood 1950; Meth. C. 1905; mines: Blue Reef *c.*1900, Growler's, Lady Jersey 1891, McGuiggan's 1874–76, McMillan's *c.*1900 and 1940, Scrub (Spicer & Co.) *c.*1900, Scrubby Plains alluvial workings 1876–86, Staples' *c.*1900, Wapping Butcher 1874–79; PO 1875–1982; RS 1893, station b. by Gerald Dalton Fetherston and Felix Edward Barbat, closed 1974; school (Brolgar till 1885, then Brolgan till 1900) 1881, repairs 1885 by William Hewson and J. Peterson, repairs 1908 by Lewis Myers, new school b. 1917 by J.M. Job, closed 1970, building moved to Middleton (Parkes), burnt down 1977; silo 1930; telephone 1907; TX 1950–65; pop. 162

(1901), 343 (1911), 219 (1933), 161 (1947), 140 (1954), 135 (1961), 232 (2006).

Tickerabil (*Co. Gloucester*) 32°28'S. 152°21'E., 15 km SE of Bulahdelah, on Myall Lake.

Tickhole (*Co. Northumberland*) see Kotara.

Tighes Hill (*Co. Northumberland*) 32°54'S. 151°45'E., 4 km NW of Newcastle, on Throsby Ck; formerly Bingle Hill; Angl. C. (All Saints') 1924; bridge (Graham Bridge) 1916 to Maryville, reinforced concrete one b. 1938 by Charles Hardy Contracting Co. Ltd, over Throsby Ck; coal loader (Port Waratah); colliery (Ferndale) o. 1877 by Bingle, White & Co., underground collapse 1886, flooded, closed 1886, defunct; Croatian Cath. C. (St Joseph's), in reused building; FB 1888, new one 1916, demolished; fibrous plaster works (J.A. Crockett), fire 1946; flood 2016; 2 foot-bridges (incl. one to Islington) over Throsby Ck; fruit and meat cannery (William Matthews) 1888; hosiery factory (Lustre Hosiery Pty Ltd); lock-up b. 1882 by M. Parkhill; PO 1872, new one b. 1937 by R.A. Keevers, closed 1997, sold and reused; Prim. Meth. C. 1871, rebuilt 1899 by W.P. Somers, d. by George Sanders & Son, reused; PS 1878, renovations and repairs 1936 by Bailey and Birrell; Rom. Cath. C. (Immaculate Conception) b. 1900 by George Taylor, extensions 1906, demolished, new one (Immaculate Heart of Mary) 1955 on new site, d. by Arthur G. Benfield and Peter Gannon; Salv. Army C., renovations 1922; school 1878, additions 1892 by John Ash & Sons; sewage pumping station 1929; smelter (copper, gold, silver) 1907–11; tannery (Richard Bryant) 1886; TC (Newcastle), E Block b. 1936–38 by Richard Seed, d. by Edward Henry Rembert, C Block b. 1938–40 by Thomas C. Whittle, d. by Cobden Parkes, D Block b. 1939–65, L Block 1952, demolished 2013, B Block 1959, refurbished 2012, F Block 1959, N Block and O Block 1959, P Block 1963, G Block 1967, J Block b. 1984 by Citra Constructions Ltd, Q Block 1984, A Block 1985, H Block 1986, became Hunter Institute of Technology, Newcastle Campus, in 1992, S. Block 1993, M Block 1997; telephone 1890; tramway (steam) to Newcastle 1894, electrified 1923, closed 1948; Unit. C. (orig. Meth.) b. 1921 by D. M'Naughton & Son, d. by Alfred Gambier Newman, re-roofed and renovated 1946, closed, sold 2012, reused 2014; univ. college (at old technical college) 1951, became univ. (Newcastle) in 1965 and moved to Callaghan 1966–71; works (BOC Gases); pop. 1,200+ (1903), 1,605 (1911), 1,483 (2006), 1,615 (2011).

Tikitere (*Co. Stapylton*) 29°02'S. 150°20'E., 47 km S. of Boggabilla; RS 1934–75.

Tikkara (*Co. Flinders*) 31°35'S. 147°05'E., 10 km W. of Nyngan; RS (Coreen till 1929) 1896–1953.

Tilbaroo Crossing (*Co. Macquarie*) 31°32'S. 152°23'E., 33 km W. of Wauchope, on Toms Ck.

Tilba Tilba (*Co. Dampier*) 36°19'S. 150°04'E., 10 km N. of Bermagui, on Tilba Tilba Ck; settled 1869 by Henry Jefferson Bate, estab. by Richard Mossop Bate, bypassed by highway 1990; goldmining till 1906, fishing, farming, fruit, maize, dairying 1830s–1970s (declined in 1930s), now tourism; Angl. C. b. 1882 by A. Mayo, new one on new site (Holy Trinity) 1896, and graveyard (5 burials 1883–98); bushfires 1919 and 1952 (12 houses destroyed); cheese factories: Mountain View (estab. by Richard Mossop Bate) 1891–1951 and Tilba Tilba Co-op. Cheese Co. Ltd (new one 1926–72, disused); dam (for hydro-electricity generation) 1932; diphtheria (woman died) 1905; fires 1908 and 1910; hydro-electricity supplied 1932 by Henry John Bate, scheme enlarged 1940, closed 1952; measles epidemic 1930; PO 1873–1977; telegraph office 1895; telephone 1888; TX 1914, automatic 1969; water supply estab. 1910 by Henry John Bate; pop. 130 (1901), 132 (1911), 154 (1921), 122 (1933), 87 (1947), 95 (1954), 71 (1961), 276 (2006).

Tilba Tilba (*Co. Dampier*) see also Central Tilba.

Tilbuster (*Co. Sandon*) 30°28'S. 151°41'E., 5 km N. of Armidale; mining; Angl. C. (St Mark's)

1925; butter factory (Nicholas Bros) 1892; goldmine (Great Britain); school 1887–1969; silver-lead mines: Endeavour and Mary Ann; TX (automatic); pop. 96 (1901), 164 (1911), 185 (1933), 186 (1947), 165 (1954), 116 (1961).

Tillegra (*Co. Durham*) 32°19'S. 151°42'E., 11 km NW of Dungog, on Williams R.; dairying; bridge (Coningalla Bridge) b. 1882 by Thomas Bell and J.B. Collerson, over Williams R.

Tillimby (*Co. Durham*) 32°35'S. 151°37'E., 18 km N. of Maitland, on Paterson R.; subdivided 1924; bushfire 1905; cemetery, closed 1843; church (Ranters' Chapel); floods 1843, 1861, 1864, 1867, 1875; school 1958–62.

Tillsbury (*Co. Westmoreland*) 33°50'S. 149°44'E., 18 km SW of Oberon, on Native Dog Ck.

Tilpa (*Co. Killara*) 30°56'S. 144°25'E., 121 km NE of Wilcannia, on Darling R.; grazing; airfield; bridge 1963 over Darling R.; bushfires 1974–75, 1976–77, 1983; cemetery; cyclone 1907; droughts 1927 and 1965; electricity 1988; floods 1950, 1955, 1956, 1971, 1974, 1976; PO 1883, new one b. 1896 by John B. Guillier, damaged 1907, closed 1988; PS 1891, new one b. 1898, closed 1936, reused till 1951, new one (incl. lock-up); punt (manual) across Darling R.; school 1920 b. by J.H. Cathcart, closed 1935; storms 1929, 1936, 1976; telegraph 1883, new office b. 1896 by John B. Guillier; TX 1915; pop. 81 (1901), 85 (1911), 64 (1933), 32 (1954), 182 (1961), 160 (2006).

Til Til (*Co. Kilfera*) 33°41'S. 143°55'E., 125 km NW of Hay; pop. 76 (1901), 24 (1933).

Timbarra (*Co. Clive*) 29°01'S. 152°11'E., 17 km E. of Tenterfield; Tableland till 1867; thrived 1861; gold (disc. 1858, gold rush 1858–59) and timber; cemetery; CH (incl. lock-up) b. 1862 by Anthony Lindall; PO 1859; PS, closed 1872; pop. 51 (1911).

Timbarra (*Co. Drake*) see Drake.

Timber Top (*Co. Fitzroy*) 30°06'S. 152°55'E., 27 km W. of Woolgoolga; RS 1924–72.

Timbery Range (*Co. Wellesley*) 36°36'S. 149°04'E., 37 km NW of Bombala; grazing; PO 1887–1942; school 1887–92; TX 1937; pop. 35 (1933), 57 (1947).

Timbillica (*Co. Auckland*) 37°22'S. 149°42'E., 38 km SW of Eden; farming; PO 1879–1930; telephone 1921.

Timbrebongie (*Co. Narromine*) 32°07'S. 148°15'E., 12 km N. of Narromine, on Macquarie R.; formerly Timbriebungie; village gaz. 1878; grazing, farming, orchards; FB; PO 1875–1931; Presb. C. o. 1888 in former Rom. Cath. C., closed, moved 1910 to Buddah; PS 1877; Rom. Cath. C. 1881; school (Timbribungie till 1892) 1880–93 and 1905–19; pop. 73 (1901), 103 (1911), 27 (1933).

Timbrebongie Falls (*Co. Ewenmar*) 32°08'S. 148°16'E., 12 km N. of Narromine, on Macquarie R.

Timbribungie (*Co. Narromine*) see Timbrebongie.

Timbriebungie (*Co. Narromine*) see Timbrebongie.

Timbumburi (*Co. Parry*) 31°13'S. 150°55'E., 13 km S. of Tamworth; school 1917, additions 1919 by J.H. Ford, additions 1969, 1982, 1993; TX (automatic); pop. 57 (1933), 389 (2011).

Timmsvale (*Co. Fitzroy*) 30°13'S. 152°52'E., 20 km NE of Dorrigo, on Little Nymboida R.; PO 1929–71; quarry; sawmill and powerhouse (Thomas B. Timms) 1923, new one 1929, burnt down 1933, rebuilt, fires 1953 and 1954; school 1941 b. by Thomas B. Timms, closed 1970; TX 1936–67; pop. 152 (1933), 130 (1947), 132 (1954), 91 (1961).

Timor (*Co. Brisbane*) 31°46'S. 151°04'E., 23 km E. of Murrurundi, on Isis R.; agric. and grazing; Angl. C. (St Peter's) 1884, renovated and restored 1983, closed, deconsecrated 2015, sold 2016; earth tremor 2014; PO 1875–1962; school 1880–90 and 1899–1911; telephone 1914; TX 1915, automatic 1954; pop. 209 (1911), 120 (1933), 75 (1947), 131 (1954), 140 (1961).

Tinapagee (*Co. Thoulcanna*) 29°26'S. 144°23'E., 164 km NW of Bourke; pop. 54 (1933).

Tindarey (*Co. Yanda*) 31°07'S. 145°50'E., 41 km N. of Cobar; pop. 104 (2006).

Tinda Tank (*Co. Cunningham*) 32°37'S. 146°52'E., 57 km NW Condobolin; farming and grazing; cemetery (13 burials, incl. 5 graves 1896+); PO 1898–1949; telephone 1916; TX 1924; pop. 34 (1933).

Tinderry (*Co. Beresford*) 35°42'S. 149°19'E., 39 km S. of Queanbeyan; goldmining (reef); pop. 10 (1866), 24 (1933).

Tingha (*Co. Hardinge*) 29°58'S. 151°13'E., 22 km SE of Inverell, on Copes Ck; Armidale Crossing till 1872; surveyed 1870; tin (disc. 1870, rush 1872, production peaked 1883) and grazing; airfield (4 km E.); Angl. C. (St Andrew's) b. 1888 by Wright, d. by John Horbury Hunt; bridges: Eastern Bridge 1987 over Copes Ck, Northern Bridge (timber beam 1883, destroyed 1955, replaced 1956 in concrete, 220 ft or 67.1 m, over Copes Ck), Eddie Walker Bridge over Darbys Ck; cemetery; CH 1874, additions 1884 by J. Anderson, repairs 1896 by Thomas and Beavan; 3 Chinese joss houses (incl. one b. 1883); clock tower 1950; cordial and condiment factory (John and E. Parker); dengue fever 1926; engineering works (W. Fulton); FB 1953; fires 1913 and 1926; floods 1916, 1954, 1955; gale 1898; hospital (cottage) b. 1906–9; measles epidemic 1940; 7 mines (incl. Beckett's and Britannia Tin Mining Co. 1871); police barracks b. 1891 by William Wilson; PO 1872, new one b. 1911 by Thomas A. Bray; pound (stock) 1877; Rom. Cath. C. 1880, closed and reused, new one (St Francis of Assisi) b. 1952 by E.J. Walker; Salv. Army C. 1889; school 1874, new one b. 1882 by J. Anderson, repairs 1895 by James M'Kay, additions 1929 by E.C. Walker, additions 1963 and 1966; telegraph 1879, new office b. 1911 by Thomas A. Bray; TX 1910; typhoid 1903, 1908, 1951; water supply augmentation 1993; Wes. Meth. C. 1887; pop. 2,424 (1881), *c.*2,500 (1887), 1,167 (1891), 727 (1901), 1,938 (1911), 1,469 (1933), 1,534 (1947), 904 (1954), 1,063 (1961), 272 (1966), 258 (1971), 868 (1976), 886 (1981), 837 (1986), 831 (1991), 732 (1996), 707 (2001), 713 (2006), 527 (2011).

Tingira Heights (*Co. Northumberland*) see Eleebana.

Tingiringi (*Co. Wellesley*) 36°54'S. 148°45'E., 42 km W. of Bombala, on Tinga Ringee Ck; grazing; PO 1899–1942; telephone 1925; TX 1929; pop. 37 (1933).

Tin Mine (*Co. Selwyn*) 36°42'S. 148°15'E., 22 km S. of Thredbo, on Tin Mine Ck.

Tin Mines (*Co. Bourke*) see Yithan.

Tin Mines (*Co. Goulburn*) 35°51'S. 147°29'E., 21 km SE of Holbrook.

Tiona (*Co. Gloucester*) 32°18'S. 152°31'E., 14 km S. of Forster, on Tasman Sea.

Tinonee (*Co. Gloucester*) 31°56'S. 152°25'E., 5 km SW of Taree, on Manning R.; orig. The Old Wharf; site reserved 1850, laid out 1853 by Henry Carmichael, village gaz. 1854, first lots sold 1855, declined 1880+, bypassed 1913 by railway; former river port, shipbuilding, maize, millet, dairying, timber; Angl. C. b. 1870 by G. Rooney, closed 1905 and bought by J. Ryan, new one (St Luke's) b. 1905 by Stewart Adolphus Levick, d. by E.H. Wright, vestry added 1916, extended 1984 by Filby; broom factories: G. Beattie & Son, Joseph E. Chapman (Nonpareil) 1897, enlarged 1898, damaged 1907, Manning River Broom Co. 1895, Montague Williams 1942, closed, sold and reused; cemetery (572 graves 1875+) 1867, incl. columbarium 2006; CH (incl. lock-up) b. 1898 by Rudolph George Ochs, d. by Walter Liberty Vernon, closed 1936, sold and reused; droughts 1923, 1927, 1928, 1929; FB; floods 1866, 1870, 1929; flour mill b. 1854 by Morgan Poole, inundated 1866, reused as sugar mill 1868–71, bought 1876 by J. McBeath and converted for flour milling and sawmilling, closed 1905; Free Presb. C. (John Knox) 1880, closed, sold and reused; PO 1855, new one b. 1887 by James Levick, additions 1899 by Henry Wilson Alcorn, burnt down 1938; PS b. 1898 by Rudolph George Ochs, d. by Walter Liberty Vernon, closed 1936, sold and reused; punt b. 1879 by D. M'Lachlan, new one 1900, to cross Manning R.; sawmills: J. Bullock (moved 1945 to Taree), Federal (estab. 1904 by Hector Gollan, burnt down 1908, rebuilt 1909, acquired 1938 by

Eriksson Bros), J. McBeath, William Smith and William Basham 1887 (destroyed 1907); school 1859, repairs 1884 by R. Howell, new building b. 1895 by Rudolph George Ochs, additions 1900 also by Ochs, additions 1991 and 2010; sewerage augmentation 1987; shipyard (Hector Gollan); storm 1907; sugar mill (Morgan Poole) 1868–71, later reverted to a flour mill, then reused as a sawmill; telegraph 1880, new office b. 1887 by James Levick; TX (automatic) 1952; Unit. C. (removed from Oxley Island) re-erected 1978, closed 2006, sold and reused; Wes. Meth. C. b. 1872 by John Watson, renovated 1898 by J.E. Boan, repairs 1907; wharves: one b. 1876 by Rudolph George Ochs, replaced, and one b. 1900 by T. Taylor for Joseph E. Chapman; pop. 74 (1856), 118 (1861), 148 (1871), *c.*300 (1891), 279 (1901), 354 (1911), *c.*300 (1924), 236 (1933), 289 (1947), 323 (1954), 276 (1961), 276 (1976), 379 (1981), 490 (1986), 579 (1991), 664 (1996), 698 (2001), 730 (2011).

Tinpot (*Co. Dampier*) 36°13'S. 149°52'E., 23 km W. of Narooma, on Tuross R.; FB (station b. 2015).

Tintenbar (*Co. Rous*) 28°48'S. 153°31'E., 8 km W. of Lennox Head on Emigrant Ck; settled *c.*1851, village gaz. 1866; orig. timber then opals (disc. 1901 by Munro, rush 1919–20), silica, sugar-cane, dairying, beef, hort.; Angl. C. (Christ) 1897; cemetery 1886; creamery b. 1897 by David and William Gillies; cyclonic storm 1940; fire 1930; mine (kaolin) estab. by Charles Ainsworth; PO 1881–1971; quarry; Rom. Cath. C. (St Matthias's) 1906, rebuilding 1940 d. by Austin McKay; schools: Tintenbar 1884, new one b. 1908, additions 1958, closed 1988 and Teven-Tintenbar 1988, re-roofed 2013; sugar mill (Toohey Bros); telegraph 1890; TX 1924, automatic 1954; water reticulation 1969; pop. 118 (1861), 148 (1871), 266 (1881), 169 (1891), 88 (1901), 492 (1911), 281 (1933), 189 (1947), 201 (1954), 160 (1961), 485 (2001), 472 (2011).

Tintinhull (*Co. Inglis*) 31°05'S. 151°00'E., 8 km E. of Tamworth; farming; PO 1880–1953; RS 1885–1961; school 1882, new buildings b. 1883 by Davies and Chaffey; telephone 1952; pop. 84 (1901), 90 (1911), 110 (1933), 80 (1947), 90 (1954), 169 (1961), 406 (2011).

Tiona (*Co. Gloucester*) 32°18'S. 152°31'E., 14 km S. of Forster, on Tasman Sea.

Tipperary (*Co. Gloucester*) 32°04'S. 152°10'E., 21 km E. of Gloucester; pop. 62 (1933), 83 (1947), 60 (1954).

Tipperary (*Co. Monteagle*) 34°16'S. 148°19'E., 5 km N. of Young; school (Tipperary Gully till *c.*1920) 1871–1934; pop. 64 (1901).

Tipperary Flat (*Co. Monteagle*) 34°16'S. 148°18'E., 5 km N. of Young; farming and orchards.

Tipperary Gully (*Co. Monteagle*) see Tipperary.

Tippereenah (*Co. Nandewar*) see Stafford.

Tipps Flat (*Co. Wellesley*) 36°59'S. 149°15'E., 7 km S. of Bombala.

Tiri (*Co. Macquarie*) 31°49'S. 152°04'E., 23 km N. of Gloucester; pop. 24 (1933).

Tirranna (*Co. Argyle*) see Tirrannaville.

Tirrannaville (*Co. Argyle*) 34°49'S. 149°41'E., 8 km SW of Goulburn, on Mulwaree R.; Terranna till 1926; gold and iron; Angl. C. (St Andrew's) 1860, closed and disused; cemetery; flood 1860; flour mill (horse powered) estab. by Andrew Gibson; PO 1927–60; quarry (A.I. & S. Co. Ltd) 1941–42 and 1945; RS 1906–41; school (Tirranna) 1869, new one b. 1889 by James Searle, closed 1906, reopened 1957; storm 1933; telephone 1960; pop. 93 (1901), 66 (1911), 49 (1933), 59 (1947).

Tirrannia Creek (*Co. Rous*) see Blakebrook.

Tirrikiba (*Co. Nothumberland*) see Mayfield.

Titania (*Co. Westmoreland*) 33°43'S. 149°55'E., 5 km E. of Oberon; Fish River Creek till 1904; farming; PO 1866–1930; school (Fish River Creek till 1904) 1868–1906; pop. 142 (1901), 21 (1933).

Titwood (*Co. Northumberland*) 33°20'S. 151°25'E., 4 km NW of Berkeley Vale, on Ourimbah Ck.

Tiverton (*Co. Harden*) 34°29'S. 148°26'E., 22 km SE of Young; farming; pop. 81 (1933).

Tiverton (*Co. Harden*) see also Currawong.

Tnononga (*Co. Waradgery*) 34°26'S. 145°12'E., 35 km E. of Hay; RS (orig. Alson's Siding) 1883, closed.

Tobermory (*Co. Clarke*) 30°11'S. 152°00'E., 32 km E. of Guyra, on Nowlands Ck; PO, closed 1971; telephone 1915; TX 1916.

Tobins Camp (*Co. Hawes*) 31°24'S. 152°06'E., 60 km W. of Wauchope; PO, closed 1930; PS 1929–30.

Tocal (*Co. Northumberland*) 32°38'S. 151°35'E., 12 km N. of Maitland; horses; agric. college (C.B. Alexander) b. 1963–65 d. by Philip Cox and Ian McKay, acquired 1970 by govt, additions 1974; bridges: first one b. 1849 by C.D. Haylock and L.G. Clements Bridge 1967; bushfire 1905; floods 1864, 1904, 2015; military barracks 1824.

Tocumwal (*Co. Denison*) 35°49'S. 145°34'E., 19 km S. of Finley, on Murray R.; laid out 1861 by Philip Francis Adams, village gaz. 1862, designated as chief town of the county; orig. river port and border customs depot, then sheep, cattle, pigs, barley, wheat, rice, grapes, citrus fruit; agric. implement works (T. Boyle); airfield (McIntyre) b. 1942 by Aust. Allied Works Council for United States Army Air Corps, taken over by RAAF later that year and used till 1960; ammunition depot (World War II); Angl. C. (St Alban's) b. 1900 by L. Jensen & Co.; brick-kiln 1886; brickworks: Tocuwal Brick & Trading Co. and Waterloo Brick & Tile Works; bridge (iron and steel, with lift span) b. 1893–95 by J. and W. Farquahson, 334 ft (101.8 m), modification for rail traffic fabricated 1907 by Mort's Dock & Engineering Co. Ltd, d. by Henry Harvey Dare and J.W. Roberts, new one (Edward Hillson Bridge) b. 1987 by Electric Power Transmission Pty Ltd, 696 ft (212 m), new one 2007, over Murray R.; bushfire 1990; cemetery (51 graves), incl. lawn cemetery; CH (incl. lock-up) b. 1893 by Fahey and Ross, but not used till 1898; container terminal (Grays); cordial factories: F. Beasley 1892, Darby Bros, Hartshorne Bros 1947 (sold 1949 to Platt and Reschke, sold 1950 to A.A. Loxton); customs-house; dust storm 1997; earth tremor 1921; engineering works estab. 1950 by D. Bate; FB (station b. 1910, new one 1952, extended and renovated 2002); fibrous plaster works; fire 1927; floods 1917, 1931, 1955, 1975, 2010; flour mills: Blake's 1897, Thye's, Wise Bros Pty Ltd 1913 (silo b. by State Monier Pipe Co., d. by Sir John Monash, fire 1945, closed 1971); hailstorm 1993; hospital 1948, fire 1950, second one 1956, third one 1992, additions 1993, fourth one 1994; irrigation channel b. 1896 by McFarlane Bros; levee 1906, strengthened 1908, raised 1983; lucerne mill (N.D. Cowan) 1947; mouse plague 1917; PO 1868, new one b. 1901 by E.A. Roe; pound (stock), relocated 1878; powerhouse 1924, demolished; Presb. C. (St David's) b. 1912 by Bell and Kidd, demolished; PS 1893, renovated 1994; pump factory (Batescrew) 1951; punt (Edward Hillson) 1872, across Murray R.; quarry (stone); railway turntable (William Sellers & Co.) 1941, 60 ft (18.3 m), removed from Mount Victoria, closed; reservoir (concrete tower) 65,000 gal. (295.5 kl); Rom. Cath. C. (St Peter's) b. 1890 by William Squires, jun.; RS 1914–87; sale-yards; sawmills: Boyle Bros and Hartshorne & Co.; school 1881, new buildings b. 1885 by J. Matthews, additions 1960; sewerage 1967; silo; telegraph (at railway station) 1937–67; TX 1910, automatic 1982; Unit. C. (orig. Wes. Meth.) b. 1890 by William Squires, jun.; water supply 1924, new chlorination plant 1979, new filtration plant 1983; wool-scour (George Frederick Sugden) 1869; pop. *c.*350 (1880), 325 (1891), 417 (1901), 788 (1911), 984 (1933), *c.*1,050 (1941), 1,341 (1947), 1,389 (1954), 1,288 (1961), 1,268 (1966), 1,132 (1971), 1,131 (1976), 1,174 (1981), 1,273 (1986), 1,587 (1991), 1,453 (1996), 1,529 (2001), 1,860 (2006), 2,154 (2011).

Toganmain (*Co. Boyd*) 34°28'S. 145°36'E., 38 km W. of Darlington Point, on Murrumbidgee R.; school 1885–89; wool-scour.

Togar (*Co. Brisbane*) 32°07'S. 150°52'E., 6 km N. of Aberdeen.

Togganoggera (*Co. Murray*) 35°39'S. 149°36'E., 29 km SW of Braidwood, on Shoalhaven R.;

grazing; airfield; quarry; telephone 1918; TX 1928–65; pop. 49 (1933).

Tolarno (*Co. Livingstone*) see Gum Lake.

Tolarno (*Co. Perry*) 32°47'S. 142°24'E., 43 km S. of Menindee, on Darling R.; pop. 77 (1911).

Tolland (*Co. Wynyard*) see Wagga Wagga.

Toll Bar Creek (*Co. Beresford*) 36°12'S. 149°13'E., 10 km NE of Cooma; school 1879–96.

Tollendool (*Co. Mitchell*) 35°15'S. 146°54'E., 17 km E. of Lockhart.

Tolwong (*Co. St Vincent*) 34°51'S. 150°08'E., 26 km SW of Bundanoon, on Tallangla Ck; mining (copper-silver-lead-arsenic lode disc. 1904 by John Sivewright); mine (Tolwong Mining Co.) 1907–12; PO 1910–11; smelters 1910–12.

Tomago (*Co. Gloucester*) 32°50'S. 151°44'E., 8 km S. of Raymond Terrace, on Hunter R.; estate subvivided 1939; formerly coalmining, then farming, later smelting; Angl. C. (St Barnabas's) b. 1924 by C.H. Boots & Sons; anti-aircraft battery, ammunition magazines and command post (World War II); bridge (lift span) to Hexham b. 1945–52 over Hunter R.; bus body factory (Volgren Aust. Pty Ltd) 2010–12; bushfires 1914 and 2018; cable factory (Midal Cables International Pty Ltd) 2014; coalmine (estab. by Robert Gordon) 1855–1864, reopened 1888, closed, reopened 1923; crematorium (Crooks and Pettigrew); gaol (periodic detention centre) 1974, additions 1996; house frame and truss factory (SBS Newcastle Pty Ltd); PO 1862–1931; rayon mill (Courtaulds Hilton Ltd) b. 1952 by F.H. Compton & Sons, d. by Percy James Gordon and J. Aubrey Kerr, closed 1976, site sold 1980 for smelter; school 1849–1926 and 1955–85; shipyards (incl. Carrington Slipways Pty Ltd); smelter (Tomago Aluminium Co. Pty Ltd) b. 1981–83, o. 1984; steel fabrication works (Allco Engineering); TX (automatic); Unit. C. (orig. Wes. Meth.) 1861, d. by Maria Windeyer and Eliza Camfield, renovated 1879, rededicated 1944 as Windeyer Memorial, restoration 1951, given to National Trust 1995, restoration 1997 by Gunter Vergens, d. by Nina Walmsley; waterworks (sandbeds) 1941, treatment plants 1959 and 1965; wharves 1874 and 1897; pop. 137 (1861), 133 (1901), 101 (1911), 102 (1933), 99 (1947), 229 (1954), 228 (1961), 271 (2011).

Tomago (*Co. St Vincent*) see Tomakin.

Tomakin (*Co. St Vincent*) 35°49'S. 150°11'E., 6 km SW of Malua Bay, on Tomaga R.; (incl. Barlings Beach); estab. *c.*1876, Tomago till 1880, later known as Sunpatch till 1978; shipbuilding and sawmilling in 1880s, then farming and dairying, now fishing; airfield; Angl. C. (St Peter's); bridge 1974, to Mossy Point, over Tomaga R.; bushfires 1915 and 1994; cemetery; cheese factory 1922; FB; marina; PO 1880–87; sawmills: Curtis and Kelsie 1883, Albert and Edward Jennings 1879 (man killed 1885), Sebbens & Co., Allen Taylor & Co. Ltd, Tomakin Sawmills Ltd, fire 1914; sewerage 1984; shipyard (Jennings Bros); telephone 1922; pop. 90 (1901), 30 (1933), 308 (1981), 473 (1986), 634 (1991), 753 (1996), 761 (2001), 793 (2006), 888 (2011).

Tomalla (*Co. Hawes*) 31°49'S. 151°30'E., 47 km NW of Gloucester; grazing; PO 1927–59; telephone 1913; TX 1916–59; pop. 56 (1933), 151 (2006).

Tomalpin (*Co. Northumberland*) 32°51'S. 151°28'E., 3 km SW of Kurri Kurri; village gaz. 1918; pop. 69 (1933), 58 (1947).

Tomanbil (*Co. Forbes*) 33°29'S. 148°15'E., 13 km SW of Eugowra, on Lachlan R.; PO 1898–1908.

Tomaree (*Co. Gloucester*) see Salamander Bay.

Tomaree Head (*Co. Gloucester*) see Shoal Bay.

Tombong (*Co. Wellesley*) 36°54'S. 148°56'E., 27 km W. of Bombala, on Tombong Ck; known as Wright's 1885–1911; grazing; cemetery; PO 1927–66; telephone 1912; TX 1923; pop. 93 (1901), 53 (1933).

Tomboye (*Co. St Vincent*) 35°15'S. 149°58'E., 26 km NE of Braidwood, on Ningee Nimble Ck; grazing; PO 1914–62; telephone 1912; TX 1917; pop. 51 (1911), 36 (1933), 54 (1947).

Tomerong (*Co. St Vincent*) 35°03'S. 150°35'E., 8 km W. of Huskisson, on Tomerong Ck; first land sold 1855; wheat till 1866, then sawmilling 1870s+, now cattle and apiculture; axe handle factory (Bradney Bros) 1920, burnt down 1924; bushfires 1868, 1869, 1884, 1894, 1900, 1902, 1909, 1919, 1926, 1929, 1939, 1952, 1956, 1965, 1968, 1971, 1980 (2 died), 2001; cemetery 1889; creamery and cheese factory estab. 1895 by Joseph Kennedy, closed 1902; electricity: South Tomerong 1946 and Tomerong 1938; FB 1939 (station b. 1991); fire 2000; floods 1870, 1925, 1938, 1958, 1959, 1974, 1978; PO 1862, new one b. 1907; pound (stock) 1873; sawmills: E.M. and T.E. Davis (became T.E. Davis Pty Ltd in 1963), P. McGuire & Son, Watt and Mathie; school 1862, additions and repairs 1882 by William Schadel, new building 1885, additions 1959 and 1995; street lighting 1966; telephone 1886; TX 1910, automatic 1969; Union C. b. 1877 by William Smith, reused, closed and demolished 1931, new one b. 1887 by Alexander Mathie, d. by Alexander Mathie and William Braithwaite, restored; water reticulation 1982; pop. 239 (1901), 165 (1911), 248 (1933), 199 (1947), 231 (1954), 264 (1961), 218 (1991), 290 (1996), 210 (2001), 295 (2006), 312 (2011).

Tomewin (*Co. Rous*) 28°15'S. 153°23'E., 10 km N. of Murwillumbah; farming, orchards, bananas, beans; PO 1927–64; school 1920–26; telephone 1916; TX 1931; pop. 75 (1933), 50 (1947), 60 (1954), 84 (1961).

Tom Groggin (*Co. Beresford*) 36°33'S. 148°08'E., 16 km W. of Thredbo, on Snowy R.; estab. 1956; gravel crushing plant.

Tomingley (*Co. Narromine*) 32°34'S. 148°13'E., 18 km N. of Peak Hill, on Gundong Ck; village gaz. 1894; mining (gold disc. 1883) till 1909, grazing, horses, farming; Angl. C. (St James's) 1896; bushfire 1926; cemetery (118 graves) 1887, incl. columbarium; dust storms 1982 and 1983; FB; fire 1902; grasshopper infestation 1907; mines: Alkane Resources Open-Cut 2013, Centenary 1888–89, Crowhurst & Sons (incl. sawmill and stamper battery) 1887–1910, Paton's or Gold Hill 1898–1914; pound (stock) 1904; PS 1897–1937; reservoir; rifle range 1909; Rom. Cath. C. (St Joseph's) 1909, closed, sold and reused; sawmill (J. Lake); school 1884 b. by James Prior Hull, demolished 1929, new one b. 1908 by George Paterson, closed 1985; stamper battery (15 head) 1883; telephone 1892; TX 1910, automatic 1962; pop. 281 (1901), 420 (1911), 147 (1933), 169 (1947), 161 (1954), 264 (1961), 230 (2006), 330 (2011).

Tomingley West (*Co. Narromine*) 32°34'S. 148°09'E., 17 km N. of Peak Hill; farming; PO 1928–52; RS 1910, station b. by T.E. Quiggin, closed 1976; silo 1929; pop. 74 (1933), 71 (1947).

Tomki (*Co. Rous*) 28°53'S. 153°08'E., 7 km E. of Casino; Angl. C. (All Saints') 1900; boiling-down works estab. 1847 by Clark Irving; creamery (NSW Creamery Butter Co. Ltd) 1897; Wes. Meth. C. 1884; pop. 177 (1901), 196 (1911), 129 (1933), 189 (1947), 118 (1954), 80 (1961).

Tomki (*Co. Rous*) see also McKees Hill.

Tomooroma (*Co. Buccleuch*) see Adjungbilly and Tumorrama.

Toms Creek (*Co. Macquarie*) 31°33'S. 152°23'E., 30 km W. of Kendall, on Toms Ck; PO, closed 1971; school 1957–68; telephone 1948; TX 1950; pop. 53 (1954), 74 (1961).

Toms Gully (*Co. Sandon*) 30°22'S. 151°33'E., 20 km NW of Armidale, on Toms Ck.

Toms Lagoon (*Co. Ashburnham*) 33°23'S. 148°03'E., 4 km E. of Forbes; school 1895, new one b. 1911 by J. Bartlett, closed 1948.

Toms Point (*Co. Sturt*) 34°28'S. 145°16'E., 39 km E. of Hay, on Murrumbidgee R.; rice.

Tonderburine (*Co. Gowen*) 31°20'S. 148°44'E., 24 km E. of Gulargambone; artesian water struck 1902; school 1957–68, moved to Tooraweenah; pop. 74 (1911), 135 (2006).

Tongarra (*Co. Camden*) 34°35'S. 150°41'E., 12 km SW of Dapto, on Tongarra Ck; farming, dairying, coal (disc. 1880); coalmine estab. 1893 by William Brownlee, further development 1908 by Owen, taken over 1943 by Excelsior Collieries, closed 1964; butter factory (Tongarra Dairy Co. Ltd) b. 1893 by Dawes Bros, closed 1908; PO 1890–1970; sawmill (Eric Bresnahan); school 1882–1919;

telephone 1926; TX 1928, automatic 1970; pop. 118 (1911).

Tongbong (*Co. Phillip*) 32°44'S. 149°55'E., 9 km NW of Rylstone, on Pinnacle Swamp Ck; school 1882–85.

Tongbong Gap (*Co. Phillip*) 32°44'S. 149°58'E., 9 km N. of Rylstone.

Toogong (*Co. Ashburnham*) 33°20'S. 148°38'E., 17 km S. of Manildra, on Boree Ck; village gaz. 1869; farming and grazing; Angl. C. (St Alban's) 1873 d. by John Hale, extended and renovated 1925 by Walter Goodacre; bridge, destroyed 1862, rebuilt 1864, new one b. 1936 by Herbert Ernest Ibbotson, new one 2001, over Boree Ck; cemetery (217 burials 1875+) 1877; CH (incl. police station) b. 1875–79 by Francis Rule and William Escher, closed 1884, reused; PO 1865–1983; PS, closed 1895; quarry; school 1881–97, 1913–24, 1957–67; telephone 1906; TX 1918–81; pop. 17 (1866), 57 (1901), 120 (1911), 142 (1933), 123 (1947), 84 (1954), 94 (1961), 371 (2006).

Toolamang (*Co. Wellington*) 32°55'S. 149°38'E., 33 km W. of Kandos, on Stinking Water Ck.

Toolaroo (*Co. Rous*) see Tullera.

Tooleaooa (*Co. Camden*) see Toolijooa.

Toolejooa (*Co. Camden*) see Toolijooa.

Tooles Creek (*Co. Wynyard*) 35°17'S. 147°31'E., 24 km SE of Wagga Wagga, on Tooles Ck; soldiers' settlement; school 1909–15; pop. 77 (1933).

Tooleybuc (*Co. Wakool*) 35°02'S. 143°20'E., 48 km SW of Balranald, on Murray R.; settled 1835, town gaz. 1866; sheep, farming, orchards, vineyards; bridge (timber trusses, and steel lift span) 1922–25, d. by Percy Allan, 293 ft (89.3 m), upgraded 2000 with steel cross girders, over Murray R.; cemetery; PO 1873; punt (Thomas Ward) 1910, ceased 1925; Rom. Cath. C. (Our Lady Help of Christians); school 1917, additions 1967, 1971, 1975; telephone 1912; TX 1914–66; pop. 90 (1933), 164 (1947), 220 (1954), 207 (1961), *c.*250 (1982), 235 (1996), 238 (2001), 180 (2006), 176 (2011).

Toolijooa (*Co. Camden*) 34°46'S. 150°47'E., 5 km SW of Gerringong; Toolejooa till 1923; farming; butter factory (Excelsior) b. 1893 by J.B. Taylor; PO 1904–71; RS (Tooleaooa till 1897) 1893, station b. by Gerald Dalton Fetherston, closed 1974; sawmill; school 1871–1951, building moved 1953 to Gerringong, reused; telephone 1925; pop. 76 (1911).

Toolmah (*Co. Wakool*) 35°21'S. 143°52'E., 39 km NW of Barham; formerly Tulmah.

Toolond (*Co. Rous*) 28°30'S. 153°23'E., 14 km NW of Mullumbimby; bananas; telephone 1936.

Toolond (*Co. Rous*)
see also Upper Main Arm.

Toolong (*Co. Selwyn*) 36°02'S. 148°16'E., 38 km SE of Tumbarumba; goldmining 1890–94.

Tooloogan (*Co. Brisbane*) 31°58'S. 150°45'E., 14 km NW of Scone, on Thompsons Ck; pop. 26 (1933), 76 (1947).

Tooloom (*Co. Buller*) 28°31'S. 152°29'E., 54 km W. of Kyogle, on Beaury Ck; orig. Tubra, then Wallaby Creek 1916–36; declined 1876+; grazing, dairying, mining (gold disc. 1858 by Billy May, gold rush 1858–59); butter factory (Tooloom & Woodenbong Co-op. Butter Factory Co. Ltd) 1909–22; cemetery (14 graves); PO 1936; school 1886–92 and 1955–61; telephone 1963; pop. *c.*50 (1903), 134 (1911), 23 (1933), 92 (1947), 67 (1961).

Tooma (*Co. Selwyn*) 35°58'S. 148°04'E., 22 km S. of Tumbarumba, on Mannus Ck; soldiers' settlement 1948; cattle; bridge b. 1879 by P. Adams, over Tumbarumba Ck; bushfire 1952; FB; flour mill (George Mair and J. Garland) 1852–75, bought by John Smeaton and removed; PO 1873–1994; pound (stock); Presb. C., burnt down 1952; PS 1896–1905; Rom. Cath. C. (Our Lady of Perpetual Succour) 1936; school 1882–93, 1929–40, 1955–80; telephone 1890; TX (automatic) 1960; Union C., additions and alterations 1889, new one 1913; pop. 98 (1901), 106 (1911), 53 (1933), 119 (1947), 199 (1954), 210 (1961), 336 (2011).

Toomelah (*Co. Stapylton*) 28°42'S. 149°47'E., 56 km W. of Boggabilla; cemetery; flood 2011; school 1940, additions 1986; pop. 226 (2011).

Toonga (*Co. Wynyard*) 35°15'S. 147°47'E., 25 km W. of Adelong; agric.

Toongi (*Co. Gordon*) 32°27'S. 148°36'E., 22 km S. of Dubbo, on Wambangalang Ck; village gaz. 1931; RS 1925–74; telephone 1933; TX 1954; pop. 75 (1933), 51 (1947), 92 (1954), 90 (1961).

Toonumbar (*Co. Rous*) 28°35'S. 152°46'E., 24 km W. of Kyogle, on Iron Pot Ck; dam 1972, 144 ft (44 m) high, on Iron Pot Ck; electricity 1960; PO 1969–71; school 1957–64; telephone 1924; pop. 39 (1933), 95 (1947), 88 (1954), 55 (1961).

Toorale (*Co. Gunderbooka*) 30°16'S. 145°24'E., 57 km W. of Bourke, on Warrego R.; PO 1869–76; wool-scour, burnt down 1929; pop. 79 (1911), 81 (1933).

Toorale East (*Co. Yanda*) 30°26'S. 145°25'E., 63 km SW of Bourke; grazing; PO 1927–72; telephone 1910; TX 1915; pop. 26 (1933).

Tooraloo Point (*Co. Wellesley*) 37°03'S. 149°04'E., 21 km SW of Bombala; airfield.

Tooraweenah (*Co. Gowen*) 31°26'S. 148°55'E., 38 km NE of Gilgandra, on Gulargambone Ck; estab. *c.*1841; orig. sheep, then cattle, pigs, goats, wheat, oats; airport (orig. Yeo, renamed Arthur Butler Memorial in 2008) 1938; Angl. C. (St Mary Magdalene) 1938, in former Union C., defunct, new one 1971, removed from Armatree; bridge 1975, over Gulargambone Ck; cemetery (18 graves 1901+) 1893; FB (station b. 2014); freezing works (Currabubula Freezing Works Co.) 1925, acquired 1927 by Amalgamated Rabbit & Skin Export Co. Ltd; lock-up b. 1913 by J.N. Lyons & Co., removed; PO 1896, new one b. 1911; Presb. C. (St Anne's) 1936 d. by C.H. Price; PS (in rented premises) 1901–61, new one b. 1961; rifle range 1909, new one 1953; Rom. Cath. C. (Immaculate Conception) b. 1926 by W. McWhirter, extended; sale-yards; school 1885, new school 1887, additions 1934 by Wallace and McGee, additions 1958 and 1966, renovations 1983; telephone 1900; TX 1911, automatic 1983; Union C. 1894–1938, reused; pop. 141 (1901), 275 (1911), 228 (1933), 330 (1947), 378 (1954), 223 (1961), *c.*150 (1981), 240 (2006), 371 (2011).

Toormina (*Co. Raleigh*) 30°21'S. 153°05'E., 2 km NW of Sawtell, on Boambee Ck; (incl. Bayldon and East Boambee); Assemblies of God C. (New Life); Bapt. C. (East Boambee) 1992; bridge (Fred Hansen Bridge) over Boambee Ck; engineering works: K.T.R. Engineering Pty Ltd 1979 and Walco Industries Pty Ltd 1970, closed and reused; Evangelical Brotherhood C. 1982; flood 2001; hailstorm 2013; PO 1980; quarry; railway bridge (Walter Harvie Bridge) over Boambee Ck; reservoirs; schools: Bayldon 1992, Toormina primary 1979, Toormina HS 1980, additions 1988; sewage works; pop. 11,522 (2011).

Toorooka (*Co. Dudley*) 30°55'S. 152°35'E., 29 km NW of Kempsey, on Macleay R.; farming and grazing; bacon factory (Upper Macleay Co-op. Dairy Co.) b. 1921 by Ben Furniful, d. by Richard Wildridge & Co.; bridge b. 1909 by Wally Boulton, 210 ft (64 m), over Macleay R.; butter factory (Upper Macleay Co-op. Dairying Co. Ltd) b. 1906 by Percy Landers, new one 1926–70; drought 1965; hailstorm 1932; PO 1908–74; TX 1924, automatic 1972; pop. 40 (1933), 73 (1954), 6,553 (2006).

Toorumbee (*Co. Dudley*) 31°02'S. 152°29'E., 33 km W. of Kempsey, on Parrabel Ck.

Tootal (*Co. Mitchell*) see Tootool.

Toothdale (*Co. Auckland*) 36°47'S. 149°45'E., 15 km SW of Bega; dairying; butter factory (J. Ramsay); cheese factories: Edward T. Doyle and Joseph Wheatley; PO 1927–59; school (Lilydale 1897–1902) 1884–1946; telephone 1907; TX 1934; pop. 136 (1933), 54 (1954).

Tootool (*Co. Mitchell*) 35°16'S. 147°00'E., 11 km W. of The Rock, on Bullenbong Ck; Tootal till 1900; village gaz. 1917; farming; airfield (World War II); Angl. C. (St John's) 1906, closed, demolished 1970; PO 1901–66; RS 1901, station b. by C. Hardy & Co., closed 1975; school (Tootal till 1900) 1897, new one b. 1928 by R.E. Mitchell, closed 1968; silo 1924; TX 1912, automatic 1966; Unit. C. (War Memorial, orig. Presb.) 1961; pop. 243 (1911), 123 (1933), 103 (1947), 96 (1954), 59 (1961).

Toowong (*Co. Durham*) see Antiene.

Toowoon Bay (*Co. Northumberland*) see Blue Bay.

Tooyal (*Co. Bourke*) 34°55'S. 147°11'E., 26 km NW of Wagga Wagga; defunct; school 1897–1925; pop. 221 (1911), 52 (1933), 67 (1947), 70 (1954), 89 (1961).

Tooyal North (*Co. Bourke*) 34°58'S. 147°11'E., 22 km NW of Wagga Wagga; telephone 1910; pop. 107 (1933).

Topar (*Co. Tandora*) 31°56'S. 142°03'E., 55 km E. of Broken Hill; pop. 27 (1933).

Top Crossing (*Co. Gough*) 29°26'S. 152°01'E., 43 km NE of Glen Innes, on Deepwater R.

Topdale (*Co. Vernon*) 31°23'S. 151°32'E., 44 km S. of Walcha, on Taylors Ck.

Topi Topi (*Co. Gloucester*) 32°22'S. 152°23'E., 17 km E. of Bulahdelah, on Shinglers Ck; farming; PO 1910–63; school 1895–1962; pop. 81 (1911), 91 (1933).

Top Woodlands (*Co. Kennedy*) 32°23'S. 147°23'E., 82 km W. of Narromine.

Torannie (*Co. Woore*) 32°36'S. 144°05'E., 136 km SE of Wilcannia; telephone 1925; TX 1937.

Torbane (*Co. Roxburgh*) 33°06'S. 150°01'E., 27 km N. of Portland, on Torbane Ck; orig. New Hartley; thrived 1883–1908, failed by 1918, dismantled 1920, razed 1926; oil-shale; brickworks (incl. 3 kilns, one b. 1908); measles epidemic 1910; miners' strikes 1911 and 1914; PO 1902–20; railway turntable 1902, 50 ft (15.2 m), replaced 1903, 60 ft (18.3 m), ruined; 40 retorts (Hall-Palmer type, for oil-shale) b. 1900 by NSW Shale & Oil Co. Ltd, acquired 1906 by Commonwealth Oil Corp. Ltd, which built a bench of 32 Pumpherston retorts, company went into liquidation 1912, retorts closed 1913, reopened 1916, closed 1918, dismantled, but experimental one (Schultz) erected 1925 by Torquay & Anglesea Oil Co.; RS 1897–1974; school 1901–20; tramway (mineral) b. 1896–1900; pop. 113 (1901), 296 (1911).

Toronto (*Co. Northumberland*) 33°01'S. 151°36'E., 7 km W. of Belmont, on Lake Macquarie; orig. Ebenezer; settled 1830 by Lancelot Edward Threlkeld, acquired 1885, subdivided and laid out 1887 by Excelsior Land, Investment, & Building Co. & Bank Ltd as tourist destination, first lots sold 1887; mining, fishing, apiculture, farming, fruit, tourism 1891+; Aboriginal mission station estab. 1831 by Lancelot Edward Threlkeld, closed 1841; ambulance station 1979; Angl. C. (Christ the King) 1901, new one (Christ) b. 1924 by H. Gane; Bapt. C. 1965, new one 2011; brickworks 1886; bridges: Fennell Bay Bridge (b. 1902, new one 1967, to Fennell Bay, over Fennell Bay) and Homer Bridge (b. 1906 to Blackalls Park, over Stony Ck); bushfire 1933; cemetery (1,813 graves 1898+), incl. lawn cemetery; CH b. 2000 by Cordukes Pty Ltd, refurbished 2011; coalmine; cordial factory (H.T. Smith); electricity (from Caledonian Colliery) 1923; FB (station b. 1931 by D.B. Hobbs, new one 1967 d. by John W. Roberts, new one 2001); Foursquare Gospel C. (New Day Christ.); Jehovah's Witnesses C.; LDS (Mormon) C.; Meth. C. b. 1909 by David Clouton, new one 1960; Newday Christ. C.; PO 1889, new one b. 1894, second one b. 1907, burnt down 1932, third one b. 1923 by Compton Bros; PS 1912, new ones 1964 and 2017; railway b. 1889–91 as a private railway to Fassifern for Excelsior Land, Investment, & Building Co. & Bank Ltd, closed 1909, acquired and reopened 1910 by govt, new station 1911, line closed 1990, reused; reservoir, 310,000 gal. (1,409.3 kl); rifle range 1916; Rom. Cath. C. (St Joseph's) b. 1915 by Frank C. D'Arcy; schools: primary b. 1890 by John Frogley, additions 1918 by P.A. Solman, additions 1972, and HS 1962, additions 1979 and 1985, fire 1994; SD Adventist C. 1941, new one 1971 on new site, burnt down 1999, new one b. 2001 by Adrian and James Grieve, d. by Stephen Rose; telephone 1894; TX 1913, automatic 1965; Unit. C.; water supply 1919; wharf b. 1925 by Bates Bros for J.R. Israel; pop. 389 (1901), 629 (1911), 1,291 (1921), 1,274 (1933), 1,962 (1947), 2,252 (1954), 5,164 (2006), 5,433 (2011).

Toronto West (*Co. Northumberland*) 33°01'S.

151°34'E., 2 km NW of Toronto, on Stony Ck; cemetery; school (Biraban since 1978) 1956, additions 1979.

Torrington (*Co. Clive*) 29°19'S. 151°42'E., 43 km SW of Tenterfield, on Catarrh Ck; The Mole till 1883; thrived in 1880s and 1920s, declined 1945+; tin (disc. 1881 by Joe Bates), wolfram (disc. 1903), bismuth, silexite, grazing, now fossicking; Angl. C. (All Saints') 1927; bushfire 1951; cemetery (186 graves); electricity 1969; FB 1964; mines: Blather Arm, Butler's, Currnow's (reef disc. by Great Britain Tin Mining Co.) 1881, The Dutchman or Hart's (lode disc. 1875, mine estab. 1877, acquired 1881 by Great Britain Tin Mining Co., 5 head stamper battery 1883), Fielders Hill, Highland Home, Scrubby Gully, Torrington (incl. 5 head stamper battery 1883) 1882, Wallaroo (reef disc. 1882 by Trewhella, mine estab. 1883, acquired *c.*1884 by Bray & Sons, then H.H. and P. Spicer 1924–36, then Cumberland Gold Mines *c.*1943, which erected 10 head stamper battery); PO 1882; PS 1910; 3 quarries; Rom. Cath. C. (Our Lady Help of Christians) 1939; school 1884–92, reopened 1900, replaced 1908, additions 1915, closed 1968; TX; pop. 140 (1891), 61 (1901), 163 (1911), 325 (1933), 316 (1947), 222 (1954), 139 (1961), *c.*200 (1972).

Torrowangee (*Co. Farnell*) 31°27'S. 141°29'E., 55 km N. of Broken Hill; known locally as Tarrawingee; surveyed 1891, defunct; grazing; PO 1892–1942; PS 1892, renovations and repairs 1918 by Michael Kenna Power, closed 1932, reused; quarries (limestone); RS 1891; school (Tarrawingie till 1916) 1892–1901 and 1911–12; telegraph 1892; tramway (to Broken Hill) b. 1891 by Baxter and Saddler for Tarrawingie Flux & Tramway Co. Ltd, closed 1932; pop. 321 (1899), 71 (1901), 104 (1911), 245 (1922), 104 (1933).

Torryburn (*Co. Durham*) 32°28'S. 151°35'E., 16 km SW of Dungog; flood 2015; winery (Allyn River) 1996; pop. 50 (1933), 173 (2011).

Torryburn (*Co. Hardinge*) 30°27'S. 151°13'E., 34 km NW of Uralla, on Back Ck; bridges: high-level one d. and b. 1927 by George Roach, 270 ft (82.3 m), over Gwydir R. and one b. 1951 by A. Bullen, over Back Ck; pop. 54 (1911), 32 (1933).

Toshs Wongy (*Co. Leichhardt*) 31°15'S. 148°37'E., 16 km NE of Gulargambone.

Tottenham (*Co. Kennedy*) 32°14'S. 147°21'E., 63 km W. of Trangie; laid out 1907 by Maurice Barlow, lots sold 1914; mining (mainly 1905–17), timber, grazing; airport, upgraded 2012; Angl. C. (St Mark's) 1928; cemetery (396 graves 1913+), incl. columbarium; CH (incl. lock-up) 1929; FB; gastroenteritis epidemic 1954; hospital (cottage) 1928, additions 1969, redeveloped 2007; Meth. C. 1927; mines: Ace (copper and silver) 1906, 1908, 1917, Bogan River (copper, silver, gold) 1905–*c.*1921, 1943, 1950–52, Effies Ace (copper) 1902–13, Mount Royal (copper, gold, silver) 1903–27, Nelson's (copper), Orange Plains (copper, silver, gold) 1884, 1900–8, 1910, Underlay (copper and silver) *c.*1903 and 1949–60, Chris Watson (copper) 1908–13; mouse plague 1956; PO 1907; PS, relocated and reused 1925, new one 1929; quarry; rabbit freezing works (Edgar Selwyn Siggers) 1931; railway coal stage, removed 1985; railway engine shed, removed 1985; railway turntable, 60 ft (18.3 m); reservoir (tower); Rom. Cath. C. (St Anthony's); RS 1916, station b. by T.E. Quiggin, closed 1974; sawmill (W.E. Watkins); school 1909, additions 1963, 1966, 1969, 1995; SD Adventist C.; sewage works; silo 1963; telephone 1907; TX 1912; Unit. C. (orig. Presb.); water supply augmentation 1994; pop. 249 (1911), 413 (1933), 367 (1947), 527 (1954), 411 (1961), 369 (1971), 383 (1976), 366 (1981), 368 (1986), 389 (1991), 341 (1996), 303 (2001), 299 (2011).

Toual (*Co. Murray*) 34°58'S. 149°05'E., 6 km E. of Murrumbateman; school 1898–1912; winery (Helm Wines) 1973.

Toubouree Lake (*Co. St Vincent*) see Tabourie Lake.

Touga (*Co. St Vincent*) 34°57'S. 150°05'E., 39 km SW of Bundanoon, on Cradle Ck; bushfires 1965 and 1977.

Toukley (*Co. Northumberland*) 33°16'S.

151°32'E., 25 km NE of Gosford, on Budgewoi Lake; (incl. Canton Beach and Wallarah Point); hort., poultry, farming, tourism; ambulance station 2019; Angl. C. (St Luke's) b. 1962 by Frank M. Treasure, d. by Mayo and Wark; bridge (Wallarah Point Bridge) 1939 to Gorokan, 570 ft (173.7 m), demolished, new one b. 1983–85, over Budgewoi and Tuggerah Lakes; FB (station b. 1970); flood 1949; Jehovah's Witnesses C.; jetty, repairs 1939; PO 1927, new one 1985; Presb. C. (St David's) 1953; PS 1956, new one 1974; sewerage 1976, augmentation 1985; squall 2017; telephone 1924; TX 1935, automatic 1951; Unit. C. (orig. Meth.) 1953 d. by R. McKinnon, extensions 1974; water reticulation 1969; wharf; pop. 320 (1947), 676 (1954), 1,275 (1961), 5,215 (2011).

Toukley (*Co. Northumberland*) see also Noraville.

Toulby (*Co. Culgoa*) 29°02'S. 146°56'E., 102 km N. of Brewarrina; pop. 26 (1933).

Towac (*Co. Wellington*) 33°20'S. 149°01'E., 8 km SW of Orange, on Molong Ck; FB; PO 1927–30; school 1881, new buildings b. 1883 by John Henry Gain, closed 1894, reopened 1910, closed 1913.

Towalbyn (*Co. Rous*) 28°53'S. 153°30'E., 6 km W. of Ballina; telephone 1917.

Towalbyn (*Co. Rous*) see also Uralba.

Towallum (*Co. Fitzroy*) 30°02'S. 152°52'E., 34 km W. of Woolgoolga, on Towallum R.; telephone 1930; TX 1935.

Towamba (*Co. Auckland*) 37°05'S. 149°42'E., 19 km W. of Eden, on Towamba R.; Sturt till 1885; settled 1840–60, lots sold 1860, village gaz. 1859 as Sturt; goldmining and farming; Angl. C. (St Paul's) 1888, relocated 1912, repairs 1930 by E. Love, restored, now a Community C.; bridge (high-level) b. 1909–11 by Charles John Foord, destroyed 1919, replaced (low-level) 1921, over Towamba R.; butter factory (Towamba Central Co-op. Creamery Co. Ltd) 1904–26; cemeteries: first one (10 burials, grave 1864) 1861, second one (147 burials) 1886; floods 1861, 1919, 2011; PO 1870–1982; PS b. 1893 by J. Malcolm, closed 1937; sawmill (Thomas Hite); school 1862–63, reopened 1882, new building b. 1888 by L.N. Bouquet; telephone 1891; TX 1915, automatic 1974; pop. 156 (1901), 242 (1911), 187 (1933), 157 (1947), 150 (1954), 73 (1991), 145 (2001), 372 (2011).

Towealgra (*Co. Lincoln*) 31°56'S. 149°20'E., 11 km NW of Dunedoo; RS 1917, station b. by John Allibone, closed.

Towgon Grange (*Co. Gresham*) 29°28'S. 152°38'E., 38 km NW of Grafton, on Clarence R.; PO 1935–66; telephone 1935; TX.

Townsend (*Co. Clarence*) 29°28'S. 153°13'E., 2 km E. of Maclean; Bapt. C. (Lower Clarence) 2000; cemetery (Maclean lawn, 3,578 plots), incl. columbaria; pop. 817 (2011).

Towradgee (*Co. Camden*) see Towradgi.

Towradgi (*Co. Camden*) 34°23'S. 150°55'E., 2 km SE of Corrimal, on Tasman Sea; orig. Towradgee; unsuccessfully subdivided 1839 by John Buckland; farming; Cong. C. 1955; PS; RS 1948, new station b. 1980 by R.N. Hughes Ltd; school 1953, additions 1956, 1959, 1962; pop. 1,611 (1954), 3,109 (1961), 3,075 (2006), 3,123 (2011).

Towradgi (*Co. Camden*) see also Fairy Meadow.

Towrang (*Co. Argyle*) 34°42'S. 149°51'E., 14 km NE of Goulburn, on Wollondilly R.; penal settlement 1833–43, village laid out 1843 by James Larmer; farming and sheep; Angl. C. 1905, demolished 1928, new one (St John the Evangelist) 1929 d. by Bertram Chisholm; boiling-down works: Benjamin and Moses 1845 and Wheatley's; bridge (masonry arch) 1839 d. by David Lennox; bushfires 1904, 1905, 1939, 1965; cemetery (3 graves) 1838–41; CH 1836; eucalyptus oil distillery (C. Farrell), burnt down 1900; FB 1939; fellmongery (W. Mills and W. Jobson) 1886; flood 1860; mine (molybdenite); PO 1881–1976; powder magazine 1836–1843, restored 1975; rifle range; RS (Mannafield till 1870) 1869–1974; school (Mannafield till 1890) 1885–1968; telephone 1913; timber carbonisation plant estab. 1899 by William Southall; toll-gate, removed 1863; TX 1924, automatic 1968; Union C.; pop. 71 (1901), 102 (1911), 119 (1933), 121 (1947), 45 (1954), 139 (1961), 314 (2011).

Towrang (*Co. Argyle*)
see also Carrick and Murrays Flats.

Trajere (*Co. Ashburnham*) 33°29'S. 148°22'E., 7 km S. of Eugowra; church, derelict; FB; RS (7 km E.) 1922–70; school 1881, new one b. 1890 by Frederick Hodgson, closed 1914; silo 1941; pop. 89 (1901), 140 (1933), 81 (1947), 100 (1954).

Trangie (*Co. Narromine*) 32°02'S. 147°59'E., 33 km NW of Narromine, on Goan Waterhole; estab. 1884 by John Campbell, village gaz. 1886; sawmilling, sheep, cattle, wheat, sorghum, maize, citrus, lucerne, safflower, cotton; agric. research station (4 km NW) 1915, additions 1974; ambulance station; Angl. C. 1890, destroyed 1926, new one (All Saints') 1935 d. by Louis Reginald Williams, closed, sold 2017; bridge b. 1899 by C.O. Bagge, new one 1998, over Goan Waterhole; bushfires 1951 and 1952; cemetery (1,020 graves 1887+) 1886, incl. lawn cemetery and columbarium; CH 1892, new one (incl. police station and lock-up) b. 1910 by R. Wills and R. Mann; cordial factory (J. Osborne); cotton gin (Namoi Cotton Co-op. Ltd); dust storms 1927 and 1938; electricity 1929; FB 1944 (station b. 1970 by Birch and Wilson); floods 1950 and 1955; grasshopper infestations 1907 and 1927; hailstorms 1927 (damaged much of town) and 1969; hospital 1954–2018; mouse plagues 1918, 1922, 1984; PO 1883, new one b. 1890, reused, second one b. 1904; powerhouse (C.E. Skinner) 1929; Presb. C. 1887, dismantled and removed 1901; reservoir (concrete), 110,000 gal. (500.1 kl); Rom. Cath. C. (St Carthage's) b. 1892 by Muller Bros; RS 1883, new station 1961, closed 1975; sale-yards b. by John Campbell, new yards 1951; sawmills: Con. Bowen and W. Lake 1899, burnt down 1909, C. Campbell, J. Duncan, fire 1900, Kelly's, Murphy's, Mathison and Smart; school 1884, new one b. 1893, additions 1902 by R. Moffatt, additions 1912 by W. Brown, additions 1956, 1959, 1966, 1972, 1978, 1984; silo; snow 1903; storm 1926; telegraph 1887; telephone 1890; tornado 1926; TX 1908; typhoid 1901; Unit. C. (St Andrew's, orig. Presb.) 1902, renovated and spire added 1959; water supply 1938; well (for locomotive water) sunk 1886 by William Muller; pop. 241 (1891), 1,003 (1901), 1,164 (1911), 958 (1933, incl. 27 on agric. research station), *c.*800 (1941), 831 (1947), 1,050 (1952), 1,400 (1954), 914 (1961), 932 (1966), 967 (1971), 1,016 (1976), 977 (1981), 966 (1986), 991 (1991), 951 (1996), 940 (2001), 866 (2006), 849 (2011).

Tranters Flat (*Co. Georgiana*) 33°59'S. 149°10'E., 46 km E. of Cowra, on Abercrombie R.; earth tremor 2006.

Trappo Flat (*Co. Vernon*) 30°47'S. 152°20'E., 57 km W. of Macksville, on Macleay R.

Treberth (*Co. Rous*) 28°25'S. 152°59'E., 22 km N. of Kyogle; RS 1942–72.

Tree Fern Vale (*Co. Fitzroy*) 30°20'S. 152°34'E., 13 km W. of Dorrigo, on Borra Ck; quarry.

Trefoil Park (*Co. Denison*) 35°37'S. 145°51'E., 5 km N. of Berrigan; formerly Woodburn.

Tregeagle (*Co. Rous*) 28°51'S. 153°21'E., 9 km SE of Lismore, on Boggy Ck; orig. Boggy Creek, then Cedar Grove from 1899; dairying then macadamia nuts; Angl. C. (St Paul's) b. 1899 by Foster and Jackson, renamed St Peter and St Paul's in 1989; PO 1905, new one b. 1928 by Leslie Gaggin, closed 1974; school 1891 b. by W.D. Foster, additions 1898 by T. Lofts, additions 1914 by T. Edwards; telephone 1908; TX 1921, automatic 1958; pop. 198 (1911), 214 (1933), 199 (1947), 208 (1954), 207 (1961), 512 (2011).

Trelawney (*Co. Arrawatta*) 29°23'S. 151°09'E., 9 km SE of Ashford.

Trelowarren (*Co. Ashburnham*) see Parkes.

Trenayr (*Co. Clarence*) 29°37'S. 152°58'E., 9 km NE of Grafton, on Alumy Ck; agric. research station; school (Millers Waterholes till 1912) 1901–70; veneer factory (Thomas Pidcock & Sons Pty Ltd).

Trendon Grange (*Co. Bathurst*) 33°33'S. 149°20'E., 8 km E. of Blayney.

Trentham Cliffs (*Co. Wentworth*) 34°15'S. 142°15'E., 8 km S. of Gol Gol, on Murray

R.; soldiers' settlement 1945+; grapes and oranges; airfield; TX (automatic); winery (Trentham Estate) estab. 1988 by Anthony and Patrick Murphy; pop. 127 (1954), 141 (1961).

Trevallyn (*Co. Durham*) 32°28'S. 151°34'E., 20 km W. of Dungog, on Allyn R.; dairying; flood 1857; flour mill (water powered) estab. by George Townshend, destroyed 1857; jam factory estab. by George Townshend; PO 1880–1965; quarry; school (Campsie till 1881) 1853–81 and 1907–35 (building moved 1944 to Ecclestone); telephone 1911; TX 1923–63; pop. 88 (1901), 48 (1933), 51 (1954), 62 (1961).

Trewilga (*Co. Narromine*) 32°47'S. 148°13'E., 8 km S. of Peak Hill; farming and gold; Angl. C. b. 1924–26; mines: Black Snake (R. Furner and F. Fairbrother) 1938, Comet 1891 and 1904–5, Happy Valley (A.G. Dow) 1936, Monte Carlo (D. Chester & Co.) 1895–97, Snake Hill, The Bluff (J. Tighe & Co.) 1890, J. Turner 1909, Who'd a Thought It *c.*1891 and 1896; PO 1913–76; RS 1914–74; school (Mingelo till 1912) 1903–51; TX; pop. 127 (1933), 88 (1947), 100 (1954), 103 (1961).

Trial Bay (*Co. Macquarie*) see Arakoon.

Triamble (*Co. Wellington*) 32°53'S. 149°16'E., 43 km SW of Mudgee, on Triamble Ck; goldmining and grazing; Angl. C. (St Matthew's) 1922; hailstorm 1870; PO 1927–30; telephone 1925; pop. 51 (1933), 53 (1954).

Triangle Flat (*Co. Bathurst*) 33°30'S. 149°03'E., 13 km SW of Millthorpe, on Flyers Ck; mines: Crows Hill (gold) and O'd (copper) *c.*1880.

Triangle Flat (*Co. Georgiana*) 33°46'S. 149°29'E., 32 km SE of Blayney, on Triangle Ck; farming and grazing; Rom. Cath. C. (Our Lady of Mount Carmel) 1927, closed, sold, moved to Rockley and reused, and graveyard (29 graves 1929–96); PO 1899–1950; school 1880, new buildings b. 1883 by James Wiburd, d. by William Edmund Kemp, closed 1910; telephone 1914; pop. 61 (1933), 87 (1947), 96 (1954), 172 (2006).

Trickett (*Co. Bourke*) 34°32'S. 147°18'E., 23 km SW of Temora; school 1891–96 and 1909–26; pop. 84 (1911).

Trida (*Co. Mossgiel*) 33°01'S. 145°00'E., 73 km NW of Hillston; village gaz. 1965; grazing; bushfire 1940; PO 1925–71; RS 1925, closed; school 1963–70; TX 1937–70; pop. 36 (1933), 60 (1947), 70 (1961).

Trigamon (*Co. Arrawatta*) 28°58'S. 150°49'E., 60 km SE of Boggabilla, on Macintyre R.; pop. 68 (1901).

Troy Junction (*Co. Lincoln*) 32°13'S. 148°37'E., 5 km N. of Dubbo, on Macquarie R.; abattoir (Ganarrin Meat Sevice, Driver Bros) b. 1930 by Wallace and McGee, d. by Alfred Norman Henry Sambrook, new one (Northern Co-op. Meatworks, incl. ice works) b. 1950–54 by Walmac Construction Pty Ltd, extended 1963, new one (Fletcher International Exports Pty Ltd) 1988; hailstorm 1884; sale-yards b. 1950 by Wallace and McGee.

Trundle (*Co. Cunningham*) 32°55'S. 147°42'E., 49 km NW of Parkes, on Yarrabandai Ck; Trundle Lagoon till 1892; surveyed 1892 by Edwin John Witts, laid out and village gaz. 1892, many lots auctioned 1913, thrived 1910–14 and late 1920s; mining (copper and gold disc. 1905), wheat, wool, mixed farming; airfield 1968; ambulance station 1956; Angl. C. (St Augustine of Canterbury) b. 1914 by A.E. Ware, demolished 1971, new one b. 1971 by J. Fullerton; Assemblies of God C.; Bapt. C. 1980; brickworks (H.O. Williams) 1922; bushfire 1926; carriage-works (F.J. Matthews); cemetery (855 graves 1891+) 1891, incl. columbarium; CH 1899, new one b. 1929 by William Raper Acret; cordial factory estab. 1897 by Alick Green, sold to Thomas Mitchell, sold 1909 to Stansfield Berry, sold 1911 to F.J. Matthews, reused; dam b. 1946 by Bowen and Lane; droughts 1919, 1940, 1944, 1946, 1959; 2 FB; fires 1907, 1923, 1933, 1955; floods 1929, 1930, 1950, 1976; hospital 1959, taken over 1968, extended 1985; joinery (M. Wynn) 1921, fire 1953, new one 1954, closed 1957, reopened by B. Thompson, closed 1964; mines: Bayley's Reward (Forbes) 1907, Cameron's 1908–10, Copper Hill (G. Berry) 1906–15, G.R. Dunn, Mordialloc (D. and C. Cameron) 1905–11, Todd's 1916–17,

Willcox's 1907–12; mouse plague 1956; PO 1889, new one b. 1914 by North, repairs 1940 by L. and F. Acret; powerhouse estab. 1935 by E.A. Curr and A.P. Townsend, burnt down 1938, replaced, disused 1951, closed 1953; Presb. C. (St Andrew's) b. 1909 by Snelling, new one b. 1919 by A.E. Ware; PS 1893, new one b. 1899 by J. Allibone, additions and alterations 1911 by J.J. Patterson; Rom. Cath. C. 1889, new one 1906 d. by John Holderness Bates, sanctuary 1908, church additions 1912 by C. Muller, also d. by Bates, demolished, replacement (St Michael's) 1962 d. by Terence A. Daly; RS 1907, station b. by Peter Herbert; sawmills: James Anderson 1911, Gault Bros, S. West; school 1890 b. by Alfred Fell, closed 1894, reopened 1900, extended 1906 and 1914, additions 1953, 1962, 1964, 1968; silo 1920; steam planing and moulding plant (Milne Bros) 1905, burnt down 1912; steel fabrication works: Trundle Steel & Joinery Works 1951 (burnt down 1953, replaced 1954, closed 1957) and Western Steel Fabrications 1952–55; storm 1928; street lighting 1922; telegraph 1892; tornado 1973; TX 1910, automatic 1980; Unit. C. (Berry Memorial, orig. Meth.) b. 1939 by James Fullerton & Son, d. by Hedley Carr; water supply 1947, augmentation 1994; pop. 78 (1901), 693 (1911), 933 (1933), 807 (1947), 873 (1954), 772 (1961), 618 (1966), 562 (1971), 547 (1976), 515 (1981), 529 (1986), 548 (1991), 491 (1996), 443 (2001), 390 (2011).

Trundle Lagoon (*Co. Cunningham*) see Trundle.

Trungley (*Co. Bland*) 34°09'S. 147°39'E., 34 km N. of Temora; pop. 85 (1933), 56 (1947).

Trungley (*Co. Bland*) see also Trungley Hall.

Trungley Hall (*Co. Bland*) 34°17'S. 147°33'E., 18 km N. of Temora, on Duck Hole Ck; orig. Duck Creek, then Trungley till 1899; German settlers arrived *c.*1890; farming; Angl. C. (St Luke's) 1913, destroyed, rebuilt 1920, closed, sold 1947, moved 1948 to Temora for reuse but demolished on arrival there; cemetery; Lutheran C. 1893, new one (Zion) 1911 d. by Richard Rahnenfuehrer, damaged 1935; PO 1914–81; squall 1948; storm 1935; TX 1924–81; pop. 86 (1933), 147 (1947), 175 (1954), 187 (1961), 9 (2011).

Trunketabella (*Co. Dampier*) 36°04'S. 150°03'E., 7 km W. of Tuross Head, on Tuross R.; bridge (timber beam spans) b. 1880 by Peter Flanagan, damaged 1891, spans replaced 1894 by Edward William Fitzgerald, centre spans collapsed 1954, temporary low-level bridge 1954, 503 ft (153.3 m), replacement (steel and concrete) fabricated by Clyde Engineering Co. Ltd, erected 1954–57 by Hornibrook McKenzie Clark Pty Ltd, 630 ft (192 m), over Tuross R.; cheese factory 1889, burnt down 1899, rebuilt, taken over 1925 by Bodalla Co-op. Cheese Society Ltd, closed 1951; punt 1864–79, removed 1893, across Tuross R.

Trunkey (*Co. Georgiana*) see Trunkey Creek.

Trunkey Creek (*Co. Georgiana*) 33°49'S. 149°19'E., 32 km S. of Blayney, on Trunkey Ck; surveyed 1869 by Richard Randolf Machattie; formerly also known as Trunkey; gold (reef disc. 1868 by Joseph Arthur), copper, silver, farming, honey, grazing; Angl. C. (Holy Spirit) 1869, new one b. 1924–26; bushfires 1900 and 1939 (largely destroyed town); cemetery (120 burials 1876+) 1873; CH (incl. lock-up) b. 1879 by Kelly and McKean, alterations 1899; cordial factory (Henry G. Chard); cyanide plant erected 1905 by Gleadow; fire 1898; mine explosions 1872 (boy killed) and 1895; mines: American Star group (Black, City of Sydney, Caledonian or Come Again, Croucher's, Easdown's, East Pioneer, Electric Spark, Pioneer, Pioneer Whip Shaft, Turner's or Crummie's) <1875, 1876–77, 1919–20, Chard and Arthur's group (Trunkey Creek Gold Mining Co., incl. Bell's or Homeward Bound or Little Wonder, Bennett's, British Lion 1894–1917, Cash's, The German Band or Germans) 1875–77, Golden Point group (incl. Evans's, Gunnas Blow, Mosquito, Noble's, Thompson's) 1908–9 and 1914, McKenzie's 1876 and 1897–99, Number Seven or Alma group (incl. Alexander's,

Bolton's, Cartwright's, Ducksbury's Jewellers Shop, J. Hunter, Murphy's, Number 5, Number 6, P. Sunderland) 1869–77, 1881–84, 1890–94, Wilson's group (incl. Benjamin's, Murray's, Prima Donna, Ranekie's, Schultz's, Wrench's) 1875–78, 1885, 1889–90, 1895–96, Wright's 1876 and 1897–99, Young Australia or Queen of Australia group (Headrick's and Tanner's) 1877, 1906, 1912, 1916–17; PO 1869, new one b. 1875, closed 1992; police barracks 1869; pound (stock) 1872; Presb. C. 1890; PS b. 1880 by Kelly and McKean, new one 1890; 3 quarries; quartz mill; sawmill (John J. Henry); school (Trunkey) 1870, new one b. 1879, repairs 1897 by W. Hargans, burnt down 1939, replaced 1940 by A.H. Baglee; snowstorms 1899, 1900, 1903, 1915; telegraph 1880; TX 1918, automatic 1984; Union C.; pop. 681 (1871), 500 (1881), 185 (1891), 219 (1901), 166 (1911), 239 (1933), 185 (1947), 235 (1954), 89 (1961), *c.*100 (1999), 123 (2006), 263 (2011).

Truscotts Flat (*Co. Georgiana*) 33°54'S. 149°37'E., 30 km SW of Oberon, on Walbrook Ck; airfield.

Trustums Hill (*Co. Richmond*) 29°06'S. 153°20'E., 3 km S. of Woodburn.

Tubbamurra (*Co. Clarke*) 30°06'S. 151°46'E., 15 km NE of Guyra; farming; PO 1911; school 1903, additions 1956, closed 1981; TX 1929; pop. 116 (1901), 153 (1911), 108 (1933), 121 (1947), 65 (1954), 78 (1961).

Tubbo (*Co. Boyd*) 34°39'S. 146°06'E., 30 km W. of Leeton; pop. 102 (1911), 45 (1933).

Tubbul (*Co. Bland*) 34°16'S. 148°00'E., 28 km W. of Young; thrived 1914; farming; cemetery 1896; PO 1891–1977; PS 1914–24; sawmill (T. Stewart) 1925; school 1889–1944 and 1955–67; telephone 1906; TX 1911, automatic 1976; Union C. (Monteagle-Bland) 1892, new one 1906; pop. 109 (1891), 128 (1901), 181 (1911), 269 (1921), 201 (1933), 278 (1947), 190 (1954), 184 (1961).

Tubbul Road (*Co. Bland*) 34°16'S. 147°56'E., 33 km W. of Young; RS 1916, station b. by W.S. Millard & Sons Ltd, closed 1977; telephone 1937; TX 1937–40.

Tubra (*Co. Buller*) see Tooloom.

Tucabia (*Co. Clarence*) 29°40'S. 153°06'E., 17 km E. of Grafton, on Coldstream R.; village gaz. 1885; sugar-cane, bananas, potatoes, maize, dairying, timber; bridge 1908, over Coldstream R.; caterpillar infestation 1948; cemetery 1886; drought 1936; FB; floods 1890 and 1921; gale 1926; PO 1914–80; sawmills: Preston Bros and Joseph Reid; school 1895, new building b. 1898 by A. Ling, alterations and additions 1941 by H.H. Thompson, damaged 1993, additions 1994; telephone 1910; tornado (damaged every building) 1993; TX 1934, automatic 1959; Union C. b. 1901 by Charles Firth, damaged 1926, destroyed 1993; water reticulation 1966; pop. 138 (1911), 200 (1933), 167 (1947), 142 (1954), 178 (1961), 236 (1991), 281 (1996), 263 (2001), 257 (2006), 287 (2011).

Tuckaburra (*Co. Rous*) see South Golden Beach.

Tuckerbil (*Co. Cooper*) see Koonadan.

Tucki Tucki (*Co. Rous*) 28°56'S. 153°19'E., 7 km NE of Coraki, on Wilsons R.; cemetery (109 graves 1898+) 1891, incl. columbarium 1999; quarry; creamery (Foley Bros) 1897; school 1882–95 and 1904–85; wharf b. 1888 by J. Walsh; pop. 88 (1901), 90 (1911), 77 (1933), 67 (1947), 101 (1954), 274 (2011).

Tucki Tucki (*Co. Rous*) see also Wyrallah.

Tucklan (*Co. Lincoln*) 32°09'S. 149°23'E., 15 km S. of Dunedoo; mining (gold disc. 1895 by Jack and Jim Marshall) 1896–1902, wheat, grazing; hailstorm 1929; PO 1897–1980; sawmill (G.H. New); school 1897–1914 and 1922–40; telephone 1924; TX 1926; pop. 154 (1901), 148 (1911), 141 (1933).

Tuckombil (*Co. Rous*) 28°49'S. 153°28'E., 4 km NE of Alstonville; school 1885–1966; butter factory (Alstonville Co-op. Refrigerating Co. Ltd) b. 1890 by A. Duncan, closed 1905; sugar mill (McPhee's) 1873; pop. 66 (1911), 57 (1933), 194 (1947), 105 (1954), 113 (1961), 267 (2011).

Tuckurimba (*Co. Rous*) 28°57'S. 153°19'E., 5 km NE of Coraki; dairying; caterpillar infestation 1919; cemetery; gale 1942; PO

1909; quarry; school 1891, new building b. 1900 by T.W. Keith, closed 1975; telephone 1909; TX 1916; pop. 125 (1911), 113 (1933), 74 (1947), 55 (1954), 51 (1961).

Tueloga (*Co. Wakool*) 35°07'S. 143°37'E., 55 km S. of Balranald; RS (Victorian railway) 1928, closed.

Tuena (*Co. Georgiana*) 34°01'S. 149°20'E., 51 km N. of Crookwell, on Tuena Ck; settled 1836 by Samuel Blackman, estab. 1852, town gaz. 1859, designated as chief town of the county; orig. mining (gold disc. 1851 by John Douglas, worked 1851–1915, also copper, silver, iron, zinc), then fruit, tobacco, wheat, sheep, cattle, potatoes; Angl. C. (St Mark's) 1886, renovations 1986, additions 1996; brewery (orig. operated by Samuel Williams) 1872–75; bridge 1940, over Limestone Ck; bushfires 1868, 1874, 1952; cemetery 1879; CH (incl. lock-up) b. 1862 by Arundel Everett and William Stephens, additions 1900 by George William Brewer, closed 1958, reused, demolished 1978; earth tremor 1890; electricity 1958; FB; foot-bridge b. 1883 by Lane, new one 1894, destroyed 1916, rebuilt, destroyed 1996, damaged and closed 2010, new one 2013; furnace 1888–89; mines: Advance 1897, Alexandria or Bald Ridge (A. McKenzie) 1902, Amos's Lucky Hit 1881–95, City of Sydney 1875, Cooper and McKenzie *c.*1890, Garnet 1898–1900, Golden Dyke 1897–98 and 1902, Markham's Hill (Hoare and Cooper) 1898–1902, W. Malone, Nuggetty Gully (Blay and Withers) 1904–5, Oliver's, Peek's Reef 1892, Penny Royal, A.V. Rigby and W.G. Ford; PO 1852; pound (stock) 1863; Presb. C. (St Margaret's) 1890, restored 1971; PS 1852, new one b. 1885 by George Horn; Rom. Cath. C. o. 1896 in former Wes. Meth. C., bought from John Hunter, closed 1934, new one (St Mary's) d. and b. 1934 by Leney and Cheverton (largely using bricks from the Cordillera mine chimney, demolished for this purpose), restored 1995; school 1860–62, 1871–73, 1879–1998, reused; stamper battery (Forwood's) erected 1895 by T. Mills; storm 1904; telegraph 1880; TX 1922, automatic 1984; Wes. Meth. C. 1870, unused, sold to John Hunter, reused 1896; pop. *c.*90 (1852), 124 (1861), 131 (1871), 213 (1881), 243 (1891), 83 (1901), 289 (1911), 125 (1933), 140 (1947), 98 (1954), 150 (1961), 50 (1996), 187 (2011).

Tuggerabach (*Co. Dowling*) 33°33'S. 146°41'E., 39 km SE of Lake Cargelligo; telephone 1926; TX 1927.

Tuggerah (*Co. Northumberland*) 33°19'S. 151°25'E., 3 km S. of Wyong, on Tuggerah Lake; (incl. Chittaway Point); Tuggerah Lakes till 1911; orig. timber, then agric., grazing, dairying, hort., orchards, fishing, tourism; airfield (World War II); Angl. C. (All Saints') 1930–33 d. and b. by J.E. Ward, closed 1979, sold and reused, dismantled 2000; Assemblies of God C.: Coastlife and Crossroads Christ. 2008; brewery (Central Coast); bridge 1906, new one (Lees Bridge) 1980, over Ourimbah Ck; clothing factory (Moderne, renamed Moonray Mills); FB; floods 1903, 1927, 1930, 1939, 2020; Meth. C. 1907; PO: Chittaway Point 1937 and Tuggerah 1894–1982; railway bridge to Wyong (5 reinforced concrete elliptical arches) over Wyong Ck; RS (formerly Tuggerah Lakes) 1890; Salv. Army C.; sawmill (Solomon Staples); school 1892 b. by William Smith, relocated, new one b. 1898, damaged 1959, additions 1960, extended 1965; sewage works (South Wyong); sewerage connected 1986; telephone: Chittaway Point 1937 and Tuggerah 1909; tornado 1959; TX (Chittaway Point) 1954; Unit. C. (orig. Union) 1907–82; wharf (stone) b. 1901 by Matthew James Woodbury, ruined; pop. 103 (1901), 527 (1911), 415 (1933), 397 (1947), 363 (1954), 474 (1961), 1,017 (2011).

Tuggerah Entrance (*Co. Northumberland*) see The Entrance.

Tuggerah Lakes (*Co. Northumberland*) see Berkeley Vale, Shelly Beach, Tuggerah and Tumbi Umbi.

Tuggerawong (*Co. Northumberland*) 33°17'S. 151°29'E., 5 km E. of Wyong, on Tuggerah Lake; Karraganbah till 1947; poultry; bushfire 1957; PO 1927; school 1957, additions 1982 and 2010; sewerage 1976; telephone 1927; TX 1928–63; wharf; pop. 58 (1933), 135 (1947), 217 (1954), 270 (1961), 1,151 (2006), 1,204 (2011).

Tuglow (*Co. Westmoreland*) 33°57'S. 149°57'E., 28 km S. of Oberon, on Tuglow R.; caves; mine (copper) 1898.

Tugrabakh (*Co. Gloucester*) 31°59'S. 151°59'E., 5 km N. of Gloucester, on Gloucester R.; RS 1922–65; pop. 70 (1933), 57 (1947).

Tulla (*Co. Wakool*) 35°29'S. 144°17'E., 22 km NE of Barham; airfield.

Tullakool (*Co. Wakool*) 35°25'S. 144°12'E., 24 km N. of Barham; soldiers' settlement 1948+, village gaz. 1956; rice; POW camp 1943–46; school 1957–63; TX (automatic); pop. 206 (1954), 208 (1961), 331 (2006).

Tullamore (*Co. Kennedy*) 32°38'S. 147°34'E., 35 km NW of Trundle; Gobondry till 1890 then Bullock Creek till 1895; orig. a private town, surveyed by Edwin John Witts, laid out 1906, founded 1910, thrived 1933; timber, wheat, sheep; Angl. C. (St John's) b. 1933 by Gordon Padey, d. by Kaberry and Chard; bushfires 1905, 1926, 1964; cemetery (373 graves 1905+), incl. columbarium; CH (incl. police station) b. 1935 by Robert Hood, closed 1980; droughts 1965 and 1968; earth tremor 1937; FB; fires 1900, 1915, 1926, 1932, 1935; flood 1959; gastroenteritis epidemic 1954; hailstorm 1962; hospital 1930, redeveloped 2007; Meth. C. 1917; mouse plague 1956; PO 1909, new one b. 1929 by W.J. Morrison; powerhouse (W.J. Colville) 1947–59; Presb. C. 1913, new one (Van der Maal Memorial); PS b. 1910 by Kerr; railway engine shed 1915, removed from Peak Hill; Rom. Cath. C. (St Mary's) b. 1928 by Norman Doyle, new one (Assumption of our Blessed Lady); RS 1908, station b. by Reid and Castles; sawmill (James Tully); school 1915, new building 1925, new building (removed from Kelvin Grove) 1950, additions 1955 by J.C. De Wol, additions 1963 and 1970; silo 1933; telephone 1912; TX 1912; pop. 104 (1911), 541 (1933), 326 (1947), 417 (1954), 337 (1961), 331 (1971), 317 (1976), 324 (1981), 319 (1986), 306 (1991), 268 (1996), 234 (2001), 210 (2011).

Tullera (*Co. Rous*) 28°46'S. 153°17'E., 5 km N. of Lismore; macadamia nuts, bananas, dairying, cattle; FB; school (Booerie till 1898, Toolaroo till 1922 then Modanville till 1923) 1891–1945; telephone 1923; TX 1927; pop. 149 (1933), 53 (1947), 120 (1954), 151 (1961), 356 (2011).

Tullibigeal (*Co. Dowling*) 33°25'S. 146°44'E., 35 km E. of Lake Cargelligo; village gaz. 1917 as Boorabil; farming and wheat; Angl. C. (St George's) b. 1937 by W.H. Geale; bushfire 1951; cemetery; FB; PO 1918; Presb. C. (Scots) 1927; PS 1927, closed; Rom. Cath. C. (St Isidore's) b. 1954 by Alan Smith; RS (Boorabil till 1918) 1917, station closed and removed 1984; sale-yards (Irvine Bros) 1943; school 1928, additions 1963 and 1985; silo 1928; telephone 1923; TX 1924; pop. 308 (1933), 259 (1947), 190 (1954), 206 (1961), 258 (2006), 384 (2011).

Tullimbar (*Co. Camden*) 34°35'S. 150°45'E., 10 km SW of Dapto, on Cooback Ck; fire 1891; PO 1872–94; school 1881 b. by John Schadel, d. by George Allen Mansfield, closed 1898, reopened 1923, closed 1942, sold and reused 1965, fire 1975, new one 2008; pop. 157 (2011).

Tulloona (*Co. Stapylton*) 28°51'S. 150°06'E., 37 km SW of Boggabilla; Angl. C. (St David's); bore (2,535 ft or 772.7 m) sunk 1899 by Hayes; school 1959; telephone 1967; TX (automatic) 1968.

Tullyangela Clearing (*Co. St Vincent*) 34°56'S. 150°09'E., 33 km SW of Bundanoon, on Tullyangela Ck.

Tullymorgan (*Co. Clarence*) 29°22'S. 153°07'E., 12 km NW of Maclean; Cormick's Creek till 1907; dairying, sugar-cane 1925; bushfire 2001; gale 1914; PO 1911; Rom. Cath. C. (St Patrick's) 1915; school (Cormick's Creek till 1899) 1888–99 and 1914–71; telephone 1908; TX 1925; pop. 154 (1911), 157 (1933), 105 (1947), 88 (1954), 70 (1961).

Tulmah (*Co. Wakool*) see Toolmah.

Tumbarumba (*Co. Selwyn*) 35°46'S. 148°01'E., 54 km S. of Tumut, on Tumbarumba Ck;

Tumberumba till 1915; settled *c.*1836, site reserved 1847, surveyed 1859 by Edward Fisher, first lots sold 1860; orig. sheep, then cattle, gold (disc. 1855, boomed in 1860s, faded by 1875, finished 1939), timber, wheat, potatoes, oats, apples, pears, plums, cherries, gooseberries, strawberries, tobacco, dairying, grapes 1988+; ambulance station 1948, new one 1954, replaced 1985; Angl. C. (St Jude's) 1875, vestry and porch added, church refurbished 1930, extended 1985; Assemblies of God C. (Community); brewery estab. 1883 by William Seymour Eaton, renamed Alpine Brewery in 1889, burnt down 1902, rebuilt by John Chapman; bridges: one b. 1882 by W. Phillips, over Tumbarumba Ck, one b. 1941 (concrete) over Pound Ck, one b. 1956, one b. 1964; bushfires 1892 and 1952; butter factory (Heinecke Bros, later Tumbarumba Co-op. Butter Factory Co. Ltd) 1907, bought 1916 by George Julius Rohr, closed, reopened as freezing works; cemetery 1864, incl. lawn cemetery; CH (incl. lock-up) b. 1867 by William Lever, new one b. 1886 by J.P. Swanston, d. by James Johnstone Barnet; cordial factory estab. by Mahon and Headley, Hogan replaced Headley in partnership, taken over by Whelan, taken over 1926 by John Austin Cowley; FB (station b. 1972); fires 1863 and 1933; floods 1909 and 2010; flour mill (Fritz Weule), burnt down 1893; 2 foot-bridges; hospital (cottage) b. 1917 by T.A. Armstrong, additions 1955 by H.O. Lyons, new one b. 2020 by Richard Crookes Constructions, d. by Peckvonhartel; lock-up b. 1885 by A. Frew; PO 1860, new one b. 1889 by Charles Hardy; pound (stock) 1860; Presb. C. (St Andrew's) b. 1889 by Hawkins, closed, sold 2018; PS, burnt down 1910, replaced; railway coal stage; railway engine shed; railway turntable, 60 ft (18.3 m), closed; reservoir 500,000 gal. (2,273 kl); rifle range 1908; Rom. Cath. C. (All Saints') b. 1905 by Charles Hardy, d. by William John Monks; RS 1921–74; sale-yards; sawmills: Alpine, Bago Timbers Pty Ltd, J. Doughty, Gaylard Bros, Hardys Pty Ltd, closed 1926, burnt down 1938, F. Hussell, Hyne & Sons, Tumbarumba Hardwood Co., reopened 1931; scarlet fever 1882; schools: primary 1868, new one b. 1872 by J. Swanston, repairs 1882 by J. Pinhorn, replacement 1938, and HS 1968, additions 1976 and 1985; sewerage 1964; snowstorm 1899; telegraph 1878; TX; typhoid 1904, 1909, 1917; Unit. C.; water supply 1939, new treatment plant d. and b. 2011 by Aquatec Maxcon Pty Ltd; pop. *c.*350 (1866), 138 (1871), 690 (1881), 496 (1891), 860 (1901), 939 (1911), 1,136 (1933), 1,196 (1947), 1,293 (1954), 1,511 (1961), 1,443 (1966), 1,391 (1971), 1,499 (1976), 1,536 (1981), 1,603 (1986), 1,548 (1991), 1,502 (1996), 1,501 (2001), 1,487 (2006), 1,455 (2011).

Tumberumba (*Co. Selwyn*) see Tumbarumba.

Tumbi Umbi (*Co. Northumberland*) 33°22'S. 151°27'E., 6 km SW of The Entrance, on Tumbi Umbi Ck; farming and citrus orchards; Angl. C. (St Christopher's), removed from The Entrance, later moved to Bateau Bay; Assemblies of God C. (Bayside); bushfire 1953; foot-bridge; hailstorm 2015; Meth. C. 1938; PO 1911, relocated 1996; pottery (Spotted Gum); Rom. Cath. C. (St John Fisher) 1988; sawmills: Killarney, Cecil George Stimson (incl. fruit case factory), Taylor and Doran (incl. fruit case factory) 1926; school (Tumbi Umbi HS till 2002, then Tuggerah Lakes Secondary College) 1997; sewerage 1975; telephone 1914; TX 1925, automatic 1968; Unit. C., closed, sold 2001 and 2018, reused, new one; pop. 143 (1933), 275 (1947), 309 (1954), 351 (1961), 4,326 (2006), 4,977 (2011).

Tumbi Umbi (*Co. Northumberland*) see also Wamberal.

Tumbleton (*Co. Monteagle*) see Garibaldi.

Tumblong (*Co. Wynyard*) 35°08'S. 148°00'E., 12 km SW of Gundagai, on Adelong Ck; Adelong Crossing Place till 1913; goldmining (alluvial), agric., grazing, dairying; Angl. C. (St James's) b. 1871 by Marshall, Neale and Wolstenholm, d. by Charles Thatcher; bushfire 1979; cemetery; earth tremor 1871; FB; fire 1906; flour mills: Henry Moon, sen. 1862 (orig. water powered, burnt down 1892) and Victoria (b. 1874 for William Williams, sen., d. by David Wilson); Meth. C. 1906; mine (Root Hog or Die Mine); PO 1864–1973; RS (Adelong Crossing till 1913) 1903, station b. by F.G. Filmer, closed 1975, demolished 1984; school (Adelong Crossing till 1913) 1870, new one b. 1886 on new site by W.H. Hilton, repairs 1893 by W.J. Ritchie, closed 1990; storm 1877; telephone 1890; TX 1913, automatic 1958; Wes. Meth. C. 1887, acquired by govt; pop. 301 (1901), 307 (1933), 265 (1947), 237 (1954), 257 (1961), 338 (2011).

Tumbulgum (*Co. Rous*) 28°17'S. 153°28'E., 9 km NE of Murwillumbah, on Tweed R.; South Tumbulgum till 1885; declined in 1880s but thrived in 1890s, bypassed by highway 1973; orig. timber, then shipbuilding, later farming, sugar-cane, bananas; Angl. C. 1888, destroyed 1943, replaced (St Peter's) 1954, closed, sold 2013 to Rob and Brenda Stuttle and reopened as Living Waters C.; bridge (Alexander Twohill Bridge) 1986; caterpillar infestation 1921; diphtheria 1914; floods 1931, 1945, 2017, 2020; PO 1885; Presb. C. (St Mark's) b. 1887 by H.H. Hawkins, closed, sold and reused; PS 1933–59; punt, ceased 1986, across Tweed R.; Rom. Cath. C. (St Joseph's) 1940, closed, sold 2008, 2015, 2018, reused; school (Tweed Junction till 1889) 1876, additions and repairs 1886 by W.J. Gillies, new building b. 1891 by Hugh Mimnow, additions 1913 by Alfred John Modini; storm 1943; sugar mill (Abbotsford) operated 1872–95 by Alexander Pringle, Thomas Shankey and Patrick Byrne; telegraph 1884; TX (automatic) 1951; wharf b. 1885 by David Rankin; pop. 166 (1901), 317 (1911), 192 (1933), 273 (1947), 285 (1954), 310 (1961), 201 (1971), 238 (1976), 249 (1981), 300 (1986), 333 (1991), 385 (1996), 360 (2001), 349 (2006), 383 (2011).

Tumbulgum (*Co. Rous*)
see also Tumbulgum North.

Tumbulgum North (*Co. Rous*) 28°15'S. 153°28'E., 11 km NE of Murwillumbah, on Tweed R.; Tweed Junction till 1881, Tumbulgum till 1885; farming, dairying, bananas; boiling-down works (A. Masterson & Son); cemetery (150+ burials 1870–1947), closed 1947, restored; cordial factory (George and Charles Henry Skinner) 1888–91, moved to Murwillumbah; distillery (Husk) estab. by Paul Messenger et al.; PO 1872, burnt down 1914; PS 1885; SD Adventist C.; telephone 1925; TX 1932–50; pop. 153 (1933), 333 (1947), 245 (1954), 190 (1961), 305 (2011).

Tumorrama (*Co. Buccleuch*) 35°10'S. 148°25'E., 23 km NE of Tumut, on Shaking Bog Ck; Margules till 1899, then Tomooroma till 1935; Angl. C. (Sacred Advent) 1923; FB 1951; PO 1899–1971; school 1905–14; telephone 1915; TX 1917; pop. 87 (1911), 84 (1933), 74 (1947), 85 (1954), 116 (1961).

Tumulla Loop (*Co. Bathurst*) 33°31'S. 149°29'E., 21 km E. of Blayney.

Tumut (*Co. Wynyard*) 35°18'S. 148°13'E., 80 km E. of Wagga Wagga, on Tumut R.; (incl. Boyd, formerly Railway End); orig. Mill Angle; settled 1830 by George Shelley, estab. 1838, surveyed 1848, laid out and first land sale 1848, village washed away 1852, moved to new site, new town proc. 1880, munic. 1887–1928, town thrived 1950s–60s; goldmining (alluvial), wheat and maize, then fruit, dairying, grazing, broom millet, tobacco, forestry (softwood) 1921+, eucalyptus oil distillation; airport (5 km N.), upgraded 1983; ambulance station; Angl. C. b. 1857 by Frederick Eberlin, new one (All Saints') b. 1876 by Thomas Brashier and Frederick Kinred, d. by Edmund Thomas Blacket, tower and spire 1881, new roof 1908 d. by Cyril Blacket, roof restoration 1928 d. by W.A. Nelson, church restoration and re-roofing 1986 by John Lusk, d. by Jackson Teece Chesterman Willis; Apostolic C. (Community); Bapt. C. 1969; box factory (T.S. Carson) 1946; breweries: Anderson's 1860–69, John Beale 1878, Thomas Sanderson 1873–1919, Tumut River Brewing Co. estab. 2013 by Tim Martin and Simon Rossato; brickworks, sold 1921 by George Emery to A.J.D. Emery; bridges: first one b. 1847 by Francis Anderson and Francis Foord, new one b. 1864, one b. 1904 by Edward William Fitzgerald, one at Punt's Crossing b. 1906 by Donaldson and Vincent, over Tumut R.; broom factories: McDonald Broom Co. (in former freezing works), burnt down 1935, and Tumut Rural Co-op. Millet Society (b. 1946 by J. Rogers and W. Dowell, taken over 1978 by Cliff Wortes, taken over by Geoff Wortes and Robert Richards); bushfires 1875, 1881, 1939, 1940; butter factories: H.W. Mason (incl. creamery) and Tumut Co-op. Butter Factory Ltd (b. 1905 by A.W. Lowe, alterations 1917, changed 1922 to Tumut Co-op. Dairy Co. Ltd, new factory b. 1924 by W.A. Whittle, d. by Richard Wildridge & Co., closed 1970, reused); carriage-works: Enterprise (James Elphick), Federal (Kindred's, burnt down 1902), W. Himsworth; cemetery 1897; CH 1846, (second) 1859, additions 1863, (third, incl. lock-up) b. 1876 by W. and D. Boston, d. by James Johnstone Barnet, repairs 1883 by W. Masters and John Cush, alterations 1893 by W.J. Ritchie, d. by Walter Liberty Vernon, repairs 1908 by C.W.M. Vernon, additions 1961, restored 2006; chaff mill (Thomas Dean); Chinese joss house; clothing factory (Dyomee Manufacturing Pty Ltd) 1946–53; cordial factories: Herbert Silvester Davy, Robert Dear, Robert Downing, Waranga (bought 1903 by James Considine from Harry Beck); diphtheria 1920; droughts 1839, 1914, 1983; earth tremors 1871, 1898, 1917; electricity 1921, then supplied from Burrinjuck 1929; engineering works (DME Engineering Services Aust. Pty Ltd) 2001; eucalyptus oil distillery; FB 1903 (station b. 1908, new one b. 1922 by Crammond and Lowther, new one 1975); fibrous plaster works; fire 1903; floods 1844, 1851, 1879, 1952, 2011; flour mills: Fred Body (b. 1853 by Hoad, orig. water powered, converted to steam, demolished 1964), G. Dunstone & Co., Francis Foord and Moore 1846, G.F. Grill (suction-gas powered), demolished 1964, L. Mandelson, Henry Moon & Sons, J. Simmers, Victoria Water Flour Mill (Hayes Bros); freezing works (William Daniel Patrick O'Brien), removed 1907 from Gilmore and enlarged by J. Patterson; gale 1875; gasworks 1882; grasshopper infestation 1931; hailstorm 1901; heatwave 1882; hospital (cottage) 1900, additions 1940, 1962, 1966; Jehovah's Witnesses C.; lock-up 1897; Lutheran C. (Pilgrim); measles epidemic 1893; particle board factory (Pyneboard Pty Ltd) b. 1967 by A.V. Jennings (Canberra) Pty Ltd, d. by Stafford, Moor and Farrington; PO 1849, new one b. 1879 by Eberlin and Hoad, renovated 1904, alterations and additions 1911 by T.G. Hastings; pound (stock) 1840; POW control centre (World War II); Presb. C. (St Stephen's) 1856, closed, sold 1876; PS b. 1874 by Thomas Hodgson, d. by James Johnstone Barnet, re-roofed and renovated; 4 quarries; railway coal stage, removed 1983; railway engine shed, fire 1910; railway turntable (William Sellers & Co.), 50 ft (15.2 m), derelict; reservoir (Telegragh Hill) 1902; rifle range (3 km SW); Rom. Cath. C. 1859, reused, new one (Immaculate Conception) b. 1875–78 by P. M'Namara and Kinred Bros (an employee killed 1877); RS 1903, station b. by F.G. Filmer, closed 1984, reused 2011; sale-yards 1932; Salv. Army C. 1889; sawmills: Stephen F. Arentz, Carson's, F.D. Lance, John J.J. Learmont, Margules Bros, Pollock's (estab. by Bill Stubbs), Charles Stokes; schools: Franklin 1976 (additions 1982 and 1993, additions 2010 by Burton Constructions Pty Ltd), Tumut 1859 (new one b. 1870 by Raeside, Eberlin, Schnokel & Co., reused, replaced 1888, new building 1954, additions 2012), Tumut HS 1961 (additions 1967, 1969, 1981); SD Adventist C.; sewerage augmentation 1996; snow 1899, 1935, 2019; squall 1885; storms 1865 and 1913; streets lit by acetylene gas 1899; TC 1976, became a campus of Riverina Institute in 1992; telegraph 1876, new office b. 1879 by Eberlin and Hoad, alterations and additions 1911 by T.G. Hastings; tobacco factory (Kentucky Tobacco Manufacturing Co.) estab. 1883 by R. McKay and D.J. Emery; trees (ornamental) planted in streets 1861 by James Carr for Barney Kelly, more planted 1901; trout hatchery 1929; TX 1909, automatic 1977; typhoid 1876, 1881, 1896 (5 died), 1900; Unit. C. (St Stephen's, orig. Presb.) b. 1878 by Thomas Brashier and Packett, d. by David Wilson, renovated 1949; watch-house b. 1939 by Charles Hardy; water supply augmentation 1986; waterworks (pumping plant erected by Tutin) 1903; Wes. Meth. C. 1871 d. by J. Francis; wool-scour (P. Rodgers); pop. 64 (1851), 256 (1856), 432 (1861), *c.*520 (1866), 555 (1871), 787 (1881), *c.*900 (1887), 980 (1891), *c.*1,300 (1895), 1,391 (1901), 2,274 (1911), 2,176 (1933), *c.*2,500 (1941), 2,725 (1947), 3,012 (1954), 3,489 (1961), 4,278 (1966), 5,525 (1971), 5,569 (1976), 5,816 (1981), 6,099 (1986), 5,955 (1991), 5,915 (1996), 6,243 (2001), 5,925 (2006), 6,086 (2011).

Tumut Plains (*Co. Buccleuch*) 35°20'S. 148°16'E., 6 km SE of Tumut, on Shelleys Ck; maize; Angl. C. (St Andrew's) 1892; bridge (Shelley Bridge, renamed Junction Bridge) b. 1893–95, McDonald timber truss, 345 ft (105.1 m), repairs 2006, over Tumut R.; caterpillar infestation 1873; FB 1943; quarry; school 1880–1953; telephone 1911; TX 1923; pop. 197 (1901), 283 (1933), 182 (1947), 165 (1954), 165 (1961), 158 (2006).

Tumut Pond (*Co. Selwyn*) 35°58'S. 148°25'E., 42 km SE of Tumbarumba, on Clear Ck; orig. Lorna Doone; orig. mining, then estab. 1950 as temporary construction camp for Snowy Mountains Hydro-Electric Scheme, defunct; barracks; 3 bridges over Clear Ck; mine (Lorna Doone Gold Mines NL); powerhouse.

Tuncester (*Co. Rous*) 28°48'S. 153°13'E., 6 km W. of Lismore, on Hanging Rock Ck; cattle, dairying, fruit; boiling-down works (Campbell's); brewery (Tooth & Co. Ltd) 1979–86; FB; Meth. C. 1904; PO 1911–71; rifle range (Lismore) 1930; RS (Tunstall till 1907) 1903–76; sawmill; school (Tunstall till 1907) 1880–81 and 1897–1972; telephone 1911; pop. 50 (1901), 179 (1911), 297 (1933), 154 (1947), 152 (1954), 126 (1961).

Tuncurry (*Co. Gloucester*) 32°11'S. 152°30'E., 1 km NW of Forster, on Wallis Lake; (incl. Jonnel Park); orig. North Shore, then North Forster till 1891; estab. 1875 by John Wright and Henry Colvin, surveyed 1892, village gaz. 1893; sawmilling, shipbuilding (started by John Wright) 1877–1954, fishing, oysters, dairying, tourism 1945+, retirement centre; ambulance station; Angl. C. (St Nicholas's); breakwater b. 1922–25, new one, 1,450 ft (442 m), 1966; bridge (47 concrete spans) to Forster, b. 1957–59 by John Holland (Constructions) Pty Ltd, 2,070 ft (631 m), over Wallis Lake; bushfire 1928; butter factory (Cape Hawke Dist. Co-op. Dairy Co. Ltd) b. 1918 by George Perkins, closed 1958; cemetery (2,748 graves 1883+) 1891, incl. lawn cemetery and columbaria; Christ. Outreach C. (Lakeside), additions and alterations 2009, damaged 2013, renovated and reopened 2014; Church of Christ; cordial factory estab. 1946 by J. Walker, taken over 1949 by J. Lanton; FB; fire 1905; floods 1894, 1927, 1962; ice works: Cape Hawke Dist. Rural Co-op. Society Ltd, Coombes's 1895, Great Lakes Ice Pty Ltd 1989, moved to Nabiac; jetty; PO 1889; powerhouse (Cape Hawke Dist. Rural Co-op. Society) 1929; prison farm (afforestation) 1913–38, reused; PS 1947, new one 1952–59; punts: diesel one across Wallamba R., pedestrian one (Charles A. Blows) 1921–59, across Wallis Lake, vehicular one (Charles A. Blows) 1924–59, across Wallis Lake; Reorganised LDS (Mormon) C. (Community of Christ) b. 1910 by Cornelius Butterworth, Stanley Wright and Frank Avery, d. by Cornelius Butterworth, vestry added 1950, fire 1969, church re-roofed and repaired, restored 1995 by Bruce Wright and Lyn Nicholson; Rom. Cath. C. 1888, (second) 1926, demolished 1968, new one (St Mary Star of the Sea) b. 1969 by P.J. Smyth, closed and sold 2016; Salv. Army C.; sawmills: Case Timbers Pty Ltd 1944, Maxwell Porter & Son 1898 (burnt down 1940), Porter and Taylor 1903, Smith Bros (fire 1951), Tuncurry Timber Trading Co. (closed 1958), John Wright 1877 (burnt down and rebuilt 1900, burnt down again

1951); schools: Tuncurry (Forster North till 1891) 1882, additions 1891, 1916, 1954, 1959, 1981 and Great Lakes College 2003; SD Adventist C.; sewerage 1969; shipyard (estab. by John Wright), closed 1958; storm (man killed) 1903; TC (North Coast Institute, Great Lakes Campus), in old public school, additions 2010 d. by Collard Maxwell; telephone 1900; TX 1911–60; Unit. C. (orig. Meth.) 1945 d. by Gaudron and Pereira, porch added 1980; water reticulation 1969; wharves: Goodlet and Smith (b. 1900 by Donaldson) and John Wright & Co.; pop. 174 (1901), 237 (1911), 517 (1933), 757 (1947), 830 (1954), 936 (1961), 6,195 (1976, incl. Forster), 9,261 (1981, incl. Forster), 11,239 (1986, incl. Forster), 14,578 (1991, incl. Forster), 15,943 (1996, incl. Forster), 17,996 (2001, incl. Forster), 18,372 (2006, incl. Forster), 18,904 (2011, incl. Forster).

Tunglebung (*Co. Drake*) 28°50'S. 152°40'E., 37 km W. of Casino, on Tunglebung Ck; school 1954–73; telephone 1925; TX 1927, automatic 1952; pop. 126 (1933), 125 (1947), 134 (1954), 115 (1961).

Tungsten (*Co. Clive*) 29°16'S. 151°40'E., 40 km SW of Tenterfield, on Bald Rock Ck; defunct; mining (wolframite); cemetery; mine (Carter's); PO 1911–26; quarry; school 1912–24; telephone 1913; pop. 322 (1911).

Tunnabutta (*Co. Wellington*) 32°42'S. 149°44'E., 18 km SW of Mudgee; school 1883 b. by Gordon and Haywood, closed 1915; storm 1862; pop. 50 (1911), 20 (1933).

Tunnel Camp (*Co. Rous*) see Cougal.

Tunstall (*Co. Rous*) see Tuncester.

Tuntabble (*Co. Rous*) see Tuntable Creek.

Tuntable Creek (*Co. Rous*) 28°38'S. 153°16'E., 6 km SE of Nimbin, on Tuntable Ck; orig. Tuntabble; popular area for communal living on small holdings in 1970s; Meth. C. b. 1907 by Robert Dunn, closed 1941 and demolished; school 1926, additions 2010; pop. 170 (1933), 153 (1947), 61 (1954), 323 (2006).

Tuntable Creek (*Co. Rous*) see also The Channon.

Tuntable Falls (*Co. Rous*) 28°35'S. 153°16'E., 6 km NE of Nimbin, on Tuntable Ck; airfield; bushfire 1951; sawmill (West and Sharpe); school 1946–56; telephone 1923; TX 1936; pop. 90 (1933), 88 (1947), 93 (1954), 54 (1961).

Tuppal (*Co. Townsend*) 35°41'S. 145°15'E., 32 km SE of Deniliquin; village gaz. 1867; school 1958–71, moved to Finley and reused; pop. 67 (1891), 51 (1901), 21 (1933).

Tura (*Co. Auckland*) 36°51'S. 149°55'E., 4 km NE of Merimbula.

Tura Beach (*Co. Auckland*) 36°52'S. 149°55'E., 3 km NE of Merimbula, on Tasman Sea; 2 reservoirs; sewage works; pop. 800 (1986), 1,415 (1991), 1,639 (1996), 2,105 (2001), 2,742 (2006), 2,921 (2011).

Turalla (*Co. Murray*) 35°14'S. 149°25'E., 4 km NW of Bungendore; airfield; cemetery; pop. 120 (1911).

Turanville (*Co. Brisbane*) 32°06'S. 150°51'E., 6 km S. of Scone, on Kingdon Ponds; bridge 1979, over Kingdon Ponds; pop. 32 (1933).

Turee (*Co. Bligh*) 31°56'S. 149°48'E., 15 km SE of Coolah, on Turee Ck; farming and grazing; Angl. C.; PO 1863–67; pop. *c.*150 (1866), 31 (1933).

Turilawa (*Co. Buckland*) 31°22'S. 150°34'E., 9 km W. of Werris Ck; RS 1925–75.

Turill (*Co. Bligh*) 32°07'S. 149°50'E., 34 km S. of Coolah, on Murrumbline Ck; Inglewood till 1892; farming and grazing; bridge over Murrumbline Ck; PO 1896–1984; PS; Rom. Cath. C. (St John the Baptist) 1899, alterations and repairs 1915, renovations 1937, closed; school (Wagoribil till 1930) 1888–91, 1903–31, 1954–76; telephone 1911; TX 1911, automatic 1984; Union C. b. 1913 by M. Duggan, closed, sold 2015 and 2017; pop. 61 (1901), 63 (1911), 76 (1933), 112 (1954), 95 (1961), 139 (2006).

Turkey Creek (*Co. Hardinge*) 30°36'S. 151°14'E., 25 km W. of Uralla; school 1889–91.

Turlinjah (*Co. Dampier*) 36°02'S. 150°05'E., 5 km NW of Tuross Head, on Tuross Lake; goldmining (reef), fishing, oysters; bridge 1953, over Smarts Ck; freezing works (Bert Cantlay); mine (Italia) estab. 1888 by Nicholas

Leoni, sold 1892 to John Holden et al.; PO 1878–1966; sawmills: Clyde Sawmilling Co., and Sly and Howard 1902; school 1880 b. by A. Anderson and R. Speer, closed 1968; telephone 1910; TX 1925; pop. 77 (1901), 106 (1911), 86 (1933), 104 (1947), 113 (1954), 78 (1961), 229 (2011).

Turners Flat (*Co. Dudley*) 31°01'S. 152°42'E., 15 km NW of Kempsey; farming and dairying; bridge (13 spans) b. 1912 by J.J. McPhillips, 451 ft (137.5 m), damaged 1949, over Macleay R.; creamery (W.G. Trees, jun. and C. Sutherland, jun.) removed 1897 from Skillion Flat; FB 1968; flood 1949; gale 1870; PO 1927–64; Prim. Meth. C. 1891, destroyed 1922; school 1882–1965; storm 1922; telephone 1921; pop. 90 (1901), 86 (1911), 79 (1933), 64 (1947), 66 (1954), 60 (1961).

Turondale (*Co. Roxburgh*) 33°06'S. 149°37'E., 39 km N. of Bathurst, on Box Ridge Ck; Box Ridge till 1899; mining (gold disc. 1866, rush 1866), grazing, bees; airfield; Angl. C. (Holy Spirit) 1924; cemetery (51 burials 1903+) 1900; mines: Gypsy Countess and Great Shakespeare; PO 1872–1981; pound (stock) estab. 1922 by Worling and Bourke; quarry; school (Box Ridge till 1899) 1881–83, 1899–1925, 1957–67; telephone 1918; TX 1928, automatic 1981; pop. 87 (1901), 82 (1911), 62 (1921), 98 (1933), 57 (1947), 72 (1954), 143 (2006).

Turon Gates (*Co. Roxburgh*) 33°10'S. 149°54'E., 22 km N. of Portland, on Turon R.; goldmining.

Tuross (*Co. Dampier*) 36°18'S. 149°31'E., 35 km E. of Cooma, on Tuross R.; sheep; PO 1927–59; telephone 1914; TX 1946; pop. 65 (1911).

Tuross Head (*Co. Dampier*) 36°04'S. 150°08'E., 17 km N. of Narooma, on Tuross Lake; founded by Hector McWilliam; formerly sheep and cattle, then maize and dairying, tourism 1945+, retirement centre; Angl. C. (St Andrew's War Memorial) 1973, extended 1987, enlarged 1988; FB; Presb. C. (St David's), removed from Nerrigundah and re-erected 1953 by Athol Hawdon; 2 reservoirs; sawmill 1865; sewerage augmentation 1986; telephone 1936; trees planted in streets 1925 by Hector McWilliam; TX 1946, automatic 1967; water supply augmentation 1987 and 1990; pop. 26 (1933), 88 (1954), 114 (1961), 249 (1971), 465 (1976), 835 (1981), 1,233 (1986), 1,632 (1991), 1,786 (1996), 2,125 (2001), 2,120 (2006), 2,148 (2011).

Turpentine (*Co. St Vincent*) 35°02'S. 150°27'E., 20 km W. of Huskisson; bushfire 1919.

Turrawan (*Co. White*) 30°27'S. 149°53'E., 18 km SE of Narrabri; surveyed by John Valentine Gorman, town gaz. 1864, never fully developed; grazing, cotton, wheat, barley, citrus; FB; flood 1864; PO 1905–81; RS (5 km NW) 1884, closed; sawmills: George Johnson and Louis A. Pheiffer; school 1957–68; telephone 1905; TX 1927–81; pop. 100 (1911), 169 (1933), 121 (1947), 123 (1954), 98 (1961).

Turrawarra (*Co. Murchison*) 29°48'S. 150°52'E., 24 km W. of Inverell; school 1905–11.

Turvey Park (*Co. Wynyard*) see Wagga Wagga.

Tweed Heads (*Co. Rous*) 28°10'S. 153°32'E., 74 km N. of Lismore, on Terranora Inlet; (incl. Greenbank Island, first lots sold 1967, and West Tweed Heads); surveyed 1886 by Edwin Johnson, village gaz. 1887 as Cooloon, first lots sold 1887; timber *c.*1844+, then sugar-cane, bananas 1909+, agric., dairying, maize, fishing, oysters, tourism, retirement centre; ambulance station; Angl. C. 1907, additions 1918, renovations 1929, new one (St Cuthbert's) 1972 d. by Trevor James Reddacliff; Assemblies of God C. (Lifeworx Christ.); boat harbour; breakwater 1902, restored 1979; bridge (Boyds Bay Bridge) to Tweed Heads South, fabricated by Goninan Ltd, erected 1934 by Birt, Bolton and Haywood, 475 ft (144.8 m), steel and concrete girder with manual lift span, replaced 1985, over Terranora Ck; butter factory (North Coast Co-op. Ltd) 1911–37, new one b. 1938 by Daniel Gallagher, demolished 1982; cemetery (918 graves) 1901; CH b. 1927 by W.J. Brown, d. by Gorrie McLeish Blair, closed, restored, reused 1985, new one 1983 on new site; Church of Christ b. 1971 by Hanna and Edmed, sold 2009; customs-house 1871; cyclones 1929 and 1951; dengue fever 1916; FB 1921 (station b. 1924, demolished, replacement b. 1966); fires 1916, 1926, 1935; floods 1938 and 2016; furniture factory (W.V. Barrett & Co.); gales 1928 and 1930; hospital (The Tweed) 1972 d. by I. Roberts, additions 2002 and 2008; jetty b. 1893 by Thomas Griffiths; lighthouse (Point Danger) b. 1970 of concrete, 66 ft (20 m), converted 1996 to laser light; Meth. C. 1906, burnt down 1910; military post 1828–29; pilot station 1870, damaged and re-roofed 1929; PO: Tweed Heads 1878, new one b. 1907 by E.A. Burgess, repairs 1925 by T.N. Mustchin, replaced 1974 by Hanna and Edmed, and West Tweed Heads 1953–76; pound (stock) 1933; Presb. C. (St Andrew's) 1910, renovated 1917, remodelled 1960; PS 1892, new one b. 1896 by Hugh Mimnow, d. by Walter Liberty Vernon, alterations 1927 d. by Gorrie McLeish Blair, new one 1983 on new site, new one 2017; punt, replaced 1934 by bridge, across Terranora Ck; Rom. Cath. C. 1918, new one (St Joseph's) 1972; RS 1903, extended 1923, closed 1961; sandfly infestation 1910; school (Point Danger till 1907) 1884, additions 1893 and 1902 by W.J. Gillies, additions 1908 by R. Thornton, additions 1923 by Lanham and Deacon, new building b. 1954 by Frank Bennett, additions 1959; SD Adventist C.; sewerage 1967, augmentation 1987 and 1990; streets electric lit 1921; telegraph 1887; TX 1910, automatic 1970; Unit. C. (orig. Meth.) 1911, alterations 1948 by Neden and Piper, closed 1988, sold, removed, restored; univ. (Southern Cross 2001, Lakeside and Riverside Campuses); water supply augmentation 1963; wharf b. 1885 by David Rankin; pop. 100 (1891), 298 (1901), 712 (1911), 1,579 (1933), 2,125 (1947), 2,467 (1954), 3,291 (1961), 3,830 (1966), 5,147 (1971, incl. Tweed Heads South and Tweed Heads West), 19,269 (1981), 22,280 (1986), 30,502 (1991), 37,775 (1996), 45,024 (2001), 51,788 (2006), 55,553 (2011).

Tweed Heads South (*Co. Rous*) 28°12'S. 153°32'E., 2 km S. of Tweed Heads, on Terranora Ck; (incl. Dry Dock, Terranora till 1915); farming, dairying, bananas; Bapt. C. (The Hub); brewery (Pickled Pig); bridge (Boyds Bay Bridge) to Tweed Heads, fabricated by Goninan Ltd, erected 1934 by Birt, Bolton and Haywood, 475 ft (144.8 m), steel and concrete girder with manual lift span, replaced 1985, over Terranora Ck; cemetery (3,462 graves) and lawn cemetery, incl. crematorium and columbaria; dry dock, 125 ft (38.1 m), b. 1899 by John Wishart & Son; FB (station refurbished 2012); PO 1950; reservoir; schools: primary 1958, additions 1962, 1964, 1968, 1971, and Tweed River HS 1961, additions 1971 and 1977; sewage works 1967; shipyard (Peter Scott) 1872; wharf, 56 ft (17.1 m), b. 1899 by John Wishart & Son; pop. 220 (1954).

Tweed Junction (*Co. Rous*) see Tumbulgum and Tumbulgum North.

Tweed River (*Co. Rous*) see Tweed Heads South.

Tweed River Junction (*Co. Rous*) see Murwillumbah.

Twelve Mile (*Co. St Vincent*) 35°10'S. 150°27'E., 13 km W. of Sussex Inlet.

Twelve Mile (*Co. Wellington*) 32°29'S. 149°16'E., 28 km SW of Gulgong, on Cudgegong R.; goldmining, farming, grazing; Angl. C. (orig. Rom. Cath.) b. 1906 by Manning; PO 1927–69; school (Ben Buckley till 1906) 1884–89, 1898–1906, 1957–58; telephone 1925; TX 1925; pop. 25 (1933).

Twelve Mile Hollow (*Co. Northumberland*) see Snodgrass Valley.

Twenty by Twelve (*Co. Gloucester*) see Blueys Beach.

Twenty-Four Mile Hollow (*Co. Cook*) see Lawson.

Twenty Mile Gums (*Co. Waradgery*) 34°20'S. 145°04'E., 28 km NE of Hay.

Twenty Mile Hollow (*Co. Cook*) see Woodford.

Twofold Bay (*Co. Auckland*) see Eden.

Two Mile Creek (*Co. Harden*) see Nubba.

Two Mile Flat (*Co. Wellington*) 32°25'S. 149°23'E., 16 km W. of Gulgong; village gaz.

1869 as Warburton; diamonds (disc. 1867), goldmining (sluicing 1933–35, shafts and drives 1935–38, dredging 1938–49), farming, grazing; mines: Cullengoral Alluvial Gold Sluicing NL 1933–49 and Two Mile Flat (diamonds) 1867; PO 1867–1980; school (Warburton till 1883) 1882–83, reopened 1900 in new school b. by Murphy and Batten, additions 1916 by F. Quinn, closed 1933; TX 1925–80; Wes. Meth. 1901; pop. 91 (1901), 69 (1911), 69 (1933), 59 (1947).

Tyagarah (*Co. Rous*) 28°36'S. 153°33'E., 7 km S. of Brunswick Heads, on Simpsons Ck; farming; airfield; boiling-down works (F.J. Powell); measles epidemic 1936; PO 1902–64; Presb. C. 1924; 5 quarries; RS 1894, station b. by William Mitchell, closed 1971; sawmills: Thomas McDermott and R.J. Roberts; school 1913–53; TX 1936, automatic 1953; pop. 162 (1901), 262 (1911), 124 (1933), 207 (1947), 174 (1954), 166 (1961), 159 (2011).

Tyagarah (*Co. Rous*) see also Ewingsdale.

Tyagong (*Co. Monteagle*) 34°03'S. 148°14'E., 19 km S. of Grenfell; goldmining (reef) *c.*1867 and farming; bushfire 1884; PO 1927–61; sawmill (Peter Cram), moved 1865 to Young; telephone 1926; TX (automatic) 1961; pop. 56 (1911), 63 (1933), 77 (1947), 93 (1954), 128 (1961).

Tyalgum (*Co. Rous*) 28°19'S. 153°25'E., 3 km NE of Murwillumbah, on Oxley R.; estab. 1904, village gaz. 1911; orig. timber and cattle then bananas and dairying; Angl. C. (St John's) 1928; bridge, destroyed 1953, replacement 1953; bushfire 1936; butter factory (North Coast Co-op. Ltd) 1913–1947, reused; cemetery (64 graves 1913+) 1906; Church of Christ 1913; flood 1974; PO 1908; Rom. Cath. C. (St Patrick's) 1927; sawmills: Brown Bros, Bryant's, Hill and Tunk, Tyalgum Sawmilling Co.; school 1908, new building b. 1910 by Walter Bray, additions 1993; telephone 1908; TX 1912, automatic 1951; water reticulation 1967; pop. 323 (1911), 427 (1933), 293 (1947), 310 (1954), 262 (1961), 211 (1981), 245 (1986), 218 (1991), 237 (1996), 224 (2006), 255 (2011).

Tyalgum Creek (*Co. Rous*) 28°21'S. 153°10'E., 22 km W. of Murwillumbah, on Tyalgum Ck; formerly Upper Tyalgum Creek; school (Upper Tyalgum Creek) 1957–63; pop. 93 (1933), 131 (1947), 98 (1954), 56 (1961).

Tyalgum Road (*Co. Rous*) see Zara.

Tyalla (*Co. Fitzroy*) see Coffs Harbour.

Tycannah (*Co. Courallie*) 29°37'S. 149°49'E., 18 km S. of Moree, on Weah Waa Ck; grazing; PO 1927–31; RS 1897, station b. by William Mitchell, closed 1974.

Tygalgah (*Co. Rous*) 28°19'S. 153°25'E., 3 km NE of Murwillumbah; sugar-cane; caterpillar infestation 1921; hailstorm 1892; pop. 162 (1901), 190 (1911), 209 (1933), 201 (1947), 149 (1954), 179 (1961), 121 (2006).

Tyldesley (*Co. Roxburgh*) 33°17'S. 150°01'E., 8 km N. of Portland; estab. 1904, defunct by *c.*1963; mining; colliery (Great Western) estab. 1904 by Great Western Mining Co. Ltd, taken over 1916 by Tyldesley Coal Mining Co. Ltd who renamed colliery as Tyldesley, strikes 1929, 1930–32, 1936, 1939, 1943, 1945, 1946, closed 1960; electricity 1942; PO 1923–59; railway (colliery siding); school 1930–63; telephone 1925; TX 1939; pop. 151 (1933), 57 (1947), 77 (1954).

Tyndale (*Co. Clarence*) 29°32'S. 153°11'E., 6 km S. of Maclean, on South Arm of Clarence R.; formerly Tynedale; farming and sugar-cane; Angl. C. (St Bartholomew's) b. 1881 by R. Till, demolished, rebuilt 1905 by F. Robertson; concrete-block plant (Patrick Sheehy); creamery (Fresh Food & Ice Co.) 1897; flood 1890; hailstorm 1964; Meth. C.; PO 1875; punt b. by Foggo; sawmill; school (Tynedale till *c.*1890) 1882, additions 1892 by Robert Forrester, new building b. 1923 by Clark and Clark, closed 1975; storm 1953; telephone 1906; TX 1916; wharf; pop. 211 (1881), 276 (1901), 192 (1911), 140 (1933), 165 (1947), 223 (1954), 167 (1961), 213 (2006), 334 (2011).

Tynedale (*Co. Clarence*) see Tyndale.

Tyraman (*Co. Durham*) 32°26'S. 151°30'E., 22 km W. of Dungog, on Paterson R.

Tyrie (*Co. Narromine*) 32°13'S. 147°32'E., 47

km SW of Trangie; FB; TX (automatic).

Tyrie Estate (*Co. Narromine*) see Narromine.

Tyringham (*Co. Fitzroy*) 30°13'S. 152°32'E., 22 km NW of Dorrigo; settled and estab. by John Perrett; timber, farming, potatoes, maize, dairying; bushfire 1935; butter factory (Tyringham Co-op. Dairy Co.) 1920, made cheese instead from 1923; cheese factory (E.V. Shaw) 1926; PO 1892–1979; sawmills: Harry E. Cooper and Dorrigo & Mt. Hyland Sawmilling & Three-Ply Co.; telephone 1916; TX 1926, automatic 1969; pop. 95 (1911), 125 (1933), 183 (1947), 99 (1954), 106 (1961).

Tyringham (*Co. Fitzroy*) see also Dundurrabin.

Tyrolean (*Co. Wallace*) 36°25'S. 148°38'E., 1 km NE of Jindabyne, on Lake Jindabyne.

Tyrone (*Co. Leichhardt*) 30°43'S. 148°17'E., 28 km N. of Coonamble, on Castlereagh R.; also known as Tahrone; telephone 1914; TX 1915–29.

Tyumba (*Co. Rous*) 28°47'S. 153°29'E., 8 km NE of Alstonville; RS 1930–49, station reused.

Tywong (*Co. Wynyard*) see Tamboolba.

U

Uarbry (*Co. Bligh*) 32°03'S. 149°46'E., 35 km E. of Dunedoo, on Talbragar R.; village gaz. 1868 as Uarby, laid out 1868 by Edward Fisher; farming; Angl. C. (St John's) 1926, burnt down 2017; bridges over Talbragar R.: Tom Bailliere Bridge (Flood Channel No. 1) 2018, Flood Channel No. 2 Bridge 1981, M'Elhone Bridge b. 1878 by Scott Bros, Pipers Bridge 1983; bushfire (largely destroyed village) 2017; cemetery (159 graves 1863–2004) 1875; PO 1870–1980; quarry; Rom. Cath. C. 1882, closed and dilapidated by 1903; school 1874–89 and 1898–1917; telephone 1914; TX 1937; pop. 101 (1901), 123 (1911), 38 (1933), 137 (1947), 26 (1954), 62 (1961), 239 (2006).

Uarby (*Co. Bligh*) see Uarbry.

Uardry (*Co. Sturt*) 34°25'S. 145°18'E., 43 km E. of Hay; rice; RS 1882–1975; pop. 41 (1933), 51 (1947), 63 (1954).

Uargon (*Co. Gowen*) 31°27'S. 148°59'E., 35 km SW of Coonabarabran, on Uargon Ck.

Uddergaul (*Co. Ashburnham*) 33°35'S. 148°30'E., 14 km W. of Canowindra, on Sandy Ck.

Ukerebagh Island (*Co. Rous*) 28°11'S. 153°33'E., 2 km S. of Tweed Heads, in Tweed R.; former Aboriginal reserve; pop. 21 (1933).

Uki (*Co. Rous*) 28°25'S. 153°20'E., 11 km SW of Murwillumbah, on Tweed R.; first lots sold 1905; timber, farming, dairying 1890s–1945, hobby farming 1980s+; Angl. C. (Holy Trinity) 1922; butter factory (North Coast Co-op. Co. Ltd) 1910 d. by Fraser, remodelled 1938 by Daniel Gallagher, additions 1940, butter production ceased 1947, reused as cream depot, closed 1961, bought by W. Taylor, reused, sold 2003; clock tower (war memorial) b. 1927 by E.E. Newell, d. by Sir John Sulman; floods 1921, 1954, 1956, 1972, 1974; Meth. C. b. 1911 by A.A. Gaggin, d. by Dakin Bros; PO 1910; rifle range 1914; Rom. Cath. C. (St Columba's) b. 1912 by Alfred John Modini, restored; sawmills: Crain & Son, Leeuwin Parker 1909 (sold 1926 by George Newell to Tanners and Peters), Joseph Priest & Co., Frederick Charles and Patrick John Stephens 1955 (sold 1956 to Henry Frederick Worley, relocated 1958, sold 1970 to Terrance Colin Faulks and Pam Jean Faulks, sold 1980 to Barry, Trevor and Paul Harding), Tweed River Timber Co., Uki Timber Co.; school 1906, additions 1912 by Alfred John Modini, additions 1991; telephone 1911; TX 1912, automatic 1941; pop. 260 (1911), 248 (1933), 313 (1947), 256 (1954), 256 (1961), 204 (1986), 214 (1991), 230 (1996), 211 (2001), 203 (2006), 214 (2011).

Ukolan (*Co. Darling*) 30°42'S. 150°50'E., 12 km NE of Manilla, on Halls Ck; Angl. C. (Christ) d. by A.W. Voysey; school 1890–96; Wes. Meth. C. 1893.

Ulamambri (*Co. Napier*) 31°20'S. 149°23'E., 13 km SE of Coonabarabran, on Castlereagh R.; village gaz. 1919; farming and grazing; Angl. C. 1929; fire 1934; PO 1922–77; RS 1917, station b. by John Allibone, closed 1976; sale-yards 1938; school 1886–92 and 1920–70; silo 1935; telephone 1919; TX 1921, automatic 1972; pop. 421 (1933), 272 (1947), 225 (1954), 118 (1961), 396 (2011).

Ulan (*Co. Bligh*) 32°17'S. 149°45'E., 22 km NE of Gulgong, on Goulburn R.; farming, grazing, coalmining; airfield; Angl. C. 1899, new one (St Cuthbert's) 1908; bridges: one over Moolarben Ck and one over Sportsmans Hollow Ck; cemetery (193 graves) 1898; collieries: Ulan No. 1 (estab. 1924 by Cunningham, closed, reopened 1942 by Key, sold 1950), and Ulan No. 2 (Hogan & Gorman Pty Ltd, taken over 1975 by White Industries); FB; PO 1893; power station 1957–69; Presb. C. b. 1919 by M.H. Bennett, renovated 1933 by William Archer; quarry; rifle range 1913; Rom. Cath. C. (St Pius X) removed from Moolarben and re-erected 1959, moved 2014 to Buckaroo; RS 1982; school 1889–94, 1908–13, reopened 1919, additions 1993; telephone 1906; TX (automatic) 1982; pop. 72 (1901), 99 (1911), 156 (1933), 158 (1947), 82 (1954), 97 (1961). (See also Old Ulan.)

Uley (*Co. Bourke*) 34°25'S. 146°54'E., 7 km S. of Ardlethan; pop. 35 (1933).

Ulgandahi Island (*Co. Clarence*) see Ulgundahi Island.

Ulgundahi Island (*Co. Clarence*) 29°26'S. 153°13'E., 3 km NE of Maclean, in Clarence R.; formerly Ulgandahi Island; Aboriginal reserve 1906; floods 1893, 1921, 1928, 1945, 1954; Presb. C. 1911, damaged 1921; pop. 47 (1933).

Ulidia (*Co. Buller*) 28°33'S. 152°43'E., 31 km W. of Kyogle, on Upper Duck Ck; telephone 1925; TX 1951.

Ulinda (*Co. Napier*) 31°35'S. 149°29'E., 35 km NW of Coolah, on Weetaliba Ck; RS 1923–75; pop. 41 (1933).

Ulinga (*Co. Northumberland*) see Cardiff.

Ulladulla (*Co. St Vincent*) 35°22'S. 150°28'E., 55 km S. of Nowra, on Tasman Sea; orig. Boat Harbour, later also known as Holy Dollar; disc. 1827 by Thomas Florance, surveyed and town gaz. 1837 as Ulludolla, munic. 1874–1948; timber seaport 1840+, shipbuilding 1840+, then wheat till 1860s, maize, pigs, vegetables, shell grit 1920s, fishing 1921+, oysters, dairying (declined 1963+), timber, honey, tourism 1950s+; ambulance station 1955; Angl. C. 1861, new one 1936, new one (St Martin's) 1988; Apostolic C. (Highway Christ.); bacon factories: Knapp's and Richard Millard; boat harbour; breakwater 1863, new ones b. 1960–64, 115 ft (35.1 m) and 525 ft (160 m); breweries: Wally and Tom Cupitt 2014 and John Hoe 1877; bridge b. 1884 by William Schadel, over Millards Ck; bushfires 1868 (many houses destroyed), 1869, 1896, 1939 (8 houses destroyed), 1948; cemetery (6 burials 1862–85) 1869; ceramics factory (Ray and Elsie Cairns) 1983; CH 1863–77; diphtheria 1875 and 1905; electricity 1948; FB (station b. 1972); flour mill b. 1861 by George Knight; foot-bridge over Millards Ck; freezing works (Angliss & Co.); Highway Christ. C.; ice works (Bennett Bros), burnt down 1939; jetties: one 1859–65 and one b. 1957, replacement b. 1971–78; lighthouse b. 1869–73 of iron by Young and Mather, d. by Edward Orpen Moriarty, 54 ft (16.5 m), relocated 1889 from breakwater to Warden Head by Isaac Banks and Enoch Whitehurst, converted to acetylene 1920 and to electricity 1964; lock-up; PO 1842, repairs 1908 by N. Mudge, new one b. 1972; pound (stock) 1859; PS 1894; reservoir; Rom. Cath. C. (Holy Family of Nazareth) b. 1937 by J.K. Owens, d. by Louis Philip Burns; sawmills: S. Braithwaite, Cashman and Seccombe (sold 1882), Clyde Sawmilling & Shipping Co. Pty Ltd, Cork and Allison, G. Goodsell, G. Ireland, Ephraim Mison 1875, Mitchell Bros 1929 (burnt down and rebuilt 1939, closed 1973); schools: primary 1861 (new one b. 1878 by John Schadel, d. by George Allen Mansfield, additions 1961, 1965, 1975), and HS 1974 (new building 1977, additions 1989, 1991, 2008, 2012, re-roofed 2014); sewage works; shipyards: naval one (sold 1950), Ulladulla Shipbuilding Co. (Kenneth Charles McLeod and Charles William Phillips, partnership dissolved 1943, then carried on alone by McLeod, in liquidation 1955), David Warden and Robert Gee 1840–61; storms 1866 and 1870; tanneries: Richard Millard 1854 (taken over 1873 by E.M. Farleigh Ltd, sold 1933 to William Henry Littlewood, closed 1939, demolished 1950) and Ulladulla Tannery Ltd (burnt down 1939); TC, additions 1985, became a campus of Illawarra Institute of Technology in 1992; telegraph 1882; TX 1913, automatic 1962; Unit. C. (orig. Meth.) b. 1964 by S.R. Robinson, extended 1983 by S.R. Robinson & Sons; watch-house 1861; water apparel factory (Hot 'n' Dry); wattle-bark mill (Craig, Mostyn & Co.); Wes. Meth. C. 1856, new one 1882; wharf (stone) b. 1863–65 by Elphinstone and Shand, 215 ft (65.5 m), replaced; winery (Griff and Rosie Cupitt); pop. *c.*300 (1856), *c.*90 (1866), 129 (1871), 1,615 (1881), 1,582 (1891), 1,765 (1901), 224 (1911), 1,415 (1933), 1,540 (1944), 1,844 (1947), 1,210 (1954), 1,458 (1961), 1,952 (1976), 6,018 (1981), 7,408 (1986), 7,381 (1991), 8,384 (1996), 9,609 (2001), 10,298 (2006), 12,137 (2011).

Ullamalla (*Co. Wellington*) 33°00'S. 149°20'E., 39 km NE of Orange, on Ulmarrah Ck; PO 1876–77.

Ulludolla (*Co. St Vincent*) see Ulladulla.

Ulmarra (*Co. Clarence*) 29°38'S. 153°02'E., 12 km NE of Grafton, on Clarence R.; formerly The Sandspit; settled 1860, estab. by Thomas Small, laid out by Wilson, munic. 1871–1956, town classified by National Trust; former river port, orig. timber and farming, then maize, sugar-cane 1865+, then dairying and fishing; Angl. C. 1865, relocated and rebuilt 1895, new one (St Paul's) b. 1909–12 by Albert Hutchby, closed, sold and reused; Bapt. C. 1878, new one 1951; bridge (Briner Bridge) 1908; butter factory (Clarence River Pioneer Dairy Co. Ltd) estab. 1892 by William McLeod et al., alterations and improvements 1899 by John M'Kay, bacon factory added 1914, butter factory rebuilt 1923 by Thackeray and Gallagher, d. by Richard Wildridge & Co., damaged 1926, amalgamated 1970 with Grafton Dairy Co. Ltd to become Grafton-Ulmarra Co-op. Dairy Co. Ltd, merged 1990 with Norco Co-op. Ltd; cemetery (908 graves 1868+) 1865; CH b. 1892 by G. Wunderlich, d. by Walter Liberty Vernon, reused; dairy factory (W. Goodyer) 1886; electricity 1924; FB; fires 1879, 1906, 1920, 1928; floods 1890 (whole town inundated), 1893, 1928, 1948, 1988, 2001, 2011, 2013; foundry (F. Foster & Son); gales 1912 and 1914; hailstorms 1925 and 1926; lock-up b. 1879 by William Kinnear; milk factory (Norco Co-op. Ltd); PO 1859, new one b. 1882 by Henry Frank Sault, additions 1892 by Holloway Bros; Presb. C. b. 1867 by William Kinnear, damaged 1890, demolished, new one (St James's) b. 1895 by Strauss Bros, closed; PS (in former court-house); punt b. 1901 by John Bichmann, to Southgate, across Clarence R.; Rom. Cath. C. (Our Lady Help of Christians) b. 1913 by R. Hayes, d. by Frederick William Conrad Schaeffer, closed 2012, sold 2015; sawmill (McMahon and Goodger); schools: East Ulmarra (Ulmarra till 1895) 1861–1904 and Ulmarra (West Ulmarra till 1895) 1891, new building b. 1920 by Till and Robertson; sugar mills: Belmore (b. 1869 by William Kinnear for Clarence Sugar Manufacturing Assoc. Ltd, sold 1870 to George Neale, closed, reopened 1877, closed 1881), Chowne's, Meston's, W. Taylor 1877; telegraph 1870, new office b. 1882 by H.S. Sault, additions 1892 by Holloway Bros; tornado 1894; TX 1910, automatic 1969; Unit. C. (orig. Meth.) b. 1935 by C. Firth, d. by Jack Strauss, closed 2010, sold 2011; water reticulation 1966; Wes. Meth. C. 1862, new one b. 1886 by F. Gran, d. by James Moyes; wharves: one b. 1882 by J. Johnstone, one b. 1891 (John See & Co.), one b. 1912 (for butter factory); pop. 997 (1871), 1,560 (1881), *c.*1,350 (1895), 1,722 (1901), 1,219 (1911), *c.*2,000 (1891–1909), 1,940 (1924), 1,985 (1933), 1,633 (1947), 1,499 (1954), 532 (1961), 358 (1971), 362 (1976), 395 (1981), 462 (1986), 508 (1991), 472 (1996), 488 (2001), 446 (2006), 435 (2011).

Ulong (*Co. Fitzroy*) 30°15'S. 152°53'E., 20 km NE of Dorrigo, on Ulong Ck; farming; plywood and veneer factory (Mulhearn Bros Ltd) 1936, closed, sold, dismantled and moved to Coffs Harbour Jetty; PO 1912; Presb. C. (St Andrew's) b. 1911 by Morris, closed, sold

1998, reused; Rom. Cath. C. (Holy Trinity) b. 1931 by C. Irving and G. Shepherd, closed, sold and reused 1992 as Community C.; RS (2 km N.) 1924–75; sawmills: G.H. Corfe & Sons and Mulhearn Bros 1928; school 1918, additions 2010; telephone 1915; TX 1926, automatic 1972; pop. 58 (1911), 128 (1933), 182 (1947), 206 (1954), 233 (1961), 130 (2006), 264 (2011).

Ulonga (*Co. Waradgery*) 34°06'S. 144°39'E., 48 km N. of Hay; pop. 65 (1911).

Ulungra Springs (*Co. Gowen*) 31°44'S. 149°06'E., 43 km NW of Dunedoo; sawmill (Hatton Bros), bought 1917 by J. Kelly and M. Houlihan.

Ulupna (*Co. Denison*) see Finley.

Umaralla (*Co. Beresford*) see Chakola and Numeralla.

Umaralla Siding (*Co. Beresford*) see Chakola.

Umbango (*Co. Wynyard*) 35°23'S. 147°46'E., 28 km W. of Adelong, on Umbango Ck; RS 1917–75, station removed 1985; school 1882, new building b. 1883 by J. M'Intosh, closed 1893; telephone 1922; pop. 50 (1911), 72 (1933), 56 (1954).

Umberumberka (*Co. Yancowinna*) see Silverton.

Umberumberka Reservoir (*Co. Yancowinna*) 31°49'S. 141°12'E., 29 km NW of Broken Hill; PS 1912–14; reservoir (incl. pumping station) b. 1911–14, d. by Ernest Macartney de Burgh, 85 ft (26 m) high, pumping station chimney (100 ft or 30.5 m) b. 1916 by Frank Saunders; pop. 121 (1911).

Umina (*Co. Northumberland*) see Umina Beach.

Umina Beach (*Co. Northumberland*) 33°31'S. 151°19'E., 4 km SE of Woy Woy, on Broken Bay; (incl. Ocean Beach); Umina till 1951; estab. 1913 as Ettalong Beach Estate by Arthur Rickard & Co. Ltd, first lot sold 1914, estab. 1917 as coastal holiday area, Ocean Beach City Estate was estab. 1918 by C.R. Staples & Co. Ltd; aeroplane crash 1950; airfield (World War II); Angl. C. 1934, new one (St Andrew's); Assemblies of God C. (Peninsula Christ. Life); bushfires 1926, 1928, 1936, 1944, 1946, 1948, 2006; Christ. Life C.; electricity 1929; gale 1952; Good News C.; Meth. C. b. 1935 by Dave Hawley; PO 1924; Rom. Cath. C. (Sacred Heart) 1964; Salv. Army C.; sawmill (Brophy and Brown); schools: Brisbane Water Secondary College (Umina HS till 2001) 1976 d. by Ian McHutchinson, additions 1979 and 2007, and Umina primary 1956 b. by A.G. Hill, additions 1961, 1986, 2007, 2010, renamed Umina Beach in 2015; telephone 1921; TX 1921; Unit. C.; pop. 246 (1933), 765 (1947), 15,394 (2006), 16,059 (2011).

Unanderra (*Co. Camden*) 34°28'S. 150°51'E., 6 km SW of Wollongong, on Charcoal Ck; (incl. Cordeaux Heights and Farmborough Heights); Charcoal Creek till 1881; settled in 1830s, town lots sold 1890; coke-making, tanning, farming, fishing, dairying; brickworks (Monier Masonry Ltd); butter factory (Unanderra Dairy Co. Ltd) 1887, taken over 1909 by Farmers & Dairymen's Milk Co., burnt down 1913; cemeteries: Berkeley pioneer (323 graves 1822+) and Wollongong memorial gardens 1959, incl. crematorium 1959; clothing factories: Bonds Wear Pty Ltd 1970–2010, sold 2015 and Delta Sportswear Pty Ltd; coke-works (orig. 20 Welsh-type ovens) b. 1888 by E. Figtree for Aust. Coke-making Co. Ltd, later increased by 72 beehive ovens, closed 1912, site abandoned 1913; colliery (Port Kembla No. 2) 1941–64; concrete products plant (Duracrete Concrete Products Co.); cordial factory (Brough Bros), closed 1979; electricity 1927; engineering works: Douglas Engineering Pty Ltd and C. & M. Leussink Engineering Pty Ltd 1977; FB (station b. 1962, upgraded 2012); floods 1914, 1952, 2017; foundry (Illawarra Metal Castings Pty Ltd); gale 1951; house frame and truss factories: Hitek Steel Framing Pty Ltd and Wadsworth Joinery; juvenile justice centre (Keelong), additions 1992, closed 2009, reused 2013; Meth. C. 1955; natural gas 1977; PO 1860; Presb. C. 1901, new one (St Stephen's) 1956; PS, closed 1931, additions 1960, new one 1973; quarry; rolling mill (stainless steel) o. 1959 by Commonwealth Steel Co. Ltd; Rom. Cath. C. (Immaculate Conception) 1954; RS 1887, station b. by Robert B. Spiers; sale-yards (John Fretus and J.N. King) 1932; Salv. Army C. 1964; schools: Farmborough Road 1956 and Unanderra (Charcoal Creek till 1888) 1878 d. by George Allen Mansfield, additions 1881 and 1899, additions 1907 by H. Williams and J.W. Poulter, damaged 1907, additions 1911, 1957, 1960, 1963, relocated 1999 to new buildings, additions 2010; storm 1907; Syrian Orthodox C. (St Thomas's); tannery (John Richards) 1860; telephone 1888; TX *c.*1905, automatic 1955; water reticulation 1909; works: Aquila Steel Co. Ltd, BHP Stainless Products, BHP Welding Products, Bisalloy Steels Pty Ltd, The Titan Manufacturing Co. Pty Ltd (founded by John Rose and known as The Titan Nail & Wire Pty Ltd); pop. 558 (1911), 782 (1947), 3,381 (1954), 6,544 (1961), 5,945 (2001), 14,576 (2011).

Underbank (*Co. Gloucester*) 32°15'S. 151°38'E., 21 km NW of Dungog, on Williams R.; farming and dairying; Angl. C. (St Paul's) b. 1901 by James Rumbel, d. by Charles Herbert Davy Button, closed 1928, sold 1935 to F.T. Cox for demolition; bridge (Tunnibuc Bridge) over Williams R.; butter factory (Ben Bosworth); Cong. C. 1924, damaged 1985; PO 1869–1951; sawmills: E. Deard and Leonard & Co.; storm 1985; telephone 1909; TX; pop. 103 (1901), 153 (1911), 99 (1933), 69 (1947), 82 (1954), 109 (1961).

Ungarie (*Co. Gipps*) 33°38'S. 146°59'E., 38 km NW of West Wyalong; Wollongough till 1889; surveyed 1893 by A. Maitland, village gaz. 1894, thrived 1924–36; grazing, wheat, farming; Angl. C. b. 1922–24 by E. Pratt, new one (St Dunstan's) 1978, closed; cemetery 1894; CH b. 1936 by R.H. Nott & Son, demolished; Community C.; dust storm 1922; electricity 1933; engineering works (estab. by Eric David and Allan Bruce Henderson, became E. & A. Henderson Pty Ltd, later R. and J. Carr) 1929; floods 1928 and 2016; gale 1960; hailstorm 1924; heatwave 1905; horse dip 1938; Lutheran C. (St Paul's) b. 1930 by J. Mitchell, d. by E.R. Laver and George Mammatt; measles epidemic 1949; Meth. C. 1933; PO 1872, new one b. 1925 by Digby Johns, burnt down 1896; pound (stock) 1928; powerhouse (Henderson Bros), burnt down 1942; Presb. C. (St Andrew's) b. 1925 by W. Hargreaves; PS (incl. lock-up) b. 1898 by J. M'Fadyean, additions and alterations 1973, new one 1995; railway coal stage 1925; reservoir (elevated tank), 100,000 gal. (454.6 kl), b. 1953 by V.G. Saunders; rifle range 1921; Rom. Cath. C., relocated 1932, additions and alterations 1932 by Arthur Edward Pereira, reopened 1932, new one (St Joseph's) 1979; RS 1917, closed and removed 1984; sawmill (E. Henderson); school 1918 b. by William Charles Hanson, additions 1920 also by Hanson, additions 1970 and 1973; sewerage 1969; silo 1928; telegraph 1895, office burnt down 1896; telephone 1901; TX 1911, automatic 1986; pop. 104 (1901), 102 (1911), 596 (1933), 367 (1947), 485 (1954), 497 (1961), 462 (1966), 455 (1971), 467 (1976), 428 (1981), 443 (1986), 373 (1991), 399 (1996), 342 (2001), 335 (2006), 322 (2011).

Unkya Creek (*Co. Raleigh*) see Eungai Creek.

Unumgar (*Co. Rous*) 28°25'S. 152°44'E., 35 km NW of Kyogle, on Richmond R.; flood 1887; PO 1870; pop. 62 (1933), 101 (1947).

Upper Adelong (*Co. Wynyard*) 35°30'S. 148°08'E., 3 km N. of Batlow; defunct; mining (alluvial gold disc. 1852); cemetery 1876; Chinese joss house; measles epidemic 1875; PO 1869–73; sawmill (Abraham Watson); school 1867–1912; snow 1865; pop. 51 (1901).

Upper Allyn (*Co. Durham*) 32°10'S. 151°29'E., 48 km W. of Gloucester; electricity 1953; sawmill: Hancock Bros and Pender and Foster 1942, bought 1964 by Earp, Woodcock, Beveridge & Co. Pty Ltd, closed 1970, demolished 1986; school 1957–70; pop. 76 (1947), 72 (1954), 77 (1961).

Upper Araluen (*Co. St Vincent*) see Araluen.

Upper Avon (*Co. Gloucester*) 32°08'S.

151°54'E., 15 km S. of Gloucester, on Clear Hill Ck.

Upper Belmore (*Co. Macquarie*) 31°07'S. 152°59'E., 9 km N. of Crescent Head, on Belmore R.; butter factory (Elijah Thurgood) 1896; PO 1927–31; school 1889–95 and 1919–69; telephone 1914; TX 1923–69.

Upper Bilambil (*Co. Rous*) 28°15'S. 153°25'E., 10 km N. of Murwillumbah; pop. 108 (1933).

Upper Bingara (*Co. Murchison*) 30°03'S. 150°39'E., 22 km S. of Bingara, on Gouron Ck; mining (gold disc. 1852 by Paddy Read and Bob Davey) and grazing; cemetery (2 graves); Chinese joss house; lock-up; mines: Bingara Gold Mines Ltd 1934 and Three Creeks Gold Mine; PO 1905–72; PS; school 1908–65; telephone 1915; TX 1945; pop. 1,905 (1861), 122 (1933), 68 (1947), 56 (1954).

Upper Botobolar (*Co. Phillip*) 32°32'S. 149°51'E., 26 km E. of Mudgee, on Stony Ck; farming and grazing; PO 1883–1931; quarry; telephone 1926; TX; pop. 33 (1933).

Upper Bowman (*Co. Gloucester*) 31°55'S. 151°47'E., 20 km NW of Gloucester, on Bowman R.; mining (gold disc. in 1870s) and dairying; mines: Bank, Birthday, Christmas Box, Federation, Germania, Gladstone, Golden Spur, Harris's, John Bright, Mint, Queen of Beauty, Saxby's; PO 1909–73; quarry; school 1907–9 and 1957–69, building moved 1977 to Gloucester and reused; stamper batteries; telephone 1916; TX 1930; pop. 97 (1933), 99 (1947), 77 (1954), 58 (1961).

Upper Brogo (*Co. Auckland*) 36°29'S. 149°46'E., 28 km W. of Bermagui; farming and dairying; bushfires 1904 and 1952 (2 died); dam (Brogo) 1976, 141 ft (43 m) high; PO 1927–42; telephone 1913; pop. 55 (1901), 52 (1933).

Upper Brungle (*Co. Buccleuch*) 35°09'S. 148°19'E., 22 km SE of Gundagai, on Brungle Ck; school (Brungle till 1885) 1882–85 and 1897–1904.

Upper Bunyah (*Co. Gloucester*) 32°08'S. 152°11'E., 31 km W. of Tuncurry.

Upper Burragorang (*Co. Camden*) 34°09'S. 150°20'E., 22 km W. of Thirlmere, on Wollondilly R. (now Lake Burragorang); surveyed by Dixon; timber, grazing, maize, oats, wheat, hort., pigs; bridge over Wollondilly R.; cheese factory 1937 d. by H.R. McCauley; flood 1910; PO 1877, burnt down 1924, replaced, closed 1957; sawmill (Edward Irwin); school 1909–29 and 1944–50; telephone 1905; TX 1917; pop. 308 (1901), 154 (1933), 167 (1947), 88 (1954).

Upper Burringbar (*Co. Rous*) 28°27'S. 153°26'E., 14 km S. of Murwillumbah, on Burringbar Ck; flood (woman died) 2017; RS 1896–1974; school 1925–75; telephone 1925; pop. 168 (1901), 158 (1933), 442 (1947), 347 (1954), 294 (1961), 283 (2011).

Upper Burrinjuck (*Co. Harden*) 34°57'S. 148°38'E., 26 km SW of Yass; PO 1941–57; school 1940–57; TX 1949; pop. 586 (1954).

Upper Bylong (*Co. Phillip*) 32°27'S. 150°08'E., 41 km SW of Merriwa; airfield; Rom. Cath. C. (Our Lady of the Sacred Heart) b. 1915 by Archer Bros, closed, sold, and graveyard (5 graves 1929–46); school 1955, new building 1975, closed 2015.

Upper Camden Haven (*Co. Macquarie*) see Lorne.

Upper Chichester (*Co. Gloucester*) 32°10'S. 151°35'E., 29 km NW of Dungog, on Chichester R.; dairying; Angl. C. (St James's) b. 1903 by W. McMurray, closed, sold 1971 to J.W. Heggarty, demolished 1972; cemetery 1889; PO 1927–31; telephone 1914; TX 1951; Unit. C.

Upper Coldstream (*Co. Clarence*) 29°38'S. 153°07'E., 19 km E. of Grafton, on Coldstream R.; farming; Angl. C. (St Philip's) 1881, rebuilt 1907; creamery (Clarence River Pioneer Dairy Co.) b. 1899 by John M'Kay; PO 1885–1963; school 1880–96; telephone 1890; TX 1916–59; Wes. Meth. C.; pop. 53 (1961).

Upper Colo (*Co. Cook*) 33°26'S. 150°44'E., 20 km NE of Kurrajong Heights, on Colo R.; Colo till 1883; farming and orchards; Angl. C. b. 1906 by Charles Frazer and Henry Burgess, d. by Charles Frazer, damaged 1953, restored 2006, and graveyard (graves 1842+);

bridge (5 spans) b. 1936 by Solomon and Duffy, replaced 2014, over Colo R.; cemetery; PO 1861–1970; school 1884–91 and 1907–47; storm 1953; TX 1940, automatic 1940; pop. 61 (1901), 90 (1933), 94 (1947), 46 (1961).

Upper Coopers Creek (*Co. Rous*) 28°36'S. 153°24'E., 11 km SW of Mullumbimby, on Coopers Ck; school 1957, additions 2010; pop. 82 (1961).

Upper Copmanhurst (*Co. Clarence*) 29°35'S. 152°45'E., 22 km NW of Grafton; Copmanhurst till 1892; farming and dairying; Angl. C. (Holy Apostles) 1871, alterations 1900 d. by Frederick William Conrad Schaeffer, damaged 1903; creamery (NSW Fresh Food & Ice Co.) 1897; hurricane (unroofed most houses) 1946; Rom. Cath. C. (St John of the Cross) 1882; PO 1865–1946; Presb. C., damaged 1903; 3 quarries; school (Smiths Flat till 1889, Copmanhurst till 1892, Upper Copmanhurst till 1894, then Urangbell till 1923) 1866–1938; squall 1914; telegraph 1879; tornado 1903; pop. 120 (1933), 77 (1947), 73 (1954).

Upper Corindi (*Co. Fitzroy*) 30°03'S. 153°08'E., 9 km W. of Arrawarra, on Corindi R.; farming; bridge (Boyles Bridge) over Corindi R.; FB; hailstorm 2013; PO 1927–31; school 1957–62; telephone 1913; TX; pop. 103 (1933), 70 (1947), 57 (1954), 59 (1961), 230 (2011).

Upper Crystal Creek (*Co. Rous*) 28°16'S. 153°18'E., 11 km NW of Murwillumbah, on Crystal Ck; bananas; bushfire 1936; sawmill; school 1957–68; telephone 1929; TX 1945; pop. 64 (1933), 118 (1947), 107 (1954), 66 (1961), 187 (2011).

Upper Dartbrook (*Co. Brisbane*) 31°56'S. 150°44'E., 18 km NW of Scone; pop. 24 (1933).

Upper Dignams Creek (*Co. Dampier*) 36°20'S. 149°58'E., 13 km NW of Bermagui, on Digmans Ck; telephone 1923.

Upper Dingo (*Co. Macquarie*) 31°40'S. 152°18'E., 23 km N. of Wingham, on Dingo Ck; telephone 1923; TX 1957.

Upper Dingo (*Co. Macquarie*) see also Kippaxs.

Upper Duck Creek (*Co. Buller*) 28°34'S. 152°41'E., 34 km W. of Kyogle, on Upper Duck Ck; electricity 1953; Plymouth Brethren C. 1927; sawmill (Joe Woodworth) 1912, later bought by Jack McGee and removed.

Upper Duncans Creek (*Co. Parry*) 31°26'S. 151°13'E., 10 km NE of Nundle, on Duncans Ck; school 1904–26.

Upper Dungay (*Co. Rous*) 28°16' 153°21'E., 9 km NW of Murwillumbah; sawmill (F.C. and P.J. Stephens), burnt down 1954; pop. 43 (1933).

Upper Dungowan (*Co. Parry*) 31°15'S. 151°10'E., 27 km SE of Tamworth; school 1881, new building b. 1884 by W.J. Davies, closed 1895, reopened 1906, closed 1918; Unit. C. (orig. Union) b. by Leslie Sprague, restored 1988, and graveyard.

Upper Duroby (*Co. Rous*) 28°15'S. 153°28'E., 11 km NE of Murwillumbah, on Duroby Ck; pop. 105 (1933).

Upper Eden Creek (*Co. Rous*) 28°32'S. 152°53'E., 15 km NW of Kyogle, on Eden Ck; formerly Edenhurst; dairying; PO 1927–31; school 1957–69; telephone 1923; TX 1929; pop. 126 (1933), 61 (1947).

Upper Eungai (*Co. Raleigh*) see Tamban.

Upper Fine Flower (*Co. Drake*) 29°16'S. 152°44'E., 51 km N. of Grafton, on Dome Mountain Ck; sawmill (Fraser Bros Ltd), burnt down 1946; pop. 223 (2006).

Upper Five Day (*Co. Dudley*) 30°40'S. 152°24'E., 42 km W. of Bowraville, on Five Day Ck; farming and grazing; sawmill, closed 1962; school (Upper Five Day Creek) 1957–62; telephone 1923; TX 1928.

Upper Five Day Creek (*Co. Dudley*) see Upper Five Day.

Upper Gilmore (*Co. Wynyard*) 35°26'S. 148°11'E., 17 km SE of Adelong, on Gilmore Ck; farming, grazing, dairying; PO 1927–31; school (Ferndale till 1926) 1882–1967; telephone 1926; TX 1928; pop. 67 (1901), 29 (1933).

Upper Grady's Creek (*Co. Rous*) see Cougal and Loadstone.

Upper Gumble (*Co. Ashburnham*) 33°04'S. 148°39'E., 13 km N. of Manildra, on Goonigal Ck; mines: Delaney Dyke Gold Mining Co. 1887–91 and Pine Hill Copper Lode 1880 and 1903.

Upper Gundaroo (*Co. Murray*) 35°05'S. 149°15'E., 26 km NW of Bungendore; Gundaroo till 1877; Angl. C. (St Luke's) 1850, restored 1913, closed, and graveyard (burials 1861–1940) 1858; PO 1848–91.

Upper Hexham (*Co. Northumberland*) see Beresfield and Tarro.

Upper Horseshoe Creek (*Co. Rous*) 28°32'S. 153°04'E., 11 km NE of Kyogle, on Horseshoe Ck; electricity 1962; school 1957–70.

Upper Horton (*Co. Murchison*) 30°08'S. 150°27'E., 31 km NW of Barraba, on Horton R.; formerly Horton; village gaz. 1896; farming and grazing; Angl. C. (Transfiguration); cemetery 1897; PO 1899–1993; PS re-erected 1898 (removed from Eulourie) by T. Potts; Rom. Cath. C. (St Anthony's); school 1900, new one b. 1909, enlarged 1930, closed 1988; telephone 1905; TX 1914; pop. 490 (1911), 229 (1933), 240 (1947), 188 (1954), 139 (1961), 207 (2011).

Upper Hunter (*Co. Brisbane*) see Brushy Hill.

Upper Kangaroo Creek (*Co. Fitzroy*) 30°01'S. 152°51'E., 37 km W. of Woolgoolga; maize; Presb. C. b. 1907 by T. Maxwell and T. Pitkin; telephone 1909.

Upper Kangaroo River (*Co. Camden*) 34°42'S. 150°36'E., 13 km NW of Berry, on Kangaroo R.; formerly Kangaroo River; farming; Angl. C. (Fern Hill) 1882, later rebuilt by Victor Cooper; butter factory (Kangaroo River Dairy Co.) 1890, moved 1913 to Glenmurray; cemetery 1876; FB; flood 1867; foot-bridge 1908, rebuilt 1924, destroyed 1974, over Kangaroo R.; PO 1892–1967; schools: Kangaroo River 1877–90 and 1896–1916, and Upper Kangaroo River (Hillcrest till 1915) 1889–1915 and 1957–69; TX 1923, automatic 1967; pop. 159 (1901), 29 (1921), 39 (1933), 35 (1947), 80 (1954), 65 (1961), 299 (2006).

Upper Kangaroo Valley (*Co. Camden*) 34°43'S. 150°35'E., 13 km NW of Berry, on Kangaroo R.; winery (Yarrawa Estate) estab. 1998 by Mark Francis and Susan Foster.

Upper Kiah (*Co. Auckland*) 37°10'S. 149°49'E., 14 km SW of Eden.

Upper Kinchela (*Co. Macquarie*) 31°02'S. 153°00'E., 16 km NE of Kempsey, on Kinchela Ck; pop. 50 (1901).

Upper Lansdown (*Co. Macquarie*) see Upper Lansdowne.

Upper Lansdowne (*Co. Macquarie*) 31°43'S. 152°28'E., 20 km NE of Wingham, on Koppin Yarratt Ck; Upper Lansdown till 1896; timber, then farming and dairying; Angl. C. (St Barnabas's); PO 1890–1980; Rom. Cath. C. 1893, closed, sold, removed and reused, new one (St Paul's) 1911, closed, sold 1978 and reused; sawmills: Cicolini's (incl. broom handle factory), Thomas MacLaughlan, Potts and Unger (bought 1907 by George Schubert); school 1901, additions 1914 by Sellick and Charton, additions 2010; storm 1934; telephone 1911; TX 1914, automatic 1971; pop. 374 (1933), 266 (1947), 241 (1954), 206 (1961), 493 (2011).

Upper Lostock (*Co. Durham*) see Lostock.

Upper Macdonald (*Co. Northumberland*) 33°16'S. 150°57'E., 41 km W. of Ourimbah, on Macdonald R.; Upper McDonald till 1924; abandoned; orig. maize; Angl. C. (St Matthew's), demolished 1931, replaced 1932, demolished; flood 1952; PO 1887–1961; Rom. Cath. C. (Our Lady of Loreto) b. 1839–42, ruined, and graveyard (graves 1836+); school (McDonald River till 1871, Lower McDonald till 1873 then McDonald River till 1879) 1868–71 and 1879–1963; telephone 1916; TX 1961; Wes. Meth. C., damaged 1964, moved 1972 to Arcadia and restored; pop. 130 (1891), 154 (1901), 142 (1911), 101 (1933), 79 (1947), 34 (1961).

Upper McDonald (*Co. Northumberland*) see Upper Macdonald.

Upper Main Arm (*Co. Rous*) 28°30'S. 153°25'E., 11 km NW of Mullumbimby; bushfire 1946; school (Toolond till 1944) 1939; TX 1945, automatic 1955; pop. 47 (1933), 192 (2011).

Upper Mangrove (*Co. Northumberland*)

33°18'S. 151°08'E., 24 km W. of Ourimbah, on Mangrove Ck; farming; Angl. C. (St Thomas's) 1866, replaced, closed, burnt down 2002, and graveyard (26 graves 1851–1949); bridge over Mangrove Ck; bushfire 2002; PO 1927; sawmill (Northern Hardwoods Ltd), burnt down 1922, rebuilt 1923; TX 1936.

Upper Manilla (*Co. Darling*) 30°38'S. 150°40'E., 14 km N. of Manilla, on Manilla R.; farming; bridges: timber one 1900, Borah Creek Bridge 1928–71, concrete one (continuous beam) 1943, Bowman Bridge 1976; caterpillar infestation 1945; fire 1921; flood 1908; foot-bridge, destroyed 1908; PO 1876–1991; railway bridge (Howe timber truss spans) 1908, over Borah Ck; Rom. Cath. C. (St Patrick's) 1884; RS 1908, station b. by W. Gawne & Sons, closed 1975, demolished 1982; school 1880, new one b. 1884 by M. Delongar, replaced 1903, closed 1968, restored and reused; telephone 1890; TX 1914, automatic 1951; Wes. Meth. C. 1892, defunct; pop. 132 (1891), 381 (1901), 230 (1933), 173 (1947), 128 (1954), 154 (1961), 266 (2006), 300 (2011).

Upper Maules Creek (*Co. Nandewar*) 30°31'S. 150°16'E., 30 km NE of Boggabri.

Upper Meroo (*Co. Wellington*) 32°45'S. 149°37'E., 19 km S. of Mudgee, on Married Mans Ck; farming and grazing; settled 1838 by George Suttor; PO 1898–1926; school 1907–29; telephone 1925; pop. 79 (1933).

Upper Missabotti (*Co. Raleigh*) 30°34'S. 152°44'E., 15 km NW of Bowraville, on Missabotti Ck; school 1957–62; TX; pop. 64 (1954), 55 (1961).

Upper Mittagong (*Co. Camden*) see Glenquarry.

Upper Mongogarie (*Co. Richmond*) 28°59'S. 152°51'E., 23 km SW of Casino, on Mongogarie Ck; dairying; bridge 1935, over Mongogarie Ck; PO 1927; sawmill (Enterprise Sawmilling Co., William Owen); school 1949–58; telephone 1917; TX 1925; pop. 89 (1933), 70 (1947), 80 (1954), 221 (2006).

Upper Monkerai (*Co. Gloucester*) 32°14'S. 151°51'E., 20 km NE of Dungog.

Upper Moore Creek (*Co. Inglis*) 30°57'S. 150°59'E., 15 km N. of Tamworth, on Moore Ck; tobacco; school 1930–41; pop. 81 (1933).

Upper Moscheto Island (*Co. Northumberland*) see Kooragang.

Upper Myall (*Co. Gloucester*) 32°16'S. 152°11'E., 17 km N. of Bulahdelah, on Myall R.; dairying; bushfire 1907; PO 1874; Rom. Cath. C. (St Mary's) b. 1940 by T. Ryan, d. by John Patrick Gannon, burnt down 1979; sawmills: Charles Dee and Arthur Harvey; school (Upper Myall River till 1891) 1883–91 and 1954–64; telephone 1924–75; TX 1928; Union C. 1905; pop. 76 (1933), 83 (1947), 76 (1954), 84 (1961).

Upper Myall River (*Co. Gloucester*) see Upper Myall.

Upper Nambucca (*Co. Raleigh*) 30°36'S. 152°42'E., 14 km NW of Bowraville, on Nambucca R.; also known as North Arm; farming; PO 1927–31; telephone 1924; TX.

Upper Nemingha (*Co. Parry*) see Piallamore.

Upper Newee Creek (*Co. Raleigh*) 30°38'S. 152°55'E., 7 km E. of Bowraville, on Newee Ck; telephone 1926.

Upper North Arm (*Co. Raleigh*) see Girralong.

Upper North Creek (*Co. Rous*) 28°49'S. 153°35'E., 6 km N. of East Ballina; farming; PO 1880–1963; telephone 1915; 3 wharves.

Upper Nulla Nulla (*Co. Dudley*) see Carcolla.

Upper Orara (*Co. Fitzroy*) 30°17'S. 153°00'E., 10 km W. of Coffs Harbour, on Orara R.; farming; Angl. C. (All Saints') b. 1910 by R. Rennie, closed; bushfire 1936; FB (old station closed and reused, new one on new site); Meth. C. 1908; PO 1890–1973; sawmills: F.J. Kerr and A. Davis 1932, Neaves Bros 1919, William Seccombe (burnt down 1926), Small and Jackson; school (Dunvegan till 1919) 1895, new one b. 1899 by Walsh and Boultwood, additions 1910 and 2010; telephone 1906; TX 1913, automatic 1972; pop. 234 (1901), 332 (1933), 234 (1947), 235 (1954), 193 (1961), 723 (2011).

Upper Pappinbarra (*Co. Macquarie*) 31°17'S.

152°26'E., 34 km NW of Wauchope, on Pappinbarra Ck; dairying; FB (station b. 2014); PO 1927–80; sawmill (C. Everett & Sons); telephone 1925; TX 1928; pop. 124 (1933), 314 (2006).

Upper Picton (*Co. Camden*) see Picton.

Upper Pigman Creek (*Co. Rous*) see Dyraaba.

Upper Pocket (*Co. Rous*) see The Pocket.

Upper Pyramul (*Co. Wellington*) see Pyramul.

Upper Quinburra (*Co. Wellesley*) see Quinburra.

Upper Rollands Plains (*Co. Macquarie*) 31°15'S. 152°37'E., 27 km SW of Kempsey, on Wilson R.; fern gathering 1914+ and farming; Free Presb. C.; hailstorm 2018; PO 1890–1969; sawmill (Thomas R. McLaughlin); school 1949, additions 2010; telephone 1914; TX 1927; Union C.; pop. 139 (1933), 132 (1947), 131 (1954), 125 (1961), 191 (2006), 379 (2011).

Upper Rouchel (*Co. Durham*) 32°07'S. 151°05'E., 19 km E. of Aberdeen, on Rouchel Brook; grazing; cemetery (Rouchel Brook, 138 graves); PO 1911–78; telephone 1911; TX 1912–69; pop. 123 (1933), 89 (1947), 102 (1954), 71 (1961), 222 (2006).

Upper Run (*Co. Westmoreland*) see Hampton.

Upper Shark Creek (*Co. Clarence*) 29°33'S. 153°12'E., 9 km S. of Maclean, on Shark Ck; Shark's Creek till 1891; sugar-cane; bridge (Hinchey Bridge) b. 1903 by J. Tully; PO 1927–31; telephone 1923.

Upper Sherwood Creek (*Co. Fitzroy*) see Athol Glen.

Upper Smiths Creek (*Co. Clarence*) 29°30'S. 152°44'E., 28 km NW of Grafton, on Smiths Ck; telephone 1924; TX.

Upper South Arm (*Co. Raleigh*) see Brierfield.

Upper Springrove (*Co. Rous*) 28°50'S. 153°07'E., 8 km NE of Casino.

Upper Stratheden (*Co. Rous*) 28°43'S. 152°56'E., 14 km SW of Kyogle.

Upper Tallawang (*Co. Darling*) 32°11'S. 149°25'E., 17 km S. of Dunedoo.

Upper Tallawang (*Co. Darling*) see also Tallawang.

Upper Tarago (*Co. Argyle*) see Tarago.

Upper Tarcutta (*Co. Wynyard*) see Tarcutta.

Upper Taylors Arm (*Co. Raleigh*) 30°46'S. 152°41'E., 23 km W. of Macksville, on Taylors Arm; pop. 258 (2006).

Upper Taylors Arm (*Co. Raleigh*) see also Taylors Arm.

Upper Temora (*Co. Bland*) see Temora.

Upper Thora (*Co. Raleigh*) 30°26'S. 152°43'E., 10 km S. of Dorrigo, on Bellinger R.; flood 2011; telephone 1923; TX 1925.

Upper Tooloom (*Co. Buller*) 28°38'S. 152°25'E., 54 km W. of Kyogle, on Tooloom Ck; gold, farming, grazing; cemetery; PO 1927–52; telephone by 1924; TX 1929; pop. 68 (1933), 143 (2006).

Upper Tooloom (*Co. Buller*) see also Cooradulla.

Upper Tuena (*Co. Georgiana*) 34°02'S. 149°21'E., 49 km N. of Crookwell, on Tuena Ck; pop. 52 (1901).

Upper Tumberumba (*Co. Wynward*) see Courabyra.

Upper Tuntable Creek (*Co. Rous*) 28°36'S. 153°16'E., 3 km E. of Nimbin.

Upper Turon (*Co. Roxburgh*) 33°07'S. 149°46'E., 35 km SW of Kandos, on Turon R.; Palmers Oaky Junction till 1872; goldmining; mines: Golden Fleece or Reef Gully, and Hilltop 1881–82, 1907–9, 1934; PO 1872–1910; 4 quarries; school 1871–85.

Upper Tyalgum Creek (*Co. Rous*) see Tyalgum Creek.

Upper Wallaby (*Co. Roxburgh*) 33°04'S. 149°37'E., 39 km N. of Bathurst, on Turon R.; bridge (Coles Bridge) over Turon R.; goldmine (Britannia, incl. stamper battery) 1877–82 and 1903–4.

Upper Williams (*Co. Durham*) see Dungog.

Upper Wilsons Creek (*Co. Rous*) 28°33'S. 153°24'E., 11 km W. of Mullumbimby, on Wilsons Ck; telephone 1924; TX 1925; pop. 422 (2006).

Upper Wybong (*Co. Brisbane*) see Kars Springs.

Upper Yarrowitch (*Co. Vernon*) 31°18'S. 151°55'E., 46 km SE of Walcha, on Yarrowitch

R.; telephone 1936; TX 1950.

Uppingham (*Co. Monteagle*) 34°03'S. 148°27'E., 33 km SW of Cowra; RS 1901, station b. by F.W. Kinch, closed 1970.

Upsalls Creek (*Co. Macquarie*) 31°38'S. 152°40'E., 5 km W. of Kendall, on Upsalls Ck; farming; bridge (Buctons Bridge) 1965, over Camden Haven R.; PO 1927–67; school (Lorne till 1918, then Kendall West) 1897–1925; telephone 1916; TX 1927; pop. 55 (1933), 68 (1961).

Urabodalla (*Co. Dampier*) see Eurobodalla.

Uradux (*Co. St Vincent*) see Euradux.

Uralba (*Co. Rous*) 28°53'S. 153°30'E., 6 km W. of Ballina, on Duck Ck; village gaz. 1866; Angl. C. (St John's) 1911, renovated 1931 by F.G. Cullen; electricity 1938; hailstorm 1951; school (Duck Creek till 1914 and Towalbyn 1922–51) 1900–67; pop. 145 (1901), 116 (1911), 98 (1933), 184 (1947), 136 (1954), 112 (1961), 208 (2011).

Uralgulla (*Co. Dudley*) see Uralgurra.

Uralgurra (*Co. Dudley*) 30°51'S. 152°33'E., 38 km NW of Kempsey, on Macleay R.; Uralgulla till 1894; estab. by Henry Davis, defunct; farming and dairying; cemetery 1892; PO 1895–1931; Prim. Meth. C.; school 1906–11; telephone 1896; TX 1944; pop. 56 (1911), 42 (1933).

Uralla (*Co. Sandon*) 30°39'S. 151°30'E., 21 km SW of Armidale, on Uralla Ck; surveyed 1849 by John James Galloway, laid out and village gaz. 1855, first lots sold 1856, munic. proc. 1882, town gaz. 1889, munic. abolished 1948; wheat, gold (disc. 1852), wool, beef, oats, fruit, potatoes; Angl. C. b. 1861 by Alexander Mitchell, new one (St John's) b. 1886–88 by William Seabrook and John Brown, d. by Blacket Bros and Turner; brass and iron foundry estab. 1872 by Henry Sheldon Goddard (iron furnace estab. 1875), bought by Christopher Andrew Young, relocated 1898, acquired 1900 by H.C. Crapp who renamed it the Phoenix Foundry, became New England Brass and Iron Lace Foundry, taken over by Les Young, sold to Peter Wright, sold 2008 to Kerry Varley; brewery (New England Brewing Co.) estab. 2013 by Ben Rylands; brickworks (D. Sharpe) 1884, defunct; bridges: bridge b. 1901 (timber beam) by W.H. Hogbin, over Rocky Ck and Shanahan's Bridge over Uralla Ck; bushfire 1905; butter factory (Uralla Co-op. Butter & Bacon Co. Ltd) 1907; causeway across Uralla Ck; cement works; cemetery (old one, 303 graves 1850s+); CH (incl. lock-up) b. 1862 by Alexander Mitchell, new one b. 1883–85 by M. and E. Scanlon, d. by James Johnstone Barnet, closed and reused; clock tower 1971; cordial factories: G.R. Borland (sold 1912 to R.W. Munsie), Joe and Albert Brissett (moved 1902 to Inverell), John Patrick Henry 1938–49, W.L. Hopkins, Pearsall's; electricity 1918; engineering works (Les Munro), enlarged 1906; FB (station b. 1962); flour mills: Kirkwood's 1856, John McCrossin (b. 1871 by Alexander Mitchell, closed, sold and reused, bought and reused again by Cooper, bought 1935 by McRae and reused again, sold 1979 and restored, reused 1982), Alex Porter & Co. 1867; foot-bridges: one over Rocky Ck and 2 over Uralla Ck; ice works (John Patrick Henry) 1938–49; lock-up 1891, additions 1910 by C.G. Cooper; measles epidemics 1936 and 1948; PO 1858, new one b. 1884 by M. and E. Scanlon, additions 1910 by John Patrick Henry; pound (stock) 1858; powerhouse estab. 1918 by John Patrick Henry, burnt down 1925, rebuilt with new engine 1925, taken over 1938 by county council; Presb. C. b. 1859 by Alexander Mitchell, new one (St David's) 1904, cement rendered 1909, closed, sold 2003, 2006, 2014, reused; rabbit freezing works (also produced ice) b. 1923 by C.G. Cooper; reservoir (Mount Mutton); rifle range 1914; Rom. Cath. C. 1861, new one 1882, reused, new one 1967 on new site (St Joseph's); RS 1882, station b. by William Seabrook and John Brown; Salv. Army C. b. 1872 as a hall by Murray, McCrossin and Maurice Carroll, closed 2001, sold and reused; sawmills: R.T. Harrison, bought 1905 by C.G. Cooper, and John Patrick Henry (incl. joinery), burnt down and rebuilt 1925; school 1862, new one

b. 1871 by Alexander Mitchell, new buildings b. 1910 by De Baskerville Edward Edwin Carden, reused 1922, replaced, additions 1931 by C.G. Cooper, additions 1959, 1967, 1982; sewerage 1968, augmentation 1995; snowstorm 1881; telegraph 1867; TX 1907, automatic 1979; Unit. C. (orig. Meth.) b. 1909 by C.G. Cooper, d. by Hugh J. Scott; water supply 1939, augmentation 1986; Wes. Meth. C. b. 1872 by Edmund Lonsdale and J.W. Moore, demolished 1909; pop. 254 (1871), *c.*300 (1874), 380 (1881), *c.*700 (1886), 819 (1891), *c.*930 (1895), 681 (1901), 1,590 (1911), 1,054 (1933), 1,186 (1947), 1,121 (1954), 1,658 (1961), 1,626 (1966), 1,746 (1971), 1,940 (1976), 2,090 (1981), 2,250 (1986), 2,324 (1991), 2,460 (1996), 2,306 (2001), 2,267 (2006), 2,388 (2011).

Urana (*Co. Urana*) 35°20'S. 146°16'E., 42 km W. of Lockhart, on Urana Ck; disc. 1842 by Augustus Morris, F.A. Gwynne and Walker, settled 1847 by Smith and O'Neill, town gaz. 1859, laid out 1859 by Hayes, first lots sold 1864; sheep and cattle, later wheat; airfield 1953; Angl. C. 1865–85, new one (St Philip's) b. 1887 by C. Martin, sanctuary added 1918, and graveyard; brewery (William Jones) 1884; bridges: one b. 1892 over Corowa Ck and one b. 1868–72, new one b. 1898 by E.W. Fitzgerald, over Urana Ck; cemetery 1869; CH b. 1880 by C. Johnson, d. by James Johnstone Barnet, repairs 1953 by A.H. Cooper, closed 1983, reused; cordial factory (George Holt) 1877, sold 1884 to W. Jones & Co.; dam b. 1887 by Burrows and Williams, strengthened 1889 and 1894; drought 1837–44; electricity 1940; FB 1903; fires 1871 and 1899; floods 1891, 1931, 1936, 1939, 1955, 1956, 2010, 2012; gales 1900 and 1923; hospital 1882, (McCaughey Memorial) b. 1936 by G.H. Dixon & Sons Ltd, additions 1938 also by Dixon's, new one 1996; lock-up b. 1864 by William Martin, new one b. 1881 by A. Frew, repairs 1953 by A.H. Cooper; PO 1861, new one b. 1879 by Brown and Pearce, d. by James Johnstone Barnet, additions 1895 by J. Huddleston and R. Liddall; pound (stock) 1861; Presb. C. 1958; PS 1865, new one b. 1881 by A. Frew, new one 1959; quarry; railway turntable, 50 ft (15.2 m), removed 1963; reservoir 1925; Rom. Cath. C. (St Fiacre's) b. 1882 by Alfred Hacker, tower added 1885, new church 1959, renovated 1984; RS 1911, station b. by John Allibone, closed 1987; saleyards (J.M. Smith & Co.) b. 1949 by Charles Gale; sawmill (Bonola's), fire 1951; school 1875, new one b. 1877 by A. Frew, additions 1885 by Charles Martin, replaced 1893 by Roe, renovations 1954, additions 1966 and 2010; silo 1920; telegraph 1861; TX 1906, automatic 1986; Unit. C. (orig. Presb.) b. 1898 by Sebastian Schuback, d. by J.B. Hotson, additions 1937; water reticulation 1926; Wes. Meth. C.; windmill (for town water supply) 1900; pop. *c.*100 (1866), 113 (1871), 398 (1881), 397 (1891), 301 (1901), 694 (1911), 620 (1933), 444 (1947), 635 (1954), 544 (1961), 500 (1966), 529 (1971), 484 (1976), 419 (1981), 400 (1986), 388 (1991), 374 (1996), 341 (2001), 336 (2006), 300 (2011).

Uranagong (*Co. Urana*) 35°24'S. 146°14'E., 48 km SW of Lockhart; RS 1912, station b. by Ernest Frederick Leggo, closed 1950.

Urandangie (*Co. Sandon*) 30°15'S. 151°42'E., 5 km SE of Guyra; trout hatchery 1926; pop. 31 (1933).

Urangbell (*Co. Clarence*)
see Upper Copmanhurst

Urangeline (*Co. Urana*) 35°27'S. 146°38'E., 25 km SW of Lockhart; farming; bushfire 1882; caterpillar infestation 1916; Lutheran C. 1929 (removed from Alma Park), new one (St Matthew's) 1965; PO 1882–1953; Rom. Cath. C. 1897, new one (St Joseph's) 1937; TX 1923, automatic 1953; pop. 106 (1911), 261 (1933), 187 (1947), 59 (1954), 132 (1961).

Urangeline (*Co. Urana*)
see also Graburn and Urangeline East.

Urangeline East (*Co. Urana*) 35°30'S. 146°42'E., 31 km W. of Henty; Bendabo till 1930; PO 1928–71; RS (orig. Urangeline) 1920–75; silo 1928, extended 1932; telephone 1925; TX 1925, automatic 1971; pop. 74 (1933), 54 (1954), 64 (1961).

Uranquinty (*Co. Mitchell*) 35°12'S. 147°15'E., 29 km NE of The Rock, on Sandy Ck; formerly Glenrouth; village gaz. 1888 as Glenrouth; soldiers' settlement after World War I; aeroplane crash 1942; air force training school 1941–47 and 1952–58; Angl. C. 1895, replacement (St Cuthbert's) 1954; bushfire (man died) 1905; cemetery 1902; chaff mills: G.R. Kleinig & Co. Ltd, and Millor and Murphy; FB; fire 1913; floods 2010 and 2012; gastroenteritis epidemic (5 babies died) 1950; Lutheran C. (Trinity) b. 1922 by Lonergan, closed 2009, reused; migrant hostel (at disused air force base) 1948–51; PO 1889, new one b. 1926 by F.H. Siebels; Presb. C. (removed from Tarcutta) re-erected 1920, demolished 1943; PS 1912, lock-up added 1914, station closed 1935, reopened 1936–39; Quintessential C. 2014 (former Lutheran C.); railway turntable, 60 ft (18.3 m), defunct; reservoir, 50,000 gal. (227.3 kl); Rom. Cath. C. (St Patrick's) 1908; RS (Sandy Creek till 1891) 1880, station b. by John Macdonald, remodelled 1888, burnt down 1934, new one 1935, closed 1984; school 1880, new one b. 1900 by C. Hardy & Co., additions 1993; SD Adventist C. (Reform Movement); silo 1918; storm 1911; telegraph 1890; TX 1912, automatic 1935; Unit. C. (St James's, orig. Presb.) 1960; pop. 457 (1911), 424 (1933), 324 (1947), 390 (1954), 421 (1961), 226 (1971), 241 (1976), 328 (1981), 477 (1986), 587 (1991), 661 (1996), 637 (2001), 695 (2011).

Urawilkie (*Co. Baradine*) 30°47'S. 148°43'E., 36 km NE of Coonamble, on Urawilkie Ck; PO 1879–87.

Urbenville (*Co. Buller*) 28°29'S. 152°33'E., 47 km W. of Kyogle, on Tooloom Ck; village gaz. 1912; timber, cattle, dairying; ambulance station 1945–49, reopened 1950; Angl. C. (St Mark the Evangelist) 1915, destroyed 1963, replaced (Anzac Memorial Church of St Mark's) 1965; bridge 1968; butter factory (North Coast Co-op. Ltd) 1909, taken over 1919 by Prescott Ltd and reused as a cheese factory, closed, sold 1924, new one b. 1927 by Thackeray and Gallagher; cemetery (262 graves), incl. columbarium; CH (building removed from Lower Acacia Creek), re-erected 1938 by J.R. Day; electricity 1958; FB; flood 2011; gale 1963; hospital b. 1942 (but o. 1945), additions 1952 and 1955, new one 1962; PO 1910; PS 1934, closed; reservoir, 200,000 gal. (909.2 kl), 1966; Rom. Cath. C. (St Joseph's) b. 1940 by G.J. Grove & Sons, closed, sold and reused 2003; sawmills: Ford Timbers Pty Ltd, W.J. Graham & Son, Stubbings Bros, burnt down and replaced 1953; school 1912, additions 1936 by L. Baker, demolished, new one 1952 on new site, additions 2010; sewerage 1981; telephone 1911; TX 1915, automatic 1961; Unit. C. (orig. Meth.) 1935, closed, sold 2015, reused; water supply 1968; pop. 123 (1911), 205 (1933), 372 (1947), 432 (1954), 420 (1961), 309 (1971), 290 (1976), 282 (1981), 291 (1986), 250 (1991), 251 (1996), 217 (2001), 245 (2006), 226 (2011).

Urisino (*Co. Ularara*) 29°44'S. 143°45'E., 207 km N. of Wilcannia; grazing; PO 1928–67; telephone 1928; TX 1957–67.

Urliup (*Co. Rous*) 28°16'S. 153°24'E., 7 km N. of Murwillumbah, on Bilambil Ck; telephone 1925; TX 1930; pop. 83 (1954), 375 (2006).

Uroly (*Co. Boyd*) see Euroley.

Urulgurra (*Co. Dudley*) see Millbank.

Urunga (*Co. Raleigh*) 30°30'S. 153°01'E., 16 km N. of Nambucca Heads, on Kalang R.; Bellinger Heads till 1909; village gaz. 1894, bypassed by highway 2016; orig. timber and shipbuilding, then dairying and hort., now fishing and tourism; ambulance station; Angl. C. 1900 d. by F.J. Board & Son, damaged 1905, new one (St Barnabas the Apostle) 1960; brick-kiln (George Ainsworth); bridge b. 1928 by A. Oxenford, demolished, new one 1972, over Kalang R.; bushfires 1905 and 1953 (man died); cemetery (828 graves) 1904, incl. columbarium; 2 FB (incl. station b. 1968); flood 2009; foot-bridge 1940, over Urunga Lagoon; hailstorm 1905; Meth. C. 1966; pilot station; PO (at pilot station) 1890–98; Presb. C. b. 1912 by Neil McPherson; PS 1903, new one b. 1921; punt, replaced 1928 with bridge, across Kalang R.; railway bridge b. 1921–23 over Kalang R.; reservoir;

rifle range 1914; river training walls (incl. Hanleys Wall); Rom. Cath. C. 1910, relocated and extended 1950, reused 1973, new one (Holy Name War Memorial) 1973; RS 1923; sawmills: Eichmann's and Smith's (operated by Ellis & Co.), burnt down 1920, rebuilt, burnt down 1927; school (Bellinger South till 1889 and Bellinger Heads till 1912) 1882, additions 1899 by A.E. Ellis, repairs 1902 by W. Atherton, additions 1908 by George Edward Moore, additions 1959 and 1991; sewerage 1970, augmentation 1989; telegraph 1884; TX (automatic); Unit. C.; wharf, additions 1891 by W.G. Boulton; pop. 327 (1901), 426 (1911), 426 (1924), 705 (1933), 781 (1947), 972 (1954), 787 (1961), 924 (1966), 1,200 (1971), 1,601 (1976), 2,045 (1981), 2,336 (1986), 2,666 (1991), 2,716 (1996), 2,704 (2001), 2,687 (2006), 2,523 (2011).

Urungie (*Co. Leichhardt*) 30°45'S. 148°32'E., 26 km NE of Coonamble.

Utungun (*Co. Raleigh*) 30°44'S. 152°50'E., 9 km W. of Macksville, on Taylors Arm; also formerly known as Boat Harbour; settled 1867 by Joseph Koenig, village gaz. 1894, never fully developed; cemetery 1894; school 1896–1947; pop. 25 (1933), 142 (1947), 80 (1954), 116 (1961).

V

Vacy (*Co. Durham*) 32°33'S. 151°35'E., 22 km N. of Maitland, on Paterson R.; former private village owned by Gilbert Cory estab. *c.*1828, subdivided and 50 lots sold 1927; orig. wheat, arrowroot, tobacco, grapes, sheep, then dairying, farming, cattle, poultry; Angl. C. 1848, renovations and repairs 1880, new one (St John's) b. 1887 by James Richardson, d. by Arthur Coe Lee, renovated 1913, re-roofed 1921, and columbarium; arrowroot factory (Thomas Cordell); boiling-down works, closed 1927; bridge 1861, burnt down 1896, new one (Allan timber truss) b. 1896–98 by Littleproud and J.J. Taylor, 213 ft (64.9 m), strengthened 2002, over Paterson R.; bushfire 1904; charcoal kilns estab. during World War II by Partridge Bros; creamery (Allbon's) b. 1892 by William Keppie and James Oldfield, acquired 1894 by William Heap, closed 1899, demolished; diphtheria 1910; electricity 1937; FB 1974 (station b. 1976, replaced 1998); fire 1896; floods 1861 and 1875; PO 1860, new one b. 1891 by J. Oldfield; sale-yards 1897; school 1859 b. by Simpson and Gosling, replacement b. 1882–84, demolished and replaced 1965, additions 2012; storm 1868; telephone 1889; tobacco factory; TX 1915, automatic 1981; water supply 1980; pop. *c.*30 (1866), 374 (1901), 379 (1911), 115 (1933), 276 (1947), 235 (1954), 237 (1961), 547 (2011).

Valentine (*Co. Northumberland*) 33°01'S. 151°38'E., 4 km NW of Belmont, on Croudace Bay; (incl. Croudace Bay); subdivided 1916 by Henry Ferdinand Halloran; bushfire 1951; collieries: Belmont (also known as Northern No. 2, o. 1957 by R.W. Miller & Co., closed 1979, except for washery), Belmont Extended, Bryantville, Cardiff Coal Co. (estab. by George Alfred Lloyd) 1863–64, Dunlock, Green Hills Coal Works, Hartley Coal Co., Shaggy (also known as Golden Egg, estab. *c.*1906 by Robertson and Fletcher, closed by fire 1955); 2 jetties; PO 1947; 3 quarries; sawmill (Cumming and Lane) 1872; school 1958, additions by R.T. Parker Pty Ltd; telephone 1948; TX 1950, automatic 1961; water supply 1948; pop. 74 (1947), 5,555 (2011).

Vale of Clwyd (*Co. Cook*) see Hartley.

Vale of Clwydd (*Co. Cook*) see Lithgow.

Valery (*Co. Raleigh*) 30°23'S. 152°57'E., 9 km NE of Bellingen, on Pine Ck; Snarebrook till 1920; farming; bridge over Pine Ck; PO 1927–64; Rom. Cath. C. (St Patrick's) 1909, closed, later sold and demolished; school (Snarebrook till 1920) 1919–60; telephone 1923; TX 1940; pop. 57 (1911), 136 (1933), 120 (1947), 98 (1954), 56 (1961).

Vales Point (*Co. Northumberland*) see Mannering Park.

Valhalla Village (*Co. Northumberland*) see Chain Valley Bay.

Valla (*Co. Raleigh*) 30°36'S. 152°58'E., 6 km NW of Nambucca Heads; Deep Creek till 1906; gold (disc. by Buckman and Dick Marshall), timber, agric., dairying, tomatoes 1924+, bananas 1927+; bridge b. by George Edward Moore over Deep Ck; bushfire 1951; PO 1892–1942; RS 1939–74; sawmills: Robert Beer (burnt down 1932), Haigh's, Frederick

Neaves (burnt down 1951); school 1880–87 and 1900–69; sewerage augmentation 1986; telephone 1914; TX 1923; Wes. Meth. C. 1879; pop. *c.*100 (1903), 75 (1911), 502 (1933, incl. 96 at goldmine), 286 (1947), 268 (1954), 170 (1961), 831 (2011).

Valla Beach (*Co. Raleigh*) 30°36'S. 153°00'E., 6 km N. of Nambucca Heads, on Tasman Sea; FB; foot-bridge over Deep Ck; reservoir (tower); school 1960–75; pop. 69 (1961), 232 (1986), 475 (1991), 731 (1996), 814 (2001), 1,054 (2006), 1,199 (2011).

Vallarca (*Co. Denison*) 35°52'S. 146°06'E., 17 km NE of Mulwala; school 1938–46.

Valley Heights (*Co. Cook*) 33°42'S. 150°35'E., 2 km E. of Springwood, on Fitzgerald Ck; Fitzgerald's Valley till 1855, then The Valley till 1907; Angl. C. (St Mark's) 1915; bushfires 1911, 1936 (3 houses destroyed), 1951 (9 houses destroyed); FB 1958; PO 1876–1976; railway coal stage, dismantled 1960; railway locomotive depot 1914–88, reused; railway round-house (10 bays) 1914–57, reused; railway turntable (third one) 1967, 60 ft (18.3 m), removed from Katoomba; RS (Eager's Platform till 1877, then The Valley till 1880) 1875, new station b. 1902 by C. Palmer, burnt down 1911, rebuilt 1912; sewage works; pop. 81 (1901), 116 (1911), 161 (1933), 206 (1947), 268 (1954), 412 (1961), 1,383 (2011).

Valley Valley (*Co. Raleigh*) see Viewmont.

Valley View (*Co. Northumberland*) see Wyoming.

Vanderville (*Co. Camden*) see The Oaks.

Vegetable Creek (*Co. Gough*) see Emmaville.

Vere (*Co. Northumberland*) 32°42'S. 151°08'E., 15 km S. of Singleton; farming and dairying; PO 1872–1920; school 1880–1927; telephone 1920; Wes. Meth. C. b. 1899 by White, d. by Anderson and White; pop. 103 (1911), 57 (1933).

Vermont Hill (*Co. Cunningham*) 32°34'S. 146°44'E., 61 km NW of Condobolin; farming; pop. 49 (1933), 90 (1947).

Verona (*Co. Dampier*) 36°28'S. 149°49'E., 23 km W. of Bermagui, on Murrah R.; dairying; cheese factory (View Mount, J. and T. Walsh); PO 1927–42; school (Cobbobra till 1890) 1882–1954; telephone 1907; TX 1928; pop. 75 (1901), 88 (1911), 70 (1933), 65 (1947), 51 (1961), 414 (2011).

Veteran Hall (*Co. Northumberland*) see Saratoga.

Veterans Flat (*Co. Northumberland*) see Maitland.

Victoria Flat (*Co. Georgiana*) 34°10'S. 149°20'E., 34 km N. of Crookwell; gold; mines: Elsinora (Junction Point Mineral Development Co.) <1907, Royal George 1875, Victoria (Staveley & Co.) 1890.

Victoria Street (*Co. Northumberland*) see Maitland East.

Viewmont (*Co. Raleigh*) 30°36'S. 152°54'E., 8 km NE of Bowraville; dairying, tomatoes, bananas; bushfire 1951; PO 1927–64; sawmill; school (Valley Valley till 1924) 1919–71; telephone 1924; TX 1928, automatic 1955; pop. 39 (1933), 93 (1947), 85 (1954), 79 (1961).

Vincentia (*Co. St Vincent*) 35°04'S. 150°41'E., 6 km NE of Sanctuary Point, on Jervis Bay; South Huskisson till 1952; village founded 1951, thrived 1970; Bapt. C. (Jervis Bay); bridge to Huskisson, over Moona Moona Ck; bushfire 2001; FB 1964 (new station b. 2014); foot-bridge 1931 to Huskisson, over Moona Moona Ck; PO 1962; PS; quarry; reservoir 1982; Rom. Cath. C. (Holy Spirit) 1983 d. by George Adams; schools: primary 1992 and HS 1993, additions 2008; sewerage augmentation 1985; water supply augmentation 1983; wharf 1842; pop. 37 (1961), 289 (1971), 726 (1976), 2,801 (2011).

Viney Creek (*Co. Gloucester*) 32°35'S. 150°06'E., 11 km NW of Tea Gardens; quarry.

Violet Hill (*Co. Camden*) see Mount Kembla.

Violet Hill (*Co. Gloucester*) 32°28'S. 152°19'E., 12 km SE of Bulahdelah, on Boolambayte Lake; formerly Bunghery.

Violet Town (*Co. Northumberland*) see Eleebana.

Vittoria (*Co. Bathurst*) 33°26'S. 149°22'E., 12 km NE of Blayney, on Neals Ck; village gaz. 1881, proposed to be developed as a new city, which never eventuated; farming and honey; brewery (Central Ranges Brewing Co.) 2012; bushfire 2009; honey processing plant (Goldfields, Grant Lockwood) 1992; PO 1867–1970; Rom. Cath. C. (St Brigid's) 1918–61, sold, derelict; school 1880–84; telephone 1923; TX 1927; pop. 12 (1891), 114 (1901), 72 (1911), 86 (1933), 84 (1947), 115 (1954), 105 (1961).

Vulcan (*Co. Roxburgh*) 33°01'S. 149°57'E., 17 km S. of Kandos; RS 1916–71; school Jan.-Dec. 1928.

Vychan (*Co. Ashburnham*) 33°28'S. 148°16'E., 25 km SE of Forbes; telephone 1951; TX 1951, automatic 1965; pop. 46 (1933).

W

Wadalba (*Co. Northumberland*) see Wyong.

Wadbilliga (*Co. Dampier*) 36°15'S. 149°39'E., 42 km W. of Narooma.

Waddi (*Co. Boyd*) 34°35'S. 145°59'E., 3 km S. of Darlington Point; village gaz. 1879; cemetery 1881.

Wade (*Co. Cooper*) see Griffith.

Wadeville (*Co. Rous*) 28°34'S. 153°08'E., 9 km NW of Nimbin, on Frenchs Ck; farming and dairying; PO 1927; telephone 1916; TX 1925; pop. 90 (1933), 74 (1947), 55 (1954), 51 (1961).

Waggalalah (*Co. King*) see Langley Park.

Wagga Wagga (*Co. Wynyard*) 35°07'S. 147°22'E., 330 km W. of Wollongong, on Murrumbidgee R.; (incl. Ashmont, Bourkelands, East Wagga Wagga, Glenfield Park, Kooringal formerly Darrung till 1960, Lloyd, Moorong, Mount Austin, Newtown, North Wagga Wagga, South Wagga Wagga, Tatton, Tolland, Turvey Park); disc. 1829 by Capt. Charles Sturt and George Macleay, settled 1832 by William Best and Charles Tompson, estab. 1847 by Michael Norton, laid out 1849 by Thomas Scott Townsend, town gaz. and first lots sold 1849, more lots sold 1850 and 1851, subdivided (Newtown) 1858, munic. proc. 1870, designated as chief town of the county, expanded 1878+, thrived 1926, city proc. 1946 (area enlarged 1951, 1968, 1981); agric. 1846, cattle, vineyards, then sheep and wheat (1860s–70s), river port (unreliable), then goldmining, dairying *c.*1900+, maize, barley, oats, rye, potatoes, tobacco, wine, fish, clothing, engineering, manufacturing; ambulance station b. 1929 by Charles Hardy Contracting Co. Ltd, d. by Eric Clarke Pitt and John Donald Morrow, new one (Turvey Park) 2016; Angl. C.: St Alban's (Kooringal) 1958 d. by Gordon Trafford Walker, St John the Evangelist (b. 1860 by Robert Nixon, d. by William Weaver and William Edmund Kemp, additions and alterations 1875–77 by Charles Hardy, enlarged 1881, extensive alterations 1905–11 also by Hardy, d. by William John Monks and Christopher Ernest Jeffs, new one b. 1933 by H.C. Buckman, d. also by Jeffs, additions and alterations, incl. spire, 1963 by H.C. Buckman & Son, d. by Harrison and Hassall), St Luke's (South Wagga Wagga) b. 1913 by C. Hardy & Co., d. by William John Monks, St Mary's (North Wagga Wagga) 1900, restoration 1936, St Paul's (Turvey Park) 1962 d. by Gordon Trafford Walker; Apostolic C. (Hope Generation); Assemblies of God C. (Kings Christ.); bacon factory (Riverina Bacon & Smallgoods Factory Ltd) 1929, sold 1933 to P.E. Riedell & Sons; Baha'i C.; Bapt. C. 1987; boiling-down works (Thomas Joseph Halloran) 1892; bond store (George Forsyth) 1868–1980; boot factory (Howard's), burnt down 1882; breweries: Albion Brewery (estab. 1889 by William Davoren and Hugh McDonnell, sold to Thomas Loughlin and James Bellair, sold 1898 to James Beattie, acquired by Robertson & Co., closed 1900), John Ball (estab. 1874, sold to Charles F. Godhard and James George Riley, acquired by J.A. Spiers, sold 1881 to Richard Heath), W.H.F. Eaton (taken over 1903 by H.S.

Headley, joined 1914 by Patrick J. Mahon, becoming Mahon and Headley, brewery then dismantled), Federal Brewery (b. 1881 by Martin Augustus Treacey and John Treacey as the Murrumbidgee Brewery, burnt down 1896, rebuilt 1899 by C. Hardy & Co. for Patrick J. Mahon, d. by William John Monks, Mahon joined in 1900 with John J. Hogan to also make cordials and brewery renamed, sold 1921 to Tooth & Co., sold 1923 to J.M. Whelan, bought back and closed 1924 by Tooth, reused), Newtown Brewery (b. by Strickland) 1866–87, Thirsty Crow Brewing Co. 2010, Wagga Wagga Brewery (estab. 1866 by George Ralston, acquired by O'Keeffe & Co., acquired 1873 by Mathew Callaghan, bought 1873 by George Wildman, bought by William Seymour Eaton and renamed Eaton & Co., closed 1914); brick-kiln (James Saul); brickworks: Bourne Brick Co. Ltd, William Fleming 1892 (man killed 1909), Hardy Brick Co., Harmon's, John Newman (operated by George Lipscombe, sold 1898 to Charles Hardy, sen.), Schnelle Brick Co., Willis Bros; bridges over Murrumbidgee R.: Company Bridge (laminated arch) b. 1862–64 by David Baillie, bought 1884 by govt, demolished, replaced by Hampden Bridge (Howe timber truss), 645 ft (196.6 m), ironwork supplied by Atlas Engineering Works, erected 1895 by Lieut. Stanley Frederick Stokes, d. by Percy Allan, renovated 1905 by G.E. Williams, demolished 2014 (bypassed 1995 by Wiradjuri Bridge), Eunony Bridge 1976, Gobbagombalin Bridge 1997, Travers Street Bridge; bushfire 1951–52; butter factories: Murrumbidgee Co-op. Dairy Co. Ltd 1923, additions and alterations 1928 by Thackeray and Gallagher, closed 1985, demolished 1991, James Stewart (Orange Tree Point) 1890–91, Wagga Wagga Co-op. Butter Factory & Chilling Co. Ltd (b. 1895 by John Gray, jun., taken over 1900 by Allen and Duncan Saxenby, bankrupt 1902, bought 1903 by George Julius Rohr, fire 1923, new freezing plant 1926, factory sold 1930 to the Murrumbidgee Co-op. Dairy Co. Ltd); CAE (Riverina) 1972, became Riverina-Murray Institute of Higher Education in 1985, became univ. (Charles Sturt, South Campus) in 1989, moved to Boorooma, site sold 2019 to Signature Care Pty Ltd, fire 2019; canvas works (W.H. Sherwood); carriage-works: Barling and Anderson, William J. Blake (sold to John Wright, who later took in Peter Rae as partner and firm became Rae and Wright by 1883), Burgess and Mitchell (partnership dissolved, Mitchell carried on, then joined by Hehir Bros till 1893, then Patrick Joseph Hehir continued alone, then Charles Douglas joined as partner, then partnership dissolved and Douglas continued alone), James Clarke, Gregory Crowther, Alfred Cullen, Douglas and Patterson, James Welsh Edney, Federal Coach Factory (estab. by W. Dunne, acquired 1889 by Bott and A.F. Hely and became Federal Coach Factory, Donnelly and Gain joined them in 1897, burnt down 1902, rebuilt, firm sold 1905 to J. Parsons & Sons, acquired 1912 by Scully and Ginger), John Gelme & Co. 1906 (burnt down 1912, became John Gelme Ltd, relocated 1913), S.J. Greer (acquired 1912 by Robert Clulow), Richard S. Heydon, A.L. Meldrum, Selwood's, Smith, Cummings and Doyle 1872; cemetery 1863; CH 1848, (second) b. 1856 by Fox, (third) b. 1862 by Charles Hardy, sen., additions 1870–72 also by Hardy, additions 1879, demolished 1901, (fourth) b. 1902 by C. Hardy & Co., d. by George John Oakeshott and Walter Liberty Vernon, used by air force during World War II, renovated and reopened 1946, additions 1982, redevelopment and expansion 2014–16 d. by Tanner, Kibble and Denton; chaff mill (Prescott's), fire 1952; Chinese joss house 1887, partly demolished 1939, partly reused 1954; Christ. Revival Crusade C. (New Life); Church of Christ 1915; clothing factory (Dunlop Weatherproofs Aust. Pty Ltd) 1944–77, reused 1980; cordial factories: James Beattie (estab. 1895 in old Phoenix Flour Mill, taken over by W.S. Eaton & Co., partnership dissolved 1901 and business carried on alone by William Henry Filmore

Eaton without William Seymour Eaton), T.S. Bell & Son 1931, Crystal 1916, Federal Brewery (Hogan and Mahon, taken over by Sheekeys Pty Ltd), Richard Heath, F.K. Lawliss (bought 1891 by Patrick Purcell), Loughlin and Bellair, Wagga Wagga Brewery & Aerated Water Manufactory (H.S. Headley), J. Webster (acquired 1875 by Samuel S. Lincoln, burnt down 1878, rebuilt); cyclone 1938; diphtheria 1931; droughts 1850–51 and 1938; dust storms 1880, 1899, 1922, 1928, 1933, 1942, 1944; earth tremors 1871, 1917, 1935, 1938, 1949; electricity: North Wagga Wagga 1925 and Wagga Wagga 1922; electroplating works (H.D. Pope) 1926; engineering works: Hepburn and Lovett, Ben Koth & Son, Nixon's, Wenk and Johnston; FB 1880 (station b. 1883, burnt down 1902, replacement b. 1903 by John Gray, jun., d. by W.J. Monks, new one b. 1927 by C. Hardy & Co., d. by William Hull McNiven, new one 1981, refurbished 2008); fibreboard plant (Laminex Group) 1982; fires 1870, 1880, 1882 (child died), 1897, 1899, 1912, 1926, 1959; floods 1852, 1853, 1864, 1867, 1869, 1870, 1872, 1891, 1894, 1900, 1906, 1917, 1925, 1931, 1947, 1950, 1952, 1956, 1974, 1991, 2010, 2012; flour mills: Britannia (estab. by John Jenkins, sold 1875 to Henry Hayes, fire 1885, sold to George Maw), John Chapman and James Brown Edney 1857, Milling Industries Ltd, Murrumbidgee Milling Co. Ltd (b. 1890 by Charles Hardy, sen., d. by William John Monks, silos 1918 and 1927, mill converted 1927 to electricity, closed), Phoenix (b. 1857 by Edward Mumford for Robert Nixon, who retired 1871, sold 1873 to James Reynolds, upgraded 1882, reused, demolished 1904), Wagga Wagga Roller Flour Mills (b. 1886 by Charles Hardy for Henry Hayes, d. by G. Sheppard), Wise Bros Pty Ltd, burnt down 1944; foot-bridge (Trail Street) 1921; foundries: John Gelme, Hanks Foundry Pty Ltd (closed 1948), Wenk and Johnston, John Whitlock (sold 1907 to Taylor Bros); gaol b. 1862 by Charles Hardy, sen. and Thomas Hodson, additions 1871, closed, demolished 1928; gasworks estab. 1878 by J.A. Wark, bought 1888 by local council, inundated 1891, new retorts 1923, fire 1927, new gasholder 1949, new gasworks 1963, natural gas 1981; Greek Orthodox C. (The Dormition of Our Lady) 1965; hospital 1865, additions 1881, 1884, 1886, new one 1910, additions 1922–24, 1936, 1938, 1940, 1955, 1962 (demolished 2016), 1978, 1988, 2015; ice-cream factory (Peters American Delicacy Co. Ltd) 1923, extended 1928 and 1933, became Peters Ice Cream Pty Ltd in 1945; ice works: E.J. Barton, Kyle and Little 1887, Murrumbidgee Dairy Co., closed 1972 and reused; Indep. Bapt. C.; Jehovah's Witnesses C.; joineries: Benchmark, Hardys Pty Ltd (estab. 1920 by Charles Hardy, demolished 1922, new one 1924), John Pendleton, R. Zanker; juvenile justice centre (Riverina) 1984, additions 1991; lamp factory (Electric Lamp Manufacturers Aust. Pty Ltd) 1942–44; levee b. 1960–62; LDS (Mormon) C.; lock-up 1847, new one b. 1870 by Charles Hardy, sen., extensions 1918 by C. Hardy & Co., d. by George McRae, additions 1981; Lutheran C. (Bethlehem); measles epidemics 1893, 1898, 1934; Meth. C.: Kooringal 1965 (and one removed 1974 from Yatheila) and Turvey Park 1951 (new one b. 1964 by D. and D. Construction Co., d. by William C. Brown); milk factory (Murrumbidgee Dairy Products Pty Ltd) 1942, bought 2006 by Fonterra & Co. and renamed Riverina Fresh, bought 2016 by Blue River; monumental stone works: Baley and Baumer, and J.S. Shephard; mouse plague 1918; munitions factory (World War II), closed 1944, sold to Dunlop Weatherproof Aust. Pty Ltd and reused; PO: Ashmont (Turvey Park till 1993) 1927, Kooringal 1954, Mount Austin 1963, North Wagga Wagga 1912, South Wagga Wagga 1911, Wagga Wagga 1849 (new one b. 1869, closed, demolished 1902, new one b. 1877 by Charles Hardy, additions and alterations 1879 also by Hardy, new one b. 1886–88, d. by James Johnstone Barnet, alterations 1896 and 1907 by C. Hardy & Co., additions and alterations 1914 by James Frizelle, alterations 1926 also by Hardy, closed 1992, sold and reused 1993, post office relocated 1993 and 1996); pounds (stock): North Wagga Wagga 1858 and South Wagga Wagga; powerhouse 1922; Presb. C.: Knox (Kooringal), St Aidan's (South Wagga Wagga) 1936, St Andrew's (b. 1869–72 by John McIntosh and Charles Hodson, renovated 1892, steeple and additions 1916 d. by Ernest E. Giles, church extended 1961); PS: North Wagga Wagga 1878, new one b. 1903 by George Huntley Dixon and William Godfrey Butterworth, and Wagga Wagga 1847, new one b. 1875 by Thomas Hodson, d. by James Johnstone Barnet, additions 1882 and 1884, repairs 1889 by Charles Hardy, replacement b. 1902 by C. Hardy & Co., d. by Walter Liberty Vernon, new building 1928, refurbished 2000 by Burton Constructions Pty Ltd, new one b. 2009 by Richard Crookes Constructions, d. by Collard Maxwell; punt estab. 1849 by William Brown, who replaced it in 1851, across Murrumbidgee R.; quarry; railway bridge (four span wrought iron lattice girder) fabricated by P. & W. MacLellan Ltd, Glasgow, Scotland, erected 1879–81 by Amos & Co. and J.S. Bennett, d. by Sir John Fowler and John Whitton, strengthened 1929, new one b. 2007 by Arenco (NSW) Pty Ltd, over Murrumbidgee R.; railway engine shed b. 1880 by W. Ball, extended 1881 by J. Johnson, moved 1893 to Harden; railway turntable, 60 ft (18.3 m); 2 railway viaducts (timber) b. 1880, replaced (in steel and concrete) 1889–1901; 6 reservoirs (incl. three on Willans Hill, 1885, 1916, 1929); rifle range (Willans Hill) 1891, new one 1917, new one (Pomingalarna) 1930; Rom. Cath. C.: Holy Trinity (Ashmont), Our Lady of Fatima (Turvey Park) 1953, St Michael's (b. 1859 by J. Wilson, closed, reused, demolished 1965, new one b. 1885–87 by Gibbs and Charles Hardy, d. by Tappin, Gilbert and Dennehy, additions 1922–25 by C. Hardy & Co., d. by William John Monks, Christopher Ernest Jeffs and Roy Ashley Shaw), St Veronica's (North Wagga Wagga) 1909; RS (South Wagga Wagga till 1882) 1878, station b. by Charles Hardy and George Shaw, refreshment rooms closed 1956; rubber works (H. Mildwater); sale-yards (A.T. Bolton) 1885, new yards (Monks') 1893; Salv. Army C. 1929, new one 1988; sawmills: Cambrian (W.G. Evans), John Gray 1872, Riverina Saw Milling Co.; scarlet fever 1876; schools: Ashmont 1966, Flowerdale 1979–87, Kooringal primary 1959, Kooringal HS 1973 (d. by Ian McHutchinson, Douglas Anderson and R. Powell, additions 1976 and 2006), Mount Austin primary 1959 (additions 2010), Mount Austin HS 1964 (additions 1967, 1971, 1976), North Wagga Wagga 1880 (new one b. 1882, additions 1913 and 1956, additions 2010 by Burton Constructions Pty Ltd), South Wagga Wagga 1892 (b. by C. Hardy & Co., d. by William Edmund Kemp, additions 1977, renamed South Wagga in 1992), Sturt 1973 (additions 1979), Tatton 1980–90, Tolland 1970 (d. by K. Thirsk and J. Lowing, additions 1975 and 1980, renamed Red Hill in 2016), Turvey Park 1953 (additions 1960, re-roofed 2013), Wagga Wagga primary 1861 (b. by John McIntosh and Andrew Cruickshank, new one b. 1872 by Charles Hardy, additions 1878, 1882, 1885, 1887, additions 1928 by Thomas Norman Grimsley, fire 2019), Wagga Wagga HS 1912 (new one b. 1917 by C. Hardy & Co., d. by Wells, additions 1931, 1956, 1961, 1972); SD Adventist C. 1939; sewerage: Wagga Wagga (works b. by William O'Brien) 1915, augmentation 1957, and Kooringal augmentation 1962; sheet metal works (Kimbell Adeney Pty Ltd); snow 1899; soap-works: W.A. Jacob 1874, Murrumbidgee Soap Works (estab. 1881 by E. and A. Janitzky), Riverine Soap Factory (estab. by William Jones, sold 1908 to A.J. Hicks); storms 1923 and 2007; street tree plantings 1885 by G. Sheppard; streets kerosene lit in Wagga Wagga 1876, gas lit in 1879, electric lit in North Wagga Wagga 1926; sugar mill (Holland's) 1871; tank works: John Gray, Hardy & Co., Stevens and Miles, R. Watts; tanneries (incl. W. Denning, burnt down

1887); TC 1943, additions 1964 and 1985, became Riverina Institute in 1992, additions 1997; teachers' college 1948, additions 1957, 1958, 1959, 1960, 1962, additions 1964 d. by David Turner and J. Nicholas, college dissolved 1972 and became CAE; telegraph 1869, new office b. 1877 by Charles Hardy, alterations 1879 and 1896 also by Hardy; telephone: Kooringal 1954, Mount Austin 1963, North Wagga Wagga 1912, South Wagga Wagga 1911; terrazzo works (Alan C. Hamblin); TX: Kooringal (automatic) 1966, South Wagga Wagga (automatic) 1951, Wagga Wagga (automatic) 1940; typhoid 1885, 1889, 1896, 1898 (boy died), 1905, 1906, 1907 (3 died), 1908, 1910, 1924; Unit. C.: Wesley (orig. Meth.) b. 1949 by H.C. Buckman, d. by Norman Welland McPherson, and Pilgrim (Glenfield Park) 2014; univ. (Charles Sturt, South Campus) 1989, fire 2007; vulcanising works (Newtown, Bert Gray); wall panelling factory (Glazite Wall Panelling Co.) 1947; water supply 1883; waterworks b. 1885 by Evans, Son and Lipscomb, additional works 1903 by C. Hardy & Co., reticulation to North Wagga Wagga 1930, filtration plant 1938; Wes. Meth. C. b. 1865 by Charles Hardy, reused, new one b. 1877 on new site also by Hardy, d. by Sheppard, Crouch and Wilson, renovated 1910 by C. Hardy & Co.; wharf 1871; whooping cough epidemic 1934; winery (John Smith); wool-scours (with fellmongeries): John Johnson 1889, acquired 1890 by Henry E. Brougham, acquired 1892 by Honeyman and Darchy, and Waratah estab. 1890 by Joseph Hayes; wool store (E.E. Collins & Co.); pop. 221 (1851), 336 (1856), 627 (1861), *c.*700 (1866), 1,858 (1871), 3,975 (1881), 4,596 (1891), *c.*4,500 (1895), 5,108 (1901), 7,446 (1911), 7,679 (1921), 11,869 (1933), 12,630 (1939), 15,569 (1947), 19,362 (1954), 22,092 (1961), 25,819 (1966), 28,905 (1971), 32,984 (1976), 36,837 (1981), 37,577 (1986), 40,875 (1991), 42,848 (1996), 44,451 (2001), 46,913 (2011). (See also Bomen, Boorooma, Estella, Forest Hill, Gumly Gumly and Lake Albert.)

Wagga Wagga North (*Co. Clarendon*) see Bomen and Wagga Wagga (*Co. Wynyard*).

Wagonga (*Co. Dampier*) 36°13'S. 150°03'E., 7 km W. of Narooma; orig. Punkalla; settled 1862, village gaz. 1866, thrived in 1880s, declined in 1890s; goldmining till 1911, butter, cheese, bacon, timber, bark, farming; Angl. C. 1886; bushfire 1919; cemetery (burials 1877+); flour mills: Coman's 1884–88 and Fuller's; PO 1863–1946; sawmills: Clyde Sawmilling & Shipping Co. Pty Ltd (closed 1914), Edward J. Coman 1884 (man killed 1885, mill leased 1886 to Perkins, Willis & Co., closed 1888), McMillan Bros (burnt down 1919); school 1884–89; stamper battery (Buckley and Hawdon's 10 head) 1884; telephone 1896; TX 1944; Wes. Meth. C. 1866; wharf b. 1893 by M'Hugh and Lynch; pop. 66 (1901), 113 (1911), 34 (1933).

Wagonga Heads South (*Co. Dampier*) see Narooma.

Wagoribil (*Co. Bligh*) see Turill.

Wagra (*Co. Goulburn*) see Wymah.

Wagragobilly (*Co. Buccleuch*) 35°06'S. 148°13'E., 10 km E. of Gundagai, on Tumut R.; farming; cemetery 1884; PO 1927–46; Rom. Cath. C. 1879, new one (St Denis's) b. 1901 on new site by William Warbrick, closed, sold and reused, and graveyard; school 1880–1900; telephone 1918; TX 1925; pop. 85 (1901), 68 (1911), 75 (1933).

Wagstaffe (*Co. Northumberland*) see Killcare.

Wagstaffe Point (*Co. Northumberland*) see Killcare.

Wahratta (*Co. Yancowinna*) 31°59'S. 141°50'E., 35 km E. of Broken Hill; RS 1924–74.

Waioma (*Co. Sandon*) 30°31'S. 151°56'E., 26 km E. of Armidale; telephone 1925; TX 1928.

Wait-A-While (*Co. Denison*) 35°40'S. 145°44'E., 8 km W. of Berrigan; RS 1898, station b. by Charles Baker, closed 1958.

Waitui (*Co. Macquarie*) 31°42'S. 152°34'E., 15 km SW of Kendall, on Stewarts R.; sawmill; school 1957–66.

Wakefield (*Co. Northumberland*) 32°58'S. 151°33'E., 6 km W. of Boolaroo, on Diega Ck; (incl. Diega Flat and Rhondda, orig. Rooty

Flat); bushfire 1951; cemetery; colliery estab. 1900 by William Laidley & Co., taken over by R.W. Miller & Co. and renamed Northern; dam (Newstan Colliery); FB; Meth. C. 1929; quarry; sawmill (Richard Colin Carroll), burnt down; school (Rhondda *c.*1905–1911) 1898 b. by W. Turnbull, new one b. 1904 by J.P. Tyler, closed 1982, burnt down 1993; telephone 1926; United Meth. Free C. 1901; pop. 123 (1901), 199 (1911), 175 (1933), 124 (1947), 179 (1954), 131 (1961), 176 (2011).

Wakool (*Co. Wakool*) 35°28'S. 144°24'E., 30 km NE of Barham; village surveyed and gaz. 1927, soldiers' settlement 1945+; orig. wheat, then rice 1942+, wool, horses, cattle; Angl. C. (St Luke's), closed; PO 1870; Rom. Cath. C. (St Joseph's); RS (1 km SW, on Victorian railway); sawmill (George Gusthart); school 1930–31, reopened 1938, additions 1960, 1972, 2010; silo (rice); TX 1928, automatic 1972; Unit. C., closed, sold 2011, 2012, 2019, reused; pop. 172 (1861), 211 (1911), 75 (1933), 80 (1947), 286 (1954), 258 (1961), 228 (1971), 250 (1976), 278 (1981), 249 (1986), 258 (1991), 224 (1996), 225 (2001), 213 (2006).

Wakool Crossing (*Co. Caira*) see Kyalite.

Wakool Junction (*Co. Caira*) 34°51'S. 143°20'E., 31 km SW of Balranald, on Murray R.

Wakool North (*Co. Wakool*) 35°28'S. 144°26'E., 34 km NE of Barham.

Walang (*Co. Roxburgh*) 33°26'S. 149°45'E., 17 km E. of Bathurst, on Saint Anthony's Ck; also known as Green Swamp; grazing, farming, orchards; copper mine (Boyd or Green Swamp or Glanmire or Walang) <1851–1910; PO 1927–51; school 1878, repairs 1901 by G.T. Clarke, new one b. 1912, closed 1941, reopened 1957–69; snowstorm 1928; telephone 1925; TX 1941; pop. 96 (1933), 76 (1947), 82 (1954), 77 (1961).

Walbrook (*Co. Georgiana*) 33°53'S. 149°40'E., 26 km SW of Oberon, on Campbells R.; school (Campbells River till 1881, then Wallbrook) 1880–93; telephone 1926.

Walbundrie (*Co. Hume*) 35°42'S. 146°43'E., 29 km W. of Culcairn, on Billabong Ck; Piney Range till 1869; laid out 1863 by James H. Wood, village gaz. 1864 as Walbundry; goldmining (reef), grazing, agric.; bridges: concrete one b. 1930 over Billabong Ck and one b. 1938 over Simmonds Ck; cemetery (2 km NW) 1880; CH 1895, new one b. 1899 by Smith and Bates; drought 1914; dust storm 1930; FB 1926; flood 1931; lock-up 1910; mouse plague 1925; PO 1861, burnt down 1914, new one b. by P.J. Fagan; Presb. C. 1910; PS 1870, replacement b. 1910 by Charles Benaud Smith, closed 1969; quarry; Rom. Cath. C. 1897, new one b. 1909 by Joe Loftus, sen., new one (Good Shepherd) b. 1931 by Geoff, Horace and Joseph Loftus; sale-yards 1912; school 1878–91, reopened 1897, extended 1914 by Joe Loftus, sen., closed and relocated, new one b. 1923 on new site by Geoff, Horace and Joseph Loftus; telegraph 1885; telephone 1909; TX 1910; Union C.; Unit. C. (St Stephen's, orig. Presb.) b. 1957 by Coombs Bros; water supply augmentation 1989; pop. 134 (1891), 220 (1901), 304 (1911), 116 (1933), 124 (1947), 322 (1954), 224 (1961), 188 (2006), 218 (2011).

Walbundrie Reefs (*Co. Hume*) see Bulgandry.

Walbundry (*Co. Hume*) see Walbundrie.

Walburton (*Co. Roxburgh*) 33°06'S. 149°43'E., 36 km SW of Kandos, on Turon R.; goldmining (alluvial); Angl. C. 1853.

Walcha (*Co. Vernon*) 30°59'S. 151°36'E., 39 km S. of Uralla, on Apsley R.; settled 1832 by Hamilton Collins Sempill, estab. 1845, surveyed 1849, laid out 1852 by John James Galloway, village gaz. and first lots sold 1852, designated as chief town of the county, munic. 1889–1955; timber, oats, wheat, gold, sheep, cattle, dairying; airfield; ambulance station 1951, closed; Angl. C. (St Paul's) b. 1862–66 by Alexander Mitchell, renamed (St Andrew's), new one 1963; bridge 1865, new one 1975, over Apsley R.; cemeteries: general (2,079 graves 1859+) 1863, incl. columbarium and Rom. Cath. (449 graves 1859+); CH 1857, new one 1873, additions 1880 by Edmund Lonsdale, renovations and repairs 1918 by Max Cooper; cordial factories: S.W. Farrell, W. Ryan 1905, E.W. Thomas and A.J. Gilmour 1914; diphtheria 1934; earth tremors

1880, 1899, 1938; electricity 1925; FB (station b. 1966); fire 1896; floods 1893, 1935, 1941, 1952, 1962; flour mills: David William Jamieson, Patrick Hamilton, Marshall's (acquired by Tom Grieve); hospital (cottage) b. 1892 by Lewis and Goman, d. by Arthur Coe Lee and James Warren Scobie, additions 1930, new one 2008; levees; PO 1850, new one b. 1884 by William Seabrook and John Brown; pound (stock) 1853; powerhouse, inundated 1935; Presb. C. b. 1854–57, closed, demolished 1888, replacement (St Mary's) b. 1888 by Duncan M'Rae, d. by Alexander Leckie Elphinstone, renamed St Paul's in 1915; PS 1857; reservoir (concrete), 500,000 gal. (2,273 kl), 1966; Rom. Cath. C. 1859, demolished, new one (St Patrick's) b. 1881 by Crowe and Furniful, extended 1955; Salv. Army C.; sawmills: Fennings and T.O. Hardaker; scarlet fever 1904; school 1859 b. by Henry Crowe, new building b. 1883 by William Seabrook and John Brown, additions and alterations 1891 by Joseph Harrison, additions 1935 by W.P. Mellefont, 1953, 1961, 1966, 1971, 1987, 1990, new one 1993 on new site; sewerage 1969; snowstorms 1892 and 1917; soap-works (A.W. Watt) 1888; streets gas lit 1892; tanneries: J.S. Dick 1872 and M.J. Walsh 1884; telegraph 1877, new office b. 1884 by William Seabrook and John Brown; TX 1906, automatic 1968; water supply augmentation 1986; Wes. Meth. C.; 2 wool-scours; pop. 19 (1839), 355 (1861), *c*.400 (1866), 246 (1871), 309 (1881), 864 (1891), *c*.1,500 (1895–99), 980 (1901), 2,192 (1911), 1,526 (1933), 1,550 (1947), 1,741 (1954), 1,585 (1961), 1,550 (1966), 1,603 (1971), 1,665 (1976), 1,674 (1981), 1,639 (1986), 1,782 (1991), 1,623 (1996), 1,488 (2001), 1,482 (2011).

Walcha Hut (*Co. Clyde*) see Brewarrina.

Walcha Road (*Co. Inglis*) 30°57'S. 151°24'E., 19 km W. of Walcha, on Surveyors Ck; grazing; bridge over Surveyors Ck; FB; PO 1882; PS b. 1886 by William Seabrook and John Brown; railway turntable 1899, 60 ft (18.3 m), removed 1972; Rom. Cath. C. (St John's) b. 1911 by J. Long, restored; RS 1882, station b. by Joseph Conlon, closed 1989; school 1884–1965; telegraph 1889; telephone 1910; TX 1913, automatic 1953; Union C. 1885, repairs 1919 by Matthew Morgan, closed and dilapidated; pop. 113 (1933), 140 (1947), 139 (1954), 158 (1961).

Waldegrave (*Co. Bathurst*) 33°26'S. 149°03'E., 12 km W. of Millthorpe, on Flyers Ck; farming; Meth. C. 1924; PO 1927–31; quarry (marble); telephone 1924; TX 1939–69; pop. 72 (1911), 54 (1933).

Waldegrave (*Co. Bathurst*) see also Forest Reefs.

Walgett (*Co. Baradine*) 30°01'S. 148°07'E., 106 km N. of Coonamble, on Namoi R.; also known as Warrena and Wingate; estab. 1851, surveyed and laid out 1859 by Arthur Dewhurst, town gaz. and first lots sold 1859, more lots sold 1867, thrived 1880–83; river port 1861+, cattle, sheep, cotton, maize, sorghum; airport (1 km SE) 1943; ambulance station; Angl. C. (St Peter's) 1893, rebuilt 1979; brewery estab. 1883 by Thomas Simpson as Castlemaine Brewery, sold and renamed Waratah Brewery in 1887, closed 1910; brickworks; bridge b. 1881 by Frederick C. Staveley, new one (Marjorie Phyllis Walford Bridge) 1981, over Namoi R.; bushfire 1951; carriage-works: Fagan Bros and McGregor's; caterpillar infestation 1939; cemetery (1,739 graves 1875+) 1863; CH (incl. lock-up) 1866, new one b. 1881 by Daniel Edwards, d. by James Johnstone Barnet, additions 1910 by A.H. Rose, repairs 1919 by Joseph Head, new building 1967, restored 1979; drought 1867; electricity 1926; 2 FB (stations b. 1918 and 1960); fires 1884, 1895, 1905, 1914, 1962, 2013, 2019; floods 1864, 1890, 1910, 1921, 1950, 1998; gale 1881; gaol b. 1882–86 by Joseph Conlon but finished by Ford, demolished 1948; heatwaves 1878, 1882, 1940; hospital b. 1881 by Daniel Edwards, additions 1969 and 1975; hurricane 1865; ice works 1899; levee b. 1961 by Phillips Construction Pty Ltd; PO 1851, new one b. 1881 by Daniel Edwards, fire 1923, reused, new one 1969; police barracks b. 1880 by Joseph Conlon, additions 1884 by Daniel Edwards; pound (stock) 1861; powerhouse; Presb. C. 1883, new one b. 1889 by Rose and Beddie, burnt down, new one (Scott Memorial) b. 1915–17 by A.H. Rose, closed, derelict, sold; PS 1860, additions 1871, additions 1907 by A.H. Rose, additions 1964, new one 1966 d. by David Turner, new one 2015; railway accidents 1926 and 1960; railway bridge 1908, over Two Mile Ck; railway coal stage, removed; railway turntable, ruined; reservoirs: 12,000 gal. (54.6 kl) and 250,000 gal. (1,136.5 kl); Rom. Cath. C. (St Mary's) 1918; RS 1908, station b. by James William Doherty, closed; sandfly infestation 1954; sawmill (Perseverance); schools: primary 1877, new one b. 1879 by Daniel Edwards, repairs 1891 by T. Harris, repairs 1900 by F.G. Williams, additions 1903 by Peter Beddie, extended 1922 by A.H. Rose, additions 1957, 1964, 1975, and HS (renamed Walgett Community College) 1972, additions 1989; sewerage 1969; soap and candle factory (Thomas Simpson) 1887; storm 1885; TC (a campus of Western Institute); telegraph 1873, new office b. 1881 by Daniel Edwards; TX; typhoid 1896 (person died), 1900 (man died), 1903; water supply (artesian bore) 1907, augmentation 1971, treatment plant 2013; wool-scours: Joe Hayes, R. Johnston, Arthur Thompson; pop. 81 (1871), *c.*100 (1877), 375 (1881), *c.*500 (1885), 742 (1891), 1,075 (1901), 1,177 (1911), 1,106 (1933), 1,141 (1947), 1,348 (1954), 1,726 (1961), 2,024 (1966), 2,284 (1971), 2,253 (1976), 2,157 (1981), 2,151 (1986), 2,091 (1991), 1,970 (1996), 1,826 (2001), 1,735 (2006), 1,625 (2011).

Walhallow (*Co. Pottinger*) 31°26'S. 150°26'E., 22 km W. of Quirindi, on Mooki R., Aboriginal reserve 1895–1962; cemetery 1903; Community C.; fire 1896; PS; school 1911; pop. 120 (1901), 188 (1911), 203 (1933, incl. 160 on Aboriginal reserve), 160 (1999).

Walhallow (*Co. Pottinger*) see also Caroona.

Walka (*Co. Northumberland*) see Oakhampton.

Walkers Hill (*Co. Cunningham*) 32°26'S. 146°46'E., 78 km NW of Condobolin.

Walkyrie (*Co. Hume*) 35°41'S. 146°50'E., 21 km W. of Culcairn; school 1914–69.

Wallabadah (*Co. Buckland*) 31°32'S. 150°50'E., 15 km E. of Quirindi, on Quirindi Ck; first lots sold 1855, declined 1877+, village gaz. 1880, town gaz. 1904, soldiers' settlement after World War II; grain, cattle, sheep, turkeys, pecan nuts; Angl. C. (Ascension) b. 1892–96, additions 1912 by George Warfield; bridge 1943, widened 1979, over Quirindi Ck; butter factory 1894; cemetery (494 graves); CH (incl. lock-up) b. 1869 by Thomas Hyndes, additions 1871, closed 1878, new one b. 1879 by J. McDonald; FB; flood 2000; hailstorms 1869 and 1900; PO 1856; pound (stock) 1857; PS, additions 1879 by J. M'Donald, closed 1888; Rom. Cath. C. 1871, replaced 1891, new one d. and b. 1905 by P.C. M'Kee, new one (St Anne's) b. 1911 by George Warfield, d. by Bishop and Alderman, closed, sold 2011 and 2018; school 1867, new building b. 1878 by Cook, additions 1882 by G. Chappel, re-roofed 1911, new building b. 1928 by E.R.S. Potter; telegraph 1874; telephone 1899; TX 1910, automatic 1958; water reticulation 1967; Wes. Meth. C. 1869, new one 1895; pop. *c.*61 (1866), 144 (1871), 172 (1881), 158 (1891), 425 (1901), 589 (1911), 263 (1933), 255 (1947), 303 (1954), 297 (1961), 229 (2011).

Wallabadah (*Co. Northumberland*) 33°03'S. 151°01'E., 30 km SW of Paxton, on Wallabadah Ck; bushfire 1994.

Wallabi Point (*Co. Gloucester*) 32°01'S. 152°34'E., 5 km SW of Old Bar, on Tasman Sea; pop. 22 (1933), 270 (1996), 317 (2001), 445 (2006), 545 (2011).

Wallaby Creek (*Co. Buller*) see Tooloom.

Wallaby Gully (*Co. Northumberland*) see Ellalong.

Wallaby Joe Flat (*Co. Macquarie*) 31°51'S. 152°20'E., 5 km NW of Wingham.

Wallaby Rocks (*Co. Roxburgh*) 33°04'S. 149°39'E., 39 km N. of Bathurst, on Turon R.; gold dredging; bridge b. 1897 by E. Taylor, d. by Percy Allan, over Turon R.; school (Bradshaws Flat) 1897–1924.

Wallaby Rocks (*Co. Wellington*) 32°50'S. 148°58'E., 31 km S. of Wellington, on Bell R.

Wallace (*Co. Clarendon*) see Wallacetown.

Wallace Town (*Co. Clarendon*) see Harefield.

Wallacetown (*Co. Clarendon*) 34°58'S. 147°27'E., 14 km SW of Junee, on Houlaghans Ck; village gaz. 1862 as Wallace; school 1882–84.

Wallaga Lake (*Co. Dampier*) 36°23'S. 150°04'E., 5 km N. of Bermagui, on Tasman Sea; pop. 111 (1911), 134 (1933), 391 (1991), 435 (1996), 526 (2011).

Wallaga Lake Heights (*Co. Dampier*) 36°22'S. 150°04'E., 6 km N. of Bermagui, on Wallaga Lake; pop. 112 (2001).

Wallagoot (*Co. Auckland*) 36°46'S. 149°55'E., 8 km SW of Tathra; surveyed 1858; dairying and cattle; cheese factory (Lake View) operated by Isaac Game; sawmill (Billy Weatherhead); school 1884–1912; telephone 1948; TX 1949–54; pop. 36 (1933), 468 (2011).

Wallalong (*Co. Durham*) 32°42'S. 151°39'E., 9 km NE of Maitland, on Paterson R.; (incl. Abbotsford and Bowthorne); farming and dairying; broom factory (Great Northern Power Broom & Brush Manufactory) estab. 1888 by Samuel Thomas Randell Foster, new one 1899, closed and reused; bushfire 1895; butter factory (Bowthorne Creamery & Refrigeration Works) estab. 1892 by John Lavis, became Bowthorne Co-op. Butter Factory Ltd in 1906, moved 1910 to Morpeth; earth tremor 1868; FB; floods 1870, 1874, 1893, 1895; gale 1938; hailstorm 1875; jam factory (Samuel Foster) 1893, burnt down 1896; Meth. C. d. and b. 1906 by W. King, new porch 1927; PO 1913; reservoir; school 1861, new one b. 1884 by J. Stuart, additions 1888 by Burg Bros, repairs 1896 by J. Stuart, closed 1954; shipyard (King's); telephone 1913; TX (automatic) 1956; Wes. Meth. C. 1846, new one 1854, inundated 1893; pop. 208 (1901), 238 (1911), 135 (1933), 77 (1947), 136 (1954), 116 (1961), 317 (1996), 363 (2001), 871 (2006), 938 (2011).

Wallambine (*Co. Northumberland*) see Fernances.

Wallambyne Creek (*Co. Northumberland*) see Fernances.

Wallamore (*Co. Parry*) 31°03'S. 150°51'E., 10 km NW of Tamworth; telephone 1925; pop. 119 (1933), 223 (2011).

Wallanbah (*Co. Gloucester*) 32°05'S. 152°06'E., 16 km SW of Gloucester; school 1955–70; TX (automatic); pop. 118 (1961).

Wallanbillan (*Co. Kennedy*) 32°26'S. 147°50'E., 44 km SW of Narromine, on Bogan R.

Wallangra (*Co. Arrawatta*) 29°15'S. 150°54'E., 20 km NW of Ashford, on Macintyre R.; grazing and lime; airfield (disused); bridge b. 1901 by John Caldow, new one b. 1922–24, over Macintyre R.; bushfire 1951; cemetery 1898; earth tremor 1870; FB 1950; PO 1888–1980; quarry; sawmill (Thomas Cook); school 1895–1916 and 1957–66; telephone 1898; TX 1916; pop. 87 (1901), 185 (1911), 77 (1933), 108 (1947), 163 (1954), 161 (1961), 229 (2006).

Wallangrive (*Co. Georgiana*) 34°10'S. 149°44'E., 42 km NE of Crookwell; formerly Paling Yards.

Wallangulla (*Co. Finch*) see Lightning Ridge.

Wallanthery (*Co. Nicholson*) 33°21'S. 145°50'E., 30 km NE of Hillston; also known as Willanthry; bridge (Coopers Bridge) 1918, Dare timber truss, 173 ft (52.7 m), over Lachlan R.; telephone 1928; TX 1928–54; pop. 24 (1866).

Wallanunnini (*Co. Gowen*) 31°31'S. 148°42'E., 23 km N. of Gilgandra.

Wallarah (*Co. Northumberland*) see Nords Wharf and Warnervale.

Wallarah Point (*Co. Northumberland*) see Toukley.

Wallaringa (*Co. Gloucester*) 32°27'S. 151°40'E., 9 km SW of Dungog; Angl. C. (St Mark's) b. 1907 by Burg, d. by J.W. Manson, closed 1970, sold to Ian Mate and removed.

Wallarobba (*Co. Durham*) 32°30'S. 151°42'E., 12 km SW of Dungog, on Wallarobba Ck; farming and dairying; bridge (St Anne's Bridge); bushfires 1880 and 1903; FB; PO 1878–1978; Presb. C. (St Anne's) 1931, closed, sold and reused; PS 1908; RS 1911, closed, station removed 1985; school 1939–

71, disused; storm 1868; telephone 1914; TX 1928, automatic 1978; Union C. 1899; pop. 126 (1901), 150 (1911), 200 (1933), 117 (1947), 137 (1954), 111 (1961), 329 (2011).

Wallaroo (*Co. Murray*) 35°10'S. 148°59'E., 38 km S. of Yass, on Murrumbidgee R.; quarry; Unit. C. (Wattle Park, orig. Wes. Meth.) 1882, vestry added 1954; wineries; pop. 35 (1933), 644 (2011).

Wallaroo Junction (*Co. Buller*) 28°42'S. 152°11'E., 42 km N. of Tenterfield.

Walla Walla (*Co. Hume*) 35°46'S. 146°54'E., 16 km SW of Culcairn; orig. Ebenezer; settled 1868 by German Lutherans, town founded 1869, subdivided 1909; farming and chaff; Bapt. C. 1910; bushfires 1905, 1926, 1951, 1952 (man died), 2009; carriage-works: G.J. Boehm and E.D. Heppner 1900, damaged 1923; cemetery 1871; chaff mills: Co-operative 1945, John Crennan & Co., J.F. Meyer, Stockman and Kleinig (b. 1915 by H.L. Eaton and J.D. Wenke, firm became A.H. Stockman & Co. Pty Ltd, mill bought by O. Przibella); electricity 1915; FB; floods 1941 and 2010; foundry (E. Heppner) 1910; Lutheran C. 1872, sold 1894, (second) 1889, closed and reused, (Zion) b. 1924 by Charles Hardy & Co., d. by Richard Rahnenfuehrer; Meth. C. 1958; PO 1878, new one b. 1940 by Lieschke Bros; pound (stock) 1870; powerhouse b. 1915 by A.J. Wenke; Presb. C. b. 1911 by H.L. Eaton and J.F. M'Farlane, d. by Campbell and Kernot, rededicated 1961 as Meth. C.; PS 1897, new building b. 1936 by R.E. Smith; reservoir, 100,000 gal. (454.6 kl); Rom. Cath. C. (St Mary's) 1921, restored 1999; RS 1892, station b. by Charles Hardy, closed 1975; scarlet fever 1941; school 1885, new one b. 1914 by Gamble Bros, additions 1967; silo 1920; silo fabrication works (Kotzur); storm 1923; telephone 1895; TX 1910, automatic 1982; water supply 1952; pop. 183 (1891), 346 (1901), 958 (1911), 396 (1933), 380 (1947), 405 (1954), 547 (1961), 403 (1966), 503 (1971), 490 (1976), 593 (1981), 670 (1986), 710 (1991), 606 (1996), 601 (2001), 581 (2006), 544 (2011).

Wallbrook (*Co. Georgiana*) see Walbrook.

Wallendbeen (*Co. Harden*) 34°32'S. 148°10'E., 18 km NE of Cootamundra, on Cunningham Ck; village gaz. and laid out 1877, first lots sold 1877, more lots sold 1882, munic. 1892–1935; sheep, cattle, wheat, canola, mustard seed; Angl. C. (St John's), relocated 1882, new one (St Clement's) 1902 d. by A. Schuler, chancel added 1911; brick-kiln (George Beattie); bridges over Cunningham Ck; butter factory (Wallendbeen Co-op. Dairy Co.) 1894, closed, bought by A.J. Chapman; carriage-works (sold by William Palmer to William James Cartwright); cemetery (264 graves 1887+) 1884; electricity 1930; FB 1905; gale 1922; floods 1975 and 2016; flour mill (Wearne & Sons), fire 1887, rebuilt 1889 as Wallendbeen Farmers' Co-op. Roller Mill, leased by Henry Jansen from Dransfield Bros, burnt down 1899; PO 1875, new one b. 1914, reused; Presb. C. b. 1882 by F. Turnrock, d. by R.M. Marnock, closed 1948; PS (incl. lock-up) b. 1907 by A. Allen, repairs 1953 by H.J. Fuller, additions 1962 and 1977; Rom. Cath. C. (St Patrick's) 1902, demolished, replaced (St Columba's) 1920, damaged 1925, renovated 1957; RS 1877, station relocated 1920; school 1881, new building b. 1885 by Thomas M'Beath, repairs 1891 by W. Pettitt, sen., additions 1911 by M. Millard; silo 1929, extended 1934; streets electric lit 1931; tannery, closed, dismantled and sold; telegraph 1880; TX 1910, automatic 1972; Unit. C. (orig. Meth.) b. 1911 by J.D. Ross, d. by Ernest Rees Laver, closed, sold 2003, reused, bought 2008 by Tim Smith and Leanne McGregor, renovated, later reused; water supply 1976; wool-scour (A.J. Chapman) 1904; pop. 189 (1891), *c.*1,225 (1895), 736 (1901), 580 (1911), 653 (1933), 430 (1947), 281 (1954), 284 (1961), 314 (2006), 305 (2011).

Wallendbeen (*Co. Harden*) see also Cullinga.

Wallerang (*Co. Wellington*) 32°51'S. 149°25'E., 33 km SW of Mudgee, on Willerang Ck.

Wallerawang (*Co. Cook*) 33°25'S. 150°04'E., 12 km NW of Lithgow, on Adams Ck; settled

1822 by James Walker; wool, apiculture, vegetables, timber (pine estab. 1932), coal; airport 1938; Angl. and Presb. C. (St John the Evangelist) b. 1881 by George Donald, d. by Blacket & Son, closed, restored and reopened 2006; box factory 1940; bushfire 1952; caterpillar infestation 1898; cemetery (767 graves 1883+) 1884, incl. lawn cemetery and columbarium; CH b. 1876 by T. Crow, G. Donald and E. Brook, closed 1978; cordial factory (W. Young); dam (Lake Wallace) 1978, 46 ft (14 m) high; diphtheria 1911; earth tremors 1903 and 1918; electricity 1930; engineering works (King's); FB (station b. 1959, demolished and replaced 2015); fire 1900; gales 1923 and 1928; mill (water powered, James Walker); PO 1871, new one b. 1912 by Albert Emanuel Ennis; power station (Delta Electricity) b. 1951–61, upgraded 1969–80, acquired 2013 by Energy Aust., closed 2014; PS b. 1876 by T. Crow, G. Donald and E. Brook; railway bridge (steel truss) 1921, 57 ft (17.4 m), over Coxs R.; pumping station (PWD); railway coal stage b. 1882 by John Briton and W. Cameron; railway engine shed b. 1882 by John Briton and W. Cameron, closed 1928; railway turntable, 50 ft (15.2 m), replaced 1901, 60 ft (18.3 m), defunct; railway viaduct (16 stone arches) b. 1871 by Patrick Higgins, replaced in brick 1923, over Coxs R.; rifle range (1 km W.) 1905; Rom. Cath. C. (removed from Lidsdale) re-erected 1921 by R. Leslie, d. by William Alfred Isley, new one (Sacred Heart) 1964; RS 1870, station b. by R. Read, refreshment room 1917, closed 1989, reused; sawmills: Thomas Groves and Neubeck Bros; school 1860, new buildings b. 1881 by G. Donald, d. by William Edmund Kemp, additions 1918 by J. Bartlett, additions 1935 by Peter Beddie and J.W. Brown, additions 1956, 1959, 1965, new one 1995 on new site; sewerage 1968, augmentation 1990; snowstorm 1910; street lighting 1930; tannery (Owen Connolly); telegraph 1883; TX 1910; Unit. C. (orig. Meth.) b. 1909 by James Short and Robert Leslie, d. by Harold Robert Hardwick; water supply 1938; Wes. Meth. C. 1874; pop. 2,307 (1881), 507 (1891), 538 (1901), 696 (1911), 631 (1933), 603 (1947), 1,285 (1954), 1,930 (1961), 1,580 (1966), 1,666 (1971), 1,658 (1976), 1,855 (1981), 1,988 (1986), 2,060 (1991), 2,045 (1996), 1,935 (2001), 1,904 (2006), 1,855 (2011).

Wallerawang (*Co. Cook*) see also Lidsdale.

Walleroobie (*Co. Bourke*) 34°30'S. 147°01'E., 20 km SE of Ardlethan; school 1916–43 and 1957–69; pop. 244 (1933), 156 (1947), 147 (1954), 86 (1961), 100 (2006).

Walli (*Co. Bathurst*) 33°40'S. 148°51'E., 20 km SE of Canowindra; farming; Angl. C. (St Cyprian's) 1901 d. by E. Lethbridge, closed, sold and dismantled; cemetery (8 graves 1898–1913) 1886; FB 1932; mines: Belubula (copper) 1845+, Fitzroy (copper) 1845+, Walli (gold); PO 1879–1972; school 1881–1925; telephone 1916; TX 1917, automatic 1972; pop. 162 (1901), 208 (1911), 93 (1933), 72 (1947), 53 (1954).

Wallis Island (*Co. Gloucester*) 32°13'S. 152°29'E., 5 km S. of Tuncurry, on Wallis Lake; airport (Forster) b. 1949–52.

Wallis Lake (*Co. Gloucester*) 32°17'S. 152°27'E., 13 km SW of Forster; cemetery 1878; telephone 1926.

Wallis' Plains (*Co. Northumberland*) see Maitland.

Walliston (*Co. Cadell*) 35°41'S. 144°42'E., 21 km NW of Mathoura; school 1962, additions 1965, closed 1972; pop. 123 (1933), 86 (1947).

Wallon (*Co. Stapylton*) see Moppin.

Wallsend (*Co. Northumberland*) 32°54'S. 151°40'E., 11 km W. of Newcastle, on Ironbark Ck; (incl. New Ballarat, Plattsburg, Whitegates); formerly Pittown and Brookstown, then Wallsend-Plattsburg 1891–1916; orig. part of the Newcastle Wallsend Coal Co.'s estate, subdivided and laid out 1860, thrived 1868, munic. 1874–1938 but became part of City of Greater Newcastle; coalmining and coke-making; abattoir (E. Young); ambulance station (in former bank, converted by J.C. Davis) 1937, new one b. 1942 by Brander Bros, d. by John William Oldham and Robert Godwin Lees; Angl.

C. (St Luke's) 1864, demolished, new one b. 1880 by William W. Humphreys, d. by Thomas Robson, remodelled 1921, renovated 1976, damaged 1989, re-roofed and renovated 1996, and columbaria; Assemblies of God C. (Newcastle, Korean); Bapt. C. 1863, (second) b. 1893 by E. Dann, d. by Frederick Burnhardt Menkens, (third) 1960; boot factory (T. M'Mullen & Co.); brick-kilns: J. Crowley and J. Slater; brickworks: G. Milgate, William Turner, Wallsend Brick & Tile Co. Ltd, Wind Brick Co.; bridge b. 1891 by Clarence Backhouse and Reginald William Laidley, 46 ft (14 m), over Ironbark Ck; bushfires 1938 (3 houses destroyed) and 1951; carriage-works (R.M. Evans); cemetery (burials 1863–97); CH b. 1878 by Robert Simpson, d. by James Johnstone Barnet, additions 1885 by J.S. Tyler, demolished 1930, new one b. 1929 on new site by W.H. Mitchell, d. by Richard McDonald Seymour Wells, additions and alterations 1961; Christ. Brethren Assemblies C.; coke-works: Co-operative Coal & Coke Co. (eventually increased to 67 beehive ovens) 1866, Newcastle-Wallsend Coal Mining Co. 1861, Wallsend Purified Coal & Coke Co. (76 beehive ovens) 1877, fire 1914; collieries: Boston, Brookstown (Andrew Sneddon), Co-operative (estab. 1861 by James Fletcher et al., o. 1862, acquired 1869 by William Laidley & Co., flooded 1889, closed 1934), Co-operative No. 2, Co-operative No. 3 (later absorbed by Wallsend Borehole) 1880, Elermore Vale 1858 (formerly A Pit of Newcastle-Wallsend Coal Co., leased 1891 to Robert Maddison et al., colliery thrived 1911–15, closed 1923), Grass Tree, Gretley (formerly Helensvale, owned by Morgan Mining & Industrial Co. Pty Ltd, later Newcastle-Wallsend Coal Co.), Jesmond (estab. 1910 by A.E. Taylor and James Sheldon, but H.C. Langwill later replaced Sheldon as Taylor's partner), Maryland No. 2, Newcastle-Wallsend Coal Co. 1860–1935, New Tunnel, Wallsend 1859 (Newcastle Wallsend Coal Co. Pty Ltd, acquired 1999 by New Wallsend Coal Co. Pty Ltd and renamed New Wallsend No. 2, closed 2002, razed), Wallsend C 1870–1934, Wallsend New Tunnel 1877–1914; cordial factories: J.T. Atkinson, W. Groves, Augustus Frederick Moore, NSW Aerated Water Pty Ltd; diphtheria 1927–31; earthquake 1989; electricity 1923; engineering works; English Cong. C. b. 1876 by George Froome; FB (old station closed, reused 1921, new one b. 1921 by Mitchell Bros, d. by William Hull McNiven, new one 2018); floods 1870, 1875, 1893, 1913, 1946, 2007, 2016; foot-bridge over Ironbark Ck; foundries: A.J. Attwood 1947, Thomas Kemp, E. Morgan, Perseverance (I. Gath) 1876, leased 1877 to Morgan; gastroenteritis epidemic 1940; gasworks (Wallsend & Plattsburg Gas Co. Ltd) 1885; hospital (mining) b. 1893 by C. Baker, d. by Frederick Burnhardt Menkens, isolation wards b. 1902 by Wooden and Frost, additions 1909 and 1925, partly demolished 1947 and 1949, new one (Wallsend Dist.) b. 1937–39, second stage b. 1946–49, closed 1991, reused; Islamic C. (in reused building b. 1875); Jehovah's Witnesses C.; Lay Meth. C. 1890; lock-up; mine subsidence 1877 and 1937; miners' strikes 1888, 1906, 1913, 1924, 1929–30; monumental stone works: J. Russell and Edward Young; plywood and veneer factory (Vencore Veneers Pty Ltd) 1948; PO: Wallsend 1861, new one b. 1882, additions and alterations 1954 by W.H. Ashmore & Sons, closed, sold and reused, and Whitegates 1949–65; police barracks b. 1883 by T.A. Bourke, closed, sold and reused; Presb. C. (St Andrew's) b. 1868 by Henderson, Laing and Wylie, d. by Suttie, re-roofed and renovated 1893 by W. Timmins, damaged 1989; Prim. Meth. C. (Devon Street) 1863, replacement (Devon Street) b. 1867 by Henderson, burnt down 1869, rebuilt 1870 by Joseph P. Tyler and Frederick Stanborough, new one (Metcalfe Street) 1867 d. by H. Rouse; Reorganised LDS (Mormon) C. b. 1889 by Henry Sutherland, d. by Cedric Hanford, closed, sold and reused, second one 1902 on new site, alterations and renovations 1928, third one (Community of Christ); PS

1878 d. by Mortimer William Lewis, jun.; reservoir, 452,500 gal. (2,057.1 kl); Rom. Cath. C. b. 1875 by Parkshill and Street, demolished 1948, new one (St Patrick's) b. 1931 by C. and F. Burg, d. by Peter Joseph Gannon; RS (Newcastle-Wallsend Coal Co.) 1889, station b. by Henry Wardell, passenger services 1922; Russian Orthodox C. (St Nicholas's); Salv. Army C. 1884, closed, sold, new one 1938; sawmill (J. Peattie, acquired by E. Osland & Sons, fire 1932); schools: Callaghan College (Wallsend HS till 2001) 1960, additions 1966, East Wallsend 1951–57, Plattsburg 1865, new buildings b. 1883 by Froome and Humphreys, repairs 1896 by A.B. Espley, repairs 1902 by M. Anderson, repairs 1907 by J.H. Patey, additions 1956, Wallsend 1862, new school b. 1870 by Yeomans and Williamson, alterations and repairs 1906 by W.J. Wooden, additions and alterations 1909 by T.E. Quiggin, additions 1959; SD Adventist C.: Newcastle Multicultural 1952 d. by G. Richardson and Newcastle Polish and International; smallpox 1915; squall 1913; storm 1883; streets (Plattsburg) gas lit 1885, Wallsend 1886, then electric lit 1923; telegraph 1875; telephone (Whitegates) 1949; tram depot 1910–32; tramway (Plattsburg to Newcastle) b. 1887 by Johnson and Billings, electrified 1925; trees planted in streets 1936; TX 1907; typhoid 1886 and 1894; Unit. C. (orig. Meth.) 1969; Welsh Cong. C.; Welsh Indep. C.; Wes. Meth. C. b. 1862 by George Froome, (second) 1867, damaged, replacement b. 1876 also by Froome, d. by James C. Cropley, damaged 1877, rebuilt 1878; pop. *c.*2,000 (1866), 2,169 (1871), 4,054 (1881), 6,945 (1891), *c.*7,170 (1895), 6,997 (1901), 5,623 (1911), *c.*6,500 (1921), 6,934 (1933), *c.*7,500 (1947), 12,683 (1954), *c.*16,100 (1961), *c.*17,500 (1966), *c.*18,500 (1971), *c.*19,300 (1976), 12,307 (2011).

Wallsend East (*Co. Northumberland*) see Wallsend.

Wallsend-Plattsburg (*Co. Northumberland*) see Wallsend.

Wallsend South (*Co. Northumberland*) see Elermore Vale.

Wallsend West (*Co. Northumberland*) 32°54'S. 151°34'E., 10 km W. of Wallsend, on Slatey Ck; (incl. O'Donnelltown); subdivided 1886, founded 1887, further subdivided 1889; Angl. C. b. 1900 by James Johnston, demolished, new one (St James's) 1959; Bapt. C. b. 1909 by Robert Hood, d. by Augustus Dixon Chater; bushfires 1929 and 1936; cemetery (1,254+ graves); collieries: Mt Sugarloaf No. 1 1949–74, Seaham No. 3 (O'Donnelltown), Tasman, Wallsend, West Wallsend (estab. 1885–87, o. 1888 by West Wallsend Coal Co. Ltd, strike 1888, acquired 1895 by Caledonian Collieries Ltd, strike 1903, man killed 1912, closed 1923); FB (station b. 1967); fire 2011; floods 1893 and 1913 (man died); measles epidemic 1893; PO 1888, new one b. 1906; Presb. C. (temporary one) 1889, new one (St Andrew's) b. 1904 by W. Turnbull, d. by Duncan M'Geachie, closed 1999, sold 2005, reused 2017; PS (in rented premises) 1889, new one b. 1951 by C.E. Hoyle, closed 2006, sold and reused; reservoir 101,800 gal. (462.8 kl); rifle range 1938; Rom. Cath. C. (Our Lady of Good Counsel) 1904; Salv. Army C. 1913; sawmill (West Wallsend Timber Trading Co.); scarlet fever 1950; schools: primary 1889 b. by Charles Baker, additions 1903 by Southon Bros, additions 1905 by C. Davis & Sons, additions 1907 by S. O'Brien, additions 1913 and 1959, and HS 1964, additions 1974 and 1979; SD Adventist C.; sewerage 1963; smallpox 1914; telephone 1891; tramway to Newcastle 1910; TX (automatic); Unit. C. (orig. Meth.) b. 1910 by James Johnson, d. by A. Parsons; United Meth. Free C. 1891; water supply 1902; pop. 795 (1891), 1,695 (1901), 2,723 (1911), 2,023 (1933), 1,683 (1947), 2,687 (1961), 1,606 (2006), 1,714 (2011).

Walls Flat (*Co. Auckland*) 36°38'S. 149°43'E., 13 km NW of Bega, on Numbugga Ck.

Walls Siding (*Co. Phillip*) see Mount Knowles.

Wallumburrawang (*Co. Gowen*) 31°34'S. 148°57'E., 32 km NE of Gilgandra.

Wallundry (*Co. Bland*) 34°22'S. 147°44'E., 20 km NE of Temora; gold; mines: Blackwell

Reef, Exhibition Lead, Perseverance Reef, Specimen Hill, Sussex Reef; school 1957–74; pop. 99 (1933).

Walmer (*Co. Gordon*) 32°40'S. 148°43'E., 23 km SW of Wellington; farming and grazing; airfield; measles epidemic 1954; PO 1899–1979; rifle range 1911; RS 1925–74; school 1928–66; silo 1935; telephone 1925; TX 1950, automatic 1959; Union C. 1935; pop. 60 (1911), 173 (1933), 148 (1947), 169 (1954), 155 (1961), 314 (2006).

Walsh Island (*Co. Northumberland*) see Kooragang.

Walters (*Co. Wellington*) 32°46'S. 149°11'E., 32 km SE of Wellington, on Lake Burrendong; school (Station Point) 1896–1900.

Wamback (*Co. Harden*) see Wombat.

Wamban (*Co. Dampier*) 35°57'S. 150°02'E., 6 km SW of Moruya, on Wamban Ck; eucalyptus oil distillation and silver mining.

Wambangalang (*Co. Gordon*) 32°28'S. 148°32'E., 25 km S. of Dubbo; sawmill (Norman Lane) 1909; school 1957–74.

Wambanumba (*Co. Monteagle*) 34°19'S. 148°21'E., 5 km E. of Young; Angl. C. (Resurrection) b. 1926 by H. Foster, sold 2007; bushfire 1905; heatwave 1905; Meth. C. 1902 (moved 1930 to Maori Farm); quarry; school 1882–1961; pop. 103 (1911), 51 (1933), 52 (1947).

Wamberal (*Co. Northumberland*) 33°26'S. 151°26'E., 9 km E. of Gosford, on Tasman Sea; orig. farming, later popular coastal holiday destination; Angl. C. (St Stephen's) 1906, additions 1908, reused; Assemblies of God C. (Shelly Beach); Bapt. C. (Calvary) 1992; bushfires 1928 and 1994; cemetery (4,996 graves) 1881; Christ. Reformed C.; electricity 1938; FB 1957; hailstorms 2015 and 2018; Jehovah's Witnesses C.; PO 1872; reservoir; school 1882 (located at Forresters Beach), new building b. 1891 by Alma Charles Watkins, school closed 1895, reopened 1910 (at Tumbi Umbi), extended 1915, new building b. 1924 by Arthur Partridge-Wall, school closed 1947, new one b. 1981 at Wamberal by Lusted Constructions Pty Ltd; storms 1974 and 2016; telephone 1905; TX 1915, automatic 1957; Unit. C. (orig. Meth.) 1917, closed, sold and resused; pop. 165 (1901), 165 (1911), 340 (1933), 440 (1947), 443 (1954), 5,712 (2006), 6,298 (2011).

Wamberal North (*Co. Northumberland*) 33°24'S. 151°27'E., 7 km SW of The Entrance; pop. 97 (1954), 55 (1961).

Wambidgee (*Co. Harden*) 34°52'S. 148°08'E., 22 km N. of Gundagai, on Muttama Ck; farming; goldmine (Booth's Reward); PO 1908–73; RS (Mooney Mooney till 1893, then Mooni Mooni till 1907) 1892, station relocated 1908, new one 1914, closed 1975, removed 1979; telephone 1912; pop. 110 (1901), 50 (1933).

Wamboin (*Co. Murray*) 35°15'S. 149°20'E., 9 km W. of Bungendore, on Yass R.; FB (station b. 1988); wineries: Gidgee Estate (Brett and Cheryl Lane) 1996 and Lambert Vineyards (Steve and Ruth Lambert) 1998; pop. 1,672 (2011).

Wambool (*Co. Roxburgh*) 33°31'S. 149°45'E., 19 km SE of Bathurst; farming; bridge (Pratt steel truss) 1896; PO 1908–70; 2 quarries; RS 1896, station relocated 1908 and 1921, closed 1974; telephone 1908; pop. 22 (1933).

Wamboota (*Co. Cadell*) see Womboota.

Wambo South (*Co. Hunter*) 32°36'S. 151°00'E., 18 km W. of Singleton, on Wollombi Brook; pop. 20 (1933).

Wamboyne (*Co. Gipps*) 33°34'S. 147°17'E., 41 km N. of West Wyalong; farming and grazing; hailstorm 1924; Meth. C. b. 1905 by J. Wyllie, removed 1958; PO 1896–1962; RS 1929–75, station removed 1984; telephone 1934; TX 1946; pop. 66 (1901), 99 (1911), 145 (1933), 62 (1954).

Wambrook (*Co. Wallace*) 36°12'S. 148°57'E., 17 km W. of Cooma, on Wambrook Ck; airfield; FB.

Waminda (*Co. Denham*) 29°56'S. 148°20'E., 22 km NE of Walgett; RS 1932–75.

Wammerawa (*Co. Leichhardt*) 30°11'S. 147°32'E., 57 km W. of Walgett; grazing; PO 1868–79; pop. *c.*20 (1903).

Wamoon (*Co. Cooper*) 34°32'S. 146°20'E., 8

km W. of Leeton; village gaz. 1921; farming; Meth. C. 1916; PO 1920; school 1916; TX 1936, automatic 1941; water supply 1951; pop. 480 (1933), 194 (1947), 249 (1954), 328 (1961).

Wanaaring (*Co. Ularara*) 29°42'S. 144°09'E., 180 km W. of Bourke, on Paroo R.; wool; airfield; cemetery 1886; CH 1881, new one b. 1908 by H.B. Howching; dust storms 1894 and 1902; heatwave 1913; PO 1879; PS b. 1908 by H.B. Howching, closed, reopened 1950; sandfly infestation 1964; school 1887, damaged and repaired 1894, new one b. 1898 by Frost and Rayward, closed 1922, reopened 1956; telegraph 1887; TX (automatic) 1991; pop. *c.*130 (1887), 220 (1891), 197 (1901), 132 (1911), 62 (1933), 76 (1947), 64 (1954), 81 (1961), *c.*50 (1999), 137 (2006), 195 (2011).

Wanatta (*Co. Auckland*) see Long Bridge.

Wanchope (*Co. Macquarie*) see Wauchope.

Wanda (*Co. Northumberland*) 33°15'S. 151°18'E., 12 km W. of Wyong, on Wyong R.; school 1906 b. by Alf Watkins and Benson, new one b. 1937, closed 1943 and removed.

Wandandian (*Co. St Vincent*) 35°05'S. 150°31'E., 11 km W. of Sanctuary Point, on Bollerang Ck; declined 1916+, revived in 1950s; formerly dairying, sawmilling 1910+, agric., grazing, now hobby farming, fruit, cattle; Angl. C. 1965 (removed from Falls Creek), closed, sold 1989; bridge 1929; bushfires 1868, 1869, 1908, 1916 (devastated town), 1929, 1939, 1952, 2001; cement works (Cleary Bros) 1982–97; cemetery; FB 1942 (station b. 1986); floods 1890 and 1971; PO 1860, burnt down 1935, replaced, closed 1990; Presb. C. 1913, closed; sawmills: Abraham Jennings 1903 (bought 1909 by Watt and Mathie, became Watt & Son, closed 1961, reopened 1963 by Golding, bought 1965 by Alf Jones & Co.), Allen Taylor & Co. Pty Ltd (sold 1908 to W.A. Caine & Co.), White Cat 1970; school (Jannung till 1890) 1880–90, 1912–46, 1956–70, building moved to St George's Basin; telephone 1904; TX 1920; water supply 1984; wharf (Allen Taylor & Co. Pty Ltd); winery (Kladis Estate Wines) estab. 1996 by Jim and Niki Kladis; pop. 74 (1901), 154 (1911), 142 (1933), 123 (1947), 121 (1954), 130 (1961), 302 (1991), 309 (1996), 440 (2011).

Wandary (*Co. Forbes*) 33°24'S. 148°05'E., 8 km E. of Forbes; pop. 63 (1954), 62 (1961).

Wandella (*Co. Dampier*) 36°20'S. 149°51'E., 28 km SW of Narooma; farming; cheese factory (NSW Creamery Butter Co. Ltd) 1897, sold 1904; PO 1879–1928; school 1885–87 and 1896–1965; telephone 1915; pop. 159 (1901), 120 (1911), 115 (1933), 88 (1947), 87 (1954), 93 (1961), 299 (2011).

Wandera (*Co. Arrawatta*) 29°40'S. 151°09'E., 13 km N. of Inverell; village gaz. 1883; bridge (Viver's Gully Bridge); cemetery 1886; 2 quarries; school 1910–24; pop. 81 (1911), 60 (1954).

Wandewoi (*Co. Brisbane*) 31°47'S. 151°17'E., 43 km E. of Murrurundi, on Pages Ck; telephone 1909.

Wandook (*Co. Townsend*) 35°27'S. 144°58'E., 10 km N. of Deniliquin; school 1879, new buildings b. 1881 by Hunter & Son, closed 1887, reopened 1957, closed 1979; TX (automatic); pop. 71 (1947).

Wandook North (*Co. Townsend*) 35°22'S. 145°05'E., 20 km NE of Deniliquin.

Wandoona (*Co. Phillip*) 32°24'S. 149°53'E., 33 km E. of Gulgong, on Cumba Ck.

Wandsworth (*Co. Hardinge*) 30°04'S. 151°31'E., 23 km NW of Guyra, on Limestone Ck; grazing, wheat, oats, potatoes, orchards, fishing; bridge 1994, over Limestone Ck; cemetery (18 graves) 1875; flour mill b. 1867 by Edward Grover; gale 1902; mine (sapphires); PO, closed 1968; pound (stock) 1873; sawmill b. 1867 by Edward Grover; school 1891–1911 and 1957–70, reused; telephone 1900; TX 1926, automatic 1952; Union C. 1886; pop. 189 (1901), 147 (1911), 142 (1933), 136 (1947), 148 (1954), 95 (1961), 78 (2006).

Wangabbri (*Co. Gresham*) 29°34'S. 152°33'E., 40 km W. of Grafton, on Mitchell R.

Wangalea (*Co. Ashburnham*) 33°04'S. 147°57'E., 22 km W. of Parkes.

Wangallo Flat (*Co. Georgiana*) 34°06'S. 149°27'E., 40 km N. of Crookwell, on Peelwood Ck.

Wangamong (*Co. Denison*) 35°38'S. 146°12'E., 45 km NW of Corowa; fire 1889; RS (Victorian railway); silo.

Wangan (*Co. Baradine*) 30°36'S. 148°59'E., 39 km N. of Baradine.

Wanganderry (*Co. Camden*) 34°21'S. 150°16'E., 20 km NW of Bowral, on Barracks Ck; sawmill (Roberts and Springett); pop. 42 (1933).

Wanganella (*Co. Townsend*) 35°12'S. 144°49'E., 38 km N. of Deniliquin, on Billabong Ck; estab. 1861 by John Innes, founded 1862 by John Dillon, town gaz. 1862 as Wangonilla, lots sold 1864; grazing; airfield; bridge 1866, new one 1970, over Billabong Ck; cemetery 1863; FB; lock-up 1909 (removed from Deniliquin); PO 1863; PS 1911–26; punt (Dillon's) 1864; school 1881–90, 1897–1947, 1957–71; TX 1926; Union C. 1876; pop. *c.*80 (1865), 94 (1901), 222 (1911), 132 (1933), 108 (1947), 103 (1954), 172 (1961), 232 (2006).

Wanganui (*Co. Rous*) 28°34'S. 153°23'E., 11 km W. of Mullumbimby, on Coopers Ck.

Wangat (*Co. Gloucester*) 32°15'S. 151°41'E., 19 km N. of Dungog, on Chichester Dam; village gaz. 1884, thrived 1880s–90s, nearly deserted by 1902, village status cancelled 1916; goldmining 1872+, then farming; cemetery 1886; dam (Chichester) b. 1918–25 d. by Ernest Macartney de Burgh, 135 ft (41 m) high, modified 1967, 1970, 1979, 1984, 1995, on Wangat R.; PO 1880–1926; school (Glenoak till 1887 then Dusodie till 1901) 1883–91, 1899–1901, 1918–43; stamper batteries (2 head and 10 head); telephone 1917; TX 1921; pop. 52 (1933).

Wangellic (*Co. Wellesely*) 36°43'S. 149°11'E., 23 km N. of Bombala; airfield.

Wangi Wangi (*Co. Northumberland*) 33°04'S. 151°35'E., 5 km NW of Swansea, on Lake Macquarie; (incl. Lakeview and Myuna Bay); settled 1829 by Edward Gostwyck Cory, land sales 1918, subdivision (Lake View Estate) 1925; fishing and tourism; anti-aircraft battery and command post (World War II); Angl. C. (St Gabriel's) 1954, relocated 1958, destroyed 1960, replacement b. 1962 by A.H. Jenkins Pty Ltd; Assemblies of God C. (Powerhouse); Bible Chapel; bushfire 1951; colliery (Myuna, Newcom Collieries Pty Ltd) estab. 1979–82; earthquake 1989; FB (station b. 1968, new one 2005); foot-bridge over Whiteheads Lagoon; 3 jetties; lock-up; PO b. 1923 by Jack McLauchlan, jun.; power station (taken over 1952 by Electricity Commission) b. 1947–58, fire 1977, closed 1986, sold 2000, fire 2017; PS 1978, closed and sold; quarry; reservoir; Rom. Cath. C. (St Patrick's), closed and moved to Kilaben Bay; sawmill (George Morton); school 1930 b. by T.C. Southon, additions 1935 by A. Ede, new one b. 1952 on new site by H. Evans, additions 1967; storm 1960; telephone 1923; TX 1924, automatic 1955; Unit. C. (orig. Meth.) 1935; water supply 1941; wharf (Little Wangi); pop. 238 (1933), 333 (1947), 908 (1954), 2,670 (2011).

Wangonilla (*Co. Townsend*) see Wanganella.

Wang Wauk (*Co. Gloucester*) 32°10'S. 152°19'E., 17 km W. of Tuncurry, on Wang Wauk R.; farming; bridge (concrete) 1936, new one 1986, over Wang Wauk R.; PO 1911–71; school 1938–59; telephone 1910; TX 1947; Union C. (Soldiers' Memorial) b. 1925 by A.E. Woodward, d. by J. Maybury; pop. 64 (1911), 87 (1933), 70 (1947), 90 (1954), 62 (1961), 238 (2006).

Waniora (*Co. Camden*) see Bulli.

Wantabadgery (*Co. Clarendon*) 35°03'S. 147°43'E., 25 km SE of Junee, on Wantiool Ck; village gaz. 1864; farming; Angl. C. 1886, new one (St Mark's War Memorial) 1959; bushfire 1902; cemetery; earth tremor 2004; PO 1927–66; flood (2 died) 1864; school 1915–71; telephone 1923; TX (automatic) 1961; pop. 35 (1891), 84 (1901), 61 (1911), 145 (1933), 118 (1947), 151 (1954), 136 (1961), 224 (2006), 299 (2011).

Wantagong (*Co. Goulburn*) 35°45'S. 147°32'E., 18 km E. of Holbrook, on Stony Ck; McLaurin till 1912; farming; PO 1927–51; telephone 1910; TX 1912; Unit. C. (McLaurin Memorial, orig. Presb.) 1936 d. by John Donald Morrow; pop. 73 (1933), 107 (1947), 99 (1954), 123 (1961), 115 (2006).

Wantiool (*Co. Clarendon*) 34°54'S. 147°41'E., 9 km E. of Junee; goldmining (alluvial and reef) and farming; measles epidemic 1893; PO 1927–31; school 1893–1903 and 1915–33; pop. 64 (1933), 66 (1947).

Wapengo (*Co. Dampier*) 36°35'S. 149°59'E., 16 km NE of Bega, on Wapengo Ck; farming and oysters; bridge over Wapengo Ck; PO 1919–71; sawmill (J. Hines) 1910; school 1882–1904 and 1912–25; TX 1939–71; pop. 54 (1901), 87 (1911), 34 (1933), 357 (2006).

Wappinguy (*Co. Brisbane*) 32°11'S. 150°26'E., 9 km SE of Merriwa; RS 1918–53.

Wapra (*Co. Gloucester*) 31°55'S. 151°54'E., 13 km NW of Gloucester, on Cravens Ck; bridge over Cravens Ck; telephone 1929; TX 1930, automatic 1952.

Warabrook (*Co. Northumberland*) 32°53'S. 151°43'E., 8 km NW of Newcastle; abattoir; Bapt. C. (Maitland Road) 1946–73, moved to Muswellbrook, reused; dam; hailstorm 2014; RS 1995; sale-yards; pop. 2,091 (2011).

Waradgery (*Co. Waradgery*) 34°32'S. 144°41'E., 15 km W. of Hay, on Murrumbidgee R.; RS 1882–96.

Waratah (*Co. Northumberland*) 32°54'S. 151°46'E., 7 km W. of Newcastle; (incl. Georgetown and West Waratah); formerly Hanbury, subdivided by Thomas Grove, estab. 1856, formerly part of the Waratah Coal Co. estate, village gaz. 1864, munic. 1871–1938 but became part of City of Greater Newcastle; coalmining, quarrying, copper smelting, brickmaking, fruit growing; abattoir, bacon factory and freezing works (Newcastle) 1916–83; ambulance station d. and b. 1936 by Lysaghts Ltd; Angl. C.: St Matthew's (Georgetown) 1953, new one 1967 and St Philip's 1869, additions 1916 by Jarrett and Broadfoot, d. by Goodwin, additions 1938 d. by Bruce Albert John Litchfield, additions 1952, church closed 2012, reused; Assemblies of God C. (International Christ.); benevolent asylum b. 1897 by Davis & Son, d. by George Sanders & Son, fire 1899, taken over 1932 by Hospitals Commission, subsequent additions; blind factory (William Montgomery), burnt down 1915; brickworks: Federal Steam Brickworks (o. 1901 by W. Woodhams & Sons, continuous-burning kiln b. 1913 by W. Hardy, closed 1940) and Robert Turton (removed 1855 from Merewether); cemetery 1863; CH 1882; Chinese joss house; Church of Christ (Georgetown) 1939, closed, sold and reused; colliery (Waratah Coal Co.) estab. 1859, o. 1862, moved 1873 to Raspberry Gully (Charlestown); confectionery factory (Llewellyn Davies) 1886; cordial factory (Sharpe Bros) 1929–39; cotton gin (British-Aust. Cotton Assoc. Ltd) 1923; earth tremor 1868; engineering works (R.H. Price and T. Miller); FB (station b. 1893 by John Scott, new one b. 1935 by George Watson, d. by William Hull McNiven, closed, sold and reused); fibrous plaster works: H.G. Dean and N. Glitheroe; floods 1908 and 1928; gasworks (munic.) 1889; hailstorm 2004; incinerator b. 1931 by Green and Stafford, d. by Edward Milton Nicholls and Walter Burley Griffin, closed 1940, demolished; iron foundry (Tighe's Hill Manufacturing Co.); joinery (W.T. Sandall & Sons) 1913; lime-works (Newcastle Lime & Cement Co. Pty Ltd), fire 1953; measles epidemic 1948; PO: Georgetown 1957, Waratah 1860, new office b. 1881 by W.H. Galbraith, additions and alterations 1901 by Thomas Candish, closed, sold and reused, West Waratah 1957–82; pottery (Waratah Steam Pottery) estab. 1865 by Alfred Plumridge and Robert Turton, additions and improvements 1879, improvements 1882 by Sidney Casey, taken over 1886 by Hall and James Silcock, closed; pound (stock) 1857; Presb. C. b. 1915 by Southon and Pearce, d. by Ernest George Yeomans; Prim. Meth. C. b. 1867 by Bowry and Street & Co.; PS (incl. lock-up) 1882 d. by James Johnstone Barnet, closed, new one b. by Adco Construction Pty Ltd; quarry (John Boyd); railway accident (3 killed) 1894; Redeemed Christ. C. (City of David); 4 reservoirs; Rom. Cath. C. (St Alphonsus's) 1906, new one (Corpus Christi) b. 1932–54, d. by Peter Joseph Gannon, extensions 1954

d. by John Patrick Gannon; RS 1858, new station b. 1891 by J. Rogers; sale-yards (Aust. Agric. Co.) b. 1913 by J. Goodwin and F. & A. Merton; scarlet fever 1932 and 1939; schools: Christo Road infants 1953–72, Newcastle Boys HS 1930–33 (in Newcastle), new school b. 1934 at Waratah by Baker and Lamb, d. by Edwin Evan Smith, became Waratah HS in 1977, then Callaghan College (Waratah Techology campus) in 2001, Waratah primary (Hanbury till 1912) 1864, new one b. 1868 by George Dart & Son, d. by George Allen Mansfield, additions and repairs 1882 by B. Mathews, extensions 1892 by Burg Bros, d. by Walter Liberty Vernon, repairs 1900 by Southon Bros, additions and repairs 1902 by B.G. Pearce, additions and alterations 1910 by Southon Bros, new building b. 1918 by P.A. Solman, new building b. 1927 by Richard Seed, new building 1976, closed, sold, reused 1997, new one on new site, West Waratah 1954, additions 1964, re-roofed 2013; smelter (Hunter River Copper Works) b. 1868 by Wallaroo Co., closed 1893; squall 1913; streets gas lit 1889; telegraph 1875, new office b. 1881 by W.H. Galbraith; telephone (Georgetown) 1957; tramway (steam) to Newcastle 1915, electrified 1925; Unit. C. (orig. Meth.) 1956, closed, sold 2002, reused; Wes. Meth. C. b. 1862–64; pop. *c.*500 (1866), 1,530 (1871), 1,714 (1881), 2,719 (1891), *c.*2,650 (1895), 3,080 (1901), 3,667 (1911), 9,441 (2011).

Waratah (*Co. Northumberland*)
see also Mayfield.

Waratah South (*Co. Northumberland*)
see Charlestown.

Waratah West (*Co. Northumberland*)
see Waratah.

Warawaralong (*Co. Cook*) 33°31'S. 150°30'E., 14 km W. of Kurrajong Heights, on Karagora Ck.

Warbro (*Co. Dudley*) 30°55'S. 152°35'E., 32 km NW of Kempsey, on Macleay R.; school 1892–1911 and 1957–72; pop. 44 (1933).

Warbrook (*Co. Selwyn*) 36°02'S. 148°02'E., 28 km S. of Tumbarumba.

Warburn (*Co. Sturt*) 34°10'S. 145°56'E., 16 km NW of Griffith; RS 1924, station relocated 1930, closed 1973; school 1955–69; telephone 1934; TX (automatic) 1969; pop. 92 (1933), 123 (1947), 92 (1954), 93 (1961).

Warburton (*Co. Wellington*) 32°24'S. 149°23'E., 14 km W. of Gulgong.

Warburton (*Co. Wellington*)
see also Two Mile Flat.

Wardell (*Co. Rous*) 28°57'S. 153°28'E., 12 km S. of Alstonville, on Richmond R.; (incl. East Wardell); orig. Blackwall, then North Wardell 1875–78; estab. 1856, laid out 1863 by Frederick Septimus Peppercorne, town gaz. 1859; orig. timber, former river port, sawmilling, maize, pigs, dairying, fishing, sugar-cane; Angl. C. b. 1879 by John Butler Ford, relocated 1897, renovated 1904, closed 1920, reused, replacement (St Barnabas's) b. 1920 by George Hampton & Son, d. by Frederick Johnson Board; bridge (steel lift span) b. 1964 by Dayal Singh Constructions Pty Ltd, d. by Maunsell & Partners, 800 ft (243.8 m), over Richmond R.; bushfire 1929; cemetery (828 graves) 1877, incl. columbarium; CH 1881, closed, sold 1887 to Johnson, new one (incl. lock-up) b. 1899 by Patrick Farrelly; creamery (NSW Creamery Butter Co. Ltd) 1896; dengue fever 1926; FB; fire 1926; floods 1893, 1945, 1954; hailstorm 1907; PO: East Wardell 1870–1918 and Wardell 1875, sold 1887 to E. Murray, new one b. 1925; pound (stock) 1891; PS (incl. lock-up) b. 1876 by Ernest Carter; punt b. 1881 by W. Yabsley, new one b. 1924 by John Kennedy, ceased 1964, to cross Richmond R.; quarry; rifle range 1927; Rom. Cath. C. b. 1879 by John Byrne, closed 1912, renovated and reused 1913, damaged 1937, demolished 1951, new one (St Patrick's) b. 1910–12 by H. Dengate & Son, d. by Eaton and Bates; sawmills: C.B. Bond, Ernest Carter (b. 1869 by Thomas Carter, burnt down 1881, rebuilt, closed), Commercial Mills (James E. James and Robert Knight) 1871, man killed 1884, Wilhelm Kirchner 1868, Duncan McIntyre, D. Sharpe; schools: East Wardell 1881–85 and Wardell 1876, repairs 1896 by J. M'Vicar, new one b. 1901 on new site by T.W. Keith & Co.; shipyard (Cook's); storm 1937; telegraph 1879, office sold 1887 to E. Murray; telephone 1909; TX 1919, automatic 1968; Unit. C. (orig. Meth.) b. 1905 by George Bale, damaged 1954, renovated 1965, closed 2012, sold 2013; wharf b. 1886 by David Rankin, dismantled 1929, rebuilt 1940; pop. 426 (1891), 390 (1901), 547 (1911), 1,697 (1924), 543 (1933), 600 (1947), 512 (1954), 423 (1961), 245 (1976), 295 (1981), 315 (1986), 425 (1991), 450 (1996), 483 (2001), 621 (2006), 648 (2011).

Ward Park (*Co. Cook*) 33°25'S. 150°44'E., 21 km NE of Kurrajong Heights, on Colo R.

Wardrop Valley (*Co. Rous*) 28°22'S. 153°27'E., 6 km SE of Murwillumbah; telephone 1929; TX 1929; pop. 48 (1933), 56 (1961).

Wardry (*Co. Dowling*) 33°04'S. 146°46'E., 36 km W. of Condobolin; pop. 28 (1933).

Wards Glen (*Co. Gloucester*) 32°10'S. 152°00'E., 18 km S. of Gloucester, on Wards R.

Wards Mistake (*Co. Clarke*) 30°08'S. 152°01'E., 35 km E. of Guyra; airfield; Rom. Cath. C. (Holy Angels), removed 1918 from Hillgrove; school 1911–36 and 1957–69; TX; pop. 103 (1911), 54 (1933), 50 (1947), 61 (1954), 56 (1961).

Wards River (*Co. Gloucester*) 32°13'S. 151°56'E., 24 km S. of Gloucester, on Wards R.; orig. timber, then farming and dairying; Angl. C. (St Peter's) 1967; cemetery 1904, disused; charcoal kilns 1942; diphtheria 1934; electricity 1936; FB; PO 1899–1918; Presb. C. (St Stephen's) 1920; RS 1913, station b. by Robert Daniel Quiggin, closed; sawmills: George and Don Mackay, and E.D. Pike & Co. Ltd (estab. 1920, sold 1924 to Turner and Ebbeck, sold 1943 to W.D. Wood Pty Ltd, sold to A.J. Fenning Pty Ltd, burnt down 1952, rebuilt, acquired by Nicholas Trading Co.); school 1887, new one b. 1892 by Eli Webber, fire 1905, new one b. 1918 on new site by Thomas Norman Grimsley, additions 1933 by T. Dunne, renovated 1971, closed 1997; telephone 1905; TX 1925; pop. 233 (1911), 205 (1933), 252 (1947), 290 (1954), 263 (1961), 237 (2006).

Wargambegal (*Co. Dowling*) 33°21'S. 146°28'E., 11 km SE of Lake Cargelligo; soldiers' settlement in 1920s, village gaz. 1931; wool and wheat; RS 1917–75; pop. 137 (1933).

Wargan Bogan (*Co. Dowling*) 33°38'S. 146°08'E., 43 km SW of Lake Cargelligo; soldiers' settlement 1923; wheat and lucerne; telephone 1929; TX 1929.

Wargeila (*Co. King*) 34°41'S. 148°54'E., 16 km N. of Yass; formerly Wargelia or Worgela; school (Wargela till *c.*1910) 1886–1923; Union C. b. 1899 by J. Newman, later only used by Anglicans; pop. 130 (1901), 100 (1911), 66 (1933), 64 (1947).

Wargela (*Co. King*) see Wargeila.

Wargelia (*Co. King*) see Wargeila.

Warge Rock (*Co. Kennedy*) 32°33'S. 147°47'E., 42 km NW of Peak Hill; PO 1892–1915.

Wargin (*Co. Bland*) 34°07'S. 147°15'E., 22 km S. of West Wyalong; RS 1925–75; silo 1934.

Warialda (*Co. Burnett*) 29°32'S. 150°35'E., 36 km N. of Bingara, on Warialda Ck; estab. 1837, surveyed 1849 by John James Galloway, village gaz. 1850, sale of lots 1853, designated as chief town of the county, more lots sold 1895, declined 1901+, munic. 1900–24; hort., agric., cattle, sheep, pigs, wheat, cotton, fossicking; airfield; ambulance station; Angl. C. 1853, new one 1902–66, third one (St Simon and St Jude's); bridges over Warialda Ck: one b. 1878 by George Carter, 222 ft (67.7 m), one b. 1900 by Sheldon Bros, one b. 1939 by B.M. Wade Ltd, Richard Bligh Bridge b. 1970 by Central Construction Pty Ltd; cemeteries: pioneer (289 burials) 1858–1901, razed, and general (1,692 graves 1885+), incl. lawn cemetery and columbarium; CH (incl. lock-up) b. 1848 by Duncan McLennan, new one 1869 d. by James Johnstone Barnet, additions 1877 by Alexander Hamilton Scouller, new one b. 1881–83 by S. Senior, d. by James Johnstone Barnet, repairs 1896 also by Senior, renovated 1938 by W.J. Axtell; cordial factories: Charles Francis Egan 1904 (burnt down 1920), Peter Gilmour, Thomas Heyden, Roger Moore 1959 (taken over 1973 by Wayne Keft), W. Power 1902, R.H. Stewart; dengue fever 1926; diphtheria 1931; dust storm 1945; engineering works (Warialda Engineering & Welding Pty Ltd, founded by Mick Davis) 1996; FB (station b. 1954); fires 1913, 1917, 1925, 1927, 1931; flood 1910; freezing works (Roger Moore) 1946; gaol b. 1907 by Sheely and Harding, closed, bought by McKay Bros and dismantled; hospital (cottage) 1862, new one 1895 d. by John Kirkpatrick, additions 1923 by Benjamin Martin Wade, d. by O'Connor and Ogilvie, alterations 1936 by William Lishman Jemison, additions 1974, 1978, 2008; meat canning works (George Wieland) 1897; PO 1848, new one b. 1878–80 by Samuel Senior, d. by James Johnstone Barnet, repairs 1889 and 1897, alterations and repairs 1903 by Amos Loseby, repairs 1913 by J. Keenan, additions and alterations 1914 by E.W. Anderson; police barracks b. 1893 by H.M. Lewis, d. by Walter Liberty Vernon; pound (stock) b. 1849 by Alexander Anderson; powerhouse (R. Moore); Presb. C. (St Stephen's) b. 1902 by W. Morris, d. by William Mark Nixon and John Shedden Adam, jun.; PS 1848, new one b. 1907 by Sheely and Harding, closed 1968; reservoir; Rom. Cath. C. (Guardian Angels) b. 1872 by Lee, new one (St Patrick's) b. 1915 by S.H. Currie, d. by John Francis O'Connor and Ogilvie; sale-yards; sawmill (South's) 1899; schools: primary 1851 b. by Patrick Reid, d. by M. Wilson, closed Dec. 1851, reopened 1861, new one b. 1880 by A. Thorley, extended 1888, additions 1923 by Anderson and Rogers, replacement d. by J. Werbeloff and HS 1976; sewerage 1969; storm 2001; street lighting 1912; telegraph 1877, new office b. 1878–80 by Samuel Senior, d. by James Johnstone Barnet; TX 1910, automatic 1986; waterworks 1954; weir on Warialda Ck; pop. 45 (1851), 65 (1856), 110 (1861), *c.*106 (1866), 131 (1871), 150 (1874), 268 (1881), 400 (1891), 875 (1901), 1,762 (1911), 848 (1921), 1,115 (1933), 1,124 (1947), 1,254 (1954), 1,294 (1961), 1,324 (1966), 1,291 (1971), 1,264 (1976), 1,340 (1981), 1,335 (1986), 1,285 (1991), 1,287 (1996), 1,201 (2001), 1,206 (2006), 1,120 (2011).

Warialda Rail (*Co. Burnett*) 29°35'S. 150°33'E., 6 km SW of Warialda, on Kellys Gully; (incl. Kellys Gully); village gaz. 1920 as Burgaria; farming; Angl. C. (first), relocated 1906, new one (St Paul's) 1911; fire 2012; flood 1910; freezing works (Joseph Moore) 1915, sold 1924 to Garratt Scandrett Freezing Companies Ltd, acquired 1927 by Amalgamated Rabbit & Skin Export Co. Ltd; PO 1900–79; railway bridge (timber truss) 1901, over Kellys Gully; RS 1901, station b. by John Allibone, refreshment rooms 1924, station closed 1979; sawmill (T. Graham), fire 1913, burnt down 1927, acquired 1950 by W.H. Stacey, relocated 1931; school (Kellys Gully till 1952 and Burgaria since 1959) 1903, additions 1914 by J. Keenan, additions 1933, closed 1971; silo 1934; telegraph 1902; TX 1926, automatic 1956; pop. 54 (1911), 495 (1933), 278 (1947), 272 (1954), 246 (1961), 201 (2011).

Warilla (*Co. Camden*) 34°33'S. 150°51'E., 9 km SE of Dapto, on Tasman Sea; founded 1951, subdivisions 1951, 1965, 1970; Angl. C. (St Luke's); Bapt. C.: North Warilla and Shellharbour City; clothing factory (Bonds Industries Ltd) 1967; FB (station b. 1965); flood 2011; foot-bridge to Barrack Point, over Little Lake; Lutheran C. (St Matthew's) 1972, reused; PO 1955, new one b. 1968 by G. Martin; PS (in rented premises) 1975, new one 1977; Salv. Army C. 1966; schools: North Warilla 1964, additions 1967 and 2010, and Warilla 1956, additions 1959, 1961, 1983; sewerage 1973; storms 1974 and 1978; TC (Illawarra Institute of Technology, Shellharbour Campus); TX (automatic) 1959; pop. 6,408 (2011).

Warilla (*Co. Camden*) see also Barrack Heights.

Warkton (*Co. Gowen*) 31°23'S. 149°15'E., 13 km S. of Coonabarabran, on Belar Ck; farming and grazing; PO 1886–1981; school 1888–1910; telephone 1914; TX (automatic); pop. 112 (1933), 104 (1954), 131 (1961).

Warkworth (*Co. Northumberland*) 32°34'S. 151°02'E., 13 km W. of Singleton, on

Wollombi Brook; surveyed *c.*1825 by Henry Dangar, laid out by George Boyle White, village gaz. 1874; agric., grazing, dairying, orchards, grapes, coalmining; airfield (World War II); Angl. C. (St Philip's) b. 1840–53, partly d. by Edmund Thomas Blacket, damaged 1955, renovated 1980, and graveyard; bridge (Cockfighter Bridge) 1836, second one 1859, third one b. 1872 by M'Kenzie, 320 ft (97.5 m), repairs 1877 by H. and H. Winsor, rebuilt 1926, severely damaged 1949, temporary replacement 1950, new one (reused plate girder spans), 637 ft (194.2 m), b. 1951–55, over Wollombi Brook; cemetery; cheese factory (Woodville) estab. 1880 by Edward Crago, burnt down 1897; collieries: Lemington (Buchanan Borehole Collieries Pty Ltd) and Wambo (Wambo Coal Pty Ltd) 1969; drought 1847; floods 1830, 1849, 1949, 1950, 1952, 1953, 1955; flour mill (William Charles Harris) b. by William Scott, burnt down 1878, Harris insolvent 1879; PO 1863–1968; school 1859–61 and 1869–1997; storm 1889; telegraph 1878–86, office unroofed 1889; telephone 1889; TX (automatic) 1957; pop. 188 (1891), 131 (1901), 177 (1911), 227 (1933), 78 (1947), 106 (1954), 132 (1961), 550 (2006).

Warmatta (*Co. Denison*) 35°43'S. 145°58'E., 16 km E. of Berrigan; Savernake till 1892; farming; PO 1892–1927; school 1906–8; telephone 1899; pop. 117 (1911), 98 (1933).

Warne (*Co. Wellington*) see Euchareena.

Warnecliffe (*Co. Wellington*) 32°59'S. 149°05'E., 24 km NE of Molong, on Nubrigyn Ck; airfield; RS 1910–58.

Warner (*Co. Northumberland*) see Warners Bay.

Warners Bay (*Co. Northumberland*) 32°58'S. 151°39'E., 7 km NE of Toronto, on Warners Bay; (incl. Lakelands); settled by Johnathan Warner, unsuccessful subdivisions 1840 and 1855, first lots sold 1885, subdivided 1927 but developed slowly; orchards, poultry, tourism; Angl. C. (St Alban's); Bapt. C.; bushfires 1936 and 1953; Church of Christ; 2 foot-bridges over North Ck; Jehovah's Witnesses C.; jetty; landslip 1950; Meth. C. 1952; PO 1927; Rom. Cath. C. 1953, reused, new one (St Mary's) 1976 d. by Terence A. Daly; sawmills: J. Cherrie, and Dewes and Foster; schools: Biddabah (Speers Point East till 1992) 1959, Warners Bay (Warner till 1933) primary b. 1904 by Charles Waters, new school 1936, additions 1956, 1960, 1963, 1966, 1973, Warners Bay HS 1966 b. by H.G. Jenkins, d. by Michael John Dysart, additions 1971, 1985, 1988, damaged 2015; sewerage augmentation 1955; storm 2015; Unit. C. (The Willows) 2010, building conversion d. by Mark Lawler; water supply 1929; pop. 115 (1901), 89 (1911), 324 (1933), 1,033 (1947), 8,573 (2006), 8,964 (2011).

Warnervale (*Co. Northumberland*) 33°15'S. 151°28'E., 6 km NE of Wyong; (incl. Halloran and Wallarah); Warnervale Railway till 1917; estab. *c.*1903 by Albert Hamlyn Warner; farming, orchards, poultry; airport 1973; Angl. C. (Blanch Memorial) 1924 d. by Edward Blanch; Assemblies of God C. (Sparks Road); brewery (Bluetongue Brewery Pty Ltd) b. 2010 by Qanstruct, closed 2014; bushfire 1928; FB; PO 1915–80; railway bridge (2 reinforced concrete spans) over Wallarah Ck; Rom. Cath. C. (Blessed Mary McKillop) 2003; RS 1907–74; sawmills: Alfred Brown and Edward Haynes, and Fleming Bros; school 1958, additions 1965, relocated 2008 to Hamlyn Terrace; telephone 1917; TX 1947; pop. 284 (1911), 225 (1933), 229 (1947), 270 (1954), 356 (1961), 989 (2011).

Warnervale (*Co. Northumberland*) see also Hamlyn Terrace and Kanwal.

Warnervale Railway (*Co. Northumberland*) see Warnervale.

Warneton (*Co. Dudley*) 31°04'S. 152°47'E., 4 km W. of Kempsey, on Macleay R., Macleay River Steam Works till 1864; farming and grazing; boiling-down works (soap and tallow) estab. 1844 by William Gard, taken over 1845 by Michael Woolley; bushfire 1895; butter factory b. 1890 by J.G. Rowe, bought 1896 by Edmund Debenham; floods 1864 and 1870; PO 1864, new one b. 1879 by

Stainer, remodelled 1898, closed 1919; Presb. C. 1901; telegraph office b. 1879 by Stainer, remodelled 1898; wharf; pop. *c.*12 (1866), *c.*50 (1903), 32 (1933).

Waroo (*Co. Irrara*) 29°05'S. 144°43'E., 162 km NW of Bourke.

Waropurra (*Co. Clive*) 29°02'S. 151°43'E., 29 km W. of Tenterfield, on Tenterfield Ck; formerly Clifton; limestone; quarry; telephone 1924; TX 1924; pop. 63 (1911), 31 (1933), 155 (1947).

Warra (*Co. Gloucester*) 32°11'S. 152°07'E., 24 km SE of Gloucester, on Upper Myall R.; also spelt as Warrah; sawmill (R.W. Brown) 1938.

Warraderry (*Co. Forbes*) 33°47'S. 148°13'E., 14 km NE of Grenfell on Warraderry Ck; defunct; gold (disc. 1899, gold rushes 1900 and 1907) and wheat; Angl. C. (St Paul's) b. 1924 by T. and E. Chessell; bushfire (woman died) 1884; mine 1917–19, 1932, 1939; PO 1900–1; school (Melyra since 1900) 1884–1904; TX (automatic); pop. 111 (1911), 81 (1933), 181 (2011).

Warragaburra (*Co. Auckland*) 36°43'S. 149°52'E., 4 km S. of Bega; bacon factory (Allen & Co.); cheese factories: A.L. Manning, Mary Manning, burnt down 1898 and C. Parbury & Sons 1933–51; creamery (NSW Creamery Butter Co.), closed 1902 and bought by A.L. Manning, relocated and reused as a cheese factory; pop. 31 (1933).

Warragai Creek (*Co. Clarence*) 29°33'S. 152°59'E., 17 km N. of Grafton; farming and dairying; PO 1927–31; RS 1905, station b. by H.W. Owen, closed 1974; telephone 1910; pop. 31 (1933).

Warragamba (*Co. Camden*) 33°53'S. 150°36'E., 14 km S. of Glenbrook, on Lake Burragorang; estab. *c.*1950; ambulance station; Angl. C. (St Paul's); Bapt. C. b. 1976 by Peter Schofield; bridge (concrete arch) 1939, over Megarritys Ck; bushfire 2001; cableway (1,610 ft or 490.7 m) b. 1950 by Perry Engineering Co. Ltd; dam b. 1948–60, 449 ft (137 m) high, raised and strengthened 1989, on Warragamba R.; FB (station b. 1967); foot-bridge (suspension) 1949, closed, damaged 2001, demolished 2005, over Warragamba R.; furniture factory (Berryman), closed, sold and reused; hydro-electric scheme (Pacific Power) 1959; PO 1938; PS; railways (for dam construction), demolished; Rom. Cath. C. (Sacred Heart) o. 1952 in relocated former town hall; sawmill; schools: Warragamba 1948, additions 1981 and 1993, and Warragamba Dam 1944–49; telephone 1938; TX 1949, automatic 1965; United C. 1950; weir, b. 1937–40, 50 ft (15.2 m) high, on Warragamba R.; pop. 494 (1947), 3,028 (1954), 1,777 (1961), 1,699 (1966), 1,646 (1971), 1,535 (1976), 1,406 (1981), 2,666 (1986, incl. Silverdale), 3,509 (1991, incl. Silverdale), 3,873 (1996, incl. Silverdale), 4,175 (2001, incl. Silverdale), 4,365 (2011, incl. Silverdale).

Warragamba Dam (*Co. Camden*) see Warragamba.

Warragoon (*Co. Denison*) 35°49'S. 146°03'E., 14 km SE of Berrigan; RS (Victorian railway).

Warragoon (*Co. Townnsend*) 35°36'S. 145°10'E., 20 km E. of Deniliquin; school 1957, additions 1961, closed 1982; TX (automatic); pop. 302 (2006).

Warragubogra (*Co. Denison*) 35°37'S. 145°47'E., 7 km N. of Berrigan; cemetery 1884.

Warrah (*Co. Buckland*) see Willow Tree.

Warrah (*Co. Gloucester*) see Warra.

Warrah Creek (*Co. Buckland*) 31°43'S. 150°40'E., 17 km W. of Murrurundi; farming and grazing; Angl. C. (St Stephen's) 1915–72, sold; PO 1917–71; school 1914–57; TX 1924, automatic 1971; Union C. 1914; pop. 79 (1933), 110 (1947), 55 (1954), 63 (1961).

Warrah Ridge (*Co. Buckland*) 31°34'S. 150°33'E., 14 km SW of Quirindi; Meth. C. 1912; PO 1879–1912; pop. 86 (1901), 160 (1911), 89 (1947).

Warrain Beach (*Co. St Vincent*) see Culburra Beach.

Warral (*Co. Parry*) 31°09'S. 150°51'E., 10 km SW of Tamworth; poultry; FB; RS (Winton Road Siding till 1911) 1910–75; silo 1934; pop. 59 (1911), 168 (1933), 195 (1947), 164 (1954), 164 (1961).

Warrambucca (*Co. St Vincent*)

see Northangera.

Warrana (*Co. Leichhardt*) 31°00'S. 148°26'E., 4 km SE of Coonamble; pop. 36 (1933).

Warrandale (*Co. Forbes*) 33°59'S. 148°29'E., 25 km SW of Cowra; school (Warrangong till 1895) 1892–95 and 1937–46.

Warrangong (*Co. Forbes*) 34°02'S. 148°29'E., 30 km SW of Cowra; RS 1901, station b. by F.W. Kinch, closed 1969; pop. 104 (1911), 23 (1933).

Warrangong (*Co. Forbes*) see also Warrandale.

Warrangunia (*Co. Roxburgh*) 32°57'S. 149°47'E., 21 km SW of Kandos, on Warrangunia Ck; wolframite (disc. 1916) and potatoes; airfield; butter factory (Poplar Grove), variously owned by I. Smith, Taylor, E.K. Wilson and A. Heath, closed 1909; school (Tabrabucca till 1889, then Warrangunyah) 1882, additions 1919 by L.O. Taylor, closed 1925.

Warrangunyah (*Co. Roxburgh*) see Warrangunia.

Warranulla (*Co. Gloucester*) 32°12'S. 152°08'E., 28 km SE of Gloucester, on Myall R.; telephone 1937.

Warratta (*Co. Tongowoko*) 29°36'S. 141°50'E., 270 km NW of Wilcannia; village gaz. 1895.

Warrawang (*Co. Roxburgh*) see Mount Lambie.

Warrawidgee (*Co. Sturt*) 34°16'S. 145°48'E., 21 km W. of Griffith; school 1957–71; TX (automatic); pop. 75 (1961).

Warrawillah (*Co. Macquarie*) 31°45'S. 152°19'E., 14 km N. of Wingham, on Mooral Ck; pop. 72 (1933).

Warrawong (*Co. Camden*) 34°29'S. 150°53'E., 2 km W. of Port Kembla, on Lake Illawarra; (incl. Lake Heights and Spoonerville); agric., then dairying *c.*1888+; ambulance station; Angl. C. (St Andrew's) b. 1940 by A.W. Anderson & Sons, d. by R. Lindsay Little, demolished 1999; Church of Christ 1950; FB; gale 1951; hospital (Port Kembla) 1966; jetty (Bob Grabham); Maronite Catholic C. (Our Lady of Lebanon); Meth. C. (Lake Heights) 1954; PO: Lake Heights 1961 and Warrawong 1936; Presb. C. 1940; quarry; Rom. Cath. C.: Warrawong (St Francis of Assisi) 1956 and Lake Heights (St Joseph the Worker) 1967; schools: Kemblawarra 1959, additions 2010 by Patterson Building Group Pty Ltd, Lake Heights 1956, additions 1964, Warrawong (Steeltown till 1946) 1935, additions 1958, 1966, 1968, 2010, Warrawong HS 1972; telephone: Lake Heights 1961 and Warrawong 1936; pop. 459 (1936), 489 (1937), 1,685 (1947), 3,520 (1954), 7,610 (1961), 4,738 (2001), 7,924 (2006), 8,023 (2011).

Warregah Island (*Co. Clarence*) 29°23'S. 153°14'E., 8 km N. of Maclean, in Clarence R.; sugar mills: A. Anderson 1879 and A. and A. McPherson; pop. 99 (1881), 67 (1911), 52 (1933), 50 (1947), 50 (1954), 184 (2011).

Warregal (*Co. Ashburnham*) 33°13'S. 148°02'E., 15 km SW of Parkes; airfield; quarry.

Warrell Creek (*Co. Raleigh*) 30°45'S. 152°54'E., 5 km S. of Macksville, on Warrell Ck; farming and dairying; Angl. C. (Christ) 1920; bridge b. 1908 by W. Boulton, destroyed 1913; PO 1914–84; RS 1919–74; sawmills: Eichmann & Co. and A.R. Neaves (burnt down 1951); school 1904, new one b. 1905 by P. Landers, closed 1978; telephone 1910; TX; Union C. 1903; wharf b. 1907 by W. Boulton; pop. 255 (1911), 220 (1933), 351 (1947), 267 (1954), 281 (1961), 250 (2011).

Warren (*Co. Oxley*) 31°42'S. 147°50'E., 62 km E. of Nyngan, on Macquarie R.; disc. 1818 by John Joseph William Molesworth Oxley, settled 1845 by William Lawson and Thomas Readford, site reserved 1853, estab. 1860 by John Readford, town surveyed 1860 by James Glen Wilson, town gaz. and first lots sold 1861, thrived 1886–90, munic. 1895–1956; orig. squatting, later sheep, cattle, horses, lucerne, millet, oats, wheat, sorghum, maize, oranges, cotton 1970s+; ambulance station; Angl. C. (St John the Baptist) b. 1903 by Stynes & Co., d. by Charles Herbert Davy Button, and graveyard; artesian water struck 1897 by Petrolia Co.; brickworks: Excelsior (H. Jordan) and Standsure Brick & Tile Works (C. Robinson) 1876; bridges: one over Gunningar Ck, one b. 1875 by J. Herrick, over Macquarie R., one b. 1909 by Edward

William Fitzgerald, over Macquarie R., one b. 1982, over Macquarie R.; bronchitis epidemic 1898; bushfire 1951; carriage-works (W.J. Parker & Sons); cemeteries: general (1,530 graves 1875+) 1872 and lawn 1992; CH (incl. lock-up) b. 1872–74 by Montague and Davis, additions 1887 by Thomas Coombs, (second) 1900, demolished 1962, (third) b. 1962 by Harry Stubbs; Chinese joss house; cordial factory (K.E. Saunders & Co.); cotton gin (Twynam Cotton Pty Ltd); droughts 1937–38 and 1965–67; dust storms 1900, 1901, 1902, 1938, 1960 (houses unroofed); electricity 1924; FB (station b. 1977); fire (razed most of town) 1899; floods 1876, 1887, 1900, 1906, 1950, 1955, 1956, 1990, 2010; gastroenteritis epidemic (4 infants died) 1928; hospital b. 1893 by Edwin Utley, extended 1899 by J.P. Ohleston, additions 1938, extended by Stan Saunders & Sons, additions 1966, extended 1972; ice works (James Struthers & Co. Ltd) 1899; measles epidemic 1898; monumental stone works; pneumonia epidemic 1898; PO 1863, new one b. 1881 by William Moffatt, additions 1899 by Kidney and Corfield, closed and disused, new one b. 1923 by Rolfe, closed 1975, reused, new one b. 1975; pound (stock) 1867; powerhouse (C.A. Saunders & Sons Pty Ltd), burnt down 1927, replaced, new one gutted 1943, replaced; Presb. C. b. 1894 by J. Webster, d. by C. Shakespeare, moved and reused, new one (St Andrew's) 1957 d. by Findlay Munro, jun.; PS 1853, new one b. 1960 by Harry Stubbs; reservoirs 1907, 1939, 1966; rifle range, upgraded 1914 by G. Cartwright, new one 1935; Rom. Cath. C. b. 1893 by James Frazer, d. by H. Murray, removed 1953, replacement (St Mary's) b. 1955 by Hutcherson Bros Pty Ltd, d. by Fowell, Mansfield and Maclurcan; RS 1898, station b. by William Mitchell, burnt down 1931, rebuilt; sale-yards; sawmills: C.A. Rankmore, and F.C. and P.W. Miller; school 1867, extended 1872, new buildings b. 1885 by James Prior Hull, additions 1896, additions 1900 by A.G. Allen, remodelled 1923 by K.J. Rolfe, additions 1937, 1956, 1962, 1967, 1969, 1983, fire-damaged and repaired 1993; sewerage 1959, augmentation 1995; silo; streets formed, drained and kerbed 1897 by Noonan and Whan; streets lit by acetylene gas 1905, electric lit 1924; TC o. 1983 in former school, became a campus of Western Institute in 1992; telegraph 1876, new office b. 1881 by William Moffatt; TX 1910, automatic *c.*1978; typhoid 1903 (2 died) and 1923; Union C. b. 1898 by Dryce; water supply (sub-artesian bores) 1890, augmentation 1995; weir 1896 on Macquarie R.; wharf; whooping cough epidemic (4 children died) 1891; wool-scour estab. 1887 by Anthill and Close; pop. *c.*70 (1866), 159 (1871), 429 (1881), 860 (1891), 1,175 (1901), 1,434 (1911), 1,567 (1933), *c.*1,600 (1941), 1,746 (1947), 1,828 (1954), 1,505 (1961), 1,678 (1966), 2,048 (1971), 2,077 (1976), 2,153 (1981), 2,030 (1986), 2,036 (1991), 1,909 (1996), 1,786 (2001), 1,654 (2006), 1,523 (2011).

Warrena (*Co. Baradine*) see Walgett.

Warrendine (*Co. Bathurst*) see Orange (*Co. Wellington*).

Warrens Crossing (*Co. Macquarie*) 31°48'S. 152°31'E., 15 km N. of Taree, on Lansdowne R.; bridge 1947, over Lansdowne R.

Warri (*Co. Bourke*) see Ardlethan.

Warri Bridge (*Co. Murray*) 35°21'S. 149°44'E., 12 km NW of Braidwood, on Shoalhaven R.; bridge b. 1874 by John Sorrie, new one (McDonald timber truss) b. 1892 by Medcalf and Watson, over Shoalhaven R.; flour mill (James Neale) 1843.

Warrigal (*Co. Oxley*) 31°36'S. 147°16'E., 8 km SE of Nyngan; meat works (Nyngan Meat Preserving & Boiling Down Co.) estab. 1890 by James and Alexander Davidson and George Cromack, modernised 1908 and renamed Nyngan Refrigerating & Boiling Down Co. Ltd, then Country Freezing Co. Ltd, then Warrigal Cold Stores; RS (Davidson's Siding till 1895) 1893–1974; school 1900, burnt down 1931; pop. 48 (1933).

Warrigundi (*Co. Buckland*) 31°18'S. 150°40'E., 6 km N. of Werris Ck; RS (Terrible Vale till 1913) 1891–1975; pop. 44 (1933).

Warrimoo (*Co. Cook*) 33°43'S. 150°36'E., 2

km N. of Blaxland; Karrabar 1881–97; Angl. C. (All Saints'); Bapt. C. 1965; bushfires 1936 (12 houses destroyed), 1944, 1951 (10 houses destroyed), 2001, 2014; FB; fire 1919; Jehovah's Witnesses C.; Meth. C. 1956; Presb. C.; RS 1918, station b. by Arthur Hand, burnt down 1951, replaced 1957; school (South Warrimoo till 1963) 1962, additions 1964 and 1981, fire 1993; SD Adventist C. 1970; telephone 1927; TX (automatic) 1953; water supply 1944; pop. 82 (1933), 305 (1947), 613 (1954), 960 (1961), 1,095 (1964), 2,346 (2011).

Warrimoo South (*Co. Cook*) see Warrimoo.

Warri Warri (*Co. Tongowoko*) 29°02'S. 141°55'E., 310 km N. of Wilcannia; town gaz. 1895.

Warriwillah (*Co. Macquarie*) 31°46'S. 152°19'E., 13 km N. of Wingham; farming; PO 1931; TX.

Warrobil (*Co. Phillip*) 32°26'S. 149°36'E., 10 km SE of Gulgong; wheat and sheep; mine (Canadian Gold Mining Co.) 1871–84; RS 1909, station b. by D.H. Reid, closed 1978.

Warroo (*Co. Gipps*) 33°20'S. 147°35'E., 39 km W. of Forbes, on Lachlan R.; Geran till 1881; bridge (Dare timber truss) b. 1909 by E.W. Fitzgerald, 206 ft (62.8 m), over Lachlan R.; PO 1880–1905; Presb. C. 1896, closed, sold 2013, reused; PS 1895, new one b. 1899 by J. Peterson and William Hewson, closed 1932; school 1894–1902 and 1957–75; telegraph 1895; telephone 1956; TX 1956, automatic 1968; Union C. built and burnt down 1894; weir on Lachlan R., raised 1901 by McPhillamy; pop. 92 (1911), 110 (1933), 56 (1947), 68 (1954), 126 (1961), 117 (2006).

Warroo (*Co. Macquarie*) 31°51'S. 152°18'E., 7 km W. of Wingham, on Dingo Ck.

Warrumbucca (*Co. St Vincent*) see Northangera.

Warrumbungle (*Co. Leichhardt*) 31°15'S. 148°48'E., 31 km E. of Gulargambone; farming and grazing; Community C.; PO 1897–1977; school 1880–88; telephone 1927; TX 1927, automatic 1972; Union C. 1900, repairs 1908 by C.E. Lyons, closed 1960; Unit. C. (orig. Presb.) 1960; pop. 55 (1911), 62 (1933), 162 (1954), 150 (1961).

Warrunga (*Co. Monteagle*) 34°03'S. 148°14'E., 18 km S. of Grenfell; school (Tyagong till 1928) 1895–1933 and 1957–66.

Warrungen (*Co. Inglis*) 31°00'S. 151°18'E., 28 km W. of Walcha, on Flag Ck.

Warwick (*Co. Bathurst*) 33°45'S. 148°36'E., 12 km NW of Cowra; school 1957–65; pop. 78 (1933), 54 (1954).

Warwick Park (*Co. Dudley*) 31°03'S. 152°49'E., 5 km NW of Kempsey; 2 sawmills.

Warwick Park (*Co. Rous*) 28°26'S. 153°32'E., 6 km SW of Pottsville; sugar-cane; quarry.

Wascoe (*Co. Cook*) see Blaxland.

Wascoes (*Co. Cook*) see Blaxland.

Wascoe's Siding (*Co. Cook*) see Glenbrook.

Washington (*Co. Narromine*) see Wyanga.

Washpool (*Co. Clive*) 28°58'S. 152°02'E., 11 km N. of Tenterfield; pop. 25 (1933).

Washpool (*Co. Drake*) 29°18'S. 152°22'E., 42 km SE of Tenterfield.

Washpool (*Co. Gloucester*) 32°22'S. 151°56'E., 16 km E. of Dungog, on Karuah R.; sheep washing; bridge b. 1891 by Matthew Murphy, new one, 330 ft (100.7 m), b. by A.R. Dickinson Construction Co. Pty Ltd, over Karuah R.; drought 1965; PO 1909; sawmill (Fenwick's), fire 1909; weir on Karuah R.; wool-scour 1832 d. by Stacey; pop. 91 (1901), 188 (1911).

Waste Point (*Co. Wallace*) 36°21'S. 148°36'E., 8 km N. of Jindabyne, on Lake Jindabyne; quarry.

Watagan (*Co. Northumberland*) 33°01'S. 151°11'E., 16 km SW of Paxton, on Watagan Ck; formerly Wattagan; timber; bridge over Watagan Ck; school (Watagon till 1868, then Wattagon) 1862–68 and 1883–94; TX.

Watagon (*Co. Northumberland*) see Watagan.

Watanobbi (*Co. Northumberland*) see Wyong.

Watego's Beach (*Co. Rous*) see Byron Bay.

Watergumben (*Co. Bathurst*) 33°38'S. 148°40'E., 7 km S. of Canowindra; school 1883–1908.

Waterhole Flats (*Co. King*) 34°35'S. 149°24'E., 15 km SW of Crookwell; formerly The Waterhole Flats; school (Gunnary till 1900)

1897–1906.

Waterloo (*Co. Gough*) 29°43'S. 151°35'E., 14 km W. of Glen Innes, on Wellingrove Ck; pop. 70 (1901).

Waterloo (*Co. Vernon*) 31°02'S. 151°43'E., 13 km SE of Walcha, on Apsley R.

Waterloo (*Co. Wellington*) 32°32'S. 149°24'E., 19 km W. of Mudgee.

Waterman's Estate (*Co. Gloucester*) see Old Bar.

Watermark (*Co. Pottinger*) 31°12'S. 150°22'E., 26 km S. of Gunnedah; RS 1911–79; school 1914–16; pop. 38 (1933).

Watertank (*Co. Cook*) see Glenbrook.

Watertank (*Co. Richmond*) see Clearfield.

Watertank (*Co. Wellington*) see Store Creek.

Watervale (*Co. Bathurst*) see Nargong.

Waterview (*Co. Clarence*) 29°41'S. 152°54'E., 3 km W. of Grafton, on Clarence R.; subdivided by Ryan; water supply augmentation 1986; pop. 177 (1947), 145 (1961).

Waterview (*Co. Monteagle*) 34°14'S. 148°20'E., 9 km N. of Young; soldiers' settlement; orchards (stone fruit); pop. 54 (1933), 70 (1947), 77 (1954), 62 (1961).

Waterview Heights (*Co. Clarence*) 29°40'S. 152°53'E., 6 km NW of Grafton; FB; pop. 762 (1996), 795 (2001), 892 (2011).

Watsonford (*Co. Bland*) see Temora.

Watsons Creek (*Co. Inglis*) 30°44'S. 151°03'E., 31 km E. of Manilla, on Watson Ck; mining (tin disc. 1872) mainly till 1953 and grazing; dredge (Ted Cleghorn), ceased 1952; mines (incl. Buchanan & Co. and Farrell Bros); PO 1906–66; sawmill (Watsons Creek Sawmilling Co.); school 1907–87; telephone 1914; TX 1927; pop. 123 (1911), 195 (1933), 183 (1947), 169 (1954), 97 (1961), 288 (2011).

Watsons Reef (*Co. Harden*) see McMahons Reef.

Wattagan (*Co. Northumberland*) see Watagan.

Wattagon (*Co. Northumberland*) see Watagan.

Wattamadara (*Co. Forbes*) see Wattamondara.

Wattamolla (*Co. Camden*) 34°44'S. 150°39'E., 7 km NW of Berry, on Brogers Ck; formerly Providential Cove; disc. 1796 by George Bass and Matthew Flinders; farming; Angl. C., closed, renovated, reopened 1939 as St Margaret's; butter factory (Wattamolla Dairy Co.) 1892–1901; cemetery, closed; FB; PO 1875–1970; school 1880, new one b. 1883 by Bernard Moss, closed 1916, reopened 1931–50; telephone 1923; TX 1925; Union C.; pop. 93 (1911), 54 (1954), 66 (1961).

Wattamondara (*Co. Forbes*) 33°56'S. 148°36'E., 14 km SW of Cowra; Wattamadara till 1903; village gaz. 1902, lots sold 1904; farming and bees; bridge b. by E.J. Brien, over Pipe Clay Ck; FB (station b. 2018); PO 1900–88; Presb. C. 1906; reservoir; Rom. Cath. C. (Our Lady Help of Christians) b. 1941 by W.E. Beetson, d. by Norman Leslie Lipman; RS 1891–1975; school (Wattamadara till 1911) 1885, additions 1924 by H.M. Hughes, closed 1974; silo 1926; telephone 1905; TX 1915; typhoid (6 died) 1933; pop. 102 (1901), 338 (1911), 313 (1933), 269 (1947), 237 (1954), 189 (1961), 267 (2011).

Wattle Flat (*Co. Argyle*) 35°04'S. 150°01'E., 47 km NE of Braidwood, on Shoalhaven R.

Wattle Flat (*Co. Georgiana*) 34°10'S. 149°27'E., 33 km N. of Crookwell, on Middle Ck.

Wattle Flat (*Co. Roxburgh*) 33°09'S. 149°41'E., 31 km N. of Bathurst; (incl. Pipers Flat); orig. Green Wattle Flat; thrived 1872; mining (gold disc. 1853), farming, orchards, grazing, honey; Angl. C. 1859, new one (Holy Trinity) b. 1871–74 d. by Cowdery Bros, closed, bought 2001 by Paul and Anne Kellett, and graveyard (73 graves 1871–2002); bushfire 1957; cemetery (2 km S.) 1884; FB; mines: Austral Cross, Baron Rothschild, Belle of Surface Hill, Belle of Wattle Flat, Bismarck, Blue Duck, Bon Accord, British Empire, Comet, El Dorado, Evening Star, Excelsior, Lion of Wattle Flat, Little Oakey 1903–18, Planet, Scotland's Glory, Solitary 1859; PO 1861, new one b. 1898 by Rigby Bros, closed 1985, reused; PS 1898–1930; Rom. Cath. C. (Sacred Heart) 1873, renovations 1922, replacement (Our Lady of the Assumption), removed from Sofala, demolished 1997, new one (St Mary of the Cross MacKillop) 1999, and graveyard (140 graves 1860+);

school 1858, new one b. 1873 by William Timothy Atkins, d. by George Allen Mansfield, additions and alterations 1882 by W. Moulsdale, d. by William Edmund Kemp, closed 1925, reopened 1957; stamper batteries: M'Cudden's, Sofala & Wattle Flat Quartz Reefing & Crushing Co. Ltd (8 head) 1861, Tompkins' 1861; storm 2002; telegraph 1889, office b. 1898 by Rigby Bros, closed 1985, reused; TX 1926; Unit. C. (orig. Meth.) 1962, and graveyard (35 graves 1863–1988); Wes. Meth. C. 1862, defunct; pop. *c.*600 (1872), 539 (1891), 671 (1901), 415 (1911), 288 (1921), 325 (1933), 212 (1947), 166 (1954), 164 (1961), *c.*240 (1965), 213 (2006), 363 (2011).

Wattle Grove (*Co. Bathurst*) 34°10'S. 149°25'E., 33 km N. of Crookwell, on Tuena Ck; school 1891–96.

Wattlegrove (*Co. Dampier*) 36°12'S. 149°54'E., 20 km W. of Dalmeny, on Tuross R.

Wattle Hill (*Co. Cooper*) see Leeton.

Wattle Ponds (*Co. Durham*) see Singleton (*Co. Northumberland*).

Wattle Town (*Co. Dampier*) see Cobargo.

Wattle View (*Co. Kennedy*) 32°41'S. 147°49'E., 35 km W. of Peak Hill; telephone 1930; TX, closed 1941.

Wattleville (*Co. Bathurst*) 33°43'S. 149°16'E., 20 km S. of Blayney; school 1889 b. by W.R. Gorringe, closed 1904, moved 1907 to Errol.

Wattley Hill (*Co. Gloucester*) 32°20'S. 152°21'E., 16 km NE of Bulahdelah; school 1957–59; telephone 1950; TX 1951; pop. 79 (1954).

Watton (*Co. Roxburgh*) 33°19'S. 149°25'E., 19 km NW of Bathurst.

Wauchope (*Co. Macquarie*) 31°28'S. 152°44'E., 17 km W. of Port Macquarie, on Hastings R.; Wanchope till 1889; settled 1836 by Capt. Robert Andrew Wauch, laid out 1841, founded 1870 by Thomas Wallace, thrived 1889; timber, cattle, pigs, maize, vegetables, dairying, apiculture; ambulance station 1954, new one 2019; Angl. C. b. 1900 by J. Pead, restored and reused, new one (St Matthew's) 1968; brickworks (W. Jones); bridge b. 1886 by Thomas Maher, over King Ck; bushfire 1905; butter factories: Aust. Dairy Co. 1892 (burnt down 1902, rebuilt 1904, burnt down 1977) and Upper Hastings Dairy Co. 1917; cemeteries: Crossroads (238 graves) and general (2,793 graves), incl. columbaria; CH (incl. police station and lock-up) b. 1902 by Thomas L. Mitchell, additions 1931 by A.W. Mackay, closed, reused; clock tower (war memorial) b. 1927–29 by Frank Brunt and James Brown; cordial factory (W. Marshall) 1926; FB (station b. 1953); fires 1896, 1916, 1937, 1940; floods 1894, 1929, 1968, 2013; Foursquare Gospel C. (Bethel); Free Presb. C. (Davis Memorial) b. 1918 by A.W.S. McKay and W. Spraggon; hospital (Hastings Memorial, became Dist. Memorial); Jehovah's Witnesses C.; LDS (Mormon) C.; measles epidemic 1924; milk factory (Hastings Co-op. Ltd); plywood and veneer factory (Veneer & Plywood Products Ltd), burnt down 1950; PO 1883, new one b. 1914, demolished 1972, replacement b. 1974 by R.J. Burg Pty Ltd; powerhouse, fire 1938, taken over 1938 by local council; Presb. C. b. 1879 by Francis Walsh, closed and demolished 1915, new one (St Stephen's) b. 1915 by Bourne Bros; PS (incl. lock-up) 1889, new one combined with court-house in 1902, new police station 1915 d. by George McRae, new one 1961; railway bridge (steel truss) 1917, fabricated by State Dockyard (Walsh Island), over Hastings R.; railway coal stage, moved 1919 to Macksville, new one 1923; reservoir; Rom. Cath. C. (St Joseph's) b. 1907 by J. Baxter, relocated 1915, rebuilt by Baxter & Sons, renamed St Mary's in 1955, reused 1971, new one (Our Lady of Lourdes) 1976 d. by Noble & Bennett Pty Ltd; RS 1915; sale-yards 1919; Salv. Army C.; sawmills: L. Bosanquet, Hastings River Sawmills Ltd, Hornsby, Lee & Sons Ltd, Roy D. McMillan (burnt down 1953), Marshall Sawmilling Co. (Balfour Ralph Logan, burnt down 1954), J. Mulhearn, R. Sutherland, James Wallace, sen.; schools: primary 1868, new one b. 1883, additions 1892 by J. Healey, new school 1918 on new site, additions 1941 by R.N. Richards, additions 1956, and HS

1954, additions 1959, 1972, 1974, 2012; SD Adventist C. 1962, relocated 1972, closed 2013; sewerage 1964, augmentation 1993; silo; steel fabrication works (Bennetts Steel) 1991; streets electric lit 1924; TC, new buildings 1967, became a campus of North Coast Institute in 1992; telegraph 1889; TX 1911; Unit. C. (orig. Meth.) 1914, extended; water supply 1939; wharves: one b. 1870 by Thomas Wallace, one b. 1885 by John Egan, one b. 1907 (for railway sleepers), one b. 1916; pop. 286 (1891), 330 (1901), 454 (1911), *c.*900 (1924), 1,479 (1933), *c.*1,650 (1941), 1,903 (1947), 2,498 (1954), 3,038 (1961), 3,173 (1966), 3,351 (1971), 3,525 (1976), 3,645 (1981), 4,181 (1986), 4,297 (1991), 4,693 (1996), 4,772 (2001), 5,503 (2006), 6,372 (2011).

Waugan (*Co. Ashburnham*) 33°27'S. 148°16'E., 10 km W. of Eugowra, on Nellies Lagoon.

Waugan Ford (*Co. Ashburnham*) 33°28'S. 148°16'E., 11 km SW of Eugowra, on Lachlan R.

Waugan Plain (*Co. Ashburnham*) 33°26'S. 148°19'E., 5 km W. of Eugowra.

Waugoola (*Co. Bathurst*) 33°43'S. 148°54'E., 24 km NE of Cowra; farming; PO 1903–74; RS (orig. Burley Jacky's, then Myalla till 1891) 1888–1974; telephone 1923; TX 1953; pop. 70 (1901), 115 (1911), 50 (1933), 58 (1961).

Waugoola (*Co. Bathurst*)
see also Woodstock.

Waukivory (*Co. Gloucester*) 32°07'S. 152°03'E., 14 km SE of Gloucester, on Waukivory Ck; dairying; FB; quarry; school 1954–78; telephone 1924; TX 1929, automatic 1969; pop. 60 (1911), 144 (1933), 133 (1947), 160 (1954), 138 (1961), 359 (2011).

Wave Hill (*Co. Cowper*) 30°28'S. 146°30'E., 68 km SE of Bourke; RS 1958–74.

Waverly (*Co. Brisbane*) 31°55'S. 151°03'E., 23 km NE of Scone; pop. 25 (1933), 241 (2006).

Way Way (*Co. Raleigh*) 30°47'S. 152°57'E., 14 km NW of South West Rocks; pop. 55 (1933), 203 (2011).

Weabonga (*Co. Parry*) 31°13'S. 151°19'E., 40 km E. of Tamworth, on Swamp Oak Ck; orig. Rywung, then Swamp Oak till 1917; town gaz. 1891 as Swamp Oak; gold (disc. 1851), manganese, timber, grazing; Angl. C. (St George's) b. 1912 by Henry H. Manuel, closed 1985; bridge 1934; caterpillar infestation 1903; cemetery (30 burials 1892–1945) 1893; electricity 1966; FB (station b. 2011); mines: Alpine, Baalgammon, Boomer, Carbine, Commotion, George Grey, Golden Belt, Golden Wedge, Great Britain, Halls Creek, Highland Mary (estab. 1890 by Brown Bros, bought 1896 by NSW Goldfields Ltd, taken over 1907 by J.K. Charlston et al., 10 head stamper battery erected 1908, mine closed 1911, reworked 1913–16 by A.H. Edwards), Hoodlum, Junction, King Bungaree, Lady Grey, Lady Sophia, Little Tichborne (incl. 5 head stamper battery, moved 1892 to Niangala, mine bought 1896 by NSW Goldfields Ltd), Little Wonder, Lord Nelson, May Lily, Mount Sheba, Mystery, Nature Lass, New Year's Gift, North Alpine, One Better, Queen of Sheba, Rainbow, Rising Moon (incl. 5 head stamper battery erected 1891), Routine Flush, South Alpine, Storm King (bought 1896 by NSW Goldfields Ltd), Storm Prince, Storm Queen, Sunlight, Surprise, Victory (bought 1896 by NSW Goldfields Ltd), Wandering Jew, Welcome; PO 1880–1961; PS 1891, new one b. 1899 by W. Steel, closed 1944, reused; Rom. Cath. C. (Our Lady of Perpetual Succour) 1929, closed and reused 1989; school (Rywung till 1916) 1892 b. by Thomas Kean, renovated 1930, closed 1968, abandoned; stamper battery (Pioneer) erected 1891 by Carter; storm 1898; telephone 1898; TX 1913; pop. 113 (1901), 233 (1911), 125 (1933), 115 (1947), 58 (1954), 85 (1961).

Wean (*Co. Nandewar*) 30°42'S. 150°18'E., 24 km E. of Boggabri; sawmill (J.F. Wearne); pop. 177 (1911), 168 (1933), 103 (1947), 136 (2006).

Wearne (*Co. Stapylton*) 28°45'S. 150°26'E., 16 km S. of Boggabilla; RS (orig. Malgarai) 1932, closed.

Weatherboard (*Co. Cook*)

see Wentworth Falls.

Weatherboard Hut (*Co. Cook*) see Wentworth Falls.

Webbers Creek (*Co. Durham*) 32°30'S. 151°23'E., 21 km E. of Singleton, on Glendon Brook.

Webbs (*Co. Narromine*) 32°15'S. 148°20'E., 8 km E. of Narromine; RS (Webb's Siding till 1925) 1894–1974; Union C.; pop. 116 (1911).

Webbs Creek (*Co. Hunter*) 33°22'S. 150°56'E., 40 km W. of Ourimbah, on Webbs Ck; farming; bridge over Webbs Ck; flood (houses destroyed) 1889; PO 1927–50; punt across Hawkesbury R.; TX 1924–25; pop. 112 (1901), 95 (1911), 51 (1933), 203 (2006).

Webb's Flat (*Co. Northumberland*) see Woy Woy.

Webb's Siding (*Co. Narromine*) see Webbs.

Webo Willows (*Co. Murray*) 34°54'S. 148°48'E., 13 km SW of Yass, on Lake Burrinjuck.

Weddin (*Co. Monteagle*) 33°57'S. 148°11'E., 7 km S. of Grenfell; orig. Seven Mile; gold (disc. 1867 by Thomas Holton, gold rush 1867), later wool and wheat; mines: Eureka, Evening Star, Exhibition, Peep of Day, St George, St Patrick; PO 1884–1911; school (Smithtown till 1880) 1876, new buildings b. 1883 by Van Idestine and Gough, closed 1937; stamper battery (Perseverance Co.) 1872; pop. 103 (1911), 20 (1933), 50 (1947).

Weddin (*Co. Monteagle*) see also Grenfell.

Weddin Mountains (*Co. Monteagle*) see Grenfell.

Wedget Plain (*Co. Dampier*) 36°05'S. 150°01'E., 9 km W. of Tuross Head, on Tuross R.

Weeamera (*Co. Hume*) 35°43'S. 146°59'E., 7 km SW of Culcairn; RS 1914, closed.

Weebo (*Co. Hume*) 35°58'S. 146°48'E., 16 km E. of Howlong; school 1882–87.

Weedallion (*Co. Bland*) 34°12'S. 147°56'E., 35 km W. of Young; RS (2 km E.) 1916, station b. by W.S. Millard & Sons Ltd, closed 1975; silo 1934; telephone 1923; TX 1927; pop. 78 (1911), 54 (1933).

Weedallion (*Co. Bland*) see also Wirrip.

Weedy Flat (*Co. St Vincent*) see Araluen.

Wee Elwah (*Co. Mossgiel*) 33°03'S. 145°15'E., 54 km NW of Hillston; RS 1919–74.

Wee Jasper (*Co. Buccleuch*) 35°07'S. 148°41'E., 37 km SW of Yass, on Goodradigbee R.; limestone caves, sheep, farming; Apostolic C.; bridge (Allan timber truss) b. 1896 by W.J. Lansdowne, 218 ft (66.5 m), rebuilt 2005, over Goodradigbee R.; mine (The Glen Copper Prospect); PO 1886; PS 1884, inundated, new one 1929 on new site, closed 1937; Rom. Cath. C. (Our Lady of the Rosary) b. 1954 by George Hall, jun., d. by Patterson; school 1918; telephone 1915; TX 1916; pop. 70 (1901), 122 (1911), 146 (1933), 93 (1947), 114 (1954), 84 (1961), *c.*100 (2001), 275 (2011).

Weekes (*Co. Raleigh*) see Fernmount.

Weelong (*Co. Forbes*) 33°32'S. 148°47'E., 26 km SW of Forbes; TX (automatic); pop. 21 (1933).

Weemelah (*Co. Benarba*) 29°01'S. 149°15'E., 26 km E. of Mungindi; wheat and wool; Angl. C. (St Jude's) 1919, damaged 1980; cemetery; flood 2009; PO, closed 1988; Rom. Cath. C. (St Anthony's) 1942; RS (Benarba till 1920) 1914, station b. by Roberts, closed 1976, destroyed 1980; school 1956–72; storm 1980; TX (automatic) 1987; pop. 103 (1933), 110 (1947), 133 (1954), 235 (1961), 139 (2006).

Weenga (*Co. Roxburgh*) 33°03'S. 149°58'E., 21 km S. of Kandos, on Oak R.; RS 1916–71.

Weeraman (*Co. Bligh*) 31°59'S. 149°36'E., 19 km E. of Dunedoo; RS 1920–68.

Weetah (*Co. Courallie*) see Marambir.

Weetalaba (*Co. Pottinger*) see Premer.

Weetaliba (*Co. Napier*) 31°39'S. 149°35'E., 22 km SE of Binnaway, on Binnia Ck; village gaz. 1926, designated as chief town of the county; PO 1938–81; RS 1923, closed; school 1954–66; telephone 1934; TX 1949, automatic 1978; pop. 62 (1911), 103 (1933), 113 (1954), 85 (1961), 168 (2006).

Weetalibah (*Co. Leichhardt*) see Gilgooma.

Weethalle (*Co. Cooper*) 33°52'S. 146°38'E., 53 km W. of West Wyalong; village gaz. 1925; gold (reef), wheat, wool; Angl. C. (St Christopher's) 1954; bridge 1938, over Popes Ck; cemetery; CH b. 1938 by E.R. Saunderson, closed; earth tremor 1945; FB;

mines: Barr's, Blue Reef, Castle and Gilbert, Gibson's 1936–38, Goddes, Smith and Pettiford; PO 1926; Presb. C. (Scots) o. 1953, in former hall; PS 1928, new one b. 1930 by W.G. Butler, closed; reservoir, 50,000 gal. (227.3 kl), 1973; Rom. Cath. C. (St Patrick's) 1937, closed; RS 1923–86, station restored and reused; school 1928; silo 1930; telephone 1925; TX 1926, automatic 1985; Unit. C.; water reticulation 1973, augmentation 1988; pop. 397 (1933), 289 (1947), 281 (1954), 195 (1961), 202 (1971), 285 (2006), 307 (2011).

Wee Waa (*Co. White*) 30°14'S. 149°27'E., 34 km W. of Narrabri, on Wee Waa Lagoon; town site reserved 1848, site surveyed 1849 by John Valentine Gorman, town surveyed by Benjamin Charles Flide and gaz. 1858, laid out 1859 by Arthur Dewhurst, first lots sold 1859; sheep, cattle, wheat, cotton 1960s+; airfield 1965; ambulance station; Angl. C. (St Augustine's) 1896, new one b. 1985 by Terry Hughes, d. by Keith Davies; Apostolic C.; bridge b. 1927 by Terence Wilson, new one 2017, over Wee Waa Lagoon; carriage-works: F. Greedy & Son and P. Scourfield; cemetery (1,404 graves 1859+) 1863, incl. columbarium; CH 1849, new one b. 1878–80 by P. Wolledge, repairs 1891 by S.J. Stead; clock tower (war memorial) b. 1938 by Walter T. Weaven, d. by R. Richardson; cordial factory (Burke's); cotton gins: Auscott Ltd, Namoi Cotton Co-op. Ltd 1963, Yarramin; electricity 1938; FB (station b. 1966); fires 1912 and 1926; floods 1864, 1897, 1908, 1910 (4 died), 1920, 1950, 1955, 1971, 1974, 1998, 2000, 2010; hailstorm 1904; heatwave 1940; hospital (cottage) 1900, burnt down 1915, replacement b. 1916 by James William Doherty, d. by E.G. Yeomans & Son, additions 1940, new one 1975; ice works (A. & L. Schwager Ltd) 1928, acquired by L. Eather, burnt down 1950; lock-up b. 1897 by G.F. Cole and W. Frost; pneumonia epidemic 1937; PO 1849, new one b. 1910; police barracks 1969; pound (stock), relocated 1861; Presb. C. b. 1889 by J.H. Findlay, relocated and reused, new one (St Andrew's) b. 1974 by Harold Freer and Robert Bye, d. by Maclurcan and Brown; PS 1847, new one 1969 d. by Rodney Connors; railway bridge over Wee Waa Lagoon; railway turntable, 50 ft (15.2 m); reservoirs; Rom. Cath. C. 1887, new one (St Mary of the Angels) b. 1898 by James William Doherty, d. by Donnelly, removed, new one (St Andrew's) b. 1957–62 by Burton and Cashman, d. by Fowell, Mansfield and Maclurcan; RS 1903, station b. by J. Bromley; sale-yards (G.J. Burns) 1948; sawmills: W.H. Burke, A. and L. Schwager (estab. 1898 and run by F.L. Schwager till 1903, acquired by L. Eather, burnt down 1950), E. Taylor, F. Underwood, Wee Waa and Merimborough; schools: primary 1878, new buildings b. 1883 by F. Beagley, new one b. 1937 by A. Mills, additions 1956, 1968, 2010, and HS 1986, additions 2013; sewerage 1973; silo; telegraph 1872; trees (ornamental) planted in streets 1947; TX; water supply augmentation 1990; winery (Seplin Estate) estab. 1998 by Seppi and Lindy Widauer; pop. 68 (1851), *c.*80 (1866), 94 (1871), 262 (1891), 775 (1901), 1,512 (1911), 988 (1933), 1,034 (1947), 1,075 (1954), 1,099 (1961), 1,488 (1966), 1,840 (1971), 1,904 (1976), 1,904 (1981), 2,106 (1986), 2,030 (1991), 1,860 (1996), 1,816 (2001), 1,689 (2006), 1,653 (2011).

Weilmoringle (*Co. Culgoa*) 29°14'S. 146°55'E., 80 km N. of Brewarrina, on Culgoa R.; grazing; cemetery; floods 1983 and 2010; PO 1911; school 1961, additions 1963 and 1965; telephone 1901; TX 1934; pop. 83 (1911), 24 (1933), 126 (1961), 155 (2011).

Weimby (*Co. Caira*) 34°43'S. 143°14'E., 31 km W. of Balranald, on Murrumbidgee R.; town gaz. 1866.

Weismantels (*Co. Gloucester*) 32°16'S. 151°55'E., 21 km NE of Dungog; Langworthy's till 1894; agric. and grazing; PO 1864–1916; Rom. Cath. C. (Our Lady and the Three Kings) 1902; RS (3 km E.) 1934–75; telephone 1905; TX; pop. 50 (1911).

Weja (*Co. Gipps*) 33°32'S. 146°49'E., 49 km SE of Lake Cargelligo; village gaz. 1919; farming; PO 1922; RS (Bellarwi till 1918) 1917–75, station removed 1982; sawmill

(Bland and Howard); silo 1934; telephone 1923; TX 1925–77; pop. 109 (1933), 53 (1947), 96 (1954), 61 (1961).

Welaregang (*Co. Selwyn*) 36°01'S. 147°58'E., 27 km S. of Tumbarumba; village gaz. 1879; designated as chief town of the county; grazing; bushfire 2009; cemetery 1890; PO 1861–73; pound (stock) 1869; PS, closed 1896; pop. *c.*20 (1866), 86 (1911), 55 (1933), 79 (1947), 75 (1954), 80 (1961), 159 (2006).

Welby (*Co. Camden*) 34°27'S. 150°25'E., 2 km W. of Mittagong, on Gibbergunyah Ck; settled 1849, village gaz. 1867 as Fitz Roy, bypassed by highway 1992; Angl. C. (St Stephen's) b. 1876–78, d. by Edmund Thomas Blacket, additions 1929; bushfires 1929, 1939, 1951, 1953; cemetery; coal washery (abandoned); dam on Nattai Ck; foot-bridge to Mittagong, over Gibbergunyah Ck; Foursquare Gospel C. (Southern Highlands) 2015; PO 1947–71; rifle range 1947; Rom. Cath. C. (St Peter's), replacement (St Michael's) 1889; winery (Howards Lane) 1991; Wes. Meth. C. 1866; pop. 90 (1891), 190 (1933), 178 (1947), 282 (1954), 299 (1961), 736 (2011).

Welcome Reef (*Co. St Vincent*) 35°10'S. 149°59'E., 35 km NE of Braidwood, on Shoalhaven R.; farming and grazing; PO 1899–1918.

Wellesley (*Co. Wellesley*) see Rowes.

Wellingrove (*Co. Gough*) 29°38'S. 151°34'E., 19 km NW of Glen Innes, on Wellingrove Ck; estab. 1846, surveyed 1851 by John James Galloway, laid out 1852, first land sales 1854, declined 1858+, town gaz. 1881, abandoned 1917, almost defunct; farming, grazing, fossicking; CH (incl. police station) 1847–58; FB; flour mill; Free Presb. C. 1866, renovations 1918 by A. Williams, closed, renovated 2014, and graveyard (22 graves 1875–1928); PO 1849–1974; school 1888–1950 and 1957–64; telephone 1915; TX 1915; pop. 71 (1856), *c.*50 (1866), 547 (1881), 112 (1891), 235 (1901), 142 (1911), 222 (1933), 164 (1947), 144 (1954), 129 (1961), 113 (2006).

Wellington (*Co. Wellington*) 32°33'S. 148°56'E., 47 km SE of Dubbo, on Bell R.; disc. 1817 by John Joseph William Molesworth Oxley, estab. 1823 as convict agric. settlement under Lieut. Percy Simpson but abandoned 1831, laid out 1846 on new site by Walker Rannie Davidson, village gaz. and first lots sold 1846, more lots laid out 1850 by Nicholson, developed 1856+, town gaz. 1879, munic. proc. 1879; wheat 1823+, then sheep, cattle, gold dredging till 1958, flour milling, oats, maize, fruit, butter, timber, tobacco, vineyards 1968+; ambulance station b. 1936 by Tom R. Sutton; Angl. C. b. 1845 by William Watson, new one (St John the Baptist) b. 1865–67, d. by Edmund Thomas Blacket, extensions 1877 d. by James Rodda, transepts added 1883, bell tower 1891 d. by James Rodda; Bapt. C. b. 1906 by Kennard Bros, d. by Arthur Hubbard; brewery estab. 1880 by W.G. Kirchner as Bell Brewery, closed 1882, extended 1882 by John Restall and Dymond, reopened, acquired 1909 by Jager and Kelly (Wellington Brewery Co.), burnt down 1932; brickworks (Ward Bros); bridges: Bell River Bridge 1875 (replacement b. 1900 by George A. Jones, over Bell R.), Duke of Wellington Bridge (to Montefiores, over Macquarie R.), Macquarie Bridge (b. 1871 by Joseph Sorrie, removed 1920, new one b. 1920 by State Monier Pipe Co., collapsed 1989, new one 1991, over Macquarie R.); butter factories: Macquarie Valley Dairying Co-op. Society Ltd 1932 and Tremain Bros 1906; carriage-works: Bennett and Crowe 1916, Charles Broderick, Robert Grimson (bought 1902 by Wellington Engineering & Carriage Co.); cemeteries: pioneer (429 burials 1825–1905), general (3,990 graves 1870s+), incl. columbarium, lawn (2,200 graves) 1969, Rom. Cath. (553 graves 1852+); CH b. 1860 by Kennard and Snow, reused, (second) b. 1871 by George Kennard, renovations 1882, (third) 1912 d. by Walter Liberty Vernon, renovations 1927; Christ. Outreach C.; cordial factories: H.C. Cosier, Excelsior (G.A. Ferguson, acquired 1917 by W.E. Heap), A.W.B. Ferguson & Sons, H.H.A. Flanagan 1914, P. Harris (taken over by James Matheson), L.N. Hyeronimus, C. Matthews, R.R. Payne, Payne and Kimbell, Volcanic Aerated Water Works (W.A. Ferguson); diphtheria 1914, 1924, 1953 (2 children died); earth tremors 1862, 1871, 1919, 1928, 1937; electricity 1927; engineering works (Freeman and Vincent); FB 1901 (station b. 1905, new one b. 1924 by S.W. and R.C. Porter, d. by William Hull McNiven); fibrous plaster works (Les G. Kew); fires 1881, 1892, 1906, 1913, 1932; floods 1823, 1867, 1870, 1926, 1950 (man died), 1955–56, 1990; flour mills: Joseph Aarons, Great Western Flour Mills (b. 1877 by Kennard and Hilton for Alexander and David Ferguson, d. by Myers, later joined by Thomas Quirk, Ferguson's share acquired 1898 by McLeod & Co., taken over 1904 by Gillespie Bros and renamed Anchor Mills, closed 1968, burnt down 1985), Henry Herman Kater 1860, E.J. Matthews (incl. sawmill) 1857, M. McLeod Pty Ltd (b. 1905 by John Dunkley, chimney demolished 1952, mill closed 1965), Roller Flour Milling Co. 1889, Wellington Farmers' Co-op. Flour Milling Co. Ltd 1910 (also known as Harvey's, demolished 1982); foundry (Phoenix), taken over 1907 by Thomas Elgar; freezing works: Country Freezing Co. Ltd and Western Freezing Co., b. 1915 by Hodge Bros, demolished 1969; furniture factory (Murray Bros), burnt down 1920; gale 1907; gaol b. 1861 by Kennard and Snow, additions 1879 by G. Harris, new one 1908, additions 1910 by Albert Arthur Folkard; gasworks b. 1902 by Donovan & Co., d. by M. Coward, improvements 1931, demolished; glove factory (A.S. Horne Ltd) 1946, sold 1949 to N.A. Hinds and reused; grasshopper infestation 1924; hailstorms 1901 and 1938; heatwave 1945; hospital 1863 d. by D.H. Dunlop, closed 1904 and reused, new one b. 1904 by F.H. Kennard, d. by Walter Liberty Vernon, additions 1908, 1923–25, 1927, 1931, 1934, 1938, 1942, 1961, 1969, 1972–75, 1977, 1980, closed 1989, fire 1993, sold 1997, reused; ice works (Lauer and Connelly) 1901; iron foundry estab. 1902 by Henry and J. Nancarrow, taken over 1907 by J.O. Noble & Co. and renamed Phoenix Foundry; Jehovah's Witnesses C.; joineries: J.W. Catts and R.J. Nelson & Sons Pty Ltd; lime-kiln; measles epidemics 1898, 1904, 1907; Meth. C. b. 1938 by Ian Wright, d. by Norman Welland McPherson; military barracks; mission station, closed 1844; monumental stone works: Phil Jewell and C.J. Shakespeare; PO 1838, new one b. 1869 by William Moffatt, d. by James Johnstone Barnet, occupied 1872, additions and alterations 1904 by James Stuart Douglas, d. by Walter Liberty Vernon, additions and alterations 1910 by J.J. Wells, renovations and repairs 1930 by W. Fuller; police barracks b. 1891 by Summerhayes Bros; pound (stock) 1860; POW control centre 1944; Presb. C. (St Andrew's) 1883, closed, sold 1907, demolished 1929; PS b. 1859 by George Kennard, new one 1908, replaced; punt (William Perkins), new one b. 1862 by Richard Pile, across Macquarie R.; rabbit freezing works: Ellis & Co. 1907 and Western Freezing Co. 1915; railway barracks b. 1885 by Rennard Bros; railway bridge (lattice girder) fabricated by Andrew Handyside & Co., Derby, England, erected 1879–81 by W. Watkins and Thomas Smithyman, d. by Sir John Fowler and John Whitton, 649 ft (197.8 m), upgraded 2014 by John Holland (Constructions) Pty Ltd, over Macquarie R.; railway coal stage; railway engine shed b. 1885 by John Ahearn, removed; railway turntable, 50 ft (15.2 m), replacement (William Sellers & Co.) 1901, 60 ft (18.3 m), defunct; railway workshops 1890–1925, dismantled and moved to Goulburn 1935; research stations: Soil Conservation Service (6 km N.) and University of NSW (3 km E.); 2 reservoirs (concrete), 400,000 gal. (1,818.4 kl) each; rifle range 1936; Rom. Cath. C. 1876 d. by Edward Gell, demolished 1899, new one b. 1893 by James Connor, d. by William Lamrock, jun., damaged and repaired 1899, demolished, new one (St Patrick's) b. 1914–17 by Hodges Bros, d. by John Francis Hennessy; RS 1880, refreshment rooms, closed 1956;

sale-yards: Oscar Smith 1938 and local council 1947; Salv. Army C. 1904, renovated 1964; sawmills: Halliday and Rose, F.A. Jones, Wellington Steam Saw & Planing Mills (estab. 1882 by Henry and J. Nancarrow, relocated 1885); scarlet fever 1907; schools: primary 1861, new buildings b. 1881 by James Prior Hull, additions 1901 by A.W. Lowe, additions 1907 by A.E. Beaumont, additions 1909 by Peter Beddie, additions 1914, 1925, 1959, 1972, 2010 and HS 1955, additions 1967, 1974, 1982; sewerage 1936, augmentation 1985; silo 1918, wheat elevator and engine house burnt down 1931, replaced 1931 by A. Guymer; small arms factory 1942–45, reused 1946; snow 1900; soap-works (W.A. Harris & Co.) 1887; stockade (convict); storm 1899; streets gas lit 1902, then electric lit 1927; TC o. 1946 in former small arms factory, became a campus of Western Institute in 1992; telegraph office b. 1869 by William Moffatt, d. by James Johnstone Barnet, additions and alterations 1904 by James Stuart Douglas, d. by Walter Liberty Vernon; TX 1905, replaced; typhoid 1903, 1908 (3 died), 1911, 1923; Unit. C.: St Andrew's (orig. Presb.) b. 1908 by H.A. Whittle and one (Aboriginal and Islander Christ. Congress, orig. Meth.) b. 1938 by Edward Martin Wright, d. by Norman Welland McPherson; waterworks b. 1898–1901 by H.T. Hill, filtration plant 1931, water supply augmentation 1990 and 1993; Wes. Meth. C. (James Callaghan Memorial) b. 1874 by James Gilland, dilapidated and demolished, replaced 1900 by A.E. Rose, enlargement 1904 also by Rose, d. by Adin Parsons; winery (Frederick Marsh); wool store (Pryke Bros), burnt down 1932; pop. 257 (1826), 29 (1851), *c.*129 (*c.*1853), 228 (1856), 175 (1861), *c.*400 (1866), 549 (1871), *c.*800 (1874), 1,340 (1881), *c.*1,400 (1886), 1,545 (1891), *c.*1,650 (1895), 2,984 (1901), 4,409 (1911), 3,924 (1921), 4,320 (1933), 4,723 (1947), 5,213 (1954), 5,599 (1961), 5,853 (1966), 5,534 (1971), 5,395 (1976), 5,280 (1981), 5,277 (1986), 5,433 (1991), 4,920 (1996), 4,674 (2001), 4,660 (2006), 4,540 (2011), *c.*4,066 (2018). (See also Montefiores.)

Wellington Vale (*Co. Gough*) 29°26'S. 151°45'E., 37 km N. of Glen Innes, on Wellington Vale Ck; Angl. C. (St Matthew's) 1912; bushfire 1934; cemetery; school 1905, new building b. 1910 by E.R.S. Potter, closed 1920; pop. 89 (1911), 75 (1933), 127 (2011).

Wells Crossing (*Co. Arrawatta*) 29°22'S. 151°08'E., 6 km SE of Ashford, on Severn R.; bridge over Severn R.

Wells Crossing (*Co. Clarence*) 29°54'S. 153°04'E., 27 km NW of Woolgoolga; 2 quarries; sawmill; pop. 302 (2011).

Welshmans Creek (*Co. Durham*) 32°31'S. 151°43'E., 13 km S. of Dungog, on Verges Ck; school 1879–1925.

Welshville (*Co. Phillip*) see Stony Creek.

Welya (*Co. Urana*) 35°19'S. 146°28'E., 25 km SW of Lockhart, on Urangeline Ck; telephone 1924; TX 1928.

Wendoree Park (*Co. Northumberland*) see Mount White.

Wenonah Head (*Co. Raleigh*) 30°33'E., 153°02'E., 5 km S. of Urunga, on Tasman Sea; mine (Valla, orig. Deep Creek) o. 1889 by Nambucca Gold & Pyrites Co. for gold, closed 1893, reopened 1917 for arsenic, taken over 1919 by Valla Gold Mining Syndicate, taken over 1921 by Victor Leggo & Co., closed 1926, reopened 1929 for gold and arsenic, closed 1933, demolished 1938; school 1934–40.

Wentworth (*Co. Wentworth*) 34°06'S. 141°55'E., 163 km W. of Balranald, on Darling R.; orig. Hawdon's Ford, then McLeod's Crossing, then The Junction till 1859; disc. 1830 by Capt. Charles Sturt, settled *c.*1840 by Bates and James McLeod, estab. 1851, founded 1856 by River Murray Navigation Co., surveyed 1858 by Philip Francis Adams, laid out 1859 by Edward Twynam, town gaz. 1859, first lots sold 1860, designated as chief town of the county, munic. proc. 1879, thrived 1883, irrigation 1890+, munic. disbanded 1956; former river port, wool, irrigation farming 1897+, citrus, dried fruit, wine; air force bombing range (World War II), 5 men killed; airport; ambulance station 2013; Angl. C. (St John the Evangelist) b. 1871 by Wright and Cummings, d. by Alberto Dias Soares, and graveyard; brewery estab. 1889 by John Dunn, closed 1898; brick and pipe works estab. 1935 by Angelo Buffon, closed 1988; bridge (with lift span) 1893, new one (steel and concrete, incl. lift span d. by Burn, Griffiths & Associates) b. 1969 by Transbridge Pty Ltd, 532 ft (162.2 m), over Darling R.; bushfire 1957; cemetery 1867; CH (incl. lock-up) b. 1864 by Edward White, reused, demolished, new one b. 1880 by Witcombe Bros, d. by James Johnstone Barnet; cordial factory (C. Lemnon), fire 1903; customs-house b. 1869 by W. Cumming, new one b. 1884 by Hogan and M'Lean, reused; diphtheria 1895 and 1916; droughts 1915, 1967, 2002; dust storms 1895 and 1902; earth tremors 1897 and 1954; electricity 1933; FB (station b. 1935); fires 1885 and 1898; floods 1870, 1890, 1917, 1931, 1939, 1952, 1955, 1956, 1964, 1974, 1981, 1989; foot-bridge; gaol b. 1879–81 by Witcombe Bros, d. by James Johnstone Barnet, closed 1927, reused; heatwave 1939; hospital 1887, fire 1918, demolished, new one b. 1946–48, additions 1955 and 1979; ice works (O. Gurd); irrigation 1890; levee 1958; lock (No. 10) b. 1924–29 on Murray R.; lock-up b. 1899 by D.G. Maclean, demolished; PO 1860, additions 1884 by Hogan and M'Lean, new one b. 1899; pound (stock) 1856; PS b. 1877 by W.T. Read, additions 1962; punt b. 1885 by J. Stuart; reservoirs (incl. one 35,000 gal. or 159.1 kl); Rom. Cath. C. (St Francis Xavier's) b. 1872 by John Webber, d. by Edward Gell, additions 1925; sawmill (A.B. Rowe & Son); school 1860, new one 1870, additions 1882 by J. Lowmer, additions 1959, 1964, 1968; sewerage 1964; streets electric lit 1931; TX; Unit. C. (St Andrew's, orig. Presb.) 1881; water supply 1888, augmentation 1990; weir d. by Boule, 384 ft (117 m), on Murray R.; Wes. Meth. C. b. 1881 by Thomas Miller & Co., demolished; wharf (200 ft or 60.9 m) b. 1879 by C.G. Millar, additions 1885 by H. West, demolished 1983, new one 1995; pop. *c.*100 (1860), 222 (1861), 445 (1871), 752 (1881), 801 (1891), 642 (1901), 702 (1911), 849 (1933), *c.*900 (1941), 2,528 (1947), 4,034 (1954), 1,154 (1961), 1,084 (1966), 1,037 (1971), 1,136 (1976), 1,180 (1981), 1,352 (1986), 1,447 (1991), 1,504 (1996), 1,435 (2001), 1,303 (2006), 1,227 (2011).

Wentworth Diggings (*Co. Bathurst*) see Lucknow.

Wentworth Falls (*Co. Cook*) 33°43'S. 150°22'E., 6 km E. of Katoomba, on Jamison Ck; (incl. Kings Tableland); Weatherboard Hut 1822–40, then Weatherboard till 1879; village gaz. 1881 as Brasfort, then gaz. 1896 as Wentworth Falls; popular mountain tourist destination for over a century; Angl. C. (Holy Trinity) b. 1889 by John Poulton, d. by Sir John Sulman, chancel added 1902; Assemblies of God C.; bushfires 1910, 1933, 1936 (2 houses destroyed), 1938, 1940, 1942, 1948, 1951, 1952, 1957, 1977, 2002, 2015; cemetery (burials 1899+, *c.*2,500 graves) 1889; Church of Christ 1948; coalmine (Bates's Tunnel); concrete products plant 1964; FB; fires 1927 and 1929; Gospel Hall C.; locomotive explosion 1882; observatory (Kings Tableland); PO 1886, new one b. 1898, replaced 1910 by Albert Arthur Folkard; Presb. C. (St Andrew's) b. 1904 by T.E. Quiggin, d. by William Mark Nixon and John Shedden Adam, jun.; PS 1913; railway dam 1878, new one b. 1903, 26 ft (8 m) high, on Jamison Ck; reservoir, 500,000 gal. (2,273 kl); rifle range, damaged 1936; Rom. Cath. C. (St Francis Xavier's) b. 1913 by J. Weidesweiler, d. by Buchanan and M'Kay, additions 1968; RS (Weatherboard till 1879) 1867, new station remodelled 1902; sanatorium (Queen Victoria Memorial) 1903 d. by George Sydney Jones, additions and alterations 1948, changed from a chest hospital to a hospital for the aged in 1958, closed 1999, bought 2000 by Longevity Management Systems (went into receivership); school 1887, additions 1914 by P. Lovett, additions 1981; sewerage 1964, augmentation 1973; TC (Western Sydney Institute, Blue Mountains

College), new buildings 2004; toll-gate 1865; TX; water supply 1940; pop. 176 (1891), 344 (1901), 753 (1911), 1,053 (1933), 1,316 (1947), 1,476 (1954), 1,683 (1961), 2,283 (1964), 5,934 (2011).

Wentworth Hills (*Co. Camden*) see Albion Park.

Werai (*Co. Camden*) 34°35'S. 150°21'E., 5 km SW of Moss Vale; farming and dairying; Angl. C. (St Margaret's) o. 1941 (in former railway building); brewery (Southern Brewing Co.) estab. 2016 by Cameron James and Ben Twomey; RS (Meryla till 1901) 1883, station relocated 1909, closed 1975; telephone 1923; pop. 52 (1911), 46 (1933), 80 (1947), 51 (1954), 97 (1961), 251 (2011).

Wereboldera (*Co. Wynyard*) 35°25'S. 148°10'E., 13 km S. of Tumut, on Gilmore Ck; RS 1923–75.

Wereid (*Co. Brisbane*) 31°58'S. 150°25'E., 20 km N. of Merriwa, on Dales Ck; telephone 1927; TX 1928.

Werombi (*Co. Camden*) 33°59'S. 150°35'E., 13 km NW of Camden, on Eagle Ck; (incl. Linns Hill); cattle, horses, deer, farming, orchards; Angl. C. 1866, new one (St Barnabas's) b. 1895 by Frank Wedesweiler, and graveyard (145 graves); bushfire 1919; PO 1881–1971; sawmill (James Rideout), man killed 1894; school 1882, new buildings b. 1883 by P.J. D'Arcy, closed 1958; telephone 1911; TX (automatic) 1969; pop. 208 (1901), 119 (1911), 163 (1933), 135 (1947), 190 (1954), 169 (1961), 673 (2001), 708 (2006), 841 (2011).

Werong (*Co. Murray*) 34°57'S. 158°59'E., 14 km SE of Yass; mine (Humewood) operated <1901 by Murrumbidgee Silver Lead Mining Co.

Werri Beach (*Co. Camden*) see Gerringong.

Werris Creek (*Co. Buckland*) 31°21'S. 150°39'E., 18 km N. of Quirindi, on Werris Ck; estab. 1877, subdivided 1883 by George Single, further subdivisions 1908, 1927, 1957; formerly grazing, horses, wheat, barley, oats, then railway town 1877+, now rural service centre; Angl. C. 1898, relocated, reused, new one (St Bede's) 1932, extended 1971; brick-kilns: Edward Auld 1922, Alfred Hudson, David Taylor; bridge 1972, over Werris Ck; cemetery (924 graves), incl. lawn cemetery 1988 and columbarium 1994; CH b. 1911 by A.J. Hulbert; clock tower (war memorial) 1975; colliery (Preston Coal Co. Pty Ltd) 1925–63; cordial factory bought 1921 by John Jenner, sen. from Walter G. Denham, taken over by John Stanley Jenner, jun., merged with Thomas Bros, closed; FB 1933 (station b. 1934); fires 1930 and 1947; flood 1955; freezing works (Thomas Bros) 1946; hailstorm 1959; heatwaves 1905 and 1945; hospital b. 1944 by W.J. Wilson, new one; meat-chilling works (Graziers' Meat Export Co.) 1894; Meth. C. b. 1902 by Burless, d. by James Hicks, closed; PO 1878, moved into rented premises 1906, new one b. 1910 by L. Whitehead, rebuilt 1953; PS 1884, closed, sold, dismantled and removed, new one b. 1911 by A.J. Hulbert, alterations 1933; rabbit freezing works (Davis Export Co.) 1931, dismantled 1936; railway accident 1907; railway barracks 1910; railway coal stage b. 1879 by J. Conlon, new one 1891; railway dam 1902; railway depot 1896, new one 1917 on new site; railway engine shed (removed from Gunnedah) re-erected 1893 by Thomas Cobban; railway gasworks b. 1888 by Gatty and Richard Flook, demolished; railway round-house 1920, rebuilt 1954; railway turntable 1883, 50 ft (15.2 m), replaced 1899, 60 ft (18.3 m), replaced 1916, 75 ft (22.9 m), replaced 1954, 105 ft (32 m); reservoir, 1,000,000 gal. (4,546 kl); Rom. Cath. C. 1886, closed, sold 1914, reused, replacement (St Thomas the Apostle) 1914, extended, new one (St Thomas More's) 1971 d. by Terry Dally; RS 1878, station b. by John McDonald, R. Moss and G. Rees, refreshment room b. 1884 by John White and Charles Coghill, new station b. 1885 by Justin McSweeney, fire 1905, refreshment room additions 1912, station additions 1926 by R. Field, station partly reused; sawmills: Malouf Bros 1959 and Cecil Marshall 1908; school 1883 b. by A. Davis, additions and repairs 1892 by W. Bryant, new one b. 1911 by Robert Hamilton Gillies, additions 1956; sewerage 1966; silo; snow 1965; storm 1996; telegraph 1879, new office b. 1910 by L. Whitehead; TX 1910; Unit. C. (St Andrew's, orig. Presb.) b. 1915 by Edward Auld, vestry added 1958; water supply 1931, filtration plant added, augmentation 1958 and 1992; pop. 329 (1891), 503 (1901), *c.*700 (1903), *c.*900 (1909), 1,083 (1911), 1,540 (1921), 2,247 (1933), 2,348 (1947), 2,409 (1954), 2,299 (1961), 2,123 (1966), 2,028 (1971), 1,999 (1976), 1,924 (1981), 1,819 (1986), 1,566 (1991), 1,484 (1996), 1,446 (2001), 1,490 (2006), 1,437 (2011).

Wertago (*Yungnulgra*) 30°58'S. 142°32'E., 108 km NW of Wilcannia; copper mining; PO 1900–1; pop. 56 (1901).

Werunda (*Co. Killara*) 31°26'S. 143°55'E., 52 km NE of Wilcannia, on Darling R.; telephone 1930; TX 1936.

Wesley Vale (*Co. King*) see Dalton.

Westbrook (*Co. Camden*) see Mount Hunter.

Westbrook (*Co. Durham*) 32°27'S. 151°18'E., 17 km NE of Singleton, on Karrakurra Ck; farming, dairying, grazing; PO 1867–1962; telephone 1914; Wes. Meth. C. 1867; pop. 95 (1901), 81 (1911), 84 (1933), 78 (1947).

Westbrook (*Co. Wynyard*) 35°32'S. 147°53'E., 23 km W. of Batlow; formerly Oberne Creek; farming and grazing; Angl. C. (St Alban's Lucas Memorial) 1915, replaced; FB; PO 1916; school 1957, additions 1963, closed 1969; telephone 1925; TX 1925–68; pop. 65 (1933), 73 (1947), 80 (1954), 196 (2006).

Westby (*Co. Mitchell*) 35°29'S. 147°25'E., 28 km N. of Holbrook, on Burkes Ck; bushfire 1952; railway turntable, 50 ft (15.2 m), replacement 1927 (removed from Eskbank depot), 60 ft (18.3 m); RS 1925–52; school 1957–69; telephone 1923; TX 1924; pop. 73 (1933), 59 (1947), 52 (1954), 71 (1961).

Westdale (*Co. Parry*)
see Tamworth (*Co. Inglis*).

West Drysdale (*Co. Robinson*) 31°10'S. 145°52'E., 35 km N. of Cobar; defunct. (See also Mount Drysdale.)

Westella (*Co. Lincoln*) 32°17'S. 148°53'E., 26 km E. of Dubbo; school 1957–66; pop. 29 (1933).

West End (*Co. Sandon*) 30°39'S. 151°29'E., 2 km W. of Uralla; pop. 166 (1933), 145 (1947), 62 (1954).

Western House (*Co. Clarence*) 29°22'S. 153°09'E., 11 km NW of Maclean.

West Haven (*Co. Macquarie*) 31°38'S. 152°47'E., 2 km NW of Laurieton, on Queens Lake; reservoir; pop. 1,120 (2011).

Westlawn (*Co. Clarence*) see Grafton.

West Lynne (*Co. Wallace*) 36°31'S. 148°34'E., 10 km SW of Jindabyne, on Grosses Plain Ck; farming and grazing; PO 1926–71; TX 1928–64.

West Maitland Marshalling Yard
(*Co. Northumberland*) see Telarah.

Weston (*Co. Northumberland*) 32°49'S. 151°28'E., 2 km W. of Kurri Kurri, on Swamp Ck; (incl. Chinamans Hollow); settled 1856 by Weston, estab. 1903; Angl. C. b. 1908 by E. Bartley, burnt down 1911, rebuilt (St Mary the Virgin) 1912, and graveyard (255 graves), incl. columbarium; bridge over Swamp Ck; bushfires 1928, 1936, 1951, 2018; cemetery (Kurri Kurri, 5,732 graves) 1903, incl. lawn cemetery and columbaria; clothing factory (Pickwick Productions) 1951; colliery (Hebburn No. 1) estab. 1901–2 by Aust. Agric. Co., o. 1903, damaged 1905, acquired 1914 by Hebburn Ltd, strikes 1914, 1916, 1917, 1924, 1926, 1927, 1932, 1934, 1941, 1942, man killed 1942, strikes 1943, 1944, 1946, 1951, 1954, closed 1958, demolished 1980; cordial factory (Healey Bros, sold to James Bros, sold to John Ellis); dam (colliery); engineering works (Joy Manufacturing Co. Pty Ltd) 1978–98; explosives factory (Southern Explosives Co. Pty Ltd) 1911; FB 1906 (station b. 1909 by A. Thorley, new one 1974); floods 1926, 1927, 1931, 1990, 2007; foot-bridge over Swamp Ck; gale 1905; ice works (Edwin George Knott, Ernest John Williams and Robert Stevenson), partnership dissolved 1942, but carried on from 1943 by Knott and Stevenson; Meth. C. 1904, new one 1939; PO 1904, new one b. 1916, closed

1996, sold and reused; Presb. C. 1912, reused 1994; PS 1904, new one b. 1929 by Montague Audet, closed 1975; quarry; railway (colliery); reservoir (Hebburn); school 1905 b. by Harry Yeo Russell, additions 1906 by Reece Lewis, additions 1908 also by Russell, burnt down 1913, replaced 1916 by Montague Audet, additions 1923 also by Audet, additions 1929 by De Baskerville Edward Edwin Carden, fire 2000, new buildings 2000; telephone 1904; typhoid 1927; Unit. C.; pop. 1,731 (1911), 3,346 (1933), 3,388 (1947), 3,201 (1954), 2,826 (1961), 3,682 (2011).

Westport (*Co. Macquarie*) see Port Macquarie.

Westville (*Co. Bathurst*) 33°46'S. 148°47'E., 12 km NE of Cowra; farming; copper mines: Bartemore and Hudsons 1873 and Cooleys Reef or Westville; PO 1903–71; RS 1898–1974; school (Milton Estate till 1927) 1914–33; telephone 1906; pop. 50 (1911), 50 (1933).

Westwood (*Co. Wynyard*) 35°24'S. 147°59'E., 12 km SW of Adelong; school 1957–61.

West Yumburra (*Co. Cowley*) 35°04'S. 148°55'E., 15 km SW of Murrumbateman, on Murrumbidgee R.; school 1885 b. by John Grace, closed 1895.

Wetuppa (*Co. Wakool*) 35°18'S. 143°49'E., 47 km NW of Barham; RS (Victorian railway) 1928, closed; pop. 31 (1933).

Weybridge Grove (*Co. Buckland*) see Jacob and Joseph Creek.

Whealbah (*Co. Franklin*) 33°39'S. 145°15'E., 32 km SW of Hillston, on Lachlan R.; bridge b. 1868 by Taylor, over Lachlan R.; PO 1877–1912; telephone 1899.

Wheatacre (*Co. Cunningham*) 32°59'S. 146°52'E., 29 km W. of Condobolin.

Wheatlands (*Co. Hume*) 35°50'S. 146°16'E., 22 km NW of Corowa.

Wheeny Creek (*Co. Cook*) see Kurrajong.

Wheeo (*Co. King*) 34°31'S. 149°18'E., 17 km SW of Crookwell; grazing and agric.; bushfire 1975; cemetery; electricity 1955; flood 1870; hailstorm 1877; PO 1856–1946; PS 1879–88; school 1880–87; Unit. C. (orig. Meth.) b. 1939 by J.A. Walton, and graveyard (29 graves 1883+); Wes. Meth. C. 1865, closed, sold and dismantled 1935; telephone 1908; TX 1915; pop. 361 (1891), 245 (1901), 356 (1911), 295 (1933), 184 (1947), 169 (1954), 210 (1961).

Wheeo North (*Co. King*) 34°27'S. 149°20'E., 13 km W. of Crookwell; school (Lost River) Jan.-Dec. 1912; telephone 1927; TX, closed 1963.

Wheoga (*Co. Bland*) 33°45'S. 147°53'E., 30 km NW of Grenfell; goldmining; mines: Croaker's Reef (B. Raymond 1884 and J. Rich 1890) and Wheoga Mountain-Sandy Creek Reefs 1888–97.

Wherrol Flat (*Co. Macquarie*) 31°47'S. 152°14'E., 17 km NW of Wingham, on Caparra Ck; formerly Little Dingo; farming; bushfire 1905; creamery (Aust. Dairying Co.) 1898; PO 1876–1976; Rom. Cath. C. 1882, burnt down and replaced (St Joseph's) 1905, closed, sold and reused; sawmill (H.G. Watson) 1950; school (Dingo Creek till 1913) 1862–1972; telephone 1914; TX 1925, automatic 1972; pop. 235 (1933), 223 (1947), 217 (1954), 187 (1961), 309 (2011).

Whian Whian (*Co. Rous*) 28°38'S. 153°19'E., 10 km SE of Nimbin, on Branch Ck; timber, farming, bananas; dengue fever 1926; PO 1911–68; sawmill (West and Sharpe); school (Rocky Creek till 1945) 1914, additions 2010; telephone 1914; TX 1930; pop. 164 (1933), 138 (1947), 144 (1954), 113 (1961).

Whian Whian (*Co. Rous*) see also Eureka.

Whick Whack (*Co. Georgiana*) 34°05'S. 149°14'E., 47 km NW of Crookwell.

Whim Plain (*Co. Irrara*) 29°07'S. 144°45'E., 157 km NW of Bourke.

Whinstone Valley (*Co. Beresford*) 35°55'S. 149°24'E., 42 km NE of Cooma; farming and grazing; PO 1873–1959; telephone 1925; TX 1929; pop. 27 (1933).

Whiporie (*Co. Richmond*) 29°17'S. 152°59'E., 28 km NW of Maclean, on Myall Ck; Myall Creek till 1907; farming, dairying, forestry; Angl. C. (St Mary the Virgin); PO 1907; RS (South Camira till 1910) 1906–74; sawmill (Alfred E. Cordener); school 1921–71; telephone 1910; TX 1926; pop. 70 (1911), 126 (1933), 101 (1947), 133 (1954), 140 (1961).

Whipstick (*Co. Auckland*) 36°57'S. 149°42'E., 15 km W. of Pambula, on Whipstick Ck; gold (disc. 1891 by Dan Crawley), molybdenum (disc. 1891, mined till 1924), bismuth, farming, wattle-bark; bushfire (only the school survived) 1929; mines: Mount Metallic, Pheasant's Nest, Turbets *c.*1916, Whipstick 1891–1927; PO 1927–29; quarry; school 1897–1912 and 1918–22; tannin mill; telephone 1914.

Whipstick (*Co. Yungnulgra*) 30°52'S. 143°00'E., 87 km NW of Wilcannia.

Whitebridge (*Co. Northumberland*) 32°59'S. 151°43'E., 9 km SW of Newcastle; poultry; bushfire 1938; Church of Christ; collieries: Burwood (o. 1883 by Burwood Coal Mining Co., strikes 1887, 1891, 1893, colliery acquired 1894 by Scottish Aust. Mining Co., strikes 1895, 1897, 1898, 1900, explosion 1901 killed 3, strikes 1902, 1905, 1908, 1909, 1910, 1912, 1913, 1915, 1917, 1924, man killed 1930, acquired 1932 by BHP, strikes 1933, 1935, 1937, 1942, 1943, 1944, man killed 1944, strikes 1945, 1947, 1949, 1950, 1953, 1954, fire 1979, closed 1979, reopened, closed 1982, razed) and Burwood No. 3; PO 1927–94; RS 1917, closed; schools: infants 1944–62 and HS 1963, additions 1966, 1976, 1985; sewerage 1959; telephone 1927; water supply 1928; pop. 366 (1933), 603 (1947), 2,496 (2006), 2,567 (2011).

White Cliffs (*Co. Yungnulgra*) 30°51'S. 143°05'E., 83 km N. of Wilcannia; disc. 1884 by Richardson and Hooley, estab. 1889, laid out 1894 by Thomas H. Bell, thrived 1899–1900 and 1902, declined 1903+; mining (opals disc. 1889 by George Hooley, Charlie Turner, Alf Richardson and Will Clouston) 1889+, peaked 1902, then declined; abattoir; airfield; Angl. C. (St Mary's) 1900; cemetery 1896; CH b. 1896–98 by Michael Kenna Power; cordial factories: Alfred Richardson 1897 and William Frederick Stanbury; dams (1895 and 1900); droughts 1889–92, 1914, 1941; dust storms 1944, 1945, 1948, 2018; earth tremor 1928; fires 1909 and 1910; flood 1898; hailstorm 1912; hospital 1901–14; Meth. C. b. 1903 by Willington, destroyed 1913; mine (open-cut), closed 1898; PO 1894, new one b. 1900 by Michael Kenna Power; pound (stock) 1895; power station (solar) 1981–2004; PS b. 1896–98 by Michael Kenna Power, additions and alterations 1981, closed, sold and reused; Rom. Cath. C. (Sacred Heart of Jesus) b. 1899 by Michael Kenna Power; school 1896, new one b. 1900, damaged 1913, repairs 1914 by Ericsson and Fiebig, additions 2010; telegraph 1898, new office b. 1900 by Michael Kenna Power; TX 1913, automatic 1986; typhoid 1894, 1895, 1898 (3 died), 1899–1900, 1902–3; water tank 1894, water supply augmentation 1986 and 1992; pop. 2,000+ (1889), *c.*1,000 (1897), *c.*3,000 (1899), 1,550 (1901), 598 (1911), *c.*30 (1914), 363 (1922), 129 (1933), 76 (1947), 33 (1954), 248 (1961), 210 (1981), 207 (1986), 219 (1991), 207 (1996), 225 (2001), 119 (2006), 103 (2011).

White Flat (*Co. Ashburnham*) 33°06'S. 148°49'E., 5 km W. of Molong, on Moss Hollow Ck; bushfire 2006; pop. 39 (1933).

Whitegates (*Co. Northumberland*) see Wallsend.

Whiteleys Flat (*Co. Wellington*) see Belgravia.

Whiteman Creek (*Co. Clarence*) 29°35'S. 152°52'E., 14 km NW of Grafton, on Whiteman Ck; farming and orchards; creamery (Fresh Food & Ice Co.) 1896; PO 1882–1962; school 1885–1904; telephone 1915; TX 1928; whooping cough epidemic 1938; pop. 58 (1901), 81 (1911), 88 (1933), 81 (1947), 70 (1954).

White Munghorn (*Co. Phillip*) 32°24'S. 149°50'E., 29 km E. of Gulgong, on Moolarben Ck.

White Rock (*Co. Roxburgh*) 33°29'S. 149°37'E., 7 km SE of Bathurst, on Macquarie R.; farming, dairying, orchards; cemetery (81 burials); Community C. 1985 (orig. Wes. Meth. 1858, renovated 1895, became Unit.) and graveyard; PO 1879; Rom. Cath. C. 1873; school 1861–1906; telephone 1938; pop. 114 (1891), 101 (1901), 94 (1911), 57 (1933), 83 (1954), 74 (1961), 446 (2006), 691 (2011).

White Rocks (*Co. Murray*) see Queanbeyan.

Whites Flat (*Co. Hardinge*) 29°54'S. 151°06'E., 12 km NW of Tingha; mine.

White Swamp (*Co. Buller*) 28°17'S. 152°30'E., 60 km NW of Kyogle, on Koreelah Ck; cemetery 1895; PO 1907–15; pop. 67 (1911), 22 (1933).

White Top (*Co. Nicholson*) 33°46'S. 145°56'E., 48 km SE of Hillston; telephone 1929; TX 1930.

Whiteville (*Co. Clarence*) 29°23'S. 152°48'E., 37 km N. of Grafton; farming; PO 1927–31; telephone 1924; TX 1928.

Whitlow (*Co. Murchison*) 29°51'S. 150°39'E., 8 km E. of Bingara, on Whitlow Ck; formerly Bobby Whitlow; goldmining; pop. 52 (1911), 25 (1933), 71 (1947).

Whittingham (*Co. Northumberland*) 32°36'S. 151°12'E., 5 km SE of Singleton, in Doughboy Hollow; surveyed by Henry Dangar, village gaz. 1881 as Wittingham; dairying; abattoir (E.C. Throsby Pty Ltd) 2000; cemetery (Angl., 2,298 graves 1833+) 1886; creamery b. 1892 by Jackson; FB; floods 1870, 1893, 1949, 1952, 1971; flour mill (James Mudie); gale 1918; PO 1879–1948; rifle range 1885; RS (Falkner's Platform till 1877) 1869, station damaged 1918, closed; school 1881, new buildings b. 1883 by G.B. Lloyd, closed 1983; storm 1912; telephone 1897; pop. 204 (1911), 150 (1933), 156 (1947), 208 (1954), 195 (1961), 576 (2011).

Whitton (*Co. Cooper*) 34°32'S. 146°11'E., 18 km E. of Darlington Point; Hulong till 1883; village gaz. 1882; rice, vegetables, summer crops; Angl. C. (St John the Evangelist) 1884–2016; bushfire 1892; cemetery 1883; CH (incl. lock-up) b. 1900 by J.H. Hanson, d. by Walter Liberty Vernon, closed 1974, reused 1988; electricity 1928; fires 1897, 1923 (destroyed most of main street buildings), 1927; lock-up 1890; PO 1883, new one b. 1899 by J.H. Hanson, additions and repairs 1905 by George Huntley Dixon and William Godfrey Butterworth; police barracks b. 1900 by J.H. Hanson; PS 1885, new one b. 1974, additions and alterations 1976; punt (manual) b. 1889 by E. Taylor; rabbit canning factory (Euroa Preserving Co. Ltd) 1897; reservoir 1987; Rom. Cath. C. (St Carthage's) b. by Frank Mirabelli, d. by Peter R. O'Halloran, closed 2016; RS (Hulong till 1883) 1881, station b. by Alexander Hamilton Scouller, closed, relocated 1983, reused 1988; school 1884, remodelled 1928 by W. O'Keefe, additions 1967, renamed Whitton-Murrami in 2015; storm 1923; telegraph 1882; TX 1910; Unit. C. (orig. Presb.) b. 1902 by George Boulton, restored; water reticulation 1957, augmentation 1988; whooping cough epidemic 1936; pop. 308 (1891), 274 (1901), 441 (1911), 528 (1933), 445 (1947), 405 (1954), 306 (1961), 293 (1971), 285 (1976), 344 (1981), 369 (1986), 340 (1991), 362 (1996), 390 (2001), 394 (2006), 379 (2011).

Whitton-Murrami (*Co. Cooper*) see Whitton.

Whoota (*Co. Gloucester*) 32°18'S. 152°29'E., 14 km S. of Forster, on Wallis Lake; telephone 1926; TX.

Whyjonta (*Co. Yantara*) 29°44'S. 142°31'E., 224 km N. of Wilcannia; TX.

Whylandra (*Co. Gordon*) 32°21'S. 148°34'E., 12 km SW of Dubbo; yellow ochre; Angl. C. (Holy Innocents) 1905; pop. 21 (1933).

Whymoul (*Co. Wakool*) 35°31'S. 144°12'E., 14 km NE of Barham; pop. 50 (1933).

Wiadra (*Co. Phillip*) 32°26'S. 149°22'E., 17 km SW of Gulgong.

Wiagdon (*Co. Roxburgh*) 33°11'S. 149°41'E., 27 km N. of Bathurst; goldmining; mines: Cox and McPeake 1896 and 1906, Mount Wiagdon, Neary and Carmichael; PS, additions 1896 by Edward Abraham Wright, closed 1905; quarry; school (Wyagdon) 1873 b. by Stanford, new buildings b. 1891 by W. Richards, closed 1913; pop. 70 (1901), 48 (1933).

Wiangaree (*Co. Rous*) 28°31'S. 152°58'E., 13 km N. of Kyogle, on Richmond R.; formerly Wyangerie; village gaz. and lots sold 1907; farming and dairying; Angl. C. (St John the Evangelist or Bundock Memorial) b. 1934 by G. Groves, closed 2009, sold and reused; bridge (Bean Tree Bridge) b. 1927 by W.F.

Oaks, 330 ft (100.6 m), Allan timber truss, dismantled 2005, new one (Jenny Constable Bridge) b. 2005 by Reed Constructions Aust. Pty Ltd, over Richmond R.; butter factory (Kyogle Dairy Co.) b. 1915 by George James Grove, bought 1925 by North Coast Co-op. Ltd, remodelled 1936 by Daniel Gallagher, closed 1947; cemetery; fire 1931; flood 1954; gale 1933; PO 1916; Presb. C. 1914, closed, relocated and reused; PS 1926–31; railway bridge over Richmond R.; Rom. Cath. C. (Our Lady Help of Christians) b. 1936 by Watt, destroyed 1954; RS 1930–75; sawmills: Fraser Bros & Co. (removed from Findon Creek), fire 1946, closed 1961, and Robert J. Randle; school (Bean Tree till 1915) 1914, new building b. 1922 by W. Tyrrell, additions 1926 by George James Grove, additions 2010; spiral railway b. 1926–30; telephone 1915; TX 1918, automatic 1966; Union C. (shared by Meth. and Presb.) o. 1929 in former Presb. C. rebuilt on new site by John Michael McHugh; pop. 148 (1911), 461 (1933), 317 (1947), 252 (1954), 220 (1961), 130 (2001), 131 (2006), 206 (2011).

Wiangaree West (*Co. Rous*) 28°33'S. 152°57'E., 10 km NW of Kyogle; gale 1933; pop. 60 (1933), 54 (1961).

Wiarborough (*Co. Georgiana*) 34°12'S. 149°55'E., 49 km NE of Crookwell, on Back Ck; telephone 1923; TX 1929; pop. 70 (1901), 41 (1933), 42 (1961).

Wickettywees (*Co. Hunter*) 32°56'S. 150°44'E., 51 km W. of Paxton; agric.

Wickham (*Co. Brisbane*) see Gungal.

Wickham (*Co. Northumberland*) 32°55'S. 151°46'E., 2 km W. of Newcastle, on Throsby Ck; (incl. Islington, Linwood, Maryville formerly Smedmore subdivided 1885 and 1905); estab. 1840, village gaz. 1857, lots sold 1868, munic. 1871–1938 but became part of City of Greater Newcastle; coalmining and engineering; abattoir (Chippendall and Fleming); Angl. C.: St James's (b. 1872 by T. Smith, d. by Joseph Backhouse, chancel added 1894, church re-roofed 1900, demolished 1973) and St Mark's (Islington, b. 1920–22 by T. Moore, d. by Frederick George and Archer Cox Castleden, extensions 1959); Assemblies of God C. (Samoan Praise); Bapt. C. (Islington) 1886, new one b. 1920 by Stratford and Burnett; boiling-down works (Henry Dangar) 1848, became Newcastle Meat Preserving Works, closed 1855; bone mill (J. Williams) 1878, sold 1883 to James Ellis, burnt down 1890; boot factory (John Kidd & Co.), removed 1884 from Newcastle, burnt down 1887, rebuilt (tannery added), strike 1894; box factory (Empire, Frederick Viggers), burnt down 1909; brewery (Park Brewery, Clarence Linden) 1887–88; 5 bridges (incl. Graham Bridge, concrete beam, 1916) over Throsby Ck; carriage-works: Butler, Wilkins and Davidson 1904 and Thomas Proctor 1870; cement works (Comel Minerals & Refractories); cereal food factory (Cereal Foods NSW Pty Ltd) b. 1939 by J. Jamieson; Christ. Outreach C. (Goodlife); clothes peg factory (Les and Herb Spencer); coke-works (Aust. Coking & By-Products Co. Ltd) estab. 1913, 48 Coppee ovens, closed 1913; collieries: Linwood 1882–90, razed, and Maryville 1884; confectionery factory (Llewellyn Davies) 1882; Cong. C. (Islington) b. 1888 by Price Bros, d. by A. Stronach; cooperage and vat works (R. Clough); cordial factories: Coleman Bros (bought by Healey Bros), J. Devereux & Co., A.W. Fisher, P.J. Harrold 1890, Mullens Cordials Pty Ltd (acquired 1961 by NSW Aerated Water & Cordial Co. Ltd), George Edward Redman, Sharpe Bros (estab. by John Sharpe) 1906, Wickham Cordial & Aerated Water Manufactory (acquired 1887 by Roberts & Co., additions 1889 d. by Peter Bennett and Ernest George Yeomans), R. Wilson (bought and removed from Newcastle 1887), Y.Y. Aerated Water Co. Ltd (b. 1937 by A.E. Young, d. by E.S. Denley); dengue fever 1926; engineering works: J.B. Barclay 1886, Dick's Engineering Co. Ltd (incl. boiler works), Engineers & Colliery Supplies Co. Ltd 1910, H. McKee, P.J. Taylor (Newcastle) Pty Ltd, Wickham Rolling Stock Works (estab. by Andrew Donald and John Moyes 1879, in liquidation 1880, sold to R.A. Ritchie & Sons and later to Hudson Bros, closed 1893, site taken over 1899 by Alfred Goninan, man killed 1904, extended 1917, strike 1941); fastener factories: Robert Beggs, Clyde A. Burgmann (b. 1941 by Baker and Lamb at Maryville), Northern Rivet & Bolt Works Pty Ltd; FB 1891 (station b. 1891, new one b. 1916 by E.L. Thorne, closed and sold 1937 to local council, remodelled 1937 by R.L. Spencer to the plans of John William Oldham and Robert Godwin Lees, and reused); fibrous plaster works (Newcastle Fibrous Manufacturing Co. Ltd); floods 1893 and 1932; foot-bridge to Tighes Hill over Throsby Ck; foundries: Jones and Bowditch, C. Pitts & Sons, James Tickle & Son Pty Ltd (fires 1926 and 1949); furniture factory (Hunter Upholstering); gate works (William C. Lynch & Co.) 1949; ice works (Newcastle & Suburban Co-op. Society Ltd); jam factory (M. Herbert); joinery (J.W. Atcheson), burnt down 1941; lock-up b. 1882 by M. Parkhill, reused; Macedonian Orthodox (St Basil the Great); oil terminals: Atlantic Union Oil Co. 1931, Caltex Aust. Petroleum Pty Ltd, Texas Oil Co. b. 1929 by A.E. Young, Vacuum Oil Co. 1928; PO: Islington 1893 and Wickham 1872, repairs 1933 by J. Monro; Presb. C. (Maryville) b. 1942 by J. Mitchell; Prim. Meth. C.: Smedmore 1891 and Wickham b. 1871 by Harvey, new one b. 1889 by Myers and Thomson; PS 1878, repairs 1897 by E. Lake & Co., renovations 1928, closed 1936; railway bridges: to Carrington (reused for road traffic) 1875, and at Islington (timber), replacement (steel Pratt truss) 1898, 73 ft (22.4 m), new one (steel truss) 1916, 73 ft (22.4 m), over Styx R.; Rom. Cath. C. (St Gabriel's) 1960–79, sold and reused; RS 1936, station demolished and new one (Newcastle Interchange) 2017 on new site; sawmills: Bibby and Tighe, Robert Cameron 1869 (man killed 1871, site acquired 1904 by Armstrong & Royse Pty Ltd, fires 1905 and 1914, demolished 1918), James Ellis, burnt down 1890, Gloucester Estate, William Henderson 1876; scarlet fever 1933; schools: Islington 1887 b. by Taylor and Eyre, additions 1891 by Burg Bros, repairs 1909 by Gow and Shearman, additions 1979, Wickham infants 1893 b. by M'Kellar and Wilson, closed, sold and reused, Wickham primary 1878, additions 1881 by John Frogley, demolished 1905, new school b. 1906 by Montague Audet, closed 1990, sold, reused 2013, Wickham Girls HS 1962–76; slipway (Lovett's); soap and candle factories: Logan's (closed 1873) and Sydney Soap & Candle Co. (estab. 1869 by William Alston Hutchinson and Charles Upfold, closed, new factory 1874); streets gas lit 1880; tannery (W.M. Jewell) 1870, taken over by Great Northern Wool Dumping Co.; telegraph 1872; telephone (Islington) 1899; tramway (Maryville to Newcastle) 1914, closed, new one (to Newcastle) 2017; Wes. Meth. C. 1877, enlarged 1889; wharf 1886; wool-scour at Islington (Northern Wool-scouring Mills) 1886; wool stores: Aust. Mercantile Land & Finance Co., New England, North, & North-west Producers' Co. Ltd (b. 1928 by Charles Davis & Sons, d. by B. Hadley, additions 1939 also by Davis), State Wool Board (b. 1940 by Stuart Bros Pty Ltd), Winchcombe, Carson Ltd (Islington, b. 1941 by Stuart Bros Pty Ltd), closed, sold and reused; pop. 398 (1871), 2,399 (1881), 6,586 (1891), *c.*6,650 (1895), 7,752 (1901), 6,056 (1911), *c.*12,200 (1921), 12,002 (1933), *c.*11,900 (1947), *c.*11,100 (1954), *c.*9,900 (1961), *c.*8,600 (1966), *c.*7,900 (1971), *c.*6,500 (1976), 4,178 (2011).

Wickhams Hill (*Co. Cooper*) see Griffith.

Wicklow (*Co. Perry*) 33°07'S. 142°21'E., 116 km N. of Wentworth; PO 1880–83.

Widden (*Co. Hunter*) 32°31'S. 150°22'E., 33 km SW of Denman, on Widden Brook; Angl. C. 1878, new one (St Luke's) 1912; bushfire 1957; landslip 1935; PO 1908–12; school 1957–82.

Wideville (*Co. Rous*) 28°34'S. 153°09'E., 8 km NW of Nimbin.

Widgelands (*Co. Flinders*) 31°56'S. 146°57'E., 47 km SW of Nyngan; telephone 1925; TX (automatic).

Widgelli (*Co. Cooper*) 34°20'S. 146°08'E., 9 km SE of Griffith; PO 1954–77; RS 1922–75; school 1957–69; telephone 1928; TX (automatic) 1966; pop. 127 (1961).

Widgiewa (*Co. Urana*) 35°03'S. 146°12'E., 45 km SW of Narrandera; farming and grazing; PO 1912–70; RS 1884–1975; school 1957–93; pop. 61 (1911), 46 (1933), 73 (1947), 86 (1961).

Wilberforce (*Co. Cook*) 33°34'S. 150°50'E., 5 km SE of Glossodia, on Hawkesbury R.; (incl. Gronos Point); settled 1809 by Thomas Rose, founded 1810 by Gov. Lachlan Macquarie, laid out 1811 by James Meehan; maize, lucerne, vegetables, dairying, orchards, turf; abattoir (Hawkesbury Valley Meat Processors); agric. implement works (George Atkins); Angl. C. b. 1820 by Capt. John Brabyn, replacement (St John's) b. 1856–59 by James Atkinson, d. by Edmund Thomas Blacket, renovated 1914, re-roofed 1950, and graveyard (graves 1804+); bushfire 1895; butter factory (J. Percival) 1890; cemetery (burials 1811+, graves 1816+); creamery b. 1898 by G. Bennett and W. Buttsworth, d. by Arthur Blacket; engineering works (Holston Engineering Products); FB; floods 1867 and 1949; flour mill (Henry Buttsworth) 1836–1907, demolished 1915; lock-up b. 1883 by Pickup and Cummins, additions 1884 also by Pickup and Cummins; Plymouth Brethren C.; PO 1856; pound (stock) 1865; PS 1883–1933, sold and reused; punts across Hawkesbury R.: Michael Nowland 1812, John Howe 1814, James Davison 1823, Grono's 1828; reservoir; school 1880 b. by J. Johnson & Son, repairs 1900 by R.W. Dunstan, new school b. 1930 by F. Walker, additions 1972, new school 1994; tannery 1881; telephone 1891; TX 1927, automatic 1954; Unit. C. (formerly Presb.) 1862, renovations 1930 by W.H. Wallis, d. by J.C.R. Mills; Wes. Meth. C. 1862; pop. 189 (1861), *c.*200 (1866), 375 (1871), 356 (1881), 482 (1891), 810 (1901), 523 (1911), 658 (1933), 630 (1947), 606 (1954), 569 (1961), 421 (1971), 532 (1976), 1,117 (1981), 1,407 (1986), 1,700 (1991), 1,960 (1996), 1,918 (2001), 1,839 (2006), 2,048 (2011).

Wilbertree (*Co. Phillip*)
see Gullamara and Wilbetree.

Wilbertree Flat (*Co. Wellington*)
see Wilbetree Flat.

Wilbetree (*Co. Phillip*) 32°30'S. 149°33'E., 11 km N. of Mudgee; formerly Wilbertree; agric. and grazing; butter factory (Wurth's) 1890; cheese factory (Thomas A. Wright) 1896–1905; dam (Gooree Dam); hailstorm 1912; PO 1864–65; rifle range; Rom. Cath. C. (Sacred Heart) 1899; school (Wilbertree till *c.*1900) 1874, additions and renovations 1904 by W. Murphy, closed 1919; pop. *c.*200 (1866), 207 (1911).

Wilbetree Flat (*Co. Wellington*) 32°31'S. 149°34'E., 10 km N. of Mudgee, on Cudgegong R.; formerly Wilbertree Flat; farming and grazing; bridge (timber beam) b. 1893 by Fitzgerald Bros, 225 ft (68.6 m), replacement 306 ft 6 in. (93.4 m), steel girders fabricated by S.E. Statham, erected 1946–48 by C. Binns and V. Packer, over Cudgegong R.; PO 1910–60; school (Menah) 1883, new one b. 1907 by G. Collyer and W. Carmichael, d. by W.S. Reay, closed 1933; telephone 1914; TX 1946; pop. 104 (1933), 69 (1947), 65 (1954).

Wilby (*Co. Stapylton*) 28°56'S. 150°24'E., 36 km S. of Boggabilla; wheat; bridge b. 1942 by T.L. Fogarty, over Mobbindry Ck.

Wilby Wilby (*Co. Finch*) 29°24'S. 147°34'E., 39 km W. of Lightning Ridge, on Narran R.; artesian water struck 1898.

Wilcannia (*Co. Young*) 31°34'S. 143°22'E., 185 km E. of Broken Hill, on Darling R.; Mount Murchison till 1868; founded 1864 by John Chadwick Woore, surveyed and first lots sold 1865, town gaz. 1866, thrived 1874 and in 1880s, declined 1900+, munic. 1883–1959; former river port, sheep, cattle, mining; airport; ambulance station; Angl. C. (St James's) b. 1883 by Cramsie, Bowden, Woodfall and Greene, damaged 1950, re-roofed and repaired 1951, restored; Assemblies of God C. (River of Life); bond stores: G.H. Doake & Co., burnt down 1889, Kirkpatrick & Co., Rich & Co.; breweries: Black Horse

Brewery (estab. 1880 by Thomas Simpson, sold 1883 to Resch, closed, burnt down 1889), Lion Brewery (estab. 1879 by Edmund and Richard Frederick Edward Nicolas Resch, Richard left partnership in 1885, closed 1930, reused), Wilcannia Brewery (estab. 1867 by James Parker, closed 1868, reopened 1871 by J.P. Tripp, closed 1873); bridge (steel, with lift span) fabricated by R. Morrison Stewart & Co., erected 1896 by William Rowe, 310 ft (94.5 m), d. by John Alexander McDonald, new one 1991, over Darling R.; carriage-works (McInnes and Marriott); cemetery 1874; CH (incl. lock-up) b. 1878–80 by D. Baillie, d. by James Johnstone Barnet, additions 1888 also d. by Barnet, alterations 1971, restored 1978; cordial factories: Sid J. Peter (sold 1912 to E.D. Peter, sold 1945 to W. Mitselburg), Edmund Resch and Richard Frederick Edward Nicolas Resch 1875, James Rodda (burnt down 1888), Thomas Simpson 1880–83, J.B. Spratt & Co., William Frederick Stanbury; customs-house b. 1887 by Edward Rice, closed 1912; diphtheria 1881; dust storms 1896, 1898, 1900, 1901, 1930, 1941, 2018; electricity 1935; fires 1880, 1889, 1894, 1897, 1899, 1900; floods 1864, 1870, 1890; gaol 1881 d. by James Johnstone Barnet, additions 1890 by Speers, additions 1895 by Patrick Smith, additions 1898 by A. Reid, closed 1916, reused; hailstorm 1950; heatwave 1940; hospital 1880 d. by Cyril Blacket, Aboriginal ward 1941, morgue 1944, hospital additions 1960, redevelopment 1998-2002 by Lahey Constructions, d. by Dillon Kombumerri; ice works: W. Mitselburg 1945 and H. Watson; PO 1860, new one b. 1868, new one b. 1880 by D. Baillie, d. by James Johnstone Barnet, repairs 1888 by R.H. M'Donald, closed, sold and reused, new building 2002; police barracks, additions 1885 by Alexander Mackay, additions 1901 by Michael Kenna Power; pound (stock) 1868; powerhouse (Provincial Electric Supply Co. Ltd), fire 1944, closed 1988; Presb. C. 1894, closed, sold, relocated and reused; PS b. 1879 by D. Baillie, additions 1899, restored 1978; punt 1874–1896, across Darling R.; 2 reservoirs (incl. elevated one b. 1885, 40,000 gal. or 181.8 kl); rifle range 1909; Rom. Cath. C. 1883 (in presbytery), new one (St John the Apostle); school 1872, repairs 1882 by R.H. M'Donald, new one 1887 d. by William Edmund Kemp, additions 1963, 1966, 1986; sewerage augmentation 1996; soap-works; storms 1907 and 1950; TC, additions 1986, became a campus of Western Institute in 1992; telegraph 1878, new office b. 1880 by D. Baillie, d. by James Johnstone Barnet; TX 1913; typhoid 1881, 1893 (2 died), 1898 (man died); Unit. C., closed, sold and reused; water pumping station 1885, upgraded 1929, burnt down 1944, replaced 1944 by prefabricated building supplied by Sidney Williams & Co. Pty Ltd, erected by T. Leggett; water supply augmentation 1986; Wes. Meth. C. 1887; wharf b. 1889 by R.H. M'Donald; wool-scour (Garland's), fire 1904; pop. 264 (1871), 1,424 (1881), 1,287 (1891), *c.*1,000 (1895), 935 (1901), 725 (1911), 623 (1933), 799 (1947), 821 (1954), 839 (1961), 800 (1966), 936 (1971), 1,023 (1976), 982 (1981), 1,048 (1986), 942 (1991), 688 (1996), 698 (2001), 596 (2006), 604 (2011).

Wild Cattle Creek (*Co. Fitzroy*) 30°09'S. 152°45'E., 22 km N. of Dorrigo; pop. 85 (1911).

Wild Cattle Flat (*Co. Murray*) 35°41'S. 149°28'E., 42 km SE of Queanbeyan, on Wild Cattle Flat Ck.

Wildes Meadow (*Co. Camden*) 34°36'S. 150°31'E., 7 km W. of Robertson, on Wildes Meadow Ck; disc. by Joseph Wilde, declined 1932+, and again 1968+; farming, dairying, hort.; bushfire 1905; butter factory (Emu) o. 1888 by Wildes Meadow & Yarrunga Dairy Co. Ltd, sold 1922 to Moss Vale Dairy Co.; cemetery; PO 1872–1970; quarry; telephone 1901; TX 1927–53; pop. 131 (1901), 189 (1911), 223 (1933), 178 (1947), 209 (1954), 205 (1961), 515 (2011).

Wildes Meadow (*Co. Camden*) see also Myra Vale.

Wiley's Flat (*Co. Northumberland*)

see Gouldsville.

Wilgamar (*Co. White*) 30°23'S. 149°28'E., 17 km S. of Wee Waa; sawmill.

Wilga Plains (*Co. Kennedy*) 32°35'S. 147°19'E., 52 km NW of Trundle; pop. 43 (1933), 65 (1954).

Wilgaroon (*Co. Yanda*) 30°52'S. 145°42'E., 89 km S. of Bourke; gold; mine (Chinaman's).

Wilgoa (*Co. Dampier*) 36°22'S. 149°51'E., 20 km W. of Bermagui; pop. 33 (1933).

Wilkurra (*Co. Perry*) 33°07'S. 143°07'E., 154 km NE of Wentworth; Clare till 1924; PO 1880–1930; telephone 1931.

Willala (*Co. Pottinger*) 30°47'S. 149°51'E., 19 km SW of Boggabri; timber and wheat; FB; Protestant Community C. (St Paul's) 1960; school 1957–99; pop. 153 (1933), 99 (1947), 104 (1954), 73 (2006).

Willandra (*Co. Franklin*) 33°12'S. 145°08'E., 48 km NW of Hillston, on Willandra Billabong; pop. 35 (1933).

Willandra (*Co. Narromine*) 32°13'S. 148°31'E., 10 km NW of Dubbo; school 1881–1911; pop. 58 (1911).

Willanthry (*Co. Nicholson*) see Wallanthery.

Willaroo (*Co. Argyle*) see Currawang South.

Willawarrin (*Co. Dudley*) 30°56'S. 152°38'E., 25 km NW of Kempsey, on Hickeys Ck; Lower Hickey's till 1899; farming; Angl. C. 1906, new one (St Thomas's) b. 1954 by Bill Lee, closed; bushfire 1970; electricity 1948; fire 1924; PO 1906; rifle range b. by John Poulton; Rom. Cath. C. (St John's) 1896; sale-yards: A.M.L. & F. Co. Ltd 1955 and Elrington's 1949; sawmill (Tom Laurence) 1949 (removed from Spencers Creek); school 1902–5, reopened 1928, additions (building removed 1983 from Comara); streets electric lit 1948; TX 1923–72; pop. 92 (1911), 97 (1933), 82 (1947), 133 (1954), 130 (1961), 304 (2011).

Willa-Willyama (*Co. Yancowinna*) see Broken Hill.

Willbriggie (*Co. Cooper*) 34°28'S. 146°01'E., 12 km N. of Darlington Point; Darlington Point Railway Station till 1882, Darlington Railway Station till 1909; PO 1881–1975; RS (Darlington till 1909) 1881, station b. by Charles Hardy, closed and demolished 1985; telephone 1912; TX 1916, automatic 1961; pop. 34 (1933), 376 (2006).

Williams Creek (*Co. Murray*) 34°59'S. 149°12'E., 30 km SE of Yass.

Williams Crossing (*Co. Bland*) 33°59'S. 147°34'E., 34 km E. of West Wyalong, on Bland Ck; bridge over Bland Ck.

Williamsdale (*Co. Murray*) 35°34'S. 149°08'E., 26 km S. of Queanbeyan, on Lobbs Hole Ck; bushfire 2003; RS 1891–1975; TX (automatic); pop. 72 (1911), 37 (1933).

Williamsville (*Co. Wentworth*) 34°06'S. 141°59'E., 4 km E. of Wentworth.

Williamtown (*Co. Gloucester*) 32°49'S. 151°51'E., 11 km SE of Raymond Terrace, on Tilligerry Ck; farming, dairying, grazing, sand mining; air force base 1941, additions 1955 by F.H. Compton & Sons, additions 2004 d. by D.W.P. Suters, additions d. and b. 2009 by John Holland (Constructions) Pty Ltd; airport (Newcastle) 1947, new terminal 1975, terminal upgraded 1996 and 2005, runway and terminal extended 2015; Angl. C. (St Saviour's) 1913; bushfire 2018; caterpillar infestation 1898; PO 1868–1993; school 1869, additions 1925 and 1958, new building 1968, closed 2010, sold; sewage works; telephone 1897; TX 1925, automatic 1963; Unit. C. (orig. Wes. Meth.) 1878, closed and sold, and columbarium 1981; Wes. Meth. C. 1854; pop. 276 (1901), 209 (1911), 262 (1933), 381 (1947), 330 (1954), 341 (1961), 826 (2006), 875 (2011).

Willie Ploma (*Co. Wynyard*) 35°07'S. 148°04'E., 7 km SW of Gundagai, on Big Ben Ck; bushfire 1979; earth tremor 1871; RS 1903, station b. by F.G. Filmer, closed 1974, removed; pop. 22 (1933).

Willigam (*Co. Argyle*) 34°29'S. 149°38'E., 14 km E. of Crookwell; RS 1926–57.

Willigobung (*Co. Wynyard*) 35°39'S. 148°02'E., 14 km N. of Tumbarumba; soldiers' settlement; fruit.

Willimbong (*Co. Cooper*) see Leeton.

Willina (*Co. Gloucester*) 32°10'S. 152°17'E., 21 km W. of Tuncurry, on Sawyers Ck; dairying;

school (Sawyers Creek till 1934) 1916–59, building moved 1963 to Bunyah; TX 1947–74; pop. 30 (1933), 62 (1947).

Willi Willi (*Co. Dudley*) 30°56'S. 152°27'E., 40 km NW of Kempsey, on Warbro Brook; copper; airfield; mine estab. *c.*1881 by H.H. Mansfield, taken over by Baker Bros, abandoned 1901 and plant removed, taken over 1907 by W.H. Trewenack; telephone 1928; TX 1941–50; pop. 26 (1933), 124 (1947).

Willow Bend (*Co. Clive*) 29°03'S. 152°01'E., 2 km N. of Tenterfield.

Willowdale (*Co. Nandewar*) 30°31'S. 150°12'E., 26 km NE of Boggabri; sawmill; pop. 50 (1947).

Willow Grove (*Co. Arrawatta*) 29°29'S. 151°05'E., 17 km S. of Ashford; school 1889–95.

Willow Point (*Co. Gloucester*) 32°07'S. 152°25'E., 11 km NW of Tuncurry, on Wallamba R.; cemetery (16+ graves 1873–1913) 1876; school 1883–86; Wes. Meth. C. 1880, demolished.

Willow Tree (*Co. Buckland*) 31°39'S. 150°44'E., 16 km NW of Murrurundi, on Borambil Ck; Warrah till 1878; estab. by Aust. Agric. Co., subdivided 1908 by Aust. Agric. Co., lots auctioned 1908; farming and grazing; Angl. C. (St Oswald's) b. 1924 by Chapple Bros; bridge (Hams Bridge) over Borambil Ck; cemeteries: Angl. (186 graves 1886+) and Rom. Cath. (58 graves 1922+); electricity 1936; FB; flood 1949; hailstorm 2015; PO 1877; PS 1877, new one (incl. lock-up) 1915; railway turntable (William Sellers & Co.), 60 ft (18.3 m); Rom. Cath. C. (St Anthony's) 1910, destroyed 1949, replacement (Immaculate Heart of Mary) 1954 on new site; RS (Warrah till 1879) 1877, station b. by W. Hudson, burnt down 1927, replaced 1929; sale-yards b. 1915 by W.I. Dick; schools: Warrah 1892–1941 and Willow Tree 1882, new buildings b. 1883 by Baker and Elsley, repairs 1891 by Turton & Co., closed 1909, reopened 1913, additions 1962; silo; toll-gate; TX 1913, automatic 1971; Unit. C. (orig. Union) 1886, and graveyard; water supply 1962; pop. 83 (1901), 248 (1911), 298 (1933), 387 (1947), 510 (1954), 352 (1961), 237 (1971), 276 (1976), 258 (1981), 263 (1986), 422 (2011). (See also Old Warrah.)

Willow Trees (*Co. Hawes*) 31°30'S. 151°21'E., 62 km E. of Quirindi.

Willow Vale (*Co. Camden*) 34°26'S. 150°28'E., 3 km NE of Mittagong, on Sheep Wash Ck; bushfire 1951; house frame and truss factories: Austruss and Custom Built Frames & Trusses; pop. 668 (2011).

Willow Vale (*Co. Camden*) 34°44'S. 150°48'E., 3 km W. of Gerringong; bushfire 1872.

Willsons Downfall (*Co. Buller*) 28°41'S. 152°05'E., 40 km N. of Tenterfield, on Wylie Ck; formerly Wilson's Downfall; tin and grazing; cemetery 1884; PO 1875–1957; PS b. 1895 by A.J. Butt, closed 1940; Rom. Cath. C. (St Joseph's); school 1882–1901; telephone 1908; TX 1917; pop. 111 (1901), 134 (1911), 54 (1933).

Willyama (*Co. Yancowinna*) see Broken Hill.

Wilmath (*Co. Kennedy*) 32°35'S. 147°04'E., 72 km NW of Trundle; mine (Mahgalore) *c.*1898.

Wilna (*Co. Bland*) 34°30'S. 147°35'E., 7 km SE of Temora; school (Yarrandale till 1930) 1907–48.

Wilpinjong (*Co. Phillip*) 32°20'S. 149°54'E., 34 km E. of Gulgong, on Wilpinjong Ck; Angl. C. (St James's) 1893; causeway across Cumbo Ck; colliery (open-cut) o. 2006 by Peabody Energy Aust. Pty Ltd; school 1881–92 and 1907–21; pop. 98 (1911), 50 (1933).

Wilson (*Co. Urana*) 35°11'S. 145°37'E., 22 km NW of Jerilderie; PO 1878–1915; school 1880–90.

Wilson (*Co. Yancowinna*) see Day Dream.

Wilson's (*Co. Cook*) see Lawson.

Wilsons Creek (*Co. Rous*) 28°34'S. 153°25'E., 7 km W. of Mullumbimby, on Wilsons R.; bananas; sawmill (Banana Growers' Federation Co-op. Ltd), fire 1948; school 1947; telephone 1950; TX 1951; pop. 164 (1933), 246 (1947), 182 (1954), 171 (1961), 317 (2011).

Wilson's Downfall (*Co. Buller*) see Willsons Downfall.

Wilsons Ridges (*Co. Rous*) 28°49'S. 153°22'E.,

8 km E. of Lismore; Angl. C. (St Paul's) 1878; cemetery (Alphadale, 432 graves) 1875.

Wilsons Ridges (*Co. Rous*) see also Goonellabah.

Wilsons Valley (*Co. Wallace*) 36°21'S. 148°32'E., 12 km NW of Jindabyne, on Sawpit Ck.

Wilton (*Co. Camden*) 34°14'S. 150°42'E., 10 km E. of Tahmoor, on Stringybark Ck; (incl. Bingara Gorge Estate); private village estab. by Major Sir Thomas Livingstone Mitchell, first lots sold 1844, thrived in 1880s; orchards, poultry, dairying, farming; airfield (Sydney Skydiving Centre); Angl. C. b. 1868–70 by John Ackroyd, d. by Edmund Thomas Blacket, new one (St Luke's) 1903, and graveyard (96 graves); bridge over Allens Ck; bushfires 1928, 1929, 1952; cemetery 1883; FB (station b. 1964); PO 1872; PS 1882; school 1871–1948, new one b. 2012 by Edwards Constructions (NSW) Pty Ltd, new building 2016; telephone 1917; TX 1920; weir (Pheasants Nest), upgraded 2010 by Christie Civil Pty Ltd, on Nepean R.; pop. 121 (1871), 170 (1891), 196 (1901), 129 (1911), 175 (1933), 130 (1947), 157 (1954), 167 (1961), 382 (1986), 445 (1991), 583 (1996), 771 (2001), 764 (2006), 935 (2011).

Wilton (*Co. Camden*) see also Maldon.

Wimbledon (*Co. Bathurst*) 33°33'S. 149°26'E., 16 km E. of Blayney; wheat, maize, lucerne, dairying, vegetables 1930s+; airfield (1 km N.); PO 1883–1962; RS (Fitzgerald's Platform till 1877) 1876–1980; school (Fitzgeralds Valley till 1894) 1881–94, reopened 1900 in building removed from Fitzgeralds Valley re-erected by Samuel F. Smith, demolished, replacement b. 1915 by F.A. Collins, closed 1953; pop. 138 (1901), 91 (1911), 87 (1933), 100 (1947), 51 (1961).

Wimborne (*Co. Darling*) 30°40'S. 150°39'E., 12 km NW of Manilla; RS 1908, station b. by W. Gawne & Sons, closed 1964.

Winburndale (*Co. Roxburgh*) 33°16'S. 149°35'E., 16 km N. of Bathurst; goldmining; dam b. 1931–33, 82 ft (25 m) high, on Winburndale Rivulet; school 1898–1917; storm 1947; woollen mill (J. Brown) 1831; pop. 44 (1933).

Winchendon Vale (*Co. Bourke*) 34°40'S. 147°20'E., 30 km NW of Junee; school 1891–1914; telephone 1916; TX 1926; pop. 55 (1911), 65 (1933), 63 (1954), 64 (1961).

Windale (*Co. Northumberland*) 33°00'S. 151°41'E., 2 km S. of Gateshead, on Scrubby Ck; (incl. Bennetts Green); Surprise Township 1892–1913, then Surprise Town till 1951; modern village founded 1949; Angl. C. (St Mark's) 1953, relocated 1977, renamed The Transfiguration in 1978; bushfires 1946, 1948, 1952; FB (station b. 1971); flood 2015; gas 1952; house frame and truss factory (Trussted Frames & Trusses); Meth. C. 1955–70, burnt down; monumental stone works (Mediterranean Stone Pty Ltd) 1901; Rom. Cath. C. (St Pius X) 1959; school 1953 b. by L.W. Dent, additions 1956, 1959, 1961, 1963; sewerage augmentation 1959; pop. 57 (1947), 2,793 (2006), 3,095 (2011).

Windang (*Co. Camden*) 34°32'S. 150°52'E., 8 km E. of Dapto, on Lake Illawarra; Lake Illawarra till 1926; subdivisions 1920, 1926, 1928, 1940, 1941; Angl. C. (St Thomas's) b. 1940 by A.W. Anderson & Sons, d. by R. Lindsay Little; bridge b. 1936–38, rebuilt 1955 by R.G. Cram, new deck and widening on existing piers b. 1973 by Peter Verheul Pty Ltd, over Lake Illawarra; bushfire 1994; floods 1943, 1984, 1991; jetty; PO 1924; PS 1961; Rom. Cath. C. (Holy Family) 1962; school 1942, new one b. 1961 by R.A. Hodge Pty Ltd, additions 1963 by G.C. North; Unit. C. (orig. Presb.) 1939; telephone 1938; TX (automatic) 1950; pop. 76 (1936), 601 (1947), 968 (1954), 1,861 (1961), 2,407 (2006), 2,598 (2011).

Winda Woppa (*Co. Gloucester*) 32°41'S. 152°10'E., 1 km S. of Tea Gardens, on Port Stephens; timber; sawmills: Aust. Export Timber Co. 1907, bought 1909 by Allen Taylor & Co. Ltd, rebuilt 1917 and renamed Birdwood Mill, closed 1953, defunct, Easeman's, Henry Grove Howard; wharf (Allen Taylor & Co. Ltd) b. 1934 by Harry Green.

Windella (*Co. Jamison*) 29°53'S. 148°54'E., 50 km SE of Collarenebri; RS 1951–75.

Windella (*Co. Northumberland*) 32°40'S. 151°28'E., 11 km E. of Branxton; pop. 483 (2006), 595 (2011).

Windellama (*Co. Argyle*) 35°01'S. 149°50'E., 33 km SE of Goulburn, on Windellama Ck; formerly goldmining, then farming and grazing; Angl. C. (St Bartholomew's) b. 1859–62 by Pinn Bros, restoration 1991, and graveyard (226 graves 1854+); bushfires 1905 and 1965; electricity 1960; FB 1943; mine (Hidden Treasure) 1883; PO 1863–1952; quarry (black marble) 1890; Rom. Cath. C. (St Colmin's) 1895, and graveyard (burials till 1955); school 1954; telephone 1915; TX 1928, automatic 1953; pop. 124 (1901), 95 (1911), 93 (1933), 98 (1947), 67 (1954), 83 (1961), 322 (2006).

Windermere (*Co. Northumberland*) 32°41'S. 151°27'E., 9 km E. of Branxton, on Hunter R.; agric.; boiling-down works: John Mitchell and C.J. Crofton, and Nott and Grenfell (taken over 1852 by John Turner); creamery (Warraba, W.L. Boyce) 1892; flour mill (John Nott) 1857; gale 1905; pop. 66 (1933), 52 (1954).

Windermere Park (*Co. Northumberland*) see Bonnells Bay.

Windeyer (*Co. Wellington*) 32°47'S. 149°33'E., 21 km S. of Mudgee, on Long Ck; Richardson's Point till 1859; surveyed by John Alexander Horatio Price and village gaz. 1859; formerly gold (disc. 1863 by Charles Leffley), then wool, orchards, fossicking; Angl. C. 1859, ruinous by 1865, new one (Holy Redeemer) b. 1866–73 by T.H. Price, d. by Henry Tebbutt, renovations 1927; bushfire 1952; cemetery (139 graves 1856+) 1863; Chinese joss house; FB; measles epidemic 1909; miners' riots 1854; mines: Bill Adams, Crystal Palace, Dog Trap Reef <1875, Jubilee, Old Gully Claim (Charles Leffley) 1863–1913, Ottis Line, South Hill; PO 1854; Presb. C. 1866; PS (incl. lock-up) 1855, closed 2007, reused; rifle range (2 km S.) 1914, abandoned; Rom. Cath. C. (St Kilian's) d. by John Job Copeman, and graveyard (87 graves 1872–2004); school 1859, additions and repairs 1885 by W. Batten, new building b. 1899 by Walter Murphy, closed 2014, sold 2015; storm 1913; telephone 1896; TX 1927, automatic 1985; pop. 594 (1871), 368 (1891), 388 (1903), 207 (1911), 167 (1933), 90 (1947), 106 (1954), 118 (1961), 441 (2011).

Windham (*Co. Auckland*) see Wyndham.

Winding Creek (*Co. Northumberland*) see Cardiff, Mount Hutton and Teralba.

Windomal (*Co. Caira*) 34°47'S. 143°21'E., 25 km SW of Balranald, on Murray R.

Windora (*Co. Lincoln*) 32°22'S. 148°56'E., 22 km N. of Wellington, on Mitchell Ck; copper and silver mine (Comobella Prospect) 1910; earth tremor 1913; PO 1905–17; Presb. C. 1905; pop. 63 (1911), 68 (1933).

Windowie (*Co. Wynyard*) 35°22'S. 148°10'E., 9 km SW of Tumut, on Gilmore Ck; bushfire 1905; RS 1923, closed; school 1878–1923 and 1941–53; TX.

Windradyne (*Co. Bathurst*) see Bathurst.

Windridge (*Co. Stapylton*) 28°58'S. 150°22'E., 39 km S. of Boggabilla; RS 1934–75.

Windrodine (*Co. Roxburgh*) 33°26'S. 149°36'E., 3 km E. of Bathurst, on Raglan Ck.

Winduella (*Co. King*) 34°27'S. 149°16'E., 19 km W. of Crookwell; Selmes till 1888; FB; PO 1888–92; school 1882–93.

Windurong (*Co. Gowen*) 31°25'S. 148°43'E., 34 km N. of Gilgandra; school 1957–68; pop. 52 (1911).

Windy (*Co. Buckland*) 31°37'S. 150°24'E., 28 km SW of Quirindi; pop. 109 (1911), 62 (1933).

Winegrove (*Co. Clarence*) 29°33'S. 152°41'E., 29 km NW of Grafton; (incl. Apple Tree Flat); farming; bridge (Lilydale) 1934, replaced 1996, over Clarence R.; PO 1927–76; school 1890–95 and 1901–32; telephone 1915; TX 1927; pop. 58 (1911), 50 (1933), 71 (1947).

Wineshanty (*Co. Richmond*) 29°05'S. 152°52'E., 30 km SW of Casino, on Myrtle Ck.

Winfold (*Co. Darling*) 30°39'S. 150°48'E., 12 km NE of Manilla, on Namoi R.

Wingadee (*Co. Leichhardt*) 30°35'S. 148°19'E., 42 km N. of Coonamble, on Nebea Ck; pop. 62 (1911), 62 (1933), 104 (1947), 55 (1961), 92 (2006).

Wingate (*Co. Baradine*) see Walgett.

Wingecarribbee (*Co. Camden*) see Bowral.

Wingello (*Co. Camden*) 34°42'S. 150°10'E., 14 km W. of Bundanoon; village gaz. 1887; farming and orchards; Angl. C. (St Andrew's) 1912, closed, sold and reused; bushfires 1895, 1936, 1965 (31 houses destroyed); cemetery; earth tremor 1930; eucalyptus oil distilleries: R. Curry, Longshaw and Bond, William John Quigg, J. Simmonds; FB 1939; PO 1885; RS 1871, station b. 1883; sawmills: William H. Bell, Ferguson Crawford & Co., 1883, fire 1885, burnt down 1895, Percy Goose, Hickson's; school 1894, additions 1901 by J. Cameron, new building b. 1918 by E. Hewson; telephone 1911; toll-gate; TX 1922, automatic 1953; pop. 125 (1901), 217 (1911), 319 (1933), 347 (1947), 256 (1954), 249 (1961), 203 (1991), 228 (1996), 295 (2001), 307 (2006), 386 (2011). (See also Old Wingello.)

Wingen (*Co. Brisbane*) 31°53'S. 150°53'E., 13 km S. of Murrurundi, on Kingdon Ponds; village gaz. 1855; dairying and grazing; Angl. C. 1883, replaced (St Peter's) 1912, reused; brickworks (J. Baker); bridge over Kingdon Ponds; cemetery (13 graves 1906–66); FB; PO 1869–1985; railway turntable 1900, 50 ft (15.2 m); Rom. Cath. C. (St Patrick's) 1893, new one 1952; RS 1871–1975; school 1880, new buildings b. 1883 by J. Johnstone, repairs 1891 by William Newman, additions 1959, closed 1968; telegraph 1880; TX 1915–74; pop. 128 (1871), 32 (1881), 251 (1901), 308 (1911), 299 (1933), 206 (1947), 179 (1954), 161 (1961), 168 (2006), 287 (2011).

Wingham (*Co. Macquarie*) 31°52'S. 152°22'E., 9 km NW of Taree, on Manning R.; estab. by William Wynter, surveyed 1843 by John Valentine Gorman, village gaz. and laid out 1844, first lots sold 1854, building commenced in 1870s, munic. 1889–1980 but became part of Taree; river port till 1938, timber, wheat, maize, then barley, oats, potatoes, tobacco, wine, cheese, bacon, sheep, beef, peas, beans, dairying till 1975; abattoir (former bacon factory) 1959; agric. implement works (P. Schneider); airport 1930; Angl. C. 1871–1902, demolished, new one (St Matthew's) b. 1902 by Silas Brewer, d. by E.H. Wright, and columbarium 1977; bacon factories: Manning River Co-op. Dairy Co. (b. 1901 by G. Bradley) and Manning Co-op. Bacon Factory Ltd (b. 1921 by James Bell & Co.); Bapt. C.; brickworks (Lincoln) b. 1952 by Schmitzer and Burg for Aubrey Baker; bridges: one b. 1869 by Rudolph George Ochs, 77 ft (23.5 m), new one b. 1896 by Worthing & Co., repairs 1954, 1965, 1976, widened 1989, new decking 1994, over Cedar Party Ck, Peter Garrett Bridge over Gorman Ck (Stoney Ck), The Bight Bridge b. 1964 by Anderson Construction Pty Ltd, 535 ft (163.1 m), over Manning R.; broom handle factory (W.G. Carter & Son); butter factory (Wingham & Upper Manning Dist. Co-op. Butter & Bacon Co.) b. 1907 by Hercules Refrigerating Co., became Wingham Rural Co-op. Society Ltd in 1924, extensive alterations 1926; carriage-works: W.J. Lambert 1903 and Victoria Iron Works & Manning River Buggy, Spring Cart, Horse Dray & Wagon Factory (John Pollock); caterpillar infestation 1909; cemetery (2,483 graves 1860+), incl. columbaria; CH b. 1859 by Butler & Co., repairs 1873 by William John Smith, repairs 1896 by A. Rye, new one b. 1909 by T.L. Mitchell, reused, new one b. 1938 by W.N. Horton, d. by Cobden Parkes, closed, sold 1991 to local council, reused 1993, restored; Church of Christ 1878, new one b. 1931 by Norman Branch and Reginald Clinch, d. by Branch, closed, sold 2014, reused; Community of Christ C.; cordial factory (P.H. Rose) 1920; droughts 1923, 1927, 1928, 1929; electricity supplied by Wingham Rural Co-op. Society Ltd 1925–41, then supply taken over by local council; engineering works: Child & Co. Pty Ltd 1981 and Ne Plus Ultra Iron Works (David Murray), buggies made from 1899; FB 1944 (station b. 1958); fires 1928, 1929, 2010; floods 1929 and

1978; foot-bridge over Cedar Party Ck; Free Presb. C. 1856–99, sold and dismantled 1899, replacement b. 1899 by George Bradley, closed, sold and reused; hailstorm 1952; horseshoe factory (Clarke Horseshoes Pty Ltd) o. 1959 in former slipper factory; hospital (Wingham and Dist. War Memorial) 1969; ice works (Wingham Rural Co-op. Society Ltd); joinery (E.A. Hodges); LDS (Mormon) C. b. 1937 by Mervyn Richards; lock-up 1859, repairs 1873 by William John Smith, repairs 1896 by A. Rye; measles epidemic 1912; PO 1853, new one b. 1884 by William T. Smith, d. by James Johnstone Barnet, additions 1905 by Silas Brewer, additions and alterations 1910 by Henry Wilson Alcorn, extended 1923, renovated 1983; pound (stock) 1859; Presb. C. (Upper Manning) 1856, new one (St Andrew's) 1961, and columbarium 1982; PS, additions and alterations 1898 by Rudolph George Ochs, new one b. 1909 by T.L. Mitchell, alterations 1938 by W.N. Horton, new one 1964; punt 1871, new one b. by S.J. Donaldson, across Manning R.; Reorganised LDS (Mormon) C. 1941; reservoirs: 360,000 gal. (1,636.6 kl), 360,000 gal. (1,636.6 kl), 2,000,000 gal. (9,092 kl); rifle range (2 km N.); Rom. Cath. C. built and burnt down 1901, replaced 1905, reused, new one (Our Lady of Perpetual Succour War Memorial) b. 1954 by Schmitzer and Burg, d. by John Patrick Gannon; RS 1913, station b. by John Allibone; sale-yards 1917, new yards (G.O. Hill) 1943; sawmills: John Brown (burnt down 1919), J.T. Chambers, F. Davies, Excelsior (estab. 1884 by John Donaldson, bought 1889 by Francis John Dennes, fire 1897, bought 1903 by Stuart J. Donaldson), R. Fittock, Graham Timber Co. Ltd (acquired 1931 by Eriksson Bros, new mill b. 1945 by James Eriksson, sold 1951 to Pat Clarke), Machin & Sons, Wingham Sawmilling Co. (burnt down 1941); schools: Wingham primary 1864 (b. by Targett, new one b. 1879 on new site by Samuel Lee, additions 1915 by T. Mitchell, new buildings b. 1926 by De Baskerville Edward Edwin Carden, additions 1933 d. by Edwin Evan Smith, additions 1948, 1954, 1958), Wingham HS 1963 (additions 1967, 1989, 1991), Wingham Brush 1987, additions 1990; SD Adventist C. 1952; sewerage 1961, augmentation 1991; slipper factory (b. by R.A.E. Babington for Wingham Investments Pty Ltd, on behalf of Felt & Textiles of Aust. Ltd) 1946–59, reused; storm 1924; streets formerly lit by acetylene gas, electric lit 1913–25 (from Donaldson's sawmill); tannery (Angus Nugent & Sons Pty Ltd) 1974; telegraph 1880, new office b. 1884 by William T. Smith, d. by James Johnstone Barnet, additions and alterations 1909 by Henry Wilson Alcorn; TX 1909; Unit. C. (orig. Meth.) b. 1908 by Silas Brewer; water reticulation 1929, augmentation 1969; wharf b. 1931 by S.J. Donaldson; pop. 31 (1856), *c.*50 (1861), *c.*90 (1866), 102 (1871), 223 (1881), 494 (1891), *c.*550 (1895), 556 (1901), *c.*900 (1909), 1,039 (1911), 1,080 (1916), 1,600 (1933), *c.*2,000 (1941), 2,097 (1947), 2,591 (1954), 2,887 (1961), 2,827 (1966), 2,917 (1971), 3,435 (1976), 3,937 (1981), 4,297 (1986), 4,407 (1991), 4,446 (1996), 4,665 (2001), 4,812 (2006), 4,518 (2011).

Wingham Brush (*Co. Macquarie*) see Wingham.

Winmalee (*Co. Cook*) 33°41'S. 150°36'E., 4 km NE of Springwood; (incl. Hawkesbury Heights); Heatherwood Village till 1963 then North Springwood till 1973; formerly farming and orchards, now residential; Angl. C. (St George's), removed from Hazelbrook; bushfires 1936, 1951 (woman died), 1968, 1994, 2001, 2013; Christ. Brethren Assemblies C. (Gospel); FB 1962; landslip (Hawkesbury Heights) 1949; PO 1963; Presb. C.; schools: North Springwood 1899–1906, Winmalee primary 1972 d. by Ian McHutchinson, additions 1977, Winmalee HS 1985, additions 1988, fire 2018; sewage works; telephone 1951; pop. 133 (1933), 372 (1947), 6,593 (2011).

Winnunga (*Co. Gipps*) 33°36'S. 146°52'E., 46 km NW of West Wyalong; farming and grazing; PO 1924–43; RS 1917–58; telephone

1923; TX 1925; pop. 89 (1933).

Winterbourne (*Co. Vernon*) 30°50'S. 151°47'E., 25 km NE of Walcha, on Winterbourne Ck; electricity 1965; sawmill (Cross's); pop. 97 (1947).

Winton (*Co. Parry*) 31°04'S. 150°43'E., 20 km W. of Tamworth, on Waterhole Gully; farming; cemetery (10 graves 1900–2004) 1898; PO 1893; school 1893–1940; telephone 1915; TX (automatic); Wes. Meth. C. 1893; pop. 247 (1901), 229 (1911), 148 (1933), 94 (1947), 130 (1954), 136 (1961), 201 (2011).

Winton Road Siding (*Co. Parry*) see Warral.

Wiradjuri (*Co. Cooper*) see Leeton.

Wirajarai (*Co. Courallie*) see Moree.

Wirega (*Co. Monteagle*) 33°55'S. 148°14'E., 8 km E. of Grenfell; RS 1901, station b. by F.W. Kinch, closed 1970; silo 1941.

Wire Gully Diggings (*Co. Bathurst*) 33°30'S. 149°00'E., 18 km W. of Millthorpe; fire (2 died) 1902; goldmine (St Jude) 1904–7, 1910, 1930, 1933–37.

Wiripaang (*Co. Northumberland*) see Gateshead.

Wiriri (*Co. Fitzroy*) 30°09'S. 152°37'E., 22 km NW of Dorrigo; sawmill (Veneer Co. Ltd).

Wirlinga (*Co. Goulburn*) 36°04'S. 147°00'E., 7 km E. of Albury, on Eight Mile Ck; Hawksview till 1928; thrived 1888; goldmining; explosives depot 1929; PO 1927–75; telephone 1928; TX 1939, automatic 1959; pop. 52 (1933), 110 (1947), 106 (1954), 398 (2011).

Wirlong (*Co. Mouramba*) 32°16'S. 145°43'E., 85 km S. of Cobar; copper mine (Star of the West); pop. 20 (1933).

Wirrabelah (*Co. Pottinger*) 31°00'S. 150°13'E., 4 km SW of Gunnedah; coalmine; school 1897 b. by Jonathan Cock, closed 1967.

Wirradgurie (*Co. Gloucester*) 31°55'S. 152°04'E., 15 km NE of Gloucester, on Gloucester R.; RS 1924–75.

Wirragulla (*Co. Durham*) 32°28'S. 151°45'E., 7 km S. of Dungog; butter factory (Butter Cup Dairy) estab. 1893 by Benjamin E. Hooke, burnt down 1895; flour mill (Thomas Walker); RS 1911, station closed and removed 1975; water pumping station; pop. 22 (1933).

Wirrah (*Co. Benarba*) 29°04'S. 149°02'E., 10 km S. of Mungindi; Angl. C. 1901; typhoid 1896.

Wirreanda (*Co. Gloucester*) see Medowie.

Wirrimah (*Co. Monteagle*) 34°07'S. 148°25'E., 24 km NE of Young; soldiers' settlement; orchards; fruit packing house; German measles epidemic 1940; PO 1927–78; prune dehydration plant 1936; school 1929–2002; telephone 1924; TX 1925; pop. 152 (1933), 121 (1947), 104 (1954), 104 (1954), 134 (1961).

Wirrimbi (*Co. Raleigh*) 30°40'S. 152°55'E., 4 km N. of Macksville, on Nambucca R.; farming and dairying; Christ. City C. (Nambucca Valley Community); meat works (Mid-Coast Co-op. Meat Society Ltd) 1941; RS 1941, closed; school 1887, additions 1898 by C. Howley and E.G. Forrester, closed 1942; telephone 1914; TX 1928; pop. 132 (1911), 53 (1933).

Wirringulla (*Co. Cooper*) 33°54'S. 146°17'E., 51 km NE of Griffith.

Wirrinya (*Co. Forbes*) 33°40'S. 147°48'E., 36 km SW of Forbes; farming and grazing; Angl. C. (All Souls') b. 1956 by Bruce Tudor and Ken Howarth; bushfire 1926; PO 1924–85; RS (Coolan till 1919) 1918–76; school 1956, new building 1967, closed 1985, sold; silo 1928; telephone 1924; TX; pop. 254 (1933), 225 (1947), 91 (1954), 274 (1961).

Wirrip (*Co. Bland*) 34°14'S. 147°53'E., 38 km W. of Young; Weedallion till 1916; telephone 1915; TX 1926.

Wisemans Creek (*Co. Westmoreland*) 33°37'S. 149°43'E., 16 km NW of Oberon, on Sawells Ck; mining (zinc, lead, copper, silver, gold), farming, grazing; Meth. C., closed 1968, removed; mines: Bell's, Blackman's or Blackfellow's <1877, 1899, 1914–15, 1935–37, Copperhill or Foran's 1907, 1911, 1914–16, Hansard, Jason's 1873–80, 1885–1907, 1941–42, 1949–51, Jocelyn 1882 and 1907, Mabel 1895–1911 and 1918, Mulhall's or Larry's Flat, Murphy's, North Wisemans or Eyrie South 1873–80, 1885–1907, 1941–42, 1949–51, Phoenix or Larry's Hill 1895–1911 and 1918,

South Wisemans 1875; PO 1886–1976; quarry; Rom. Cath. C. (St Alphonsus Liguori's) 1888, closed; smelter 1876; telephone 1925; Wes. Meth. C., demolished 1947; pop. 115 (1901), 126 (1911), 25 (1933), 71 (1947), 66 (1954), 52 (1961). (See also Glenburn.)

Wittenbra (*Co. Baradine*) 31°02'S. 149°05'E., 10 km S. of Baradine; RS 1923–61.

Wittingham (*Co. Northumberland*) see Whittingham.

Wittitrin (*Co. Dudley*) 31°06'S. 152°39'E., 18 km W. of Kempsey, on Dungay Ck; farming; PO 1927–31; telephone 1925; TX 1956; pop. 58 (1933), 183 (2006), 308 (2011).

Woerden (*Co. Durham*) 32°33'S. 151°44'E., 17 km S. of Dungog, on Wolleroo Ck; PO 1929–31; school 1892–1934; telephone 1929; pop. 59 (1911).

Wogamia (*Co. St Vincent*) 34°53'S. 150°31'E., 9 km W. of Nowra, on Shoalhaven R.; flood 1870; pop. 56 (1911).

Wog Wog (*Co. St Vincent*) 35°17'S. 150°03'E., 29 km NE of Braidwood, on Wog Wog Ck; Muskgrove till 1894; bushfires 1926 and 1982.

Wolgan (*Co. Cook*) see Newnes.

Wollar (*Co. Phillip*) 32°22'S. 149°57'E., 40 km E. of Gulgong, on Wollar Ck; estab. 1867, village gaz. 1868; farming and grazing, oil shale disc. 1927 by Edmund Edward Mancq; Angl. C. 1876, enlarged 1895, new one (St Luke's) b. 1915 by Babbage Bros, d. by Harold Robert Hardwick, closed 2009, and graveyard (101 burials 1865+); butter factory (Wollar Dairy Co.) 1893; causeway across Wollar Ck; cemetery (252 graves 1875+) 1875; CH; fire 1960; flood 2010; PO 1874–1985; PS 1875, additions and repairs 1913 by William J. Kelman, new one b. 1936 by W.N. Horton, closed 1966; retort (Schultz) erected 1931 by Aust. Imperial Shale Oil Co.; Rom. Cath. C. 1873, new one (St Laurence O'Toole's) b. 1905 by John S. Nutt, d. by Harold Robert Hardwick, closed; school 1881, additions 1927 by A.H. Baglee; telephone 1900; TX 1927, automatic 1985; pop. 76 (1901), 162 (1911), 115 (1933), 132 (1947), 97 (1954), 61 (1961), 260 (2011).

Wollogorang (*Co. Argyle*) 34°53'S. 149°31'E., 23 km SW of Goulburn; quarry; pop. 33 (1933), 63 (1954), 54 (1961).

Wolloman (*Co. Bligh*) see Bulbudgeree.

Wollomba (*Co. Gloucester*) see Nabiac.

Wollombi (*Co. Northumberland*) 32°56'S. 151°09'E., 14 km W. of Paxton, on Wollombi Brook; soldiers' settlement *c.*1830, surveyed *c.*1832, laid out by Major Sir Thomas Livingstone Mitchell and village gaz. 1833, first lots sold 1838, thrived in 1860s, declined *c.*1911+; orig. timber, then wheat till 1863, tobacco, butter, beef, pigs, maize, barley, oats, potatoes, oranges, beans, wattle-bark, wine, now some farming and grazing, but mainly tourism; Angl. C. (St John the Evangelist) b. 1846–49 by Philip Galway, d. by Edmund Thomas Blacket, enlarged 1864 by Edward Miles and George Elliott, inundated 1867, and graveyard; bridges: Cuneens Bridge b. 1896 by A.J. and R.J. Keevers over Wollombi Brook and Gleghorns Bridge 1969 over Watagan Ck; cemetery (802 graves 1846+); CH 1841 (incl. lock-up), new one b. 1866 by T.H. Wright, d. by Mortimer William Lewis, jun., additions 1881 by R. Jurd, damaged 1923, closed 1950, restored and reused 1970; FB; floods 1856, 1857, 1867, 1893, 1949, 2007; flour mills: George Chapman 1845, modernised 1898 by Henry Simon, burnt down 1908 and Thomas Crothers 1856; gale 1923; PO 1839, new one b. 1892 by Elliot and Halliday; pound (stock) 1841; PS 1866 d. by Mortimer William Lewis, jun., closed, reused 1970, new one 1970; Rom. Cath. C. (St Michael the Archangel) b. 1840–43 by Maurice Callaghan, largely destroyed 1893, rebuilt 1894 on new site, d. by Frederick Burnhardt Menkens, sold 1991, restored 1993, and graveyard; sale-yards (J.A. Thompson) 1918; sawmills: Craft Bros and Richard Sweetman; school 1852, new one b. 1881, enlarged 1913 by James Ryan, closed 2014; telegraph 1860, new office b. 1892 by Elliot and Halliday; TX; Wes. Meth. C. 1845, destroyed 1867, new one 1869, and graveyard; wharf b. 1897 by W. Avery; wineries: Undercliff 1993, Wollombi Village

Vineyard estab. 1996 by Alan and Maria Roe, Wollombi Wines estab. 1994 by Hoft; pop. 76 (1846), 105 (1851), 176 (1856), 233 (1861), 222 (1871), 211 (1881), 177 (1891), 146 (1901), 406 (1911), 156 (1933), 97 (1947), 130 (1954), 151 (1961), *c.*150 (1987), 265 (2006).

Wollombi Road (*Co. Northumberland*) see Farley.

Wollomombi (*Co. Clarke*) 30°31'S. 152°03'E., 36 km E. of Armidale, on Wollomombi R.; estab. *c.*1881; sheep, cattle, oats; bridge (Allan timber truss) 1897, 182 ft (55.5 m), over Wollomombi R.; PO 1879, new one b. 1920 by Con McShane; Presb. C. (St John's) 1926; sawmill (W.A. Baker); telephone 1889; TX (automatic) 1967; pop. 54 (1901), 185 (1911), 141 (1933), 93 (1947), 214 (1954), 299 (1961), 147 (2006).

Wollondibby Valley (*Co. Wallace*) 36°27'S. 148°32'E., 9 km W. of Jindabyne; cemetery 1848; pop. 63 (1901).

Wollondilly (*Co. Argyle*) see Goulburn.

Wollondilly (*Co. Camden*) see Kareela.

Wollongbar (*Co. Rous*) 28°49'S. 153°24'E., 4 km NW of Alstonville; (incl. Brewers Hill); estab. 1870; farming and dairying; Angl. C. (St Paul's) b. 1878 by John Stephen Lumley, new one b. 1905 by J. Barron, d. by F. West, closed 1989, reused; butter factory (Spring Hill Co-op. Butter Co.) b. 1889 by Duncan for John Seccombe; caterpillar infestation 1896; Christ. Community C.; cyclonic storm 1940; electricity 1935; experiment farm (incl. creamery) 1894, additions 1901, damaged 1940, extensive rebuilding programme, renamed Wollongbar Agricultural Institute in 1990, dairy closed 2005, renamed Wollongbar Primary Industries Institute in 2008; FB; gale 1942; PO 1876; quarry; reservoir; school 1900, additions 1903, remodelled 1947, additions 1964, later relocated, new one 1995; TC 1981, additions 1991, became a campus of North Coast Institute in 1992, additions 1993, 1995, 2004; telephone 1906; TX (automatic) 1953; Union C. b. 1909 by A. Thorburn and Marshall, d. by Frederick Johnson Board, renovated 1955 and 1957, closed 1976, reused; water supply augmentation 1991; pop. 265 (1901), 318 (1911), 236 (1933), 162 (1947), 152 (1954), 223 (1961), 477 (1981), 707 (1986), 1,266 (1991), 1,858 (1996), 1,959 (2001), 1,846 (2006), 2,116 (2011).

Wollongong (*Co. Camden*) 34°25'S. 150°54'E., 67 km SW of Sydney, on Tasman Sea; (incl. Millbrook, North Wollongong, West Wollongong); explored 1797, unofficially settled 1815 by Charles Throsby, first land grants 1816, garrison estab. 1826 under Capt. Peter Bishop, officially settled 1829, surveyed 1829 by Edward James Howse Knapp, sen. and 1832–33 by William Romaine Govett and Phillip Elliott, laid out 1834 by Major Sir Thomas Livingstone Mitchell, town gaz. 1834, lots sold 1835, Illawarra Dist. Council 1843–50, munic. proc. 1859, town thrived 1880s–1890s, city proc. 1942, City of Greater Wollongong proc. 1947, migrants arrived 1947, city council in administration 2008–11; logging 1815–30, then cattle 1830+, dairying 1840s+, wheat till 1861, maize 1866–1908, potatoes till 1881, orchards 1886+, shipbuilding, major seaport till 1948, commercial centre; ambulance station b. 1912 by J.A. Waters, d. by John Alfred Ford, second one b. 1934 by Margeson Bros, also d. by Ford, third one 1969; Angl. C.: St John's (West Wollongong) 1906, damaged 1940, moved to Gwynneville, St Mark and St Michael's (b. 1840, reused, new one 1847 d. by Edmund Thomas Blacket, demolished 1859, replaced by St Michael's, b. 1859 by Patrick Lahiff, d. by Edmund Thomas Blacket), St Mark's (West Wollongong) 1943, replaced 1963, steeple removed 2018 and replaced 2019; Antiochian Orthodox C. (St Elias's); Apostolic C. (Gateway City), in former theatre b. 1957; Assemblies of God C.: Citylife and Lighthouse (in former clothing factory, renovated 2006 by Manteena Pty Ltd); Bapt. C. 1840, new one 1937, enlarged 1972, closed, sold 2013, new one 2013 on new site; bond store (Charles Throsby Smith); boot factory (F. Rowen); breakwater 1868, damaged 1895, 1896, 1903, new one 1968;

breakwater light b. 1872 by Joseph Mather, d. by Edward Orpen Moriarty, 42 ft (12.8 m), converted to acetylene 1916, later converted to electricity, closed 1974, restored 2000; breweries: Five Barrel (Phillip O'Shea) 2016, Mackie's 1839, George Young 1869; bridge (Ghosts Ck), defunct; carriage-works: Buckland & Co., William Dwyer (burnt down 1905, rebuilt, burnt down 1915), Exhibition Coach Factory (W.J. Wiseman), Illawarra Coach & Buggy Factory (G.W. Commens, joined in 1881 by J.R. M'Donald); cemetery (11,079 graves) 1867; CH b. 1835 by George Brown, (second) b. 1858 by William Stoddart, d. by Alexander Dawson, extended 1866, closed and reused 1885, repairs 1910 by F.W. Beaumont, repairs 1913 by Ernest Frederick Leggo, additions 1938, restored 1998–2002, (third) b. 1883–85 on new site by Wilson and Walker, d. by James Johnstone Barnet, clock tower 1890 d. by Walter Liberty Vernon, court-house extended 1951, additions 1967–69 by Hughes Bros, d. by Andrew Andersons, new wing 1992, renovated 2015; Christ. City C.; Christ. Revival Crusade C. (Lighthouse) 1970; Christ. Science C. 1954; Christ. Spiritualist C.; Church of Christ 1941, new one 1981 (in converted hall), expanded 1984; clothing factories: E. Bell, Berlei Ltd 1945, Crystal Clothing Industries Pty Ltd 1948, L.E. Isaacs Pty Ltd (b. 1945 by S. Boyle & Son, d. by A. Macintosh, reused), Richard Moore, Silknit Wollongong Pty Ltd 1943, R. Whitmont; coke-works: Federal Coke Co. Ltd (45 McLanahan ovens) 1901–71, Flagstaff Point (4 beehive ovens b. 1878 by William Ahearn and James Osborne, taken over 1879 by William M. Ashley who built 2 more ovens in 1885, closed 1890, demolished 1892), Mount Pleasant No. 1 (4 ovens estab. 1889 by Figtree and Robshaw, became Figtree & Sons, increased to 14 ovens by 1901, closed 1910, dismantled), Mount Pleasant No. 2 (40 McLanahan ovens estab. 1910 by Figtree & Sons, sold 1920 to Federal Coke Co., closed 1978); Cong. C. b. 1857 by James Orphin, d. by George Waring, vestry added 1860, gallery added 1865, church renovated 1882, restored 1988; convict stockade 1837; cordial factories: Louis Chandler 1881 (sold 1882 to Charles Robert Hill and Edward Barrett Gurdon), Crystal Fountain (estab. 1883 by James Parkinson, relocated twice, bought 1966 by Shelleys, closed 1978), Harrold and Harrold 1897 (sold 1905 to Albert William Hickman), Headly's, John Mellor, Railway Aerated Waters & Cordial Manufactory (estab. 1878 by William Osborne, acquired by J.T. Duhigg, became Illawarra Aerated & Cordial Co. in 1889), Sharpe Bros 1919, Wheeldon and Marks (acquired by H. Tribolet, bought 1951 by Parkinson); customs-house (in former court-house) 1885–1902; diphtheria 1910; droughts 1815, 1827, 1829, 1832; dust storm 1889; electricity 1921; FB 1870 (station burnt down 1902, new one b. 1915 by Frederick Lemm, d. by Alfred Spain, Thomas Frame Cosh and Robert Smith Dods, closed, sold 1963, new one 1962, major upgrades 1989, 1996, 2018); fibrous plaster works: R.C. Barbee, Lininite, Reginald Bradley Henry Wilton and Charles Thomas McCloy; fires 1895, 1906, 1924, 1925, 1927, 1928, 1930, 1950; floods 1833, 1834, 1918, 1998, 2017; flour mills: King's and Palmer's 1840, burnt down 1847; forts: Battery Park 1890, Flagstaff Point b. 1889–91 by James Russell & Co., gun removed 1937, closed, Smiths Hill 1893–1947, restored 1988; foundries: David Bros Pty Ltd (closed 1973), Hit or Miss, Lilleshall (William Davies) 1882, incl. engineering works, extended 1887 and enlarged 1900; Free Serbian Orthodox C. (St John the Baptist); gales 1895, 1896, 1903, 1909, 1911, 1936, 1951; gaol b. 1859 by McBeath and Bloomfield, additions 1861 also by Bloomfield, decl. a lock-up 1873, additions 1885 by Wilson and Walker, additions and repairs 1908 by T.J. Stead, repairs 1910 by H. Williams & Co., demolished 1920; gasworks: first works (Benjamin Fawcett) 1864, and new works b. 1883 by Montagu Coward for Wollongong Gaslight Co. Ltd, improvements 1929 by J.F. Thomson & Co., fire 1950; Greek Orthodox

C.: Holy Cross and St Nektarios Autocephalic; harbour basin b. 1837–44, d. by Capt. George Barney, Belmore Basin b. 1861–68 by Patrick Lahiff, d. by Edward Orpen Moriarty; hospital (Albert Memorial) b. 1864 by S. Chambers, d. by Joseph Backhouse, extensions 1889 by John Francis Tabrett and William P. Draper, d. by Harry Chambers Kent, closed and sold 1908, demolished, new one (Wollongong Dist.) b. 1907 on new site by W. Holloway, additions 1925, 1933, 1937, new building b. 1951 by F.C.W. Powell, additions 1964, 1967, 1991, 1994, additions 2003 by John Holland (Constructions) Pty Ltd, d. by McConnel Smith and Johnson, additions 2009 d. by D.W.P. Suters, additions 2013 by Edwards Constructions (NSW) Pty Ltd, additions 2014; ice works: South Coast Meat Co. Ltd, Streets Ice Cream Pty Ltd, Wollongong Ice Works; jetty 1856, replaced 1880 by J.K. Taylor, new one 1987; joinery (Rosemont Joinery Works, Charles Thomas); LDS (Mormon) C. 1964; lighthouses: Belmore Basin b. 1869–72 of iron by Young and Mather, 56 ft (17.1 m), d. by Edward Orpen Moriarty, converted 1883 to gas, converted 1921 to electricity, closed 1936, and Flagstaff Point b. 1937 of concrete, 83 ft (25.3 m), converted 1938 from acetylene to electricity; lime-works (South Coast Lime & Mortar Co.); Lutheran C.: St John's (Estonian) 1946, new one 1968, and St Peter's; Macedonian Orthodox C. (St Dimitrija Solunski), rebuilt 1997; marble works (Frederick W. Rose); Maronite Catholic C. (Our Lady of Lebanon); Meth. C. 1933, remodelling 1940 by J. Kennedy, d. by Norman Welland McPherson, new one 1959; military barracks b. 1830 by C. O'Brien, closed 1832, reused; mine (coal) 1849; monumental stone works (F.W. Rose); pilot station 1872; PO: Crown Street 1930, Millbrook 1963–92, West Wollongong 1925, Wollongong 1832 (new one b. 1870, additions 1882 by George Billings, d. by James Johnstone Barnet, closed 1892, reused, new one b. 1890–92 on new site by Isaac Banks and Enoch Whitehurst, extensions 1914, alterations and renovations 1918, renamed East Wollongong in 1968, restored 1988, closed 2000, sold and reused, new one, Wollongong, b. 1968 by A.F. Little Pty Ltd, closed 2001); police barracks (in former military barracks) 1832, new barracks b. 1899 by G.L. Thompson; pound (stock) 1865; Presb. C. 1839 d. by James Hume, tower, spire and porch added 1843, church closed, sold 1936 to Woolworths and demolished, replacement (St Andrew's) b. 1938 on new site by H.W. Thompson & Co., d. by Joseph Fearis Munnings; Prim. Meth. C. (Market Street) b. 1869 by John Brown, closed and sold, second one (Campbell Street) 1882, third one b. 1892 by Hudson, Howland and Money, and graveyard; PS b. 1889 by Birks, closed and reused, new one b. 1951–53 by R.L. Morris, additions and alterations 1973, new one 1992; railway coal stage 1922; railway turntable 1907 (William Sellers & Co.), 60 ft (18.3 m), replaced 1954, 75 ft (22.9 m); reservoir (concrete) 400,000 gal. (1,818.4 kl) 1902; rifle range 1911; Rom. Cath. C.: first one 1836, St Francis Xavier's (West Wollongong) b. 1840–49, additions 1878, renovations 1891, additions 1906 by Jones and Thorn, d. by James Nangle, additions 1922, extensions and renovations 1933 by T. Kiernan, alterations 1960 and 1985, renovations 2010, and 2 graves 1983 and 2013, incl. columbaria, St Therese, the Little Flower (West Wollongong) b. 1939 by H.A. Taylor, d. by Clement Glancey; RS: North Wollongong 1915 (station upgraded 2007 by Manteena Pty Ltd, d. by Caldis Cook Pty Ltd) and Wollongong 1887 (station b. by Alexander Hamilton Scouller, refreshment rooms 1890, station redeveloped 2002); salt-works (Courtney Puckey) 1895; Salv. Army C. 1905, new ones 1923 and 1955 (William McKenzie Memorial), extended 1980, sold 1995, new one o. 1996 in reused building on new site, additions 2012; schools: Lindsay Park 1959, additions 1965 and 2010, Smiths Hill HS 1944, additions 1966 and 1985, West

Wollongong 1925, new buildings 1928 and 1954, additions 1963, 1967, 2010, Wollongong 1851, new one 1885 d. by William Edmund Kemp, repairs 1892 by Frank Bevan, additions 1900 by H.A. Baglee, repairs 1906 by A. Harris, additions 1910 by J.A. Waters, new building b. 1913 and others remodelled by Ernest Frederick Leggo, additions 1923, new buildings b. 1925 by Kent and Kent, d. by Richard McDonald Seymour Wells, additions 2010 by Patterson Building Group Pty Ltd; SD Adventist C. 1941 d. by Royal Brandstater; Serbian Orthodox C. (St John the Baptist) 1976; sewerage 1929; shipyard estab. by John Cunningham; slipway 1856; Spiritualist C.; squalls 1891 and 1899; storms 1898 and 1952; streets gas lit 1883, then by electricity 1911–17, and 1921+; tannery (Robert Haworth); TC 1908, additions 1952, 1962, 1974, 1979, 1981, 1985, 1991, became Illawarra Institute of Technology in 1992, additions 1994; telegraph office b. 1865 by Stephen Evangelist Bloomfield, new one 1882 d. by James Johnstone Barnet, additions 1885 by Andrew Herd; telephone: Crown Street 1930, Millbrook 1963, West Wollongong 1924, Wollongong 1904; tramway (horse drawn) b. 1859–61, for Robson & Co., from Mount Keira colliery; TX 1905, automatic 1952; Ukrainian Catholic C. (St Volodymyr the Great) 1978; Union C. (Rosemont) b. 1919 by Gardner and Winley, used from 1926 by Angl. C., additions 1930; Unit. C.: Keiraview (West Wollongong) and Wesley (orig. Wes. Meth.) b. 1880–82 by George Osborne, d. by Robert Boyd, re-roofed 1902, additions and alterations 1930 by C.A. Bullivant, d. by Arthur Lanyon Clark; United Pentecostal C. (Bible); univ. (Wollongong, Innovation Campus) b. 2006–8 by Baulderstone Hornibrook Pty Ltd, new building 2009; watch-house b. 1889 by Thomas Birks; water reticulation 1901, extended 1911 by M'Donald Bros; Wes. Meth. C.: Keira Street 1842 and Crown Street 1855; pop. (figures since World War II relate to Greater Wollongong and include many places outside Wollongong itself and are therefore not comparable with earlier figures) 13 (1828), 831 (1841), 515 (1846), 501 (1851), 864 (1856), 1,397 (1861), 1,297 (1871), *c.*1,600 (1875), 1,635 (1881), *c.*2,500 (1887), 3,041 (1891), *c.*3,400 (1895), 3,545 (1901), 4,125 (1908), 4,725 (1911), 5,300 (1916), 6,708 (1921), 7,580 (1926), 10,800 (1931), 11,403 (1933), 12,660 (1936), *c.*19,000 (1939), 18,300 (1941), 17,080 (1946), 18,116 (1947), 21,331 (1954), 131,754 (1961), 162,153 (1966), 199,048 (1971), 200,141 (1976), 208,651 (1981), 206,803 (1986), 211,417 (1991), 219,761 (1996), 228,846 (2001), 234,482 (2006), 245,942 (2011). (See separate entries for surrounding suburbs.)

Wollongong (*Co. Camden*)
see also Gwynneville and Mount Ousley.

Wollongong South (*Co. Camden*)
see Coniston.

Wollongough (*Co. Gipps*) see Ungarie.

Wollumben (*Co. Rous*) see Kynnumboon.

Wollumbin (*Co. Rous*)
see Eungella and Murwillumbah.

Wollun (*Co. Sandon*) 30°50'S. 151°26'E., 22 km NW of Walcha, on St Helena Ck; farming and grazing; airfield; Angl. C. (St Martin's) 1923; PO 1914–77; RS 1883–1975; school 1893–1915 and 1957–64; TX 1916, automatic 1953; pop. 55 (1901), 89 (1911), 115 (1933), 92 (1947), 111 (1954), 90 (1961).

Wolonga Camp (*Co. Burnett*) 29°00'S. 150°27'E., 45 km S. of Boggabilla.

Wolseley Park (*Co. Selwyn*) 35°43'S. 147°53'E., 13 km NW of Tumbarumba; farming and grazing; cheese factory (Wolseley Park Co-op. Dairying Co. Ltd) b. 1906 by Otto Brown, closed 1915; PO 1910–56; RS 1927–68; telephone 1900; TX 1921; wool-scour (James Hudson); pop. 78 (1933), 111 (1947), 73 (1954), 53 (1961).

Wolseleys Gap (*Co. Selwyn*) 36°04'S. 148°14'E., 38 km SE of Tumbarumba; also known as Port Phillip.

Wolumla (*Co. Auckland*) 36°50'S. 149°49'E., 11 km NW of Merimbula; orig. also known as The Waterholes; mining (gold disc. 1896 by Christy Momsen) 1896–1930s, grazing, farming, dairying; Angl. C. 1888, demolished and replaced (St Luke's) 1925; bushfires 1909 and 1926; cemetery (3 km NW) 1874; CH (incl. lock-up) b. 1904 by Olaf Rye Lassen; cheese factory (Eureka) estab. by J.J. Smith; crematorium (Clavering Park Memorial Gardens); FB; gale 1898; hailstorms 1879 and 1925; mines: Black Ghost, Lammy's Farewell, Nancy Lee, Mount Momsen Gold & Silver Mining Syndicate 1897, man killed 1899, closed 1902 and 1913–20, New Venture 1911–15, North Pacific, Pacific 1903–15 and 1922–37, Wolumla; PO 1864, new one b. 1884; Presb. C. 1904; PS 1883, new one b. 1903 by J. Burnett; quarry; reservoir; Rom. Cath. C. (All Saints') 1890; sawmill: A.B. Grealey 1921, and Smith Bros and White; school (Three Mile Waterhole till 1900) 1882, new one b. 1883 by L.N. Bouquet, closed and reused 1912, new school b. 1912 by Olaf Rye Lassen, additions 2009; scarlet fever 1882; tannery (Pitt, Walsh & Co.) 1883; telegraph 1883; TX 1915; water supply 1952; pop. 352 (1881), 511 (1891), 441 (1901), 450 (1911), 273 (1921), 176 (1933), 131 (1947), 166 (1954), 155 (1961), 269 (1991), 310 (1996), 363 (2001), 366 (2011).

Wolumla (*Co. Auckland*) see also Kanoona.

Wolumla North (*Co. Auckland*) see Kanoona.

Wolumla South (*Co. Auckland*) 36°49'S. 149°46'E., 15 km NW of Merimbula; farming and dairying; butter factory (South Wolumla Creamery Co. Ltd) o. 1893 in Cochrane's old butter factory, relocated to new factory on new site, became South Wolumla Co-op. Creamery Co. Ltd in 1927, new factory 1930; cemetery (1 km E.); hailstorm 1925; PO 1904, burnt down 1927; school 1866, new one b. 1910 by A. Wright, closed 1960; telephone 1914; TX 1926; Union C. 1873; pop. 116 (1933), 131 (1947), 92 (1954), 75 (1961).

Wombah (*Co. Clarence*) see Woombah.

Wombat (*Co. Harden*) 34°26'S. 148°15'E., 13 km SW of Young, on Wombat Ck; orig. Wamback; village gaz. 1870; goldmining, wheat, sheep, orchards; Angl. C. (St Matthew's) b. 1874 by William Sharp, d. by Alberto Dias Soares; cemetery (205 graves 1881+) 1877; FB; mines: Barnes Reef, Demondrille Creek, New Chum, Wombat Creek; PO 1862–91; pound (stock) 1881; Presb. C. 1904; PS b. 1863 by John Leeder and David Van Iderstein, new one b. 1910 by A. Allen, closed 1934; rifle range 1917; Rom. Cath. C. (St Columbanus's) 1875, additions 1921; scarlet fever 1917; school 1870; telephone 1908; TX 1911, automatic 1972; Wes. Meth. C. 1870; pop. 235 (1871), 319 (1881), 329 (1891), 392 (1901), *c.*430 (1903), 516 (1911), 260 (1933), 204 (1947), 236 (1954), 175 (1961), *c.*150 (1987), 247 (2011).

Wombateeni Brush (*Co. Macquarie*) 31°49'S. 152°17'E., 11 km NW of Wingham, on Beitibombi Ck.

Wombeyan Caves (*Co. Westmoreland*) 34°19'S. 149°58'E., 39 km NW of Berrima, on Wombeyan Ck; grazing and tourism (caves disc. 1828 by John Joseph William Molesworth Oxley, first explored 1842 by Denning, o. to tourists 1865, lit by electricity 1928); fire 1934; PO 1927–78; telephone 1909; TX 1916; pop. 56 (1901), 73 (1911), 70 (1933), 65 (1947), 72 (1954), 263 (2011).

Wombiana (*Co. Bathurst*) 33°30'S. 149°15'E., 3 km N. of Blayney; RS 1903–66.

Womboota (*Co. Cadell*) 35°54'S. 144°36'E., 28 km NW of Moama; village gaz. 1880; farming and grazing; PO 1899–1979; Rom. Cath. C. (St Paul's) 1929; school (Wamboota till 1914) 1880, repairs 1896 by Freeman and Rofe, additions 1915 by W. Moore & Sons, closed 1973; telephone 1907; TX 1907, automatic 1974; winery (Old School Winery & Meadery); pop. 240 (1911), 221 (1933), 196 (1947), 172 (1954), 135 (1961), 341 (2006).

Womboota East (*Co. Cadell*) 35°55'S. 144°40'E., 22 km NW of Moama; village gaz. 1928; RS (Victorian railway).

Wombo Sawmill (*Co. Baradine*) 30°30'S. 148°46'E., 57 km NW of Baradine.

Wombramurra (*Co. Parry*) 31°31'S. 151°04'E., 35 km NE of Murrurundi.

Womelguy (*Co. Durham*) see Woolooma.

Womleroi (*Co. Hunter*) 32°33'S. 151°02'E., 12

km W. of Singleton, on Wollombi Brook.

Wommara (*Co. Northumberland*) see Belmont North.

Wonboyn Lake (*Co. Auckland*) 37°15'S. 149°55'E., 20 km S. of Eden, on Wonboyn Lake; Moomaga till 1926; oysters; cemetery; PO 1925–77; telephone 1926; TX 1945, automatic 1971; pop. 72 (1991), 85 (1996), 86 (2001).

Wonboyn North (*Co. Auckland*) 37°14'S. 149°55'E., 18 km S. of Eden, on Wonboyn R.

Wondabyne (*Co. Northumberland*) 33°30'S. 151°16'E., 6 km W. of Woy Woy, on Mullet Ck; (incl. Cogra Bay, subdivided 1911); bushfire 2006; PO 1927, burnt down 1928; quarry (Gosford Quarries Pty Ltd) 1922; railway bridge (7 Baltimore truss spans), 2,912 ft (887.6 m), b. 1886–89 by S.V. Ryland and E.K. Morse for Union Bridge Co., Buffalo, New York, USA, strengthened 1926–31, dismantled, replacement (4 Pratt trusses, 2 K-trusses and 2 shore spans) b. 1939–46, 2,764 ft (842.5 m), d. by Albert Cecil Fewtrell and Keith King, over Hawkesbury R.; railway tunnels: Mullet Ck (484 yds or 442.9 m) and Woy Woy b. 1884–87 by George Blunt (1,957 yds or 1,789.4 m); RS (Mullet Creek Junction till 1890, then Hawkesbury Cabin till 1891) 1889, station relocated 1910, 1918, 1939; wharf.

Wondalga (*Co. Wynyard*) 35°25'S. 148°07'E., 13 km N. of Batlow, on Adelong Ck; Middle Adelong till 1908; village gaz. 1863 as Middle Adelong, town gaz. 1864; goldmining and grazing; Angl. C. (St Alban's) 1910; bridge (Carter's Bridge) b. 1876 by Boston Bros, 35 ft (10.7 m); bushfire 1940; FB 1959; PO 1901–71; sawmill (estab. by Austin & Co., bought by Watson, burnt down 1879); school 1875–84, 1898–1922, 1945–60; snow 1865; telephone 1910; TX 1925, automatic 1968; pop. 122 (1901), 82 (1911), 71 (1933), 90 (1947), 56 (1961), 283 (2011).

Wonga (*Co. Urana*) 34°55'S. 145°33'E., 51 km N. of Jerilderie.

Wongabi (*Co. Fitzroy*) 29°58'S. 153°01'E., 20 km NW of Arrawarra, on Sherwood Ck; telephone 1925.

Wongabinda (*Co. Courallie*) 29°23'S. 150°04'E., 24 km E. of Moree; RS (2 km NW) 1932–75.

Wongagong (*Co. Forbes*) see Wongajong.

Wonga Hut (*Co. Clarke*) 30°06'S. 152°08'E., 47 km E. of Guyra.

Wongajong (*Co. Forbes*) 33°25'S. 148°02'E., 4 km SE of Forbes, on Lachlan R.; formerly Wongagong; bushfires 1880 and 1906; school 1882, closed 1884, new one b. 1896 by Charles Weaver, new one b. 1902 by Mitchell and Dodd, closed 1965; silo; pop. 109 (1911).

Wongalea (*Co. Ashburnham*) 33°04'S. 147°57'E., 22 km W. of Parkes; farming; school 1918–70, sold 1971, moved to Parkes; telephone 1915; TX 1915–26; pop. 41 (1933), 67 (1954).

Wongarbon (*Co. Lincoln*) 32°20'S. 148°45'E., 17 km SE of Dubbo; Murrumbidgerie till 1908; wheat and wool; Angl. C. (All Saints') 1906; brick-kiln (Alf Smith); cemetery (42 graves 1895–2005) 1889; dust storm 1938; FB; fire 1932; PO 1877; PS 1926; reservoir; rifle range 1915; Rom. Cath. C. (St Joseph's) b. 1902 by G. Heaney, closed, sold and reused; RS (Murrumbidgerie till 1908) 1881, station b. by James Stuart Douglas, closed 1975; sale-yards 1910; sawmill (Alwyn Armstrong); school (Murrumbidgerie till 1908) 1887, new one b. 1911 by Devitt Bros, additions 1994; telegraph 1890; telephone 1911; TX (automatic) 1949; Unit. C. (orig. Meth.), closed, sold 2011, reused; water supply augmentation 2000; pop. 251 (1901), 457 (1911), 299 (1933), 260 (1947), 243 (1954), 225 (1961), 271 (1981), 292 (1986), 308 (1991), 392 (1996), 352 (2001), 449 (2006), 525 (2011).

Wongavale (*Co. Rous*) 28°42'S. 153°09'E., 14 km SW of Nimbin, on Leycester Ck; Boveedy till 1925; sawmill (B. Muldoon); school (Chelmsford till 1925) 1916–64; telephone 1923; TX 1923; pop. 40 (1933), 107 (1947), 122 (1954), 64 (1961).

Wongawilli (*Co. Camden*) 34°29'S. 150°46'E., 4 km NW of Dapto, on Robins Ck; (incl. Horsley, subdivided 1954+, and Huntley);

coalmining, dairying, farming; bushfire 1939; cheese factory (John Lindsay); coalmine estab. 1907 by Alexander Lang, sold 1916 to G. & C. Hoskins Ltd and named Wongawilli Colliery, powerhouse 1917, strike 1918, colliery closed 1918–20, acquired 1928 by BHP, strikes 1935, 1937, 1942, 1945, became Nebo Colliery in 1946, washery closed and demolished 1948, renamed Elouera Colliery in 1993, operated by BHP Billiton Illawarra Coal till 2005 when it was redeveloped as Dendrobium Colliery by Dendrobium Coal Pty Ltd, sold 2007 to Gujarat NRE FCGL Ltd and renamed Wongawilli Colliery; coke-works (20 rectangular beehive ovens b. 1917 by G. & C. Hoskins Ltd, closed 1918–20, acquired 1920 by Hoskins Iron & Steel Co. Ltd, another 60 ovens b. 1924, taken over 1928 by Aust. Iron & Steel Ltd, man killed 1936, closed 1945, demolished); FB; quarry; PO, closed 1978; railway (Aust. Iron & Steel Ltd); RS 1916–60; schools: Dapto 1852 (reopened 1875, new one b. 1877, new one b. 1928 on new site by Carden Bros, additions 1958 and 1968, removed 2004 from Dapto) and Wongawilli 1928–76; telephone 1943; pop. 168 (1947), 151 (1954), 213 (1961).

Wongo Creek (*Co. Darling*) 30°42'S. 150°31'E., 21 km W. of Manilla, on Wongo Ck; school 1886–96; pop. 105 (1911), 104 (1933), 99 (1947), 138 (1954).

Wongoni (*Co. Lincoln*) 31°52'S. 149°17'E., 19 km NW of Dunedoo; RS 1917, station b. by John Allibone, closed 1967; pop. 22 (1933).

Wongwibinda (*Co. Clarke*) 30°18'S. 152°10'E., 49 km E. of Guyra, on Kangaroo Ck; airfield (3 km NE); rifle range 1910; school 1957–2009, sold; pop. 28 (1933), 108 (1947), 115 (1954).

Wongy (*Co. Gowen*) 31°17'S. 148°42'E., 23 km E. of Gulargambone, on Baronne Ck; school 1884–89.

Wonnaminta (*Co. Mootwingee*) 30°38'S. 142°18'E., 144 km NW of Wilcannia; pop. 31 (1933).

Woodberry (*Co. Northumberland*) 32°47'S. 151°41'E., 7 km SW of Raymond Terrace, on Woodberry Swamp; schools: Francis Greenway HS 1966, additions by R.T. Parker Pty Ltd, and Woodberry 1972 d. by John Rabong, additions 2010; window frame factory (Beresfield Aluminium); pop. 31 (1933), 52 (1947), 69 (1954), 62 (1961), 3,155 (2011).

Woodburn (*Co. Denison*) see Trefoil Park.

Woodburn (*Co. Richmond*) 29°04'S. 153°21'E., 10 km NW of Evans Head, on Richmond R.; South Woodburn till 1935; settled 1863 by William Cravigan, estab. 1868 by William Gollan, village gaz. 1869, thrived 1882; timber, shipbuilding 1847+, sugar-cane 1871+, dairying, agric., cattle, sand mining; ambulance station; Angl. C. 1912 d. by J.G. Popplewell and J. Sykes, new one 1948 d. by Louis Reginald Williams, new one (St Alban's) 1961, closed, reused 2010; brewery (Arthur Pedley) 1887; bridge (concrete) b. 1981 by Transbridge Contractors, over Richmond R.; bushfire 1952; butter factory (Excelsior, estab. by O.H. and A.J.B. Gollan, inundated 1893, cheese factory added 1909) 1889–1916; cemetery (531 graves 1873+) 1873; CH (incl. lock-up) b. 1885 by Wheeler and Brown, additions 1888; cordial factory (J.J. Devney) 1912, acquired by L.G. Olive, burnt down 1929; creamery (Woodburn Co-op. Creamery Butter Co. Ltd) 1898; FB; floods 1870, 1892, 1893, 1948, 1954, 1967, 1980, 2001, 2008; hailstorms 1886, 1907, 1945 (damaged most buildings), 1951; ice works; Meth. C. 1903, new one 1962 (removed from Empire Vale); mineral sand separation plant estab. 1956 by Rusan Minerals Pty Ltd; PO 1883, inundated 1892, damaged 1945; Presb. C. 1869, new one 1889; PS 1876, new one b. 1885 by Wheeler and Brown, additions 1899, damaged 1945; punt b. 1884 by T. West, to cross Richmond R., sunk 1893; 4 quarries; rifle range; Rom. Cath. C. d. and b. 1904 by R. Tyler, enlarged, new one 1925, destroyed 1945, replacement (All Saints') b. 1953 by Frank Eastoe, d. by James Starkey; Salv. Army C. 1926; sawmills: James Butler (taken over 1909 by Malcolm M'Donald, J. Morgan and J. Casey, jun.), W. Gray 1928, Sly Bros (burnt down 1942); school 1876, new one b. 1881 by G. Finlay, new buildings 1949, 1954, 1959, 1966; sewerage 1971; storms 1891, 1938, 2012; sugar mills: Albert (William Gollan, sen.) 1882, inundated 1893, McLaren Bros (horse powered) 1871, Meston and King 1876 (damaged 1893, closed 1905), Woodford & Co. 1874; telegraph 1883; telephone 1905; trees planted in streets 1935; TX 1910, automatic 1969; water supply 1963; wharves: one b. 1882 by R. Fenwick and one b. 1903 for Davis Bros; pop. 842 (1891), 585 (1901), 853 (1911), 135 (1933), 654 (1947), 781 (1954), 510 (1961), 530 (1966), 697 (1971), 610 (1976), 647 (1981), 602 (1986), 592 (1991), 607 (1996), 612 (2001), 618 (2006), 633 (2011).

Woodburn (*Co. Rous*) see Woodburn North.

Woodburn (*Co. St Vincent*) 35°22'S. 150°22'E., 8 km SW of Milton; Meth. C.; school 1866–67; pop. 76 (1947).

Woodburn North (*Co. Rous*) 29°04'S. 153°21'E., opposite Woodburn, on Richmond R.; Woodburn till 1935; lots sold 1881; dairying; FB; PO 1868–1961; telegraph 1879; water supply 1964; wharf b. 1882 by R. Fenwick, demolished 1932; pop. 218 (1933), 201 (1947), 159 (1954), 165 (1961), 100 (2006).

Woodburn South (*Co. Richmond*) see Woodburn.

Woodenbong (*Co. Buller*) 28°23'S. 152°37'E., 46 km NW of Kyogle, on Tooloom Ck; subdivided and first lots sold 1907; dairying, timber, cattle, potatoes, maize; Angl. C. (St Margaret of Scotland) 1941, and columbarium; cemetery (209 graves), incl. columbarium; cheese factory (Prescott Ltd) 1919; electricity 1958; FB; PO 1905; Presb. C. (Gateway) 1935; PS (incl. lock-up) b. 1888 by Dunsmore and Walton; reservoir; Rom. Cath. C. (Sacred Heart) 1947, and graveyard; sawmills: Harold Duke 1929 (bought 1933 by Lance Sly Pty Ltd, relocated 1942, converted 1958 from steam to electricity, sold 1968 to Ford Timbers Pty Ltd), W.J. Graham & Son, W.B. Standing Sawmilling Co.; school 1924, additions 1960 and 1966, new one b. 1977; telephone 1911; TX 1920, automatic 1961; water supply 1968; pop. 147 (1911), 362 (1933), 515 (1947), 559 (1954), 469 (1961), 395 (1971), 380 (1976), 409 (1981), 392 (1986), 349 (1991), 377 (1996), 326 (2001), 333 (2006), 310 (2011)

Woodend (*Co. Mitchell*) 35°24'S. 146°56'E., 18 km NW of Henty; Lutheran C. (St Peter's) 1952; school 1935–68.

Woodfield (*Co. Murray*) see Amungula.

Woodford (*Co. Cook*) 33°44'S. 150°29'E., 3 km SE of Hazelbrook, on Garnet Ck; Twenty Mile Hollow 1814–56, then Buss's; settled by William James; Angl. C. (St Paul's) 1919 d. by T.O. Thomas; Buddhist C. (Bo Moon Sa); bushfires 1909, 1928, 1938, 1944 (22 houses destroyed), 1978, 2001; convict stockade (Bull's camp) 1835–44; FB 1948; lock-up b. 1855 by Thomas Boland; Meth. C. 1906, closed and reused; PO 1896, closed; Presb. C. (Pioneer Memorial) 1965; quarry; reservoir 1928, modified 1948, 59 ft (18 m) high; RS (Buss's Platform till 1871) 1868, (second one on new site) 1877, (third one on new site) 1880, (fourth) 1902; school (Haddon Hall) Jan.-Dec. 1951; Society of Friends (Quakers) C.; TX 1916–57; Unit. C. (orig. Meth.) b. 1911 by G. and T. Hastings, d. by Alfred Gambier Newman, closed, sold 2009, reused; water supply 1940, augmentation 1966; pop. 996 (1891), 53 (1901), 158 (1911), 295 (1921), 234 (1933), 331 (1947), 394 (1954), 472 (1961), 392 (1964), 460 (1966), 762 (1976), 1,470 (1986), 1,842 (2011).

Woodford (*Co. Northumberland*) see Thornton.

Woodford Dale (*Co. Clarence*) 29°32'S. 153°07'E., 11 km SW of Maclean, on Clarence R.; farming and dairying; electricity 1931; flood 1890; fruit case mill; PO 1905–71; Presb. C., re-roofed and renovated 1897; school 1867, additions and repairs 1888 by Dugald Macdonald, new building b. 1911 by William Herd, closed 1933, reopened 1957, closed 2012, sold 2014 to Vicki Munro; telephone 1906; wharf b. 1896 by John Walsh; pop. 121 (1901), 91 (1933), 117 (1947), 86 (1954), 80 (1961).

Woodford Leigh (*Co. Clarence*) 29°29'S.

153°08'E., 7 km SW of Maclean, on Clarence R.; sugar-cane, maize, vegetables, then pigs and dairying; cyclone (man killed) 1904; flood 1890; gale 1914; hailstorm 1894; PO 1882–1971; school 1869, new buildings b. 1881 by Hermann Schaeffer, inundated 1890, repairs 1915 by J. Baneroft and T.G. Castles, closed 1956; storm 1953; sugar mill (Dyraaba) b. 1881 for J.A. M'Aulay and J. M'Leod, sold 1893 to Buss; telephone 1910; TX 1916, automatic 1959; wharf; pop. 115 (1901), 178 (1933), 164 (1947), 141 (1954), 129 (1961), 254 (2006).

Woodglen (*Co. Wellesley*) 36°59'S. 148°52'E., 34 km W. of Bombala; school 1954–76.

Woodhill (*Co. Camden*) 34°43'S. 150°41'E., 6 km N. of Berry; farming; butter factory (Woodhill Co-op. Dairy Co. Ltd) b. 1901 by A. Johnston, closed 1913; cemetery; FB; Meth. C. 1919; PO 1885–1971; sawmill (George Saunders); school 1896–1907; TX 1924–71; Wes. Meth. C. 1870; pop. 58 (1911).

Woodhouselee (*Co. Argyle*) 34°34'S. 149°38'E., 19 km SE of Crookwell, on Pejar Ck; orig. farming, later grazing; Angl. C. (St James's) b. 1883 by John Campbell and Dalton, d. by Thomas Wilson Parrott, restored 1932, closed, sold 2013; PO 1862–1968; 2 quarries; railway bridge (timber truss) 1902, over Pejar Ck; RS 1902–75; school 1879–1942; storm (man killed) 1901; telephone 1907; TX 1908; pop. *c.*30 (1866), 202 (1901), 122 (1911), 92 (1933), 65 (1947), 55 (1954).

Woodlands (*Co. Brisbane*) see Sparkes Creek.

Woodlands (*Co. Camden*) 34°26'S. 150°22'E., 6 km NW of Bowral, on Nattai Ck; quarry.

Woodlands (*Co. Canbelego*) 31°26'S. 147°00'E., 24 km NW of Nyngan.

Woodlands (*Co. Clive*) 29°00'S. 152°05'E., 10 km NE of Tenterfield.

Woodlands (*Co. Flinders*) 32°25'S. 147°08'E., 74 km N. of Condobolin.

Woodlands (*Co. Narromine*) 32°14'S. 148°19'E., 7 km E. of Narromine.

Woodlands (*Co. St Vincent*) 35°48'S. 150°11'E., 5 km W. of Malua Bay.

Woodlands (*Co. Windeyer*) 33°17'S. 141°53'E., 92 km N. of Wentworth.

Woodlands (*Co. Yanda*) 30°29'S. 145°14'E., 81 km SW of Bourke.

Woodlawn (*Co. Rous*) 28°47'S. 153°19'E., 5 km NE of Lismore, on Wilsons Ck; farming and dairying; PO 1927–42; RS 1894, station b. by Alexander Hamilton Scouller, closed 1974; school 1881 b. by G. Crawford, closed 1894, reopened 1904, closed 1912; pop. 56 (1933).

Woodleigh (*Co. Rous*) 28°38'S. 152°58'E., 3 km W. of Kyogle, on Richmond R.; sawmill.

Woodonga (*Co. Monteagle*) 34°17'S. 148°21'E., 6 km NE of Young; creamery (Young Butter & Dairy Products Co-op. Factory Co. Ltd) 1894; Unit. C. (orig. Meth.) 1918, closed, sold 2007 and 2018, reused; Wes. Meth. C. 1898 (former Angl. C. removed from Monteagle).

Woodonga (*Co. Monteagle*) see also Shirrenden Hill.

Woodport (*Co. Northumberland*) see Erina.

Woodrising (*Co. Northumberland*) see Booragul.

Woods Flat (*Co. Bathurst*) 33°47'S. 148°53'E., 18 km E. of Cowra, on Waugoola Ck; estab. 1868, declined *c.*1885; mining (gold disc. 1868) 1868–76, 1880–83, 1932–37; drought 1877; pop. 21 (1933).

Woodside (*Co. Clive*) 29°08'S. 151°50'E., 20 km SW of Tenterfield; pop. 50 (1947).

Woodside (*Co. Macquarie*) 31°54'S. 152°12'E., 16 km W. of Wingham, on Manning R.; farming and grazing; PO 1867–1916; sugar mill (Joseph Andrews) 1869, burnt down 1871; telephone 1891; TX; Union C. 1866, defunct; pop. 110 (1911), 42 (1933).

Woodside (*Co. Urana*) 35°09'S. 145°40'E., 24 km N. of Jerilderie.

Woods Reef (*Co. Darling*) 30°23'S. 150°45'E., 13 km E. of Barraba, on Nangahrah Ck; mining (asbestos 1919–23 and 1972–83, chromite 1911, copper, gold) and grazing; Angl. C. (St John's) 1923; cemetery 1897; mine (open-cut) and mill (Chrysotile Corp. of Aust.) 1972–83, derelict; PO 1861–68 and 1895–1961; Presb. C.; school 1897–99, reopened 1912, additions 1914 by William Acheson, closed 1965, building moved to Barraba; stamper battery;

telephone 1913; pop. *c.*120 (1866), 96 (1911), 176 (1933), 278 (2006).

Woodstock (*Co. Bathurst*) 33°45'S. 148°51'E., 18 km NE of Cowra, on Noyeau Hollow; surveyed and first lots sold 1890; copper mining, sheep, pigs, linseed, peas, agric.; Angl. C. (St Matthew's) b. 1904 by Albert Emanuel Ennis, d. by John Job Copeman, and columbarium; bore (119 ft or 36.3 m) 1917; cemetery 1889; dam (Noyeau); FB 1932; Meth. C. b. 1903 by Henry Hugh Suttor Francis, d. by John Job Copeman, vestry added 1927, chancel b. 1937 by F.J. Reynolds, d. by Norman Welland McPherson, church closed; mines: Belmore or Mount Jack or Webbs 1867, Burly Jack 1877–1911, Woods Flat 1868–76, 1880–83, 1932–37; PO 1888, new one b. 1911 by John Baker, repairs 1940 by W.G. Thomas; PS 1895, new one b. 1910 by J.J. Wells, new one 1970 d. by Margaret Watson; quarry; reservoir 1955; rifle range; Rom. Cath. C. (Sacred Heart) 1892, renamed St Brigid's, additions 1907, demolished, replacement 1956 d. by E.R. Green & Sons; RS 1888, station b. by Charles Palmer and William Lewis, closed, restored 1990; school (Waugoola till 1893, then Noyeau till 1907) 1879, new buildings b. 1892 by Atkins and Cunningham, additions 1910 by W.J. Bailey; silo 1931; telegraph 1889; TX 1910; water reticulation 1956; pop. 133 (1891), 433 (1901), 908 (1911), 690 (1933), 521 (1947), 466 (1954), 381 (1961), 358 (1971), 283 (1976), 266 (1981), 263 (1986), 287 (1991), 262 (1996), 249 (2001), 263 (2006), 276 (2011).

Woodstock (*Co. Camden*) see Jamberoo.

Woodstock (*Co. St Vincent*) 35°20'S. 150°25'E., 3 km SW of Milton; cheese factory (Ulludulla Refrigerating Butter Co.) b. 1909 by Nicholas Mudge, jun., rebuilt 1927, closed 1942, sold 1946 to Cynthia and Ruby Warden, acquired 1979 by Country Women's Assoc., bought by Jack Wallace, sold to Bloomfield, sold 2000 to Michael and Jane Crowle, renovated and reused 2001–3; Cong. graveyard (48 burials, 15 graves) 1875–1915.

Woodton (*Co. Buckland*) 31°38'S. 150°51'E., 15 km N. of Murrurundi.

Woodview (*Co. Richmond*) 28°52'S. 152°57'E., 9 km W. of Casino; dairying; creamery (NSW Creamery Butter Co.); FB; PO 1924–72; quarry; school (Wooroowoolgan till 1916) 1913–75; telephone 1911; TX 1924; pop. 98 (1911), 135 (1933), 98 (1947), 109 (1954), 103 (1961), 247 (2011).

Woodville (*Co. Camden*) see Burragorang.

Woodville (*Co. Durham*) 32°41'S. 151°37'E., 8 km NE of Maitland, on Paterson R.; (incl. Iona); estab. in 1850s; farming, poultry, dairying; Angl. C. (All Saints') 1864, restoration 1922, additions 1925, closed, sold 2003, 2007, 2008; bridge (sliding opening span) b. 1865 by Francis Bell, repairs 1875 by W.S. Congdor, demolished, replacement (Dunmore Bridge) b. 1899 by Samuel McGill, overhead braced Allan timber trusses (lift span now inoperative, replaced 2003), 428 ft (130.5 m), over Paterson R.; floods 1874, 1875, 1893, 1895, 1949, 1955, 2015; PO 1864; poultry processing plant (Steggles Poultry Ltd); punt till 1863; schools: Iona 1853, new one b. 1879 by Pritchard, new one b. 1946, additions 2010 and Woodville 1850–51; telephone 1890; toll-gate b. 1867 by John Paton; Wes. Meth. C. 1878; pop. 339 (1901), 366 (1911), 397 (1933), 269 (1947), 276 (1954), 222 (1961), 553 (2006), 604 (2011).

Woodville (*Co. Nicholson*) 33°49'S. 145°49'E., 45 km SE of Hillston.

Woodville (*Co. Northumberland*) see Hamilton.

Woodville (*Co. Sandon*) 30°39'S. 151°32'E., 2 km SE of Uralla; pop. 117 (1947), 123 (1954).

Woody Head (*Co. Clarence*) 29°22'S. 153°22'E., 4 km N. of Iluka, on Coral Sea; reservoir (30,000 gal. or 136.4 kl) 1973; water reticulation 1973; pop. 30 (1961).

Woogoolga (*Co. Fitzroy*) see Woolgoolga.

Woolabra (*Co. Jamison*) see Bellata.

Woolaman (*Co. Bligh*) see Wuuluman.

Woola Woola (*Co. Macquarie*) see Kolodong.

Woolbrook (*Co. Inglis*) 30°58'S. 151°21'E., 24 km W. of Walcha, on Macdonald R.; Macdonald River till 1891; sheep; airfield;

bridge b. 1914 by J.A. Jackson, new one 2014, over Macdonald R.; cemetery (140 burials) 1902; electricity 1955; FB; PO 1889–1990; Presb. C. b. 1928 by Pickles and Smith, d. by Frederick James Bishop; rabbit freezing works (Woolbrook Freezing Co. Ltd) 1916, taken over by Garratt Scandrett Freezing Companies Ltd, acquired 1927 by Amalgamated Rabbit & Skin Export Co. Ltd; railway bridge (lattice girder) fabricated by J.O. and C.E. Brettell, Worcester, England, erected 1882 by A. and R. Amos and J.S. Bennett, d. by Sir John Fowler and John Whitton, over Macdonald R.; RS (Macdonald River till 1891) 1882–1985, station demolished 1987; sawmill (Macdonald River Timber Co.); school (Railway Crossing till 1881, then Maluerindi till 1900) 1880, additions 2010; TX *c.*1947; Union C. 1897; pop. 59 (1901), 225 (1911), 331 (1933), 225 (1947), 275 (1954), 298 (1961), 221 (2006), 248 (2011).

Woolenget (*Co. Jamison*) 30°05'S. 149°48'E., 27 km N. of Narrabri, on Middle Gully; RS (Edgeroi Wool Siding till 1904) 1901–51.

Wooleybah (*Co. Baradine*) 30°46'S. 148°48'E., 43 km NE of Coonamble; formerly Dead Man's Waterhole; sawmill (Colin and Mervyn Head) 1992; school 1955–67; pop. 67 (1954).

Woolgarlo (*Co. Harden*) 34°54'S. 148°42'E., 17 km W. of Yass, on Lake Burrinjuck; mining (copper, silver, lead); flood 1870; furnaces (copper); lime-kiln; mines: Bunyip, Dickson's, Emma Belle, Good Hope (Scottish Aust. Mining Co.) 1859–62, 1875, 1896, 1904, 1908, 1968, Sime and Armstrong *c.*1900, Wheal Maria, Wheal Matilda, Woolgarlo or Emma Jane (Woolgarlo Lead Mining Co.) 1867 and 1915–18; PO 1870–72; stamper battery (10 head); pop. *c.*90 (1870), 22 (1933), 56 (1947).

Woolgoolga (*Co. Fitzroy*) 30°07'S. 153°12'E., 22 km N. of Coffs Harbour, on Tasman Sea; settled 1880 by Thomas Small, surveyed 1885 by James Ogle Burgess, village gaz. 1888 as Woogoolga, first lots sold 1890, more sold 1893, regazetted 1966 as Woolgoolga, bypassed by highway 2013; orig. timber, sugar-cane, maize, then bananas 1930+, vegetables, mineral sand mining, blueberries; ambulance station o. 1967 (in rented premises, new one 1972; Angl. C. (St Augustine's) 1900, vestry added 1911 by R. Wells, church demolished and replaced 1973; Assemblies of God C. (All Nations) o. 2010 in former Presb. C., became Lifehouse C. in 2015; bridges: one b. 1958 over Woolgoolga Ck and one b. 1959 over Poundyard Ck; bushfires 1946, 1951, 1968 (3 died); butter factory (Woolgoolga Co-op. Dairying & Refrigerating Co. Ltd) 1922; case mills: Arthur Cavey (gutted 1951), Herb Clouten (taken over by Sid Moller and later Parbury Henty & Co. Pty Ltd), Clarrie Gray, Hoys', Freddie Morgan, Harold Turner; cemeteries: general (630 graves 1904+) 1888 and lawn (340 plots), incl. columbarium; 2 FB (incl. station b. 1977); foot-bridge over Woolgoolga Ck; gales 1894, 1914, 1937, 1950, 1952; ice works (Woolgoolga Co-op. Dairying & Refrigerating Co. Ltd); jetties: public jetty b. 1890–92 by Kerr and Cronin, 1,561 ft (475.8 m), crane erected 1892 by J.S. Rodgers & Sons, jetty repairs 1896 and 1904, crane erected 1908 by E.W. Fitzgerald, tram loop laid 1910 by D. McNaughton, jetty closed and steam loading cranes removed 1952, demolished 1952–61, and inclined plane (William Toft Pullen) 1883; measles epidemic 1946; Meth. C. b. 1906 by M. Auld, d. by W.M. Shaw, damaged 1955, relocated; PO 1884, new ones 1898, 1975, 1997; Presb. C. (St Stephen's) 1965–77, sold 1979, reused 1980, new one b. 1992 on new site, closed, reused 2010; PS b. 1891 by John A. Rowsell, renovations 1911, repairs 1919 by Frank Bolton, alterations and renovations 1931 by H.J. Little, new one 1994; reservoirs: 100,000 gal. (454.6 kl), 1966, and 1,000,000 gal. (4,546 kl), 1966; Rom. Cath. C. (St Francis Xavier's) 1968 d. by J.L. Toomey, alterations 1987; sawmills: British Aust. Timber Co. (incl. steam tramway) 1907, Great Northern Timber Co. (incl. steam tramway) 1915, Johnson Bros, George William Nicoll (acquired 1905 by North Coast Steam Navigation Co. Ltd),

E.D. Pike & Co. Ltd, William Toft Pullen 1884, Saxton & Sons, Smith & Ellis Pty Ltd, Allen Taylor & Co. Ltd (burnt down 1955), Harry Turner; schools: primary 1889 b. by Taylor and Baker, new one b. 1908 by Charles Benaud Smith, repairs 1919 by Bull and Perring, additions 1956, 1961, 1970, additions 1976 by E.E. Lahey Constructions Pty Ltd, additions 1980, HS 1981 d. by Chris Johnson; shipwreck (The Buster) 1893; sewerage augmentation 1975; signal station 1887; Sikh C. 1968, second one (New Guru Nanak Sikh Gurudwara) 1970 d. by Trevor James Reddacliff; sugar mill (William Toft Pullen) 1884–93; telegraph 1890; telephone 1896; TX 1915, automatic 1950; Unit. C. (orig. Meth.) 1957; water reticulation 1967, augmentation 1980; whooping cough epidemic 1941; pop. 246 (1892), 75 (1901), 406 (1911), 514 (1933), 915 (1947), 1,304 (1954), 1,109 (1961), 1,199 (1966), 1,311 (1971), 1,601 (1976), 2,081 (1981), 2,346 (1986), 3,660 (1991), 3,772 (1996), 3,795 (2001), 4,356 (2006), 4,718 (2011).

Wooli (*Co. Clarence*) 29°52'S. 153°16'E., 23 km N. of Arrawarra, on Wooli Wooli R.; village gaz. 1923; fishing and oysters; Angl. C. (St Margaret's), removed from Ulmarra; FB; ice works (C.W. King), bought 1948 by Clarence River Fishermen's Co-op. Ltd; 4 jetties; PO 1943; PS; reservoir; school 1945; telephone 1925; TX 1937, automatic 1973; water reticulation 1966, augmentation 1996; pop. 231 (1947), 173 (1954), 160 (1961), 253 (1971), 345 (1976), 457 (1981), 463 (1986), 524 (1991), 573 (1996), 561 (2001), 502 (2006), 493 (2011).

Woollamia (*Co. St Vincent*) 35°01'S. 150°39'E., 2 km NW of Huskisson, on Currumbene Ck; farming; wharf 1988; pop. 53 (1947), 64 (1954), 68 (1961), 404 (2011).

Woolla Woolla (*Co. Macquarie*) see Kolodong.

Woolli (*Co. Clarence*) see Yamba.

Woolners Arm (*Co. Rous*) 28°42'S. 152°51'E., 18 km SW of Kyogle, on Woolners Arm Ck; farming; PO 1927–61; school 1930–74; pop. 156 (1933), 113 (1947), 88 (1954), 81 (1961).

Wooloban (*Co. Parry*) 31°21'S. 151°16'E., 39 km SE of Kootingal; school 1888–1905.

Woolomin (*Co. Parry*) 31°18'S. 151°09'E., 31 km SE of Tamworth, on Peel R.; estab. 1858, town gaz. 1860; tobacco *c.*1926, grazing, lucerne, potatoes, dairying, fruit, fossicking, fishing; Angl. C. b. 1900 by Tom Smith, new one (St Mary's) 1934; bridge 1926, destroyed 1955; cemetery; FB; floods 1910, 1911, 1955, 1971, 2000; milk factory (Peel Valley Milk) estab. by Peter Rose; PO 1889–1974; sawmill (Carl J. Butten); school 1885, sold, replacement b. 1890 by James White and George Alderman, closed 1892, reopened 1899, new one b. 1907 by Thomas Moran, additions 2010; snow 1949 and 1984; telephone 1903; TX 1926, automatic 1971; Union C. b. 1905 by George Hannaford; pop. 104 (1901), 146 (1911), 226 (1933), 145 (1947), 157 (1954), 108 (1961), 308 (2011).

Woolomol (*Co. Inglis*)
see Hallsville and Tamworth.

Woolooma (*Co. Durham*) 32°00'S. 151°14'E., 34 km E. of Scone, on Stewarts Brook; mining (gold disc. in 1890s) and grazing; PO 1917–74; sawmill (Ted Bromley) 1946, burnt down 1962; school (Womelguy till 1920) 1916–22 and 1957–74; telephone 1915; TX 1916; pop. 73 (1933), 79 (1947), 69 (1954), 83 (1961).

Wooloweyah (*Co. Clarence*) 29°29'S. 153°21'E., 5 km S. of Yamba, on Wooloweyah Lagoon; FB; pop. 342 (1991), 414 (1996), 420 (2001), 436 (2006), 410 (2011).

Woolport (*Co. Clarence*) see Grafton.

Woolshed Flat (*Co. Wallace*) 36°21'S. 148°42'E., 11 km NE of Jindabyne, on Ironpot Ck.

Woomargama (*Co. Goulburn*) 35°50'S. 147°15'E., 14 km SW of Holbrook, on Mountain Ck; village gaz. 1869, bypassed by highway 2011; agric. (mainly wheat) and grazing; Angl. C. (St Mark's) 1888, extensions and restoration 1923, additions 1936; bushfire 1873; cemetery 1880; FB; PO 1875; Presb. C. (St Andrew's) b. 1888 by P.H. Stewart & Son, destroyed 1935; Rom. Cath. C. 1887; sawmill (Edward Schultz); school 1873–1997, reused; storm 1935; telephone 1896; TX 1917, automatic 1956; pop. 44 (1881), 65 (1901), 217

(1911), 155 (1933), 136 (1947), 148 (1954), 149 (1961), 214 (2011).

Woombah (*Co. Clarence*) 29°22'S. 153°17'E., 9 km NW of Iluka, on Clarence R. (North Arm); formerly Jinabiby, also known as Wombah; village gaz. 1883; farming and fishing; bridge to Goodwood Island, over Clarence R. (North Arm); cemetery 1884; FB; PO 1927–31; reservoirs: 50,000 gal. (227.3 kl), 1967 and 10,000 gal. (45.5 kl), 1973; school (Wombah) 1876–1953; sugar mills: J. Bale 1871, Kempnich's, J. Schaefer; telephone 1916; water reticulation 1973; pop. 107 (1881), 260 (1901), 129 (1911), 54 (1933), 738 (2006), 745 (2011).

Woongarrah (*Co. Northumberland*) see Charmhaven.

Woonona (*Co. Camden*) 34°21'S. 150°55'E., 3 km N. of Corrimal, on Tasman Sea; (incl. Belnona, East Woonona, Russell Vale, Woonona Heights); estab. 1857, subdivided 1889; timber, fruit, dairying, farming, coalmining; Angl. C. (St Paul's) b. 1926 by S.B. Anderson, d. by John Burcham Clamp and Clifford Horace Finch; Bapt. C. 1908; brickworks: Illawarra Fireclay & Brick Co. 1909 and Pendlebury & Son 1901 (these two firms merged in 1946); bridge (Jeffreys Bridge) b. 1898 by W. Clarke, over Collins Ck; catamaran factory (Seawind Group Holdings Pty Ltd), upgraded 2008; cemetery (Bulli, *c.*3,500 burials, graves 1869+); coke-works (Belnona), 115 rectangular beehive ovens b. 1901 by BHP, taken over 1915 by Associated Smelters' Co., closed and abandoned 1935, demolished; colliery (Blackball) 1905–8 and 1920–23; cordial factories: Ball Bros (acquired 1922 by E.H. Holmes Ltd), Hedley & Co. 1916–35, Lockett Bros (bought 1935 by J. Parkinson Ltd), J. Pallier 1902; creamery (Woronora Creamery Co.) 1894; fire 1906; Meth. C. b. 1909 by G.H. Waters; mines rescue station (Southern); PO: East Woonona 1953 (in rented premises), Russell Vale 1963, Woonona 1859 (new one b. 1903 by E. Fraser); Presb. C. 1864, new one b. 1871 by P. Gavine, replacement b. 1916 by G. Haberley, and graveyard (razed); PS; quarry (clay); RS 1919; Salv. Army C. 1960, new one 1978; sawmill (Molloy & Sons), burnt down 1906; schools: East Woonona 1964, additions 2010, Russell Vale 1954 b. by Hodge and Norman, additions 1961, Woonona 1882, new one b. 1885, additions 1890, alterations 1910 by J. Myles & Co., demolished and replaced 1928, additions 1914–23 and 1964, Woonona HS 1964, additions 1972 and 1976; telephone: East Woonona 1953, Russell Vale 1963, Woonona 1891; toll-gate 1871–81; Unit. C.; Wes. Meth. C. 1868, new one 1885; pop. 1,226 (1891), 1,758 (1901), 2,456 (1911), 2,920 (1921), 3,289 (1933), 4,093 (1947), 5,700 (1954), 6,254 (1961), 12,960 (2011).

Woonona Heights (*Co. Camden*) see Woonona.

Wooram (*Co. Richmond*) see Tatham.

Wooroowoolgan (*Co. Richmond*) 28°51'S. 153°00'E.; 7 km W. of Casino; cheese factory estab. 1889 by G. Neville Griffiths, leased 1897 to NSW Creamery Butter Co. Ltd; school (The Bend) 1904–54; pop. 108 (1911), 27 (1933), 69 (1947), 281 (1991), 283 (1996), 355 (2001), 451 (2006), 590 (2011).

Wooroowoolgan (*Co. Richmond*) see also Woodview.

Wootton (*Co. Gloucester*) 32°18'S. 152°18'E., 16 km NE of Bulahdelah, on Coolongolook R.; timber and dairying; Angl. C. (St Mary the Virgin) 1927–96, sold 1996 and reused; 4 bridges (incl. one b. 1959) over Coolongolook R.; FB; flood 2016; PO 1913–77; sawmill; school 1917, additions 1941 by Richards and Maybury, closed 1978, reused; telephone 1915; tramway (timber); TX 1923, automatic 1975; winery (Great Lakes) 1990; pop. 67 (1911), 251 (1933), 267 (1947), 197 (1954), 174 (1961), 218 (2011).

Wooyung (*Co. Rous*) 28°27'S. 153°32'E., 8 km S. of Pottsville, on Crabbes Ck; formerly known as Newhaven; thrived 1917; sugar-cane; school 1920–24 and 1957–74.

Woram (*Co. Richmond*) 28°55'S. 153°07'E., 9 km SE of Casino, on Shannon Brook; boiling-down works estab. 1847 by Edward

Hamilton and Alfred Denison; flood 1870; pop. 86 (1901).

Worgela (*Co. King*) see Wargeila.

Worragee (*Co. St Vincent*) see Nowra.

Worrigee (*Co. St Vincent*) see Nowra.

Worrowing Heights (*Co. St Vincent*) 35°05'S. 150°38'E., 3 km N. of Sanctury Point.

Wowagin (*Co. Argyle*) see Strathaird.

Wowagin (*Co. Georgiana*) 34°25'S. 149°42'E., 22 km E. of Crookwell, on Wowagin Ck; farming and grazing; PO 1883–93 and 1927–31; sawmill (Andrew J. Toole); telephone 1931; TX 1938; pop. 56 (1901), 69 (1911).

Wowingragon (*Co. Forbes*) 33°26'S. 147°55'E., 10 km SW of Forbes; PO 1881–82; school 1899–1941, building moved to Gunning Gap; pop. 88 (1911), 27 (1933).

Woy Woy (*Co. Northumberland*) 33°29'S. 151°20'E., 7 km S. of Gosford, on Woy Woy Inlet; (incl. South Woy Woy); formerly known as Sandy Point, Cox's Flat and Webb's Flat; settled by Samuel Coulter, estab. by James Paul Gee Cox II, subdivided and first lots sold 1903, subdivided again 1904, thrived 1906, further subdivided 1912 (Cox Estate); orig. shell digging, lime burning and timber, oysters 1884+, then popular summer fishing and boating holiday location 1891+, clothing; abattoir (F.C. Nicholls Wholesale Meat Pty Ltd), closed 2003, reused 2011 by Margins Mushrooms; airfield (World War II); Angl. C. 1904, reused, new one (St Luke's) 1970; bridge to Koolewong, 265 ft (80.8 m), b. 1941 by D. and H. Woodward, replacement (concrete) 1985, over Woy Woy Inlet; bushfires 1909, 1918, 1928; CH 1973; cordial factory (Hubert Charles Margin), also made ice and ice-cream; electricity (from Newcastle) 1929; Evangelical C. (Peninsula); FB: Umina (station b. 2001) and Woy Woy 1934 (station b. 1935, reused, new one 1989); fire 1928; flood 1927; foot-bridge (Spike Milligan Bridge) 2008, to Koolewong, d. by Jim Alexander, 279 ft (85 m), over Woy Woy Inlet; gale 1910; hospital 1971, additions 2013; Jehovah's Witnesses C.; Meth. C. d. and b. 1937 by Hawley; PO: South Woy Woy 1927 and Woy Woy 1884, new one b. 1911 by H.J. Piper, new one b. 1922, demolished and replaced 1976; Presb. C. (St David's) b. 1908–10, renovated 1963; PS (in rented premises) 1883–88, new one b. 1947 by C. Davis & Sons Pty Ltd, additions 1970; quarry (Basalt Quarries Ltd) 1927–29; railway bridge to Koolewong (3 steel spans on concrete piers) over Woy Woy Inlet; railway tunnel b. 1884–86 by George Blunt, 1,957 yds (1,789.4 m), accident (killed 4 men) 1940; Rom. Cath. C. b. 1914 by Dengate & Son, d. by Buchanan and McKay, closed and reused, new one (St John the Baptist) b. 2007 by Kingston Building Aust. Pty Ltd, d. by Randall Lindstrom; RS 1889; sawmill (S. Davis); schools: Brisbane Water Secondary College (Woy Woy HS till 2001) 1962 (extended 1965, 1970, 1973, 1975, 1979, 1988, major upgrade 1990), Railway Camp 1884–88, South Woy Woy 1964 (in leased premises), new school 1966, additions 1968, 1970, 1977, Woy Woy (Blackwall till 1912) 1894, new buildings b. 1922 by F. Packenham & Son, additions 1955 by F.P. Butt; SD Adventist C.; sewage works (South Woy Woy); sewerage augmentation 1982 and 1984; slipper factory (C.P. and R. Nielsen), reused 1957 by Osti Knitting Industries Pty Ltd; telegraph 1906; telephone (South Woy Woy) 1925; TX 1910, automatic 1968; water supply augmentation 1964; wharves: Brick b. 1885 by Rock Davis, Brick Wharf Road b. 1899 by George Lawson, Commercial, Fishermen's, Pier Street, public, Rawson Road; pop. 126 (1901), 660 (1911), 1,059 (1933), 1,710 (1947), 7,396 (1954), 9,982 (2006), 10,114 (2011).

Woy Woy Bay (*Co. Northumberland*) 33°29'S. 151°18'E., 1 km W. of Woy Woy, on Woy Woy Bay; (incl. Horsfield Bay, and Phegans Bay formerly Burrawong Bay); bridge (Bulls Hill Bridge) b. by George Frost and Gordon Beattie, over Woy Woy Ck; bushfires 1994 and 2006; electricity (from Newcastle) 1929; FB (Phegans Bay); PO: Phegans Bay 1927 and Woy Woy Bay 1917–74; quarry (Bulls Hill); telephone: Phegans Bay 1920 and Woy Woy Bay 1916; water reticulation 1979; 2 wharves; pop. 109 (1933), 160 (1947), 150 (1954), 229

(1961), 432 (2011).

Wright's (*Co. Wellesley*) see Tombong.

Wrights Beach (*Co. St Vincent*) 35°07'S. 150°40'E., 2 km SE of Erowal Bay, on St Georges Basin; subdivision (Federation) planned by Henry F. Halloran & Co., but never developed.

Wrights Creek (*Co. Northumberland*) 33°19'S. 151°00'E., 37 km W. of Ourimbah, on Wrights Ck; pop. 29 (1933).

Wrightville (*Co. Robinson*) 31°32'S. 145°52'E., 5 km SE of Cobar; village gaz. 1895; copper mining; Angl. C. b. 1910 by H. Davies and Ratcliffe; brick-kiln (Gudgeon and Clifton) 1899; Meth. C. 1904; PO 1897, fire 1901, closed 1958; PS 1900–22; Rom. Cath. C., closed; RS 1901–31; school 1897, new one b. 1904 by E.P. Frost & Co., closed 1924; stamper battery (100 head); telephone 1931; typhoid (man died) 1897; pop. *c.*1,200 (1904), 1,385 (1911), 60 (1933), 203 (1947).

Wubbera (*Co. Courallie*) 29°33'S. 150°09'E., 31 km E. of Moree; RS (Pallamallawa till 1909) 1902, station closed and removed 1972.

Wumbulgal (*Co. Cooper*) 34°22'S. 146°13'E., 17 km SE of Griffith; container terminal (Western Riverina) 2015; RS 1922, closed; school 1955, additions 1968, closed 1971, bought by Ron and Betty Carlon, moved 1972 to Griffith and reused; pop. 56 (1933).

Wunba (*Co. Wynyard*) see Wybalena.

Wunglebung (*Co. Drake*) 29°13'S. 152°15'E., 29 km SE of Tenterfield, on Timbarra R.; mining (molybdenite-wolfram-bismuth).

Wunnamurra (*Co. Urana*) 35°25'S. 145°42'E., 7 km S. of Jerilderie; RS 1896–1951.

Wunnamurra South (*Co. Urana*) 35°26'S. 145°42'E., 9 km S. of Jerilderie; quarry; RS 1923–62.

Wuuluman (*Co. Bligh*) 32°32'S. 149°05'E., 15 km E. of Wellington, on Wuuluman Ck; Woolaman till 1882 then Alma till 1889; mining (gold and silver), farming, sheep; mines: Federal (Wuuluman Gold Reefs NL, acquired by Federal Gold & Silver Mining Co. NL) 1902, 1905–13, 1925, 1933, 1936–39, Kelly's Perseverance or Welcome Mick (Mt Boppy Co. and Perseverance Mining Co. NL) 1920–21 and 1926–27; PO 1882–1940; Presb. C. 1905; Rom. Cath. C. (St Joseph's) b. 1906 by W.A. Daw, closed, sold and reused; pop. 99 (1901), 107 (1911), 95 (1933), 61 (1961).

Wyagdon (*Co. Roxburgh*) see Wiagdon.

Wyaldra (*Co. Bligh*) see Birriwa.

Wyaldra (*Co. Phillip*) 32°20'S. 149°34'E., 5 km NE of Gulgong, on Wialdra Ck; village gaz. 1879; school (Broadfield 1911–17) 1882–83 and 1893–1927; pop. 158 (1911).

Wyalong (*Co. Bland*) 33°56'S. 147°14'E., 3 km E. of West Wyalong; orig. The Township; surveyed 1894 by J. Richmond, town gaz. 1894, munic. proc. 1899; goldmining 1894–1920, wheat, hay; Angl. C. 1896, enlarged 1897, moved to Yalgogrin 1919, replacement (All Saints') b. 1919 by John Stephenson, d. by Ernest Rees Laver; brewery (estab. by Alphonso Tewksbury and James Bellair) 1894–1901; brickworks (Marshall Bros) 1893; cemetery (burials 1894+) 1895; CH 1894, new one b. 1899 by Albert Brown, d. by Walter Liberty Vernon, repairs 1919 by C.M. Daniel, closed, reused 2011; Chinese joss house; cordial factory (George Craig); 2 cyanide plants (incl. Duncan and Channon); dust storms 1914 and 1915; electricity 1937; fires 1897, 1903, 1908, 1913; foundry (Frisken and Atkinson) estab. 1901 by David Balfour Frisken, closed 1904; gale 1904; hospital 1895, new wing 1901, closed 1934; lock-up b. 1897 by Kidney and Corfield, d. by Walter Liberty Vernon, additions 1899 by William Charles Hanson, also d. by Vernon, additions 1922 d. by George McRae; metallurgical works (Sully's); mines: Called Back 1895–96, Klink's 1894 and 1916, Klondyke (owned by Tyler 1896–1909) 1894–1914, Pine Hill *c.*1898, Pine Ridge (Leathery) 1895–1900, Pioneer 1894–1900, Santa Claus 1894 and 1916, Summergill's 1895–1900; PO 1894, new one b. 1896 by Charles Baker, burnt down 1899, replacement b. 1899–1901 by S. Corfield, d. by Walter Liberty Vernon, reused, replaced; PS 1894, new one b. 1897, closed and reused; Rom. Cath. C. (St Patrick's) 1896;

RS: Central Wyalong (Wyalong till 1908) 1903, closed, and South Wyalong 1908–75; sawmills: Neil Bland, R.J. King, Pioneer Steam Saw & Planing Mills (Clarke & Sons); scarlet fever 1896; school 1894 b. by James Finney, additions by W. Hanson; sewerage augmentation 1987; stamper batteries: James Channon, Duncan, Noyes & Co., Neeld & Son (15 head) 1899; telegraph 1894; typhoid 1894 and 1895 (man died); water supply 1929; Wes. Meth. C. 1894, replaced 1898; whooping cough epidemics 1899 and 1900; pop. 1,515 (1901), 3,301 (1911), 964 (1933), *c.*850 (1941), 524 (1947), 604 (1954), 578 (1961), 540 (2011).

Wyalong (*Co. Bland*)
see also Barmedman and Wyalong West.

Wyalong West (*Co. Gipps*) 33°55'S. 147°12'E., 65 km NW of Temora; Main Camp and The Camp till 1895; estab. 1894 by Joseph Neeld et al., surveyed 1895 by J. Richmond, laid out 1895 by V.F. Tozer; orig. mining (gold disc. 1893 by Fred, Joseph G., Harry C., George W. and Ernest A. Neeld, gold rush 1894, production peaked 1899) 1894–1921, then wheat, sheep, cattle, hay, pigs, eucalyptus oil 1907+, manufacturing; airport 1949; ambulance station b. 1951 by Les Carr; Angl. C. 1901, enlarged 1909, new one (St Barnabas's) b. 1938 by Wallace and McGee, d. by Louis Reginald Williams, tower added 1960; Assemblies of God C. (Generocity, formerly Kings Christ.); brickworks (Herridge's); cemetery 1896; CH b. 1908 by C. Hansen, new one 1993; Chinese joss house; 2 chlorination plants (incl. Sully's); Christ. Revival Crusade C.; cordial factories: H.J. Ausburn and Goldfields Aerated Water & Cordial Works (B. Coan, bought 1904 by William Graff, new factory 1906); 7 cyanide plants (incl. Plumb and Channon 1896, Speirs & Sons, John Stephenson, Sully's, D. West 1899); dust storms 1915 and 1923; earth tremor 2014; electricity 1920; eucalyptus oil distilleries: Beckett and Skidmore, Dallon Doone Eucalyptus Co., Matthews & Co.; FB (station b. 1924 by Lowther and Horrocks); fibrous plaster works (Charles A. Stephenson); fires 1896, 1907, 1909, 1912; flour mill (F. Crago & Sons Pty Ltd) b. 1912 by Henry Simon Aust. Ltd, burnt down 1914, rebuilt, burnt down again 1943, reopened 1945 by J.J. Duff; hospital b. 1933–35 by N.R. Morris, additions 1977; ice works (E.A. Moore), taken over 1934 by Gordon Butler; Jehovah's Witnesses C.; lock-up; Lutheran C. (Immanuel) 1968; miners' strike 1908; mines: Ante-up, Balaclava 1895–96, Bantam and Lady Grace Amalgamated, Barrier 1894–1916, Brick Kiln (owned by Nelson and Suthern 1911–1914), Christmas Gift, Coronation, Crampton's, Crawley's, Currajong 1894–1916, Daisy, Dawson's, Dead Rabbit or Easter Gift 1895–97, Early Morn, Erin's Isle, Fletcher's, Gatlan's, Harry's Find, Hill Top 1894–1916, Homeward Bound, Junction, Keep it Dark (formerly Golden Fleece, closed 1920), Iron Bark, Irwin's Blow, Keen's, Lady Hampden, Lady Mary 1895–96, Lighthouse, Lucknow (Bolte's), Maiee, Mallee Bull 1893–1920, Miner's Right 1895–1900, Molloy's, Mouse Trap 1894–1916, Napoleon, Neeld's No. 1 (taken over 1917 by J. Channon), Perry's 1894–1916, Perseverance, Prince of Wales, Princess, Prospector's, Red Flag, Rothacker's, Shamrock and Thistle (P. Conway), Stanley's Blow 1895–1900, Star of Peace, True Blue (estab. 1894 by James Cusack and John Jones, taken over 1917 by J. Channon, closed 1920), Victoria, Waratah, Welcome Stranger, Western 1894–1916, While Reef, Young Australia; PO o. 1876 as Wyalong (moved 8 km away to Ada Reef in 1882 and renamed Barmedman), replacement b. 1894 by Henry Hardy, new one b. 1900 by S. Corfield, alterations 1927; POW control centre 1944; powerhouse b. 1920 by William Charles Hanson; Presb. C. 1899, new one (Pioneer Memorial) b. 1938 by Frank Mitchell, d. by John Reid & Son; PS b. 1906 by G.E. Fraser, additions and renovations 1934 by W.G. Butler, renovations 1953 by C. Clancy; railway coal stage; railway engine shed, removed 1985; railway turntable, replaced 1938; 2 reservoirs (incl. one b.

1937); rifle range b. 1902 by T. McDermott, fire 1907; Rom. Cath. C. 1894, new one 1912, replacement (St Mary's) b. 1929 by John Dunton, d. by William Patrick Conolly; RS (West Wyalong) 1917, closed; sale-yards b. 1928 by T.G. Taylor; Salv. Army C. 1916, new one 2001; sausage casing factory (A.R. Clark); sawmills: William Charles Hanson, burnt down 1917 and S. McFadzean; schools: primary 1894 b. by C. Hardy & Co., additions 1895 by Edward Mills, additions 1897 by I. McMullen, additions 1899 by Robertson and Anderson, additions 1924 by John Stephenson, additions 1933 by R. Lockhart, additions 1959, 1972, 1978, and HS 1963, additions 1972 and 1985; sewerage 1938, augmentation 1987; silo 1922; soap-works (Janitzky and Fraser) 1902; stamper batteries: Ashcroft's, Cox's, Gough's (25 head), Government (5 head), Plumb and Channon 1894, Auguste Nicolas and Joseph Bernard Reymond (35 head), Speir's, West's (10 head); TC (a campus of Riverina Institute), additions by New England Constructions Pty Ltd; telegraph 1894; TX 1900, new one b. 1955 by Sommer and Libner; typhoid 1900; Unit. C. (orig. Meth.) b. 1911 by William Charles Hanson, d. by Alfred Gambier Newman, additions 1926, renovated 1958; vulcanising works (E.J. Wood) 1926; water supply 1929, augmentation 1969; Wes. Meth. C. 1896; pop. 1,696 (1901), 2,460 (1933), 2,520 (1947), 2,490 (1954), 2,399 (1961), 3,534 (1976), 3,778 (1981), 3,700 (1986), 3,458 (1991), 3,419 (1996), 3,331 (2001), 3,191 (2006), 2,643 (2011).

Wyan (*Co. Richmond*) 29°04'S. 152°52'E., 28 km SW of Casino, on Busbys Ck; settled by T.E. Smith; dairying; Angl. C. (St Aidan's) 1898, enlarged 1904 by R. Hayes; cemetery (graves 1875–1957); PO 1955–60; school (Wyan Hogarth till *c.*1920) 1907–23 and 1957–84; telephone 1915; TX 1929; pop. 112 (1911), 130 (1933), 110 (1947), 88 (1954), 54 (1961).

Wyan Creek (*Co. Richmond*) 29°08'S. 152°47'E., 40 km SW of Casino; sawmill (J.S. and J.C. Bennett) 1943, fire 1945; school 1957–58.

Wyanga (*Co. Narromine*) 32°28'S. 148°08'E., 27 km S. of Narromine; farming and grazing; PO 1915–72; RS (Washington till 1911) 1910, station b. by T.E. Quiggin, closed 1974; silo 1929; telephone 1917; TX 1928, automatic 1967; pop. 96 (1933), 68 (1961).

Wyangala (*Co. Bathurst*) 33°58'S. 148°57'E., 28 km SE of Cowra, on Wyangala Dam; estab. 1929; Angl. C. (St Barnabas's) 1930; bridge b. 2014 by John Holland (Constructions) Pty Ltd, over Lachlan R.; dam b. 1928–35, 272 ft (83 m) high, enlarged 1961–71, on Lachlan R.; FB; PO 1929; power station (hydro-electric) 1947, new one 1992; PS 1929, new one 1963–69; Rom. Cath. C. 1929, demolished, replacement (St Vincent's) 1954; school (Wyangala Dam) 1930; telephone 1911; TX 1930; pop. 932 (1933), 116 (1947), 91 (1954), 140 (1961), 227 (2011).

Wyangala Dam (*Co. Bathurst*) see Wyangala.

Wyangerie (*Co. Rous*)
see Kilgra and Wiangaree.

Wyangle (*Co. Buccleuch*) 35°13'S. 148°18'E., 12 km NE of Tumut; gold; pop. 63 (1911), 60 (1961).

Wyan Hogarth (*Co. Richmond*) see Wyan.

Wybalena (*Co. Wynyard*) 35°30'S. 148°10'E., 3 km N. of Batlow; RS (Wunba till 1924) 1923–75.

Wybong (*Co. Brisbane*) 32°16'S. 150°38'E., 15 km N. of Denman, on Wybong Ck; dairying, agric., grazing, wine; Angl. C. (St Mark's) 1873; bridge (Allan timber truss) 1924, 209 ft (63.7 m); cemetery; grasshopper infestation 1871; PO 1873–1968; quarry; Rom. Cath. C. (St Thomas Aquinas's) 1919, closed and dilapidated; sawmill (Hogan's); school (Wybong Creek) 1880, new building b. 1883 by E. Cowan, closed 1889; telephone 1907; TX 1916; winery (Dalwood Estate) 1967; pop. 238 (1901), 300 (1911), 250 (1933), 164 (1947), 166 (1954), 157 (1961), 456 (2006).

Wybong Creek (*Co. Brisbane*) see Wybong.

Wybung (*Co. Northumberland*)
see Frazer Park.

Wyee (*Co. Northumberland*) 33°11'S. 151°29'E., 8 km S. of Morisset, on Mannering Ck; (incl. Kiar and Wyee Point, formerly Ramsgate); town gaz. 1891; farming and citrus orchards; bridge over Wyee Ck; cemeteries: Bethshan (435 graves 1920+), incl. columbaria, and general (96 graves 1910+) 1892; Community C. (Bethshan); dam; 2 FB; foot-bridge over Mannering Ck; marina; PO 1890; railway dam 1913; RS (Norahville till 1888) 1887, station b. by G.R. and F.H. Harrison, relocated 1896; sawmills: Alexander Melville and James Robert Summerhayes, and Wakefield's; schools: Hue Hue 1893–1912 and Wyee 1886, buildings removed and re-erected 1893 on new site by H.J. Taylor, additions 1895, new building b. 1912 by Cock, additions 1936, 1968, 2010; SD Adventist C.; TX 1916; Union C. b. 1908 by Wood; 2 wharves; pop. 179 (1901), 496 (1911), 249 (1933), 287 (1947), 397 (1954), 447 (1961), 259 (1971), 433 (1976), 526 (1981), 525 (1986), 1,330 (1991), 1,760 (1996), 1,861 (2001), 2,325 (2006), 2,665 (2011).

Wyee Bay (*Co. Northumberland*) 33°09'S. 151°31'E., 2 km NW of Mannering Park, on Lake Macquarie.

Wyee Point (*Co. Northumberland*) see Wyee.

Wyembah (*Co. Raleigh*) 30°33'S. 152°43'E., 17 km NW of Bowraville, on Kalang R.; telephone 1924.

Wygelmar (*Co. Phillip*) 32°29'S. 150°05'E., 43 km SW of Merriwa; telephone 1915.

Wylie Creek (*Co. Buller*) 28°32'S. 152°09'E., 57 km N. of Tenterfield, on Wylie Ck; tin (alluvial), grazing, dairying; airfield; cemetery; cheese factory (Tenterfield Dairy Co.); PO 1911–72; TX 1923; pop. 98 (1911), 83 (1933), 59 (1947).

Wylies Flat (*Co. Durham*) 32°35'S. 151°07'E., 6 km W. of Singleton, on Hunter R.; agric.; school 1853–59; pop. 22 (1933).

Wymah (*Co. Goulburn*) 36°02'S. 147°17'E., 34 km E. of Albury, on Murray R.; Wagra till 1912; mining (wolfram), farming, grazing; Angl. C. (St Clement's) 1885, closed, moved 1936 to Victoria and reused; bushfire 1926; cemetery 1900; electricity 1950; PO 1879–1952; punt b. 1892 by E. Taylor, new one (3 car capacity) 1946, new one 2013, across Murray R.; Rom. Cath. C. (St John's) 1885, demolished; school (Wagra till 1912) 1875, new building 1883, burnt down 1884, replaced 1885 by Jackson and Neill, relocated 1888 by Baker Vincent, closed and sold to Robert A. Hoare, new school b. 1899 by Albert Schuler, closed 1946, reopened 1956, closed 1985, reused 2013; storm 1935; telephone 1893; TX (automatic) 1952; pop. 146 (1901), 124 (1911), 72 (1933), 99 (1947), 70 (1954), 109 (1961), 204 (2006).

Wyndella (*Co. Sandon*) 30°25'S. 151°34'E., 15 km NW of Armidale; farming and grazing; PO 1927–31; school (Eversleigh till 1892) 1888–1908; telephone 1924; pop. 69 (1911).

Wyndham (*Co. Auckland*) 36°56'S. 149°39'E., 20 km W. of Pambula, on Mataganah Ck; surveyed 1856 by Spencer Lasinby Bransby, land sales 1856 and 1860, village gaz. 1856 as Windham; mining, timber, agric., grazing, dairying; Angl. C. (Holy Trinity) 1888; brick-kiln; bushfires 1905 (two killed), 1909, 1929; cemetery (burials 1881+); CH 1885, new one 1898; eucalyptus oil distillery (J.T. Whitby); PO 1880; pound (stock) 1885; Presb. C. b. 1889 by Thomas Waterson; PS 1885, new one (incl. lock-up) b. 1898, closed 1966; Rom. Cath. C. (St Joseph's) 1898, restored 2012; sawmill estab. 1907 by George Sydney Rayner; school 1880, new one b. 1881 by A. Hammond; telegraph 1889; TX 1924, automatic 1980; typhoid (man died) 1900; pop. 391 (1891), 282 (1901), 281 (1911), 240 (1933), 222 (1947), 208 (1954), 162 (1961), 95 (1991), 113 (1996), 103 (2001), 367 (2006), 610 (2011).

Wyneden (*Co. Rous*) 28°33'S. 152°55'E., 12 km NW of Kyogle, on Eden Ck; Burmpabank till 1933; measles epidemic 1939; telephone 1923; TX 1933.

Wynnefield (*Co. Bathurst*) 33°44'S. 148°39'E., 13 km N. of Cowra; farming; earth tremor 2002; PO 1927–30; school (Glenlogan) 1880–93; pop. 80 (1933).

Wyoming (*Co. Macquarie*) 31°52'S. 152°10'E.,

20 km W. of Wingham; PO 1913–16; sawmill (W.J. Hawkins), fire 1922; sugar mill (Charles Richardson) 1869; telephone 1911; TX, closed 1922.

Wyoming (*Co. Northumberland*) 33°25'S. 151°22'E., 3 km N. of Gosford, on Wingello Ck; settled 1825 by Frederick Augustus Hely, subdivided 1881, but not sold till 1887; orchards; Angl. C. (Holy Family) 1982; Christ. Outreach C.; Church of Christ 1954; electricity 1938; FB (station b. 1983); granary (Hely's); LDS (Mormon) C.; lock-up; PO 1945; railway gatehouse, burnt down 1934; Rom. Cath. C. (Our Lady of the Rosary) 1966; sawmills: Eric William Hawkins and Charles Tilbury Parson, destroyed 1913 by explosion; schools: Valley View 1980 b. by G.M. Pluim Construction Pty Ltd and Wyoming 1955, new building b. 1969 on new site, additions 1971, 1974, 1982; SD Adventist C.; Unit. C. (Narara) 1984; pop. 117 (1933), 267 (1947), 577 (1954), 8,783 (2006), 9,904 (2011).

Wyoming (*Co. Oxley*) 32°04'S. 147°27'E., 50 km W. of Trangie.

Wyong (*Co. Northumberland*) 33°17'S. 151°26'E., 18 km NE of Gosford, on Wyong R.; (incl. North Wyong, Wadalba, Watanobbi subdivided 1966, lots surveyed by John Hunter); settled by William Cape, estab. by Charles Alison, subdivisions 1893, 1920s, 1930s; timber 1830+, dairying, vegetables, orchards, poultry, fishing, tourism 1895+; airfield (Parry's) 1971, closed; ambulance station 1952; Angl. C. b. 1906 by William Thomas Trevitt, d. by R. Wilkins, fire 1994, new one (St James's) 1998; Assemblies of God C. (Crossroads); Bapt. C.; bridges: one over Porters Ck and one (composite truss) b. 1901 by Taylor, Murphy & Co., d. by Henry Harvey Dare, removed, new one 1963, over Wyong R.; bushfires 1909 and 1940; butter factory (Wyong Co-op. Dairy Co. Ltd) b. 1907 by A. Duncan, burnt down and replaced 1921, with ice works, closed 1994, sold and reused; cemetery 1887; CH 1925–91, sold and reused, new one 1992 d. by Lindsay Kelly and Rebecca Hearty; cheese factory (Little Creek Cheese Pty Ltd); chocolate factory (Luka's) 2014; cordial factory (George, William and Henry Bell, sold to B.T. Dunk, later sold to Hubert Charles Margin) 1909; electricity 1929; FB (station b. 1936, new one 1962); fibreglass products factory (Exatal), bought 1977 by Vickers Aust. and became Vickers Exatal; fires 1903, 1904 (destroyed most of town), 1906, 1913, 1914; floods 1927 (3 died), 1946, 1949; food factory (Cordina Food Co.) 2014; fruit packing house (Wyong Co-op. Citrus Packing Shed) 1923, burnt down 1937; grist mill (D'Arcy Rose Pty Ltd) 1953; hailstorms 1902 and 1993; house frame and truss factories: Fleetwood Timber Pty Ltd 1994 and Heyden Frame & Truss; Islamic. C.; Jehovah's Witnesses C.; Meth. C. b. 1907 by Parker and Dixon, renovated 1926, closed; PO: North Wyong 1958 and Wyong 1889 (new one b. 1892 by J. Hopkins, second one b. 1911 by C. Parker and William Daniel Ponton, replaced 1980); pound (stock) 1920; Presb. C. 1909; PS 1889, new one (incl. lock-up) b. 1901 by William Frederick Gazzard, additions and renovations 1910 by Thomas Curran, additions 1931, 1961, 1971, 1973, closed, sold and reused, new one b. 2009–12 by Adco Construction Pty Ltd, d. by D.W.P. Suters; punt 1891–1901, across Wyong Ck; railway bridge to Tuggerah (5 reinforced concrete elliptical arches) over Wyong Ck; railway duplication 1912; railway turntable (75 ft or 22.9 m) 1951; reservoirs: Chapmans Hill 1929, Wadalba, Wyong Hill; Rom. Cath. C. (St Cecilia's) b. 1908 by Norbert A. O'Leary, d. by Joseph Ignatius Sheerin and John Francis Hennessy, damaged 1920, enlarged 1926 by G. Dixon, and again in 1935 and 1950; RS 1887, station b. by G.R. and F.H. Harrison; sawmills: Charles Alison (taken over by O'Neill and Goldsmith, bought 1917 by Wilson and Flood, closed 1929), P.J. Farrell, Stewart's; schools: Wyong primary 1888 (new one b. 1889 by Louis Le Breton & Son, additions 1906, new building b. 1910 by D. M'Donald, additions 1963, closed 1979, sold and reused, replaced (at

Watanobbi), inundated 2007), Wyong HS 1950 (b. by Davis Bros, additions 1964, 1971, 1979, 1985, alterations 1987), Wyong Grove 1981 (additions 2010 and 2012, closed 2013, reused 2014, sold 2015); sewerage 1969, augmentation 1983, completion 1990; shoe factory (Van Eden) 1965, closed; steel fabrication works (Amarcon Group) 2009; storm 1920; TC b. 1982 by G.M. Pluim Construction Ltd, additions 1988 and 1990, became a campus of Hunter Institute of Technology in 1992; textile factory (Moderne Knitwear Co.) 1948; telegraph 1891, new office b. 1892 by J. Hopkins, second one b. 1911 by C. Parker and William Daniel Ponton; TX 1910; Unit. C. (St Andrew's, orig. Presb.); water reticulation 1930; water supply augmentation 1969 and 1994; wharves 1908; pop. 194 (1891), *c.*200 (1898), 405 (1901), 1,193 (1911), 1,188 (1933), 1,324 (1947), 1,582 (1954), 1,907 (1961), 3,679 (1976), 3,902 (1981), 9,182 (2011).

Wyongah (*Co. Northumberland*) see Kanwal.

Wyong Creek (*Co. Northumberland*) 33°16'S. 151°22'E., 6 km W. of Wyong, on Wyong R.; farming, dairying, turf, nuts; Angl. C. (St Silas's) 1886, destroyed 1900; bridges: Dixon Kings Bridge over Chandlers Ck, Kidmans Bridge over Wyong Ck, Woodburys Bridge over Wyong R.; FB; gale 1900; Meth. C. b. 1920 by Reuben Greentree (moved 1926 to Kangy Angy); PO 1877–1967; quarry; sawmills: Thomas Cantrell Bradley (later moved to Brush Creek), Shem Davis 1921, E.J. Flood, Andrew Herks, H. Levett, O'Neill and Goldsmith, E.J. Richter; school (Lower Wyong Creek till 1888) 1884, new buildings b. 1893 by James Prior Hull; telephone 1911; TX 1915; pop. 403 (1901), 333 (1933), 249 (1947), 217 (1954), 216 (1961), 387 (2011).

Wyong Creek (*Co. Northumberland*) see also Yarramalong.

Wyong East (*Co. Northumberland*) see Tacoma.

Wyong Grove (*Co. Northumberland*) see Wyong.

Wyora (*Co. Buccleuch*) 35°17'S. 148°42'E., 42 km E. of Tumut, on Sandy Flat Ck; earth tremor 2012; telephone 1926; TX 1930.

Wyrallah (*Co. Rous*) 28°53'S. 153°18'E., 9 km S. of Lismore, on Wilsons R.; estab. in 1860s; timber, shipbuilding, maize, sugar-cane, dates, yams, peanuts, ginger, arrowroot, dairying, apiculture, fruit; Angl. C. (St Thomas's) 1910 d. by Charles Rosenthal; bushfire 1902; cemetery 1869; creamery (NSW Creamery Butter Co. Ltd) 1897; FB; floods 1917, 1921, 1931; Free Presb. C. (John Knox's) b. 1880 by J. Bannatyne; gales 1886 and 1942; PO 1869–1982; Presb. C. b. 1888 by Brown and Jolly; punt; quarry; sawmills: James and John Breckenridge 1865 and John Keep & Sons 1862; school (Tucki Tucki till 1871) 1867, repairs 1914 by J.W. Snars, additions 2010; sugar mill (Thompson's), moved 1879 to Broadwater; telegraph 1888; telephone 1886; TX 1922, automatic 1938; Unit. C. (orig. Wes. Meth.) 1885; pop. 307 (1901), 391 (1911), 274 (1933), 239 (1947), 221 (1954), 248 (1961), 446 (2011).

Wyrallah Road (*Co. Rous*) see Lismore.

Wyrra (*Co. Gipps*) 33°49'S. 147°16'E., 13 km N. of West Wyalong; RS 1929, station closed and removed 1972.

Wytaliba (*Co. Gough*) 29°41'S. 152°06'E., 35 km E. of Glen Innes, on Mann R.; school 1984, burnt down 2019.

Wyuna Downs (*Co. Cowper*) 30°30'S. 146°29'E., 70 km SE of Bourke; RS 1901–58.

Wyweera (*Co. Clive*) 29°00'S. 151°55'E., 11 km NW of Tenterfield, on Sunnyside Ck; telephone 1924; TX 1936–73.

Y

Yadboro Flat (*Co. St Vincent*) 35°20'S. 150°13'E., 20 km W. of Milton, on Clyde R.

Yaddra (*Co. Dowling*) 33°15'S. 146°38'E., 24 km E. of Lake Cargelligo; school 1930–37 and 1961–65; telephone 1926; pop. 127 (1933).

Yagobe (*Co. Burnett*) 29°32'S. 150°15'E., 30 km W. of Warialda, on Gwydir R. farming and grazing; PO 1906–34; quarry; RS 1900, station b. by E.W. Rowland, closed 1975; telephone 1912; TX 1916; pop. 52 (1933).

Yagon (*Co. Gloucester*) 32°27'S. 152°29'E., 27 km E. of Bulahdelah, on Tasman Sea.

Yahoo Brush (*Co. Macquarie*) 31°52'S. 152°20'E., 4 km W. of Wingham, on Dingo Ck; pumping station on Dingo Ck.

Yalama (*Co. Townsend*) 35°42'S. 144°55'E., 20 km S. of Deniliquin; village gaz. 1864; pop. 54 (1911).

Yalbraith (*Co. Georgiana*) 34°18'S. 149°45'E., 31 km NE of Crookwell, on Yalbraith Ck; farming and grazing; butter factory (Ptarmigan) b. 1891 by C. Ross and J. Pollock; PO 1901–81; Presb. C. 1882, renovated 1889; telephone 1913; TX 1927, automatic 1981; pop. 157 (1901), 56 (1911), 78 (1933), 55 (1947), 68 (1954).

Yalcogrin (*Co. Gowen*) 31°39'S. 148°40'E., 8 km N. of Gilgandra; school 1884–88.

Yalgogrin (*Co. Cooper*) 34°09'S. 146°47'E., 25 km NW of Ardlethan; formerly South Yalgogrin; grazing, agric., gold, tin; PO 1927, burnt down 1953; school 1884–88; telephone 1925; TX 1925; pop. 129 (1947), 53 (1954), 58 (1961).

Yalgogrin (*Co. Gipps*) 33°50'S. 146°50'E., 36 km W. of West Wyalong; formerly North Yalgogrin; village gaz. 1895; orig. gold (disc. 1893), then sheep, wheat, eucalyptus oil; Angl. C., removed from Wyalong 1919, o. as St Mary the Virgin, closed and dismantled 1977, new one (St Mary's) o. 1977 in former school; cemetery 1898; CH, moved 1927 to Tallimba; eucalyptus oil distillery (S. Chandler); lock-up, moved 1927 to Tallimba; mines: Adelaide (H. Huntley 1897–1900 and R.O. Moffat 1932–40), Autocrat (W. Thompson 1897 and C.E. Anderson 1900–2), Black Angel, Black Coon or Coon 1896–1910, Bottrell's (J. Bottrell and W.H. Waldron) 1900–3, Bursted Boulder (T. McCarten and J. Steppe) 1903–5, Cherry Tree or Wild Cherry, Democrat 1893–1914, Eureka 1887–1912 and 1931–40, Great Central (M. Foley and W.H. Waldron) 1896–99, Great Eastern (C. Skelly 1893 and J. Ottnad 1896–1900), Perry's (M. Perry 1900–2 and H. Huntley 1904–5), Picaninny 1896–1903 and 1934–54, Scoop Holes 1907–9, 1915–17, 1936–39, Shelly's (C. Shelly, F.E. Welby, W.T. Coonan) 1895–1900, Surprise (J.E. McGeach) 1897–99, True Blue (E. Miller) 1894, Try Again (H. Huntley 1897–1899 and D.J. Mulcahy 1914–15), Yalgogrin North (J. Bottrell 1896–1900, R.O. Moffatt 1922–26, T.H. Beattie 1922–26); PO 1894–1985; PS 1896–1927, moved to Tallimba; school 1896, burnt down 1923, rebuilt, closed 1970 (building reused 1977 as Angl. C.); telephone 1898; TX 1911; pop. 138 (1901), 379 (1911), 221 (1933), 129 (1947), 102 (1954), 117 (1961).

Yalgogrin North (*Co. Gipps*) see Yalgogrin.

Yalgogrin South (*Co. Cooper*) see Yalgogrin.

Yallah (*Co. Camden*) 34°32'S. 150°47'E., 4 km S. of Dapto, on Lake Illawarra; (incl. Avondale and Haywards Bay); dairying 1860–90; breakwater; bridge 1858, replaced 1909, new one (concrete) b. 1971 by P.H. Koshemakin & Co., 377 ft (114.9 m), over Macquarie Rivulet; collieries: Avondale (estab. 1884, o. 1911 by Illawarra Steam & Coal Co. Ltd, closed 1920, reopened 1938 by George Brunero, acquired 1955 by S.A. Brunero, closed 1982, sealed 1993, reopened 2006 by Gujarat NRE Coking Coal Ltd) and Huntley (estab. 1946 by William, Philip and Frank Waugh, bought 1951 by Joint Coal Board, powerhouse 1954, colliery bought 1955 by Electricity Commission, closed 1989, sealed 1993); creamery (Avondale, Fresh Food & Ice Co.) 1894–1902; meat works (Parrish Meat Supplies) 1945–91; PO 1927–31 and 1946–71; power station (Tallawarra) b. 1948–61, d. by Edward Herbert Farmer, closed 1989, demolished, new one b. 2006–9 by Tru-Energy; railway (power station) 1951; 2 reservoirs (Mt Brown); RS (Albion Park till 1888) 1887–1974, reused; SD Adventist C.; TC, additions 1987 and 1990, became a campus of Illawarra Institute of Technology in 1992; telephone 1923; pop. 124 (1911), 118 (1947), 136 (1954), 140 (1961).

Yallakool (*Co. Cadell*) 35°33'S. 144°27'E., 31 km E. of Barham; PO 1927–64; RS (2 km N., on Victorian railway); telephone 1927; TX 1928; pop. 38 (1933).

Yallambie (*Co. Northumberland*) 33°02'S. 151°08'E., 20 km SW of Paxton, on Wollombi Brook; grazing, dairying, orchards; bridge over Wollombi Brook; quarry; telephone 1916; TX 1928.

Yallaroi (*Co. Burnett*) 29°07'S. 150°29'E., 48 km N. of Warialda, on Yallaroi Ck; wheat; Angl. C. (St Simon and St Jude's) 1966; bridge (Belmore Bridge) 1989, d. by Ron Trevallion, over Yallaroi Ck; drought 1965–66; PO 1901–4; school 1885–1903 and 1958–69; TX (automatic); pop. 64 (1901), 58 (1911), 32 (1933), 67 (1947), 111 (2006).

Yallock (*Co. Goulburn*) 35°42'S. 147°37'E., 26 km E. of Holbrook; mines: Four Mile Creek (Anglo-American Minnie Quartz Reef), Just-In-Time (Yourns and Whip Shaft), Perseverance 1875–81.

Yallock (*Co. Mossgiel*) 32°25'S. 144°49'E., 140 km SW of Cobar.

Yalpunga (*Co. Tongowoko*) 29°01'S. 142°03'E., 309 km NW of Wilcannia, on Wampah Ck; grazing; PO 1890–1947; pop. 37 (1933).

Yalwal (*Co. St Vincent*) 34°56'S. 150°23'E., 20 km W. of Nowra, on Danjera Ck; declined 1900+, submerged 1972 under Danjera Dam; mining (alluvial gold disc. 1860, sluicing 1870+, reef gold disc. 1871 by J. Sivewright and E. Curtis) till 1920s and farming; bridge b. 1894 by S. Brown, over Yarramunmun Ck; bushfires 1939 (man killed and fire almost completely destroyed village and mines), 1953 (3 houses destroyed), 2001; cemetery (15 graves 1854+) 1892, restored 1988; cyanide plants: Homeward Bound 1900 and Pioneer Co. 1898; dam 1971, 125 ft (38 m) high, on Danjera Ck; diphtheria 1911; FB; flood 1871; foot-bridge b. 1892 by Thomas Atkinson, over Danjera Ck; mines: Albion or GL 26, Black Lode, Bruce, Caledonian or GL 20 (estab. 1885, amalgamated 1887 with Star), Coolangatta or GL 39, Daydawn or GL 23, Eclipse or No. 2 1874, Fountainhead 1934–37, Golden Crown or GL 1 1924, Golden Quarry, Hidden Treasure, Homeward Bound (estab. 1872–74 by West and Harvey, sold 1890 to J. Hanson, acquired by Yalwal Consolidated Gold Mines Ltd, equipment dismantled and sold 1916), Paul's, Pincombe's, Pinnacle or No. 1 1871–1938, Pioneer (disc. 1872 by E. Aldis and J. Caddle, sold 1890, acquired by Yalwal Consolidated Gold Mines Ltd, sold 1892, equipment dismantled and sold 1916), Poor Man (disc. 1880 by E. Curtis and E. Fletcher, closed 1887), Sawpit Gully, Sir Julian's Leg, Spencer's, Star (estab. 1883, acquired 1900 by H. Martin), Thomas's Cut, Usher or GL 17, Victory; PO 1883, burnt down 1953, replaced, closed 1961; PS

1894–1910; school 1882, additions 1892 by W. Bryce, closed 1917; stamper batteries: Eclipse 10 head 1878, Homewood Bound 10 head 1887, 20 head 1889, 20 head 1892, J. MacArthur & Co. 5 head 1875, Pinnacle 15 head 1881, Pioneer 40 head 1891, public 5 head 1875; telephone 1890; TX 1950; pop. 315 (1891), 350 (1901), 106 (1911), 61 (1933).

Yamba (*Co. Clarence*) 29°26'S. 153°22'E., 49 km NE of Grafton, on Clarence R.; (incl. Yamba Shores Estate and Yamba Waters); Clarence River Heads till 1885, formerly also known as Woolli; disc. 1799 by Matthew Flinders, laid out 1861 by William Albert Braylesford Greaves, town gaz. 1864; orig. oysters, then fishing, seaport, farming, grazing, mineral sand mining 1934–43 and 1968–70, tourism *c.*1919+; Angl. C. 1897, relocated 1914, replacement (All Saints') 1972 d. by J.W. Costa; Assemblies of God C. (Wellspring Christ. Life); boat harbour 1985; breakwater: first section b. 1862–89 by J.H. White, d. by Edward Orpen Moriarty, second section b. 1893–1903, third section b. 1950–71; bushfires 1952 (2 houses destroyed) and 2001; cemetery 1891; customs-house; electricity 1931; FB (station b. 1957); floods 1890, 2001, 2009; lighthouse (Clarence River) 1866, replacement b. 1880 by William Kinnear, d. by James Johnstone Barnet, 24 ft (7.3 m), converted 1920 to automatic acetylene, demolished 1956, new one b. 1955 of concrete, 60 ft (18.3 m); lock-up; Meth. C.; pilot station 1854; PO 1862, new one b. 1949; Presb. C. 1910, replaced 1921 and 1958; PS b. 1879 by W. Kinnear, new one b. 1903 by Crimson, additions 1904 by Hattersley, extended 2007; quarry; reservoir; river training wall; Rom. Cath. C. 1931, new one (St James's) b. 1975 by C. and N. Pyke; school 1883, new one b. 1891 by George Wunderlich, additions 1893, alterations 1914, renovations 1949, additions 1962, 1966, 1971, new one 1990; sewerage 1972, augmentation 2014; squalls 1886, 1891, 1939; storms 1902, 1936, 1950; TC 2019; telegraph 1877; TX 1910, automatic 1977; water reticulation 1967; wharf b. 1880 by J.A. Pashley; pop. *c.*200 (1862), 60 (1866), 35 (1876), 68 (1881), 288 (1891), *c.*350 (1893), 214 (1901), 306 (1911), 419 (1933), 815 (1947), 861 (1954), 853 (1961), 694 (1966), 1,274 (1971), 1,649 (1976), 2,528 (1981), 2,880 (1986), 3,707 (1991), 4,721 (1996), 5,660 (2001), 5,514 (2006), 6,032 (2011).

Yamba Shores Estate (*Co. Clarence*) see Yamba.

Yamba Waters (*Co. Clarence*) see Yamba.

Yambla (*Co. Goulburn*) see Table Top.

Yamble (*Co. Wellington*) 32°24'S. 149°20'E., 19 km W. of Gulgong, on Cudgegong R.; defunct; bridge 1879, repairs 1907 by J. Bedford, destroyed 1910, replacement (Dare timber truss) b. 1912 by John Bedford & Co., 388 ft (118.3 m), over Cudgegong R.; freezing works (Yamble Freezing Co. Ltd) 1917, taken over 1921 by Garratt Scandrett Freezing Companies Ltd, acquired 1927 by Amalgamated Rabbit & Skin Export Co. Ltd; telephone 1900; pop. 23 (1933).

Yambulla (*Co. Auckland*) 37°13'S. 149°33'E., 36 km SW of Eden; goldmining; cemetery; mines: Bungalow and Pedley, Duchess of York, Pola; PO 1900–18; school 1901–18; stamper battery (10 head) erected 1900 by J. Haugh; telephone 1906; pop. 210 (1911).

Yamma (*Co. Ashburnham*) 33°25'S. 148°12'E., 18 km E. of Forbes, on Lachlan R.; school 1886–92 and 1906–17; pop. 135 (1911), 26 (1933).

Yammatree (*Co. Harden*) 34°55'S. 147°58'E., 21 km NW of Gundagai; bushfires 1946 and 1979; PO 1879–89; school 1882–87; pop. 24 (1933).

Yammatree (*Co. Harden*) see also Burra Creek.

Yancannia (*Co. Yantara*) 30°15'S. 142°47'E., 156 km NW of Wilcannia, on Yacannia Ck; flood 1971; wool-scour; pop. 77 (1911).

Yanco (*Co. Cooper*) 34°36'S. 146°24'E., 5 km S. of Leeton, on Gogeldrie Branch Canal; The Quarries till 1883, North Yanco till 1892, then Yanko till 1928; housing by WC & IC began 1911, irrigation began 1912 by Frank H. Brewster, village gaz. 1913; rice 1915+, fruit, pigs, sheep, cattle, dairying; abattoir and bacon factory o. 1915 by WC & IC, acquired 1921 by Murrumbidgee Irrigation Dairy Farmers' Co-op. Society Ltd, acquired and enlarged 1963 by A.J. Bush & Sons (Yanco) Pty Ltd as a meat works; Angl. C. (St Mary's) 1936; Assemblies of God C. (Bethel Christ.); brickworks: Leslie Alexander and R.W. Cooper; bridge 1986, over Gogeldrie Branch Canal; experiment farm estab. 1908 by Department of Agric., expanded 1911–20, became the Riverina Welfare Farm in 1928, new buildings b. 1933–36, fire 1936, closed 1942, became POW camp in 1942, became returned soldiers' training facility in 1947, became agric. research station in 1961, renamed agric. institute, agric. college o. 1963, additions 1970, renamed Murrumbidgee College of Agric. in 1980, closed 2003, o. 2013 as Murrumbidgee Rural Studies Centre; FB; hailstorm 1911; meat works (South-West Co-op. Stock Treatment Works Ltd) 1950; Meth. C. 1913; PO 1888, new one 1926, closed 2000, sold and reused 2002; POW camp and control centre (World War II); powerhouse (WC & IC) 1914, additions 1915, extended 1937, closed 1958, sold, renovated and reused; Presb. C. 1914, closed, sold, extended and reused; PS (temporary) 1915, new one 1923, sold and reused 2006; reservoir (elevated) 1912; Rom. Cath. C. (St Patrick's) 1923–70, moved 1976 to Leeton; RS (Yanko till 1889) 1882, new station 1902, relocated 1925; sawmill (WC & IC) 1912–25; school 1913, burnt down and replaced 1936, additions 1964, 1967, 1979; sewerage augmentation 1981; silo; telegraph 1890; telephone 1913; TX (automatic) 1974; pop. 331 (1911), 853 (1933 incl. 186 at welfare farm for boys), 824 (1947), 649 (1954), 738 (1961), 429 (1971), 457 (1976), 415 (1981), 408 (1986), 651 (1991), 576 (1996), 601 (2001), 572 (2006), 505 (2011).

Yanco (*Co. Cooper*)
see also Euroley (*Co. Boyd*).

Yanco Glen (*Co. Yancowinna*) 31°44'S. 141°34'E., 27 km N. of Broken Hill; dust storm 1944; RS (railway to take limestone to Broken Hill) 1891.

Yanco North (*Co. Cooper*) see Yanco.

Yanda (*Co. Cowper*) 30°17'S. 145°39'E., 36 km SW of Bourke.

Yandama (*Co. Evelyn*) 29°40'S. 141°26'E., 280 km NW of Wilcannia; pop. 59 (1911).

Yanderra (*Co. Camden*) 34°19'S. 150°34'E., 4 km S. of Bargo, on Hornes Ck; orchards; bushfires 1939 (house destroyed), 1952, 2013; explosion (3 killed) 1941; FB 1969; Meth. C. (United Fellowship) b. 1937 by I. France; PO 1935–70; RS 1924, station b. by Arthur Rickard & Co., closed 1975, demolished; school 1957, additions 1993; telephone 1935; TX; Unit. C.; pop. 75 (1933), 108 (1947), 112 (1954), 89 (1961), 354 (1986), 493 (1991), 498 (1996), 536 (2001), 561 (2006), 683 (2011).

Yanga (*Co. Caira*) 34°43'S. 143°36'E., 9 km SE of Balranald, on Yanga Lake; sheep; pop. 56 (1961).

Yangalake (*Co. Caira*) 34°42'S. 143°38'E., 10 km SE of Balranald; RS (Victorian railway), closed.

Yango Creek (*Co. Northumberland*) 33°00'S. 151°06'E., 21 km SW of Paxton, on Yango Ck; school 1890–95; telephone 1925; pop. 94 (1911), 68 (1933).

Yangy Angy (*Co. Northumberland*) see Mardi.

Yankees Flat (*Co. Auckland*) 36°31'S. 149°35'E., 29 km NW of Bega, on Yankees Ck.

Yanko (*Co. Cooper*) see Yanco.

Yanko Station (*Co. Urana*) 35°10'S. 145°47'E., 22 km N. of Jerilderie, on Yanko Ck; pop. 87 (1961).

Yannawah (*Co. Bland*) 34°24'S. 148°00'E., 27 km N. of Cootamundra; telephone 1926; TX 1926–66; pop. 115 (1933), 84 (1947), 57 (1954), 94 (1961).

Yannergee (*Co. Pottinger*) 31°27'S. 150°02'E., 56 km SW of Gunnedah; farming and grazing; PO 1927–67; RS 1923, closed; telephone 1925; TX 1930; pop. 42 (1933).

Yans Crossing (*Co. Buccleuch*) 35°41'S. 148°27'E., 33 km SE of Batlow, on Yarrangobilly R.

Yantabulla (*Co. Irrara*) 29°20'S. 145°00'E., 125 km NW of Bourke; village gaz. 1886;

grazing; cemetery 1893; PO 1896–1982; pound (stock) 1899; telephone 1899; TX 1915; pop. 56 (1901), 69 (1911), 35 (1933), 74 (1947), 69 (1961), 17 (2006).

Yaouk (*Co. Cowley*) 35°49'S. 148°48'E., 52 km NW of Cooma, on Murrumbidgee R.; farming and grazing; bridge b. 1902 by J.M. Dodd; bushfire 2003; PO 1927–71; telephone 1925; TX 1926.

Yarara (*Co. Goulburn*) 35°44'S. 147°39'E., 32 km W. Tumbarumba, on Vyners Ck; pop. 54 (1901).

Yard Flat (*Co. Clarke*) 30°38'S. 152°14'E., 56 km SW of Dorrigo, on Georges R.

Yarmawl (*Co. Cooper*) 34°24'S. 146°16'E., 25 km SE of Griffith; RS 1937–75.

Yarra (*Co. Argyle*) 34°47'S. 149°38'E., 9 km SW of Goulburn, on Run O' Waters Ck; farming and grazing; Angl. C. (St Mary's, orig. St Bartholomew's Prim. Meth., till 1902) b. 1868 by Richard Benjamin Clewett, largely destroyed 1986, and graveyard (graves 1878+); bushfire 1986; Meth. C. b. 1910 by F. Barker, closed and sold, second one b. 1925 (from dismantled church removed from Thornford); PO 1885–1970; RS (Collector till 1878) 1875, station relocated 1912, closed 1975, defunct; school (Run of Water till 1906) 1886–1970, defunct; telephone 1905; TX 1917, automatic 1964; pop. 194 (1901), 155 (1911), 153 (1933), 102 (1947), 117 (1954), 85 (1961).

Yarrabandai (*Co. Cunningham*) 33°08'S. 147°35'E., 26 km SW of Trundle; farming; PO 1913–80; RS 1898, closed; school 1957–66; silo 1932; telephone 1914; TX 1915; pop. 106 (1911), 223 (1933), 158 (1947), 79 (1954), 166 (1961).

Yarrabandini (*Co. Dudley*) 30°57'S. 152°50'E., 14 km N. of Kempsey; Angl. C. (St George's); flood 1863; gale 1870.

Yarrabin (*Co. Wellington*) 32°35'S. 149°19'E., 27 km W. of Mudgee, on Yarraman Ck; Merrendee till 1859, then Merindee till 1923; goldmining, grazing, tomatoes; Angl. C., renovated 1941; cemetery (42 burials); FB; mines: Royal Mint, Verity, West of England; PO 1859–1965; school 1935–50 and 1957–63; storm 1877; telephone 1923; TX 1928; pop. 152 (1861), *c.*120 (1866), 110 (1901), 125 (1911), 160 (1933), 97 (1947), 64 (1954), 101 (1961).

Yarraford (*Co. Gough*) see Yarrowford.

Yarragal (*Co. Bligh*) 32°36'S. 149°04'E., 13 km SE of Wellington, on Wuuluman Ck; mining (gold disc. 1901) and dredging; mines: Commonwealth 1901–12 and 1920–30, Hare and Marshall's, Railway, Stringers or Independent or Yarragal (disc. 1906) 1921 and 1936–37, Wall and Stockwell's, Welcome Jack 1908–9, 1920–21, 1935–37; telephone 1928; pop. 111 (2006).

Yarragee (*Co. Dampier*) 35°54'S. 150°04'E., 3 km NW of Moruya, on Moruya R.; settled 1844 by Timothy Gannon; flood 1863.

Yarragrin (*Co. Gowen*) 31°39'S. 149°04'E., 32 km SW of Binnaway; TX (automatic).

Yarragundry (*Co. Mitchell*) 35°07'S. 147°13'E., 13 km W. of Wagga Wagga, on Sandy Ck; farming and dairying; PO 1927–67; school 1880, new one b. 1928 by Roebuck and Mueller, closed 1959; TX 1926; pop. 99 (1911), 127 (1933), 39 (1947), 58 (1954), 51 (1961), 437 (2006).

Yarrahapinni (*Co. Dudley*) 30°50'S. 152°57'E., 11 km NW of South West Rocks; cattle, fruit, nuts; cemetery 1895; cheese factory 1920; school 1883 b. by R. Kirkwood, closed 1972; Unit. C. (orig. Meth.), removed from Jerseyville, rebuilt 1951 by John Gillies; pop. 92 (1911), 81 (1933), 111 (1947), 148 (1954), 171 (1961), 308 (2006), 349 (2011).

Yarramalong (*Co. Northumberland*) 33°13'S. 151°17'E., 15 km NW of Wyong, on Wyong R.; settled 1856 by William Stinson and Ezekiel Waters; orig. timber then wheat and maize, later honey, citrus orchards, horses; Angl. C. 1871, new one b. 1885 by James Bailey, new one (St Barnabas's) 1920–77, reopened, and graveyard (79 graves 1887+); arrowroot grinding mill (James Waters); bridge (Stevenson Bridge) b. 1888 by Matthew James Woodbury, over Wyong R.; bushfires 1905 and 1994; cemetery (202 graves 1865+) 1888; electricity 1956; FB; 2

felloe works (incl. Waters Bros); floods 1905 (man died), 1927, 1951, 2016; Meth. C. 1909; PO 1881–1968; Rom. Cath. C. 1914; sawmills: R. Campbell, R.F. Greentree, O'Neill and Goldsmith, Mervin H. Smith, Stinson's (sold 1921 to Shem Davis, sold to Frederick J. Carson, moved 1926), Waters Bros 1880, inundated 1905; school (Wyong Creek till 1888) 1883, new one b. 1891 by George Donald, replacement b. by John Cook, closed 2010, reused 2016; snow 1965; sugar mill (James Waters); telephone 1911; TX 1923, automatic 1957; pop. 157 (1901), 246 (1911), 171 (1933), 138 (1947), 130 (1954), 116 (1961), 340 (2006), 468 (2011).

Yarraman (*Co. Courallie*) 29°26'S. 149°51'E., 4 km N. of Moree, on Gwydir R.; bridge (Pioneer Bridge) over Gwydir R.; school 1905–11; wool-scour (Stanley Crossley); pop. 41 (1933), 63 (1947), 213 (1961).

Yarraman (*Co. Pottinger*) 31°36'S. 150°11'E., 47 km W. of Quirindi, on Yarraman Ck; formerly North Yarraman; grazing; Angl. C. (St Aidan's) b. 1914 by J.H. Pengilley, moved 1966 to Blackville; PO 1868–1955; telephone 1915; TX 1915; Union C. 1884; pop. 201 (1911), 46 (1933), 131 (1954), 107 (1947).

Yarraman North (*Co. Pottinger*) see Yarraman.

Yarraman Park (*Co. Pottinger*) 31°34'S. 150°13'E., 44 km W. of Quirindi, on Yarraman Ck.

Yarrambah (*Co. Jamison*) see Yarranbah.

Yarramundi (*Co. Cook*) 33°37'S. 150°40'E., 7 km SW of North Richmond, on Nepean R.; Angl. C. (St Paul's) 1893; bushfires 1951 and 1994; FB; floods 1867, 1897, 1900, 1925, 1949; flour mills: water-mill (George Howell), destroyed 1867 and steam mill (Howell's), burnt down; Presb. C. b. 1886 by Crisford and Boughton, d. by William Lamrock, jun.; quarry (Boral); pop. 62 (1961), 468 (2011).

Yarranbah (*Co. Jamison*) 29°59'S. 149°15'E., 31 km NW of Wee Waa; Yarrambah till 1898; PO 1868; pop. 38 (1933).

Yarranbella (*Co. Raleigh*) 30°43'S. 152°48'E., 11 km W. of Macksville; dairying and bananas; PO 1927–38; school (Grays Crossing till 1921) 1912, additions 1965, closed 1972; TX 1928; pop. 68 (1933), 80 (1947), 70 (1954), 304 (2006), 322 (2011).

Yarrandale (*Co. Bland*) see Wilna.

Yarrandale (*Co. Gowen*) 31°26'S. 148°37'E., 15 km SE of Gulargambone; sawmill (F. Jones).

Yarran Farm (*Co. Narromine*) see Backwater.

Yarrangobilly (*Co. Buccleuch*) 35°39'S. 148°28'E., 31 km SE of Batlow, on Yarrangobilly R.; defunct; agric., mining (copper), timber, grazing; bridge b. 1909 by James M'Evoy, over Yarrangobilly R.; bushfire 1965; cemetery; PO 1902–69; PS 1886–1909 and 1916–1923; sawmills: Bridge and Dunne 1908, Harrison and Clark, W.W. Gillespie 1902 (burnt down 1904, rebuilt 1905); school 1901–14; telephone 1905; TX 1921; pop. 142 (1901), 138 (1911), 51 (1933).

Yarrangobilly Caves (*Co. Buccleuch*) 35°43'S. 148°30'E., 38 km SE of Batlow; disc. 1834 by John Bowman; grazing; hydro-electricity 1926; PO 1912–66; sawmill (Norman Buchanan); telephone 1899; TX; pop. 51 (1933).

Yarranjerry (*Co. Bourke*) 34°29'S. 147°04'E., 20 km SE of Ardlethan, on Methul Ck; telephone 1916; TX 1917.

Yarrans (*Co. Gipps*) 33°46'S. 146°56'E., 30 km NW of West Wyalong, on Euglo Ck; telephone 1929; TX 1929–42.

Yarranung (*Co. Auckland*) 36°38'S. 149°49'E., 5 km NW of Bega; butter factory (NSW Creamery Butter Co. Ltd) 1894–1903, reused; cheese factory (Tarraganda, Wren & Son) in rented premises; floods 1851 and 1925; pop. 32 (1933).

Yarrara (*Co. Goulburn*) 35°45'S. 147°40'E., 30 km E. of Holbrook, on Vyners Ck; goldmining; Yarrara Reefs till 1878; PO 1874–1905; PS 1876; school 1957–66.

Yarrara Reefs (*Co. Goulburn*) see Yarrara.

Yarrari (*Co. Nandewar*) 30°50'S. 150°19'E., 30 km SE of Boggabri; FB; school 1919–49.

Yarras (*Co. Macquarie*) 31°25'S. 152°19'E., 40 km W. of Wauchope, on Hastings R.; mining (copper) and farming; PO 1875–1981;

sawmills: Oakley and Ball, and Oxley's; school 1955–2004; telephone 1915; TX 1915, automatic 1981; Union C. 1910; pop. 121 (1933), 231 (1947), 207 (1954), 186 (1961).

Yarras (*Co. Roxburgh*) 33°23'S. 149°40'E., 9 km NE of Bathurst; grazing; flood 1930; storm 1950.

Yarravel (*Co. Dudley*) 31°04'S. 152°45'E., 9 km W. of Kempsey, on Macleay R.; pop. 775 (2006), 1,049 (2011).

Yarrawa (*Co. Hunter*) 32°24'S. 150°36'E., 9 km W. of Denman, on Yarrawa Ck; bushfire 1957; school 1957–59; pop. 118 (1911), 99 (1933), 80 (1947), 92 (1954), 62 (1961). (See also Old Yarrawa.)

Yarrawah (*Co. Camden*) see Robertson.

Yarrawin (*Co. Clyde*) 30°16'S. 147°14'E., 47 km SE of Brewarrina, on Marra Ck; pop. 24 (1933), 61 (1954), 57 (1961).

Yarrawonga Estate (*Co. Lincoln*) see Dubbo.

Yarrawonga Park (*Co. Northumberland*) see Balcolyn.

Yarra Yarra (*Co. Goulburn*) 35°43'S. 147°25'E., 10 km E. of Holbrook; sawmill (M'Laurin Bros) 1904; pop. 110 (1901).

Yarra Yarra Junction (*Co. Goulburn*) 35°43'S. 147°27'E., 12 km E. of Holbrook, on Yarra Yarra Ck; cemetery (1 km S.).

Yarric (*Co. Gloucester*) 32°20'S. 152°29'E., 17 km S. of Forster.

Yarrie Lake (*Co. White*) 30°22'S. 149°31'E., 17 km S. of Wee Waa, on Yarrie Lake; pop. 45 (1933), 56 (1947), 262 (2011).

Yarrigan (*Co. Baradine*) 31°00'S. 148°59'E., 8 km SW of Baradine.

Yarrow Creek (*Co. Gough*) 29°51'S. 151°56'E., 24 km SE of Glen Innes, on Yarrow R.; Angl. C. (St Michael and All Angels') 1903; bridge (3 spans) b. 1913 by Arthur Butt, damaged 1928, over Yarrow R.; flood 1928; Rom. Cath. C. (St Joseph's) b. 1964 by Hardy Marr Constructions Pty Ltd, d. by Terence A. Daly, and graveyard (9 graves); school 1899–1905; pop. 22 (1933).

Yarrowford (*Co. Gough*) 29°40'S. 151°46'E., 10 km NE of Glen Innes, on Beardy Waters; formerly Yarraford; bridge b. 1875 by John Strauss and Edward F. Wright, 170 ft (51.8 m), new one b. 1901 by Arthur J. Butt, new one (concrete and steel) 1967, 172 ft (52.4 m), over Beardy Waters; mill (water powered, Archibald Boyd); mine (sapphires); RS 1886–1959; sawmill (John Louis Schwenke); school (Yarraford) 1888–1927; telephone 1936; TX 1936; pop. 88 (1911), 64 (1933), 158 (2006).

Yarrowitch (*Co. Vernon*) 31°16'S. 151°58'E., 48 km SE of Walcha, on Stace Ck; Angl. C. 1921; bushfire 2013; FB; PO 1899–1979; school 1893, burnt down 1898, replacement b. 1898 by James Davis, removed 1924, new one b. 1923 by A. Hitchcoe, closed 1927, reopened 1951; telephone 1924; TX 1927; pop. 126 (1901), 178 (1911), 257 (1933), 166 (1947), 162 (1954), 160 (1961), 125 (2006), 167 (2011).

Yarrowitch Mills (*Co. Vernon*) 31°19'S. 151°54'E., 45 km SE of Walcha; sawmill (Thorsbys Ltd), in liquidation 1912.

Yarrowyck (*Co. Hardinge*) 30°28'S. 151°22'E., 30 km W. of Armidale, on Gwydir R.; estab. in 1870s; grazing; FB; floods 1916 and 1949; Meth. C. b. 1910 by J.S. and W.A. Crapp; PO 1888–1954; school 1886, additions 1928, closed 1931; telephone 1908; TX (automatic) 1954; pop. 221 (1911), 188 (1933), 101 (1947), 77 (1954), 92 (1961), 135 (2006), 219 (2011).

Yarrunga (*Co. Camden*) 34°35'S. 150°26'E., 7 km SE of Moss Vale; Yurrunga till 1918; bushfire 1905; earth tremor 1897; PO 1882; sawmills: McCleery's Ltd and Seery, Haytor & Co. 1892; school (Elmwood) 1888–1914, reopened 1955, additions 1967, closed 1972; telephone 1914; TX 1915; pop. 23 (1933).

Yarrunga (*Co. Camden*) see also Avoca.

Yarrunga North (*Co. Camden*) 34°36'S. 150°26'E., 8 km SE of Moss Vale; North Yurrunga till 1918; hort. and dairying; PO 1897–1925; sawmill (Southern Hardwoods Steam Sawmill) 1922; telephone 1924; TX 1928–40; pop. 44 (1933), 55 (1954).

Yass (*Co. Murray*) 34°51'S. 148°54'E., 64 km NW of Queanbeyan, on Yass R.; (incl. Hattons Corner and North Yass); estab. *c.*1830, founded by Francis Allman, old site surveyed and first lots sold 1834, new site surveyed 1836, town gaz. 1837, first lots sold 1838 at new site, laid out 1840 by Henry O'Brien, more lots sold 1854, designated as chief town of the county, munic. 1873–1979, bypassed by highway 1994; wheat 1830s–1927, fruit 1880s+, flour milling till 1950, maize, barley, oats, rye, potatoes, tobacco, now wool, cattle, horses, goats, wine; airfield; ambulance station b. 1955 by Hall and McDermott, d. by Toohey, Miller & Co., new one 2019 on new site; Angl. C. (temporary one) 1841, burnt down 1850, new one (St Clement's) b. 1847–50 by John Gunning, d. by Edmund Thomas Blacket, tower and spire added 1859, church extensions 1877–79 also d. by Blacket, and graveyard (closed 1869); Apostolic C. (Eagles Nest); Bapt. C. (orig. Wes. Meth.) closed, sold 1994, new one (Community) 2009; boiling-down works estab. by Hamilton Hume, Henry O'Brien and Cornelius O'Brien; boot factory (Hume Footwear) 1946–47; breweries: Star Brewery (estab. by Edward Heap) 1882–87 and Yass Brewery (estab. by Milne and Woodman) 1864–65; brickworks: W. Burden and W.J. Gorman; bridge (Hume Bridge) b. 1854 by William Henry Downey, d. by William Weaver, repairs 1859 by Barry, repairs 1862 by Vaughan, collapsed 1867, destroyed 1870, replacement (iron lattice), 179 ft or 54.4 m, fabricated 1869 by P.N. Russell & Co., erected 1870 by Musson and Down, severely damaged 1870, reconstructed 1871 by Thomas Smithyman and T. Bartholomew, extended 1878, re-decked 1888, extended 1933, new one 1977, over Yass R.; bushfires 1858, 1909, 1939, 1940, 1944, 1951, 1952, 1957; carriage-works (Cusack and Palmer); 2 cemeteries (incl. lawn cemetery); CH 1837 d. by Mortimer William Lewis, renovations 1858 and 1860, alterations 1863 by William Kinnear, replacement b. 1878–80 by Frederick Horn, d. by James Johnstone Barnet, additions 1883 by R. Beverley, also d. by Barnet; chenille factory (Pacific Chenille Craft Pty Ltd) 1948–52; cordial factories: T.J. Sheekey Ltd 1874 and Times (T.P. Williamson); cyclone 1891; dam 1927, 39 ft (12 m) high, on Yass R.; diphtheria 1907; droughts 1838, 1862, 1966; dust storms 1882, 1902, 1903; earth tremors 1852, 1860, 1871, 1923, 1924, 1930, 1932, 1935, 1949; electricity 1927, supplied from Burrinjuck 1929; FB 1901 (station b. 1928 by D.L. Lawrence, d. by William Hull McNiven); fellmongery, bought 1895 by Beaumont, damaged 1900; fires 1926 and 1927; floods 1836, 1850, 1852, 1864, 1867, 1870, 1899, 1900, 1906, 1915, 1923, 1925, 1948, 1959; flour mills: Crago Bros Pty Ltd 1882–1952 (bought 1952 by Winchcombe Carson Ltd), Hayes Bros, Rees Jones, Triggs's 1898 (sold 1899 to P.T. Crago), John Watson (acquired by Ernest Barber, destroyed 1870, replaced 1871); foundry (Scurr's) 1870; freezing works (Country Freezing Co. Ltd); furniture factories: Stan Cusack, sold 1937 and Pridecraft 1967; gaol 1838, new one b. 1862–64 by Charles Hardy and Thomas Hodson, additions 1878 by M'Kinley and M'Lean, additions 1879 by William Sharp, additions 1888 by Lansdown Bros, demolished; gasworks b. 1892 by McGill & Son, d. by J.C. Alexander, new retorts erected 1929 by James Hurll & Co. Ltd, works upgraded 1943; hailstorm 1869; heatwave 1839; hospital b. 1847 by Gunning and Peter Davis, new one 1889, additions 1898, additions 1904 by D.J. Grogan, additions 1909, remodelled 1929, additions 1936, 1937, 1938, 1946, 1950, 1975; joinery (W. Burden); leathergoods factory (E.E. Smith); lock-up b. 1890 by A. Scoller, d. by James Johnstone Barnet; monumental stone works: B. Doman, Scott Dickson, Joseph Robert Throwden 1898; PO: North Yass 1947–71 and Yass 1835 (new one b. 1882–84 by W. Bundock, d. by James Johnstone Barnet, clock turret 1888, post office repairs 1890 by E. Quartly); police barracks 1841, inundated 1864; pounds (stock): North Yass 1865 and Yass 1899; powerhouse 1927 d. by Crompton & Co. Ltd, closed 1929; Presb. C. (St Andrew's) b. 1865 by Charles Hardy and William Henry Downey, d. by William Carson, damaged

1891, demolished 1908; PS, destroyed 1870, replacement b. 1878–80 by William Duncan, d. by James Johnstone Barnet, alterations and repairs 1904 by Samuel Stead; 2 quarries; railway (from Yass Junction) b. 1890–92 by Kerr and Cronin, closed to passengers 1958, closed to goods 1988; railway bridge (Pratt truss), 210 ft (64 m), fabricated by O. McMasters, erected 1892 by McGill & Son, d. by C. Fischer, over Yass R., abandoned; railway coal stage; railway engine shed b. by Taylor and McClune, damaged 1900; 2 reservoirs, 330,000 gal. (1,500.2 kl) each; rifle range (5 km S.); Rom. Cath. C. b. 1838–43 by James Walsh, enlargement and alterations 1860, renovations 1888, tower extended 1890, church closed 1956, reused, restored 1988, new one (St Augustine's) b. 1954–56; RS: Meehan Street 1893, station b. by Thompson and Bates, closed 1958, North Yass 1903–58, Rossi Street 1892–1958, School Gates 1892–1958, Yass (station b. 1892 by Thompson and Bates, platform b. 1917, closed 1988, station restored and reused); sale-yards (Mellersh & Co.) 1887, new yards 1929; Salv. Army C.; schools: Berinba 1972 d. by Douglas Anderson (additions 1995), North Yass 1865–68, Yass 1879 b. by R. Beverley, d. by George Allen Mansfield (alterations 1906, additions 1908 by A. Allen, additions 1959 and 1964), Yass HS 1961 (additions 1972, fire 2012, additions 2014); SD Adventist C.; sewage pumping station b. 1939 by Hardy Davis Pty Ltd, augmentation 1988; shoe factory (Yasco) estab. 1944 by Edward E. Smith, additions 1949 d. by John K. Noller; silo; snow 1899, 1900, 1929; snowstorms 1878 and 1881; soap-works: Myers and Alexander, and Rees Jones; streets were gas lit 1892; tanneries: one destroyed 1850 and Robinson's; TC, additions 1983, became a campus of Illawarra Institute of Technology in 1992; telegraph 1858, new office b. 1861, inundated 1870, additions 1871 by P. M'Namara, repairs 1890 by E. Quartly; TX 1907, automatic 1967; typhoid 1903 (man died) and 1914 (man died); Unit. C. (St Andrew's, orig. Presb.) b. 1906 by T.G. Hastings, d. by William Mark Nixon and John Shedden Adam, jun.; water supply 1927, extended 1956, augmentation 1970 and 1990; weir on Yass R.; Wes. Meth. C. 1859 d. by Hilly and Mansfield, demolished 1869, new one b. 1871 by David Howell, d. by Thomas Rowe, additions 1908, renovated 1936, closed, sold to Bapt. C. and reused; pop. 37 (1837), 173 (1841), 274 (1846), 653 (1851), 660 (1856), 1,123 (1861), 1,167 (1871), 1,804 (1881), 1,770 (1891), 2,220 (1901), 2,243 (1911), 2,866 (1933), *c.*3,100 (1941), 3,254 (1947), 3,662 (1954), 3,909 (1961), 4,100 (1966), 4,240 (1971), 4,247 (1976), 4,283 (1981), 4,529 (1986), 4,828 (1991), 4,840 (1996), 4,909 (2001), 5,333 (2006), 5,591 (2011).

Yass Junction (*Co. King*) 34°49'S. 148°55'E., 4 km N. of Yass, on Bango Ck; Yass Railway Station till 1892; PO 1889–1953; railway dam 1903, on Bango Ck; RS 1876, station b. by Frederick Horn, refreshment room (closed 1956), station restored; telephone 1913; winery (Benfield Estate) 1979.

Yass Railway Station (*Co. King*) see Yass Junction.

Yass River (*Co. King*) 34°55'S. 149°07'E., 20 km SE of Yass; pop. 38 (1933), 64 (1961).

Yates's Flat (*Co. Drake*) see Alice.

Yathella (*Co. Clarendon*) 34°56'S. 147°28'E., 12 km SW of Junee, on Houlaghans Ck; school 1881–90; Union C. 1937, closed, moved 1974 to Kooringal; pop. 51 (1933).

Yathong (*Co. Urana*) see North Yathong.

Yatnaville (*Co. Monteagle*) see Shirrenden Hill.

Yattalunga (*Co. Northumberland*) see Saratoga.

Yatteyattah (*Co. St Vincent*) 35°16'S. 150°26'E., 6 km N. of Milton, on Currowar Ck; formerly known as Armstrong Forest; farming and dairying; Angl. C. 1876, defunct; bushfire 1953; creamery (Yatteyattah Co-op. Dairy Co.) 1898, converted to butter factory 1903, converted to cheese factory (Yatteyattah Co-op. Cheese Factory Ltd) 1907 by Nicholas Mudge, jun., rebuilt 1927, closed 1942, reused; FB; Meth. C. 1925; PO 1874–1973; Rom. Cath. C. 1866–79, demolished, and graveyard (76 burials) 1869; school 1879, new one b. 1884 by J. Poole, repairs 1907 by S.J. Butson, closed 1959; telephone 1914; TX 1926; pop. 112 (1911), 125 (1954), 96 (1961).

Yaven Creek (*Co. Wynyard*) 35°30'S. 147°56'E., 24 km SW of Adelong, on Yaven Yaven Ck; farming and grazing; bridge b. 1901 by W. Archer, over Yaven Yaven Ck; FB 1953; PO 1927–30; school 1955–63; TX 1974; pop. 74 (1911), 33 (1933), 99 (1947), 109 (1954), 90 (1961).

Yaven Yaven (*Co. Wynyard*) 35°22'S. 147°57'E., 12 km SW of Adelong; school 1881–84.

Yaypo Brush (*Co. Gloucester*) see The Bight.

Yeagerton (*Co. Rous*) 29°00'S. 153°17'E., 3 km SE of Coraki; Bapt. C. 1885, demolished; sawmill (Oaklands) estab. 1882 by William Tudor Yeager, closed 1921, chimney demolished 1932, sawmill largely defunct; school (Oaklands till 1894, then Oakland till 1914) 1886–1968; wharf; pop. 147 (1901), 141 (1911), 109 (2006).

Yearinan (*Co. Baradine*) 31°11'S. 149°11'E., 14 km NW of Coonabarabran; village gaz. 1931; PO, closed 1967; RS 1923–74; telephone 1951; TX; pop. 89 (1933), 96 (1947).

Yelgun (*Co. Rous*) 28°29'S. 153°31'E., 7 km NW of Brunswick Heads, on Billinudgel Ck; farming; PO 1927–74; RS 1922–72; sawmill (Alfred Bashforth, jun.); school 1947–65; telephone 1955; pop. 99 (1933), 127 (1947), 144 (1954), 101 (1961).

Yelkin (*Co. Dowling*) 33°28'S. 146°23'E., 18 km S. of Lake Cargelligo; wheat; TX 1926; pop. 109 (1933).

Yellow Bog (*Co. Selwyn*) 36°02'S. 148°12'E., 34 km SE of Tumbarumba, on Yellow Bog Ck.

Yellow Crossing (*Co. Richmond*) 29°08'S. 153°10'E., 20 km W. of Woodburn, on Bungawalbin Ck; 2 tea-tree stills.

Yellowin (*Co. Selwyn*) 35°31'S. 148°15'E., 9 km E. of Batlow, on Yellowin Ck; fruit, farming, dairying; bridge 1933–52, replaced 1953; FB 1945; flood 1952; PO 1927–31; telephone 1912; TX 1930–46; pop. 54 (1901), 58 (1911), 21 (1933), 51 (1947).

Yellow Pinch (*Co. Auckland*) 36°52'S. 149°49'E., 18 km W. of Merimbula, on Merimbula Ck; dam 1987, 131 ft (40 m) high; earth tremor 1866; pop. 609 (2001).

Yellow Rock (*Co. Camden*) 34°36'S. 150°44'E., 11 km SW of Dapto, on Yellow Rock Ck; coal and farming; bushfires 1936, 1942, 1954; coalmine 1940; colliery (Austen & Butta Pty Ltd) 1970–88; creamery 1890–1903; PO 1892–1930; telephone 1926; TX 1926; pop. 88 (1911), 267 (2006), 415 (2011).

Yellow Rock (*Co. Cook*) 33°42'S. 150°38'E., 6 km E. of Springwood, on Nepean R.; nurseries; bushfires 1951, 2001, 2013; FB (station burnt down 2013, replaced 2015); pop. 503 (1996), 593 (2001), 600 (2006), 916 (2011).

Yellow Tank (*Co. Narromine*) 32°25'S. 148°13'E., 20 km S. of Narromine.

Yellow Waterhole (*Co. Wellesley*) 36°51'S. 149°26'E., 19 km NE of Bombala, on Coolumbooka R.

Yellow Waterholes (*Co. Fitzroy*) 30°11'S. 153°09'E., 9 km S. of Woolgoolga, on Skinners Ck.

Yelma (*Co. Phillip*) 32°43'S. 149°58'E., 11 km N. of Rylstone; telephone 1915; TX 1923.

Yenda (*Co. Cooper*) 34°15'S. 146°11'E., 14 km E. of Griffith, on Main Canal; soldiers' settlement, village gaz. 1916; fruit, wine, wheat, rice, sheep, vegetables; ammunition factory (Bronzewing Ammunition Pty Ltd) estab. 2011 by Marcello Casella; Angl. C. (St George's) 1927; brewery (Aust. Beer Co.) 2013; bridge 2006, over Main Canal; cemetery; cyclone 1931; electricity (WC & IC) 1913; engineering works; FB (station b. 1959); fire 1939; floods 1931, 1974, 2012; fruit packing house (Producers' Co-op. Society), burnt down 1938; gale 1922; Meth. C. (damaged during construction) 1923; PO 1919, new one b. 1928; PS 1920, new one 1922, new one b. 1934 by N.R. Morris; reservoir (concrete), 50,000 gal. (227.3 kl); rice mills: C.S. Hall & Co. 1933, burnt down 1936, and Creamota Ltd 1949, bought 1952 by Ricegrowers' Co-op. Mills Ltd; Rom. Cath. C. (St Therese's), damaged 1931, alterations

1938; RS 1916, station b. by Ernest Frederick Leggo, closed, removed 1984; school 1870, new building b. 1920 by F. Mitchell, additions 1965; silo 1936; telephone 1922; TX 1923, automatic 1972; water supply 1936, augmentation 1985; wineries: Berton's 1945 (acquired 2005 by Southcorp), Casella (estab. 1965–69 by Filippo and Maria Casella), McManus Wines, McWilliam's Wines Pty Ltd (sold to Casella), St Peter's (formerly Wilton Estate), Terrel Estate, Wynvale 1959 (became a public company in 1970, taken over by Tooheys in 1972 and then by Penfolds in 1985), Yarran Wines Pty Ltd; pop. 1,407 (1933), 1,373 (1947), 596 (1954), 666 (1961), 544 (1966), 656 (1971), 667 (1976), 697 (1981), 836 (1986), 923 (1991), 1,058 (1996), 1,073 (2001), 1,064 (2006), 1,021 (2011).

Yeola (*Co. Camden*) 34°39'S. 150°36'E., 16 km NW of Berry, on Kangaroo R.

Yeoval (*Co. Gordon*) 32°45'S. 148°39'E., 35 km SW of Wellington, on Buckinbah Ck; (incl. North Yeoval); Buckinbah till 1882; laid out by William Butler Simpson, village gaz. 1886; copper, gold, wheat, wool; Angl. C. (St Luke's) 1925, closed, sold 2013; Bapt. C. b. 1954 by Armstrong; bridges: one (timber beam) b. 1937 by L. Delatorre, over Buckinbah Ck and Williamson Bridge, over Sandy Ck; caterpillar infestation 1914; cemetery (448 graves 1894+) 1888; dust storm 1983; FB 1928; freezing works (Country Freezing Co. Ltd) b. 1917 by Male, closed 1918; hailstorm 1924; mines: AI and AI South 1907, Cyclops 1907–8, Freehold (J.W.S. Small) 1907–8 and 1936–37, Suntop, Timbie Hill 1930, 1934, 1939, Yeoval and Lady Lizzie (Williams and Taylor) 1907; PO 1881, new one b. 1928 by E.R. Greenfield; PS 1924, additions 1987; rabbit processing works (Purex Meat Extract Co.) b. 1917 by Joseph F. Walker; reservoir, 100,000 gal. (454.6 kl), 1964; Rom. Cath. C. (St David's) b. 1906 by James Murray, new one (Our Lady) b. 1974 by Walmac Construction Pty Ltd; RS 1925, closed; sale-yards (L.C. Wykes & A.J. Schilling & Co.) 1950; sawmill (Reg Barnes), burnt down 1942; school 1884, new building b. 1914 by J. Job, additions 1956, 1965, 1982; silo 1928; telephone 1913; TX 1916, switchboard enlarged 1950; Union C. b. 1908 by T. March; Unit. C. (orig. Union) b. 1955 by J. Rodgers, d. by Ron Swane; water pumping station, chlorination and reticulation 1964; whooping cough epidemic 1927; pop. 96 (1901), 329 (1911), 753 (1933), 582 (1947), 774 (1954), 574 (1961), 325 (1971), 306 (1976), 288 (1981), 293 (1986), 303 (1991), 317 (1996), 310 (2001), 292 (2006), 386 (2011).

Yeo Yeo (*Co. Bland*) 34°30'S. 147°57'E., 18 km N. of Cootamundra; town gaz. 1861; RS 1893, station b. by Franklin and Finlay, closed 1975; school 1885, new one b. 1893 by Falconer Bros, closed 1896; pop. 36 (1933).

Yerong Creek (*Co. Mitchell*) 35°23'S. 147°04'E., 14 km S. of The Rock; farming, wheat, barley; bushfires 1901, 1902, 1951; cemetery 1892; electricity 1950; FB (station b. 1955, extended 1977); fires 1922 and 1929; flood 1891; horse dip 1937; lock-up 1893; Lutheran C. (Trinity) 1965–2006, bought 2007 by Nicholas Stone, renovated and reused; PO 1882, new one b. 1926 by Hardy Bros, closed, sold and reused; Presb. C. 1888, closed and reused, new one (Trinity) 1960; PS b. 1893 by Jabez Stanton, additions 1980, closed and sold; reservoir, 100,000 gal. (454.6 kl); rifle range 1914; Rom. Cath. C. (St Ignatius's) 1891; RS 1880, station b. by John Macdonald, renovated 1954, closed 1984, removed 1985; sale-yards b. 1891 by Thompson, Manning and Jeremy; scarlet fever 1944; school 1881, new buildings b. 1883 by G. Dobbyns, school burnt down 1891, replaced 1892, additions 1965; silo 1923; snow 1899; telegraph 1891; TX 1914, automatic 1958; water supply 1947; pop. 206 (1891), 297 (1901), 587 (1911), 248 (1933), 628 (1947), 446 (1954), 244 (1961), 176 (1967), 179 (1981), 517 (2011).

Yerranderie (*Co. Westmoreland*) 34°07'S. 150°13'E., 37 km W. of Picton; (incl. East Yerranderie or govt town, Newtown, Quigtown, West Yerranderie or private town); orig. The Peaks; settled by Harold Clyde Manning, estab. 1898, laid out and lots sold 1907, further subdivision and land sales 1910, thrived 1907–14, bought by L.J. Hooker *c.*1952, last lots sold 1957, abandoned 1959, private town bought 1972 by Valerie Anne Lhuede, whole town and mines classified by National Trust, private town acquired 2011 by govt; mining (silver-lead disc. 1871 by Billy George and Billy Russell) 1897–1930; airfield; Angl. C. (St James's) b. 1910 by Reg Smee, closed 1958; bushfires 1926 and 1936; cemetery 1906; CH 1904, closed, restored 1986; cordial factory (Mich Guerin); drought 1907; fire 1908; lock-up; Meth. C. 1908; miners' strikes 1925 and 1928; mines: Burragorang or Nelson's (incl. Kerry's Shaft and Lance Shaft) 1911–22, Coffey's, Colon Peaks or Bartlett's (James Vigar Bartlett) 1898, Feldsworth (Dunn's) 1900–28, Golden Gates (I. Sant), Great Peak 1906, Great Western or Nevada or Peaks 1900–15, Lady Manning (I. Sant), Maye's Shaft, Myall Ridge, Robert Nelson 1900, New Burragorang, North Yerranderie, Piece of Pork (Norris and Brough), St George 1898–1929, Sheritt's (Maddock and Taylor), Silver King 1900–12, Silver Peak or Bore Block 1904, Silver Star or Terni, W. Webb, Wollondilly or Hilder's (formerly Yerranderie, estab. by Thomas Hilder, operated by Yerranderie Silver Mining Co. 1901–22, sold 1923) 1899, Wonga (formerly Tonalli) 1911–26; PO 1899, closed, sold, restored and reused; PS 1904–40; Rom. Cath. C. (St Senan's) b. 1911 by W. Peters & Co., d. by Buchanan and McKay, closed 1956, reused; sawmill (Tonalli) estab. by Litchfield and Fletcher, burnt down; school 1906, alterations 1908 and 1912, closed 1950, demolished 1964; telephone 1905; TX 1905; pop. 105 (1899), 100 (1901), 426 (1905), 820 (1908), 840 (1911), 231 (1933), 82 (1947), 25 (1955), 27 (2001).

Yerrinbool (*Co. Camden*) 34°22'S. 150°32'E., 5 km SW of Hill Top, on Bargo R.; subdivided and first lots sold 1920; orchards and poultry; bushfires 1902 and 1936; FB; fire 1934; PO 1927–77, defunct; quarry; RS 1919; sawmill 1921, demolished; school 1923–62, defunct; telephone 1922; TX 1926, automatic 1953; pop. 71 (1933), 137 (1947), 133 (1954), 162 (1961), 367 (1986), 604 (1991), 834 (1996), 973 (2001), 1,033 (2006), 1,088 (2011).

Yerriong (*Co. St Vincent*) see Yerriyong Vale.

Yerriyong (*Co. St Vincent*) see Yerriyong Vale.

Yerriyong Vale (*Co. St Vincent*) 34°58'S. 150°30'E., 13 km SW of Nowra; Yerriong till 1905; farming; FB; PO 1927–30; sawmill (Les H. De Foy); school (Yerriyong) 1883–95; pop. 90 (1901).

Yessabah (*Co. Dudley*) 31°05'S. 152°41'E., 15 km W. of Kempsey; lime; quarry (limestone) developed 1949 by Co-op. Lime Society, taken over 1961 by K. Fisher and E. Berrigan, acquired 1969 by Petrie's Produce; pop. 40 (1933).

Yethera (*Co. Kennedy*) 32°32'S. 147°35'E., 45 km N. of Trundle; farming; PO 1927–40; RS 1916–74; telephone 1925; pop. 22 (1933).

Yetholme (*Co. Roxburgh*) 33°27'S. 149°49'E., 18 km SW of Portland, on Frying Pan Ck; Frying Pan till 1865; village gaz. 1863; farming and orchards; Angl. C. (St Paul's) b. 1868 by David Jones, and graveyard (161 graves 1873+) 1867; PO 1860–1974; quarry; sawmill (Aliston), damaged 1925; school (Kirkconnell till 1895) b. 1858 by W.C. Knight, d. by William Kerr and Andrew Rae, closed 1916, sold 1973 to Brian and Robyn Costello, restored and reused; snowstorms 1911 and 1914; storm 1925; telephone 1911; TX (automatic) 1953; pop. *c.*250 (1866), 149 (1891), 81 (1901), 128 (1911), 189 (1933), 187 (1947), 189 (1954), 189 (1961), 253 (2011).

Yetman (*Co. Arrawatta*) 28°54'S. 150°47'E., 52 km SE of Boggabilla, on Macintyre R.; settled by Richard Holmes, village gaz. 1863; orig. cattle and horses, then sheep and timber, wheat 1950s+, fishing; Angl. and Presb. C. 1882, damaged 1916, renovated 1933, replacement (St Andrew's) b. 1938 by Benjamin Martin Wade, d. by Castleden and Sara, and graveyard; bridge (Richard Coventry Bridge) 1981, 660 ft (201.3 m), over Macintyre R.; bushfire 1953; cemetery 1870; CH 1876–1925, replaced 1925 by B.M. Wade;

cyclone 1964; dengue fever 1943; electricity 1963; FB; fire 1870; floods 1890, 1933, 1935, 1950, 1952, 1976; hospital (Wellard Memorial) b. 1938 by George Graham; PO 1867; PS 1874, additions, alterations and repairs 1899, new building b. 1918 by K.E. Smith, new one b. 1925 by B.M. Wade; reservoir; Rom. Cath. C. (St Joseph the Worker) b. 1971 by Clarrie Robinson; sawmills: A.E. Head & Sons (estab. by A. Ernest Head and Albert E. Rope), Holdfast (W.E. Armstrong), Martin Bros 1943 (sold 1946 to Ken Gollan, burnt down 1957, rebuilt), W.H. Stacey, burnt down; school 1887, new building b. 1918 by K.E. Smith; telegraph 1888; tornadoes 1891 and 1916 (damaged many buildings); TX 1914; water reticulation 1969; pop. 148 (1901), 356 (1954), 285 (1961), 348 (2011).

Yeurabar (*Co. Rous*) 28°49'S. 153°14'E., 5 km W. of Lismore; school 1881–86.

Yiddah (*Co. Bland*) 34°02'S. 147°19'E., 17 km SE of West Wyalong; Bapt. C. b. 1912 by D. Lee and N. Daniels; horse dip (S.E. Ford); RS 1903–75; silo; pop. 85 (1911), 86 (1933), 129 (1947).

Yithan (*Co. Bourke*) 34°20'S. 146°52'E., 5 km NW of Ardlethan; also known as Ardlethan Tin Mines and Tin Mines; village gaz. 1919; mining (tin disc. 1912 by James Joseph Keogh) till 1932, then 1964+; gale 1923; Meth. C. 1920, destroyed 1923; mine fatalities 1924, 1929, 1933; mines: Ardlethan Tin Mining Co. 1964, Carpathia Tin Mining Co., Cherry, New Venture, New White Crystal, North Cherry, Southern Cross Tin Mining Co., Vegetable Creek Tin Mining Co., Wild Cherry, White Crystal Tin Mining Co.; PO 1913; school (Ardlethan Tin Mines) 1917, additions 1919 by Knox and Dacey, closed 1941; telephone 1914; typhoid (person died) 1919.

Yongurra (*Co. Rous*) 28°38'S. 153°00'E., 2 km S. of Kyogle; airfield; RS 1926, station b. by George James Grove, closed; sawmill.

Yoogali (*Co. Cooper*) 34°18'S. 146°05'E., 4 km E. of Griffith; village gaz. 1921; rice, grapes, oranges; flood 2012; Gurdwara Singh Sabha Sikh C.; PO 1924–91; Rom. Cath. C. (Our Lady of Pompeii) b. 1940 by Antonio Ceccato, d. by Ceccato and G.W.A. Welsh; RS 1928–75; school 1919 b. by C.B. Chitts, additions 1930 by B.A. Bennetts; winery (Peter Mogliotti) 1945; pop. 529 (1933), 556 (1947), 723 (1954), 523 (1961), *c.*350 (1990), 927 (2011).

Yoogali (*Co. Cooper*) see also Yoogali East.

Yoogali East (*Co. Cooper*) 34°19'S. 146°07'E., 8 km SE of Griffith, on Mirrool Ck Branch Canal; RS (Yoogali till 1928) 1923–75.

Yoolarai (*Co. Nicholson*) 33°51'S. 145°52'E., 50 km N. of Griffith; farming; FB; PO 1927–31; school 1956–70; telephone 1926; TX 1927.

Yooroonah (*Co. Clarke*) 30°30'S. 152°15'E., 46 km W. of Dorrigo; grazing; mine (tin) *c.*1890; PO 1914–58; sawmill (Wright Bros); school 1957–60; tank traps 1942; telephone 1913; TX 1927; pop. 91 (1933).

Yorkey's Corner (*Co. Wellington*) see Ophir.

Yorklea (*Co. Richmond*) 28°57'S. 153°04'E., 9 km S. of Casino, on Deep Ck; dairying; Angl. C. (St Agatha, Virgin and Martyr) b. 1926 by E.C. Rayner, destroyed and rebuilt 1931; gale 1931; PO 1924–29; sawmill; school 1897, additions 1966, closed 1972; telephone 1914; TX 1947; pop. 212 (1933), 219 (1947), 154 (1954), 196 (1961), 446 (2011).

Yosemite Park (*Co. Cook*) see Katoomba.

Yosemite Valley (*Co. Cook*) see Katoomba.

Youdales Hut (*Co. Vernon*) 31°05'S. 152°18'E., 51 km W. of Kempsey.

Young (*Co. Monteagle*) 34°19'S. 148°18'E., 64 km SW of Cowra, on Burrangong Ck; (incl. South Young); Lambing Flat till 1863; settled 1826 by James White, surveyed and laid out 1861 by Philip Francis Adams, first lots sold 1861, town gaz. 1864, designated as chief town of the county, munic. 1882–1980; mining (gold disc. 1860, gold rush 1860–61) till 1866, wheat, sheep, cattle, maize, barley, oats, rye, lucerne, potatoes, stone fruit 1890s+, grapes 1880s–1930s, wine 1900–30s, cherries, apples, pears, oranges, prunes, strawberries, eggs, pigs, poultry, manufacturing, fabrication; abattoir (Burrangong Meat Processors Pty Ltd) 1985, fire 2004, closed 2010, sold 2010 to B.E. Campbell, refurbished and reopened in 2014 as Hilltop Meats; ambulance station 1954; Angl. C. (temporary one) 1861, new one b. 1865 by Leeder, Nash & Co., d. by Sir Robert William Edis, demolished 1913, new one (St John the Evangelist) 1914 d. by Henry Laker, extensions 1927–29 d. by Louis Reginald Williams; Assemblies of God C. (Christ. Life); ball lightning 1882 and 1933; Bapt. C. 1965; bicycle works (George Bailey & Son, sold 1905 to Bennett and Barkell); boot factory and tannery (W.H. Thomas); breweries: Crystal Spring Brewery (George A. Cranfield) 1885–1916 and Young Brewery (b. by G.W. Fisher for Frederick Gleich and William J. Hills, sold to Frederick Sibbald and Henry Simmond, sold to Harry Tovey) 1874–97; brickworks: H.R. Blackett & Son, Hilton Frost & Son, W.S. Millard & Sons Ltd (man killed 1924); bridges: one b. 1862 by Halliday, collapsed 1875, replaced 1876, over Main Ck, one b. 1864, replaced 1900 by R.J. Madden, over Burrangong Ck, one b. 1885 by Thomas Brooks, over Burrangong Ck, one b. 1931 by Burns Bros, over Burrangong Ck; bushfires 1883, 1900, 1926, 1944; butter factory (Young Butter & Dairy Products Co-op. Factory Co. Ltd) b. 1894 by William Samuel Millard, d. by Charles C. Lance, acquired 1896 by NSW Creamery Butter Co. Ltd, acquired 1900 by Fresh Food & Ice Co., closed; calcining works (Causmag Ore Co.) 1952; carriage-works: Burrangong Coach & Buggy Building Factory (estab. by Barnett Phillips, taken over 1875 by John Rogan and George Lancashire) and M. O'Brien; cemetery (5,133 graves 1856+) 1863, incl. lawn cemetery; CH b. and burnt down 1861, (second) 1862–73, (third) b. 1874–78 by William Sharp, (fourth) b. 1884–86 by John George Gough, d. by James Johnstone Barnet, repairs 1900 by W.S. Stead & Co., alterations and repairs 1912 by Hugh Robert Blackett, closed, reused 1925, (fifth) 1928, new building b. 1936 by E.R. Greenfield; chaff mill (J. McLellan); chilling works: Young & Dist. Meat Export & Storage Co. (o. 1893, acquired by Pastoral Finance Assoc., closed, leased to Country Freezing Co. Ltd, sold 1923) and Young Poultry Chilling Co. Pty Ltd 1949–79; Chinese joss house; clothing factory (Aust. Silknit Ltd) o. 1944 in former small arms factory, orig. for military clothing, then civilian clothing; Cong. C. 1861, destroyed 1876; cordial factories: Crystal Spring (George A. Cranfield), W. Edwards, McVeigh Pty Ltd (estab. 1863 by David McVeigh), Sheekey's (estab. 1875 by Patrick and Cornelius Sheekey, acquired 1875 by Frank Hickey); distillery (Bluestill), in former jam factory; dust storm 1915; earth tremors 1871, 1886, 1898, 1902, 1910, 1949, 2013; electricity 1889; eucalyptus oil distillery 1892; FB 1876–85, reformed 1905 (station b. 1921), second FB 1930 (station b. 1938 by A.G. Brown, d. by Ross); fires 1874, 1877, 1897, 1898, 1907, 1915, 1922, 1940; floods 1912, 1927, 2010; flour mills: Thomas P. Chapman and Edward Taylor (sold 1908 to Young Co-op. Roller Flour Mill Co. Ltd), Peter Cram 1875 (demolished 1894), Watson Bros (b. 1866 by James and Joseph Smithers Hayes, upgraded 1878, sold 1888, closed 1895, reused, demolished 1917), Young Co-op. Roller Flour Mill Co. Ltd (b. 1891 by Holworthy and Rennie, upgraded 1895, bought 2012 by Quayle Milling Pty Ltd); 3 foot-bridges over Burrangong Ck; foundry (John Rogan); fruit cool stores (Young Cool Stores Rural Co-op. Society) b. 1930 by A.G. Brown, burnt down 1940; gaol (lock-up proc. gaol 1870) b. 1876–78 by William Duncan, d. by James Johnstone Barnet, additions and repairs 1898 by D. Rintoul, closed, reopened 1918, closed 1923, mostly demolished 1932, some parts reused; grasshopper infestation 1931; hailstorms 1953 and 2016; heatwaves 1929 and 1932; hospital (Burrangong) 1862, replaced 1870, extended 1880, new one (Burrangong Dist.) b. 1901 on new site by William Samuel Millard, extended 1921 by W.S. Millard & Sons Ltd, additions 1938 and 1940; hurricane 1863; ice works: Frank Hickey 1876 and Thomas McVeigh;

ironworks (S.G. Hawkins); jam factories: JD's (bought 2008 from Jan Donges by Mark and Lisa Smith), reused and Poppa's (Kevin and Vicki Powderly) 2004; Jehovah's Witnesses C.; joineries: Steam Cabinet Factory (William Samuel Millard), burnt down 1927 and John George Gough and Holworthy 1887; milk factory (Neville Young) 1967, new one b. 1970, sold to Braun, then sold to Ronald Charles Prosser; mines: Sawpit Gully, Spring Creek, Victoria Hill or Victoria Gully; monumental stone works: H.R. Blackett & Son, E.M. Downes, Joseph Robert Throwden 1900; PO: South Young, closed 1971 and Young 1861 (new one b. 1862 by James Moore, replacement b. 1876–78, d. by James Johnstone Barnet, additions and repairs 1903 by G. M'Gee, additions and alterations 1955 by Donnelly and Millay); poultry chilling works 1943; pound (stock) 1861; powerhouse (steam powered) 1889, new one (suction gas) b. 1916 by Hugh Robert Blackett, diesel generation 1923, closed 1928 and hydro-electricity from Burrinjuck supplied town instead; Presb. C. 1872, closed, converted 1923 and reused, new one (St Paul's) b. 1921 on new site by Hugh Robert Blackett, d. by William H. Campbell; Prim. Meth. C. 1864, new one 1879; prune store (Young Dist. Co-op. Producers' Assoc.) 1937; PS b. 1861 by Johnson and Viers, new one b. 1885 by William Sharp, additions 1900 by William Samuel Millard, demolished 1935, new one (incl. lock-up) b. 1921 on new site by W.S. Millard & Sons Ltd, additions and repairs 1935 by Stanley Gordon Lipscombe and Len Price, additions and alterations 1973; 2 quarries; reservoir, 500,000 gal. (2,273 kl); rifle range; riots (anti-Chinese) 1860 and 1861; Rom. Cath. C. (bark chapel) 1861, replacement b. 1863 by Leeder van Iderstein & Co., new one (St Mary's) b. 1874–76, d. by Andrea Giovanni Stombuco, extensions 1908 by W.S. Millard & Sons, d. by John Francis Hennessy and Joseph Ignatius Sheerin, tower and steeple 1931 also d. by Hennessy, church enlarged and renovated 1963 by A. Donnelly, refurbished and modernised 1986, and North Young (St Anne's) b. 1959 by J. Lehane, d. by Norman Leslie Lipman; RS 1885, station b. by John George Gough, closed 1989, reused; sale-yards (C.H. Ellerman & Co.) 1932; Salv. Army C. 1916, new one 1939; sawmills: Burrangong Steam Sawmills (estab. 1861 by Cadell & Co.), Peter Cram (removed from Tyagong) 1865, John George Gough and Holworthy 1887, Joseph Robert Throwden); scarlet fever 1917; schools: North Young 1953 (additions 1958, 1960, 1982), Young primary 1861 (new one b. 1863, additions 1873 by William Sharp, demolished 1884, replacement b. 1884 by Charles Hardy, d. by William Edmund Kemp, additions 1936 and 1959, reused 1978, new school 1976 on new site), Young HS 1946 (additions 1960, 1963, 1983, 1990); SD Adventist C. b. 1934 by Mitchell and Behrins; sewerage 1938; silo; small arms factory 1943, reused 1944; snowstorm 1929; soap-works (W. Wright), fire 1903; storms 1876, 1877, 1924, 1933; streets formerly kerosene lit, electric lit 1889; TC o. 1941 (in former gaol), additions 1992, became a campus of Riverina Institute in 1992, upgraded 2017; telegraph 1864, new office b. 1865, replacement b. 1876–78, d. by James Johnstone Barnet, additions and repairs 1903 by G. M'Gee; telephone (South Young) 1968; TX (automatic) 1969; typhoid 1906; Unit. C. (orig. Meth.) b. 1909 by Joseph Robert Throwden, d. by Alfred Gambier Newman; vulcanising works: Dean's, Para Rubber Co., William Charles Reece, Les Smith; water supply 1935, augmentation 1955, 1958, 1969; 3 weirs (incl. Capt. Cook), damaged 2010, on Burrangong Ck; Wes. Meth. C. 1865, reused, (second) 1880, (third) 1886; wineries: Chalker's Crossing Pty Ltd 2000 and Grove Estate 1886; wool-scour (Taylor Bros); pop. 792 (1871), 1,517 (1881), 2,746 (1891), 2,755 (1901), 3,619 (1911), *c.*3,281 (1921), 4,011 (1933), *c.*4,538 (1941), 4,320 (1944), 4,656 (1947), 5,503 (1954), 5,448 (1961), 5,754 (1966), 6,062 (1971), 6,459 (1976), 6,906 (1981), 6,797 (1986), 6,798 (1996), 6,835

(2001), 6,960 (2011).

Youngareen (*Co. Gipps*) 33°39'S. 146°51'E., 43 km NW of West Wyalong; RS 1929–75, station removed 1985; pop. 23 (1933).

Youngville (*Co. Durham*) 32°12'S. 151°19'E., 39 km E. of Aberdeen.

Young Wallsend (*Co. Northumberland*) see Edgeworth.

Yourie (*Co. Dampier*) see Yowrie.

Yowaka (*Co. Auckland*) 36°58'S. 149°53'E., 4 km SW of Pambula Beach, on Pambula Lake; (incl. Greigs Flat); agric. and mining (gold disc. 1888) 1889; bridge b. 1892 by J.W. Page, repairs 1904 by G. Phillips, repairs 1906 by Jakob Nybeck, destroyed 1930, replacement (4 concrete spans) b. 1934–36 by Maclean Construction Co., 214 ft (65.2 m), widened 1994, damaged 1999, over Yowaka R.; mines: Brassknocker Mine (closed 1939), Diorite Mine (closed 1915), Hidden Treasure Co., Mount Gahan Co. (closed 1906), Pambula Gold Mining Co. (closed 1902); PS 1891; 2 quarries; school (Greigs Flat till 1942) 1889–1944; 3 stamper batteries; pop. 286 (1891).

Yowrie (*Co. Dampier*) 36°19'S. 149°44'E., 37 km W. of Narooma, on Yowrie R.; formerly Yourie; farming; cemetery 1894; eucalyptus oil distilleries: C. Gough and Sylvie Sutherland; PO 1927–78; school 1907–29; telephone 1909; TX 1919; pop. 64 (1901), 53 (1933), 396 (2001).

Yow Yow Estate (*Co. Northumberland*) see Davistown.

Ystington (*Co. Buckland*) 31°43'S. 150°26'E., 35 km SW of Quirindi, on Yarramanbah Ck; telephone 1925; TX 1932.

Yuglamah (*Co. Auckland*) see New Buildings.

Yulgilbar (*Co. Drake*) 29°13'S. 152°34'E., 56 km E. of Tenterfield, on Clarence R.; lots sold 1923; gold (rush 1873) and mercury (disc. 1895) processed 1899–1903 by Great Australian Quicksilver Mining Co. Ltd, now cattle; bridge 1926 d. by R.C. Braithwaite, replaced 1966, over Clarence R.; drought 1926; flour mill (Ogilvie's); pop. 153 (1901), 55 (1911), 43 (1933).

Yullundry (*Co. Gordon*) 32°51'S. 148°43'E., 31 km NW of Molong, on Buckinbah Ck; largely defunct; Angl. C. (St David's), renovated 1899; bushfire 1901; cemetery, razed; grasshopper infestation 1904; PO 1873–87; RS 1925–74; school 1880–93; silo 1935; Union C. 1882, new one 1955; pop. 70 (1947).

Yuluma (*Co. Urana*) 35°10'S. 146°29'E., 22 km W. of Lockhart; farming; RS (Mucra till 1913) 1910–75; school 1960–68; silo 1935; pop. 95 (1933), 62 (1947), 85 (1961).

Yurammie (*Co. Auckland*) 36°50'S. 149°41'E., 22 km SW of Bega; school 1885–1931; pop. 85 (1911).

Yurrunga (*Co. Camden*) see Yarrunga.

Yurrunga North (*Co. Camden*) see Yarrunga North.

Yuulong (*Co. Gordon*) see Dubbo West.

Z

Zara (*Co. Rous*) 28°19'S. 153°16'E., 14 km W. of Murwillumbah; Tyalgum Road till 1905; farming and bananas; PO 1906–31; sawmill (John Lowe, jun.); telephone 1908; pop. 48 (1933).

Zara (*Co. Rous*) see also Chillingham.

Zig Zag (*Co. Cook*) see Oakey Park.